EVIDENCE

CASES AND MATERIALS

Seventh Edition

By

Kenneth S. Broun
Henry Brandis Professor of Law, University of North Carolina

Robert P. Mosteller
Harry R. Chadwick, Sr. Professor of Law, Duke University

Paul C. Giannelli
Albert J. Weatherhead, III & Richard W. Weatherhead Professor of Law
Case Western Reserve University

AMERICAN CASEBOOK SERIES®

Mat # 40470590

610 Opperman Drive
P.O. Box 64526
St. Paul, MN 55164–0526
1–800–328–9352

ISBN–13: 978–0–314–16879–5
ISBN–10: 0–314–16879–6

To

Margie

(K.S.B.)

Elizabeth

(R.P.M.)

Susan

(P.C.G.)

*

Introduction to the Seventh Edition

The strengths of this book have always been in its insight into the origins of the evidence rules, which was a particular strength of its original authors Edward W. Cleary and John W. Strong. The new authors have built upon that strength at the same time we strive to give attention to contemporary issues in evidence law.

The most pronounced change in this edition was the result of the revolution in Confrontation Clause jurisprudence occasioned by the Supreme Court's decisions in *Crawford v. Washington* (2004) and *Davis v. Washington* (2006). The confrontation section of the book in Chapter 13 is completely revised and substantially expanded. Extensive notes describe the operation of the earlier system of confrontation analysis and the immediate impact and areas of continuing uncertainty under *Crawford* and *Davis*.

A number of new cases have been added in this edition although fewer than to the Sixth Edition, which in particular greatly revamped the treatment of scientific evidence. New cases concerning scientific evidence have been added in this edition as well because of the dynamic nature of that particular area of evidence law. Indeed, throughout the text, an occasional new case and more frequently additions to notes have been made to bring a modern perspective to the discussion, but the pattern and flow of cases should feel familiar to those who have used the Sixth Edition.

In recognition of the importance of the Federal Rules of Evidence and state rules based upon them, principal cases and notes are largely directed to the application of those rules. Where possible, we have selected cases that illustrate how major issues are being dealt with under those rules. Where state law diverges significantly from Federal Rule treatment, notes generally examine the differences, although in a few situations a principal case illustrating the different treatment is included.

We also recognize the impact that modern technology has had both on the law of evidence and in the trial process. For the most part, the courts have not had much trouble adapting to new technologies, such as e-mail, computer simulations, and the internet. However, they have changed the way people live their lives and cases are tried. As a result, we have attempted to acknowledge those changes and illustrate the application of doctrine with new technologies by our selection of cases and more generally by the discussion in the accompanying notes.

The current authors of the casebook owe a great debt to Professors Cleary and Strong, and we hope both in the continuity reflected in the book and its treatment of new areas we have lived up to the best tradition of their scholarly instincts and their keen interest in teaching.*

K.S.B.
R.P.M.
P.C.G.

*In an effort to make cases more readable, we have universally omitted all indication of the denial of certiorari and made similar minor alterations without notation.

Summary of Contents

TOPIC IV. COMMUNICATING DATA TO THE TRIER OF FACT

TOPIC V. THE HEARSAY RULE

TOPIC VI. PRIVILEGE

*

Table of Contents

TOPIC IV. COMMUNICATING DATA TO THE TRIER OF FACT

TOPIC V. THE HEARSAY RULE

TOPIC VI. PRIVILEGE

Table of Cases

The principal cases are in bold type. Cases cited or discussed in the text are roman type. References are to pages. Cases cited in principal cases and within other quoted materials are not included.

*

Table of Federal Rules of Evidence

FEDERAL RULES OF EVIDENCE

FEDERAL RULES OF EVIDENCE

EVIDENCE

CASES AND MATERIALS

Seventh Edition

*

Topic I

AN INTRODUCTION TO THE ADVERSARY SYSTEM

Chapter 1[1]

CHARACTERISTICS OF THE ADVERSARY SYSTEM

SECTION A. THE ROLES OF THE JUDGE AND JURY

UNITED STATES v. BEATY

United States Court of Appeals, Third Circuit, 1983.
722 F.2d 1090.

JAMES HUNTER, III, CIRCUIT JUDGE:

Defendants John Ballouz and William Beaty appeal from their convictions on a number of drug-related offenses. The principal question presented in both cases is whether the trial judge, by his conduct, deprived the defendants of a fair trial. * * * After carefully reviewing the trial transcript, we conclude that the judge's conduct with regard to defendant Beaty, while sometimes unfortunate, did not rise to the level of prejudicial error. With respect to defendant Ballouz, however, we conclude that the trial judge's conduct was prejudicial. We will therefore reverse Ballouz's conviction and remand his case for a new trial.

* * *

I. FACTS

A brief recital of the evidence adduced at trial is helpful in considering defendants' claims. According to the Government, William Beaty asked a longtime friend, John Clark, if he would be interested in helping Beaty smuggle hashish into the United States. Clark was interested. Beaty explained that he needed a boat and a crew to ferry the hashish from the "mother ship" to shore. Clark arranged for Beaty to meet Robert Soleau, a commercial fisherman. Soleau agreed to provide the *Falcon* to carry the hashish, and a "safe boat," the *Tanqueray,* to carry people to count the bales of hashish and then return those people to shore separately from the drugs.

1. In the cases and materials throughout the chapter, some footnotes have been omitted and others have been renumbered. [Ed.]

The operation was carried out on the night of October 9, 1981. Government witnesses testified that Ballouz was on the *Falcon* and Beaty was on the *Tanqueray.* Due to a combination of factors, the operation was unsuccessful. The weather was bad, the sea was rough, and the *Falcon* was overloaded. Eventually, after its crew was transferred to the *Tanqueray,* the *Falcon* sank. Government witnesses testified that Beaty was subsequently involved in two unsuccessful attempts to salvage the lost hashish.

Defendant Beaty presented no evidence. Defendant Ballouz presented an alibi defense. He testified that he lived in California, but had come to New Jersey the week of October 9th to surprise his parents for his birthday. He discovered only after his arrival that they had gone to California to surprise him. He testified that he could not have been on the *Falcon* because he spent the evening of October 9th having dinner with Mrs. Axelson, an old friend. He presented Mrs. Axelson, his father and brother, and Mr. Rumolo, an old friend, as witnesses.

II. The Trial Judge's Conduct: Defendant Beaty

Beaty claims that the judge "chilled" his counsel, thereby denying Beaty effective assistance of counsel, by showing "favoritism" to the Government while constantly criticizing Beaty's counsel. He also claims that the judge's "favoritism" communicated the judge's belief in Beaty's guilt to the jury, thereby prejudicing Beaty and depriving him of a fair trial.

The law governing judicial participation in trials, while easy to state, is difficult to apply. On the one hand, it is clear that "[i]n a trial by jury in a federal court, the judge is not a mere moderator, but is the governor of the trial. * * *" *Quercia v. United States,* 289 U.S. 466, 469 * * * (1933). Indeed, this court has emphasized that:

> We have long abandoned the adversary system of litigation which regards opposing lawyers as players and the judge as a mere umpire whose only duty is to determine whether infractions of the rules of the game have been committed. A trial is not a contest but a search for the truth so that justice may properly be administered. For the purpose of eliciting the germane facts, a judge may on his own initiative and within his sound discretion interrogate witnesses.

Riley v. Goodman, 315 F.2d 232, 234 (3d Cir.1963) * * *. On the other hand, a judge must not "abandon his proper role and assume that of an advocate. * * *" *United States v. Green,* 544 F.2d 138, 147 (3d Cir. 1976). We have cautioned that "[t]he judge's participation must never reach the point where 'it appears clear to the jury that the court believes the accused is guilty.'" *United States v. Nobel,* 696 F.2d 231, 237 (3d Cir.1982) (quoting *United States v. Robinson,* 635 F.2d 981, 984 (2d Cir.1980).

Unfortunately, "the manner in which interrogation should be conducted and the proper extent of its exercise are not susceptible of formulation in a rule." *United States v. Green,* 544 F.2d at 147 * * *.

The task of an appellate court asked to review a trial judge's conduct is therefore a difficult one. We approach this case cautiously, aware that "no absolute, rigid rule exists. Each case must be viewed in its own setting. The pattern of due process is picked out of the facts and circumstances of each case." *Riley v. Goodman,* 315 F.2d at 234 * * *.

The judge's conduct of this trial undeniably left much to be desired. Whether or not his conduct was ideal, however, is not the issue before us. We must determine whether his conduct was so prejudicial as to deprive defendant Beaty of a fair, as opposed to a perfect, trial. *See United States v. Parodi,* 703 F.2d 768, 776 (4th Cir.1983); *United States v. Robinson,* 635 F.2d at 984. A careful and detailed review of this trial record of more than 1600 pages satisfies us that, while the decision is not an easy one, Beaty has not made a sufficient showing of prejudice to require a new trial.

Initially, we note that the court's rebukes of Beaty's counsel, serious as some of them were,[2] occupy but a small portion of the extensive trial court record. Furthermore, the bulk of these rebukes occurred out of the presence of the jury. The record also reveals that these reprimands were far from unprovoked. Beaty's lawyer apparently believed that he should be allowed to elicit otherwise inadmissible hearsay on the grounds of relevance. He also believed that he could ask questions tending to impugn the veracity of the prosecution's witnesses without any good faith basis. The trial judge, quite correctly, flatly disagreed. The record reveals a judge who was increasingly frustrated by counsel's repeated attempts to do that which he had properly been forbidden to do.

When considered in this context, the only really serious altercation between the judge and Beaty's counsel is less troubling. The judge essentially cross-examined Beaty's counsel in the jury's presence concerning counsel's basis for a question that intimated that a prosecution witness was lying. We cannot condone the judge's conduct or say that the ensuing colloquy would not better have been conducted outside the jury's presence. But "misconduct by defense counsel may properly be taken into account by us in determining whether a defendant was prejudiced by the judge's response." *United States v. Robinson,* 635 F.2d at 985 * * *. In *United States v. Weiss,* 491 F.2d 460, 468 (2d Cir.1974), the Second Circuit recognized that, "Judges, while expected to possess more than the average amount of self-restraint, are still only human. They do not possess limitless ability, once passion is aroused, to resist

2. For example, when Beaty's counsel, during cross-examination of a government witness, sought to question the witness as to whether he had lied under oath in an earlier, unrelated bankruptcy proceeding, the district court judge, after ruling that the question was improper, continued by asking Beaty's counsel: "Do you know he [the prosecutor] can put you on the stand and ask you the basis for the question?" Beaty's counsel charged that this suggestion by the court intimidated and chilled him. While we do not quarrel with the court's substantive ruling in the context in which it appears, we question the need for the district court judge to threaten defense counsel with taking the stand and responding to questioning by the prosecutor. Nor was this the only occasion on which the district court expressed itself in this same fashion.

provocation." We likewise reject any suggestion that defense counsel may inject reversible error into a trial by baiting the trial judge.

In considering Beaty's claim we also consider whether the judge exhibited partisanship by favoring Government trial counsel or holding them to lesser standards than those applied to counsel for the defendant. *See United States v. Robinson,* 635 F.2d at 985. He did not. The judge appeared to resolve all doubts concerning the admissibility of evidence in favor of the defense and repeatedly sustained defense objections to the prosecutor's questions. On occasion, he expressed disapproval of the prosecutor's conduct and, in general, he expected her to conform to a very high standard. Although we do not approve of the judge's rebukes of counsel, his relatively even-handed treatment of Government and defense counsel persuades us that his admonitions of Beaty's counsel did not convey a belief in Beaty's guilt to the jury.

Furthermore, we are persuaded that Beaty was not denied effective assistance of counsel because Beaty's counsel never acted as though he felt chilled. He zealously represented Beaty throughout. He extensively and vigorously cross-examined each prosecution witness. He pursued every possible avenue in testing their credibility and recollections. He frequently objected during the prosecutor's examinations. In sum, the record reveals no evidence that Beaty's counsel was chilled.

Beaty also claims that the judge frequently "rehabilitated" prosecution witnesses, and in so doing, conveyed to the jury his belief that they were credible. The questions complained of were designed to clarify testimony and pertained to no ultimate issue of fact for the jury. As such, they were proper unless they conveyed to the jury the judge's belief on the proper outcome of the trial. *Riley v. Goodman,* 315 F.2d at 235. Only one instance of questioning presents a sufficiently serious possibility of prejudice to merit further discussion. Defense counsel extensively elicited during cross-examination that Robert Soleau had previously lied under oath. At certain points in this lengthy cross-examination, Soleau's testimony became confused. The judge interrupted cross-examination to ask such questions as: "Did you tell any other lies to the Grand Jury other than trying to protect the names of the two men that you just gave?"; and "Did you at any time tell any lies to the authorities and falsely accuse anybody?" Given the extreme sensitivity of these questions, it might have been better for the judge to refrain altogether from asking them. Certainly he should have waited until after the prosecutor had had an opportunity on redirect examination to clear up any confusion. It may well have been error for the judge to interrupt cross-examination in this fashion. If it was, however, we do not believe that it rose to the level of prejudicial error.

We are unpersuaded that these questions implied to the jury that the judge believed Soleau. *See United States v. Parodi,* 703 F.2d at 776; *United States v. Robinson,* 635 F.2d at 986. Considered in isolation, they are nevertheless troublesome because a jury might think that a witness would be more likely to tell the truth to the judge than to counsel. The record reveals, however, that Beaty's counsel skillfully disproved any such inference. After Soleau told the judge that he had not lied other than to protect the names of "two men," Beaty's counsel impeached the witness by pointing out that he had actually lied to protect the names of three men. Thus neutralized, we do not believe that these questions prejudiced Beaty.

The sheer length of this two week trial makes us cautious about investing any but the most inflammatory isolated statements with critical importance. We do not believe that a few summary questions or intemperate remarks assumed the same importance in the jury's mind as they naturally have in counsel's while preparing this appeal. *See United States v. Weiss,* 491 F.2d at 468. Although we acknowledge that this question is an uncomfortably close one, when the length of the trial and the overwhelming evidence of Beaty's guilt[3] are considered, we are convinced that Beaty was not prejudiced by the judge's conduct.

III. The Trial Judge's Conduct: Defendant Ballouz

We cannot reach the same conclusion with respect to defendant Ballouz. The judge's conduct, always troublesome, became clearly prejudicial when he lengthily questioned three of Ballouz's four witnesses in a manner which Ballouz fairly labels as "cross-examination."[4] The court's vigorous participation in examining the defendant's witnesses, especially when contrasted with the complete freedom from hostile interruption of the prosecution's witnesses, must certainly have conveyed the judge's skepticism about Ballouz's alibi to the jury. *See United States v. Nazzaro,* 472 F.2d 302, 310 (2d Cir.1973). " 'A trial judge's isolated questioning to clarify ambiguities is one thing; however, a trial judge cannot assume the mantle of an advocate and take over the cross-examination for the government to merely emphasize the government's proof or question the credibility of the defendant and his witnesses.' " *United States v. Singer,* 710 F.2d 431, 436–37 (8th Cir.1983) (in banc) (quoting *United States v. Bland,* 697 F.2d 262, 265–66 (8th Cir.1983) * * *.

We are particularly disturbed by the court's examination of Mrs. Axelson, the witness who testified that Ballouz spent the evening of October 9th with her. This exchange is reprinted in full in the Appendix to this opinion. Mrs. Axelson was the only witness (other than the defendant) whose testimony could not have been harmonized with the prosecution's version of the truth. She was therefore a "key" witness, and the jury's verdict ultimately rested on the jurors' evaluation of her credibility.[5] We have long held that a judge must be extremely careful,

3. In sum, the evidence, some of which came from uninvolved persons, strongly indicates that Beaty was deeply enmeshed in all aspects of the smuggling attempt.

4. For example, counsel for Ballouz called Ballouz's father as a witness. The entire direct examination dealing with the father's visit to San Francisco was transcribed in only four pages of testimony. The cross-examination took no more than one page. The court's examination, which occurred during redirect, consumed over eight pages of transcript.

5. At oral argument, even the government conceded that if the jury believed the testimony of the alibi witness, John Ballouz's conviction could not be sustained.

especially when dealing with a key witness, to "minimize its own questioning * * * to the end that any such judicial departure from the normal course of trial be merely helpful in clarifying the testimony rather than prejudicial in tending to impose upon the jury what the judge seems to think about the evidence." *Groce v. Seder,* 267 F.2d 352, 355 (3d Cir.1959). In this instance, the judge's questions cannot possibly be construed as "clarifying." They were completely unrelated to the offenses with which Ballouz was charged, the alibi which Ballouz offered, and the substance of Mrs. Axelson's testimony. Rather the judge asked Mrs. Axelson again and again how she had come to be a witness in the case. This lengthy cross-examination, which occupies four pages in the trial transcript, was a frontal attack on her credibility. The jury could not have helped but conclude that the judge simply did not believe Mrs. Axelson.

It is true that the judge instructed the jurors that, "I am not a partisan either way. I have no view. And you are to treat any questions put by me as though they had been put by anybody else." He also admonished them that they were the sole triers of fact and determiners of credibility. We do not believe, however, that the damaging impression created by the judge's questions was mitigated by these instructions. "[S]uch admonitions may offset [only] brief or minor departures from strict judicial impartiality." *United States v. Nazzaro,* 472 F.2d at 312–13 (quoting *United States v. Brandt,* 196 F.2d 653, 656 (2d Cir.1952)); *cf. United States v. Anton,* 597 F.2d 371, 375 (3d Cir.1979) ("Where a court has expressed its opinion on a pivotal issue in the case, and has expressed that opinion in a strong, unequivocal and one-sided fashion, abstract instructions regarding the jury's role as fact finder are not a sufficient remedy.").

The judge's overzealous examination was error. Because the evidence of Ballouz's guilt, in contrast to that of Beaty's guilt, was far from overwhelming we cannot conclude that this error did not prejudice Ballouz.[6] In such circumstances, the only remedy for the prejudice suffered by the defendant is to reverse the conviction and grant him a new trial. *See, e.g., United States v. Nazzaro,* 472 F.2d at 313; *United States v. Grunberger,* 431 F.2d 1062 (2d Cir.1970).

* * *

V. Conclusion

The conviction of defendant William Beaty will be affirmed. The conviction of defendant John Ballouz will be reversed, and his case remanded for a new trial.

6. The testimony against John Ballouz consisted of the testimony of four co-conspirators and telephone toll records showing contact between Ballouz and Beaty, who were old friends. Three of the witnesses did not know Ballouz, and claim to have seen him only briefly on the evening of the rendezvous. The only witness who claimed to know Ballouz had not seen him for ten years before seeing him briefly on the night of the operation—when the witness was admittedly sick and drinking.

APPENDIX

Axelson—cross

THE COURT: How did you come to be a witness in this case, Ma'am?

THE WITNESS: How did I come to be an [sic] witness in this case?

THE COURT: That's what I asked you.

THE WITNESS: Because of the lawyer coming and asking me to be, which was telling the truth.

THE COURT: Oh, I see.

Was the first contact made from him to you or from you to him?

THE WITNESS: No. From the lawyer to me.

THE COURT: Did Mr. John Ballouz contact you before the lawyer did, or was it [sic] lawyer the first one?

THE WITNESS: Well, I had seen John before.

THE COURT: That isn't what I asked you, Ma'am.

THE WITNESS: I'm sorry.

THE COURT: Who first spoke to you about being a witness in this case?

THE WITNESS: Well, I think I approached them about that.

THE COURT: Oh, you approached somebody first?

THE WITNESS: Oh, yes, I managed to [sic] job. Gee, we were at the restaurant. I'd [sic] be willing to go as a witness.

THE COURT: You reached out for John Ballouz?

THE WITNESS: Yes.

THE COURT: Where was he when you reached out for him, Ma'am?

THE WITNESS: At my home.

THE COURT: He was in your home at that time?

THE WITNESS: Yes, he was.

THE COURT: Was he staying there?

THE WITNESS: No, no.

THE COURT: Was he just visiting you?

THE WITNESS: Visiting.

THE COURT: Who was he visiting there?

THE WITNESS: Me.

THE COURT: You?

THE WITNESS: Yes.

THE COURT: Not your daughter?

THE WITNESS: No. My daughter is married now.

THE COURT: When was it that he was visiting you that you mentioned to him about being a witness for him?

THE WITNESS: As I said, he always visited my home when he came to New Jersey.

THE COURT: Yes, but on what occasion was this? What month was this?

THE WITNESS: When he came home for the arraignment.

THE COURT: When was that?

THE WITNESS: The 1st of October—I don't know exactly when it was.

THE COURT: And where was he living when he came home for the arraignment?

THE WITNESS: Sausalito, California.

THE COURT: Did he stay overnight here in New Jersey, to your knowledge?

THE WITNESS: At his parents', probably. Not my home.

THE COURT: But he paid you a visit?

THE WITNESS: Yes.

THE COURT: The purpose of that was simply to come to see you?

THE WITNESS: Yes. Just to come to see us, which he always did.

THE COURT: Whenever he was in New Jersey?

THE WITNESS: Yes. Definitely.

THE COURT: When he happened to drop in you mentioned to him you could be a witness for him?

THE WITNESS: Yes.

THE COURT: Did you know the critical dates at that time?

THE WITNESS: I started from his birthday. It all sort of worked down. In the month of October it was a very specific month for me.

THE COURT: Yes, I know that you remember his birthday; is that correct?

THE WITNESS: I never forget helps [sic] birthday.

THE COURT: No. But do you also, at the time of his arraignment a year later, remember the day when the Falcon went down?

THE WITNESS: I don't know anything about the Falcon.

THE COURT: How did you know that you can be a witness for him, Ma'am, or that you would have anything useful to say?

THE WITNESS: Only that, you know—

THE COURT: I don't.

THE WITNESS:—if he was involved with this thing, how can he been there and at my home—be at the restaurant, too?

THE COURT: Be where, Ma'am?

THE WITNESS: Whatever this thing that is going with—

THE COURT: What did you know about this thing going with when you first spoke to him?

THE WITNESS: What I read in the newspaper.

THE COURT: You read it in the newspaper?

THE WITNESS: Yes.

THE COURT: Did you read the dates in the newspaper?

THE WITNESS: No.

THE COURT: Did you know what dates were important in this case?

THE WITNESS: No.

THE COURT: Did you know whether or not you could be of use to him as a witness?

THE WITNESS: Not then, really.

THE COURT: When you first spoke to him and told him that you would be a witness, did you have any idea whether you had any evidence to offer?

THE WITNESS: No. Not really.

THE COURT: All right. Thank you.

Notes and Questions

1. *Judicial Questioning*. Federal Rule 614(b) specifically approves interrogation of witnesses by the court. It does not, however, authorize questioning that demonstrates the court's partiality in the matter. See United States v. Tilghman, 134 F.3d 414, 416 (D.C.Cir.1998) ("Because juries, not judges, decide whether witnesses are telling the truth, and because judges wield enormous influence over juries, judges may not ask questions that signal their belief or disbelief of witnesses."); United States v. Filani, 74 F.3d 378, 385 (2d Cir.1996) ("these inquiries targeted the defendant's credibility and challenged his story more in the manner of a prosecutor than an impartial judge"). Also, while permitting counsel to delay objection to the court's questioning until a time when the jury is not present, Rule 614(c) does not eliminate the requirement that an objection be made.

See also ABA Civil Trial Practice Standard 10(a) & (c) (1998) ("Generally, the court should not question a witness about subject matter not raised by any party with that witness, unless the court has provided the parties an opportunity, outside the hearing of the jury, to explain the omission. If the court believes that questioning on the subject is necessary, the court should afford the parties an opportunity to develop the subject on further examination prior to questioning the witness itself. * * * Except in unusual circumstances, the court should not seek to impeach or to rehabilitate a witness, nor seek to emphasize or de-emphasize the importance of any witness or testimony.").

2. *Reversals rare.* As one may gather from *Beaty,* it is the extraordinary case where judicial action, even if apparently slanted strongly in favor of one party, produces a reversal. While the same standard—whether the trial is unfair—is generally applied in both criminal and civil contexts, reversals are rarer in civil cases. See, e.g., Handgards, Inc. v. Ethicon, Inc., 743 F.2d 1282, 1289 (9th Cir.1984) (very few cases outside criminal area find judicial misconduct); Ward v. Westland Plastics, Inc., 651 F.2d 1266, 1271 (9th Cir.1980) (new trial denied in discrimination case under Title VII, even though judge demeaned quality and relevance of plaintiff's evidence, suggested his own nondiscriminatory reasons for defendant's behavior, and disparaged congressional wisdom in creating cause of action). But cf. Maheu v. Hughes Tool Co., 569 F.2d 459, 471–72 (9th Cir.1977) ("glowing" comments by judge constituted personal character reference of plaintiff, whose credibility was crucial, denied defendant fair trial).

3. *View from above.* In ruling on the claim of improper judicial intervention, the appellate court's characterization of the purpose and effect of the judge's questioning is far from objectively certain. See, e.g., State v. Riley, 140 A.2d 543 (N.J.App.Div.), rev'd, 145 A.2d 601 (N.J.1958), where the intermediate appellate court ordered a new trial in the defendant's rape prosecution. The court concluded that the trial judge improperly assumed the role of an advocate in questioning the complaining witness and thereby communicated his opinion of the defendant's guilt. The state supreme court disagreed and affirmed the guilty verdict, characterizing the same questioning as necessary intervention by the judge who, because of his position, was particularly able to elicit sordid details from an anguished victim.

For an interesting effort at empirical analysis of the transmission of judicial influence or beliefs to the factfinders, see Note, 38 Stan.L.Rev. 89 (1985). See also Note, 53 Fordham L.Rev. 1333 (1985) (arguing for automatic reversal where reviewing court determines trial judge indicated belief in defendant's guilt).

4. *Expressive conduct.* What should counsel do in a jury case if the judge shook her head during a witness' examination in a manner indicating disbelief? See Note, 61 Va.L.Rev. 1266 (1975); Annot., 49 A.L.R.3d 1186. In United States v. Michienzi, 630 F.2d 455 (6th Cir.1980), a conviction was reversed because at the conclusion of an important government witness' testimony the judge shook his hand and told the jury he was an old friend. The problems of making an appropriate record of such conduct must not be overlooked. How should such a record be made? See Section B, infra.

5. *Bench trials.* The absence of a jury would seem to eliminate, or at least reduce, the harm caused by undue participation by the judge. On what theory might undue participation by the judge call for reversal? See State v. Lawrence, 123 N.E.2d 271 (Ohio 1954); Note, 30 Notre Dame L.Rev. 689 (1955).

6. *Jury questioning.* The Federal Rules neither explicitly authorize nor disallow the practice of juror questions. Rule 611(a) provides the only guidance by way of the statement that the court is to "exercise reasonable control over the mode and order of interrogating witnesses." In United States v. Feinberg, 89 F.3d 333, 336 (7th Cir.1996), the court wrote: "The permissibility of witness questioning by jurors is a matter of first impression

in this circuit. Every circuit to consider the practice has found it permissible in some circumstances. However, those same courts have expressed grave concerns about the practice. We agree that the practice is acceptable in some cases, but do not condone it. We share the reservations expressed by other courts.'' The court went on to note:

> Although questioning by jurors is "deeply entrenched" in American jurisprudence, concern over the practice is warranted. Witness questioning by jurors is fraught with risks. If permitted to go too far, examination by jurors may convert the jurors to advocates, compromising their neutrality. Jurors also may begin premature deliberation. Further, the practice "will often impale attorneys on the horns of a dilemma." Attorneys are faced with objecting to questions proffered by the arbiters that the attorneys are attempting to influence. The risk that an objection will alienate a jury is rather obvious. In cases such as this one, where jurors are permitted to blurt out their questions, the district court almost invites a mistrial. The district court leaves open the possibility that a juror will ask an impermissibly prejudicial question to which the witness responds before the judge is able to intervene. In the event of such a mishap, the entire trial may be rendered nothing more than a lesson in futility.

Id. at 336–37. See also United States v. Bush, 47 F.3d 511, 516 (2d Cir.1995) ("(1) jurors should be instructed to submit their questions in writing to the judge; (2) outside the presence of the jury, the judge should review the questions with counsel, who may then object; and (3) the court itself should put the approved questions to the witnesses."); Morrison v. State, 845 S.W.2d 882 (Tex.Crim.App.1992) (juror questioning disallowed in criminal cases); ABA Civil Trial Practice Standard 4 (1998) (setting forth procedure and jury instructions for juror questioning).

Empirical research has sparked interest in permitting some two-way communication between jurors and witnesses. See Penrod & Heuer, Tweaking Commonsense: Assessing Aids to Jury Decision Making, 3 Psychol.Pub.Pol'y & L. 259 (1997); Heuer & Penrod, Increasing Jurors' Participation in Trials: A Field Experiment with Jury Notetaking and Question Asking, 12 Law & Hum.Behav. 231 (1988); Sand & Reiss, A Report on Seven Experiments Conducted by District Court Judges in the Second Circuit, 60 N.Y.U.L.Rev. 423 (1985).

7. *Court witnesses.* Rule 614(a) authorizes the trial judge to call witnesses. See generally Saltzburg, The Unnecessarily Expanding Role of the American Trial Judge, 64 Va.L.Rev. 1 (1978). However, as with questioning witnesses, there are some, albeit largely undefinable, limits. In the extraordinary case when a judge crosses the boundary between the appropriate, though limited, role as a searcher for the truth and becomes a partisan, aiding one side by calling witnesses, such conduct becomes improper. See People v. Arnold, 772 N.E.2d 1140, 1145 (N.Y.2002) ("Although it does not appear from the record that the Trial Judge intended to give an advantage to either side, he abused his discretion in calling Sergeant Miller on a key issue when both parties chose not to. By calling Sergeant Miller, the court deprived defendant of the ability to request that the trier of fact draw a negative inference from the People's failure to produce an ESU [Emergency

Services Unit] officer during its case. Loss of that inference, coupled with the generally damaging testimony of Sergeant Miller, create a significant probability that the verdict would have been affected had the error not occurred."). Rule 706 also permits the trial court to appoint an expert witness, who the judge can then call as a witness under Rule 614(a). See Saltzburg, supra.

8. *Comparative law.* Professor Mirjan Damaska has written extensively comparing the "inquisitorial" and "adversary" systems: The Faces of Justice and State Authority: A Comparative Approach to the Legal Process (1986); Structures of Authority and Comparative Criminal Procedure, 84 Yale L.J. 480 (1975); Presentation of Evidence and Factfinding Precision, 123 U.Pa. L.Rev. 1083 (1975); Evidentiary Barriers to Conviction and Two Models of Criminal Procedure: A Comparative Study, 121 U.Pa.L.Rev. 506 (1973). Empirical efforts to evaluate the effectiveness and accuracy of the adversary system reach conflicting conclusions. Compare Thibaut, Walker & Lind, Adversary Presentation and Bias in Legal Decisionmaking, 86 Harv.L.Rev. 386 (1972); Lind, Thibaut & Walker, A Cross–Cultural Comparison of the Effect of Adversary and Inquisitorial Processes on Bias in Legal Decisionmaking, 62 Va.L.Rev. 271 (1976), with Vidmar & Laird, Adversary Social Roles: Their Effects on Witnesses' Communication of Evidence and the Assessments of Adjudicators, 44 J. Personality & Soc.Psychol. 888 (1983); Sheppard & Vidmar, Adversary Pretrial Procedures and Testimonial Evidence: Effects of Lawyer's Role and Machiavellianism, 39 J. Personality & Soc. Psychol. 320 (1980). As one might imagine, our adversary system has its critics, see, e.g., Van Kessel, Adversary Excesses in the American Criminal Trial, 67 Notre Dame L.Rev. 403 (1992), and defenders, see, e.g., Landsman, The Adversary System: A Description and Defense (1984).

CRANE v. KENTUCKY

Supreme Court of the United States, 1986.
476 U.S. 683.

JUSTICE O'CONNOR delivered the opinion of the Court.

* * *

On August 7, 1981, a clerk at the Keg Liquor Store in Louisville, Kentucky, was shot to death, apparently during the course of a robbery. A complete absence of identifying physical evidence hampered the initial investigation of the crime. A week later, however, the police arrested petitioner, then 16 years old, for his suspected participation in an unrelated service station holdup. According to police testimony at the suppression hearing, "just out of the clear blue sky," petitioner began to confess to a host of local crimes, including shooting a police officer, robbing a hardware store, and robbing several individuals at a bowling alley. App. 4. Their curiosity understandably aroused, the police transferred petitioner to a juvenile detention center to continue the interrogation. After initially denying any involvement in the Keg Liquors shooting, petitioner eventually confessed to that crime as well.

Subsequent to his indictment for murder, petitioner moved to suppress the confession on the grounds that it had been impermissibly coerced in violation of the Fifth and Fourteenth Amendments to the Federal Constitution.[7] At the ensuing hearing, he testified that he had been detained in a windowless room for a protracted period of time, that he had been surrounded by as many as six police officers during the interrogation, that he had repeatedly requested and been denied permission to telephone his mother, and that he had been badgered into making a false confession. Several police officers offered a different version of the relevant events. Concluding that there had been "no sweating or coercion of the defendant" and "no overreaching" by the police, the court denied the motion. *Id.*, at 21.

The case proceeded to trial. In his opening statement, the prosecutor stressed that the Commonwealth's case rested almost entirely on petitioner's confession and on the statement of his uncle, who had told the police that he was also present during the holdup and murder. Tr. 10–14. In response, defense counsel outlined what would prove to be the principal avenue of defense advanced at trial—that, for a number of reasons, the story petitioner had told the police should not be believed. The confession was rife with inconsistencies, counsel argued. For example, petitioner had told the police that the crime was committed during daylight hours and that he had stolen a sum of money from the cash register. In fact, counsel told the jury, the evidence would show that the crime occurred at 10:40 p.m. and that no money at all was missing from the store. Beyond these inconsistencies, counsel suggested, "[t]he very circumstances surrounding the giving of the [confession] are enough to cast doubt on its credibility." *Id.*, at 16. In particular, she continued, evidence bearing on the length of the interrogation and the manner in which it was conducted would show that the statement was unworthy of belief.

In response to defense counsel's opening statement, and before any evidence was presented to the jury, the prosecutor moved *in limine* to prevent the defense from introducing any testimony bearing on the circumstances under which the confession was obtained. Such testimony bore only on the "voluntariness" of the confession, the prosecutor urged, a "legal matter" that had already been resolved by the court in its earlier ruling. App. 27. Defense counsel responded that she had no intention of relitigating the issue of voluntariness, but was seeking only to demonstrate that the circumstances of the confession "cas[t] doubt on its validity and its credibility." *Ibid.* Rejecting this reasoning, the court granted the prosecutor's motion. Although the precise contours of the ruling are somewhat ambiguous, the court expressly held that the defense could inquire into the inconsistencies contained in the confession, but would not be permitted to "develop in front of the jury" any evidence about the duration of the interrogation or the individuals who were in attendance. *Id.*, at 28.

7. [In many jurisdictions, an objection to the admissibility of evidence based on constitutional grounds must be made before trial as a motion to suppress. The Supreme Court had long held that an "involuntary" (coercive) confession violated due process. Ed.]

After registering a continuing objection, petitioner invoked a Kentucky procedure under which he was permitted to develop a record of the evidence he would have put before the jury were it not for the court's evidentiary ruling. That evidence included testimony from two police officers about the size and other physical characteristics of the interrogation room, the length of the interview, and various other details about the taking of the confession. *Id.*, at 45–53.

The jury returned a verdict of guilty, and petitioner was sentenced to 40 years in prison. The sole issue in the ensuing appeal to the Kentucky Supreme Court was whether the exclusion of testimony about the circumstances of the confession violated petitioner's rights under the Sixth and Fourteenth Amendments to the Federal Constitution. Over one dissent, the court rejected the claim and affirmed the conviction and sentence. 690 S.W.2d 753 (1985). The excluded testimony "related solely to voluntariness," the court reasoned. *Id.*, at 754. * * *

II

The holding below rests on the apparent assumption that evidence bearing on the voluntariness of a confession and evidence bearing on its credibility fall in conceptually distinct and mutually exclusive categories. Once a confession has been found voluntary, the Supreme Court of Kentucky believed, the evidence that supported that finding may not be presented to the jury for any other purpose. This analysis finds no support in our cases, is premised on a misconception about the role of confessions in a criminal trial, and, under the circumstances of this case, contributed to an evidentiary ruling that deprived petitioner of his fundamental constitutional right to a fair opportunity to present a defense. *California v. Trombetta*, 467 U.S. 479, 485 (1984).

It is by now well established that "certain interrogation techniques, either in isolation, or as applied to the unique characteristics of a particular suspect, are so offensive to a civilized system of justice that they must be condemned under the Due Process Clause of the Fourteenth Amendment." *Miller v. Fenton*, 474 U.S. 104, 109 (1985). To assure that the fruits of such techniques are never used to secure a conviction, due process also requires "that a jury [not] hear a confession unless and until the trial judge [or some other independent decisionmaker] has determined that it was freely and voluntarily given." *Sims v. Georgia*, 385 U.S. 538, 543–544 (1967). See generally *Jackson v. Denno*, 378 U.S. 368 (1964).

In laying down these rules the Court has never questioned that "evidence surrounding the making of a confession bears on its credibility" as well as its voluntariness. *Id.*, at 386, n.13 * * *. [T]o the extent the Court has addressed the question at all, it has expressly assumed that evidence about the manner in which a confession was secured will often be germane to its probative weight, a matter that is exclusively for the jury to assess.

The decisions in both *Jackson* and *Lego* [v. Twomey, 404 U.S. 477 (1972)], while not framed in the language of constitutional command, reflect the common-sense understanding that the circumstances surrounding the taking of a confession can be highly relevant to two separate inquiries, one legal and one factual. The manner in which a statement was extracted is, of course, relevant to the purely legal question of its voluntariness, a question most, but not all, States assign to the trial judge alone to resolve. * * * But the physical and psychological environment that yielded the confession can also be of substantial relevance to the ultimate factual issue of the defendant's guilt or innocence. Confessions, even those that have been found to be voluntary, are not conclusive of guilt. And, as with any other part of the prosecutor's case, a confession may be shown to be "insufficiently corroborated or otherwise * * * unworthy of belief." *Lego v. Twomey, supra,* 404 U.S., at 485–486 * * *. Indeed, stripped of the power to describe to the jury the circumstances that prompted his confession, the defendant is effectively disabled from answering the one question every rational juror needs answered: If the defendant is innocent, why did he previously admit his guilt? Accordingly, regardless of whether the defendant marshaled the same evidence earlier in support of an unsuccessful motion to suppress, and entirely independent of any question of voluntariness, a defendant's case may stand or fall on his ability to convince the jury that the manner in which the confession was obtained casts doubt on its credibility.

This simple insight is reflected in a federal statute, 18 U.S.C. § 3501(a), the Federal Rules of Evidence, Fed. Rule Evid. 104(e), and the statutory and decisional law of virtually every State in the Nation. See, *e.g.,* Mont.Code Ann. § 46–13–301(5) (1983); * * *

Whether rooted directly in the Due Process Clause of the Fourteenth Amendment, * * * or in the Compulsory Process or Confrontation clauses of the Sixth Amendment, * * * the Constitution guarantees criminal defendants "a meaningful opportunity to present a complete defense." *California v. Trombetta,* 467 U.S., at 485 * * *. We break no new ground in observing that an essential component of procedural fairness is an opportunity to be heard. * * * That opportunity would be an empty one if the State were permitted to exclude competent, reliable evidence bearing on the credibility of a confession when such evidence is central to the defendant's claim of innocence. In the absence of any valid state justification, exclusion of this kind of exculpatory evidence deprives a defendant of the basic right to have the prosecutor's case encounter and "survive the crucible of meaningful adversarial testing." *United States v. Cronic,* 466 U.S. 648, 656 (1984). * * *

Under these principles, the Kentucky courts erred in foreclosing petitioner's efforts to introduce testimony about the environment in which the police secured his confession. As both *Lego* and *Jackson* make clear, evidence about the manner in which a confession was obtained is often highly relevant to its reliability and credibility. Such evidence was especially relevant in the rather peculiar circumstances of this case.

Petitioner's entire defense was that there was no physical evidence to link him to the crime and that, for a variety of reasons, his earlier admission of guilt was not to be believed. To support that defense, he sought to paint a picture of a young, uneducated boy who was kept against his will in a small, windowless room for a protracted period of time until he confessed to every unsolved crime in the county, including the one for which he now stands convicted. We do not, of course, pass on the strength or merits of that defense. We do, however, think it plain that introducing evidence of the physical circumstances that yielded the confession was all but indispensable to any chance of its succeeding. Especially since neither the Supreme Court of Kentucky in its opinion, nor respondent in its argument to this Court, has advanced any rational justification for the wholesale exclusion of this body of potentially exculpatory evidence, the decision below must be reversed.

* * *

So ordered.

Notes and Questions

1. *"Admissibility v. weight."* Rule 104 allocates certain decisions to the trial judge. The judge decides issues of admissibility, which often include factual issues. For example, the admissibility of statements falling within the hearsay exception for declarations against interest, Rule 804(b)(3), depends upon the unavailability of the declarant—a question of fact if unavailability is based on the death of the declarant. Admissibility also depends upon whether the statement "possesses the required against-interest characteristics"—the application of a legal standard. Fed.R.Evid. 104 advisory committee's note. Once the court decides to admit the evidence, the jury decides what "weight" the evidence is to be accorded. *Crane* and Rule 104(e) preserve a party's right to challenge the evidence before the jury.

2. *Applicability of rules of evidence.* Should the judge, in taking evidence to aid in deciding questions of fact, be governed by the rules of evidence? Rule 104(a) states explicitly that in determining preliminary questions concerning the admissibility of evidence the judge is not bound by evidentiary rules with the exception of privilege. See Bourjaily v. United States, 483 U.S. 171 (1987) (court may consider alleged coconspirator statement itself in determining whether conspiracy exists preliminary to admissibility of the statement).

3. *Standard of proof.* Rule 104(a) does not specify the standard of proof to be observed in determining such preliminary questions. However, *Bourjaily*, note 2, supra, resolved that issue, holding that it must be established by a "preponderance of proof." 483 U.S. at 175–76.

4. *Overlapping functions.* Sometimes the allocation of responsibility between judge and jury presents overlapping roles. For example, the hearsay exemption for coconspirator statements, Rule 801(d)(2)(E), requires the judge to determine the existence of a conspiracy as a prerequisite to admitting the statement; the "preponderance of evidence" standard applies. If the defendant is also charged with a substantive count of conspiracy, the

jury will have to decide the existence of a conspiracy—using the "beyond a reasonable doubt" standard applicable in criminal trials. The judge does not inform the jury of the basis of the admissibility decision.

5. *Out-of-court hearings.* Rule 104(c) requires that hearings on the admissibility of a confession shall be conducted outside the presence of the jury. The court has discretion to hold hearings to determine other preliminary questions under Rule 104 outside the presence of the jury. In exercising this discretion, the primary concern of the judge will be the potential for prejudice inherent in the evidence that will be produced by the parties on the preliminary question.

HUDDLESTON v. UNITED STATES

Supreme Court of the United States, 1988.
485 U.S. 681.

CHIEF JUSTICE REHNQUIST delivered the opinion of the Court.

Federal Rule of Evidence 404(b) provides:

> "Other crimes, wrongs, or acts.—Evidence of other crimes, wrongs, or acts is not admissible to prove the character of a person in order to show action in conformity therewith. It may, however, be admissible for other purposes, such as proof of motive, opportunity, intent, preparation, plan, knowledge, identity, or absence of mistake or accident."

This case presents the question whether the district court must itself make a preliminary finding that the Government has proved the "other act" by a preponderance of the evidence before it submits the evidence to the jury. We hold that it need not do so.

Petitioner, Guy Rufus Huddleston, was charged with one count of selling stolen goods in interstate commerce, 18 U.S.C. § 2315, and one count of possessing stolen property in interstate commerce, 18 U.S.C. § 659. The two counts related to two portions of a shipment of stolen Memorex videocassette tapes that petitioner was alleged to have possessed and sold, knowing that they were stolen.

The evidence at trial showed that a trailer containing over 32,000 blank Memorex videocassette tapes with a manufacturing cost of $4.53 per tape was stolen from the Overnight Express yard in South Holland, Illinois, sometime between April 11 and 15, 1985. On April 17, 1985, petitioner contacted Karen Curry, the manager of the Magic Rent-to-Own in Ypsilanti, Michigan seeking her assistance in selling a large number of blank Memorex videocassette tapes. After assuring Curry that the tapes were not stolen, he told her he wished to sell them in lots of at least 500 at $2.75 to $3 per tape. Curry subsequently arranged for the sale of a total of 5,000 tapes, which petitioner delivered to the various purchasers—who apparently believed the sales were legitimate.

There was no dispute that the tapes which petitioner sold were stolen; the only material issue at trial was whether petitioner knew they were stolen. The District Court allowed the Government to introduce evidence of "similar acts" under Rule 404(b), concluding that such evidence had "clear relevance as to [petitioner's knowledge]." App. 11. The first piece of similar act evidence offered by the Government was the testimony of Paul Toney, a record store owner. He testified that in February 1985, petitioner offered to sell new 12 black and white televisions for $28 apiece. According to Toney, petitioner indicated that he could obtain several thousand of these televisions. Petitioner and Toney eventually traveled to the Magic Rent-to-Own, where Toney purchased 20 of the televisions. Several days later, Toney purchased 18 more televisions.

The second piece of similar act evidence was the testimony of Robert Nelson, an undercover FBI agent posing as a buyer for an appliance store. Nelson testified that in May 1985, petitioner offered to sell him a large quantity of Amana appliances—28 refrigerators, 2 ranges, and 40 icemakers. Nelson agreed to pay $8,000 for the appliances. Petitioner was arrested shortly after he arrived at the parking lot where he and Nelson had agreed to transfer the appliances. A truck containing the appliances was stopped a short distance from the parking lot, and Leroy Wesby, who was driving the truck, was also arrested. It was determined that the appliances had a value of approximately $20,000 and were part of a shipment that had been stolen.

Petitioner testified that the Memorex tapes, the televisions, and the appliances had all been provided by Leroy Wesby, who had represented that all of the merchandise was obtained legitimately. Petitioner stated that he had sold 6,500 Memorex tapes for Wesby on a commission basis. Petitioner maintained that all of the sales for Wesby had been on a commission basis and that he had no knowledge that any of the goods were stolen.

[The Court explained that the circuit courts had divided on the issue. Some applied the "preponderance of evidence" standard, some the "clear and convincing evidence" standard, and still others applied a prima facie standard based on Rule 104(b).]

* * *

Federal Rule of Evidence 404(b)—which applies in both civil and criminal cases—generally prohibits the introduction of evidence of extrinsic acts that might adversely reflect on the actor's character, unless that evidence bears upon a relevant issue in the case such as motive, opportunity, or knowledge. Extrinsic acts evidence may be critical to the establishment of the truth as to a disputed issue, especially when that issue involves the actor's state of mind and the only means of ascertaining that mental state is by drawing inferences from conduct. The actor in the instant case was a criminal defendant, and the act in question was "similar" to the one with which he was charged. Our use of these terms is not meant to suggest that our analysis is limited to such circumstances.

Before this Court, petitioner argues that the District Court erred in admitting Toney's testimony as to petitioner's sale of the televisions. The threshold inquiry a court must make before admitting similar acts evidence under Rule 404(b) is whether that evidence is probative of a material issue other than character. The Government's theory of relevance was that the televisions were stolen, and proof that petitioner had engaged in a series of sales of stolen merchandise from the same suspicious source would be strong evidence that he was aware that each of these items, including the Memorex tapes, was stolen. As such, the sale of the televisions was a "similar act" only if the televisions were stolen. Petitioner acknowledges that this evidence was admitted for the proper purpose of showing his knowledge that the Memorex tapes were stolen. He asserts, however, that the evidence should not have been admitted because the Government failed to prove to the District Court that the televisions were in fact stolen.

Petitioner argues from the premise that evidence of similar acts has a grave potential for causing improper prejudice. For instance, the jury may choose to punish the defendant for the similar rather than the charged act, or the jury may infer that the defendant is an evil person inclined to violate the law. Because of this danger, petitioner maintains, the jury ought not to be exposed to similar act evidence until the trial court has heard the evidence and made a determination under Federal Rule of Evidence 104(a) that the defendant committed the similar act. Rule 104(a) provides that "[p]reliminary questions concerning the qualification of a person to be a witness, the existence of a privilege, or the admissibility of evidence shall be determined by the court, subject to the provisions of subdivision (b)." According to petitioner, the trial court must make this preliminary finding by at least a preponderance of the evidence.

We reject petitioner's position, for it is inconsistent with the structure of the Rules of Evidence and with the plain language of Rule 404(b). Article IV of the Rules of Evidence deals with the relevancy of evidence. Rules 401 and 402 establish the broad principle that relevant evidence—evidence that makes the existence of any fact at issue more or less probable—is admissible unless the Rules provide otherwise. Rule 403 allows the trial judge to exclude relevant evidence if, among other things, "its probative value is substantially outweighed by the danger of unfair prejudice." Rules 404 through 412 address specific types of evidence that have generated problems. Generally, these latter Rules do not flatly prohibit the introduction of such evidence but instead limit the purpose for which it may be introduced. Rule 404(b), for example, protects against the introduction of extrinsic act evidence when that evidence is offered solely to prove character. The text contains no intimation, however, that any preliminary showing is necessary before such evidence may be introduced for a proper purpose. If offered for such a proper purpose, the evidence is subject only to general strictures limiting admissibility such as Rules 402 and 403.

Petitioner's reading of Rule 404(b) as mandating a preliminary finding by the trial court that the act in question occurred not only superimposes a level of judicial oversight that is nowhere apparent from the language of that provision, but it is simply inconsistent with the legislative history behind Rule 404(b). The Advisory Committee specifically declined to offer any "mechanical solution" to the admission of evidence under 404(b). Advisory Committee's Notes on Fed.Rule Evid. 404(b), 28 U.S.C.App., p. 691. Rather, the Committee indicated that the trial court should assess such evidence under the usual rules for admissibility: "The determination must be made whether the danger of undue prejudice outweighs the probative value of the evidence in view of the availability of other means of proof and other factors appropriate for making decisions of this kind under Rule 403." *Ibid.* see also S.Rep. No. 93–1277, p. 25 (1974) ("[I]t is anticipated that with respect to permissible uses for such evidence, the trial judge may exclude it only on the basis of those considerations set forth in Rule 403, *i.e.* prejudice, confusion or waste of time").

Petitioner's suggestion that a preliminary finding is necessary to protect the defendant from the potential for unfair prejudice is also belied by the Reports of the House of Representatives and the Senate. The House made clear that the version of Rule 404(b) which became law was intended to "plac[e] greater emphasis on admissibility than did the final Court version." H.R.Rep. No. 93–650, p. 7 (1973). The Senate echoed this theme: "[T]he use of the discretionary word 'may' with respect to the admissibility of evidence of crimes, wrongs, or other acts is not intended to confer any arbitrary discretion on the trial judge." S.Rep. No. 93–1277, *supra,* at 24. Thus, Congress was not nearly so concerned with the potential prejudicial effect of Rule 404(b) evidence as it was with ensuring that restrictions would not be placed on the admission of such evidence.

We conclude that a preliminary finding by the court that the Government has proved the act by a preponderance of the evidence is not called for under Rule 104(a).[8] This is not to say, however, that the Government may parade past the jury a litany of potentially prejudicial similar acts that have been established or connected to the defendant only by unsubstantiated innuendo. Evidence is admissible under Rule 404(b) only if it is relevant. "Relevancy is not an inherent characteristic of any item of evidence but exists only as a relation between an item of evidence and a matter properly provable in the case." Advisory Committee's Notes on Fed.Rule Evid. 401, 28 U.S.C.App., p. 688. In the Rule

8. Petitioner also suggests that in performing the balancing prescribed by Federal Rule of Evidence 403, the trial court must find that the prejudicial potential of similar acts evidence substantially outweighs its probative value unless the court concludes by a preponderance of the evidence that the defendant committed the similar act. We reject this suggestion because Rule 403 admits of no such gloss and because such a holding would be erroneous for the same reasons that a preliminary finding under Rule 104(a) is inappropriate. We do, however, agree with the Government's concession at oral argument that the strength of the evidence establishing the similar act is one of the factors the court may consider when conducting the Rule 403 balancing. Tr. of Oral Arg. 26.

404(b) context, similar act evidence is relevant only if the jury can reasonably conclude that the act occurred and that the defendant was the actor. See *United States v. Beechum,* 582 F.2d 898, 912–913 (C.A.5 1978) (en banc). In the instant case, the evidence that petitioner was selling the televisions was relevant under the Government's theory only if the jury could reasonably find that the televisions were stolen.

Such questions of relevance conditioned on a fact are dealt with under Federal Rule of Evidence 104(b). *Beechum, supra,* at 912–913; see also E. Imwinkelried, Uncharged Misconduct Evidence § 2.06 (1984). Rule 104(b) provides:

> "When the relevancy of evidence depends upon the fulfillment of a condition of fact, the court shall admit it upon, or subject to, the introduction of evidence sufficient to support a finding of the fulfillment of the condition."

In determining whether the Government has introduced sufficient evidence to meet Rule 104(b), the trial court neither weighs credibility nor makes a finding that the Government has proved the conditional fact by a preponderance of the evidence. The court simply examines all the evidence in the case and decides whether the jury could reasonably find the conditional fact—here, that the televisions were stolen—by a preponderance of the evidence. See 21 C. Wright & K. Graham, Federal Practice and Procedure § 5054, p. 269 (1977). The trial court has traditionally exercised the broadest sort of discretion in controlling the order of proof at trial, and we see nothing in the Rules of Evidence that would change this practice. Often the trial court may decide to allow the proponent to introduce evidence concerning a similar act, and at a later point in the trial assess whether sufficient evidence has been offered to permit the jury to make the requisite finding. If the proponent has failed to meet this minimal standard of proof, the trial court must instruct the jury to disregard the evidence.

We emphasize that in assessing the sufficiency of the evidence under Rule 104(b), the trial court must consider all evidence presented to the jury. "[I]ndividual pieces of evidence, insufficient in themselves to prove a point, may in cumulation prove it. The sum of an evidentiary presentation may well be greater than its constituent parts." *Bourjaily v. United States,* 483 U.S. 171, 179–180 (1987). In assessing whether the evidence was sufficient to support a finding that the televisions were stolen, the court here was required to consider not only the direct evidence on that point—the low price of the televisions, the large quantity offered for sale, and petitioner's inability to produce a bill of sale—but also the evidence concerning petitioner's involvement in the sales of other stolen merchandise obtained from Wesby, such as the Memorex tapes and the Amana appliances. Given this evidence, the jury reasonably could have concluded that the televisions were stolen, and the trial court therefore properly allowed the evidence to go to the jury.

We share petitioner's concern that unduly prejudicial evidence might be introduced under Rule 404(b). See *Michelson v. United States,*

335 U.S. 469, 475–476 (1948). We think, however, that the protection against such unfair prejudice emanates not from a requirement of a preliminary finding by the trial court, but rather from four other sources: first, from the requirement of Rule 404(b) that the evidence be offered for a proper purpose; second, from the relevancy requirement of Rule 402—as enforced through Rule 104(b); third, from the assessment the trial court must make under Rule 403 to determine whether the probative value of the similar acts evidence is substantially outweighed by its potential for unfair prejudice, see Advisory Committee's Notes on Fed.Rule Evid. 404(b), 28 U.S.C.App., p. 691; S.Rep. No. 93–1277, at 25; and fourth, from Federal Rule of Evidence 105, which provides that the trial court shall, upon request, instruct the jury that the similar acts evidence is to be considered only for the proper purpose for which it was admitted. See *United States v. Ingraham,* 832 F.2d 229, 235 (C.A.1 1987).

Affirmed.

Notes

1. *Conditional relevance.* When dealing with a matter of "conditional relevancy," as in *Huddleston*, the judge still has a role, albeit a somewhat limited one, in determining whether the foundation evidence is sufficient for the jury to reasonably find the condition fulfilled. In performing this function, the court may consider only evidence admissible under the rules of evidence since the jury will have only such evidence before it when it makes the final determination of the existence of the fact. 1 Graham, Handbook of Federal Evidence § 104.2 (6th ed. 2006).

2. *State positions.* Some jurisdictions have rejected the result in the *Huddleston* case with regard to application of Rule 104(b) either by judicial decision, see, e.g., People v. Garner, 806 P.2d 366 (Colo.1991) (adopts preponderance of evidence standard), and Robinson v. United States, 623 A.2d 1234 (D.C.App.1993) (clear and convincing evidence required), or by amendment of state Rule 404(b), see, e.g., Minn.R.Evid. 404(b) (1989) ("such evidence shall not be admitted unless the other crime, wrong, or act and the participation in it by a relevant person are proven by clear and convincing evidence"). The American Bar Association House of Delegates has endorsed a recommendation from its Criminal Justice Section that *Huddleston* be reversed and a clear and convincing standard adopted. 44 Crim.L.Rptr. (BNA) 2376 (Feb. 22, 1989). See also discussion in Ordover, Balancing the Presumptions of Guilt and Innocence: Rules 404(b), 608(b) and 609(a), 38 Emory L.J. 135 (1989).

3. *Reference.* See generally Callen, Rationality and Relevancy: Conditional Relevancy and Constrained Resources, 2003 Mich.St.L.Rev. 1243.

Note on Plain–Meaning Jurisprudence

Beginning in the late 1980s, the Supreme Court employed a plain-meaning standard in interpreting the Federal Rules of Evidence. Such a method of "statutory interpretation" requires courts to follow a Rule's literal language unless ambiguous. Its primary interpretative tool is the statutory text itself, giving those words their ordinary meaning.

This mode of analysis is exemplified by *Huddleston*, where the Court held that Rule 104(b)'s very lenient standard of proof governed the determination of the defendant's involvement in other crimes that were offered by the government under Rule 404(b) to establish his guilty knowledge in the charged crime. Finding that imposing a higher standard of proof was inconsistent with the structure of the Rules and the "plain language" of Rule 404(b), the Court rejected substantial authority from the federal circuit courts that imposed special admission standards on other crimes evidence because of their special dangers of prejudice. Similarly, in Bourjaily v. United States, 483 U.S. 171 (1987), the Court used plain-meaning analysis in ruling that, contrary to longstanding pre-Rules practice, a putative coconspirator statement could be considered by the trial court in finding the existence of a conspiracy involving the person making the statement. The effect of the ruling was to permit the statement to be employed to help establish its own admissibility under Rule 801(d)(2)(E). See also United States v. Owens, 484 U.S. 554 (1988) (using plain meaning to interpret "subject to cross-examination" language of Rule 801(d)(1)).

However, despite the apparent dominance of this mode of analysis championed by Justice Scalia, the Court has occasionally used quite traditional methodology, suggesting that it is not yet fully committed to plain-meaning analysis. See Old Chief v. United States, 519 U.S. 172 (1997) (citing advisory committee notes); Tome v. United States, 513 U.S. 150, 160 (1995) ("Our conclusion that Rule 801(d)(1)(B) embodies the common-law premotive requirement is confirmed by an examination of the Advisory Committee's Notes to the Federal Rules of Evidence. We have relied on those well-considered Notes as a useful guide in ascertaining the meaning of the Rules."); Green v. Bock Laundry Machine Co., 490 U.S. 504 (1989) (extensive examination of legislative history materials undertaken to determine whether Rule 403 applies in deciding if witness in civil case could be impeached with prior conviction under Rule 609(a)(1)).

The general effect of the plain-meaning method of interpreting the Federal Rules is to diminish the importance of extrinsic interpretative aids such as common law history, pre-Rules precedent, and general policy. See generally Becker & Orenstein, The Federal Rules of Evidence After Sixteen Years—The Effect of "Plain Meaning" Jurisprudence, the Need for an Advisory Committee on the Rules of Evidence, and Suggestions for Selective Revision of the Rules, 60 Geo.Wash.L.Rev. 857 (1992); Imwinkelried, A Brief Defense of the Supreme Court's Approach to the Interpretation of the Federal Rules of Evidence, 27 Ind.L.Rev. 267 (1993); Jonakait, The Supreme Court, Plain Meaning, and the Changed Rules of Evidence, 68 Tex.L.Rev. 745 (1990); Weissenberger, The Supreme Court and the Interpretation of the Federal Rules of Evidence, 53 Ohio St.L.J. 1307 (1992).

UNITED STATES v. ZOLIN

Supreme Court of the United States, 1989.
491 U.S. 554.

JUSTICE BLACKMUN delivered the opinion of the Court.

This case arises out of the efforts of the Criminal Investigation Division of the Internal Revenue Service (IRS) to investigate the tax returns of L. Ron Hubbard, founder of the Church of Scientology * * *.

[In the course of its investigation, the IRS sought access to documents that had been filed under seal in state court in connection with a suit by the Church of Scientology against one its former members. The suit charged that the former member had obtained documentary materials relating to Church activities, including two tapes, by unlawful means. The Church objected to production of the documents, *inter alia*, on the ground of attorney-client privilege. The IRS argued that the tapes fell within the crime-fraud exception to the privilege and urged the district court to listen to the tapes in making its privilege determination. Both the district court and the Ninth Circuit refused to apply the crime-fraud exception, finding no independent evidence to support it.]

* * * The specific question presented is whether the applicability of the crime-fraud exception must be established by "independent evidence" (i.e., without reference to the content of the contested communications themselves), or, alternatively, whether the applicability of that exception can be resolved by an *in camera* inspection of the allegedly privileged material. * * *

* * *

III

Questions of privilege that arise in the course of the adjudication of federal rights are "governed by the principles of the common law as they may be interpreted by the courts of the United States in the light of reason and experience." Fed.Rule Evid. 501. We have recognized the attorney-client privilege under federal law, as "the oldest of the privileges for confidential communications known to the common law." *Upjohn Co. v. United States*, 449 U.S. 383, 389 (1981). Although the underlying rationale for the privilege has changed over time, see 8 J. Wigmore, Evidence § 2290 (McNaughton rev. 1961),[9] courts long have viewed its central concern as one "to encourage full and frank communication between attorneys and their clients and thereby promote broader public interests in the observance of law and administration of justice." *Upjohn*, 449 U.S., at 389. That purpose, of course, requires that clients be free to "make full disclosure to their attorneys" of past wrongdoings, *Fisher v. United States*, 425 U.S. 391, 403 (1976), in order that the client

9. See also Hazard, An Historical Perspective on the Attorney–Client Privilege, 66 Calif.L.Rev. 1061 (1978); Developments in the Law–Privileged Communications, 98 Harv.L.Rev. 1450, 1455–1458 (1985).

may obtain "the aid of persons having knowledge of the law and skilled in its practice," *Hunt v. Blackburn*, 128 U.S. 464, 470 (1888).

The attorney-client privilege is not without its costs. Cf. *Trammel v. United States*, 445 U.S. 40, 50 (1980). "[S]ince the privilege has the effect of withholding relevant information from the factfinder, it applies only where necessary to achieve its purpose." *Fisher*, 425 U.S., at 403. The attorney-client privilege must necessarily protect the confidences of wrongdoers, but the reason for that protection—the centrality of open client and attorney communication to the proper functioning of our adversary system of justice—"ceas[es] to operate at a certain point, namely, where the desired advice refers *not to prior wrongdoing, but to future wrongdoing*." 8 Wigmore, § 2298, p. 573 (emphasis in original); see also *Clark v. United States*, 289 U.S. 1, 15 (1933). It is the purpose of the crime-fraud exception to the attorney-client privilege to assure that the "seal of secrecy," ibid., between lawyer and client does not extend to communications "made for the purpose of getting advice for the commission of a fraud" or crime. *O'Rourke v. Darbishire*, [1920] A.C. 581, 604 (P.C.).

* * *

A

We consider first the question whether a district court may ever honor the request of the party opposing the privilege to conduct an *in camera* review of allegedly privileged communications to determine whether those communications fall within the crime-fraud exception. We conclude that no express provision of the Federal Rules of Evidence bars such use of *in camera* review, and that it would be unwise to prohibit it in all instances as a matter of federal common law.

(1)

At first blush, two provisions of the Federal Rules of Evidence would appear to be relevant. Rule 104(a) provides: "Preliminary questions concerning the qualification of a person to be a witness, *the existence of a privilege*, or the admissibility of evidence shall be determined by the court * * *. In making its determination it is not bound by the rules of evidence *except those with respect to privileges*." (Emphasis added.) Rule 1101(c) provides: "The rule with respect to privileges applies at all stages of all actions, cases, and proceedings." Taken together, these Rules might be read to establish that in a summons-enforcement proceeding, attorney-client communications cannot be considered by the district court in making its crime-fraud ruling: to do otherwise, under this view, would be to make the crime-fraud determination without due regard to the existence of the privilege.

Even those scholars who support this reading of Rule 104(a) acknowledge that it leads to an absurd result.

> "Because the judge must honor claims of privilege made during his preliminary fact determinations, many exceptions to the rules of

privilege will become 'dead letters,' since the preliminary facts that give rise to these exceptions can never be proved. For example, an exception to the attorney-client privilege provides that there is no privilege if the communication was made to enable anyone to commit a crime or fraud. There is virtually no way in which the exception can ever be proved, save by compelling disclosure of the contents of the communication; Rule 104(a) provides that this cannot be done." 21 C. Wright & K. Graham, Federal Practice & Procedure: Evidence § 5055, p. 276 (1977) (footnote omitted).

We find this Draconian interpretation of Rule 104(a) inconsistent with the Rule's plain language. The Rule does not provide by its terms that all materials as to which a "clai[m] of privilege" is made must be excluded from consideration. In that critical respect, the language of Rule 104(a) is markedly different from the comparable California evidence rule, which provides that "the presiding officer may not require disclosure of information *claimed to be privileged* under this division in order to rule on the claim of privilege." Cal.Evid.Code Ann. § 915(a) (West Supp.1989) (emphasis added). There is no reason to read Rule 104(a) as if its text were identical to that of the California rule.

* * *

We see no basis for holding that the tapes in this case must be deemed privileged under Rule 104(a) while the question of crime or fraud remains open. Indeed, respondents concede that "if the proponent of the privilege is able to sustain its burden only by submitting the communications to the court" for *in camera* review, Brief for Respondents 14–15 (emphasis in original), the court is not required to avert its eyes (or close its ears) once it concludes that the communication would be privileged, if the court found the crime-fraud exception inapplicable. Rather, respondents acknowledge that the court may "then consider the same communications to determine if the opponent of the privilege has established that the crime-fraud exception applies." *Id.*, at 15. Were the tapes truly deemed privileged under Rule 104(a) at the moment the trial court concludes they contain potentially privileged attorney-client communications, district courts would be required to draw precisely the counterintuitive distinction that respondents wisely reject. We thus shall not adopt a reading of Rule 104(a) that would treat the contested communications as "privileged" for purposes of the Rule, and we shall not interpret Rule 104(a) as categorically prohibiting the party opposing the privilege on crime-fraud grounds from relying on the results of an *in camera* review of the communications.

(2)

Having determined that Rule 104(a) does not prohibit the *in camera* review sought by the IRS, we must address the question as a matter of the federal common law of privileges. See Rule 501. We conclude that a complete prohibition against opponents' use of *in camera* review to establish the applicability of the crime-fraud exception is inconsistent with the policies underlying the privilege.

We begin our analysis by recognizing that disclosure of allegedly privileged materials to the district court for purposes of determining the merits of a claim of privilege does not have the legal effect of terminating the privilege. Indeed, this Court has approved the practice of requiring parties who seek to avoid disclosure of documents to make the documents available for *in camera* inspection, *see Kerr v. United States District Court for Northern District of Cal.*, 426 U.S. 394, 404–405 (1976), and the practice is well established in the federal courts. *See, e.g., In re Antitrust Grand Jury*, 805 F.2d 155, 168 (C.A.6 1986); *In re Vargas*, 723 F.2d 1461, 1467 (C.A.10 1983); *United States v. Lawless*, 709 F.2d 485, 486, 488 (C.A.7 1983); *In re Grand Jury Witness*, 695 F.2d 359, 362 (C.A.9 1982). Respondents do not dispute this point: they acknowledge that they would have been free to request *in camera* review to establish the fact that the tapes involved attorney-client communications, had they been unable to muster independent evidence to serve that purpose. Brief for Respondents 14–15.

Once it is clear that *in camera* review does not destroy the privileged nature of the contested communications, the question of the propriety of that review turns on whether the policies underlying the privilege and its exceptions are better fostered by permitting such review or by prohibiting it. In our view, the costs of imposing an absolute bar to consideration of the communications *in camera* for purpose of establishing the crime-fraud exception are intolerably high. * * *

B

We turn to the question whether *in camera* review at the behest of the party asserting the crime-fraud exception is always permissible, or, in contrast, whether the party seeking *in camera* review must make some threshold showing that such review is appropriate. In addressing this question, we attend to the detrimental effect, if any, of *in camera* review on the policies underlying the privilege and on the orderly administration of justice in our courts. We conclude that some such showing must be made.

Our endorsement of the practice of testing proponents' privilege claims through *in camera* review of the allegedly privileged documents has not been without reservation. This Court noted in *United States v. Reynolds*, 345 U.S. 1 (1953), a case which presented a delicate question concerning the disclosure of military secrets, that "examination of the evidence, even by the judge alone, in chambers" might in some cases "jeopardize the security which the privilege is meant to protect." *id.*, at 10. Analogizing to claims of Fifth Amendment privilege, it observed more generally: "Too much judicial inquiry into the claim of privilege would force disclosure of the thing the privilege was meant to protect, while a complete abandonment of judicial control would lead to intolerable abuses." *id.*, at 8. * * *

We think that the following standard strikes the correct balance. Before engaging in *in camera* review to determine the applicability of the crime-fraud exception, "the judge should require a showing of a factual basis adequate to support a good faith belief by a reasonable person," *Caldwell v. District Court*, 644 P.2d 26, 33 (Colo.1982), that *in camera* review of the materials may reveal evidence to establish the claim that the crime-fraud exception applies. * * *

C

The question remains as to what kind of evidence a district court may consider in determining whether it has the discretion to undertake an *in camera* review of an allegedly privileged communication at the behest of the party opposing the privilege. Here, the issue is whether the partial transcripts may be used by the IRS in support of its request for *in camera* review of the tapes.

The answer to that question, in the first instance, must be found in Rule 104(a), which establishes that materials that have been determined to be privileged may not be considered in making the preliminary determination of the existence of a privilege. * * *

* * * We conclude that the party opposing the privilege may use any nonprivileged evidence in support of its request for *in camera* review, even if its evidence is not "independent" of the contested communications as the Court of Appeals uses that term.[10]

D

In sum, we conclude that a rigid independent evidence requirement does not comport with "reason and experience," Fed.Rule Evid. 501, and we decline to adopt it as part of the developing federal common law of evidentiary privileges. We hold that *in camera* review may be used to determine whether allegedly privileged attorney-client communications fall within the crime-fraud exception. We further hold, however, that before a district court may engage in *in camera* review at the request of the party opposing the privilege, that party must present evidence sufficient to support a reasonable belief that *in camera* review may yield evidence that establishes the exception's applicability. Finally, we hold that the threshold showing to obtain *in camera* review may be met by using any relevant evidence, lawfully obtained, that has not been adjudicated to be privileged. * * *

It is so ordered.

10. In addition, we conclude that evidence that is not "independent" of the contents of allegedly privileged communications—like the partial transcripts in this case—may be used not only in the pursuit of *in camera* review, but also may provide the evidentiary basis for the ultimate showing that the crime-fraud exception applies. We see little to distinguish these two uses: in both circumstances, if the evidence has not itself been determined to be privileged, its exclusion does not serve the policies which underlie the attorney-client privilege. See generally Note, The Future Crime or Tort Exception to Communications Privileges, 77 Harv.L.Rev. 730, 737 (1964).

JUSTICE BRENNAN took no part in the consideration or decision of this case.

Notes and Questions

1. *In camera review.* As *Zolin* demonstrates, when the preliminary question to be decided involves the existence of a privileged relationship, the determination becomes complicated because of the simultaneous demands to protect the arguably privileged information and to determine fairly whether any valid privilege exists. A delicate compromise between honoring and breaching the privilege often results. The Court's conclusion that an *in camera* review "does not destroy the privilege," 491 U.S. at 569, is critical in permitting this delicate compromise to proceed. In determining whether to conduct an *in camera* review, the court need not consider information offered by the party opposing review. In re Grand Jury Subpoena 92–1(SJ), 31 F.3d 826, 829–30 (9th Cir.1994).

2. *Sources.* For general treatments of the process of determining preliminary questions of fact, see Maguire & Epstein, Preliminary Questions of Fact in Determining the Admissibility of Evidence, 40 Harv.L.Rev. 392 (1927); Morgan, Functions of Judge and Jury in the Determination of Preliminary Questions of Fact, 43 Harv.L.Rev. 165 (1929); Morgan & Maguire, Looking Backward and Forward at Evidence, 50 Harv.L.Rev. 909, 913–18 (1937); Kaplan, Of Mabrus and Zorgs—An Essay in Honor of David Louisell, 66 Calif.L.Rev. 987 (1978). As to conditional relevancy, see Allen, The Myth of Conditional Relevance, 25 Loy.L.A.L.Rev. 871 (1992); Ball, The Myth of Conditional Relevancy, 14 Ga.L.Rev. 435 (1980); Nance, Conditional Relevance Reinterpreted, 70 B.U.L.Rev. 447 (1990); Seidelson, Conditional Relevancy and Federal Rule of Evidence 104(b), 47 Geo.Wash.L.Rev. 1048 (1979).

3. The attorney-client privilege and the crime-fraud exception to that privilege, which were at issue in *Zolin*, are examined in Chapter 15, Section B, infra.

SECTION B. PARTY RESPONSIBILITY

(1) OBJECTIONS: FEDERAL RULE 103(a)(1)

WILSON v. WILLIAMS

United States Court of Appeals, Seventh Circuit, En Banc, 1999.
182 F.3d 562.

EASTERBROOK, CIRCUIT JUDGE.

* * *

Jackie Wilson alleges in this suit under 42 U.S.C. § 1983 that James Williams, a guard at the Cook County Jail, attacked him without provocation and inflicted serious injuries. Williams contends that Wilson was the aggressor and that the force used in defense was reasonable under the circumstances. * * *

[Andrew Wilson, the plaintiff's brother, shot and killed two police officers. The plaintiff was an accomplice. Both Wilsons were serving terms of life imprisonment without possibility of parole, and both filed § 1983 suits contending that they were beaten (in separate incidents) while in custody before their convictions.] Andrew recovered a substantial judgment, Wilson v. Chicago, 120 F.3d 681 (7th Cir.1997), though he had trouble receiving a fair trial because the defendants harped on the nature of the crime he had committed. See Wilson v. Chicago, 6 F.3d 1233 (7th Cir.1993) (reversing an initial jury verdict in defendants' favor because the district judge failed to control inappropriate use of Andrew's criminal history).

Before the second trial of his civil suit began, Jackie Wilson asked the district judge to prevent Williams from informing the jury that he had been convicted of killing a police officer. * * * Nonetheless, the judge denied the motion *in limine*,[11] and when the trial began Wilson tried to make the best of his situation. His lawyer told the jury during his opening statement why Wilson was in custody and tried to use this to Wilson's advantage by arguing that Williams attacked Wilson because of the nature of Wilson's crime. Although Wilson's lawyer used the nature of the crime circumspectly, Williams's counsel had no reservations about the subject and invited the jury to rule against Wilson on emotional grounds. Practically the first words of counsel's opening statement were:

> I'd like to reintroduce the litigant, Jackie Wilson, cop killer, murdered a Chicago police officer who was on duty, Officer O'Brien. He also robbed Officer O'Brien. He was convicted of that. He also robbed Officer O'Brien's partner, Officer Fahey. He was also convicted of that. And, yes, that is the crime he was waiting trial on back in 1988 in the Cook County Jail.

Throughout the trial, Williams's lawyer did not miss an opportunity to remind the jury that Wilson had committed a despicable offense, and therefore must be a despicable person who should not collect a dime. Defense counsel was not satisfied with a suggestion that the jury should consider the conviction in connection with Wilson's credibility as a witness. The nature of the crime colored the trial. "Cop killer" was the refrain; defense counsel was inflammatory throughout; neutral language such as "criminally accountable because he participated in a robbery during which his brother Andrew shot two men" did not pass counsel's lips.

* * *

First in sequence is the question whether an objection at trial was necessary, given the district court's pretrial ruling that Williams would be allowed to inform the jury that Wilson had been convicted, not simply of murder, but of killing a police officer. As the panel recognized, this

11. [A motion *in limine* is a pretrial motion to exclude or admit evidence. "*In limine*" means "at the threshold." Ed.]

court's precedents are in conflict. [An amendment to Fed.R.Evid. 103, adopted in 2000, states that a definitive pretrial ruling is sufficient to preserve the issue for appeal.]

One good example of a conditional [nondefinitive] ruling is a judge's statement that, if a litigant testifies, then the adverse party will be entitled to cross-examine in such-and-such a way. Until the condition has been satisfied by the testimony, the ruling has no effect. * * * Similarly, if the judge's pretrial ruling is tentative—if, for example, the judge says that certain evidence will be admitted unless it would be unduly prejudicial given the way the trial develops—then later events may lead to reconsideration, and the litigant adversely affected by the ruling must raise the subject later so that the judge may decide whether intervening events affect the ruling. An appeal in such a case without an objection at trial would bushwhack both the judge and the opponent. Objections alert the judge at critical junctures so that errors may be averted. When a judge has made a conditional, contingent, or tentative ruling, it remains possible to avert error by revisiting the subject.

Definitive rulings, however, do not invite reconsideration. When the judge makes a decision that does not depend on how the trial proceeds, then an objection will not serve the function of ensuring focused consideration at the time when decision is best made. A judge who rules definitively before trial sends the message that the right time has come and gone. An objection is unnecessary to prevent error, and it may do little other than slow down the trial. Sometimes an objection or offer of proof will alert the jury to the very thing that should be concealed. * * * Motions *in limine* are designed to avoid the delay and occasional prejudice caused by objections and offers of proof at trial; they are more useful if they can serve these purposes, which they do only if objections (and offers of proof) can be foregone safely.

Treating a definitive ruling as sufficient to preserve the litigant's position for appeal also avoids laying a trap for unwary counselors. Many lawyers suppose that it is enough to raise an issue once and receive a definitive ruling. They may believe that raising the question again may annoy the judge. * * *

Conclusive pretrial rulings on evidence serve another useful end: they permit the parties to adjust their trial strategy in light of the court's decisions. Wilson wanted to keep the occupation of his victim out of the case, but if this could not be accomplished he wanted to introduce the evidence himself, if only to draw its sting. Sensible adaptations could not be accomplished if Wilson had to wait until Williams offered the evidence, and then raise an objection, acting in the jury's eyes as if he had something to hide. Waiting, objecting, and only then trying to make something of the subject not only would divest Wilson of the initiative but also would deprive him of an alternative theory of the case.

* * *

A vital qualification is implicit in this way of putting the conclusion. Only arguments that were actually presented to the district court before trial are preserved for appeal—and then only if the district judge came to a definitive conclusion. A judge who expresses a tentative or conditional ruling can by that step require the parties to raise the issue again at trial. District judges thus are fully in charge of the process; they can require or excuse further exchanges on a subject by the way they express their rulings. A judge would do well to explain in the decision proper (or in the final pretrial conference) whether the conclusion is definitive, and whether consideration at trial is required, appropriate, or forbidden * * * ; but if the judge does not elaborate, then we assume that an apparently unconditional ruling is conclusive.

Even if the ruling is unconditional, however, it resolves only the arguments actually presented. That much is clear from Fed.R.Evid. 103(a)(1), which requires a litigant to state a specific ground for an objection to evidence; grounds not presented cannot be raised later, else both judge and adversary are sandbagged (and preventable errors occur). There's a corollary to this point: a pretrial objection to and ruling on a particular *use* of evidence does not preserve an objection to a different and inappropriate use. Thus if the judge decides before trial that particular evidence can be used for impeachment, then there is no need to object at trial to this use; but a completely different use of the evidence is not covered by the ruling, and therefore fresh attention at trial (prompted by an objection) is essential if the error-prevention function of the contemporaneous-objection rule is to be achieved.

This is where Wilson's appeal founders. The district judge, asked before trial to forbid *all* reference to the occupation of the murder victims, said no. This meant at a minimum that Wilson could be cross-examined about the conviction when he testified on his own behalf. It also implied that Williams could present the testimony of another guard, Officer Cavallone, that Wilson stated during a trip to the infirmary after the altercation: "[Y]ou should have killed me when you had the chance. I already killed two Chicago police officers. My attorney is going to have a field day with this. I have no respect for the law. And the next thing we are going to do is take care of the blue shirts [guards] inside the jail." Williams offered this statement to corroborate his view that Wilson had a hostile and aggressive attitude, and either initiated the altercation or planned to invent a story for his attorney to have a "field day" with. Wilson denies saying any such thing to Cavallone, and he wanted the line "I already killed two Chicago police officers" redacted. The judge did not require this step. But beyond permitting Cavallone to testify to the full version of the statement, and permitting the use of the conviction to call Wilson's credibility as a witness into question, the ruling *in limine* did not sanction any particular use of evidence. In particular, the judge did not give Williams's counsel permission to introduce Wilson as a "cop killer," to describe the details of the crime, to seek sympathy for Wilson's victims, or to imply that people who commit heinous offenses are fair game in prison—all of which Williams's lawyer did, and without objection. The pretrial ruling did not say or imply that such uses (or misuses) of the evidence would be allowed. We reversed the verdict for defendants in the first trial of Andrew Wilson's § 1983 action precisely because defense counsel harped on the details of the murders and sought an emotional rather than reasoned evaluation of the facts. The defense strategy in Jackie Wilson's second trial was similar to that in Andrew Wilson's first—but the big difference is that Andrew Wilson's lawyers objected, and Jackie Wilson's did not. *Misuse* of evidence that has a proper use cannot be argued on appeal without a specific objection. See Fed.R.Evid. 103(a)(1).

A pretrial ruling is definitive only with respect to subjects it covers. Details of usage were not raised or resolved before trial. If the only problem were that Williams's counsel once said "cop killer" rather than a more neutral formulation, or repeated the statement when using the conviction for impeachment, we would be reluctant to say that objection has been forfeited. Misuse of evidence is a matter of degree, and litigants receive the benefit of the doubt in grey areas. But defense counsel strummed on "cop killer" as if it were a guitar rather than a bit of evidence; whatever line there was between proper and improper use was overstepped; objection never came, so forfeiture occurred and the plain-error standard governs. Fed.R.Evid. 103(d).

Plain error means an error that not only is clear in retrospect but also causes a miscarriage of justice. United States v. Olano, 507 U.S. 725, 736 * * * (1993). Wilson has not persuaded us that justice miscarried in his trial because of the way Williams used Wilson's crime. Blatant efforts to manipulate jurors' emotions and persuade them to ignore the facts and instructions often backfire. Wilson may have withheld objection in the hope that jurors would deem that Williams had overplayed his hand. Moreover, Wilson might have thought that Williams's efforts to hammer away on the cop-killer theme showed animus, and thus made Wilson's accusation against Williams more credible. Wilson had a weak case on damages, and success on liability depended on the resolution of a credibility contest. How the balance of advantage from the overuse of the cop-killer theme plays out in such a trial is difficult to say. The effects are not so inevitably baleful to the truth-finding function of trial that the problem must be deemed "plain error."

At last, in what must appear to be an afterthought, we tackle the issue that *has* been preserved: whether the district judge should have ruled before trial that the nature of Wilson's crime is inadmissible. As the Supreme Court observed in *Old Chief*,[12] the precise identity of a crime often creates a potential for prejudice that overwhelms its constructive value. Any legitimate use of the conviction by the defense would have been served by informing the jury that Wilson has been convicted of murder and sentenced to life imprisonment. The judge thus

12. [Citing Old Chief v. United States, 519 U.S. 172 (1997), discussed in Chapter 7, Section B, infra. Ed.]

abused his discretion in denying the motion outright. But at oral argument before the court en banc, Wilson's lawyer disclaimed any contention that the district judge should have barred Cavallone from testifying that Wilson said "I already killed two Chicago police officers." With this statement in evidence, the district judge's error with the *Old Chief* issue is harmless. Williams's harping on the subject, and his implication that "cop killers" are not entitled to damages when guards behave as vigilantes, could not be thought harmless, but the lack of objection means that the misuse of the evidence has not been preserved for appellate review. As a result, the judgment is

AFFIRMED.

[Opinion of MANION, CIRCUIT JUDGE, concurring in part, dissenting in part, and concurring in judgment is omitted.]

WOOD, CIRCUIT JUDGE, with whom RIPPLE, CIRCUIT JUDGE, joins, dissenting in part.

While I agree with the *en banc* majority on the larger issues of law that this case presents, I am unable to concur with its finding that the errors that infected this trial do not require reversal. * * *

* * *

The place where I part company with the majority is in its application of these rules. To begin with, it is important to remember that there are two separate potential sources of reversible error in this case: the introduction of evidence concerning the victims of Wilson's crimes and the misuse of this evidence. With respect to the latter, because Wilson's failure to object to the improper use of the victim identity evidence led him to forfeit this point, * * * the question is how his appeal fares under the plain error standard of review of Fed.R.Evid. 103(d). A review of this transcript leaves no doubt that the error is clear in retrospect, and I do not understand the majority to assert otherwise. That leaves the question whether this was an error that "seriously affect[ed] the fairness, integrity, or public reputation of judicial proceedings," and thereby caused a miscarriage of justice. See United States v. Olano, 507 U.S. 725, 736 * * * (1993) (internal quotations deleted). In a brisk paragraph, the majority concludes that it did not, based solely on the fact that Wilson succeeded in finding a strategic use for the offensive information. * * * But this conclusion loses sight of the very point that lies behind the finding of forfeiture: far more was going on here than the simple act of making sure the jury knew what Wilson had done. Instead, defense counsel openly, repeatedly, and blatantly urged the jury to find against Wilson because of what lay in his past. The misuse of the evidence was so extreme and so pervasive that, even though Wilson forfeited his objection, I would find plain error and reverse on this ground.

Even if the misuse of the victim identity evidence did not rise to the level of plain error, there would remain the question whether the district court committed reversible error in permitting defense counsel to use the evidence at all. Here too, I agree with the majority at the beginning of its analysis, but not at the end. The district court abused its discretion in denying the motion *in limine* outright, because as the majority points out, any legitimate use of the conviction would have been served by informing the jury that Wilson had been convicted of murder and sentenced to life imprisonment. * * * Nevertheless, according to the majority, the fact that Wilson's lawyer at oral argument was not urging us to find that the judge should have barred Officer Cavallone from testifying that Wilson had proclaimed "I already killed two Chicago police officers," means that the district court's error was harmless. * * * In my view, however, this misunderstands the scope of counsel's comment at oral argument. The question we must ask is whether counsel would have objected to that part of Officer Cavallone's account if the judge had granted the motion *in limine* at the outset. To do otherwise would undermine the central holding of the majority opinion, that an objection at trial is unnecessary to preserve for appeal an issue addressed in a definitive *in limine* ruling. Given the wording of the *in limine* motion, I believe that the damaging statement would have been improper. Wilson's lawyers asked that "all evidence of Wilson's criminal conviction for Murder, together with all reference to those criminal proceedings and to any of the underlying conduct" be excluded from the trial. Accordingly, if the motion *in limine* had been granted (even if it had been limited to references to victim identity), as it should have been, Wilson's lawyer would have had a ground on which to object to Officer Cavallone's statement and likely would have done so. There is no question that Wilson's lawyer would have preferred to have tried this case without any mention at all, through Officer Cavallone or anyone else, about the identity of Wilson's victim. Under the proper perspective, I do not regard the error as harmless. Furthermore, again harking back to the theme of most of the majority's opinion, there is an important distinction between a single mention of the identity of the victim and an incessant mantra. From that perspective as well, the error that opened the door to the mantra cannot be regarded as harmless.

* * *

Notes and Questions

1. *Waiver or forfeiture?* See United States v. Olano, 507 U.S. 725, 733 (1993) ("Whereas forfeiture is the failure to make the timely assertion of a right, waiver is the 'intentional relinquishment or abandonment of a known right.' "). Nevertheless, courts and lawyers often do not make this distinction.

2. *Specific v. general objections.* In Hafner Mfg. Co. v. City of St. Louis, 172 S.W. 28, 31 (Mo.1914), Justice Lamm paid his respects to the "three i's," incompetent, irrelevant and immaterial: "We think the time has come when, for the convenience of apt designation, this stereotyped objection may, without lowering the dignity of our case, be termed the '*3 i's.*' On a similar ground we may say these '*i's,*' like the mere germinating eyes of the potato, see not, and are of little or no sensible use in the administration of justice."

Probably the all time record for generality of objection was set by the Kansas lawyer who objected "on all the grounds ever known or heard of." Johnston v. Clements, 25 Kan. 376, 379 (1881).

3. *Specificity requirement—wrong grounds.* Wigmore asserts, "a specific objection sustained (like a general objection) is sufficient, though naming an untenable ground, if some other tenable ground existed." 1 Wigmore, Evidence § 18, at 831 (Tillers rev. 1983). See also Hamling v. United States, 418 U.S. 87, 108 n.10 (1974) (suggesting that trial court's exclusion of expert testimony might be erroneous on grounds stated but sustainable on lack of expert qualifications); People v. Brown, 94 P.3d 574, 579 (Cal.2004) ("If a judgment rests on admissible evidence it will not be reversed because the trial court admitted that evidence upon a different theory, a mistaken theory, or one not raised below."). But compare 1 McCormick, Evidence § 52 (6th ed. 2006) (arguing that new trial appropriate where correct objection, if made, could have been obviated); Morgan, Basic Problems of Evidence 54 (1962) (same). The case authority is divided.

4. *Specificity requirement—parts.* With documents, the specificity requirement further demands that counsel indicate which particular portions are objectionable. See State v. Fox, 12 N.E.2d 413, 417 (Ohio 1938) ("Whenever evidence is offered which is only partially objectionable, the complaining party must point out the objectionable portion specifically."). Cf. Old Chief v. United States, 519 U.S. 172, 179 n.4 (1997) ("We see no impediment in general to a district court's determination, after objection, that some sections of a document are relevant within the meaning of Rule 401, and others irrelevant and inadmissible under Rule 402.").

5. *Continuing objections.* See State v. Henness, 679 N.E.2d 686, 693 (Ohio 1997) ("At times, a continuing objection is enough to preserve error. * * * However, it was not sufficient in this case. The existence of the marital privilege turns on the specific circumstances surrounding each allegedly privileged communication, e.g., whether a third party was present. Thus, appellant had to object specifically so the circumstances could be determined.").

6. *"Apparent from the context" exception.* Rule 103(a)(1) recognizes an exception to the objection requirement where the ground for the objection is "apparent from the context." See United States v. Musacchia, 900 F.2d 493, 496–97 (2d Cir.1990) (exception invoked where review of transcript revealed counsel had specifically objected to similar questioning of another witness and asked that objection be deemed continuing). Can trial counsel ever assume that an appellate court will later find that the grounds for an objection were apparent from the context?

7. *Timeliness requirement.* Ordinarily, objections must be made as soon as grounds to object become apparent, which is usually when the question is asked. Counsel cannot, as the courts are fond of saying, gamble on a favorable answer to an objectionable question and then move to strike if the result is disappointing. If circumstances prevent counsel from objecting before the witness answers, as where an objectionable answer is not responsive to the question or where the response is hastily given, a motion to strike is appropriate. Normally, in that situation counsel should also request and

the court should give an instruction to the jury to disregard the inadmissible evidence. See 1 McCormick, Evidence § 52 (6th ed. 2006).

8. *Judicial explanation.* If counsel is unable to understand the ground upon which his or her opponent objects to admission of evidence and asks for specification, the judge should indicate the ground specifically or require objecting counsel to do so. United States v. Dwyer, 539 F.2d 924 (2d Cir.1976); Colburn v. Chicago, St. P., M. & O. Ry. Co., 85 N.W. 354 (Wis.1901).

9. *Common law "exceptions."* At common law, a party wishing to appeal an unfavorable ruling had a further obligation—i.e., to "except" to the ruling. Federal Civil Rule 46 and Criminal Rule 51, which are identical, provide, *inter alia,* that a party need not take a formal "exception" in order to review rulings or orders of the court.

10. *Making the record.* Even the best of offers or objections are obviously of no avail on appeal unless they appear in the record. United States v. Johnson, 542 F.2d 230, 234 n.8 (5th Cir.1976):

> Appellant's manner of preserving the point for appeal was irregular. No objection was ever made on the record. Instead, the objection was made and overruled in chambers with the court reporter absent. Later, the trial judge put into the record his recollection of the objection and his reason for overruling it.
>
> Because appellant failed in his obligation to make the record for appeal, he came dangerously close to losing his chance to argue to us his evidentiary point. Had appellant gone by the book, we would have had before us four items: (1) the original objection, (2) the government's response attempting to bring the elicited testimony within one or more of the exceptions to the bar against "other crimes" evidence, (3) the appellant's response to the government's position, and (4) the trial judge's ruling based on the arguments of both sides.
>
> Here we have only a general objection as restated by the trial judge and his decision to overrule based on the impeachment exception to the general rule of exclusion.
>
> If it is necessary to hear an objection outside the presence of the jury, this can be done without depriving this court of a record upon which to base its holding.

See also State v. Goodwin, 703 N.E.2d 1251, 1260 (Ohio 1999) ("[The defendant] did not make a pretrial motion to record all sidebars, nor does the record show that counsel for [the defendant] requested that all pretrial or bench conferences be recorded. In the absence of such a request, any possible error is waived."); State v. Keenan, 689 N.E.2d 929, 938 (Ohio 1998) (47 unrecorded sidebars).

11. *"Connecting up."* See Huddleston v. United States, 485 U.S. 681, 690 (1988) ("Often the trial court may decide to allow the proponent to introduce evidence concerning a similar act, and at a later point in the trial assess whether sufficient evidence has been offered to permit the jury to make the requisite finding. If the proponent has failed to meet this minimal standard of proof, the trial court must instruct the jury to disregard the

evidence."). Is it the court's or opposing counsel's responsibility to raise the issue?

12. *Plain error.* Courts have been largely incapable of giving any concrete meaning to "plain error." See 3A Wright, Federal Practice and Procedure: Criminal § 856, at 337 & n.8 (2d ed. 1982) (the best that can be said is that they, like Justice Stewart on obscenity, "know it when they see it"). See also Tompkins v. Cyr, 202 F.3d 770, 779 (5th Cir.2000) ("There are four prerequisites to a finding that the district court committed plain error in admitting specified evidence: (1) an error; (2) that is clear and obvious under current law; (3) that affects the defendant's substantial rights; and (4) that would seriously affect the fairness, integrity or public reputation of judicial proceedings if left uncorrected.").

13. *Harmless error.* Although properly preserved, a technical infraction of the rules of evidence may prove unavailing because deemed harmless. See, e.g., Federal Civil Rule 61:

> No error in either the admission or the exclusion of evidence * * * is ground for granting a new trial or for setting aside a verdict * * * unless refusal to take such action appears to the court inconsistent with substantial justice. The court at every stage of the proceeding must disregard any error or defect in the proceeding which does not affect the substantial rights of the parties.

See also Federal Criminal Rule 52(a) (Any error, defect, irregularity or variance which does not affect substantial rights shall be disregarded). Rule 103(a) is intended to leave these principles concerning harmless error unchanged. See Fed.R.Evid. 103(a) advisory committee's note.

14. *Sources.* Traynor, The Riddle of Harmless Error (1970) (discussing mainly evidentiary rulings). Constitutional errors are discussed in Field, Assessing the Harmlessness of Federal Constitutional Error—A Process in Need of a Rationale, 125 U.Pa.L.Rev. 15 (1976); Goldberg, Harmless Error: Constitutional Sneak Thief, 71 J.Crim.L. & Criminology 421 (1980); Meltzer, Harmless Error and Constitutional Remedies, 61 U.Chi.L.Rev. 1 (1994); Monaghan, Harmless Error and the Valid Rule Requirement, 1989 S.Ct.Rev. 195; Ogletree, *Arizona v. Fulminante*: The Harm of Applying Harmless Error to Coerced Confessions, 105 Harv.L.Rev. 152 (1991); Saltzburg, The Harm of Harmless Error, 59 Va.L.Rev. 988 (1973); Stacy, The Search for the Truth in Constitutional Criminal Procedure, 91 Colum.L.Rev. 1369 (1991); Stacy & Dayton, Rethinking Harmless Constitutional Error, 88 Colum.L.Rev. 79 (1988).

WILLIAMS v. STATE

Texas Court of Criminal Appeals, 1977.
549 S.W.2d 183.

DALLY, COMMISSIONER.

This is an appeal from a conviction for the offense of robbery by firearm under the former penal code; the punishment is imprisonment for 25 years.

* * *

The appellant was represented by a court-appointed attorney at trial; however, he filed six pro se motions on his own behalf plus a pro se brief. In one pro se motion the appellant requested permission to "pick my own jury" and cross-examine the complaining witness. The trial court granted both requests. The appellant conducted the cross and direct examination of three witnesses and his attorney questioned the other witnesses. The appellant also made closing arguments to the jury at the guilt-innocence phase of the trial.

Appellant contends the court erred in failing to grant a mistrial after the complaining witness alluded to a prior extraneous offense allegedly committed by him. The appellant complains of the following testimony that occurred during the examination of the complaining witness:

"Q. (By Prosecutor): Except for the occasion when he came into your store once previously, before October the 24th of 1973, had you ever seen the man before?

"A. Yes, sir, I had.

"Q. Where?

"A. He had robbed me once before.

"Q. Well, that's not what I wanted.

"Okay. He has robbed you once before then? Is that true?

"A. Yes, sir.

"Q. And when did that happen?

"A. I don't remember the exact date.

"Q. And is that why you recognized him when he came back to rob you the second time?

"A. That is why.

"THE DEFENDANT: Objection, Judge, Your Honor.

"THE COURT: Sustained."

Testimony concerning this first robbery was brought out numerous other times before the jury without objection. The appellant himself questioned the complainant extensively concerning the first robbery. The court's charge instructed the jury not to consider testimony regarding other offenses that appellant may have committed unless it found beyond a reasonable doubt that the appellant committed the offenses and then only for the purpose of showing a common plan or systematic course of action, or in determining the identity, intent, motive, or malice of the defendant.

Appellant's only objection to this testimony was a general objection which does not preserve error for review. *Smith v. State*, 513 S.W.2d 823 (Tex.Crim.App.1974). Furthermore, appellant's objection was untimely and testimony concerning this first robbery was elicited by the appellant himself on cross-examination of the complainant. *Randolph v. State*, 502

S.W.2d 138 (Tex.Crim.App.1973). Appellant's objection was sustained and no further relief was requested; nothing is presented for review. *Fuller v. State*, 501 S.W.2d 112 (Tex.Crim.App.1973); *Weedon v. State*, 501 S.W.2d 336 (Tex.Crim.App.1973).

Appellant's counsel on appeal argues in this ground of error that this Court should take into consideration the appellant's ignorance, as a layman, of the rules of evidence and procedure concerning preserving error and the rules excluding extraneous offenses. Appellate counsel recognizes that the appellant requested and was granted the right to conduct his own defense, but urges that permitting the appellant to conduct his own defense denied him a fair and impartial trial.

The United States Supreme Court has decided that an accused has the absolute right under the United States Constitution to defend himself without the benefit of counsel. *Faretta v. California*, 422 U.S. 806 * * * (1975). In footnote 46 of *Faretta*, the Court said:

> "The right of self-representation is not a license to abuse the dignity of the courtroom. Neither is it a license not to comply with relevant rules of procedural and substantive law. Thus, whatever else may or may not be open to him on appeal, a defendant who elects to represent himself cannot thereafter complain that the quality of his own defense amounted to a denial of 'effective assistance of counsel.' "

The rules of evidence, procedure, and substantive law will be applied the same to all parties in a criminal trial whether that party is represented by counsel or acting pro se. *Cf. Webb v. State*, 533 S.W.2d 780 (Tex.Crim.App.1976). Grounds of error number one and three are overruled.

* * *

The judgment is affirmed.

Opinion approved by the Court.

Notes and Questions

1. *Pro se defendants*. Why was the court in *Williams* not more inclined to protect the defendant, who was representing himself, from his own errors? What potential systemic problems might result from liberally forgiving procedural defaults in such circumstances?

2. *Plain error*. A possible escape from the harshness of strict enforcement of procedural defaults exemplified in *Williams* may be found in the doctrine of "plain error." See the *Leech* case, Chapter 2, infra, and the notes following it. However, plain error with all its uncertainties is a woefully inadequate alternative to "protecting the record" by a properly made objection.

3. *Contemporaneous objection rule*. The requirement that a party object in a timely fashion at trial is known generally as the contemporaneous objection rule. For a discussion of its merits, particularly in criminal habeas

corpus litigation, see the majority and dissenting opinions in Wainwright v. Sykes, 433 U.S. 72 (1977).

(2) OFFERS OF PROOF: FEDERAL RULE 103(a)(2)

UNITED STATES v. ADAMS

United States Court of Appeals, Tenth Circuit, 2001.
271 F.3d 1236.

KELLY, CIRCUIT JUDGE.

Defendant–Appellant Dale L. Adams was found guilty by a jury of possession of a firearm by a felon in violation of 18 U.S.C. § 922(g)(1), and sentenced to 51 months and three years supervised release. At trial, the government relied upon a series of incriminating statements made by Mr. Adams immediately following his arrest. On appeal, he contends that the district court's exclusion of expert testimony by a clinical psychologist denied his right to due process and a fair trial. * * * [The expert reported that Adams's low neurocognitive functioning and dependent personality structure strongly raised "the possibility, *given the conflicting explanations made by Mr. Adams and others,* that he was not telling the truth when he made incriminating statements to Wichita Police Officers and ATF agents. His statements that he was 'protecting a girlfriend' when he confessed to possession of the firearm is consistent with his personality and cognitive state, and indicative of his difficulty making appropriate and reasoned choices."]

* * *

Mr. Adams tried again at the onset of trial to admit the psychologist's report, claiming that it was relevant to Mr. Adams's mental condition and education, factors that could be considered in judging the credibility of his incriminating statements. Again, the government objected to the substance and timing of the evidence and again the court excluded it.

At trial, the government relied heavily on the incriminating statements that Mr. Adams made to the officers immediately following his arrest. Mr. Adams testified at trial, denying the veracity of his earlier confessions, and claiming that he lied to protect his girlfriend from incrimination. Nevertheless, the jury returned a guilty verdict.

DISCUSSION

A. Adequacy of the Offer of Proof

At the outset we are faced with the question of whether Mr. Adams made an offer of proof to the trial court adequate to preserve the claimed error of excluding the psychologist's testimony. "Error may not be based on a ruling excluding evidence unless 'the substance of the evidence was made known to the court by offer [of proof] or was apparent from the context within which questions were asked.'" Inselman v. S & J Operating Co., 44 F.3d 894, 896 (10th Cir.1995) (quoting Fed.R.Evid. 103(a)(2)).

On numerous occasions we have held that " 'merely telling the court the content of * * * proposed testimony' is not an offer of proof." Polys v. Trans–Colorado Airlines, Inc., 941 F.2d 1404, 1407 (10th Cir.1991) * * *. In order to qualify as an adequate offer of proof, the proponent must, first, describe the evidence and what it tends to show and, second, identify the grounds for admitting the evidence. Phillips v. Hillcrest Med. Ctr., 244 F.3d 790, 802 (10th Cir.2001); *Polys,* 941 F.2d at 1407. If the proponent's offer of proof fails this standard, then this court can reverse only in instances of plain error that affected appellant's substantial rights. *Phillips*, 244 F.3d at 802; Fed.R.Evid. 103(d).

A twofold purpose underlies these required showings. First, an effective offer of proof enables the trial judge to make informed decisions based on the substance of the evidence. *Polys*, 941 F.2d at 1406. Second, an effective offer of proof creates "a clear record that an appellate court can review to 'determine whether there was reversible error in excluding the [testimony].' " Id. at 1407 * * *.

Federal Rule of Evidence 103(a)(2) does not mandate a particular form for offers of proof. Instead, the rule invests the trial judge with discretion in determining the form of the offer. Fed.R.Evid. 103(b). There are at least four ways to make an offer of proof of testimony and achieve the purposes underlying the rule. 1 *McCormick on Evidence* § 51, at 216 n.9 (John W. Strong, 5th ed.1999). First, and most desirable from all standpoints except cost, the proponent may examine the witness before the court and have the answers reported on the record. *Id.;* 21 Charles Alan Wright & Kenneth W. Graham, *Federal Practice and Procedure* § 5040, at 214 (1977). The question and answer method necessitates excusing a jury, but this concern is not present when the offer of proof is made, as here, at a pretrial motion hearing. When the proponent proffers testimony in this manner, opposing counsel may be permitted "to cross-examine the witness to develop any factors which would put the proffered testimony in its true light." Wright & Graham § 5040, at 214.

The second, and least favorable, method for making an offer of proof of testimony is a statement of counsel as to what the testimony would be. *Id.* at 215. In this case, the colloquy between counsel and the district court was so lacking in detail that it is difficult to decipher why exclusion of the evidence might be error. During the hearing on the motion in limine, defense counsel stated that he had asked the examining psychologist to "look into whether or not [Mr. Adams's] personality, mental makeup, however you want to put it, would he be so inclined—given the testing that's done, would there be a possibility that he would give a false statement to the police." R.O.A. Supp. Vol. I, at 4. Counsel then proffered that the examining psychologist had "suggested in one of the paragraphs [of the report] * * * that his personality certainly is one that could have been—statements to the police could have been false." *Id.*

An offer of proof of testimony by counsel is the least favored method because of its potential to fall short of the standard required by the rules of evidence as well as the standard set out in *Phillips* and *Polys.* Defense counsel's offer of proof made during the colloquy with the judge illustrates the potential pitfalls of this method. Specificity and detail are the hallmarks of a good offer of proof of testimony, Wright & Graham § 5040, at 213, and conclusory terms, especially when presented in a confused manner, mark poor ones. * * *. Defense counsel hardly met the baseline requirement of " 'merely telling the court the content of * * * [the] proposed testimony.' " *Polys*, 941 F.2d at 1407. As for the additional requirements set out in *Phillips* and *Polys,* counsel did not explain the significance of the proposed evidence or what he expected the evidence to show. *Phillips*, 244 F.3d at 802; *Polys*, 941 F.2d at 1407. Nor did counsel clearly identify "the grounds for which [he] believes the evidence to be admissible." *Id.*

Documentary offers of proof comprise the third and fourth proper forms of proffering anticipated testimony. McCormick § 51, at 216 n.9. The first of these, and least common, is a statement written by examining counsel describing the answers the proposed witness would give if permitted to testify. *Id.* More common, and relevant to this case, the proponent of the evidence may introduce a "written statement of the witness's testimony signed by the witness and *offered as part of the record.*" *Id.* (emphasis added). In using either method of documentary proffer for anticipated testimony, "[i]t is suggested * * * that the writing be marked as an exhibit and introduced into the record for proper identification on appeal." *Id.* * * * Indeed the primary, formal reason for an offer of proof is "to preserve the issue for appeal by including the proposed answer and expected proof *in the official record of trial.*" McCormick § 51, at 216 n.9 (emphasis added).

On the morning of the pretrial hearing, counsel for Mr. Adams apparently sent a facsimile of the psychologist's report directly to the district court judge, who referred to the report during the hearing. * * * The report was not marked as an exhibit. "Documents and other exhibits are usually marked for identification and become part of the record on appeal, even if excluded." Wright & Graham § 5040, at 213. Nor was it filed as an exhibit to a pleading. The report is not part of the record below.

Merely sending a facsimile of the psychologist's report to the judge on the morning before the hearing unfortunately does not guarantee that the faxed item will actually be marked as an exhibit or filed and become part of the record. Our rules anticipate that when an appeal is based upon the challenge to the admission or exclusion of evidence, we be furnished not only with pertinent transcript excerpts, but also with pertinent trial exhibits that are part of the record. 10th Cir. R. 10.3(D)(1) & (2).

Mr. Adams has moved to supplement the record. The appellate rules allow supplementation of the record on appeal in instances where "anything material * * * is omitted from or misstated in the record by error or accident." Fed. R.App. P. 10(e)(2). Because the district court judge did make passing reference to a recently faxed psychologist's report, R.O.A. Supp. Vol. I, at 8, and because counsel as an officer of the court represents that this is the same report that was before the district court, and because the government does not oppose it, we will grant the motion. We remind counsel, however, of the importance of a valid, properly presented, detailed, and recorded offer of proof when testimony is involved and of the importance of insuring that supporting documentary evidence be made part of the record.

* * *

[The court then upheld the exclusion of the evidence, in part because the prosecution was not notified until three days before trial, in violation of a discovery order.]

Notes and Questions

1. *Completeness of offer of proof.* See United States v. Crockett, 435 F.3d 1305, 1311–12 (10th Cir.2006) ("The proponent of excluded evidence does not satisfy his burden to make an offer of proof merely by telling the trial court the content of the proposed testimony. Rather, the proponent must explain what [he] expects [the evidence] to show and the grounds for which the party believes the evidence to be admissible.").

2. *"Apparent from the context" exception.* Rule 103(a)(2) recognizes an exception to the offer of proof requirement where the substance of the evidence is "apparent from the context within which questions were asked." See Beech Aircraft Corp. v. Rainey, 488 U.S. 153, 174 (1988) (nature of proposed testimony of plaintiff on cross-examination by his own counsel "was abundantly apparent from the very questions" asked). Can trial counsel ever assume that an appellate court will later find that the substance of the offer is apparent from the context?

3. *Cross-examination.* See Ohio R.Evid. 103(A)(2) (providing that an "offer of proof is not necessary if evidence is excluded during cross-examination"); 1 McCormick, Evidence § 51, at 250 n.14 (6th ed. 2006) ("On cross-examination, the examining counsel is ordinarily assumed not to have had an advance opportunity to learn how the witness will answer, and the requirement of an offer will not usually be applied.").

4. *Pretrial hearings.* Sometimes extensive pretrial hearings are required. DNA evidence is illustrative. See United States v. Yee, 134 F.R.D. 161, 168 (N.D.Ohio 1991) ("hearings were held for approximately six weeks"); People v. Castro, 545 N.Y.S.2d 985, 986 (Sup.Ct.1989) ("This hearing took place over a twelve week period producing a transcript of approximately five thousand pages.").

5. *Talking objections.* Some judges prohibit "talking" objections and offers of proof in front of the jury. See United States v. Henderson, 409 F.3d 1293, 1298 (11th Cir.2005) (Defendant "argues that he could not have made an offer of proof at trial because the district judge did not permit bench conferences, requiring parties to reserve issues they did not wish to discuss before the jury to a time when the jurors were not required to be present in court. Moreover, he indicates that the district judge also forbade 'speaking

objections,' where the objecting party explains the basis for its objection, allowing the objecting party to voice only a very abbreviated basis for its complaint."). How should counsel deal with such a practice?

(3) APPEALS

LUCE v. UNITED STATES

Supreme Court of the United States, 1984.
469 U.S. 38.

CHIEF JUSTICE BURGER delivered the opinion of the Court.

We granted certiorari to resolve a conflict among the Circuits as to whether the defendant, who did not testify at trial, is entitled to review of the District Court's ruling denying his motion to forbid the use of a prior conviction to impeach his credibility.

I

Petitioner was indicted on charges of conspiracy, and possession of cocaine with intent to distribute, in violation of 21 U.S.C. §§ 846 and 841(a)(1). During his trial in the United States District Court for the Western District of Tennessee, petitioner moved for a ruling to preclude the Government from using a 1974 state conviction to impeach him if he testified. There was no commitment by petitioner that he would testify if the motion were granted, nor did he make a proffer to the court as to what his testimony would be. In opposing the motion, the Government represented that the conviction was for a serious crime—possession of a controlled substance.

The District Court ruled that the prior conviction fell within the category of permissible impeachment evidence under Federal Rule of Evidence 609(a).[13] The District Court noted, however, that the nature and scope of petitioner's trial testimony could affect the court's specific evidentiary rulings; for example, the court was prepared to hold that the prior conviction would be excluded if petitioner limited his testimony to explaining his attempt to flee from the arresting officers. However, if petitioner took the stand and denied any prior involvement with drugs, he could then be impeached by the 1974 conviction. Petitioner did not testify, and the jury returned guilty verdicts.

II

The United States Court of Appeals for the Sixth Circuit affirmed. 713 F.2d 1236 (1983). The Court of Appeals refused to consider petition-

13. Rule 609(a) provides:

"General Rule.—For the purpose of attacking the credibility of a witness, evidence that he has been convicted of a crime shall be admitted if elicited from him or established by public record during cross-examination but only if the crime (1) was punishable by death or imprisonment in excess of one year under the law under which he was convicted, and the court determines that the probative value of admitting this evidence outweighs its prejudicial effect to the defendant, or (2) involved dishonesty or false statement, regardless of the punishment."

er's contention that the District Court abused its discretion in denying the motion *in limine* without making an explicit finding that the probative value of the prior conviction outweighed its prejudicial effect. The Court of Appeals held that when the defendant does not testify, the court will not review the District Court's *in limine* ruling.

Some other Circuits have permitted review in similar situations;[14] we granted certiorari to resolve the conflict. 466 U.S. 903 (1984). We affirm.

III

It is clear, of course, that had petitioner testified and been impeached by evidence of a prior conviction, the District Court's decision to admit the impeachment evidence would have been reviewable on appeal along with any other claims of error. The Court of Appeals would then have had a complete record detailing the nature of petitioner's testimony, the scope of the cross-examination, and the possible impact of the impeachment on the jury's verdict.

A reviewing court is handicapped in any effort to rule on subtle evidentiary questions outside a factual context.[15] This is particularly true under Rule 609(a)(1), which directs the court to weigh the probative value of a prior conviction against the prejudicial effect to the defendant. To perform this balancing, the court must know the precise nature of the defendant's testimony, which is unknowable when, as here, the defendant does not testify.[16]

Any possible harm flowing from a district court's *in limine* ruling permitting impeachment by a prior conviction is wholly speculative. The ruling is subject to change when the case unfolds, particularly if the actual testimony differs from what was contained in the defendant's proffer. Indeed even if nothing unexpected happens at trial, the district judge is free, in the exercise of sound judicial discretion, to alter a previous *in limine* ruling. On a record such as here, it would be a matter of conjecture whether the District Court would have allowed the Government to attack petitioner's credibility at trial by means of the prior conviction.

When the defendant does not testify, the reviewing court also has no way of knowing whether the Government would have sought to impeach with the prior conviction. If, for example, the Government's case is strong, and the defendant is subject to impeachment by other means, a

14. *See, e.g., United States v. Lipscomb,* 226 U.S.App.D.C. 312, 332, 702 F.2d 1049, 1069 (1983) (en banc); * * * The Ninth Circuit allows review if the defendant makes a record unequivocally announcing his intention to testify if his motion to exclude prior convictions is granted, and if he proffers the substance of his contemplated testimony. See *United States v. Cook,* 608 F.2d 1175, 1186 (1979) (en banc).

15. Although the Federal Rules of Evidence do not explicitly authorize *in limine* rulings, the practice has developed pursuant to the district court's inherent authority to manage the course of trials. See generally Fed.Rule Evid. 103(c); cf. Fed.Rule Crim.Proc. 12(e).

16. Requiring a defendant to make a proffer of testimony is no answer; his trial testimony could, for any number of reasons, differ from the proffer.

prosecutor might elect not to use an arguably inadmissible prior conviction.

Because an accused's decision whether to testify "seldom turns on the resolution of one factor," *New Jersey v. Portash,* 440 U.S. 450, 467 (1979) (BLACKMUN, J., dissenting), a reviewing court cannot assume that the adverse ruling motivated a defendant's decision not to testify. In support of his motion a defendant might make a commitment to testify if his motion is granted; but such a commitment is virtually risk free because of the difficulty of enforcing it.

Even if these difficulties could be surmounted, the reviewing court would still face the question of harmless error. See generally *United States v. Hasting,* 461 U.S. 499 (1983). Were *in limine* rulings under Rule 609(a) reviewable on appeal, almost any error would result in the windfall of automatic reversal; the appellate court could not logically term "harmless" an error that presumptively kept the defendant from testifying. Requiring that a defendant testify in order to preserve Rule 609(a) claims will enable the reviewing court to determine the impact any erroneous impeachment may have had in light of the record as a whole; it will also tend to discourage making such motions solely to "plant" reversible error in the event of conviction.

Petitioner's reliance on *Brooks v. Tennessee,* 406 U.S. 605 (1972), and *New Jersey v. Portash, supra,* is misplaced. In those cases we reviewed Fifth Amendment challenges to state-court rulings that operated to dissuade defendants from testifying. We did not hold that a federal court's preliminary ruling on a question not reaching constitutional dimensions—such as a decision under Rule 609(a)—is reviewable on appeal.

However, JUSTICE POWELL, in his concurring opinion in *Portash,* stated essentially the rule we adopt today:

> "The preferred method for raising claims such as [petitioner's] would be for the defendant to take the stand and appeal a subsequent conviction. * * * Only in this way may the claim be presented to a reviewing court in a concrete factual context." 440 U.S., at 462.

We hold that to raise and preserve for review the claim of improper impeachment with a prior conviction, a defendant must testify. Accordingly, the judgment of the Court of Appeals is

Affirmed.

JUSTICE STEVENS took no part in the consideration or decision of this case.

JUSTICE BRENNAN, with whom JUSTICE MARSHALL joins, concurring.

I join the opinion of the Court because I understand it to hold only that a defendant who does not testify at trial may not challenge on appeal an *in limine* ruling respecting admission of a prior conviction for purposes of impeachment under Rule 609(a) of the Federal Rules of Evidence. The Court correctly identifies two reasons for precluding appellate review unless the defendant testifies at trial. The careful weighing of probative value and prejudicial effect that Rule 609(a) requires of a district court can only be evaluated adequately on appeal in the specific factual context of a trial as it has unfolded. And if the defendant declines to testify, the reviewing court is handicapped in making the required harmless-error determination should the district court's *in limine* ruling prove to have been incorrect.

I do not understand the Court to be deciding broader questions of appealability *vel non* of *in limine* rulings that do not involve Rule 609(a). In particular, I do not read the Court's quotation of JUSTICE POWELL's concurring opinion in *New Jersey v. Portash,* 440 U.S. 450, 462 (1979), * * * as intimating a determination with respect to a federal court's *in limine* ruling concerning the constitutionality of admitting immunized testimony for impeachment purposes. In that case, and others in which the determinative question turns on legal and not factual considerations, a requirement that the defendant actually testify at trial to preserve the admissibility issue for appeal might not necessarily be appropriate. The appellate court's need to frame the question in a concrete factual context would be less acute, and the calculus of interests correspondingly different, than in the Rule 609(a) case the Court decides today.

Notes and Questions

1. *Extending Luce.* The lower courts have been rather quick to extend *Luce* to situations outside of Rule 609 where the propriety of anticipated impeachment is challenged. See United States v. Coumaris, 399 F.3d 343, 348 (D.C. Cir.2005) ("Coumaris clearly waived his objection to the district court's *in limine* ruling by failing to call the character witnesses to testify. * * * We see no reason—and Coumaris has not suggested any—why [the *Luce*] considerations are not equally applicable when it is a character witness, rather than the defendant himself, who might have testified but for the *in limine* ruling."); United States v. Bond, 87 F.3d 695, 700 (5th Cir.1996) ("Bond also attacks the magistrate judge's statements from the bench, in effect a ruling on a motion in limine, that if Bond took the stand to testify regarding the terms of his plea bargain, he would waive his privilege against self-incrimination with regard to all grounds asserted in his motion to withdraw. We hold that Bond has failed to preserve this issue for appellate review, [citing *Luce*]. * * * This case does not involve Rule 609(a), but courts have refused to limit *Luce* to Rule 609(a) cases and have instead applied its principles to analogous contexts."). Should *Luce* be inapplicable when impeachment would violate constitutional principles as suggested by Justice Brennan? Compare United States ex rel. Adkins v. Greer, 791 F.2d 590, 593–94 (7th Cir.1986) (*Luce* inapplicable to ruling on impeachment with unconstitutionally obtained confession), with Jordan v. State, 591 A.2d 875, 878 (Md.1991) (*Luce* applicable to claim that confession was involuntary). See also People v. Boyd, 682 N.W.2d 459, 466–67 (Mich. 2004) ("[D]efendant was required to testify to preserve for review his challenge to the trial court's ruling in limine allowing the prosecutor to admit evidence of defendant's exercise of his *Miranda* right to remain silent. Because the statement

at issue in this case would have been properly admissible in one context, defendant's failure to testify precludes us from being able to determine whether the trial court's ruling was erroneous and, if so, whether the error requires reversal.'').

2. *Rejecting Luce.* Some state courts have declined to follow *Luce*. See, e.g., Warren v. State, 124 P.3d 522, 527 (Nev.2005) (''But states declining to follow *Luce* maintain that the problem of meaningful review is unfounded when the record sufficiently demonstrates, through an offer of proof, the nature of the defendant's proposed testimony and that the defendant refrained from testifying when faced with impeachment by a prior conviction. Under such conditions, a reviewing court would have a sufficient record to conduct a harmless error analysis.''); State v. Whitehead, 517 A.2d 373 (N.J.1986) (impeachment with prior conviction reviewable without defendant testifying); State v. Lamb, 365 S.E.2d 600, 607–08 (N.C.1988) (erroneous decision to permit impeachment of defendant with bad acts preserved for review in spite of defendant's decision not to testify).

3. Does *Luce* mean that, in order to preserve an issue of improper impeachment for appeal, the defendant or witness must in all cases have testified before the jury? The Supreme Court's concerns (1) that a trial court must know the precise nature of the defendant's testimony, which is unknowable when he or she does not testify, and (2) that the ruling remains tentative and subject to changes occasioned by later developments during trial prior to the moment of the defendant's testimony, may be met without the evidence being revealed to the jury. See United States v. Griffin, 818 F.2d 97, 105 (1st Cir.1987); United States v. Wexler, 657 F.Supp. 966, 970–71 (E.D.Pa.1987). What about the court's concern that the defendant in bad faith will ''plant'' error in the record, never intending to testify? Is this danger, which the Court suggests is not subject to remedy because of the difficulty of enforcing any commitment by the defendant to testify, limited to criminal litigation and specifically to impeachment of the defendant?

OHLER v. UNITED STATES

Supreme Court of the United States, 2000.
529 U.S. 753.

CHIEF JUSTICE REHNQUIST delivered the opinion of the Court.

* * *

Maria Ohler drove a van from Mexico to California in July 1997. As she passed through the San Ysidro Port of Entry, a customs inspector noticed that someone had tampered with one of the van's interior panels. Inspectors searched the van and discovered approximately 81 pounds of marijuana. Ohler was arrested and charged with importation of marijuana and possession of marijuana with the intent to distribute. Before trial, the Government filed motions *in limine* seeking to admit Ohler's prior felony conviction as character evidence under Federal Rule of Evidence 404(b) and as impeachment evidence under Rule 609(a)(1). The District Court denied the motion to admit the conviction as character evidence, but reserved ruling on whether the conviction could be used for impeachment purposes. On the first day of trial, the District Court ruled that if Ohler testified, evidence of her prior conviction would be admissible under Rule 609(a)(1). * * * She testified in her own defense, denying any knowledge of the marijuana. She also admitted on direct examination that she had been convicted of possession of methamphetamine in 1993. The jury found Ohler guilty of both counts * * *.

On appeal, Ohler challenged the District Court's *in limine* ruling allowing the Government to use her prior conviction for impeachment purposes. The Court of Appeals for the Ninth Circuit affirmed, holding that Ohler waived her objection by introducing evidence of the conviction during her direct examination.169 F.3d 1200 (C.A.9 1999). We granted certiorari to resolve a conflict among the Circuits regarding whether appellate review of an *in limine* ruling is available in this situation. * * * We affirm.

Generally, a party introducing evidence cannot complain on appeal that the evidence was erroneously admitted. See 1 J. Weinstein & M. Berger, Weinstein's Federal Evidence § 103.14, 103–30 (2d ed.2000). Cf. 1 J. Strong, McCormick on Evidence § 55, p. 246 (5th ed. 1999) ("If a party who has objected to evidence of a certain fact himself produces evidence from his own witness of the same fact, he has waived his objection."). Ohler seeks to avoid the consequences of this well-established commonsense principle by invoking Rules 103 and 609 of the Federal Rules of Evidence. But neither of these Rules addresses the question at issue here. Rule 103 sets forth the unremarkable propositions that a party must make a timely objection to a ruling admitting evidence and that a party cannot challenge an evidentiary ruling unless it affects a substantial right. The Rule does not purport to determine when a party waives a prior objection, and it is silent with respect to the effect of introducing evidence on direct examination, and later assigning its admission as error on appeal.

Rule 609(a) is equally unavailing for Ohler; it merely identifies the situations in which a witness' prior conviction may be admitted for impeachment purposes. The Rule originally provided that admissible prior conviction evidence could be elicited from the defendant or established by public record during cross-examination, but it was amended in 1990 to clarify that the evidence could also be introduced on direct examination. According to Ohler, it follows from this amendment that a party does not waive her objection to the *in limine* ruling by introducing the evidence herself. However, like Rule 103, Rule 609(a) simply does not address this issue. There is no question that the Rule authorizes the eliciting of a prior conviction on direct examination, but it does no more than that.

Next, Ohler argues that it would be unfair to apply such a waiver rule in this situation because it compels a defendant to forgo the tactical advantage of preemptively introducing the conviction in order to appeal the *in limine* ruling. She argues that if a defendant is forced to wait for evidence of the conviction to be introduced on cross-examination, the jury will believe that the defendant is less credible because she was trying to conceal the conviction. The Government disputes that the defendant is unduly disadvantaged by waiting for the prosecution to introduce the conviction on cross-examination. First, the Government argues that it is debatable whether jurors actually perceive a defendant to be more credible if she introduces a conviction herself. Brief for United States 28. Second, even if jurors do consider the defendant more credible, the Government suggests that it is an unwarranted advantage because the jury does not realize that the defendant disclosed the conviction only after failing to persuade the court to exclude it. *Ibid.*

Whatever the merits of these contentions, they tend to obscure the fact that both the Government and the defendant in a criminal trial must make choices as the trial progresses. For example, the defendant must decide whether or not to take the stand in her own behalf. If she has an innocent or mitigating explanation for evidence that might otherwise incriminate, acquittal may be more likely if she takes the stand. Here, for example, petitioner testified that she had no knowledge of the marijuana discovered in the van, that the van had been taken to Mexico without her permission, and that she had gone there simply to retrieve the van. But once the defendant testifies, she is subject to cross-examination, including impeachment by prior convictions, and the decision to take the stand may prove damaging instead of helpful. A defendant has a further choice to make if she decides to testify, notwithstanding a prior conviction. The defendant must choose whether to introduce the conviction on direct examination and remove the sting or to take her chances with the prosecutor's possible elicitation of the conviction on cross-examination.

The Government, too, in a case such as this, must make a choice. If the defendant testifies, it must choose whether or not to impeach her by use of her prior conviction. Here the trial judge had indicated he would allow its use, but the Government still had to consider whether its use might be deemed reversible error on appeal. This choice is often based on the Government's appraisal of the apparent effect of the defendant's testimony. If she has offered a plausible, innocent explanation of the evidence against her, it will be inclined to use the prior conviction; if not, it may decide not to risk possible reversal on appeal from its use.

Due to the structure of trial, the Government has one inherent advantage in these competing trial strategies. Cross-examination comes after direct examination, and therefore the Government need not make its choice until the defendant has elected whether or not to take the stand in her own behalf and after the Government has heard the defendant testify.

Petitioner's submission would deny to the Government its usual right to decide, after she testifies, whether or not to use her prior conviction against her. She seeks to short-circuit that decisional process by offering the conviction herself (and thereby removing the sting) and still preserve its admission as a claim of error on appeal.

But here petitioner runs into the position taken by the Court in a similar, but not identical, situation in Luce v. United States, 469 U.S. 38 (1984), that "[a]ny possible harm flowing from a district court's *in limine* ruling permitting impeachment by a prior conviction is wholly speculative." Id., at 41. Only when the government exercises its option to elicit the testimony is an appellate court confronted with a case where, under the normal rules of trial, the defendant can claim the denial of a substantial right if in fact the district court's *in limine* ruling proved to be erroneous. In our view, there is nothing "unfair," as petitioner puts it, about putting petitioner to her choice in accordance with the normal rules of trial.

Finally, Ohler argues that applying this rule to her situation unconstitutionally burdens her right to testify. She relies on Rock v. Arkansas, 483 U.S. 44 (1987), where we held that a prohibition of hypnotically refreshed testimony interfered with the defendant's right to testify. But here the rule in question does not prevent Ohler from taking the stand and presenting any admissible testimony which she chooses. She is of course subject to cross-examination and subject to impeachment by the use of a prior conviction. In a sense, the use of these tactics by the Government may deter a defendant from taking the stand. But, as we said in McGautha v. California, 402 U.S. 183, 215 (1971):

> "It has long been held that a defendant who takes the stand in his own behalf cannot then claim the privilege against cross-examination on matters reasonably related to the subject matter of his direct examination * * *. It is not thought overly harsh in such situations to require that the determination whether to waive the privilege take into account the matters which may be brought out on cross-examination. It is also generally recognized that a defendant who takes the stand in his own behalf may be impeached by proof of prior convictions or the like. * * * Again, it is not thought inconsistent with the enlightened administration of criminal justice to require the defendant to weigh such pros and cons in deciding whether to testify."

For these reasons, we conclude that a defendant who preemptively introduces evidence of a prior conviction on direct examination may not on appeal claim that the admission of such evidence was error.

The judgment of the Court of Appeals for the Ninth Circuit is therefore affirmed.

It is so ordered.

JUSTICE SOUTER, with whom JUSTICE STEVENS, JUSTICE GINSBURG, and JUSTICE BREYER join, dissenting.

The majority holds that a testifying defendant perforce waives the right to appeal an adverse *in limine* ruling admitting prior convictions for impeachment. The holding is without support in precedent, the rules of evidence, or the reasonable objectives of trial, and I respectfully dissent.

The only case of this Court that the majority claims as even tangential support for its waiver rule is *Luce v. United States* * * *.

This case is different, there being a factual record on which Ohler's claim can be reviewed. She testified, and there is no question that the *in limine* ruling controlled her counsel's decision to enquire about the earlier conviction; defense lawyers do not set out to impeach their own witnesses, much less their clients. Since analysis for harmless error is made no more difficult by the fact that the convictions came out on direct examination, not cross-examination, the case raises none of the practical difficulties on which *Luce* turned, and *Luce* does not dictate today's result.

In fact, the majority's principal reliance is not on precedent but on the "commonsense" rule that "a party introducing evidence cannot complain on appeal that the evidence was erroneously admitted." * * * But this is no more support for today's holding than *Luce* is, for the common sense that approves the rule also limits its reach to a point well short of this case. The general rule makes sense, first, when a party who has freely chosen to introduce evidence of a particular fact later sees his opponent's evidence of the same fact erroneously admitted. He suffers no prejudice. * * * The rule makes sense, second, when the objecting party takes inconsistent positions, first requesting admission and then assigning error to the admission of precisely the same evidence at his opponent's behest. "The party should not be permitted 'to blow hot and cold' in this way." 1 J. Strong, McCormick on Evidence § 55, p. 246, n.14 (5th ed.1999).

Neither of these reasons applies when (as here) the defendant has opposed admission of the evidence and introduced it herself only to mitigate its effect in the hands of her adversary. Such a case falls beyond the scope of the general principle, and the scholarship almost uniformly treats it as exceptional. See, *e.g.,* 1 J. Wigmore, Evidence § 18, p. 836 (P. Tillers rev. 1983) ("[A] party who has made an unsuccessful motion in limine to exclude evidence that he expects the proponent to offer may be able to first to offer that same evidence without waiving his claim of error") * * *. The general thrust of the law of evidence, then, not only fails to support the majority's approach, but points rather clearly in the other direction.

With neither precedent nor principle to support its chosen rule, the majority is reduced to saying that "there is nothing 'unfair' * * * about putting petitioner to her choice in accordance with the normal rules of trial." * * * Things are not this simple, however.

Any claim of a new rule's fairness under normal trial conditions will have to stand or fall on how well the rule would serve the objects that trials in general, and the Rules of Evidence in particular, are designed to achieve. Thus the provisions of Federal Rule of Evidence 102, that "[t]hese rules shall be construed to secure fairness in administration, elimination of unjustifiable expense and delay, and promotion of growth and development of the law of evidence to the end that the truth may be ascertained and proceedings justly determined." A judge's job, accordingly, is to curb the tactics of the trial battle in favor of weighing evidence calmly and getting to the most sensible understanding of whatever gave rise to the controversy before the court. The question is not which side gains a tactical advantage, but which rule assists in uncovering the truth. Today's new rule can make no such claim.

Previously convicted witnesses may testify honestly, but some convictions raise more than the ordinary question about the witness's readiness to speak truthfully. A factfinder who appreciates a heightened possibility of perjury will respond with heightened scrutiny, and when a defendant discloses prior convictions at the outset of her testimony, the jury will bear those convictions in mind as she testifies, and will scrutinize what she says more carefully. The purpose of Rule 609, in making some convictions admissible to impeach a witness's credibility, is thus fully served by a defendant's own testimony that the convictions occurred.

It is true that when convictions are revealed only on cross-examination, the revelation also warns the factfinder, but the timing of their disclosure may do more. The jury may feel that in testifying without saying anything about the convictions the defendant has meant to conceal them. The jury's assessment of the defendant's testimony may be affected not only by knowing that she has committed crimes in the past, but by blaming her for not being forthcoming when she seemingly could have been. Creating such an impression of current deceit by concealment is very much at odds with any purpose behind Rule 609, being obviously antithetical to dispassionate factfinding in support of a sound conclusion. The chance to create that impression is a tactical advantage for the Government, but only in the majority's dismissive sense of the term; it may affect the outcome of the trial, but only if it disserves the search for truth.

Allowing the defendant to introduce the convictions on direct examination thus tends to promote fairness of trial without depriving the Government of anything to which it is entitled. There is no reason to discourage the defendant from introducing the conviction herself, as the majority's waiver rule necessarily does.

Notes and Questions

1. *Rejecting Ohler.* Some state courts have declined to follow *Ohler.* E.g., State v. Swanson, 707 N.W.2d 645, 654 (Minn.2006) ("We recently rejected similar reasoning, stating that '[i]t is inconsistent with our precedent and with our notion of fairness to conclude that once a defendant chooses to stipulate to evidence he was unsuccessful in getting excluded he has waived the opportunity to argue on appeal that the court erred in admitting the evidence.' "); Pineda v. State, 88 P.3d 827, 831 (Nev.2004) ("States that have rejected *Ohler* have done so because a trial court is fully aware of the proposed evidence and law when ruling on such evidence in limine, and it is a poor trial tactic for defense attorneys to wait for the

prosecution to introduce such evidence on cross-examination. Given the nature of this tactical dilemma, these courts have held that a defendant may under such circumstances appeal a trial court's preliminary ruling conditionally admitting prior bad acts or convictions for impeachment purposes.'').

2. *Invited error*. See All American Life & Cas. Co. v. Oceanic Trade Alliance Council Int'l, Inc., 756 F.2d 474, 479–80 (6th Cir.1985) (''Under the 'invited error' doctrine, it is an accepted matter of law that where the injection of allegedly inadmissible evidence is attributable to the action of the party seeking to exclude that evidence, its introduction does not constitute reversible error.''); State v. Campbell, 738 N.E.2d 1178, 1188 (Ohio 2000) (''This court has found invited error when a party asked the court to take some action later claimed to be erroneous, or affirmatively consented to a procedure the trial judge proposed. But defense counsel did not suggest, request, or affirmatively consent to this procedure. * * * But invited error must be more than mere 'acquiesence in the trial judge's erroneous conclusion.' ''); State v. Gary M.B., 676 N.W.2d 475, 480 (Wis.2004) (''Under the doctrine of strategic waiver, also known as invited error, '[a] defendant cannot create his own error by deliberate choice of strategy and then ask to receive benefit from that error on appeal.' '').

3. *''Fighting fire with fire.''* Cross-examination on a matter, or introducing evidence to rebut it, has occasionally been held to waive objections to the matter previously made and overruled. See, e.g., State v. McKinney, 190 S.E.2d 30 (S.C.1972) (unless the objection is expressly reserved, cross-examination waives objection). However, the vast weight of authority is contra. 1 Wigmore, Evidence § 18, at 838 n.37 (Tillers rev. 1983). Parties objecting to admission may be held to waive the objection if they go beyond cross-examination and rebuttal of the evidence and affirmatively rely upon the inadmissible evidence and introduce similar evidence through their own witnesses. 1 Graham, Handbook of Federal Evidence § 103.4 (6th ed. 2006). Is this concept of waiver consistent with the Federal Rules of Evidence? Even if not held to waive the initial objection, introduction of other favorable evidence that is also inadmissible may render the initial error harmless. 21 Wright & Graham, Federal Practice and Procedure: Evidence § 5039, at 202–03 (1977).

4. *''Opening the door.''* The above concepts are related to, but are analytically distinct from, other situations that are sometimes included under the opening-the-door label. In this category, parties may, by their decision to open a specific issue such as character, permit response by an opponent that would have been barred absent their action under general concepts of relevancy or specific application of a rule, such as Rule 404(a) governing evidence of the character of the accused. See Chapter 8, Section C, infra. See 21 Wright & Graham, note 3, supra, § 5039, at 199–200. The distinction between this ''door opening'' concept and those discussed above is that there is nothing improper here about introduction of the new issue into the case. As a result, the analysis is a much more straightforward application of concepts of probativity weighed against prejudice, confusion, and consumption of time, rather than the equitable concern of rough justice that infuses what passes for analysis under the other concepts.

When the first inquiry on an issue occurs during cross-examination, the door-opening principle does not operate because cross-examiners are not permitted to open the door for themselves. United States v. Mariani, 539 F.2d 915, 923–24 (2d Cir.1976). This limitation, however, is not generally applicable to matters "plainly within the scope of" direct examination or "reasonably suggested by" it. United States v. Havens, 446 U.S. 620, 627 (1980).

(4) LIMITED ADMISSIBILITY: FEDERAL RULE 105

CARBO v. UNITED STATES

United States Court of Appeals, Ninth Circuit, 1963.
314 F.2d 718.

[Carbo and others were convicted of extortion affecting commerce and of conspiracy. The case arose out of their efforts to secure managerial control of Don Jordan, a welterweight fighter, by bringing pressure to bear upon his manager, Donald Nesseth, and a local promoter, Jackie Leonard.]

MERRILL, CIRCUIT JUDGE.

* * *

Sica * * * objected to the introduction of testimony by Leonard and Nesseth to the effect that by reputation they knew of Sica as an "underworld" man and a "strong-arm" man. The objection was overruled. Sica assigns error in these respects.

In discussing the admissibility of evidence of bad moral character the Supreme Court in Michelson v. United States, 1948, 335 U.S. 469, 475 * * *, states:

> "Courts that follow the common-law tradition almost unanimously have come to disallow resort by the prosecution to any kind of evidence of a defendant's evil character to establish a probability of his guilt. * * * "

* * *

The nature of Sica's reputation was not introduced into the case for the purpose of characterizing him as a bad man likely to resort to the conduct with which he is charged. This was not the source of its relevance.

Instead the prosecution relied on the reputation of Sica as a probative fact enabling the jury to infer that Sica had intervened with Leonard and Nesseth knowing that his presence would instill fear in them and intending to manipulate this fear for the benefit of Carbo and Palermo; and further, to conclude that Carbo and Palermo had secured Sica's participation with full realization that his effectiveness was based upon the fear his reputation could inspire in the victims.

In cases of extortion based upon fear of violence the facts of fear, actual or anticipated, and of its reasonableness, are vital factors. To prove a substantive act of extortion it is essential to show the generation of fear in the victim. To prove a substantive act of attempted extortion it is necessary to prove an attempt to instill fear. To prove a conspiracy to extort it is necessary to show a plan to instill fear.

Here Sica stood in the position of a dangerous weapon to be used to strike fear into the hearts of Leonard and Nesseth. It was part of the prosecution's case to charge and to prove that the conspirators considered Sica to occupy this position. That Leonard and Nesseth considered him to be dangerous and that fear reasonably resulted from his appearance because of his reputation constituted relevant facts upon this part of the prosecution's case. * * *

It is true that (despite the precautionary steps taken by the judge as later discussed) the jury may have permitted this evidence to bear upon the probability of Sica's guilt. The question is whether this possibility renders such evidence unduly prejudicial and inadmissible. If so, the United States is precluded from establishing a material part of its case.

The question then is not whether the United States may use Sica's reputation as a sword against him, but whether he may himself make use of it as a shield to immunize himself from proof of the means by which the conspirators planned to frighten their victims into submission. If he may, then all who are known to live by violence are free to extort by the tacit threat of violence conveyed by their reputations; for the reasonableness of the resulting fear, as determined by its cause, may not be presented to the jury.

We cannot accept this result as a sound balance of the conflicting interests involved.

This, in our judgment (with such safeguards as were taken by the trial judge), is a proper case for application of what has been termed the "multiple admissibility doctrine." As stated in 1 Wigmore, Evidence (3d Ed., 1940), § 13, page 300:

> "When an evidentiary fact is offered for one purpose, and becomes admissible by satisfying all the rules applicable to it in that capacity, it is not inadmissible because it does not satisfy the rules applicable to it in some other capacity, and because the jury might improperly consider it in the latter capacity. This doctrine, although involving certain risks, is indispensible [sic] as a practical rule."

* * *

To avoid confusion of issues and to foreclose the jury from using the reputation evidence to convict defendants on the "bad man" theory, the court below, upon admitting the testimony in question, instructed the jury as to the limited consideration which might be given. The subject was again dealt with in the court's charge to the jury. We have no doubt but that to the maximum extent possible, prejudice flowing from any confusion of issues by the jury was eliminated.

* * *

We conclude that the district court did not err in * * * in admitting the evidence of Sica's reputation.

SHERMAN v. BURKE CONTRACTING, INC.

United States Court of Appeals, Eleventh Circuit, 1990.
891 F.2d 1527.

PER CURIAM:

Willie Lewis Sherman brought this suit against his former employer, Burke Contracting, Inc., and its president and principal owner, William Burke, (collectively Burke) seeking recovery for two acts of racial discrimination. * * * [After leaving Burke, Sherman] found work with another contractor, Palmer Construction Co. (Palmer). [He alleges] that Burke, in retaliation against him for complaining to the EEOC, persuaded Palmer to fire him.

* * *

To prove that Burke caused Palmer to fire him, Sherman introduced into evidence a tape recording of a conversation he had with Wade Palmer, the owner of Palmer Construction, a few weeks after he left Palmer's employ. In that conversation, which Sherman recorded without Wade Palmer's knowledge, Wade Palmer stated that William Burke had urged him to fire Sherman for complaining about Burke to the EEOC.[17]

Burke contends that the district court erred in permitting the recording to come before the jury because the recording was inaudible and its contents were hearsay. We find no error.

The controversy concerning the admissibility of the recording arose during Sherman's case-in-chief[18] when his attorney called Wade Palmer to the witness stand and asked him if William Burke had spoken to him

17. The tape recording contains the following exchange: Sherman: "Alright sir, Mr. Wade you know when you were telling me about [how] Mr. Bill and Mr. John told you not to work me. [pause] You remember I was working that week with you and you were telling me * * *." Palmer: "Un, un, that ain't what I told you they didn't tell me not to work you. They said if they was me, they wouldn't work you, you turning it around. They can't tell me who to work and who not to work. They just said if I was you, he sued us and done us like he did, if I was you, I wouldn't. * * * Like he didn't tell me I couldn't work you, he just told me if it was him and you done sued him like you did, and all, you might turn around and sue me."

18. The controversy actually began prior to trial when Burke's counsel moved the court in limine to prevent Sherman from mentioning the tape recording in the jury's presence; counsel argued that the recording's contents were hearsay. The court reserved decision on the matter until trial, at which time Burke could renew his objection. As the text indicates, infra, after the court admitted the tape recording for purposes of impeachment, Burke objected on the ground that the recording was inaudible. Under the circumstances, we do not consider the motion in limine; rather, we review the objection made at trial and the court's ruling thereon.

about Sherman at any time during Sherman's employment with Palmer Construction. Counsel hoped that Palmer would say that a conversation had taken place and that William Burke had urged him to fire Sherman for complaining to the EEOC; this testimony would have been admissible as nonhearsay under Fed.R.Evid. 801(d)(2) (admission by party-opponent). When Palmer responded that there had been no such conversation, Sherman's attorney approached the bench and asked to discuss a matter out of the jury's presence. After the jury had been excused, counsel informed the court that Palmer had told Sherman that such a conversation had, in fact, taken place; that Sherman had surreptitiously recorded Palmer's statement to this effect; and that counsel wished to impeach Palmer by playing the recording before the jury.

The court concluded that the recording might be admissible as impeachment evidence and suggested that the proper course would be for counsel to call Sherman to the stand, in the jury's absence, and have him identify the recording. *See generally* Fed.R.Evid. 901. If Sherman identified it, he could then recall Palmer to the stand and confront him with the recording. Defense counsel made no objection to this procedure. Accordingly, with the jury still out, Sherman took the stand and identified the recording as the one he had made of his conversation with Wade Palmer a few weeks after the company had fired him.

At this point, Sherman's counsel argued that a sufficient predicate had been laid to introduce the recording into evidence for purposes of impeaching Palmer's statement that William Burke had not spoken to him about Sherman. Defense counsel objected, however, on the ground that portions of the recording were inaudible. The court found that the recording adequately revealed the relevant portion of the conversation between Sherman and Palmer and therefore overruled counsel's objection. The defense raised no objection on hearsay grounds; nor did counsel request a limiting instruction to inform the jury that the recording was admitted solely to impeach Palmer's testimony. The trial then resumed, with Sherman taking the stand and identifying the tape recording. The court admitted the recording into evidence and played it before the jury without any limiting instruction. * * *

Burke's second claim is that the recording was hearsay. We agree, as did the district court, which admitted the recording only for impeachment purposes. *See generally* Fed.R.Evid. 801(c). The court, however, gave no limiting instruction, and the defense failed to raise any objection on that point. In effect, then, the recording was received for the truth of its contents, and Sherman's counsel used it for that purpose—without any objection from the defense—in his closing argument to the jury. We believe that had defense counsel requested a limiting instruction, the court would have given one, having already recognized that the recording's sole value was as impeachment evidence. Burke now asks us to hold that its attorney had no duty to request a limiting instruction but that the court had a duty to give such an instruction on its own initiative. We refuse to so hold.

The relevant rule of evidence, Fed.R.Evid. 105, provides: "When evidence which is admissible as to one party or for one purpose but not admissible as to another party or for another purpose is admitted, the court, *upon request*, shall restrict the evidence to its proper scope and instruct the jury accordingly." (Emphasis added.) Under this rule, the court had a duty to instruct only "upon request." Since the court had no duty to give a limiting instruction in the absence of a request, we may reverse only if we conclude that the court's failure to give the instruction constituted plain error. *See United States v. Garcia*, 530 F.2d 650, 656 (5th Cir.1976).

We have found no civil case in which a federal appellate court has labelled as plain error a trial judge's failure to give a limiting instruction with respect to evidence that is admissible for some purpose.[19] Indeed, we have uncovered only a single case even addressing the issue. In that case, *Herndon v. Seven Bar Flying Serv., Inc.*, 716 F.2d 1322 (10th Cir.1983), the appellant argued that plain error occurred when a trial judge failed sua sponte to instruct a jury that evidence of subsequent remedial measures was not admissible to prove negligence. The Tenth Circuit recognized that such an instruction would have been appropriate if requested but held that, without such a request, reversal would be improper unless the trial court's failure to instruct constituted plain error. *Id.* at 1330. The court then concluded that the absence of an instruction in that case did not constitute plain error because it resulted in no manifest "miscarriage of justice." *Id.*; *cf. Wilson v. Attaway*, 757 F.2d 1227, 1242–43 (11th Cir.1985) (finding no plain error in trial judge's failure sua sponte to exclude relevant evidence on ground that danger of unfair prejudice outweighed probative value based on his holding that admission resulted in no manifest "miscarriage of justice"). Lawyers frequently choose for strategic reasons not to request limiting instructions. In order to find plain error in this context, therefore, a court must conclude that, as a matter of law, counsel's strategic choice resulted in a manifest miscarriage of justice. We cannot reach such a conclusion here. We therefore find no plain error in the trial court's decision to admit the tape-recorded statement for its nonhearsay purpose without a cautionary instruction.

* * *

AFFIRMED in part, REVERSED in part, and VACATED in part.

[CHIEF JUDGE TJOFLAT and SENIOR JUDGE ATKINS concurred specially on another issue.]

Notes and Questions

1. *Limiting instructions.* Concerning the problem of limiting and curative instructions, America's most famous trial lawyer once wrote:

19. Appellants concede that the challenged evidence was admissible to impeach the credibility of relevant testimony: whether Palmer had talked with William Burke about Sherman while Sherman was an employee of Palmer Construction was pertinent to the merits of Sherman's case against Burke.

> Few judges are psychologists, or they would realize that nothing can be stricken out of a human consciousness after being once let in. Judges seem to be quite unaware that it is a hard task to put anything into the average mind, and, once in, an impossible one to take it out. * * * If, after days or weeks or months of taking testimony, the judge decides that some item was not [admissible], he coolly tells the jury that they are to ignore this, that, and the other thing, probably without at all explaining his meaning of "ignore." The jury is so instructed, regardless of the fact that no one is able to know all the specific things that enter into his opinion, or take away, from an opinion already formed, any of the special facts, circumstances, guesses, or prejudices that go into its making.

Darrow, The Story of My Life 145 (Grosset's Universal ed.1960).

In O'Rear v. Fruehauf Corp., 554 F.2d 1304, 1309 (5th Cir.1977), after counsel had repeatedly brought out prejudicial matter contrary to court rulings, the judge put it more picturesquely: "You can throw a skunk into the jury box and instruct the jurors not to smell it, but it doesn't do any good."

2. *Multiple parties*. Problems of limited admissibility also arise when evidence is admissible against one party but not against a co-party. In Delli Paoli v. United States, 352 U.S. 232 (1957), the trial judge admitted a confession by one defendant which implicated his codefendant even though it was inadmissible against the codefendant. The Supreme Court held that no error was committed since the jury was instructed to consider the confession only against the confessing defendant. However, in Bruton v. United States, 391 U.S. 123 (1968), *Delli Paoli* was expressly overruled. The Court concluded that the risk that the jury would not follow the instruction was too great, and since the confessing defendant elected not to testify, the right of the nonconfessing defendant to confront the witnesses against him under the Sixth Amendment was violated. The Court described the confession as "powerfully incriminating" and "devastating." See also Gray v. Maryland, 523 U.S. 185, 192 (1998) ("Redactions that simply replace a name with an obvious blank space or a word such as 'deleted' or a symbol or other similarly obvious indications of alteration * * * leave statements that * * * so closely resemble *Bruton's* unredacted statements that, in our view, the law must require the same result.").

What is the reach of the decision when the impact of the codefendant's confession is less direct or where its independent impact is diminished by the admission of the defendant's own confession? For some answers to these questions, see Richardson v. Marsh, 481 U.S. 200 (1987) (Confrontation Clause not violated where direct references to nontestifying defendant omitted from codefendant's confession even though defendant is indirectly linked to the confession by other evidence); Cruz v. New York, 481 U.S. 186 (1987) (Confrontation Clause violated when codefendant's confession naming defendant is introduced even though defendant's own interlocking confession admitted, but since defendant's own confession properly admitted error may be rendered harmless). For further examination of confrontation issues, see Chapter 13, Section C, infra.

(5) NON–JURY TRIALS

CLARK v. UNITED STATES

United States Court of Appeals, Eighth Circuit, 1932.
61 F.2d 695, aff'd, 289 U.S. 1 (1933).

[Genevieve Clark was accepted and acted as a juror in a celebrated mail fraud case. After a seven week trial, the jury deliberated one week and was unable to reach a verdict. Throughout the deliberations the vote was eleven for conviction and one for acquittal, the lone vote being Mrs. Clark's. She was then adjudged guilty of contempt for withholding, on voir dire examination, information as to her previous associations with the accused and other aspects of bias and prejudice. On appeal, one of the grounds of error asserted was the admission in evidence of the deliberations in the jury room.]

KENYON, CIRCUIT JUDGE.

* * * There is no question here of impeaching the verdict of a jury. The question is the misconduct of one chosen as a juror. * * *

The testimony admitted of other jurors as to the statements and conduct of appellant in the jury room were admissible as bearing on the question of the falsity of answers given by her on the voir dire examination. No public policy requires the proceedings in the jury room to be kept secret under the circumstances here presented.

Assuming, however, that such testimony should have been excluded, there is exclusive thereof sufficient evidence in this record in our judgment to sustain the finding of the trial court as to criminal contempt. * * *

The fact that immaterial evidence may have been admitted does not necessarily require the reversal of a case where a court sits without a jury as a trier of fact, as there is a presumption that it acts only upon the basis of proper evidence. If there is not sufficient evidence to sustain the trial court if the improper evidence is disregarded, the presumption of course breaks down. In Swepston v. United States (C.C.A.) 251 F. 205, 209, referring to this question, the court said: "It is to be presumed that the court at last considered only the facts and circumstances that were in reality admissible and also calculated to support the judgments claimed; and this was in accord with settled rules of practice in cases tried without a jury." In Sinclair v. United States, 279 U.S. 749, 767 * * *, the court said: "Objections are offered to the admission of certain evidence. In answer, we need only refer to what was said in United States v. King, 7 How. 833, 854, 855 (12 L.Ed. 934): 'In some unimportant particulars, the evidence objected to was not admissible. But where the court decides the fact and the law without the intervention of a jury, the admission of illegal testimony, even if material, is not of itself a ground for reversing the judgment, nor is it properly the subject of a bill of exceptions. If evidence appears to have been improperly admitted, the appellate court will reject it, and proceed to decide the case as if it was not in the record.' " In Oates v. United States (C.C.A.) 233 F. 201, 205, it is said: "When a judge hears a case without a jury, he is supposed to act only on proper evidence, and if on review it is found that the evidence properly admitted justifies the decree it ought to be affirmed, and if not it ought to be reversed. * * * In all these and many other cases the rule laid down by Chief Justice Marshall in Field v. United States, 9 Pet. 202, 9 L.Ed. 94, has been followed: 'As the cause was * * * not tried by a jury, the exception to the admission of evidence was not properly the subject of a bill of exceptions. But if the District Court improperly admitted the evidence, the only effect would be that this court would reject that evidence, and proceed to decide the cause as if it were not on the record. It would not, however, of itself constitute any ground for a reversal of the judgment.' "

* * * The judgment of the court as to the contempt is affirmed, but the sentence is set aside and the case remanded to the trial court only for the purpose of resentencing.

Remanded.

GARDNER, CIRCUIT JUDGE (dissenting).

* * *

Finally, it is said in the majority opinion that the fact that immaterial evidence may have been admitted does not necessarily require a reversal of the case where the court sits without a jury, because there is a presumption that it acts only on the basis of proper evidence. There are two answers to this suggestion: First, if this evidence be excluded, there is no substantial evidence to sustain the judgment of the trial court, and the evidence is not only immaterial but is incompetent; and, second, that while it will ordinarily be presumed that the court sitting without a jury considers only the material and competent evidence, yet this is only a presumption, and it affirmatively appears in this case that the court did consider and did rely upon this very evidence. In the opinion of the trial court it is said: "During the deliberations of the jury, after the case was finally submitted, she announced that, since Mr. Horowitz had been unable to convince her of the guilt of the defendants, the other jurors could hardly expect to do so. She virtually closed her ears to the arguments of other jurors, and made a statement with respect to the government witness Cobel, the effect of which was to charge him with having given perjured testimony in a case in the South in an attempt to convict an innocent man. * * * Mrs. Clark, during the deliberations of the jury, expressed a wish that she might consult with her husband and secure his advice. She also made statements to the effect that she could not vote to send seven men to the penitentiary. The jury were out for approximately one week, and stood eleven for conviction, and one (Mrs. Clark) for acquittal." In another part of the opinion the court refers to the appellant's "unyielding attitude" in the jury room.

This conclusively shows that the trial court did not disregard nor exclude this incompetent evidence, and it is elementary that when facts appear presumptions vanish. A presumption cannot be weighed in the balance as against facts. * * *

Notes and Questions

1. *Reversals rare.* While, as *Clark* teaches, reversal will rarely result from admission of questionable evidence in a bench trial, the erroneous exclusion of evidence is treated the same in bench and jury trials. A professional finder of fact is no better able than a jury to consider evidence that was excluded. However, the greater danger of reversal when evidence is excluded from a bench trial does not mean that it is always foolish to object. Parties do not need to worry about reversal on appeal unless they won below, and exclusion of persuasive, albeit inadmissible, evidence may be critical to a victory in the trial court. This is true even when the finder of fact is a judge, equipped with a sophisticated legal mind that we presume is capable of ignoring improperly admitted evidence.

2. *Federal Rules.* The position set forth in *Clark* continues under the Federal Rules. See Tampa Bay Shipbuilding & Repair Co. v. Cedar Shipping Co., 320 F.3d 1213, 1216 (11th Cir.2003) ("A district court's evidentiary rulings are not subject to reversal on appeal absent a clear abuse of discretion. This standard of deference is even greater when the objected-to evidentiary ruling is made during a bench trial because it is presumed that the district judge will rely only upon properly admitted and relevant evidence.").

3. *Sources.* Levin & Cohen, The Exclusionary Rules in Nonjury Criminal Cases, 119 U.Pa.L.Rev. 905 (1971); Davis, An Approach to Rules of Evidence for Nonjury Cases, 50 A.B.A.J. 723 (1964).

4. The admissibility of evidence to impeach verdicts is considered in more detail in Chapter 16, Section B, infra.

Chapter 2[1]

LIMITATIONS OF THE ADVERSARY SYSTEM

NAPUE v. ILLINOIS

Supreme Court of the United States, 1959.
360 U.S. 264.

MR. CHIEF JUSTICE WARREN delivered the opinion of the Court.

At the murder trial of petitioner the principal state witness, then serving a 199–year sentence for the same murder, testified in response to a question by the Assistant State's Attorney that he had received no promise of consideration in return for his testimony. The Assistant State's Attorney had in fact promised him consideration, but did nothing to correct the witness' false testimony. The jury was apprised, however, that a public defender had promised "to do what he could" for the witness. The question presented is whether on these facts the failure of the prosecutor to correct the testimony of the witness which he knew to be false denied petitioner due process of law in violation of the Fourteenth Amendment to the Constitution of the United States.

The record in this Court contains testimony from which the following facts could have been found. The murder in question occurred early in the morning of August 21, 1938, in a Chicago, Illinois, cocktail lounge. Petitioner Henry Napue, the witness George Hamer, one Poe and one Townsend entered the dimly lighted lounge and announced their intention to rob those present. An off-duty policeman, present in the lounge, drew his service revolver and began firing at the four men. In the melee that followed Townsend was killed, the officer was fatally wounded, and the witness Hamer was seriously wounded. Napue and Poe carried Hamer to the car where a fifth man, one Webb, was waiting. In due course Hamer was apprehended, tried for the murder of the policeman, convicted on his plea of guilty and sentenced to 199 years. Subsequently, Poe was apprehended, tried, convicted, sentenced to death and executed. Hamer was not used as a witness.

1. In the cases and materials throughout the chapter, some footnotes have been omitted and others have been renumbered. [Ed.]

Thereafter, petitioner Napue was apprehended. He was put on trial with Hamer being the principal witness for the State. Hamer's testimony was extremely important because the passage of time and the dim light in the cocktail lounge made eyewitness identification very difficult and uncertain, and because some pertinent witnesses had left the state. On the basis of the evidence presented, which consisted largely of Hamer's testimony, the jury returned a guilty verdict and petitioner was sentenced to 199 years.

Finally, the driver of the car, Webb, was apprehended. Hamer also testified against him. He was convicted of murder and sentenced to 199 years.

Following the conviction of Webb, the lawyer who, as former Assistant State's Attorney, had prosecuted the Hamer, Poe and Napue cases filed a petition in the nature of a writ of error *coram nobis* on behalf of Hamer. In the petition he alleged that as prosecuting attorney he had promised Hamer that if he would testify against Napue, "a recommendation for a reduction of his [Hamer's] sentence would be made and, if possible, effectuated."[2] The attorney prayed that the court would effect "consummation of the compact entered into between the duly authorized representatives of the State of Illinois and George Hamer."

* * *

This *coram nobis* proceeding came to the attention of Napue, who thereafter filed a post conviction petition, in which he alleged that Hamer had falsely testified that he had been promised no consideration for his testimony,[3] and that the Assistant State's Attorney handling the case had known this to be false. A hearing was ultimately held at which the former Assistant State's Attorney testified that he had only promised to help Hamer if Hamer's story "about being a reluctant participant" in

2. In relevant part, his petition read as follows:

"After Hamer was sentenced your petitioner [the Assistant State's Attorney] well knowing that identification of Poe, Napue and Webb if and when apprehended would be of an unsatisfactory character and not the kind of evidence upon which a jury could be asked to inflict a proper, severe penalty, and being unable to determine in advance whether Poe, Napue and Webb would make confessions of their participation in the crime, represented to Hamer that if he would be willing to cooperate with law enforcing officials upon the trial of [*sic*] trials of Poe, Napue and Webb when they were apprehended, that a recommendation for a reduction of his sentence would be made and, if possible, effectuated.

"Before testifying on behalf of the State and against Napue, Hamer expressed to your petitioner a reluctance to cooperate any further unless he were given definite assurance that a recommendation for reduction of his sentence would be made. Your petitioner, feeling that the interests of justice required Hamer's testimony, again assured Hamer that every possible effort would be made to conform to the promise previously made to him."

3. The alleged false testimony of Hamer first occurred on his cross-examination:

"Q. Did anybody give you a reward or promise you a reward for testifying?

"A. There ain't nobody promised me anything."

On redirect examination the Assistant State's Attorney again elicited the same false answer.

"Q. [by the Assistant State's Attorney] Have I promised you that I would recommend any reduction of sentence to anybody?

"A. You did not."

the robbery was borne out, and not merely if Hamer would testify at petitioner's trial. He testified that in his *coram nobis* petition on Hamer's behalf he "probably used some language that [he] should not have used" in his "zeal to do something for Hamer" to whom he "felt a moral obligation." The lower court denied petitioner relief on the basis of the attorney's testimony.

On appeal, the Illinois Supreme Court affirmed on different grounds over two dissents. 13 Ill.2d 566, 150 N.E.2d 613. It found, contrary to the trial court, that the attorney had promised Hamer consideration if he would testify at petitioner's trial, a finding which the State does not contest here. It further found that the Assistant State's Attorney knew that Hamer had lied in denying that he had been promised consideration. It held, however, that petitioner was entitled to no relief since the jury had already been apprised that someone whom Hamer had tentatively identified as being a public defender "was going to do what he could" in aid of Hamer, and "was trying to get something did" for him.[4] We granted certiorari to consider the question posed in the first paragraph of this opinion. * * *

First, it is established that a conviction obtained through use of false evidence, known to be such by representatives of the State, must fall under the Fourteenth Amendment, Mooney v. Holohan, 294 U.S. 103; Pyle v. Kansas, 317 U.S. 213 * * *. The same result obtains when the State, although not soliciting false evidence, allows it to go uncorrected when it appears. Alcorta v. Texas, 355 U.S. 28. * * *

4. The following is Hamer's testimony on the subject:

"Q. [on cross-examination] And didn't you tell him [one of Napue's attorneys] that you wouldn't testify in this case unless you got some consideration for it?

"A. * * * Yes, I did; I told him that. * * *

"Q. What are you sentenced for?

"A. One Hundred and Ninety-Nine Years.

"Q. You hope to have that reduced, don't you?

"A. Well, if anybody would help me or do anything for me, why certainly I would.

"Q. Weren't you expecting that when you came here today?

"A. There haven't no one told me anything, no more than the lawyer. The lawyer come in and talked to me a while ago and said he was going to do what he could.

"Q. Which lawyer was that?

"A. I don't know; it was a Public Defender. I don't see him in here.

"Q. You mean he was from the Public Defender's office?

"A. I imagine that is where he was from, I don't know.

"Q. And he was the one who told you that?

"A. Yes, he told me he was trying to get something did for me.

"Q. * * * And he told you he was going to do something for you?

"A. He said he was going to try to. * * *

"Q. And you told them [police officers] you would [testify at the trial of Napue] but you expected some consideration for it?

"A. I asked them was there any chance of me getting any. The man told me he didn't know, that he couldn't promise me anything.

"Q. Then you spoke to a lawyer today who said he would try to get your time cut?

"A. That was this Public Defender. I don't even know his name. * * * "

The principle that a State may not knowingly use false evidence, including false testimony, to obtain a tainted conviction, implicit in any concept of ordered liberty, does not cease to apply merely because the false testimony goes only to the credibility of the witness. The jury's estimate of the truthfulness and reliability of a given witness may well be determinative of guilt or innocence, and it is upon such subtle factors as the possible interest of the witness in testifying falsely that a defendant's life or liberty may depend. As stated by the New York Court of Appeals in a case very similar to this one, People v. Savvides, 1 N.Y.2d 554, 557, 154 N.Y.S.2d 885, 887, 136 N.E.2d 853, 854–855:

> "It is of no consequence that the falsehood bore upon the witness' credibility rather than directly upon defendant's guilt. A lie is a lie, no matter what its subject, and, if it is in any way relevant to the case, the district attorney has the responsibility and duty to correct what he knows to be false and elicit the truth. * * * That the district attorney's silence was not the result of guile or a desire to prejudice matters little, for its impact was the same, preventing, as it did, a trial that could in any real sense be termed fair."

Second, we do not believe that the fact that the jury was apprised of other grounds for believing that the witness Hamer may have had an interest in testifying against petitioner turned what was otherwise a tainted trial into a fair one. As Mr. Justice Schaefer, joined by Chief Justice Davis, rightly put it in his dissenting opinion below, 13 Ill.2d 566, 571, 150 N.E.2d 613, 616:

> "What is overlooked here is that Hamer clearly testified that no one had offered to help him except an unidentified lawyer from the public defender's office. The jury could have concluded, and probably did conclude, that such an offer of help was unlikely to influence Hamer."

Had the jury been apprised of the true facts, however, it might well have concluded that Hamer had fabricated testimony in order to curry the favor of the very representative of the State who was prosecuting the case in which Hamer was testifying, for Hamer might have believed that such a representative was in a position to implement (as he ultimately attempted to do) any promise of consideration. That the Assistant State's Attorney himself thought it important to establish before the jury that no official source had promised Hamer consideration is made clear by his redirect examination, which was the last testimony of Hamer's heard by the jury:

> "Q. Mr. Hamer, has Judge Prystalski [the trial judge] promised you any reduction of sentence?
>
> "A. No, sir.
>
> "Q. Have I promised you that I would recommend any reduction of sentence to anybody?
>
> "A. You did not. [That answer was false and known to be so by the prosecutor.]

"Q. Has any Judge of the criminal court promised that they [*sic*] would reduce your sentence?

"A. No, sir.

"Q. Has any representative of the Parole Board been to see you and promised you a reduction of sentence?

"A. No, sir."

"Q. Has any representative of the Government of the State of Illinois promised you a reduction of sentence?

"A. No, sir."

We are therefore unable to agree with the Illinois Supreme Court that "there was no constitutional infirmity by virtue of the false statement." * * *

Reversed.

Notes and Questions

1. *Imputed knowledge.* In Giglio v. United States, 405 U.S. 150, 154 (1972), one assistant United States Attorney promised a key government witness that he would not be prosecuted if he cooperated with the government. Another assistant, who tried the case, stated in summation that no promises had been made, after the witness testified to that effect. In reversing defendant's conviction and remanding for a new trial, the Court said:

> In the circumstances shown by this record neither [the first assistant's] authority nor his failure to inform his superiors or his associates is controlling. Moreover, whether the nondisclosure was a result of negligence or design, it is the responsibility of the prosecutor. The prosecutor's office is an entity and as such it is the spokesman for the Government.

2. *Extent of obligation.* In Commonwealth of N. Mariana Islands v. Bowie, 243 F.3d 1109, 1113 (9th Cir.2001), the police seized the following letter from one of six defendants charged with murder and kidnapping:

> Hey brod I want you to help me please for this problem that were facing right now because if they know that Im the one that did this theyre gonna put me in jail for life. I tried this before. Brah this Is what we gonna do listen carefully okay if we go to court on Thursday and they ask us questions how the murder happens and who kill the philipino just say J.J. because I already talk to John and Brasslley before I was arrested but anyway don't worry about Lucas because I talk to Lucas that don't tell the detectives that Im the one that did this things. You know what brah, don't worry about this case because well win this just imagine four against one I I even lied to my lawyer about the incedent.

The letter was unsigned. Despite the letter, the prosecution went ahead and entered into plea agreements with four of the defendants, which required their testimony against the other two defendants. The court held that turning the letter over to the defense was insufficient—that the prosecutor had an independent constitutional and ethical duty to investigate. The failure to discharge this obligation deprived the defendant of due process. Citing *Napue*, the court wrote: "This duty is not discharged by attempting to finesse the problem by pressing ahead without a diligent and a good faith attempt to resolve it. A prosecutor cannot avoid this obligation by refusing to search for the truth and remaining willfully ignorant of the facts." Id. at 1118. The court elaborated:

> Never has it been more true than it is now that a criminal charged with a serious crime understands that a fast and easy way out of trouble with the law is not only to have the best lawyer money can buy or the court can appoint, but to cut a deal at someone else's expense and to purchase leniency from the government by offering testimony in return for immunity, or in return for reduced incarceration. * * *
>
> [B]ecause of the perverse and mercurial nature of the devils with whom the criminal justice system has chosen to deal, each contract for testimony is fraught with the real peril that the proffered testimony will not be truthful, but simply factually contrived to "get" a target of sufficient interest to induce concessions from the government. Defendants or suspects with nothing to sell sometimes embark on a methodical journey to manufacture evidence and to create something of value, setting up and betraying friends, relatives, and cellmates alike. Frequently, and because they are aware of the low value of their credibility, criminals will even go so far as to create corroboration for their lies by recruiting others into the plot, a circumstance we appear to confront in this case.

Id. at 1123. The author of *Bowie*, Judge Trott, had previously written on this subject. See Trott, Words of Warning for Prosecutors Using Criminals as Witnesses, 47 Hastings L.J. 1381 (1996). See also Note, Dealing with the Devil: An Examination of the FBI's Troubled Relationship With Its Confidential Informants, 34 Colum.J.L. & Soc.Probs. 301 (2001).

3. *Access to witnesses.* See ABA Model Rules 3.4(f) ("A lawyer shall not: * * * (f) request a person other than a client to refrain from voluntarily giving relevant information to another party unless * * * "). See also United States v. Hyatt, 565 F.2d 229, 232 (2d Cir.1977) ("[W]e shall not tolerate the view that the government has some special right or privilege to control access to trial witnesses."); Gregory v. United States, 369 F.2d 185, 188 (D.C.Cir.1966) ("Witnesses, particularly eye witnesses, to a crime are the property of neither the prosecution nor the defense. Both sides have an equal right, and should have an equal opportunity, to interview them. * * * But we know of nothing in the law which gives the prosecutor the right to interfere with the preparation of the defense by effectively denying defense counsel access to the witnesses except in his presence.").

4. *Defense counsel.* The obligations of defense counsel are discussed in Pye, The Role of Counsel in the Suppression of Truth, 1978 Duke L.J. 921. Should they be coextensive with those of the prosecutor? See Mosteller, Discovery Against the Defense: Tilting the Adversarial Balance, 74 Cal. L.Rev. 1567 (1986) (criticizing tendency to move toward equal disclosure requirements under vague concept of "litigative fairness").

Circumstances that may require defense disclosure of evidence arise in a number of contexts. Many problems center on the perjurious defendant. See Brazil, Unanticipated Client Perjury and the Collision of Rules of Ethics, Evidence, and Constitutional Law, 44 Mo.L.Rev. 601 (1979); Callan & David, Professional Responsibility and the Duty of Confidentiality: Disclosure of Client Misconduct in an Adversary System, 29 Rutgers L.Rev. 332 (1976); Lefstein, Client Perjury in Criminal Cases: Still in Search of an Answer, 1 Geo.J. Legal Ethics 521 (1988); Rutherglen, Dilemmas and Disclosures: A Comment on Client Perjury, 19 Am.J.Crim.L. 267 (1992). See also Nix v. Whiteside, 475 U.S. 157 (1986) (right to effective assistance of counsel not violated when counsel refused to cooperate with defendant's presentation of perjured testimony). Counsel may also be permitted or obligated to disclose information to prevent a client from committing a future crime. See Mosteller, Child Abuse Reporting Laws and Attorney–Client Confidences: The Reality and the Specter of Lawyer as Informant, 42 Duke L.J. 203, 244–55 (1992). Similar issues face lawyers with civil clients who either commit perjury or plan future frauds. Goldberg, Heaven Help to Lawyer for a Civil Liar, 2 Geo.J. Legal Ethics 885 (1989); Hazard, Lawyers and Client Fraud: They Still Don't Get It, 6 Geo.J. Legal Ethics 701 (1993).

Possession of potentially incriminating physical evidence also presents difficult issues concerning the obligation of disclosure. See, e.g., People v. Meredith, 631 P.2d 46 (Cal.1981) (statements by defendant concerning location of incriminating physical evidence privileged but privilege waived if defense counsel removes the evidence); Hitch v. Pima County Superior Court, 708 P.2d 72 (Ariz.1985) (where defense attorney receives incriminating physical evidence from source other than client and reasonably believes it may be destroyed if returned, counsel is obligated to give evidence to authorities). See generally 1 Hazard et al., The Law and Ethics of Lawyering 40–57 (3d ed. 1999); Lefstein, Incriminating Physical Evidence, The Defense Attorney's Dilemma, and the Need for Rules, 64 N.C.L.Rev. 897 (1986).

UNITED STATES v. BAGLEY

Supreme Court of the United States, 1985.
473 U.S. 667.

JUSTICE BLACKMUN announced the judgment of the Court and delivered an opinion of the Court except as to Part III.

In *Brady v. Maryland,* 373 U.S. 83, 87 (1963), this Court held that "the suppression by the prosecution of evidence favorable to an accused upon request violates due process where the evidence is material either to guilt or punishment." The issue in the present case concerns the standard of materiality to be applied in determining whether a conviction should be reversed because the prosecutor failed to disclose requested evidence that could have been used to impeach Government witnesses.

I

In October 1977, respondent Hughes Anderson Bagley was indicted in the Western District of Washington on 15 charges of violating federal narcotics and firearms statutes. On November 18, 24 days before trial, respondent filed a discovery motion. The sixth paragraph of that motion requested:

> "The names and addresses of witnesses that the government intends to call at trial. Also the prior criminal records of witnesses, and any deals, promises or inducements made to witnesses in exchange for their testimony." App. 18.

The Government's two principal witnesses at the trial were James F. O'Connor and Donald E. Mitchell. O'Connor and Mitchell were state law-enforcement officers employed by the Milwaukee Railroad as private security guards. Between April and June 1977, they assisted the federal Bureau of Alcohol, Tobacco and Firearms (ATF) in conducting an undercover investigation of respondent.

The Government's response to the discovery motion did not disclose that any "deals, promises or inducements" had been made to O'Connor or Mitchell. In apparent reply to a request in the motion's ninth paragraph for "[c]opies of all Jencks Act material," the Government produced a series of affidavits that O'Connor and Mitchell had signed between April 12 and May 4, 1977, while the undercover investigation was in progress. These affidavits recounted in detail the undercover dealings that O'Connor and Mitchell were having at the time with respondent. Each affidavit concluded with the statement, "I made this statement freely and voluntarily without any threats or rewards, or promises of reward having been made to me in return for it."

Respondent waived his right to a jury trial and was tried before the court in December 1977. At the trial, O'Connor and Mitchell testified about both the firearms and the narcotics charges. On December 23, the court found respondent guilty on the narcotics charges, but not guilty on the firearms charges.

In mid–1980, respondent filed requests for information pursuant to the Freedom of Information Act and to the Privacy Act of 1974, 5 U.S.C. §§ 552 and 552a. He received in response copies of ATF form contracts that O'Connor and Mitchell had signed on May 3, 1977. Each form was entitled "Contract for Purchase of Information and Payment of Lump Sum Therefor." * * * Each form contained the following typewritten description of services:

> "That he will provide information regarding T–I and other violations committed by Hughes A. Bagley, Jr.; that he will purchase evidence for ATF; that he will cut [*sic*] in an undercover capacity for ATF; that he will assist ATF in gathering of evidence and testify against the violator in federal court." [App. 22 and 23.]

The figure "$300.00" was handwritten in each form on a line entitled "Sum to Be Paid to Vendor."

Because these contracts had not been disclosed to respondent in response to his pretrial discovery motion, respondent moved under 28 U.S.C. § 2255 to vacate his sentence. He alleged that the Government's failure to disclose the contracts, which he could have used to impeach O'Connor and Mitchell, violated his right to due process under *Brady v. Maryland, supra.*

The motion came before the same District Judge who had presided at respondent's bench trial. An evidentiary hearing was held before a Magistrate. * * * Although the ATF case agent who dealt with O'Connor and Mitchell testified that these payments were compensation for expenses, the Magistrate found that this characterization was not borne out by the record. * * *

The District Court adopted each of the Magistrate's findings except for the last one * * * [finding] it was "probable" that O'Connor and Mitchell expected to receive compensation, in addition to their expenses, for their assistance, "though perhaps not for their testimony." * * *

The District Court found beyond a reasonable doubt, however, that had the existence of the agreements been disclosed to it during trial, the disclosure would have had no effect upon its finding that the Government had proved beyond a reasonable doubt that respondent was guilty of the offenses for which he had been convicted. * * * The testimony of O'Connor and Mitchell concerning the narcotics charges was relatively very brief, [and] tended to be favorable to respondent. Thus, the claimed impeachment evidence would not have been helpful to respondent and would not have affected the outcome of the trial. * * *

The United States Court of Appeals for the Ninth Circuit reversed. * * * In particular, it disagreed with the Government's—and the District Court's—premise that the testimony of O'Connor and Mitchell was exculpatory on the narcotics charges, and that respondent therefore would not have sought to impeach "his own witness." [719 F.2d,] at 1464, n.1.

The Court of Appeals apparently based its reversal, however, on the theory that the Government's failure to disclose the requested *Brady* information that respondent could have used to conduct an effective cross-examination impaired respondent's right to confront adverse witnesses. * * * In the last sentence of its opinion, the Court of Appeals concluded: "we hold that the government's failure to provide requested *Brady* information to Bagley so that he could effectively cross-examine two important government witnesses requires an automatic reversal." 719 F.2d, at 1464.

We * * * now reverse.

II

The holding in *Brady v. Maryland* requires disclosure only of evidence that is both favorable to the accused and "material either to guilt or punishment." 373 U.S., at 87. See also *Moore v. Illinois,* 408 U.S. 786, 794–795 (1972). The Court explained in *United States v. Agurs,* 427 U.S. 97, 104 (1976): "A fair analysis of the holding in *Brady* indicates that implicit in the requirement of materiality is a concern that the suppressed evidence might have affected the outcome of the trial." The evidence suppressed in *Brady* would have been admissible only on the issue of punishment and not on the issue of guilt, and therefore could have affected only Brady's sentence and not his conviction. Accordingly, the Court affirmed the lower court's restriction of Brady's new trial to the issue of punishment.

The *Brady* rule is based on the requirement of due process. Its purpose is not to displace the adversary system as the primary means by which truth is uncovered, but to ensure that a miscarriage of justice does not occur.[5] Thus, the prosecutor is not required to deliver his entire file to defense counsel,[6] but only to disclose evidence favorable to the accused that, if suppressed, would deprive the defendant of a fair trial:

> "For unless the omission deprived the defendant of a fair trial, there was no constitutional violation requiring that the verdict be set aside; and absent a constitutional violation, there was no breach of the prosecutor's constitutional duty to disclose. * * *

"* * * But to reiterate a critical point, the prosecutor will not have violated his constitutional duty of disclosure unless his omission is of sufficient significance to result in the denial of the defendant's right to a fair trial." 427 U.S., at 108.

In *Brady* and *Agurs,* the prosecutor failed to disclose exculpatory evidence. In the present case, the prosecutor failed to disclose evidence that the defense might have used to impeach the Government's witnesses by showing bias or interest. Impeachment evidence, however, as well as exculpatory evidence, falls within the *Brady* rule. See *Giglio v. United States,* 405 U.S. 150, 154 (1972). Such evidence is "evidence favorable to an accused," *Brady,* 373 U.S., at 87, so that, if disclosed and used effectively, it may make the difference between conviction and acquittal. Cf. *Napue v. Illinois,* 360 U.S. 264, 269 (1959) ("The jury's estimate of the truthfulness and reliability of a given witness may well be determinative of guilt or innocence, and it is upon such subtle factors as the possible interest of the witness in testifying falsely that a defendant's life or liberty may depend").

5. By requiring the prosecutor to assist the defense in making its case, the *Brady* rule represents a limited departure from a pure adversary model. The Court has recognized, however, that the prosecutor's role transcends that of an adversary: he "is the representative not of an ordinary party to a controversy, but of a sovereignty * * * whose interest * * * in a criminal prosecution is not that it shall win a case, but that justice shall be done." *Berger v. United States,* 295 U.S. 78, 88 (1935). See *Brady v. Maryland,* 373 U.S., at 87–88.

6. See *United States v. Agurs,* 427 U.S. 97, 106, 111 (1976); *Moore v. Illinois,* 408 U.S. 786, 795 (1972). See also *California v. Trombetta,* 467 U.S. 479, 488, n.8 (1984). An interpretation of *Brady* to create a broad, constitutionally required right of discovery "would entirely alter the character and balance of our present systems of criminal justice." *Giles v. Maryland,* 386 U.S. 66, 117 (1967) (dissenting opinion). Furthermore, a rule that the prosecutor commits error by any failure to disclose evidence favorable to the accused, no matter how insignificant, would impose an impossible burden on the prosecutor and would undermine the interest in the finality of judgments.

The Court of Appeals treated impeachment evidence as constitutionally different from exculpatory evidence. According to that court, failure to disclose impeachment evidence is "even more egregious" than failure to disclose exculpatory evidence "because it threatens the defendant's right to confront adverse witnesses." 719 F.2d, at 1464. Relying on *Davis v. Alaska,* 415 U.S. 308 (1974), the Court of Appeals held that the Government's failure to disclose requested impeachment evidence that the defense could use to conduct an effective cross-examination of important prosecution witnesses constitutes " 'constitutional error of the first magnitude' " requiring automatic reversal. 719 F.2d, at 1464 (quoting *Davis v. Alaska, supra,* 415 U.S., at 318).

This Court has rejected any such distinction between impeachment evidence and exculpatory evidence [citing *Giglio v. United States, supra*]. * * *

Moreover, the court's reliance on *Davis v. Alaska* for its "automatic reversal" rule is misplaced. In *Davis,* the defense sought to cross-examine a crucial prosecution witness concerning his probationary status as a juvenile delinquent. * * * Pursuant to a state rule of procedure and a state statute making juvenile adjudications inadmissible, the trial judge prohibited the defense from conducting the cross-examination. This Court reversed the defendant's conviction * * *.

The present case, in contrast, does not involve any direct restriction on the scope of cross-examination. * * * The constitutional error, if any, in this case was the Government's failure to assist the defense by disclosing information that might have been helpful in conducting the cross-examination. As discussed above, such suppression of evidence amounts to a constitutional violation only if it deprives the defendant of a fair trial. Consistent with "our overriding concern with the justice of the finding of guilt," *United States v. Agurs,* 427 U.S., at 112, a constitutional error occurs, and the conviction must be reversed, only if the evidence is material in the sense that its suppression undermines confidence in the outcome of the trial.

III

A

It remains to determine the standard of materiality applicable to the nondisclosed evidence at issue in this case. Our starting point is the framework for evaluating the materiality of *Brady* evidence established in *United States v. Agurs.* The Court in *Agurs* distinguished three situations involving the discovery, after trial, of information favorable to the accused that had been known to the prosecution but unknown to the defense. The first situation was the prosecutor's knowing use of perjured testimony or, equivalently, the prosecutor's knowing failure to disclose that testimony used to convict the defendant was false. The Court noted the well-established rule that "a conviction obtained by the knowing use of perjured testimony is fundamentally unfair, and must be set aside if there is any reasonable likelihood that the false testimony could have affected the judgment of the jury." 427 U.S., at 103 (footnote omitted).[7] Although this rule is stated in terms that treat the knowing use of perjured testimony as error subject to harmless-error review,[8] it may as easily be stated as a materiality standard under which the fact that testimony is perjured is considered material unless failure to disclose it would be harmless beyond a reasonable doubt. The Court in *Agurs* justified this standard of materiality on the ground that the knowing use of perjured testimony involves prosecutorial misconduct and, more importantly, involves "a corruption of the truth-seeking function of the trial process." *Id.*, at 104.

At the other extreme is the situation in *Agurs* itself, where the defendant does not make a *Brady* request and the prosecutor fails to disclose certain evidence favorable to the accused. The Court rejected a harmless-error rule in that situation, because under that rule every nondisclosure is treated as error, thus imposing on the prosecutor a constitutional duty to deliver his entire file to defense counsel. *Id.*, at 111–112. At the same time, the Court rejected a standard that would require the defendant to demonstrate that the evidence if disclosed probably would have resulted in acquittal. *Id.*, at 111. The Court reasoned: "If the standard applied to the usual motion for a new trial based on newly discovered evidence were the same when the evidence was in the State's possession as when it was found in a neutral source, there would be no special significance to the prosecutor's obligation to serve the cause of justice." *Ibid.* The standard of materiality applicable in the absence of a specific *Brady* request is therefore stricter than the

7. In fact, the *Brady* rule has its roots in a series of cases dealing with convictions based on the prosecution's knowing use of perjured testimony. In *Mooney v. Holohan,* 294 U.S. 103 (1935), the Court established the rule that the knowing use by a state prosecutor of perjured testimony to obtain a conviction and the deliberate suppression of evidence that would have impeached and refuted the testimony constitutes a denial of due process. The Court reasoned that "a deliberate deception of court and jury by the presentation of testimony known to be perjured" is inconsistent with "the rudimentary demands of justice." *Id.*, at 112. The Court reaffirmed this principle in broader terms in *Pyle v. Kansas,* 317 U.S. 213 (1942), where it held that allegations that the prosecutor had deliberately suppressed evidence favorable to the accused and had knowingly used perjured testimony were sufficient to charge a due process violation.

The Court again reaffirmed this principle in *Napue v. Illinois,* 360 U.S. 264 (1959). In *Napue,* the principal witness for the prosecution falsely testified that he had been promised no consideration for his testimony. The Court held that the knowing use of false testimony to obtain a conviction violates due process regardless of whether the prosecutor solicited the false testimony or merely allowed it to go uncorrected when it appeared. The Court explained that the principle that a State may not knowingly use false testimony to obtain a conviction—even false testimony that goes only to the credibility of the witness—is "implicit in any concept of ordered liberty." *Id.*, at 269. * * *

8. The rule that a conviction obtained by the knowing use of perjured testimony must be set aside if there is any reasonable likelihood that the false testimony could have affected the jury's verdict derives from *Napue v. Illinois,* 360 U.S. at 271. *Napue* antedated *Chapman v. California,* 386 U.S. 18 (1967), where the "harmless beyond a reasonable doubt" standard was established.

It is [clear], that this Court's precedents indicate that the standard of review applicable to the knowing use of perjured testimony is equivalent to the *Chapman* harmless-error standard.

harmless-error standard but more lenient to the defense than the newly discovered evidence standard.

The third situation identified by the Court in *Agurs* is where the defense makes a specific request and the prosecutor fails to disclose responsive evidence. The Court did not define the standard of materiality applicable in this situation, but suggested that the standard might be more lenient to the defense than in the situation in which the defense makes no request or only a general request. *Id.,* at 106. The Court also noted: "When the prosecutor receives a specific and relevant request, the failure to make any response is seldom, if ever, excusable." *Ibid.*

The Court has relied on and reformulated the *Agurs* standard for the materiality of undisclosed evidence in * * * subsequent cases arising outside the *Brady* context. * * *

[I]n *Strickland v. Washington,* 466 U.S. 668 (1984), the Court held that a new trial must be granted when evidence is not introduced because of the incompetence of counsel only if "there is a reasonable probability that, but for counsel's unprofessional errors, the result of the proceeding would have been different." *Id.,* at 694.[9] The *Strickland* Court defined a "reasonable probability" as "a probability sufficient to undermine confidence in the outcome." *Ibid.*

We find the *Strickland* formulation of the *Agurs* test for materiality sufficiently flexible to cover the "no request," "general request," and "specific request" cases of prosecutorial failure to disclose evidence favorable to the accused: The evidence is material only if there is a reasonable probability that, had the evidence been disclosed to the defense, the result of the proceeding would have been different. A "reasonable probability" is a probability sufficient to undermine confidence in the outcome.

The Government suggests that a materiality standard more favorable to the defendant reasonably might be adopted in specific request cases. See Brief for United States 31. The Government notes that an incomplete response to a specific request not only deprives the defense of certain evidence, but has the effect of representing to the defense that the evidence does not exist. In reliance on this misleading representation, the defense might abandon lines of independent investigation, defenses, or trial strategies that it otherwise would have pursued. *Ibid.*

We agree that the prosecutor's failure to respond fully to a *Brady* request may impair the adversary process in this manner. And the more specifically the defense requests certain evidence, thus putting the prosecutor on notice of its value, the more reasonable it is for the defense to assume from the nondisclosure that the evidence does not exist, and to make pretrial and trial decisions on the basis of this assumption. This possibility of impairment does not necessitate a differ-

9. In particular, the Court explained in *Strickland:* "When a defendant challenges a conviction, the question is whether there is a reasonable probability that, absent the errors, the factfinder would have had a reasonable doubt respecting guilt." 466 U.S., at 695.

ent standard of materiality, however, for under the *Strickland* formulation the reviewing court may consider directly any adverse effect that the prosecutor's failure to respond might have had on the preparation or presentation of the defendant's case. The reviewing court should assess the possibility that such effect might have occurred in light of the totality of the circumstances and with an awareness of the difficulty of reconstructing in a post-trial proceeding the course that the defense and the trial would have taken had the defense not been misled by the prosecutor's incomplete response.

B

In the present case, we think that there is a significant likelihood that the prosecutor's response to respondent's discovery motion misleadingly induced defense counsel to believe that O'Connor and Mitchell could not be impeached on the basis of bias or interest arising from inducements offered by the Government. * * * Accordingly, we reverse the judgment of the Court of Appeals and remand the case to that court for a determination whether there is a reasonable probability that, had the inducement offered by the Government to O'Connor and Mitchell been disclosed to the defense, the result of the trial would have been different.

It is so ordered.

JUSTICE POWELL took no part in the decision of this case.

JUSTICE WHITE, with whom THE CHIEF JUSTICE and JUSTICE REHNQUIST join, concurring in part and concurring in the judgment.

I agree with the Court that respondent is not entitled to have his conviction overturned unless he can show that the evidence withheld by the Government was "material," and I therefore join Parts I and II of the Court's opinion. * * * Given the flexibility of the standard and the inherently factbound nature of the cases to which it will be applied, however, I see no reason to attempt to elaborate on the relevance to the inquiry of the specificity of the defense's request for disclosure, either generally or with respect to this case. * * *

JUSTICE MARSHALL, with whom JUSTICE BRENNAN joins, dissenting.

When the Government withholds from a defendant evidence that might impeach the prosecution's *only witnesses,* that failure to disclose cannot be deemed harmless error. Because that is precisely the nature of the undisclosed evidence in this case, I would affirm the judgment of the Court of Appeals and would not remand for further proceedings. * * *

II

Instead of affirming, the Court today chooses to reverse and remand the case for application of its newly stated standard to the facts of this case. While I believe that the evidence at issue here, which remained undisclosed despite a particular request, undoubtedly was material under the Court's standard, I also have serious doubts whether the Court's definition of the constitutional right at issue adequately takes account of the interests this Court sought to protect in its decision in *Brady v. Maryland,* 373 U.S. 83 (1963).

A

* * *

When the State does not disclose information in its possession that might reasonably be considered favorable to the defense, it precludes the trier of fact from gaining access to such information and thereby undermines the reliability of the verdict. Unlike a situation in which exculpatory evidence exists but neither the defense nor the prosecutor has uncovered it, in this situation the State already has, resting in its files, material that would be of assistance to the defendant. With a minimum of effort, the State could improve the real and apparent fairness of the trial enormously, by assuring that the defendant may place before the trier of fact favorable evidence known to the Government. * * *

This recognition no doubt stems in part from the frequently considerable imbalance in resources between most criminal defendants and most prosecutors' offices. Many, perhaps most, criminal defendants in the United States are represented by appointed counsel, who often are paid minimal wages and operate on shoestring budgets. In addition, unlike police, defense counsel generally is not present at the scene of the crime, or at the time of arrest, but instead comes into the case late. Moreover, unlike the Government, defense counsel is not in the position to make deals with witnesses to gain evidence. Thus, an inexperienced, unskilled, or unaggressive attorney often is unable to amass the factual support necessary to a reasonable defense. When favorable evidence is in the hands of the prosecutor but not disclosed, the result may well be that the defendant is deprived of a fair chance before the trier of fact, and the trier of fact is deprived of the ingredients necessary to a fair decision. This grim reality, of course, poses a direct challenge to the traditional model of the adversary criminal process, and perhaps because this reality so directly questions the fairness of our longstanding processes, change has been cautious and halting. Thus, the Court has not gone the full road and expressly required that the State provide to the defendant access to the prosecutor's complete files, or investigators who will assure that the defendant has an opportunity to discover every existing piece of helpful evidence. But cf. *Ake v. Oklahoma,* 470 U.S. 68 (1985) (access to assistance of psychiatrist constitutionally required on proper showing of need). Instead, in acknowledgment of the fact that important interests are served when potentially favorable evidence is disclosed, the Court has fashioned a compromise, requiring that the prosecution identify and disclose to the defendant favorable material that it possesses. This requirement is but a small, albeit important, step toward equality of justice.[10]

10. Indeed, this Court's recent decision stating a stringent standard for demonstrating ineffective assistance of counsel makes an effective *Brady* right even more

B

* * *

Once the prosecutor suspects that certain information might have favorable implications for the defense, either because it is potentially exculpatory or relevant to credibility, I see no reason why he should not be required to disclose it. After all, favorable evidence indisputably enhances the truth-seeking process at trial. And it is the job of the defense, not the prosecution, to decide whether and in what way to use arguably favorable evidence. In addition, to require disclosure of all evidence that might reasonably be considered favorable to the defendant would have the precautionary effect of assuring that no information of potential consequence is mistakenly overlooked. By requiring full disclosure of favorable evidence in this way, courts could begin to assure that a possibly dispositive piece of information is not withheld from the trier of fact by a prosecutor who is torn between the two roles he must play. A clear rule of this kind, coupled with a presumption in favor of disclosure, also would facilitate the prosecutor's admittedly difficult task by removing a substantial amount of unguided discretion. * * *

C

The Court, however, offers a complex alternative. It defines the right not by reference to the possible usefulness of the particular evidence in preparing and presenting the case, but retrospectively, by reference to the likely effect the evidence will have on the outcome of the trial. Thus, the Court holds that due process does not require the prosecutor to turn over evidence unless the evidence is "material," and the Court states that evidence is "material" "only if there is a reasonable probability that, had the evidence been disclosed to the defense, the result of the proceeding would have been different." * * * Although this looks like a post-trial standard of review, see, *e.g., Strickland v. Washington,* 466 U.S. 668 (1984) (adopting this standard of review), it is not. Instead, the Court relies on this review standard to define the contours of the defendant's constitutional right to certain material prior to trial. By adhering to the view articulated in *United States v. Agurs,* 427 U.S. 97 (1976)—that there is no constitutional duty to disclose evidence unless nondisclosure would have a certain impact on the trial—the Court permits prosecutors to withhold with impunity large amounts of undeniably favorable evidence, and it imposes on prosecutors the burden to identify and disclose evidence pursuant to a pretrial standard that virtually defies definition. * * *

crucial. Without a real guarantee of effective counsel, the relative abilities of the state and the defendant become even more skewed, and the need for a minimal guarantee of access to potentially favorable information becomes significantly greater. See *Strickland v. Washington,* 466 U.S. 668 (1984); *id.,* at 712–15 (Marshall, J., dissenting); Babcock, [Fair Play: Evidence Favorable to an Accused and Effective Assistance of Counsel, 34 Stan.L.Rev. 1133, 1163–1174 (1982)] (discussing the interplay between the right to *Brady* material and the right to effective assistance of counsel).

JUSTICE STEVENS, dissenting.

* * *

[T]he Court's analysis reduces the significance of deliberate prosecutorial suppression of potentially exculpatory evidence to that merely of one of numerous factors that "may" be considered by a reviewing court. * * * Such suppression is far more serious than mere nondisclosure of evidence in which the defense has expressed no particular interest. * * * Such silence actively misleads in the same way as would an affirmative representation that exculpatory evidence does not exist when, in fact, it does (*i.e.,* perjury) * * *.

Notes and Questions

1. *Later Supreme Court cases.* In Kyles v. Whitley, 514 U.S. 419 (1995), the Court reversed a first degree murder conviction due to a *Brady* violation, noting that in *Bagley* it had "disavowed any difference between exculpatory and impeachment evidence for *Brady* purposes, and it abandoned the distinction between the second and third *Agurs* circumstances, i.e., the 'specific-request' and 'general-or no-request' situations." Id. at 432. The Court went on to explain that *Bagley* had addressed four aspects of the "materiality" requirement. First, that requirement did not mean that the defendant had to show that the undisclosed evidence would have resulted in an acquittal. Second, the *Bagley* materiality requirement is "not a sufficiency of evidence test. A defendant need not demonstrate that after discounting the inculpatory evidence in light of the undisclosed evidence, there would not have been enough left to convict." Third, once a reviewing court has found constitutional error, "there is no need for further harmless-error review." Id. at 435. Fourth, the materiality standard focuses on the "suppressed evidence considered collectively, not item-by-item." Id. at 436. The Court also observed: "On the one side, showing that the prosecution knew of an item of favorable evidence unknown to the defense does not amount to a *Brady* violation, without more. But the prosecution, which alone can know what is undisclosed, must be assigned the consequent responsibility to gauge the likely net effect of all such evidence and make disclosure when the point of 'reasonable probability' is reached. This in turn means that the individual prosecutor has a duty to learn of any favorable evidence known to the others acting on the government's behalf in the case, including the police." Id. at 437. If in doubt, the prosecutor should disclose: "This means, naturally, that a prosecutor anxious about tacking too close to the wind will disclose a favorable piece of evidence * * *. This is as it should be." Id. at 439. See also Wood v. Bartholomew, 516 U.S. 1, 10 (1995) (per curiam) ("Disclosure of the polygraph results, then, could have had no direct effect on the outcome of trial, because respondent could have made no mention of them either during argument or while questioning witnesses.").

In Strickler v. Greene, 527 U.S. 263 (1999), the Court found that the suppressed evidence was exculpatory. The materials consisted of notes taken by a detective during his interviews with an eyewitness and letters written by the witness to the detective. "They cast serious doubt on [the witness'] confident assertion of her 'exceptionally good memory.' " Id. at 273. The

Court held, however, that the added a significant comment: "We certainly do not criticize the prosecution's accused had not satisfied the materiality requirement. Nevertheless, the Court use of the open file policy. We recognize that this practice may increase the efficiency and the fairness of the criminal process. We merely note that, if a prosecutor asserts that he complies with *Brady* through an open file policy, defense counsel may reasonably rely on that file to contain all materials the State is constitutionally obligated to disclose under *Brady*." Id. at 283 n.23.

In Banks v. Dretke, 540 U.S. 668 (2004), the State did not disclose that one of the prosecution's essential witnesses was a paid police informant, nor did it disclose a pretrial transcript revealing that another witness' trial testimony had been intensively coached by prosecutors and law enforcement officers. In addition, the prosecution failed to correct false statements by these witnesses. The Court reversed.

2. *Preservation of evidence. Brady's* due process disclosure requirement has been extended to encompass the right to have evidence preserved, at least under limited circumstances. If the evidence is not preserved, it cannot be disclosed to the defense. In Arizona v. Youngblood, 488 U.S. 51 (1988), the Supreme Court addressed the issue in a case involving the failure to preserve semen in a sexual assault case. The evidence was critical. While bad faith is not a requirement in the *Brady* suppression cases, the Court nevertheless ruled it determinative in a failure to preserve situation. The Court wrote: "The failure of the police to refrigerate the clothing and to perform tests on the semen samples can at worst be described as negligent." Numerous state courts have rejected the bad-faith test as a matter of state law because the importance of the evidence is not a consideration under that test. As one court observed: "Apparently only Arizona and California * * * have concluded that their state charters offer the same limited degree of protection as the federal constitution." State v. Morales, 657 A.2d 585, 594 n.20 (Conn.1995). The court went on to reject *Youngblood* as a matter of state constitutional law: "Like our sister states, we conclude that the good or bad faith of the police in failing to preserve potentially useful evidence [semen stains that could have been tested for DNA] cannot be dispositive of whether a criminal defendant has been deprived of due process of law. Accordingly, we, too, reject the litmus test of bad faith on the part of the police, which the United States Supreme Court adopted under the federal constitution in *Youngblood*."

The *Youngblood* test provides no incentive for police departments to adopt standard operating procedures that ensure the proper collection and preservation of evidence—procedures that in all likelihood would benefit the prosecution more in the long run. After having spent nine years in prison, Larry Youngblood was exonerated through DNA testing. Dr. Edward Blake, a DNA scientist, told a reporter: "We now have before us a flawed legal precedent that stands on the shoulders of an innocent man * * *. For those organizations that are poorly run or mismanaged or don't give a damn, * * * the Youngblood case was a license to let down their guard and be lazy. The effect that had was generally to lower the standards of evidence collection." Whiteaker, DNA Frees Inmate Years After Justices Rejected Plea, N.Y. Times, Aug. 11, 2000, at A12.

3. *Sources*. For an interesting analysis of the place of the *Brady* doctrine in our adversary system, see Babcock, Fair Play: Evidence Favorable to an Accused and Effective Assistance of Counsel, 34 Stan.L.Rev. 1133 (1982). See also 5 LaFave, Israel & King, Criminal Procedure § 24.3(b) (2d ed. 1999); Whitebread & Slobogin, Criminal Procedure § 24.04 (4th ed. 2000); Dewar, Note, A Fair Trial Remedy for *Brady* Violations, 115 Yale L.J. 1450 (2006); Joy & McMunigal, Disclosing Exculpatory Material in Plea Bargaining, 16 Crim. Just. 41 (Fall 2001); Weeks, No Wrong Without a Remedy: The Effective Enforcement of the Duty of Prosecutors to Disclose Exculpatory Evidence, 22 Okla.City U.L.Rev. 833 (1997); Note, *Brady v. Maryland* and the Search for Truth in Criminal Trials, 63 U.Chi.L.Rev. 1673 (1996).

4. *DNA Exonerations*. Would a prosecutor have an obligation under *Brady* or ethical standards to assist in having post-conviction DNA testing performed at the request of a defendant. The experience of the Cardozo Law School Innocence Project is not encouraging: "[I]n nearly half the sixty-four [DNA] exonerations, local prosecutors refused to release crime evidence for DNA tests until litigation was threatened or filed." Scheck et al., Actual Innocence: Five Days to Execution, and Other Dispatches From the Wrongly Convicted xvi (2000). In contrast, the San Diego District Attorney adopted a different approach. Sterngold, San Diego District Attorney Offering Free DNA Testing, N.Y. Times, July 28, 2000, at A12.

5. *Ethical duty*. Does the prosecution have an ethical duty to disclose exculpatory information to the defense and what sanctions are appropriate for a violation of any such duty? See Zacharias, Structuring the Ethics of Prosecutorial Trial Practice: Can Prosecutors Do Justice?, 44 Vand.L.Rev. 45 (1991) (criticizing the difficulty of enforcing the present "do justice" ethical standard); Rosen, Disciplinary Sanctions Against Prosecutors for *Brady* Violations: A Paper Tiger, 65 N.C.L.Rev. 693 (1987) (sanctions illusory). If DNA evidence undercuts the prosecution's case, is it ethical to oppose a new trial based on theories that were never presented to the jury? See Ritter, Note, It's the Prosecution's Story, But They're Not Sticking to It: Applying Harmless Error and Judicial Estoppel to Exculpatory Post–Conviction DNA Testing, 74 Fordham L.Rev. 825 (2005).

HOLMES v. SOUTH CAROLINA

United States Supreme Court, 2006.
547 U.S. ___, 126 S.Ct. 1727.

JUSTICE ALITO delivered the opinion of the Court.

This case presents the question whether a criminal defendant's federal constitutional rights are violated by an evidence rule under which the defendant may not introduce proof of third-party guilt if the prosecution has introduced forensic evidence that, if believed, strongly supports a guilty verdict.

I

On the morning of December 31, 1989, 86–year-old Mary Stewart was beaten, raped, and robbed in her home. She later died of complications stemming from her injuries. Petitioner was convicted by a South Carolina jury of murder, first-degree criminal sexual conduct, first-degree burglary, and robbery, and he was sentenced to death. * * * Upon state postconviction review * * *, petitioner was granted a new trial. * * *

At the second trial, the prosecution relied heavily on the following forensic evidence:

> "(1) [Petitioner's] palm print was found just above the door knob on the interior side of the front door of the victim's house; (2) fibers consistent with a black sweatshirt owned by [petitioner] were found on the victim's bed sheets; (3) matching blue fibers were found on the victim's pink nightgown and on [petitioner's] blue jeans; (4) microscopically consistent fibers were found on the pink nightgown and on [petitioner's] underwear; (5) [petitioner's] underwear contained a mixture of DNA from two individuals, and 99.99% of the population other than [petitioner] and the victim were excluded as contributors to that mixture; and (6) [petitioner's] tank top was found to contain a mixture of [petitioner's] blood and the victim's blood." * * *

In addition, the prosecution introduced evidence that petitioner had been seen near Stewart's home within an hour of the time when, according to the prosecution's evidence, the attack took place. * * *

As a major part of his defense, petitioner attempted to undermine the State's forensic evidence by suggesting that it had been contaminated and that certain law enforcement officers had engaged in a plot to frame him. * * * Petitioner's expert witnesses criticized the procedures used by the police in handling the fiber and DNA evidence and in collecting the fingerprint evidence. * * * Another defense expert provided testimony that petitioner cited as supporting his claim that the palm print had been planted by the police. * * *

Petitioner also sought to introduce proof that another man, Jimmy McCaw White, had attacked Stewart. * * * At a pretrial hearing, petitioner proffered several witnesses who placed White in the victim's neighborhood on the morning of the assault, as well as four other witnesses who testified that White had either acknowledged that petitioner was " 'innocent' " or had actually admitted to committing the crimes. * * * One witness recounted that when he asked White about the "word * * * on the street" that White was responsible for Stewart's murder, White "put his head down and he raised his head back up and he said, well, you know I like older women." * * * According to this witness, White added that "he did what they say he did" and that he had "no regrets about it at all." * * * Another witness, who had been incarcerated with White, testified that White had admitted to assaulting Stewart, that a police officer had asked the witness to testify falsely against petitioner, and that employees of the prosecutor's office, while soliciting the witness' cooperation, had spoken of manufacturing evidence against petitioner. * * * White testified at the pretrial hearing and denied making the incriminating statements. * * * He also provided an alibi for the time of the crime, but another witness refuted his alibi. * * *

The trial court excluded petitioner's third-party guilt evidence citing *State v. Gregory,* 198 S.C. 98, 16 S.E.2d 532 (1941), which held that such evidence is admissible if it " 'raise[s] a reasonable inference or presumption as to [the defendant's] own innocence' " but is not admissible if it merely " 'cast[s] a bare suspicion upon another' " or " 'raise[s] a conjectural inference as to the commission of the crime by another.' " * * * On appeal, the South Carolina Supreme Court found no error in the exclusion of petitioner's third-party guilt evidence. Citing both *Gregory* and its later decision in *State v. Gay,* 343 S.C. 543, 541 S.E.2d 541 (2001), the State Supreme Court held that "where there is strong evidence of an appellant's guilt, especially where there is strong forensic evidence, the proffered evidence about a third party's alleged guilt does not raise a reasonable inference as to the appellant's own innocence." * * * Applying this standard, the court held that petitioner could not "overcome the forensic evidence against him to raise a reasonable inference of his own innocence." * * * We granted certiorari. * * *

II

"[S]tate and federal rulemakers have broad latitude under the Constitution to establish rules excluding evidence from criminal trials." *United States v. Scheffer,* 523 U.S. 303, 308 (1998); see also *Crane v. Kentucky,* 476 U.S. 683, 689–690 (1986); *Marshall v. Lonberger,* 459 U.S. 422, 438, n.6 (1983); *Chambers v. Mississippi,* 410 U.S. 284, 302–303 (1973) * * *. This latitude, however, has limits. "Whether rooted directly in the Due Process Clause of the Fourteenth Amendment or in the Compulsory Process or Confrontation clauses of the Sixth Amendment, the Constitution guarantees criminal defendants 'a meaningful opportunity to present a complete defense.' " * * * This right is abridged by evidence rules that "infring[e] upon a weighty interest of the accused" and are " 'arbitrary' or 'disproportionate to the purposes they are designed to serve.' " *Scheffer, supra,* at 308 (quoting *Rock v. Arkansas,* 483 U.S. 44, 58, 56 (1987)).

This Court's cases contain several illustrations of "arbitrary" rules, *i.e.,* rules that excluded important defense evidence but that did not serve any legitimate interests. In *Washington v. Texas,* 388 U.S. 14 (1967), state statutes barred a person who had been charged as a participant in a crime from testifying in defense of another alleged participant unless the witness had been acquitted. As a result, when the defendant in *Washington* was tried for murder, he was precluded from calling as a witness a person who had been charged and previously convicted of committing the same murder. Holding that the defendant's right to put on a defense had been violated, we noted that the rule embodied in the statutes could not "even be defended on the ground that it rationally sets apart a group of persons who are particularly likely to commit perjury" since the rule allowed an alleged participant to testify if he or she had been acquitted or was called by the prosecution. *Id.,* at 22–23 * * *.

A similar constitutional violation occurred in *Chambers v. Mississippi, supra.* A murder defendant called as a witness a man named McDonald, who had previously confessed to the murder. When McDonald repudiated the confession on the stand, the defendant was denied permission to examine McDonald as an adverse witness based on the State's " 'voucher' rule," which barred parties from impeaching their own witnesses. * * * In addition, because the state hearsay rule did not include an exception for statements against penal interest, the defendant was not permitted to introduce evidence that McDonald had made self-incriminating statements to three other persons. Noting that the State had not even attempted to "defend" or "explain [the] underlying rationale" of the "voucher rule," * * * this Court held that "the exclusion of [the evidence of McDonald's out-of-court statements], coupled with the State's refusal to permit [the defendant] to cross-examine McDonald, denied him a trial in accord with traditional and fundamental standards of due process," *id.*, at 302.

Another arbitrary rule was held unconstitutional in *Crane v. Kentucky, supra.* There, the defendant was prevented from attempting to show at trial that his confession was unreliable because of the circumstances under which it was obtained, and neither the State Supreme Court nor the prosecution "advanced any rational justification for the wholesale exclusion of this body of potentially exculpatory evidence." * * * *Id.*, at 691.

In *Rock v. Arkansas, supra,* this Court held that a rule prohibiting hypnotically refreshed testimony was unconstitutional because "[w]holesale inadmissibility of a defendant's testimony is an arbitrary restriction on the right to testify in the absence of clear evidence by the State repudiating the validity of all post-hypnotic recollections." * * * By contrast, in *United States v. Scheffer, supra,* we held that a rule excluding all polygraph evidence did not abridge the right to present a defense because the rule "serve[d] several legitimate interests in the criminal trial process," was "neither arbitrary nor disproportionate in promoting these ends," and did not "implicate a sufficiently weighty interest of the defendant." *Id.* at 309.

While the Constitution thus prohibits the exclusion of defense evidence under rules that serve no legitimate purpose or that are disproportionate to the ends that they are asserted to promote, well-established rules of evidence permit trial judges to exclude evidence if its probative value is outweighed by certain other factors such as unfair prejudice, confusion of the issues, or potential to mislead the jury. See, *e.g.,* Fed. Rule Evid. 403; Uniform Rule of Evid. 45 (1953); ALI, Model Code of Evidence Rule 303 (1942); 3 J. Wigmore, Evidence §§ 1863, 1904 (1904). Plainly referring to rules of this type, we have stated that the Constitution permits judges "to exclude evidence that is 'repetitive

* * *, only marginally relevant' or poses an undue risk of 'harassment, prejudice, [or] confusion of the issues.' " *Crane, supra,* at 689–690 * * *.

A specific application of this principle is found in rules regulating the admission of evidence proffered by criminal defendants to show that someone else committed the crime with which they are charged. See, *e.g.,*41 C.J.S., Homicide § 216, pp. 56–58 (1991) ("Evidence tending to show the commission by another person of the crime charged may be introduced by accused when it is inconsistent with, and raises a reasonable doubt of, his own guilt; but frequently matters offered in evidence for this purpose are so remote and lack such connection with the crime that they are excluded"); 40A Am.Jur.2d, Homicide § 286, pp. 136–138 (1999) ("[T]he accused may introduce any legal evidence tending to prove that another person may have committed the crime with which the defendant is charged * * *. [Such evidence] may be excluded where it does not sufficiently connect the other person to the crime, as, for example, where the evidence is speculative or remote, or does not tend to prove or disprove a material fact in issue at the defendant's trial" (footnotes omitted)). Such rules are widely accepted, and neither petitioner nor his *amici* challenge them here.

In *Gregory,* the South Carolina Supreme Court adopted and applied a rule apparently intended to be of this type, given the court's references to the "applicable rule" from Corpus Juris and American Jurisprudence:

> " '[E]vidence offered by accused as to the commission of the crime by another person must be limited to such facts as are inconsistent with his own guilt, and to such facts as raise a reasonable inference or presumption as to his own innocence; evidence which can have (no) other effect than to cast a bare suspicion upon another, or to raise a conjectural inference as to the commission of the crime by another, is not admissible* * *. [B]efore such testimony can be received, there must be such proof of connection with it, such a train of facts or circumstances, as tends clearly to point out such other person as the guilty party.' " * * *

In *Gay* and this case, however, the South Carolina Supreme Court radically changed and extended the rule. In *Gay,* after recognizing the standard applied in *Gregory,* the court stated that "[i]n view of the strong evidence of appellant's guilt—especially the forensic evidence—* * * the proffered evidence * * * did not raise 'a reasonable inference' as to appellant's own innocence." *Gay,* 343 S.C., at 550 * * *. Similarly, in the present case, as noted, the State Supreme Court applied the rule that "where there is strong evidence of [a defendant's] guilt, especially where there is strong forensic evidence, the proffered evidence about a third party's alleged guilt" may (or perhaps must) be excluded. * * *

Under this rule, the trial judge does not focus on the probative value or the potential adverse effects of admitting the defense evidence of third-party guilt. Instead, the critical inquiry concerns the strength of the prosecution's case: If the prosecution's case is strong enough, the evidence of third-party guilt is excluded even if that evidence, if viewed independently, would have great probative value and even if it would not pose an undue risk of harassment, prejudice, or confusion of the issues.

Furthermore, as applied in this case, the South Carolina Supreme Court's rule seems to call for little, if any, examination of the credibility of the prosecution's witnesses or the reliability of its evidence. Here, for example, the defense strenuously claimed that the prosecution's forensic evidence was so unreliable (due to mishandling and a deliberate plot to frame petitioner) that the evidence should not have even been admitted. The South Carolina Supreme Court responded that these challenges did not entirely "eviscerate" the forensic evidence and that the defense challenges went to the weight and not to the admissibility of that evidence. * * * Yet, in evaluating the prosecution's forensic evidence and deeming it to be "strong"—and thereby justifying exclusion of petitioner's third-party guilt evidence—the South Carolina Supreme Court made no mention of the defense challenges to the prosecution's evidence.

Interpreted in this way, the rule applied by the State Supreme Court does not rationally serve the end that the *Gregory* rule and its analogues in other jurisdictions were designed to promote, *i.e.,* to focus the trial on the central issues by excluding evidence that has only a very weak logical connection to the central issues. The rule applied in this case appears to be based on the following logic: Where (1) it is clear that only one person was involved in the commission of a particular crime and (2) there is strong evidence that the defendant was the perpetrator, it follows that evidence of third-party guilt must be weak. But this logic depends on an accurate evaluation of the prosecution's proof, and the true strength of the prosecution's proof cannot be assessed without considering challenges to the reliability of the prosecution's evidence. Just because the prosecution's evidence, *if credited,* would provide strong support for a guilty verdict, it does not follow that evidence of third-party guilt has only a weak logical connection to the central issues in the case. And where the credibility of the prosecution's witnesses or the reliability of its evidence is not conceded, the strength of the prosecution's case cannot be assessed without making the sort of factual findings that have traditionally been reserved for the trier of fact and that the South Carolina courts did not purport to make in this case.

The rule applied in this case is no more logical than its converse would be, *i.e.,* a rule barring the prosecution from introducing evidence of a defendant's guilt if the defendant is able to proffer, at a pretrial hearing, evidence that, if believed, strongly supports a verdict of not guilty. In the present case, for example, the petitioner proffered evidence that, if believed, squarely proved that White, not petitioner, was the perpetrator. It would make no sense, however, to hold that this proffer precluded the prosecution from introducing its evidence, including the forensic evidence that, if credited, provided strong proof of the petitioner's guilt.

The point is that, by evaluating the strength of only one party's evidence, no logical conclusion can be reached regarding the strength of contrary evidence offered by the other side to rebut or cast doubt. Because the rule applied by the State Supreme Court in this case did not heed this point, the rule is "arbitrary" in the sense that it does not rationally serve the end that the *Gregory* rule and other similar third-party guilt rules were designed to further. Nor has the State identified any other legitimate end that the rule serves. It follows that the rule applied in this case by the State Supreme Court violates a criminal defendant's right to have " 'a meaningful opportunity to present a complete defense.' " *Crane,* 476 U.S., at 690 * * *.

III

For these reasons, we vacate the judgment of the South Carolina Supreme Court and remand the case for further proceedings not inconsistent with this opinion.

It is so ordered.

Notes and Questions

1. *Right to present a defense. Holmes* is the latest in a line of cases often classified under the rubic "the right to present a defense." In *Washington v. Texas*, Chapter 12 (A), infra, 388 U.S. at 19, the Court first recognized this right:

> The right to offer the testimony of witnesses, and to compel their attendance, if necessary, is in plain terms the right to present a defense, the right to present the defendant's version of the facts as well as the prosecution's to the jury so it may decide where the truth lies. Just as an accused has the right to confront the prosecution's witnesses for the purpose of challenging their testimony, he has the right to present his own witnesses to establish a defense. This right is a fundamental element of due process of law.

Washington rested on the Compulsory Process Clause. The Court's next case, *Chambers v. Mississippi*, was based on due process. See also California v. Trombetta, 467 U.S. 479, 485 (1984) (In finding a qualified right for the preservation of evidence in the government's control, the Court stated: "We have long interpreted [the due process] standard of fairness to require that criminal defendants be afforded a meaningful opportunity to present a complete defense."); note 5 following *Old Chief v. United States*, Chapter 7, Section C, infra. *Crane v. Kentucky*, Chapter 1(A), supra, cited several different constitutional provisions. Does it matter where among these provisions the right is anchored?

2. *Right to jury trial.* Why didn't the Court base its decision on the right to a jury trial as one amicus brief argued? The Court has recently reinvigorated that right. See Apprendi v. New Jersey, 530 U.S. 466, 490 (2000) ("Other than the fact of a prior conviction, any fact that increases the penalty for a crime beyond the prescribed statutory maximum must be submitted to a jury, and proved beyond a reasonable doubt."). See also

Blakely v. Washington, 542 U.S. 296 (2004). Isn't the South Carolina rule a direct invasion of the jury trial right? Does the exclusion of such evidence undercut the prosecution's burden of proof? See Imwinkelried, The Reach of *Winship*: Invalidating Evidentiary Admissibility Standards that Undermine the Prosecution's Obligation to Prove the Defendant's Guilt Beyond a Reasonable Doubt, 70 U.M.K.C.L.Rev. 865 (2002).

3. *Perry Mason?* The most comprehensive treatment of third-party guilt evidence is found in McCord, "But Perry Mason Made It Look So Easy!": The Admissibility of Evidence Offered by a Criminal Defendant to Suggest That Someone Else is Guilty, 63 Tenn.L.Rev. 917, 919 (1996). Professor McCord notes that "the law is much less favorable to criminal defendants than one might expect, given the unassailable logic that a defendant should be able to defend by offering proof that someone else committed the crime." He labels the most prevalent view, cited in *Holmes*, as the "direct connection" doctrine. Does a prosecutor have to satisfy such a burden when introducing evidence? Also, several states permit third-party guilt evidence only if the prosecution's case is entirely circumstantial. Would such a rule survive *Holmes*?

4. *Polygraph evidence*. In United States v. Scheffer, 523 U.S. 303 (1998), the Supreme Court upheld the military's per se exclusionary rule of polygraph results in face of the same constitutional challenge that was made in *Holmes*. For a discussion of *Scheffer*, see Giannelli, The Supreme Court's "Criminal" *Daubert* Cases, 33 Seton Hall L.Rev. 1071 (2003).

5. *Other evidence rules*. At least two other evidence rules potentially raise third-party guilt issues. Federal Rule 804(b)(3) recognizes a hearsay exception for statements against penal interest and explicitly mentions evidence "offered to exculpate the accused." See Chapter 14(J), infra. In addition, evidence of "other acts" may be offered to establish third-party guilt. See Chapter 8(C), infra, after *Robinson*.

LEECH v. PEOPLE

Supreme Court of Colorado, 1944.
146 P.2d 346.

Burke, Justice. Plaintiff in error, hereinafter referred to as defendant, was convicted of the theft of an automobile and sentenced to the penitentiary for a term of fifteen months to two years. To review that judgment he prosecutes this writ and asks that it be made a supersedeas. He further requests, for good cause appearing, that final disposition be had on this application and in that request the people join. We proceed accordingly. * * *

November 18, 1940, defendant bought a new Pontiac automobile of the Kenyon Company of Cortez. For an unpaid balance on the purchase price he gave his note for approximately $1,000, secured by a mortgage on the car. Title was registered in defendant but in January following (without consideration) it was transferred to his wife. The car carried insurance. The Kenyon Company assigned to the Intermountain Finance Company of Durango. December 12, 1941, with installments on said note delinquent and another in the immediate offing, defendant and one Holman took the car from the former's residence to a place some miles distant where they concealed it out of sight of the main highway. The next morning defendant reported the car stolen and search was begun. December 24, 1941, apparently fearful of discovery, defendant sought the further aid of Holman and together they transferred it to a point near Egnar, concealed it in a clump of trees about 150 feet from the highway, and removing and taking with them the wheels and tires they departed. The automobile was later stripped of almost everything detachable. The insurance company, on the theory of actual theft, paid the policy. Eventually the stripped carcass was discovered, report made to the sheriff and an investigation started which resulted in the filing of an information against defendant and Holman. When the cause came on for trial, Holman entered a plea of guilty, his sentence was postponed, and he testified against defendant. He claimed to have first been hired to help with the concealment of the car, later coerced into assisting in its transfer and a promise to return and burn it, and finally, having quarreled with defendant, apparently over his failure to burn, defendant's failure to pay, and the stripping and disposition of accessories he went to the police. A further detail of evidence is not essential. Suffice it to say that the jurors were entitled to believe the foregoing, and that while this was the theory of the people[,] that of defendant was that most of the testimony of Holman was false, that he was the actual thief, and that his evidence was motivated by the fact that he was unable to extricate himself from the net in which he was caught and determined, as a measure of revenge, to carry defendant down with him. There was evidence to support a verdict to that effect had the jurors elected to accept defendant's theory. * * *

Let it here be borne in mind that Holman's testimony was indispensable to support the verdict, that Holman had been originally informed against jointly with defendant and that he had entered a plea of guilty. Now, called as a witness for the people, Holman was asked by the district attorney, on direct examination:

> "Q. You have been charged with the same crime as Mr. Leech is being tried for now, have you? A. Yes, sir.
>
> "Q. Have you entered a plea of guilty to the charge? A. Yes, sir.
>
> "Q. Do you desire to testify now concerning what you know about this case? A. Yes, sir."

This was neither incidental nor accidental. It was no by-product of cross examination. It did not come from the witness as a voluntary statement. It was the fifth question propounded by the prosecution on direct examination and apparently came with the most careful deliberation. We have held this prejudicial error. Paine v. People, 106 Colo. 258, 103 P.2d 686.[11]

11. ["Our cases clearly establish that a defendant is entitled to have the question of his guilt determined upon the evidence against him, not on whether a codefendant

But, say the people, no objection was interposed, hence the error need not be noticed. True, but it is equally true that when such an error appears and justice requires its consideration this court will not ignore it. Reppin v. People, 95 Colo. 192, 34 P.2d 71.

Is this such a case? We need but call attention to one disclosure of this record to so demonstrate. In addition to the two foregoing errors at least several minor ones appear. Yet here is a record of 230 pages in an important criminal case in which sixteen instructions were given to the jury and from first to last not a single objection on the part of counsel for defendant appears. There was no instruction tendered for defendant and no objection made to any instruction given. Ignoring the failure to object to the Holman testimony, as noted above, it is a test on credulity to believe that defendant's interests called for no faint protest from beginning to end. In the face of such a record justice certainly requires that we note serious prejudicial error and act accordingly. We should here observe that counsel who appear for defendant in this court did not represent him on the trial.

The judgment is reversed and the cause remanded for a new trial.

Notes and Questions

1. *Federal Rule 103.* Important and obvious errors not objected to at trial may be reviewed under the principle of plain error. See Fed.R.Evid. 103(d). See discussion in Chapter 1, Section B, supra.

2. *Sources.* The extent to which courts have been willing to ignore the general rule of the adversary system that issues must be raised in the trial court to be reviewed on appeal is examined in Campbell, Extent to Which Courts of Review Will Consider Questions Not Properly Raised and Preserved (Parts 1–3), 7 Wis.L.Rev. 91, 160 (1932), 8 Wis.L.Rev. 147 (1933); Martineau, Considering New Issues on Appeal: The General Rule and the Gorilla Rule, 40 Vand.L.Rev. 1023 (1987); Vestal, Sua Sponte Consideration in Appellate Review, 27 Fordham L.Rev. 477 (1958–59); Note, 64 Ind.L.J. 985 (1989).

3. *Ineffective assistance of counsel.* Claims of plain error will to some extent overlap with claims of inadequate representation of counsel. If counsel's failure to object is the result of ineffective assistance of counsel, the failure to object will not bar review either in state court or in federal court on collateral attack. See Murray v. Carrier, 477 U.S. 478, 488 (1986). See also Jeffries & Stuntz, Ineffective Assistance and Procedural Default in Federal Habeas Corpus, 57 U.Chi.L.Rev. 679 (1990). However, the showing required to sustain a claim of ineffective assistance of counsel is very substantial. See Strickland v. Washington, 466 U.S. 668, 686 (1984) (counsel's conduct must both violate an objective reasonableness standard and also create a reasonable probability that but for counsel's errors the result would have been different). And success in establishing ineffectiveness is

or government witness has been convicted on the same charge." United States v. Miranda, 593 F.2d 590, 594 (5th Cir.1979). Ed.]

relatively infrequent. See Colbert, Thirty–Five Years After *Gideon*: The Illusory Right to Counsel at Bail Proceedings, 1998 U.Ill.L.Rev. 1. The difficulty of establishing ineffectiveness of counsel has received most attention in capital cases. See Beck & Shumsky, A Comparison of Retained and Appointed Counsel in Cases of Capital Murder, 21 Law & Hum.Behav. 525 (1997); Langfitt & Nolas, Ineffective Assistance of Counsel in Death Penalty Cases, 26 Litigation 6 (Summer 2000); White, Effective Assistance of Counsel in Capital Cases: The Evolving Standard of Care, 1993 U.Ill.L.Rev. 323.

The general inadequacy of an ineffectiveness claim as a method of reviewing trial errors is illustrated by State v. Weaver, 295 S.E.2d 375 (N.C.1982). In *Weaver,* the defendant, who was charged with rape, was represented by two members of the public defender office—one senior counsel, the other without prior jury trial experience. At the time for closing arguments, senior counsel was absent because of a family medical emergency. Co-counsel requested a continuance so that senior counsel, who had planned to give the bulk of the closing argument, could be present. The trial court denied the request, and after a recess of several hours, junior counsel was required to proceed. On appeal, defendant claimed that the closing argument was ineffective. However, because counsel had failed to ask that the court reporter transcribe the argument, no record of the closing existed, and the defendant conceded that he was unable to demonstrate its incompetence. The appellate court ruled that failure to request recording of the closing argument did not per se demonstrate ineffectiveness and counsel's inexperience standing alone did not entitle the defendant to relief. The conviction was affirmed.

HOUSE v. BELL

United States Supreme Court, 2006.
547 U.S. ___, 126 S.Ct. 2064.

JUSTICE KENNEDY delivered the opinion of the Court.

Some 20 years ago in rural Tennessee, Carolyn Muncey was murdered. A jury convicted petitioner Paul Gregory House of the crime and sentenced him to death, but new revelations cast doubt on the jury's verdict. House, protesting his innocence, seeks access to federal court to pursue habeas corpus relief based on constitutional claims that are procedurally barred under state law. Out of respect for the finality of state-court judgments federal habeas courts, as a general rule, are closed to claims that state courts would consider defaulted. In certain exceptional cases involving a compelling claim of actual innocence, however, the state procedural default rule is not a bar to a federal habeas corpus petition. See *Schlup v. Delo,* 513 U.S. 298, 319–322 (1995). After careful review of the full record, we conclude that House has made the stringent showing required by this exception; and we hold that his federal habeas action may proceed.

I

[Mrs. Muncey was last seen the evening before her body was discovered. She told a neighbor (Luttrell) that she was going to make her husband take her fishing the next day. Later her daughter Lora (age 10) said she thought she heard a horn blow, and somebody with a deep voice asked if her father was home and said that he had been in a wreck. She also heard her mother going down the steps crying. Another witness claimed to have seen House, a neighbor, "come out from under a bank, wiping his hands on a black rag" near where the body was later discovered, although when and where he saw House, and how well he could have observed him, were disputed at trial. When questioned by the sheriff, House falsely claimed that he had spent the entire evening with his girlfriend, Donna Turner, at her trailer. After initially supporting House's alibi, Turner informed authorities that House had left her trailer around 10:30 or 10:45 p.m. to go for a walk. According to Turner's trial testimony, House returned later—she was not sure when—"hot and panting, missing his shirt and his shoes." House told her that while he was walking on the road near her home, a vehicle pulled up beside him and somebody inside "called him some names and then they told him he didn't belong here anymore." A fight ensued and House ran away. Turner's trailer was located just under two miles by road, through hilly terrain, from the Muncey residence. FBI testing showed that semen consistent with House's was present on Mrs. Muncey's nightgown and panties, and that small bloodstains consistent with her blood appeared on his jeans.

The Tennessee Supreme Court affirmed House's conviction, finding the evidence "circumstantial" but quite strong. House filed but lost a state postconviction relief application. A second application was then filed. The Tennessee Supreme Court held that House's claims were barred under a state statute providing that claims not raised in prior postconviction proceedings are presumptively waived. House next sought federal habeas relief, asserting numerous claims of ineffective assistance of counsel and prosecutorial misconduct. The district court deemed House's claims procedurally defaulted but held an evidentiary hearing to determine whether House fell within the "actual innocence" exception to the procedural default rule.]

IV

As a general rule, claims forfeited under state law may support federal habeas relief only if the prisoner demonstrates cause for the default and prejudice from the asserted error. * * * The rule is based on the comity and respect that must be accorded to state-court judgments. * * * The bar is not, however, unqualified. In an effort to "balance the societal interests in finality, comity, and conservation of scarce judicial resources with the individual interest in justice that arises in the extraordinary case," *Schlup,* 513 U.S., at 324, the Court has recognized a miscarriage-of-justice exception. * * *

In *Schlup,* the Court adopted a specific rule to implement this general principle. It held that prisoners asserting innocence as a gateway to defaulted claims must establish that, in light of new evidence, "it is more likely than not that no reasonable juror would have found petitioner guilty beyond a reasonable doubt." 513 U.S., at 327. * * *

* * *

With this background in mind we turn to the evidence developed in House's federal habeas proceedings.

DNA Evidence

First, in direct contradiction of evidence presented at trial, DNA testing [not available at the time of trial] has established that the semen on Mrs. Muncey's nightgown and panties came from her husband, Mr. Muncey, not from House. The State, though conceding this point, insists this new evidence is immaterial. At the guilt phase at least, neither sexual contact nor motive were elements of the offense, so in the State's view the evidence, or lack of evidence, of sexual assault or sexual advance is of no consequence. We disagree. In fact we consider the new disclosure of central importance.

From beginning to end the case is about who committed the crime. When identity is in question, motive is key. The point, indeed, was not lost on the prosecution, for it introduced the evidence and relied on it in the final guilt-phase closing argument. Referring to "evidence at the scene," the prosecutor suggested that House committed, or attempted to commit, some "indignity" on Mrs. Muncey that neither she "nor any mother on that road would want to do with Mr. House." * * * Particularly in a case like this where the proof was, as the State Supreme Court observed, circumstantial, * * * we think a jury would have given this evidence great weight. Quite apart from providing proof of motive, it was the only forensic evidence at the scene that would link House to the murder.

Law and society, as they ought to do, demand accountability when a sexual offense has been committed, so not only did this evidence link House to the crime; it likely was a factor in persuading the jury not to let him go free. At sentencing, moreover, the jury came to the unanimous conclusion, beyond a reasonable doubt, that the murder was committed in the course of a rape or kidnaping. The alleged sexual motivation relates to both those determinations. This is particularly so given that, at the sentencing phase, the jury was advised that House had a previous conviction for sexual assault.

A jury informed that fluids on Mrs. Muncey's garments could have come from House might have found that House trekked the nearly two miles to the victim's home and lured her away in order to commit a sexual offense. By contrast a jury acting without the assumption that the semen could have come from House would have found it necessary to establish some different motive, or, if the same motive, an intent far more speculative. When the only direct evidence of sexual assault drops out of the case, so, too, does a central theme in the State's narrative linking House to the crime. In that light, furthermore, House's odd evening walk and his false statements to authorities, while still potentially incriminating, might appear less suspicious.

Bloodstains

The other relevant forensic evidence is the blood on House's pants, which appears in small, even minute, stains in scattered places. As the prosecutor told the jury, they were stains that, due to their small size, "you or I might not detect[,] [m]ight not see, but which the FBI lab was able to find on [House's] jeans." App. 11. The stains appear inside the right pocket, outside that pocket, near the inside button, on the left thigh and outside leg, on the seat of the pants, and on the right bottom cuff, including inside the pants. Due to testing by the FBI, cuttings now appear on the pants in several places where stains evidently were found. (The cuttings were destroyed in the testing process, and defense experts were unable to replicate the tests.) At trial, the government argued "nothing that the defense has introduced in this case explains what blood is doing on his jeans, all over [House's] jeans, that is scientifically, completely different from his blood." *Id.,* at 105. House, though not disputing at this point that the blood is Mrs. Muncey's, now presents an alternative explanation that, if credited, would undermine the probative value of the blood evidence.

During House's habeas proceedings, Dr. Cleland Blake, an Assistant Chief Medical Examiner for the State of Tennessee and a consultant in forensic pathology to the TBI for 22 years, testified that the blood on House's pants was chemically too degraded, and too similar to blood collected during the autopsy, to have come from Mrs. Muncey's body on the night of the crime. The blood samples collected during the autopsy were placed in test tubes without preservative. Under such conditions, according to Dr. Blake, "you will have enzyme degradation. You will have different blood group degradation, blood marker degradation." * * * The problem of decay, moreover, would have been compounded by the body's long exposure to the elements, sitting outside for the better part of a summer day. In contrast, if blood is preserved on cloth, "it will stay there for years," *ibid.;* indeed, Dr. Blake said he deliberately places blood drops on gauze during autopsies to preserve it for later testing. The blood on House's pants, judging by Agent Bigbee's tests, showed "similar deterioration, breakdown of certain of the named numbered enzymes" as in the autopsy samples. *Id.,* at 110. "[I]f the victim's blood had spilled on the jeans while the victim was alive and this blood had dried," Dr. Blake stated, "the deterioration would not have occurred," *ibid.,* and "you would expect [the blood on the jeans] to be different than what was in the tube," *id.,* at 113. Dr. Blake thus concluded the blood on the jeans came from the autopsy samples, not from Mrs. Muncey's live (or recently killed) body.

Other evidence confirms that blood did in fact spill from the vials. It appears the vials passed from Dr. Carabia, who performed the autopsy, into the hands of two local law enforcement officers, who transported it to the FBI, where Agent Bigbee performed the enzyme tests. The blood was contained in four vials, evidently with neither preservative nor a proper seal. The vials, in turn, were stored in a styrofoam box, but nothing indicates the box was kept cool. Rather, in what an evidence protocol expert at the habeas hearing described as a violation of proper procedure, the styrofoam box was packed in the same cardboard box as other evidence including House's pants (apparently in a paper bag) and other clothing (in separate bags). The cardboard box was then carried in the officers' car while they made the 10–hour journey from Tennessee to the FBI lab. Dr. Blake stated that blood vials in hot conditions (such as a car trunk in the summer) could blow open; and in fact, by the time the blood reached the FBI it had hemolyzed, or spoiled, due to heat exposure. By the time the blood passed from the FBI to a defense expert, roughly a vial and a half were empty, though Agent Bigbee testified he used at most a quarter of one vial. Blood, moreover, had seeped onto one corner of the styrofoam box and onto packing gauze inside the box below the vials.

In addition, although the pants apparently were packaged initially in a paper bag and FBI records suggest they arrived at the FBI in one, the record does not contain the paper bag but does contain a plastic bag with a label listing the pants and Agent Scott's name—and the plastic bag has blood on it. The blood appears in a forked streak roughly five inches long and two inches wide running down the bag's outside front. Though testing by House's expert confirmed the stain was blood, the expert could not determine the blood's source. Speculations about when and how the blood got there add to the confusion regarding the origins of the stains on House's pants.

Faced with these indications of, at best, poor evidence control, the State attempted to establish at the habeas hearing that all blood spillage occurred after Agent Bigbee examined the pants. Were that the case, of course, then blood would have been detected on the pants before any spill—which would tend to undermine Dr. Blake's analysis and support using the bloodstains to infer House's guilt. In support of this theory the State put on testimony by a blood spatter expert who believed the "majority" of the stains were "transfer stains," that is, stains resulting from "wip[ing] across the surface of the pants" rather than seeping or spillage. * * * Regarding the spillage in the styrofoam box, the expert noted that yellow "Tennessee Crime Laboratory" tape running around the box and down all four sides did not line up when the bloodstains on the box's corner were aligned. The inference was that the FBI received the box from Tennessee authorities, opened it, and resealed it before the spillage occurred. Reinforcing this theory, Agent Bigbee testified that he observed no blood spillage in the styrofoam box and that had he detected such signs of evidence contamination, FBI policy would have required immediate return of the evidence.

* * *

In sum, considering " 'all the evidence,' " *Schlup,* 513 U.S., at 328 * * * on this issue, we think the evidentiary disarray surrounding the blood, taken together with Dr. Blake's testimony and the limited rebuttal of it in the present record, would prevent reasonable jurors from placing significant reliance on the blood evidence. We now know, though the trial jury did not, that an Assistant Chief Medical Examiner believes the blood on House's jeans must have come from autopsy samples; that a vial and a quarter of autopsy blood is unaccounted for; that the blood was transported to the FBI together with the pants in conditions that could have caused vials to spill; that the blood did indeed spill at least once during its journey from Tennessee authorities through FBI hands to a defense expert; that the pants were stored in a plastic bag bearing both a large blood stain and a label with TBI Agent Scott's name; and that the styrofoam box containing the blood samples may well have been opened before it arrived at the FBI lab. Thus, whereas the bloodstains, emphasized by the prosecution, seemed strong evidence of House's guilt at trial, the record now raises substantial questions about the blood's origin.

A Different Suspect

Were House's challenge to the State's case limited to the questions he has raised about the blood and semen, the other evidence favoring the prosecution might well suffice to bar relief. There is, however, more; for in the post-trial proceedings House presented troubling evidence that Mr. Muncey, the victim's husband, himself could have been the murderer. * * *

[Two weeks before the murder Mrs. Muncey's brother received a frightened phone call from his sister indicating that she and Mr. Muncey had been fighting, that she was scared, and that she wanted to leave him. Moreover, the brother once saw the husband smack her. In addition, multiple sources suggested that Mr. Muncey regularly abused his wife. Another witness (Atkins) saw him hit Mrs. Muncey at a dance on the night of the murder. Still another witness (Lawson) testified that Mr. Muncey visited her the morning after the murder, before the body was found, and asked her to tell anyone who inquired that he had breakfasted at her home at 6 o'clock that morning. Mr. Muncey had not been with her so early. Moreover, Kathy Parker and her sister Penny Letner, testified at the habeas hearing that, around the time of House's trial, Mr. Muncey when intoxicated confessed to the crime, claiming he did not mean to kill her. He said that his wife was "bitching him out," he smacked her, she fell and hit her head. Letner, who was then 19 years old, testified she was scared and kept silent because she thought no one would believe her. Parker claimed she went to the Sherriff's Department, but no one would listen. Other evidence suggested Mr. Muncey had the opportunity to commit the crime.]

In the habeas proceedings, then, two different witnesses (Parker and Letner) described a confession by Mr. Muncey; two more (Atkins and Lawson) described suspicious behavior (a fight and an attempt to construct a false alibi) around the time of the crime; and still other witnesses described a history of abuse.

As to Parker and Letner, the District Court noted that it was "not impressed with the allegations of individuals who wait over ten years to come forward with their evidence," especially considering that "there was no physical evidence in the Munceys' kitchen to corroborate [Mr. Muncey's] alleged confession that he killed [his wife] there." * * * Parker and Letner, however, did attempt to explain their delay coming forward, and the record indicates no reason why these two women, both lifelong acquaintances of Mr. Muncey, would have wanted either to frame him or to help House. Furthermore, the record includes at least some independent support for the statements Parker and Letner attributed to Mr. Muncey. The supposed explanation for the fatal fight—that his wife was complaining about going fishing—fits with Mrs. Muncey's statement to Luttrell earlier that evening that her husband's absence was "all right, because she was going to make him take her fishing the next day" * * *. And Dr. Blake testified, in only partial contradiction of Dr. Carabia, that Mrs. Muncey's head injury resulted from "a surface with an edge" or "a hard surface with a corner," not from a fist. * * * (Dr. Carabia had said either a fist or some other object could have been the cause.)

Mr. Muncey testified at the habeas hearing, and the District Court did not question his credibility. Though Mr. Muncey said he seemed to remember visiting Lawson the day after the murder, he denied either killing his wife or confessing to doing so. Yet Mr. Muncey also claimed, contrary to Constable Wallace's testimony and to his own prior statement, that he left the dance on the night of the crime only when it ended at midnight. Mr. Muncey, moreover, denied ever hitting Mrs. Muncey; the State itself had to impeach him with a prior statement on this point.

It bears emphasis, finally, that Parker's and Letner's testimony is not comparable to the sort of eleventh-hour affidavit vouching for a defendant and incriminating a conveniently absent suspect that Justice O'Connor described in her concurring opinion in [Herrera v. Collins, 506 U.S. 390 (1993)] as "unfortunate" and "not uncommon" in capital cases, 506 U.S., at 423; nor was the confession Parker and Letner described induced under pressure of interrogation. The confession evidence here involves an alleged spontaneous statement recounted by two eyewitnesses with no evident motive to lie. For this reason it has more probative value than, for example, incriminating testimony from inmates, suspects, or friends or relations of the accused.

The evidence pointing to Mr. Muncey is by no means conclusive. If considered in isolation, a reasonable jury might well disregard it. In combination, however, with the challenges to the blood evidence and the lack of motive with respect to House, the evidence pointing to Mr. Muncey likely would reinforce other doubts as to House's guilt.

Other Evidence

Certain other details were presented at the habeas hearing. First, Dr. Blake, in addition to testifying about the blood evidence and the victim's head injury, examined photographs of House's bruises and scratches and concluded, based on 35 years' experience monitoring the development and healing of bruises, that they were too old to have resulted from the crime. In addition Dr. Blake claimed that the injury on House's right knuckle was indicative of "[g]etting mashed"; it was not consistent with striking someone. * * * (That of course would also eliminate the explanation that the injury came from the blow House supposedly told Turner he gave to his unidentified assailant.)

The victim's daughter, Lora Muncey (now Lora Tharp), also testified at the habeas hearing. She repeated her recollection of hearing a man with a deep voice * * * and a statement that her father had had a wreck down by the creek. She also denied seeing any signs of struggle or hearing a fight between her parents, though she also said she could not recall her parents ever fighting physically. The District Court found her credible, and this testimony certainly cuts in favor of the State.

Finally, House himself testified at the habeas proceedings. He essentially repeated the story he allegedly told Turner about getting attacked on the road. The District Court found, however, based on House's demeanor, that he "was not a credible witness." * * *

Conclusion

This is not a case of conclusive exoneration. Some aspects of the State's evidence—Lora Muncey's memory of a deep voice, House's bizarre evening walk, his lie to law enforcement, his appearance near the body, and the blood on his pants—still support an inference of guilt. Yet the central forensic proof connecting House to the crime—the blood and the semen—has been called into question, and House has put forward substantial evidence pointing to a different suspect. Accordingly, and although the issue is close, we conclude that this is the rare case where—had the jury heard all the conflicting testimony—it is more likely than not that no reasonable juror viewing the record as a whole would lack reasonable doubt.

V

In addition to his gateway claim under *Schlup,* House argues that he has shown freestanding innocence and that as a result his imprisonment and planned execution are unconstitutional. In *Herrera,* decided three years before *Schlup,* the Court assumed without deciding that "in a capital case a truly persuasive demonstration of 'actual innocence' made after trial would render the execution of a defendant unconstitutional, and warrant federal habeas relief if there were no state avenue open to process such a claim." 506 U.S., at 417; see also *id.,* at 419 (O'Connor, J., concurring) ("I cannot disagree with the fundamental legal principle that executing the innocent is inconsistent with the Constitution"). "[T]he threshold showing for such an assumed right would necessarily be extraordinarily high," the Court explained, and petitioner's evidence there fell "far short of that which would have to be made in order to trigger the sort of constitutional claim which we have assumed, *arguen-*

do, to exist." *Id.*, at 417, 418–419 * * *. House urges the Court to answer the question left open in *Herrera* and hold not only that freestanding innocence claims are possible but also that he has established one.

We decline to resolve this issue. We conclude here, much as in *Herrera,* that whatever burden a hypothetical freestanding innocence claim would require, this petitioner has not satisfied it. * * *

[CHIEF JUSTICE ROBERTS, with JUSTICE SCALIA and JUSTICE THOMAS, concurred in the judgment in part and dissented in part on the grounds that House had not met his burden of proof under *Schlup*. JUSTICE ALITO took no part in the decision. The Chief Justice made a number of points, including that the majority essentially disregarded the district court's role in assessing the reliability of House's new evidence. He also pointed out that the jury had been informed that Mrs. Muncey's body was found fully clothed. He stressed that the Munceys' daughter had heard a deep-voiced perpetrator arrive at the Muncey home late at night and tell Mrs. Muncey that her husband had been in a wreck near the creek. He concluded: "Surely a reasonable juror would give the fact that an alibi had been made up and discredited significant weight. People facing a murder charge, who are innocent, do not make up a story out of concern that the truth might somehow disturb their parole officer. And people do not lie to the police about which jeans they were wearing the night of a murder, if they have no reason to believe the jeans would be stained with the blood shed by the victim in her last desperate struggle to live."]

Notes and Questions

1. *Procedural default.* Procedural default is just one aspect of habeas corpus law. See 3 LaFave, Israel & King, Criminal Procedure § 28.4 (2d ed. 1999). The changes in federal habeas law that began in the late 1970s have had the effect of dramatically restricting its scope from that enjoyed during the Warren Court era. These changes have generated an extensive body of largely critical commentary. See, e.g., Arkin, The Prisoner's Dilemma: Life in the Lower Federal Courts after *Teague v. Lane*, 69 N.C.L.Rev. 371 (1991); Fallon & Meltzer, New Law, Non–Retroactivity and Constitutional Remedies, 104 Harv.L.Rev. 1731 (1991); Friedman, Habeas and Hubris, 45 Vand. L.Rev. 797 (1992); Hoffman, Is Innocence Sufficient? An Essay on the U.S. Supreme Court's Continuing Problems with Federal Habeas Corpus and the Death Penalty, 68 Ind.L.J. 817 (1993); Liebman, Apocalypse Next Time?: The Anachronistic Attack on Habeas Corpus/Direct Review Parity, 92 Colum.L.Rev. 1997 (1992); Liebman, More Than "Slightly Retro:" The Rehnquist Court's Rout of Habeas Corpus Jurisdiction in *Teague v. Lane*, 18 N.Y.U.Rev.L. & Soc. Change 537 (1991); Weisberg, A Great Writ While It Lasted, 81 J.Crim.L. & Criminology 9 (1990); Woolhandler, Demodeling Habeas, 45 Stan.L.Rev. 575 (1993). Congress further limited the availability of habeas review. See Whitebread & Slobogin, Criminal Procedure § 33.03, at 1002 (4th ed. 2000) ("For capital cases, the 1996 Antiterrorism and Effective Death Penalty Act appears to have radically changed the

cause/prejudice/actual innocence framework the Supreme Court had developed.").

2. *Retroactivity.* Even assuming that the claim was properly raised at trial, a defendant does not necessarily benefit from a new constitutional rule. This is because newly established constitutional rights are not given full retroactive application, which the Supreme Court first recognized in Linkletter v. Walker, 381 U.S. 618 (1965). Abandoning a substantial and complex body of precedent, the Court eventually settled upon an overall approach for determining which cases will receive the benefit of new constitutional rulings. In a series of cases beginning with United States v. Johnson, 457 U.S. 537 (1982), and culminating in Griffith v. Kentucky, 479 U.S. 314 (1987), it held that a new constitutional rule applies to all cases pending review on direct appeal at the time the new principle is established. Then in Teague v. Lane, 489 U.S. 288 (1989), the Court ruled that, with very limited exceptions, a defendant on collateral attack whose direct appeal was complete could not benefit from a new constitutional rule. Obviously the definition of what constitutes a new rule is important to determining the force of *Teague*, and in Butler v. McKellar, 494 U.S. 407 (1990), the Court applied the "new rule" principle expansively, putting real teeth into the *Teague* rule. See generally 1 LaFave, Israel & King, Criminal Procedure § 2.9 (2d ed. 1999); Whitebread & Slobogin, Criminal Procedure § 29.06 (4th ed. 2000).

3. *Innocence.* As *House* suggests, the power of DNA evidence to exonerate convicted prisoners is having a significant impact on the criminal justice system. According to the Innocence Project, DNA analysis has exonerated over 180 convicts, 14 of whom had been on death row, by the summer of 2006. Another study identified 340 exonerations, 196 of which did not involve DNA evidence. Gross et al., Exonerations in the United States: 1989 Through 2003, 95 J.Crim.L. & Criminology 523, 524 (2005). Many states enacted post-conviction DNA testing laws, as did Congress in the Innocence Protection Act of 2004, 18 U.S.C. § 3600, which was part of major crime legislation, the Justice for All Act, Public Law 108–405. As a result of the exonerations, commentators began to examine the causes of these miscarriages of justice. See Barry Scheck et al., Actual Innocence: Five Days to Execution and Other Dispatches from the Wrongly Convicted 246 (2000): (1) mistaken eyewitnesses (84%), police misconduct (50%), prosecutorial misconduct (42%), tainted or fraudulent science (33%), ineffective defense counsel (27%), false confessions (24%), and jailhouse snitches (21%). The ABA House of Delegates passed a number of resolutions addressing these issues, including recommendations for videotaping all interrogations, accrediting crime laboratories, conducting double blind lineups, and requiring corroboration in all cases involving jailhouse snitches. Report of the ABA Criminal Justice Section's Ad Hoc Innocence Committee to Ensure the Integrity of the Criminal Process, Achieving Justice: Freeing the Innocent, Convicting the Guilty (Giannelli & Raeder eds., 2006).

4. *Victim's Rights.* Rape shield laws, which are discussed in Chapter 8(C), infra, can be viewed as privileges that often exclude defense evidence. They are reflective of the growing recognition in modern criminal proceedings of a role for the crime victim, who may have specific interests that differ from those of the party prosecuting the case, the state or federal government. The movement to give recognition to "victim rights" has produced a

substantial body of legislation to compensate and protect victims and to give them more say in the conduct of the prosecution. See, e.g., Victim and Witness Protection Act of 1982, 18 U.S.C. §§ 1501 et seq.; Justice for All Act of 2004, Public Law 108–405, with victim's rights provisions codified in 18 U.S.C.A. § 3771. Here too there is a growing body of scholarly commentary. See Cassell, Recognizing Victims in the Federal Rules of Criminal Procedure: Proposed Amendment in Light the Crime Victims' Rights Act, 2005 BYU L.Rev. 835; Henderson, The Wrongs of Victim's Rights, 37 Stan.L.Rev. 937 (1985); Mosteller, Victim's Rights and the Constitution: An Effort to Recast the Battle in Criminal Litigation, 85 Geo.L.J. 1691 (1997); Mosteller, Victim's Rights and the Constitution: Moving from Guaranteeing Participatory Rights to Benefitting the Prosecution, 29 St. Mary's L.J. 1053 (1998); Welling, Victim Participation in Plea Bargains, 65 Wash.U.L.Q. 301 (1987); Symposium, Crime Victims' Rights in the Twenty–First Century, 1999 Utah L.Rev. 285–552; Symposium, Victims' Rights, 11 Pepperdine L.Rev. 1–182 (1984).

5. *Jury Nullification.* This chapter has explored a few of the limitations on our adversary system. Jury nullification, the jury's ability to acquit in the face of law and facts demonstrating guilt, constitutes another theoretically important check upon the "efficient" operation of that system. While the jury is consistently recognized to have the power to nullify, does it have that "right"? With extremely rare exceptions, American courts hold that the jury is not to be instructed regarding its ability to nullify. Why is that position held? See, e.g., United States v. Dougherty, 473 F.2d 1113 (D.C.Cir. 1972). See also United States v. Abbell, 271 F.3d 1286, 1302 (11th Cir.2001) ("Because of the danger that a dissenting juror might be excused under the mistaken view that the juror is engaging in impermissible nullification, we must apply a tough legal standard. In these kind of circumstances, a juror should be excused only when no 'substantial possibility' exists that she is basing her decision on the sufficiency of the evidence."); People v. Williams, 21 P.3d 1209, 1222 (Cal.2001) ("It is striking that the debate over juror nullification remains vigorous after more than a hundred years. But it is equally significant that, during this time, no published authority has restricted a trial court's authority to discharge a juror when the record demonstrates that the juror is unable or unwilling to follow the court's instructions."). See generally Conrad, Jury Nullification: The Evolution of a Doctrine (1998); Brown, Jury Nullification Within the Rule of Law, 81 Minn.L.Rev. 1149 (1997); Butler, Racially Based Jury Nullification: Black Power in the Criminal Justice System, 105 Yale L.J. 677 (1995); Horowitz & Willging, Changing Views of Jury Power: The Nullification Debate, 1787–1988, 15 Law & Hum.Behav. 165 (1991); Leipold, Rethinking Jury Nullification, 82 Va.L.Rev. 253 (1996); Saks, Judicial Nullification, 68 Ind.L.J. 1281 (1993); Wiener et al., The Social Psychology of Jury Nullification: Predicting When Jurors Disobey the Law, 21 J. Applied Soc.Psychol. 1379 (1991); Note, License to Nullify: The Democratic and Constitutional Deficiencies of Authorized Jury Lawmaking, 106 Yale L.J. 2563 (1997).

Topic II
THE FRAMEWORK OF DECISION

Chapter 3

ALLOCATING THE CASE

CLEARY, PRESUMING AND PLEADING: AN ESSAY ON JURISTIC IMMATURITY[1]

12 Stanford Law Review 5 (1959).

* * *

THE SUBSTANTIVE LAW

Since all are agreed that procedure exists only for the purpose of putting the substantive law effectively to work, a preliminary look at the nature of substantive law, as viewed procedurally, is appropriate.

Every dog, said the common law, is entitled to one bite. This result was reached from reasoning that man's best friend was not in general dangerous, and hence the owner should not be liable when the dog departed from his normally peaceable pursuits and inflicted injury. Liability should follow only when the owner had reason to know of the dangerous proclivities of his dog, and the one bite afforded notice of those proclivities. So the formula for holding a dog owner liable at common law is: + *ownership* + *notice of dangerous character* + *biting*.

This rule of law becomes monotonous to postmen. Hence the postmen cause to be introduced in the legislature a bill making owners of dogs absolutely liable, i.e., eliminating notice from the formula for liability. At the hearing on the bill, however, the dog lovers appear and, while admitting the justness of the postmen's complaint, point out that a dog ought at least to be entitled to defend himself against human aggression. Then the home owners' lobby points out the usefulness of dogs in guarding premises against prowlers. Balancing these factors, there emerges a statute making dog owners liable for bites inflicted except upon persons tormenting the dog or unlawfully on the owner's premises. The formula for liability now becomes: + *ownership* + *biting* − *being tormented* − *unlawful presence on the premises.*

1. Copyright © 1959–1960 by the Trustees of the Leland Stanford Junior University. Reprinted by permission. Some footnotes have been omitted, and the remainder have been renumbered. [Ed.]

So in any given situation, the law recognizes certain elements as material to the case, and the presence or absence of each of them is properly to be considered in deciding the case. Or, to rephrase in somewhat more involved language, rules of substantive law are "statements of the specific factual conditions upon which specific legal consequences depend. * * * Rules of substantive law are conditional imperatives, having the form: *If* such and such *and* so and so, *etc.* is the case, *and unless* such and such *or unless* so and so, *etc.* is the case, *then* the defendant is liable * * *."[2] Now obviously the weighing and balancing required to determine what elements ought to be considered material cannot be accomplished by any of the methodologies of procedure. The result is purely a matter of substantive law, to be decided according to those imponderables which travel under the name of jurisprudence.

This view of the substantive law may seem unduly Euclidean, yet some system of analysis and classification is necessary if the law is to possess a measure of continuity and to be accessible and usable.

Prima Facie Case and Defense

Under our adversary method of litigation a trial is essentially not an inquest or investigation but rather a demonstration conducted by the parties.

Since plaintiff is the party seeking to disturb the existing situation by inducing the court to take some measure in his favor, it seems reasonable to require him to demonstrate his right to relief. How extensive must this demonstration be? Should it include every substantive element, which either by its existence or nonexistence may condition his right to relief? If the answer is "yes," then plaintiff under our dog statute would be required to demonstrate each of the elements in the formula: + *ownership* + *biting* − *tormenting* − *illegal presence on the premises.*

In the ordinary dog case this would not be unduly burdensome, but if the suit is on a contract and we require plaintiff to establish the existence or nonexistence, as may be appropriate, of every concept treated in Corbin and Williston, then the responsibility of plaintiff becomes burdensome indeed and the lawsuit itself may include a large amount of unnecessary territory. Actually, of course, the responsibility for dealing with every element is not placed on plaintiff. Instead we settle for a "prima facie case" or "cause of action," consisting of certain selected elements which are regarded as sufficient to entitle plaintiff to recover, *if* he proves them and *unless* defendant in turn establishes other elements which would offset them. Thus in a simple contract case, by establishing + *offer* + *acceptance* + *consideration* + *breach,* plaintiff is entitled to recover, unless defendant establishes + *accord and satisfac-*

2. [Michael & Adler, *The Trial of an Issue of Fact: I,* 34 Colum.L.Rev. 1224, 1241 (1934).]

tion or + *failure of consideration* or + *illegality* or—*capacity to contract,* and so on.

Observe that the plus and minus signs change, in accord with proper mathematical rules, when we shift elements to the defendant's side of the equation as "defenses." For example, if plaintiff were required to deal with capacity to contract, it would become + *capacity to contract* as a part of his case, rather than the—*capacity to contract* of defendant's case.

Defenses, too, may be prima facie only and subject to being offset by further matters produced by plaintiff, as in the case of the defense of release, offset by the further fact of fraud in the inducement for the release. The entire process is the familiar confessing and avoiding of the common law.

Allocating the Elements

The next step to be taken is the determination whether a particular material element is a part of plaintiff's prima facie case or a defense. Or, referring back to the statement that rules of substantive law are "conditional imperatives, having the form: *If* such and such *and* so and so, *etc.,* is the case * * * *then* the defendant is liable,"[3] should the element in question be listed as an *if* or as an *unless?*

In some types of situations, the test has been purely mechanical, with the mechanics in turn likely to be accidental and casual. Thus, in causes of action based on statute, if an exception appears in the enacting clause, i.e., the clause creating the right of action, then the party relying on the statute must show that the case is not within the exception; otherwise the responsibility for bringing the case within an exception falls upon the opposite party. The principle is widely recognized, but the vagaries of statutory draftsmanship detract largely from its certainty of application. Returning to our dogs, two statutes will serve as illustrations.

> If any dog shall do any damage to either the body or property of any person, the owner * * * shall be liable for such damage, unless such damage shall have been occasioned to the body or property of a person who, at the time such damage was sustained, was committing a trespass or other tort, or was teasing, tormenting or abusing such dog. Mass.Ann.Laws ch. 140, § 155 (1950).
>
> Every person owning or harboring a dog shall be liable to the party injured for all damages done by such dog; but no recovery shall be had for personal injuries to any person when they [sic] are upon the premises of the owner of the dog after night, or upon the owner's premises engaged in some unlawful act in the day time. Ky.Laws 1906, ch. 10, at 25, Ky.Stats.1936, § 68a–5.

The Massachusetts statute was construed as imposing on a two and one quarter year old plaintiff the burden of establishing that he was not

3. Michael & Adler, supra note [2].

teasing, tormenting or abusing the dog,[4] while under the Kentucky statute a plaintiff was held to have stated a prima facie case by alleging only that he was bitten by a dog owned by defendant, leaving questions of presence on the premises at night or unlawful activities in the day time to be brought in as defenses.[5] The difference in result can scarcely be regarded as calculated but is typical. Unfortunately, the statute which states in so many words the procedural effects of its terms is a rarity.

Exceptions in contracts receive similar treatment. If the words of promising are broad, followed by exceptions, the general disposition is to place on defendant the responsibility of invoking the exception. Of course, many of the cases involve insurance policies, with all that implies. In Munro, Brice & Co. v. War Risks Ass'n,[6] during World War I one underwriter insured plaintiffs' ship against loss due to hostilities and another underwriter insured it against perils of the sea except consequences of hostilities. The ship was lost, and plaintiffs sued on both policies. The King's Bench Division held that as regards the first policy plaintiffs must show the loss to have been due to hostilities, but that under the second policy merely establishing the loss was sufficient, leaving it to the underwriter to bring in loss by hostilities as a defense. Since evidence of the cause of loss was wholly lacking, the loss fell on the second underwriter.

Julius Stone commented as follows:

> Every qualification of a class can equally be stated without any change of meaning as an exception to a class not so qualified. Thus the proposition "All animals have four legs except gorillas", and the proposition "all animals which are not gorillas have four legs", are, so far as their meanings are concerned, identical. * * *
>
> If the distinction between an element of the rule and an exception to it does not represent any distinction in meaning, it may still remain a valid distinction for legal purposes. In that case, however, it must turn upon something other than the meaning of the propositions involved. It may turn, for instance, merely upon their relative form or order.[7]

So in a few kinds of cases the answer to the question of allocation is found in the structure of a statute or contract, perhaps with some tenuous reference to intent, either of the legislature or of the contracting parties. But what of the great bulk of the cases, involving neither exception in a statute nor limitation upon words of promising? What general considerations should govern the allocation of responsibility for the elements of the case between the parties?

Precedent may settle the manner in a particular jurisdiction, but precedent as such does nothing for the inquiring mind. Thayer was of

4. Sullivan v. Ward, 304 Mass. 614, 24 N.E.2d 672, 130 A.L.R. 437 (1939).

5. Bush v. Wathen, 104 Ky. 548, 47 S.W. 599 (1898).

6. [1918] 2 K.B. 78.

7. Stone, *Burden of Proof and the Judicial Process,* 60 L.Q.Rev. 262, 280–81 (1944).

the view that questions of allocation were to be referred to the principles of pleading, or perhaps to analysis of the substantive law, and "one has no right to look to the law of evidence for a solution of such questions as these. * * * "[8] Books about pleading, however, have not been numerous in recent years, except for the local practice works; and aside from a brief but provocative treatment by Judge Clark[9] they offer slight assistance. The substantive law texts, when they deal with the matter at all, tend to describe results rather than reasons.

Despite Thayer's strictures, his descendants in the field of writing about evidence, by assuming to deal with problems of burden of proof as an aspect of the law of evidence, have found themselves inevitably enmeshed in the problems of allocation and have contributed most of the literature on the subject, although in an introductory and incidental fashion.

Before trying to establish some bench marks for allocation, let us note, though only for the purpose of rejecting them, two which are sometimes suggested. (a) That the burden is on the party having the affirmative; or, conversely stated, that a party is not required to prove a negative. This is no more than a play on words, since practically any proposition may be stated in either affirmative or negative form. Thus a plaintiff's exercise of ordinary care equals absence of contributory negligence, in the minority jurisdictions which place this element in plaintiff's case. In any event, the proposition seems simply not to be so. (b) That the burden is on the party to whose case the element is essential. This does no more than restate the question.

Actually the reported decisions involving problems of allocation rarely contain any satisfying disclosure of the *ratio decidendi*. Implicit, however, seem to be considerations of policy, fairness and probability. None affords a complete working rule. Much overlap is apparent, as sound policy implies not too great a departure from fairness, and probability may constitute an aspect of both policy and fairness. But despite the vagueness of their generality, it is possible to pour enough content into these concepts to give them some real meaning.

(1) *Policy.* As Judge Clark remarks, "One who must bear the risk of getting the matter properly set before the court, if it is to be considered at all, has to that extent the dice loaded against him."[10] While policy more obviously predominates at the stage of determining what elements are material, its influence may nevertheless extend into the stage of allocating those elements by way of favoring one or the other party to a particular kind of litigation. Thus a court which is willing to permit a recovery for negligence may still choose to exercise restraints by imposing on plaintiff the burden of freedom from contributory negligence, as a

8. Thayer, A Preliminary Treatises on Evidence at the Common Law 371 (1898). * * *

9. Clark, Code Pleading § 96, at 606–11 (2d ed. 1947). * * *

10. Clark, Code Pleading § 96, at 609 (2d ed. 1947).

theoretical, though perhaps not a practical, handicap. Or the bringing of actions for defamation may in some measure be discouraged by allocating untruth to plaintiff as an element of his prima facie case, rather than by treating truth as an affirmative defense. And it must be apparent that a complete lack of proof as to a particular element moves allocation out of the class of a mere handicap and makes it decisive as to the element, and perhaps as to the case itself. In Summers v. Tice[11] plaintiff was hunting with two defendants and was shot in the eye when both fired simultaneously at the same bird. The court placed on each defendant the burden of proving that his shot did not cause the injury. To discharge this burden was impossible, since each gun was loaded with identical shot. In Munro, Brice & Co. v. War Risks Ass'n[12] the absence of proof of the cause of the ship's loss meant that the party on whom that burden was cast lost the case. In these cases the admonition of Julius Stone is particularly apt: "the Courts should not essay the impossible task of making the bricks of judge-made law without handling the straw of policy."[13]

(2) *Fairness.* The nature of a particular element may indicate that evidence relating to it lies more within the control of one party, which suggests the fairness of allocating that element to him. Examples are payment, discharge in bankruptcy, and license, all of which are commonly treated as affirmative defenses. However, caution in making any extensive generalization is indicated by the classification of contributory negligence, illegality, and failure of consideration also as affirmative defenses, despite the fact that knowledge more probably lies with plaintiff. Certainly in the usual tort cases, knowledge of his own wrongdoing rests more intimately in defendant, though the accepted general pattern imposes this burden on plaintiff.

(3) *Probability.* A further factor which seems to enter into many decisions as to allocation is a judicial, i.e., wholly nonstatistical, estimate of the probabilities of the situation with the burden being put on the party who will be benefited by a departure from the supposed norm.

The probabilities may relate to the type of situation out of which the litigation arises or they may relate to the type of litigation itself. The standards are quite different and may produce differences in result. To illustrate: If it be assumed that most people pay their bills, the probabilities are that any bill selected at random has been paid; therefore, a

11. 33 Cal.2d 80, 199 P.2d 1, 5 A.L.R.2d 91 (1948). Like presumptions, liberal party joinder provisions appear to be no more than procedural in nature. However, they may encourage courts to impose blanket responsibility upon a group of defendants, leaving each to extricate himself as he can. Thus they may have a significant role in extending the substantive law of liability. See McCoid, *Negligence Actions Against Multiple Defendants,* 7 Stan.L.Rev. 480 (1955).

12. [1918] 2 K.B. 78. * * *

13. Stone, *Burden of Proof and the Judicial Process,* 60 L.Q.Rev. 262, 283 (1944).

Compare: "where natural logic is insufficient the state is disposed to discard it and to adopt other procedures for arriving at a decision; and so by means of ingenious procedural mechanisms, it creates a kind of 'artificial' or 'official' logic that serves to resolve all questions at issue, even those that common reason would call insoluble." Calamandrei, Procedure and Democracy 6 (1956).

plaintiff suing to collect a bill would be responsible for nonpayment as an element of his prima facie case. If, however, attention is limited to bills upon which suit is brought, a contrary conclusion is reached. Plaintiffs are not prone to sue for paid bills, and the probabilities are that the bill is unpaid. Hence payment would be an affirmative defense. Or again, "guest" statutes prohibit nonpaying passengers from recovering for the negligence of the driver. If most passengers are nonpaying, then the element of compensation for the ride would belong in the prima facie case of the passenger-plaintiff. If, however, most passengers in the litigated cases ride for compensation, then absence of compensation would be an affirmative defense. In the payment-of-a-bill situation the probabilities are estimated with regard to the litigated situation, payment being regarded generally as an affirmative defense, while in the guest situation they are estimated with regard to such situations generally and not limited to those which are litigated, status as a nonguest being a part of plaintiff's prima facie case. No reason for the shift is apparent, and it may be unconscious. The litigated cases would seem to furnish the more appropriate basis for estimating probabilities.

Matters occurring after the accrual of the plaintiff's right are almost always placed in the category of affirmative defenses. Examples are payment, release, accord and satisfaction, discharge in bankruptcy, and limitations. A plausible explanation is that a condition once established is likely to continue; hence the burden ought to fall on the party benefited by a change.

In the cases of complete absence of proof, a proper application of the probability factor is calculated to produce a minimum of unjust results, and the same is true, though less impressively, even if proof is available.

The Role of Pleading

Determining what elements are relevant to a case and allocating them between the parties does not of necessity have to be done at any particular stage of litigation. These questions can be left suspended in mid-air like Mohammed's coffin until the very end of the case, when it can be decided what are the responsibilities of each party and whether he has discharged them. This is the practice followed in small claims cases. However, decision prior to trial helps to eliminate uncertainties and lends direction and assurance to preparation and presentation. This is one of the useful functions of pleadings. Unhappily, certain characteristics of the legal mind at times enter in to divorce the pleadings from the realities.

* * *

On the whole, however, the pleadings can and do constitute reasonably accurate blueprints of the trial which is to follow, except as their accuracy may be impaired by the workings of presumptions, which will be treated hereinafter. * * *

* * *

Notes

1. *More recent articles.* Professor Cleary's classic article has withstood the test of time. In the almost 50 years since its publication, its analysis has essentially gone unchallenged. More recent articles have put forth similar ideas, particularly with regard to the importance of the probability of an event occurring, although the analysis is presented in the language of law and economics. The premises of these writers is that the allocation of the burdens of proof is based or at least ought to be based in substantial measure on minimizing the costs of litigation—a premise with which Professor Cleary would likely have been very comfortable. See Hay, Allocating the Burden of Proof, 72 Ind.L.J. 651 (1997); Hay & Spier, Burdens of Proof in Civil Litigation: An Economic Perspective, 26 J. Legal Stud. 413 (1997); Lee, Pleading and Proof: The Economics of Legal Burdens, 1997 B.Y.U.L.Rev. 1.

2. *Criminal cases.* The problem of allocating responsibility for proof of the elements of a criminal case between prosecution and defense obviously entails considerations not pertinent in civil litigation. While one or more of the factors noted in the above discussion would clearly tend to support the allocation of certain elements of criminal cases to the defendant, nevertheless it may easily be seen that a wholesale allocation of elements to the defendant would render the time–honored presumption of innocence largely nugatory and radically alter the traditional form of the Anglo–American criminal proceeding. Indeed, as we shall see in the next two chapters, any allocation of a burden to the defendant, especially the burden of persuasion, will present serious constitutional issues.

Chapter 4[1]

BURDEN OF PROOF

The preceding chapter sketched briefly the problem of allocating between the respective parties to litigation the responsibility for proof of the various elements in the case. Ordinarily this allocation will be at least preliminarily made at a relatively early stage of the lawsuit and, at the optimum, will be reflected by the pleadings in the case. The next question, then, and the one to be considered in the present section, is the nature of the responsibility, or "burden of proof," so allocated. Of what does this responsibility or burden consist, and how is it to be successfully fulfilled or discharged?

By way of introduction it should be noted that analysis of these and related problems has been plagued by an essentially semantic difficulty. The commonly used phrase "burden of proof," being singular, might suggest that party responsibility for proof is a single, integral responsibility. Analytically, however, as was first pointed out by the great Professor James Bradley Thayer,[2] party responsibility is not single and integral, but instead consists of two interrelated but quite distinguishable responsibilities.

The first of these distinguishable responsibilities or burdens which a party may initially be allocated (or to which he may fall heir during the course of the trial) is that of producing evidence sufficient to enable a jury, acting reasonably, to find the existence or nonexistence of a particular element. The fulfillment or nonfulfillment of this burden by a party possessing it is generally deemed a question for determination by the court, and nonfulfillment is sanctionable, depending upon local practice, by a directed verdict, involuntary nonsuit, or peremptory instruction.

The second burden obliges the party possessing it, in the ordinary civil case, actually to persuade the trier of fact that the existence or nonexistence of a particular element is more probable than not. In certain other types of cases this second burden will be more onerous,

1. In the cases and materials throughout this chapter, some footnotes have been omitted; others have been renumbered. Notes 1–8 are editor's notes. [Ed.]

2. Thayer, Preliminary Treatise on Evidence 353–89 (1898).

requiring persuasion of the trier of fact that the existence or nonexistence of a given element is much more probable than not, or that it exists or does not exist beyond a reasonable doubt.[3] Whether this second burden has been satisfied by the party possessing it will, as already indicated, be determined by the trier of fact, and imposition of the burden will, in the jury case, be accomplished by an instruction requiring the trier, unless persuaded to the requisite level, to find against the burdened party.

Since the time of Thayer's writing it has become fairly common, in the interest of precision, to denominate the first of the above described burdens as the "burden of going forward," or the "burden of producing evidence," and the second as the "burden of persuasion." Unfortunately terminology has not become standardized, nor has the practice entirely disappeared of referring indiscriminately to either or both of the two burdens as the "burden of proof."[4]

SECTION A. THE BURDEN OF GOING FORWARD

According to one definition previously suggested, the burden of producing evidence is the obligation of a party to produce evidence sufficient to enable a jury, acting reasonably, to find the existence or nonexistence of an element of the case. This same burden has also been defined as the obligation of a party to produce evidence when necessary to avoid a directed verdict against her. Taken together, these definitions suggest that recognition of a burden of producing evidence means simply that juries are not to be allowed to render verdicts on grounds which are without reasonable support in the evidence, and that courts will, through use of various devices, see to it that they do not do so.

The basic problem suggested, then, is to articulate a general test by which it may be determined that a jury, in a given situation, would be acting unreasonably in returning a given verdict. Over the years the courts have devoted their best efforts toward the articulation of such a general standard, but with limited success. It is common ground, of course, that a total absence of evidence upon an essential element of the case is fatal to the party assigned the burden of production as to that element. Again, it is at least commonly agreed today, that a "mere

3. The formulations here adopted for the various burdens of persuasion are substantially those recommended by McBaine, Burden of Proof: Degrees of Belief, 32 Cal. L.Rev. 242 (1944). It should be noted, however, that the device of instructing the trier of fact on the burden of persuasion in terms of probabilities is a relatively recent suggestion, and has been vigorously rejected by a number of courts. See, e.g., Lampe v. Franklin American Trust Co., 339 Mo. 361, 96 S.W.2d 710 (1936). The more traditional formulations are, of course, "by a preponderance of the evidence," "by clear and convincing evidence," and "beyond a reasonable doubt."

4. Thayer himself viewed as Utopian the possibilities of banishing the phrase "burden of proof" from the language, or of standardizing its usage, and contented himself with an exhortation which remains good advice today: "[A]dopt other terms where it is necessary to mark the discrimination between one meaning and the other." Thayer, Preliminary Treatise on Evidence 386–87 (1898).

scintilla" of evidence on an essential element will not suffice to support a verdict for the burdened party. Beyond this point, a plethora of differing formulations, already familiar from readings in other courses, may be found currently in use by appellate courts across the country. Whatever the abstraction used, the rub comes, as is usual in the law, in its concrete application. The materials which follow therefore focus upon the propriety of judicially determined results where the evidence presents one or another of certain commonly recurring patterns.

As a general point of reference throughout this section, consider to what extent the various rules of sufficiency encountered reflect assumptions, explicit or implicit, concerning the relative areas of competence of juries and judges respectively. At the end of the section, you might well ask yourself whether today's juries are given too much or too little to do. There is respectable modern authority for either conclusion you may reach.

Notes

1. *History.* The concept of a burden of going forward, owing its very existence to the power of the court to evaluate the sufficiency of evidence by some legal standard, was of relatively recent origin. As late as 1670 Chief Justice Vaughn, in the celebrated decision of Bushell's case, granted habeas corpus to a juror who had been imprisoned for refusing to follow the direction of the trial court to return a verdict against William Penn. As one ground for his decision, Vaughn indicated that the court should not have directed a verdict since:

> Being return'd of the vicinage, where the cause of action ariseth, the law supposeth them [the jury] thence to have sufficient knowledge to try the matter in issue (and so they must) though no evidence were given on either side in Court, but to this evidence the Judge is a stranger.

Vaughn 135, 124 Eng.Rep. 1006 (C.P.1670).

Thus, before the end of the 17th century, no device equivalent to today's directed verdict was available in the English courts.[5] At that time, however, there were at least two devices available by which certain questions concerning the sufficiency of one's opponent's evidence might be raised. These were the demurrer to the evidence and the motion for a new trial. A demurrer to the evidence was substantially similar to a demurrer to the pleadings and, if joined in by the opponent, resulted in a decision of the case by the court. The demurrer to the evidence, however, possessed serious deficiencies from the standpoint of the demurrant. First, the party to whose evidence the demurrer was interposed might avoid a decision by the court by refusing to join in the demurrer. Moreover, the decision of the court on a demurrer to the evidence resulted in a final judgment. Thus where the demurrer was ill-founded the case was concluded by a ruling to that effect, and the demurrant

5. For fuller accounts of the history here synopsized, see Blume, Origin and Development of the Directed Verdict, 48 Mich. L.Rev. 555 (1950); Galloway v. United States, 319 U.S. 372 (1943).

was precluded from rebutting the evidence of the proponent with evidence of his own.[6]

The motion for a new trial, on the other hand, possessed quite different but no less significant inadequacies from the standpoint of a party wishing to challenge the sufficiency of his opponent's proof. While the motion for a new trial did not of course entail loss of the challenging party's right to introduce evidence, neither did it serve as a device for obtaining a final adjudication by the court. Then, as now, the only relief obtainable on such a motion was the opportunity to try again before a different jury.

The gradual abandonment, following Bushell's case, of the notion that juries might predicate verdicts upon facts known to them but not established by evidence removed one major conceptual objection to final determinations of litigation by the courts on grounds of insufficiency of the evidence. The English courts seem to have begun to "direct verdicts" in scattered cases shortly before the beginning of the 18th century, and the device appeared in the United States at least as early as 1850.[7] As developed in both England and the United States, the directed verdict allowed challenge of the legal sufficiency of an opponent's evidence without waiver of the right to rebut, and usually permitted such a challenge to be interposed even after rebutting evidence had been introduced.[8] As the preceding materials have suggested, however, no unanimity has been achieved either as to the proper standard for evaluating sufficiency, or as to whether rebutting evidence should or should not be considered in the evaluation. The classic article on the directed verdict in the federal courts is Cooper, Directions for Directed Verdicts: A Compass for Federal Courts, 55 Minn.L.Rev. 903 (1971).

2. *Judgments notwithstanding the verdict.* As its name would suggest, the directed verdict in its original form consisted of an instruction by the court to the jury to return a verdict in favor of one of the parties. Thus, while the directed verdict in substance represented a determination by the court, it was in form a determination by the jury, and of necessity had to be moved for and granted, if at all, prior to the jury's return of its verdict.

The judge may, even after the jury's return of a verdict, set aside that verdict and enter judgment for the opposing party. A judgment of this kind is called, variously, a judgment notwithstanding the verdict, a judgment *non obstante veredicto,* or a judgment n.o.v. Where the judgment n.o.v. or its equivalent is recognized, the standard employed for passing upon motions for judgment of this sort is generally the same as that applied in ruling on motions for directed verdicts. In fact, in the federal courts since 1991, the two motions share the same name, a motion for judgment as matter of law. See 9 Moore's Federal Practice ¶ 50.03(3d ed. 2001); 9A Wright & Miller, Federal Practice and Procedure § 2521 (1995). If the identical issue is raised,

6. Conversely, the introduction of evidence waived the right to demur.

7. Parks v. Ross, 52 U.S. (11 How.) 362 (1850).

8. The constitutionality of the device, as embodied in Fed.R.Civ.P. 50, was challenged, and upheld, in Galloway v. United States, supra note 5. The essence of the petitioner's argument in *Galloway* was that the device, not having existed at the time of the ratification of the 7th Amendment, offended against that amendment's guarantee of trial by jury.

what justification exists for permitting the court to delay its ruling until after return of the jury verdict? See James, Hazard & Leubsdorf, Civil Procedure § 7.30 (5th ed. 2001).

(1) DIRECT EVIDENCE

CALIFORNIA EVIDENCE CODE

§ 410. Direct Evidence

As used in this chapter, "direct evidence" means evidence that directly proves a fact, without an inference or presumption, and which in itself, if true, conclusively establishes that fact.

§ 411. Evidence of One Witness Sufficient to Prove Fact

Except where additional evidence is required by statute, the direct evidence of one witness who is entitled to full credit is sufficient for proof of any fact.

Note

As in California under § 411, throughout the United States, direct evidence by a single witness affirming the existence of an elemental fact in the case will generally be sufficient to satisfy the burden of going forward. A corroboration requirement exists in a few instances, generally in criminal cases. Most notably, corroboration is required in treason and perjury cases. James, Hazard & Leubsdorf, Civil Procedure § 7.19, at 437 (5th ed. 2001). In addition to these kinds of cases, it is frequently required that certain types of evidence in a criminal prosecution be corroborated in order to support a conviction. Among the most noteworthy rules of this type are those requiring corroboration of: the extrajudicial confession or admission of a criminal defendant, Annot., 45 A.L.R.2d 1316; the testimony of an accomplice to the crime with which the defendant is charged, 7 Wigmore, Evidence §§ 2056–2060 (Chadbourn rev. 1978); the testimony of the complaining witness in a prosecution for rape, Annot., 31 A.L.R.4th 120 (now abandoned in most jurisdictions).

Of the few analogous requirements enjoying widespread currency in civil cases, perhaps the most common are the requirements of corroboration of the testimony of the petitioner in a divorce or separate maintenance proceeding. See Annots., 15 A.L.R.2d 170, 100 A.L.R.2d 612. The requirement of corroboration will also occasionally be resounded in certain highly specialized contexts. Price v. Symsek, 988 F.2d 1187 (Fed.Cir.1993) (in patent law, uncorroborated testimony of inventor insufficient to prove conception), and finally, some of the so-called "Dead Man's Acts" necessitate corroboration by prohibiting judgment against the personal representative of a deceased person on the uncorroborated testimony of his adversary. Annot., 21 A.L.R.2d 1013.

SCOTT v. HANSEN

Supreme Court of Iowa, 1940.
289 N.W. 710.

[Plaintiff brought suit to recover for personal injuries sustained when defendant's automobile, in which plaintiff was riding as a guest, collided with a cow that was crossing the highway. Defendant's auto was proceeding west at the time of the collision. Plaintiff alleged defendant's operation of the car at the time of the collision was reckless, and that such reckless operation was the proximate cause of plaintiff's injuries. The jury returned a verdict for the plaintiff, and defendant appeals.]

RICHARDS, JUSTICE.

* * *

At the conclusion of the evidence defendant moved for a directed verdict. One of the grounds was that in the record there was no competent evidence to show that defendant was guilty of recklessness in the operation of the car which was the proximate cause of the collision and injuries to plaintiff. Defendant claims that upon this ground the motion should have been sustained and that consequently the court erred in ordering that it be overruled. Plaintiff specified that there was reckless operation in that defendant failed to reduce the speed of the car as he approached the cattle and continued to drive into the cattle at an excessive and reckless rate of speed. Whether there was competent evidence showing that there was such failure and such continued manner of driving into the cattle as plaintiff specified, and if so whether in view of the attendant facts and surrounding circumstances a jury would have been warranted in finding that when the accident happened defendant was driving at a rate of speed that evidenced recklessness of operation of the car, appear to be the questions raised by the above stated ground. In seeking the answers it seems needful that we review the evidence.

* * * [The court here summarized the evidence introduced by the plaintiff relating to the situs of the accident and to the respective conditions of car and cow following the collision.] Plaintiff also adduced from his witnesses the fact that there were black tire marks four or five inches in width having the appearance of brake marks or skid marks that extended east from the point of the collision. One of these witnesses testified that measurements of these marks were taken by him and others, and that the marks extended for a distance of 354 feet east from the point where the cow was struck. All these matters plaintiff fully developed in either his own testimony or upon his quite extended direct examination of the witnesses he produced.

At this point the query obtrudes itself whether, in deciding upon the ruling on the motion, we should eliminate from any consideration on our part, as plaintiff says we should, certain unfavorable portions of the showing plaintiff himself made as a part of his case as set out in the foregoing paragraph. It seems to be plaintiff's thought that in viewing the evidence in a light that is favorable to him it becomes our duty to consign to oblivion the physical facts and some other matters that plaintiff not only conceded but affirmatively and intentionally established, and concerning which there is no contradiction by any witness. Then, according to plaintiff, we should determine the right of the controversy upon certain other testimony in the record the salient features of which are the following. One of plaintiff's witnesses testified he saw the car hit the cow. Then, says this witness, "The cow just spun around and around and around and went up the pavement as it threw her a ways. She flew pretty near up thirty feet without touching the pavement at all; and then she hit the pavement and bounced better than five feet; then she hit the pavement again and bounced again to where she laid." It was like a rubber ball, the witness explained to the jury. The bounce of five feet or more was a bounce of ten or more feet the witness related later in his testimony. He reiterated that preceding this bounce he had seen the cow "fly through the air thirty feet." His testimony was also to the effect that the cow's flying weight when she took off was 1200 pounds. What car velocity and weight would have been required to develop the foot-pounds this witness allegedly saw expended would be a worthwhile if possible calculation. Plaintiff's own testimony was that he was almost sure that defendant at no time applied the brakes and that in his opinion the speed was about seventy or seventy-five miles per hour when the car struck the cow. At another place in his testimony he says it was eighty miles per hour. One of the tenants, as plaintiff's witness, stated "as near as I can say the car was coming down the hill seventy-five to eighty miles per hour and did not slow up so far as I could see." This was the witness to whom it appeared that the cow performed so amazingly like a rubber ball. The other tenant testified that there was an awful roar and that "it never slowed down until they struck the cattle." This was the witness who also testified concerning the measurement of the black tire marks that extended 354 feet. The rate of speed as estimated by plaintiff and his two witnesses together with the manner in which, allegedly, the cow was catapulted, was sufficient and effective, in plaintiff's opinion, to generate jury questions respecting the specifications that (1) defendant failed to reduce his speed and (2) drove into the cattle at seventy to eighty miles per hour. But defendant urges, and it appears to us, that this testimony of plaintiff and his witnesses is so wholly inconsistent with the undisputed and established physical facts, related in the preceding paragraph, that the inevitable conclusion is that plaintiff and his witnesses were mistaken. In connection with what defendant urges, plaintiff was undoubtedly entitled to have his evidence viewed in a light as favorable to his contention as is reasonably possible. But one should not be unmindful of the element of reasonableness that inheres in this rule, or of the fact that the scintilla of evidence doctrine does not obtain in this jurisdiction. The estimates of the rate of speed at the time of the collision as stated by plaintiff and his witnesses, together with the testimony concerning the exhibition of levitation credited to the cow by one witness, were in such conflict with incontestable [sic] facts that plaintiff established as verities, including plaintiff's showing that the brakes were being applied for 354 feet, that we are of the opinion that such testimony of said witnesses was so lacking in probative force or effect that a jury finding that the car's speed as it approached the cattle was not reduced, would be unwarranted. * * *

[The court then considered and rejected, plaintiff's contention that the evidence was sufficient to show that defendant drove into the cattle at an excessive rate of speed.]

* * * The court erred in not sustaining the motion for a directed verdict upon the ground that has been discussed. The judgment is reversed.

Reversed.

STIGER, MILLER, SAGER, and HALE, JJ., concur.

HAMILTON, C.J., dissents.

Notes and Questions

1. *Evidence contradicted by physical facts.* In connection with the principal case, consider the following statement:

> It is generally agreed by all courts that the jury will not be permitted to believe testimony that is contradicted by physical facts. Were a witness to testify that the sun rose at midnight in Chicago, no one would argue that the jury might believe him. This is the sort of "physical fact" that is within the realm of judicial notice. The difficult questions arise when the physical facts must be established in some other way.

Dow, Judicial Determination of Credibility, 38 Neb.L.Rev. 835, 854–55 (1959).

In *Scott v. Hansen* were the items of testimony relied upon by the plaintiff to establish unabated speed by the defendant contradicted by physical facts of which the court took judicial notice, or by facts established in some other way? To what extent might it be said that facts of both varieties figured in the court's determination? If "facts" of the latter sort were involved, on what basis were these facts deemed to be established?

2. *Evidence contrary to law of nature.* Cases involving evidence judicially determined to be incredible as contrary to some scientific principle or law of nature are collected in Annot., 21 A.L.R. 141. The doctrine of judicial notice, which is more frequently seen operating to assist rather than to baffle the discharge of the burden of going forward, is treated more fully in Chapter 9, infra.

(2) CIRCUMSTANTIAL EVIDENCE

UNITED STATES v. NELSON

United States Court of Appeals, Ninth Circuit, 1969.
419 F.2d 1237.

BROWNING, CIRCUIT JUDGE: Roy Arthur Nelson and Frank Brewton were indicted for robbery of a federally-insured institution in violation of 18 U.S.C.A. § 2113(a) (1964). Brewton was found incompetent to stand trial. Nelson was tried separately and convicted. He has appealed on three grounds, all of which relate to the use of circumstantial evidence to secure his conviction.

The government offered direct evidence of the following facts. Brewton entered a bank and presented a teller with a written demand for money. The teller handed Brewton $627 in currency, including five marked $20 bills. Meanwhile, an unidentified person was observed sitting in a car in an adjacent parking lot, racing the engine. Brewton fled from the bank to the waiting car and entered on the passenger side. The car immediately sped away. Shortly thereafter, a police officer, alerted to these incidents, observed the car, with two male occupants, at an intersection some blocks away. The car fled. The officer pursued at high speed. After a chase the car slowed down, defendant alighted from the driver's side and ran, and was captured. Currency in the amount of $125 was taken from his person. The car, driverless, crashed into a tree. Brewton emerged from the wreck, and was arrested after attempting to conceal $502 in currency, including the marked bills taken from the bank, under an adjacent building. Ten to fifteen minutes elapsed between the robbery of the bank and defendant's flight from the car.

Defendant asserts that since he was charged as a principal in the bank robbery rather than as an accessory after the fact, the government was required to prove that he had actual knowledge that Brewton intended to rob the bank. We assume, arguendo, that proof of precisely that specific knowledge was required.

Defendant contended below, and in this court, that such proof was lacking. He argued that if such knowledge could be inferred at all, the inference must be based upon the prior inference that he was the man waiting in the car while the robbery occurred—and such an "inference upon an inference" was precluded by law. Further, he argued that even if the jury were permitted to infer that he knowingly acted as the "get-away" driver, there was no evidence that he knew Brewton planned to commit a robbery, as distinguished from some other illegal act, or planned to rob the bank, and not one of the several stores and offices in the area, and that circumstantial evidence which does not "exclude every hypothesis but that of guilt" is insufficient as a matter of law.

The court denied a motion for acquittal based on these grounds, and rejected proposed instructions embodying the theories that a conviction could not be based upon inferences drawn from other inferences, or upon circumstances "which while consistent with guilt, are not inconsistent with innocence."

The legal theories upon which defendant relies, although clearly wrong, are repeatedly asserted in the trial courts of this circuit and in fruitless appeals to this court. It would be a boon to both the parties and the courts if they could be laid finally to rest.

I

For at least a third of a century this court has rejected the notion that it is improper to infer a fact at issue from other facts which have been established by circumstantial evidence. E.K. Wood Lumber Co. v. Andersen, 81 F.2d 161, 166 (9th Cir.1936).[9] * * * As Professor Wigmore has said, "[t]here is no such orthodox rule; nor can be. If there were, hardly a single trial could be adequately presented." 1 Wigmore, Evidence, § 41, at 435 (3rd ed. 19 40).

The error in this discredited doctrine is clearly reflected in the defendant's formulation:[10] it assumes that a fact established by circumstantial evidence is not a "proven fact." But as we have repeatedly said, circumstantial evidence is not inherently less probative than direct evidence. Under some conditions it may even be more reliable, as this case illustrates.

The intermediate fact at issue here was whether defendant was the driver of the car waiting in the parking lot. That fact was established to a moral certainty by circumstances proven by uncontradicted and unquestioned testimony. Unless defendant was Brewton's accomplice waiting in the get-away car, it is all but inconceivable that he would have been driving that car with Brewton as a passenger a few minutes after Brewton ran from the bank to the car and was driven from the scene; that he would have had part of the stolen currency in his possession, and Brewton the rest; and that upon seeing the police officer he would have driven away at high speed, and later fled from the office[r] on foot.

If none of this circumstantial evidence had been available and the only evidence offered had been a courtroom identification of the defendant by a witness who had a fleeting glimpse of the driver as the car stood in the parking lot, the truth of the fact that defendant was that man would not have been established with equal certainty.[11]

Of course either direct or circumstantial evidence may fail to prove the fact in issue—direct evidence because the credibility of the witness is destroyed; circumstantial evidence for that reason, or because the infer-

9. A significant number of footnotes, primarily those containing citations to cases, have been omitted from this opinion. [Ed.]

10. The following instruction was requested and refused:

"Permissible inferences from the evidence must be based upon proven facts and one inference may not be based upon another inference to support a conclusion of fact."

11. As the Supreme Court pointed out in United States v. Wade, 388 U.S. 218 * * * (1967), "the annals of criminal law are rife with instances of mistaken [eyewitness] identifications." 388 U.S. at 228 * * * . * * *

ence from the proven circumstances to the fact in issue is too speculative, or remote. Whether such a failure has occurred is an appropriate inquiry in any case—be the evidence direct, circumstantial, or both. But since under some conditions circumstantial evidence may be equally or more reliable than direct evidence, it would be wholly irrational to impose an absolute bar upon the use of circumstantial evidence to prove any fact, including a fact from which another fact is to be inferred.

The trial court therefore properly refused to instruct the jury that "one inference may not be based upon another inference to support a conclusion of fact." It would be error for the jury, the trial court, or this court, to apply such an arbitrary formula in the performance of their respective roles in the fact-finding process.

II

It is also clear that the court properly rejected defendant's proposed instruction embodying a variation on the theme that circumstantial evidence must exclude every hypothesis but that of guilt.[12]

This much, at least, is settled by Holland v. United States, 348 U.S. 121 * * * (1955). * * *

* * *

III

One question remains: Did the district court properly overrule the motion for acquittal?

Defendant contends that whether or not he was entitled to the proposed jury instruction, this court, in reviewing the sufficiency of the evidence, must ask "whether reasonable minds could find that the evidence excludes every hypothesis but that of guilt."

The test to be applied by the trial court in deciding a motion for acquittal in a criminal case, and the test to be applied by this court in reviewing that decision, are, as a practical matter, identical. 8 J. Moore, Federal Practice ¶ 29.06, at 29–19 (1968). It is also undisputed that the evidence must be taken in the light most favorable to the verdict—that it is the exclusive function of the jury to determine the credibility of witnesses, resolve evidentiary conflicts, and draw reasonable inferences from proven facts. Therefore the reviewing court must assume that the jury resolved all such matters in a manner which would support the verdict. 4 Barron, Federal Practice and Procedure, § 2221, at 235 (1951). Beyond this, however, the substance of the standard to be applied is subject to much confusion and dispute.

12. Defendant proposed the following instruction:

"You may not base a finding of the existence of any fact in issue upon the basis of circumstantial evidence, if the circumstances relied upon are consistent with another conclusion, even if they are consistent with a conclusion of the truth of the fact in issue.

"Proof of circumstances which while consistent with guilt, are not inconsistent with innocence, will not support a conviction."

The opinions of our court dealing with this issue combine various threads of doctrine in such a wide variety of ways that no simple analysis can accurately reflect their content. Nonetheless, it is convenient to deal with the issues as involving two different, though overlapping, questions.

The first is whether the test of the sufficiency of the evidence in a criminal case is the same as that applied in civil cases—namely, whether there is substantial evidence to support a judgment adverse to the moving party—or whether a different test is to be applied in criminal cases reflecting the burden of establishing guilt beyond a reasonable doubt.

Some courts, led by the Court of Appeals for the Second Circuit, apply the substantial evidence test in criminal as well as civil cases. There is language in Supreme Court opinions, and in opinions of this court, supporting this approach.

However, other courts—indeed, most courts—"have included the standard of persuasion as part of their criterion of sufficiency." A. Goldstein, The State and the Accused: Balance of Advantage in Criminal Procedure, 69 Yale L.J. 1149, 1157 (1960). Thus, in American Tobacco Co. v. United States, 328 U.S. 781, 787 n.4 * * * (1946), the Supreme Court stated: "The verdict in a criminal case is sustained only when there is relevant evidence from which the jury could properly find or infer, *beyond a reasonable doubt,* that the accused is guilty. Mortensen v. United States, 322 U.S. 369 * * * ." (Emphasis added.) Similar expressions appear in an overwhelming majority of our opinions reviewing the sufficiency of the evidence in criminal cases.

The function which the court performs in passing upon a motion for acquittal suggests that this latter view is correct. That function is to determine whether the jury in arriving at the verdict has acted within the bounds of its authority. Since it is the jury's duty to acquit unless guilt is established beyond a reasonable doubt, the reviewing court may properly inquire whether the evidence, considered most favorably to the government, was such as to permit a rational conclusion by the jury that the accused was guilty beyond a reasonable doubt.

The second question is that specifically raised by the defendant, namely, whether the court is also to inquire whether the evidence "excludes every hypothesis but that of guilt."

Precisely as put, the test is unquestionably wrong. Although we have frequently stated the rule as defendant does, it has never been held that the evidence must exclude "*every* hypothesis," as distinguished from every reasonable hypothesis, of innocence. Furthermore, in applying the test, the question is not whether the court itself would find that every reasonable hypothesis of innocence had been excluded, but rather whether the jurors could reasonably arrive at the conclusion.

Thus, as first stated in this court in Stoppelli v. United States, 183 F.2d 391, 393 (9th Cir.1950), the test was as follows:

"The testimony * * * was sufficient to go to the jury if its nature was such that reasonable minds could differ as to whether inferences other than guilt could be drawn from it. It is not for us to say that the evidence was insufficient because we, or any of us, believe that inferences inconsistent with guilt may be drawn from it. To say that would make us triers of the fact. We may say that the evidence is insufficient to sustain the verdict only if we can conclude *as a matter of law* that reasonable minds, as triers of the fact, must be in agreement that reasonable hypotheses other than guilt could be drawn from the evidence."

This formulation, commonly condensed to "whether 'reasonable minds could find the evidence excludes every hypothesis but that of guilt,' " appears frequently in our opinions.

Yet this is precisely the standard which was rejected by the Supreme Court in Holland v. United States, supra, 348 U.S. at 139 * * * , as a guide for the jury, on the ground that it was "confusing and incorrect." Id. at 140 * * *. Our opinions demonstrate that it is equally confusing as a guide for the reviewing court. Moreover, if it is "incorrect" as an instruction defining the jury's duty, it must be equally "incorrect" as a test for determining whether the jury has performed its duty within the limits fixed by the instructions. Accordingly, most courts have held that its use as a test of the sufficiency of the evidence on review is inconsistent with *Holland*.

The "reasonable hypothesis" test was formulated for the evaluation of circumstantial evidence; it is often referred to as the "circumstantial evidence test." See, e.g., Comment, *Sufficiency of Circumstantial Evidence in a Criminal Case,* 55 Colum.L.Rev. 549 (1955). * * * [T]he Supreme Court rejected the test in *Holland* on the premise that there is no essential difference in the mental processes required of the jury in weighing direct and circumstantial evidence. As to both, "the jury must use its experience with people and events in weighing the probabilities. If the jury is convinced beyond a reasonable doubt, we can require no more." Holland, 348 U.S. at 140 * * * .

The key word is "probabilities." The jury cannot determine that a proposition is true or false but only that it is more or less probable. Guilt "is proved beyond a reasonable doubt if it proved not only to be more probable than its contradictory but much more probable than its contradictory." Adler & Michael, *The Trial of an Issue of Fact I,* 34 Colum.L.Rev. 1224, 1256 (1934). The required degree of probability is reached if the jury is free of "the kind of doubt that would make a person hesitate to act" in the more serious and important affairs of his own life. Holland v. United States, supra, 348 U.S. at 140 * * * .

It adds only an illusion of certainty, and is both misleading and wrong, to attempt to describe this broad exercise of practical judgment in abstract generalizations borrowed from the terminology of formal logic.

The "reasonable hypothesis" test does not reflect what juries and reviewing courts in reality do. Juries constantly convict, and the convictions are duly affirmed, on evidence upon which none would hesitate to act but which cannot be said to exclude as a matter of inexorable logic, every reasonable hypothetical consistent with innocence.

Moreover, the impression left by appellate court opinions is that the "reasonable hypothesis" standard may lead to serious departures from the proper appellate role in evaluating the sufficiency of evidence. Courts following the rule exhibit a noticeable tendency to divide the evidence into separate lines of proof, and analyze and test each line of proof independently of others rather than considering the evidence as an interrelated whole. The sufficiency of the evidence is often tested against theoretical and speculative possibilities not fairly raised by the record, and inferences are sometimes considered which, though entirely possible or even probable, are drawn from evidence which the jury may have disbelieved.

We affirm the denial of the motion for acquittal in this case because we are satisfied that the jurors reasonably could decide that they would not hesitate to act in their own serious affairs upon factual assumptions as probable as the conclusion that defendant planned and executed the robbery of the bank as a joint venture with Brewton in which each carried out a prearranged role.

Affirmed.

Notes and Questions

1. *Only reasonable hypothesis test.* The "only reasonable hypothesis" test for determining the sufficiency of circumstantial evidence relied on by the state in a criminal case still commands a following. See, e.g., State v. Nichols, 725 S.W.2d 927 (Mo.Ct.App.1987). A number of jurisdictions, however, while continuing to use the "only reasonable hypothesis" language, have reconstrued the standard as something other than a test for legal sufficiency.

> Whether or not in a given case circumstances are sufficient to exclude every reasonable hypothesis save the guilt of the accused, is primarily a question for determination by the jury. This of necessity is so, for we have no legal yardstick by which we can ordinarily determine what in a given case is a reasonable hypothesis, save the opinion of twelve upright and intelligent jurors.

Townsend v. State, 195 S.E.2d 474, 476 (Ga.Ct.App.1972). How does the view of the Georgia court compare with that expressed in the principal case?

For an argument for a reinvigorated "only reasonable hypothesis" test as a standard of sufficiency, see Gregory, Whose Reasonable Doubt? Reconsidering the Appropriate Role of the Reviewing Court in the Criminal Decision Making Process, 24 Am.Crim.L.Rev. 911 (1987).

2. *Standard for sufficiency in criminal cases.* Note the statement of the *Nelson* court, that "the reviewing court may properly inquire whether the evidence, considered most favorably to the government, was such as to permit a rational conclusion by the jury that the accused was guilty beyond a

reasonable doubt." In Jackson v. Virginia, 443 U.S. 307 (1979), the Supreme Court held that the articulated standard is not only proper but is the standard constitutionally required to be applied in reviewing the sufficiency of evidence to support state convictions in federal habeas corpus proceedings. The *Jackson* case effectively ended the debate that had raged for decades concerning the desirability and feasibility of differentiating between the standards of sufficiency in criminal as opposed to civil cases. See the classic article, McNaughten, Burden of Production of Evidence: A Function of a Burden of Persuasion, 68 Harv.L.Rev. 1382 (1955) (arguing for differing standards). However, the precise formulation and application of the higher standard remains problematic. See, for example, Newman, Beyond "Reasonable Doubt," 68 N.Y.U.L.Rev. 979 (1993).

3. *Inference on an inference.* Though the court in the principal case concurs with Dean Wigmore that there is not, and could not be, a rule prohibiting the predication of an inference upon a previous inference, the conception that there is such a rule has proved extremely difficult to eradicate. Decisions variously adopting, rejecting, and discussing the "non-rule" are compendiously collected in Annot., 5 A.L.R.3d 100. Kindred problems are raised by the attempted predication of a presumption on a presumption or a presumption on an inference.

What significance, if any, should be attached to the *Nelson* court's statement that any inference other than that defendant was the driver waiting in the parking lot would be "all but inconceivable?" In Voelker v. Combined Ins. Co., 73 So.2d 403 (Fla.1954), it was held that inferences may be predicated upon prior inferences if every inference other than the last is "inescapable" as the only reasonable theory. Compare Vaccarezza v. Sanguinetti, 163 P.2d 470, 477 (Cal.Ct.App.1945): "In a civil case, if the first inference is a reasonably probable one it may be used as a basis for a succeeding inference."

Consider the bearing of the following mathematical hypothetical on the problem. Suppose that in seven-tenths of the cases in which fact A exists fact B will exist, and further that in seven-tenths of the cases in which fact B exists fact C will exist. Should proof of fact A alone be sufficient to support a finding of the existence of fact C?

For an interesting fictional inquiry into the question of whether a succession of inferences, each reasonable when viewed in isolation, may lead to a false conclusion, see Harry Kemmelman's short detective story, The Nine Mile Walk, reprinted in Barzun, Delights of Detection (1961).

SMITH v. BELL TEL. CO. OF PENNSYLVANIA

Supreme Court of Pennsylvania, 1959.
153 A.2d 477.

McBride, Justice. This case is here on plaintiff's appeal from the refusal of the court below to take off a compulsory non-suit.

In 1948 defendant, Counties Contracting and Construction Company, under contract to defendant, Bell Telephone Company of Pennsylvania, constructed an underground conduit to carry telephone lines along

Baltimore Avenue in Lansdowne, Pennsylvania. In 1950, after an inspection which revealed no structural or other defects, plaintiff purchased a house on Baltimore Avenue. Sometime prior to March 25, 1951, he discovered seepage in his basement, which proved to be sewage backed up from the sewer lateral running from his home to the street. He made efforts several times that summer with varying degrees of success, to find the cause and cure the trouble. These efforts continued from time to time until September 1956, when, in desperation, plaintiff and a friend tunnelled under the sidewalk, found that the telephone conduit had crushed the sewer lateral and was blocking it. Plaintiff brought suit September 19, 1957 and, after presenting evidence, met with a compulsory non-suit which the court later refused to take off. The refusal was based on two grounds:

(1) That plaintiff had not made out a prima facie case,

* * *

In support of the judgment of non-suit the court below applied the standard that where plaintiff's case is based on circumstantial evidence and inferences to be drawn therefrom, such evidence must be so conclusive as to exclude any other reasonable inference inconsistent therewith, and that plaintiff did not produce such evidence. Indeed, he did not, but did he have to?

A variety of formulae for determining the sufficiency of circumstantial evidence to sustain a verdict may be found, including: "such as to satisfy reasonable and well balanced minds". Connor v. Hawk, 1957, 387 Pa. 480, 483, 128 A.2d 566; Rowles v. Evanuik, 1944, 350 Pa. 64, 68, 38 A.2d 255; Ferry v. Philadelphia Rapid Transit Co., 1911, 232 Pa. 403, 406, 81 A. 426. "[The facts and inferences] must so preponderate in favor of the basic proposition he is seeking to establish as to exclude any equally well-supported belief in any inconsistent proposition", Wagner v. Somerset County Memorial Park, 1953, 372 Pa. 338, 342, 93 A.2d 440, 442; Polk v. Steel Workers Organizing Committee, 1949, 360 Pa. 631, 634, 62 A.2d 850. Although some of the formulations appear to be mutually inconsistent, they have sometimes been used together. See Stauffer v. Railway Express Agency, 1946, 355 Pa. 24, 47 A.2d 817. The formula that "the circumstances must be so strong as to preclude the possibility of injury in any other way and provide as the only reasonable inference the conclusion plaintiff advances" is not a correct statement of the rule to be applied by the judge on deciding a motion for either a non-suit or binding instructions. If that were the rule what would be the province of the jury? In no case where there was more than one reasonable inference would the jury be permitted to decide. Insofar as this rule is stated in our cases it is disapproved.

We have said many times that the jury may not be permitted to reach its verdict merely on the basis of speculation or conjecture, but that there must be evidence upon which logically its conclusion may be based. Schofield v. King, 1957, 388 Pa. 132, 136, 130 A.2d 93; Connor v. Hawk, 1957, 387 Pa. 480, 482, 128 A.2d 566; Ebersole v. Beistline, 1951,

368 Pa. 12, 16, 82 A.2d 11. Clearly this does not mean that the jury may not draw inferences based upon all the evidence and the jurors' own knowledge and experiences, for that is, of course, the very heart of the jury's function. It means only that the evidence presented must be such that by reasoning from it, without resort to prejudice or guess, a jury can reach the conclusion sought by plaintiff, and not that conclusion must be the *only* one which logically can be reached.

It is not necessary, under Pennsylvania law, that every fact or circumstance point unerringly to liability; it is enough that there be sufficient facts for the jury to say reasonably that the preponderance favors liability. The judge cannot say as a matter of law which are facts and which are not unless they are admitted or the evidence is inherently incredible. Also, it is beyond the power of the court to say whether two or more reasonable inferences are "equal". True enough the trial judge has to do something like this in deciding a motion for new trial based on the weight of the evidence but no such rule governs him in deciding whether a case is submissible to the jury. The facts are for the jury in any case whether based upon direct or circumstantial evidence where a reasonable conclusion can be arrived at which would place liability on the defendant. It is the duty of plaintiff to produce substantial evidence which, if believed, warrants the verdict he seeks. The right of a litigant to have the jury pass upon the facts is not to be foreclosed just because the judge believes that a reasonable man might properly find either way. A substantial part of the right to trial by jury is taken away when judges withdraw close cases from the jury. Therefore, when a party who has the burden of proof relies upon circumstantial evidence and inferences reasonably deducible therefrom, such evidence, in order to prevail, must be adequate to establish the conclusion sought and must so preponderate in favor of that conclusion as to outweigh in the mind of the fact-finder any other evidence and reasonable inferences therefrom which are inconsistent therewith. This rule has been applied in substance in many cases. See Miller v. Hickey, 368 Pa. 317, 81 A.2d 910, Rockey v. Ernest, 367 Pa. 538, 541, 80 A.2d 783; Turek v. Pennsylvania R. Co., 361 Pa. 512, 64 A.2d 779; Randolph v. Campbell, 360 Pa. 453, 62 A.2d 60.

To the court below it seems that all plaintiff had proved was "the happening of an accident", and that the best that could be said for plaintiff's case was that "the collapse of the conduit may have been the consequence of defendant's negligence." It would seem however, that plaintiff has proved more than that; enough more, in fact, that he should have been permitted to have the jury pass upon the problem. We are not here faced with a case relying on circumstantial evidence to show both the happening of the accident and the defendants' negligence. It is clear that the injury was caused by the conduit crushing the sewer lateral. The question is, did defendants' negligence cause the conduit so to behave?

* * *

Plaintiff has fairly shown that defendants buried a heavy conduit over his sewer lateral, and that after about three years the conduit crushed the lateral. It is hard to see how a plaintiff in these circumstances could prove more.

A likely inference under the conditions described is that the soil was normal and the crushing of the pipe was due to defendants' negligence in not supporting a conduit which passed over plaintiff's lateral with less than six inches clearance. It is also possible, as defendants suggest, though perhaps not as likely, that the clearance was adequate for normal conditions or that piers were installed and that the mischief resulted from abnormal soil conditions, or from subterranean waters. The difficulty with that hypothesis for defendants is that it too presents a strong probability of negligence since it seems unlikely that soil conditions could have changed very much in what was apparently an established community in the short space of three years or less. If the condition of the soil at the time of installation of the conduit was subnormal, defendants were bound to support their conduit accordingly, and not to proceed on the basis of ideal or average soil conditions. To suggest that the collapse which broke the sewer lateral occurred through the undermining action of sewage flowing from the break would be patently absurd.

Under the conditions described, it is entirely reasonable for the jury to find that the accident resulted from the negligence of the defendants. Of course, if the jury is not convinced of that fact by the preponderance of the evidence, they may not conclude that negligence was the cause. But that decision is for the jury, and neither the trial judge nor this Court may assume it. * * *

* * *

Judgment reversed and a new trial ordered.

BELL, JUSTICE (concurring).

I cannot agree with some parts of the Court's opinion, hence this concurring opinion. We agree that mere conjecture or guess do not amount to proof, and a jury's verdict cannot be supported if it is based upon conjecture, guess or sympathy. Whenever a party has the burden of proving certain facts, his evidence tending to prove such facts cannot prevail if, in the opinion of either the Court or of the jury, it is so uncertain, or inadequate, or equivocal, or ambiguous, or contradictory as to make findings or legitimate inferences therefrom a mere conjecture. * * *

Since the Court has decided to change, in cases of circumstantial evidence, "the only reasonable inference rule" which had been reiterated in at least 18 cases in the last few years, we should attempt to make certain that the new test is accurately expressed. In my judgment that has not been done in the majority opinion. The adequacy of the evidence is first of all a matter for the Court and if it passes that test it is then a matter for the jury. In my judgment it would be more accurate if the new rule read as follows:

When a party who has the burden of proof relies—not upon direct evidence, but—upon circumstantial evidence, such evidence, together with all inferences reasonably deducible therefrom, must, in order to prevail, be adequate to establish the conclusion sought and must so *preponderate* in favor of that conclusion as to outweigh any other *reasonable* or possible inference or deduction inconsistent therewith. * * *

Whether the evidence, if believed, is legally sufficient to satisfy this test is in the first instance for the Court's determination; if the Court is of the opinion that the evidence, if believed, is sufficient, then the Court must submit to the jury the determination of what evidence to believe, and whether in its mind the person who relies on the circumstantial evidence has met and satisfied his burden of proof.

* * *

Notes and Questions

1. *Judge or jury?* Note the way in which Justice Bell, concurring, would prefer to have the new rule of sufficiency in civil cases formulated. Is this preference merely a matter of semantics, or does it reflect a view of the respective roles of court and jury in the fact-finding process which differs substantially from that taken by the majority? Formulations such as Justice Bell's have been strongly criticized as suggesting an improper focus for judicial evaluation of questions of sufficiency. See, e.g., Tennant v. Peoria & P. U. Ry. Co., 321 U.S. 29 (1944); McCarty v. National Life & Acc. Ins. Co., 129 S.E.2d 408 (Ga.Ct.App.1962). In considering the legitimacy of this criticism, consider the following statement by one state supreme court in the process of applying a test like that suggested by Justice Bell:

> We cannot support our belief by mathematical proof that the probabilities favor the plaintiff's contention. * * * We have only our own experiences, observations and understanding of what commonly happens from which to judge whether the inferences drawn from the circumstances connect up defendant's conduct to the injury more strongly than the conduct of some other person.

Eitel v. Times, Inc., 352 P.2d 485, 490 (Or.1960).

Whose decision-making qualifications rather than its own might the court appear to be describing? Is the rule of sufficiency enunciated by the majority in *Smith* to be preferred on the ground that it will exert a retarding influence upon the phenomenon observed by Lord Bramwell, that "one-third of a judge is a common-law juror if you get beneath his ermine"?[13]

Judicial recognition that evidence might reasonably convince a jury though it does not convince the court is clearly essential to the preservation of a substantial role for the jury in the fact-finding process. Does the

13. Quoted in J. Frank, Courts on Trial 180 (1949).

distinction between potentially convincing evidence and evidence actually convincing to the judge have any utility where the court sits without a jury? Stated another way, may the court sitting as trier of fact direct a verdict against a party who has made out a prima facie case? Should it? Cases are collected in Annot., 55 A.L.R.3d 272.

2. *Expert testimony.* Suppose that the evidence relied upon to establish a material proposition is not only circumstantial but of a sort which may only be interpreted by an "expert witness," a person viewed as having special competency by virtue of special training or experience. Will the expert testimony, if relied upon by the party with the burden of going forward on the proposition, need to assume any particular form if a directed verdict is to be avoided? See Dobbs, The Law of Torts § 246 (2000). Reconsider this question after reading *Toy v. Mackintosh*, Chapter 12, Section D(1).

COLTHURST v. LAKE VIEW STATE BANK

United States Court of Appeals, Eighth Circuit, 1927.
18 F.2d 875.

OTIS, DISTRICT JUDGE. April 19, 1924, the Lake View State Bank of Chicago, an Illinois corporation, herein referred to as the plaintiff, filed in the District Court for the Southern District of Iowa its petition, thereafter amended, in which, as amended, it alleged it was the holder in due course, for value, and without notice of any defense thereto, of a note in the principal amount of $3,200, with interest at 6 per cent., dated December 16, 1918, due in one year, and signed by the plaintiff in error, herein referred to as the defendant. The answer charged procurement of the note by fraud and denied that the bank held it in due course.

Upon the trial, having heard the testimony offered by the plaintiff to the effect that it had purchased the note February 20, 1919, for $3,234.67 (being the principal plus the interest then due) from the then holder, one W.F. Van Buskirk, to whom the note had been indorsed by a prior indorsee, and that it had no knowledge of any defenses existing in favor of the maker of the note, the District Court directed the defendant to put on his evidence in this order: First, any evidence he had tending to show that the bank was not a holder in due course and without notice; and, second, after such evidence (but not otherwise) any evidence he had tending to show that the note in the first instance was obtained by fraud.

* * * [The trial court excluded the only evidence, referred to in the opinion as the Van Buskirk letters, offered by the defendant to show that the plaintiff was not a holder in due course.]

The District Court directed a verdict for the plaintiff. It is contended that the court erred therein, first, because the Van Buskirk letters showed that the bank did not receive the note before maturity and therefore was not a holder in due course; second, because, even if the Van Buskirk letters properly were excluded, facts and circumstances in evidence tended to show the bank was not a holder in due course; and, third, because, in any event, it was for the jury to pass upon the credibility of the witnesses for the plaintiff.

* * * [The court here held that the Van Buskirk letters were properly excluded by the trial court.]

2. It is true, of course, that even if there were no direct testimony tending to show that the bank had knowledge of defenses existing against the note when it obtained possession of it, if in the evidence there were facts and circumstances from which such a conclusion reasonably could be inferred then a verdict should not have been directed. In our view, however, there were not in evidence any facts or circumstances which, whether considered separately or together, furnish any basis for such an inference.

3. The contention of defendant that even in the absence of any disproof of the prima facie case made by the plaintiff it was still the duty of the court to submit the case to the jury solely upon the matter of credibility is not tenable. Even if on that question the decisions of the Iowa Supreme Court were controlling, and it is on them the defendant bases his argument, they do not support the contention. Earlier decisions by that court apparently did. Arnd v. Aylesworth, 136 Iowa 297, 111 N.W. 407; Connelly v. Greenfield, 192 Iowa 876, 185 N.W. 887. But not so its later pronouncements.

In First National Bank of Montour v. Brown, 197 Iowa 1376, 199 N.W. 272, the Supreme Court of Iowa said:

> "To sustain the proposition advanced by the appellant in the instant case, we would be compelled to say that the defendant has an inherent right to have a jury pass upon his claim, or that the credibility of an uncontradicted and unimpeached witness in all cases presents a jury question. We cannot make such a pronouncement."

Again in First National Bank v. Dutton, 199 Iowa 468, 202 N.W. 228, the same court said:

> "We have intimated, if not decided, in some of our cases, such as Connelly v. Greenfield Sav. Bank, 192 Iowa, 876, 185 N.W. 887, and Arnd v. Aylesworth, 136 Iowa 297, 111 N.W. 407, and kindred cases, that although the officers specifically denied notice, yet at least its credibility is for the jury, hence making a jury question. If these pronouncements were followed to the conclusion contended for by appellant, then, in every case, where prima facie case of fraud is made by defendant, thereby casting the burden on the plaintiff to show that it was an innocent purchaser, it would have to go to the jury on the question of the credibility of witnesses tendered to establish that plaintiff was an innocent purchaser. We refuse to acquiesce in any such construction of that line of cases."

Our conclusion is that the action of the court below in directing a verdict for the plaintiff was right. Accordingly the judgment is affirmed.

Notes and Questions

1. *Shifting burdens.* "In contrast with the accepted view that the burden of persuasion remains on the same party throughout the trial, it is everywhere agreed that the other burden, i.e., the burden of producing evidence * * * may and often does shift back and forth between the parties like a tennis ball in play." Ray, Burden of Proof and Presumptions, 13 Tex.L.Rev. 33, 44 (1933).

In *Colthurst v. Lake View State Bank*, did the plaintiff succeed not only in discharging the burden of going forward but also in shifting that burden to the defendant? If the view were adopted that "the credibility of an uncontradicted and unimpeached witness in all cases presents a jury question" might the burden of going forward ever be shifted? By the introduction of what type of evidence? See Gardner v. Linwedel, 192 S.W.2d 613, 617 (Mo.Ct.App.1946); Sunderland, Directing a Verdict for the Party Having the Burden of Proof, 11 Mich.L.Rev. 198, 203–06 (1912).

2. On the propriety of directing a verdict in favor of the party with the burden of persuasion, see James, Hazard & Leubsdorf, Civil Procedure § 7.19, at 442 (5th ed. 2001).

SECTION B. THE BURDEN OF PERSUASION

DELAWARE COACH CO. v. SAVAGE

United States District Court, District of Delaware, 1948.
81 F.Supp. 293.

RODNEY, DISTRICT JUDGE. This was an action brought as a result of a collision in the City of Wilmington, Delaware between a trolley coach of the plaintiff and a truck and trailer of the defendants. As a result of the collision the driver of the trolley coach was killed and his widow received from the plaintiff compensation for his death, and this suit is brought pursuant to the subrogation provisions of the Delaware Workmen's Compensation Act. Rev.Code Del.1935, § 6108. Recovery was also sought for the damage sustained to the trolley coach. Jurisdiction is based upon diversity of citizenship. The case was tried to the court without the intervention of a jury, and separate findings of fact and conclusions of law have been filed. This comment is collateral to such findings and conclusions.

The collision was a right angle collision and happened at the intersection of two paved and well-travelled highways. The accident happened in broad daylight when the weather was clear and the roadways dry and in good condition. The intersection was protected by traffic lights upon all four corners operating in unison and controlling traffic in all four directions. The traffic lights were activated by treadles in each street placed at varying distances from the intersection.

It was established that when a green light or "Go" signal is shown, the "traffic facing such signal may proceed except that vehicular traffic and coaches proceeding under such signal shall yield the right of way to pedestrians, vehicles and coaches lawfully within a crosswalk or the intersection at the time such signal was exhibited."

It was also established that when a red light or "Stop" signal is shown the "traffic facing the signal shall stop before entering the nearest crosswalk at the intersection or at such other point as may be plainly and officially designated by authority of the Street and Sewer Department, and remain standing until green or 'Go' is shown alone."

The plaintiff, in support of its allegation of the negligence of the defendants, produced several highly intelligent and entirely disinterested witnesses who were in a position to see the traffic lights just prior to the accident, as well as the collision itself. They testified that the traffic lights were favorable to the trolley coach of the plaintiff and against the truck and trailer of the defendants.

The defendants, in support of their denial of their own negligence and in support of their allegations of contributory negligence of the plaintiff, produced an even greater number of disinterested witnesses who were in an equally favorable position to see and to know the conditions just prior to the accident. These witnesses testified unequivocally that the red or unfavorable traffic signal was shown toward the trolley coach of the plaintiff and that, notwithstanding such adverse signal, the trolley coach entered the intersection and the collision ensued.

The court found that the accident was not an unavoidable accident, but was caused by the negligence of at least one of the drivers of the motor vehicles involved. The evidence was in direct and irreconcilable conflict with witnesses on both sides who were disinterested, intelligent and entitled to credence. The court found that there was no preponderance on behalf of the plaintiff of the evidence of negligence of the defendants, but that such evidence was in equipoise and as a legal consequence the plaintiff had not sustained its burden and judgment must be entered for the defendants.

Jurisdiction being based upon the diversity of citizenship, it is essential that the law of Delaware be ascertained.

* * *

The burden of proof rests upon the party asserting the affirmative of an issue, such as, in this case, the negligence of the defendants. If an allegation, such as the negligence of the defendant, be alleged, the party asserting such fact must prove it by a preponderance of the evidence. The burden of proof of such fact continues throughout the case and this burden of proof never shifts. The burden of going forward with the evidence may shift from time to time during a trial after the establishing of a prima facie case or due to some other development in the case, but the burden of proof of the main fact remains with the party who alleged such main fact.

Upon the establishment of a prima facie case the burden of evidence or the burden of going forward with the evidence shifts to the defensive party. It then becomes incumbent upon such defensive party to meet the prima facie case which has been established. For this purpose the defensive party need not produce evidence which preponderates or outweighs or surpasses the evidence of his adversary, but it is sufficient if such evidence is co-equal, leaving the proof in equilibrium. If the defensive party, either by a preponderance of evidence or evidence sufficient to establish equilibrium, has met and answered the prima facie case, then the burden of going forward with the evidence returns to the original proponent charged with the burden of proof who must in turn, by a preponderance or greater weight of evidence, overcome the equilibrium thus established, or otherwise support his burden of proof by a preponderance of the evidence. This is true whether the original prima facie case is founded upon affirmative evidence or established by the doctrine of res ipsa loquitur or other presumption or inference of law. Sweeney v. Erving, 228 U.S. 233 * * * . As said in Commercial Molasses Corporation v. New York Tank Barge Corporation, 314 U.S. 104, 111 * * * , an inference or presumption "does no more than require the [defensive party,] if he would avoid the inference, to go forward with evidence sufficient to persuade that the nonexistence of the fact, which would otherwise be inferred, is as probable as its existence. It does not cause the burden of proof to shift, and if the [defensive party] does go forward with evidence enough to raise doubts as to the validity of the inference, which the trier of facts is unable to resolve, the [proponent] does not sustain the burden of persuasion which upon the whole evidence remains upon him, where it rested at the start." The court cited, inter alia, the opinion of Judge Woolley in Tomkins Cove Stone Co. v. Bleakley Transp. Co., 3 Cir., 40 F.2d 249. * * *

Wigmore in his elaborate treatise shows the shifting and progressive nature of the burden of producing evidence for the satisfaction of the judge as well as the permanent and non-shifting nature of the burden of proof (the non-persuasion of the jury), which remains at all times with the proponent of the issue, to be established by a preponderance of the evidence. 9 Wigmore on Evidence, 3d Ed., Sec. 2485–2489. See also 2 Chamberlayne, Modern Law of Evidence, Sec. 940, etc.; McKelvey on Evidence, 75.

In Board of Education v. Makely, 139 N.C. 31, 51 S.E. 784, and Shepard v. Western Union Telegraph Co., 143 N.C. 244, 55 S.E. 704, 118 Am.St.Rep. 796, is cited a terse and apt quotation from 1 Elliott on Evidence, as follows: "The burden of the issue, that is, the burden of proof, in the sense of ultimately proving or establishing the issue or case of the party upon which such burden rests, as distinguished from the burden or duty of going forward and producing evidence, never shifts, but the burden or duty of proceeding or going forward often does shift from one party to the other, and sometimes back again. Thus, when the actor has gone forward and made a prima facie case, the other party is compelled in turn to go forward or lose his case, and in this sense the burden shifts to him. So the burden of going forward may, as to some particular matter, shift again to the first party in response to the call of a prima facie case or presumption in favor of the second party. But the party who has not the burden of the issue is not bound to disprove the actor's case by a preponderance of the evidence, for the actor must fail if, upon the whole evidence, he does not have a preponderance, no matter whether it is because the weight of evidence is with the other party, or because the scales are equally balanced."

Because, in this case, the plaintiff did not sustain its burden toward the fact-finding tribunal and show the negligence of the defendants by a preponderance of the evidence, judgment must be entered for the defendants.

On Motion for Reargument

Subsequent to the filing of the court's opinion in this case, plaintiff moved for reargument, grounding such motion upon an alleged failure by the court to apply the principle of law that all facts and circumstances must be weighed by the trier of facts in reaching its decision, especially in determining the credibility of witnesses and the probabilities of a case. The motion is supported by a memorandum in which plaintiff sets forth three cases as authorities for the principle urged by plaintiff. One of the three cases, Le Fevre v. Crossan, 3 Boyce 379, 26 Del. 379, 396, 84 A. 128, was cited by the court in its opinion.

The court is in complete agreement with plaintiff's contention and indicated as much in its opinion. Indeed, the very procedure which plaintiff contends must be followed by the trier of facts was, in fact, followed by the court in the instant case.

It is only necessary to add that courts of Delaware have uniformly set forth to juries certain aids or means of assistance when the testimony presented has been in conflict. Quite uniformly have juries been told that when the testimony is in conflict the juries should consider all the facts of the case and take into consideration the demeanor of the witnesses on the stand, their apparent fairness in giving their testimony, their opportunities for knowing the facts about which they have testified, any bias or interest they may have in the outcome of the litigation, and any other matters appearing from the evidence and having a bearing upon the reliability or unreliability of the testimony.

Where, as in this case, all those means of establishing the burden of proof have been exhausted and the trier of facts is still confronted with an equilibrium of testimony, as is here found, the plaintiff must be adjudged to have failed in its burden of proof.[14]

The motion for reargument is denied.

14. Model Code of Evidence, p. 3.

Problem

If *Delaware Coach Co. v. Savage* had been tried to a jury rather than to the court, how should the jury have been instructed with respect to the burden of persuasion? Prepare a jury instruction which could properly (and helpfully) have been given in the case. With your result, compare O'Malley, Grenig & Lee, Federal Jury Practice & Instructions § 104.01 (2000). See also, the Uniform Jury Instructions cited in the next case.

RILEY HILL GENERAL CONTRACTOR, INC. v. TANDY CORP.

Supreme Court of Oregon, 1987.
737 P.2d 595.

JONES, JUDGE.

Plaintiff, Riley Hill General Contractor, Inc., sought compensatory and punitive damages on claims labeled "fraud," "breach of warranty" and "negligence" against defendant, Tandy Corporation, arising out of plaintiff's purchase of a computer that was manufactured and sold by defendant doing business as Radio Shack. Defendant answered with a general denial of the claims and raised an affirmative defense of contributory fault. The trial court instructed the jury that:

"You are instructed that the law recognizes a presumption against fraud and this presumption against fraud must be overcome by clear and convincing evidence." The Party alleging fraud must thus bring forth evidence to prove it, and may not rely upon mere suspicious circumstances or equivocal conduct. "Thus, there must be a certain quality of evidence to overcome the presumption against fraud even though the burden of proof remains in this case as in all civil cases, proof by a preponderance of the evidence." (Emphasis added.)

Defendant excepted to these instructions. The jury returned a verdict for plaintiff. Defendant appealed, and the Court of Appeals reversed and remanded for a new trial because of the inconsistency in the trial court's jury instructions on the burden of proof. Riley Hill General Contractor v. Tandy Corp., 82 Or.App. 458, 728 P.2d 577 (1986). We allowed review to decide whether the burden of persuasion[15] for common law deceit should be by "clear and convincing evidence," by a "preponderance of the evidence" or by a combination of both concepts. We hold that the burden of persuasion for common law deceit requires the proponent to prove each of the elements of deceit by clear and convincing evidence, but that general or punitive damages arising out of that deceit need be proved only by a preponderance of the evidence. The Court of Appeals is affirmed.

* * *

At the conclusion of the trial, the judge gave the above-quoted instruction to the jury. The Court of Appeals reversed the trial court,

15. OEC [Oregon Evidence Code] 305 provides: "A party has the burden of persuasion as to each fact the existence or nonexistence of which the law declares essential to the claim for relief or defense the party is asserting."

holding that the instructions were inconsistent because the jury was told that the burden of proof in "fraud" cases is by both clear and convincing evidence and by a preponderance of the evidence. As mentioned, the Court of Appeals held that the instruction was reversible error, because it was not possible to tell from the verdict whether the jury used the correct clear and convincing evidence standard or the incorrect preponderance of the evidence standard. 82 Or.App. at 461, 728 P.2d 577.

Before we set forth the level of proof required in civil actions for deceit, we address the origins and meanings of the terms "preponderance of evidence" and "clear and convincing evidence."

THE ORIGINS AND MEANINGS OF "PREPONDERANCE" AND "CLEAR AND CONVINCING" EVIDENCE

"Preponderance" derives from the Latin word "praeponderare," which translates to "outweigh, be of greater weight." 8 Oxford English Dictionary 1289 (1933). With regard to the burden of proof or persuasion in civil actions, it is generally accepted to mean the greater weight of evidence. At one time in the history of English law, the translation received a literal interpretation, with heads of witnesses being counted on each side, and each item of testimony receiving a quantitative value or weight. See Millar, in Engelmann, History of Continental Civil Procedure 41–49 (1927); 9 Wigmore, Evidence 424–31, § 2498 (Chadbourn rev 1981); 1 Holdsworth, History of English Law 302–04 (3d ed 1922). The term suggests to the jury that the evidence should be weighed on a scale and, frequently, trial judges will speak of weights and scales in explaining to jurors under this standard that they cannot speculate or guess what happened but that a party with the burden of persuasion in a civil case must prove what probably occurred. Uniform Jury Instructions (Civil), Nos. 21.01, 21.02 (Oregon CLE 1986), read, respectively:

"A party has the burden of proving by a preponderance of the evidence any claim made in that party's pleadings. In the absence of such proof, the party cannot prevail as to that claim."

" 'Preponderance of the evidence' means the greater weight of evidence. It is such evidence that, when weighed with that opposed to it, has more convincing force and is more probably true and accurate. If, upon any question in the case, the evidence appears to be equally balanced, or if you cannot say upon which side it weighs heavier, you must resolve that question against the party upon whom the burden of proof rests."[16]

Mellinkoff, in his extensive work, The Language of the Law (1963), does not specifically trace the origins of the terms "preponderance of the evidence" or "clear and convincing evidence." However, he asserts that certain words, such as "plaintiff," "defendant," "fee simple" and "lessee," are terms of art with a specific meaning, id. at 17, but that other

16. We note that the uniform jury instruction still refers to the former usage, "burden of proof." Since January 1, 1982, the statutory terminology is "burden of persuasion." OEC 305, set out ante at note [15]. [Was the change warranted? Ed.]

language of the law is better characterized as equivocal because "there is a deliberate choice of the flexible," id. at 21. Among a sample of words and phrases which are often used "because they are flexible or despite their flexibility," are the words "clear and convincing," id. at 21, and he lists among "the cats and dogs of law language, defined and redefined, but not more precise for all of that," the words "preponderance of the evidence," id. at 385. Thus, he tells us what we already know, that these terms are not precise standards but are words that do no more than characterize evidence. See Byers v. Santiam Ford, Inc., 281 Or. 411, 420, 574 P.2d 1122 n.2 (1978) (Lent, J., specially concurring).

We now examine why there are two somewhat parallel words, "clear" and "convincing," for a separate standard of proof. Mellinkoff traces this repetition of words to the origins of the English language. * * * . He writes:

One of the sources of tautology [that is, a needless repetition of words] is the prolonged presence of two languages side by side. England, for example, is peppered with place names which would read Hill-hill, or worse, except that the first hill is Celtic (bre or cruc or penn) and the other Old English (hyll), for instance, names like Breedon-on-the-Hill, Churchill, Penhill, Pendle Hill. * * *

* * *

He then comments that, sometimes for clarity, sometimes for emphasis and sometimes in keeping with the bilingual fashion of the day, English lawyers joined synonyms. A sampling of bilingual synonyms coupled in the law are:

fit and proper (OE; F)

free and clear (OE; F)

give, devise, and bequeath (OE; F; OE)

goods and chattels (OE: F)

* * *

peace and quiet (F; L)

* * *

will and testament (OE; L)

Such a combination of languages is found in the "clear and convincing" standard of proof, although this pair of words does not repeat a single concept. Outside the law, a proposition may be very clear but unconvincing, and murky statements may be persuasive in the absence of criticism or contrary assertions. In short, "clear" describes the character of unambiguous evidence, whether true or false; "convincing" describes the effect of evidence on an observer.

"Clear" is a Norman French word which means "of words, statements, explanations, meanings: Easy to understand, fully intelligible, free from obscurity of sense; of a vision, concept, notion, view, memory, etc.; Distinct, unclouded, free from confusion." 2 Oxford English Dictionary, supra at 475. The use of the term "clear" by itself after the Norman Conquest could have created great confusion due to its close association with the native English word "clean," which meant "without anything left or omitted, without any exception that may vitiate the statement, without qualification wholly, entirely, quite absolutely." Id. at 482.

"Convincing" is an English word derived from the Latin "convincere." It means "to overcome, to conquer, convict; to overcome (a person) in argument, to prove wrong, confute; to cause (a person) to admit, as establish to his satisfaction, that which is advanced in argument; that which convinces, that convicts, proves guilty, that which brings conviction to the mind." Id. at 950–51.

The use of similar terms, one Norman French, one English, arose in English history around the time of William the Conqueror and the Norman Conquest in 1066. King William I encouraged and maintained the loyalty and obligations system which had bound subjects to the kings of England. He made great use of certain trusted Norman followers, but these prelates were required to rule within a native English framework of law and custom * * * .

* * * In furtherance of his use of the jury system, and as part of his assimilation policy, William I directed that, where possible, Norman French words be joined with Anglo–Saxon words for purposes of effectuating the law. 1 Pollock & Maitland, The History of English Law, chs 2, 3 (1895).

In trying to understand the Norman French and English terms, of course, we need to examine not only their origins but also the usage given to them by judicial decisions.

The Use of the Terms

Historically, the "clear and convincing" standard of proof

> "was first applied in equity to claims which experience had shown to be inherently subject to fabrication, lapse of memory, or the flexibility of conscience. Conceding the validity of policies which the parol evidence rule and the Statutes of Wills and Frauds were designed to carry out, the chancery courts compromised between becoming a mecca for the trumped-up prayer for relief and refusing altogether to mitigate the stern fulfillment of these policies in the law courts, by granting relief only in cases where the evidence in support of this type of claim was 'clear and convincing.' * * * " Note, Appellate Review in the Federal Courts of Findings Requiring More than a Preponderance of the Evidence, 60 Harv.L.Rev. 111, 112 (1946).

The author of the above-quoted law review article notes that in jury trials of civil actions at law, the clear and convincing rule was applied to actions for fraud or deceit as well as to equitable defenses based on fraud or mistake. He concludes that one method of enforcing the demand for clear and convincing evidence available in appeals from jury verdicts is the approval of a charge to the jury which directs them to apply that level of proof or reversal for error where the charge does not incorporate it. Id. at 116–17, nn.43 & 44 (citing Fidelity & Casualty Co. of N.Y. v. Genova, 90 F.2d 874 (C.C.A.6th.1937); Kuhn v. Chesapeake & Ohio Ry., 118 F.2d 400 (C.C.A.4th.1941)).

Many courts have recognized that the intermediate standard of "clear and convincing" evidence is applicable in appropriate civil cases. Then Chief Justice Warren Burger, in Addington v. Texas, 441 U.S. 418, 424 * * * (1979), wrote that this

> " 'intermediate standard, which usually employs some combination of the words "clear," "cogent," "unequivocal," and "convincing," is less commonly used, but nonetheless is no stranger to the civil law.' One typical use of the standard is in civil cases involving allegations of fraud or some other quasi-criminal wrongdoing by the defendant. The interests at stake in those cases are deemed to be more substantial than mere loss of money and some jurisdictions accordingly reduce the risk to defendant of having his reputation tarnished erroneously by increasing the plaintiff's burden of proof." Citing Woodby v. INS, 385 U.S. 276, 285 * * * (1966); McCormick Evidence § 320 (1954); 9 Wigmore, Evidence § 2498 (3d ed. 1940).

Application of this intermediate standard permeates a line of United States Supreme Court decisions declaring that "clear and convincing" evidence is required in various quasi-criminal proceedings or where the proceedings threaten the individual involved with a significant deprivation of liberty or with a stigma.

The Levels of Proof in Oregon

Since the time of the first Deady Code, Oregon statutes have set forth the level of proof required in civil and criminal actions. See General Laws of Oregon, ch. 9, § 835, pp. 355–56 (Deady 1845–1864). Those standards are now codified at ORS 10.095(5) and (6), as follows: "The jury, subject to the control of the court, in the cases specified by statute, are the judges of the effect or value of evidence addressed to them, except when it is thereby declared to be conclusive. They are, however, to be instructed by the court on all proper occasions:" * * *

> "(5) That in civil cases the affirmative of the issue shall be proved, and when the evidence is contradictory, the finding shall be according to the preponderance of evidence;
>
> (6) That in criminal cases a person is innocent of a crime or wrong until the prosecution proves otherwise, and guilt shall be established beyond reasonable doubt;" (Emphasis added.)

Plaintiff contends that, under ORS 10.095(5), in a civil action, a plaintiff's burden can never be more than a preponderance of the evidence. We disagree.

In Cook v. Michael, 214 Or. 513, 526–27, 330 P.2d 1026 (1958), this court stated that there are three standards of proof: "a preponderance," "clear and convincing" and "beyond a reasonable doubt." Proof by a "preponderance of the evidence" means that the jury must believe that the facts asserted are more probably true than false. To be "clear and convincing," evidence must establish that the truth of the facts asserted is "highly probable." "Beyond a reasonable doubt" means that the facts asserted are almost certainly true. This part of the Cook opinion has been endorsed repeatedly by this court. See, e.g., Mutual of Enumclaw Ins. v. McBride, 295 Or. 398, 405–06, 667 P.2d 494 (1983). * * *

In Mutual of Enumclaw Ins. v. McBride, supra, this court signaled that

> "[t]he time may come when it is proper to address the question of the requirement of a higher level of proof in actions for common law fraud; but we decline to do so here because we disagree that the statutory provisions of fraud and false swearing are sufficiently similar to common law fraud as urged by defendants, nor do we think that to be the proper basis on which to decide this case." 295 Or. at 403, 667 P.2d 494.

Acknowledging that "skepticism [is] often voiced regarding the practical importance of an intermediate measure of proof," this court nonetheless stated that

> "ORS 10.095 requires the court 'on all proper occasions' to instruct the jury '[t]hat in civil cases * * * the finding shall be according to the preponderance of evidence' while 'in criminal cases guilt shall be established beyond reasonable doubt.' ORS 10.095(5), (6). The 'proper occasion' for interpolating an intermediate measure of proof is in cases that are between 'civil' and 'criminal' and where what is to be established is akin to 'guilt.' " Id. at 405, 667 P.2d 494.

One reason for imposing the higher "clear and convincing" standard in a claim based on deceit is that the defendant is branded with something akin to guilt. In Mutual of Enumclaw, after conceding that setting the clear and convincing standard for "fraud" was dictum in Cook v. Michael, an assault case, this court said:

> "So well established is this rule that the commentary to OEC 305 states, '[i]n actions that allege fraud or gift, for example, the trier of fact must be persuaded by "clear and convincing evidence," which means that the truth of the facts asserted must be highly probable,' citing Cook v. Michael, supra. This is repeated in L. Kirkpatrick, Oregon Evidence 51 (1982). The dictum of Cook v. Michael has become the accepted practice in Oregon. Thus, while the preponderance standard is the rule in most civil cases, an

exception to the standard is applied in civil cases of common law fraud." Mutual of Enumclaw, 295 Or. at 403, 667 P.2d 494.

* * *

A party who is found "guilty" of deceit is not found merely negligent in deceiving the victim. That party must have intended to deceive the victim or acted in reckless disregard for the truth. The type of interest protected by the law of deceit is the interest in formulating business judgments without being misled by others—in short, in not being cheated. See U.S. National Bank v. Fought, supra, 291 Or. at 220, 630 P.2d 337. A person who has been found "guilty" of deceiving or cheating someone certainly has been found "guilty" of conduct which carries the same stigma of guilt whether the conduct is a criminal or civil act of deceit.

As mentioned in Mutual of Enumclaw v. McBride, supra, ORS 10.095 is not cast in absolute terms. It requires the jury be instructed to apply the "preponderance" standard "on all proper occasions," thus leaving some discretion for this court to decide which cases are proper for such an instruction and which are not.

We conclude that the standard of proof in a civil action for common law deceit must be "clear and convincing." As our discussion above of the origins of the words points out, the evidence must be free from confusion, fully intelligible, distinct and establish to the jury that the defendant intended to deceive the plaintiff or did so with a reckless disregard for the truth. To be both clear and convincing, the truth of the facts asserted must be highly probable. Cook v. Michael, supra, 214 Or. at 527, 330 P.2d 1096. A trial judge should not tell a jury in a deceit case that it must be convinced by clear and convincing evidence. This misuse of parallel words would thrust us back to the dark ages. As Justice O'Connell cautioned in Cook v. Michael, 214 Or. at 528, 330 P.2d 1096.

> "when the proposition to be proved must be established by clear and convincing evidence, we regard it as improper for the trial court to use the word 'preponderance' in any of the instructions relating to that proposition. * * * "

However, as this court held in Dizick v. Umpqua Comm. College, supra, 287 Or. at 311, 599 P.2d 444, even though "fraud" must be proved by "clear and convincing evidence," the extent of damages need only be proved by a preponderance of the evidence. See also Byers v. Santiam Ford, Inc., supra, 218 Or. at 418, 574 P.2d 1122 (Lent, J., specially concurring).

In sum, in a common law deceit action the trial judge, when referring to the basic elements of the claim, should tell the jury that proof by clear and convincing evidence is required, which means that the truth of the facts is highly probable. However, when considering the issue of damages, be they general or punitive, the judge should instruct the jury that the proponent need only prove those damages by a preponderance, or greater weight of the evidence.[17]

We agree with the Court of Appeals' disposition as to defendant's assignment of error in the submission of the jury verdict form, which inferred that punitive damages could be allowed for simple negligence. Other assignments of error raised by defendant are not meritorious.

* * *

Note and Question

While most jurisdictions recognize the existence of a burden of persuasion intermediate between that applicable in an ordinary civil case and a criminal prosecution, unanimity is lacking with respect to the types of issues as to which the burden should be imposed. What types of considerations are suggested by the issues to which the Supreme Court of the United States has held the standard constitutionally required? See Rivera v. Minnich, 483 U.S. 574 (1987) (finding no constitutional requirement of the clear and convincing standard in a state paternity proceeding.)

IN RE WINSHIP

Supreme Court of the United States, 1970.
397 U.S. 358.

MR. JUSTICE BRENNAN delivered the opinion of the Court. Constitutional questions decided by this Court concerning the juvenile process have centered on the adjudicatory stage at "which a determination is made as to whether a juvenile is a 'delinquent' as a result of alleged

17. The court should not instruct the jury that deceit is not presumed or make any reference that a presumption must be overcome by evidence. In a properly tried civil case, the term "presumption" should not be heard by a jury. The legislative commentary to OEC 308 reads in part: "Under ORE 308, once a party invoking a presumption establishes the basic facts giving rise to it, the burden of establishing the nonexistence of the presumed fact shifts to the opposing party. Plaintiff, for example, may raise the presumption that a letter duly addressed and mailed was received in the regular course of the mail. See Rule 311(1)(h). The judge in such a case would determine whether the evidence is sufficient to support a finding of the existence of the basic facts: that the letter was properly addressed, that it was mailed, and that it was not returned. If so, the judge would instruct the jury that if they find the basic facts to be true, then the burden is on defendant to prove by a preponderance of the evidence that the letter was not received. The jury should never hear the word 'presumption' during this instruction. * * * The Legislative Assembly decided to change Oregon practice on presumptions for several reasons. First, it is extremely difficult to phrase a jury instruction without conveying the impression that the presumption itself is evidence. That proposition has long been discredited. Second, under the current approach to presumptions, the jury must weigh the force of the legal conclusion mandated by the presumption against the testimony of witnesses and other direct evidence. That is a difficult or impossible task. Finally, the considerations of fairness, policy and probability, which underlie the creation of presumptions, are not satisfied by giving them any lesser effect. The approach set forth in this rule is simple and workable, and gives due consideration to the policies behind the creation of presumptions. All presumptions, whether legislatively or judicially created, must be treated in the manner prescribed by this section." Evidence 4–8 to 4–9, § 4.13 (Oregon CLE 1986) (emphasis in original; citations omitted).

misconduct on his part, with the consequence that he may be committed to a state institution." In re Gault, 387 U.S. 1, 13 (1967). *Gault* decided that, although the Fourteenth Amendment does not require that the hearing at this stage conform with all the requirements of a criminal trial or even of the usual administrative proceeding, the Due Process Clause does require application during the adjudicatory hearing of " 'the essentials of due process and fair treatment.' " Id., at 30. This case presents the single, narrow question whether proof beyond a reasonable doubt is among the "essentials of due process and fair treatment" required during the adjudicatory stage when a juvenile is charged with an act which would constitute a crime if committed by an adult.

Section 712 of the New York Family Court Act defines a juvenile delinquent as "a person over seven and less than sixteen years of age who does any act which, if done by an adult, would constitute a crime." During a 1967 adjudicatory hearing, conducted pursuant to § 742 of the Act, a judge in New York Family Court found that appellant, then a 12–year–old boy, had entered a locker and stolen $112 from a woman's pocketbook. The petition which charged appellant with delinquency alleged that his act, "if done by an adult, would constitute the crime or crimes of Larceny." The judge acknowledged that the proof might not establish guilt beyond a reasonable doubt, but rejected appellant's contention that such proof was required by the Fourteenth Amendment. The judge relied instead on § 744(b) of the New York Family Court Act which provides that "[a]ny determination at the conclusion of [an adjudicatory] hearing that a [juvenile] did an act or acts must be based on a preponderance of the evidence."[18] During a subsequent dispositional hearing, appellant was ordered placed in a training school for an initial period of 18 months, subject to annual extensions of his commitment until his 18th birthday—six years in appellant's case. The Appellate Division of the New York Supreme Court, First Judicial Department, affirmed without opinion, 30 A.D.2d 781, 291 N.Y.S.2d 1005 (1968). The New York Court of Appeals then affirmed by a four-to-three vote, expressly sustaining the constitutionality of § 744(b), 24 N.Y.2d 196, 299 N.Y.S.2d 414, 247 N.E.2d 253 (1969).[19] We noted probable jurisdiction, 396 U.S. 885 (1969). We reverse.

18. The ruling appears in the following portion of the hearing transcript:

Counsel: "Your Honor is making a finding by the preponderance of the evidence."

Court: "Well, it convinces me."

Counsel: "It's not beyond a reasonable doubt, Your Honor."

Court: "That is true * * * Our statute says a preponderance and a preponderance it is."

19. * * * Legislative adoption of the reasonable-doubt standard has been urged by the National Conference of Commissioners on Uniform State Laws and by the Children's Bureau of the Department of Health, Education, and Welfare's Social and Rehabilitation Service. See Uniform Juvenile Court Act § 29(b) (1968); Children's Bureau, Social and Rehabilitation Service, U.S. Department of Health, Education and Welfare, Legislative Guide for Drafting Family and Juvenile Court Acts § 32(c) (1969). Cf. the proposal of the National Council on Crime and Delinquency that a "clear and convincing" standard be adopted. Model Rules for Juvenile Courts, Rule 26, p. 57 (1969). See generally Cohen, The Standard of Proof in Juvenile Proceedings: Gault Beyond a Reasonable Doubt, 68 Mich.L.Rev. 567 (1970).

I

The requirement that guilt of a criminal charge be established by proof beyond a reasonable doubt dates at least from our early years as a Nation. The "demand for a higher degree of persuasion in criminal cases was recurrently expressed from ancient times, [though] its crystallization into the formula 'beyond a reasonable doubt' seems to have occurred as late as 1798. It is now accepted in common law jurisdictions as the measure of persuasion by which the prosecution must convince the trier of all the essential elements of guilt." C. McCormick, Evidence § 321, pp. 681–682 (1954); see also 9 J. Wigmore, Evidence, § 2497 (3d ed. 1940). Although virtually unanimous adherence to the reasonable-doubt standard in common-law jurisdictions may not conclusively establish it as a requirement of due process, such adherence does "reflect a profound judgment about the way in which law should be enforced and justice administered." Duncan v. Louisiana, 391 U.S. 145, 155 (1968).

Expressions in many opinions of this Court indicate that it has long been assumed that proof of a criminal charge beyond a reasonable doubt is constitutionally required. * * * Mr. Justice Frankfurter stated that "[i]t is the duty of the Government to establish * * * guilt beyond a reasonable doubt. This notion—basic in our law and rightly one of the boasts of a free society—is a requirement and a safeguard of due process of law in the historic, procedural content of 'due process.'" Leland v. Oregon, supra, 343 U.S., at 802–803 (dissenting opinion). In a similar vein, the Court said in Brinegar v. United States, supra, 338 U.S., at 174, that "[g]uilt in a criminal case must be proved beyond a reasonable doubt and by evidence confined to that which long experience in the common-law tradition, to some extent embodied in the Constitution, has crystallized into rules of evidence consistent with that standard. These rules are historically grounded rights of our system, developed to safeguard men from dubious and unjust convictions, with resulting forfeitures of life, liberty and property." Davis v. United States, supra, 160 U.S., at 488 stated that the requirement is implicit in "constitutions * * * [which] recognize the fundamental principles that are deemed essential for the protection of life and liberty." In *Davis* a murder conviction was reversed because the trial judge instructed the jury that it was their duty to convict when the evidence was equally balanced regarding the sanity of the accused. This Court said: "On the contrary, he is entitled to an acquittal of the specific crime charged, if upon all the evidence, there is reasonable doubt whether he was capable in law of committing crime. * * * No man should be deprived of his life under the forms of law unless the jurors who try him are able, upon their consciences, to say that the evidence before them * * * is sufficient to show beyond a reasonable doubt the existence of every fact necessary to constitute the crime charged." Id., at 484, 493.

The reasonable-doubt standard plays a vital role in the American scheme of criminal procedure. It is a prime instrument for reducing the risk of convictions resting on factual error. The standard provides concrete substance for the presumption of innocence—that bedrock "axiomatic and elementary" principle whose "enforcement lies at the foundation of the administration of our criminal law." Coffin v. United States, supra, 156 U.S., at 453. As the dissenters in the New York Court of Appeals observed, and we agree, "a person accused of a crime * * * would be at a severe disadvantage, a disadvantage amounting to a lack of fundamental fairness, if he could be adjudged guilty and imprisoned for years on the strength of the same evidence as would suffice in a civil case." 24 N.Y.2d, at 205, 299 N.Y.S.2d, at 422, 247 N.E.2d, at 259.

The requirement of proof beyond a reasonable doubt has this vital role in our criminal procedure for cogent reasons. The accused during a criminal prosecution has at stake interest of immense importance, both because of the possibility that he may lose his liberty upon conviction and because of the certainty that he would be stigmatized by the conviction. Accordingly, a society that values the good name and freedom of every individual should not condemn a man for commission of a crime when there is reasonable doubt about his guilt. As we said in Speiser v. Randall, supra, 357 U.S., at 525–526: "There is always in litigation a margin of error, representing error in factfinding, which both parties must take into account. Where one party has at stake an interest of transcending value—as a criminal defendant his liberty—this margin of error is reduced as to him by the process of placing on the other party the burden of * * * persuading the factfinder at the conclusion of the trial of his guilt beyond a reasonable doubt. Due process commands that no man shall lose his liberty unless the Government has borne the burden of * * * convincing the factfinder of his guilt." To this end, the reasonable-doubt standard is indispensable, for it "impresses on the trier of fact the necessity of reaching a subjective state of certitude of the facts in issue." Dorsen & Rezneck, In Re Gault and the Future of Juvenile Law, 1 Family Law Quarterly, No. 4, pp. 1, 26 (1967).

Moreover, use of the reasonable-doubt standard is indispensable to command the respect and confidence of the community in applications of the criminal law. It is critical that the moral force of the criminal law not be diluted by a standard of proof that leaves people in doubt whether innocent men are being condemned. It is also important in our free society that every individual going about his ordinary affairs have confidence that his government cannot adjudge him guilty of a criminal offense without convincing a proper factfinder of his guilt with utmost certainty.

Lest there remain any doubt about the constitutional stature of the reasonable-doubt standard, we explicitly hold that the Due Process Clause protects the accused against conviction except upon proof beyond a reasonable doubt of every fact necessary to constitute the crime with which he is charged.

II

We turn to the question whether juveniles, like adults, are constitutionally entitled to proof beyond a reasonable doubt when they are charged with violation of a criminal law. The same considerations that demand extreme caution in factfinding to protect the innocent adult apply as well to the innocent child. We do not find convincing the contrary arguments of the New York Court of Appeals. *Gault* rendered untenable much of the reasoning relied upon by that court to sustain the constitutionality of § 744(b). * * *

Nor do we perceive any merit in the argument that to afford juveniles the protection of proof beyond a reasonable doubt would risk destruction of beneficial aspects of the juvenile process.[20]

* * *

We conclude, as we concluded regarding the essential due process safeguards applied in *Gault,* that the observance of the standard of proof beyond a reasonable doubt "will not compel the States to abandon or displace any of the substantive benefits of the juvenile process." *Gault,* supra, at 21.

Finally, we reject the Court of Appeals' suggestion that there is, in any event, only a "tenuous difference" between the reasonable-doubt and preponderance standards. The suggestion is singularly unpersuasive. In this very case, the trial judge's ability to distinguish between the two standards enabled him to make a finding of guilt that he conceded he might not have made under the standard of proof beyond a reasonable doubt. Indeed, the trial judge's action evidences the accuracy of the observation of commentators that "the preponderance test is susceptible to the misinterpretation that it calls on the trier of fact merely to perform an abstract weighing of the evidence in order to determine which side has produced the greater quantum, without regard to its effect in convincing his mind of the truth of the proposition asserted." Dorsen & Rezneck, supra, at 26–27.[21]

III

In sum, the constitutional safeguard of proof beyond a reasonable doubt is as much required during the adjudicatory stage of a delinquency proceeding as are those constitutional safeguards applied in *Gault*—notice of charges, right to counsel, the rights of confrontation and examination, and the privilege against self-incrimination. We therefore hold, in agreement with Chief Judge Fuld in dissent in the Court of

20. Appellee, New York City, apparently concedes as much in its Brief, page 8, where it states:

> "A determination that the New York law unconstitutionally denies due process because it does not provide for use of the reasonable doubt standard probably would not have a serious impact if all that resulted would be a change in the quantum of proof." * * *

21. Compare this Court's rejection of the preponderance standard in deportation proceedings, where we ruled that the Government must support its allegations with "clear, unequivocal, and convincing evidence." Woodby v. Immigration and Naturalization Service, 385 U.S. 276, 285 (1966). Although we ruled in *Woodby* that deportation is not tantamount to a criminal conviction, we found that since it could lead to "drastic deprivations," it is impermissible for a person to be "banished from this country upon no higher degree of proof than applies in a negligence case." Ibid.

Appeals, "that, where a 12–year–old child is charged with an act of stealing which renders him liable to confinement for as long as six years, then, as a matter of due process * * * the case against him must be proved beyond a reasonable doubt." 24 N.Y.2d, at 207, 299 N.Y.S.2d, at 423, 247 N.E.2d, at 260.

Reversed.

MR. JUSTICE HARLAN, concurring. No one, I daresay, would contend that state juvenile court trials are subject to *no* federal constitutional limitations. Differences have existed, however, among the members of this Court as to *what* constitutional protections do apply. See In re Gault, 387 U.S. 1 (1967).

The present case draws in question the validity of a New York statute that permits a determination of juvenile delinquency, founded on a charge of criminal conduct, to be made on a standard of proof that is less rigorous than that which would obtain had the accused been tried for the same conduct in an ordinary criminal case. While I am in full agreement that this statutory provision offends the requirement of fundamental fairness embodied in the Due Process Clause of the Fourteenth Amendment, I am constrained to add something to what my Brother Brennan has written for the Court, lest the true nature of the constitutional problem presented become obscured or the impact on state juvenile court systems of what the Court holds today be exaggerated.

I

Professor Wigmore, in discussing the various attempts by courts to define how convinced one must be to be convinced beyond a reasonable doubt, wryly observed: "The truth is that no one has yet invented or discovered a mode of measurement for the intensity of human belief. Hence there can be yet no successful method of communicating intelligibly * * * a sound method of self-analysis for one's belief," 9 J. Wigmore, Evidence 325 (3d ed. 1940).[22]

Notwithstanding Professor Wigmore's skepticism, we have before us a case where the choice of the standard of proof has made a difference: the juvenile court judge below forthrightly acknowledged that he believed by a preponderance of the evidence, but was not convinced beyond a reasonable doubt, that appellant stole $112 from the complainant's pocketbook. Moreover, even though the labels used for alternative standards of proof are vague and not a very sure guide to decisionmaking, the choice of the standard for a particular variety of adjudication does, I think, reflect a very fundamental assessment of the comparative social costs of erroneous factual determinations.[23]

To explain why I think this so, I begin by stating two propositions, neither of which I believe can be fairly disputed. First, in a judicial

22. See also Paulsen, *Juvenile Courts and the Legacy of '67,* 43 Ind.L.J. 527, 551–552 (1968).

23. For an interesting analysis of standards of proof see Kaplan, *Decision Theory and the Factfinding Process,* 20 Stan.L.Rev. 1065, 1071–1077 (1968).

proceeding in which there is a dispute about the facts of some earlier event, the factfinder cannot acquire unassailably accurate knowledge of what happened. Instead, all the factfinder can acquire is a belief of what *probably* happened. The intensity of this belief—the degree to which a factfinder is convinced that a given act actually occurred—can, of course, vary. In this regard, a standard of proof represents an attempt to instruct the factfinder concerning the degree of confidence our society thinks he should have in the correctness of factual conclusions for a particular type of adjudication. Although the phrases "preponderance of the evidence" and "proof beyond a reasonable doubt" are quantitatively imprecise, they do communicate to the finder of fact different notions concerning the degree of confidence he is expected to have in the correctness of his factual conclusions.

A second proposition, which is really nothing more than a corollary of the first, is that the trier of fact will sometimes, despite his best efforts, be wrong in his factual conclusions. In a lawsuit between two parties, a factual error can make a difference in one of two ways. First, it can result in a judgment in favor of the plaintiff when the true facts warrant a judgment for the defendant. The analogue in a criminal case would be the conviction of an innocent man. On the other hand, an erroneous factual determination can result in a judgment for the defendant when the true facts justify a judgment in plaintiff's favor. The criminal analogue would be the acquittal of a guilty man.

The standard of proof influences the relative frequency of these two types of erroneous outcomes. If, for example, the standard of proof for a criminal trial were a preponderance of the evidence rather than proof beyond a reasonable doubt, there would be a smaller risk of factual errors that result in freeing guilty persons, but a far greater risk of factual errors that result in convicting the innocent. Because the standard of proof affects the comparative frequency of these two types of erroneous outcomes, the choice of the standard to be applied in a particular kind of litigation should, in a rational world, reflect an assessment of the comparative social disutility of each.

When one makes such an assessment, the reason for different standards of proof in civil as opposed to criminal litigation becomes apparent. In a civil suit between two private parties for money damages, for example, we view it as no more serious in general for there to be an erroneous verdict in the defendant's favor than for there to be an erroneous verdict in the plaintiff's favor. A preponderance of the evidence standard therefore seems peculiarly appropriate for, as explained most sensibly,[24] it simply requires the trier of fact "to believe that the existence of a fact is more probable than its nonexistence before [he]

24. The preponderance test has been criticized, justifiably in my view, when it is read as asking the trier of fact to weigh in some objective sense the quantity of evidence submitted by each side rather than asking him to decide what he believes most probably happened. See J. Maguire, Evidence, Common Sense and Common Law 180 (1947).

may find in favor of the party who has the burden to persuade the [judge] of the fact's existence."[25]

In a criminal case, on the other hand, we do not view the social disutility of convicting an innocent man as equivalent to the disutility of acquitting someone who is guilty. As Mr. Justice Brennan wrote for the Court in Speiser v. Randall, 357 U.S. 513, 525–526 (1958):

> "There is always in litigation a margin of error, representing error in factfinding, which both parties must take into account. Where one party has at stake an interest of transcending value—as a criminal defendant his liberty—this margin of error is reduced as to him by the process of placing on the other party the burden * * * of persuading the fact-finder at the conclusion of the trial of his guilt beyond a reasonable doubt."

In this context, I view the requirement of proof beyond a reasonable doubt in a criminal case as bottomed on a fundamental value determination of our society that it is far worse to convict an innocent man than to let a guilty man go free. It is only because of the nearly complete and long-standing acceptance of the reasonable-doubt standard by the States in criminal trials that the Court has not before today had to hold explicitly that due process, as an expression of fundamental procedural fairness, requires a more stringent standard for criminal trials than for ordinary civil litigation.

II

When one assesses the consequences of an erroneous factual determination in a juvenile delinquency proceeding in which a youth is accused of a crime, I think it must be concluded that, while the consequences are not identical to those in a criminal case, the differences will not support a distinction in the standard of proof. * * * I therefore agree that a juvenile court judge should be no less convinced of the factual conclusion that the accused committed the criminal act with which he is charged than would be required in a criminal trial.

III

I wish to emphasize, as I did in my separate opinion in *Gault,* 387 U.S. 1, that there is no automatic congruence between the procedural requirements imposed by due process in a criminal case, and those imposed by due process in juvenile cases.

* * *

MR. CHIEF JUSTICE BURGER, with whom MR. JUSTICE STEWART joins, dissenting.

[The dissenting opinion of MR. CHIEF JUSTICE BURGER is omitted.]

25. F. James, Civil Procedure 250–251 (1965); see E. Morgan, Some Problems of Proof Under the Anglo–American System of Litigation 84–85 (1956).

Notes and Questions

1. *Jury instructions.* How the jury should be instructed as to the "reasonable doubt" standard is a question which has received considerable judicial attention. One definition which has received extensive usage in jury charges is that found in Commonwealth v. Webster,[26] 59 Mass. (5 Cush.) 295, 320 (1850):

> It is not a mere possible doubt; because everything relating to human affairs and depending on moral evidence, is open to some possible or imaginary doubt. It is that state of the case, which, after the entire comparison and consideration of all the evidence, leaves the minds of the jurors in that condition that they cannot say they feel an abiding conviction, to a moral certainty, of the truth of the charge.

Charges drawing largely upon *Webster*, including references to "moral certainty," were upheld against constitutional attack in Victor v. Nebraska, 511 U.S. 1 (1994), although the Court made clear its view that such phraseology is less than optimum. What formulation would be preferable? Justice Ginsburg, concurring in *Victor,* characterizes the following as "clean, straight forward, and accurate:"

> [T]he government has the burden of proving the defendant guilty beyond a reasonable doubt. Some of you may have served as jurors in civil cases, where you were told that it is only necessary to prove that a fact is more likely true than not true. In criminal cases, the government's proof must be more powerful than that. It must be beyond a reasonable doubt.
>
> Proof beyond a reasonable doubt is proof that leaves you firmly convinced of the defendant's guilt. There are very few things in this world that we know with absolute certainty, and in criminal cases the law does not require proof that overcomes every possible doubt. If, based on your consideration of the evidence, you are firmly convinced that the defendant is guilty of the crime charged, you must find him guilty. If on the other hand, you think there is a real possibility that he is not guilty, you must give him the benefit of the doubt and find him not guilty. Federal Judicial Center, Pattern Criminal Jury Instructions 17–18 (1987) (instruction 21).

511 U.S. at 27.

For a more recent discussion of reasonable doubt instructions, see Sheppard, The Metamorphoses of Reasonable Doubt: How Changes in the Burden of Proof Have Weakened the Presumption of Innocence, 78 Notre Dame L.Rev. 1165 (2003).

2. *Probabilities.* In light of Justice Harlan's comment, concurring *In re Winship*, that all the factfinder can acquire is a belief as to what probably happened, would it be desirable (and constitutional) to define "reasonable

26. In addition to its legal significance, the *Webster* case constitutes a fascinating piece of Americana which has been of continuing interest to historians. See Borowitz, The Janitor's Story: An Ethical Dilemma in the Harvard Murder Case, 66 A.B.A.J. 1540 (1980); Thomson, Murder at Harvard (1971). [Ed.]

doubt" in terms of probabilities? What degree of probability? For a challenging proposal admitted by the author to be somewhat heretical, see Ball, Probability Theory: The Moment of Truth, 14 Vand.L.Rev. 807 (1961).

More recent attempts to utilize probability theory with respect to burdens of persuasion include Cohen, Confidence in Probability: Burdens of Persuasion in a World of Imperfect Knowledge, 60 N.Y.U.L.Rev. 385 (1985); Kaye, Do We Need a Calculus of Weight to Understand Proof Beyond a Reasonable Doubt, 66 B.U.L.Rev. 657 (1986). See also Chambers, Reasonable Certainty and Reasonable Doubt, 81 Marq.L.Rev. 655 (1998). For an argument that the standard of proof under the rubric of reasonable doubt can and should vary with the kind of case, see Lillquist, Recasting Reasonable Doubt: Decision Theory and the Virtues of Variability, 36 U.C. Davis L.Rev. 85 (2002).

3. *Error in instructions.* There is no federal constitutional requirement that the phrase "beyond a reasonable doubt" be defined for the jury, and some authority exists for the proposition that any attempt to do so will constitute reversible error. Note, Defining Reasonable Doubt: To Define or Not to Define, 90 Colum.L.Rev. 1716 (1990). If an instruction is given which misdescribes the standard under federal constitutional law, the Supreme Court has held that the error is "structural" and thus not susceptible to harmless error analysis. Sullivan v. Louisiana, 508 U.S. 275 (1993). See also Note, Reasonable Doubt: An Argument Against Definition, 108 Harv.L.Rev. 1955 (1995).

4. *Circumstantial evidence cases.* Where the state relies upon circumstantial evidence, it is common for the defense to request an instruction in effect equating reasonable doubt with any reasonable hypothesis consistent with the circumstances and inconsistent with guilt. In Holland v. United States, 348 U.S. 121, 139–40 (1954), discussed by the court in *United States v. Nelson, supra,* in reference to the standard on review, the Supreme Court stated:

> The petitioners assail the refusal of the trial judge to instruct that where the Government's evidence is circumstantial it must be such as to exclude every reasonable hypothesis other than that of guilt. There is some support for this type of instruction in the lower court decisions, * * * but the better rule is that where the jury is properly instructed on the standards for reasonable doubt, such an additional instruction on circumstantial evidence is confusing and incorrect * * *.
>
> Circumstantial evidence in this respect is intrinsically no different from testimonial evidence. Admittedly, circumstantial evidence may in some cases point to a wholly incorrect result. Yet this is equally true of testimonial evidence. In both instances, a jury is asked to weigh the chances that the evidence correctly points to guilt against the possibility of inaccuracy or ambiguous inference. In both, the jury must use its experience with people and events in weighing the probabilities. If the jury is convinced beyond a reasonable doubt, we can require no more.

But see State v. Ohler, 134 N.W.2d 265 (Neb.1965) (suggesting such an instruction is not only proper but required).

See also Rosenberg & Rosenberg, " 'Perhaps What Ye Say Is Based Only on Conjecture'—Circumstantial Evidence, Then and Now," 31 Hous.L.Rev. 1371 (1995).

5. *Difference in civil and criminal standards.* In the principal case, the majority "rejects" the suggestion that there is only a "tenuous difference" between the reasonable doubt and preponderance standards, noting in support of its position that the trial judge was clearly cognizant of a distinction. In this connection, see Simon & Mahan, Quantifying Burdens of Proof, 5 Law & Soc.Rev. 319, 329 (1971) (reporting the results of an empirical study of jury and judge behavior): "For the judges a preponderance means a little more than half; for the jurors it means a probability almost indistinguishable from the standard applied in criminal trials." See also Stoffelmayr & Diamond, The Conflict Between Precision and Flexibility in Explaining "Beyond a Reasonable Doubt," 6 Psychol.Pub.Pol'y & L. 769 (2000).

6. *Affirmative defenses.* The implications of the *Winship* decision for "affirmative defenses"—particularly rules that assign the burden of persuasion to the defendant—in criminal cases deserve note. Though some states decline to impose the burden of persuasion upon the defendant as to any element of a criminal case, it has long been assumed, in light of Leland v. Oregon, 343 U.S. 790 (1952), that there is no general federal constitutional barrier to the practice. In *Leland* the Supreme Court upheld an Oregon statute which required an accused pleading insanity to establish that defense beyond a reasonable doubt. See also Martin v. Ohio, 480 U.S. 228 (1987) (constitutional to allocate burden of persuasion on self defense to accused).

But there are some limitations on the placement of the burden of persuasion on the defense although the exact nature of those limitations is not entirely clear. Compare Mullaney v. Wilbur, 421 U.S. 684 (1975) (holding unconstitutional to place burden on defendant to show that he acted in the heat of passion on sudden provocation), with Patterson v. New York, 432 U.S. 197 (1977) (ruling not unconstitutional to require defendant to prove that he acted under the influence of "extreme emotional disturbance" and distinguishing *Mullaney* as dealing with a situation which the defendant was asked to disprove an essential element of the prosecution's case). See discussion in 2 McCormick, Evidence §§ 346–348 (6th ed. 2006). See also Allen, Restructuring Jury Decision Making in Criminal Cases: A Unified Constitutional Approach to Evidentiary Devices, 94 Harv.L.Rev. 321 (1980); Garfield, Back to the Future: Does *Apprendi* Bar a Legislature's Power to Shift the Burden of Proof Away from the Prosecution by Labeling an Element of a Traditional Crime as an Affirmative Defense?, 35 Conn.L.Rev. 1351 (2003); Rosenberg, *Winship* Redux: 1970 to 1990, 61 Tex.L.Rev. 109 (1990); Saltzburg, Burdens of Persuasion in Criminal Cases: Harmonizing the Views of the Justices, 20 Am.Crim.L.Rev. 393 (1983); Sundby, The Reasonable Doubt Rule and the Meaning of Innocence, 40 Hastings L.J. 457 (1989).

Chapter 5

PRESUMPTIONS[1]

McNULTY v. CUSACK

District Court of Appeal of Florida, 1958.
104 So.2d 785.

ALLEN, ACTING CHIEF JUDGE. This is an appeal from a final judgment in a negligence action, entered after a directed verdict for plaintiff as to liability. Annie B. Cusack sued F. Jerome McNulty as the result of a rear-end collision between a car driven by plaintiff and another driven by defendant. Defendant's car ran into the rear of plaintiff's car at an intersection. The jury brought in a verdict for plaintiff in the amount of $16,000.

* * *

We state the principal question involved here as follows:

> "Whether the showing of a rear-end collision and the circumstances under which it occurred, in the absence of explanation, gives rise to a presumption of negligence so as to authorize a directed verdict, or whether it only gives rise to an inference of negligence sufficient for presentation to the jury."

There is a split of authority on whether or not a rear-end collision, coupled with circumstances under which it occurs, gives rise to an inference or a presumption of negligence. [Some] * * * authorities hold that a presumption arises and that the burden of going forward with the evidence is on the person who ran into the preceding car from the rear * * *.

The Rhode Island court, in the case of Douglas v. Silvia, supra, said:

> "We agree with the rule established by the cases of O'Donnell v. United Electric Rys. Co., 48 R.I. 18, 134 A. 642 and Riccio v. Ginsberg, 49 R.I. 32, 139 A. 652, 62 A.L.R. 967, that proof of a rear-end collision makes a prima facie case of negligence against the driver of the car in the rear. This does not mean, however, that the driver of an automobile which is following another is to be held

1. Throughout the cases and materials in this chapter some footnotes have been omitted; others have been renumbered. [Ed.]

liable under all conditions and irrespective of existing circumstances. When a prima facie case is made out by proving that the plaintiff was damaged in a rear-end collision, the duty of going forward with evidence of due care falls upon the defendant. If the testimony then shows a conflict of evidence from which different conclusions may reasonably be drawn by ordinarily prudent persons, then the question becomes one of fact for the jury to determine under proper instructions from the court. The burden of proof[2] in such a case still remains with the plaintiff."

* * *

The case of Harvey v. Borg, 1934, 218 Iowa 1228, 257 N.W. 190, 193, indicates the logic of those cases which hold that only an inference of neglect arises from the fact that a rear-end collision occurred and, therefore, it becomes a matter for the jury.

In Harvey v. Borg, supra, the Supreme Court of Iowa said:

"It is universally agreed that no inference of negligence arises from the mere fact that a collision occurred. A collision of two motor vehicles might result without negligence upon the part of the operator of either of them. The facts and circumstances surrounding the occurrence must be considered. It is certainly the general rule that a truck driven by a careful and prudent driver would not ordinarily crash with the rear of a forward moving vehicle of any kind. The inference recognized in such cases is by no means conclusive and may be readily dissipated by an explanation on the part of the party causing the injuries by evidence in the usual way. Appellant [sic] did not see fit to offer any explanation or to present testimony in their behalf. Appellee made out a prima facie case of negligence, and, in the absence of explanation on the part of defendant or of other evidence, an issue was presented for the jury."

* * *

The record shows that the sole testimony as to negligence in the case was that of the plaintiff. After the plaintiff rested, the defendant also rested, so there was no explanation on the part of the defendant of his actions of crashing his car into the rear-end of plaintiff's car. * * *

We, therefore, have the testimony of the plaintiff that she had stopped her car at a street intersection where the traffic light showed red and was waiting for the light to change to green, that while still sitting there, the defendant's car crashed into the back of her car; and in addition, that the defendant rushed up and apologized to her and when she stated to him that he had wrecked her car, he remarked that that could be fixed.

Was there sufficient evidence before the court to create a presumption of negligence on the part of the defendant so as to require him to go forward with testimony to show that he was not legally at fault in

2. [In what sense is the court here using the phrase "burden of proof?" Ed.]

crashing into the back of plaintiff's car? We agree with the circuit judge that the facts above stated created a presumption of negligence and not an inference of negligence and that, in the absence of an explanation from the defendant, a verdict should have been directed by the lower court in favor of the plaintiff. We think the court could take judicial notice of the fact that it was the duty of both the plaintiff and the defendant to stop at the intersecting street when a traffic light was showing red. In this day of heavy motor traffic all over the nation, the youngest or the most careless motorist knows that it is negligence to go through a red light. In addition, the rules of the road would require the defendant, as he approached the intersection, to have his car under control so that he would not drive into the rear-end of a motorist obeying traffic signals by waiting for the red light to turn green. If the defendant had a justifiable reason for not observing traffic rules, then it was his duty to go forward with the evidence to show that he was not negligent and thus, permit the case to go to a jury for the jury's determination on conflicting theories or facts.

* * *

The judgment is affirmed.

SHANNON, J., concurs.

GERALD, LYNN, ASSOCIATE JUDGE, dissents.

Notes and Questions

1. *"Real presumptions."* "[I]t must be kept in mind that the peculiar effect of a presumption 'of law' (that is, the real presumption) is merely to invoke a rule of law compelling the jury to reach the conclusion *in the absence of evidence to the contrary* from the opponent." 9 Wigmore, Evidence § 2491 (Chadbourn rev. 1981).

Under the above classic and widely accepted definition, the dubious distinction of being designated a presumption is denied to a rule of law which declares merely that a party's burden of producing evidence as to fact A is sufficiently met by proof of facts B and C without calling for the further consequence that the trier of fact *must* find A from B and C in the absence of contrary evidence. In light of the multiplicity and importance of rules of this latter sort, however, it would seem expedient to have a name for them. Most of the older decisions, and many recent ones, denominate these rules "presumptions of fact" as distinguished from "presumptions of law" (the latter being Wigmore's "real" presumptions). Somewhat in vogue more recently has been the terminology of Professor McCormick who urged that the term presumption should be considered a generic one, embracing both "permissive" and "mandatory" presumptions which "have in common the most important advantage that a presumption, however defined, could give, namely [that of enabling] the proponent to 'get to the jury.' " McCormick, Evidence § 308, at 640–641 (1st ed. 1954). Compare 2 McCormick, Evidence § 342 (6th ed. 2006).

2. *Res ipsa loquitur.* Should facts sufficient to invoke the doctrine of *res ipsa loquitur* be considered to raise a presumption, or merely a permissi-

ble inference? Though the question has been heatedly debated, it currently appears that a large majority of jurisdictions accord the doctrine only the latter effect. Dobbs, The Law of Torts § 156 (2000). Is *McNulty v. Cusack* inconsistent with this majority view? For a criticism of the *McNulty* decision on this basis, see Note, 13 U.Miami L.Rev. 236 (1958).

THE BASES OF PRESUMPTION

What considerations underlie the creation and recognition of presumptions? One of the better judicial statements on the subject is contained in the opinion in Watkins v. Prudential Ins. Co., 173 A. 644, 648 (Pa.1934):

> Presumptions arise as follows: They are either (1) a procedural expedient, or (2) a rule of proof production based upon the comparative availability of material evidence to the respective parties, or (3) a conclusion firmly based upon the generally known results of wide human experience, or (4) a combination of (1) and (3). The presumption as to the survivorship of husband and wife meeting death in a common disaster is a procedural expedient. It is not based upon extensive data arising from human experience. An unexplained absence for seven years raises the presumption of the death of the absentee upon the expiration of the last day of the period. This also is a procedural expedient—an arbitrary but necessary rule for the solution of problems arising from unexplained absences of human beings. An example of (2) is the rule requiring persons on trial for doing certain acts which are illegal if done without a license to produce evidence that they belong to the class privileged by license. See Com. v. Wenzel, 24 Pa.Super.Ct. 467. The following are examples of (3): (a) An envelope properly addressed and stamped will reach the addressee if the latter is alive; (b) a child born during the wedlock of its parents is legitimate; (c) a person who drives across a railroad crossing will show due care. If the driver is killed at such a crossing, the presumption that he showed due care shifts the burden of proof to the party who defends the action on the ground of the victim's want of care. (In this example, the presumption of the victim's due care is merely the converse of the statement that the burden of proof rests on the asserter of the victim's negligence.) A presumption that a debt is paid after a lapse of a definite long period of time is both a procedural expedient (1) and a conclusion based on the results of wide human experience (3).

To the list of reasons for creating presumptions set forth by the Pennsylvania court, most authorities would make at least one addition, that of social policy.

> [N]otions, usually implicit rather than expressed, of social and economic policy incline the courts to favor one contention by giving it the benefit of a presumption, and correspondingly to handicap the disfavored adversary. A classic instance is the presumption of owner-

ship from possession, which tends to favor the prior possessor and to make for the stability of estates.

2 McCormick, Evidence § 343, at 437–38 (6th ed. 2006). For a more elaborate list of considerations underlying the creation of various presumptions, see Morgan, Presumptions, 12 Wash.L.Rev. 255 (1937).

Questions

Upon which one or more of the reasons for raising presumptions did the court rely in recognizing a presumption in *McNulty v. Cusack*? Which, if any, of these considerations would you view as supporting the following commonly recognized presumptions? (1) The presumption that the driver of a motor vehicle is the agent of the owner, acting in the scope of his employment. See Malone v. Hanna, 156 So.2d 626 (Ala.1963). Compare Judson v. Bee Hive Auto Serv. Co., 297 P. 1050, 1052 (Or.1931). (2) The presumption that goods bailed in good condition and returned in damaged condition were damaged through the fault of the bailee. See Richmond Sand & Gravel Corp. v. Tidewater Constr. Corp., 170 F.2d 392 (4th Cir.1948). Compare Wyatt v. Baughman, 239 P.2d 193 (Utah 1951). (3) The presumption that a lost will has been revoked. See In re Givens' Estate, 119 N.W.2d 191 (Iowa 1963).

O'BRIEN v. EQUITABLE LIFE ASSUR. SOC'Y

United States Court of Appeals, Eighth Circuit, 1954.
212 F.2d 383.

COLLET, CIRCUIT JUDGE. This is an action to recover double indemnity insurance for the alleged accidental death of plaintiff's husband. From a directed verdict for the defendant insurance company at the close of all the evidence, plaintiff appeals. The sole question for review is whether plaintiff established a prima facie case warranting its submission to the jury. It is conceded that the law of Missouri is controlling.

The policy provided for the payment of $10,000 upon the death of the insured. That has been paid and is not in dispute. In addition, the policy provided for the payment of an additional $10,000 in the event of accidental death, with certain qualifications. Whether those qualifications, only one of which is now involved, constituted an integral part of the definition of coverage for accidental death, or were exceptions to coverage, is given considerable importance by the parties. The definition of coverage and the qualifications appear in the policy in the following language:

> "The Society agrees, subject to the provisions hereinafter stated, to increase the amount payable under said policy by a sum equal to the face amount thereof upon receipt of due proof, as herein required, that
>
> "(1) the death of the Insured resulted from bodily injuries caused directly and independently of all other causes by external, violent and purely accidental means,
>
> * * *

"(3) such death was not the result of or caused by * * * (d) committing or attempting to commit an assault or felony * * *"

The insured was shot and instantly killed by Robert Jackson on the evening of October 27, 1951, at the home of Virginia Jackson, his wife, from whom he was temporarily separated. There were no witnesses to the shooting and what transpired immediately theretofore except the Jacksons and the deceased. The Jacksons' testimony constitutes substantial but not clear, positive and unequivocal evidence that the insured was at the time of his death committing an assault or a felony, or both, and that that was the cause and reason for the shooting. The husband, Robert Jackson, testified that he heard an outcry from his father's home some 300 feet away, saw something flit by a window, and got his father's revolver, went to the house, found the insured in bed with his wife, and opened fire. Several shots were fired, one of them taking effect in the hips of Virginia Jackson. She substantiated his testimony and testified that she was forced into the bedroom and onto the bed but does not remember what happened after that until the first shot was fired. There was some uncertainty on the part of both Jacksons concerning the number of times they had been married to each other and divorced, but both were sure that at the time in question they were married. There is no conflict in the evidence on that point.

The plaintiff offered in evidence the policy, made proof of death by gunshot wounds inflicted by another, and rested. A motion for a directed verdict was made and denied. The defendant then offered the evidence heretofore referred to, which is uncontradicted and which, as heretofore stated, showed that death occurred while the insured was committing an assault or felony or both. Plaintiff then offered some evidence tending to create the inference that robbery might have been the motive for the shooting. Whether that evidence, together with the other evidence on plaintiff's behalf, was sufficient to make out a submissible case in plaintiff's favor will be alluded to later. At the close of all of the evidence the trial court sustained defendant's motion for a directed verdict.

As stated, this case is to be determined upon principles of law consonant with the law of Missouri. Before considering the legal principles which, in view of the facts, must govern the propriety or impropriety of the directed verdict, it is necessary to keep in mind those double indemnity provisions of the policy, heretofore quoted, which give rise to the instant litigation. It is plaintiff's contention that her burden of establishing a submissible, prima facie case of accidental death was satisfied upon the mere showing of the insurance agreement and the violent death of the insured at the hands of another. Plaintiff insists that defendant had the burden of proving its "affirmative defense" that the insured was engaged in the commission of a felony at the time of his death. Thus it is argued, not without logic, that plaintiff's prima facie case and defendant's affirmative defense should have been submitted to the trier of the facts.

It is fundamental that in cases involving double indemnity benefits the burden of proving accidental death rests firmly upon the plaintiff seeking recovery. * * *

Just what are the evidentiary demands at trial necessary to meet this initial and never shifting burden is obscured considerably by a broad procedural utilization of legal presumptions. To illustrate more graphically, it is said that the burden of proving accidental death rests unswervingly upon the plaintiff, yet, due to recognized human propensities, we will presume that there is so strong a love of life in the human breast that death by one's own hand or by invitation is lacking, in the absence of evidence to the contrary. Sellars v. John Hancock Mutual Life Ins. Co., Mo.App.1941, 149 S.W.2d 404. In this way a prima facie case of accidental death arises from the presumption against nonaccidental death, thereby satisfying plaintiff's burden of proof. Some courts have said that death by accident is not presumed, but merely follows, so to speak, from the presumption *against* suicide or death by invitation. Perringer v. Metropolitan Life Ins. Co., Mo.App.1951, 244 S.W.2d 607. But whether it is said an unexplained violent death will be presumed accidental, or, instead, a showing of violent death merely raises a presumption *against* suicide or invited injury, we think the difference is one without legal distinction. Suffice it to say, an unexplained death by violence is alone sufficient to make out a prima facie case of "accidental death", whether the presumption utilized is one in *favor* of death by accident or *against* death by suicide. Sellars v. John Hancock Mutual Life Ins. Co., supra; cf. Perringer v. Metropolitan Life Ins. Co., supra. As stated in the Sellars case, 149 S.W.2d loc. cit. 405:

> "* * * where no more is shown than the fact of the insured's violent death without the benefit of any of the explanatory circumstances, then such fact, considered in the light of the presumption of love of life which obtains in the case of the normal individual, is so repugnant to the idea of death by intention or invitation as to afford the presumption that death was by accident or accidental means, and thereby satisfy the plaintiff's initial burden of proof upon such issue."

In effect, plaintiff argues that once this "prima facie" case is established, the burden thereafter rests with defendant to prove its affirmative defense on the excepted risk which, whatever the testimony, creates a question of fact submissible to the jury. In so arguing, plaintiff ignores the legal import of the procedural presumption utilized which, unlike the substantive presumption in a res ipsa loquitur case, is not indestructably immune from the effects of refutatory testimony. The presumption of accidental death, while accomplishing the function of evidence in so far as plaintiff's initial burden of going forward is concerned, nevertheless is not evidence of the fact presumed and is merely a rule of procedure or "rebuttable legal presumption". It casts upon defendant the burden of going forward with substantial evidence to the contrary which, if adduced, destroys the procedural presumption on which plaintiff had relied as an evidentiary substitute. As so strikingly quoted by Justice Lamm of the Missouri Supreme Court in Mackowik v. Kansas City, St. J. & C.B.R. Co., 1906, 196 Mo. 550, 94 S.W. 256, 262, " 'Presumptions * * * may be looked on as the bats of the law, flitting in the twilight, but disappearing in the sunshine of actual facts'." The significance of the procedural presumption relates then only to the burden of going forward with testimony, not to the burden of proof. Though the burden of going forward may frequently shift during the course of a trial, the burden of proof remains upon the plaintiff to establish his substantive case.

Where a plaintiff's "prima facie" case vitally depends upon a rebuttable presumption, which is destroyed, then, too, must the "prima facie" case collapse with the presumption, thereby placing upon plaintiff the burden of going forward with evidence sufficient to avoid a directed verdict. Once the presumption is destroyed it is no longer a question of plaintiff's prima facie case versus defendant's affirmative defense, but rather has plaintiff made out a continuing prima facie case at all. Where a rebuttable procedural presumption has been utilized, as in the instant case, at most plaintiff makes out but a "rebuttable" prima facie case which is procedurally but not substantively significant.

With this in mind, we can more easily understand plaintiff's contention that the burden is upon defendant to show facts negating accidental death heretofore presumed. The pitfall lies, however, in confusing this burden, which is one of going *forward* procedurally, with the underlying substantive burden of *proof* which lies constantly with the plaintiff throughout the course of trial. In a limited sense, the insured's commission of a felony or even suicide is always a risk excepted from accident coverage, in that it is incumbent upon defendant initially to bring the issue forth. But the burden is one dictated by the presumption against death from misconduct which, when removed by substantial testimony, shifts the burden of going forward back to plaintiff to establish by evidence what had formerly been presumed. This is entirely consistent with the underlying burden of proof cast upon plaintiff to establish recoverable accidental death within the meaning of the policy.

* * *

In the instant case appellee proffered the direct testimony of Robert and Virginia Jackson relating the manner of and circumstances surrounding the death of the insured. In view of the authorities cited herein, we are convinced that such testimony amply destroyed any presumption of "accidental death" theretofore arising from plaintiff's bare showing of death by violence. The only question remaining is whether the state of the evidence, when viewed in light of plaintiff's underlying burden of proof and absent presumptions, justified a directed verdict. The test to be used has been variously stated. In the Sellars case, the court held, 149 F.2d loc. cit. 406:

> "When contrary facts appear, the presumption [of accidental death] disappears; * * * if the plaintiff, in rebuttal, adduces countervailing evidence supporting the conclusion that death resulted from a cause within the coverage of the policy, then the ultimate

question is one of fact to be determined by the jury as in the case of any other factual issue."

By the foregoing it is not meant that in an action of this kind *any* rebuttal testimony, however, feeble, will suffice to avoid a directed verdict on behalf of the defending insurance company. The "scintilla of evidence" doctrine is no longer the law of Missouri. Hardwick v. Kansas City Gas Co., 1944, 352 Mo. 986, 180 S.W.2d 670. To hold otherwise would be to ignore a plaintiff's burden to establish his case, no longer aided by presumption. Unless the plaintiff produces some substantial evidence negativing the excepted misconduct and thereby brings the death within the coverage of the policy, a directed verdict will be proper. Ray v. Mutual Life Ins. Co. of New York, Mo.App.1949, 218 S.W.2d 986.

In the instant case the only positive evidence proffered was that at the time of his death the insured was committing an assault or a felony. It is only by inference and innuendo that plaintiff suggests that the insured may have been the victim of robbery and foul play. Although plaintiff testified that the insured had some $200 on his person the morning of the fatal day, it would be patently improper to assume that the absence of this money from his personal effects proves thievery claimed his life. To do so we would have to infer that not only did O'Brien have this money with him when he called at the Jackson residence many hours later, but we would have to infer further that theft of this purportedly missing money brought about this tragedy. It requires the citation of no authority that such an inference upon an inference is entitled to no evidentiary consideration. The fact, as testified to by plaintiff, that the insured's trousers were missing is of no substantial evidentiary significance in furthering plaintiff's burden of proving accidental death.

Viewing the circumstances surrounding the insured's death most favorably to plaintiff's hypothesis, we have at most inferences arising which are as consistent with a theory of death while in the commission of a felony as with death by accident. Though plaintiff's initial burden of going forward with the evidence was obviated by a procedural presumption of accidental death, this presumption was destroyed, by the positive, substantial testimony of the two Jacksons, thereby casting upon plaintiff the burden, *ab initio,* of going forward with evidence sufficient to sustain her unshifting and underlying burden of proof on the issue. With this in mind, plaintiff offers only the violent death of the insured from gunshot wounds received at the Jackson residence, and the absence of money, eyeglasses, and certain items of clothing from the personal effects of the insured. Can it be reasonably said that such facts, assuming them to be true, even approach to support plaintiff's burden of proof that the insured was not in the commission of an assault or felony? We think not. The inferences to be gleaned from such evidence are as consistent with defendant's theory of death (which is supported by positive testimony) as they are with plaintiff's. As this court said in New York Life Ins. Co. v. King, 93 F.2d 347, 353:

> "* * * evidence which is equally consistent with two hypotheses, under one of which a defendant is liable, and under the other of which it is not liable, supports neither hypothesis."

Cf., Christianson v. Metropolitan Life Ins. Co., Mo.App.1937, 102 S.W.2d 682; Stafford v. New York Life Ins. Co., Mo.App.1952, 248 S.W.2d 76. Consequently we are convinced the trial court below properly directed a verdict for the defendant.

In view of the foregoing considerations and their decisive effect upon the propriety of the trial court's action, it is unnecessary to consider other grounds advanced by defendant in support of the judgment.

Judgment affirmed.

Notes and Questions

1. *The Thayer doctrine.* Of the many difficult questions concerning presumptions, perhaps none has proven so troublesome as the question of what, if any, continuing effect a presumption should be given once evidence contrary to the presumption has been introduced. The view taken by the court in the principal case, i.e., that a presumption once countered disappears like a "bat of the twilight," is commonly called the Thayer or Thayer–Wigmore doctrine of presumptions. It is today applied by many, perhaps a majority, of the American courts. Annot., 5 A.L.R.3d 19.

2. *Disappearing presumptions.* What, properly, should be understood from the statement that a presumption, once met by counter evidence, disappears? What was the consequence of the disappearance of the presumption involved in *O'Brien v. Equitable Life Assur. Soc.*? Should the same consequence flow whenever a presumption is met by counter evidence and irrespective of what particular presumption is involved? With the principal case, compare Schlichting v. Schlichting, 112 N.W.2d 149, 155–56 (Wis.1961), where the court stated:

> In the instant case, a presumption of undue influence arose from the part which John played in the transaction, the confidential relationship in which John stood to his father, and the advanced age of the father. Christian's testimony * * * does have a tendency to rebut the presumption. However, the introduction of such evidence did not remove from the case the inference upon which such presumption was grounded. Therefore, plaintiff father and his conservator were not thereby reduced to the position where, in order to prevail and set aside the conveyance, they were required to adduce further proof of the four constituent elements of undue influence. Without offering further evidence, they were entitled to judgment if the trial court, in weighing the evidence adduced which tended to negative undue influence against the inference of undue influence arising by reason of the presumption, could reasonably conclude that the weight of the evidence was in favor of a finding of undue influence. * * *
>
> We have no hesitancy in upholding the trial court's finding that the conveyance from Herman to Christian was the result of undue influence exercised by John. The court could reasonably conclude that the evi-

dence adduced to rebut the presumption was too weak to overcome the inference embodied in the presumption.

3. *Life beyond the presumption.* It has been urged that the Thayer doctrine of presumptions, correctly applied, rarely necessitates a result such as that reached in the *O'Brien* case. See Laughlin, In Support of the Thayer Theory of Presumptions, 52 Mich.L.Rev. 195 (1953). Would this thesis seem to be supported by the following statement: "Presumptions in the law are almost invariably crystallized inferences of fact"? In re Estate of Wood, 132 N.W.2d 35, 42 (Mich.1965). See also Widmayer v. Leonard, 373 N.W.2d 538 (Mich.1985) (*Wood* abandoned as to its holding that the trier of fact must be instructed as to the existence of a presumption; however, court notes that "almost all presumptions are made up of permissible inferences").

SAMPLE RULES DEALING WITH THE EFFECT OF PRESUMPTIONS

Model Code of Evidence, Rule 704 (1942). Effect of Presumptions.

(1) * * * when the basic fact of a presumption has been established in an action, the existence of the presumed fact must be assumed unless and until evidence has been introduced which would support a finding of its nonexistence or the basic fact of an inconsistent presumption has been established.

(2) * * * when the basic fact of a presumption has been established in an action and evidence has been introduced which would support a finding of the nonexistence of the presumed fact or the basic fact of an inconsistent presumption has been established, the existence or nonexistence of the presumed fact is to be determined exactly as if no presumption had ever been applicable in the action.

Uniform Rule of Evidence 14 (1953). Effect of Presumptions.

* * * (a) if the facts from which the presumption is derived have any probative value as evidence of the existence of the presumed fact, the presumption continues to exist and the burden of establishing the non-existence of the presumed fact is upon the party against whom the presumption operates, (b) if the facts from which the presumption arises have no probative value as evidence of the presumed fact, the presumption does not exist when evidence is introduced which would support a finding of the non-existence of the presumed fact, and the fact which would otherwise be presumed shall be determined from the evidence exactly as if no presumption was or had ever been involved.

Federal Rule of Evidence 301. Presumptions in General in Civil Actions and Proceedings.

In all civil actions and proceedings not otherwise provided for by Act of Congress or by these rules, a presumption imposes on the party against whom it is directed the burden of going forward with evidence to rebut or meet the presumption, but does not shift to such party the burden of proof in the sense of the risk of nonpersuasion, which remains throughout the trial upon the party on whom it was originally case.

Uniform Rule of Evidence 302(a) (1999). Effect of Presumptions in Civil Cases.

* * * In a civil action of proceeding, unless otherwise provided by statute, judicial decision, or these rules, a presumption imposes on the party against whom it is directed the burden of proving that the nonexistence of the presumed fact is more probable than its existence.

California Evidence Code

§ 603. Presumption affecting the burden of producing evidence defined.

A presumption affecting the burden of producing evidence is a presumption established to implement no public policy other than to facilitate the determination of the particular action in which the presumption is applied.

§ 604. Effect of presumption affecting burden of producing evidence.

The effect of a presumption affecting the burden of producing evidence is to require the trier of fact to assume the existence of the presumed fact unless and until evidence is introduced which would support a finding of its nonexistence, in which case the trier of fact shall determine the existence or nonexistence of the presumed fact from the evidence and without regard to the presumption. Nothing in this section shall be construed to prevent the drawing of any inference that may be appropriate.

§ 605. Presumption affecting the burden of proof defined.

A presumption affecting the burden of proof is a presumption established to implement some public policy other than to facilitate the determination of the particular action in which the presumption is applied, such as the policy in favor of establishment of a parent and child relationship, the validity of marriage, the stability of titles to property, or the security of those who entrust themselves or their property to the administration of others.

§ 606. Effect of presumption affecting burden of proof.

The effect of a presumption affecting the burden of proof is to impose upon the party against whom it operates the burden of proof as to the nonexistence of the presumed fact.

North Carolina Rule of Evidence 301(a). Presumptions in General in Civil Actions and Proceedings.

* * * In all civil actions and proceedings when not otherwise provided for by statute, by judicial decision, or by these rules, a presumption imposes on the party against whom it is directed the burden of going forward with evidence to rebut or meet the presumption, but does not shift to such party the burden of proof in the sense of the risk of

nonpersuasion, which remains throughout the trial upon the party on whom it was originally cast. The burden of going forward is satisfied by the introduction of evidence sufficient to permit reasonable minds to conclude that the presumed fact does not exist. If the party against whom a presumption operates fails to meet the burden of producing evidence, the presumed fact shall be deemed proved, and the court shall instruct the jury accordingly. When the burden of producing evidence to meet a presumption is satisfied, the court must instruct the jury that it may, but is not required to, infer the existence of the presumed fact from the proved fact.

Notes and Questions

1. *The academic debate.* The above samples illustrate some of the many approaches to the question of the effect of presumptions. The debate has been a long and heated one in academic circles. Professor Edmund M. Morgan had long been a critic of the Thayer view of presumptions when he was appointed Reporter for the American Law Institute's (ALI) Model Code of Evidence. As Reporter, Professor Morgan to a limited extent incorporated his own views on presumptions into a draft rule submitted for the Institute's consideration at its 1941 meeting. The ALI rejected his views and instead adopted the rule set forth above. Professor Morgan was later successful in having his views incorporated into the Uniform Rules of Evidence promulgated in 1953 by the Commissioners on Uniform State Laws. In 1954, the ALI withdrew its endorsement of the Model Code and recommended adoption of the Uniform Rules of Evidence.

The rule proposed by Professor Morgan to the American Law Institute and ultimately adopted by the drafters of the Uniform Rules distinguished between presumptions the basic facts of which have probative value as evidence of the presumed fact and presumptions the basic facts of which have no such probative value. This distinction was thought by Professor Morgan to be necessitated by constitutional considerations deriving from Western & Atlantic R.R. v. Henderson, 279 U.S. 639 (1929). See ALI, Model Code of Evidence, Foreword by Edmund M. Morgan 69 (1942). For additional interpretations of the *Henderson* decision, see Keeton, Statutory Presumptions—Their Constitutionality and Effect, 10 Tex.L.Rev. 34 (1931); Note, Constitutionality of Rebuttable Statutory Presumptions, 55 Colum.L.Rev. 527 (1955). The draftsmen of recent codifications of Evidence law have concluded that the *Henderson* case would not today impose any restriction upon implementation of the Morgan treatment of presumptions in civil cases. See Fed.R.Evid. 301 advisory committee's note, 56 F.R.D. 183, 209 (1972); Report of the New Jersey Supreme Court Committee on Evidence 50 (1963). See also 2 McCormick, Evidence § 345 (6th ed. 2006). Constitutional limitations on the creation and effect of presumptions clearly continue to persist in the criminal area. See *County Court of Ulster County v. Allen*, set forth later in this chapter.

Proposed Federal Rule 301 as promulgated by the Supreme Court followed Morgan and the Uniform Rule approach for all presumptions, but a Thayer rule was substituted by the Congress and became Rule 301 set forth above. In 1975, however, the Uniform Commissioners adopted the Court's Morgan rule. This adoption was reaffirmed by the Commissioners in their 1999 amendments.

While rules on presumptions are classifiable as Thayer or Morgan depending upon whether or not they operate upon the burden of persuasion, it should be noted that each generic rule comes in several variants. For an exhaustive analysis and comparison of the Thayer and Morgan rules and their respective subspecies, see Mueller, Instructing the Jury Upon Presumptions in Civil Cases: Comparing Federal Rule 301 with Uniform Rule 301, 12 Land & W.L.Rev. 219 (1977). For an assessment of which type of Thayer rule is embodied in Rule 301, see Louisell, Construing Rule 301: Instructing the Jury on Presumptions in Civil Actions and Proceedings, 63 Va.L.Rev. 281 (1977). A general treatment of presumptions is Ladd, Presumptions in Civil Cases, 1977 Ariz.St.L.J. 275.

The states are divided as to whether they adopt the Federal Rules approach allocating only the burden of producing evidence to the party against whom the presumption is directed or the Uniform Rules approach allocating the burden of persuasion to that party. Compare Colo.R.Evid. 301 (burden of producing evidence allocated), with Wis.Stat.Ann. 903.01 (burden of persuasion allocated). As set forth above, California gives a different effect to different kinds of presumptions. Compare the California approach to that of the original Uniform Rules of Evidence. Isn't the approach the exact opposite? Which approach better reflects the policy behind presumptions?

2. *Elimination of the term "presumption."* Some authors have argued for elimination of the term "presumption." One has called for the replacement of the functions which it serves with direct allocations of the burdens of proof and by judicial comment describing the logical implications of certain facts. Allen, Presumptions, Inferences and Burden of Proof in Federal Civil Actions—An Anatomy of Unnecessary Ambiguities and a Proposal for Reform, 76 Nw.U.L.Rev. 892 (1982); Allen, Presumptions in Civil Actions Reconsidered, 66 Iowa L.Rev. 843 (1981). See also Cleary, Presuming and Pleading: An Essay on Juristic Immaturity, 12 Stan.L.Rev. 5 (1959). See discussion in 2 McCormick, Evidence § 344 (6th ed. 2006).

3. *Statutory presumptions.* In addition to the classic debate directed primarily to common law presumptions, there has been considerable controversy over legislative intent, especially congressional intent, in dealing with statutory presumptions. The public policy debate has raged with special fervor in the field of employment discrimination. See Texas Dep't of Community Affairs v. Burdine, 450 U.S. 248 (1981); St. Mary's Honor Ctr. v. Hicks, 509 U.S. 502 (1993); Note, Developments in the Law—Employment Discrimination, 109 Harv.L.Rev. 1579 (1996).

4. *Use of the term "presumption" in jury instructions.* Judge Learned Hand wrote, in Alpine Forwarding Co. v. Pennsylvania R.R., 60 F.2d 734, 736 (2d Cir.1932), that "if the trial is properly conducted the presumption will not be mentioned [to the jury] at all." What, if anything, is objectionable in the contrary view taken by some courts that a presumption constitutes "evidence" which the jury may be instructed to weigh against other countervailing evidence? Do any difficulties with this approach appear if the presumption involved is not a pure probability presumption but is based, wholly

or partially, upon considerations of social policy or procedural convenience? See McBaine, Presumptions, Are They Evidence?, 26 Cal.L.Rev. 519 (1938). Some states have specifically provided for the jury to be told something about the presumption. The Alaska rule is similar to the North Carolina rule set forth above but at the same time prohibits the judge from using the word presumption. See Alaska R.Evid. 301(a). The next principal case raises additional questions with regard to instructions on presumptions.

5. *The Shakespeare authorship debate*. For an interesting application of the law of burdens of proof and presumptions to the debate over who wrote the works attributed to William Shakespeare, see Causey, Burden of Proof and Presumptions in the Shakespeare Authorship Debate, 72 Tenn.L.Rev. 93 (2004).

STATE OF MARYLAND v. BALTIMORE TRANSIT CO.

United States Court of Appeals, Fourth Circuit, 1964.
329 F.2d 738.

J. SPENCER BELL, CIRCUIT JUDGE. The plaintiffs' intestate was killed at a street corner in the city of Baltimore when struck by a bus owned by the defendant Transit Company and driven by the individual defendant. Judgment was entered for the defendants upon a general verdict. Plaintiffs allege that the court erred in charging the jury as follows:

> "I instruct you that ordinarily, a decedent is presumed to have exercised ordinary care for his own safety in accordance with the natural instinct of human beings to guard against danger, but where as here, evidence has been offered to show that the decedent failed to exercise ordinary care in a number of respects, you shall consider the proof which has been offered and determine whether you are persuaded by a preponderance of the evidence that he failed to exercise ordinary care, and you are not to reply upon the presumption."

Both parties to this appeal concede, and we agree, that the federal courts are bound in diversity cases by the applicable state rules with respect to the effect to be given to presumptions, "since the effect accorded these presumptions may substantially affect the rights of the parties and there is nothing in the Federal Rules to the contrary." 5 Moore's Federal Practice § 43.08. The plaintiffs had submitted a written request for an instruction to the jury that they might consider the presumption of due care in connection with the other evidence. The court rejected the request and instructed the jury as above set out. In this we find fatal error.

The principal Maryland case on this point is Grier v. Rosenberg, 213 Md. 248, 131 A.2d 737 (1957). In that case the plaintiff, a passenger, was injured by the sudden stopping of the bus. She sued the bus company, the bus driver, and one Rosenberg, who was the owner of an automobile which, the bus driver testified, cut sharply across his path and caused him to come to a sudden stop. The jury rendered a verdict for all three defendants. The plaintiff appealed from a judgment for the car owner, Rosenberg. The Court of Appeals of Maryland reversed the judgment and remanded the case for a new trial. In doing so the court pointed out that the plaintiff had offered evidence from which the jury could find ownership of the car in the defendant Rosenberg. She had asked for an instruction that from this evidence, if believed, a presumption arose that the car was being driven by the owner or by the owner's agent about the owner's business. The trial court refused to give the instruction because the defendant had offered evidence which conflicted with the presumption. The appellate court held failure to give the instruction was fatal. In a careful review of the Maryland decisions and authorities in the field of Evidence, Judge Prescott said that the presumption prevails and the jury should have been so instructed despite the fact that countervailing evidence was adduced upon the disputed presumption. The court said:

> "In cases of this nature, after the plaintiff has offered proof of the ownership of the automobile in the defendant, if the defendant does not offer any evidence on the issue of agency, the Court should instruct the jury that if they find as a fact that the defendant owned the car, they must find that he is responsible for the negligence (if any) of the driver. If the defendant does present evidence to show that the alleged driver was engaged on business or a purpose of his own, it may be so slight that the Court will rule it is insufficient to be considered by the jury in rebuttal of the presumption, in which case the Court should grant the same instruction it would have granted if the defendant had offered no evidence on the issue. The evidence may be so conclusive that it shifts the burden or duty of going forward with the evidence back to the plaintiff, in which event the defendant would be entitled to a directed verdict, if the plaintiff does not produce evidence in reply, unless there is already evidence in the case tending to contradict defendant's evidence. Erdman v. Horkheimer & Co., supra, 169 Md. [204] 207, 181 A. 221; Fowser Fast Freight v. Simmont, supra, 196 Md. [584] 588, 78 A.2d 178. The evidence, however, may fall between the two categories mentioned above, in which event the issue of agency should be submitted to the jury. Cf. 3 Md.Law Rev. 287, 288. It would be difficult, if not impossible, to lay down a rule, that would apply in all cases, as to when the evidence is so slight that it is insufficient to be considered by the jury in rebuttal of the presumption of agency, or so conclusive as to require a directed verdict for the defendant. These matters must depend upon, and be decided by, the facts developed in each individual case."

The defendant in this appeal argues that Grier v. Rosenberg is not applicable because the evidence there offered in rebuttal of the presumption was so slight that the trial court would have been justified in holding that it was insufficient to be submitted to the jury in the face of the presumption, but such was not the holding of the court. Indeed, the appellant in the Grier case made the point in an effort to secure a reversal instead of a remand for a new trial, but the argument was rejected. The court expressly held that the conflicting evidence was enough to take the case to the jury.

The defendant here also argues that the presumption in Grier v. Rosenberg is different from the presumption of due care here considered and thus that case may not be taken as a precedent. With this argument we must also disagree, because first, we can find no case in Maryland which makes any such distinction and second, in reaching its decision the court reviewed and cited cases involving the presumption of due care in negligence cases in support of its opinion.

Our dissenting Brother similarly misinterprets Grier v. Rosenberg and would unduly restrict its rule. We perceive no basis in law or in logic for the suggested distinction; but more importantly, Judge Prescott, speaking for the Maryland Court, explicitly pointed out that the precedents in that State recognize no basis for any distinction between the presumption that the decedent exercised due care for his self-preservation and the presumption of agency arising from the fact of ownership. And this observation of Judge Prescott is immediately followed by the very sensible question, "[I]ndeed, if the instruction be not granted, how is the jury to know of the presumption?"

* * *

We are * * * aware that in many states the rule as to presumptions is to the contrary—that is, that the presumption survives only until conflicting evidence is offered. This is the rule suggested in the American Law Institute's Model Code of Evidence, Rule 704. It is the rule attributed to Thayer and suggested by Wigmore. But we are bound by the law of Maryland, and we might add that the Maryland rule is strongly supported by such eminent authorities as McCormick, Evidence §§ 316, 317 (1954), and by the writings of Professor Morgan, who, contrary to his expressed opinions, finally acceeded [sic] to the wishes of the committee in drafting the Model Code.

* * *

We are unable to acquiesce in the final suggestion in our colleague's dissenting opinion, that the presumption in Maryland that the decedent acted with due care stands on a parity with the presumption that the defendant was free from negligence and that therefore the district court should tell the jury at the retrial that the presumption as to the disposition to act in self-preservation applies equally to the defendant's driver. The comment is then added that the result would be a radical distortion, and perversion. This comment would indeed be true, if the trial judge were to permit such a confusing double instruction, linking and treating as equal two entirely disparate and unequal ideas. The presumption with which we are concerned in this case may be invoked only where the injured person is unavailable because of the injuries suffered or because of death. Such incapacity is the just reason for the presumption; the premise upon which the presumption rests is lacking in the situation of this defendant.

* * *

Reversed and remanded.

HAYNSWORTH, CIRCUIT JUDGE (dissenting).

I am unpersuaded that Maryland would attribute any such evidentiary effect to the presumption as the majority conclude on the basis of an opinion of the Maryland Court of Appeals dealing with a different presumption in a very dissimilar context.

* * *

The question of the office of the presumption arises in this case under the following circumstances. Witnesses for the plaintiff testified that her decedent was crossing a street in downtown Baltimore at an intersection and in a marked pedestrian crosswalk, with the invitation and the protection of an electric "walk" signal, when he was struck by the bus. Witnesses for the defendant, however, testified that the decedent undertook to cross the street some distance from the intersection and the pedestrian crosswalk and without the invitation or protection of an electric signal. The evidence was sharply conflicting, but there was no dearth of it. Resolution by the jury of the factual question on the contributory negligence issue depended simply upon whether the jurors believed the one set of witnesses or the other. No presumption artificially endowed with evidentiary weight was needful or useful to them in resolving the simple issue of credibility which was presented to them.

The District Court, of course, instructed the jury that the defendant had the burden of proving by a preponderance of the evidence that the decedent was contributorily negligent. On this question of fact, the Court clearly and unequivocally placed the burden of persuasion upon the defendant. If the jury, under its instructions, was unable to decide the issue of credibility upon which its finding of the decedent's conduct depended, if its mind was in equipoise, it was required to find for the plaintiff. If, then, my brothers are correct that under the Maryland law the jury should have been allowed to consider as evidence the presumption of due care, then the office of the presumption was not merely to place upon the defense the burden of producing evidence sufficient to support a finding inconsistent with the presumed fact; it was not merely to place upon the defendant the burden of persuasion on the factual question underlying the contributory negligence issue; it is to require that the defendant carry the burden of persuasion by a measure of proof greater than a mere preponderance of the evidence. How much greater the burden placed upon the defense to prove its contention beyond a preponderance of evidence, the majority does not specify, but it would invite them to apply a standard of proof akin to that applicable in criminal cases, that they must be persuaded beyond all reasonable doubt, for jurors are not unaware of the existence of that standard.

Having in mind the circumstances in which the question now arises and the practical effect of the instruction which my brothers now require, it is appropriate to turn to Grier v. Rosenberg upon which my brothers' hats are hung.

* * *

Maryland's Court of Appeals held in Grier that the jury should have been instructed that a presumption that Rosenberg, or one of his authorized employees, was driving the car arose out of proof of his ownership of it which they might consider along with the defendant's testimony indicating that it was not.

In Grier, of course, unlike the present case, there was a dearth of proof. Beyond proof of the basic fact of Rosenberg's ownership of the offending vehicle, the plaintiff had no source of reliable information. The ultimate fact was peculiarly within the knowledge of her adversary, and the kind of general disclaimer he entered was not susceptible to direct contradiction. There was thus a compelling need for some instruction to inform the jury that it need not accept Rosenberg's self-serving testimony as conclusive of the plaintiff's rights.

The two presumptions are in sharp contrast. That with which the court was concerned in Grier arose out of proof of basic, evidentiary facts which were logically related to it. In the absence of some instruction, there was grave danger that the jury would not appreciate the evidentiary value of the basic, proven facts. The presumption of due care, however, is not dependent upon proof of any basic fact or facts. There is in this case no circumstantial evidence, the utility of which might go unnoticed by the jury in the absence of some instruction which would draw their attention to it.

Grier's formulation may be offensive to Thayerian purists, but clearly the circumstances there called for some instruction which would inform the jurors that they were not bound to accept Rosenberg's self-serving testimony. The jury could have been told that a permissible inference that Rosenberg, or his authorized servant, was driving the offending automobile might be drawn from proof of his ownership of it, and that it was for the jury to determine, after consideration of Rosenberg's denials, whether or not his automobile at the time was being driven by him or one of his employees engaged in Rosenberg's business. An instruction in terms of the presumption would have no other practical effect.

Thus in Grier, reference to the presumption of the identity and authority of the driver arising out of proof of ownership of the vehicle did not place upon Rosenberg a greater burden of persuasion than proof by a preponderance of the evidence. * * *

That a court holds under certain circumstances that a jury should be informed of the existence of a particular presumption, is far from persuasive authority that a different presumption having a wholly different relationship to the basic fact out of which it arises should be mentioned to a jury under different circumstances and with wholly different consequences. Indeed, it is trite now to repeat what everyone addressing himself to the subject has said that so much of the confusion over presumptions springs from failure to distinguish between different presumptions and the different situations out of which the problems regarding their use arise.

The occasion seems inappropriate for entry upon the controversy over the relative merits of any particular theory about the employment of presumptions and their offices. Since my brothers read Grier as taking Maryland out of the main stream of the prevailing current of thought, I may briefly refer to those authorities which my brothers adroitly, but it seems to me inexactly, align on one side or the other, for I can give Grier no such reading.

Thayer thought that presumptions of the sort with which the Maryland Court was concerned in Grier should have no other office than to shift the burden of producing enough evidence to support a finding inconsistent with the fact sought to be presumed. When such evidence comes into the case, the presumption disappears. This is the theory adopted by the American Law Institute's Model Code of Evidence in Rule 704.

Professor Edmund Morgan, when he first began to write about presumptions, expounded a complicated theory which would attribute to some presumptions a larger effect, but he, himself, withdrew from that suggestion long before he began to work as Reporter for the American Law Institute in the formulation of the Model Code of Evidence. When he approached that task, he was firmly of the view that such a presumption should not only shift the burden of production of evidence but should fix the ultimate burden of persuasion. He thought it should have no other office. * * * As we have indicated, the Court in this case clearly placed the burden of persuasion upon the defendant, which is all that Professor Morgan would require. Even his earliest writings ascribed no such undefined and unbounded evidentiary effect to presumptions as the majority would attribute to this one.

Wigmore, in general, supports the Thayerian view, but he clearly recognizes that there are times and circumstances calling for mention to a jury of a presumption, though he would not have that word employed by the court. In the circumstances of Grier v. Rosenberg, Wigmore advocates an instruction to the jury that it is bound by no rule of law in deciding the issue, but it may give special weight, in its discretion, to the fact that in the course of experience automobiles not shown to have been stolen are usually driven by their owners or their authorized servants. This is plainly stated in ¶ 21 under Remedies in § 2498a.[3]

I find in McCormick on Evidence nothing which lends support to what the majority does here. In §§ 316 and 317, to which the majority opinion refers, Professor McCormick is principally concerned with the

3. IX Wigmore on Evidence, 3d ed., pages 340–341. See, also, ¶ 41 on page 343 and the illuminating comments of others on pages 348–350.

preservation of the practical utility of circumstantial evidence in the face of inconsistent evidence, however incredible, going directly to the ultimate fact and the mechanics of telling the jury how to resolve the issue when the basic facts upon which the presumption rests are in dispute. In the first mentioned aspect of the problem he is dealing with the Grier v. Rosenberg situation. * * * McCormick may be searched in vain for any hint that a presumption may be used to place a heavier, undefined burden of persuasion on the presumption's opponent, or that a presumption having no evidentiary basis may be given evidentiary value.

* * * What the Maryland Court of Appeals did in Grier v. Rosenberg, and all that it did, was to leave in the case a permissible inference inconsistent with the defendant's weak, self-serving denial of the ultimate fact. If, in the courts of a state whose trial judges are not allowed to comment upon the evidence, this must be done in terms of a presumption rather than in terms of a permissible inference, the effect is the same.

Far from being a departure from the current course of thought about presumptions, Grier v. Rosenberg is a specific application of the affirmatively expressed teachings of Wigmore. That decision is no premise for a conclusion that it is a rejection of what it embraces. What my brothers do is certainly a rejection of Wigmore's theory,[4] as they recognize, but Grier v. Rosenberg, the platform upon which they stand, was not.

* * *

Finally, it may be observed that in Maryland the presumption that the decedent acted with due care for his own self-protection is no stronger and stands on no higher basis than the presumption that the driver of the bus that killed him acted with due care for the safety of pedestrians and others using the streets. Indeed, Maryland's Court of Appeals has spoken of the two presumptions in the same breath.[5] If, therefore, upon a new trial, the District Court is to be required to inform the jury of the one and permit it to weigh it as evidence, surely it must inform the jury of the other and permit it to weigh that one as evidence, too. The result will be a radical distortion and perversion of the burden of persuasion, but if the burden of persuasion resting on the defendant on the contributory negligence question is to be enlarged to confusing proportions, it cannot logically or fairly be said that the burden of persuasion resting upon the plaintiff as to the primary negligence

4. The presumption of due care, as we have noted, is not dependent upon proof of any basic fact or facts. If it be given no substantive, evidentiary value, it leaves no base of proven facts from which an inference of due care might conceivably be drawn. The presumption is wholly unlike those which Wigmore and McCormick think require some instruction to the jury in some situations, and the difference is critical. We have here no problem of preservation of the practical utility of circumstantial evidence; the jury was here called upon only to resolve, on conflicting, direct evidence, a simple question of credibility.

5. P.W. & B.R.R. Co. v. Stebbing, 62 Md. 504 (1884); State, for Use of Chenoweth v. Baltimore Contracting Co., 177 Md. 1, 6 A.2d 625 (1939).

question is not similarly enlarged to undefined proportions by the identical presumption of due care.

* * *

I thus do not understand that Maryland has held, or even suggested, that the presumption of due care is to be given evidentiary effect if the actor is dead, but not if alive. Though, here, the plaintiff's decedent is unavailable as a witness while the defendant's bus driver presumably is available. I do not think those circumstances warrant disparate treatment of the concomitant presumptions.

Unconvinced that Maryland's Court of Appeals would apply to the presumption of due care the undefined evidentiary weight attributed to it by my brothers, I respectfully dissent.

Notes and Questions

1. *The Maryland aftermath.* In 1994, Maryland sought to codify the approach to presumptions taken in Grier v. Rosenberg, 131 A.2d 737 (Md.1957), the case upon which the majority in the principal case relies, by enacting Rule of Evidence 5–301. See Note, Court of Appeals Standing Committee on Practice and Procedure to Rule 5–301. The rule provides, with regard to all presumptions that shift the burden of going forward: "If the party introduces evidence tending to disprove the presumed fact, the presumption will retain the effect of creating a question to be decided by the trier of fact unless the court concludes that such evidence is legally insufficient or is so conclusive that it rebuts the presumption as a matter of law." The Rule has not been construed as mandating an instruction with regard to the presumption of due care in a situation like that in the *Baltimore Transit Co.* case. Indeed the question of whether to instruct or not is more complex than ever. See McQuay v. Schertle, 730 A.2d 714 (Md.Ct.Spec.App.1999) (trial judge had discretion not to instruct the jury on decedent's due care where there was eyewitness testimony about the decedent's conduct immediately before the accident).

Washington, another jurisdiction in which contributory negligence is an affirmative defense, finally abandoned the giving of the presumption instruction discussed in the principal case. For thoughtful analysis and discussion, see Falknor, Notes on Presumptions, 15 Wash.L.Rev. 71 (1940), and Comment, 29 Wash.L.Rev. 79 (1954) in Selected Writings on Evidence and Trial 1020, 1032 (Fryer ed. 1957).

2. *One rule for all presumptions?* On what basis does Judge Haynsworth, dissenting in the principal case, refuse to view *Grier v. Rosenberg* as controlling authority? In connection with Judge Haynsworth's discussion consider the following statement: "The theoretically sound view, therefore is that 'the procedural effect of each presumption should depend upon the reasons which induced the courts to create or enforce it, [but it] has met with little favor, principally because of the practical difficulties of applying it at the trial.' " Gausewitz, Presumptions in a One Rule World, 5 Vand.L.Rev. 324, 330 (1952). See also Broun, The Unfulfillable Promise of One Rule for All Presumptions, 62 N.C.L.Rev. 697 (1984); Hjelmaas, Stepping Back from

the Thicket: A Proposal for the Treatment of Rebuttable Presumptions and Inferences, 42 Drake L.Rev. 427 (1993). Note that the existence of Federal 301 has not prevented the federal courts from giving some presumptions stronger effects where so desired. See, e.g., Fazio v. Heckler, 760 F.2d 187 (8th Cir.1985) (Social Security Act); ACS Hospital Systems, Inc. v. Montefiore Hosp., 732 F.2d 1572 (Fed.Cir.1984) (validity of a patent). What practical difficulties might be involved in the attempt to attach varying procedural effects to different presumptions depending upon the reasons for their creation? See Maguire, Evidence, Common Sense and Common Law 188 (1947). If these difficulties are critical [and at least one court has intimated that they are not, see O'Dea v. Amodeo, 170 A. 486 (Conn.1934)], are they of such a nature as to be obviated by a legislative rather than a judicial attack on the problem?

3. *Conflicting presumptions.* It will sometimes occur that each of two adverse contentions as to the same fact is supported by a different presumption, raising the problem of what are generally called "conflicting presumptions." Under this definition would it be improper to refer to the two presumptions arguably applicable in the principal case as "conflicting"? How should a conflict of presumptions, when one exists, be resolved? See Turro v. Turro, 120 A.2d 52 (N.J.Super.Ct.App.Div.1956).

4. The court's decision in the principal case to follow Maryland law with regard to the effect to be given to presumptions is consistent with current law. See Federal Rule 302.

COUNTY COURT OF ULSTER COUNTY v. ALLEN

Supreme Court of the United States, 1979.
442 U.S. 140.

MR. JUSTICE STEVENS delivered the opinion of the Court.

A New York statute provides that, with certain exceptions, the presence of a firearm in an automobile is presumptive evidence of its illegal possession by all persons then occupying the vehicle. The United States Court of Appeals for the Second Circuit held that respondents may challenge the constitutionality of this statute in a federal habeas corpus proceeding and that the statute is "unconstitutional on its face." * * * We granted certiorari to review these holdings and also to consider whether the statute is constitutional in its application to respondents. * * *

Four persons, three adult males (respondents) and a 16–year–old girl (Jane Doe, who is not a respondent here), were jointly tried on charges that they possessed two loaded handguns, a loaded machinegun, and over a pound of heroin found in a Chevrolet in which they were riding when it was stopped for speeding on the New York Thruway shortly after noon on March 28, 1973. The two large-caliber handguns, which together with their ammunition weighed approximately six pounds, were seen through the window of the car by the investigating police officer. They were positioned crosswise in an open handbag on either the front floor or the front seat of the car on the passenger side where Jane Doe was sitting. Jane Doe admitted that the handbag was hers. The machinegun and the heroin were discovered in the trunk after the police pried it open. The car had been borrowed from the driver's brother earlier that day; the key to the trunk could not be found in the car or on the person of any of its occupants, although there was testimony that two of the occupants had placed something in the trunk before embarking in the borrowed car. The jury convicted all four of possession of the handguns and acquitted them of possession of the contents of the trunk.

Counsel for all four defendants objected to the introduction into evidence of the two handguns, the machinegun, and the drugs, arguing that the State had not adequately demonstrated a connection between their clients and the contraband. The trial court overruled the objection, relying on the presumption of possession created by the New York statute. * * * Because that presumption does not apply if a weapon is found "upon the person" of one of the occupants of the car, * * * the three male defendants also moved to dismiss the charges relating to the handguns on the ground that the guns were found on the person of Jane Doe. Respondents made this motion both at the close of the prosecution's case and at the close of all evidence. The trial judge twice denied it, concluding that the applicability of the "on the person" exception was a question of fact for the jury. * * *

At the close of the trial, the judge instructed the jurors that they were entitled to infer possession from the defendants' presence in the car. He did not make any reference to the "upon the person" exception in his explanation of the statutory presumption, nor did any of the defendants object to this omission or request alternative or additional instructions on the subject.

Defendants filed a post-trial motion in which they challenged the constitutionality of the New York statute as applied in this case. The challenge was made in support of their argument that the evidence, apart from the presumption, was insufficient to sustain the convictions. The motion was denied, * * * and the convictions were affirmed by the Appellate Division without opinion. * * *

The New York Court of Appeals also affirmed. It rejected the argument that as a matter of law the guns were on Jane Doe's person because they were in her pocketbook. Although the court recognized that in some circumstances the evidence could only lead to the conclusion that the weapons were in one person's sole possession, it held that this record presented a jury question on that issue. Since the defendants had not asked the trial judge to submit the question to the jury, the Court of Appeals treated the case as though the jury had resolved this fact question in the prosecution's favor. It therefore concluded that the presumption did apply and that there was sufficient evidence to support the convictions. * * * It also summarily rejected the argument that the presumption was unconstitutional as applied in this case. * * *

Respondents filed a petition for a writ of habeas corpus in the United States District Court for the Southern District of New York contending that they were denied due process of law by the application of the statutory presumption of possession. The District Court issued the writ, holding that respondents had not "deliberately bypassed" their federal claim by their actions at trial and that the mere presence of two guns in a woman's handbag in a car could not reasonably give rise to the inference that they were in the possession of three other persons in the car. * * *

The Court of Appeals for the Second Circuit affirmed, but for different reasons. First, the entire panel concluded that the New York Court of Appeals had decided respondents' constitutional claim on its merits rather than on any independent state procedural ground that might have barred collateral relief. Then, the majority of the court, without deciding whether the presumption was constitutional as applied in this case, concluded that the statute is unconstitutional on its face because the "presumption obviously sweeps within its compass (1) many occupants who may not know they are riding with a gun (which may be out of their sight), and (2) many who may be aware of the presence of the gun but not permitted access to it." Concurring separately, Judge Timbers agreed with the District Court that the statute was unconstitutional as applied but considered it improper to reach the issue of the statute's facial constitutionality. * * *

The State's petition for a writ of certiorari presented three questions: (1) whether the District Court had jurisdiction to entertain respondents' claim that the presumption is unconstitutional; (2) whether it was proper for the Court of Appeals to decide the facial constitutionality issue; and (3) whether the application of the presumption in this case is unconstitutional. We answer the first question in the affirmative, the second two in the negative. We accordingly reverse.

I

[In this section of its opinion, the Court concluded that the decisions of the New York courts had not been based upon independent state grounds, and that the case was therefore properly before the federal courts.]

II

Although § 2254 authorizes the federal courts to entertain respondents' claim that they are being held in custody in violation of the Constitution, it is not a grant of power to decide constitutional questions not necessarily subsumed within that claim. * * *

A party has standing to challenge the constitutionality of a statute only insofar as it has an adverse impact on his own rights. As a general rule, if there is no constitutional defect in the application of the statute to a litigant, he does not have standing to argue that it would be unconstitutional if applied to third parties in hypothetical situations. Broadrick v. Oklahoma, 413 U.S. 601, 610 (and cases cited). A limited exception has been recognized for statutes that broadly prohibit speech protected by the First Amendment. Id., at 611–616. This exception has been justified by the overriding interest in removing illegal deterrents to the exercise of the right of free speech. E.g., Gooding v. Wilson, 405 U.S. 518, 520; Dombrowski v. Pfister, 380 U.S. 479, 486. That justification, of course, has no application to a statute that enhances the legal risks associated with riding in vehicles containing dangerous weapons.

In this case the Court of Appeals undertook the task of deciding the constitutionality of the New York statute "on its face." Its conclusion that the statutory presumption was arbitrary rested entirely on its view of the fairness of applying the presumption in hypothetical situations—situations, indeed, in which it is improbable that a jury would return a conviction, or that a prosecution would ever be instituted. We must accordingly inquire whether these respondents had standing to advance the arguments that the Court of Appeals considered decisive. An analysis of our prior cases indicates that the answer to this inquiry depends on the type of presumption that is involved in the case.

Inferences and presumptions are a staple of our adversarial system of factfinding. It is often necessary for the trier of fact to determine the existence of an element of the crime—that is, an "ultimate" or "elemental" fact—from the existence of one or more "evidentiary" or "basic" facts. * * * The value of these evidentiary devices, and their validity under the Due Process Clause, vary from case to case, however, depending on the strength of the connection between the particular basic and elemental facts involved and on the degree to which the device curtails the factfinder's freedom to assess the evidence independently. Nonetheless, in criminal cases, the ultimate test of any device's constitutional validity in a given case remains constant: the device must not undermine the factfinder's responsibility at trial, based on evidence adduced by the State, to find the ultimate facts beyond a reasonable doubt. See In re Winship, 397 U.S. 358, 364; Mullaney v. Wilbur, 421 U.S. 684, 702–703 n.31.

The most common evidentiary device is the entirely permissive inference or presumption, which allows—but does not require—the trier of fact to infer the elemental fact from proof by the prosecutor of the basic one and that places no burden of any kind on the defendant. See, e.g., Barnes v. United States, 412 U.S., at 840 n.3. In that situation the basic fact may constitute prima facie evidence of the elemental fact. See, e.g., Turner v. United States, 396 U.S. 398, 402 n.2. When reviewing this type of device, the Court has required the party challenging it to demonstrate its invalidity as applied to him. * * * Because this permissive presumption leaves the trier of fact free to credit or reject the inference and does not shift the burden of proof, it affects the application of the "beyond a reasonable doubt" standard only if, under the facts of the case, there is no rational way the trier could make the connection permitted by the inference. For only in that situation is there any risk that an explanation of the permissible inference to a jury, or its use by a jury, has caused the presumptively rational factfinder to make an erroneous factual determination.

A mandatory presumption is a far more troublesome evidentiary device. For it may affect not only the strength of the "no reasonable doubt" burden but also the placement of that burden; it tells the trier that he or they *must* find the elemental fact upon proof of the basic fact, at least unless the defendant has come forward with some evidence to rebut the presumed connection between the two facts. * * *[6] In this situation, the Court has generally examined the presumption on its face to determine the extent to which the basic and elemental facts coincide. * * * To the extent that the trier of fact is forced to abide by the presumption, and may not reject it based on an independent evaluation

6. This class of more or less mandatory presumptions can be subdivided into two parts: presumptions that merely shift the burden of production to the defendant, following the satisfaction of which the ultimate burden of persuasion returns to the prosecution; and presumptions that entirely shift the burden of proof to the defendant. The mandatory presumptions examined by our cases have almost uniformly fit into the former subclass, in that they never totally removed the ultimate burden of proof beyond a reasonable doubt from the prosecution. E.g., Tot v. United States, supra, at 469. See Roviaro v. United States, 353 U.S. 53, 63, describing the operation of the presumption involved in *Turner, Leary,* and *Romano.*

To the extent that a presumption imposes an extremely low burden of production—e.g., being satisfied by "any" evidence—it may well be that its impact is no greater than that of a permissive inference and it may be proper to analyze it as such. See generally Mullaney v. Wilbur, supra, 421 U.S., at 703 n.31.

In deciding what type of inference or presumption is involved in a case, the jury instructions will generally be controlling, although their interpretation may require recourse to the statute involved and the cases decided under it. Turner v. United States, supra, provides a useful illustration of the different types of presumptions. It analyzes the constitutionality of two different presumption statutes (one mandatory and one permissive) as they apply to the basic fact of possession of both heroin and cocaine, and the presumed facts of importation and distribution of narcotic drugs. The jury was charged essentially in the terms of the two statutes.

The importance of focusing attention on the precise presentation of the presumption to the jury and the scope of that presumption is illustrated by a comparison of United States v. Gainey, 380 U.S. 63, with United States v. Romano, 382 U.S. 136. Both cases involved statutory presumptions based on proof that the defendant was present at the site of an illegal still. In *Gainey* the Court sustained a conviction "for carrying on" the business of the distillery in violation of 26 U.S.C. § 5601(a)(4), whereas in *Romano,* the Court set aside a conviction for being in "possession, custody, and * * * control" of such a distillery in violation of § 5601(a)(1). The difference in outcome was attributable to two important differences between the cases. Because the statute involved in *Gainey* was a sweeping prohibition of almost any activity associated with the still, whereas the *Romano* statute involved only one narrow aspect of the total undertaking, there was a much higher probability that mere presence could support an inference of guilt in the former case than in the latter.

Of perhaps greater importance, however, was the difference between the trial judge's instructions to the jury in the two cases. In *Gainey* the judge had explained that the presumption was permissive; it did not require the jury to convict the defendant even if it was convinced that he was present at the site. On the contrary, the instructions made it clear that presence was only "a circumstance to be considered along with all the other circumstances in the case." As we emphasized, the "jury was thus specifically told that the statutory [presumption] was not conclusive." 380 U.S., at 69–70. In *Romano* the trial judge told the jury that the defendant's presence at the still "shall be deemed sufficient evidence to authorize conviction." 382 U.S., at 138. Although there was other evidence of guilt, that instruction authorized conviction even if the jury disbelieved all of the testimony except the proof of presence at the site. This Court's holding that the statutory presumption could not support the *Romano* conviction was thus dependent, in part, on the specific instructions given by the trial judge. Under those instructions it was necessary to decide whether, regardless of the specific circumstances of the particular case, the statutory presumption adequately supported the guilty verdict.

of the particular facts presented by the State, the analysis of the presumption's constitutional validity is logically divorced from those facts and based on the presumption's accuracy in the run of cases.[7] It is for this reason that the Court has held it irrelevant in analyzing a mandatory presumption, but not in analyzing a purely permissive one, that there is ample evidence in the record other than the presumption to support a conviction.* * *

Without determining whether the presumption in this case was mandatory, the Court of Appeals analyzed it on its face as if it were. In fact, it was not, as the New York Court of Appeals had earlier pointed out. 40 N.Y.2d, at 510–511, 387 N.Y.S.2d, at 100, 354 N.E.2d, at 840.

The trial judge's instructions make it clear that the presumption was merely a part of the prosecution's case, that it gave rise to a permissive inference available only in certain circumstances, rather than a mandatory conclusion of possession, and that it could be ignored by the jury even if there was no affirmative proof offered by defendants in rebuttal. The judge explained that possession could be actual or constructive, but that constructive possession could not exist without the intent and ability to exercise control or dominion over the weapons. He also carefully instructed the jury that there is a mandatory presumption of innocence in favor of the defendants that controls unless it, as the exclusive trier of fact, is satisfied beyond a reasonable doubt that the defendants possessed the handguns in the manner described by the judge. In short, the instructions plainly directed the jury to consider all the circumstances tending to support or contradict the inference that all four occupants of the car had possession of the two loaded handguns and

7. In addition to the discussion of *Romano* in n. [6], supra, this point is illustrated by Leary v. United States, supra. In that case, Dr. Timothy Leary, a professor at Harvard University was stopped by customs inspectors in Laredo, Texas as he was returning from the Mexican side of the international border. Marihuana seeds and a silver snuff box filled with semirefined marihuana and three partially smoked marihuana cigarettes were discovered in his car. He was convicted of having knowingly transported marihuana which he knew had been illegally imported into this country in violation of 21 U.S.C.A. § 176a. That statute includes a mandatory presumption: "possession shall be deemed sufficient evidence to authorize conviction [for importation] unless the defendant explains his possession to the satisfaction of the jury." Leary admitted possession of the marihuana and claimed that he had carried it from New York to Mexico and then back.

Justice Harlan for the Court noted that under one theory of the case, the jury could have found direct proof of all of the necessary elements of the offense without recourse to the presumption. But he deemed that insufficient reason to affirm the conviction because under another theory the jury might have found knowledge of importation on the basis of either direct evidence or the presumption, and there was accordingly no certainty that the jury had not relied on the presumption. 395 U.S., at 31–32. The Court therefore found it necessary to test the presumption against the Due Process Clause. Its analysis was facial. Despite the fact that the defendant was well educated and had recently traveled to a country that is a major exporter of marihuana to this country, the Court found the presumption of knowledge of importation from possession irrational. It did so not because Dr. Leary was unlikely to know the source of the marihuana but instead because "a majority of possessors" were unlikely to have such knowledge. Id., at 53. Because the jury had been instructed to rely on the presumption even if it did not believe the government's direct evidence of knowledge of importation (unless, of course, the defendant met his burden of "satisfying" the jury to the contrary), the Court reversed the conviction.

to decide the matter for itself without regard to how much evidence the defendants introduced.[8]

* * *

Our cases considering the validity of permissive statutory presumptions such as the one involved here have rested on an evaluation of the presumption as applied to the record before the Court. None suggests that a court should pass on the constitutionality of this kind of statute "on its face." It was error for the Court of Appeals to make such a determination in this case.

III

As applied to the facts of this case, the presumption of possession is entirely rational. Notwithstanding the Court of Appeals' analysis, respondents were not "hitch-hikers or other casual passengers," and the guns were neither "a few inches in length" nor "out of [respondents'] sight." * * * The argument against possession by any of the respondents was predicated solely on the fact that the guns were in Jane Doe's pocketbook. But several circumstances—which, not surprisingly, her counsel repeatedly emphasized in his questions and his argument, * * * made it highly improbable that she was the sole custodian of those weapons.

Even if it was reasonable to conclude that she had placed the guns in her purse before the car was stopped by police, the facts strongly suggest that Jane Doe was not the only person able to exercise dominion over them. The two guns were too large to be concealed in her handbag. The bag was consequently open, and part of one of the guns was in plain view, within easy access of the driver of the car and even, perhaps, of the other two respondents who were riding in the rear seat.

Moreover, it is highly improbable that the loaded guns belonged to Jane Doe or that she was solely responsible for their being in her purse. As a 16–year–old girl in the company of three adult men she was the least likely of the four to be carrying one, let alone two, heavy handguns. It is far more probable that she relied on the pocketknife found in her brassiere for any necessary self-protection. Under these circumstances, it was not unreasonable for her counsel to argue and for the jury to infer that when the car was halted for speeding, the other passengers in the car anticipated the risk of a search and attempted to conceal their weapons in a pocketbook in the front seat. The inference is surely more likely than the notion that these weapons were the sole property of the 16–year–old girl.

8. The verdict announced by the jury, clearly indicates that it understood its duty to evaluate the presumption independently and to reject it if it was not supported in the record. Despite receiving almost identical instructions on the applicability of the presumption of possession to the contraband found in the front seat and in the trunk, the jury convicted all four defendants of possession of the former but acquitted all of them of possession of the latter. See n. [8], supra.

Under these circumstances, the jury would have been entirely reasonable in rejecting the suggestion—which, incidentally, defense counsel did not even advance in their closing arguments to the jury—that the handguns were in the sole possession of Jane Doe. Assuming that the jury did reject it, the case is tantamount to one in which the guns were lying on the floor or the seat of the car in the plain view of the three other occupants of the automobile. In such a case it is surely rational to infer that each of the respondents was fully aware of the presence of the guns and had both the ability and the intent to exercise dominion and control over the weapons. The application of the statutory presumption in this case therefore comports with the standard laid down in Tot v. United States, 319 U.S. 463, 467, and restated in Leary v. United States, supra, 395 U.S., at 36. For there is a "rational connection" between the basic facts that the prosecution proved and the ultimate fact presumed, and the latter is "more likely than not to flow from" the former.

Respondents argue, however, that the validity of the New York presumption must be judged by a "reasonable doubt" test rather than the "more likely than not" standard employed in *Leary*. Under the more stringent test, it is argued that a statutory presumption must be rejected unless the evidence necessary to invoke the inference is sufficient for a rational jury to find the inferred fact beyond a reasonable doubt. See Barnes v. United States, 412 U.S. 837, 842–843. Respondents' argument again overlooks the distinction between a permissive presumption on which the prosecution is entitled to rely as one not-necessarily-sufficient part of its proof and a mandatory presumption which the jury must accept even if it is the sole evidence of an element of the offense.[9]

In the latter situation, since the prosecution bears the burden of establishing guilt, it may not rest its case entirely on a presumption unless the fact proved is sufficient to support the inference of guilt beyond a reasonable doubt. But in the former situation, the prosecution may rely on all of the evidence in the record to meet the reasonable doubt standard. There is no more reason to require a permissive statutory presumption to meet a reasonable doubt standard before it may be permitted to play any part in a trial than there is to require that degree of probative force for other relevant evidence before it may be admitted. As long as it is clear that the presumption is not the sole and sufficient basis for a finding of guilt, it need only satisfy the test described in *Leary*.

The permissive presumption, as used in this case, satisfied the *Leary* test. And, as already noted, the New York Court of Appeals has conclud-

9. The dissenting argument rests on the assumption that "the jury [may have] rejected all of the prosecution's evidence concerning the location and origin of the guns." * * * Even if that assumption were plausible, the jury was plainly told that it was free to disregard the presumption. But the dissent's assumption is not plausible; for if the jury rejected the testimony describing where the guns were found, it would necessarily also have rejected the only evidence in the record proving that the guns were found in the car. The conclusion that the jury attached significance to the particular location of the handguns follows inexorably from the acquittal on the charge of possession of the machineguns and heroin in the trunk.

ed that the record as a whole was sufficient to establish guilt beyond a reasonable doubt.

The judgment is reversed.

[The concurring opinion of MR. CHIEF JUSTICE BURGER is omitted.]

MR. JUSTICE POWELL, with whom MR. JUSTICE BRENNAN, MR. JUSTICE STEWART, and MR. JUSTICE MARSHALL join dissenting.

I agree with the Court that there is no procedural bar to our considering the underlying constitutional question presented by this case. I am not in agreement, however, with the Court's conclusion that the presumption as charged to the jury in this case meets the constitutional requirements of due process as set forth in our prior decisions. On the contrary, an individual's mere presence in an automobile where there is a handgun does not even make it "more likely than not" that the individual possesses the weapon.

I

In the criminal law presumptions are used to encourage the jury to find certain facts, with respect to which no direct evidence is presented, solely because other facts have been proved.[10] See, e.g., Barnes v. United States, 412 U.S. 837, 840 n.3 (1973); United States v. Romano, 382 U.S. 136, 138 (1965). The purpose of such presumptions is plain: Like certain other jury instructions, they provide guidance for jurors' thinking in considering the evidence laid before them. Once in the juryroom, jurors necessarily draw inferences from the evidence—both direct and circumstantial. Through the use of presumptions, certain inferences are commended to the attention of jurors by legislatures or courts.

Legitimate guidance of a jury's deliberations is an indispensible part of our criminal justice system. Nonetheless, the use of presumptions in criminal cases poses at least two distinct perils for defendants' constitutional rights. The Court accurately identifies the first of these as being the danger of interference with "the factfinder's responsibility at trial, based on evidence adduced by the State, to find the ultimate facts beyond a reasonable doubt." * * * If the jury is instructed that it must infer some ultimate fact (that is, some element of the offense) from proof of other facts unless the defendant disproves the ultimate fact by a preponderance of the evidence, then the presumption shifts the burden of proof to the defendant concerning the element thus inferred.[11]

10. Such encouragement can be provided either by statutory presumptions, see, e.g., 18 U.S.C.A. § 1201(b), or by presumptions created in the common law. See, e.g., Barnes v. United States, 412 U.S. 837 (1973). Unless otherwise specified, "presumption" will be used herein to "permissible inferences," as well as to "true" presumptions. See F. James, Civil Procedure § 7.9 (1965).

11. The Court suggests that presumptions that shift the burden of persuasion to the defendant in this way can be upheld provided that "the fact proved is sufficient to support the inference of guilt beyond a reasonable doubt." * * * As the present case involves no shifting of the burden of persuasion, the constitutional restrictions on such presumptions are not before us, and I express no views on them.

But I do not agree with the Court's conclusion that the only constitutional difficulty with presumptions lies in the danger of lessening the burden of proof the prosecution must bear. As the Court notes, the presumptions thus far reviewed by the Court have not shifted the burden of persuasion * * * ; instead they either have required only that the defendant produce some evidence to rebut the inference suggested by the prosecution's evidence, see Tot v. United States, 319 U.S. 463 (1943), or merely have been suggestions to the jury that it would be sensible to draw certain conclusions on the basis of the evidence presented.[12] See Barnes v. United States, supra 412 U.S. at 840 n.3. Evolving from our decisions, therefore, is a second standard for judging the constitutionality of criminal presumptions which is based—not on the constitutional requirement that the State be put to its proof—but rather on the due process rule that when the jury is encouraged to make factual inferences, those inferences must reflect some valid general observation about the natural connection between events as they occur in our society.

This due process rule was first articulated by the Court in Tot v. United States, supra, in which the Court reviewed the constitutionality of § 2(f) of the Federal Firearms Act. That statute provided in part that "possession of a firearm or ammunition by any * * * person [who has been convicted of a crime of violence] shall be presumptive evidence that such firearm or ammunition was shipped or transported [in interstate or foreign commerce]." As the Court interpreted the presumption, it placed upon a defendant only the obligation of presenting some exculpatory evidence concerning the origins of a firearm or ammunition, once the Government proved that the defendant had possessed the weapon and had been convicted of a crime of violence. Noting that juries must be permitted to infer from one fact the existence of another essential to guilt, "if reason and experience support the inference," id., at 467, the Court concluded that under some circumstances juries may be guided in making these inferences by legislative or common-law presumptions, even though they may be based "upon a view of relation broader than that a jury might take in a specific case," 319 U.S., at 468. To provide due process, however, there must be at least "a rational connection between the facts proved and the fact presumed"—a connection grounded in "common experience." Id., at 467. In *Tot,* the Court found that connection to be lacking.

It may well be that even those presumptions that do not shift the burden of persuasion cannot be used to prove an element of the offense, if the facts proved would not permit a reasonable mind to find the presumed fact beyond a reasonable doubt. My conclusion in Part II, infra, makes it unnecessary for me to address this concern here.

12. The Court suggests as the touchstone for its analysis a distinction between "mandatory" and "permissive" presumptions. * * * For general discussions of the various forms of presumptions, see Jeffries & Stephan, Defenses, Presumptions, and Burden of Proof in the Criminal Law, 88 Yale L.J. 1325 (1979); F. James, Civil Procedure § 7.9 (1965). I have found no recognition in the Court's prior decisions that this distinction is important in analyzing presumptions used in criminal cases. Cf. F. James, Civil Procedure, ibid. (distinguishing true "presumptions" from "permissible inferences").

Subsequently, in Leary v. United States, 395 U.S. 6 (1969), the Court reaffirmed and refined the due process requirement of *Tot* that inferences specifically commended to the attention of jurors must reflect generally accepted connections between related events. At issue in *Leary* was the constitutionality of a federal statute making it a crime to receive, conceal, buy, or sell marihuana illegally brought into the United States, knowing it to have been illegally imported. The statute provided that mere possession of marihuana "shall be deemed sufficient evidence to authorize conviction unless the defendant explains his possession to the satisfaction of the jury." After reviewing the Court's decisions in Tot v. United States, supra, and other criminal presumption cases, Mr. Justice Harlan, writing for the Court, concluded "that a criminal statutory presumption must be regarded as 'irrational' or 'arbitrary,' and hence unconstitutional, unless it can be said with substantial assurance that the presumed fact is more likely than not to flow from the proved fact on which it is made to depend." 395 U.S., at 36 * * *. The Court invalidated the statute, finding there to be insufficient basis in fact for the conclusion that those who possess marihuana are more likely than not to know that it was imported illegally.[13]

Most recently, in Barnes v. United States, supra, we considered the constitutionality of a quite different sort of presumption—one that suggested to the jury that "[p]ossession of recently stolen property, if not satisfactorily explained, is ordinarily a circumstance from which you may reasonably draw the inference * * * that the person in possession knew the property had been stolen." Id., 412 U.S. at 840 n.3. After reviewing the various formulations used by the Court to articulate the constitutionally required basis for a criminal presumption, we once again found it unnecessary to choose among them. As for the presumption suggested to the jury in *Barnes,* we found that it was well founded in history, common sense, and experience, and therefore upheld it as being "clearly sufficient to enable the jury to find beyond a reasonable doubt" that those in the unexplained possession of recently stolen property know it to have been stolen. Id., at 845.

In sum, our decisions uniformly have recognized that due process requires more than merely that the prosecution be put to its proof.[14] In addition, the Constitution restricts the court in its charge to the jury by requiring that, when particular factual inferences are recommended to the jury, those factual inferences be accurate reflections of what history, common sense, and experience tell us about the relations between events in our society. Generally this due process rule has been articulated as

13. Because the statute in Leary v. United States, 395 U.S. 6 (1969), was found to be unconstitutional under the "more likely than not" standard, the Court explicitly declined to consider whether criminal presumptions also must follow "beyond a reasonable doubt" from their premises, if an essential element of the crime depends upon the presumption's use. Id., at 36 n.64 * * * The Court similarly avoided this question in Turner v. United States, 396 U.S. 398, 416 (1970).

14. The Court apparently disagrees, contending that "the factfinder's responsibility * * * to find the ultimate facts beyond a reasonable doubt" is the only constitutional restraint upon the use of criminal presumptions at trial. * * *

requiring that the truth of the inferred fact be more likely than not whenever the premise for the inference is true. Thus, to be constitutional a presumption must be at least more likely than not true.

II

In the present case, the jury was told that,

> "Our Penal Law also provides that the presence in an automobile of any machine gun or of any handgun or firearm which is loaded is presumptive evidence of their unlawful possession. In other words, [under] these presumptions or this latter presumption upon proof of the presence of the machine gun and the hand weapons, you may infer and draw a conclusion that such prohibited weapon was possessed by each of the defendants who occupied the automobile at the time when such instruments were found. The presumption or presumptions is effective only so long as there is no substantial evidence contradicting the conclusion flowing from the presumption, and the presumption is said to disappear when such contradictory evidence is adduced."

Undeniably, the presumption charged in this case encouraged the jury to draw a particular factual inference regardless of any other evidence presented: to infer that respondents possessed the weapons found in the automobile "upon proof of the presence of the machine gun and the hand weapon" and proof that respondents "occupied the automobile at the time such instruments were found." I believe that the presumption thus charged was unconstitutional because it did not fairly reflect what common sense and experience tell us about passengers in automobiles and the possession of handguns. People present in automobiles where there are weapons simply are not "more likely than not" the possessors of those weapons.

Under New York law, "to possess" is "to have physical possession or otherwise to exercise dominion or control over tangible property." N.Y.Penal Law § 10.00(8). Plainly the mere presence of an individual in an automobile—without more—does not indicate that he exercises "dominion or control over" everything within it. As the Court of Appeals noted, there are countless situations in which individuals are invited as guests into vehicles the contents of which they know nothing about, much less have control over. Similarly, those who invite others into their automobile do not generally search them to determine what they may have on their person; nor do they insist that any handguns be identified and placed within reach of the occupants of the automobile. Indeed, handguns are particularly susceptible to concealment and therefore are less likely than are other objects to be observed by those in an automobile.

In another context, this Court has been particularly hesitant to infer possession from mere presence in a location, noting that "[p]resence is relevant and admissible evidence in a trial on a possession charge; but absent some showing of the defendant's function at [the illegal] still, its connection with possession is too tenuous to permit a reasonable inference of guilt—'the inference of the one from proof of the other is arbitrary * * *.' Tot v. United States, 319 U.S. 463, 467." United States v. Romano, 382 U.S. 136, 141 (1965). We should be even more hesitant to uphold the inference of possession of a handgun from mere presence in an automobile, in light of common experience concerning automobiles and handguns. Because the specific factual inference recommended to the jury in this case is not one that is supported by the general experience of our society. I cannot say that the presumption charged is "more likely than not" to be true. Accordingly, respondents' due process rights were violated by the presumption's use.

As I understand it, the Court today does not contend that in general those who are present in automobiles are more likely than not to possess any gun contained within their vehicles. It argues, however, that the nature of the presumption here involved requires that we look, not only to the immediate facts upon which the jury was encouraged to base its inference, but to the other facts "proved" by the prosecution as well. The Court suggests that this is the proper approach when reviewing what it calls "permissive" presumptions because the jury was urged "to consider all the circumstances tending to support or contradict the inference." * * *

It seems to me that the Court mischaracterizes the function of the presumption charged in this case. As it acknowledges was the case in *Romano,* supra, the "instruction authorized conviction even if the jury disbelieved all of the testimony except the proof of presence" in the automobile.[15] * * * The Court nevertheless relies on all of the evidence introduced by the prosecution and argues that the "permissive" presumption could not have prejudiced defendants. The possibility that the jury disbelieved all of this evidence, and relied on the presumption, is simply ignored.

I agree that the circumstances relied upon by the Court in determining the plausibility of the presumption charged in this case would have made it reasonable for the jury to "infer that each of the respondents was fully aware of the presence of the guns and had both the ability and the intent to exercise dominion and control over the weapons." But the jury was told that it could conclude that respondents possessed the weapons found therein from proof of the mere fact of respondents' presence in the automobile. For all we know, the jury rejected all of the prosecution's evidence concerning the location and origin of the guns,

15. In commending the presumption to the jury, the court gave no instruction that would have required a finding of possession to be based on anything more than mere presence in the automobile. Thus, the jury was not instructed that it should infer that respondents possessed the handguns only if it found that the guns were too large to be concealed in Jane Doe's handbag * * * ; that the guns accordingly were in the plain view of respondents * * * ; that the weapons were within "easy access of the driver of the car and even, perhaps, of the other two respondents who were riding in the rear seat," ibid; that it was unlikely that Jane Doe was solely responsible for the placement of the weapons in her purse, id.; or that the case was "tantamount to one in which the guns were lying on the floor or the seat of the car in the plain view of the three other occupants of the automobile." * * *.

and based its conclusion that respondents possessed the weapons solely upon its belief that respondents had been present in the automobile.[16] For purposes of reviewing the constitutionality of the presumption at issue here, we must assume that this was the case. * * *

The Court's novel approach in this case appears to contradict prior decisions of this Court reviewing such presumptions. Under the Court's analysis, whenever it is determined that an inference is "permissive," the only question is whether, in light of all of the evidence adduced at trial, the inference recommended to the jury is a reasonable one. The Court has never suggested that the inquiry into the rational basis of a permissible inference may be circumvented in this manner. Quite the contrary, the Court has required that the "evidence *necessary to invoke the inference* [be] sufficient for a rational juror to find the inferred fact * * *." Barnes v. United States, 412 U.S. 837 (1973) (emphasis supplied). See Turner v. United States, 396 U.S. 398, 407 (1970). Under the presumption charged in this case, the only evidence necessary to invoke the inference was the presence of the weapons in the automobile with respondents—an inference that is plainly irrational.

In sum, it seems to me that the Court today ignores the teaching of our prior decisions. By speculating about what the jury may have done with the factual inference thrust upon it, the Court in effect assumes away the inference altogether, constructing a rule that permits the use of any inference—no matter how irrational in itself—provided that otherwise there is sufficient evidence in the record to support a finding of guilt. Applying this novel analysis to the present case, the Court upholds the use of a presumption that it makes no effort to defend in isolation. In substance, the Court—applying an unarticulated harmless error standard—simply finds that the respondents were guilty as charged. They may well have been but rather than acknowledging this rationale, the Court seems to have made new law with respect to presumptions that could seriously jeopardize a defendant's right to a fair trial. Accordingly, I dissent.

Notes and Questions

1. *Mandatory presumptions.* In the same term as the principal case, the Supreme Court decided Sandstrom v. Montana, 442 U.S. 510 (1979). In *Sandstrom*, the Court found that a jury instruction in a homicide case that the "law presumes that a person intends the ordinary consequences of his

16. The Court is therefore mistaken in its conclusion that, because "respondents were not 'hitch-hikers or other casual passengers,' and the guns were neither 'a few inches in length' nor 'out of [respondents'] sight,'" reference to these possibilities is inappropriate in considering the constitutionality of the presumption as charged in this case. * * * To be sure, respondents' challenge is to the presumption as charged to the jury in this case. But in assessing its application here, we are not free, as the Court apparently believes, to disregard the possibility that the jury may have disbelieved all other evidence supporting an inference of possession. The jury may have concluded that respondents—like hitchhikers—had only an incidental relationship to the auto in which they were traveling, or that, contrary to some of the testimony at trial, the weapons were indeed out of respondents' sight.

voluntary acts'' could have been interpreted either as creating a conclusive presumption or as shifting the burden of persuasion with regard to the question of intent to the defendant. The Court held that such a shift of the burden would be constitutionally impermissible, citing, among others, the *Ulster County* case. See also Francis v. Franklin, 471 U.S. 307 (1985), where the Court rejected another ''mandatory'' presumption. Are ''mandatory'' presumptions ever constitutionally permissible in a criminal case? What about a ''mandatory'' presumption which simply shifts the burden of production? The Court in the *Francis* case expressly reserved the question of the treatment of such a presumption. Id. at 314 n.3. For discussions and criticism of the Court's treatment of presumptions in criminal cases, see Allen & De Grazia, The Constitutional Requirement of Proof Beyond a Reasonable Doubt in Criminal Cases: A Comment Upon Incipient Chaos in the Lower Courts, 20 Am.Crim.L.Rev. 1 (1982); Note, The Improper Use of Presumptions in Recent Criminal Law Adjudication, 38 Stan.L.Rev. 423 (1986); 2 McCormick, Evidence §§ 347, 348 (6th ed. 2006).

2. *Presumptions or affirmative defenses?* To what extent is the problem in the principal case related to the question of what elements of a criminal case may be allocated to the accused as affirmative defenses? See Jeffries & Stephan, Defenses, Presumptions and the Burden of Proof in the Criminal Law, 88 Yale L.J. 1325 (1979); 2 McCormick, Evidence § 348 (6th ed. 2006). Related discussions include: Allen, Structuring Jury Decisionmaking in Criminal Cases: A Unified Constitutional Approach to Evidentiary Devices, 94 Harv.L.Rev. 321 (1980); Allen, More on Constitutional Process-of-Proof Problems in Criminal Cases, 94 Harv.L.Rev. 1795 (1981); Ashford & Risinger, Presumptions, Assumptions and Due Process in Criminal Cases: A Theoretical Overview, 79 Yale L.J. 165 (1969); Ranney, Presumptions in Criminal Cases, 41 Mont.L.Rev. 21 (1980). See also the concurring opinions of Judge Phillips in Rook v. Rice, 783 F.2d 401 (4th Cir.1986), and Davis v. Allsbrooks, 778 F.2d 168 (4th Cir.1985).

3. *Harmless error.* May a jury instruction which puts an impermissible burden of persuasion on the defendant ever be harmless error? If so, is it enough that there is evidence in the record, independent of the presumption, to support the verdict? In Yates v. Evatt, 500 U.S. 391 (1991), the Court held that, in order for the error to be harmless, all of the evidence in the case must have been of such compelling force to show beyond a reasonable doubt that the presumption must have made no difference in reaching the verdict.

Chapter 6[1]

THE ORDER OF PROOF

LIPTAK v. SECURITY BENEFIT ASS'N

Supreme Court of Illinois, 1932.
183 N.E. 564.

STONE, J. The appellee, as widow of Julius Liptak, brought suit in the circuit court of Madison county against appellant, a fraternal benefit society, on a benefit certificate issued to Liptak on November 26, 1921, in the amount of $1,000. To the declaration appellant filed no plea of general issue but a special plea setting out certain sections of its by-laws and alleging that before his death the insured became suspended for failure to pay premium assessments in accordance with the provisions of those by-laws. There was a trial by jury and a verdict for plaintiff in the sum of $1,000. Judgment entered thereon was affirmed by the Appellate Court.

The special plea relied on was to the effect that under the by-laws of the society Liptak's policy had lapsed by reason of his failure to pay the assessment for June, 1929, before the last day of that month. The appellant asserts that thereafter, in July of that year, Liptak, or some one for him, attempted to reinstate him by payment of assessments for the months of June and July, but that this payment was made to one not authorized by the society to receive it, and as a result Liptak was not reinstated. It further states that he was not in good health at that time and could not have been reinstated. * * *

The dispute in the case arises over the payment during June, 1929, of the assessment and dues for that month. Liptak died on November 13, 1929. He was ill from the spring of that year, and it is conceded that if he became suspended in June his health was such as to prevent his reinstatement. The testimony of appellee and her witnesses is to the effect that one John R. De Bow, an officer of the association, came to the house of appellee, at her request, on the 29th of June and received the payment for that month on the certificate of Julius Liptak and other members of the family who were likewise members of the society. De Bow was an officer of appellant having a sort of supervision over certain

1. Throughout the cases and materials in this chapter some footnotes from the originals have been omitted; others have been renumbered. [Ed.]

lodges, or councils as they were styled, including the one holding Liptak's membership. It does not appear that he was the "financier" of the local council of this society, but that he had at times taken dues and assessments of various members of the council and signed the receipt books therefor. Appellant's evidence is a denial of the presence of De Bow at the house of appellee during the month of June and of his authority to accept dues. That evidence tends to show that De Bow received the June and July assessments from appellee on July 23, with the request that he try and have Julius Liptak reinstated. He testified that he agreed to do what he could in that behalf. This is denied on rebuttal by appellee. Concerning this payment there is sharp dispute in the evidence, and it is on this evidence that the case turns.

When the case was called for trial counsel for appellant stated to the court that under the pleadings in the case they admitted the issuance of the certificate, the relationship of the parties, the correctness of the by-laws referred to in the certificate and declaration, admitted the death of the insured and receipt of proof of death, and moved the court to be permitted to take the lead in the examination of the jury on account of the fact that under the pleadings the burden of proof was upon the defendant. This motion was denied. It was for the same reason renewed before the taking of evidence and again before the arguments to the jury were had. In each case it was denied, and the ruling of the court in that matter is here urged as error. Counsel for appellee argues that it was necessary that she introduce proof in support of her case in chief and that therefore she had a right to open and close, and whether this be so or not, the matter of opening and closing lay in the discretion of the trial court. The right to open and close is a substantial right coexistent with the burden of proof and is corollary thereto. Whenever the plaintiff has anything to prove in order to secure a verdict, the right to open and close belongs to him. It is generally held that the right to open and close is not a matter resting merely in the discretion of the trial judge, but is a substantial right in the person who must introduce proof to prevent judgment against him. The party who asserts the affirmative of an issue is entitled to begin and reply. * * * If appellee was, under the pleadings and admissions of appellant, entitled to judgment, in the absence of proof supporting the special plea, appellant carried the burden to go forward in the offer of proof and was entitled to open and close the evidence and arguments. No plea of general issue was on file. The only controversy in the case was that raised on the affirmative special plea. This threw the burden of proof upon appellant. The issue of fact raised by that plea was sharply controverted. The right of appellant to open and close was a substantial right. In a trial before a jury, where the pivotal fact is in sharp dispute, the advantage of opening and closing the evidence and arguments becomes one controlled by rules of law defining rights, and is not left to the discretion of the judge.

* * *

For the error in denying appellant the right to open and close the case, the judgments of the appellate and circuit courts are reversed, and the cause remanded to the circuit court for a new trial.

Reversed and remanded.

SEGUIN v. BERG

Supreme Court of New York, Appellate Division, 1940.
21 N.Y.S.2d 291.

HEFFERNAN, JUSTICE. On January 2, 1938, the automobiles of plaintiff and defendants collided on the state highway connecting Lake Placid and Saranac Lake as a result of which both cars were damaged. Each of the owners of the respective vehicles charged the other with negligence in causing the collision.

Plaintiff instituted this action to recover a money judgment for the damages to his car. Defendants interposed an answer denying liability and also asserted a counterclaim against plaintiff for the damages to their car. After a trial of the issues the jury rendered a verdict in favor of defendants on their counterclaim and plaintiff has appealed.

Only a question of law relating to practice is presented for our determination. In support of his cause of action plaintiff offered his own testimony and that of the mechanic who repaired his car and rested. At the conclusion of defendants' proof plaintiff called as witnesses three persons—passengers in his car—who saw the collision and sought to obtain their version as to how it occurred. Upon objection of defendants the evidence was excluded on the ground that it was not proper rebuttal.

The proper administration of justice requires some regular method of procedure in the trial of an action. No rule for the conduct of trials is more familiar than that a plaintiff must put in all his evidence before he rests. He must exhaust all of his testimony in support of the issue on his side before the proof of his adversary is heard. The defendant should then produce his evidence, and finally the evidence in rebuttal is received. Marshall et al. v. Davies, 78 N.Y. 414; Richardson on Evidence, Fifth Edition, § 537. Plaintiff cannot put in merely enough evidence to make out a prima facie case and reserve the rest to meet the emergency of later needs. He has no right to reopen his case after defendants have closed theirs although he may introduce proof in rebuttal. He may not however under the guise of rebuttal put in evidence tending to support the allegations of his pleading. Notwithstanding the general rule that a party holding the affirmative is bound to introduce all the evidence on his side before he closes the trial court in the exercise of its discretion and for sufficient reason may allow a departure from the rule and permit a party to reopen and supply defects in the evidence which have inadvertently occurred. The order of proof may be varied as occasion requires being a matter resting in the discretion of the trial court.

If we were not dealing with a case involving a counterclaim we would have no hesitancy in sustaining the ruling of the learned trial justice. We are convinced, however, that the decision under review is erroneous. The Civil Practice Act, § 424, provides that where a defendant interposes a counterclaim and demands an affirmative judgment against the plaintiff the mode of trial of an issue of fact arising thereupon is the same as if it arose in an action brought by defendant against the plaintiff for the cause of action stated in the counterclaim and demanding the same judgment.

In the case before us plaintiff had the right to offer such testimony as he desired in support of his cause of action. It is true that the evidence which he sought to introduce in rebuttal, and which was excluded, would have been competent as part of his affirmative case. He was not obliged however to avail himself of it for that purpose. It seems clear to us that he had the right to offer the proof, not to establish his case, but to defeat the cause of action which defendants were asserting against him. The evidence was clearly admissible in rebuttal for the purpose of contradicting the evidence on the part of defendants to the effect that the collision was due solely to plaintiff's negligence. Evidence which would have been proper as part of plaintiff's affirmative case, and which he has no right to introduce as affirmative evidence after the defendants had rested, may still be offered by the plaintiff if it tends to impeach or discredit the testimony of defendants. Winchell v. Winchell et al., 100 N.Y. 159, 2 N.E. 897; Ankersmit et al. v. Tuch, 114 N.Y. 51, 20 N.E. 819. Rebutting evidence "means, not merely evidence which contradicts the witnesses on the opposite side and corroborates those of the party who began, but evidence in denial of some affirmative fact which the answering party has endeavored to prove." Marshall et al. v. Davis, supra.

For these reasons we think plaintiff is entitled to have the evidence which was excluded considered by the jury and hence the judgment and order appealed from should be reversed on the law and a new trial granted with costs to appellant to abide the event.

Judgment and order reversed on the law, and new trial granted, with costs to appellant to abide the event.

HILL, P.J., and BLISS and FOSTER, JJ., concur.

CRAPSER, J., dissents, and votes to affirm.

Questions

1. Would it have been permissible for the plaintiff in *Seguin v. Berg* to begin the presentation of his case in chief by offering the testimony of the mechanic who repaired his car? See 6 Wigmore, Evidence § 1869 (Chadbourn rev. 1976).

2. P sues D for negligence. In his answer, D denies P's allegations with respect to negligence and further raises the affirmative defense that P had executed a release of his claim. May P, as a part of his case in chief, introduce evidence tending to show that D obtained the release by fraud?

DURAN v. NEFF

District Court of Appeal of Florida, 1979.
366 So.2d 169.

In a medical malpractice action, the plaintiff sought and received the right to have her case presented first on a Monday morning before the trial court. On Monday afternoon, at 5:10 P.M., counsel for the plaintiff suggested that the court take a short recess before permitting him to put on an expert witness, whose examination would be lengthy. The court declined to do this and recessed until the next day. Plaintiff was unable to produce the expert witness on the following day and directed verdict was rendered against the plaintiff.

The plaintiff appeals and urges error in the trial judge's refusal to take her expert's testimony late on the first day. We find no abuse of discretion in the trial court's ruling. It is elementary that a trial judge must be given broad latitude in the control of causes before him, particularly jury cases, and on this record there is certainly no abuse of discretion demonstrated. * * *

Therefore, the final judgment based on the directed verdict is affirmed.

Affirmed.

Note

While the trial judge's discretion to control the timing and order of proof is generally held to be very broad, it should not be considered to be totally unfettered. With the principal case, compare Loinaz v. EG & G, Inc., 910 F.2d 1 (1st Cir.1990) (reversible error to refuse defendant's request to present main witness during plaintiff's case, where result was to force defendant to resort to witness' deposition).

ATKINSON v. SMITH

Supreme Court of New Brunswick, 1859.
9 N.B. 309.

Trespass for breaking and entering the plaintiff's close and cutting down a mill-dam. Plea—not guilty; with a notice of defense, that the locus in quo was a branch of the Buctouche river, which was a public navigable river for driving logs and lumber; that it was obstructed by a mill-dam built across it, and that the defendants having occasion to pass down the river with their lumber, were obliged to remove a part of the dam to enable them to pass. There was another notice stating the river to be a public highway and navigable stream, and that the defendants removed the dam to enable their lumber to pass down.

At the trial before Parker, J., at the last Kent circuit, the defendants' counsel proposed on the cross-examination of one of the plaintiff's witnesses, to ask certain questions connected with the justification, which had not been enquired into on the examination in chief, and were not available on the general issue; but the learned Judge ruled that the evidence could not be gone into till the defendants had opened their case. * * * The jury found that the justification was proved, but gave a verdict for the plaintiff for £25, for the excessive damage in cutting the dam.

A rule nisi for a new trial having been granted on the ground of the improper rejection of evidence,

D.S. Kerr shewed cause in Hilary term. He contended that since the case of Browne v. Murray[2], the rule was, that the plaintiff might either go into his whole case in the first instance, or merely prove his prima facie case and leave the defendant to answer it. That case was confirmed in Shaw v. Beck[3], which shewed that the particular period of the cause when evidence should be received, was in the discretion of the Judge. The defendant had no right to prove a justification until the plaintiff's case was closed, unless the plaintiff went into the whole case in the first instance.

A.J. Smith, contra. It was a matter of right for the defendant to extract from the plaintiff's witnesses on cross-examination, all they know about the case. The witness was sworn to tell the whole truth, and he was bound to answer all questions put to him, if when answered they would be legal evidence. It is not a matter in the Judge's discretion at all, but a matter of right. [PARKER, J. I thought the defendants had no right to go into evidence on cross-examination, of any matter that did not constitute a defence under the general issue.] The recent alteration in the law, allowing the parties to give evidence, required that the old practice should be relaxed, and that the defendant should be allowed to prove his case by cross-examination of the plaintiff's witnesses.

PARKER, J., now delivered the judgment of the Court. The only point on which the rule was granted in this case was, the rejection of evidence—the rejection not amounting to an exclusion, but a postponement of the evidence tendered, until a later stage of the trial. No injustice seems to have been done by the ruling, even if wrong, for the defendants, though somewhat irregularly, have had the benefit of their justification of which they went into proof, damages having only been given for the excess; but as the point has now come distinctly up, it is very important for our future guidance that it should be settled, especially as there has not hitherto been an entire uniformity of practice, though the deviations from what we all believe to be the true rule, have not been frequent. The question is, has the defendants' counsel a right on the cross-examination of the plaintiff's witnesses, and before he has opened the defence, to prove a special justification of which notice has been given under the Act of Assembly, and the affirmative of which, if pleaded and traversed, would lie on the defendant—a right not to be controlled by the discretion of the Judge, and where the plaintiff's counsel has carefully and advisedly abstained from leading to it by the examination

2. R. & M. 254.

3. 20 Eng.R. 309; 8 Exch. 392.

in chief? It appears to the Judges present (and I should add we have not been able to confer with His Honour the Chief Justice on the point) that the defendant has no such right, and that the ruling at the trial was quite correct; indeed, we think it would be almost impossible fairly to try causes if a right existed to the extent claimed. The difficulties attendant on trials at Nisi Prius by the generality of pleading, and which it has been the policy of the Legislature of the mother country of late years to contract, have been much enhanced by recent legislation in this Province, to compensate for which, whatever the benefits may be in other respects, certainly relief to the Judges is no part of the equivalent. It would be impossible for the Judges to decide on the relevancy of many questions put by the defendant's counsel, and it would be in the power of an ingenious counsel to multiply discussion to almost any extent. It would be most inconvenient, and often positively unjust, to interrupt the course of the examination of the plaintiff's witnesses while constantly recurring arguments were gone into on the admissibility of proof under the notice of defence, to be at once heard and decided on, which would be found afterwards when the real defence, if any, was opened, to be utterly useless, except for the purpose of making difficulties and causing ruinous delay. The Judge's notes would become a mass of confusion; and no better illustration could be given than a case before us at the last term, where, in an action of slander, charging theft and false swearing, the defendant justified under a notice of over a dozen larcenies in different places, and half a dozen perjuries. Until the defendant's case was opened, what question could a Judge say might not be directly or indirectly applicable to some part of such matter? The discretion which is exercised by the Judge would in reality be shifted to the defendant's counsel, who, under the prompting of a crafty client, would find his duty much more arduous than it is at present.

* * *

Rule discharged.

Notes

1. *Cross-examination for impeachment.* The rule restricting cross-examination to the scope of the direct, recognized in a large majority of American jurisdictions, does not apply to cross-examination for purposes of impeachment. Cross-examination to impeach is treated in Chapter 12, Section E, infra. In England and in a few states the cross-examiner is free to question about any issue relevant to the case. See 1 McCormick, Evidence § 21 (6th ed. 2006).

2. *Trial court discretion.* Cross-examination to impeach possesses considerable potential for injecting confusion of, and distracting attention from, the issues. In Howard v. United States, 389 F.2d 287, 292 (D.C.Cir.1967), the court spoke of the judge's authority to control this aspect of cross-examination.

> Although opportunity to cross-examine is a fundamental right demanding great respect, the courts have recognized that regulation of the

extent and scope of cross-examination must generally be within the discretion of the trial court, and reversal is warranted only when an abuse of discretion leads to prejudice. * * * We will not reverse the judge for cutting off what he reasonably believed * * * was a fruitless endeavor that would succeed only in proliferating and confusing the issues. This is all the more so since the questions posed were designed solely to test * * * general credibility. A trial court has much more leeway with respect to cross-examination for that purpose than with cross-examination on subjects raised in direct.

BOLLER v. COFRANCES

Supreme Court of Wisconsin, 1969.
166 N.W.2d 129.

This is an appeal from a judgment of the circuit court for LaCrosse county, which, after a jury verdict assessing the negligence of each driver at 50 percent, dismissed the complaint of Virginia M. Boller, the administratrix of Henry W. Boller, deceased.

The action arose out of an automobile accident that occurred in the city of LaCrosse on May 23, 1965. Henry W. Boller and his passenger, Catherine Case, were both killed in the accident.

* * *

In motions after verdict, the plaintiff, Virginia M. Boller, asked for a new trial because of errors in the instructions, prejudicial conduct on the part of defendant's counsel, and in the interest of justice. These motions were denied, and judgment on the verdict was entered for the defendant. The plaintiff has appealed to this court.

HEFFERNAN, JUSTICE.

Is a new trial warranted because of defendant's counsel's conduct in asking an allegedly improper question that indelibly prejudiced the jury despite the admonitions of the trial judge?

The plaintiff argues that a new trial should be granted because Virginia Boller was asked the following question on cross-examination by defense counsel:

"Q. Were you aware of the affair that your husband was having with Mrs. Case [the passenger in the car]?

"MR. ARNESON: I object to this, Your Honor, as improper cross examination. There's no foundation for any kind of questioning about that. It's beyond the scope of direct examination in every respect.

"THE COURT: *Beyond the scope,* Mr. Crosby. Objection sustained. [Emphasis supplied.]

"MR. ARNESON: And I ask that the jury be instructed to disregard it.

"THE COURT: Jury will be instructed to disregard it.

"MR. CROSBY: That's all."

* * *

In the instant case plaintiff's counsel, although he objected to the question, was at the time satisfied with the judge's order to strike the question and with his direction to the jury to disregard it. It was only after the disappointing verdict that the plaintiff, who could well have been benefitted by the question, claimed it to be prejudicial. His claim is not only without merit, but it is also untimely.

Was it error to exclude the question in regard to Henry Boller's affair with Mrs. Case?

While the trial judge excluded the question, "Were you [Virginia Boller] aware of the affair that your husband was having with Mrs. Case?"—and the plaintiff assumes that such ruling was correct—the defendant on this appeal stoutly contends that the question was proper and Virginia Boller's answer should have been admitted into evidence. Defendant points out in his brief that the plaintiff on direct examination testified, "that she and her husband had a close relationship and were very happily married."

When defendant's counsel asked his question, it was objected to and that objection was sustained on the grounds that it was *beyond the scope of the direct* examination. We do not agree with the ruling of the trial judge. One of the major issues to be resolved by the jury was the evaluation, to the extent possible, of the loss Virginia Boller sustained by losing the society and companionship of Henry Boller. Certainly, the existence of an "affair" with another woman and Virginia Boller's knowledge of it were probative of the value to be placed upon Virginia Boller's loss. Moreover, the question was directly related to, and in impeachment of, her testimony on direct examination. We are satisfied that the question was relevant to the questions posed on direct examination and was within its scope. Of course, despite its probativeness, it is within the discretion of the trial judge to exclude evidence if its probativeness is offset by possible jury prejudice. * * * Here, however, such discretion was not in fact exercised, and in view of the state of the record, such evidence should not have been excluded. While we find the disputed question to be within the scope of the direct examination, we have grave doubts that such rule of exclusion should be followed, particularly when the witness on the stand is a party and subject to be called, in a civil case at least, by the opponent. * * * The rule against questioning any witness "beyond the scope of direct examination" has no intrinsic merit and does not demonstrably assist in the search for the truth. Rather, by encouraging pettifogging objections that go to form and not substance, the rule is likely to be disruptive of trial procedure and results in appeals that basically have no merit.

The only claimed virtue for the rule is that it ensures the orderly presentation of evidence, i.e., that a plaintiff's witness should not be expected to help make the defendant's case on cross-examination. But why shouldn't he? If the question is relevant and is otherwise admissible and the information solicited is within the knowledge of the witness, it should be within the sound discretion of the trial judge to determine whether or not questions on cross-examination prevent an orderly and cogent presentation of the evidence. They well might, and usually would, contribute to the intelligent search for the truth.[4]

This test, which leaves the admission or exclusion to the discretion of the trial judge, is infinitely preferable to the artificial and meaningless rule that excludes all evidence whether it should then logically come into the record or not, simply because it is "beyond the scope." The Model Code of Evidence recommends the following rule to supplant the present practice:

> "Rule 105. Control of Judge over Presentation of Evidence. The judge controls the conduct of the trial to the end that the evidence shall be presented honestly, expeditiously and in such form as to be readily understood, and in his discretion determines, among other things, * * *
>
> "(h) to what extent and in what circumstances a party cross-examining a witness may be forbidden to examine him concerning material matters not inquired about on a previous examination by the judge or by an adverse party."

Wigmore points out that the present rule, as practiced in Wisconsin, is a recent one, and that the historical or orthodox rule permitted:

> "* * * the opposite party * * * not only [to] cross-examine him in relation to the point which he was called to prove, but he may examine him as to any matter embraced in the issue. He may establish his defence by him without calling any other witnesses. If he is a competent witness to the jury for any purpose, he is so for all purposes." 6 Wigmore, Evidence (3d ed.) sec. 1885, p. 532, quoting Sutherland, J., Fulton Bank v. Stafford, 2 Wend. 483, 485.

Wigmore in that volume, sec. 1885 ff., discusses in detail the shortcomings of the present rule. In his Students' Textbook, Wigmore on Evidence, he summarizes the effect of the present rule:

> "Cross examination is the greatest engine for getting at the truth; * * * and a rule which needlessly hampers its exercise as this one does cannot be a sound one."

4. In the recent case of Neider v. Spoehr (March 4, 1969), Wis., 165 N.W.2d 171, Mr. Justice Beilfuss, speaking for the Court, pointed out that it is within the discretion of the trial judge to control cross-examination:

> "* * * the right of * * * cross-examination * * * can be controlled by the trial court so that the trial proceeds in an orderly and fair manner. The exercise of discretion by the trial court to deny or restrict cross-examination must be dependent upon the circumstances of the trial. This court will not reverse unless it clearly appears that the trial court abused its discretion and that the error affected a substantial right of the complaining party and probably affected the result of the trial."

This statement is valid under the rule we herein adopt and expresses the rationale of the Model Code of Evidence that discretion in this respect is properly vested in the trial court.

McCormick, in his treatise on Evidence (hornbook series), sec. 27, p. 51, points out that, when all relevant factors are considered, "the balance [is] overwhelmingly in favor of the wide-open rule." He points out that:

> "The restrictive practice in all its forms * * * is productive * * * of continual bickering over the choice of the numerous variations of the 'scope of the direct' criterion, and of their application to particular cross-questions. These controversies are often reventilated on appeal, and reversals for error in their determination are frequent. Observance of these vague and ambiguous restrictions is a matter of constant and hampering concern to the cross-examiner. If these efforts, delays and misprisions were the necessary incidents to the guarding of substantive rights or the fundamentals of fair trial, they might be worth the cost. As the price of the choice of an obviously debatable regulation of the order of evidence, the sacrifice seems misguided."

McCormick also emphasizes the deleterious effect of the present rule in the prosecution of criminals:

> "* * * the accused may limit his direct examination to some single aspect of the case, such as age, sanity or alibi, and then invoke the court's ruling that the cross-examination be limited to the matter thus opened. Surely the according of a privilege to the accused to select out a favorable fact and testify to that alone, and thus get credit for testifying but escape a searching inquiry on the whole charge, is a travesty on criminal administration * * *"

"In jurisdictions following the wide-open practice there is of course no obstacle to cross-examining the accused upon any matters relevant to any issue in the entire case." Sec. 26, pp. 49, 50.

While the Wisconsin cases appear to allow greater latitude in the cross-examination of a criminal defendant, they appear to permit examination of all facets of an alleged crime only when the defendant has opened the door on direct by testifying on the merits of the case. Sprague v. State (1925), 188 Wis. 432, 206 N.W. 69.

We are satisfied that the wide-open rule should be adopted by this court. The appeal herein is founded upon the exclusion from the record of relevant evidence on the grounds that it elicited information not covered by, or within, the scope of the direct evidence. The evidence, in reason, ought not to have been excluded. Because the plaintiff, by invoking the spurious "beyond the scope" rule, contends that the jury made use of improper and inadmissible evidence, he has brought a patently specious appeal. The exclusion of the evidence on the basis of the restrictive rule is founded in neither reason nor the interest of justice. It is productive of confusion and super-technical appeals similar to the one brought in this instance.

Had the rule been the one permitting wide-open cross-examination, the answer to the question would have been clearly admissible and the subsequent bickering would have been avoided. Of course, as stated above, otherwise admissible evidence can still be excluded in the discretion of the trial judge if its harmful effects on the legal process outweigh its probative value. In such event, e.g., had it been clearly admissible under the wide-open rule, the question would have hinged upon the question of abuse of discretion by the trial judge and not upon a mechanistic rule of evidence.

We conclude that in the instant case the plaintiff failed to preserve his right to review the judge's instructions to the jury. We also conclude that the disputed question properly should have been allowed as eliciting evidence relevant to the issue or an impeachment. On both scores the answer would be admissible even under the restrictive rule heretofore in use. It would without a doubt have been a proper question under the wide-open rule which we herein adopt. Under this rule the trial judge shall exercise discretion to assure an orderly and intelligible presentation of the facts without the requirement of slavish compliance with the "beyond the scope" rule.

We conclude that the plaintiff was not prejudiced by the proceedings and the apportionment of negligence is supported by substantial evidence. The interest of justice would not be secured by a new trial.

Judgment affirmed.

Notes and Questions

1. *Support for wide-open cross-examination.* Scholarly opinion has long inclined heavily to the views espoused in the principal case. See, e.g., McCormick, The Scope and Art of Cross Examination, 47 Nw.L.Rev. 177 (1952); Degnan, Non–Rules Evidence Law: Cross–Examination, 6 Utah L.Rev. 322 (1959); Note, The Limiting Effect of Direct Examination upon the Scope of Cross-examination, 37 Colum.L.Rev. 1373 (1937). And the ABA Committee for the Improvement of the Law of Evidence for 1937–38 commented:

> The rule limiting cross-examination to the precise subject of direct examination is probably the most frequent rule (except the opinion rule) leading in trial practice today to refined and technical quibbles which obstruct the trial, confuse the jury, and give rise to appeal on technical grounds only.

But despite occasional defections such as that in the principal case, the restrictive American rule continues as the law in the great majority of jurisdictions.

2. *Broad interpretations of the restrictive view.* Some jurisdictions have interpreted the American rule in a manner that leaves enormous discretion in the trial court judge. See, e.g., Eno v. Adair County Mut. Ins. Ass'n, 294 N.W. 323, 327 (Iowa 1940) ("where the testimony of a witness on direct examination makes a prima facie case, or creates a presumption or inference as to the existence of a fact not directly testified to, the witness may be cross-examined to rebut such prima facie proof, presumption or inference"). Does such a rule restrict cross-examination in any significant way?

3. *Rule 611(b).* The history of Federal Rule 611(b) reflects the strenuous disagreement on the subject within the profession. The original Advisory Committee draft embodied the restrictive majority rule. Preliminary Draft of Proposed Rules of Evidence for United States District Courts, 46 F.R.D. 161, 302 (1969). The wide-open rule was substituted in the version of the rules approved by the Supreme Court. Proposed Rule of Evidence 611(b), 56 F.R.D. 183, 273 (1972). The final congressionally enacted version restores the orthodoxy. Arizona, Maine, Michigan, Mississippi, New Hampshire, North Carolina, Ohio, South Carolina, Tennessee, West Virginia, and Wisconsin, though adopting counterparts of the Federal Rules, have opted for wide-open cross-examination.

Although Rule 611(b) adopts the American approach, in operation the Rule leaves a great deal of discretion and flexibility in the trial court judge. The following case is illustrative.

UNITED STATES v. LARA

United States Court of Appeals, First Circuit, 1999.
181 F.3d 183.

SELYA, CIRCUIT JUDGE.

A federal grand jury indicted a coterie of defendants, including the six appellants (Giovanni "King G" Lara, George "King Paradise" Sepulveda, Terrence "King Bullet" Boyd, Shariff "King Biz" Roman, George "King Animal" Perry, and Eryn "King Guy" Vasquez) for a multiplicity of crimes arising out of their involvement in the Providence chapter of the Almighty Latin King Nation. Following a 44–day trial, each appellant was convicted on one or more of the following charges: racketeering, 18 U.S.C. § 1962(c); conspiracy to commit racketeering, *id.* § 1962(d); violent crime in aid of racketeering (including two murders and two attempted murders), *id.* § 1959(a)(1) & (5); carjacking, *id.* § 2119(3); witness intimidation, *id.* § 1512(b); use or carriage of a firearm during a crime of violence, *id.* § 924(c); and being a felon in possession of a firearm, *id.* § 922(g). The district court sentenced five of the appellants to life imprisonment and the sixth, Vasquez, to 100 months in prison. These appeals followed. We affirm.

I. BACKGROUND

We offer a thumbnail sketch of the interrelationship between the appellants and the Latin Kings, taking the information contained in the record in the light most congenial to the jury's verdict. *See United States v. Houlihan,* 92 F.3d 1271, 1277 (1st Cir.1996). We eschew an exposition of the other evidence, preferring to discuss that evidence in the body of the opinion as it pertains to our consideration of particular points raised by the appellants.

The Latin Kings originated in Chicago in the 1940s. Over time, the street gang's influence spread to other venues. The movement migrated east to Providence in the early 1990s. Though some chapters of the Latin Kings, called Charter Nations, require Hispanic descent as a condition of membership, others (like the Providence chapter) allow persons of all races and ethnicities to join.

Members of the Latin Kings signal their affiliation by sporting beads and other accouterments (including tattoos) in the gang's colors—black and gold. They pay dues, attend weekly meetings, and undertake "missions" (a euphemism that covers an array of activities ranging from running errands to committing violent crimes) when directed by gang leaders. Respect and security rank among the gang's paramount concerns: the Latin Kings routinely discipline members for disrespectful behavior or for discussing Latin King business with outsiders. Discipline runs a lengthy gamut from the "silent treatment" (suspension of all communications with other gang members), to revocation of drug use privileges, to a "bounce" (a time-controlled beating limited to certain areas of the body), to death.

The Almighty Latin King Nation is a hierarchical organization, and each of the appellants held one or more leadership positions within the Providence chapter. Sepulveda served as the group's president (sometimes called "Inca"). Boyd served as the vice-president (sometimes called "Cacique"), and later succeeded Sepulveda as president. Roman served as the chief enforcer (a position previously held by Lara and subsequently held by Perry), and replaced Boyd as vice-president. Vasquez functioned as the group's philosopher and then graduated to the post of investigator.

* * *

C. Scope of Cross–Examination

Perry, who testified at trial in his own defense, strives to persuade us that the district court gave the government too free rein in cross-examination. We are unconvinced.

Perry's thesis is that the challenged cross-examination exceeded the scope of direct examination and, therefore, should have been foreclosed. This thesis rests primarily on the first sentence of Fed.R.Evid. 611(b), which reads: "Cross-examination should be limited to the subject matter of the direct examination and matters affecting the credibility of the witness." Perry notes that his direct examination consisted of only ten questions, restricted to the Vandergroen carjacking and its sequelae. * * * Yet, the trial court allowed the prosecutor, over objection, to cross-question Perry not only about the carjacking, but also about other crimes of which he and his codefendants were accused (including the Mendez murder and two attempted homicides charged as predicate acts in the RICO conspiracy count), and about a draft of a letter seized from his jail cell in which he accused his former girlfriend of "snitching" and requested that she be silenced.

We review district court rulings anent the scope of cross-examination solely for abuse of discretion. *See United States v. Smith,* 145 F.3d 458, 462 (1st Cir.1998); *United States v. Morla–Trinidad,* 100 F.3d 1, 4

(1st Cir.1996). We find none here. It is standard fare for cross-examiners to inquire into issues not mentioned on direct examination, but related to and made relevant by that examination. *See McGautha v. California,* 402 U.S. 183, 215 * * * (1971). It is equally standard—and equally proper—for a cross-examiner to delve into matters which, although not mentioned on direct examination, bear on the witness's credibility. *See id.* Collectively, these two categories envelop the questions that Perry challenges. We explain briefly.

The indictment charged the Vandergroen carjacking as a predicate act within the RICO conspiracy and as a violent crime in aid of racketeering. At trial, the government asserted that Vandergroen's disrespect of Perry offended the Latin King code and led Perry to target him. During the government's case in chief, at least two witnesses testified in support of this theory. Because Perry's direct examination included a denial that the Vandergroen incident had anything to do with the Latin Kings, the government was entitled to test the veracity of this denial. One way of doing so was to interrogate Perry about other crimes that he had committed under the organization's auspices.

In his direct testimony, Perry also endeavored to exonerate Lara, portraying him on direct examination as unaware—until it was too late—that either the carjacking or the killing would transpire. On cross-examination, the government sought to show that this version of events conflicted with Perry's earlier statement to the police and to suggest that he was covering for Lara as part of his perceived duty as a Latin King not to "rat" on fellow gang members. It was in this context that the prosecutor asked about the correspondence in which Perry solicited punishment for his loose-lipped girlfriend. Thus, we detect no abuse of discretion in Judge Lisi's determination that these lines of cross-questioning were not beyond the scope of Perry's direct examination.

We hasten to add that, even were we to conclude that the challenged questions exceeded the scope of direct examination, we nonetheless would uphold the judge's rulings. Perry's animadversions largely overlook the second sentence of Rule 611(b), which empowers trial courts, "in the exercise of discretion, [to] permit inquiry into additional matters as if on direct examination." Fed.R.Evid. 611(b). This authorization confers discretion on trial judges to disregard the first sentence of Rule 611(b) and allow cross-examination to extend into areas not explored on direct. *See Losacco v. F.D. Rich Constr. Co.,* 992 F.2d 382, 385 (1st Cir.1993); *United States v. Arnott,* 704 F.2d 322, 324 (6th Cir.1983); *United States v. Raper,* 676 F.2d 841, 846–47 (D.C.Cir.1982). *But cf. Lis v. Robert Packer Hosp.,* 579 F.2d 819, 823 (3d Cir.1978) (confining the exercise of a district court's discretion under the second sentence of Rule 611(b) to "special circumstances"). In this instance, the challenged questions occupied only a fraction of the cross-examination and bore a close relationship to major trial issues. Thus, whether or not the questions fell within the scope of the direct examination, we could not say that the trial judge's overruling of Perry's objections constituted an abuse of discretion.

* * *

Affirmed.

Notes and Questions

1. *Liberal construction of Rule 611(b).* The liberal construction of Rule 611(b) is further illustrated by statements such as the widely quoted one from United States v. Arnott, 704 F.2d 322, 324 (6th Cir.1983): "[Rule 611(b)] has been liberally construed to include all inferences and implications arising from [direct examination] testimony." Based upon such statements, as well as the application of the rule in *Lara,* is there much left of the American rule in the federal courts? See also United States v. Chance, 306 F.3d 356 (6th Cir.2002) (no abuse of discretion to permit testimony on recross examination about the competency of all employees where redirect examination had elicited testimony about four specific employees).

2. *Limiting cross-examination.* Despite the broad discretion in the trial judge to open cross-examination to matters only remotely related to those covered on direct examination, discretion is perhaps not as broad when the decision has been to limit the examination, particularly on questions of credibility. See, e.g., Harbor Ins. Co. v. Schnabel Foundation Co., 946 F.2d 930 (D.C.Cir.1991). But see United States v. Route, 104 F.3d 59 (5th Cir.1997) (trial judge properly exercised discretion in limiting defendant's cross-examination of government witness); United States v. Mikutowicz, 365 F.3d 65 (1st Cir.2004) (court did not abuse its discretion in limiting cross-examination of IRS agent with regard to tax court opinions).

3. *The accused as witness.* Particularly troublesome questions are raised when the witness being cross-examined is the accused in a criminal case who has elected to testify on the merits. With the dictum in the principal case, compare Tucker v. United States, 5 F.2d 818 (8th Cir.1925). See also Carlson, Cross–Examination of the Accused, 52 Cornell L.Q. 705 (1967); 1 McCormick, Evidence § 26 (6th ed. 2006). It is to be noted that the problem does not arise where the accused testifies solely on a preliminary matter, such testimony having been held not to open the witness to cross-examination on the entire case. Simmons v. United States, 390 U.S. 377 (1968).

BOMMER v. STEDELIN

St. Louis Court of Appeals, Missouri, 1951.
237 S.W.2d 225.

HOUSER, COMMISSIONER. This is a bailment case involving a claim for damages to an automobile delivered to a public parking lot for storage and parking.

This appeal involves the propriety of the action of the trial court in directing a verdict for defendants at the close of plaintiff's evidence and in refusing plaintiff's request to reopen the case to present additional evidence.

* * *

The testimony showed that plaintiff's wife, intending to shop in downtown St. Louis, took plaintiff's automobile to the parking lot at 8th and Delmar, turned the car over to an attendant, received "a little stub", paid "a quarter" and the attendant drove the car "away"; that the parking lot was "two or three stories high and it has no sides". Plaintiff testified that it was "a three story steel affair". Upon returning for the car later in the day plaintiff's wife went to the office on the premises, gave the stub "to the boy, and he went and rang it out on a time card and went and got it for me"; that he went upstairs; that "he got on some kind of a little elevator and went on some kind of a lift." She was standing about 30 or 40 feet from the ramp down which the automobile was driven. She heard and saw the car coming down the ramp. She testified "It sounded like wheels squeaking, and the brakes squeaking and whistling."

"Q. What happened to your car? A. It come on down and hit into a parked car and part of the building, one of those big girders.

"Q. A steel girder? A. Yes, sir.

"Q. Did it stop against the girder or this other automobile? A. Oh, yes."

She testified that "some young fellow" was driving the car down the ramp. She could not say whether or not he was the one to whom she had given the ticket or with whom she had left the car.

The "whole front end" of the automobile was damaged. It looked like the engine was pushed back under the seat. Plaintiff was called to the scene and when he arrived his car was "laying against a big, new car and the balance of it was against the steel girder."

Plaintiff's wife testified that a gentleman who identified himself as Mr. Stedelin came to the parking lot after the occurrence; that he was "in charge there"; that after her husband arrived Stedelin said he did not own the parking lot; that it was owned by the Glueck Realty Company. "Q.—Did he indicate to you or to your husband what capacity he held, if any? A. Well, I don't know whether he was in charge or vice-president or president of it."

Plaintiff testified that he had a conversation with Jerome Stedelin; that plaintiff wanted to know "who was in charge"; that Stedelin said "he was the manager of the parking lot under the Glueck Realty Company at 1103 North Third Street, were the owners of the lot"; that Stedelin did not disclose to plaintiff his capacity with the company.

Plaintiff's proof of damages is not challenged.

When defendants' counsel requested a directed verdict at the close of the plaintiff's evidence, the trial judge indicated he would direct a verdict, whereupon plaintiff's counsel requested leave to reopen the case "in order to bring in additional witnesses to testify with respect to ownership and operation of the parking lot * * * by bringing in the officers of the Glueck Realty Company" stating he could "within an hour" produce evidence to "further show to the court the ownership of this parking lot by the defendants." Leave to reopen was denied.

* * *

Defendants moved for a directed verdict "for the reason that plaintiff wholly failed to identify the ownership and management of the parking lot mentioned in evidence, with either or both the said defendants." Since that motion was sustained the court must have based its action on failure of proof in this connection. Since as we shall see the case must be retried we will not weigh the sufficiency of the proof in this regard, but will consider now the question whether the trial court abused its discretion.

Although a trial judge is vested with a wide latitude and broad discretion in the allowance or denial of leave to reopen a case for additional testimony, that discretion must be a sound judicial discretion. It cannot be exercised in an arbitrary manner. The record shows that the request was made at 6 minutes before 1:00 o'clock P.M.; that the jury was recessed until 2:00 o'clock; that counsel assured the court that he could produce the required evidence "within an hour". There was no showing of surprise to defendants or of inconvenience to the court, parties, counsel, or jury or that the adverse party would have been deceived or prejudiced in any manner by granting the leave. The ruling on the motion for a directed verdict had not yet been made. The court denied plaintiff the opportunity to offer evidence to prove that defendants owned and operated the parking facility, while at the same time directing a verdict against plaintiff for failure to prove such fact. This constituted an abuse of discretion. * * *

For the reasons stated the Commissioner recommends that the judgment of the circuit court be reversed and the cause remanded.

PER CURIAM.

The foregoing opinion of HOUSER, C., is adopted as the opinion of the court.

The judgment of the circuit court is, accordingly, reversed and the cause remanded.

Note

It is commonly held that the trial court may, in its sound discretion, permit reopening of the evidence after both parties have formally rested. At what stage of the proceedings should the court's discretion to permit reopening expire? See United States v. Nunez, 432 F.3d 573 (4th Cir.2005) (district court abused its discretion in permitting the government to reopen its case after summation and after jury deliberations began to present report summarizing interview with defendant; by admitting the report at that point, the report "gained distorted importance, prejudiced the appellants' case," and precluded an adequate opportunity to meet the additional evidence offered). See also 6 Wigmore, Evidence §§ 1876–81 (Chadbourn rev. 1976); Annot., 87 A.L.R.2d 849.

Topic III
RELEVANCY AND ITS LIMITS

Chapter 7

THE CONCEPT OF RELEVANCY

A. INTRODUCTION

JAMES, RELEVANCY, PROBABILITY AND THE LAW[1]

29 California Law Review 689, 690–91 (1941).

Relevancy, as the word itself indicates, is not an inherent characteristic of any item of evidence but exists as a relation between an item of evidence and a proposition sought to be proved. If an item of evidence tends to prove or to disprove any proposition, it is relevant to that proposition. If the proposition itself is one provable in the case at bar, or if it in turn forms a further link in a chain of proof the final proposition of which is provable in the case at bar, then the offered item of evidence has probative value in the case. Whether the immediate or ultimate proposition sought to be proved is provable in the case at bar is determined by the pleadings, by the procedural rules applicable thereto, and by the substantive law governing the case. Whether the offered item of evidence tends to prove the proposition at which it is ultimately aimed depends upon other factors, shortly to be considered. But because relevancy, as used by Thayer and in the Code, means tendency to prove a proposition properly provable in the case, an offered item of evidence may be excluded as "irrelevant" for either of these two quite distinct reasons: because it is not probative of the proposition at which it is directed, or because that proposition is not provable in the case.[2]

1. Copyright by Fred B. Rothman & Co. Reprinted by permission. Throughout the cases and materials in this chapter some footnotes from the originals have been omitted; others have been renumbered. [Ed.]

2. Henceforth, for brevity, propositions of ultimate fact properly provable in a case under the pleadings and substantive law will be referred to as "material propositions"; the characterization "relevant" will be reserved for propositions of evidence which, whether or not material themselves, tend to prove other propositions which are material. "Irrelevant" and "immaterial" are of course the contraries of the two first terms, as defined. * * *

Notes and Questions

1. *Discussions.* Other helpful treatments of the nature of relevancy include: Crump, On the Uses of Irrelevant Evidence, 34 Hous.L.Rev. 1 (1997); Ladd, Determination of Relevancy, 31 Tul.L.Rev. 81 (1956); Lempert, Modeling Relevance, 75 Mich.L.Rev. 1021 (1977); Lyon & Koehler, The Relevance Ratio: Evaluating the Probative Value of Expert Testimony in Child Abuse Cases, 82 Cornell L.Rev. 43 (1996); Trautman, Logical or Legal Relevancy—A Conflict in Theory, 5 Vand.L.Rev. 385 (1952).

2. *Materiality.* As indicated in the quotation from James, the admissibility of evidence often depends upon the substantive law, which governs whether a proposition is properly in the case. Thus an allegation in a complaint that a promissory note was given for "a valuable consideration" would not be provable by evidence that it was given for an antecedent debt in a jurisdiction where that did not constitute a valuable consideration. The evidence is immaterial under that classic but seldom observed concept and irrelevant under the looser definition in Federal Rule 401. Accordingly, in diversity cases the admissibility of evidence in federal courts may depend upon state substantive law.

3. *Standard.* By what standard should the probative value of offered evidence be judged in determining whether to admit it? At least two possibilities will come to mind: (1) evidence to be relevant must render the fact sought to be proved more probable than not, and (2) evidence to be relevant must help to render the fact sought to be proved more probable than would be so in the absence of the evidence. The first standard, which, as suggested by the materials of Topic II, is commonly used in evaluating the sufficiency of evidence, has also sometimes been employed by courts in the present context. These applications would appear unfortunate. Not only will the standard, if rigorously applied, exclude a great deal of helpful evidence, but it also entirely fails to take into account the fact that it is frequently possible to establish a material proposition by a conjunction of evidentiary items, none of which would alone suffice. To extend Professor McCormick's metaphor, a brick is not a wall, but many bricks may make one.

The second standard noted above is most commonly applied. See Rule 401. It allows the legal mind to display a tremendous sweep of ingenuity in attacking problems of proof, but it also entails problems of its own. The cases of the present section, all dealing with the same generic type of evidence, will serve to illustrate both facets of the standard, and also to suggest the relative nature of relevancy itself.

4. *Federal Rules of Evidence.* Rules 401–403 deal with the general question of relevancy and the exclusion of relevant evidence on grounds of prejudice, confusion, or waste of time. For discussion of these rules see Dolan, Rule 403: The Prejudice Rule in Evidence, 49 S.Cal.L.Rev. 220 (1976); Gold, Federal Rule of Evidence 403: Observations on the Nature of Unfairly Prejudicial Evidence, 58 Wash.L.Rev. 497 (1983); Travers, An Essay on the Determination of Relevancy Under the Federal Rules of Evidence, 1977 Ariz.St.L.J. 327; Weinstein & Berger, Basic Rules of Relevancy in the Proposed Federal Rules of Evidence, 4 Ga.L.Rev. 43 (1969).

5. *Rule 403.* Rule 403 recognizes the problems which arise from taking the broad view of relevancy reflected by Rule 401. Should identical effect be

given to each of the various factors which may weigh against the admissibility of relevant evidence? If Justice Holmes was correct in saying that the exclusion of evidence which would unduly consume time is "a concession to the shortness of life," Reeve v. Dennett, 11 N.E. 938, 944 (Mass.1887), then the admission of such evidence can scarcely be more than harmless error. Is this true of evidence which may involve the other factors enumerated by the Rule?

B. AN ILLUSTRATION OF RELEVANCY RULES: EVIDENCE OF FINANCIAL WORTH

CITY OF CLEVELAND v. PETER KIEWIT SONS' CO.

United States Court of Appeals, Sixth Circuit, 1980.
624 F.2d 749.

WEICK, CIRCUIT JUDGE.

* * *

I

Dock 34, the dock in question, was originally constructed in the year 1908. In recent years, because of its deterioration and lack of repair, it was no longer used for its original purpose and only a small portion of which was being used chiefly as a parking lot for nearby sporting events, and for the mooring of a schoolship and a pleasure boat. In 1973, Peter Kiewit Sons' Co., a contracting firm headquartered in Omaha, Nebraska (and incorporated in that state), was engaged in performing dike construction and dike modification at another place in the Cleveland Harbor, pursuant to a contract with the Corps of Engineers. Kiewit entered into the permit agreement with the City whereby Kiewit was permitted to use a portion of the dock to load blast furnace slag on barges to be transported to the dike project. Under the agreement, Kiewit was permitted to occupy and use a 100 – 400 foot portion of the southwest corner of the dock from July 9, 1973, to and including October 12, 1973 (except for six days in late July when the area would be occupied by a carnival). Kiewit agreed to pay the City therefor $2,000 a month.

Kiewit actually occupied the dock site from July 16 to and including October 6 (except for the period from July 21 through July 30 when it was used by the carnival); the dock was used for the slag loading operation from August 1 to October 6. The slag loading operation consisted of trucking slag to the dock, where the slag was piled and then loaded onto barges for transportation to the breakwall some distance away. The operations were concluded, and Kiewit vacated the dock on October 8, 1973.

On October 24, 1973, after Kiewit had surrendered possession to the City, portions of the dock collapsed. The portion that collapsed included only a small section of the area which had been leased to Kiewit; the major portion of the area which collapsed was not within the section that had been leased to and used by Kiewit.

The City of Cleveland filed suit against Kiewit in the Court of Common Pleas of Cuyahoga County in a three-count complaint. The three causes of action alleged reflected different theories of law under which the plaintiff sought to impose liability on defendant for the collapses of the dock. The action was removed on the basis of diversity of citizenship to the United States District Court for the Northern District of Ohio on August 28, 1974. The City sought recovery of $350,000 in compensatory damages plus interest. Following a November 1976 trial which lasted six days, the jury[3] returned a general verdict in favor of the City and against Kiewit in the amount of $350,000. Judgment was entered thereon plus costs. Kiewit then filed a timely motion for judgment notwithstanding the verdict, or, in the alternative, for a new trial, alleging misconduct of counsel for the City as one of the three grounds that "the remarks, argument and questioning of witnesses by plaintiff's counsel regarding liability insurance and defendant's financial resources, considered in total, were prejudicial."

The District Judge ordered a remittitur of $175,000, and stated that, if the remittitur were not accepted within thirty days, he would grant a new trial on the issue of damages. * * * The City thereafter advised the District Court that it would decline to accept the remittitur, and would instead proceed to a new trial on the issue of damages. The court then ordered a new trial solely on the issue of damages, with the trial date to be set following this appeal.

The comments which are at issue here began early in the City's opening statement to the jury, when Nick DeVito, an Assistant Law Director of the City, stated that "the defendant is Peter Kiewit and Sons, a corporation whose headquarters are in Omaha, Nebraska * * * Peter Kiewit is one of the largest construction corporations." Counsel for Kiewit promptly objected; the Court explained that "if they (plaintiff) can prove that in their evidence, I will overrule the objection, but if they can't, I will then admonish the jury to disregard it." Mr. DeVito then proceeded to tell the jury that "Peter Kiewit Co. is one of the largest construction corporations in the United States * * * it has international operations throughout the world. Its marine division is headquartered in New Jersey, and * * * you will have * * * testimony * * * from some of its executives from that part of the country." Mr. DeVito then stated that Kiewit, in 1973, "was awarded approximately a $9 million contract with the United States Corps of Army Engineers." Kiewit's attorney objected, but was overruled by the Court. Counsel for the City then repeated his statement about the $9 million contract. At the conclusion of the plaintiff's opening statement, the court admonished the jury as to Mr. DeVito's remarks that Kiewit was one of the nation's largest

3. Of the six members of the jury, three were residents of the City of Cleveland, and the other three resided in Cuyahoga County.

construction companies, and that the defendant had a $9 million contract with the Corps. The court instructed the jury that "these two statements standing by themselves are not be considered in your deliberations * * * the fact that they were large or that they had a large monetary contract with the United States government has no bearing on the case whatsoever."

During direct examination of Robert Jones, a witness for the City, Mr. DeVito, referring to Kiewit, inquired "How big a company is that?" Counsel for Kiewit promptly objected, but the Court permitted Jones to answer that defendant had "a rather large, good credit rating" and was a large corporation. Mr. DeVito asked where Kiewit was headquartered, and Jones responded "Omaha, Nebraska." Mr. DeVito also inquired whether Kiewit had a marine division, and where it was headquartered; Jones replied that defendant's marine division headquarters was located in Tenafly, New Jersey. Counsel for the City then asked: "Do you know the size of the contract that they had with the federal government?" Kiewit's attorney objected immediately, and was sustained.

During cross-examination of William Bogas, a witness for the City, the attorney representing Kiewit asked several questions concerning a provision of the permit agreement, under the terms of which Kiewit was obligated to take out a general public liability insurance policy in the amount of $300,000 and $100,000. The witness acknowledged that the City was named as an additional insured, so that the insurance protected the City as well as Kiewit from liability to third persons. The witness testified that he did not know whether the City had made any claims under the policy for damage to the dock.

Later, on redirect, the following exchange between Mr. DeVito and witness Bogas transpired:

Q. Are you aware of the contract between Peter Kiewit and the Corps of Engineers?

A. Yes.

Q. Do you know approximately the amount of that contract?

Counsel for Kiewit immediately objected, and the court sustained the objection.

Jack Frakes, a Kiewit employee who testified on behalf of the defendant, was asked on direct examination about the permit agreement's insurance provisions. Frakes acknowledged that the City had drafted the provisions, calling for a general public liability insurance policy with $100,000 and $300,000 limits, and, further, that Kiewit complied with the provisions and obtained said insurance which, as required by the contract, named the City as an additional insured.

On cross-examination, DeVito asked Frakes whether Kiewit "is a pretty big corporation?" Frakes answered: "It is a fair-sized corporation." DeVito then inquired "how large" Kiewit was in the field of marine engineering. The trial court permitted the witness to answer over objection. DeVito persisted in asking "how big" the defendant was, and finally the court interrupted: "I have already admonished the jury that the largeness of the company doesn't make any difference as far as the verdict is concerned in this case."

Subsequently during the cross-examination of Frakes, the following exchange occurred:

Q. You talked about insurance. You did take out insurance?

A. Yes, sir.

Q. And you did have the City of Cleveland as an additional insured?

A. Yes, sir.

Q. And wasn't that in relation to claims from third parties?

A. Yes, sir, liability insurance.

Keenen (counsel for Kiewit): Objection, your Honor.

Court: Are you talking about liability insurance?

DeVito: Yes. I mean, Mr. Keenen represents an insurance company, doesn't he?

Keenen: Objection, your Honor.

Court: Objection sustained.

DeVito: Well, you tell me: Is there insurance involved in this particular case?

Keenen: Objection, your Honor.

Court: Objection sustained.

Keenen: I think that is highly prejudicial, your Honor, He asked three times.

Court: I will ask the jury to disregard that. Whether there is or not has no bearing on this lawsuit.

DeVito: Now, Peter Kiewit has many claims against it in various places throughout the world?

A. No.

Keenen: Objection.

Court: Objection sustained.

DeVito: Are you familiar with various claims and lawsuits against Peter Kiewit Co.?

Keenen: Objection.

Court: Sustained.

During cross-examination of defense witness Saada, the following transpired:

DeVito: Now, you talked about insurance just briefly. You said that you can only get insurance—

Court: Just one minute.

Denny (counsel for Kiewit): Objection.

Court: I don't recall anything about insurance.

Keenen: I can't recall anything about it. It is prejudicial at this point anyway. This is the third or fourth time he has done that.

Court: I am going to sustain the objection, and I am going to admonish counsel that he is not to talk about it.

DeVito: I would like to approach the bench.

Court: No. You can take exception.

DeVito: I am not talking about insurance in this case.

Court: I am not going to permit you to ask these questions.

Q. You have talked about buildings and you talked about buildings having a useful life; is that correct?

A. Yes, sir.

Q. And you also talked about the limit to which someone could acquire insurance on a building, is that correct?

A. The limits. My statement went something like that. I doubt very much anybody would give you insurance for something built for more than 50 years.

DeVito: Your Honor, if I may and I do not mean to be disrespectful to the Court, this is something he testified to earlier, and this is what I was going to ask him about.

Court: That you may do.

During his closing argument, Mr. DeVito again mentioned that Kiewit had undertaken a "seven or eight million dollar job, whatever it was that they were doing for the Corps of Engineers." Counsel for Kiewit promptly objected to the mention of said contract, which had not been admitted into evidence, and the Court admonished Mr. DeVito "not to comment on it."

During his summation, Mr. Keenen, representing Kiewit, said:

> As far as the insurance permit that opposing counsel says is in the contract, read it for yourself. You will find that the City is the named insured, so that if there is any coverage under that contract for Peter Kiewit, the same coverage belongs to the City, and they could collect fully the limit in that policy.

The following colloquy ensued:

DeVito: Your Honor, I am going to object. That insurance was for third—

Court: I will sustain the objection. The insurance in the contract, so there will be no misunderstanding, is with reference to third party liability, and not as between the parties.

DeVito: That insurance does not extend between Peter Kiewit and the City, your Honor.

Court: They can read the contract for themselves.

In his rebuttal, Mr. DeVito stated that Kiewit was "a $75 million corporation in the marine engineering field." Mr. Keenen objected, and the Court, in sustaining the objection, admonished DeVito: "Now, you have done this before, Mr. DeVito, and I am going to have to reprimand you. I have said the size of the corporation makes no difference."

Finally, in concluding his summation, Mr. DeVito told the Jury:

> I respectfully request that you discharge your responsibility in your own conscience as best you can and that you find for the City of Cleveland and that you make us whole and hold Peter Kiewit responsible for the damage that they have caused to the taxpayers of the City of Cleveland.

In his charge to the jury, Judge Green instructed:

> This case should be considered and decided by you as an action between persons of equal standing in the community, of equal worth, and holding the same or similar stations in life. Both the plaintiff, a municipal corporation, and the defendant, a private corporation, stand equal before the law, and are to be dealt with as equals in a court of justice.

II

Kiewit was entitled to a fair trial but, as we have pointed out, did not receive it because of the pervasive misconduct of counsel for the City.

* * *

In the case at bar, counsel for the City almost continuously sought to plant the seed in the minds of the jurors that Kiewit was a very large corporation with international operations. In addition to the comments recounted above, Mr. DeVito made several other remarks, and asked other questions designed to convey to the jury the image of the defendant as a giant in the field of marine engineering. For example, plaintiff's trial counsel managed to inform the jury that defendant's headquarters was located at "1000 Kiewit Plaza" leaving it for the jurors to draw the inevitable inference that defendant was a huge corporation. Similarly, Mr. DeVito suggested that Kiewit employed several attorneys at its headquarters. Since the Kiewit name is not, among the general public, synonymous with a "corporate giant," as, for example, IBM or General Motors would be, it is unlikely that the jurors would have been aware of defendant's size had Mr. DeVito not strived to so inform them at every opportunity. It was obviously an appeal to passion and prejudice.

The City has advanced the contention that its comments about Kiewit's stature were intended to show that defendant's ability and experience would enable it to determine the condition of the dock in advance of entering the agreement and beginning operations. Indeed, the court below noted that "there was a tenable argument that defendant's size was relevant to the question of its expertise which in turn could be relevant to its knowledge of conditions pertaining to the dock." Yet, the trial court emphasized that "it was not necessary to make mention of defendant's status as a leader in the field of marine engineering in the manner and with the frequency that plaintiff's counsel did." It seems clear that plaintiff could have demonstrated defendant's knowledge and expertise in a much less prejudicial (and perhaps an even more direct and effective) manner.

This court has said, in a diversity case governed by Ohio law, that "evidence as to the poverty or wealth of a party to an action is inadmissible in a negligence action." Eisenhauer v. Burger, 431 F.2d 833, 837 (6th Cir.1970). "Appealing to the sympathy of jurors through references to financial disparity is improper." Draper v. Airco, Inc., 580 F.2d 91, 95 (3d Cir.1978). The Third Circuit in *Draper* explained that:

> The cumulative thrust of plaintiff's counsel's argument * * * was that because the defendants were rich (giants of the industrial world) and because the plaintiff was poor, the jury should base its verdict in favor of plaintiff on this financial disparity. But justice is not dependent upon the wealth or poverty of the parties and a jury should not be urged to predicate its verdict on a prejudice against bigness or wealth.

In *Draper,* plaintiff's counsel repeatedly referred to a $7 million contract between defendant Airco and U.S. Steel.

In Ohio, a "great number of cases * * * have condemned arguments of counsel contrasting the wealth and poverty or strength and weakness, of the opposing litigants, appealing to prejudice against a party to an action because it is a corporation, or corporation of a particular class * * * " 53 Ohio Jur.2d Section 270, pp. 185–186. The Supreme Court of Ohio articulated the general rule in Hudock v. Ry. Co., 164 Ohio St. 493, 498–499, 132 N.E.2d 108 (1956):

> * * * in damage actions in which compensatory damages only are recoverable, evidence is not admissible, directly or indirectly, to show the wealth or financial standing of either the plaintiff or the defendant, except in those exceptional cases, such as actions for defamation or injury to reputation, where the position or wealth of the parties is necessarily involved in determining the damages sustained. It has ever been the theory of our government and a cardinal principle of our jurisprudence that the rich and poor stand alike in courts of justice and that neither the wealth of one nor the poverty of the other shall be permitted to affect the administration of law.

See Book v. Erskine & Sons, Inc., 154 Ohio St. 391, 399–401, 96 N.E.2d 289, 293 (1951) (statements relating to the poverty of one of the parties or the wealth of the other "are clearly calculated to direct the jury's attention to the need of an injured party for compensation rather than the real issues in the case" and have been held to be prejudicial error).

Counsel for the City, as noted above, also made several comments, and asked several questions, which were intended to inform and emphasize that Kiewit had its corporate "residence in another state." Smith v. Travelers Insurance Company, 438 F.2d 373, 375 (6th Cir.1971). Here, as in *Smith,* "[T]he remarks were * * * obviously designed to prejudice the jurors. Taken alone the statements may well have been prejudicial." Id.

The other topic about which counsel for the City made improper and prejudicial references was insurance. Although it is true that it was counsel for Kiewit who first brought up the subject of insurance, the insurance to which he referred was the general public liability insurance policy required under the permit agreement with the City, which protected both Kiewit and the City from claims by third parties. The Court below correctly observed that this "mention of insurance was inevitable in the course of the trial by reason of the fact that matters of insurance coverage were included in the contracts between the parties." However, it was counsel for the plaintiff who interjected the subject of *another* insurance policy—one covering Kiewit in the instant litigation, and one under which Mr. Keenen was allegedly representing Kiewit at trial. * * * As the Court in Radinsky v. Ellis, 167 F.2d 745, 746 (D.C.Cir. 1948), stated:

> In a case such as this, when the existence of insurance protection in favor of the defendant is shown to the jury, a mistrial should be declared forthwith. * * *

In light of the foregoing, the curative instructions which the trial court eventually chose to give were plainly, "not sufficient to remove the probability of prejudice." *Draper,* supra at 97. As the Fifth Circuit has so accurately observed:

> * * * the bench and bar are both aware that cautionary instructions are effective only up to a certain point. There must be a line drawn in any trial where, after repeated exposure of a jury to prejudicial information, * * * cautionary instructions will have little, if any, effect in eliminating the prejudicial harm. O'Rear v. Fruehauf Corp., 554 F.2d 1304, 1309 (5th Cir.1977).

Furthermore, the excessive size of the verdict demonstrates the prejudicial effect of counsel's comments. * * * This Court is likewise of the opinion that the remittitur ordered below does not, and cannot, erase the prejudicial error deliberately injected by plaintiff's counsel. In *Draper,* supra * * * at 97, the Court explained:

> A jury which is prejudiced with respect to its finding of liability is not likely to be free from prejudice in awarding damages. Because there is a substantial probability that the error which affected the liability verdict also affected the determination of damages, the new trial must deal with both liability and damages.

This Court believes that the spillover of prejudice discussed in *Draper* may also occur in a case such as this: since the jury was prejudiced with respect to its award of damages, it cannot be said that its finding of liability was free from prejudice. Thus, on remand, "the new trial must deal with both liability and damages." * * *

* * * Since the prejudicial error here cannot be corrected by remittitur, this Court reverses and remands for a new trial on all issues.

Notes and Questions

1. What was the court's basis for condemning the injection into the case of defendant's financial condition? Of the existence of liability insurance covering the claim? What arguments can be made in support of the relevance of each of them? In a negligence case?

2. At an earlier day, forays into the financial condition of the parties tended to be more colorful. E.g., Louisville & N.R. Co. v. Hull, 68 S.W. 433, 436 (Ky.1902), an action for delay in shipment of the corpse of plaintiff's wife. Plaintiff's lawyer in final argument declared, "We were in the magnificent depot of defendant in Nashville * * * which is more magnificent than Soloman's [sic] Temple. The ticket office there cost more than this court house, I reckon; and the doors of that station, more than plaintiff asked for his damages in this case, I imagine."

3. *Determining prejudice.* How does a court determine what is prejudicial? Under rules such as Rule 403, how does a court compare the probative value of evidence against its danger of unfair prejudice, etc.? See Teitelbaum, Sutton–Barbere & Johnson, Evaluating the Prejudicial Effect of Evidence: Can Judges Identify the Impact of Improper Evidence on Juries? 1983 Wis.L.Rev. 1147, and Gold, Federal Rule of Evidence 403: Observations on the Nature of Unfairly Prejudicial Evidence, 58 Wash.L.Rev. 497 (1983).

4. The cases in the present section of the casebook develop the concept of relevancy by considering varying aspects of the financial condition of parties as evidence. Liability insurance is considered following *Reed v. General Motors Corp.*, which appears later in this section.

5. See Annots., 122 A.L.R. 1408 and 65 A.L.R.2d 945, as to admissibility of evidence of a party's financial condition.

PLUMB v. CURTIS

Supreme Court of Errors of Connecticut, 1895.
33 A. 998.

[Plaintiff, Hanford C. Plumb, sued Lewis F. Curtis for building materials allegedly purchased by the latter through his agent Simeon Plumb. Plaintiff had furnished materials for three houses, on Simeon Plumb's order, and defendant admitted responsibility therefor. Thereafter plaintiff furnished materials for an additional five houses, also on Simeon Plumb's order, and defendant denied liability, claiming the materials had been sold to Simeon Plumb. The jury returned a verdict for plaintiff, and defendant appeals from the judgment entered thereon.]

BALDWIN, J. * * * The plaintiff was allowed, against the defendant's objection, to testify that Simeon Plumb was a man of no property, so far as he knew. It was not disputed that all the goods charged to the defendant had been ordered by Simeon Plumb, and sold on credit. The plaintiff claimed that he had extended this credit to the defendant, and was justified by the circumstances in so doing. The defendant denied that Simeon Plumb had any authority to buy on his credit the goods charged in 1891; and the main controversy was as to this point.

Unless excluded by some rule or principle of law, any fact may be proved which logically tends to aid the trier in the determination of the issue. Evidence is admitted not because it is shown to be competent, but because it is not shown to be incompetent. No precise and universal test of relevancy is furnished by the law. The question must be determined in each case according to the teachings of reason and judicial experience. Thayer's Cases on Evidence, 2, 3. "If the evidence offered conduces in any reasonable degree to establish the probability or improbability of the fact in controversy, it should go to the jury." Insurance Company v. Weide, 78 U.S. 438, 20 L.Ed. 197, 11 Wall. 438, 440. The question as to its admission or rejection addresses itself to the court as one to be answered with a view to practical rather than theoretical considerations. The guiding principle is well stated in Stephen's Digest of the Law of Evidence (Chap. 1, p. 36) in these words: "The word 'relevant' means that any two facts to which it is applied are so related to each other, that according to the common course of events one either taken by itself or in connection with other facts proves or renders probable the past, present, or future existence or non-existence of the other."

The jury, in the case at bar, were to determine whether it was probable that the plaintiff, after charging all the materials furnished on the order of Simeon Plumb, for the construction of three houses in Bridgeport, to the defendant as the principal for whom Plumb acted, and for whom it was not denied that he had authority to act, proceeded to furnish like materials for the construction of five other houses in Bridgeport on the order of Plumb, and to charge them to the defendant, when he really gave credit to Plumb and dealt with him as the only party to the transaction. According to the common course of human conduct, a merchant is not likely to continue for several months to make almost daily sales on credit, of goods worth in the aggregate several hundred dollars, to a man who, so far as he knows, is destitute of any means to pay for them. Inglis v. Usherwood, 1 East, 515, 524; O'Brien v. Norris, 16 Md. 122, 77 Am.Dec. 284. If he has been selling to him the same line of goods previously, as an agent for a responsible principal, and claims that the sales in question were made in the same way, and under the same circumstances, any evidence which renders a change of credit improbable, is relevant to an inquiry as to whether such a change was made. We think the plaintiff's testimony, taken in connection with the other evidence already in the case, fairly tended to throw light on the matter in controversy, and was properly received. * * *

There was no error in the judgment of the trial court.

Notes and Questions

1. If plaintiff had not introduced evidence that Simeon was without means, should defendant have been allowed to introduce evidence that Simeon was a man of means? How many definitions of relevancy does the opinion contain?

2. *Payment defense.* If the defense of payment were raised, would evidence of the financial condition of the parties be admissible? See Horicon v. Langlois' Estate, 66 A.2d 16 (Vt.1949).

3. *Will contest.* In a will contest on grounds of testamentary incapacity, should evidence be admitted of the financial condition of the various "natural objects of the testator's bounty"? See Norris v. Bristow, 236 S.W.2d 316 (Mo.1951).

STATE v. MATHIS

Supreme Court of New Jersey, 1966.
221 A.2d 529.

WEINTRAUB, C.J.

Defendant was convicted of murder in the first degree, and the jury not having recommended life imprisonment, he was sentenced to die. He appeals directly to this Court. R.R. 1:2–1(c).

The deceased, Stanley Caswell, had an insurance debit route which took him to North Ninth Street in Kenilworth. The residents there knew him as "the insurance man."

There are two houses at 218–220 North Ninth Street, one behind the other. Defendant's father occupied an apartment in the rear house. On February 12, 1965 Mr. Caswell was at the premises. Defendant, too, was there, to see his father on some matter. One State's witness placed defendant outside the house at about 6:00 P.M. on a course on which defendant and Mr. Caswell would have met. Moments later, one occupant heard two reports, like those of exploding firecrackers.

James Faines, who also lived at 220 North Ninth Street, testified that he and his friend, Lewis Clark, were working in the driveway on Faines' automobile; that he saw defendant pushing a man into the back seat of a red Renault which belonged to the insurance man; that he looked into the car and saw that it was the insurance man; that blood was coming from the victim's forehead and he was moaning; and that defendant struck Faines with his arm, saying "Get away from here, boy." Faines left, remarking to Clark that "It looks like Marvin was rolling the guy." Clark testified substantially to the same effect, although he did not look into the Renault and could not say who the victim was.

The testimony shows the Renault was then driven a short distance to a wooded area; that two further shots were fired; and the car then set afire. When the blaze was extinguished, the badly charred body of the deceased was found.

The autopsy revealed that death was due to four shots fired from a .22 caliber gun. There was testimony that late on the day of the murder or early the next morning, defendant tried to sell a small gun and a box of shells.

Defendant admitted being at his father's home at the time of the murder, but denied all knowledge of it. He said he did not know Mr. Caswell and did not see the red Renault. He denied trying to sell a gun. He said that on the 13th, the day after the crime, he heard his wife was in police custody and that he was wanted as a "material witness." He said his brother-in-law advised him to lose himself in Harlem for a while, in the hope that the culprit would meanwhile be found, and this because defendant had a criminal record. Defendant did go to New York City, but on the 15th he called the F.B.I., identified himself, and was taken into custody.

I

* * *

* * * Mrs. Caswell testified the deceased wore a wristwatch, a wedding ring, and a Masonic lapel pin, none of which were recovered. Mr. Brady, a chemist, testified that his analysis of the charred remnants revealed no evidence of gold beyond that usually found in ordinary dirt or debris. There was no direct proof of the loss of money, for the deceased had apparently secreted his wallet in the car where it was found by the police, and some change, totaling less than two dollars, was still in his trousers. But the debit book was found, and an audit of it indicated a shortage of $3.93. There was also testimony that the right rear pocket of deceased's trousers was turned inside out.

* * *

V

The prosecutor cross-examined defendant as to how much money he had and when he last worked. The examination suggested strongly that the State might be urging that defendant was in financial need, and hence was likely to commit a robbery. The trial court interrupted to say it would not permit proof of a financial need, unless the State was in a position to show also that things of value were stolen and that thereafter the defendant was affluent. Cf. State v. Schuck, 96 N.J.L. 154, 114 A. 562 (E. & A.1921). This the State could not do.

Prior to that ruling the prosecutor had asked defendant when he last worked and in response defendant said he had from time to time assisted his father in the repair of automobiles at his father's home. The prosecutor wished to pursue that matter, and in order to take it outside the trial court's ban against inquiry into financial need, the prosecutor said his inquiry was directed solely at "credibility," that the inquiry

> "* * * was intended for purposes of testing the validity of the defendant's testimony and his credibility in that, if I recall correctly,

> he said that he never saw the insurance man, for one thing. Now, if he was working with any degree of regularity at 220 North Ninth Street, he may have seen the insurance man on one or more occasions. That is an element of testing the credibility of this witness. And also the other element that may arise out of such testimony involving pure and simple credibility."

The court permitted the inquiry on "your representation that the question goes to the credibility of the defendant and is not a part of a designed attempt to picture as one critically in need of funds." The prosecutor then drew from defendant a statement of the number of times he had worked with his father on the repair of automobiles.

If the State's purpose remained only to show defendant was there with such frequency as to make it likely he knew the deceased, defendant's testimony that he was thus at his father's home would not have been challenged. But the State proceeded to call two neighbors of the father to testify they never saw defendant working there; and in summation the prosecutor asked why defendant had not called his father or his sister-in-law, who also lived there, to support his testimony. Thus instead of proving defendant was at the premises, the State in essence undertook to prove that he was not. The State was no longer trying to show that defendant visited his father's home so often that he probably knew the deceased. Rather the State's rebuttal testimony had to mean that defendant lied when he said he had worked with his father, *ergo,* his financial needs must have been met in some other way.

* * *

Whether defendant did or did not work with his father was of course not an issue in the case. Nor would it directly bear upon credibility, for surely there is nothing about working with one's father, or not working with one's father, which suggests a man cannot be a trustworthy witness. Thus the rebuttal evidence was not germane to the case, either with respect to the triable issues or as to defendant's reliability as a witness. His testimony therefore could not be contradicted. If no more were involved than an infraction of the rules relating to collateral issues, the irregularity might be of no moment. But what emerged was something more than a mere trial of something extraneous. The point the State in truth made by its rebuttal witnesses was that defendant lied when he said he worked for his father, and hence he did not earn money that way, and being otherwise essentially unemployed, he must have been destitute and therefore he likely would rob. Thus, in ultimate effect, the State made the very point which the trial court said was impermissible.

Undoubtedly a lack of money is logically connected with a crime involving financial gain. The trouble is that it would prove too much against too many. As said in 2 Wigmore, Evidence (3d ed. 1940), § 392, p. 341:

> "The *lack of money* by A might be relevant enough to show the probability of A's desiring to *commit a crime* in order to obtain money. But the practical result of such a doctrine would be to put a poor person under so much unfair suspicion and at such a relative disadvantage that for reasons of fairness this argument has seldom been countenanced as evidence of the graver crimes, particularly of violence."

The relationship between the deceased and defendant of creditor and debtor may be competent as to motive, see State v. Rogers, 19 N.J. 218, 116 A.2d 37 (1955), but, in general terms, there must be something more than poverty to tie a defendant into a criminal milieu. Hence we are satisfied the trial court was correct in its approach to this subject. The State, however, transgressed that ruling when by its cross-examination of defendant and its rebuttal testimony it again projected before the jury the forbidden theme that defendant had no apparent means of income and hence was likely to commit a crime for dollar gain. This was improper and injurious.

The judgment is reversed [on this and other grounds] and the matter remanded for a new trial.

For reversal: CHIEF JUSTICE WEINTRAUB and JUSTICES JACOBS, FRANCIS, PROCTOR, HALL and SCHETTINO—6.

For affirmance: None.

Notes and Questions

1. *Affluence after a crime.* Would the principle of *Mathis* foreclose the prosecution in a bank robbery case from introducing evidence that the accused had been without means prior to the robbery and exhibited affluence after the robbery? See United States v. Weller, 238 F.3d 1215 (10th Cir. 2001); State v. Kane, 492 N.W.2d 209 (Iowa Ct.App.1992).

2. *Evidence of poverty.* Evidence that an accused person is poor is generally excluded when offered to prove motive for a crime involving financial gain. See United States v. Reed, 700 F.2d 638 (11th Cir.1983); Vitek v. State, 453 A.2d 514 (Md.1982); 2 Wigmore, Evidence § 392 (Chadbourn rev. 1979). However, note the following: United States v. Hawkins, 360 F.Supp.2d 689 (E.D.Pa. 2005) (evidence of financial condition admitted in fraud and perjury case where it bore directly on transaction relevant to the indictment); State v. Delahoussaye, 534 So.2d 76 (La.Ct.App.1988) (couple's financial condition and insurance policies on husband admissible in case where wife claimed shooting of husband was accidental); United States v. Reed, 639 F.2d 896 (2d Cir.1981) (securities fraud trial, letter threatening foreclosure of defendant's home held admissible); United States v. Hernandez, 588 F.2d 346 (2d Cir.1978) (unlawful importation of cocaine by airline steward; not error to admit evidence that accused was having problems with alimony and debts; court noted absence of evidence that he was a poor person); Commonwealth v. Johnson, 225 N.E.2d 360 (Mass.1967) (robbery murder; not error to admit evidence that accused needed but did not have money for down payment on automobile); State v. Schieving, 535 P.2d 1232

(Utah 1975) (embezzlement; not error to admit evidence of heavy indebtedness and poor financial condition). In addition, compare United States v. Saniti, 604 F.2d 603 (9th Cir.1979) (bank robbery; proper to admit evidence of $250–a–day heroin habit to show motive), with State v. LeFever, 690 P.2d 574 (Wash.1984) (robbery; prejudicial effect of evidence of $125–a–day heroin habit overwhelmed any probative value to show motive).

HALL v. MONTGOMERY WARD & CO.

Supreme Court of Iowa, 1977.
252 N.W.2d 421.

UHLENHOPP, JUSTICE.

This appeal involves a jury award of damages in an action by plaintiff Thomas C. Hall against defendant Montgomery Ward & Company for mental anguish caused by threatening language by Wards' representatives. We view the evidence in the light most favorable to the verdict. Jacobson v. Benson Motors, Inc., 216 N.W.2d 396 (Iowa).

Hall, a borderline mental retardate with an intelligence quotient of 69, worked as a maintenance man in Wards' store at Cedar Falls, Iowa. He "borrowed" Wards' floor scrubber to moonlight by cleaning tavern floors, and also took cleaning material for the scrubber. He testified he did not take other items.

A security officer of Wards came from Chicago and, with the local store manager, interrogated Hall in the manager's office. The officer threatened Hall with jail, among other statements, and emerged from the interrogation with four documents signed by Hall. A clinical psychologist testified that some of the words in the documents were beyond Hall's comprehension and that Hall would probably sign anything in a stressful situation to extricate himself. Hall testified he signed the documents because of the threats of jail. The documents were a consent that Wards' representatives could detain and interview Hall on company business as long as they deemed necessary, a list of items Hall allegedly took from the store (such as shorts, knife, belt, brush), a confession to the theft of store merchandise worth $5000, and a promissory note to Wards for $5000. The store manager testified the items listed in the second document as stolen would come to $25 to $35 but the list did not cover everything and the figure $5000 was Hall's estimate.

Hall testified to his mental anguish from the incident. He stated several times that he had recurring dreams from the incident and that the incident affected his relationship with his family. The psychologist testified that Hall reacted as though the incident was "the end of the world," and Wards' officer testified he had to assure Hall at the conclusion of the interrogation that the situation was not the end of the world. Hall did not introduce evidence of physical injury or of financial loss or expense.

Hall testified regarding the pitifully small amount of property possessed by himself and his wife, as tending to show he did not have the property Wards contended he stole. Over Wards' objection of irrelevant, immaterial, and prejudicial, overruled by the trial court, Hall also introduced Wards' balance sheet and operating statement showing inter alia assets of $1,964,822,000 and net annual sales of $2,640,122,000.

The trial court overruled a motion for directed verdict by Wards. The jury found for Hall and awarded him $12,500 actual and $50,000 exemplary damages.

Wards moved for judgment notwithstanding verdict and alternatively for a new trial. The trial court overruled the former motion but sustained the latter one on the ground that the court erred in overruling Wards' objection to admission of the exhibit containing the balance sheet and operating statement which, according to the court, Hall's attorney used to make a "devastating" jury argument.

Hall appealed from the new trial award. Wards cross appealed from the court's failure to sustain its motions for directed verdict and for judgment notwithstanding verdict. The appeal and cross appeal present several issues.

* * *

III. Hall contends that the trial court erred in granting a new trial for admitting Wards' balance sheet and operating statement into evidence. The rule in this jurisdiction has been that with certain exceptions not involved here, a defendant's pecuniary condition may not be shown although the plaintiff asks smart money. Guengerech v. Smith, 34 Iowa 348; Bailey v. Bailey, 94 Iowa 598, 63 N.W. 341. This view has the support of a few courts, which state that if pecuniary condition is shown the fact finder will tend to get off on the relative poverty or affluence of the parties; despite trial-court instructions to juries, the issues of liability and damages will become intermixed. Wilson v. McLendon, 225 Ga. 119, 166 S.E.2d 345; Givens v. Berkley, 108 Ky. 236, 56 S.W. 158; Texas Public Utilities Corp. v. Edwards, 99 S.W.2d 420 (Tex.Civ.App.).

The great weight of authority today, however, holds the other way where the plaintiff seeks and the evidence supports exemplary damages. Many of the decisions are gathered in Annotations, 16 A.L.R. 838 and 123 A.L.R. 1136. See also Jones on Evidence, § 4:50 at 486 (6th ed.); 22 Am.Jur.2d Damages § 322 at 422; 25 C.J.S. Damages § 126 at 1168–1170. The rationale employed in these decisions is that the jury needs to know the extent of the defendant's holdings in order to know how large an award of damages is necessary to make him smart. E.g. Suzore v. Rutherford, 35 Tenn.App. 678, 684, 251 S.W.2d 129, 131 ("what would be 'smart money' to a poor man would not be, and would not serve as a deterrent, to a rich man").

We are impressed by the large number of courts which have arrived at the conclusion that generally the rule of admissibility is the better one. We are more impressed by the actual need of jurors, in connection with exemplary damages, to have evidence about the defendant's poverty or wealth. We thus overrule the *Guengerech* and *Bailey* decisions and hold that the trial court properly admitted the exhibit and erroneously sustained Wards' motion for new trial. In adopting the rule of admissibility, we caution trial courts to confine plaintiffs carefully to the proper use of such evidence—to the issue of the amount of exemplary damages which is necessary to punish the particular defendant.

* * *

The trial court should have overruled Wards' motion for new trial and it properly overruled Wards' motion for judgment notwithstanding verdict. Its rulings at trial were correct in the first instance. We thus return the case to district court for reinstatement of the verdict and judgment thereon.

Reversed and Remanded.

Notes and Questions

1. Should the evidence be of actual or reputed wealth? Should it make any difference that the action is for slander or breach of promise to marry? Is there an effective control against excessive awards? Should the financial condition be that at the time of the injury or that at the time of trial? May defendant introduce evidence of his own poverty? Only in rebuttal? Is the financial condition discoverable in advance of trial? See Annot., 32 A.L.R. 4th 432, as to the necessity of determining or showing liability for punitive damages before discovery or reception of evidence of defendant's wealth.

2. *Absence of evidence of financial condition.* May the jury consider and award exemplary damages in the absence of evidence of defendant's financial condition? Compare Rinaldi v. Aaron, 314 So.2d 762 (Fla.1975) (yes), with City of El Monte v. Superior Court, 34 Cal.Rptr.2d 490 (Ct.App.1994) (no). See also Annot., 87 A.L.R. 4th 141.

REED v. GENERAL MOTORS CORP.

United States Court of Appeals, Fifth Circuit, 1985.
773 F.2d 660.

ALVIN B. RUBIN, CIRCUIT JUDGE:

This personal injury suit arising out of an automobile accident was prosecuted against two individual defendants and their insurers. Because the district court admitted evidence of the amount of liability insurance carried by the defendants and because we are unable to conclude that this was not prejudicial both on the question of the defendants' liability and the amount of damages awarded, we reverse the judgment in favor of the plaintiffs. We conclude that there was, however, sufficient evidence to warrant a verdict that both defendants were negligent even though the plaintiffs' car was struck only by the vehicle driven by one of the defendant drivers and affirm the district court's denial of a directed verdict. We, therefore, remand the case for a new trial.

One Saturday night in May, 1982, David Reed, his wife, Patricia Loretta, his mother, Ardell, and his fifteen-year-old brother, Keith, were traveling west on Interstate Highway 10 in David Reed's Chevrolet Monza. They had left their home in Alabama earlier that day and were traveling to Texas. Near Lafayette, Louisiana, Ardell Reed began to suffer from cramps so David stopped the car to adjust her seat and thus ease her discomfort. David parked the car, with its emergency lights flashing, on the right shoulder of the highway, when it was violently struck in the rear by a Pontiac Trans Am driven by Brent Boudreaux. All of the passengers in the Reed auto were seriously injured.

At the time of the accident, Boudreaux and his friend, John Fontenot, were returning home to Kaplan, Louisiana from the Breaux Bridge Crawfish Festival. Some of their friends had left earlier, en route through Lafayette to Kaplan, and Boudreaux was trying to catch up with them. Soon after he left Breaux Bridge, Boudreaux's vehicle was passed on the right shoulder of the road by a 1981 Chevrolet ¾–ton pick-up truck, driven at a high rate of speed by Gerard Meche. With encouragement from Fontenot, Boudreaux followed Meche onto the shoulder of the highway, driving equally fast and passing vehicles proceeding in the same direction. The two vehicles at times speeded to over ninety miles an hour. There was testimony that Boudreaux merely followed Meche but there was also testimony that at times Boudreaux passed Meche and took the lead. The evidence warranted, although it certainly did not compel, the inference that Meche knew what Boudreaux was doing and that the two were engaged in racing or some other sort of rivalry.

As the two vehicles approached the Reed vehicle, Meche passed an automobile by traveling on the right shoulder of the road and returned to the right lane of the highway. Boudreaux attempted to follow Meche's example. As his car moved onto the shoulder it struck the rear of the Reed vehicle.

Invoking diversity jurisdiction, the four Reeds sued Boudreaux and Meche, and, as the Louisiana Direct Action Statute permits, their insurers, Insured Lloyds and Casualty Reciprocal Exchange. After trial on the merits, the jury returned a verdict in favor of each of the plaintiffs and against all of the defendants jointly.

In response to special interrogatories, the jury found that (1) both drivers had been negligent; and (2) Meche had caused, assisted, or encouraged Boudreaux in the commission of an unlawful act that had proximately caused the plaintiffs' injuries. The jury attributed fault under the Louisiana Comparative Negligence Act 70% to Boudreaux and 30% to Meche. It awarded damages totalling $450,000. Under Louisiana law, Meche and his insurer are solidarily liable with Boudreaux and his insurer for the full award. The determination that Boudreaux was 70% negligent does not reduce Meche's exposure to the plaintiffs, but serves only to fix the liability for contribution between the codefendants. Only Meche and his insurer, Casualty Reciprocal Exchange, appeal.

At the time this case was tried, Louisiana courts permitted a defendant to try to mitigate the damages that might be assessed against him by introducing evidence of his poverty and inability to pay a large verdict. For this purpose, Boudreaux sought to introduce evidence of the limits of his insurance coverage, $5,000 per person and $10,000 per accident, amounts clearly inadequate to compensate any of the plaintiffs. To accord the plaintiffs supposed equal treatment, the district court permitted them to introduce evidence of Meche's coverage, $500,000.

The Louisiana inability-to-pay doctrine originated in an 1886 Louisiana Supreme Court decision, *Williams v. McManus.*[4] In that case, the court reduced an award for slander, in part because the defendant was "a laborer of general good demeanor and of limited means."[5] Twelve years later, in *Loyacano v. Jurgens,*[6] the Louisiana court held: "A party's circumstances may not improperly be considered to a reasonable extent in estimating damages to be awarded in a case like this, where defendant personally was not at fault."

The inability-to-pay rule was founded on equitable considerations explained by a Louisiana Court of Appeal a half century later:

> It has never been considered good policy to bankrupt one to pay another even though the award granted is not in line with other cases involving the same injuries and might not fully compensate the plaintiff for the injuries he received. Fair justice between both parties must be arrived at.

The propriety of the rule, however, had been questioned by some Louisiana appellate judges, and the Louisiana Supreme Court had held the doctrine inapplicable in suits involving solvent and insolvent joint tortfeasors.

After this case was tried, the Louisiana Supreme Court reversed entirely the jurisprudential line that admitted evidence of inability to pay. In *Rodriguez v. Taylor,*[7] the court stated: "[T]he wealth or poverty of a party to a lawsuit is not a proper consideration in the determination of compensatory damages."[8] The defendants argue that *Rodriguez* should be given retroactive effect and applied here, but we need not decide that issue. There is a more fundamental reason why Louisiana's inability-to-pay doctrine should not have been applied in this federal action.

The inability-to-pay doctrine was not a defense. It did not bar recovery; it merely allowed evidence concerning the defendant's pecuniary condition to be considered in arriving at the measure of damages. Although the *Erie* rule requires federal courts sitting in diversity to follow substantive state law, they apply federal procedural rules. Because the inability-to-pay doctrine was evidentiary in nature, it was not applicable in federal actions. The Federal Rules of Evidence, rather than state rules, therefore govern the admissibility of evidence in diversity cases, including questions of the admissibility of evidence of insurance.

4. 38 La.Ann. 161 (1886).

5. *Id.* at 164.

6. 50 La.Ann. 441, 23 So. 717, 718 (1898).

7. 468 So.2d 1186 (La.1985).

8. *Id.* at 1188.

Rule 411 of the Federal Rules of Evidence proscribes the admission of evidence that a person was or was not insured against liability "upon the issue whether he acted negligently or otherwise wrongfully." However, "[e]vidence of insurance against liability" is not barred, it continues, "when offered for another purpose, such as proof of agency, ownership, or control, or bias or prejudice of a witness."

The jury knew, of course, that Casualty Reciprocal Exchange insured Meche because it was named as a defendant. The fact that each party was insured had "independent, substantive evidentiary relevance," as we held in *Dicks v. Cleaver.*[9] But the fact that the existence of insurance was admissible, did not mean that the court was bound, or even permitted, to admit the amount of coverage. There was no issue to which the amount of either Meche's or Boudreaux's insurance was relevant. Therefore, the limits of coverage should have been excluded pursuant to the dictates of Rule 411. As the Ninth Circuit observed in *Geddes v. United Financial Group,*[10] consideration of "the ability of a defendant to pay the necessary damages injects into the damage determination a foreign, diverting, and distracting issue which may effectuate a prejudicial result."

The parties had stipulated that Boudreaux and Meche were both insured and the names of their insurers; this established the predicate for a judgment against the insurers, as named defendants, if judgment were rendered against their respective insureds. However, even in a Louisiana court, it would have been error to admit evidence of the amount of Meche's insurance, for as a Louisiana appellate court held in *Ponder v. Groendyke Transport, Inc.*[11] "[t]he financial status of a defendant is irrelevant unless he places it at issue by claiming inability to pay." Even under the now discarded Louisiana rule, when there were solvent and insolvent joint tortfeasors, evidence of the insolvent defendant's inability to pay was inadmissible, and might not be considered in determining the amount of damages to be awarded or in apportioning the damages.

The parties' stipulation in the pretrial order that Meche's policy was the best evidence of its contents did not make the amount of insurance relevant or make the entire policy admissible. The failure of the insurance company to object to admissibility at some time before the day of trial does not constitute a waiver of its objections in the absence of pretrial proceedings that required it to take a position.

The trial court's admonitions to the jurors at the trial's conclusion that they were not to consider the liability limits of the parties' insurance policies in determining who, if anyone, was negligent, did not suffice to cure the error. The jury could not be expected to ignore the fact that, if it found only Boudreaux liable, the seriously injured plaintiffs would share only $10,000 but, if it found both Boudreaux and

9. 433 F.2d 248, 254 (5th Cir.1970).

10. 559 F.2d 557, 560 (9th Cir.1977).

11. 454 So.2d 823, 831 (La.App. 3d Cir. 1984).

Meche liable, a deeper pocket would be available. We may speculate that the evidence of Meche's negligence was so overwhelming that the liability verdict was not tainted, but we cannot be sure. The wisdom of experience is embodied in the aphorism that the scent of a skunk thrown into the jury box cannot be wiped out by a trial court's admonition to ignore the smell. The reference to insurance coverage was not accidental or fleeting. The plaintiffs' counsel argued for admissibility of the limits in Meche's policy, persuaded the district court, and made a deliberate effort to inform the jury of the amount. Considering how important the matter was considered to be, we cannot overlook it now as harmless even as to the issue of Meche's liability.

* * *

[Reversed and remanded.]

Notes and Questions

1. For what purpose did Louisiana permit evidence of inability to pay? If admitted on the issue of damages, is not the evidence relevant under Rule 401 and not precluded under Rule 411? Is there another basis, other than by application of Rule 411, for excluding this evidence?

2. *Direct action statutes.* Statutes permitting direct action against a liability insurer are extremely rare. In addition to the Louisiana procedure, see also Wis.Ann.Stat. § 803.04. For an analysis of evidentiary problems under the Louisiana statute, see Comment, Admissibility of Insurance Policy Limits, 45 La.L.Rev. 1299 (1985).

3. *Common law rulings.* The courts at common law generally agreed that evidence that the defendant carried liability insurance is not admissible for the purpose of proving that he acted negligently. Annot., 4 A.L.R.2d 761, 767; Annot., 71 A.L.R. 4th 1025 (medical malpractice cases); for federal cases, see Annot., 40 A.L.R.Fed. 541. Correspondingly, evidence that a defendant is not insured against liability has been excluded. King v. Starr, 260 P.2d 351 (Wash.1953); Piechuck v. Magusiak, 135 A. 534 (N.H.1926); Annot., 68 A.L.R. 4th 954. In general, see Calnan, The Insurance Exclusionary Rule Revisited: Are Reports of its Demise Exaggerated, 52 Ohio St.L.J. 1177 (1991); 1 McCormick, Evidence § 201 (6th ed. 2006); Leonard, The New Wigmore: Selected Rules of Limited Admissibility § 6.1 to 6.13 (2002).

4. *Exceptions.* The similarity to evidence of financial condition is readily apparent, and a similar set of exceptions has evolved. See Rule 411. Illustrative cases are: Oliveira v. Jacobson, 846 A.2d 822, 828 (R.I.2004) (proper to ask expert testifying as to absence of medical malpractice about his payments as a board member of medical malpractice insurance company and his omission of that position from his curriculum vitae); Maggard Truck Line, Inc. v. Deaton, Inc., 573 F.Supp. 1388 (N.D.Ga.1983) (action between shipping broker and motor carrier; evidence of insurance admissible as tending to prove the existence of agreement to shift liability for loss of goods); People v. Steele, 37 N.Y.S.2d 199 (Erie County Ct.1942) (error to exclude evidence that defendant had liability insurance when offered to prove lack of motivation to commit the offense of leaving the scene of an

accident); Filloon v. Stenseth, 498 N.W.2d 353 (N.D.1993) (error to exclude evidence that witness who testified that plaintiff was out of the cross-walk had become adjuster for defendant's insurance carrier); Pinckard v. Dunnavant, 206 So.2d 340 (Ala.1968) (admissible to prove who had management and maintenance of premises, which was disputed).

5. *Modern applications.* In general, the tendency now is to take a less serious view of the disclosure of the existence of liability insurance of the plaintiff, or conversely the absence of coverage of defendant, than formerly, and reversals are rare unless the disclosure is viewed as a deliberate invitation to the jury to base its decision on the presence or absence of insurance. E.g., Ouachita Nat'l Bank v. Tosco Corp., 686 F.2d 1291 (8th Cir.1982), aff'd on rehearing, 716 F.2d 485 (8th Cir.1983); Anchor Coatings, Inc. v. Marine Indus. Residential Insulation, Inc., 490 So.2d 1210 (Miss. 1986). But see Calnan, supra note 3. In ruling on questions involving the admissibility of insurance, should weight be accorded the consideration that jurors, like other people, today know that carrying liability insurance is common practice? See Bott v. Wendler, 453 P.2d 100 (Kan.1969); Notman, Insurance Nondisclosure: The "Hush, Hush" Game, 53 Ill.B.J. 896 (1965). What if the particular jurisdiction involved makes the carrying of certain types of liability insurance mandatory? See Uy v. Shapmor, Inc., 257 N.Y.S.2d 208 (Sup.App.Term 1965).

6. *Punitive damages.* Questions that arise as to the admissibility of liability insurance in cases where punitive damages are sought are discussed in King, The Insurability of Punitive Damages: A New Solution to an Old Dilemma, 16 Wake Forest L.Rev. 345 (1980); Powell & Leiferman, Results Most Embarrassing: Discovery and Admissibility of Net Worth of the Defendant, 40 Baylor L.Rev. 527 (1988). Contrast Fleegel v. Estate of Boyles, 61 P.3d 1267 (Alaska 2002) (evidence of insurance relevant to defendant's financial condition as it related to punitive damages), with City of West Allis v. Wisconsin Elec. Power Co., 635 N.W.2d 873 (Wis.Ct.App.2001) (evidence of insurance inadmissible as a factor in assessing punitive damages).

7. *Jury selection.* In jury selection, should a plaintiff be allowed to ask a prospective juror about his or her connection either with the defendant's liability insurer or with the insurance industry generally? Compare Langley v. Turner's Exp., Inc., 375 F.2d 296 (4th Cir.1967), with Kiernan v. Van Schaik, 347 F.2d 775 (3d Cir.1965). Is not the more sensible practice to require prospective jurors to furnish information concerning any connections with the insurance industry prior to being called for duty in a particular case? See Calnan, supra note 3; Vetter, Voir Dire II: Liability Insurance, 29 Mo.L.Rev. 305 (1964).

C. SPECIAL APPLICATIONS OF RULE 403

Since the balance between the probative value of a given type of evidence and its capacity for raising the countervailing considerations cited by Rule 403 will vary with the nature of the case, the issue sought to be proved, and the specific evidentiary item offered, might all questions of relevancy best be left for ad hoc determination by the trial judge under the guidance of the general propositions embodied in Rules 401 and 403? See James, Relevancy, Probability and the Law, 29 Cal.L.Rev. 689 (1941).

While any attempt to strike the balance suggested by Rule 403 a priori for every conceivable type of evidence which may be offered to prove a material fact would obviously be doomed to failure, certain questions of relevancy have occurred with sufficient frequency for more or less specific rules to evolve. For example, the drafters of the Federal Rules did not leave the admissibility of evidence of liability insurance to prove negligence for ad hoc resolution, but specifically declared such evidence inadmissible by Rule 411. Is this treatment of the question justified? Which factor enumerated by Rule 403 would the admission of such evidence preeminently entail?

OLD CHIEF v. UNITED STATES

Supreme Court of the United States, 1997.
519 U.S. 172.

[Defendant was prosecuted under 18 U.S.C. § 922(g)(1), possession of a firearm by a person with a prior felony conviction. The defendant offered to stipulate to the prior-conviction element of the crime and argued that such a stipulation meant that the probative value of evidence of the prior conviction (for assault causing serious bodily injury) was necessarily substantially outweighed by the danger of unfair prejudice under Rule 403. The Government refused to join in the stipulation and was permitted to introduce the judgment record for the prior conviction. The court of appeals affirmed defendant's conviction.]

JUSTICE SOUTER delivered the opinion of the Court.

* * *

II

A

As a threshold matter, there is Old Chief's erroneous argument that the name of his prior offense as contained in the record of conviction is irrelevant to the prior-conviction element, and for that reason inadmissible under Rule 402 of the Federal Rules of Evidence. Rule 401 defines relevant evidence as having "any tendency to make the existence of any fact that is of consequence to the determination of the action more probable or less probable than it would be without the evidence." Fed. Rule Evid. 401. To be sure, the fact that Old Chief's prior conviction was for assault resulting in serious bodily injury rather than, say, for theft was not itself an ultimate fact, as if the statute had specifically required proof of injurious assault. But its demonstration was a step on one evidentiary route to the ultimate fact, since it served to place Old Chief within a particular sub-class of offenders for whom firearms possession is outlawed by § 922(g)(1). A documentary record of the conviction for that named offense was thus relevant evidence in making Old Chief's

§ 922(g)(1) status more probable than it would have been without the evidence.

Nor was its evidentiary relevance under Rule 401 affected by the availability of alternative proofs of the element to which it went, such as an admission by Old Chief that he had been convicted of a crime "punishable by imprisonment for a term exceeding one year" within the meaning of the statute. The 1972 Advisory Committee Notes to Rule 401 make this point directly:

> "The fact to which the evidence is directed need not be in dispute. While situations will arise which call for the exclusion of evidence offered to prove a point conceded by the opponent, the ruling should be made on the basis of such considerations as waste of time and undue prejudice (see Rule 403), rather than under any general requirement that evidence is admissible only if directed to matters in dispute." Advisory Committee's Notes on Fed. Rule Evid. 401, 28 U.S.C.App., p. 859.

If, then, relevant evidence is inadmissible in the presence of other evidence related to it, its exclusion must rest not on the ground that the other evidence has rendered it "irrelevant," but on its character as unfairly prejudicial, cumulative or the like, its relevance notwithstanding.

B

The principal issue is the scope of a trial judge's discretion under Rule 403, which authorizes exclusion of relevant evidence when its "probative value is substantially outweighed by the danger of unfair prejudice, confusion of the issues, or misleading the jury, or by considerations of undue delay, waste of time, or needless presentation of cumulative evidence." Fed. Rule Evid. 403. Old Chief relies on the danger of unfair prejudice.

1

The term "unfair prejudice," as to a criminal defendant, speaks to the capacity of some concededly relevant evidence to lure the factfinder into declaring guilt on a ground different from proof specific to the offense charged. See generally 1 J. Weinstein, M. Berger, & J. McLaughlin, Weinstein's Evidence ¶ 403[03] (1996) (discussing the meaning of "unfair prejudice" under Rule 403). So, the Committee Notes to Rule 403 explain, " 'Unfair prejudice' within its context means an undue tendency to suggest decision on an improper basis, commonly, though not necessarily, an emotional one." Advisory Committee's Notes on Fed. Rule Evid. 403, 28 U.S.C.App., p. 860.

Such improper grounds certainly include the one that Old Chief points to here: generalizing a defendant's earlier bad act into bad character and taking that as raising the odds that he did the later bad act now charged (or, worse, as calling for preventive conviction even if he should happen to be innocent momentarily). As then-Judge Breyer put it, "Although * * * 'propensity evidence' is relevant, the risk that a jury will convict for crimes other than those charged—or that, uncertain of guilt, it will convict anyway because a bad person deserves punishment—creates a prejudicial effect that outweighs ordinary relevance." *United States v. Moccia,* 681 F.2d 61, 63 (C.A.1 1982). Justice Jackson described how the law has handled this risk:

> "Courts that follow the common-law tradition almost unanimously have come to disallow resort by the prosecution to any kind of evidence of a defendant's evil character to establish a probability of his guilt. Not that the law invests the defendant with a presumption of good character, *Greer v. United States,* 245 U.S. 559 * * *, but it simply closes the whole matter of character, disposition and reputation on the prosecution's case-in-chief. The state may not show defendant's prior trouble with the law, specific criminal acts, or ill name among his neighbors, even though such facts might logically be persuasive that he is by propensity a probable perpetrator of the crime. The inquiry is not rejected because character is irrelevant; on the contrary, it is said to weigh too much with the jury and to so overpersuade them as to prejudge one with a bad general record and deny him a fair opportunity to defend against a particular charge. The overriding policy of excluding such evidence, despite its admitted probative value, is the practical experience that its disallowance tends to prevent confusion of issues, unfair surprise and undue prejudice." *Michelson v. United States,* 335 U.S. 469, 475–476 * * * (1948) (footnotes omitted).

Rule of Evidence 404(b) reflects this common-law tradition by addressing propensity reasoning directly: "Evidence of other crimes, wrongs, or acts is not admissible to prove the character of a person in order to show action in conformity therewith." Fed. Rule Evid. 404(b). There is, accordingly, no question that propensity would be an "improper basis" for conviction and that evidence of a prior conviction is subject to analysis under Rule 403 for relative probative value and for prejudicial risk of misuse as propensity evidence. Cf. 1 J. Strong, McCormick on Evidence 780 (4th ed. 1992) (hereinafter McCormick) (Rule 403 prejudice may occur, for example, when "evidence of convictions for prior, unrelated crimes may lead a juror to think that since the defendant already has a criminal record, an erroneous conviction would not be quite as serious as would otherwise be the case").

As for the analytical method to be used in Rule 403 balancing, two basic possibilities present themselves. An item of evidence might be viewed as an island, with estimates of its own probative value and unfairly prejudicial risk the sole reference points in deciding whether the danger substantially outweighs the value and whether the evidence ought to be excluded. Or the question of admissibility might be seen as inviting further comparisons to take account of the full evidentiary context of the case as the court understands it when the ruling must be made. This second approach would start out like the first but be ready to go further. On objection, the court would decide whether a particular item of evidence raised a danger of unfair prejudice. If it did, the judge would go on to evaluate the degrees of probative value and unfair prejudice not only for the item in question but for any actually available substitutes as well. If an alternative were found to have substantially the same or greater probative value but a lower danger of unfair prejudice, sound judicial discretion would discount the value of the item first offered and exclude it if its discounted probative value were substantially outweighed by unfairly prejudicial risk. As we will explain later on, the judge would have to make these calculations with an appreciation of the offering party's need for evidentiary richness and narrative integrity in presenting a case, and the mere fact that two pieces of evidence might go to the same point would not, of course, necessarily mean that only one of them might come in. It would only mean that a judge applying Rule 403 could reasonably apply some discount to the probative value of an item of evidence when faced with less risky alternative proof going to the same point. Even under this second approach, as we explain below, a defendant's Rule 403 objection offering to concede a point generally cannot prevail over the Government's choice to offer evidence showing guilt and all the circumstances surrounding the offense. * * *

The first understanding of the Rule is open to a very telling objection. That reading would leave the party offering evidence with the option to structure a trial in whatever way would produce the maximum unfair prejudice consistent with relevance. He could choose the available alternative carrying the greatest threat of improper influence, despite the availability of less prejudicial but equally probative evidence. The worst he would have to fear would be a ruling sustaining a Rule 403 objection, and if that occurred, he could simply fall back to offering substitute evidence. This would be a strange rule. It would be very odd for the law of evidence to recognize the danger of unfair prejudice only to confer such a degree of autonomy on the party subject to temptation, and the Rules of Evidence are not so odd.

Rather, a reading of the companions to Rule 403, and of the commentaries that went with them to Congress, makes it clear that what counts as the Rule 403 "probative value" of an item of evidence, as distinct from its Rule 401 "relevance," may be calculated by comparing evidentiary alternatives. The Committee Notes to Rule 401 explicitly say that a party's concession is pertinent to the court's discretion to exclude evidence on the point conceded. Such a concession, according to the Notes, will sometimes "call for the exclusion of evidence offered to prove [the] point conceded by the opponent * * *." Advisory Committee's Notes on Fed. Rule Evid. 401, 28 U.S.C.App., p. 859. As already mentioned, the Notes make it clear that such rulings should be made not on the basis of Rule 401 relevance but on "such considerations as waste of time and undue prejudice (see Rule 403) * * *." *Ibid.* The Notes to Rule 403 then take up the point by stating that when a court considers "whether to exclude on grounds of unfair prejudice," the "availability of other means of proof may * * * be an appropriate factor." Advisory Committee's Notes on Fed. Rule Evid. 403, 28 U.S.C.App., p. 860. The point gets a reprise in the Notes to Rule 404(b), dealing with admissibility when a given evidentiary item has the dual nature of legitimate evidence of an element and illegitimate evidence of character: "No mechanical solution is offered. The determination must be made whether the danger of undue prejudice outweighs the probative value of the evidence in view of the availability of other means of proof and other facts appropriate for making decision of this kind under 403." Advisory Committee's Notes on Fed. Rule Evid. 404, 28 U.S.C.App., p. 861. Thus the notes leave no question that when Rule 403 confers discretion by providing that evidence "may" be excluded, the discretionary judgment may be informed not only by assessing an evidentiary item's twin tendencies, but by placing the result of that assessment alongside similar assessments of evidentiary alternatives. See 1 McCormick 782, and n.41 (suggesting that Rule 403's "probative value" signifies the "marginal probative value" of the evidence relative to the other evidence in the case); 22 C. Wright & K. Graham, Federal Practice and Procedure § 5250, pp. 546–547 (1978) ("The probative worth of any particular bit of evidence is obviously affected by the scarcity or abundance of other evidence on the same point").

2

In dealing with the specific problem raised by § 922(g)(1) and its prior-conviction element, there can be no question that evidence of the name or nature of the prior offense generally carries a risk of unfair prejudice to the defendant. That risk will vary from case to case, for the reasons already given, but will be substantial whenever the official record offered by the Government would be arresting enough to lure a juror into a sequence of bad character reasoning. Where a prior conviction was for a gun crime or one similar to other charges in a pending case the risk of unfair prejudice would be especially obvious, and Old Chief sensibly worried that the prejudicial effect of his prior assault conviction, significant enough with respect to the current gun charges alone, would take on added weight from the related assault charge against him.

The District Court was also presented with alternative, relevant, admissible evidence of the prior conviction by Old Chief's offer to stipulate, evidence necessarily subject to the District Court's consideration on the motion to exclude the record offered by the Government. Although Old Chief's formal offer to stipulate was, strictly, to enter a formal agreement with the Government to be given to the jury, even without the Government's acceptance his proposal amounted to an offer to admit that the prior-conviction element was satisfied, and a defendant's admission is, of course, good evidence. See Fed. Rule Evid. 801(d)(2)(A).

Old Chief's proffered admission would, in fact, have been not merely relevant but seemingly conclusive evidence of the element. The statutory language in which the prior-conviction requirement is couched shows no congressional concern with the specific name or nature of the prior offense beyond what is necessary to place it within the broad category of qualifying felonies, and Old Chief clearly meant to admit that his felony did qualify, by stipulating "that the Government has proven one of the essential elements of the offense." App. 7. As a consequence, although the name of the prior offense may have been technically relevant, it addressed no detail in the definition of the prior-conviction element that would not have been covered by the stipulation or admission. Logic, then, seems to side with Old Chief.

3

There is, however, one more question to be considered before deciding whether Old Chief's offer was to supply evidentiary value at least equivalent to what the Government's own evidence carried. In arguing that the stipulation or admission would not have carried equivalent value, the Government invokes the familiar, standard rule that the prosecution is entitled to prove its case by evidence of its own choice, or, more exactly, that a criminal defendant may not stipulate or admit his way out of the full evidentiary force of the case as the Government chooses to present it. The authority usually cited for this rule is *Parr v. United States,* 255 F.2d 86 (CA5 1958), in which the Fifth Circuit explained that the "reason for the rule is to permit a party 'to present to the jury a picture of the events relied upon. To substitute for such a picture a naked admission might have the effect to rob the evidence of much of its fair and legitimate weight.'" 255 F.2d, at 88 (quoting *Dunning v. Maine Central R. Co.,* 91 Me. 87, 39 A. 352, 356 (1897)).

This is unquestionably true as a general matter. The "fair and legitimate weight" of conventional evidence showing individual thoughts and acts amounting to a crime reflects the fact that making a case with testimony and tangible things not only satisfies the formal definition of an offense, but tells a colorful story with descriptive richness. Unlike an abstract premise, whose force depends on going precisely to a particular step in a course of reasoning, a piece of evidence may address any number of separate elements, striking hard just because it shows so much at once; the account of a shooting that establishes capacity and causation may tell just as much about the triggerman's motive and intent. Evidence thus has force beyond any linear scheme of reasoning, and as its pieces come together a narrative gains momentum, with power not only to support conclusions but to sustain the willingness of jurors to draw the inferences, whatever they may be, necessary to reach an honest verdict. This persuasive power of the concrete and particular is often essential to the capacity of jurors to satisfy the obligations that the law places on them. Jury duty is usually unsought and sometimes resisted, and it may be as difficult for one juror suddenly to face the findings that can send another human being to prison, as it is for another to hold out conscientiously for acquittal. When a juror's duty does seem hard, the evidentiary account of what a defendant has thought and done can accomplish what no set of abstract statements ever could, not just to prove a fact but to establish its human significance, and so to implicate the law's moral underpinnings and a juror's obligation to sit in judgment. Thus, the prosecution may fairly seek to place its evidence before the jurors, as much to tell a story of guiltiness as to support an inference of guilt, to convince the jurors that a guilty verdict would be morally reasonable as much as to point to the discrete elements of a defendant's legal fault. Cf. *United States v. Gilliam,* 994 F.2d 97, 100–102 (CA2 1993).

But there is something even more to the prosecution's interest in resisting efforts to replace the evidence of its choice with admissions and stipulations, for beyond the power of conventional evidence to support allegations and give life to the moral underpinnings of law's claims, there lies the need for evidence in all its particularity to satisfy the jurors' expectations about what proper proof should be. Some such demands they bring with them to the courthouse, assuming, for example, that a charge of using a firearm to commit an offense will be proven by introducing a gun in evidence. A prosecutor who fails to produce one, or some good reason for his failure, has something to be concerned about. "If [jurors'] expectations are not satisfied, triers of fact may penalize the party who disappoints them by drawing a negative inference against that party." Saltzburg, A Special Aspect of Relevance: Countering Negative Inferences Associated with the Absence of Evidence, 66 Calif. L.Rev. 1011, 1019 (1978) (footnotes omitted). Expectations may also arise in jurors' minds simply from the experience of a trial itself. The use of witnesses to describe a train of events naturally related can raise the prospect of learning about every ingredient of that natural sequence the same way. If suddenly the prosecution presents some occurrence in the series differently, as by announcing a stipulation or admission, the effect may be like saying, "never mind what's behind the door," and jurors may well wonder what they are being kept from knowing. A party seemingly responsible for cloaking something has reason for apprehension, and the prosecution with its burden of proof may prudently demur at a defense request to interrupt the flow of evidence telling the story in the usual way.

In sum, the accepted rule that the prosecution is entitled to prove its case free from any defendant's option to stipulate the evidence away rests on good sense. A syllogism is not a story, and a naked proposition in a courtroom may be no match for the robust evidence that would be used to prove it. People who hear a story interrupted by gaps of abstraction may be puzzled at the missing chapters, and jurors asked to rest a momentous decision on the story's truth can feel put upon at being asked to take responsibility knowing that more could be said than they have heard. A convincing tale can be told with economy, but when economy becomes a break in the natural sequence of narrative evidence, an assurance that the missing link is really there is never more than second best.

* * *

This recognition that the prosecution with its burden of persuasion needs evidentiary depth to tell a continuous story has, however, virtually no application when the point at issue is a defendant's legal status, dependent on some judgment rendered wholly independently of the concrete events of later criminal behavior charged against him. As in this case, the choice of evidence for such an element is usually not between eventful narrative and abstract proposition, but between propositions of slightly varying abstraction, either a record saying that conviction for some crime occurred at a certain time or a statement admitting the same thing without naming the particular offense. The issue of substituting one statement for the other normally arises only when the record of conviction would not be admissible for any purpose beyond proving status, so that excluding it would not deprive the prosecution of evidence with multiple utility; if, indeed, there were a justification for receiving evidence of the nature of prior acts on some issue other than status (*i.e.,* to prove "motive, opportunity, intent, preparation, plan, knowledge, identity, or absence of mistake or accident," Fed. Rule Evid. 404(b)), Rule 404(b) guarantees the opportunity to seek its admission. Nor can it be argued that the events behind the prior conviction are proper nourishment for the jurors' sense of obligation to vindicate the public interest.

The issue is not whether concrete details of the prior crime should come to the jurors' attention but whether the name or general character of that crime is to be disclosed. Congress, however, has made it plain that distinctions among generic felonies do not count for this purpose; the fact of the qualifying conviction is alone what matters under the statute. * * * The most the jury needs to know is that the conviction admitted by the defendant falls within the class of crimes that Congress thought should bar a convict from possessing a gun, and this point may be made readily in a defendant's admission and underscored in the court's jury instructions. Finally, the most obvious reason that the general presumption that the prosecution may choose its evidence is so remote from application here is that proof of the defendant's status goes to an element entirely outside the natural sequence of what the defendant is charged with thinking and doing to commit the current offense. Proving status without telling exactly why that status was imposed leaves no gap in the story of a defendant's subsequent criminality, and its demonstration by stipulation or admission neither displaces a chapter from a continuous sequence of conventional evidence nor comes across as an officious substitution, to confuse or offend or provoke reproach.

Given these peculiarities of the element of felony-convict status and of admissions and the like when used to prove it, there is no cognizable difference between the evidentiary significance of an admission and of the legitimately probative component of the official record the prosecution would prefer to place in evidence. For purposes of the Rule 403 weighing of the probative against the prejudicial, the functions of the competing evidence are distinguishable only by the risk inherent in the one and wholly absent from the other. In this case, as in any other in which the prior conviction is for an offense likely to support conviction on some improper ground, the only reasonable conclusion was that the risk of unfair prejudice did substantially outweigh the discounted probative value of the record of conviction, and it was an abuse of discretion to admit the record when an admission was available. What we have said shows why this will be the general rule when proof of convict status is at issue, just as the prosecutor's choice will generally survive a Rule 403 analysis when a defendant seeks to force the substitution of an admission for evidence creating a coherent narrative of his thoughts and actions in perpetrating the offense for which he is being tried.

The judgment is reversed, and the case is remanded to the Ninth Circuit for further proceedings consistent with this opinion.

It is so ordered.

JUSTICE O'CONNOR, with whom THE CHIEF JUSTICE, JUSTICE SCALIA, and JUSTICE THOMAS join, dissenting.

The Court today announces a rule that misapplies Federal Rule of Evidence 403 and upsets, without explanation, longstanding precedent regarding criminal prosecutions. I do not agree that the Government's introduction of evidence that reveals the name and basic nature of a defendant's prior felony conviction in a prosecution brought under 18 U.S.C. § 922(g)(1) "unfairly" prejudices the defendant within the meaning of Rule 403. Nor do I agree with the Court's newly minted rule that a defendant charged with violating § 922(g)(1) can force the Government to accept his concession to the prior conviction element of that offense, thereby precluding the Government from offering evidence on this point. I therefore dissent.

I

Rule 403 provides that a district court may exclude relevant evidence if, among other things, "its probative value is substantially outweighed by the danger of unfair prejudice." Certainly, Rule 403 does not permit the court to exclude the Government's evidence simply because it may hurt the defendant. As a threshold matter, evidence is excludable only if it is "unfairly" prejudicial, in that it has "an undue tendency to suggest decision on an improper basis." * * * The evidence tendered by the Government in this case—the order reflecting petitioner's prior conviction and sentence for assault resulting in serious bodily injury, in violation of 18 U.S.C. § 1153 and 18 U.S.C. § 113(f) (1988 ed.)—directly proved a necessary element of the § 922(g)(1) offense, that is, that petitioner had committed a crime covered by § 921(a)(20). Perhaps petitioner's case was damaged when the jury discovered that he previously had committed a felony and heard the name of his crime. But I cannot agree with the Court that it was *unfairly* prejudicial for the Government to establish an essential element of its case against petitioner with direct proof of his prior conviction.

The structure of § 922(g)(1) itself shows that Congress envisioned jurors' learning the name and basic nature of the defendant's prior offense. Congress enacted § 922(g)(1) to prohibit the possession of a firearm by any person convicted of "a crime punishable by imprisonment for a term exceeding one year." Section 922(g)(1) does not merely prohibit the possession of firearms by "felons," nor does it apply to all prior felony convictions. Rather, the statute excludes from § 922(g)(1)'s coverage certain business crimes and state misdemeanors punishable by imprisonment of two years or less. § 921(a)(20). Within the meaning of § 922(g)(1), then, "a crime" is not an abstract or metaphysical concept. Rather, the Government must prove that the defendant committed a *particular* crime. In short, under § 922(g)(1), a defendant's prior felony conviction connotes not only that he is a prior felon, but also that he has engaged in specific past criminal conduct.

Even more fundamentally, in our system of justice, a person is not simply convicted of "a crime" or "a felony." Rather, he is found guilty of a specified offense, almost always because he violated a specific statutory prohibition. For example, in the words of the order that the Government offered to prove petitioner's prior conviction in this case, petitioner "did knowingly and unlawfully assault Rory Dean Fenner, said assault resulting in serious bodily injury, in violation of Title 18 U.S.C. §§ 1153 and 113(f)." App. 18. That a variety of crimes would have satisfied the prior conviction element of the § 922(g)(1) offense does not detract from the fact that petitioner committed a specific offense. The name and basic nature of petitioner's crime are inseparable from the fact of his earlier conviction and were therefore admissible to prove petitioner's guilt.

The principle is illustrated by the evidence that was admitted at petitioner's trial to prove the other element of the § 922(g)(1) offense—possession of a "firearm." The Government submitted evidence showing that petitioner possessed a 9-mm. semiautomatic pistol. Although petitioner's possession of any number of weapons would have satisfied the requirements of § 922(g)(1), obviously the Government was entitled to prove with specific evidence that petitioner possessed the weapon he did. In the same vein, consider a murder case. Surely the Government can submit proof establishing the victim's identity, even though, strictly speaking, the jury has no "need" to know the victim's name, and even though the victim might be a particularly well loved public figure. The same logic should govern proof of the prior conviction element of the § 922(g)(1) offense. That is, the Government ought to be able to prove, with specific evidence, that petitioner committed a crime that came within § 922(g)(1)'s coverage.

* * *

Any incremental harm resulting from proving the name or basic nature of the prior felony can be properly mitigated by limiting jury instructions. Federal Rule of Evidence 105 provides that when evidence is admissible for one purpose, but not another, "the court, upon request, shall restrict the evidence to its proper scope and instruct the jury accordingly."

Indeed, on petitioner's own motion in this case, the District Court instructed the jury that it was not to " 'consider a prior conviction as evidence of guilt of the crime for which the defendant is now on trial.' " * * * The jury is presumed to have followed this cautionary instruction, see *Shannon v. United States,* 512 U.S. 573, 585 (1994) * * *.

* * *

III

The Court manufactures a new rule that, in a § 922(g)(1) case, a defendant can force the Government to accept his admission to the prior felony conviction element of the offense, thereby precluding the Government from offering evidence to directly prove a necessary element of its case. I cannot agree that it "unfairly" prejudices a defendant for the Government to prove his prior conviction with evidence that reveals the name or basic nature of his past crime. Like it or not, Congress chose to make a defendant's prior criminal conviction one of the two elements of the § 922(g)(1) offense. Moreover, crimes have names; a defendant is not convicted of some indeterminate, unspecified "crime." Nor do I think that Federal Rule of Evidence 403 can be read to obviate the well accepted principle, grounded in both the Constitution and in our precedent, that the Government may not be forced to accept a defendant's concession to an element of a charged offense as proof of that element. I respectfully dissent.

Notes and Questions

1. *The defense perspective.* In excluding evidence as to defendant's "status" in light of the defendant's offer to stipulate, while still emphasizing the prosecution's entitlement in most cases to "prove its case by evidence of its own choice," has the Court made it more or less difficult for a defendant to invoke Rule 403 to limit prosecution proof in the ordinary case? See Note, The Supreme Court—Leading Cases, 111 Harv.L.Rev. 197, 360 (1997). See also Risinger, John Henry Wigmore, Johnny Lynn Old Chief, and "Legitimate Moral Force"—Keeping the Courtroom Safe for Heartstrings and Gore, 49 Hastings L.J. 403 (1998).

2. *Photographs.* The Court in *Old Chief* distinguishes "status" evidence from evidence of "what the defendant is charged with thinking and doing to commit the current offense." Would photographs of a victim's body be evidence going to "what the defendant is charged with thinking and doing to commit the current offense?" Most courts admit such photographs despite defendant's attempts to stipulate to the ultimate facts to which they may be relevant. See, e.g., State v. Fisher, 445 S.E.2d 866 (N.C.1994) (autopsy photographs properly admitted despite defendant's offer to stipulate as to the identity of the victim, that the cause of death was multiple stab wounds, and that defendant was the individual who inflicted the wounds).

3. *Limitations of Old Chief holding.* Federal courts have been reluctant to extend the holding in *Old Chief* beyond its facts. See, e.g., United States v. Becht, 267 F.3d 767 (8th Cir.2001) (defendant's stipulation that images

seized from his computer depicted child pornography did not negate probative value of images on issue of defendant's knowledge of the images); United States v. Crowder, 141 F.3d 1202 (D.C.Cir.1998) (defendant's offer of a stipulation with regard to intent insufficient to preclude admission of prior crimes evidence). The issue of a stipulation tendered to preclude an aspect of prosecution proof occurs with some frequency in connection with prosecution efforts to introduce evidence of prior crimes to prove intent. Some courts have held that a stipulation as to the existence of intent is effective under Rule 403 to preclude the admission of prior crimes; most have said not. The issue is revisited in connection with evidence admitted under Rule 404(b). See *United States v. Hernandez*, Chapter 8, Section C, infra.

4. *Judicial discretion.* How much discretion does a trial judge have under Rule 403 to exclude relevant evidence? See Gold, Limiting Judicial Discretion to Exclude Prejudicial Evidence, 18 U.C.Davis L.Rev. 59 (1984); Waltz, Judicial Discretion in the Admission of Evidence Under the Federal Rules of Evidence, 79 Nw.U.L.Rev. 1097 (1985).

5. *Constitutional limitations on the exclusion of defense evidence.* The exclusion of evidence offered by the defense for reasons other than the absence of logical relevance or the possibility of undue prejudice may raise constitutional issues. In Holmes v. South Carolina, 126 S.Ct. 1727 (2006), the Court overturned a conviction under a state rule that precluded the defendant from introducing evidence that another person had committed the crime in the face of "strong forensic evidence" of defendant's guilt. The Court noted (126 S.Ct. at 1734):

> Under this rule, the trial judge does not focus on the probative value or the potential adverse effects of admitting the defense evidence of third-party guilt. Instead, the critical inquiry concerns the strength of the prosecution's case: If the prosecution's case is strong enough, the evidence of third-party guilt is excluded even if that evidence, if viewed independently, would have great probative value and even if it would not pose an undue risk of harassment, prejudice, or confusion of the issues.

Viewed this way, the South Carolina rule resulted in a denial of defendant's right to present a complete defense. The *Holmes* decision is found in Chapter 2 with further discussion of constitutional limitations on the defendant's right to introduce evidence.

6. The succeeding chapter deals with other frequently occurring questions of relevancy. In reading about them, attempt not only to extract those more or less specific rules which the courts have evolved but also to gain the ability to predict the probable application of the doctrine embodied in Rule 403 to more unusual methods of proof.

Chapter 8[1]

FORMALIZED APPLICATIONS OF THE RELEVANCY CONCEPT

SECTION A. OTHER HAPPENINGS

CITY OF BLOOMINGTON v. LEGG

Supreme Court of Illinois, 1894.
37 N.E. 696.

This was an action on the case to recover damages for the death of Silas M. Legg, son of appellee. The declaration charges that the City of Bloomington erected a fountain on North Main street, to be used for drinking purposes and for watering horses. That around the fountain was a basin, into which water was conducted by two spouts; that the spouts were placed where the heads and bridles of the horses would come when drinking. That the spouts projected out several inches over the basin, and then bent, forming a hook, so that horses in drinking and after drinking, in lifting their heads, were liable to catch or break their bridles, of which the city had notice.

Silas M. Legg, on September 10, 1889, was driving a team of horses, hitched to an oil wagon, on which he was riding, on said street, and while exercising due care and diligence for his own safety, and permitting the horses to drink from the basin of the fountain, the bridle of one of the horses caught upon a curved or bent spout and was pulled off, and the horses ran away without his fault, threw him off, and the wagon on to him, thereby causing his death. * * *

A trial by jury resulted in a verdict for plaintiff, and damages assessed at the sum of $1,000, on which judgment was rendered. That judgment was affirmed by the Appellate Court, and this appeal is prosecuted by the city, it assigning error in allowing evidence to go to the jury that other accidents had occurred on account of the fountain spouts, and that it was error to allow evidence to show other accidents

1. Throughout this chapter some footnotes from the cases and materials have been omitted; others have been renumbered. [Ed].

when the spouts were not in the same condition as at the time of the accident, and that instructions for plaintiff were erroneous.

MR. JUSTICE PHILLIPS delivered the opinion of the Court:

The declaration contained several counts, some of which alleged that the spouts of the fountain turned downward at an angle at the end, whilst other counts charged the spouts as projecting straight out.

Evidence was admitted, over the defendant's objection, that other accidents had occurred of a similar character to that which resulted in injury to the deceased. Evidence of other accidents occurring from the same cause is by many courts held incompetent.

This court has held such evidence competent, not for the purpose of showing independent acts of negligence, but as tending to show the common cause of these accidents is a dangerous, unsafe thing. Where an issue is made as to the safety of any machinery or work of man's construction which is for practical use, the manner in which it has served that purpose, when put to that use, would be a matter material to the issue, and ordinary experience of that practical use, and the effect of such use, bear directly upon such issue. It no more presents a collateral issue than any other evidence that calls for a reply which bears on the main issue. Such evidence is held competent by the weight of authority. * * * The same rule is adopted in Georgia, Alabama, Connecticut, Minnesota, Michigan, and other States. In addition to being evidence material to the issue to show a dangerous condition, it is also evidence material as tending to show notice. City of Chicago v. Powers, Admx., supra. The frequency of such accidents would create a presumption of knowledge, and would be material to the question of diligence used to obviate the cause of injury.

The further point is made that plaintiff was permitted to show, over the objection of defendant, that other accidents occurred on account of the fountain spouts, when they were not in the same condition as they were at the time of injury to the deceased. The rule is clear, that to render evidence of similar accidents, resulting from the same cause, competent, it must appear, or the evidence must reasonably tend to show that the instrument or agency which caused the injury was in substantially the same condition at the time such other accidents occurred, as at the time the accident complained of was caused. The fountain spouts, when the fountain was first erected, projected two or three inches from the standard, and an elbow was screwed on to the outer end, which, in position, was perpendicular to the end of the spout, and projected downward. That elbow was removed, and that was the changed condition. It is not possible for a trial court to know the fact to be testified to by a particular witness, and whenever a witness was inquired of as to other accidents, the court, when the question was objected to, ruled in the presence of the jury that such evidence, if there were changed conditions, could not be considered to the prejudice of the city. And on the trial the court instructed the jury that they were not "to consider any testimony regarding accidents or trouble with horses, occurring at the fountain in question, at a time or times when you believe from the evidence the spouts complained of were in a materially different condition from what they were at the time of the injury complained of in this case."

Considering the instruction, and what was said by the court in ruling on the objection, we are not disposed to hold there was such error in the admission of that evidence that this judgment should be reversed. * * *

Judgment affirmed.

Notes and Questions

1. *Earlier rulings.* The principal case is in accord with modern treatments of evidence of other happenings. The courts were not always so tolerant of such of evidence. Compare Diamond Rubber Co. v. Harryman, 92 P. 922, 924 (Colo.1907), which involved a claim that plaintiff had tripped on a "goose-neck" placed in the sidewalk by defendant and used to inflate bicycle and automobile tires. The court held that the evidence had been improperly admitted, stating:

> Testimony that other persons had tripped upon this "goose-neck" was clearly not admissible for the purpose of establishing negligence of the defendants, or that the "goose-neck" was dangerous. If the fact that others had tripped upon the obstruction could be shown for the purpose of establishing negligence, then there would necessarily be as many distinct issues injected into the case, as there were persons called as witnesses who had passed over the sidewalk in the vicinity of the "goose-neck." The care they had exercised and the conditions under which they had tripped upon the obstruction would be a subject of inquiry. If such evidence was admissible, then it would be proper to show that persons had passed along the sidewalk and had not tripped upon the obstruction; and, again, the care they had exercised and the conditions under which they had passed by the "goose-neck" could be gone into; and thus the case would be confused by a great number of collateral issues which would not aid in determining whether or not the obstruction was dangerous. * * *

2. *Cases of inadmissibility.* Despite the generally more tolerant recent attitude toward this kind of evidence, it is not always admitted. See, e.g., Coate v. State, 306 S.W.2d 727 (Tex.Crim.App.1957), commented upon in 36 Tex.L.Rev. 664 (1958), and Smith v. City of Rock Island, 161 N.E.2d 369 (Ill.App.Ct.1959). In the former, a negligent homicide case, the accused offered evidence of prior collisions at the same intersection. In the latter, defendant city, being sued for failure to maintain a proper stop sign at the intersection where plaintiff was injured, offered evidence of collisions at other intersections having proper stop signs. In both cases the evidence was ruled inadmissible.

3. *Rebutting extreme claims.* The court of appeals opted for admissibility of testimony of three one-eyed marine carpenters that they were successfully employed at their trade, offered to rebut plaintiff-marine carpenter's

claim in admiralty that loss of an eye had rendered him unemployable. Rapisardi v. United Fruit Co., 441 F.2d 1308 (2d Cir.1971).

4. *Degree of similarity.* The degree of similarity of circumstances required may depend upon the purpose for which the evidence is offered. Strict similarity is likely to be required where the evidence is offered to show the dangerousness of the condition; a lesser showing of similarity may be required where the evidence is offered to show notice. Why? Compare Kelsay v. Consolidated Rail Corp., 749 F.2d 437 (7th Cir.1984) (evidence of prior railroad crossing accidents excluded as too remote and dissimilar), with Young v. Illinois Cent. Gulf R. Co., 618 F.2d 332 (5th Cir.1980) (evidence of recent prior accidents admissible to show notice of an arguably dangerous railroad crossing without a "trial of the details and circumstances of those prior accidents").

5. *Examples of treatments of other happenings.* For treatments of other happenings in a variety of situations, see Annots., 26 A.L.R.2d 136, prior escapes of gas; 45 A.L.R.2d 1121, explosion damage to other properties; 46 A.L.R.2d 935, other failures of railroad crossing devices; 21 A.L.R.4th 472, prior accidents at same place; 42 A.L.R.3d 780, other accidents to prove dangerous nature of product. See generally 2 Imwinkelried, Uncharged Misconduct Evidence §§ 7:13–7:26 (1999).

6. *Federal Rule 404(b).* A strong argument can be made that evidence of other happenings in civil cases should be considered under Rule 404(b) as evidence of "other crimes, wrongs, or acts." See, e.g., Imwinkelried, note 5, supra, §§ 7:12, 7:23, 7:26. Many courts considering the question under the Federal Rules have ignored Rule 404(b) and relied instead either on common law principles or on Rule 403. See, e.g., *Kelsay v. Consolidated Rail Corp.*, note 4, supra (trial court properly excluded evidence of two prior accidents at railroad crossing, one 30 years and one 12 years before, on grounds of remoteness and dissimilarity of conditions). Might the application of Rule 404(b) make any difference in such cases?

JONES v. PAK–MOR MANUFACTURING CO.

Supreme Court of Arizona, En Banc, 1985.
700 P.2d 819.

FELDMAN, JUSTICE.

Jerry Jones (plaintiff) was injured on January 27, 1979, while working on a machine manufactured by Pak–Mor Manufacturing Company (defendant). In the product liability action which followed, plaintiff alleged improper design and sought recovery on theories of negligence and strict liability. Before trial, plaintiff moved to exclude all evidence of the absence of prior, similar accidents. The trial court granted plaintiff's motion, ruling that such evidence was inadmissible under Arizona law. After verdict and judgment for plaintiff, defendant appealed, claiming, *inter alia,* that the exclusion ruling was in error. The court of appeals affirmed. *Jones v. Pak–Mor Manufacturing Co.,* 145 Ariz. 132, 700 P.2d 830 (1984). * * * We accepted review only on the issue pertaining to admissibility of evidence of the absence of prior accidents.

* * *

Plaintiff was employed by SCA Services of Arizona, Inc. On January 27, 1979, plaintiff was injured while working on a side-loading refuse compaction and collection machine on a route serviced by SCA.

[Plaintiff, a worker on the machine, seriously injured his leg when he was caught between the vehicle and a fence. The trial involved his claims of negligence and strict liability against the manufacturer of the vehicle based upon its design of the standing space on the machine.]

* * *

[T]he evidence indicates that no material change in the design occurred and that the compactor on which plaintiff was riding was a model which had been used without relevant change for a period of twenty-six years.

At the beginning of trial, plaintiff moved to exclude any evidence that the machine had been in use for twenty-six years without report of similar accidents. In opposing the motion, defendant offered to prove that the product had been designed and put into use in 1947, that the relevant portion of the design had not been changed, that thousands of machines with the same design had been sold, that they had been used under widely varying conditions, and that there had been no report of claims to or against defendant based on any injury sustained in a manner similar to that alleged by plaintiff. Defendant was prepared to offer this evidence through the testimony of its president. It argued that the evidence was relevant to show that the design was not defective, that the product was not unreasonably dangerous, and that the defendant had no notice of any defect or danger.

While recognizing that there is authority from other jurisdictions supporting the admission of evidence relating to the absence of prior accidents in both negligence and strict liability actions, both the trial judge and the court of appeals correctly noted the existence of Arizona decisions "admit[ting] evidence of prior accidents, but exclud[ing] evidence of the absence of prior accidents." (*Jones v. Pak–Mor,* at 123, 700 P.2d at 821.) As the court of appeals further noted, in Arizona the rule is "applied mechanically." (*Id.*) Although the trial court has discretion to admit evidence of prior accidents, the rule relating to inadmissibility of evidence of the absence of prior accidents is a *per se* rule. *Hlavaty v. Song,* 107 Ariz. 606, 491 P.2d 460 (1971). Evidence of the absence of prior accidents under similar conditions is inadmissible to prove lack of defect, lack of danger, or similar issues. * * *

The rule of *per se* inadmissibility was first adopted by this court in *Fox Tucson Theaters Corp. v. Lindsay,* 47 Ariz. 388, 56 P.2d 183 (1936). * * *

1. The Basis for Rejection

The reason given in *Lindsay* for the rule of inadmissibility was that

> * * * it is apparent that such testimony, could the parties be prepared to meet it, might introduce into the case numerous collat-

> eral issues bearing only remotely on the main issue, which would tend to greatly protract the trial, distract the attention of the jury from the issues involved in the suit, and impose great and unnecessary expense on the parties.

Fox Tucson Theaters Corp. v. Lindsay, 47 Ariz. at 395, 56 P.2d at 186, quoting from the seminal case of *Anderson v. Taft,* 20 R.I. 362, 39 A. 191, 192 (1898). A second reason sometimes given for the *per se* rule of inadmissibility in some of the earlier literature was that

> Litigants should be protected against surprise * * *. [S]afety-history evidence is not closely confined in time, and sometimes not in space. Therefore, opposing counsel may be unprepared to meet fraudulent, partial, or mistaken testimony about accidents other than the principal one, or about long periods of safe use.

Morris, *Proof of Safety History in Negligence Cases,* 61 Harv.L.Rev. 205, 210 (1948). A final consideration was that jurors would be misled or prejudiced by such evidence. Thus, jurors impressed by the defendant's good record might be swayed in his favor and fail to see that he had lowered his standards. *Id.* at 210–11.

While some of these objections may still be viable, recent cases indicate that the rule of *per se* inadmissibility is "manifestly incompatible with modern principles of evidence." *Simon v. Town of Kennebunkport,* 417 A.2d 982, 985 (Me.1980). In *Simon* the court rejected a *per se* rule of inadmissibility of evidence of other accidents and stated:

> Whatever the continued vitality * * * of an absolute prohibition against other-accident evidence, it is clear that such a rule did not survive the adoption of our new Rules of Evidence * * *.

Id. at 986; *see also Sturm v. Clark Equipment Co.,* 547 F.Supp. 144, 145 (W.D.Mo.1982), *aff'd,* 732 F.2d 161 (8th Cir.1984) (noting that under the Federal Rules of Evidence the absence of prior accidents is "relevant and admissible, assuming an adequate foundation is established regarding comparability of circumstances").

We note also that the rule of *per se* inadmissibility, adopted in *Fox Tucson Theaters Corp. v. Lindsay* and followed in other cases, has been criticized by most, if not all, evidence scholars. *See McCormick on Evidence* § 200 at 590–92 (E. Cleary ed.1984); M. Udall & J. Livermore, *Arizona Law of Evidence* § 85 at 190 (2d ed.1982); 2 Wigmore, *Evidence* § 443–44 at 528–32 (Chadbourn rev.1979). Observing that few recent decisions have applied a general rule of exclusion, McCormick has criticized the lack of symmetry in the rule allowing a judge discretion to admit proof of other accidents but not proof of the absence of other accidents:

> One might think that if proof of similar accidents is admissible in the judge's discretion to show that a particular condition or defect exists, or that the injury sued for was caused in a certain way, or that a situation is dangerous, or that defendant knew or should have known of the danger, then evidence of the absence of accidents

> during a period of similar exposure and experience likewise would be receivable to show that these facts do not exist in the case at bar. Indeed, it would seem perverse to tell a jury that one or two persons besides the plaintiff tripped on defendant's stairwell while withholding from them the further information that another thousand persons descended the same stairs without incident.

McCormick, *supra,* § 200 at 590. Similarly, Wigmore has rejected as unsound a fixed rule of admissibility or inadmissibility, favoring instead a general rule of judicial discretion:

> It is much wiser and more practical to leave the possible inconvenience to be determined by the tribunal best fitted to determine it, the trial court, and to sanction the reception of all such relevant evidence subject to this exclusionary discretion based on inconvenience.

2 Wigmore, *supra,* § 444 at 532.

Whatever the debate waged in the courts and by the authors of articles and treatises, we believe that our position should be compatible with the rules of evidence which we adopted in 1977. A blanket rule of inadmissibility is essentially a rule of relevancy. As a matter of law it declares the evidence inadmissible either because it lacks probative value with regard to the issues presented or because its probative value is outweighed by the danger of prejudice and the problems associated with inquiry into collateral matters, such as time wasted, expense, and the like. *See Simon v. Town of Kennebunkport,* 417 A.2d at 986.

2. The Rules of Evidence

We turn, then, to an examination of the rules of evidence. Rule 401 defines "relevant evidence" as that "having any tendency to make the existence of any fact that is of consequence to the determination of the action more probable or less probable than it would be without the evidence." The essence of a negligence action based on defective design is that defendant distributed a product when it was reasonably foreseeable that its design presented an unreasonable risk of harm. W. Prosser & W. Keeton, *The Law of Torts* §§ 96, 99 at 688–89, 698–702 (5th ed.1984). In a strict liability action, the plaintiff must prove that the product was defective and unreasonably dangerous. Restatement (Second) of Torts § 402A. The factors which bear upon this determination in a defective design case were considered by us in *Byrns v. Riddell, Inc.,* 113 Ariz. 264, 550 P.2d 1065 (1976). One of those factors is the likelihood that the product, as designed, will cause serious injury. *Id.* at 267, 550 P.2d at 1068. Thus, in product liability actions based on defective design, relevant issues may include whether defendant should have foreseen the potential for danger from use of the product as designed, whether a defect existed, and whether a particular danger was unreasonable—including the likelihood of its causing serious injury. Safety-history, including the presence or absence of prior accidents under similar use, is evidence which may make these ultimate facts "more probable or less probable than [they] would be without the evidence." Rule 401, Ariz.R.Evid., 17A A.R.S. * * * There can be no doubt that evidence of safety-history is relevant.

Once evidence is shown to be relevant, Rule 402 provides that it is admissible unless "otherwise provided" by constitutional provision, statute, or rule. Several rules of evidence provide for *per se* inadmissibility, subject to enumerated exceptions. *See* Rules 404 and 407–411. No specific rule of evidence mandates rejection of evidence of safety-history. The one rule that applies to safety-history evidence is Rule 403, which covers the concerns expressed by this court in *Fox Tucson Theaters Corp. v. Lindsay, supra,* and described by Wigmore as "considerations of auxiliary probative policy." 2 Wigmore, *supra,* § 443 at 528. Rule 403 permits exclusion of evidence when

> [a]lthough relevant, * * * its probative value is substantially outweighed by the danger of unfair prejudice, confusion of the issues, or misleading the jury, or by considerations of undue delay, waste of time, or needless presentation of cumulative evidence.

Rule 403 is not a rule of *per se* inadmissibility, but one which gives the court discretion to reject relevant evidence upon the grounds stated. 1 *Weinstein's Evidence* § 403[01] (1982). It is essentially a rule which requires the court to weigh and balance the benefit to be gained by admission against the harm which may result from admission. It is the rule applicable to evidence showing the existence of prior accidents. *Simon v. Town of Kennebunkport,* 417 A.2d at 986. It is the rule which defendant claims logically should apply to evidence of the absence of prior accidents in cases involving alleged negligent or defective design. For this proposition defendant cites a number of recent cases holding that the trial court has discretion under Rule 403 to admit evidence of the absence of prior accidents. * * *

3. Characterization of Evidence of the Absence of Prior Accidents

There is little logic in the proposition that the trial court may admit evidence of other accidents but may never admit evidence of their absence. *See* McCormick, *supra,* § 200 at 590. Nevertheless, experience teaches us that the problems of prejudice, inability of the opposing party to meet the evidence, and the danger of misleading the jury are substantial. We are aware, also, that defendant's "lack of notice" of injury does not establish the fact that no injuries had occurred, and that a "long history of good fortune" may not preclude the conclusion that the product was defective and unreasonably dangerous. *Tucson Industries, Inc. v. Schwartz,* 108 Ariz. 464, 468, 501 P.2d 936, 940 (1972).

We believe that the true problem underlying the rejection of evidence of the lack of prior accidents is more evidentiary than substantive in nature. The essential nature of evidence of the absence of prior accidents is different from evidence of the existence of prior accidents. It is harder to prove that something did not happen than to prove that it did happen. When a witness testifies that he knows of no prior accidents, there are two possible explanations. The first is that there have been no prior accidents; the second is that there have been prior accidents but the witness does not know about them. This problem, however, is not peculiar to safety-history evidence in product liability cases. It is, we believe, a variant of the "negative evidence" problem. *See* M. Udall & J. Livermore, *supra,* § 65 at 120; 2 Wigmore, *supra,* § 664. The response of most courts to this problem has been that testimony that a witness did not see an event (knows of no prior accident) "has, in and of itself no probative force sufficient to prove that the event did not occur." *Byars v. Arizona Public Service Co.,* 24 Ariz.App. 420, 424, 539 P.2d 534, 538 (1975). *See also State v. Jeffers,* 135 Ariz. 404, 661 P.2d 1105 (1983). Generally, courts hold that such negative evidence is inadmissible, unless testimony that the witness did not see the event or does not know of it is coupled with further evidence that the witness was in such a position or has such sources of knowledge that if the event had occurred, he would have seen it or would have known about it. M. Udall & J. Livermore, *supra,* § 65 at 120; 2 Wigmore, *supra,* § 664 at 907.

All of these factors indicate the path that should be taken. If the *per se* rule is rejected, the trial court will apply Rule 403, weigh the auxiliary probative problems, and balance them against the value of the evidence. The trial judge should be aware of the difficulty of meeting an allegation that there have been no prior accidents. If a product is very widely distributed, it will be almost impossible for the plaintiff to rebut such a contention when the real issue is simply whether, among millions of users, a few each year may have used the product in a way which produced serious injuries. The trial judge must remember that where plaintiff alleges that a particular use of the product has produced a prior injury, he is put to his proof of the specific instance. The existence of a specific prior occurrence, the question of similarity, and other questions of specific proof are all much easier to meet than the general assertion that there have been no prior accidents. These factors, then, should weigh in the trial judge's determination of admissibility under Rule 403.

Other matters also should be considered. One of these is the plain nature of the danger. An open hole in a sidewalk poses a patent, unreasonable danger to pedestrians. Evidence of the lack of prior accidents is no more than evidence that the plaintiff was the first to fall in the hole. It creates a considerable risk of misleading the jury with respect to the purpose for which the evidence is admitted. Further considerations are similarity of use and length of exposure to the particular danger. *See Darrough v. White Motor Co.,* 74 Ill.App.3d at 565, 30 Ill.Dec. at 472, 393 N.E.2d at 125. The foundation should include evidence that the product experience which the proponent seeks to prove "is so extensive as to be sure to include an adequate number of similar situations." McCormick, *supra,* § 200 at 591.

We come, then, to the important consideration of the characterization of the evidence. The character of the evidence which might be admissible is determined by the issue on which it is offered. The ultimate issue is not whether lawsuits have been filed, nor whether claims have been made, nor whether the witness is aware of any accidents. The relevance of safety-history evidence is to establish evidentiary facts from which it may be inferred that there have been no prior accidents, thus warranting the ultimate inference that the product was neither defective and unreasonably dangerous nor the cause of the injury. Thus, the proponent of the evidence must establish that if there had been prior accidents, the witness probably would have known about them. This portion of the evidentiary predicate will, in most cases, be formidable. It is not, however, insurmountable. The defendant may have established a department or division to check on the safety of its products and may have a system for ascertaining whether accidents have occurred from the use of its products. The defendant or its insurers may have made a survey of its customers and the users of its product to determine whether particular uses of the product have produced particular types of injuries. Information may have been compiled by and obtained from governmental agencies such as the Consumer Product Safety Commission, the FAA, the FDA, or the FTC. Defendant may have established a system with its insurers, distributors, or retailers whereby retail customers are encouraged to report accidents, accidents are investigated, and data is compiled. Any of these methods, or others, may produce facts with which the proponent of the evidence may establish that if there had been accidents or near-accidents when the product was used in a relevant manner, defendant probably would have learned of the information and would have it available. Thus, if the import of the evidence is no more than testimony that no lawsuits have been filed, no claims have been made, or "we have never heard of any accidents," the trial judge generally should refuse the offered evidence since it has very little probative value and carries much danger of prejudice.

We are cognizant, also, that in the ordinary case (*see Fox Tucson Theaters Corp. v. Lindsay, supra*) involving the design or construction of buildings or intersections, the evidentiary predicate which we have described will militate strongly against admission of the evidence. Where, for instance, plaintiff alleges that premises were negligently designed or maintained, the mere fact that no prior accidents have been reported is incomplete. It does not tell us how many near-accidents, nor how many fortuitous escapes from injury, may have occurred, and it leaves the opponent of the evidence no method to ascertain and identify those who may have passed by the area, under what conditions, and with what risks or experience. In such a case, the scales tip strongly in favor of rejection of the evidence. However, in product design defect cases, the focus is on the inherent nature and quality of all products of similar design. If the design is "defective," then all units have the same defect. *See* R. Hursh & H. Bailey, 1 *American Law of Products Liability* § 1.21 at 66–67 (2d ed.1974). In such cases, the accumulation of relevant data is possible if the defendant, its insurers, distributors, customers, or some governmental agency has undertaken appropriate steps to acquire and compile information on safety-history. Under such circumstances, we believe that the problem of trial preparation is manageable. Once either party learns, through appropriate discovery, of the other's intent to offer evidence of safety-history, the opponent usually will be in a position to undertake some type of discovery or investigation to meet the assertion, so long as the offer is specific and not merely "we know of no claims." In these cases, the balancing test required by Rule 403 may well tip toward admission.

One further consideration must be examined. Plaintiff argues that the policy of product liability law should be to foster the manufacture and distribution of safe products and to discourage the distribution of unsafe products. Therefore, plaintiff maintains that we should continue to follow a policy of admission of proof of prior accidents under similar circumstances and *per se* exclusion of relevant evidence of lack of prior accidents, even though this rule has been criticized. We agree with the premise but not with the conclusion. We have recognized safety incentive as a factor in the evolution of Arizona law of product liability. *Salt River Project v. Westinghouse,* 143 Ariz. 368, 694 P.2d 198 (1984). We disagree, however, with the assumption made by the plaintiff. Safety is not promoted by giving manufacturers, sellers, and distributors an incentive to refrain from learning about their products. The present rule, providing for discretionary admission of evidence of prior accidents and automatic exclusion of evidence of the lack of prior accidents, does just that. We believe the law is better served by a rule which gives manufacturers and distributors the utmost incentive to acquire, record, and maintain information regarding the performance of their products.

We hold, therefore, that in product liability cases involving a claim of defective design, whether based on negligence, strict liability, or both, the trial court has discretion under Rule 403 to admit evidence of safety-history concerning both the existence and the nonexistence of prior accidents, provided that the proponent establishes the necessary predicate for the evidence.[2] The evidence of safety-history is admissible on issues pertaining to whether the design caused the product to be defective, whether the defect was unreasonably dangerous, whether it was a cause of the accident, or—in negligence cases—whether the defendant should have foreseen that the design of the product was not reasonably safe for its contemplated uses.

In the case at bench, the trial court held that evidence of the lack of prior accidents was *per se* inadmissible. The court of appeals affirmed that holding. We turn, then, to determine whether that ruling constituted reversible error.

[Despite its rejection of the *per se* rule, the court affirmed the lower court decision. It found that the defendant's offer of proof was insufficient to establish that its evidence would have been admissible. The

2. We emphasize that this is a rule applicable to defective design cases and not those involving a manufacturing flaw. Cases involving a manufacturing flaw do not implicate the inherent design or quality of the entire line of products in question, but only the quality of a particular unit or number of units of that product. In such cases, the fact that the product as a whole has a demonstrated safety-history is irrelevant.

defendant had simply stated that, over the past 26 years, it had had no reports of injuries like those to the plaintiff. The court responded:

> * * * the absence of claims and reports is not the relevant fact, nor even one which justifies an inference of the relevant fact (that there have been no accidents), absent a showing that if there had been accidents the witness would have known of them either from the system utilized to track safety-history or from the investigation made at the sources of such information. There may have been no lawsuits filed against defendant, but we have no way of knowing what workers' compensation claims were filed with appropriate administrative bodies nor any way of knowing what injuries were sustained but not pursued. * * *]

Note

For a more recent case adopting an approach similar to that in the *Pak-Mor* case see Forrest v. Beloit Corp., 424 F.3d 344 (3d Cir.2005) (evidence not admitted where no records of injuries or accidents involving same model were kept; thorough discussion of problems that may exist where proof of absence of accidents is offered). See also Evans v. State, 18 P.3d 227 (Idaho Ct.App.2001) (evidence of infrequency of accidents resulting from dives from platform properly admitted); Spino v. John S. Tilley Ladder Co., 696 A.2d 1169 (Pa.1997) (evidence of prior claims properly admitted in design defect product liability case); Bazzano v. Killington Country Village, Inc., 830 A.2d 24 (Vt. 2003) (evidence of no prior falls down stairs properly admitted to show absence of defect). See generally Morris, Proof of Safety History in Negligence Cases, 61 Harv.L.Rev. 205 (1948); 1 McCormick, Evidence § 200 (6th ed. 2006); Annots., 10 A.L.R.5th 371; 42 A.L.R.2d 1055.

REDFIELD v. IOWA STATE HIGHWAY COMM'N

Supreme Court of Iowa, 1959.
99 N.W.2d 413.

GARRETT, JUSTICE. In February, 1956 plaintiffs-appellants purchased 97.2 acres of land near the north edge of Des Moines for contemplated development as a residential sub-division. In November, 1957 the State Highway Commission filed notice of proceedings to condemn the north 77.2 acres of said land in connection with the construction of limited access interstate highway number 80. On December 10, 1958 the condemnation commission filed its report fixing plaintiffs' damages at $70,000. On December 26, 1957 the highway commission took possession of said condemned property and proceeded to complete the construction of said highway.

Within the proper time plaintiffs filed suit in the district court seeking damages in the amount of $198,925. The case was tried to a jury which gave plaintiffs a verdict for $60,000. They, being dissatisfied, have appealed to this court. * * *

Appellants' four witnesses testified to values as follows:

	Before	After	Difference
Redfield	$195,000.	$20,000.	$175,000.
Ashby	179,500.	20,000.	159,500.
Holden	143,000.	20,000.	123,000.
Neal	169,750.	20,000.	149,750.

Appellee's witnesses testified to values as follows:

Froning	66,000.	10,000.	56,000.
Donahoe	80,000.	8,000.	72,000.
Brandt	76,050.	11,550.	64,500.

It is enlightening to observe the extreme differences between the values placed on the subject property by the witnesses for the respective sides. All witnesses on value showed outstanding training and experience but when experts differ so widely on a proposition they profess to know all about, it lends force to appellants' claim that the actual records of sales of comparable properties from which the witnesses gained their knowledge are more reliable evidence than mere opinions of the experts. * * *

Appellants assign as error the striking of the testimony of their witness Ashby on direct examination regarding the price paid in a sale he used in arriving at his opinion of the value of appellants' property. This assignment has reference to a tract referred to as follows: "Also the piece inside the city limits on Merle Hay purchased by the water works, 360 by 360 for $15,000.00". On motion the amount of the purchase price was stricken. The witness had testified this was a comparable sale which he took into consideration in fixing the value of plaintiffs' property. After describing other sales he said, "All of these sales, I have informed myself as to the sales price and can give accurate details. Most of the properties were raw land and most of it sub-division land."

It appeared at that stage the court would continue to rule against the admission on direct examination of evidence of the prices paid for other similar properties. * * *

Under the rule heretofore prevailing in Iowa, such evidence would not be admissible. We have been asked by appellants to review our former decisions and to change the rule in this state to conform with the majority rule. * * *

We do not hold the view that the majority is always right but in this instance, after considering the advantages and disadvantages of each rule, being aided by well considered opinions of learned courts on both sides of the question, we feel it is advisable now to join those who adhere to the Massachusetts rule and we now adopt that rule. We quote from the Annotation, 118 A.L.R. 869, 870 * * * "The view is taken in a majority of jurisdictions that evidence of the sale price of other real property is admissible upon the issue of the value of other real property where the conditions with respect to the other land and the sale thereof are similar to those involved in the case at bar." Cases from many states following the above rule are cited as are also cases from states holding contra. At page 387 of 174 A.L.R. will be found an extensive annotation listing additional cases sustaining both views. It is stated this annotation supplements the one above from which we quoted. For the evidence to be admitted it must be shown that the conditions are similar. "Similar does not mean identical, but having a resemblance; and property may be similar in the sense in which the word is here used though each possess various points of difference." Forest Preserve Dist. of Cook County v. Lehmann Estate, Inc., 388 Ill. 416, 58 N.E.2d 538, 544. Size, use, location and character of the land, time, mode and nature of the sale all have a bearing on the admissibility of such evidence.

The futility, if not the absurdity of the rule under which we now operate is well described in an opinion in a California case before that court adopted the majority rule. "Everyone recognizes that the first thing a prospective buyer of any kind of property wants to know is what other people have paid for like property in the recent past. * * * But when the valuation of realty is the problem, court and jury are suddenly cut off from informative sources and forced to rely (theoretically) upon opinions based principally upon undisclosed prices of other sales. * * * The main objective of the rule—avoidance of collateral issues—has proved abortive and the procedural aspect of the trial has changed for the worse. * * * Ever since adoption of the rule excluding other sales on direct it has been stated repeatedly that such sales, though the prices are given on cross-examination, are not evidence of value, are to be considered only upon the imputation of lack of information or trustworthiness of the witness. The jurors are so instructed. They know that sales are the basis on which mankind universally values properties; they have many of the pertinent sales before them; when they hear the judge instruct that those sales are not any evidence of value the jurors who are still listening begin to wonder what is the matter with the judge; * * * That such an instruction must be given is well settled in the law of this state." County of Los Angeles v. Faus, Cal.App., 304 P.2d 257, 269.

On appeal of the above case to the Supreme Court of California the decision was reversed and California in 1957 adopted the majority rule. In County of Los Angeles v. Faus, (Decided June 21, 1957) 48 Cal.2d 672, 312 P.2d 680, 684 the court said: "In taking this position it is recognized that we are overruling a line of decisions in this state that announce a contrary rule. The former rule was contrary to logic, unrealistic, and followed in only a few other states. It was merely a rule of procedure. Therefore, it becomes our duty not to follow decisions that we are convinced are erroneous and obsolete." * * * That court then taking the view that neither contract nor property rights had vested in either party by reason of its prior decision, stated: "The rule now announced is available to both parties upon a retrial." We make the same pronouncement in this case.

New York, formerly on uncertain ground, is now aligned with those states which hold evidence of sales of comparable properties admissible as substantive proof of the value of the property under condemnation. Village of Lawrence v. Greenwood, 300 N.Y. 231, 90 N.E.2d 53. Utah and Nebraska are among the large number of states now following this rule. State, By and Through Its Engineering Comm. v. Peek, 1 Utah 2d 263, 265 P.2d 630; City of Lincoln v. Marshall, 161 Neb. 680, 74 N.W.2d 470; 2 Wigmore on Evidence, 3rd Edition, 503 to 507, Section 463.

Much must necessarily be left to the sound discretion of the trial court as to whether or not the conditions are met which make the admissibility rule applicable. * * *

Reversed and remanded.

LARSON, C.J., and THORNTON, PETERSON, HAYS, BLISS and GARFIELD, JJ., concur.

THOMPSON and OLIVER, JJ., dissent.

Notes and Questions

1. *Another example.* In Hays v. State, 342 S.W.2d 167 (Tex.Civ.App. 1960), a discrepancy of as much as eight to one between values given by experts for the landowners and those for the condemnor was emphasized as influencing the court to adopt the rule admitting evidence of similar sales.

2. *Discussions.* Broad discussions of valuation evidence are found in Note, Methods of Proving Land Values, 43 Iowa L.Rev. 270 (1958), and Note, Valuation Evidence in California Condemnation Cases, 12 Stan.L.Rev. 766 (1960). Cases on similar sales are collected in Annot., 85 A.L.R.2d 110. With regard to the requirement of similarity see Patterson v. City of Lincoln, 550 N.W.2d 650 (Neb.1996); Duke Power Co. v. Winebarger, 265 S.E.2d 227 (N.C.1980).

3. *Forced sales and offers.* Consider the admissibility of foreclosure sales, sales to a body having the power of eminent domain, and partition sales. Should offers to buy or sell be admitted? See, e.g., Arkansas State Highway Comm'n v. Barker, 931 S.W.2d 138 (Ark.1996) (condemnation sale improperly admitted); Samonek v. Norvell Township, 527 N.W.2d 24 (Mich. Ct.App.1994) (evidence of forced sales inadmissible).

CARPENTER v. KURN

Supreme Court of Missouri, 1941.
157 S.W.2d 213.

TIPTON, P.J.—Respondent brought this action as widow of Reuben Carpenter, deceased, to recover damages for alleged wrongful death of her husband, which occurred on May 25, 1937, near Henryetta, Oklahoma. She brought this action for the benefit of herself and deceased's four minor children. This action was first tried in the Circuit Court of Barry County, Missouri, where respondent obtained a judgment for $18,000. We reversed that judgment for error in respondent's instruction; our opinion is reported in 345 Mo. 877, 136 S.W.2d 997, where a full statement of the facts may be found. Thereafter, the case was sent to

Henry County, Missouri, on a change of venue, where a judgment of $20,000 was obtained by respondent. The appellants have duly appealed from that judgment. * * *

The appellants assigned as error the testimony of witnesses Sherman Gipson and Luther Houk, who testified that on two occasions following the accident, they, with others, made certain tests for the purpose of ascertaining the distance one standing on the track could tell that a person sitting in the same position and dressed the same as deceased was a human being. The conditions under which these tests were made were the same as existed when deceased was struck by appellants' train, except that persons making the observation were on foot instead of being in the cab of a moving engine.

The appellants contend this testimony is inadmissible; first, for the reason that these witnesses knew in advance the object on the track when the tests were made was a man and just how he was dressed, and second, that these witnesses were on foot, while the engineer was in a moving engine attended with much vibration and lateral motion.

> "'* * * But, if the evidence shows that the experiment was made under circumstances similar, or approximately similar, to those which surround the original transaction, and such experiment would serve to shed any light upon that transaction, we can see no reason for the exclusion of such experiment, although it might not have been made under exactly similar conditions as attended the original transaction. The dissimilarity would not exclude, but would go to, its weight before the jury. * * *'" [Amsbary v. Grays Harbor Ry. & Light Co., 78 Wash. 379, 139 Pac. 46, l. c. 51, 8 A.L.R. 1.]

The above quotation was approved by this court in the case of Griggs v. Kansas City Rys. Co. (Mo.), 228 S.W. 508, l. c. 512. In that case, we held: "The difference in the conduct of such an experiment arising from the fact that the experimenter looks for what he is expected to see, while the engineer or motorman is expected only to watch for any object that might appear upon the track, and has his attention more or less engaged in operating his car or engine, is not a difference of condition sufficient to warrant the exclusion of the evidence. Its weight is a matter for the jury." To the same effect is the case of Norfolk & W. Ry. Co. v. Henderson, 132 Va. 297, 111 S.E. 277. We, therefore, overrule appellants' first objection to this testimony.

The question next arises, were the conditions when the witnesses were standing on the track making the experiments substantially the same as those when the engineer was in the cab of his engine, when the accident occurred resulting in deceased's death? Respondent's witness Ruskoski testified that an engineer could not see as far when the engine was running as when it was standing still, but he did testify that the engineer on a moving engine could see as well as a man standing on the ground and that the lateral motion of the cab impairs the view of an engineer looking down the track "very little, if any," and is not noticeable. Respondent's witness Wilson testified that side-sway "didn't have any material effect on your vision, and that you could see as far looking through one of those plate glasses as you could if you were standing on the ground."

The Supreme Court of Arkansas, in ruling almost the same question in the case of St. Louis, I.M. & S. Ry. Co. v. McMichael, 115 Ark. 101, 171 S.W. 115, l. c. 121, said:

> "We are of the opinion that the court did not err in holding that the conditions under which the experiments were made by the witnesses on behalf of the appellee were substantially the same. It is true that the witnesses who made these observations were not on an engine moving at a speed of 35 or 40 miles an hour, but there was testimony of expert passenger engineers to the effect that one accustomed to the movements of an engine could see a man as plainly from an engine going 35 or 40 miles per hour as one standing or walking on the track. This testimony, although contradicted by expert passenger engineers testifying for appellant, was nevertheless sufficient to render the testimony of the witnesses for appellee competent, so far as the essential similarity of viewpoints was concerned."

* * *

[Affirmed, subject to remittitur of excessive damages.]

Notes and Questions

1. *Purpose of offer.* In the experiment cases, as in cases involving other happenings generally, a fair amount of confusion may be engendered by failure to make clear the exact purpose for which the evidence is offered. In the visibility cases, is the experiment calculated to determine a "normal" human reaction under the circumstances, what actually happened, or merely to establish some physical fact or facts? With the principal case, compare Handley v. Erb, 41 N.E.2d 222 (Ill.App.Ct.1942), upholding exclusion of evidence of experiments to determine the visibility of a rope stretched across a street because the subject of the experiment knew that the rope was there while defendant at the time of the occurrence did not.

2. *The human factor.* When an experiment involving human participants is probative of some material fact despite dissimilarities between the persons involved in the experiment and those involved in the actual occurrence in litigation, may admission of evidence of the experiment nevertheless constitute error? In Spurlin v. Nardo, 114 S.E.2d 913 (W.Va.1960), the plaintiff was injured when defendant's car, in which plaintiff was riding, descended a hill out of control as a result of failure of the foot brake. Plaintiff offered evidence of experiments by an expert automotive mechanic with thirty-five years driving experience, conducted in a like-model car on the same hill, to prove that the car could have been stopped by alternative means. The evidence was admitted by the trial court. On appeal, held: *Reversed.* While the evidence was proper to show "what the machine could do," nevertheless "where a human element is involved [in an experiment], such experiments should be excluded or the human element separated." Id.

at 920. What did the court mean by "separating the human element"? How do you suppose the court felt this might have been accomplished in the *Spurlin* case? Are there problems even where the same driver is involved in the experiment? See First Midwest Trust Co. v. Rogers, 701 N.E.2d 1107 (Ill.App.Ct.1998) (experiment improperly admitted).

3. *Danger.* Situations involving disastrous or fatal consequences to human beings may present practical problems of securing a suitable subject for experimentation. However, in Louisville Gas and Elec. Co. v. Duncan, 31 S.W.2d 915 (Ky.1930), involving the electrocution of a miner, the superintendent induced another employee to assume the same position as the deceased.

4. *Other cases.* Experiment cases are collected in Annots., 26 A.L.R.2d 892, ballistics; 54 A.L.R.2d 922, damages from electricity; 76 A.L.R.2d 354, chemical or physical qualities; 76 A.L.R.2d 402, explosions; 78 A.L.R.2d 152, visibility; 78 A.L.R.2d 218, skidding of vehicles; 64 A.L.R.4th 125, defect in motor vehicle; 11 A.L.R.5th 497, distance of gun fired at victim. Absence of the accused from the site does not generally render the results of experiments inadmissible. Annot., 17 A.L.R.2d 1078.

FOSTER v. AGRI–CHEM, INC.

Supreme Court of Oregon, 1963.
385 P.2d 184.

DENECKE, JUSTICE.

[One of] the primary problems in this case involve[s] the admissibility of evidence of out-of-the-courtroom experiments. * * *

The defendant contracted to sell and apply liquid nitrogen fertilizer on the plaintiffs' wheatlands. The defendant agreed to apply not more than 50 pounds of fertilizer per acre. Plaintiffs contend that 64 pounds per acre were applied and the application was performed in an unhusbandlike manner. They allege that because of this negligence the land yielded 10,550 bushels of wheat less than it would have yielded had the fertilizer been performed according to the contract.

The defendant denied excessive or improper application; alleged plaintiffs were contributorily negligent in improperly applying the fertilizer; and contended plaintiffs waived any claim for damages by paying for the entire amount of fertilizer. The jury returned a verdict for the defendant.

A crucial question was whether or not the application of 64 pounds of fertilizer per acre caused the yield to decrease 10,550 bushels or in any substantial amount. The claimed loss was approximately 11 bushels of wheat per acre. Plaintiffs' evidence was that in the crop year involved, 1959, their wheatland produced an average of 46 bushels per acre. (The crop year of 1959 means the crop is harvested in the summer of 1959, but seeded and fertilized in the fall of 1958.) To prove that the application of 64 pounds of fertilizer adversely affected their yield, the plaintiffs introduced evidence of the amount of fertilizer used by their neighbors and the crop yield of their neighbors. The evidence was that plaintiffs' neighbors used a maximum of 45 pounds per acre and had yields of no less than 58 bushels per acre.

To counteract this testimony defendant offered the testimony of two experts, Mr. Oveson, superintendent of the Pendleton Branch, Oregon Agricultural Experiment Station, and Mr. Gassett, supervisor of the research laboratory of Pendleton Grain Growers, a large farmers cooperative. Both of these witnesses testified that in the course of their work they had conducted various tests to determine the effect of nitrogen fertilizer upon wheat. They testified these tests indicated that the application of 60, 90, and 120 pounds of liquid nitrogen fertilizer had not substantially reduced the yield of wheat. Evidence of specific test results was admitted. Plaintiffs objected to the introduction of these test results upon the ground that the results of experiments cannot be introduced without evidence that they were made under conditions substantially similar to those present in the matter in dispute.

As a general proposition an experiment is admissible only if the experiment is performed under conditions substantially similar to those existing in the case being tried. See Western Feed Co. v. Heidloff, 230 Or. 324, 347, 370 P.2d 612 (1962). It is also a general principle that the trial court has wide discretion in the admission of the results of experiments. Loibl v. Niemi, 214 Or. 172, 181, 327 P.2d 786 (1958).

There was testimony that the type of soil and the amount and time of rainfall on the test plots were the same as those on the Foster ranch. The time when seeding was done is unknown as to either plaintiffs' land or the test crops. Mr. Oveson, one of the testers, stated this was immaterial. He also stated it was immaterial whether or not the land had been fallow or had a previous crop of peas or grain.

The tests conducted by these two witnesses are not the usual kind of "experiments" as that term is used in decisions on the admissibility of evidence. The usual "experiment" consists of the arranging of conditions approximating those attendant upon the fact in issue and observing data emanating from such arranged conditions. The sole purpose of such an "experiment" is to obtain information for use in a particular lawsuit. The tests here had no relation to any lawsuit and were for the sole purpose of obtaining scientific knowledge. No decisions have been found pointing up this distinction. However, because this type of evidence is free from the taint of interest or bias that might accompany the usual "experiment" evidence, we believe greater latitude should be shown in admitting such evidence.[3]

Therefore, for these two reasons, that it is within the discretion of the trial court to admit the usual "experiment" if as much similarity of

3. The same kind of evidence may have been visualized in the statement at 361, § 169, McCormick, Evidence (1954): "It seems also that experiments designed to show the general traits and capacities of materials involved in the controversy might often reasonably be admitted in evidence without confining such experiments to the conditions surrounding the litigated situation."

conditions is shown as was here, and that these were not "experiments for trial," the trial court's admission of the evidence is approved.

* * *

[Reversed on other grounds.]

Notes and Questions

1. *Other decisions.* Other decisions illustrative of the distinction between experiments calculated to show what happened in the particular case and experiments to develop principles, physical or chemical characteristics and the like, include: Pandit v. American Honda Motor Co., 82 F.3d 376 (10th Cir.1996) (operation of charge warning light system on automobile); Osborne v. United States, 542 F.2d 1015 (8th Cir.1976) (time required to drive automobile between two points); Gardner v. Q.H.S., Inc., 448 F.2d 238 (4th Cir.1971) (flammability test of hair rollers); Millers' Nat'l Ins. Co. v. Wichita Flour Mills Co., 257 F.2d 93 (10th Cir.1958) (principles of dust explosions); Walden v. Dep't of Transp., 27 P.3d 297, 306 (Alaska 2001) (traits and capacities of "Willow sand" on the coefficient of friction on a road). Would relaxation of the similar condition requirement appear warranted with respect to experiments of the latter sort even when they are conducted at the request of one of the parties and in contemplation of use in litigation? See discussion in Gladhill v. General Motors Corp., 743 F.2d 1049 (4th Cir.1984) (court held that test of braking went beyond demonstrating general principles so as to constitute a re-enactment of the accident). But see Van Steemburg v. General Aviation, Inc., 611 N.E.2d 1144 (Ill.App.Ct.1993) (evidence of test flight admissible; lower standard for similarity of conditions where no attempt to re-enact accident, even where test conducted by party in contemplation of use in litigation).

2. *Ex parte experiments.* Despite the obvious preferability of experimental evidence free from the taint of interest or bias, ready-made evidence of this sort will usually be unavailable. Thus, it is generally held that whatever bias inheres in the pure ex parte experiment does not in and of itself require exclusion of the experiment. Might any benefit nevertheless accrue from inviting participation by the adversary? See United States v. Love, 482 F.2d 213 (5th Cir.1973).

3. *Physical facts.* Under the "physical facts" rule, evidence contrary to unquestionably established physical facts will be disregarded. A very high degree of accuracy and neutrality in testing has been indicated when test results are sought to be qualified as "physical facts." Fortunato v. Ford Motor Co., 464 F.2d 962 (2d Cir.1972).

SECTION B. PERSONALITY TRAITS AND BEHAVIOR PATTERNS—CIVIL CASES

RUMBAUGH v. McCORMICK

Supreme Court of Ohio, 1909.
88 N.E. 410.

[McCormick and Blair filed separate actions against Rumbaugh for injuries allegedly inflicted upon their respective sheep by a dog owned by Rumbaugh. Each plaintiff recovered judgment, and defendant appeals, assigning errors which include admitting evidence "as to the propensity of the dog to attack sheep."]

PRICE, J. * * * In the Blair case the following questions and answers appear on page 28 of the record: "What do you know about that dog as to having a habit of running and killing sheep?" An objection to the question was sustained. Later, on page 33, the following was propounded to the same witness: "Do you know whether or not this dog is in the habit of attacking sheep?" Objection was overruled and witness answered: "Yes, sir." Again, he was asked: "Do you know whether or not in the fall of 1903 and spring of 1904 this dog was in the habit of attacking sheep?" Answer: "Yes, sir, he was." But the witness was not permitted to tell what or whose sheep had been attacked.

In each case evidence was given that this dog had been driven away from plaintiff's sheep on several occasions prior to the time of the particular injuries sued for. The above covers all we can find in the Blair case as to prior assaults, and as to the habits of the dog. No evidence of reputation was offered and none given. Hence the wasted time spent in the brief, discussing the question of dog reputation.

It is well to state a fact or two before considering the legal question said to be involved. Defendant Rumbaugh urged in each case an *alibi* for the canine; that he was at home either tied up, or under close surveillance of the family. Again, defendant gave some evidence tending to prove that McCormick owned a dog bearing a strong resemblance to the other, and that witnesses might be mistaken about the animal which perpetrated the mischief—a case of mistaken identity. Intimate acquaintance with the accused animal could be properly shown—such as seeing him frequently about defendant's premises, at his house and in his company and under his control. And if the plaintiff's familiarity was partly made up of having seen the dog at his sheep on former occasions, when he was driven away to prevent injury, that would aid in the matter of identification, and for that reason evidence of such former assaults was competent. In both cases there is direct and positive evidence of the several forays made by the dog including those in which the damages were inflicted. No better means of qualification as to the identity of the guilty animal can be suggested than frequently seeing him upon the sheep of the two plaintiffs from which it was necessary to drive him away. He was a close neighbor's dog and the means of establishing his identity were entirely legitimate. It was the same dog still after the same sheep, in both cases. Whether the knowledge of these former raids was the foundation for the answer made to the foregoing questions as to the habits of the dog, we are not able to say, but we think the answers were competent evidence, when considered in their relation to the other testimony. It tended to prove that this particular canine was viciously disposed towards the neighbor's sheep, and had a propensity to chase, worry and kill them. Such a disposition in an animal moved by instinct and not by reason, may be shown in corroboration of direct testimony where there is conflict as to his identity. We have examined such authorities as can be found on this subject, and are satisfied they justify the preceding questions. Some of these authorities are text-books, among which is Wigmore on Evidence. In Section 201, Volume 1, and the appended notes, we find the view taken by that author, and several illustrations of the application of the rule are given as well as a reference to the decided cases. In Section 68 of the same volume, the author says, "The character or disposition of an animal is no less relevant than that of a human being, as indicating his probable conduct on a particular occasion, and it is open to none of the objections of auxiliary policy which affect the use of a party's character. It is therefore commonly conceded to be admissible. The hesitation sometimes observed in the rulings has been due to the *time* at which the disposition is predicated in the offer; but here, as with human character, the existence of a trait at a given time is evidence that it existed also for a reasonable time before and afterwards, and within liberal limits should therefore be received." See also footnotes on same page. In Maggi v. Cutts, 123 Mass. 535, it is held "that in an action for personal injuries, caused by an obstruction in the highway, where the evidence is conflicting as to the cause of the accident and the character of the horse which plaintiff was driving at the time of the accident, evidence of the character and habits of the horse, as well after as before the accident, is admissible." In Broderick v. Higginson, 169 Mass. 482, it is held that "it is competent to prove that a dog has a habit of attacking passing teams, in support of a disputed allegation that he attacked a passing team on a particular occasion."

Without quoting from other authorities, we have concluded that no error was committed in admitting evidence of habit of the animal, and his vicious propensity towards sheep at and preceding the time when the injuries complained of were inflicted.

Finally, we observe that this sheep loving dog has had "his day in court"—yea, in four courts—although uniformly condemned.

We will let the judgment stand.

Judgments affirmed.

SUMMERS, SPEAR and SHAUCK, JJ., concur.

Notes and Questions

1. Compare Kelly v. Alderson, 37 A. 12, 13 (R.I.1896), a dog-bite action under a statute imposing strict liability:

> It is further argued that testimony as to the character of the dog was admissible to show that it was improbable that the dog would have attacked the plaintiff without being first assaulted by the plaintiff himself. This would set up the character of the dog against the plaintiff's oath. We think that the inference of probability is too remote and inconclusive. Dogs have often bitten persons when they have not been known to bite before, and the statute takes account of this fact by giving a remedy in such a case, if it be upon a highway.

2. *Bloodhounds.* In a criminal prosecution, should it be admissible for the state to introduce evidence that bloodhounds brought to the scene of the crime shortly after its commission led their handlers to the home of the defendant? If defendant testifies that he was not at the scene, is the evidence objectionable as setting up the character of the dogs against the oath of the defendant? See Blair v. Commonwealth, 204 S.W. 67, 68 (Ky.1918), upholding the admission of the evidence and citing Sir Walter Scott's Talisman in which Richard I is represented as preferring the mute testimony of Roswell the hound to the knightly word of Conrade, Marquis of Montserrat. For a more recent discussion of the admission of canine scent evidence see Brooks v. People, 975 P.2d 1105 (Colo.1999). See also Rex v. Trupedo, 1920 A.D. 58 (S.Af.1920) (prejudicial error to admit evidence that dog identified accused based on scent left in room). Cases dealing with the admissibility of evidence of trailing by dogs are collected in Annot., 81 A.L.R.5th 563.

3. For a more recent case involving animal character, see Durst v. Newby, 685 F.Supp. 250, 252 n.2 (S.D.Ga.1988) ("the wanderlust of cows is simply a relevant fact not relating to the character of a party or witness").

BEACH v. RICHTMYER

Supreme Court of New York, Appellate Division, 1949.
90 N.Y.S.2d 332.

HEFFERNAN, JUSTICE. At about nine o'clock in the evening of October 11, 1947, a collision occurred on the state highway near Cobleskill between an automobile truck owned and operated by defendant Richtmyer and an automobile owned by defendant Carpenter and operated by Glenn W. Harris, her chauffeur.

At the time of the accident the plaintiffs, Mr. and Mrs. Beach, the latter a sister of Harris, were passengers in the Carpenter car as were also Ethel E. Morrison, the mother of Harris and a Mrs. Smith. As a result of the collision Harris and Mrs. Smith lost their lives and the other occupants of the car were seriously injured.

Thereafter these plaintiffs instituted actions against defendants Richtmyer, Carpenter and Wildove as administrator of the estate of Harris, for the recovery of the damages which they sustained on the theory that the operators of both vehicles were negligent.

The actions were tried together and the jury found a verdict in favor of Mrs. Beach in the sum of $20,000 against defendants Carpenter and Wildove as administrator and a verdict in her husband's favor in the sum of $8000, against the same defendants. The jury's verdicts exonerated defendant Richtmyer.

From judgments entered on these verdicts and from orders denying their motions to vacate them defendants Carpenter and Wildove have come to this court. * * *

After a careful review of the record before us we cannot escape the conviction that the negligence of Harris is the sole cause of this tragic occurrence. Neither defendant contends otherwise and no claim is made by either of them that the plaintiffs were at fault in any respect. It should also be noted that neither defendant asserts that the verdicts are excessive.

The interests of these two defendants are adverse.

Two points are urged by defendant Carpenter to be relieved of liability. She asserts that Harris had no permission, either express or implied, to use her car on the night of the accident and that the admission of evidence on behalf of defendant Wildove pertaining to the good character of Harris was prejudicial and constitutes reversible error.

Although defendant Wildove has appealed from the judgments against him in his representative capacity his brief is devoted to a justification of the good character evidence of his decedent and he is asking us to affirm both judgments and orders.

We now come to the only remaining questions in these cases—the contentions of defendant Carpenter. In her testimony she emphatically denied that her chauffeur had any authority to use her car on the night in question. She was a vitally interested witness. Her testimony is uncorroborated. Death has sealed the lips of Harris and he could not contradict her. Although uncontradicted her credibility was exclusively for the jury. The question before us is whether this defendant produced substantial evidence to rebut the statutory presumption that the car was in use with her consent. It would serve no useful purpose to discuss in detail the evidence relating to this question. There is ample evidence in this record from which the triers of the facts might conclude that Harris' use of the car at the time of the accident was not unlawful. Either he had defendant's permission to use it then, as he had frequently used it theretofore, or he was guilty of larceny. Defendant's evidence, when read in connection with the other evidence in the case, and with all the surrounding circumstances, is not sufficient in law to destroy the presumption of responsibility.

Mr. Kniffen, a lawyer of repute in Schoharie County, and the president of a local bank, was sworn as a witness on behalf of plaintiffs. On his cross-examination by counsel for defendant, Wildove, he was interrogated as to the general moral character of Harris. He was asked the following questions and made the following answers:

> "Q. You may answer this question yes or no. Did you know his general reputation from the speech of people in the community in which he resided as to his general moral character? A. Why, I would say that I did.
>
> "Q. And was it good or bad? A. I would say that it was good."

Like testimony was given by the police justice of Cobleskill, by the pastor of the Methodist Church and by the mayor of the village.

All this evidence was received over the objection and exception of defendant Carpenter.

In our opinion this evidence should have been excluded by the trial judge. The credibility of Harris had not been impeached. He was neither a party nor a witness and for obvious reasons could not be.

In civil actions the character or reputation of a party is not a proper subject of inquiry. The courts of this State are committed to the doctrine that evidence of the character or reputation of a party to a civil action, where character is not at issue, is generally irrelevant and inadmissible, * * *

Mr. Ford in his excellent work on Evidence, Volume 3, § 244–a states the rule as follows:

> "In a civil action the general rule is that evidence of character is inadmissible as a probative fact to show that a party did or did not do an act which is the subject of the issue."

In 32 C.J.S., Evidence, § 423, it is said:

> "As a general rule the character of a party to a civil action is not a proper subject of inquiry, for, while it is recognized that ground for an inference of some logically probative force as to whether or not a person did a certain act may be furnished by the fact that his character is such as might reasonably be expected to predispose him toward or against such an act, this consideration is outweighed by the practical objections to opening the door to this class of evidence."

We may not say as a matter of law that the reception of this testimony did not prejudice the rights of defendant Carpenter. It is presumptively injurious. To justify this court in disregarding the erroneous admission of this evidence it is not enough to say that possibly the result would have been the same if the improper evidence had been excluded, nor even that it is probable that defendant sustained no injury by the error. It must appear that the evidence could not by any possibility have affected the result.

The plaintiffs had no part in the introduction of the incompetent testimony. It is unfortunate that they should suffer because of the act of one of the defendants.

The judgments and orders in favor of defendant Richtmyer are affirmed without costs. The judgments and orders in favor of plaintiffs against the codefendants are reversed on the law and new trials granted in each action with costs to abide the event. The findings of fact implicit in the judgments are affirmed.

Notes and Questions

1. *Discussions.* See generally Ladd, Techniques and Theory of Character Testimony, 24 Iowa L.Rev. 498 (1939); Leonard, In Defense of the Character Evidence Prohibition: Foundation of the Rule Against Trial by Character, 73 Ind.L.J. 1161 (1998); Reed, The Pushy Ox: Character Evidence in Pennsylvania Civil Actions, 58 Temple L.Q. 623 (1985); Slough, Relevancy Unraveled—Character and Habit, 5 U.Kan.L.Rev. 404 (1957); 1 McCormick, Evidence ch. 17 (6th ed. 2006); 1 Wigmore, Evidence § 64 (Tillers rev. 1983).

2. *When alleged acts are crimes.* Evidence of character to prove conduct, as will be seen in the next section, is quite freely admitted in criminal prosecutions where offered by the defendant. Would the fact, noted by the court in the principal case, that if Harris was not driving the car with permission he was guilty of larceny, have provided a rationale for admitting the evidence of character? Courts have generally rejected the suggestion. In Greenberg v. Aetna Ins. Co., 235 A.2d 582 (Pa.1967), an action to recover on a policy of fire insurance to which the defense of arson by the insured was raised, plaintiff offered testimony of his exemplary service record during World War II. Admission of the testimony was held improper, the court noting that "the fact that the act in question is indictable if proved, or that fraud is charged in the pleadings is not sufficient" as a basis for admitting character evidence. Occasional cases, however, notably involving civil assault, have held in favor of admission, particularly where punitive damages have been sought. See Annot., 154 A.L.R. 121.

3. *Federal Rule 404.* Rule 404(a)(1) was amended in 2006 to make certain what most federal courts had held—evidence of character is inadmissible in civil cases to prove a propensity to act in a particular way. See 1 Saltzburg, Martin & Capra, Federal Rules of Evidence Manual, Rule § 404.02 [3], at 404–11 (9th ed. 2006). Rule 404(a)(2), providing that the accused may introduce evidence of a pertinent character trait of the victim of a crime and that, in a homicide case, the prosecutor may introduce evidence of the peacefulness of the victim in order to rebut evidence that the victim was the first aggressor, was amended at the same time to clarify that its provisions do not apply in civil cases. Some federal and state cases have held to the contrary. See Perrin v. Anderson, 784 F.2d 1040 (10th Cir.1986) (police officer charged in civil case with shooting victim entitled to protection of Rule 404(a)(2)); Feliciano v. City and County of Honolulu, 611 P.2d 989 (Haw.1980) (character of both victim and assailant admissible on issue of who was the first aggressor). But see Palmquist v. Selvik, 111 F.3d 1332 (7th Cir.1997) (victim's death wish inadmissible in civil rights action against police for shooting him).

Rule 404(b), which provides for admissibility of other crimes, wrongs, or acts if probative of something other than the character of a person to show that he acted in conformity therewith, is applicable to civil as well as criminal cases. E.g., Macsenti v. Becker, 237 F.3d 1223 (10th Cir.2001) (evidence of dentist's erratic behavior admissible in malpractice case). See generally 2 Imwinkelried, Uncharged Misconduct Evidence ch. 7 (1999); Annot., 171 A.L.R.Fed. 483.

SCHAFER v. TIME, INC.

United States Court of Appeals, Eleventh Circuit, 1998.
142 F.3d 1361.

BIRCH, CIRCUIT JUDGE:

* * *

This appeal * * * presents a number of evidentiary questions, most notably whether specific instances of misconduct are admissible to prove character under Federal Rule of Evidence 405(b) in an action for libel under Georgia law. The plaintiff-appellant challenges the district court's decision to admit character evidence pursuant to Rule 405(b) * * *. Although these evidentiary issues are not dispositive given our decision to reverse the district court on the grounds mentioned above, they may well arise at a second trial.

* * *

On December 21, 1988, Pan Am Flight 103 exploded in mid-flight over Lockerbie, Scotland, causing the death of everyone on board. A terrorist's bomb was then, and is now, widely suspected to be the source of that explosion. On April 20, 1992, defendant-appellee, Time, Inc. ("Time"), published a cover story entitled "The Untold Story of Pan Am 103." The article purported to debunk the then-prevailing theory that the government of Lybia [sic] had sponsored the attack on Pan Am 103. Instead, the article posited that a Palestinian group, with connections to Syrian drug traffickers, had targeted Pan Am 103 to eliminate several of the passengers who were members of a United States counter terrorism team attempting to rescue United States hostages in Lebanon. The article claims that these passengers had discovered an unsavory, covert relationship between the Syrian drug traffickers and a unit of the United States Central Intelligence Agency and intended to expose it upon their return to the United States.

The article further stated that an American agent, David Lovejoy, had become a double agent and had leaked information regarding the team's travel plans to forces hostile to the United States. The article included a photograph of a man identified by the following caption:

> David Lovejoy, a reported double agent for the U.S. and Iran, is alleged to have told Iranian officials that McKee [one of the U.S. agents] was booked on Flight 103.

* * * The article went on to imply that the information Lovejoy disclosed to hostile forces led to the attack on Pan Am 103.

The photograph in question apparently became associated with the Pam Am 103 bombing in connection with a civil case filed by the families of the Pan Am 103 victims. The families' law suit claimed that Pan Am had failed to take adequate security precautions to prevent the bombing. One of Pan Am's lawyers in that case, James Shaughnessy, filed a sworn affidavit that contained a variety of assertions about the attack that he hoped to explore through discovery in the Pan Am litigation. Shaughnessy's affidavit alleged that unnamed sources had identified Lovejoy, the double agent whose treachery facilitated the attack on Pan Am 103, as the man in an attached photograph. The man in the photograph, however, is Michael Schafer, the plaintiff-appellant in this case.

Time's article, therefore, erroneously identified Schafer, then working in his family's janitorial business in Austell, Georgia, both as a traitor to the United States government and a player in the bombing of Pan Am 103.

Upon discovering his picture in the magazine, Schafer demanded and eventually received a retraction from Time. Schafer filed suit against Time, making claims under Georgia's libel laws. A jury returned a verdict in Time's favor, finding no liability for the error. After filing a motion for a new trial, which the district court denied, Schafer filed this timely appeal. Schafer challenges a number of the district court's evidentiary rulings as well as the court's recharge to the jury on the definition of "malicious" under Georgia's libel statute. He also challenges both the district court's refusal to instruct the jury that the republication of a libelous depiction constitutes libel under Georgia law and the court's decision not to charge the jury on Georgia's retraction statute.

* * *

Schafer also argues that the district court committed reversible error by permitting Time's counsel to question Schafer regarding a number of "specific acts of misconduct" during cross-examination and by excluding from evidence a memorandum discussing the credibility of Time's sources for the Pan Am 103 article. We review the district court's legal decision to apply a particular rule of evidence *de novo* but its decision to admit or exclude particular evidence under that rule for an abuse of discretion. *Cf.* Carmichael v. Samyang Tire, Inc., 131 F.3d 1433, 1435 (11th Cir.1997). We will not overturn an evidentiary ruling unless the complaining party has shown a "substantial prejudicial effect." *See* Judd v. Rodman, 105 F.3d 1339, 1341 (11th Cir.1997).

* * *

Evidence of a person's character is viewed with some suspicion under the law and generally is disfavored in the Federal Rules of Evidence. *See* Fed.R.Evid. 404 (character evidence generally inadmissible to prove conforming conduct). In an action for defamation or libel, however, the issue of the plaintiff's reputation and character scarcely can be avoided because the plaintiff typically seeks to recover compensation for damage to his or her reputation. Even in such cases, however, the rules of evidence prescribe particular methods for broaching the issue of character. *See* Fed.R.Evid. 405 ("Methods of Proving Character").

Before trial, the district court instructed the parties that Time would not be permitted to introduce and explore a number of specific acts and events in Schafer's life as they were irrelevant to the issues before the jury. At that time, however, the district court warned both parties that the court would revisit the character issue to the extent that particular acts and events were shown to be relevant to the question of damages or how Schafer's picture might have become associated with the Pan Am case. During the course of the trial, the district court made a preliminary ruling permitting Time to explore selective incidents and acts in Schafer's background but excluding evidence of others. Specifically, the district court ruled that Time would be permitted to question Schafer about a felony conviction, a possible violation of his subsequent parole, convictions for driving under the influence, an arrest for writing a bad check, failure to file tax returns, failure to pay alimony and child support, and evidence concerning Schafer's efforts to change his name and social security number. Schafer attacks the district court's ruling and argues that these specific acts were inadmissible.

The Federal Rules of Evidence detail the circumstances under which character evidence is admissible and the methods available for presenting such evidence. In all cases in which character evidence is admissible a party may offer reputation or opinion testimony on the issue of a person's character. *See* Fed. R. Evid. 405(a). Only in cases in which a person's character is "an essential element of a charge, claim or defense," however, may a party offer evidence of specific instances of conduct. *See* Fed.R.Evid. 405(b).[4]

Character evidence does not constitute an "essential element" of a claim or charge unless it alters the rights and liabilities of the parties under the substantive law. *See* United States v. Keiser, 57 F.3d 847, 856 & n.20 (9th Cir.1995); Perrin v. Anderson, 784 F.2d 1040, 1045 (10th Cir.1986) (citing McCormick on Evidence § 187 at 551 (3d ed.1984)). Our determination of whether character constitutes an essential element requires us to examine the "authoritative statutory or common law statement of the elements of the prima facie case and defenses." Keiser, 57 F.3d at 856 n.20. The advisory committee's notes to the Federal Rules of Evidence provide two examples in which character evidence constitutes such an essential element: "[1] the chastity of a victim under a statute specifying her chastity as an element of the crime of seduction, or [2] the competency of the driver in an action for negligently entrusting a motor vehicle to an incompetent driver." Fed.R.Evid. 404(a) adv. comm. note (explaining that Rule 404 does not exclude such evidence because it is not offered to prove conduct consistent with character). In addition to

4. The advisory committee notes to Rule 405 provide some insight as to the rule's limitations on the use of specific acts to prove character:

> Of the three methods of proving character provided by the rule, evidence of specific instances of conduct is the most convincing. At the same time it possesses the greatest capacity to arouse prejudice, to confuse, to surprise, and to consume time. Consequently the rule confines the use of evidence of this kind to cases in which character is, in the strict sense, in issue and hence deserving of a searching inquiry. Fed.R.Evid. 405, adv. comm. note.

these examples, a charge of defamation or libel commonly makes damage to the victim's reputation or character an essential element of the case. *See e.g.*, Johnson v. Pistilli, No. 95 C 6424, 1996 WL 587554 (N.D.Ill. Oct. 8, 1996) ("It is rare that character is an essential element. The typical example of such a case is defamation where injury to reputation must be proven."); *see also* Michael H. Graham, Handbook of Federal Evidence § 405.2 (4th ed.1996). Georgia law confirms that an assertion of damage to reputation in a libel case makes the plaintiff's character an issue under the substantive law. *See* Ajouelo v. Auto–Soler Co., 61 Ga.App. 216, 6 S.E.2d 415, 419 (1939) ("It is generally held that the foundation of an action for defamation is the injury done to the reputation, that is, injury to character in the opinion of others arising from publication * * *."); Redfearn v. Thompson, 10 Ga.App. 550, 555, 73 S.E. 949 (1912) (permitting the jury to consider plaintiff's bad reputation in mitigation of damages). Since the plaintiff's character is substantively at issue in a libel case under Georgia law, Rule 405(b) permits the admission of evidence regarding specific instances of the plaintiff's conduct on that issue.[5] *See* Perrin, 784 F.2d at 1045; Government of the Virgin Islands v. Grant, 775 F.2d 508, 511 n.4 (3d Cir.1985); *cf.* Longmire v. Alabama State Univ., 151 F.R.D. 414, 419 (M.D.Al.1992) (permitting discovery regarding specific incidents because the libel plaintiff put his character in issue); *accord* Ex Parte Healthsouth Corp., Nos. 1961758, 1970010, 2–3, 1997 WL 778837 (Ala.1997) (permitting discovery of such evidence in a libel case under a state rule of evidence identical to Fed.R.Evid. 405(b)); Daniels v. Wal–Mart Stores, Inc., 634 So.2d 88, 93 (Miss.1993) (making a similar observation in dicta). Given the plain language of Rule 405(b), Schafer's arguments that specific acts remain inadmissible to prove character in an action for libel are unpersuasive.[6]

5. Schafer's argument that this analysis puts "the horse before the cart" because Rule 404 governs the question of whether character evidence is admissible is unavailing. Rule 404 forbids the use of character evidence to prove "action in conformity therewith on a particular occasion," or as the advisory committee's notes describe it, the "circumstantial" use of character evidence. *See* Fed.R.Evid. 404(a) adv. comm. notes. Rule 404 does not bar the admission of character evidence when character or a particular character trait is actually at issue. *Id.* Rule 404 permits the character evidence in dispute here, and Rule 405 governs the acceptable methods for introducing it. For the sake of completing the analysis, however, we note that even though evidence of specific acts is admissible to prove character in a libel case under Rule 405(b), a district court must still determine whether such acts pass muster under Federal Rule of Evidence 401 (relevance) and Federal Rule of Evidence 403 (prejudice). *See* United States v. Barry, 814 F.2d 1400, 1403–04 & n.6 (9th Cir.1987). The district court's decision to admit the evidence at issue here cannot be said to constitute an abuse of discretion under these rules.

6. Schafer cites Butts v. Curtis Publ'g Co., 225 F.Supp. 916 (N.D.Ga.1964) *aff'd*, 351 F.2d 702 (5th Cir.1965), 388 U.S. 130 * * * (1967), a case decided before the Federal Rules of Evidence entered into effect on July 1, 1973, for the proposition that specific incidents of prior conduct are not admissible to prove character in a libel case. Although the district court in that case confirmed that character was an essential issue in a libel case under Georgia law and that a defendant could demonstrate that the "plaintiff's general character is bad," it held that both federal and state case law prevented the defendant from relying on specific acts or general rumors to do so. *Id.* at 921. The plain language of Rule 405(b), however, contradicts *Butts* by expressly permitting the admission of specific acts when character is an essential element of the

Accordingly, we find no error in Time's exploration of these and other issues of character during its cross-examination of Schafer. To the extent that Time strayed from the specific issues of character enumerated in the district court's preliminary ruling, including Time's questions regarding Schafer's work for *Soldier of Fortune* magazine, Time's questions fell within the scope of Federal Rules of Evidence 405(a) and 608(b). We cannot say that the district court's decisions on these matters rose to the level of an abuse of discretion, nor can we say that Schafer suffered a "substantial prejudicial effect." *See* Rodman, 105 F.3d at 1341.

* * *

[The court reversed and remanded the case based on its holding with regard to an error in jury instructions.]

Notes and Questions

1. *Instances in which character is an essential element.* The instances in which character will actually be an essential element of a charge, claim, or defense are very limited. The court in the principal case refers to the examples of seduction and negligent entrustment cases. Seduction cases are now rare to nonexistent. Negligent entrustment is somewhat more common. For an example of the application of the rule in such a case see Guedon v. Rooney, 87 P.2d 209 (Or.1939). Are there other instances in which character is an essential element of a claim or defense? Could character be an essential element of a criminal charge? See Robinson v. California, 370 U.S. 660 (1962) (statute criminalizing addiction unconstitutional).

2. *Federal Rule 405.* Under Rule 405(b), when character is an essential element, it may be shown by specific acts. The court in *Schafer* notes that it can also be proved by reputation or opinion proof. Is the rule as clear as it could be on that point?

3. *Character or reputation?* Are the terms character and reputation as used in the principal case synonymous? Is reputation simply one of the ways by which character can be shown? Is evidence going solely to character without reference to reputation relevant to the issue of damages in a defamation case?

MISSOURI–KANSAS–TEXAS R.R. v. McFERRIN

Supreme Court of Texas, 1956.
291 S.W.2d 931.

CALVERT, JUSTICE. This is a suit for damages for wrongful death brought against the petitioner Railroad by respondent, Ruth Adele McFerrin, for herself and as next friend for the minor children of herself and her deceased husband, R.T. McFerrin, who was killed in a crossing accident. * * * [The fireman testified that decedent failed to stop, but merely slowed down and drove onto the crossing.]

case. Schafer's citation to Sharon v. Time, Inc., 103 F.R.D. 86 (S.D.N.Y.1984), a case that does not refer to Rule 405(b), does not require a different result.

Mrs. McFerrin testified, over the objection of petitioner, that on occasions when she was in the car with him her husband never crossed the crossing in question without first stopping the car and looking and listening for trains. The objection was that what the deceased did on other occasions or what his habit and custom was with respect to stopping before proceeding over the crossing would not be evidence as to whether he stopped on this particular occasion. The question briefed here is whether evidence of habit and custom is admissible to prove care or negligence on a particular occasion. The sufficiency of the predicate laid for the testimony of habit is not questioned.

On the question presented the decided cases in this state, like those in some of the other states, are conflicting. * * *

With respect to the state of the decided cases in other jurisdictions, the following definite statements, as drawn from the authorities listed, may be made. 1. Where there are eyewitnesses to the accident, the overwhelming weight of authority is that evidence of habit or custom of care or negligence is not admissible. 2. Where there is no eyewitness to the accident, the weight of authority is that evidence of habit or custom is admissible. 3. In a few jurisdictions habit and custom evidence is admitted in all cases, even those in which there is an eyewitness to the accident, and in a few it is not admitted in any case, even those in which there is no eyewitness. * * * In the few cases in which the question has been considered, it is held that the fact that the only witness may be an employee of the opposite party or that his veracity is under attack does not let in habit or custom evidence. * * *

With the exception of the writer and Associate Justice Smith, all members of the Court are in agreement that this Court should adopt and follow the majority rule that habit evidence should not be admitted where there is an eyewitness to the accident, even though the eyewitness be an employee of the opposite party. What is now to be said on the subject is said in support of the writer's position that such evidence has probative force and therefore should be admitted under circumstances to be noted.

Habit evidence to prove care or negligence is not usually excluded because wholly lacking in probative value, but for reasons such as those given by the court in Zucker v. Whitridge, 205 N.Y. 50, 98 N.E. 209, 213, 41 L.R.A., N.S., 683, where it is said:

> "* * * Habit is an inference from many acts, each of which presents an issue to be tried, and necessarily involves direct, and naturally invites, cross examination. The circumstances surrounding each act present another issue, and thus many collateral issues would be involved which would not only consume much time, but would tend to distract the jury and lead them away from the main issue to be decided. From the want of previous notice, the other party would not be prepared to meet such evidence; and after all the testimony of this character was in the fact would remain that, as no one is always careful, the subject of inquiry, although careful on

many occasions, might have been careless on the occasion in question."

Wigmore suggests that "there is no reason why such a habit should not be used as evidential,—either a habit of negligent action or a habit of careful action", and states that "such evidence often is of probative value and is not attended by the inconveniences of character evidence." 1 Wigmore on Evidence, Third Edition, § 97, pp. 530 and 532.

The American Law Institute's Model Code of Evidence has not been adopted in this state and of course does not control our decisions. On the other hand, the Model Code was prepared by and with the advice of many of this country's outstanding lawyers, judges and teachers in the field of evidence, and the rules suggested in the Model Code are entitled to serious consideration in deciding any evidence question which is still open in this state. By Rule 307(2) of the Model Code it is stated: "Evidence of a habit of a person is admissible as tending to prove that his behavior on a specified occasion conformed to the habit." It is then suggested, by way of example, that if in an action for the wrongful death of X at a railway crossing "W offers to testify for P that he had on numerous occasions been with X when X crossed the track in question and that on such occasions X had stopped and looked in both directions before entering the crossing" the testimony should be admitted; whereas, if the offer is that each of ten witnesses will testify that he was with X on one separate occasion and that on that occasion X stopped and looked in both directions before entering the crossing, the testimony should be excluded. No doubt the basis of the distinction is that in the first example the probative value of the evidence is thought to outweigh the slight inconvenience that would be caused by the examination and cross-examination of one witness on a somewhat collateral matter, while in the second example the inconvenience to the court of examining and cross-examining ten witnesses as to ten different incidents would outweigh the value of the evidence.

If it be conceded that habit evidence has any probative value (and most courts concede that it has) and it can be obtained from one witness, it is my opinion that it should be admitted even though there was an eyewitness to the accident. * * *

[Reversed and remanded.]

The writer and Associate Justice Smith dissent from the judgment. * * * We * * * believe the judgment of the courts below should be affirmed. * * *

Notes and Questions

1. *Eyewitnesses.* The principal case is commented upon in 10 Vand. L.Rev. 447 (1957). See also Snell, Eying the Iowa No Eyewitness Rule, 43 Iowa L.Rev. 57 (1957); Annot., 28 A.L.R.3d 1293. Federal Rule 406 specifically makes the presence of eyewitnesses an irrelevant consideration in dealing with the admissibility of habit evidence. Although the number of states

requiring that there be no eyewitnesses in order for habit evidence to be introduced has dropped significantly with state adoptions of Rule 406, the concept is not entirely dead. Compare Isbell v. Union Pac. R.R., 745 N.E.2d 53 (Ill.App.Ct.2001) (habit testimony inadmissible where there are eyewitnesses), with Alvarado v. Goepp, 663 N.E.2d 63 (Ill.App.Ct.1996) (admissibility of habit testimony not dependent on absence of eyewitnesses).

2. *Sources.* Concerning the use of habit evidence generally, see Lewan, The Rationale of Habit Evidence, 16 Syracuse L.Rev. 39 (1964); Schroeder, Evidence of Habit and Routine Practice, 29 Loy.U.Chi.L.J. 385 (1998).

3. *Business habit.* Can evidence that a person has done business in a particular way in the past constitute habit proof? Compare Hollingham v. Head, 4 C.B.(N.S.) 388, 140 Eng.Rep. 1135 (1858) (terms of other sales contracts inadmissible), and Turpin v. Branaman, 58 S.E.2d 63 (Va.1950) (past business dealings inadmissible), with Whittemore v. Lockheed Aircraft Corp., 151 P.2d 670 (Cal.Ct.App.1944) (evidence that plaintiff's intestate had on other occasions flown planes from the factory for delivery to his employer, admissible to prove that he, rather than a factory pilot, was flying plane when it crashed en route for delivery).

REYES v. MISSOURI PACIFIC R.R.

United States Court of Appeals, Fifth Circuit, 1979.
589 F.2d 791.

JAMES C. HILL, CIRCUIT JUDGE:

In this diversity case plaintiff-appellant challenges the admission into evidence of his four prior misdemeanor convictions for public intoxication, introduced for the purpose of showing that he was intoxicated on the night that he was run over by defendant-appellee's train. We agree with appellant, finding the evidence of his prior convictions to be inadmissible under Rule 404(a) of the Federal Rules of Evidence; therefore, we reverse and remand the case for a new trial.

I.

Shortly after midnight on June 17, 1974, appellant Reyes was run over by appellee-railroad's train as he lay on the railroad tracks near a crossing in Brownsville, Texas. Reyes brought this diversity suit against the railroad, alleging negligence on the part of the railroad's employees in failing to discover plaintiff as he lay on the tracks and stop the train in time to avoid the accident. The railroad answered by claiming that Reyes, dressed in dark clothing that night, was not visible from the approaching train until it was too late for its employees to avert the accident. Moreover, the railroad alleged that Reyes was contributorily negligent because he was intoxicated on the night of the accident and passed out on the tracks before the train arrived. Reyes explained his presence on the railroad tracks by claiming that he was knocked unconscious by an unknown assailant as he walked along the tracks.

Reyes made a motion *in limine* to exclude the evidence relating to his prior misdemeanor convictions for public intoxication. The railroad opposed this motion, arguing that the convictions were admissible to show that Reyes was intoxicated on the night of the accident. The district court agreed and refused to grant Reyes' motion.

In an attempt to minimize the damaging effects of his prior convictions, Reyes brought them out on direct examination. In answering a special interrogatory submitted to them, the jury found the plaintiff more negligent than the defendant; under Texas law, this finding precluded Reyes from recovering against the railroad. *See* 7 Tex.Civ.Code Ann. Art. 2212a, § 1 (Vernon).

II.

Rule 404 of the Federal Rules of Evidence embodies the well-settled principle that evidence of a person's character is usually not admissible for the purpose of proving that the person acted in conformity with his character on a particular occasion. Fed.R.Evid. 404, 28 U.S.C.A. *See also McCormick on Evidence* § 188 (2d ed. 1972). This general rule of exclusion, applicable to both civil and criminal proceedings, is based upon the assumption that such evidence is of slight probative value yet very prejudicial.

An analysis of the admissibility of character evidence necessarily begins, then, with an examination of the purposes for which the evidence is proffered. If the evidence is introduced for the purpose of showing that a person acted in accordance with his character on a given occasion, then the evidence is inadmissible unless it falls within one of the exceptions noted in Rule 404.

The record in this case makes clear that the railroad intended for Reyes' prior convictions to show that he was intoxicated on the night of the accident. Indeed, that purpose was the only possible one for which the evidence could be offered. Moreover, the trial judge specifically noted in the motion *in limine* hearing that evidence of the prior convictions would be relevant to the issue of whether Reyes was intoxicated on the night of the accident. Because the evidence of Reyes' prior convictions was admitted for the sole purpose of showing that he had a character trait of drinking to excess and that he acted in conformity with his character on the night of the accident by becoming intoxicated, we conclude that the prior convictions were inadmissible character evidence under Rule 404.

III.

The suggestion that the prior convictions constituted evidence of Reyes' "habit" of excessive drinking is equally unpersuasive. Rule 406 allows the introduction of evidence of the habit of a person for the purpose of proving that the person acted in conformity with his habit on a particular occasion. Fed.R.Evid. 406, 28 U.S.C.A. *See generally McCormick on Evidence* § 195 (2d ed. 1972); 1 *Wigmore on Evidence* § 92 (3d ed. 1940). Habit evidence is considered to be highly probative and therefore superior to character evidence because "the uniformity of one's response to habit is far greater than the consistency with which one's conduct conforms to character or disposition." *McCormick on Evidence* § 195 at 463 (2d ed. 1972).

Perhaps the chief difficulty in deciding questions of admissibility under Rule 406 arises in trying to draw the line between inadmissible character evidence and admissible habit evidence. Quite often the line between the two may become blurred.

Character and habit are close akin. Character is a generalized description of one's disposition, or one's disposition in respect to a general trait, such as honesty, temperance, or peacefulness. "Habit," in modern usage, both lay and psychological, is more specific. It describes one's regular response to a repeated specific situation. If we speak of character for care, we think of the person's tendency to act prudently in all the varying situations of life, in business, family life, in handling automobiles and in walking across the street. A habit, on the other hand, is the person's regular practice of meeting a particular kind of situation with a specific type of conduct, such as the habit of going down a particular stairway two stairs at a time, or of giving the hand-signal for a left turn, or of alighting from railway cars while they are moving. The doing of the habitual acts may become semi-automatic. *McCormick on Evidence* § 195 at 462–63 (2d ed. 1972). Although a precise formula cannot be proposed for determining when the behavior may become so consistent as to rise to the level of habit, "adequacy of sampling and uniformity of response" are controlling considerations. *Notes of Advisory Committee on Proposed Rules,* Fed.R.Evid. 406, 28 U.S.C.A. at p. 153. *See also Wilson v. Volkswagen of America,* 561 F.2d 494 (4th Cir.1977). Thus, the probative force of habit evidence to prove intoxication on a given occasion depends on the "degree of regularity of the practice and its coincidence with the occasion." *McCormick on Evidence* § 195 n.16 (2d ed. 1972).

We do not undertake here to prescribe the precise quantum of proof necessary to transform a general disposition for excessive drinking into a "habit" of intemperance; we simply find that four prior convictions for public intoxication spanning a three and one-half year period are of insufficient regularity to rise to the level of "habit" evidence. Consequently, we hold the evidence to be inadmissible under Rule 406 as well.

IV.

A principle purpose behind the exclusion of character evidence, as we have said, is the prejudicial effect that it can have on the trier of fact. This concern is especially compelling here where the character evidence relates to one of the critical issues in the case, *i.e.,* the contributory negligence of Reyes. Finding the introduction of the prior convictions to be extremely prejudicial, we feel that the error affected the substantial rights of Reyes, thus requiring a new trial. Fed.R.Civ.P. 61, 28 U.S.C.A. * * *

Reversed and Remanded.

Note

Contrast the holding in *Reyes* with those in Loughan v. Firestone Tire & Rubber Co., 749 F.2d 1519 (11th Cir.1985) (evidence of extensive drinking over a 6–year period, including proof that plaintiff regularly carried a cooler of beer on his truck, sufficient to establish habit under Rule 406), and Keltner v. Ford Motor Co., 748 F.2d 1265 (8th Cir.1984) (court permitted cross-examination of plaintiff under Rule 406 to the effect that he drank a six pack of beer four nights a week). Cases on evidence of intemperate habits in accident litigation are collected in Annot., 46 A.L.R.2d 103; for federal cases, see Annot., 53 A.L.R.Fed. 703. See also Tillers, The Death of a Youth and of a Drunkard: A Remarkable Story of Habit and Character in New Jersey, in Evidence Stories 29 (Lempert ed., 2006).

EATON v. BASS

United States Court of Appeals, Sixth Circuit, 1954.
214 F.2d 896.

[Wrongful death action in which defendant trucking company was charged with operating a truck with defective brakes. Plaintiffs appeal from a judgment rendered on a verdict in favor of the trucking company.]

MILLER, CIRCUIT JUDGE. * * *

Hunter Mir, shop foreman for Hoover Motor Express Company, testified for the appellees, over objection of appellants, that he was in charge of safety checking the trucks before they went out on the highway; that it was the custom of the company to check every unit that went out to see that it was safe to put on the road; that the trucks were driven through three lanes in the shop; that the mechanics tried the brakes and the safety equipment, lights, horn and anything pertaining to the safety of the operation of the equipment; that if any defect is found it is repaired or the unit is cut out and replaced by another; and that no equipment went out on the road without it having been checked through his department. He had no records or personal knowledge about the check which was given the particular truck involved in the accident.

Appellants contend that evidence of custom or usage is not admissible to prove the exercise of due care by one charged with negligence, in that what ought to be done is fixed by a standard of reasonable prudence, whether it usually is complied with or not, and that in any event such custom must be a general custom among others acting under similar circumstances, rather than the usage or custom of a single person. Texas & Pacific Ry. Co. v. Behymer, 189 U.S. 468, 470 * * * ; Standard Oil Co. v. Swan, 89 Tenn. 434, 15 S.W. 1068, 10 L.R.A. 366. The rule is not an unqualified one, Brigham Young University v. Lillywhite, 10 Cir., 118 F.2d 836, Annotation, 137 A.L.R. 611, and in any event is not applicable to the present case.

The evidence was not received for the purpose of proving that appellees were not negligent because they followed a custom generally in use in the particular industry. It was offered and received for the purpose of proving the existence of a particular fact, namely, that the truck was inspected in a certain way, leaving open the question whether such inspection, if it did take place, was sufficient to constitute due care. No evidence was offered or received pertaining to the custom of other truck operators, with which the particular inspection by the appellees would be compared. We think the District Judge ruled correctly in admitting the evidence on the ground that it had probative value on the issue of what, if any, inspection the truck received before being sent out on the highway, but at the same time pointing out that it was not conclusive that the particular truck was so inspected, and that whether it was or was not so inspected was still a question for the jury. Knickerbocker Life Ins. Co. v. Pendleton, 115 U.S. 339, 344–347 * * * ; Thorn v. Aler, 92 W.Va. 290, 114 S.E. 741, 28 A.L.R. 536, 542. See Atlanta Coco–Cola [sic] Bottling Co. v. Shipp, 170 Ga. 817, 154 S.E. 243, 71 A.L.R. 1295. * * *

The judgments are affirmed.

Notes and Questions

1. *Sufficiency.* Was the testimony of the shop foreman in *Eaton* sufficient to establish that the inspection was in fact made? See also United States v. Cornett, 484 F.2d 1365 (6th Cir.1973), where a clerk who sold defendant a gun and filled in the answers on a required form that he signed testified that she always read the questions "word by word" to the purchaser. Cases on a notary's usual practice are collected in Annot., 59 A.L.R.3d 1327.

2. *Establishing habit.* Federal Rule 406 contains no guidance as to how a habit or routine practice is to be established. An earlier version of the Rule had a subsection (b) which provided that proof could be "in the form of an opinion or by specific instances of conduct sufficient in number to warrant a finding that the habit existed or that the practice was routine." The House Committee on the Judiciary deleted the section, stating that the method of proof should be dealt with on a "case-by-case" basis. H.R.Rep. No. 650, 93d Cong., 1st Sess. 5 (1973). One witness' testimony in the form of an opinion has been held sufficient under Rule 406 to establish a routine practice. See, e.g., Envirex, Inc. v. Ecological Recovery Assoc., Inc., 454 F.Supp. 1329 (M.D.Pa.1978), aff'd, 601 F.2d 574 (3d Cir.1979) (single witness established routine business practice of sending complete proposals to all general contractors with whom business contracted).

3. *Mailing.* Many of the cases of evidence of the practice or routine of a business organization involve proving mailing. Some courts at common law hold that, in addition to proving a routine of mailing, there must be a showing that a "part of the routine was followed." Others find proof of a routine mailing sufficient in itself. Compare Consolidated Motors v. Skousen, 109 P.2d 41 (Ariz.1941) (need to show that part of routine followed), with General Mills, Inc. v. Zerbe Bros., Inc., 672 P.2d 1109 (Mont.1983) (routine sufficient). See cases cited in Annot., 45 A.L.R.4th 476. Does Federal Rule 406 do away with the need for proof in addition to the routine by its

elimination of the requirement of corroboration? See 2 Mueller & Kirkpatrick, Federal Evidence § 126 (2d ed. 1994).

SECTION C. PERSONALITY TRAITS AND BEHAVIOR PATTERNS—CRIMINAL CASES

(1) ACCUSED'S CHARACTER: FEDERAL RULE 404(a)(1)

STATE v. RENNEBERG

Supreme Court of Washington, En Banc, 1974.
522 P.2d 835.

BRACHTENBACH, ASSOCIATE JUSTICE.

Virginia Sue [Renneberg] LaVanway was charged with and convicted of grand larceny. Her codefendant, Milton V. LaVanway, whom she married after they were charged with these crimes, was charged with and convicted of aiding and abetting grand larceny. The Court of Appeals affirmed the convictions and we granted review.

The defendant wife had been employed by a restaurant but had been discharged from that employment. In the early evening of June 24, 1970, the defendants visited the restaurant to obtain her final paycheck. The defendants went to the rest rooms in the rear of the restaurant and then returned to the front where defendant wife used the telephone which was located next to the cash register. Defendant husband stood near the restaurant door where he paced back and forth, looked about and kept moving around, according to the witnesses. The restaurant employee who was the only one operating the cash register that evening heard the register bell, indicating the register was being opened, and went toward the cash register. He saw defendant wife facing the cash register, then the defendants left the restaurant. A witness reported to the employee that his son had seen a young woman at the register with a stack of money bills in her hand. An immediate tally of the register disclosed a shortage of approximately $250.

The first issue arises from the following testimony elicited by the prosecutor:

> Q. Mrs. LaVanway, is it true that in June of this year you were addicted to or were using a narcotic drug? A. Yes. Q. Mrs. LaVanway, is it true that on July 14th, you went onto a methadone program to cure a narcotic addiction or use? A. Yes.

It appears that the question of admissibility of this testimony was discussed in chambers before the trial started. Apparently, although it is not clear from the record, the court indicated that testimony as to drug addiction would be inadmissible in the state's case. Only after defendant wife took the stand and testified as to her character, as described later, did the court allow this testimony. Admissibility of evidence of prior drug addiction can be considered on at least two distinctly different grounds.

First, that it relates to the witness' credibility and second, that it is an unrelated act of misconduct, admissible to contradict character evidence. It is obvious that there is an immense difference between the practical effect of the two theories of admissibility. If it is admissible to attack credibility, it will come in whenever a defendant testifies while, if it is restricted to countering character evidence, it will only be used against that defendant who chooses to put his or her character into evidence. As to admissibility relating to credibility, there is a division of authority. *See* 3A J. Wigmore, Evidence § 934 (J. Chadbourn rev. 1970); 52 A.L.R.2d 848 (1957).

We note that we are not confronted with a situation where it is contended that the witness was under the influence of drugs at the time of the events to which he testifies as in Doe v. State, 487 P.2d 47 (Alaska 1971), or that the witness is under the influence at the time of testifying such as in State v. Reyes, 99 Ariz. 257, 408 P.2d 400 (1965).

The Court of Appeals recognized the division in the authorities but felt bound by our decision in Lankford v. Tombari, 35 Wash.2d 412, 213 P.2d 627 (1950), wherein a terse holding concluded that drug use or addiction is relevant to veracity. In view of society's deep concern today with drug usage and its consequent condemnation by many if not most, evidence of drug addiction is necessarily prejudicial in the minds of the average juror. Additionally there is no proof before the court connecting addiction to a lack of veracity. If such medical or scientific proof were made, it might well be admissible as relevant to credibility. Absent such proof its relevance on credibility or veracity is an unknown factor while its prejudice is within common knowledge. The Lankford v. Tombari decision is limited accordingly by our view herein.

However, the alternate and more restrictive ground of character impeachment dictates admissibility here. The defendant wife voluntarily put her character before the jury. She testified to her work experience, that she had attended college, that she had been a candidate in the Miss Yakima pageant, that she had participated in a glee club, drill team, pep club and was the treasurer of a science club. Implicit in such testimony is the painting of a picture of a person most unlikely to commit grand larceny. While the character of defendant husband was not so clearly put into evidence, it was introduced sufficiently to subject the defendant husband to the same questions as recited above which were asked of the wife. There was testimony as to his occupation as a professional photographer, as to his physical dress on the day in question, as to his somewhat lengthy engagement and subsequent marriage to the defendant wife whose character had been so vividly pictured, as to his working in his garden at home and as to the planned attendance at a family barbecue on the day of the alleged crime. The state was entitled to complete the tapestry with his admitted drug addiction.

This court has consistently followed the rule stated in State v. Emmanuel, 42 Wash.2d 1, 14, 253 P.2d 386, 393 (1953), that: "[I]f a defendant puts his prior conduct into issue by testifying as to his own past good behavior, he may be cross-examined as to specific acts of misconduct unrelated to the crime charged." * * *

The court instructed the jury that evidence of prior misconduct was to be considered only as bearing on credibility and on the weight to be given to the witness' testimony. That instruction was proposed by the defendants. The record discloses that the defendants felt the instruction was necessary to lessen the impact of the evidence. Defendants had a choice to propose no instruction, to propose one relating to credibility or one relating to character. The choice was made and cannot now be urged as error. * * *

Notes and Questions

1. *Relevance.* What was defendant wife's purpose in testifying to her work experience, that she had attended college, that she had been a candidate in the Miss Yakima pageant, etc., or of comparable testimony from the defendant husband?

2. *"Opening the door" by the defense.* A number of cases have held that a defendant may put his or her character "in issue" by door-opening testimony, which the prosecution is then entitled to rebut. For example, in United States v. Castillo, 181 F.3d 1129, 1132 (9th Cir.1999), a drug prosecution, the trial court initially ruled that the defendant's prior arrest for cocaine possession was inadmissible:

> On direct examination, Castillo testified that he worked with disadvantaged children, and would not have smuggled drugs "for a million dollars." Castillo portrayed himself as an anti-drug counselor who taught kids to "stay away from drugs." He added that he had never used drugs and would not touch them. Castillo's sweeping denial of any association with drugs was volunteered and often not responsive to questions posed by his lawyer. After hearing Castillo's testimony, the district court advised the parties it was reconsidering its earlier ruling excluding evidence of the 1997 arrest for cocaine possession. * * * Explaining that Castillo had portrayed himself as a "paragon of virtue" and "quintessential model citizen" who would never have anything to do with drugs, the district court concluded that the 1997 cocaine arrest "bears directly on [Castillo's] credibility" and admitted extrinsic evidence concerning the earlier arrest to impeach Castillo.

See also United States v. Chance, 306 F.3d 356, 387 (6th Cir.2002) ("The phrase 'competent hard-working people' suggests that the persons identified were wholesomely industrious citizens. We do not think that wholesomely industrious law enforcement officers plant evidence, mistake flour for cocaine, or swear out false affidavits in support of search and arrest warrants."); United States v. Adamson, 665 F.2d 649 (5th Cir.1982) (in misapplication of bank funds, defendant testified as to his career, personal history, family and business ties, medical problems, personal philosophy and civil contributions); Hattaway v. United States, 416 F.2d 1178, 1180 (5th Cir. 1969) (defendant in Mann Act prosecution testified that "she had been raised in a very Christian home and had always been concerned about the children's welfare").

3. *"Opening the door" by the prosecution.* While the courts have been sensitive to attempts by prosecutors themselves to open up character on cross-examination, United States v. Gilliland, 586 F.2d 1384 (10th Cir.1978) (prosecution could not convert defense eyewitness into character witness by asking what kind of man defendant was), and Martin v. People, 162 P.2d 597 (Colo.1945) (improper cross-examination of defendant challenging him to put his character in issue), the risk that a defendant may volunteer a "good character" statement on cross-examination is graphically illustrated in United States ex rel. Johnson v. Johnson, 531 F.2d 169, 175 n.17 (3d Cir.1976). See also *Castillo*, note 2, supra, 181 F.3d at 1133–34 ("Courts are more willing to permit, and commentators more willing to endorse, impeachment by contradiction where * * * testimony is volunteered on direct examination. The distinction between direct and cross-examination recognizes that opposing counsel may manipulate questions to trap an unwary witness into 'volunteering' statements on cross-examination. * * * The distinction also recognizes that, as a practical matter, it is often difficult to determine whether testimony is invited or whether it is volunteered on cross-examination.").

4. *Other ways to insinuate character into a trial.* E.g., Belmar v. State, 621 S.E.2d 441 (Ga.2005) (photograph of appellant's right upper back displaying a tattoo reading "12 gauge" where a 12–gauge shotgun was the murder weapon); State v. Breedlove, 271 N.E.2d 238, 241 (Ohio 1971) ("[W]e believe it unjustifiable for the state, on direct examination, to present police mug shots, bearing police identification numbers, from which a reasonable inference can be drawn that the defendant, at some indefinite time in the past had had trouble with the law."); State v. McMillan, 590 N.E.2d 23, 26 (Ohio Ct.App.1990) (profile of sex abusers improper "group character evidence"); State v. Pargeon, 582 N.E.2d 665, 666 (Ohio Ct.App.1991) (In a domestic violence prosecution, evidence that the accused's wife is a battered woman "really serves as evidence of the prior bad acts from which the inference may be drawn that appellant has the propensity to beat his wife and that he beat her on this particular occasion. This is precisely the prohibited inference that is excluded under [Ohio] Evid. R. 404(B).").

5. *Character on issue of credibility.* The question of the introduction of evidence with regard to the credibility of a witness, the accused or any other witness, is considered more completely in Chapter 12, Section E, infra.

6. *What is character?* The law obviously assumes there is something called "character"? But is there such a thing? See Sanchirico, Character Evidence and the Object of Trial, 101 Colum.L.Rev. 1227, 1233, 1240–41 (2001) ("Personality psychologists are now in general agreement that individuals do have identifiable cross situational attributes that, along with situation specific factors, help to determine individual behavior. * * * Current research suggests that a defendant's cross situation attributes, as evidence by past acts, may be quite probative of conduct in the case at hand. * * * Several influential studies specifically maintain that the stability of criminal and tortious behavior is due to the stability of certain personality features, such as 'low empathy' or lack of 'self-control.' "). Professor Sanchirico further argues that the character rules only make sense when viewed as a mechanism to regulate behavior outside the courtroom. But see Imwinkelried, The Dubiety of Social Engineering Through Evidence: A Reply to

Professor Sanchirico's Recent Article on Character Evidence, 51 Drake L.Rev. 283 (2003).

EDGINGTON v. UNITED STATES

Supreme Court of the United States, 1896.
164 U.S. 361.

At the March term, 1895, in the District Court of the United States for the Southern District of Iowa, Avington A. Edgington was tried and found guilty of the crime of making a false deposition on April 13, 1894, in aid of a fraudulent pension claim on behalf of his mother, Jennie M. Edgington, claiming to be the widow of Francis M. Edgington. * * *

MR. JUSTICE SHIRAS, after stating the case, delivered the opinion of the court. * * *

We are constrained to sustain the assignments which complain of the exclusion of testimony offered to show defendant's general reputation for truth and veracity. It is not necessary to cite authorities to show that, in criminal prosecutions, the accused will be allowed to call witnesses to show that his character was such as would make it unlikely that he would be guilty of the particular crime with which he is charged. And as here the defendant was charged with a species of the *crimen falsi,* the rejected evidence was material and competent. This, indeed, is conceded in the brief for the government; but it is argued that, as the learned judge, in overruling the offer of the evidence, observed that the testimony might "become proper later on," he was merely passing on the order of proof, his discretion in respect to which is not reversible. It is possible, as suggested, that the judge thought that such evidence should not be offered until it appeared that the defendant had himself testified. But this would show a misconception of the reason why the evidence was competent. It was not intended to give weight to the defendant's personal testimony in the case, but to establish a general character inconsistent with guilt of the crime with which he stood charged; and the evidence was admissible whether or not the defendant himself testified. When testimony, competent and material, has been offered and erroneously rejected, the error is not cured by a conjecture that if offered at a subsequent period in the trial the evidence might have been admitted. It should also be observed that when a subsequent offer to the same effect was made the judge rejected it without qualification. * * *

Whatever may have been said in some of the earlier cases, to the effect that evidence of the good character of the defendant is not to be considered unless the other evidence leaves the mind in doubt, the decided weight of authority now is that good character, when considered in connection with the other evidence in the case, may generate a reasonable doubt. The circumstances may be such that an established reputation for good character, if it is relevant to the issue, would alone create a reasonable doubt, although, without it, the other evidence would be convincing.

The judgment of the court below is reversed and the cause remanded with directions to set aside the verdict and award a new trial.

MR. JUSTICE BREWER concurred in the judgment.

MR. JUSTICE BROWN dissented.

Notes and Questions

1. *Pertinent trait.* If the accused was tried for assault or murder, what would be the pertinent trait? For larceny? For perjury? Both the common law and the Federal Rules limit character evidence to traits pertinent to the crime in question. See, e.g., State v. Howland, 138 P.2d 424 (Kan.1943) (proper to exclude evidence of character of accused for truth and veracity to meet a charge of statutory rape). What about law-abiding character? E.g., United States v. Angelini, 678 F.2d 380 (1st Cir.1982) (accused's character as law-abiding citizen always admissible); United States v. Hewitt, 634 F.2d 277 (5th Cir.1981) (same).

2. *Prosecution rebuttal.* The "pertinence" requirement is particularly significant when the prosecution seeks to rebut the accused's evidence of good character. See United States v. Reed, 700 F.2d 638 (11th Cir.1983) (introduction of character evidence on truth and veracity did not open the door for questions to the accused with regard to marijuana use); State v. Kramp, 651 P.2d 614 (Mont.1982) (character evidence as to truth, integrity, honesty and veracity did not open door to evidence of traffic or drinking offenses). But see United States v. Diaz, 961 F.2d 1417, 1419 (9th Cir.1992) ("Diaz's proneness to criminal activity is an admissible character trait encompassed under [the] general definition of 'law-abidingness.' ").

3. *Reputation testimony.* The bulk of the common law decisions limited proof of character as proof of conduct to reputation evidence. Several problems may arise in connection with the proof of character by reputation. For example, should a reputation witness be required to be a resident of the same community? Should an investigator be allowed to testify to the results of his inquiries? See United States v. Lewin, 467 F.2d 1132 (7th Cir.1972). What geographical and social factors should be considered in determining the "community" in which a reputation exists? See United States v. Oliver, 492 F.2d 943 (8th Cir.1974) (college roommates of seven weeks' acquaintance). In United States v. Straughan, 453 F.2d 422 (8th Cir.1972), allowing a police officer to testify that defendant had two reputations, a good one in the community where he lived and a bad one in state law-enforcement circles, was held error. Should a witness who has not heard the person's reputation discussed nevertheless be allowed to testify concerning it? See People v. Van Gaasbeck, 82 N.E. 718, 722 (N.Y.1907) (ruling that a witness could testify to the good reputation of the defendant without ever hearing anything said of his character if the witness has lived a considerable time in the defendant's community since "one's character does not get talked about until there is some fault to be found with it").

4. *Opinion testimony.* The rationale for rejecting opinion testimony at common law was typically expressed in language such as the following:

> An opinion as to reputation, however, (although composed of numerous individual subjective opinions) is essentially an objective fact about a defendant, thus subject to reasonably limited cross-examination. A witness can be accurate or inaccurate as to reputation, but his opinion as to character is essentially his own personal estimate.

United States v. White, 225 F.Supp. 514, 522 (D.D.C.1963).

Wigmore argued strongly in favor of enlarging the scope of character proof to include opinion, contrasting such proof with "the secondhand, irresponsible product of multiplied guesses and gossip which we term 'reputation.' " 7 Wigmore, Evidence § 1986 (Chadbourn rev. 1978). Federal Rule 405(a) specifically permits opinion evidence. What about the problems with opinion suggested by the language in the *White* case?

5. *Expert testimony.* The removal of the prohibition against opinion evidence gave rise to the possibility that expert testimony with regard to character might be introduced. See United States v. Roberts, 887 F.2d 534, 536 (5th Cir.1989) (expert testimony that defendant's "naive and autocratic" personality traits were consistent with his claimed activity as a self-appointed vigilante should not have been excluded); United States v. Hill, 655 F.2d 512 (3d Cir.1981) (psychologist's testimony as to defendant's susceptibility was relevant to defense of entrapment and should not have been excluded); United States v. Staggs, 553 F.2d 1073 (7th Cir.1977) (psychologist's testimony that defendant's impulsive acts are more likely to be directed inwardly than outwardly should not have been excluded); State v. Hood, 346 N.W.2d 481 (Iowa 1984) (expert testimony that co-defendant in homicide prosecution was a "passive-dependent" individual who will allow others to assume responsibility was properly admitted). But cf. United States v. MacDonald, 688 F.2d 224, 227 (4th Cir.1982) (upholding trial judge's discretion under Rule 403 to exclude psychiatric evidence that the defendant had "a personality configuration inconsistent with the outrageous and senseless murder of his family."). At least one state adopting rules based upon the Federal Rules has attempted specifically to exclude expert testimony of this kind. See N.C.R.Evid. 405(a).

6. *Specific acts.* Even under modern practice, the accused may not attempt to prove his good character by evidence of specific instances, United States v. Benedetto, 571 F.2d 1246 (2d Cir.1978) (honesty of meat inspector charged with taking bribes not provable by testimony of other packers that he did not solicit bribes from them), or by religious beliefs, Government of Virgin Islands v. Petersen, 553 F.2d 324 (3d Cir.1977) (proper to exclude evidence of membership in Rastafarians, who believe in nonviolence). Is this position justifiable? See Uviller, Evidence of Character to Prove Conduct: Illusion, Illogic, and Injustice in the Courtroom, 130 U.Pa.L.Rev. 845 (1982).

7. *Character instruction.* The *Edgington* opinion contains the following statement: "The circumstances may be such that an established reputation for good character, if it is relevant to the issue, would alone create a reasonable doubt, although, without it, the other evidence would be convincing." See also Michelson v. United States, 335 U.S. 469, 476 (1948) ("Such testimony alone, in some circumstances, may be enough to raise a reasonable doubt of guilt."). Defense attorneys frequently request that these sentiments be incorporated into a jury instruction. However, most federal courts hold

that the "standing alone-reasonable doubt" instruction need not be given. E.g., United States v. Pujana–Mena, 949 F.2d 24, 28 n.2 (2d Cir.1991) ("Seven circuits have held that a defendant is not entitled to a 'standing alone' charge. In addition, the Seventh Circuit has held that the 'standing alone' instruction is improper in a case where the defendant testifies, but has left open the question whether the charge should be forbidden in all cases. The Fourth and Tenth Circuits similarly have held that the 'standing alone' charge need not always be given, but may be necessary when defendant relies solely on evidence of good character. The District of Columbia Circuit is the only circuit still requiring a 'standing alone' instruction in all cases in which a defendant offers character evidence."). Should trial counsel request such an instruction?

BROYLES v. COMMONWEALTH

Kentucky Court of Appeals, 1954.
267 S.W.2d 73.

COMBS, JUSTICE. George Richard Broyles appeals from a sentence of life imprisonment imposed after a jury found him guilty of the murder of Billy D. Smithers. He urges as grounds for reversal: (1) Improper cross-examination of defense witnesses by the Assistant Commonwealth's Attorney * * *.

The appellant introduced several witnesses who testified that his reputation for peace and quietude was good. These witnesses were asked on cross-examination if they knew appellant had been arrested and convicted on separate occasions for drunken driving, for reckless driving, and for disorderly conduct. One witness admitted to having knowledge of these convictions; the others disavowed such knowledge. Appellant contends the questions were improper because they related to a trait of character not involved in the crime with which he was charged.

Broadly speaking, it is the rule in this state that where the defendant introduces evidence of his good reputation, the witness so testifying may be asked on cross-examination whether he has heard reports of particular acts of misconduct by the defendant. * * * But the rule is not absolute. When there is an objection to such evidence or a motion to limit its effect, the court is required to admonish the jury that it is admitted only for the purpose of testing the accuracy and credibility of the witness' testimony and not as substantive evidence of defendant's guilt. * * * Moreover, inquiry may be made only about those acts of misconduct having some relation to the particular trait of character which the defendant has put in issue. * * *

Another limitation to the rule, but one with which we are not here concerned, is that the attorney for the Commonwealth may not deliberately inject into the case the issue of previous acts of misconduct by the defendant without some basis for his questions. * * *

The question here is whether one who is guilty of drunken driving, reckless driving, and disorderly conduct thereby evinces a trait of character inconsistent with a good reputation for peace and quietude. Courts in other jurisdictions have answered the question in the affirmative and have permitted questions designed to test the witness' knowledge of the other offenses. * * *

We find no Kentucky case directly in point, but an examination of related cases reveals that this court has taken a cautious attitude toward the introduction of such testimony. In Smith v. Commonwealth, 206 Ky. 728, 268 S.W. 328, the defendant, being tried for murder, introduced witnesses who testified that his reputation for peace and quietude was good. The witnesses were asked on cross-examination if they had heard that defendant had an illegitimate child by his sister-in-law; that he had taken another man's wife to Tennessee and lived with her, and that he had been convicted for the illegal sale of whisky. It was held that the questions should not have been permitted because responsive answers would have thrown no light on defendant's reputation for peace and quietude.

In Albertson v. Commonwealth, 312 Ky. 68, 226 S.W.2d 523, the defendant, under charge of murder, introduced witnesses who testified to his good reputation for peace and quietude. The witnesses were asked on cross-examination if they knew the defendant had engaged in the illegal traffic of whisky. This was held to be reversible error on the ground that a responsive answer to the question would have had no bearing on defendant's reputation for peace and quietude.

Although we are of the opinion the practice should be indulged in cautiously and that the rule should be kept within strict limitations, it seems to us that a conviction for drunken driving, or reckless driving, or disorderly conduct has some reasonable connection with a man's reputation for peace and quietude. In the legal sense, peace and quietude signify obedience to law, public quiet, good order and tranquility. A jury might reasonably infer that a propensity to drunken driving, reckless driving, or disorderly conduct is evidence of an attitude of disrespect for the law inconsistent with a good reputation for peace and quietude. It should be kept in mind that such evidence is never competent unless the defendant himself puts his reputation in issue; and even then it is competent only for the purpose of testing the witness' credibility, and not as substantive evidence. It is noted that proper admonition to this effect was given by the trial judge in this case. We conclude that the court properly permitted the attorney for the state to ask the defendant's character witnesses whether they had heard reports of his previous conviction for drunken driving, reckless driving, or disorderly conduct.

* * *

The judgment is reversed because of the improper argument of the attorney for the Commonwealth.

Notes and Questions

1. *Purpose of cross-examination.* See Michelson v. United States, 335 U.S. 469, 479 n.16 (1948) ("A classic example in the books is a character

witness in a trial for murder. She testified she grew up with defendant, knew his reputation for peace and quiet, and that it was good. On cross-examination she was asked if she had heard that the defendant had shot anybody and, if so, how many. She answered, 'Three or four,' and gave the names of two but could not recall the names of the others. She still insisted, however, that he was of 'good character.' The jury seems to have valued her information more highly than her judgment and convicted."). See also Mueller, Of Misshapen Stones and Compromises: *Michelson* and the Modern Law of Character Evidence, in Evidence Stories 75 (Lempert ed., 2006).

2. *Form of question.* Observe that the court at the beginning of *Broyles* describes the cross-examination as inquiring into whether the witness *knew* of the arrests and convictions, while at the conclusion the questions are described as inquiring into whether the witness has *heard*. The opinion in *Michelson*, note 1, supra, says that with respect to reputation witnesses "the form of inquiry, 'Have you heard?' has general approval, and 'Do you know?' is not allowed." 335 U.S. at 482. Since Federal Rule 405(a) now permits opinion evidence to prove character, the restriction in *Michelson*, which flowed from only reputation being admissible, is not applicable to such a character witness. Moreover, the Advisory Committee note indicates that the second sentence of the rule was designed to eliminate this distinction—hear/know—in formulating questions for either reputation or opinion.

3. *Good faith requirement.* As Wigmore observed: "This method of inquiry or cross-examination is frequently resorted to by counsel for the very purpose of injuring by indirection a character which they are forbidden directly to attack in that way; they rely upon the mere putting of the question (not caring that it is answered negatively) to convey their covert insinuation." 3A Wigmore, Evidence § 988, at 921 (Chadbourn rev. 1970).

4. *Guilt assuming hypotheticals.* Should a cross-examiner be permitted to ask a reputation or opinion character witness questions that refer to the crime on trial or some element of it? E.g., United States v. Candelaria-Gonzalez, 547 F.2d 291, 293 n.2 (5th Cir.1977) ("Would his reputation with your firm be affected if he were convicted of trafficking in narcotics [the charged crimes]?"). See also United States v. Shwayder, 312 F.3d 1109, 1121 (9th Cir.2002) ("Following almost every other circuit that has addressed the question, we now hold that the use of guilt assuming hypotheticals undermines the presumption of innocence and thus violates a defendant's right to due process.").

5. *Scope of cross-examination.* Under rules such as Rule 405, can a witness who has testified with regard to the *reputation* of an accused be cross-examined with regard to matters which might affect his or her *opinion* of the accused? See United States v. Curtis, 644 F.2d 263 (3d Cir.1981).

(2) VICTIM'S CHARACTER: FEDERAL RULE 404(a)(2)

EVANS v. UNITED STATES

United States Court of Appeals, District of Columbia, 1960.
277 F.2d 354.

BAZELON, CIRCUIT JUDGE.

Appellant was convicted of second-degree murder. The homicide occurred on the sidewalk of a street in Washington about 5:30 a.m., on May 1, 1955. The Government called three disinterested eyewitnesses, none of whom observed all the events surrounding the homicide. When pieced together, however, their testimony showed that appellant was in the company of two other women and a man; that they hailed the deceased, who was walking on the other side of the street, and he joined the group; and that a few moments later, tussling and fighting began in the group, in the course of which appellant inflicted mortal wounds with a knife. There was also strong evidence that the deceased was drunk. The Government advanced no motive for the killing and none appears. Since appellant and the deceased were total strangers and money on his person was undisturbed, there is no basis for imputing a personal or a robbery motive.

Appellant took the stand and testified that she killed the deceased in defending herself from a sexual assault. She said that she was returning home alone; that the decedent came up from behind and asked whether she was "out for some sporting"; that when she rebuffed this and other obscenities, he grabbed her, ripping some of her clothing. Appellant admitted that in the course of the ensuing struggle she stabbed the decedent with a knife which she carried for protection.

Able counsel appointed by this court urge only one ground for reversal. It is that the trial court erred in rejecting the defendant's proffer of testimony by the deceased's wife that he

> "was ill mentally, not insane * * * a lost soul who wanted to be with people, get along with the rest, and did not know how to do it; that at times, that he would like to drink and at times on drinking and otherwise he would even go to the extent of being psychotic, perhaps, and with her at least she would know—acted belligerent and in a really bellicose type of manner."

Appellant's counsel contend that upon a plea of self-defense, evidence of the deceased's "character and belligerency," though unknown to the defendant, is admissible in corroboration of the defendant's testimony that the deceased was the aggressor. They say this is but a logical extension of the rule of Griffin v. United States, 1950 [183 F.2d 990, 992], that "evidence of uncommunicated threats of the deceased against the defendant is admissible." We agree. The reasons for our view are well summarized by Professor Wigmore:

> "When the issue of self-defense is made in a trial for homicide, and thus a controversy arises *whether the deceased was the aggres-*

sor, one's persuasion will be more or less affected by the character of the deceased; it may throw much light on the probabilities of the deceased's action:

* * *

> "[The] additional element of communication is unnecessary; for the question is what the deceased probably did, not what the defendant probably thought the deceased was going to do. The inquiry is one of objective occurrence, not of subjective belief." I Wigmore, Evidence § 63, at 467, 470–471 (3d ed. 1940). See also 2 id. § 246, at 54.

Although the proffer in this case was inartful, we think that, at the very least, it adequately apprised the trial judge that the evidence would show that the deceased was aggressive when drunk. Since it is clear that the deceased was drunk, such testimony was relevant in corroborating appellant's contention that she was attacked. Moreover, the proffer, broadly construed, purported to explain the deceased's general character and reputation. We think that, in the circumstances of this case, almost any evidence showing what kind of man the decedent was would be highly relevant in helping the jury to determine whether appellant's story of a sexual assault was truthful, and would therefore serve the interests of justice.

We cannot say that the error in excluding this testimony was harmless. It is true that three disinterested prosecution witnesses testified that appellant was not alone at the time of the incident, and that this adversely affected her credibility. But none of the Government's witnesses could say who instigated the fight. Consequently even if the jury believed all that the Government's witnesses said, it still could have found that appellant acted in self-defense if it believed her uncontradicted statement that the deceased was the aggressor. We think the proffered evidence might have led the jury to believe that statement, notwithstanding its apparent doubts as to appellant's credibility on other phases of her testimony.

Finally, but equally important, even if it convincingly appeared that the excluded testimony could not induce the jury to acquit, evidence suggesting that he was the aggressor might well have induced the jury to convict appellant for the lesser included offense of manslaughter, instead of second-degree murder.

Reversed and remanded.

FAHY, CIRCUIT JUDGE (dissenting).

The defense offered was the need to kill deceased in resisting a sexual assault. In my view the proffered testimony was too tenuous in corroborative relationship to this particular defense to justify reversal because of rejection of the proffer, especially when all the evidence as to the manner in which the homicide occurred is considered. It follows from this view that I attach no significance to the circumstance that the jury could convict of manslaughter.

Notes and Questions

1. *Method of proof.* See United States v. Bautista, 145 F.3d 1140, 1152 (10th Cir.1998) ("evidence of the victim's aggressive character may be admissible * * * to establish that the victim was the aggressor. * * * However, Fed. R. Evid. 405 limits the type of character evidence to reputation or opinion evidence * * *. Therefore, Bautista could have introduced evidence of Carrillo's reputation for aggressiveness, but he could not introduce specific instances of aggressive conduct.").

2. *Homicide cases.* Rule 404(a)(2) contains a special rule in homicide cases. *Any* evidence that the victim was the first aggressor in a homicide case triggers the prosecution's right to introduce rebuttal evidence of the victim's peaceful character. For example, if the accused testifies that the victim was the first aggressor, but does not introduce character evidence on this issue, the prosecution may nevertheless introduce evidence of the victim's peaceful character in rebuttal. This rule does not apply in assault cases in which self-defense is raised. Why not?

3. *Accused's character.* A 2000 amendment to Rule 404(a)(1) permits the prosecutor to introduce evidence of the accused's character if the accused offers evidence of the victim's character.

4. *Communicated character.* "Whether evidence concerning the victim is admissible to prove self-defense depends upon the type of evidence being offered. Typically, such evidence falls into two general categories: (1) testimony concerning the victim offered to demonstrate the defendant's state of mind at the time of the incident, and (2) testimony about the victim's character offered to prove that the victim was more likely the aggressor." State v. Baker, 623 N.E.2d 672, 674 (Ohio Ct.App.1993). The first use does not involve character-as-proof-of-conduct, and hence, the restriction on methods of proof found in Rule 405(a) are not applicable. In reversing petitioner's conviction on the basis that exclusion of evidence violated due process, the court in DePetris v. Kuykendall, 239 F.3d 1057, 1058–59 (9th Cir.2001) stated:

> Petitioner Kelly DePetris shot and killed her husband Dana DePetris while he was asleep in bed. At trial, she claimed 'imperfect self-defense'—that is, she claimed to have had an actual, honest belief that she was in imminent danger even if such a belief was objectively unreasonable. Under California law, imperfect self-defense is not a complete defense to homicide; however, if established, it negates malice and reduces murder to voluntary manslaughter. To prove her claim that she acted out of an actual fear that her husband would make good on his threats to kill her and their baby that night, petitioner attempted (1) to offer into evidence Dana's handwritten journal and (2) to testify herself about how having read the journal contributed to her belief that Dana's threats were to be taken seriously. The journal contained Dana's chilling account of his violent behavior toward his first wife and others. The trial court excluded as irrelevant the journal and petitioner's testimony about having read it.

(3) VICTIM'S CHARACTER: FEDERAL RULE 412

DOE v. UNITED STATES

United States Court of Appeals, Fourth Circuit, 1981.
666 F.2d 43.

BUTZNER, CIRCUIT JUDGE:

These appeals concern the district court's evidentiary ruling in a pre-trial proceeding held pursuant to rule 412 of the Federal Rules of Evidence. The court held that evidence concerning the past sexual behavior and habits of the prosecutrix was admissible in the rape trial of Donald Robert Black. We conclude that we have jurisdiction to hear her appeal, and we affirm in part and reverse in part the order of the district court.

I

The appellant is the alleged victim and chief government witness in the impending rape trial of Black. Pursuant to rule 412 of the Federal Rules of Evidence, Black made a pre-trial motion to admit evidence and permit cross-examination concerning the victim's past sexual behavior. After a hearing, the district court ruled that Black could introduce the evidence which he proffered.

Several days later, the district court granted Black's motion for the issuance of subpoenas for individuals who were to testify about the victim's sexual history. These included the victim's former landlord, a social worker who had previously investigated the victim, a sexual partner of the victim, and two people who claimed to be aware of the victim's reputation for promiscuity.

Thereafter, the victim instituted a civil action seeking the permanent sealing of the record of the rule 412 proceedings and other relief. During the course of this civil action, the court learned that the rape victim had not received notice of the earlier proceeding as mandated by subsection (c) (1) of rule 412. Consequently, it reopened the rule 412 hearing. The court then reaffirmed its prior ruling in the criminal case and entered summary judgment in favor of the defendants in the civil action. The victim appeals from the orders in both the civil and criminal actions.

II

Black asserts that this court lacks jurisdiction to entertain the victim's appeal from the district court's order in the rule 412 proceeding. Resolution of this issue requires an examination of the procedural provisions of the rule.

Rule 412 places significant limitations on the admissibility of evidence concerning the past sexual behavior of a rape victim. The rule provides the additional safeguard of a hearing in chambers to determine the admissibility of such evidence. These provisions were adopted "to protect rape victims from the degrading and embarrassing disclosure of intimate details about their private lives." 124 Cong.Rec. at H 11945 (1978). To effectuate this purpose, subsections (c) (1) and (2) of the rule require that rape victims receive notice of the evidentiary hearing and a copy of the defendant's motion and offer of proof. Additionally, subsection (c) (2) makes provision for the victim's testimony at the evidentiary hearing.

The text, purpose, and legislative history of rule 412 clearly indicate that Congress enacted the rule for the special benefit of the victims of rape. The rule makes no reference to the right of a victim to appeal an adverse ruling. Nevertheless, this remedy is implicit as a necessary corollary of the rule's explicit protection of the privacy interests Congress sought to safeguard. *Cf. Cort v. Ash,* 422 U.S. 66 * * * (1975). No other party in the evidentiary proceeding shares these interests to the extent that they might be viewed as a champion of the victim's rights. Therefore, the congressional intent embodied in rule 412 will be frustrated if rape victims are not allowed to appeal an erroneous evidentiary ruling made at a pre-trial hearing conducted pursuant to the rule.

Section 1291 of title 28 U.S.C. confers on courts of appeals jurisdiction to review final decisions of the district courts. The Supreme Court has held that this finality requirement should be "given a 'practical rather than a technical construction.'" *Gillespie v. U.S. Steel Corp.,* 379 U.S. 148, 152 * * * (1964). The Court also has instructed that the most important considerations for determining whether an order is final are "the inconvenience and costs of piecemeal review on the one hand and the danger of denying justice by delay on the other." *Dickinson v. Petroleum Corp.,* 338 U.S. 507, 511 * * * (1950).

In this case the balancing of these factors weighs heavily in favor of a conclusion of finality. The inconvenience and costs associated with permitting the victim to appeal are minimal. Certainly, they are no greater than those resulting from government appeals of suppression orders that are authorized by 18 U.S.C. § 3731. Because the rule provides for pre-trial evidentiary hearings, appeals are unlikely to involve significant postponements of criminal trials. Indeed, in this case, we heard the appeal and filed an order resolving the issues without any delay of the criminal trial.

On the other hand, the injustice to rape victims in delaying an appeal until after the conclusion of the criminal trial is manifest. Without the right to immediate appeal, victims aggrieved by the court's order will have no opportunity to protect their privacy from invasions forbidden by the rule. Appeal following the defendant's acquittal or conviction is no remedy, for the harm that the rule seeks to prevent already will have occurred. Consequently, we conclude that with respect to the victim the district court's order meets *Gillespie*'s test of practical finality, and we have jurisdiction to hear this appeal.

III

At the pre-trial rule 412 evidentiary hearing, Black presented several witnesses who told about the victim's past sexual behavior and reputation. Black testified that although he had talked on the phone with the victim several times, he did not meet her until the night of the alleged crime. Several men previously had told him the victim was promiscuous, and he had read a love letter she had written to another man.

At the conclusion of the hearing, the district court ruled that the following evidence was admissible:

(1) evidence of the victim's "general reputation in and around the Army post * * * where Mr. Black resided;"

(2) evidence of the victim's "habit of calling out to the barracks to speak to various and sundry soldiers;"

(3) evidence of the victim's "habit of coming to the post to meet people and of her habit of being at the barracks at the snack bar;"

(4) evidence from the victim's former landlord regarding "his experience with her" alleged promiscuous behavior;

(5) evidence of what a social worker learned of the victim;

(6) telephone conversations that Black had with the victim;

(7) evidence of the defendant's "state of mind as a result of what he knew of her reputation * * * and what she had said to him."

Black argues that all of the evidence delineated in items 1–7 is admissible to support his claim that the victim consented, to show the reasonableness of his belief that she consented, and to corroborate his testimony. He relies on the rule's provision for the admission of constitutionally required evidence. Exclusion of the evidence, he maintains, will deprive him of the rights secured by the due process clause of the fifth amendment and the right of confrontation and compulsory process guaranteed by the sixth amendment.

Rule 412 restricts the admission of evidence in several respects. Subsection (a) excludes reputation or opinion evidence of the past sexual behavior of the victim. Subsection (b) provides that evidence of past sexual behavior, other than reputation and opinion, is only admissible in three circumstances: first, the defendant may introduce this evidence when it is constitutionally required, 412(b) (1); second, when the defendant claims that he was not the source of semen or injury, he may introduce evidence of the victim's relations with other men, 412(b) (2) (A); and third, when the defendant claims the victim consented, he may testify about his prior relations with the victim, 412(b) (2) (B).

The evidence delineated in items 1–5 of the district court's order clearly falls within the proscription of subsection (a) of the rule. Though sometimes couched in terms of habit, this evidence is essentially opinion or reputation evidence. Consequently, the exceptions set forth in subsection (b) do not render it admissible.

The constitutional justification for excluding reputation and opinion evidence rests on a dual premise. First, an accused is not constitutionally entitled to present irrelevant evidence. Second, reputation and opinion concerning a victim's past sexual behavior are not relevant indicators of the likelihood of her consent to a specific sexual act or of her veracity. *Privacy of Rape Victims: Hearings on H.R. 14666 and Other Bills Before the Subcomm. on Criminal Justice of the Committee on the Judiciary,* 94th Cong., 2d Sess. 14–15 (1976). Indeed, even before Congress enacted rule 412, the leading federal case on the subject, *United States v. Kasto,* 584 F.2d 268, 271–72 (8th Cir.1978), stated that in the absence of extraordinary circumstances:

> evidence of a rape victim's unchastity, whether in the form of testimony concerning her general reputation or direct or cross-examination testimony concerning specific acts with persons other than the defendant, is ordinarily insufficiently probative either of her general credibility as a witness or of her consent to intercourse with the defendant on the particular occasion * * * to outweigh its highly prejudicial effect.

State legislatures and courts have generally reached the same conclusion. We are not prepared to state that extraordinary circumstances will never justify admission of such evidence to preserve a defendant's constitutional rights. The record of the rule 412 hearing in this case, however, discloses no circumstances for deeming that the rule's exclusion of the evidence classified in items 1–5 is unconstitutional.

The evidence described in items 6 and 7 of the district court's ruling is admissible. Certainly, the victim's conversations with Black are relevant, and they are not the type of evidence that the rule excludes. Black's knowledge, acquired before the alleged crime, of the victim's past sexual behavior is relevant on the issue of Black's intent. *See* 2 Weinstein and Berger, *Evidence* ¶ 412(01). Moreover, the rule does not exclude the production of the victim's letter or testimony of the men with whom Black talked if this evidence is introduced to corroborate the existence of the conversations and the letter.

The legislative history discloses that reputation and opinion evidence of the past sexual behavior of an alleged victim was excluded because Congress considered that this evidence was not relevant to the issues of the victim's consent or her veracity. *Privacy of Rape Victims: Hearings on H.R. 14666 and Other Bills Before the Subcomm. on Criminal Justice of the Committee on the Judiciary,* 94th Cong., 2d Sess. 14–15, 45 (1976). There is no indication, however, that this evidence was intended to be excluded when offered solely to show the accused's state of mind. Therefore, its admission is governed by the Rules of Evidence dealing with relevancy in general. Knowledge that Black acquired after the incident is irrelevant to this issue.

* * *

Notes and Questions

1. *Rape shield laws.* Rule 412 is known as the federal rape shield law. It was adopted in 1978, after many states had already enacted such laws. See 1 McCormick, Evidence § 193, at 777 (6th ed. 2006) ("In the 1970s, however, nearly all jurisdictions enacted criminal 'rape shield' laws * * *."). The federal rule was amended in 1994 to extend the rule (1) to all criminal cases (e.g., kidnaping), (2) impeachment, and (3) to civil cases (such as sexual harassment).

Why should the evidence precluded under the rape shield act be inadmissible generally in criminal cases, except for some narrowly prescribed circumstances, and, in civil cases, admissible whenever its "probative value substantially outweighs the danger of harm to any victim and of unfair prejudice to any party?" Given the protections afforded defendants in criminal cases, should it not be easier for an accused to have such evidence admitted than a party in a civil case?

2. *Common law approach.* In the not-too-distant past, evidence of prior sexual activity was offered either for substantive purposes, i.e., as evidence going to a defense of consent, or as evidence going to the credibility of the complaining witness. Given the fact that the victim of a sexual assault is usually the principal witness for the prosecution, it was most frequently offered for both purposes. In the absence of a rape shield statute, would the evidence excluded by the court in the principal case be admitted? For substantive purposes? For credibility? See Rule 608(b), discussed in Chapter 12, Section E(7), infra.

The following statement was written long before the adoption of rape shield laws, but is still contained in 3A Wigmore, Evidence § 924a, at 736 (Chadbourn rev. 1970):

> There is, however, at least one situation in which chastity may have a direct connection with veracity, viz. when a woman or young girl testifies as complainant against a man charged with a sexual crime. * * * Modern psychiatrists have amply studied the behavior of errant young girls and women coming before the courts in all sorts of cases. Their psychic complexes are multifarious, distorted partly by inherent defects, partly by diseased derangements or abnormal instincts, partly by bad social environment, partly by temporary physiological or emotional conditions. One form taken by these complexes is that of contriving false charges of sexual offenses by men. The unchaste (let us call it) mentality finds incidental but direct expression in the narration of imaginary sex incidents of which the narrator is the heroine or the victim. The real victim, however, too often in such cases is the innocent man; for the respect and sympathy naturally felt by any tribunal for a wronged female helps to give easy credit to such a plausible tale.

Does this statement accurately reflect the attitudes of the past? Does it reflect current attitudes? For a criticism of Wigmore's scientific methodology see Bienen, A Question of Credibility: John Henry Wigmore's Use of Scientific Authority in Section 924(a) of the Treatise on Evidence, 19 Cal.W.L.Rev. 235 (1983). For an interesting account of a defense lawyer's struggle with the issues involved in attacking the credibility of a complaining witness in a rape case by use of prior sexual activity, see Mortimer, Rumpole of the Bailey, "Rumpole and the Honourable Member" 79–105 (Penguin Books 1986).

3. *Mens rea issue.* The principal case is strongly criticized in Spector & Foster, Rule 412 and the Doe Case: The Fourth Circuit Turns Back the Clock, 35 Okla.L.Rev. 87 (1982), for admitting evidence going to the reasonableness of the defendant's belief. The authors argue that such an exception violates congressional intent. The case receives somewhat more favorable treatment in Galvin, Shielding Rape Victims in the State and Federal Courts: A Proposal for the Second Decade, 70 Minn.L.Rev. 763 (1986). See also United States v. Saunders, 943 F.2d 388, 392 (4th Cir.1991) ("The rule manifests the policy that it is unreasonable for a defendant to base his belief of consent on the victim's past sexual experiences with third persons, since it is intolerable to suggest that because the victim is a prostitute, she automatically is assumed to have consented with anyone at any time. If we were to require admission of Smith's testimony about his affair with Duckett, we would eviscerate the clear intent of the rule to protect victims of rape from being exposed at trial to harassing or irrelevant inquiry into their past sexual behavior, an inquiry that, prior to the adoption of the rule, had the tendency to shield defendants from their illegal conduct by discouraging victims from testifying.").

4. *Prostitution.* Courts have differed on the admissibility of evidence that an alleged victim engaged in prostitution. Compare State v. DeJesus, 856 A.2d 345, 355 (Conn.2004) ("[E]vidence of the victim's prior history of prostitution and the defendant's knowledge of that history was sufficiently material to the issue of consent that its exclusion violated the defendant's constitutional rights."), with Commonwealth v. Jones, 826 A.2d 900, 909 (Pa.Super.Ct.2003) (en banc) ("[T]he Rape Shield Law's purpose would not be served in the instant case by permitting Appellee to explore any of the complainant's prostitution convictions solely to show she has a propensity to engage in sexual activity for hire. * * * It is possible that a situation may arise during trial that would place this evidence within some recognized exception to the Rape Shield Law."). See also Bryant v. United States, 859 A.2d 1093, 1104 (D.C.2004) ("To admit evidence of sexual activity [as a prostitute] after the date of the offenses in this case would tend only to suggest that because Ms. Williams continued to have sex at some point after being raped, she therefore consented on the night in question. That is exactly the type of speculation that the law seeks to prevent."). When should such evidence be admissible?

5. *Demise of instruction recommending skepticism in rape cases.* A related rule was based on Sir Matthew Hale's text—i.e., rape "is an accusation easily made and hard to be proved, and harder to be defended by the party accused, tho never so innocent." 1 Hale, History of the Pleas of the Crown 634 (1st Am. ed. 1847). Why aren't similar instructions given in one-on-one robbery cases? See Hardin v. State, 840 A.2d 1217, 1223 (Del.2003) ("Lord Hale's caution has grown increasingly out of favor in other jurisdictions. The major movement to abandon the caution began in 1975 with California, closely followed by Iowa and Arizona. Several other courts have subsequently held that the instruction is improper. Additionally, in the

1980s, Colorado, Minnesota, Nevada and Pennsylvania all enacted statutes abolishing Lord Hale's caution as an instruction to the jury."). See also Baker, Once a Rapist? Motivational Evidence and Relevancy in Rape Law, 110 Harv.L.Rev. 563, 584 (1997) ("Lord Hale had it precisely backwards: rape allegations are not easily made, and they are very easy to defend against."); Morris, Note, The Empirical, Historical and Legal Case Against the Cautionary Instruction, 1988 Duke L.J. 154, 167–68.

UNITED STATES v. AZURE

United States Court of Appeals, Eighth Circuit, 1988.
845 F.2d 1503.

LARSON, SENIOR DISTRICT JUDGE.

Defendant Anthony Damian Azure was convicted by a jury of carnal knowledge of a female under the age of sixteen, in violation of 18 U.S.C. §§ 1153 and 2032. This Court reversed defendant's initial conviction because we found the district court had improperly admitted expert opinion testimony on the credibility of the victim. *United States v. Azure,* 801 F.2d 336, 341 (8th Cir.1986). On retrial, a jury again found the defendant guilty as charged. Defendant has again appealed to this Court, arguing his subsequent conviction must be reversed because the district court erred in (1) excluding evidence of the victim's past sexual behavior under Fed.R.Evid. 412; * * * We affirm.

I. BACKGROUND

Azure was charged with having had sexual intercourse on or about December 8, 1984, with Wendy Lozensky, one of the daughters of Azure's common law wife, Patty Lozensky. Wendy was ten years old at the time. She testified at trial concerning the events surrounding the December 8th incident, and also testified that Azure had been abusing her since she was eight years old. Wendy's sisters, Melissa Lozensky and Michelle Faine, testified that they had seen Azure take Wendy into his bedroom alone when their mother Patty was gone. They also corroborated Wendy's testimony concerning the events on the evening of December 8th.

According to the girls' testimony, Wendy, Melissa, and Michelle were staying with their two younger siblings at Mary Lou Caine's house on December 8, 1984, while Azure and their mother went out drinking. Azure and Patty had a fight and Patty went to her mother's house. Later that evening, Azure returned alone to Mary Lou Caine's house to pick up the children. He was angry and drunk and Caine did not want the children to leave with him. Azure hit Wendy and gave her a bloody nose. When Wendy went outside to put some snow on her nose, Azure grabbed her and took her back to their house. He attempted to have sexual intercourse with her in his pickup truck on the way home and again when they got home. He also forced her to have oral sex. In the morning, Wendy called Mary Lou Caine and asked if she would pick her up and take her with the rest of the children to their grandmother's house.

Caine agreed, and met Wendy across the road from Azure's home. Azure was still sleeping when Wendy left, and she asked Bill Berceir, who also lived with them, not to tell Azure where she was going.

When Wendy and Melissa went to stay with their father for Christmas, he brought them to social services personnel because he suspected they were being physically abused. Social worker Linda Heilman interviewed Wendy in late December, 1984, and Wendy told her about the episodes of sexual abuse. At Heilman's request, Wendy was examined by Dr. Warren Keene on December 31, 1984. The examination revealed that Wendy had a three centimeter healing laceration on the side wall of her vagina, which Dr. Keene testified would have resulted from some recent, painful penetration to the vaginal wall; a vaginal opening of two centimeters, which Dr. Keene stated was twice the size one would anticipate in a child of Wendy's age; and a stretched hymenal ring. Wendy also tested positive for gonorrhea.[7] Wendy told Dr. Keene that Azure had sexually abused her and that "the last time Damian did that to me was 2 or 4 weeks ago." Keene offered his opinion, based on his medical examination, that Wendy was in fact a victim of sexual abuse.

II. Discussion

A. *Exclusion of Wendy's Alleged Past Sexual Activities*

Prior to trial, defendant sought to introduce evidence of past sexual relations between Wendy and a boy named David Malterre under Fed. R.Evid. 412. Rule 412 provides that evidence of a victim's past sexual behavior is not admissible except in certain narrow situations. The relevant exception in this case states that, subject to the procedural and relevancy requirements of subdivision (c), evidence of specific instances of an alleged victim's past sexual behavior is admissible if offered "upon the issue of whether the accused was or was not, with respect to the alleged victim, the source of semen or injury." Fed.R.Evid. 412(b) (2) (A).

We have previously applied Rule 412 in the context of child abuse cases. *See United States v. Shaw,* 824 F.2d 601, 602–04 (8th Cir.1987). In *Shaw,* we affirmed the district court's exclusion of evidence of prior sexual behavior on the ground that the victim's stretched hymen did not constitute an "injury" within the meaning of Rule 412(b) (2) (A). *Id.* at 605. In this case, the victim suffered from a healing laceration on her vaginal wall; an "injury" sufficient to trigger subdivision (b) (2) (A)'s exception. The district court nonetheless excluded defendant's proffered evidence of Wendy's past sexual behavior on the ground that it was not relevant to the source of this injury. We agree.

7. Dr. Robert ten Bensel, a pediatrician and an expert on child abuse, also interviewed Wendy and reviewed the medical records in the case. He testified that in his opinion Wendy was the victim of sexual abuse, and confirmed Dr. Keene's testimony that only repeated or chronic penetration would cause the stretched hymenal ring and the two centimeter vaginal opening which was observed in Wendy. Ten Bensel also confirmed that the laceration on Wendy's vaginal wall would have been very painful; something a child would not have submitted to voluntarily.

Following defendant's Rule 412 motion, the district court held an in camera hearing at which Malterre and Patty Lozensky testified. Malterre's testimony was vague and at times contradictory. He stated that he had had consensual sexual intercourse with Wendy, but could not remember how many times. He testified it could have been between one and four times over a one and one half year period. He also could not remember any specific dates; he could only recall that the first time was when he was thirteen years old. He denied having sex with Melissa and then minutes later stated that he had had sex with Melissa. He nonetheless clearly testified that he never forced or hurt Wendy, and she never cried. At the time of trial, Malterre was living with Rose Azure, defendant's mother. Malterre had previously denied any sexual contact with Wendy and admitted at the hearing that he would like to help the defendant if he could. Lozensky testified only that Malterre had recently told her of his alleged past sexual contact with Wendy.

We believe the district court properly excluded this evidence as irrelevant to the source of the three centimeter laceration on Wendy's vaginal wall. Malterre testified that all contacts he had had with Wendy were consensual; that he never hurt her. Both Dr. Keene and Dr. ten Bensel unequivocally testified that the laceration Dr. Keene observed would be very painful; that it was an indication of force.[8] Moreover, Malterre was unable to testify that his contact with Wendy occurred during the time the laceration was received.[9] Under these circumstances, we cannot say the district court abused its discretion in excluding evidence of Wendy's alleged prior sexual activities.[10]

Defendant also claims the evidence of Wendy's alleged contact with Malterre should have been admitted for "impeachment purposes," since Wendy had previously denied any contact with Malterre, and to demonstrate Wendy's capability to fabricate a story. These are not recognized exceptions under Rule 412. As we have previously stated, the effect of Rule 412 is "to preclude the routine use of evidence of specific instances of a rape victim's prior sexual behavior." *United States v. Shaw,* 824 F.2d at 607 (citing 124 Cong.Rec. 34913 (1978) (statement of Rep. Mann)). Defendant's arguments to the contrary must be rejected.

* * *

8. Wendy testified at trial that her contacts with Azure were painful. Dr. ten Bensel also testified that Wendy told him "that there was [pain]. Every time over the length of the time that there were these alleged sexual abuses that there was pain."

9. Only a vague "guess" by Melissa when social workers questioned her about the alleged contact placed one of the incidents in November, 1984.

10. Defendant also refers in his brief to testimony by Patty Lozensky that Wendy came home from school one day in the summer of 1984 bleeding from her vagina and admitted the injury stemmed from an attempt to masturbate with a bottle. This testimony was not mentioned in defendant's Rule 412 motion and hence was not properly before the *United States v. Shaw,* 824 F.2d 601, 603 n.2 (8th Cir.1987); Fed. R.Evid. 412(c) (1). Even assuming it was, we find no error in the district court's exclusion of any references to the alleged incident since, as the court found, there was no showing that it could have caused the injury Dr. Keene observed in December, 1984.

III. Conclusion

For all of the foregoing reasons, the judgment of the district court is affirmed.

Notes

1. *Statutory exceptions.* Where rape shield laws enumerate exceptions, the most frequent are those specifically set forth in Rule 412: (1) prior sexual activity with the accused and (2) evidence going to the source of semen or injury. Yet, the possibilities for exceptions are seemingly endless. Many of the cases are discussed in Galvin, Shielding Rape Victims in the State and Federal Courts: A Proposal for the Second Decade, 70 Minn.L.Rev. 763 (1986). Cases in which the defense seeks to set up a pattern of prior conduct are perhaps the most frequent. See, e.g., People v. Hackett, 365 N.W.2d 120 (Mich.1985). Attempts to show that the victim was likely to have fantasized the event (as suggested by Wigmore) also are frequent. See, e.g., State v. Clarke, 343 N.W.2d 158 (Iowa 1984). North Carolina specifically makes such evidence an exception to the rule if offered as the basis of expert opinion. N.C.Evid.R. 412(b)(4).

2. *Types of rape shield statutes.* Galvin, note 1, supra, thoroughly describes and analyses the current statutes by dividing them into several groups. In addition to the Federal Rule pattern with both its specific and catch-all exceptions (followed in seven jurisdictions), she identifies: (1) the "Michigan" group which prohibits the introduction of sexual conduct evidence subject to certain enumerated exceptions (25 states); (2) the "Texas" group under which the trial judge, after an in camera hearing, has nearly unfettered discretion to admit sexual conduct under traditional relevancy standards (11 states); (3) the "California" group where evidence is categorized either as substantive or credibility evidence and then excluded generally subject to a few exceptions (7 states). Contrast the state of the law in the Galvin article published in 1986, with its more than 150 pages of discussion of current rape shield statutes, with the leading piece on this question published in 1977: Berger, Man's Trial, Woman's Tribulation: Rape Cases in the Courtroom, 77 Colum.L.Rev. 1 (1977). See also Althouse, Thelma and Louise and the Law: Do Rape Shield Rules Matter?, 25 Loy.L.A.L.Rev. 757 (1992); Ordover, Admissibility of Patterns of Similar Sexual Conduct: The Unlamented Death of Character for Chastity, 63 Cornell L.Rev. 90 (1977).

3. *Exception for accused-complaint conduct.* The courts have not always admitted evidence of prior sexual conduct with the defendant. See, e.g., United States v. Ramone, 218 F.3d 1229, 1238 (10th Cir.2000) (In a case involving armed aggravated assault and sexual abuse, the court stated: "[I]t is difficult to discern what relevance the testimony could have to Ramone's consent defense. We can not agree with the defendant that evidence of prior consensual use of inanimate objects during sex is probative of whether sex after a brutal beating was consensual."); State v. Hopkins, 377 N.W.2d 110, 116–17 (Neb.1985) (ruling that evidence of the victim's prior sexual conduct with the defendant was not admissible where the defendant failed at the in camera hearing to introduce any evidence that the victim had consented to the sexual act at issue in the case).

REDMOND v. KINGSTON

United States Court of Appeals, Seventh Circuit, 2001.
240 F.3d 590.

POSNER, CIRCUIT JUDGE.

* * * The petitioner, Redmond, a counselor at an institution for drug-and alcohol-abusing minors, was convicted of statutory rape of Heather, a 15-year-old resident of the institution. The specific charge was that he had traded cocaine to her for sex. The state acknowledged at argument that the principal evidence of the offense was Heather's testimony and that of another resident, Michelle, who, however, merely repeated what Heather had told her had happened. There was also evidence that Heather had tested positive for cocaine after the alleged offense but that she had a long history of using cocaine and might have gotten it from someone other than Redmond or for something other than sex.

Eleven months before the alleged offense, Heather had told her mother that she had been forcibly raped, and she had offered her torn clothes as evidence. She had repeated the story of the rape, with many circumstantial details, to a hospital nurse and to a police officer investigating the incident, but later had admitted making up the story (and ripping her clothes herself) in order to get her mother's attention. Her new story was that she had had sex with the man she had accused of forcible rape, but that it had been with her consent. Since she was underage, the police continued to investigate the incident as a crime. The man was never found, and there is no evidence other than Heather's say-so that the incident actually occurred. There is no serious doubt that her recantation of the forcible-rape story was truthful. Redmond offered more than thirty police reports of the investigation of Heather's claim that she had been forcibly raped, convincingly demonstrating its falsity, and in addition the district attorney had instituted contempt charges against Heather. * * *

Redmond wanted to bring out her lie on cross-examination in order to show that Heather would lie about a sexual assault in order to get attention, and thus had a motive to accuse him falsely. The trial judge, seconded by the Wisconsin court of appeals, refused to permit this cross-examination. The court of appeals held that although the state's rape-shield law makes an exception for a prior false charge of sexual assault, Wis. Stat. § 972.11(2) (b)3, Heather's false charge did not have "sufficient probative value to outweigh its inflammatory and prejudicial nature," and therefore, under another section of the statute, § 971.31(11), it was inadmissible. The court thought the false charge merely "cumulative of other evidence which went to Heather's credibility," namely that she had begun using drugs at the age of 12, had stolen and occasionally danced (!) to obtain money for cocaine, had run away from the institution, had skipped school, and had told lies in the past. Furthermore, the court thought the evidence of the false charge might have "confused the issue" since "the initial recantation involved consent which was not an element of the current charges," and also that it might have misled the jury "into focusing on Heather's willingness to have sexual intercourse with a complete stranger, instead of on the charges against Redmond." State v. Redmond, 1996 WL 485095, at *10 (Wis.App.1996).

With all due respect, we believe that the court of appeals' analysis and conclusion cannot be considered a reasonable application of the Supreme Court's confrontation doctrine. * * * The evidence of the false charge of forcible rape was not cumulative of other evidence bearing on Heather's credibility, because none of the other evidence either involved a false charge of being sexually assaulted or furnished a motive for such a charge. The fact that a teenage girl has a disordered past and lies a lot (who doesn't?) does not predict that she will make up stories about having sex. To indulge such an assumption would be to place such persons largely beyond the protection of the law. But the fact that the girl had led her mother, a nurse, and the police on a wild goose chase for a rapist merely to get her mother's attention supplied a powerful reason for disbelieving her testimony eleven months later about having sex with another man, by showing that she had a motive for what would otherwise be an unusual fabrication. * * *

The evidence thus was not cumulative, or otherwise peripheral, considering that testimony by Heather was virtually the only evidence of Redmond's guilt that the prosecution had. Nor was the evidence of her previous false charge of rape prejudicial to the state, except insofar as its prejudicial effect was a function of its probative weight, which of course is not the relevant meaning of prejudice. * * * The prejudice that offsets probative weight has to inhere in some extraneous fact, such as embarrassing but irrelevant details or, as the court believed, in the potential of the evidence to confuse the trier of fact. But in concluding that there was a danger of confusion the court committed a fatal analytical mistake. It assumed that Heather would be required or permitted to testify that she had had consensual sex with the alleged rapist, evidence barred by the rape-shield law. The only evidence that was relevant to her credibility in Redmond's case, however, the only evidence she would or should have been permitted to give on that subject, was that within the preceding year she had made up a story about being forcibly raped. Whether or not she had had sex with the alleged rapist was irrelevant, since Redmond was not prepared to try to prove that she had not. For unexplained reasons the Wisconsin court of appeals thought that if Redmond's lawyer had been permitted to ask Heather whether she had ever made a false charge of forcible sexual assault, the door would have been opened to an inquiry into whether she had had sex on that occasion at all. We cannot think of any reason why. The state could not have used the "fact" that Heather had had sex with the alleged forcible rapist to show that she fabricates only tales of being *forcibly* raped, because, all objections based on the rape-shield statute to one side, the state can no more show that Heather had sex with the alleged rapist than Redmond can show the contrary.

And thus the court's ruling, though ostensibly based on the rape-shield statute, derives no support from that statute. The statute protects complaining witnesses in rape cases (including statutory-rape cases) from being questioned about their sexual conduct, but a false charge of rape is not sexual conduct. See Wis. Stat. § 972.11(2) (a) (defining such conduct); * * * . The false-charge "exception" to the rape-shield statute is not really an exception, but rather a reminder of the limited meaning of "sexual conduct" as defined in the statute. The only basis for the court's ruling was the general principle of the law of evidence, which is codified for federal trials in Fed.R.Evid. 403 but is equally a principle of Wisconsin's law of evidence, see Wis. Stat. § 904.03, that relevant evidence may be excluded if its probative value is substantially outweighed by its prejudicial (confusing, or cumulative) effect. When that unexceptionable rule is applied as it was here to exclude highly probative, noncumulative, nonconfusing, nonprejudicial evidence tendered by a criminal defendant that is vital to the central issue in the case (Heather's credibility), the defendant's constitutional right of confrontation has been infringed. Olden v. Kentucky, 488 U.S. 227, 232 * * * (1988) (per curiam) * * *.

Olden is factually very similar to the present case, which eliminates any question about the scope of the applicable federal doctrine declared by the Supreme Court, while cases such as Hogan v. Hanks, 97 F.3d 189, 191 (7th Cir.1996), and United States v. Bartlett, 856 F.2d 1071, 1087–89 (8th Cir.1988), which upheld the exclusion from evidence of false rape charges, are readily distinguishable. They are cases in which the defendant wanted to use the falsity of the charges to demonstrate that the complaining witness was a liar, rather than to demonstrate that she had a motive to lodge a false accusation against the defendant. The use of evidence that a person has lied in the past to show that she is lying now is questionable, quite apart from rape-shield laws, since very few people, other than the occasional saint, go through life without ever lying, unless they are under oath. Cf. Fed.R.Evid. 404(b), 608(b); Hogan v. Hanks, supra, 97 F.3d at 191; * * *. The probative value of such evidence when used for such a purpose is small and may be outweighed by the prejudicial effect of revealing that the witness had made such a serious charge falsely. United States v. Bartlett, supra, 856 F.2d at 1088–89. But while "generally applicable evidentiary rules limit inquiry into specific instances of conduct through the use of extrinsic evidence and through cross-examination with respect to general credibility attacks, * * * no such limit applies to credibility attacks based upon motive or bias," Quinn v. Haynes, 234 F.3d 837, 845 (4th Cir.2000)—as in this case.

* * *

Reversed.

Notes

1. *Constitutional issues.* The limitations placed by rape shield statutes on the accused's ability to cross-examine the prosecution's principal witness have given rise to frequent constitutional challenges both to the rape shield statutes on their face and to particular applications of those laws. The language of Rule 412 is obviously an attempt to circumvent such attacks. For a discussion of the constitutional problems generally, see Tanford & Bocchino, Rape Victim Shield Laws and the Sixth Amendment, 128 U.Pa.L.Rev. 544 (1980); Comment, 1985 Wis.L.Rev. 1219. Most courts have upheld the constitutionality of the statutes. See, e.g., Bell v. Harrison, 670 F.2d 656 (6th Cir.1982); People v. Hackett, 365 N.W.2d 120 (Mich.1985). But see State v. Jalo, 557 P.2d 1359 (Or.Ct.App.1976) (en banc).

2. *Olden v. Kentucky.* In Olden v. Kentucky, 488 U.S. 227 (1988) (per curiam), an alleged rape victim testified that Olden had tricked her into leaving a bar, raped her, and then drove her to the house of Bill Russell, where she was released. Russell, also a prosecution witness, testified that he had seen the victim leave Olden's car and that she had immediately complained of rape. The defense claimed consent, arguing that the victim and Russell were involved in an extramarital relationship and that the victim fabricated the rape story to explain to Russell why she was in the defendant's car. By the time of trial, the victim and Russell were living together, but the trial judge refused to permit cross-examination on this fact. The judge believed that this information would prejudice the jury against the victim because she was white and Russell was African American. The Supreme Court reversed. Olden had consistently maintained that the alleged victim lied because she feared jeopardizing her relationship with Russell. Thus, her current living arrangement with Russell was relevant to impeachment, and foreclosure of this line of inquiry violated the right of confrontation.

3. *False accusations of rape.* Several courts have taken the position that evidence of past accusations of sexual assault is not protected under rape shield rules. See, e.g., Miller v. State, 779 P.2d 87 (Nev.1989). The Advisory Committee note to amended Federal Rule 412 states: "Evidence offered to prove allegedly false prior claims by the victim is not barred by Rule 412. However, this evidence is subject to the requirements of Rule 404." A rape accusation could be false for either of two reasons: first, there was never any sexual intercourse, or second, there was intercourse but it was consensual. The latter situation involves sexual history and could come within a rape shield law depending the law's scope. If such evidence is admissible, most courts hold that the prior allegation must have been demonstrably false. See People v. Weiss, 133 P.3d 1180, 1187 (Colo.2006) ("[T]hese provisions require[] the defense, in its offer of proof affidavit, to articulate facts which, if demonstrated at the evidentiary hearing, would show that the alleged victim made multiple prior or subsequent reports of sexual assault that were in fact false. An allegation that charges were not brought as a result of these sexual assault reports is insufficient * * *."); State v. West, 24 P.3d 648, 655 (Haw.2001) ("[N]early every jurisdiction

addressing this question has consistently required a preliminary determination of falsity prior to the admission of allegedly false statements of unrelated sexual assaults. * * * Furthermore, as some courts have explained, where the truth or falsity of a statement regarding an unrelated sexual assault is unknown, it falls within the purview of the rape shield statute and must be analyzed accordingly.").

4. *Bias v. untruthful character.* In Boggs v. Collins, 226 F.3d 728, 739–40 (6th Cir.2000), the court drew a distinction between bias, which is often admissible under the Confrontation Clause, and a more general attack on character, which is not. It stated:

> [W]e must reject Boggs's primary argument because it improperly blurs the precise distinctions drawn in Confrontation Clause jurisprudence. Not having articulated an argument sounding in motive, bias or prejudice, Boggs instead seeks to elevate his purpose—attacking Berman's general credibility—into a constitutionally mandated right. * * * No matter how central an accuser's credibility is to a case—indeed, her credibility will almost always be the cornerstone of a rape or sexual assault case, even if there is physical evidence—the Constitution does not *require* that a defendant be given the opportunity to wage a general attack on credibility by pointing to individual instances of past conduct.

5. *Alternate sources of knowledge.* See LaJoie v. Thompson, 217 F.3d 663, 673 (9th Cir.2000) (Constitution required admissibility of evidence of prior rape to show that victim could have learned about sexual acts and male genitalia from source other than defendant accused of rape); State v. Rolon, 777 A.2d 604 (Conn.2001) (exclusion violated right of confrontation); State v. Grovenstein, 530 S.E.2d 406, 410 (S.C.Ct.App.2000) ("Other jurisdictions have concluded that evidence of a young victim's sexual history is relevant where the defendant seeks to admit the evidence to show a source for the victim's sexual knowledge. Specifically, these courts found the evidence relevant to rebut the inference that a child victim could not describe the sexual acts unless the defendant had committed the alleged acts."). See also State v. Bass, 465 S.E.2d 334 (N.C.Ct.App.1996) (upholding trial court's exclusion of evidence of a child/victim's past sexual abuse but reversing because state had argued to the jury that child would have had no prior knowledge of the types of conduct she had testified about).

6. *Notice requirement.* See United States v. Rouse, 111 F.3d 561, 569 (8th Cir.1997) ("The Rule has strict procedural requirements, including a timely offer of proof delineating what evidence will be offered and for what purpose, and an *in camera* hearing at which the victim may respond. Defendants' vague notice fell far short of complying with the Rule, and the district court properly excluded this evidence.").

7. *Sanctions.* In Michigan v. Lucas, 500 U.S. 145 (1991), the United States Supreme Court ruled that the exclusion of defense evidence for failing to comply with the notice provision of a rape shield statute was not per se unconstitutional. The Court indicated, however, that exclusion in a particular case may be unconstitutional.

(4) ACCUSED'S CHARACTER: FEDERAL RULES 413–15

UNITED STATES v. LEMAY

United States Court of Appeals, Ninth Circuit, 2001.
260 F.3d 1018.

TROTT, CIRCUIT JUDGE:

Fred LeMay appeals his convictions for two counts of child molestation * * *. LeMay lived on the Fort Peck Reservation from 1991 to 1998, and intermittently resided at the home of his sister, Justine Shields, and her husband, Daniel Renz. Shields and Renz had several young children, for whom LeMay often babysat. One such instance occurred during the summer of 1997. Shields and Renz had gone out for the evening, leaving LeMay to watch their children D.R. and A.R., two boys ages five and seven.

LeMay made both children orally copulate with him while their parents were away and threatened to beat them up if they told anyone. Undeterred, the boys informed their mother of the abuse the next morning. Although Shields refused to let LeMay babysit for her children after that, she did not report the incident, look for evidence, or take the boys to a doctor or a counselor. Two years later, however, law enforcement authorities got wind of LeMay's abuse of the children and investigated the allegations. LeMay was eventually arrested and charged with child molestation.

Before trial, the prosecutor gave notice of her intent to introduce evidence of LeMay's prior acts of sexual misconduct under Rule 414 of the Federal Rules of Evidence. * * *

As in the 1997 incident for which LeMay was charged, LeMay sexually abused the children while babysitting for them [in 1989]. Francine LeMay returned from the grocery store to find her two-year old daughter upset and bruised. Upon confrontation, Francine LeMay extracted an admission from LeMay that he had "put his penis in" the older child's mouth. Francine LeMay also found a cream-like substance in her infant's vagina when she changed her diaper, and implied that this substance was semen. In a subsequent juvenile adjudication, LeMay was found guilty of rape. * * *

At trial, the prosecution called both A.R. and D.R., who by that time were seven and nine years old. Both boys remembered the incidents and testified consistently. The prosecution also called the boys' mother, Justine Shields. Because Shields had not informed anyone that LeMay had molested her children, the prosecution was unable to offer any forensic, medical, or psychological evidence that the boys had been abused, and the case therefore rested on their testimony.

LeMay took advantage of this lack of evidence in his opening statement, arguing that no eyewitnesses or medical or scientific experts would corroborate the testimony of A.R. and D.R. Further, in cross-examining the boys, LeMay's counsel attempted to call into question their ability to remember events accurately. He also suggested that the boys might have a motive to lie because they were currently in foster care, and that they might have thought that accusing LeMay of molesting them would be a way to be reunited with their parents. * * *

[The prosecutor] first called Francine LeMay, who testified about the defendant's abuse of her children in Oregon in 1989. Ms. LeMay, who began her testimony in tears, described generally how she had discovered that LeMay had abused her daughters and how she had gotten him to admit to that abuse. The prosecution's final witness established that LeMay had been found guilty of rape in a juvenile adjudication. After these witnesses, the prosecution closed its case.

* * *

The jury found LeMay guilty of both counts of molestation, and the district judge sentenced him to 405 months in prison.* * *

B. Due Process

Prior to 1994, when Rules 413 through 415 were passed, admission of a defendant's prior crimes or acts was governed by Rule 404(b), which disallows such evidence when used to prove "the character of a person in order to show action in conformity therewith." * * *

The Supreme Court has held that the primary guide for determining whether a rule is so "fundamental" as to be embodied in the Constitution is historical practice. * * * In this case, however, evidence of historical practice does not lead to a clear conclusion. On the one hand, it seems clear that the general ban on propensity evidence has the requisite historical pedigree to qualify for constitutional status. *See, e.g.,* McKinney v. Rees, 993 F.2d 1378, 1384–85 (9th Cir.1993) (holding in the context of a murder prosecution that "[t]he character rule is based on * * * a 'fundamental conception of justice' and the 'community's sense of fair play and decency' "); Old Chief v. United States, 519 U.S. 172, 182 * * * (1997) (stating in dicta that "[t]here is * * * no question that propensity would be an 'improper basis' for conviction"); Michelson v. United States, 335 U.S. 469, 475–76 * * * (1948) (noting in dicta that "[c]ourts that follow the common-law tradition almost unanimously have come to disallow resort by the prosecution to any kind of evidence of a defendant's evil character to establish a probability of his guilt").

On the other hand, courts have routinely allowed propensity evidence in sex-offense cases, even while disallowing it in other criminal prosecutions. In many American jurisdictions, evidence of a defendant's prior acts of sexual misconduct is commonly admitted in prosecutions for offenses such as rape, incest, adultery, and child molestation. *See, e.g.,* 2 JOHN H. WIGMORE, WIGMORE ON EVIDENCE, §§ 398–402. As early as 1858, the Michigan Supreme Court noted that "courts in several of the States have shown a disposition to relax the rule [against propensity evidence] in cases where the offense consists of illicit intercourse between the sexes." People v. Jenness, 5 Mich. 305, 319–20, 1858 WL 2321 at *8 (Mich.1858). Today, state courts that do not have evidentiary rules comparable to Federal Rules 414 through 415 allow this evidence either by stretching traditional 404(b) exceptions to the ban on character evidence or by resorting to the so-called "lustful disposition" exception, which, in its purest form, is a rule allowing for propensity inferences in sex crime cases. * * * Thus, "the history of evidentiary rules regarding a criminal defendant's sexual propensities is ambiguous at best, particularly with regard to sexual abuse of children." United States v. Castilló, 140 F.3d 874, 881 (10th Cir.1998). * * *

The historical evidence in this case thus leads to no clear conclusion. In holding that Rule 414 is constitutional, we therefore do not rely solely on the fact that courts have historically allowed propensity evidence to reach the jury in sex offense cases. Because LeMay has the burden of proving that the ban on propensity evidence is a matter of fundamental fairness, the divergence in historical evidence does cut against his position. * * * Yet while we recognize the importance of historical practice in determining whether an evidentiary rule is embodied in the Due Process Clause, in this case, we find it necessary to conduct an independent inquiry into whether allowing propensity inferences violates fundamental ideas of fairness. * * *

With the protections of the Rule 403 balancing test still in place, LeMay's due-process challenge to Rule 414 loses much of its force. The evidence that he had sexually molested his cousins in 1989 was indisputably relevant to the issue of whether he had done the same thing to his nephews in 1997. *See, e.g.,* Michelson, 335 U.S. at 475 * * * (noting that defendant's prior crimes or ill name "might logically be persuasive that he is by propensity a probable perpetrator of the crime"). The introduction of relevant evidence, by itself, cannot amount to a constitutional violation. * * *

The introduction of such evidence can amount to a constitutional violation only if its prejudicial effect far outweighs its probative value. In *McKinney*, we granted a writ of habeas corpus and overturned a murder conviction where the petitioner's trial had been infused with highly inflammatory evidence of almost no relevance. *See* McKinney, 993 F.2d at 1384–85. LeMay, of course, emphasizes that *McKinney* held that the ban on propensity evidence is of constitutional magnitude. What he misses, however, is the fact that we held that such evidence will only *sometimes* violate the constitutional right to a fair trial, if it is of no relevance, or if its potential for prejudice far outweighs what little relevance it might have. Potentially devastating evidence of little or no relevance would have to be excluded under Rule 403. Indeed, this is exactly what Rule 403 was designed to do. We therefore conclude that as long as the protections of Rule 403 remain in place so that district judges retain the authority to exclude potentially devastating evidence, Rule 414 is constitutional. * * *

C. Rule 403

* * * Rule 403 provides that relevant evidence may be excluded, among other reasons, if "its probative value is substantially outweighed

by the danger of unfair prejudice." FED. R. EVID. 403. In *Glanzer*, we stated that "[b]ecause of the inherent strength of the evidence that is covered by [Rule 414], when putting this type of evidence through the [Rule 403] microscope, a court should pay 'careful attention to both the significant probative value and the strong prejudicial qualities' of that evidence." [United States v.] Glanzer, 232 F.3d at 1268 (quoting United States v. Guardia, 135 F.3d 1326, 1330 (10th Cir.1998)). We also articulated several factors that district judges must evaluate in determining whether to admit evidence of a defendant's prior acts of sexual misconduct. These factors are: (1) "the similarity of the prior acts to the acts charged," (2) the "closeness in time of the prior acts to the acts charged," (3) "the frequency of the prior acts," (4) the "presence or lack of intervening circumstances," and (5) "the necessity of the evidence beyond the testimonies already offered at trial." Id. We also stated that this list of factors is not exclusive, and that district judges should consider other factors relevant to individual cases. Id.

We had not decided *Glanzer* at the time of LeMay's trial and so the district judge did not explicitly consider each of the factors we articulated there in making his 403 ruling. However, the district judge did conduct just the sort of searching inquiry we deemed necessary in *Glanzer*. He held an extensive pre-trial hearing, at which he grilled the prosecutor about all aspects of Rule 414, and questioned her as to why she needed the prior acts evidence and how she intended to introduce it. The judge also reserved the Rule 403 decision until after the prosecution had introduced all its other evidence, in order to get a feel for the evidence as it developed at trial before ruling on whether LeMay's prior acts of child molestation could come in. After hearing the opening statements and the prosecutor's case, the judge concluded that the prior molestations were relevant to bolster the credibility of D.R. and A.R., and to rebut the suggestion that there was no evidence to corroborate their testimony. Finally, the district court reminded the jury in its final instructions that, while it could consider the prior acts evidence for any matter which it deemed relevant, it could only convict LeMay for the charged crimes. In short, although the district judge did not discuss the specific factors we deemed relevant in *Glanzer*, the record reveals that he exercised his discretion to admit the evidence in a careful and judicious manner.

We also conclude that admitting LeMay's prior acts of molestation was proper in light of the factors we discussed in *Glanzer* and others relevant to this particular case. We begin by noting, as the district judge did, that the evidence of LeMay's prior acts of child molestation was highly relevant. The 1989 molestations were very similar to the charged crimes. Each case involved forced oral copulation. In each case the victims were young relatives of LeMay, and each instance occurred while LeMay was babysitting them.

Moreover, as the district judge suggested, the prior acts evidence was relevant to bolster the credibility of the victims after LeMay suggested they could be fabricating the accusations. The evidence also countered

LeMay's claim that there was no evidence corroborating the testimony of D.R. and A.R.

We recognize that this characterization of the evidence is essentially a veiled propensity inference. *See, e.g.,* Wright & Graham, 22 FEDERAL PRACTICE AND PROCEDURE § 5248 (noting that use of prior act evidence to "corroborate" testimony of victims is propensity evidence if it "depends upon an inference to the defendant's character"). However, it is also exactly the sort of use of prior acts evidence that Congress had in mind when enacting Rule 414. *See* 140 Cong. Rec. H8991–92 (August 21, 1994) (statement of Rep. Molinari) (noting that child molestation cases "require reliance on child victims whose credibility can readily be attacked in the absence of substantial corroboration"). The case against LeMay rested on testimony of D.R. and A.R. Both children were very young at the time of the incidents, and two years had passed before LeMay was tried. LeMay attacked their credibility and suggested that there was not enough evidence to prove their allegations. That this case made use of the prior acts evidence in precisely the manner Congress contemplated strongly indicates that its admission was not an abuse of discretion.

Additionally, the evidence of LeMay's prior abuse of his cousins was also highly reliable. LeMay had been convicted of at least one of the rape charges arising from the incidents in Oregon. Because LeMay had admitted to abusing his cousins, Francine LeMay's testimony fell within a well-established exception to the hearsay rule. To the extent that allowing the evidence permitted a propensity inference, it was an inference based on proven facts and LeMay's own admissions, not rumor, innuendo, or prior uncharged acts capable of multiple characterizations. Thus, although we do not suggest that district courts may *only* introduce prior acts of molestation for which a defendant has been tried and found guilty, we hold that the extent to which an act has been proved is a factor that district courts may consider in conducting the Rule 403 inquiry.

We must also consider the remoteness in time of LeMay's prior acts of molestation, the frequency of prior similar acts, and whether any intervening events bear on the relevance of the prior similar acts. *See* Glanzer, 232 F.3d at 1268. The "intervening events" factor seems to have little relevance in the present case, and the other two cut in favor of the government. About eleven years had passed between LeMay's abuse of his nieces and his trial for the abuse of D.R. and A.R. We have held, in the context of Rule 404(b), that the lapse of twelve years does not render the decision to admit relevant evidence of similar prior acts an abuse of discretion. *See* United States v. Rude, 88 F.3d 1538, 1550 (9th Cir.1996). The "frequency of events" factor discussed in *Glanzer* also cuts in favor of the government. Although it was not introduced at trial, the government also had evidence of a third incident in which LeMay had sexually abused his young relatives. True, this incident occurred even before the 1989 abuse of his cousins when LeMay himself was extremely young, and, as the prosecutor noted, was "triple hearsay."

However, that there was evidence of a third similar incident suggests that LeMay's abuse of his cousins in 1989 was not an isolated occurrence.

Glanzer also instructs that courts must consider whether the prior acts evidence was necessary to prove the case. This factor also supports the government's position and indicates that the district judge did not abuse his discretion in admitting the evidence. The prosecution's case rested on the testimony of A.R. and D.R. No other scientific, forensic, medical, or psychological witness was available. LeMay had attacked the credibility of the boys and capitalized on the lack of eyewitness and expert testimony. That the prosecutor claimed that she could get a conviction without introducing LeMay's prior acts of molestation does not suggest that the evidence was not "necessary." Prior acts evidence need not be *absolutely necessary* to the prosecution's case in order to be introduced; it must simply be helpful or *practically necessary.*

Finally, Francine LeMay's testimony was necessary to establish that LeMay's 1989 molestations were very similar, and thus relevant, to the charged crimes. We reject the idea that the district court should have limited the prosecution to merely proving that LeMay had been convicted of rape eleven years before. The relevance of the prior act evidence was in the details. Establishing the simple fact of conviction would leave out the information that LeMay had been convicted of sexually abusing his young relatives, by forced oral copulation, while they were in his care. Francine LeMay's testimony was necessary to fill in the details that made the prior rape conviction relevant. Therefore, the "necessity" factor favors the government in all respects.

Several factors do admittedly favor LeMay. LeMay himself was only twelve years old at the time of the 1989 molestations. And foremost, of course, is the emotional and highly charged nature of Francine LeMay's testimony. Although we, as an appellate court, are not in a position to evaluate how great an effect Francine LeMay's testimony had on the jury, we do not doubt that it was powerful. Francine LeMay began her testimony in tears, and certainly, her suggestion that LeMay had raped her infant daughter would have been particularly shocking. However, evidence of a defendant's prior acts of molestation will always be emotionally charged and inflammatory, as is the evidence that he committed the charged crimes. Thus, that prior acts evidence is inflammatory is not dispositive in and of itself. Rather, district judges must carefully evaluate the potential inflammatory nature of the proffered testimony, and balance it with that which the jury has already heard, the relevance of the evidence, the necessity of introducing it, and all the other relevant factors discussed above. The record here shows that the district judge did just that. Therefore, admitting LeMay's prior acts of molestation was not an abuse of discretion.

All in all, the record shows that the district judge struck a careful balance between LeMay's rights and the clear intent of Congress that evidence of prior similar acts be admitted in child molestation prosecutions.

* * * [The court also rejected equal protection and other arguments.]

Affirmed.

PAEZ, CIRCUIT JUDGE, concurring in part and dissenting in part:

I concur in all but Discussion § C of the majority's decision. I respectfully dissent from the majority's holding that the district court did not abuse its discretion in admitting the evidence under Fed.R.Evid. 403. I would reverse the district court's Rule 403 ruling and remand for reconsideration in light of our decision in Doe by Rudy–Glanzer v. Glanzer, 232 F.3d 1258 (9th Cir.2000) (hereinafter *Glanzer*). * * *

Rules 413, 414, and 415 were extraordinarily controversial at the time of their passage. The Judicial Conference Advisory Committee on Evidence Rules and the Judicial Conference Committee on Rules of Practice and Procedure both voted overwhelmingly to oppose the rules because they "would permit the introduction of unreliable but highly prejudicial evidence * * *." Fed.R.Evid. 413 hist. notes. The report submitted by the Judicial Conference to Congress expressed "significant concern" about the "danger of convicting a criminal defendant for past, as opposed to charged, behavior or for being a bad person." *Id.*

Nevertheless, there are benefits to these rules. As members of Congress repeatedly recognized, "[i]n most rape or molestation cases, it is the word of the defendant against the word of the victim. If the defendant has committed similar acts in the past, the claims of the victim are more likely to be considered truthful if there is substantiation of other assaults." 140 Cong. Rec. H5437–03, *H5439 (daily ed. June 29, 1994) (statement of Rep. Kyl). This case, with two child victims and no other witnesses, is precisely the type of case for which Fed.R.Evid. 414 was designed.

As courts, we are left to balance the public's interest in convicting those charged with sexual abuse crimes, as expressed in these evidentiary rules, with the right of the accused to be convicted only for the crime charged, and not his previous acts. LeMay served his sentence for his previous criminal acts, and he may not be punished again, unless the government can prove that he committed new crimes as well. The best way for district courts to balance these competing interests is to conduct the Rule 403 analysis on the record, carefully considering each of the factors, and others as necessary, identified by this court in *Glanzer*. * * *

In this case, the district court made no record of its Rule 403 analysis at all. Unlike *Glanzer*, there was much more the district court could—and should—have done. In fact, the district court did not even identify the probative value of the evidence, only describing it as "relevant." There is a marked difference between describing evidence as relevant and describing it as having probative value significant enough to outweigh any unfair prejudicial effect. * * *

In this case, the district court found that evidence of LeMay's prior conviction was "relevant" to bolstering the child witnesses' credibility and to rebutting the suggestion that there was no proof that a crime actually occurred. But the district court later made an explicit factual finding that the two victims were "extremely credible," that their testimony was clear, and that they testified with certitude and impressive demeanor. This, combined with the prosecution's own assertion that the children's testimony alone was sufficient for a conviction, suggests that the prior acts evidence had minimal probative value. That minimal probative value should have been weighed against the risk of unfair prejudice to LeMay.

Because the district court did not conduct the 403 balancing on the record and consider the *Glanzer* factors, I would find that it abused its discretion. * * *

Notes and Questions

1. *Legislative history.* The congressional enactment of Rules 413–415 was delayed for 150 days in order to permit the Judicial Conference to submit recommendations with regard to the admissibility of such evidence. The Conference urged Congress to reconsider these rules: "[T]he new rules, which are not supported by empirical evidence, could diminish significantly the protections that have safeguarded persons accused in criminal cases and parties in civil cases against undue prejudice. These protections form a fundamental part of American jurisprudence and have evolved under long-standing rules and case law. A significant concern identified by the [Standing] committee was the danger of convicting a criminal defendant for past, as opposed to charged, behavior or for being a bad person. In addition, * * * because prior bad acts would be admissible even though not the subject of a conviction, mini-trials within trials concerning those acts would result when a defendant seeks to rebut such evidence." Report of the Judicial Conference on the Admission of Character Evidence in Certain Sexual Misconduct Cases, 159 F.R.D. 51, 53 (1995). Congress enacted the rules without change.

2. *Change in law.* See United States v. LeCompte, 131 F.3d 767, 768 (8th Cir.1997) ("The admissibility of T.T.'s testimony has been considered by this Court once before. In LeCompte's first trial, the government offered the evidence under Rule 404(b). It was not then able to offer the evidence under Rule 414 because of its failure to provide timely notice of the offer, as required by Rule 414. The District Court admitted the evidence, and the jury convicted LeCompte. On appeal, this Court held that the District Court's admission of the evidence under Rule 404(b) was improper, and reversed LeCompte's conviction. United States v. LeCompte, 99 F.3d 274 (8th Cir. 1996). We now consider the admissibility of T.T.'s testimony in LeCompte's retrial, under Rule 414, the government having given timely notice the second time around." The court ruled the evidence admissible.).

3. *Recidivism rationale.* Is recidivism a convincing rationale for treating character evidence differently in sexual assault or child molestation cases

than in other cases? See Baker, Once a Rapist? Motivational Evidence and Relevancy in Rape Law, 110 Harv.L.Rev. 563, 578 (1997) ("A 1989 Bureau of Justice Statistics recidivism study found that only 7.7% of released rapists were rearrested for rape. In contrast, 33.5% of released larcenists were rearrested for larceny; 31.9% of released burglars were rearrested for burglary; and 24.8% of drug offenders were rearrested for drug offenses."). Are molestation cases different? See Prentky et al., Recidivism Rates Among Child Molesters and Rapists: A Methodological Analysis, 21 Law & Hum.Behav. 635 (1997).

4. *Equal Protection.* See United States v. Mound, 149 F.3d 799, 801 (8th Cir.1998) ("Promoting the effective prosecution of sex offenses is a legitimate end. The legislative history of Rule 413 indicates good reasons why Congress believed that the rule was 'justified by the distinctive characteristics of the cases it will affect.' 140 Cong. Rec. H8991 (daily ed. Aug. 21, 1994) (statement of Rep. Molinari). These characteristics included the reliance of sex offense cases on difficult credibility determinations that 'would otherwise become unresolvable swearing matches,' as well as, in the case of child sexual abuse, the 'exceptionally probative' value of a defendant's sexual interest in children.").

5. *Due process and Rule 403.* See United States v. Enjady, 134 F.3d 1427, 1433 (10th Cir.1998) ("Considering the safeguards of Rule 403, we conclude that Rule 413 is not unconstitutional on its face as a violation of the Due Process Clause."); United States v. Castillo, 140 F.3d 874, 883 (10th Cir.1998) ("The due process violation that the defendant alleges here is that Rule 414 evidence is so prejudicial that it violates the defendant's fundamental right to a fair trial. Application of Rule 403, however, should always result in the exclusion of evidence that has such a prejudicial effect.").

6. *Rule 403 balancing.* Compare United States v. Guardia, 135 F.3d 1326, 1331 (10th Cir.1998) (Rule 413 "contains no language that supports an especially lenient application of Rule 403."), with United States v. Meacham, 115 F.3d 1488, 1492 (10th Cir.1997) ("Rule 403 balancing is still applicable, * * * but clearly under Rule 414 the courts are to 'liberally' admit evidence of prior uncharged sex offenses."). See also Orenstein, Deviance, Due Process, and the False Promise of Federal Rule of Evidence 403, 90 Cornell L.Rev. 1487, 1519, 1520 (2005) ("Propensity shifted from being the quintessential example of unfair prejudice to being a permissible—and indeed officially endorsed—method of proving guilt. * * * In practice, despite their dicta to the contrary, the courts have weakened Rule 403 by tending to admit evidence of prior sexual offenses automatically under a pro forma approach to Rule 403 ['403–lite'].").

7. *Relevant factors.* Other courts have proposed different factors. See United States v. Enjady, 134 F.3d 1427, 1433 (10th Cir.1998) ("1) how clearly the prior act has been proved; 2) how probative the evidence is of the material fact it is admitted to prove; 3) how seriously disputed the material fact is; [4)] whether the government can avail itself of any less prejudicial evidence[;] * * * [5)] how likely it is such evidence will contribute to an improperly-based jury verdict; [6)] the extent to which such evidence will distract the jury from the central issues of the trial; and [7)] how time consuming it will be to prove the prior conduct.").

8. *Remoteness.* See United States v. Larson, 112 F.3d 600, 605 (2d Cir.1997) ("In the present case, the Stevens testimony covered events 16–20 years prior to trial. Those events closely paralleled the events complained of by Furs, taking place in the same geographic locations, with Larson using the same enticements for both boys, plying both with alcohol, and engaging both in similar progressions of sexual acts. The similarity of the events clearly demonstrated the Stevens testimony's relevance. The court was entitled to view both the traumatic nature of the events and their repetition over a span of four years as strong indicators of the reliability of the witness's memory. We see no abuse of discretion in the admission of this testimony."); United States v. LeCompte, 131 F.3d 767, 769–70 (8th Cir. 1997) ("The sexual offenses committed against T.T. were substantially similar to those allegedly committed against C.D. By comparison, the differences were small. In particular, the District Court itself acknowledged that the time lapse between incidents 'may not be as significant as it appears at first glance, because defendant was imprisoned for a portion of the time between 1987 and 1995, which deprived defendant of the opportunity to abuse any children.' ").

9. *Record.* See United States v. Castillo, 140 F.3d 874, 884 (10th Cir.1998) ("As we said in a similar case: '[T]he district court's summary disposition of this issue renders it impossible for us to review the propriety of its decision * * *. Without any reasoned elaboration by the district court we have no way of understanding the basis of its decision * * *. As an appellate court, we are in no position to speculate about the possible considerations which might have informed the district court's judgment. Instead, we require an on the record decision by the court explaining its reasoning in detail.' ").

10. *"Consent" cases.* Should Rules 413–15 be limited to the issue of consent in rape cases? See Bryden & Park, Other Crimes Evidence in Sex Offense Cases, 78 Minn.L.Rev. 529 (1994). What is the difference between "consent" and "identity" cases?

11. *Method of proof.* See United States v. Enjady, 134 F.3d 1427, 1434 (10th Cir.1998) ("But here the government established that B had filed a contemporaneous police report and it presented the investigating officer's testimony about why the alleged rape of B was not prosecuted."). Should these Rules be limited to situations where there is a prior conviction? See Orenstein, note 6, supra, at 1541–42 ("By allowing propensity evidence only where there is a prior conviction, we significantly enhance the likelihood that the prior offense occurred * * * [and avoid mini-trials]. * * * Because the accused has already been punished, the jury is less likely to want to punish him again.").

12. *State cases and rules.* See Alaska Evid.R. 404(b)(3) ("In a prosecution for a crime of sexual assault in any degree, evidence of other sexual assaults or attempted sexual assaults by the defendant against the same or another person is admissible if the defendant relies on a defense of consent. In a prosecution for a crime of attempt to commit sexual assault in any degree, evidence of other sexual assaults or attempted sexual assaults by the defendant against the same or another person is admissible."); Ariz.R.Evid. 404(c); Cal.Evid. Code § 1108; Tex.Crim.Proc. Code § 38.37 (when victim is

a minor). Other jurisdictions have created similar rules by court decision. Some states limit this "lustful disposition" exception to cases involving the same victim, to cases in which the victim is a minor, or to incest cases. See People v. Donoho, 788 N.E.2d 707, 717–18 (Ill.2003) (discussing various positions). See also State v. Kennedy, 803 So.2d 916, 921 (La.2001) ("[W]e have consistently restricted this judicially-recognized 'lustful disposition' exception to Article 404(B) to evidence of other sexual crimes committed by the defendant against the same prosecuting victim, whether child or adult.").

13. *Sources.* Baker, Once a Rapist? Motivational Evidence and Relevancy in Rape Law, 110 Harv.L.Rev. 563 (1997) (arguing that there are different motivations for different types of rape (e.g., date rape, gang rape, spousal rape, opportunistic rape during the course of a robbery, etc.), and this should affect admissibility decisions); Ojala, Propensity Evidence Under Rule 413: The Need for Balance, 77 Wash.U.L.Q. 947 (1999); Symposium, Perspectives on Proposed Federal Rules of Evidence 413–15, 22 Fordham Urban L.J. 265 (1995).

(5) "OTHER ACTS" EVIDENCE: FEDERAL RULE 404(b)

UNITED STATES v. ROBINSON

United States Court of Appeals, Seventh Circuit, 1998.
161 F.3d 463.

KANNE, CIRCUIT JUDGE.

* * *

I. HISTORY

A federal grand jury returned a four-count indictment against Richard Robinson on charges stemming from two armed bank robberies. Counts one and two of the indictment alleged that on April 8, 1997, Robinson robbed the Americana Bank in Anderson, Indiana, and that he used a firearm during the commission of this offense. Counts three and four of this same indictment alleged that ten days later, on April 18, 1997, Robinson committed another armed robbery with a firearm, this time robbing Harrington Bank in Fishers, Indiana. The cities of Anderson and Fishers are separated by approximately twenty-five miles. Robinson pleaded guilty to the later armed robbery of Harrington Bank and went to trial on the charges stemming from the earlier Americana Bank robbery. Because the government offered evidence of the April 18 Fishers robbery at Robinson's trial, it is necessary to review the facts of both robberies when considering the issues before us. * * *

[Following the April 18th robbery, a high speed pursuit of Robinson ensued, at times exceeding speeds of 100 miles per hour. Evidence indicated that he disregarded traffic signals, operated his vehicle on the wrong side of the road, nearly caused numerous traffic accidents, and evaded a road block that had been set up by police before his Chevrolet Cavalier was eventually disabled. In addition, numerous local police officers were required to subdue him after a prolonged struggle. Robinson assaulted one and drove his car into a sheriff.]

II. Analysis

A. *Admission of Evidence of the Harrington Bank Robbery and the Subsequent Chase*

Robinson contends that the District Court abused its discretion by allowing the government to admit evidence of his plea of guilty to the charges stemming from the April 18 armed bank robbery at his trial for the April 8 armed bank robbery. The evidence of the April 18 armed bank robbery included evidence tending to demonstrate the similarities between the two robberies, evidence of the high speed chase and Robinson's struggle with police subsequent to the chase, and the materials recovered from Robinson's vehicle following his apprehension, including the orange ski mask, the distinctive duffle bag [''Louis Vuitton''-brand] containing money from the April 18 armed bank robbery, and the handgun used in both robberies. Prior to trial, the District Court conducted an evidentiary hearing on the admissibility of this evidence and, over Robinson's objections, ruled that the admission of this evidence was not prohibited by Rule 404(b) of the Federal Rules of Evidence. The admission of evidence under Rule 404(b) by a district court is reviewed only for an abuse of discretion. * * *

* * *

The categories that appear in the text of Rule 404(b) are not exclusive. Indeed, Rule 404(b) does not require the party offering the evidence to force the evidence into a particular listed category, but simply to show *any* relevant purpose other than proving conduct by means of a general propensity inference. We have held that evidence may be admissible under Rule 404(b) to demonstrate *modus operandi*. * * * Evidence of *modus operandi* is evidence that shows a defendant's distinctive method of operation. Such evidence may be properly admitted pursuant to Rule 404(b) to prove identity. Id. In addition, some courts have interpreted the admission of evidence establishing consciousness of guilt as coming within the identity exception to Rule 404(b). *See, e.g.,* United States v. Sims, 617 F.2d 1371, 1378 (9th Cir.1980) (''Flight immediately after the commission of a crime, especially where the person learns that he may be a suspect * * * supports an inference of guilt * * *. It was therefore relevant under the identity exception to Rule 404(b).''). Irrespective of whether such evidence may be admitted specifically to show identity, we have held that evidence demonstrating consciousness of guilt may be properly admitted under Rule 404(b). *See* United States v. Acevedo, 28 F.3d 686, 688 (7th Cir.1994) * * *.

We have fashioned a four-prong test to determine the appropriateness of admitting evidence of other crimes, wrongs, or acts. Under this test, the admissibility of the evidence is dependant [sic] upon whether: (1) the evidence is directed toward establishing a matter in issue other than the defendant's propensity to commit the crime charged; (2) the evidence shows that the other act is similar enough and close enough in time to be relevant to the matter in issue; (3) the evidence is sufficient to support a jury finding that the defendant committed the similar act; and (4) the evidence has probative value that is not substantially outweighed by the danger of unfair prejudice. * * * The fourth prong of this test incorporates Rule 403, which provides for the exclusion of relevant evidence on grounds of prejudice, confusion, or waste of time. Though not specifically stated as such, the primary thrust of Robinson's argument, both before the District Court during the evidentiary hearing and before this Court on appeal, is that the second and fourth prongs of this test were not met with respect to the District Court's admission of evidence relating to the April 18 armed bank robbery.

* * *

When considering the second and fourth prongs—whether the evidence shows that the other act is similar enough and close enough in time to be relevant to the matter in issue and whether the evidence has a probative value that is not substantially outweighed by the danger of unfair prejudice—it is helpful to consider the evidence of the similarities between the two armed bank robberies first and then to turn our attention to the evidence of flight and Robinson's struggle with the police.

As stated, the evidence demonstrating the similarities between the two crimes amounts, in essence, to evidence demonstrating *modus operandi*. We have cautioned that "[i]f defined broadly enough, *modus operandi* evidence can easily become nothing more than the character evidence that Rule 404(b) prohibits." Smith, 103 F.3d at 603. To ensure that the evidence at issue is not merely offered to establish the defendant's propensity to commit certain conduct, we require that *modus operandi* evidence bear "a singular strong resemblance to the pattern of the offense charged," United States v. Shackleford, 738 F.2d 776, 783 (7th Cir.1984) * * *, and that the similarities between the crimes be "sufficiently idiosyncratic to permit an inference of pattern for purposes of truth." United States v. Hudson, 884 F.2d 1016, 1021 (7th Cir.1989) (quoting Shackleford, 738 F.2d at 783 * * *)). "Thus, we must first determine whether there are sufficient similarities between the other crime evidence and the charged crime that clearly distinguish the defendant from other criminals committing bank robberies." Moore, 115 F.3d at 1355.

There are numerous similarities between the armed bank robberies of April 8 and April 18 that make them "clearly distinctive from the thousands of other bank robberies committed each year." Moore, 115 F.3d at 1355 (quoting Smith, 103 F.3d at 603). In both cases, the robber donned an orange ski mask prior to entering the bank, and he entered the bank carrying a distinctive duffle bag in one hand and brandishing a handgun in the other. Once inside the banks, the robber vaulted over the teller counter and demanded money. The robber emptied the teller drawers at each bank by himself, but only after placing the handgun down. The getaway vehicle in both cases was identified as a blue Chevrolet Cavalier. Furthermore, the robberies occurred within ten days and twenty-five miles of each other. This proximity in both time and location has significant bearing on the determination of whether the robberies are sufficiently idiosyncratic so as to permit an inference of pattern when considered in conjunction with the distinctive characteristics of each robbery. *See* Smith, 103 F.3d at 603 (noting the one month interval and 40 mile distance between two bank robberies when viewed in light of the rural locations of the banks in Wisconsin was relevant to demonstrating *modus operandi*). It is clear that sufficient similarities exist with respect to the April 8 and the April 18 robberies to identify Robinson as the individual responsible for committing these robberies.

Given the similarities between the two robberies, it cannot be said that the probative value of evidence demonstrating these similarities is substantially outweighed by the danger of unfair prejudice. Moreover, any risk of unfair prejudice was lessened by the jury instruction given by the District Court that the evidence offered by the government relating to the April 18 bank robbery was relevant only to the purposes contemplated by Rule 404(b). * * *

The government's theory for the admission of evidence of the chase and Robinson's struggle with the police following the April 18 armed bank robbery, however, is somewhat more troublesome. During the evidentiary hearing before the District Court, the government argued that the evidence of the chase and subsequent struggle demonstrated Robinson's consciousness of guilt with respect to the April 8 armed bank robbery. The government explained that the motivation prompting flight and struggle on April 18 was twofold—Robinson was fleeing from the most recent armed bank robbery and he also knew that he possessed evidence connecting him to the April 8 armed bank robbery. Thus, he had a dual purpose in fleeing from law enforcement after the April 18 armed bank robbery. The government argued that the fervor with which he attempted to escape from the police was proportional to Robinson's consciousness of guilt, and, therefore, the magnitude of Robinson's resistance was directly related to Robinson's consciousness that he possessed evidence connecting him with not one, but two armed bank robberies. In short, the government asserted that Robinson was fleeing, in effect, from both armed bank robberies. * * *

In the instant case, Robinson's conduct in attempting to elude police after the April 18 armed bank robbery certainly constituted flight. It cannot be seriously disputed that this flight was the result of consciousness of guilt. The degree of confidence with which the jury could reasonably draw inferences from Robinson's flight to an ultimate finding of his guilt with respect to the April 8 armed bank robbery is also substantial. The relative proximity in time between the crime charged and Robinson's flight and the fact that at the time he fled from police he possessed considerable evidence linking him to the April 8 armed bank robbery are sufficient to establish a reasonable inference that he fled because of consciousness of guilt stemming from both the April 8 and the April 18 armed bank robberies.

Despite Robinson's arguments to the contrary, evidence of flight from the April 18 bank robbery is not merely generalized evidence offered to establish Robinson's character or his propensity to commit criminal acts. By establishing that Robinson fled from the April 18 armed bank robbery and struggled with police while in possession of evidence linking him to both that robbery and an armed bank robbery occurring a mere ten days before that date, the government was able to offer proof that Robinson possessed a culpable state of mind. As we have explained, "[t]his is a legitimate use of such evidence, whether one conceives of it as outside the scope of Rule 404(b) because of the evidence's 'intrinsic' value deriving from its specific relationship to the facts of the offense or as countenanced by Rule 404(b) because of its relevance in proving a non-character-related consequential fact—consciousness of guilt." Acevedo, 28 F.3d at 688. Under either theory, the evidence is probative of Robinson's state of mind in a manner entirely separate from how it reflects upon his character.

While it may be tempting to conclude Robinson's flight from the April 18 armed bank robbery has no bearing on his consciousness of guilt with respect to the April 8 armed bank robbery, and, indeed, Robinson argues as much, this position can be dispensed with if one considers two scenarios not far removed from the instant case. Under Rule 404(b), evidence of flight certainly would be admissible to show consciousness of guilt of a defendant who knew he was in possession of evidence demonstrating his involvement in an armed bank robbery if that defendant fled from or struggled with police even if the police were attempting to stop him for a mere routine traffic violation, such as a broken taillight, shortly after the commission of the bank robbery. *Cf.* United States v. Dierling, 131 F.3d 722, 731 (8th Cir.1997) (concluding that evidence of a defendant's flight and struggle with a police officer attempting to arrest the defendant for violation of a domestic protection order was admissible as evidence of consciousness of guilt with respect to a conviction for conspiracy to distribute narcotics and stating that "[t]he intended purpose of the attempted stop need not be related to the conspiracy * * *. The real question is what is in the mind of the person who flees and whether there is sufficient evidence to allow the inference that the flight was prompted by consciousness of guilt."). Similarly, if a defendant committed a string of five armed bank robberies and was pursued by police after robbing a sixth, it can hardly be said that evidence of flight could not be admitted to show consciousness of guilt with respect to the other five robberies based on the contention that he was merely fleeing from his latest endeavor to plunder a bank. *Cf.* United States v. Clark, 45 F.3d 1247, 1251 (8th Cir.1995) ("The existence of other possible reasons for flight does not render the inference [of guilt] impermissible or irrational."). And so it is with this case. Robinson had knowledge that he committed acts proscribed by law on both April 8 and April 18. This knowledge was manifested in his efforts to evade police after the robbery on April 18. In such a case, it is not the role of the District Court to parse the mind of a defendant to determine which act may have created a higher consciousness of guilt on a given occasion when the defendant is in possession of evidence linking him to both robberies and when the underlying crimes are virtually identical and separated by a mere ten days.

To the extent that the evidence at issue falls outside the scope of Rule 404(b), we will not deprive a party from presenting evidence when its exclusion leaves a conceptual or chronological void. *See* United States v. Lahey, 55 F.3d 1289, 1295–96 (7th Cir.1995); *see also* United States v. King, 126 F.3d 987, 995 (7th Cir.1997) ("[A] court may admit evidence of other criminal conduct that is inextricably intertwined with a charged offense or that completes the story of the charged offense."). The government needed the evidence of the chase and Robinson's struggle to present a complete picture of the events transpiring between the short time separating the April 8 armed bank robbery and Robinson's capture on April 18. Beyond merely establishing consciousness of guilt, this evidence explains the circumstances surrounding Robinson's arrest and how the government came into possession of the orange ski mask, the distinctive duffle bag, and the handgun—three pieces of evidence of paramount importance to the government's case. "While prosecutorial need alone does not mean probative value outweighs prejudice, the more essential the evidence, the greater its probative value, and the less likely that a trial court should order the evidence excluded." Jackson, 886 F.2d at 847. * * *

Notes and Questions

1. *"Signature" quality.* What features make the two robberies similar? See United States v. Luna, 21 F.3d 874, 881 (9th Cir.1994) (generic "take-over" bank robberies not sufficiently distinctive); State v. Bey, 709 N.E.2d 484, 491 (Ohio 1999) ("[T]he 'other act' evidence established a 'behavioral fingerprint' linking [the defendant] to the [other] crime due to the common features shared by the [prior] homicide and the [present] homicide. The deaths of [the two victims] occurred under practically identical circumstances.").

2. *Subsequent acts.* See United States v. Dickerson, 248 F.3d 1036, 1046 (11th Cir.2001) (As to cocaine distribution almost two years after the last overt act in the alleged conspiracy, the court stated: "It is well-settled in this circuit that 'the principles governing what is commonly referred to as other crimes evidence are the same whether the conduct occurs before or after the offense charged, and regardless of whether the activity might give rise to criminal liability.").

3. *Defense proffer.* See United States v. Wilson, 307 F.3d 596, 601 (7th Cir.2002) ("Under what has come to be known as 'reverse 404(b) evidence,' a defendant can introduce evidence of someone else's conduct if it tends to negate the defendant's guilt. The trial court is entitled to exclude this kind of evidence if, upon a balancing of the evidence's probative value against

considerations such as prejudice, undue waste of time, and confusion of the issues under Rules 401 and 403 * * *, it concludes that the evidence would not be beneficial."); People v. Primo, 753 N.E.2d 164, 168 (N.Y.2001) (As to evidence that a person who had been present at the shooting had used the same gun in an unrelated crime two months later, the court stated: "The better approach, we hold, is to review the admissibility of third-party culpability evidence under the general balancing analysis that governs the admissibility of all evidence."); McCord, "But Perry Mason Made It Look So Easy!": The Admissibility of Evidence Offered by a Criminal Defendant to Suggest That Someone Else is Guilty, 63 Tenn.L.Rev. 917, 936 (1996).

4. *Noncriminal conduct.* See United States v. Rubio–Gonzalez, 674 F.2d 1067, 1075 (5th Cir.1982) ("The fact that the records did not show that appellant's prior conduct was criminal is immaterial. Rule 404(b) authorizes the admission of prior 'acts' as well as 'crimes' and 'wrongs.' ").

5. *Civil cases.* See Udemba v. Nicoli, 237 F.3d 8, 14 (1st Cir.2001) ("The facts are straightforward. The appellant himself set the stage for the admission of the evidence that he now seeks to challenge. In elaboration of his claimed damages, he told on direct examination about his humiliation when news of his arrest appeared in the local newspaper and emphasized the mental anguish that followed. Since the appellant did not testify to a closed period of emotional distress, defense counsel sought to minimize this open-ended claim by inquiring about a subsequent arrest that evoked the same sort of newspaper publicity. The district court allowed this cross-examination for the limited purpose of assisting the jury in determining the extent of damages suffered for mental anguish and emotional distress."); Turley v. State Farm Mut. Auto. Ins. Co., 944 F.2d 669, 672–75 (10th Cir.1991) (evidence of prior insurance scams admissible).

6. *Inextricably intertwined.* See United States v. Bowie, 232 F.3d 923, 927 (D.C.Cir.2000) ("Courts have denominated evidence of the same crime 'intrinsic' and evidence of 'other' crimes 'extrinsic.' As a practical matter, it is hard to see what function this interpretation of Rule 404(b) performs. If the so-called 'intrinsic' act is indeed part of the crime charged, evidence of it will, by definition, always satisfy Rule 404(b). * * * So far as we can tell, the only consequences of labeling evidence 'intrinsic' are to relieve the prosecution of Rule 404(b)'s notice requirement and the court of its obligation to give an appropriate limiting instruction upon defense counsel's request. *See* Fed.R.Evid. 404(b) advisory committee's note on the 1991 amendment (indicating that the notice requirement does not apply to 'intrinsic' evidence); Fed.R.Evid. 105 (mandating, upon request, limiting instruction for multi-purpose evidence) * * *.").

7. *Flight evidence.* See United States v. Levine, 5 F.3d 1100, 1107 (7th Cir.1993) ("The probative value of flight as evidence of a defendant's guilt depends on the degree of confidence with which four inferences can be drawn: (1) from behavior to flight; (2) from flight to consciousness of guilt; (3) from consciousness of guilt to consciousness of guilt concerning the crime charged; and (4) from consciousness of guilt concerning the crime charged to actual guilt of the crime charged.").

8. *Rule 403.* The mere fact that the prosecutor states that other crimes evidence is offered for one of the purposes listed in Rule 404(b) does not

guarantee admissibility. The evidence must also meet the test of relevancy. Under Rule 403, relevant evidence is admissible so long as its probative value is not "substantially outweighed by the danger of unfair prejudice" etc. The Rule places the burden of showing unfair prejudice on the opponent of the evidence. Should a different test be applied when considering other crimes evidence? See discussion in Kuhns, The Propensity to Misunderstand the Character of Specific Acts Evidence, 66 Iowa L. Rev. 777 (1981). What other factors should be considered by the judge? See Gleason v. State, 57 P.3d 332, 342 (Wyo.2002) (One factor is the "comparative enormity of the charged crime and the prior bad act. When the prior act is a more serious offense than the charged crime, the introduction of that act will tend to place the defendant in a different and unfavorable light.").

9. *California.* In 1982, California's voters approved an amendment to the state constitution which, *inter alia,* virtually abolished the common law rules on character proof in criminal cases. The former rules are replaced with a broad grant of judicial discretion similar to Federal Rule 403. For a criticism of the amendment and a discussion of its likely impact in California, see Mendez, California's New Law on Character Evidence: Evidence Code Section 352 and the Impact of Recent Psychological Studies, 31 UCLA L.Rev. 1003 (1984).

10. A classic example of other acts evidence is Whitty v. State, 149 N.W.2d 557 (Wis.1967). In *Whitty*, the defendant was charged with taking indecent liberties with a 10–year-old girl. The state's evidence showed that the accused approached the victim and asked for help in finding a black and white rabbit which he had lost. She went with him to a house where the indecent liberties were taken. The Wisconsin Supreme Court held that evidence had been properly admitted that the accused had approached an 8–year-old girl on the evening before the incident in question and told her he was looking for a black and white rabbit and was about to take indecent liberties with her when he was frightened off. For what purpose or purposes might such evidence have been admitted? How much proof of the earlier occurrence should have been required?

UNITED STATES v. HERNANDEZ

United States Court of Appeals, Fourth Circuit, 1992.
975 F.2d 1035.

BUTZNER, SENIOR CIRCUIT JUDGE:

Xiomaro E. Hernandez appeals a judgment entered on the verdict of a jury convicting her of conspiracy to distribute and to possess with intent to distribute cocaine. She alleges that the district court abused its discretion by admitting extraneous evidence of bad acts or crimes under Federal Rule of Evidence 404(b). We hold that the district court erred in admitting the challenged evidence over her lawyer's objection. Because we cannot conclude that the error was harmless, we vacate the judgment and remand the case for a new trial.

I

Xiomaro Hernandez, a native of the Dominican Republic, came to the United States in 1976 and is now a naturalized citizen. She lived at first in Puerto Rico and Miami, then moved to New York City where she worked in a travel agency owned by her family. She then moved with Rodolfo Fernandez to the District of Columbia where they shared an apartment. She testified that she supported herself during this time by traveling to New York, buying clothes, and bringing them back to Washington for resale.

The charges against Hernandez arose out of an undercover operation run by a joint task force set up by the Drug Enforcement Agency (DEA) and local police in northern Virginia. A DEA Special Agent, Frank Shroyer, obtained an introduction to a suspected drug dealer named Naikin DeLaCruz Duran (DeLaCruz). On August 23, 1990, Shroyer arranged to purchase powder cocaine and a sample of cocaine base, or crack cocaine, from DeLaCruz. One week later, Shroyer solicited DeLaCruz to sell him crack. After this conversation, task force officers observed DeLaCruz entering the apartment building where Hernandez lived with Fernandez. After DeLaCruz left the building, he met Shroyer at a metro station and gave him the promised crack. On September 10, 1990, Shroyer sought to purchase a substantial amount of crack from DeLaCruz. DeLaCruz stated that he would go to the District, get the drug, and return to Virginia to sell it to Shroyer. A surveillance team saw DeLaCruz enter the same building, then exit in the company of Fernandez. DeLaCruz delivered the drug to Shroyer in the parking lot outside DeLaCruz's apartment building. Federal agents and police immediately arrested DeLaCruz and then entered his apartment, where they found and arrested Fernandez.

DeLaCruz negotiated a plea agreement requiring him to cooperate with the government in its prosecution of Fernandez, Hernandez, and a third person, Victor "Shorty" Liriano. * * *

* * *

Romulo DeLeon, who was testifying pursuant to a plea agreement in an unrelated drug case, related that he had met Hernandez at the clothing store where he worked. The meeting occurred more than six months before the acts alleged in the indictment. He testified that Hernandez had told him that she knew a special recipe for cooking crack "to make more quantity while you are cooking it." He said she had told him that she knew the recipe because "she used to do that, sell that in New York."

The government offered DeLeon's testimony as part of the government's case in chief, not in rebuttal to Hernandez's defense. Counsel for Hernandez objected to the testimony. * * *

Hernandez testified that she was out of town during the first two drug transactions and that she had left Hotke, an acquaintance whom she had met in Puerto Rico, in charge of her apartment during her absence. She stated that she had never had more than minimal contact with DeLaCruz and that she had "[n]ever in my life" sold him crack or drugs. She did not testify that she had no knowledge of crack or that she had never been exposed to or involved with drugs in general but only that, on the occasions alleged in the indictment, she was not involved in or aware of the drug transactions at issue.

* * *

II

* * * "This court has held that Rule 404(b) is an inclusive rule that allows admission of evidence of other acts relevant to an issue at trial except that which proves only criminal disposition." *United States v. Watford,* 894 F.2d 665, 571 (4th Cir.1990). The decision to admit evidence of other acts under Rule 404(b) is within the discretion of the trial court. * * *

Some trouble and confusion in applying this rule are only to be expected, for it is designed to exclude evidence that many both within and without the legal system intuitively find powerful and useful. * * *

* * * In this circuit, we have evolved a test for evidence proffered pursuant to Rule 404(b). "Under Rule 404(b) * * * prior bad acts are admissible if they are (1) relevant to an issue other than character; (2) necessary, and (3) reliable." *United States v. Rawle,* 845 F.2d 1244, 1247 (4th Cir.1988) * * *. Evidence that passes this test is not automatically admissible, however. Rule 403 requires the trial judge to determine that its probative value outweighs the danger of undue prejudice to the defendant. * * * In this circuit, unlike others, the trial court is not required to make an explicit statement of the purpose for which the evidence is admitted. *Rawle,* 845 F.2d at 1247. The use of limiting instructions setting out the purpose for which the evidence is admitted and admonishing the jury against considering it as improper evidence of guilt will do much to alleviate difficulties raised by its admission. * * *

III

Under the doctrine of *Rawle,* we must begin by considering what, if any, relevance the challenged testimony bears to the issue for which it was offered. * * * "In order for evidence to be relevant, it must be sufficiently related to the charged offense." *Rawle,* 845 F.2d at 1247 n.3.

Judged by this standard, the relevance of DeLeon's testimony was at best small. It was offered as evidence of the intent with which Hernandez engaged in the charged conspiracy. The testimony did not establish anything about her conduct or mental state during the course of the conspiracy alleged in the indictment. Hernandez offered as her defense the contention that she had not sold the crack in question to DeLaCruz. She did not testify that she had in some way sold or handled the crack but without the requisite knowledge or intent; nor did she testify that she had never touched crack or did not know what it was. The DeLeon testimony showed that, before her move from New York to Washington, Hernandez had learned a special recipe for making crack and that she had made and apparently sold it in New York at that time. The testimony did not show that she intended to engage in crack distribution in Washington or that she had continued to deal in crack after leaving New York. Nor did it show that she intended to engage in crack distribution with Fernandez, or even that she intended to engage in future crack dealing at all.

It is a truism that a plea of "not guilty" to a charge requiring intent places that mental state in issue and that the state may offer evidence of other bad acts to address that issue. * * * This principle, however, does not permit any sort of uncharged bad act to be brought to bear against defendants charged with intentional crimes. Most crimes involve some level of intent, but all evidence of other intentional acts or crimes does not for this reason become relevant. Evidence to show intent is not admissible when the unrelated bad act is "tenuous and remote in time from the charges in the indictment." *United States v. Cole,* 491 F.2d 1276, 1279 (4th Cir.1974). For example, evidence of a prior stabbing by the defendant is not relevant to show intent in a later encounter with a different victim when the defendant admitted stabbing the victim but pleaded self-defense. *United States v. Sanders,* 964 F.2d 295, 298–99 (4th Cir.1992).

A plausible interpretation of the rule holds that evidence of other crimes may not be offered when the defendant unequivocally denies committing the acts charged in the indictment. *See United States v. Ortiz,* 857 F.2d 900, 904 (2d Cir.1988). This circuit has no similar precept. Our cases examine the use for which intent evidence is offered in each instance, following the admonition that "the rule and the exceptions should be considered with meticulous regard to the facts of each case." *United States v. Baldivid,* 465 F.2d 1277, 1290 (4th Cir.1972) (Sobeloff, J., concurring in part and dissenting in part). We have admitted evidence of other acts on the issue of intent, for example, where the defendant claimed that "he was present but innocent" during the sale of the drugs, and he elicited false testimony that he had no prior involvement in any cocaine transaction, *United States v. Rhodes,* 779 F.2d 1019, 1030–31 (4th Cir.1985); where the defendant contended he had merely obtained a truck for friends without knowing it would be used to transport stolen property, *Hadaway,* 681 F.2d at 217; where intent was a "key issue" because the defendant was "sharply contesting the sufficiency of the government's proof of lascivious intent" in a child-molestation case, *United States v. Beahm,* 664 F.2d 414, 417 (4th Cir.1981); and where the defendant has sought "to depict herself as one whose essential philosophy and habitual conduct in life is completely at odds with the possession of a state of mind requisite to guilt of the offense charged. * * * " *United States v. Johnson,* 634 F.2d 735, 737 (4th Cir.1980).

The government insists that because intent and knowledge are essential elements of the charge against Hernandez, which were placed in issue by her plea of not guilty, the DeLeon testimony about prior bad acts is admissible. For this proposition it relies on *Mark,* 943 F.2d at 448. But reliance on *Mark* for this sweeping ground for admission is unwarranted. The evidence must still be relevant. In *Mark* the trial court pointed out that the evidence of prior bad acts disclosed how the defendant got the drugs that he was charged with selling. 943 F.2d at 448. Consequently, *Mark* is well within the mainstream of our cases that have admitted evidence of prior similar acts to show intent and knowledge. Because *Mark* differs significantly from the case before us, it does not support the government's contention that DeLeon's evidence was relevant.

Necessity is the second part of the *Rawle* test. In some sense all evidence that tends to make conviction more likely is necessary, particularly in a case like this one where the other evidence of guilt is tenuous. Our cases dictate a more sophisticated inquiry: "The evidence is necessary and admissible where it is an essential part of the crimes on trial * * * or where it 'furnishes part of the context of the crime.' " *Rawle,* 845 F.2d at 1247 n.4 * * *. DeLeon's testimony serves no such purpose. It bears at best a slight relationship to the acts charged in the indictment. Indeed, its principal value relates not to the crime but to the alleged criminal. The charged acts become more plausible when the defendant has admitted involvement with crack on other occasions. But this, once again, is precisely the criminal propensity inference Rule 404(b) is designed to forbid.

As for the third part of the test, reliability, *see Rawle,* 845 F.2d at 1247, this evidence barely passes muster. Admissible prior acts testimony is sometimes corroborated by a judgment of conviction, *King,* 768 F.2d at 587; by other testimony as to the time and place at which the prior acts allegedly occurred, *Mark,* 943 F.2d at 449 * * *; or by audio-or videotaped evidence, *DiZenzo,* 500 F.2d at 266. Such corroboration, however, is not required; the weight and credibility of uncorroborated testimony of defendants testifying pursuant to plea agreements is largely for the jury. However, "the convincingness of the evidence that other crimes were committed is a factor that should be weighed in the decision to admit such evidence." *Cole,* 491 F.2d at 1279. In this case, careful consideration of reliability might not in itself require barring the testimony, but it surely does not generate a compelling argument for its admission.

IV

Even assuming the DeLeon testimony did not fail the *Rawle* test, it still was inadmissible unless it could be held more probative than prejudicial. *Rawle,* 845 F.2d at 1247. * * * In this case, the trial record does not reflect that the district court engaged in an explicit balancing of the probative value of the evidence against prejudice. However, "[a]s long as the record as a whole indicates appropriate judicial weighing, we will not reverse for a failure to recite mechanically the appropriate balancing test." *United States v. Lewis,* 780 F.2d 1140, 1142 (4th Cir.1986).

In *Lewis* the record disclosed that the attorneys presented lengthy arguments on the balancing test and that the probative value of the evidence was high. Based on these factors the court was able to conclude on appeal that the trial court had complied with the admonition to balance the probative value of prior extraneous culpability with its prejudicial effect. But in Hernandez's case the record is silent about the balancing test, and there is no mention of Rule 403. Perhaps balancing was accomplished at an unreported bench conference. Here—unlike *Lewis*—the probative value of the evidence is slight. Hernandez's "cooking" recipe and her sale of crack in New York at some indefinite time are in no way connected to the cocaine she is charged with conspiring to sell in this case. The evident effect, if not the purpose, of DeLeon's testimony relating Hernandez's statement about her activities in New York was to bolster DeLaCruz's testimony about her acts in Washington by depicting her as an experienced crack dealer. But this is precisely the effect Rules 403 and 404(b) seek to avoid. Upon consideration of all the circumstances, we think the balance so one-sided that admission of the evidence was error.

* * *

The judgment is vacated, and the case is remanded for retrial consistent with this opinion.

Notes and Questions

1. *Relevance.* What is the relevance of the prior crime to prove intent? See State v. Sullivan, 679 N.W.2d 19, 29 (Iowa 2004) ("The State's inherent argument for admitting the evidence was based on the character theory that if Sullivan entertained the intent to deliver during a similar prior incident, he probably harbored the same intent at the time of the charged offense. The evidence was therefore not admissible * * *.").

2. *Disputed issues.* The principal case refers to *United States v. Ortiz*, a Second Circuit decision that requires intent to be a disputed issue before "other acts" evidence may be admitted. See also United States v. Williams, 577 F.2d 188, 191 (2d Cir.1978) ("other crimes evidence is inadmissible to prove intent when that issue is not really in dispute"); Robbins v. State, 88 S.W.3d 256, 260 (Tex.Crim.App.2002) ("[I]n Texas a simple plea of not guilty usually does not make issues such as intent a relevant issue of consequence for purposes of determining the admissibility of relationship evidence under Rule 404(b)."). Other courts, however, reject this approach. See United States v. Matthews, 431 F.3d 1296, 1311–12 (11th Cir.2005) ("Matthews's 1991 arrest for distribution of cocaine was relevant to the intent at issue in the charged conspiracy to distribute cocaine."; The "precise difficulty of proving intent in conspiracies is what creates the presumption that intent is always at issue."); United States v. Miller, 725 F.2d 462, 466 (8th Cir.1984) (prosecution need not await the defendant's denial of intent before offering evidence of similar acts). See Leonard, The Use of Uncharged Misconduct Evidence to Prove Knowledge, 81 Neb.L.Rev. 115, 148 (2002) ("Though weak judicial analysis of the admissibility of uncharged misconduct to prove knowledge can be found in many types of case, it is perhaps most commonly represented in drug-related prosecutions, particularly those charging possession of illegal drugs with intent to distribute.").

If the prosecution is always entitled to introduce other crimes evidence to show intent, how much is left of the other crimes rule? See discussion in Thompson v. United States, 546 A.2d 414 (D.C.1988); Imwinkelried, The Use of Evidence of an Accused's Uncharged Misconduct to Prove *Mens Rea*: The Doctrines Which Threaten to Engulf the Character Evidence Prohibition, 51 Ohio St. L.J. 575 (1990).

3. *Stipulations*. See United States v. Jemal, 26 F.3d 1267, 1274 (3d Cir.1994) ("District courts should generally deem prior bad acts evidence inadmissible to prove an issue that the defendant makes clear he is not contesting. * * * [H]owever, * * * to succeed, the defendant's proffer to stipulate must be comprehensive and unreserved, completely eliminating the government's need to prove the point it would otherwise try to establish using 404(b) evidence.").

4. *Stipulations revisited.* In *Old Chief v. United States*, discussed in Chapter 7, Section B, supra, the Supreme Court wrote: "[If] there were a justification for receiving evidence of the nature of prior acts on some issue other than status (i.e., to prove motive, opportunity, intent, preparation, plan, knowledge, identity, or absence of mistake or accident), Rule 404(b) guarantees the opportunity to seek its admission." 519 U.S. at 190. See also United States v. Williams, 238 F.3d 871, 876 (7th Cir.2001) (In a case involving intent to distribute cocaine, the court stated: "[A]s the other circuits to consider this issue after *Old Chief* have held, we believe that *Old Chief* counsels that a defendant's offer to stipulate unequivocally to an element of an offense, such as those demonstrating knowledge or intent, does not render the Government's evidence of prior crimes that are relevant to those elements inadmissible under Rule 404(b)."); United States v. Bowie, 232 F.3d 923, 931 (D.C.Cir.2000) ("Far from a choice between 'propositions of slightly varying abstraction,' the choice in this case was between concrete evidence of the defendant's actions giving rise to natural and sensible inferences, and abstract stipulations about hypothetical persons not on trial.").

5. *Instructions.* One federal appellate court stated that the trial judge "must carefully identify, in its instructions to the jury, the specific factor named in the rule that is relied upon to justify admission of the other acts evidence, explain why that factor is material, and warn the jurors against using the evidence to draw the inferences expressly forbidden in the first sentence of Rule 404(b)." United States v. Spikes, 158 F.3d 913, 929 (6th Cir.1998). Can a jury follow such an instruction?

6. *Malice (drunk driving).* See United States v. Tan, 254 F.3d 1204, 1209 (10th Cir.2001) ("[I]ntent is at issue here. In fact, it appears to be *the* issue. In addition, there is no evidence in this case from which Defendant's malice can be readily inferred other than his numerous prior drunk driving convictions."); United States v. Fleming, 739 F.2d 945, 949 (4th Cir.1984) ("[T]he driving record was relevant to establish that defendant had grounds to be aware of the risk his drinking and driving while intoxicated presented to others. It thus was properly admitted."). What about lesser offenses? See United States v. Leonard, 439 F.3d 648 (10th Cir.2006) (in a vehicular homicide case, court upheld use of 15 traffic citations, including 9 for driving

with a suspended license, 2 for failing to appear for traffic citation hearings, and 2 for moving violations).

7. *Lack of accident.* See United States v. Bowie, 232 F.3d 923, 930 (D.C.Cir.2000) ("Evidence that Bowie possessed and passed counterfeit notes on a prior occasion was relevant because it decreased the likelihood that Bowie accidentally or innocently possessed the counterfeit notes on May 16.").

8. *Inconsistent results?* In United States v. Curtin, 443 F.3d 1084 (9th Cir.2006), the accused was convicted of traveling across state lines with intent to have sex with a minor (14–year-old girl) and use of the Internet to attempt to persuade a minor to have sex. When he was arrested approaching a police decoy, his PDA contained over 140 stories about adults having sex with children. The court held the evidence inadmissible because possession of lawful reading material is not the type of conduct contemplated by Rule 404(b) and possession of lawful reading material was not similar to the actual criminal conduct charged. The court distinguished an earlier case, United States v. Allen, 341 F.3d 870 (9th Cir.2003), in which the defendants were charged with violating federally protected rights on the basis of race and religion. The court upheld the admissibility of "skinhead and white supremacist evidence," including color photographs of the defendant's tattoos (e.g., swastikas), Nazi-related literature, group photographs including some of the defendants (e.g., in "Heil Hitler" poses and standing before a swastika that they later set on fire), and other skinhead paraphernalia. Are there meaningful differences between *Curtin* and *Allen*?

UNITED STATES v. WOODS

United States Court of Appeals, Fourth Circuit, 1973.
484 F.2d 127.

WINTER, CIRCUIT JUDGE:

Martha L. Woods was found guilty by a jury of murder in the first degree and seven other charges of assault with intent to murder, attempt to murder, and mistreatment of her eight-month-old pre-adoptive foster son, Paul David Woods. [Federal jurisdiction was based on the claim that the alleged crimes took place on an army base.]

* * *

Beginning August 4, 1969, a bizarre series of events occurred. Twice on that date, and once again on August 8, August 13, and August 20, Paul suffered instances of gasping for breath and turning blue from lack of oxygen. Each time he responded to mouth-to-mouth resuscitation, except on August 20, when he went into a coma which persisted until September 21, when he died at an age of slightly more than seven months. On each of these occasions the evidence indicated that Paul had been in Mrs. Woods' custody, and only Mrs. Woods had had access to him. On each occasion prior to August 20, Paul was taken to the hospital. On the first occasion, he was immediately released because an examination disclosed that he was apparently well. On the other occasions, even after several days' observation, no reason for his cyanosis or respiratory difficulties could be discovered.

To prove that Paul's death was neither accidental nor the result of natural causes, the government presented the testimony of a forensic pathologist, Dr. DiMaio, who, based upon Paul's medical history, the records of his various hospitalizations, and the results of an autopsy which the pathologist had performed after Paul's death stated that Paul's death was not suicide or accident and that he found no evidence of natural death. Dr. DiMaio expressed his opinion as one of seventy-five percent certainty that Paul's death was homicide caused by smothering. Dr. DiMaio explained his twenty-five percent degree of doubt as being the possibility that Paul died naturally from a disease currently unknown to medical science, and he agreed that his doubt was a "reasonable doubt" within the standard definition given by the court.

Next, the government showed that beginning in 1945 Mrs. Woods had had custody of, or access to, nine children who suffered a minimum of twenty episodes of cyanosis. Seven children died, while five had multiple episodes of cyanosis. * * *

* * *

Defendant's contention that the government failed to prove the corpus delicti beyond a reasonable doubt rests upon the three propositions that (a) proof of the corpus delicti for culpable homicide requires proof of death of the alleged victim *and* proof that that death occurred by means other than suicide, accident or natural causes, in short, that death occurred by a criminal act, (b) evidence of other crimes is not admissible to show that the death of the alleged victim occurred by homicide, but (c) even if admissible, the proof of other crimes presented by the government in the instant case was not so clear and convincing as to permit the jury to find that Paul's death was homicide.

* * *

* * * [W]e proceed directly to discuss whether proof of the prior events concerning the other children was legally admissible to prove that (a) Paul's death was the result of culpable homicide and not of natural causes, and (b) defendant was the perpetrator of the crime.

We state, at the outset, that if otherwise legally admissible, we have no doubt about the relevance of the proof and its probative effect to establish both propositions. The evidence of what happened to the other children was not, strictly speaking, evidence of other crimes. There was no evidence that defendant was an accused with respect to the deaths or respiratory difficulties of the other children, except for Judy. Simultaneously with her trial for crimes alleged against Paul, defendant was being tried for crimes alleged against Judy, but there was no direct proof of defendant's guilt and the district court ruled that the circumstantial evidence was insufficient for the government to have proved its case. Thus, with regard to no single child was there any legally sufficient proof that defendant had done any act which the law forbids. Only when all of the evidence concerning the nine other children and Paul is considered collectively is the conclusion impelled that the probability that some or all of the other deaths, cyanotic seizures, and respiratory deficiencies were accidental or attributable to natural causes was so remote, the truth must be that Paul and some or all of the other children died at the hands of the defendant. We think also that when the crime is one of infanticide or child abuse, evidence of repeated incidents is especially relevant because it may be the only evidence to prove the crime. A child of the age of Paul and of the others about whom evidence was received is a helpless, defenseless unit of human life. Such a child is too young, if he survives, to relate the facts concerning the attempt on his life, and too young, if he does not survive, to have exerted enough resistance that the marks of his cause of death will survive him. Absent the fortuitous presence of an eyewitness, infanticide or child abuse by suffocation would largely go unpunished. See Minnesota v. Loss, 295 Minn. 271, 204 N.W.2d 404 (1973).

B. *Admissibility of Evidence Generally.* The government and the defendant agree that evidence of other crimes is not admissible to prove that an accused is a bad person and therefore likely to have committed the crime in question. Indeed, the rule is beyond dispute: Michelson v. United States, 335 U.S. 469, 475–476 (1948) * * *. Defendant argues that while there are certain recognized exceptions to this rule, the instant case cannot be fitted into any of them, emphasizing that corpus delicti is not an exception. McCormick on Evidence § 190 (Cleary Ed.1972). The government, in meeting this approach, contends that the evidence was admissible on the theory that it tended to prove (a) the existence of a continuing plan,[11] (b) the handiwork or signature exception,[12] (c) that the acts alleged in the indictment were not inadvertent, accidental, or unintentional, and (d) the defendant's identity as the perpetrator of the crime. We are inclined to agree with the defendant that the evidence was not admissible under the scheme or continuing plan exception because there was no evidence that defendant engaged in any scheme or plan, or, if so, the objective or motive. The evidence may have been admissible under the lack of accident exception, although ordinarily that exception is invoked only where an accused admits that he did the acts charged but denies the intent necessary to constitute a crime, or contends that he did the acts accidentally. McCormick, p. 450. However, in State v. Lapage, 57 N.H. 245, 294 (1876), there was dictum that under certain circumstances where several children of the same mother had died, evidence of the previous deaths ought to be admissible

11. Makin v. Attorney General of New South Wales, [1894] A.C. 57 (P.C.1893) (N.S.Wales) and Regina v. Roden, 12 Cox Cr. 630 (1874) support this view. *Makin* was a prosecution for infanticide by a professional foster parent. Evidence that the bodies of twelve other infants, who had been entrusted to him with inadequate payment for their support, was held admissible. In *Roden,* a prosecution for infanticide by suffocation, evidence that three of defendant's other children died in her lap, was held admissible.

12. Rex. v. George Joseph Smith, [1914–15] All.E.R.Rep. 262 ("Brides of Bath" case) and People v. Peete, 28 Cal.2d 306, 169 P.2d 924 (1946) permitted proof of unique methods of previous homicides to establish guilt of the accused.

because of the unlikelihood of such deaths being accidental. Finally, the identity exception is not really an exception in its own right, but rather is spoken of as a supplementary purpose of another exception. McCormick, p. 451.

The handiwork or signature exception is the one which appears most applicable, although defendant's argument that cyanosis among infants is too common to constitute an unusual and distinctive device unerringly pointing to guilt on her part would not be without force, were it not for the fact that so many children at defendant's mercy experienced this condition. In the defendant's case, the "commonness" of the condition is outweighed by its frequency under circumstances where only defendant could have been the precipitating factor.

While we conclude that the evidence was admissible generally under the accident and signature exceptions, we prefer to place our decision upon a broader ground. Simply fitting evidence of this nature into an exception heretofore recognized is, to our minds, too mechanistic an approach.

McCormick, in listing the instances in which evidence of other crimes may be admissible, cautions "that the list is not complete, for the range of relevancy outside the ban is almost infinite * * *." Id. 448. And then, McCormick states:

> [S]ome of the wiser opinions (especially recent ones) recognize that the problem is not merely one of pigeon-holing, but one of balancing, on the one side, the actual need for the other crimes evidence in the light of the issues and other evidence available to the prosecution, the convincingness of the evidence that the other crimes were committed and that the accused was the actor, and the strength or weakness of the other crimes evidence in supporting the issue, and on the other, the degree to which the jury will probably be roused by the evidence to overmastering hostility.

Id. p. 453. This approach is one which finds support in [numerous cases including Dirring v. United States, 328 F.2d 512 (1 Cir.1964)]. These cases stand for the proposition that evidence of other offenses may be received, if relevant, for any purpose other than to show a mere propensity or disposition on the part of the defendant to commit the crime, provided that the trial judge may exclude the evidence if its probative value is outweighed by the risk that its admission will create a substantial danger of undue prejudice to the accused.

As we stated at the outset, we think that the evidence would prove that a crime had been committed because of the remoteness of the possibility that so many infants in the care and custody of defendant would suffer cyanotic episodes and respiratory difficulties if they were not induced by the defendant's wrongdoing, and at the same time, would prove the identity of defendant as the wrongdoer. Indeed, the evidence is so persuasive and so necessary in case of infanticide or other child abuse by suffocation if the wrongdoer is to be apprehended, that we think that its relevance clearly outweighs its prejudicial effect on the jury. We reject defendant's argument that the proof was not so clear and convincing that its admissibility should not be sustained. As we stated at the outset, if the evidence with regard to each child is considered separately, it is true that some of the incidents are less conclusive than others; but we think the incidents must be considered collectively, and when they are, an unmistakable pattern emerges. That pattern overwhelmingly establishes defendant's guilt.

C. *Admissibility of Evidence to Prove Corpus Delicti.* For the reasons stated, the sufficiency of the evidence of (a) what happened to the other children, (b) proof of the fact of Paul's death, and (c) the government's expert testimony of the probable cause of death, to prove the corpus delicti was apparent. Defendant argues strenuously, however, that even if admissible for other purposes, the law does not permit evidence of prior acts to be employed to prove the corpus delicti * * *.

Counsel have not cited, nor have we found, any case which considers whether or not prior acts can be used to establish the corpus delicti of murder, but the law seems clear that prior acts can be proved to establish the corpus delicti of arson,[13] and also that a confession may be relied upon to prove the corpus delicti if there is other corroborating evidence, short of independent proof of the corpus delicti, to prove the reliability of the confession. The rule in cases of arson would seem equally applicable in cases of murder, and the rule with regard to confessions bears a close analogy to the use of other acts to prove murder. We therefore hold that in the instant case proof of the incidents involving other children was admissible to prove the corpus delicti of murder and other acts of child abuse.

* * *

Affirmed.

WIDENER, CIRCUIT JUDGE (dissenting):

I respectfully dissent from the majority opinion as it relates to evidence of incidents concerning other children, and especially as it holds such evidence may be considered proof of the *corpus delicti* (which may include the criminal agency of the accused). * * *

While I do not agree with the majority that the evidence of prior occurrences was admissible under either the signature exception or to show lack of accident, since the majority gives no reason for its holding, the reason for my dissent will not be further mentioned here. * * *

13. State v. Schleigh, 210 Or. 155, 310 P.2d 341, 348 (1957) (repeated fires by spontaneous combustion unlikely; eight fires along one country road immediately after defendant, his father and others drove by show "a deliberate plan to set them"); State v. Smith, 221 S.W.2d 158 (Mo.1949) (proof of prior fire was admissible to show that fire charged in indictment was incendiary); People v. Wolf, 334 Ill. 218, 165 N.E. 619 (1929) (proof of separate fires admissible to prove corpus delicti); State v. Ritter, 288 Mo. 381, 231 S.W. 606 (1921) (proof of prior fires admissible to prove the corpus delicti); People v. Jones, 123 Cal. 65, 55 P. 698 (1898) (proof of burning of other buildings admissible to prove corpus delicti). Contra: Kahn v. State, 182 Ind. 1, 105 N.E. 385 (1914).

I am convinced that the defendant here did not receive a fair trial because the evidence of prior occurrences, fitting no recognized exception to the general rule, was so highly inflammatory and prejudicial, as well as being neither plain, nor clear, nor convincing, that it should not have been admitted for any purpose, much less for all purposes.

* * *

In applying a balancing test, the considerations confronting the district court may be summarized succinctly: assuming an exception to the rule is applicable, before admitting evidence of prior acts or crimes, the court should determine, first, whether the evidence is relevant; secondly, whether the evidence is unduly prejudicial notwithstanding its relevancy; and, thirdly, having met both prior tests, whether the evidence is truly needed by the prosecution.[14]

* * *

Notes and Questions

1. *Doctrine of chances.* How many other incidents is sufficient? In the "Brides in the Bath" case, cited in a footnote in *Woods*, two other wives had drowned while taking baths. Compare the principal case with Tucker v. State, 412 P.2d 970 (Nev.1966):

> On May 7, 1957, Horace Tucker telephoned the police station and asked a detective to come to the Tucker home in North Las Vegas. Upon arrival the detective observed that Tucker had been drinking, was unshaven, and looked tired. Tucker led the detective to the dining room where one, Earl Kaylor, was dead on the floor. Kaylor had been shot several times. When asked [what] had happened, Tucker said that he (Tucker) had been sleeping in the bedroom, awakened, and walked to the dining room where he noticed Kaylor lying on the floor. Upon ascertaining that Kaylor was dead, Tucker telephoned the police station. He denied having killed Kaylor. A grand jury conducted an extensive investigation. Fifty-three witnesses were examined. However, an indict-

14. The majority alters the balance by weighing the relevance of the evidence plus the need for the evidence against the prejudice resulting to the defendant. It also applies the test without first finding an exception to gain admissibility. The infirmity in this formulation is that as the need for the evidence increases, the probative value may decrease and still the evidence will be admissible. This new test given effect by today's ruling, elevates need, if accompanied by the slightest probative value, to the status of an exception in compelling cases. This, of course, coupled with the absence of a limiting instruction, gives no protection to the defendant in a case already clouded with emotional issues.

Indeed, I find that such emphasis on need comes perilously close to a rule in the law of evidence that the end may justify the means, and my inhibition at such a departure from the common law tradition is at the root of my dissent. While the executive branch of government must frequently, of necessity, make the decision as to need as against consequences in securing evidence, such a balance should not be given dignity by the courts in ascertaining admissibility absent an exception to the general rule. The use of need in any balancing test properly ought to be limited to applying, in a negative sense, an exclusionary rule, not to bolstering admissibility. McCormick on Evidence, 1954 Ed. § 157, clearly points this out, and advocates that the test be used as a further limit on admissibility, not as an extension of it.

ment was not returned as the grand jury deemed the evidence inconclusive. No one, including Tucker, has ever been charged with that killing.

On October 8, 1963, Horace Tucker telephoned the police and asked a sergeant to come to the Tucker home in North Las Vegas; that there was an old man dead there. Upon arrival the sergeant noticed that Tucker had been drinking. The body of Omar Evans was dead on the couch in the living room. Evans had been shot. Tucker stated that he (Tucker) had been asleep, awakened, and found Evans dead on the couch. Subsequently Tucker was charged with the murder of Evans. * * *

See also Imwinkelried, *United States v. Woods*: A Story of the Triumph of Traditions, in Evidence Stories 59 (Lempert ed., 2006).

2. *Unenumerated purposes.* Should evidence of other acts be admitted which purportedly is not offered for the purpose of proving that the accused acted in conformity with his character, but is not within any of the purposes listed in Rule 404(b)? Judge Widener in his dissent in *Woods* used the term "exclusionary" rule. Is that still good law? See United States v. Tan, 254 F.3d 1204, 1208 (10th Cir.2001) ("The list of proper purposes is illustrative, not exhaustive, and Rule 404(b) is considered to be 'an inclusive rule, admitting all evidence of other crimes or acts except that which tends to prove *only* criminal disposition.' "). For examples of cases in which evidence has been admitted other than for an enumerated purpose see United States v. Tafoya, 757 F.2d 1522 (5th Cir.1985) (tax evasion prosecution; evidence of three attempted killings for hire admitted to show that the accused "did something to earn the income * * * he failed to report"); State v. Jeffers, 661 P.2d 1105 (Ariz.1983) (prior murder attempt upon victim offered in homicide prosecution to rebut opening statement claim by counsel that the accused had an "abiding love" for the victim which would not allow him to cause her harm). There are a few crimes, such as domestic violence, that make the victim's state of mind an essential element of the offense and prior other acts may be relevant for this purpose. E.g., State v. Drake, 734 N.E.2d 865, 868 (Ohio Ct.App.1999) ("The act of previously putting Eva Drake's arm in a cast is admissible to show Eva Drake's state of mind when appellant made the threats in this case. The second statement also goes to Eva Drake's state of mind. The third statement is directly relevant to the threat to put Eva Drake in the river. These two previous threatening statements and one prior act are not generalized bad acts from appellant's past.").

3. *Defendant's involvement in the other act.* In Huddleston v. United States, 485 U.S. 681 (1988), the Supreme Court held that proof that the accused participated in the other act is governed by Rule 104(b) (conditional relevance). In other words, only a prima facie case need to shown. The Court rejected cases that had required the "preponderance of evidence" or "clear and convincing evidence" standard. *Huddleston* is in Chapter 1, Section A, supra. Some states have rejected *Huddleston*. See Minn.R.Evid. 404(b) (1989) ("such evidence shall not be admitted unless the other crime, wrong, or act and the participation in it by a relevant person are proven by clear and convincing evidence"). See also United States v. Dickerson, 248 F.3d 1036, 1047 (11th Cir.2001) (" 'the uncorroborated word of an accomplice

* * * provides a sufficient basis for concluding that the defendant committed extrinsic acts admissible under Rule 404(b)' ").

4. *Acquittal.* May the prosecution introduce evidence of an alleged past crime where the defendant has been acquitted of that crime? While the United States Supreme Court has held there is no constitutional impediment to the use of such evidence, Dowling v. United States, 493 U.S. 342 (1990), some courts have nevertheless refused to permit its admission. See, e.g., State v. Scott, 413 S.E.2d 787 (N.C.1992). If there is no constitutional impediment, on what grounds might such evidence be excluded? What about the application of Rule 403? Collateral estoppel? With regard to the application of collateral estoppel, see discussion in State v. Aparo, 614 A.2d 401 (Conn.1992).

5. *Notice.* Should there be a requirement that the prosecution give notice of its intent to use evidence falling under Rule 404(b)? A provision to this effect was added to Federal Rule 404(b) in 1991. See also Ky.R.Evid. 404(c) (notice required in criminal cases).

6. *Reform proposal.* Ross, "He Looks Guilty": Reforming Good Character Evidence to Undercut the Presumption of Guilt, 65 U.Pitt.L.Rev. 227 (2004) (arguing for both the reduction of Rule 404(b) evidence and the expansion of good character evidence by the defense).

SECTION D. THE INTERSECTION OF RELEVANCY AND ANCILLARY POLICY CONSIDERATIONS

INTRODUCTORY NOTE

Two rationales generally support Rules 407–410. Take, as an example, offers of compromise under Rule 408. One rationale is that the evidence is of marginal relevancy. See 4 Wigmore, Evidence § 1061, at 36 (Chadbourn rev. 1972) ("The true reason for excluding an offer of compromise is that it does not ordinarily proceed from and *imply a specific belief that the adversary's claim is well-founded,* but rather a belief that the further prosecution of that claim, whether well-founded or not, would in any event cause such annoyance as is preferably avoided by the sum offered.") But see Advisory Committee Note to Rule 408 ("The validity of this position will vary as the amount of the offer varies in relation to the claim and may also be influenced by other circumstances."). The second is that the admission of the evidence would contravene some important ancillary policy—here the promotion of settlement of suits short of trial that would be discouraged if offers of compromise were freely admissible. See 2 McCormick, Evidence § 266, at 231 (6th ed. 2006). What are the ancillary policy considerations behind Rules 407, 409 and 410?

A hearsay issue arises regarding evidence covered by Rules 407–410, although it is typically easily resolved. Often the evidence is nonhearsay because the actor or declarant had no intention to make an assertion (see Rule 801(a)). In other circumstances, where an intention to assert may be found, the evidence is treated as an admission (see Rule 801(d)(2)). In both situations, the hearsay objection is overcome, see Chapter 13, infra, and admissibility depends upon relevancy and ancillary policy questions. Nevertheless, the status of such evidence as admissions has caused some legal scholars to treat the questions raised in this section as part of the study of hearsay. See 2 McCormick, Evidence ch. 25 (6th ed. 2006).

IN RE AIR CRASH DISASTER

United States Court of Appeals, Sixth Circuit, 1996.
86 F.3d 498.

[In August 1987, a Northwest Airlines flight crashed during takeoff from the airport in Detroit, Michigan killing all passengers and crew and two bystanders. Plaintiffs sued Northwest Airlines and McDonnell Douglas, the plane's manufacturer. The airline and manufacturer filed claims against each other for contribution and indemnity. A jury found Northwest one hundred percent liable, and the trial court permitted McDonnell Douglas to recover money it paid to settle certain claims. Northwest appealed, and the Sixth Circuit affirmed.]

BOGGS, CIRCUIT JUDGE.

* * *

We now address Northwest's claims that it is entitled to a new trial because the district court erred by excluding various items of evidence from the jury's consideration.

EXCLUDING EVIDENCE OF NORTHWEST'S POST-ACCIDENT REWIRING OF THE CENTRAL AURAL WARNING SYSTEM

Northwest claims that the district court erred in excluding evidence relating to its post-accident rewiring of the plane's Central Aural Warning System ("CAWS"). After the accident, Northwest rewired all of its fleet of MD–80 aircraft (the model that crashed) so that the CAWS Fail Light would illuminate upon loss of input power. Northwest sought to introduce the fact of this rewiring as circumstantial evidence that the system had been unsafe.

The district court granted McDonnell Douglas's Motion *in Limine* No. 3 and excluded the evidence. The court reasoned that Northwest's post-accident rewiring of the CAWS was inadmissible under Fed.R.Evid. 407 as a subsequent remedial measure offered to prove culpable conduct of a tortfeasor. Order, October 30, 1989, at 11.

According to Northwest, the court erred in excluding the evidence of the rewiring because it was relevant and not excludable under Rule 407. Northwest contends that its rewiring evidence was not precluded under Rule 407 "because [the Rule] does not apply to subsequent measures taken by a third party." Northwest Br. at 51. Inasmuch as Northwest is not a third party to this suit, its claim appears to be that Rule 407 does not bar evidence of subsequent remedial measures taken by a party other than the one with primary responsibility for the subject of the remedial measures (a "non-responsible party"). Northwest also argues that even if the court's Rule 407 ruling was correct, later developments at trial opened the door to admission of the CAWS rewiring.

We agree with Northwest that its rewiring of the CAWS fell within the federal rules' broad definition of relevance. Fed.R.Evid. 401. Under Rule 401, evidence is relevant if it has "any tendency to make the existence of any fact that is of consequence to the determination of the action more probable or less probable than it would be without the evidence." Whether the CAWS was improperly wired was an issue of consequence in this case. Northwest's rewiring of the CAWS is circumstantial evidence, if only of a weak and suspect sort, that the CAWS as it existed at the time of the accident was not foolproof.

However, it is not clear that the court erred by excluding the fact of the rewiring under Rule 407 as a subsequent remedial measure. There is nothing in the text of Rule 407 that limits its application to measures by a "responsible" party—i.e., measures by a party against whom the evidence is offered. The Rule provides,

> When, after an event, measures are taken which, if taken previously, would have made the event less likely to occur, evidence of the subsequent measures is not admissible to prove negligence or culpable conduct in connection with the event. This rule does not require the exclusion of evidence of subsequent measures when offered for another purpose, such as proving ownership, control, or feasibility of precautionary measures, if controverted, or impeachment.

Fed.R.Evid. 407. Although the Rule specifically removes from its reach evidence of remedial measures offered for purposes other than to prove negligence or culpable conduct, it nowhere embraces the limitation Northwest urges. By its terms, the Rule seems to exclude evidence of remedial measures regardless of who undertook them.

It is true that exceptions to the Rule have developed. *E.g., Werner v. Upjohn Co., Inc.,* 628 F.2d 848, 855 (4th Cir.1980). Northwest cites several cases in which courts declined to exclude evidence of subsequent remedial measures. Some cases contain language saying that "Rule 407 applies only to subsequent remedial measures taken voluntarily *by the defendant.*" *Raymond v. Raymond Corp.,* 938 F.2d 1518, 1524 (1st Cir.1991). *Accord Middleton v. Harris Press & Shear, Inc.,* 796 F.2d 747, 751 (5th Cir.1986). In each of these cases, however, the remedial measure was taken, not by a plaintiff, but by someone who was not a party to the suit. * * * There is no direct support for Northwest's argument that it should have been able to introduce evidence of its own voluntary remedial measures to prove the culpability of an adversary.

Courts have been wary to restrict the scope of Rule 407. "[W]e should not be too quick to read new exceptions into the rule because by doing so there is a danger of subverting the policy underlying the rule." *Werner,* 628 F.2d at 856. In this case, there is neither clear textual authority nor legislative history supporting an exception. *See Bradley v. Austin,* 841 F.2d 1288, 1293 (6th Cir.1988) (unambiguous language in a statute is conclusive of its meaning).

One might argue that the purpose of Rule 407, at least as that purpose is commonly understood, is not directly served by the application of the rule to the present circumstances. Allowing evidence of subsequent remedial measures by someone suing the manufacturer of an allegedly faulty product does not *deter* subsequent safety precautions. In fact, allowing such evidence might *encourage* subsequent precautions, as the value of a subsequent remedial measure to the buyer of the faulty product would include its safety effect *and* its tactical advantage during litigation.

However, it would be wrong to construe the function of Rule 407 so narrowly. Independent of its effect on safety upgrades by alleged tortfeasors, the rule bars a class of evidence that is very poor proof of negligence or defectiveness. 2 Weinstein's Evidence § 407, 13–14 (finding in the unreliability of such evidence a primary purpose of the rule). There is nothing that makes evidence of a subsequent remedial measure by a plaintiff (or someone in the position of a plaintiff, like Northwest) better proof of culpable conduct than evidence of a remedial measure by a defendant. Indeed, measures taken by a plaintiff—especially one contemplating litigation—strike us as *more* dubious because of the possibility that the plaintiff is only "repairing" an item in order to create helpful evidence.

We believe that the district court's interpretation of Rule 407 was correct and that the rule can encompass situations like the one presented here. The text of the rule is unqualified, and there is precedent cautioning us from creating exceptions. Furthermore, although applying the rule to measures taken by plaintiffs does not serve the rule's purpose to encourage safety precautions, it does serve the rule's purpose of excluding inherently unreliable evidence. Therefore, we hold that the district court did not err by excluding the evidence of the CAWS rewiring.

Northwest's argument that later developments at trial opened the door to admission of the CAWS rewiring evidence is also unpersuasive. Northwest contends that MDC opened the door in its cross-examination of Northwest witness Rodney Peters. Our review of the record indicates that while McDonnell Douglas examined Peters about Northwest's "fleet campaign" to remove and replace all CAWS circuit breakers from its MD–80s, it did not question Peters about the rewiring of the CAWS. Northwest argues that the replacement of the circuit breakers was nonetheless sufficiently related to the rewiring of the CAWS to open the door to the use of the CAWS rewiring evidence. In our view, however, the replacement of the breakers and the rewiring of the CAWS to warn the crew when the system is not receiving any power are not so related that McDonnell Douglas's examination of Peters on the former opens the door to Northwest's examination of him on the latter. Therefore, we agree with the district court that McDonnell Douglas did not open the door to admission of Northwest's rewiring of the CAWS.[15]

We note that, even if the exclusion of the rewiring evidence was an error, the error was harmless. The parties stipulated into evidence the feasibility of rewiring the CAWS Fail Light. 199 Transcript 130–32 (jury instructions). Furthermore, the court permitted Northwest to introduce factual and expert opinion testimony critical of McDonnell Douglas's wiring scheme. *See* Northwest Br. at 10 (summarizing).

Excluding Evidence that the Flight Director Was Defective

Northwest claims that the court erred in excluding from evidence Exhibits 1106, 1107, 1123–29, and 1138, which related to the Honeywell flight directors used on MD–83, MD–87, and MD–88 aircraft. According to Northwest, the court erred in excluding these exhibits because they were relevant to its case and not otherwise inadmissible.

The court granted in part MDC's Motion *in Limine* No. 8 and excluded the exhibits as irrelevant, unduly prejudicial, and, except as to Exhibit 1126, concerned with subsequent remedial measures. Order, October 30, 1990, at 12–13. The court held that the exhibits were irrelevant under Rule 401, because they related to different model flight directors used on heavier planes with different engines. For much the same reason, the court excluded the exhibits on grounds that they would confuse the jury and result in an unwarranted expenditure of time, under Rule 403. Furthermore, the court held that the exhibits (except for Exhibit 1126) were inadmissible under Rule 407 on grounds that "remedial measures taken before an accident are excludable for the same policy considerations involved in a standard Rule 407 ruling." *Ibid.*

In disagreement with the district court's holding, we believe that the exhibits at issue have at least minimal relevance. Although many of the exhibits related to different and newer models of flight directors than the model aboard flight 255, what the parties call the "control laws," or computer program, for the takeoff mode of all the flight directors were identical. 177 Transcript at 57. The exhibits lent at least some support to Northwest's claim that the flight director was defective.

Nor do we agree with the district court that Rule 407 bars the exhibits' admission. Rule 407 bars the admission of evidence of remedial measures taken after an event that would have made the event less likely to occur. Fed.R.Evid. 407. Here, however, the evidence was of

15. Although the court did not exclude the evidence of Northwest's rewiring the CAWS under Rule 403, we believe that exclusion of this evidence may alternatively be affirmed under that Rule. Rule 403 provides that "evidence may be excluded if its probative value is substantially outweighed by the danger of unfair prejudice, confusion of the issues, or misleading the jury * * *." In our view, the danger of unfair prejudice from this evidence was great—especially because the repairs in question were made by a non-responsible party in whose interest it was to minimize its liability and maximize the liability of its codefendant—and substantially outweighed the minimal probative worth of the evidence. *See Bauman v. Volkswagenwerk Aktiengesellschaft,* 621 F.2d 230, 233 (6th Cir.1980) (noting extent of prejudice caused by evidence of remedial measures).

measures taken *after* the design of a product but *before* the accident. Inasmuch as the exhibits related to pre-accident changes to the flight director, they fell outside the reach of Rule 407. * * *

Moreover, Rule 407 does not preclude evidence of subsequent measures offered for purposes of impeachment. Fed.R.Evid. 407*; see Patrick v. South Cent. Bell Tel. Co.,* 641 F.2d 1192, 1196–97 (6th Cir.1980). McDonnell Douglas's flight director expert, Jean–Jacques LeBlond, testified that the flight director was not defective and represented the state of the art, 76 Transcript at 56–57, and that there was no reason for McDonnell Douglas to advise operators about any "error" in the control laws operating immediately after takeoff, 79 Transcript at 72. In our view, Northwest was entitled to impeach LeBlond's testimony by showing that McDonnell Douglas, in later models, modified the design of the flight director aboard Flight 255 to correct deficiencies. *See Muzyka v. Remington Arms Co., Inc.,* 774 F.2d 1309, 1313–14 (5th Cir.1985) (originally excluded evidence of post-accident design change should have been admitted for impeachment purposes once the nature of the evidence presented by defendant manufacturer became apparent).

In the final analysis, however, we cannot conclude that the district court abused its discretion in excluding the exhibits under Rule 403 because their probative value was substantially outweighed by the danger of unfair prejudice, confusion of the issues, or misleading the jury. Though not irrelevant, the exhibits in question were of marginal probative value, because they related to different model flight directors used on heavier planes with different engines. The exhibits would have complicated the proceedings, and could easily have confused the jury.[16]

EXCLUDING AN INTERNAL MEMORANDUM FROM MCDONNELL DOUGLAS

Northwest claims that the court erred in excluding Exhibit 297, an internal memorandum from McDonnell Douglas dated two months after the crash. The short memorandum says that McDonnell Douglas recommended to the buyers of DC–10 planes that they should perform a "takeoff warning system check" prior to takeoff. The memorandum says that this recommendation was made in response to "the Chicago Accident"—a reference to the crash on takeoff of an American Airlines DC–10 in Chicago in 1979. The memorandum also says that a "takeoff warning system check" was not recommended to buyers of MD–80 planes because the CAWS Fail Light should catch similar problems.

The district court excluded the exhibit on two grounds. We agree with Northwest that one reason given by the court—that the memorandum, because it mentioned the Chicago accident, was more prejudicial than probative under Fed.R.Evid. 403—was improper. It may be true that the jury would have been swayed unfairly by the fact that another McDonnell Douglas plane crashed on takeoff. It may also be true that

16. [The court also ruled that if exclusion under Rule 403 was erroneous, it was harmless. Ed.]

the fact that a "takeoff warning systems check" was not recommended is of little probative value—both because other systems checks were recommended and not performed by the Crew, and because there was evidence that the Crew pulled the circuit breaker connected to the CAWS. However, the district court did not consider the possibility that the memorandum could be redacted. We find this a minor error.

The error made no difference in the case, however. First, the court's other reason for excluding the exhibit is legitimate: Rule 407. The memorandum, written shortly after the crash, explains why the additional check was not recommended for the MD–80 model. It is obvious that the memorandum is part of a discussion about whether McDonnell Douglas should recommend the check in the future—and such a change in policy is a subsequent remedial measure within the meaning of Fed.R.Evid. 407. *Hall v. American Steamship Co.,* 688 F.2d 1062, 1066 (6th Cir.1982) (steamship's choice to follow new safety policy after an accident not admissible evidence of negligence under Rule 407). Second, the probative value of the memorandum, as mentioned above, is minimal. Even if one of the precautions neglected by the flight crew was not necessary, others certainly were. Our review of the record indicates that the neglect of these other, far more important, precautions constituted the heart of McDonnell Douglas's case, and the crux of the jury's verdict.

* * *

It is impossible to summarize completely in a concluding paragraph the results of the legal system's effort to cope with a tragedy of this magnitude. The deaths of 156 people resulted in five years of proceedings below, nineteen months of trial, 199 volumes of trial transcript, over 4000 evidentiary exhibits, and more than 3000 record entries reproduced in 77 volumes of Joint Appendix in our court, comprising 18,922 pages and eight videocassettes.

At the end of the day, however, we are firmly convinced that Chief Judge Cook and the jury provided a fair trial based on permissible rulings of law. In the words of Justice Minton, "There must be an end to litigation someday * * *." *Ackermann v. United States,* 340 U.S. 193, 198 * * * (1950). The judgment of the district court is AFFIRMED.

Notes and Questions

1. *Applicability of rule to actions of others or involuntary remedial measures by defendant.* The first issue examined by *Air Crash Disaster* is whether Rule 407 excludes subsequent remedial measures other than those done voluntarily by the defendant. The conduct by another party to the suit, Northwestern, presented the issue in an unusual situation. More commonly the action is taken by an entity that is not party to the suit, where courts often find the Rule inapplicable. See Diehl v. Blaw–Knox, 360 F.3d 426, 429–30 (3d Cir.2004) (finding policy argument and therefore Rule inapplicable to conduct of non-parties); Buchanna v. Diehl Mach., Inc., 98 F.3d 366, 370–71 (8th Cir.1996) (same). Also, when the change is made by the defendant but

done involuntarily, such as when ordered by a "superior authority," such as a government agency, courts sometimes also find Rule 407 inapplicable. See State v. Elementis Chem., Inc., 887 A.2d 1133, 1139 (N.H.2005) (observing that for identical state rule to apply the act must be voluntarily undertaken by the defendant). The law is in some conflict. Compare O'Dell v. Hercules, 904 F.2d 1194 (8th Cir.1990) (adopting exception), with Werner v. Upjohn, 628 F.2d 848 (4th Cir.1980) (rejecting exception). Finally, as *Air Crash Disaster* illustrates, when the conduct at issue is that of a third party, its relevance may be more problematic, and it may be excluded for that reason. See, e.g., Raymond v. Raymond Corp., 938 F.2d 1518, 1524–25 (1st Cir.1991).

2. *Meaning of "event."* In *Air Crash Disaster*, which was decided in 1996, the court was construing a Rule that stated "[w]hen, after an event, [remedial] measures are taken * * *." It concluded that a remedial measure taken after the design of the product but before the accident was not covered by Rule 407 as a "subsequent" remedial measure. It defined the critical "event" as the accident, not the design. In 1997, Rule 407 was amended consistent with this ruling. It now begins, "[w]hen after an injury or harm allegedly caused by an event, [remedial] measures are taken * * *." The Advisory Committee Note explains: "Evidence of measures taken by the defendant prior to the 'event' do not fall within the exclusionary scope of Rule 407 even if they occurred after the manufacture or design of the product."

3. *Scope of "impeachment" exception. Air Crash Disaster* acknowledges that Rule 407 lists impeachment among the purposes for which evidence of subsequent remedial measures may be received. Given the broad potential scope of impeachment, including the right of parties to impeach their own witnesses, the impeachment exception, if construed liberally, could constitute a particularly effective means of circumventing the protections of the Rule. Commentators and courts, as a consequence, argue for a narrow application of this exception. As distinguished from simple contradiction where the limited probative value is typically outweighed by the risk of prejudice and confusion, testimony in terms of "superlatives—e.g., 'this is the safest product on the market—' * * * provides a more direct and probative form of impeachment, which justifies a limited exception to the Rule." 2 Saltzburg, Martin & Capra, Federal Rules of Evidence Manual § 407.02[8], at 407–11—407–12 (9th ed. 2006); Doe v. Wal–Mart Stores, Inc., 558 S.E.2d 663, 677 (W.Va.2001) (recognizing the danger in permitting impeachment, but holding it proper under the circumstances because of the extreme claim that no greater care was possible).

4. *Practices admitted under common law.* Under common law development, the general rule excluding evidence of subsequent remedial measures was subject to numerous exceptions, e.g., evidence of subsequent installation of crossing flasher admitted to rebut defendant's contention that wigwag signal was safest, Daggett v. Atchison, T. & S.F.Ry., 313 P.2d 557 (Cal.1957); evidence of design modification admitted to show feasibility of using safeguard or changing design, Boeing Airplane Co. v. Brown, 291 F.2d 310 (9th Cir.1961); evidence admitted that defendant road contractor put out warning signs after accident to show defendant was in control of locus, Powers v. J.B. Michael & Co., 329 F.2d 674 (6th Cir.1964). Exceptions of these type are continued by the final sentence of the Rule. Indeed, as Professor Michael

Graham put it, "In practice the exception to Rule 407 may fairly be said to come close to swallowing up the rule—evidence as to the subsequent remedial repair is very frequently brought to the attention of the jury for a purpose other than to establish negligence or culpable conduct. Since the efficiency of * * * a limiting instruction, Rule 105, is extremely suspect, policy considerations underlying Rule 407 are greatly compromised." 1 Graham, Handbook of Federal Evidence § 407.1, at 962 n.9 (6th ed. 2006).

5. *"When controverted."* Rule 407 states that evidence of subsequent remedial measures may be admitted to prove feasibility "if controverted," but the federal courts are divided on the meaning of that term. Compare In re Joint Eastern District & Southern District Asbestos Litigation, 995 F.2d 343, 345–46 (2d Cir.1993) (defendant did not affirmatively contest feasibility issue so it was not controverted), with Meller v. Heil Co., 745 F.2d 1297, 1300 n.7 (10th Cir.1984) (absent stipulation as to feasibility, it was controverted).

6. *Self-critical analysis.* In *Air Crash Disaster*, a memorandum that the court described as "part of a discussion about whether McDonnell Douglas should recommend the [takeoff warning check] in the future" was excluded because such a change in policy is a protected remedial measure. Protecting this memorandum resembles protection sometimes given by courts to an organization's post-accident internal investigative report, labeled self-critical analysis. The Massachusetts Supreme Court ruled that such reports should not be treated differently than the remedial measures they help bring about because "[t]o do so would discourage potential defendants from conducting such investigations, and so preclude safety improvements, and frustrate the salutary public policy under the rule." Martel v. Massachusetts Bay Transp. Auth., 525 N.E.2d 662, 664 (Mass.1988). Whether such investigatory reports should be protected by the Rule is the subject of lively debate in federal and state courts, although the weight of authority appears to oppose such an extension of the Rule. See, e.g., Granberry v. Jet Blue Airways, 228 F.R.D. 647, 650–51 (N.D.Cal.2005); City of Bethel v. Peters, 97 P.3d 822, 825–27 (Alaska 2004); Fox v. Kramer, 994 P.2d 343, 355–61 (Cal.2000). For discussion of self-critical analysis "privilege," see generally 2 Imwinkelried, The New Wigmore: Evidentiary Privileges § 7.8 (2002) (noting three schools of thought on the scope of a self-critical analysis privilege: first, a broad privilege to be invoked by any entity (§ 7.8.1), second, a more limited privilege for medical peer review (§ 7.8.2), and third, a more limited privilege for environmental audits (§ 7.8.3)).

7. *Broad construction of "remedial measure."* Other situations comparable to subsequent remedial measures, in that either it is unclear whether the conduct or statement may fairly be construed as an admission or their evidentiary use may discourage desirable conduct, are fairly numerous. This is probably the true rationale of cases excluding evidence of the discharge of an employee after an accident. See, e.g., Rynar v. Lincoln Transit Co., 30 A.2d 406 (N.J.1943). Indeed, the broad language of Rule 407 protects not only subsequent repairs but also installation of safety devices, changes in company rules, and the discharge of employees. 2 McCormick, Evidence § 267, at 239–40 (6th ed. 2006). By contrast, company rules in effect at the time of the occurrence have generally been held admissible against the company. Most of the cases involve railroad companies, and the quasi-public

nature of their rules likely affected the decisions. Danbois v. New York Central R.R., 189 N.E.2d 468 (N.Y.1963); Winters, The Evidentiary Value of Defendant's Safety Rules in a Negligence Action, 38 Neb.L.Rev. 906 (1959).

8. *Application to product liability cases.* In 1997, Federal Rule 407 was amended to make clear that it applied to product liability cases in addition to those based on negligence. Where the Rule had previously excluded evidence to prove "negligence or culpable conduct," it now excludes evidence that proves "negligence, culpable conduct, a defect in a product, a defect in a product design, or a need for a warning or instruction." Prior to the amendment, most of the federal circuit courts had already adopted this position. By contrast, a number of state courts, although apparently a dwindling number, follow the lead of the California Supreme Court in Ault v. International Harvester Co., 528 P.2d 1148 (Cal.1974), and do not extend the protection of their version of Rule 407 to product liability cases. See 23 Wright & Graham, Federal Practice and Procedure: Evidence § 5282.1, at 40 (Supp. 2005) (asserting that majority of state drafters and courts have taken the view that the Rule's policy does not justify expansion to strict liability cases); but see First Premier Bank v. Kolcraft Enters., Inc., 686 N.W.2d 430, 449–52 (S.D.2004) (applying the Rule to products liability case and describing the shift in the states against the result in *Ault*).

In Forma Scientific, Inc. v. Biosera, Inc., 960 P.2d 108, 115–16 (Colo. 1998), the Colorado Supreme Court articulates the rationales for non-application to strict liability cases:

> We agree with the reasoning expressed in *Ault* as well as in pre-amendment decisions of the Eighth and Tenth Circuits. We decline to follow the newly amended Rule 407 which is now in direct opposition to our reading of CRE 407 and the Colorado Committee Comment following that rule.
>
> The explicit language of CRE 407—that "evidence of the subsequent measures is not admissible to prove negligence or culpable conduct"—does not permit the exclusion of evidence of remedial actions in strict liability claims premised on design defect. This is true because the manufacturer's conduct, whether culpable or negligent, is not germane in a strict liability action. *See Camacho v. Honda Motor Co.,* 741 P.2d 1240, 1246 n.7 (Colo.1987) ("[I]n accordance with one of the underlying goals of strict liability of easing the burden of proof for a plaintiff injured by a defective product, the plaintiff is relieved of the requirement of proving the manufacturer's negligence."). What is germane in such a case is the nature of the manufactured product itself. *See id.* at 1246. ("The primary focus must remain upon the nature of the product under all relevant circumstances rather than upon the conduct of either the consumer or the manufacturer."). Thus, any attempt to stretch the meaning of "culpable conduct" or negligence to include design defect products liability claims would be disingenuous at best.
>
> Next, we agree with *Ault* and its progeny that the public policy rationale underlying CRE 407—not to discourage entities from taking safety precautions—is largely inapplicable in the context of today's mass manufacturers. It is unreasonable to presume that a mass manufacturer of goods takes its cue from evidentiary rules rather than considerations

of consumer safety and/or the safety of consumer property. Even taking a less rosy view, recognizing that not all manufacturers necessarily place the best interests of their consumers at the forefront, market forces generally operate to compel manufacturers to improve their products. This is amply demonstrated by the actions taken here by Forma to protect its consumers' property interests by lessening the risk of inadvertent shut offs of its ultra-cold temperature freezers.

See generally Carver, Subsequent Remedial Measures 2000 and Beyond, 27 Wm. Mitchell L.Rev. 583 (2000).

McINNIS v. A.M.F., INC.

United States Court of Appeals, First Circuit, 1985.
765 F.2d 240.

PETTINE, SENIOR DISTRICT JUDGE.

The plaintiff * * * claims that the trial judge erred in admitting evidence that Patricia McInnis had released Florence Poirier from liability for the accident prior to instituting suit against the defendants. She argues that the release was offered to show that Mrs. Poirier, not the defendants, had in fact caused the amputating injury to her leg. Such evidence, she urges, is barred by Federal Rule of Evidence 408, which precludes admission of settlement agreements to prove the validity or invalidity of a claim or its amount. The defendants counter that the admission of the release does not prove the "invalidity" of the plaintiff's claim against them, but rather "narrows the issues" to allow the jury to determine what injuries were actually caused by the defendants. * * * We concur with the plaintiff/appellant and hold that the trial court erred in admitting the release. We further find that this error was prejudicial, and therefore necessitates a new trial.

* * *

[McInnis] asserted that the defendants were liable for her injuries on theories of negligent design of the motorcycle's clutch housing, negligent failure to warn, and strict products liability. Specifically, plaintiff claimed that when Poirier struck her motorcycle, it fell on its left side where the clutch housing is located. When it fell, she argued, the clutch housing shattered, exposing her leg to the sharp jagged edges and whirring gears which caused the almost complete severance of her limb. A.M.F. * * * defended the action in part on the theory that the plaintiff's severe injury was actually and immediately caused by the impact with the bumper of the Poirier vehicle, and had already occurred before the motorcycle fell.

* * *

The Trial Court Erred in Admitting the Release

Rule 408 of the Federal Rules of Evidence governs the admissibility of evidence of compromise offers or agreements in federal trials. * * * The exclusion of evidence of settlement offers is justifiable on two grounds. First, the rule illustrates Congress' desire to promote a public policy favoring the compromise and settlement of claims by insulating potential litigants from later being penalized in court for their attempts to first resolve their dispute out of court. Second, such evidence is of questionable relevance on the issue of liability or the value of a claim, since settlement may well reflect a desire for peaceful dispute resolution, rather than the litigants' perceptions of the strength or weakness of their relative positions. *See* Fed.Rule of Evid. 408, advisory committee note.

In analyzing the impact of Rule 408 on the admissibility of the Poirier release, we shall initially allay any doubts that the Rule applies to cases which are posturally like the one now before us. The settlement agreement at issue here was entered into between a litigant and a third party, rather than between the two litigants themselves. The Advisory Committee Note clearly acknowledges that the policies underlying the exclusionary rule are equally applicable to such a situation. The note states that:

> While the rule is ordinarily phrased in terms of offers of compromise, it is apparent that a similar attitude must be taken with respect to completed compromises when offered against a party thereto. *The latter situation will not, of course, ordinarily occur except when a party to the present litigation has compromised with a third person.* * * * (emphasis added).

In the context of settlements between a litigant and a third party, it is true that Rule 408 is more commonly invoked to bar the admission of agreements between a defendant and a third party to compromise a claim arising out of the same transaction as the one being litigated. * * * If the policies underlying Rule 408 mandate that settlements may not be admitted against a defendant who has recognized and settled a third party's claim against him, it is axiomatic that those policies likewise prohibit the admission of settlement evidence against a plaintiff who has accepted payment from a third party against whom he has a claim. The admission of such evidence would discourage settlements in either case. In addition, the relevance of the settlement to the validity of the claim cannot logically be considered stronger in the former instance than in the latter. * * * A number of recent federal cases have adopted this position, holding that Rule 408 bars evidence of settlements between plaintiffs and third party joint tortfeasors or former co-defendants. *See Quad/Graphics, Inc. v. Fass,* 724 F.2d 1230, 1235 (7th Cir.1983) (evidence of plaintiff's settlement with two defendants in contract action not admissible at trial of remaining defendants) * * *.

Although Rule 408 bars the admission of evidence of settlement to prove liability or the validity of a claim, it expressly allows such evidence offered for other purposes. * * * A critical inquiry in the instant case, therefore, is for what purpose the Poirier release was admitted at trial. We think it evident from a reading of the trial transcript that the district judge admitted the evidence as tending to prove that it was Mrs.

Poirier's collision with the plaintiff, not the shattering of the motorcycle clutch housing, that in fact severed the plaintiff's leg.

The defendants began their case in chief at trial by calling Patricia McInnis to the stand. Their attorney, over strenuous objection by the plaintiff, entered the release into evidence and questioned McInnis at length about its significance. The objective of his line of questioning was manifest—he was attempting to elicit an admission from McInnis that she received $60,000 from Florence Poirier because it was Mrs. Poirier alone who caused her injury. While McInnis persistently maintained that she had received the money because Mrs. Poirier had been responsible for setting the accident in motion, defense counsel repeatedly suggested that the $60,000 represented compensation for the full extent of her injuries. * * *

The trial judge's comments in overruling the plaintiff's objection to the admission of the release further illuminate the purpose of that evidence. The judge stated:

> It seems to me that there's an issue in this case which relates to the question of who caused what, what injuries were sustained as a result of the contact with the Poirier vehicle, and what injuries the plaintiff had were the responsibilities of the defendants in this case; and it may well be that the reliance [sic] represents an admission on the part of the plaintiff. I don't see that it comes within 408 because it's not offered to prove liability or invalidity of the claims or its amount. I'm going to allow it. You may have an exception. * * *

From this record it is apparent that the release was admitted as relevant to the issue of causation in fact.

* * *

Having concluded that the Poirier release was offered as relevant to the issue of causation, we have no difficulty in ruling that the evidence of causation or non-causation is fully subsumed under Rule 408's meaning of validity or invalidity of a claim. Causation in fact is an integral component of a tort claim; without causation there can be no liability. In the instant case, it is obvious that the defendants wanted the jury to infer that Mrs. Poirier would not have paid the significant sum of $60,000 to the plaintiff unless it was she, *and not the defendants,* who had caused the plaintiff's injury. Whether cast in terms of "causation", "responsibility", or the "validity of the claim", the defendants wanted the jury to conclude from the fact of settlement that the defendants could not be held liable for the amputation of the plaintiff's leg. This clearly flouts the most basic policies underlying Rule 408.

Other federal courts have held in closely analogous situations that this type of jury inference is unquestionably improper under the Federal Rule. In *McHann v. Firestone Tire and Rubber Co.,* 713 F.2d 161 (5th Cir.1983), for example, the Fifth Circuit reversed the trial court's admission of a covenant not to sue given by a plaintiff in a products liability action to a third party service station owner. The plaintiff had sued the defendant Firestone Tire for injuries he sustained when a tire on his vehicle exploded, alleging that the defendant had negligently designed and manufactured the tire. *Id.* at 162–3. Firestone introduced evidence at trial that the plaintiff had previously given a covenant not to sue to a service station owner whose employee had mounted the tire. The Fifth Circuit held the covenant inadmissible under Rule 408, since the evidence "might lead the jury to deny [plaintiff's] claim against Firestone on the perception that Green Oaks Exxon would not have paid the substantial sum of $27,000 if it * * * were not the party at fault." *Id.* at 166.

The *McHann* case illustrates the applicability of the policies underlying rule 408 to a situation such as the one now before us. Certainly, the admission of settlement evidence to prove or disprove causation would discourage a plaintiff from settling with one of several potential defendants. In addition, the fact of settlement, as the Advisory Committee has observed, is of questionable relevance to the issue. An innocent third party may settle, even for a large amount, merely to avoid the burdens of litigation. In the instant case, in fact, the Poirier release is even more doubtfully relevant to the causation issue than was the covenant not to sue in *McHann.* Since neither of the parties contests the fact that the Poirier vehicle negligently struck the plaintiff's motorcycle, Mrs. Poirier is liable for the ultimate injury to the plaintiff, whether or not the collision itself was the immediate cause. Under elementary principles of proximate cause, Mrs. Poirier is legally responsible for any harm that could foreseeably result from her tortious act. * * * We think it obvious that it is reasonably foreseeable that once struck by a car, a motorcycle may crash, causing serious bodily injury to its driver. * * * The fact that Poirier settled or the amount she paid, therefore, cannot reasonably be indicative of the harm that was in fact caused by the collision between her car and the motorcycle as opposed to that which was in fact caused by the shattering of the clutch housing.

* * *

The defendants also suggest that they introduced the Poirier release for a purpose other than proving causation—to impeach McInnis' testimony. Specifically, they sought to undermine her assertion that the injury to her leg occurred only after the clutch housing shattered. They wanted the jury to infer that if Patricia McInnis accepted $60,000 from Mrs. Poirier, it was because she believed her to be responsible for the injury. The introduction of the release, then, would allegedly discredit her present claim against the defendants.

Even if the record were not clear, as it is, that the release was admitted to prove causation, the defendants' deft paralogism would still fail. The use of the settlement for this purpose implicitly requires the jury to infer some indicia of causation in fact from the existence of the release; otherwise it would be of no logical relevance to the issue of McInnis' credibility. We cannot permit the defendants to avoid the policies of rule 408 by merely recasting the issue of who caused the injury as an issue of who the plaintiff believed caused it.[17] * * *

Notes and Questions

1. *Bias. McInnis* excluded a settlement by the plaintiff with a third party, which the court concluded was being used as evidence of the validity of the plaintiff's claim against the remaining defendant. Such settlements with third parties are more frequently encountered when offered "for another purpose" allowed under the Rule—bias. The argument is typically that a witness who is testifying "for" the party with whom the settlement was made was influenced to give favorable testimony by a generous settlement. See Miller v. Marymount Med. Ctr., 125 S.W.3d 274, 278–82 (Ky.2004) (ruling that settlement could be admitted to show bias where expert witnesses changed opinion regarding defendant's liability after settlement). However, while using settlements for this purpose is not prohibited by the Rule, admission is not always permitted. See Graber v. City of Ankeny, 616 N.W.2d 633, 638–41 (Iowa 2000) (use of evidence to show witness' bias held improper based on analysis of circumstances of settlement, effect on testimony, and potential for prejudice). Admissibility is determined by the balancing process of Rule 403.

2. *Protection for statement of facts beyond the offer.* One of the most significant differences between the protection offered under Rule 408 and its common law antecedents is the treatment of admissions of fact made during settlement efforts. Under common law doctrine, statements of fact, unless either made hypothetically or inseparably connected with the offer, were admissible. Federal Rule 408 excludes "[e]vidence of conduct or statements made in compromise negotiations" because lack of protection for statements of facts had the tendency to discourage open communications important to successful settlement efforts. See 2 McCormick, Evidence § 266, at 233 (6th ed. 2006). *Affiliated Manufacturers*, which follows, reflects a liberal application of such protection by shielding internal documents related to settlement negotiations. Is such an extension warranted or wise?

AFFILIATED MANUFACTURERS, INC. v. ALUMINUM CO. OF AMERICA

United States Court of Appeals, Third Circuit, 1995.
56 F.3d 521.

RESTANI, JUDGE.

Following a trial in this action brought by plaintiff-appellant Affiliated Manufacturers, Inc. ("AMI") alleging additional money was due on a contract, the jury returned a verdict in favor of defendant-appellee

17. We also note that the existence of the Poirier release could not have been legally relevant to the issue of McInnis' credibility. As we have already discussed, Mrs. Poirier, by colliding with the motorcycle and instigating the crash, was a proximate, legal cause of the plaintiff's ultimate injury. Since she was jointly liable for the harm, if any, that was caused by the shattering of the clutch housing, the fact that the plaintiff settled with her is hardly inconsistent with a claim that the motorcycle crash in fact caused the amputating injury.

Aluminum Company of America ("Alcoa") on its counterclaim for failure to satisfy contract specifications and breach of warranties. AMI appeals from the district court's grant of a motion *in limine* brought by Alcoa to exclude certain documents and deposition testimony as evidence of settlement negotiations under Fed.R.Evid. 408. For the reasons set forth herein, we affirm the judgment of the district court.

I.

* * *

The dispute between AMI and Alcoa arose from a contract for design and fabrication of an automated greenline handling system ("the system"). The system built under this contract was never put into production. During the construction of the system, AMI submitted to Alcoa invoices for work not included in the contract. Upon receipt, Alcoa processed the invoices for payment. The parties disagree concerning one unpaid invoice for hardware costs (four screen printers) totalling $280,000, and another unpaid invoice for $208,130 in software costs. These two invoices were submitted by AMI at the end of the project, on April 5, 1990, to the attention of Thomas Pollak ("Pollak"), Alcoa's procurement manager.

Pollak consulted with Alcoa employees Earle Lockwood ("Lockwood") and Phil Kasprzyk ("Kasprzyk") concerning the invoices, because both were closely involved with the project. In memoranda, Lockwood and Kasprzyk each evaluated one of the two invoices from AMI. At a meeting between Pollak, Lockwood and AMI's president, Benson Austin ("Austin"), on May 2, 1990, one topic of discussion was the issue of unpaid invoices, as reflected in handwritten contemporaneous notes.

Alcoa's original motion *in limine* sought exclusion of portions of the Lockwood and Kasprzyk memoranda and a letter from Austin dated June 26, 1990, as well as portions of the meeting notes from May 2, deposition exhibits and transcripts that were not specifically described. At the request of the district court, Alcoa supplied an additional submission detailing twelve items (meeting notes, deposition testimony and letters) for which Alcoa also sought portions excluded from admission at trial. * * *

[The district court ruled portions of thirteen items inadmissible. AMI challenges these rulings.]

II.

* * *

A district court's ruling as to admissibility of evidence is reviewed under an abuse of discretion standard, where the question presented involves the application of the Federal Rules of Evidence. *See In re Paoli R.R. Yard PCB Litig.,* 35 F.3d 717, 749 (3d Cir.1994). To the extent the district court's ruling turns upon an interpretation of Rule 408, it is subject to plenary review. *Id.* Where the trial court has made a factual finding in determining admissibility of evidence, the clearly erroneous standard is applied. *United States v. 68.94 Acres of Land,* 918 F.2d 389, 392 (3d Cir.1990) * * *.

III.

A. FED.R.EVID. 408

1. Evidence of negotiations to settle a disputed claim

AMI contends that the district court erred in its interpretation and application of Rule 408. AMI alleges that the court took an extreme view of the meaning of "settlement negotiations" as contemplated within the rule. AMI asserts that the district court incorrectly found that even an "apparent difference of opinion between the parties" could trigger an exclusion under the rule. *See* [*Affiliated Mfrs., Inc. v. Aluminum Co. of America, Civ. No. 91–2877, at 7 (D.N.J. Dec. 23, 1993) ("AMI I")*] at 6 * * *. Further, AMI argues that the district court erred in its factual finding that a dispute existed between the parties.

* * * The application of [Rule 408] is limited to evidence concerning settlement or compromise of a claim, where the evidence is offered to establish liability, or the validity or amount of the claim. Additionally, Rule 408 has been interpreted as applicable to an actual dispute, or at least an apparent difference of view between the parties concerning the validity or amount of a claim. 2 Jack B. Weinstein & Margaret A. Berger, *Weinstein's Evidence* ¶ 408[01] at 408–12 (1994); Kenneth S. Brown et al., *McCormick on Evidence* § 266, at 466 (John William Strong ed., 4th ed. 1992). The policy behind Rule 408 is to encourage freedom of discussion with regard to compromise. *See Weinstein's Evidence, supra,* ¶ 408[01] at 408–10.

AMI argues that the case law clearly delineates distinctions as to what constitutes "a claim which was disputed," and characterizes the excluded documents at issue as merely evidencing discussions that had not yet reached the "dispute" stage for Rule 408 purposes. Thus, AMI maintains that Rule 408 is inapplicable here, arguing that the intended construction of Rule 408 is that there must be a threat or contemplation of litigation, that goes beyond conduct or statements made to resolve differences of opinion as to the validity or amount of a claim. AMI relies chiefly upon the holdings from other circuits to support its view that the district court misinterpreted the term "dispute" and misapplied the rule. Alcoa responds that AMI has mischaracterized these decisions, as well as the district court's reasoning, in its discussion of relevant precedent.

In reaching its conclusion to apply the Rule 408 exclusion, the district court reasoned that the Tenth Circuit's application of Rule 408, in *Big O Tire Dealers, Inc. v. Goodyear Tire & Rubber Co.,* 561 F.2d 1365 (10th Cir.1977), was too restrictive in its establishment of "the point of threatened litigation [as] a clear cut-off point" for application. *AMI I* at 5 (quoting *Big O Tire,* 561 F.2d at 1373). Instead, the district court adopted the view articulated by the court in *Alpex,* 770 F.Supp. at 164–

65, finding that the *Alpex* court "considered factors apart from any indicia of threatened litigation." *AMI I* at 5–6. * * *

In *Big O Tire,* a small tire manufacturer that had used the term "Big Foot" in its business was approached by Goodyear Tire, who wished to use the same term for a national ad campaign for a new product. 561 F.2d at 1368. Both parties participated in a series of discussions about how to proceed, and Goodyear sought assurance from Big O Tire that it would not object to such use. *Id.* * * * The district court in *Big O Tire* determined that phone and letter communications between the parties prior to litigation concerning use of the trademark did not fall within the Rule 408 exclusion, as the calls and letters were merely "business communications." *See id.* at 1368, 1372–73. The Court of Appeals for the Tenth Circuit concluded that the district court did not commit manifest error in finding the disputed statements were business communications because the discussions at issue "had not crystallized to the point of threatened litigation." *Id.* at 1373.

To the extent *Big O Tire* establishes a strict standard for application of Rule 408, it was rejected by *Alpex. See* 770 F.Supp. at 164. The plaintiff in *Alpex* held certain rights relating to a patent for video games and pursued a program to combat infringement by sending letters from counsel offering certain alleged infringers the opportunity to settle what plaintiff viewed as meritorious infringement claims. *Id.* at 162. * * * The *Alpex* court determined that certain license agreements reached in the absence of litigation fell within the purview of the Rule 408 exclusion. *Id.* at 165. In its analysis, the *Alpex* court examined various factors in addition to indicia of threat of litigation, that might call for application of the exclusion. *Id.* at 164–65.

We believe that AMI has oversimplified the *Big O Tire* and *Alpex* holdings. Regarding the issue of when a "dispute" between parties exists, the *Alpex* court acknowledged that litigation need not have commenced for Rule 408 to apply. 770 F.Supp. at 164; *see North Am. Biologicals, Inc. v. Illinois Employers Ins.,* 931 F.2d 839, 841 (11th Cir.1991) (finding letter written prior to suit excludable under Rule 408 as offer of settlement). * * * Furthermore, the *Alpex* court did not, as AMI asserts, adopt *in toto* the view that a dispute must "crystallize [ ] to the point of threatened litigation" before evidence of settlement negotiations are excludable. Rather, *Alpex* and other courts make clear that the Rule 408 exclusion applies where an actual dispute or a difference of opinion exists, rather than when discussions crystallize to the point of threatened litigation. *See Alpex,* 770 F.Supp. at 163; *Dallis v. Aetna Life Ins. Co.,* 768 F.2d 1303, 1307 (11th Cir.1985) (citing *Weinstein's Evidence, supra,* ¶ 408[01]) (affirming admission of testimony involving settlement of similar claim between party to action and third party, where no evidence that validity or amount of payment had been in dispute).

Accordingly, we hold that the district court's construction of Rule 408 did not constitute legal error. As a matter of interpretation, the meaning of "dispute" as employed in the rule includes both litigation and less formal stages of a dispute, and this meaning "is unchanged by the broader scope of Rule 408." *Weinstein's Evidence, supra,* ¶ 408[01] at 408–12. The district court properly interpreted the scope of the term "dispute" to include a clear difference of opinion between the parties here concerning payment of two invoices.

The facts of each case bear upon the trial court's exercise of discretion to apply the exclusion. *See Alpex,* 770 F.Supp. at 164–65; *Bradbury v. Phillips Petroleum Co.,* 815 F.2d 1356, 1364 (10th Cir.1987) (holding if application of Rule 408 exclusion doubtful, better practice is to exclude evidence of compromise negotiations). Admittedly, it can be difficult to discern whether an "offer" was made to attempt to "compromise a claim." The existence of a disputed claim as well as the timing of the offer are relevant to making this determination. *Pierce v. F.R. Tripler & Co.,* 955 F.2d 820, 827 (2d Cir.1992). The district court here found that inherent in each of the documents presented for exclusion was the parties' disagreement or dispute as to the amount and the validity of the invoice presented for payment. *AMI I* at 6–14.

The district court found that when viewed in context, the April 5, 1990 letter from Austin at AMI was evidence of a dispute concerning the printer design and software programming. *See id.* at 2–3, 6. As this letter was not among the disputed documents, we need not consider whether a dispute arose as early as April 5. Following receipt of the April 5 letter and invoices, Kasprzyk described to Pollak in his May 1, 1990 memorandum his evaluation of the amount billed by AMI for software and his assessment of the merits of AMI's claim. This is the earliest document in dispute. In this memorandum, Kasprzyk concluded that

> [s]ince the original purchase order for the line did not thoroughly specify the capability of the line, I feel that AMI has a legitimate claim to some software compensation. I feel that AMI should only be compensated for 1/3 of the requested amount since the line does not meet [certain specifications]. I also feel that this is appropriate due to the AMI's overall inferior performance on system software.

AMI characterizes this memorandum as an "evaluation," implying that it did not evidence a dispute under Rule 408. * * * We also need not reach the question of whether the mere existence of an internal evaluation such as this memorandum provides evidence of a dispute. In his deposition Pollak stated that "[i]n preparation for [a May 2 settlement] meeting, I asked Phil Kasprzyk, an Alcoa engineer familiar with the project, his view of the disputed invoices."[18] That Kasprzyk's evaluation was written in order to prepare Pollak for a meeting to discuss a possible compromise necessarily demonstrates that at least as of May 1 there was a dispute. We cannot say that the district court erred in concluding that

18. In an affidavit, Austin denied Pollak's statement that one purpose of the May 2 meeting was to attempt settlement of the dispute. As we previously indicated, however, the notes of the May 2 meeting contained mathematical calculations, as well as the terms "software proposal" and "above settlement proposal by Alcoa unacceptable."

a dispute existed as of May 1 and that the documents at issue evidenced attempts to compromise the dispute.

2. *Exclusion of internal memoranda*

AMI's second argument is that the district court erred in applying the Rule 408 exclusion to internal memoranda that were a part of the fifteen items offered for exclusion under Rule 408. AMI argues that the rule only protects conduct and statements during negotiations, and does not protect internal memoranda, or deposition testimony concerning these memoranda. Alcoa responds that such an interpretation and application of Rule 408 would contradict the rule's purpose, serving instead to discourage open settlement discussions.

The district court found both the Lockwood and Kasprzyk memoranda, and testimony concerning these documents, to be eligible for exclusion under Rule 408. *AMI I* at 8–9. The district court declined to adopt the reasoning in *Blue Circle Atl., Inc. v. Falcon Materials, Inc.,* 760 F.Supp. 516, 522 (D.Md.1991), *aff'd without op.,* 960 F.2d 145 (4th Cir.1992), which interpreted Rule 408 to require communication of internal memoranda to an opposing party, and instead relied upon the holding in *Ramada Dev. Co. v. Rauch,* 644 F.2d 1097 (5th Cir.1981). The Court of Appeals for the Fifth Circuit in *Ramada* upheld the district court's exclusion of an internal report "made in the course of an effort to compromise." *Id.* at 1106–07. The Fifth Circuit quoted the text of Rule 408, that *"[e]vidence of conduct or statements made in compromise negotiations is likewise not admissible."* *Id.* at 1106. In construing this language, the district court here determined that the

> failure of Alcoa to communicate the internal memoranda to AMI is not dispositive in the context of a Rule 408 analysis; rather, any statements prepared by Alcoa representatives that function as the basis for compromise negotiations demonstrate 'evidence of conduct' in compromise negotiations.

AMI I at 8–9. The district court further found that the memoranda served as a basis for calculation of compromise figures. Thus, the court concluded that the Rule 408 exclusion applied. *Id.* at 9.

First, AMI argues that the legislative history of Rule 408 suggests a different result and that the district court has incorrectly broadened the language of the rule. Second, AMI asserts that the district court should have followed *Blue Circle,* and that the court disregarded an important fact in *Ramada* that narrows its application.

Under the common law, offers of compromise were excluded from evidence, but the exclusion did not extend to "admissions of fact, even though made in the course of compromise negotiations, unless hypothetical, stated to be 'without prejudice,' or so connected with the offer as to be inseparable from it." 10 James Wm. Moore, *Moore's Federal Practice* § 408.01[9] (Daniel R. Coquillette et al. eds., 2d ed. 1995) (Advisory Committee's Note on Proposed Rule 408). Thus, AMI argues, Rule 408 was intended to remedy the common law rule by expanding it merely to include evidence of conduct or statements, but not internal memoranda. *Id.* While Rule 408 was specifically designed to cover admissions of fact, its language is considerably broader than that necessary to accomplish this change.

Next, in *Ramada,* the report sought to be excluded was generated by an architect hired for the purpose of preparing an analysis of defects in the construction of a motel that plaintiff had contracted to have built. 644 F.2d at 1099, 1106. Testimony in *Ramada* indicated that the architect was "commissioned by Ramada to prepare a report that would function as a basis of settlement negotiations regarding the alleged defects in the motel." *Id.* at 1107. Thus, the Fifth Circuit determined that because the report had been prepared as a tool for settlement negotiations, it fell within the scope of Rule 408. *Id.*

In contrast to *Ramada,* the District Court of Maryland in *Blue Circle* interpreted Rule 408 as inapplicable to internal memoranda, unless they were communicated to the other side in an attempt at settlement. 760 F.Supp. at 523, citing 23 Charles Alan Wright & Kenneth W. Graham, Jr., *Federal Practice and Procedure* § 5303 (1980). We reject this interpretation of Rule 408 as too broad, and find that the district court in *Blue Circle* overstated the meaning of the treatise citation.[19]

* * *

The court notes that the Eleventh Circuit's decision in *Blu-J, Inc. v. Kemper C.P.A. Group,* 916 F.2d 637, 642 (11th Cir.1990), reinforces the reasoning in *Ramada.* In *Blu-J,* the Eleventh Circuit upheld the exclusion of evidence of an accountant's evaluation "prepared by mutual agreement of [the parties] as part of their settlement negotiations." *Id.* at 641. This independent evaluation in *Blu-J* was found to fall within the Rule 408 exception, and the holding in *Ramada,* because although the parties disagreed as to whether "an offer was on the table" during "negotiations," both parties agreed that the evaluation was done to promote settlement of a dispute. *Id.* at 642. Here, the district court found the Alcoa memoranda was prepared as a basis for compromise negotiations, particularly because the memoranda appeared to be intended to assist in calculation of compromise figures discussed subsequently. *AMI I* at 9. The district court's analysis is consistent with the view of Rule 408 expressed in the *Ramada* and *Blu-J* decisions of our sister

19. The treatise states that "[o]f course, the mere fact that information may be useful in compromise negotiations does not mean that it is privileged where it was never communicated to the opponent." *Federal Practice and Procedure, supra,* § 5303, at 179 n.26 (citing *United States v. Reserve Mining Co.,* 412 F.Supp. 705, 711–12 (D.C.Minn.1976)). * * *

Reserve Mining does not define clearly a rule for treatment of internal memoranda, as *Blue Circle* implies. Rather, the *Reserve Mining* court noted that the party's request for Rule 408 exclusion, if granted, would permit the exclusion of studies done long before any dispute arose. See 412 F.Supp. at 711–12. Such is not the case here, as the Kasprzyk memorandum was written immediately before, and in preparation for, the first meeting in which the settlement of the dispute over invoices was discussed. The Lockwood memorandum was formulated after a number of correspondence concerning settlement figures.

circuits, which we find persuasive. Thus, we hold that the district court did not abuse its discretion in excluding internal memoranda prepared for use in discussion of settlement of AMI invoice amounts.

IV.

The district court properly interpreted and applied the Rule 408 exclusion to suppress portions of the documents and testimony discussed herein. Further, the court's factual finding as to the existence of a dispute between the parties was not clearly erroneous. Thus, the district court did not err in its denial of the motion for new trial on the basis of its rulings as to evidentiary exclusions. The judgment of the district court is affirmed.

Notes and Questions

1. *Dispute as to either validity or amount.* Rule 408 protects statements made in efforts to settle a claim that is "disputed as to either validity or amount." However, as the Advisory Committee's Note makes clear, it does not protect efforts to settle an admitted debt for a lesser sum. Judge Weinstein provides an interesting example of the type of delicate judgments still required under the Rule:

> [A] careful distinction [must be made] between a frank disclosure during the course of negotiations—such as "All right, I was negligent. Let's talk about damages" (inadmissible)—and the less frequent situation in which the validity of the claim and the amount of damages are admitted—"Of course, I owe you the money, but unless you're willing to settle for less, you'll have to sue me for it" (admissible).

2 Weinstein's Federal Evidence § 408.06 (2d ed. 2006).

2. *Existence of dispute and beginning of negotiations.* As *Affiliated Manufacturers* discusses, major issues under Rule 408 are whether a dispute exists and whether and when compromise negotiations have commenced. See Johnson v. Land O' Lakes, Inc., 181 F.R.D. 388, 390–93 (N.D.Iowa 1998) (discussing different approaches to the applicability of Rule 408). For the Rule to have full effectiveness, a dispute must be considered to exist prior to the filing of a formal complaint. Should it operate to protect an unsolicited partial payment? Judge Weinstein argues that it should because such initial efforts create a favorable atmosphere for successful compromise negotiations. 2 Weinstein & Berger, Weinstein's Evidence ¶ 408[01], at 16 (1994). But see Deere & Co. v. International Harvester Co., 710 F.2d 1551, 1557–58 (Fed.Cir.1983) (Rule 408 inapplicable to offer to license a patent since there was not at the time of the offer any dispute or contest concerning the patent); Wal–Mart Stores, Inc. v. Londagin, 37 S.W.3d 620, 625 (Ark.2001) (Rule inapplicable where store apologized and took full responsibility for paying the entire claim).

3. *Impeachment not a permitted other purpose.* In 2006, Rule 408 was amended to make explicit that offers of compromise or statements made during such negotiations could not be used to impeach as a prior inconsistent statement or contradiction. As the Advisory Committee noted, " 'Use of statements made in compromise negotiations to impeach the testimony of a

party * * * is fraught with danger of misuse of the statement to prove liability, threatens frank interchange of information during negotiations * * *.' 2 McCormick, Evidence § 266, at 186 & n.25 (5th ed. 1999)." This amendment eliminates what was sometimes a difficult matter of legislative interpretation for the courts. In contrast, Rule 407 specifically lists "impeachment" as one of those other purposes not excluded by that Rule.

4. *Obstruction of justice not protected.* Compromise negotiations that constitute an effort to obstruct a criminal investigation or prosecution, such as buying off the complaining witness, are not protected under the explicit terms of the Rule 408. Another element of the 2006 amendment to Rule 408 was intended to clarify that as a general matter Rule 408's exclusion is applicable when the evidence is offered in a criminal case outside the obstruction-of-justice area. Prior to the revision, courts disagreed as to whether Rule 408 should be applicable at all in criminal cases. Some found Rule 408 applicable in criminal cases to bar admission of civil compromise efforts. See, e.g., United States v. Arias, 431 F.3d 1327, 1336–38 (11th Cir.2005); United States v. Bailey, 327 F.3d 1131, 1144–46 (10th Cir.2003); State v. Gano, 988 P.2d 1153, 1160 (Haw.1999). Others found the Rule applicable only to civil proceedings. See, e.g., Manko v. United States, 87 F.3d 50, 54–55 (2d Cir.1996); United States v. Logan, 250 F.3d 350, 367 (6th Cir.2001); State v. O'Connor, 119 P.3d 806, 809–813 (Wash.2005) (construing identical state provision). The revision to Rule 408, however, means that in federal court the evidence is clearly excluded in most criminal cases, the exception applying only when the defendant negotiated in a related civil case with a public office or agency.

5. *Interaction with mediation proceedings and emerging debate on privilege.* As several of the articles in Note 6 demonstrate, the protections of Rule 408 often intersect with the developing privilege for mediation proceedings. See Folb v. Motion Picture Indus. Pension & Health Plans, 16 F.Supp.2d 1164, 1180 (C.D.Cal.1998) (defining the boundary between and interaction of mediation privilege and Rule 408 protections). Whether outside the formal mediation context there is a privilege that would prevent third party discovery of settlement negotiations is in dispute. Compare Goodyear Tire & Rubber Co. v. Chiles Power Supply, Inc., 332 F.3d 976, 979–82 (6th Cir.2003) (recognizing privilege), with In re Subpoena Issued to Commodity Futures Trading Commission, 370 F.Supp.2d 201 (D.D.C.2005) (rejecting privilege).

6. *Sources.* Brazil, Protecting the Confidentiality of Settlement Negotiations, 39 Hastings L.J. 955 (1988); Ehrhardt, Confidentiality, Privilege and Rule 408: The Protection of Mediation Proceedings in Federal Court, 60 La.L.Rev. 91 (1999); Rambo, Impeaching Lying Parties with their Statements During Negotiation: Demysticizing the Public Policy Rationale Behind Evidence Rule 408 and the Mediation–Privilege Statutes, 75 Wash.L.Rev. 1037 (2000); Leonard, The New Wigmore: Selected Rules of Limited Admissibility § 3.7 (2000).

Rule 409

1. *Contrast to Rule 408.* Two differences should be noted between Rule 409, which excludes payments of or offers to pay medical expenses, and Rule 408, examined above. First, Rule 409 requires no dispute concerning the

validity of any claim in order to be applicable. On this dimension, Rule 409 is less demanding than Rule 408, which requires a dispute as to either the claim's validity or its amount. Second, Rule 409 provides no protection to "conduct or statements not a part of the act of furnishing or offering or promising to pay." Advisory Committee Note on Rule 409. Such communications are protected under Rule 408. Under Rule 409, communications are not considered essential to the provision of medical services to an injured party. In contrast, a full and frank exchange of information is seen as critical to the negotiation of settlements under Rule 408. Id.

2. *Statements that go beyond protections of rule.* The meager case law construing Federal Rule 409 and its counterparts in the states disagree as to when statements are "not a part of the act of furnishing or offering or promising to pay." Compare Port Neches Indep. Sch. Dist. v. Soignier, 702 S.W.2d 756, 757 (Tex.Ct.App.1986) (letter stating that future bills should be submitted to insurance company and acknowledging insurance coverage was admissible under Texas Rule 409 in that it admitted coverage), with Holguin v. Smith's Food King Properties, Inc., 737 P.2d 96, 100 (N.M.Ct.App.1987) (statement on insurance form that defendant would "take full responsibility" was inadmissible as part of offer to pay medical bills).

3. *Other (unstated) purposes.* Although it does not list other purposes for which the evidence remains admissible, Rule 409, like the other rules considered in this section, does not exclude statements or conduct offered for a purpose other than proving liability. See Savoie v. Otto Candies, Inc., 692 F.2d 363, 370 n.7 (5th Cir.1982) (evidence of maintenance payments after injury admissible as circumstantial evidence to prove plaintiff's employment status as seaman).

Rule 410

1. *Prohibition of impeachment by rule but not by agreement.* While the final sentence of Rule 410 specifies certain circumstances where statements made in connection with plea discussions may be introduced, impeachment of the subsequent testimony of the defendant is not one of them. United States v. Lawson, 683 F.2d 688, 693 (2d Cir.1982) (legislative history demonstrates "Congress' explicit intention to preclude use of statements made in plea negotiations for impeachment purposes"). However, in United States v. Mezzanatto, 513 U.S. 196 (1995), the Supreme Court held that the general prohibition in Rule 410 and Federal Rule of Criminal Procedure 11(e)(6) against use for impeachment of statements made in the course of unsuccessful plea negotiations could be waived by the defendant and that waiver required by the prosecutor as a condition of entering into plea negotiations was valid. Justice Souter in dissent, id. at 215–16, argued that allowing waiver would largely eliminate this general restriction because most defendants lack the bargaining power to refuse the condition. Lower courts have interpreted *Mezzanatto* agreements quite broadly. See 2 McCormick, Evidence § 266, at 238 n.44 (6th ed. 2006). See generally Naftalis, "Queen For A Day" Agreements and the Proper Scope of Permissible Waiver of the Federal Plea–Statement Rules, 37 Colum.J.L. & Soc.Probs. 1 (2003); Slobogin, The Story of Rule 410 and *United States v. Mezzanatto*, in Evidence Stories 103 (Lempert ed., 2006).

2. *Protecting only negotiations with prosecuting attorney.* In 1980, Rule 410 was amended to make explicit that, in order to fall within the protections of the Rule, plea negotiations must be made with an *attorney* for the prosecution. The original language of the Rule had been interpreted to cover statements made by suspects to law enforcement officers who might be incapable of reaching a plea agreement where the defendant "made the statements during the course of a conversation in which he sought concessions from the government in return for a guilty plea." United States v. Herman, 544 F.2d 791, 798 (5th Cir.1977). Such statements to law enforcement officials are now clearly outside the potential protection of modified Rule 410. See People v. Hart, 828 N.E.2d 260, 266–72 (Ill.2005) (giving state law provision similar interpretation).

3. *Permitted use of valid guilty and nolo contendere pleas.* Rule 410 protects statements made in connection with unsuccessful guilty plea negotiations and withdrawn guilty pleas. However, an unwithdrawn plea constitutes a binding admission in the case in which it is made and would also be admissible in other litigation. By contrast, Rule 410 generally prohibits use of an extant, still valid, nolo contendere plea when offered in relevant civil litigation. Convictions based on nolo contendere pleas have, however, been held admissible under Rule 609 for impeachment, see, e.g., Brewer v. City of Napa, 210 F.3d 1093, 1096 (9th Cir.2000), and occasionally for very limited substantive purposes. See Olsen v. Correiro, 189 F.3d 52 (1st Cir.1999) (admissible to show valid conviction and sentence).

*

Topic IV

COMMUNICATING DATA TO THE TRIER OF FACT

Chapter 9[1]

JUDICIAL NOTICE

STATE v. MANN

New Mexico Supreme Court, 2002.
39 P.3d 124.

Serna, Chief Justice.

Defendant William Mark Mann appeals his conviction for intentional child abuse resulting in death. * * * Defendant argues that he is entitled to a new trial based on juror misconduct during deliberations. We affirm Defendant's conviction.

I. Facts and Background

* * *

The victim was the six-year-old son of Defendant and Rita Yancher. Yancher had primary custody of the victim, and the victim usually spent every other weekend with Defendant and Patricia St. Jeor Mann, at the time, Defendant's girlfriend. On August 29, 1996, the victim was present at Defendant's house. At about 11:00 p.m., Defendant and Yancher argued during a telephone conversation regarding the victim staying with him through Saturday as well as late child support payments. At approximately 1 a.m., on August 30th, St. Jeor awoke and saw Defendant going to the victim's room to take him to the bathroom. She heard a noise from the victim, followed by a loud crash and a scream. She ran to the bathroom and saw the victim, apparently having a seizure, on the floor with Defendant cushioning his head. St. Jeor called 911 and reported that the victim was injured. She returned to the bathroom and saw the victim on his back with a screwdriver protruding from his chest. St. Jeor testified that the victim was trying to move himself and Defendant was cupping the screwdriver. St. Jeor, a nurse, attempted to attend the victim, but Defendant punched her in the eye, grabbed her by her hair and by the back of the neck and "slammed" her through the door into the opposite wall. She again called 911, telling them that Defendant attacked her.

* * *

1. Throughout this chapter some footnotes from the cases and materials have been omitted; others have been renumbered. [Ed.]

The victim's cause of death was the stab wound in his chest. Almost the entire screwdriver's blade, approximately four inches, was embedded in his chest; an autopsy revealed that the screwdriver was wedged between the sternum and the second and third ribs. * * *

Defendant was also charged with child abuse for a head injury the victim suffered in 1994. The State's pathologist testified regarding the victim's earlier skull fracture. He concluded that the brain injuries he observed were inconsistent with a simple fall from a bar stool as described by Defendant.

Defendant testified that he got up around 1 a.m. and realized that he had not taken the victim to the bathroom, a routine occurrence. He woke up the victim and walked him into the bathroom. Defendant testified that he was standing in the bathroom doorway when he saw the victim trip on a rug, put out his arms and knock the items on the hamper, and then fall to the floor. Defendant testified that he turned the victim over and saw the screwdriver. Defendant said he grabbed the screwdriver to prevent the victim from pulling it out in order to minimize the injuries. Defendant testified that St. Jeor came back in and that he thought that she would try to move him, so he pushed her from him and told her to get away. He testified that he did not remember hurting her.

Defendant presented the testimony of Dr. Alan Watts, a physicist, regarding the possibility of the victim impaling himself on the screwdriver consistent with Defendant's explanation of events. He performed several calculations in the courtroom relating to the angle at which the screwdriver may have landed and the amount of force which the victim's body would have exerted upon it on impact, as well as videotaped and live demonstrations for the jury. The videotape consisted of Dr. Watts performing experiments in which he dropped a metal rod, which simulated the victim's body, and a screwdriver onto the concrete floor of his garage. Dr. Watts analogized how a screwdriver might bounce if it hits a solid object with the randomness of throwing dice. Dr. Watts testified that the occurrence of an impalement such as that described by Defendant has "a relatively small overall probability." He stated that, based on the "probability aspects of this," it would be a "freakish accident." Dr. Watts said that "[i]t is a probability calculation" and he offered an example for comparison to "Monte Carlo [codes] because basically you roll the dice."

The State did not present rebuttal testimony, but instead cross-examined Defendant's expert. * * * The prosecutor asked if Dr. Watts could calculate "the probability of [Defendant's] explanation of the stab wound." Dr. Watts testified that he did not calculate the probability of impaling oneself on a screwdriver because "the whole issue that [he] was asked to address was can this happen, and the answer is, yes, it can." He said that the probability would be "finite," but "never zero." Dr. Watts testified that if he "were to run every option possible, [he'd] come to the conclusion that on average you won't stab yourself by falling on a screwdriver, but there is nevertheless a finite possibility it can happen." * * *

Defendant filed a motion for a new trial, arguing that the verdict was tainted by juror misconduct. Defense counsel interviewed several jurors and was told that Juror 7 [an engineer] presented probability calculations to the other members of the jury regarding the chances of a child and a screwdriver falling in such a manner as to result in impalement. Defendant identified several jurors who he believed had information regarding Juror 7.

* * *

Juror 7 told the trial court that he did not do any calculations or experiments at home. He contended that he did not dispute or discredit Dr. Watts' testimony but believed that Dr. Watts' testimony consisted of "fine calculations and [he] would agree with the calculations." Juror 7 thought that the testimony did not "[answer] the right question" because he did not accept the "logical tie" between the testimony and Defendant's story. Juror 7 completed a probability calculation to "verify [his] own gut feeling," beginning with Dr. Watts' calculations which were presented during the trial. He stated that he used his "professional judgment" and a "fairly simple five-step probability" calculation with five events from Defendant's description of the event: first, whether "the screwdriver land[ed] in the correct orientation" or "solid angle" perpendicular to the victim's falling body; second, whether the screwdriver landed with the blade facing up; third, whether the screwdriver separated itself, as it fell, from other items that had been knocked off the hamper; fourth, where it landed on the floor; and fifth, whether its orientation caused the wound path. He recounted, "I simply multiplied the numbers, one over 10 times one over two times 1 over 100 three times, and the number you get is basically five times ten to minus 8 or in what most of us think about, one in a 20 million chance."

* * *

II. Discussion

As discussed below, we conclude that Juror 7's statements constituted proper deliberations based upon his professional and educational experience. Defendant argues that Juror 7 injected new evidentiary facts which contradicted defense testimony rather than expressing opinions, views or beliefs about the evidence. We disagree. Defendant concedes that Juror 7 began with Dr. Watts' testimony, but he asserts that Juror 7 "added his own testimony of probability and physics." * * * Juror 7, albeit with greater understanding than the average person, was engaging in deliberation of the evidence presented at trial. * * *

In order to provide expert testimony supporting Defendant's version of events, Dr. Watts described basic physics principles, completed extensive calculations, and performed both in-court and videotaped demonstrations with a screwdriver and other materials. Dr. Watts testified that the occurrence of an accidental impalement consistent with Defendant's theory has "a relatively small overall probability." * * * Defendant himself placed probability calculations regarding his accidental impalement theory in evidence before the jury.

Juror 7 articulated his own thought process as to what this "finite" probability calculation would be, based on the evidence presented in court and based on Dr. Watts' testimony. * * * Juror 7's deliberations properly took their content from the evidence and testimony presented at trial. His calculation, as well as several other jurors' calculations, expressed the probability, introduced into evidence by Defendant, as one in several million. The jury's deliberation was an attempt to review and evaluate Defendant's expert testimony. Juror 9 rejected the conclusion of Defendant's expert, and decided that "Not in a zillion billion years did that happen." Juror 4 estimated the probability of Defendant's accident occurring as "one in 10 million." Defendant concedes that this type of opinion is proper. * * * Juror 7, because of his life experience, occupation, and education, verbalized a similar opinion as other jurors based on evidence and testimony presented at trial in a more complex manner, explaining the basis behind the conclusion that Defendant finds permissible. Concluding that Defendant's theory has a less than one in twenty million chance, rather than Dr. Watts' characterization of a "freak accident," is not a new evidentiary fact. The jury, including Juror 7, carefully considered Defendant's theory but was ultimately persuaded that the State demonstrated that Defendant was guilty beyond a reasonable doubt; thus, the jury performed its duty. * * * Defendant wishes to be allowed, and in fact, was properly allowed, to present expert physics testimony regarding the ultimate conclusion of the probability of impalement to the jury (possible but extremely unlikely), but now strenuously objects to the jury actually deliberating on this very issue. It would be inordinately bad policy to single out a juror who thoughtfully and conscientiously engaged in deliberation and presented his conclusion to the jury because he was able to express exactly why he came to that conclusion based on the evidence at trial, rather than more simply state the theory as one in a million.

* * *

"In deciding every case, jurors must necessarily take into consideration their knowledge and impressions founded upon experience in their everyday walks of life, and the fact that these things affect them in reaching their verdict cannot be reversible error, because, indeed, jurors without possessing such knowledge and impressions could not be had." *State v. Dascenzo,* 30 N.M. 34, 37, 226 P. 1099, 1100 (1924). The trial court did not abuse its discretion by denying Defendant's motion for a new trial under New Mexico precedent. Cases from other jurisdictions also support this conclusion. *See, e.g., Wagner v. Doulton,* 112 Cal.App.3d 945, 169 Cal.Rptr. 550, 552–53 (1980) (concluding that an engineer juror's map, drawn based on his understanding of the testimony and used during deliberations, did not constitute extraneous evidence); *State v. Heitkemper,* 196 Wis.2d 218, 538 N.W.2d 561, 563–64 (App.1995) (concluding that a pharmacist juror's remark that he disbelieved a witness regarding drugs she ingested because the quantities should have knocked her out did not constitute extraneous information). "A juror's common sense and experience, including expertise in particular subjects, is not extrinsic information warranting relief if used during deliberations." *State v. Dickens,* 187 Ariz. 1, 926 P.2d 468, 483 (1996) (en banc) (holding that a mechanic juror's statement that he did not believe the defendant's claim that his truck overheated based on his expertise did not constitute extraneous information).

Remarks made by the jurors in the present case illustrate the problematic application of a broad definition that communication of specific knowledge from a particular juror to others constitutes extraneous prejudicial information. Juror 9 described how another juror discussed that juror's experience with his own child falling from a tree and how that experience related to his understanding of the child abuse charge stemming from the victim's 1994 head injury. Both Juror 9 and Juror 7 mentioned that two jurors who were nurses discussed their opinion regarding the expert medical testimony, based on their educational and professional experience. Finally, Juror 7 described another juror recounting a previous experience in which the juror fell straight forward and sustained an injury to her chin. All of this information was not subject to cross-examination regarding the similarity or dissimilarity to the charges in the present case; it could be considered extraneous under this definition. * * *

Defendant argues that the Court of Appeals opinion will result in the "dumbing down" of juries because attorneys will remove individuals such as Juror 7. We disagree. We do not believe that because an individual has particular professional experience or is well-educated one can assume that he or she is biased in favor of any particular party. As discussed above, venire members who express experiences which would affect their ability to be unbiased can be dismissed through cause challenges during voir dire. * * *

Notes and Questions

1. *"Jury notice."* Obviously it is not feasible for every judicial inquiry to begin from the Cartesian postulate *cogito, ergo sum.* In order for the trial of factual issues to proceed with anything like dispatch, indeed for them to proceed at all, it must be assumed that the trier of fact comes to his or her task already apprised of the multitude of nonevidence or background facts which will enable him or her to comprehend and utilize the additional data communicated to him or her by the formal introduction of evidence. Thus, as one writer has stated, "[i]t is considered appropriate that a judge or juror be permitted to employ, inconspicuously and interstitially in his elementary process of understanding and reasoning, his beliefs (though they are not in evidence) which he reasonably thinks he shares with other intelligent persons as to the general nature of things—the meanings of ordinary words,

typical modes of human behavior, causal relations between commonplace events, and the like. * * * [T]his category of judicial notice is often referred to by the somewhat misleading name 'jury notice.' " McNaughton, Judicial Notice—Excerpts Relating to the Morgan–Wigmore Controversy, 14 Vand. L.Rev. 779, 789–90 (1961). See also Davis, A System of Judicial Notice Based on Fairness and Convenience, in Perspectives of Law 69 (1964); Thayer, A Preliminary Treatise on Evidence at the Common Law 279–80 (1898). Lest the jury feel any hesitancy in this regard, the notion is commonly conveyed to it by instruction.

2. *Jury special knowledge.* In *Mann*, is there a difference between Jurors 4 and 9' colloquial expressions and Juror 7's calculations? Do these calculations differ from comments of the nurse jurors concerning the expert medical testimony? Compare Hunt v. State, 603 S.W.2d 865 (Tex.Crim.App. 1980), in which a juror enlightened his fellow jurors concerning the use of ligatures to cause death, based upon his Marine training years previously. The court held this incident to be "improper" and to entitle defendant to a new trial.

3. *The imprecise line between background facts and adjudicatory facts.* In Palestroni v. Jacobs, 73 A.2d 89 (Bergen County Ct.1950), the jurors used a standard dictionary, during their deliberations, in order to determine the meaning of the word "wainscot", which was used in the evidence. The trial court found no error: "Since jurors may take judicial notice of the commonly accepted meaning of all English words used in the evidence, they are entitled to have the use of a standard English dictionary to aid their understanding by refreshing their recollection of the meaning of any English word used in the evidence, where no unusual, special, or legal significance of its use is involved. Therefore, it is not improper for a jury to have the use of a standard English dictionary during its deliberations." On review, the appellate court reversed, 77 A.2d 183 (N.J.App.Div.1950). Judge Brennan (later a Supreme Court Justice) stated that "even if the word was employed in the specification with its ordinary meaning, defendant was denied the chance to challenge the completeness of the definition given in the dictionary used. Here counsel might have properly suggested that another dictionary containing a more comprehensive definition was appropriate * * *." Id. at 185. Does the specific meaning of a word like "wainscot" that is ordinarily outside the concern of judicial notice of adjudicative facts take on a more sensitive status in a contract case where the issue involves the adequacy of wainscoting? Was the problem the specific definition of the term or a procedural defect in failing to provide an opportunity to contest the definition provided?

4. *The theory of the dividing line.* At what points other than during jury deliberations are "background facts" inevitably going to be assumed and used by various participants in the trial process? Should jury notice of background facts for one or more of these purposes be regulated in some way? How? For a discussion of these questions suggesting the imposition of some strictures on jury notice, see Mansfield, Jury Notice, 74 Geo.L.J. 395 (1985). Professor Mansfield's thesis is strenuously criticized by Fraher, Adjudicative Facts, Non–Evidence Facts, and Permissible Jury Background Information, 62 Ind.L.J. 333 (1987), in part on the ground that such strictures are not feasible. Among the points discussed by Mansfield is the

extent to which the jury notice principle applies to argument by counsel which draws upon facts or propositions which have not been supported by evidence. For an excellent earlier discussion of this question, see Levin & Levy, Persuading the Jury with Facts Not in Evidence: The Fiction–Science Spectrum, 105 U.Pa.L.Rev. 139 (1956).

STATE v. CANADY

Court of Appeals of North Carolina, 1993.
431 S.E.2d 500.

GREENE, JUDGE.

Appeal by defendant from judgment and commitment to fourteen years imprisonment entered 3 March 1992, after jury verdict convicting him of voluntary manslaughter. N.C.G.S. § 14–18 (1986).

The State's evidence tends to show, *inter alia,* that defendant stabbed George Bullard (Bullard), who was romantically involved with defendant's estranged wife, to death on the evening of 24 May 1990 at the mobile home where defendant's estranged wife was living. One of the State's witnesses, Mrs. Nunnery, testified that her house was approximately 150 feet from Mrs. Canady's mobile home and that she could see Mrs. Canady's mobile home and front yard from her porch. On the evening Bullard was killed, Mrs. Nunnery received a telephone call from Mrs. Canady. Mrs. Nunnery heard a "scuffle" on the phone, and Mrs. Canady asked her to "call the law," which Mrs. Nunnery did. As she hung up the telephone, Mrs. Canady came into her house.

Mrs. Nunnery then went out onto the front porch and observed Bullard and defendant. She saw Bullard standing beside defendant's car with no weapon in his hand. Defendant was inside the car at the time, but the driver's door was open and defendant's leg was outside the door. Mrs. Nunnery observed that Bullard was attempting to get defendant into his car, and heard Bullard say "[g]et your leg in and go on. I don't want to fight you." Mrs. Nunnery then went back inside her house. She returned to the front porch minutes later and observed both Bullard and defendant standing outside the car, neither one armed. Mrs. Nunnery returned inside, and then heard defendant call out that an ambulance should be called. Mrs. Nunnery was the only witness, other than defendant, to the altercation. Mrs. Nunnery testified that when she was watching defendant and Bullard "[i]t was still daylight. It was getting toward dusk * * *. [T]here was good light."

Defendant's evidence, consisting primarily of statements made to officers at the scene, tended to establish that he killed Bullard in self-defense, and conflicted with the testimony of Mrs. Nunnery. Defendant did not testify, but claimed in statements made to the police that it was dark when he arrived at the mobile home. Defendant's counsel moved in writing that the trial court take judicial notice of the fact that the sunset on 24 May 1990 occurred at 8:19 p.m., and that there was a new moon on that date. Defendant offered verification of these facts in the form of the reports published daily in *The Fayetteville Observer.* The trial court refused defendant's request. The jury returned a verdict finding defendant guilty of voluntary manslaughter.

Defendant contends that the evidence of the time of sunset and presence of a new moon was critical to his case because such information casts doubt on Mrs. Nunnery's testimony that there was sufficient daylight by which to see the exchanges between defendant and Bullard. Thus, defendant claims, he was prejudiced when the trial court wrongfully refused to take judicial notice of the information offered. The State contends that the information in *The Fayetteville Observer* is not official, and therefore not the proper subject for judicial notice.

The dispositive issue is whether the trial court is required to take judicial notice of the time of the sunset and the phase of the moon as reported in *The Fayetteville Observer*.

The Rules of Evidence provide that the trial "court shall take judicial notice [of adjudicative facts] if requested by a party and supplied with the necessary information." N.C.G.S. § 8C–1, Rule 201(d) (1992). Once a request to take judicial notice is made and accompanied by supporting data, the trial court "is entitled to pass upon the sufficiency of the data." 1 Henry Brandis, Jr., *Brandis on North Carolina Evidence* § 11 (3d ed. 1988) (footnote omitted). The trial court weighs the sufficiency of the data by determining whether the fact put forth for judicial notice is

> one not subject to reasonable dispute in that it is either (1) generally known within the territorial jurisdiction of the trial court or (2) capable of accurate and ready determination by resort to sources whose accuracy cannot reasonably be questioned.

N.C.G.S. § 8C–1, Rule 201(b) (1992). To warrant judicial notice under the second part of this test, the source from which the data is drawn must be "a document of such indisputable accuracy as [would] justif[y] judicial reliance." State v. Dancy, 297 N.C. 40, 42, 252 S.E.2d 514, 515 (1979). It is the responsibility of counsel seeking to have a fact judicially noticed to supply the trial court with such information, and "[t]he trial judge is not required to make an independent search for data of which he may take judicial notice." Id.

The exact time of sunset and the current phase of the moon on a particular date are not facts "generally known." They are, however, facts which are "capable of accurate and ready determination by resort to sources whose accuracy cannot reasonably be questioned." Thus, it was the responsibility of defendant's counsel, upon his request that the trial court take judicial notice of the moon phase and time of sunset, to provide that information to the trial court in "a document of such indisputable accuracy as [would] justif[y] judicial reliance." Dancy, 297 N.C. at 42, 252 S.E.2d at 515. *The Fayetteville Observer* is not such a document. We note that the newspaper excerpt does not even identify the source of its data. We believe that, in the case of facts such as the time of sunset and the phase of the moon, a document of "indisputable accuracy" contemplates material from a primary source in whose hands the gathering of such information rests. Our Supreme Court has approved this view in *Dancy*, refusing to find error in the trial court's failure to take judicial notice of the phase of the moon when the source was *The Ladies Birthday Almanac,* but taking judicial notice on its own initiative of the same fact as found in the records of the U.S. Naval Observatory. Id.

Accordingly, the trial court did not err in failing to take judicial notice of the facts put forth by defendant.

Notes and Questions

1. *Morgan-Wigmore Debate.* Guidice & Kraft, Comment, The Presently Expanding Concept of Judicial Notice, 13 Villanova L.Rev. 528, 534–36 (1968)[2]:

> The scope of judicial notice of fact has been traditionally considered in the context of the Morgan–Wigmore, indisputable-disputable controversy. On the one side, Professors Morgan and McNaughton contend that the primary purpose of judicial notice is to prevent wasteful litigation of moot questions of fact. Therefore, they maintain that judicial notice should be confined to indisputables, that is, those facts which are so notorious or so universally known or so easily and accurately verifiable that they cannot reasonably be disputed. They reason that since judicial notice, by their definition, applies only to indisputables, once such an indisputable proposition is properly noticed, it should not be allowed to be controverted. In other words, judicial notice is conclusive, so that in a jury trial, once a judge judicially notices a fact, he should give the jury binding instructions to find the fact as noticed, and no evidence may be introduced in an effort to persuade the jury to make a finding contrary to the noticed fact. The parties may, however, present informal 'information' to the judge, before or after his ruling, in an effort to convince him that the fact is not indisputable.
>
> On the other side of the dispute, Professors Wigmore and Thayer contend that a judge may notice facts unlikely to be challenged as well as those considered to be absolutely indisputable. Under their definition, judicial notice operates in the way of a presumption. Says Thayer:
>
> > Taking judicial notice does not import that the matter is indisputable. It is not necessarily anything more than a *prima facie* recognition, leaving the matter still open to controversy. * * * In very many cases * * * taking judicial notice of a fact is merely presuming it, i.e., assuming it until there shall be reason to think otherwise.
>
> Under the Wigmore–Thayer approach, as under the Morgan approach, the parties may initially present information to the court to help it decide whether or not it should take judicial notice of the particular

fact in question. If the judge decides to notice the fact, he will instruct the jury that they *may* find the noticed fact to be true even though no evidence has been introduced in its support. The opponent of the fact, at this point, has the option of producing material in an effort to convince the *judge* that he has decided incorrectly—that he should not have noticed the fact because the fact was not unlikely to be challenged. Having failed to dissuade the judge as to the propriety of taking notice, or not having attempted to do so, the opponent of the fact may yet introduce evidence directed at rebutting the presumption and persuading the *jury* to find that the noticed fact is not true.

Which theory does Federal Rule 201 adopt?

2. *Types of facts.* "Historical facts fall within the doctrine, such as the dates upon which wars began and terminated. Geographical facts are involved, particularly with reference to the boundaries of the state in which the court is sitting and of the counties, districts and townships thereof, as well as the location of the capital of the state and the location and identity of the county seats. Whether common knowledge or not, courts notice the identity of the principal officers of the national government and the incumbents of principal state offices." 2 McCormick, Evidence § 330, at 441–42 (6th ed. 2006). See also Disabled Rights Action Committee v. Las Vegas Events, Inc., 375 F.3d 861, 866 n.1 (9th Cir.2004) ("Under Federal Rule of Evidence 201, we may take judicial notice of the records of state agencies and other undisputed matters of public record."); Dippin' Dots, Inc. v. Frosty Bites Distribution, LLC, 369 F.3d 1197, 1205 (11th Cir.2004) ("[T]he district court took judicial notice of the fact that color is indicative of flavor in ice cream. This fact is adjudicative in nature and is generally known among consumers."); Denius v. Dunlap, 330 F.3d 919, 926 (7th Cir.2003) ("[T]he fact that the [National Personnel Records Center] maintains medical records of military personnel is appropriate for judicial notice because it is not subject to reasonable dispute.").

3. *Political facts.* See Namo v. Gonzales, 401 F.3d 453, 458 (6th Cir.2005) ("[W]e recognize that the situation in Iraq has changed due to the demise of the regime of Saddam Hussein. This court may take judicial notice of changed circumstances."); Singh v. Ashcroft, 393 F.3d 903, 905 (9th Cir.2004) ("We can notice that the government of India exists. We can notice that the office of the Prime Minister of India exists. We can notice that a part of the Prime Minister of India's office is the RAW [Research and Analysis Wing]."); Gafoor v. Immigration and Naturalization Serv., 231 F.3d 645, 656 (9th Cir.2000) ("We do not exceed our authority by taking judicial notice of dramatic foreign developments * * *."); Ivezaj v. INS, 84 F.3d 215, 219 (6th Cir.1996) (taking judicial notice of persecution of Albanians by Serbs).

4. *Authoritative sources.* See Morgan, Basic Problems in Evidence 10 (1962) ("If the issue is whether a matter falls within the scope of judicial notice, neither judge nor counsel will be hampered by the rules of evidence."); 9 Wigmore, Evidence § 2568a, at 538 (3d ed. 1940) ("any source whatever that suffices to satisfy [the judge's] mind in making a ruling" is acceptable; listing "official records, encyclopedias, any books or articles" as examples); Cal.Evid.Code § 454(a)(1) ("Any source of pertinent information,

including the advice of persons learned in the subject matter, may be consulted or used."). In the principal case, what was wrong with the *Fayetteville Observer*? Would the newspaper have been admissible? See Federal Rules 803(17) and 902(6).

5. *Timing of judicial notice.* Rule 201(f) authorizes the taking of judicial notice at any stage of the proceeding. See Dippin' Dots, Inc. v. Frosty Bites Distribution, LLC, 369 F.3d 1197, 1204 (11th Cir.2004) ("A court may take judicial notice * * * at the summary judgment stage."). This would include appeals. However, in Jespersen v. Harrah's Operating Co., Inc., 444 F.3d 1104 (9th Cir.2006), a sex discrimination suit based on a requirement that female bar tenders wear makeup ("face powder, blush and mascara must be worn and applied neatly in complimentary colors, and lip color must be worn at all times"), the appellate court refused to take judicial notice of the fact that it costs more money and takes more time for a woman to comply with the makeup requirement than it takes for a man to comply with the requirement that he keep his hair short because such facts lack a high degree of indisputability. The dissent rejoined:

> Harrah's policy requires women to apply face powder, blush, mascara and lipstick. You don't need an expert witness to figure out that such items don't grow on trees. Nor is there any rational doubt that application of makeup is an intricate and painstaking process that requires considerable time and care. Even those of us who don't wear makeup know how long it can take from the hundreds of hours we've spent over the years frantically tapping our toes and pointing to our wrists. It's hard to imagine that a woman could "put on her face," as they say, in the time it would take a man to shave—certainly not if she were to do the careful and thorough job Harrah's expects. Makeup, moreover, must be applied and removed every day; the policy burdens men with no such daily ritual. While a man could jog to the casino, slip into his uniform, and get right to work, a woman must travel to work so as to avoid smearing her makeup, or arrive early to put on her makeup there.

Is there another basis for the majority opinion? Is it fair to permit a party to do through judicial notice on appeal what that party should have done at trial? See Colonial Leasing Co. v. Logistics Control Group Int'l, 762 F.2d 454, 461 (5th Cir.1985) ("[W]hen Logistics declined to produce evidence, it relied on Colonial's failure to establish its prima facie case. When the district court subsequently took notice of the only fact necessary to complete Colonial's prima facie proof, Logistics was deprived of the opportunity to adduce evidence on a critical fact.").

STATE v. VEJVODA

Supreme Court of Nebraska, 1989.
438 N.W.2d 461.

SHANAHAN, JUSTICE.

In a bench trial in the county court for Hall County, Mark Vejvoda was convicted of drunk driving and received an enhanced sentence as the result of his second conviction for drunk driving. * * * On appeal, the district court affirmed Vejvoda's conviction and sentence. Vejvoda contends that the evidence is insufficient to sustain his conviction for drunk driving and that the State failed to prove that Hall County was the venue for his trial because the court improperly took judicial notice that locations mentioned in Vejvoda's trial were within Hall County.

* * *

The only testimony regarding venue was that of Edwards', a Grand Island police officer, who observed Vejvoda's car at "7th and Vine Streets" and later apprehended Vejvoda on a street called "Oak." Edwards never identified the city or county where he observed and apprehended Vejvoda. As this court noted in *State v. Bouwens*, 167 Neb. 244, 247, 92 N.W.2d 564, 566 (1958), the fact that a defendant was arrested by policemen to a particular city "is not proof that the offense was committed within the jurisdiction * * * of the city * * *." When the judicial notice in question is disregarded, the evidence offered in Vejvoda's case fails to establish that either a Vine Street or an Oak Street exists in Grand Island or Hall County.

Judicial Notice

Neb.Evid.R. 201(2), Neb.Rev.Stat. § 27–201(2) (Reissue 1985), pertains to judicial notice of adjudicative facts and states: "A judicially noticed fact must be one not subject to reasonable dispute in that it is either (a) generally known within the territorial jurisdiction of the trial court or (b) capable of accurate and ready determination by resort to sources whose accuracy cannot reasonably be questioned."

A fact is adjudicative if the fact affects the determination of a controverted issue in litigation, or, as one author has characterized adjudicative facts:

> When a court or an agency finds facts concerning the immediate parties—who did what, where, when, how, and with what motive or intent—the court or agency is performing an adjudicative function, and the facts so determined are conveniently called adjudicative facts * * *.
>
> Stated in other terms, the adjudicative facts are those to which the law is applied in the process of adjudication. They are the facts that normally go to the jury in a jury case. They relate to the parties, their activities, their properties, their businesses.

Davis, *Judicial Notice*, 55 Colum.L.Rev. 945, 952 (1955).

* * *

Judicial Notice: A Species of Evidence

Judicial notice of an adjudicative fact is a species of evidence, which, if relevant as an ultimate fact or a fact from which an ultimate fact may be inferred, is received without adherence to the Nebraska Evidence Rules otherwise applicable to admissibility of evidence and established a fact without formal evidentiary proof. * * * *National Aircraft Leasing v.*

American Airlines, 74 Ill.App. 3d 1014, 1017, 31 Ill.Dec. 268, 394 N.E.2d 470, 474 (1979): "Judicial notice is an evidentiary concept which operates to admit matters into evidence without formal proof * * *." Although Neb.Evid.R. 201 does not expressly require relevance for judicial notice, an irrelevant fact cannot be validly classified as an "adjudicative fact," the only type of fact noticeably under Neb.Evid.R. 201. * * *

Judicial Notice v. A Judge's Personal Knowledge

Judicial notice, however, is not the same as extrajudicial or personal knowledge of a judge. "What a judge knows and what facts a judge may judicially notice are not identical data banks * * *. [A]ctual private knowledge by the judge is no sufficient ground for taking judicial notice of a fact as a basis for a finding or a final judgment * * *." McCormick on Evidence § 329 at 922–23 (E. Cleary 3d ed. 1984). As Wigmore observes:

> There is a real but elusive line between the judge's *personal knowledge* as a private man and these matters of which he takes judicial notice as a judge. The latter does not necessarily include the former; as a judge, indeed, he may have to ignore what he knows as a man and contrariwise.
>
> * * *
>
> It is therefore plainly accepted that the judge is not to use from the bench, under the guise of judicial knowledge, that which he knows *only as an individual* observer outside of court. The former is in truth "known" to him merely in the fictional sense that it is known and notorious to all men, and the dilemma is only the result of using the term "knowledge" in two senses. Where to draw the line between knowledge by notoriety and knowledge by personal observation may sometimes be difficulty but the principle is plain.

(Emphasis in original.) 9 J. Wigmore, Evidence in Trials at Common Law § 2569(a) at 722–23 (J. Chadbourn rev. 1981). * * *

Judicial Notice in Criminal Cases

In function and effect, judicial notice in a civil action is fundamentally different from judicial notice in a criminal case. "In a civil action or proceeding, the judge shall instruct the jury to accept as conclusive any fact judicially noticed. In a criminal case, the judge shall instruct the jury that it may, but is not required to, accept as conclusive any fact judicially noticed." Neb.Evid.R. 201(7). In a civil action, the adjudicative fact judicially noticed is conclusively established and binds the jury, whereas in a criminal case a jury ultimately has the freedom to find that an adjudicative fact has not been established notwithstanding judicial notice by the trial court. If the conclusive effect of judicial notice in a civil action were transposed to the trial of a criminal case, judicial notice might supply proof of an element in the charge against an accused and thereby have the practical effect of a directed verdict on the issue of the defendants guilt * * *.

* * *

In *U.S. v. Mentz*, 840 F.2d 315 (6th Cir.1988), the government prosecuted Mentz in a jury trial on charges of bank robbery. To convict Mentz, the government had to prove that Mentz robbed a financial institution insured by the federal Deposit Insurance Corporation. * * * When Mentz moved for dismissal of the charges at the close of the government's case, claiming that evidence failed to establish that the banks were FDIC-insured at the time of the robberies, the court overruled Mentz' motion and, although there was no evidence of FDIC insurance, instructed the jury that each of the banks, which Mentz was accused of robbing, was "insured by the Federal Deposit Insurance Corporation at the time of the offense alleged in the indictment." * * * In reversing Mentz' conviction, the court stated:

> Regardless of how overwhelming the evidence may be, the Constitution delegates to the jury, not to the trial judge, the important task of deciding guilt or innocence. "[The jury's] overriding responsibility is to stand between the accused and a potentially arbitrary or abusive Government that is in command of the criminal sanction. For this reason, a trial judge is prohibited from entering a judgment of conviction or directing the jury to come forward with such a verdict, regardless of how overwhelming the evidence may point in that direction. The trial judge is thereby barred from attempting to override or interfere with the jurors' independent judgment in a manner contrary to the interests of the accused." *United States v. Martin Linen Supply Co.* [430 U.S. 564 (1977)] * * *.

* * *

Specifically referring to judicial notice under Fed.R.Evid. 201(g), the counterpart to Neb.Evid.R. 201(7), the court concluded in *Mentz*:

> In a criminal case, a trial court that takes judicial notice of an adjudicative fact must "instruct the jury that it may, but is not required to, accept as conclusive any fact judicially noticed." Rule 201(g), Fed.R.Evid. This provision "contemplates that the jury in a criminal case [will] pass upon facts which are judicially noticed." *United States v. Jones*, 580 F.2d 219, 224 (6th Cir.1978). As so construed, Rule 201(g) preserves the jury's "traditional prerogative to ignore even uncontroverted facts in reaching a verdict," and thereby prevents the trial court from transgressing the spirit, if not the letter, of the Sixth Amendment right to a jury trial by directing a partial verdict as to the facts. * * *

As one commentator has remarked concerning judicial notice and Fed.R.Evid. 201(g), which remark is equally applicable to Neb.Evid.R. 201(7):

> With respect to criminal cases, Rule 201(g) apparently contemplates that contrary evidence is admissible, which of course means that evidence, if any, in support of the fact judicially noticed may also be admitted. Problems arising with respect to the court considering inadmissible evidence in determining the propriety of taking judicial notice coupled with the confusion that naturally would be expected to rise in the jury's mind when presented with judicial notice accompanied by conflicting evidence, makes resort to judicial notice in criminal cases where the opposing party is prepared to introduce contrary evidence highly undesirable.

M. Graham, Handbook of Federal Evidence § 201.7 at 83 (2d ed. 1986).

Judicial Notice in A Bench Trial

Potential problems from judicial notice in a bench trial are discussed in 21 C. Wright & K. Graham, Federal Practice and Procedure § 5104 at 488 (1977):

> [T]he high degree if indisputability required before a fact can be judicially noticed applies to both forms of litigation [jury trials and court or bench trials]. However, the procedural context in which notice is taken makes the process quite different in court trials. Since the judge is not insulated, as the jury is, from the material consulted in deciding whether or not to take notice, it may make little difference whether he takes formal judicial notice based on the material or whether he is simply convinced of the fact as a result of having examined the sources. Technically, the source material is not in evidence, and thus a finding that was without other support in the record could not stand unless the matter was properly noticeable; but otherwise, the line between judicial notice and proof-taking is blurred in court trials.

From all the foregoing observations, we believe, and for that reason suggest, that judicial notice should be sparingly used in a criminal case lest prejudicial error result form denial of a defendant's constitutional or statutory rights in the trial of a criminal case.

Judicial Notice in Vejvoda's Case

Under the Nebraska Evidence Rules, the trial court's sua sponte judicial notice was permissible at the point in Vejvoda's trial where adduction of evidence has been concluded and the case was ready for submission to the factfinding process. See Neb.Evid.R. 201(4): "A judge or court shall take judicial notice if requested by a party and supplied with the necessary information." See, also, Neb.Evid.R. 201(6): "Judicial notice may be taken at any stage of the proceeding."

However, from the record in Vejvoda's case, one cannot conclude that the location of the municipal microcosm known as Vine Street or 8th and Oak Streets was known throughout the length and breadth of Hall County and, therefore, a fact "known within the territorial jurisdiction of the trial court." Neb.Evid.R. 201(2)(a). Consequently, we must focus on the alternative expressed in Neb.Evid.R. 201(2)(b), that is, whether the location of Vine and Oak streets in Grand Island and the site of Vejvoda's arrest are adjudicative facts "capable of accurate and ready determination by resort to sources whose accuracy cannot reasonably be questioned."

For resolution of Vejvoda's claim regarding the impropriety of the trial court's judicial notice, we must first identify and characterize the scope of the trial court's "judicial notice," which actually has two components: (1) Vine, Oak, 7th, and 8th Streets exist in Grand Island, which is located in Hall County, and (2) Vejvoda's drunk driving occurred at 8th and Oak in Grand Island. Thus, existence of Grand Island streets is inferentially correlated with Edwards' testimony, producing a conclusion judicially noticed by the trial court, namely, the judicially noticed streets are the same streets mentioned in Edwards' testimony, and, therefore, Vejvoda was arrested in Grand Island.

An inference may be entirely reasonable, yet nevertheless an improper subject for judicial notice. * * *

* * *

When a fact is not generally known within the territorial jurisdiction of the trial court, judicial notice may be taken only if an adjudicative fact can be verified by "sources whose accuracy cannot reasonably be questioned." Neb.Evid.R. 201(2)(b).

* * *

In Vejvoda's case, the trial court could properly take judicial notice that Grand Island, which is wholly within Hall Country, has streets named "Vine" and "Oak." Furthermore, by simply referring to a map of Grand Island, the court could properly take judicial notice that the intersection of 7th and Vine Streets is within two blocks of the intersection of 8th and Oak Streets. At that point the site of the offense was an issue submissible to the trier of fact.

Although the location of streets within Grand Island is readily verifiable by reference to a city map, a source capable of ready certification and a cartographic source of information which cannot reasonably be questioned, the county court took another and impermissible step by judicially noticing the inference that Vejvoda was driving in Grand Island. The court's locational inference necessary for venue was not an adjudicative fact "capable of accurate and ready determination by resort to sources whose accuracy cannot reasonably be questioned." The county court erred in taking judicial notice of the inference that Vejvoda was driving in Grand Island and, therefore, that Vejvoda's drunk driving occurred in Grand Island.

If Vejvoda had been convicted in a jury trial, we would reverse Vejvoda's conviction on account of the trial court's invasion of the factfinding process within a jury's province in the trial of a criminal case. However, as mentioned, Vejvoda's case was tried to the court. Although

Vejvoda's arrest by Edwards, a Grand Island police officer, does not establish venue, Edwards' official affiliation as a Grand Island police officer was a circumstance bearing on the issue of venue. When combined with other evidence, namely, the trial court's judicial notice of "Vine" and "Oak" as street in Grand Island, Edwards' testimony supplied a sufficient evidentiary basis for a fact finder's determination that Vejvoda's drunk driving occurred in Grand Island, Hall County, Nebraska. "Harmless error exists in a jury trial of a criminal case when there is some incorrect conduct by the trial court which, on review of the entire record, did not materially influence the jury in a verdict adverse to a substantial right of the defendant." *State v. Watkins*, 227 Neb. 677, 686, 419 N.W.2d 660, 666 (1988). The preceding principle applicable in a jury trial of a criminal case is equally applicable to a judgment embodying factfinding in the bench trial of a criminal case.

Therefore, the trial court's error in judicially noticing the inferential location of Vejvoda's conduct, namely, drunk driving, is harmless error beyond a reasonable doubt. Vejvoda's conviction is affirmed.

Affirmed.

Notes and Questions

1. *Criminal cases.* In United States v. Dior, 671 F.2d 351, 358 n.11 (9th Cir.1982), the prosecution failed to enter the Canadian–American exchange rate into evidence to establish the value of transported property. The court declined to take judicial notice on appeal:

> [T]o take judicial notice of an adjudicative fact after a jury's discharge in a criminal case would cast the court in the role of a fact-finder and violate defendant's Sixth Amendment right to trial by jury * * *. Indeed, for a trial court (in a post-verdict motion) or an appellate court to take judicial notice of an adjudicative fact in a criminal case would frustrate the policies Congress sought to achieve in providing in F.R. Evid. 201(g) that a jury is not required to accept as conclusive a judicially noticed fact. These policies are to preserve the jury's traditional prerogative, in a criminal case, to ignore even uncontroverted facts in reaching a verdict and to prevent the trial court from violating the spirit of the Sixth Amendment * * * by directing a partial verdict as to facts.

See also United States v. Herrera–Ochoa, 245 F.3d 495, 501 (5th Cir.2001) ("Taking judicial notice in this case of an essential element of the crime * * * potentially infringes on Herrera's right to have each element proved beyond a reasonable doubt."); United States v. Jones, 580 F.2d 219, 224 (6th Cir.1978) ("As enacted by Congress, Rule 201(g) plainly contemplates that the jury in a criminal case shall pass upon facts which are judicially noticed. This it could not do if this notice were taken for the first time * * * on appeal.") (status of phone company as "common carrier" not established at trial).

For a survey and analysis of federal results under Rule 201(g), see Turner, Judicial Notice and Federal Rule of Evidence 201—A Rule Ready for Change, 45 U.Pitt.L.Rev. 181 (1983). Professor Turner concludes that the congressional effort to vindicate the right to trial by jury through Rule 201(g) is ineffective, unnecessary, and should be rescinded.

Nevertheless, the Supreme Court's reinvigoration of the right to jury trial suggests that caution is in order when taking any issue away from the jury. See Apprendi v. New Jersey, 530 U.S. 466, 490 (2000) ("Other than the fact of a prior conviction, any fact that increases the penalty for a crime beyond the prescribed statutory maximum must be submitted to a jury, and proved beyond a reasonable doubt."). See also Blakely v. Washington, 542 U.S. 296 (2004). One commentator has argued that taking judicial notice of jurisdictional facts in federal trials in unconstitutional. See Carter, "Trust Me, I'm a Judge": Why Binding Judicial Notice of Jurisdictional Facts Violates the Right to Jury Trial, 68 Mo.L.Rev. 649 (2003). See also Comment, Proper Venue as a Jury Issue in Federal Criminal Cases: The "in issue" Approach to When Venue Presents a Fact Question for the Jury as Opposed to a Question of Law for the Court, 76 Temp.L.Rev. 883 (2003).

2. *Ambiguous status of generalized knowledge.* Central to the application of rules patterned upon Fed.R.Evid. 201 is the question of what types of facts are "adjudicative facts" subject to the strictures of the rule. For example, are the principles underlying X-rays, fingerprinting, various tests for intoxication, radar, and ballistics adjudicative facts? These and other scientific principles are frequently "noticed" by courts[3] with the consequence that the foundation necessary for the introduction of evidence obtained through their application can be abbreviated somewhat. But does judicial notice taken for such a purpose fall within Rule 201? Clearly the advisory committee originally charged with drafting the Federal Rules did not consider such "facts" as adjudicative facts.

> While judges use judicial notice of "propositions of generalized knowledge" in a variety of situations: determining the validity and meaning of statutes, formulating common law rules, deciding whether evidence should be admitted, assessing the sufficiency and effect of evidence, all are essentially nonadjudicative in nature. * * * It is not believed that judges now instruct juries as to "propositions of generalized knowledge" derived from encyclopedias or other sources, or that they are likely to do so, or indeed, that it is desirable that they do so. There is a vast difference between ruling on the basis of judicial notice that radar evidence of speed is admissible and explaining to the jury its principles and degree of accuracy, or between using a table of stopping distances of automobiles at various speeds in a judicial evaluation of testimony and telling the jury its precise application in the case.

Fed.R.Evid. 201 advisory committee's note.

Concerning the judicial use of "background facts" in passing on questions of relevancy and sufficiency, see Mansfield, Jury Notice, 74 Geo.L.J. 395 (1985).

3. See Daubert v. Merrell Dow Pharm., Inc., 509 U.S. 579, 593 n.11 (1993) ("[T]heories that are so firmly established as to have attained the status of scientific law, such as the laws of thermodynamics, properly are subject to judicial notice under Fed. Rule Evid. 201.").

POTTS v. COE

United States Court of Appeals, District of Columbia, 1944.
145 F.2d 27.

ARNOLD, ASSOCIATE JUSTICE. This is a motion to vacate our decision in the case of *Louis M. Potts and Teletype Corporation v. Conway P. Coe, Commissioner of Patents*,[4] and to withdraw the opinion filed in support of that decision. The moving parties had appealed from a judgment dismissing their complaint brought under Section 4915, R.S., 35 U.S.C.A. § 63, to require the Patent Office to grant patents on certain claims relating to an automatic stock quotation board capable of giving nation-wide service. Our decision affirmed the order of the court below dismissing the complaint. The ground for the present motion to vacate is that in affirming the District Court we raised and decided a question not presented by the record and based our opinion on facts found in investigations authorized by Congress.

* * *

We will restate the principle on which our decision rests and which appellants claim was improperly injected into the case. Where a corporation, as assignee of one of its employees, seeks a patent on a discovery made in the course of its organized technical research it must assume a different burden of proof from that imposed where the discovery is the product of independent inventive genius. The corporation, which in substance is seeking the patent, must show that (1) the employee is the real inventor, and (2) the discovery is above the level of the art current in its own corporate laboratory and other corporate laboratories with which it has connections and affiliations. Such a burden is not met merely by showing that the discovery is an advance over the art shown in technical literature outside the laboratory or in previous patent application by others.

We believe this result is compelled if we apply the fundamental principles of the patent law to the actual facts of the complex modern technology of corporate research laboratories. These principles are (1) that a discovery which is the result of step-by-step experimentation does not rise to the level of invention; (2) that invention must rise above the level of accomplishment of the ordinary skilled technicians engaged in the art; (3) that the patent law must be so administered as to promote science and the useful arts. These three somewhat overlapping principles are questioned by no one.

Our opinion holds that in applying these principles to discoveries which arise out of the experimentation of modern organized corporate research we must take judicial notice of the character of that kind of enterprise. Unless we do so the patent law may become a cloak under which a corporate group may prevent the independent use of modern technical information by obtaining patents on the step-by-step progress of scientific knowledge. The methods employed by successful corporate research are well known. It has become a device by which a corporation

4. [140 F.2d 470 (D.C.Cir.1944)].

may get a patent on what has been called "know how", which means the technical skill which large groups of men acquire through extensively financed experimentation and cooperation. By taking an assignment in advance from each employee the corporation appears to satisfy the requirement that there be an individual inventor. But the corporation is the real applicant, and the man whose name appears on the patent is only a nominal party. Furthermore, though the discovery may appear to be a startling innovation, actually it is frequently the product of years of research by many men who come and go, who consult each other and the employees of other corporations with which their own employer has affiliations and agreements. The result is a gradual advance in scientific knowledge made possible because large funds have been spent on research—not an invention. The use of this accumulating body of technical information is denied to the public and to new enterprise whenever a patent is granted on this kind of "discovery". Corporate patenting of this character gives the first private group that trains its employees in a modern industrial technique the right to prevent others from using the same knowledge which they may obtain by similar methods. For that reason acquisition of control over technical education acquired by years of routine experimentation has become a major patent policy of domestic and international cartels.

* * *

Today, when the strangling effects on industrial progress and the promotion of patent cartels, through the growth of the fiction under which corporate patenting has been inadvertently approved, are written large in the investigations authorized by Congress, appellants argue that we have no right to consider such public hearings in applying the principles of the patent law to corporate research. This argument is not worthy of serious consideration. The purpose of economic investigations by Congress is not only to promote sensible legislation; it is also to aid in the intelligent interpretation and administration of the law. Facts brought out by such investigations are particularly important in construing the patent law since it must effectuate the broad economic purpose defined in the Constitution as the promotion of science and the useful arts. Furthermore, we have used Congressional investigations only to illustrate characteristics of organized research that are obvious without their support. The patent law is designed to encourage competition among inventors by giving a patent to the ingenious individual who wins in a race for discovery. The modern corporate research laboratory is a negation of this principle because it is compelled to suppress competition between individuals. Instead the race is between the financial interests that organize the laboratories. The result is that a corporation, by successfully eliminating competition for prior discovery between individuals, receives the statutory reward offered to encourage the individual effort which it has suppressed. A court which grants patents on an assumption contrary to these facts[5] is guilty of affirmatively promoting a

5. What we believe to be the view of the Supreme Court has been adequately summarized by Mr. Justice Brandeis as follows: "The judge came to the bench unequipped with the necessary knowledge of social and economic science, and his judg-

fiction which inevitably leads to the monopoly grants to corporations on the technical education of our time.

We suspect that the underlying reason for appellants' objection to our opinion is not that it is based on judicial notice of the facts of industrial research. It is rather that it lays down a principle of law which is not acceptable to appellants. Leaders in corporate research have argued that corporate patenting of technical information is in the public interest. Their contention is that corporate research is so expensive that the financing of research would stop if corporations were not offered a monopoly on the information for which they spend their funds. Independent innovators like Henry Kaiser and Edsel Ford repudiate this notion. The argument justifying corporate control of technical information is simply a variation of the larger argument justifying the protection of the investments and dominating position of cartels to insure orderly production and full employment. To those who believe in the economics of free enterprise this position is both unsound and dangerous. But a debate on these opposing economic philosophies is not relevant here because our legislative policy is clearly committed to the proposition that public interest can only be protected through freedom of competitive enterprise to use the technology of our time. It is sufficient, therefore, to say that the policy of the patent law gives no support whatever to monopolies on step-by-step experimentation however expensive that process may be.

* * *

The motion is denied.

Notes and Questions

1. *Legislative facts.* For what purpose does the court utilize judicial notice in *Potts v. Coe*? Due primarily to the ideas advanced by Professor Kenneth Culp Davis, first set out in Davis, An Approach to Problems of Evidence in the Administrative Process, 55 Harv.L.Rev. 364 (1942), it has become common among commentators, and more recently among courts, to distinguish between "adjudicative" and "legislative" facts.

> * * * [A]djudicative facts are those to which the law is applied in the process of adjudication. They are the facts that normally go to the jury in a jury case. They relate to the parties, their activities, their properties, their businesses. Legislative facts are those which help the

ment suffered likewise through lack of equipment in the lawyers who presented the cases to him. For a judge rarely performs his functions adequately unless the case before him is adequately presented. Thus were the blind led by the blind. It is not surprising that under such conditions the laws as administered failed to meet contemporary economic and social demands. * * * The court reawakened to the truth of the old maxim of the civilians, Ex factor jus oritur. It realized that no law, written or unwritten, can be understood without a full knowledge of the facts out of which it arises and to which it is to be applied. * * * " Address before the Chicago Bar Association January 3, 1916, in The Brandeis Guide to the Modern World, edited by Alfred Lief (1941), pp. 100–101.

> tribunal to determine the content of law and policy and to exercise its judgment or discretion in determining what course of action to take. Legislative facts are ordinarily general and do not concern the immediate parties. In the great mass of cases decided by courts and by agencies, the legislative aspect is either absent, unimportant, or interstitial, because in most cases the applicable law and policy have been previously established. But whenever a tribunal is engaged in the creation of law or of policy, it may need to resort to legislative facts, whether or not those facts have been developed on the record.

Davis, Judicial Notice, 55 Colum.L.Rev. 945, 952 (1955).

Note that the term "legislative" facts is not restricted to facts developed and relied upon by a legislature in the process of formulating statutory law, but extends to all facts utilized by the courts in determining what the law, either statutory or decisional, is or should be. See Rogers v. Tennessee, 532 U.S. 451, 461 (2001) ("In the context of common law doctrines (such as the year and a day rule), there often arises a need to clarify or even to reevaluate prior opinions as new circumstances and fact patterns present themselves. Such judicial acts, whether they be characterized as 'making' or 'finding' the law, are a necessary part of the judicial business in States in which the criminal law retains some of its common law elements.").

2. *Judicial notice of likely correct but disputable legislative facts.* Professor Davis vigorously criticized both the Model Code and the original Uniform Rules of Evidence, neither of which drew any distinction between "legislative" and "adjudicative" facts, on the ground that judicial notice of "legislative" facts should not be, and is not in fact, confined to facts which are indisputable. Davis, Judicial Notice, 55 Colum.L.Rev. 945 (1955). Federal Rule 201 does draw such a distinction since it purports to regulate only judicial notice of "adjudicative facts." Professor Davis proved almost equally critical of the federal rule, however, on the ground that it left legislative facts out of account. For Davis' criticisms and the rule which he would prefer, see Davis, Judicial Notice, 1969 Law & Soc.Ord. 513.

3. *Sources for judicial notice of legislative facts.* Assuming, as implied by Rule 201, notice of legislative facts is not to be regulated by the same strictures and standards applicable to adjudicative facts, by what means may a court apprise itself of the pertinent facts? In Chastleton Corp. v. Sinclair, 264 U.S. 543, 548 (1924), Justice Holmes stated that "the Court may ascertain as it sees fit any fact that is merely a ground for laying down a rule of law * * *." In *Chastleton*, the appropriate mode of ascertainment was deemed to be a remand of the case to the district court, apparently for the reception of further evidence. Adopting the same expedient, see Borden's Farm Products Co. v. Baldwin, 293 U.S. 194 (1934). Are legislative facts always susceptible to satisfactory development through traditional evidentiary channels? See Roberts, Preliminary Notes Toward a Study of Judicial Notice, 52 Cornell L.Q. 210, 225 (1967).

4. *Another type of legislative fact that is far from indisputable.* A method by which a party may undertake to apprise the court of "legislative" facts is that of the so-called "Brandeis Brief," the prototype of which was authored by Louis Brandeis, in the case of Muller v. Oregon, 208 U.S. 412 (1908), before his elevation to the Supreme Court. In attempting to support

the constitutionality of an Oregon statute regulating the employment of women, Brandeis devoted virtually his entire brief to a monumental collection of social and economic data tending to demonstrate the factual realities of the problem at which the statute was directed. The Brandeis Brief was originally conceived as a method of supporting the constitutionality of legislation, usually social legislation, attacked as having no reasonable basis in fact and therefore arbitrary and capricious. When used for this purpose is it necessary that the court take judicial notice of the "truth" of the data adduced, or only of the fact that the data exist? See the dissenting opinion of Justice Brandeis in Jay Burns Baking Co. v. Bryan, 264 U.S. 504, 519–20 (1924).

5. *Sources of legislative facts.* Where the proposed use of legislative facts logically requires not only that the data exist but that they be accurate, troublesome questions arise concerning how the reliability of the data should be assessed. A novel and potentially valuable approach to this problem is suggested by Monahan & Walker, Social Authority: Obtaining, Evaluating, and Establishing Social Science in Law, 134 U.Pa.L.Rev. 477 (1986). The authors of this article argue that much of the product of social science research might more appropriately and usefully be analogized to legal precedent than to evidentiary fact. What assessment methodologies are suggested by this new analogy?

More traditional treatments of the same problem include: Roberts, Preliminary Notes Toward a Study of Judicial Notice, 52 Cornell L.Q. 210 (1967); Currie, Appellate Courts Use of Facts Outside the Record by Resort to Judicial Notice and Independent Investigation, 1960 Wis.L.Rev. 39; Laughlin, Judicial Notice, 40 Minn.L.Rev. 365 (1956); Morgan, Judicial Notice, 57 Harv.L.Rev. 269 (1944).

Chapter 10[1]

REAL AND DEMONSTRATIVE EVIDENCE

SMITH v. OHIO OIL CO.

Appellate Court of Illinois, 1956.
134 N.E.2d 526.

SCHEINEMAN, JUSTICE. Plaintiff, W.R. Smith, suffered personal injuries when his truck was run into by a truck of the Ohio Oil Company, driven by its employee, Maurice M. Smedley. In a suit against these parties, plaintiff recovered a judgment on a verdict of $50,000 and the defendants have appealed.

* * *

During the testimony of a medical witness for plaintiff, the court permitted the use of a plastic model of a human skeleton to assist the explanations. This is assigned as error on the ground that it was unnecessary to an understanding of the issues, was gruesome, and tended only to arouse emotion rather than explain anything.

The use of physical objects before a jury falls into two categories: 1, real evidence, which Wigmore calls "adoptive," and 2, demonstrative evidence. The tests for the proper use of either are substantially similar, i.e., the object must be relevant to some issue in the case, and it must also be actually explanatory of something which it is important for the jury to understand. If these tests are met, the courts do not seem to be greatly concerned with the question whether the object is gruesome.

Real evidence involves the production of some object which had a direct part in the incident, and includes the exhibition of injured parts of the body. * * *

Demonstrative evidence (a model, map, photograph, X-ray, etc.) is distinguished from real evidence in that it has no probative value in itself, but serves merely as a visual aid to the jury in comprehending the verbal testimony of a witness. Wigmore, Evid. Sec. 790 et seq. It is said its great value lies in the human factor of understanding better what is

1. Throughout this chapter some footnotes from the original cases and materials have been omitted; others have been renumbered. [Ed.]

seen than what is heard. Wigmore favors the use of any aid modern science may provide, to the end that the jury may have the best possible understanding of matters it must decide. The limitations are: that the evidence must be relevant and the use of the object actually explanatory. Sometimes the question of accuracy of an exhibit is pertinent, but this seems to be a phase of its explanatory function, since it may be misleading if inaccurate.

Similar views have been expressed by the courts. Reinke v. Sanitary District, 260 Ill. 380, 103 N.E. 236; 20 Am.Jur.Evid. § 740; 9 A.L.R.2d 1044, note. The skeleton of a human foot was held properly used by physicians in explanation of their testimony. Chicago & A. Ry. Co. v. Walker, 217 Ill. 605, 75 N.E. 520. It was proper to use a model skeleton where it was of assistance to the jury. Carnine v. Tibbetts, 158 Or. 21, 74 P.2d 974. But where its use would not aid a jury, trial court properly excluded it. Dameron v. Ansbro, 39 Cal.App. 289, 178 P. 874.

Articles by law professors and trial attorneys in various law reviews have pointed out that the very fact people learn and understand better with the eyes than with the ears, makes it possible to abuse demonstrative evidence by giving a dramatic effect, or undue emphasis to some issue at the expense of others. There is obvious merit in these criticisms and the courts must be alert to eliminate such abuse. Apparently the enthusiasm of Wigmore, Greenleaf, and other writers for demonstrative evidence is shared by the courts, and the desirability of giving the jury the best possible understanding of the subject on which they are to pass seems to have outweighed other factors.

As a result, the use of such evidence is usually left to the discretion of the trial court, and expressions of disapproval are generally based on irrelevance, or that the model, picture, etc., was misleading or not explanatory. Therefore, this court will not announce any flat rule that a skeletal model may never be used, but holds that its use must be actually explanatory of some relevant issue in the case.

This court holds that the determination of relevancy and explanatory value of demonstrative evidence is primarily within the discretion of the trial court, but, to curtail abuses, is subject to review as to the actual use made of the object. If it appears that the exhibit was used for dramatic effect, or emotional appeal, rather than factual explanation useful to the reasoning of the jury, this should be regarded as reversible error, not because of abuse of discretion, but because actual use proved to be an abuse of the ruling.

Applying these tests to the actual use in the case at bar, it appears that the model was not used at all during the physician's testimony as to injuries he found, operations performed, methods of treatment, etc. Not until he proceeded to describe the present condition of plaintiff was the model exhibited. This involved the pelvic area, which is probably the part of the body most difficult for the average person to visualize.

In reply to questions by the court, the witness stated the model would assist his explanation, and that it was an excellent reproduction of a normal human skeleton. Permission was given to use the model. The witness then pointed to displacement of bones of the pelvis in a recent X-ray of plaintiff, and pointed to the model to illustrate normal alignment. Witness also explained the muscular arrangement and how the weight of the upper torso is transmitted to the lower extremities. He pointed out where excess strain would occur because of damaged ligaments and bone displacement, and how this would affect the ability to balance, or to stoop over. This was important as an explanation of the doctor's statement that a built-up shoe would not remedy the condition.

From consideration of testimony of the witness, this court concludes that the explanation was relevant, legitimate and helpful, and contained nothing emotional or dramatic in character. The rulings of the court thereon were correct. * * *

Judgment affirmed.

BARDENS, P.J., and CULBERTSON, J., concur.

Notes and Questions

1. *Sources*. The increased interest in recent years in real and demonstrative evidence has produced a wealth of periodical literature on the subject. Some classic articles dealing basically with the efficacy of tangible evidence as a vehicle of persuasion and the range of possibilities for its use include: Belli, Demonstrative Evidence and the Adequate Award, 22 Miss.L.J. 284 (1951); Dooley, Demonstrative Evidence—Nothing New, 42 Ill.B.J. 136 (1953); Hinshaw, Use and Abuse of Demonstrative Evidence: The Art of Jury Persuasion, 40 A.B.A.J. 479 (1954); Spangenberg, The Use of Demonstrative Evidence, 21 Ohio St.L.J. 178 (1960). For more recent treatments see Imwinkelried, Evidentiary Foundations (6th ed. 2005); Lubet, Modern Trial Advocacy ch. 10 (3d ed. 2004); Mauet, Trial Techniques ch. VI (6th ed.2002).

2. *Directly involved exhibits*. The court in the principal case follows Wigmore in citing models, maps and photographs as examples of demonstrative, rather than real, evidence. No great effort, however, is required to imagine numerous possible situations in which, e.g., a map or photograph will have "had a direct part in the incident." The problems of classifying and labeling types of evidence other than oral testimony are treated in Michael & Adler, Real Proof, 5 Vand.L.Rev. 344 (1952); Nokes, Real Evidence, 65 L.Q.Rev. 57 (1949), reprinted in Selected Writings on Evidence and Trial 668 (Fryer ed.1957).

3. *Classification as "real" or "demonstrative."* What practical difference will it make whether a particular item is properly classified as "real" or merely "demonstrative" evidence? In contrast to the principal case, one Texas trial judge is said to have excluded a proffered skeleton on the ground that it did not comprise the "very bones" of the plaintiff. See Cady, Objections to Demonstrative Evidence, 32 Mo.L.Rev. 333, 338 (1967). Where, as is generally the case, the admissibility of both real and demonstrative evidence is viewed as depending upon whether it will assist the understanding of the jury, one importance of classification may be to determine the foundation which will be required for introduction of the item. For other

practical differences in consequence, see 1 Giannelli & Imwinkelried, Scientific Evidence ch. 7 (3d ed. 1999); Graham, Relevancy and Exclusion of Relevant Evidence—Real Evidence, 18 Crim.L.Bull. 333 (1982); 2 McCormick, Evidence § 212 (6th ed. 2006).

Sometimes a physical object will be offered as demonstrative evidence because the actual item involved in the incident is no longer available. See United States v. Aldaco, 201 F.3d 979, 986 (7th Cir.2000) (replica of destroyed shotgun properly admitted as demonstrative evidence).

Had you represented the plaintiff in *Smith v. Ohio Oil Co.*, what foundation would you have sought to lay through the testimony of your expert medical witness prior to offering the skeleton in evidence? Prepare a series of questions calculated to elicit such foundation testimony. With your result, compare that suggested in Lay, Use of Real Evidence, 37 Neb.L.Rev. 501, 513 (1958).

4. *Which federal rule?* Which, if any, of the Federal Rules deals with the issues involved in the admission of real or demonstrative evidence?

GALLAGHER v. PEQUOT SPRING WATER CO.

Circuit Court of Connecticut, Appellate Division, 1963.
199 A.2d 172.

KOSICKI, JUDGE. The plaintiff sued the defendant, a bottler and vendor of grape soda, for injuries sustained by her after consuming soda sold by the defendant, because of the presence in it of a foreign substance. The complaint was in two counts, one sounding in negligence and the other for breach of an implied warranty as to the merchantability of the soda and as to its fitness for the intended use. The jury returned a general plaintiff's verdict for $2500. On motion to set aside the verdict, the court ordered a remitter of $1000, which was filed, and judgment was entered on the verdict as modified. * * *

The following facts are not in dispute. The plaintiff was married on August 26, 1961, and a wedding reception was held at the Mount Carmel Hall. There were approximately 150 guests present, of whom about thirty were children. At the wedding dinner, the plaintiff's father poured for her some of the soda sold by the defendant. There were approximately fifteen people seated at the bride's table. The plaintiff consumed the soda as her father poured the remaining contents of the bottle for others at the table. While he was pouring, some of those at the table, other than the plaintiff and her mother, who were the only witnesses to testify for the plaintiff, exclaimed excitedly over a foreign substance which they variously described, within hearing of the plaintiff, as a "bloodsucker" or "cockroach." Neither the plaintiff nor her mother saw what was in the bottle. On trial, there was no identification of the substance other than a characterization of it by a defendant's witness as a "mold." The plaintiff became ill and retired to the ladies' room, where she vomited. She was unable to eat her dinner and left before the grand march took place. According to custom, the guests are expected to make gifts of money to the bride and groom in the course of the grand march, but because of the early departure of the plaintiff many of the guests also left and consequently some of the expected gifts failed to materialize. Because of her illness, the plaintiff abstained from the joyous incidents of the nuptial night, abandoned the plans for her honeymoon, and a few days later returned to work.

Among the errors assigned by the defendant is error in the ruling of the court admitting in evidence, as exhibit 1 a soda bottle containing some unidentified substance. If the exhibit was admitted improperly, the error would be material because the jury then would have been permitted to accept as true the very fact which the plaintiff needed in order to establish the defendant's liability on either count. The exhibit was offered through Mrs. Alaimo, the plaintiff's mother, who, in the course of her direct examination, testified that the bottle was the one opened by her husband at the table where she sat about twelve feet from him. The defendant objected, stating as reasons that the substance in the bottle had not been identified, that there was no proof that the substance was in the bottle at the time of the alleged occurrence, that custody and care of the bottle until the date of trial had not been accounted for, and that a proper foundation had not been laid for admitting this item of evidence. The objection was overruled and the bottle admitted as a full exhibit. Upon further questioning, the witness testified as follows: "Q.—Now, did anything unusual happen while he was pouring from the bottle? A.—Yes, everybody—well, as he was pouring, they noticed this object in the bottle was moving around and they got up and there was quite a commotion. They was wondering what was in the bottle. The court: And while he was pouring this, some people noticed something? A.—Well, yes—you know—they were facing her table and as he was pouring it, someone nearby said something about a cockroach being in the bottle, or something, and they named other bugs and then the people sitting in back walked up. They wanted to see what was in the bottle. Q.—Now, Mrs. Alaimo, can you tell me what actually this object in the bottle was? A. I don't know, I mean—Q.—Did you know at that time? A.—Everybody was saying different things—Mr. Higgins: Objection, Your Honor. She is just not answering the question. The court: She doesn't know. Q.—Do you know at this time? A.—Well, I don't know—do you mean do I know what's in the bottle? Q.—Yes. A.—No, I don't know. I know something is in the bottle, but I don't know what it is. Q.—But this is the bottle as you saw it there? A.—Yes it is." On cross-examination, the witness stated that after the wedding reception her husband took the bottle home and later turned it over to a lawyer. Her husband had died some time before the trial.

The plaintiff, during her testimony, identified the bottle as being the one from which she had consumed soda poured by her father. "Q.—What did you do with the soda when you got it? A.—I drank it. Q.—Right away? A.—Yes. Q.—Now, did any incident occur while your father was pouring the soda in other people's cups? A.—Yes, it started an uproar. They saw something shaking around in the bottle, they said there was a bloodsucker, cockroaches, there was a lot of comments about what was in the bottom of the bottle. Q.—Now it's true that you don't know what is in that bottle now, isn't it? A.—No. Q.—Is that right? A.—Yes. Q.—And you didn't know what was in it—supposedly in it—at the reception, is that right? A.—No, that's right. Q.—And you consumed a cup of grape soda at the reception? A.—Yes. Q.—And thereafter, didn't you testify that some people around there saw something in the bottle? A.—Splashing around in the bottle. Q.—And they started making remarks? A.—Yes. Q.—And isn't that what upset you? A.—No, that wasn't what upset me, no."

We have set down the testimony verbatim and at considerable length so that all of the evidence material to the issue raised by the defendant's objection may be examined in the light most favorable to the plaintiff. In laying a foundation for the receipt in evidence of the thing claimed to have caused the injury, it is ordinarily sufficient for the witness having knowledge of the object to identify it. See Lestico v. Kuehner, 204 Minn. 125, 283 N.W. 122, Exhibit 1 was admitted on identification of the bottle. It was not introduced to prove the identity of the bottle which had contained the beverage consumed but as real evidence of the purported substance which allegedly the beverage contained and which caused the plaintiff's illness and suffering. See 1 Wigmore, Evidence (3d Ed.) § 24. In order to justify its admission for that purpose, it was necessary first to show that it was the substance it purported to be, that is, that it was present in the bottle at the time of the occurrence, in a condition reasonably the same as that viewed at the trial, eighteen months later. The plaintiff had the burden of proving as a preliminary matter that the substance allegedly contained in the bottle at the time it was first opened was the same substance, without any material change, as that found in the bottle when it was offered as an exhibit. See Wieland v. C.A. Swanson & Sons, 223 F.2d 26 (2d Cir.). This is usually accomplished by showing original apperception of the object and then its care and custody under circumstances which would reasonably exclude any tampering with or material alteration in it so as to render the exhibit misleading—or, as in this case, the probability of chemical changes or organic growth resulting from environmental factors such as air, moisture and temperature. See Jasper Coca Cola Bottling Co. v. Breed, 40 Ala.App. 449, 452, 115 So.2d 126; 32 C.J.S. Evidence §§ 601, 602, 607. The rule, however, is not so rigid as to render things sometimes called unique inadmissible unless absolute continuity of possession and the absence of tampering are first established. Pasadena Research Laboratories, Inc. v. United States, 169 F.2d 375, 380 (9th Cir.); Anheuser-Busch, Inc. v. Southard, 191 Ark. 107, 84 S.W.2d 89; Coca-Cola Bottling Co. of Arkansas v. Adcox, 189 Ark. 610, 74 S.W.2d 771. It is enough if the object offered in evidence has been reasonably identified as that sought to be proved, by someone who can testify of his own knowledge that the object proffered is the one claimed to have caused the result.

The questioned exhibit consists of a dark green quart bottle with a roughened surface, some liquid therein, and a substance described by one witness as a "mold." To see this substance at all requires observation at very close range in good light. It is plain that neither witness who identified the bottle had any knowledge of what was in it, other than soda, at the time the plaintiff partook of the contents. Neither of them examined the bottle at that time; they relied on what they heard, not on what they saw; no testimony was offered as to care and custody of the bottle and its contents; and no evidence supports the conclusion, obviously reached by the jury, that the substance they observed was the same as that which was allegedly present in the bottle when the soda was consumed by the plaintiff. * * *

The objection of the defendant was well taken; a sufficient foundation had not been laid for the admission of exhibit 1 and its examination by the jury; and the error was harmful and prejudicial to the defendant.

* * *

There is error, the judgment is set aside and a new trial is ordered.

In this opinion DEARINGTON and KINMONTH, JJ., concurred.

Notes and Questions

1. *Differences in testimony.* Would you expect the holding of the principal case to have been different: (a) had either the plaintiff or her mother been able to testify as to the contents of the bottle at the time of the wedding supper, or (b) if the attorney to whom the bottle was subsequently delivered had been called to testify as to what he did with it?

2. *Chain of custody.* The exactitude with which the "chain of custody" of a tangible object must be traced as a precondition to its admission will frequently vary with the nature of the object. Thus, an object which is more or less readily identifiable by observation and relatively impervious to change or alteration will frequently be admitted without perfect tracing of the chain. See, e.g., State v. Sugimoto, 614 P.2d 386 (Haw.1980) (check held properly admitted without complete chain because identifiable and relatively impervious to change); Brown v. State, 518 P.2d 898 (Okla.Crim.App.1974) (jack properly admitted despite broken chain of custody which would have been of "grave concern" had evidence been a specimen for chemical analysis). And some courts expressly consider "identification" testimony a complete alternative to establishing a chain of custody, at least where identifiable objects are concerned. Cooper v. Eagle River Mem. Hosp., 270 F.3d 456 (7th Cir. 2001) (authentication sufficient without chain of custody where reference number on pathology slide matched the specimen number in pathology report); State v. Emery, 688 P.2d 175 (Ariz.1984) (linen taken from victim's bed properly authenticated without chain of custody by police officer's tags). For a clear statement of the relativity of foundation requirements, see Loza v. State, 325 N.E.2d 173 (Ind.1975).

3. *Strictness of showing chain.* A showing sufficient to preclude the possibilities of tampering or unintentional interchange or contamination is frequently said to be necessary to the introduction of more fungible items, particularly in criminal cases. One authority, however, has contended that

such standards are not always applied with the strictness with which they are enunciated. See 1 Giannelli & Imwinkelried, Scientific Evidence ch. 7 (3d ed. 1999) (a thorough treatment of the subject).

SEMET v. ANDORRA NURSERIES, INC.

Supreme Court of Pennsylvania, 1966.
219 A.2d 357.

BELL, CHIEF JUSTICE. * * *

On May 22, 1962, plaintiff was sent by his employer Milton Sugerman (an electric contractor) to a construction site owned by defendant, Andorra Nurseries, Inc. Plaintiff was to string a temporary line from an electric service box in the basement of a sample home to the chimney of the sample home and then to poles for the purpose of carrying electric current to the job site. Plaintiff instructed an employee of Andorra Nurseries to place an aluminum 34–foot extension ladder against the left side of the chimney of the sample home. This employee went to the top of the ladder and came down without any unusual incident occurring. Plaintiff made certain that the ladder was straight and settled. He then climbed to the top of the ladder and took some wire off his shoulder. While on the upper portion of the ladder it began to slip downward, and telescoping into the lower portion, as a result of which plaintiff fell and was severely injured. The lower Court entered a compulsory nonsuit which the Court en banc refused to take off. Plaintiff thereafter appealed to this Court.

* * *

52 days after this accident Martin Alkon, a registered Engineer, went to the scene and examined a ladder to which he had been directed by *unnamed* employees of defendant Andorra Nurseries, Inc. Photographs were taken of this ladder. Plaintiff offered Alkon's testimony and the photographs for the purposes of explaining the mechanical function of the ladder and the reasons for the ladder's collapse. The lower Court properly held that this testimony and the accompanying photographs were inadmissible. There was no legally admissible testimony that the ladder examined by Alkon and the ladder photographed was the ladder from which plaintiff fell. Moreover, even if this were proven to be the same ladder, the proffered evidence would still be inadmissible. 52 days passed before the ladder was examined. There was no testimony that the condition of the ladder had not changed from the time of the accident. In Brandon v. Peoples Natural Gas Co., 417 Pa. 128, at pages 133–134, 207 A.2d 843, at page 846, the Court said:

> "* * * 'Whenever the condition of a particular place or thing at a certain time is in question, evidence of its condition at a prior or subsequent time is admissible if accompanied by proof that it has not changed in the meanwhile.' "

Plaintiff attempted to have the photograph admitted into evidence on the ground that it was authenticated by him. Plaintiff was not present when the photograph was taken. A photograph may be proven at the trial of a case without calling the person who took it. Commonwealth v. White, 160 Pa.Super. 522, 52 A.2d 360 (1947). Nevertheless, the photograph must be shown to be a faithful and accurate reproduction of the object in question. Puskarich v. Trustees of Zembo Temple, 412 Pa. 313, 194 A.2d 208. There is nothing in the record which indicates plaintiff had the kind of familiarity with the ladder in question which would enable him to examine a picture of a common two-part metal ladder and verify it as a faithful and accurate reproduction of the ladder which caused his injuries. Plaintiff was injured on or prior to May 22, 1962. The time of his injury was the only instance he saw the ladder. His recollection of the ladder at the time of the trial, over three years from the time of the accident, was extremely dim. We therefore must conclude that plaintiff's vague knowledge and recollection makes it impossible for him to establish that the photographs offered in evidence by him accurately depicted the ladder from which he fell.

In Puskarich v. Trustees of Zembo Temple, 412 Pa. 313, 194 A.2d 208, supra, the Court said (at page 317, 194 A.2d at page 211) quoting from Nyce v. Muffley, 384 Pa. 107, 119 A.2d 530 (1956):

> "The admission of photographs is a matter largely within the discretion of the trial Judge. A photograph must be verified either by the testimony of the person who took it or by another person with sufficient knowledge to state that it fairly and accurately represents the object or place reproduced as it existed at the time of the accident, or if there is a difference or change, the difference or change is specifically pointed out and is readily capable of being clearly understood and appreciated by the jury: Taylor v. Modena Borough, 370 Pa. 100, 87 A.2d 195; Beardslee v. Columbia Township, 188 Pa. 496, 41 A. 617." The lower Court correctly excluded this evidence.

The Order of the lower Court refusing to take off the nonsuit is affirmed.

MUSMANNO, J., dissents.

EAGEN and ROBERTS, JJ., concur in the result.

Notes and Questions

1. *Purpose of offer.* The theory upon which photographs are usually offered, i.e., that they serve "to illustrate or explain" oral testimony, makes for rather liberal admission of this type of evidence. Why did the theory not suffice in the principal case? Would the following rule have provided ancillary support to the plaintiff's argument for admissibility? "Where only the generic characteristics of the item are significant no objection would appear to exist to the introduction of a substantially similar 'duplicate'." 2 McCormick, Evidence § 213, at 17 (6th ed. 2006), citing People v. Jordan, 10 Cal.Rptr. 495 (Cal.Ct.App.1961).

2. *Modern technology.* For discussions of some of the problems that arise as a result of modern technology see Madison, Seeing Can be Deceiv-

ing: Photographic Evidence in a Visual Age—How Much Weight Does It Deserve, 25 Wm. & Mary L.Rev. 705 (1984); Note, A Picture is Worth a Thousand Lies: Electronic Imaging and the Future of the Admissibility of Photographs into Evidence, 18 Rutgers Computer & Tech.L.J. 365 (1992); Witkowski, Can Juries Really Believe What They See? New Foundational Requirements for the Authentication of Digital Images, 10 Wash. U.J.L. & Pol'y 267 (2002). For cases dealing with specific problems related to photographic evidence, see Annots., 9 A.L.R.2d 899 (photos generally); 72 A.L.R.2d 308 (enlargements); 53 A.L.R.2d 1102 (colored slide projection); 85 A.L.R.5th 671(aerial photographs); 19 A.L.R.2d 877 (posed photographs).

CLARK v. ST. THOMAS HOSPITAL

Court of Appeals of Tennessee, 1984.
676 S.W.2d 347.

OPINION

TODD, PRESIDING JUDGE (Middle Section).

Plaintiff has appealed from a jury verdict and judgment dismissing his suit for injuries sustained in a fall in defendant's hospital. The sole issue presented on appeal is the admission in evidence of a video tape of a reenactment of the occasion of his injury.

The background facts are undisputed.

Plaintiff entered the defendant hospital as a patient on October 7, 1977, and was discharged on November 12, 1977. On October 25, 1977, plaintiff's left kidney and spleen were surgically removed. On November 12, 1977, plaintiff was taken to the x-ray room where an x-ray picture was to be taken in a standing position. While standing for the picture, plaintiff fell and was injured.

The principal issue of fact relates to whether plaintiff was attended at the time of his fall. Plaintiff asserted that the x-ray technician was some distance away when she ordered him to move slightly; and, when he endeavored to do so without assistance, he fell. The technician testified that she went to plaintiff and was assisting him in a slight change of position when his knees began to buckle and she lowered him to the floor.

The video tape depicts a reenactment of the events just stated in which the technician performs her version of her actions and a third party performs the movements of plaintiff as described by the technician in her testimony. The technician testified that the movie was a fair representation of the events narrated in her testimony.

Appellant argues:

> Appellant contends that it is grossly unfair, inappropriate, judicially unsound and factually inaccurate to allow either party to a lawsuit to make an obviously rehearsed out of court movie of that party's version of how the alleged negligent act occurred for presentation to the jury. Should such a procedure be approved, the obvious

> next step in every major lawsuit would be to have a theatrical production shown for the jury. The convincing effect of such a production would be in excess of credibility ordinary testimony concerning the matter would be given and jury verdicts would be based, not on the true facts but, on a party's ability to glamorize their versions of the facts.

This Court respectfully disagrees with the foregoing argument as applied to the present case.

First, the admission of the questionable evidence was not grossly unfair. Frequently witnesses are permitted to reenact before the jury the actions of the witness described in the testimony. Sometimes the reenactment requires a second person to represent the other participant in the actions. Such evidence is not original evidence, but is illustrative evidence and is valid for consideration only to the extent that it illustrates facts otherwise shown by sworn testimony. Of such character was the evidence in question. The fundamental evidence to be considered by the jury was the sworn oral testimony of the witness who also swore that the reenactment was the same as her testimony. See *McCormick on Evidence* 2nd Edition, § 212, p. 527.

There is no unfairness in the fact that defendant's witness was supported by illustrative evidence, while plaintiff's testimony was not. There was no reason why plaintiff could not have reenacted the events by videotape or in person during his testimony. He did not see fit to do so. Actually, it would have been even simpler for plaintiff to illustrate his testimony. His version of the incident was that he was alone.

Appellant's fears about the ultimate result of allowing reenactments are unfounded, because the sound discretion of trial judges will prevent the abuse of the device in specific cases and in limiting the subject matter to facts stated in the sworn testimony being illustrated.

Appellant cites *Mize v. Skeen,* 63 Tenn.App. 37, 468 S.W.2d 733 (1971) which involved a motion picture depicting the static condition of an intersection and a vehicle moving in the manner in which testimony had shown the defendant's vehicle was moving at the time of the accident. In that opinion, this Court said:

> The general rule is that the admissibility of photographs is to be determined by the trial judge in the exercise of his sound discretion. *Monday v. Millsaps,* 37 Tenn.App. 371, 264 S.W.2d 6 [1953]; *Strickland Transp. Co. v. Douglas,* 37 Tenn.App. 421, 264 S.W.2d 233 [1953]. We know of no reason for a different rule to be applied to motion pictures. Generally the courts in other jurisdictions have held motion pictures to be admissible in the discretion of the trial court when they are shown to be relevant and properly authenticated. See annotation in 62 A.L.R.2d 688. (at 46)

Appellant is largely but not completely correct in stating that the moving picture was confined to static conditions in *Lampley v. Waygood* 57 Tenn.App. 610, 422 S.W.2d 708 (1967). One of the issues in that case was the visibility of a vehicle as it rounded a curve and traversed a crest as it approached an intersection. The moving pictures were made from the position of the eyes of the driver of a vehicle about to enter the intersection from a side street and showed another vehicle approaching over the crest. The movement of the vehicle did illustrate the manner in which the approaching vehicle came into the view of the driver waiting at the intersection. In the cited opinion, this Court said:

> The question whether a photograph is helpful or instructive to the jury on any material issue in the case, is generally a preliminary question to be determined by the Trial Judge, and the fact that a photograph is incorrect in some particulars does not render it inadmissible as evidence but merely affects the weight thereof.
>
> Considering the specific instructions of the Trial Judge to the jury regarding the introduction of these motion pictures, and considering all the other matters hereinabove referred to, we are of opinion that there is no reversible error shown in this record, * * * (at 620, 422 S.W.2d 708).

Appellant cites *Summit County Development Corporation v. Bagnoli*, 1968, 166 Colo. 27, 441 P.2d 658, which is distinguishable on its facts. One of the issues in that case was the safety of the speed of the movement of a ski lift, and there was no evidence that the speed shown in the movie was the same as the speed at the time of the injury. Speed of movement has no such relation to the present issues which involve manner of fall, i.e. unassisted or assisted. Also, in the cited case it was held that the trial court did not abuse its discretion in excluding the evidence.

Appellant's textual quotations from *Wigmore, McCormick* and Am Jur are reasonable and correct, but not applicable, for they appear to refer to original evidence as to which the rules of accuracy are more strict. As previously pointed out, in the present case the exhibit was illustrative and its admissibility was based upon its conformity to sworn testimony.

Appellant complains that the movie was not subject to cross examination. The witness whose testimony was illustrated was present for cross examination, and this was sufficient.

As early as 1912, the Tennessee Supreme Court recognized the value and admissibility of posed still pictures to illustrate the testimony of an eyewitness to the facts depicted. *Hughes v. State*, 126 Tenn. 40, 148 S.W. 543 (1912). In the present case, no reason is seen for applying a different standard to a movie which did not distort or embellish sworn testimony.

For an extensive collection of authorities from other jurisdictions, see 32 C.J.S., Evidence, § 715, pp. 1016–1018 notes 76 and 76.5.

The admission of the challenged evidence was clearly within the proper scope of the discretionary powers of the Trial Judge. Any fears of the plaintiff as to prejudicial effect might have been readily relieved by a proper request for instructions to the jury as to the consideration of the evidence.

Appellant's sole issue is found to be without merit. The judgment of the Trial Court is affirmed. Costs of this appeal are taxed against appellant. The cause is remanded for such further proceedings as may be necessary and proper.

Affirmed & Remanded.

Lewis and Cantrell, JJ.

Notes and Questions

1. *Motion pictures and videotapes.* The theory of admissibility utilized by the court in the principal case was first advanced to facilitate the introduction of motion pictures. See Paradis, The Celluloid Witness, 37 Colo.L.Rev. 235 (1965). That theory, now widely accepted by the courts, is readily applicable to videotapes despite the fact that the latter are created through a different technology. For a comprehensive collection of authorities relating to the use of videotapes, see Joseph, Modern Visual Evidence (2001).

2. *Reconstructions or reenactments.* Note the distinction drawn in *Clark* between videotapes (or motion pictures) of the actual event in litigation and those of reconstructions or reenactments. To what extent is the court justified in stating that "the rules of accuracy are more strict" with respect to the former? If exact accuracy is not to be required of the latter are any other precautions appropriate? See Balian v. General Motors, 296 A.2d 317 (N.J.Super.1972); Note, Videotaped Reenactments in Civil Trials: Protecting Probative Evidence from the Trial Judge's Unbridled Discretion, 24 J. Marshall L.Rev. 433 (1991).

COMMONWEALTH v. SERGE

Supreme Court of Pennsylvania, 2006.
896 A.2d 1170.

Justice Newman. Michael Serge (Appellant) appeals the sentence of life imprisonment entered by the Court of Common Pleas of Lackawanna County (trial court) following his conviction for first-degree murder * * * . We granted allowance of appeal in this case to consider the admissibility of a computer-generated animation (CGA) illustrating the Commonwealth's theory of the homicide. For the reasons discussed herein, we hold that the trial court properly admitted the CGA as demonstrative evidence. * * *

On the morning of January 15, 2001, Appellant shot his wife, Jennifer Serge (Victim), three times, killing her inside their home in Scott Township, Lackawanna County. Appellant was arrested that morning and charged with one count of first-degree murder, * * * and one count of third-degree murder * * * .

On June 18, 2001, prior to trial, the Commonwealth filed a Motion *in limine,* seeking to present the prosecution's theory of the fatal shooting through a CGA based on both forensic and physical evidence.[2] On September 14, 2001, following an evidentiary hearing, the trial court granted the Commonwealth's Motion in limine provided that certain evidentiary foundations were established at trial.[3] * * * The trial court required the Commonwealth to authenticate the animation as both a fair and accurate depiction of expert reconstructive testimony and exclude any inflammatory features that may cause unfair prejudice. To safeguard against potential prejudice, the trial court required the pre-trial disclosure of the CGA.

At his jury trial held January 29, 2002 to February 12, 2002, Appellant alleged that he had acted in self-defense as his wife attacked him with a knife. He further asserted that he should be acquitted on the grounds of justifiable self-defense. Alternatively, Appellant argued that his extreme intoxication at the time of the shooting rendered him incapable of formulating the specific intent to kill.

2. A CGA is a drawing, or drawings, created by a computer that, when assembled frame-by frame, produce the image of motion. The image is merely a graphic representation depicting the previously formed opinion of a witness or witnesses, in this case the Commonwealth experts. F. Galves, *Where the Not So Wild Things Are: Computers in the Courtroom, the Federal Rules of Evidence, and the Need for Institutional Reform and More Judicial Acceptance,* 13 Harv. J.L. & Tech. 161, 227–30 (2000). Presently, the CGA is akin to the traditionally permitted drawings used by crime scene reconstructionists to show bullet path trajectory. Accordingly, a CGA is only as credible as the underlying testimony that it represents and the computer plays no part in calculating an outcome or presenting its own conclusions. Conversely, computer-generated simulations do not depict witness opinion; rather, the computer program, based upon the data entered, draws a conclusion. As such, a computer simulation presents not only the testimony of an expert regarding the programming and data input but also a conclusion of the computer based upon the formulas programmed to use the raw data entered. For example, scientists use computer simulations to predict the effects of earthquakes on a building's structure by inputting factors such as: (1) wind; (2) magnitude of earthquake; (3) proximity of earthquake; (4) building materials; (5) building height; (6) amplitude of the earthquakes waves; and so forth. However, the simulation creates a result that nobody can testify to with personal knowledge nor is it the representation of an individual's opinion. Rather it is the outcome of the program's mathematical formulas based on the various inputted data and the laws of physics as entered by the programmers. As noted by Justice Castille in his concurring Opinion, the program used for either a CGA or a simulation is a human product and may be subjected to scrutiny regarding its programming bias and soundness in principles of both math and physics. At that point, a proper determination of the appropriate weight to be assigned to its output can occur. Further, as discussed *infra,* jury instructions may help in reducing or eliminating the potential for a jury to assign undue weight to a CGA by clarifying that it is, in actuality, a graphic representation of biased testimony of one party and not a product of neutral infallible artificial intelligence. Today, we address only the admissibility of CGA evidence as defined above and not that of computer simulations.

3. Chief Justice Cappy urges this Court to adopt a standard in which the Commonwealth would be required to file a pre-trial motion *in limine* whenever CGA evidence is involved. Although this is a recommended procedure to reduce potential prejudice, we hold that the moving party, be it the Commonwealth or a defendant, should file a motion *in limine* and seek permission of the trial court to admit the evidence as soon as possible, even if after the start of trial. It is conceivable that a party may find, after the start of trial, that a CGA would be helpful to rebut evidence or new testimony set forth by the opposing party. Should a party discover that a CGA would be helpful at that point in time that party should not be precluded from asking the trial court to admit a CGA into evidence. The timing of the request must be weighed along with the various other factors involved in determining if the prejudicial effect of the CGA outweighs its probative value. * * *

The Commonwealth countered that the killing was intentional, and that Appellant, a former Lieutenant of Detectives with the Scranton Police Department, "used his decades of experience as a police officer to tamper with the crime scene to stage a self-defense setting." * * * In particular, the Commonwealth asserted that Appellant had moved his wife's body and strategically positioned her near a knife that he had placed on the floor, as depicted in the CGA.

On February 7, 2002, during its case-in-chief, the Commonwealth presented a CGA as demonstrative evidence to illustrate the expert opinions of its forensic pathologist, Gary W. Ross, M.D. (Dr. Ross), and crime scene reconstructionist, Trooper Brad R. Beach (Trooper Beach). The CGA showed the theory of the Commonwealth based upon the forensic and physical evidence, of how Appellant shot his wife first in the lower back and then through the heart as she knelt on the living room floor of their home. More importantly, the animation showed the location of Appellant and his wife within the living room, the positioning of their bodies, and the sequence, path, trajectory, and impact sites of the bullets fired from the handgun.

The trial court thoroughly instructed the jury of the purely demonstrative nature of the CGA both before the animation was presented and during the jury charge prior to deliberation. In particular, the court noted that the CGA was a demonstrative exhibit, not substantive evidence, and it was being offered solely as an illustration of the Commonwealth's version of the events as recreated by Dr. Ross and Trooper Beach. Finally, the court informed the jury that they should not confuse art with reality and should not view the CGA as a definitive recreation of the actual incident.

On February 12, 2002, the jury found Appellant guilty of first-degree murder and the trial court immediately sentenced him to life imprisonment. Appellant filed a timely appeal, challenging several of the jury instructions and evidentiary rulings of the trial court. * * * On August 25, 2004, we granted allowance of appeal limited solely to the issue of whether the admission of the CGA depicting the Commonwealth's theory of the case was proper. The admissibility of a CGA is an issue of first impression in the Commonwealth. * * *

We determine that, for the reasons below, a CGA is admissible evidence in this Commonwealth. In particular, CGA evidence must be weighed by the same criteria of admissibility; namely, probative value versus prejudicial effect to which all other evidence is subject. Notably, certain concerns prior to admission carry more weight and deserve closer scrutiny when admitting CGA evidence than more traditional forms of evidence.

Appellant argues that the trial court erred in allowing the Commonwealth to present a CGA, which was used to introduce evidence of the Commonwealth's theory of the killing. Appellant alleges that the Commonwealth's use of the CGA: (1) lacked proper authentication; (2) lacked proper foundation; and (3) was, essentially, cumulative and unfairly prejudicial. The Commonwealth counters this argument and posits that the trial court properly admitted the CGA as demonstrative evidence used to explain or illustrate the testimony of its expert witnesses and should be subject to the same rules of admissibility as any other demonstrative evidence.

Society has become increasingly dependent upon computers in business and in our personal lives. With each technological advancement, the practice of law becomes more sophisticated and, commensurate with this progress, the legal system must adapt. Courts are facing the need to shed any technophobia and become more willing to embrace the advances that have the ability to enhance the efficacy of the legal system. However, before we are too quick to differentiate CGA's or create a special test for their admission, it must be noted that the rules for analyzing the admission of such evidence have been previously established. In particular, a CGA should be treated equivalently to any other demonstrative exhibit or graphic representation and, thus, a CGA should be admissible if it satisfies the requirements of Pa.R.E. 401, 402, 403, and 901.[4] See *State v. Tollardo,* 134 N.M. 430, 77 P.3d 1023, 1029 (Ct.App.2003) (opining that, "[w]hen the [CGA] is used to illustrate an opinion that an expert has arrived at without using the computer, the fact that the visual aid was generated by a computer * * * does not matter because the witness can be questioned and cross-examined concerning the perceptions or opinions to which the witness testifies. In that situation, the computer is no more or less than a drafting device."); *People v. McHugh,* 124 Misc.2d 559, 476 N.Y.S.2d 721, 722 (N.Y.Sup. Gen. Term 1984) ("Whether a diagram is hand drawn or mechanically drawn by means of a computer is of no importance.").

There are three basic types of evidence that are admitted into court: (1) testimonial evidence; (2) documentary evidence; and (3) demonstrative evidence. 2 McCormick on Evidence § 212 (5th ed. 1999). Presently, at issue is demonstrative evidence, which is "tendered for the purpose of rendering other evidence more comprehensible to the trier of fact." *Id.* As in the admission of any other evidence, a trial court may admit demonstrative evidence whose relevance outweighs any potential prejudicial effect. *Commonwealth v. Reid,* 571 Pa. 1, 811 A.2d 530, 552 (2002), *cert. denied,* 540 U.S. 850 * * * (2003). The offering party must authenticate such evidence. "The requirement of authentication or identification as a condition precedent to admissibility is satisfied by evidence sufficient to support a finding that the matter in question is what its

4. Because a CGA is a graphic illustration of an expert's reconstruction rather than a simulation based upon scientific principles and computerized calculations, it is not subject to the *Frye* test governing the admissibility of scientific evidence in Pennsylvania. *See Frye v. United States,* 293 F. 1013 (D.C.Cir.1923). Of course, the underlying expert opinion that the animation seeks to illustrate must satisfy Pa.R.E. 702 and be premised upon principles and methodology that are generally accepted in the relevant scientific community. Moreover, in accordance with Pa.R.E. 703, the facts or data on which the expert has relied in forming the opinion, which is illustrated by the computer animation, must be "of a type reasonably relied upon by experts in the particular field." *Id.* However, the issue of applying the *Frye* test to a computer simulation must await another day.

proponent claims." Pa.R.E. 901(a). Demonstrative evidence may be authenticated by testimony from a witness who has knowledge "that a matter is what it is claimed to be." Pa.R.E. 901(b)(1). Demonstrative evidence such as photographs, motion pictures, diagrams, and models have long been permitted to be entered into evidence provided that the demonstrative evidence fairly and accurately represents that which it purports to depict. *See Nyce v. Muffley,* 384 Pa. 107, 119 A.2d 530, 532 (1956).

The overriding principle in determining if any evidence, including demonstrative, should be admitted involves a weighing of the probative value versus prejudicial effect. We have held that the trial court must decide first if the evidence is relevant and, if so, whether its probative value outweighs its prejudicial effect. *Commonwealth v. Hawk,* 551 Pa. 71, 709 A.2d 373, 376 (1998). This Commonwealth defines relevant evidence as "having any tendency to make the existence of any fact that is of consequence to the determination of the action more probable or less probable than it would be without the evidence." Pa.R.E. 401. Relevant evidence may nevertheless be excluded "if its probative value is outweighed by the danger of unfair prejudice, confusion of the issues, or misleading the jury, or by considerations of undue delay, waste of time, or needless presentation of cumulative evidence." Pa.R.E. 403.

At issue is both the basis and form of the demonstrative evidence offered. An expert witness may offer testimony other than opinions. Pa.R.E. 702 provides that an expert witness may testify "in the form of an opinion **or otherwise.**" (Emphasis added). An important function of an expert witness is to educate the jury on a subject about which the witness has specialized knowledge but the jury does not. * * * To help perform the function of educating a jury, an expert witness may use various forms of demonstrative evidence.

Demonstrative evidence continues to evolve as society advances technologically. Medical witnesses use computerized axial tomography, i.e. CAT scans, and magnetic resonance imaging instead of, or with, traditional x-rays. Forensic pathologists previously used only blood types in an attempt to bolster their testimony and implicate a defendant, but now use specific DNA matches to prove the statistical probability that a defendant was, by virtue of biological evidence at the scene of a crime, present at some point in time. *See Commonwealth v. Blasioli,* 552 Pa. 149, 713 A.2d 1117 (1998) (accepting the use of DNA matching of blood and semen to prove the statistical probability that the blood and semen found on the victim after an alleged rape was that of the defendant).

The law has been flexible enough to accommodate scientific progress and technological advances in all fields, and should continue to do so.[5]

5. CGA evidence has been admitted in most states that have considered the matter, including in the criminal context. *See Pierce v. State,* 718 So.2d 806 (Fla.App. 1997) (holding that a CGA of an automobile accident was admissible when the testimony of three accident-reconstruction experts established that the: (1) computer program used was accepted in engineering field as one of the leading computer-aided design

Pa.R.E. 702 permits expert testimony if it "will assist the trier of fact to understand the evidence or to determine a fact in issue [.]" Such expert testimony is not limited to that which is purely verbal; rather, it includes pertinent illustrative adjuncts that help explain the testimony of one or more expert witnesses.

Presently, had the Commonwealth's experts, a crime scene reconstructionist and a pathologist, used traditional methods, they may have drawn chalk diagrams or sketches on a blackboard to help explain the basis for their opinions. Instead, they used a CGA to more concisely and more clearly present their opinion. The difference is one of mode, not meaning. The law does not, and should not, prohibit proficient professional employment of new technology in the courtroom. This is, after all, the twenty-first century. As such, we must turn to the traditional factors considered in determining if a particular CGA is admissible.

Therefore, despite the relative novelty of CGA evidence, the evaluation of its admissibility relates back to this longstanding evaluation of probative value versus prejudicial value. G. Joseph, *A Simplified Approach to Computer–Generated Evidence and Animations,* 43 N.Y.L. Sch. L.Rev. 875 (1999–2000) (stating that, "[a]t its simplest, an animation is merely a sequence of illustrations that, when filmed, videotaped or computer-generated, creates the illusion that the illustrated objects are in motion. Traditionally—because they are drawings—animations have been subjected to the fair-and-accurate-portrayal test and have been admitted, within the trial judge's discretion, generally for illustrative purposes.") As a preliminary matter, a CGA should be deemed admissible as demonstrative evidence if it: (1) is properly authenticated pursuant to Pa.R.E. 901 as a fair and accurate representation of the evidence it purports to portray; (2) is relevant pursuant to Pa.R.E. 401 and 402; and (3) has a probative value that is not outweighed by the danger of unfair prejudice pursuant to Pa.R.E. 403. However, new factors must be considered when evaluating a CGA. In particular, in determining the admissibility of a CGA the courts must address the additional dangers and benefits this particular type of demonstrative evidence presents as compared with more traditional demonstrative evidence.[6] As a result, the court must, as discussed *infra,* issue limiting instructions to the jury explaining the nature of the specific CGA.

programs in the world; (2) CGA fairly and accurately reflected expert opinion of how accident occurred; (3) CGA was fair and accurate representation of what it purported to depict; and (4) data, information, and evidence utilized was of type reasonably relied upon by experts in field of forensic animation) * * * .

6. Appellant argues that a CGA or computer simulation has the potential to influence unduly a jury due to its visual impact. However, at least one controlled study suggests that a CGA, although helpful, has a negligible measurable impact upon a jury when the CGA does not present new information. R. Bennett, Jr., J. Leibman, R. Fetter, *Seeing is Believing; or is it? An Empirical Study of Computer Simulations as Evidence,* 34 Wake Forest L.Rev. 257, 285 (1999) ("[T]he extraordinary possibilities inherent in computer animations and computer simulations raised hopes—and fears—that juries would find computer-generated displays more persuasive or convincing than other forms of evidence. These hopes and fears seem to be unwarranted, at least within the context of the empirical results of this study. In other words, computer-generated evidence is not a "silver bullet" which guarantees victory.").

It should be noted that conspicuously absent among the factors to be considered in determining the relevancy and prejudice of evidence is the potency of the evidence. Thus, although the use of illustrative demonstrative evidence by an expert, such as a CGA, may help explain his or her opinion and make the testimony more persuasive than it otherwise might have been, it is not proper grounds for excluding this relevant evidence.

Here, both the trial court and the Superior Court determined that the Commonwealth had satisfied all foundational requirements for admitting the animation and therefore it was properly admitted as demonstrative evidence. After applying the three-prong test noted above, we agree.

Appellant initially argues that the Commonwealth did not properly authenticate the CGA. Pa.R.E. 901(a) provides, "The requirement of authentication or identification as a condition precedent to admissibility is satisfied by evidence sufficient to support a finding that the matter in question is what its proponent claims." *See also* A. Albrecht, *Laying a Proper Foundation for Computer–Generated Demonstrative Evidence,* 90 Ill. B.J. 261 (2002) (stating that "courts have said that computer-generated demonstrative evidence must be relevant and authenticated by testimony that (a) the witness has personal knowledge of the exhibit's subject matter and (b) the exhibit is accurate. * * * To lay a proper foundation for computer-generated visual evidence, the proponent must first establish through witness testimony the accuracy of the exhibit's portrayal of the substantive information in question.")

In authenticating the CGA, the Commonwealth presented the testimony of multiple individuals, including: (1) Randy Matzkanin (Matzkanin), the Director of Operations for 21st Century Forensic Animations; (2) Trooper Beach; and (3) Dr. Ross. Additionally, Patrolman Jared Ganz, Patrolman Joseph Zegalia, Trooper George Scochin, Trooper Connie Devens, and Trooper Gustas testified at trial concerning the physical evidence and the measurements taken at the crime scene, both of which were used in creating the CGA. Further, the creator of the CGA testified at the Motion *in limine* hearing that the CGA was a graphical presentation of another expert's opinion, not the conclusions or calculations of a computer or himself. * * *

Matzkanin described the process employed in making the animation and testified that it was a strict depiction of the Commonwealth's forensic evidence and expert opinions. Matzkanin stated that he used the expert opinions provided by Trooper Beach and Dr. Ross as well as the measurements gathered at the crime scene. * * * Moreover, Matzkanin discussed both the computer software and hardware that created the three dimensional CGA drawings and their general use in the field. * * * Matzkanin, at the questioning of the Commonwealth, carefully explained the differences between a CGA and a simulation. * * * Matzkanin stated that he began working on the project at the end of January 2001, or beginning of February 2001, and continued until December 20, 2001.

* * * During his testimony, Matzkanin explained that photos are used to reconstruct the room, including color and the like, but the major factor in recreation is the measurements.* * * However, Matzkanin explained that the character depictions are more difficult because of the stock models used by the company to represent people. * * * He further testified that the models do not represent the defendants. * * * Next, the CGA is created in a rough draft and sent to the Commonwealth for further input. Matzkanin could not recall the exact number of versions created but specified that many changes were made to ensure that the CGA conformed to the opinions of Trooper Beach and Dr. Ross. Matzkanin further explained that drawings are recorded in time intervals of thirty frames per second and thereafter transferred onto a DVD or video tape to create the image of motion. * * *

[The court analyzed the record and found that the depictions within the CGA were supported by the evidence. Defendant had the opportunity in cross examination of the experts to bring the credibility of the animation and the opinions of the experts to the attention of the jury.]

The CGA is not meant to represent the theories of both parties; rather, as noted by both the trial court and Matzkanin, the sole purpose of the CGA and role of Matzkanin was to represent the findings of Trooper Beach and Dr. Ross. Matzkanin made no active decisions, rather, he merely interpreted the data and made corrections to the CGA based on the recommendations given to him by the two experts. The CGA is, ultimately, a representation of the expert opinions and demonstrative evidence. The line of questions presented by Appellant highlighted the alleged uncertainty regarding specific facts within the CGA and alerted the jury to the possible lack of credibility of Trooper Beach, Dr. Ross, and, by extension, the CGA. However, the jury ultimately found the testimony of the Commonwealth experts, and the CGA, to be credible. As such, the foundation was properly laid and the CGA was, in fact, what the Commonwealth purported it to be, a depiction of the various testimonies of the Commonwealth witnesses concerning their theory about the chain of events. * * *

Because the CGA was properly authenticated, we must turn to the second prong of the three-part test, which involves a question of its relevancy. The CGA was relevant because it clearly, concisely, and accurately depicted the Commonwealth's theory of the case and aided the jury in the comprehension of the collective testimonies of the witnesses without use of extraneous graphics or information.

Appellant argues that, in the alternative, even if the CGA is relevant, it is cumulative. However, as noted by the Superior Court, although the evidence did not offer anything inherently original, it presented a clear and precise depiction of the Commonwealth's theory and evidence as presented by its experts. Pursuant to * * * demonstrative depictions of the testimony of an expert have long been allowed into evidence, including drawings or depictions of bullet trajectories as here. Therefore, the cumulative argument carries no weight. Rather, the question is whether the evidence presented by the CGA is relevant and whether its probative value outweighs its prejudicial effect. Pa.R.E. 401, 403.

Accordingly, we must turn to the third and final prong, prejudice. It is within this prong that a CGA has the potential danger due to the visual nature of the presentation. Various jurisdictions that have been faced with the issue of CGA-evidence have noted the potentially powerful impact based upon its visual nature, but, nonetheless, have permitted CGA evidence. * * * Despite this potential power,[7] even inflammatory evidence may be admissible if it is relevant and helpful to a jury's understanding of the facts and the probative value outweighs the prejudicial effect. * * *

Presently, the content of the CGA was neither inflammatory nor unfairly prejudicial. Any prejudice derived from viewing the CGA resulted not from the on-screen depiction of the Commonwealth's theory, but rather was inherent to the reprehensible act of murder. The possible unnecessary and prejudicial aspects of a CGA were not present. In particular, the CGA did not include: (1) sounds; (2) facial expressions; (3) evocative or even life-like movements; (4) transition between the scenes to suggest a story line or add a subconscious prejudicial effect; or (5) evidence of injury such as blood or other wounds. Instead, much like a two-dimensional hand drawing of bullet trajectories, the CGA merely highlighted the trajectory of the three bullets fired, concluding from ballistics and blood splatter that the body had been moved after the victim died as part of Appellant's attempt to stage his self-defense. The CGA was devoid of drama so as to prevent the jury from improperly relying on an emotional basis. *See People v. Hood,* 53 Cal.App.4th 965, 972, 62 Cal.Rptr.2d 137 (1997) (permitting a CGA in a murder trial, in part because "[t]he animation was clinical and emotionless. This, combined with the instruction given the jurors about how they were to utilize both animations, persuades us that the trial court did not [err in permitting the CGA].") The major difference between a traditional chart or drawing of bullet trajectories and the instant presentation lays in the three-dimensional nature that enabled the Commonwealth experts to present their exact theory and the underlying mathematics used in formulating its case. In particular, the ability to rotate the view allowed the Commonwealth's experts to explain the exact path of the bullets and show why the evidence suggested that it was not a killing in self-defense. As such, it was a clearly relevant and helpful tool for an expert to present an informed opinion to the jury. *See* Pa.R.E. 703.

Within his argument concerning prejudice, Appellant, in this appeal, additionally raises the issue that public policy should prevent the presentation of a CGA, which, allegedly, costs between $10,000.00 and

7. At least one empirical study * * * has shown that the use of CGA evidence is not the deciding factor for a jury. Rather, the evidence and opinions underlying the CGA are the ultimate determinants of the jury's decision. The CGA merely facilitates the jury's understanding of the evidence and opinions without shifting the weight a jury assigns to the presenting side's testimony.

$20,000.00 to make.[8] He notes that his entire defense fund, provided by the Commonwealth due to his *in forma pauperis* status, was limited to $10,000.00. (Brief of Appellant, p. 44). Any additional expenditure would then come from Appellant.[9]

This argument is waived because it was not raised at the trial court level. * * * (stating that issues not raised in the lower court are waived and cannot be raised for the first time on appeal). However, Appellant argues that we should consider this factor because of the implications of permitting the Commonwealth to present expensive CGA productions at trial against an indigent defendant. * * * [The court cited United States Supreme Court and Pennsylvania decisions it characterized as holding that the defense is entitled to access to expert testimony only in limited situations and that the decision is ordinarily within the discretion of the trial court.]

Similarly, there can be no obligation to provide the defendant the finances necessary to create a CGA of his or her own. Chief Justice Cappy's concurring Opinion accurately summarizes the ultimate concerns regarding the economic disparity between the Commonwealth and an indigent defendant. * * * Thus, we ultimately conclude that the relative monetary positions of the parties are relevant for the trial court to consider when ruling on whether or not to admit a CGA into evidence. Such a question and determination are within the province of the trial court and should not be overturned absent an abuse of discretion. In particular, the trial court sitting with all facts before it, including the monetary disparity of the parties, must determine if the potentially powerful effect of the CGA and the inability of a defendant to counter with his or her own CGA should lead to its preclusion. Nevertheless, as noted above, this specific argument is waived in the instant matter.

It is argued that the uniquely dangerous aspect of a CGA is in its visual appeal to a jury resulting in an acceptance of the CGA as fact. However, such a danger is vitiated by thorough cautionary instructions that educate the jury on the exact nature and role of a CGA. Presently, the trial court safeguarded against the possibility of jury confusion over the animation or potential prejudice by supplying a thorough and extensive cautionary instruction before playing the CGA. * * *

Although limiting instructions may not be necessary, such cautionary instructions limit the prejudice or confusion that could surround a

8. As noted previously, Appellant did not raise the issue of cost in the courts below and, therefore, it is waived. Pa.R.A.P. 302(a). As a result, the record was not developed on this issue and does not contain the exact final cost. However, both Appellant's brief and the Commonwealth during oral argument before this Court indicated the cost to be between $10,000.00 and $20,000.00. * * *

9. However, although cost is a consideration, this issue will lessen over time because of the inevitable reduction in cost as technology advances. This fact has been acknowledged from the inception of CGA usage. *See* R. Sherman, *Moving Graphics: Computer Animation Enters Criminal Cases,* Nat'l L.J., p. 32 (Apr. 6, 1992) (noting that, in 1992, the overall cost of computer animations had already dropped dramatically, thereby increasing their usage, including in criminal trials).

CGA. *See Harris,* 13 P.3d at 495 (requiring cautionary jury instructions when using a CGA and noting South Carolina's requirement of the same in *Clark, supra*). Additionally, the trial court reiterated the same concerns and instructions during its closing jury charge. In so doing, the trial court duly minimized any possible prejudice by insisting that the jury not make more of the CGA than what it was—an illustration of expert witness testimony. The repetition of the instructions in the case *sub judice* ensured that the jury comprehended the nature of the CGA and would not mistake it for fact, but could only rely upon it to the extent they credited the underlying testimony. * * *

In a question of first impression in this Commonwealth, we hold that a CGA is potentially admissible as demonstrative evidence, as long as the animation is properly authenticated, it is relevant, and its probative value outweighs the danger of unfair prejudice or confusion. Therefore, because in the instant matter: (1) the Commonwealth satisfied all of the foundational requirements for admitting the CGA as demonstrative evidence; (2) the CGA was relevant evidence that enabled the Commonwealth experts to illustrate their opinions and educate the jury on the forensic and physical data; and (3) the alleged prejudicial effect of the CGA does not outweigh its relevance, we conclude that the admission of this evidence was proper. Hence, the admission of a CGA depicting the theory of the Commonwealth in this case was proper. Accordingly, we affirm the decision of the Superior Court.

[The concurring opinions of Chief Justice Cappy and Justices Castille and Eakin are omitted.]

Notes and Questions

1. *Computer generated simulations distinguished.* The court distinguishes the kind of exhibit involved in *Serge*, a computer generated animation, from a computer generated simulation. It notes that simulations would be subject to the rules governing scientific evidence. See Chapter 12, Section D. For a case rejecting a computer generated simulation for failure to meet the requirements for admission of scientific evidence, see State v. Sipin, 123 P.3d 862 (Wash.Ct.App.2005). Why should there be a difference between the two types of computer generated exhibits? For a further discussion of the differences and the policy behind the different treatment, see 2 McCormick, Evidence § 218 (6th ed. 2006).

2. *The foundation for admission of computer generated animations.* Might it be useful to require a more significant analysis of the scientific basis for the creation of computer generated animations than was required by the court in *Serge?* Certainly, there are possibilities for jury misuse of the exhibits, including inadequate sophistication of software to accurately depict technical data input and the injection of programmer creativity or personal assumptions about the evidence. See Fiedler, Note, Are Your Eyes Deceiving You?: The Evidentiary Crisis Regarding the Admissibility of Computer Generated Evidence, 48 N.Y.L.Sch.L.Rev. 295 (2003); Weinreb, Note, "Counselor, Proceed With Caution": The Use of Integrated Evidence Presentation

System and Computer–Generated Evidence in the Courtroom, 23 Cardozo L.Rev. 393 (2001). Is it sufficient simply to leave such matters to for cross-examination of the expert presenting the animation?

3. *Requiring pretrial motions.* The court in *Serge* rejected the requirement of a pre-trial motion *in limine* in favor of a more flexible approach. For an example of a rule governing the procedure for admission of computer generated evidence, including a requirement of pre-trial disclosure, see Md. Rule 2–504.3.

FISHER v. STATE

Court of Appeals of Arkansas, 1982.
643 S.W.2d 571.

COOPER, JUDGE.

This is a criminal case in which the appellant was charged with theft of property having a value of over $100.00, but less than $2,500.00. After a trial by jury, she was found guilty.* * * On appeal, the appellant challenges the sufficiency of the evidence, and alleges that the trial court erred in ruling that certain portions of a video tape recording were properly admitted into evidence. We find no merit to either contention, and therefore we affirm.

THE FACTS

The appellant and her two daughters were employed by M & W Thriftway in Nashville, Arkansas to clean the store. On August 12, 1981, the appellant and her daughters arrived at the store for the purpose of cleaning it. The manager and owner of the store had installed a video tape camera on the premises, prior to the time that the appellant and her daughters arrived. He testified that he adjusted the camera, started it, and then left the building, leaving the camera unattended. He testified that he started the video tape camera at approximately 9:15 p.m. and that he returned at approximately midnight. He testified that he replaced the tape in the camera, since the first tape was about to run out. The manager testified that at approximately 1:30 to 2:00 a.m., he returned to get the tapes. When he arrived at the store, he found law enforcement officers on the scene, and, pursuant to their instructions, he removed the video tapes. He testified that he had safeguarded those tapes until the time of trial.

The sheriff of Howard County, Dick Wakefield, testified that he observed the appellant's daughters removing groceries in paper sacks from the back door of the store. The sheriff had the individuals arrested. * * *

THE ADMISSIBILITY OF THE VIDEO TAPE RECORDING

The appellant argues that the trial court erred in admitting in evidence a video tape recording[10], since no witness testified that the

10. A video tape recording is an electronic means of recording sound and action on tape for subsequent playback in the form of a sound motion picture. 1 C. Scott, Pho-

photographic evidence was a fair and accurate representation of the subject matter.

Immediately prior to the trial, the trial court conducted a hearing on the appellant's motion *in limine* which sought to preclude the State from introducing the video tapes. The trial court required the State to present the foundational facts which would support its claim that the video tapes were admissible. The manager of the store, Mr. Moore, testified that he had positioned the video tape camera on a tripod on top of an ice machine, so as to provide a view of the back door. He testified that he loaded the tape into the camera, started it, and checked to make sure that it was operating properly, prior to the time that he left the store. He testified that at the time he left the store, no one else was present in the store. He further testified that he changed the tape approximately two hours later and that he had continuous custody of the tapes, since the date of the alleged theft.

Mr. Moore further testified regarding the contents of the tapes, that the camera worked properly at all times, and that there were no gaps in the tapes. He testified that, when he returned to the store, the camera had not been moved or tampered with in any way, and that that fact could be verified, since the tapes would have shown movement had the camera been moved. He testified that in order to turn the camera off or to change the tapes, he had to pose in front of the camera and that his image appeared on the video tapes. He also testified that, once the camera had been turned on, the controls could not be approached, without a picture of that approach being made.

The trial court held that a proper foundation had been presented, and that the video tape was admissible. He found that the video tape fairly represented the situation that existed at the store, and he further noted that any question regarding the tapes went more to their credibility, rather than to admissibility. He noted it was for the jury to determine whether any criminal activity was taking place by virtue of the events which were shown on the video tape. The tape showed appellant and her daughters sacking groceries, and removing them.

The admissibility of photographic evidence is based on two different theories. One theory is the "pictorial testimony" theory. Under this theory, the photographic evidence is merely illustrative of a witness' testimony and it only becomes admissible when a sponsoring witness can testify that it is a fair and accurate representation of the subject matter, based on that witness' personal observation. Obviously, the photographic evidence in this case is not admissible under such a theory, since no person could verify that the video tape accurately represented what occurred at the store, based on personal observation. A second theory under which photographic evidence may be admissible is the "silent

tographic Evidence § 87 (2d ed. 1969). Video tape recordings are admissible in evidence on the same basis as sound motion picture films. 3 C. Scott, Photographic Evidence § 1294 (2d ed. Supp.1980).

witness" theory. Under that theory, the photographic evidence is a "silent witness" which speaks for itself, and is substantive evidence of what it portrays independent of a sponsoring witness. *See,* 2 C. Scott, Photographic Evidence § 1021 (2d ed. Supp.1980); 3 J. Wigmore, Evidence § 790 (Chadbourn rev. 1970).

In Arkansas, photographic evidence is admissible under the "pictorial testimony" theory, when a sponsoring witness testifies that it is a fair and accurate representation of the subject matter. *Martin v. State,* 258 Ark. 529, 527 S.W.2d 903 (1975) * * *.

The question presented on this appeal has never been answered in Arkansas. A video tape recording and a film produced by an automatic camera have been admitted into evidence in two cases. However, the precise objection made in the case at bar was not raised in either case. *See, French v. State,* 271 Ark. 445, 609 S.W.2d 42 (1980); *Lunon v. State,* 264 Ark. 188, 569 S.W.2d 663 (1978).

This case presents the question of whether photographic evidence may be admitted as substantive evidence under the "silent witness" theory. We hold that the trial court correctly ruled that the video tape recording was admissible.

The Uniform Rules of Evidence, Rule 901(a), Ark.Stat.Ann. § 28–1001 (Repl.1979), provides that authentication is a condition precedent to the admissibility of evidence and that this requirement is met by a showing of evidence sufficient to support a finding that the matter in question is what its proponent claims. Section (b) lists various illustrations, showing methods of authentication or identification. The Uniform Rules of Evidence, Rule 1001(2), Ark.Stat.Ann. § 28–1001 (Repl.1979), provides that "photographs" includes photographs, x-ray films, video tapes, and motion pictures.

X-ray films are admissible in Arkansas, subject to proper authentication. *Oxford v. Villines,* 232 Ark. 103, 334 S.W.2d 660 (1960); *Arkansas Amusement Corporation v. Ward,* 204 Ark. 130, 161 S.W.2d 178 (1942); *Prescott & N.W.R. Co. v. Franks,* 111 Ark. 83, 163 S.W. 180 (1914); *Miller v. Minturn,* 73 Ark. 183, 83 S.W. 918 (1904). Obviously, it is impossible for a witness to testify that an x-ray film is a fair and accurate representation of the subject matter, based on that witness' personal observation. Therefore, x-rays could never be admissible under the "pictorial testimony" theory. 3 C. Scott, Photographic Evidence § 1262 (2d ed. 1969). Every jurisdiction admits x-ray films as substantive evidence upon a sufficient showing of authentication, thus utilizing the "silent witness" theory, even if unintentionally.[11] We note that Rule 1001(2) treats x-rays, photographs, video tapes, and motion pictures, as one and the same.

11. Some jurisdictions treat x-rays as scientific evidence, and not photographic evidence. *See, Howard v. State,* 264 Ind. 275, 342 N.E.2d 604 (1976). Professor Wigmore treats the admissibility of x-rays as scientific evidence, even though admitting that the "silent witness" theory may be a "more satisfactory rationale." 3 J. Wigmore, Evidence § 795 n.1 (Chadbourn rev. 1970).

Photographic evidence is the best available means of preserving the appearance of a scene at a given time. It is superior to eyewitness testimony in certain respects. Eyewitness testimony is subject to errors in perception, memory lapse, and a witness' problem of adequately expressing what he observed in language so that the trier of fact can understand. *See,* 1 C. Scott, Photographic Evidence § 41–54 (2d ed. 1969). Photographic evidence can observe a scene in detail without interpreting it, preserve the scene in a permanent manner, and transmit its message more clearly than the spoken word.

We hold that photographic evidence is admissible where its authenticity can be sufficiently established in view of the context in which it is sought to be admitted.[12] Obviously, the foundational requirements for the admissibility of photographic evidence under the "silent witness" theory are fundamentally different from the foundational requirements under the "pictorial testimony" theory. It is neither possible nor wise to establish specific foundational requirements for the admissibility of photographic evidence under the "silent witness" theory, since the context in which the photographic evidence was obtained and its intended use at trial will be different in virtually every case. It is enough to say, that adequate foundational facts must be presented to the trial court, so that the trial court can determine that the trier of fact can reasonably infer that the subject matter is what its proponent claims. The trial court determines the preliminary questions regarding the admissibility of evidence, and the appellate court reviews those determinations only for an abuse of discretion. Uniform Rules of Evidence, Rule 104(a), (b), Ark.Stat.Ann. § 28–1001 (Repl.1979); *Wilson v. City of Pine Bluff,* 6 Ark.App. 286, 641 S.W.2d 33 (1982). Our holding in this case in no way affects the admissibility of, or the foundational requirements for, photographic evidence used as demonstrative evidence under the "pictorial testimony" theory.

In adopting the "silent witness" theory, we join the overwhelming majority of other jurisdictions that have decided this issue. [Citations from 20 states and three federal circuits omitted.]

[The court here held that the state's evidence was sufficient to prove appellant guilty of theft.]

Affirmed.

Notes and Questions

1. *Other silent witness evidence.* Several modern photographic techniques, infra red photography, surveillance cameras, and self-timing mechanisms, are calculated to produce products which cannot be said to "illustrate" the testimony of anyone and are therefore impossible to introduce

12. Photographic evidence is subject to the same rules as other evidence. Thus, even if photographic evidence is properly authenticated, it may still be excluded because it is not relevant or because its probative value is substantially outweighed by the danger of unfair prejudice, confusion of the issues, or misleading the jury. Uniform Rules of Evidence, Rules 401, 402, 403, Ark.Stat.Ann. § 28–1001 (Repl.1979).

under conventional doctrine. Comment, Photographic Evidence—Is There a Recognized Basis for Admissibility?, 8 Hast.L.J. 310 (1957).

2. *Silent witness or scientific evidence?* What practical difference does it make whether a jurisdiction admits X-rays under the "silent witness" theory or as scientific evidence? Are these two theories mutually exclusive, as the court's discussion in *Fisher* might seem to suggest, or is a scientific foundation only one of several possible avenues to the introduction of "silent witness" photographic evidence? See McNeal, Silent Witness Evidence in Relation to the Illustrative Evidence Foundation, 35 Okla.L.Rev. 219 (1984). What is the characteristic which distinguishes illustrative from "silent witness" photographs? For a case applying the Federal Rules in a silent witness situation and reaching a result similar to that in *Fisher*, see United States v. Rembert, 863 F.2d 1023 (D.C.Cir.1988).

Notes on Real and Demonstrative Evidence Appealing to Nonvisual Senses

1. *Evidence involving other senses.* Though the great bulk of real and demonstrative evidence introduced in litigation is of a visual nature, it should not be assumed that the senses other than sight cannot or should not be appealed to when occasion presents itself. Thus, jurors have not infrequently been permitted to hear, taste, feel, and smell evidence in appropriate cases. See, e.g., Dowling v. Peyroux, 126 So. 270 (La.Ct.App.1930) (children's band known as "The Kiddies" whose practice sessions were alleged to constitute a nuisance allowed to perform in court); People v. Kinney, 83 N.W. 147 (Mich.1900) (jury allowed to taste cider to determine whether it was "hard" or "soft"); McAndrews v. Leonard, 134 A. 710 (Vt.1926) (jurors allowed to feel plaintiff's skull).

2. *Sound recordings.* Next to evidence appealing to the visual sense, probably the most frequently encountered type of real or demonstrative evidence today is the sound recording. Is a sound recording, given its nature and possible points of relevancy, more likely to be offered as illustrative or as substantive evidence? When offered as the latter, sound recordings will present foundational problems analogous to "silent witness" photographs. See United States v. McKeever, 169 F.Supp. 426 (S.D.N.Y.1958), which lays down a set of foundational requirements that has been widely followed. But compare State v. Lavers, 814 P.2d 333 (Ariz.1991) (upholding admission of tape recording apparently made by homicide victim on basis of "flexible" test which requires only that trial judge be satisfied that the recording is accurate, authentic, and generally trustworthy). Cases concerning the admissibility of sound recordings generally are collected in Annot., 58 A.L.R.2d 1024. For cases involving taped 911 calls, see Annot., 3 A.L.R.5th 784. Where the recording is of human speech as opposed to mere sounds or noise, the recording may raise problems traditionally associated with written evidence. Such questions are treated in the next chapter.

3. *Juror squeamishness.* Jurors today are generally given little choice with respect to what they are required to see and hear even when the evidence is extremely unpleasant. Should the juror have an option as to what he or she is required to touch? See Curry v. American Enka, Inc., 452 F.Supp. 178 (E.D.Tenn.1977).

EVANSVILLE SCHOOL CORP. v. PRICE

Appellate Court of Indiana, 1965.
208 N.E.2d 689.

PRIME, PRESIDING JUSTICE. This action was commenced by Alfred Price, father of Alfred Lee Price (deceased), against the Evansville School Corporation, to recover damages for wrongful death allegedly sustained as the result of the decedent, Alfred Lee Price, being injured while a spectator attending a baseball game at Bosse Field in the City of Evansville, Indiana. The boy, age 11, was struck on the head with a baseball on May 27, 1960, and died as a result of said injuries on May 29, 1960.

The case was originally filed in the Vanderburgh Probate Court and subsequently venued to the Warrick Circuit Court where it was tried by a jury on the issues as formed by the appellee's amended complaint and the amended answer of the appellant thereto. The jury returned a verdict favorable to the plaintiff-appellee, awarding him the sum of $14,500.00, and the court rendered judgment on the verdict. The appellant filed its motion for a new trial, said motion was overruled by the trial court, and appellant appeals from this adverse ruling.

At the trial the appellee offered in evidence a color photograph designated Plaintiff's Exhibit No. 5. It depicted the deceased youth lying in his casket, after preparation by a mortician, and prior to interment. The photograph shows the white satin interior of the casket and that portion of the body exposed to public view. The decedent's face bears a deep tan, and he is clothed in a white sport coat and a blue shirt open at the neck. The photograph is not gruesome, nor does it depict any physical markings, wounds, defects or other bodily abnormalities. The appellant objected to the admission of Exhibit No. 5 for a number of reasons. First, appellant objected on the ground that the pleadings admitted the fact that the decedent died as a result of injuries sustained on May 27, 1960, and therefore, no issue was presented to the jury concerning the fact or cause of death. Second, that Exhibit No. 5 could only serve to inflame the minds of the jury or excite their feelings rather than to enlighten them as to any of the facts in issue. Third, Exhibit No. 5 is not material to any issue involved in the case.

Appellee alleged that the photograph was being offered into evidence to show the physical characteristics of the boy, and to corroborate testimony that the boy was a "nice looking and healthy chap." It was also offered into evidence to establish the fact that the parents incurred funeral expenses for the boy, and "that he was properly interred."

Appellant further objected to the admission of Exhibit No. 5 into evidence on the grounds that there was testimony in the record of two witnesses concerning the boy's health prior to his death, and that a picture of a person after death could not establish the person's condition of health prior to death, especially in light of the fact that the body had been prepared for burial by a mortician. Appellant also objected on the ground that the fact that the boy was "nice looking" or handsome does not constitute an admissible item of evidence because the measure of damages is limited to the pecuniary loss sustained by the parent.

Appellant's objections were overruled and the photograph was admitted into evidence. The appellant predicates error on this ruling by the trial court, for the reasons stated in the objections.

It is the rule in Indiana that the admission or rejection of photographs in evidence lies largely within the discretion of the trial court, and will not be disturbed unless an abuse of discretion is shown to have occurred. Dill v. Dill (1949), 120 Ind.App. 61, 65, 88 N.E.2d 396 (Transfer denied). It is also the law in this state that in order for a photograph to be admissible in evidence, it must first be accepted by the trial court as *material and relevant,* and must tend to prove or disprove some material fact in issue. Kiefer v. State (1958), 239 Ind. 103, 153 N.E.2d 899. See also: St. Lukes Hospital Asso. v. Long (1952), 125 Colo. 25, 240 P.2d 917, 31 A.L.R.2d 1120; 3 Wigmore, Evidence 3d ed. § 792.

Relevancy is determined by an inquiry into whether or not a witness would be permitted to describe the objects photographed. Hawkins v. State (1942), 219 Ind. 116, 37 N.E.2d 79. Photographs should assist and enlighten the members of the jury, and not confuse or unduly prejudice them. Kiefer v. State, supra.

The fact that a photograph might arouse the passions of the jury and prejudice them against one of the parties is not a sufficient ground to justify its exclusion if the photograph is *material and relevant.* Kiefer v. State, supra.

The above stated rules are applicable, whether the judicial proceedings involved are criminal or civil in nature, and whether the photograph of the deceased is taken during his lifetime, or after death. State of New Jersey v. Bucanis, 26 N.J. 45, 138 A.2d 739, 73 A.L.R.2d 760, 769; Elliott v. Black River Electric Cooperative, 233 S.C. 233, 104 S.E.2d 357, 74 A.L.R.2d 907, 928.

In the case at bar appellee argues primarily that Exhibit No. 5 was offered to corroborate the testimony of certain witnesses with respect to the decedent's physical characteristics prior to his death. This testimony was to the effect that the decedent was in excellent health, practically never sick, and was a good looking boy with a husky build. Further, that the boy was about 5 feet tall, weighed about 115 pounds, blond haired and blue eyed. Appellee asserts that the photograph accurately depicted the decedent's appearance before his death as well as after his death. It is difficult for us to see how Exhibit No. 5 could possibly be construed to establish the physical conditions and characteristics of this boy during his lifetime. This picture was not only taken after death, but also after the boy's body had been prepared for burial by a mortician.

Appellee also argued that Exhibit No. 5 was being offered into evidence to prove that the parents incurred funeral expenses for the boy, and "that he was properly interred." Again, we fail to see how this photograph of the decedent, lying in his casket, showing only a part of the interior of the casket, could aid the jury in deciding the question of funeral expenses. There was testimony concerning the amount of expenses incurred, and a copy of the funeral bill was introduced into evidence without objection as Plaintiff's Exhibit No. 19.

It appears to us that the only legitimate purpose for admitting this photograph would have been to establish the fact of death, and this fact was admitted by virtue of the pleadings.

Therefore, we are of the opinion that Plaintiff's Exhibit No. 5 should not have been admitted into evidence, and the trial court abused its discretion in permitting it to be admitted and exhibited to the jury. In the Kiefer case at page 107, of 239 Ind. at page 900, of 153 N.E.2d our Supreme Court said:

> "As a general rule a photograph that is 'entirely irrelevant and immaterial to any issue in the cause and which is of such a character as to divert the minds of the jury to improper or irrelevant considerations should be excluded from evidence.' 20 Am.Jur., Evidence, § 729, p. 609; Underhill's Cr. Evidence, 5th Ed., § 117, p. 16 (1958 Supp.)."

In our opinion Exhibit No. 5 was immaterial and irrelevant to any of the material facts in issue, and was prejudicial to the defendant.

Again we refer to the *Kiefer* case, wherein it is stated at pages 117 and 118, at page 905, of 153 N.E.2d:

> " * * * [T]o introduce evidence only for the purpose of arousing the passions and prejudices of the jury, in such a manner as to cause them to abandon any serious consideration of the facts of the case and give expression only to their emotions, is clearly outside the scope of such duty * * * ." (Referring to a duty of counsel to present relevant and material facts to the jury.)

Judgment reversed with instructions to sustain appellant's motion for a new trial.

Notes and Questions

1. *Wrongful death cases.* It has sometimes been held that an ante mortem picture of the deceased is relevant to the issue of damages in an action for wrongful death. Drinon v. Wilson, 113 F.2d 654 (2d Cir.1940). Compare Roberts v. Stevens Clinic Hosp., Inc., 345 S.E.2d 791 (W.Va.1986), a medical malpractice case brought to recover damages for the death of a 2½ year old child. Plaintiff was allowed to introduce a professionally prepared videotape which combined home videos and still pictures of the deceased with his family, combined with a sound track of child's singing and mother and child talking. The tape was said by the court to demonstrate that the deceased was a healthy, intelligent, enthusiastic, and well-loved child; admission was held discretionary. The jury award was $10,000,000, although the

West Virginia Supreme Court of Appeals required a remittitur of $7,000,000 of that amount.

2. *Admissions in pleadings.* Did the admission by pleading of decedent's death in the principal case render the offered photograph irrelevant? The traditional answer has been in the negative. Dunning v. Maine Central R.R., 39 A. 352 (Me.1897). It has been argued, however, that admission of the fact sought to be proved alters the balance required by Rule 403. Dolan, Rule 403: The Prejudice Rule in Evidence, 49 S.Cal.L.Rev. 220 (1976). The potential value of such an approach to the defendant in a criminal case is discussed in Fortune, Judicial Admissions in Criminal Cases: Blocking the Introduction of Prejudicial Evidence, 17 Crim.L.Bull. 101 (1981). But many courts continue to discern points of relevancy for such evidence beyond those which have been stipulated or otherwise admitted. See, e.g., State v. Clabourne, 690 P.2d 54 (Ariz.1984); State v. Schneider, 736 S.W.2d 392 (Mo. 1987); State v. Broberg, 677 A.2d 602 (Md.1996). See also Note, North Carolina's "Test for Excess": The Prejudicial Use of Photographic Evidence in Criminal Prosecutions After *State v. Hennis,* 67 N.C.L.Rev. 1367 (1989).

3. *Paternity cases.* Should the prosecution in a paternity proceeding be allowed to exhibit the illegitimate child to the jury for the purpose of showing its resemblance to the defendant? See Annot., 55 A.L.R.3d 1087. To what extent is the problem analogous to that in the principal case? To what extent does it raise additional difficulties?

ENSOR v. WILSON

Supreme Court of Alabama, 1987.
519 So.2d 1244.

BEATTY, JUSTICE

Appeal by Herman Ensor, M.D. and Ensor, Baccus & Williamson, P.A., from a judgement for plaintiff, Misty Wilson, a minor suing by her next friend, based upon a jury verdict that awarded plaintiff $2.5 million. The action was based upon allegations of malpractice.

Plaintiff is a child who was born prematurely, suffering a degree of brain damage and retardation * * * .

II.

Did the trial court err in permitting an in-court demonstration between Misty and a special education therapist? We quote from defendants' brief for an understanding of this issue:

> "Over the numerous and vigorous objections of defendant's counsel * * * , the court permitted a demonstration of Misty's *physical and mental abilities* and limitations to be conducted by Ms. Holland, a special education therapist, in the presence of the jury. During the course of that demonstration, Misty cried out, laughed, and called for her mother * * * . Ms. Holland repeatedly admonished her not to fall over as she walked and moved about on the mat which Ms. Holland admitted was not stable for walking on by anyone * * * . Presenting an adorable six-year-old child to the jury

in this manner served no useful purpose other than to win the sympathy of the jurors for Misty and to substantially prejudice the defendants. Further, Ms. Holland testified on cross-examination that the demonstration was not necessary to explain Misty's physical and mental limitations to the jury—only that it would make it 'easier' or more 'graphic.' * * *

"As noted in the objections raised prior and subsequent to the demonstration * * *, the exhibition of Misty in this fashion put the defendants at an unwarranted and unjust disadvantage. There was no opportunity during the demonstration to cross-examine Misty, she was not placed under oath, she was not competent to testify, and there were no adequate means for preserving for appeal purposes the effect of such a demonstration upon the jury. Indeed, to fully comprehend the impact of this demonstration upon the jury and all present in the courtroom, one had to have been there. All of these reasons justify the reversal of this case." (Emphasis added.)

In considering this issue, we note that the therapist, Dr. Francine Holland, the holder of a Ph.D. in education, was sworn as a witness and was subjected to a searching cross-examination. The trial court, moreover, required her examination to be previewed outside the jury's presence. It is clear, also, that the plaintiff's cognitive, as well as physical, ability was in issue on the matter of damages.

In his order denying the defendants' post-trial motions, the trial court made the following observations:

"The defendants also contend that the in-court demonstration of the child by plaintiff's expert, Dr. Holland, was highly prejudicial and inflammatory. Undersigned Judge observed the witnesses and the child on a preliminary run-through outside the presence of the jury and again observed all concerned when the jury was present. In the court's view the demonstration fully comported with due process and modern standard personal injury lawsuit procedure. The minor plaintiff sat with her parents in the courtroom during an all-day voir dire, in the full presence of the jury, with no objection of any kind from the defendant's attorneys. In the court's opinion, the child appeared more animated in the Dr. Holland demonstration than she did while simply lying, almost comatose, with the parents during the voir dire."

The exhibition of injuries, usually by photograph or like means, see *Occidental Life Ins. Co. of California v. Nichols,* 266 Ala. 521, 97 So.2d 879 (1957); C. Gamble, *McElroy's Alabama Evidence,* § 207.01(5) at 461–2 (3d ed. 1977), is permissible in the measurable discretion of the trial court. While we have been unable to find a case directly on point, an Ohio case, *Heidbreder v. Northhampton Township Trustees,* 64 Ohio App.2d 95, 411 N.E.2d 825, 829 (1979), approved the demonstration in open court of an infant who allegedly had suffered brain damage:

"The infant, Jonathan Heidbreder, remained outside the courtroom during the entire trial except for the period of demonstration.

He was brought before the jury to demonstrate the extent of his motor paralysis and *ability to communicate and do simple tasks.* This evidence was relevant to the issue of damages and peripherally so to the liability issue. Prior to this demonstration, an in-camera hearing was held and the proposed demonstration enacted for the trial court. The trial court specifically found that the evidentiary value of the appearance would not be outweighed by its prejudicial effect. We find no error in permitting the jury to see the demonstration and view the infant * * * ." (Emphasis added.)

It is not clear from *Heidbreder* that the demonstration held in that case contained questions and answers between the demonstrator and the demonstratee, or that, as here, the demonstration was conducted by a testifying witness or by counsel. Nevertheless, under the control of the trial judge, the demonstration in the present case was not different in theory and practice from the relevant exhibition of wounds, movement, articulation, and the like, whether by the witness himself or through the use of the medium of photography, which, after all, is in effect another witness. Indeed, it would be difficult to exhibit cognition without a demonstration of vocal expression, physical response, or a combination of both, and thus it would not be, as a matter of law, erroneous to have such a demonstration guided by a witness skilled in ascertaining such relevant responses and explaining their meaning. The accuracy of such a demonstration, of course, is to be tested by the requirements of relevancy, and such a demonstration is to be disallowed when its probative worth is exceeded by its capacity for prejudice. In this case, we find no abuse in the trial court's permitting the demonstration.

* * *

Let the judgment be affirmed.

Notes and Questions

1. *Presence in the courtroom.* In the principal case the plaintiff was allowed to sit with her parents all day without objection. What if objection had been made? What would be the bearing of a rule such as Rule 615 on the question? See Bremner v. Charles, 821 P.2d 1080 (Or.1991).

2. *Day in the life films.* An evidentiary development of recent years now encountered is the so-called "day in the life" film or videotape, in which a substantially incapacitated plaintiff is pictured carrying out his or her daily routine. To what extent are the evidentiary questions raised by such films similar to those in the principal case? To what extent do such films raise additional questions? See Bannister v. Town of Noble, 812 F.2d 1265 (10th Cir.1987), for a discussion of the frequently raised concerns with regard to such films or videotapes. See also 2 McCormick, Evidence § 216 (6th ed. 2006); Note, Beyond Words: The Evidentiary Status of Day in the Life Films, 66 B.U.L.Rev. 133 (1986).

3. Cases involving demonstrations to show the effect of injury are collected in Annot., 82 A.L.R.4th 980.

McDOWELL v. SCHUETTE

Missouri Court of Appeals, 1980.
610 S.W.2d 29.

STEWART, JUDGE.

Plaintiffs, David and Donna McDowell, who are in the construction business, brought an action in two counts against defendants. In the first count they sought to recover the balance due under a contract for construction of a house for defendants. The second count was in quantum meruit for labor and materials furnished defendants that were not within the terms of the contract. Defendants filed a counterclaim in two counts alleging inter alia that they had been damaged because the house was not completed in "a good and workmanlike manner" and because the work was not timely completed. Judgment was entered upon a jury verdict for plaintiffs on both counts of their petition that assessed damages at $14,150 on Count I and $5,280 on Count II. Defendants were awarded $2,600 on Count I of their counterclaim. Defendants appeal from the judgment.

We affirm. * * *

As we understand defendants' next point they contend that the court erred when it told the jury that it had decided to allow the jury to view the home of defendants, how they were to be transported and who would be present, and then admonished them not to discuss the case or their view of the premises with anyone. Defendants claim that this was an oral instruction which should have been reduced to writing and given to the jury before they viewed the building.

The statement made by the court reads as follows:

> "Ladies and gentlemen of the Jury, it's my determination that after hearing evidence for two days that a view of the premises involved would not be inappropriate and therefore I am going to rule that you be allowed to view the house in question. However, I want to do this with some very strict guidelines, within some strict guidelines.
>
> You will be taken to the, to the home in a van, with a chauffeured driver. Eleven of you can go with that driver. I'm going to order the Bailiff to accompany you to the home. The Bailiff will take the twelfth juror to the home.
>
> I will allow any of the parties, Mr. and Mrs. Schuette or Mr. and Mrs. McDowell, to go in their own separate vehicles. I will not allow the attorneys to accompany either the Jury, the parties or the Bailiff.
>
> When you get to the home I want you to remember the caution that we have given you before. Do not discuss this case among yourselves or with anyone. If any of the parties, the Bailiff, the driver, if anyone, or a member of your own Jury, attempts to

emphasize some portion of the house or to point something out to you, I want to know about it immediately.

You are to go to the home, view the home, and then return to the jury room; you are to do no more, no less.

Now, I hope we understand one another."

While it is true that Rule 70.02(a) requires that "all instructions shall be submitted in writing and shall be given or refused by the court according to the law and the evidence in the case" not every statement of the court to the jury is an instruction within the meaning of the rule. An oral direction or cautionary remark not a part of the law of the case need not be in writing. *State v. Jordan,* 506 S.W.2d 74, 78 (Mo.App. 1974).

The first three paragraphs of the statement made by the court contain no instruction to the jury. In this portion of the statement the court announced its ruling upon plaintiffs' request that the jury be permitted to view the house and explained the manner in which this would be accomplished.

* * *

In any event the court was not required to give any written instructions to the jury before they viewed the premises. Written instructions are given to the jury only at the close of the case. Rule 70.02(a).

The defendants contend that the court erred when it did not grant a new trial because most of the jurors were transported to view the house in a bus owned by plaintiffs and driven by one of their employees. Defendants' counsel made an affidavit that he had learned of this alleged impropriety after the jury returned its verdict. In this case the jurors were cautioned not to speak with anyone including the driver of the vehicle and to report any attempt by anyone to emphasize any portion of the house.

Defendants made no attempt to produce any evidence which might show any impropriety on the part of the driver or the jurors. There is no evidence that the jurors even knew that the vehicle had been furnished by plaintiffs or that the driver was Mr. Cook, an employee of plaintiffs.

The action of the trial court in matters such as this requires the exercise of sound discretion on the part of the trial court. We find no abuse of discretion in this instance. *Kelley v. Prince,* 379 S.W.2d 508, 513 (Mo.1964).

We consider defendants' next two subpoints together because they are premised upon defendants' contention that the jury's view of the premises constituted evidence.

Defendants argue that it was error to bar counsel for the parties and the court reporter from the inspection of the house because their absence prevented objections to and preservation of evidence presented by the jury view. Defendants also claim that plaintiffs' introduction of expert testimony was an admission that laymen (the jury) could not understand the defects in the house. Thus, defendants believe the jury view improperly allowed evidence of lay opinion.

These subpoints are answered by the court's holding in *Koplar v. State Tax Comm'n,* 321 S.W.2d 686, 696 (Mo.1959):

> "While a view may be taken by the triers of the fact to enable them to understand the evidence, such view cannot be substituted for evidence, nor can it constitute evidence in the case. We think its purpose is well stated in *Cowan v. Bunting Glider Co.,* 159 Pa.Super. 573, 49 A.2d 270, 271, as follows: 'Triers of fact, be they judges, jurors, viewers, board or commissions, may always visit and inspect the locus in quo to secure a better understanding of the evidence and to enable them to determine the relative weight of conflicting testimony. But a view cannot replace testimony; the visual observations of the trier cannot be substituted for testimony; and the only legitimate purpose of an inspection is to illustrate the evidence and provide a base for understanding and comprehending testimony upon the record.' "

The record indicates the court's comments to the jury regarding the disparity of the testimony served as the basis for the jury view of the house. The court allowed the view in order to determine the relative weight of the conflicting testimony as suggested in the *Koplar* case. Because the jury view did not constitute evidence, defendants' argument that the view was evidence of lay opinion fails.

The question of whether to permit an inspection of the premises is a matter within the discretion of the trial court. We find no abuse of discretion in this case. *State ex inf. McKittrick v. Jones,* 353 Mo. 900, 185 S.W.2d 17, 22 (1945).

Other issues sought to be raised with respect to the inspection of the premises have not been preserved for our review because the defendants did not raise them at the time the court made its ruling. *Germann v. City of Kansas City,* 577 S.W.2d 54, 55[1] (Mo.App.1978). * * *

Finding no reversible error, the judgment of the trial court is affirmed.

KELLY, P.J., and SNYDER, J., concur.

Notes and Questions

1. *Views as evidence.* The position taken by the court in the principal case, that a jury view does not constitute evidence, has generally been criticized by the commentators. See, e.g., Hardman, The Evidentiary Effect of a View: Stare Decisis or Stare Dictis, 53 W.Va.L.Rev. 103 (1951); Wendorf, Some Views on Jury Views, 15 Baylor L.Rev. 379 (1963); 2 McCormick, Evidence § 219 (6th ed. 2006). Some courts have been moved to promote the view to evidentiary status. In an especially thoughtful opinion, the court in State v. Pauline, 60 P.3d 306, 322–30 (Haw.2002), rejected the former

Hawaii rule that a view was not evidence, noting, among other things, that technological advances permit the view to be recorded and included in the record. See also United States v. Gray, 199 F.3d 547, 549 (1st Cir.1999); Moore, Kelly & Reddish, Inc. v. Shannondale, Inc., 165 S.E.2d 113 (W.Va. 1968). Other recent decisions have persisted in finding that a view is not evidence. See, e.g., Stephenson v. State, 742 N.E.2d 463 (Ind.2001). Should the practice of treating the view as evidence be subject to any restrictions or limitations? In light of its ruling that the view would be considered evidence, the court in *Pauline* suggested a number of procedural safeguards including the presence of counsel and the judge, a full and accurate recording of the view and the presence of the defendant. See generally Keele, Note, When Mohamed Goes to the Mountain: The Evidentiary Value of a View, 80 Ind.L.J. 1091 (2005).

2. *Attendance by accused.* Does the suggestion in *Pauline* that the defendant be present rise to a constitutional level? In Snyder v. Massachusetts, 291 U.S. 97 (1934), the Supreme Court held, four Justices dissenting, that due process had not been denied a defendant who was refused the opportunity to be present at a view. The Court, however, carefully limited its holding in *Snyder* to the facts of the case. These included the fact that a view is not deemed evidence in Massachusetts, that no oral testimony was taken at the view, and that the judge, court reporter, and also defendant's counsel were present.

Despite the trend toward recognizing the view as itself evidence, the defendant's right to be present is frequently seen as dependent upon whether testimony was taken. See 2 McCormick, Evidence § 219 (6th ed. 2006). In the various states, the question is commonly treated by statute. E.g., N.Y. Crim. Pro. § 270.50; N.C. Gen. Stat. § 15A–1229.

3. *Eminent domain proceedings.* In some jurisdictions a jury view is a matter of right in an eminent domain proceeding. Assume that in such a proceeding both the condemnor and the condemnee present expert testimony as to the value of the land taken, the highest expert valuation being $25,000 and the lowest $19,000. The jury is also allowed to view the premises. If the jury thereafter returns a verdict in favor of the condemnee for $28,000 should such a verdict be allowed to stand? Would you expect the answer to turn upon whether or not the particular jurisdiction holds that a jury view constitutes "evidence?" What significance, if any, should be accorded the fact that in virtually every American jurisdiction only a qualified "expert" may give testimony as to the monetary value of real property? See Annot., 1 A.L.R.3d 1397.

GEO. C. CHRISTOPHER & SON, INC. v. KANSAS PAINT & COLOR CO.

Supreme Court of Kansas, 1974.
523 P.2d 709.

OWSLEY, JUSTICE: This action was based on the breach of an implied warranty to furnish a suitable paint to prime steel. In a jury trial the plaintiff prevailed, resulting in an appeal by defendant.

* * *

In support of its motion for a new trial, defendant filed the affidavit of one of its attorneys stating he had conferred with several jury members following the verdict and that the foreman of the jury had performed certain tests on a paint sample panel submitted as evidence. The foreman scraped paint from plaintiff's exhibit with a pocket knife and discussed these results with the jury; no such tests were performed on defendant's exhibits. The affidavit contends jurors admitted these tests were influential factors in their decision for plaintiff. The trial court denied the motion for new trial saying the facts stated in the affidavit were insufficient grounds upon which to order a new trial. There was no questioning of the jurors themselves, but the facts in the affidavit were not disputed and were accepted as true although held insufficient.

Misconduct of jurors *per se* does not necessitate a new trial, but misconduct which results in prejudice to a litigant and impairs his right to a fair and impartial trial requires a new trial. (Baker v. Western Casualty & Surety Co., 196 Kan. 345, 411 P.2d 711; Furstenberg v. Wesley Medical Center, 200 Kan. 277, 436 P.2d 369.) It is for the trial court to determine in the first instance whether misconduct on the part of the jury has resulted in prejudice to a litigant, and its judgment thereon will not be overturned unless abuse of discretion is manifest. (Walker v. Holiday Lanes, 196 Kan. 513, 413 P.2d 63; Furstenberg v. Wesley Medical Center, supra.) Defendant contends the action of the jury in independently testing only plaintiff's paint panel exhibit was prejudicial to it and cites several Kansas cases in support of its argument. The cases are not relevant because they involve jury gathering of evidence either outside the physical surroundings of the courtroom or outside the scope of the evidence and issues presented for jury consideration. In Kaminski v. Kansas City Public Service Co., 175 Kan. 137, 259 P.2d 207, several jurors visited the scene of the collision and measured distances; in Kincaid v. Wade, 196 Kan. 174, 410 P.2d 333, jurors followed the woman defendant in a motor accident and reported to other jurors on her driving habits; in Barajas v. Sonders, 193 Kan. 273, 392 P.2d 849, one juror used a slide rule to determine the point of impact and other computations; in Walker v. Holiday Lanes, supra, a juror went to the bowling alley, the scene of a slip and fall incident, and reported the results of his independent investigation. These were instances of prejudicial jury conduct because, as the court said in *Kaminski:*

> "* * * Litigants have a right to expect that with respect to evidence juries will confine themselves to the evidence introduced, and that members of a jury will not engage in any 'extra curricular' activities such as were indulged in here." (175 Kan. p. 140, 259 P.2d p. 210.)

In the case at bar, the jurors duplicated tests performed in the courtroom on exhibits sent with them to the jury room. This instance more closely resembles or parallels the circumstances in State v. Levin, 117 Kan. 739, 232 P. 1020, where the jury's thorough examination of a still produced half a pint of the forbidden product. When defendant claimed he was prejudiced, the court said:

> "Obviously the object of sending exhibits to the jury is to enable the jurors to make a more thorough examination of them than it was possible to make when the exhibits were offered in evidence. * * *" (p. 741, 232 P. p. 1022.)

An even closer parallel is presented by Taylor v. Reo Motors, Inc., 275 F.2d 699 (10th Cir.1960). A poorly manufactured heat exchanger was the alleged cause of a fire. The device was admitted into evidence and went with the jury to the jury room. During their deliberations, members of the jury took the device apart and put it back together, using pocket knives, nail clippers, and other pocket tools. Defendant claimed this was jury misconduct prejudicial to it and moved for a new trial. The court commented on the action of the jurors as follows:

> "The salient question is whether the experiment or investigation made by the jury out of the presence of the parties, and while they were deliberating, can be said to be within the scope or purview of the evidence introduced at the trial, or whether it amounts to the taking of evidence outside the presence of the parties. See Annotation 80 A.L.R. 108. If the experiment or demonstration was conducted by the jury for the purpose of testing the truth of the statements made concerning the functioning of the heat exchanger, it was proper. The heat exchanger was offered in evidence. It had been disassembled and reassembled in open court by experts for the purpose of demonstrating negligence or lack of negligence in its manufacture or assemblage. The exhibit was before the jury, and it was permissible to take it to the jury room and examine it for the purpose of testing the validity of statements made in open court in respect thereto. If it had been a written document in fine print, we do not suppose that it would have been improper for the jury to use a magnifying glass in possession of one of them for the purpose of scrutinizing critical language. It therefore does not seem improper for the jury to disassemble this exhibit for the purpose of deciding the issues presented to them." (pp. 705, 706.)

The conduct of the jurors in this case passes the test of *Kaminski* in that they did not stray beyond the confines of the evidence presented to them with their tests, and it also passes the test of *Taylor* because the purpose of the test was to check the validity of evidence presented in open court. An experiment or demonstration is proper when conducted by the jury with the use of exhibits properly submitted to it for the purpose of testing the truth of statements made by witnesses or duplicating tests made by witnesses in open court.

The trial court correctly denied defendant's motion for a new trial based on alleged jury misconduct.

Affirmed.

Notes and Questions

1. *Exhibits in the jury room.* American authority generally supports the sending of formally offered and admitted tangible exhibits with the jury upon its retirement, subject in some jurisdictions to discretionary control of the practice by the court. See 2 McCormick, Evidence § 220 (6th ed. 2006). Federal criminal cases are collected in Annot., 62 A.L.R.Fed. 950. Cases relating to jury acquisition of items not formally admitted are collected in Annot., 37 A.L.R.2d 662.

2. *Juror testimony.* If the attorney's affidavit as to the jury conduct had been disputed, would it have been proper to question the jurors themselves as to what they did? The long-standing rule is that "a juror may not impeach his own verdict," but jurisdictions are divided on the application of this rule to facts such as those in the principal case. As to the effect of Rule 606(b) on the question, see Note, The Room Without a View: Inquiries Into Jury Misconduct After the Adoption of Texas Rule of Evidence 606(b), 38 Baylor L.Rev. 965 (1986). Federal Rule 606(b) was amended in 2006 to deal with instances of mistakes in filling out a verdict form, but with no effect on this question. See also Chapter 16, Section B. Cases involving experimentation by jurors are collected in Annot., 31 A.L.R.4th 566. Unauthorized jury views raise similar questions. See Annot., 11 A.L.R.3d 918.

Chapter 11[1]

WRITINGS AND RELATED MATTERS

SECTION A. AUTHENTICATION

UNITED STATES v. SKIPPER

United States Court of Appeals, Fifth Circuit, 1996.
74 F.3d 608.

DUHÉ, CIRCUIT JUDGE:

John Derrick Skipper appeals his conviction for possession of crack cocaine with intent to distribute, in violation of 21 U.S.C. § 841(a)(1). Finding insufficient evidence to support the jury's verdict, we reverse, vacate the sentence and remand for sentencing on the lesser included offense of simple possession. * * *

While patrolling Interstate Highway 10, Deputy Sheriff Todd Richards and criminal justice student Benny Soileau observed a Nissan automobile changing lanes erratically. Officer Richards closed on the Nissan and activated the lights of his patrol car. As the Nissan moved to the right lane, Richards and Soileau observed a small plastic bag fly from the driver's side of the car.

After pulling over to the shoulder, John Derrick Skipper, the driver and owner of the Nissan, exited his car and approached the police car. Officer Richards immediately placed Skipper under arrest. Richards then went to the Nissan, where he found a passenger, Jerome Cutright, seated in the car. Officer Richards next placed Skipper in the patrol car and drove to retrieve the bag from the side of the road. The bag contained 2.89 grams of crack cocaine. Richards also searched the Nissan and found one straight-edge razor between the front two seats.

At trial, pursuant to Federal Rule of Evidence 404(b), the district court admitted into evidence two state-court convictions for crimes allegedly committed by Skipper. Government Exhibit #3 was a certified copy of a judgment against "John Derrick Skipper" indicating that

1. Throughout this chapter some footnotes from the original cases and materials have been omitted; others have been renumbered. [Ed.]

Appellant pled guilty to possession of a controlled substance. An expert testified that the fingerprints on this conviction matched Appellant's fingerprints. Government Exhibit #2 was a certified copy of a deferred adjudication order indicating that "John D. Skipper" was placed on ten years probation for possession of a controlled substance. However, this order did not bear any fingerprints, and the government did not otherwise identify Appellant as the person named in the order.

The jury convicted Skipper of possession of crack cocaine with intent to distribute, in violation of 21 U.S.C. § 841(a)(1). On appeal, Skipper challenges the sufficiency of the evidence and also argues that the district court erred by admitting the deferred adjudication order. * * *

> We review the admission of evidence only for an abuse of discretion. United States v. Eakes, 783 F.2d 499, 506–07 (5th Cir.1986). Furthermore, even if we find an abuse of discretion in the admission or exclusion of evidence, we review the error under the harmless error doctrine. United States v. Scott, 678 F.2d 606, 612 (5th Cir.1982). Finally, we must affirm evidentiary rulings unless they affect a substantial right of the complaining party. Fed.R.Evid. 103(a); *Foster v. Ford Motor Co.,* 621 F.2d 715, 721 (5th Cir.1980).

The district court admitted into evidence a deferred adjudication order indicating that a "John D. Skipper" was placed on ten years probation for possession of a controlled substance. However, the court erred in admitting this evidence because the government should have been required to produce evidence proving that Appellant was the actual "John D. Skipper" named in the deferred adjudication order. Rule 901(a) of the Federal Rules of Evidence provides: "The requirement of authentication or identification as a condition precedent to admissibility is satisfied by evidence sufficient to support a finding that the matter in question is what its proponent claims." We hold that the mere similarity in name between a criminal defendant and a person named in a prior conviction alone does not satisfy Rule 901's identification requirement.

[The court found the error to be harmless.]

Note and Question

Is the fact that there was a John D. Skipper placed on probation logically relevant to this prosecution? Is the authentication rule simply a specific application of Rule 403 guarding against the admission of evidence that may be logically relevant where admission of that evidence runs the danger of unfair prejudice? Why should there be an additional rule? Are there specific considerations involved in the requirement of authentication that make a separate rule a good idea? See generally Imwinkelried, Evidentiary Foundations (6th ed. 2005); 2 McCormick, Evidence § 221 (6th ed. 2006).

BUCKINGHAM CORP. v. EWING LIQUORS CO.

Appellate Court of Illinois, 1973.
305 N.E.2d 278.

STAMOS, PRESIDING JUSTICE. Defendant, Ewing Liquors Co., appeals from an order granting plaintiff a permanent injunction. The trial court found that plaintiff's Cutty Sark scotch whiskey is sold in Illinois pursuant to a valid fair trade agreement, and that on December 13, 1971, defendant knowingly sold Cutty Sark scotch whiskey at a price below plaintiff's fair trade price in contravention of the Illinois Fair Trade Act.[2] The order permanently enjoined defendant from advertising, offering for sale or selling plaintiff's products in Illinois at prices less than those stipulated by plaintiff from time to time pursuant to the fair trade agreement. Plaintiff's fair traded products and their current prices were also set forth in the order.

On appeal defendant contends that:

1. Plaintiff failed to prove the execution of the fair trade agreement;

2. Plaintiff failed to prove knowledge by defendant of its fair trade prices;

* * *

Plaintiff filed a verified complaint alleging that Cutty Sark scotch whiskey is in free and open competition in Illinois; that plaintiff imports and distributes this product to wholesale distributors in Illinois; that plaintiff has entered into fair trade contracts in Illinois wherein it is provided that Cutty Sark shall not be sold, advertised or offered for sale at prices below the prices stipulated by plaintiff; that defendant had due notice of the stipulated prices; that on December 13, 1971 defendant sold a fifth of Cutty Sark scotch whiskey at a price of $5.99 whereas the fair trade price was $6.59; and that defendant is continuing knowingly to sell Cutty Sark scotch whiskey at prices below the fair trade prices.[3]

Defendant filed a verified answer denying plaintiff's material allegations, and raising various affirmative defenses. Plaintiff then filed a reply to defendant's answer, and attached an affidavit of Ted Herbik, an employee of Buckingham Distributors, a letter from plaintiff to all Illinois liquor retailers informing them of amended fair trade prices effective December 1, 1969, and a page from the December, 1969 issue of the *Illinois Beverage Journal* reproducing plaintiff's letter to Illinois retailers.

2. Ill.Rev.Stat.1971, ch. 121½, par. 188 et seq.

3. Defendant did not contract with plaintiff to sell plaintiff's products at fair trade prices. However, under the Illinois Fair Trade Act, defendant is a "non-signer" (one who is not a party to a fair trade agreement), and is also prohibited from "wilfully and knowingly advertising, offering for sale or selling" plaintiff's products at less than plaintiff's stipulated prices. Ill. Rev.Stat.1971, ch. 121½, par. 189; Kinsey Distilling Sales Co. v. Foremost Liquor Stores, Inc., 15 Ill.2d 182, 154 N.E.2d 290.

At the hearing for a temporary injunction, the parties stipulated that they would proceed with a hearing for a permanent injunction. A private detective testified that on December 13, 1971 he entered defendant's store and purchased a fifth of Cutty Sark scotch whiskey at a price of $5.99. He testified that the fair trade price schedule which he received from plaintiff's attorney listed the fair trade price as $6.59 per fifth. His report was introduced into evidence.

The managing editor of the *Illinois Beverage Journal* testified that the *Journal* is a trade publication which advertises, lists trade prices and publishes news of interest in the industry. He stated that the *Journal* conducted a mailing of price schedules for Buckingham Corporation in November, 1969, and that defendant was on that mailing list. The witness admitted on cross-examination that he had no personal knowledge of whether defendant received the letter, or indeed of whether in fact the letter had actually been mailed to defendant, because the mailing was handled by the *Journal's* mailing service. However, the witness did receive an attestation from the mailing service that the mailing was being conducted. On redirect examination the witness stated that the mailing service handled 4 or 5 mailings per month other than the *Journal,* and had been reliable for 17 years. In addition, defendant was a subscriber to the *Journal* in December, 1969, and plaintiff's price schedule was reproduced in that issue of the *Journal.* Reproductions of the price list as it was mailed, and as it was reproduced in the *Journal,* were introduced into evidence.

Evidence of the fair trade agreement was then adduced. A Chicago liquor retailer acknowledged his signature on a fair trade agreement dated July 30, 1969 between himself and Buckingham Corporation. Ted Herbik, a marketing director of Buckingham Distributors, testified that he recognized the signature of William Gallagan, plaintiff's vice-president, and he identified Gallagan's signature on the July 30, 1969 agreement. He stated that he was familiar with Gallagan's signature because he had received correspondence from him in the past; he admitted that he had never seen Gallagan sign his name. The fair trade agreement was then introduced into evidence.

* * *

Defendant contends that plaintiff failed to adequately prove an essential element of its cause of action—the existence of a fair trade agreement. Defendant's answer demanded strict proof of all allegations of plaintiff's complaint, and one of defendant's affirmative defenses stated that defendant had no knowledge of plaintiff's alleged fair trade agreement. Plaintiff was therefore required to prove the execution, existence and authenticity of the agreement before it was admitted into evidence. Dick v. Halun, 344 Ill. 163, 176 N.E. 440; Crosier v. Crosier, 201 Ill.App. 406; 18 I.L.P. Evidence, §§ 234, 235.

It has long been the rule in Illinois that handwriting may be proved by a witness's show of familiarity with it. This familiarity may be gained from having seen the party actually write, or from having been acquainted with the handwriting in the course of business dealings. (Riggs v. Powell, 142 Ill. 453, 32 N.E. 482; Gard, Illinois Evidence Manual, Rule 316; Cleary, Evidence (2d Ed.) § 11.14.) The extent of the knowledge of the witness goes to the weight to be given his opinion.

The evidence adduced as to the execution and authenticity of the fair trade agreement was the testimony of the liquor retailer and plaintiff's employee, Herbik. The retailer identified his signature on the agreement dated July 30, 1969; he was not asked whether he saw plaintiff's vice-president, William Gallagan, sign the agreement. Herbik testified on direct examination that he had personal knowledge of Gallagan's signature from having seen it on documents sent to him in the regular course of business. Upon the objection of defendant's counsel, his testimony that Gallagan also had told him that he had signed the agreement was stricken from the record as hearsay. On cross-examination, however, the following colloquy occurred:

> Defendant's Counsel: So, your testimony as to Mr. Gallagan's signature is the result of what he said in Siegel's office while you were present, is that right?
>
> Witness: That is right.
>
> Defendant's Counsel: Which I objected to. You heard me object to that, didn't you?
>
> Witness: I have no objection of your objections.

It is clear that, although Herbik's hearsay testimony was stricken from the record on direct examination, counsel for defendant allowed the same testimony to be entered into the record on his cross-examination of the witness. It is elementary that hearsay evidence is competent if not objected to (Town of Cicero v. Industrial Commission, 404 Ill. 487, 89 N.E.2d 354; Potato Growers' Exchange v. Wignall–Moore Co., 249 Ill. App. 34). Therefore, this testimony was competent evidence of Herbik's knowledge of Gallagan's signature in addition to the testimony regarding Herbik having seen the signature on correspondence in the regular course of business. In any event, the trial court was in a superior position to observe and hear the witness and determine the weight to be given this testimony. (First National Bank of Elgin v. Dierking, 87 Ill.App.2d 4, 230 N.E.2d 520.) Therefore, we will not disturb the trial court's finding that plaintiff adequately proved the execution of the fair trade agreement.

[The court nevertheless reversed on the basis that the plaintiff failed to prove an essential element of its case in failing adequately to prove notice of the fair trade price to defendant. It noted that the plaintiff had not established that the *Illinois Beverage Journal* was commonly relied upon by retailers for notice of fair trade prices, nor had plaintiff adequately proved that a copy of the *Journal* was actually mailed to the defendant.]

Notes and Questions

1. *Lay witness authentications.* In accord with the principal case, identification of signature by a lay witness is generally held sufficient to authenticate. 2 McCormick, Evidence § 223 (6th ed. 2006). While the courts have varied as to the degree of familiarity which the authenticating witness must be shown to have with the purported author's writing, the requirements in this regard have tended to be minimal. See, e.g., State v. Freshwater, 85 P. 447 (Utah 1906) (single observation of writing sufficient to confer familiarity); Morgan v. First Pennsylvania Bank, 541 A.2d 380 (Pa.Super.1988) (familiarity through correspondence). See also the authenticating testimony of the witness set out in footnote 5 of the next principal case. As to the inherent unreliability of lay witness handwriting identification, see Inbau, Lay Witness Identification of Handwriting (An Experiment), 34 Ill.L.Rev. 433 (1939). What purpose, if any, is served by the exaction of such testimony?

2. *Familiarity not acquired for litigation.* Under Rule 901(b)(2) nonexpert opinion of the genuineness of handwriting cannot be based on familiarity acquired for purposes of the litigation. What should constitute the "litigation"? See United States v. Scott, 270 F.3d 30 (1st Cir.2001) (IRS agent properly permitted to authenticate handwriting based upon knowledge of defendant's handwriting over the course of several years of investigating his activities).

3. *Authenticating relationships.* Authentication most commonly involves the introduction of evidence tending to show authorship. The substantive law, however, frequently declares many other types of relationship between individuals and things to be legally significant. The prima facie establishment of relationships such as ownership, publication, manufacture, and distribution may also constitute authentication.

4. *Trademarked items.* Was the testimony of the private detective that he purchased a bottle of "Cutty Sark" potentially objectionable for lack of sufficient authentication? Authentication of trademarked items has traditionally been required, usually with untoward results. See, e.g., Keegan v. Green Giant Co., 110 A.2d 599 (Me.1954) (directed verdict against plaintiff who testified that she suffered injury to teeth while eating peas (and a stone) from a can bearing Green Giant label). Compare, however, State v. Rines, 269 A.2d 9 (Me.1970). The problem is now resolved in those jurisdictions adopting Federal Rule 902(7), which renders trademarked items self-authenticating.

5. *Newspapers and periodicals.* Consider also the copy of the Illinois Beverage Journal admitted in the principal case. Was the copy itself authenticated? If so, what of the plaintiff's listed fair trade price? See the comment of Wigmore, a zealot for authentication: "There is usually available as much evidence of the act of * * * handing to a printer as there would be of any other act, such as chopping a tree or building a fence." 7 Wigmore, Evidence § 2150, at 608 (Chadbourn rev. 1978). Are either or both of these problems resolved by the provisions of Rule 902(6) applying the principle of self-authentication to "newspapers and periodicals?" For an interesting ap-

plication of Rule 902(6), see Boim v. Quranic Literacy Inst., 340 F.Supp.2d 885 (N.D.Ill.2004) (interview published in well-known Arabic language newspaper was self-authenticating).

UNITED STATES v. AMERICAN RADIATOR & STANDARD SANITARY CORP.

United States Court of Appeals, Third Circuit, 1970.
433 F.2d 174.

[Appellants were convicted by a jury of certain violations of section 1 of the Sherman Act. The indictment charged, among other things, that the appellants and other indicted and non-indicted co-conspirators had met at various "official" conventions of the Plumbing Fixtures Manufacturers Association (hereinafter PFMA) and entered into various specified illegal agreements, including one to discontinue the manufacture of regular enameled cast iron plumbing fixtures which were lower-priced than acid-resistant enameled cast iron plumbing fixtures. One of the alleged meetings was held at the Palm Beach Biltmore Hotel. The Crane Company, referred to in the opinion, was indicted as a defendant in the action, but was not a party to the present appeal.]

SEITZ, CIRCUIT JUDGE:

* * *

EVIDENTIARY RULINGS

Appellants argue they were prejudiced by certain rulings on government evidence. They first challenge the propriety of the admission of Government Exhibits 551 through 556 (HCA notes). As we have noted, the elimination of regular enamel products and the fixing of acid resistant enamel prices was the fourth alleged event in the criminal conspiracy charged by the government. A part of the government's evidence on this aspect of the conspiracy concerned events at an informal session after the PFMA meeting at the Palm Beach Biltmore on March 28, 1963. As evidence of the agreement to eliminate regular enamel and to fix acid resistant fixture prices, the government offered two documents. One was an American Standard worksheet entitled "Acid–Resisting Enamel Prices" dated March 1, 1963. The other consisted of six pages of undated and unsigned handwritten notes on the stationery of the Hotel Corporation of America (HCA notes), which echoed figures and statements on the American Standard price worksheet. The appellants claim the admission of the HCA notes was reversible error.

They first argue that the notes were inadequately identified in that there was insufficient evidence concerning their author for them to be admitted in evidence. The government's contention is that Raymond Pape, a Crane official, wrote the notes at the Palm Beach meeting. In support of their position, government counsel introduced a stipulation by all counsel that the HCA notes were found in Crane's files and were stapled together. The government also called a former secretary in

Pape's department to make a lay handwriting identification of the notes.[4] She testified that she had done work for Pape and had been familiar with his handwriting "at times." She identified the handwriting on four of the six pages as resembling Pape's. She could not identify the writing on the two remaining pages.[5]

Appellants contend that since a substantial danger of a wrongful attribution of guilt existed if these documents were erroneously identified, no less than a "positive, unequivocal identification of the handwriting must be required." In fact the weight of authority requires only that a prima facie case of the alleged author's identity be established for the documents to be admitted. See generally 3 Wigmore, Evidence § 693 et seq. (1940); McCormick, Evidence § 189 (1954). The ultimate issue of their authorship and the probative weight to be afforded them is for the jury. We conclude upon a reading of the record that the requisite prima facie case as to the four pages identified by the secretary was established. Thus, we hold that the trial judge did not abuse his discretion in admitting them.

Two of the pages were admitted without any handwriting identification. The jury was instructed that these pages might be compared with the other four pages for handwriting similarities should the other four be determined to be Pape's. Appellants challenge the propriety of allowing the jury to make such a comparison. They assert that the standard for comparison—the four pages—must be "admitted or proved" to be genuine before they may be used for comparison purposes. They further assert that the evidence was insufficient for the trial judge to properly determine the genuineness of the handwriting on the four pages so that they could be used as a standard of comparison.

Where documents are admitted for purposes other than handwriting comparison, they may be used by the jury as a standard for handwriting comparison if the handwriting is admitted or proved to be that of the alleged author. Williams v. Conger, 125 U.S. 397, 411–415 * * * (1888); cf. 28 U.S.C.A. § 1731. The vast weight of authority requires that the trial judge determine whether the genuineness of the handwriting on the

4. The government represents in its brief that although Pape himself was technically available to be called as a witness, he was not called to identify the HCA notes because of the precarious state of his health. Indeed, Pape filed a motion to quash the government's subpoena to him on this ground. Although his motion was denied, the trial judge indicated his intention to take all possible measures short of granting Pape's motion to protect him. Moreover, the government represented to the trial judge that it would avoid calling Pape if at all possible. Pape died of heart failure shortly after the trial ended.

5. The witness testified as follows concerning each of the six pages:

(1) GX–551: "As I remember, it looks as if it could be Mr. Pape's but I can't be sure right now."

(2) GX–552: "[I]t resembles Mr. Pape's."

(3) GX–553: "It looks like it could be Mr. Pape's."

(4) GX–554: "There really isn't too much handwriting on here to say too much about it." * * * "I can't really say."

(5) GX–555: "That appears to be Mr. Pape's."

(6) GX–556: "I can't be sure about this one."

documents to be used as the standard is sufficiently proved. E.g., United States v. Swan, 396 F.2d 883 (2d Cir.1968); Citizens' Bank & Trust Co. of Middlesboro, Ky. v. Allen, 43 F.2d 549 (4th Cir.1930); 7 Wigmore, Evidence § 2020 (1940). In those jurisdictions where the trial judge is required to make the initial determination of genuineness the courts have adopted differing standards of proof. We believe the proper standard requires that there be sufficient evidence so that a jury finding of genuineness would not be subject to reversal as against the weight of the evidence. See United States v. Swan, supra.

In view of the present state of the law as developed above, we are convinced that the trial judge, had he considered this question directly, could only have properly held that the four pages were appropriate for jury use as a handwriting standard.[6] We say this because the evidence supplied by the lay handwriting witness, a former Crane employee, in conjunction with the fact that the HCA notes were subpoenaed from Crane's PFMA file, were stapled together, and were internally consistent in content convince us that a jury finding that the four pages were in Pape's hand would be fairly supported by the evidence. Thus, we conclude the four pages were properly before the jury for use as a handwriting standard.

The appellants challenge the judge's instruction on the HCA notes in this connection as well. They contend that the instruction assumed that the four pages to be used as a handwriting standard were in Pape's hand when in fact that very issue was in dispute. We have read the instruction and do not find that it contains such an assumption.

* * *

[Affirmed.]

Notes and Questions

1. *Exemplars.* Authentication by comparison of handwriting may be made by experts or, as the principal case indicates, by the trier of fact, but not by lay witnesses. The early cases limited the use of specimens (exemplars) for comparison purposes to those already in the case for some other purpose. That rule was modified by statutes and decisions so as to permit use of exemplars admitted to be genuine or proved to be genuine to the satisfaction of the court. For an excellent opinion tracing the evolution of the law in one state, see State v. LeDuc, 291 S.E.2d 607 (N.C.1982) (holding *inter alia*, that jury may compare exemplars and contested writings even in absence of expert testimony.) Rule 901(b)(3) adopts the same standard for authentication of handwriting exemplars as for documents generally. See

6. In view of our disposition of this issue, we need not decide at this time whether the requirement of an initial determination of genuineness by the trial judge ought to be eliminated and the question of genuineness both as to the standard and the other documents be left solely to the jury. Such a course has been suggested by some commentators. See Committee on Rules of Practice and Procedure of the Judicial Conference of the United States, Preliminary Draft of Proposed Rules of Evidence for the United States District Courts and Magistrates, Article IX, Rule 9–01 (March 1969).

United States v. Mangan, 575 F.2d 32 (2d Cir.1978) (income tax returns in government files admitted as exemplars on basis of presumption of genuineness under statute). Cases dealing with the establishment of exemplars as genuine are collected in Annot., 41 A.L.R.2d 575. Should any distinction be made between exemplars prepared for use in the case and those preexisting? Between those prepared to demonstrate similarity and those prepared to demonstrate dissimilarity? See United States v. Pastore, 537 F.2d 675 (2d Cir.1976).

2. *Court or jury?* As to the respective roles of court and jury in the process of authentication, see United States v. Goichman, 547 F.2d 778 (3d Cir.1976).

3. *Required attesting witnesses.* While most writings may be authenticated by the testimony of any witness having the requisite familiarity with the handwriting of the signatory, different rules were evolved by the courts for writings whose execution is required to be attested by witnesses. Thus, the attesting witnesses must be called or shown to be unavailable before other evidence of authenticity could be resorted to. 2 McCormick, Evidence § 222 (6th ed. 2006). But compare Rule 903.

4. *Expert testimony.* The sufficiency based upon a comparison of the offered item with an authenticated sample of expert testimony to authenticate handwritten evidence has long been accepted doctrine. It is embodied in Rule 901(b)(3). The reliability of the "science," however, is seriously questioned by Risinger, Denbeaux & Saks, Exorcism of Ignorance as a Proxy for Rational Knowledge: The Lessons of Handwriting Identification "Expertise," 137 U.Pa.L.Rev. 731 (1989). This article and another by two of the same authors, Risinger & Saks, Science and Nonscience in the Courts: *Daubert* Meets Handwriting Identification Expertise, 82 Iowa L.Rev. 21 (1996), sparked a lively debate. See also Mnookin, Scripting Expertise: The History of Handwriting Identification Evidence and the Judicial Construction of Reliability, 87 Va.L.Rev. 1723 (2001); Moenssens, Handwriting Identification Evidence in the Post-*Daubert* World, 66 U.M.K.C.L.Rev. 251 (1997); Risinger, Denbeaux & Saks, Brave New "Post-*Daubert* World"—A Reply to Professor Moenssens, 29 Seton Hall L.Rev. 405 (1998). Another species of expert testimony bearing on the authenticity *vel non* of writings seems to be emerging. This is expert testimony based upon the comparison of linguistic patterns exhibited by exemplars of known authorship and the disputed document. See Estate of Ciaffoni, 446 A.2d 225 (Pa.1982). The case is the subject of Annot., 36 A.L.R.4th 598. See also Comment, Stylistics Evidence in the Trial of Patricia Hearst, 1977 Ariz.St.L.J. 387.

UNITED STATES v. SUTTON

United States Court of Appeals, District of Columbia Circuit, 1969.
426 F.2d 1202.

SPOTTSWOOD W. ROBINSON, III, CIRCUIT JUDGE. This appeal, from convictions by a jury of first degree murder and the unlicensed carrying of a dangerous weapon, presents [the question] whether four writings,  three purportedly authored by appellant, were sufficiently authenticated by their interrelated contents, the circumstances under which they were discovered, and a connecting note found on appellant's person to qualify them for admission into evidence at his trial. * * *

[The government's evidence included the testimony of two eyewitnesses to the effect that they observed the appellant and the victim, Mrs. Matilda Glass, emerge from an automobile and embrace momentarily, after which appellant fired a shot and Mrs. Glass fled. Appellant pursued her and, when she fell to the ground, turned her over and fired two or three shots at her at point-blank range. These witnesses rushed to obtain assistance.] When they returned once more, police officers were there, and an assessment of the gruesome details was begun.

Mrs. Glass, struck by three bullets, either then was dead or died very shortly thereafter. Lying wounded nearby was appellant, a revolver under his right hand containing five expended cartridges and one that was live. Appellant was removed to a hospital, where seven more live cartridges were discovered in a pocket of his trousers.

Found also, beside Mrs. Glass' body, was an envelope bearing these notations:[7]

> From Alexander Sutton to daughter, Frances D. Sutton, JA 26671. Wife, Birdie Mal Sutton, 587–2456. Call them at once. Fort Launderdale, Florida. My mother JA 22779.

Inside the envelope were four notes, three of which were received in evidence.[8] The lengthiest of the three notes mentioned difficulties between the writer and "Matilda,"[9] and indicated plainly enough that an ominous event was about to occur.[10] This note also detailed dispositions

7. These quotations, as well as others from the documentary evidence, are as they appear in the trial transcript. The original exhibits were not transmitted with the record on appeal. Slight variations respecting names may perhaps be accounted for by Government counsel's explanation to the court and the jury that he experienced some difficulty in deciphering the handwriting when he undertook to read the documents into the record.

8. One of the enclosures was not introduced into evidence because its sole significance lay in its reference to a note stationed in appellant's locker at his place of work. The latter note also remained outside the evidence, and all references to it in other Government exhibits were deleted.

9. As stated in the text, this was the deceased's forename.

10. This note read as follows:

To my daughter. Call her at Florida, JA 26671 587–2456. Frances D. Sutton, Fort Lauderdale Florida.

The car note is paid until April 12. It is paid until then until it paid for March 12. Send it on the 13th Frances, don't worry about what happened. You all just keep the car. I am sick. Let me say this. I might not get a chance to paid, but it might be in my pocket and the card where I send the money over to you all I have the most of the thing fix up.

I have some money on my job. I would not have done this but Matilda made me do this. Now we will both are in bad shape. I have no other choice at all. I have something pack. All of the lamps of mine, two floor lamps, one table lamp, Frances, the car may be paid for. These are the people that owe me where I work at the Shoreham West. These are the number.

Mr. Mazor, L614, $25. Mrs. Sherling or Sherring, L2517, $125. Mr. Birch, L312.

Just a few days there are two snow tires put in the receiving room. One way or the other, it will be two of some kind left in there. The diamond ring, give it to Jal on my finger. The watch for Lloyd, my son. I have spent hundred of dollars on this woman. But the Judge will not believe it of the jury.

There are some checks to show and the rest in cash. Hub Furniture Store and we

of personal estate the writer desired to make, and designated relatives of the writer by names and telephone numbers identical to those appearing on the envelope.[11] These features pointed to appellant as the penman, in a degree which was later to be judicially gauged. Another writing placed in evidence, also purportedly written by appellant, began with the words "[r]ead this other note," and identified one "Arthur" as the party who had "carr[ied] her home Sunday night."[12] The third writing received, clearly not appellant's creation, was an amorous note ostensibly from "Arthur" to an unnamed addressee.[13]

There was, at the hospital to which appellant had been removed, another discovery which was to assume special importance at the trial. In the pocket of appellant's trousers was still another note, also let into evidence, which, as read into the trial transcript,[14] was as follows:

> Call Fort Lauderdale, Florida, JA 22779. Mother, Bessie Sutton, 587–2456. Wife, Birdie Neal Sutton. Daughter, Frances Sutton [more numbers].[15]

The Government's proffer of the envelope and the notes in evidence was strenuously resisted on the ground, inter alia, that they were not properly authenticated. The trial judge, after entertaining extensive argument by counsel, overruled the objection and allowed the prosecutor to read the envelope's inscription and three of the notes to the jury.[16] The judge also denied appellant's motion for a judgment of acquittal, presented at the conclusion of the Government's case in chief, and appellant then proceeded with his defense.

* * *

The jury, as we have stated, returned verdicts finding appellant guilty of murder in the first degree and carrying a dangerous weapon. The jury could not, however, agree on the punishment to be imposed on the murder conviction. The trial judge sentenced appellant to life impris-

will put a hundred on the house which was my money. I have live with her for at least five or five and a half months. She were treated better than my wife or any other woman. There is $40 of $47 in my pocket.

Bessie Sutton, mother, Fort Lauderdale Florida, Ja 22779. Birdie Sutton, wife, Fort Lauderdale, Florida 587–2456. My daughter, Frances Sutton, JA 26671.

11. See note [10], supra.

12. March 13, 1967, the day of the alleged homicide, was a Monday.

13. In overall tone, this note, dated August 30, 1966, was something of a temporary farewell to the addressee. In it, "Arthur" stated, among other things, "that I will always cherish the moments and time that I have spent with you and even today I have the same feeling in respect for you that I had the day I stopped you in the Shoreham driveway." Later, he said that "[i]f this comes out okay someday later, I hope I can make you real happy like we used to be, at least for one day, anyhow." He concluded: "But always remember I do love you regardless of what or who. Please be careful and don't do anything to get yourself in trouble."

14. See note [7], supra.

15. We are not benefited by information respecting the other numbers. Government counsel, reading this note to the jury, stated simply that "there are some numbers appearing at the bottom which seem to have no relevancy."

16. The notes read were those quoted, wholly or partially in text supra following notes [7] and [15], and in notes [10] and [13], supra.

onment on that conviction, and to a concurrent one-year term of imprisonment on the other. This appeal followed.

II

Ordinarily, documentary evidence possesses no self-authenticating powers; unaided by an operable presumption, its reliability is not automatically assumed. The legal requirement obtaining in normal contexts is that its genuineness be shown independently before it is accepted as proof. The contention is vigorously pressed upon us that the communications purportedly written by appellant and "Arthur" were not sufficiently authenticated prior to their submission for consideration by the jury. Our scrutiny of the record in the light of the authorities leads us to conclude that the writings were properly received in evidence.

Indubitably, the sufficiency of a showing of authenticity of a document sought to be introduced into evidence is a matter residing in the sound discretion of the trial judge. As is always true with discretionary exercises there are discernible limits which judges must not transcend, but the judge's assessment of admissibility is vulnerable only if the error is clear. The applicable test to determine error is not whether the evidence of genuineness induces a belief beyond a reasonable doubt that the document is the handiwork of its alleged drafter, but whether, if it is uncontradicted, a reasonable mind might—though not necessarily would—fairly conclude favorably to the fact of authorship. In the case at bar, the contents of the questioned notes, conjoined with the circumstances surrounding their discovery, fashioned an adequate basis for the ruling admitting them in evidence.

We abide fully the usual judicial concession "that the mere *contents of a written communication,* purporting to be a particular person's, are of themselves not sufficient evidence of genuineness."[17] Such a rule serves meaningfully as a protective device minimizing the occasion for fraud on the innocent and imposition on the courts. At the same time, we recognize the general proposition that authorship of writings may be shown by circumstantial evidence, among the components of which the contents of the writing may play a significant role. Circumstances beyond the four corners of a document may point with sufficient certitude to the person whose pen created it. Moreover, "in special circumstances, where the contents reveal a *knowledge* or other trait peculiarly referable to a single person, * * * the contents alone [may] suffice,"[18] and where a document, purportedly that of a particular person, makes reference to facts peculiarly known to him, the "manifest probabilities" that the document is his permit a logical conclusion that in actuality he is in fact the composer. The receipt of otherwise unauthenticated writings in evidence under such conditions adequately safeguards the policy considerations underlying the broad rule disfavoring authentication of writings solely on the basis of what they contain.

17. 7 J. Wigmore, Evidence § 2148 (3d ed. 1940) (emphasis in original).

18. 7 J. Wigmore, Evidence § 2148 (3d ed. 1940) (emphasis in original).

III

The situation before us is interlaced with artifacts pointing to appellant's hand in the generation and placement of the questioned writings.[19] The envelope and the notes inside it were found beside the body of the deceased at the site of the macabre events that gave birth to the prosecution. The envelope bore the name of appellant as the addressor, and designated three persons, all described as close relatives, as the intended addressees. Full names, including the surname "Sutton," were supplied for two of the latter, as were telephone numbers for each of the three. Inscribed on the face of the envelope was the single entreaty "[c]all them at once."

One of the envelope's enclosures, beginning "[r]ead this other note," named "Arthur" as the man who had taken "her" home on a Sunday night, which could have been the night before the homicide. Another, signed "Arthur," contained enough to explain why someone—perhaps our appellant—might have become upset over "Arthur's" affair with "her." A third note gave the names and telephone numbers of three persons, each with the surname "Sutton" and otherwise denominated kinfolk, and requested that they be contacted. In names, telephone numbers and specifications of kinship, these designations matched exactly those appearing on the covering envelope.

Additionally, the latter note discussed intimate business and personal affairs which, if true, would have been peculiarly within the writer's knowledge. Included were references to the author's difficulties with "Matilda," and expressions of despondency over the deterioration of his own relationship with her. Included, too, were a summary statement of the status of the writer's financial affairs, and the dispositions he desired of his worldly estate. We do not suggest that appellant's authorship of this note was sufficiently denoted to qualify it for admission simply on the basis that such matters would normally reside solely within appellant's knowledge, for here there was no attempt by the Government to prove their accuracy.[20] This shortcoming is overcome, however, by its

19. We test the trial judge's ruling accepting the envelope and notes in evidence without regard to appellant's subsequent testimonial admissions, which alone might have warranted the conclusion that he had previously possessed the note from "Arthur" and had himself written the others. Compare Harrison v. United States, 392 U.S. 219 * * * (1968).

20. It is obvious that one's authorship of a document is not connoted simply by its reference to what supposedly is a fact known only to him unless the so-called fact is shown to be actually true. A note giving the combination of a safe exclusively within A's knowledge indicates that A wrote it. The indication is lacking if the safe defies opening when the dial is spun strictly in accordance with the information in the note, however much that information had seemed to be the combination.

While some of the matters discussed in the note in suit, if factually accurate, tended to earmark appellant as the author, there is little or nothing to show that they were accurate. The record does not explain why no effort was made in that direction at trial, or why there was no resort to a handwriting analysis. Nonetheless, if the Government's demonstration on authenticity sufficed legally for the purpose, it is immaterial that the authenticity requirement might have been better met by another method. "It is not ground for complaint that the Government chose instead to stake the prosecution on evidence that appellant regards as proof of a distinctly lower order." Powell v. United States, 135 U.S.App.

other evidentiary virtues, particularly its clairvoyant qualities in terms of personal history that was yet to be made.

The writer forecasted portentous events. His words clearly contemplated suicide and probably murder as well. This latter thought is revealed not merely by the statement that "[n]ow we will both are in bad shape," but is bolstered by the moribund mood permeating the note. Its tenor indicates an author who expected that his life would soon be terminated. It also suggests that the deceased's conduct was the driving force to that end, and intimates that she too was doomed. These are thoughts uniquely within the mind of the one planning a murder-suicide, a deed which, as things eventuated, seemingly was partially accomplished. Appellant came to the death scene with a loaded gun and seven more live cartridges in his pocket. He fired several shots at the deceased at close range, and then wounded himself. These were facts of record at the time introduction of the note was sought. A jury could reasonably feel that only by irrationally defying the probabilities could one say that the author of the note was not describing the events later witnessed by Hall and Brock.

Not only were there these indicia of a connection between appellant and the interrelated documents at the scene, but further indication of such a nexus was supplied by another note found in appellant's pocket after his admittance to the hospital. The probability of genuineness of that note is enhanced by its discovery in appellant's possession, an unchallenged factor increasing the prospect that he was the scrivener.[21] And the note listed the same persons—by the same names, the same familial relationships, and in two instances the same telephone numbers—as were furnished by the writings beside the deceased's body. The documents found in the two locations bore obvious similarities in subject matter and style, and in common pled that the named relatives be called. While the interrelation of all of the documents was such that each tended to afford reassurance of the authenticity of the others, the most important single welding agent was perhaps the in-pocket note. For it strengthened both the already close integration of the on-scene writings and their tie to appellant; indeed, the trial judge considered it to be the clinching item.

In our view, the aggregated circumstances forged such links between the questioned writings and appellant as reasonably to enable findings by the jury that he was a prior possessor of the note from "Arthur" and

D.C. 254, 258, 418 F.2d 470, 474 (1969) (footnote omitted).

21. We find a close analogy in cases permitting the introduction into evidence of writings found in the possession of an accused as exemplars for purposes of expert comparison with the handwriting in a disputed document. The courts have frequently sanctioned receipt of the exemplar when there were additional circumstances supporting its authenticity. See Dean v. United States, 246 F. 568 (5th Cir.1917) (handwriting taken from defendant's memorandum book); People v. Davis, 65 Cal.App.2d 255, 150 P.2d 474 (1944) (application for bank loan taken from defendant's wallet); Little v. Rogers, 99 Ga. 95, 24 S.E. 856 (1896) (possession of notes coupled with fact that the deceased paid them). In at least a few cases, possession alone was deemed sufficient. * * *

the author of the remainder. By the same token, we conclude that the trial judge did not exceed his authority in letting the writings in. Indeed, we applaud his identification and synthesis of the relevant factors, his sensitivity to the need for a firm circumstantial foundation for admission, and the caution with which he proceeded to his ruling. We hold that the disputed exhibits were properly accepted in evidence, and were entitled to such consideration as the jury was inclined to give them. * * *

[Affirmed.]

Notes and Questions

1. *Location as authenticating circumstance.* The location in which writings were found, plus contents reflecting peculiar knowledge on the part of the scrivener, have been held to authenticate even where the circumstances do not point to any particular individual as the author. United States v. Helmel, 769 F.2d 1306 (8th Cir.1985) (illegal gambling; ledgers reflecting intimate acquaintance with organization found at one of defendants' homes held authenticated); United States v. De Gudino, 722 F.2d 1351 (7th Cir. 1983) ("pollo" lists of smuggled aliens with dates and payment records found at headquarters of operation); United States v. Wilson, 532 F.2d 641 (8th Cir.1976) (notebooks revealing familiarity with drug operations found at apartment frequented by defendants). What was the "connection" which constituted authentication in these cases?

2. *Standardized rulings.* Obviously, as pointed out in the principal case, circumstantial evidence to authenticate may vary extensively and must, in many cases, be evaluated for sufficiency on an ad hoc basis. Like the field of relevancy of which it is analytically a subpart, however, authentication has a double aspect. While a broad general rule is required to accommodate the wide variety of questions which may arise, it has also proved true that certain specific problems recur with great frequency. The next case deals with one of the most significant of the crystallized applications of the general rule that have been developed to deal with these recurrent problems.

PEOPLE v. LYNES

Court of Appeals of New York, 1980.
401 N.E.2d 405.

FUCHSBERG, JUDGE.

Defendant Julius Lynes was convicted, after a jury trial, of rape in the first degree, sodomy in the first degree, robbery in the first degree and burglary in the first degree. His conviction was affirmed by the Appellate Division. The issues on which the present appeal turns are the admissibility at trial of (1) a telephone conversation between a police detective and a caller who identified himself as the defendant * * *

Police attention in this case was directed at defendant after the complainant, happening to observe him with a group of young men on a congested street in the Harlem section of Manhattan, recognized him as her assailant. When the defendant ran into a nearby tenement house, other people who had been standing with him told the complainant that the man was nicknamed Speedy. Acting on her relay of this information to the police, a detective, Donald Longo, repaired to the building into which the man had disappeared, where, in the course of his inquiries of tenants, he came upon a man who identified himself as Speedy's brother and provided the information that defendant's formal name was Julius Lynes. However, the man denied knowing where Speedy was at the time and, when he asked why the detective was seeking his brother, was advised that it was in connection with the investigation of an old warrant. Before departing, Longo requested that Speedy telephone him and, for that purpose, left with the brother a slip of paper bearing the detective's name and telephone number at the Manhattan Sex Crimes Squad. This sets the stage for the call which gives rise to the first of the two evidentiary points with which we treat here.

For, only hours later, Longo picked up a telephone receiver at the other end of which was an unfamiliar male voice that asked for him by name. According to the record, the detective, having then inquired who was calling, received the response, "Speedy—Julius Lynes" and then, "What are you looking for me for?" In reply, the detective said, "Your knife was found in an apartment", to which the voice was then heard to say "Oh no, oh no". When the detective thereupon asked if the man who had identified himself as Julius Lynes would come in and talk to the police, the caller refused, saying "you are going to have to find me" and then hung up. It is this conversation which was introduced at trial over the defense's vigorous objection that Longo admittedly was unfamiliar with the voice and therefore could not personally identify it as that of the defendant. The trial court's ruling was based generally on the rationale that other circumstances provided sufficient corroboration of the identity of the caller.

Prefatory to focusing on the question so raised, we note that the problem was fundamentally one of authentication, i.e., not merely whether the sound of the voice was recognizable as that of the defendant, but, more broadly, whether a sufficient foundation had been laid to permit a finding that the conversation was one with the party against whom it was offered. Putting the issue another way, in this case was the proof such that a jury could find that defendant was indeed the caller? (See *People v. Dunbar Contr. Co.,* 215 N.Y. 416, 422, 109 N.E. 554, 555 [Cardozo, J.]; *Carbo v. United States,* 9 Cir., 314 F.2d 718, 743.)

The question of authentication, of course, presents no great legal difficulty when the witness testifies that he recognizes the voice of the caller, and that is irrespective of whether the familiarity was acquired before or after the conversation (*People v. Dunbar Contr. Co., supra,* p. 422, 109 N.E. p. 555; *People v. Strollo,* 191 N.Y. 42, 61, 83 N.E. 573, 580). At the opposite end, it goes without saying that, without more, a mere self-serving statement of identity by a caller whose voice is unknown to the listener is not enough to permit it to go in (*Murphy v. Jack,* 142 N.Y. 215, 36 N.E. 882; 7 Wigmore, Evidence [Chadbourn rev.

ed.], § 2155, p. 760). But that defect need not be fatal where alternative indices of reliability are to be found in surrounding facts and circumstances (see *People v. McKane,* 143 N.Y. 455, 38 N.E. 950; *Van Riper v. United States,* 2 Cir., 13 F.2d 961, 968).

Thus, in part on the theory that the customary mode of operation of telephone users provides some assurance of reliability, in some instances the placing of a call to a number listed in a directory or other similarly responsible index of subscribers, coupled with an unforced acknowledgment by the one answering that he or she is the one so listed, has been held to constitute an adequate showing (see, e.g., *Mankes v. Fishman,* 163 App.Div. 789, 149 N.Y.S. 228; *Van Riper v. United States, supra*). In other cases, the substance of the conversation itself has furnished confirmation of the caller's identity, as, for example, when subsequent events indicated that the party whose identity is sought to be established had to have been a conversant in the telephone talk (see *Ottida, Inc. v. Harriman Nat. Bank & Trust Co. of City of N.Y.,* 260 App.Div. 1008, 24 N.Y.S.2d 63; *United States v. Frankel,* 2 Cir., 65 F.2d 285, 286–287) or when the caller makes reference to facts of which he alone is likely to have knowledge (see *Levine & Co. v. Wolf's Package Depot,* 29 Misc.2d 1085, 1088, 138 N.Y.S.2d 427, 431; *Dege v. United States,* 308 F.2d 534; *State v. Bassano,* 67 N.J.Super. 526, 171 A.2d 108). From all this emerges the rule that, while in each case the issue is one to be decided upon its own peculiar facts, in the first instance the Judge who presides over the trial must determine that the proffered proof permits the drawing of inferences which make it improbable that the caller's voice belongs to anyone other than the purported caller (see *United States v. Lo Bue,* 180 F.Supp. 955, 956–957; see, generally, Comment, 11 N.C.L.Rev. 344).

So measured, it was not error for the court to overrule the objection. The call was made to the detective after he had made a specific request that the defendant call and had left his name and telephone number for that very purpose with a man purporting to be defendant's brother. The promptness of the call—within a few hours of this invitation—can be said to impart a quality of reflexiveness that tends to undermine the chance that the invitation and the response are connected by only a *post hoc ergo propter hoc* rationalization (see *People v. Conway,* 3 Ill.App.3d 69, 278 N.E.2d 852; *People v. Kroeger,* 61 Cal.2d 236, 37 Cal.Rptr. 593, 390 P.2d 369). Moreover, aside from the immediacy of the response, the court could weigh such factors as the caller's seeming ability to track the message left for the defendant, specifically in asking to speak to Detective Longo and in using his own formal name as provided by the brother as well as the more informal appellation "Speedy". And, since the record reveals no attempt by Detective Longo to communicate with Lynes other than on the occasion when he left the request to call, the court also was entitled to view defendant's subsequent admission, made to another police officer, that he knew the detective was looking for him as additional confirmation that the message was delivered intact to its intended recipient. Beyond this, the substance of the conversation supplies further criteria of reliability. Not only did the caller indicate that he knew the detective had been searching for him, but, perhaps above all, what could be found to be his dismayed and spontaneous reaction to the information that the complainant's attacker had left a knife behind—a fact which Longo had not communicated to the brother—could be taken as telltale evidence that the caller indeed was Speedy.

Moreover, the question here was whether the conversation was admissible and not whether, standing alone, it would suffice to support a finding of guilt beyond a reasonable doubt. In that connection, it is well to remember that the complainant directly described the details of the criminal event and identified the defendant as its perpetrator on the basis of her personal observations at the time of its commission.

In sum, taking these facts and inferences in various combinations or in concert, it cannot be said as a matter of law that the Trial Judge erred in leaving it to the jury—aided as it could be by the instruments of cross-examination, counsels' arguments and other fact-finding tools available at the trial level—to decide whether, as Learned Hand put it, "The chance that these circumstances should unite in the case of some one [other than the defendant] seems * * * so improbable that the speaker was sufficiently identified" (*Van Riper v. United States,* 13 F.2d 961, 968, *supra*). * * *

Notes and Questions

1. *Reply letter doctrine.* The rule applied in the principal case has an analogue in the area of written evidence known as the "reply letter doctrine." Under the latter, if it is proved that a communication was properly dispatched to a certain addressee and a response duly received by the sender purporting to be from the addressee, the authenticity of the latter communication will be considered as sufficiently established to permit admission. See Whelton v. Daly, 37 A.2d 1 (N.H.1944).

2. *Subsequent voice familiarity.* Voice familiarity for purposes of identifying a telephoner may be acquired subsequently to the conversation in question. McGuire v. State, 92 A.2d 582 (Md.1952); State v. McGee, 83 S.W.2d 98 (Mo.1935); Annot., 79 A.L.R.3d 79. See Rule 901(b)(5).

3. *Outgoing telephone calls.* The identity of a speaker, answering the telephone and giving his first name, has been held sufficiently established as that of the person with the same first name, in whose name the number called was listed. United States v. Scully, 546 F.2d 255 (9th Cir.1976). When the listed number is that of a business, the person answering is generally presumed to have authority to speak for the enterprise. 2 McCormick, Evidence § 228 (6th ed. 2006). See also Rule 901(b)(6).

4. *Caller identification.* Should evidence that a number appeared on a caller identification device be sufficient to authenticate the call as coming from that number? The courts have found such information to be "reliable." See, e.g., State v. Lucier, 887 A.2d 129 (N.H.2005); Tatum v. Commonwealth, 440 S.E.2d 133 (Va.Ct.App.1994). Would the evidence be sufficient to authenticate the call as coming from a particular person?

5. *Sound recordings.* The issues involving the introduction of sound recordings generally were discussed in Chapter 10. If such recordings are of the human voice, additional questions are raised similar to those involving telephone calls. Under most circumstances, in addition to the other foundational requirements, there must also be an identification of the voice on the recording, either through a witness who can identify the voice or by circumstantial evidence. See Williams v. Butler, 746 F.2d 431, 441 (8th Cir.1984) (identification of voices by person with knowledge and by circumstantial evidence); State v. Stager, 406 S.E.2d 876 (N.C.1991) (audiotape of murder victim's statements expressing concerns about accused's conduct admissible based upon voice identification and circumstances of finding of tape). Cases are collected in Annot., 58 A.L.R.2d 1024.

UNITED STATES v. SIDDIQUI

United States Court of Appeals, Eleventh Circuit, 2000.
235 F.3d 1318.

GEORGE, DISTRICT JUDGE: Mohamed Siddiqui appeals his convictions for fraud and false statements to a federal agency, and obstruction in connection with a federal investigation. Siddiqui challenges the district court's admission into evidence of e-mail and foreign depositions.

I. BACKGROUND

The National Science Foundation ("NSF") is a congressionally established federal agency. The NSF presents the Waterman Award annually to an outstanding scientist or engineer, and consists of a $500,000 research grant. To become eligible for the Waterman Award, candidates are nominated by a nominator who completes and submits a form to the NSF, and recruits four outside references to support the candidate. The nominator identifies the references on the form, and sends forms to the references for letters to be submitted on behalf of the nominee.

On December 15, 1996, Susan Fannoney, Executive Secretary of the Waterman Award, received a form indicating that Dr. Hamuri Yamada was nominating Mohamed Siddiqui, an Indian citizen, and at that time a visiting professor at the University of South Alabama, for the award. The nomination form listed three references, Dr. von Gunten, James Westrick and Dr. Mysore. Along with the nomination form, Ms. Fannoney received a reference form apparently signed by von Gunten, recommending Siddiqui for the Waterman Award. In addition, Fannoney received by fax a letter of reference from James Westrick.

On January 14, 1997, Fannoney received a letter from von Gunten addressed to the Waterman Awards Committee. The letter stated that von Gunten had received confirmation for a letter of recommendation in support of Siddiqui, but that he had never sent such a letter. Fannoney alerted the Inspector General's office, which began an investigation. On February 7, 1997, Fannoney received a fax from Siddiqui stating that he was withdrawing his name from consideration for the award.

On February 18, 1997, Jodi Saltzman, a special agent with the NSF interviewed Siddiqui at Siddiqui's office at the University of South Alabama. During the interview, Siddiqui signed a statement admitting that he had nominated himself for the Waterman Award, but that he had permission from Yamada and von Gunten to submit forms on their behalf. Siddiqui also acknowledged in the statement that Westrick had recommended Siddiqui for a different award, the PECASE Award, but that Siddiqui had changed the wording of the letter to apply to the Waterman Award. Siddiqui was indicted on April 29, 1997.

* * *

Yamada's deposition was taken in Japan on March 6, 1998. At government expense, Siddiqui's counsel attended the deposition and cross-examined the witness, but was not in telephonic contact with Siddiqui during the deposition. Yamada testified that on February 1, 1997, she received an e-mail stating that if she received a phone call from the NSF to "please tell good words about me." Yamada testified that she knew the e-mail was from Siddiqui because the name on the e-mail had Siddiqui's sender address, and it ended with the name "Mo" which Siddiqui had previously told her was his nickname, and which he had used in previous e-mail.

Yamada further testified that she never signed or submitted a Waterman Award form on behalf of Siddiqui, nor had she given Siddiqui permission to sign her name to the form. On February 22, 1997, Yamada received another e-mail from Siddiqui requesting that she prepare a letter indicating that she had permitted Siddiqui to sign the nomination form on her behalf. Yamada testified that during that time period Siddiqui had also contacted her by phone making the same request, and that she recognized his voice. On February 28, 1997, Yamada sent an e-mail to Agent Saltzman stating that she had permitted Siddiqui to sign on her behalf. Yamada later admitted to Saltzman that she had not given Siddiqui permission to sign, but had made the earlier representation because she thought Siddiqui would go to jail.

During cross-examination of Yamada at the deposition, Siddiqui's counsel introduced an e-mail from Yamada to Siddiqui. This e-mail contained the same e-mail address for Siddiqui as the e-mail received by Yamada and von Gunten apparently from Siddiqui.

Von Gunten's video deposition was taken in Switzerland. At government expense, Siddiqui's counsel attended the deposition and cross-examined von Gunten. During the deposition, Siddiqui was in communication with his counsel by telephone. Von Gunten testified at the deposition that he had not submitted a letter of recommendation in favor of Siddiqui for the Waterman Award, and that he had not given Siddiqui permission to submit such a letter in his name.

Von Gunten further testified that on February 24, 1997, he received an e-mail from what appeared to be Siddiqui's e-mail address asking him to tell the NSF that Siddiqui had permission to use von Gunten's name.

Von Gunten replied by e-mail to the address that he could not tell the NSF anything but the truth. Von Gunten also testified that during the same time period as the exchange of e-mail he spoke with Siddiqui by phone two or three times. In those conversations, in which Siddiqui identified himself and von Gunten recognized his voice, Siddiqui urged von Gunten to change the statements that he had made to the NSF that Siddiqui did not have permission to use von Gunten's name. Von Gunten refused those requests.

During trial, the district court allowed the depositions to be read into evidence, and admitted the e-mail into evidence.

II. Discussion

Siddiqui * * * claims that the district court abused its discretion by allowing the government to offer the e-mail into evidence without proper authentication * * *.

* * *

A. Authentication of the E-mail

Under Fed.R.Evid. 901(a), documents must be properly authenticated as a condition precedent to their admissibility "by evidence sufficient to support a finding that the matter in question is what its proponent claims." A document may be authenticated by "[a]ppearance, contents, substance, internal patterns, or other distinctive characteristics, taken in conjunction with circumstances." Fed.R.Evid. 901(b)(4); *United States v. Smith,* 918 F.2d 1501, 1510 (11th Cir.1990) ("[t]he government may authenticate a document solely through the use of circumstantial evidence, including the document's own distinctive characteristics and the circumstances surrounding its discovery"). A district court has discretion to determine authenticity, and that determination should not be disturbed on appeal absent a showing that there is no competent evidence in the record to support it. *United States v. Munoz,* 16 F.3d 1116, 1120–21 (11th Cir.1994).

In this case, a number of factors support the authenticity of the e-mail. The e-mail sent to Yamada and von Gunten each bore Siddiqui's e-mail address *"msiddiquo@jajuar1.usouthal.edu"* at the University of South Alabama. This address was the same as the e-mail sent to Siddiqui from Yamada as introduced by Siddiqui's counsel in his deposition cross-examination of Yamada. Von Gunten testified that when he replied to the e-mail apparently sent by Siddiqui, the "reply-function" on von Gunten's e-mail system automatically dialed Siddiqui's e-mail address as the sender.

The context of the e-mail sent to Yamada and von Gunten shows the author of the e-mail to have been someone who would have known the very details of Siddiqui's conduct with respect to the Waterman Award and the NSF's subsequent investigation. In addition, in one e-mail sent to von Gunten, the author makes apologies for cutting short his visit to EAWAG, the Swiss Federal Institute for Environmental Science and

Technology. In his deposition, von Gunten testified that in 1994 Siddiqui had gone to Switzerland to begin a collaboration with EAWAG for three or four months, but had left after only three weeks to take a teaching job.

Moreover, the e-mail sent to Yamada and von Gunten referred to the author as "Mo." Both Yamada and von Gunten recognized this as Siddiqui's nickname. Finally, both Yamada and von Gunten testified that they spoke by phone with Siddiqui soon after the receipt of the e-mail, and that Siddiqui made the same requests that had been made in the e-mail. Considering these circumstances, the district court did not abuse its discretion in ruling that the documents were adequately authenticated.

* * *

Affirmed.

Notes and Questions

1. *The internet.* Despite vast technological differences between various computer aided communications and what has become known as snail-mail, the courts have had little trouble applying long established authentication principles to the age of the internet. For examples of other such applications, see the annotated cases collected in 5 Saltzburg, Martin & Capra, Federal Rules of Evidence Manual § 901.03[1][i], at 901–45 (9th ed. 2006). The paucity of cases dealing with authentication problems in connection with e-mails is some indication of the general comfort level with such exhibits. As in *Siddiqui*, the courts may look to the content of the e-mail to bolster authentication. See Massimo v. State, 144 S.W.3d 210 (Tex.App.2004). For a comprehensive treatment of the evidentiary issues involving e-mail, see Robins, Evidence at the Electronic Frontier: Introducing E–Mail at Trial in Commercial Litigation, 29 Rutgers Computer & Tech.L.J. 219 (2003).

2. *Ancient documents.* On the other side of the modernity spectrum, Rule 901(b)(8) codifies the common law doctrine authenticating "ancient documents," i.e., those that have been in existence 20 years or more. For an application of the common law rule, see Town of Ninety Six v. Southern Ry. Co., 267 F.2d 579 (4th Cir.1959). As illustrated by that case, mere authentication of such a document does not necessarily guarantee admissibility. Other rules of evidence, especially the hearsay rule, may come into play.

3. *Public documents.* Among those documents that are self-authenticating under the Federal Rules are various types of public documents and certified copies of public records. See Rule 902(1), (2), (3) and (4). What is the relationship between authentication and certification? Compare Rule 901(b)(7) and Rule 902(4). Why are both rules necessary?

4. *Records of regularly conducted activities.* The Federal Rules of Evidence were amended in 2000 to provide for self-authentication of domestic or foreign records of regularly conducted activities certified as such by the custodian. See Rules 902(11) & (12). For the hearsay implications of such authentication, see Chapter 14, Section E. Does such self-authentication expand dramatically the kinds of documents as to which there need be no

supporting testimony from a witness? See 2 McCormick, Evidence § 229.1 (6th ed. 2006).

5. *Computerized records.* As to proving computerized public records, see Annot., 71 A.L.R.3d 232. Higher standards in the authentication of computer records generally are advocated in Peritz, Computer Data and Reliability: A Call for Authentication of Business Records Under the Federal Rules of Evidence, 80 Nw.U.L.Rev. 956 (1986).

Note on Alternatives to Authentication

Given the inconvenience and expense frequently entailed in authenticating items of evidence in the ways suggested by the foregoing materials, it will obviously be desirable whenever possible to utilize alternative methods to the same end. One clearly available method which is in fact commonly used with reference to questions of authentication is the stipulation. In addition, the Federal Rules of Civil Procedure and their state counterparts afford additional options which may prove effective even where the opponent initially refuses to stipulate. Federal Rules of Civil Procedure of particular utility in this regard include Fed.R.Civ.P. 10(c), 16(c)(3), 26(a)(1)(B), 26 (a)(3)(C), 33, 36, and 37(c). The general subject of alternatives to authentication is discussed in 2 McCormick, Evidence § 229 (6th ed. 2006).

Note on the Rule of Completeness

The so-called rule of completeness allows the opposite party to introduce other parts of a recorded conversation or document or series thereof insofar as pertinent to a part already introduced by her adversary. Sometimes this result is reached on the broad ground that statements ought to be considered in context. At other times principles governing the scope of cross-examination are invoked. In either event, the original authentication is an incidental benefit to the party calling for the additional matter.

The rule of completeness does not ordinarily extend to bringing out matters in violation of a positive rule of exclusion when no inseparable connection appears. Illustrative are Derrick v. Rock, 236 S.W.2d 726 (Ark. 1951), and Jeddeloh v. Hockenhull, 18 N.W.2d 582 (Minn.1945) (references to liability insurance in conversations following automobile collision). But see Nance, A Theory of Verbal Completeness, 80 Iowa L.Rev. 825 (1995).

The longer the time which intervenes between the introduction of the original portion and the introduction of the remainder, the less the impact of the latter. Hence rather than requiring a wait until cross-examination or even until the party is putting in the party's own case, Federal Rule of Civil Procedure 32(a)(4) provides:

> If only part of a deposition is offered in evidence by a party, an adverse party may require the offeror to introduce any other part which ought in fairness to be considered with the part introduced, and any party may introduce any other parts.

See also Rule 106.

SECTION B. PROOF OF CONTENTS (THE "BEST EVIDENCE" RULE)

UNITED STATES v. DUFFY

United States Court of Appeals, Fifth Circuit, 1972.
454 F.2d 809.

WISDOM, CIRCUIT JUDGE: The defendant-appellant James H. Duffy was convicted by a jury of transporting a motor vehicle in interstate commerce from Florida to California knowing it to have been stolen in violation of 18 U.S.C.A. § 2312. He was sentenced to imprisonment for a term of two years and six months. On this appeal, Duffy complains of error in the admission of certain evidence and of prejudice resulting from members of the jury having been present during a sentencing in an unrelated case. We affirm.

At the trial, the Government established that Duffy was employed in the body shop of an automobile dealership in Homestead, Florida; that the stolen vehicle was taken by the dealership as a trade-in on the purchase of a new car; that the vehicle was sent to the body shop for repair; and that the vehicle and the defendant disappeared over the same weekend. The Government also presented testimony as to the discovery of the car in California including the testimony of (1) a witness who was found in possession of the vehicle and arrested and who testified he had received the vehicle from the defendant, (2) a San Fernando, California police officer who made the arrest and recovered the automobile, and (3) an F.B.I. agent who examined the vehicle, its contents, and the vehicle identification number. The defense stipulated to the authenticity of fingerprints, identified as Duffy's found on the rear-view mirror of the vehicle. The defense sought, through the testimony of three witnesses including the defendant, to establish that Duffy had hitchhiked to California and that, although he had worked on the stolen vehicle in the automobile dealership in Florida, he had not stolen it and had not transported it to California.

Both the local police officer and the F.B.I. agent testified that the trunk of the stolen car contained two suitcases. Found inside one of the suitcases, according to the witnesses, was a white shirt imprinted with a laundry mark reading "D–U–F". The defendant objected to the admission of testimony about the shirt and asked that the government be required to produce the shirt.[22] The trial judge overruled the objection and admitted the testimony. This ruling is assigned as error.

The appellant argues that the admission of the testimony violated the "Best Evidence Rule". According to his conception of the "Rule", the

22. It is undisputed that the shirt was available to be produced and that there was no reason for failure to produce the shirt.

Government should have been required to produce the shirt itself rather than testimony about the shirt. This contention misses the import of the "Best Evidence Rule." The "Rule", as it exists today, may be stated as follows:

> [I]n proving the terms of *a writing*, where such terms are material, the original writing must be produced, unless it is shown to be unavailable for some reason other than the serious fault of the proponent. (Emphasis supplied.)

McCormick, Evidence 409 (1954).[23] See also United States v. Wood, 1840, 10 L.Ed. 527, 14 Pet. 430; 4 Wigmore, Evidence §§ 1173–1282 (3rd ed. 1940). Although the phrase "Best Evidence Rule" is frequently used in general terms, the "Rule" itself is applicable only to the proof of the contents of a writing. See 2 Wharton's Criminal Evidence 476 (1955) and cases cited therein; McCormick, Evidence 408–410 (1954); United States v. Waldin, 3 Cir.1958, 253 F.2d 551; Dicks v. United States, 5 Cir.1958, 253 F.2d 713; Burney v. United States, 5 Cir.1964, 339 F.2d 91.[24] McCormick summarizes the policy-justifications for the rule preferring the original writing:

> (1) * * * precision in presenting to the court the exact words of the writing is of more than average importance, particularly as respects operative or dispositive instruments, such as deeds, wills and contracts, since a slight variation in words may mean a great difference in rights, (2) * * * there is a substantial hazard of inaccuracy in the human process of making a copy by handwriting or typewriting, and (3) as respects oral testimony purporting to give from memory the terms of a writing, there is a special risk of error, greater than in the case of attempts at describing other situations generally. In the light of these dangers of mistransmission, accompanying the use of written copies or of recollection, largely avoided through proving the terms by presenting the writing itself, the preference for the original writing is justified.

McCormick, Evidence 410 (1954).

The "Rule" is not, by its terms or because of the policies underlying it, applicable to the instant case. The shirt with a laundry mark would not, under ordinary understanding, be considered a writing and would not, therefore, be covered by the "Best Evidence Rule". When the disputed evidence, such as the shirt in this case, is an object bearing a mark or inscription, and is, therefore, a chattel *and* a writing, the trial judge has discretion to treat the evidence as a chattel or as a writing. See 4 Wigmore, Evidence § 1182 and cases cited therein; McCormick, Evi-

23. Wharton states the "Rule" as follows:

> [I]f the primary evidence of a fact is a writing, that writing must be produced in evidence as the best evidence of that fact, and * * * secondary evidence may only be produced when the nonproduction of the primary writing is explained and excused.

2 Wharton's Criminal Evidence 475–476 (1955).

24. For a discussion of the other uses of the phrase, see 4 Wigmore, Evidence 302–303 (3rd ed. 1940).

dence 411–412 and cases cited therein. In reaching his decision, the trial judge should consider the policy-consideration behind the "Rule". In the instant case, the trial judge was correct in allowing testimony about the shirt without requiring the production of the shirt. Because the writing involved in this case was simple, the inscription "D–U–F", there was little danger that the witness would inaccurately remember the terms of the "writing". Also, the terms of the "writing" were by no means central or critical to the case against Duffy. The crime charged was not possession of a certain article, where the failure to produce the article might prejudice the defense. The shirt was collateral evidence of the crime. Furthermore, it was only one piece of evidence in a substantial case against Duffy.

The appellant relies on Watson v. United States, 5 Cir.1955, 224 F.2d 910 for his contention that the testimony was inadmissible without production of the shirt. *Watson* involved a prosecution for possession of liquor without internal revenue stamps affixed to the containers in violation of what was then 26 U.S.C.A. § 2803(a). This Court held that admission of testimony that there were no revenue stamps on seized containers without requiring production of the containers was erroneous. This case, however, does not provide support for appellant's assertion. First, the only case cited in *Watson* in support of application of the "Best Evidence Rule" to an object was a 1917 Ninth Circuit case involving a writing and not an object. See Simpson v. United States, 9 Cir.1917, 245 F. 278. Second, the containers in *Watson* were critical to the proof of the crime. Possession of the containers was an element of the crime. As mentioned above, the shirt in the instant case, was not critical and possession of the shirt was not an element of the crime. Finally, *Watson,* although it has never been specifically overruled, has been distinguished into oblivion by this and other courts. See Atkins v. United States, 5 Cir.1957, 240 F.2d 849 at 852; Dicks v. United States, 5 Cir.1958, 253 F.2d 713; West v. United States, 5 Cir.1958, 259 F.2d 868; Palmquist v. United States, 5 Cir.1960, 283 F.2d 758; Chandler v. United States, 10 Cir.1963, 318 F.2d 356; United States v. Alexander, 4 Cir. 1964, 326 F.2d 736; Burney v. United States, 5 Cir.1964, 339 F.2d 91; O'Neal v. United States, 5 Cir.1965, 341 F.2d 581. Where *Watson* has been followed, a writing has been involved. See Daniel v. United States, 5 Cir.1956, 234 F.2d 102; United States v. Maxwell, 2 Cir.1967, 383 F.2d 437. In *Burney,* we held that oral testimony describing the contents of two containers as distilled spirits was admissible without producing the containers or their contents.

> The Watson decision is a minority decision on this point. As far as we are able to ascertain, the Watson case is the only case in all of the Circuits which does not confine the scope of the best evidence rule to the production of original documents or writings whenever feasible.

339 F.2d at 93.

In sum, the admission of the testimony in the instant case did not violate the "Best Evidence Rule".

* * *

Affirmed.

Notes and Questions

1. *Inscribed chattels.* There is almost universal agreement that the rule applies only to writings and not to chattels generally. 4 Wigmore, Evidence § 1181 (Chadbourn rev. 1972). The proper treatment of inscribed chattels within this dichotomy is further discussed in 2 McCormick, Evidence § 233 (6th ed. 2006). The *Duffy* case was decided before the adoption of the Federal Rules of Evidence. Would the result in the case have been different had the Rules been in effect? See United States v. Marcantoni, 590 F.2d 1324 (5th Cir.1979), where the court treated two $10 bills, found but not seized during a search of the defendants' residence and bearing the serial numbers included in the list of "bait money" taken in the robbery in question, as within the best evidence rule.

2. *"Proving the terms of" or "identifying" a writing.* How legitimate is the distinction sometimes drawn between proving the terms of a writing and identifying it? Can one "identify" a license to sell liquor or firearms without proving its terms? See Reyna v. State, 477 S.W.2d 564 (Tex.Crim.App.1972). Can one "identify" identification cards as the property of a given individual without proving terms? See People v. Prince, 275 N.E.2d 181 (Ill.App.Ct. 1971).

3. *Sound recordings.* Issues involved in the admission of sound recordings have already been discussed in connection with the Chapter 10 material on real and demonstrative evidence and the material earlier in this chapter dealing with authentication. Such recordings also present best evidence rule problems. See United States v. Workinger, 90 F.3d 1409 (9th Cir.1996), where the court applied the rule to a transcript of a tape recording but indicated that it would not have applied the rule to testimony from someone who had heard the conversation recorded. Why this difference? Consider this question in light of the next case. On the subject of sound recordings and the best evidence rule generally, see cases collected in Annot., 58 A.L.R.3d 598.

4. *Applications to modern technology.* For an example of the application of the rule to readings from a global positioning satellite (GPS), see United States v. Bennett, 363 F.3d 947, 952–53 (9th Cir.2004). The court held that testimony about what a custom's officer had found on the "back-track" feature of the GPS concerning the route of defendant's boat violated the best evidence rule. The testimony "was analogous to proffering testimony describing security camera footage of an event instead of introducing the footage itself."

MEYERS v. UNITED STATES

United States Court of Appeals, District of Columbia Circuit, 1948.
171 F.2d 800.

[Defendant Lamarre testified before a committee of the United States Senate investigating fraud and corruption in the conduct of World War II that he, and not General Bennett Meyers, was the actual owner of Aviation Electric Corporation. The Corporation had held numerous lucrative contracts with the Army Air Force. Meyers was deputy chief procurement officer for the Army Air Force. Lamarre was indicted for perjury, and Meyers was indicted for suborning the perjury of Lamarre. Lamarre pleaded guilty, and Meyers was found guilty after trial.]

WILBUR K. MILLER, CIRCUIT JUDGE. * * *

At the opening of the dissent it is said, "The testimony given by Lamarre before the Senate Committee was presented to the jury upon the trial in so unfair and prejudicial a fashion as to constitute reversible error."

The reference is to the fact that the William P. Rogers, chief counsel to the senatorial committee, who had examined Lamarre before the subcommittee and consequently had heard all the testimony given by him before that body, was permitted to testify as to what Lamarre had sworn to the subcommittee. Later in the trial the government introduced in evidence a stenographic transcript of Lamarre's testimony at the senatorial hearing.

In his brief here the appellant characterizes this as a "bizarre procedure" but does not assign as error the reception of Rogers' testimony. The dissenting opinion, however, asserts it was reversible error to allow Rogers to testify at all as to what Lamarre had said to the subcommittee, on the theory that the transcript itself was the best evidence of Lamarre's testimony before the subcommittee.

That theory is, in our view, based upon a misconception of the best evidence rule. As applied generally in federal courts, the rule is limited to cases where the contents of a writing are to be proved. Here there was no attempt to prove the contents of a writing; the issue was what Lamarre had said, not what the transcript contained. The transcript made from shorthand notes of his testimony was, to be sure, evidence of what he had said, but it was not the only admissible evidence concerning it. Rogers' testimony was equally competent, and was admissible whether given before or after the transcript was received in evidence. Statements alleged to be perjurious may be proved by any person who heard them, as well as by a reporter who recorded them in shorthand.

A somewhat similar situation was presented in Herzig v. Swift & Co., 146 F.2d 444, decided by the United States Court of Appeals for the Second Circuit in 1945. In that case the trial court had excluded oral testimony concerning the earnings of a partnership on the ground that the books of account were the best evidence. After pointing out the real nature and scope of the best evidence rule, the court said, 146 F.2d at page 446: " * * * Here there was no attempt to prove the contents of a writing; the issue was the earnings of a partnership, which for convenience were recorded in books of account after the relevant facts occurred. Generally, this differentiation has been adopted by the courts. On the precise question of admitting oral testimony to prove matters that are contained in books of account, the courts have divided, some holding the oral testimony admissible, others excluding it. The federal courts have generally adopted the rationale limiting the 'best evidence rule' to cases where the contents of the writing are to be proved. We hold, therefore, that the district judge erred in excluding the oral testimony as to the earnings of the partnership." * * *

As we have pointed out, there was no issue as to the contents of the transcript, and the government was not attempting to prove what it contained; the issue was what Lamarre actually had said. Rogers was not asked what the transcript contained but what Lamarre's testimony had been.

After remarking, " * * * there is a line of cases which holds that a stenographic transcript is not the best evidence of what was said. There is also a legal cliche that the best evidence rule applies only to documentary evidence", the dissenting opinion asserts that the rule is outmoded and that "the courts ought to establish a new and correct rule." We regard the principle set forth in the cases which we have cited as being, not a legal cliche, but an established and sound doctrine which we are not prepared to renounce.

With the best evidence rule shown to be inapplicable, it is clearly seen that it was neither "preposterously unfair", as the appellant asserts, nor unfair at all, to permit the transcript of Lamarre's evidence to be introduced after Rogers had testified. Since both methods of proving the perjury were permissible, the prosecution could present its proof in any order it chose.

There is no substance in the criticism, voiced by the appellant and in the dissent, of the fact that Rogers testified early in the unduly protracted trial and the transcript was introduced near its close. Appellant's counsel had a copy of the transcript from the second day of the trial, and had full opportunity to study it and to cross-examine Rogers in the light of that study. The mistaken notion that, had the transcript been first put in evidence, Rogers' testimony would have been incompetent is, of course, based on the erroneous idea that the best evidence rule had application.

* * *

Affirmed.

PRETTYMAN, CIRCUIT JUDGE (dissenting).

I am of strong opinion that the judgment in this case should be reversed. I think so for two reasons.

I. The testimony given by Lamarre before the Senate Committee was presented to the jury upon the trial in so unfair and prejudicial a fashion as to constitute reversible error.

Lamarre testified before the Committee in executive session, only Senators, Mr. William P. Rogers, who was counsel to the Committee, the clerk, the reporter, and the witness being present. An official stenographic record was made of the proceedings. The testimony continued for two days, and the transcript is 315 typewritten pages. * * *

The notable characteristics of this testimony of Rogers are important. In each instance, the "substance" was a short summation, about half a printed page in length. The witness did not purport to be absolute in his reproduction but merely recited his unrefreshed recollection, and his recollection on each of the three matters bears a striking resemblance to the succinct summations of the indictment. It is obvious that what the witness gave as "substance" was an essence of his own distillation and not an attempt to reproduce the whole of Lamarre's testimony. * * *

In my view, the court iterates an error when it says that the best evidence rule is limited to cases where the contents of a writing are to be proved. The purpose of offering in evidence a "written contract" is not to prove the contents of the writing. The writing is not the contract; it is merely evidence of the contract. The contract itself is the agreement between the parties. Statutes such as the statute of frauds do not provide that a contract be in writing; they provide that the contract be evidenced by a writing, or that a written memorandum of it be made. The writing is offered as evidence of an agreement, not for the purpose of proving its own contents. A deed to real estate is different, being actually the instrument of conveyance, although there is authority that it too is merely evidence of the agreement between the parties. * * *

From the theoretical point of view, the case poses this question: Given both (1) an accurate stenographic transcription of a witness' testimony during a two-day hearing and (2) the recollection of one of the complainants as to the substance of that testimony, is the latter admissible as evidence in a trial of the witness for perjury? I think not. To say that it is, is to apply a meaningless formula and ignore crystal-clear actualities. The transcript is, as a matter of simple, indisputable fact, the best evidence. The principle and not the rote of the law ought to be applied.

I do not suggest that a stenographer's report is unimpeachable; that question is not here. * * *

Notes and Questions

1. *Coincidental recordings.* For another example of the distinction made by the majority in the principal case, see Forrester v. State, 167 A.2d 878 (Md.1961) (disallowing testimony of what was contained in a "dictabelt" recording of conversation as not the best evidence), with United States v.

Rose, 590 F.2d 232 (7th Cir.1978), and People v. Sica, 247 P.2d 72 (Cal.Ct. App.1952) (proper to allow officers to testify to telephone conversations overheard by them though conversations had been recorded). An alternative approach to the problem is suggested in 2 McCormick, Evidence § 234 (6th ed. 2006), where the author suggests a rule based upon the centrality of the writing to the litigation. Despite such criticism, the orthodoxy is well entrenched. See, e.g., R & R Associates, Inc. v. Visual Scene, Inc., 726 F.2d 36 (1st Cir.1984) (testimony as to cost of items admissible without necessity for records); Jackson v. State, 411 N.E.2d 609 (Ind.1980) (semble; videotape); State v. Hill, 505 P.2d 704 (Kan.1973) (testimony of witness to contents of oral statement by defendant admissible though transcript was taken); Naranjo v. Paull, 803 P.2d 254 (N.M.Ct.App.1990) (IRS forms did not necessitate exclusion of other evidence of partnership income).

2. *Writings that become the act.* From the situation in the principal case, distinguish cases in which an act may be done only in writing, and the writing in effect becomes the act, e.g., the judgment of a court of record. 9 Wigmore, Evidence § 2453 (Chadbourn Rev. 1981). What about corporate minutes. See Annot., 48 A.L.R.2d 1259, 1260. What writings would Judge Prettyman place in this category?

3. *Collateral writings.* Another escape from the rule is via a holding that, although a writing is concerned, its contents are not of sufficient importance or likely enough to be controverted as to require application of the rule. Judicial language commonly describes these situations as involving the writing only "collaterally." Illustrative cases are: United States v. Beebe, 467 F.2d 222 (10th Cir.1972) (prosecution for making false statement to obtain a firearm from a licensed dealer; dealers allowed to testify as to licensing without producing licenses); Farr v. Zoning Bd. of Appeals, 95 A.2d 792 (Conn.1953) (parties to zoning appeal allowed to testify they were town landowners without producing documentary evidence of titles); Chicago City Ry. v. Carroll, 68 N.E. 1087 (Ill.1903) (testimony of plaintiff that he was a passenger admissible without production of or accounting for streetcar transfer). See also Rule 1004(4).

4. *Admissions.* The possibility of proving the contents of a document by the admission of a party-opponent should also be noted. Slatterie v. Pooley, 6 M. & W. 664, 151 Eng.Rep. 579 (Exch.1840), held in favor of proof by an oral admission without production of the original. The Federal Rules restrict the principle to admissions made by testimony or deposition, or in writing. Rule 1007.

STATE v. NANO

Supreme Court of Oregon, In Banc, 1975.
543 P.2d 660.

DENECKE, JUSTICE.

Defendant was convicted of the theft of a box of calculators. The Court of Appeals reversed on the ground that the trial court erred in admitting evidence which did not satisfy the best evidence rule. Or.App., 531 P.2d 750 (1975). We granted the state's petition for review.

To prove that the calculators were taken by criminal means the prosecutor sought to eliminate other possibilities which would account for the disappearance. He asked the merchandise manager for the division selling calculators, "* * * were they sold?" The witness answered, "They were not sold, because by checking our sales record we have not * * *." Defense counsel objected, "I am going to object again under the best evidence rule—checking the sales records." The trial court remarked, "Well, he testified they weren't sold. That's sufficient."

We granted the petition for review because of doubt about the Court of Appeals' application of the "best evidence rule."

We have previously expressed our belief that the "best evidence rule" is an ambiguous principle. *Lumbermens Mut. Cas. v. Jamieson,* 251 Or. 608, 610, 447 P.2d 384 (1968). The statutes, ORS 41.610, 41.640(1), are not particularly helpful in defining the scope of the rule.

McCormick has stated the best evidence rule:

> "* * * [I]n proving the terms of a writing, where the terms are material, the original writing must be produced unless it is shown to be unavailable for some reason other than the serious fault of the proponent." McCormick, Evidence § 230 (2d ed. 1972).

Most scholars believe the rule serves at least two purposes. First, it is aimed at preventing fraud. Second, due to the central position which the written word occupies in the law, the production of the original writing is essential to an accurate determination of the rights of the parties. McCormick, Evidence, 561, § 231 (2d ed. 1972). Cleary and Strong, *The Best Evidence Rule: An Evaluation in Context,* 51 Iowa L.Rev. 825, 826–831 (1966). Restated, certain documents, particularly operative or dispositive instruments, must be interpreted with "unusual precision." Comment, 21 Rutgers L.Rev. 526, 528–530 (1967). The rule accomplishes these two objectives by requiring production of the original, thereby preventing a wilful or unintentional mistransmission of the contents of the writing.

Wigmore believed that the prevention of fraud is a spurious rationale for the rule. 4 Wigmore, Evidence, 417, § 1180 (Chadbourn rev. 1972). Arguably, if this objective were controlling, all oral testimony would be excluded if nonoral evidence existed. In any event, the prevention of fraud is not the sole purpose of the best evidence rule.

Based upon the importance of the written word in the law and the consequent need for unusual precision, it is apparent when the contents of writings, such as deeds, contracts and wills, are in issue the writing itself must be in evidence. To accurately determine the intention of the parties, the exact word, phrase and punctuation must be brought before the court. In these cases, the crucial determination is the precise wording of the language in the document. For example, did the deed recite "the northwest quarter" or "the north half of the northwest quarter?"

The case of *Hammons v. Schrunk,* 209 Or. 127, 138, 305 P.2d 405, 410 (1956), relied upon by the Court of Appeals, is illustrative. Plaintiff brought an action against the defendant sheriff claiming that the sheriff had failed to serve a summons and complaint before the statute of limitations had run. At issue was whether the defendant in the original action was financially able to satisfy any judgment which might have been rendered against him. "The defendant objected to the examination of the witness relative to the surrender value of his life insurance, because the policy itself was the best evidence." We held that the trial court erred in allowing the oral testimony. Under these circumstances it is essential that the court have the policy before it to determine the exact cash surrender value of the property. The precise terms or contents of the policy were decisive facts in the case.

As McCormick points out, the best evidence rule is actually misnamed and should be referred to as the "original document rule."

The key words in McCormick's statement of the rule * * * are "the terms of a writing," because the rule should only apply when the material issue in a case is the precise wording of the document.

In the present case the witness testified to what the document did not contain; that is, the sales records did not show any sales of the calculators. Literally, this is not proof of the terms of a document. More importantly, this is not testimony in which "the smallest variation in words may be of importance." Wigmore, Evidence, supra, at 574.

We previously adopted the rule that testimony that a record did not contain certain entries was admissible and did not violate the best evidence rule. *State v. Whiteaker,* 118 Or. 656, 663, 247 P. 1077 (1926). Whiteaker was convicted of selling securities without a license. We stated:

> "Error is predicated in permitting A.E. Gebhart, then attorney for the state Corporation Commission, and familiar with its records, to testify that an examination of the same disclosed no permit to sell 'securities' had been issued to defendant Whiteaker. Appellant contends that the records of the commission is the best evidence. It is not necessary, indeed it is frivolous, to produce a record for the purpose of establishing the nonexistence of something. * * *." 118 Or. at 663, 247 P. at 1080.

Wigmore cites *State v. Whiteaker,* supra, 118 Or. 656, 247 P. 1077, and many other cases (including a few to the contrary) for the proposition:

> "On the other hand, the fact that an *entry* in a record or account book *does not exist,* while in a sense it involves the document's terms, yet is usually and properly regarded as not requiring the books' production for proof * * *." Wigmore, Evidence, supra, at 579.

We hold the testimony was not received in violation of the best evidence rule.[25]

25. The state relied upon *State v. Lenhardt,* 152 Or. 372, 374, 53 P.2d 720 (1936). The Court of Appeals was of the opinion that if *Hammons v. Schrunk,* supra, 209

Reversed with instructions to the Court of Appeals to reinstate the judgment of conviction.

Note and Questions

The weight of authority supports the holding of the principal case that a witness may testify to the absence of a particular entry based on his examination of records without producing the records themselves. See, e.g., State v. Phillips, 259 P.2d 185 (Kan.1953). Given the rationale supporting the best evidence rule, how supportable is this non-application of it? Might such testimony better be considered as a "summary" of documents and subjected to the requirements for admission of such a summary? See *United States v. Stephens*, infra. See also 2 McCormick, Evidence § 234 (6th ed. 2006).

WILSON v. STATE

Court of Appeals of Indiana, 1976.
348 N.E.2d 90.

GARRARD, JUDGE.

Appellant Wilson was charged with robbery and was subsequently convicted of theft. His appeal challenges the introduction of certain evidence at trial and asserts the prosecution was barred because he was subjected to double jeopardy. We affirm the conviction.

* * *

[Charges against Wilson had stemmed from an incident occurring in a township poor relief office. While Wilson was discussing a problem with a township employee, the employee's paycheck was delivered to her. Shortly thereafter Wilson allegedly knocked the employee from her chair, took the paycheck, and attempted to flee. He was subdued by other employees.]

Wilson next claims error over the introduction into evidence of a Xerox copy of the payroll check. The objection was that no proper foundation had been laid to excuse the requirement that the state produce the original.

It is suggested that the copy was capable of introduction pursuant to IC 1971, 34–1–17–7 which provides:

Or. 127, 305 P.2d 405, was in conflict with *State v. Lenhardt,* supra, 152 Or. 372, 53 P.2d 720, *Hammons* would prevail as it is a more recent case.

Earlier in this opinion we pointed out the rationale for the ruling in *Hammons v. Schrunk,* supra, 209 Or. 127, 305 P.2d 405. This rationale is not applicable to the facts in *State v. Lenhardt,* supra, 152 Or. 372, 53 P.2d 720. Lenhardt was convicted of robbing the cash register of a store. The manager of the store testified he examined the cash register and it was short of what it should have contained as shown by the cash register tape. We held the testimony was admissible and it was not necessary to produce the tape. We have not relied upon that decision as the only reason stated by this court for its ruling was that the defendant did not demand that the witness produce the tape. We are not casting doubt upon the correctness of the decision, but we do have doubt about the reasoning used in reaching the decision.

> "Exemplifications or copies of records, and records of deeds and other instruments, or of office books or parts thereof, and official bonds which are kept in any public office in this state, shall be proved or admitted as legal evidence in any court or office in this state, by the attestation of the keeper of said records, or books, deeds or other instruments, or official bonds, that the same are true and complete copies of the records, bonds, instruments or books, or parts thereof, in his custody, and the seal of office of said keeper thereto annexed if there be a seal, and if there be no official seal, there shall be attached to such attestation, the certificate of the clerk, and the seal of the circuit or superior court of the proper county where such keeper resides, that such attestation is made by the proper officer."

While we doubt that the paycheck in question qualifies as a public record within the purview of this statute, we need not so decide. The statute requires an attestation and it is undisputed that none was appended to the exhibit in question. The copy was not allowable under this statute.

We are also aware of IC 1971, 34–3–15–1, 2 and 3 which provide:

> "Any business may cause any or all records kept by such business to be recorded, copied or reproduced by any photographic, photostatic or miniature photographic process which correctly, accurately and permanently copies, reproduces or forms a medium for copying or reproducing the original record on a film or other durable material, and such business may thereafter dispose of the original record."
>
> "Any such photographic, photostatic or miniature photographic copy or reproduction shall be deemed to be an original record for all purposes and shall be treated as an original record in all courts or administrative agencies for the purpose of its admissibility in evidence. A facsimile, exemplification or certified copy of any such photographic copy or reproduction shall, for all purposes, be deemed a facsimile, exemplification or certified copy of the original record."
>
> "For purposes of this act [34–3–15–1—34–3–15–3] 'business' shall mean and include such business, bank, industry, profession, occupation and calling of every kind."

The primary thrust of this statute is to permit businesses to substitute copies for original records. Such copies may then be used as originals. There was no evidence in the case before us qualifying the exhibit as a photographic, etc., copy maintained by the business under this statute.

We return then to the objection made. As commonly stated, the rule prohibits introduction in evidence of a copy of a document or writing unless and until the absence of the original is accounted for on some reason other than the serious fault of the proponent. The purpose of the rule is to ensure trustworthiness. In earlier times a "copy" was a handmade reproduction. It was amenable not only to deliberate falsification but to scrivener's error and, in some instances, a "sure" recollection which was in fact not sure at all. That the rule has been so premised and has had sufficient flexibility to respond to circumstances where its application is uncalled for, may be readily determined from our prior decisions.

In *Federal Union Surety Co. v. Indiana, etc., Mfg. Co.* (1911), 176 Ind. 328, 95 N.E. 1104, the Court considered the admissibility of one of three copies of an order prepared on an "autographic register." Holding the document admissible without the others having been accounted for, the Court stated:

> "Each of the three slips was printed by a single mechanical impression. There is a distinction between letterpress copies of writing, and triplicate writings produced as was the slip in controversy. The law does not require the doing of unnecessary things. The slip delivered to the contractor was of necessity exactly like the slip admitted, and may be regarded as a triplicate original and no useful purpose would be subserved by requiring a notice for the production of the slip delivered to the contractor." 176 Ind. 328, 331, 95 N.E. 1104, 1106.

The Court similarly ruled in *Pittsburgh, C.C. & St. L. Ry. Co. v. Brown* (1912), 178 Ind. 11, 98 N.E. 625, that a copy of a bill of lading was admissible without accounting for a duplicate original. (The offering party's original was shown to have been lost.) While the facts of the case are not as strong, the language chosen by the Court is:

> "Where duplicates are produced by mechanical means, all are duplicate originals and any of them may be introduced in evidence without accounting for the nonproduction of the other." 178 Ind. 11, 30, 98 N.E. 625.

In *Watts v. Geisel* (1935), 100 Ind.App. 92, 194 N.E. 502, the Appellate Court approved the introduction in evidence of an apparently unsigned carbon copy of a letter. The court stated that in absence of proof that it was not a true copy, it was primary evidence and admissible.

The court again allowed admission of a carbon copy in *Town of Frankton v. Closer* (1939), 107 Ind.App. 193, 202, 20 N.E.2d 216, 220. Significantly, the court stated:

> "No objection was made (nor was there any effort to show) that the copy offered in evidence was not a carbon copy of the original. In the absence of such showing we may fairly infer that the typewritten copies prepared by the attorney were carbon copies or duplicate originals and as such they may be introduced in evidence without accounting for any other impressions of the writing." [Citations omitted. Parentheses added for clarification.]

While it may be noted that these decisions all involved copies produced simultaneously, the importance of that fact is not the time of production. Under the technology of the times, it was the assurance of trustworthiness. *See, e.g.,* McCormick On Evidence (2nd Ed.) §§ 231, 236.

Thus, McCormick points out that with the advent of modern technology in the production of facsimiles, no good reason exists for excluding such copies under the rule unless there is raised some issue of authenticity which might be resolved by requiring presentation of the original. McCormick, *supra,* p. 569.[26] In this connection, it should also be noted that modern ability to secure discovery of documents greatly reduces the opportunity for surprise or injustice through the production at trial of a thitherto undisclosed written exhibit.

Similarly, the Federal Rules of Evidence now permit use of duplicates without accounting for the "original" unless authenticity is in issue or it would be unfair under the circumstances to permit use of a duplicate. Federal Rules of Evidence, Rules 1001–1003.

We think the position taken by McCormick and the federal rules is proper and clearly supported by the decisions of the Supreme and Appellate Court of this state.

We therefore hold that a "duplicate" of a document or other writing is a counterpart produced by the same impression as the original, or from the same matrix, or by means of photography, including enlargements and miniatures, or by mechanical, electronic or chemical reproduction or other equivalent technique which accurately reproduces the original.[27] Such duplicates are admissible in evidence to the same extent as an original unless a genuine issue is raised as to the authenticity of the original, or under the circumstances existing it would be unfair to admit the duplicate as an original. By this latter qualification, we refer primarily to circumstances affecting the trustworthiness of the duplicate for the purpose for which it is offered. Such circumstances might occur where the duplicate is not fully legible or where only a portion of the total original document is offered and the remainder would be useful for cross examination, or might qualify the portion offered, or otherwise be useful to the opposing party.

In the case before us no question was presented regarding authenticity of the original check or its contents, nor was any other reason advanced for rejection of the duplicate, except that it was not the original. There was no error in admitting the duplicate.

* * *

The judgment is affirmed.

26. For example, identification of watermarks, types of paper and inks used in the document may aid in determining its genuineness. On the other hand, we also take note of the common practice of the parties in moving the court for permission to substitute copies for the record once the original has been produced. While this practice retains whatever guarantee of trustworthiness use of the original provides, it appears to be a useless formality when genuineness or completeness are not in issue.

27. This tracks the language of the federal rule applicable to writings. F.R.E. § 1001(4).

STATON, P.J., concurs.

HOFFMAN, J., concurs in result with opinion.

HOFFMAN, JUDGE (concurring).

I concur in result since I do not agree with the reasoning permitting the admission of a photograph of a check into evidence.

The photograph of the check was admissible since it was proved to be a true representation of that which it purports to represent and it was competent evidence because the witness could testify to give a verbal description of the check.

The check was the object stolen and it could have been verbally described by a witness. *Hawkins v. State* (1941), 219 Ind. 116, 37 N.E.2d 79; *Highshew v. Kushto* (1956), 126 Ind.App. 584, 131 N.E.2d 652 (transfer denied, 235 Ind. 505, 134 N.E.2d 555).

Notes and Questions

1. *Duplicates and duplicate originals.* Consider the distinction between a duplicate and a duplicate original. See Rules 1001(3) & (4). See Thompson v. State, 488 A.2d 995 (Md.Ct.Spec.App.1985) (discussing the distinction and holding that a search warrant created by filling in blanks on a mass produced form, then photocopying the form and having it signed in multiple copies by the issuing magistrate qualified for admission both as an original and as a duplicate).

2. *Raising a question of authenticity or unfairness.* What is required to raise a question of authenticity under Rule 1003? When would unfairness result from admission of a duplicate? On both questions, see Equitable Life Assur. Soc. v. Starr, 489 N.W.2d 857 (Neb.1992). On the question of authenticity, see United States v. Mulinelli–Navas, 111 F.3d 983 (1st Cir. 1997) (objection as to authenticity insufficient). On the question of fairness, see United States v. Sinclair, 74 F.3d 753 (7th Cir.1996) (no abuse of discretion in admitting duplicates). See also a case predating the Federal Rules, Toho Bussan Kaisha, Ltd. v. American President Lines, Ltd., 265 F.2d 418 (2d Cir.1959) (photostats of parts of records properly excluded).

3. *Computer printouts.* A similar pattern has very recently emerged with respect to the admissibility of computer printouts. See Annot., 7 A.L.R.4th 8. As to the admissibility of computer maintained public records, see Annot., 71 A.L.R.3d 232. Rule 1001(3) resolves the question by defining printouts as originals, but the adequacy of the solution is questioned in Peritz, Computer Data and Reliability: A Call for Authentication of Business Records Under the Federal Rules of Evidence, 80 Nw.U.L.Rev. 956 (1986).

4. *Digitally enhanced copies.* Special problems may exist where copies have been digitally enhanced. See United States v. Seifert, 351 F.Supp.2d 926 (D.Minn.2005) (enhanced version changed from analog to digital format and made other changes; court found enhanced version to be fair and accurate and admitted as a duplicate).

5. *Copies as originals.* Although an item may appear to be a "copy" from the point of view of the means used to produce it, is there any reason

why a person may not by his treatment of it constitute it an original? United States v. Gerhart, 538 F.2d 807 (8th Cir.1976) (in support of allegedly false loan application defendant submitted to bank photocopies of checks claimed to be due him from other sources); United States v. Manton, 107 F.2d 834 (2d Cir.1939) (copies of items passing through bank, kept as record); Chicago & E.I.R. Co. v. Zapp, 70 N.E. 623 (Ill.1904) (letterpress copies of reports, retained by local weather bureau).

UNITED STATES v. STEPHENS

United States Court of Appeals, Fifth Circuit, 1985.
779 F.2d 232.

Before RUBIN, RANDALL and WILLIAMS, CIRCUIT JUDGES.

JERRE S. WILLIAMS, CIRCUIT JUDGE.

Columbus Schalah Stephens, Jr. appeals his conviction on one count of falsifying information on a Farmers' Home Administration (FmHA) loan application, 18 U.S.C. § 1014, and five counts of mail fraud, 18 U.S.C. § 1341. He contends on appeal: * * * (4) government summary exhibits were erroneously admitted into evidence, * * * We reject the defendant's arguments and affirm his convictions.

Stephens complains that the district court erred in admitting into evidence on the government's proffer certain charts which constituted summaries of evidence already received. He asserts the charts did not qualify for admission under Fed.R.Evid. 1006 and that he was further severely prejudiced when the court allowed the charts to accompany the jury into the jury room.

This contention involves six summary charts which the government introduced in evidence through a witness who was a special agent with the office of the Inspector General of the United States Department of Agriculture. The witness had prepared them. A separate chart illustrated each of the five counts of mail fraud, and the sixth chart summarized the disposition of the entire loan funds. The charts were approximately three feet by five feet in size and consisted of simple flow charts tracing Stephens' use of the loan proceeds. The sixth chart categorized Stephens' expenditures as either "questioned" or "not questioned." The witness defined "questioned" to mean that as an investigator he questioned the particular use of the loan funds. It is clear that all the records upon which the charts were based were also in evidence.

The trial court overruled Stephens' objections to the admission of the charts in evidence. The court expressly found that the charts were summaries of "voluminous writings and records which have been introduced into evidence and which cannot be conveniently examined in court by this jury" and thus were properly admitted under Rule 1006. As each chart was introduced, the court instructed the jury that the summary charts did not in themselves constitute evidence in the case, the real evidence was the underlying documents. The judge repeated this instruction in his general charge to the jury, and then the court allowed the summary charts to go into the jury room with the jury. The defendant also had introduced a summary chart, and it as well accompanied the jury into the jury room.

Stephens attacks on two fronts the introduction of the charts into evidence under Fed.R.Evid. 1006. First, he argues that the charts were merely pedagogical devices, not proper Rule 1006 summaries, and second, the charts were argumentative. This Court has noted the importance of distinguishing between charts or summaries as evidence pursuant to Rule 1006, *United States v. Smyth,* 556 F.2d 1179, 1184 (5th Cir.1977) (summaries admitted pursuant to Rule 1006 are evidence) and charts or summaries as pedagogical devices. In *Pierce v. Ramsey Winch Co.,* 753 F.2d 416, 431 (5th Cir.1985), we recognized that pedagogical charts are not themselves evidence, and, absent the consent of all parties, they should not be sent to the jury room with the other exhibits. Relying on *Pierce,* Stephens argues that the charts were pedagogical because they summarize and organize data already in evidence. It is his contention that Rule 1006 is restricted to summaries of writings that cannot feasibly be admitted into evidence.

We reject Stephens' reading of Rule 1006. The language of Rule 1006 is not so restrictive. Rule 1006 does not require that "it be literally impossible to examine the underlying records" before a summary chart may be introduced. *United States v. Scales,* 594 F.2d 558, 562 (6th Cir.1978). The fact that the underlying documents are already in evidence does not mean that they can be "conveniently examined in court." *United States v. Lemire,* 720 F.2d 1327, 1347 (D.C.Cir.1983). Stephens' reading of Rule 1006 is also clearly inconsistent with one proper method of laying a foundation for admission of summary charts—admitting the documentation on which the summary is based. 5 J. Weinstein & M. Berger, Weinstein's Evidence ¶ 1006[03], p. 1006–7 (1983).

Stephens' reliance on *Pierce* is misplaced. *Pierce* did not hold that charts based upon documents already in evidence are always pedagogical charts and ineligible under Rule 1006. The party in *Pierce* seeking to admit the charts into evidence did not offer the charts pursuant to Rule 1006, so Rule 1006 was not even an issue in the case. Stephens' position runs counter to our decisions that do deal with Rule 1006 charts. In *United States v. Means,* 695 F.2d 811 (5th Cir.1983), we held that a chart based on documents in evidence was properly admitted under Rule 1006. To the same effect are *United States v. Evans,* 572 F.2d 455 (5th Cir.1978) and *United States v. Smyth,* 556 F.2d 1179 (5th Cir.1977).

Rule 1006 requires (1) the underlying writings be voluminous and (2) in-court examination not be convenient. *Scales,* 594 F.2d at 562. The decision of the trial judge to admit the charts is subject only to an abuse of discretion standard of review. *United States v. Means,* 695 F.2d 811, 817 (5th Cir.1983). There is no abuse of discretion in this case. The evidence was undisputably complex as it involved hundreds of exhibits. Stephens does not question that the underlying documentation was voluminous. Examination of the underlying materials would have been inconvenient without the charts utilized by the government. *See United States v. Evans,* 572 F.2d at 491; *United States v. Howard,* 774 F.2d 838, 844 (7th Cir.1985).

We also find no merit to Stephens' contention that the charts were argumentative. Stephens objects to the "questioned" and "unquestioned" characterization used in the sixth chart. He claims that the word "questioned" appeared to establish conclusively that the use of the loan funds was questioned. The use of the term, he maintains, improperly shifted the burden of proof to him.

This case is similar to *United States v. Smyth,* 556 F.2d 1179 (5th Cir.1977). The government introduced computer printout summaries that contained "original data", "classified data", "falsified data summarized" and "difference between original/false" headings to illustrate how the defendant used forged time cards to overbill the government. The trial court admitted the computer printout into evidence and instructed the jury that the underlying documents were the evidence and that the computer printout summaries were not evidence. We stated, "[I]n light of appellants' objections to the characterizations the Government utilized in the summary headings the cautionary instruction given by the trial judge was entirely appropriate, if not necessary, for it neutralized their possible prejudicial effect." 556 F.2d at 1184.

Like the court in *Smyth,* the court admitted the summary charts into evidence and instructed the jury that the charts were not to be considered as the evidence in the case,[28] and thus, neutralized the possible prejudicial effect of the headings. Moreover, "questioned" falls far short of being as argumentative as "falsified". The use of the term "questioned" is no more than accurate in a case dealing with alleged conversion of loan proceeds. In sum, we find that the judge properly admitted the summary charts into evidence under Rule 1006, and consequently there was no error in allowing the charts to go into the jury room with the jury. * * *

Affirmed.

Note

Given the increasingly complex nature of the business world and, consequently, business litigation, the use of summaries in such trials has become routine. See cases collected in 5 Saltzburg, Martin & Capra, Federal Rules of Evidence Manual § 1006.03, at 1006–7—1006–30 (9th ed. 2006).

SEILER v. LUCASFILM, LTD.

United States Court of Appeals, Ninth Circuit, 1986.
808 F.2d 1316.

FARRIS, CIRCUIT JUDGE:

Lee Seiler, a graphic artist and creator of science fiction creatures, alleged copyright infringement by George Lucas and others who created

28. This practice is consistent with our other cases. *See, e.g., United States v. Evans,* 572 F.2d 455, 495 (5th Cir.1978).

and produced the science fiction movie "The Empire Strikes Back." Seiler claimed that creatures known as "Imperial Walkers" which appeared in The Empire Strikes Back infringed Seiler's copyright on his own creatures called "Garthian Striders." The Empire Strikes Back appeared in 1980; Seiler did not obtain his copyright until 1981.

Because Seiler wished to show blown-up comparisons of his creatures and Lucas' Imperial Walkers to the jury at opening statement, the district judge held a pre-trial evidentiary hearing. At the hearing, Seiler could produce no originals of his Garthian Striders nor any documentary evidence that they existed before The Empire Strikes Back appeared in 1980. The district judge, applying the best evidence rule, found that Seiler had lost or destroyed the originals in bad faith under Fed.R.Evid. 1004(1) and denied admissibility of any secondary evidence, even the copies that Seiler had deposited with the Copyright Office. With no admissible evidence, Seiler then lost at summary judgment, 613 F.Supp. 1253.

FACTS

Seiler contends that he created and published in 1976 and 1977 science fiction creatures called Garthian Striders. In 1980, George Lucas released The Empire Strikes Back, a motion picture that contains a battle sequence depicting giant machines called Imperial Walkers. In 1981 Seiler obtained a copyright on his Striders, depositing with the Copyright Office "reconstructions" of the originals as they had appeared in 1976 and 1977.

Seiler contends that Lucas' Walkers were copied from Seiler's Striders which were allegedly published in 1976 and 1977. Lucas responds that Seiler did not obtain his copyright until one year after the release of The Empire Strikes Back and that Seiler can produce no documents that antedate The Empire Strikes Back.

Because Seiler proposed to exhibit his Striders in a blow-up comparison to Lucas' Walkers at opening statement, the district judge held an evidentiary hearing on the admissibility of the "reconstructions" of Seiler's Striders. Applying the "best evidence rule," Fed.R.Evid. 1001–1008, the district court found at the end of a seven-day hearing that Seiler lost or destroyed the originals in bad faith under Rule 1004(1) and that consequently no secondary evidence, such as the post-Empire Strikes Back reconstructions, was admissible. In its opinion the court found specifically that Seiler testified falsely, purposefully destroyed or withheld in bad faith the originals, and fabricated and misrepresented the nature of his reconstructions. The district court granted summary judgment to Lucas after the evidentiary hearing.

On appeal, Seiler contends 1) that the best evidence rule does not apply to his works, 2) that if the best evidence rule does apply, Rule 1008 requires a jury determination of the existence and authenticity of his originals, and 3) that 17 U.S.C. § 410(c) of the copyright laws overrides the Federal Rules of Evidence and mandates admission of his secondary evidence.

* * *

Discussion

1. Application of the best evidence rule.

The best evidence rule embodied in Rules 1001–1008 represented a codification of longstanding common law doctrine. Dating back to 1700, the rule requires not, as its common name implies, the best evidence in every case but rather the production of an original document instead of a copy. Many commentators refer to the rule not as the best evidence rule but as the original document rule.

Rule 1002 states: "To prove the content of a writing, recording, or photograph, the original writing, recording, or photograph is required, except as otherwise provided in these rules or by Act of Congress." Writings and recordings are defined in Rule 1001 as "letters, words, or numbers, or their equivalent, set down by handwriting, typewriting, printing, photostating, photographing, magnetic impulse, mechanical or electronic recording, or other form of data compilation."

The Advisory Committee Note supplies the following gloss:

> Traditionally the rule requiring the original centered upon accumulations of data and expressions affecting legal relations set forth in words and figures. This meant that the rule was one essentially related to writings. Present day techniques have expanded methods of storing data, yet the essential form which the information ultimately assumes for usable purposes is words and figures. Hence the considerations underlying the rule dictate its expansion to include computers, photographic systems, and other modern developments.

Some treatises, whose approach seems more historical than rigorously analytic, opine without support from any cases that the rule is limited to words and figures. 5 *Weinstein's Evidence* (1983), ¶ 1001(1)[01] at 1001–11; 5 Louisell & Mueller, § 550 at 285.

We hold that Seiler's drawings were "writings" within the meaning of Rule 1001(1); they consist not of "letters, words, or numbers" but of "their equivalent." To hold otherwise would frustrate the policies underlying the rule and introduce undesirable inconsistencies into the application of the rule.

In the days before liberal rules of discovery and modern techniques of electronic copying, the rule guarded against incomplete or fraudulent proof. By requiring the possessor of the original to produce it, the rule prevented the introduction of altered copies and the withholding of originals. The purpose of the rule was thus long thought to be one of fraud prevention, but Wigmore pointed out that the rule operated even in cases where fraud was not at issue, such as where secondary evidence is not admitted even though its proponent acts in utmost good faith. Wigmore also noted that if prevention of fraud were the foundation of the rule, it should apply to objects as well as writings, which it does not. 4 Wigmore, *Evidence* § 1180 (Chadbourn rev. 1972).

The modern justification for the rule has expanded from prevention of fraud to a recognition that writings occupy a central position in the law. When the contents of a writing are at issue, oral testimony as to the terms of the writing is subject to a greater risk of error than oral testimony as to events or other situations. The human memory is not often capable of reciting the precise terms of a writing, and when the terms are in dispute only the writing itself, or a true copy, provides reliable evidence. To summarize then, we observe that the importance of the precise terms of writings in the world of legal relations, the fallibility of the human memory as reliable evidence of the terms, and the hazards of inaccurate or incomplete duplication are the concerns addressed by the best evidence rule. *See* 5 Louisell & Mueller, *Federal Evidence,* § 550 at 283; *McCormick on Evidence* (3d ed. 1984) § 231 at 704; Cleary & Strong, *The Best Evidence Rule: An Evaluation in Context,* 51 Iowa L.Rev. 825, 828 (1966).

Viewing the dispute in the context of the concerns underlying the best evidence rule, we conclude that the rule applies. McCormick summarizes the rule as follows:

> [I]n proving the terms of a writing, where the terms are material, the original writing must be produced unless it is shown to be unavailable for some reason other than the serious fault of the proponent.

McCormick on Evidence § 230, at 704.

The contents of Seiler's work are at issue. There can be no proof of "substantial similarity" and thus of copyright infringement unless Seiler's works are juxtaposed with Lucas' and their contents compared. Since the contents are material and must be proved, Seiler must either produce the original or show that it is unavailable through no fault of his own. Rule 1004(1). This he could not do.

The facts of this case implicate the very concerns that justify the best evidence rule. Seiler alleges infringement by The Empire Strikes Back, but he can produce no documentary evidence of any originals existing before the release of the movie. His secondary evidence does not consist of true copies or exact duplicates but of "reconstructions" made after The Empire Strikes Back. In short, Seiler claims that the movie infringed his originals, yet he has no proof of those originals.

The dangers of fraud in this situation are clear. The rule would ensure that proof of the infringement claim consists of the works alleged to be infringed. Otherwise, "reconstructions" which might have no resemblance to the purported original would suffice as proof for infringement of the original. Furthermore, application of the rule here defers to the rule's special concern for the contents of writings. Seiler's claim depends on the content of the originals, and the rule would exclude reconstituted proof of the originals' content. Under the circumstances here, no "reconstruction" can substitute for the original.

Seiler argues that the best evidence rule does not apply to his work, in that it is artwork rather than "writings, recordings, or photographs." He contends that the rule both historically and currently embraces only words or numbers. Neither party has cited us to cases which discuss the applicability of the rule to drawings.[29]

To recognize Seiler's works as writings does not, as Seiler argues, run counter to the rule's preoccupation with the centrality of the written word in the world of legal relations. Just as a contract objectively manifests the subjective intent of the makers, so Seiler's drawings are objective manifestations of the creative mind. The copyright laws give legal protection to the objective manifestations of an artist's ideas, just as the law of contract protects through its multifarious principles the meeting of minds evidenced in the contract. Comparing Seiler's drawings with Lucas' drawings is no different in principle than evaluating a contract and the intent behind it. Seiler's "reconstructions" are "writings" that affect legal relations; their copyrightability attests to that.

A creative literary work, which is artwork, and a photograph whose contents are sought to be proved, as in copyright, defamation, or invasion of privacy, are both covered by the best evidence rule. *See* McCormick, § 232 at 706 n. 9; Advisory Committee's Note to Rule 1002; 5 Louisell & Mueller, § 550 at 285 n. 27. We would be inconsistent to apply the rule to artwork which is literary or photographic but not to artwork of other forms. Furthermore, blueprints, engineering drawings, architectural designs may all lack words or numbers yet still be capable of copyright and susceptible to fraudulent alteration. In short, Seiler's argument would have us restrict the definitions of Rule 1001(1) to "words" and "numbers" but ignore "or their equivalent." We will not do so in the circumstances of this case.

Our holding is also supported by the policy served by the best evidence rule in protecting against faulty memory. Seiler's reconstructions were made four to seven years after the alleged originals; his memory as to specifications and dimensions may have dimmed significantly. Furthermore, reconstructions made after the release of the Empire Strikes Back may be tainted, even if unintentionally, by exposure to the movie. Our holding guards against these problems.

29. Lucas argues that Seiler's work, involving painting and photographic processes, is photography and therefore under the explicit reach of rule 1001. But the pleadings, Lucas' memoranda in opposition to summary judgment, and the district judge's initial references all characterize Seiler's work as drawings.

2. *Rule 1008.*

As we hold that the district court correctly concluded that the best evidence rule applies to Seiler's drawings, Seiler was required to produce his original drawings unless excused by the exceptions set forth in Rule 1004. The pertinent subsection is 1004(1), which provides:

> The original is not required, and other evidence of the contents of a writing, recording, or photograph is admissible if—
>
> (1) Originals lost or destroyed. All originals are lost or have been destroyed, unless the proponent lost or destroyed them in bad faith;

In the instant case, prior to opening statement, Seiler indicated he planned to show to the jury reconstructions of his "Garthian Striders" during the opening statement. The trial judge would not allow items to be shown to the jury until they were admitted in evidence. Seiler's counsel reiterated that he needed to show the reconstructions to the jury during his opening statement. Hence, the court excused the jury and held a seven-day hearing on their admissibility. At the conclusion of the hearing, the trial judge found that the reconstructions were inadmissible under the best evidence rule as the originals were lost or destroyed in bad faith. This finding is amply supported by the record.

Seiler argues on appeal that regardless of Rule 1004(1), Rule 1008 requires a trial because a key issue would be whether the reconstructions correctly reflect the content of the originals. Rule 1008 provides:

> When the admissibility of other evidence of contents of writings, recordings, or photographs under these rules depends upon the fulfillment of a condition of fact, the question whether the condition has been fulfilled is ordinarily for the court to determine in accordance with the provisions of rule 104. However, when an issue is raised (a) whether the asserted writing ever existed, or (b) whether another writing, recording, or photograph produced at the trial is the original, or (c) whether other evidence of contents correctly reflects the contents, the issue is for the trier of fact to determine as in the case of other issues of fact.[30]

Seiler's position confuses admissibility of the reconstructions with the weight, if any, the trier of fact should give them, after the judge has ruled that they are admissible. Rule 1008 states, in essence, that when the *admissibility* of evidence other than the original depends upon the fulfillment of a condition of fact, the trial judge generally makes the determination of that condition of fact. The notes of the Advisory Committee are consistent with this interpretation in stating: "Most preliminary questions of fact in connection with applying the rule preferring the original as evidence of contents are for the judge * * * [t]hus the question of * * * fulfillment of other conditions specified in

30. Lucas conceded the originals existed and Seiler conceded the items he sought to introduce were not the originals. Hence, as subsections (a) and (b) are not in issue, Seiler is arguing that 1008(c) requires that the case be submitted to the jury.

Rule 1004 * * * is for the judge." In the instant case, the condition of fact which Seiler needed to prove was that the originals were not lost or destroyed in bad faith. Had he been able to prove this, his reconstructions would have been admissible and then their accuracy would have been a question for the jury. In sum, since admissibility of the reconstructions was dependent upon a finding that the originals were not lost or destroyed in bad faith, the trial judge properly held the hearing to determine their admissibility.

[The court then held that § 410(c)[31] of the Copyright Act does not mandate the admissibility of copies of a work deposited at the Copyright Office.]

Affirmed.

Notes and Questions

1. *Excuses for non-production.* The "best evidence" rule, it is said, is a rule of preference only. In Thompson v. State, 488 A.2d 995, 1006 (Md.Ct. Spec.App.1985), the essence of the rule is said to be captured in the statement, "You always have to produce the original document * * * unless you can't."[32] In Hernandez v. Pino, 482 So.2d 450 (Fla.Dist.Ct.App.1986), a malpractice plaintiff was unable to produce dental x-rays which had been lost after their release to plaintiff's attorney. The x-rays had already been reviewed by defendant's expert prior to their release. Should plaintiff be allowed to present expert testimony as to what they showed? Other circumstances in addition to inadvertent loss or destruction which have traditionally been accepted as excuses for failing to produce the original of a document include possession by a third person beyond the reach of the court's process, and failure of an adversary having possession to produce after being given notice. See 2 McCormick, Evidence § 237 (6th ed. 2006). These excuses are recognized by Rule 1004.

2. *Notice.* How is notice to an adversary to produce to be proved? "Every written notice is, for the best of all reasons, to be proved by a duplicate original; for if it were otherwise, the notice to produce the original could be proved only in the same way as the original notice itself; and thus a fresh necessity would be constantly arising, *ad infinitum,* to prove notice of the preceding notice; so that the party would, at every step, be receding instead of advancing." Eisenhart v. Slaymaker, 14 Serg. & R. 153, 156 (Pa.1826), allowing a notice to quit to be proved by a "duplicate original" without proof of service of notice to produce the original. Is the reasoning suggested in the quotation valid except as to proving notice to produce the original? Compare McDonald v. Hanks, 113 S.W. 604 (Tex.Civ.App.1908), holding carbons of letters written by attorneys to relatives of alleged grantor

31. Section 410(c) of the act provides as follows:

In any judicial proceedings the certificate of a registration made before or within five years after first publication of the work shall constitute prima facie evidence of the validity of the copyright and of the facts stated in the certificate. The evidentiary weight to be accorded the certificate of a registration made thereafter shall be within the discretion of the court. [Ed.]

32. The statement is attributed by the court to the late Professor Irving Younger. [Ed.]

in order to lay foundation for proof of contents of lost deed not admissible without accounting for nonproduction of the original letters.

DOE D. GILBERT v. ROSS

7 M. & W. 102, 151 Eng.Rep. 696 (Exch. of Pleas 1840).

EJECTMENT by the lessors of the plaintiff, who claimed as coheiresses-at-law of Arthur Gramer Miller. At the trial before Lord Denman, Ch. J., at the Warwickshire Spring Assizes, 1840, it appeared that, in 1779, the father of A.G. Miller had devised the property to A.G. Miller for life, with remainder as he should by deed or will appoint, with remainder, in default of and until appointment, to the heirs of his body, with remainders over. A.G. Miller died in 1832 without issue, and it therefore became necessary for the lessors of the plaintiff, who claimed as his collateral heirs, to prove that he had acquired the fee-simple of the property before the time of his death. For this purpose they sought to give evidence of the marriage settlement of A.G. Miller, executed by him in 1789, after his father's death, in order to show that he had acquired the fee by exercising the power of appointment. This settlement was in the possession of Mr. Baxter, the defendant's attorney, who had been subpoenaed to produce it: and upon his examination, he stated that he had received it from a Mr. Weetman, who was in possession of another part of the property, and against whom the lessors of the plaintiff had previously brought an ejectment, which was tried at the Summer Assizes of 1838, before Lord Abinger, C.B., and in which the lessors of the plaintiff were nonsuited. Mr. Baxter stated that he claimed a lien on the deeds for professional business done for Mr. Weetman, and he declined to produce it on this ground. Mr. Weetman himself was in Court, but was not examined, or called on to produce the deed.

Upon Mr. Baxter's refusal to produce the deed, the lessors of the plaintiff proposed to give secondary evidence of its contents. This was objected to on the part of the defendants, but Lord Denman ruled that such evidence was admissible. The lessors of the plaintiff then tendered in evidence a copy of the deed; but upon examination it appeared that this had been made an attested copy, and was unstamped, and it was consequently rejected. It was then proposed to read, as secondary evidence of the contents of the deed, a short-hand writer's notes of the proceedings of the trial in the former action, when the settlement had been produced and proved by the then defendant Weetman. This evidence was objected to, but Lord Denman allowed it to be admitted, and the short-hand writer's notes were read; but it appeared from them that the deed had not been actually read by the officer of the Court, but that its contents were stated by the defendant's junior counsel. It was objected that this statement could not be received, but Lord Denman considered that it was substantially the same as if the deed had been read by the officer, and accordingly the note of this statement was read, and it thereby appeared that A.G. Miller had exercised the appointment in favour of himself and his heirs in fee, subject to a life interest in part of the estate to his wife, who died before him. * * *

Adams, Serjt., in Easter Term last, moved for a nonsuit or a new trial, on several grounds:

> 1st, that secondary evidence of the settlement was altogether inadmissible. 2ndly, that even if secondary evidence was receivable, the short-hand writer's notes were not admissible evidence. 3rdly, that at all events they were not receivable, when it appeared that a copy of the settlement was in existence. * * * The Court granted a rule on all the points except the third, which was disposed of on the application. Adams, Serjt., urged in support of this point, that, assuming that the short-hand writer's notes might have been evidence if no better evidence had been in existence, it appeared here that better evidence did exist, viz. the attested copy, which the lessors of the plaintiff might have produced if they had procured it to be stamped. The short-hand writer's notes, at best, amount to nothing more than mere parol evidence. * * *

PARKE, B.: You must contend then, that there is to be primary, secondary, and tertiary evidence. If an attested copy is to be one degree of secondary evidence, the next will be a copy not attested; and then an abstract: then would come an inquiry, whether one man has a better memory than another, and we should never know where to stop.

LORD ABINGER, C.B.: There can be no rule upon this point. Upon examination of the cases, and upon principle, we think there are no degrees of secondary evidence. The rule is, that if you cannot produce the original, you may give parol evidence of its contents. If indeed the party giving such parol evidence appears to have better secondary evidence in his power, which he does not produce, that is a fact to go to the jury, from which they might sometimes presume that the evidence kept back would be adverse to the party withholding it. But the law makes no distinction between one class of secondary evidence and another. In cases where the contents of public records and documents are to be proved, examined copies are allowed as primary evidence; but this is upon public grounds; for in these cases, the law, for public convenience, gives credit to the sworn testimony of any witness who examines the entry, and produces the copy.

Note

A majority of American jurisdictions at one time rejected the "English" view espoused in the principal case in favor of a hierarchical system of preference between types of secondary evidence. See 4 Wigmore, Evidence § 1275 (Chadbourn rev. 1972). However, the Federal and Revised Uniform Rules of Evidence contain no provision for "degrees" of secondary evidence. Rule 1004. See also United States v. Gerhart, 538 F.2d 807 (8th Cir.1976).

Chapter 12[1]

TESTIMONIAL EVIDENCE

SECTION A. COMPETENCY OF WITNESSES

The term "competent," with reference to witnesses, is generally used to describe a person who is free of personal characteristics which would disable him from giving testimony before a court of law. In times gone by, questions relating to the competency of witnesses bulked extremely large in the law of Evidence. "Under the English common law, at various times and in various instances, a person might be disqualified to be a witness because of race, color, sex, relationship by blood or marriage [to a party or interested person], infancy, interest, mental derangement, conviction of crime, or self-confessed moral turpitude."[2] By a gradual process of judicial decision and legislative enactment, however, early begun and greatly accelerated during the 19th century, this extensive list of incompetencies was greatly constricted, so that Thayer, writing in 1898, could state with some justification that "as to rules for the exclusion of witnesses, they have nearly disappeared. Little remains except what reason requires, namely, the exclusion of persons too young to be trusted, or too deficient in intelligence."[3] The materials which follow will deal briefly with the present significance of those characteristics which formerly served to render a witness incompetent, and with certain vestigial remnants of the rules of incompetency themselves.

(1) GENERAL REQUIREMENT: FEDERAL RULE 601

WASHINGTON v. TEXAS

Supreme Court of the United States, 1967.
388 U.S. 14.

MR. CHIEF JUSTICE WARREN delivered the opinion of the Court.

We granted certiorari in this case to determine whether the right of a defendant in a criminal case under the Sixth Amendment to have

1. Throughout this chapter some footnotes from cases and materials have been omitted; others have been renumbered. [Ed.]

2. American Law Institute, Model Code of Evidence Rule 101, Comment (1942).

3. Thayer, Preliminary Treatise on Evidence 526 (1898).

compulsory process for obtaining witnesses in his favor is applicable to the States through the Fourteenth Amendment, and whether that right was violated by a state procedural statute providing that persons charged as principals, accomplices, or accessories in the same crime cannot be introduced as witnesses for each other.

[At his trial, petitioner sought to introduce the testimony of one Fuller, which was excluded. However, for purposes of the record, petitioner established that if allowed to testify Fuller would have substantiated petitioner's version of the facts leading up to the homicide.]

It is undisputed that Fuller's testimony would have been relevant and material, and that it was vital to the defense. Fuller was the only person other than petitioner who knew exactly who had fired the shotgun and whether petitioner had at the last minute attempted to prevent the shooting. Fuller, however, had been previously convicted of the same murder and sentenced to 50 years in prison, and he was confined in the Dallas County jail. Two Texas statutes provided at the time of the trial in this case that persons charged or convicted as coparticipants in the same crime could not testify for one another, although there was no bar to their testifying for the State. On the basis of these statutes the trial judge sustained the State's objection and refused to allow Fuller to testify. Petitioner's conviction followed, and it was upheld on appeal by the Texas Court of Criminal Appeals. 400 S.W.2d 756. * * * We reverse.

I.

We have not previously been called upon to decide whether the right of an accused to have compulsory process for obtaining witnesses in his favor, guaranteed in federal trials by the Sixth Amendment, is so fundamental and essential to a fair trial that it is incorporated in the Due Process Clause of the Fourteenth Amendment. At one time, it was thought that the Sixth Amendment had no application to state criminal trials. That view no longer prevails, and in recent years we have increasingly looked to the specific guaranties of the Sixth Amendment to determine whether a state criminal trial was conducted with due process of law. We have held that due process requires that the accused have the assistance of counsel for his defense,[4] that he be confronted with the witnesses against him,[5] and that he have the right to a speedy[6] and public[7] trial.

The right of an accused to have compulsory process for obtaining witnesses in his favor stands on no lesser footing than the other Sixth Amendment rights that we have previously held applicable to the States. * * *

4. Gideon v. Wainwright, 372 U.S. 335 (1963).

5. Pointer v. State of Texas, 380 U.S. 400 (1965).

6. Klopfer v. North Carolina, 386 U.S. 213 (1967).

7. In re Oliver, 333 U.S. 257 (1948).

The right to offer the testimony of witnesses, and to compel their attendance, if necessary, is in plain terms the right to present a defense, the right to present the defendant's version of the facts as well as the prosecution's to the jury so it may decide where the truth lies. Just as an accused has the right to confront the prosecution's witnesses for the purpose of challenging their testimony, he has the right to present his own witnesses to establish a defense. This right is a fundamental element of due process of law.

II.

Since the right to compulsory process is applicable in this state proceeding, the question remains whether it was violated in the circumstances of this case. The testimony of Charles Fuller was denied to the defense not because the State refused to compel his attendance, but because a state statute made his testimony inadmissible whether he was present in the courtroom or not. We are thus called upon to decide whether the Sixth Amendment guarantees a defendant the right under any circumstances to put his witnesses on the stand, as well as the right to compel their attendance in court. The resolution of this question requires some discussion of the common-law context in which the Sixth Amendment was adopted.

Joseph Story, in his famous Commentaries on the Constitution of the United States, observed that the right to compulsory process was included in the Bill of Rights in reaction to the notorious common-law rule that in cases of treason or felony the accused was not allowed to introduce witnesses in his defense at all.[8] Although the absolute prohibition of witnesses for the defense had been abolished in England by statute before 1787,[9] the Framers of the Constitution felt it necessary specifically to provide that defendants in criminal cases should be provided the means of obtaining witnesses so that their own evidence, as well as the prosecution's, might be evaluated by the jury.

Despite the abolition of the rule generally disqualifying defense witnesses, the common law retained a number of restrictions on witnesses who were physically and mentally capable of testifying. To the extent that they were applicable, they had the same effect of suppressing the truth that the general proscription had had. Defendants and codefendants were among the large class of witnesses disqualified from testifying on the ground of interest.[10] A party to a civil or criminal case was not allowed to testify on his own behalf for fear that he might be tempted to lie. Although originally the disqualification of a codefendant appears to have been based only on his status as a party to the action, and in some

8. 3 Story, Commentaries on the Constitution of the United States §§ 1786–1788 (1st ed. 1833).

9. By 1701 the accused in both treason and felony cases was allowed to produce witnesses who could testify under oath. See 2 Wigmore, Evidence § 575, at 685–686 (3d ed. 1940).

10. See generally 2 Wigmore §§ 575–576. We have discussed elsewhere the gradual demise of the common-law rule prohibiting defendants from testifying in their own behalf. See Ferguson v. State of Georgia, 365 U.S. 570 (1961).

jurisdictions coindictees were allowed to testify for or against each other if granted separate trials, other jurisdictions came to the view that accomplices or coindictees were incompetent to testify at least in favor of each other even at separate trials, and in spite of statutes making a defendant competent to testify in his own behalf. It was thought that if two persons charged with the same crime were allowed to testify on behalf of each other, "each would try to swear the other out of the charge."[11] This rule, as well as the other disqualifications for interest, rested on the unstated premises that the right to present witnesses was subordinate to the courts' interest in preventing perjury, and that erroneous decisions were best avoided by preventing the jury from hearing any testimony that might be perjured, even if it were the only testimony available on a crucial issue.[12]

The federal courts followed the common-law restrictions for a time, despite the Sixth Amendment. In United States v. Reid, 53 U.S. 361 (1852), the question was whether one of two defendants jointly indicted for murder on the high seas could call the other as a witness. Although this Court expressly recognized that the Sixth Amendment was designed to abolish some of the harsh rules of the common law, particularly including the refusal to allow the defendant in a serious criminal case to present witnesses in his defense, it held that the rules of evidence in the federal courts were those in force in the various States at the time of the passage of the Judiciary Act of 1789, including the disqualification of defendants indicted together. The holding in United States v. Reid was not satisfactory to later generations, however, and in 1918 this Court expressly overruled it, refusing to be bound by "the dead hand of the common law rule of 1789," and taking note of "the conviction of our time that the truth is more likely to be arrived at by hearing the testimony of all persons of competent understanding who may seem to have knowledge of the facts involved in a case, leaving the credit and weight of such testimony to be determined by the jury or by the court * * *." Rosen v. United States, 245 U.S. 467, 471 (1918).

Although Rosen v. United States rested on nonconstitutional grounds, we believe that its reasoning was required by the Sixth Amendment. * * *

The rule disqualifying an alleged accomplice from testifying on behalf of the defendant cannot even be defended on the ground that it rationally sets apart a group of persons who are particularly likely to commit perjury. The absurdity of the rule is amply demonstrated by the exceptions that have been made to it. For example, the accused accomplice may be called by the prosecution to testify against the defendant. Common sense would suggest that he often has a greater interest in lying in favor of the prosecution rather than against it, especially if he is

11. Benson v. United States, 146 U.S. 325, 335 (1892).

12. "Indeed, the theory of the common law was to admit to the witness stand only those presumably honest, appreciating the sanctity of an oath, unaffected as a party by the result, and free from any of the temptations of interest. The courts were afraid to trust the intelligence of jurors." Benson v. United States, 146 U.S. 325, 336 (1892).

still awaiting his own trial or sentencing. To think that criminals will lie to save their fellows but not to obtain favors from the prosecution for themselves is indeed to clothe the criminal class with more nobility than one might expect to find in the public at large. Moreover, under the Texas statutes, the accused accomplice is no longer disqualified if he is acquitted at his own trial. Presumably, he would then be free to testify on behalf of his comrade, secure in the knowledge that he could incriminate himself as freely as he liked in his testimony, since he could not again be prosecuted for the same offense. The Texas law leaves him free to testify when he has a great incentive to perjury, and bars his testimony in situations when he has a lesser motive to lie.

We hold that the petitioner in this case was denied his right to have compulsory process for obtaining witnesses in his favor because the State arbitrarily denied him the right to put on the stand a witness who was physically and mentally capable of testifying to events that he had personally observed, and whose testimony would have been relevant and material to the defense.[13] The Framers of the Constitution did not intend to commit the futile act of giving to a defendant the right to secure the attendance of witnesses whose testimony he had no right to use. The judgment of conviction must be reversed. It is so ordered.

Reversed.

[The opinion of JUSTICE HARLAN, concurring in the result, is omitted.]

Notes and Questions

1. *Common law.* In the absence of specific legislative abrogation, many of the common law incompetencies have shown surprising hardiness. For example, the common law rule prohibiting the defendant in a criminal prosecution from testifying in his own behalf continued to be enforced in most jurisdictions until legislatively abolished. To the credit of the bench, however, it can be noted that judicial patience with the rule sometimes snapped somewhat earlier, as witness the following anecdote concerning Charles Doe, one-time Chief Justice of the Supreme Court of New Hampshire:

> As a trial judge, Doe broke with the established common law rule that a party was incompetent to testify in his own behalf. This rule provided the basis for numerous eloquent lamentations by counsel for clients clearly guilty that innocence could easily be shown but for the fact that the clients' lips were sealed. Eventually Doe lost his patience with such orations and interrupted one lawyer to tell him he could put his clients on the stand.

13. Nothing in this opinion should be construed as disapproving testimonial privileges, such as the privilege against self-incrimination or the lawyer-client or husband-wife privileges, which are based on entirely different considerations from those underlying the common-law disqualifications for interest. Nor do we deal in this case with nonarbitrary state rules that disqualify as witnesses persons who, because of mental infirmity or infancy, are incapable of observing events or testifying about them.

> The astonished lawyer at first couldn't believe his ears. Finally, after Doe repeated himself, the lawyer sensing that the jig was up, turned to his colleague and whispered, "Well, John, we shall have to put the rascals on * * * "

Geisler, Book Review, Harvard Law Record, Oct. 19, 1967, at 11. The incompetency of the criminally accused has now been abolished in all states, Georgia being the last in 1962.

2. *Right to present a defense. Washington* is the seminal case in establishing a right to present a defense. In Holmes v. South Carolina, 126 S.Ct. 1727, 1232 (2006), the Court held that a defendant's constitutional rights were violated by an evidence rule under which the defendant may not introduce proof of third-party guilt if the prosecution has introduced forensic evidence that, if believed, strongly supports a guilty verdict. See Chapter 2, supra. See also Chambers v. Mississippi, 410 U.S. 284, 313 (1973) (Mississippi's "voucher rule" and hearsay rule prevented the defendant from introducing out-of-court admissions by a third party admitting to the murder that Chambers was charged with committing. The Court concluded that, "[i]n these circumstances, where constitutional rights directly affecting the ascertainment of guilt are implicated, the hearsay rule may not be applied mechanistically to defeat the ends of justice.").

(2) OATH REQUIREMENT: FEDERAL RULE 603

GORDON v. IDAHO

United States Court of Appeals, Ninth Circuit, 1985.
778 F.2d 1397.

PREGERSON, CIRCUIT JUDGE:

* * *

George K. Gordon filed a *pro se* complaint alleging constitutional violations under 42 U.S.C. § 1983 against the State of Idaho, Ada County, several state and county officials, and other individuals. In his federal civil rights complaint, Gordon asserts that the defendants violated his First Amendment rights during the course of state civil proceedings by imprisoning him for twelve days for civil contempt for refusal to take an oath or affirmation.

The defendants in the instant federal civil rights action served Gordon with a Notice of Taking Deposition Duces Tecum and an Amended Notice of Taking Deposition Duces Tecum requiring him to appear at a deposition and testify under oath. Gordon appeared at the deposition but, because of his religious beliefs, refused to swear under oath or make an alternative affirmation. The defendants thereafter moved the district court to compel discovery. The district court granted that motion and specifically ordered Gordon either to swear or affirm before testifying at the rescheduled deposition. At the second deposition, Gordon again refused both to swear under oath or to affirm before testifying. The defendants thereafter filed a motion to dismiss pursuant to Fed.R.Civ.P. 37(b)(2)(C) for failure to comply with the court's order.

Following a hearing on the motion, the district court dismissed Gordon's federal civil rights action with prejudice. Gordon timely filed this appeal. Our jurisdiction is based on 28 U.S.C. § 1291.

We review the district court's imposition of sanctions under Fed. R.Civ.P. 37(b)(2)(C) for abuse of discretion. * * *

* * *

Fed.R.Civ.P. 37(b)(2)(C) authorizes district courts to use the sanction of dismissal if a party fails to obey an order to provide or permit discovery under Rule 37(a). It is inappropriate for a district court to use the dismissal sanction, however, unless non-compliance with its discovery order results from the willfulness, bad faith, or fault of the noncomplying party. * * * Where failure to comply with a discovery order results from the disobedient party's inability to comply or from circumstances beyond its control, the dismissal sanction should not be imposed. * * *

In this case, the district court ordered Gordon to take an oath or to make an alternative affirmation before giving his deposition. The court's order specified the precise language that such an oath or alternative affirmation was to take, despite Gordon's religious objection to taking an oath or using the word "affirmation." The court abused its discretion in insisting that Gordon use either the word "swear" or "affirm" in light of Gordon's sincere religious objections.

The First Amendment's guarantee of the free exercise of religion requires that our procedural rules be interpreted flexibly to protect sincerely-held religious beliefs and practices. In *Callahan v. Woods,* 736 F.2d 1269, 1273 (9th Cir.1984), we set forth factors that courts must consider in determining whether a neutrally based statute violates the First Amendment guarantee of the free exercise of religion. We stated that the "government must shoulder a heavy burden to defend a regulation affecting religious actions." *Id.* at 1272. And we emphasized that it is "the 'least restrictive means' inquiry which is the critical aspect of the free exercise analysis." *Id.* The specific verbal formula offered by the district court was not the least restrictive means of assuring that Gordon testify truthfully at his deposition.

Courts that have considered issues involving oaths and affirmations have interpreted procedural rules flexibly to accommodate religious objections. In *Moore v. United States,* 348 U.S. 966 * * * (1955) (per curiam), for example, the Supreme Court ruled that the trial court erred by refusing to allow a witness to testify because of his refusal to use the word "solemnly" in his affirmation. The Court held that there "is no requirement that the word 'solemnly' be used in the affirmation." *Id.* at 966 * * *. The Fourth Circuit has also noted that "all that the common law requires [of a criminal defendant testifying at trial on his own behalf] is a form of statement which impresses upon the mind and conscience of a witness the necessity for telling the truth." *United States v. Looper,* 419 F.2d 1405, 1407 (4th Cir.1969). *See also Baynes v.*

Ossakow, 336 F.Supp. 386, 388 (E.D.N.Y.1972) (plaintiff's handwritten "affirmation" made expressly under penalty of perjury deemed a sufficient affidavit for purposes of defeating summary judgment motion).

Fed.R.Civ.P. 30(c) requires that deponents be placed under oath, and Fed.R.Civ.P. 43(d) allows the substitution of a "solemn affirmation" in lieu of an oath. We have found no authority insisting on the use of the word "affirm" in such alternative affirmations.

The Federal Rules of Evidence, which contain a provision parallel to Fed.R.Civ.P. 43(d), are also instructive on the need of the courts to protect minority religious views about oaths and affirmations. Fed. R.Evid. 603 states that every witness "shall be required to declare that he will testify truthfully, by oath or affirmation administered in a form calculated to awaken his conscience and impress his mind with his duty to do so." The advisory committee notes to Rule 603 illustrate that an affirmation need take no particular form: "The rule is designed to afford the flexibility required in dealing with religious adults, atheists, conscientious objectors, mental defectives, and children. Affirmation is simply a solemn undertaking to tell the truth; no special verbal formula is required." Fed.R.Evid. 603 advisory committee note.

This reasoning should also apply to affirmations at depositions under the Federal Rules of Civil Procedure. We therefore conclude that any statement indicating that the deponent is impressed with the duty to tell the truth and understands that he or she can be prosecuted for perjury for failure to do so satisfies the requirement for an oath or affirmation under Fed.R.Civ.P. 30(c) and 43(d). Deponents, furthermore, need not raise their hand when they state the words necessary to satisfy Fed.R.Civ.P. 30(c) and 43(d) if to do so impinges on sincerely-held religious beliefs. This flexible approach is consistent with the constitutional obligation to protect the free exercise of religious beliefs by using the least restrictive means to further compelling state interests that impinge on such free exercise. * * *

Gordon has demonstrated that raising his right hand and swearing an oath or making an affirmation violates his sincerely-held religious beliefs. The district court, therefore, should have explored the least restrictive means of assuring that Gordon would testify truthfully at his deposition. At oral argument before our court, Gordon said that before his deposition is taken he is willing to state: "I understand that I must tell the truth. I agree to testify under penalty of perjury. I understand that if I testify falsely I may be subject to criminal prosecution."[14] This statement, we believe, would satisfy Fed.R.Civ.P. 30(c) and 43(d). By failing to explore less restrictive means of assuring truthful deposition testimony, the district court abused its discretion when it dismissed Gordon's federal civil rights action. The court, therefore, erred in dis-

14. Because of his religious beliefs, Gordon also stated at oral argument that he would prefer to say: "I understand that I must accurately state the facts" in place of "I understand that I must tell the truth." That would also suffice, so long as Gordon acknowledges that he understands he is testifying under penalty of perjury.

missing the action with prejudice for failure to comply with the discovery order directing Gordon to take an oath or make an affirmation.

Reversed.

WEIGEL, DISTRICT JUDGE, dissenting:

I respectfully dissent.

The alternative of affirming testimony (as distinguished from swearing to it) has been provided for all witnesses who, for religious or other reasons, object to oath taking. * * *[15]

Appellant seeks to assert claimed rights in the federal courts. He should not be permitted to disregard reasonable Federal Rules of Procedure because of his insistence, however sincere, that his esoteric interpretation of one of those rules must prevail over the interpretation established by the federal courts.[16]

Appellant's demand trivializes the vital purposes of the free exercise clause. Moreover, yielding to appellant's demand in this case tends to invite demands for special formulations in future cases and thus cause needless delay in the administration of justice.

The trial court's dismissal of appellant's action should be affirmed.

Notes and Questions

1. *Common law.* The common law's rigid insistence upon definite religious belief is parodied in Charles Dickens' *Bleak House,* a work more commonly cited as a biting indictment of the delays of the 19th century Courts of Chancery. At an inquest into the death of a personage known as the "law-writer" it transpires that the only person having any knowledge concerning the victim is the boy, Jo, who is summoned with the following results:

> "Here he is, very muddy, very hoarse, very ragged. Now, boy!—But stop a minute. Caution. This boy must be put through a few preliminary paces.

15. The majority's reliance on *Callahan v. Woods,* 736 F.2d 1269 (9th Cir.1984) is, it seems to me, not well taken. The objection on religious grounds in that case was to the requirement of obtaining a Social Security number in order to receive public assistance benefits. No alternative was provided to that requirement.

16. Neither of the statements approved by the majority satisfies an important purpose of requiring oath or affirmation, i.e., to insure that the witness makes a conscious commitment to tell the truth. (*See Looper, supra;* * * * ; *A Reconsideration of the Sworn Testimony Requirement: Securing Truth in the Twentieth Century,* 75 Mich. L.R. 1681 (1977).) To say that "I understand that I must tell the truth" or that "I understand I must accurately state the facts" is not a *promise* to tell the truth nor accurately to state the facts. Appellant was aware of this as shown by his statements at oral argument that

> " * * * Now the scripture says 'Let God be true though every man be a liar.' I'm simply saying that since we've all lied in the past and we've lied once or twice today and we're going to lie in the future, why kid ourselves by saying we tell the truth when in fact we do not. It's my position I would be guilty of perjury the moment I said 'Do you swear to tell the truth, the whole truth and nothing but the truth so help you God' and I say 'I do' I'm committing a lie."

"Name, Jo. Nothing else he knows on * * * Knows a broom's a broom, and knows it's wicked to tell a lie. Don't recollect who told him about the broom, or about the lie, but knows both. Can't exactly say what'll be done to him after he's dead if he tells a lie to the gentlemen here, but believes it'll be something very bad to punish him, and serve him right—and so he'll tell the truth.

" 'This won't do, gentlemen!,' says the Coroner, with a melancholy shake of his head.

" 'Don't you think you can receive his evidence, sir?' asks an attentive Juryman.

" 'Out of the question,' says the Coroner. 'You have heard the boy. "Can't exactly say" won't do, you know. We can't take *that,* in a Court of Justice, gentlemen. It's terrible depravity. Put the boy aside!' "

2. *Rule 603.* Despite flexibility in the form of the oath, "testimony taken from a witness who has not given an oath or affirmation to testify truthfully is inadmissible." United States v. Hawkins, 76 F.3d 545, 551 (4th Cir.1996). See also United States v. Odom, 736 F.2d 104, 116 (4th Cir.1984) (holding that right to object on appeal to the failure to swear witnesses is waived when the objecting party voluntarily and knowingly refused to object at trial).

(3) CHILD WITNESSES

EVANS v. STATE

Supreme Court of Nevada, 2001.
28 P.3d 498.

BECKER, J.:

In 1994 appellant Vernell Ray Evans was convicted of burglary and four counts of first-degree murder and sentenced to death. * * *

Around 1:00 a.m. on May 1, 1992, officers of the Las Vegas Metropolitan Police Department responded to a report of a shooting at a Wardelle Street apartment. They discovered four people shot to death: Jermaine Woods, Steven Walker, Lisa Boyer, and Samantha Scotti. Scotti and her eighteen-month-old son, Francois, were residents of the apartment.

Four-year-old Adriana Ventura (Adriana) and her mother and infant sister also resided at the apartment. Adriana witnessed the murders and testified at trial to the following. Two men entered the apartment carrying guns. Adriana referred to the men as "Scary Eyes" and "Little Ray." The intruders first shot the two men already in the apartment, Woods and Walker. They then shot Scotti, who was in the bathroom, and Boyer, who was in the bedroom. Adriana could not remember how many times the two women were shot or which one of the intruders fired the shots, and she did not see how the men left the apartment. Sometime thereafter, Adriana's mother, Alicia Ventura (Ventura), called the apartment. Adriana answered and told her mother that Scotti was dead. After that, Adriana went to the apartment next door and told the neighbor that everyone had been killed.

Adriana testified that she did not know "Scary Eyes," but she had seen "Little Ray" before at the apartment. Adriana was unable to identify Evans as "Little Ray" either in court or in a lineup at the jail. However, [Alicia] Ventura testified that Adriana usually referred to Evans as either "Little Ray" or "Uncle Ray."

* * *

Adriana Ventura was four at the time of the murders and six when she testified. At trial, the prosecutor first questioned Adriana about her family, the difference between the truth and lies, and the need to tell the truth. Adriana then testified regarding the murders.

According to Evans, before her trial testimony Adriana testified at a preliminary hearing, a grand jury hearing, and a federal sentencing hearing and was questioned repeatedly about the crimes by her mother, neighbors, a detective, a child psychologist, and the media. Her grandfather allowed reporters to tape her telling her story on several occasions. Evans argues that there was great potential that the child's testimony was contaminated, particularly by her mother.

Evans also asserts that Adriana's testimony shows that she was not competent to testify. For example, she was unable to remember whether she lived in a house or an apartment at the time of the murders or the name of the other child who was present. Evans also claims that Adriana could not remember whether the murderers left through the door or jumped out of a window, but this claim is mistaken. Adriana actually said they could have done either, but she did not know because she did not watch them leave. Our review of Adriana's trial testimony shows that she readily admitted whenever she did not know or could not remember something and did not appear to make up information just to answer a question. For example, she had apparently told defense counsel before trial that each killer had shot a specific victim. She acknowledged this on cross-examination but maintained, as she had on direct examination, that she actually did not know who shot whom. The material facts which Adriana did remember and provide, such as where each victim was when shot, were consistent with the evidence at the crime scene.

A child is competent to testify if he or she is able to receive just impressions and relate them truthfully. Courts must evaluate a child's competency on a case-by-case basis, but relevant considerations include:

> (1) the child's ability to receive and communicate information; (2) the spontaneity of the child's statements; (3) indications of "coaching" and "rehearsing;" (4) the child's ability to remember; (5) the child's ability to distinguish between truth and falsehood; and (6) the likelihood that the child will give inherently improbable or incoherent testimony.[17]

17. [Felix v. State, 849 P.2d 220, 235 (Nev.1993). Ed.]

This court will not disturb a finding of competency absent a clear abuse of discretion. A child's testimony supports a finding of competency if it is clear, relevant, and coherent. Inconsistencies in the testimony go to the weight of the evidence.

We conclude that Adriana's testimony indicates that she was competent. Her basic account of the crimes remained coherent and consistent, even under cross-examination. Her testimony reflected none of the serious problems—inability to differentiate between fact and fantasy, confusion between truth and falsehood, inherently improbable testimony, suggestions of coaching, inability to recall recent events—which in other cases have prompted this court to overturn the district court's finding of competency.

Evans also contends that the district court violated this court's directive requiring trial courts to examine a child under ten years of age before permitting her to testify. He cites this court's decision in *Felix v. State*, which stands for this rule. However, at least part of the foundation for the rule no longer exists. *Felix* followed a line of authority that relied on former NRS 48.030(2), which provided that children under ten years of age could not be witnesses if they appeared "incapable of receiving just impressions of the facts * * * or of relating them truly." Nevada's statutes no longer treat the competency of witnesses younger than ten as a special case. Even assuming the rule still retains its full force, the district court's failure to examine Adriana before she testified was prejudicial only if she indeed lacked competency. We conclude that her testimony shows she was competent.

Nevertheless, Evans's allegations regarding possible contamination of Adriana's testimony arguably warranted an evidentiary hearing. Roughly two years had passed since the crimes occurred, and she had apparently talked with a number of people about the murders. On the other hand, the mere fact that Adriana spoke with people about her experience does not establish that her testimony was improperly influenced. Evans has not pointed to any particular behavior by Adriana or to inconsistencies in her statements—or to any words or conduct by anyone else—that indicate her testimony was deliberately or inadvertently tainted. Evans stresses that a detective suspected that Adriana's mother, Ventura, knew that Scotti was going to be murdered, but he does not explain why this suggests that Ventura manipulated her daughter's account of the crimes. We conclude that the district court could have reasonably found that Evans's allegations on this issue were insufficient to warrant an evidentiary hearing.

Adriana was competent to testify * * *.

Notes and Questions

1. *Rule 601.* Most states provide that a witness is incompetent to testify if she does not have the intelligence to make it worthwhile to hear her or if she does not feel a duty to tell the truth. See 1 McCormick, Evidence

§ 62 (6th ed. 2006). In contrast, Federal Rule 601 provides that every person is "competent to be a witness," with exceptions for the application of other rules and instances in which state law governs. The Advisory Committee Note emphasizes that "no mental or moral qualifications for testifying as a witness are specified." Yet, several federal cases decided since the enactment of the Rules have suggested that a witness may be disqualified if he "does not have the capacity to recall, or that he does not understand the duty to testify truthfully." United States v. Lightly, 677 F.2d 1027 (4th Cir.1982). The matter is left in the discretion of the trial judge. What basis is there for such a statement? Does Rule 403 come into play?

2. *Presumption of competency.* As the principal case indicates, in some jurisdictions children of ten years of age or older are made "presumptively competent" by statute. Under such statutes children under the statutory age may still be found competent by the trial court in its discretion, but generally a voir dire examination of the child will be conducted. See Ohio R. Evid. 601 ("Every person is competent to be a witness except: (A) * * * children under ten years of age, who appear incapable of receiving just impressions of the facts and transactions respecting which they are examined, or of relating them truly."); State v. Clark, 644 N.E.2d 331, 334 (Ohio 1994) (A child witness under ten years of age "is not presumed incompetent, but rather, the proponent of the witness's testimony bears the burden of proving that the witness" is competent.); State v. Frazier, 574 N.E.2d 483, 487 (Ohio 1991) (During the voir dire examination, the "trial judge has the opportunity to observe the child's appearance, his or her manner of responding to the questions, general demeanor and any indicia of ability to relate the facts accurately and truthfully. Thus, the responsibility of the trial judge is to determine through questioning whether the child of tender years is capable of receiving just impressions of facts and events and to accurately relate them."). See also State v. Woods, 114 P.3d 1174, 1178 (Wash.2005) (in a molestation case against a father, children ages 3 and 5 at time of abuse were competent because they "were able to provide details of contemporaneous events and circumstances which demonstrated that they had the mental capacity to receive accurate impressions"); 1 McCormick, Evidence § 62, at 305 (6th ed. 2006) ("Children as young as three years old have been ruled competent as witnesses.").

3. *Child abuse cases.* More recent statutes have focused on child sexual abuse cases. See Utah Code Ann. § 76–5–410 ("A child victim of sexual abuse under the age of ten is a competent witness and shall be allowed to testify without prior qualification in any judicial proceeding. The trier of fact shall determine the weight and credibility of the testimony."). See also State v. Webb, 779 P.2d 1108, 1113–14 (Utah 1989) (holding that trial court erred by assuming that an 18–month old child was unavailable due to immaturity without interviewing the child or taking expert testimony regarding the capability of the child, then two years old, to testify in court).

4. *Oath requirement.* Many courts have undertaken to evaluate the competency of witnesses, particularly children of tender years, by whether the witness "understands the nature and obligation of an oath." Does this constitute a viable standard? For an excellent judicial discussion, see State v. Walton, 179 A.2d 78 (N.J.Super.Ct.Law Div.1962) (holding competent a ten-year-old girl who stated she did not believe in God). See also Del.Code Ann.

tit. 10, § 4302 ("No child under the age of 10 years may be excluded from giving testimony for the sole reason that such child does not understand the obligation of an oath. Such child's age and degree of understanding of the obligation of an oath may be considered by the trier of fact in judging the child's credibility."); N.Y.Crim.Proc.Law § 60.20(2) ("A witness less than nine years old may not testify under oath unless the court is satisfied that he or she understands the nature of an oath. If in either case the court is not so satisfied, the witness may nevertheless be permitted to give unsworn evidence if the court is satisfied that the witness possesses sufficient intelligence and capacity to justify the reception thereof. A witness understands the nature of an oath if he or she appreciates the difference between truth and falsehood, the necessity for telling the truth, and the fact that a witness who testifies falsely may be punished."); Id. § 60.20(3) ("A defendant may not be convicted of an offense solely upon unsworn evidence given pursuant to subdivision two.").

5. *Interviewing techniques.* "An emerging consensus in the case law relies upon scientific studies to conclude that suggestibility and improper interviewing techniques are serious issues with child witnesses, and that expert testimony on these subjects is admissible * * *." Washington v. Schriver, 255 F.3d 45, 57 (2d Cir.2001). Other courts use "taint" hearings to determine competency. *See* Commonwealth v. Delbridge, 859 A.2d 1254, 1256 (Pa.2004) ("[A]n allegation of taint raises a legitimate question of witness competency in cases involving complaints of sexual abuse by young children. Because taint implicates the ability of a child to distinguish real memories of an event from falsely implanted suggestions, we found that taint could infect the mental capacity of the child witness to independently recall the event and truthfully testify."). For a discussion of the problems raised by offers of the testimony of children, see Ceci & Friedman, The Suggestibility of Children: Scientific Research and Legal Implications, 86 Cornell L.Rev. 33 (2000).

6. *Parental objection.* What if the parents object to having the child testify? See State v. Iban C., 881 A.2d 1005, 1031 (Conn.2005) (in a prosecution of an uncle for sexual abuse, trial court appointed a guardian ad litem for a 5 year old child when parents resisted having child testify; court held parents were entitled to a hearing, notice, and representation by counsel at the appointment hearing).

UNITED STATES v. SNYDER

United States Court of Appeals, Seventh Circuit, 1999.
189 F.3d 640.

BAUER, CIRCUIT JUDGE.

James W. Snyder was convicted of producing, receiving, and distributing child pornography, as well as possessing child pornography with intent to sell. On appeal, he argues that: (1) the district court should have granted his request for a psychological examination to determine the competency of the victim * * *. [The victim, referred to as Michael Doe, was an eleven-year-old boy who had engaged in sex with Snyder and another man. Pornographic images of Doe were projected over the Internet.]

A. Competency Examination

Children are presumed to be competent to testify. 18 U.S.C. § 3509(c)(2). Accordingly, a "competency examination regarding a child may be conducted only if the court determines, on the record, that compelling reasons exist," 18 U.S.C. § 3509(c)(4), and "only upon written motion and offer of proof of incompetency by a party," 18 U.S.C. § 3509(c)(3). Furthermore, "[p]sychological and psychiatric examinations to assess the competency of a child witness shall not be ordered without a showing of compelling need." 18 U.S.C. § 3509(c)(9). As long as a witness has the capacity to testify truthfully, it is best left to the fact-finder to determine whether he in fact did so. *See* Fed.R.Evid. 601, Advisory Notes (noting that unless witness is wholly without capacity, the question is one of credibility and weight); United States v. Zizzo, 120 F.3d 1338, 1347 (7th Cir.1997) ("Rather than rendering him incompetent to testify without some sort of psychiatric examination, [a witness'] penchant for perjury simply provide[s] the defense with an ample opportunity to undermine [the witness'] credibility on cross-examination."). The district court held that Snyder had shown neither a compelling reason to hold a hearing, nor a compelling need to order a psychological evaluation. We review for abuse of discretion. *See id.* at 1347 ("Whether a witness should be forced to endure a psychiatric examination before being allowed to testify is a matter best left to the discretion of the district court.").

Snyder's motion for a psychological examination stated simply that Doe's prior statements demonstrated that he could not differentiate between truth and fantasy, and that "[u]pon information and belief," Doe was being treated with anti-depressants that "can have extreme side effects on individuals which could make the witness incompetent to testify at trial." These assertions, even if true, did not establish a compelling reason or need for a competency examination. First, the fact that some of Doe's statements were unfounded does not show that he was unable to differentiate between reality and fantasy. Second, Snyder stated only that Doe was taking medication that could render him incompetent to testify; he did not assert that the medication had in fact made Doe incompetent. Finally, the reliability of Doe's testimony was predictably (and effectively) called into question on cross examination, when Snyder's attorney elicited detailed descriptions of imaginary events from Doe. Under these circumstances, the district court was safely within its discretion when it refused to order a psychological evaluation of Doe. Indeed, we have found no abuse of discretion in situations where the competency of a witness was much more questionable. *See e.g. United States v. Gutman*, 725 F.2d 417, 420 (7th Cir.1984) (witness had "bouts of serious mental illness in the year before the trial"). * * *

For the foregoing reasons, we AFFIRM Snyder's conviction and sentence.

UNITED STATES v. ROUSE

United States Court of Appeals, Eighth Circuit, 1997.
111 F.3d 561.

LOKEN, CIRCUIT JUDGE.

[The defendants, the victims' uncles, appealed their convictions for sexual abuse of young children.] * * *

B. VICTIM TESTIMONY BY CLOSED CIRCUIT TELEVISION.

Prior to trial, the government filed a motion to permit all child witnesses to testify by closed circuit television. At a hearing on this motion, therapist Kelson testified that the victims were afraid of defendants—"They still believe if they walked in the courtroom today that their uncles would attack them." The district court denied the motion without prejudice, concluding there had not been a sufficient showing that the children could not testify due to fear of the defendants.

At trial, when three of the victims were called as witnesses and appeared to be emotionally unable to testify in open court, the district court questioned each child in chambers, in the presence of defense counsel, one prosecutor, the child's guardian ad litem, and a court reporter. *See* 18 U.S.C. § 3509(b)(1)(C). Five-year-old J.R. was unable to speak when called to testify and stated in chambers that she was afraid to speak in front of her uncles. Considering this statement along with Kelson's pretrial testimony, the court found that defendants' presence in the courtroom would "more than anything else prevent her from testifying." The court made similar findings after questioning six-year-old R. R., who was found sobbing outside the courtroom and affirmed in chambers that she was crying out of fear of her uncles; and nine-year-old T. R., who became so fearful before testifying that "the guardian ad litem would have had to physically pull her into the courtroom." Defendants argue that the district court erred in permitting these three victims to testify by closed circuit television. (The other two child witnesses were able to testify in open court.)

The Sixth Amendment's Confrontation Clause "guarantees the defendant a face-to-face meeting with the witnesses appearing before the trier of fact." *Coy v. Iowa,* 487 U.S. 1012, 1016 * * * (1988). However, this right is not absolute and must accommodate the State's "compelling" interest in "the protection of minor victims of sex crimes from further trauma and embarrassment." *Globe Newspaper Co. v. Superior Court,* 457 U.S. 596, 607 * * * (1982). Accordingly, "where necessary to protect a child witness from trauma that would be caused by testifying in the physical presence of the defendant, at least where such trauma would impair the child's ability to communicate, the Confrontation Clause does not prohibit use of a procedure" which preserves "the essence of effective confrontation"—testimony by a competent witness, under oath, subject to contemporaneous cross-examination, and observable by the judge, jury, and defendant. *Maryland v. Craig,* 497 U.S. 836, 851, 857 * * * (1990). Testimony by closed circuit television is a procedure now authorized by statute. *See* 18 U.S.C. § 3509(b).

Before invoking such a procedure, the district court must find that the child "would be traumatized, not by the courtroom generally, but by the presence of the defendant." *Hoversten v. Iowa,* 998 F.2d 614, 616 (8th Cir.1993), quoting *Craig,* 497 U.S. at 856 * * *. *See* 18 U.S.C. § 3509(b)(1)(B)(i) (child may testify by closed circuit television "if the court finds that the child is unable to testify in open court in the presence of the defendant * * * because of fear"). In this case, the district court made specific "because of fear" findings for three victims. Our review of the children's responses to the court's questions in chambers and the prior testimony by therapist Kelson persuades us these findings are not clearly erroneous. * * *

Defendants argue that the district court's findings are inadequate because they were not based upon the expert testimony required by § 3509(b)(1)(B)(ii). However, the statute does not require an expert to support a "because of fear" finding. That finding may be based upon the court's own observation and questioning of a severely frightened child. "[O]nce the trial has begun, the court may judge with its own eyes whether the child is suffering the trauma required to grant the requested order." H.R.Rep. No. 101–681(I), 101st Cong., 2nd Sess. (1990), *reprinted in* 1990 U.S.C.C.A.N. 6472, 6574. We also reject defendants' contention that the closed circuit television system infringed their Sixth Amendment rights because defense counsel could not see the jury while cross examining the sequestered witnesses.[18] * * *

The judgments of the district court are affirmed.

Notes and Questions

1. *Fair trial.* The protective procedures in *Rouse* have the potential to prejudice the right of the defendant to have his guilt fairly assessed by suggesting that even in court he threatens to do the victim harm. Are the protective mechanism used in the child sexual abuse cases based on the assumption of the defendant's guilt? Do they shift the balance of advantage by altering evidentiary rules that normally would control the admission of probative evidence and govern attacks on the credibility of witnesses? Are they justified by important social policies that overcome legitimate objections to altering the balance? Cf. Coy v. Iowa, 487 U.S. 1012 (1988) (in child sex abuse case, screen blocking complaining witnesses' view of defendant during their testimony violated Sixth Amendment confrontation rights in absence of individualized showing that screen necessary to protect them from trauma; claim not reached that screen violated due process by creating appearance of defendant's guilt).

18. The system included five monitors in the courtroom for the judge, jury, defense expert, and defendants to view the child testifying in chambers; a monitor for the child witness to view defendants as she testified; and separate communication lines permitting each defendant to confer with his attorney.

2. *Related issues*. Fear of testifying in front of a jury or in a large room is not sufficient to permit closed-circuit television. See United States v. Bordeaux, 400 F.3d 548, 555 (8th Cir.2005) ("The district court's findings did not satisfy the *Craig* standard. The district court found that AWH's fear of the defendant was only one reason why she could not testify in open court; it did not find that AWH's fear of the defendant was the dominant reason."). See also United States v. Etimani, 328 F.3d 493, 501 (9th Cir.2003) ("§ 3509 does not require that the television monitor in the witness room be located directly in the child's field of vision while she testifies. Rather, it is sufficient (1) if the presence of the monitor has been called to the child's attention, (2) if the child can see the monitor, if she wishes, with little effort from where she is seated while testifying, and (3) if the jury is able to observe whether or not the child looks at the monitor during her testimony.").

3. *Videotape*. In United States v. Miguel, 111 F.3d 666 (9th Cir.1997), the victim was allowed to give testimony via a videotaped deposition, while the defendant watched from another room via closed circuit television. The judge did not allow the defendant to communicate by telephone with counsel during the deposition, but only during breaks. After viewing the complete tape, defense counsel would have the opportunity to make additional objections before trial. However, the federal statute provides that the defendant be allowed "contemporaneous communication" with his counsel "during the deposition." The court found that, under the statute, a defendant must be allowed to communicate instantly during the deposition. Although counsel could request a recess to communicate with the defendant, the right to communicate belongs to the defendant. It may distress the victim if the defense counsel talks to the defendant during the deposition; however, "section 3509 represents a careful compromise of highly important rights." Id. at 670. While the defendant loses the right to face to face confrontation, he retains "some of the protections inherent in the confrontation of witnesses." Id. In this case, however, the error was harmless.

4. *Methods of testimony*. See State v. Johnson, 528 N.E.2d 567 (Ohio Ct.App.1986) (court permitted child to testify while sitting on a relative's lap). See generally ABA Criminal Justice Section's Task Force, Child Witnesses in Criminal Cases (2002).

5. *Hearsay exceptions*. Child abuse cases have caused several jurisdictions to adopt new exceptions to the hearsay rule permitting out-of-court statements of children to be introduced. See Mosteller, Remaking Confrontation Clause and Hearsay Doctrine Under the Challenge of Child Sexual Abuse Prosecutions, 1993 U.Ill.L.Rev. 691. For further discussion, see Chapter 13, Section C, infra.

(4) ABILITY TO COMMUNICATE

BYNDOM v. STATE

Supreme Court of Arkansas, 2001.
39 S.W.3d 781.

HANNAH, JUSTICE.

Appellant Gregory Charles Byndom appeals his rape conviction, arguing that the trial court erred in finding the victim, Shaneani Mason, competent to testify at trial. * * *

Mason is a twenty-five-year-old woman with cerebral palsy and mental retardation caused by suffering strokes as a child due to Sickle Cell disease. Mason lived with Byndom's girlfriend, Rita Bealer, who was paid a stipend by the State to help care for Mason because Mason cannot care for herself, stand or move without assistance, or speak without the assistance of a Dynavox computer, an augmented speaking device.

* * *

* * * [T]he focus in such a case is on the witness's ability to communicate thoughts, impressions, feelings, and beliefs, and here Mason was able to do all of that by virtue of her gestures, facial expressions, ability to sign "yes" and "no," and by the limited use of the yes/no function key on her Dynavox computer. To hold otherwise would render a segment of society incompetent merely because they cannot communicate as effectively and in the same manner as those who can speak through oral, written, or signed language. Furthermore, * * * the trial court actually allowed Mason to return to using the Dynavox computer during cross-examination as long as the icons did not appear on the projection screen set up behind her for the jury to see. This ruling properly recognized that the Dynavox computer did not constitute hearsay evidence where the user, Mason, could directly answer a question with an answer only she could choose from thousands of words and phrases programmed into the computer. As such, the defendant's assertion that Mason could not communicate effectively suffers a devastating blow when it is apparent that the defense had the opportunity to elicit more detailed responses from Mason through the Dynavox computer. However, the defense continued to mostly ask yes/no questions of Mason even after the trial court allowed Mason to utilize her computer to render more thorough responses.

Notes and Questions

1. *Other cases.* What are the problems associated with this method of communication? See United States v. Bell, 367 F.3d 452, 463 (5th Cir.2004) ("George Cotton is deaf and mute. He is able to effectively communicate through a form of sign language, a system of grunts and gestures, that is understood by family and friends familiar with him. The district court held a competency hearing before Bell's trial to determine whether George would be able to testify and who should serve as interpreter when George testified."); People v. White, 238 N.E.2d 389 (Ill.1968) (a partially paralyzed and bed-ridden mute person could communicate by raising the right knee to answer affirmatively and remaining still to answer negatively; reversed); People v. Spencer, 457 N.E.2d 473 (Ill.App.Ct.1983) (thirty-one-year-old deaf-mute woman rape victim who was mildly to moderately retarded could communicate through gestures and references to anatomically-correct dolls,

picture symbols, numbers, colors, and the alphabet; defense objection on confrontation grounds rejected).

2. *Interpreters.* If the witness does not speak English, the obvious expedient is to appoint an interpreter. The competency of interpreters is covered by Federal Rule 604. See also Court Interpreters Act, 28 U.S.C 1827. Federal Civil Rule 43 and Criminal Rule 28 authorize appointment and compensation for interpreters.

3. *Accuracy of translation.* Ensuring that the interpreter provides a literal translation of testimony and does not embellish upon the testimony is a significant problem. E.g., United States v. Gomez, 908 F.2d 809, 811 (11th Cir.1990) (improper embellishment); Valladares v. United States, 871 F.2d 1564, 1566 (11th Cir.1989) (perfect translation not required).

4. *Right to an interpreter.* What about the defendant? See United States v. Carrion, 488 F.2d 12, 14 (1st Cir.1973) ("Clearly, the right to confront witnesses would be meaningless if the accused could not understand their testimony, and the effectiveness of cross-examination would be severely hampered. * * * If the defendant takes the stand in his own behalf, but has an imperfect command of English, there exists the additional danger that he will either misunderstand crucial questions or that the jury will misconstrue crucial responses. The right to an interpreter rests most fundamentally, however, on the notion that no defendant should face the Kafkaesque spectre of an incomprehensible ritual which may terminate in punishment."). Accord United States ex rel. Negron v. New York, 434 F.2d 386, 389 (2d Cir.1970).

5. *Transcripts of tape recordings.* See United States v. Rrapi, 175 F.3d 742, 746 (9th Cir.1999) ("Generally, the Court reviews the following steps taken to ensure the accuracy of the transcripts: (1) whether the court reviewed the transcripts for accuracy, (2) whether defense counsel was allowed to highlight alleged inaccuracies and to introduce alternative versions, (3) whether the jury was instructed that the tape, rather than the transcript, was evidence, and (4) whether the jury was allowed to compare the transcript to the tape and hear counsel's arguments as to the meaning of the conversations. The third factor (instruction that the tape, not the transcript, is evidence) does not apply with foreign language tapes."); United States v. Fuentes–Montijo, 68 F.3d 352, 355 (9th Cir.1995) ("when faced with a taped conversation in a language other than English and a disputed English translation transcript, the usual admonition that the tape is the evidence and the transcript only a guide is not only nonsensical, it has the potential for harm").

(5) MENTAL COMPETENCY

UNITED STATES v. HEINLEIN

United States Court of Appeals, District of Columbia Circuit, 1973.
490 F.2d 725.

McGowan, Circuit Judge: [Defendants were convicted of felony-murder and assault with intent to rape while armed.] * * *

All of the participants in the events giving rise to these appeals appear to have lived in the nether world of chronic alcoholism, and the events themselves are of a singularly squalid nature. Because of this, as well as the difficulties of reconstructing—through the imperfect instrument of a chronic alcoholic—what happened in this instance in that confused and cloudy environment, this was obviously a difficult and distasteful case to try, both for judge and jury. * * *

I

Appellants chose not to testify at trial. Accordingly, the only purportedly eyewitness version of the events in question was given by Mr. James Harding, a chronic alcoholic. On the morning of April 13, 1968, so Harding testified, he and Marie McQueen, the murder victim, were released after overnight incarceration for drunkenness. After buying some wine, they met Bernard Heinlein and the Walker brothers, David and Frank, on the street. The five of them then went to an apartment occupied by the Walkers to drink the wine. Heinlein told McQueen that he wanted to have sexual relations with her, and the Walkers both voiced support of this proposal. When McQueen refused, the three appellants seized her, held her down, and began to remove her clothing. During the struggle, McQueen slapped Heinlein in the face. His response was to take a knife from his pocket and stab her, inflicting what proved to be a fatal wound. McQueen was then carried down into the basement by her assailants, and Harding last saw her lying on the floor there, apparently just barely alive.

Harding testified that he was a friend of the deceased, but that paralysis of the left side of his body prevented him from helping her during the brutal assault. Harding was arrested for drunkenness again a few hours later but made no report of the incident. Appellants were also arrested for drunkenness later that day. The body of the deceased was discovered two days later by a neighbor. One day after that, Harding made a statement to the police which implicated appellants.

[The court here reviewed the circumstantial evidence presented by the prosecution which tended to corroborate the testimony of the witness Harding.]

The defense put forward at trial was an effort to demolish Harding's credibility. This was based upon asserted inconsistencies between his testimony at trial and prior statements made by him to the police, at the preliminary hearing, and to the grand jury. A witness was produced in the person of Dr. Prochazka, a psychiatric resident at St. Elizabeths, who testified that she examined Harding in October of 1967 and made a diagnosis then of chronic brain syndrome associated with alcoholic intoxication, with moderate to severe memory defect. The District Court also permitted Harding's credibility to be impeached by prior convictions consisting of 42 prior drunk convictions, a 1950 conviction of assault with intent to commit rape, two 1953 convictions for forgery and uttering, and a 1968 larceny conviction.

II

A principal claim of error advanced on behalf of all the appellants is that Harding was not a competent witness. In particular, it is urged that the District Court erred in failing to grant appellants' motion that Harding be subjected to a psychiatric examination with respect to his competency.

The trial began on April 28, 1969. On the second day Harding completed his direct examination, and was cross-examined at great length by counsel for Heinlein. At the beginning of the third day of trial, appellants' motion was made. In support of it, it was argued that Harding had displayed confusion in his testimony on the previous day. Counsel also reported that, at the end of the preceding day, St. Elizabeths' records had been subpoenaed which indicated a medical basis for Harding's allegedly inadequate performance on the stand. It was also said that an expert examination would take into account the fact that Harding had been drinking at the time of the events described by him. The court's ruling was couched in these terms:

> "THE COURT: As far as this witness is concerned, he has shown confusion and he has shown different statements at different times, primarily about matters that really don't go to the crux of this case, and that is as to where he went and what order immediately after this thing went on.
>
> He may have been inexpertly questioned. We have seen from the stand that he has to be questioned very carefully; otherwise he gets the wrong impression of the question and gives an answer that might be considered at variance with another answer he has given.
>
> But his testimony is primarily important, as I see it, to put these people at the scene of this crime, and in this he has never varied, never varied.
>
> The jury is perfectly competent to weigh the testimony of this witness.
>
> As a matter of fact, that is one of the two chief functions of a jury. One is to weigh the testimony of witnesses, the other of course is to decide the facts.
>
> And the jury is perfectly competent to do this.
>
> I have observed nothing in this man to indicate other than that he is an alcoholic, that his memory is clouded as to certain events, it doesn't appear to have been clouded as to others as far as putting these people at the scene of the crime. That he has never been shaken in by any statement that I know of.
>
> I don't believe that the interest of justice demands such a psychiatric examination, which I don't believe would be the slightest help.
>
> I think the jury in this matter is altogether competent to judge the effect of this man's testimony, and I will deny your motion."

It is apparent from the foregoing that the trial court did not regard Harding as a particularly impressive witness, as indeed he was not—a fact upon which appellants presumably relied when they decided not to take the witness stand, and which was argued vigorously by their counsel to the jury as a reason for rejecting his story *in toto*. In this jurisdiction as elsewhere, however, the "competency of the witness to testify before the jury is a threshold question of law committed to the trial court's discretion;" and the decision as to whether a court should order a psychiatric examination in order to aid it in resolving the issue of competency "must be entrusted to the sound discretion of the trial judge in light of the particular facts (footnote omitted)." United States v. Benn & Hunt, 155 U.S.App.D.C. 180, 476 F.2d 1127 (1973).

In United States v. Butler, 156 U.S.App.D.C. 356, 481 F.2d 531 (1973), this court has quite recently said:

> The question of when a trial judge should order a physical and psychiatric examination of a prosecution witness was directly considered by this court in United States v. Benn & Hunt. * * * We there explained that such an examination "may seriously impinge on a witness' right to privacy; * * * the examination itself could serve as a tool of harassment;" and the likelihood of an examination could deter witnesses from coming forward. * * * The resultant presumption against ordering an examination must be overcome by a showing of need.

In both *Benn* and *Butler,* this court, speaking through Chief Judge Bazelon, sustained the action of the District Court in failing to order a psychiatric examination of a key Government witness.

* * *

The scope of our review of that ruling is limited—and necessarily so—by the fact that it was the trial court, in contrast to ourselves, which had the opportunity to observe Harding at first hand. * * *

The arguments urged upon the trial court in support of the motion stressed (1) what was said to be the highly confusing character of Harding's testimony as given, and (2) the suggestion in the St. Elizabeths' records that Harding had a clinical history which rendered him wholly unreliable. As to the former, the trial court, as we have seen, readily recognized that there had been elements of confusion in Harding's story. A prominent one of these had been his apparent inability to differentiate between the Walker brothers by name, which resulted in the court's fashioning the expedient of having Harding refer to one brother as "the tall one" and the other as the "heavy-set one;" and it is by no means certain from the transcript that even this device was uniformly successful. * * *

Cross-examination on the first day of trial had also exposed discrepancies and gaps in Harding's statements to the police, his appearance at the preliminary hearing, and his testimony before the grand jury. But the court, noting that Harding's various statements, despite some differences, related essentially to the same event and described all three appellants as active participants, concluded that these differences were not such as to shake significantly Harding's all-important account of what happened to Marie McQueen. Although subjected to severe defense challenge, as the only prosecution witness purporting to have direct knowledge of what went on in the Walkers' apartment, Harding's story in that regard held together in a way not indicative of incompetency.

The second aspect of the defense argument was that Harding was essentially lacking in capacity to recall past events accurately, and that any effort on his part at historical reconstruction could only be pure confabulation. At the time the motion was argued, the defense had two things to go on in this regard. One was the St. Elizabeths' records.[19] The other was the fact that Harding's account of his movements during the several hours immediately succeeding the alleged slaying was plainly untrue, as the official records showed that he had again been arrested and detained for intoxication during the afternoon of the day in question. It was argued that, if this latter account was a fabrication, then so must be the tale of the Walkers' apartment.

The difference, however, is that Harding's friend, McQueen, was subsequently found dead under circumstances corroborative of Harding's version of the events culminating in her death. This hard fact stands against any claim that, because Harding may, although with no apparent incentive to do so, have lied about where he was and what he did later in the fatal day, he also lied about the events of the morning. In any event, it leaves us unable to say that the trial court abused its discretion in refusing to treat Harding as a witness of actual or potential incompetency.

* * *

Notes and Questions

1. *Another example.* In United States v. Hicks, 389 F.2d 49 (3d Cir. 1968), the defendant asserted as error the admission against him of the

19. Counsel pressed upon the trial court certain entries made in 1961 and 1967. In the former year a clinical report characterized Harding in these terms:

> "The patient drank excessively, had domestic problems and had a feeling that when he walked down the streets people were looking at him and wanted to harm him."

In 1967 one clinical report said of Harding that he "was only fairly well oriented." Two others referred to memory difficulties; and the eventual diagnosis was couched in these terms:

> "Acute brain syndrome associated with alcohol intoxication and chronic brain syndrome associated with alcohol intoxication without qualifying phase."

One of the examining physicians in 1967, Dr. Martha Prochazka, testified later in the trial for the defense. Her testimony was generally to the effect that Harding's mental problems were caused by excessive use of alcohol. She suggested that Harding might be suffering from something known as Korsakoff's Psychosis—a condition in which a person conceals his inability to remember by fabrication. She could not make a positive diagnosis of such a condition without further neurological examination. The motion for psychiatric examination was not, however, renewed during or at the close of the defense testimony.

Hicks

testimony of a witness alleged to be incompetent by virtue of a combination of factors, specifically, *inter alia*, that the witness used narcotics, that she heard voices telling her that "they" would take her to Hell, that she was scheduled for a mental examination in a state hospital, that she was a prostitute, and that she was being supported by a burglar who had shot the defendant. *Held:* The trial court did not err in admitting the witness' testimony in light of the lucidity of the testimony and the witness' expression of an appreciation of the obligation to tell the truth.

2. *Trial court discretion.* The discretion of the trial court to admit the testimony of a witness alleged to be incompetent is very broad. Compare, however, People v. McCaughan, 317 P.2d 974, 981–82 (Cal.1957), where the testimony of certain inmates of a mental institution was admitted by the trial court in a prosecution of a hospital attendant for manslaughter. The witnesses were shown to have histories of delusions relating to mistreatment by hospital personnel. Reversing on other grounds, the Supreme Court of California stated: "It is universally recognized that the competency of a witness is to be determined by the trial court in the exercise of its discretion * * *. Manifestly, however, sound discretion demands the exercise of great caution in qualifying as competent a witness who has a history of insane delusions relating to the very subject of inquiry in a case in which the question is not simply whether or not an act was done but, rather, the manner in which it was done and in which testimony as to details may mean the difference between conviction and acquittal."

3. *Psychiatric examinations.* The determination of a witness' competency will generally be made by the trial judge solely on the basis of his or her own observation of the witness on the stand. However, "the judge has discretion to admit extrinsic evidence on the question [of competency], to use mental and psychological tests, and to hear opinion evidence of psychiatric experts." Weihofen, Testimonial Competence and Credibility, 34 Geo. Wash.L.Rev. 53, 55 (1964). See also Conrad, Mental Examination of Witnesses, 11 Syracuse L.Rev. 149, 153–56 (1960). And discretion, it would seem, is most frequently exercised against compelling the examination. See United States v. Jackson, 576 F.2d 46 (5th Cir.1978); United States v. Gutman, 725 F.2d 417 (7th Cir.1984). What if the trial court orders an examination but the witness refuses to cooperate? Compare State v. Franklin, 229 A.2d 657 (N.J.1967), with State v. Miller, 151 N.W.2d 157 (Wis. 1967).

For historical interest, see Hutchins & Slesinger, Some Observations on the Law of Evidence—The Competency of Witnesses, 37 Yale L.J. 1017 (1928). In this article, the authors advocate the employment of simple intelligence tests in determining competency. They also note, to support the growing acceptance of intelligence testing in 1928: "Even the law schools are becoming interested. One of the leading law schools in the East has just announced that it will base its system of entrance henceforth partly on a 'capacity test.' "

4. *Attorney competence.* There is no express provision in the Federal Rules of Evidence governing the competency of attorneys as witnesses. Therefore, the language of Rule 601 would seem to permit their testimony. However, some judges have refused to permit such testimony, presumably

based on the court's inherent power to control attorneys and the trial. In addition, an attorney should also be aware of the provisions of Model Rule of Professional Conduct 3.7, which provides, with limited exceptions, that a "lawyer shall not act as advocate at a trial in which the lawyer is likely to be a necessary witness." See Gonzalez v. State, 117 S.W.3d 831, 837–38 (Tex.Crim.App.2003) ("Counsel may be disqualified under the disciplinary rules when the opposing party can demonstrate actual prejudice resulting from opposing counsel's service in the dual role of advocate-witness. Allegations of one or more violations of the disciplinary rules or evidence showing only a possible future violation are not sufficient.").

5. *Hypnotically-refreshed testimony.* Some courts have held that the testimony of a witness who has been hypnotized is incompetent, at least with regard to matters not contained in statements given prior to the hypnotic session. The question is discussed in connection with refreshing the recollection of witnesses, Section B(4), infra.

(6) DEAD MAN'S STATUTES

RAY, DEAD MAN'S STATUTES

24 Ohio State Law Journal 89 (1963).[20]

At common law in England and the United States, parties to a lawsuit and all other persons having a direct pecuniary or proprietary interest in the outcome of the action were excluded from testifying in the case. A party could not testify in his own behalf nor could he be required to testify if called by his adversary. The rule was thus a combination of disqualification and privilege. The theory of the disqualification was that self-interest would probably cause such persons to perjure themselves; therefore, they should be prevented from giving testimony.[21] Defenders of the rule of exclusion realized, of course, that perjury would not always result from self-interest and that by silencing truthful persons the rule threatened honest litigants with injustice, but they argued that the rule did more good than harm.[22] No justification was advanced for the privilege. Jeremy Bentham, the great English Reformer, made a determined attack upon the rule in his Treatise on Evidence published in 1827 and, in the words of Wigmore, "first furnished the arsenal of arguments for transforming public opinion."[23] The unanswerable arguments that pecuniary interest did not make it probable that parties and witnesses would commit perjury, that the rule underestimated the ability of the judge and jurors to detect perjury, and that it created intolerable injustice, were taken up by such reformers as Denman and Brougham

21. Gilbert, Evidence 119 (1727). Baron Gilbert's words were: "The law removes them from testimony to prevent their sliding into perjury."

22. Starkie, Evidence 83 (1832): "The law must prescribe general rules; and experience proves that more mischief would result from the general reception of interested witnesses than is occasioned by their exclusion."

23. 2 Wigmore § 576. Bentham's attack is found in his Rationale of Judicial Evidence, book IX, pt. III, ch. III and pt. V, ch. I.

who led the assault on the disqualification. Through their efforts and those of others, professional opinion was gradually brought to the realization that the disqualification created more injustice than it prevented. In 1843 a statute was enacted by Parliament abolishing the disqualification of interested persons.[24] And in 1851 another statute swept away the disqualification of parties and those on whose behalf a suit was brought or defended.[25] These reforms spread to the United States, and the English statutes served as models for legislation here. As in England the change was brought about in two steps: the first qualifying interested nonparties and the second qualifying parties. Unfortunately most of the states which enacted similar statutes departed from the English model in a most significant respect. They retained a portion of the old disqualification as an exception to the new rule of qualification. At the time when the first statutes abolishing the interest disqualification were offered to the state legislatures in this country, the objection was made that if parties and interested persons were allowed to testify in cases involving contracts and transactions where one party had died and the other survived, this would work a hardship on the estate of the deceased. Since the lips of one party to the transaction were sealed by death, the suggestion was that the living party's lips should be sealed by excluding his testimony.[26] This compromise was accepted in most of the early statutes and became the pattern of legislation in this country. Today in most jurisdictions the statutes contain a general statement to the effect that no person shall be disqualified because he is a party to a suit or proceeding or interested in the issue to be tried. But they add a provision to the effect that in suits brought or defended by an executor or administrator, such persons shall remain incompetent to testify concerning a communication with the testator or intestate. While this is the most common type of statute, there are many which vary substantially from this in certain respects * * * The statutes usually provide that the surviving party or interested person may testify if called by the opposite party, thus doing away with the privilege feature of the common-law rule. These statutes which retain the common-law interest disqualification of parties and interested persons with respect to testimony as to transactions with decedents are popularly known as "Dead Man's Statutes" * * *.[27] They vary greatly in their wording and coverage, and the attitudes of the courts differ as to their interpretation, even where similar provisions are involved. Consequently, precedents from one state may be of little value in another jurisdiction. * * *

24. Lord Denman's Act, 6 & 7 Vict., c. 85 (1843).

25. Lord Brougham's Act, 13 & 14 Vict., c. 99 (1851).

26. Owens v. Owen's Adm'r, 14 W.Va. 88, 95 (1878): "The temptation to falsehood and concealment in such cases is considered too great, to allow the surviving party to testify in his own behalf. Any other view of this subject, I think, would place in great peril the estates of the dead, and would in fact make them an easy prey for the dishonest and unscrupulous, which with due deference to the views and opinions of others, it seems to me, the Legislature never intended."

27. [Professor Ray cited 34 states as having "Dead Man's Acts" at the time his article appeared in 1963. By 2006, the number had shrunk to less than a dozen. Ed.].

Notes

1. *Choice of law issues.* The language in Rule 601, providing for the application of state competency rules when state substantive law governs, may have a significant impact in a case in which the state law would apply a Dead Man's Act.

2. *Sources.* See Barnard, The Dead Man's Act Rears its Ugly Head Again, 72 Ill.Bar J. 420 (1984); Johnson & Hanzman, Construing Florida's Dead Man Statute: Let the Dead Speak in Will Contests, 60 Fla. Bar J. 35 (1986); Wallis, An Outdated Form of Evidentiary Law: A Survey of Dead Man's Statutes and a Proposal for Change, 53 Clev.St.L.Rev. 75 (2005); Comment, The Deadman's Statutes—Who is an Interested Party in Wisconsin?, 87 Marq.L.Rev. 1025 (2004).

SECTION B. ELICITATION OF TESTIMONY

(1) EXCLUSION OF WITNESSES: FEDERAL RULE 615

UNITED STATES v. RHYNES

United States Court of Appeals, Fourth Circuit, En Banc, 2000.
218 F.3d 310.

KING, CIRCUIT JUDGE:

Michael Rhynes and several co-defendants were tried before a jury in the Western District of North Carolina on a number of drug-related charges. * * *

* * *

On September 24, 1996, at the commencement of the trial in Charlotte, North Carolina, a lawyer for one of Rhynes's co-defendants moved for sequestration of the Government's witnesses. In response, the district court entered its sequestration order from the bench. The Government then noted that its "case agent" and a "summary witness" were in the courtroom and intended to "sit[ ] in on the testimony prepared to testify at the end of the trial [.]" * * * The district court granted the Government's request that two of its witnesses be excepted from the sequestration order and another motion that the defense witnesses be sequestered. Thereafter, the lawyer for one of Rhynes's co-defendants sought to have his investigator excepted from the sequestration order, and the court granted the exception "[s]o long as your investigator observes Rule 615 and does not talk to the witnesses about testimony that has just concluded or testimony that has concluded." * * *

During the Government's case-in-chief, it presented the testimony of witness D.S. Davis. Davis is a convicted felon and was, at the time of trial, serving a seven-year sentence for participating in a drug conspiracy. Davis testified, *inter alia,* that he first met [Corwin] Alexander in

1990, when he (Davis) asked Alexander to serve as an intermediary in a drug transaction between Davis and Michael Rhynes.

* * *

During Rhynes's defense, he testified on his own behalf; then, he called a single witness to corroborate his testimony: Corwin Alexander. Alexander testified on a number of subjects * * * before he was asked about the Government's earlier witness, Davis. Alexander explained that, at a meeting between the two, Davis told Alexander that the Government had offered Davis a deal in exchange for information about Rhynes. Alexander then stated, "And he [(Davis)] went off to do his time, and I hear from Tuesday he got up and said—," whereupon the Government objected and requested a bench conference. * * *

At the bench, Mr. Scofield [defense counsel] advised the district court that he had discussed Davis's testimony with Alexander: "I specifically told him about that testimony and told him I was going to ask him about that, Your Honor. And I don't think that violates the sequestration order." * * * The district court indicated its belief that the sequestration order had been violated. Mr. Scofield then responded, "I'm sorry then, Your Honor. I've done wrong then because I don't know how else I can prepare him to testify. I told him that that guy told him that he was a drug dealer." * * *

The district court nonetheless granted the Government's motion to strike Alexander's testimony and to exclude him as a witness. * * *

* * * It is clear from the plain and unambiguous language of Rule 615 that lawyers are simply not subject to the Rule. This Rule's plain language relates only to "witnesses," and it serves only to exclude witnesses from the courtroom. Thus, Rule 615 did not prohibit Mr. Scofield from discussing D.S. Davis's testimony with Corwin Alexander.

The district court's bald Rule 615 order was then extended by the statement that "the witnesses shall not discuss one with the other their testimony." Of course, nothing on the face of this extending language addresses the conduct of lawyers in any way. Moreover, the relevant authorities interpreting Rule 615, including court decisions and the leading commentators, agree that sequestration orders prohibiting discussions between witnesses should, and do, permit witnesses to discuss the case with counsel for either party: "Sequestration requires that witnesses not discuss the case among themselves or anyone else, *other than the counsel for the parties.*" United States v. Walker, 613 F.2d 1349, 1354 (5th Cir.1980) * * *.

D.

The Government has conceded that neither the plain language of the district court's order, nor the provisions of Rule 615, prohibit any conduct by lawyers * * *. Nonetheless, the Government asserts that the "purpose and spirit" of the sequestration order were compromised by Mr. Scofield's discussion with Alexander. Specifically, the Government contends that the "truth-seeking" process would be hindered if lawyers were permitted to reveal testimony in the manner exercised by Mr. Scofield. This is basically an argument that Rule 615, the extending language, or the policies underlying sequestration implicitly proscribed Mr. Scofield's conduct; we reject the argument for several reasons.

We have properly recognized the purpose and spirit underlying witness sequestration: it is "designed to discourage and expose fabrication, inaccuracy, and collusion." Opus 3 Ltd. v. Heritage Park, Inc., 91 F.3d 625, 628 (4th Cir.1996). Put differently, sequestration helps to smoke out lying witnesses: "It is now well recognized that sequestering witnesses 'is (next to cross-examination) one of the greatest engines that the skill of man has ever invented for the detection of liars in a court of justice.' " Id. (citing 6 *Wigmore on Evidence* § 1838, at 463).

To the extent that the Government asserts that Mr. Scofield frustrated the purpose and spirit of sequestration, we disagree. The Government asserts that Mr. Scofield's actions undermined the truthfulness of Alexander's testimony, which, in the Government's view, is surely an act that runs afoul of the sequestration order. On the contrary, lawyers are not like witnesses, and there are critical differences between them that are dispositive in this case. Unlike witnesses, lawyers are officers of the court, and, as such, they owe the court a duty of candor, *Model Rules of Professional Conduct* Rule 3.3 (1995) ("Model Rules"). Of paramount importance here, that duty both forbids an attorney from knowingly presenting perjured testimony and permits the attorney to refuse to offer evidence he or she reasonably believes is false. *Id.* Rule 3.3(a)(4), (c). Similarly, an attorney may not "counsel or assist a witness to testify falsely." *Id.* Rule 3.4(b). And, if an attorney believes that a non-client witness is lying on the witness stand about a material issue, he is obliged to "promptly reveal the fraud to the court." *Id.* Rule 3.3, cmt. 4. The Supreme Court has emphasized the importance of attorneys' duty of candor: "Any violation of these strictures would constitute a most serious breach of the attorney's duty to the court, to be treated accordingly." Geders v. United States, 425 U.S. 80, 90 n.3 * * * (1976) (citing to parallel provisions of *Model Code of Professional Responsibility*). Consequently, lawyers' ethical obligations to the court distinguish them from trial witnesses.

Moreover, the purpose and spirit underlying sequestration are not absolute; indeed, we have aptly recognized that even the "powerful policies behind sequestration" must bend to the dictates of the Constitution. Opus 3 Ltd., 91 F.3d at 628.[28] Thus, to the extent that they are

28. It is important to note that the language of Rule 615 does not require exclusion of *all* witnesses from the courtroom. While an absolute rule might further promote the truth-seeking policy behind Rule 615, constitutional considerations have required that exceptions be built into the Rule itself. Opus 3 Ltd., 91 F.3d at 628 ("confrontation and due process considerations" drive Rule 615's exceptions). Parties or their representatives, as well as expert witnesses, are authorized by Rule 615 to remain in the courtroom, hear testimony, and subsequently testify. Fed.R.Evid. 615(1)-(3). In criminal cases these exceptions are applied to allow the prosecution's

implicated in this case, the policies and spirit of sequestration must yield to the constitutional and ethical duties Mr. Scofield sought to effectuate here.[29] That is, in the context of a criminal trial like this one, a defense attorney's duty to his client assumes constitutional stature: "In all criminal prosecutions, the accused shall * * * have the Assistance of Counsel for his defence." U.S. Const. amend. VI. To all clients, an attorney owes competence. *Model Rules* Rule 1.1. To fulfill this basic duty, the attorney must prepare carefully for the task at hand: "Competent representation requires * * * thoroughness and preparation reasonably necessary for the representation." *Id.* Rule 1.1(a).

Thorough preparation demands that an attorney interview and prepare witnesses before they testify. No competent lawyer would call a witness without appropriate and thorough pre-trial interviews and discussion. In fact, more than one lawyer has been punished, found ineffective, or even disbarred for incompetent representation that included failure to prepare or interview witnesses. United States v. Tucker, 716 F.2d 576 (9th Cir.1983) (defense counsel ineffective for failing to interview witnesses); McQueen v. Swenson, 498 F.2d 207 (8th Cir.1974) (same); In re Warmington, 212 Wis.2d 657, 668, 568 N.W.2d 641 (1997) (lawyer disbarred for, among other things, "failing to supervise the preparation of an expert witness"); In re Wolfram, 174 Ariz. 49, 847 P.2d 94, 96 (1993) (failure to interview witnesses cited among reasons for suspending attorney).

In this context, Mr. Scofield's actions were necessary in the exercise of his duties, both constitutional and ethical, as a lawyer. First, when the Government called Davis as a witness and began asking him questions about Alexander, Mr. Scofield made clear that he was unaware that Alexander had been implicated as a co-conspirator. * * * Although Davis's subsequent testimony did not implicate Alexander in any specific drug deal, the import of Davis's allegation was clear: Alexander was serving as an intermediary between drug buyers and Rhynes. Faced with an allegation that his prime supporting witness, Alexander, had been assisting, or participating in, a drug conspiracy with Rhynes, Mr. Sco-

case agent to remain at counsel table with the prosecutor, hear the other witnesses testify, and nevertheless testify on behalf of the prosecution. In this very case, moreover, the district court's sequestration order specifically exempted the Government's FBI case agent as well as its summary witness. * * *

29. While it is unnecessary for us to reach the issue in this case, we observe that sequestration orders that prevent attorneys from performing their duties as counsel, including discussing trial proceedings with future witnesses, may well violate a criminal defendant's Sixth Amendment rights. The Supreme Court has explicitly forbidden some sequestration orders that prohibit a defendant-witness from conferring with counsel. Geders v. United States, 425 U.S. [at 91] * * *. And at least one court has extended this reasoning to sequestration orders preventing counsel from discussing prior testimony with non-defendant witnesses:

> It has been held that to deprive a party * * * of the right to consult with counsel as the trial proceeds is to infringe its right to due process of law. This court believes that similar considerations apply to the right of a party to have his counsel free to discuss with prospective witnesses developments in the case, *including the testimony of other witnesses.*

United States v. Scharstein, 531 F.Supp. 460, 463–64 (E.D.Ky.1982) (emphasis added).

field had ethical (and possibly constitutional) duties to investigate these allegations with Alexander before he put Alexander on the stand. Mr. Scofield was thus compelled to ascertain, if possible: (1) whether Davis's allegations were untrue (or, if true, whether Alexander intended to invoke his Fifth Amendment rights); (2) whether Alexander's denials were credible; and (3) why Davis would make potentially false allegations against Alexander. Put simply, Mr. Scofield needed to fully assess his decision to call Alexander as a witness, and, to fulfill his obligations to his client, Scofield was compelled to discuss Davis's testimony with Alexander. *See Chandler v. Jones,* 813 F.2d 773 (6th Cir.1987) (finding counsel's performance deficient for (1) failing to prepare witness for trial; (2) improperly using leading questions; and (3) calling witness who was expected to invoke the Fifth Amendment).

In response, the Government claims that Mr. Scofield did not violate the sequestration order by merely speaking with Alexander; instead, it was Mr. Scofield's informing Alexander of Davis's testimony that violated the order. Based on this view, the Government asserts that counsel had ample room to interview and prepare witnesses without running afoul of the sequestration order. But this conclusion begs the question, "How was counsel to discern the limits of the sequestration order?" Those limits—as declared after the fact by the district court—did not appear on the face of the order, in Rule 615, in controlling precedent, or even in persuasive authorities. In fact, adoption of the Government's position would make it virtually impossible for counsel to know whether they have "ample room" to perform essential tasks without violating an order. This argument thus fails to persuade us.

Further, sequestration is not the only technique utilized to ensure the pursuit of truth at trial. Indeed, if an attorney has inappropriately "coached" a witness, thorough cross-examination of that witness violates no privilege and is entirely appropriate and sufficient to address the issue. * * *

In short, the Government's position requires the implication that by discussing prior trial testimony with Corwin Alexander, Mr. Scofield necessarily coached Alexander or made it likely that Alexander would commit perjury.[30] To the contrary, we must trust and rely on lawyers' abilities to discharge their ethical obligations, including their duty of candor to the court, without being policed by overbroad sequestration orders. Furthermore, we are confident that, if an attorney is lax in his duty of candor, that laxness will normally be exposed—even exploited—by skillful cross-examination. * * *

III.

Even if Mr. Scofield had violated a sequestration rule or order, we would still hold, in the context of this case, that the sanction imposed—

30. For the sake of clarification, we note that nothing in the record even remotely suggests that Mr. Scofield improperly coached Alexander or encouraged him to commit perjury.

exclusion of Alexander's testimony—constituted reversible error. "Because exclusion of a defense witness impinges upon the right to present a defense, we are quite hesitant to endorse the use of such an extreme remedy." United States v. Cropp, 127 F.3d 354, 363 (4th Cir.1997). Under these circumstances, we conclude that exclusion of Alexander's testimony in its entirety was unduly severe.

At the outset, sanction analysis must encompass proportionality, and sanctions as extreme as witness exclusion must be proportional to the offense. * * * In this case, when the district court excluded Alexander's testimony, it was aware, through Mr. Scofield's representations, that Alexander had been exposed to Davis's accusation that Alexander was involved in drug deals. However, the district court conducted no examination of Alexander to determine exactly what he had been told; neither did the court attempt to ascertain through Mr. Scofield what he had revealed to Alexander.

More importantly, the proffer of Alexander's testimony covered at least six other Government witnesses and a number of other topics that were crucial to Rhynes's defense. Mr. Scofield specifically represented that, "Your Honor, I do not believe, as I stand here and think about it, that I mentioned anybody else's testimony other than D.S. Davis." * * * Notwithstanding this representation, the district court determined that Alexander's testimony relating to each of the other Government witnesses and other subjects was tainted by the same "coaching" as the testimony relating to D.S. Davis. * * *

* * *

We are also cognizant that although the alleged violation of the sequestration order was effected by Mr. Scofield, the sanction imposed inured to the defendant.[31] There was, of course, no requirement that Rhynes be sanctioned for his lawyer's conduct; indeed, a lawyer may be personally sanctioned for violations of court orders. If, however, a defendant is being sanctioned for his lawyer's conduct, courts should impose the least severe sanction justified under the circumstances. The district court had alternative sanctions at its disposal; we have endorsed at least two others: "sanction of the witness; [and] instructions to the jury that they may consider the violation toward the issue of credibility." Cropp, 127 F.3d at 363. Further, there were many other possible corrective measures that could have been taken, including: limiting the scope of the witness's testimony, *see English,* 92 F.3d at 913 (endorsing limitation of witness's testimony following violation of sequestration order); permitting broad cross-examination into the alleged "coaching," * * * ; or any other sanction appropriate under the circumstances. There is no doubt that, under facts like these, the district court could have imposed a less severe sanction.

* * *

31. There has been no allegation that Rhynes participated in this alleged violation in any way.

Vacated and Remanded.

[WILKINS, CIRCUIT JUDGE concurred in part and concurred in the judgment.]

WILKINSON, CHIEF JUDGE, dissenting:

* * * The district court should be commended, not chastised, for refusing to recognize an exception to Rule 615 that does not exist and for acting to preserve trial proceedings as a means of ascertaining truth.

* * *

Scofield's conduct * * * utterly thwarted the sequestration order. * * * It has no conceivable object other than to prevent prospective witnesses from knowing the testimony of prior witnesses before taking the stand themselves. * * * Yet Scofield's actions accomplished this prohibited end as surely as if Alexander had heard Davis' testimony in the courtroom himself. This was a matter of no small concern to the district court. Davis' testimony was extremely problematic for Alexander, because Davis had linked Alexander to Rhynes' drug-dealing activities. Foreknowledge of Davis' testimony would enable Alexander to counter these allegations with greater credibility, specificity, and force. The district court was understandably troubled when it learned that Scofield had related Davis' testimony to Alexander. The court was not compelled to countenance Scofield's conduct any more than it was required to permit Alexander to hire a courtroom scribe to record prior testimony, *see McMahon,* 104 F.3d 638, or read trial transcripts of what earlier witnesses said, *see Miller v. Universal City Studios, Inc.,* 650 F.2d 1365 (5th Cir.1981).

Nor did the district court's ruling impair Scofield's ability to discharge his professional obligations to thoroughly prepare his witnesses. * * * To argue that the district court's ruling impermissibly ties attorneys' hands is both gross overstatement and a red herring. Indeed, Scofield himself commendably acknowledged to the district court that attorneys may fully prepare witnesses without revealing the details of prior testimony in contravention of a sequestration order * * *.

[NIEMEYER, CIRCUIT JUDGE, dissenting opinion omitted.]

Notes and Questions

1. *Recent example.* In the prosecution for the 9/11 terrorist attacks, the trial judge barred the testimony of government aviation officials because a Transportation Security Administration official, who was assisting prosecutors, sent e-mails coaching these officials, including transcripts of the opening statements and the testimony of an FBI agent. Lewis, Judge Penalizes Moussaoui Prosecutors by Barring Major Witnesses, N.Y.Times, Mar. 15, 2006, at A23.

2. *Scope of rule.* See United States v. Hargrove, 929 F.2d 316, 320–21 (7th Cir.1991) ("The testimony of Baker did not contravene [Rule 615's] purpose. Baker was a surprise witness whom the government did not intend

to call until Michael Beckett testified that the police pressured him to falsely identify Hargrove as his source for cocaine. The government called Baker solely to testify to the lack of police coercion and not to the substance of what Michael Beckett had said about Hargrove.").

3. *Exception: Parties.* In Portuondo v. Agard, 529 U.S. 61 (2000), the prosecutor, in her summation, called the jury's attention to the fact that the defendant had the opportunity to hear all other witnesses testify and to tailor his testimony accordingly. The defendant argued that these comments burdened his Sixth Amendment right to be present at trial and to be confronted with the witnesses against him, as well as his Fifth and Sixth Amendment rights to testify on his own behalf. The Court rejected these arguments. Some courts distinguish between different types of comments, permitting comment only when there is specific evidence of tailoring. Generic accusations are prohibited. See State v. Daniels, 861 A.2d 808, 819 (N.J.2004) (The latter "occur when the prosecutor, despite no specific evidentiary basis that defendant has tailored his testimony, nonetheless attacks the defendant's credibility by drawing the jury's attention to the defendant's presence during trial and his concomitant opportunity to tailor his testimony.").

4. *Exception: Designated representatives.* The Senate Judiciary Committee construed this exception to permit an "investigative agent" to remain during trial notwithstanding the possibility that the agent may be called as a witness. "The investigative agent's presence may be extremely important to government counsel, especially when the case is complex or involves some specialized subject matter. The agent, too, having lived with the case for a long time, may be able to assist in meeting trial surprises where the best-prepared counsel would otherwise have difficulty." S. Rep. No. 1277, 93d Cong., 2d Sess., reprinted in 1974 U.S.C.C.A.N. 7051, 7072. But see In re United States, 584 F.2d 666, 667 (5th Cir.1978) (trial court has authority under Rule 611(a) to require the investigative agent to testify "at an early stage of the government's case if he remains the government's designated representative under Rule 615"); Carter v. State, 610 S.E.2d 181, 183–84 (Ga.Ct.App.2005) ("We have reached a point where the prosecution acts as though it has an absolute right to have its witness present for the duration of trial. An empty assertion that the prosecution simply 'needs' a witness during trial to assist in the orderly presentation of its case, without more, should not be the kind of assertion upon which discretion can be granted.").

5. *Exception: Essential persons.* This exception "contemplates such persons as an agent who handled the transaction being litigated or an expert needed to advise counsel in the management of the litigation." Fed.R.Evid. 615 advisory committee's note.

6. *Exception: Statutes.* Federal statutes recognize a crime victim's right to be present unless the victim's testimony would be materially affected by attendance. 42 U.S.C. § 10606(b)(4). Many state provisions are more specific. See Ala.R.Evid. 615 ("This rule does not authorize exclusion of * * * (4) a victim of a criminal offense or the representative of a victim who is unable to attend, when the representative has been selected by the victim, the victim's guardian, or the victim's family."); Fla.Stat.Ann. § 90.616(d) (recognizing an exception: "In a criminal case, the victim of the crime, the victim's next of

kin, the parent or guardian of a minor child victim, or a lawful representative of such person, unless, upon motion, the court determines such person's presence to be prejudicial."). See also Mosteller, The Unnecessary Victims' Rights Amendment, 1999 Utah L.Rev. 443, 457–62 (discussing Rule 615 issues and victims' rights).

7. *Separation of attorney and client.* In Geders v. United States, 425 U.S. 80 (1976), a sequestration order so broad that it prohibited the accused from consulting with his counsel during a 17–hour overnight recess violated the Sixth Amendment. But see Perry v. Leeke, 488 U.S. 272 (1989) (proper for trial court to order accused not to talk to anyone, including counsel, during a 15–minute recess between direct and cross-examination). At what point is an order not to confer with counsel too broad?

8. *Sanctions.* "Sanctions for violations of sequestration orders fall into three general categories: (1) citing the witness for contempt; (2) permitting counsel or the court to comment to the jury on the witness's non-compliance as a reflection on his or her credibility; and (3) precluding the witness's testimony." People v. Melendez, 102 P.3d 315, 319 (Colo.2004). May an accused who has failed to list a witness prior to trial, as required by applicable discovery rules, be prevented from calling that witness at trial? See Taylor v. Illinois, 484 U.S. 400 (1988) (preclusion of testimony proper under certain circumstances).

9. *"Coaching."* Where the issue is what constitutes improper coaching and tailoring of testimony, the answer may not be as easily answered as would first appear. Can a lawyer practice cross-examination with the witness? Suggest the language to be used by the witness in testimony? Can the lawyer bring to the witness' attention facts not initially mentioned by the witness but instead learned from another witness, and if upon hearing the fact the witness wishes to include it in his or her testimony, may the lawyer ethically elicit such testimony? See Opinion 79, Legal Ethics Committee of the District of Columbia Bar, 108 Daily Washington L.Rptr. 285 (1980); Joy & McMunigal, Witness Preparation: When Does it Cross the Line?, 17 Crim.Just. 48 (Fall 2002).

(2) NARRATIVE TESTIMONY: FEDERAL RULE 611(a)

NORTHERN PAC. R.R. v. CHARLESS

United States Court of Appeals, Ninth Circuit, 1892.
51 Fed. 562.

MORROW, DISTRICT JUDGE. This action was brought by Hugh Charless, defendant in error, the plaintiff below, to recover the sum of $25,000 for damages for personal injuries alleged to have been received by him while in the employ of the Northern Pacific Railroad Company, defendant in error, as a section hand engaged at work on the line of the road at a point near Cheney, then in the territory, now in the state, of Washington. The case was tried before a jury, and the plaintiff had a verdict and judgment for $18,250 and costs. A motion for a new trial was made and denied, and thereupon the company sued out this writ of error. * * *

* * *

It is next claimed as error that the plaintiff was allowed on the trial to make a statement in narrative form, as a witness in his own behalf, without being specially interrogated by his counsel in reference to the particular matters involved in the case; that the statement was made in such a way as to afford the defendant no opportunity of making any objection to any particular portion, and was allowed to be made over the general objection that it contained matters immaterial to the issues, and incompetent as being hearsay and not the best evidence. It appears from the record that after a few preliminary questions the plaintiff was asked the following question by his counsel: "Turn to the jury, and tell them the facts in this case, commencing at the time of your employment with the Northern Pacific Railroad Company, and tell them the complete story." To this question no objection was made. The plaintiff therefore proceeded to relate the facts in the case requested. After stating the particulars of his employment, the use of a hand car, the method of stopping it, and the breaking of one of its wheels, counsel for defendant objected to the course in which the taking of the testimony was proceeding, claiming that the witness was making a statement of matters immaterial to the issues involved in the case, and incompetent as being hearsay, and not the best evidence, and that he desired to interpose such objections, but that, owing to the fact that the testimony was being given in a narrative form, no opportunity was given counsel to properly interpose such objection. The court replied to this objection that the taking of the witness' testimony in the narrative form would be the best way of getting at what he knew or could state concerning the matter at issue; that it would save time to proceed in that way, and would perhaps furnish to the jury a more connected statement of the matter to be told as it occurred and took place. It was within the discretion of the court to allow the witness to give his testimony in a narrative form. Thomp. Trials, § 354. In general, this practice is commended by text writers. Mr. Chitty, in speaking of this method of examining witnesses, says:

> "It is certainly the practice, when the time and place of the scene of action have once been fixed, to desire the witness *to give his own account of the matter,* directing him, when not a professional person to omit, as he proceeds, account of what he has only heard from others and not seen or heard himself, and which he is apt to suppose is quite as material as that which he himself has seen."

* * *

But if, in the giving of such testimony, the witness states matters irrelevant or immaterial or incompetent as being hearsay, it is the right and duty of counsel objecting to such testimony to interpose and arrest the narrative by calling the attention of the court particularly to the objectionable matter, and by a motion to strike it out obtain a ruling of the court excluding such testimony from the case. * * * It does not appear that counsel for defendant was deprived of an opportunity to make such a motion, and the proceedings cannot be considered as error.

* * *

Judgment affirmed.

Notes

1. *Policy.* It has long been assumed that narrative testimony is likely to result in a more complete presentation of the facts, a consideration which, if true, would go far to outweigh the objections to such testimony noted in the principal case. See Wigmore, The Science of Judicial Proof § 264 (3d ed. 1937). The traditional assumption, however, may be a questionable one. See Marshall, Marquis & Oskamp, Effects of Kind of Question and Atmosphere of Interrogation in Accuracy and Completeness of Testimony, 84 Harv.L.Rev. 1620 (1971); Tanford, An Introduction to Trial Law, 51 Mo.L.Rev. 623 (1986).

2. *Federal cases.* See United States v. Pless, 982 F.2d 1118, 1123 (7th Cir.1992) ("Fed. R. Evid. 611(a) provides district judges with authority to allow testimony in narrative form rather than as answers to specific questions."); United States v. Garcia, 625 F.2d 162, 169 (7th Cir.1980) ("[T]here is * * * nothing particularly unusual, or incorrect, in a procedure of letting a witness relate pertinent information in a narrative form as long as it stays within the bounds of pertinency and materiality."). Despite this discretion, many judges require that counsel ask specific questions because of the opportunity that such a format gives to the opposing party to object. See discussion in Tanford, The Trial Process 336 (1983). An objection to narrative testimony is likely to be effective only where counsel can suggest some real prospect of harm that cannot be cured by striking testimony and instructing the jury to disregard or where testimony may concern a matter inadmissible on constitutional grounds. See 1 McCormick, Evidence § 5 (6th ed. 2006); Tanford, note 1, supra, at 665.

3. *Other "objections."* Numerous common objections are not based on any Federal Rule: (1) argumentative questions, (2) asked and answered, (3) assuming facts not in evidence, (4) misleading questions, (5) compound questions, and (6) nonresponsive answers. The entire catalog of possible objections to the form of questions is discussed in Denbeaux & Risinger, Questioning Questions: Objections to Form in the Interrogation of Witnesses, 33 Ark.L.Rev. 439 (1980).

(3) LEADING QUESTIONS: FEDERAL RULE 611(c)

UNITED STATES v. CLINICAL LEASING SERV., INC.

United States Court of Appeals, Fifth Circuit, 1992.
982 F.2d 900.

GARZA, CIRCUIT JUDGE:

The government brought suit against defendants, Melvin Soll and Leroy Brinkley, seeking to hold them personally liable for fines imposed against their corporation, Clinical Leasing Service, Inc. ("Clinical"), for violations of the Federal Controlled Substances Act ("FCSA"), 21 U.S.C. § 842 et seq. (1988). A jury found Soll and Brinkley liable for the corporation's fines on the grounds that Clinical was the alter ego of Soll and Brinkley, and that Clinical was used by them to frustrate a legislative purpose. * * *

Lastly, Soll and Brinkley claim that they were denied a fair trial. During trial, the district court terminated Soll's direct examination because of leading questions. * * *

"The conduct of a fair trial is vested in the sound discretion of the trial judge." *Cranberg v. Consumers Union of U.S., Inc.,* 756 F.2d 382, 391 (5th Cir.1985). "On review, this conduct will be measured against a standard of fairness and impartiality." *Id.* Soll and Brinkley contend that the district court abused its discretion in terminating Soll's direct testimony "without any explanation." * * * We disagree. When the district court terminated Soll's direct testimony, the court sustained a specific objection by government's counsel to leading questions.[32] Therefore, we find that the district court adequately explained its actions.

In addition, the exclusion of Soll's direct testimony was within the sound discretion granted the district court by Fed.R.Evid. 611. The record indicates that Soll's counsel attempted to elicit direct testimony from Soll through leading questions. * * * A few minutes before terminating direct testimony, the district court specifically warned Soll's attorney not to lead the witness. * * * The record further indicates that the district court warned Soll's attorney about leading questions on at least seven previous occasions. * * * Under these circumstances, we find no abuse of discretion in the district court's termination of Soll's direct testimony.

Notes and Questions

1. *Rationale.* See Stine v. Marathon Oil, 976 F.2d 254, 266 (5th Cir.1992) ("We urge the trial court * * * to limit the use of leading questions to non-controversial or background areas—leading questions must not be allowed in controverted substantive areas where the jury must weigh the evidence and make credibility determinations. As we all are fully aware, any good trial advocate who is allowed leading questions can both testify for the witness and argue the client's case by the use of leading questions. This practice must not be allowed."); Fed.R.Evid. 611 advisory committee's note ("The rule continues the traditional view that the suggestive powers of the leading question are as a general proposition undesirable.").

32. Soll's testimony immediately preceding termination was:

BY MR. KERRIGAN [Soll's counsel]:

Q. Did you [Soll] also have, as Mr. Brinkley did in his office, a computer terminal at your home?

A. Yes.

Q. Is that where you[r] law office is or was?

A. That's correct.

Q. So, information that was available from the clinic on the things that the other witnesses have talked about were available to you at your own—

MR. WATSON [government's counsel]: Objection, Your Honor. He's continuing to lead.

THE COURT: I sustain the objection. We're going to cut the questions now. You can't raise them properly. Sorry. Let's go on. * * *

2. *Exceptions.* Rule 611(c) contains a general prohibition against leading questions "except as may be necessary to develop the witness' testimony." As was the case at common law, the question is left clearly within the discretion of the trial judge. Leading questions are permitted in a variety of circumstances. See United States v. Grassrope, 342 F.3d 866, 869 (8th Cir.2003) ("It is not uncommon that the precise physiological details of sexual assault must be elicited by focused questioning. We have repeatedly upheld the use of leading questions to develop the testimony of sexual assault victims, particularly children."); United States v. Salameh, 152 F.3d 88, 128 (2d Cir.1998) ("The challenged question was necessary to develop Igiri's testimony and elicit information from a nervous witness."); United States v. Goodlow, 105 F.3d 1203, 1207 (8th Cir.1997) (witness suffering from mental retardation); United States v. Ajmal, 67 F.3d 12, 16 (2d Cir.1995) ("a non-English speaking witness testifying through a translator").

3. *Sanction.* At the trial level the prohibition against leading questions may, as in the principal case, preclude the admission of evidence. A good attorney, however, will often merely rephrase the question and the witness, now alerted by the suggestion, will provide the desired information. Is the purpose of the rule adequately served by sustaining an objection to the suggestive question?

What if counsel does not stop? United States v. Gant, 487 F.2d 30, 35 (10th Cir.1973), had occasion to rule on the question:

> Counsel for Gant also argues that the trial court should have prevented the attorney for codefendant Doyle from asking excessive leading questions. From the record it appears that a genuine effort was made by the trial court to prevent this and the judge finally gave up, apparently being of the opinion that counsel for Doyle was unable to ask a question which was not leading.[33] We are at a loss to know what a trial court can do when faced with this condition. The judge sought to prevent it and to help the attorney, and he did everything short of taking over the examination himself. We fail to see this as a source of error on the judge's part, and we fail also to see that there was any prejudice to the appellant arising from this.

See also United States v. Meza–Urtado, 351 F.3d 301, 303 (7th Cir.2003) ("[A]n objection to a question as 'leading' is only an objection to the 'form' of the question. If an objection is offered and sustained, the examiner simply

33. The trial court reproached counsel for Rebecca Doyle as follows:

> Well look, you are just completely leading this witness, and for a day and a half I have been trying to tell you how you should do it, and, please, please, this is a sensitive area, now, don't lead the witness. Let the witness testify.

He further commented:

> I am criticizing you because you are asking her leading questions. You are testifying in effect, counsel. Let the witness testify.

Again he explained:

> Well now you are leading her. Do you know what a leading question is?

And again:

> * * * you don't put words in her mouth. I have told you and told you and told you.

Finally, in response to an objection by counsel, for defendant-appellant, that the questions were still leading, the trial judge acknowledged:

> I know it, but he can't do it any differently. Go on.

rephrases the question and draws the desired information from the witness. Any reasonably good lawyer worth his salt can accomplish this little trick. Without a sustained objection, an examiner would never have a chance to rephrase his question. For this reason, we think error, plain or otherwise, could never be identified in a case where only the form of a question to which no objection is made is challenged on appeal.'').

Is it fair to conclude that the rule is lacking in substance? See Cleary, Evidence as a Problem in Communicating, 5 Vand.L.Rev. 277, 287 (1952).

Types of Leading Questions

1. *Leading questions defined.* Leading questions are ones that suggest the answer, and they are often less obvious than the one in the principal case. For instance, the inflection of the voice could turn a neutral question into a leading question.

2. *Yes or no answer.* A question that calls for a "yes" or "no" answer "may or may not be leading." See 3 Wigmore, Evidence § 772(1), at 164 (Chadbourn rev. 1970); State v. Scott, 149 P.2d 152, 153 (Wash.1944) ("Even though the question may call for a yes or a no answer, it is not leading for that reason, unless it is so worded that, by permitting the witness to answer yes or no, he would be testifying in the language of the interrogator rather than in his own.").

3. *Alternative forms.* A question put in the alternative form may be leading. See Wigmore, note 2, supra, § 772(2), at 164 ("The alternative form of question ('State whether or not you said that you refused,' 'Did you or did you not refuse?') is free from this defect of form, because both affirmative and negative answers are presented for the witness' choice. Nevertheless, such a question may become leading, in so far as it rehearses lengthy details which the witness might not otherwise have mentioned, and thus supplies him with full suggestions which he incorporates without any effort, by the simple answer, 'I did,' or 'I did not.' Accordingly, the sound view is that such a question may or may not be improper, according to the amount of palpably suggestive detail which it embodies.").

4. *Conduct.* Accompanying conduct may make a question leading. See United States v. Warf, 529 F.2d 1170, 1173–74 (5th Cir.1976) ("[W]ithout Hartman's testimony it was * * * a very dubious identification * * *. The prosecutor assisted Hartman both verbally and by pointing. The explanation made to the District Court that he was pointing at the table where Warf was seated rather than at Warf individually is no explanation at all. The trial judge's statement that Hartman would have picked out Warf eventually was speculative, and, in any event, delay or indecision by Hartman in making an identification might have diminished the effect of his testimony.").

UNITED STATES v. BROWN

United States Court of Appeals, First Circuit, 1979.
603 F.2d 1022.

BOWNES, CIRCUIT JUDGE.

Defendant-appellant, John T. Brown, appeals from a jury conviction of stealing sixteen birds in violation of 18 U.S.C.A. § 659 and 18

U.S.C.A. § 2. [Appellant assigned several errors on appeal, among them the District Court's permitting one Jerome Proulx to be examined as a hostile witness.] * * *

* * * The government here had to prove beyond a reasonable doubt that on or about April 27, 1977, the defendant stole sixteen birds worth more than $100 from the Delta Airlines air freight terminal at Logan Airport which had been shipped from Virginia to Massachusetts. The evidence, which has a Damon Runyon flavor, viewed from the government's vantage, was as follows. Nancy Pancoast who, along with her husband, operates Blue Ridge Aviaries in Lowesville, Virginia, received an order from a pet store in Somerville, Massachusetts, called Big Fish Little Fish for eight male and four female cockatiels and one yellow headed Amazon parrot. A cockatiel is a small Australian parrot. The value of the birds was in excess of $100.

Appellant and two friends, Roland Coyne and Jerome Proulx, went to Big Fish Little Fish sometime during the evening of April 27, 1977. Proulx was a frequent visitor to the store and was called Gerry the Canary. While at the store, appellant was in a position to hear a clerk, Lester Thomson, acknowledge a telephone message from Delta Airlines that a shipment of birds addressed to the store had arrived at the airport. The clerk put the information down on paper and then called the owner of the store and repeated the message. Appellant was also in a position to hear this. The message could be understood to state that the birds were cockatoos, a variety of parrot, described accurately, if not scientifically, at the trial as the kind that sits on Baretta's shoulder in the TV show of the same name. A cockatoo is much larger and more expensive than a cockatiel. Appellant sometime later asked Proulx if he would be interested in some cockatoos and said that he would have no trouble picking them up.

After leaving the store, the three men, accompanied by Proulx's wife, went to appellant's home from where he made a phone call. Appellant then suggested to Proulx and his wife that they take a ride with him and his wife to the airport. On the way, appellant borrowed $20 from Proulx. Coyne did not go to the airport. At the airport, appellant, his wife, and Proulx's wife got out of the station wagon and went into one of the buildings. When they returned, appellant had a box with him that he put in the back of the station wagon. Appellant laughed all the way home. Proulx testified that he did not see what was in the box or hear any chirping.

* * *

Based on the evidence, the jury could find beyond a reasonable doubt that appellant overheard at least one of the telephone conversations relative to the arrival of the birds at Delta's air freight terminal. There was evidence from which it could find that appellant decided to steal the birds and that he called Delta to confirm the shipment and ascertain the shipping charges. There is little question that appellant went to the airport and picked up a box there. The jury was not bound to believe Proulx's testimony that he did not see what was in the box or hear any chirping; * * * Proulx, the chief witness for the government, was a hesitant, confused and very reluctant witness, but the jury had the right to pick and choose from what he said, and he said enough to make the picking and choosing easy. * * *

* * *

3. Whether the District Court Abused Its Discretion in Ruling That Jerome Proulx Should Be Treated As Hostile Pursuant to Federal Rule of Evidence 611(c).

It has long been established that in the use of leading questions "much must be left to the sound discretion of the trial judge who sees the witness and can, therefore, determine in the interest of truth and justice whether the circumstances justify leading questions to be propounded to a witness by the party producing him." St. Clair v. United States, 154 U.S. 134, 150 * * * (1894). * * *

The record does not bear out appellant's contention that witness Proulx was not adverse, evasive or hostile. Proulx and appellant were close friends. The evidence strongly suggests that Proulx was a participant in the crime. His testimony is replete with lapses of memory attributed to alcohol and drugs. He stressed several times his susceptibility to suggestion by the last person who talks to him. Appellant talked to Proulx at length about the case right up to the trial. While Proulx was not hostile in the sense of being contemptuous or surly, he was both evasive and adverse to the government.

It is true that the prosecutor did not move to have Proulx declared a hostile witness. This was a decision made by the court on its own initiative, but only after a lengthy direct examination (twenty-five transcript pages) during which all leading questions were excluded. It had become painfully clear that the district court was faced with a witness whose apparent lapses of memory, failure to understand what he had said or written on prior occasions, as well as the questions asked and his general air of confusion, made his testimony prolix and difficult to comprehend. The trial judge had a duty to see to it that the case be tried with reasonable dispatch and that the testimony of Proulx be presented as coherently as possible. We find no abuse of discretion in the ruling by the district judge that the prosecutor be allowed to use leading questions in his remaining direct examination of Proulx. * * *

Affirmed.

Notes

1. *Another example.* United States v. Meza–Urtado, 351 F.3d 301, 303 (7th Cir.2003) (The leading questions "all were necessary as Farias obviously became conveniently 'forgetful' despite his agreement to help the government. In this situation, had the government asked, he could have been treated as a hostile witness and asked leading questions until the cows came home.").

2. *Witnesses identified with adverse parties.* Leading questions are also permitted in examining a "witness identified with an adverse party." See Chonich v. Wayne County Community College, 874 F.2d 359, 368 (6th Cir.1989) ("court designated Drs. Waters and Callaghan [employees], as witnesses identified with an adverse party under F.R.E. 611(c) and allowed plaintiffs' counsel to use leading questions on direct examination"); United States v. Hicks, 748 F.2d 854, 859 (4th Cir.1984) ("permitting government to ask two leading questions of girlfriend, who was called as a government witness"); United States v. Tsui, 646 F.2d 365, 368 (9th Cir.1981) ("Tsui argues that he should have been allowed to ask leading questions of investigator Ono as an adverse witness. There is some merit to this contention.").

(4) REFRESHING RECOLLECTION: FEDERAL RULE 612

WARD v. MORR TRANSFER & STORAGE CO.

Kansas City Court of Appeals, Missouri, 1906.
95 S.W. 964.

Ellison, J. The defendant is a general storage and warehouse company in Kansas City, Mo., and the plaintiff, then residing at that place, on March 11, 1903, stored with it a lot of household goods, which she charged it with converting, and brought this action for conversion. She prevailed in the trial court by a judgment for $434.75.

[The court here concluded that certain errors in the instructions of the trial court to the jury necessitated a new trial of the action.]

There were a number of objections to evidence made by the defendant during the trial. * * * There was one much insisted upon, which arose in different forms. It involved the right of the plaintiff to refer to a list of the articles which she claimed were stored with defendant. Her receipt from defendant named, among other things, boxes, barrels, and tubs. These were filled with a great variety of articles of household goods and kitchen ware. The list was not made at the time she packed them, nor at the time she delivered them to defendant. It was made on separate pieces of paper at different times, when the article or articles would come into her memory as being a part of the goods stored. She said, "Just as I would remember things I would jot them down." Before the trial she arranged these various memoranda, thus made, in an orderly way, and had them copied into one list on a typewriter. It made a list of two or three pages of printed matter. It was from the list thus made she proposed using, not as evidence to be read to the jury, but to look at in the course of her testimony in order to bring different articles to her memory. On objection to the typewritten list, she was permitted by the court to use the original slips made by her. These were also objected to.

We think it was proper for her to use either the typewritten list or the slips for that purpose. Either reminded her of things to which and about which she testified, just as anything else may bring to the mind of

an individual a fact, distinctly remembered as a fact, when once the mind was brought to bear upon it. The memoranda, in such case, are not evidence; but the memory of the witness is. * * * It is a case of testimony from knowledge and present memory, and it is of no consequence, so far as being admissible is concerned, what circumstance or train of circumstances brought about a recollection. Every one knows what trivial incidents will cause immediate consciousness of matters of which one was temporarily unconscious. It is the right of the opposite party to cross-examine as to how a witness comes to remember anything to which he has testified. * * * 1 Wigmore's Ev. pp. 829, 830, § 735 * * * quotes from Davis v. Field, 56 Vt. 426, as follows: "* * * There seem to be two classes of cases on this subject: (1) Where the witness by referring to the memorandum has his memory quickened and refreshed thereby, so that he is enabled to swear to an actual recollection; (2) where the witness, after referring to the memorandum, undertakes to swear to the fact, yet not because he remembers it, but because of his confidence in the correctness of his memorandum. In both cases the oath of the witness is the primary, substantive evidence relied upon; in the former the oath being grounded on actual recollection, and in the latter on the faith reposed in the verity of the memorandum." * * *

The judgment will be reversed and cause remanded. All concur.

Notes and Questions

1. *What may be used to refresh memory?* One court said "a song, a face, or a newspaper item," Jewett v. United States, 15 F.2d 955, 956 (9th Cir.1926), may be the source of the awakened memory, while another court pointed out that it "may be a line from Kipling or the dolorous strain of the 'Tennessee Waltz'; a whiff of hickory smoke; the running of the fingers across a swatch of corduroy; the sweet carbonation of a chocolate soda; [or] the sight of a faded snapshot in a long-neglected album." Baker v. State, 371 A.2d 699, 705 (Md.Ct.Spec.App.1977).

In N.L.R.B. v. Federal Dairy Co., 297 F.2d 487, 489 (1st Cir.1962), the court took strong exception to the proposition that any writing whatsoever may be used for the purpose of refreshing recollection:

> [W]e must express disapproval of the advocated practice of preparing a written account for the purpose of testifying under the principle that "anything" may be used to refresh recollection. This is, of course, not to say that when recollection is exhausted a witness may not be shown a paper. But he should not bring into court specially prepared extensive testimonial notes to use over objection instead of the original records. One may well ask why there should be strictures against leading questions if a witness is free to have a prepared answer before him in any event.

But see United States v. Church, 970 F.2d 401, 409 (7th Cir.1992) (approving district court's decision to permit a government informant to testify while referring to notes prepared by government agent who interviewed him after his undercover drug buys).

2. *Recorded recollection distinguished.* The quote from *Davis v. Field* in the principal case refers to "two classes of cases." The second type involves a hearsay exception for recorded recollection, Rule 803(5), which is treated in Chapter 14, Section D, infra. For an able opinion distinguishing the two doctrines, see United States v. Riccardi, 174 F.2d 883 (3d Cir.1949).

3. *Lack of memory requirement.* Courts often state that a witness' recollection must be totally exhausted before she is to be permitted to look at a writing to refresh her recollection. Furthermore, many courts similarly state that a witness, once having stated that his recollection is refreshed by a writing, must testify independently of it. See 1 McCormick, Evidence § 9 (6th ed. 2006). What about the witness who can remember some portions of a long list of events but not the details without reference to notes? Courts in fact exercise considerable flexibility with regard to such testimony. See, e.g., United States v. Rinke, 778 F.2d 581 (10th Cir.1985) (permissible to use notes even though witness had some recollection of events); Bankers Trust Co. v. Publicker Industries, Inc., 641 F.2d 1361 (2d Cir.1981) (permissible to refer to chronology of events as long as not used as script). What latitude should be given expert witnesses such as physicians who may have to recall a large number of patients with complex histories? What about police officers?

WINTERS v. WINTERS

Court of Civil Appeals of Texas, Amarillo, 1955.
282 S.W.2d 749.

PITTS, CHIEF JUSTICE. This is an appeal from a judgment denying a divorce upon a jury verdict returned in the trial court. Appellant, Dorothye K. Winters, filed suit against her husband, appellee, Elmer Winters, seeking a divorce on alleged grounds of harsh, cruel and unkind treatment. * * * Appellee denied generally appellant's alleged grounds for divorce and charged that appellant's association with a man by the name of Carl Maberry was the sole cause of any and all troubles between appellant and appellee.

[The case was submitted to a jury upon special issues which the jury found in favor of the appellee.]

* * *

The witness, Ray Converse, Jr., testified that appellee employed him on June 3, 1954, to follow, watch and observe the acts and conduct of appellant in connection with her association with Carl Maberry and that he began his professional observances of them on the following day and continued them for some time thereafter. As a witness he related seven different instances when he observed the said parties together. He further testified in effect that at each time he saw them he made written notes or memoranda of his observations of the said parties on each occasion and had such notes with him when he testified. In his direct testimony the witness used his said notes or memoranda to refresh his memory in giving testimony. After giving his direct testimony appellant asked permission to see, examine and use the same notes and memoranda in cross-examination of the witness, to which request appellee objected. The trial court sustained appellee's objections and refused to permit appellant or her attorney to examine or use such notes or memoranda in the cross-examination of the witness. Appellant charges that such a ruling of the trial court constituted reversible error. * * *

* * *

In our opinion the issue or question here presented is more clearly answered as a result of a similar situation reported by the Fifth Circuit * * * [in Montgomery v. United States, 203 F.2d 887]. In that case a special government agent was investigating appellant's activities in connection with his income tax returns, during which time he contacted appellant 12 or 15 times about the matter. On each occasion the said agent made notes concerning what transpired and transcribed said notes later. The said agent as a witness began using the said notes to refresh his memory in giving direct testimony in the case. Appellant's counsel objected to such use of the said notes unless appellant would have the privilege of examining the said notes and using them upon cross-examination of the witness. Such objection was overruled by the trial court and the witness continued using the notes. After the direct examination was completed and before cross-examination of the witness, appellant again requested the right to examine the said notes but was again overruled. Concerning this matter the appellate court said in part:

> "The law is now well settled that where a witness while he is on the stand uses any paper or memoranda to refresh his memory in giving his testimony, the opposing side, upon proper demand, has a right to see and examine that paper or memoranda and to use the same in cross-examination of the witness. * * * "

The court there held that to deny the opposing party the right to examine and use such notes or memoranda under such circumstances to cross-examine the witness constituted reversible error.

* * *

In our opinion since an employed detective as a witness in the case at bar apparently made the notes or memoranda he was using for the purpose of testifying from them and giving minute details of the place, hour and minute he saw appellant and Maberry holding clandestine meetings on various occasions and since the witness brought such notes or memoranda with him to the trial court and did so use such notes so made, it is our opinion under the record here presented and the authorities cited that appellant should have been permitted in the case at bar to have examined the said notes and memoranda so made and to have used them, if desired, upon cross-examining the witness. There may be other different situations arising under different circumstances wherein notes, memoranda or records used to refresh the memory of a witness should not be examined by an adversary, particularly if such examination would reveal secret matters about other different transactions which bore no relation to the matters being considered and which should not be revealed, but such was not shown to be true in the case at bar.

Because of the errors shown in the trial court procedure the judgment of the trial court is reversed and the cause is remanded.

Notes and Questions

1. *Policy.* What is the rationale for a right of inspection?

2. *Jencks Act.* 18 U.S.C.A. § 3500, referenced in Federal Rule 612, is known as the Jencks Act. Federal Criminal Rules 26.2 and 17(h) have supplanted the statute.

3. *Pretrial refreshment.* Few trial attorneys will call a crucial witness to the stand for direct examination without first having had the witness "refresh her recollection" by reading over her previous statements as the attorney possesses. The version of Rule 612 originally proposed by the drafting committee adopted the growing minority state view that such writings, even though used for refreshment only out of court, should be available to the cross-examiner as of right. The final version of the rule makes the matter one for judicial discretion. Even so limited, the rule has demonstrated a potential for invasion of the traditionally protected "work product" area. See 1 McCormick, Evidence § 9, at 45 (6th ed. 2006) ("[T]he clear trend in the federal cases has been to hold that Rule 612 overrides all privileges claims, at least when the witness consulted the writing pretrial for the specific purpose of freshening his memory in order to testify.").

4. *Verbal refreshment.* What if the form of the matter used to refresh is not susceptible to inspection by anyone, court or adversary? See State v. Schmelz, 111 A.2d 50 (N.J.1955) (witness refreshing recollection by speaking on the telephone during trial recess).

BORAWICK v. SHAY

United States Court of Appeals, Second Circuit, 1995.
68 F.3d 597.

WALKER, CIRCUIT JUDGE:

* * *

Borawick, who is currently thirty-eight years old and a citizen of California, brought a diversity tort action alleging that her aunt and uncle, Christine and Morrie Shay, Connecticut citizens, sexually abused her in the summers of 1961 and 1964, when she visited them at their home at the ages of four and seven, respectively. At the time, she lived in Seattle. Borawick had no memory of the alleged abuse for more than twenty years.

During the fall of 1984, Borawick began to experience panic attacks. [When they continued, she received psychological treatment. She also received treatment] for chronic physical illness with Dr. Ronald Peters, a medical doctor and part owner of the Pacific Medical Center ("PMC") in Santa Monica, California. PMC's clientele was largely composed of people from the entertainment industry.

After reviewing Borawick's medical history of chronic illness, Dr. Peters referred Borawick to Valerian St. Regis, a hypnotist who worked under Peters's supervision, since "problems in childhood" sometimes cause chronic illness and are susceptible to recall through hypnosis. Borawick underwent twelve to fourteen hypnotic sessions with St. Regis from the summer of 1987 through the fall of 1988. Before and immediately following these sessions, she had no recollection of abuse, much less of any abuse by these defendants.

When deposed in 1993, St. Regis testified that he had no permanent records relating to the hypnosis of Borawick; however, prior to his deposition, he had read a portion of Borawick's deposition. St. Regis maintained that, before hypnotizing Borawick, he had no expectation of the type of information that the hypnosis would reveal. He explained that he used "regression therapy" to take Borawick back to the age of between three and five years old. St. Regis also testified that, in general, instead of using hypnotic suggestion with Borawick, he asked broad questions such as "what happened?," "what do you remember?," or "what do you recall?."

St. Regis testified that Borawick revealed under hypnosis that her aunt, defendant Christine Shay, persuaded Borawick, at age four, to strip and engage in "ritual dancing." St. Regis further stated that during hypnosis Borawick described anal object penetration by Christine Shay, as well as another incident in which her aunt inserted a "cap pistol in [Borawick's] vagina." St. Regis also testified that during hypnotic sessions, Borawick disclosed that her uncle, defendant Morrie Shay, anally raped her. St. Regis did not know whether the alleged anal rape involved penile insertion or object insertion.

St. Regis testified that he did not reveal to Borawick what she had described during the sessions, because, in his opinion, such revelations would have been "devastating" and would probably surface in time. Borawick attended her last session with St. Regis in the fall of 1988.

Borawick testified in her deposition that during the second week of February, 1989, several months after her final hypnotic session, she experienced her first non-hypnotic memory of sexual abuse by her father, who is not a defendant in this case. Following this initial recollection, according to Borawick, subsequent memories surfaced in "bits and pieces." Her first memory concerning defendant Christine Shay allegedly occurred on February 10, 1989. On that date, Borawick first recalled her aunt vaginally raping her with a pistol. In late 1990 or early 1991, she first remembered an incident when Christine Shay forced "a broomstick into [Borawick's] vagina." Borawick also stated that she regained memory of being naked in the presence of her aunt and "having to dance around."

Borawick testified that her memory of being anally raped by defendant Morrie Shay surfaced in 1990. In addition to recalling sexual abuse by her father, aunt, and uncle, Borawick also claims sexual abuse by numerous others, including family members and her father's friends.

More detailed references to these individuals and their various "rituals" and other alleged abusive conduct are described in the sealed portion of the appendix.

* * * On November 4, 1992, defendants filed a motion in limine seeking to exclude the plaintiff's testimony. [The motion was subsequently granted.]

* * *

I. Admissibility of Post-Hypnotic Testimony

This circuit has yet to address the admissibility of post-hypnotic testimony of memories elicited as a result of hypnosis. While numerous state and federal courts have considered this issue, nearly all of them dealt with recall in the context of hypnosis that was specifically intended to enhance a memory of a particular known or suspected occurrence. The parties have not cited, nor are we aware of, any case concerning the specific issue before us: the admissibility of testimony about memories of childhood sexual abuse that are recalled for the first time in adulthood following the use of hypnosis as part of psychotherapy.

* * *

D. What is Hypnosis?

While "[t]here is no single, generally accepted theory of hypnosis, [or] consensus about a single definition," Council on Scientific Affairs, "Scientific Status of Refreshing Recollection by the Use of Hypnosis," 253 JAMA 1918, 1919 (1985) [hereinafter, Scientific Affairs], " 'there is considerable consensus at the descriptive level' as to how the [phenomenon] manifests itself in the hypnotized individual," 27 Charles A. Wright & Victor J. Gold, Federal Practice and Procedure: Evidence § 6011, at 116 (1990) * * * The American Medical Association has described hypnosis as a

> temporary condition of altered attention in the subject which may be induced by another person and in which a variety of phenomena may appear spontaneously or in response to [verbal] or other stimuli. These phenomena include alterations in consciousness and memory, increased susceptibility to suggestion, and the production in the subject of responses and ideas unfamiliar to him in his usual state of mind.

People v. Zayas, 131 Ill.2d 284, 137 Ill.Dec. 568, 546 N.E.2d 513, 515–16 (1989) (alteration in original) (quotations omitted).

As early as 1958, the American Medical Association recognized hypnosis as a valid therapeutic technique. Council on Medical Health of the American Medical Association, "Medical Uses of Hypnosis," 168 JAMA 186, 187 (1958). It has been found useful in psychotherapy, in the treatment of psychosomatic illness, to alleviate pain or as a substitute for anesthesia, and for memory recall. * * * It has sometimes been useful in developing leads in criminal investigations. *See Harker v. Maryland,* 800

F.2d 437, 440 (4th Cir.1986) * * * Despite these successes, many in the field remain skeptical of the reliability of hypnosis as a technique for refreshing or restoring memory. * * * Empirical studies calling into question the ability of hypnosis to restore memory effectively have engendered "considerable controversy" concerning the validity of using hypnosis for that purpose. Scientific Affairs, *supra,* at 1918. Thus, "[t]he popular belief that hypnosis guarantees the accuracy of recall is as yet without established foundation," *Rock v. Arkansas,* 483 U.S. 44, 59 * * * (1987), and no consensus has been reached regarding the ability of hypnosis to enhance memory, Scientific Affairs, *supra,* at 1918.

The controversy over the effectiveness of hypnosis in memory enhancement centers in large part on disagreements concerning theories of memory. Those scientists who are most optimistic about the role of hypnosis in memory recall conceptualize a process whereby the brain records and stores sensory input accurately, much like a videotape. Recall is the ability to "play back" that tape, and loss of memory is the inability to retrieve that information. [Citations omitted.] Under this theory, hypnosis simply enhances the retrieval process.

Many scientists reject this theory, however. They view memory recall as "much more complex and much less accurate than previously thought." *State v. Tuttle,* 780 P.2d 1203, 1210 (Utah 1989) * * * Instead, they espouse a "construction theory" of memory, which holds that a memory is formed and influenced by numerous factors when the mind creates and integrates the information from an event "into the memory representation of that event." *Valdez,* 722 F.2d at 1200. The composite created by this process is malleable and evolves over time as additional input is received. In fact, a leading proponent of this theory has written that memory is " 'being continually remade [and] reconstructed in the interest of the present.' " F. Bartlett, Remembering 213 (reprint 1964) (1932) * * *.

The "constructivists" are highly skeptical of any view that hypnosis can effectively and accurately enhance memory. They believe that because hypnosis has the power to contribute to memory reconstruction, it can create inaccurate memories. In other words, if present events can contribute to a construction of a memory that differs from that which was originally perceived and if the process of hypnosis is such an event, then hypnosis may distort memory.

The courts have identified several problems with the reliability of hypnotically-refreshed recall. First, a person undergoing hypnosis becomes more susceptible to suggestion. The subject may be influenced by verbal and nonverbal cues, intentionally or unintentionally planted by the hypnotist. This suggestibility may be enhanced by the perception that hypnosis will refresh one's memory and by a wish to please the hypnotist. * * *

In addition, a hypnotized person may "confabulate," that is, fill in the gaps in her memory to make it comprehensible. The added details may be derived from irrelevant or unrelated facts or from pure fantasy.

* * * Like suggestibility, confabulation can occur as a result of the subject's desire to please the hypnotist by coming up with complete and coherent memories. * * *

A third problem with hypnotically-refreshed recall is "memory hardening," a phenomenon which gives the subject enhanced confidence in the facts remembered, whether they be true or false. * * * Even as inaccurate recollections increase, the subject's confidence is likely to remain constant or even to increase. * * * The lack of correlation between the accuracy of recall and the subject's confidence in the accuracy makes it more difficult for a jury or even an expert to judge the credibility of hypnotically-enhanced testimony, * * * and makes cross-examination difficult * * *.

Finally, after undergoing hypnosis to refresh memory, individuals may lose the ability to assess their memory critically and be more prone to speculation than if they had relied only on normal memory recall. * * * The subject becomes less able "to discriminate between accurate and inaccurate recollections." Scientific Affairs, *supra,* at 1921. He or she may also experience "source amnesia," believing that a statement heard prior to hypnosis was a product of his or her own memory. * * *

As a result of the foregoing phenomena, the "hypnotically recalled memory is apt to be a mosaic of (1) appropriate actual events, (2) entirely irrelevant actual events, (3) pure fantasy, and (4) fantasized details supplied to make a logical whole." Bernard L. Diamond, "Inherent Problems in the Use of Pretrial Hypnosis on a Prospective Witness," 68 Cal.L.Rev. 313, 335 (1980); *see* Scientific Affairs, *supra,* at 1921. In the worst case, someone who has undergone hypnosis might "inaccurately reconstruct the memory * * * and * * * then become convinced of the absolute accuracy of the reconstruction through memory hardening." *Harker,* 800 F.2d at 441. The "constructionist" views, supported as they are in the scientific community, have considerable force. * * *

E. Various Approaches to the Admissibility Question

The state and federal courts that have been faced with the admissibility of hypnotically-refreshed testimony have followed four different approaches. Some courts treat all such testimony as per se admissible under the theory that hypnosis does not render the witness incompetent, but goes to the question of credibility. * * * This position depends in considerable part on one's faith in the jury's ability to evaluate the testimony accurately in light of cross-examination, expert testimony relating to hypnosis, and jury instructions. * * * Such an approach was particularly favored when courts were just beginning to address the admissibility of hypnotically-refreshed testimony, *see Tuttle,* 780 P.2d at 1208, but it "has sparsely been followed since 1980," *Zayas,* 137 Ill.Dec. at 571, 546 N.E.2d at 516.

Courts at the other end of the spectrum have found that post-hypnotic testimony is per se inadmissible because the witness is incompetent to testify regarding such matters. * * * The common thread running through these cases is that the possible distorting effects of hypnosis on memory are impossible to circumvent and are so substantial that "the game is not worth the candle." *Shirley,* 181 Cal.Rptr. at 256, 723 P.2d at 1366. * * * Reasoning that no safeguard can adequately ensure reliability, these courts deem the evidence inadmissible. * * * A number of courts apply a modified version of the rule by confirming the witness's testimony to matters recalled before undergoing hypnosis. * * *

In *Rock v. Arkansas,* * * * the Supreme Court reviewed Arkansas's rule that a criminal defendant's hypnotically-refreshed testimony was per se inadmissible. While the Court recognized the problems with hypnosis, it concluded that certain procedural safeguards could reduce the potential inaccuracies of post-hypnotic testimony. * * * Focusing on the due process right of criminal defendants to testify in their own defense, * * * the Sixth Amendment right to call witnesses in the defendant's favor, * * * and the Fifth Amendment guarantee against compelled testimony, * * * the Court concluded that the rule of per se inadmissibility was an "arbitrary restriction on the [criminal defendant's] right to testify in the absence of clear evidence by the State repudiating the validity of all post-hypnosis recollections," *id.* at 61 * * *. Consequently, the Court deemed Arkansas's prohibition unconstitutional. The Court, however, explicitly limited the reach of its holding by refusing to express an opinion as to the appropriate rule of admissibility "of testimony of previously hypnotized witnesses other than criminal defendants." *Id.* at 58 n.15 * * *.

The third and fourth approaches occupy a middle ground. These attempt to balance the competing concerns that animate the per se positions. The third approach, articulated by the New Jersey Supreme Court in the oft-cited *State v. Hurd,* 86 N.J. 525, 432 A.2d 86 (1981), requires adherence to a list of prescribed safeguards intended to ensure the reliability of hypnotically-refreshed testimony. The court concluded that "a rule of per se inadmissibility is unnecessarily broad and will result in the exclusion of evidence that is as trustworthy as other eyewitness testimony." *Id.,* 432 A.2d at 94.

In light of recommendations offered by a frequent expert witness, Dr. Martin Orne, the court adopted the following procedural requirements:

> First, a psychiatrist or psychologist experienced in the use of hypnosis must conduct the session. This professional should also be able to qualify as an expert in order to aid the court in evaluating the procedures followed * * *.
>
> Second, the professional conducting the hypnotic session should be independent of and not regularly employed by the prosecutor, investigator or defense * * *.
>
> Third, any information given to the hypnotist by law enforcement personnel or the defense prior to the hypnotic session must be recorded, either in writing or another suitable form * * *.

> Fourth, before inducing hypnosis the hypnotist should obtain from the subject a detailed description of the facts as the subject remembers them [without] * * * asking structured questions or adding new details.
>
> Fifth, all contacts between the hypnotist and the subject must be recorded * * *.
>
> Sixth, only the hypnotist and the subject should be present during any phase of the hypnotic session, including the pre-hypnotic testing and the post-hypnotic interview.

Id., 432 A.2d at 96–97 (footnote omitted).

* * *

Finally, the approach most frequently taken by the federal courts, Federal Practice, *supra,* § 6011, at 173, is a so-called case-by-case or totality-of-the-circumstances approach, *see, e.g., McQueen v. Garrison,* 814 F.2d 951, 958 (4th Cir.1987) * * *. While recognizing the benefits of the *Hurd* guidelines, these courts conclude that the district court should be given discretion to balance all of the factors to determine the reliability of the evidence and the probative versus prejudicial effect of the testimony. They note that even though the safeguards required by other courts

> represent[ ] the type of general reliability inquiry that must be made[,] * * * a court cannot necessarily rest solely on the reliability *vel non* of the hypnosis procedures in ruling on the admissibility of the proffered testimony. Even though all of the *Hurd* safeguards might be employed, the defendant may still be able to demonstrate by expert testimony that a witness' memory has been irreparably distorted by hypnosis. On the other hand, even if the hypnosis procedures are flawed, a trial or appellate court might discern that a witness' testimony was nonetheless independent of the dangers associated with hypnosis.

McQueen, 814 F.2d at 958 (citations omitted). As the foregoing summary indicates, the law continues to be in a state of flux regarding the reception of hypnotically-enhanced testimony. *See* Federal Practice, *supra,* § 6011, at 123.

F. Hypnosis as a Therapeutic Tool

The existing caselaw concerning the admissibility of post-hypnotic testimony, while helpful to our analysis, is grounded in fact situations where the hypnosis is specifically directed to the witness's recollections of known events, rather than where repressed memories of past traumas previously unknown simply emerge following hypnosis. Borawick, relying heavily on a law review article, Kanovitz, *supra,* at 1213,[34] argues that hypnosis functions differently and more reliably when it results in the

34. [Kanovitz, Hypnotic Memories and Civil Sexual Abuse Trials, 45 Vand.L.Rev. 1185 (1992). Ed.]

retrieval of repressed memories of traumatic events than when it is used to refresh one's memory of eye-witnessed events and therefore testimony relating to the former should be admitted on a per se basis.

The research on hypnosis only uses subjects with normal memory function who are exposed to simulations of real-life events to "replicate eyewitness situations," *id.* at 1212, 1223, since for practical and ethical reasons, it is impossible to design effective controlled studies to test the ability of hypnosis to retrieve accurate, suppressed memories of childhood trauma, *id.* at 1221–22. The Kanovitz article sets forth some arguments in support of the view that hypnosis may be better able to retrieve memories "kept out of conscious awareness by ego-defenses that protect the psyche from trauma," *id.* at 1194, than hypnosis used for normal memory recall. In the clinical setting, hypnosis may overcome the psychological barriers to remembering past traumas because it induces profound relaxation and calmness, intensifies concentration, and focuses the subject's attention inward. *Id.* at 1213. In addition, the clinical literature "abounds with case histories of spectacular memory successes." *Id.* at 1225. Finally, repressed memories of events that have a traumatic impact upon the witness may, even if unconscious, tend to remain fixed and survive longer than memories of events witnessed quickly, in the context of a great deal of other sensory information. *Id.* at 1231–32.

* * *

While we appreciate the force of many of these arguments, the fact remains that the literature has not yet conclusively demonstrated that hypnosis is a consistently effective means to retrieve repressed memories of traumatic, past experiences accurately. For example, the Council on Scientific Affairs has pointed out that the case histories of "spectacular memory successes" are anecdotal and difficult to verify independently and there are no controlled studies confirming these reports. Scientific Affairs, *supra,* at 1919. In addition, some in the clinical community express reservations concerning the theory of memory repression, or at least the phenomenon's prevalence. *See* Julie M. Murray, "Repression, Memory, and Suggestibility," 66 U.Colo.L.Rev. 477, 505–08 (1995). Furthermore, we are highly skeptical of the belief in the clinician's ability to "weed out most patently groundless claims" because childhood sexual abuse often "fits like a tailor-made glove" to certain psychiatric disorders. Kanovitz, *supra,* at 1242. Some therapists may be too eager to find patterns of behavior demonstrative of childhood sexual abuse. *See* Murray, 66 U.Colo.L.Rev. at 507–08. *But cf.* Colette M. Smith, "Recovered Memories of Alleged Sexual Abuse," 18 Seattle Univ.L.Rev. 51, 61 (1994) (noting that Harvard Medical School psychiatrist Judith Herman "believes that therapists rarely wield enough power over patients to impose false memories on them"). Therefore, even though there may be important distinctions between the use of hypnosis to enhance memories of witnessed events and the use of hypnosis to retrieve repressed memories, given the lack of empirical studies as to the latter and the complicated nature of hypnotically-induced recall, we are not willing to assume that the risks of suggestibility, confabulation, and memory hardening are significantly reduced when the hypnosis that triggers the testimony is used for therapeutic purposes.

G. *Totality-of-the-Circumstances Approach*

Based on our review of the literature and the caselaw, we conclude that the district court was correct to reject a per se rule of admissibility or inadmissibility. A per se rule of exclusion or inclusion is too blunt a tool with which to address the concerns regarding the reliability of post-hypnotic testimony or the concerns that people who have been sexually abused may lose an opportunity to bring suit against their abusers.

To be sure, the exclusion of such testimony in every case avoids the problems of unreliability, but it ignores Federal Rule of Evidence 601, which "abolished almost all grounds for witness disqualification based on new assumptions that took a more optimistic view of witness reliability and jury perceptiveness." Federal Practice, *supra,* § 6011, at 124, 129. In addition, we believe that it risks the elimination of reliable testimony. *See State v. Iwakiri,* 106 Idaho 618, 624, 682 P.2d 571, 577 (1984).

On the other hand, to admit all such testimony without pause, even if the jury is informed of the risks of the potential problems of hypnotically-enhanced testimony, creates the danger of having a lay jury speculate as to the effects of the hypnosis in the case before it. As a result, such an approach seems to us inadequate to protect defendants from unfounded charges in either criminal or civil suits. * * * While we appreciate the care and sensitivity with which the district court chose its methodology, we nevertheless find its approach too rigid and restrictive and prefer a "totality-of-the-circumstances" approach. * * *

In conducting a case-by-case analysis, the district court should consider the following non-exclusive list of factors. First, it should evaluate the purpose of the hypnosis: whether it was to refresh a witness's memory of an accident or crime or whether it was conducted as part of therapy. In the former instance, the subject may feel pressured to remember details, to aid the criminal investigation, whereas when the subject has undergone therapy to explore the sources of her psychological ailments, she may be less inclined to confabulate or describe a complete coherent story. In the latter case, however, the court should be mindful of the possibility that the subject may have received subtle suggestions from her therapist that abuse or other traumas could be at the root of her problems. Thus, a second important consideration is whether the witness received any suggestions from the hypnotist or others prior to or during hypnosis such as a theory of the cause of the subject's ailments or key information relevant to the investigation for which she underwent hypnosis. A third and related factor is the presence or absence of a permanent record, which can help the court ascertain whether suggestive procedures were used. Ideally, the session should be videotaped or audiotaped. Fourth, a court should consider whether the hypnotist was appropriately qualified by training in psychology or psychiatry. A fifth factor is whether corroborating evidence exists to support the reliability of the hypnotically-refreshed memories. Sixth, evidence of the subject's hypnotizability may also be relevant. A highly hypnotizable subject may be more prone to confabulate and more susceptible to suggestion. Seventh, the court should consider any expert evidence offered by the parties as to the reliability of the procedures used in the case. Finally, a pretrial evidentiary hearing is highly desirable to enable the parties to present expert evidence and to test credibility through cross-examination.

After consideration of all of the relevant circumstances, the trial court should weigh the factors in favor and against the reliability of the hypnosis procedure in the exercise of its discretion whether to admit the post-hypnotic testimony. Finally, we add that the party attempting to admit the hypnotically-enhanced testimony bears the burden of persuading the district court that the balance tips in favor of admissibility. *Hurd,* 432 A.2d at 97.

H. Application of Admissibility Approach to this Case

* * * Since in our view the factors before the district court weighed decisively against the admissibility of Borawick's testimony, we are convinced that if the district court had followed our test, it would have necessarily reached the same conclusion. We see no point in remanding the case so that the district court can reach the same finding.

First, Borawick's assertions notwithstanding, it is beyond question that St. Regis lacked adequate professional qualifications as a hypnotist. While a panoply of academic qualifications is not necessary in all circumstances for one to qualify as an expert, there should be a general presumption in favor of appropriate academic credentials. The district court's finding that St. Regis was not properly qualified finds ample support in the record: his formal education ended with a high school diploma; he had no formal training in psychiatry or psychotherapy; his hypnotic technique used an experimental cranial electronic stimulator; he did not read the professional literature; and his work experience prior to being a hypnotist at Pacific Medical Center was intermittent. The fact that Dr. Peters, a medical doctor, self-servingly stated that he considered St. Regis to be qualified is not enough to disturb the district court's determination.

There was also no permanent record of the procedures that St. Regis used; no videotapes, audiotapes, or even contemporaneously-drafted medical reports existed. * * * As a result, the district court was not provided with any means, independent of St. Regis's testimony, to determine whether or not he was inadvertently suggestive in his approach or otherwise used suspect techniques in conducting the hypnosis. Without such a record, expert testimony would have been of little value, since experts similarly would have had no basis on which to evaluate the actual procedures St. Regis used.

Finally, we receive no comfort from the fact that St. Regis read excerpts from Borawick's deposition transcript prior to testifying himself. Given that he is not qualified and that the record lacks any basis on which to assess the reliability of the procedures he used, this circumstance further undermines the value, if any, of his testimony.

Our conclusion is reinforced by the inherent incredibility of Borawick's allegations. In this case, Borawick has levelled fanciful accusations of sexual abuse against numerous persons other than the defendants in this matter that include persons both familiar and unfamiliar to her. For example, Borawick allegedly recalls being raped and sexually abused at the age of three during rituals by men whom she believed to be members of the Masons. She also purports to recollect several incidents in which she was drugged by injection as well as an incident in which she was forced to drink blood at a ritual involving a dead pig, incense, chanting, and people dressed in black gowns. Several additional incidents of a similarly unlikely nature involving sexual abuse by others are included in the sealed record. That Borawick has made these far-fetched, uncorroborated accusations against others, in addition to the defendants, erodes our confidence in the allegations against Morrie and Christine Shay and properly weighs against the admissibility of her hypnotically-induced memories.

* * *

Notes and Questions

1. *Various approaches.* While the federal courts and some states follow the "totality of the circumstances" approach as indicated in the principal case, the majority of courts have adopted the per se exclusion rule, at least in criminal cases. See 1 Giannelli & Imwinkelried, Scientific Evidence ch. 12 (3d ed. 1999); Webert, Are The Courts in a Trance? Approaches To The Admissibility of Hypnotically Enhanced Witness Testimony in Light of Empirical Evidence, 40 Am.Crim.L.Rev. 1301 (2003). However, these jurisdictions recognize two exceptions. See notes 2 and 3 infra. In State v. Moore, 902 A.2d 1212 (N.J.2006), the N.J. Supreme Court rejected its earlier position in *Hurd* (cited in the principal case) and adopted the per se exclusion approach, which the court stated was followed by 26 other states.

2. *Exception for prehypnotic testimony.* In State ex rel. Collins v. Superior Court, 644 P.2d 1266, 1295 (Ariz.1982), several rape victims were hypnotized in an attempt to discover more information about the identity of their assailant. Although no new information developed from this process, the defendant was later apprehended as he approached a police decoy. The defense moved to disqualify the victims as witnesses. On appeal, the Arizona Supreme Court reaffirmed its earlier position, ruling that the testimony of a hypnotized witness is inadmissible. On a motion for rehearing, however, the court modified this ruling:

> [A] witness will be permitted to testify with regard to those matters which he or she was able to recall *and* relate prior to hypnosis. Thus, for example, the rape victim would be free to testify to the occurrence of the

crime, the lack of consent, the injury inflicted and the like, assuming that such matters were remembered and related to the authorities prior to use of hypnosis.

Collins II represents the prevailing view on this issue. Are there problems with this approach?

3. *Exception for the accused.* In Rock v. Arkansas, 483 U.S. 44 (1987), cited in the principal case, the Court held that an accused who has been hypnotized cannot be barred from testifying under a rule making hypnotically enhanced testimony per se inadmissible. What about other defense witnesses? See Burral v. State, 724 A.2d 65, 65 (Md.1999) ("The exclusion of hypnotically-enhanced testimony was stated in the form of a per se exclusion; it did not depend on who the witness was, who called the witness to testify, or the circumstances of the case."). See Giuliana, Between *Rock* and a *Hurd* Place: Protecting the Criminal Defendant's Right to Testify After Her Testimony Has Been Hypnotically Refreshed, 65 Fordham L.Rev. 2151 (1997).

4. *Right of confrontation.* Compare State v. Mena, 624 P.2d 1274, 1280 (Ariz.1981) ("[T]here is a strong belief among several authorities that hypnotism of a witness renders subsequent cross-examination ineffective * * *. Until the general scientific reliability of hypnotism * * * [is] established and/or the barriers which it raises to effective cross-examination are somehow overcome, we think the confrontation clause of the Sixth Amendment * * * requires [exclusion]."), with Bundy v. Dugger, 850 F.2d 1402, 1415 (11th Cir.1988) (*Rock* "teaches that, although hypnosis may make effective cross-examination more difficult, it does not always make it impossible, thereby preserving the opportunity for effective cross-examination safeguarded by the Sixth Amendment.").

5. *Nonforensic hypnosis.* In McGlauflin v. State, 857 P.2d 366, 378 (Alaska Ct.App.1993), the court considered the admissibility of a child abuse victim's testimony. The hypnotic session was intended to focus on her weight problem. The court ruled that there is no presumption of unreliability in this type of case because "the circumstances and results of the hypnosis session make it likely that the witness's memories have not been enhanced or altered by hypnosis." See also Franklin v. Duncan, 884 F.Supp. 1435, 1441 (N.D.Cal.1995) (defendant's daughter recalled murder 20 years later; reversed on other grounds), aff'd, 70 F.3d 75, 78 (9th Cir.1995).

6. *Nonhypnotic recall.* In Commonwealth v. Crawford, 718 A.2d 768 (Pa.1998), an arrest for a murder was not made until 20 years after the victim's body had been found. The witness claimed that his "flashback" occurred when he saw a person who resembled the victim when he was shopping. The Pennsylvania Supreme Court upheld the exclusion of a defense expert's testimony on the grounds that it would have invaded the jury's province in evaluating credibility. The expert would have testified that the witness' memory was inaccurate. The Court also noted that the prosecution had not introduced expert testimony on revived memory and had not sought to establish the scientific validity of repressed memory.

7. *Repressed memories.* See Shahzade v. Gregory, 923 F.Supp. 286, 287 (D.Mass.1996) (finding the theory of repressed memory reliable under *Daubert*); Logerquist v. McVey, 1 P.3d 113 (Ariz.2000) (in a civil case, ruling

expert testimony on repressed memories admissible; plaintiff claimed that she did not remember for 20 years that her pediatrician had sexually abused her); Doe v. Shults–Lewis Child and Family Services, Inc., 718 N.E.2d 738, 748–49 (Ind.1999) (before testimony admitted, trial judge must be satisfied that the expert testimony is based on reliable scientific principles); State v. Quattrocchi, 681 A.2d 879, 883–84 (R.I.1996) (when repressed memory testimony offered, trial judge "should exercise a gatekeeping function and hold a preliminary evidentiary hearing outside the presence of the jury in order to determine whether such evidence is reliable").

For further discussion, see Porter et al., The Nature of Real, Implanted, and Fabricated Memories for Emotional Childhood Events: Implications for the Recovered Memory Debate, 23 Law & Hum.Behav. 517, 529 (1999) ("Over repeated interviews, one fourth of participants came to report that they experienced a stressful emotional childhood incident which actually had been contrived by the researchers. The 'recovered' memories included a serious medical procedure, getting lost, getting seriously harmed by another child, a serious animal attack, and serious outdoor accident. These findings cast doubt on the argument against false memories for highly emotional events."); Fletcher, Repressed Memories: Do Triggering Methods Contribute to Witness Testimony Reliability?, 13 Wash.U.J.L. & Pol'y 335 (2003).

SECTION C. LAY WITNESSES

(1) FIRSTHAND KNOWLEDGE: FEDERAL RULE 602

KEMP v. BALBOA

United States Court of Appeals, Eighth Circuit, 1994.
23 F.3d 211.

FRIEDMAN, SENIOR CIRCUIT JUDGE.

In this case, a state prisoner filed suit under 42 U.S.C. § 1983 (1988), accusing a prison guard of improperly confiscating his medication used to control his epilepsy, resulting in the prisoner's having epileptic fits, which injured him. The jury found for the prisoner, but awarded him only nominal damages of $1.00 and punitive damages of the same amount. The prisoner challenges the award of only nominal damages as based upon inadmissible evidence, and the guard appeals from the award of attorney fees against him. We hold that the district court improperly admitted testimony by a lay witness who lacked personal knowledge of the matter about which she testified, in violation of Fed.R.Evid. 602, and remand for a new trial on the issue of damages only. We vacate the attorney fee award.

* * *

Vicki Maness, a licensed practical nurse at the Center, testified that Kemp failed to pick up his medication from the prison infirmary on seven separate occasions. She testified that she had reviewed portions of Kemp's medical file relating to the dispensing of medication. * * * Maness read from the records three dates during June and July, 1989 on which Kemp allegedly failed to pick up his epilepsy medication from the prison infirmary.

Kemp objected repeatedly to Maness' reading of these records while she was testifying on direct examination. * * * Maness then testified that Kemp failed to procure his medication on three occasions in September 1989, and one time in October 1989.

On cross examination, Maness stated she was not on duty on the days that Kemp allegedly failed to obtain his medication, and that her only knowledge of the subject came from her reviewing the medical charts, which someone else had prepared. Upon completion of the cross examination, Kemp moved to strike Maness' testimony on the ground that Maness' had no personal knowledge of Kemp's failure to pick up his medication, since her testimony was based solely on her review of Kemp's medical file. The district court denied the motion to strike. * * *

Unlike an expert witness, who may give his or her opinion about a matter within the witness' expertise (Fed.R.Evid. 703), a lay witness may testify only about matters within his or her personal knowledge. * * * Rule 602 prohibits a lay witness from testifying about matters that are not within the personal knowledge of the witness. * * *

Maness was not tendered and did not testify as an expert witness. She testified only as a lay witness to present factual evidence that Kemp had failed to pick up his medication from the Center infirmary. As her testimony on cross examination brought out, however, she had no personal knowledge of these facts, since she was not on duty on the days on which she stated Kemp failed to pick up his medication. Her testimony was based not upon her personal knowledge of the facts about which she testified, but solely upon what she had read in the medical records prepared by others.

Those medical records themselves were not introduced in evidence. According to the district court and Balboa, however, the records were properly used to refresh Maness' recollection. Since Maness had no personal knowledge of the facts, however, she had no recollection that was capable of being refreshed. * * *

[The court held the error was not harmless.] Maness' testimony that Kemp had failed to pick up his medication might have lead the jury to conclude that it was Kemp's own indifference to his medical needs rather than Balboa's confiscation of his medication that was primarily the cause of Kemp's increased seizures. Indeed, based on Maness' testimony, the jury might have believed that Kemp, himself, sometimes failed to take his own medication. The probable impact of Maness' testimony on the jury is further suggested by the jury's request to see the medical files Maness read from during her testimony. The court denied the request, but instructed the jury to use its "collective recollection" of Maness' testimony regarding the contents of the medical logs.

* * *

Notes and Questions

1. *Time of acquiring firsthand knowledge.* It is the witness' knowledge at the time of trial, not necessarily at the time of the event, that is determinative; a witness could gained new personal knowledge after an accident or crime. See Cleveland Terminal & Valley R.R. v. Marsh, 58 N.E. 821, 822 (Ohio 1900); Strickland Transp. Co. v. Ingram, 403 S.W.2d 192, 195 (Tex.Ct.App.1966) ("A witness may testify in accordance with his knowledge at the time his testimony is offered; he is not restricted to his knowledge at the time the event occurred.").

2. *Hearsay overlap.* As *Kemp* illustrates, there is an overlap between the lack of firsthand knowledge and hearsay rule. Although hearsay, the records may have been admissible under the public records or business records exceptions to the hearsay rule. See Chapter 14, infra.

3. *Basis of knowledge.* See United States v. Doe, 960 F.2d 221, 223 (1st Cir.1992) (In a case involving possession of a firearm shipped interstate, the court stated: "Doe claims that the district court should have excluded the sports shop owner's testimony that he 'knows' Taurus pistols are 'manufactured in Brazil,' on the ground that the witness did not have 'personal knowledge' of that fact. Evidence proving personal knowledge may, however, 'consist of the witness' own testimony,' and that knowledge includes inferences and opinions, so long as they are grounded in personal observation and experience. * * * A reasonable trier of fact could believe that the sports shop owner had firsthand knowledge from which he could infer that the pistol was made outside of Massachusetts, indeed in Brazil, particularly since his testimony to this effect was unchallenged."). Is the basis sufficient or is the lack of objection determinative?

4. *Controlled drug buy.* A lack of firsthand knowledge on the part of police officers, combined with the suspect credibility of drug informants, sometimes make proof in drug buys tricky. The police have developed procedures for dealing with these issues. See United States v. Beal, 279 F.3d 567, 571–72 (8th Cir.2002) ("The officers testified that they searched Booker's person prior to the controlled buy, though they did not conduct a body cavity search. The officers further testified that the transaction occurred in Beal's car on a public street, that it was monitored by audiotape, and that it lasted less than one minute. Most notably, Booker was under constant surveillance by several officers * * *. The government further demonstrated that the cocaine went from Booker to Officer Troy Smith (who had searched Booker before the buy and provided money for the purchase) to Officer Randy McDowell, who forwarded it to the DEA laboratory where it was received and analyzed by Khrishna James.").

JACKSON v. LEACH

Court of Appeals of Maryland, 1931.
152 A. 813.

ADKINS, J. This is a suit for damages for injuries to the plaintiff resulting from a collision between the automobile of the plaintiff and that of Howard W. Jackson, one of the defendants, while being driven by Riall Jackson, the other defendant. The accident occurred at the intersection of Ellamont street and Clifton avenue in Baltimore city. The plaintiff was driving northerly on Ellamont street and Riall Jackson westwardly on Clifton avenue.

* * *

* * * This appeal is from a judgment on a verdict in favor of the plaintiff.

There was no evidence of negligence on the part of the defendants except as to excessive speed; and the only direct testimony as to that was given by the witness, Hall. It is contended by the appellants that his testimony should have been stricken out on motion duly made, because, according to his own statement, he did not see defendants' car except at the moment of the collision, when he was walking north on the east side of Ellamont street half a block away, and therefore his opinion as to the speed was merely an inference, as in Dashiell v. Jacoby, 142 Md. 330, 336, 120 A. 751, and was not based on his actual observation of the car while running. Hall's testimony on this point was substantially as follows:

"Q. Did you see the other car (referring to the Jackson car)? Ans. I saw it when it hit it.

"Q. You saw it coming up the street then? Ans. At a terrific speed.

"Q. Did you see Mr. Jackson's car at any time before the collision? Ans. I saw the car when it hit.

"Q. Of course you couldn't see around the corner? Ans. No, Oh, no.

"Q. You didn't see around the corner, but when you first saw Mr. Jackson's car how far was it away from the east side of Ellamont street? Ans. You see, I was going extreme north and it was just fortunately my eyes were looking straight ahead, and all of a sudden, right smack off, like that (snapping fingers), just like a shot out of a cannon.

"Q. What attracted your attention, the crash? Ans. No, my eyes just happened to catch the accident.

"Q. Well, you just caught a flashing glance of the machines as they came together, that's right, isn't it? Ans. I got the full view when they came together.

"Q. But you didn't see Mr. Jackson's machine when it was any distance away from Mr. Leach's machine, did you? Ans. It was impossible, on account of the speed.

"Q. You mean it was going so fast you couldn't see it? Ans. Well, you see, the corner covers your view.

"Q. You couldn't see around the corner? Ans. No, sir, And it was on an incline.

"Q. And you didn't see the Jackson car at any time before the accident? Just when they came together, you saw it? Ans. That's right."

The witness further testified as to the position of the car before and after the collision.

And then he was asked:

"All you remember about this accident is that you saw two machines when they came together? Ans. Yes, sir.

"Q. An instantaneous appearance, that is what you saw, isn't it? Ans. Well, the excitement was so great the first thing I thought of was the people in the automobile."

Can we say from all this as a matter of law that the testimony of the witness as to speed was without probative force? It is not like the case of Dashiell v. Jacoby [142 Md. 330, 120 A. 751], relied on by the appellants, where the testimony excluded was an inference merely. Nor is it like the case of Taxicab Co. v. Ottenritter, 151 Md. 525, 135 A. 587, cited by appellee, where the court was asked to exclude testimony on the ground of its incredibility. Here the question is, Was the observation of the car which the witness had immediately before the collision sufficient to give him any information as to the speed of the car? In this connection it should be noted that there was a clear space of twenty-six feet from the building line on the east side of Ellamont street to the gutter in which there was at least a momentary view of the car before the collision. While under the circumstances it might be well argued that the weight to be given to the testimony was slight, we are unable to say that, as a matter of law, it was without any probative force, and that it should have been stricken out. * * *

Finding no error in the rulings presented for review the judgment must be affirmed.

Judgment affirmed, with costs to appellee.

Notes and Questions

1. *Basis of knowledge.* Virtually all courts will today admit testimony concerning the speed of vehicles given by a lay witness demonstrated to have had a sufficient opportunity to observe the vehicle in motion. Holdings concerning what opportunity is to be deemed "sufficient," however, have varied. See, e.g., Hicks v. Reavis, 337 S.E.2d 121 (N.C.Ct.App.1985), where the court held that witnesses who heard, but did not see, vehicles before the accident could testify in relative terms as to speed (for example, "fast," "high rate of speed," etc.) but could not give an opinion of speed in miles per hour, and Keyes v. Amundson, 391 N.W.2d 602 (N.D.1986), where the court permitted testimony as to speed (40 to 45 mph) by witnesses who saw and heard a motorcycle for three seconds before an accident, noting that noise of a vehicle may be a factor is assessing speed. See also cases collected in Note, Lay Opinion in Civil Cases—Speed of Motor Vehicles, 4 Vill.L.Rev. 245 (1959).

2. *Uncertainty.* Many witnesses, even those testifying as to phenomena observed by them under relatively favorable conditions, will feel obliged to qualify their testimonial assertions by such prefatory statements as, "I believe," "my impression was," or "as nearly as I could tell." Should qualifications of this sort preclude admissibility of the statements so qualified? It is generally held that absolute certainty is not required and that admissibility will not be affected unless, judging from the witness' testimony as a whole, the uncertainty appears to stem from a basic lack of opportunity to observe the matter related. See State v. Thorp, 72 N.C. 186 (1875); 1 McCormick, Evidence § 10 (6th ed. 2006).

3. *Negative testimony.* It is sometimes broadly asserted that testimony that a particular event did not occur ("negative" testimony) is of a relatively weak and unsatisfactory character, and further that as between negative and positive evidence the latter should control. Does this rule have any relevance when a witness shown to have been in a position to observe an event if it had occurred testifies that it did not occur? Should the foundation required for the introduction of negative testimony differ from that required when the witness proposes to testify positively that the event did occur? See South v. National R.R. Passenger Corp., 290 N.W.2d 819 (N.D.1980). The positive-negative rule is discussed in Dow, Judicial Determination of Credibility in Jury Tried Actions, 38 Neb.L.Rev. 835 (1959).

(2) OPINION RULE: FEDERAL RULE 701

PARKER v. HOEFER

Supreme Court of Vermont, 1953.
100 A.2d 434.

SHERBURNE, CHIEF JUSTICE. This is an action for alienation of affections by enticement and criminal conversation. It comes here upon the defendant's exceptions after a verdict and judgment for the plaintiff.

* * *

We next have exceptions to the admission of evidence, and to the refusal of the court to strike out answers to questions, mainly relating to opinion testimony. * * * [The plaintiff] testified that Parker stayed out many nights very late, and came in from four to eight in the morning, and sometimes didn't come in until a day later. That this caused her concern and the effect upon her was such that she became very tired waiting up all night and very lonely and unhappy. That the further effect of his not coming home regularly was that she lost weight, had no sleep, became very nervous and she had a doctor's care. That she noticed the defendant's actions in regard to her husband, noticed her interest, her taking him aside and that there was great intimacy between them. That she noticed that the defendant was absorbed in him. That she noticed that her husband's appearance was abnormal, he was exhausted and had lipstick on his collar, he smelled as though he had been drinking and he looked very haggard. That the plaintiff visited her husband's room in the

Gibson Hotel and noticed pictures of the defendant and Tina Thomson,[35] women's gloves, perfume, cigarettes with lipstick on them, flowers. The defendant argues that this evidence relative to what the plaintiff noticed about how the defendant appeared and acted and about how Parker appeared were inadmissible as opinions and conclusions, and that no proper foundation had been laid for its admission.

As a general rule witnesses are to state facts and not give their inferences or opinions; but this rule is subject to the exception that "where the facts are of such a character as to be incapable of being presented with their proper force to anyone but the observer himself so as to enable the triers to draw a correct or intelligent conclusion from them without the aid of the judgment or opinion of the witness who had the benefit of personal observation, he is allowed to a certain extent, to add his conclusion, judgment or opinion." Bates v. Town of Sharon, 45 Vt. 474, 481.

Under this exception to the rule, it is permissible for a witness to testify that a horse appeared tired * * * ; that a man appeared worried * * * ; that two persons were very intimate * * * ; that a person was domineering * * * ; that there was nothing peculiar in one's talk or action * * * ; the expression of the respondent's face and eyes * * * ; that the respondent was under the influence of intoxicating liquor * * * ; that cattle were not strong * * *. In this connection we quote State v. Felch, [92 Vt. 477, 105 A. 27]: "So, too, it is held that a witness may testify that one spoke affectionately of another * * * ; that a respondent acted 'sneaky' * * * ; and that one was affectionate toward another * * *. And speaking generally, an ordinary observer may be allowed to state that one appeared pleased, angry, excited, friendly, insulting, affectionate, or the like. * * * The raising of an eyebrow, the wave of a handkerchief, or the flash of an eye may give character to an act otherwise too trivial to notice."

As to laying a foundation for the admission of this evidence it is not pointed out in what respect the witness could have stated more facts than she did. * * *

The defendant also excepted to questions calling for similar testimony from Mr. and Mrs. Grant Titsworth, long time friends and acquaintances of the plaintiff and Parker. * * *

On an earlier occasion before the plaintiff and Parker had first separated Mrs. Titsworth, with the plaintiff and Parker and five other guests, attended a dinner at the home of the defendant * * *. She was asked: "Can you describe for us the attitude of Mrs. Thomson toward Mr. Parker?" to which was added "during the course of that evening?", and she answered: "Well, they kept cozying off into the corners. I don't know how to say it." She was then asked what she observed of her conduct toward Parker, and how she acted, and she answered: "She was attracted by him." She was then asked: "Tell us what she did if you

35. [Defendant had been married successively to one Thomson, to Parker whose affections were the subject of the instant litigation, and to one Hoefer. Ed.]

observed anything. If you didn't just tell us that?" and she answered: "She would separate herself and him from the rest of the group and talk together off in either a corner of one room or go into one of the other living rooms and be alone with him rather than with the rest of the guests". Having testified that she had known the plaintiff since their marriage, and that on the occasion of her visit at the Parkers' at the time of this dinner she had noticed a change in their relations toward one another, she was asked: "What change, if any, did you note?", and she answered: "Mr. Parker wasn't as kind and considerate as he had been before."

The exceptions along these lines are not sustained.

Exceptions were taken to questions asked witnesses who were acquainted with the plaintiff and her husband as to their observation of the physical and mental condition of the plaintiff before and after her husband became acquainted with the defendant. Exceptions were also taken to questions asked the plaintiff about the family life, the affection of her husband and the kind of provider he had been. Considerable testimony is set out in the brief and it is claimed generally that the evidence was inadmissible because calling for conclusions. These exceptions are not sustained. The rule stated in Bates v. Town of Sharon, supra, applies.

* * *

Judgment affirmed.

Notes and Questions

1. *Firsthand knowledge.* The term "opinion" has numerous meanings, many of which are not governed by Rule 701. Suppose "that as the witness was leaving a room in which A, B and others remained, he saw A advance toward B with clenched fist, and on his return to the room later, he saw B wiping blood from his nose and lips and A with skinned knuckles, his statement that A struck B would be the result of a conscious deduction from what he saw to what had happened." Morgan, Basic Problems in Evidence 216 (1962). What evidence rule governs this type of "conscious deduction," opinion, inference, or conclusion? Rule 602 or Rule 701?

2. *Fact-opinion dichotomy.* Is it valid to assume that a clear-cut distinction exists between facts perceived by the witness' senses and opinions, inferences and conclusions drawn from such facts?

> Suppose, for instance, that the witness says that he saw John Jones on the street. No court would reject his testimony on the ground that it is opinion, but, of course, it is just that. To require a minute description of the real John Jones and then to require the witness to describe the man whom he saw in order that the jury could form the opinion as to whether the man was John Jones or not, would be complete nonsense. And so it is with many of the objections to opinion testimony as experience will demonstrate.

Gard, Illinois Evidence Manual 246 (1963). For discussion and illustrations of the relativity of what constitutes fact as opposed to opinion, see King and Pillinger, Opinion Evidence in Illinois (1942); see also 7 Wigmore, Evidence § 1919 (Chadbourn rev. 1978); 1 McCormick, Evidence § 11 (6th ed. 2006). Are the difficulties attendant upon determining what shadings of grays are too gray justified by the considerations supporting the rule? See Ladd, Expert Testimony, 5 Vand.L.Rev. 414, 415–16 (1952).

3. *Shorthand rendition exception.* The rule applied in the principal case, variously called the "collective facts," "congeries of circumstances," or "shorthand rendition" doctrine, clearly constitutes a limited recognition of the extent to which "opinion" or "inference" pervades all human thought and communication. Where liberally applied, the exception has frequently made substantial inroads on the opinion rule itself. See Tyree, The Opinion Rule, 10 Rutgers L.Rev. 601, 604–05 (1956). However, some courts have limited the operation of the rule to instances where the expression of an opinion by the witness is necessarily due to the "impossibility" of expressing the matter in any other form. See, e.g., People v. Manoogian, 75 P. 177, 179 (Cal.1904). Where the rule has been too narrowly applied, the result has been like that described by Judge Learned Hand in Central R.R. v. Monahan, 11 F.2d 212, 213 (2d Cir.1926): "Every judge of experience in the trial of causes has again and again seen the whole story garbled, because of insistence upon a form with which the witness cannot comply, since, like most men, he is unaware of the extent to which inference enters into his perceptions. He is telling the 'facts' in the only way that he knows how, and the result of nagging and checking him is often to choke him altogether, which is, indeed, usually its purpose."

4. *Further inferences.* What if the question posed calls not only for the witness' "shorthand rendition" of his or her own perceptions but for an additional inference concerning what might have been or was perceived by another under the same or similar circumstances? In McVay v. State, 14 So. 862 (Ala.1894), a prosecution for using obscene language, the witness was held properly to have been allowed to state that in his opinion certain females standing nearby could have heard the defendant's cursing. The collective facts doctrine is frequently, but not invariably, held applicable to such opinion. See cases collected in Annot., 10 A.L.R.3d 258.

KRUEGER v. STATE FARM MUT. AUTO. INS. CO.

United States Court of Appeals, Eighth Circuit, 1983.
707 F.2d 312.

* * *

On April 16, 1979, in the early afternoon, Florence and Joseph Krueger were driving in a westerly direction on Missouri State Highway 50, at a point near Union, Missouri. As they approached their home, located on the south side of Highway 50, Mrs. Krueger, who was driving the automobile, noticed that a pick-up truck was parked in their driveway. She therefore pulled her car off the roadway and onto the north shoulder of the highway, just west of the driveway.

The pick-up truck in the driveway was occupied by Anthony Castelli, who had stopped by the Krueger house to discuss the purchase of hay with Mr. Krueger.

Once Florence Krueger had stopped her vehicle, Joseph Krueger exited and walked around the back of the car in order to proceed across Highway 50 to speak to Mr. Castelli.

At that particular location, Highway 50 consists of two, twelve-foot wide travel lanes running east and west. There is also a center left-turn lane and two ten-foot wide shoulders.

At this same time, Gladys Batchman was driving her car in an easterly direction on Highway 50 at a rate of speed of approximately 50 to 55 miles-per-hour. Miss Batchman first noticed Mr. Krueger on the opposite shoulder of the road standing behind his car. At this point, she was approximately 439 feet from him.

Soon after seeing Mr. Krueger, Gladys Batchman took her foot off of her vehicle's accelerator. At about the same time, Mr. Krueger began to proceed, on foot, across the westbound lane, stopping in the center turn lane. He then began to run across the eastbound lane after looking straight at Miss Batchman's vehicle. At the time he started across the eastbound lane, the Batchman vehicle was approximately 150 feet away. Mr. Krueger ran into the path of the Batchman vehicle and was impinged thereby. Miss Batchman applied her brakes either simultaneously with, or immediately after the impact. Mr. Krueger died soon thereafter as a result of the injuries he sustained.

* * *

The second issue raised by appellant deals with the trial court's exclusion of a portion of the testimony of Anthony Castelli, a witness to the collision. Mr. Castelli testified as to his estimate of the distances and speeds involved, but was not allowed to testify as to whether Miss Batchman had enough time to avoid hitting Joseph Krueger once he ran into her lane of traffic. Appellant argues that the Magistrate erred in sustaining appellee's objection to the following question propounded at trial by plaintiff-appellant's counsel: "After you saw Mr. Krueger start to run, did the operator of the car have enough time to stop?" Transcript at 95.[36]

Appellant contends that Mr. Castelli was qualified, pursuant to *Fed.R.Civ.P.* 701, to render such an opinion, and should have been allowed to testify as to his perception of Miss Batchman's ability to avoid hitting Mr. Krueger. Rule 701 provides:

> If the witness is not testifying as an expert, his testimony in the form of opinions or inferences is limited to those opinions or inferences which are (a) rationally based on the perception of the

36. Thereafter, the plaintiff's attorney made an offer of proof that, if allowed to testify, Mr. Castelli would have opined that Gladys Batchman could have stopped, slowed, or swerved in such a way as to avoid the accident. Transcript at 95–96.

> witness and (b) helpful to a clear understanding of his testimony or the determination of a fact in issue.

The trial court sustained the defendant's objection to the question and to the subsequent offer of proof.

We decline to reverse here for three reasons. First, although it appears that Mr. Castelli's opinion might have been rationally based on his perceptions, it would not have been helpful to a clear understanding of his testimony or the determination of a fact in issue. The jury had before it evidence, including testimony by Mr. Castelli, as to the distances, speeds, and conditions which set the stage for the collision. The Seventh Circuit has held that:

> in order to conclude that such testimony is admissible, the court must find that the witness' testimony is based upon his or her personal observation and recollection of concrete facts * * * , and that those facts cannot be described in sufficient detail to adequately convey to the jury the substance of the testimony.

United States v. Jackson, 688 F.2d 1121, 1124 (7th Cir.1982) (citations omitted). We find that Mr. Castelli could and did describe the facts of which he was aware to the jury in sufficient detail to adequately convey what he perceived on the afternoon of April 16, 1979. There was no need to provide the jury with a "short-hand rendition" of the total situation, when he could describe the entire situation. * * * His further conclusions would have been superfluous at best.

Second, we note that Rule 701 is designed to give the trial court wide latitude in determining the admissibility of lay opinion testimony. "[H]ow far a witness may go in stating an opinion or conclusion is for the practical discretion of the trial court." *United States v. Freeman,* 514 F.2d 1184, 1191 (10th Cir.1975) (citations omitted). " '[T]he decision as to the admissibility [of a lay opinion] is within the sound discretion of the trial judge and the issues involved are peculiarly suited to his determination.' *Bohannon v. Pegelow,* 652 F.2d 729, 732 (7th Cir.1981). There must be a clear abuse of discretion to justify reversal of the trial court's decision. *Id.*" *United States v. Ness,* 665 F.2d 248, 250 (8th Cir.1981). No such abuse of discretion is apparent here.

Finally, even if we were to find that the exclusion of Mr. Castelli's opinions was error, we would not reverse here, since it is clear that no prejudice has befallen plaintiff. "Taken together, there was sufficient evidence upon which the jury could make an informed decision." *Scheib v. Williams–McWilliams Co.,* 628 F.2d 509, 511 (5th Cir.1980).

Since the trial court's ruling was obviously based upon *Fed.R.Evid.* 701, it is unnecessary to deal with appellant's arguments under *Fed. R.Evid.* 704.

* * *

Affirmed.

Notes and Questions

1. *Rule 701.* The movement for substantial modification of the opinion rule culminated in the adoption of Rule 701. The rule has been described as a rule of "preference" rather than admissibility. 1 McCormick, Evidence § 11 (6th ed. 2006). Why?

2. *Helpfulness standard.* Despite the limitations on the application of Rule 701 noted in the principal case, the federal courts have generally been flexible in its application. See, e.g., United States v. Espino, 317 F.3d 788, 798 (8th Cir.2003) ("[T]he jury heard specific testimony from witnesses, who all had substantial experience in the use and trade of illegal drugs, regarding the weight of the methamphetamine Espino sold."); United States v. Vega–Figueroa, 234 F.3d 744, 755 (1st Cir.2000) (no abuse of discretion "in allowing Gotay to state her opinion as to why her sister was killed"); United States v. Figueroa–Lopez, 125 F.3d 1241, 1246 (9th Cir.1997) (testimony "that the movements of the Monte Carlo were 'suspicious' "); Government of Virgin Islands v. Knight, 989 F.2d 619, 630 (3d Cir.1993) ("[A]n eyewitness' testimony that Knight fired the gun accidentally would be helpful to the jury. The eyewitness described the circumstances that led to his opinion. It is difficult, however, to articulate all of the factors that lead one to conclude a person did not intend to fire a gun. Therefore, the witness' opinion that the gunshot was accidental would have permitted him to relate the facts with greater clarity, and hence would have aided the jury."); United States v. De Peri, 778 F.2d 963 (3d Cir.1985) (interpretation of a conversation); United States v. McCullah, 745 F.2d 350 (6th Cir.1984) (stolen tractor was "hidden" under some trees); United States v. Johnson, 805 F.2d 753 (7th Cir.1986) (value of stolen property).

3. *State cases.* See Markgraf v. State, 12 P.3d 197, 200 (Alaska Ct.App. 2000) ("lay witness may testify that another person seemed scared"); State v. McKee, 744 N.E.2d 737, 742 (Ohio 2001) ("[S]ince the adoption of the Rules of Evidence, both on the state and federal levels, many courts have used an Evid.R. 701 analysis and have allowed lay witnesses to testify about the identity of a drug. * * * [However, the] evidence was insufficient to show that the girls were qualified to testify as lay witnesses. Their testimony was sketchy and conclusory."); Osbourn v. State, 92 S.W.3d 531, 537 (Tex.Crim.App.2002) ("It does not take an expert to identify the smell of marihuana smoke. * * * While smelling the odor of marihuana smoke may not be an event normally encountered in daily life, it requires limited, if any, expertise to identify.").

4. *Speech.* See United States v. Jankowski, 194 F.3d 878, 881 (8th Cir.1999) (person spoke Polish on the telephone); United States v. Bostic, 713 F.2d 401, 404 (8th Cir.1983) (robbery witnesses testify that, based on manner and content of speech, robbers were African American); United States v. Card, 86 F.Supp.2d 1115, 1117 (D.Utah 2000) (ethnic identity based on speech admissible). See also Clifford v. Chandler, 333 F.3d 724 (6th Cir.2003) (ruling that racial identification of voice did not violate due process). See also Purnell et al., Perceptual and Phonetic Experiments on American English Dialect Identification, 18 J.Language & Soc.Psychol. 10 (1999) (In a study involving 421 graduate and undergraduate students at

Stanford University, the participants were asked to identify the racial or ethnic background of twenty different speakers. They correctly identified the African–American males' voices approximately 88% of the time.).

RUPERT v. PEOPLE

Supreme Court of Colorado, 1967.
429 P.2d 276.

McWILLIAMS, JUSTICE. Rupert was charged with the crime of kidnapping, to which charge he first entered a plea of not guilty by reason of insanity. Upon trial of this particular issue a jury determined that Rupert was sane at the time the alleged offense was committed.

Rupert thereafter entered a general plea of not guilty. Upon trial of the issues raised by this plea the trial court, sitting without a jury, adjudged Rupert guilty of the crime of kidnapping and sentenced him to a term in the state penitentiary of from fifteen to twenty years. By this writ of error Rupert now seeks reversal of the judgment and sentence thus imposed.

* * *

Rupert contends that the judgment and sentence must be reversed upon any one of the following grounds:

1. that during the course of the sanity trial the trial court erred when it permitted Durham, a lay witness, to express an opinion as to Rupert's sanity;

* * *

3. that in the sanity trial the trial court also erred in its refusal to direct the jury to return a verdict finding Rupert insane at the time of the alleged commission of the crime; and

* * *

As concerns the propriety of permitting a lay witness to express an opinion as to the sanity of another, in Turley v. People, 73 Colo. 518, 216 P. 536, we declared as follows:

> "A nonexpert witness may never, in response to purely hypothetical questions stating the facts, be permitted to give an opinion on the question of sanity. But by the great weight of authority one who, in the opinion of the trial court, shows adequate means of becoming acquainted with the person whose mental condition is in issue, after detailing the facts and circumstances concerning his acquaintance and the acts, conduct, and conversation upon which his conclusion is based, may give his opinion on the question of sanity. The weight of that opinion is for the jury. * * *
>
> "This rule, supported by the weight of authority and better reasoning, has been adopted by the courts in this jurisdiction. * * * "

Application of the foregoing rule compels the conclusion that the trial court committed no error in permitting Durham to express his opinion as to Rupert's sanity. Durham did relate in considerable detail the facts and circumstances concerning his acquaintance with Rupert, as well as the "acts, conduct and conversation" upon which his opinion was based. Under these circumstances, then, his opinion as to Rupert's sanity was admissible, with the weight to be accorded his opinion being a matter to be determined by the jury. * * *

* * *

The contention that at the conclusion of the sanity trial the trial court committed error when it refused to direct the jury to return a verdict of insanity is without merit. There is, at the outset, a presumption of sanity. The People then introduced the testimony of the lay witness, Durham, to the effect that Rupert was sane. It is quite true that thereafter, by way of defense, a psychiatrist did testify that in his opinion Rupert was insane as of the date of the alleged commission of the crime. But all this did was pose a disputed issue of fact to be resolved by the trier of the facts. The instant factual situation is somewhat akin to that found in Arridy v. People, 103 Colo. 29, 82 P.2d 757. In that case we held that there was sufficient evidence to support a jury's determination that Arridy was sane, even though the medical testimony was to the contrary. And in the *Arridy* case, as in the instant one, the supporting evidence came from lay witnesses, as opposed to expert testimony.

* * *

The judgment is affirmed.

Notes and Questions

1. *Difference between expert and lay opinion testimony.* See Ladd, Expert Testimony, 5 Vand.L.Rev. 414, 419 (1952) ("The lay witness is using his opinion as a composite expression of his observations otherwise difficult to state, whereas the expert is expressing his scientific knowledge through his opinions.").

2. *Procedural differences.* The 2000 amendment added the following phrase to Rule 701: "and (3) not based on scientific, technical, or other specialized knowledge within the scope of Rule 702." Rule 702 governs expert testimony. See United States v. Peoples, 250 F.3d 630, 641 (8th Cir.2001) ("What is essentially expert testimony, however, may not be admitted under the guise of lay opinions. Such a substitution subverts the disclosure and discovery requirements of Federal Rules of Criminal Procedure 26 and 16 and the reliability requirements for expert testimony as set forth in [*Daubert* and *Kumho*]."). Also Rule 704(b), prohibiting opinion testimony on mental states, applies only to expert testimony. See discussion of Rule 704 in Section D(4), infra.

3. *Legal terms.* See Torres v. County of Oakland, 758 F.2d 147, 151 (6th Cir.1985) (exclusion of lay opinion testimony containing terms which have "a separate, distinct, and specialized meaning in the law different from

that present in the vernacular," such as "fiduciary relationship," "unreasonably dangerous," and "discriminated against because of * * * national origin"; employment discrimination case; witness improperly asked whether plaintiff had been discriminated against; question asking whether national origin "motivated" hiring decision would have been proper). What other legal terms may prove troublesome?

4. *Mental condition.* Lay opinion concerning mental condition is currently admitted in virtually all American jurisdictions. See, e.g., L. Richardson Mem'l Hosp., Inc. v. Allen, 325 S.E.2d 40 (N.C.Ct.App.1985) (intensive care nurses who watched decedent through video monitor could testify as to her mental competency), and In re Belanger's Estate, 433 N.E.2d 39 (Ind.Ct. App.1982) (nurses could not testify as to mental capacity based upon only 20 minutes contact). Admissibility is generally subject to the requirement that where the opinion is of insanity it must be preceded by a recitation of the "facts" giving rise to the opinion. Cases are collected in 7 Wigmore, Evidence; § 1938 (Chadbourn rev. 1978). In a number of jurisdictions no such recitation is required where the opinion supports sanity. With the principal case compare, e.g., Singleton v. Carmichael, 305 S.W.2d 379 (Tex.Civ.App. 1957); State v. Riggle, 298 P.2d 349 (Wyo.1956). What considerations, if not sufficient to justify the distinction, may serve to explain its genesis? What recitation should be required under Rule 701?

5. *Sufficiency of evidence.* The view that a verdict of sanity is sufficiently supported by lay testimony even where expert testimony to the contrary is offered continues to be followed by many American courts. See Bowker v. State, 373 P.2d 500 (Alaska 1962) (noting that defendant bore the burden of persuasion on the insanity issue in this jurisdiction); Yates v. State, 703 P.2d 197 (Okla.Crim.1985) (relying on Oklahoma evidence rule based on Federal Rule 701). At the same time, a large number of courts, while unwilling to lay down a rule that expert must be countered by expert, have reversed cases where such rebuttal was not forthcoming. See, e.g., Brock v. United States, 387 F.2d 254 (5th Cir.1967) (citing a number of federal cases).

SECTION D. EXPERT TESTIMONY

(1) SUBJECT MATTER REQUIREMENT: FEDERAL RULE 702

In his 1947 book, *Evidence: Common Sense and Common Law* 30 (1947), Professor Maguire commented on the subject matter of expert testimony:

> The field of expertness is bounded on one side by the great area of the *commonplace*, supposedly within the ken of every person of moderate intelligence, and on the other by the even greater area of the *speculative and uncertain.* Of course both these boundaries constantly shift, as the former area enlarges and the latter diminishes. Only a few years ago it would have been necessary to take expert evidence on issues with respect to the operation of motor cars, airplanes, or radio which are now so completely inside the domain of popular understanding that such evidence would be rejected as

superfluous. A century ago purportedly expert evidence on these topics would have been rejected as visionary.

A chart illustrates these two aspects of the subject matter requirement:

speculative-uncertain	expert testimony	commonplace
	A	B

Boundaries A and B raise distinct issues, and thus the evidentiary standards for these two boundaries are different.

TOY v. MACKINTOSH

Supreme Judicial Court of Massachusetts, 1916.
110 N.E. 1034.

CROSBY, J. This is an action to recover damages for the alleged negligence of the defendant in allowing a tooth to fall into the plaintiff's throat during an operation performed on January 7, 1913, for the extraction of several teeth by the defendant which was performed while the plaintiff was under an anaesthetic. The plaintiff contended that the tooth which fell into his throat ultimately lodged in his lung. There was evidence to show that the plaintiff was in good health before the teeth were extracted and that soon afterwards he had a cough accompanied by a severe pain in his side; that later he became dizzy and felt a numbness in his right arm and leg and was affected by partial loss of speech, and that this condition continued up to the time of the trial except that the condition of his speech had slightly improved.

It appeared that nine weeks after the operation the plaintiff coughed up a tooth which he produced in evidence. He testified that "his coughing was relieved immediately thereafter."

The record recites that the plaintiff offered no dental or medical evidence, nor any further evidence to show "whether the symptoms which it appeared he had were or could have been caused by the tooth."

The defendant's evidence tended to show that he was a dentist of experience and skill. He also offered expert testimony to show that under the conditions attending the extraction of the plaintiff's teeth, it was not carelessness on his part if a tooth was inhaled by the plaintiff during the operation, but was entirely consistent with due care. Four medical experts called by the defendant testified that in their opinion the plaintiff had two shocks soon after his teeth were extracted; that the symptoms from that time on were consistent with hemiplegia[37]; and that the tooth, wherever it had lodged during the nine weeks, had nothing to do with his condition.

1. The jury properly could not have been instructed that upon the evidence their verdict must be for the defendant. Accordingly the defendant's first request was refused rightly. The jury were not obliged to

37. [Hemiplegia is the paralysis of one side of the body. Ed.]

believe the expert testimony, offered by the defendant, that to allow the tooth to fall into the plaintiff's throat was consistent with due care, although such testimony was not contradicted. * * * We are of opinion that the question whether the defendant was negligent in permitting the tooth to be inhaled by the plaintiff when he was in an unconscious condition was for the jury.

2. The defendant's second request was that "There is no evidence justifying the jury in finding that the plaintiff's loss of speech, weakened condition of body, partial paralysis and inability to work were in any way caused by the inhaling of his tooth."

We are of opinion that this instruction, in substance at least, should have been given. The connection between the negligent act of the defendant and the plaintiff's condition afterwards was necessary to be established by a fair preponderance of the evidence in order that he might recover. The burden of proof rested upon the plaintiff to show by competent evidence that his condition after the negligent act of the defendant, if that was established, was the effect in part at least of such negligence. Whether such causal connection existed depended upon proof and could not be left to conjecture or speculation. * * * The burden was upon the plaintiff to satisfy the jury that the illness and disabilities from which he has suffered since he was operated upon by the defendant were caused either wholly or in part by the defendant's negligence. Whether these diseases and disabilities could have been the result of inhaling a tooth was not a matter of common knowledge and observation but depended upon affirmative proof. The jury were not bound to believe the expert evidence coming from the defendant's witnesses that the tooth had nothing to do with the plaintiff's condition afterwards; and while this testimony could have been disregarded, still proof was wanting to support the contention that hemiplegia, aphasia,[38] and the plaintiff's weakened condition and inability to work were due to the inhaling of the tooth. In the absence of such evidence, the jury were not warranted in finding that the tooth caused the disabilities with which the plaintiff afterwards was afflicted and for that reason we think that the defendant's second request in substance should have been given. [Citations omitted.]

Under the instructions of the presiding judge the jury were allowed to determine whether the physical ailments from which they found the plaintiff suffered after the operation, and his present condition, were due to the inhaling of the tooth.

We are of opinion that this instruction was wrong, and that the jury were not justified in finding that the plaintiff's condition after the operation was due to the alleged negligence of the defendant in the absence of any proof to that effect. * * *

Exceptions sustained.

38. [Aphasia is the loss of the capacity to speak or understand speech due to brain injury. Ed.]

Notes and Questions

1. *Causation.* On what element of the plaintiff's case did the court hold that specialized information was indispensable? Had the plaintiff offered the testimony of an expert witness on this element what form would that testimony be required to take in order to preserve the plaintiff from suffering a directed verdict? See note 2, following *Smith v. Bell Tel. Co. of Pennsylvania*, Chapter 4, supra.

2. *Standard of care.* In malpractice actions generally, the great weight of authority requires expert testimony for the purpose of establishing the appropriate standard by which the defendant's actions are to be measured. Dobbs, The Law of Torts § 242 (2000). Relaxations of the general rule, such as that in the principal case, are frequently, though perhaps somewhat inaptly, explained with the label res ipsa loquitur. As to the problems of proof in malpractice actions generally, see Selected Writings on the Law of Evidence and Trial 529–42 (Fryer ed. 1957).

3. *Obscenity prosecutions.* In passing upon the constitutionality of state regulation of obscene films, the Supreme Court held that expert testimony was not necessary to the state's case and questioned the propriety of using it except when the materials were directed to a bizarre deviant group beyond the experience of the trier of fact. Paris Adult Theatre I v. Slaton, 413 U.S. 49 (1973). In Kaplan v. California, 413 U.S. 115, 121 (1973), the Court observed that the defense should be free to introduce "appropriate" expert testimony. Evidently the considerations involved in obscenity cases have served to remove them from the mine run of cases involving use of expert testimony. See United States v. Thoma, 726 F.2d 1191 (7th Cir.1984) (expert testimony not required even in cases involving pedophilic material). Brigman, The Controverted Role of the Expert in Obscenity Litigation, 7 Capital U.L.Rev. 519 (1978).

PEOPLE v. KELLY

Supreme Court of California, 1976.
549 P.2d 1240.

RICHARDSON, JUSTICE.

* * *

Defendant was convicted of extortion (Pen.Code, §§ 518–520) arising out of a series of anonymous, threatening telephone calls to Terry Waskin. The police, acting with Waskin's consent, tape recorded two of these calls (the extortion tapes). An informant familiar with defendant's voice subsequently listened to these tapes and tentatively identified defendant as the caller. Thereafter, the officers obtained a tape recording of defendant's voice during a telephone call (the control tape). Copies of the extortion tapes and the control tape were then sent to Lieutenant Ernest Nash of the Michigan State Police for spectrographic analysis. On the basis of his examination, Nash concluded that the voices on these tapes were those of the same person.

Nash * * * testified that among those who were familiar with and used voice identification analysis the technique was considered reliable. No other expert testimony was presented by either side.

* * *

Defendant attacks his conviction arguing that (1) the People failed to establish that voiceprint techniques have reached the requisite degree of general acceptance in the scientific community, (2) Nash was not qualified to express an expert opinion regarding the judgment of scholars and experts and (3) the testing procedures employed in identifying defendant's voice were not conducted in a fair and impartial manner. Finding ourselves in general agreement with defendant's first two contentions, we do not reach the third.

1. The Voiceprint Technique

Voiceprint analysis is a method of identification based on the comparison of graphic representations or "spectrograms" made of human voices. The method utilizes a machine known as a spectrograph which separates the sounds of human voices into the three component elements of time, frequency and intensity. Using a series of lines or bars, the machine plots these variables across electronically sensitive paper. The result is a spectrogram of the acoustical signal of the speaker, with the horizontal axis representing time lapse, the vertical axis indicating frequency, and the thickness of the lines disclosing the intensity of the voice. * * * Spectrograms are taken of certain cue words, such as "the," "me," "on," "is," "I," and "it," spoken by a known voice and an unknown voice. An examiner then visually compares the spectrograms of the same words, as spoken, and also listens to the two voices. Based upon these visual and aural comparisons, the examiner states his opinion whether or not the voices, known and unknown, are the same. * * * Since the identification process is essentially an exercise in pattern matching, the examiner's opinion is to a large extent a subjective one based upon the relative aural similarity or dissimilarity of the two voices and visual comparison of their spectrograms. * * * In some instances, the examiner is unable to declare positively either that there is a match or nonmatch of the sample tests, in which event no opinion is rendered. * * *

2. General Principles of Admissibility

* * *

The test for determining the underlying reliability of a new scientific technique was described in the germinal case of Frye v. United States (1923) 54 App.D.C. 46, 293 F. 1013, 1014, involving the admissibility of polygraph tests: "Just when a scientific principle or discovery crosses the line between the experimental and demonstrable stages is difficult to define. Somewhere in this twilight zone the evidential force of the principle must be recognized, and while courts will go a long way in admitting expert testimony deduced from a well-recognized scientific principle or discovery, the thing from which the deduction is made must be *sufficiently established to have gained general acceptance in the particular field in which it belongs.*" (Italics added.)

We have expressly adopted the foregoing *Frye* test and California courts, when faced with a novel method of proof, have required a preliminary showing of general acceptance of the new technique in the relevant scientific community. * * * Some criticism has been directed at the *Frye* standard, primarily on the ground that the test is too conservative, often resulting in the prevention of the admission of relevant evidence (see United States v. Sample (E.D.Pa.1974) 378 F.Supp. 43, 53 [voiceprints admissible in probation revocation proceeding]; McCormick, Evidence (2d ed. 1972) § 203, pp. 490–491). * * *

Arguably, the admission of such evidence could be left, in the first instance, to the sound discretion of the trial court, in which event objections, if any, to the reliability of the evidence (or of the underlying scientific technique on which it is based) might lessen the weight of the evidence but would not necessarily prevent its admissibility. This has not been the direction taken by the California courts or by those of most states. *Frye,* and the decisions which have followed it, rather than turning to the trial judge have assigned the task of determining reliability of the evolving technique to members of the scientific community from which the new method emerges. As stated in a recent voiceprint case, United States v. Addison, supra, 498 F.2d 741, 743–744: "The requirement of general acceptance in the scientific community assures that *those most qualified to assess the general validity of a scientific method will have the determinative voice.* Additionally, the *Frye* test protects prosecution and defense alike by assuring that a minimal reserve of experts exists who can critically examine the validity of a scientific determination in a particular case." (Italics added.)

Moreover, a beneficial consequence of the *Frye* test is that it may well promote a degree of uniformity of decision. Individual judges whose particular conclusions may differ regarding the reliability of particular scientific evidence, may discover substantial agreement and consensus in the scientific community. * * *

The primary advantage, however, of the *Frye* test lies in its essentially conservative nature. For a variety of reasons, *Frye* was deliberately intended to interpose a substantial obstacle to the unrestrained admission of evidence based upon new scientific principles. "There has always existed a considerable lag between advances and discoveries in scientific fields and their acceptance as evidence in a court proceeding." (People v. Spigno, [156 Cal.App.2d at p. 289]) Several reasons founded in logic and common sense support a posture of judicial caution in this area. Lay jurors tend to give considerable weight to "scientific" evidence when presented by "experts" with impressive credentials. We have acknowledged the existence of a " * * * misleading aura of certainty which often envelops a new scientific process, obscuring its currently experimental nature." (Huntingdon v. Crowley, supra, 64 Cal.2d at p. 656] * * * As stated in *Addison,* supra, in the course of rejecting the admissibility of voiceprint testimony, "scientific proof may in some instances assume a posture of mystic infallibility in the eyes of a jury * * *." (United States v. Addison, supra, 498 F.2d at p. 744.) * * *

* * * [W]e are persuaded by the wisdom of, and reaffirm our allegiance to, the *Frye* decision and the "general acceptance" rule which that case mandates. In the matter before us, the People attempted to satisfy the *Frye* test by reliance upon prior decisions of the courts of this state and sister states, and upon Lieutenant Nash's testimony. Yet, as discussed below, none of these sources provide satisfactory proof of the reliability of voiceprint evidence.

3. The Voiceprint Cases

Our review of the applicable authorities reveals no uniform or established trend either for or against the admissibility of voiceprint evidence. * * *

4. Lieutenant Nash's Testimony

* * *

As indicated, Lieutenant Nash was *the sole witness* testifying on the reliability issue. The record discloses that Nash has been associated with the voiceprint technique since 1967, having been trained in voiceprint analysis by Kersta, the pioneer in this field. At the time of trial, Nash was employed by the Michigan State Police as head of its voice identification unit. Nash studied audiology and speech sciences at Michigan State University, and completed courses in anatomy and the physiology of speech. Although Nash had received approximately 50 hours of college credit in these subjects, he had not attained a formal degree.

Lieutenant Nash testified that since 1967 he has prepared or reviewed 180,000 voice spectrograms. As noted above, he worked with Dr. Tosi in preparing the design for the 1968–1970 Michigan State University study which Dr. Tosi conducted, and he assisted Tosi in drafting the final report of the study. According to Nash, the Tosi study demonstrated a high degree of reliability. It was a "controlled experimental situation" based on examination and identification of the voices of students and other nonsuspect persons, rather than a forensic, in-the-field, study of the reliability of voiceprint analysis in identifying criminals.

Lieutenant Nash stated that among members of the scientific community involved in voiceprint analysis there is general acceptance of the technique as "extremely" reliable. Nash admitted, however, that those persons who are actually involved in voiceprint work are primarily voiceprint examiners "connected with a government agency of some kind," i.e., law enforcement officers such as Nash himself.

Our analysis of Nash's testimony discloses at least three infirmities which, in combination, are fatal to the People's claim that they established that voiceprint analysis is generally accepted as reliable by the scientific community. First, we think it questionable whether the testimony of a single witness alone is ever sufficient to represent, or attest to, the views of an entire scientific community regarding the reliability of a new technique. Ideally, resolution of the general acceptance issue would require consideration of the views of a typical cross-section of the scientific community, including representatives, if there are such, of those who oppose or question the new technique. * * *

* * *

We are troubled by a second feature of the evidentiary record before us. In addition to the trial court's reliance solely upon Nash's testimony to the exclusion of other, possibly adverse, expert witnesses, a serious question existed regarding Nash's ability fairly and impartially to assess the position of the scientific community. Nash has had a long association with the development and promotion of voiceprint analysis. His qualifications in this somewhat limited area cannot be doubted. In addition to his work with Dr. Tosi, Nash was the chief of the Michigan State Police Voice Identification Unit, a position which led him to testify as a voiceprint expert in numerous cases throughout the country. Further, Nash is either a founder or member of four other organizations which promote the use of voiceprint analysis.

Nash's background thus discloses that he is one of the leading proponents of voiceprint analysis; he has virtually built his career on the reliability of the technique. This situation is closely akin to that in People v. King, [266 Cal.App.2d 437] in which Kersta, a pioneer in the field, was the chief prosecution witness supporting the admissibility of voiceprint evidence. The court in *King* rejected Kersta's testimony regarding the scientific basis of voiceprint analysis and warned that "[b]efore a technique or process is generally accepted in the scientific community, self-serving opinions should not be received which invade the province of the trier of fact." (Id., at p. 458 * * *) Likewise, Nash, a strong advocate of the voiceprint technique, may be too closely identified with the endorsement of voiceprint analysis to assess fairly and impartially the nature and extent of any opposing scientific views. A more detached and neutral observer might more fairly do so. In the absence of additional and impartial evidence regarding general acceptance, the trial court was in a similar position to that presented in *King,* in which "a court could only receive Kersta's opinion on faith." (People v. King, supra, 266 Cal.App.2d at p. 456, 72 Cal.Rptr. at p. 490.)

A third objection to Nash's testimony pertains to his qualifications as an expert in the field of voiceprint analysis. Substantial doubt exists whether Nash possessed the necessary academic qualifications which would have enabled him to express a competent opinion on the issue of the general acceptance of the voiceprint technique in the scientific community.

* * *

The record in the instant case reveals that Nash has an impressive list of credentials in the field of voiceprint analysis. However, these qualifications are those of *a technician and law enforcement officer, not a scientist.* Neither his training under Kersta, his association with the Tosi study, his limited college study in certain speech sciences, his membership in organizations promoting the use of voiceprints, nor his former position as head of the Michigan State Police Voice Identification Unit, necessarily qualifies Nash to express an informed opinion on the view of the scientific community toward voiceprint analysis. This area may be one in which only another scientist, in regular communication with other colleagues in the field, is competent to express such an opinion.

Nash was allowed to testify in a dual role, both as a technician and a scientist, in order to show both that the voiceprint technique is reliable and that it has gained general acceptance in the scientific community. From the demonstrably wide technical experience of Nash, it does not necessarily follow that academic and scientific knowledge are present as well. * * * In considering the position of the scientific community, a court is found to let scientists speak for themselves. Nash's undoubted qualifications as a technician, like Kersta's, do not necessarily qualify him as a scientist to express an opinion on the question of general scientific acceptance. * * *

6. Conclusion

We conclude that the People failed to carry their burden of establishing the reliability of voiceprint evidence. We emphasize, however, that our decision is not intended in any way to foreclose the introduction of voiceprint evidence in future cases. * * * Although the present record is insufficient to justify the admissibility of voiceprint evidence, the future proponent of such evidence may well be able to demonstrate in a satisfactory manner that the voiceprint technique has achieved that required general acceptance in the scientific community.

The judgment is reversed.

Notes and Questions

1. *Identifying the issue.* The reliability of evidence derived from a scientific theory or principle depends upon three factors: (1) the validity of the underlying theory, (2) the validity of the technique applying that theory, and (3) the proper application of the technique on a particular occasion. In short, neither an invalid technique nor a valid technique improperly applied will produce reliable results. The first two factors—the validity of the underlying theory and validity of the technique—are distinct issues. One could accept, for example, the validity of the premise underlying "voiceprint" identification—voice uniqueness—but still question whether the voiceprint technique can identify that uniqueness. Similarly, the underlying psychological and physiological principles of polygraph testing could be acknowledged without endorsing the proposition that a polygraph examiner can detect deception by means of the polygraph technique. The validity of a

scientific principle and the validity of the technique applying that principle may be established through judicial notice, legislative recognition, stipulation, or the presentation of evidence, including expert testimony.

The third requirement—the proper application of a scientific technique on a particular occasion—raises a number of additional issues: (a) the condition of any instrumentation used in the technique, (b) adherence to proper procedures, and (c) the qualifications of both the person conducting the procedure and the person interpreting the results. See Giannelli, The Admissibility of Novel Scientific Evidence: *Frye v. United States*, a Half-Century Later, 80 Colum.L.Rev. 1197 (1980).

2. *Frye survives.* The *Frye* test was the majority rule until 1993, when the United States Supreme Court rejected it. Nevertheless, it is still followed in a dozen or so jurisdictions, including California, Florida, Illinois, Maryland, Minnesota, New Jersey, New York, Pennsylvania, and Washington. See 1 Giannelli & Imwinkelried, Scientific Evidence § 1–15 (3d ed. 1999). These populous states try a large number of criminal and civil cases.

3. *Voiceprint report.* In 1976, the FBI requested the National Academy of Sciences (NAS) to evaluate the validity of voiceprint evidence. The Academy appointed a Committee on Evaluation of Sound Spectrograms, which published its report in 1979. The Report concluded:

> The practice of voice identification rests on the assumption that intraspeaker variability is less than or different from interspeaker variability. However, at present the assumption is not adequately supported by scientific theory and data. Viewpoints about probable errors in identification decisions at present result mainly from various professional judgments and fragmentary experimental results rather than from objective data representative of results in forensic applications.
>
> The Committee concludes that the technical uncertainties concerning the present practice of voice identification are so great as to require that forensic applications be approached with great caution.

National Research Council, On the Theory and Practice of Voice Identification 2 (1979). In another passage the Committee wrote: "Estimates of error rates now available pertain to only a few of the many combinations of conditions encountered in real-life situations. These estimates do not constitute a generally adequate basis for a judicial or legislative body to use in making judgments concerning the reliability and acceptability of aural-visual voice identification in forensic applications." Id. at 60.

4. *Later cases.* Prior to this report, many courts had admitted voiceprint evidence. Even after the report, some courts continued to admit voiceprint evidence. See State v. Williams, 446 N.E.2d 444 (Ohio 1983) (did not mention report); State v. Wheeler, 496 A.2d 1382, 1389 (R.I.1985) (same).

In United States v. Smith, 869 F.2d 348 (7th Cir.1989), the court found that the voiceprint technique had been generally accepted by the scientific community, despite the NAS report. The court discounted the report by pointing out that the report had taken no position on the admissibility issue. In United States v. Maivia, 728 F.Supp. 1471, 1478 (D.Haw.1990), the court also admitted voiceprint evidence. In this case, an FBI examiner testified (against FBI policy, but required by subpoena) for the prosecution after the court ruled that the defense could introduce voiceprint evidence through its expert. The court wrote: "Thus it would appear that inasmuch as the admissibility of spectrographic evidence to identify voices has received general judicial recognition, it is no longer considered novel within the *Frye* test and consequently the test is inapplicable." On what scientific basis could these opinions be based?

In *Smith*, the federal prosecutor argued that voiceprint evidence was reliable. The court found that the "government presented ample evidence of the reliability of spectrographic voice identification at trial." 869 F.2d at 353. In *Maivia*, a different federal prosecutor moved to exclude voiceprint evidence "because spectrographic analysis is a novel scientific technique which has not gained sufficient acceptance in its field." 728 F.Supp. at 1473. The only difference between the two cases was the offering party—the defendant proffered the evidence in *Maivia*. In sum, Assistant U.S. Attorneys, both representing the Department of Justice, argued both for and against admissibility in these cases. Compare United States v. Bahena, 223 F.3d 797, 810 (8th Cir.2000) (voiceprint analysis rejected); United States v. Angleton, 269 F.Supp.2d 892, 902 (S.D.Tex. 2003) (same); State v. Morrison, 871 So.2d 1086, 1086–87 (La.2004) (same), with State v. Coon, 974 P.2d 386 (Alaska 1999) (admitting voiceprint evidence).

5. *Defense experts.* One court noted that in 80% of the voiceprint cases no opposing expert had testified on the issue of reliability and general acceptability of the technique. People v. Chapter, 13 Crim.L.Rptr. (BNA) 2479 (Cal.Super.1973). The NAS Report also took note of this fact: "A striking fact about the trials involving voicegram evidence to date is the very large proportion in which the only experts testifying were those called by the state." NAS Report, note 3, supra, at 49.

DAUBERT v. MERRELL DOW PHARMACEUTICALS, INC.

Supreme Court of the United States, 1993.
509 U.S. 579.

JUSTICE BLACKMUN delivered the opinion of the Court.

In this case we are called upon to determine the standard for admitting expert scientific testimony in a federal trial.

I

Petitioners Jason Daubert and Eric Schuller are minor children born with serious birth defects. They and their parents sued respondent in California state court, alleging that the birth defects had been caused by the mothers' ingestion of Bendectin, a prescription anti-nausea drug marketed by respondent. Respondent removed the suits to federal court on diversity grounds.

After extensive discovery, respondent moved for summary judgment, contending that Bendectin does not cause birth defects in humans and that petitioners would be unable to come forward with any admissible evidence that it does. In support of its motion, respondent submitted an affidavit of Steven H. Lamm, physician and epidemiologist, who is a well-credentialed expert on the risks from exposure to various chemical substances. Doctor Lamm stated that he had reviewed all the literature on Bendectin and human birth defects—more than 30 published studies involving over 130,000 patients. No study had found Bendectin to be a human teratogen (*i.e.,* a substance capable of causing malformations in fetuses). On the basis of this review, Doctor Lamm concluded that maternal use of Bendectin during the first trimester of pregnancy has not been shown to be a risk factor for human birth defects.

Petitioners did not (and do not) contest this characterization of the published record regarding Bendectin. Instead, they responded to respondent's motion with the testimony of eight experts of their own, each of whom also possessed impressive credentials. These experts had concluded that Bendectin can cause birth defects. Their conclusions were based upon "in vitro" (test tube) and "in vivo" (live) animal studies that found a link between Bendectin and malformations; pharmacological studies of the chemical structure of Bendectin that purported to show similarities between the structure of the drug and that of other substances known to cause birth defects; and the "reanalysis" of previously published epidemiological (human statistical) studies.

[The District Court granted respondent's motion for summary judgment. Given the vast body of epidemiological data concerning Bendectin, the court held, expert opinion which is not based on epidemiological evidence is not admissible to establish causation. Thus, the animal-cell studies, live-animal studies, and chemical-structure analyses on which petitioners had relied could not raise by themselves a reasonably disputable jury issue regarding causation. Petitioners' epidemiological analyses, based as they were on recalculations of data in previously published studies that had found no causal link between the drug and birth defects, were ruled to be inadmissible because they had not been published or subjected to peer review. The court of appeals affirmed, citing the *Frye* general acceptance test.]

We granted certiorari * * * in light of sharp divisions among the courts regarding the proper standard for the admission of expert testimony. * * *

II

A

In the 70 years since its formulation in the *Frye* case, the "general acceptance" test has been the dominant standard for determining the admissibility of novel scientific evidence at trial. * * * Although under increasing attack of late, the rule continues to be followed by a majority of courts, including the Ninth Circuit.

The *Frye* test has its origin in a short and citation-free 1923 decision concerning the admissibility of evidence derived from a systolic blood pressure deception test, a crude precursor to the polygraph machine.

* * *

The merits of the *Frye* test have been much debated, and scholarship on its proper scope and application is legion.[39] Petitioners' primary attack, however, is not on the content but on the continuing authority of the rule. They contend that the *Frye* test was superseded by the adoption of the Federal Rules of Evidence.[40] We agree. * * *

Frye, of course, predated the Rules by half a century. * * *

* * *

Nothing in the text of this Rule[41] establishes "general acceptance" as an absolute prerequisite to admissibility. Nor does respondent present any clear indication that Rule 702 or the Rules as a whole were intended to incorporate a "general acceptance" standard. The drafting history makes no mention of *Frye,* and a rigid "general acceptance" requirement would be at odds with the "liberal thrust" of the Federal Rules and their "general approach of relaxing the traditional barriers to 'opinion' testimony." * * * See also Weinstein, Rule 702 of the Federal Rules of Evidence is Sound; It Should Not Be Amended, 138 F.R.D. 631, 631 (1991) ("The Rules were designed to depend primarily upon lawyer-adversaries and sensible triers of fact to evaluate conflicts"). Given the Rules' permissive backdrop and their inclusion of a specific rule on expert testimony that does not mention "general acceptance," the assertion that the Rules somehow assimilated *Frye* is unconvincing. *Frye* made "general acceptance" the exclusive test for admitting expert scientific testimony. That austere standard, absent from and incompatible with the Federal Rules of Evidence, should not be applied in federal trials.

B

That the *Frye* test was displaced by the Rules of Evidence does not mean, however, that the Rules themselves place no limits on the admissibility of purportedly scientific evidence.[42] Nor is the trial judge disabled

39. *See, e.g.,* Green, Expert Witnesses and Sufficiency of Evidence in Toxic Substances Litigation: The Legacy of *Agent Orange* and Bendectin Litigation, 86 Nw. U.L.Rev. 643 (1992); * * * Giannelli, The Admissibility of Novel Scientific Evidence: *Frye v. United States,* a Half–Century Later, 80 Colum.L.Rev. 1197 (1980); * * * Indeed, the debates over *Frye* are such a well-established part of the academic landscape that a distinct term—"*Frye*-ologist"—has been advanced to describe those who take part. See Behringer, Introduction, Proposals for a Model Rule on the Admissibility of Scientific Evidence, 26 Jurimetrics J., at 239, quoting Lacey, Scientific Evidence, 24 Jurimetrics J. 254, 264 (1984).

40. Like the question of *Frye*'s merit, the dispute over its survival has divided courts and commentators. Compare, *e.g., United States v. Williams,* 583 F.2d 1194 (C.A.2 1978) (*Frye* is superseded by the Rules of Evidence), with *Christopherson v. Allied–Signal Corp.,* 939 F.2d 1106, 1111, 1115–1116 (C.A.5 1991) (en banc) (*Frye* and the Rules coexist), 3 J. Weinstein & M. Berger, Weinstein's Evidence ¶ 702[03], pp. 702–36 to 702–37 (1988) (hereinafter Weinstein & Berger) (*Frye* is dead), and M. Graham, Handbook of Federal Evidence § 703.2 (2d ed. 1991) (*Frye* lives). See generally P. Gianelli & E. Imwinkelried, Scientific Evidence § 1–5, pp. 28–29 (1986 & Supp.1991) (citing authorities).

41. [The Court quoted Rule 702, as it existed before 2001. Ed.]

42. THE CHIEF JUSTICE "do[es] not doubt that Rule 702 confides to the judge some gatekeeping responsibility," * * * but would neither say how it does so, nor explain what that role entails. We believe the

from screening such evidence. To the contrary, under the Rules the trial judge must ensure that any and all scientific testimony or evidence admitted is not only relevant, but reliable.

The primary locus of this obligation is Rule 702, which clearly contemplates some degree of regulation of the subjects and theories about which an expert may testify. "*If scientific,* technical, or other specialized *knowledge will assist the trier of fact* to understand the evidence or to determine a fact in issue" an expert "may testify *thereto.*" The subject of an expert's testimony must be "scientific * * * knowledge." The adjective "scientific" implies a grounding in the methods and procedures of science. Similarly, the word "knowledge" connotes more than subjective belief or unsupported speculation. The term "applies to any body of known facts or to any body of ideas inferred from such facts or accepted as truths on good grounds." Webster's Third New International Dictionary 1252 (1986). Of course, it would be unreasonable to conclude that the subject of scientific testimony must be "known" to a certainty; arguably, there are no certainties in science. See, *e.g.,* Brief for Nicolaas Bloembergen et al. as *Amici Curiae* 9 ("Indeed, scientists do not assert that they know what is immutably 'true'—they are committed to searching for new, temporary theories to explain, as best they can, phenomena"); Brief for American Association for the Advancement of Science and the National Academy of Sciences as *Amici Curiae* 7–8 ("Science is not an encyclopedic body of knowledge about the universe. Instead, it represents a *process* for proposing and refining theoretical explanations about the world that are subject to further testing and refinement") (emphasis in original). But, in order to qualify as "scientific knowledge," an inference or assertion must be derived by the scientific method. Proposed testimony must be supported by appropriate validation—*i.e.,* "good grounds," based on what is known. In short, the requirement that an expert's testimony pertain to "scientific knowledge" establishes a standard of evidentiary reliability.[43]

Rule 702 further requires that the evidence or testimony "assist the trier of fact to understand the evidence or to determine a fact in issue." This condition goes primarily to relevance. "Expert testimony which does not relate to any issue in the case is not relevant and, ergo, nonhelpful." 3 Weinstein & Berger ¶ 702[02], p. 702–18. See also *United States v. Downing,* 753 F.2d 1224, 1242 (C.A.3 1985) ("An additional consideration under Rule 702—and another aspect of relevancy—is whether expert testimony proffered in the case is sufficiently tied to the facts of the case that it will aid the jury in resolving a factual dispute"). The consideration has been aptly described by Judge Becker as one of "fit." *Ibid.* "Fit" is not always obvious, and scientific validity for one purpose is not necessarily scientific validity for other, unrelated pur-

better course is to note the nature and source of the duty.

43. We note that scientists typically distinguish between "validity" (does the principle support what it purports to show?) and "reliability" (does application of the principle produce consistent results?). * * * In a case involving scientific evidence, *evidentiary reliability* will be based upon *scientific validity.*

poses. * * * The study of the phases of the moon, for example, may provide valid scientific "knowledge" about whether a certain night was dark, and if darkness is a fact in issue, the knowledge will assist the trier of fact. However (absent creditable grounds supporting such a link), evidence that the moon was full on a certain night will not assist the trier of fact in determining whether an individual was unusually likely to have behaved irrationally on that night. Rule 702's "helpfulness" standard requires a valid scientific connection to the pertinent inquiry as a precondition to admissibility.

That these requirements are embodied in Rule 702 is not surprising. Unlike an ordinary witness, see Rule 701, an expert is permitted wide latitude to offer opinions, including those that are not based on first-hand knowledge or observation. See Rules 702 and 703. Presumably, this relaxation of the usual requirement of first-hand knowledge—a rule which represents "a 'most pervasive manifestation' of the common law insistence upon 'the most reliable sources of information,'" Advisory Committee's Notes on Fed.Rule Evid. 602 (citation omitted)—is premised on an assumption that the expert's opinion will have a reliable basis in the knowledge and experience of his discipline.

C

Faced with a proffer of expert scientific testimony, then, the trial judge must determine at the outset, pursuant to Rule 104(a), whether the expert is proposing to testify to (1) scientific knowledge that (2) will assist the trier of fact to understand or determine a fact in issue.[44] This entails a preliminary assessment of whether the reasoning or methodology underlying the testimony is scientifically valid and of whether that reasoning or methodology properly can be applied to the facts in issue. We are confident that federal judges possess the capacity to undertake this review. Many factors will bear on the inquiry, and we do not presume to set out a definitive checklist or test. But some general observations are appropriate.

Ordinarily, a key question to be answered in determining whether a theory or technique is scientific knowledge that will assist the trier of fact will be whether it can be (and has been) tested. "Scientific methodology today is based on generating hypotheses and testing them to see if they can be falsified; indeed, this methodology is what distinguishes science from other fields of human inquiry." Green, at 645. See also C. Hempel, Philosophy of Natural Science 49 (1966) ("[T]he statements constituting a scientific explanation must be capable of empirical test"); K. Popper, Conjectures and Refutations: The Growth of Scientific

44. Although the *Frye* decision itself focused exclusively on "novel" scientific techniques, we do not read the requirements of Rule 702 to apply specially or exclusively to unconventional evidence. Of course, well-established propositions are less likely to be challenged than those that are novel, and they are more handily defended. Indeed, theories that are so firmly established as to have attained the status of scientific law, such as the laws of thermodynamics, properly are subject to judicial notice under Fed.Rule Evid. 201.

Knowledge 37 (5th ed. 1989) ("[T]he criterion of the scientific status of a theory is its falsifiability, or refutability, or testability").

Another pertinent consideration is whether the theory or technique has been subjected to peer review and publication. Publication (which is but one element of peer review) is not a *sine qua non* of admissibility; it does not necessarily correlate with reliability, see S. Jasanoff, The Fifth Branch: Science Advisors as Policymakers 61–76 (1990), and in some instances well-grounded but innovative theories will not have been published, see Horrobin, The Philosophical Basis of Peer Review and the Suppression of Innovation, 263 J.Am.Med.Assn. 1438 (1990). Some propositions, moreover, are too particular, too new, or of too limited interest to be published. But submission to the scrutiny of the scientific community is a component of "good science," in part because it increases the likelihood that substantive flaws in methodology will be detected. See J. Ziman, Reliable Knowledge: An Exploration of the Grounds for Belief in Science 130–133 (1978); Relman and Angell, How Good Is Peer Review?, 321 New Eng.J.Med. 827 (1989). The fact of publication (or lack thereof) in a peer-reviewed journal thus will be a relevant, though not dispositive, consideration in assessing the scientific validity of a particular technique or methodology on which an opinion is premised.

Additionally, in the case of a particular scientific technique, the court ordinarily should consider the known or potential rate of error, see, *e.g., United States v. Smith,* 869 F.2d 348, 353–354 (C.A.7 1989) (surveying studies of the error rate of spectrographic voice identification technique), and the existence and maintenance of standards controlling the technique's operation. See *United States v. Williams,* 583 F.2d 1194, 1198 (C.A.2 1978) (noting professional organization's standard governing spectrographic analysis).

Finally, "general acceptance" can yet have a bearing on the inquiry. A "reliability assessment does not require, although it does permit, explicit identification of a relevant scientific community and an express determination of a particular degree of acceptance within that community." *United States v. Downing,* 753 F.2d, at 1238. See also 3 Weinstein & Berger ¶ 702[03], pp. 702–41 to 702–42. Widespread acceptance can be an important factor in ruling particular evidence admissible, and "a known technique that has been able to attract only minimal support within the community," *Downing, supra,* at 1238, may properly be viewed with skepticism.

The inquiry envisioned by Rule 702 is, we emphasize, a flexible one. Its overarching subject is the scientific validity—and thus the evidentiary relevance and reliability—of the principles that underlie a proposed submission. The focus, of course, must be solely on principles and methodology, not on the conclusions that they generate.

Throughout, a judge assessing a proffer of expert scientific testimony under Rule 702 should also be mindful of other applicable rules. Rule 703 provides that expert opinions based on otherwise inadmissible hearsay are to be admitted only if the facts or data are "of a type reasonably relied upon by experts in the particular field in forming opinions or inferences upon the subject." Rule 706 allows the court at its discretion to procure the assistance of an expert of its own choosing. Finally, Rule 403 permits the exclusion of relevant evidence "if its probative value is substantially outweighed by the danger of unfair prejudice, confusion of the issues, or misleading the jury* * *." Judge Weinstein has explained: "Expert evidence can be both powerful and quite misleading because of the difficulty in evaluating it. Because of this risk, the judge in weighing possible prejudice against probative force under Rule 403 of the present rules exercises more control over experts than over lay witnesses." Weinstein, 138 F.R.D., at 632.

III

We conclude by briefly addressing what appear to be two underlying concerns of the parties and *amici* in this case. Respondent expresses apprehension that abandonment of "general acceptance" as the exclusive requirement for admission will result in a "free-for-all" in which befuddled juries are confounded by absurd and irrational pseudoscientific assertions. In this regard respondent seems to us to be overly pessimistic about the capabilities of the jury, and of the adversary system generally. Vigorous cross-examination, presentation of contrary evidence, and careful instruction on the burden of proof are the traditional and appropriate means of attacking shaky but admissible evidence. See *Rock v. Arkansas,* 483 U.S. 44, 61 (1987). Additionally, in the event the trial court concludes that the scintilla of evidence presented supporting a position is insufficient to allow a reasonable juror to conclude that the position more likely than not is true, the court remains free to direct a judgment, Fed.Rule Civ.Proc. 50(a), and likewise to grant summary judgment, Fed.Rule Civ.Proc. 56. Cf., *e.g., Turpin v. Merrell Dow Pharmaceuticals,* to find it more probable than not that defendant caused plaintiff's injury); *Brock v. Merrell Dow Pharmaceuticals, Inc.,* 874 F.2d 307 (C.A.5 1989) (reversing judgment entered on jury verdict for plaintiffs because evidence regarding causation was insufficient) * * *. These conventional devices, rather than wholesale exclusion under an uncompromising "general acceptance" test, are the appropriate safeguards where the basis of scientific testimony meets the standards of Rule 702.

Petitioners and, to a greater extent, their *amici* exhibit a different concern. They suggest that recognition of a screening role for the judge that allows for the exclusion of "invalid" evidence will sanction a stifling and repressive scientific orthodoxy and will be inimical to the search for truth. See, *e.g.,* Brief for Ronald Bayer et al. as *Amici Curiae.* It is true that open debate is an essential part of both legal and scientific analyses. Yet there are important differences between the quest for truth in the courtroom and the quest for truth in the laboratory. Scientific conclusions are subject to perpetual revision. Law, on the other hand, must resolve disputes finally and quickly. The scientific project is advanced by broad and wide-ranging consideration of a multitude of hypotheses, for those that are incorrect will eventually be shown to be so, and that in itself is an advance. Conjectures that are probably wrong are of little use, however, in the project of reaching a quick, final, and binding legal judgment—often of great consequence—about a particular set of events in the past. We recognize that in practice, a gatekeeping role for the judge, no matter how flexible, inevitably on occasion will prevent the jury from learning of authentic insights and innovations. That, nevertheless, is the balance that is struck by Rules of Evidence designed not for the exhaustive search for cosmic understanding but for the particularized resolution of legal disputes.[45]

IV

To summarize: "general acceptance" is not a necessary precondition to the admissibility of scientific evidence under the Federal Rules of Evidence, but the Rules of Evidence—especially Rule 702—do assign to the trial judge the task of ensuring that an expert's testimony both rests on a reliable foundation and is relevant to the task at hand. Pertinent evidence based on scientifically valid principles will satisfy those demands.

The inquiries of the District Court and the Court of Appeals focused almost exclusively on "general acceptance," as gauged by publication and the decisions of other courts. Accordingly, the judgment of the Court of Appeals is vacated and the case is remanded for further proceedings consistent with this opinion.

It is so ordered.

CHIEF JUSTICE REHNQUIST, with whom JUSTICE STEVENS joins, concurring in part and dissenting in part.

* * * The Court concludes, correctly in my view, that the *Frye* rule did not survive the enactment of the Federal Rules of Evidence, and I therefore join Parts I and II–A of its opinion. The second question presented in the petition for certiorari necessarily is mooted by this holding, but the Court nonetheless proceeds to construe Rules 702 and 703 very much in the abstract, and then offers some "general observations." * * *

"General observations" by this Court customarily carry great weight with lower federal courts, but the ones offered here suffer from the flaw common to most such observations—they are not applied to deciding whether or not particular testimony was or was not admissible, and therefore they tend to be not only general, but vague and abstract. This is particularly unfortunate in a case such as this, where the ultimate legal question depends on an appreciation of one or more bodies of knowledge not judicially noticeable, and subject to different interpre-

45. This is not to say that judicial interpretation, as opposed to adjudicative fact-finding, does not share basic characteristics of the scientific endeavor: "The work of a judge is in one sense enduring and in another ephemeral* * *. In the endless process of testing and retesting, there is a constant rejection of the dross and a constant retention of whatever is pure and sound and fine." B. Cardozo, The Nature of the Judicial Process 178, 179 (1921).

tations in the briefs of the parties and their *amici*. Twenty-two *amicus* briefs have been filed in the case, and indeed the Court's opinion contains no less than 37 citations to *amicus* briefs and other secondary sources.

* * *

I defer to no one in my confidence in federal judges; but I am at a loss to know what is meant when it is said that the scientific status of a theory depends on its "falsifiability," and I suspect some of them will be, too.

I do not doubt that Rule 702 confides to the judge some gatekeeping responsibility in deciding questions of the admissibility of proffered expert testimony. But I do not think it imposes on them either the obligation or the authority to become amateur scientists in order to perform that role. I think the Court would be far better advised in this case to decide only the questions presented, and to leave the further development of this important area of the law to future cases.

Notes and Questions

1. *Legislative history.* The *Frye* issue was not addressed in the Advisory Committee's Notes, the congressional committee reports, or the hearings on the Federal Rules. Giannelli, *Daubert*: Interpreting the Federal Rules of Evidence, 15 Cardozo L.Rev. 1999 (1994). See also Caudill & LaRue, No Magic Wand: The Idealization of Science in Law (2006); Giannelli, The *Daubert* Trilogy and the Law of Expert Testimony, in Evidence Stories 181 (Lempert ed., 2006).

2. *Relevancy approach.* In addition to the *Frye* general acceptance test and the *Daubert* reliability test, a third test, known as the relevancy test, is followed in some jurisdictions. In his 1954 text, Professor McCormick rejected the *Frye* test, stating: "Any relevant conclusions which are supported by a qualified expert witness should be received unless there are other reasons for exclusion. Particularly, its probative value may be overborne by the familiar dangers of prejudicing or misleading the jury, unfair surprise and undue consumption of time." McCormick, Evidence 363–64 (1954). Wisconsin follows this rule. See State v. Donner, 531 N.W.2d 369, 374 (Wis.Ct.App.1995) ("[B]efore *Daubert*, the *Frye* test was not the law in Wisconsin. To that extent, Wisconsin law and *Daubert* coincide. Beyond that, Wisconsin law holds that 'any relevant conclusions which are supported by a qualified witness should be received unless there are other reasons for exclusion.' Stated otherwise, expert testimony is admissible in Wisconsin if relevant and will be excluded only if the testimony is superfluous or a waste of time.").

3. *Death penalty cases.* In Barefoot v. Estelle, 463 U.S. 880 (1983), a capital murder case, the prosecution offered psychiatric testimony concerning Barefoot's future dangerousness in the penalty phase. One psychiatrist, Dr. James Grigson, without ever examining Barefoot, testified that there was a " '*one hundred percent and absolute*' chance that Barefoot would commit future acts of criminal violence." In an amicus brief, the American Psychiatric Association (APA) stated that the "large body of research in this

area indicates that, even under the best of conditions, psychiatric predictions of long-term dangerousness are wrong in at least two out of every three cases." In a later passage, the brief notes that the "unreliability of [these] predictions is by now an established fact within the profession." A substantial body of research supported the APA position.

Nevertheless, the Court rejected Barefoot's challenge to the expert testimony. According to the Court, "[n]either petitioner nor the [APA] suggests that psychiatrists are always wrong with respect to future dangerousness, only most of the time." In one passage the Court set forth the relevancy approach:

> [T]he rules of evidence generally extant at the federal and state levels anticipate that relevant, unprivileged evidence should be admitted and its weight left to the factfinder, who would have the benefit of cross-examination and contrary evidence by the opposing party.
>
> * * * We are not persuaded that such testimony is almost entirely unreliable and that the factfinder and the adversary system will not be competent to uncover, recognize, and take due account of its shortcomings.

See Dix, The Death Penalty, "Dangerousness," Psychiatric Testimony, and Professional Ethics, 5 Am.J.Crim.L. 151, 172 (1977) (Court admitted evidence "at the brink of quackery"); Huber, Galileo's Revenge: Junk Science in the Courtroom 220 (1991) (One could favor the death penalty and "yet still recoil at the thought that a junk science fringe of psychiatry * * * could decide who will be sent to the gallows."). Why would a higher standard (*Daubert*) apply in a civil case than in a capital case?

4. *Which is the better approach: Frye* or *Daubert*? In State v. Copeland, 922 P.2d 1304, 1314 (Wash.1996) (en banc), the court commented: "The State maintains that this court should abandon *Frye* and adopt *Daubert*. The State argues that *Frye* is difficult to apply. While *Frye* may be difficult to apply in some contexts, this is a result of the complexity of the particular science at issue, the extent to which the scientific community has made its view known, and the extent of any dispute in the scientific community. The same, or similar problems, arise under *Daubert*, including questions of testability, the extent to which the scientific technique or method is accepted by the scientific community, and drawing the line between legitimate science and 'junk' science, along with other questions. Questions of admissibility of complex, controversial scientific techniques or methods, like those involving DNA evidence, are going to be difficult under either standard."

5. *Peer review.* An amici brief in *Daubert*, filed on behalf of several scientists, questioned the peer review system. Brief of Amici Curiae Daryl E. Chubin et al., Daubert v. Merrell Dow Pharmaceuticals, Inc., 509 U.S. 579 (1993), at 28 ("[T]he peer review system should not be regarded as more rigorous and reliable than the jury system's use of cross-examination.") In their view, the peer review system is not intended to yield "the truth" and publication does not mean that an article's content is "generally accepted" or represents a "consensus" position of the relevant academic community. In addition, they noted that peer review journals do not replicate or verify experiments; nor do they warrant that the information contained in an article is valid or otherwise amounts to "good science." They also pointed

out that often only two referees are selected and that these individuals spend on average "2.4 hours" reviewing each manuscript. Is cross-examination really as good?

6. *Error rates.* The *Daubert* Court cited United States v. Williams, 583 F.2d 1194 (2d Cir.1978), for specifying the "rate of error." In that case, the Second Circuit had rejected the *Frye* rule and admitted voiceprint evidence. The court recognized "the potential rate of error" as "[o]ne indicator of evidential reliability." Citing a Michigan State study, the court noted that the false identification error rate was 6.3%, a rate reduced to 2.4% when doubtful comparisons are eliminated. However, in note 3 following *People v. Kelly*, supra, a subsequent National Academy of Sciences Report on voiceprints undermined these error rates.

7. *Litigation science.* On remand, the Ninth Circuit again excluded the plaintiff's evidence; this time on the ground that the underlying research had been conducted in anticipation of litigation, which undercut its validity. The court saw an important difference where experts were "proposing to testify about matters naturally and directly out of research they have conducted independent of the litigation, or whether they have developed their opinions expressly for purposes of testifying." Daubert v. Merrell Dow Pharmaceuticals, Inc., 43 F.3d 1311, 1317 (9th Cir.1995).

8. *Appellate review.* In General Elec. Co. v. Joiner, 522 U.S. 136 (1997), a city electrician, who suffered from lung cancer, brought action against the manufacturer of polychlorinated biphenyls (PCBs) and manufacturers of electrical transformers and dielectric fluid, alleging strict liability, negligence, fraud, and battery. The district court ruled that Joiner's experts had failed to show that there was a link between exposure to PCBs and small-cell lung cancer. The Eleventh Circuit reversed, holding that "[b]ecause the Federal Rules of Evidence governing expert testimony display a preference for admissibility, we apply a particularly stringent standard of review to the trial judge's exclusion of expert testimony."

In an opinion by Chief Justice Rehnquist, the Court reversed, holding that a stringent standard of review was not required: "Thus, while the Federal Rules of Evidence allow district courts to admit a somewhat broader range of scientific testimony than would have been admissible under *Frye*, they leave in place the 'gatekeeper' role of the trial judge in screening such evidence. A court of appeals applying 'abuse-of-discretion' review to such rulings may not categorically distinguish between rulings allowing expert testimony and rulings disallowing it." Unlike *Daubert*, the Court's analysis involved a close scrutiny of the scientific evidence offered at the trial level. The Court found significant problems with both the animal[46] and epidemiological studies.[47]

46. The Court wrote: "The infant mice in the studies had had massive doses of PCB's injected directly into their peritoneums or stomachs. Joiner was an adult human being whose alleged exposure to PCB's was far less than the exposure in the animal studies. The PCB's were injected into the mice in a highly concentrated form. The fluid with which Joiner had come into contact generally had a much smaller PCB concentration of between 0–to–500 parts per million. The cancer that these mice developed was alveologenic adenomas; Joiner had developed small-cell carcinomas. No study demonstrated that adult mice developed cancer after being exposed to PCB's. One of the experts admitted that no study had demonstrated that PCB's lead to cancer in any other species."

47. The Court commented that the "authors [of one study] noted that lung cancer

The Court also addressed the "methodology/conclusion" dichotomy that had been cited in *Daubert*: "Respondent points to *Daubert's* language that the 'focus, of course, must be solely on principles and methodology, not on the conclusions that they generate.' * * * He claims that because the District Court's disagreement was with the conclusion that the experts drew from the studies, the District Court committed legal error and was properly reversed by the Court of Appeals. But conclusions and methodology are not entirely distinct from one another. Trained experts commonly extrapolate from existing data. But nothing in either *Daubert* or the Federal Rules of Evidence requires a district court to admit opinion evidence that is connected to existing data only by the *ipse dixit* of the expert. A court may conclude that there is simply too great an analytical gap between the data and the opinion proffered. * * * That is what the District Court did here, and we hold that it did not abuse its discretion in so doing."

Other courts have taken a different approach to the standard of review issue. For example, the Massachusetts Supreme Judicial Court has stated that "[i]n considering the issue of scientific validity, our review is de novo because a trial judge's conclusion will have applicability beyond the facts of the case before him." Commonwealth v. Vao Sok, 683 N.E.2d 671, 677 (Mass.1997). *See* Faigman, Appellate Review of Scientific Evidence Under *Daubert* and *Joiner*, 48 Hastings L.J. 969 (1997). Does an abuse-of-discretion standard mean one trial court could find polygraph evidence reliable and another court find the same evidence unreliable?

KUMHO TIRE CO. v. CARMICHAEL

Supreme Court of the United States, 1999.
526 U.S. 137.

JUSTICE BREYER delivered the opinion of the Court.

* * *

This case requires us to decide how *Daubert* applies to the testimony of engineers and other experts who are not scientists. We conclude that *Daubert's* general holding—setting forth the trial judge's general "gatekeeping" obligation—applies not only to testimony based on "scientific" knowledge, but also to testimony based on "technical" and "other specialized" knowledge. See Fed. Rule Evid. 702. We also conclude that a trial court *may* consider one or more of the more specific factors that

deaths among ex-employees at the plant were higher than might have been expected, but concluded that 'there were apparently no grounds for associating lung cancer deaths (although increased above expectations) and exposure in the plant.' * * * Given that [the authors] were unwilling to say that PCB exposure had caused cancer among the workers they examined, their study did not support the experts' conclusion that Joiner's exposure to PCB's caused his cancer." Similarly, another a second study was also problematic: "The authors of [a second study] found that the incidence of lung cancer deaths among these workers was somewhat higher than would ordinarily be expected. The increase, however, was not statistically significant and the authors of the study did not suggest a link between the increase in lung cancer deaths and the exposure to PCB's." The Court also found drawbacks in two more studies.

Daubert mentioned when doing so will help determine that testimony's reliability. * * *

I

On July 6, 1993, the right rear tire of a minivan driven by Patrick Carmichael blew out. In the accident that followed, one of the passengers died, and others were severely injured. In October 1993, the Carmichaels brought this diversity suit against the tire's maker and its distributor, whom we refer to collectively as Kumho Tire, claiming that the tire was defective. The plaintiffs rested their case in significant part upon deposition testimony provided by an expert in tire failure analysis, Dennis Carlson, Jr., who intended to testify in support of their conclusion.

Carlson's depositions relied upon certain features of tire technology that are not in dispute. A steel-belted radial tire like the Carmichaels' is made up of a "carcass" containing many layers of flexible cords, called "plies," along which (between the cords and the outer tread) are laid steel strips called "belts." Steel wire loops, called "beads," hold the cords together at the plies' bottom edges. An outer layer, called the "tread," encases the carcass, and the entire tire is bound together in rubber, through the application of heat and various chemicals. * * * The bead of the tire sits upon a "bead seat," which is part of the wheel assembly. That assembly contains a "rim flange," which extends over the bead and rests against the side of the tire. See M. Mavrigian, Performance Wheels & Tires 81, 83 (1998) (illustrations).

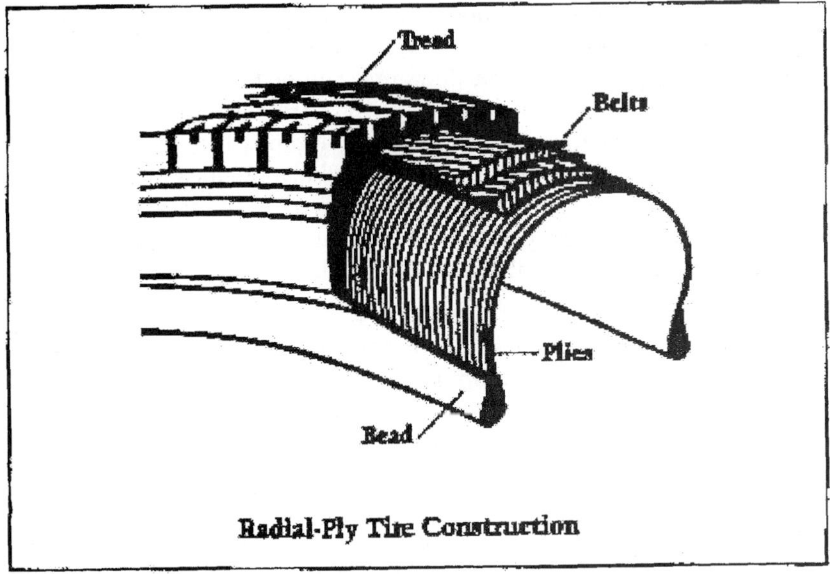

Radial-Ply Tire Construction

Carlson's testimony also accepted certain background facts about the tire in question. He assumed that before the blowout the tire had traveled far. (The tire was made in 1988 and had been installed some time before the Carmichaels bought the used minivan in March 1993; the Carmichaels had driven the van approximately 7,000 additional miles in the two months they had owned it.) Carlson noted that the tire's tread depth, which was 11/32 of an inch when new, * * * had been worn down to depths that ranged from 3/32 of an inch along some parts of the tire, to nothing at all along others. * * * He conceded that the tire tread had at least two punctures which had been inadequately repaired. * * *

Despite the tire's age and history, Carlson concluded that a defect in its manufacture or design caused the blowout. He rested this conclusion in part upon three premises which, for present purposes, we must assume are not in dispute: First, a tire's carcass should stay bound to the inner side of the tread for a significant period of time after its tread depth has worn away. * * * Second, the tread of the tire at issue had separated from its inner steel-belted carcass prior to the accident. * * * Third, this "separation" caused the blowout. * * *

Carlson's conclusion that a defect caused the separation, however, rested upon certain other propositions, several of which the defendants strongly dispute. First, Carlson said that if a separation is *not* caused by a certain kind of tire misuse called "overdeflection" (which consists of underinflating the tire or causing it to carry too much weight, thereby generating heat that can undo the chemical tread/carcass bond), then, ordinarily, its cause is a tire defect. * * * Second, he said that if a tire has been subject to sufficient overdeflection to cause a separation, it should reveal certain physical symptoms. These symptoms include (a) tread wear on the tire's shoulder that is greater than the tread wear along the tire's center, * * * ; (b) signs of a "bead groove," where the beads have been pushed too hard against the bead seat on the inside of the tire's rim, * * * (c) sidewalls of the tire with physical signs of deterioration, such as discoloration, * * * ; and/or (d) marks on the tire's rim flange * * *. Third, Carlson said that where he does not find *at least two* of the four physical signs just mentioned (and presumably where there is no reason to suspect a less common cause of separation), he concludes that a manufacturing or design defect caused the separation. * * *

Carlson added that he had inspected the tire in question. He conceded that the tire to a limited degree showed greater wear on the shoulder than in the center, some signs of "bead groove," some discoloration, a few marks on the rim flange, and inadequately filled puncture holes (which can also cause heat that might lead to separation). * * * But, in each instance, he testified that the symptoms were not significant, and he explained why he believed that they did not reveal overdeflection. For example, the extra shoulder wear, he said, appeared primarily on one shoulder, whereas an overdeflected tire would reveal equally abnormal wear on both shoulders. * * * Carlson concluded that the tire did not bear at least two of the four overdeflection symptoms, nor was there any less obvious cause of separation; and since neither overdeflection nor the punctures caused the blowout, a defect must have done so.

Kumho Tire moved the District Court to exclude Carlson's testimony on the ground that his methodology failed Rule 702's reliability requirement. [The district court granted the motion on the ground that the evidence did not meet the *Daubert* reliability standard. The Eleventh Circuit reversed, holding that *Daubert* did not apply to non-scientific evidence.]

II

A

In *Daubert*, this Court held that Federal Rule of Evidence 702 imposes a special obligation upon a trial judge to "ensure that any and all scientific testimony * * * is not only relevant, but reliable." 509 U.S. [at 589]. The initial question before us is whether this basic gatekeeping obligation applies only to "scientific" testimony or to all expert testimony. * * *

* * *

[Rule 702] makes no relevant distinction between "scientific" knowledge and "technical" or "other specialized" knowledge. It makes clear that any such knowledge might become the subject of expert testimony. In *Daubert*, the Court specified that it is the Rule's word "knowledge," not the words (like "scientific") that modify that word, that "establishes a standard of evidentiary reliability." 509 U.S. [at 589–590]. Hence, as a matter of language, the Rule applies its reliability standard to all "scientific," "technical," or "other specialized" matters within its scope. We concede that the Court in *Daubert* referred only to "scientific" knowledge. But as the Court there said, it referred to "scientific" testimony "because that [wa]s the nature of the expertise" at issue. Id. [at 590 n.8]

Neither is the evidentiary rationale that underlay the Court's basic *Daubert* "gatekeeping" determination limited to "scientific" knowledge. *Daubert* pointed out that Federal Rules 702 and 703 grant expert witnesses testimonial latitude unavailable to other witnesses on the "assumption that the expert's opinion will have a reliable basis in the knowledge and experience of his discipline." Id. [at 592] (pointing out that experts may testify to opinions, including those that are not based on firsthand knowledge or observation). The Rules grant that latitude to all experts, not just to "scientific" ones.

Finally, it would prove difficult, if not impossible, for judges to administer evidentiary rules under which a gatekeeping obligation depended upon a distinction between "scientific" knowledge and "technical" or "other specialized" knowledge. There is no clear line that divides the one from the others. Disciplines such as engineering rest upon scientific knowledge. Pure scientific theory itself may depend for its development upon observation and properly engineered machinery. And conceptual efforts to distinguish the two are unlikely to produce clear legal lines capable of application in particular cases. * * *

Neither is there a convincing need to make such distinctions. Experts of all kinds tie observations to conclusions through the use of what Judge Learned Hand called "general truths derived from * * * specialized experience." Hand, Historical and Practical Considerations Regarding Expert Testimony, 15 Harv. L.Rev. 40, 54 (1901). And whether the specific expert testimony focuses upon specialized observations, the specialized translation of those observations into theory, a specialized theory itself, or the application of such a theory in a particular case, the expert's testimony often will rest "upon an experience confessedly foreign in kind to [the jury's] own." *Ibid.* * * *

We conclude that *Daubert's* general principles apply to the expert matters described in Rule 702. * * *

B

Petitioners ask more specifically whether a trial judge determining the "admissibility of an engineering expert's testimony" *may* consider several more specific factors that *Daubert* said might "bear on" a judge's gatekeeping determination. [listing *Daubert* factors] Emphasizing the word "may" in the question, we answer that question yes.

Engineering testimony rests upon scientific foundations, the reliability of which will be at issue in some cases. * * * In other cases, the relevant reliability concerns may focus upon personal knowledge or experience. As the Solicitor General points out, there are many different kinds of experts, and many different kinds of expertise. See Brief for United States as *Amicus Curiae* 18–19, and n.5 (citing cases involving experts in drug terms, handwriting analysis, criminal *modus operandi,* land valuation, agricultural practices, railroad procedures, attorney's fee valuation, and others). Our emphasis on the word "may" thus reflects *Daubert's* description of the Rule 702 inquiry as "a flexible one." 509 U.S. [at 594]. *Daubert* makes clear that the factors it mentions do *not* constitute a "definitive checklist or test." Id. [at 593]. And *Daubert* adds that the gatekeeping inquiry must be " 'tied to the facts' " of a particular "case." Id. [at 591]. We agree with the Solicitor General that "[t]he factors identified in *Daubert* may or may not be pertinent in assessing reliability, depending on the nature of the issue, the expert's particular expertise, and the subject of his testimony." Brief for United States as *Amicus Curiae* 19. The conclusion, in our view, is that we can neither rule out, nor rule in, for all cases and for all time the applicability of the factors mentioned in *Daubert,* nor can we now do so for subsets of cases categorized by category of expert or by kind of evidence. Too much depends upon the particular circumstances of the particular case at issue.

Daubert itself is not to the contrary. It made clear that its list of factors was meant to be helpful, not definitive. Indeed, those factors do not all necessarily apply even in every instance in which the reliability of scientific testimony is challenged. It might not be surprising in a particular case, for example, that a claim made by a scientific witness has never been the subject of peer review, for the particular application at issue may never previously have interested any scientist. Nor, on the other hand, does the presence of *Daubert's* general acceptance factor help show that an expert's testimony is reliable where the discipline itself lacks reliability, as, for example, do theories grounded in any so-called generally accepted principles of astrology or necromancy.

At the same time, and contrary to the Court of Appeals' view, some of *Daubert's* questions can help to evaluate the reliability even of experience-based testimony. In certain cases, it will be appropriate for the trial judge to ask, for example, how often an engineering expert's experience-based methodology has produced erroneous results, or whether such a method is generally accepted in the relevant engineering community. Likewise, it will at times be useful to ask even of a witness whose expertise is based purely on experience, say, a perfume tester able to distinguish among 140 odors at a sniff, whether his preparation is of a kind that others in the field would recognize as acceptable.

We must therefore disagree with the Eleventh Circuit's holding that a trial judge may ask questions of the sort *Daubert* mentioned only where an expert "relies on the application of scientific principles," but not where an expert relies "on skill-or experience-based observation." 131 F.3d, at 1435. We do not believe that Rule 702 creates a schematism that segregates expertise by type while mapping certain kinds of questions to certain kinds of experts. Life and the legal cases that it generates are too complex to warrant so definitive a match.

To say this is not to deny the importance of *Daubert's* gatekeeping requirement. The objective of that requirement is to ensure the reliability and relevancy of expert testimony. It is to make certain that an expert, whether basing testimony upon professional studies or personal experience, employs in the courtroom the same level of intellectual rigor that characterizes the practice of an expert in the relevant field. Nor do we deny that, as stated in *Daubert*, the particular questions that it mentioned will often be appropriate for use in determining the reliability of challenged expert testimony. Rather, we conclude that the trial judge must have considerable leeway in deciding in a particular case how to go about determining whether particular expert testimony is reliable. That is to say, a trial court should consider the specific factors identified in *Daubert* where they are reasonable measures of the reliability of expert testimony.

C

The trial court must have the same kind of latitude in deciding *how* to test an expert's reliability, and to decide whether or when special briefing or other proceedings are needed to investigate reliability, as it enjoys when it decides *whether or not* that expert's relevant testimony is reliable. Our opinion in *Joiner* makes clear that a court of appeals is to apply an abuse-of-discretion standard when it "review[s] a trial court's decision to admit or exclude expert testimony." 522 U.S. [at 138–39].

That standard applies as much to the trial court's decisions about how to determine reliability as to its ultimate conclusion. Otherwise, the trial judge would lack the discretionary authority needed both to avoid unnecessary "reliability" proceedings in ordinary cases where the reliability of an expert's methods is properly taken for granted, and to require appropriate proceedings in the less usual or more complex cases where cause for questioning the expert's reliability arises. Indeed, the Rules seek to avoid "unjustifiable expense and delay" as part of their search for "truth" and the "jus[t] determin[ation]" of proceedings. Fed. Rule Evid. 102. Thus, whether *Daubert's* specific factors are, or are not, reasonable measures of reliability in a particular case is a matter that the law grants the trial judge broad latitude to determine. See *Joiner*, [at 143]. And the Eleventh Circuit erred insofar as it held to the contrary.

III

We further explain the way in which a trial judge "may" consider *Daubert's* factors by applying these considerations to the case at hand, a matter that has been briefed exhaustively by the parties and their 19 *amici.* The District Court did not doubt Carlson's qualifications, which included a masters degree in mechanical engineering, 10 years' work at Michelin America, Inc., and testimony as a tire failure consultant in other tort cases. Rather, it excluded the testimony because, despite those qualifications, it initially doubted, and then found unreliable, "the methodology employed by the expert in analyzing the data obtained in the visual inspection, and the scientific basis, if any, for such an analysis." * * * In our view, the doubts that triggered the District Court's initial inquiry here were reasonable, as was the court's ultimate conclusion.

For one thing, and contrary to respondents' suggestion, the specific issue before the court was not the reasonableness *in general* of a tire expert's use of a visual and tactile inspection to determine whether overdeflection had caused the tire's tread to separate from its steel-belted carcass. Rather, it was the reasonableness of using such an approach, along with Carlson's particular method of analyzing the data thereby obtained, to draw a conclusion regarding *the particular matter to which the expert testimony was directly relevant.* That matter concerned the likelihood that a defect in the tire at issue caused its tread to separate from its carcass. The tire in question, the expert conceded, had traveled far enough so that some of the tread had been worn bald; it should have been taken out of service; it had been repaired (inadequately) for punctures; and it bore some of the very marks that the expert said indicated, not a defect, but abuse through overdeflection. * * * The relevant issue was whether the expert could reliably determine the cause of *this* tire's separation.

Nor was the basis for Carlson's conclusion simply the general theory that, in the absence of evidence of abuse, a defect will normally have caused a tire's separation. Rather, the expert employed a more specific theory to establish the existence (or absence) of such abuse. Carlson testified precisely that in the absence of *at least two* of four signs of abuse (proportionately greater tread wear on the shoulder; signs of grooves caused by the beads; discolored sidewalls; marks on the rim flange), he concludes that a defect caused the separation. And his analysis depended upon acceptance of a further implicit proposition, namely, that his visual and tactile inspection could determine that the tire before him had not been abused despite some evidence of the presence of the very signs for which he looked (and two punctures).

For another thing, the transcripts of Carlson's depositions support both the trial court's initial uncertainty and its final conclusion. Those transcripts cast considerable doubt upon the reliability of both the explicit theory (about the need for two signs of abuse) and the implicit proposition (about the significance of visual inspection in this case). Among other things, the expert could not say whether the tire had traveled more than 10, or 20, or 30, or 40, or 50 thousand miles, adding that 6,000 miles was "about how far" he could "say with any certainty." * * * The court could reasonably have wondered about the reliability of a method of visual and tactile inspection sufficiently precise to ascertain with some certainty the abuse-related significance of minute shoulder/center relative tread wear differences, but insufficiently precise to tell "with any certainty" from the tread wear whether a tire had traveled less than 10,000 or more than 50,000 miles. And these concerns might have been augmented by Carlson's repeated reliance on the "subjective[ness]" of his mode of analysis in response to questions seeking specific information regarding how he could differentiate between a tire that actually had been overdeflected and a tire that merely looked as though it had been. * * * They would have been further augmented by the fact that Carlson said he had inspected the tire itself for the first time the morning of his first deposition, and then only for a few hours. (His initial conclusions were based on photographs.) * * *

Moreover, prior to his first deposition, Carlson had issued a signed report in which he concluded that the tire had "not been * * * overloaded or underinflated," not because of the absence of "two of four" signs of abuse, but simply because "the rim flange impressions * * * were normal." * * * That report also said that the "tread depth remaining was 3/32 inch," * * * though the opposing expert's (apparently undisputed) measurements indicate that the tread depth taken at various positions around the tire actually ranged from .5/32 of an inch to 4/32 of an inch, with the tire apparently showing greater wear along *both* shoulders than along the center * * *.

Further, in respect to one sign of abuse, bead grooving, the expert seemed to deny the sufficiency of his own simple visual-inspection methodology. He testified that most tires have some bead groove pattern, that where there is reason to suspect an abnormal bead groove he would ideally "look at a lot of [similar] tires" to know the grooving's significance, and that he had not looked at many tires similar to the one at issue. * * *

Finally, the court, after looking for a defense of Carlson's methodology as applied in these circumstances, found no convincing defense. Rather, it found (1) that "none" of the *Daubert* factors, including that of "general acceptance" in the relevant expert community, indicated that Carlson's testimony was reliable * * * ; (2) that its own analysis "revealed no countervailing factors operating in favor of admissibility which could outweigh those identified in *Daubert*" * * * ; and (3) that the "parties identified no such factors in their briefs" * * *. For these three reasons *taken together,* it concluded that Carlson's testimony was unreliable.

Respondents now argue to us, as they did to the District Court, that a method of tire failure analysis that employs a visual/tactile inspection is a reliable method, and they point both to its use by other experts and to Carlson's long experience working for Michelin as sufficient indication that that is so. But no one denies that an expert might draw a conclusion from a set of observations based on extensive and specialized experience. Nor does anyone deny that, as a general matter, tire abuse may often be identified by qualified experts through visual or tactile inspection of the tire. * * * As we said before, * * * the question before the trial court was specific, not general. * * *

The particular issue in this case concerned the use of Carlson's two-factor test and his related use of visual/tactile inspection to draw conclusions on the basis of what seemed small observational differences. We have found no indication in the record that other experts in the industry use Carlson's two-factor test or that tire experts such as Carlson normally make the very fine distinctions about, say, the symmetry of comparatively greater shoulder tread wear that were necessary, on Carlson's own theory, to support his conclusions. Nor, despite the prevalence of tire testing, does anyone refer to any articles or papers that validate Carlson's approach. * * * Indeed, no one has argued that Carlson himself, were he still working for Michelin, would have concluded in a report to his employer that a similar tire was similarly defective on grounds identical to those upon which he rested his conclusion here. Of course, Carlson himself claimed that his method was accurate, but, as we pointed out in *Joiner*, "nothing in either *Daubert* or the Federal Rules of Evidence requires a district court to admit opinion evidence that is connected to existing data only by the *ipse dixit* of the expert." 522 U.S. [at 146].

* * *

In sum, Rule 702 grants the district judge the discretionary authority, reviewable for its abuse, to determine reliability in light of the particular facts and circumstances of the particular case. The District Court did not abuse its discretionary authority in this case. Hence, the judgment of the Court of Appeals is *Reversed.*

JUSTICE SCALIA, with whom JUSTICE O'CONNOR and JUSTICE THOMAS join, concurring.

I join the opinion of the Court, which makes clear that the discretion it endorses—trial-court discretion in choosing the manner of testing expert reliability—is not discretion to abandon the gatekeeping function. I think it worth adding that it is not discretion to perform the function inadequately. Rather, it is discretion to choose among *reasonable* means of excluding expertise that is *fausse* and science that is junky. Though, as the Court makes clear today, the *Daubert* factors are not holy writ, in a particular case the failure to apply one or another of them may be unreasonable, and hence an abuse of discretion.

[JUSTICE STEVENS, concurring in part and dissenting in part, argued that whether the trial judge had abused his discretion required a study of the record that could be performed more efficiently by the court of appeals.]

Notes and Questions

1. *Indication of "exacting standards."* Is the *Daubert* standard less stringent than *Frye*? See Weisgram v. Marley Co., 528 U.S. 440, 445 (2000) (In ruling on summary judgment motion in wrongful death action against the manufacturer of allegedly defective baseboard heater, the Court stated: "Since *Daubert*, moreover, parties relying on expert evidence have had notice of the exacting standards of reliability such evidence must meet.").

2. *Civil v. criminal cases.* A Rand Institute study of civil cases concluded that since *Daubert*, judges have examined the reliability of expert evidence more closely and have found more evidence unreliable as a result. See Dixon & Gill, Changes in the Standards of Admitting Expert Evidence in Federal Civil Cases Since the *Daubert* Decision, 8 Psychol., Pub.Pol'y & L. 251, 298 (2002). Some federal courts have demanded stringent epidemiological studies in toxic tort cases. See Rider v. Sandoz Pharm. Corp., 295 F.3d 1194, 1202 (11th Cir.2002) ("The district court, after finding that the plaintiffs' evidence was unreliable, noted that certain types of other evidence may have been considered reliable, including peer-reviewed epidemiological literature, a predictable chemical mechanism, general acceptance in learned treatises, or a very large number of case reports."). Many cases do not even survive summary judgment, and some commentators have argued that the standards are too strict. See Kassierer & Cecil, Inconsistency in Evidentiary Standards for Medical Testimony: Disorder in the Courts, 288 J.Am. Med.Ass'n 1382, 1382 (2002) ("In some instances, judges have excluded medical testimony on cause-and-effect relationships unless it is based on published, peer-reviewed, epidemiologically sound studies, even though practitioners rely on other evidence of causality in making clinical decisions, when such studies are not available.").

In contrast, admissibility standards in criminal litigation appear unchanged. An extensive study of reported criminal cases found that "the *Daubert* decision did not impact on the admission rates of expert testimony at either the trial or appellate court levels." Groscup et al., The Effects of *Daubert* on the Admissibility of Expert Testimony in State and Federal Criminal Cases, 8 Pyschol., Pub.Pol'y & L. 339, 364 (2002).

3. *Jury mistrust.* Are stringent admissibility standards needed because jurors are incapable of dealing with expert testimony? The petitioners in *Kumho* stressed the jury's deficiencies in their briefs. An amicus brief, filed by experts in jury research, attempted to educate the Court on this issue, advising that the Court should *not* decide the case "based on the Petitioners' unsupported or flawed assertions that juries fail to critically evaluate expert testimony, that they are overawed by experts, that they have a 'natural tendency' to defer to experts, and that they have pro-plaintiff and anti-business biases. The heavy preponderance of data from more than a quarter century of empirical jury research points to just the opposite view of jury behavior." Brief Amici Curiae of Neil Vidmar et al., Kumho Tire Co. v. Carmichael, 526 U.S. 137 (1999).

4. *Amended Rule 702.* The following clause was added to Rule 702 in 2000: "if (1) the testimony is based upon sufficient facts or data, (2) the testimony is the product of reliable principles and methods, and (3) the witness has applied the principles and methods reliably to the facts of the case." In Rudd v. General Motors Corp., 127 F.Supp.2d 1330, 1336–37 (M.D.Ala.2001), the court wrote that "the new Rule 702 appears to require a trial judge to make an evaluation that delves more into the facts than was recommended in *Daubert*, including as the rule does an inquiry into the sufficiency of the testimony's basis ('the testimony is based upon sufficient facts or data') and an inquiry into the application of a methodology to the facts ('the witness has applied the principles and methods reliably to the facts of the case'). Neither of these two latter questions that are now *mandatory* under the new rule * * * were expressly part of the former admissibility analysis under *Daubert*."

The Advisory Committee Note to amended Rule 702 lists a number of additional reliability factors: (1) whether the underlying research was conducted independently of litigation, (2) whether the expert unjustifiably extrapolated from an accepted premise to an unfounded conclusion, (3) whether the expert has adequately accounted for obvious alternative explanations, (4) whether the expert was as careful as she would be in her professional work outside of paid litigation, and (5) whether the field of expertise claimed by the expert is known to reach reliable results.

5. *Findings.* See United States v. Velarde, 214 F.3d 1204, 1209 (10th Cir.2000) ("While we recognize that the trial court is accorded great latitude in determining how to make *Daubert* reliability findings before admitting expert testimony, *Kumho* and *Daubert* make it clear that the court must, on the record, make some kind of reliability determination. * * * The record in this case reveals no such reliability determination.").

6. *Pretrial hearings.* See United States v. Alatorre, 222 F.3d 1098, 1100, 1104 (9th Cir.2000) ("[T]rial courts are not compelled to conduct pretrial hearings in order to discharge the gatekeeping function. * * * Here the court adopted a practical procedure, well within its discretion, when it allowed Alatorre to explore Jacobs's qualifications and the basis for his testimony at trial via voir dire and then, following voir dire, rejected his renewed objections to the testimony regarding wholesale and retail value [of drugs].").

Note on Daubert and Kumho in the States

Tracing the effects of *Daubert* in the states is somewhat complex. First, although many states rejected *Frye* in favor of *Daubert,* they did not necessarily adopt *Joiner* or *Kumho.* See Bernstein & Jackson, The *Daubert* Trilogy in the States, 44 Jurimetrics J. 351, 365 (Spring 2004).

Second, *Daubert's* impact on the *Frye* test has clouded the distinction between the two standards. Terms such as gatekeeper, testability, and peer review have crept into the *Frye* lexicon. Indeed, some *Frye* cases look like *Daubert* in disguise. For instance, in Ramirez v. State, 810 So.2d 836, 844 (Fla.2001), the Florida Supreme Court rejected the testimony of five experts who claimed general acceptance for a process of matching a knife with a cartilage wound in a murder victim—a type of "toolmark" comparison. The court emphasized the lack of testing, the paucity of "meaningful peer review", the absence of a quantified error rate, and the failure to develop objective standards.

Third, *Frye*, which had been limited to criminal cases, has been extended to toxic tort litigation, see Bernstein, *Frye, Frye*, Again: The Past, Present, and Future of the General Acceptance Test, 41 Jurimetrics J. 385, 394 (Spring 2001), and a recent study "found no evidence that *Frye* or *Daubert* makes a difference" in toxic tort litigation. Cheng & Yoon, Does *Frye* or *Daubert* Matter? A Study of Scientific Admissibility Standards, 91 Va.L.Rev. 471, 511 (2005) (using removal rates).

Fourth, *Daubert's* effect on the third approach to scientific evidence, the relevancy approach, may have been the most profound development. A number of courts had rejected *Frye* before *Daubert* was decided. Many of these courts now claim that *Daubert* is consistent with their former approach. This is true in some instances but not in others. Many of these jurisdictions had, in practice, adopted the relevancy approach, and their movement toward *Daubert* raises their standard of admissibility.

Finally, there has always been strict and lax *Frye* jurisdictions. Well-reasoned *Frye* decisions manifest far more than a superficial "nose-counting"—these cases demonstrate an understanding of the underlying science. See *Kelly*, supra. In contrast, an Illinois court admitted "lip print" comparisons, somehow finding them generally accepted. People v. Davis, 710 N.E.2d 1251 (Ill.App.Ct.1999). The same dichotomy can now be observed with *Daubert*. Compare the majority opinion (lax application) in United States v. Crisp, 324 F.3d 261 (4th Cir.2003) (admitting fingerprint and handwriting comparisons), with the dissent (strict application). See also Lee v. Martinez, 96 P.3d 291, 297 (N.M.2004) (admitting polygraph results under *Daubert*). As a British scholar commented, "The choice is not between easy *Frye* and difficult *Daubert*; it is between strict and lax scrutiny." Mike Redmayne, Expert Evidence and Criminal Justice 113 (2001).

UNITED STATES v. HINES

United States District Court, D. Massachusetts, 1999.
55 F.Supp.2d 62.

GERTNER, DISTRICT JUDGE.

This case raises questions concerning the application of Daubert v. Merrell Dow Pharmaceuticals, Inc., * * * and Kumho Tire Co. v. Carmichael * * * to technical fields, that are not, strictly speaking, science. Two fields are involved: The first is an "old" field, handwriting analysis, which has been the subject of expert testimony for countless years. The second is a comparatively "new" field, the psychology of eyewitness identification. The government maintained that handwriting analysis is "science," meeting the *Daubert* and *Kumho* tests, while the psychology of eyewitness identification is not. Not surprisingly, the defendant insisted that the opposite is true.

Johannes Hines ("Hines") is charged under 18 U.S.C. § 2113 for allegedly robbing the Broadway National Bank in Chelsea, Massachusetts on January 27, 1997. The government's principal evidence consisted of the eyewitness identification of the teller who was robbed, Ms. Jeanne Dunne, and the handwriting analysis of the robbery note. In connection with the latter, the government offered Diana Harrison ("Harrison"), a document examiner with the Federal Bureau of Investigations, to testify as to the authorship of a "stick-up" note found at the scene of the crime.

Hines sought to exclude the handwriting analysis. This testimony, defense claims, notwithstanding its venerable history, does not meet the standards of *Daubert* and *Kumho*. In the alternative, if the court permitted the jury to hear the handwriting testimony, Hines sought to have his expert—Professor Mark Denbeaux ("Denbeaux")—testify as to the weaknesses of the methodology and the basis of Harrison's conclusions. The government, on the other hand, argued for its handwriting expert under the applicable tests, and rejects Denbeaux.

* * *

This trial ended in a hung jury (as did the first). Since the issues noted in this memorandum will recur in the next trial, I outline my reasoning * * *

Kumho extended *Daubert* to non-scientific fields. * * *

Again, a mixed message: Apply *Daubert* to technical fields, even though the scientific method may not *really* fit, but be flexible. Moreover, in this setting, because few technical fields are as firmly established as traditional scientific ones, the new science/old science comparison is less clear. The court is plainly inviting a reexamination even of "generally accepted" venerable, technical fields.

A. *Handwriting*

Handwriting analysis is one such field. The Harrison testimony may be divided into two parts: Part 1 is Harrison's testimony with respect to similarities between the known handwriting of Hines, and the robbery note. Part 2 is Harrison's testimony with respect to the author of the note, that the author of the robbery note was indeed Hines. I concluded that Harrison could testify only as to the former. * * *

Hines challenges Harrison's testimony under *Daubert/Kumho*. If I were to give special emphasis to "general acceptance" or to treat *Daubert/ Kumho* as calling for a rigorous analysis only of new technical fields, not traditional ones, then handwriting analysis would largely pass muster. Handwriting analysis is perhaps the prototype of a technical field regularly admitted into evidence. But, if I were to apply the *Daubert/ Kumho* standards rigorously, looking for such things as empirical testing, rate of error, etc., the testimony would have serious problems. *See* U.S. v. Starzecpyzel, 880 F.Supp. 1027, 1036 (S.D.N.Y.1995) (finding that if the court had to apply *Daubert* to the preferred handwriting testimony, it would have to be excluded).

According to Denbeaux, handwriting analysis by experts suffers in two respects. It has never been subject to meaningful reliability or validity testing, comparing the results of the handwriting examiners' conclusions with actual outcomes. There is no peer review by a "competitive, unbiased community of practitioners and academics." Starzecpyzel, 880 F.Supp. at 1038. To the extent that it has been "generally accepted," it is not by a "financially disinterested independent community, like an academic community," Id.; only other handwriting analysts have weighed in. It has never been shown to be more reliable than the results obtained by lay people. Some tests have been done, but all lacked a control or comparison group of lay persons. Thus, Denbeaux concludes, there is no need for expert testimony on handwriting analysis. Lay people can do as well. In this regard, I accept Denbeaux's testimony, and the article supporting it.

I do not believe that the government's expert, Kam, and the studies he has cited suggest otherwise. While Kam has conducted several interesting and important tests, purporting to validate handwriting analysis, they are not without criticism. They cannot be said to have "established" the validity of the field to any meaningful degree.

There is no question that lay witnesses are permitted to draw inferences of authorship from handwriting. Where the lay witness is familiar with the handwriting, he or she can testify about it. No expert testimony is necessary. But just because lay witnesses can evaluate handwriting in some circumstances, does not necessarily mean that they can do it as well as an expert can in all.

Handwriting analysis typically involves reviewing two samples, a known sample and an unknown one, to determine if they are similar. Both defense and government experts agree that unlike DNA or even fingerprints, one's handwriting is not at all unique in the sense that it remains the same over time, or uniquely separates one individual from another. Everyone's handwriting changes from minute to minute, day to day. At the same time, our handwriting is sufficiently similar to one another so that people can read each other's writing. Given that variability, the "expert" is obliged to make judgments—these squiggles look more like these, these lines are shaped more like these, etc. And those judgments are, as Harrison conceded, subjective.

When a lay witness, the girlfriend of the defendant for example, says "this is my boyfriend's writing," her conclusion is based on having been exposed to her paramour's handwriting countless times. Without a lay witness with that kind of expertise, the government is obliged to offer the testimony of "experts" who have looked at, and studied handwriting for years. These are, essentially, "observational" experts, taxonomists—arguably qualified because they have seen so many examples over so long. It is not traditional, experimental science, to be sure, but *Kumho*'s gloss on *Daubert* suggests this is not necessary. I conclude that Harrison can testify to the ways in which she has found Hines' known handwriting similar to or dissimilar from the handwriting of the robbery note; part 1 of her testimony.

Part 2 of the Harrison testimony is, however, problematic. There is no data that suggests that handwriting analysts can say, like DNA experts, that this person is "the" author of the document. There are no meaningful, and accepted validity studies in the field.[48] No one has shown me Harrison's error rate, the times she has been right, and the times she has been wrong. There is no academic field known as handwriting analysis. This is a "field" that has little efficacy outside of a courtroom. There are no peer reviews of it. Nor can one compare the opinion reached by an examiner with a standard protocol subject to validity testing, since there are no recognized standards. There is no agreement as to how many similarities it takes to declare a match, or how many differences it takes to rule it out. * * *

Moreover, the issue here is not only the validity and reliability of the expert testimony, but its validity and reliability in the context of this lay proceeding. Harrison's account of what is similar or not similar in the handwriting of Hines and the robber can be understood and evaluated by the jury. The witness can be cross examined, as she was, about why this difference was not considered consequential, while this difference was, and the jury can draw their own conclusions. This is not rocket science, or higher math.[49]

48. Kam, the government's proposed expert agrees that "[s]urprisingly, there are only a few studies that examine the reliability of writer screening by document examiners." Kam, et al., *Proficiency of Document Examiners in Writer Identification,* 39 J. Forensic Sci. at 5 * * *). Kam also concluded that "[i]t is very likely that many examiner decisions and associations are difficult to verbalize, and that some verbal explanations are post factum re-creations of the reasoning process." *Id.* at 12.

49. In United States v. Buck, 1987 WL 19300 (S.D.N.Y.1987), an opinion predating both *Kumho* and *Daubert,* the court observed that "the ability of jurors to perform the crucial visual comparisons relied upon by handwriting experts cuts against the danger of undue prejudice from the mystique attached to 'experts.' " Id. at *3. Denbeaux suggests that it is precisely because the jury can so easily draw their own conclusions that expert testimony even in this limited area is not at all necessary. I am not willing to come to that conclusion—on this record at this time. I am persuaded for now that the testimony involves more than just identifying what is similar and what is dif-

Her conclusion of authorship, however, has a difference resonance: "Out of all of my experience, and training, I am saying that he is the one, the very author." That leap may not at all be justified by the underlying data; and in the context of this case, is extraordinarily prejudicial.

The Court faced a similar issue in *United States v. McVeigh*, (D.Colo. Trans.) [Oklahoma City bombing case] (citing to *Starzecpyzel*, supra):

> [T]here is a great difference between a witness who has the requisite training and skill saying, 'Look, I've compared this handwriting on this exhibit with this exemplar and I've used the techniques of microscoping (sic) and, you know, all of those things that are often involved in that kind of comparison, and these are the things I find,' and 'I see these similarities and these dissimilarities and so forth' but does not go on to reach any sort of ultimate conclusion that this was written by the same person or expresses some probability or degree of confidence.
>
> The problem with * * * handwriting is that there is no testing of the—no verification-type testing of these opinion results; and in addition, there has never been within the discipline of people who practice this skill—there has never been any agreement on how to express the results. There is no standardized nomenclature, you know. Therefore, it seems to me that we should draw the distinction between somebody getting on the stand and saying 'Yeah, written by the same person,' or 'no, not written by the same person,' vs. 'these are the similarities or these are the dissimilarities'; and the jury can decide.

I find Harrison's testimony meets Fed.R.Evid. 702's requirements to the extent that she restricts her testimony to similarities or dissimilarities between the known exemplars and the robbery note. However, she may not render an ultimate conclusion on who penned the unknown writing. * * *

B. Eyewitness Identification

The government offered the testimony of Jeanne Dunne ("Dunne"), the teller. Dunne, a white woman, gave the following identification moments after the robbery occurred: She identified the man as black with dark skin, a wide nose, and a medium build.[50] Her description was as close to a generic identification of an African American man as one can imagine. Dunne was unable to identify Hines from a book of photographs of African American men shortly after the robbery.[51] She

ferent in the same way a lay person would. It involves taking the next step—that this or that similarity matters, that it equals a general pattern. Presumably, the expert is helped in drawing general patterns by the numbers of exemplars she has seen, just like the spouse identifies the husband's handwriting because she has seen it numbers of times.

50. She also noted that he had on a blue jacket, and a baseball cap.

51. Another witness, a customer at the bank, was unable to effect any identification.

picked out a few photographs, but none of them were as "dark black" as the robber. Working with a police artist, she helped construct a sketch of the robber. Immediately following, she was shown eight photographs, including one of Hines, and indicated that the Hines photograph "resembled" the robber, that it "looked like him," but she was still not sure. (Since the robber was wearing a hat, she tried to envision the man in the photograph with a baseball cap.) Months later Dunne picked Hines out of a lineup.

Hines offered the testimony of Kassin, a psychologist studying human perception at Williams College with substantial credentials, and trial experience. The government offered a similarly credentialed expert, Ebbesen. I allowed the testimony of both.

The Kassin testimony was offered to show, inter alia, the following: the decreased accuracy of cross-racial identification relative to same-race identification, the effect of stress on identification, the effect of time on memory as it relates to identification, the "confidence-accuracy" phenomenon which suggests the absence of any correlation between the amount of confidence expressed by an eyewitness in his or her memory and the accuracy of that witness' identification, the suggestiveness of subtle aspects of the identification process, such as the darkness of a particular photo as compared to others in the array, the fact that the eyewitness knows there is a suspect in the mix, the transference phenomenon by which a witness may believe that a face looks familiar but is unable to say whether her familiarity comes from seeing a previous mug shot, or from the robbery, etc.

On direct examination, Kassin identified those factors in the Dunne identification that were implicated in the studies with which he was familiar, and could undermine accuracy—the cross racial issues, the differences between the photographs of the other men and Hines' in the photo array,[52] the differences between Hines and the other men in the lineup.[53] He noted problems with what he called relative, comparative judgments: The witness would like to resolve the case and so compares the photographs of one man to another in the array, rather than attempting to compare the photographs to the man she saw. On cross, the government brought up the factors that enhanced accuracy, the nature of the lighting, the distance from the robber, the instructions that were given to the witness, especially at the lineup. The government questioned Kassin about the instructions given to Dunne at the lineup. Kassin agreed that those instructions were "ideal."

52. Kassin testified that Hines' photograph was the darkest of the eight in the array. Moreover, the numbering for his photograph was different from the others. All the others were 6 numbers, beginning with 96, Hines' number was 1234.

53. The defense pointed out that in the photograph taken of the lineup, which Dunne had indicated was a fair and accurate representation of it, Hines was the darkest man. Furthermore, Dunne could have inferred from the presence of a defense attorney that one of the men in the lineup was a suspect.

Unlike handwriting analysis, there is no question as to the scientific underpinnings of Kassin's testimony. They are based on experimental psychological studies, testing the acquisition of memory, retention, and retrieval of memory under different conditions. Indeed, the central debate before the jury, eloquently articulated by Ebbesen, the government's expert, is the polar opposite of the debate in the handwriting field—whether conclusions obtained in an experimental, academic, setting with college students should be applied to a real life setting. * * * Kassin and others believe that these conclusions are appropriately applied to eyewitness identifications in court. Ebbesen disagreed.

The government claimed that the jury did not need this testimony at all, that it was not necessary under Fed.R.Evid. 702 to assist the trier of fact. I disagree. While jurors may well be confident that they can draw the appropriate inferences about eyewitness identification directly from their life experiences, their confidence may be misplaced, especially where cross-racial identification is concerned. See *id.* at 1137; *United States v. Smith,* 736 F.2d, 1103, 1106 (6th Cir.1984) (such testimony would "not only 'surpass' common-sense evaluation, it would question common-sense evaluation.") Indeed, in this respect the rationale for the testimony tracks that for battered women syndrome experts. The jury, for example, may fault the victim for not leaving an abusive spouse, believing that they are fully capable of putting themselves in the shoes of the defendant. In fact, psychological evidence suggests that the "ordinary" response of an "ordinary" woman are not in play in situations of domestic violence where the victim suffers from "battered women syndrome." *See e.g., People v. Day,* 2 Cal.App.4th 405, 2 Cal.Rptr.2d 916, 924 (1992). Common sense inferences thus may well be way off the mark.

Nor do I agree that this testimony somehow usurps the function of the jury. The function of the expert here is not to say to the jury—"you should believe or not believe the eyewitness." (Indeed, it has far fewer pretensions to conclusions than does handwriting analysis, with far more science attached to it.) All that the expert does is provide the jury with more information with which the jury can then make a more informed decision.[54] And only the expert can do so. In the absence of an expert, a defense lawyer, for example, may try to argue that cross racial identifications are more problematic than identifications between members of the

54. In this respect, it is analogous to expert testimony on Rape Trauma Syndrome, *see* Roger B. Handberg, *Expert Testimony on Eyewitness Identification: A New Pair of Glasses for the Jury,* 32 Am.Crim. L.Rev. 1013, 1017 (1995), or pseudologia fantastica. *See United States v. Thomas Shay,* 57 F.3d 126, 129–35 (1st Cir.1995). Pseudologia fantastica is categorized as a factitious disorder in the Diagnostic and Statistical Manual of Mental Disorders and is sometimes referred to as Munchausen's Disease. *See id.* at 129 n.1. This disorder is a variant of lying, often characterized as an extreme form of pathological lying. *See id.* (citing R. Sharrock and M. Cresswell, *Pseudologia Fanastica: A Case Study of a Man Charged with Murder,* 29 Med.Sci.Law. 323, 323 (1989)). People who suffer from this condition present falsifications that are "disproportionate to any discernable end." *Id.* Pseudologues represent fantasies as real occurrences. *See id.*

same race, or that stress may undermine accuracy, but his voice necessarily lacks the authority of the scientific studies Kassin cited.

Finally, the fact that the expert has not interviewed the particular eyewitness makes it less likely that the jury will merely accept the expert testimony and more likely that the testimony will be appropriately cabined. The witness can only be providing the jury with the tools to analyze the eyewitness; he has no more specific information. The science makes no pretensions that it can predict whether a particular witness is accurate or mistaken.

In my judgment, the accuracy of these proceedings was enormously enhanced by treating the jury to all sides of the eyewitness debate, rather than assuming there was no controversy, that the issue, notwithstanding this literature is clear. * * *

Notes and Questions

1. *Handwriting.* Several trial courts have excluded handwriting testimony. United States v. Lewis, 220 F.Supp.2d 548, 554 (S.D.W.Va.2002) ("[Expert's] bald assertion that the 'basic principle of handwriting identification has been proven time and time again through research in [his] field,' without more specific substance, is inadequate to demonstrate testability and error rate."); United States v. Fujii, 152 F.Supp.2d 939, 940 (N.D.Ill.2000) (expert testimony concerning Japanese handprinting inadmissible; "Handwriting analysis does not stand up well under the *Daubert* standards. Despite its long history of use and acceptance, validation studies supporting its reliability are few, and the few that exist have been criticized for methodological flaws."). However, most appellate court have not even imposed the limitation found in *Hines.* See United States v. Prime, 363 F.3d 1028, 1033 (9th Cir.2004); United States v. Crisp, 324 F.3d 261 (4th Cir.2003). See also Mnookin, Scripting Expertise: The History of Handwriting Identification Evidence and the Judicial Construction of Reliability, 87 Va.L.Rev. 1723 (2001); Risinger et al., Exorcism of Ignorance as a Proxy for Rational Knowledge: The Lessons of Handwriting Identification "Expertise," 137 U.Pa.L.Rev. 731 (1989).

2. *Fingerprints.* In United States v. Havvard, 117 F.Supp.2d 848 (S.D.Ind.2000), aff'd, 260 F.3d 597 (7th Cir.2001), the court ruled that fingerprint identification satisfied the standards announced in *Daubert* and *Kumho* without citing any scientific research: "First, the methods of latent print identification can be and have been tested. They have been tested for roughly 100 years. They have been tested in adversarial proceedings with the highest possible stakes—liberty and sometimes life. * * * Next, the methods of identification are subject to peer review. As just stated, any other qualified examiner can compare the objective information upon which the opinion is based and may render a different opinion if warranted. In fact, peer review is the standard operating procedure among latent print examiners." Is this a proper application of the *Daubert* factors? See also United States v. Abreu, 406 F.3d 1304, 1307 (11th Cir.2005) (admitting evidence); United States v. Mitchell, 365 F.3d 215, 247 (3d Cir.2004) (same).

Assuming that every finger is unique does not mean that this uniqueness is transferred to a surface in a particular case. Typically, only a partial impression is transferred (often only a fifth of the record print), and distortion due to pressure inevitably affects the impression. The examination, although based on physical characteristics, is basically subjective. There is no minimum number of points of similarity required before a conclusion of identity may be reached. Moreover, because there are frequently "dissimilarities" between the crime scene and record prints, the examiner must decide whether there is a *true* dissimilarity, in which case there is an exclusion ("no match"), or whether the dissimilarity is due to distortion or an artifact.

In the terrorist bombing of a train in Madrid on March 11, 2004, which killed 191 and injured 2,000, the FBI misidentified Brandon Mayfield, a Portland lawyer, as the source of the crime scene prints. See Kershaw, Spain and U.S. at Odds on Mistaken Terror Arrest, N.Y.Times, June 5, 2004, at A1 (Spanish authorities cleared Mayfield and matched the fingerprints to an Algerian national); Stacey, A Report on the Erroneous Fingerprint Individualization in the Madrid Train Bombing Case, 54 J. Forensic Identification 707 (2004). For other misidentifications, see Cole, More Than Zero: Accounting for Error in Latent Fingerprint Identification, 95 J.Crim.L. & Criminology 985 (2005) (discussing 22 misidentifications).

3. *Firearms Identifications ("ballistics").* Judge Gertner applied her *Hines* analysis to cartridge case comparison evidence, once again limiting the scope of the testimony. United States v. Green, 405 F.Supp.2d 104, 107 (D.Mass.2005) ("O'Shea declared that this match could be made 'to the exclusion of every other firearm in the world.' * * * That conclusion, needless to say, is extraordinary, particularly given O'Shea's data and methods."). She also wrote that "the standards should be higher than were met in this case, and than have been imposed across the country. The more courts admit this type of toolmark evidence without requiring documentation, proficiency testing, or evidence of reliability, the more sloppy practices will endure; we should require more." Compare United States v. Hicks, 389 F.3d 514, 526 (5th Cir.2004) ("the matching of spent shell casings to the weapon that fired them has been a recognized method of ballistics testing in this circuit for decades"), with United States v. Monteiro, 407 F.Supp.2d 351 (D.Mass.2006) (testimony ruled inadmissible because expert failed to follow standards—i.e., no documentation (sketches or photographs) and no technical review by second examiner).

4. *Rape trauma syndrome.* In People v. Bledsoe, 681 P.2d 291, 300 (Cal.1984), the court noted that "rape trauma syndrome was not devised to determine the 'truth' or 'accuracy' of a particular past event—i.e., whether, in fact, a rape in the legal sense occurred—but rather was developed by professional rape counselors as a therapeutic tool, to help identify, predict and treat emotional problems experienced by the counselors' clients or patients." Thus, although generally accepted by the scientific community for a therapeutic purpose, expert testimony on RTS was not generally accepted "to prove that a rape, in fact, occurred." The court commented:

> [A]s a rule, rape counselors do not probe inconsistencies in their clients' descriptions of the facts of the incident, nor do they conduct independent investigations to determine whether other evidence corroborates or

> contradicts their clients' renditions. Because their function is to help their clients deal with the trauma they are experiencing, the historical accuracy of the client's descriptions of the details of the traumatizing events is not vital in their task.

The court, however, approved the admissibility of RTS evidence where the defendant suggests to the jury that the conduct of the victim after the incident is inconsistent with the claim of rape. In this situation, the court wrote, "expert testimony on rape trauma syndrome may play a particularly useful role by disabusing the jury of some widely held misconceptions about rape and rape victims, so that it may evaluate the evidence free of popular myths." Id. at 299. Most courts accept this position. For example, expert testimony has been admitted to explain a victim's (1) passive resistance during a rape, (2) delay in reporting the crime, (3) failure to attempt to escape, and (4) calm demeanor after an attack.

Should the same result apply to Child Sexual Abuse Accommodation Syndrome? See United States v. Bighead, 128 F.3d 1329, 1330 (9th Cir.1997) (In rebuttal, an expert "testified about 'delayed disclosure' and 'script memory,' which are typical characteristics she has observed among the more than 1300 persons she has interviewed who say they are victims of child abuse.").

5. *Battered women syndrome.* See Smith v. State, 486 S.E.2d 819, 822 (Ga.1997) ("[T]he battered person syndrome is not a separate defense, but * * * evidence of battered person syndrome is relevant in a proper case as a component of justifiable homicide by self-defense. * * * [E]vidence that a defendant suffered from battered person syndrome is only another circumstance which, if believed by the jury, would authorize a finding that a reasonable person, who had experienced prior physical abuse such as was endured by the defendant, would reasonably believe that the use of force against the victim was necessary, even though that belief may have been, in fact, erroneous.").

If the legal context is not self-defense, should BWS evidence be admissible? See Dunn v. Roberts, 963 F.2d 308 (10th Cir.1992) (accused entitled to expert assistance to raise duress defense); Arcoren v. United States, 929 F.2d 1235 (8th Cir.1991) (defendant charged with aggravated sexual abuse; his estranged wife reported the assault but then recanted her grand jury testimony at trial; BWS evidence admissible); Barrett v. State, 675 N.E.2d 1112 (Ind.Ct.App.1996) (BWS evidence relevant to a neglect-of-dependent charge).

6. *Modus operandi experts.* The courts have been receptive to expert testimony concerning criminal operations. E.g., United States v. Burchfield, 719 F.2d 356, 358 (11th Cir.1983) (counterfeiting); United States v. Scavo, 593 F.2d 837, 843–44 (8th Cir.1979) (bookmaking); United States v. Jackson, 425 F.2d 574, 576–77 (D.C.Cir.1970) (pickpocketing); United States v. Locascio, 6 F.3d 924, 936 (2d Cir.1993) ("inner workings of the Gambino Family" in the John Gotti trial); United States v. Pungitore, 910 F.2d 1084, 1148–49 (3d Cir.1990) (structure and organization of La Cosa Nostra).

The most frequent use of this type of testimony involves drug trafficking. Expert testimony has been admitted about the operation of clandestine laboratories, the street value of drugs, the amount of drugs consistent with distribution rather than personal use, strategies of deception, as well as other aspects of the drug trade. In addition, expert testimony on various "tools of the drug trade," including the use of beepers, code words, weapons, duct tape, and the like has been admitted.

Are there problems with this type of testimony? In United States v. Cruz, 981 F.2d 659 (2d Cir.1992), the expert testified about the use of intermediaries or brokers in the drug trade. The court questioned whether such testimony was useful: "That drug traffickers may seek to conceal their identities by using intermediaries would seem evident to the average juror from movies, television crime dramas, and news stories." Id. at 662. Moreover, the court believed that the expert's testimony was directed at another purpose: "[T]he credibility of a fact-witness may not be bolstered by arguing that the witness's version of events is consistent with an expert's description of patterns of criminal conduct, at least where the witness's version is not attacked as improbable or ambiguous evidence of such conduct." Id. at 663.

7. *Laboratory fraud.* A judicial investigation into the conduct of Fred Zain, the former head serologist of the West Virginia State Police crime laboratory, found the following problems with his work: "(1) overstating the strength of results; (2) overstating the frequency of genetic matches on individual pieces of evidence; (3) misreporting the frequency of genetic matches on multiple pieces of evidence; (4) reporting that multiple items had been tested, when only a single item had been tested; (5) reporting inconclusive results as conclusive; (6) repeatedly altering laboratory records; (7) grouping results to create the erroneous impression that genetic markers had been obtained from all samples tested; (8) failing to report conflicting results; (9) failing to conduct or to report conducting additional testing to resolve conflicting results; (10) implying a match with a suspect when testing supported only a match with the victim; and (11) reporting scientifically impossible or improbable results." In re Investigation of the W. Va. State Police Crime Lab., Serology Div., 438 S.E.2d 501, 516 (W.Va.1993).

A team from the American Society of Crime Lab Directors found that "when in doubt, Zain's findings would always inculpate the suspect." Id. at 512 n.9. After Zain left to accept a position in the San Antonio crime lab, prosecutors continued to send evidence to him for retesting. One serologist testified that at least twice after Zain left the lab, evidence on which that serologist had been unable to obtain genetic markers was subsequently sent to Texas for testing by Zain, "who again was able to identify genetic markers." Id. at 512.

8. *CSI Effect—Expectations of definitive proof?* Scholars, practitioners, and judges have raised the possibility that the recent expansion and popularization of powerful types of forensic proof is having an effect on how jurors perceive and evaluate evidence, particularly in criminal cases. This phenomenon is termed the "CSI effect." CSI stands for *Crime Scene Investigation*, a popular set of television shows. The theory is that jurors learn through popular media about the power of such proof to definitively establish guilt or innocence and come to expect it in all cases, becoming skeptical of a claim where it is not supported by such proof.

Clearly, advances in science and technology have made it possible to extract usable physical trace evidence when it was previously unavailable and to link those physical traces to a particular individual. For example, only a few decades ago tests in rape cases on semen samples could often say no more than that the suspect, the perpetrator, and 20% of the population share a genetic characteristic; now the chances of a random match with a DNA profile may be 1 in a million. Similarly, increases in computing capacity and the growth of databases has allowed identification of the source of that evidence where previously matches were practical only when particular individuals were recognized as suspects. In addition, the ubiquitousness of older technologies, such as photography, in the form of surveillance cameras and camera phones carried by a growing percentage of the population is making another type of "trace" evidence—electronic trace evidence—available in a growing number of prosecutions. These advances can have profound effects on cases where such proof is available. On the other hand, in the huge volume of criminal cases, limits on law enforcement investigative resources, ordinary human failures of imagination and technique, and the fact that trace evidence is often not left, preserved, or collected mean that evidence of this type is frequently unavailable even in prosecutions with clear merit. See Mosteller, Evidence History, the New Trace Evidence, and Rumblings in the Future of Proof, 3 Ohio St.Crim.L.J. 523 (2006).

However, beyond noting that much has changed in recent decades in the quality of forensic proof, that these changes are occurring with increasing speed, and that they have caught popular attention, not much can be said about the reality of the CSI effect on jurors, or if there is such a phenomenon precisely what effect it has on the evaluation of evidence. See Tyler, Viewing CSI and the Threshold of Guilt: Managing Truth and Justice in Reality and Fiction, 115 Yale L.J. 1050 (2006) (noting uncertainty of phenomenon and questioning who benefits if it exists).

Note on Eyewitness Identifications

As the Supreme Court noted nearly 40 years ago: "The vagaries of eyewitness identification are well-known; the annals of criminal law are rife with instances of mistaken identification." United States v. Wade, 388 U.S. 218, 228 (1967). Decades earlier, before serving on the Supreme Court, Justice Frankfurter questioned the identifications in the Sacco and Vanzetti case. See Frankfurter, The Case of Sacco and Vanzetti 30 (1927) ("What is the worth of identification testimony even when uncontradicted? The identification of strangers is proverbially untrustworthy."). The DNA exoneration cases have vividly documented the problem. Eyewitness misidentifications are the greatest cause of wrongful convictions. "In 1999, the Innocence Project reconstructed sixty-two cases * * * to determine what factors had been prevalent in the wrongful convictions. Mistaken eye-witnesses were a factor in 84 percent of the convictions * * *." Scheck et al., Actual Innocence: Five Days to Execution and Other Dispatches from the Wrongly Convicted 246 (2000).

Research has identified a number of causes for these misidentifications. Many eyewitnesses believe, at least subconsciously, that their assailant

> "must be" in the lineup or photo spread. Accordingly, they often guess at a choice rather than truly recognize that person as the perpetrator. They make their guess using "relative judgment processes," that is, by selecting the person in the lineup or photo spread who looks most like the wrongdoer, rather than picking someone whom they are convinced is an exact match. Moreover, the detective administering an identification procedure can unwittingly encourage a guess, for example, by smiling or nodding the head slightly or even just widening the eyes as the witness focuses attention toward the suspect. Further, cross-racial identifications are also more likely than intraracial ones to be mistaken. In addition, if "foils"—those persons other than the suspect appearing in the lineup or photo spread—are selected to look more like one another than like the witness's description of the attacker, or if their appearance is significantly different from the suspect's, an additional risk of error is introduced. Witness certainty likewise tends to rise over time. Thus, witnesses making a tentative identification at a lineup but told that they selected the "right man" become supremely confident of their identification at trial. Finally, juries tend to give great weight to confident identifications, even though the research shows that there is often little, if any, correlation between eyewitness confidence and eyewitness accuracy. Indeed, the research suggests juries, because of their unawareness of the sources of error and the limited evidence enabling them fairly to recreate the circumstances of the lineup or photo spread, find it hard to judge when well-meaning eyewitnesses are just plain wrong.

Report of the ABA Criminal Justice Section's Ad Hoc Innocence Committee to Ensure the Integrity of the Criminal Process, Achieving Justice: Freeing the Innocent, Convicting the Guilty xvii-xviii (Giannelli & Raeder eds., 2006).

Expert testimony. As shown by *Hines*, the use of expert testimony is one approach to the problem. See United States v. Langan, 263 F.3d 613, 621 (6th Cir.2001):

> The use of expert testimony in regard to eyewitness identification is a recurring and controversial subject. Trial courts have traditionally hesitated to admit expert testimony purporting to identify flaws in eyewitness identification. Among the reasons given to exclude such testimony are that the jury can decide the credibility issues itself; that experts in this area are not much help and largely offer rather obvious generalities; that trials would be prolonged by a battle of experts; and that such testimony creates undue opportunity for confusing and misleading the jury.
>
> Several courts, however, including our own, have suggested that such evidence warrants a more hospitable reception. *See United States v. Smithers,* 212 F.3d 306, 314 (6th Cir.2000) (holding that "the district court abused its discretion in excluding [the eyewitness identification expert's] testimony, without first conducting a hearing pursuant to *Daubert*") * * *. Moreover, such testimony has been allowed in with increasing frequency where the circumstances include "cross-racial identification, identification after a long delay, identification after observation under stress, and [such] psychological phenomena as * * * uncon-

scious transference." *See United States v. Harris,* 995 F.2d 532, 535 (4th Cir.1993). Nonetheless, each court to examine this issue has held that the district court has broad discretion in, first, determining the reliability of the particular testimony, and, second, balancing its probative value against its prejudicial effect.

See also United States v. Lester, 254 F.Supp.2d 602, 612 (E.D.Va.2003) ("[T]he problem of cross-race recognition, the phenomenon of weapon focus, the relationship of different levels of stress on eyewitness perception, and the correlation (or lack thereof) between confidence and accuracy * * * do seem to fall outside the common sense of the average juror."); Johnson, Cross–Racial Identification Errors in Criminal Cases, 69 Cornell L.Rev. 934, 938–39 (1984) ("The impairment in ability to recognize black faces is substantial."); Natarajan, Racialized Memory and Reliability: Due Process Applied to Cross-racial Eyewitness Identifications, 78 N.Y.U.L.Rev. 1821 (2003); Wells & Murray, "Eyewitness Confidence," in Eyewitness Testimony: Psychological Perspectives 155, 165 (Wells & Loftus eds., 1984) ("the eyewitness accuracy-confidence relationship is weak under good laboratory conditions and functionally useless in forensically representative settings").

While there does appear to be something of a trend, certainly in the appellate case law, supportive of greater admission of eyewitness expert testimony, it appears that the evidence is more often excluded by the exercise of trial court discretion. See Mosteller, Syndromes and Politics in Criminal Trials and Evidence Law, 46 Duke L.J. 461, 495 (1996) ("[D]espite lip service to the inherent weakness of eyewitness identification evidence, courts do not believe that innocent defendants are frequently convicted as a result of such evidence. The greater perceived danger is that such expert testimony would too often produce acquittals of the guilty; this fear has led to its general exclusion."). See also Overbeck, Note, Beyond Admissibility: A Practical Look at the Use of Eyewitness Expert Testimony in the Federal Courts, 80 N.Y.U.L.Rev. 1895 (2005).

Jury instructions. Some courts have attempted to deal with eyewitness identification problems by requiring special cautionary jury instructions. The leading case is United States v. Telfaire, 469 F.2d 552 (D.C.Cir.1972), which sets forth a recommended instruction. There are three different approaches in the cases: (1) courts requiring the *Telfaire* instruction; (2) courts leaving the decision on whether to instruct to the discretion of the trial court; and (3) courts rejecting *Telfaire*-like instructions and holding that the general instructions on credibility are sufficient. However, the effectiveness of special instructions is debatable. See Penrod & Cutler, Eyewitness Expert Testimony and Jury Decisionmaking, 52 Law & Contemp.Probs. 43, 82 (Aut.1989); Ramirez et al., Judge's Cautionary Instructions on Eyewitness Testimony, 14 Am.J. Forensic Psych. 31 (1996). Indeed, some instructions may mislead. In Brodes v. State, 614 S.E.2d 766, 771 (Ga.2005), the court ruled that, in light of the documented lack of correlation between a witness' certainty in his or her identification, it could "no longer endorse an instruction authorizing jurors to consider the witness's certainty in his/her identification as a factor to be used in deciding the reliability of that identification."

Lineup and photo spread procedures. Several proposed reforms focus on the police procedures used to produce an identification. These include the use of double-blind procedures, increasing the number of foils, and employing sequential (rather than simultaneous) procedures. How do these proposals address the concerns mentioned above? Are there other possible reforms? See Wells et al., Eyewitness Identification Procedures: Recommendations for Lineups and Photospreads, 22 Law & Hum.Behav. 603 (1998).

UNITED STATES v. VEYSEY[55]

United States District Court, N.D. Illinois.
No. 99 CR 381, October 23, 2000.

JUDGE PALLMEYER.

Defendant John T. Veysey, III is charged with engaging in various schemes to intentionally cause losses to his property and to individuals in order to collect the insurance proceeds. As part of this scheme, Defendant is charged with starting fires at his own residences. The government proposes to offer the testimony of Charles McClenahan, an actuarian, that the odds of an individual's suffering four serious house fires in a 106 month period of time at random is one in 1.7 trillion. Defendant moves *in limine* to bar this testimony under Federal Rules of Evidence 701, 702, 704 and 403.

* * *

In reaching his conclusion, McClenahan consulted the residential fire rate in the United States for the period 1988 to 1997. * * * He assumed that each of the four fires at Defendant's residences was a serious fire, that is, one which results in a loss of more than 20% of the dwelling value. * * * To calculate the probability that four or more "serious" fires would occur randomly during a continuous period of 106 months, McClenahan used a binomial model based upon monthly fire probabilities, using recognized statistical software. * * * From these calculations, McClenahan determined that the odds that an individual would suffer four residential fires at random are one in 1.7 trillion. * * *

A. EXPERT TESTIMONY

Before turning to the specific issue of the admissibility of probability statistics, the court addresses Veysey's threshold objections to any expert testimony in this area. * * *

Defendant Veysey has offered no specific objections to McClenahan's qualifications as an expert. He does argue, however, that McClenahan's testimony is not relevant because it speaks only to whether the four fires were random events when, according to Defendant, the defense has never suggested that the fires were random events. * * * Defendant therefore contends that such evidence should only be admitted, if at all, as rebuttal evidence in the event that Defendant claims at trial that the fires were random events. The court disagrees. The Government must

55. http://pub.bna.com/cl/99cr381.htm, cited at 68 Crim.L.Rptr. (BNA) 107 (Nov. 8, 2000). See also United States v. Veysey, 2001 WL 1617217 (N.D. Ill. 2001) (post trial motions). [Ed.]

prove beyond a reasonable doubt that the fires that occurred in 1996 and 1998 were intentionally started by Defendant and must prove that the 1993 fire was intentionally set one as part of Defendant's plan to fraudulently collect insurance proceeds for that property. McClenahan's testimony, if believed, shows that there is almost no possibility that the four fires were random events, which supports the Government's theory that the fires were intentional, thereby qualifying as relevant evidence. *See* Fed.R.Evid. 401 * * *

Defendant argues next that, even if relevant, such evidence does not call for expert testimony because the fact that the chances are low that one person would have numerous house fires in an eight year period "is * * * easily * * * comprehended [by] people of common understanding." * * * Certainly most people understand that the chance of having four serious house fires in 106 months is rare, but the proposed expert testimony would help the jury to understand just how rare such a situation is, rather than leaving the jury to simply speculate on its own. * * *

B. Admissibility of Statistical Probability Evidence

Recognizing the importance of the issue in this case, the court has considered the circumstances in which statistical evidence has been admitted in other trials. At least four Courts of Appeals have recognized the admissibility of such evidence. *See, e.g., United States ex rel. DiGiacomo v. Franzen*, 680 F.2d 515, 519 (7th Cir.1982) (allowing statistical probability evidence of two hairs matching); *United States v. Kandiel*, 865 F.2d 967, 971 (8th Cir.1989) (admitting probability evidence of genetic testing); *United States v. Gwaltney*, 790 F.2d 1378, 1382 (9th Cir.1986) (admitting statistical evidence concerning incidence of certain seminal characteristics of population); *United States v. Gerry*, 515 F.2d 130, 134, 142 (2d Cir.1975) (allowing testimony of mathematician on probabilities to establish betting patterns). The Seventh Circuit has cautioned, however, that "the interjection into the criminal trial process of sophisticated theories of mathematical probability raises a number of serious concerns." *Franzen*, 680 F.2d at 518. One of those concerns is the danger that the evidence will be used improperly. *Id.* * * *. Another concern is that, even when the evidence is used in accordance with generally accepted principles, the possibility of prejudice remains because "[t]estimony expressing opinions or conclusions in terms of statistical probabilities can make the uncertain seem all but proven, and suggest, by quantification, satisfaction of the requirement that guilt be established 'beyond a reasonable doubt.' " 680 F.2d at 518 (quoting Laurence H. Tribe, *Trial by Mathematics: Precision and Ritual in the Legal Process,* 84 Harv.L.Rev. 1329 (1971)).

To answer these concerns, courts have excluded probability evidence when it is not supported by a proper foundation. For example, in *United States v. Massey*, 594 F.2d 676, 680–1 (8th Cir.1979), an expert witness testified that hair samples taken from the defendant matched a hair sample found in a ski mask allegedly used in a bank robbery. *Id.* at 679.

The expert himself did not attempt to introduce probability statistics as to his own accuracy rate of determining hair matches, but he did estimate that he had been unable to distinguish the hair of individuals only twice in approximately 2,000 cases. The Eighth Circuit found that prejudicial error occurred when the prosecutor, in his closing argument, converted this testimony into a "better than 99.44% chance" that the defendant was guilty. *Id.*

Similarly, in *People v. Collins*, 68 Cal.2d 319, 438 P.2d 33 (1968), the California Supreme Court reversed a conviction based on probability evidence that was not supported by a proper foundation. In *Collins*, the victim was robbed by a white woman with a pony tail, who, according to eye-witnesses, fled to a yellow car driven by a black man wearing a beard and mustache. *Id.* at 321, 438 P.2d at 34. At trial, a mathematician testified that, assuming the eyewitnesses were accurate, there was an overwhelming probability that the crime was committed by any couple answering such distinctive characteristics. *Id.* at 325, 438 P.2d at 36. The expert reached this conclusion after the prosecutor directed the expert to assume probability factors for the various characteristics (*e.g.* for example, the expert assumed that the probability of an interracial couple in a car was one in 1,000) "without presenting any statistical evidence whatsoever in support of the probabilities for the factors selected." *Id.* at 325, 438 P.2d at 36–37. The court reversed the conviction, finding that "the specific technique presented through the expert's testimony and advanced by the prosecutor suffered both from an inadequate evidentiary foundation and an inadequate proof of statistical independence." *Id.* at 327, 438 P.2d at 38.

Courts have also warned that probability evidence cannot be admitted solely to express the odds that the defendant is guilty or innocent. *See id; compare State v. Pankow*, 144 Wis.2d 23, 39, 422 N.W.2d 913, 918 (Wis.Ct.App.1988) (admitting evidence of the probability of having two SIDS deaths in one family after determining that the prosecutor did not use this number "to assign a number to the probability of guilt or innocence"); *Gwaltney*, 790 F.2d at 1382 (probability evidence admissible when there was no support for the defendant's implication that the government used these statistics to assign a number to the chance of defendant being guilty).

In contrast to these situations, courts allow expert testimony on statistical probabilities when (1) the expert's statistics are based on a proper foundation of accepted scientific studies or data, rather than mere speculation and (2) the evidence meets or rebuts some theory advanced by the defense. *See, e.g., Davis v. State*, 476 N.E.2d 127, 135 (Ind.Ct.App. 1985) (no foundational error where the probability calculations tending to show that defendants were the parents of abandoned child were based upon accepted scientific tables); *United States v. Gerry*, 515 F.2d 130, 134, 142 (2d Cir.1975) (admitting probability evidence of betting patterns to meet defense's theory that defendant's success was due to his handicapping skills). Indeed, when statistical evidence is based on scientific methods, the Seventh Circuit has explained that limiting such testimony could rob the government of the full probative value of its evidence. *Franzen*, 680 F.2d at 519 (allowing expert to testify that odds of hair samples matching defendant's by chance were one in 4,500).

In the case before this court, the proposed expert has based his analysis on a proper foundation of accepted studies rather than mere speculation. McClenahan is an actuary who has relied on the documented residential fire rates in the United States to reach his conclusion. His report determining the probability of four random fires clearly explains how he calculated the results from these numbers using a binomial model and then ran that calculation using a BASIC computer program. McClenahan has established a proper foundation for his results.

Defendant argues, however, that this case differs from those in which courts have admitted statistics relating to science. * * * In Defendant's view, statistics concerning the likelihood of certain events are an improper means of placing "mathematical probability on the ultimate issue to be decided by the jury" rather than just meeting an issue of the defense's theory. *Id.* Defendant emphasizes *U.S. v. Massey*, 594 F.2d 676, where the prosecutor referred to statistical evidence as establishing that the odds of defendant's guilt was "better than 99.44%." *Id.*

Indeed, Veysey is correct that few cases deal directly with statistics that explain the probability of a particular *occurrence*; those that do deal with such issues, however, have uniformly allowed such evidence to be admitted when those statistics are derived from a proper foundation. In *United States v. Abdelhaq*, 98 CR 146 (N.D. Ill. Feb. 2, 1999),[56] Judge Lindberg of this court admitted probability occurrence statistics offered by the government to refute the defendant's claim that both of her children had died from Sudden Infant Death Syndrome ("SIDS"). * * * The expert in that case, a pediatric forensic pathologist, testified that the SIDS rate in 1995 was one in a thousand births and, because there is no genetic predisposition to SIDS, the chances that a second child will die of SIDS is one in one million. *Id.* at 1106, 1108, 1110.

Similarly, in *State v. Pankow*, 144 Wis. 2d 23, 422 N.W.2d at 914, the defendant was convicted on two counts of second-degree murder, after three different children in her care died in her home over a five year period, purportedly of sudden infant death syndrome. The court allowed expert testimony from a sociological statistician, Dr. Robert Hauser, regarding the improbability of three occurrences of SIDS in the same household within five years. *Id.* at 39, 422 N.W.2d at 918. Using a binomial distribution method, Dr. Hauser determined the probability that the three children had died of SIDS was one thousand times smaller than 9.1 in one trillion, or, that such an event would occur by chance only once in 600,000 years. *Id.* at 37–38, 422 N.W.2d at 918. The court held that such evidence was admissible, reasoning that it "was not

56. [United States v. Abdelhaq, 246 F.3d 990 (7th Cir.2001) (affirming conviction). Ed.]

introduced * * * to prove identity nor to prove cause. The sole purpose was to meet Pankow's defense theory that the deaths were attributable to SIDS." *Id.* at 38, 422 N.W.2d at 918. The court overruled Pankow's objection that the statistical evidence would establish a cause for the deaths, reasoning, "[i]t does not follow that the evidence amounted to an opinion as to the cause of death merely because it demonstrated the improbability of SIDS as a cause." *Id.* at 39, 422 N.W.2d at 918. The court found that this evidence did not assign a number to the probability of guilt or innocence and, therefore, did not invade the province of the jury.

Statistical evidence of probability occurrence was also admitted in *Rachals v. State*, 184 Ga.App. 420, 361 S.E.2d 671, 673–75 (Ga.Ct.App. 1987), *aff'd*, 258 Ga. 48, 364 S.E.2d 867 (1988), where the defendant nurse was charged with intentionally causing cardiac arrests by administering potassium chloride to her patients. *Id.* at 673. The court allowed testimony of an epidemiologist concerning the mathematical probability of cardiac arrest while the defendant was on duty. The expert testified that it was "26.6 times more likely that a cardiac arrest would occur while [the defendant] was on duty" than when she was not on duty. *Id.* at 422, 361 S.E.2d at 74. According to the expert, the probability of the number of cardiac arrests increasing in the way it did "by chance alone" while the defendant was on duty was "less than one in a trillion." *Id.* at 422, 361 S.E.2d at 674. The court reasoned that the potential for analytical error was not an issue where, as here, hospital records were used to provide data for the expert's analysis. The court also noted that despite the statistics, the evidence did not invade the province of the jury because the evidence might still be "totally rejected by the jury." *Id.* at 424, 361 N.E.2d at 675.

* * * Rather tha[n] being offered as evidence of Veysey's guilt, the McClenahan testimony will be offered to show that there is almost no chance that all four of the fires were random as opposed to intentionally started by someone. The Government will then still have to meet its burden to prove beyond a reasonable doubt that the three fires were intentionally set and that Defendant was involved in setting those fires. Additionally, the jury is still free to reject the probability evidence in making its final decision. In *United States v. Massey*, 594 F.2d 676 (8th Cir.1979), on which Veysey relies, the Eighth Circuit found reversible error where the prosecutor erroneously translated an expert's estimates of how often he was unable to determine hair matches into a "better than 99.44% chance" that the defendant was guilty. *Id.* at 679–81. Here, in contrast, the court will not permit McClenahan to speculate on Defendant's guilt, nor will the Government be permitted to argue that there is a one in 1.7 trillion chance that the Defendant is not guilty. McClenahan's evidence will be limited to the probability of having four random fires. As long as the Government does not improperly use this evidence to opine on the probability of Defendant's guilt, such evidence is admissible.

C. FRE 403: The Potential for Prejudice and Confusion

Finally, Defendant argues that even if evidence of statistical probabilities is admissible, this evidence should be excluded in his case because the extreme numbers reached by the expert (one in 1.7 trillion) will be confusing to the jury and prejudicial to Defendant. * * * Fed.R.Evid. 403. Many courts that have considered the admissibility of statistical probability evidence have recognized this potential for jury confusion. Nevertheless, most jurisdictions find that, even when dealing with very extreme numbers, the prejudicial value does not substantially outweigh the probative value of such statistics. * * *

Only one jurisdiction has concluded that admitting probability calculations, even when based upon a proper foundation, is so prejudicial as to outweigh any probative value. *See, State v. Carlson*, 267 N.W.2d 170 (Minn.1978); *State v. Boyd*, 331 N.W.2d 480 (Minn.1983). In *Carlson*, an expert witness testified there was a "1 in 800 chance" and a "1 in 4,500 chance" that pubic hair and head hair samples did not belong to the accused. *Id.* at 175. The Supreme Court of Minnesota expressed concern over the potentially exaggerated impact of those numbers on the trier of fact. *Id.* at 176. Although the court acknowledged the ability of diligent cross-examination to minimize the confusion, the psychological impact of mathematical precision was found to be too compelling to admit such testimony. *Id.* The court nonetheless upheld the conviction because the testimony was cumulative of another expert witness's testimony that the samples were similar. *Id.*

This court does not find, however, that the testimony is so prejudicial that diligent cross examination and a limiting instruction from the judge cannot overcome any jury confusion as to the meaning of the statistics. * * * In order to avoid confusion, the court will give a limiting instruction to the jury explaining that McClenahan's statistics speak only to the issue of whether the four fires were random and do not in any way purport to address the odds that the Defendant is or is not guilty. * * * The jury will also be instructed that they are free to reject or accept these statistics as they see fit. Finally, Defendant will be able to limit the statistics to their meaning through cross examination. For these reasons, the court finds that the risk of confusion to the jury is not so great as to hold this evidence inadmissible.

Notes and Questions

1. *Probability of guilt.* What is the difference between the probability of a random match and the probability of guilt? In the ABO blood system, the probability of someone in the general population having type O is 45%, A is 42%, B is 10%, and AB is 3%. If blood at a murder scene is AB and this "matches" the defendant's type (and assuming the victim's blood in not AB), is there a 97% probability of guilt? In a community of one million people? See also Broun & Kelly, Playing the Percentages and the Law of Evidence, 1970 U.Ill.L.Rev. 23.

2. *Minnesota rule.* As the principal case indicates, the Minnesota cases, *Carlson* and *Boyd*, ban the use of statistics. What will the jury do with evidence of a "match" without a statistical figure?

3. *Independence.* In *Collins,* cited in the principal case, a mathematician testified in effect that the chances were one in twelve million that a robbery had been committed by a couple other than the two defendants: woman with a pony tail (1 in 10); woman with blond hair (1 in 3); yellow car (1 in 10); man with mustache (1 in 4); African American man wearing a beard (1 in 10); and interracial couple (1 in 1000). Does the product rule work here? See generally Fisher, Green Felt Jungle: The Story of *People v. Collins*, in Evidence Stories 7 (Lempert ed., 2006).

There may also be a similar problem in the SIDs cases. See Wilson v. State, 803 A.2d 1034, 1044 (Md.2002) ("[T]he trial court erred in admitting expert testimony based on the product rule because a condition necessary to the proper application of the product rule was lacking: there was inadequate proof of the independence of [siblings] Brandi and Garrett's deaths. As evidenced by the authorities above cited, there is not general agreement in the scientific community as to the relationship between SIDS deaths within a single family. Stated another way, there is not general agreement in the medical community that multiple SIDS deaths in a single family are genetically unrelated.").

4. *Underlying data.* Is the statistic (1 in 4,500) used in the hair cases valid? See Smith & Goodman, Forensic Hair Comparison Analysis: Nineteenth Century Science or Twentieth Century Snake Oil?, 27 Colum.Hum.Rts.L.Rev. 227, 231 (1996) ("If the purveyors of this dubious science cannot do a better job of validating hair analysis than they have done so far, forensic hair comparison analysis should be excluded altogether from criminal trials.").

5. *Bayes' theorem.* Through a mathematical rule of unquestioned validity known as Bayes' theorem, experts are able to show how data showing the frequency of an occurrence in the population should increase a previously established probability that the defendant is the person who left an incriminating trace. For example, if the jury believed that there was a 25% probability of guilt and then heard new evidence that a trace left at the crime scene was found in only 1% of the population and that the defendant was part of that population, Bayes' rule would provide that there should now be a 97% chance of guilt. See Finkelstein & Fairley, A Bayesian Approach to Identification Evidence, 83 Harv.L.Rev. 489, 500 (1970). Should the jury be told about Bayes' rule so that they can make their own determinations of guilt in a more scientific way? What problems would such evidence present for the accused? In addition to the Finkelstein and Fairley article, see Tribe, Trial by Mathematics: Precision and Ritual in the Legal Process, 84 Harv. L.Rev. 1329 (1971); Finkelstein & Fairley, A Comment on "Trial by Mathematics," 84 Harv.L.Rev. 1801 (1971); Kaye, The Law of Probability and the Laws of the Land, 47 U.Chi.L.Rev. 34 (1979).

COMMONWEALTH v. ROSIER

Supreme Judicial Court of Massachusetts, 1997.
685 N.E.2d 739.

GREANEY, JUSTICE.

A jury in the Superior Court convicted the defendant, Adam Rosier, of murder in the first degree (by reason of deliberate premeditation and extreme atrocity or cruelty) of sixteen year old Kristal Hopkins. [The defendant challenged the admissibility of DNA test results.[57]]

* * *

* * * The Commonwealth engaged Cellmark Diagnostics (Cellmark), a recognized forensic laboratory located in Germantown, Maryland, to perform DNA testing on two blood stains taken from the undercarriage of the automobile, one blood stain from the front tire on the passenger side, one blood stain taken from the passenger side quarter panel, the threadlike substance that appeared to be human tissue found on the undercarriage, a blood sample taken from the victim, and one taken from the defendant. Cellmark completed the testing using the polymerase chain reaction (PCR) method, and submitted a written report to the State police. The report concluded that PCR-based testing disclosed * * * that the approximate frequencies in the Caucasian and African–American populations between the genotypes analyzed in the sample, when compared with the same genotypes obtained from the victim's blood sample, were 1 in 770,000 for the Caucasian population and 1 in 7.5 million for the African–American population.

* * *

We turn now to the issues involving the DNA evidence. As has been indicated, the samples submitted by the State police for DNA analysis

57. [DNA (deoxyribonucleic acid) is a chemical messenger of genetic information, a code that gives both common and individual characteristics to people. DNA is found in packages called chromosomes. Humans have 23 pairs of chromosomes, half of which are inherited from each parent. DNA is composed of a chain of nucleotide bases twisted into a double helix structure, resembling a twisted ladder. Each rung of the helix is a "base pair." The order of the base pairs on the DNA ladder is known as the DNA sequence; it constitutes the "genetic code." Except for identical twins, no two individuals share the same DNA profile.

DNA is found in every body cell with a nucleus. With few exceptions, DNA does not vary from cell to cell. Each cell contains the entire genetic code, although each cell reads only the part of the code that it needs to perform its job. Thus, blood obtained from a suspect can be compared with semen, sweat, saliva, or hair cells from a crime scene.

Approximately 99% of the base pairs found in humans are the same. A single DNA molecule contains roughly three billion base pairs. It is the area of base pair variation that is used in DNA analysis. These base pairs are called "polymorphisms." Approximately three million base pairs are thought to be polymorphic. Examining every polymorphic site on the DNA molecule is not practical. In other words, DNA analysis does not examine an individual's entire genome, but rather a snapshot of a specific area. The analysis focuses on a number of sites (loci) that are highly polymorphic, which are examined to determine whether the evidence and suspect samples contain matching alleles. The more loci used, the more significant the "matches." Note that a non-match at any loci excludes the subject as the source. Ed.]

were examined by the PCR method,[58] and Cellmark performed DQA1, PM, and STR testing, using three commercial kits.[59] We have explained the PCR method and the process of testing at the DQA1 and PM loci in Commonwealth v. Vao Sok, 425 Mass. 787, 683 N.E.2d 671 (1997). We need to explain STR testing.[60] STR is an acronym for short tandem repeat. A tandem repeat involves multiple copies of identical DNA sequence arranged in direct succession in a particular region of a chromosome. A short tandem repeat is a tandem repeat in which the repeat units are three, four, or five base pairs (a base pair has two complementary nucleotides). Loci containing STRs are scattered throughout the chromosomes in enormous numbers. Such loci have a fairly large number of alleles and are usually capable of unique identification. Cellmark tested at three STR loci,[61] which, in combination with the testing at the DQA1 and PM loci, gave results from nine different loci. The STR testing became important in the case because Cellmark had done prior DNA testing on the samples submitted examining only the DQA1 and PM loci and had concluded, based on results from those loci, that the population frequencies between the victim and the Caucasian and African–American population were 1 in 5,500 and 1 in 11,000 respectively. The additional testing of the STR loci, when considered with the results of the DQA1 and PM testing, increased the probabilities to 1 in 770,000 (Caucasian) and 1 in 7.5 million (African–American). As Dr. Basten agreed, STR analysis made a "significant difference" in terms of the frequency in which the genetic markers would be expected to be seen within a population. As the judge found: "At the CSF1PO locus, scientists have observed nine different alleles, giving rise to 45 possible genotypes. At the TP0X locus, seven different alleles have been observed, giving rise to 28 possible genotypes. At the TH01 locus, eight different alleles have been observed, giving rise to 36 possible genotypes."

At the hearing on the motion in limine, the defendant did not specifically challenge the collection and preservation of the samples submitted to Cellmark for DNA testing, the quality control and assurance standards at the laboratory,[62] the use of the PCR method, the

58. The PCR method was utilized because the samples were too small to be tested by the Restriction Fragment Length Polymorphism (RFLP) method, which requires larger samples of investigatory materials before profiling can be satisfactorily done. See Commonwealth v. Vao Sok, 425 Mass. 787, 683 N.E.2d 671 (1997)

59. The AmpliType HLA DQa Forensic DNA Amplification and Typing Kit, the AmpliType PM PCR Amplification and Typing Kit, and GenePrint STR Systems. The DQA1 and PM kits appear to be the same kits that were used by the Center for Blood Research, the laboratory that did the DNA testing in Commonwealth v. Vao Sok, supra at 790–94, 683 N.E.2d at 674–75.

60. All the information that follows as to STR testing is taken from the 1996 report of the National Research Council entitled, The Evaluation of Forensic DNA Evidence (1996 NRC Report).

61. The STR loci tested were at chromosomes identified as CSF1PO, TPOX, and TH01 using GenePrint STR systems.

62. Cellmark is accredited for forensic work by the American Society of Crime Laboratory Directors and for paternity testing by the American Association of Blood Banks. The accreditations are the result of audits of Cellmark's work by these accrediting groups and regular proficiency and quality assurance testing. The testing and other safeguards adhered to by Cellmark

reliability of the three test procedures or the accuracy of the test results obtained from the use of the typing kits. * * *

The PCR method is scientifically valid, and testing at the DQA1 and PM loci is scientifically reliable, if properly done. Commonwealth v. Vao Sok, supra at 799, 683 N.E.2d at 679. The defendant's appellate counsel appears to suggest that STR testing is unreliable because it is too new. No specific scientific or forensic evidence or literature is offered to support that suggestion. The judge heard testimony that, in 1991, several years before the STR kit became commercially available, Cellmark, working under contract to the United States government, used STR testing to identify the remains of soldiers killed in Operation Desert Storm, and that, by the time of the hearing, Cellmark had performed STR analysis in approximately fifty cases and had been permitted to testify as to its test results in at least five cases.[63] While we have not been directed to any decisional law approving STR testing, an authoritative scientific study, the 1996 report of the National Research Council entitled, The Evaluation of Forensic DNA Evidence (1996 NRC Report), has concluded (*id.* at 71) that STR testing is "coming into wide use," that "STR loci appear to be particularly appropriate for forensic use" (*id.* at 117), and that "STRs can take their place along with VNTRs as forensic tools" (*id.* at 35). The latter comment appears to recognize that STR testing is similar in principle to the RFLP (or VNTR) method, which has been found to be reliable. See Commonwealth v. Daggett, 416 Mass. 347, 350 n.1, 622 N.E.2d 272 (1993). Based on the evidence before him and his careful analysis of the subject, the judge properly concluded that the methodology underlying the PCR-based tests in this case, including the STR testing, was scientifically valid and relevant to a fact at trial. * * *

The defendant's principal attack on the DNA results is focused on the evidence pertaining to the statistical significance of the match found by the three tests between the DNA in the blood stains and tissue taken from the automobile and the victim's DNA. Evidence of a match based on correctly used testing systems is of little or no value without reliable evidence indicating the "significance of the match, that is, evidence of the probability of a random match of [the victim's or] the defendant's DNA in the general population." Commonwealth v. Lanigan, supra at 20, 641 N.E.2d 1342. To obtain the relevant statistical results in this case, Cellmark used a database it had developed using samples taken from paternity studies done at Cellmark.[64] At the time of the hearing, Cellmark's database was the only one that used samples from the same

comply with the guidelines set out by the Technical Working Group on DNA Analysis Methods (TWGDAM), a group of forensic DNA analysts from government and private laboratories who are considered authoritative in the field.

63. Dr. Word testified that, prior to using STR testing in forensic cases, Cellmark had conducted extensive validation tests to evaluate the reliability and sensitivity of STR testing, as well as how much DNA was needed to get results and the development of other "testing parameters."

64. The database consisted of one hundred blood samples from Caucasian persons and one hundred blood samples from African-American persons.

persons for all of the nine loci analyzed under the DQA1, PM, and STR tests used by Cellmark. The statistical results were calculated by means of the product rule. "Under the product rule, the frequency in the population base of each allele disclosed in the DNA test is multiplied to produce the frequency of the combination of all the alleles found." Commonwealth v. Lanigan, supra at 21, 641 N.E.2d 1342, citing Commonwealth v. Curnin, 409 Mass. 218, 224 n.10, 225 n.11, 565 N.E.2d 440 (1991). The defendant argues that Cellmark's database is too small and, for various other reasons, unreliable.

The judge acted properly in rejecting the defendant's arguments. He accepted the expert testimony that the Cellmark database was adequate and common within the field and that a database larger than Cellmark's would produce "no significant difference in the result." There was expert and scientific evidence that the Cellmark database met two factors critical to the reliability of a database. The first factor, "linkage equilibrium" (LE), establishes that the various chromosomal loci identified in a database occur randomly in proportion to one another, thus assuring that results related to one locus are not affected by, nor predictive of, the results related to another.[65] The second factor is "Hardy–Weinberg equilibrium" (HW). A database is considered to be "in HW" when the predicted values for the various loci within the database actually correspond to those found in the population, assuming mates are randomly chosen. Thus, it was properly found that the Cellmark database was both in LE and in HW. The database and statistical results reached by Cellmark were also independently verified by Dr. Basten through calculations of "confidence intervals"[66] and a comparison of Cellmark's results with other databases that achieved statistically comparable results.[67] Dr. Basten also concluded that the methods used by Cellmark to generate statistical results are "generally accepted" within the field of population genetics, and that the statistical results they produce are reliable and accurate.

At the motion hearing, the defendant did not make any argument that Cellmark's use of the product rule to reach its conclusions about

65. There was evidence that the Cellmark database, better than any combination of available databases, allowed for proper testing for LE to determine whether the identified alleles are genetically independent, because it used the same persons for testing results in each of its systems.

66. Dr. Basten's process of "confidence intervals" involved the selection of individuals at random from Cellmark's database to create a new database and then utilizing a computer to repeat the procedure 1,000 times so that 1,000 new databases of one hundred individuals each were produced. A complicated statistical analysis then followed (which is set forth in the judge's memorandum and need not be described here) to arrive at a statistical result that, according to Dr. Basten, verified Cellmark's results and frequency conclusions. The fact that the proportions derived by Dr. Basten from the confidence intervals differed from Cellmark's proportions did not throw the latter into doubt, because, as the judge noted, Dr. Basten was conducting a verification test and not a test designed to express an opinion as to the actual frequency of genotypes derived from the crime scene samples in the population at large.

67. Three other databases were consulted by Dr. Basten: one developed by the Federal Bureau of Investigation (FBI) and published in the Journal of Forensic Science; and two others as reported at the Fifth International Symposium on Human Identification.

population frequencies was wrong. We think it is appropriate, however, to discuss the product rule to assure completeness in the examination of this phase of the case. In Commonwealth v. Lanigan, supra at 21, 641 N.E.2d 1342, we stated that "[t]he product or multiplication rule is based on the assumption that the population does not contain subpopulations with distinct allele frequencies, and, therefore, each person's alleles constitute statistically independent random selections from a common gene pool." We went on to state that "[t]he validity of the use of the multiplication rule thus depends on the absence of population substructure. If there is population substructure, the assumption of complete statistical independence of alleles is not valid." Id. To ameliorate this problem, we accepted the recommendation that population frequencies be calculated by use of "the ceiling principle," which was "adopted to make irrelevant the dispute among population geneticists over the question whether the product rule may properly be used to express numerically the probability of finding a DNA match in a random selection of the appropriate population." Id. at 26, 641 N.E.2d 1342. The ceiling principle was recommended by the National Research Council in its 1992 Report on The Evaluation of Forensic DNA Evidence to help quiet the significant debate over potential problems arising out of population substructuring.[68]

It is fair to say that the controversy has been resolved in large part. The 1996 NRC Report notes (*id.* at 53) that "information is now available from a number of relevant populations, so that experts can usually base estimates on an appropriate database." In considering the same question, the admissibility of statistical evidence calculated under the product rule, the Supreme Court of Washington cited a major Federal Bureau of Investigation (FBI) study of VNTR frequency data from around the world entitled, VNTR Population Data: A Worldwide Study (Feb.1993) (Worldwide Study), which concluded that the product rule is reliable and valid.[69] State v. Copeland, 130 Wash.2d 244, 267–268,

68. The 1996 NRC Report describes the "ceiling principle" and the "interim ceiling principle" as follows:

> "The 1992 report * * * recommended the use of an ad hoc approach for the calculation of an upper bound on the frequencies that would be found in any real population; this approach used what was termed the 'ceiling principle.' The report recommended that population frequency data be collected on homogeneous populations from 15–20 racial and ethnic groups. The highest frequency of a marker in any population, or 5%—whichever was higher, was to be used for calculation. Until the highest frequencies were available an 'interim ceiling principle' was to be used. That would assign to each marker the highest frequency value found in any population database (adjusted upward to allow for statistical uncertainty) or 10%—whichever was higher. The result would be a composite profile frequency that did not depend on a specific racial or ethnic database and would practically always exceed the frequency calculated from the database of the reference populations."

Id. at 52.

69. The Worldwide Study study, *supra* at 2, concluded as follows:

> "(1) that there are sufficient population data available to determine whether or not forensically significant differences might occur when using different population databases; (2) that subdivision, either by ethnic group or by U.S. geographic region, within a major population group does not substantially affect forensic estimates of the likelihood of occurrence of a DNA profile; (3) that estimates of the likelihood of occurrence of a DNA profile using major population group da-

922 P.2d 1304 (1996), quoting Worldwide Study, *supra* at 2. That report has been supported by other studies that have similarly concluded that differences of allelic distribution are not forensically significant,[70] and courts that have examined the question have agreed that challenges to the use of the product rule have been sufficiently resolved. [Citations omitted.]

It is important to note as well: "The ceiling principles were intended for VNTRs with many alleles, no one of which has a very high frequency [and t]hey are not applicable to PCR-based systems." 1996 NRC Report at 158.[71] We agree with the conclusions of the 1996 NRC Report that "both the ceiling principle and the interim ceiling principle are unnecessary," (*id.* at 162) and that "[i]n general, the calculation of a profile frequency should be made with the product rule," (*id.* at 5) both for VNTR and PCR-based systems.[72] Thus, the use of the product rule by Cellmark in connection with its PCR-based testing in this case was scientifically acceptable.

* * *

Judgment affirmed.

Notes and Questions

1. *The science.* As the principal case indicates, DNA profiling involves two fields: molecular biology and population genetics. Thus, the process involves two corresponding steps—first, determining whether the genetic markers at different loci "match." If there is a "no match" at any locus, the suspect is excluded.

tabases (e.g., Caucasian, Black, and Hispanic) provide a greater range of frequencies than would estimates from subgroups of a major population category; therefore, the estimate of the likelihood of occurrence of a DNA profile derived by the current practice of employing the multiplication rule and using general population databases for allele frequencies is reliable, valid, and meaningful, without forensically significant consequences; and (4) that the data do not support the need for alternate procedures, such as the ceiling principle approach."

70. See, e.g., Budowle, The Assessment of Frequency Estimates of Hae III–Generated VNTR Profiles in Various Reference Databases, 39 J. Forensic Sci. 319 (1994); Budowle, Evaluation of Hinf I–Generated VNTR Profile Frequencies Determined Using Various Ethnic Databases, 39 J. Forensic Sci. 988 (1994); Shui The Development of DNA Profiling Database in an HAE III Based RFLP System for Chinese, Malays, and Indians in Singapore, 38 J. Forensic Sci. 874 (1993).

71. The judge noted that the ceiling principle arose in the context of RFLP testing, the technological limitations of which made it impossible to recognize specific allele types. Because PCR-based testing identifies specific alleles and genotypes at specific loci, the arguments voiced by critics of the product rule as applied to RFLP testing do not apply to PCR-based testing.

72. The 1996 NRC Report also recommends that "[i]f the race of the person who left the evidence sample DNA is known, the database for the person's race should be used; if the race is not known, calculations for all the racial groups to which possible suspects belong should be made." 1996 NRC Report at 5 (Recommendation 4.1 of the Recommendations for Estimating Random–Match Probabilities). Recommendations 4.2, 4.3, and 4.4 suggest calculation methodologies for cases where a subpopulation is involved (4.2), where the source of the DNA sample is from a subpopulation for which no database exists (4.3), and where all possible contributors of the sample include relatives of the subject (4.4), situations that complicate the application of the product rule. 1996 NRC Report at 5–6.

If there are "matches" at all the tested loci, the significance of these matches must be determined. Once a match is declared, a probability is computed that estimates the chances that someone randomly selected from the population would have the same genetic marker (allele) as the forensic sample. Because a number of people will have the same genetic markers at one locus, more than one locus is tested. The frequencies of the individual alleles are multiplied together (according to the "product rule"), and an aggregate probability estimate is computed. For the calculations to be reliable, all the loci tested must be independent. For this assumption to be true, individuals must reproduce randomly so that distinct subgroups (population substructure) are absent.

2. *The procedures.* There have been three generations of DNA tests. The first type was based on Restriction Fragment Length Polymorphism (RFLP). The second was polymerase chain reaction (PCR) for specific alleles. PCR permits amplification of DNA ("molecular photocopying"). Thus, it requires far less biological material than RFLP technologies. In many instances, the forensic sample may be too small, or too damaged by environmental conditions, for RFLP testing. Also, unlike RFLP, this procedure focused on the presence or absence of alleles at a specific locus, such as the DQ alpha locus. In the beginning, this procedure was far less discriminating than RLFP. The third technique is Short Tandem Repeats (STR).

Currently, STR testing is typically based on thirteen loci. See People v. Shreck, 22 P.3d 68, 72 (Colo.2001) (probability that the contributor was not the defendant but a random third person was 1 in 5.3 quadrillion); State v. Butterfield, 27 P.3d 1133, 1137 (Utah 2001) (probability of a random individual other than the victim matching the blood on Butterfield's undershirt was 215 billion to 1). See also Imwinkelried & Kaye, DNA Typing: Emerging or Neglected Issues, 76 Wash.L.Rev. 413 (2001).

3. *Mitochondrial DNA.* In addition to nuclear DNA, mitochondrial DNA testing may be used when nuclear DNA is unavailable (e.g., hair without a root or bone without marrow). See United States v. Beverly, 369 F.3d 516, 531 (6th Cir.2004); State v. Underwood, 518 S.E.2d 231 (N.C.Ct. App.1999); State v. Council, 515 S.E.2d 508, 518 (S.C.1999). It is not as discriminating as nuclear DNA.

4. *Nonhuman DNA evidence.* DNA is found in all living organisms. See United States v. Boswell, 270 F.3d 1200 (8th Cir.2001) (in a false statement prosecution, DNA used to compare swine blood); State v. Bogan, 905 P.2d 515 (Ariz.Ct.App.1995) (in murder case, DNA of seed pods from palo verde trees at scene compared to those found in Bogan's truck); State v. Schmidt, 699 So.2d 448 (La.Ct.App.1997) (in attempted murder by injection of HIV virus, expert testified that HIV from two persons were "closely related"). But see State v. Leuluaialii, 77 P.3d 1192 (Wash.Ct.App.2003) (canine DNA match between sample obtained from defendant and murder victim's dog not generally accepted).

5. *Presenting DNA Evidence.* How should trial counsel offer DNA Evidence before a jury? One experienced DNA prosecutor recommends the K.I.S.S. principle: "Keep it short and simple." Wooley, Presentation of DNA Evidence at Trial: The K.I.S.S. Principle, 1 Profiles in DNA 3 (May 1997).

See also Schklar & Diamond, Juror Reactions to DNA Evidence: Errors and Expectancies, 23 Law & Hum.Behav. 159 (1999).

6. *DNA Wars.* DNA evidence was the subject of fierce debates when first introduced. See People v. Castro, 545 N.Y.S.2d 985, 996 (Sup.Ct.1989) ("In a piercing attack upon each molecule of evidence presented, the defense was successful in demonstrating to this court that the testing laboratory failed in its responsibility to perform the accepted scientific techniques and experiments."). The FBI's top DNA expert, Dr. Budowle, later acknowledged the early deficiencies. Lander & Budowle, DNA Fingerprinting Dispute Laid to Rest, 371 Nature 735, 735 (Oct. 27, 1994) ("The initial outcry over DNA typing standards concerned laboratory problems: poorly defined rules for declaring a match; experiments without controls; contaminated probes and samples; and sloppy interpretation of autoradiograms. Although there is no evidence that these technical failings resulted in any wrongful convictions, the lack of standards seemed to be a recipe for trouble."). See generally Mnookin, *People v. Castro*: Challenging the Forensic Use of DNA Evidence, in Evidence Stories 207 (Lempert ed., 2006).

7. *Lab errors.* Despite the power of DNA evidence, some problems have been exposed in its use. See Madigan, Houston's Troubled DNA Crime Lab Faces Growing Scrutiny, N.Y.Times, Feb. 9, 2003 (operations suspended in December after an audit found numerous problems including poor calibration and maintenance of equipment, improper record keeping, and a lack of safeguards against contamination; "Among other problems, a leak in the roof was found to be a potential contaminant of samples on tables below."); Liptak & Blumenthal, New Doubt Cast on Crime Testing in Houston Cases, N.Y.Times, Aug. 5, 2004 ("[P]rosecutors in Mr. Sutton's case had used [DNA] to convict him, submitting false scientific evidence asserting that there was a solid match between Mr. Sutton's DNA and that found at the crime scene. In fact, 1 of every 8 black people, including Mr. Sutton, shared the relevant DNA profile. More refined retesting cleared him.").

8. *Testimony without statistics?* Young v. State, 879 A.2d 44, 56–57 (Md.2005) ("[T]here exist methods of DNA analysis employing certain markers that, when tested along a minimum number of loci, yield DNA profiles with an astonishingly small random match probability. When the random match probability is sufficiently minuscule, the DNA profile may be deemed unique. In such circumstances, testimony of a match is admissible without accompanying contextual statistics. In place of the statistics, the expert may inform the jury of the meaning of the match by identifying the person whose profile matched the profile of the DNA evidence as the source of that evidence; *i.e.* the expert may testify that in the absence of identical twins, it can be concluded to a reasonable scientific certainty that the evidence sample and the defendant sample came from the same person.").

9. *DNA evidence without corroboration.* In State v. Toomes, 191 S.W.3d 122, 131 n.4 (Tenn.Crim.App.2005), the court upheld a conviction based on DNA alone but with a caution: "By our holding, we are not announcing an iron-clad princip[le] that DNA evidence, without corroboration, is always sufficient to support a conviction. Practically infinite factual variations can arise, and we do not intend by our opinion to prejudge other factual scenarios. For instance, this case has an unusual feature in that two

separate DNA comparisons were performed. The first comparison identified the twin's DNA, and the second comparison identified the twin's and the defendant's DNA, which were identical, thereby reinforcing the integrity of the comparisons. In our opinion, it is quite sufficient in this case to recognize and respect the admissibility of DNA evidence and to conclude that the evidence was sufficient to support the defendant's aggravated rape conviction."

10. *Databases*. A national system of computer-based databanks is run by the FBI. Most states require convicted sex offenders to provide samples for this system. A majority require all felons. Should everyone be a contributor? See Kaye & Imwinkelried, Is a DNA Identification Database in Your Future?, 16 Crim. Just. 4 (Fall 2001).

11. *Cold hits.* Matches produced by DNA databases are called "cold hits" because the police have no suspects. There is a major debate about how to calculate the statistics in such cases. See People v. Johnson, 43 Cal.Rptr.3d 587, 600 (Cal.Ct.App.2006) ("[T]he fact that many profiles have been searched increases the probability of finding a match, so that conceptually, the more populated the database, the less impressive the match. Appellant contends that there is broad scientific consensus concerning the need to determine differently the statistical significance of profile matches in a cold hit case versus a confirmation case, but says that the means of determining the statistical value of a cold hit 'is a matter of continuing and strident debate.' ").

(2) QUALIFICATION REQUIREMENT

ELCOCK v. KMART CORP.

United States Court of Appeals, Third Circuit, 2000.
233 F.3d 734.

BECKER, CHIEF JUDGE.

This is an appeal by defendant Kmart from a judgment entered on a $650,000 jury verdict in favor of plaintiff Carmelita Elcock ("Elcock") for personal injuries [lower back injuries from a slip and fall] and economic loss that she suffered as the result of a slip and fall at a Kmart store in Frederiksted, U.S. Virgin Islands. Kmart concedes its liability and acknowledges that Elcock's fall caused her some quantum of harm. However, Kmart challenges several evidentiary rulings that relate to the proof of Elcock's damages, and contends that the $650,000 award, which consisted of $300,000 for pain and suffering and $350,000 for loss of future earnings and earning capacity, was excessive.

The most important questions on appeal relate to the testimony of Dr. Chester Copemann, who was proffered by Elcock, *inter alia*, as an expert in vocational rehabilitation,[73] and whose vocational rehabilitation

73. [Elsewhere in the opinion, the court wrote: "A vocational rehabilitationist assesses the extent of an individual's disability, evaluates how the disability affects the individual's employment opportunities, and assists the individual's re-entry into the labor market."]

presentation substantially informed the large award for loss of future earnings and earning capacity. [Copermann opined that she was 50–60% vocationally disabled.] * * *

II. The Evidentiary Issues Relating to Copemann's Qualifications

Before trial and again during trial, Kmart sought to exclude Copemann's vocational rehabilitation testimony on the grounds that he was not qualified as an expert in the field. The District Court conducted a *voir dire* on Copemann's qualifications, during which Copemann testified regarding his credentials, and Kmart's vocational rehabilitation expert gave testimony that called those credentials into question. The District Court considered the qualifications issue raised by Kmart a "close call," but ultimately found that Copemann was qualified to testify about vocational rehabilitation. Kmart challenges this decision. We review the District Court's decision to qualify Copemann for abuse of discretion. *See* Waldorf v. Shuta, 142 F.3d 601, 627 (3d Cir.1998).

* * * Before an expert witness may offer an opinion pursuant to Rule 702, he must first be qualified by virtue of specialized expertise. * * * In *Waldorf v. Shuta*, * * * , we articulated the standard for qualifying an expert:

> Rule 702 requires the witness to have "specialized knowledge" regarding the area of testimony. The basis of this specialized knowledge "can be practical experience as well as academic training and credentials." We have interpreted the specialized knowledge requirement liberally, and have stated that this policy of liberal admissibility of expert testimony "extends to the substantive as well as the formal qualification of experts." However, "at a minimum, a proffered expert witness * * * must possess skill or knowledge greater than the average layman * * *."

Id. at 625 (citations omitted).

Even under the liberal standard described in *Waldorf*, Copemann's qualifications as a vocational rehabilitationist are thin. In contending that Copemann possessed skill or knowledge "greater than the average layman," Elcock focuses primarily on Copemann's experience. Specifically, Elcock points to (1) Copemann's general training in "assessing" individuals, which he received while earning his Ph.D. in psychology; (2) his experience, twenty years previous, helping drug addicts reenter the workforce; (3) his experience primarily in the last two years dealing with the Virgin Islands Division of Workers' Compensation, which he had advised regarding the ability of approximately fifty to sixty-five disabled employees to return to their previous jobs; (4) his past experience as an expert witness making lost earning capacity assessments; (5) his attendance at two seminars regarding vocational rehabilitation, and his stated familiarity with the literature in the area; (6) his membership in two vocational rehabilitation organizations, both of which place no restrictions on membership; and (7) the fact that when Copemann was in school, a degree in vocational rehabilitation therapy was not available, but that he received similar training nonetheless. This last fact, Elcock argues, explains why Copemann did not possess the degrees or formal training one would ordinarily associate with an expert.

In response, Kmart emphasizes several factors that significantly undermine Copemann's purported qualifications. First, during Kmart's *voir dire*, Copemann admitted that he had neither the academic training nor the standard credentials that would ordinarily qualify one as an expert in vocational rehabilitation. Moreover, Kmart argues that nothing prevented Copemann from either receiving formal training in vocational rehabilitation after he left school or from earning a related degree or certificate while he was in school. Second, Copemann conceded that his experience dealing with the workers' compensation board consisted primarily of diagnosing whether patients were so disabled that they could not return to a particular job; this experience did not include assessing what range of jobs those injured individuals were capable of performing. Third, Kmart adduced evidence suggesting that not only was Copemann's experience as a counselor for drug addicts dated, but that it did not include performing assessments of which jobs the recovered addicts would be able to perform. Fourth, although Copemann maintained that there was no difference between a psychologist and a vocational rehabilitationist, Kmart's vocational rehabilitation therapist testified that despite a common psychological diagnostic component in both jobs, the vocational rehabilitationist's expertise entails a distinct speciality: the capacity to "translate" psychological *and* physical impairments into the "ability to work, earn income, [and] get a job * * *."

Kmart's forceful argument all but persuaded the District Court. Given Copemann's lack of credentials and limited experience, the District Court twice expressed its reluctance to qualify Copemann as an expert in vocational rehabilitation. However, after two attempts by Elcock's counsel to qualify him, the Court eventually admitted Copemann's testimony. The Court relied heavily on the fact that a formal degree in vocational rehabilitation therapy was not available when Copemann attended school, and the fact that the training of psychologists was functionally similar to that of vocational rehabilitationists at the time. The Court also relied on Copemann's practical experience evaluating the ability of injured employees to return to work.

B.

This court has had, for some time, a generally liberal standard of qualifying experts. * * * However, we have also set a floor with respect to an expert witness's qualifications. For example, in Aloe Coal Co. v. Clark Equipment Co., 816 F.2d 110 (3d Cir.1987), we held that a district court abused its discretion in allowing a tractor sales representative to testify as an expert regarding the cause of a tractor fire. *See* id. at 114. In making this determination we stated:

> Drewnoski [the expert witness] was not an engineer. He had no experience in designing construction machinery. He had no knowl-

> edge or experience in determining the cause of equipment fire. He had no training as a mechanic. He had never operated construction machinery in the course of business. He was a salesman, who at times prepared damage estimates.

Id. (citations omitted); *see also Waldorf*, 142 F.3d at 625 ("Even though we apply Rule 702 liberally, we have not pursued a policy of qualifying *any* proffered witness as an expert.").

Our decision in *Waldorf* provides guidance for our assessment of Copemann's qualifications. In *Waldorf*, the district court qualified an expert [Rizzo] with credentials similar to Copemann's * * *.

What drove the *Waldorf* panel's decision to affirm on this issue was not the impressiveness of Rizzo's credentials or experience, but the standard of review governing our review of Rule 702 qualification rulings:

> Waldorf has a heavy burden in challenging this decision because, absent an abuse of discretion, we will not substitute our own judgment for that of the trial court regarding the admission or exclusion of expert testimony. Of course, an abuse of discretion means much more than that the appellate court disagrees with the trial court. Rather, a trial court's determination whether to admit or exclude expert testimony will be upheld "unless manifestly erroneous."

* * *

Copemann, like Rizzo, has no formal training in vocational rehabilitation and Elcock must therefore rely on Copemann's practical experience to demonstrate that he "possessed the minimum qualifications necessary to testify as an expert." Id. at 627. In support of Copemann's qualifications, Elcock points to Copemann's experience in helping drug addicts return to employment and to his work with the Virgin Islands Division of Workers' Compensation. Based on this background, one can presume that Copemann has learned about the difficulties disabled individuals face in employment, and has accumulated some experience in evaluating whether they can return to a particular job. Nonetheless, the most fundamental problem with Copemann's experience in this area is that he seems most qualified to testify on a micro-level regarding the ability of a disabled individual to return to a specific job; he does not appear particularly qualified to testify on the macro-level regarding the number of jobs in the national or local economy that the disabled individual is able to perform.

On the other hand, Copemann claims to have kept abreast of the relevant literature in his field, and to have consulted the Dictionary of Occupational Titles, a standard tool of the vocational rehabilitationist. In addition, Copemann possesses a degree in a field tangentially related to the one about which he testified, and he has also attended conferences regarding vocational rehabilitation. Finally, in the process of testifying as an expert in similar matters, Copemann has no doubt performed his brand of vocational rehabilitation assessments.[74] Though his efforts in this regard are not grounded in formal training, when taken together with his review of the literature in the field and his attendance at conferences, we must acknowledge that he has "substantially more knowledge than an average lay person regarding employment opportunities for disabled individuals." Id. at 627.

We consider *Waldorf* to be at the outer limit of this court's generally liberal approach to reviewing the qualifications of experts. We also suspect that, had the district court in *Waldorf* ruled the witness unqualified, the panel would have affirmed. While Copemann seems but marginally qualified to perform a vocational rehabilitation assessment, and a district judge would be free to decline to qualify him, we recognize that Copemann's qualifications fall within Waldorf's outer bounds. Despite misgivings, because we are not prepared to say that the District Court, acting "on the spot" and exercising considerable care in its approach to this question, abused its discretion, we will affirm the Court's decision to qualify Copemann as an expert. * * *

Notes and Questions

1. *Standard.* Does Rule 702 comport with Wigmore's view. He wrote that the witness' expertise "may have been attained, so far as legal rules go, in any way whatever; all the law requires is that it should have been attained." 2 J. Wigmore, Evidence § 556, at 751 (Chadbourn rev. 1979). The federal drafters wrote: "[T]he expert is viewed, not in a narrow sense, but as a person qualified by 'knowledge, skill, experience, training or education.' Thus within the scope of the rule are not only experts in the strictest sense of the word, e.g. physicians, physicists, and architects, but also the large group sometimes called 'skilled' witnesses, such as bankers or landowners testifying to land values." Fed.R.Evid. 702 advisory committee's note.

2. *Examples.* United States v. Kunzman, 54 F.3d 1522, 1530 (10th Cir.1995) ("Experience alone can qualify a witness to give expert testimony"; banker for 20 years interpreting numbers and bank stamps on checks to show they cleared interstate banking system); Davis v. United States, 865 F.2d 164, 168 (8th Cir.1988) ("Rule 702 does not state a preference for academic training over demonstrated practical experience."); United States v. Barker, 553 F.2d 1013, 1024 (6th Cir.1977) ("An expert need not have certificates of training, nor memberships in professional organizations * * *. Nor need he be, as the trial court apparently required, an outstanding practitioner in the field in which he professes expertise."); United States v. Madoch, 935 F.Supp. 965, 972 (N.D.Ill.1996) ("[O]ne expert need not hold the exact same set of qualifications to rebut another expert's testimony.

74. We note that the mere fact that Copemann was previously admitted as an expert witness qualified to give testimony on vocational rehabilitation is irrelevant to the determination whether he is qualified to give such testimony in this case. *See* Thomas J. Kline, Inc. v. Lorillard, Inc., 878 F.2d 791, 800 (4th Cir.1989) ("[I]t would be absurd to conclude that one can become an expert simply by accumulating experience in testifying."). Moreover, while any expertise he may have gained in performing vocational rehabilitation assessments in these cases would be relevant, the crucible of litigation makes for a poor classroom.

* * * This Court need not analyze, as Defendant contends it should, whether a psychologist or psychiatrist is more qualified to testify as to the psychological condition of a patient at the time of the offense.").

See also McConnell v. Budget Inns, 718 N.E.2d 948, 955 (Ohio Ct.App. 1998) (In receiving expert testimony of a woodworker on chair construction, the court stated: "The witness, a long-time owner of a woodworking company in New York, testified that he had approximately thirty-six years of woodworking experience that included the design, repair, manufacture, and construction of wood furniture, including wood chairs used in commercial settings and chairs of the type involved in the accident herein. These qualifications gave [the witness] knowledge of chair construction and mechanical failure therein superior to that possessed by the average juror.").

3. *Hired guns?* Is the qualification standard set forth in the principal case too low? See the footnote in the principal case. See also In re Air Crash Disaster at New Orleans, 795 F.2d 1230, 1234 (5th Cir.1986) ("experts whose opinions are available to the highest bidder have no place testifying in a court of law"); Chaulk v. Volkswagen of Am., Inc., 808 F.2d 639, 644 (7th Cir.1986) ("There is hardly anything, not palpably absurd on its face, that cannot now be proved by some so-called 'experts.' "). For an insightful discussion of the "hired gun" problem, see Gross, Expert Evidence, 1991 Wis.L.Rev. 1113 (proposing several changes to ensure the appointment of neutral experts).

4. *Criminal cases.* See United States v. Johnson, 575 F.2d 1347, 1360 (5th Cir.1978) (An experienced user, who "had smoked marijuana over a thousand times," was permitted to testify that certain marijuana came from Colombia. "He based his identification upon the plant's appearance, its leaf, buds, stems, and other physical characteristics, as well as upon the smell and the effect of smoking it."); State v. Barnes, 597 So.2d 1109, 1112 (La.Ct.App. 1992) (defense expert concerning a pellet dispersion pattern test excluded; He "became a gunsmith after completing a correspondence course. He had never received training in forensic science, firearms identification or ballistics. He had never testified as an expert in any area. He worked as a sales clerk at a hardware store and in his own gun repair business."); Hooten v. State, 492 So.2d 948, 958 (Miss.1986) (dissenting opinion) ("If this witness has indeed testified over 300 times as an *expert* on discovering spurious handwriting as she claimed, it is an astonishing indictment on the gullibility of lawyers and judges.").

5. *Certification.* See United States v. Bourgeois, 950 F.2d 980, 986 (5th Cir.1992) (upholding exclusion of the testimony of an "expert" who was not a member of the American Board of Forensic Document Examiners, who practiced graphotherapy in addition to handwriting comparison, and who acquired a masters degree in graphoanalysis and a Ph.D. in metaphysics and religion by correspondence). See also MacDonald, The Making of an Expert Witness: It's in the Credentials, Wall Street J., Feb. 8, 1999, at B1 (Article discussing the American College of Forensic Examiners (ACFE), which makes $2.2 million a year certifying experts. The roots of this organization, according to its founder, can be traced to the *Daubert* decision, which was intended to tighten the standards for expert testimony.); Hansen, Expertise to Go, 86 A.B.A.J. 44, 45 (Feb. 2000) ("certification" mill; cost $350 to be

certified, dial 1–800–4A–Expert; "ACFE is the biggest credentialing body in forensic science and the only one that credentials experts in many specialties. It has 13,000 members and nearly 17,000 board-certified diplomates.").

6. *Stipulations.* In State v. Colwell, 790 P.2d 430, 434 (Kan.1990), the trial court required defense counsel to accept the prosecution's offer to stipulate to the qualifications of the defense pathologist. Consequently, the jury was deprived of learning the credentials of the expert, who had a "national reputation" in the field of forensic pathology. In contrast, eleven pages of the transcript were needed to record the qualifications of the prosecution's expert. The court reversed: "We conclude that an offer by the State to stipulate to the qualifications of an expert witness called by the defendant is merely an offer unless accepted by the defendant. Absent such acceptance, the defendant has the right to present the witness' qualifications to the jury."

7. *Informing jury.* See Luttrell v. Commonwealth, 952 S.W.2d 216, 218 (Ky.1997) ("Great care should be exercised by a trial judge when the determination has been made that the witness is an expert. If the jury is so informed such a conclusion obviously enhances the credibility of that witness in the eyes of the jury. All such rulings should be made outside the hearing of the jury and there should be no declaration that the witness is an expert."); Richey, Proposals to Eliminate the Prejudicial Effect of the Use of the Word "Expert" Under the Federal Rules of Evidence in Civil and Criminal Jury Trials, 154 F.R.D. 537, 554 (1994); ABA Civil Trial Practice Standard 17 (1998) ("Except in ruling on an objection, the court should not, in the presence of the jury, declare that a witness is qualified as an expert or to render an expert opinion, and counsel should not ask the court to do so.").

WHEELING PITTSBURGH STEEL CORP. v. BEELMAN RIVER TERMINALS, INC.

United States Court of Appeals, Eighth Circuit, 2001.
254 F.3d 706.

HANSEN, CIRCUIT JUDGE.

In this breach of a bailment contract action brought by Wheeling Pittsburgh Steel Corporation (a manufacturer of steel coils and sheet steel) (Wheeling) against Beelman River Terminals, Inc., (a warehouseman) (Beelman) for damages to approximately 3,000 tons of Wheeling's steel held in Beelman's warehouse during the Mississippi River flood of 1993 * * *.

* * *

To begin with, we agree with the district court that Dr. Curtis, a hydrologist specializing in flood risk management [who testified for Beelman], easily qualifies as an expert under Federal Rule of Evidence 702. The real question is, what is he an expert about? Though eminently qualified to testify as an expert hydrologist regarding matters of flood risk management, Dr. Curtis sorely lacked the education, employment, or other practical personal experiences to testify as an expert specifically regarding safe warehousing practices. Dr. Curtis did not study warehousing practices during his formal education, he has not written about warehousing practices in any of his sixty-plus published articles, and he has never been employed by a warehouseman during any of the twenty-one projects on which he has worked. Although he has worked with entire communities and shopping centers, he has never prepared emergency response plans specifically for storage facilities or warehouses. Furthermore, he did not compensate for his lack of education or experience about warehousing by, for example, determining or studying the actions of other warehousemen along the Mississippi River in response to this or any other flood.

After carefully examining the transcript of his trial testimony, we conclude that the district court erred in allowing Dr. Curtis to testify beyond the scope of his expertise and that the inadmissible opinions expressed by him prejudiced Wheeling. Dr. Curtis repeatedly offered opinion testimony outside of his area of expertise on ultimate issues of fact that the jury was required to answer—namely, whether Beelman's actions met the required standard of care for warehousemen.

There is no doubt that Dr. Curtis was qualified to testify that Beelman was diligent and reasonable in assessing available river data in historical context, in making judgments about reasonably foreseeable river levels and the risks they posed to the warehouse in light of the available information. But that does not make Dr. Curtis qualified to testify as an expert regarding what specific efforts and specific levels of protection are consistent with good warehousing practices, which he repeatedly did during the trial. * * * Furthermore, Dr. Curtis's improper opinions went to the primary issue upon which the jury had to make a judgment. We are convinced that the district court abused its discretion in allowing Dr. Curtis to give opinions specifically about warehousing practices and that Wheeling was prejudiced as a result. *See* Weisgram v. Marley Co., 169 F.3d 514, 517–21 (8th Cir.1999) (holding that portions of testimony from three different expert witnesses each lacked a sufficient foundation because they had exceeded the scope of the witness's expertise and thus were unreliable under Rule 702, and therefore it was an abuse of discretion to allow the testimony), *aff'd,* 528 U.S. 440 * * * (2000); Robertson, 148 F.3d at 907–08 (ordering new trial after manufacturing/ceramics/materials expert offered opinions as to the adequacy of grinding wheel warnings because the opinion was not sufficiently reliable under *Daubert* due to the expert's lack of training, research, practical knowledge, or experience with respect to warning labels); *see also* Redman v. John D. Brush & Co., 111 F.3d 1174, 1179 (4th Cir.1997) (holding it was error for metallurgical engineer to give opinion testimony that a particular safe met industry standards for burglar deterrence when no industry standard for burglar deterrent safes was ever established and the expert had no personal knowledge about or experience with the industry).

Notes

1. *Technicians.* See People v. King, 72 Cal.Rptr. 478, 491 (Cal.Ct.App. 1968) (courts must "differentiate between ability to operate an instrument or perform a test and the ability to make an interpretation drawn from use of the instrument"). Compare People v. Williams, 5 Cal.Rptr.2d 130, 135 (Cal.Ct.App.1992) ("[The officer's] opinion that appellant was under the influence of alcohol, to the extent it was based on the nystagmus test, rests on scientific principles well beyond his knowledge, training, or education. Without some understanding of the processes by which alcohol ingestion produces nystagmus, how strong the correlation is, how other possible causes might be masked, what margin of error has been shown in statistical surveys, and a host of other relevant factors, [the officer's] opinion on causation, notwithstanding his ability to recognize the symptom, was unfounded."), with People v. Ojeda, 275 Cal.Rptr. 472, 474 (Cal.Ct.App.1990) ("The gaze nystagmus test, as do other commonly used field sobriety tests, requires only the personal observation of the officer administering it.").

2. *False credentials.* In United States v. Williams, 233 F.3d 592, 593 (D.C.Cir.2000), the prosecution called an expert on drug distribution to testified that the heroin in the defendant's possession was intended for more than personal use. The witness told the jury he was "a Board-certified pharmacist. I receive, maintain [,] compound and dispense narcotic as well as non-narcotic substances per prescription." After conviction, the defense attorney learned that the expert "was not a pharmacist and had no degree in pharmacology, facts unknown to the prosecution during the trial." In fact, this expert reportedly testified in thousands of cases, misrepresenting his credentials for at least 16 years. See Groner, Your Expert Lied—for 16 Years * * * , Legal Times, July 3, 2000, at 8. The government has lost some cases because of this witness but not *Williams* because the D.C. Circuit held that the perjury did not change the outcome of the trial. See also United States v. Davis, 113 F.Supp.2d 1, 3 (D.D.C.2000) (defense attorney not ineffective in failing to discover the false credentials of the same expert because the accused could not show prejudice). Many defense attorneys had stipulated to this expert's qualifications, thus erecting another barrier to obtaining a new trial. See also Starrs, Mountebanks Among Forensic Scientists, in 2 Forensic Science Handbook 1, 7, 20–29 (Saferstein ed., 1988) (noting that one firearms expert took some credit for "the development of penicillin, the 'Pap' smear, and to top it all off, the atomic bomb").

(3) BASIS OF EXPERT OPINION: FEDERAL RULES 703 & 705

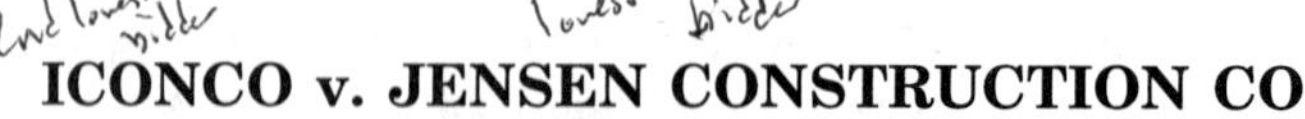

ICONCO v. JENSEN CONSTRUCTION CO.

United States Court of Appeals, Eighth Circuit, 1980.
622 F.2d 1291.

ARNOLD, CIRCUIT JUDGE.

This is a diversity case. Iconco, the plaintiff below, was the second lowest bidder on a small-business "set aside" construction contract let by the [Army] Corps of Engineers.[75] Jensen Construction Company, the low bidder, was awarded the contract. Iconco filed suit in the United States District Court for the Southern District of Iowa claiming that Jensen, in making its bid, falsely certified that it was a small business under federal law and was awarded the contract based upon that certification. Iconco claimed damages and lost profits based upon fraud and unjust-enrichment theories under Iowa law. The jury awarded Iconco $61,503 on its unjust-enrichment claim, and $10,000 actual damages and $30,000 punitive damages for fraud. The District Court, the Hon. Donald E. O'Brien, entered judgment in the amount of $61,503, but set aside the award for fraud, finding insufficient evidence to support the verdict. We affirm.

* * *

Jensen next argues that Iconco is not entitled to recover because, as a matter of law, it cannot prove that it was entitled to be awarded the contract. Under the provisions of the Armed Services Procurement Act, 10 U.S.C. § 2301 et seq., the award of the contract to the low bidder, or to any bidder, is not automatic * * *.

* * * Jensen argues that since the contracting officer can award the contract only to a "responsible" bidder whose bid is most advantageous to the government, and may reject all bids, no bidder, even the lowest one, has the right to expect that it will be awarded the contract. Jensen argues, in essence, that a claim for lost profits under these circumstances is speculative and improper.

The more logical approach, in our view, is to put the unsuccessful bidder to its proof; if it proves by a preponderance of the evidence that it would have received the contract award absent the successful bidder's wrongdoing, we find no persuasive reasons why recovery should be denied.

Here, Colonel Walter H. Johnson, the Corps of Engineers contracting officer for the Saylorville project, testified on Iconco's behalf. He was ultimately responsible for the awarding of the contract, and if it had not been awarded to Jensen, he would have been the one to decide to whom the award would be made.

According to Colonel Johnson, the standard procedure at bid opening, which was followed on the Saylorville contract, is to rank the bidders by amount of bid and then announce the apparent low bidder. Contractors are required as a matter of course to submit a bid bond along with their bid. If the low bidder submitted the appropriate bid bond, the contracting officer would declare it the apparent low bidder and then direct an investigation known as a "pre-award survey." The purpose of the survey is to determine whether the low bidder is "responsible," in other words, whether it has the financial resources, physical

75. [The bid invitation was for the removal of structures and the building of barricades in connection with the construction of the Saylorville Reservoir in central Iowa. Ed.]

capacity, and skill to perform the contract in a competent and timely fashion. The survey is conducted in accordance with the provisions of 32 C.F.R. §§ 1.903, 1.904, and 1.905 (1974).

Colonel Johnson testified that the overriding consideration in determining contractor responsibility is whether it can provide a performance bond; other important factors regarding responsibility, in his view, are the prior record of the contractor on similar jobs and apparent ability to concentrate sufficient resources on the job to perform the contract competently and in a timely fashion, factors which would require an evaluation of office organization, financial resources, organizational capability, and adequacy of equipment. The Saylorville job, according to Colonel Johnson, was not technically difficult, mostly "mule work" by his characterization. In his view, any contractor who had responsibly performed heavy work of any kind, including the demolition of heavy structures, could have done the job.

* * *

At trial, Iconco propounded a lengthy hypothetical question to Colonel Johnson. Colonel Johnson was asked to assume that the low bidder on the Saylorville contract was not a small business, that the second low bidder was and submitted a bid which was reasonable in amount (roughly 50% of the amount estimated by the Corps as necessary to perform the contract), that the second low bidder could obtain a performance bond and had successfully completed in its ten years experience several other similar contracts, and that it met other requirements of the pre-award survey in terms of financial ability, licensing, organization, experience, equipment, integrity, and reputation. Assuming these facts, Colonel Johnson was asked for an opinion about whether the contract would have been awarded to the second low bidder. His answer was yes. * * *

The standards by which a hypothetical question is to be judged are well-settled in this Circuit. The form of the question "must be left largely to the discretion of the trial court." United States v. Kiliyan, 456 F.2d 555, 561 (8th Cir.1972). The question need not include all facts shown by the evidence or pertinent to the ultimate issue, but it should be in such a form as not to mislead or confuse the jury. Id. A hypothetical should include only such facts as are supported by the evidence, and "(*o*)nly the basic facts need be assumed in the hypothesis," Twin City Plaza, Inc. v. Central Surety & Ins. Corp., 409 F.2d 1195, 1200 (8th Cir.1969), but "a question which omits any material fact essential to the formation of a rational opinion is * * * incompetent." Harris v. Smith, 372 F.2d 806, 812 (8th Cir.1967). Accord, Fed.R.Evid. 705, which eliminates the mandatory preliminary statement of all the facts underlying an expert's opinion. Jensen argues that the hypothetical omitted some of the findings material to the determination of responsibility by the contracting officer, but we think the question fairly characterized the material considerations. Colonel Johnson's testimony in response to other questions made clear his opinion that any experienced contractor could have performed the Saylorville job, and we evaluate the hypothetical in that context.

Jensen also argues that the hypothetical asked Colonel Johnson to assume facts which were not in evidence. We cannot agree. Iconco's first witness at trial was Richard Joseph Diven, Iconco's president since 1973. He testified to a number of contracts involving the demolition of bridges performed by Iconco satisfactorily before the Saylorville bid was submitted. Diven stated further that the company had obtained hundreds of bid bonds without difficulty. John E. Weber, Iconco's secretary, testified after Colonel Johnson. Mr. Weber described several of the other contracts which Iconco had performed adequately, some of which were more sophisticated and difficult than the Saylorville job. According to Weber, Iconco had never been denied a performance bond, and no one had ever questioned the integrity of the company or its financial capacity. At the time of the award of the Saylorville contract, Iconco had a qualified superintendent and the equipment necessary to do the job. In Weber's view, Iconco complied with the requirements of the pre-award survey in all respects.

* * *

The judgment of the District Court is affirmed in all respects.

Notes and Questions

1. *Value of hypothetical question.* If the jury does not accept the facts on which the expert's opinion is based, it should reject the opinion. Does the hypothetical question assist the jury in this regard? The principal case cites *Harris v. Smith* for the proposition that the omission of "any material fact" from the hypothetical question makes the opinion "incompetent." Should such defects in the hypothetical question be left to cross-examination?

2. *Criticisms.* The hypothetical question as a vehicle for eliciting the expert's opinion upon facts as to which the expert has no personal knowledge has received extensive criticism from every quarter—judges, attorneys, commentators, and the experts themselves. Dieden & Gasparich, Psychiatric Evidence and Full Disclosure in the Criminal Trial, 52 Cal.L.Rev. 543, 556 (1964), contains the following observations:

> Unfortunately the hypothetical question has been the traditionally accepted method of adducing expert testimony. It even has been characterized as one of the truly scientific features of the rules of evidence in that it is designed to reveal all of the pertinent facts in the most logical order to support the expert opinion. In fact, its objectives have never been realized and the method has been uniformly criticized by the authorities, as well as the California courts which have commented on the undue length and complexity of hypothetical questions and the slanting of their hypotheses. Medical men have also been outspoken in expressing their disdain for the technique.

3. *Optional use.* Mandatory use of the hypothetical question has now been abandoned in virtually all jurisdictions, often by the adoption of rules

based upon Federal Rules 703 and 705. What language in those rules frees the examiner from the need to phrase questions to experts in the form of hypothetical questions? Is use of the hypothetical question still permitted? If so, might trial counsel ever elect to use such a question? Might a trial judge, in his or her discretion, require use of a hypothetical question? At least one state has specifically provided, in its version of Rule 705, that the trial judge cannot require the use of a hypothetical question. N.C.R.Evid. 705. With regard to the use of hypothetical questions under the Federal Rules, see McElhaney, Expert Witnesses and the Federal Rules of Evidence, 28 Mercer L.Rev. 463 (1977).

4. *Problems?* In United States v. Mancillas, 183 F.3d 682, 705 (7th Cir.1999), the prosecution presented a hypothetical to a testifying DEA agent, regarding a person possessing a plastic bag containing 400 grams of marijuana, a slip of paper bearing the notation '420 g,' a handgun, a scale, two pagers, a cellular phone and $2440 in cash. After setting forth these hypothetical facts, the government asked the agent whether, in his opinion, the marijuana was being held for distribution or personal consumption. The agent testified that, in his opinion, the marijuana was being held for distribution. Is there a problem with this type of testimony? What if the hypothetical facts "mirror" the facts in the case?

THOMAS v. METZ

Supreme Court of Wyoming, 1986.
714 P.2d 1205.

BROWN, JUSTICE.

This is a medical malpractice action brought by appellant Phyllis Thomas against appellee Albert Metz, Jr., M.D. Appellant claimed she was damaged as a result of improper back surgery performed by appellee. Trial to a jury resulted in a verdict for appellee. Appellant presents the following issues:

> "It was reversible error for the trial court to admit expert opinions of defendant's witnesses which were based upon defendant doctor's deposition and the opinions of other experts when this type of facts or data is not of the type reasonably relied upon by experts in the field.
>
> "It was reversible error for the trial court to refuse to require disclosure of the underlying facts or data upon which the opinions of the defendant's experts were based prior to the giving of the opinions, or once having allowed the opinions, refusing to strike the opinions when it was disclosed that the facts or data was not of that type reasonably relied upon by experts in the field."

We will affirm.

The facts show that on April 17, 1982, appellant rolled over in bed and experienced pain in her back between her shoulder blades. She was admitted to the hospital that same day, complaining of pain between her shoulder blades, pain in her left arm, and numbness in the left thumb, index finger and middle finger. After consultation and testing by Dr. James Maddy and Dr. Malvin Cole, it was concluded that appellant was suffering a disc herniation at the Cervical 6/Cervical 7 (C–6/C–7) level, primarily on the left side. Neurosurgical consultation was then sought from appellee, who, after evaluation, confirmed the findings of Drs. Maddy and Cole, and recommended that surgery be performed to remove disc fragments that were pressing on the spinal cord and the left C–7 nerve root.

After obtaining appellant's consent, appellee performed surgery to remove the disc fragments. A bone plug was then removed from appellant's hip and placed in the spine to fuse the two vertebral bodies. After surgery, appellant experienced pain on her right side, similar to that previously experienced on the left side. Further testing revealed the bone plug was encroaching upon the C–7 nerve root on the right side. Additional surgery was performed to alleviate the condition on April 27, 1982.

When appellant continued to experience pain, she consulted several physicians in Denver during the months of May and June, 1982. In June of 1982, appellant underwent further surgery in Denver. This surgery was performed by another physician, and consisted of removal of the first right thoracic rib.

The pain persisted. An expert witness for appellant, Dr. John Williams, testified appellant now suffers from a condition known as "hysterical conversion"—where pain is a stress reaction and has no medical, anatomical or physiological basis. Dr. Robert Kelso, a clinical psychologist, examined and evaluated appellant and concluded that he believed "this disorder should show significant improvement within a 12–month period."

Appellant filed the present action on January 25, 1983. As noted above, trial to the jury resulted in a verdict for appellee.

We will consider both of appellant's issues together. Basically, appellant claims the trial court erred by admitting the testimony of appellee's expert witnesses, alleging such witnesses improperly based their testimony upon appellee's apparent discovery deposition and previous opinions given by other physicians.

We have heretofore recognized the need for expert testimony in medical malpractice actions. * * *

The two expert witnesses who testified on behalf of appellee were Drs. Federico Mora and Philip Gordy. * * *

* * * Appellant's main objection to the testimony of both expert witnesses is that such testimony was improperly based on material not reasonably relied upon by experts. Specifically, appellant claims it was improper for Dr. Mora to rely upon appellee's discovery deposition in giving his opinion at trial. Appellant further claims it was also error for Dr. Gordy to base his opinion upon appellee's discovery deposition, as well as Dr. Mora's deposition.

Rules 702 and 703, Wyoming Rules of Evidence, are pertinent to this case * * *

It is significant to note that appellee's deposition was only one of several sources of information Dr. Mora relied upon to base his opinion. When asked what materials he had reviewed to form his opinion, Dr. Mora testified:

> "Basically what I examined is I looked over the hospital records of Ms. Thomas here when she was treated in Casper. I have also looked at hospital records and personal notes of physicians who treated her when she went to Denver later on. Furthermore, I have read the depositions that were given by Dr. Metz, by Ms. Thomas, and by Dr. Williams, two that come to mind."

And when asked if he felt the surgery performed by appellee was appropriate, Dr. Mora answered:

> "Well, basing myself on the hospital record and the review of the X rays, the operation was appropriate."

Dr. Gordy based his opinion upon a review of hospital records, as well as appellee's deposition and depositions from the other physicians. He was then asked:

> "Q. Doctor, based upon the information you have reviewed, have you an opinion as to whether or not the surgery performed on April 23, 1982, upon Plaintiff here by Dr. Metz was necessary? Answer yes or no.
>
> "A. Yes, I have an opinion.
>
> "Q. And what is that opinion?
>
> "A. It was absolutely necessary."

Trial counsel for appellant made an objection to the basis for Dr. Mora's expert testimony. After a conference at bench, the trial court ruled that counsel's objection was in the nature of impeachment and counsel would be allowed to thoroughly cross-examine the witness. * * *

Ordinarily, it is within the sound discretion of the trial court whether voir dire of a witness will be allowed, or whether counsel must wait until cross-examination to attack the credibility of an expert witness. Such rulings will not be overturned on appeal absent a showing of prejudicial error. * * *

Appellant's trial counsel was allowed to thoroughly cross-examine both expert witnesses, and attack the bases of their opinions for impeachment purposes. [quoting Rule 705]

Appellant contends the court erred in refusing to require disclosure of facts upon which the experts based their opinions. But as we have already pointed out, the experts did state what records they had reviewed in making their conclusions. Therefore, the experts did disclose the basis of their opinions. * * *

It is then within the province of the trier of fact to give whatever credence they may to the expert testimony as well as all the evidence in reaching a verdict.

> "* * * The trier of fact must decide what weight is to be given to expert testimony, and it still remains the duty of the trier of the factual issues, whether jury or judge, to determine the credibility of all witnesses, including expert witnesses, and to evaluate the testimony of each in reaching its verdict. [Citations.]" *Reed v. Hunter,* supra, at 518.

We are not able to find prejudicial error inasmuch as appellee's two expert witnesses based their opinions *in part* upon the deposition of appellee. Appellant has failed to show how such prejudiced her or how such affected the jury's verdict. Both of the witnesses were qualified as experts and possessed a great deal of expertise in the area of neurosurgery.

> "It is common practice for a prospective witness, in preparing himself to express an expert opinion, to pursue pretrial studies and investigations of one kind or another. Frequently, the information so gained is hearsay or double hearsay, insofar as the trier of the facts is concerned. This, however, does not necessarily stand in the way of receiving such expert opinion in evidence. It is for the trial court to determine, in the exercise of its discretion, whether the expert's sources of information are sufficiently reliable to warrant reception of the opinion. If the court so finds, the opinion may be expressed. If the opinion is received, the court may, in its discretion, allow the expert to reveal to the jury the information gained during such investigations and studies. Wide latitude in cross-examination should be allowed." *Standard Oil Co. of California v. Moore,* 251 F.2d 188, 222 (9th Cir.1957).

* * *

We have carefully reviewed the issues raised by appellant and are unable to find the trial court committed reversible error in allowing the testimony of appellee's expert witnesses.

Affirmed.

Notes and Questions

1. *Hearsay.* When an expert witness testifies to facts upon which she based her opinion that are not otherwise admissible in evidence, are such facts admissible for all purposes or only as the basis of the expert's opinion? Does Rule 703 in effect create a new exception to the hearsay rule? See Chapters 13 and 14, infra. A 2000 amendment to Rule 703 added the following sentence: "Facts or data that are otherwise inadmissible shall not be disclosed to the jury by the proponent of the opinion or inference unless the court determines that their probative value in assisting the jury to evaluate the expert's opinion substantially outweighs their prejudicial ef-

fect." See Carlson, Is Revised Expert Witness Rule 703 a Critical Modernization for the New Century?, 52 Fla.L.Rev. 715 (2000).

2. *Background hearsay.* What was the basis of Dr. Mora's opinion in the principal case? Are these sources used differently than the "pretrial studies and investigations" in the quotation from *Standard Oil*, which is cited in the principal case? In Wells v. Miami Valley Hosp., 631 N.E.2d 642, 654 (Ohio Ct.App.1993), a physician testified that Wells "probably died of a cardiac tamponade." This expert "indicated that the factual basis of his testimony was his review of the medical records and the autopsy report." He also read scholarly medical articles on cardiac tamponade risks from CVP catheter placement. Are the medical records and autopsy report the "facts or data in the particular case" within the meaning of Rule 703? Are the scholarly articles read during the expert's research? See Maguire, Evidence: Common Sense and Common Law 29 (1947) ("Progress of expert knowledge demands reliance upon the learning of the past. Almost invariably this learning is recorded in hearsay form. No individual can ever make himself into an expert without absorbing much hearsay—lectures by his teachers, statements in textbooks, reports of experiments and experiences of others in the same field.").

3. *Other cases.* See United States v. Bramlet, 820 F.2d 851 (7th Cir.1987) (notes and reports of non-professional staff at mental institution); United States v. Lundy, 809 F.2d 392, 395 (7th Cir.1987) (Arson expert based his opinion on his firsthand inspection of the scene and on interviews with witnesses at the scene. "[H]earsay and third-party observations that are of a type normally relied upon by an expert in the field are properly utilized by such an expert in developing an expert opinion * * *. [The expert] presented uncontroverted evidence that interviews with many witnesses to a fire are a standard investigatory technique in cause and origin inquiries."); United States v. 1,014.16 Acres of Land, 558 F.Supp. 1238 (W.D.Mo.1983) (opinion of other real estate appraisers as to the value of land), aff'd, 739 F.2d 1371 (8th Cir.1984).

4. *Admissibility decision.* If an expert testifies that her opinion is based on facts not within her own perception or in evidence at the trial, how much of an inquiry into either the general use of such information by similar experts or the reasonableness of such reliance should the court conduct? There are two different approaches to the judge's role. One approach requires the court to make an independent assessment of the reasonableness of the expert's reliance: "[T]he court may not abdicate its independent responsibilities to decide if the bases meet minimum standards of reliability as a condition of admissibility * * *. If the underlying data are so lacking in probative force and reliability that no reasonable expert could base an opinion on them, an opinion which rests entirely upon them must be excluded." In re "Agent Orange" Product Liability Litigation, 611 F.Supp. 1223, 1245 (E.D.N.Y.1985), aff'd, 818 F.2d 187 (2d Cir.1987).

The other approach limits the judge's role to determining what experts in the field consider reasonable. The "proper inquiry is not what the court deems reliable, but what experts in the relevant discipline deem it to be." Zenith Radio Corp. v. Matsushita Elec. Indus. Co., 723 F.2d 238, 276 (3d Cir.1983), rev'd on other grounds, 475 U.S. 574 (1986). The Third Circuit added: "In substituting its own opinion as to what constitutes reasonable reliance for that of the experts in the relevant fields the trial court misinterpreted Rule 703." Id. at 277. However, the Third Circuit changed positions after the Supreme Court decided the *Daubert* case. The court noted that its "former view is no longer tenable in light of *Daubert*." In re Paoli R.R. Yard PCB Litigation, 35 F.3d 717, 748 (3d Cir.1994). The court wrote:

> [I]t is the judge who makes the determination of reasonable reliance, and that for the judge to make the factual determination under Rule 104(a) that an expert is basing his or her opinion on a type of data *reasonably* relied upon by experts, the judge must conduct an independent evaluation into reasonableness. The judge can of course take into account the particular expert's opinion that experts reasonably rely on that type of data, as well as the opinions of other experts as to its reliability, but the judge can also take into account other factors he or she deems relevant.

See also Imwinkelried, The Meaning of "Facts or Data" in Federal Rule of Evidence 703: The Significance of the Supreme Court's Decision to Rely on Federal Rule 702 in *Daubert v. Merrell Dow Pharmaceuticals, Inc.*, 54 Md.L.Rev. 352 (1995).

5. *Supervising chemist.* In Reardon v. Manson, 806 F.2d 39, 42 (2d Cir.1986), a toxicologist testified based on tests performed by a chemist. The Second Circuit upheld the practice: "Expert reliance upon the output of others does not necessarily violate the confrontation clause where the expert is available for questioning concerning the nature and reasonableness of his reliance * * *. This is particularly true where the defendants have access to the same sources of information through subpoena or otherwise." The expert, however, worked at a laboratory staffed by three doctorate-level toxicologists and 24 chemists with lesser credentials. With an annual volume of 20,000 tests, the toxicologists had an average of "only a few minutes per day to attend to any given test. Is this adequate involvement to justify testifying to the findings?" Saks & Van Duizend, The Use of Scientific Evidence in Litigation 49 (1983).

Do special problems exist in criminal cases because of the confrontation clause? See Carlson, Experts as Hearsay Conduits: Confrontation Abuses in Opinion Testimony, 76 Minn.L.Rev. 859 (1992); Faigman, Commentary: A Response to Professor Carlson—Struggling to Stop the Flood of Unreliable Expert Testimony, 76 Minn.L.Rev. 877 (1992). See also Minn.R.Evid. 703(b) (underlying data must be independently admissible in order to be received on direct examination; exception for "particularly trustworthy" data in civil cases).

6. Has the liberalization of the common law rules governing expert testimony gone too far? Is adequate trustworthiness insured by the new rules? See Huber, Galileo's Revenge: Junk Science in the Courtroom (1991); Giannelli, "Junk Science": The Criminal Cases, 84 J.Crim.L. & Criminology 105 (1993); Graham, Expert Witness Testimony and the Federal Rules of Evidence: Insuring Adequate Assurance of Trustworthiness, 1986 U.Ill. L.Rev. 43.

(4) ULTIMATE ISSUE RULE: FEDERAL RULE 704

CARR v. RADKEY

Supreme Court of Texas, 1965.
393 S.W.2d 806.

GREENHILL, JUSTICE. This is a will contest. Upon a finding by the jury that Miss Hattie Hewlett did not have testamentary capacity, the trial court denied probate to her holographic wills of April 17 and December 28, 1936. The only serious contest was and is over the instrument of December 28, 1936. Except for procedural problems later noticed, this opinion will deal only with the December 28 will.

The State[76] appealed on the ground that it (and those aligned with it in support of the will) had not been given a fair trial because of the exclusion of what they regarded as their most important evidence, the testimony of Dr. Sam Hoerster, an expert in mental illnesses. The evidence which was excluded was Dr. Hoerster's opinion, in answer to a hypothetical question, as to whether Miss Hewlett, when she wrote her will, had sufficient ability to understand the business in which she was engaged, the effect of her acts in making the will, realized what she was doing, knew her people and relatives, and knew the property she owned. Also excluded was his answer to a question as to whether Miss Hewlett wrote the will during a lucid interval. Outside the hearing of the jury, in completing a bill of exceptions, Dr. Hoerster answered both questions in such a way as to support the probate of the will.

* * *

Miss Hewlett wrote the will when she was 62 years of age, while in the Brown Rest Home in Austin. Before she became mentally ill, she had supported herself and had been in charge of the safety deposit boxes at the American National Bank in Austin. She lived close to the university's campus. She had made investments in Austin real estate, some of them relatively close to the time of her mental illness, which proved to be profitable. Her estate was appraised at $240,000 upon her death in 1960.

* * *

After being * * * qualified [as an expert in mental illnesses], Dr. Hoerster was asked a hypothetical question. As a predicate to the question, counsel reviewed the evidence about Miss Hewlett, including the fact that she had been taken to a rest home in the latter part of 1936. He was told of her periods of excitement and depression. He was told that her brother, David Hewlett, had died, and that she was informed of his death on December 28, 1936, the same day on which her

76. [The State was involved in the case in defense of the will because, as noted in an omitted portion of the opinion, the will contained a residuary bequest to establish scholarships for worthy students in certain disciplines (including law) at the University of Texas. Ed.]

will is dated; she showed no emotion. Her will was read to Dr. Hoerster. Assuming these facts, he was asked whether Miss Hewlett, when she wrote the will, "had sufficient ability to understand the business in which she was engaged, the effects of her acts in making the will, realized what she was doing, knew her people and her relatives, and knew the property she owned." He was not permitted to answer. The court also sustained objections to other questions breaking down the larger question into various elements.

* * *

The question of a witness, lay or expert, being allowed to answer questions regarding the capacity of a testator has been given considerable attention by persons regarded as authorities in the field. They have considered and discussed the objections to the admission of the testimony which fall into these general categories: (1) it invades the province of the jury; (2) the witness is asked to answer a question the jury must answer, or the ultimate issue; and (3) the witness, lay or expert, may not have in mind the same definition of capacity to execute an instrument as is contained in the legal definition of capacity. These textwriters and authorities are almost uniform in their criticism of using "invasion of the province of the jury" as a reason for excluding testimony in this area. The function of the witness is to give information which will be helpful to the jury. The province of the jury is to believe or disbelieve, weigh evidence, and to evaluate it. The witness could not invade that province if he wanted to. Wigmore says the phrase "is so misleading, as well as so unsound, that it should be entirely repudiated. It is a mere bit of empty rhetoric." 7 Wigmore, Evidence 17 (3d ed. 1940). McCormick says the phrase if taken literally is absurd. It suggests that the jury may forego independent analysis and bow too readily to the opinion of an expert or otherwise influential witness. * * * This indicates a mistrust of the mentality and capacity of jurors to decide matters for themselves.* * *

Regarding the second objection, that the juror is asked the ultimate question the jury must answer, Mr. Justice Smedley held for this Court in Federal Underwriters Exchange v. Cost, 132 Tex. 299, 123 S.W.2d 332 (1938), discussed above, that there are many occasions on which a witness may be asked the same question the jury must answer. For example as in *Cost*, a doctor was permitted to give his opinion as to whether an incapacity of a workman would be permanent. Again, an automobile intersection case may turn on whether a party ran a red light, failed to stop at a sign, gave a particular signal, and the like. In all of these, witnesses may testify, if they know, that the person did or did not do these things; and the jury is then asked the same question. Many authorities would permit questions even on an ultimate issue. * * * It is when the question involves a legal definition and a conclusion based on the definition that Brown v. Mitchell and Lindley v. Lindley, 384 S.W.2d 676 (Tex.1964) are offended.

It is the third objection listed above which is the basis for the holdings of Brown v. Mitchell [88 Tex. 350, 31 S.W. 621 (1895)] and Lindley v. Lindley [384 S.W.2d 676 (Tex.Sup.1964)]. A witness may not be asked whether a person had the [legal] capacity to execute a deed, or was acting under an insane delusion when he executed his will, because these concepts involve legal definitions. As stated in Lindley, the doctor's or lay witness's definition or understanding of capacity to perform the act in a legal manner may be different from the legal standard.[77] * * *

It is our conclusion that the jury in cases such as these should be given all relevant and competent testimony with regard to the mental condition of the testatrix; and in our opinion, competent evidence about her mental condition and mental ability or lack of it which does not involve legal definitions, legal tests, or pure questions of law should be admitted. This is in accord with the modern trend in this field. * * *

This has also been the trend of the better cases in Texas. In Chambers v. Winn, 137 Tex. 444, 154 S.W.2d 454 (1941), several witnesses were asked if they thought the testator was of sound or unsound mind. Objection was sustained. This Court reversed, saying that "[t]he courts below failed * * * to observe the distinction between evidence bearing on the mental condition of the testator and that bearing on his legal capacity to make a will." * * *

* * * Our holding is that a witness may not be asked whether a testator had the mental capacity to make and publish a will because, under Brown v. Mitchell, whether a person has mental capacity to execute a will involves a legal definition and a legal test. A witness may be asked, assuming he knows or is a properly qualified expert, whether the testator knew or had the capacity to know the objects of his bounty, the nature of the transaction in which he was engaged, the nature and extent of his estate, and similar questions.

The particular question here was whether Miss Hewlett, when she wrote her will, had sufficient ability to understand the business in which she was engaged, the effect of her acts in making a will, realized what she was doing, and knew the property she owned. The trial court erred in excluding the question and the answer thereto.

We are also of the opinion that the error was harmful. While Dr. Hoerster, the only medically trained expert tendered by either party, did get in bits of testimony here and there, he was never permitted to develop his testimony, the Petitioner's side of the lawsuit * * *. At least three of Respondents' witnesses were permitted to testify that in their opinion Miss Hewlett was of unsound mind, giving their reasons. Mrs. Radkey had been permitted to testify that in her opinion the testatrix was not mentally capable of knowing or understanding her acts. Similarly, Mrs. Brown was permitted to testify that Miss Hewlett was not

77. It has been argued by many of the authorities set out above that any difference of definition could be brought out by proper cross examination; and so the question and answer should be allowed if it would be helpful to the jury. Nevertheless, this Court's position is stated in Brown v. Mitchell and followed in Lindley.

mentally capable of knowing the nature and effect of her acts. The Petitioner was entitled to meet that evidence with Dr. Hoerster's testimony.

* * *

The judgments of the courts below are reversed and the case is remanded to the district court for a new trial.

Notes and Questions

1. *Criticism.* Critical opinion has almost universally condemned exclusion of opinions solely on the ground that they are upon the "ultimate issue," but some commentators have, like the court in the principal case, expressed reservations as to whether liberalization should be carried to the point of allowing such opinion to be expressed in legal terms of art. McCoid, Opinion Evidence and Expert Witnesses, 2 UCLA L.Rev. 356, 360–61 (1955); Stoebuck, Opinions on Ultimate Facts: Status, Trends, and a Note of Caution, 41 Denv.L.C.J. 226, 236–38 (1964). See also Strong, Language and Logic in Expert Testimony: Limiting Expert Testimony by Restrictions of Function, Reliability, and Form, 71 Or.L.Rev. 349 (1992).

2. *Mental states.* The Federal Rules, as originally adopted, completely eliminated the ultimate issue rule. What is now Rule 704(a) stood alone, without the qualification of Rule 704(b). As originally adopted, the Rule constituted a culmination of a common law trend toward total abrogation of the ultimate issue rule, illustrated by cases such as *Carr.* However, Congress took a major step back from this position in 1984 by the enactment of Rule 704(b), which specifically applies the ultimate issue rule to testimony concerning the mental state of a defendant in a criminal case. See California Penal Code § 29 for a state provision with the same effect. The amendment to the Federal Rule arose out of the national concern over the prosecution of John Hinckley for attempting to assassinate President Reagan. The amendment was part of a package of legislation intended to make it more difficult for an accused successfully to assert the insanity defense.

> The purpose of this amendment is to eliminate the confusing spectacle of competing expert witnesses testifying to directly contradictory conclusions as to the ultimate legal issue to be found by the trier of fact. Under this proposal, expert psychiatric testimony would be limited to presenting and explaining their diagnosis, such as whether the defendant had a severe mental disease or defect and what the characteristics of such a disease or defect, if any, may have been.

H.Rep.No. 98–1030, 98th Cong., 2d Sess. 224, 232, U.S.C.C.A.N. 1984, at 1.

Another portion of the legislative history gives further insight into congressional thinking:

> When, however, "ultimate issue" questions are formulated by the law and put to the expert witness who must then say "yea" or "nay" then the expert witness is required to make a leap in logic. He no longer addresses himself to medical concepts but instead must infer or intuit what is in fact unspeakable, namely, the probable relationship between

> medical concepts and legal or moral constructs such as free will. These impermissible leaps in logic made by expert witnesses confuse the jury.

S.Rep.No. 225, 98th Cong., 1st Sess. 231, quoting American Psychiatric Association Statement on the Insanity Defense, Dec. 1982, at 18.

Are there likely to be problems with this congressional resurrection of the ultimate issue rule? Some have already arisen, such as the difficulty of distinguishing between testimony concerning diagnosis and testimony concerning the ultimate decision. See United States v. Edwards, 819 F.2d 262 (11th Cir.1987) (psychiatrist's testimony that the defendant was "frantic" over financial situation held not to violate Rule 704(b)). See generally Note, Resurrection of the Ultimate Issue Rule: Federal Rule of Evidence 704(b) and the Insanity Defense, 72 Cornell L.Rev. 620 (1987).

To what extent does Rule 704(b) apply in cases other than those involving the insanity defense? See United States v. Campos, 217 F.3d 707, 711 (9th Cir.2000) ("While Congress primarily targeted subdivision (b) towards limiting the use of psychiatric expert testimony on whether a defendant is sane or insane, * * * Rule 704(b) is not limited in 'its reach to psychiatrists and other mental health experts,' but rather, extends to all expert witnesses. * * * Rule 704(b) clearly applies to expert polygraph testimony on ultimate issues. * * * The polygraph examiner's testimony that Campos was truthful in stating that she did not know that she was transporting marijuana leaves no room for inference, but rather, compels the conclusion that she did not possess the requisite knowledge."); United States v. Morales, 108 F.3d 1031, 1036, 1037 (9th Cir.1997) ("The language of Rule 704(b) is perfectly plain. It does not limit its reach to psychiatrists and other mental health experts. Its reach extends to all expert witnesses. * * * [The accountant] was not going to state an opinion or draw an inference that Morales did not intend to make false entries [the ultimate issue]. Rather, she was going to state her opinion as to a predicate matter—that Morales had a weak grasp of bookkeeping principles.").

(5) RIGHT TO EXPERT ASSISTANCE

In Ake v. Oklahoma, 470 U.S. 68 (1985), the accused was charged with capital murder. At arraignment, his conduct was "so bizarre" that the trial judge ordered, sua sponte, a mental evaluation. Ake was found incompetent to stand trial but later recovered due to antipsychotic drugs. When the prosecution resumed, Ake's attorney requested a psychiatric evaluation at state expense to prepare an insanity defense. The trial court refused. Thus, although insanity was the only contested issue at trial, no psychiatrists testified on this issue, and Ake was convicted. In the penalty stage, the prosecution relied on state psychiatrists, who testified that Ake was "dangerous to society," in seeking the death sentence. This testimony stood unrebutted because Ake could not afford an expert.

The Supreme Court overturned Ake's conviction on due process grounds, commenting that "when a State brings its judicial power to bear on an indigent in a criminal proceeding, it must take steps to assure that the defendant has a fair opportunity to present his defense." Id. at

76. This fair opportunity mandates that an accused be provided with the "basic tools of an adequate defense." In another passage, the Court elaborated on what it meant by a "fair opportunity" and "basic tools" for an adequate defense: "We hold that when a defendant has made a preliminary showing that his sanity at the time of the offense is likely to be a significant factor at trial, the Constitution requires that a State provide access to a psychiatrist's assistance on this issue, if the defendant cannot otherwise afford one." Id. at 74. See generally Giannelli, *Ake v. Oklahoma*: The Right to Expert Assistance in a Post–*Daubert*, Post–DNA World, 89 Cornell L.Rev. 1305 (2004).

While the *Ake* decision settled the core issue by recognizing a right to expert assistance, it left a number of important issues unresolved:

Noncapital cases. Compare Isom v. State, 488 So.2d 12, 13 (Ala. Crim.App.1986) ("*Ake* does not reach noncapital cases."), with Taylor v. State, 939 S.W.2d 148, 152 (Tex.Crim.App.1996) ("[W]e have also extended—at least implicitly—the due process protections recognized in *Ake* beyond the capital context.").

Nonpsychiatric experts. Compare Ex parte Grayson, 479 So.2d 76, 82 (Ala.1985) ("[T]here is nothing contained in the *Ake* decision to suggest that the United States Supreme Court was addressing anything other than psychiatrists and the insanity defense."), with Little v. Armontrout, 835 F.2d 1240, 1243 (8th Cir.1987) (en banc) (In finding error to fail to appoint hypnotist, the court stated: "[T]here is no principled way to distinguish between psychiatric and nonpsychiatric experts. The question in each case must be not what field of science or expert knowledge is involved, but rather how important the scientific issue is in the case, and how much help a defense expert could have given.").

Role of expert. Compare Granviel v. Lynaugh, 881 F.2d 185, 191 (5th Cir.1989) (a "court-appointed psychiatrist, whose opinion and testimony is available to both sides, satisfies [the accused's] rights. * * * The state is not required to permit defendants to shop around for a favorable expert. * * * He has no right to the appointment of a psychiatrist who will reach biased or only favorable conclusions."), with United States v. Sloan, 776 F.2d 926, 929 (10th Cir.1985) ("That duty [to appoint a psychiatrist] cannot be satisfied with the appointment of an expert who ultimately testifies contrary to the defense on the issue of competence. The essential benefit of having an expert in the first place is denied the defendant when the services of the doctor must be shared with the prosecution.").

Standard. In Volson v. Blackburn, 794 F.2d 173, 176 (5th Cir.1986), the court noted that "the *Ake* decision fails to establish a bright line test for determining when a defendant has demonstrated that sanity at the time of the offense will be a significant factor at the time of trial." Some reasonable threshold showing is necessary because the system cannot afford defense experts on "demand." For example, in State v. Mason, 694 N.E.2d 932 (Ohio 1998), a capital case, the defendant received state funds for the services of a private investigator, a forensic psychiatrist, a forensic pathologist, and for DNA and blood testing services. He requested, but did not receive, funds to hire a soils and trace evidence expert, a shoeprint expert, an eyewitness identification expert, a homicide investigation expert, a mass media expert, a forensic psychologist, a statistical DNA expert, and a firearms expert. However, if the threshold standard is set too high, the defendant is placed in a "Catch–22" situation, in which the standard "demand[s] that the defendant possess already the expertise of the witness sought." State v. Moore, 364 S.E.2d 648, 657 (N.C. 1988).

Statutory provisions. Under 18 U.S.C. § 3006(A), an indigent person may obtain expert assistance. The Act limits expenses for expert services to $1,000.00 unless the court certifies that a greater amount is "necessary to provide fair compensation for services of an unusual character or duration." Until 1986 the maximum had been $300. Many states have comparable provisions. See Minn.Stat.Ann. § 611.21 ($1,000 maximum).

Court-appointed experts. Although not frequently used, Rule 706 has been employed in a variety of situations. See, e.g., Students of Cal. Sch. for Blind v. Honig, 736 F.2d 538 (9th Cir.1984) (in case involving seismic safety of new campus of school for blind, after lengthy and conflicting evidence, court appointed expert under Rule 706). The question of the appointment of an impartial expert is within the discretion of the trial court judge. See Oklahoma Natural Gas Co. v. Mahan & Rowsey, Inc., 786 F.2d 1004, 1007 (10th Cir.1986). Might frequent use of Rule 706 present problems for the adversary system? See Cecil & Willging, Court–Appointed Experts: Defining the Role of Experts Appointed under Federal Rule of Evidence 706 (Fed. Judicial Center 1993): Choy, Judicial Education After *Markman v. Westview Instruments, Inc.*: The Use of Court-appointed Experts, 47 UCLA L.Rev. 1423 (2000); Thorpe, Oelhafen & Arnold, Court–Appointed Experts and Technical Advisors, 26 Litigation 31 (Summer 2000); Note, Improving Judicial Gatekeeping: Technical Advisors and Scientific Evidence, 110 Harv.L.Rev. 941 (1997).

Civil litigation. May the impecunious civil party plaintiff (who unlike the criminal defendant may improve his financial situation by the litigation) obtain expert testimony by means of an agreement with the expert under which the expert's right to receive a fee is conditioned upon success in the litigation? See, e.g., Barnes v. Boatmen's Nat'l Bank, 156 S.W.2d 597 (Mo.1941) (contract upheld against contention that it was against public policy). But see also Model Rule of Prof'l Conduct R. 3.4 cmt. ("The common law rule in most jurisdictions is * * * that it is improper to pay an expert witness a contingent fee.").

SECTION E. CREDIBILITY: BOLSTERING, IMPEACHMENT AND REHABILITATION

The credibility of a witness is a quintessential jury issue. For present purposes, credibility may be defined as a witness' worthiness of belief. The evidentiary rules governing credibility can be viewed in three stages: (1) bolstering of credibility, (2) impeachment of credibility, and (3) rehabilitation of credibility. Impeachment is the elicitation or presentation of any matter *for the purpose* of impairing or destroying the credibility of a witness in the estimation of the trier of fact. Note that bolstering and rehabilitation both involve attempts to support the credibility of a witness. The difference is one of timing: Bolstering involves attempts to support credibility before it has been attacked or impeached. In contrast, rehabilitation comes after impeachment. Different rules apply to bolstering and rehabilitation.

Credibility issues cover matters for which there may not be a specific Federal Rule. How many methods are in the following statute?

Cal. Evid. Code § 780

General rule as to credibility. Except as otherwise provided by statute, the court or jury may consider in determining the credibility of a witness any matter that has any tendency in reason to prove or disprove the truthfulness of his testimony at the hearing, including but not limited to any of the following:

(a) His demeanor while testifying and the manner in which he testifies.

(b) The character of his testimony.

(c) The extent of his capacity to perceive, to recollect, or to communicate any matter about which he testifies.

(d) The extent of his opportunity to perceive any matter about which he testifies.

(e) His character for honesty or veracity or their opposites.

(f) The existence or nonexistence of a bias, interest, or other motive.

(g) A statement previously made by him that is consistent with his testimony at the hearing.

(h) A statement made by him that is inconsistent with any part of his testimony at the hearing.

(i) The existence or nonexistence of any fact testified to by him.

(j) His attitude toward the action in which he testifies or toward the giving of testimony.

(k) His admission of untruthfulness.

(1) BOLSTERING

It is not unusual to find statements stating that bolstering the credibility of witnesses is impermissible: United States v. Cosentino, 844 F.2d 30, 32–33 (2d Cir.1988) ("It is well settled that absent an attack, no evidence may be admitted to support a witness' credibility."). Consumption of time and confusion of issues are the principal reasons for this rule. See United States v. LeFevour, 798 F.2d 977, 983 (7th Cir.1986)

("To bolster a witness's credibility in advance is improper. It not only has the potential for extending the length of trials enormously, but asks the jury to take the witness's testimony on faith; it may therefore reduce the care with which jurors listen for inconsistencies and other signs of falsehood or inaccuracy.").

Prominent examples of this rule are (1) the prohibition on the admissibility of evidence of a witness' truthful character prior to attack, Rule 608(a), and (2) the prohibition on the admissibility of prior consistent statements prior to attack. See also Rule 801(d)(1)(B) (altering the common law rule to admit as substantive evidence). See Chapter 13, Section B(1), infra.

UNITED STATES v. THORNTON

United States Court of Appeals, Seventh Circuit, 1999.
197 F.3d 241.

Terence T. Evans, Circuit Judge.

Major federal drug cases these days follow a fairly familiar pattern. They are centered in big cities, and they usually involve a wide-ranging drug distribution network that has been operating for several years. The drug of choice is invariably cocaine, often in its most addictive form as crack. * * * The typical case has a dozen or more defendants (many with multiple and often creative nicknames), and other counts in the indictment specifically charge some of them with individual acts of possession of cocaine with intent to distribute at various times and places. * * *

When these cases arrive in court they follow a predictable pattern. Some of the defendants jump ship, make deals with the government, and become principal witnesses against those defendants who do not elect "to cooperate." "Cooperating" defendants usually do not receive a complete pass; instead they are permitted to wrap up their cases on more favorable terms based on their acceptance of responsibility under the federal sentencing guidelines and a motion for a downward departure based on the assistance given to the government. * * *

The facts in this case and the issues raised on appeal are typical of the usual federal drug conspiracy prosecution we have just described. The case involves a 20–count indictment against 14 defendants which grew out of a conspiracy to distribute cocaine in the cities of Indianapolis and Chicago. Today we consider the appeals of three defendants who went to trial and were convicted * * *.

* * *

Third, Harris, Jackson, and Reynolds all fault the trial court for allowing into evidence the government's proffer letters to cooperating witnesses and for not allowing cross-examination of these witnesses to delve into polygraph testing. The admission of proffer letters is an evidentiary decision reviewed for abuse of discretion. United States v. Lewis, 110 F.3d 417, 422 (7th Cir. * * * 1997). * * *

The government introduced into evidence plea agreements for the nine cooperating witnesses, as well as proffer letters for most of those witnesses. Each of the proffer letters makes three references[78] to truthfulness and each of the plea agreements makes five references[79] to truthfulness. Just as defense counsel have every right to attack the credibility of witnesses who get deals, the prosecution is entitled to get into evidence the fact that the deals are conditioned upon truthful testimony. "[O]n direct examination, the prosecutor may elicit testimony regarding the witness' plea agreement and actually introduce the plea agreement into evidence." Lewis, 110 F.3d at 421 (internal quotations and citations omitted). Contrary to the defendants' claims, the admission of these agreements does not constitute government vouching for the credibility of the witnesses. Two types of "vouching" are forbidden: a prosecutor may not express her personal belief in the truthfulness of a witness, and a prosecutor may not imply that facts not before the jury lend a witness credibility. United States v. Renteria, 106 F.3d 765, 767 (7th Cir.1997). Neither sin was committed here. The proffer letters and plea agreements merely laid out the terms and conditions of the agreements. * * * Each side could urge competing inferences—as indeed the defendants' did—but the jury's role as independent fact finder was not undermined. Renteria, 106 F.3d at 767.

The documents in this case closely track the language of the proffer letters and plea agreements that were allowed in Lewis, 110 F.3d at 421. Likewise, the judge's jury instructions here[80] resemble the judge's instructions in that case. Lewis said that the admission of proffer letters and plea agreements was not an attempt to enhance the credibility of the witnesses and that the judge's instructions should have dispelled any

78. The three references to truthful testimony in the proffer letters pertained to the following topics: (1) providing "false" information could result in prosecution for perjury or giving a false statement; (2) the grant of use immunity is conditioned on the indictee's "complete and candid compliance" with the terms of the agreement and any violation could result in prosecution for perjury, false statements, or obstruction of justice; (3) after the indictee provides the proffer the government "will assess the value of the information provided, your honesty, candor and special circumstances."

79. The five references to truthful testimony in the plea agreements pertained to the following topics: (1) the codefendant agreed to provide "complete, total and truthful debriefings" regarding criminal activity to the government; (2) the codefendant agreed to provide "complete, total and truthful" testimony before grand juries and at trials; (3) the government agreed not to bring criminal charges against the codefendant for the "full, complete and truthful information and testimony" the codefendant provided; (4) the government reserved the right to prosecute for perjury or false statements if the codefendant testified "falsely"; (5) breach of the agreement, such as the failure to provide "full, complete and truthful information and testimony," could result in the agreement being withdrawn.

80. The judge told the jury that "[y]ou are the sole judges of the credibility—that is, the believability—of the witnesses." The judge said the jury "should draw no inferences" based on the government's exercise of its discretion to enter into plea bargains and emphasized that "[y]ou may give this testimony such weight as you feel it deserves, keeping in mind that such testimony is always to be received with caution and weighed with great care." The judge noted that "[y]ou have heard testimony from witnesses who received immunity, that is a promise from the government that any testimony or other information he or she provided would not be used against him or her in a criminal case. You may give this testimony such weight as you feel it deserves, keeping in mind that it must be considered with caution and great care."

harmful effects. Id. at 421–22. The same logic applies here, and we reach the same result.

However, some words of wisdom to the wise: This decision should not be read as an enthusiastic endorsement for the admission of all proffer letters and all plea agreements at all times and in all places. We approve the admission in this case in light of the judge's jury instructions and in light of the overwhelming evidence that would render any erroneous admission harmless. But for more than a decade we have been warning prosecutors to "avoid unnecessarily repetitive references to truthfulness if it wishes to introduce the agreements into evidence." Id. at 421; * * *. Three references to truthfulness in the proffer letters and five references in the plea agreements comes perilously close to being unnecessarily repetitive. * * *

The admission of the proffer letters, in particular, strikes us as overkill. The plea agreements' references to truthfulness were repetitive enough—admitting the proffer letters, with their own repetitive references to truthfulness, compounded the problem. The government confidently states that "while the immunity letters and plea agreements contained similar language concerning truthfulness, they were executed at different times and fulfilled distinct purposes." But this does not explain what distinct evidentiary purpose the admission of the proffer letters served at trial. The plea agreements explained the conditions under which the cooperating codefendants were testifying. The proffer letters, which memorialize the framework under which the codefendants agreed to talk in the first place, seem of scant relevance at trial when a subsequent, superseding plea agreement has been reached. * * *

At the defendants' request, the district judge redacted from all of the cooperating witnesses' plea agreements a sentence in which the witness consented to submit to a polygraph examination upon the government's request. (The government never made any requests and none of the cooperating witnesses ever took a polygraph test.) However, proffer letters to two witnesses, Renee Yvette Booker and Valarie Sanders, also mentioned the possibility of a polygraph test. While cross-examining Sanders, Reynolds' counsel exhibited to the jury the proffer letter containing the polygraph test reference. The judge cut off this line of cross-examination. Later, the judge decided to admit into evidence Booker's proffer letter without redacting the polygraph reference. Admitting the polygraph reference was a mistake. Unlike in United States v. Bursten, 560 F.2d 779, 785 (7th Cir.1977), defense counsel were not permitted to cross-examine the witness on this subject. Unlike in Lewis, 110 F.3d at 421 n.2, defense counsel were not responsible for the admission of the polygraph reference as to Booker. However, the judge cured any problem by instructing the jury not to pay attention to whether Booker might have taken a polygraph test.[81] Furthermore, two

81. The judge told the jury: "[O]ne of the things that you may have heard, or picked up somewhere, is that there are references now and again in these proffer agreements, and sometimes even in plea agreements, to lie detector tests. Now, you

passing references to the possibility of polygraph tests for two witnesses was harmless in a jury trial that lasted 19 days, involved 60 witnesses and contained strong evidence of the defendants' guilt.

On a related note, the defendants claim their Sixth Amendment right to confrontation was violated because the district judge prohibited them from bringing out in cross-examination the fact that none of the government's witnesses took lie detector tests. Since the polygraph test statement in Booker's proffer letter was admitted, defense counsel should have been permitted to cross-examine her on this subject. * * *

* * *

For these reasons, the judgments of conviction of Harris, Jackson and Reynolds—as well as of Thornton—are affirmed.

Notes and Questions

1. *The issue.* What is the problem with introducing the plea agreements and proffer letters during the direct examination if they could be introduced after the witnesses have been impeached for bias on cross-examination?

2. *Permissive approach.* In United States v. Spriggs, 996 F.2d 320, 323 (D.C.Cir.1993), the D.C. Circuit explained:

> We think the majority position is the better reasoned. Simply put, we are not persuaded that evidence of the contents of a cooperation agreement unduly bolsters the credibility of a Government witness. First, insofar as the agreement provides that if the witness lies the agreement is revocable, that the witness is liable to prosecution for perjury, and that his perjurious testimony may be used against him, it adds nothing to the law—as the defense is free to bring out upon cross-examination. Therefore, the agreement provides no special incentive for the Government witness to testify truthfully; hence, the jury is not likely to place special credence in the witness merely because of the terms of the agreement. Furthermore, that the Government may (obviously) impose a sanction upon the witness if he lies does nothing to enhance the Government's ability to detect whether he is in fact lying; again the terms of the cooperation agreement should do nothing to enhance the witness's credibility. Finally, at least in the present case there is nothing in the agreement or in the prosecutor's direct examination on that subject to "imply that the government had special knowledge" of the witness's veracity.

3. *Restrictive approach.* In United States v. Cosentino, 844 F.2d 30, 33–34 (2d Cir.1988), the Second Circuit wrote:

> Because of the bolstering potential of cooperation agreements, however, we have permitted such agreements to be admitted in their

are not to draw any inference from that as to whether a particular individual either took or didn't take a lie detector test or passed or didn't pass a lie detector test. Everybody understand that? No speculation about that, no inferences to be drawn from that."

entirety only after the credibility of the witness has been attacked. This restriction proceeds from our view that "the *entire* cooperation agreement bolsters more than it impeaches." Thus, although the prosecutor may inquire into impeaching aspects of cooperation agreements on direct, bolstering aspects such as promises to testify truthfully or penalties for failure to do so may only be developed to rehabilitate the witness after a defense attack on credibility. Such an attack may come in a defendant's opening statement. If the opening sufficiently implicates the credibility of a government witness, we have held that testimonial evidence of bolstering aspects of a cooperation agreement may be introduced for rehabilitative purposes during direct examination. (Citations omitted.)

4. *Plea reduction motions.* In United States v. Harlow, 444 F.3d 1255, 1263 (10th Cir.2006), the prosecution introduced Criminal Rule 35(b) motions and sentence reduction orders in addition to the plea agreement. The court reversed: "[One] provision [of the agreement] coupled with the introduction of the government's Rule 35(b) motion implies that the government has verified the truthfulness of the witness and believes that his ongoing testimony is truthful, which is why it made a motion for a sentence reduction. The jury could reasonably infer that the government would not have recommended such a downward departure if it had not independently verified the truthfulness of the testimony. * * * [These documents] amount[ ] to prosecutorial vouching. Section 13 only compounds the matter. Not only does it reiterate the role of the government in recommending sentence reductions for truthful testimony, it also implicates the judge in the verification process."

5. *Polygraph evidence.* A majority of states still follow the traditional rule, holding polygraph evidence per se inadmissible. This exclusionary rule extends to evidence that a person was willing to take, took, or refused to take an examination. A substantial minority of jurisdictions admit polygraph results upon stipulation. A third group leaves the admissibility issue to the trial judge. At one time most federal circuit courts followed the per se approach. However, the *Daubert* decision changed this result. See United States v. Posado, 57 F.3d 428, 429 (5th Cir.1995) ("[T]he rationale underlying this circuit's per se rule against admitting polygraph evidence did not survive *Daubert* * * *."). Most federal courts, however, have exercised their discretion to exclude polygraph evidence. See 1 Giannelli & Imwinkelried, Scientific Evidence ch. 8 (3d ed. 1999) (polygraph evidence).

6. *Fresh complaint.* Many jurisdictions recognize an exception to the rule against bolstering in rape cases, where evidence of an alleged victim's "fresh complaint" is admissible to corroborate or bolster her testimony. See State v. Rolon, 777 A.2d 604, 625 (Conn.2001) ("The constancy of accusation doctrine is well established in Connecticut and recently has been reaffirmed by this court. * * * [W]e restricted the doctrine so that a constancy of accusation witness could testify only to the fact and the timing of the victim's complaint. Even so limited, the evidence would be admissible solely for corroboration of the victim's testimony, and not for substantive purposes."). In Commonwealth v. King, 834 N.E.2d 1175, 1197 (Mass.2005), the court changed the rule from the "fresh complaint" to the "first complaint"

rule. Why? See generally Stanchi, The Paradox of the Fresh Complaint Rule, 37 B.C.L.Rev. 441 (1996).

7. *Pretrial identifications*. Another exception to the rule against bolstering involved testimony concerning a pretrial identification (e.g., lineup, showup, or photographic display) once an in-court identification had been made. See also Rule 801(d)(1)(C) (altering the common law rule to admit as substantive evidence). See Chapter 13, Section B(1), infra.

(2) IMPEACHMENT: WHO MAY IMPEACH[82]

STATE v. GREEN

Supreme Court of Washington, 1967.
428 P.2d 540.

[Defendant was charged with burglary after having been apprehended by police officers while fleeing from the scene of the crime. Defendant contended that the burglary had been undertaken by two companions of defendant's, Gaither and Wilkerson, while defendant, ignorant of the others' purpose, waited in a car. He further asserted that he subsequently left the car and was protesting against his friends' activities when the police arrived. Defendant was convicted by a jury and appealed.]

HALE, JUDGE.

* * *

Defendant claims reversible error when the prosecution impeached state's witness Gaither, an admitted participant in the burglary. It came about in this way: Charles Gaither, called by the state in its case in chief, testified at the outset that he had participated in the Medical Center Pharmacy burglary on the night of March 10th; then he testified:

Q. All right. I will ask you whether or not the Defendant Nathaniel Leon Green participated with you and aided you in the commission of that burglary? A. No.

He repeated this negative answer after a lengthy colloquy in the jury's absence, and the state, claiming that Gaither had made earlier statements inconsistent with the exonerating testimony, sought to impeach him.

The prosecuting attorney had not interviewed Gaither before trial, nor otherwise ascertained if he intended to contradict the statement. On receiving from the state's witness the exculpatory answer that the defendant was innocent, the state claimed surprise and unexpected hostility from the witness, and laid a foundation for impeachment by establishing that the witness had earlier made a written statement

82. Remember that in the majority of American jurisdictions, cross-examination is limited to the subject matter of the direct. All jurisdictions permit cross-examination on matters of impeachment regardless of the scope of the direct examination. Review the materials in Chapter 6, Order of Proof, particularly *Atkinson v. Smith*, *Boller v. Cofrances*, and *United States v. Lara*, supra.

describing the crime and incriminating defendant as an accomplice. When shown this confession on the stand, Gaither denied that the written statement referred to the defendant, Nathaniel Leon Green, asserting that it referred to another man variously mentioned in the statement as Green, Nathaniel, or Nat.

Having thus laid a proper predicate for impeachment by first showing that Gaither denied having incriminated defendant in his confession and meant a different person, the state then impeached the witness through the testimony of a police officer who testified that, throughout the entire statement-taking process, both orally and when reducing it to writing, the witness, in referring to a Nat, Nathaniel or Green at all times identified and referred to the defendant, Nathaniel Leon Green * * *.

* * * [T]he assignment of error focuses directly on the questions of surprise and hostility. Could the prosecuting attorney legitimately claim surprise when he had not interviewed Gaither, nor otherwise made inquiries as to whether he would adhere to his statement concerning the defendant?

* * *

One of the basic obligations resting on everyone living under the protection of our constitutions is that, when called upon to give evidence in court he will, without reservation, speak the truth; that he will not avoid or evade this duty through fear, malice, or hope or promise of reward. The court and every party to a judicial proceedings—indeed, society itself—has a right to assume that the duty to give truthful evidence will be discharged and it need not be anticipated that that duty will be betrayed. Thus, the law—with several notable exceptions, of course—assumes that a party calling one as a witness not only believes the witness to be truthful, but represents him to be truthful. One is thus held to vouch for the credibility of the witnesses he presents. Having called the witness to testify and thereby vouching for his truthfulness—although he may present other evidence of a contradictory nature through other witnesses—a party may not impeach his own witness unless without warning the witness tells a story different than the one the party calling him had a reasonable right to expect of him.

But what if the party's faith in his witness is betrayed?

The law has a protective device for this betrayal through a corollary rule which allows a party to impeach his own witness in event of genuine surprise and hostility. Both the rule as to credibility and impeachment are essential to elicit the truth. If one were not held to vouch for the credibility of witnesses called by him, he could present one lying witness after another in the hope of establishing facts favorable to his cause. Contrarily, if there were no exception or corollary to this rule, a party to a judicial proceedings would be left in a position of hopeless betrayal by a witness upon whom he had good reason to rely and for whose credibility he had vouched.

At the time the state called Gaither, the prosecuting attorney had in hand a detailed statement of the crime signed by Gaither and describing defendant as one of two accomplices. Made by the witness without duress, coercion or fear, the statement recited at firsthand Gaither's and his accomplices' step-by-step participation in the burglary, and corroborated in detail the mass of other evidence which the prosecuting attorney intended to offer in the state's case in chief. Gaither had never, to the prosecuting attorney's knowledge, repudiated the statement nor had he ever intimated to the prosecuting attorney at any time before being put on the witness stand that he intended to do so.

* * *

Gaither's acknowledged guilt did not absolve him from his duty to give truthful evidence. * * * The prosecution had a right to undo this damage by attempting to impeach the witness and thus cancel the effect of this surprisingly hostile testimony. The court properly allowed the impeachment.

* * *

Affirmed.

Notes and Questions

1. *Voucher rule.* The two most commonly cited bases for the rule against impeaching one's own witness are (a) the "vouching" theory expounded in the principal case, and (b) the contention that a party "should not have the power to coerce his own witness." Does either of these theories have modern validity?

2. *Bound by testimony.* Another aspect of the voucher rule concerned whether a party was bound by the testimony of its own witnesses. For example, in Becker v. Eisenstodt, 158 A.2d 706, 708 (N.J.Super.Ct.App.Div.1960), a malpractice case, the plaintiff called the defendant-doctor in its case-in-chief and asked him the following questions:

> "Q. Doctor, on December 27, 1957, when Arlene Becker came to your office, you inserted into her nose, the right nostril of her nose, a pledget or a piece of cotton saturated with a ten percent solution of cocaine? A. That's right, sir.
>
> "Q. And nothing else? A. That's right."

There was no cross-examination. On appeal, the defendant stressed the fact that plaintiff called defendant as his own witness, and argued that he was therefore bound by his testimony. The appellate court disagreed, writing

> Such a rule, so broadly stated, ill serves the cause of justice. It is a relic of the earliest system of trial, where those who attended on behalf of the parties were not witnesses, as we understand the word, but "oath-helpers," whose mere oath, when taken by the prescribed number of persons and in the proper form, determined the issue. Ordinarily, these persons were relatives and adherents of either party, clearly partisan. As Wigmore observes, so long as this traditional notion of a witness

persisted, it was inconceivable that a party should gainsay his own witness. If a witness failed to swear for him, it was his loss—he should have chosen a better person for his purpose. Accordingly, a party was not allowed to dispute what his witness said. This "primitive" concept of the role of witnesses persisted long after the time when their function had ceased to be that of mere oath-taker and had become that of a testifier to the facts. 3 Wigmore on Evidence (3d ed. 1940), § 896, p. 383.

3. *Exception: Surprise.* The exception to the voucher rule where the calling party is "surprised" by the witness' testimony has received varying interpretations by the courts. May surprise within the meaning of the exception exist if the calling party, in possession of a prior statement of the witness, receives notice that the witness does not intend to testify in accord with the statement? Compare Hooks v. United States, 375 F.2d 212 (5th Cir.1967), with Wheeler v. United States, 211 F.2d 19 (D.C.Cir.1953).

4. *Exception: Affirmative damage.* Should more than surprise, however defined, be required? For example, in the principal case would impeachment of the witness Gaither by the state have been allowed if Gaither had testified that he did not recall what the defendant's activities had been while the robbery was in progress? See United States v. Coppola, 479 F.2d 1153 (10th Cir.1973) (surprise not lacking simply by virtue of prior notice of changed story, but impeachment not allowable where calling party's case not affirmatively damaged); Commonwealth v. Strunk, 293 S.W.2d 629, 630 (Ky.1956) (damage defined as "where the witness testifies positively to the existence of a fact prejudicial to the party, or to a fact clearly favorable to the adverse party").

5. *Exception: Court witnesses.* An alternative escape from the common law voucher rule is potentially afforded by the power of the trial court to call its own witnesses. 3A Wigmore, Evidence § 918 (Chadbourn rev. 1970). The witness is not then in theory that of either party. The utility of this escape has been considerably limited by appellate reminders that the trial courts should use the power sparingly, although United States v. Karnes, 531 F.2d 214 (4th Cir.1976), seems to stand alone in holding that the calling by the judge of two essential prosecution witnesses was a denial of due process.

6. *Due process.* In Chambers v. Mississippi, 410 U.S. 284 (1973), the defendant sought in vain to have the court call a witness who had repeatedly confessed out of court to the murder with which defendant was charged. The Supreme Court reversed, concluding that the combined effect of Mississippi's voucher rule and its hearsay rule served to deny petitioner due process of law.

7. *New approach.* The law in Washington has now moved away from the traditional common law view illustrated in the principal case by the adoption of that state's Rule 607, based upon Federal Rule 607, which abolishes the voucher rule. See State v. Lavaris, 721 P.2d 515 (Wash.1986).

UNITED STATES v. WEBSTER

United States Court of Appeals, Seventh Circuit, 1984.
734 F.2d 1191.

POSNER, CIRCUIT JUDGE.

The defendant, Webster, was convicted of aiding and abetting the robbery of a federally insured bank and receiving stolen bank funds, was sentenced to nine years in prison, and appeals. Only one issue need be discussed. The government called the bank robber, King (who had pleaded guilty and been given a long prison term), as a witness against Webster. King gave testimony that if believed would have exculpated the defendant, whereupon the government introduced prior inconsistent statements that King had given the FBI inculpating Webster. Although the court instructed the jury that it could consider the statements only for purposes of impeachment, Webster argues that this was not good enough, that the government should not be allowed to get inadmissible evidence before the jury by calling a hostile witness and then using his out-of-court statements, which would otherwise be inadmissible hearsay, to impeach him.

Rule 607 of the Federal Rules of Evidence provides: "The credibility of a witness may be attacked by any party, including the party calling him." But it would be an abuse of the rule, in a criminal case, for the prosecution to call a witness that it knew would not give it useful evidence, just so it could introduce hearsay evidence against the defendant in the hope that the jury would miss the subtle distinction between impeachment and substantive evidence—or, if it didn't miss it, would ignore it. The purpose would not be to impeach the witness but to put in hearsay as substantive evidence against the defendant, which Rule 607 does not contemplate or authorize. We thus agree that "impeachment by prior inconsistent statement may not be permitted where employed as a mere subterfuge to get before the jury evidence not otherwise admissible." *United States v. Morlang,* 531 F.2d 183, 190 (4th Cir.1975). Although *Morlang* was decided before the Federal Rules of Evidence became effective, the limitation that we have quoted on the prosecutor's rights under Rule 607 has been accepted in all circuits that have considered the issue. * * *

But it is quite plain that there was no bad faith here. Before the prosecutor called King to the stand she asked the judge to allow her to examine him outside the presence of the jury, because she didn't know what he would say. The defendant's counsel objected and the voir dire was not held. We do not see how in these circumstances it can be thought that the prosecutor put King on the stand knowing he would give no useful evidence. If she had known that, she would not have offered to voir dire him, as the voir dire would have provided a foundation for defense counsel to object, under *Morlang,* to the admission of King's prior inconsistent statements.

Webster urges us, on the authority of Graham, Handbook of Federal Evidence § 607.3 (1981 and Supp.1983), to go beyond the good-faith standard and hold that the government may not impeach a witness with his prior inconsistent statements unless it is surprised and harmed by the witness's testimony. But we think it would be a mistake to graft such a requirement to Rule 607, even if such a graft would be within the power of judicial interpretation of the rule. Suppose the government called an adverse witness that it thought would give evidence both helpful and harmful to it, but it also thought that the harmful aspect could be nullified by introducing the witness's prior inconsistent statement. As there would be no element of surprise, Professor Graham would forbid the introduction of the prior statements; yet we are at a loss to understand why the government should be put to the choice between the Scylla of forgoing impeachment and the Charybdis of not calling at all a witness from whom it expects to elicit genuinely helpful evidence. The good-faith standard strikes a better balance; and it is always open to the defendant to argue that the probative value of the evidence offered to impeach the witness is clearly outweighed by the prejudicial impact it might have on the jury, because the jury would have difficulty confining use of the evidence to impeachment. See Fed.R.Evid. 403.

The judgment of conviction is

Affirmed.

Notes and Questions

1. *Criticism.* The approach rejected in the *Webster* case is set forth in 2 Graham, Handbook of Federal Evidence § 607.3 (6th ed. 2006). Graham notes that under Federal Rule 801(d)(1)(A), statements made by a person testifying as a witness, which are inconsistent with his testimony at trial and which were given under oath, subject to the penalty of perjury, at a trial, hearing, or other proceeding or in a deposition, are admissible as nonhearsay. He argues that it was the congressional intent to have such statements admitted without satisfying the common law tests of surprise and affirmative harm, but that there was no such intent with regard to prior statements not falling within Rule 801(d)(1)(A). Graham adds:

> * * * If the witness does not give affirmatively damaging testimony, i.e., testimony of positive aid to the adversary, the party simply does not need to attack his credibility. If the witness' testimony does not surprise the party, the litigant should not be permitted to impeach his testimony by placing before the jury the witness' prior statement because he could have refrained from eliciting the statement he seeks to impeach. The requirement of surprise would prevent the party from consciously introducing affirmatively damaging testimony under the only circumstances in which he would do so—when the potential effect on the jury of the prior inconsistent statement outweighs the affirmatively damaging effect of the elicited testimony. (Id. at 462)

Graham responds to the rejection of his position in the *Webster* case as follows:

> Judge Posner misses a very simple point. The government is not put to the choice he presents. It may elicit the helpful testimony without eliciting the known harmful testimony as well. If the defendant chooses to elicit the harmful testimony, the government can impeach with the prior inconsistent statement. If the defendant does not elicit such testimony, the prior inconsistent statement will never be presented to the jury. The only reason the government has to elicit the harmful testimony in the first instance is its belief that the effect of impeachment will more than nullify the harmful effect. (Id. at 468 n.17)

Who is right, Professor Graham or Judge Posner? Irrespective of the wisdom or lack of wisdom of Graham's position, he himself recognizes that the federal courts have interpreted Rule 607 literally and have not grafted on a surprise and affirmative harm limitation. But see Ohio R. Evid. 607(A) (requiring surprise and affirmative damage when a party impeaches its own witness with a prior inconsistent statement).

2. *Balancing.* The court in the principal case recognizes the rule that the prosecution may not call a witness for the primary purpose of using an inconsistent statement to impeach that witness' credibility. However, despite frequent statements of agreement with this rule, invocation of the rule has seldom resulted in a reversal. See, e.g., United States v. Crouch, 731 F.2d 621 (9th Cir.1984) (harmless error); United States v. Hogan, 763 F.2d 697 (5th Cir.1985) (witness not called as a subterfuge); State v. Lavaris, 721 P.2d 515 (Wash.1986) (same). But see United States v. Logan, 121 F.3d 1172, 1175–76 (8th Cir.1997) ("Although some courts focus on determining the 'true' purpose of the government in introducing testimony, we think that the relevant question is simply whether the evidence is admissible under Fed. R. Ev. 403. * * * Our assessment of the prior statements as creating a danger of unfair prejudice and jury confusion is reinforced by the fact that the government elicited, through the state police officer's testimony, additional inculpatory statements that Ms. Carlen allegedly made to the officer. * * * The only possible relevance that testimony could have had was as substantive evidence, yet it was clearly hearsay for those purposes. See Fed. R. Ev. 801(c). It was therefore manifestly inadmissible.").

(3) IMPEACHMENT: BIAS

ALFORD v. UNITED STATES

Supreme Court of the United States, 1931.
282 U.S. 687.

MR. JUSTICE STONE delivered the opinion of the Court. Petitioner was convicted in the District Court for southern California of using the mails to defraud in violation of section 215 of the Criminal Code (18 U.S.C.A. § 338). * * *

In the course of the trial the government called as a witness a former employee of petitioner. On direct examination he gave damaging testimony with respect to various transactions of accused, including conversations with the witness when others were not present, and statements of accused to salesmen under his direction, whom the witness did not identify. Upon cross-examination questions seeking to elicit the witness's place of residence were excluded on the government's objection that they were immaterial and not proper cross-examination. Counsel for the defense insisted that the questions were proper cross-examination, and that the jury was entitled to know "who the witness is, where he lives and what his business is." Relevant excerpts of the record are printed in the margin.[83]

Later, the jury having been excused, counsel for the defense urged, as an "additional" ground for asking the excluded questions, that he had been informed that the witness was then in the custody of the federal authorities, and that such fact might be brought out on cross-examination "for the purpose of showing whatever bias or prejudice he may have." But the court adhered to its previous rulings, saying that if the witness had been convicted of a felony that fact might be proved, but not that he was detained in custody.

* * *

Cross-examination of a witness is a matter of right. * * * Its permissible purposes, among others, are that the witness may be identified with his community so that independent testimony may be sought

83. Q. Where do you live, Mr. Bradley?

Mr. Armstrong: That is objected to as immaterial and not proper cross-examination.

The Court: I cannot see the materiality.

Mr. Friedman: Why, I think the jury has a perfect right to know who the witness is, where he lives and what his business is, and we have the right to elicit that on cross-examination. I may say that this is the first witness the Government had called that they have not elicited the address from.

The Court: I will sustain the objection.

Q. By Mr. Friedman: What is your business, Mr. Bradley? A. My profession is an accountant, public accountant.

Q. What is your occupation now? A. I am not doing anything at the present time on account of this case.

Q. On account of this case? A. Yes.

Q. Do you live in Los Angeles?

Mr. Armstrong: That is objected to as immaterial and invading the Court's ruling.

The Court: I have ruled on that question.

Mr. Friedman: I will temporarily pass on to something else. I would like leave to submit authorities on my right to develop that on cross-examination. I haven't them with me.

The Court: All right. * * *

The jury were thereupon excused by the court until 9:30 o'clock on the morning of July 24, 1929, whereupon the jury retired after which the following proceedings were had relative to the materiality of the testimony, as to the residence and place thereof of Cameron Bradley.

The Court: So ordered. In what particular do you think that evidence is material?

Mr. Friedman: I think it is material for this purpose, first, not only on the general grounds I urged in asking the question, but on the additional grounds that I have been informed and caused to believe that this witness himself is now in the custody of the Federal authorities.

Mr. Armstrong: You mean Mr. Bradley? You mean by the Federal authorities here?

Mr. Friedman: I don't know by what authorities, but that is my impression, that he is here in the custody of the Federal authorities. If that is so, I have a right to show that for the purpose of showing whatever bias or prejudice he may have.

The Court: No; I don't think so. If you can prove he has ever been convicted of a felony, that is a different thing.

Mr. Friedman: I realize that is the rule. I may impeach him if he has been convicted of a felony.

The Court: No. You may prove that fact as going to his credibility, but you can't merely show that he is detained or in charge of somebody. Everybody is presumed to be innocent until proven guilty. * * *

and offered of his reputation for veracity in his own neighborhood * * * ; that the jury may interpret his testimony in the light, reflected upon it by knowledge of his environment * * * ; and that facts may be brought out tending to discredit the witness by showing that his testimony in chief was untrue or biased * * *.

Counsel often cannot know in advance what pertinent facts may be elicited on cross-examination. For that reason it is necessarily exploratory; and the rule that the examiner must indicate the purpose of his inquiry does not, in general, apply. * * * It is the essence of a fair trial that reasonable latitude be given the cross-examiner, even though he is unable to state to the court what facts a reasonable cross-examination might develop. Prejudice ensues from a denial of the opportunity to place the witness in his proper setting and put the weight of his testimony and his credibility to a test, without which the jury cannot fairly appraise them. * * * To say that prejudice can be established only by showing that the cross-examination, if pursued, would necessarily have brought out facts tending to discredit the testimony in chief, is to deny a substantial right and withdraw one of the safeguards essential to a fair trial. ** * In this respect a summary denial of the right of cross-examination is distinguishable from the erroneous admission of harmless testimony. * * *

The present case, after the witness for the prosecution had testified to uncorroborated conversations of the defendant of a damaging character, was a proper one for searching cross-examination. The question, "Where do you live?" was not only an appropriate preliminary to the cross-examination of the witness, but on its face, without any such declaration of purpose as was made by counsel here, was an essential step in identifying the witness with his environment, to which cross-examination may always be directed. * * *

But counsel for the defense went further, and in the ensuing colloquy with the court urged, as an additional reason why the question should be allowed, not a substitute reason, as the court below assumed, that he was informed that the witness was then in court in custody of the federal authorities, and that that fact could be brought out on cross-examination to show whatever bias or prejudice the witness might have. The purpose obviously was not, as the trial court seemed to think, to discredit the witness by showing that he was charged with crime, but to show by such facts as proper cross-examination might develop, that his testimony was biased because given under promise or expectation of immunity, or under the coercive effect of his detention by officers of the United States, which was conducting the present prosecution. * * * Nor is it material, as the Court of Appeals said, whether the witness was in custody because of his participation in the transactions for which petitioner was indicted. Even if the witness were charged with some other offense by the prosecuting authorities, petitioner was entitled to show by cross-examination that his testimony was affected by fear or favor growing out of his detention. * * *

The extent of cross-examination with respect to an appropriate subject of inquiry is within the sound discretion of the trial court. It may exercise a reasonable judgment in determining when the subject is exhausted. * * * But no obligation is imposed on the court, such as that suggested below, to protect a witness from being discredited on cross-examination, short of an attempted invasion of his constitutional protection from self incrimination, properly invoked. There is a duty to protect him from questions which go beyond the bonds of proper cross-examination merely to harass, annoy, or humiliate him. * * * But no such case is presented here. The trial court cut off in limine all inquiry on a subject with respect to which the defense was entitled to a reasonable cross-examination. This was an abuse of discretion and prejudicial error. * * *

Reversed.

Notes and Questions

1. *Federal rule.* There is no federal rule on bias impeachment, although other rules refer to it. See Rule 411 (evidence of liability insurance inadmissible except if offered for another purpose such as "bias or prejudice"); Rule 801(d)(1)(B) (prior consistent statements admissible if "offered to rebut an express or implied charge against the declarant of recent fabrication or improper influence or motive"); Fed.R.Evid. 608(a) advisory committee's note ("corruption"). Should there be a federal rule? Other jurisdictions have such a rule. See Unif.R.Evid. 616 (rev. 1999); Haw.R.Evid. 609.1; Ohio R.Evid. 616(A); Utah R.Evid. 608(c); Mil.R.Evid. 608(c).

In United States v. Abel, 469 U.S. 45, 52 (1984), the Supreme Court held that the prosecution had properly been permitted to show that the defendant and a defense witness were both members of a secret prison organization whose members would lie, cheat, steal, and kill to protect each other. A full description of the organization was held to be justified as showing the source and strength of the witness' bias. The Court also stated that "proof of bias is almost always relevant because the jury, as finder of fact and weigher of credibility, has historically been entitled to assess all evidence which might bear on the accuracy and truth of a witness' testimony."

2. *Types of bias.* Other terms for bias are interest, partiality, and corruption. Facts which will suggest bias or interest on the part of a witness are so various as to defy cataloging. For illustrative listings see 3A Wigmore, Evidence §§ 948–969 (Chadbourn rev. 1970). See also *Abel*, note 1, supra, 469 U.S. at 52 ("Bias may be induced by a witness' like, dislike, or fear of a party, or by the witness' self-interest."); United States v. Keys, 899 F.2d 983, 987 (10th Cir.1990) ("Keys' statement that he controlled sixty soldiers in the prison system who would do him favors, including breaking the law, is relevant to show that Kinnison's and Ward's testimony might have been influenced by their fear of Keys and his gang.").

3. *Extrinsic evidence.* As held in the *Abel* case, note 1, supra, the courts have admitted extrinsic evidence (e.g., other witnesses) of bias as "noncollateral." 469 U.S. at 52 ("The 'common law of evidence' allowed the showing of bias by extrinsic evidence."). Does Rule 403 now replace the common law?

4. *Foundation requirement.* Must a foundation for such evidence be laid by asking the witness about his bias on cross-examination? Apparently a majority of the courts say yes. See 1 McCormick, Evidence § 39 (6th ed. 2006). Is such an inquiry necessary under the Federal Rules? See United States v. Betts, 16 F.3d 748, 764 (7th Cir.1994) ("[T]he weight of authority supports the proposition that when a party seeks to prove bias through extrinsic evidence of a witness' prior statement, he must first give the witness the opportunity to explain or deny that statement, even though Rule 613(b) is not strictly applicable."). Rule 613 governs prior inconsistent statements.

5. *Right of confrontation.* The necessity of allowing reasonable scope for exercise of the right of cross-examination is constantly emphasized in the decisions. See Douglas v. Alabama, 380 U.S. 415, 418 (1965) ("Our cases construing the confrontation clause hold that a primary interest secured by it is the right of cross-examination.").

In Davis v. Alaska, 415 U.S. 308, 320 (1974), a defendant was prohibited from cross-examining a prosecution witness concerning that witness' status as a juvenile probationer. This curtailment of cross-examination was based on a state statute designed to protect the confidentiality of juvenile adjudications. The Supreme Court reversed: "The State's policy interest in protecting the confidentiality of a juvenile offender's record cannot require yielding of so vital a constitutional right as the effective cross-examination for bias of an adverse witness."

The Supreme Court, however, has recognized some limitations on the right of cross-examination: "It does not follow, of course, that the Confrontation Clause of the Sixth Amendment prevents a trial judge from imposing any limits on defense counsel's inquiry into the potential bias of a prosecution witness. On the contrary, trial judges retain wide latitude insofar as the Confrontation Clause is concerned to impose reasonable limits on such cross-examination based on concerns about, among other things, harassment, prejudice, confusion of the issues, the witness' safety, or interrogation that is repetitive or only marginally relevant." Delaware v. Van Arsdall, 475 U.S. 673, 679 (1986).

6. *Other causes for deprivation of right to cross-examine.* Loss of the opportunity to cross-examine can stem from causes other than judicial action. Occasionally a witness will die or become physically incapacitated during the interval between direct and cross-examination. See Best v. Tavenner, 218 P.2d 471 (Or.1950); State v. Bigham, 131 S.E. 603 (S.C.1926); Note, 11 Okla.L.Rev. 452 (1958). More commonly, a claim of privilege by the witness during cross-examination precludes inquiry into otherwise appropriate matters. Although the matter has been said to be in the discretion of the trial judge, see United States v. Stubbert, 655 F.2d 453 (1st Cir.1981), the direct testimony of the witness may be stricken at least where the claim of privilege is shown to be unfounded. See Klein v. Harris, 667 F.2d 274 (2d Cir.1981). What if the privilege claim is valid? See United States v. Cardillo, 316 F.2d 606 (2d Cir.1963). Under what circumstances should the direct examination be stricken? See 1 McCormick, Evidence § 19 (6th ed. 2006).

7. *Harassment.* In accord with the principal case, it is commonly said that cross-examination cannot be used merely to humiliate, annoy, or

disgrace the witness. See Rule 611(a). Would it be proper to inquire of a witness whether he had had an illicit relationship with one of the parties? See Annot., 25 A.L.R.3d 537. To go further and ask whether the witness was married at the time? See Ryan v. McEvoy, 315 N.E.2d 38 (Ill.App.Ct.1974). Would your answer to the first question be different if the relationship was homosexual? See Salgado v. United States, 278 F.2d 830 (1st Cir.1960).

8. *Broken witnesses?* In the popular lay view, effective cross-examination is equated with a broken witness crying *mea culpa* from the stand, or at the very least with the exposure by the cross-examiner of some powerful motive for prevarication on the part of the witness. Compare the following comments of one noted cross-examiner:

> No cause reaches the stage of litigation unless there are two sides to it. If the witnesses on one side deny or qualify the statements made by those on the other, which side is telling the truth? Not necessarily which side is offering perjured testimony,—there is far less intentional perjury in the courts than the inexperienced would believe. But which side is honestly mistaken,—for, on the other hand, evidence itself is far less trustworthy than the public usually realizes. The opinions of which side are warped by prejudice or blinded by ignorance? Which side has had the power or opportunity of correct observation? How shall we tell, how make it apparent to a jury of disinterested men who are to decide between the litigants? Obviously, by the means of cross-examination.

Wellman, The Art of Cross–Examination 27 (1st Collier ed. 1962). What potentially fruitful lines of cross-examination, other than inquiry into possible bias and interest, do Mr. Wellman's observations suggest? See generally Lezak, Some Psychological Limitations on Witness Reliability, 20 Wayne L.Rev. 117 (1973).

EDE v. ATRIUM SOUTH OB–GYN, INC.

Supreme Court of Ohio, 1994.
642 N.E.2d 365.

PFEIFER, JUSTICE.

This is a medical malpractice/wrongful death action brought by the plaintiff-appellant, Charles Ede, as administrator of the estate of his wife, Sheri Ede, who died on August 28, 1989. The defendants-appellees are George R. Dakoske, M.D., and the corporation of which he is the president, Atrium South OB–GYN, Inc. Dr. Dakoske performed surgery on Sheri Ede on August 24, 1989. Sheri had been scheduled to undergo an abdominal hysterectomy, but during that procedure Dakoske discovered a cancerous tumor on Sheri's right ovary which required further surgery. Sheri died four days later. Appellant alleges that Dakoske's negligent post-operative care caused Sheri's death. [Dr. Schneider testified on behalf of Dr. Dakoske.]

* * *

* * * The trial court in this case pointed to Evid.R. 403 in determining that the issue of the commonality of interests between Drs. Dakoske

and Schneider could not be demonstrated through evidence of a common insurance carrier. The trial court ruled that the danger of prejudice outweighed the probative value of such testimony. We find that determination to be unreasonable, and therefore reversible error, for two reasons.

First, the trial court did not appreciate the probative value of establishing that Dakoske and Schneider were both insured by PIE [Physicians' Mutual Insurance Company.]. The trial court focused its inquiry on only one thing—whether a doctor's premiums could be raised by PIE if the doctor refused to testify on behalf of another PIE-insured doctor. Thus, the trial court sought to determine whether PIE coerced Schneider's testimony, but did not seem to consider Schneider's personal bias resulting from his insurance relationship. Satisfied by Dakoske's attorney's assurance that Schneider was not being coerced by PIE, the trial court failed to consider other possible biases created by Schneider's relationship with PIE. The trial court was not responsive to appellant's argument that as a fractional part-owner of PIE, Schneider's own premiums might fluctuate due to the result of the case. Such testimony would have been probative of bias.

Second, the trial court erred by grossly overestimating to what extent testimony that Dakoske was insured would prejudice the jury. The second sentence of Evid.R. 411 exists for a reason—it recognizes that testimony regarding insurance is not always prejudicial. However, too often courts have a Pavlovian response to insurance testimony—immediately assuming prejudice. It is naive to believe that today's jurors, bombarded for years with information about health care insurance, do not already assume in a malpractice case that the defendant doctor is covered by insurance. The legal charade protecting juries from information they already know keeps hidden from them relevant information that could assist them in making their determinations. Our Rules of Evidence are designed with truth and fairness in mind; they do not require that courts should be blind to reality.

* * *

Given the sophistication of our juries, the first sentence of Evid.R. 411 ("[e]vidence that a person was or was not insured against liability is not admissible upon the issue [of] whether he acted negligently or otherwise wrongfully") does not merit the enhanced importance it has been given. Instead of juries knowing the truth about the existence and extent of coverage, they are forced to make assumptions which may have more prejudicial effect than the truth.

Thus, the second sentence of Evid.R. 411, which allows courts to operate in a world free from truth-stifling legal fictions, ought to be embraced. In such instances as the case at hand, truth should win out over a naively inspired fear of prejudice.

Therefore, we hold that in a medical malpractice action, evidence of a commonality of insurance interests between a defendant and an expert witness is sufficiently probative of the expert's bias as to clearly outweigh any potential prejudice evidence of insurance might cause. Thus, in the present case, the trial court acted unreasonably in excluding evidence regarding the commonality of insurance interests of Drs. Dakoske and Schneider. * * *

Judgment reversed and cause remanded.

Notes and Questions

1. *Other cases on insurance.* See Bernal v. Lindholm, 727 N.E.2d 145, 172 (Ohio Ct.App.1999) ("We find that *Ede* is distinguishable from the case at hand because, in that case, the expert was insured by the same company as the doctor for whom he was testifying. Additionally, in *Ede*, the doctors participated in a mutual insurance company. Hence, because the expert and the defendant doctor for whom he was testifying shared in a common pool of liability loss, the expert stood to suffer an economic loss should the defendant doctor lose at trial. In this case, however, there is no evidence that Dr. Kunin shared a commonality of interest with any appellee with respect to insurance or otherwise."). See also Vasquez v. Rocco, 836 A.2d 1158, 1163–64 (Conn.2003) ("The majority of courts that have addressed this issue apply a 'substantial connection' test to determine whether evidence of an expert witness' relationship to the defendant's insurer is more probative of potential bias than it is prejudicial.").

2. *Expert compensation.* It may be assumed that the majority of experts appearing as witnesses in litigation today will receive compensation from the party calling them in addition to the statutory witness fee. Ford & Holmes, Exposure of Doctors' Venal Testimony, 32 Ins.C.J. 221 (1965). How may cross-examining counsel be expected to phrase a question inquiring as to compensation?

Should it be permissible to bring out, if such is the fact, that the expert regularly testifies in litigation? That his testimony is always offered by plaintiffs rather than defendants, or vice versa? Compare Traders & Gen. Ins. Co. v. Robinson, 222 S.W.2d 266 (Tex.Civ.App.1949), with Schoolfield v. Witkowski, 203 N.E.2d 460 (Ill.Ct.App.1964). See also Collins v. Wayne Corp., 621 F.2d 777, 783 (5th Cir.1980) ("Counsel then brought out that the plaintiffs were paying Severy $95 an hour for his testimony, and that Severy had been testifying in accident cases for 20 years. Based on earlier deposition testimony that he worked around 12 hours a day, six days a week, counsel asked whether Severy earned $343,480 per year for testifying. * * * [C]ross-examination of an expert about fees earned in prior cases is not improper. The parties have not cited and our research has not uncovered any federal cases on this point. Cases from the state courts are split.").

3. *Religious belief.* Rule 610 provides that the "nature" of a witness' religious beliefs or opinions is not admissible either to impeach or support the witness' credibility. However, the federal drafters stated: "While the rule forecloses inquiry into the religious beliefs or opinions of a witness for the purpose of showing that his character for truthfulness is affected by their nature, an inquiry for the purpose of showing interest or bias because of them is not within the prohibition. Thus disclosure of affiliation with a

church which is a party to the litigation would be allowable under the rule." Fed.R.Evid. 610 advisory committee's note.

(4) IMPEACHMENT: MENTAL OR SENSORY CAPACITY

UNITED STATES v. HEINLEIN

United States Court of Appeals, District of Columbia Circuit, 1973.
490 F.2d 725.

[The opinion in United States v. Heinlein appears in Section A(5), supra].

Notes and Questions

1. *Heinlein case*. Note particularly in the principal case that despite the court's finding that the expert testimony concerning Harding's mental condition was insufficient to render him incompetent, the defense was allowed to present that testimony to the jury as potentially affecting credibility.

2. *Federal rule*. Like bias, there is no explicit provision in the Federal Rules for this type of impeachment. But see Ohio R.Evid. 616(B) ("A defect of capacity, ability, or opportunity to observe, remember, or relate may be shown to impeach the witness either by examination of the witness or by extrinsic evidence.").

3. *Other cases*. United States v. Sasso, 59 F.3d 341, 347–48 (2d Cir. 1995) ("Evidence of a witness's psychological history may be admissible when it goes to her credibility. *See* Fed.R.Evid. 611(b). In assessing the probative value of such evidence, the court should consider such factors as the nature of the psychological problem, see, e.g., *Chnapkova v. Koh* (paranoid and delusional condition likely to be probative), the temporal recency or remoteness of the history, *see, e.g., id.* at 81–82 (paranoid delusions five years earlier not too remote); *United States v. Bari* (more than 10 years too remote); *United States v. Glover,* (12 years too remote), and whether the witness suffered from the problem at the time of the events to which she is to testify, so that it may have affected her 'ability to perceive or to recall events or to testify accurately'.").

4. *Contra cases*. United States v. Butt, 955 F.2d 77, 82 (1st Cir.1992) ("For over forty years, federal courts have permitted the impeachment of government witnesses based on their mental condition at the time of the events testified to. *See United States v. Hiss,* 88 F.Supp. 559, 559–60 (S.D.N.Y.1950). * * * 'The readily apparent principle is that the jury should, within reason, be informed of all matters affecting a witness's credibility * * *.' *United States v. Partin,* 493 F.2d 750, 762 (5th Cir.1974). * * * Despite this precedent, we are aware of no court to have found relevant an informally diagnosed depression or personality defect. Rather, federal courts appear to have found mental instability relevant to credibility only where, during the time-frame of the events testified to, the witness exhibited a pronounced disposition to lie or hallucinate, or suffered from a severe illness, such as schizophrenia, that dramatically impaired her ability to perceive and

tell the truth."); United States v. Bari, 750 F.2d 1169, 1178–79 (2d Cir.1984) (finding no abuse of discretion when trial judge would not permit cross-examination on witness' prior hospitalization for schizophrenia); United States v. Falcon, 245 F.Supp.2d 1239, 1245 (S.D.Fla.2003) ("Only in rare cases, where there is temporally relevant and reliable documentation that a witness' capacity for perception and recollection is severely hampered, will a court permit an expert to testify to the witness' mental incapacity.").

5. *Psychiatric examinations.* Psychiatric opinion testimony to impeach, as well as to determine competency, has sometimes been admitted. Weihofen, Testimonial Competence and Credibility, 34 Geo.Wash.L.Rev. 53, 68 (1965) ("Because modern practice admits as competent to testify persons proved or conceded to be mentally ill to some degree, a liberal admission policy for evidence on the effect of mental conditions upon credibility is needed."). Helpful treatments of the question include: Juviler, Psychiatric Opinion as to Credibility, 48 Cal.L.Rev. 648 (1960); Slovenko, Witnesses, Psychiatry and the Credibility of Testimony, 19 Fla.L.Rev. 1 (1966). A significant countervailing consideration is the invasion of the privacy of the witness. See Nobrega v. Commonwealth, 628 S.E.2d 922, 926 (Va.2006) (rejecting a "compelling need" test that has been adopted in other jurisdictions, "a trial court has no authority to order a complaining witness in a rape case to undergo a psychiatric or psychological evaluation").

6. *Memory issues.* United States v. Love, 329 F.3d 981, 985 (8th Cir.2003) ("Here the nature of the psychological problem in question is memory loss—a condition that implicates Thomas's ability 'to comprehend, know and correctly relate the truth.' "); United States v. Ciocca, 106 F.3d 1079, 1083 (1st Cir.1997) ("Ciocca was able to place before the jury ample evidence regarding Caporino's ability to remember the events that transpired prior to and after his accident.").

7. *Other capacities.* See Grimes v. Mazda North American Operations, 355 F.3d 566, 573 (6th Cir.2004) ("As to Gutierrez, the driver, the court ruled that the evidence of her drug and alcohol use on the night of the accident went to the credibility of her testimony describing the accident."); United States v. Gonzalez–Maldonado, 115 F.3d 9, 14–15 (1st Cir.1997) ("It is well established that a witness' mental state can be relevant to the issue of the witness' credibility. * * * Dr. Fumero would have testified that Robles, as a result of his illness, was prone to exaggeration.").

(5) IMPEACHMENT: UNTRUTHFUL CHARACTER, FEDERAL RULE 608(a)

STATE v. BAKER

Supreme Court of Wisconsin, 1962.
114 N.W.2d 426.

BROWN, JUSTICE. The complaint was signed by a police officer on information and belief. At the trial the only evidence of defendant's guilt was the uncorroborated testimony of James A., a fifteen year old boy, that defendant took James into a shed behind defendant's filling station and there they cooperated in the indecent liberties with which defendant was charged. Defendant denied James' accusations in every particular, and had a number of witnesses whose testimony tended to throw doubt on James' narrative.

Successful prosecution of the case, and likewise successful defense, depends completely on the jury's belief or disbelief in James' veracity. After the State had rested and the attorney for the defendant had called a number of witnesses whose evidence to some extent impeached James' story of his presence in the shed at the time in question, defendant's attorney called Rev. Clarence J. Schouten and then there occurred the following:

> "DIRECT EXAMINATION BY MR. TIERNEY:
>
> "I am the pastor of St. Joseph's Church which is one block north of the Baker filling station. I have been the pastor there since June, 1955.
>
> "Q. Do you know Jimmy A.?
>
> "A. I do.
>
> "Q. And how long have you known him?
>
> "A. I would say from September of '55.
>
> "Q. Did he go to your school?
>
> "A. He did.
>
> "Q. Do you know what Jimmy A.'s reputation in the community there is as for truth and veracity?
>
> "MR. MIECH: I am going to object; that's highly immaterial and irrelevant and its calling for a conclusion so far as the State's witness is concerned.
>
> "THE COURT: Sustained."

* * *

On this appeal the State concedes that the court was in error in sustaining the objection, so no extensive research by us on the question is required for the purposes of this appeal. * * *

In our own state we find Duffy v. Radke (1909), 138 Wis. 38, 40, 119 N.W. 811, wherein we said:

> "The contention that the court erred in the admission of evidence to impeach the defendant cannot be sustained. The record shows that a foundation for the reception of such evidence was properly laid by showing that the witnesses based their conclusions upon their knowledge of defendant's general reputation among those with whom he resided and the form of inquiry was properly restricted to the inquiry whether, in view of defendant's general reputation for truth and veracity the witness would believe him under oath."

When the court permitted the State to shut out evidence bearing upon James' reputation for truthfulness under the circumstances of the

trial it was an error going to the heart of defendant's guilt or innocence. The State's present contention is that this acknowledged error was cured, or at least rendered innocuous, by the failure of defendant's counsel after the recess to convince the court of its error, in which case it could be presumed that the court would reverse its erroneous ruling. We do not think the State can throw upon defendant the onus of the error made at the instance of the State. Proper objection being made, the error is not cured because defendant was unable to persuade the court that error was committed.

* * *

Order reversed and cause remanded for a new trial.

Notes and Questions

1. *Character trait.* Where character evidence is offered for the purpose of impeaching credibility, most courts require that the evidence relate to the traits of truthfulness and veracity. A few jurisdictions, however, permit a witness to be impeached with regard to his morality generally. See 1 McCormick, Evidence § 43 (6th ed. 2006). Why would an offeror of character proof ever prefer the latter formulation to the former? See State v. Scott, 58 S.W.2d 275 (Mo.1933).

2. *Federal rule.* As with character evidence introduced for substantive purposes under Rules 404 and 405, the practice with regard to character proof for impeachment purposes has been liberalized by the adoption of the Federal Rules. Rule 608(a) allows impeaching evidence as to truthfulness to be given in terms of the witness' personal opinion. Testimony as to reputation for truthfulness remains admissible. A foundation must be laid to show the character witness' familiarity either with the witness and the relevant community in the case of reputation proof or with the witness himself or herself in the case of opinion evidence. See United States v. Turning Bear, 357 F.3d 730, 734 (8th Cir.2004) ("Such a foundation is laid by demonstrating that the opinion witness knows the relevant witness well enough to have formed an opinion. * * * Because Ms. Odens had had daily contact with N.T.B. over the four-to-six-month period that he lived in her home, she knew him well enough to have formed an opinion about his character for untruthfulness that was more than a 'bare assertion' or 'conclusory observation.' ").

3. *Impeaching the accused.* United States v. McMurray, 20 F.3d 831, 834 (8th Cir.1994) ("McMurray next argues that the district court erred in allowing the government's rebuttal witness, Marjorie Carper, to express a negative opinion as to McMurray's truthfulness after he had testified in his own behalf at trial. We disagree. The credibility of a defendant who testifies may be attacked in the same manner as that of any other witness. * * * The prosecutor asked Mrs. Carper whether she would believe McMurray's testimony under oath, based upon her opinion as to his truthfulness. This questioning is consistent with Rule 608(a).").

(6) IMPEACHMENT: CONVICTION OF CRIME, FEDERAL RULE 609

Pre-Rules law. In an article written prior to the adoption of the Federal Rules, Professor Slough, while noting wide agreement on allowing convictions to be introduced to affect credibility, found no agreement on the type of conviction receivable. He summarized the variations as follows:

> One formula adheres to common law terminology and requires the conviction to have been for an "infamous crime." Another formula limits scope of examination to conviction for "felonies" or "crimen falsi."[84] A third formula admits evidence of conviction for "felony" or "crime involving moral turpitude."[85] Finally, there are jurisdictions that allow evidence of conviction to enter without limitation, meaning that conviction of any crime will satisfy.[86] There is an increasing tendency to bar reference to traffic court convictions, and a declaration of delinquency in juvenile court will not ordinarily be classified with conviction for purposes of impeachment.

Slough, Impeachment of Witnesses: Common Law Principles and Modern Trends, 34 Ind.L.J. 1, 22 (1958).

If an accused is charged with driving while intoxicated, should the prosecutor be permitted to impeach the accused with a prior conviction for the same offense? See State v. Murdock, 174 N.E.2d 543 (Ohio 1961) (upholding use of any prior felony or misdemeanor for impeachment). What does a DUI conviction tell us about the witness' character for truthfulness?

Federal Rule 609. "In drafting Rule 609(a), Congress was torn between two conflicting interests. On the one hand, there was the interest in letting the jury have information regarding a prior conviction to the extent that it might bear on a defendant's credibility as a witness. On the other hand, there was the desire to avoid deterring the defendant, because of the obvious prejudice that might be caused by the jury's learning of his prior conviction, from testifying in his own defense, which might preclude the jury from having the benefit of his version of events." United States v. Ortiz, 553 F.2d 782, 785 (2d Cir.1977) (Mansfield, J., dissenting). The congressional compromise that was finally reached recognized two types of convictions: (1) those punishable by death or imprisonment for more that one year, and (2) those involving dishonesty or false statement ("crimen falsi").

UNITED STATES v. ALEXANDER

United States Court of Appeals, Ninth Circuit, 1995.
48 F.3d 1477.

DAVID R. THOMPSON, CIRCUIT JUDGE: These are the consolidated appeals of defendants Gary Edward Alexander, Jonathan Harrington,

84. Commonwealth v. Kostan, 349 Pa. 560, 37 A.2d 606 (1944). "Crimen falsi" is a general designation of a class of offenses including those which involve deceit or falsification or affect the public administration of justice. Forgery, counterfeiting, and perjury are common examples.

85. A * * * decision in Maine defines moral turpitude as being akin to baseness, vileness, or depravity. * * * State v. Jenness, 143 Me. 380, 62 A.2d 867 (1948).

86. Way v. State, 224 Ind. 280, 66 N.E.2d 608 (1946) (convictions for speeding and disorderly conduct allowed despite slight probative values; discretion of lower court stressed); Fritch v. State, 199 Ind. 89, 155 N.E. 257 (1927) (cross-examination not confined to convictions for felony or infamous crimes); * * *

Anthony F. Hicks and Willie James Harris. The defendants appeal their convictions for conspiracy to commit robbery, [armed bank robbery, and use of a firearm during commission of a crime of violence].

* * *

Before trial, defendant Hicks filed a motion *in limine* to exclude evidence of his prior felony convictions for residential robbery and possession of rock cocaine for sale. The district court denied the motion, ruling that, if Hicks elected to testify, the evidence would be admissible for impeachment purposes, under Federal Rule of Evidence 609(a)(1), because its probative value outweighed its prejudicial effect. At trial, Hicks chose to take the stand and present an alibi defense. He testified that he was in the vicinity of the arrests on the day of the robbery because he was scheduled to meet a friend there. He also said he ran away when he heard sirens and saw police cars because he was afraid of being arrested on two outstanding warrants for traffic violations. Purportedly for the same reason, he also gave the arresting officer a false name. At the conclusion of his direct examination, Hicks again moved to exclude the evidence of his prior convictions. The district court adhered to its original ruling and denied the motion. On cross examination, the prosecution elicited testimony from Hicks regarding the nature and dates of both prior convictions.

Hicks contends the district court erred in allowing the jury to hear evidence of his prior convictions. With regard to his prior robbery conviction, he argues United States v. Brackeen, 969 F.2d 827, 830 (9th Cir.1992) (en banc) (per curiam), stands for the proposition that a prior robbery conviction cannot be used to attack a defendant's credibility. We disagree. Federal Rule of Evidence 609(a) provides, in pertinent part, that evidence of prior convictions is admissible for purposes of attacking the credibility of a witness if the crime "(1) was [a felony], and the court determines the probative value of admitting this evidence outweighs its prejudicial effect to the defendant, or (2) involved dishonesty or false statement* * *." *Brackeen* held only that, in this circuit, bank robbery is not per se a crime of dishonesty, and therefore prior robbery convictions are not admissible for impeachment purposes under Rule 609(a)(2). *Brackeen,* 969 F.2d at 829. We did not foreclose in *Brackeen* the admission of a prior robbery conviction under the balancing test of Rule 609(a)(1). Here, the government explicitly stated it intended to introduce both of Hicks's prior convictions under Rule 609(a)(1), and the district court specifically ruled on that basis by applying the appropriate balancing test. If the district court did not abuse its discretion * * * , the evidence of both of his prior convictions was properly admitted. *United States v. Browne,* 829 F.2d 760, 762 (9th Cir.1987) (noting that a district court's decision to admit evidence of prior convictions is reviewed for an abuse of discretion).

In *United States v. Cook,* 608 F.2d 1175, 1185 n.8 (9th Cir.1979) (en banc), we outlined five factors that should be considered in balancing the probative value of a prior conviction against its prejudicial impact for purposes of Rule 609(a)(1): (1) the impeachment value of the prior crime; (2) the point in time of conviction and the defendant's subsequent history; (3) the similarity between the past crime and the charged crime; (4) the importance of the defendant's testimony; and (5) the centrality of the defendant's credibility. The government bears the burden of showing, based on these factors, that the proffered evidence's probative value substantially outweighs its prejudicial effect. * * * Hicks does not dispute that the first factor favors admission of both his prior convictions. We have previously stated that "prior convictions for robbery are probative of veracity." *United States v. Givens,* 767 F.2d 574, 580 (9th Cir.1985). The same is true of prior convictions for drug offenses. Hicks stipulates that both his prior crimes were sufficiently recent to satisfy the second *Cook* factor. He was convicted of residential robbery, and was sentenced to a four-year prison term, in 1987. Shortly after his parole in 1988, he committed the drug offense, for which he received another four-year prison sentence. Less than a year later, he was arrested for the present crime. "By its terms, Rule 609 allows for admissibility of such * * * prior conviction[s] even where the defendant has been released for up to ten years." *Browne,* 829 F.2d at 763. *See* Fed.R.Evid. 609(b).

Hicks concedes that, as to his prior drug offense, the third factor is satisfied because the drug offense is sufficiently different from the present bank robbery. With regard to the prior residential robbery, the district court held that offense was similar to the charged bank robbery and, therefore, the third factor weighed in favor of excluding it. However, we have held that even "a prior 'bank robbery conviction [is] not inadmissable per se, merely because the offense involved was identical to that for which [the defendant] was on trial.' " *Browne,* 829 F.2d at 763 * * *. What matters is the balance of all five factors. Hicks contends that, contrary to the district court's determination, the related fourth and fifth factors weigh against admission of his prior convictions. He contends his trial testimony was not particularly important and his credibility was not central to the case, because other evidence corroborated his alibi defense.[87] We disagree. When a defendant takes the stand and denies having committed the charged offense, he places his credibility directly at issue. * * *

In *United States v. Bagley,* 772 F.2d 482, 488 (9th Cir.1985), we held that admission of the defendant's prior robbery convictions was an abuse of the district court's discretion. But in that case we emphasized "the record [was] devoid of any evidence that [the defendant] intended to misrepresent his character or to testify falsely as to his prior criminal record." *Id.* Here, Hicks testified he ran from the police because he was afraid of being arrested on outstanding warrants for traffic violations.

87. At trial, Hicks's attorney told the district court that Hicks's testimony was "central."

This testimony could reasonably have misled the jury into believing that, with the exception of some minor traffic infractions, Hicks had no previous trouble with the police. As we said in *Cook:*

> [I]t is not surprising that the [district] court was unwilling to let a man with a substantial criminal history misrepresent himself to the jury, with the government forced to sit silently by, looking at a criminal record which, if made known, would give the jury a more comprehensive view of the trustworthiness of the defendant as a witness.

Cook, 608 F.2d at 1187.

We conclude that the district court properly balanced all five *Cook* factors and did not abuse its discretion * * *.

Notes and Questions

1. *Impeachment value of prior offense.* Remember that the most probative offenses (e.g., perjury) fall within Rule 609(a)(2) (crimes of dishonesty or false statement) and not this Rule. What is left? Burglary? Robbery? Drug offenses? See United States v. Brito, 427 F.3d 53, 64 (1st Cir.2005) ("Prior drug-trafficking crimes are generally viewed as having some bearing on veracity."); United States v. Ortiz, 553 F.2d 782, 784 (2d Cir.1977) ("a narcotics trafficker lives a life of secrecy and dissembling in the course of that activity, being prepared to say whatever is required by the demands of the moment, whether the truth or a lie").

2. *Similarity.* In the principal case, which way does the similarity of the past crime (residential robbery) and the charged crime cut? In favor of probative value or in showing unfair prejudice? See United States v. Brito, 427 F.3d 53, 63 (1st Cir.2005) ("The offenses underlying the appellant's prior convictions are not similar to the offenses charged in this case. That is relevant because convictions for dissimilar crimes are customarily thought to be less prejudicial than convictions for similar crimes (which may run a risk of implying a propensity to commit the crime).").

3. *Rule 609 balancing.* How does the balancing in Rule 609(a) regarding the accused's prior convictions differ from the Rule 403 balancing that applies to all other witnesses? Which of the *Cook* factors would be relevant in the latter context? See United States v. Tse, 375 F.3d 148, 164 (1st Cir.2004) ("[T]he prior convictions of a government witness are unlikely to inflame the jury or invite a propensity inference: The probability that prior convictions of an ordinary government witness will be unduly prejudicial is low in most criminal cases.").

4. *Record findings.* How much of a record of its balancing process under Rule 609(a)(1) must a trial court make? Some courts have strongly recommended explicit findings if the evidence of convictions is admitted. See United States v. Mahone, 537 F.2d 922 (7th Cir.1976). Despite desires such as those expressed in the *Mahone* case, the appellate courts have generally not imposed a requirement of explicit findings on trial judges in connection with Rule 609(a) rulings. The matter is left in the discretion of the trial court judge, with or without explicit findings. See, e.g., United States v.

Givens, 767 F.2d 574 (9th Cir.1985); United States v. Love, 746 F.2d 477 (9th Cir.1984). Such discretion will be held to have been abused if it is clear that the trial judge did not even consider the prejudice to the accused. See United States v. Mehrmanesh, 689 F.2d 822 (9th Cir.1982).

5. *State adoptions.* Many jurisdictions have adopted impeachment rules based on the balancing approach of Federal Rule 609, although there are variations. Other jurisdictions have blanket rules, which also vary significantly. Compare Mont.R.Evid. 609 ("For the purpose of attacking the credibility of a witness, evidence that the witness has been convicted of a crime is not admissible."), with N.C.R.Evid. 609(a) (all felonies and many misdemeanors, including simple assault and even some speeding convictions, shall be admitted).

6. *Ten-year rule.* In accord with the specific language of Rule 609(b), the courts have imposed a requirement of explicit findings in connection with rulings on the admissibility of convictions that are more than ten years old. See United States v. Portillo, 699 F.2d 461 (9th Cir.1982). Rule 609(b)'s relatively strict balancing test applies to all convictions more than ten years old—both "felony" convictions under Rule 609(a)(1) and otherwise automatically admissible "crimen falsi" convictions under Rule 609(a)(2).

The context of the witness' testimony may be a significant factor in weighing the probative value of the prior conviction against the prejudice to the defendant. This is particularly true in cases involving convictions which are more than ten years old. The testimony of the defendant on direct examination may open the door for a finding that the probative value of the conviction substantially outweighs its prejudicial effect. See United States v. Ebner, 782 F.2d 1120 (2d Cir.1986) (defendant opened door to introduction of prior convictions by testifying that his conduct was attributable to advice from his lawyers).

7. *"Other acts" evidence.* In United States v. Valencia, 61 F.3d 616, 618–19 (8th Cir.1995), a prosecution for conspiracy, intent to distribute cocaine, and money laundering, the district court ruled that a prior conviction of the accused for unlawful possession for sale and purchase for sale of a controlled substance was inadmissible under Rule 404(b) ("other acts") evidence but was admissible under Rule 609. The accused appealed. The Eighth Circuit commented:

> The appellant contends that Rule 609(a)'s internalized balancing test is stricter in terms of admissibility in that a prior conviction is not admissible against the accused for impeachment purposes unless the probative value of the evidence outweighs its prejudicial effect. Appellant's argument is that after finding that the prejudice of the prior conviction *substantially* outweighed the probative value under 404(b), the district court abused its discretion in admitting the same evidence under Rule 609, where it would be excluded if the prejudice *merely* outweighed its probative effect. We disagree.
>
> * * * In a criminal setting, evidence offered under Rule 404(b) is substantive evidence against the accused, i.e., it is part of the government's case offered to prove his guilt beyond a reasonable doubt. Rule 609 evidence on the other hand has to do with the accused's ability to tell the truth when testifying on his or her own behalf. While both rules

speak of "probative value" and "prejudice," it is critical to note that evidence offered under the respective rules is probative as to different matters. The probative character of evidence under Rule 609 has to do with credibility of a witness, while 404(b) "probativeness" essentially goes to the question of whether or not the accused committed the crime charged. Any similarity or overlap in the standards of admissibility under the respective rules is irrelevant because the rules apply to completely distinct situations.

ALTOBELLO v. BORDEN CONFECTIONARY PRODUCTS, INC.

United States Court of Appeals, Seventh Circuit, 1989.
872 F.2d 215.

POSNER, CIRCUIT JUDGE.

Guy Altobello brought this suit against his former employer, Borden, charging that Borden had fired him because of his age, in violation of the Age Discrimination in Employment Act, 29 U.S.C. §§ 621 *et seq.* The jury brought in a verdict for the defendant at the end of a five-day trial. The evidence at trial had been in sharp conflict, with Borden presenting evidence that it had fired Altobello because he was a malingerer, and Altobello responding with evidence that his alleged malingering was merely the pretext for a discharge motivated by his age. The only issue on appeal that merits discussion is Altobello's claim that the district court erred in allowing Borden to impeach his credibility as a witness by asking him on the stand: "Mr. Altobello, in 1978 [ten years before the trial] you were convicted of the crime of tampering with electric meters of Commonwealth Edison, weren't you?"—to which Altobello had replied, "Yes."

* * * Rule 609(a)(2)—the provision applicable to this case—allows the witness to be impeached by proof that he was convicted of a crime that "involved dishonesty or false statement, regardless of the punishment," i.e., regardless of whether it was a felony or a misdemeanor. Altobello's conviction of meter tampering was a misdemeanor conviction, and therefore admissible if at all only under Rule 609(a)(2).

At trial Altobello argued that the conviction should be excluded under Fed.R.Evid. 403, which directs the exclusion of evidence the prejudicial effects of which substantially outweigh its probative value. Yet we held in *Campbell v. Greer,* 831 F.2d 700, 705–07 (7th Cir.1987), decided before the trial of this case, that Rule 403 is inapplicable to Rule 609(a)(2). On appeal, Altobello has abandoned Rule 403, and argues instead that Borden was obliged to show that the specific acts of meter tampering for which he was convicted involved dishonesty in the sense of a deceptive act—that, in an older jargon, the crime of which he was convicted was *crimen falsi.* * * *

Altobello's argument begins with the proposition that unless Borden is required to show that the specific acts for which Altobello was convicted involved dishonesty in the sense of deception, subsection (a)(2) of Rule 609 would swallow up (a)(1), making *any* misdemeanor conviction—any conviction, period—usable for impeachment regardless of how prejudice and probative value balanced out; for every crime is in a sense a dishonest act and 609(a)(2) contains no balancing test. But although acquisitive crimes are indeed dishonest, not all crimes are acquisitive, and those that are not are not "dishonest" unless honest and law-abiding are treated as synonyms. A man who kills his wife's lover *in flagrante delicto* is violent and lawless, but not necessarily dishonest as that word is normally understood, and there may be less reason to expect him to lie on the stand in a suit unrelated to his crime than to expect a lesser criminal, but one who has a history of seeking to enrich himself at others' expense, to lie on the stand.

The suggestion in short is that greed or *pleonexia* (wanting more than your fair share) is more highly correlated with willingness or propensity to lie under oath than wrath or passion is. Well, maybe; but a more plausible distinction—and the one that most courts have accepted * * * is between crimes that do not involve an element of deception and crimes that do. * * * It seems plausible (no stronger statement is possible) that a person who has used deceit to commit a crime is more likely than either another type of criminal or a law-abiding person to perceive the witness stand as an attractive site for further deceit—especially when as in this case he is a party to the suit in which he is testifying.

In the case of some crimes, such as perjury, deceit is an element of the crime; conviction of the crime therefore imports the use of deceit. In the case of other crimes, deceit is not an element, but the manner in which the witness committed the offense may have involved deceit, and if that is shown the conviction is admissible under Rule 609(a)(2). * * * The trial judge must not allow himself to be sidetracked into the details of the earlier conviction, but where as in this case the deceitful nature of the crime is admitted or is plain on the face of the indictment of other official record, the fact that the same type of offense can be committed in a manner not involving deceit does not make the conviction inadmissible.

Altobello was convicted of a crime in the second category—the category of crimes that may or may not involve deceit, depending on the circumstances. In Altobello's case it was misdemeanor theft, which can be committed by obtaining property through deception, but alternatively by obtaining it through threat or force, or by receiving stolen property. See Ill.Rev.Stat. ch. 38, ¶ 16–1.

Which was it here? All the record discloses on this score is "tampering with electric meters of Commonwealth Edison." Apparently what happened is that Altobello helped several McDonald's franchisees in the Chicago area to alter the electric meters in their restaurants, in order to reduce their electric bills; but this was only told to us at argument and the record is limited to the bare question asked him at trial, to an unilluminating sidebar discussion of admissibility, and to the indictment, which is no more informative. There was nevertheless an adequate foundation for the admission of the conviction. An electric meter is not like a vending machine or a pay telephone, which you can jimmy to get out the coins. Tampering with an electric meter means altering the meter so that it records less use than the user is actually making of it. Meter tampering is *necessarily* a crime of deception; the goal is *always* to deceive the meter reader. It is therefore securely within the scope of Rule 609(a)(2).

The other errors claimed by Altobello are signally devoid of merit and require no discussion. The judgment is

Affirmed.

Notes and Questions

1. *Crimen falsi.* The 2006 amendment added the following phrase: "if it readily can be determined that establishing the elements of the crime required proof or admission of an act of dishonesty or false statement by the witness." See note 2, infra. The Advisory Committee also took the occasion to further define the term "crimen falsi":

> The amendment provides that Rule 609(a)(2) mandates the admission of evidence of a conviction only when the conviction required the proof of (or in the case of a guilty plea, the admission of) an act of dishonesty or false statement. Evidence of all other convictions is inadmissible under this subsection, irrespective of whether the witness exhibited dishonesty or made a false statement in the process of the commission of the crime of conviction. Thus, evidence that a witness was convicted for a crime of violence, such as murder, is not admissible under Rule 609(a)(2), even if the witness acted deceitfully in the course of committing the crime.
>
> The amendment is meant to give effect to the legislative intent to limit the convictions that are to be automatically admitted under subdivision (a)(2). The Conference Committee provided that by "dishonesty and false statement" it meant "crimes such as perjury, subornation of perjury, false statement, criminal fraud, embezzlement, or false pretense, or any other offense in the nature of *crimen falsi*, the commission of which involves some element of deceit, untruthfulness, or falsification bearing on the [witness's] propensity to testify truthfully." Historically, offenses classified as *crimina falsi* have included only those crimes in which the ultimate criminal act was itself an act of deceit. *See* Green, *Deceit and the Classification of Crimes: Federal Rule of Evidence 609(a)(2) and the Origins of* Crimen Falsi, 90 J. Crim. L. & Criminology 1087 (2000).

In United States v. Mejia–Alaracon, 995 F.2d 982, 989–90 (10th Cir.1993), the court wrote that "crimes like burglary, robbery, and theft are not automatically admissible under Rule 609(a)(2)." Why doesn't "theft" fall within the Rule?

2. *Going beyond the record.* The Advisory Committee provided the following guidance on the new language:

Evidence of crimes in the nature of *crimina falsi* must be admitted under Rule 609(a)(2), regardless of how such crimes are specifically charged. For example, evidence that a witness was convicted of making a false claim to a federal agent is admissible under this subdivision regardless of whether the crime was charged under a section that expressly references deceit (e.g., 18 U.S.C. § 1001, Material Misrepresentation to the Federal Government) or a section that does not (e.g., 18 U.S.C. § 1503, Obstruction of Justice).

The amendment requires that the proponent have ready proof that the conviction required the factfinder to find, or the defendant to admit, an act of dishonesty or false statement. Ordinarily, the statutory elements of the crime will indicate whether it is one of dishonesty or false statement. Where the deceitful nature of the crime is not apparent from the statute and the face of the judgment—as, for example, where the conviction simply records a finding of guilt for a statutory offense that does not reference deceit expressly—a proponent may offer information such as an indictment, a statement of admitted facts, or jury instructions to show that the factfinder had to find, or the defendant had to admit, an act of dishonesty or false statement in order for the witness to have been convicted. * * * But the amendment does not contemplate a "mini-trial" in which the court plumbs the record of the previous proceeding to determine whether the crime was in the nature of *crimen falsi*.

Is *Altobello* still good law?

3. *Pardons.* What effect does a pardon have on the use of a conviction for impeachment purposes? Does it matter why the pardon was given? See Rule 609(c).

4. *Juvenile adjudications.* See Rule 609(d), but see also *Davis v. Alaska*, note 5, following *Alford* v. *United States*, supra.

5. *Appeals.* Rule 609(e) is in accord with the generally held rule that the usability of a prior conviction to impeach is unaffected by the fact that the conviction is being appealed at the time the question is asked. See Suggs v. State, 250 A.2d 670 (Md.Ct.Spec.App.1969). But if the conviction has already been reversed a different result obtains. See State v. Hill, 520 P.2d 618 (Wash.1974). As to use of convictions on which judgment or sentence has not been imposed, see Annot., 28 A.L.R.4th 647.

6. *Method of proof.* One common technique of impeachment by showing prior conviction of crime is to inquire of the witness concerning the fact of conviction on cross-examination and, if the conviction is denied, thereafter to establish the conviction by a certified record of the judgment or other extrinsic evidence. See, e.g., Mead v. State, 86 So.2d 773 (Fla.1956).

7. *Foundation requirement.* Most jurisdictions hold that no foundation for producing documentary or other evidence of conviction need be laid, and that the evidence may be introduced without first having elicited a denial of the conviction from the witness. 1 McCormick, Evidence § 42 (6th ed. 2006). Should it be permissible, conversely, for a cross-examiner to inquire whether a witness has previously been convicted of crime without being prepared to

introduce documentary or other evidence of such convictions in the event of a denial? See Ciravolo v. United States, 384 F.2d 54 (1st Cir.1967).

8. *Details of crime.* In the event the witness concedes the fact of conviction in the first instance, it is generally held that additional questions concerning the nature and circumstances of the conviction are limited to those matters which are shown by the record of conviction. See Young v. James Green Management, Inc., 327 F.3d 616, 625–26 (7th Cir.2003) ("As a general rule, we have held that 'all that is needed to serve the purpose of challenging the witness's veracity is the elicitation of the crime charged, the date, and the disposition' and that 'it is error to elicit any further information for impeachment purposes.' "). See discussion in 1 McCormick, Evidence § 42 (6th ed. 2006).

9. *Appellate review.* In Luce v. United States, 469 U.S. 38 (1984), the United States Supreme Court ruled that an accused had to take the stand and testify in order to preserve the issue of admissibility for appeal. In Ohler v. United States, 529 U.S. 753 (2000), the Court held that bringing out the conviction on direct examination ("taking out the sting") also waived the issue for appellate purposes. Both cases are found in Chapter 1, Section B, supra.

(7) IMPEACHMENT: UNTRUTHFUL CONDUCT, FEDERAL RULE 608(b)

STATE v. MORGAN

Supreme Court of North Carolina, 1986.
340 S.E.2d 84.

Before Owens, J., at the 15 October 1984 Criminal Session of Superior Court, Rutherford County, defendant was convicted of first-degree murder. Defendant appeals his sentence of life imprisonment as a matter of right * * *. * * *

MEYER, JUSTICE.

Defendant brings forth three assignments of error. First, defendant contends that the trial court committed reversible error in allowing the prosecutor, over objection, to cross-examine the defendant concerning a specific instance of prior assaultive conduct that was not probative of truthfulness or veracity. * * * For the reasons stated below, we find no reversible error.

* * *

Defendant's theory of the case was that he had shot Harrell in self-defense; that he reasonably felt it necessary to shoot Harrell in order to protect himself from Mr. Harrell, a 6–3, 280–pound manic depressive who was coming at him through the doorway of his home and business threatening to kill him. Defendant admitted on cross-examination, however, that at the time he shot Harrell, Harrell did not have a weapon in his hand.

During recross-examination of the defendant at trial, the following exchange took place:

> Q. Mr. Morgan, do you recall that on April 26th, 1984, less than three months before this incident, that you assaulted Mike Hall with a deadly weapon, a shotgun, by pointing it at Mr. Hall and stating that you would cut him in two with the shotgun there at this same place of business, did you not do that did you not do that [sic] with Mike Hall?
>
> MR. MITCHELL: Objection.
>
> THE COURT: Objection overruled.
>
> A. Mike Hall followed me from the station and come into my store [sic], yes sir, I remember that.
>
> Q. And then when Roger Poteat, the CHief [sic] of Police of Alexander Mills, came to serve the Warrant, did you not point the shotgun at Roger Poteat?
>
> A. No sir, I did not. I showed Roger the gun and it wouldn't [sic] even loaded.

The trial judge thus allowed the prosecutor to question defendant on cross-examination about a prior act of assaultive conduct not charged in the indictment upon which he was being tried. * * * Before analyzing the propriety of the trial judge's ruling here, we must be clear about what the transcript reveals.

This colloquy took place on recross-examination of the defendant by the prosecutor. The defendant had just testified on his own behalf and had admitted shooting Mr. Harrell but claimed he had done so in self-defense. Defendant testified that he would not have shot Mr. Harrell if he had not been afraid of him. During direct and redirect examination, defendant had testified as to Mr. Harrell's often violent behavior and his drinking during the days preceding his death. Apparently without having requested a ruling on admissibility prior to trial, the prosecutor on recross-examination then inquired of defendant whether he had engaged in a specific act of misconduct, which involved the same type of conduct (use of a shotgun at defendant's place of business) as that resulting in the charges for which defendant was being tried, but directed toward unrelated third parties at a time three months prior to the Harrell incident. Defendant admitted pointing the shotgun at Mike Hall but denied pointing the shotgun at Police Chief Poteat. The prosecutor did not then seek to further prove this conduct by extrinsic evidence; thus the record does not reveal the specific circumstances surrounding the 26 April 1984 incident. In the record before us, there is no indication why defendant pointed a gun at Mr. Hall, whether Chief Poteat ever served the warrant or even what or for whom the warrant was issued, or whether defendant was ever charged and convicted of pointing a gun at either man. For purposes of this discussion, we shall assume that defendant was not convicted of either alleged previous assault. Thus, this exchange informed the jury that defendant, at his place of business, may have pointed a shotgun at two men other than Mr. Harrell within three months of the 4 July tragedy when similar conduct resulted in Mr. Harrell's death and defendant's arrest therefor.

* * * Defendant argues that the prosecutor's questions were improper under N.C.G.S. § 8C–1, Rule 608(b) (evidence of specific instances of conduct for the purpose of proving credibility of witness or lack thereof). The State contends that the evidence was properly admitted pursuant to Rule 404(b) (evidence of specific instances of a party's conduct for the purpose of proving motive, opportunity, etc.) as well as Rule 608(b).

Although both rules concern the use of specific instances of a person's conduct, the two rules have very different purposes and are intended to govern entirely different uses of extrinsic conduct evidence.[88] * * * Our task on appellate review is complicated by the fact that there is nothing in the record indicating under which rule the prosecutor was proceeding or under which rule the trial judge overruled the objection. We must therefore consider the admissibility of the evidence under both Rule 404(b) and Rule 608(b).

Defendant correctly argues that the evidence of his alleged prior act of misconduct was inadmissible pursuant to Rule 608(b) (evidence of specific instances of conduct for the purpose of proving credibility of a witness or lack thereof). * * *

Rule 608(b) represents a drastic departure from the former traditional North Carolina practice which allowed a defendant to be cross-examined for impeachment purposes regarding *any* prior act of misconduct not resulting in conviction so long as the prosecutor had a good-faith basis for the questions. *E.g., State v. Dixon,* 77 N.C.App. 27, 334 S.E.2d 433 (1985).

Rule 608(b) addresses the admissibility of specific instances of conduct (as opposed to opinion or reputation evidence) only in the very narrow instance where (1) the *purpose* of producing the evidence is to impeach or enhance credibility by proving that the witness' conduct indicates his character for truthfulness or untruthfulness; and (2) the conduct in question *is in fact probative* of truthfulness or untruthfulness and is not too remote in time; and (3) the conduct in question did *not result in a conviction*; and (4) the inquiry into the conduct *takes place during cross-examination.* If the proffered evidence meets these four enumerated prerequisites, before admitting the evidence the trial judge must determine, in his discretion, pursuant to Rule 403, that the probative value of the evidence is not outweighed by the risk of unfair prejudice, confusion of issues or misleading the jury, and that the questioning will not harass or unduly embarrass the witness. Even if the trial judge allows the inquiry on cross-examination, extrinsic evidence of

88. "Extrinsic conduct evidence" refers to evidence of a specific prior or subsequent act, not charged in the indictment, which may be criminal but, as applied in Rule 608(b), does not result in a conviction. Criminal convictions are included in Rule 404(b).

the conduct is not admissible. N.C.G.S. § 8C–1, Rule 608(b) and Commentary.

Because the only purpose for which this evidence is sought to be admitted is to impeach or to bolster the credibility of a witness, the only character trait relevant to the issue of credibility is veracity or the lack of it. The focus, then, is upon whether the conduct sought to be inquired into is of the type which is indicative of the actor's character for truthfulness or untruthfulness. Among the types of conduct most widely accepted as falling into this category are "use of false identity, making false statements on affidavits, applications or government forms (including tax returns), giving false testimony, attempting to corrupt or cheat others, and attempting to deceive or defraud others." 3 D. Louisell & C. Mueller, Federal Evidence § 305 (1979) (footnotes omitted). On the other hand, evidence routinely disapproved as irrelevant to the question of a witness' general veracity (credibility) includes specific instances of conduct relating to "sexual relationships or proclivities, the bearing of illigitimate [sic] children, the use of drugs or alcohol, * * * *or violence against other persons.*" *Id.* (footnotes omitted) (emphasis added). *See also* 3 J. Weinstein & M. Berger, Weinstein's Evidence ¶ 608[05] (1985) ("crimes primarily of force or intimidation * * * or crimes based on malum prohibitum are not included."). For example, in *United States v. Alberti,* 470 F.2d 878 (2d Cir.1972), cross-examination of a witness regarding a prior assault was properly disallowed because "the conduct involved does not relate to truthfulness or untruthfulness." *Id.* at 882. *See also United States v. Hill,* 550 F.Supp. 983 (E.D.Pa.1982), *aff'd*, 716 F.2d 893 (3d Cir.1983) ("acts of assault, force, or intimidation do not directly indicate an impairment of a witness' character for veracity." *Id.* at 990); *United States v. Kelley,* 545 F.2d 619 (8th Cir.1976) (evidence tending to show defendant had directed threats and violence toward these victims in the past properly excluded under Rules 607, 608, 609; court intimates that had defendant asserted self-defense at trial, the evidence might have been admissible under Rule 404(b)).

We conclude that the prosecutor's cross-examination of defendant in this case concerning an alleged specific instance of misconduct, i.e., two assaults by pointing a gun at two people during the same incident, was improper under Rule 608(b) because extrinsic instances of assaultive behavior, standing alone, are not in any way probative of the witness' character for truthfulness or untruthfulness.

[The court went on to hold that the evidence of the prior assaults was also inadmissible under Rule 404(b), but that the admission of the evidence in violation of both Rules 608(b) and 404(b) was harmless error under the facts of the case. A dissent by Exum, J. on the question of harmless error is omitted.]

Notes and Questions

1. *Other jurisdictions.* Although impeachment by prior misconduct is permitted by Rule 608 and state rules based on it, a number of American

jurisdictions prohibit such impeachment. See 1 McCormick, Evidence § 41 (6th ed. 2006). What considerations might be suggested to support this minority view?

2. *Other examples.* United States v. Dawson, 434 F.3d 956 (7th Cir. 2006) (within trial court's discretion to permit defense counsel to ask government agents whether a judge had ever disbelieved them in a previous case); United States v. Thiongo, 344 F.3d 55, 60 (1st Cir.2003) ("Defendant's willingness to serve as a legal witness to a sham marriage designed to avoid immigration laws is fairly probative of Defendant's truthfulness."); Young v. James Green Management, Inc., 327 F.3d 616, 627 (7th Cir.2003) ("Stealing is probative of untruthfulness; therefore, the district court acted within the bounds of its discretion in allowing counsel to inquire on cross-examination with respect to this incident.").

3. *Rule 403 balancing.* Should the balancing test of Rule 403 be applied to evidence of misconduct offered under Rule 608(b)? See United States v. Thiongo, 344 F.3d 55, 59 (1st Cir.2003) ("The admissibility of such evidence is determined by weighing several factors including whether the instances of prior conduct bear some similarity to the conduct at issue, whether they were recent or remote in time, and whether the evidence is cumulative of other evidence.").

4. *Extrinsic evidence.* As noted in the principal case, extrinsic evidence of misconduct not the subject of a conviction is not admissible. Obviously, if trials are ever to reach an end, it is not possible to permit contradictory evidence concerning every conceivable fact on which a witness may testify falsely or inaccurately. Thus the doctrine of "collateral facts," which precludes such contradictory proof unless the fact's importance looms large enough to justify the time required for contradiction. See State v. Long, 140 S.W.3d 27, 30–31 (Mo.2004) ("The bar on extrinsic evidence of prior, specific acts of misconduct furthers the general policy focusing the fact-finder [on] the most probative facts and conserving judicial resources by avoiding mini-trials on collateral issues. In some cases, however, the rule excluding extrinsic evidence of prior false allegations fails to serve this purpose by shielding the fact-finder not from collateral issues, but from a central issue in the case. An issue is not collateral if it is a 'crucial issue directly in controversy.' ").

5. *Good faith.* The Fourth Circuit found a due process violation where a prosecutor's questions concerning prior bad acts, offered to impeach the defendant, lacked a sufficient evidentiary foundation. Watkins v. Foster, 570 F.2d 501 (4th Cir.1978).

(8) IMPEACHMENT: SPECIFIC CONTRADICTION

UNITED STATES v. OPAGER

United States Court of Appeals, Fifth Circuit, 1979.
589 F.2d 799.

JOHN R. BROWN, CHIEF JUDGE:

On February 23, 1977, appellant Patricia Lynn Opager made the regrettable mistake of selling a pound of 90.4% [p]ure cocaine to three buyers, two of whom happened to be law enforcement officers, and the third a government informant and acquaintance of Opager. As a result of this incident, Opager was convicted by a jury of knowingly and intentionally possessing cocaine with the intent to distribute and knowingly and intentionally distributing cocaine * * *.

* * *

At her trial, Opager attempted to establish an entrapment defense. Opager took the stand, testifying that she had never sold cocaine before and that she was pressured into this sale by the informant, Phillip Posner, and the two police officers. In turn, Posner testified to show Opager's "predisposition" to sell cocaine. He stated that he had observed her engage in cocaine transactions in the past. On cross-examination, Posner explained that he had worked at a beauty salon (the Clipper) with defendant in 1974 and again in 1976 and that during both times he had seen her use and sell cocaine. To impeach Posner's testimony, Opager presented five witnesses to attack Posner's character. By questioning witnesses and by attempting to offer into evidence business records from the beauty salon,[89] she also sought to prove that she and Posner had not worked together in 1974. The District Court ruled that the records were inadmissible under F.R.Evid. 608(b) as extrinsic evidence of a specific instance of conduct introduced to discredit the witness's testimony. * * *

Although the District Court refused to admit the records, the Court did indicate that it would accept into evidence two cancelled checks from the beauty salon to show when Opager started work there. Record at 375. The Record does not specify which checks these were. They apparently were not offered into evidence.

Applicability of F.R.Evid. 608(b)

The District Court erred in applying F.R.Evid. 608(b) to determine the admissibility of the business records. The application of Rule 608(b) to exclude extrinsic evidence of a witness's conduct is limited to instances where the evidence is introduced to show a witness's general character for truthfulness. * * *

In this case, we are convinced that the records were not offered for such a purpose. The documents show and would permit the jury to find that, contrary to Posner's testimony, Posner and Opager did not work together in 1974 and that therefore Posner did not witness any of the drug transactions he described as occurring at that time. Thus, the records do more than indicate Posner's capacity to lie, about which five witnesses had testified. Instead, as Opager's counsel strenuously argued at trial. The records were introduced to disprove a specific fact material to Opager's defense. * * *

89. The documentary evidence consisted of cancelled checks, appointment books, various tax forms, and other business records of the beauty salon.

We consider Rule 608(b) to be inapplicable in determining the admissibility of relevant evidence introduced to contradict a witness's testimony as to a material issue. So long as otherwise competent, such evidence is admissible. McCormick, Evidence § 47 (2d ed. 1972); 3A Wigmore, Evidence §§ 1000–1005 (Chadbourn rev. 1970). This was long the rule in this Circuit prior to the enactment of the Federal Rules of Evidence. * * *

In making this determination, we find helpful the Ninth Circuit's opinion in United States v. Batts, 558 F.2d at 513. In that case, the defendant on cross-examination testified that he had no knowledge of cocaine or its uses. To rebut this testimony, the trial court allowed the government to introduce evidence showing that the defendant had in fact recently sold a large amount of cocaine to an undercover agent. * * *

* * *

That the payroll records are relevant evidence is unmistakable. * * * Posner's testimony that he saw Opager deal in cocaine in 1974 was a factor in establishing Opager's criminal "predisposition," itself a matter clearly of consequence to her case. Hence, the payroll records, "as indicative that a fact in issue did or did not exist," were clearly relevant. United States v. Allison, 5 Cir., 1973, 474 F.2d 286, 289 * * *.

Reversed.

Notes

1. *No federal rule.* Because there is no Federal Rule on specific contradiction, it was often confused with other methods of impeachment, especially Rule 608(b), which prohibits the use of extrinsic evidence. Rule 608(b) was amended—substituting the phrase "character for untruthfulness" for the term "credibility"—to eliminate this confusion. See Fed.R.Evid. 608 advisory committee's note (2003) ("The amendment restores the Rule to its original intent, which was to impose an absolute bar on extrinsic evidence only if the sole purpose of offering the evidence was to prove the witness' character for veracity."). Specific contradiction involves present conduct (e.g., lying at trial), while Rule 608(b) concerns prior conduct (e.g., lying on an earlier occasion). Specific contradiction would also apply if the witness was simply mistaken at trial.

2. *Other examples.* In United States v. Crockett, 435 F.3d 1305, 1312 (10th Cir.2006), the defendant was charged with defrauding the government of taxes and of assisting others to do the same. He testified on direct examination that he would never advise anyone to cheat on his or her taxes. On cross-examination, he conceded that he had earned income assisting individuals in preparing trusts but had not filed federal income tax returns. According to the court, "when a defendant makes a false statement during direct testimony, the prosecution is allowed to prove, either through cross-examination or by rebuttal witnesses, that the defendant lied as to that fact. * * * This is so even if the evidence elicited by the prosecution ordinarily

might be collateral or otherwise inadmissible. * * * This principle of cross-examination is known as the doctrine of 'specific contradiction.' "

In United States v. Lopez, 979 F.2d 1024, 1034 (5th Cir.1992), which involved the sale of 432 pounds of marihuana, Lopez asserted on direct examination that he never had seen and could not recognize marihuana. The government contradicted this testimony by introducing a 1974 conviction for possession of marihuana. Objections were raised pursuant to Rules 608(b) and 609. On appeal, however, the court stated: "Extrinsic evidence, which includes prior convictions, is admissible under the general standards of Rules 402 and 403 to contradict specific testimony, as long as the evidence is relevant and its probative value is not substantially outweighed by the danger of unfair prejudice."

In State v. Eddy, 895 A.2d 162, 165 (Vt.2006), an alibi witness (Labelle) testified that neither defendant nor his confederate committed burglary because they were both with her at the time. The prosecution called the confederate who admitted pleading guilty to the crime. The court held: "Ritchie's guilty plea was introduced not to show that Labelle was generally untrustworthy, but rather to contradict Labelle's assertion that neither Ritchie nor defendant could have committed the crime. Rule 609 simply does not address the use of a prior conviction for the purpose of impeachment by contradiction."

3. *Extrinsic evidence.* The Advisory Committee Note, note 1, supra, also addressed the admissibility of extrinsic evidence to prove specific contradiction:

> By limiting the application of the Rule [608(b)] to proof of a witness' character for truthfulness, the amendment leaves the admissibility of extrinsic evidence offered for other grounds of impeachment (such as contradiction, prior inconsistent statement, bias and mental capacity) to Rules 402 and 403. *See, e.g., United States v. Winchenbach*, 197 F.3d 548 (1st Cir.1999) (admissibility of a prior inconsistent statement offered for impeachment is governed by Rules 402 and 403, not Rule 608(b); *United States v. Tarantino*, 846 F.2d 1384 (D.C.Cir.1988) (admissibility of extrinsic evidence offered to contradict a witness is governed by Rules 402 and 403); *United States v. Lindemann*, 85 F.3d 1232 (7th Cir.1996) (admissibility of extrinsic evidence of bias is governed by Rules 402 and 403). Rules 402 and 403 displace the common-law rules prohibiting impeachment on "collateral" matters. * * *

4. *Sources.* Gilligan & Imwinkelried, Bringing the "Opening the Door" Theory to a Close: The Tendency to Overlook the Specific Contradiction Doctrine in Evidence Law, 41 Santa Clara L.Rev. 807 (2001); McMunigal & Sharpe, Reforming Extrinsic Impeachment, 33 Conn.L.Rev. 363 (2001).

(9) IMPEACHMENT: PRIOR INCONSISTENT STATEMENTS, FEDERAL RULE 613

CENTRAL MUT. INS. CO. v. NEWMAN

District Court of Appeal of Florida, Third District, 1960.
117 So.2d 41.

BARNS, PAUL D., ASSOCIATE JUDGE. Judgment was entered against the appellant-defendant in an action against it as insurer on a jewelry "floater" policy. Appeal was taken from the final judgment entered after trial to the judge and the exclusion of evidence was assigned as error. We find error and reverse.

STATEMENT OF THE CASE

The case was tried by the Court without a jury. The parties stipulated that the sole issue was the credibility of the Plaintiff to be determined by the Court from the evidence. The Court found for the Plaintiff and judgment was entered in the sum of $5,812, including costs and attorneys' fees. During the trial, the Defendant offered into evidence prior inconsistent statements of the Plaintiff, consisting of a sworn statement given by the Plaintiff to Defendant's counsel pursuant to provisions of the policy, and marked as Defendant's Exhibit A–2 for identification, and a signed statement of the Plaintiff marked as Defendant's Exhibit A–1 for identification. Both offers were refused by the Court which refusals are assigned as error.

STATEMENT OF FACTS

The policy covered seven pieces of jewelry owned by the Plaintiff and his wife. Four of the insured pieces allegedly disappeared in a manner unknown to the Plaintiff. The loss was alleged to have occurred sometime between July 20 and July 22, 1958, while the Plaintiff, according to his allegations and testimony, was on a business trip to Atlanta, Georgia.

The Plaintiff was a liquidator of distressed and closed-out, etc., merchandise and resided in Miami, Florida. About a week before the loss, the Plaintiff was having lunch with a group of men and one of the members of this luncheon group told him of several businesses in Atlanta that had merchandise for sale. At the trial, the Plaintiff testified that this lunch took place at a restaurant named "Wolfie's", while in a sworn statement given by him previously, he said that this group was having lunch at a restaurant called the "Great Gables". He could not remember the name of the man who told him of the businesses in Atlanta, nor could he remember the names or name of the persons with whom he was having lunch at this time.

The unknown friend had written down the names and addresses of the businesses in Atlanta and the Plaintiff carried them in his pocket for about several days or a week before making the trip. Then the Plaintiff allegedly made a trip for the purpose of inspecting this merchandise. He did not remember the names of the places of business he went to see in

Atlanta, and he either did not remember or was uncertain of the name of the street on which they were located.

The Plaintiff's testimony and previous statements as to the day and the date upon which he allegedly made this trip to Atlanta are inconsistent. On July 25, 1958, a few days after this alleged trip, Mr. Matou, an agent of the Defendant, took a statement from the Plaintiff concerning some of the trip. On October 2, 1958, Mr. Gotthardt, counsel for the Defendant, took a sworn statement from him concerning the details of the trip. After instituting suit, his deposition was taken on November 21, 1958. His previous statements and testimony at the trial, which was held on April 8, 1959, are inconsistent in many details concerning his trip to Atlanta.

The jewelry which was lost or stolen was kept in a brown pouch. Some of the jewelry which he carried with him on his trip belonged to his wife. Despite the fact that he had opened the pouch while in Atlanta to remove and return jewelry to it, he stated that he did not know that his wife's jewelry was in the pouch until his wife told him. She did not testify. The testimony does not reveal how many of the seven pieces insured were in the bag.

The subject matter of the loss was in the exclusive control of the Plaintiff and the facts surrounding the alleged loss were virtually within his exclusive knowledge, and therefore, were not subject to being controverted by testimony offered by the Defendant. The only defense upon which the Defendant could rely is that the Plaintiff's story is inherently improbable, illogical, and unworthy of credit.

Conclusions

Concerning the impeachment of the testimony of a witness by the use of prior self-contradictory statements, III Wigmore on Evidence, 3d ed. § 1017, p. 684, states:

> "*Theory of Relevancy.* The end aimed at by the present sort of impeaching evidence [self-contradiction] is the same as that of the preceding sort, [specific contradiction] namely, to show the witness to be in general capable of making errors in his testimony (ante, § 1000); for upon perceiving that the witness has made an erroneous statement upon one point, we are ready to infer that he is capable of making an error upon other points. But the method of showing this is here slightly different; for, instead of invoking the assertions of other witnesses to prove his specific error [contradiction], we resort simply to witness' own prior statements, in which he has given a contrary version. We place his contradictory statements side by side, and, as both cannot be correct, we realize that in at least one of the two he must have spoken erroneously. Thus, we have detected him in one specific error, from which may be inferred a capacity to make other errors. * * *
>
> (1) The general end attained is the same indefinite end attained by the preceding method [specific contradiction], i.e., some unde-

fined capacity to err; it may be a moral disposition to lie, it may be partisan bias, it may be faulty observation, it may be defective recollection, or any other quality. No specific defect is indicated; but each and all are hinted at. It has been often said that a Prior Self–Contradiction shows a defect either in the memory or in the honesty of the witness. * * * "

McCormick on Evidence, p. 63, citing Wigmore, supra, states:

* * *

"The theory of attack by prior inconsistent statements is not based on the assumption that the present testimony is false and the former statement true but rather upon the notion that talking one way on the stand and another way previously is blowing hot and cold, and raises a doubt as to the truthfulness of both statements."

We find error in refusing to admit the prior statements of the plaintiff and the cause is remanded for trial to the judge unless on motion a trial to a jury is awarded. * * *

Reversed.

Notes and Questions

1. *Inconsistency requirement.* By definition, a prior inconsistent statement must be inconsistent with the testimony of the witness at the trial. Is a direct contradiction required? See United States v. Gravely, 840 F.2d 1156, 1163 (4th Cir.1988) ("The Federal Rules of Evidence, however, reject the view that the prior testimony must flatly contradict trial testimony. * * * It is enough if the 'proffered testimony, taken as a whole, either by what it says or by what it omits to say' affords some indication that the fact was different from the testimony of the witness whom it sought to contradict.").

2. *Lack of knowledge.* See United States v. Shoupe, 548 F.2d 636, 638–39 (6th Cir.1977) ("Adkins credibility as a witness was also challenged by the defense. He was confronted with prior grand jury testimony in which he had stated unequivocally that he had no recollection of finding a ski mask included in the contents of the duffle bag and that his agreement with Willison called for him to receive a fee for the use of his apartment which differed from the sum which he mentioned at trial.").

3. *Lack of memory.* See United States v. Knox, 124 F.3d 1360, 1364 (10th Cir.1997) ("A well-settled body of case law holds that where a declarant's memory loss is contrived it will be taken as inconsistent * * *."); United States v. Strother, 49 F.3d 869, 874 (2d Cir.1995) ("Under certain circumstances, a witness's prior silence regarding critical facts may constitute a prior inconsistent statement where failure to mention those matters * * * conflicts with that which is later recalled. Where the belatedly recollected facts merely augment that which was originally described, the prior silence is often simply too ambiguous to have any probative force. * * * It would have been natural for Wollschleager to include Strother's request in her earlier statement.").

4. *Opinion rule.* It will frequently occur that a prior and allegedly inconsistent statement made by a witness will be phrased in terms which, if made on the stand, would violate the rule against opinions where it still prevails. May such a statement be used for impeachment? See Miller v. Lint, 404 N.E.2d 752 (Ohio 1980); Grady, The Admissibility of a Prior Statement of Opinion for Purposes of Impeachment, 41 Cornell L.Q. 224 (1956). Would exclusion of an opinion be consistent with the rationale underlying Federal Rule 701?

UNITED STATES v. HUDSON

United States Court of Appeals, First Circuit, 1992.
970 F.2d 948.

YOUNG, DISTRICT JUDGE.

Richard B. Hudson, Sr. ("appellant") here appeals from his conviction on two separate counts, each charging him with conspiracy to possess with intent to distribute in excess of five hundred grams of cocaine. * * * The first count alleged that during late 1986 and continuing through 1987, appellant engaged in a cocaine conspiracy with Henry Cormier, Robert Johnson, and others. The second count alleged another cocaine conspiracy, this one commencing in late 1988 and continuing through 1989, involving appellant with his brother, James Hudson, and others. [Cromier, Johnson, and the accused's brother, James Hudson, all testified pursuant to plea agreements. They all implicated the accused in the charged incidents.] * * *

Throughout, defense counsel had ably sought to impugn the motives of the government witnesses for testifying in a manner which inculpated appellant and had painted each of the government witnesses in the darkest possible hue. Defense counsel now prepared to present appellant's affirmative case.

At this point, the Assistant United States Attorney asked to approach the side bar and asked the Court to require defense counsel to make a proffer and to hear the testimony of the two defense witnesses outside the presence of the jury as it was "from the government's view, rank hearsay." Defense counsel represented that the two witnesses, Paul Whitten and Gregory Benson, were inmates in the South Windham Correctional Center where Henry Cormier and James Hudson had been held. Defense counsel said that onc of the two witnesses would testify that he heard Cormier tell James Hudson that appellant "had nothing to do with drugs" but that he was angry with appellant over a gambling debt. What follows next in this side bar conference is vital to an understanding of appellant's claim here. We set forth the relevant colloquy * * *:

THE COURT: How do you overcome the hearsay?

DEFENSE COUNSEL: I think it's a situation—

CO-DEFENSE COUNSEL: I think it's evidence of impeachment of bias and motive for a witness who has previously testified that he doesn't have any bias, that he is telling the truth.

THE COURT: How do you get over the hearsay?

CO–DEFENSE COUNSEL: Prior inconsistent statement.

* * *

Whitten testified [on voir dire examination] that Cormier had told James Hudson that he "didn't believe that Dick Hudson had anything to do with drugs" but that Cormier was upset with appellant because "Dick had beat him in a game of gin and it cost him $5,000." Gregory Benson then testified that he had overheard the same conversation and that Cormier had said to James Hudson, "I never really thought your brother sold drugs but me and Robbie * * * said he did because he beat us out of a lot of money playing cards, gambling." Benson further testified that James Hudson "said he wanted to make sure the bastard got what he deserved" because "Dick was supposed to take care of [my] family and he never did." [The court sustained the government's hearsay objection.]

I.

Appellant first contends that the district court erred in excluding the testimony of the defense witnesses, Paul Whitten and Gregory Benson, contending that this aspect of the appeal is controlled by our decision in *United States v. Barrett,* 539 F.2d 244, 253–56 (1st Cir.1976).

* * *

Next, the government contends that the foundation for admitting extrinsic evidence through Benson about James Hudson's prior statement was never properly laid pursuant to Fed.R.Evid. 613(b), since James Hudson was never "afforded an opportunity to explain or deny [his earlier statement]." The government urges us to reconsider our ruling in *Barrett* in which we explained that the foundation requirements of 613(b) do not require that the witness be confronted with the statement while on the witness stand, but rather, only that the witness be available to be recalled in order to explain the statement during the course of the trial. *Barrett,* 539 F.2d at 254–56. The government properly notes that the Fifth, Ninth, and Tenth Circuits have upheld the refusal to admit proof through extrinsic evidence of prior inconsistent statements unless the witness has first been afforded the opportunity to deny or explain those statements. [Citations omitted.] The Eighth Circuit has followed suit, at least in circumstances in which there are considerable logistical difficulties in arranging for the recall of inmate witnesses sought to be impeached through extrinsic evidence of prior inconsistent statements. *United States v. Lynch,* 800 F.2d 765, 770 (8th Cir.1986). We decline the invitation. Assuming without deciding that James Hudson's expression of bias against appellant constituted a prior inconsistent statement with respect to his trial testimony, we reaffirm our earlier analysis as set forth in *Barrett.* The approach there taken is wholly consistent with the requirements of Fed.R.Evid. 613(b), as explained by the notes of the Advisory Committee: "the traditional insistence that the attention of the witness be directed to the statement on cross examination is relaxed in favor of simply providing the witness an opportunity to explain and the opposite party an opportunity to examine the statement, with no specification of any particular time or sequence," and is supported by the great weight of authority. * * *

Here, as in *Barrett,* we have no basis for assuming that James Hudson, a federal prisoner, was not available for recall or that the government would have been prejudiced by admission of the statement without the opportunity for adequate rebuttal and examination. Even though the district court possesses a substantial measure of discretion under Fed.R.Evid. 613(b), it would resurrect the now-discredited procedure laid down in *Queen Caroline's Case,* 2 Brod. & Bing. 284, 313, 129 Eng.Rep. 976 (1820), if we excluded James Hudson's statement on the ground of an inadequate evidentiary foundation when the district court acted without any evaluation of the availability of the witness sought to be impeached or, alternatively, without any expressed consideration of whatever delay or inconvenience might have been caused by defense counsel's failure to confront James Hudson, on cross-examination, with his allegedly inconsistent statement.[90] * * *

[Appellant's conviction on Count I was affirmed on harmless error grounds. The conviction on Count II was vacated and remanded for further proceedings.]

SELYA, CIRCUIT JUDGE (concurring).

* * * I concur in the judgment. I write separately, however, to express my thoughts as to why *Barrett* bears overruling and as to how Fed.R.Evid. 613(b) was meant to operate.

This court decided *Barrett* soon after the Federal Rules of Evidence took effect. Since that time, most (though not all) of the circuits have rejected *Barrett*'s rationale, deciding instead that the adoption of Rule 613(b) did not abolish the traditional common law requirement of laying a suitable foundation prior to the introduction of impeachment evidence. [Citations omitted.] In my estimation, the majority rule is sounder than the view espoused in *Barrett.* It works to avoid unfair surprise, gives the target of the impeaching evidence a timely opportunity to explain or

90. We think it is important to note that, both in *Barrett* and in the present case, the trial court's fundamental error lay not in a mistaken interpretation of Rule 613(b) but in its failure to exercise its discretion. Even if a proponent is not always required to lay a prior foundation under Rule 613(b), a trial court is free to use its informed discretion to exclude extrinsic evidence of prior inconsistent statements on grounds of unwarranted prejudice, confusion, waste of time, or the like. *See, e.g., Nachtsheim v. Beech Aircraft Corp.,* 847 F.2d 1261, 1276–77 (7th Cir.1988) (suggesting that trial court has discretion under Fed.R.Evid. 403 to exclude evidence not excluded by Fed.R.Evid. 613 [b]); * * * Moreover, *Barrett* notwithstanding, Fed.R.Evid. 611(a) allows the trial judge to control the mode and order of interrogation and presentation of evidence, giving him or her the discretion to impose the common-law "prior foundation" requirement when such an approach seems fitting. *See Nachtsheim,* 847 F.2d at 1276–77 (suggesting that trial court has broad discretion under Rules 611 and 403 to exclude evidence not barred by Rule 613[b]); *United States v. Marks,* 816 F.2d 1207, 1210–11 (7th Cir.1987) (stating that Rule 613 was not intended to eliminate trial judge's discretion to manage the trial in a way designed to promote accuracy and fairness). Here, however, there is no sign that the trial judge sought to exercise these powers.

deny the alleged inconsistency, facilitates judges' efforts to conduct trials in an orderly manner, and conserves scarce judicial resources. At the same time, insistence upon a prior foundational requirement, subject, of course, to relaxation in the presider's discretion if "the interests of justice otherwise require," Fed.R.Evid. 613(b), does not impose an undue burden on the proponent of the evidence. * * *

Notes and Questions

1. *Hearsay.* The principal case and these notes concern statements offered for purposes of impeachment. Note that certain prior inconsistent statements are admissible as nonhearsay under Rule 801(d)(1)(A). See discussion in Chapter 13, Section B(1), infra.

2. *Written statements.* When the prior inconsistent statement with which the witness is sought to be impeached is a statement in writing, should the cross-examiner be required to show the statement to the witness before interrogating him concerning it? Such a requirement is commonly thought to have been laid down in The Queen's Case, 129 Eng.Rep. 976 (C.P.1820), and was widely applied in this country, at least prior to the adoption of the Federal Rules of Evidence. For an explanation and evaluation of the rule, see Ladd, Impeachment of Witness, 52 Cornell L.Q. 239, 246–77 (1967). As the principal case indicates, Rule 613(a) abolished this requirement. See Rush v. Illinois Cent. R. Co., 399 F.3d 705, 716, 720 (6th Cir.2005) (Defendant sought to impeach Lockett's direct testimony that he never saw "anybody running to get on the back of the train" with his post-accident statement that "Johnathan was running alongside the train trying to get on." "Although unnecessary under the current version of Rule 613, defense counsel took the additional step of revealing the prior inconsistent statement to Lockett during cross-examination and afforded Lockett with the opportunity to explain the apparent inconsistency.").

3. *Extrinsic evidence.* The common law rule prohibiting contradicting a witness on collateral matters by extrinsic evidence applied to prior inconsistent statements. Thus, although wide latitude was generally given on cross-examination with regard to the subject matter of prior inconsistent statements, extrinsic evidence of such statements was inadmissible unless the statement concerned facts relevant to the issues in the case or facts which themselves would be provable by extrinsic evidence, such as those involving bias or facts about which the witness would not be mistaken if his story were true. The classic case is Attorney–General v. Hitchcock, 154 Eng.Rep. 38 (1847). Has this requirement survived the Federal Rules? See discussion in 1 McCormick, Evidence §§ 36, 45, 49 (6th ed. 2006). See also the discussion of this topic when specific contradiction is employed in the notes following *Opager*, Subsection 8, supra.

4. *Constitutional issues.* Evidence obtained by the state in violation of the constitutional rights of a criminal accused is inadmissible as substantive evidence of the accused's guilt. Should such evidence be admissible for purposes of impeachment if the defendant chooses to testify in his own defense? In Walder v. United States, 347 U.S. 62 (1954), it was held proper, where the defendant testified that he had never possessed narcotics, to

impeach him by evidence that an illegal search had disclosed the defendant in possession of narcotics. The Court qualified its holding by stating that the defendant "must be free to deny all the elements of the case against him without thereby giving leave to the Government to introduce by way of rebuttal evidence illegally secured by it * * *." Id. at 65.

Subsequent to *Miranda v. Arizona*, it was widely supposed that, *Walder* notwithstanding, statements obtained from a criminal accused in the absence of *Miranda* warnings would be inadmissible for impeachment as well as for substantive purposes. See, e.g., United States v. Fox, 403 F.2d 97 (2d Cir.1968). However, in Harris v. New York, 401 U.S. 222 (1971), the Supreme Court revived the *Walder* doctrine and arguably expanded it beyond its original compass. In *Harris,* the police had obtained certain statements from the defendant concerning two alleged narcotics sales, concededly without giving antecedent *Miranda* warnings. The state made no attempt to introduce these statements as part of its case in chief, but when defendant took the stand, denied one sale and asserted the other was of baking powder rather than heroin, the prosecution was allowed to use the statements for impeachment. A majority of the Court found no "difference in principle" between *Walder's* allowance of impeachment on a collateral matter and the instant case where the contradiction was as to facts relevant to the charge being tried. If there is no such difference, of what continuing significance is the statement in *Walder* that the defendant "must be free to deny all elements of the case against him?" See an able analysis of this and related questions in a Comment, The Impeachment Exception to the Constitutional Exclusionary Rules, 73 Colum.L.Rev. 1476 (1973). However, an involuntary (coercive) confession may not be used to impeach, Mincey v. Arizona, 437 U.S. 385 (1978), nor may silence following the giving of *Miranda* warnings, Doyle v. Ohio, 426 U.S. 610 (1976).

The exclusionary rule may also come into play where the prosecution seeks to impeach the testimony of a defense witness by use of accused's tainted statements. See James v. Illinois, 493 U.S. 307 (1990).

(10) IMPEACHMENT: LEARNED TREATISE

FRESHWATER v. SCHEIDT

Supreme Court of Ohio, 1999.
714 N.E.2d 891.

DOUGLAS, J.

[Plaintiff underwent surgery to remove her gallbladder. She subsequently filed a malpractice action against Dr. Scheidt, who had performed the laparoscopic cholecystectomy.]

Shortly after surgery, Kathleen had noticeable swelling of her body and severe abdominal pain. Kathleen was eventually transported by ambulance to another hospital, where she underwent further surgery to repair a perforation to her small bowel. The perforation occurred as a result of the laparoscopic procedure performed by Scheidt. During this time, Kathleen became seriously ill and almost died. She was hospitalized for seventy-seven days, the majority of which was spent in the intensive-care unit. She also incurred extensive medical bills.

* * *

Also at trial, Dr. Karl A. Zucker, an expert witness for appellees, testified that Scheidt did not deviate from accepted standards of medical care in removing Kathleen's gallbladder. Upon cross-examination of Zucker, counsel for appellants attempted to question Zucker about statements contained in a book entitled "Surgical Laparoscopy," which had been edited and written in part by Zucker. The statements were in a chapter entitled "Open Laparoscopy," written in part by a colleague of Zucker's, Dr. Fitzgibbons. Additionally, appellants' counsel also sought to cross-examine Zucker with respect to other medical literature authored by Fitzgibbons. This additional literature had apparently been referred to by Zucker in some of Zucker's other publications. When questioned about the writings that Fitzgibbons had authored, Zucker avoided answering whether Fitzgibbons was an "authority" in the field and he further refused to acknowledge whether the medical literature authored by Fitzgibbons was "authoritative" in nature:

"Q. When you have written articles on laparoscopic surgery, have you frequently cited Dr. Fitzgibbons as an authority on the open laparoscopic technique?

"A. I'm not sure the word 'authority' is one I'd use; but he's a colleague, a personal friend, my kids play with his kids. So he's a respected colleague, and I often will quote him. I think he's very honorable and honest individual with very good experience.

"Q. And you value his opinion?

"A. Yes.

"Q. And when you put out your book, he's the one who wrote the chapter with another doctor or two on open laparoscopic?

"A. Yes. * * *

"Q. * * * Doctor, I have—did you quote Dr. Fitzgibbons because you believed he was an authority in the area of open laparoscopic surgery?

"A. As I said, I'm not sure I used the word 'authority.'

"Q. Well, that's my question, though. It's of some legal significance as to the questions I can ask you or cannot ask you, and I'd like to know if you consider him an authority in the area of open laparoscopic surgery. * * *

"Q. * * * Have you relied upon Dr. Fitzgibbons at all in your profession of informing other doctors as to the open Hasson technique?

"A. I've quoted Dr. Fitzgibbons; but I don't always, you know, agree with his writing or what he advocates.

"Q. Did you rely upon, did you think he was authoritative enough to write a chapter in your book?

"A. Again, I'm not sure about the word 'authoritative,' but I value his opinion and his expertise. I invited him to write a chapter in a textbook that I wrote on laparoscopic surgery.

"Q. Did you rely upon the materials presented in that chapter of your book for any part of your testimony today?

"A. I certainly, I used part of that in coming up to my opinions and every day practice as well as in this testimony.

"Q. Did you rely upon his part of the chapter that dealt with complications and risk factors of not using the open technique? * * *

"Q. Did you rely upon any studies or statistics that he had as to the open Hasson technique versus the closed technique in coming to your conclusions for trial today?

"A. Well, as I said, I agree with some of the things and I disagree with other parts of his writings * * *."

The trial court prevented counsel for appellants from cross-examining Zucker with respect to statements in Zucker's book. * * *

* * *

The central issue in this case concerns the extent to which statements from learned treatises and other publications may be used to impeach the testimony of expert witnesses. * * * In *Hallworth v. Republic Steel Corp.* (1950), 153 Ohio St. 349 * * * the court held that learned treatises, even though properly identified, authenticated, and recognized as standard authority, are not admissible in evidence to prove the truth of the matter asserted therein. Rather, "learned treatises are considered hearsay, may not be used as substantive evidence, and are specifically limited to impeachment purposes only." Ramage v. Cent. Ohio Emergency Serv. Inc. (1992), 64 Ohio St.3d 97 * * *.

Later, in *Stinson v. England* (1994), 69 Ohio St.3d 451, 633 N.E.2d 532, this court set forth the conditions under which learned treatises can be used to impeach the credibility of expert witnesses. Counsel may use a learned treatise to impeach a testifying expert by establishing that the expert is either unaware of the text or unfamiliar with its contents. * * * Additionally, the substance of a learned treatise can be used to impeach the credibility of an expert witness if the expert has relied upon the treatise in forming his or her opinion or the expert has acknowledged the authoritative nature of the treatise. * * *

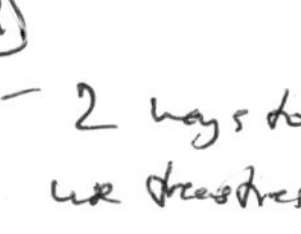

* * *

In the case at bar, both the trial court and court of appeals ruled that *Stinson* prevented appellants' counsel from cross-examining Scheidt and Zucker about the medical literature in question. On cross-examination, both Scheidt and Zucker would not explicitly concede the "authoritative" nature of the literature. Nevertheless, although Scheidt and Zucker refused to explicitly acknowledge the authoritative nature of the medical literature, they implicitly conceded as much. * * * Scheidt

testified that he "hardly [knew] how to define authority," but that his teachers in the area of laparoscopic surgery were "helpful and useful," and that he looked to his teachers for "helpful suggestions." He also stated that the courses pertaining to laparoscopic cholecystectomies "were certainly helpful to me." With respect to Zucker, he testified that Fitzgibbons was a "respected colleague," "I often will quote him," and that he was "a very honorable and honest individual with very good experience." Zucker further stated that he valued Fitzgibbons's "opinions and his expertise," and had "invited him to write a chapter in a textbook that I wrote on laparoscopic surgery." Zucker also testified that he had relied upon materials presented in the chapter in that he "used part of that [chapter] in coming up to my opinions in everyday practice as well as in this testimony."

In *Stinson*, we determined that it was error to allow the medical treatise to be used for impeachment purposes because a proper foundation had not been laid establishing the text as a reliable authority. However, *Stinson* was not intended to allow testifying experts to adroitly evade cross-examination simply by avoiding such words as "rely" or "authority" or any forms of those words. Indeed, if an expert witness relies upon published medical literature in forming his or her opinion, or the expert provides testimony sufficient to establish that the literature is reliable authority, or the literature is part of the expert's own publication, statements contained in the literature can be used for purposes of impeachment. The requisite reliance upon published medical literature or its authoritative nature can be established without an express acknowledgement by the testifying expert that he or she had relied upon the literature or that it is authoritative.

The testimony of Scheidt and Zucker established that the medical literature at issue was reliable authority. Moreover, testimony and other evidence in the record indicate that Scheidt and Zucker also relied upon the literature in forming their opinions. The literature was not offered by appellants' counsel as substantive evidence. Instead, the literature was intended to call into question the weight to be attached by the fact finder to the testimony of Scheidt and Zucker. In this regard, the restricted cross-examination of Scheidt and Zucker by the trial court harmed the fact-finding process and prevented the jury from adequately assessing the credibility of the witnesses. * * *

Judgment reversed and cause remanded.

Note and Questions

At the time *Freshwater* was decided, Ohio had a rule limiting the use of learned treatises to impeachment, which reflected the common law approach. The Ohio rule was based on Michigan Rule 707. In 2006, Ohio adopted the approach found in the Federal Rules, which create a hearsay exception for learned treatises. Under Rule 803(18), statements contained in treatises called to an expert's attention during cross-examination or relied upon in direct examination may be admissible as substantive evidence. By creating an exception to the hearsay rule, the Federal Rules avoid the awkwardness and futility of an instruction which tells the jury to consider the substance of the statement in the treatise for purposes of impeachment only.

Following the lead of the United States Supreme Court in Reilly v. Pinkus, 338 U.S. 269 (1949), Rule 803(18) provides that the authoritativeness of the treatise may be established by the testimony of the witness, by expert testimony or by judicial notice. Why must statements in authoritative treatises be called to the attention of an expert? Why not simply admit them on their own merit?

(11) REHABILITATION

THOMAS, CROSS-EXAMINATION AND REHABILITATION OF WITNESSES[91]

14 Defense Law Journal 247, 261 (1965).

* * *

REHABILITATING THE CROSS-EXAMINED WITNESS

Many of us have experienced instances where a devastating or skillful cross-examination has apparently made a shambles or wreckage of the "star witness" or other witnesses. The question then arises for the advocate, who vouches for said witness, to determine whether Humpty Dumpty really had a "great fall," and if he did, whether he can be "put together again," on re-direct or re-examination. For some unknown reason, the subject of re-direct examination, or rehabilitation of witnesses, has received but scant attention from the writers, yet it is here that we have a good indication of a trial lawyer's general ability and certainly an excellent test as to whether he has well prepared the facts of his case.

Admittedly, the proper function and scope of re-direct examination is to rebut, explain or avoid the effect of new matter brought out on cross-examination. Occasionally, in the discretion of the court, it has been utilized to propound forgotten questions.

LEAVING WELL ENOUGH ALONE MAY BE BEST

At the outset, trial counsel must decide whether to proceed on re-direct. He should be mindful of the adage, "Let well enough alone" if his witness has not been seriously damaged, for he can over-try his case, and so doing "open the door" for a real time bomb. If the cross-examination has fallen short of the mark in reaching any material part of the story on direct, most skilled lawyers will waive re-direct, and seek to take care of his witness in summation if counsel opposite try to turn the spotlight on these immaterial contradictions or fallacies. * * *

91. Copyright by the publisher, The Allen Smith Company, Indianapolis 46202. Reprinted by permission. [Ed.]

Notes and Questions

1. *Limitations.* Having once made the determination that rehabilitation of a witness is essential, what evidence is admissible for the purpose? Few helpful generalizations are possible in the area, but if the courts recognize one cardinal principle it is that the permissible rehabilitation of a witness is a function of the type of impeachment to which that witness has been subjected. Therefore, since it is impossible to answer the general question, "How may a witness be rehabilitated?," it is fruitful only to inquire how a witness who has been impeached in a certain specific manner may be rehabilitated. The succeeding materials therefore follow the same general organizational pattern as have preceding materials on impeachment.

2. *Bolstering.* The first derivative of the proposition that rehabilitation is a function of impeachment is the universal rule that the credibility of an unimpeached witness cannot be supported. See material on bolstering at beginning of this Section.

3. *Sources.* As to rehabilitation generally, see Ladd, Techniques and Theory of Character Testimony, 24 Iowa L.Rev. 498 (1939); Orfield, Impeachment and Support of Witnesses in Federal Criminal Cases, 11 Kan. L.Rev. 477 (1963); Note, 36 Minn.L.Rev. 724 (1952); Mauet, Fundamentals of Trial Techniques 172 (1980).

RODRIGUEZ v. STATE

Court of Criminal Appeals of Texas, 1957.
305 S.W.2d 350.

Woodley, Judge. The offense is aggravated assault; the punishment, 9 months in jail and a fine of $750.

Appellant, aged 66 years, came to the home of Ramon Gavia on a Sunday afternoon to see Gavia.

Gavia was not at home and appellant was invited by Gavia's daughter, Cathalina, to wait for her father.

Cathalina Gavia testified that she left the room for a few minutes and upon her return appellant and her seven year old foster daughter were on the couch and appellant was holding one hand on the child's mouth and was taking her pants off, and she ran and got the child and called some friends who notified the officers.

The child was found not to be competent to testify.

Appellant testified and denied any assault was made on the child. His version was that the little girl went to the bathroom and returned with her panties down, and he called her to him to assist her in pulling them up which he was doing when Cathalina Gavia came into the room, ordered him to leave and called the officers.

Appellant further testified that on the previous day he had seen Cathalina in a car on a country road and a man was "lying down on her legs"; that when he came to see Cathalina's father, he spoke to her about what he had seen and she denied it and got mad, and shortly thereafter charged him with assaulting the child.

Cathalina was then recalled and denied that she had been on any country road or with a man on Saturday, and further denied that appellant had spoken to her about any such incident at her home on Sunday.

* * *

After the testimony above mentioned had been given by appellant and by the State's witness Cathalina Gavia, the State was permitted over objection to prove that Cathalina's reputation in the community for truth and veracity was good.

We are cited to the rule that where there is no evidence to impeach the testimony of a witness except contradictory evidence, it is not permissible to bolster the testimony of the witness by proof of his good reputation for truth and veracity. Jones v. State, 52 Tex.Cr.R. 206, 106 S.W. 126; Zysman v. State, 42 Tex.Cr.R. 432, 60 S.W. 669.

This rule has no application here for where an attack is made upon the veracity of a witness, such as by evidence that the witness has conspired with another to falsely accuse the defendant, or where it is attempted to be shown that the witness is testifying under corrupt motives, or is fabricating testimony, it is proper to permit testimony that the witness has a good reputation for truth and veracity. * * *

No reversible error appearing, the judgment is affirmed.

Notes and Questions

1. *Explaining or denying bias*. In accord with the principal case, facts alleged to have given rise to bias or interest may generally be denied or explained. 1 McCormick, Evidence § 47 (6th ed. 2006); 4 Wigmore, Evidence § 1119 (Chadbourn rev. 1970).

2. *Truthful character*. Should charges of bias or interest invariably authorize rebuttal in the form of evidence of good reputation for truth and veracity? What if the bias is alleged to arise from a familial relationship with a party? Lassiter v. State, 47 So.2d 230 (Ala.Ct.App.1950). See United States v. Medical Therapy Sciences, Inc., 583 F.2d 36 (2d Cir.1978), for discussion of when evidence of bias is an attack on truthful character. See also Renda v. King, 347 F.3d 550, 554 (3d Cir.2003) ("The reason that evidence of bias does not open the door for evidence of good character for truthfulness is because evidence of bias only relates to a motive to lie in the particular case, not a general predisposition to lie.").

UNITED STATES v. PLANTE

First Circuit, 1973.
472 F.2d 829.

ALDRICH, SENIOR JUDGE.

[The defendants were convicted of bank robbery.]

* * *

Plante next complains of the cross-examination of his witness Kedian. Kedian admitted a conviction for mail fraud on direct examination.

On cross-examination, over objection, the government was permitted to inquire as to the details of the offense.[92] Certain formalized rules apply to impeachment of a witness. * * * [W]hile a conviction may be shown, it is generally not permissible to rehabilitate a witness by having him deny his guilt. The conventional reasons given for this are that the question is collateral, * * * and the opponent of the witness should not have to be prepared to try the criminal case. * * * *Contra*: United States v. Boyer, 1945, 80 U.S. App.D.C. 202, 150 F.2d 595. The frequent statement that the conviction is "conclusive," * * * merely states the rule, not the reason.

Within the limits of not disputing the offense, occasionally the opponent of the witness, and occasionally the proponent, wish to go into the details in order to enhance, or diminish the effect of the conviction. There is a split of authority as to whether the proponent may do so. Dryden v. United States, 5 Cir., 1956, 237 F.2d 517 (proponent may give brief explanatory or mitigating statement); United States v. Crisafi, 2 Cir., 1962, 304 F.2d 803 (proponent may explain, in court's discretion); Lamoureux v. New York, N. H. & H. RR., 1897, 169 Mass. 338, 47 N.E. 1009 (proponent may not); Rogers v. Baltimore & Ohio RR. Co., 6 Cir., 1963, 325 F.2d 134, 137 (proponent may not). The *Lamoureux* court reasoned that the opponent of the witness would normally not be in a position to contradict the explanation. We find this persuasive, although we note that the same reasoning would not apply to prevent the opponent of a witness asking the witness for the details. However, such decisions as there are appear to be uniform that the opponent of the witness may not do this. * * * We believe that neither party should be able to develop the details. To permit the opponent to do so tends unduly to prejudice the witness, * * * and in all cases it leads to a collateral issue, with frequently one party or the other being at a disadvantage.

In the present case we find no prejudice. In the first place, the witness was only a witness, and not the defendant. Secondly, the details of the witness' particular offense * * * seem very low on the scale of what a jury would normally consider mail fraud to constitute, and hence no threat to the evaluation of the witness' testimony. * * *

Notes and Questions

1. *Trial court discretion.* While some decisions support the admissibility of evidence in extenuation of a witness' prior conviction, exercise of trial court discretion to exclude is rarely held reversible error. See United States v. Crisafi, 304 F.2d 803, 804 (2d Cir.1962) ("No case has been called to our

92. The witness was not very specific, but apparently he had purchased, through the mail, a book of checks bearing the printed name of a fictitious person.

attention, and we have discovered none, in which a federal court has ever reversed a conviction against a defendant witness because he was not permitted to explain his [prior] conviction.").

2. *Double-edged sword?* Are there dangers in such an explanation? See United States v. Swanson, 9 F.3d 1354, 1357 (8th Cir.1993) ("Although we acknowledge the general rule of impropriety of inquiry by the prosecutor into specific details surrounding prior convictions, [a] different situation is presented when an accused, on direct examination, attempts to explain away the effect of the conviction or to minimize his guilt. In such cases, the defendant may be cross-examined on any facts which are relevant to the direct examination.").

3. *Truthful character.* Under Federal Rule 608(a)(2), evidence of truthful character is admissible "after the character of the witness for truthfulness has been attacked by opinion or reputation evidence or otherwise." Thus, evidence of good reputation for truthfulness is generally held admissible to rehabilitate a witness impeached by the showing of a prior conviction. 1 McCormick, Evidence § 47 (6th ed. 2006). See also United States v. Thomas, 768 F.2d 611, 618 (5th Cir.1985) ("Vigorous cross-examination and/or the fact that a witness is contradicted by other evidence in the case does not constitute such an attack.").

BRADFORD v. STATE

Court of Appeals of Alabama, 1956.
90 So.2d 96.

Bone, Judge. This appellant's jury trial on an indictment charging murder in the first degree resulted in his conviction of manslaughter in the first degree and a sentence of imprisonment in the state penitentiary for a term of ten years.

* * *

There were four witnesses who testified that they were eyewitnesses to the incidents and circumstances surrounding the actual shooting made the basis of the charges embodied in the indictment against the appellant. One was the wife of the deceased, another a friend and employee of the deceased, and the third was a witness called by the State.

One David Earl Trammell, the fourth witness, was the only one of the four testifying on behalf of the appellant. There was direct conflict between the testimony of Trammell on direct examination and the testimony of the other three witnesses. The testimony of Trammell on direct examination, if believed by the jury, corroborated the testimony of the appellant with respect to the evidence surrounding and leading up to the shooting and made out a case of self-defense. During cross-examination Trammell was asked twice if he did not tell Mr. Troy Tate that he was not at the scene of the homicide, and in both instances the witness answered in the affirmative.

On redirect examination of Trammell the following transpired:

"Q. (By Mr. Beddow): When Mr. Tate came to your brother's home was he at home? A. Yes, sir.

"Q. What did he have on? A. A gun.

"Q. Did you know he was an officer of the law? A. Yes, sir.

"Q. Had you heard that Jack Tate was his nephew? A. Yes, sir.

"Q. Now, were you afraid when Troy came there?

"Mr. Deason: Wait a minute. We object to that.

"The Court: Yes, sustain the objection.

"Mr. Beddow: We except.

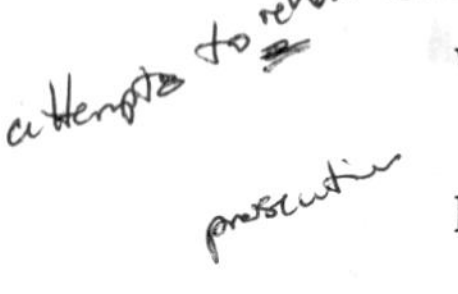

"Q. I will ask you this question: Why did you tell him that you were not there?

"Mr. Deason: Don't answer that. We object to that, if the court please.

"The Court: Sustain the objection.

"Mr. Beddow: We except. Judge, I will call your attention to the case of Williams v. The State of Alabama, if this boy told Tate he wasn't there and didn't see anything, I think we have got a right to show the circumstances, that he was afraid, Troy Tate was armed, he knew this boy was kin to him, he knew he was his uncle, and we offer to show he was afraid.

"Mr. Deason: We object to that, if the court please.

"The Court: I have already ruled.

"Mr. Beddow: We except.

"Mr. Deason: Wait a minute, Roderick.

"The Court: Don't consider any of it, gentlemen.

"Mr. Deason: All right.

"The Court: Don't consider that for any purpose whatsoever."

Appellant's attorneys contend that: "Where, upon cross examination of the witness, he admitted having made statements which are contradictory to his testimony, he may on re-direct examination show what his motive or reason was for having made the statements even though his testimony is of an uncommunicated mental state."

Dean Wigmore states the rule in the following words: "The impeached witness *may always* endeavor to explain away the effect of the supposed inconsistency by relating whatever circumstances would naturally remove it." (Emphasis supplied.) 3 Wigmore on Evidence 1044, p. 737 (3rd ed. 1940).

* * *

One hundred and three years ago Chief Justice Chilton said: "It is a well established rule of law, that where a witness has been cross examined respecting his former statements with a view of impairing his credit, the counsel who called him has the right to reexamine him, so as to afford him an opportunity of explaining such statements, and it is also said by the same authority that he may be asked what induced him to give to the person or persons to whom he made the communication the account which he has stated in the cross examination." Campbell v. State, 23 Ala. 44, 76.

The principle involved, testimonial rehabilitation, is not only the law of Alabama, but it is elementary hornbook law as well. A Student's Textbook of the Law of Evidence, Wigmore, Sec. 175 (1935 Ed.).

* * *

Seneca once said: "He who decides a case without hearing the other side, though he decide justly, cannot be considered just." He might have added that where one side only is heard it is highly unlikely that the case will be decided justly. In the instant case the reason for the rule is well illustrated. The denial of the right to rehabilitate the witness could well have been the reason for the adverse verdict.

Ever mindful of Canon 5 of the Professional Ethics of the American Bar Association, which reads in part, "The primary duty of a lawyer engaged in public prosecution is not to convict, but to see that justice is done", and taking into consideration both the elementary principle involved and the expense involved in appealing a case, we are frankly shocked that error was not confessed by the prosecuting officers in this cause.

For the error of the court below in sustaining the objection of the State to the appellant's attorney's questions on redirect examination, the judgment is reversed and the cause remanded.

Reversed and remanded.

HARWOOD, P.J., and PRICE, J., concur in the conclusion.

Note

Truthful character. Although the witness may deny or explain the inconsistency, evidence of truthful character is generally not admissible to rehabilitate the witness. See United States v. Drury, 396 F.3d 1303, 1316 (11th Cir.2005) ("[T]he prosecution's questioning the veracity of the accused's testimony and calling attention to inconsistencies therein does not constitute an attack on the accused's reputation for truthfulness permitting rehabilitative testimony."); Renda v. King, 347 F.3d 550, 554 (3d Cir.2003) ("[P]rior inconsistent statements do not open the door for evidence of good character for truthfulness because there can be a number of reasons for the error, such as defects in knowledge or memory, a bias or interest to lie in this particular instance, or a general character trait for untruthfulness.").

Note on Prior Consistent Statements

When the credibility of a witness has been attacked, may credibility be buttressed through the introduction of prior statements consistent with his or her trial testimony? The great weight of state authority severely limits the use of such statements. Usually admissibility is limited to statements offered to rebut an express or implied charge of recent fabrication or improper motive, or to statements made relatively near the time of an alleged inconsistent statement that the witness has denied making. Certainly, the relevancy of consistent statements not offered for such purposes is questionable. See 4 Wigmore, Evidence § 1126 (Chadbourn rev. 1972); 1 McCormick, Evidence § 47 (6th ed. 2006). A few states broadly admit consistent statements. For a discussion of the wide latitude in one such state, see 1 Brandis & Broun, North Carolina Evidence §§ 162–65 (6th ed. 2004).

Most of the current questions involving prior consistent statements arise as a result of Rule 801(d)(1)(B) and identical state rules which provide that a statement is not hearsay if the declarant testifies at the trial and the statement is "consistent with the declarant's testimony and is offered to rebut an express or implied charge against the declarant of recent fabrication or improper influence or motive." In essence, Rule 801(d)(1)(B) makes these consistent statements substantive evidence, rather than evidence simply affecting the credibility of the witness. What is the significance of that distinction? What is the status of consistent statements not falling within Rule 801(d)(1)(B)? Such issues are best developed in connection with a discussion of Rule 801. See Chapter 13, infra.

Topic V
THE HEARSAY RULE

Chapter 13[1]

FOUNDATIONS OF THE HEARSAY RULE AND CONFRONTATION

SECTION A. DEFINITION AND RATIONALE: STATEMENTS FOR THE TRUTH OF THE MATTER ASSERTED

FEDERAL RULE 801(a)–(c)

MOORE v. UNITED STATES

Supreme Court of the United States, 1976.
429 U.S. 20.

PER CURIAM.

John David Moore, Jr., was convicted in a bench trial of possession of heroin with intent to distribute it, in violation of 21 U.S.C. § 841(a)(1). * * *

In early January 1975, police officers received a tip from an informant that Moore and others were in possession of heroin at "Moore's apartment." The police obtained a search warrant and entered the apartment, where they found Moore lying face down near a coffee table in the living room. Also present in the apartment was a woman who was sitting on a couch in the same room. Bags containing heroin were found both on top of and beneath the coffee table, and they were seized along with various narcotics paraphernalia.

At a consolidated hearing on Moore's motion to suppress evidence and on the merits, the prosecution adduced no admissible evidence showing that Moore was in possession of the heroin in the apartment in which he and the woman were found other than his proximity to the

1. In the cases and materials throughout the chapter, some footnotes have been omitted and others have been renumbered. [Ed.]

narcotics at the time the warrant was executed. Indeed, one police officer testified that he did not find "any indications of ownership of the apartment." In his closing argument on the merits, however, the prosecutor placed substantial emphasis on the out-of-court declaration of the unidentified informant:

> "[A] confidential informant came to Detective Uribe and said, 'I have information or I have—through personal observation, know[ledge] that John David Moore resides at a certain apartment here in El Paso, Texas, and he is in possession of a certain amount of heroin.' "

In adjudging Moore guilty, the trial court found that he had been in close proximity to the seized heroin, that he was the tenant of the apartment in question, and that he had, therefore, been in possession of the contraband. In making these findings, the court *expressly* relied on the hearsay declaration of the informant * * *.

There can be no doubt that the informant's out-of-court declaration that the apartment in question was "Moore's apartment," either as related in the search warrant affidavit or as reiterated in live testimony by the police officers, was hearsay and thus inadmissible in evidence on the issue of Moore's guilt. Introduction of this testimony deprived Moore of the opportunity to cross-examine the informant as to exactly what he meant by "Moore's apartment," and what factual basis, if any, there was for believing that Moore was a tenant or regular resident there. Moore was similarly deprived of the chance to show that the witness' recollection was erroneous or that he was not credible. The informant's declaration falls within no exception to the hearsay rule recognized in the Federal Rules of Evidence, and reliance on this hearsay statement in determining petitioner's guilt or innocence was error.

* * *

The petition for a writ of certiorari is granted, the judgment of the Court of Appeals is vacated, and the case is remanded to that court so it may determine whether the wrongful admission of the hearsay evidence was harmless error.

It is so ordered.

TRIBE, TRIANGULATING HEARSAY[2]

87 Harv.L.Rev. 957, 958–59 (1974).

THE TESTIMONIAL TRIANGLE

The basic hearsay problem is that of forging a reliable chain of inferences, from an act or utterance of a person not subject to contemporaneous in-court cross-examination about that act or utterance, to an event that the act or utterance is supposed to reflect. Typically, the first

2. Copyright © 1974 by the Harvard Law Review Association. Reprinted by permission of the Association and the author. [Ed.]

link in the required chain of inferences is the link from the act or utterance to the belief it is thought to express or indicate. It is helpful to think of this link as involving a "trip" into the head of the person responsible for the act or utterance (the declarant) to see what he or she was really thinking when the act occurred. The second link is the one from the declarant's assumed belief to a conclusion about some external event that is supposed to have triggered the belief, or that is linked to the belief in some other way. This link involves a trip out of the head of the declarant, in order to match the declarant's assumed belief with the external reality sought to be demonstrated.

The trier must obviously employ such a chain of inferences whenever a witness testifies in court. But the process has long been regarded as particularly suspect when the act or utterance is not one made in court, under oath, by a person whose demeanor at the time is witnessed by the trier, and under circumstances permitting immediate cross-examination by counsel in order to probe possible inaccuracies in the inferential chain. These inaccuracies are usually attributed to the four testimonial infirmities of ambiguity, insincerity, faulty perception, and erroneous memory. In the absence of special reasons, the perceived untrustworthiness of such an out-of-court act or utterance has led the Anglo–Saxon legal system to exclude it as hearsay despite its potentially probative value.

There exists a rather simple way of schematizing all of this in terms of an elementary geometric construct that serves to structure its several related elements. The construct might be called the Testimonial Triangle. By making graphic the path of inferences, and by functionally grouping the problems encountered along the path, the triangle makes it easier both to identify when a hearsay problem exists and to structure consideration of the appropriateness of exceptions to the rule that bars hearsay inferences.

The diagram is as follows:

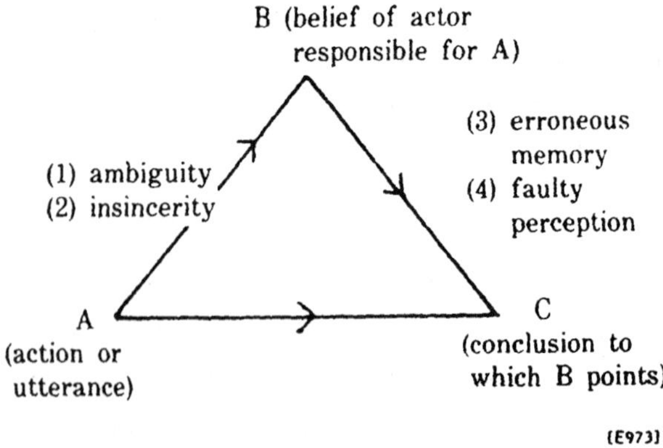

If we use the diagram to trace the inferential path the trier must follow, we begin at the lower left vertex of the triangle (A), which represents the declarant's (X's) act or assertion. The path first takes us to the upper vertex (B), representing X's belief in what his or her act or assertion suggests, and then takes us to the lower right vertex (C), representing the external reality suggested by X's belief. When "A" is used to prove "C" along the path through "B," a traditional hearsay problem exists and the use of the act or assertion as evidence is disallowed upon proper objection in the absence of some special reason to permit it.

It is of course a simple matter to locate the four testimonial infirmities on the triangle to show where and how they might impede the process of inference. To go from "A" to "B," the declarant's belief, one must remove the obstacles of (1) ambiguity and (2) insincerity. To go from "B" to "C," the external fact, one must further remove the obstacles of (3) erroneous memory and (4) faulty perception.

Notes and Questions

1. *Oral and written statements.* As *Moore* demonstrates, hearsay may be either oral (testimony of police officers) or written (affidavit). Indeed, it may be presented in additional form, such as a tape recording or the audio component of a videotape.

2. *Hearsay for probable cause.* In *Moore,* the out-of-court declarations of the unidentified informant were admitted on both the issue of probable cause to search and the issue of Moore's guilt of heroin possession. While inadmissible on the issue of guilt, no objection was raised to its use to establish probable cause, a limited purpose for which it is generally admissible. See, e.g., United States v. Wilkes, 451 F.2d 938 (2d Cir.1971) (probable cause for arrest), and United States v. Cruz, 478 F.2d 408 (5th Cir.1973) (grand jury indictment).

3. *Different diagrams.* Other evidence scholars have offered modifications to Professor Tribe's method of diagraming hearsay. See Friedman, Route Analysis of Credibility and Hearsay, 96 Yale L.J. 667 (1987); Graham, "Stickperson Hearsay": A Simplified Approach to Understanding the Rule Against Hearsay, 1982 U.Ill.L.Rev. 887; Lempert, Gross & Liebman, A Modern Approach to Evidence 497–501 (3d ed. 2000); Reutlinger, Evidence: Essential Terms and Concepts 65 (1996); 3 Graham, Handbook of Federal Evidence § 801.1, at 542–46 (6th ed. 2006).

4. *Edification, not agreement.* By helping to identify the hearsay dangers present in a particular out-of-court statement, Professor Tribe's diagram is useful in analyzing whether the statement is hearsay, and if hearsay, whether it should nevertheless be admitted under an exception to the rule. However, use of the diagram does not insure agreement on the appropriate definition of hearsay.

Tribe, for instance, interprets the Federal Rule definition to exclude a statement from hearsay when it is "seemingly nonassertive," thereby apparently, at least, reducing the sincerity concern on the left leg of the triangle. Tribe, Triangulating Hearsay, at 972. He disagrees, however, with this result since only one of the four hearsay dangers is eliminated or substantially reduced. Id. Professor Graham agrees with Tribe's view of how hearsay should be defined but disagrees that the Federal Rule definition has the effect Tribe ascribes to it. Under his view, only when all four hearsay dangers are eliminated is a statement not hearsay under that definition. 3 Graham, Handbook of Federal Evidence § 801.1, at 545 & § 801.7 (6th ed. 2006). Professors Lempert, Gross, and Liebman, on the other hand, contend that a statement is properly classified as not hearsay even if it depends upon the belief of the declarant as long as its relevance does not require that belief accurately to reflect reality. In such a situation, the dangers located on the left leg of the triangle are unaffected, but those on the right leg are eliminated, which they contend properly renders it not hearsay. Lempert, Gross & Liebman, A Modern Approach to Evidence 505–07 (3d ed. 2000).

5. *Sources.* For a general analysis of the definition of hearsay and the basis of the rule against admission of hearsay, see Ireland, Deconstructing Hearsay's Structure: Toward a Witness Recollection Definition of Hearsay, 43 Vill.L.Rev. 529 (1998); Morgan, Hearsay Dangers and the Application of the Hearsay Concept, 62 Harv.L.Rev. 177 (1948); Mueller, Post–Modern Hearsay Reform: The Importance of Complexity, 76 Minn.L.Rev. 367 (1992); Nesson, The Evidence or the Event? On Judicial Proof and the Acceptability of Verdicts, 98 Harv.L.Rev. 1357 (1985); Park, The Hearsay Rule and the Stability of Verdicts: A Response to Professor Nesson, 70 Minn.L.Rev. 1057 (1986); Park, McCormick on Evidence and the Concept of Hearsay: A Critical Analysis Followed by Suggestions to Law Teachers, 65 Minn.L.Rev. 423 (1981); Park, A Subject Matter Approach to Hearsay Reform, 86 Mich.L.Rev. 51 (1987); Swift, A Foundation Fact Approach to Hearsay, 75 Cal.L.Rev. 1339 (1987); Swift, Abolishing the Hearsay Rule, 75 Cal.L.Rev. 495 (1987); Weissenberger, Reconstructing the Definition of Hearsay, 57 Ohio St.L.J. 1525 (1996); Wellborn, The Definition of Hearsay in the Federal Rules of Evidence, 61 Tex.L.Rev. 49 (1982); Symposium on Hearsay Reform, 76 Minn.L.Rev. 363 (1992).

SILVER v. NEW YORK CENT. R.R.

Supreme Judicial Court of Massachusetts, 1952.
105 N.E.2d 923.

WILKINS, JUSTICE.

On January 14, 1948, Frances Silver became a passenger, bound from Boston to Cincinnati, on a train operated by the defendant railroad. The following morning the Pullman car in which she had a berth was detached at Cleveland and stood for nearly four hours in the yard to await connection with the next train to Cincinnati. She was suffering from a circulatory ailment known as Raynaud's disease. The temperature in the car became too cold for her, and she experienced ill effects. Mrs. Silver * * * brought this action against the defendant railroad and the Pullman Company. * * * The judge found for the plaintiff against the railroad. * * * The exceptions of the railroad * * * are to the denial of certain of its requests for rulings and to the exclusion of evidence.

Certain basic facts are not in dispute. The plaintiff, who was 58 years of age, boarded the train at Boston, on January 14, 1948, at 4:50

p.m. She occupied a lower berth in the rear car, which was the only through car to Cincinnati. The train was scheduled to arrive in Cleveland at 6:20 a.m. the following day, but did not do so until 8:40 a.m., too late for the intended connection for Cincinnati. This necessitated a layover in Cleveland until the next train for Cincinnati, which left at 12:30 p.m. In Cleveland the weather bureau records show that the temperature at 5:35 a.m. was one degree below zero Fahrenheit and 26 degrees above zero at 9 p.m. The plaintiff reached Cincinnati without further event, but because of her tendency to develop Raynaud's syndrome and the exposure to cold in Cleveland the condition of her hands required that she be hospitalized. * * *

Findings as to the plaintiff's experience at Cleveland could have been based upon statements she had made before suit was brought. She woke up about 9 a.m. because she was cold. She rang for the porter but no one came. She was alone in the car, which was standing in the yard and not at a platform. The station was inaccessible. She went to the washroom and got dressed. She "had to bundle up with her coat and furs," and put on a pair of woolen gloves. She rang twice more. Still no one came. She thought that the temperature was below freezing. She was extremely cold. She went back into her berth. The car remained in the same condition until connected with the Cincinnati train after 12 [noon]. At that time the temperature outside was 10 to 15 degrees, and the car had been "without any heat whatsoever" for about three hours with that temperature outside. * * *

We * * * turn to questions of evidence that may arise again. * * * The porter in the plaintiff's car was rightly allowed to testify as to the temperature conditions in that car. Leopold v. Van Kirk, 29 Wis. 548, 553–554. He was giving at first hand his experience with the same conditions which confronted the plaintiff. * * * But he was not permitted to give evidence that eleven other passengers in that car made no complaint to him as to the temperature while at Cleveland. This is a somewhat different proposition, as it was sought to draw from the silence of those passengers a deduction that the car was not too cold, otherwise they would have spoken. In certain courts evidence of absence of complaints by customers has been excluded on the issue of defective quality of goods sold, and the hearsay rule has been relied upon or referred to. * * * In Menard v. Cashman, 94 N.H. 428, 433–434, 55 A.2d 156, which was an action of tort arising out of a fall on a defective stairway in a business block, it was held proper to exclude testimony of a tenant that none of her customers had ever complained of any defects, the court saying that the testimony had the characteristics of hearsay, and that if it was not hearsay, it was only evidence of inconclusive silence, which might be excluded in the discretion of the trial judge.

Evidence as to absence of complaints from customers other than the plaintiff has been admitted in four cases, all relating to breach of warranty in the sale of food, in this Commonwealth. In three of them the testimony was apparently received without objection. Gracey v. Waldorf System, Inc., 251 Mass. 76, 78, 146 N.E. 232; Monahan v. Economy

Grocery Stores Corp., 282 Mass. 548, 550, 185 N.E. 34; Schuler v. Union News Co., 295 Mass. 350, 352, 4 N.E.2d 465. In Landfield v. Albiani Lunch Co., 268 Mass. 528, 168 N.E. 160, the plaintiff alleged that he had been made ill by eating beans purchased at the defendant's restaurant. Subject to his exception, evidence was admitted that on that day and on the day preceding no complaint as to the beans was made by any other customer. In upholding the ruling on evidence, it was said, 268 Mass. at page 530, 168 N.E. at page 160: "The fact that others than the plaintiff ate of the food complained of without ill effects is competent evidence that it was not unwholesome. * * * There is a reasonable inference based on common experience that one who ate and suffered as he believed in consequence would make complaint. There is a further reasonable inference, based on logic, that if no one complained no one suffered. Obviously, the latter conclusion is not convincing that the food was wholesome, unless one is satisfied that both plaintiff and others ate of it. Evidence of no complaint is too remote and should not be admitted unless, in addition to the fact that no complaints were made, there is evidence of circumstances indicating that others similarly situated ate and had opportunity for complaining."

It has often been said that where collateral issues may be opened, much must rest in the discretion of the trial judge. * * * In the case at bar, should the circumstances of the plaintiff and of the other passengers as to exposure to the cold be shown to be substantially the same, the negative evidence that none of the others spoke of it to the porter might properly be admitted. The evidence would not be equivocal, and would then be offered on the basis of a common condition which all in the car encountered. The porter's duties should be shown to include the receipt of that sort of complaints from those passengers. It should appear that he was present and available to be spoken to, and that it was not likely that complaints were made by those passengers to other employees of the railroad or the sleeping car company. This would not seem to be a situation where one might prefer to remain silent rather than to make any statement. Indeed, if the car was too cold, ordinary prudence might seem to require that one speak out. There would be no ambiguity of inference. There would be at least as strong a case for admissibility as in the food cases, and a far stronger one than those relating to the sale of allegedly defective goods in which little may be known of the terms of sale to the noncomplaining buyers. Unlike the unknown users of a stairway in a business block, the uniform result of silence in the cases of a large number of passengers, here apparently eleven, would not be inconclusive. See Falknor, Silence as Hearsay, 89 U. of Pa.L.Rev. 192.

Exceptions sustained.

Notes and Questions

1. *"Assertion."* Under the Rule 801, conduct that is nonverbal is not defined as hearsay unless it is intended as an assertion. The Advisory Committee Note places the burden on the party contending that an intention

to assert is present: "The rule is so worded as to place the burden upon the party claiming that the intention existed; ambiguous and doubtful cases will be resolved against him and in favor of admissibility."

2. *Fainting rather than asserting.* People v. Clark, 86 Cal.Rptr. 106 (Cal.Ct.App.1970), provides a vivid example of nonassertive conduct. There a woman's partially decomposed body was discovered in an orchard. Witnesses reported that several days earlier they had been approached by a man seeking help in having his car pulled from a ditch near the orchard. They described the man, *inter alia,* as wearing a coat with a fur-lined collar. Clark was arrested at his home on the night the body was discovered. The court described the arrest as follows:

> The officers advised defendant of his constitutional rights and searched the premises and defendant's automobile. Traces of blood were found on defendant's shoes, and blood tracings were found in the interior of his automobile. Then, Sergeant Tabler asked defendant if he had a jacket with a fur-lined collar. Defendant turned to his wife and queried, "I don't have one like that, do I dear?" His wife fainted.

Id. at 108. Defendant's hearsay objection to Sergeant Tabler's description of Mrs. Clark's conduct was rejected by the court.

> The reaction of defendant's wife to this question was relevant to prove that defendant owned a coat with a fur-lined collar and that he had worn it on the night of the murder; and because it was nonassertive conduct it was not objectionable hearsay * * *.

Id. at 112.

3. *Other hearsay dangers.* Assuming that dangers of insincerity are reduced when nonverbal, nonassertive conduct is involved, what other hearsay dangers remain and may even be exacerbated? See Blakey, You Can Say That If You Want—The Redefinition of Hearsay in Rule 801 of the Proposed Federal Rules of Evidence, 35 Ohio St.L.J. 601, 615–16 (1974) (criticizing the result in *Clark*).

4. *Conduct and silence as assertions.* Conduct can clearly be intended as an assertion. See, e.g., United States v. Aspinall, 389 F.3d 332, 342 (2d Cir.2004) (concluding that giving items to a police agent in response to the agent's inquiry was an assertive act); Clabon v. State, 111 S.W.3d 805, 808 (Tex.Ct.App.2003) (treating stabbing motion to the chest as asserting witness' knowledge about murders). When, if ever, will silence be assertive?

5. *Nonassertive nonverbal conduct and implied assertions.* Some commentators who question broad exclusion of assertive verbal conduct from the Federal Rules under the concept of implied assertions, discussed in the remainder of this section, view the exclusion of nonassertive nonverbal conduct more favorably. See, e.g., Graham, "Stickperson Hearsay": A Simplified Approach to Understanding the Rule Against Hearsay, 1982 U.Ill. L.Rev. 887, 909; Rice, Should Unintended Implications of Speech Be Considered Nonhearsay? The Assertive/Nonassertive Distinction under Rule 801(a) of the Federal Rules of Evidence, 65 Temp.L.Rev. 529 (1992); Wellborn, The Definition of Hearsay in the Federal Rules of Evidence, 61 Tex.L.Rev. 49, 63–64 (1982); 3 Graham, Handbook of Federal Evidence § 801.3 (6th ed. 2006). When nonassertive nonverbal conduct is involved, the hearsay dan-

gers of memory and perception are theoretically reduced. This is because the "declarant" has an enhanced incentive to verify the accuracy of perception and memory when translating his thoughts into action that is likely to carry more substantial consequences than typical speech alone. Lempert, Gross & Liebman, A Modern Approach to Evidence 519 (3d ed. 2000). Moreover, by definition, if the conduct is truly not intended as an assertion, the hearsay danger of insincerity is greatly reduced.

PLAYER v. THOMPSON

Supreme Court of South Carolina, 1972.
193 S.E.2d 531.

[Bobby Thompson furnished an automobile to his then-estranged wife Geraldine, who entrusted the car to Nancy Carder. Plaintiff, a passenger in the car driven by Carder, was injured when the car skidded on wet pavement. She sued Carder and the Thompsons, and was nonsuited.]

PER CURIAM:

* * *

Inasmuch as the case must be tried again, we will rule upon evidentiary questions raised by plaintiff's exceptions. The complaint alleged:

(1) That Nancy Carder was heedless and reckless in driving the motor vehicle which she *"knew, or should have known, had worn and defective tires,* upon a wet and slippery street;" (emphasis added)

(2) That Geraldine Thompson was negligent, careless, reckless, wilful and wanton in providing an automobile to a driver when she *"knew or should have known, that the tires on said motor vehicle were worn, slippery, and in a defective condition."* (emphasis added)

Section 46–611, as amended, of the Code of Laws of South Carolina, requires that tires on motor vehicles "shall be in a safe operating condition." Section 46–644.1 makes it an offense to operate a vehicle not having a current inspection sticker issued by the State Highway Department. The stickers are issued by authorized inspection stations throughout the State. Stickers are not issued for cars with defective or slick tires.

Subsequent to the collision and prior to suit, Carder gave a statement (to a representative of plaintiff's counsel) which was sworn to and recorded, concerning Geraldine Thompson and the car she was driving. In essence, she stated that she (Carder) went with Geraldine Thompson, two or three weeks before the collision, to a motor vehicle inspection station. She said that the inspector refused Mrs. Thompson a sticker because "she needed two tires." She stated she heard the inspector "tell her [Mrs. Thompson] and she [Mrs. Thompson] told me."—"The man told her that * * * she needed two more to pass inspection."

As a part of plaintiff's case in chief, counsel attempted to introduce the statement, or in the alternative call the court reporter who took the statement, to testify as to Carder's statement or read the questions and answers to the jury. Counsel conceded that "no portion of the statement is relevant as to the Thompsons." He stated: "I therefore in my proffer of proof have eliminated all references to the Thompsons and the portions that I now read includes only those words that I would think would be appropriate as to Miss Carder."

The proffer was refused because Carder had no personal knowledge of the tires being slick; because the inspection station incident was too remote in point of time; and because it was "hearsay against Thompson" and "prejudicial to Thompson."

There was testimony by Charles Player tending to prove that the tires on the car were slick when examined after the collision. We do not agree that evidence concerning the tires being defective two or three weeks before the collision was too remote in point of time.

It often happens that a statement which is inadmissible for one purpose is admissible for other purposes. We have held and we think it is indispensable that when a statement is admissible against one defendant and not against others, that the trial judge must admit the statement against the defendant and instruct the jury to disregard it as to the other defendants. Eberhardt v. Forrester, 241 S.C. 399, 128 S.E.2d 687 (1962); 1 Wigmore on Evidence § 13 (3d ed. 1940). The trial judge was in error in excluding the admission because it was hearsay against the Thompsons and prejudicial to them.

The admission as it affects Carder should not have been excluded because Carder did not have personal knowledge that the tires were slick. The rule is that personal knowledge of the person making an admission is immaterial. 4 Wigmore on Evidence § 1053 (3d ed. 1940).

At the new trial, if the statement can be dissected so as to eliminate mention of the Thompsons, its admission in that form would be the best procedure; on the other hand, if it cannot be dissected, the judge should admit the statement and charge the jury that it must not be considered against the Thompsons.

After the trial judge declined to admit the statement in evidence, counsel for plaintiff called defendant Carder as a witness. He attempted to ask her about the inspection station incident in an effort to show that both she (Carder) and Mrs. Thompson had notice of the slick tires. Defense counsel's objection was sustained on the ground that it was hearsay.

In C. McCormick, Law of Evidence § 225 (1954) hearsay evidence is defined:

"Hearsay evidence is testimony in court or written evidence, of a statement made out of court, such statement being offered as an

assertion to show the truth of matters asserted therein, and thus resting for its value upon the credibility of the out-of-court asserter."

Our Court has recognized this sound and very basic proposition in Watson v. Wall, 239 S.C. 109, 121 S.E.2d 427 (1961). Also see 5 Wigmore on Evidence § 1361 (3d ed. 1940).

> "If, then, an utterance can be used as circumstantial evidence, i.e. without inferring from it as an assertion to the fact asserted, the Hearsay rule does not oppose any barrier, because it is not applicable." 6 Wigmore on Evidence § 1788 (3d ed. 1940).

It would not be improper in this case for the plaintiff to elicit testimony from Nancy Carder that a filling station attendant stated to both Mrs. Thompson and her that the automobile had bad tires. It would be receivable, not as a testimonial assertion by the attendant to prove the fact of slick tires, but as indicating that Nancy Carder and Mrs. Thompson obtained knowledge of the slick tires, the fact of slick tires being proved by other evidence.

Inasmuch as the testimony was not offered to prove the truth of the matter stated, but solely to prove notice, which is a state of mind, the hearsay rule does not apply. Whether one is negligent or heedless or reckless in providing a car with slick tires to another or in driving a car with slick tires, depends at least to some degree on one's knowledge of the condition of the tires. Carder's testimony should have been admitted as it affects both Geraldine Thompson's and Carder's notice of slick tires. * * *

Reversed and remanded.

Notes and Questions

1. *Change the hypothetical.* Consider in each of the following situations whether hearsay is involved.

(a) The inspector, being called as a witness, testifies:

(i) He examined the tires, and they were slick;

(ii) He told Ms. Carder and Ms. Thompson that the tires were slick.

(b) Ms. Carder's statement to the adjuster is offered. It states:

(i) The inspector told Ms. Thompson and her that the tires were slick;

(ii) Ms. Thompson told her that the inspector said the tires were slick.

(c) Ms. Carder, being called as a witness, testifies:

(i) The inspector told them that the tires were slick;

(ii) Ms. Thompson told her that the inspector said the tires were slick.

2. *Hearsay and nonhearsay together.* For other cases in which the extrajudicial statement is admissible for a nonhearsay purpose and also contains an "assertion," see Rinehimer v. Cemcolift, Inc., 292 F.3d 375, 383 (3d Cir.2002) (finding statement as to what company doctor told manager about condition not hearsay because it explained why plaintiff employee was not permitted to return to his job as a working foreman and wear a respirator); Emich Motors Corp. v. General Motors Corp., 181 F.2d 70 (7th Cir.1950), rev'd on other grounds, 340 U.S. 558 (1951) (complaining letters from customers offered to show that cancellation of dealer's franchise was not motivated by dealer's refusal to finance car sales through defendant's finance affiliate).

In what ways can the evidence in these cases be used improperly? Can misuse be prevented by an instruction to the jury?

3. *Statements made in the presence of a party.* In *Player,* the statements were admissible because they were made in the presence of a party to the litigation to provide notice. Occasionally in other circumstances, statements are admissible because they were made in the presence of a party, as when they are adopted by the failure of the party to protest. See infra Section B. There is, however, no general basis for the objection, remarkably entrenched in the folklore of the profession, that extrajudicial statements should be excluded if not made in the presence of the party against whom offered. See Adkins v. Brett, 193 P. 251, 252 (Cal.1920); People v. Carpenter, 190 N.E.2d 738, 741 (Ill.1963).

UNITED STATES v. GIBSON

United States Court of Appeals, Ninth Circuit, 1982.
690 F.2d 697.

Reinhardt, Circuit Judge:

Wilford R. Gibson was found guilty of * * * mail fraud, wire fraud, and inducing people to travel in interstate commerce for purposes of fraud. * * *

Background and Proceedings

In 1973, defendant incorporated Gibson Marketing International, Inc. (GMI), named himself president and chairman of that entity, and retained its entire capital stock. From its Phoenix, Arizona headquarters, GMI began a business of selling franchises and franchise distributorship rights ("area distributorships") to fast food restaurants which it called either "Burgher Haus" or "Kelly's Basket."

GMI's selling procedure was as follows. The company placed advertisements in newspapers and certain circulars for single unit franchises. Prospective investors dialed the toll free number printed in the ads and received an invitation to come to the Phoenix headquarters for a "personal interview." At these "personal interviews," GMI salesmen, sometimes including Gibson, urged investors to purchase "area distributorships" rather than the less expensive, single unit franchises. GMI personnel also outlined the "Burgher Haus" and/or "Kelly's Basket" programs. They promised that GMI would provide certain business services including personnel training, local advertising, site location and approvals and discounted national material purchasing accounts. * * *

Unfortunately, GMI did not provide certain of the promised business services. For example, in the course of its "site approval" service, for which it charged some investors a $1,000 fee, GMI approved a piece of unimproved underwater swamp land submitted as a test by a wary New York investor. * * * In addition, the evidence showed that Gibson spent substantial amounts of GMI's money in various Las Vegas gambling spots, [and] there was evidence that Gibson instructed GMI personnel to convey false information to complaining investors.

THE HEARSAY ARGUMENT

Gibson contends that the district court erred in admitting the testimony of investors regarding statements made by GMI's employees/salesmen. * * *

The Federal Rules of Evidence define hearsay as: "[A] statement, other than one made by the declarant while testifying at the trial or hearing, offered in evidence to prove the truth of the matter asserted." Fed.R.Evid. 801(c). The government argues that the disputed testimony was not "offered in evidence to prove the truth of the matter asserted."

In their testimony, the investors related their discussions with GMI personnel. One witness testified that Gibson's brother, a GMI employee, told her that there were over 80 "Burgher Haus" restaurants in operation. Another witness said a GMI employee told him that GMI would finance 80% of his building and equipment costs. Other witnesses related assurances from GMI salesmen and officials regarding, *inter alia,* GMI's financial assets, the allegedly low failure rate of the restaurants, and the projected financial return on a franchise investment.

The investors' testimony was offered to prove the *existence* of a scheme; the statements were not offered for their truthfulness. The purpose of the testimony was solely to establish the fact that the salesmen and employees had made the statements. That fact was relevant to support the government's allegation that a scheme existed.[3]

* * *

We hold that these statements were not hearsay * * *.

[Affirmed.]

Notes and Questions

1. *Threats.* With regard to the "verbal act" element of *Gibson,* consider also United States v. Jones, 663 F.2d 567, 568–69, 571 (5th Cir.1981), a prosecution for threatening the lives of a federal judge and prosecutor:

3. Ultimately of course, the truth or falsity of the statements was important to the outcome of the case. However, the fact that the statements were made was not used to prove the truth of the content of the statements. Instead, the government sought to show their falsity through independent evidence.

On May 4, 1979, appellant Lloyd Jones stood before the United States District Court, Northern District of Georgia, for sentencing in connection with his conviction for murder committed at the Atlanta Federal Penitentiary. Judge William C. O'Kelley addressed Jones, who appeared with counsel, to determine whether Jones wished to be heard on matters bearing upon his sentence. Jones responded:

> Yes, sir. I'd like to say that * * * I don't think you passed sentence on me, you know, like, I think, during the process of the trial that I was totally insane, you know, which I also think that you should have looked over into the matter when I told you that them people out there was threatening me and stuff, which you said you would but you never have. But now today you bring me down here to pass sentence on me. It's nothing really too much I could do about it. When you can't beat them you join them. *So, Judge O'Kelley, U.S. Attorney, Mr. Bostic, I pass sentence on you, the sentence would be death, you and all your relatives.* Now you can pass your sentence. *It is death to you, you, and you, and all your relatives by gunshot wound.* Now do as you please. I don't give a * * * if you throw the whole Empire State building at me, the whole State of Georgia.

* * *

The statement at issue is paradigmatic nonhearsay; it was offered because it contains threats made against officers of the federal courts, i.e., it contains the operative words of this criminal action. It was not "offered in evidence to prove the truth of the matter asserted," [Fed. R.Evid.] 801(c).

2. *"Performative" utterances.* During trial, a marshal overheard the defendant state, "it's going to be $10,000," to a co-participant in crime who had earlier entered a guilty plea and testified that the defendant was innocent. Judge Posner accepted the government's position that the statement was a "verbal act," providing the following explanation:

> The [remaining issue] * * * is the admissibility of the marshal's testimony that Dodd had told Montana that the price of Dodd's favorable testimony was $10,000. The government argues that it was admissible as a "verbal act" * * *, thus echoing the linguist's distinction between performative and illocutionary utterances. The latter narrate, describe, or otherwise convey information, and so are judged by their truth value (information is useful only if true—indeed is information only if it is true); the former—illustrated by a promise, offer, or demand—commit the speaker to a course of action. Performative utterances are not within the scope of the hearsay rule, because they do not make any truth claims. Had the marshal overheard Dodd tell Montana, "your father has promised me $10,000," Dodd's overheard statement would have been hearsay, because its value as evidence would have depended on its being truthful, that is, on such a promise having actually been made. But what in fact was overheard was merely a demand—in effect, "give me $10,000"—and so the only issue of credibility was whether the marshal was reporting the demand correctly, and his testimony was not hearsay.

United States v. Montana, 199 F.3d 947, 950 (7th Cir.1999).

3. *False statements.* Some constructions of the hearsay definition might mean that a statement that is false cannot be hearsay. Although this position may be too strong, when false statements are admitted, it is typically because they are introduced for another purpose than proving the matter asserted, which supports nonhearsay treatment even if not per se determinative of the issue. A false statement that is being admitted as a "verbal act" because it is false (e.g., a fraudulent sales offer in a fraud case or the false statement made under oath in a perjury prosecution) is nonhearsay based on its falsity. However, if the statement depends for its significance upon an inference about the reasons for the declarant's insincerity, as when false alibi testimony is given by the defendant's spouse, nonhearsay treatment is not as clear. Compare Anderson v. United States, 417 U.S. 211 (1974), and United States v. Hackett, 638 F.2d 1179 (9th Cir.1980), with Park, McCormick on Evidence and the Concept of Hearsay: A Critical Analysis Followed by Suggestions to Law Teachers, 65 Minn.L.Rev. 423, 426 (1981), and Graham, "Stickperson Hearsay": A Simplified Approach to Understanding the Rule Against Hearsay, 1982 U.Ill.L.Rev. 887, 898–99. In this latter situation, all hearsay dangers are not eliminated and the evaluation involved is similar to that of "implied assertions,"discussed later in this Section.

Professor Park has usefully categorized hearsay definitions as either assertion oriented, which "focuses on whether an out-of-court assertion will be used to prove the truth of what it asserts" or declarant oriented, which "focuses on whether the use of the utterance will require reliance on the credibility of the out-of-court declarant." 65 Minn.L.Rev. at 424. Under which of these categories would false statements be more broadly excluded from the hearsay rule?

4. *Major categories of nonhearsay.* Statements that are not hearsay because they are not offered for the truth of the matter asserted may be grouped under several general categories: (1) Some statements are relevant because of their effect on the hearer or reader. Common examples are statements providing notice or motive, or those showing reasonableness or good faith or the reason for taking action. (2) Verbal acts are statements that have operative legal effect. Examples include words of contract, slander, threats to do bodily harm, and the granting of authority to act as an agent. See 2 McCormick, Evidence § 249, at 133 (6th ed. 2006). Closely related to verbal acts are verbal parts of acts. These are words that accompany and characterize otherwise ambiguous nonverbal conduct, taking on with the act operative legal significance. The most common example is the words that accompany the handing over of money and characterize it as a loan, a bribe, a gift, etc. See id. at 101; 3 Graham, Handbook of Federal Evidence § 801.5, at 577–78 (6th ed. 2006); 5 Weinstein's Federal Evidence § 801.11[4] (2d ed. 2006). (3) A prior consistent or inconsistent statement of a witness likewise is not hearsay when offered for its impact upon the witness' credibility by showing that the witness previously made such a statement. See, e.g., United States v. Hudson, 970 F.2d 948, 956–57 (1st Cir.1992) (inconsistent statement not hearsay when used to affect credibility). Critically, the theory of impeachment does not depend on the premise that the testimony is false and the prior statement true but rather that the fact of an inconsistency

("blowing hot and cold") raises doubts as to the credibility of both statements. See 1 McCormick, Evidence § 34, at 151 (6th ed. 2006).

5. *Common misuse of nonhearsay argument.* One area of frequent misuse of the argument that a statement is not used for the truth occurs when arresting or investigating officers recite what they were told about the crime as a reason why they came to the scene of a crime or why they conducted a specific type of investigation. The argument has obvious validity if properly applied. For example, officers should not be put in the misleading position of appearing to have happened upon the scene and therefore should be entitled to provide some explanation for their presence and conduct. They should not, however, be allowed to relate historical aspects of the case. The need for this evidence is slight, and the likelihood of misuse great, see Rule 403, particularly since a statement that an officer acted "upon information received," or words to that effect, would suffice. See, e.g., United States v. Silva, 380 F.3d 1018, 1019–20 (7th Cir.2004) (rejecting government argument that statements incriminating the defendant could be admitted as nonhearsay to show why the police investigated the defendant). Another ploy that should be ineffective is to offer an indirect version of hearsay statements. If the purpose or effect of testimony is to prove the truth of facts indirectly stated, an objection to the hearsay nature of the underlying facts cannot be eliminated by eliciting the content in summary form as "information received" or the result of investigation. See, e.g., United States v. Baker, 432 F.3d 1189, 1209 (11th Cir.2005) (investigator's statement about what he learned upon arrival at the scene of a shooting was inadmissible hearsay).

LOETSCH v. NEW YORK CITY OMNIBUS CORP.

Court of Appeals of New York, 1943.
52 N.E.2d 448.

THACHER, JUDGE.

Appeal by defendant from the nonunanimous judgment of the Appellate Division affirming a judgment of the Supreme Court, New York County, in favor of plaintiff in a wrongful death action.

Upon the trial of this action counsel for defendants-appellants offered in evidence the will of the decedent dated December 2, 1940, for the purpose of proving the statement of the decedent with respect to her relations with her husband. The statement was as follows: "Whereas I have been a faithful, dutiful, and loving wife to my husband, Dean Yankovich, and whereas he reciprocated my tender affections for him with acts of cruelty and indifference, and whereas he has failed to support and maintain me in that station of life which would have been possible and proper for him, I hereby limit my bequest to him to one dollar."

On plaintiffs' objection the will was excluded from evidence, and the exception taken presents the only question for our consideration. The will, executed within four months prior to decedent's death, was relevant to an understanding of the relations which existed between the decedent and her husband. It is always proper to make proof of the relations of the decedent to the person for whose benefit the action is maintained, because such proof has a bearing upon the pecuniary loss suffered by the person entitled to the recovery, and this is true whether the beneficiary is the surviving husband or wife or one or more of the next of kin. * * *

The measure of loss is to be determined solely from the standpoint of the surviving spouse and is strictly limited to compensation for pecuniary loss. Decedent Estate Law, § 132, Consol.Laws, c. 13. Accordingly, the amount recoverable in any particular case must be very largely influenced by the nature of the relationship between the beneficiary and the deceased. When the deceased is one who was under no legal obligation to provide support for the beneficiary during life, his or her disposition voluntarily to do so is of essential importance to the jury in determining pecuniary loss. Evidence showing such a disposition or the lack of it should not be excluded.

Question remains as to the character of the proof offered, which was a declaration in writing of the decedent made within four months of her death. Such declarations are evidence of the decedent's state of mind and are probative of a disposition on the part of the declarant which has a very vital bearing upon the reasonable expectancy, or lack of it, of future assistance or support if life continues. This expectancy, disappointed by death, is the basis of recovery * * * and is the measure of pecuniary loss for which the jury must award fair and just compensation. No testimonial effect need be given to the declaration, but the fact that such a declaration was made by the decedent, whether true or false, is compelling evidence of her feelings toward, and relations to, her husband. As such it is not excluded under the hearsay rule but is admissible as a verbal act. * * *

The judgments should be reversed and a new trial granted, with costs to the appellant to abide the event.

Notes and Questions

1. *"Whether or not true, that wasn't nice to say."* What does the court mean when it says, "No testimonial effect need be given to the declaration"? See State v. Newell, 710 N.W.2d 6, 18 (Iowa 2006) (ruling that derogatory names were not hearsay because not used to prove that victim was what the defendant called her). Note that what is being proven is the declarant's feelings or state of mind rather than the truth of some external fact, which is a key to the validity of the nonhearsay argument.

2. *A transition category.* The category created in *Loetsch* of nonhearsay statements can be viewed as something of a transition between different forms of statements not offered for their truth. We earlier examined statements that are nonhearsay because they are not offered for their truth in what might be considered the "strong sense"—e.g., verbal acts, statements that have impact on the hearer, and inconsistent statements offered to impeach. In the two following cases, we examine a "weaker sense" of the not-for-the-truth-of-the-matter-asserted argument, labeled "implied assertions." These statements, the argument goes, are nonhearsay because they

are not admitted for the truth of what is specifically asserted, but instead to prove some other fact that may be inferred from the asserted fact.

WRIGHT v. DOE DEM. TATHAM

Exchequer Chamber, 1837.
7 Adolph. & E. 313, 112 Eng.Rep. 488.

[In an ejectment action, the plaintiff's lessor claimed as heir, and the defendant, an employee, claimed through the will of John Marsden. The case hinged upon the testamentary capacity of Marsden. In support of competency, the defendant offered several letters received by Marsden from persons who had died by the time of trial. The first letter was from a cousin, describing his voyage to America and conditions found there; the second from Rev. Marton, vicar, asking that Marsden have his attorney propose terms of agreement as to an undescribed matter in dispute between Marsden and the parish; the third was a letter of gratitude from Rev. Ellershaw upon resigning a curacy to which Marsden had appointed him. The letters were excluded. A verdict was returned for plaintiff's lessor. On appeal, the judgment was affirmed by the Exchequer Chamber on an equally divided vote. The House of Lords also affirmed. 5 Cl. & F. 670, 47 Rev.Rep. 136 (1838). The following extract by Baron Parke in the Exchequer Chamber is selected from the numerous opinions delivered in the two courts of review.]

PARKE, B. * * * It is argued that the letters would be admissible because they are evidence of the treatment of the testator as a competent person by individuals acquainted with his habits and personal character, not using the word treatment in a sense involving any conduct of the testator himself; that they are more than mere statements to a third person indicating an opinion of his competence by those persons; they are acts done towards the testator by them, which would not have been done if he had been incompetent, and from which, therefore a legitimate inference may, it is argued, be derived that he was so.

Each of the three letters, no doubt, indicates that in the opinion of the writer the testator was a rational person. He is spoken of in respectful terms in all. Mr. Ellershaw describes him as possessing hospitality and benevolent politeness; and Mr. Marton addresses him as competent to do business to the limited extent to which his letter calls upon him to act, and there is no question but that, if any one of these writers had been living, his evidence, founded on personal observation, that the testator possessed the qualities which justified the opinion expressed or implied in his letters, would be admissible on this issue. * * *

But the question is, whether the contents of these letters are evidence of the fact to be proved upon this issue,—that is, the actual existence of the qualities which the testator is, in those letters, by implication, stated to possess: and those letters may be considered in this respect to be on the same footing as if they had contained a direct and positive statement that he was competent. For this purpose they are mere hearsay evidence, statements of the writers, not on oath, of the truth of the matter in question with this addition, that they have acted upon the statements on the faith of their being true, by their sending the letters to the testator. That the so acting cannot give a sufficient sanction for the truth of the statement is perfectly plain; for it is clear that, if the same statements had been made by parol or in writing to a third person, that would have been insufficient; and this is conceded by the learned counsel for the plaintiff in error. Yet in both cases there has been an acting on the belief of the truth, by making the statement, or writing and sending a letter to a third person; and what difference can it possibly make that this is an acting of the same nature by writing and sending the letter to the testator? It is admitted, and most properly, that you have no right to use in evidence the fact of writing and sending a letter to a third person containing a statement of competence, on the ground that it affords an inference that such an act would not have been done unless the statement was true, or believed to be true, although such an inference no doubt would be raised in the conduct of the ordinary affairs of life, if the statement were made by a man of veracity. But it cannot be raised in a judicial inquiry; and, if such an argument were admissible, it would lead to the indiscriminate admission of hearsay evidence of all manner of facts.

Further, it is clear that an acting to a much greater extent and degree upon such statements to a third person would not make the statements admissible. For example, if a wager to a large amount had been made as to the matter in issue by two third persons, the payment of that wager, however large the sum, would not be admissible to prove the truth of the matter in issue. You would not have had any right to present it to the jury as raising an inference of the truth of the fact, on the ground that otherwise the bet would not have been paid. It is, after all, nothing but the mere statement of that fact, with strong evidence of the belief of it by the party making it. Could it make any difference that the wager was between the third person and one of the parties to the suit? Certainly not. The payment by other underwriters on the same policy to the plaintiff could not be given in evidence to prove that the subject insured had been lost. Yet there is an act done, a payment strongly attesting the truth of the statement, which it implies, that there had been a loss. To illustrate this point still further, let us suppose a third person had betted a wager with Mr. Marsden that he could not solve some mathematical problem, the solution of which required a high degree of capacity; would payment of that wager to Mr. Marsden's banker be admissible evidence that he possessed that capacity? The answer is certain; it would not. It would be evidence of the fact of competence given by a third party not upon oath.

Let us suppose the parties who wrote these letters to have stated the matter therein contained, that is, their knowledge of his personal qualities and capacity for business, on oath before a magistrate, or in some judicial proceeding to which the plaintiff and defendant were not parties. No one could contend that such statement would be admissible on this issue; and yet there would have been an act done on the faith of the statement being true, and a very solemn one, which would raise in the ordinary conduct of affairs a strong belief in the truth of the statement, if the writers were faith-worthy. The acting in this case is of much less importance, and certainly is not equal to the sanction of an extra-judicial oath.

Many other instances of a similar nature, by way of illustration, were suggested by the learned counsel for the defendant in error, which, on the most cursory consideration, any one would at once declare to be inadmissible in evidence. Others were supposed on the part of the plaintiff in error, which, at first sight, have the appearance of being mere facts, and therefore admissible, though on further consideration they are open to precisely the same objection. Of the first description are the supposed cases of a letter by a third person to any one demanding a debt, which may be said to be a treatment of him as a debtor, being offered as proof that the debt was really due; a note, congratulating him on his high state of bodily vigour, being proposed as evidence of his being in good health; both of which are manifestly at first sight objectionable. To the latter class belong the supposed conduct of the family or relations of a testator, taking the same precautions in his absence as if he were a lunatic; his election, in his absence, to some high and responsible office; the conduct of a physician who permitted a will to be executed by a sick testator; the conduct of a deceased captain on a question of seaworthiness, who, after examining every part of the vessel, embarked in it with his family; all these, when deliberately considered, are, with reference to the matter in issue in each case, mere instances of hearsay evidence, mere statements, not on oath, but implied in or vouched by the actual conduct of persons by whose acts the litigant parties are not to be bound.

The conclusion at which I have arrived is that proof of a particular fact, which is not of itself a matter in issue, but which is relevant only as implying a statement or opinion of a third person on the matter in issue, is inadmissible in all cases where such a statement or opinion not on oath would be of itself inadmissible; and, therefore, in this case the letters which are offered only to prove the competence of the testator, that is the truth of the implied statements therein contained, were properly rejected, as the mere statement or opinion of the writer would certainly have been inadmissible. * * *

Notes and Questions

1. *Dangers perhaps reduced, not eliminated.* Are the hearsay dangers realistically present in the *Tatham* situation? Are they unquestionably absent?

2. *Is Tatham good law?* How should the issues in *Tatham* be decided under the Federal Rules of Evidence? For an answer, see the next principal case, *United States v. Zenni*, and the notes following that case.

3. *Metaphors, indirect statements, and delicate analysis.* Assertive conduct under the Federal Rules is not hearsay if not offered in evidence to

prove "the truth of the matter asserted." Clearly, however, more is covered by the hearsay definition than direct, literal assertions of the matter to be proved. For example, "it will stop raining in an hour," if offered to prove that it was raining at the time of the statement, is hearsay because the matter to be proved is a "necessary implication" of the statement made. Wellborn, The Definition of Hearsay in the Federal Rules of Evidence, 61 Tex.L.Rev. 49, 75 (1982). Similarly, metaphorical speech must be included: A statement that the "sky is on fire" would be hearsay to prove that the sun was setting. Id. at 78.

Moving beyond these easy and somewhat unusual examples, when is a statement that is assertive for one proposition not hearsay because it is offered to prove another proposition? One potential way of addressing this question is to use the declarant's intent, or some objective manifestation of it, to determine what the statement asserts. Commentators have attempted various formulations of an intent-based test. Professor Saltzburg argues that "a statement should be treated as hearsay whenever it is offered to prove the truth of an express or implied assertion, so long as the Trial Judge finds that the declarant intended to communicate that assertion when he made the statement." 4 Saltzburg, Martin & Capra, Federal Rules of Evidence Manual § 801.02[1][i], at 801–23 (9th ed. 2006). Professor Park suggests a somewhat similar, albeit differently focused, approach: "If helpfulness depends on the trier's belief that the declarant intended to assert a fact that supports the proponent's case, then the court should consider the statement hearsay * * * ." Park, "I Didn't Tell Them Anything About You": Implied Assertions as Hearsay Under the Federal Rules of Evidence, 74 Minn.L.Rev. 783, 800 (1990). These analytic methods are consistent with a view that the Federal Rules' definition of hearsay at least partially overrules *Tatham*. See generally 2 McCormick, Evidence § 250, at 144–46 (6th ed. 2006) (examining likelihood of purposeful deception in implied assertion).

By contrast, Professor Graham attempts to reconcile the Federal Rules' definition of hearsay with the result in *Tatham* by interpreting differently and more broadly when a statement is offered to prove the truth of the matter asserted. He contends that, if the truth of the matter directly asserted must be assumed in order for the nonasserted inference to be drawn, then the statement is offered for the truth of the matter asserted and is therefore properly considered hearsay under Rule 801's definition. 3 Graham, Handbook of Federal Rules of Evidence § 801.7, at 640–43 (6th ed. 2006). See also Rice, Should Unintended Implications of Speech Be Considered Nonhearsay? The Assertive/Nonassertive Distinction under Rule 801(a) of the Federal Rules of Evidence, 65 Temp.L.Rev. 529, 538–39 (1992) (assertion/nonassertion distinction should apply only to conduct that the actor did not intend to communicate anything).

4. *Sources on a lively debate.* The academic debate on the proper treatment of implied assertions has continued since the time of *Tatham*, and the enactment of the Federal Rules has done little to diminish its vigor. In addition to the sources cited in the preceding note, see Callen, Hearsay and Informal Reasoning, 47 Vand.L.Rev. 43 (1994); Falknor, The "Hear–Say" Rule as a "See–Do" Rule: Evidence of Conduct, 33 Rocky Mt.L.Rev. 133 (1966); Finman, Implied Assertions as Hearsay: Some Criticisms of the Uniform Rules of Evidence, 14 Stan.L.Rev. 682 (1962); Kirgis, Meaning,

Intention, and the Hearsay Rule, 43 Wm. & Mary L.Rev. 275 (2001); Maguire, The Hearsay System: Around and Through the Thicket, 14 Vand. L.Rev. 741 (1961); Milich, Re-examining Hearsay Under the Federal Rules: Some Method for Madness, 39 Kan.L.Rev. 893 (1991); Seidelson, Implied Assertions and Federal Rule of Evidence 801: A Quandary for Federal Courts, 24 Duq.L.Rev. 741 (1986).

UNITED STATES v. ZENNI

United States District Court, Eastern District of Kentucky, 1980.
492 F.Supp. 464.

BERTELSMAN, DISTRICT JUDGE.

This prosecution for illegal bookmaking activities presents a classic problem in the law of evidence, namely, whether implied assertions are hearsay. The problem was a controversial one at common law, the discussion of which has filled many pages in the treatises and learned journals.[4] Although the answer to the problem is clear under the Federal Rules of Evidence, there has been little judicial treatment of the matter, and many members of the bar are unfamiliar with the marked departure from the common law the Federal Rules have effected on this issue.

FACTS

The relevant facts are simply stated. While conducting a search of the premises of the defendant, Ruby Humphrey, pursuant to a lawful search warrant which authorized a search for evidence of bookmaking activity, government agents answered the telephone several times. The unknown callers stated directions for the placing of bets on various sporting events. The government proposes to introduce this evidence to show that the callers believed that the premises were used in betting operations. The existence of such belief tends to prove that they were so used. The defendants object on the ground of hearsay.

COMMON LAW BACKGROUND

At common law, the hearsay rule applied "only to evidence of out-of-court statements[5] offered for the purpose of proving that the facts are as asserted in the statement."[6]

On the other hand, not all out-of-court expression is common law hearsay. For instance, an utterance offered to show the publication of a

4. *See e.g., McCormick on Evidence* § 250 (2d Ed. 1972) [*hereinafter McCormick*]; Morgan, *Basic Problems of Evidence* (1976); *Weinstein's Evidence* ¶ 801 [hereinafter *Weinstein*]. Falknor, *The "Hear-Say" Rule as a "See-Do" Rule: Evidence of Conduct,* 33 Rocky Mt.L.Rev. 133 (1961) [hereinafter Falknor] contains a particularly penetrating and succinct analysis. (*See also* authorities in note [11], *infra.*)

5. It should be noted at the outset that the word *statement* as used in the Federal Rules of Evidence has a more restricted meaning than as used at common law. F.R.Ev. 801(a). See further discussion below.

6. *McCormick supra* note [4], § 250.

slander, or that a person was given notice of a fact, or orally entered into a contract, is not hearsay.[7]

In the instant case, the utterances of the absent declarants are not offered for the truth of the words,[8] and the mere fact that the words were uttered has no relevance of itself.[9] Rather they are offered to show the declarants' belief in a fact sought to be proved. At common law this situation occupied a controversial no-man's land. It was argued on the one hand that the out-of-court utterance was not hearsay, because the evidence was not offered for any truth stated in it, but for the truth of some other proposition inferred from it. On the other hand, it was also argued that the reasons for excluding hearsay applied, in that the evidence was being offered to show declarant's belief in the implied proposition, and he was not available to be cross-examined. Thus, the latter argument was that there existed strong policy reasons for ruling that such utterances were hearsay.

* * *

The court in *Wright v. Tatham* [7 Adolph. & E. 313, 112 Eng.Rep. 488 (Exchequer Chamber 1837)] held that implied assertions[10] of this kind were hearsay. * * * This was the prevailing common law view, where the hearsay issue was recognized. But frequently, it was not recognized. * * *

THE FEDERAL RULES OF EVIDENCE

The common law rule that implied assertions were subject to hearsay treatment was criticized by respected commentators for several reasons. A leading work on the Federal Rules of Evidence, referring to the hotly debated question whether an implied assertion stands on better ground with respect to the hearsay rule than an express assertion, states:

> "By the time the federal rules were drafted, a number of eminent scholars and revisers had concluded that it does. Two principal arguments were usually expressed for removing implied assertions from the scope of the hearsay rule. First, when a person acts in a way consistent with a belief but without intending by his act to communicate that belief, one of the principal reasons for the

7. *Ibid.* at 596–97.

8. That is, the utterance, "Put $2 to win on Paul Revere in the third at Pimlico," is a direction and not an assertion of any kind, and therefore can be neither true nor false.

9. *Cf. United States v. McLennan,* 563 F.2d 943 (9th Cir.1977), in a criminal case, the defense was advice of counsel. Statements made by counsel to the defendant were not hearsay, because it was relevant what the advice was. Of a similar nature would be a policeman's statement. "Go through the stop sign," if it were illegal to go through it unless directed by an officer. Other examples of expression admissible as non-hearsay, because they are verbal acts, relevant merely because they occurred, are "I agree" offered to show a contract was made; or "He took a bribe," offered to show a slander was published.

10. The problem is the same whether the relevant assertion is implied from verbal expression, such as that of the betters in the instant case or the letter writers in *Wright,* or from conduct, as in the sea captain example. *See* F.R.Ev. 801(a); Falknor, *supra* note [4], at 134.

hearsay rule—to exclude declarations whose veracity cannot be tested by cross-examination—does not apply, because the declarant's sincerity is not then involved. In the second place, the underlying belief is in some cases self-verifying:

> 'There is frequently a guarantee of the trustworthiness of the inference to be drawn * * * because the actor has based his actions on the correctness of his belief, i.e. his actions speak louder than words.' "[11]

In a frequently cited article the following analysis appears:

"But ought the hearsay rule be deemed applicable to evidence of conduct? As McCormick has observed, the problem 'has only once received any adequate discussion in any decided case,' *i.e.,* in *Wright v. Tatham,* already referred to. And even in that case the court did not pursue its inquiry beyond the point of concluding that evidence of an 'implied' assertion must necessarily be excluded wherever evidence of an 'express' assertion would be inadmissible. But as has been pointed out more than once (although I find no *judicial* recognition of the difference), the 'implied' assertion is, from the hearsay standpoint, not nearly as vulnerable as an express assertion of the fact which the evidence is offered to establish.

"This is on the assumption that the conduct was 'nonassertive;' that the passers-by had their umbrellas up for the sake of keeping dry, not for the purpose of telling anyone it was raining; that the truck driver started up for the sake of resuming his journey, not for the purpose of telling anyone that the light had changed; that the vicar wrote the letter to the testator for the purpose of settling the dispute with the latter, rather than with any idea of expressing his opinion of the testator's sanity. And in the typical 'conduct as hearsay' case this assumption will be quite justifiable.

"On this assumption, it is clear that evidence of conduct must be taken as freed from at least one of the hearsay dangers, *i.e.,* mendacity. A man does not lie to himself. Put otherwise, if in doing what he does a man has no intention of asserting the existence or non-existence of a fact, it would appear that the trustworthiness of evidence of this conduct is the same whether he is an egregious liar or a paragon of veracity. Accordingly, the lack of opportunity for cross-examination in relation to his veracity or lack of it, would seem to be of no substantial importance. Accordingly, the usual judicial disposition to equate the 'implied' to the 'express' assertion is very questionable."[12]

The drafters of the Federal Rules agreed with the criticisms of the common law rule that implied assertions should be treated as hearsay

11. *Weinstein* ¶ 801(a)[01], at 801–55. * * *

12. Falknor, *supra* note [4], at 136. The context makes clear that the author would apply the same analysis "where the conduct, although 'verbal,' is relevant, not as tending to prove the truth of what was said, but circumstantially, that is, as manifesting a belief in the existence of the fact the evidence is offered to prove." *Id.* at 134.

and expressly abolished it.[13] They did this by providing that no oral or written expression was to be considered as hearsay, unless it was an "assertion" concerning the matter sought to be proved and that no nonverbal conduct should be considered as hearsay, unless it was intended to be an "assertion" concerning said matter.[14] The relevant provisions are:

> **Rule 801.** "(a) Statement.—A *'statement'* is (1) an oral or written *assertion* or (2) nonverbal conduct of a person, if it is *intended by him as an assertion.* * * *
>
> (c) Hearsay. 'Hearsay' is a *statement,* other than one made by the declarant while testifying at the trial or hearing, offered in evidence to prove the truth of the matter asserted." * * *

"Assertion" is not defined in the rules, but has the connotation of a forceful or positive declaration.[15]

The Advisory Committee note concerning this problem states:

> "The definition of 'statement' assumes importance because the term is used in the definition of hearsay in subdivision (c). *The effect of the definition of 'statement' is to exclude from the operation of the hearsay rule all evidence of conduct, verbal or nonverbal, not intended as an assertion. The key to the definition is that nothing is an assertion unless intended to be one.*
>
> "It can scarcely be doubted that an assertion made in words is intended by the declarant to be an assertion. Hence verbal assertions readily fall into the category of 'statement.' Whether nonverbal conduct should be regarded as a statement for purposes of defining hearsay requires further consideration. Some nonverbal conduct, such as the act of pointing to identify a suspect in a lineup, is clearly the equivalent of words, assertive in nature, and to be regarded as a statement. Other nonverbal conduct, however, may be offered as evidence that the person acted as he did because of his belief in the existence of the condition sought to be proved, from which belief the existence of the condition may be inferred. This sequence is, arguably, in effect an assertion of the existence of the condition and hence properly includable within the hearsay concept. *See* Morgan, "Hearsay Dangers and the Application of the Hearsay Concept," 62 Harv.L.Rev. 177, 214, 217 (1948), and the elaboration in Finman,

13. *See Weinstein,* ¶ 801(a)[01] at 801–55—801–56; Lewis, *Federal Rules of Evidence,* ¶ 6.5 (Ill.Inst. for C.L.E.1977).

14. *See* the sea captain illustration discussed, *supra.* In an unpublished ruling this court recently held admissible as non-hearsay the fact that a U.S. mining inspector ate his lunch in an area in a coal mine now alleged to have been unsafe, and that other inspectors who observed operations prior to a disastrous explosion issued no citations, when it would have been their duty to do so, if there had been safety violations. These non-assertive acts would have been hearsay under the rule of *Wright v. Tatham* but are not hearsay under Rule 801 of the Federal Rules of Evidence, because the inspectors did not intend to make assertions under the circumstances. *Boggs v. Blue Diamond Coal Company (E.D.Ky. No. 77–69, Pikeville Division).*

15. Random House *Dictionary of the English Language* (1969 Ed.).

"Implied Assertions as Hearsay: Some Criticisms of the Uniform Rules of Evidence," 14 Stan.L.Rev. 682 (1962). Admittedly evidence of this character is untested with respect to the perception, memory, and narration (or their equivalents) of the actor, *but the Advisory Committee is of the view that these dangers are minimal in the absence of an intent to assert and do not justify the loss of the evidence on hearsay grounds.* No class of evidence is free of the possibility of fabrication, but the likelihood is less with nonverbal than with assertive verbal conduct. The situations giving rise to the nonverbal conduct are such as virtually to eliminate questions of sincerity. Motivation, the nature of the conduct, and the presence or absence of reliance will bear heavily upon the weight to be given the evidence. Falknor, "The 'Hear–Say' Rule as a 'See–Do' Rule: Evidence of Conduct," 33 Rocky Mt.L.Rev. 133 (1961). *Similar considerations govern nonassertive verbal conduct and verbal conduct which is assertive but offered as a basis for inferring something other than the matter asserted,* also excluded from the definition of hearsay by the language of subdivision (c)." (Emphasis added).

This court, therefore, holds that, "Subdivision (a)(2) of Rule 801 removes implied assertions from the definition of statement and consequently from the operation of the hearsay rule."[16]

Applying the principles discussed above to the case at bar, this court holds that the utterances of the betters telephoning in their bets were nonassertive verbal conduct, offered as relevant for an implied assertion to be inferred from them, namely that bets could be placed at the premises being telephoned. The language is not an assertion on its face, and it is obvious these persons did not intend to make an assertion about the fact sought to be proved or anything else.[17]

As an implied assertion, the proffered evidence is expressly excluded from the operation of the hearsay rule by Rule 801 of the Federal Rules of Evidence, and the objection thereto must be overruled. An order to that effect has previously been entered.

Notes and Questions

1. *Some dissenting voices.* Although *Zenni* rather than *Tatham* clearly represents the majority position in American jurisdictions that implied

16. *Weinstein,* ¶ 801(a)[01] at 801–56; *McCormick* § 250 at 599.

17. A somewhat different type of analysis would be required by words non-assertive in form, but which under the circumstances might be intended as an assertion. For example, an inspector at an airport security station might run a metal detector over a passenger and say "go on through." In the absence of the inspector, would testimony of this event be objectionable hearsay, if offered for the proposition that the passenger did not have a gun on him at that time? Although Rule 801(a) does not seem to require a preliminary determination by the trial court whether verbal conduct is intended as an assertion, it is submitted that such a determination would be required in the example given. If an assertion were intended the evidence would be excluded. If not, it would be admissible. This result is implicit in the policy of the drafters of the Federal Rules of Evidence that the touchstone for hearsay is the intention to make an assertion. *See* S. Saltzburg and K. Redden, Federal Rules of Evidence Manual 456 (2d ed. 1977).

assertions are nonhearsay, see Mueller, Post–Modern Hearsay Reform: The Importance of Complexity, 76 Minn.L.Rev. 367, 413 n.133 (1992), there are occasionally explicitly dissenting voices. See Stoddard v. State, 887 A.2d 564 (Md.2005) (holding that question by 18–month-old child to her mother whether the defendant was "going to get" her was hearsay).

2. *Tatham's only recent demise in England.* In Regina v. Kearley, 2 App.Cas. 228, 2 W.L.R. 656, 2 All E.R. 345 (H.L.1992), the House of Lords, adhered to the *Tatham* decision and reached the opposite conclusion from *Zenni*. It held that a series of calls asking to purchase drugs received by the police at the defendant's flat were hearsay and therefore inadmissible to prove the implied assertion that he was selling drugs. See generally Symposium on Hearsay and Implied Assertions: How Would (or Should) the Supreme Court Decide the *Kearley* Case?, 16 Miss.C.L.Rev. 1 (1995). However, that result was changed by provisions of the Criminal Justice Act of 2003. See Regina v. Singh, [2006] EWCA Crim. 660 (ruling that the legislation creates "a new rule against hearsay which does not extend to implied assertions" and would admit what was said by the callers in *Kearley*).

3. *Linguistically not assertive or an implied assertion?* How is the result in *Zenni* that the phone calls are not hearsay best explained? Is it a linguistic explanation that they are "directions" that are not hearsay because they are not assertive under Rule 801(a)? See United States v. Bailey, 270 F.3d 83, 87 (1st Cir.2001) (holding telephone call which summoned recipient to rendezvous point but did not by content identify the recipient, was a direction and not hearsay). Or are these calls more properly examined as assertions but not hearsay under an implied assertion analysis under Rule 801(c)? Is it significant that several calls were received? Is there anything about the fact in *Zenni* that makes it more like conduct than the typical hearsay statement that is pure conversational speech?

HEADLEY v. TILGHMAN

United States Court of Appeals, Second Circuit, 1995.
53 F.3d 472.

McLaughlin, Circuit Judge:

[Headley was charged with possession of narcotics with intent to distribute and conspiracy to distribute narcotics.]

[At issue were statements from an unidentified Jamaican caller, which the trial court admitted as those of a co-conspirator made during and in furtherance of the conspiracy. The appellate court concluded that it did not need to struggle with the difficult co-conspirator argument because it could affirm on the alternative ground that "the statements were perfectly admissible as non-hearsay" under United States v. Oguns, 921 F.2d 442, 448–49 (2d Cir.1990).]

In Oguns, a police officer answered a telephone call while searching the defendant's house pursuant to a valid warrant. The unidentified caller asked, "Have the apples arrived there?" Id. at 448. The district court allowed the officer to recount this question, and admitted additional evidence demonstrating that narcotics traffickers often use code words when discussing drugs on the telephone. Id. at 445, 449. We affirmed, reasoning that:

> [t]he government legitimately used the phone call as circumstantial evidence of Oguns' knowledge and intent regarding the importation and distribution charges. The fact that an out-of-court statement is used to provide circumstantial evidence of a conspiracy does not require that the statement be analyzed under the co-conspirator exception to the hearsay rule.

Id. at 449 * * *.

Here, as in Oguns, the questions asked by the unidentified Jamaican caller—"Are you up? Can I come by? Are you ready?"—were not admitted for their truth, but rather as circumstantial evidence that Headley used his beeper to receive requests for drugs. Evidence scholars are wont to characterize such statements as "mixed acts and assertions," see generally 4 Christopher B. Mueller & Laird C. Kirkpatrick, Federal Evidence 101–12 (2d ed. 1994), and admissibility is won by emphasizing the performance aspect of the statement. Thus, the question implies the speaker's belief that he is talking to a drug dealer; and that belief is regarded as circumstantial evidence of the nature of the business. By intellectual corner-cutting, the cases treat this as an assumption by the speaker that he has reached a drug den, rather than a direct assertion by him that "you are a drug dealer," an assertion that would surely trigger the hearsay rule, with its risks of insincerity, distorted perception, imperfect memory, and ambiguity of utterance. An assumption has a fair claim to be treated as non-hearsay since the attendant risks are not as intensively implicated as when the idea is directly enunciated in a statement. See United States v. Long, 905 F.2d 1572, 1579–80 (D.C.Cir.1990).

Accordingly, the questions are non-hearsay, the exclusion of which is not mandated by any other evidentiary rule. In addition, although, as in Oguns, the caller's questions were seemingly innocuous, Manzi's expert opinion that the caller was seeking to purchase cocaine provided an alternative interpretation based upon his experience eavesdropping on numerous drug deals between Jamaican individuals. The jury was free to reject the government's interpretation in favor of the defense's construction that the caller was merely asking Headley to go out for the night.

UNITED STATES v. SUMMERS

United States Court of Appeals, Tenth Circuit, 2005.
414 F.3d 1287.

PAUL KELLY, JR., CIRCUIT JUDGE.

[Marvin Thomas appealed his conviction for bank robbery and aiding and abetting * * * and conspiracy to commit bank robbery * * *.]

BACKGROUND

* * * [After investigation,] [t]he officers conducted a felony stop, handcuffing and frisking the four occupants of the vehicle. * * * The

occupants were identified as Mr. Summers, Mr. Thomas, Mohammed, and Frazier. A search of the vehicle revealed evidence linked to the bank robbery. Officers discovered $5,142.10 in cash in Mr. Thomas's pockets, including ten "bait bills" subsequently identified by the Bank of America. * * * Mr. Thomas also possessed a key to Apartment 2013. * * * Officers also discovered zippered bank bags containing significant quantities of cash or cash equivalents, clothing and latex gloves resembling those used in the robbery, a purple pillowcase containing cash and coins, and a large amount of cash in the cargo area. * * *

Although Messrs. Summers and Thomas were apparently silent during the stop and search, Mohammed cannot be described as reticent. When an officer asked Mohammed to identify suspicious items in his front pocket during a pat down, Mohammed replied: "What do you think? It's bank money." * * * Later, while being led to a police car, Mohammed inquired of an attending officer: "How did you guys find us so fast?" * * *

Discussion

Hearsay Issues

Mr. Thomas first complains that the admission of a hearsay statement by co-defendant Mohammed violated his Sixth Amendment confrontation right. As noted above, over defense objection the district court permitted the following colloquy between the prosecution and Officer Daniel Wolf of the Albuquerque Police Department describing events immediately following the stop of the red Ford Escape:

* * *

> Q. And as you walked him over to the patrol car, did he say anything?
>
> A. Yes, sir, he did.
>
> Q. And tell the ladies and gentlemen of the jury what he said.
>
> A. He stated, "How did you guys find us so fast? "

* * *

A. *Whether Mohammed's Question, "How Did You Guys Find Us So Fast?," Was Hearsay*

[In ruling on the constitutional challenge under the Confrontation Clause], [w]e must first ascertain whether the question, "How did you guys find us so fast?," is properly considered hearsay. It hardly needs stating that the admission of hearsay is frowned upon and generally inadmissible at trial. Fed.R.Evid. 802. Under the Federal Rules of Evidence, hearsay "is a statement, other than one made by the declarant while testifying at the trial or hearing, offered in evidence to prove the truth of the matter asserted." Fed.R.Evid. 801(c). A statement "is (1) an oral or written assertion or (2) nonverbal conduct of a person, if it is intended by the person as an assertion." *Id.* 801(a). The term "assertion" is not defined in Rule 801. "Assert" is generally defined as "to state or declare positively and often forcefully or aggressively" or "to demonstrate the existence of." *Webster's Ninth New Collegiate Dictionary* 109 (1991). To further guide our inquiry, the advisory notes to Rule 801 indicate that "[t]he key to the definition [of a statement] is that nothing is an assertion unless intended to be one." The government limits its argument on appeal to the contention that Mohammed's declaration is not hearsay because the declarant did not intend to make an assertion by uttering the words. We disagree.

In *United States v. Jackson,* 88 F.3d 845 (10th Cir.1996), we addressed for the first time whether the admission into evidence of a question posited by a non-testifying witness constituted hearsay within the meaning of Rules 801(c) and 802. In that case, officers recovered the pager of a suspected carjacker during a foot pursuit. *Id.* at 846. While an officer filled out a report on the carjacking, the pager went off and displayed a telephone number. *Id.* The officer called the displayed number and heard a voice say, "Is this Kenny?" The question was admitted over objection through the testimony of the officer, and the defendant was convicted of carjacking and related firearm offenses. *Id.* As in this case, the government argued that there was no error in the admission of the declaration because, as a question lacking assertive quality, it did not constitute hearsay under Rule 801(a)(1) and (c). *Id.* at 847. In determining that the question, "Is this Kenny?," did not constitute hearsay, we emphasized that such a declaration could not "reasonably be construed to be an assertion, either express or implied." *Id.* at 848. We explained that in analyzing the question, we found "it hard to believe in this case that the declarant *intended* to assert that Mr. Jackson was in possession of the pager and that he was responding to her call." *Id.* (emphasis added). We did not, however, foreclose the possibility that a question might indeed be construed as an assertion, either express or implied.

Our decision in *Jackson* relied in part on the District of Columbia Circuit's decision in *United States v. Long,* 905 F.2d 1572 (D.C.Cir.1990). In *Long,* the defendant was charged with various firearms and narcotics charges after a police search of the apartment in which Keith Long was arrested revealed a plethora of evidence related to the charged criminal conduct. *Id.* at 1575. While officers were searching the apartment, a telephone rang and police answered it. *Id.* at 1579. The unidentified caller first asked to speak with "Keith" and then inquired whether Keith "still had any stuff." *Id.* When queried as to the meaning of this question, the caller responded by indicating a quantity of crack cocaine. *Id.* Over defense objection, the police officer was permitted to testify concerning the conversation at trial. *Id.* Long argued that the caller's questions contained implicit assertions of his involvement in narcotics distribution and that the government introduced the statements to prove the truth of those assertions. *Id.* Writing for the court, then Circuit Judge Clarence Thomas rejected Long's argument. Noting that "[i]t is difficult to imagine any question, or for that matter any act, that does not in some way convey an implicit message," the court focused squarely on the intent of the caller. *Id.* at 1580. The court found that Long had failed to provide any evidence to suggest that the unidentified caller actually intended to assert that he was involved in narcotics distribution. *Id.*

Taken together, *Jackson* and *Long* do not foreclose the possibility that a declaration in the form of a question may nevertheless constitute an assertion within the meaning of Rule 801(a) and (c). Rather, both cases properly focus the inquiry on the declarant's intent. Furthermore, it is the party challenging admission of the declaration that bears the burden of demonstrating the declarant's requisite intent. *Jackson,* 88 F.3d at 848; *Long,* 905 F.2d at 1580; Rule 801 advisory committee's note ("The rule is so worded as to place the burden upon the party claiming that the intention existed; ambiguous and doubtful cases will be resolved against him and in favor admissibility.").

Turning to the facts of the instant case, we hold that Mr. Thomas has met his burden of demonstrating that by positing the question, "How did you guys find us so fast?," Mohammed intended to make an assertion. Unlike the rather innocuous and ambiguous question in *Jackson,* Mohammed's question clearly contained an inculpatory assertion. It begs credulity to assume that in positing the question Mohammed was exclusively interested in modern methods of law enforcement, including surveillance, communication, and coordination. Rather, fairly construed the statement intimated both guilt and wonderment at the ability of the police to apprehend the perpetrators of the crime so quickly. This in turn is distinguished from the questions in *Long* that were designed to elicit information and a response, rather than assert the defendant's involvement in criminal activity. Thus, on the face of the record, we hold that Mohammed's intent to make an assertion was apparent and that his question directed to police officers on the scene constituted hearsay for purposes of Rule 802.

[The court concluded admission of the hearsay violated the defendant's rights under the Confrontation Clause, and it reversed Mohammed's conviction but affirmed that of Thomas, finding the error harmless.]

Notes and Questions

1. *Almost a categorical exclusion for questions.* Although some courts treat questions as if they were categorically excluded from hearsay because not assertions, as *Summers* demonstrates, a more nuanced treatment may be appropriate. In what way is the effective inquiry similar to that involved in determining whether an implied assertion should be considered hearsay?

2. *Context and reducing hearsay dangers.* How might the context of these questions add critically to their superiority to the typical declarative sentence? See Park, The Definition of Hearsay: To Each His Own, 16 Miss.C.L.Rev. 125, 136–37 (1995).

UNITED STATES v. MUSCATO

United States District Court, Eastern District of New York, 1982.
534 F.Supp. 969.

MEMORANDUM AND ORDER

WEINSTEIN, CHIEF JUDGE.

Defendant was found guilty of conspiracy to unlawfully manufacture firearms and of related crimes. [Only the] claim that hearsay was improperly admitted [warrants discussion.] For the reasons stated below, this claim is rejected.

I. FACTS

The story begins with Walter Gollender, a self-styled part-time talent promotor. Though a fastidious and intelligent man, Gollender had been forced to leave the teaching profession by a psychiatric disability. In need of protection from Newark's dangers, real and imagined, he purchased a small, single shot firearm of simple design, in appearance resembling a large pen.

Gollender revealed his purchase to an acquaintance named Stanley Szostek, Jr., a former Newark police officer, who assisted his father in operating a neighborhood liquor and food store. In turn, Szostek showed the pen gun to his friend and business partner, Joseph Kirchner, a truck driver who delivered soft drinks to the store. Together, this enterprising pair had contrived to provide their community with a variety of services. They had invested in a rock concert, conducted a desultory loan-sharking business, and sold patent remedies as illicit drugs. Upon observing the simple construction of Gollender's weapon and learning that he had paid $40.00 for it, they decided to enter the arms trade.

Szostek took the prototype to a friend on the Newark police force, the defendant, John Muscato. Despairing of ever making the down payment for a new home on a modest policeman's salary, Muscato was moonlighting as a machinist in his father's basement. Muscato agreed to make copies of the pen gun in commercial quantities.

One problem with this plan was that it left Gollender defenseless. Accordingly, Muscato temporarily lent Gollender a twenty-five calibre pistol to replace his pen gun. Awed by the complexity and dangers of this new acquisition, Gollender carefully marked the pistol with a gummed label to indicate the safety position and the firing position. * * * After the model pen gun had served its purpose, it was returned to him and he relinquished the pistol to Szostek.

As Muscato began producing pen guns, Szostek and Kirchner began casting about for markets for their product. * * * To this end they contacted a business acquaintance, Patrick Monteforte. * * * He began looking for potential buyers of pen guns on Staten Island. * * * It was Monteforte's fortune to land as a customer one of the world's major armaments purchasers, the United States Government. Though presenting himself as the representative of a large New York area crime syndicate, the buyer was in fact Special Agent Matthew Raffa of the United States Treasury Department, Bureau of Alcohol, Tobacco and Firearms. As quickly as the basement factory could produce the pen guns, the Treasury Department bought them. Eventually, the government placed an order for 1,000 at $20,000. * * *

Delivery of the final shipment was arranged to be in neutral territory, a diner in the shadow of the George Washington Bridge, in Fort Lee, New Jersey. Szostek and Kirchner were armed and present. They were accompanied by a new recruit to the conspiracy, another former Newark policeman named Charles McDonald, now a hopeless alcoholic. His role was described as "riding shotgun," i.e., providing extra security. Muscato hid in the background with a high-powered rifle to "watch the deal go down."

To the surprise of Kirchner, Szostek and McDonald, instead of enriching them by $20,000, Raffa and his colleagues arrested them. From McDonald the federal agents recovered a .25 calibre pistol, bearing the remnants of a gummed label at the safety catch.

Eventually, all of the conspirators were rounded up and Kirchner, Gollender, Kasper and Monteforte agreed to testify for the government. During his debriefing by government officials, Gollender chanced to describe the gun that he claimed he had received from Muscato and returned to Szostek, recalling that he had placed a gummed label at the safety catch. At this point, the government agents retrieved from a safe the pistol found on McDonald. Gollender promptly identified it as the same pistol he had described.

Muscato did not cooperate with the United States Attorney. He was charged in a six count indictment [largely related to the unlawful manufacture and distribution of firearms.]

The evidence against Muscato at trial was overwhelming. He was directly implicated by Kirchner, Kasper and Gollender. Their testimony was corroborated by extensive circumstantial evidence, including damaged pen gun parts from the basement arsenal.

The defense consisted of a denial of criminal intent. The hypothesis suggested to the jury was that Muscato was a law-abiding policeman who had been making the various pen gun parts independently without knowing what they were or how they fit together. * * * [A]fter the jury had been exposed to pen guns in assembled and unassembled form over a period of days, they were probably predisposed to reject both Muscato's testimony that he was making parts without knowing their purpose and his attorney's argument that a reasonable policeman-machinist might believe he was helping manufacture pocket flashlights.

The defense position was, as noted, seriously undercut by the testimony of the other conspirators. Now, if these witnesses were not quite your run-of-the-mill mobsters, neither were they particularly solid citizens, and the defense attacked their credibility on cross-examination with considerable gusto.

Given Gollender's psychiatric history, he was by no means an ideal witness and the defense attorney had a field day with him on cross-examination. Particularly stressed was Gollender's difficulty in distinguishing reality from fancy and his suggestibility. The following exchanges are typical:

Mr. Richman: * * *

Q. You have many inordinate fears? * * *

A. I have had, yes. * * *

Q. * * * You have strong feelings of inadequacy and a terror that you will lose control of yourself?

A. Not ultimate control, but I have feelings like that, similar to those. Not total control, no. I have some good judgment I think sometimes.

Q. And it is true that * * * Dr. Howard Davidman, said that you have a great need to be noticed and appreciated which sometimes leads you to bizarre behavior? * * *

A. It has happened on occasion, yes.

Q. And on those occasions you don't know whether you behavior is bizarre or not, isn't that correct?

A. I would hope it would not be, but maybe perhaps it has been.

Q. You can't distinguish sometimes from reality to perhaps not so reality?

A. I can distinguish from reality but I can't always predict what effect my behavior would have on other people.

Q. Sometimes you become panicky and overdo some things, isn't that correct? * * *

A. Sometimes.

Given this attack on Gollender's credibility, one piece of real proof took on added weight. Linking Muscato to the conspiracy was the pistol he allegedly lent Gollender, which ultimately turned up in the hands of McDonald at the time of his arrest. Gollender identified the pistol in open court as follows:

Mr. [A.U.S.A.] Kirby: Did you have any conversation with Mr. Muscato at that time?

A. No, I did not. Except he gave me a .25 calibre gun while we were in the car. He came to an intersection in Irvington and he stopped and gave me the pistol. * * *

Q. Mr. Gollender, I show you what has been marked as Government's Exhibit 12.

Would you take a look at that object and tell the Court and jury whether you recognize it?

A. Yes, it's the gun.

Q. I'm sorry?

A. Yes, I recognize it as the .25 caliber pistol.

Q. How do you recognize it as such?

A. It has the same marking on it, same scuff mark and mainly the remnants of the gum label I marked it with, safe or unsafe. It still has a piece of the paper indicating how it was safe or unsafe.

The fact that Gollender had provided an accurate description of the pistol prior to his being shown it or being told that it had been discovered on the person of Charles McDonald provided important confirmation of his testimony. The government [received] permission to elicit this fact from Special Agent Raffa. (It was clear that Muscato would deny from the witness stand Gollender's testimony about the source of the pistol.) The defense objected on the ground of hearsay. * * *

II. Law * * *

B. Hearsay * * *

1) Was the extrajudicial declaration hearsay under the Federal Rules?

For purposes of analysis one way of treating the case with respect to the gun might be to consider only the following testimony: One member of the conspiracy testified that he had received a gun from the defendant, an alleged coconspirator, that this gun had a unique characteristic, observable upon examination, and that he had returned the gun to a third conspirator. The arresting officer testified that he had obtained a gun with the same unique characteristic from an alleged fourth conspirator. The jury could examine the gun, which had been admitted as an exhibit, to help it determine if the two witnesses were describing the same object. This part of the case presents no hearsay problem. Both witnesses testified with respect to characteristics and events they themselves observed.

The evidence was significant in two respects. First, the prosecution's ability to produce a gun matching Gollender's description lent circumstantial support to Gollender's story of having received such a gun from the defendant in furtherance of the conspiracy. Second, the fact that this gun was found on the person of another conspirator while engaged in acts furthering the conspiracy linked Muscato to the conspiracy.

What made the production of the gun useful as corroboration of Gollender's story is the improbability of his describing a gun with such a unique characteristic if he had not seen it. The physical evidence of the gun provided some assurance (unless the jury believed that this real evidence was fabricated by the prosecution) that the tale was not cut out of whole cloth. It did not by itself insure that Gollender saw the gun under the circumstances he related. If he first described the gun after having identified it while it was in the agent's possession, much of the effect of this line of proof would have been eroded. If, on the other hand, he described the gun before being shown it by a law enforcement official, production of the gun would have a substantial corroborative effect.

If we then add to the case the extrajudicial declaration of Gollender to the agent we have 1) testimony revealing the existence of a memory in the mind of a witness (a description of a gun with unique characteristics and its source), 2) a physical object matching that memory, and 3) an extrajudicial declaration made under circumstances indicating that the reported memory was acquired in a manner consistent with the witness' testimony.

It is the third leg which involved a hearsay danger since it depended on the truth of an extrajudicial declaration to the agent by Gollender. Gollender said outside of court, in essence, "the gun given to me by Muscato had a unique characteristic; this is that gun." On its face, thus parsed, his statement to the agent would appear to fall squarely within the definition of hearsay provided in rule 801(c) of the Federal Rules of Evidence:

> "Hearsay" is a statement, other than one made by the declarant while testifying at the trial * * * offered in evidence to prove the truth of the matter asserted.

The fact that the extrajudicial declarant, like his auditor, was a witness subject to cross examination does not eliminate the hearsay problem. While many writers proposed treating extrajudicial declarations by witnesses as non-hearsay or as falling within a broad hearsay exception [citing authorities], the Federal Rules reject this approach except in special cases. *See* F.R.Evid. 801(d)(1); 803(5). * * *[18]

Despite the fact that it could be analyzed as hearsay under the Federal Rules of Evidence, this extrajudicial declaration posed minimal hearsay dangers; it was highly probative while being essentially corroborative in function. Admitting it may be justified under a number of different theories: that it was circumstantial rather than testimonial evidence and, therefore, was not hearsay; that it was offered on the issue of credibility rather than for its truth as evidence-in-chief; and that it was admissible under Rule 803(24).

2) The extrajudicial declaration as circumstantial evidence

One way of characterizing the extrajudicial declaration in this case is as "circumstantial non-assertive use" of the utterance "to show state of mind." Statements used in this way, according to Professor McCormick, need not be denominated hearsay. This, he wrote, is especially true

18. [The court rejected application of the hearsay exception for declarations offered as evidence of a mental state. Federal Rule 803(3) admits statements showing then existing mental states but explicitly prohibits use "to prove the facts remembered," and Gollender's statement to the agent was probative of the remembered fact that he received a unique gun from the defendant. Ed.]

of "declarations evincing knowledge, notice, consciousness or awareness of some fact, which fact is established by other evidence in the case." McCormick, Evidence, § 249, p. 592 (2nd Cleary Ed. 1972). According to this analysis, the extrajudicial declaration was offered not to prove the truth of the proposition asserted—the description of the gun—but to prove that the declarant had knowledge of the truth of that proposition. Because McCormick's discussion of the "trace" on the mind theory has had great influence, it is set forth in its entirety:

> When the existence of knowledge is sought to be used as the basis for a further inference, caution is required lest the hearsay rule be infringed upon. Thus, in a Wisconsin case [*Bridges v. State,* 247 Wis. 350, 19 N.W.2d 529 (1945)] * * * evidence was received in a trial for mistreatment of a little girl, that the girl in reporting the incident gave a description of the house and its surroundings and of the room and its furnishings, where the mistreatment occurred. Other evidence showed that this description fitted exactly the house and room where the defendant lived. Morgan suggested that this evidence depended for its value upon "the observation, memory and veracity" of the girl and thus shared the hazards of hearsay. [Morgan, Evidence 1941–1945, 59 Harv.L.Rev. 481, 544 (1946). * * * It seems, however, that the testimony had value without regard to her veracity. Other witnesses had described the physical characteristics of the house. Her testimony was not relied on for that, but to show her knowledge as a "trace," as it were, on her mind of her visit at the time of the crime. Significantly the undisputed proof excluded the possibility of other means by which she could have acquired the knowledge, and thus the hearsay dangers were eliminated.

The evidence before us is much like the extrajudicial declaration at issue in *Bridges v. State,* 247 Wis. 350, 19 N.W.2d 529, 534 (1945), the case McCormick cited as the paradigm. A seven year old child described to a police officer several exterior and interior details of the house in which she was allegedly assaulted. Subsequently, it was discovered that this description closely fit defendant's home. The court, relying on 6 Wigmore §§ 1788, 1790, 1791 (3rd Ed. 1940), reasoned that the statement to the police officer was circumstantial evidence of the child's state of mind which, in turn, was evidence of what caused that state of mind.

Additional support for such treatment of extrajudicial declarations (or behavior) evincing knowledge may be sought in *Kinder v. Commonwealth,* 306 S.W.2d 265 (Kentucky Court of Appeals, 1957), in which a defendant was convicted of larceny on the basis of his young son's knowledge of the location of the cache of stolen goods. Another such case is *State v. Galvan,* 297 N.W.2d 344 (Iowa Supreme Court, 1980), a murder case in which the court approved admission of a description by defendant's ex-wife of their two year old daughter's apparent unreflective re-enactment of the killing while the youngster was at play. While the *Galvan* court based its ruling on a "res gestae exception," *id.* at 347, and rejected the *Bridges* rationale, the fact pattern places the case in the *Bridges–Kinder* line. * * *

The *Bridges* approach to cases of this sort cuts the gordian knot of hearsay. Not surprisingly, however, it leaves a few loose ends.

First, it involves an oversimplification of the function of the declaration involved. It is not quite accurate to characterize the extrajudicial declarations in any of these cases as mere descriptions of places or things or of "traces" on the mind. They are essentially accounts of events implicating criminal defendants and, ultimately, they will be used by the trier in support of the accounts they suggest, even if, as an intermediate step, they indicate only states of mind consistent with the truth and accuracy of these implied accounts. Thus, there is a sense in which they are offered to prove the proposition asserted.

Second, it does not sufficiently distinguish between the use of an extrajudicial declaration as evidence of past state of mind and its use as evidence of current state of mind. Yet there may be a difference in reliability between these two uses of an extrajudicial declaration. Where a prior statement is adduced to show the basis of a current memory trace, it can be checked and tested against the current statement. This is not necessarily the case for evidence such as that offered in *Bridges* or *Galvan,* concerning an ephemeral mental impression. In the present case, the extrajudicial declaration corroborates in-court testimony. In a case like *Galvan,* where the extrajudicial declarant is unavailable to testify, that is not the situation. This is cause for a sense of disquiet which cannot be adequately dispelled since there can be no in-court current explanation and testing of the declarant.

Third, and most important, a rule admitting all such material ignores important distinctions in reliability. There are dangers implicit in allowing into evidence material like that offered in *Bridges, Kinder* and *Galvan*—dangers which McCormick acknowledges but which the trier may fail to give proper weight. The ability of declarants to recall details observed in incriminating situations, before being exposed to those details by law enforcement officials or others, is bound to impress a trier. The probative force of such evidence, however, is dependent on the assumption that the extrajudicial declarant had no other way of learning the details described than by having witnessed the events described. If declarants in such cases were exposed to the objects they identified in some fashion other than one which squares with their implied account, or if the information was otherwise suggested to them, as by the form of questioning or what they inadvertently overheard, then their extrajudicial descriptions have little probative force. There is always a danger that even the least suggestible auditor will read into a conversation details put forward by one party and adopted by the other as his own thoughts. *See, e.g.,* E. Loftus, Eyewitness Testimony, 98 ff. (1979) ("highly credible people can manipulate others more readily"); Hofstadter, "About Two Kinds of Inquiry," 246 Scientific American 18, 23 (1982) ("the same system [of thought based on intelligent use of context and memory] that enables us to creatively find meanings and to make new discoveries also makes us extremely vulnerable. * * * [T]he manipulator may be conscious of his deception; but often he too is a victim of personal validation.").

Where the assumption that the extrajudicial declarant has not been previously exposed to the objects or events in question or their description remains unchecked by vigorous cross-examination or other evidence tested under adversarial fire, dangerous consequences can result. A well-documented Swedish case presented facts analogous to those in *Bridges* but with a twist. While a young boy claiming to be the victim of an assault could accurately identify the interior of the accused's apartment, it turned out that he had been previously exposed to an identical apartment. Then further investigation demonstrated inconsistencies in the boy's story that revealed that the accusation was fabricated in an attempt to deflect attention from the child's own disobedience. Trankell, "Was Lars Sexually Assaulted?", 56 Journal of Abnormal and Social Psychology, 385 ff. (1958); A. Trankell, Reliability of Evidence, 106 ff. (1972).

One way of coping with the incompleteness of the *Bridges* approach is to turn to criteria of admissibility other than the hearsay rule—i.e., those of Rule 403—for evaluating circumstantial non-assertive uses of extrajudicial declarations. *See, e.g.,* Note, Theoretical Foundations of the Hearsay Rule, 93 Harv.L.Rev. 1786 (1980). A federal court following this approach in a case with the *Galvan* fact pattern would exclude testimony about the daughter's extrajudicial behavior because it lacked such supplementary guarantees of reliability, even though Rule 801(a) excluded it from the Federal definition of hearsay. * * * While the mother in *Galvan* was a witness at the trial, even assuming she was credible, there may be too many unexplorable nuances and possibilities of error through unconscious suggestion to run the risk of allowing the young child's indirect hearsay as evidence-in-chief. Children of that age are all ears and may overhear adult conversations which they may be unable to differentiate from their own original sense impressions.

Bridges is halfway between *Galvan* and the instant case because in *Bridges* the seven-year-old testified, although the testimony of such a youngster must usually be treated skeptically in view of the added problems of influencing such a witness. *Cf., e.g., Hollaris v. Jankowski,* 315 Ill.App. 154, 42 N.E.2d 859 (1942) (court refused to hear eight-year-old child because of suggestibility; he had heard so many conversations about the event that he could not differentiate what he had heard from what he had seen). Much would, of course, depend upon the court's evaluation of the witness. Moreover, in *Bridges* the circumstances were such as to make it highly unlikely that the details of the description could have been derived from anything but the child's experience of the event in question.

The same court that would exclude in *Galvan* and would be *dubitante* in *Bridges* would admit the extrajudicial declaration in the case now before us. The out-of-court declaration is accompanied by the declarant's in-court identification and availability for cross examination as well as the auditor's testimony respecting the declarant's limited opportunities for prior contact with the object identified.

[The court proceeded to analyze the admissibility of the statement under two alternative bases. First, it considered the statement as a prior consistent statement excluded from the definition of hearsay either under Rule 801(d)(1)(B) or more generally under 801(c) because it is not offered for its truth but for the impact on credibility that flows from the fact that such a statement was previously made. Second, it considered admissibility under the Rule 803(24), the catchall provision.]

III. CONCLUSION

Gollender's out-of-court statement was properly admitted. Whether or not this extrajudicial declaration is denominated hearsay turns on how one characterizes its function in the development of the government's case. It may be viewed as admissible hearsay, non-hearsay evidence-in-chief, or non-hearsay insofar as it is admissible on the issue of credibility. Admission of evidence of this sort does not derive its ultimate justification from any one theory, but from notions of reliability and the ability of the trier to properly evaluate probative force.

Absent a constitutional issue of confrontation—and there is none here—the central question is whether the jury could accurately evaluate the probative value of Gollender's out-of-court statement. Essentially this is an issue implicated in Rules 401 to 403, requiring the court's exercise of sound judgment and discretion. *See, e.g., United States v. Barbati,* 284 F.Supp. 409, 413 (E.D.N.Y.1968) ("We cannot permit the mechanical and unreasoned application of the hearsay rule to deny evidence vital for our search for the truth."). In the circumstances of this case there can be no doubt that admitting this evidence enhanced the search for the truth without any possible unfairness or prejudice to the defendant. Motion for a new trial denied.

Notes and Questions

1. *Narrowing, not eliminating interpretative disagreement.* As the preceding cases make clear, enactment of the Federal Rules of Evidence has not eliminated major disagreements as to when a statement is not hearsay. See also United States v. Reynolds, 715 F.2d 99, 103 (3d Cir.1983) (finding a codefendant's statement that "I didn't tell them anything about you" hearsay under the theory that implied assertions are hearsay under the Federal Rules). While federal courts frequently analyze implied assertions as did *Zenni* and treat them broadly as nonhearsay, others have either ignored the issue or, like *Reynolds*, have refused to recognize that the Federal Rules changed the result in *Tatham*. Callen, Hearsay and Informal Reasoning, 47 Vand.L.Rev. 43, 47 (1994). They have generally avoided decisions based on a literalistic distinction of how the utterance was phrased. Park, "I Didn't Tell Them Anything About You": Implied Assertions as Hearsay Under the Federal Rules of Evidence, 74 Minn.L.Rev. 783, 827–28 (1990).

2. *Brain teasers.* Consider whether hearsay is involved in each of the following cases: United States v. Sells, 496 F.2d 912 (7th Cir.1974) (name seen on driver's license to show identity of possessor); United States v. Snow, 517 F.2d 441 (9th Cir.1975) (defendant's name on tape affixed to gun case found on premises frequented by defendant as proof that he knowingly possessed firearm contained in case). Although typically considered not hearsay, the results are not always consistent. Compare Bernadyn v. State, 887 A.2d 602, 606–12 (Md.2005) (medical bill found at crime scene addressed to defendant considered hearsay as implied assertion), with United States v. Mejias, 552 F.2d 435, 446 (2d Cir.1977) (hotel receipt seized from defendant not hearsay when used to show defendant stayed at hotel but rather circumstantial evidence to connect him to that place).

3. *Some things can't be cross-examined.* A hearsay objection is sometimes made to "statements" by machines or animals, such as speed detecting devices or bloodhounds. In City of Webster Groves v. Quick, 323 S.W.2d 386, 390 (Mo.Ct.App.1959), the court rejected such a challenge to a speed detecting device:

> Evidence is called hearsay when its probative force depends, in whole or in part, on the competency and credibility of some person other than the witness by whom it is sought to be produced. * * * The hearsay rule cannot be applied to what the witness, on the stand and subject to cross-examination, observed, either through his own senses or through the use of scientific instruments.

See also United States v. Hamilton, 413 F.3d 1138, 1142–43 (10th Cir.2005) (ruling that header attached to photograph not hearsay when automatically created by computer without human input).

SECTION B. OTHER STATEMENTS THAT ARE NOT HEARSAY

(1) PRIOR STATEMENTS OF THE WITNESS

FEDERAL RULE 801(d)(1)

COMMONWEALTH v. DAYE

Supreme Judicial Court of Massachusetts, 1984.
469 N.E.2d 483.

ABRAMS, JUSTICE.

We granted further appellate review to consider the Commonwealth's request that we adopt Proposed Mass.R.Evid. 801(d)(1)(A),[19] permitting the introduction of limited categories of prior inconsistent statements for their probative worth.

* * *

19. Proposed Mass.R.Evid. 801(d)(1)(A) reads as follows: "(d) Statements which are not hearsay. A statement is not hearsay if— (1) Prior statement by witness. The declarant testifies at the trial or hearing and is subject to cross-examination concerning the statement, and the statement is (A) inconsistent with his testimony and was given under oath subject to the penalty of perjury at a trial, hearing, or other proceeding, or in a deposition." Grand jury testimony falls within the "other proceeding" category.

The evidence implicating the defendant consisted principally of one in-court identification of him as the gunman by an eyewitness who admitted on cross-examination that earlier he had identified a codefendant, Michael Prochilo as the gunman during a lineup conducted several days after the shooting. The victim and five other witnesses present at the scene of the shooting were unwilling or unable to identify the defendant in court.[20] There was evidence that three of those witnesses, including the victim, also identified Prochilo as the gunman prior to trial. Statements elicited from some of the witnesses at trial suggest that their testimony may have been colored by fear of reprisals if they made an identification at trial.

The evidentiary issues we are asked to decide are affiliated with the Commonwealth's attempts to demonstrate that witnesses who did not identify the defendant at trial had done so from pretrial photographic arrays and before the grand jury.

[After concluding that the trial court committed reversible error by admitting testimony by a police officer concerning pretrial identifications of the defendant by two witnesses who denied at trial making such identifications, the court considered admission of identifications testimony given by one of those witnesses, Ciambelli, before the grand jury.]

2. *Grand jury testimony.* After Ciambelli denied making a pretrial photographic identification of the defendant as the gunman, and stated that "I didn't know what he [the shooter] looks like," the prosecutor questioned him about his grand jury testimony. Over the defendant's objection, Ciambelli was permitted to read from the grand jury transcript that he had stated to the grand jury that he had identified Dennis Daye as the gunman. After reading the defendant's name from the transcript, Ciambelli volunteered that "I don't know Dennis Daye and I never seen him. That's just a name that was going around." Ciambelli stated he did not see Dennis Daye in the court room.

At side bar, the prosecutor specifically stated he did not intend to use the grand jury testimony for purposes of impeachment, but argued instead its probative admissibility as past recollection recorded. Admission of the testimony on that basis over the defendant's objection without a limiting instruction was error. We have previously expressed "serious doubt" whether grand jury testimony is admissible under the "past recollection recorded" exception to the hearsay rule. *Commonwealth v. Bookman,* 386 Mass. 657, 664–665, 436 N.E.2d 1228 (1982). We need not decide that question, however, because it is plain that the requirements of that exception are not met in this case. When a witness has no current recollection of a particular event, the witness may incorporate in his testimony "a writing expressive of his past knowledge," *Bendett v. Bendett,* 315 Mass. 59, 64, 52 N.E.2d 2 (1943), provided

20. One witness, whose testimony is not at issue on this appeal, asserted that, at a pretrial photographic array, he had selected Dennis Daye's photograph as representative of the gunman, but that the defendant at trial did not look like the man in the photograph.

the witness, "having firsthand knowledge of the facts recorded in the memorandum, [is] able to testify that the memorandum written or observed by him was true at the time it was made." *Commonwealth v. Bookman, supra* 386 Mass. at 663, 436 N.E.2d 1228. See P.J. Liacos, Massachusetts Evidence 92–94 (5th ed. 1981). Ciambelli, however, denied at trial both first hand knowledge of the defendant's involvement in the crime and the truth of his statement to the grand jury implicating the defendant. Cf. *Commonwealth v. Greene,* 9 Mass.App. 688, 690, 404 N.E.2d 110 (1980).[21]

3. *Probative use of prior inconsistent statements.* On the basis of the errors described above, we conclude that a new trial is required. We are unpersuaded by the Commonwealth's argument that any evidentiary errors relating to extrajudicial identifications of the defendant by Ciambelli and O'Connor should be treated as harmless because the identifications were cumulative of other evidence implicating the defendant. In this case, only one witness identified the defendant in court as the gunman, and that identification was impeached by evidence of a prior identification by the same witness of another person as the gunman. The evidence, although sufficient to justify verdicts against the defendant, was not overwhelming. We are not persuaded that, in this context, it was harmless to permit the jury to consider at probative value evidence of independent identifications by other witnesses of the defendant as the gunman. * * *

The settled rule in this Commonwealth is the "orthodox" one that prior inconsistent statements, though admissible for the limited purpose of impeaching the credibility of a witness's testimony at trial, are inadmissible hearsay when offered to establish the truth of the matters asserted. [Citation omitted.] By contrast, Fed.R.Evid. 801(d)(1)(A), incorporated verbatim in Proposed Mass.R.Evid. 801(d)(1)(A), permits probative use of inconsistent grand jury testimony, as well as other categories of inconsistent statements given under oath, in instances where "[t]he declarant testifies at the trial * * * and is subject to cross-examination concerning the statement." * * *

The orthodox view against probative admissibility of prior inconsistent statements is founded on the general rationale for the exclusion of hearsay, namely, that the reliability of a prior inconsistent statement "rests on the credit of the declarant, who was not (1) under oath, (2) subject to cross-examination, or (3) in the presence of the trier, when the statement was made." McCormick, Evidence § 251, at 601 (2d ed. 1972). This rationale for exclusion has come under attack from numerous

21. Ciambelli's grand jury testimony was likewise inadmissible as present recollection refreshed. A writing may be used to revive a witness's recollection of events observed by the witness, but, so utilized, the writing has no evidentiary value and should not be read to the jury. *Commonwealth v. Parrotta,* 316 Mass. 307, 312, 55 N.E.2d 456 (1944). *Bendett v. Bendett, supra,* 315 Mass. at 63, 52 N.E.2d 2. P.J. Liacos, Massachusetts Evidence, *supra* at 87. Moreover, it must be clear that when, assisted by the writing, the witness testifies in the presence of the jury, the witness is testifying from present memory rather than reciting the contents of the writing. *Commonwealth v. Hoffer,* 375 Mass. 369, 376, 377 N.E.2d 685 (1978).

prominent commentators, who think the dangers the hearsay rule was designed to protect against are dissipated to a large extent when, as in the case of prior inconsistent statements, the extrajudicial declarant is present at trial. See, e.g., 3A J. Wigmore, *supra* at 996; Morgan, Hearsay Dangers and the Application of the Hearsay Concept, 62 Harv.L.Rev. 177, 192 (1948); McCormick, The Turncoat Witness: Previous Statements as Substantive Evidence, 25 Tex.L.Rev. 573 (1947). Some proponents of the "modern view" advocate probative use of all prior inconsistent statements on the grounds that the oath is not a significant safeguard of reliability and that counsel's opportunity to cross-examine the declarant at trial, and the jury's opportunity to view the declarant's demeanor at trial, satisfy the other concerns. See Comment, Prior Inconsistent Statements: Conflict Between State and Federal Rules of Evidence, 34 Mercer L.Rev. 1495, 1498–1500 (1983). A less extreme "modern" position, reflected in the rule the Commonwealth advises us to adopt, accepts at probative value only those prior inconsistent statements given under oath in instances where a record of the statement is likely to be available.

The schism between adherents of the "orthodox" and "modern" doctrines is accounted for in large part by divergent viewpoints as to the validity of the premise that the presence of the extrajudicial declarant at trial constitutes adequate protection for the lack of contemporaneous cross-examination of the declarant at the time the subsequently disavowed statement was made.[22] Supporters of the modern view argue that, at least where the witness at trial does not disclaim memory of the circumstances under which the prior statement was made, the reliability of the statement can be tested notwithstanding the witness's recantation. "Cross-examination [at trial] can probe the witness' perception and memory and can develop all the reasons why the witness made a statement which he now insists was not true." 4 J. Weinstein & M. Berger, Evidence ¶ 801(d)(1)(A)[03] at 801–92. See McCormick, The Turncoat Witness: Previous Statements as Substantive Evidence, 25 Tex.L.Rev. 573, 577 (1947) (questioning at trial "will lay bare the sources of the change of face, in forgetfulness, carelessness, pity, terror or greed, and thus reveal which is the true story and which the false"). Partisans of the orthodox view retort that prior inconsistent statements, if admitted for probative purposes, are endowed with an "indestructible" quality superior to that of testimony at trial. "Nothing that happens to the witness inside the courtroom can deprive the fact finder of the right to believe the [extrajudicial statement]. Indeed, if the witness inside the courtroom were to be attacked with the usual devices of the cross-examiner and shown to be untrustworthy, that would merely make it all

22. If the witness affirms the truth of the prior statement, he adopts it and no hearsay problem is presented. 4 J. Weinstein & M. Berger, *supra,* ¶ 801(d)(1)(A)[02] at 801–90 to 801–91. Questions concerning the probative admissibility of prior inconsistent statements arise in instances where the witness denies, or asserts a lack of memory with regard to, the making of a statement or its veracity. See *Ruhala v. Roby,* 379 Mich. 102, 124, 150 N.W.2d 146 (1967); 4 J. Weinstein & M. Berger, *supra.* * * *

the more likely that the fact finder would decide to believe the [extrajudicial statement]." Blakey, Substantive Use of Prior Inconsistent Statements Under the Federal Rules of Evidence, 64 Ky.L.J. 3, 44–45 (1975–1976). A fact finder's disbelief of a witness's contradiction of a prior statement at trial, it is argued, "sheds no direct light on the accuracy of [the] pretrial statement," *California v. Green,* 399 U.S. 149, 193 * * * (1970) (Brennan, J., dissenting), and does not, therefore, adequately ensure the reliability of the extrajudicial statement's factual content.

The proponents of the modern view argue that doubts as to the effectiveness of cross-examination at trial should, as a matter of public policy, be resolved in favor of probative use of prior inconsistent statements because a contrary rule encourages witness intimidation and deprives the prosecution of evidence necessary to prove cases against criminal defendants in instances where key witnesses recant their testimony. To this policy argument is added the pragmatic argument that juries cannot, and perhaps should not, be expected to discriminate between impeachment and probative use of a prior inconsistent statement, and that formally conferring probative status to such statements does no more than legitimize current practice.

The orthodox view, on the other hand, is defended on the ground that a witness may recant former statements for reasons other than intimidation, see Blakey, *supra* at 46, and that probative use of prior inconsistent statements permits convictions based on ex parte statements to prosecutorial authorities that may be fabricated, distorted, or erroneous. See *State v. Spadafore,* 159 W.Va. 236, 220 S.E.2d 655 (1975). Further, the distinction between probative and impeachment use of prior inconsistent statements, it is argued, even if elusive to some jurors, is one of importance to the courts in adjudicating issues relating to sufficiency of the evidence. See *California v. Green, supra,* 399 U.S. at 194 n.6 * * * (Brennan, J., dissenting).

The history of Fed.R.Evid. 801(d)(1)(A) illuminates the controversy over the evidentiary status of prior inconsistent statements. In 1970, the United States Supreme Court, although not called on to decide, as between the orthodox and modern views, "which of these positions, purely as a matter of the law of evidence, is the sounder," *California v. Green, supra* at 155 * * *, held that, as a Federal constitutional matter, acceptance of prior inconsistent statements for their probative value does not violate the Sixth Amendment Confrontation Clause "as long as the declarant is testifying as a witness and subject to full and effective cross-examination." *Id.* at 158 * * *. See *Nelson v. O'Neil,* 402 U.S. 622 * * * (1971).

As drafted in the Proposed Federal Rules of Evidence promulgated by the Supreme Court in 1972, Fed.R.Evid. 801(d)(1)(A) would have sanctioned, as an evidentiary matter, the probative admissibility of prior inconsistent statements to the full extent constitutionally permissible. Rules of Evidence for United States Courts and Magistrates, 56 F.R.D. 183, 293 (1972). Although the United States Senate favored adoption of the Supreme Court rule, permitting probative use of prior inconsistent statements irrespective of the circumstances under which they were made, S.Rep. No. 1277, 93d Cong., 2d Sess. 13 (1974), reprinted in 1974 U.S.Code Cong. & Ad.News 7051, 7062–7063, the House Judiciary Committee advocated a stricter rule admitting only those statements made under oath and subject to cross-examination, H.R.Rep. No. 650, 93d Cong., 2d Sess. 13 (1974), reprinted in 1974 U.S.Code Cong. & Ad.News 7075, 7086–7087. Under the House version, inconsistent grand jury testimony would have remained within the hearsay category. As adopted, Fed.R.Evid. 801(d)(1)(A) constitutes a compromise between the two positions. The House requirement that the statement have been made under oath was retained, thereby eliminating the risk of manufactured third-party testimony by restricting probative admissibility to situations in which there is likely to be a written transcript or tape recording providing "overwhelming proof that the witness did in fact make the prior inconsistent statement," Blakey, *supra* at 10. The compromise version eliminated the requirement of contemporaneous cross-examination, however, thereby allowing the probative use of inconsistent grand jury testimony.

In the wake of the adoption of Fed.R.Evid. 801(d)(1)(A), other jurisdictions remain divided over the probative admissibility of prior inconsistent statements. At the present time, other States can be categorized in roughly equal numbers into groups following, respectively, the Federal rule, the more expansive Supreme Court version, and the orthodox rule.[23] A majority of States permit the probative use of inconsistent grand jury testimony.

We take note of these developments and are persuaded that the reasoning favoring use of inconsistent grand jury statements as probative evidence is sound. * * * With regard to inconsistent grand jury statements, we are satisfied that the truth-seeking function of trials may be enhanced rather than diminished if consideration of their probative value is permitted. Where the presence of the declarant at trial creates an opportunity fully to explore the circumstances under which a grand jury statement was made and the veracity of its factual content, the absence of contemporaneous cross-examination does not in our opinion so impair the statement's reliability as to mandate that the fact finder be deprived of the right to accept the statement for its probative worth. "The jury is alerted by the inconsistency in the stories, and its attention is sharply focused on determining either that one of the stories reflects

23. Fifteen States, by statute or common law, follow, at least in criminal cases, rules identical or substantially identical to Fed.R.Evid. 801(d)(1)(A). Sixteen States espouse, with minor variation, the more expansive rule initially proposed by the United States Supreme Court, permitting substantive use of all prior inconsistent statements of a witness available for cross-examination at trial. Sixteen States adhere to the orthodox rule precluding any substantive use. Two States have adopted the House version, conditioning substantive admissibility on a showing that the declarant was under oath and subject to cross-examination at the time the statement was made. See 4 J. Weinstein & M. Berger, Evidence, ¶ 801(d)(1)(A)[09] at 801–111 to 801–116 (1981 & Supp.1983) (State by State listing); 3A J. Wigmore, Evidence § 1018(b) at 998–1007 n.3 (Chadbourn rev. 1970 & Supp.1983) (same).

the truth or that the witness who has apparently lied once, is simply too lacking in credibility to warrant its believing either story." *California v. Green, supra* 399 U.S. at 160 * * *. We believe that a fact finder should be permitted to prefer a grand jury statement made closer in time to the events at issue over contradictory trial testimony that the passage of time and intervening influences may have affected. The prior statement will have been made in an atmosphere of formality impressing upon the declarant the need for accuracy, and will be memorialized in a manner eliminating subsidiary inquiries into whether the statement was actually made that would unacceptably attenuate the statement's probative worth.

Permitting probative use of an inconsistent grand jury statement also eliminates an unnecessary and unseemly legal fiction. "The rule limiting the use of prior statements by a witness subject to cross-examination to their effect on his credibility has been described by eminent scholars and judges as 'pious fraud,' 'artificial,' 'basically misguided,' 'mere verbal ritual,' and an anachronism 'that still impede[s] our pursuit of the truth.' * * * [T]o tell a jury it may consider the prior testimony as reflecting on the veracity of the later denial of relevant knowledge but not as the substantive evidence that alone would be pertinent is a demand for mental gymnastics of which jurors are happily incapable." *United States v. DeSisto,* 329 F.2d 929, 933 (2d Cir.1964).

* * *

* * * Today, we do little more than harmonize the legal treatment of prior inconsistent statements with the practical effect of permitting the jury to consider such statements under the guise of impeachment. * * *[24]

Although we today hold that inconsistent grand jury testimony may be admitted in limited circumstances for its probative worth, we will not permit convictions based exclusively on inconsistent extrajudicial testimony to stand. See *California v. Green, supra,* 399 U.S. at 170 and n.19. In this case the Commonwealth must produce identification evidence in addition to a prior inconsistent statement in order to meet its burden of proof. * * *

* * * The judgments of the Superior Court are reversed, the verdicts set aside, and the case is remanded for a new trial. * * *

24. [The court articulated two restrictions on the use of inconsistent statements that are not typically imposed. First, it required an "opportunity for effective cross-examination" of the declarant at trial, which would preclude admission when the witness at trial had no recollection of the events to which the statement relates. Second, it mandated that the grand jury statement must clearly be the statement of the witness rather than the interrogator and therefore not the product either of a series of "yes" or "no" answers to leading questions or prosecutorial coercion. Contra United States v. Dennis, 625 F.2d 782, 795 (8th Cir.1980) (statements before the grand jury qualify for admission under 801(d)(1)(A) "even if the statements were elicited by means of leading questions"). Ed.]

Notes and Questions

1. *The meaning of "other proceeding."* As *Daye* notes, grand jury proceedings satisfy the requirement of Rule 801(d)(1)(A) that the statement must be made "at a trial, hearing, or other proceeding." A number of courts have excluded statements given to investigative agents "under informal circumstances tantamount to a station house interrogation setting." United States v. Day, 789 F.2d 1217, 1222 (6th Cir.1986). See also United States v. Livingston, 661 F.2d 239 (D.C.Cir.1981); Santos v. Murdock, 243 F.3d 681, 684 (2d Cir.2001); United States v. Lloyd, 10 F.3d 1197, 1217 (6th Cir.1993). In United States v. Castro–Ayon, 537 F.2d 1055 (9th Cir.1976), the Ninth Circuit took a rather expansive view of what "other proceedings" would meet the requirements of the Rule. It held admissible statements taken under oath by a Border Patrol Agent in tape recorded interrogations during an "immigration proceeding." Compare State v. Smith, 651 P.2d 207 (Wash. 1982) (holding admissible under the "other proceeding" requirement a notarized statement taken by a police detective where the court found the statement reliable under the particular circumstances of its making), with State v. Smith, 573 So.2d 306, 314–16 (Fla.1990) (rejecting Washington's approach).

2. *Inconsistency requirement flexibly applied.* Rule 801(d)(1)(A) requires that to be admissible, the statement must be "inconsistent with [the witness'] testimony." Courts have generally interpreted the inconsistency requirement very flexibly. United States v. Dennis, 625 F.2d 782, 795 (8th Cir.1980), is reflective of the majority position: "The trial judge has considerable discretion in determining whether testimony is 'inconsistent' with prior statements; inconsistency is not limited to diametrically opposed answers but may be found in evasive answers, inability to recall, silence, or changes of position." A very well-settled body of case law treats a contrived memory loss as inconsistent, see, e.g., United States v. Knox, 124 F.3d 1360, 1364 (10th Cir.1997), but there is no requirement that the trial court determine that the witness is lying about lack of memory, see United States v. Gajo, 290 F.3d 922, 930–32 (7th Cir.2002).

3. *Requiring little more than a human presence.* Rule 801(d)(1) generally requires that the declarant "testifies at trial * * * and is subject to cross-examination concerning the statement." The meaning of the term "subject to cross-examination" requires interpretation in the situation where a witness lacks memory of the prior statement and/or the underlying event or claims to have no memory. In United States v. Owens, 484 U.S. 554 (1988), the Supreme Court, in ruling admissible a prior statement of identification under Rule 801(d)(1)(C), provided a rather extreme interpretation of the term that largely eliminates the memory issue:

> Ordinarily a witness is regarded as "subject to cross-examination" when he is placed on the stand, under oath, and responds willingly to questions. Just as with [the Confrontation Clause], limitations on the scope of examination by the trial court or assertions of privilege by the witness may undermine the process to such a degree that meaningful cross-examination within the intent of the rule no longer exists. But that effect is not produced by the witness' assertion of memory loss—which * * * is often the very result sought to be produced by cross-examination, and can be effective in destroying the force of the prior

> statement. Rule 801(d)(1)(C) [like 801(d)(1)(A)], which specifies that the cross-examination need only "concer[n] the statement," does not on its face require more.

484 U.S. at 561–62. *Owens'* definition of "subject to cross-examination" allows extraordinarily few exceptions. United States v. Torrez–Ortega, 184 F.3d 1128, 1132–35 (10th Cir.1999), which found a witness who erroneously but persistently claimed the Fifth Amendment privilege did satisfy the Rule, represents one of those unusual situations. See related discussion in Section C, infra.

4. *Sufficiency.* Admissibility of prior inconsistent statements as substantive evidence under the Rule does not necessarily mean that such statements alone are sufficient to sustain a conviction. See United States v. Bahe, 40 F.Supp.2d 1302, 1308–10 (D.N.M.1998) (describing the weight of authority that a prior inconsistent statement standing alone is insufficient to sustain a guilty verdict).

5. *Limits on statements admissible for impeachment only.* In spite of Rule 801(d)(1)(A), many prior inconsistent statements will remain admissible only for impeachment purposes because, to be substantively admissible, the prior inconsistent statements must have been made under oath, subject to penalty for perjury, and in certain types of proceedings. Where they are not substantively admissible, the basic principle remains that "[t]he prosecution may not call a witness it knows to be hostile for the *primary* purpose of eliciting otherwise inadmissible impeachment testimony, for such a scheme serves as a subterfuge to avoid the hearsay rule." United States v. Hogan, 763 F.2d 697, 702 (5th Cir.1985).

6. *Sources.* Bein, Prior Inconsistent Statements: The Hearsay Rule, 801(d)(1)(A) and 803(24), 26 UCLA L.Rev. 967 (1979); Goldman, Guilt by Intuition: The Insufficiency of Prior Inconsistent Statements to Convict, 65 N.C.L.Rev. 1 (1986).

TOME v. UNITED STATES

Supreme Court of the United States, 1995.
513 U.S. 150.

JUSTICE KENNEDY delivered the opinion of the Court, except as to Part IIB.

Various federal Courts of Appeals are divided over the evidence question presented by this case. At issue is the interpretation of a provision in the Federal Rules of Evidence bearing upon the admissibility of statements, made by a declarant who testifies as a witness, that are consistent with the testimony and are offered to rebut a charge of a "recent fabrication or improper influence or motive." Fed. Rule Evid. 801(d)(1)(B). The question is whether out-of-court consistent statements made after the alleged fabrication, or after the alleged improper influence or motive arose, are admissible under the Rule.

I

Petitioner Tome was charged in a one-count indictment with the felony of sexual abuse of a child, his own daughter, aged four at the time of the alleged crime. * * *

Tome and the child's mother had been divorced in 1988. A tribal court awarded joint custody of the daughter, A.T., to both parents, but Tome had primary physical custody. In 1989 the mother was unsuccessful in petitioning the tribal court for primary custody of A.T., but was awarded custody for the summer of 1990. * * * On August 27, 1990, the mother contacted Colorado authorities with allegations that Tome had committed sexual abuse against A.T.

The prosecution's theory was that Tome committed sexual assaults upon the child while she was in his custody and that the crime was disclosed when the child was spending vacation time with her mother. The defense argued that the allegations were concocted so the child would not be returned to her father. At trial A.T., then six and one half years old, was the Government's first witness. For the most part, her direct testimony consisted of one-and two-word answers to a series of leading questions. Cross-examination took place over two trial days. The defense asked A.T. 348 questions. On the first day A.T. answered all the questions posed to her on general, background subjects.

The next day there was no testimony, and the prosecutor met with A.T. When cross-examination of A.T. resumed, she was questioned about those conversations but was reluctant to discuss them. Defense counsel then began questioning her about the allegations of abuse, and it appears she was reluctant at many points to answer. As the trial judge noted, however, some of the defense questions were imprecise or unclear. The judge expressed his concerns with the examination of A.T., observing there were lapses of as much as 40–55 seconds between some questions and the answers and that on the second day of examination the witness seemed to be losing concentration. The trial judge stated, "We have a very difficult situation here."

After A.T. testified, the Government produced six witnesses who testified about a total of seven statements made by A.T. describing the alleged sexual assaults: A.T.'s babysitter recited A.T.'s statement to her on August 22, 1990, that she did not want to return to her father because he "gets drunk and he thinks I'm his wife"; the babysitter related further details given by A.T. on August 27, 1990, while A.T.'s mother stood outside the room and listened after the mother had been unsuccessful in questioning A.T. herself; the mother recounted what she had heard A.T. tell the babysitter; a social worker recounted details A.T. told her on August 29, 1990 about the assaults; and three pediatricians, Drs. Kuper, Reich and Spiegel, related A.T.'s statements to them describing how and where she had been touched by Tome. All but A.T.'s statement to Dr. Spiegel implicated Tome. * * *

A.T.'s out-of-court statements, recounted by the six witnesses, were offered by the Government under Rule 801(d)(1)(B). The trial court admitted all of the statements over defense counsel's objection, accepting the Government's argument that they rebutted the implicit charge that A.T.'s testimony was motivated by a desire to live with her mother.

* * * Following trial, Tome was convicted and sentenced to 12 years imprisonment.

On appeal, the Court of Appeals for the Tenth Circuit affirmed, adopting the Government's argument that all of A.T.'s out-of-court statements were admissible under Rule 801(d)(1)(B) even though they had been made after A.T.'s alleged motive to fabricate arose. The court reasoned that "the pre-motive requirement is a function of the relevancy rules, not the hearsay rules" and that as a "function of relevance, the pre-motive rule is clearly too broad * * * because it is simply not true that an individual with a motive to lie always will do so." 3 F.3d 342, 350 (C.A.10 1993). "Rather, the relevance of the prior consistent statement is more accurately determined by evaluating the strength of the motive to lie, the circumstances in which the statement is made, and the declarant's demonstrated propensity to lie." *Ibid.* * * * Applying this balancing test to A.T.'s first statement to her babysitter, the Court of Appeals determined that although A.T. might have had "some motive to lie, we do not believe that it is a particularly strong one." 3 F.3d, at 351. The court held that the district judge had not abused his discretion in admitting A.T.'s out-of-court statements. * * *

II

The prevailing common-law rule for more than a century before adoption of the Federal Rules of Evidence was that a prior consistent statement introduced to rebut a charge of recent fabrication or improper influence or motive was admissible if the statement had been made before the alleged fabrication, influence, or motive came into being, but it was inadmissible if made afterwards. As Justice Story explained: "[W]here the testimony is assailed as a fabrication of a recent date * * * in order to repel such imputation, proof of the *antecedent* declaration of the party may be admitted." *Ellicott v. Pearl*, 35 U.S. 412, 439 (1836) (emphasis supplied). See also *People v. Singer*, 300 N.Y. 120, 124–125, 89 N.E.2d 710, 712 (1949).

McCormick and Wigmore stated the rule in a more categorical manner: "[T]he applicable principle is that the prior consistent statement has no relevancy to refute the charge unless the consistent statement was made before the source of the bias, interest, influence or incapacity originated." E. Cleary, McCormick on Evidence § 49, p. 105 (2d ed. 1972) (hereafter McCormick). See also 4 J. Wigmore, Evidence § 1128, p. 268 (J. Chadbourn rev. 1972) (hereafter Wigmore) ("A consistent statement, at a *time prior* to the existence of a fact said to indicate bias * * * will effectively explain away the force of the impeaching evidence" (emphasis in original)). The question is whether Rule 801(d)(1)(B) embodies this temporal requirement. We hold that it does.

A

Rule 801 * * * defines prior consistent statements as nonhearsay only if they are offered to rebut a charge of "recent fabrication or improper influence or motive." Fed. Rule Evid. 801(d)(1)(B). Noting the "troublesome" logic of treating a witness prior consistent statements as hearsay at all (because the declarant is present in court and subject to cross-examination), the Advisory Committee decided to treat those consistent statements, once the preconditions of the Rule were satisfied, as nonhearsay and admissible as substantive evidence, not just to rebut an attack on the witness's credibility. See Advisory Committee Notes on Fed. Rule Evid. 801(d)(1), 28 U.S.C.App., p. 773. * * *

The Rules do not accord this weighty, nonhearsay status to all prior consistent statements. To the contrary, admissibility under the Rules is confined to those statements offered to rebut a charge of "recent fabrication or improper influence or motive," the same phrase used by the Advisory Committee in its description of the "traditiona[l]" common law of evidence, which was the background against which the Rules were drafted. See Advisory Committee Notes, *supra*, at 773. Prior consistent statements may not be admitted to counter all forms of impeachment or to bolster the witness merely because she has been discredited. In the present context, the question is whether A.T.'s out-of-court statements rebutted the alleged link between her desire to be with her mother and her testimony, not whether they suggested that A.T.'s in-court testimony was true. The Rule speaks of a party rebutting an alleged motive, not bolstering the veracity of the story told.

This limitation is instructive, not only to establish the preconditions of admissibility but also to reinforce the significance of the requirement that the consistent statements must have been made before the alleged influence, or motive to fabricate arose. That is to say, the forms of impeachment within the Rule's coverage are the ones in which the temporal requirement makes the most sense. Impeachment by charging that the testimony is a recent fabrication or results from an improper influence or motive is, as a general matter, capable of direct and forceful refutation through introduction of out-of-court consistent statements that predate the alleged fabrication, influence or motive. A consistent statement that predates the motive is a square rebuttal of the charge that the testimony was contrived as a consequence of that motive. By contrast, prior consistent statements carry little rebuttal force when most other types of impeachment are involved. McCormick § 49, p. 105 ("When the attack takes the form of impeachment of character, by showing misconduct, convictions or bad reputation, it is generally agreed that there is no color for sustaining by consistent statements. The defense does not meet the assault." (footnote omitted)); see also 4 Wigmore § 1131, p. 293 ("The broad rule obtains in a few courts that consistent statements may be admitted after impeachment of any sort—in particular after any impeachment by cross-examination. But there is no reason for such a loose rule" (footnote omitted)).

There may arise instances when out-of-court statements that postdate the alleged fabrication have some probative force in rebutting a charge of fabrication or improper influence or motive, but those statements refute the charged fabrication in a less direct and forceful way. Evidence that a witness made consistent statements after the alleged motive to fabricate arose may suggest in some degree that the in-court testimony is truthful, and thus suggest in some degree that that testimony did not result from some improper influence; but if the drafters of Rule 801(d)(1)(B) intended to countenance rebuttal along that indirect inferential chain, the purpose of confining the types of impeachment that open the door to rebuttal by introducing consistent statements becomes unclear. If consistent statements are admissible without reference to the time frame we find imbedded in the Rule, there appears no sound reason not to admit consistent statements to rebut other forms of impeachment as well. Whatever objections can be leveled against limiting the Rule to this designated form of impeachment and confining the rebuttal to those statements made before the fabrication or improper influence or motive arose, it is clear to us that the drafters of Rule 801(d)(1)(B) were relying upon the common-law temporal requirement.

The underlying theory of the Government's position is that an out-of-court consistent statement, whenever it was made, tends to bolster the testimony of a witness and so tends also to rebut an express or implied charge that the testimony has been the product of an improper influence. Congress could have adopted that rule with ease, providing, for instance, that "a witness' prior consistent statements are admissible whenever relevant to assess the witness's truthfulness or accuracy." The theory would be that, in a broad sense, any prior statement by a witness concerning the disputed issues at trial would have some relevance in assessing the accuracy or truthfulness of the witness's in-court testimony on the same subject. The narrow Rule enacted by Congress, however, cannot be understood to incorporate the Government's theory.

* * *

The language of the Rule, in its concentration on rebutting charges of recent fabrication, improper influence and motive to the exclusion of other forms of impeachment, as well as in its use of wording which follows the language of the common-law cases, suggests that it was intended to carry over the common-law pre-motive rule. * * *

B

Our conclusion that Rule 801(d)(1)(B) embodies the common-law premotive requirement is confirmed by an examination of the Advisory Committee Notes to the Federal Rules of Evidence. We have relied on those well-considered Notes as a useful guide in ascertaining the meaning of the Rules. * * *

* * *

Throughout their discussion of the Rules, the Advisory Committee Notes rely on Wigmore and McCormick as authority for the common-law approach. In light of the categorical manner in which those authors state the premotive requirement, * * * it is difficult to imagine that the drafters, who noted the new substantive use of prior consistent statements, would have remained silent if they intended to modify the premotive requirement. As we observed with respect to another provision of the Rules, "[w]ith this state of unanimity confronting the drafters of the Federal Rules of Evidence, we think it unlikely that they intended to scuttle entirely [the common-law requirement]." *United States v. Abel,* 469 U.S. 45, 50 (1984). Here, we do not think the drafters of the Rule intended to scuttle the whole premotive requirement and rationale without so much as a whisper of explanation.

Observing that Edward Cleary was the Reporter of the Advisory Committee that drafted the Rules, the Court has relied upon his writings as persuasive authority on the meaning of the Rules. See *Daubert v. Merrell Dow Pharmaceuticals, Inc.,* 509 U. S. 579 (1993); *Abel, supra,* at 51–52. Cleary also was responsible for the 1972 revision of McCormick's treatise, which included an examination of the changes introduced by the proposed federal rules to the common-law practice of impeachment and rehabilitation. The discussion, which occurs only three paragraphs after the treatise's categorical description of the common-law premotive rule, also lacks any indication that the proposed rules were abandoning that temporal limitation. See McCormick § 50, p. 107.

* * *

That Rule 801(d)(1)(B) permits prior consistent statements to be used for substantive purposes after the statements are admitted to rebut the existence of an improper influence or motive makes it all the more important to observe the preconditions for admitting the evidence in the first place. The position taken by the Rules reflects a compromise between the views expressed by the "bulk of the case law * * * against allowing prior statements of witnesses to be used generally as substantive evidence" and the views of the majority of "writers * * * [who] ha[d] taken the opposite position." [See Advisory Committee Notes on Rule 801(d)(1), 28 U.S.C.App., p. 773]. That compromise was one that the Committee candidly admitted was a "judgment * * * more of experience than of logic." *Ibid.*

C

The Government's final argument in favor of affirmance is that the common-law premotive rule advocated by petitioner is inconsistent with the Federal Rules' liberal approach to relevancy and with strong academic criticism, beginning in the 1940's, directed at the exclusion of out-of-court statements made by a declarant who is present in court and subject to cross-examination. This argument misconceives the design of the Rules' hearsay provisions.

* * * To be sure, certain commentators in the years preceding the adoption of the Rules had been critical of the common-law approach to hearsay, particularly its categorical exclusion of out-of-court statements offered for substantive purposes. See, e.g., Weinstein, The Probative Force of Hearsay, 46 Iowa L.Rev. 331, 344–345 (1961) (gathering sources). * * * As an alternative, they suggested moving away from the categorical exclusion of hearsay and toward a case-by-case balancing of

the probative value of particular statements against their likely prejudicial effect. See Weinstein, *supra*, at 338; Ladd, The Relationship of the Principles of Exclusionary Rules of Evidence to the Problem of Proof, 18 Minn.L.Rev. 506 (1934). The Advisory Committee, however, was explicit in rejecting this balancing approach to hearsay: "The Advisory Committee has rejected this approach to hearsay as involving too great a measure of judicial discretion, minimizing the predictability of rulings, [and] enhancing the difficulties of preparation for trial." Advisory Committee's Introduction, *supra*, at 771 (emphasis added). * * *

The statement-by-statement balancing approach advocated by the Government and adopted by the Tenth Circuit creates the precise dangers the Advisory Committee noted and sought to avoid: It involves considerable judicial discretion; it reduces predictability; and it enhances the difficulties of trial preparation because parties will have difficulty knowing in advance whether or not particular out-of-court statements will be admitted. See Advisory Committee's Introduction, *supra*, at 771.

D

The case before us illustrates some of the important considerations supporting the Rule as we interpret it, especially in criminal cases. If the Rule were to permit the introduction of prior statements as substantive evidence to rebut every implicit charge that a witness' in-court testimony results from recent fabrication or improper influence or motive, the whole emphasis of the trial could shift to the out-of-court statements, not the in-court ones. The present case illustrates the point. In response to a rather weak charge that A.T.'s testimony was a fabrication created so the child could remain with her mother, the Government was permitted to present a parade of sympathetic and credible witnesses who did no more than recount A.T.'s detailed out-of-court statements to them. Although those statements might have been probative on the question whether the alleged conduct had occurred, they shed but minimal light on whether A.T. had the charged motive to fabricate. At closing argument before the jury, the Government placed great reliance on the prior statements for substantive purposes but did not once seek to use them to rebut the impact of the alleged motive.

* * *

[Reversed and remanded.]

[JUSTICE SCALIA's opinion, in which he disagrees with the "authoritative" weight given to the Advisory Committee Notes in Part IIB, is omitted.]

JUSTICE BREYER, with whom THE CHIEF JUSTICE, JUSTICE O'CONNOR and JUSTICE THOMAS join, dissenting.

The basic issue in this case concerns, not hearsay, but relevance. As the majority points out, the common law permitted a lawyer to rehabilitate a witness (after a charge of improper motive) by pointing to the fact that the witness had said the same thing earlier—but only if the witness made the earlier statement before the motive to lie arose. The reason for the time limitation was that, otherwise, the prior consistent statement had no relevance to rebut the charge that the in-court testimony was the product of the motive to lie. * * *

The majority believes that a hearsay-related rule, Federal Rule of Evidence 801(d)(1)(B), codifies this absolute timing requirement. I do not. Rule 801(d)(1)(B) has nothing to do with relevance. Rather, that Rule carves out a subset of prior consistent statements that were formerly admissible only to rehabilitate a witness (a nonhearsay use that relies upon the fact that the statement was made). It then says that members of that subset are "not hearsay." This means that, if such a statement is admissible for a particular rehabilitative purpose (to rebut a charge of recent fabrication, improper influence or motive), its proponent now may use it substantively, for a hearsay purpose (i.e., as evidence of its truth), as well.

The majority is correct in saying that there are different kinds of categories of prior consistent statements that can rehabilitate a witness in different ways, including statements (a) placing a claimed inconsistent statement in context; (b) showing that an inconsistent statement was not made; (c) indicating that the witness' memory is not as faulty as a cross-examiner has claimed; and (d) showing that the witness did not recently fabricate his testimony as a result of an improper influence or motive. See *United States v. Rubin*, 609 F.2d 51, 68 (C.A.2 1979) (Friendly, J., concurring). But, I do not see where, in the existence of several categories, the majority can find the premise, which it seems to think is important, that the reason the drafters singled out one category (category (d)) was that category's special probative force in respect to rehabilitating a witness. Nor, in any event, do I understand how that premise can help the majority reach its conclusion about the common-law timing rule.

* * *

Assuming Rule 801(d)(1)(B) does not codify the absolute timing requirement, I must still answer the question whether, as a relevance matter, the common-law statement of the premotive rule stands as an absolute bar to a trial court's admission of a postmotive prior consistent statement for the purpose of rebutting a charge of recent fabrication or improper influence or motive. * * *

[O]ne can find examples where the timing rule's claim of "no relevancy" is simply untrue. A post-motive statement is relevant to rebut, for example, a charge of recent fabrication based on improper motive, say, when the speaker made the prior statement while affected by a far more powerful motive to tell the truth. A speaker might be moved to lie to help an acquaintance. But, suppose the circumstances also make clear to the speaker that only the truth will save his child's life. Or, suppose the postmotive statement was made spontaneously, or when the speaker's motive to lie was much weaker than it was at trial. In these and similar situations, special circumstances may indicate that the prior statement was made for some reason other than the alleged improper motivation; it may have been made not because of, but despite, the improper motivation. Hence, postmotive statements can, in appropriate circumstances, directly refute the charge of fabrication based on improper motive, not because they bolster in a general way the witness' trial testimony, * * * but because the circumstances indicate that the statements are not causally connected to the alleged motive to lie.

* * *

Accordingly, I would hold that the Federal Rules authorize a district court to allow (where probative in respect to rehabilitation) the use of postmotive prior consistent statements to rebut a charge of recent fabrication, improper influence or motive (subject of course to, for example, Rule 403). * * *

Notes and Questions

1. *Substantial room for interpretation.* In an omitted portion of the opinion, Justice Kennedy acknowledges that determining precisely when a particular corrupting influence arose will sometimes be difficult. To what extent does *Tome* leave the lower courts free to shape admissibility through that factual determination? Compare United States v. Montague, 958 F.2d 1094, 1096–98 (D.C.Cir.1992) (warning that if consistent statements must predate the corrupting motive, statements made by accomplices during police interrogation will generally be inadmissible to support their testimony when testifying for the prosecution), with United States v. Prieto, 232 F.3d 816, 819–22 (11th Cir.2000) (rejecting bright-line rule that any statement after arrest is inadmissible because a motive to fabricate necessarily and automatically attaches, reasoning that determination regarding motive to fabricate is to be made on the basis of the circumstances of the individual case by the trial court, and concluding voluntary statement made after arrest and before any discussion of possible cooperation with the government was untainted by improper motive).

2. *Consistent statements still admissible to rehabilitate.* As Justice Breyer states in his dissent, prior consistent statements can rehabilitate a witness whose credibility has been attacked in several different ways. On this point, Breyer cites Judge Friendly's concurring opinion in United States v. Rubin, 609 F.2d 51, 68–70 (2d Cir.1979). Judge Friendly argued in *Rubin* that the specific timing requirement of Rule 801(d)(1)(B) was applicable exclusively to those prior consistent statements offered for their truth after an attack charging recent fabrication or improper motive or influence. When used only to rehabilitate after other types of attacks on credibility, such as when a consistent statement taken nearer the event is used to rehabilitate an attack based on poor memory, the statement is admissible under Rule 801(c) for the limited purpose of affecting credibility rather than for the truth of the statement, and Friendly contended the timing restrictions of Rule 801(d)(1)(B) were inapplicable. In such circumstances, no improper influence or motive is alleged, and the prior statement need not precede it. Judge Friendly's position is generally accepted in the federal courts. See United States v. Simonelli, 237 F.3d 19, 27–28 (1st Cir.2001) (consistent

statements offered only for credibility are not governed by restrictions in Rule 801 but must have rebuttal force beyond mere fact that consistent statement was made). The most clearly accepted use of a prior consistent statement to rehabilitate is to clarify or rebut the impeaching effect of a prior inconsistent statement that was used to impeach the witness. See United States v. Santiago, 199 F.Supp.2d 101, 106–07 (S.D.N.Y.2002) (allowing government to admit statement to correct misleading impeaching claim regarding its contents).

3. *Common law's perspective of the limited significance of typical prior consistent statement.* In determining whether a prior consistent statement is admissible when offered to rehabilitate, one should be cognizant of the common law position that mere repetition is valueless: "The witness is not helped by it; for, even if it is an improbable or untrustworthy story, it is not made more probable or more trustworthy by any number of repetitions of it." 4 Wigmore, Evidence § 1124, at 255 (Chadbourn rev. 1972). A simple example may be helpful in understanding this perspective. Learning that a witness gave the same version of her story moments before taking the witness stand would not be admissible regarding credibility; it would be excluded under Rule 403. In other situations, however, the particular circumstances under which the statement was made and its timing can make it sufficiently valuable in restoring credibility to satisfy the relevancy concerns of Rules 401 and 403.

4. *Sources.* Bullock & Gardner, Prior Consistent Statements and the Premotive Rule, 24 Fla.St.U.L.Rev. 509 (1997); Friedman, Prior Statements of a Witness: A Nettlesome Corner of the Hearsay Thicket, 1995 Sup.Ct.Rev. 277.

UNITED STATES v. LEWIS

United States Court of Appeals, Second Circuit, 1977.
565 F.2d 1248.

FEINBERG, CIRCUIT JUDGE:

After a jury trial in the United States District Court for the Eastern District of New York before Thomas C. Platt, J., appellant Frank Tillman Lewis was convicted of armed bank robbery and conspiracy to commit that crime * * * .

THE PHOTOGRAPHIC IDENTIFICATION

In his thorough brief and argument, appellant's counsel maintains that the district judge committed a number of errors of law. The most substantial arguments on appeal stem from Norma Sharpe's pre-trial identification of appellant from a display of photographs. At trial, Mrs. Sharpe was unable to identify appellant in the courtroom and mistakenly picked out a Deputy United States Marshal instead. When Mrs. Sharpe was then shown the photographic display, she testified that she had previously identified one of the bank robbers from the group of pictures, and she then picked out the photograph she had earlier selected. This picture, which was of appellant, was then admitted into evidence. After Mrs. Sharpe's testimony, FBI Agent Leo Farrell testified as to the way in which he had prepared the photographic spread. He also confirmed that Mrs. Sharpe had selected appellant's picture shortly after the bank robbery. * * *

Appellant next argues that the identification testimony should have been excluded as hearsay, and is not permitted by the new Federal Rules of Evidence. Appellant directs our attention to Rule 801(d), which contains various definitions, and provides in relevant part that:

> (d) Statements which are not hearsay. A statement is not hearsay if—
>
> (1) Prior statement by witness. The declarant testifies at the trial or hearing and is subject to cross-examination concerning the statement, and the statement is (A) inconsistent with his testimony, and was given under oath subject to the penalty of perjury at a trial, hearing, or other proceeding, or in a deposition, or (B) consistent with his testimony and is offered to rebut an express or implied charge against him of recent fabrication or improper influence or motive, or (C) *one of identification of a person made after perceiving him* ; * * * (Emphasis supplied).

Appellant argues that Agent Farrell's testimony should have been excluded because "identification of a person made after perceiving him" contemplates only corporeal, not photographic, identification; and because it was improper to allow Farrell to testify in the absence of an in-court identification by Mrs. Sharpe. Appellant also claims that Mrs. Sharpe's testimony about her prior identification after she erroneously identified someone else in court amounted to testimony about a prior inconsistent statement not made under oath, rendering it improper under subsection (A), which overrides subsection (C).

Subsection (C) of Rule 801(d)(1), the focal point of appellant's arguments, appeared in its present form in the Rules as promulgated by the Supreme Court in November 1972. However, the Senate deleted the subsection before the Rules were approved by Congress in December 1974. Not long thereafter, the subsection was resurrected in an amendment to Rule 801, effective October 31, 1975. The Senate Report on the 1975 amendment attributed the initial opposition to the subsection to concern over convicting a defendant solely on "unsworn, out-of-court testimony."[25] The Report noted, however, that the Rule required the identifier to be available for cross-examination at the trial, and in support of the view that such evidence should be admissible, cited, among other recent decisions, the Supreme Court's discussion in *Gilbert v. California,* 388 U.S. 263, 272 n.3 * * * (1967), the opinion of Judge Friendly in *United States v. Miller,* 381 F.2d 529, 538 (2d Cir.1967), and the en banc decision of the Court of Appeals for the District of Columbia, *Clemons v. United States,* 408 F.2d 1230 (1968). The controversy over, and the rationale of, subsection (C) are both admirably summarized in 4

25. S.Rep. No. 199, 94th Cong., 1st Sess. 2 (1975), hereafter "Senate Report." See also S.Rep. No. 1277, 93rd Cong., 2d Sess. (1974).

Weinstein's Evidence, 801–3ff., ¶ 801(d)(1)(C)[01]. We agree with the observation there made that

> Congress has recognized, as do most trial judges, that identification in the courtroom is a formality that offers little in the way of reliability and much in the way of suggestibility. The experienced trial judge gives much greater credence to the out-of-court identification.

Id. at 801–103. This court recently pointed out that "[t]he purpose of the rule was to permit the introduction of identifications made by a witness when memory was fresher and there had been less opportunity for influence to be exerted upon him." *United States v. Marchand,* 564 F.2d 983, 996 (2d Cir.1977).

With these considerations in mind, we turn to appellant's specific contentions. The legislative history makes clear that Congress intended "nonsuggestive * * * photographic," as well as lineup, identifications to be covered by subsection (C). Senate Report, at 2.[26] This conclusion is confirmed by our recent holding in *United States v. Marchand,* supra, 564 F.2d at 996. We can see no sound principle for construing "identification of a person" to exclude identification by a photograph. True, there are dangers peculiar to photographic identification and these, like the dangers of a lineup or even those of an on-the-spot identification, must be taken into account in assessing reliability. But they do not justify a limiting construction of subsection (C).

Appellant's second argument on this point is that the failure of Mrs. Sharpe to identify appellant in court made inadmissible Agent Farrell's evidence that she had identified appellant a month or two earlier. Appellant may be confusing this situation with that posed by the failure or refusal of the identifying witness to recall in court the earlier identification, which is discussed in Judge Weinstein's treatise from which appellant's brief extensively quotes. In that situation, testimony like Agent Farrell's might well raise questions concerning the adequacy of cross-examination and the right to confront the original identifying witness. In this case, however, Mrs. Sharpe did recall her prior identification and so testified. Even before the new Rule, we approved of admitting evidence of prior identification, albeit corporeal, by the declarant's "own testimony and also by that of others corroborating his version of the details," see *United States v. Miller,* supra, 381 F.2d at 538, cited by the Senate Report in support of subsection (C). Cf. *United States v. Jenkins,* 496 F.2d 57, 68–70 (2d Cir.1974) (declarant could not recall prior photographic nonidentification of Jenkins and identification of another; evidence of same through third party excluded). If appellant is suggesting that under the new Rule testimony like Agent Farrell's may only be used to bolster an accurate in-court identification, we disagree. It seems clear both from the text and the legislative history of

26. See, also the House Report on subsection (C), H.Rep. No. 355, 94th Cong., 1st Sess. 2–3 (1975) hereafter "House Report."

the amended Rule that testimony concerning extra-judicial identifications is admissible regardless of whether there has been an accurate in-court identification. The Senate Report recognizes the possibility that there may be a "discrepancy * * * between the witness's in-court and out-of-court testimony,"[27] and the House Report praises the amended Rule as a means of ensuring that "delays in the criminal justice system do not lead to cases falling through because the witness can no longer recall the identity of the person he saw commit the crime."[28] The occurrence of the very contingency foreseen by the Congress will obviously not serve, of itself, to bar the Farrell testimony.

Appellant's final point seems to be that subsection (C) does not apply at all when the identifier has made an erroneous in-court identification because the prior identification is inconsistent with it and was not given under oath, as required by subsection (A). The Government responds that since appellant's appearance had changed significantly by the time of trial, there was no inconsistency. More significantly, even though Rule 801(d)(1) embraces subsection (C), the latter is not limited by the earlier subsections. Subsection (C) represents a legislative decision to admit statements of identification provided the declarant "testifies at * * * trial * * * and is subject to cross-examination concerning the statement." These conditions were met here, and we do not think that subsection (C) is rendered inoperative by Mrs. Sharpe's misidentification in court.

* * *

Judgment affirmed.

Notes and Questions

1. *Antecedents.* Prior to the enactment of the Federal Rules of Evidence, a number of courts had held pretrial identification evidence admissible as an "exception" to the hearsay rule. The most influential of these decisions was People v. Gould, 354 P.2d 865 (Cal.1960). There the Supreme Court of California recognized the superiority of pretrial identification testimony to the suggestive and unpersuasive in-court identification typically occurring at trial. This reliability would support an exception to the hearsay rule. *Gould* also concluded that "the principal danger of admitting hearsay is not present since the witness is available at the trial for cross-examination," which is the justification of the Federal Rules for treating prior identifications as falling outside the hearsay rule. Id. at 867.

2. *Improper and unconstitutional police identification methods.* In addition to the hearsay concern, the reliability of eyewitness identifications is the subject of great concern, particularly when the identification may be the product of improper police methods. The suggestiveness of pretrial identification procedures are at least partially addressed by a series of United States Supreme Court cases. See Manson v. Brathwaite, 432 U.S. 98 (1977);

27. Senate Report, supra * * * at 2.

28. House Report, supra * * * at 3.

Simmons v. United States, 390 U.S. 377 (1968); Neil v. Biggers, 409 U.S. 188 (1972); United States v. Wade, 388 U.S. 218 (1967); Gilbert v. California, 388 U.S. 263 (1967); Stovall v. Denno, 388 U.S. 293 (1967). They guarantee a criminal defendant the right to counsel at pretrial identification procedures conducted after the initiation of formal adversarial proceedings, *Wade*, and exclude identification evidence where it is the result of suggestive police procedures that give rise to a "very substantial likelihood of irreparable misidentification." *Simmons,* 390 U.S. at 384. Despite these protections, commentators continue to question the reliability of eyewitness identifications. See, e.g., Loftus, Eyewitness Testimony (1979).

3. *"Subject to cross-examination" requirement.* Rule 801(d)(1)(C), which governs admission of prior statements of identification, like Rule 801(d)(1)(A) for prior inconsistent statements, requires that the declarant be subject to cross-examination. Here too issues of the adequacy of cross-examination arise if the witness claims at trial to have no memory. In United States v. Owens, 484 U.S. 554 (1988), the Supreme Court held that the victim of an assault, which resulted in severe memory impairment, was "subject to cross-examination" within the meaning of the Rule. While the victim remembered at trial previously identifying the defendant, he could not recall seeing his attacker or the circumstances of the identification. The Court reasoned broadly that "[o]rdinarily a witness is regarded as 'subject to cross-examination' when he is placed on the stand, under oath, and responds willingly to questions. * * * [Absent limitations on cross-examination or assertion of privilege,] Rule 801(d)(1)(C) * * * does not * * * require more." 484 U.S. at 562.

4. *Composite drawing.* How should a composite drawing of the suspect prepared at the direction of the victim be treated? Compare State v. Motta, 659 P.2d 745 (Haw.1983) (drawing admissible under Rule for prior identifications), with United States v. Moskowitz, 581 F.2d 14 (2d Cir.1978) (drawing treated as nonhearsay; statements by victim identifying it admissible under instant Rule). How should statements describing the perpetrator be treated? See Morris v. United States, 398 A.2d 333 (D.C.1978) (treating victim's prior description of perpetrator as falling under the common law exception for identifications).

5. *Covering identification procedures, not prior statements that the witness knows the perpetrator.* A few courts have erroneously ignored the purpose and language of the Rule as to testimony about an identification of the defendant through an out-of-court identification procedure and instead allowed testimony that a certain person, known to the witness, committed a crime. See Bugh v. Mitchell, 329 F.3d 496, 505 n.2 (6th Cir.2003); (noting Ohio's brief use of the Rule in this fashion); United State v. Lopez, 271 F.3d 472, 484 (3d Cir.2001). The Rule should not be employed in this fashion. See United States v. Kaquatosh, 242 F.Supp.2d 562, 565–67 (E.D.Wis.2003). It is also not a proper way to introduce details of the crime. See Randolph v. United States, 882 A.2d 210, 220 (D.C.2005).

6. *Sources.* Mauet, Prior Identifications in Criminal Cases: Hearsay and Confrontation Issues, 24 Ariz.L.Rev. 29 (1982); Seidelson, Third–Party Testimony About Prior Identifications and the Federal Rule of Evidence 801(d)(1)(C): A Petition for Rehearing, 8 Rev.Litig. 259 (1989).

(2) ADMISSION OF THE PARTY OPPONENT

FEDERAL RULE 801(d)(2)

2 EDMUND M. MORGAN, BASIC PROBLEMS OF EVIDENCE 266

(1962)[29]

The admissibility of an admission made by the party himself rests not upon any notion that the circumstances in which it was made furnish the trier means of evaluating it fairly, but upon the adversary theory of litigation. A party can hardly object that he had no opportunity to cross-examine himself or that he is unworthy of credence save when speaking under sanction of an oath. His adversary may use against him anything which he has said or done. Originally he had no chance to make an explanation, but since about the middle of the 1800's, he has been competent as a witness and can furnish the trier with all pertinent information within his knowledge. Consequently the orthodox decisions refuse to apply to evidence of personal admissions restrictions usually applicable to testimonial evidence.

OLSON v. HODGES

Supreme Court of Iowa, 1945.
19 N.W.2d 676.

[Personal injury action by passenger against driver of automobile. Defendant contends that his driving was not "reckless" within the meaning of the state's guest statute and appeals from a judgment entered on a verdict in favor of plaintiff.]

BLISS, JUSTICE. * * * As a part of plaintiff's cross-examination, defendant introduced a statement signed by plaintiff on March 14, 1944—nine days after the accident. In part it is as follows:

> "It is my understanding Hodges was going to Denison. My buddy, Clarence Salisbury, asked me to go along. He told me he would make it worth my while if I would go along to help lift a small piano out of the car. They made arrangements for the trip between themselves but in my presence.
>
> "At any rate we started for Denison. Just before the accident occurred the car started to skid, the back end started to slide around, and before Hodges could get the car under control it had skidded into a bridge bannister.
>
> "It was about five P.M. It was snowing a little. I had not noticed the pavement being slick. Hodges was a good, careful driver. He had not been driving fast or carelessly. He was only going twenty-seven

29. Copyright 1963 by The American Law Institute. Reprinted with the permission of the American Law Institute–American Bar Association Committee on Continuing Professional Education. [Ed.]

or twenty-eight miles per hour when the accident happened. It happened right in front of some farm buildings and a drive into this place. There had been some dirt pulled out on the pavement, which caused the car to start skidding.

"We were all sober, we had only a couple of beers. Neither of us were intoxicated in any way. * * *

"Have you read this statement? Yes. Is it true? Yes."

Plaintiff's explanation of the statements in this writing which are contrary to his testimony was that a stranger, whom he supposed was an adjuster, interviewed him at the hospital, but he didn't remember what he told him, and he didn't read the statement which the man wrote, and it was not read to him, and he was in great pain and had been taking considerable opiates during that first month. * * *

II. Appellant assigned error because the court in instructing upon the signed statement of appellee, heretofore referred to, told the jury that it could be considered only as bearing upon the credibility of the plaintiff as a witness and not as proving any substantive fact. The instruction was duly excepted to. This statement was admitted generally without any restriction as to its consideration, over plaintiff's objection that it was incompetent. The instruction unduly and improperly limited the consideration of the statement by the jury. It was proper for the jury to consider it not only in its bearing upon plaintiff's credibility as a witness, because inconsistent with his testimony but since it was a deliberate statement over his own signature, it was admissible not merely as discrediting the testimony of plaintiff, if the statement was believed by the jury, but as substantive evidence against him, and as bearing upon the worthiness of his whole claim. Castner v. Chicago, B. & Q.R. Co., 126 Iowa 581, 585, 586, 102 N.W. 499. The plaintiff was not only a witness but a party-opponent of appellant, and even though he had not taken the stand as a witness, the statement was admissible against him and his case, as based upon his pleadings and the testimony relied upon him, as a discrediting inconsistency on his part. 2 Wigmore on Evidence, 2d Ed., §§ 1048, 1053. The giving of the instruction was reversible error.

Notes and Questions

1. *Confession of liability or simply inconsistent position.* One could imagine that to constitute an "admission" a statement had to fully or at least substantially admit of liability or guilt. However, the only requirements are that the statement be inconsistent with the party's position at trial and that it be offered by the opponent, and there is no additional requirement concerning the degree of inconsistency between the prior statement and the party's present position. See United States v. Reed, 227 F.3d 763, 770 (7th Cir.2000) (stating that admission need not be "incriminating, inculpatory, against interest, nor otherwise inherently damaging to the declarant's case" but merely be statements made by one party and offered as evidence by the opponent).

2. *Offered by the opponent.* An admission must be made by one party and offered by the opposing party. See United States v. McDaniel, 398 F.3d 540, 545 & n.2 (6th Cir.2005) (refusing to receive defendant's own statement as admission because not offered by party-opponent, observing that to receive such a statement would create an "end run" around the adversarial system).

3. *Admission "against interest"?* While most admissions are against the interest of the party making them at the time they were made (as opposed to the time of trial), there is no requirement for admissions that the statement must have been against interest when made. See 2 McCormick, Evidence § 254, at 181–82 (6th ed. 2006). Sometimes admissions are called "admissions against interest," which is an inaccurate label. Statements against interest are examined in Chapter 14, Section J, and the differences between that exception and the admission exclusion should then be noted. Cf. Globe Savings Bank, F.S.B. v. United States, 61 Fed.Cl. 91, 94–95 (Fed.Cl.2004) (finding that deposition by party-opponent is admission and therefore unavailability is not required).

4. *Foundation requirement.* The final sentence of Rule 613(b) makes inapplicable to admissions the general requirement for inconsistent statements that a foundation must be laid before statements are admitted.

5. *Sharp practices in obtaining statements.* In some states, statutes deal with a side aspect of *Olson*, the taking of statements from persons in injured condition. See, e.g., Minn.Stat.Ann. § 602.01 (West 2000) (statement obtained from injured person within 30 days after injury presumably fraudulent).

6. *Examining another issue.* Refer to *Player v. Thompson*, Section A, supra, for its treatment of the out-of-court statement of Ms. Carder as an admission against her alone.

UNITED STATES v. McKEON

United States Court of Appeals, Second Circuit, 1984.
738 F.2d 26.

WINTER, CIRCUIT JUDGE:

Following a trial before Judge Platt and a jury, appellant Bernard McKeon was convicted in the Eastern District of New York on one count of conspiracy to export firearms in violation of 18 U.S.C. § 371. McKeon was acquitted of eight substantive counts concerning the illegal exportation of firearms. The trial was McKeon's third on these charges, the first two having ended in mistrials. At issue on appeal is Judge Platt's admission into evidence at the third trial of portions of the opening statement made by McKeon's lawyer at the second trial and the resulting disqualification of that lawyer.

We affirm.

BACKGROUND

On October 31, 1979, Irish police in Dublin found firearms in crates sent from New York supposedly containing electric paper drills. The alleged shipper of the crates, "Standard Tools," was a fictitious New York corporation which gave as its address a building in Queens, New York, owned by Bernard McKeon.

Officials of the United States Customs Service investigated the origin of the seized shipment and unearthed several shipping and warehousing documents relating to the shipment signed by one "John Moran." On at least one of these documents, which bore the Standard Tools letterhead, they discovered fingerprints of McKeon and his wife, Olive McKeon. * * *

McKeon's first trial on federal firearms charges took place in December, 1982 and ended in a mistrial when the jury was unable to reach a verdict. Prior to McKeon's second trial, a government handwriting and photocopy expert concluded that warehousing and shipping documents supposedly prepared by representatives of Standard Tools, were photocopies produced on the xerox machine located in the bank in which Olive McKeon worked. The defense was apprised both of the expert's identity and his conclusions. In his opening statement at the second trial, Michael Kennedy, McKeon's lawyer told the jury that the evidence would show that McKeon had innocently helped build packing crates for his tenant, John Moran, and that Moran alone was responsible for the Standard Tools' shipment of weapons. Kennedy then declared:

> With reference to the place where Olive McKeon works, expert testimony is going to be brought in to show that the Xerox machine * * * where Mrs. McKeon worked is not—I repeat—is not the same kind of Xerox machine that prepared any of the Standard Tools Xeroxed documents.
>
> The evidence will also indicate that Mrs. McKeon had absolutely nothing to do with this case other than doing what many wives do, which is, picking up mail and opening it. That is the extent, the sum and substance of her involvement.

The second trial ended in a mistrial before the conclusion of the prosecution's case-in-chief when the defense moved for access to classified documents regarding alleged foreign wiretaps. As a consequence, the expert testimony promised by Kennedy in his opening statement was never offered.

Kennedy's opening statement at the third trial depicted Olive McKeon's role in the events differently than had his opening statement at the second trial. At the third trial, Kennedy told the jury that Bernard McKeon gave his wife the warehouse receipt and some Standard Tools stationery so that she might make two photocopies on the stationery using the bank's xerox machine. This was done, Kennedy said, as a favor to John Moran. He thus continued to picture Bernard McKeon as the innocent dupe of John Moran.

The next day, outside the presence of the jury, the prosecution moved to introduce as evidence the above-quoted portion of Kennedy's opening statement from the second trial. Arguing that the statement was the admission of a party-opponent under Fed.R.Evid. 801(d)(2), the prosecution suggested that it should be imputed to McKeon for any of the following reasons: (i) it was a statement in which McKeon had "manifested his adoption or belief in its truth," *id.* 801(d)(2)(B); (ii) it was "a statement by a person authorized by [McKeon] to make a statement concerning the subject," *id.* 801(d)(2)(C); and (iii) it was "a statement made by [McKeon's] agent * * * concerning a matter within the scope of his agency," *id.* 801(d)(2)(D). The government argued that the inconsistencies in Kennedy's statements were relevant to prove McKeon's consciousness of guilt under Fed.R.Evid. 404(b). Judge Platt ruled that Kennedy's opening statement at the second trial was admissible as an admission under Rule 801(d)(2).

* * *

As part of its case-in-chief, the government introduced the above-quoted portions of Kennedy's opening statement from the second trial. It also put on its expert witness in photocopying, James Kelly, who testified that between the second and third trials he met a former student, Jim Horan, and told him that he, Kelly, had been hired by the prosecution to testify at the third McKeon trial. Horan had been hired as the expert witness for the defense; until his meeting with Kelly, the defense had believed that the prosecution's expert witness would be one Peter Tytell, another former Kelly student. In summation, the prosecution argued that so long as the defense believed that Horan and Tytell would offer conflicting testimony about the xerox machine on which the copies were produced, it was prepared to contend that Olive McKeon did not xerox the warehouse receipt. Once it discovered that the teacher, Kelly, would dispute his pupil, Horan, at the third trial, the defense elected to present a different version of the facts—*viz.* that the receipt had been xeroxed by Olive McKeon at her workplace but for innocent reasons. The prosecution's summation dwelt at length on the change in stories as manifested by the opening statements, arguing that it established McKeon's consciousness of guilt.

This appeal followed McKeon's conviction on a single count of conspiracy.

Discussion

1. *The Admissibility of the Opening Statement*

The parties agree that the evidentiary use against a criminal defendant of his counsel's argument to a jury in an earlier trial is without direct precedent. Although guidance is found in the rules and underlying policies of the law of evidence, the issue raises a number of difficulties since it touches upon numerous sensitive areas including: communications between criminal defendants and their attorneys, the privilege against self-incrimination, fear of impeachment by a prior conviction, the work product, legal theories and trial tactics of the attorney, the freedom of the attorney to engage in uninhibited and robust advocacy, the right to counsel of one's choice, and the usual issues of relevance, confusion and unfair prejudice as well.

We begin with the general proposition that "[s]tatements made by an attorney concerning a matter within his employment may be admissible against the party retaining the attorney," *United States v. Margiotta,* 662 F.2d 131, 142 (2d Cir.1981), a proposition which extends to arguments to a jury. The binding effect on a party of a clear and unambiguous admission of fact made by his or her attorney in an opening statement was acknowledged by the Supreme Court in *Oscanyan v. Arms Co.,* 103 U.S. 261, 263 * * * (1880) and has been frequently recognized in subsequent lower court decisions involving civil cases. *See, e.g., Rhoades, Inc. v. United Air Lines,* 340 F.2d 481, 484 (3d Cir.1965); *Collins v. Texas Company,* 267 F.2d 257, 258 (5th Cir.1959). An admission by a defense attorney in his opening statement in a criminal trial has also been held to eliminate the need for further proof on a given element of an offense, *Dick v. United States,* 40 F.2d 609, 611 (8th Cir.1930) (attorney's opening statement that defendant previously had been convicted of an offense involving sale of liquor sufficient evidence as to that fact).

The general admissibility of an attorney's statements, as well as the binding effect of an opening statement within the four corners of a single trial, are thus well established. The specific issue before us, however, is somewhat different. It involves not the binding effect of an attorney's statements within a trial, but rather the evidentiary use against a criminal defendant of an attorney's seemingly inconsistent statement at an earlier trial to prove that fundamental portions of the defendant's present case are fabricated. Authority on this specific issue is scant, although in at least one civil action it has been suggested that while a previous opening statement is not binding on a litigant, the statement can, under certain circumstances be considered by the trier of fact.[30] *Beyer Co. v. Fleischmann Co.,* 15 F.2d 465, 466 (6th Cir.1926).

We believe that prior opening statements are not *per se* inadmissible in criminal cases. To hold otherwise would not only invite abuse and sharp practice but would also weaken confidence in the justice system itself by denying the function of trials as truth-seeking proceedings. That function cannot be affirmed if parties are free, wholly without explanation, to make fundamental changes in the version of facts within their personal knowledge between trials and to conceal these changes from the final trier of fact.

Support for this conclusion may be found in the analogous issue of the admissibility of superseded pleadings in civil litigation. The law is

30. A distinction is generally recognized between an attorney's judicial admissions, which, like any stipulation, can bind a party within a given lawsuit, and an attorney's less formal evidentiary admissions, which are statements made as a party's agent and which the trier of fact may evaluate as it sees fit. Note, *Judicial Admissions,* 64 Colum.L.Rev. 1121, 1121 (1964). We are of course concerned only with evidentiary admissions since no one claims that the opening statement from the second trial estopped McKeon from claiming that his wife had photocopied the receipts at his request.

quite clear that such pleadings constitute the admissions of a party-opponent and are admissible in the case in which they were originally filed as well as in any subsequent litigation involving that party. *Contractor Utility Sales Co. v. Certain–Teed Products Corp.*, 638 F.2d 1061, 1084 (7th Cir.1981); *Raulie v. United States,* 400 F.2d 487, 526 (10th Cir.1968); D. McCormick, *Handbook of the Law of Evidence* 633–36 (2d ed. 1972). A party thus cannot advance one version of the facts in its pleadings, conclude that its interests would be better served by a different version, and amend its pleadings to incorporate that version, safe in the belief that the trier of fact will never learn of the change in stories. As was explained in *Kunglig Jarnvagsstyrelsen v. Dexter & Carpenter, Inc.*, 32 F.2d 195, 198 (2d Cir. * * * (1929) by Judge Swan,

> Error is now assigned to the receipt in evidence of the original complaint, which was offered by the defendant both as evidence of agency, and as a formal ratification of the contract. One ground of objection to its admission was lack of proof of authority of the [party's] attorney to bind his client by the averments of the pleading. Such an objection is clearly not sustainable. A pleading prepared by an attorney is an admission by one presumptively authorized to speak for his principal.
>
> * * *
>
> A further objection was based upon the fact that the complaint had been superseded by an amended pleading. This objection is likewise unavailing. When a pleading is amended or withdrawn, the superseded portion ceases to be a conclusive judicial admission; but it still remains as a statement once seriously made by an authorized agent, and as such it is competent evidence of the facts stated, though controvertible, like any other extra-judicial admission made by a party or his agent. * * * If the agent made the admission without adequate information, that goes to its weight, not to its admissibility. There was no error in receiving the original complaint in evidence.

Although we by no means equate the admissibility of inconsistent pleadings with the admissibility of inconsistent opening statements, we believe the analogy is correct insofar as consideration of whether a *per se* rule against the admission of the latter exists.[31]

We conclude, therefore, that there is no absolute rule preventing use of an earlier opening statement by counsel as an admission against a criminal defendant in a subsequent trial. We are not willing, however, to subject such statements to the more expansive practices sometimes

31. This principle is not inconsistent with the long-established federal rule that a withdrawn guilty plea is not admissible in subsequent civil or criminal proceedings. Fed.R.Evid. 410; *Kercheval v. United States,* 274 U.S. 220 * * * (1927). The *Kercheval* rule is intended to permit a criminal defendant to exercise his right to a trial without imposing on that right conditions which make its exercise meaningless, *id.* at 224 * * *. A criminal defendant's right to a trial does not carry with it a right to present in multiple trials contradictory versions of the facts that vary according to the nature of the prosecution's case.

permitted under the rule allowing use of admissions by a party-opponent. The rule itself has caused a substantial expenditure of ink by legal commentators seeking a coherent doctrinal theory explaining the use of admissions, D. McCormick, *supra* at 628–31, and has resulted in "a lengthy academic dispute in which most courts have evinced little interest." 4 J. Weinstein & M. Berger, *Evidence* 801–135 (rev.perm.ed. 1981).

Although we share that lack of interest, we note that the admissions rule is itself something of an anomaly since it is in some respects an exception to the general proposition that probative value and reliability are the touchstone of the law of evidence where non-privileged matters are concerned. Admissions may thus be used even though the statement was plainly self-serving when made, was not based upon the personal knowledge of the speaker and is in a form which would otherwise be inadmissible. D. McCormick, *supra* at 631–33; J. Weinstein & M. Berger, *supra* at 801–136. Why probative value and reliability carry so little weight in the case of the admissions rule is not clear, particularly since the use of admissions may be the trial equivalent of a deadly weapon. In all probability, these aspects of the rule are derived vestigially from an older, rough and ready view of the adversary process which leaves each party to bear the consequences of its own acts, no matter how unreliable these acts may be as proof. Whatever its derivation, however, we conclude that the evidentiary use of prior jury argument must be circumscribed in order to avoid trenching upon other important policies.

* * *

Before permitting such use, the district court must be satisfied that the prior argument involves an assertion of fact inconsistent with similar assertions in a subsequent trial. Speculations of counsel, advocacy as to the credibility of witnesses, arguments as to weaknesses in the prosecution's case or invitations to a jury to draw certain inferences should not be admitted. The inconsistency, moreover, should be clear and of a quality which obviates any need for the trier of fact to explore other events at the prior trial. The court must further determine that the statements of counsel were such as to be the equivalent of testimonial statements by the defendant. The formal relationship of the lawyer as agent and the client as principal by itself will rarely suffice to show this since, while clients authorize their attorneys to act on their behalf, considerable delegation is normally involved and such delegation tends to drain the evidentiary value from such statements. Some participatory role of the client must be evident, either directly or inferentially as when the argument is a direct assertion of fact which in all probability had to have been confirmed by the defendant.

Finally, the district court should, in a Fed.R.Evid. 104(a) hearing outside the presence of the jury, determine by a preponderance of the evidence that the inference the prosecution seeks to draw from the inconsistency is a fair one and that an innocent explanation for the inconsistency does not exist. Where the evidence is in equipoise or the preponderance favors an innocent explanation, the prior opening statement should be excluded. We impose this requirement so as to allow leeway for advocacy and to lessen the burden of choice between the defendant's not explaining the inconsistency to the jury or sacrificing other valuable rights.

* * *

Applying these principles to the present case, we conclude that the prior opening statement was properly admitted against McKeon under Fed.R.Evid. 801(d)(2)(B) and (C). The expert testimony about the xerox machine promised by Kennedy in the opening statement at the second trial was in support of a factual claim that Olive McKeon had not copied the documents. Kennedy's opening argument at the third trial, stating that Olive McKeon had indeed copied the documents at the request of her husband, was facially and irreconcilably at odds with the earlier assertion.

* * *

Affirmed.

Notes and Questions

1. *Special concern for counsel in criminal cases.* The Second Circuit has wavered regarding its admonition in *McKeon* that in criminal cases care should be exercised lest the admissions by counsel concept that is expansively applied in the civil context impair the criminal defendant's constitutional rights under the Fifth and Sixth Amendments. Compare United States v. Valencia, 826 F.2d 169 (2d Cir.1987) (statements by defense counsel during informal conversations with a prosecutor not admissible as statements of an agent), with United States v. Arrington, 867 F.2d 122, 127–28 (2d Cir.1989) (no special procedures need be followed or analysis performed as prerequisite to evidentiary use of out-of-court statements by defense counsel). See generally Humble, Evidentiary Admissions of Defense Counsel in Federal Criminal Cases, 24 Am.Crim.L.Rev. 93 (1986).

2. *Equal treatment.* The principle in *McKeon* may also be applied to statements by the prosecutor from a former trial. Hoover v. State, 552 So.2d 834, 840 (Miss.1989).

3. *"Judicial" versus "evidentiary" admission.* A basic distinction exists between the "solemn judicial admission," which places the matter outside the area of controversy in the case, and the "evidentiary admission," which is admissible but not necessarily conclusive. In the "judicial admission" category fall admissions contained in the effective pleadings in the case, Foxmeyer Corp. v. General Elec. Capital Corp., 286 B.R. 546, 567–68 (Bankr.D.Del.2002), through a failure to deny under Fed.R.Civ.P. 8(d), admissions by stipulation, and admissions made pursuant to requests under Fed.R.Civ.P. 36. Superseded pleadings in the same case and pleadings in other cases may be admitted but are given only the effect of evidentiary admissions. Annot., 52 A.L.R.2d 516. Similarly, a superseded bill of particulars in a criminal case may be received as an evidentiary admission of the

government. United States v. GAF Corp., 928 F.2d 1253, 1258–62 (2d Cir.1991).

4. *Is party legally or practically "bound" by an admission?* Some courts treat a party's own statement at trial as conclusive on the issue, rather than as a simple evidentiary admission. See Bell v. Harmon, 284 S.W.2d 812 (Ky.1955) (party's statement in testimony concerning facts directly observed by him and establishing unequivocally that opponent was not negligent constitutes binding "judicial admission"). Cf. Fox v. Taylor Diving & Salvage Co., 694 F.2d 1349, 1355–56 (5th Cir.1983) (finding testimony of expert that was inconsistent with recovery under one theory held binding against plaintiff as adoptive admission because of high potential for jury prejudice likely from what the court viewed as a manipulative trial strategy). McCormick finds treating statements of a party as simple evidentiary admissions "preferable in policy and most in accord with the tradition of jury trial." 2 McCormick, Evidence § 258, at 191 (6th ed. 2006).

5. *Movement from evidentiary to judicial admission.* Answers to interrogatories have received the same treatment as a party's own testimony. Freed v. Erie Lackawanna Ry., 445 F.2d 619 (6th Cir.1971); Smith v. Trans World Airlines, Inc., 358 S.W.2d 91 (Mo.Ct.App.1962). In Ridley v. Young, 253 P.2d 433 (Colo.1953), the court permitted the defendant to contradict his response to an interrogatory admitting that he was driving the automobile that caused plaintiff's injuries even though it was a matter within the defendant's knowledge about which he could not be mistaken. Accordingly, a formal request to admit may be appropriate once an admission is obtained by deposition or interrogatory. See Fed.R.Civ.P. 36(b).

6. *Witness statements not admissions.* The fact that testimony given by a party's witnesses at a former trial was in conflict with testimony given by other witnesses now presented by the party is not admissible, much less binding upon the party. However, if the witnesses are the same, inconsistent testimony may be used for impeachment. Annot., 74 A.L.R.2d 521.

7. *Guilty plea as evidentiary admission.* A guilty plea in a criminal case may be received as a non-binding evidentiary admission where relevant in a civil case involving the party. See, e.g., State Farm Mut. Automobile Ins. Co. v. Worthington, 405 F.2d 683 (8th Cir.1968); Smith v. Southern Nat'l Life Ins. Co., 134 So.2d 337 (La.Ct.App.1961). Guilty pleas involving non-parties may be admissible under Rule 804(b)(3) as a statement against penal interest, discussed in Chapter 14, Section J.

8. *Exclusion under Rule 410.* A plea of nolo contendere, a withdrawn guilty plea, and statements made to prosecuting attorneys in conjunction with plea negotiations are generally inadmissible for policy reasons. See Rule 410. See also Kercheval v. United States, 274 U.S. 220 (1927).

9. *Impact of liberal pleading rules.* A few courts have accepted policy-based arguments that alternative and amended pleadings should not be admitted since to do so may thwart the liberal intent of modern civil pleading practices. See 2 McCormick, Evidence § 257, at 188 (6th ed. 2006).

10. *Admissibility of some criminal judgments.* Even without a guilty plea, a judgment of guilty rendered by a judge or jury of a crime punishable by imprisonment in excess of one year may be introduced in civil cases under

Rule 803(22) as an exception to the hearsay rule to prove any fact essential to sustain the judgment. The effect of the judgment is similar to an admission; it has evidentiary, not conclusive, effect.

11. *Treatment of guilty pleas in traffic cases.* In terms of the principle of an admission, a plea of guilty to a traffic offense is no different than a plea of guilty to any other offense; it is admissible as evidence of the commission of the act in question in a companion civil case arising from the same event. However, the argument that people plead guilty to traffic charges for reasons of convenience and with little regard to guilt or the collateral consequences has led some commentators to argue for exclusion. See 3 Graham, Handbook of Federal Evidence § 801.17, at 777–78 (6th ed. 2006) (arguing that Rule 803(22), which excludes offenses punishable by less than a year, supports excluding pleas of guilty to minor traffic offenses). However, courts tend to admit such pleas as admissions. See 2 McCormick, Evidence § 257, at 189 (6th ed. 2006).

12. *Civil judgment not admission.* The admissibility of a prior civil judgment and its effect is largely a matter of the substantive law of res judicata and collateral estoppel. See generally Motomura, Using Judgments as Evidence, 70 Minn.L.Rev. 979 (1986).

MAHLANDT v. WILD CANID SURVIVAL & RESEARCH CENTER, INC.

United States Court of Appeals, Eighth Circuit, 1978.
588 F.2d 626.

VAN SICKLE, DISTRICT JUDGE.

This is a civil action for damages arising out of an alleged attack by a wolf on a child. The sole issues on appeal are as to the correctness of three rulings which excluded conclusionary statements against interest. Two of them were made by a defendant, who was also an employee of the corporate defendant; and the third was in the form of a statement appearing in the records of a board meeting of the corporate defendant.

On March 23, 1973, Daniel Mahlandt, then 3 years, 10 months, and 8 days old, was sent by his mother to a neighbor's home on an adjoining street to get his older brother, Donald. Daniel's mother watched him cross the street, and then turned into the house to get her car keys. Daniel's path took him along a walkway adjacent to the Poos' residence. Next to the walkway was a five foot chain link fence to which Sophie had been chained with a six foot chain. In other words, Sophie was free to move in a half circle having a six foot radius on the side of the fence opposite from Daniel.

Sophie was a bitch wolf, 11 months and 28 days old, who had been born at the St. Louis Zoo, and kept there until she reached 6 months of age, at which time she was given to the Wild Canid Survival and Research Center, Inc. It was the policy of the Zoo to remove wolves from the Children's Zoo after they reached the age of 5 or 6 months. Sophie was supposed to be kept at the Tyson Research Center, but Kenneth Poos, as Director of Education for the Wild Canid Survival and Research

Center, Inc., had been keeping her at his home because he was taking Sophie to schools and institutions where he showed films and gave programs with respect to the nature of wolves. Sophie was known as a very gentle wolf who had proved herself to be good natured and stable during her contacts with thousands of children, while she was in the St. Louis Children's Zoo.

Sophie was chained because the evening before she had jumped the fence and attacked a beagle who was running along the fence and yapping at her.

A neighbor who was ill in bed in the second floor of his home heard a child's screams and went to his window, where he saw a boy lying on his back within the enclosure, with a wolf straddling him. The wolf's face was near Daniel's face, but the distance was so great that he could not see what the wolf was doing, and did not see any biting. Within about 15 seconds the neighbor saw Clarke Poos, about seventeen, run around the house, get the wolf off of the boy, and disappear with the child in his arms to the back of the house. Clarke took the boy in and laid him on the kitchen floor.

Clarke had been returning from his friend's home immediately west when he heard a child's cries and ran around to the enclosure. He found Daniel lying within the enclosure, about three feet from the fence, and Sophie standing back from the boy the length of her chain, and wailing. An expert in the behavior of wolves stated that when a wolf licks a child's face that it is a sign of care and not a sign of attack; that a wolf's wail is a sign of compassion, and an effort to get attention, not a sign of attack. No witness saw or knew how Daniel was injured. Clarke and his sister ran over to get Daniel's mother. She says that Clarke told her, "a wolf got Danny and he is dying." Clarke denies that statement. The defendant, Mr. Poos, arrived home while Daniel and his mother were in the kitchen. After Daniel was taken in an ambulance, Mr. Poos talked to everyone present, including a neighbor who came in. Within an hour after he arrived home, Mr. Poos went to Washington University to inform Owen Sexton, President of Wild Canid Survival and Research Center, Inc., of the incident. Mr. Sexton was not in his office so Mr. Poos left the following note on his door:

> Owen, would call me at home, 727–5080? Sophie bit a child that came in our back yard. All has been taken care of. I need to convey what happened to you. (Exhibit 11)

Denial of admission of this note is one of the issues on appeal.

Later that day, Mr. Poos found Mr. Sexton at the Tyson Research Center and told him what had happened. Denial of plaintiff's offer to prove that Mr. Poos told Mr. Sexton that, "Sophie had bit a child that day," is the second issue on appeal.

A meeting of the Directors of the Wild Canid Survival and Research Center, Inc., was held on April 4, 1973. Mr. Poos was not present at that meeting. The minutes of that meeting reflect that there was a "great deal of discussion * * * about the legal aspects of the incident of Sophie biting the child." Plaintiff offered an abstract of the minutes containing that reference. Denial of the offer of that abstract is the third issue on appeal.

Daniel had lacerations of the face, left thigh, left calf, and right thigh, and abrasions, and bruises of the abdomen and chest. Mr. Mahlandt was permitted to state that Daniel had indicated that he had gone under the fence. Mr. Mahlandt and Mr. Poos, about a month after the incident, examined the fence to determine what caused Daniel's lacerations. Mr. Mahlandt felt that they did not look like animal bites. The parallel scars on Daniel's thigh appeared to match the configuration of the barbs or tines on the fence. The expert as to the behavior of wolves opined that the lacerations were not wolf bites or wounds caused by wolf claws. Wolves have powerful jaws and a wolf bite will result in massive crushing or severing of a limb. He stated that if Sophie had bitten Daniel there would have been clear apposition of teeth and massive crushing of Daniel's hands and arms which were not injured. Also, if Sophie had pulled Daniel under the fence, tooth marks on the foot or leg would have been present, although Sophie possessed enough strength to pull the boy under the fence.

The jury brought in a verdict for the defense.

The trial judge's rationale for excluding the note, the statement, and the corporate minutes, was the same in each case. He reasoned that Mr. Poos did not have any personal knowledge of the facts, and accordingly, the first two admissions were based on hearsay; and the third admission contained in the minutes of the board meeting was subject to the same objection of hearsay, and unreliability because of lack of personal knowledge.

The Federal Rules of Evidence became effective in July 1975 (180 days after passage of the Act). Thus, at this time, there is very little case law to rely upon for resolution of the problems of interpretation.

The relevant rule here is: [801(d)(2)] * * * (A) his own statement, in either his individual or representative capacity or

> (B) a statement of which he has manifested his adoption or belief in its truth, or
>
> (C) a statement by a person authorized by him to make a statement concerning the subject, or
>
> (D) a statement by his agent or servant concerning a matter within the scope of his agency or employment, made during the existence of the relationship * * *.

So the statement in the note pinned on the door is not hearsay, and is admissible against Mr. Poos. It was his own statement, and as such was clearly different from the reported statement of another. Example, "I was told that * * *." See Cedeck v. Hamiltonian Fed. Sav. & L. Ass'n, 551 F.2d 1136 (8th Cir.1977). It was also a statement of which he had manifested his adoption or belief in its truth. And the same observations may be made of the statement made later in the day to Mr. Sexton that, "Sophie had bit a child * * *."

Are these statements admissible against Wild Canid Survival and Research Center, Inc.? They were made by Mr. Poos when he was an agent or servant of the Wild Canid Survival and Research Center, Inc., and they concerned a matter within the scope of his agency, or employment, i.e., his custody of Sophie, and were made during the existence of that relationship.

Defendant argues that Rule 801(d)(2) does not provide for the admission of "in house" statements; that is, it allows only admissions made to third parties.

The notes of the Advisory Committee on the Proposed Rules * * * discuss the problem of "in house" admissions with reference to Rule 801(d)(2)(C) situations. This is not a (C) situation because Mr. Poos was not authorized or directed to make a statement on the matter by anyone. But the rationale developed in that comment does apply to this (D) situation. Mr. Poos had actual physical custody of Sophie. His conclusions, his opinions, were obviously accepted as a basis for action by his principal. See minutes of corporate meeting. As the Advisory Committee points out in its note on (C) situations.

> * * * communication to an outsider has not generally been thought to be an essential characteristic of an admission. Thus a party's books or records are usable against him, without regard to any intent to disclose to third persons. V Wigmore on Evidence § 1557.

Weinstein's discussion of Rule 801(d)(2)(D) (Weinstein's Evidence § 801(d)(2)(D)(01), p. 801–137), states that:

> Rule 801(d)(2)(D) adopts the approach * * * which, as a general proposition, makes statement made by agents within the scope of their employment admissible * * *. Once agency, and the making of the statement while the relationship continues, are established, the statement is exempt from the hearsay rule so long as it relates to a matter within the scope of the agency.

After reciting a lengthy quotation which justifies the rule as necessary, and suggests that such admissions are trustworthy and reliable, Weinstein states categorically that although an express requirement of personal knowledge on the part of the declarant of the facts underlying his statement is not written into the rule, it should be. He feels that is mandated by Rules 805 and 403.

Rule 805 recites, in effect, that a statement containing hearsay within hearsay is admissible if each part of the statement falls within an exception to the hearsay rule. Rule 805, however, deals only with hearsay exceptions. A statement based on the personal knowledge of the declarant of facts underlying his statement is not the repetition of the statement of another, thus not hearsay. It is merely opinion testimony. Rule 805 cannot mandate the implied condition desired by Judge Weinstein.

Rule 403 provides for the exclusion of relevant evidence if its probative value is substantially outweighed by the danger of unfair prejudice, confusion of the issues, or misleading the jury, or by consideration of undue delay, waste of time, or needless presentation of cumulative evidence. Nor does Rule 403 mandate the implied condition desired by Judge Weinstein.

Thus, while both Rule 805 and Rule 403 provide additional bases for excluding otherwise acceptable evidence, neither rule mandates the introduction into Rule 801(d)(2)(D) of an implied requirement that the declarant have personal knowledge of the facts underlying his statement. So we conclude that the two statements made by Mr. Poos were admissible against Wild Canid Survival and Research Center, Inc.

As to the entry in the records of a corporate meeting, the directors as primary officers of the corporation had the authority to include their conclusions in the record of the meeting. So the evidence would fall within 801(d)(2)(C) as to Wild Canid Survival and Research Center, Inc., and be admissible. The "in house" aspect of this admission has already been discussed, Rule 801(d)(2)(D), supra.

But there was no servant, or agency, relationship which justified admitting the evidence of the board minutes as against Mr. Poos.

None of the conditions of 801(d)(2) cover the claim that minutes of a corporate board meeting can be used against a non-attending, non-participating employee of that corporation. The evidence was not admissible as against Mr. Poos.

There is left only the question of whether the trial court's rulings which excluded all three items of evidence are justified under Rule 403. He clearly found that the evidence was not reliable, pointing out that none of the statements were based on the personal knowledge of the declarant.

Again, that problem was faced by the Advisory Committee on Proposed Rules. In its discussion of 801(d)(2) exceptions to the hearsay rule, the Committee said:

> The freedom which admissions have enjoyed from technical demands of searching for an assurance of trustworthiness in some against-interest circumstances, and from the restrictive influences of the opinion rule and the rule requiring first hand knowledge, when taken with the apparently prevalent satisfaction with the results, calls for generous treatment of this avenue to admissibility. * * *

So here, remembering that relevant evidence is usually prejudicial to the cause of the side against which it is presented, and that the prejudice which concerns us is unreasonable prejudice; and applying the spirit of Rule 801(d)(2), we hold that Rule 403 does not warrant the exclusion of the evidence of Mr. Poos' statements as against himself or Wild Canid Survival and Research Center, Inc.

But the limited admissibility of the corporate minutes, coupled with the repetitive nature of the evidence and the low probative value of the minute record, all justify supporting the judgment of the trial court under Rule 403.

The judgment of the District Court is reversed and the matter remanded to the District Court for a new trial consistent with this opinion.

Notes and Questions

1. *No firsthand knowledge requirement.* As *Mahlandt* asserts, admissions under the Federal Rules are received despite lack of firsthand knowledge. This result represents the majority position under the common law. Annot., 54 A.L.R.2d 1069. But see Bein, Parties' Admissions, Agents' Admissions: Hearsay Wolves in Sheep's Clothing, 12 Hofstra L.Rev. 393 (1984) (proposing firsthand knowledge requirement for employee admissions). Regarding *Mahlandt*, see generally Swift, The Story of *Mahlandt v. Wild Canid Survival & Research Center, Inc.*, in Evidence Stories 239 (Lempert ed., 2006).

2. *Freedom from lay opinion rule.* The rule against opinions is another familiar landmark that disappears in connection with admissions. An admission couched in the form of an opinion is not objectionable. Cox v. Esso Shipping Co., 247 F.2d 629 (5th Cir.1957); 2 McCormick, Evidence § 256, at 184 (6th ed. 2006) (opinion rule is designed to "promote the concreteness of answers on the stand" and "is grotesquely misapplied to out-of-court statements such as admissions where the declarant's statements are made without thought of the form of courtroom testimony").

3. *Changes in rules on statements by agents.* Conventional doctrine has determined the admissibility of agents' statements to third persons by referring to the scope of authority of the agent. Bristol Wholesale Grocery Co. v. Municipal Lighting Plant Comm'n of Taunton, 200 N.E.2d 260 (Mass.1964). That view is continued in Rule 801(d)(2)(C), but the range of admissions of agents expanded dramatically in 801(d)(2)(D).

> Rule 801(d)(2)(C), unlike 801(d)(2)(D), requires that a statement be "by a person authorized by him to make a statement concerning the subject." Rule 801(d)(2)(D), however, says nothing about an agent having authority to make a statement on a particular subject. After the fact of the agency is established, Rule 801(d)(2)(D) requires only that the statement "concern a matter within the scope of [the] agency or employment." * * * Rule 801(d)(2)(D) takes the broader view that an agent or servant who speaks on any matter within the scope of his agency or employment during the existence of that relationship, is unlikely to make statements damaging to his principal or employer unless those statements are true.

Nekolny v. Painter, 653 F.2d 1164, 1171 (7th Cir.1981). The scope of the agency relates to the authority "to speak" under Rule 801(d)(1)(C) and the scope of the individual's duties "to act" under Rule 801(d)(1)(D). As to the latter, see, e.g., Skay v. St. Louis Parking Co., 130 S.W.3d 22, 27 (Mo.Ct.App. 2004) (finding statement of employee not an admission because that employee had no responsibilities for operating sprinkler system, which was the subject of the statement).

4. *Alternate theory of respondeat superior.* Logically, when liability of the principal is predicated on respondeat superior, any evidence that would establish the liability of the agent should be acceptable, including any admissions by the agent. Madron v. Thomson, 419 P.2d 611 (Or.1966). However, some courts, apparently believing that this view would undermine their rule that unauthorized statements are not admissible against the principal, have insisted that the agent's liability be established by evidence also admissible against the principal. Annot., 27 A.L.R.2d 966.

5. *Privity not recognized.* Under common law analysis, some courts treated declarations by persons in "privity," such as persons jointly liable or interested with others, as another form of vicarious admission. See Belfield v. Coop, 134 N.E.2d 249 (Ill.1956). The Federal Rules contain no provision specifically governing privity-based admissions, which has been interpreted to omit from admissions statements made by those in privity or jointly interested with a party. See Calhoun v. Baylor, 646 F.2d 1158, 1162–63 (6th Cir.1981); Huff v. White Motor Corp., 609 F.2d 286, 290–91 (7th Cir.1979); In re Ty.B., 878 A.2d 1255, 1261–63 (D.C.2005) (ruling that privity concept inapplicable so that admission by mother improperly received against father under "privity of obligation"); 2 McCormick, Evidence § 260, at 208 (6th ed. 2006). However, many of the most powerful statements that would previously have been admitted under the privity concept will still be received as admissions by an agent (801(d)(2)(D)) or statements against interest (804(b)(3)) or admitted under the catchall exception (807).

6. *Agents for some, but not for all.* As *Mahlandt* indicates, not all statements made by corporate officers are admissible against other individuals in the corporation. For example, in United States v. Young, 736 F.2d 565, 567–68 (10th Cir.1983), rev'd on other grounds, 470 U.S. 1 (1985), the court noted that a statement of one corporate employee is not admissible against another simply because the latter is higher in the corporate chain of authority. Courts have looked instead for evidence of regular supervisory control. Lippay v. Christos, 996 F.2d 1490, 1498–99 (3d Cir.1993).

7. *Indirect importance of firsthand knowledge.* While firsthand knowledge is not required even for vicarious admissions, that fact does not relieve the party seeking to introduce the statement from demonstrating that the statements were made "concerning a matter within the scope of the agency or employment," which may have the effect of eliminating some putative admission where an employee has no personal knowledge. In this regard, consider Litton Systems, Inc. v. American Tel. & Tel. Co., 700 F.2d 785, 816–17 (2d Cir.1983):

> A Litton attorney, Norman Roberts, made notes of his interviews with various Litton employees during the course of [an internal] investigation. * * * AT & T's claim that Roberts' notes—which summarized what various Litton employees recounted to him about wrongdoing on the part of other Litton employees—were admissible because the multiple levels of hearsay were all made in the course and scope of employment, is not persuasive. * * * The fact that Roberts summarized what some Litton employees said about other employees in the course of his investigation does not bring the events he summarized within the "scope of his agency or employment" under 801(d)(2)(D). See J. Wein-

stein, 4 Evidence 801–164 (1981) ("Gossip does not become reliable merely because it is heard in an office rather than a home.") The hearsay which he summarized may well have been inadmissible even if testified to by the employees interviewed.

The principle in *Litton* is recognized as limited and does not generally reimpose a firsthand knowledge requirement for vicarious admissions. See Brookover v. Mary Hitchcock Mem'l Hosp., 893 F.2d 411, 415–18 (1st Cir.1990).

8. *Law enforcement personnel as agents.* Most courts do not treat the statements of law enforcement officials in criminal cases as admissions under Rule 801(d)(2)(D) as they would be if the statements had been made by employees of a corporate party. In United States v. Kampiles, 609 F.2d 1233, 1246 (7th Cir.1979), the court observed:

> Prior to adoption of the Federal Rules of Evidence, admissions by government employees in criminal cases were viewed as outside the admissions exception to the hearsay rule. * * * Because the agents of the Government are supposedly disinterested in the outcome of a trial and are traditionally unable to bind the sovereign * * *, their statements seem less the product of the adversary process and hence less appropriately described as admissions of a party. Nothing in the Federal Rules of Evidence suggests an intention to alter the traditional rule. * * *

However, in United States v. Morgan, 581 F.2d 933 (D.C.Cir.1978), the court held that a statement of a government agent was admissible against the government as an adoptive admission under Rule 801(d)(2)(B). There the statement of the agent was approved by an Assistant United States Attorney and presented as part of an affidavit to a magistrate to justify issuance of a warrant. Moreover, the court questioned whether special treatment of government admission survived generally under the Federal Rules: "As in the case of Rule 801(d)(2)(B), there is no indication in the history of the Rules that the draftsmen meant to except the government from operation of Rule 801(d)(2)(D) in criminal cases." 581 F.2d at 938 n.15. See Imwinkelried, Of Evidence and Equal Protection: The Unconstitutionality of Excluding Government Agents' Statements Offered as Vicarious Admissions Against the Prosecution, 71 Minn.L.Rev. 269 (1986). Perhaps the two positions can be reconciled by basing admissibility on whether the statement was made by an attorney (admissible) rather than an investigative agent (inadmissible). See United States v. Yildiz, 355 F.3d 80, 81–82 (2d Cir.2004) (setting out briefly majority view of the federal courts that excludes statements by informants and admits formally submitted statements by government attorneys); 2 McCormick, Evidence § 259, at 205–06 (6th ed. 2006); 5 Weinstein's Federal Evidence § 801.33[3] (2d ed. 2001) (noting admission particularly of statements by government attorneys).

9. *Expert reports as admissions of agents?* Occasionally experts are considered agents so that the expert's analysis constitutes an admission of the party. See Collins v. Wayne Corp., 621 F.2d 777 (5th Cir.1980) (deposition of expert hired to investigate accident and to report conclusions constituted admission of party under Rule 801(d)(2)(C) that could be identified with party in presentation to jury); Budden v. United States, 748 F.Supp.

1374, 1378–79 (D.Neb.1990) (same). Cf. Rollins v. Bd. of Governors for Higher Educ., 761 F.Supp. 939, 942 (D.R.I.1991) (report of board of inquiry regarding accident treated as admission of principal). But statements by independent contractors or outside consultants typically do not qualify as admissions of the principal. See, e.g., Columbia First Bank, FSB v. United States, 58 Fed.Cl. 333 (Fed.Cl.2003); Dora Homes, Inc. v. Epperson, 344 F.Supp.2d 875, 885 (E.D.N.Y.2004); Powers v. Coccia, 861 A.2d 466, 470–71 (R.I.2004).

WILSON v. CITY OF PINE BLUFF

Court of Appeals of Arkansas, 1982.
641 S.W.2d 33.

COOPER, JUDGE.

The appellant was convicted of criminal trespass * * * and was fined $75.00, plus costs. From that decision, comes this appeal.

THE FACTS

On June 13, 1981, two Pine Bluff police officers, in response to radio instructions, went to a residence at 5704 Cheatham Street in Pine Bluff. Upon their arrival, they observed an injured woman being placed in an ambulance for transport to a hospital. The officers entered the residence to investigate the situation.

Inside the residence, the officers found the appellant and an unidentified woman. The officers testified that the woman claimed to live in the residence, and that she wanted the appellant to leave. They stated that the appellant did not respond to the woman's statement concerning her occupancy of the residence, even though he heard it. They further testified that the appellant stated that he was not going to leave the residence.

The officers testified that they explained to the appellant that if the woman wanted him to leave, then he would have to do so, or be arrested for criminal trespass. The officers verified that the woman did want the appellant to leave, and they requested that he do so on several occasions. The appellant refused to leave, and he was arrested for criminal trespass. The testimony shows that the appellant never claimed any possessory or ownership right to the premises.

THE ADMISSIBILITY OF THE EVIDENCE

[C]riminal trespass is committed when an individual purposely enters or remains unlawfully on the premises of another person. The appellant argues that the only evidence which proved that the premises belonged to another person was the hearsay testimony of the officers concerning the woman's statements, and that this testimony was inadmissible hearsay. The appellant made a timely objection to the testimony, and the trial court ruled that the statements made by the woman, as testified to by the officers, were admissible as an adoptive admission of a party-opponent.

The Uniform Rules of Evidence, Rule 801(d)(2)(ii), Ark.Stat.Ann. § 28–1001 (Repl.1979), provides that a statement is not hearsay if the statement is offered against a party and is a statement of which that party has manifested his adoption or belief in its truth. Prior to the adoption of this rule, Arkansas law recognized a "tacit admission" as an exception to the hearsay rule. Under that exception, proof of damaging statements against an accused, made in his presence, were admissible in evidence, on the theory that the jury might find that the silence of the accused in the face of the accusation was a tacit admission. * * * Before hearsay evidence of an implied admission could fit within this exception, it must have been shown that the accused heard the statement, that he understood it, and that he failed to deny it.

The sole question in determining whether statements made by another person are admissible against a party as an admission by silence or acquiescence is whether a reasonable person, under the circumstances, would naturally have been expected to deny them, if the statements were untrue.[32] Some of the factors which should be considered in determining whether a party has impliedly admitted the statements are:

> (1) The statement must have been heard by the party against whom it is offered;
>
> (2) it must have been understood by him;
>
> (3) the subject matter must have been within his personal knowledge;
>
> (4) he must have been physically and psychologically able to speak;
>
> (5) the speaker or his relationship to the party or event must be such as to reasonably expect a denial; and
>
> (6) the statement itself must be such that, if untrue, under the circumstances, it would have been denied.

Other factors besides these may need to be considered, depending on the facts of a particular case. *See,* 4 J. Wigmore, Evidence §§ 1071–1073 (Chadbourn rev. 1972); C. McCormick, The Law of Evidence § 270 (2d ed. 1972).

The Uniform Rules of Evidence, Rule 801(d)(2)(ii), as adopted by the State of Arkansas, is identical to the Federal Rules of Evidence, Rule 801(d)(2)(B). The manner in which the federal courts have applied their rule is helpful.

The federal cases indicate that before a statement can fall under the adoptive admission rule, the trial court must find that sufficient founda-

32. Silence by an accused or a claim of his Fifth Amendment right to remain silent made in response to a police accusation during custodial interrogation is inadmissible. *Doyle v. Ohio,* 426 U.S. 610 * * * (1976). Even silence by an accused in response to incriminating statements made by a third person, while he was in police custody and before he was advised of his Fifth Amendment right to remain silent, is inadmissible. *Kagebein v. State,* 254 Ark. 904, 496 S.W.2d 435 (1973).

tional facts have been introduced so that the jury can reasonably infer that the accused heard and understood the statement and that the statement was such that, under the circumstances, if the accused were innocent he would normally respond. *United States v. Fortes,* 619 F.2d 108 (1st Cir.1980); *United States v. Moore,* 522 F.2d 1068 (9th Cir.1975). Once a foundation has been established, the question is left to the jury to determine whether the accused acquiesced in the statement.[33] *United States v. Moore, supra.*

The procedure used by the federal courts in applying rule 801 is appropriate to use in applying our rule, since it is entirely consistent with the approach followed in applying the "tacit admission" exception to the hearsay rule under prior Arkansas law. *Moore v. State, supra.*

In the case at bar, the testimony indicates that the appellant was present, and in fact was within two feet of the officers and the woman, when the statements were made. Further, he made no comment or objection to the woman's claim of right to occupy the residence. On these facts, adequate foundational facts were presented to the trial court so as to render the statements admissible. The trier of fact could reasonably infer that the appellant heard and understood the woman's statements, and that, had her statements been untrue, he would have responded with either a denial or an explanation.

Preliminary questions regarding the admissibility of evidence are decided by the trial court, and the appellate court will affirm such a decision unless it constitutes an abuse of discretion. Uniform Rules of Evidence, Rule 104(a, b), Ark.Stat.Ann. § 28–1001 (Repl.1979); *Derring v. State,* 273 Ark. 347, 619 S.W.2d 644 (1981). We hold that the trial court did not abuse his discretion by ruling that the officer's testimony was admissible.

* * *

The judgment appealed from is affirmed.

Affirmed.

Notes and Questions

1. *Scope of concept.* Adoptive admissions may occur in a variety of situations. See generally Heller, Admissions by Acquiescence, 15 U. Miami L.Rev. 161 (1960); Annots., 87 A.L.R.3d 706, 48 A.L.R.Fed. 721.

2. *Ambiguity of custodial silence.* When the declarant is aware of the presence of the police, separate from the constitutional concerns, silence may be considered too ambiguous to constitute an admission. United States v. Williams, 577 F.2d 188, 193–94 (2d Cir.1978), provides a useful discussion of the issues:

33. Even though a statement may be admissible under the adoptive admission rule, the trial court may still exclude such a statement if he finds that the probative value of the statement is substantially outweighed by the danger of unfair prejudice, confusion of the issues, or misleading the jury. Uniform Rules of Evidence, Rule 403, Ark.Stat.Ann. § 28–1001 (Repl.1979).

In United States v. Flecha, [539 F.2d 874, 876–77 (2d Cir.1976)], this court addressed a situation in which one of several co-defendants under arrest apparently turned to another and said in Spanish, "Why so much excitement? If we are caught, we are caught." We there concluded that in light of the custodial circumstances it was not likely that the appellant would have responded to such a vaguely phrased comment and that, therefore, Rule 801(d)(2)(B) was inapplicable. Here, however, Williams and Simmons met in the street. If appellant had truly been an innocent bystander, it is more probable than not that he would have vigorously asserted his non-involvement in the conspiracy when told that, unlike those already arrested, he was in the clear because his larcenous participation had not been betrayed to the authorities. Since this natural reply was not forthcoming, we hold that the conversation constituted an adoptive admission within the circumscribed purview of Rule 801(d)(2)(B). * * *

3. *Application of Rules 104(a) or 104(b) to preliminary issues.* Whether the preliminary factual issues involved in adoptive admissions are questions of preliminary fact for the trial judge under Rule 104(a) or matters of conditional relevance under Rule 104(b) is subject to some disagreement. Among the various views on how these issues should be allocated between the judge and jury, *Wilson* clearly gives the principal role to the jury. See 5 Weinstein's Federal Evidence § 801.31[3][d] (2d ed. 2006) (treating issues of whether individual heard, understood, and acquiesced as matters of conditional relevance). Nevertheless, it allows for judicial control by authorizing the exclusion of evidence by balancing probativity versus prejudice under Rule 403. Other courts give the trial court a more substantial and direct role in deciding whether hearsay policy has been satisfied by placing these issues under the judge's determination through Rule 104(a). State v. Carlson, 808 P.2d 1002, 1007–09 (Or.1991). For an intermediate view, see 3 Graham, Handbook of Federal Evidence § 801.21, at 792–95 (6th ed. 2006) (whether the statement was made in the person's hearing, whether he or she understood it, and whether the person had an opportunity to reply are matters of conditional relevance decided under Rule 104(b), while the question of whether the ordinary pattern of human behavior would have called for a response if the person believed the statement to be untrue is a preliminary question of fact decided by the court under Rule 104(a)).

4. *Not responding to accusatory letters.* Closely akin to the failure to respond to an oral accusation is the failure to respond to an accusatory letter or one that otherwise demands a response. Southern Stone Co., Inc. v. Singer, 665 F.2d 698 (5th Cir.1982), provides an example. There the court held inadmissible the failure of one of the defendants to respond to a letter by Southern Stone's counsel. The letter set out various allegations concerning the defendant's activities on behalf of a then defunct company and ended with the statement, "If any of the above is incorrect, please advise me." Id. at 702 n.4. Failure to respond to a letter constitutes an admission under Rule 801(d)(1)(B) only if "it was reasonable under the circumstances for the sender to expect the recipient to respond and correct the erroneous assertions." Id. at 703. The recipient testified that he did not respond because he was no longer involved with or concerned about the company, which he considered nonexistent. See also United States v. Ordonez, 737 F.2d 793,

800–01 (9th Cir.1983) (mere possession of a document does not constitute an adoptive admission).

5. *Forms of adoption.* Other actions manifesting adoption or belief, such as republication of material written by another, may qualify as an admission under this provision. See Wagstaff v. Protective Apparel Corp. of Am., Inc., 760 F.2d 1074, 1078 (10th Cir.1985) (newspaper articles received as adoptive admission in fraud case under theory that, "[b]y reprinting the newspaper articles and distributing them to persons with whom defendants were doing business, defendants unequivocally manifested their adoption of the inflated statements made in the newspaper articles"); Agriculture Ins. Co. v. Ace Hardware Corp., 214 F.Supp.2d 413, 416 (S.D.N.Y.2002) (drawing inferences from information provided by others constitutes adoption whereas merely repeating information may not).

6. *Constitutional considerations as to silence.* In *Wilson,* at the time the defendant made the adoptive admission, he was in the presence of the police but not in "custody." The Fifth Amendment right of the criminal defendant to remain silent after arrest under Miranda v. Arizona, 384 U.S. 436 (1966), means that constitutional principles must be considered before adoptive admissions are received. In Doyle v. Ohio, 426 U.S. 610 (1976), the Supreme Court held that once the defendant is warned of his *Miranda* rights "silence is insolubly ambiguous," and given the implicit assurance in the warnings that silence will carry no penalty, "it would be fundamentally unfair and a deprivation of due process to allow the arrested person's silence to be used to impeach." Id. at 617–18.

Silence after arrest while in police custody may not be used in the prosecution's case-in-chief in the absence of *Miranda* warnings and waiver. However, the Supreme Court has held that when the defendant's silence occurs before he or she is taken into custody and given *Miranda* rights, use of that silence to impeach offends neither the Fifth Amendment nor due process. Jenkins v. Anderson, 447 U.S. 231 (1980). Moreover, in Fletcher v. Weir, 455 U.S. 603, 607 (1982), the Court held that, where the defendant had been arrested but had not been advised of his rights, the absence of the "affirmative assurances" contained in *Miranda* warnings meant due process would not be offended by impeaching a defendant with his silence. For a general critique of the basic soundness of failure to deny as an admission, see Gamble, The Tacit Admission Rule: Unreliable and Unconstitutional—A Doctrine Ripe for Abandonment, 14 Ga.L.Rev. 27 (1980).

7. *Flight.* Flight has generally been received as evidence of guilt. However, a distinction should be drawn between flight from custody or disappearance from one's usual haunts, which is offered to prove consciousness of guilt, and flight from the scene of the crime itself, which helps to connect the accused physically to the crime scene. In civil cases, flight from the scene of an accident has been admitted as proof of belief of fault as well. Harrington v. Sharff, 305 F.2d 333 (2d Cir.1962). The inference of a consciousness of guilt can be drawn from other conduct as well, such as changing appearance. See, e.g., United States v. Felix–Gutierrez, 940 F.2d 1200, 1207–08 (9th Cir.1991) (removal of distinctive tattoo and cosmetic surgery). See generally 2 McCormick, Evidence § 263 (6th ed. 2006).

In discussing flight as evidence of guilt, the courts and writers have been prone to quote the Old Testament adage, "the wicked flee when no one pursues." Proverbs 28:1 (New Rev. Standard). See, e.g., Alberty v. United States, 162 U.S. 499, 509 (1896); 2 Wigmore, Evidence § 276, at 122 (Chadbourn rev. 1979). But with regard to silence as an admission, compare Matthew 27:11–14 (Christ stood silent before his accusers).

8. *Spoliation.* "Admissions" by conduct also may occur in the form of "spoliation." This rubric includes fabrication of evidence, subornation of perjury, destruction of evidence, bribery, intimidation or other influences on a witness to testify favorably or to avoid testifying. The theory is that, by resorting to these means, the party demonstrates a belief that the case is weak or that he or she is at fault or guilty. See generally 2 McCormick, Evidence § 265 (6th ed. 2006). Should a sanction more severe than admission of spoliation evidence be imposed?

9. *Missing evidence.* Whether counsel should be permitted to argue to the jury that the failure of a party to produce witnesses or evidence within the party's control gives rise to an unfavorable inference and whether the court should instruct the jury on such an inference are hotly contested issues in many jurisdictions. If either is permitted, a number of additional issues arise, such as what the nature and effect of such an inference is and under what circumstances it may properly be drawn. See generally 2 McCormick, Evidence § 264 (6th ed. 2006). Compare United States v. Erb, 543 F.2d 438 (2d Cir.1976), with United States v. Busic, 587 F.2d 577 (3d Cir.1978), rev'd on other grounds, 446 U.S. 398 (1980).

UNITED STATES v. CORNETT

United States Court of Appeals, Fifth Circuit, 1999.
195 F.3d 776.

DENNIS, CIRCUIT JUDGE:

This direct criminal appeal arises from the conviction following jury trial of Appellants Wendell Alboyd Cornett ("Cornett") and Mary Martillea Galloway ("Galloway") for conspiracy to distribute and possess with intent to distribute cocaine and cocaine base * * *. For the reasons assigned, we affirm the convictions and sentences of Appellant Cornett and reverse the conviction and sentence of Appellant Galloway and remand Galloway's case to the district court for further proceedings consistent with this opinion.

I. FACTS AND PROCEDURAL HISTORY

This case presents a complicated set of facts that involve allegations of drug possession and distribution, money-laundering, tax evasion, police corruption and exploitation. The grand jury indicted ten co-conspirators as being part of an elaborate drug conspiracy. Appellants Cornett and Galloway were tried together and convicted of performing various roles in the drug conspiracy. * * *

Cornett owned and operated multiple businesses in the Houston area. Specifically, Cornett owned an automotive detailing shop called the

House of Colors and a bowling alley pro shop. Galloway was one of Cornett's girlfriends. The government, believing that Cornett was running an elaborate drug smuggling operation behind the fronts of his legitimate businesses, began a three-year undercover investigation of Cornett and other suspects. In doing so, the government used undercover agents, cooperating witnesses, electronic monitoring and wire taps to gather evidence of Cornett's drug smuggling operation. * * *

Cornett used his wife and several girlfriends to assist his drug enterprise. Specifically, his girlfriend Kim Boutte ("Boutte") arranged drug transactions with customers and counted the cash receipts. Gradually Cornett used Boutte less and less, however, as his trust and interest in her waned. The government contends that Cornett then recruited Galloway to oversee the counting and storing of the drug money.

The facts surrounding Galloway's involvement in the drug conspiracy are disputed. The government's witnesses testified as to circumstantial evidence ambiguously suggesting differing degrees of Galloway's involvement with Cornett and his activities. Testimony from [several witnesses] suggested that Galloway was responsible for counting the money involved in the drug transactions. Specifically, one witness testified that, when he went to the hair salon where Galloway and Cornett worked for a rendezvous with Cornett, Galloway let him in the front door and escorted him to an upstairs room. He said he entered the room without Galloway and found Cornett counting, in his estimation, over $400,000. An audiotaped statement of a co-conspirator reported that Cornett had made a statement to her in which he mentioned Galloway in connection with "$500,000." Another witness testified that Cornett had told him that Galloway had a money counting machine and had accurately counted sums in excess of $21,000 for him. In an attempt to connect Galloway to the drug money, the government introduced evidence that Galloway received several expensive presents from Cornett, including a fur coat, a custom designed diamond ring and a Mercedes Benz; co-signed an automobile credit application as a reference for Cornett; and on two occasions wrote checks on her own account (for which Cornett supplied the cash) to pay Cornett's creditors. Galloway denied her involvement in the conspiracy, claiming that she had never seen more than $1,000 in cash in her life and that she never owned a money counting machine. It is undisputed, however, that she knew how to operate such a machine from her experience as a bank employee. She testified to her belief that any money or presents she had received from Cornett came from the operations of his legitimate businesses. Galloway's experience in bookkeeping and familiarity with Cornett's legitimate businesses tends to show that she knew Cornett's legal income from them was not sufficient to support their lifestyles.

As Cornett continued to engage in the drug conspiracy, the government arranged for cooperation with several of the participants. * * * Through its network of cooperating witnesses and undercover agents, the government compiled evidence of the drug conspiracy—recording over 100 audio tapes of conversation between the participants. The government argued at the end of the trial that one of these tapes, Exhibit 1.165, directly implicated Galloway in the conspiracy. Exhibit 1.165 involves a discussion between Boutte and a cooperating witness at the bowling alley pro shop. On the tape they discussed several topics—mostly limited to bowling scores and the appearance of persons on the scene. Part of the tape consisted of Boutte's laments over Cornett's exclusion of her from some of the drug activities and Cornett's relationship with Galloway. While mostly unintelligible, the government contends that this tape directly implicates Galloway because Boutte suggests her belief that Cornett had entrusted Galloway with storing and counting $500,000 of Cornett's drug money. Galloway's counsel objected to the admission of this tape, but the district court allowed the tape to be admitted as statements of co-conspirators in furtherance of the conspiracy under Federal Rules of Evidence 801(d)(2)(e).

* * * Galloway was convicted on the sole count of conspiracy and sentenced to sixty months imprisonment. * * *

2. Co–Conspirator Statements

* * *

Hearsay is not admissible under the Federal Rules of Evidence unless it fits an exception. Fed.R.Evid. 802. However, Rule 801 provides that certain statements which would otherwise constitute excludable hearsay under the general rule of Rule 801(c) are not hearsay by definition. One such definitional non-hearsay is found in Rule 801(d)(2)(e), which provides:

> A statement is not hearsay if * * * the statement is offered against a party and is * * * a statement by a coconspirator of a party during the course and in furtherance of the conspiracy.

Under Rule 801(d)(2)(e), the proponent of admittance must prove by a preponderance of the evidence (1) the existence of the conspiracy (2) the statement was made by a co-conspirator of the party, (3) the statement was made during the course of the conspiracy, and (4) the statement was made in furtherance of the conspiracy. *See United States v. Broussard,* 80 F.3d 1025, 1038 (5th Cir.1996) (citing *Bourjaily v. United States,* 483 U.S. 171, 175 * * * (1987)); *United States v. Means,* 695 F.2d 811, 818 (5th Cir.1983). There is no dispute as to the existence of the conspiracy, that the statements made in Exhibit 1.165 were made by a co-conspirator or that they were made during the course of the conspiracy—the only issue properly before the court is whether the statement was "in furtherance" of the conspiracy.

The legal standards that define the "in furtherance" requirement are well-established. A statement must be "in furtherance" of the conspiracy in order to fit within the non-hearsay definition of Rule 801(d)(2)(e). However, this Circuit has consistently held that the "in furtherance" requirement is not to be construed too strictly lest the purpose of the exception be defeated. *See United States v. Lechuga,* 888

F.2d 1472, 1480 (5th Cir.1989); *United States v. Ascarrunz,* 838 F.2d 759, 763 (5th Cir.1988). This rule is not without its limits, however; a statement is not in furtherance of the conspiracy unless it advances the ultimate objects of the conspiracy. *See United States v. Snyder,* 930 F.2d 1090, 1095 (5th Cir.1991). "Mere idle chatter", even if prejudicial and made among co-conspirators, is not admissible under Rule 801(d)(2)(e). *See Means,* 695 F.2d at 818. Thus, while the in furtherance requirement is not a strict one, it is a necessary one, and the proponent of admissibility must satisfy it by a preponderance of the evidence. *See Broussard,* 80 F.3d at 1038; *see also United States v. Doerr,* 886 F.2d 944, 951 (7th Cir.1989).

Exhibit 1.165 involves a discussion between Boutte and a confidential informant that took place at the bowling alley pro shop. The tape is over 50 minutes long and the conversation recorded covers many topics. A significant portion of the tape involves discussions between the two co-conspirators on such diverse issues as the bowling prowess of certain friends and relatives, the appearance of some of the patrons at the bowling alley, the merits of certain designer outfits and the respective talents of certain exotic dancers. Amid these conversations, however, occurred the following dialogue which, although mostly unintelligible, was offered to connect Galloway to the conspiracy:

Boutte: Somebody taking me away from him.

Informant: Thought you was supposed to be his ace.

* * *

Boutte: ya'll can't be mad cause what's her name never stole for me

* * *

Informant: If you going to bring * * * half a million dollars. Right ain't going to steal from you and he done counted it * * *

Boutte: Now she * * * because she take x amount of dollars with her * * * always comparing me to her likeness * * * he thought she was an angel.

* * *

Informant: She don't know what she's buying into * * * when I called up there yesterday I thought that was you.

Boutte: He told me he feel like I was just, he feels like I'm using him. What the hell am I using him * * *

Informant: It ain't all peach and cream * * *

Boutte: That's what I told him * * * me and Kevin ain't got no business sitting around talking about his business * * *

* * *

Boutte: [apparently quoting Cornett]—I don't trust nobody but my wife * * * well I mean there is other ladies I trust but I ain't got to tell you that cause we gonna get into it * * * Mary.

Informant: Mary.

The government contends that this interchange was intended to further the conspiracy in that it was meant to convey to a purchaser of the drugs that he should contact a new person (Galloway) for future drug deals because Boutte had lost favor with Cornett and Galloway had taken her place. The prosecution argued that this message is evidenced by the references to Galloway in connection with the drug money. In finding that the tape was admissible under Rule 801(d)(2)(e) the district court stated:

> The tape says that, essentially, Boutte feels like she's being compared to the woman who Cornett bought a Mercedes for. I hear the word "Mercedes" in there and then they say "who" and they say "Mary." And this was all in connection with the half-million dollars.

It is well-settled that a statement made among conspirators for the purpose of describing proper sources, avenues or conduits to promote the conspiracy is "in furtherance" for purposes of Rule 801(d)(2)(e). *See United States v. Lechuga,* 888 F.2d at 1480 (holding that during a conversation arranging a drug transaction, a reference to a "Wisconsin Source" as the source of the drugs in question was in furtherance of the conspiracy). However, in the cases in which a statement was found to be "in furtherance", either the statement itself or the conversation as a whole was intended to advance, facilitate or promote the ultimate conspiratorial objective. By way of contrast, conversations that represent "mere idle chatter" or which are mere narratives of past conduct are not in furtherance of the conspiracy because the statement and the conversation were not intended to further the conspiracy, regardless of whether an individual co-conspirator was implicated in the conversation. *See Means,* 695 F.2d at 818; *see also United States v. Phillips,* 664 F.2d 971, 1027 (5th Cir.1981) (abrogation on other grounds recognized by *United States v. Huntress,* 956 F.2d 1309 (5th Cir.1992)). The distinction between conversations in furtherance of the conspiracy and prejudicial statements made in conversations not in furtherance of the conspiracy has been recognized in other circuits as well. *See, e.g., United States v. Lieberman,* 637 F.2d 95, 102 (2d Cir.1980) ("The conversation * * * smacks of nothing more than casual conversation about past events. It is difficult to envision how it would have furthered the conspiracy"); *United States v. Santos,* 20 F.3d 280, 286 (7th Cir.1994) ("These statements are best described as narrative discussions of past events, which do not satisfy the 'in furtherance' requirement of Rule 801(d)(2)(E)"); *United States v. Roberts,* 14 F.3d 502, 514–515 (10th Cir.1993) ("mere narratives between co-conspirators or narrative declarations of past events are not in furtherance"); *United States v. Urbanik,* 801 F.2d 692, 698 (4th Cir.1986) ("We think that this statement can fairly be treated only as the sort of idle conversation which though it touches upon, does not 'further' a conspiracy").

In this respect, the present case is factually similar to the one addressed by the Fourth Circuit in *Urbanik.* In *Urbanik,* two co-conspirators conducted a conversation in furtherance of the conspiracy. Once they finished the business of the conspiracy, the two co-conspirators moved to a different part of the house and began lifting weights. During this weight lifting session one of the co-conspirators implicated a third co-conspirator. The Fourth Circuit held that this statement was inadmissible hearsay in that the statement was not in furtherance of the conspiracy. It was evident that the conversation was between two co-conspirators and that it was made during the course of the conspiracy in that they had just finished conducting the business of the conspiracy. However, it was also clear that the co-conspirators had ceased the operations of the conspiracy and had begun engaging in "mere idle chatter" as they pursued an unrelated activity. In the words of the Fourth Circuit:

> The statement identifying Urbanik as Pelino's "connection" for marijuana was merely a casual aside to the discussion of Urbanik the weight-lifter. In no sense but a most speculative one could it be thought to have been made to further the purposes of the conspiracy. Haselhuhn himself testified that this identification of Pelino's marijuana supplier could have had no effect on the conspiratorial relationship between him and Pelino. We think that this statement can fairly be treated only as the sort of idle conversation which though it touches upon, does not "further," a conspiracy, and which accordingly should not be admitted under Rule 801(d)(2)(E). *See United States v. Means,* 695 F.2d 811, 818 (5th Cir.1983); *United States v. Lieberman,* 637 F.2d 95, 102 (2d Cir.1980); *United States v. Eubanks,* 591 F.2d 513, 520 (9th Cir.1979). The requirement that the statements have been in furtherance of the conspiracy is designed both to assure their reliability and to be consistent with the presumption that the coconspirator would have authorized them* * *. The requirement is not satisfied by a conversation * * * which amounted to no more than idle chatter.

Urbanik, 801 F.2d at 698 * * *.

In the present case, the context of the admitted statements is that Boutte and the Informant were discussing a variety of subjects, which did not concern the conspiracy. The subject of whether Galloway enjoyed the confidence of Cornett arose out of a conversation about relationships and trust in relationships—the conversation turning to the specific trouble in Boutte's relationship with Cornett. The reference to the half-million dollars and then to Mary cannot reasonably be construed to convey to the Informant the message that future business in the conspiracy was to be conducted through Galloway instead of Boutte. Rather, the reference to Galloway and $500,000 was "a mere casual aside" in the conversation about Boutte the spurned lover and Galloway the other woman. That an allusion to the half-million dollars and Galloway was made in the statement is irrelevant for purposes of Rule 801(d)(2)(e) because the possible connection was not made in furtherance of the conspiracy and the statement was not part of a conversation that itself was in furtherance of the conspiracy. While this may be the kind of conversation that touches upon the conspiracy, it cannot fairly be said that it furthered the conspiracy and thus its admissibility was not authorized by Rule 801(d)(2)(e).

[The court found the error was not harmless and reversed Galloway's conviction, stating *inter alia*: "The government's evidence against Galloway was 'thin' as the trial judge observed, because no item of evidence directly linked Galloway to the conspiracy. Further, the government relied heavily on the ambiguous audiotape Exhibit 1.165 to give meaning to all of its evidence concerning Galloway."]

Notes and Questions

1. *Kinship of "in furtherance" statements to verbal act. Cornett* deals extensively with the meaning and application of the requirement of Rule 801(d)(2)(E) that coconspirator statements must have been made "in furtherance" of the conspiracy. United States v. Hassell, 547 F.2d 1048, 1052 (8th Cir.1977), suggests that when statements are made in furtherance of the conspiracy they are not hearsay at all but are rather verbal acts. Indeed, in United States v. Balthazard, 360 F.3d 309, 318 (1st Cir.2004), the court held that statements from one conspirator to another regarding the care and feeding of marijuana plants were not admissions but rather are nonhearsay verbal acts, or if in written form, real evidence of the crime. Is this an appropriate way to view the effect of the "in furtherance" requirement or does the in-furtherance requirement extend farther to include statements less directly involved in the conspiracy but facilitating its purpose?

2. *Narratives of past events and "idle chatter."* Under the "in furtherance" requirement, the narratives of past events are not generally admissible but may be admitted in appropriate circumstances. The test is whether they further the conspiracy, and in some types of conspiracies and under some circumstances, they will. See, e.g., United States v. Haldeman, 559 F.2d 31 (D.C.Cir.1976) (en banc) (narratives of past events were in furtherance of the Watergate cover-up because they were necessary for planning strategy). Moreover, as *Cornett* notes, courts typically apply the "in furtherance" requirement generously. See United States v. Shores, 33 F.3d 438, 444 (4th Cir.1994) (admissible if subject to alternative interpretations that include some reasonable basis to conclude statement intended to move conspiracy closer to its objectives). Thus, to be excluded, the narratives of past events must be viewed roughly as "idle chatter." The history of the "in furtherance" requirement is recounted in United States v. Harris, 546 F.2d 234, 237–38 (8th Cir.1976), and United States v. Perez, 989 F.2d 1574, 1577–79 (10th Cir.1993) (en banc).

3. *Statements themselves usable but not sufficient to establish admissibility.* In Bourjaily v. United States, 483 U.S. 171 (1987), the Supreme Court held that under Rule 104(a) the trial judge is entitled to consider the purported hearsay statement in determining under Rule 801(d)(2)(E) the existence of a conspiracy and the participation in that conspiracy of the declarant and the defendant. The Court left undecided whether the statement standing alone was sufficient to establish these issues. A 1997 amendment to the Rule codified the admissibility holding in *Bourjaily* and extended it to establishing the declarant's authority as a "speaking" agent under

subdivision (C) and the agency or employment relationship and its scope under subdivision (D). The amendment also resolved the undecided sufficiency issue, stating that the contents of the statement "are not alone sufficient" to prove these facts.

4. *Bourjaily* holds that Rule 104(a) should be used in determining the existence of a conspiracy and its membership and that these facts are to be established by a preponderance of the evidence. As noted in Chapter 1, Section A, proof under Rule 104(a) is by a "preponderance of proof." How does this square with the requirement of proof beyond a reasonable doubt in criminal cases where coconspirator statements are typically admitted?

BLECHA v. PEOPLE

Supreme Court of Colorado, 1998.
962 P.2d 931.

JUSTICE BENDER delivered the Opinion of the Court.

We granted certiorari to review the court of appeals' decision in *People v. Blecha,* 940 P.2d 1070 (Colo.App.1996), to determine whether the hearsay statement of a previously acquitted co-defendant, Roger Younger (Younger), was properly admitted at the trial of the defendant-appellant, Clifton Blecha (Blecha). A jury convicted Blecha of first degree murder and conspiracy to commit first degree murder of a fellow inmate at the Limon Correctional Facility. The court of appeals held that the admission of Younger's statements was erroneous since the statements [did not qualify] as co-conspirator hearsay * * * [but found the error harmless and affirmed].

I. FACTS

At the trial, an inmate eyewitness to the murder, Joseph Bates (Bates), testified to two hearsay statements made by a previously acquitted co-defendant, Younger. These statements form the basis of Blecha's appeal * * *.

On July 13, 1992 at approximately 9:15 p.m., staff members of the Limon Correctional Facility (LCF) found inmate Daniel Shettler (the victim) dead in his cell, lying under the covers of his upper bunk bed. The staff members discovered the body as the result of a "lockdown" of the facility that occurred at 7:00 p.m. An investigation revealed that the victim was strangled by a ligature surrounding his neck, and that the time of death was approximately between 6:00 p.m. and 9:30 p.m. on July 13, 1992. * * *

The victim lived in a three-tiered pod that housed approximately fifty inmates, including Blecha, Younger, and Green. On the day of the murder, all fifty inmates were permitted to move freely throughout the pod between a lockdown that occurred at 4:00 p.m. and the lockdown that occurred at 7:00 p.m. In the days following the murder, investigators questioned all fifty inmates. During these interviews, the investigators learned of a rumor among the prisoners that the victim was killed because he was an informant in a murder that occurred six months earlier at a different prison, the Fremont Correctional Facility (FCF). Three inmates * * * told investigators that Blecha, Younger, and Green killed the victim. Another inmate, Michael Ford (Ford), implicated three other inmates. * * *

In August of 1992, Bates told the chief investigating officer that shortly after the murder, Younger threatened his life and told him to keep his mouth shut. The officer's opinion was that Bates feared for his life from the day of the murder until he was subsequently transferred from LCF to another facility.

In October of 1992, Blecha, Younger, and Green were charged with murder and conspiracy to commit murder. Blecha moved to exclude Younger's hearsay statements from trial, contending that the admission of these statements was prohibited by [Colorado hearsay rules] and by the confrontation clauses of the United States and Colorado Constitutions.

After a hearing, the district court ruled that Younger's statements were admissible as the nonhearsay statements of a co-conspirator under CRE 801(d)(2)(E).[34] The district court then addressed Blecha's assertion that admission of these statements violated the confrontation clauses of the United States and Colorado Constitutions under the two-part test articulated in *Ohio v. Roberts,* 448 U.S. 56, 65 * * * (1980). First, the district court found that Younger was not available to testify at trial because, at the time of the pre-trial hearing, Younger was protected by the Fifth Amendment privilege against self-incrimination due to the pending murder and conspiracy charges against him. Second, the district court determined that Younger's statements possessed sufficient independent indicia of reliability to overcome the presumption of unreliability that attaches to hearsay statements. Thus, the district court held that the admission of Younger's statements was appropriate under the Colorado and federal constitutions.

After this hearing, the district court severed the trials of each of the three co-defendants. In August of 1993, Younger was acquitted of all charges. Blecha's case proceeded to trial in November of 1993.

At Blecha's trial, the prosecution submitted the results of the investigation, set forth above, into evidence. The prosecution's theory was that the victim was killed pursuant to the order of the vice-president of the Aryan Brotherhood, a prison gang. Mike Schneider * * *, the vice-president of the gang and an inmate at FCF, believed that the victim was an informant in the unrelated prison murder that occurred at FCF. The defense's theory was that Blecha was in the gymnasium when the murder occurred, that the investigation overlooked inmate Ford's information that pointed to other suspects, and that the prosecution's case was based solely on the testimony of "liars, thieves and murderers."

34. [Like Federal Rule 801(d)(2)(E), the Colorado Rule limits coconspirator statements to those "made during the course of and in furtherance of the conspiracy." Ed.]

Bates, who lived a few cells away from the victim, testified that on the evening of the murder he saw Younger, Green, and Blecha enter the victim's cell and shut the door. Bates testified that he walked by the victim's cell and saw Younger holding the victim in a headlock, Blecha standing in front of the victim with his hands up in the air, and Green standing behind Blecha holding a cord. Bates went to inmate Heath Pinion's * * * cell and told him "they were doing Danny." Bates returned to the victim's cell and saw Green, Blecha, and Younger putting the victim on the top bunk bed. Bates then informed three additional inmates * * * as to what he saw, and unsuccessfully attempted to rouse the victim by kicking the door to the victim's cell.

Bates further testified that the day after the murder Younger motioned to Bates by raising his index finger to his lips, indicating to Bates to be quiet. Three or four days after this incident, Younger told Bates that "[h]e knew I seen it, and he didn't want me to say anything."

[The court recounted testimony by several other witness that incriminated defendant Blecha as well as some testimony offered by the defense pointing to another group of inmates.]

II. Co-Conspirator Hearsay

Hearsay statements are out-of-court declarations offered into evidence for the truth of the matter asserted. *See* CRE 801(c). Hearsay statements are presumptively unreliable since the declarant is not present to explain the statement in context. Moreover, since the declarant is not subjected to cross-examination, the truthfulness of the statement is questionable. *See* Paul Marcus, *Prosecution and Defense of Criminal Conspiracy Cases* § 5.04[1], at 5–16 (1996). Due to this presumptive unreliability, hearsay statements are generally not admissible as evidence at trial. *See Bourjaily v. United States,* 483 U.S. 171, 179 * * * (1987). However, the out-of-court declarations of criminal conspirators "made during the course of and in furtherance of the conspiracy" are deemed non-hearsay under CRE 801(d)(2)(E) and may be admissible against all of the participants in the conspiracy.

The scope of the co-conspirator exception is narrow, *see Krulewitch v. United States,* 336 U.S. 440, 444 * * * (1949), and the requirement that the co-conspirator's statement be made during the course of and in furtherance of the conspiracy is a "prerequisite to admissibility" that must be "scrupulously observed." *Id.* The proponent must demonstrate the existence of both of these factors to overcome the presumption of unreliability that is the basis of the prohibition against the admission of hearsay. *See Williams v. People,* 724 P.2d 1279, 1285 (Colo.1986).

CRE 801(d)(2)(E)'s provision for the admission of co-conspirator statements is based on a theory of agency. Each conspirator is considered the agent of the other conspirators when acting or speaking to promote the conspiracy. *See* 5 Jack B. Weinstein & Margaret A. Berger, *Weinstein's Evidence* § 801.30, at 801–59 (Joseph M. McLaughlin, ed., 2d ed. 1998); *United States v. Perez,* 989 F.2d 1574, 1577 (10th Cir.1993).

However, just as an agent's responsibilities end upon the termination of the agency relationship, "all such responsibility is at an end when the conspiracy ends." *Fiswick v. United States,* 329 U.S. 211, 217 * * * (1946); *see also People v. Armstrong,* 704 P.2d 877, 879 (Colo.App.1985). "There can be no furtherance of a conspiracy that has ended." *Lutwak v. United States,* 344 U.S. 604, 617–18 * * * (1953).

Thus, it is well-settled under Colorado and federal law that co-conspirator statements made after the conspirators attain the object of the conspiracy are not admissible under this exception unless the proponent demonstrates "an express original agreement among the conspirators to continue to act in concert in order to cover up, for their own self-protection, traces of the crime after its commission." *Grunewald v. United States,* 353 U.S. 391, 404 * * * (1957); *see also Villafranca v. People,* 194 Colo. 472, 474, 573 P.2d 540, 542 (1978). The proponent can satisfy this requirement by showing that the objectives of the original conspiracy include such an agreement or that there exists a separate conspiracy to conceal. *See Kolkman v. People,* 89 Colo. 8, 18, 300 P. 575, 579 (1931).

It is also well-settled that "secrecy plus overt acts of concealment" do not establish an express agreement to act in concert in order to conceal the crime. *Grunewald,* 353 U.S. at 403 * * *. Acts of concealment occur in every conspiracy case, *see id.* at 404 * * *, and admission of hearsay statements on this basis would impermissibly expand the narrow scope of the co-conspirator exception and further dilute the general prohibition against hearsay statements. *See Krulewitch,* 336 U.S. at 444 * * * (holding that statements aimed at preventing detection and punishment were not admissible under the co-conspirator exception). As the United States Supreme Court articulated in *Grunewald v. United States:*

> [A] subsidiary conspiracy to conceal may not be implied from circumstantial evidence showing merely that the conspiracy was kept a secret and that the conspirators took care to cover up their crime in order to escape detection and punishment* * *. Acts of covering up, even though done in the context of a mutually understood need for secrecy, cannot themselves constitute proof that concealment of the crime after its commission was part of the initial agreement among the conspirators* * *. [E]very conspiracy will inevitably be followed by actions taken to cover the conspirators' traces. Sanctioning the Government's theory would for all practical purposes wipe out the statute of limitations in conspiracy cases, as well as extend indefinitely the time within which hearsay declarations will bind co-conspirators.

Grunewald, 353 U.S. at 401–02 * * *. We adopted this view in *Villafranca v. People,* when we stated:

> Not every conspiracy continues beyond the time of the occurrence of the crime that is the object of the conspiracy. There must be some specific evidence of a plan or agreement of concealment to demon-

strate the pendency of the conspiracy at the time that the statements were made.

Villafranca, 194 Colo. at 474, 573 P.2d at 542.

Applying these principles to the facts of this case, the prosecution sought the admission of two hearsay statements made by Younger after the commission of the murder. Such statements are admissible only if the prosecution demonstrates the existence of an express agreement among the conspirators to continue to act in concert in order to conceal the crime.

The record shows that the conspirators disposed of the murder weapon and placed the victim's body in a manner that would give the appearance that the victim was asleep. "[A]cts of covering up, even though done in the context of a mutually understood need for secrecy, cannot themselves constitute proof that concealment of the crime after its commission was part of the initial agreement among the conspirators." *Grunewald,* 353 U.S. at 402 * * * (holding that conspirators' efforts to conceal irregularities in documents and attempts to silence witnesses were insufficient evidence of an explicit agreement to conceal the crime). The record also shows that in the days following the murder, Younger made two statements to Bates that could be construed as an attempt to silence Bates. While these statements may demonstrate Younger's purpose to conceal the murder conspiracy, they are not evidence that the murder conspiracy included the further agreement to conceal. *See Lutwak,* 344 U.S. at 616 * * * (explaining that statements "in the nature of an afterthought by the conspirator for the purpose of covering up" do not constitute evidence of an agreement to conceal). Other conspirators did not similarly attempt to silence witnesses. Review of the record discloses no evidence that concealment was an explicit objective of the murder conspiracy and no evidence of a separate conspiracy with the explicit objective of concealing the murder. Hence, we hold that Younger's statements were not admissible under the co-conspirator exception because they were not made during the course of and in furtherance of the conspiracy to murder as required by CRE 801(d)(2)(E), and we affirm the court of appeals' ruling that the district court's admission of these statements was error.

[Blecha argued that Younger's statements acknowledging that Bates witnessed the murder indirectly admitted Younger's guilt thereby bolstering Bates' credibility and contributing to Blecha's conviction. The Colorado Supreme Court nevertheless found admission of the statements harmless error because of the strength of the independent evidence linking Younger to the crime, other corroboration of Bates' account, and the relative lack of importance of Younger's statement to the prosecution's case.]

Notes and Questions

1. *Frequently admitted.* In both *Cornett* and *Blecha*, the courts found error (albeit harmless error in *Blecha*) in the admission of the coconspirator statements. Those results should not be read to suggest a general reticence of courts to receive such hearsay, which the Supreme Court observed "apparently is the most frequently used exception to the hearsay rule." United States v. Inadi, 475 U.S. 387, 398 (1986).

2. *Determining when primary conspiracy ends.* Under Federal Rule 801(d)(2)(E), a coconspirator's statements must have been made in the course of the conspiracy and later concealment activities are not automatically included. Nevertheless, difficult issues arise concerning concealment because of the nature of some conspiracies, and in ordinary conspiracies dividing the primary conspiracy from concealment is often not obvious. Certainly some acts of concealment are treated as part of the "main" conspiracy in some cases. The Court in Grunewald v. United States, 353 U.S. 391, 405 (1957), gave the following examples: "Kidnapers in hiding, waiting for ransom, commit acts of concealment in furtherance of the objectives of the conspiracy itself, just as repainting a stolen car would be in furtherance of a conspiracy to steal; in both cases the successful accomplishment of the crime necessitates concealment." In a typical conspiracy, "in the course of" would more likely include dividing up the spoils of the crime (see United States v. Hickey, 596 F.2d 1082, 1089–90 (1st Cir.1979)) or a participant collecting payment for his part in the criminal enterprise (see United States v. Schwanke, 598 F.2d 575, 581–82 (10th Cir.1979)) than the subsequent arson of the getaway car (see United States v. Floyd, 555 F.2d 45, 48 (2d Cir.1977)).

Withdrawal from a conspiracy under the substantive criminal law test also has the effect of eliminating admissibility of statements by coconspirators against the withdrawing party. United States v. Pratt, 239 F.3d 640, 644 (4th Cir.2001).

3. *Concealment phase under state rules.* While federal evidentiary law will not permit admission of statements made during a broadly defined concealment phase, some states take a different view. See, e.g., State v. Helmick, 495 S.E.2d 262, 269 (W.Va.1997) ("we are persuaded by those jurisdictions that hold that '[a] conspiracy to commit a crime does not necessarily end with the commission of the crime' "). Moreover, the Federal Rule limitation is not constitutionally required. Dutton v. Evans, 400 U.S. 74 (1970) (affirming the constitutionality of admission of coconspirator statement from state (Georgia) that automatically included concealment phase).

4. *Conspiracy need not be charged.* A formal conspiracy charge is not required in order to admit the statement of a coconspirator. 2 McCormick, Evidence § 259, at 204 (6th ed. 2006).

5. *Admission despite acquittal.* The acquittal of a coconspirator does not usually require exclusion of his or her statement because the standard of proof for admissibility is less demanding than proof beyond a reasonable doubt required for conviction. See United States v. Peralta, 941 F.2d 1003,

1006–07 (9th Cir.1991); United States v. Gil, 604 F.2d 546, 549 (7th Cir.1979).

6. *Extending an established conspiracy.* Some courts continue to state, despite the rather obvious flaw, that only slight evidence is required to connect a coconspirator once a conspiracy is established. See, e.g., United States v. Andrews, 585 F.2d 961 (10th Cir.1978). But see United States v. Malatesta, 590 F.2d 1379 (5th Cir.1979) (banishing the rule).

7. *Sources.* Davenport, The Confrontation Clause and the Co-conspirator Exception in Criminal Prosecutions: A Functional Analysis, 85 Harv. L.Rev. 1378 (1972); Klein, Conspiracy—The Prosecutor's Darling, 24 Brooklyn L.Rev. 1 (1957); Levie, Hearsay and Conspiracy, 52 Mich.L.Rev. 1159 (1954); Mueller, The Federal Coconspirator Exception: Action, Assertion, and Hearsay, 12 Hofstra L.Rev. 323 (1984).

SECTION C. CONFRONTATION

CALIFORNIA v. GREEN

Supreme Court of the United States, 1970.
399 U.S. 149.

MR. JUSTICE WHITE delivered the opinion of the Court.

Section 1235 of the California Evidence Code, effective as of January 1, 1967, provides that "[e]vidence of a statement made by a witness is not made inadmissible by the hearsay rule if the statement is inconsistent with his testimony at the hearing and is offered in compliance with Section 770."[35] In *People v. Johnson,* 68 Cal.2d 646, 441 P.2d 111 (1968), the California Supreme Court held that prior statements of a witness that were not subject to cross-examination when originally made, could not be introduced under this section to prove the charges against a defendant without violating the defendant's right of confrontation guaranteed by the Sixth Amendment and made applicable to the States by the Fourteenth Amendment.

* * *

The origin and development of the hearsay rules and of the Confrontation Clause have been traced by others and need not be recounted in detail here. It is sufficient to note that the particular vice that gave impetus to the confrontation claim was the practice of trying defendants on "evidence" which consisted solely of *ex parte* affidavits or depositions secured by the examining magistrates, thus denying the defendant the opportunity to challenge his accuser in a face-to-face encounter in front of the trier of fact. Prosecuting attorneys "would frequently allege matters which the prisoner denied and called upon them to prove. The proof was usually given by reading depositions, confessions of accomplices, letters, and the like; and this occasioned frequent demands by the

35. * * * Section 770 merely requires that the witness be given an opportunity to explain or deny the prior statement at some point in the trial. * * *

prisoner to have his 'accusers,' *i.e.* the witnesses against him, brought before him face to face * * *."[36]

But objections occasioned by this practice appear primarily to have been aimed at the failure to call the witness to confront personally the defendant at his trial. So far as appears, in claiming confrontation rights no objection was made against receiving a witness' out-of-court depositions or statements, so long as the witness was present at trial to repeat his story and to explain or repudiate any conflicting prior stories before the trier of fact.

* * *

This conclusion is supported by comparing the purposes of confrontation with the alleged dangers in admitting an out-of-court statement. Confrontation: (1) insures that the witness will give his statements under oath—thus impressing him with the seriousness of the matter and guarding against the lie by the possibility of a penalty for perjury; (2) forces the witness to submit to cross-examination, the "greatest legal engine ever invented for the discovery of truth"[37]; (3) permits the jury that is to decide the defendant's fate to observe the demeanor of the witness in making his statement, thus aiding the jury in assessing his credibility.

It is, of course, true that the out-of-court statement may have been made under circumstances subject to none of these protections. But if the declarant is present and testifying at trial, the out-of-court statement for all practical purposes regains most of the lost protections. If the witness admits the prior statement is his, or if there is other evidence to show the statement is his, the danger of faulty reproduction is negligible and the jury can be confident that it has before it two conflicting statements by the same witness. Thus, as far as the oath is concerned, the witness must now affirm, deny, or qualify the truth of the prior statement under the penalty of perjury; indeed, the very fact that the prior statement was not given under a similar circumstance may become the witness' explanation for its inaccuracy—an explanation a jury may be expected to understand and take into account in deciding which, if either, of the statements represents the truth.

Second, the inability to cross-examine the witness at the time he made his prior statement cannot easily be shown to be of crucial significance as long as the defendant is assured of full and effective

36. 1 J. Stephen, A History of the Criminal Law of England 326 (1883). See also 9 [W.] Holdsworth, [A History of English Law] 225–228 [(3d ed. 1944)].

A famous example is provided by the trial of Sir Walter Raleigh for treason in 1603. A crucial element of the evidence against him consisted of the statements of one Cobham, implicating Raleigh in a plot to seize the throne. Raleigh had since received a written retraction from Cobham, and believed that Cobham would now testify in his favor. After a lengthy dispute over Raleigh's right to have Cobham called as a witness, Cobham was not called, and Raleigh was convicted. See 1 Stephen, *supra,* at 333–336; 9 Holdsworth, *supra,* at 216–217, 226–228. At least one author traces the Confrontation Clause to the common-law reaction against these abuses of the Raleigh trial. See F. Heller, The Sixth Amendment 104 (1951).

37. 5 [J.] Wigmore [, Evidence] § 1367.

cross-examination at the time of trial. The most successful cross-examination at the time the prior statement was made could hardly hope to accomplish more than has already been accomplished by the fact that the witness is now telling a different, inconsistent story, and—in this case—one that is favorable to the defendant. * * *

The defendant's task in cross-examination is, of course, no longer identical to the task that he would have faced if the witness had not changed his story and hence had to be examined as a "hostile" witness giving evidence for the prosecution. This difference, however, far from lessening, may actually enhance the defendant's ability to attack the prior statement. For the witness, favorable to the defendant, should be more than willing to give the usual suggested explanations for the inaccuracy of his prior statement, such as faulty perception or undue haste in recounting the event. Under such circumstances, the defendant is not likely to be hampered in effectively attacking the prior statement, solely because his attack comes later in time.

Similar reasons lead us to discount as a constitutional matter the fact that the jury at trial is foreclosed from viewing the declarant's demeanor when he first made his out-of-court statement. The witness who now relates a different story about the events in question must necessarily assume a position as to the truth value of his prior statement, thus giving the jury a chance to observe and evaluate his demeanor as he either disavows or qualifies his earlier statement. * * *

It may be true that a jury would be in a better position to evaluate the truth of the prior statement if it could somehow be whisked magically back in time to witness a gruelling cross-examination of the declarant as he first gives his statement. But the question as we see it must be not whether one can somehow imagine the jury in "a better position," but whether subsequent cross-examination at the defendant's trial will still afford the trier of fact a satisfactory basis for evaluating the truth of the prior statement. On that issue, neither evidence[38] nor reason convinces us that contemporaneous cross-examination before the ultimate trier of fact is so much more effective than subsequent examination that it must be made the touchstone of the Confrontation Clause.

Finally, we note that none of our decisions interpreting the Confrontation Clause requires excluding the out-of-court statements of a witness who is available and testifying at trial. The concern of most of our cases has been focused on precisely the opposite situation—situations where

38. The California Supreme Court in its earlier decision on this issue stated that "[t]his practical truth [the importance of immediate cross-examination] is daily verified by trial lawyers, not one of whom would willingly postpone to both a later date and a different forum his right to cross-examine a witness against his client." *People v. Johnson,* 68 Cal.2d 646, 655, 441 P.2d 111, 118 (1968). The citations that follow this sentence are to books on trial practice that shed little empirical light on the actual comparative effectiveness of subsequent, as opposed to timely, cross-examination. As the text suggests, where the witness has changed his story at trial to favor the defendant he should, if anything, be more rather than less vulnerable to defense counsel's explanations for the inaccuracy of his former statement.

statements have been admitted in the absence of the declarant and without any chance to cross-examine him at trial.

* * *

We find nothing, then, in either the history or the purposes of the Confrontation Clause, or in the prior decisions of this Court, that compels the conclusion reached by the California Supreme Court concerning the validity of California's § 1235. Contrary to the judgment of that court, the Confrontation Clause does not require excluding from evidence the prior statements of a witness who concedes making the statements, and who may be asked to defend or otherwise explain the inconsistency between his prior and his present version of the events in question, thus opening himself to full cross-examination at trial as to both stories.

[The Court remanded the case to the California courts to consider the narrow question of whether Porter's statement to Officer Wade, which had not been the subject of prior cross-examination, was inadmissible because of the witness' apparent memory lapse and the resulting limitation on cross-examination at trial.]

[In an omitted portion of the case, the Court approves admission of statements made by Porter at the preliminary hearing where he had been cross-examined by Green's counsel.]

Notes and Questions

1. *On remand.* In *Green*, the Supreme Court remanded to the state court the determination of whether Melvin Porter's claim that he could not remember the critical events covered by his prior statement to a police officer so affected Green's right of cross-examination as to deny effectively his confrontation rights. On remand, in People v. Green, 479 P.2d 998 (Cal.1971), the California court ruled that Porter's testimony amounted to an implied denial that defendant had furnished him with the marijuana and thus was inconsistent with his prior statements within the meaning of California Evidence Code. The court also held that the purposes of the Confrontation Clause had been satisfied, relying particularly upon the fact that Green's counsel had the opportunity to test the witness' memory concerning the prior statement but declined to take advantage of that opportunity.

2. *Availability for cross-examination, but not much more, required.* The Court in *Green* reserved judgment on whether the Confrontation Clause is violated if a witness who made a prior inconsistent statement is unable at trial to recall the underlying event to which the statement refers. Similar issues arise when a witness has a memory of the underlying event but either has no memory of the prior statement or denies making it. See generally Graham, The Confrontation Clause, the Hearsay Rule, and the Forgetful Witness, 56 Tex.L.Rev. 151 (1978).

In United States v. Owens, 484 U.S. 554 (1988), the Court swept these various issues aside. It adopted the position of Justice Harlan in his concurring opinion in *Green* that "a witness's inability to 'recall either the underlying events that are the subject of an extra-judicial statement or previous testimony or recollect the circumstances under which the statement was given, does not have Sixth Amendment consequences.'" Id. at 558 (quoting *Green,* 399 U.S. at 188). See also United States v. Milton, 8 F.3d 39, 47 (D.C.Cir.1993) (prior statement receivable despite failure to remember both the events underlying statement and prior statement itself). *Owens* means that almost no matter what the witness' testimonial limitations, the physical availability and willing response to questions satisfies the Confrontation Clause. Compare United States ex rel. Hamilton v. Ellingsworth, 692 F.Supp. 356, 359 (D.Del.1988) (ruling that despite amnesia witness was "available"), with United States v. Spotted War Bonnet, 933 F.2d 1471, 1474 (8th Cir.1991) (stating that although a child's substantial forgetfulness regarding events or prior statement does not render opportunity for cross-examination constitutionally inadequate, simply putting child on stand who is so young that she could not be cross-examined at all would deny confrontation right). See similar discussion in Section(B)(1), supra.

3. *Calling witness or making available?* In order for *Green*'s rationale to apply, is it necessary that the prosecution call the declarant to testify on direct examination and the defendant then be given an opportunity for cross-examination, or is it sufficient if the prosecution simply produces the declarant and permits the defendant to conduct an examination? Compare People v. Bastien, 541 N.E.2d 670 (Ill.1989) (witness must be called as witness by state), with State v. Schaal, 806 S.W.2d 659 (Mo.1991) (en banc) (making witness available for examination is constitutionally sufficient).

4. *Part of the "new" system.* In *Crawford v. Washington*, infra, the Supreme Court established a new Confrontation Clause analysis that differs dramatically from its earlier analysis, particularly the general system described in *Ohio v. Roberts*, which is the next principal case. However, the theory of *California v. Green*, applicable when the declarant testifies at the current trial and is available for cross-examination about prior statements, remains valid under *Crawford.*

OHIO v. ROBERTS

Supreme Court of the United States, 1980.
448 U.S. 56.

MR. JUSTICE BLACKMUN delivered the opinion of the Court.

This case presents issues concerning the constitutional propriety of the introduction in evidence of the preliminary hearing testimony of a witness not produced at the defendant's subsequent state criminal trial.

I

Local police arrested respondent, Herschel Roberts, on January 7, 1975, in Lake County, Ohio. Roberts was charged with forgery of a check in the name of Bernard Isaacs, and with possession of stolen credit cards belonging to Isaacs and his wife Amy.

A preliminary hearing was held in Municipal Court on January 10. The prosecution called several witnesses, including Mr. Isaacs. Respondent's appointed counsel had seen the Isaacs' daughter, Anita, in the courthouse hallway, and called her as the defense's only witness. Anita Isaacs testified that she knew respondent, and that she had permitted him to use her apartment for several days while she was away. Defense counsel questioned Anita at some length and attempted to elicit from her an admission that she had given respondent checks and the credit cards without informing him that she did not have permission to use them. Anita, however, denied this. Respondent's attorney did not ask to have the witness declared hostile and did not request permission to place her on cross-examination. The prosecutor did not question Anita. * * *

Between November 1975 and March 1976, five subpoenas for four different trial dates were issued to Anita at her parents' Ohio residence. The last three carried a written instruction that Anita should "call before appearing." She was not at the residence when these were executed. She did not telephone and she did not appear at trial.

In March 1976, the case went to trial before a jury in the Court of Common Pleas. Respondent took the stand and testified that Anita Isaacs had given him her parents' checkbook and credit cards with the understanding that he could use them. Tr. 231–232. Relying on Ohio Rev.Code Ann. § 2945.49 (1975), which permits the use of preliminary examination testimony of a witness who "cannot for any reason be produced at the trial," the State, on rebuttal, offered the transcript of Anita's testimony. Tr. 273–274.

Asserting a violation of the Confrontation Clause and indeed, the unconstitutionality thereunder of § 2945.49, the defense objected to the use of the transcript. The trial court conducted a *voir dire* hearing as to its admissibility. Tr. 194–199. Amy Isaacs, the sole witness at *voir dire,* was questioned by both the prosecutor and defense counsel concerning her daughter's whereabouts. Anita, according to her mother, left home for Tucson, Ariz., soon after the preliminary hearing. About a year before the trial, a San Francisco social worker was in communication with the Isaacs about a welfare application Anita had filed there. Through the social worker, the Isaacs reached their daughter once by telephone. Since then, however, Anita had called her parents only one other time and had not been in touch with her two sisters. When Anita called, some seven or eight months before trial, she told her parents that she "was traveling" outside Ohio, but did not reveal the place from which she called. Mrs. Isaacs stated that she knew of no way to reach Anita in case of an emergency. App. 9. Nor did she "know of anybody who knows where she is." *Id.* at 11. The trial court admitted the transcript into evidence. Respondent was convicted on all counts.

The Court of Appeals of Ohio reversed. * * * The Supreme Court of Ohio * * * affirmed * * *. It first held that * * * Anita was * * * unavailable. *Barber v. Page* was distinguished as a case in which "the government knew where the absent witness was," whereas Anita's "whereabouts were entirely unknown." 55 Ohio St.2d, at 194, 378 N.E.2d, at 495, "[T]he trial judge could reasonably have concluded from

Mrs. Isaacs' *voir dire* testimony that due diligence could not have procured the attendance of Anita Isaacs"; he "could reasonably infer that Anita had left San Francisco"; and he "could properly hold that the witness was unavailable to testify in person." *Id.,* at 195, 378 N.E.2d, at 495–496.

The court, nonetheless, held that the transcript was inadmissible. Reasoning that normally there is little incentive to cross-examine a witness at a preliminary hearing, where the "ultimate issue" is only probable cause, *id.,* at 196, 378 N.E.2d, at 496 * * * the court held that the mere opportunity to cross-examine at a preliminary hearing did not afford constitutional confrontation for purposes of trial. * * * Since Anita had not been cross-examined at the preliminary hearing and was absent at trial, the introduction of the transcript of her testimony was held to have violated respondent's confrontation right. * * *

II

A

The Court here is called upon to consider once again the relationship between the Confrontation Clause and the hearsay rule with its many exceptions. The basic rule against hearsay, of course, is riddled with exceptions developed over three centuries. These exceptions vary among jurisdictions as to number, nature, and detail. But every set of exceptions seems to fit an apt description offered more than 40 years ago: "an old-fashioned crazy quilt made of patches cut from a group of paintings by cubists, futurists and surrealists." Morgan & Maguire, Looking Backward and Forward at Evidence, 50 Harv.L.Rev. 909, 921 (1937).

The Sixth Amendment's Confrontation Clause, made applicable to the States through the Fourteenth Amendment, *Pointer v. Texas,* 380 U.S. 400, 403–405 (1965) * * *, provides: "In all criminal prosecutions, the accused shall enjoy the right * * * to be confronted with the witnesses against him." If one were to read this language literally, it would require, on objection, the exclusion of any statement made by a declarant not present at trial. See *Mattox v. United States,* 156 U.S. 237, 243 (1895) ("[T]here could be nothing more directly contrary to the letter of the provision in question than the admission of dying declarations"). But, if thus applied, the Clause would abrogate virtually every hearsay exception, a result long rejected as unintended and too extreme.

The historical evidence leaves little doubt, however, that the Clause was intended to exclude some hearsay. See *California v. Green,* 399 U.S., at 156–157, and nn.9 and 10; see also McCormick § 252, p. 606. Moreover, underlying policies support the same conclusion. The Court has emphasized that the Confrontation Clause reflects a preference for face-to-face confrontation at trial, and that "a primary interest secured by [the provision] is the right of cross-examination." *Douglas v. Alabama,* 380 U.S. 415, 418 (1965).[39] In short, the Clause envisions

> "a personal examination and cross-examination of the witness, in which the accused has an opportunity, not only of testing the recollection and sifting the conscience of the witness, but of compelling him to stand face to face with the jury in order that they may look at him, and judge by his demeanor upon the stand and the manner in which he gives his testimony whether he is worthy of belief." *Mattox v. United States,* 156 U.S., at 242–243.

These means of testing accuracy are so important that the absence of proper confrontation at trial "calls into question the ultimate 'integrity of the fact-finding process.' " *Chambers v. Mississippi,* 410 U.S. 284, 295 (1973), quoting *Berger v. California,* 393 U.S. 314, 315 (1969). * * *

B

The Confrontation Clause operates in two separate ways to restrict the range of admissible hearsay. First, in conformance with the Framers' preference for face-to-face accusation, the Sixth Amendment establishes a rule of necessity. In the usual case (including cases where prior cross-examination has occurred), the prosecution must either produce, or demonstrate the unavailability of, the declarant whose statement it wishes to use against the defendant. See *Mancusi v. Stubbs,* 408 U.S. 204 (1972); *Barber v. Page,* 390 U.S. 719 (1968). * * *

The second aspect operates once a witness is shown to be unavailable. Reflecting its underlying purpose to augment accuracy in the factfinding process by ensuring the defendant an effective means to test adverse evidence, the Clause countenances only hearsay marked with such trustworthiness that "there is no material departure from the reason of the general rule." *Snyder v. Massachusetts,* 291 U.S., at 107. The principle recently was formulated in *Mancusi v. Stubbs*:

> "The focus of the Court's concern has been to insure that there 'are indicia of reliability which have been widely viewed as determinative of whether a statement may be placed before the jury though there is no confrontation of the declarant,' *Dutton v. Evans, supra,* at 89 and to 'afford the trier of fact a satisfactory basis for evaluating the truth of the prior statement,' *California v. Green, supra,* 399 U.S., at 161. It is clear from these statements, and from numerous

39. See also * * * *California v. Green,* 399 U.S., at 158 (cross-examination is the " 'greatest legal engine ever invented for the discovery of truth,' " quoting 5 J. Wigmore, Evidence § 1367 (3d ed. 1940)). Of course, these purposes are interrelated, since one critical goal of cross-examination is to draw out discrediting demeanor to be viewed by the factfinder. See *Government of Virgin Islands v. Aquino,* 378 F.2d 540, 548 (C.A.3 1967).

Confrontation at trial also operates to ensure reliability in other ways. First, "[t]he requirement of personal presence * * * undoubtedly makes it more difficult to lie against someone, particularly if that person is an accused and present at trial." 4 J. Weinstein & M. Berger, Weinstein's Evidence ¶ 800[01], pp. 800–10 (1979). See also Note, 54 Iowa L.Rev. 360, 365 (1968). Second, it "insures that the witness will give his statements under oath—thus impressing him with the seriousness of the matter and guarding against the lie by the possibility of a penalty for perjury." *California v. Green,* 399 U.S., at 158.

prior decisions of this Court, that even though the witness be unavailable his prior testimony must bear some of these 'indicia of reliability.' " 408 U.S., at 213.

The Court has applied this "indicia of reliability" requirement principally by concluding that certain hearsay exceptions rest upon such solid foundations that admission of virtually any evidence within them comports with the "substance of the constitutional protection." *Mattox v. United States,* 156 U.S., at 244. This reflects the truism that "hearsay rules and the Confrontation Clause are generally designed to protect similar values," *California v. Green,* 399 U.S., at 155, and "stem from the same roots," *Dutton v. Evans,* 400 U.S. 74, 86 (1970). It also responds to the need for certainty in the workaday world of conducting criminal trials.

In sum, when a hearsay declarant is not present for cross-examination at trial, the Confrontation Clause normally requires a showing that he is unavailable. Even then, his statement is admissible only if it bears adequate "indicia of reliability." Reliability can be inferred without more in a case where the evidence falls within a firmly rooted hearsay exception. In other cases, the evidence must be excluded, at least absent a showing of particularized guarantees of trustworthiness.

III

We turn first to [the adequacy of Anita's cross-examination]. Resolution of this issue requires a careful comparison of this case to *California v. Green, supra.*[40]

A

In *Green,* at the preliminary hearing, a youth named Porter identified Green as a drug supplier. When called to the stand at Green's trial, however, Porter professed a lapse of memory. Frustrated in its attempt to adduce live testimony, the prosecution offered Porter's prior statements. The trial judge ruled the evidence admissible, and substantial portions of the preliminary hearing transcript were read to the jury. This Court found no error. * * * It reasoned:

> "Porter's statement at the preliminary hearing had already been given under circumstances closely approximating those that surround the typical trial. Porter was under oath; respondent was represented by counsel—the same counsel in fact who later represented him at the trial; respondent had every opportunity to cross-examine Porter as to his statement; and the proceedings were conducted before a judicial tribunal, equipped to provide a judicial record of the hearings." 399 U.S., at 165.

40. [This element of the *Green* decision was omitted from the earlier treatment of the case. Ed.]

These factors, the Court concluded, provided all that the Sixth Amendment demands: "substantial compliance with the purposes behind the confrontation requirement." *Id.,* at 166.

This passage and others in the *Green* opinion suggest that the *opportunity* to cross-examine at the preliminary hearing—even absent actual cross-examination—satisfies the Confrontation Clause. Yet the record showed, and the Court recognized, that defense counsel in fact had cross-examined Porter at the earlier proceeding. *Id.,* at 151. * * *

We need not decide whether the Supreme Court of Ohio correctly dismissed statements in *Green* suggesting that the mere opportunity to cross-examine rendered the prior testimony admissible. * * * Nor need we decide whether *de minimis* questioning is sufficient, for defense counsel in this case tested Anita's testimony with the equivalent of significant cross-examination.

B

Counsel's questioning clearly partook of cross-examination as a matter of *form.* His presentation was replete with leading questions, the principal tool and hallmark of cross-examination. In addition, counsel's questioning comported with the principal *purpose* of cross-examination: to challenge "whether the declarant was sincerely telling what he believed to be the truth, whether the declarant accurately perceived and remembered the matter he related, and whether the declarant's intended meaning is adequately conveyed by the language he employed." Davenport, The Confrontation Clause and the Co–Conspirator Exception in Criminal Prosecutions: A Functional Analysis, 85 Harv.L.Rev. 1378 (1972). Anita's unwillingness to shift the blame away from respondent became discernible early in her testimony. Yet counsel continued to explore the underlying events in detail. He attempted, for example, to establish that Anita and respondent were sharing an apartment, an assertion that was critical to respondent's defense at trial and that might have suggested ulterior personal reasons for unfairly casting blame on respondent. At another point, he directly challenged Anita's veracity by seeking to have her admit that she had given the credit cards to respondent to obtain a television. When Anita denied this, defense counsel elicited the fact that the only television she owned was a "Twenty Dollar * * * old model." App. 21. Cf. *Davis v. Alaska,* 415 U.S. 308, 316–317 (1974). * * *

In sum, we perceive no reason to resolve the reliability issue differently here than the Court did in *Green.* "Since there was an adequate opportunity to cross-examine [the witness], and counsel * * * availed himself of that opportunity * * *." 408 U.S., at 216.

IV

[Respondent also contends that the State] failed to lay a proper predicate for admission of the preliminary hearing transcript by its failure to demonstrate that Anita Isaacs was not available to testify in person at the trial. * * *

A

The basic litmus of Sixth Amendment unavailability is established: "[A] witness is not 'unavailable' for purposes of the * * * exception to the confrontation requirement unless the prosecutorial authorities have made a *good-faith effort* to obtain his presence at trial." *Barber v. Page,* 390 U.S., at 724–725 (emphasis added). * * *

Although it might be said that the Court's prior cases provide no further refinement of this statement of the rule, certain general propositions safely emerge. The law does not require the doing of a futile act. Thus, if no possibility of procuring the witness exists (as, for example, the witness' intervening death), "good faith" demands nothing of the prosecution. But if there is a possibility, albeit remote, that affirmative measures might produce the declarant, the obligation of good faith *may* demand their effectuation. "The lengths to which the prosecution must go to produce a witness * * * is a question of reasonableness." *California v. Green,* 399 U.S., at 189, n.22 (concurring opinion, citing *Barber v. Page, supra*). The ultimate question is whether the witness is unavailable despite good-faith efforts undertaken prior to trial to locate and present that witness. As with other evidentiary proponents, the prosecution bears the burden of establishing this predicate.

B

On the facts presented we hold that the trial court and the Supreme Court of Ohio correctly concluded that Anita's unavailability, in the constitutional sense, was established.

At the *voir dire* hearing, called for by the defense, it was shown that some four months prior to the trial the prosecutor was in touch with Amy Isaacs and discussed with her Anita's whereabouts. It may appropriately be inferred that Mrs. Isaacs told the prosecutor essentially the same facts to which she testified at *voir dire*: that the Isaacs had last heard from Anita during the preceding summer; that she was not then in San Francisco, but was traveling outside Ohio; and that the Isaacs and their other children knew of no way to reach Anita even in an emergency. This last fact takes on added significance when it is recalled that Anita's parents earlier had undertaken affirmative efforts to reach their daughter when the social worker's inquiry came in from San Francisco. This is not a case of parents abandoning all interest in an absent daughter.

The evidence of record demonstrates that the prosecutor issued a subpoena to Anita at her parents' home, not only once, but on five separate occasions over a period of several months. In addition, at the *voir dire* argument, the prosecutor stated to the court that respondent "witnessed that I have attempted to locate, I have subpoenaed, there has been a *voir dire* of the witness' parents, and they have not been able to locate her for over a year." App. 12.

Given these facts, the prosecution did not breach its duty of good-faith effort. To be sure, the prosecutor might have tried to locate by telephone the San Francisco social worker with whom Mrs. Isaacs had spoken many months before and might have undertaken other steps in an effort to find Anita. One, in hindsight, may always think of other things. Nevertheless, the great improbability that such efforts would have resulted in locating the witness, and would have led to her production at trial, neutralizes any intimation that a concept of reasonableness required their execution. We accept as a general rule, of course, the proposition that "the possibility of a refusal is not the equivalent of asking and receiving a rebuff." *Barber v. Page,* 390 U.S., at 724, quoting from the dissenting opinion in that case in the Court of Appeals (381 F.2d 479, 481 (C.A.10 1966)). But the service and ineffectiveness of the five subpoenas and the conversation with Anita's mother were far more than mere reluctance to face the possibility of a refusal. It was investigation at the last-known real address, and it was conversation with a parent who was concerned about her daughter's whereabouts.

Barber and *Mancusi v. Stubbs, supra,* are the cases in which this Court has explored the issue of constitutional unavailability. Although each is factually distinguishable from this case, *Mancusi* provides significant support for a conclusion of good-faith effort here,[41] and *Barber* has no contrary significance. Insofar as this record discloses no basis for concluding that Anita was abroad, the case is factually weaker than *Mancusi*; but it is stronger than *Mancusi* in the sense that the Ohio prosecutor, unlike the prosecutor in *Mancusi,* had no clear indication, if any at all, of Anita's whereabouts. In *Barber,* the * * * prosecution knew where the witness [who was incarcerated in a federal penitentiary in a neighboring state] was, procedures existed whereby the witness could be brought to the trial, and the witness was not in a position to frustrate efforts to secure his production. Here, Anita's whereabouts were not known, and there was no assurance that she would be found in a place from which she could be forced to return to Ohio.

We conclude that the prosecution carried its burden of demonstrating that Anita was constitutionally unavailable for purposes of respondent's trial.

The judgment of the Supreme Court of Ohio is reversed * * *.

41. In *Mancusi,* the declarant "who had been born in Sweden but had become a naturalized American citizen, had returned to Sweden and taken up permanent residence there." 408 U.S., at 209. While in this country, he had testified against Stubbs at his Tennessee trial for murder and kidnaping. Stubbs was convicted, but obtained habeas corpus relief 10 years later, and was retried by Tennessee. Before the second trial, the prosecution sent a subpoena to be served in Texas, the declarant's last place of residence in this country. It could not be served. The Court rejected Stubbs' assertion that the prosecution had not undertaken good-faith efforts in failing to do more. "Tennessee * * * was powerless to compel his attendance * * * either through its own process or through established procedures." *Id.,* at 212.

MR. JUSTICE BRENNAN, with whom MR. JUSTICE MARSHALL and MR. JUSTICE STEVENS join, dissenting.

* * *

In the present case, I am simply unable to conclude that the prosecution met its burden of establishing Anita Isaacs' unavailability. From all that appears in the record—and there has been no suggestion that the record is incomplete in this respect—the State's *total* effort to secure Anita's attendance at respondent's trial consisted of the delivery of five subpoenas in her name to her parents' residence, and three of those were issued after the authorities had learned that she was no longer living there. At least four months before the trial began, the prosecution was aware that Anita had moved away; yet during that entire interval it did nothing whatsoever to try to make contact with her. It is difficult to believe that the State would have been so derelict in attempting to secure the witness' presence at trial had it not had her favorable preliminary hearing testimony upon which to rely in the event of her "unavailability." The perfunctory steps which the State took in this case can hardly qualify as a "good-faith effort." In point of fact, it was no effort at all. * * *

Notes and Questions

1. *Constitutional unavailability. Roberts* treatment of prior cross-examined hearsay when the declarant is unavailable, like present cross-examination of the declarant about prior statements under *California v. Green*, remains solid precedent. The Constitution as explicated by *Barber v. Page* requires that, before a witness outside the jurisdiction (or inside the jurisdiction but not readily findable) is determined to be unavailable, reasonable efforts must be made to secure the witness' presence, but as *Mancusi v. Stubbs* indicates, not all possible efforts are required. Indeed, the facts of *Roberts* suggest that a limited effort may be sufficient. Nevertheless, the constitutional requirement has teeth beyond mere inability to subpoena the witness. See, e.g., State v. Nobles, 584 S.E.2d 765, 770 (N.C.2003) (failure of prosecution to at least attempt to contact out-of-state witness and request presence violated requirement).

2. *The Roberts system. Roberts* is best known for the general system for handling hearsay under the Confrontation Clause. That system lasted almost a quarter of a century until it was replaced in substantial part by *Crawford v. Washington*, the next principal case. To understand the historical context that *Crawford* dramatically altered, and because *Roberts* may remain valid outside of the core area of Confrontation Clause concern covered by *Crawford*, the general dimensions of its system are set out.

Roberts' general statement for Confrontation Clause treatment of hearsay is:

> In sum, when a hearsay declarant is not present for cross-examination at trial, the Confrontation Clause normally requires a showing that he is unavailable. Even then, his statement is admissible only if it bears adequate "indicia of reliability." Reliability can be inferred without

> more in a case where the evidence falls within a firmly rooted hearsay exception. In other cases, the evidence must be excluded, at least absent a showing of particularized guarantees of trustworthiness.

This produced two areas of analysis for statements—(1) reliability and (2) unavailability.

3. *Reliability—"Firmly rooted" hearsay.* Under *Roberts*, the "indicia of reliability" necessary for a hearsay statement to meet the Confrontation Clause is automatically established if the statement falls within a "firmly rooted" hearsay exception. For a time after *Roberts*, courts and commentators debated the basis for judging an exception to be "firmly rooted"—does it relate to the inherent reliability of the statement or to the exception's longevity and widespread acceptance? See Goldman, Not So "Firmly Rooted": Exceptions to the Confrontation Clause, 66 N.C.L.Rev. 1 (1987). In Bourjaily v. United States, 483 U.S. 171, 183 (1987), the Court adopted the latter view. See also Idaho v. Wright, 497 U.S. 805, 817 (1990) ("Admission under a firmly rooted hearsay exception satisfies the constitutional requirement of reliability because of the weight accorded longstanding judicial and legislative experience in assessing the trustworthiness of certain types of out-of-court statements.").

Bourjaily provided a particularly difficult test for the proposition that all "firmly rooted" exceptions or exemptions are to be deemed sufficiently trustworthy to satisfy the Confrontation Clause. This is because the coconspirator exemption, like other admissions, "has never been justified primarily upon reliability or trustworthiness grounds and its reliability safeguards are not extensive." 483 U.S. at 201 (Blackmun, J, dissenting). Indeed, for this reason, many courts had read *Roberts* to require that in addition to meeting the coconspirator rule, the statement had to be shown to have independent indicia of reliability. The Supreme Court majority laid this argument to rest: "We think that the co-conspirator exception to the hearsay rule is firmly enough rooted in our jurisprudence that, under this Court's holding in *Roberts,* a court need not independently inquire into reliability of such statements." 483 U.S. at 183.

4. *Reliability—Occasionally a firmly rooted hearsay exception is troublesome. Bourjaily* gave a strong indication that the Court did not want to fine-tune reliability analysis once it was determined that the hearsay fell within a "firmly rooted" hearsay exception. However, resolving reliability concerns by reference to whether a statement fit within an established hearsay exception proved to have some limits. In Lilly v. Virginia, 527 U.S. 116 (1999), the Court found that admission of statements that fell within Virginia's exception for statements against interest, a long-standing and broadly adopted hearsay rule (see Federal Rule 804(b)(3)), nevertheless violated the Confrontation Clause. A plurality of the Court concluded that statements against penal interest were not firmly rooted when they were "accomplice's statements that shift or spread blame" to co-participants. Id. at 130–34. Additional members of the Court concluded that the particular statements violated the Confrontation Clause because they were not in fact against interest and were part of a custodial confession. Id. at 146–48. Thus, at least some portions of some traditional exceptions are not firmly rooted. See also Mosteller, The Maturation and Disintegration of the Hearsay

Exception for Statements for Medical Examination in Child Sexual Abuse Cases, 65 Law & Contemp. Probs., Winter 2002, at 47, 52 & 94 (arguing that statements under Rule 803(4) that are made solely for the purpose of diagnosis without any treatment motivation are not "firmly rooted"). For further development of the issue, see the notes after *Williamson*, Chapter 14, Section J, infra.

5. *Reliability—External corroboration not useable as indicia of trustworthiness.* When a hearsay statement does not fall within a "firmly rooted" exception, *Roberts* holds that the Confrontation Clause requires a showing of "particularized guarantees of trustworthiness." In Idaho v. Wright, 497 U.S. 805, 819–23 (1990), the Supreme Court ruled that such guarantees could not be shown by corroborating of the truth of the hearsay statement. Writing for the majority, Justice O'Connor reasoned:

> [Our conclusion that] the relevant circumstances include only those that surround the making of the statement and that render the declarant particularly worthy of belief * * * derives from the rationale for permitting exceptions to the general rule against hearsay:
>
> > "The theory of the hearsay rule * * * is that the many possible sources of inaccuracy and untrustworthiness which may lie underneath the bare untested assertion of a witness can best be brought to light and exposed, if they exist, by the test of cross-examination. But this test or security may in a given instance be superfluous; it may be sufficiently clear, in that instance, that the statement offered is free enough from the risk of inaccuracy and untrustworthiness, so that the test of cross-examination would be a work of supererogation." 5 J. Wigmore, Evidence § 1420, p. 251 (J. Chadbourn rev. 1974).
>
> In other words, if the declarant's truthfulness is so clear from the surrounding circumstances that the test of cross-examination would be of marginal utility, then the hearsay rule does not bar admission of the statement at trial. The basis for the "excited utterance" exception, for example, is that such statements are given under circumstances that eliminate the possibility of fabrication, coaching, or confabulation, and that therefore the circumstances surrounding the making of the statement provide sufficient assurance that the statement is trustworthy and that cross-examination would be superfluous. See, e.g., 6 Wigmore, supra, §§ 1745–1764 * * *.
>
> We think the "particularized guarantees of trustworthiness" required for admission under the Confrontation Clause must likewise be drawn from the totality of circumstances that surround the making of the statement and that render the declarant particularly worthy of belief. Our precedents have recognized that statements admitted under a "firmly rooted" hearsay exception are so trustworthy that adversarial testing would add little to their reliability. * * * Because evidence possessing "particularized guarantees of trustworthiness" must be at least as reliable as evidence admitted under a firmly rooted hearsay exception, * * * we think that evidence admitted under the former requirement must similarly be so trustworthy that adversarial testing would add little to its reliability. * * *

> * * * To be admissible under the Confrontation Clause, hearsay evidence used to convict a defendant must possess indicia of reliability by virtue of its inherent trustworthiness, not by reference to other evidence at trial. * * * "[T]he Clause countenances only hearsay marked with such trustworthiness that 'there is no material departure from the reason of the general rule.'" Roberts, supra, 448 U.S., at 65 (quoting Snyder v. Massachusetts, 291 U.S. 97, 107 (1934)). A statement made under duress, for example, may happen to be a true statement, but the circumstances under which it is made may provide no basis for supposing that the declarant is particularly likely to be telling the truth—indeed, the circumstances may even be such that the declarant is particularly unlikely to be telling the truth. In such a case, cross-examination at trial would be highly useful to probe the declarant's state of mind when he made the statements; the presence of evidence tending to corroborate the truth of the statement would be no substitute for cross-examination of the declarant at trial.
>
> In short, the use of corroborating evidence to support a hearsay statement's "particularized guarantees of trustworthiness" would permit admission of a presumptively unreliable statement by bootstrapping on the trustworthiness of other evidence at trial, a result we think at odds with the requirement that hearsay evidence admitted under the Confrontation Clause be so trustworthy that cross-examination of the declarant would be of marginal utility.

Justice Kennedy, for four dissenters, argued that there is "no constitutional justification for this decision to prescind corroborating evidence from consideration of the question whether a child's statements are reliable. It is a matter of common sense for most people that one of the best ways to determine whether what someone says is trustworthy is to see if it is corroborated by other evidence." 497 U.S. at 828.

Wright means that the trustworthiness of a hearsay statement cannot be corroborated by other evidence such as physical proof of the crime. See, e.g., State v. Matsamas, 808 P.2d 1048, 1055 (Utah 1991) (evidence of sexually transmitted disease cannot be used to corroborate child's statement of sexual abuse). But while *Wright* eliminates use of external corroborating evidence for the purpose of satisfying the Confrontation Clause, such evidence may be used to show that any error in admitting the hearsay was harmless. 497 U.S. at 823.

6. *The Catchall Hearsay Exception—Use of external corroboration to establish trustworthiness.* When the Confrontation Clause is inapplicable or otherwise satisfied (e.g., the declarant is available for cross-examination), can corroboration that under *Wright* may not be used to establish trustworthiness under the Confrontation Clause be employed to establish trustworthiness for the purposes of hearsay analysis under the residual hearsay exception, Federal Rule 807? See the notes after *Bohler-Uddeholm America, Inc. v. Ellwood Group, Inc.*, Chapter 14, Section L, infra.

7. *Unavailability—Frequently need not be shown.* In United States v. Inadi, 475 U.S. 387 (1986), as to coconspirator statements, and in White v. Illinois, 502 U.S. 346 (1992), as to excited utterances and statements for medical treatment, the Court ruled that unavailability need not be shown

under *Roberts* because the statements fell within these hearsay exceptions. It reasoned that the circumstances of the making of those out-of-court statements and/or the motivation of the declarant gave them "independent evidentiary significance," *Inadi*, 475 U.S. at 394, that could not likely be replicated if the declarant was asked to make the same statement in court. These cases noted that, while *Roberts* stated the unavailability requirement as generally applicable, it relied exclusively on cases involving hearsay admitted under a single hearsay exception—prior testimony.

After *White*, *Roberts'* "unavailability" requirement was transformed, and unavailability was not required for any of the specific hearsay exceptions contained in Federal Rule 803. Under the theory that placed each of these exceptions within Rule 803, where the availability of the declarant is considered irrelevant, the out-of-court statement is in some way superior to or at least equivalent to in-court testimony, which under the *Inadi/White* theory eliminates any constitutional requirement that unavailability be shown. A few questions remained, such as whether the Confrontation Clause under *Roberts* required that unavailability be demonstrated for any or all of the statements admitted under Rule 807, the residual or catchall exception, and whether there was a relationship between an exception not being "firmly rooted" and the unavailability requirement? See Stuart v. Wilson, 442 F.3d 506, 514–21 (6th Cir.2006) (finding confrontation law not clearly established as to whether unavailability need be shown for child's hearsay statement admitted under catchall exception).

8. *Confrontation challenge under Roberts typically resolved by hearsay admissibility.* After the clarifying cases, Confrontation Clause analysis under *Roberts* and admission under the hearsay rules largely merged into a single inquiry for most hearsay statements. The sole issue was whether the statement was admissible under an established hearsay exception. Statements admitted under newly created exceptions or through the residual or catchall exception still had to be independently and individually examined. However, for most hearsay, if the statement was admissible under an established evidentiary rule, the Confrontation Clause provided no additional barrier.

This was the state of the law when *Crawford v. Washington*, which follows, was decided.

CRAWFORD v. WASHINGTON

Supreme Court of the United States, 2004.
541 U.S. 36.

JUSTICE SCALIA delivered the opinion of the Court.

Petitioner Michael Crawford stabbed a man who allegedly tried to rape his wife, Sylvia. At his trial, the State played for the jury Sylvia's tape-recorded statement to the police describing the stabbing, even though he had no opportunity for cross-examination. The Washington Supreme Court upheld petitioner's conviction after determining that Sylvia's statement was reliable. The question presented is whether this procedure complied with the Sixth Amendment's guarantee that, "[i]n all criminal prosecutions, the accused shall enjoy the right * * * to be confronted with the witnesses against him."

I

On August 5, 1999, Kenneth Lee was stabbed at his apartment. Police arrested petitioner later that night. After giving petitioner and his wife *Miranda* warnings, detectives interrogated each of them twice. Petitioner eventually confessed that he and Sylvia had gone in search of Lee because he was upset over an earlier incident in which Lee had tried to rape her. The two had found Lee at his apartment, and a fight ensued in which Lee was stabbed in the torso and petitioner's hand was cut.

Petitioner gave the following account of the fight:

"Q. Okay. Did you ever see anything in [Lee's] hands?

"A. I think so, but I'm not positive.

"Q. Okay, when you think so, what do you mean by that?

"A. I coulda swore I seen him goin' for somethin' before, right before everything happened. He was like reachin', fiddlin' around down here and stuff * * * and I just * * * I don't know, I think, this is just a possibility, but I think, I think that he pulled somethin' out and I grabbed for it and that's how I got cut * * * but I'm not positive. I, I, my mind goes blank when things like this happen. I mean, I just, I remember things wrong, I remember things that just doesn't, don't make sense to me later." (punctuation added).

Sylvia generally corroborated petitioner's story about the events leading up to the fight, but her account of the fight itself was arguably different—particularly with respect to whether Lee had drawn a weapon before petitioner assaulted him:

"Q. Did Kenny do anything to fight back from this assault?

"A. pausing) I know he reached into his pocket * * * or somethin' * * * I don't know what.

"Q. After he was stabbed?

"A. He saw Michael coming up. He lifted his hand * * * his chest open, he might [have] went to go strike his hand out or something and then (inaudible).

"Q. Okay, you, you gotta speak up.

"A. Okay, he lifted his hand over his head maybe to strike Michael's hand down or something and then he put his hands in his * * * put his right hand in his right pocket * * * took a step back * * * Michael proceeded to stab him * * * then his hands were like * * * how do you explain this * * * open arms * * * with his hands open and he fell down * * * and we ran (describing subject holding hands open, palms toward assailant).

"Q. Okay, when he's standing there with his open hands, you're talking about Kenny, correct?

"A. Yeah, after, after the fact, yes.

"Q. Did you see anything in his hands at that point?

"A. (pausing) um um (no)." *Id.,* at 137 (punctuation added).

The State charged petitioner with assault and attempted murder. At trial, he claimed self-defense. Sylvia did not testify because of the state marital privilege, which generally bars a spouse from testifying without the other spouse's consent. See Wash. Rev.Code § 5.60.060(1) (1994). In Washington, this privilege does not extend to a spouse's out-of-court statements admissible under a hearsay exception, see *State v. Burden,* 120 Wash.2d 371, 377, 841 P.2d 758, 761 (1992), so the State sought to introduce Sylvia's tape-recorded statements to the police as evidence that the stabbing was not in self-defense. Noting that Sylvia had admitted she led petitioner to Lee's apartment and thus had facilitated the assault, the State invoked the hearsay exception for statements against penal interest, Wash. Rule Evid. 804(b)(3) (2003).

Petitioner countered that, state law notwithstanding, admitting the evidence would violate his federal constitutional right to be "confronted with the witnesses against him." Amdt. 6. According to our description of that right in *Ohio v. Roberts,* 448 U.S. 56 (1980), it does not bar admission of an unavailable witness's statement against a criminal defendant if the statement bears "adequate 'indicia of reliability.'" *Id.,* at 66. To meet that test, evidence must either fall within a "firmly rooted hearsay exception" or bear "particularized guarantees of trustworthiness." *Ibid.* The trial court here admitted the statement on the latter ground, offering several reasons why it was trustworthy: Sylvia was not shifting blame but rather corroborating her husband's story that he acted in self-defense or "justified reprisal"; she had direct knowledge as an eyewitness; she was describing recent events; and she was being questioned by a "neutral" law enforcement officer. The prosecution played the tape for the jury and relied on it in closing, arguing that it was "damning evidence" that "completely refutes [petitioner's] claim of self-defense." The jury convicted petitioner of assault.

The Washington Court of Appeals reversed. It applied a nine-factor test to determine whether Sylvia's statement bore particularized guarantees of trustworthiness, and noted several reasons why it did not: The statement contradicted one she had previously given; it was made in response to specific questions; and at one point she admitted she had shut her eyes during the stabbing. The court considered and rejected the State's argument that Sylvia's statement was reliable because it coincided with petitioner's to such a degree that the two "interlocked." The court determined that, although the two statements agreed about the events leading up to the stabbing, they differed on the issue crucial to petitioner's self-defense claim: "[Petitioner's] version asserts that Lee may have had something in his hand when he stabbed him; but Sylvia's version has Lee grabbing for something only after he has been stabbed."

The Washington Supreme Court reinstated the conviction, unanimously concluding that, although Sylvia's statement did not fall under a firmly rooted hearsay exception, it bore guarantees of trustworthiness: " '[W]hen a codefendant's confession is virtually identical [to, *i.e.,* interlocks with,] that of a defendant, it may be deemed reliable.' " * * *. The court explained:

> "Although the Court of Appeals concluded that the statements were contradictory, upon closer inspection they appear to overlap * * *.
>
> "[B]oth of the Crawfords' statements indicate that Lee was possibly grabbing for a weapon, but they are equally unsure when this event may have taken place. They are also equally unsure how Michael received the cut on his hand, leading the court to question when, if ever, Lee possessed a weapon. In this respect they overlap.
>
> "[N]either Michael nor Sylvia clearly stated that Lee had a weapon in hand from which Michael was simply defending himself. And it is this omission by both that interlocks the statements and makes Sylvia's statement reliable." 147 Wash.2d, at 438–439, 54 P.3d, at 664 (internal quotation marks omitted).[42]

We granted certiorari to determine whether the State's use of Sylvia's statement violated the Confrontation Clause. 539 U.S. 914 (2003).

II

The Sixth Amendment's Confrontation Clause provides that, "[i]n all criminal prosecutions, the accused shall enjoy the right * * * to be confronted with the witnesses against him." We have held that this bedrock procedural guarantee applies to both federal and state prosecutions. *Pointer v. Texas,* 380 U.S. 400, 406 (1965). As noted above, *Roberts* says that an unavailable witness's out-of-court statement may be admitted so long as it has adequate indicia of reliability—*i.e.,* falls within a "firmly rooted hearsay exception" or bears "particularized guarantees of trustworthiness." 448 U.S., at 66. Petitioner argues that this test strays from the original meaning of the Confrontation Clause and urges us to reconsider it.

A

The Constitution's text does not alone resolve this case. One could plausibly read "witnesses against" a defendant to mean those who actually testify at trial, cf. *Woodsides v. State,* 3 Miss. 655, 664–665 (1837), those whose statements are offered at trial, see 3 J. Wigmore, Evidence § 1397, p. 104 (2d ed.1923) (hereinafter Wigmore), or some-

42. The court rejected the State's argument that guarantees of trustworthiness were unnecessary since petitioner waived his confrontation rights by invoking the marital privilege. It reasoned that "forcing the defendant to choose between the marital privilege and confronting his spouse presents an untenable Hobson's choice." * * * The State has not challenged this holding here. The State also has not challenged the Court of Appeals' conclusion (not reached by the State Supreme Court) that the confrontation violation, if it occurred, was not harmless. We express no opinion on these matters.

thing in-between, see *infra,* at 52–53. We must therefore turn to the historical background of the Clause to understand its meaning.

The right to confront one's accusers is a concept that dates back to Roman times. * * *. The founding generation's immediate source of the concept, however, was the common law. English common law has long differed from continental civil law in regard to the manner in which witnesses give testimony in criminal trials. The common-law tradition is one of live testimony in court subject to adversarial testing, while the civil law condones examination in private by judicial officers. See 3 W. Blackstone, Commentaries on the Laws of England 373–374 (1768).

Nonetheless, England at times adopted elements of the civil-law practice. Justices of the peace or other officials examined suspects and witnesses before trial. These examinations were sometimes read in court in lieu of live testimony, a practice that "occasioned frequent demands by the prisoner to have his 'accusers,' *i.e.* the witnesses against him, brought before him face to face." 1 J. Stephen, History of the Criminal Law of England 326 (1883). In some cases, these demands were refused. See 9 W. Holdsworth, History of English Law 216–217, 228 (3d ed.1944); *e.g., Raleigh's Case,* 2 How. St. Tr. 1, 15–16, 24 (1603) * * *.

Pretrial examinations became routine under two statutes passed during the reign of Queen Mary in the 16th century, 1 & 2 Phil. & M., c. 13 (1554), and 2 & 3 *id.,* c. 10 (1555). These Marian bail and committal statutes required justices of the peace to examine suspects and witnesses in felony cases and to certify the results to the court. It is doubtful that the original purpose of the examinations was to produce evidence admissible at trial. See J. Langbein, Prosecuting Crime in the Renaissance 21–34 (1974). Whatever the original purpose, however, they came to be used as evidence in some cases, see 2 M. Hale, Pleas of the Crown 284 (1736), resulting in an adoption of continental procedure. See 4 Holdsworth, *supra,* at 528–530.

The most notorious instances of civil-law examination occurred in the great political trials of the 16th and 17th centuries. One such was the 1603 trial of Sir Walter Raleigh for treason. Lord Cobham, Raleigh's alleged accomplice, had implicated him in an examination before the Privy Council and in a letter. At Raleigh's trial, these were read to the jury. Raleigh argued that Cobham had lied to save himself: "Cobham is absolutely in the King's mercy; to excuse me cannot avail him; by accusing me he may hope for favour." 1 D. Jardine, Criminal Trials 435 (1832). Suspecting that Cobham would recant, Raleigh demanded that the judges call him to appear, arguing that "[t]he Proof of the Common Law is by witness and jury: let Cobham be here, let him speak it. Call my accuser before my face * * *." 2 How. St. Tr., at 15–16. The judges refused, *id.,* at 24, and, despite Raleigh's protestations that he was being tried "by the Spanish Inquisition," *id.,* at 15, the jury convicted, and Raleigh was sentenced to death.

One of Raleigh's trial judges later lamented that " 'the justice of England has never been so degraded and injured as by the condemnation of Sir Walter Raleigh.' " 1 Jardine, *supra,* at 520. Through a series of statutory and judicial reforms, English law developed a right of confrontation that limited these abuses. For example, treason statutes required witnesses to confront the accused "face to face" at his arraignment. *E.g.,* 13 Car. 2, c. 1, § 5 (1661); see 1 Hale, *supra,* at 306. Courts, meanwhile, developed relatively strict rules of unavailability, admitting examinations only if the witness was demonstrably unable to testify in person. See *Lord Morley's Case,* 6 How. St. Tr. 769, 770–771 (H.L.1666); 2 Hale, *supra,* at 284; 1 Stephen, *supra,* at 358. Several authorities also stated that a suspect's confession could be admitted only against himself, and not against others he implicated. See 2 W. Hawkins, Pleas of the Crown c. 46, § 3, pp. 603–604 (T. Leach 6th ed. 1787) * * *.

B

Controversial examination practices were also used in the Colonies. Early in the 18th century, for example, the Virginia Council protested against the Governor for having "privately issued several commissions to examine witnesses against particular men *ex parte,*" complaining that "the person accused is not admitted to be confronted with, or defend himself against his defamers." A Memorial Concerning the Maladministrations of His Excellency Francis Nicholson, reprinted in 9 English Historical Documents 253, 257 (D. Douglas ed.1955). A decade before the Revolution, England gave jurisdiction over Stamp Act offenses to the admiralty courts, which followed civil-law rather than common-law procedures and thus routinely took testimony by deposition or private judicial examination. See 5 Geo. 3, c. 12, § 57 (1765); Pollitt, The Right of Confrontation: Its History and Modern Dress, 8 J. Pub.L. 381, 396–397 (1959). Colonial representatives protested that the Act subverted their rights "by extending the jurisdiction of the courts of admiralty beyond its ancient limits." Resolutions of the Stamp Act Congress § 8th (Oct. 19, 1765), reprinted in Sources of Our Liberties 270, 271 (R. Perry & J. Cooper eds.1959). John Adams, defending a merchant in a high-profile admiralty case, argued: "Examinations of witnesses upon Interrogatories, are only by the Civil Law. Interrogatories are unknown at common Law, and Englishmen and common Lawyers have an aversion to them if not an Abhorrence of them." Draft of Argument in *Sewall v. Hancock* (1768–1769), in 2 Legal Papers of John Adams 194, 207 (K. Wroth & H. Zobel eds.1965).

Many declarations of rights adopted around the time of the Revolution guaranteed a right of confrontation [1776—Virginia, Pennsylvania, Delaware, Maryland, North Carolina; 1777 Vermont; 1780—Massachusetts; 1783—New Hampshire]. The proposed Federal Constitution, however, did not. At the Massachusetts ratifying convention, Abraham Holmes objected to this omission precisely on the ground that it would lead to civil-law practices: "The mode of trial is altogether indetermined; * * * whether [the defendant] is to be allowed to confront the witnesses, and have the advantage of cross-examination, we are not yet told * * *. [W]e shall find Congress possessed of powers enabling them to institute judicatories little less inauspicious than a certain tribunal in Spain, * * * the *Inquisition.*" 2 Debates on the Federal Constitution 110–111 (J. Elliot 2d ed. 1863). Similarly, a prominent Antifederalist writing under the pseudonym Federal Farmer criticized the use of "written evidence" while objecting to the omission of a vicinage right: "Nothing can be more essential than the cross examining [of] witnesses, and generally before the triers of the facts in question * * *. [W]ritten evidence * * * [is] almost useless; it must be frequently taken ex parte, and but very seldom leads to the proper discovery of truth." R. Lee, Letter IV by the Federal Farmer (Oct. 15, 1787), reprinted in 1 Schwartz, *supra,* at 469, 473. The First Congress responded by including the Confrontation Clause in the proposal that became the Sixth Amendment.

Early state decisions shed light upon the original understanding of the common-law right. *State v. Webb,* 2 N.C. 103 (1794) *(per curiam),* decided a mere three years after the adoption of the Sixth Amendment, held that depositions could be read against an accused only if they were taken in his presence. Rejecting a broader reading of the English authorities, the court held: "[I]t is a rule of the common law, founded on natural justice, that no man shall be prejudiced by evidence which he had not the liberty to cross examine." *Id.,* at 104.

Similarly, in *State v. Campbell,* 1 Rich. 124, 1844 WL 2558 (S.C. 1844), South Carolina's highest law court excluded a deposition taken by a coroner in the absence of the accused. * * * Many other decisions are to the same effect. Some early cases went so far as to hold that prior testimony was inadmissible in criminal cases *even if* the accused had a previous opportunity to cross-examine. See *Finn v. Commonwealth,* 26 Va. 701, 708 (1827) * * *. Most courts rejected that view, but only after reaffirming that admissibility depended on a prior opportunity for cross-examination. See *United States v. Macomb,* 26 F.Cas. 1132, 1133 (No. 15,702) (CC Ill. 1851); *State v. Houser,* 26 Mo. 431, 435–436 (1858) * * *.

III

This history supports two inferences about the meaning of the Sixth Amendment.

A

First, the principal evil at which the Confrontation Clause was directed was the civil-law mode of criminal procedure, and particularly its use of *ex parte* examinations as evidence against the accused. It was these practices that the Crown deployed in notorious treason cases like Raleigh's; that the Marian statutes invited; that English law's assertion of a right to confrontation was meant to prohibit; and that the founding-era rhetoric decried. The Sixth Amendment must be interpreted with this focus in mind.

Accordingly, we once again reject the view that the Confrontation Clause applies of its own force only to in-court testimony, and that its application to out-of-court statements introduced at trial depends upon "the law of Evidence for the time being." 3 Wigmore § 1397, at 101; accord, *Dutton v. Evans,* 400 U.S. 74, 94 (1970) (Harlan, J., concurring in result). Leaving the regulation of out-of-court statements to the law of evidence would render the Confrontation Clause powerless to prevent even the most flagrant inquisitorial practices. Raleigh was, after all, perfectly free to confront those who read Cobham's confession in court.

This focus also suggests that not all hearsay implicates the Sixth Amendment's core concerns. An off-hand, overheard remark might be unreliable evidence and thus a good candidate for exclusion under hearsay rules, but it bears little resemblance to the civil-law abuses the Confrontation Clause targeted. On the other hand, *ex parte* examinations might sometimes be admissible under modern hearsay rules, but the Framers certainly would not have condoned them.

The text of the Confrontation Clause reflects this focus. It applies to "witnesses" against the accused—in other words, those who "bear testimony." 1 N. Webster, An American Dictionary of the English Language (1828). "Testimony," in turn, is typically "[a] solemn declaration or affirmation made for the purpose of establishing or proving some fact." *Ibid.* An accuser who makes a formal statement to government officers bears testimony in a sense that a person who makes a casual remark to an acquaintance does not. The constitutional text, like the history underlying the common-law right of confrontation, thus reflects an especially acute concern with a specific type of out-of-court statement.

Various formulations of this core class of "testimonial" statements exist: "*ex parte* in-court testimony or its functional equivalent—that is, material such as affidavits, custodial examinations, prior testimony that the defendant was unable to cross-examine, or similar pretrial statements that declarants would reasonably expect to be used prosecutorially," Brief for Petitioner 23; "extrajudicial statements * * * contained in formalized testimonial materials, such as affidavits, depositions, prior testimony, or confessions," *White v. Illinois,* 502 U.S. 346, 365 (1992) (THOMAS, J., joined by SCALIA, J., concurring in part and concurring in judgment); "statements that were made under circumstances which would lead an objective witness reasonably to believe that the statement would be available for use at a later trial," Brief for National Association of Criminal Defense Lawyers et al. as *Amici Curiae* 3. These formulations all share a common nucleus and then define the Clause's coverage at various levels of abstraction around it. Regardless of the precise articulation, some statements qualify under any definition—for example, *ex parte* testimony at a preliminary hearing.

Statements taken by police officers in the course of interrogations are also testimonial under even a narrow standard. Police interrogations bear a striking resemblance to examinations by justices of the peace in England. The statements are not *sworn* testimony, but the absence of oath was not dispositive. Cobham's examination was unsworn, see 1 Jardine, Criminal Trials, at 430, yet Raleigh's trial has long been thought a paradigmatic confrontation violation, see, *e.g., Campbell,* 1 Rich., at 130. Under the Marian statutes, witnesses were typically put on oath, but suspects were not. See 2 Hale, Pleas of the Crown, at 52. Yet Hawkins and others went out of their way to caution that such unsworn confessions were not admissible against anyone but the confessor. See *supra,* at 45.

That interrogators are police officers rather than magistrates does not change the picture either. Justices of the peace conducting examinations under the Marian statutes were not magistrates as we understand that office today, but had an essentially investigative and prosecutorial function. See 1 Stephen, Criminal Law of England, at 221; Langbein, Prosecuting Crime in the Renaissance, at 34–45. England did not have a professional police force until the 19th century, see 1 Stephen, *supra,* at 194–200, so it is not surprising that other government officers performed the investigative functions now associated primarily with the police. The involvement of government officers in the production of testimonial evidence presents the same risk, whether the officers are police or justices of the peace.

In sum, even if the Sixth Amendment is not solely concerned with testimonial hearsay, that is its primary object, and interrogations by law enforcement officers fall squarely within that class.[43]

B

The historical record also supports a second proposition: that the Framers would not have allowed admission of testimonial statements of a witness who did not appear at trial unless he was unavailable to testify, and the defendant had had a prior opportunity for cross-examination. The text of the Sixth Amendment does not suggest any open-ended exceptions from the confrontation requirement to be developed by the courts. Rather, the "right * * * to be confronted with the witnesses against him," Amdt. 6, is most naturally read as a reference to the right of confrontation at common law, admitting only those exceptions established at the time of the founding. See *Mattox v. United States,* 156 U.S. 237, 243 (1895); cf. *Houser,* 26 Mo., at 433–435. As the English authorities above reveal, the common law in 1791 conditioned admissibility of an absent witness's examination on unavailability and a prior opportunity to cross-examine. The Sixth Amendment therefore incorporates those limitations. The numerous early state decisions applying the same test confirm that these principles were received as part of the common law in this country.

We do not read the historical sources to say that a prior opportunity to cross-examine was merely a sufficient, rather than a necessary,

43. We use the term "interrogation" in its colloquial, rather than any technical legal, sense. Cf. *Rhode Island v. Innis,* 446 U.S. 291, 300–01 (1980). Just as various definitions of "testimonial" exist, one can imagine various definitions of "interrogation," and we need not select among them in this case. Sylvia's recorded statement, knowingly given in response to structured police questioning, qualifies under any conceivable definition.

condition for admissibility of testimonial statements. They suggest that this requirement was dispositive, and not merely one of several ways to establish reliability. This is not to deny, as THE CHIEF JUSTICE notes, that "[t]here were always exceptions to the general rule of exclusion" of hearsay evidence. * * * Several had become well established by 1791. See 3 Wigmore § 1397, at 101; Brief for United States as *Amicus Curiae* 13, n.5. But there is scant evidence that exceptions were invoked to admit *testimonial* statements against the accused in a *criminal* case.[44] Most of the hearsay exceptions covered statements that by their nature were not testimonial—for example, business records or statements in furtherance of a conspiracy. We do not infer from these that the Framers thought exceptions would apply even to prior testimony. Cf. *Lilly v. Virginia,* 527 U.S. 116, 134 (1999) (plurality opinion) ("[A]ccomplices' confessions that inculpate a criminal defendant are not within a firmly rooted exception to the hearsay rule").[45]

IV

Our case law has been largely consistent with these two principles. Our leading early decision, for example, involved a deceased witness's prior trial testimony. *Mattox v. United States,* 156 U.S. 237 (1895). In allowing the statement to be admitted, we relied on the fact that the defendant had had, at the first trial, an adequate opportunity to confront the witness: "The substance of the constitutional protection is preserved to the prisoner in the advantage he has once had of seeing the witness face to face, and of subjecting him to the ordeal of a cross-examination. This, the law says, he shall under no circumstances be deprived of * * *." *Id.,* at 244.

Our later cases conform to *Mattox's* holding that prior trial or preliminary hearing testimony is admissible only if the defendant had an adequate opportunity to cross-examine. See *Mancusi v. Stubbs,* 408 U.S. 204, 213–16 (1972); *California v. Green,* 399 U.S. 149, 165–68 (1970); *Pointer v. Texas,* 380 U.S., at 406–08; cf. *Kirby v. United States,* 174 U.S.

44. The one deviation we have found involves dying declarations. The existence of that exception as a general rule of criminal hearsay law cannot be disputed. See, *e.g., Mattox v. United States,* 156 U.S. 237, 243–44 (1895); *King v. Reason,* 16 How. St. Tr. 1, 24–38 (K.B.1722); 1 D. Jardine, Criminal Trials 435 (1832); Cooley, Constitutional Limitations, at *318; 1 G. Gilbert, Evidence 211 (C. Lofft ed. 1791); see also F. Heller, The Sixth Amendment 105 (1951) (asserting that this was the *only* recognized criminal hearsay exception at common law). Although many dying declarations may not be testimonial, there is authority for admitting even those that clearly are. See *Woodcock, supra,* at 501–504, 168 Eng. Rep., at 353–354; *Reason, supra,* at 24–38; Peake, Evidence, at 64; cf. *Radbourne, supra,* at 460–462, 168 Eng. Rep., at 332–333. We need not decide in this case whether the Sixth Amendment incorporates an exception for testimonial dying declarations. If this exception must be accepted on historical grounds, it is *sui generis.*

45. We cannot agree with THE CHIEF JUSTICE that the fact "[t]hat a statement might be testimonial does nothing to undermine the wisdom of one of these [hearsay] exceptions." *Post,* at 74. Involvement of government officers in the production of testimony with an eye toward trial presents unique potential for prosecutorial abuse—a fact borne out time and again throughout a history with which the Framers were keenly familiar. This consideration does not evaporate when testimony happens to fall within some broad, modern hearsay exception, even if that exception might be justifiable in other circumstances.

47, 55–61 (1899). Even where the defendant had such an opportunity, we excluded the testimony where the government had not established unavailability of the witness. See *Barber v. Page,* 390 U.S. 719, 722–25 (1968); cf. *Motes v. United States,* 178 U.S. 458, 470–71 (1900). We similarly excluded accomplice confessions where the defendant had no opportunity to cross-examine. See *Roberts v. Russell,* 392 U.S. 293, 294–95 (1968) *(per curiam); Bruton v. United States,* 391 U.S. 123, 126–28 (1968); *Douglas v. Alabama,* 380 U.S. 415, 418–20 (1965). In contrast, we considered reliability factors beyond prior opportunity for cross-examination when the hearsay statement at issue was not testimonial. See *Dutton v. Evans,* 400 U.S., at 87–89 (plurality opinion).

Even our recent cases, in their outcomes, hew closely to the traditional line. *Ohio v. Roberts,* 448 U.S., at 67–70, admitted testimony from a preliminary hearing at which the defendant had examined the witness. *Lilly v. Virginia, supra,* excluded testimonial statements that the defendant had had no opportunity to test by cross-examination. And *Bourjaily v. United States,* 483 U.S. 171, 181–84 (1987), admitted statements made unwittingly to an FBI informant after applying a more general test that did *not* make prior cross-examination an indispensable requirement.[46]

Lee v. Illinois, 476 U.S. 530 (1986), on which the State relies, is not to the contrary. There, we *rejected* the State's attempt to admit an accomplice confession. The State had argued that the confession was admissible because it "interlocked" with the defendant's. We dealt with the argument by rejecting its premise, holding that "when the discrepancies between the statements are not insignificant, the codefendant's confession may not be admitted." *Id.,* at 545. Respondent argues that "[t]he logical inference of this statement is that when the discrepancies between the statements *are* insignificant, then the codefendant's statement *may* be admitted." Brief for Respondent 6. But this is merely a possible inference, not an inevitable one, and we do not draw it here. If *Lee* had meant authoritatively to announce an exception—previously unknown to this Court's jurisprudence—for interlocking confessions, it would not have done so in such an oblique manner. Our only precedent on interlocking confessions had addressed the entirely different question whether a limiting instruction cured prejudice to codefendants from admitting a defendant's own confession against him in a joint trial. See

46. One case arguably in tension with the rule requiring a prior opportunity for cross-examination when the proffered statement is testimonial is *White v. Illinois,* 502 U.S. 346 (1992), which involved, *inter alia,* statements of a child victim to an investigating police officer admitted as spontaneous declarations. *Id.,* at 349–351. It is questionable whether testimonial statements would ever have been admissible on that ground in 1791; to the extent the hearsay exception for spontaneous declarations existed at all, it required that the statements be made "immediat[ely] upon the hurt received, and before [the declarant] had time to devise or contrive any thing for her own advantage." *Thompson v. Trevanion,* Skin. 402, 90 Eng. Rep. 179 (K.B.1694). In any case, the only question presented in *White* was whether the Confrontation Clause imposed an unavailability requirement on the types of hearsay at issue. See 502 U.S., at 348–49. The holding did not address the question whether certain of the statements, because they were testimonial, had to be excluded *even if* the witness was unavailable. We "[took] as a given * * * that the testimony properly falls within the relevant hearsay exceptions." *Id.,* at 351, n.4.

Parker v. Randolph, 442 U.S. 62, 69–76 (1979) (plurality opinion), abrogated by *Cruz v. New York,* 481 U.S. 186 (1987).

Our cases have thus remained faithful to the Framers' understanding: Testimonial statements of witnesses absent from trial have been admitted only where the declarant is unavailable, and only where the defendant has had a prior opportunity to cross-examine.[47]

V

Although the results of our decisions have generally been faithful to the original meaning of the Confrontation Clause, the same cannot be said of our rationales. *Roberts* conditions the admissibility of all hearsay evidence on whether it falls under a "firmly rooted hearsay exception" or bears "particularized guarantees of trustworthiness." 448 U.S., at 66. This test departs from the historical principles identified above in two respects. First, it is too broad: It applies the same mode of analysis whether or not the hearsay consists of *ex parte* testimony. This often results in close constitutional scrutiny in cases that are far removed from the core concerns of the Clause. At the same time, however, the test is too narrow: It admits statements that *do* consist of *ex parte* testimony upon a mere finding of reliability. This malleable standard often fails to protect against paradigmatic confrontation violations.

Members of this Court and academics have suggested that we revise our doctrine to reflect more accurately the original understanding of the Clause. See, *e.g., Lilly,* 527 U.S., at 140–43 (BREYER, J., concurring); *White,* 502 U.S., at 366 (THOMAS, J., joined by SCALIA, J., concurring in part and concurring in judgment); A. Amar, The Constitution and Criminal Procedure 125–131 (1997); Friedman, Confrontation: The Search for Basic Principles, 86 Geo. L.J. 1011 (1998). They offer two proposals: First, that we apply the Confrontation Clause only to testimonial statements, leaving the remainder to regulation by hearsay law—thus eliminating the overbreadth referred to above. Second, that we impose an absolute bar to statements that are testimonial, absent a prior

47. THE CHIEF JUSTICE complains that our prior decisions have "never drawn a distinction" like the one we now draw, citing in particular *Mattox v. United States,* 156 U.S. 237 (1895), *Kirby v. United States,* 174 U.S. 47 (1899), and *United States v. Burr,* 25 F.Cas. 187 (No. 14,694) (CC Va.1807) (Marshall, C. J.). * * * But nothing in these cases contradicts our holding in any way. * * * That the two cases did not extrapolate a more general class of evidence to which that criterion applied does not prevent us from doing so now. * * * THE CHIEF JUSTICE fails to identify a single case (aside from one minor, arguable exception [*White*]), where we have admitted testimonial statements based on indicia of reliability other than a prior opportunity for cross-examination. If nothing else, the test we announce is an empirically accurate explanation of the results our cases have reached.

Finally, we reiterate that, when the declarant appears for cross-examination at trial, the Confrontation Clause places no constraints at all on the use of his prior testimonial statements. See *California v. Green,* 399 U.S. 149, 162 (1970). * * * The Clause does not bar admission of a statement so long as the declarant is present at trial to defend or explain it. (The Clause also does not bar the use of testimonial statements for purposes other than establishing the truth of the matter asserted. See *Tennessee v. Street,* 471 U.S. 409, 414 (1985).)

opportunity to cross-examine—thus eliminating the excessive narrowness referred to above.

In *White,* we considered the first proposal and rejected it. 502 U.S., at 352–53. Although our analysis in this case casts doubt on that holding, we need not definitively resolve whether it survives our decision today, because Sylvia Crawford's statement is testimonial under any definition. This case does, however, squarely implicate the second proposal.

A

Where testimonial statements are involved, we do not think the Framers meant to leave the Sixth Amendment's protection to the vagaries of the rules of evidence, much less to amorphous notions of "reliability." Certainly none of the authorities discussed above acknowledges any general reliability exception to the common-law rule. Admitting statements deemed reliable by a judge is fundamentally at odds with the right of confrontation. To be sure, the Clause's ultimate goal is to ensure reliability of evidence, but it is a procedural rather than a substantive guarantee. It commands, not that evidence be reliable, but that reliability be assessed in a particular manner: by testing in the crucible of cross-examination. The Clause thus reflects a judgment, not only about the desirability of reliable evidence (a point on which there could be little dissent), but about how reliability can best be determined. Cf. 3 Blackstone, Commentaries, at 373 ("This open examination of witnesses * * * is much more conducive to the clearing up of truth"); M. Hale, History and Analysis of the Common Law of England 258 (1713) (adversarial testing "beats and bolts out the Truth much better").

The *Roberts* test allows a jury to hear evidence, untested by the adversary process, based on a mere judicial determination of reliability. It thus replaces the constitutionally prescribed method of assessing reliability with a wholly foreign one. In this respect, it is very different from exceptions to the Confrontation Clause that make no claim to be a surrogate means of assessing reliability. For example, the rule of forfeiture by wrongdoing (which we accept) extinguishes confrontation claims on essentially equitable grounds; it does not purport to be an alternative means of determining reliability. See *Reynolds v. United States,* 98 U.S. 145, 158–59 (1879).

The Raleigh trial itself involved the very sorts of reliability determinations that *Roberts* authorizes. In the face of Raleigh's repeated demands for confrontation, the prosecution responded with many of the arguments a court applying *Roberts* might invoke today: that Cobham's statements were self-inculpatory, 2 How. St. Tr., at 19, that they were not made in the heat of passion, *id.,* at 14, and that they were not "extracted from [him] upon any hopes or promise of Pardon," *id.,* at 29. It is not plausible that the Framers' only objection to the trial was that Raleigh's judges did not properly weigh these factors before sentencing him to death. Rather, the problem was that the judges refused to allow

Raleigh to confront Cobham in court, where he could cross-examine him and try to expose his accusation as a lie.

Dispensing with confrontation because testimony is obviously reliable is akin to dispensing with jury trial because a defendant is obviously guilty. This is not what the Sixth Amendment prescribes.

B

The legacy of *Roberts* in other courts vindicates the Framers' wisdom in rejecting a general reliability exception. The framework is so unpredictable that it fails to provide meaningful protection from even core confrontation violations.

Reliability is an amorphous, if not entirely subjective, concept. There are countless factors bearing on whether a statement is reliable; the nine-factor balancing test applied by the Court of Appeals below is representative. See, *e.g., People v. Farrell,* 34 P.3d 401, 406–407 (Colo. 2001) (eight-factor test). Whether a statement is deemed reliable depends heavily on which factors the judge considers and how much weight he accords each of them. Some courts wind up attaching the same significance to opposite facts. For example, the Colorado Supreme Court held a statement more reliable because its inculpation of the defendant was "detailed," *id.,* at 407, while the Fourth Circuit found a statement more reliable because the portion implicating another was "fleeting," *United States v. Photogrammetric Data Servs., Inc.,* 259 F.3d 229, 245 (C.A.4 2001). The Virginia Court of Appeals found a statement more reliable because the witness was in custody and charged with a crime (thus making the statement more obviously against her penal interest), see *Nowlin v. Commonwealth,* 40 Va.App. 327, 335–338, 579 S.E.2d 367, 371–372 (2003), while the Wisconsin Court of Appeals found a statement more reliable because the witness was *not* in custody and *not* a suspect, see *State v. Bintz,* 2002 WI App. 204, ¶ 13, 257 Wis.2d 177, 187, 650 N.W.2d 913, 918. Finally, the Colorado Supreme Court in one case found a statement more reliable because it was given "immediately after" the events at issue, *Farrell, supra,* at 407, while that same court, in another case, found a statement more reliable because two years had elapsed, *Stevens v. People,* 29 P.3d 305, 316 (Colo.2001).

The unpardonable vice of the *Roberts* test, however, is not its unpredictability, but its demonstrated capacity to admit core testimonial statements that the Confrontation Clause plainly meant to exclude. Despite the plurality's speculation in *Lilly,* 527 U.S., at 137, that it was "highly unlikely" that accomplice confessions implicating the accused could survive *Roberts,* courts continue routinely to admit them. See *Photogrammetric Data Servs., supra,* at 245–246; *Farrell, supra,* at 406–408; *Stevens, supra,* at 314–318 * * *. One recent study found that, after *Lilly,* appellate courts admitted accomplice statements to the authorities in 25 out of 70 cases—more than one-third of the time. Kirst, Appellate Court Answers to the Confrontation Questions in *Lilly v. Virginia,* 53 Syracuse L.Rev. 87, 105 (2003). Courts have invoked *Roberts* to admit other sorts of plainly testimonial statements despite the absence of any opportunity to cross-examine. See *United States v. Aguilar,* 295 F.3d 1018, 1021–1023 (C.A.9 2002) (plea allocution showing existence of a conspiracy) * * *.

To add insult to injury, some of the courts that admit untested testimonial statements find reliability in the very factors that *make* the statements testimonial. As noted earlier, one court relied on the fact that the witness's statement was made to police while in custody on pending charges—the theory being that this made the statement more clearly against penal interest and thus more reliable. *Nowlin, supra,* at 335–338, 579 S.E.2d, at 371–372. Other courts routinely rely on the fact that a prior statement is given under oath in judicial proceedings. *E.g., Gallego, supra,* at 168 (plea allocution); *Papajohn, supra,* at 1120 (grand jury testimony). That inculpating statements are given in a testimonial setting is not an antidote to the confrontation problem, but rather the trigger that makes the Clause's demands most urgent. It is not enough to point out that most of the usual safeguards of the adversary process attend the statement, when the single safeguard missing is the one the Confrontation Clause demands.

C

Roberts' failings were on full display in the proceedings below. Sylvia Crawford made her statement while in police custody, herself a potential suspect in the case. Indeed, she had been told that whether she would be released "depend[ed] on how the investigation continues." * * * In response to often leading questions from police detectives, she implicated her husband in Lee's stabbing and at least arguably undermined his self-defense claim. Despite all this, the trial court admitted her statement, listing several reasons why it was reliable. In its opinion reversing, the Court of Appeals listed several *other* reasons why the statement was *not* reliable. Finally, the State Supreme Court relied exclusively on the interlocking character of the statement and disregarded every other factor the lower courts had considered. The case is thus a self-contained demonstration of *Roberts'* unpredictable and inconsistent application.

Each of the courts also made assumptions that cross-examination might well have undermined. The trial court, for example, stated that Sylvia Crawford's statement was reliable because she was an eyewitness with direct knowledge of the events. But Sylvia at one point told the police that she had "shut [her] eyes and * * * didn't really watch" part of the fight, and that she was "in shock." * * * The trial court also buttressed its reliability finding by claiming that Sylvia was "being questioned by law enforcement, and, thus, the [questioner] is * * * neutral to her and not someone who would be inclined to advance her interests and shade her version of the truth unfavorably toward the defendant." *Id.,* at 77. The Framers would be astounded to learn that *ex parte* testimony could be admitted against a criminal defendant because it was elicited by "neutral" government officers. But even if the court's assessment of the officer's motives was accurate, it says nothing about

Sylvia's perception of her situation. Only cross-examination could reveal that. * * *

We readily concede that we could resolve this case by simply reweighing the "reliability factors" under *Roberts* and finding that Sylvia Crawford's statement falls short. But we view this as one of those rare cases in which the result below is so improbable that it reveals a fundamental failure on our part to interpret the Constitution in a way that secures its intended constraint on judicial discretion. Moreover, to reverse the Washington Supreme Court's decision after conducting our own reliability analysis would perpetuate, not avoid, what the Sixth Amendment condemns. The Constitution prescribes a procedure for determining the reliability of testimony in criminal trials, and we, no less than the state courts, lack authority to replace it with one of our own devising.

We have no doubt that the courts below were acting in utmost good faith when they found reliability. The Framers, however, would not have been content to indulge this assumption. They knew that judges, like other government officers, could not always be trusted to safeguard the rights of the people; the likes of the dread Lord Jeffreys were not yet too distant a memory. They were loath to leave too much discretion in judicial hands. Cf. U.S. Const., Amdt. 6 (criminal jury trial); Amdt. 7 (civil jury trial); *Ring v. Arizona,* 536 U.S. 584, 611–12 (2002) (SCALIA, J., concurring). By replacing categorical constitutional guarantees with open-ended balancing tests, we do violence to their design. Vague standards are manipulable, and, while that might be a small concern in run-of-the-mill assault prosecutions like this one, the Framers had an eye toward politically charged cases like Raleigh's—great state trials where the impartiality of even those at the highest levels of the judiciary might not be so clear. It is difficult to imagine *Roberts'* providing any meaningful protection in those circumstances. * * *

Where nontestimonial hearsay is at issue, it is wholly consistent with the Framers' design to afford the States flexibility in their development of hearsay law—as does *Roberts,* and as would an approach that exempted such statements from Confrontation Clause scrutiny altogether. Where testimonial evidence is at issue, however, the Sixth Amendment demands what the common law required: unavailability and a prior opportunity for cross-examination. We leave for another day any effort to spell out a comprehensive definition of "testimonial."[48] Whatever else the term covers, it applies at a minimum to prior testimony at a preliminary hearing, before a grand jury, or at a former trial; and to police interrogations. These are the modern practices with closest kinship to the abuses at which the Confrontation Clause was directed.

48. We acknowledge THE CHIEF JUSTICE's objection * * * that our refusal to articulate a comprehensive definition in this case will cause interim uncertainty. But it can hardly be any worse than the status quo. * * * The difference is that the *Roberts* test is *inherently,* and therefore *permanently,* unpredictable.

In this case, the State admitted Sylvia's testimonial statement against petitioner, despite the fact that he had no opportunity to cross-examine her. That alone is sufficient to make out a violation of the Sixth Amendment. *Roberts* notwithstanding, we decline to mine the record in search of indicia of reliability. Where testimonial statements are at issue, the only indicium of reliability sufficient to satisfy constitutional demands is the one the Constitution actually prescribes: confrontation.

The judgment of the Washington Supreme Court is reversed, and the case is remanded for further proceedings not inconsistent with this opinion.

CHIEF JUSTICE REHNQUIST, with whom JUSTICE O'CONNOR joins, concurring in the judgment.

I dissent from the Court's decision to overrule *Ohio v. Roberts,* 448 U.S. 56 (1980). I believe that the Court's adoption of a new interpretation of the Confrontation Clause is not backed by sufficiently persuasive reasoning to overrule long-established precedent. Its decision casts a mantle of uncertainty over future criminal trials in both federal and state courts, and is by no means necessary to decide the present case.

The Court's distinction between testimonial and nontestimonial statements, contrary to its claim, is no better rooted in history than our current doctrine. Under the common law, although the courts were far from consistent, out-of-court statements made by someone other than the accused and not taken under oath, unlike *ex parte* depositions or affidavits, were generally not considered substantive evidence upon which a conviction could be based.[49] See, *e.g., King v. Brasier,* 1 Leach 199, 200, 168 Eng. Rep. 202 (K.B.1779) * * *. Testimonial statements such as accusatory statements to police officers likely would have been disapproved of in the 18th century, not necessarily because they resembled *ex parte* affidavits or depositions as the Court reasons, but more likely than not because they were not made under oath. See *King v. Woodcock,* 1 Leach 500, 503, 168 Eng. Rep. 352, 353 (1789) * * *. Without an oath, one usually did not get to the second step of whether confrontation was required. * * *

49. Modern scholars have concluded that at the time of the founding the law had yet to fully develop the exclusionary component of the hearsay rule and its attendant exceptions, and thus hearsay was still often heard by the jury. See Gallanis, The Rise of Modern Evidence Law, 84 Iowa L.Rev. 499, 534–535 (1999); Mosteller, Remaking Confrontation Clause and Hearsay Doctrine Under the Challenge of Child Sexual Abuse Prosecutions, 1993 U. Ill. L.Rev. 691, 738–746. In many cases, hearsay alone was generally not considered sufficient to support a conviction; rather, it was used to corroborate sworn witness testimony. See 5 J. Wigmore, Evidence, § 1364, pp. 17, 19–20, 19, n.33 (J. Chadbourn rev.1974) * * * ; see also J. Langbein, Origins of Adversary Criminal Trial 238–239 (2003). Even when unsworn hearsay was proffered as substantive evidence, however, because of the predominance of the oath in society, juries were largely skeptical of it. See Landsman, Rise of the Contentious Spirit: Adversary Procedure in Eighteenth Century England, 75 Cornell L.Rev. 497, 506 (1990) (describing late 17th-century sentiments); Langbein, Criminal Trial before the Lawyers, 45 U. Chi. L.Rev. 263, 291–293 (1978). In the 18th century, unsworn hearsay was simply held to be of much lesser value than were sworn affidavits or depositions.

I therefore see no reason why the distinction the Court draws is preferable to our precedent. Starting with Chief Justice Marshall's interpretation as a Circuit Justice in 1807, 16 years after the ratification of the Sixth Amendment, *United States v. Burr,* 25 F.Cas. 187, 193 (No. 14,694) (CC Va.1807), continuing with our cases in the late 19th century, *Mattox v. United States,* 156 U.S. 237, 243–44 (1895); *Kirby v. United States,* 174 U.S. 47, 54–57 (1899), and through today, *e.g., White v. Illinois,* 502 U.S. 346, 352–53 (1992), we have never drawn a distinction between testimonial and nontestimonial statements. And for that matter, neither has any other court of which I am aware. I see little value in trading our precedent for an imprecise approximation at this late date.

I am also not convinced that the Confrontation Clause categorically requires the exclusion of testimonial statements. * * * Between 1700 and 1800 the rules regarding the admissibility of out-of-court statements were still being developed. * * * It is one thing to trace the right of confrontation back to the Roman Empire; it is quite another to conclude that such a right absolutely excludes a large category of evidence. It is an odd conclusion indeed to think that the Framers created a cut-and-dried rule with respect to the admissibility of testimonial statements when the law during their own time was not fully settled. * * *

In choosing the path it does, the Court of course overrules *Ohio v. Roberts,* 448 U.S. 56 (1980), a case decided nearly a quarter of a century ago. * * * The Court grandly declares that "[w]e leave for another day any effort to spell out a comprehensive definition of 'testimonial,' " *ante,* at 68. But the thousands of federal prosecutors and the tens of thousands of state prosecutors need answers as to what beyond the specific kinds of "testimony" the Court lists, see *ibid.,* is covered by the new rule. They need them now, not months or years from now. Rules of criminal evidence are applied every day in courts throughout the country, and parties should not be left in the dark in this manner.

[Moreover, the Court's change is] * * * not in the least necessary to reverse the judgment of the Supreme Court of Washington in this case. The result the Court reaches follows inexorably from *Roberts* and its progeny without any need for overruling that line of cases. * * * A citation to *Idaho v. Wright,* [497 U.S. 805 (1990)], would suffice. For the reasons stated, I believe that this would be a far preferable course for the Court to take here.

DAVIS v. WASHINGTON & HAMMON v. INDIANA

Supreme Court of the United States, 2006.
547 U.S. ___, 126 S.Ct. 2266.

JUSTICE SCALIA delivered the opinion of the Court.

These cases require us to determine when statements made to law enforcement personnel during a 911 call or at a crime scene are "testimonial" and thus subject to the requirements of the Sixth Amendment's Confrontation Clause.

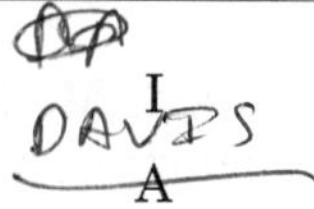

The relevant statements in *Davis v. Washington,* No. 05–5224, were made to a 911 emergency operator on February 1, 2001. When the operator answered the initial call, the connection terminated before anyone spoke. She reversed the call, and Michelle McCottry answered. In the ensuing conversation, the operator ascertained that McCottry was involved in a domestic disturbance with her former boyfriend Adrian Davis, the petitioner in this case:

"911 Operator: Hello.

"Complainant: Hello.

"911 Operator: What's going on?

"Complainant: He's here jumpin' on me again.

"911 Operator: Okay. Listen to me carefully. Are you in a house or an apartment?

"Complainant: I'm in a house.

"911 Operator: Are there any weapons?

"Complainant: No. He's usin' his fists.

"911 Operator: Okay. Has he been drinking?

"Complainant: No.

"911 Operator: Okay, sweetie. I've got help started. Stay on the line with me, okay?

"Complainant: I'm on the line.

"911 Operator: Listen to me carefully. Do you know his last name?

"Complainant: It's Davis.

"911 Operator: Davis? Okay, what's his first name?

"Complainant: Adran[.]

"911 Operator: What is it?

"Complainant: Adrian.

"911 Operator: Adrian?

"Complainant: Yeah.

"911 Operator: Okay. What's his middle initial?

"Complainant: Martell. He's runnin' now." * * *

As the conversation continued, the operator learned that Davis had "just r[un] out the door" after hitting McCottry, and that he was leaving in a car with someone else. *Id.,* at 9–10. McCottry started talking, but the operator cut her off, saying, "Stop talking and answer my questions." *Id.,* at 10. She then gathered more information about Davis (including his birthday), and learned that Davis had told McCottry that his purpose in coming to the house was "to get his stuff," since

McCottry was moving. *Id.,* at 11–12. McCottry described the context of the assault, *id.,* at 12, after which the operator told her that the police were on their way. "They're gonna check the area for him first," the operator said, "and then they're gonna come talk to you." *Id.,* at 12–13.

The police arrived within four minutes of the 911 call and observed McCottry's shaken state, the "fresh injuries on her forearm and her face," and her "frantic efforts to gather her belongings and her children so that they could leave the residence." 154 Wash.2d 291, 296, 111 P.3d 844, 847 (2005) (en banc).

The State charged Davis with felony violation of a domestic no-contact order. "The State's only witnesses were the two police officers who responded to the 911 call. Both officers testified that McCottry exhibited injuries that appeared to be recent, but neither officer could testify as to the cause of the injuries." *Ibid.* McCottry presumably could have testified as to whether Davis was her assailant, but she did not appear. Over Davis's objection, based on the Confrontation Clause of the Sixth Amendment, the trial court admitted the recording of her exchange with the 911 operator, and the jury convicted him. The Washington Court of Appeals affirmed, 116 Wash.App. 81, 64 P.3d 661 (2003). The Supreme Court of Washington, with one dissenting justice, also affirmed, concluding that the portion of the 911 conversation in which McCottry identified Davis was not testimonial, and that if other portions of the conversation were testimonial, admitting them was harmless beyond a reasonable doubt. 154 Wash.2d, at 305, 111 P.3d, at 851. * * *

B

In *Hammon v. Indiana,* No. 05–5705, police responded late on the night of February 26, 2003, to a "reported domestic disturbance" at the home of Hershel and Amy Hammon. 829 N.E.2d 444, 446 (Ind.2005). They found Amy alone on the front porch, appearing " 'somewhat frightened,' " but she told them that " 'nothing was the matter,' " *id.,* at 446, 447. She gave them permission to enter the house, where an officer saw "a gas heating unit in the corner of the living room" that had "flames coming out of the * * * partial glass front. There were pieces of glass on the ground in front of it and there was flame emitting from the front of the heating unit." * * *

Hershel, meanwhile, was in the kitchen. He told the police "that he and his wife had 'been in an argument' but 'everything was fine now' and the argument 'never became physical.' " 829 N.E.2d, at 447. By this point Amy had come back inside. One of the officers remained with Hershel; the other went to the living room to talk with Amy, and "again asked [her] what had occurred." Ibid. * * * Hershel made several attempts to participate in Amy's conversation with the police, see *id.,* at 32, but was rebuffed. The officer later testified that Hershel "became angry when I insisted that [he] stay separated from Mrs. Hammon so that we can investigate what had happened." *Id.,* at 34. After hearing Amy's account, the officer "had her fill out and sign a battery affidavit."

Id., at 18. Amy handwrote the following: "Broke our Furnace & shoved me down on the floor into the broken glass. Hit me in the chest and threw me down. Broke our lamps & phone. Tore up my van where I couldn't leave the house. Attacked my daughter." *Id.*, at 2.

The State charged Hershel with domestic battery and with violating his probation. Amy was subpoenaed, but she did not appear at his subsequent bench trial. The State called the officer who had questioned Amy, and asked him to recount what Amy told him and to authenticate the affidavit. Hershel's counsel repeatedly objected to the admission of this evidence. * * *. At one point, after hearing the prosecutor defend the affidavit because it was made "under oath," defense counsel said, "That doesn't give us the opportunity to cross examine [the] person who allegedly drafted it. Makes me mad." *Id.,* at 19. Nonetheless, the trial court admitted the affidavit as a "present sense impression," *id.,* at 20, and Amy's statements as "excited utterances" that "are expressly permitted in these kinds of cases even if the declarant is not available to testify." *Id.,* at 40. The officer thus testified that Amy

> "informed me that she and Hershel had been in an argument. That he became irrate [sic] over the fact of their daughter going to a boyfriend's house. The argument became * * * physical after being verbal and she informed me that Mr. Hammon, during the verbal part of the argument was breaking things in the living room and I believe she stated he broke the phone, broke the lamp, broke the front of the heater. When it became physical he threw her down into the glass of the heater. * * *
>
> "She informed me Mr. Hammon had pushed her onto the ground, had shoved her head into the broken glass of the heater and that he had punched her in the chest twice I believe." *Id.,* at 17–18.

The trial judge found Hershel guilty on both charges, *id.,* at 40, and the Indiana Court of Appeals affirmed in relevant part, 809 N.E.2d 945 (2004). The Indiana Supreme Court also affirmed, concluding that Amy's statement was admissible for state-law purposes as an excited utterance, 829 N.E.2d, at 449; that "a 'testimonial' statement is one given or taken in significant part for purposes of preserving it for potential future use in legal proceedings," where "the motivations of the questioner and declarant are the central concerns," *id.,* at 456, 457; and that Amy's oral statement was not "testimonial" under these standards, *id.,* at 458. It also concluded that, although the affidavit was testimonial and thus wrongly admitted, it was harmless beyond a reasonable doubt, largely because the trial was to the bench. * * *

II

The Confrontation Clause of the Sixth Amendment provides: "In all criminal prosecutions, the accused shall enjoy the right * * * to be confronted with the witnesses against him." In *Crawford v. Washington,* 541 U.S. 36, 53–54 (2004), we held that this provision bars "admission of testimonial statements of a witness who did not appear at trial unless he was unavailable to testify, and the defendant had had a prior opportunity for cross-examination." A critical portion of this holding, and the portion central to resolution of the two cases now before us, is the phrase "testimonial statements." Only statements of this sort cause the declarant to be a "witness" within the meaning of the Confrontation Clause. See *id.,* at 51. It is the testimonial character of the statement that separates it from other hearsay that, while subject to traditional limitations upon hearsay evidence, is not subject to the Confrontation Clause.

Our opinion in *Crawford* set forth "[v]arious formulations" of the core class of " 'testimonial' " statements, *ibid.,* but found it unnecessary to endorse any of them, because "some statements qualify under any definition," *id.,* at 52. Among those, we said, were "[s]tatements taken by police officers in the course of interrogations," *ibid.;* see also *id.*, at 53. The questioning that generated the deponent's statement in *Crawford*—which was made and recorded while she was in police custody, after having been given *Miranda* warnings as a possible suspect herself—"qualifies under any conceivable definition" of an " 'interrogation,' " 541 U.S., at 53, n.4. We therefore did not define that term, except to say that "[w]e use [it] * * * in its colloquial, rather than any technical legal, sense," and that "one can imagine various definitions * * *, and we need not select among them in this case." *Ibid.* The character of the statements in the present cases is not as clear, and these cases require us to determine more precisely which police interrogations produce testimony.

Without attempting to produce an exhaustive classification of all conceivable statements—or even all conceivable statements in response to police interrogation—as either testimonial or nontestimonial, it suffices to decide the present cases to hold as follows: Statements are nontestimonial when made in the course of police interrogation under circumstances objectively indicating that the primary purpose of the interrogation is to enable police assistance to meet an ongoing emergency. They are testimonial when the circumstances objectively indicate that there is no such ongoing emergency, and that the primary purpose of the interrogation is to establish or prove past events potentially relevant to later criminal prosecution.[50]

III

A

In *Crawford,* it sufficed for resolution of the case before us to determine that "even if the Sixth Amendment is not solely concerned

50. Our holding refers to interrogations because, as explained below, the statements in the cases presently before us are the products of interrogations—which in some circumstances tend to generate testimonial responses. This is not to imply, however, that statements made in the absence of any interrogation are necessarily nontestimonial. The Framers were no more willing to exempt from cross-examination volunteered testimony or answers to open-ended questions than they were to exempt answers to detailed interrogation. (Part of the evidence against Sir Walter Raleigh was a letter from Lord Cobham that was plainly *not* the result of sustained questioning. *Raleigh's Case,* 2 How. St. Tr. 1, 27 (1603).) And of course even when interrogation exists, it is in the final analysis the declarant's statements, not the interrogator's questions, that the Confrontation Clause requires us to evaluate.

with testimonial hearsay, that is its primary object, and interrogations by law enforcement officers fall squarely within that class." *Id.*, at 53. Moreover, as we have just described, the facts of that case spared us the need to define what we meant by "interrogations." The *Davis* case today does not permit us this luxury of indecision. The inquiries of a police operator in the course of a 911 call[51] are an interrogation in one sense, but not in a sense that "qualifies under any conceivable definition." We must decide, therefore, whether the Confrontation Clause applies only to testimonial hearsay; and, if so, whether the recording of a 911 call qualifies.

The answer to the first question was suggested in *Crawford,* even if not explicitly held:

> "The text of the Confrontation Clause reflects this focus [on testimonial hearsay]. It applies to 'witnesses' against the accused—in other words, those who 'bear testimony.' 1 N. Webster, An American Dictionary of the English Language (1828). 'Testimony,' in turn, is typically 'a solemn declaration or affirmation made for the purpose of establishing or proving some fact.' *Ibid.* An accuser who makes a formal statement to government officers bears testimony in a sense that a person who makes a casual remark to an acquaintance does not." 541 U.S., at 51.

A limitation so clearly reflected in the text of the constitutional provision must fairly be said to mark out not merely its "core," but its perimeter.

We are not aware of any early American case invoking the Confrontation Clause or the common-law right to confrontation that did not clearly involve testimony as thus defined. Well into the 20th century, our own Confrontation Clause jurisprudence was carefully applied only in the testimonial context. See, *e.g., Reynolds v. United States,* 98 U.S. 145, 158, 25 L.Ed. 244 (1879) (testimony at prior trial was subject to the Confrontation Clause, but petitioner had forfeited that right by procuring witness's absence); *Mattox v. United States,* 156 U.S. 237, 240–244 (1895) (prior trial testimony of deceased witnesses admitted because subject to cross-examination); *Kirby v. United States,* 174 U.S. 47, 55–56 (1899) (guilty pleas and jury conviction of others could not be admitted to show that property defendant received from them was stolen); *Motes v. United States,* 178 U.S. 458, 467, 470–471 (1900) (written deposition subject to cross-examination was not admissible because witness was available); *Dowdell v. United States,* 221 U.S. 325, 330–331 (1911) (facts regarding conduct of prior trial certified to by the judge, the clerk of court, and the official reporter did not relate to defendants' guilt or innocence and hence were not statements of "witnesses" under the Confrontation Clause).

911 operators agent of law enforcement

51. If 911 operators are not themselves law enforcement officers, they may at least be agents of law enforcement when they conduct interrogations of 911 callers. For purposes of this opinion (and without deciding the point), we consider their acts to be acts of the police. As in *Crawford v. Washington,* 541 U.S. 36 (2004), therefore, our holding today makes it unnecessary to consider whether and when statements made to someone other than law enforcement personnel are "testimonial."

Even our later cases, conforming to the reasoning of *Ohio v. Roberts,* 448 U.S. 56 (1980),[52] never in practice dispensed with the Confrontation Clause requirements of unavailability and prior cross-examination in cases that involved testimonial hearsay, see *Crawford,* 541 U.S., at 57–59 (citing cases), with one arguable exception, see *id.,* at 58, n.8 (discussing *White v. Illinois,* 502 U.S. 346 (1992)). Where our cases did dispense with those requirements—even under the *Roberts* approach—the statements at issue were clearly nontestimonial. See, *e.g., Bourjaily v. United States,* 483 U.S. 171, 181–184 (1987) (statements made unwittingly to a Government informant); *Dutton v. Evans,* 400 U.S. 74, 87–89 (1970) (plurality opinion) (statements from one prisoner to another).

Most of the American cases applying the Confrontation Clause or its state constitutional or common-law counterparts involved testimonial statements of the most formal sort—sworn testimony in prior judicial proceedings or formal depositions under oath—which invites the argument that the scope of the Clause is limited to that very formal category. But the English cases that were the progenitors of the Confrontation Clause did not limit the exclusionary rule to prior court testimony and formal depositions, see *Crawford, supra,* at 52, and n.3. In any event, we do not think it conceivable that the protections of the Confrontation Clause can readily be evaded by having a note-taking policeman *recite* the unsworn hearsay testimony of the declarant, instead of having the declarant sign a deposition. Indeed, if there is one point for which no case—English or early American, state or federal—can be cited, that is it.

The question before us in *Davis,* then, is whether, objectively considered, the interrogation that took place in the course of the 911 call produced testimonial statements. When we said in *Crawford, supra,* at 53, that "interrogations by law enforcement officers fall squarely within [the] class" of testimonial hearsay, we had immediately in mind (for that was the case before us) interrogations solely directed at establishing the facts of a past crime, in order to identify (or provide evidence to convict) the perpetrator. The product of such interrogation, whether reduced to a writing signed by the declarant or embedded in the memory (and perhaps notes) of the interrogating officer, is testimonial. It is, in the terms of the 1828 American dictionary quoted in *Crawford,* " '[a] solemn declaration or affirmation made for the purpose of establishing or proving some fact.' " 541 U.S., at 51. (The solemnity of even an oral declaration of relevant past fact to an investigating officer is well enough established by the severe consequences that can attend a deliberate falsehood. See, *e.g., United States v. Stewart,* 433 F.3d 273, 288 (C.A.2 2006) (false statements made to federal investigators violate 18 U.S.C. § 1001); *State v. Reed,* 2005 WI 53, ¶ 30, 280 Wis.2d 68, 695 N.W.2d 315,

52. "*Roberts* condition[ed] the admissibility of all hearsay evidence on whether it falls under a 'firmly rooted hearsay exception' or bears 'particularized guarantees of trustworthiness.' " Crawford, 541 U.S., at 60 (quoting *Roberts,* 448 U.S., at 66). We overruled *Roberts* in *Crawford* by restoring the unavailability and cross-examination requirements.

323 (state criminal offense to "knowingly giv[e] false information to [an] officer with [the] intent to mislead the officer in the performance of his or her duty").) A 911 call, on the other hand, and at least the initial interrogation conducted in connection with a 911 call, is ordinarily not designed primarily to "establis[h] or prov[e]" some past fact, but to describe current circumstances requiring police assistance.

The difference between the interrogation in *Davis* and the one in *Crawford* is apparent on the face of things. In *Davis,* McCottry was speaking about events *as they were actually happening,* rather than "describ [ing] past events," *Lilly v. Virginia,* 527 U.S. 116, 137 (1999) (plurality opinion). Sylvia Crawford's interrogation, on the other hand, took place hours after the events she described had occurred. Moreover, any reasonable listener would recognize that McCottry (unlike Sylvia Crawford) was facing an ongoing emergency. Although one *might* call 911 to provide a narrative report of a crime absent any imminent danger, McCottry's call was plainly a call for help against bona fide physical threat. Third, the nature of what was asked and answered in *Davis,* again viewed objectively, was such that the elicited statements were necessary to be able to *resolve* the present emergency, rather than simply to learn (as in *Crawford*) what had happened in the past. That is true even of the operator's effort to establish the identity of the assailant, so that the dispatched officers might know whether they would be encountering a violent felon. See, *e.g., Hiibel v. Sixth Judicial Dist. Court of Nev., Humboldt Cty.,* 542 U.S. 177, 186 (2004). And finally, the difference in the level of formality between the two interviews is striking. Crawford was responding calmly, at the station house, to a series of questions, with the officer-interrogator taping and making notes of her answers; McCottry's frantic answers were provided over the phone, in an environment that was not tranquil, or even (as far as any reasonable 911 operator could make out) safe.

We conclude from all this that the circumstances of McCottry's interrogation objectively indicate its primary purpose was to enable police assistance to meet an ongoing emergency. She simply was not acting as a *witness;* she was not *testifying.* What she said was not "a weaker substitute for live testimony" at trial, *United States v. Inadi,* 475 U.S. 387, 394 (1986), like Lord Cobham's statements in *Raleigh's Case,* 2 How. St. Tr. 1 (1603), or Jane Dingler's *ex parte* statements against her husband in *King v. Dingler,* 2 Leach 561, 168 Eng. Rep. 383 (1791), or Sylvia Crawford's statement in *Crawford.* In each of those cases, the *ex parte* actors and the evidentiary products of the *ex parte* communication aligned perfectly with their courtroom analogues. McCottry's emergency statement does not. No "witness" goes into court to proclaim an emergency and seek help.

Davis seeks to cast McCottry in the unlikely role of a witness by pointing to English cases. None of them involves statements made during an ongoing emergency. In *King v. Brasier,* 1 Leach 199, 168 Eng. Rep. 202 (1779), for example, a young rape victim, "immediately on her coming home, told all the circumstances of the injury" to her mother.

Id., at 200, 168 Eng. Rep., at 202. The case would be helpful to Davis if the relevant statement had been the girl's screams for aid as she was being chased by her assailant. But by the time the victim got home, her story was an account of past events.

This is not to say that a conversation which begins as an interrogation to determine the need for emergency assistance cannot, as the Indiana Supreme Court put it, "evolve into testimonial statements," 829 N.E.2d, at 457, once that purpose has been achieved. In this case, for example, after the operator gained the information needed to address the exigency of the moment, the emergency appears to have ended (when Davis drove away from the premises). The operator then told McCottry to be quiet, and proceeded to pose a battery of questions. It could readily be maintained that, from that point on, McCottry's statements were testimonial, not unlike the "structured police questioning" that occurred in *Crawford,* 541 U.S., at 53, n.4. This presents no great problem. Just as, for Fifth Amendment purposes, "police officers can and will distinguish almost instinctively between questions necessary to secure their own safety or the safety of the public and questions designed solely to elicit testimonial evidence from a suspect," *New York v. Quarles,* 467 U.S. 649, 658–659 (1984), trial courts will recognize the point at which, for Sixth Amendment purposes, statements in response to interrogations become testimonial. Through *in limine* procedure, they should redact or exclude the portions of any statement that have become testimonial, as they do, for example, with unduly prejudicial portions of otherwise admissible evidence. Davis's jury did not hear the *complete* 911 call, although it may well have heard some testimonial portions. We were asked to classify only McCottry's early statements identifying Davis as her assailant, and we agree with the Washington Supreme Court that they were not testimonial. That court also concluded that, even if later parts of the call were testimonial, their admission was harmless beyond a reasonable doubt. Davis does not challenge that holding, and we therefore assume it to be correct.

B

Determining the testimonial or nontestimonial character of the statements that were the product of the interrogation in *Hammon* is a much easier task, since they were not much different from the statements we found to be testimonial in *Crawford.* It is entirely clear from the circumstances that the interrogation was part of an investigation into possibly criminal past conduct—as, indeed, the testifying officer expressly acknowledged * * *. There was no emergency in progress; the interrogating officer testified that he had heard no arguments or crashing and saw no one throw or break anything. When the officers first arrived, Amy told them that things were fine, and there was no immediate threat to her person. When the officer questioned Amy for the second time, and elicited the challenged statements, he was not seeking to determine (as in *Davis*) "what is happening," but rather "what happened." Objectively viewed, the primary, if not indeed the sole, purpose of the interrogation was to investigate a possible crime—which is, of course, precisely what the officer *should* have done.

It is true that the *Crawford* interrogation was more formal. It followed a *Miranda* warning, was tape-recorded, and took place at the station house, see 541 U.S., at 53, n.4. While these features certainly strengthened the statements' testimonial aspect—made it more objectively apparent, that is, that the purpose of the exercise was to nail down the truth about past criminal events—none was essential to the point. It was formal enough that Amy's interrogation was conducted in a separate room, away from her husband (who tried to intervene), with the officer receiving her replies for use in his "investigat[ion]." * * * What we called the "striking resemblance" of the *Crawford* statement to civil-law *ex parte* examinations, 541 U.S., at 52, is shared by Amy's statement here. Both declarants were actively separated from the defendant—officers forcibly prevented Hershel from participating in the interrogation. Both statements deliberately recounted, in response to police questioning, how potentially criminal past events began and progressed. And both took place some time after the events described were over. Such statements under official interrogation are an obvious substitute for live testimony, because they do precisely *what a witness does* on direct examination; they are inherently testimonial.[53]

Both Indiana and the United States as *amicus curiae* argue that this case should be resolved much like *Davis*. For the reasons we find the comparison to *Crawford* compelling, we find the comparison to *Davis* unpersuasive. The statements in *Davis* were taken when McCottry was alone, not only unprotected by police (as Amy Hammon was protected), but apparently in immediate danger from Davis. She was seeking aid, not telling a story about the past. McCottry's present-tense statements showed immediacy; Amy's narrative of past events was delivered at some remove in time from the danger she described. And after Amy answered

53. The dissent criticizes our test for being "neither workable nor a targeted attempt to reach the abuses forbidden by the [Confrontation] Clause," * * * (opinion of THOMAS, J.). As to the former: We have acknowledged that our holding is not an "exhaustive classification of all conceivable statements—or even all conceivable statements in response to police interrogation," * * * but rather a resolution of the cases before us and those like them. For *those* cases, the test is objective and quite "workable." The dissent, in attempting to formulate an exhaustive classification of its own, has not provided anything that deserves the description "workable"—unless one thinks that the distinction between "formal" and "informal" statements * * * qualifies. * * *

As for the charge that our holding is not a "targeted attempt to reach the abuses forbidden by the [Confrontation] Clause," which the dissent describes as the depositions taken by Marian magistrates, characterized by a high degree of formality * * *: We do not dispute that formality is indeed essential to testimonial utterance. But we no longer have examining Marian magistrates; and we do have, as our 18th-century forebears did not, examining police officers, see L. Friedman, Crime and Punishment in American History 67–68 (1993)—who perform investigative and testimonial functions once performed by examining Marian magistrates, see J. Langbein, The Origins of Adversary Criminal Trial 41 (2003). It imports sufficient formality, in our view, that lies to such officers are criminal offenses. Restricting the Confrontation Clause to the precise forms against which it was originally directed is a recipe for its extinction. Cf. *Kyllo v. United States,* 533 U.S. 27 (2001).

the officer's questions, he had her execute an affidavit, in order, he testified, "[t]o establish events that have occurred previously." * * *

Although we necessarily reject the Indiana Supreme Court's implication that virtually any "initial inquiries" at the crime scene will not be testimonial, see 829 N.E.2d, at 453, 457, we do not hold the opposite—that *no* questions at the scene will yield nontestimonial answers. We have already observed of domestic disputes that "[o]fficers called to investigate * * * need to know whom they are dealing with in order to assess the situation, the threat to their own safety, and possible danger to the potential victim." *Hiibel,* 542 U.S., at 186. Such exigencies may *often* mean that "initial inquiries" produce nontestimonial statements. But in cases like this one, where Amy's statements were neither a cry for help nor the provision of information enabling officers immediately to end a threatening situation, the fact that they were given at an alleged crime scene and were "initial inquiries" is immaterial. Cf. *Crawford, supra,* at 52, n.3.[54]

IV

Respondents in both cases, joined by a number of their *amici,* contend that the nature of the offenses charged in these two cases—domestic violence—requires greater flexibility in the use of testimonial evidence. This particular type of crime is notoriously susceptible to intimidation or coercion of the victim to ensure that she does not testify at trial. When this occurs, the Confrontation Clause gives the criminal a windfall. We may not, however, vitiate constitutional guarantees when they have the effect of allowing the guilty to go free. Cf. *Kyllo v. United States,* 533 U.S. 27 (2001) (suppressing evidence from an illegal search). But when defendants seek to undermine the judicial process by procuring or coercing silence from witnesses and victims, the Sixth Amendment does not require courts to acquiesce. While defendants have no duty to assist the State in proving their guilt, they *do* have the duty to refrain from acting in ways that destroy the integrity of the criminal-trial system. We reiterate what we said in *Crawford:* that "the rule of forfeiture by wrongdoing * * * extinguishes confrontation claims on essentially equitable grounds." 541 U.S., at 62 (citing *Reynolds,* 98 U.S., at 158–159). That is, one who obtains the absence of a witness by wrongdoing forfeits the constitutional right to confrontation.

We take no position on the standards necessary to demonstrate such forfeiture, but federal courts using Federal Rule of Evidence 804(b)(6), which codifies the forfeiture doctrine, have generally held the Govern-

54. Police investigations themselves are, of course, in no way impugned by our characterization of their fruits as testimonial. Investigations of past crimes prevent future harms and lead to necessary arrests. While prosecutors may hope that inculpatory "nontestimonial" evidence is gathered, this is essentially beyond police control. Their saying that an emergency exists cannot make it be so. The Confrontation Clause in no way governs police conduct, because it is the trial *use* of, not the investigatory *collection* of, *ex parte* testimonial statements which offends that provision. But neither can police conduct govern the Confrontation Clause; testimonial statements are what they are.

ment to the preponderance-of-the-evidence standard, see, *e.g., United States v. Scott,* 284 F.3d 758, 762 (C.A.7 2002). State courts tend to follow the same practice, see, *e.g., Commonwealth v. Edwards,* 444 Mass. 526, 542, 830 N.E.2d 158, 172 (2005). Moreover, if a hearing on forfeiture is required, *Edwards,* for instance, observed that "hearsay evidence, including the unavailable witness's out-of-court statements, may be considered." *Id.,* at 545, 830 N.E.2d, at 174. The *Roberts* approach to the Confrontation Clause undoubtedly made recourse to this doctrine less necessary, because prosecutors could show the "reliability" of *ex parte* statements more easily than they could show the defendant's procurement of the witness's absence. *Crawford,* in overruling *Roberts,* did not destroy the ability of courts to protect the integrity of their proceedings.

We have determined that, absent a finding of forfeiture by wrongdoing, the Sixth Amendment operates to exclude Amy Hammon's affidavit. The Indiana courts may (if they are asked) determine on remand whether such a claim of forfeiture is properly raised and, if so, whether it is meritorious.

* * *

We affirm the judgment of the Supreme Court of Washington * * *. We reverse the judgment of the Supreme Court of Indiana * * *, and remand the case to that Court for proceedings not inconsistent with this opinion.

[Justice Thomas' concurring and dissent opinion is omitted.]

Notes and Questions

1. *The "Crawford" rule.* If the statement is "testimonial" and confrontation is not provided, *Crawford* interposes a huge "STOP SIGN" barring its admission in the absence of one of a few limited exceptions.

Crawford makes the key determination whether the statement is "testimonial." It described some testimonial statements: "Whatever else the term covers, [testimonial] applies at a minimum to prior testimony at a preliminary hearing, before a grand jury, or at a former trial; and to police interrogations." In the course of the opinion, the Court also included "plea allocution[s] showing existence of a conspiracy," which presumably includes all statements during guilty pleas, known as plea allocutions. In *Davis & Hammon*, the Court added to the testimonial category statements made during police interrogation "when the circumstances objectively indicate that there is no * * * ongoing emergency, and that the primary purpose of the interrogation is to establish or prove past events potentially relevant to later criminal prosecution."

Although not technically an exception to the right of confrontation under *Crawford*, if the statement is determined not to be "testimonial," then the strong command to exclude absent confrontation is not triggered. Thus, the dimensions of the definition of testimonial and the determination of whether the statement falls within the definition are of paramount importance.

2. *Paradigm shift from focus on hearsay exceptions.* Under *Roberts*, the a critical determination in most cases in satisfying the Confrontation Clause was the determination that a statement fit within a "firmly rooted" hearsay exception. *Crawford*'s critical determination of the testimonial character of the statement is, by contrast, based on a very different model, which does not rest on hearsay exceptions and their guarantees of trustworthiness. The testimonial determination may sometimes overlap with hearsay theory as when the *Crawford* Court stated that "[m]ost of the hearsay exceptions covered statements that by their nature were not testimonial—for example, business records or statements in furtherance of a conspiracy." The statements in these hearsay categories are, however, not excluded from the testimonial category because they are within hearsay exceptions, but rather because statements within these categories are generally made for other purposes beside creating testimony. The Court indicated that White v. Illinois, 502 U.S. 346 (1992), where a firmly rooted excited utterance to a police officer was admitted, may have been wrongly decided. Indeed, in *Hammon*, the Court treated the state court's determination that the statement was an excited utterance as irrelevant to its conclusion that it was testimonial and violated the Constitution.

3. *The exceptions: (A) Present confrontation. Crawford* reaffirmed that the principles of *California v. Green* and *United States v. Owens* were valid in meeting the Confrontation Clause even as to testimonial statements. Accordingly, whether the hearsay statement is testimonial or nontestimonial, the Confrontation Clause is satisfied if the person who made the out-of-court statement is present in court, testifies, and is subject to cross-examination.

4. *The exceptions: (B) Prior confrontation* ***and*** *unavailability. Crawford* also reaffirmed that if the witness has previously been subject to confrontation and is currently unavailable, then the prior testimonial statements may be received. Thus, the method of satisfying the Confrontation Clause illustrated by *Roberts*, where the preliminary hearing testimony of the defendant's unavailable former friend was received, remains sound.

5. *The exceptions: (C) Forfeiture by wrongdoing. Crawford* recognized an exception to the right of confrontation for "forfeiture by wrongdoing." That doctrine, which had been recognized in a nineteenth century decision, is largely undeveloped as a confrontation principle. Unlike the often used exceptions described in the previous two notes, it must now be fleshed out. In *Davis & Hammon*, the Court invited attention to this task, suggesting that a preponderance-of-the-evidence standard applied and that the hearsay statements of the unavailable witness could be considered in making the determination.

Whether forfeiture under the Confrontation Clause will require an intent to make the witness unavailable as the new federal hearsay exception, Rule 804(b)(6), does remains to be seen. Several post-decisions concluded that murdering the victim, albeit without intent to silence that person as a witness, constituted "forfeiture by wrongdoing" under the Confrontation Clause. See United States v. Garcia–Meza, 403 F.3d 364, 370 (6th Cir.2005); State v. Meeks, 88 P.3d 789, 794–95 (Kan.2004). How expansively this doctrine will be interpreted is a significant unresolved question, particularly as to witnesses who do not testify apparently because of fear of the defendant, as frequently happens in domestic violence and child abuse cases. Finally, the Court in *Crawford* did not independently decide whether the defendant's act of invoking a privilege that barred his wife's testimony should have resulted in a forfeiture of his Confrontation Clause right. Instead, because the prosecution had not challenged that ruling on appeal, it deferred to the decision of the lower courts without deciding the issue. Should the defendant invoking a privilege that renders the witness unavailable forfeit the right even though this action is not "wrongdoing"?

6. *The exceptions: (D) Statements not offered for the "truth of the matter asserted."* In *Crawford*, the Court stated that even if testimonial, statements were not barred if not offered for their truth. It cited the example of Tennessee v. Street, 471 U.S. 409 (1985), where a clearly testimonial confession by the codefendant was ruled admissible to refute a claim by the defendant. The defendant testified at trial that he had confessed only because the sheriff had told him to do so and had instructed him to "say the same thing" as the codefendant. The prosecution introduced the codefendant's statement, which contained quite different information, to refute the defendant's claim, and the trial court had given a limiting instruction that the jury was only to use it for that purpose. The Court in *Street* found the Confrontation Clause was not violated, id. at 411, 413–14, and *Crawford* explicitly approved this result.

7. *The exceptions: (E) (Perhaps) dying declarations.* In *Crawford*, the Court noted that at the time the Constitution was adopted, historical practice was to admit dying declarations as an exception to the principle of confrontation, which might mean it would be an exception to the Confrontation Clause. But it stated, "[i]f this exception must be accepted on historical grounds, it is *sui generis*."

8. *The exceptions: (F) Admissions by the defendant.* Although not mentioned by the Supreme Court, there can be no doubt that the defendant's own admissions, even if testimonial, are not barred by the Confrontation Clause. The explanation is the same as given by Morgan for receiving admissions when objected to on hearsay grounds: A party may not complain about not being able to cross-examine herself. See Section B(2), supra.

9. *Additional examples of testimonial and nontestimonial statements.* "An off-hand, overheard remark" may be a good candidate for exclusion under the hearsay rule, according to the Court, but bears little resemblance to the abuses that were the target of the Confrontation Clause. "An accuser who makes a formal statement to government officers bears testimony in a sense that a person who makes a causal remark to an acquaintance does not."

10. *Still waiting for a general definition.* The Court in *Crawford* refused to give a definition of testimonial, and working out the dimensions of that definition will be one of the most important tasks facing lower courts until the Supreme Court speaks expansively. The Court provided three possible definitions:

> *ex parte* in-court testimony or its functional equivalent—that is, material such as affidavits, custodial examinations, prior testimony that the defendant was unable to cross-examine, or similar pretrial statements

> that the declarant would reasonably expect to be used prosecutorially (Petitioner's Brief);
>
> extrajudicial statements * * * contained in formalized testimonial materials, such as affidavits, depositions, prior testimony, or confessions (Justice Thomas' concurring opinion in White v. Illinois, 502 U.S. 346, 365 (1992)); and
>
> statements that were made under circumstances which would lead an objective witness reasonably to believe that the statement would be available for use at a later trial (Defense Lawyers Amicus Brief).

In what ways do these definitions differ? Which would be more likely to produce clarity in application?

In *Davis & Hammon*, the Court apparently rejected the formality of the second definition. It did not use the language of either of the other two possible definitions and again declined to give "an exhaustive classification" of all statements or even all police interrogations. It did, however, give some general guidance in the area of police interrogations, whether at the stationhouse or in the field:

> Statements are nontestimonial when made in the course of police interrogation under circumstances objectively indicating that the primary purpose of the interrogation is to enable police assistance to meet an ongoing emergency. They are testimonial when the circumstances objectively indicate that there is no such ongoing emergency, and that the primary purpose of the interrogation is to establish or prove past events potentially relevant to later criminal prosecution.

testimony guidelines

11. *Police "interrogation" and "structured questioning."* In *Crawford*, the Court used the terms "interrogation" and "structured questioning" to characterize the questioning of Sylvia Crawford but did not define or indicate the significance of either term in determining whether a response is testimonial. In *Davis & Hammon*, the Court used the term interrogation, but stated while such questioning "in some circumstances tend to generate testimonial responses," it is not a requirement: "The Framers were no more willing to exempt from cross-examination volunteered testimony or answers to open-ended questions than they were to exempt answers to detailed interrogations."

12. *Significance of government involvement.* The Court in *Crawford* noted that government involvement in the creation of evidence is a particularly salient feature: "The involvement of government officers in the production of testimony with an eye toward trial presents *unique potential* for prosecutorial abuse—a fact borne out time and again throughout a history with which the Framers were keenly aware." (emphasis added). However, it did not state that government involvement in the creation of the evidence was required. In *Davis*, it treated 911 operators as agents of law enforcement, and thereby avoided deciding "whether and when" statements made to non-law enforcement personnel would be testimonial. Would it matter if the videotaped statement of a victim of domestic violence was made by a privately funded group rather than by a police officer responding to the victim's home an hour after the apparent assault or whether a child's statement regarding sexual abuse is made to a government doctor, or to a

private doctor who works as part of a sexual abuse investigative team, or to the child's pediatrician during a routine exam?

13. *Declarant's knowledge of government involvement.* Must the statement be made with knowledge that the declarant is talking to a police or government officer? Apparently such knowledge may be an important factor at least in some contexts. In both *Crawford* and *Davis & Hammon*, the Court noted that the coconspirator statement in Bourjaily v. United States, 483 U.S. 171 (1987), which it considered correctly admitted, involved a statement "made unwittingly" to a government informant. Is the lack of knowledge of the speaker that the conversation is with a government agent dispositive in making the statement nontestimonial when the "primary purpose of the interrogation is to establish or prove past events potentially relevant to later criminal prosecution," which under *Davis & Hammon* would ordinarily make it testimonial? Is this lack of knowledge that the apparent coconspirator is in fact a government agent the reason for excluding coconspirator statements from the testimonial category, or is it rather that the statement is made for the purpose of aiding the conspiracy ("in furtherance of") rather than for a testimonial purpose?

14. *Likely class of nontestimonial statements.* Privately made statements without an intention for use at trial are unlikely to be considered testimonial, even if highly incriminating to another. See, e.g., State v. Rivera, 844 A.2d 191, 202 (Conn.2004) (concluding "statement in confidence and on [the declarant's] own initiative to a close family member, almost eighteen months before the defendant was arrested and more than four years before his own arrest" not testimonial).

15. *Elimination of manipulation by police failure to formally record.* The *Crawford* opinion had left open the possibility that the formality of the statement might be given dispositive weight in determining its testimonial status, which could lead to manipulation by investigative officers in their decision to record a statement or to recite it from memory or informal notes. See Mosteller, *Crawford v. Washington*: Encouraging and Ensuring the Confrontation of Witnesses, 39 U.Rich.L.Rev. 511, 555 (2005). In *Davis & Hammon*, the Supreme Court eliminated that concern: "[W]e do not think it conceivable that the protections of the Confrontation Clause can readily be evaded by having a note-taking policeman *recite* the unsworn hearsay testimony of the declarant instead of having the declarant sign a deposition. * * * The product of [police interrogation to prove or establish past crime], whether reduced to a writing signed by the declarant or embedded in the memory (and perhaps notes) of the interrogating officer is testimonial."

16. *Problematic effect on some prosecutions: Domestic violence.* In general, *Crawford* has had a deleterious effect on domestic violence prosecutions. See generally Lininger, Prosecuting Batterers after *Crawford*, 91 Va.L.Rev. 747 (2005). As the facts of *Davis & Hammon* illustrate, emergency operators and police are frequently involved with frantic victims shortly after the incident, but some of these victims fail to appear at the time of trial or are unwilling witnesses against their partners or spouses. Prior to *Crawford*, many jurisdictions built prosecutions around 911 tapes, other excited utterances made to emergency workers and police, and special exceptions that relied on *Roberts'* individual indicia of reliability. After *Crawford*, some or all of that evidence was placed in doubt. *Davis & Hammon* opens the door to many 911 calls, but closes it to many statements

on the scene of a past assault made to the police. As *Davis & Hammon* note, domestic violence advocates sought greater flexibility for admission of hearsay under the testimonial definition, but the Court declined, offering instead the forfeiture by wrongdoing exception to the Confrontation Clause when silence is procured or coerced from victims and witnesses.

17. *Problematic effect on some prosecutions: Child sexual abuse cases.* For children's cases, many of the most serious being child sexual abuse prosecutions, clarity of *Crawford*'s application may exist for those statements clearly solicited for the purpose of admission at trial. See State v. Snowden, 867 A.2d 314 (Md. 2005) (finding testimonial a statement obtained by social worker for express purpose of developing testimony under special hearsay exception). However, the coverage of the term testimonial is up in the air for many types of statements by children. The early revelations to parents and doctors may be good candidates for being considered nontestimonial, but after *Davis & Hammon* not some statements to the police. The decisive factors in rendering the statement testimonial are not clear. Whose intent regarding the purpose of the statement matters, the aware police or the perhaps unaware child? Will government involvement be required, and if so, to what degree? Did the expansion of Federal Rule 803(4) to cover statements made, not for treatment purposes, but exclusively for diagnosis mean that all such statements are testimonial since that expansion was intended to admit statements made to doctors whose only function is to give trial testimony?

18. *The future of Roberts. Crawford* sharply criticized *Roberts* but stated for nontestimonial statements that the flexibility of *Roberts* was consistent with the Framers' design "as would an approach that exempted such statements from Confrontation Clause scrutiny altogether." The continued viability of *Roberts* was not directly at issue in *Davis & Hammon. Hammon* was in the same posture as *Crawford* in that the statements were inadmissable as testimonial, rendering the *Roberts* inquiry inconsequential. *Roberts'* continued application to the nontestimonial statements in *Davis* was likewise inconsequential since the statements involved in the case fell within the "firmly rooted" excited utterance exception and were admissable under *Roberts* as they are under *Crawford* analysis. Nevertheless, the Court again signaled its displeasure and indeed *Roberts'* apparent demise: "It is the testimonial character of the statement that separates it from other hearsay that, while subject to traditional limitations upon hearsay evidence, is not subject to the Confrontation Clause." Also, referring to its focus on testimonial hearsay in *Crawford*, the Court stated in *Davis & Hammon*, "A limitation so clearly reflected in the text of the constitutional provision must fairly be said to mark out not merely its 'core,' but its perimeter." Quite arguably *Davis & Hammon* laid *Roberts* to rest and declared the Confrontation Clause inapplicable to hearsay that is not testimonial.

Because *Crawford* did not overrule *Roberts* for nontestimonial statement, *Roberts* was generally treated by the courts as applicable to such hearsay statements when offered against the criminal defendant. Whether it will survive the dicta in *Davis & Hammon* is unclear. Compare United States v. Thomas, 453 F.3d 838, 844 & n.2 (7th Cir. 2006) (stating *Roberts* continues to apply to nontestimonial statements), with United States v. Tolliver, 454 F.3d 660 (7th Cir. 2006) (assuming *Roberts* eliminated for such statements). Whether it will survive future Supreme Court decisions is perhaps even more uncertain. Interestingly, one of the *Roberts'* cases not mentioned at all by Justice Scalia in either *Crawford* or *Davis &*

Hammon is Idaho v. Wright, 497 U.S. 805 (1990), which excluded in a child sexual abuse case accusatory hearsay made in response to leading questions by a pediatrician. If not considered testimonial, would additional screening under the Confrontation Clause through *Roberts* be appropriate for some problematic types of statements like that in *Wright* or for hearsay generally? Is it consistent with the modern Confrontation Clause?

19. *Alternatives of face-to-face confrontation at trial for children: Apparently unaffected by Crawford.* Child abuse cases raise other special Confrontation Clause issues. One of those concerns is the mode of presenting testimony: Where a child-witness would suffer psychological trauma from testifying in the presence of the criminal defendant, does the Constitution permit use of techniques that will eliminate the face-to-face confrontation? In Maryland v. Craig, 497 U.S. 836 (1990), the Court, over Scalia's dissent, concluded that the Confrontation Clause permitted a child-witness to testify outside the physical presence of the defendant upon a case-specific showing that the child would suffer trauma interfering with the ability to testify that is not *de minimis*. See generally Marsil et al., Child Witness Policy: Law Interfacing with Social Science, 65 Law & Contemp.Probs., Winter 2002, at 209. This aspect of Confrontation Clause doctrine is apparently unaffected by *Crawford*, although its general approach was indirectly criticized in another recent Sixth Amendment case. See United States v. Gonzalez–Lopez, 126 S.Ct. 2557, 2562 (2006) ("abstract[ing] from the right to its purposes, and then eliminat[ing] the right"). See also Chapter 12, Section A(3), supra.

20. *General sources.* Berger, The Deconstitutionalization of the Confrontation Clause: A Proposal for a Prosecutorial Restraint Model, 76 Minn. L.Rev. 557 (1992); Counseller & Rickett, The Confrontation Clause after *Crawford v. Washington*: Smaller Mouth, Bigger Teeth, 57 Baylor L.Rev. 1 (2005); Douglass, Beyond Admissibility: Real Confrontation, Virtual Cross–Examination, and the Right to Confront Hearsay, 67 Geo.Wash.L.Rev.191 (1999); Friedman & McCormack, Dial–In Testimony, 150 U. Pa.L.Rev. 1171 (2002); Friedman, Confrontation: The Search for Basic Principles, 86 Geo. L.J. 1011 (1998); Friedman, The Story of *Crawford*, in Evidence Stories 335 (Lempert ed., 2006); Jonakait, Restoring the Confrontation Clause to the Sixth Amendment, 35 UCLA L.Rev. 557 (1988); Jonakait, "Witnesses" in the Confrontation Clause: *Crawford v. Washington,* Noah Webster, and Compulsory Process, 79 Temp.L.Rev. 155 (2006); Lininger, Prosecuting Batterers after *Crawford*, 91 Va.L.Rev. 747 (2005); Massaro, The Dignity Value of Face-to-Face Confrontations, 40 U.Fla.L.Rev. 863 (1988); Mendez, *Crawford v. Washington*: A Critique, 57 Stan.L.Rev. 569 (2004); Mosteller, *Crawford v. Washington*: Encouraging and Ensuring the Confrontation of Witnesses, 39 U.Rich.L.Rev. 511 (2005); Mosteller, Remaking Confrontation Clause and Hearsay Doctrine under the Challenge of Child Sexual Abuse Prosecutions, 1993 U.Ill.L.Rev. 691; Reed, *Crawford v. Washington* and the Irretrievable Breakdown of A Union: Separating the Confrontation Clause from the Hearsay Rule, 56 S.C.L.Rev. 185 (2004); Tuerkheimer, *Crawford* Triangle: Domestic Violence and the Right of Confrontation, 85 N.C.L.Rev. 1 (2006); Symposium: *Crawford* and Hearsay—One Year Later, 20 Crim.Just. 1 (Summer 2005); Symposium: *Crawford* and Beyond, 71 Brooklyn L.Rev. 1 (2005).

Chapter 14[1]

EXCEPTIONS TO THE HEARSAY RULE

SECTION A. PRESENT SENSE IMPRESSIONS AND EXCITED UTTERANCES

FEDERAL RULES 803(1) & (2)

UNITED STATES v. CAIN

United States Court of Appeals, Fifth Circuit, 1979.
587 F.2d 678.

JAMES C. HILL, CIRCUIT JUDGE:

This appeal is from a conviction of interstate transportation of a stolen vehicle under the Dyer Act, 18 U.S.C. § 2312. The appellant seeks reversal of his conviction [, *inter alia*, on the ground that his] conviction was prejudiced by the trial judge's improperly receiving into evidence inadmissible hearsay. We find * * * that * * * his third argument is well-taken. Appellant's conviction is, therefore, reversed.

The appellant and a companion escaped from federal prison in Texarkana, Texas, during the early hours of August 21, 1977. On the following morning a pickup truck was reported missing from a residence approximately one mile from the prison.

At about the same time, a state trooper responding to a motorist's call on a citizens band radio concerning an abandoned truck found the pickup, with a khaki shirt and a tee shirt in it, on a bridge in Louisiana. A second unidentified "CB'er," responding to the state trooper's request for information, reported having seen two white, shirtless males walking from the place where the truck had been abandoned and attempting to hitch a ride toward the east. A call to police headquarters revealed that

1. In the cases and materials throughout the chapter, some footnotes have been omitted and others have been renumbered. [Ed.]

the truck had not been reported stolen, and the trooper then concluded that the truck had probably given out of gas. He sought, by way of a call on his CB, to determine the present whereabouts of the two shirtless men so that he could help them remove the truck from the bridge, where it was blocking a lane of traffic. Other unidentified "CB'ers" informed him that two shirtless, white males were seen walking five to six miles east of the truck's location. Realizing that if these two men were from the truck, they had passed several service stations, the trooper used his police radio to request that anyone seeing them stop them for questioning. A deputy sheriff who was in the area where the two men had been reported to be walking was, at that moment, watching two shirtless, white males walk toward him. As it turned out, these two men were the appellant and his fellow escaped prisoner.

At the deputy sheriff's request, the appellant and his companion entered the deputy's car and were taken to the service station where the state trooper waited with the truck, which had been towed there. When the men refused to answer questions concerning their identity, their clothing, and their connection to the abandoned truck, they were transported to the parish jail, where it was learned that the pickup truck had been stolen in Texarkana and that the two men had escaped from the Texarkana prison.

* * *

Appellant's * * * third argument regarding the improper admission of hearsay into evidence requires that his conviction be reversed. The state trooper was allowed to testify, over objection, concerning the CB radio transmission he received regarding two white, shirtless males leaving the abandoned truck. There is no doubt and the government concedes that the statement constituted hearsay testimony, since it was offered for the truth of the matter therein. No limiting instruction regarding consideration of the statement for any purpose other than its truth was given. *See United States v. Gomez,* 529 F.2d 412, 416 (5th Cir.1976). The government contends that the statement was admissible under Rule 803(1) of the Federal Rules of Evidence and that no confrontation rights of the appellant were infringed. The trial judge agreed with the prosecutor's assertion that the "CB'er's" statement was admissible under the "present sense impression" exception to the hearsay rule. That exception reads as follows:

> (1) Present sense impression. A statement describing or explaining an event or condition made while the declarant was perceiving the event or condition or immediately thereafter.

Id. The appellant correctly points out, however, that his position five miles away within a few minutes of the statement contradicts the possibility that he could have been seen leaving the pickup truck at about that same time. Indeed, for the "CB'er" to have seen the appellant leave the truck immediately prior to his statement, one must make the unlikely assumption that Cain and his companion were transported at high speed immediately upon leaving the truck and resumed walking five miles later just prior to being observed by the deputy sheriff. The distances and time lapses involved make it impossible to determine whether the declaration by the "CB'er" was made immediately following the observation or not, but the chances that it was are slim. The exception to the hearsay rule found in Rule 803(1) is, therefore, inapplicable. The District of Columbia Circuit recently reached a similar conclusion in a case involving a hearsay statement that was calculated to have been made fifteen to forty-five minutes after the subject observation.

> This time span hardly qualifies as 'immediately' after the accident as that term is used in Rule 803(1), particularly in view of the commentary on that Rule contained in the Advisory Committee Notes. This states that the 'most significant practical difference [between 803(1) and 803(2)] will lie in the time lapse allowable between event and statement,' and that 803(1) 'recognizes that in many, if not most, instances, *precise contemporaneity* is impossible, and hence a *slight lapse* is allowable.' 56 F.R.D. 187, 304 (1973) (emphasis added). The thrust of this commentary is that in a circumstance such as that before us, an out-of-court statement made at least fifteen minutes after the event it describes is not admissible unless the declarant was still in a state of excitement resulting from the event.

Hilyer v. Howat Concrete Co., Inc., 578 F.2d 422, 426 n.7 (D.C.Cir.1978). *Accord, United States v. Kehoe,* 562 F.2d 65, 70 (1st Cir.1977); *United States v. Medico,* 557 F.2d 309 (2d Cir.1977). Since the declarant in this case had no reason to be in a state of excitement when he observed the two men or when he spoke and apparently was not in such a state, the "excited utterance" exception provided by Rule 803(2) is also inapplicable.

[The court also held that the evidence is inadmissible under the residual exception of Rule 803(24), now Rule 807.]

We conclude that the statement was inadmissible under the Federal Rules of Evidence and that, viewing the evidence as a whole, there is a significant possibility that the testimony had a substantial impact on the verdict of the jury. *See United States v. Gomez,* 529 F.2d 412, 416–17 (5th Cir.1976). The statement was the only evidence directly linking Cain to the pickup truck. It remains to be seen whether a new jury will consider the remaining evidence, circumstantial in nature, sufficient to connect Cain to the stolen truck and establish his guilt. Having reversed on the basis of the improper admission of hearsay testimony, we consider it unnecessary to decide whether or not Cain's confrontation rights were infringed.

Reversed.

Notes and Questions

1. *Time limitation.* The difference in time spans allowable where a statement is offered under the present sense impression as compared with

the excited utterance exception is shown in Hilyer v. Howat Concrete Co., 578 F.2d 422 (D.C.Cir.1978), cited in *Cain.* Mr. Hilyer, a construction worker, was killed when he was struck by a concrete mixer truck. A fellow worker stated, somewhere between 15 and 45 minutes after the occurrence, that decedent had "backed into" the truck, a statement that supported defendant's contention that the decedent was contributorily negligent. The court expressed doubt that the statement could qualify under Rule 803(1), given the time span, but held the statement admissible as an excited utterance under Rule 803(2). Courts have not, however, required precise contemporaneity. See, e.g., Miller v. Crown Amusements, Inc., 821 F.Supp. 703, 706–07 (S.D.Ga.1993) (call made "in all likelihood, less than 10 minutes after the incident" received as present sense impression). A statement that involves the operation of memory is not admissible. See United States v. Hamilton, 948 F.Supp. 635, 639 (W.D.Ky.1996) (because it requires memory of what was previously seen, a photographic identification does not satisfy the exception). See generally McFarland, Present Sense Impressions Cannot Live in the Past, 28 Fla.St.L.Rev. 907 (2001).

2. *Subject matter.* The exception for present sense impressions ("statement describing or explaining an event or condition") is also more limited than the excited utterance exception ("statement relating to" an event or condition) in terms of the subject matter of the statement. As with the temporal element, the distinction between the two exceptions is based upon the theory that spontaneity has a more limited reach with regard to the statement's subject matter because the statement is not produced by an exciting event. 2 McCormick, Evidence § 271, at 252–54 (6th ed. 2006).

3. *Corroboration.* Some commentators have argued that an additional requirement of the present sense exception is corroboration through the testimony of the declarant or another witness who perceived the events. Waltz, The Present Sense Impression Exception to the Rule Against Hearsay: Origins and Attributes, 66 Iowa L.Rev. 869 (1981). See also United States v. Blakey, 607 F.2d 779, 785 (7th Cir.1979) (noting the argument that corroboration is required). However, court rulings have not embraced such a requirement. See United States v. Ruiz, 249 F.3d 643, 647 (7th Cir.2001); 2 McCormick, Evidence § 271, at 254 (6th ed. 2006). Occasionally courts have required some corroboration. See People v. Hendrickson, 586 N.W.2d 906, 909–10 (Mich.1998) (rejecting "strict" requirement of percipient witness but requiring some corroboration of foundation facts).

MILLER v. KEATING

United States Court of Appeals, Third Circuit, 1985.
754 F.2d 507.

STERN, DISTRICT JUDGE:

The district court admitted into evidence a statement, made by an unidentified declarant at the scene of an automobile accident, amounting to an accusation that the accident was the fault of plaintiff Carol Miller. The district judge admitted the statement as "*res gestae,*" without making reference to any of the hearsay exceptions in Fed.R.Evid. 803, or any findings of fact on the issue of admissibility. Fed.R.Evid. 104(a). We conclude that the district judge erred.

I.

On January 18, 1982, Carol Miller was driving her white Ford LTD east on U.S. Route 22, a limited access highway, near Easton, Pennsylvania. She carried a passenger named Annette Vay. It is undisputed that Miller and Vay were traveling behind a UPS truck and that both vehicles switched into the lefthand lane to avoid a stalled vehicle in the righthand lane near the 25th Street exit ramp. It is also undisputed that, soon thereafter, the Miller car was struck from behind by defendant Texaco's tractor-trailer driven by co-defendant Lawrence Keating. The force of the collision propelled the Miller car first into the side of a car stopped in the righthand lane and then into the rear of the UPS truck. Mrs. Miller sustained serious injuries in the collision. The driver of the car stopped in the righthand lane was Kenneth Parris. His wife, Elfriede Parris, was a passenger.

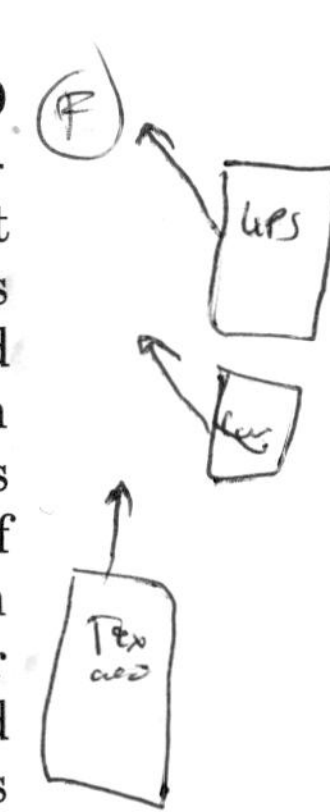

One dispute at trial was over the amount of time that elapsed between the moment when Mrs. Miller pulled into the lefthand lane and the moment when her car was struck from the rear. Another conflict focused on whether the Miller car was stopped behind the UPS truck or was still moving when it was hit by the Texaco tractor-trailer.

Both Mrs. Miller and her passenger, Annette Vay, testified at trial that Miller had completely stopped her car before being rammed by the Texaco truck.[2] According to Vay, the Miller car was stopped in the lefthand lane for "a few seconds" before the accident. Later, she testified that the time period could have been longer than "a second or two." Lawrence Keating testified, however, that he was driving his Texaco tractor-trailer in the lefthand lane, slowing down in order to stop, and there was no vehicle between him and the UPS truck. He testified that he never saw the Miller car pull in front of him, and the first time he saw it was when it was in his lane. He said he saw only a "white blur" half or three-quarters of the way into his lane. He claimed that by the time he saw the Miller car in his lane, he was too close to it to avoid the collision.

There were other inconsistencies at trial of less relevance to the issue here, but several deserve mention because they illustrate the profusion of accounts before the jury. Mrs. Vay, who testified at length at the trial, had previously told police officer Young that she could not tell him what had happened, "[t]hat she did not know." The Parrises, who were stopped in the right lane, both testified that the Texaco truck had come to a full stop in the left lane behind the Parris car (and two car lengths behind the UPS truck, according to Mr. Parris), before the Miller car pulled in front of it. However, both Keating and the UPS driver, Neil Rasmussen, Jr., who was watching out of his side view mirror, depicted the Texaco truck as moving continuously toward the rear of the UPS truck. The UPS driver said, "it looked like I had better give Mr. Texaco all of the room he can have, you know, for stopping." And Keating said he was making "a gradual rolling stop."

2. Citations to the record have been omitted. [Ed.]

There is also a dispute as to when the Parris car arrived alongside the Miller car. Vay and Miller both testified that the Parris car pulled up next to the Miller car during the few seconds it was stopped before being rammed by the Texaco truck. But the Parrises testified that they were stopped in the right lane for "several minutes" or "two minutes" before the accident.

It is the testimony of the Parrises about an incident occurring after the accident that gives rise to this appeal. After being hit in the left side, Mr. Parris pulled his car over. He testified that he left his car, comforted one of the victims in the Miller car, then walked to the rear of the Miller car where his wife was writing down the license plate number of the Miller car. At that point, a man approached and said, "the bastard tried to cut in." In somewhat inconsistent testimony, Mrs. Parris stated that she and her husband "were running towards the car, and I heard this person that was driving—running towards us—* * * [a]nd said the s.o.b. or some words like that, tried to cut in." Mr. Parris could not identify the declarant beyond saying that he was a white male. Mrs. Parris could do no better. There is no indication in the record why she thought the declarant was a driver or which vehicle he drove. Mr. Parris testified that he did not know what vehicle the declarant was driving.

Over objections, the trial judge allowed the Parrises to relate their versions of the declaration to the jury. He admitted the statements as "*res gestae.*" Parenthetically, we note that this terminology is inappropriate. As the trial judge implicitly recognized in his opinion denying post-trial relief, there is no such exception to the prohibition against hearsay. If admissible, the declaration must qualify under one of the genuine exceptions to the hearsay rule. The old catchall, "*res gestae,*" is no longer part of the law of evidence.[3]

As the trial judge also recognized, the excited utterance exception of Fed.R.Evid. 803(2) provides the most likely basis for admitting the statement. The question before us, therefore, is whether that statement by the unknown declarant should have been admitted under Fed.R.Evid. 803(2), which defines "excited utterance" as "[a] statement relating to a startling event or condition made while the declarant was under the stress of excitement caused by the event or condition."

II.

A.

[The court determined that admission of the statement was not harmless error because in] the thicket of conflicting accounts of the accident, the jurors may well have relied heavily on this apparent assignment of blame, made by an unknown person who was not under a

3. As Wigmore notes, "*res gestae*" means literally "the thing done" and properly applies only to words that accompany and aid in giving legal significance to the act. Such words are treated as "verbal acts." Before adoption of the Federal Rules of Evidence, courts applied "*res gestae*" with much confusion to hearsay statements of various sorts. 6 J. Wigmore, *Evidence* § 1745 (J. Chadbourn rev. 1976).

duty to speak truthfully and who can never be confronted about his statement.

B.

The next question is whether the excited utterance exception may ever authorize the admission of a statement by an anonymous declarant. Fed.R.Evid. 806 provides that whenever a hearsay statement is admitted, the declarant's credibility may be attacked through cross-examination and the introduction of evidence of inconsistent statements. The rule confers no absolute right to cross-examination, because hearsay statements may often be admitted despite the unavailability of the declarant. For example, Fed.R.Evid. 804 defines various situations where hearsay testimony comes in even though the declarant is unavailable. Among these are dying declarations, former testimony, and declarations against interest. The unifying trait of all the Rule 803 exceptions is a circumstantial guarantee of trustworthiness sufficient to justify nonproduction of the declarant, whether available or not.[4] Although Rule 806 cannot be read to confer a right to any particular form of attack on the credibility of a hearsay declarant, it does confer a generalized right that is significantly diminished when the hearsay declarant is not only unavailable, but is also unidentified, and the party against whom the hearsay declarant's statement is introduced is thus deprived not only of the right to cross-examine, but of any meaningful prospect of finding evidence of inconsistency or bias.

We do not conclude, however, that statements by unidentified declarants are ipso facto inadmissible under Fed.R.Evid. 803(2). Such statements are admissible if they otherwise meet the criteria of 803(2). But unlike unavailability, which is immaterial to admission under Rule 803, the unidentifiability of the declarant is germane to the admissibility determination. A party seeking to introduce such a statement carries a burden heavier than where the declarant is identified to demonstrate the statement's circumstantial trustworthiness.

At minimum, when the declarant of an excited utterance is unidentified, it becomes more difficult to satisfy the established case law requirements for admission of a statement under Fed.R.Evid. 803(2). Wigmore defines these requirements as: (1) a startling occasion, (2) a statement relating to the circumstances of the startling occasion, (3) a declarant who appears to have had opportunity to observe personally the events, and (4) a statement made before there has been time to reflect and fabricate. 6 J. Wigmore, *Evidence* §§ 1750–51 (J. Chadbourn rev. 1976). *See* Fed.R.Evid. 803 advisory committee note; S. Saltzburg & K. Redden,

4.
"The present rule proceeds upon the theory that under appropriate circumstances a hearsay statement may possess circumstantial guarantees of trustworthiness sufficient to justify nonproduction of the declarant at trial even though he may be available. The theory finds vast support in the many exceptions to the hearsay rule developed by the common law in which unavailability of the declarant is not a factor."

Fed.R.Evid. 803 advisory committee note.

Federal Rules of Evidence Manual 574–75 (3d ed. 1982); J. Weinstein, *Evidence* ¶ 803(2)[01] (1984). There is no doubt that the present case presents a startling occasion and little doubt that the declarant's statement relates to the circumstances of the occurrence. Partly because the declarant is unidentified, however, problems arise with the last two requirements: personal knowledge and spontaneity.

The first of these expresses the familiar principle that a witness may not testify about a subject without personal knowledge. Fed.R.Evid. 602. This rule applies with equal force to hearsay statements. *Kornicki v. Calmar Steamship Corporation,* 460 F.2d 1134, 1138 (3d Cir.1972). To be admissible, the declarant of an excited utterance must personally observe the startling event. *McLaughlin v. Vinzant,* 522 F.2d 448, 451 (1st Cir.1975). The burden of establishing perception rests with the proponent of the evidence. *David v. Pueblo Supermarkets of St. Thomas, Inc.,* 740 F.2d 230, 235 (3d Cir.1984). As in all questions of admissibility, the resolution of any dispute of fact necessary to the question is confided to the trial judge to be decided by a preponderance of the evidence. And while the trial judge is not confined to legally admissible evidence in making the determination, Fed.R.Evid. 104(a), still he must make the findings necessary to support admissibility.

Direct proof of perception, or proof that forecloses all speculation is not required. On the other hand, circumstantial evidence of the declarant's personal perception must not be so scanty as to forfeit the "guarantees of trustworthiness" which form the hallmark of all exceptions to the hearsay rule. Fed.R.Evid. 803 advisory committee note. When there is no evidence of personal perception, apart from the declaration itself, courts have hesitated to allow the excited utterance to stand alone as evidence of the declarant's opportunity to observe. *Garrett v. Howden,* 73 N.M. 307, 387 P.2d 874, 876–78 (1963); *Beck v. Dye,* 200 Wash. 1, 92 P.2d 1113, 1117 (1939). In some cases, however, the substance of the statement itself does contain words revealing perception. A statement such as, "I saw that blue truck run down the lady on the corner," might stand alone to show perception if the trial judge finds, from the particular circumstances, that he is satisfied by a preponderance that the declarant spoke from personal perception.

In this regard, we recognize that we are construing the foundation for Rule 803(2) excited utterances differently than the foundation necessary for admitting co-conspirators' statements as non-hearsay under Rule 801(d)(2)(E). Most courts will not admit a co-conspirator's statement unless there is independent proof, aliunde, of membership in a conspiracy. *In re Japanese Electronic Products Antitrust Litigation,* 723 F.2d 238, 261 (3d Cir.1983). In other words, the statement itself can form no part of evidence establishing admissibility against a non-declarant. By contrast, we find that the statement offered as an excited utterance may itself be a piece of the mosaic establishing its own admissibility.

In the present case, however, the record is empty of any circumstances from which the trial court could have inferred, by a preponderance, that the declarant saw Miller "cut in." The disputed declaration itself does not proclaim it. Indeed, the district judge acknowledged as much in his opinion denying plaintiffs' motion for a new trial. Nevertheless, he drew an inference of perception, reasoning that "the declarant would have made the declaration only if he was in a position to observe the collision." Yet the statements reported by the Parrises—"the bastard tried to cut in" and "the s.o.b., or some words like that, tried to cut in"—alone, do not show more likely than not that the declarant saw the event. The declarant might have been drawing a conclusion on the basis of what he saw as he approached the scene of the accident. He might have been hypothesizing or repeating what someone else had said. It is even possible that the declarant was talking about some other driver who had just cut in front of him. It is far from unlikely that the declarant was a participant in the accident, for the Parrises could never identify or exclude anyone as the speaker. And the tenor of the declaration, i.e., "the bastard tried to cut in," suggests at least the possibility that the declarant was a participant with a natural degree of bias. The self-serving exclamation by a participant in an auto accident "it was the other guy's fault," is hardly likely to qualify as trustworthy.

The circumstances external to the statement itself not only fail to demonstrate that the declarant was in a position to have seen what happened, they also fail to show that the declarant was excited when he spoke. No one so testified, and the trial judge made no finding of excitement. Thus, this last prong of the test for admissibility is also unsatisfied. The assumption underlying the hearsay exception of Rule 803(2) is that a person under the sway of excitement temporarily loses the capacity of reflection and thus produces statements free of fabrication. *See, e.g., Kornicki,* 460 F.2d at 1138; *see also* 6 J. Wigmore *Evidence* § 1747 (Chadbourn rev. 1976). Since lack of capacity to fabricate is the justification for excited utterances, courts have recognized that the length of time separating the event from the statement may be considerably longer than for statements qualifying under the present sense impression exception of Rule 803(1), which is based on the lack of time to fabricate. *See* J. Weinstein, *Evidence* ¶ 803(2)[01] (1984). In *McCurdy v. Greyhound Corporation,* 346 F.2d 224, 226 (3d Cir.1965), for example, this Court approved admission of a statement made ten or fifteen minutes after an accident, recognizing that there can be no arbitrary time limits on the operation of Rule 803(2). Thus, even if several minutes elapsed between the exciting event and the utterance, it is not necessarily an abuse of discretion to admit the statement so long as the trial court explicitly finds it was not the product of conscious reflection. There is no such finding in this case.

We have considered appellants' other contentions and find them to be without merit. The judgment of the district court will be reversed and the case remanded for a new trial.

Notes and Questions

1. *Spontaneity*. Numerous criteria have been suggested as bearing upon the spontaneity of the utterance: lapse of time, place, content of the utterance, physical or mental condition of the declarant, whether made in response to an inquiry, and presence or absence of a motive to fabricate. See United States v. Iron Shell, 633 F.2d 77, 85–86 (8th Cir.1980), Section C, infra. Spontaneity is a preliminary question of fact for the trial judge, and the number of factors to be considered necessarily vests the judge with considerable discretion. 2 McCormick, Evidence § 272, at 259 (6th ed. 2006).

2. *Time requirement, children.* Where children are involved, a number of courts have liberally interpreted the allowable period of time between the exciting event and the child's description of it. See *Iron Shell*, 633 F.2d at 86; State v. Smith, 337 S.E.2d 833, 841–43 (N.C.1985). The theory is that the psychological characteristics of young children tend, as a general matter, to extend the period that is free of the dangers of conscious fabrication. *Smith,* 337 S.E.2d at 842; State v. Padilla, 329 N.W.2d 263, 266 (Wis.Ct.App.1982). In Morgan v. Foretich, 846 F.2d 941, 947 (4th Cir.1988), the court developed a new theory for further expansion of the time limitation for statements involving children. It looked, not to the time lapse since the abuse, but to the time lapse from the child's first opportunity to report it. Cf. United States v. Donaldson, 58 M.J. 477, 482–84 (C.A.A.F.2003) (finding period of 11–12 hours allowable, *inter alia*, because the defendant threatened to kill the victim and family members if she reported the abuse). Occasionally, courts generally question this broad expansion of exception to children, see Reed v. Thalacker, 198 F.3d 1058, 1062 (8th Cir.1999), or as applied to older children, see United States v. Marrowbone, 211 F.3d 452, 455 (8th Cir.2000), but the general pattern is expansive, see United States v. Hefferon, 314 F.3d 211, 222–23 (5th Cir.2002).

Approximately half of the states have enacted specific hearsay exceptions covering the statements of child-victims. Mosteller, Remaking Confrontation Clause and Hearsay Doctrine under the Challenge of Child Sexual Abuse Prosecutions, 1993 Ill.L.Rev. 691, 697. In State v. Myatt, 697 P.2d 836 (Kan.1985), the Supreme Court of Kansas noted that without a separate exception for statements by children, some courts had stretched the limits of existing hearsay exceptions, particularly the time limitation of the excited utterance exception, and had thereby undercut the certainty and integrity of the excited utterance exception. Id. at 842.

3. *Perhaps a narrowing of exception and maybe new life for the res gestae concept?* Although, as the court in *Miller v. Keating* notes, the term "res gestae" has been criticized for leading to confusion, this historical relic may get new life by virtue of the Supreme Court's decision in Crawford v. Washington, 541 U.S. 36 (2004). *Crawford* observed that to the extent that a hearsay exception for excited utterances existed at all at the time of the framing of the Constitution and Bill of Rights, "it required that the statements be made 'immediat[ely] upon the hurt received, and before [the declarant] had time to devise or contrive any thing for her own advantage.' " *Id.* at 58 n.8 (quoting Thompson v. Trevanion, Skin. 402, 90 Eng. Rep. 179 (K.B.1694)). Shortly after *Crawford*, the New Jersey Supreme Court re-

interpreted and restricted its excited utterance hearsay exception with emphasis on its historical roots in the res gestae concept. *See* State v. Branch, 865 A.2d 673, 682–92 (N.J.2005) (excluding statements made while children were excited because there was opportunity to deliberate before making the statement). *See also* Friedman & McCormack, Dial–In Testimony, 150 U.Pa.L.Rev. 1171, 1209–25 (2002) (describing and criticizing expansion of excited utterance exception under Wigmore's influence).

4. *Independent evidence.* In *Miller,* the occurrence of a startling event was established independently of the statements by other witnesses. If this evidence had not been introduced, could the occurrence of a startling event be proved by the utterance of the witness alone? (Similarly, under Rule 803(1), does there need to be any proof beyond the statement that the described event in fact occurred?) Prior to the adoption of the Federal Rules of Evidence, there was considerable theoretical debate on this issue. See Slough, Res Gestae, 2 Kan.L.Rev. 41, 253–56 (1954) (noting the dangers to the hearsay rule in abolition of all corroboration requirements but recognizing that a substantial number of cases, particularly those involving workmen's compensation, admit excited utterances when the only evidence of the happening of the event is the utterance). Under Rule 104(a), contested evidence itself may be considered by the court in ruling upon admissibility. Bourjaily v. United States, 483 U.S. 171 (1987). Accordingly, the theoretical question of admissibility of the statement to prove the event has been resolved. Is the statement standing alone sufficient proof? "Under generally prevailing practice, the statement itself is taken as sufficient proof of the exciting event." 2 McCormick, Evidence § 272, at 256–57 (6th ed. 2006). See also United States v. Brown, 254 F.3d 454, 459–60 (3d Cir.2001).

A similar question is presented as to whether the words of the statement such as "I saw" are by themselves sufficient to prove the declarant's observation of the event. As *Miller* suggests, it will often be found adequate. Cf. State v. Phillips, 461 S.E.2d 75, 84 (W.Va.1995) (sufficiently descriptive statement may prove knowledge under identical requirements of Rule 803(1)).

5. *Subject matter requirement.* The utterance must relate to the startling event. This terminology covers more than merely a description or explanation of the event, and courts have construed it quite liberally. 2 McCormick, Evidence § 272, at 260 (6th ed. 2006). See United States v. Moore, 791 F.2d 566, 572 (7th Cir.1986) (statements reflecting past events admissible under the exception if the subject matter likely evoked by the event). See also Murphy Auto Parts Co. v. Ball, 249 F.2d 508 (D.C.Cir.1957) (admitting a statement of agency by a driver following a collision, the court suggesting that whether the statement goes beyond a description of the exciting occurrence is merely another factor to be weighed in determining the existence of spontaneity).

6. *Unidentified declarant.* Excited utterances are not generally excluded because the declarant was a bystander rather than a participant. The declarant only has to be affected by the event, not involved in it. In most cases, the identity of the bystander is known, and he or she is often a witness at trial. As demonstrated in *Miller,* when the witness' identity is unknown, the cases show more reluctance to admit the declaration. See also

State v. Harris, 531 S.E.2d 340, 345–46 (W.Va.2000) (court should ordinarily conclude statement does not satisfy requirements of rule in criminal case). But cf. Miller v. Crown Amusements, Inc., 821 F.Supp. 703 (S.D.Ga.1993) (statement by unidentified caller to 911 regarding accident admissible under similar requirements of Rule 803(1) where circumstantial evidence and content of call provided basis to satisfy requirements).

7. *Competency requirement.* Some courts find that for children excitement, which theoretically eliminates the concern about fabrication, also eliminates competency concerns related to truthfulness. See Morgan v. Foretich, 846 F.2d 941, 946–47 (4th Cir.1988) (nature of the utterance obviates the usual sources of untrustworthiness); State v. Bingham, 776 P.2d 424, 431 (Idaho 1989) (same). However, this logic should not apply to other sources of incompetency related to youthfulness.

8. *Other hearsay dangers ignored.* Excited utterances are received against a hearsay objection on the basis that the excitement temporarily reduces the capacity for reflection and thereby eliminates the danger of conscious fabrication. Long ago Hutchins and Slesinger pointed out the tendency of emotional stress, on the other hand, to increase another of the hearsay dangers by impairing the accuracy of perception. Some Observations on the Law of Evidence—Spontaneous Exclamations, 28 Colum.L.Rev. 432 (1928). Why should an exception be recognized where one hearsay danger is increased by the operation of the same factor that reduces another danger? In terms of Professor Tribe's hearsay triangle, is it more important to strengthen the left leg or may a hearsay exception rest on the presence of one strong leg, no matter which one it is?

9. *Sources.* Miller, A Shock to the System: Analyzing the Conflict Among Courts Over Whether and When Excited Utterances May Follow Subsequent Startling Events in Rape and Sexual Assault Cases, 12 Wm. & Mary J. Women & L. 49 (2005); Moorehead, Compromising the Hearsay Rule: The Fallacy of Res Gestae Reliability, 29 Loy.L.A.L.Rev. 203 (1995); Orenstein, "My God!": A Feminist Critique of the Excited Utterance Exception to the Hearsay Rule, 85 Cal.L.Rev. 159 (1997).

SECTION B. EXISTING MENTAL, EMOTIONAL, OR PHYSICAL CONDITION

FEDERAL RULE 803(3)

WILKINSON v. SERVICE

Supreme Court of Illinois, 1911.
94 N.E. 50.

MR. JUSTICE CARTER delivered the opinion of the court:

Plaintiff in error, Carrie E. Wilkinson, filed her bill in the superior court of Cook county to set aside the will of her father, Charles D. Hews, on the ground that he was not of sound mind and memory when it was executed. A trial before a jury resulted in a verdict that the writing was the last will and testament of the testator, made while he was of sound mind and memory. A decree to that effect was thereafter entered and the bill dismissed for want of equity. From that decree this writ of error is sued out.

Charles D. Hews was a physician and resided and practiced in Chicago for many years. The plaintiff in error was his daughter and only child. At the time of the trial she had been married for some years and resided in St. Paul. By his will, dated March 23, 1909, Hews gave his small amount of household furniture and surgical and medical material to Dr. James W. Kelly, an intimate personal friend, and the remainder of his property, substantially all real estate, estimated by different witnesses to be worth from $8,000 to $12,000, to his sister, Mary J. Service, one of the defendants in error. The plaintiff in error received nothing under the will. * * *

It is further insisted that portions of the evidence of this witness [the lawyer who drew the will] as to conversations with testator were inadmissible on the ground that they were hearsay, especially the statement of the testator that plaintiff in error's husband had written a letter in which he had directed the doctor not to communicate with the daughter in any way, the letter further stating that the testator had never treated his daughter right, and that when she wanted his assistance he was spending his money on whisky and fast women. The letter was also introduced in evidence. The rule is well established in this State that the declarations of the testator are competent, in a contest involving the validity of his will, to show the state of his mind but not to prove the facts stated. * * * Whatever is material to prove the state of a person's mind or what is passing in it, and what were his intentions, may be shown by his declarations and statements. The truth or falsity of such statements is of no consequence. They are to be used only as showing the condition of his mind. Declarations, prior to the execution of the will, that certain of the testator's children were wanting in natural affection are properly considered as showing his state of mind. * * * The testimony as to the doctor's feeling towards his daughter, and the causes for it, was properly admitted to show the condition of his mind at the time the will was executed. This evidence, taken in connection with the fact that he had several years before drawn two other wills, one giving his daughter $50 and the other $5, and also in connection with other declarations that he had given his divorced wife (the plaintiff in error's mother) quite an amount of property which she could give to plaintiff in error, was properly admitted as tending to show his reasons for disposing of his property as he did, under the will here in question.

* * *

Decree affirmed.

Notes and Questions

1. *Significance of indirect statement?* For the purpose of classification as hearsay, would it make any practical difference whether the testator's statement was, "My daughter does not love me," or "I believe that my daughter does not love me"? From the point of view of being classed as hearsay, is there any difference between the testimony of the lawyer about what the testator told him about the letter and the letter itself?

2. *Emotional condition v. its cause(s).* The principle that the mental or emotional condition of a person may be proved by his or her contemporaneous declarations is firmly established. Further illustration may be found in the alienation of affections cases. Declarations of the alienated spouse are inadmissible hearsay for the purpose of proving the actions of the defendant that are claimed to have resulted in alienation, but they are admissible to prove the state of mind of the alienated spouse before the separation, the effect produced on the alienated spouse, and the reason why the alienated spouse left. Adkins v. Brett, 193 P. 251 (Cal.1920); Glatstein v. Grund, 51 N.W.2d 162 (Iowa 1952).

3. *Alternative forms of expression.* Hinton, States of Mind and the Hearsay Rule, 1 U.Chi.L.Rev. 394 (1934), lists many states of mind and emotion and suggests various possible means of proving their existence: testimony of the person, proof of events conducive to the state, nonverbal conduct (kicking the cat), an assertive statement not offered to prove the truth of the matter asserted ("I am Napoleon" in a competency case), or an assertive statement of an existing state. Consider whether each of the above types of evidence is hearsay, and, if hearsay, whether it comes within the instant exception. See also Hutchins & Slesinger, Some Observations on the Law of Evidence: State of Mind in Issue, 29 Colum.L.Rev. 147 (1929).

4. *Complexity through inferences.* In most cases, rather than being directly relevant, a party is seeking to draw an inference from the existence of the state of mind. The inferences to be drawn increase in complexity in the following cases. See generally Weissenberger, Hearsay Puzzles: An Essay on Federal Evidence Rule 803(3), 64 Temp.L.Rev. 145 (1991).

MUTUAL LIFE INS. CO. v. HILLMON

Supreme Court of the United States, 1892.
145 U.S. 285.

[Liability under policies insuring the life of Hillmon depended upon whether he was in fact dead. Plaintiff claimed that Hillmon was shot accidentally at Crooked Creek, about 175 miles west of Wichita, on March 18. The insurance companies contended that the person killed at Crooked Creek was one Walters, that Hillmon was still alive, and that he and others were engaged in a fraudulent conspiracy. Evidence as to the identity of the body was conflicting. The trial court excluded evidence offered by the insurance companies, consisting of letters written by Walters to his sister and to his fiancée stating that he planned to leave Wichita early in March for Colorado with Hillmon. Defendant insurance companies appeal from judgments rendered on verdicts against them.]

Mr. Justice Gray.

* * *

Much conflicting evidence had been introduced as to the identity of the body. The plaintiff had also introduced evidence that Hillmon and one Brown left Wichita in Kansas on or about March 5, 1879, and travelled together through Southern Kansas in search of a site for a cattle ranch, and that on the night of March 18, while they were in camp at Crooked Creek, Hillmon was accidentally killed, and that his body was taken thence and buried. The defendants had introduced evidence, without objection, that Walters left his home and his betrothed in Iowa in March, 1878, and was afterwards in Kansas until March, 1879; that during that time he corresponded regularly with his family and his betrothed; that the last letters received from him were one received by his betrothed on March 3 and postmarked at Wichita March 2, and one received by his sister about March 4 or 5, and dated at Wichita a day or two before; and that he had not been heard from since.

The evidence that Walters was at Wichita on or before March 5, and had not been heard from since, together with the evidence to identify as his the body found at Crooked Creek on March 18, tended to show that he went from Wichita to Crooked Creek between those dates. Evidence that just before March 5 he had the intention of leaving Wichita with Hillmon would tend to corroborate the evidence already admitted, and to show that he went from Wichita to Crooked Creek with Hillmon. Letters from him to his family and his betrothed were the natural, if not the only attainable, evidence of his intention.

* * * A man's state of mind or feeling can only be manifested to others by countenance, attitude or gesture, or by sounds or words, spoken or written. The nature of the fact to be proved is the same, and evidence of its proper tokens is equally competent to prove it, whether expressed by aspect or conduct, by voice or pen. When the intention to be proved is important only as qualifying an act, its connection with that act must be shown, in order to warrant the admission of declarations of the intention. But whenever the intention is of itself a distinct and material fact in a chain of circumstances, it may be proved by contemporaneous oral or written declarations of the party.

The existence of a particular intention in a certain person at a certain time being a material fact to be proved, evidence that he expressed that intention at that time is as direct evidence of the fact, as his own testimony that he then had that intention would be. After his death there can hardly be any other way of proving it; and while he is still alive, his own memory of his state of mind at a former time is no more likely to be clear and true than a bystander's recollection of what he then said, and is less trustworthy than letters written by him at the very time and under circumstances precluding a suspicion of misrepresentation.

The letters in question were competent, not as narratives of facts communicated to the writer by others, nor yet as proof that he actually went away from Wichita, but as evidence that, shortly before the time when other evidence tended to show that he went away, he had the intention of going, and of going with Hillmon, which made it more probable both that he did go and that he went with Hillmon, than if there had been no proof of such intention. In view of the mass of conflicting testimony introduced upon the question whether it was the body of Walters that was found in Hillmon's camp, this evidence might properly influence the jury in determining that question.

* * *

Upon principle and authority, therefore, we are of opinion that the two letters were competent evidence of the intention of Walters at the time of writing them, which was a material fact bearing upon the question in controversy; and that for the exclusion of these letters, as well as for the undue restriction of the defendants' challenges, the verdicts must be set aside, and a new trial had. * * *

Judgment reversed, and case remanded to the Circuit Court, with directions to set aside the verdict and to order a new trial.

Notes and Questions

1. *Threats.* The authorities cited by the Court to support its decision have been omitted for brevity. Strangely enough, none of these authorities involves the admissibility of evidence of threats by an accused to prove that the acts threaten were taken, which involves a similar use of state of mind and whose admissibility has never been doubted. 1A Wigmore, Evidence § 105 (Tillers rev. 1983); 6 Wigmore, Evidence § 1732 (Chadbourn rev. 1976). Similarly, to support a claim of self-defense in a homicide case, evidence is admissible that the victim made threats against the accused, although the accused had no knowledge of them. 1A Wigmore, Evidence § 110 (Tillers rev. 1983). It should be noted that a quite distinct theory—impact on the hearer that renders the statement nonhearsay because not offered for the truth of the matter asserted under Rule 801(c)—supports the admission of threats actually communicated by the victim to the accused.

2. *Relevancy v. hearsay.* Once the soundness of establishing mental state by contemporaneous declarations is conceded, the next step in a *Hillmon* situation is relatively simple. As a matter of relevancy, the conclusion is difficult to escape that a person who intends to do an act is more likely to do so than one who has no such intent. 2 McCormick, Evidence § 275, at 273 (6th ed. 2006). While objections are often noted concerning the strength of such evidence given the possibility of intervening circumstances or changed intentions, these are more appropriately considered as issues involving relevancy rather than hearsay. See Lempert, Gross & Liebman, A Modern Approach to Evidence 589 (3d ed. 2000). The hazard of giving the inference too great an effect is a real one. See United States v. Moore, 571 F.2d 76 (2d Cir.1978) (evidence of a statement by one of the defendants that

kidnap victim would be taken out of the state held insufficient to prove interstate transportation).

3. *Dangers in backward-looking hearsay.* If a person's mental state in the form of a statement of intention to do an act in the future is admissible to prove the subsequent doing of an act, why should not the declarant's state of mind in the form of memory be admissible as evidence of the happening of the event? Are statements that a person intends to take action more reliable than statements that he or she has done so? Which is subject to greater hearsay dangers?

In general, while the *Hillmon* doctrine has permitted the use of state of mind to prove the declarant's future conduct, the proposition that a declaration of state of mind may be used to prove the happening of a prior act has been rejected, particularly the prior act of another person. One reason for this result is practical. In Shepard v. United States, 290 U.S. 96 (1933), the Supreme Court ruled inadmissible the statement of Mrs. Shepard that "Dr. Shepard has poisoned me" offered by the government under the state of mind exception. It noted, "[d]eclarations of intention, casting light upon the future, have been sharply distinguished from declarations of memory, pointing backwards to the past. There would be an end, or nearly that, to the rule against hearsay if the distinction were ignored." Id. at 105–06. The theoretical distinction is that when statements relate to an intention of the declarant to do a future act, the hearsay dangers of faulty memory and misperception are eliminated. In terms of Professor Tribe's hearsay triangle, the dangers located on the right leg are eliminated. Lempert, Gross & Liebman, A Modern Approach to Evidence 585–86 (3d ed. 2000). Rule 803(3) writes this limitation into the text of the Rule through the provision "not including a statement of memory or belief to prove the fact remembered or believed."

4. *A piece of history.* A rich literature on the *Hillmon* case has developed. See Hutchins & Slesinger, Some Observations on the Law of Evidence—State of Mind to Prove an Act, 38 Yale L.J. 283 (1929); Maguire, The *Hillmon* Case—Thirty-three Years After, 38 Harv.L.Rev. 709 (1925); Payne, The *Hillmon* Case—An Old Problem Revisited, 41 Va.L.Rev. 1011 (1955); McFarland, Dead Men Tell Tales: Thirty Times Three Years of the Judicial Process After *Hillmon,* 30 Vill.L.Rev. 1 (1985). The history of the *Hillmon* case is described in Wigmore, The Science of Judicial Proof 970 (3d ed. 1937); later in MacCracken, The Case of the Anonymous Corpse, 19 American Heritage 51 (No. 4, June 1968); and most recently in Wesson, The *Hillmon* Case, The Supreme Court, and The McGuffin, in Evidence Stories 277 (Lempert ed., 2006).

UNITED STATES v. DAY

United States Court of Appeals, District of Columbia Circuit, 1978.
591 F.2d 861.

["Beanny" Day and Eric Sheffey were indicted for the murder of Gregory Williams, who was killed by a shotgun blast fired from a person inside a parked car. Prior to trial, the district judge excluded proposed testimony by Mason, a government witness, that Williams, a few minutes before he was killed, gave Mason a slip of paper on which he had written "Beanny, Eric 635–3135" and told Mason "if he [Williams] wasn't back home by three the next day to call the police and tell them what he had told me and give them the number." The ruling also excluded testimony by Mason that at the same time Williams told him that Williams and "Beanny" had a fight over [stolen] guns and coats and that "Beanny" and "his boy" were trying to "get out on him." The government appealed.[5]]

MacKinnon, Circuit Judge

* * *

We turn first to the Government's contention in their brief and at oral argument that the following testimony should be admitted: * * * the contemporaneous statement that if he (Williams) was not home by 3:00 o'clock the next day, Mason should call the police, tell them what he had said, and give them the number.

The Government, in arguing this point, does not seek to have admitted the content of "what he (Williams) had said," concerning the statements made prior to giving Mason the slip of paper about the fight and the dispute between him and Day, the robbery, and the location of the guns.

In arguing that the statement which immediately accompanied the delivery of the slip of paper is not hearsay, the Government states: "All that is sought to be proven in connection with the statement now under consideration, is that it was *in fact* made." Govt.Br. at 31 (emphasis in original). But in actuality, the Government seeks to have something more inferred from the content of the statement. The jury is being asked to infer from Williams' words that Day bore ill will toward Williams and had reason to cause him harm. Because this inference attaches to Williams' statement, the Government is seeking to use the statement for more than the mere fact that it was made.

The Government also contends that this statement is admissible as an utterance contemporaneous with a non-verbal act which relates to and elucidates that event, i.e., the giving of the piece of paper. Govt.Br. at 31 n.41. Professor Wigmore has described the limitations which attended the use of utterances forming the verbal part of an act. The first limitation is:

> [T]he conduct that is to be made definite must be independently material and provable under the issues, either as a fact directly in issue or as incidentally or evidentially relevant to the issue. The use of the words is wholly subsidiary and appurtenant to the use of the conduct. The former without the latter have no place in the case, and could only serve as a hearsay assertion in direct violation of the rule * * *.

5. [A federal statute, 18 U.S.C.A. § 3731, allowed the prosecution to appeal before trial certain rulings excluding or suppressing evidence to avoid the bar that the Double Jeopardy Clause imposes on appeals by the government after acquittal. Ed.]

VI Wigmore on Evidence, § 1773, at 268 (Chadbourn rev. 1976). In this case, the conduct to be made definite is that Williams gave Mason a slip of paper. Had Williams said "take this slip," that utterance would have been "wholly subsidiary and appurtenant" to the conduct. Here, Williams said more, and the inference from those words is not wholly incidental to the conduct. We conclude that the statement accompanying the delivery of the paper is inadmissible hearsay.

Our analysis does not end here, as Rule 803(3) provides an exception for evidence of state of mind. That rule provides: * * *

> (3) Then existing mental, emotional, or physical condition. A statement of the declarant's then existing *state of mind,* emotion, sensation, or physical condition (such as intent, plan, motive, design, *mental feeling,* pain, and bodily health), but not including a statement of memory or belief to prove the fact remembered or believed unless it relates to the execution, revocation, identification, or terms of declarant's will. [Emphasis added.]

We briefly summarized the purpose of the exception in United States v. Brown, 160 U.S.App.D.C. 190, 490 F.2d 758 (1973):

> [T]he state of mind exception to the hearsay rule allows the admission of extrajudicial statements to show the state of mind of the declarant at that time *if that is the issue in the case.* * * * It also allows such statements to show a future intent of the declarant to perform an act if the occurrence of that act is at issue.

160 U.S.App.D.C. at 194, 490 F.2d at 762 (emphasis added). We noted that such statements invariably contain some extraneous factual elements which necessitate limiting instructions to ensure that the statements are considered solely on the issue of the declarant's mental state and not for the truth of the matters contained therein. 160 U.S.App.D.C. at 195, 490 F.2d at 763. We also noted that whether such evidence is admissible is subject to the rule of extrinsic policy, which is now embodied in Rule 403:

> [*S*]*ome* evidence, while bearing some *logical* relevance to the case, may in the discretion of the judge nevertheless be excluded where its probative value is substantially outweighed by the danger of *unfair* prejudice, confusion or delay.

Id. (emphasis in original except "unfair").[6] While Williams' statements to Mason are some indication of his state of mind, i.e., to fear of the

6. We elaborated upon these dangers later in the opinion:

> Quite a number of courts have confronted facts similar to those here involving hearsay statements made by the victim of a homicide which inferentially implicate the defendant. Such statements by the victims often include previous threats made by the defendant towards the victim, narrations of past incidents of violence on the part of the defendant or general verbalizations of fear of the defendant. While such statements are admittedly of some value in presenting to the jury a complete picture of all the facts and circumstances surrounding the homicide, it is generally agreed that their admissibility must be determined by a careful balancing of their probative value against their prejudicial effect. Courts

future, there is a danger that the jury would misuse such evidence. We described the nature of the balancing process at length in *Brown,* supra, and we need not restate that discussion here.

We think that the inference to be drawn from Williams' statement to Mason which accompanied his handing over of the slip of paper, involving as it did somewhat of a prophecy of what might happen to him, has too great a potential for *unfair* prejudice, and we do not think that a limiting instruction can correct that deficiency. As was the case in *Brown,* the prejudicial dangers in the statement in question are substantial. Had Williams referred to prior harmful acts or threats by Day, such statements would be even more unfairly prejudicial, but even here "a palpable danger exists" that the jury will infer from the statement, "if anything happens to me, call the police and give them the names on this slip [i.e., Day and Sheffey]," that Day and Sheffey were capable of murder, or that they had done things in the past to justify Williams' apprehension. Such inferences insofar as they reflect on defendants' intentions or past conduct would be improperly drawn. See 160 U.S.App. D.C. at 210, 490 F.2d at 778. In fact, on the present record, Williams' state of mind, from which such inferences would be drawn, is immaterial. Of course, the situation will be different if the defendant seeks to adduce evidence tending to show self-defense or accident. Under the present circumstances of this case, we find the proffered evidence in this regard to be inadmissible at the outset of the Government's case in chief, and we would doubt the efficacy of a limiting instruction.

[The court held that the slip of paper itself with the names and telephone number on it was admissible because it was not offered for its truth under Rule 801(c). It likewise concluded that Mason could testify that sometime in the hour before the shooting Williams gave him the slip of paper. The act of handing over the paper, while potentially communicative, was not assertive of a crime and was therefore admissible.]

* * * The ruling of the district court excluding the testimony of Kerry Mason is affirmed in part and reversed in part, as set forth in this opinion.

Judgment accordingly.

SPOTTSWOOD W. ROBINSON, III, CIRCUIT JUDGE, dissenting in part:

* * *

I am in complete accord with the court's application of Judge MacKinnon's perceptive opinion in *Brown* to the bulk of the statements made by Williams to Mason. I cannot, however, reconcile *Brown* with admission of (a) the slip bearing appellees' names and a telephone number, (b) testimony by Mason that when Williams turned the slip over he made a statement or (c), evidence that Mason called the police after

have recognized that such statements are fraught with inherent dangers and require the imposition of rigid limitations. 160 U.S.App.D.C. at 197–98, 490 F.2d at 765–66.

the shooting and gave them the information on the slip—when it is combined with the first two.

* * *

Notes and Questions

1. *Why relevant?* An obvious condition of the admission of statements showing directly or circumstantially the declarant's state of mind is that such state of mind be relevant to the issues in the litigation. The declarant's fear is rarely directly relevant. In certain fact patterns, it may be indirectly useful in showing the declarant's likely conduct, which *Hillmon* shows is generally a permissible use of the exception. United States v. Green, 680 F.2d 520, 523 (7th Cir.1982), provides an example. There the victim's statements showing fear of the defendant were relevant to help prove she did not accompany him voluntarily, which was relevant to proving a kidnapping charge. See also United States v. Adcock, 558 F.2d 397 (8th Cir.1977) (victim's fear crucial in extortion cases). *Day* states that the admissibility decision would be "different if the defendant seeks to adduce evidence tending to show self-defense or accident." In those two situations, the declarant's fear of the defendant would be relevant to show that it was unlikely, given his fear, that he attacked the defendant and the defendant responded in self-defense or that he was, for example, inspecting the defendant's gun collection and accidentally shot himself with defendant's gun.

In *Day*, other than to show indirectly that the victim had reasons to fear the defendants and thereby to communicate indirectly the historical facts that gave rise to his fear, fear had no relevance. As discussed in the notes following the *Hillmon* case, Rule 803(3) prohibits use of statements admissible under Rule 803(3) to prove past facts. Therefore, statements of fear relevant only to prove those past facts are inadmissible. Furthermore, if the jury is not inferring the defendant's likely future conduct from those past facts as proved through the declarant's fear, fear should be inadmissible as speculative, unless clairvoyance is accepted. It is important to note that under other hearsay exceptions, such as Rules 803(2)(excited utterances) or 804(b)(2) (dying declarations) that rely on other theories of trustworthiness, statements may prove events and the actions of others in the past.

2. *Fear and domestic violence.* Statements of fear of a domestic partner are often found in domestic violence cases and are generally excluded to prove the perpetrator's identity. See State v. Canaday, 911 P.2d 104, 111–12 (Haw.Ct.App.1996). See also Commonwealth v. Laich, 777 A.2d 1057, 1060–61 (Pa.2001) (victim's prior statements regarding "state of the relationship" not admissible to show defendant's intent). In part in response to exclusion of a statement of this sort by Nicole Brown Simpson, California created a new hearsay exception for statements of past threats made by presently unavailable declarants that are recorded in writing or electronically or made to police officers. See Cal.Evid. Code § 1370. Without the benefit of a special rule, the North Carolina Supreme Court has repeatedly admitted statements of fear and related statements by those who later became victims under Rule 803(3) to establish the actions and intent of the defendant in domestic assaults, frequently homicides. See, e.g., State v. Alston, 461 S.E.2d 687

(N.C.1995). That analysis has been sharply criticized as a matter of both relevancy and hearsay theory. See 2 McCormick, Evidence § 276, at 282 n.24 (6th ed. 2006).

3. *Events rather than emotions.* In *Day,* the declarant's state of mind could be inferred from his statements of fact, and the issue was whether the likely misuse of those statements in spite of a limiting instruction required their exclusion under Rule 403. A similar problem also frequently encountered is that even when the declarant has made direct statements of his or her state of mind or emotion, those statements are accompanied by descriptions of the event that gave rise to those feelings. See Adkins v. Brett, 193 P. 251 (Cal.1920) (in alienation of affection case, wife's admissible statements of feelings contained inadmissible statements concerning automobile rides, dinners, and gifts involving defendant). With the exception of statements related to the declarant's last will, where admission is based on practical rather than theoretical grounds, Federal Rule 803(3) excludes statements concerning the cause of the state of mind.

United States v. Cohen, 631 F.2d 1223 (5th Cir.1980), provides a typical example of the operation of this restriction. Cohen defended on the ground of duress in that his alleged coconspirator, Galkin, had forced him to cooperate in the illegal scheme. The court upheld the exclusion of testimony under Rule 803(3) of Cohen's hearsay statements regarding Galkin's threats.

> [T]he state-of-mind exception does not permit the witness to relate any of the declarant's statements as to why he held the particular state of mind, or what he might have believed that would have induced the state of mind. If the reservation in the text of the rule is to have any effect, it must be understood to narrowly limit those admissible statements to declarations of condition—"I'm scared"—and not belief—"I'm scared because Galkin threatened me." Cohen's witnesses were permitted to relate any direct statements he had made concerning his state of mind but were prevented only from testifying to his statements of belief—that he believed that Galkin was threatening him.

Id. at 1225. *See also* United States v. Samaniego, 345 F.3d 1280, 1282–83 (11th Cir.2003) (finding an apology would be admissible to show the emotion of remorse, but inadmissible to prove why he was remorseful).

STATE v. TERROVONA

Supreme Court of Washington, En Banc, 1986.
716 P.2d 295.

ANDERSEN, JUSTICE.

FACTS OF CASE

At issue in this case is the admissibility of much of the State's evidence against the defendant, James R. Terrovona, who is appealing his conviction for the first degree murder of his stepfather, Gene Patton.

At about 8:15 p.m. on February 26, 1984, the decedent, Gene Patton, received a telephone call at his home. He told his girl friend that the phone call was from the defendant. He said that the defendant had apparently run out of gas on 116th in Marysville and wanted his (the decedent's) assistance. The decedent also said that he (the decedent) must be crazy, but left for the avowed purpose of helping the defendant.

At about 8:30 p.m., a passerby found a body lying alongside a car on 116th Street. Shortly after 9:00 p.m. Snohomish County deputies identified the deceased. He had been severely beaten and shot. The subsequent autopsy revealed that the cause of death was gun shots to the head and abdomen. * * *

ISSUE ONE. Did the trial court err in admitting hearsay evidence of the statements the decedent made as he left home to meet his death? * * *

CONCLUSION. Under ER 803(a)(3), the decedent's statements to his girl friend were admissible in evidence because they evinced his then state of mind.

A statement made out of court that is offered in court to prove the truth of the matter stated is inadmissible hearsay evidence unless it falls within one of the exceptions to the hearsay rule. One exception to the hearsay rule allows evidence of a declarant's state of mind * * * is ER 803(a)(3) * * *. This rule is in accord with previous Washington law providing that statements of a declarant's then existing state of mind are admissible in evidence if there is need for their use and if there is substantial probability of their trustworthiness.

Fed.R.Evid. 803(3) is the same as ER 803(a)(3). Under both rules, hearsay evidence is admissible if it bears on the declarant's state of mind and if that state of mind is an issue in the case.[7] Under the federal rule, the state of mind exception has also been held to authorize admission of evidence of a party's intentions as circumstantial evidence that he acted according to those intentions. This extension of the state of mind exception is known as the "*Hillmon* doctrine."[8]

Long before the present evidentiary rules were adopted, the United States Supreme Court examined the state of mind rule in *Mutual Life Ins. Co. v. Hillmon,* 145 U.S. 285 * * * (1892). The issue in *Hillmon* was the identity of a body found at a campsite. The plaintiffs in that case contended that the body was that of a Mr. Hillmon. The defendants contended the body was that of a Mr. Walters and sought to introduce letters Walters had written stating that he intended to go to the area of the campsite with Hillmon. The Supreme Court found the letters admissible for two purposes:

> The letters in question were competent, * * * as evidence that, * * * [Walters] had the intention of going, and of going with Hillmon, which made it more probable both that he did go and that he went with Hillmon, than if there had been no proof of such intention.

7. *United States v. Pheaster,* 544 F.2d 353, 376 (9th Cir.1976); *State v. Parr,* 93 Wash.2d 95, 98–99, 606 P.2d 263 (1980).

8. *Pheaster,* at 376; *United States v. Stanchich,* 550 F.2d 1294, 1297 n.1 (2d Cir. 1977).

Hillmon, at 295–96 * * *.

Although *Hillmon* was a civil case, the Court cited with approval a number of criminal cases in support of its decision.

One such case was *Hunter v. State,* 40 N.J.L. 495 (1878). In that case, Hunter was indicted for the murder of Armstrong. At issue was the admissibility of Armstrong's letters and statements, conveyed to his wife and son on the date of his death, to the effect that he was going on a business trip with Hunter. The Court quoted as follows from *Hunter,* at 538:

> In the ordinary course of things, it was the usual information that a man about leaving home would communicate, for the convenience of his family, * * * At the time it was given, such declarations could * * * mean harm to no one; * * * If it is legitimate to show by a man's own declarations that he left his home to be gone a week, or for a certain destination, which seems incontestable, why may it not be proved in the same way that a designated person was to bear him company? * * * If it was in the ordinary train of events for this man to leave word or to state where he was going, it seems to me it was equally so for him to say with whom he was going.

Hillmon, at 299 * * *. A similar fact pattern, and much the same analysis, is found in *State v. Vestal,* 278 N.C. 561, 180 S.E.2d 755 (1971).

Under *Hillmon,* therefore, a declarant's statement of future intent is admissible to prove: (1) that the declarant went to the place indicated by his or her statement of intention, and (2) that the declarant went there with the other named party.[9]

Most courts have expanded the "*Hillmon* doctrine" to admit hearsay statements of intent that implicate a third party's conduct.[10] This expansion is commonly used in murder trials, where courts admit a decedent's hearsay statements that implicate the defendant in the murder.[11] Courts use such evidence despite conflicting guidance in the comments to Fed.R.Evid. 803(3). That rule itself makes no reference to *Hillmon,* but the comments contain this statement by the Advisory Committee: " 'The rule of *Mutual Life Ins. Co. v. Hillmon* * * *, allowing evidence of intention as tending to prove the doing of the act intended, is, of course, left undisturbed.' "[12] Following this observation is one from the House Judiciary Committee: " 'the Committee intends that the Rule be construed to limit the doctrine of [*Hillmon*], so as to render statements of intent by a declarant admissible only to prove *his* future conduct, not the future conduct of another person.' "[13] * * *

9. *Clark v. United States,* 412 A.2d 21, 29 (D.C.Ct.App.1980); *see also United States v. Astorga–Torres,* 682 F.2d 1331, 1335–36 (9th Cir.1982); *State v. Abernathy,* 265 Ark. 218, 222, 577 S.W.2d 591 (1979).

10. *See* Note, *Federal Rule of Evidence 803(3) and the Criminal Defendant: The Limits of the Hillmon Doctrine,* 35 Vand. L.Rev. 659, 683 (1982); *see also Astorga–Torres,* at 1335–36; *Stanchich,* at 1297 n.1.

11. Note, 35 Vand.L.Rev. at 686 * * *.

12. Note, 35 Vand.L.Rev. at 681.

13. Note, 35 Vand.L.Rev. at 681–82.

The defendant argues that under *State v. Parr,* 93 Wash.2d 95, 606 P.2d 263 (1980), the decedent's statements as to the defendant's phone call to him are inadmissible to show that the defendant met the decedent on 116th Street. At issue in *Parr* was the admissibility of a decedent's statements that she feared Parr and that he once threatened her. This evidence was introduced to rebut a claim that the defendant accidentally shot the victim in self-defense.[14] We observed there that the inference to be drawn from such testimony was that the defendant wanted to and did kill the victim and was unduly prejudicial. *Parr* held that ER 803(a)(3) "permits statements reporting the declarant's state of mind, but does not permit statements reporting the conduct of another which might have induced that state of mind."[15]

Parr is distinguishable from the case before us. Here, the decedent's statements concerning his intention to take a certain action shortly before he was killed necessarily implicated the defendant's future conduct. The decedent said that because the defendant had called him, he (the decedent) was going to meet the defendant on 116th Street. Unlike *Parr,* the State is not relying on past incidents to prove the defendant's subsequent conduct.

The Ninth Circuit recognized that state of mind evidence used to prove subsequent conduct of the declarant and a third party is not foolproof, but concluded that any unreliability goes to the weight of the evidence rather than to its admissibility.

> Even where no actions by other parties are necessary in order for the intended act to be performed, a myriad of contingencies could intervene to frustrate the fulfillment of the intention. The fact that the cooperation of another party is necessary if the intended act is to be performed adds another important contingency, but the difference is one of degree rather than kind. The possible unreliability of the inference to be drawn from the present intention is a matter going to the weight of the evidence which might be argued to the trier of fact, but it should not be a ground for completely excluding the admittedly relevant evidence.

United States v. Pheaster, 544 F.2d 353, 376 n.14 (9th Cir.1976). We agree.

One New York court has found a greater degree of reliability in using *Hillmon* evidence to prove the conduct of a third person.

> Everyday experience confirms that people frequently express an intent to see another under circumstances that make it extremely likely that such a meeting will occur. Indeed, it is not uncommon for such expressions of intent to be more trustworthy evidence that the meeting took place than many statements of intent with regard to the performance of acts not involving any inference with regard to another person.

14. *Parr,* at 98, 606 P.2d 263.

15. *Parr,* at 104 n.1, 606 P.2d 263.

People v. Malizia, 92 A.D.2d 154, 460 N.Y.S.2d 23, 27 (1983), *aff'd,* 62 N.Y.2d 755, 476 N.Y.S.2d 825, 465 N.E.2d 364 * * * (1984).

The decedent's statements, made before leaving his house, about the phone call from the defendant and his intention to go help him, constituted the State's strongest evidence of the defendant's guilt. Neither this defendant's nor the decedent's states of mind were at issue in the trial. Under the "*Hillmon* doctrine", however, the decedent's intentions were admissible to infer that he acted according to those intentions, and that he acted with the person he mentioned. The conduct of the decedent and the defendant after the phone call was definitely at issue in the trial. The decedent's statements under the circumstances here created a trustworthy inference that the defendant met him on 116th Street where he was killed within a half hour of receiving the phone call and leaving his home. Those statements were properly admitted into evidence, the weight of such evidence being for the jury. * * *

Affirmed.

Notes and Questions

1. *Future actions of another.* The problem of admissibility was greatly simplified in *Hillmon* because the parties agreed that Hillmon went to Crooked Creek. The question was whether Walters went there. Some courts have reached the result in *Terrovona* by allowing the evidence of intention to show such things as opportunity, with a limiting instruction not to use the evidence as proof of any act by the nondeclarant. Can and will a jury make the distinction? See People v. Alcalde, 148 P.2d 627 (Cal.1944) (declarations by the murder victim that she was going out with the accused on the night of the killing admitted with a limiting instruction that the statement showed only decedent's intention). Is the limitation imposed in *Alcalde* that the statement shows only the intent of the declarant meaningful or valid? The Second Circuit permits the statement of intention of the declarant to establish the nature of the transaction contemplated where the third party's participation is proven by independent evidence. United States v. Cicale, 691 F.2d 95, 103–04 (2d Cir.1982). A minority of courts have excluded state of mind evidence when offered to show another person's conduct directly or indirectly through the intent of the declarant. See Clark v. United States, 412 A.2d 21, 29–30 (D.C.1980) (such statements excluded because inconsistent with theory of state of mind exceptions and because only reliable as to declarant's own intention).

2. *Will cases and other expansions of the doctrine.* Despite the limitation announced in Shepard v. United States, 290 U.S. 96 (1933), that the state of mind exception could not be used to show past acts, numerous decisions admitted subsequent declarations of testators to show an "influenced" state of mind, Annot., 148 A.L.R.1225, and to show genuineness or due execution of a will, Annot., 62 A.L.R.2d 855. Rule 803(3) explicitly continues this practice of admitting statements of memory or belief to prove past acts in cases relating to wills. Other exceptions were also created under common law analysis, including subsequent declarations of intent relative to deliveries of deeds by grantors, Annot., 34 A.L.R.2d 588, subsequent declara-

tions of agents to show knowledge, People v. One 1948 Chevrolet Convertible Coupe, 290 P.2d 538 (Cal.1955). Whether these additional exceptions survive adoption of evidence rules that do not explicitly codify them is unclear. See generally McFarland, Dead Men Tell Tales: Thirty Times Three Years of the Judicial Process After *Hillmon,* 30 Vill.L.Rev. 1 (1985) (arguing that the *Hillmon* doctrine has continued to expand and threatens the integrity of the hearsay doctrine).

UNITED STATES v. VELTMANN

United States Court of Appeals, Eleventh Circuit, 1993.
6 F.3d 1483.

FAY, CIRCUIT JUDGE:

Defendants Chris Veltmann and Carl Veltmann were convicted of matricide and uxoricide[16] respectively. Each defendant was also found guilty on twenty eight counts of mail and wire fraud based on insurance claims arising from Elizabeth Veltmann's death and fire damage to the family home [and were sentenced to life in prison]. Defendants appeal their convictions based, [*inter alia*] on the trial court's * * * exclusion of state-of-mind evidence * * *. We REVERSE * * *.

FACTS

Elizabeth Veltmann ("Elizabeth") died the evening of January 7, 1990 during a fire in the home she shared with her husband, Carl Veltmann ("Carl"). The couple had just returned from a week-long honeymoon cruise with Elizabeth's son, Christopher Veltmann ("Chris"), and his new bride.

The fire was caused by arson; the crux of the case is the identity of the arsonist(s). The government theorized that Carl and Chris set fire to the house with the knowledge that Elizabeth was inside and with intent to recover proceeds under various insurance policies. Defendants argued that Elizabeth, beset with fiscal worries and physical maladies, committed suicide after setting fire to the home. To evaluate the sufficiency of the evidence and harmlessness of evidentiary rulings, we must review in some detail the relevant facts pertaining to the fire, Elizabeth's state of mind, and the circumstantial case against the defendants.

I. The Fire

On January 7, 1990, at 9:41 p.m., a neighbor called 911 after hearing an alarm and seeing smoke and flames coming from a second floor window of the Veltmann's three story residence. Firefighters broke into the house through the locked front door and found Elizabeth unconscious in the third floor master bedroom. She could not be revived. No one else was found in the home.

The investigation revealed the fire had three separate points of origin. The majority of damage was caused by a fire in the first floor

16. [The murder of a wife by her husband. Ed.]

foyer. * * * The second fire was in the garage and the third in the dumbwaiter in the second floor kitchen. * * *

There was no forced entry into the house other than that made by firefighters. Although numerous people had access to keys, there were apparently no suspects other than Carl and Chris who had both access to the house and knowledge of the home protection systems.

II. Elizabeth Veltmann's State-of-Mind

The defense's case rested on proof that Elizabeth was suicidal. Elizabeth's autopsy revealed that her blood-alcohol level at death was .149, with a .33 level of Dalmane, a prescription sedative, in her system. Carbon monoxide test samples yielded a 73 to 75 percent result evidencing the cause of death as acute carbon monoxide intoxication from the inhalation of smoke and gases. The physician testified he did not consider suicide because it was not suggested by the police. Although Elizabeth was discovered two feet away from the sliding glass door, there is no forensic evidence that she was attempting to escape because her feet were not analyzed for soot deposits. She was found lying face down on the floor, clutching a tissue or handkerchief, nearby bills, bank statements, and family photos strewn across the floor. Approximately a year and a half after her death, Carl found an undated suicide note written by Elizabeth. The authenticity of the note was not challenged.

Contradictions permeate evidence of Elizabeth's physical and psychological condition. Elizabeth and Carl were married for twenty-five years, were business partners, and were described by a number of witnesses as a loving and devoted couple. Elizabeth was happy about Chris' recent marriage and excited about the honeymoon cruise. But numerous indicators point to Elizabeth's deep distress over her medical and financial problems.

Elizabeth suffered from a variety of physical maladies. She was treated for years with a variety of pain killers, and eventually became a prescription drug addict. In 1987, Elizabeth suffered respiratory arrest as a result of a self-induced drug overdose. Psychiatrists suspected a suicide attempt, but Elizabeth steadfastly refused to admit she was depressed and checked out of the hospital against medical advice. An addictionologist concluded that Elizabeth eventually became desperate for drugs as evidenced by stockpiling her supply, forging a prescription, obtaining drugs in her father's name, and trying to manipulate a nurse and another friend into providing her with drugs illegally. The expert postulated that she took most or all of the drugs in her system near the time of death. He concluded that the sudden infusion of alcohol and prescription drugs was consistent with suicide by overdose. But with a delay of fifteen to sixty minutes between taking the drugs and becoming incapacitated by their effect, considering her tolerance level, Elizabeth was probably able to set a simple fire and negotiate the stairs in the house (or operate the elevator) for some period of time after taking the drugs. The government's expert believed that given her level of drug intoxication, Elizabeth was not ambulatory during the time in which the fire must have been set.

In addition to being chemically dependent, Elizabeth was deeply troubled about what seemed to be impending financial ruin. She needed money for drugs and was trying to keep her dependency a secret. The Veltmann's corporation filed for bankruptcy in December, 1989. Their home, built in 1985 with Elizabeth as general contractor, was on the market. In the months preceding her death, Elizabeth tried to borrow money from a number of people.

The most telling indicator of Elizabeth's monetary dilemma and mental state was not admitted into evidence. In a videotaped deposition, Carl Engstrom testified that Elizabeth extracted $500,000 from him over the past twenty-five to thirty years. She was apparently blackmailing him based on their brief affair that took place when she was married to her first husband. Engstrom believed that Elizabeth would eventually pay him back because she frequently promised to do so. A few months before she died, Elizabeth talked to Engstrom about the possibility of her death, and instructed him to see Chris about being paid when she was gone. She mentioned suicide several times. In early December, 1989, Engstrom sent money which Elizabeth never picked up. She called him again for money on December 31 or January 1st, from Miami, where she was waiting to board the cruise ship. She called him collect from the Cayman Islands on January 6th, again demanding money. He refused. * * *

An addictionologist testified that suicidal ideation typically develops over two or three years, and that Elizabeth's earlier suicide threats to Engstrom were evidence of suicidal thinking. In the expert's view, Engstrom's cutting off of funds that Elizabeth could use for drugs was the "major precipitating event" in her suicide.

The financial picture was not entirely gloomy. The Veltmanns were willing to accept an incoming offer of $1,200,000 for the house and an adjacent lot. Carl testified that this money would be used to pay off mortgages with the balance infused into their failing corporation. But Elizabeth told friends that she did not want to live any longer, and that no one would have her house after she was gone; she believed Carl would remarry after her death, but "another Mrs. Veltmann" would not have what she had. Elizabeth said she would destroy everything.

III. The Evidence Against Carl and Chris Veltmann

* * * The government argued that the arson and murder were motivated by greed, and that defendants had the opportunity and knowledge to commit the crime. * * * David Meehan, Chris' cellmate, testified to admissions allegedly made by Chris while in custody. * * * Terry Price, Carl's cellmate, testified that Carl told him the fire was set with lighter fluid, but that he left for Montana the day before the fire and was hunting when the fire started. * * * Price testified that Carl said he dated the suicide note "January 7, 1990" because the insurance

companies would not pay off otherwise; presumably Carl believed that the note should be dated, and that the date of death was most likely to promote payment by the insurers. * * * [Other incriminating evidence was also offered by the government.] Carl denied having anything to do with the arson to his residence and with the death of his wife. * * *

DISCUSSION

* * *

The Evidentiary Rulings

A. *State of Mind Evidence*

Defendants appeal the trial court's exclusion of Carl Engstrom's videotaped deposition. Defendants offered the deposition as relevant hearsay, admissible pursuant to Fed.R.Evid. 803(3), reflecting Elizabeth's state-of-mind. The government objected, claiming that decedent did not threaten suicide in the last phone call with Engstrom, and that threats of suicide in months preceding her death were inadmissible hearsay and irrelevant. The district court agreed with the government, also finding the information cumulative and collateral, and excluded the deposition testimony. We believe the trial court erred. The deposition was admissible under the state of mind exception, and while conceivably cumulative, its import was such that exclusion violated defendants' right to put on a defense. This abuse of discretion requires reversal.

Rule 803(3) of the Federal Rules of Evidence allows the admission of "* * *[a] statement of the declarant's then existing state of mind, emotion, sensation or physical condition (such as intent, plan, motive, design, mental feeling, pain and bodily health) * * *." The declarant's statement of mind must be relevant to some issue in the case before such testimony can be admitted under Rule 803(3). * * *

A homicide victim's state of mind is unquestionably relevant to the defense theory that she committed suicide. The government maintains that Elizabeth's earlier suicide threats and references to dying were too remote to make Engstrom's testimony relevant. The time lag between Elizabeth's references to dying and her death warrants further examination.

In *In re Fill,* 68 B.R. 923 (Bankr.S.D.N.Y.1987), an action to avoid allegedly fraudulent transfers, the transferee was permitted to offer state of mind hearsay evidence of the debtor's declarations that he intended to repay the loans even though such statements were made six years before actual repayment. The court discussed a continuity of time concept relevant to the state of mind inquiry, quoting a leading commentator as follows:

> Although it is required that the statement describe a state of mind or feeling existing at the time of the statement, the evidentiary effect of the statement is broadened by the notion of the continuity of time in states of mind * * *. Since, however, the duration of state of mind or emotion varies with the particular attitudes or feelings at

> issue and with the cause, it is reasonable to require as a condition of invoking the continuity notion that the statement mirror a state of mind which, *in light of all the circumstances* including proxity [sic] in time, has some probability of being the same condition existing at the material time * * *.

Id. at 928, *citing McCormick,* Evidence, § 294, at 844–45 (Cleary, 3d ed. 1984) (emphasis added).

The court noted that substantial weight must be given to the "significant number of years between the making of the statement that the loans would be repaid and the actual repayment of the loans * * *." *Id.*

The temporal relationship between Elizabeth's statements and her death is far less attenuated than the six year time lag analyzed in *Fill.* Where one threatens suicide, talks about what should be done in event of her death, and dies within months under suspicious circumstances including the presence of a suicide note and other witnesses corroborating her depression and suicidal ideation, we do not believe uncertainty over the exact date of the suicide threats should preclude admission of those statements to show state of mind.

The totality of the circumstances convinces us that Engstrom's testimony was relevant, admissible hearsay under the state of mind exception for another reason. Elizabeth was dependent on him for money. Five hours before she died, after a quarter of a century of responding to her demands, Engstrom told Elizabeth he would not give her any more money.[17] Engstrom was asked how Elizabeth responded. He answered:

> She said, "Well, I'm all washed up then," or some words to that effect. She couldn't—she had to have money to go, continue operation.

The extent of Elizabeth's financial dependence on Engstrom figured prominently in her mental state on January 7th. We hold that Engstrom's deposition was relevant, admissible state of mind evidence because it contained not merely references to suicide, but information pertinent to decedent's desperate mental condition regarding finances on the date of her death.

However, our inquiry is not over. The trial court ruled that the testimony was cumulative and collateral. Defendants argue that exclusion of crucial, relevant, admissible evidence violated their constitutional right to present a defense. *Rock v. Arkansas,* 483 U.S. 44, 52 * * * (1987). The Engstrom deposition, they say, provided Elizabeth's motive for self-destruction. * * *

We move, then, to a brief review of admitted testimony to determine if Engstrom's deposition was, in fact, cumulative or collateral. Elizabeth's relationship with Engstrom figured prominently in the conclu-

17. Engstrom did testify that he had refused Elizabeth before, but agreed that he was cutting her off in no uncertain terms in the January 7th call.

sions of the defenses' addictionologist. The expert testified that Engstrom's cutting off of funds that Elizabeth could use to buy drugs was the "major precipitating event" in her suicide. Nonetheless, his only direct reference to Engstrom was as follows:

> Q. * * * Did you find precipitating events in the case of Elizabeth Veltmann that would lead to suicide?
>
> A. Rejection by Mr. Ingstrom [sic] and his—the apparent finality of this, you are getting no more money. That's got to be perceived by her as an enormous threat because, how am I going to pay for these drugs? * * * R.16–53.

We cannot find, nor has counsel brought to our attention any other references to Engstrom in testimony or evidence heard by the jury.

"Although the trial court has discretion to exclude testimony and will not be reversed absent an abuse of discretion, the trial court's discretion does not extend to exclusion of crucial relevant evidence." *United States v. Ethridge,* 948 F.2d 1215, 1218 (11th Cir.1991) (citation omitted). Although a number of witnesses talked about Elizabeth's depression, threat to destroy her house, drug addiction, and financial straits, no witness brought to the jury that aspect of decedent's financial desperation arising from the end of a successful, long-term, blackmail. We find that exclusion of this evidence impaired defendants' right to fully present their defense, requiring reversal and remand for new trial.

* * *

Notes and Questions

1. *Limitations recognized.* Although expanding the reach of the exception, two basic limitations described earlier are honored by *Veltmann*. First, the statement describes a then existing state of mind. Second, the statement is used to prove the conduct of the declarant in the future rather than past conduct or conduct of others.

2. *Sincerity as a requirement?* May a trial court exclude a statement of the declarant's then existing state of mind as not falling within Rule 803(3) because it doubts the sincerity of the statement? The court in United States v. DiMaria, 727 F.2d 265, 272 (2d Cir.1984), held that it was improper to exclude the defendant's exculpatory statement of his reason for being in possession of stolen cigarettes immediately upon his arrest by officers who had the location of the cigarettes under surveillance. Speaking specifically as to Rule 803(3), it stated:

> [T]he scheme of the Rules is to determine that issue [a particular guarantee of credibility] by categories; if a declaration comes within a category defined as an exception, the declaration is admissible without any preliminary finding of probable credibility by the judge, save for the "catch-all" exceptions * * * and the business records exceptions of Rule 803(6) ("unless the source of the information or the method or circumstance of preparation indicate lack of trustworthiness").

United States v. Ponticelli, 622 F.2d 985, 991–92 (9th Cir.1980), appears to take a different position:

> In making the foundational inquiry on admissibility under * * * [803(1), 803(2), and 803(3)], the court must evaluate three factors: contemporaneousness, chance for reflection, and relevance. The state of mind declaration has probative value, because the declarant presumably knows what his thoughts and emotions are at the time of his declarations. * * * The state of mind declaration also has probative value, because the declarant presumably has no chance for reflection and therefore for misrepresentation. * * * The greater the circumstances for misrepresentation, the less reliable is the declaration. * * *
>
> In weighing these factors, the trial court did not abuse its discretion in concluding that Ponticelli had a chance for reflection and misrepresentation in making the proffered statements. Ponticelli's declarations came after his arrest; thus, he was aware that he was under investigation and that anything he said could be used against him. Since, in proffering this testimony, Ponticelli's trial attorney did not advise the court how much time elapsed between the arrest and the statements, the court was entitled to conclude that Ponticelli had sufficient time * * * to concoct an explanation * * *. Finally, Ponticelli made the statement while consulting an attorney. This fact implies that Ponticelli was considering the legal significance of his declarations at the time he made them.

Some courts have tried to reconcile *DiMaria* and *Ponticelli*. See United States v. Cardascia, 951 F.2d 474, 497–88 (2d Cir.1991); United States v. Hogan, 886 F.2d 1497, 1512 (7th Cir.1989). One difference between the cases is the timing. However, even statements of intent made during a criminal conspiracy may not be admitted if they are construed as backward looking to characterize past acts rather than viewed as statements of current state of mind. See United States v. Cianci, 378 F.3d 71, 106–07 (1st Cir.2004).

Courts can exclude evidence under the concepts of relevance and prejudice contained in Rules 401–403. Rule 403 may provide an alternate way for courts to accomplish the result prohibited in *DiMaria* when it questions the trustworthiness of a self-serving statement. See United States v. Peak, 856 F.2d 825, 834 (7th Cir.1988); United States v. Yu, 697 F.Supp. 635, 637–38 (E.D.N.Y.1988); 2 McCormick, Evidence § 270, at 249–50 (6th ed. 2006) (suggesting use of Rule 403 to exclude as a preferable, although still somewhat controversial, approach).

3. *Physical condition.* In addition to mental and emotional conditions, Rule 803(3) covers statements of sensation and physical condition such as pain and bodily health. These statements, unlike those covered by Rule 803(4), need not be made to a physician or for the purpose of medical treatment or diagnosis. On the other hand, since contemporaneity is the guarantee of trustworthiness, statements concerning past sensations or conditions are inadmissible. Does contemporaneity provide sufficient protections against contrived statements? Should the exception be limited to admit only statements of sudden pain rather than reports of a chronic condition? Is there a realistic alternative to receiving such statements in spite of the dangers of conscious contrivance to establish the presence and effects of

chronic pain? Issues of whether statements are self-serving and contrived arise not only in situations where intent is at issue but also in those where the declarant's statements establish existing physical condition. The general answer provided by *DiMaria* regarding statements of mental conditions applies to physical conditions as well.

4. *Limited trustworthiness.* Exceptions to the hearsay rules are generally seen as based on some very rough mix of trustworthiness and necessity. See, e.g., *Dallas County v. Commercial Union Assur. Co.*, Section L, infra. For statements under Rule 803(3), how impressive is the guarantee of trustworthiness?

SECTION C. STATEMENTS FOR PURPOSE OF MEDICAL DIAGNOSIS OR TREATMENT

FEDERAL RULE 803(4)

UNITED STATES v. IRON SHELL

United States Court of Appeals, Eighth Circuit, 1980.
633 F.2d 77.

STEPHENSON, CIRCUIT JUDGE.

Defendant, John Louis Iron Shell, appeals from a jury conviction of assault with intent to commit rape in violation of the Major Crimes Act, 18 U.S.C. § 1153 (1970).

* * *

The indictment in this case arose out of the defendant's acts on July 24, 1979, in the community of Antelope, which is within the Rosebud Indian Reservation and near Mission, South Dakota. The defense conceded at trial that Iron Shell had assaulted Lucy, a nine-year-old Indian girl. The key questions at trial concerned the nature of the assault and the defendant's intent.

* * *

Dr. Mark Hopkins, a physician with the Indian Health Service, examined Lucy at about 8:20 p.m. on the night of the assault. During his examination the doctor elicited a series of statements from Lucy concerning the cause of her injuries. Dr. Hopkins was only aware that Lucy was allegedly a rape victim and was not told of the details surrounding the assault. During the examination, in response to questions posed by the doctor, Lucy told Dr. Hopkins she had been drug into the bushes, that her clothes, jeans and underwear, were removed and that the man had tried to force something into her vagina which hurt. She said she tried to scream but was unable because the man put his hand over her mouth and neck.[18] The doctor, over objection, repeated Lucy's statement at trial.

18. Out of the presence of the jury, the doctor testified that he first asked Lucy "what happened" and she didn't answer. He asked whether she was in any pain and

Dr. Hopkins' examination also revealed that there was a small amount of sand and grass in the perineal area but not in the vagina. He also found superficial abrasions on both sides of Lucy's neck and testified that they were consistent with someone grabbing her but qualified his statement by adding that he could not absolutely determine that they were so caused. Dr. Hopkins also testified that there was no physical evidence of penetration, the hymen was intact and no sperm was located.

Lucy was able to add little and could only partially confirm the above record at trial. Lucy, a nine-year-old, was able to answer a number of preliminary questions demonstrating her ability to understand and respond to counsel but was unable to detail what happened after she was assaulted by the defendant. She did testify that she remembered something happening near the bushes and that a man had pushed her down. Lucy also said at trial that the man told her if she "didn't shut up he would choke me." In response to a series of leading questions she confirmed that the man had put his hand over her neck, hit her on the side of the face, held her down, taken her clothes off and that Mae Small Bear had scared the man, making him leave.[19] On cross-examination defense counsel did not explore any of the substantive issues, nor did he examine Lucy concerning the statement she made to Dr. Hopkins, although he had the opportunity.

Dr. Hopkins' Testimony

* * *

she pointed to her vaginal area. He asked if she hurt anywhere else and she didn't answer. Dr. Hopkins again asked "what happened" and Lucy said she had been drug into the bushes. The doctor then asked if the man "had taken her clothes off." She said yes, and then related the facts set out above. Dr. Hopkins testified that he was not "badgering" the patient, nor "dragging information out," but was asking "simple questions."

19. The following is a representative sample of the prosecutor's direct examination of Lucy:

Q. What did the man do when he pushed you down, Lucy?

A. (Long hesitation)

Q. What did he do?

A. (Long hesitation)

Q. Did he hurt you any place?

A. (Long hesitation)

Q. Do you remember that?

A. (Long hesitation)

Q. Where did he put his hand, did he put his hand on your neck?

A. Yes

Q. Did you get hit on the side of the face?

A. Yes.

Q. When he pushed you down, did he hold you down?

A. Yes.

Q. Did you start crying?

A. Yes.

THE COURT: As much as you can, phrase your questions in a way to avoid any unnecessary leading.

Q. What else happened when he had you down, Lucy; did he say anything to you, do you remember?

A. (Long hesitation)

Q. What did he say to you, can you tell me? Tell me what he said?

A. (Long hesitation)

Q. Could you do that for me?

A. Yes.

Q. Okay, tell me what he said?

A. If I didn't shut up he would choke me.

Defendant challenges the admission of statements made by Lucy to Dr. Hopkins during his examination. The prosecution offered this testimony admittedly as hearsay but within the exception expressed in Rule 803(4). The rule states: * * *

> (4) * * * Statements made for purposes of medical diagnosis or treatment and describing medical history, or past or present symptoms, pain, or sensations, or the inception or general character of the cause or external source thereof insofar as reasonably pertinent to diagnosis or treatment.

Fed.R.Evid. 803(4). The defendant argues that the questions asked by Dr. Hopkins and the information received in response to those questions were not "reasonably pertinent" to diagnosis or treatment. The defense stresses Dr. Hopkins' question in which he asked Lucy whether the man had taken her clothes off and suggests that this was asked by one in the role of an investigator, seeking to solve the crime, rather than a doctor treating or diagnosing a patient. The defendant also asserts that the doctor's examination would have been the same whether or not this extra information had been received. The defense argues that this point supports his claim that the questions were not pertinent to treatment or diagnosis because they had no affect on the doctor's examination. Lastly, the defendant urges that the doctor was employed for the specific purpose of qualifying as an expert witness and as such his testimony should be more suspect.

It is clear that Rule 803(4) significantly liberalized prior practice concerning admissibility of statements made for purposes of medical diagnosis or treatment. *See* Notes of Advisory Committee on Proposed Rules, Rule 803 * * *. Rule 803(4) admits three types of statements: (1) medical history, (2) past or present sensations, and (3) inception or general cause of the disease or injury. All three types are admissible where they are "reasonably pertinent to diagnosis or treatment." The rule changed prior law in two main points. First, the rule adopted an expansive approach by allowing statements concerning past symptoms and those which related to the cause of the injury. Second, the rule abolished the distinction between the doctor who is consulted for the purpose of treatment and an examination for the purpose of diagnosis only; the latter usually refers to a doctor who is consulted only in order to testify as a witness.[20] *See* Weinstein & Berger, *supra,* at 803–125.

Lucy's statements fall primarily within the third category listed by 803(4).[21] The key question is whether these statements were reasonably

20. This is the first Eighth Circuit opinion to consider the effect of 803(4) on its pre–1975 case law. This circuit had followed the majority rule which prevented admission of testimony concerning the cause of the injury as not connected with treatment and excluded statements made to a physician who examined the patient solely for the purpose of testifying. * * * Some courts had also held that a physician could repeat a patient's statement regarding medical history or past symptoms for the limited purpose of explaining the basis of an opinion and not in order to prove the truth of the out-of-court declarations. This distinction was likewise rejected by the federal rules. Notes of Advisory Committee on Proposed Rules * * *.

21. Dr. Hopkins testified that Lucy said she was experiencing pain in her vaginal

pertinent to diagnosis or treatment. The rationale behind the rule has often been stated. It focuses upon the patient and relies upon the patient's strong motive to tell the truth because diagnosis or treatment will depend in part upon what the patient says. It is thought that the declarant's motive guarantees trustworthiness sufficiently to allow an exception to the hearsay rule. *See Meaney v. United States,* 112 F.2d 538 (2d Cir.1940). Judge Weinstein, in his treatise, suggests another policy ground. He writes that "a fact reliable enough to serve as the basis for a diagnosis is also reliable enough to escape hearsay proscription." Weinstein & Berger, *supra,* at 803–129. This principle recognizes that life and death decisions are made by physicians in reliance on such facts and as such should have sufficient trustworthiness to be admissible in a court of law. This rationale closely parallels that underlying rule 703 and suggests a similar test should apply, namely—is this fact of a type reasonably relied upon by experts in a particular field in forming opinions. *See* Fed.R.Evid. 703 (Basis of Opinion Testimony by Experts). Thus, two independent rationales support the rule and are helpful in its application. A two-part test flows naturally from this dual rationale: first, is the declarant's motive consistent with the purpose of the rule; and second, is it reasonable for the physician to rely on the information in diagnosis or treatment.

We find no facts in the record to indicate that Lucy's motive in making these statements was other than as a patient seeking treatment. Dr. Hopkins testified that the purpose of his examination was two-fold. He was to treat Lucy and to preserve any evidence that was available. There is nothing in the content of the statements to suggest that Lucy was responding to the doctor's questions for any reason other than promoting treatment. It is important to note that the statements concern what happened rather than who assaulted her. The former in most cases is pertinent to diagnosis and treatment while the latter would seldom, if ever, be sufficiently related.[22] *See United States v. Nick,* 604 F.2d 1199, 1201–02 (9th Cir.1979). All of Lucy's statements were within the scope of the rule because they were related to her physical condition and were consistent with a motive to promote treatment. The age of the patient also mitigates against a finding that Lucy's statements were not within the traditional rationale of the rule. The trial court placed special

area. This expression of a present symptom falls within the second category of 803(4) and would also be excepted from the hearsay rule under rule 803(3) covering a then existing physical condition. Fed.R.Evid. 803(3). The remainder of Lucy's statement concerns the general character and nature of the cause of the injury. Because of the result we reach in this case, it is not necessary to discuss this distinction at length.

22. The advisory committee notes on 803(4) provide that statements as to fault would not ordinarily qualify. The notes use this example: "a patient's statement that he was struck by an automobile would qualify but not his statement that the car was driven through a red light." Advisory Committee Notes, *supra,* at 585. Another example concludes that a statement by a patient that he was shot would be admissible but a statement that he was shot by a white man would not. *United States v. Narciso,* 446 F.Supp. 252, 289 (E.D.Mich.1977). And the fact that a patient strained himself while operating a machine may be significant to treatment but the fact that the patient said the machine was defective may not. *See Stewart v. Baltimore & O.R. Co.,* 137 F.2d 527, 530 (2d Cir.1943).

emphasis on this factor and we likewise find that it is important to our holding.

During an extensive examination outside the presence of the jury, Dr. Hopkins explained in detail the relevancy of his questions to the task of diagnosis and treatment. He testified that a discussion of the cause of the injury was important to provide guidelines for his examination by pinpointing areas of the body to be examined more closely and by narrowing his examination by eliminating other areas. It is not dispositive that Dr. Hopkins' examination would have been identical to the one he performed if Lucy had been unable to utter a word. The doctor testified that his examination would have been more lengthy had he been unable to elicit a description of the general cause, although he stated the exam would have been basically the same. The fact that in this case the discussion of the cause of the injury did not lead to a fundamentally different exam does not mean that the discussion was not pertinent to diagnosis. It is enough that the information eliminated potential physical problems from the doctor's examination in order to meet the test of 803(4). Discovering what is not injured is equally as pertinent to treatment and diagnosis as finding what is injured. Dr. Hopkins also testified, in response to specific questions from the court, that most doctors would have sought such a history and that he relied upon Lucy's statements in deciding upon a course of treatment.[23]

Weinstein & Berger, *supra,* at 803–130 (footnotes omitted). It is not necessary to find, and we do not hold in this case, that the fact that the doctor took the information is prima facie evidence that it was pertinent. Rather, we conclude that a close examination of the facts and circumstances in each case is required.

In light of this analysis we hold that it was not an abuse of discretion to admit the doctor's testimony. * * *

Affirmed.

Notes and Questions

1. *Three changes.* As *Iron Shell* notes, Rule 803(4) changed prior law in three ways: first, it admits statements concerning past symptoms; second, it permits admission of statements of causation of the condition or injury; and third, it abolishes the distinction between statements to a doctor consulted for the purpose of treatment and one who is consulted for the purpose of

23. Judge Weinstein approached the problem as follows:

> Much depends on the doctor's analysis. The doctor may or may not need to know that his patient was struck by a train and what caused him to fall under the train since dizziness before the accident may bear on diagnosis. A doctor consulted after the patient was involved in an automobile accident may need to know that the accident was precipitated when the patient fainted while driving. Since doctors may be assumed not to want to waste their time with unnecessary history, the fact that a doctor took the information is prima facie evidence that it was pertinent. Courtroom practice has tended to let in medical records and statements to nurses and doctors fairly freely, leaving it to the jury to decide probative force.

diagnosis only. These developments are considered in turn in the notes below.

2. *Past symptoms.* On the admission of past symptoms, the Federal Rule followed the progressive trend of cases such as Peterson v. Richfield Plaza, Inc., 89 N.W.2d 712 (Minn.1958). As *Peterson* stated:

> [I]f the statements of the patient are deemed trustworthy for the reason that proper treatment rests on the truth of such statements, it is difficult to distinguish between the reliability of statements made in the doctor's presence as to subjective symptoms existing at that time and statements made which relate to similar symptoms, pertaining to the injury or ailment which the doctor seeks to diagnose, that the patient has experienced before coming to the doctor's office.

Id. at 721. See also 2 McCormick, Evidence § 277, at 285 (6th ed. 2006) (past symptoms received based on assurance of reliability arising from patient's belief that effective treatment requires accuracy as to past, as well as current, symptoms). This ability to receive evidence of past events under Rule 803(4) is one of the major differences between this exception and Rule 803(3) as applied to statements of physical and mental condition.

3. *Causation.* Admitting statements of causation under the Rule constituted a more substantial change in existing law. The tradition had been to exclude the patient's statement regarding the cause of his or her condition on the theory that it was not relevant to diagnosis and treatment and thus not within the guarantee of trustworthiness. See, e.g., Clark v. People, 86 P.2d 257 (Colo.1939) (error to admit statement of deceased to physician that abortion had been performed by defendant). See also 6 Wigmore, Evidence § 1722 (Chadbourn rev. 1976). However, some cases reflected a trend to recognize that the manner in which an injury was sustained, short of excursions into fault and responsibility, could be relevant to diagnosis and treatment. See, e.g., Shell Oil Co. v. Industrial Comm'n, 119 N.E.2d 224 (Ill.1954) (proper to admit statement of claimant that he slipped and hurt his back while pulling pipe). Rule 803(4) includes statements of general causation under the theory that the guarantee of trustworthiness extends to such statements when reasonably pertinent to diagnosis or treatment. See State v. Cookson, 837 A.2d 101, 109 (Me.2003) (admitting statement by depressed patient to nurse practitioner that defendant had been following and stalking her as describing external source of depression and pertinent to treatment); State v. Momplaisir, 815 A.2d 65, 72 (R.I.2003) (admitting statement that injured patient had been struck by a club as medically pertinent).

4. *Fault.* However, as *Iron Shell* notes, while statements as to cause are admitted under this theory, statements as to fault or identity of the perpetrator are generally not. This is because statements in the second category would generally fail to satisfy either of the rationales for the exception. First, such statements are not likely to be motivated by the patient's selfish interest in facilitating proper treatment. Second, they are seldom, if ever, sufficiently related to proper diagnosis and treatment to be reasonably relied upon by the doctor. See also Cook v. Hoppin, 783 F.2d 684, 690 (7th Cir.1986) (putting prime emphasis on whether statements of fault

are reasonably pertinent to diagnosis or treatment and observing that "much will depend on the treating physician's own analysis").

5. *Identifying statements.* A substantial number of cases have recognized an exception to the general rule excluding statements that identify the perpetrator in cases involving sexual abuse of children where, the theory is, knowledge of identity may be relevant to the child's placement, see United States v. Renville, 779 F.2d 430, 436–39 (8th Cir.1985); Goldade v. State, 674 P.2d 721, 726 (Wyo.1983), or treatment of continuing psychological problems, see Hawkins v. State, 72 S.W.3d 493, 498 (Ark.2002); State v. Robinson, 735 P.2d 801, 810 (Ariz.1987). But see Cassidy v. State, 536 A.2d 666, 682–83 (Md.Ct.Spec.App.1988) (finding child's placement outside scope of exception).

6. *Diagnosis-only statements.* The third change made by the Rule, which is probably the most dramatic, is to admit statements made to physicians consulted only for the purpose of diagnosis, which generally means a doctor who is consulted solely to testify at trial. Under traditional analysis, judicial attitudes changed radically when the physician to whom the statement was made was not the treating physician but one who makes an examination for the purpose of testifying. In the latter situation, it was recognized that the declarant/"patient" might be motivated to embellish or fabricate symptoms and therefore trustworthiness was lacking. Although such statements were not admitted for their truth, statements made to a testifying physician were admissible as the basis for an opinion, a distinction in use that required a considerable intellectual feat by jurors. It was perceived futility of admitting testimony for the limited purpose of providing the basis of the doctor's diagnosis along with trust in medical experts to screen out unreliable statements that caused the drafters of the Federal Rule to admit statements made for diagnosis only as a hearsay exception. See Advisory Committee Note.

Are these sufficient justifications for admission of hearsay? Note that, when made for diagnosis only, the declarant's "selfish treatment interest" does not necessarily support the reliability of the statement since inaccurate declarations will not result in erroneous treatment because none is contemplated. Does acceptance of this rationale mean that statements received under Rule 703 to support the basis of the expert's opinion are also substantively admissible? Should the 2000 amendment to Rule 703 that restricts receipt of otherwise inadmissible evidence have any effect on this exception? Does the skill of the person who hears the statement provide a basis for admission of hearsay in any other situations? See generally Perrin, Expert Witnesses under Rules 703 and 803(4) of the Federal Rules of Evidence: Separating the Wheat from the Chaff, 72 Ind.L.J. 939 (1997).

Some jurisdictions differ from the Federal Rule and have limited the exception to situations where treatment is contemplated. See, e.g., State v. Hinnant, 523 S.E.2d 663, 669 (N.C.2000) (requiring satisfaction of common law treatment motivation); Pa.R.Evid. 803(4) ("medical diagnosis in contemplation of treatment"). See generally Mosteller, The Maturation and Disintegration of the Hearsay Exception for Statements for Medical Examination in Child Sexual Abuses Cases, 65 Law & Contemp.Probs., Winter 2002, at 47.

7. *Admissibility of statements to non-physicians.* The exception admits statements when made for the purpose of medical diagnosis even when not made to a physician. Such statements may be made directly by the patient to persons who are not doctors. See State v. Smith, 337 S.E.2d 833, 839–40 (N.C.1985) (statements of child sex victims to grandmother describing past assault and physical trauma admissible under this exception since children cannot independently seek medical treatment but must rely on their caretakers). Similarly, the motivation of the patient to speak truthfully to a treating physician is readily extended to include statements of parents or close family members relating the symptoms of a child. See United States v. Yazzie, 59 F.3d 807, 813 (9th Cir.1995) (in most circumstances, statements by parent of injured child to doctor will qualify); First Premier Bank v. Kolcraft Enters., Inc., 686 N.W.2d 430, 449 (S.D.2004) (admitting statement by parents as to cause of injury to child). As noted above, if the statement is one of current physical condition, it may be admitted regardless of to whom made under Rule 803(3).

8. *Meaning of "medical."* The exception admits statements made for the purpose of "medical" diagnosis or treatment. What range of professionals should be considered to provide "medical" services? In addition to medical doctors and nurses, courts have often included in this group psychologists and social workers. See Mosteller, Child Sexual Abuse and Statements for the Purpose of Medical Diagnosis or Treatment, 67 N.C.L.Rev. 257, 282–83 (1989). However, a minority has been unwilling to move beyond statements to physicians. See, e.g., State v. Zimmerman, 829 P.2d 861, 864 (Idaho 1992) (statements to psychologists inadmissible); State v. Huntington, 575 N.W.2d 268, 278 (Wis.1998) (statements to social workers and counselors inadmissible). See generally Capowski, An Interdisciplinary Analysis for Statements to Mental Health Professionals under the Diagnosis or Treatment Hearsay Exception, 33 Ga.L.Rev. 353 (1999).

9. *Statements to psychiatrists.* When the declarant is consulting a psychiatrist, almost all statements may be relevant to diagnosis or treatment. In this situation, the commentators note the discretion of the judge to exclude statements or to limit their admissibility for the purpose of supporting the diagnosis. See 5 Weinstein's Federal Evidence § 803.06[7] (2d ed. 2006); 2 McCormick, Evidence § 277, at 285 n.8 (6th ed. 2006).

10. *Interplay with Confrontation Clause and Impact of Crawford v. Washington.* Before *Crawford*, some courts restricted the exception under Ohio v. Roberts, 448 U.S. 56 (1980), on questions such as whether a treatment motivation had to be exhibited by the child. See United States v. Turning Bear, 357 F.3d 730, 738–39 (8th Cir.2004) (requiring understanding of treatment purpose in examination before statements of child admitted as firmly rooted hearsay exception). The impact of *Crawford*'s new mode of analysis, see Chapter 13, Section C, supra, is yet to be determined. However, statements made solely for diagnosis without a treatment purpose, which the Advisory Committee described as being made "only for the purpose of enabling him to testify," would seem to be almost definitionally testimonial and therefore excluded by *Crawford*. See Mosteller, *Crawford v. Washington*: Encouraging and Ensuring the Confrontation of Witnesses, 39 U.Rich.L.Rev. 511, 600–11(2005).

11. *Importance in child sexual abuse cases.* As the above notes suggest, the expansions of this hearsay exception by the Federal Rules have seen frequent use and legal challenge in child sexual abuse cases. See generally Mosteller, Child Sexual Abuse and Statements for the Purpose of Medical Diagnosis or Treatment, 67 N.C.L.Rev. 257 (1989); Mosteller, The Maturation and Disintegration of the Hearsay Exception for Statements for Medical Examination in Child Sexual Abuses Cases, 65 Law & Contemp.Probs., Winter 2002, at 47; Symposium: Hearsay Testimony in Trials Involving Child Witnesses, 5 Psychol.Pub. Pol'y & L. 251 (1999); Symposium: What Have We Learned About Children as Victims and Witnesses in Criminal Trials?, 65 Law & Contemp.Probs., Winter 2002, at 1.

SECTION D. RECORDED RECOLLECTION

FEDERAL RULE 803(5)

UNITED STATES v. BOOZ

United States Court of Appeals, Third Circuit, 1971.
451 F.2d 719.

SEITZ, CHIEF JUDGE. At around 8:30 a.m. on April 18, 1967, two armed men robbed the Dublin, Pennsylvania branch of the Bucks County Bank & Trust Company of $8,950.75. The appellant is alleged by the government to be one of the robbers; no other suspect has been charged. Included in the stolen money were twenty-five so-called bait bills, i.e., those whose serial numbers had been recorded. On June 12, 1967, the appellant deposited a large sum of money in the Girard Trust Bank which included eighteen of the bait bills. On June 14, 1967, FBI Agents executed a search warrant at appellant's home but apparently obtained no additional evidence. Approximately fourteen months later, in August, 1968, appellant was indicted by a grand jury for violating the Federal Bank Robbery Act, 18 U.S.C.A. § 2113 (1970). In January, 1971, approximately two years and five months after indictment, appellant was brought to trial, convicted by a jury and sentenced to fifteen years imprisonment. This appeal followed. The government's evidence showed that appellant had substantial opportunity to become acquainted with the pre-opening procedures of the bank's personnel, including the opening of the bank vault; that appellant's financial distress at about the time of the crime might have induced him to take this drastic step; that unusual activity in the area between appellant's home and the bank tended to place the perpetrators in that general area and hence, near appellant's home; and that appellant was seen in this area a few days after the robbery, perhaps to retrieve a hat, earlier found left at the scene. It was introduced in evidence and subsequently identified at trial as having been worn by one of the robbers.

* * *

Several witnesses testified about the movements of a tan car in the area of the bank and appellant's home in the early morning hours of the day of the robbery. Mrs. Kaprolet, who lived in the area, testified on behalf of the government to seeing the car around 8:00 a.m. However, FBI Agent Bass was called by the government to testify that Mrs. Kaprolet told him, on April 21, 1967, she had seen the tan car near her home twice, once at around 8:00 a.m. and a second time about 45 minutes later. Mrs. Kaprolet's testimony was important because a field search of this area turned up the hat allegedly worn by one of the robbers. We think it was error to permit the FBI agent to relate this hearsay statement of Mrs. Kaprolet. * * *

A farmer, Mr. Kulp, who also lived in this area, related that on April 21, 1967, he observed a white pickup truck stop where Mrs. Kaprolet said she had seen the tan car. A man got out of the truck, looked around and then left. Mr. Kulp recorded the license plate number, and FBI Agent Bass testified from his investigatory notes that Mr. Kulp gave him the number S0633. The evidence showed appellant owned two pickup trucks with plate numbers S6003R and S6002R.

* * *

Alleged Hearsay Nature of the License Number Evidence

A Mr. Kulp, who was a farmer living in the general vicinity of the crime, testified for the government that, on April 21, 1967, he observed a man in a white pickup truck stop and look around in the area where the farmer had seen police activity several days before. The hat allegedly worn by one of the robbers had been found there. This testimony was critical to the prosecution's case. If it could be established that the appellant was the man who searched the area on April 21, it would be if unexplained, a very strong circumstantial indication of appellant's involvement in the crime. The following colloquy occurred in the direct examination of Mr. Kulp:

"Q. Now, were you subsequently interviewed by an agent from the FBI?

"A. The FBI, yes.

"Q. Did you give him a license number that you had seen?

"A. Yes.

"Q. You did, all right. Now this was a little less than four years ago. Do you today remember that license plate number as you gave it to the FBI?

"A. No, I wouldn't remember that license number.

"Q. Did we discuss this matter within the past hour?

"A. What's that?

"Q. Did we discuss this matter of your testifying within the past hour up in my office?

"A. Yes.

"Q. Did I read you a report from the FBI regarding their interviewing you?

"A. That's right.

"Q. And did I read you that license number that was in that report?

"A. Yes, you did. I don't remember that number.

"Q. All right. The license number that I read to you from that report, did that jibe with your recollection of what you reported to the FBI?

"DEFENSE COUNSEL: I object, sir.

"A. That's right.

"THE COURT: Overruled.

"DEFENSE COUNSEL: He has already testified that he doesn't remember.

"THE COURT: Overruled. That is not the question.

"PROSECUTOR: Your Honor, I ask leave of the Court to tender to the witness the FBI report.

"THE COURT: No. You can call the FBI Agent if you wish."

After Mr. Kulp's cross-examination, FBI Agent Bass was called by the prosecution. Bass testified that Mr. Kulp had given him a license number. Using the written FBI report to refresh his recollection, Bass testified the license number was S0633. Subsequent testimony revealed that defendant's two trucks bore plate numbers S6003R and S6002R.

The objection to this part of the prosecution's case raised here by appellant is that FBI Agent Bass impermissibly testified as to hearsay, i.e., Mr. Kulp's oral statement to Agent Bass. The only question for us is whether one or more of the many exceptions to the hearsay rule applies.

Witnesses may use any aid to refresh their recollections. Reading Kulp's answer to the prosecution's question whether the report "jibed" with his recollection, it might be concluded that the witness' memory of the plate number was thereby revived. If so, Kulp should then have gone on to relate his revived memory of the number. In such circumstances, there was no need to admit the FBI report into evidence or to bring the Agent to the stand. The rule in cases of refreshed recollection is that the writing may not be admitted into evidence or its contents even seen by the jury. 3 Wigmore, Evidence § 763, (Chad.Rev.1970) and cases cited at 142 n.1.

It is not entirely clear on this record whether Kulp's memory had, in fact, been refreshed. If not, resort must be had by the prosecution to the hearsay exception for past recollection recorded. If Mr. Kulp's memory is not revived by the FBI Report, he may nevertheless testify from its contents if certain conditions are met. A prerequisite of such testimony is ascertaining the identity and accuracy of the record used. 3 Wigmore, Evidence § 747, supra. If Kulp had testified that he read the report over after the FBI Agent made it and was, at that time, satisfied that it was correct, sufficient proof of the report's accuracy would have been made out. Since Kulp did not so testify, the more difficult question is whether there is any other basis for admitting the license plate number.

Some courts and textwriters have taken the view that where as here, a record is the joint product of two individuals, one who makes an oral statement and one who embodies it in a writing, if both parties are available to testify at trial as to the accuracy with which each performed his role, the recollection may be admitted. See, e.g., Swart v. United States, 394 F.2d 5 (9th Cir.1968); 3 Wigmore, Evidence § 751, supra; Morgan, *The Relation Between Hearsay and Preserved Memory,* 40 Harv.L.Rev. 712, 720 (1927). We think such an exception to the hearsay rule is sound and adopt it here. If Agent Bass can verify the accuracy of his transcription and if Kulp can testify he related an accurate recollection of the number to Agent Bass, we believe that, even though Kulp may not have read the report, sufficient indicia of its accuracy exist to let the evidence go to the jury. If the appropriate evidentiary basis is established at the retrial we think that the appellant would be entitled to an instruction on this point to the effect that in view of the elapsed time since Kulp reported to the FBI, the jurors should cautiously consider the degree of reliability the offered recollection deserves and that no more weight should be accorded it than such degree dictates.

* * *

[The defendant's conviction was reversed on other grounds and the case remanded to the trial court for examination of an unrelated issue.]

Notes and Questions

1. *Continuity of interpretation.* Rule 803(5) continues to receive two-party statements like the one discussed in *Booz.* See United States v. Hernandez, 333 F.3d 1168, 1178–79 (10th Cir.2003) (admitting two-party statement despite noting that most logical reading of Rule's language "made or adopted by the witness" would exclude such statements); 2 McCormick, Evidence § 283, at 300–01 (6th ed. 2006).

2. *Refreshing recollection.* The related but distinct doctrine of refreshing recollection is examined in Chapter 12, Section B(4), supra.

UNITED STATES v. FELIX–JEREZ

United States Court of Appeal, Ninth Circuit, 1982.
667 F.2d 1297.

SKELTON, SENIOR JUDGE:

In this case the facts are not in dispute and are generally as follows. Miguel Felix–Jerez (defendant) had been convicted in another proceeding of having entered the United States illegally and was sentenced to ninety days in prison and three years probation for that offense. He was serving his sentence as an inmate of the Federal Prison Camp at Stafford [sic],

Arizona, when the events giving rise to the instant case occurred. The record shows that the defendant was arrested and indicted for escaping from the prison camp in violation of 18 U.S.C. § 751, and was convicted by a jury * * *. Because of the error of the court in admitting a hearsay statement into evidence over the timely objection of defendant, we reverse.

The prison camp at Stafford [sic] is a minimum security prison with no fences or enclosures and no armed guards. The prisoners are free to walk about the premises of the prison. While it was against the rules of the prison for the prisoners to leave the prison grounds without permission, the testimony of prison guards at the trial revealed that it was common knowledge at the prison that prisoners frequently went to a restaurant and bar about one-half mile from the camp to buy cigarettes, food and alcoholic beverages without obtaining permission to do so. On November 5, 1980, during a 10:00 P.M. head count at the camp it was discovered that the defendant was not present, although he had not obtained permission to leave the prison grounds. He was discovered the next day walking along a road about 10 miles from the camp by an off-duty prison guard. The guard notified the local sheriff who arrested the defendant and returned him to the prison. At the time of his arrest, the defendant had two bottles of wine in his possession, one of which was unopened and the other was partly filled. He made no statement at the time he was picked up.

The next day, November 7th, the defendant was interrogated by Deputy United States Marshal Larry Hardeman at the prison. Because the defendant did not speak English and Hardeman did not speak Spanish, a camp guard named Daniel Tolavera served as an interpreter. The defendant was advised in Spanish of his *Miranda* rights and he waived them by signing a written form printed in Spanish.

The interrogation was conducted by Hardeman's asking questions in English which were translated into Spanish by Tolavera. The defendant answered the questions in Spanish and Tolavera translated the answers into English. Hardeman made notes of the questions and translated answers. Sometime later, after the interview had been concluded, Hardeman typed a statement containing the questions and translated answers as shown by his notes. As far as the record shows, the defendant was not present when the statement was typed by Hardeman, it was not read to him in Spanish, he did not sign it, and obviously did not know of its existence until the day of the trial.

At the trial, Tolavera was called as a witness. He testified that he acted as an interpreter at the interview between Hardeman and defendant in the manner described above because he spoke both Spanish and English, but that he had no independent recollection of the questions and answers and could not testify what they were. He said that his translations were accurate and that he had no difficulty in understanding the defendant's Spanish. He made no notes of the questions and answers.

The prosecutor then called Hardeman as a witness. He testified that he conducted the interrogation of the defendant as a United States Marshal with the assistance of camp guard Tolavera as an interpreter in the manner aforesaid. He said he did not know Spanish and did not know what the answers were that the defendant gave to Tolavera in Spanish, nor whether Tolavera correctly translated them into English. He testified further that he made notes of the questions and translated answers and later typed them himself in the form of a statement. He then compared the statement with his original notes and said that the statement was a true and accurate record and transcript of his original notes of the conversation with defendant. The prosecutor then offered the statement as evidence without asking Hardeman if he had an independent recollection of the questions he asked the defendant and of the answers the defendant gave, nor whether he could testify from his recollection what the questions and answers were. The defense counsel objected to the introduction of the statement on the ground that it was hearsay. The court overruled the objection and admitted the statement into evidence without giving any reason for his ruling. The statement was then read to the jury.

The questions and answers in the statement Hardeman had typed and which was read to the jury showed that the defendant had planned from the beginning of his incarceration at the Stafford [sic] prison camp to escape, and that he did escape on November 5, 1980, and that after drinking two six-packs of beer he bought at the nearby bar, he decided to remain away, and that he had no intention of returning to the camp.

After a careful review of the entire record and consideration of the briefs, argument of counsel and applicable authorities, we conclude that the Hardeman statement that was read to the jury was hearsay and inadmissible as evidence under Rule 802 of the Federal Rules of Evidence, unless it met the requirements of one of the 24 exceptions to the hearsay rule which are set forth in Rule 803(1)–(24).

[The court first concluded that the written statement did not constitute an adoptive admission of the defendant because he never saw, read, nor signed it. The court felt the involvement of a guard as a translator made treating the statement as an admission even more problematic.]

* * * We have carefully examined each of these exceptions in connection with the facts in this case and have concluded that none of them are applicable so as to make the Hardeman statement admissible as a non-hearsay document, except *arguendo* sub-paragraph (5) which provides:

> (5) Recorded recollection. A memorandum or record concerning a matter about which a witness once had knowledge but now has insufficient recollection to enable him to testify fully and accurately, shown to have been made or adopted by the witness when the matter was fresh in his memory and to reflect that knowledge correctly. If admitted, the memorandum or record may be read into

evidence but may not itself be received as an exhibit unless offered by an adverse party.

The notes of the Advisory Committee found at the end of Rule 803 contain the following statement, in pertinent part, regarding this exception:

> The principal controversy attending the exception has centered, not upon the propriety of the exception itself, but upon the question whether a preliminary requirement of impaired memory on the part of the witness should be imposed. The authorities are divided. * * * Nevertheless, the absence of the requirement, it is believed, would encourage the use of statements carefully prepared for purposes of litigation under the supervision of attorneys, investigators, or claim adjusters. Hence the example includes a requirement that the witness not have "sufficient recollection to enable him to testify fully and accurately." * * * Title 28 U.S.C.A. Rule 803 at p. 586.

This circuit follows the rule set forth above that before a prior hearsay statement of a witness who is testifying can be admitted into evidence under this exception, it must first be shown that the witness does not now have sufficient recollection as to the matters contained in the statement to enable him to testify fully and accurately regarding them. See *United States v. Edwards,* 539 F.2d 689 (9 Cir.1976), where we held:

> Appellant also claims the trial court erred in admitting evidence of Newman's signed statement describing the events leading to the crime. At trial Newman denied any present recollection of the facts in question and the written statement was offered and admitted under the recorded recollection exception to the hearsay rule. F.R.Evid. 803(5).
>
> Documents admitted pursuant to this rule must meet three requisites: (1) The document must pertain to matters about which the witness once had knowledge; (2) The witness must now have an insufficient recollection as to such matters; (3) The document must be shown to have been made by the witness and reflect his knowledge when the matters were fresh in his memory. 539 F.2d at 691–692.

It is clear that the second requirement set forth above in *Edwards* was not complied with in this case. Witness Hardeman did not testify that he now had an insufficient recollection as to the matters contained in the statement so as to be able to testify regarding them. In fact, he was not even asked if he now had an insufficient recollection as to such matters. The proper predicate was not laid for the introduction of the statement. Hardeman was on the witness stand and, as far as the record shows, he could have testified about the facts contained in the statement. Under these circumstances there was no need to introduce the statement, and it was error to do so.

Long before Rule 803(5) was adopted the Supreme Court set forth the substance of the rule in the case of *Vicksburg & Meridian R.R. Co. v. O'Brien,* 119 U.S. 99 * * * (1886). In that case, a physician was testifying as to the injuries to the plaintiff's wife in a railroad accident. The plaintiff offered a prior statement of the physician which he had made at the time of the accident regarding the wife's injuries. The court allowed the statement to be read to the jury over the hearsay objection of the defendant. There was no prior showing that the physician had no recollection of the facts so as to be able to testify regarding the facts in the statement. The Supreme Court held that it was error to read the hearsay statement to the jury under these circumstances, saying:

> We are of the opinion that this ruling cannot be sustained, upon any principle recognized in the law of evidence. The authorities are uniform in holding that a witness is at liberty to examine a memorandum prepared by him under the circumstances in which this one was, for the purpose of refreshing or assisting his recollection as to the facts stated in it. * * *
>
> There are, however, other cases, to the effect that where the witness states, under oath, that the memorandum was made by him presently after the transaction to which it relates, for the purpose of perpetuating his recollection of the facts, and that he knows it was correct when prepared, although after reading it he cannot recall the circumstances so as to state them alone from memory, the paper may be received as the best evidence of which the case admits.
>
> The present case does not require us to enter upon an examination of the numerous authorities upon this general subject; for, it does not appear here but that at the time the witness testified he had, without even looking at his written statement, a clear, distinct recollection of every essential fact stated in it. If he had such present recollection, there was no necessity whatever for reading that paper to the jury. Applying, then, to the case the most liberal rule announced in any of the authorities, the ruling by which the plaintiffs were allowed to read the physician's written statement to the jury as evidence, in itself, of the facts therein recited, was erroneous. 119 U.S. at 102 * * *.

See also United States v. Riccardi, 174 F.2d 883 (3 Cir.1949) * * * and *United States v. Judon,* 567 F.2d 1289 (5 Cir.1978).

The decision in the *Judon* case, *supra,* contains a good discussion of Rule 803(5) and the reasoning therein is particularly applicable to our case. There a witness was present when a savings and loan branch was robbed. He wrote down on a piece of paper a description of the robber's car and its license number. The witness testified at the trial and his memorandum aforesaid was introduced into evidence over a hearsay objection and a further objection that a proper predicate had not been laid for its admission. The court held this was error, saying:

> The admissibility of this document is governed by Fed.R.Evid. 803(5), which prescribes the conditions under which recorded recol-

lection qualifies as an exception to the hearsay rule * * *. It is clear from the second sentence of this rule that the admission of this memorandum as an exhibit was error. The drafters precluded the receipt of recorded recollection as an exhibit of the proponent of the memorandum in order to prevent the trier of fact from being overly impressed by the writing. 11 J. Moore, Federal Practice § 803(5)[5] (1976).

This memorandum may have qualified as a hearsay exception; however, the record reveals no proper predicate had been laid to show its admissibility as such. In particular, there was no showing that the witness had insufficient recollection to enable him to testify fully and accurately at trial. The Advisory Committee deemed this requirement desirable, since its absence "would encourage the use of statements carefully prepared for purposes of litigation under the supervision of attorneys, investigators, or claim adjusters." *See* 11 J. Moore, Federal Practice § 803(5)[4] (1976). Additionally, we note that there was no specific testimony that the recording reflected the witness' knowledge correctly when the matter was fresh in his memory.

This failure to adhere to the requirements of the Federal Rules of Evidence compounds the error in admitting the documents in evidence. (Emphasis supplied). 567 F.2d at 1294.

As stated in the notes of the Advisory Committee, and as repeated and approved by the court in the *Judon* case, the absence of a showing that the witness had insufficient recollection to enable him to testify fully and accurately at the trial, "would encourage the use of statements carefully prepared for purposes of litigation under the supervision of attorneys, investigators, or claim adjusters." That is exactly what happened in the instant case. Marshal Hardeman was an investigator. He prepared the statement for the express purpose of using it to prosecute the defendant. This is a classic example of the vice the Advisory Committee sought to prohibit by requiring proof of insufficient recollection by a witness before his hearsay statement can be admitted into evidence.

We conclude that the admission of Hardeman's statement into evidence without the proper predicate having been laid did not meet the requirements of Rule 803(5).

* * *

[The court concluded that the error was not harmless, and it reversed and remanded.]

Notes and Questions

1. *Requirement of some failure of memory.* Wigmore notes two rationales for receiving recorded recollections. The first is that receipt of the memorandum is necessary because "there is not available a present actual

recollection in the specific witness." The second is that "in the usual case a faithful record of past recollection, if it exists, is more trustworthy and desirable than a present recollection of greater or less vividness." 3 Wigmore, Evidence § 738, at 90 (Chadbourn rev. 1970). The second rationale, which was favored by Wigmore, id. at 91, would support admission of recorded recollections even when the witness claims no memory loss. Prior to the adoption of the Federal Rules, several states followed this second rationale. See State v. Sutton, 450 P.2d 748 (Or.1969), overruled, Elam v. Soares, 577 P.2d 1336 (Or.1978); Jordan v. People, 376 P.2d 699 (Colo.1962). However, of the over forty states that have enacted rules of evidence based on the Federal Rules, it appears that only Colorado omits a requirement of some failure of present recollection. See Colo.R.Evid. 803(5).

2. *Impaired not exhausted.* As explained in *Felix–Jerez,* Rule 803(5) requires some demonstration of impaired memory but does not require that it be totally exhausted. For a criticism of the federal approach, see Blakely, Past Recollection Recorded: Restrictions on Use as Exhibit and Proposals for Change, 17 Hous.L.Rev. 411 (1980).

3. *Proving document's accuracy.* As a conceptual matter, witnesses may specifically remember that a statement they made about an event was accurate without remembering the event itself, but as a matter of everyday experience, one might assume witnesses who have forgotten the event, which is likely more memorable, would likewise have forgotten precisely what they said about it as well. One might suspect that sometimes the claims of a specific memory about the accuracy of the statement are overstated. McCormick notes that such an attestation is not inevitably required.

> [I]f present memory is inadequate, the requirement may be met by testimony that the declarant knows [the document] is correct because of a habit or practice to record such matters accurately or to check them for accuracy. At the extreme, some courts find sufficient testimony that the individual recognizes his or her signature and believes the statement correct because the witness would not have signed it if he or she had not believed it true at the time.

2 McCormick, Evidence § 283, at 298–99 (6th ed. 2006). Some courts have been particularly liberal in finding an acknowledgment of accuracy with a reluctant witness. See United States v. Porter, 986 F.2d 1014, 1016–17 (6th Cir.1993); Isler v. United States, 824 A.2d 957, 960–61 (D.C.2003); State v. Gorman, 854 A.2d 1164, 1173 (Me.2004); State v. Marcy, 680 A.2d 76, 79 (Vt.1996).

4. *Timeliness requirement.* The Rule requires that the memorandum must have been made or adopted when the matter was fresh in the witness' memory but provides no specific guidelines as to the degree of contemporaneity required. The courts have interpreted this requirement extremely generously. See, e.g., United States v. Smith, 197 F.3d 225, 231 (6th Cir.1999) (holding that trial court did not abuse its discretion in admitting statement made after fifteen months delay).

5. *Prohibition on admitting document.* Rule 803(5) specifies that if admitted, the memorandum or record may be read into evidence but that the document itself can be received only if it is offered by the adverse party. Why

does the Rule impose this restriction on admission of the document? Is it wise? See *Blakely*, note 2, supra.

6. *Translators.* How to treat translated statements under the hearsay rules, raised in the *Felix-Jerez* case, presents an interesting question. Most courts consider the translator, even when not selected by the declarant, to be his or her agent, which allows the translation to be received as a vicarious admission where the declarant is a party. See, e.g., State v. Felton, 412 S.E.2d 344, 353–55 (N.C.1992). Other courts treat the translation as not hearsay at all, considering the interpreter as merely a "language conduit." See, e.g., United States v. Cordero, 18 F.3d 1248, 1253 (5th Cir.1994). A third, albeit rarely used, approach admits the translation under the hearsay exception for present sense impressions. United States v. Kramer, 741 F.Supp. 893, 896 (S.D.Fla.1990).

SECTION E. RECORDS OF REGULARLY CONDUCTED ACTIVITY

FEDERAL RULES 803(6) & (7)

TRACY, THE INTRODUCTION OF DOCUMENTARY EVIDENCE

24 Iowa L.Rev. 436, 454 (1939).[24]

Business Records

To understand thoroughly the problems attendant upon the authentication of business records there must be borne in mind the development of the law as to the admissibility of such entries as an exception to the hearsay rule.

Under the rule which formerly excluded the testimony of interested parties, it was impossible for a tradesman doing business alone to prove even a simple case for goods sold and delivered. To remedy this situation, the courts developed the so-called "shop-book" rule, by which the tradesman's books of account were admissible in evidence to prove the facts stated therein, provided that the tradesman kept no clerk. At the same time this rule was being developed, the courts were confronted with other cases where the accounts of third parties and of tradesmen who did keep clerks were involved. In the first of these cases the tradesman was not ineligible as a witness, because he was not interested, and in the second class of cases the account could be proved by the clerks of the plaintiff, who also were not ineligible. In both classes of cases, however, the testimony of the person who knew about the transaction, whether proprietor or clerk, was often unobtainable because of death. In those cases the courts were able to work out a real exception to the hearsay rule, based on the necessity element arising from death. There thus grew up, side by side, two bodies of law, one for parties' books, where no clerks were employed, and the other as to the use of books of account in other cases. When the statutes were passed abolishing the

24. Copyright © by the State University of Iowa. Reprinted by permission. [Ed.]

disqualification of interest and making parties eligible to testify, the reasons for the shop-book rule vanished and the use of all book entries came to be governed by the same set of rules, except in a very few jurisdictions where legislation recognizing the shop-book rule has never been repealed.

ROBERTSON v. CARLSON

Appellate Court of Illinois, First District, 1913.
181 Ill.App. 251.

MR. JUSTICE FITCH delivered the opinion of the court. By this writ of error the defendant seeks to have reversed a judgment against him in the Municipal Court for $104.70 for work, labor and material furnished by defendants in error in repairing an automobile. It appears that defendant's automobile broke down near the garage of defendants in error. Hans Robertson was requested to look at it and found the crank case was broken and that the "rocker arm" had become loose. Defendant asked him if he could repair it, and upon receiving a reply in the affirmative, the machine was towed to plaintiffs' garage and left there for repairs. One of the witnesses testified that in order to make the repairs it was necessary to take the engine apart and have the crank case taken out and welded. Plaintiffs found they could not weld the crank case themselves and sent it to a welding company. Considerable delay resulted, and when it was returned to plaintiffs it did not fit perfectly, and a number of the engine parts had to be filed and readjusted, and the machine put together in running order. To prove the time spent in doing this, the workmen's time books were offered in evidence. They were objected to by defendant on the ground that no proper foundation had been laid, and this is the chief objection urged.

Some of the time books were properly identified by the workmen themselves as containing original entries made by them in the ordinary course of business contemporaneously with the doing of the work for which the charges were made. These books were properly admitted on the authority of House v. Beak, 141 Ill. 290, 296. The remainder were admitted in evidence after the foreman had testified that the books were in the handwriting of workmen who were no longer in plaintiffs' employ and whom he could not find, that he had made inquiries at the last known place of residence or at the last working places of these workmen, and that "the only thing he found was—no one knows where they are, most of them are out of town." As to the workman Reed, there is some evidence that he was in California at the time of the trial. Under § 3 of chapter 51 of the Revised Statutes it was necessary, in order to make the books kept by the absent workmen admissible, that there should be proof that the entries therein were made "by a deceased person, or by a disinterested person, a non-resident of the state at the time of the trial." We find no competent evidence in the record to the effect that the entries in the time books kept by Peterson, Price, Forslund and Rachan were made by persons who were either dead or non-residents of the state at the time of the trial. It was, therefore, error to admit such books. The total number of hours included in the entries made by those workmen is sixty-six hours, the charge for which, at sixty cents an hour, amounts to $39.60. The witness Siddons, another workman, admitted that eight hours of his time, out of the nine and one-half hours charged against defendant, were employed in doing work having no connection with the repairs ordered, and the witness Hepburn admitted a similar overcharge of twelve hours. These items, at the same rate, amount to $12. Subtracting the sum of these two items from the amount of the judgment leaves $53.10 as the amount which is supported by a preponderance of competent evidence.

If, therefore, the defendants in error will remit within ten days the sum of $51.60, the judgment for the remainder, $53.10, will be affirmed; otherwise the cause will be reversed and remanded for a new trial.

Affirmed on remittitur; otherwise reversed and remanded.

Notes and Questions

1. *Historical perspective.* The excerpt from Tracy and *Robertson* provide some historical perspective on the modern "business records" exception found in Rule 803(6). See generally 2 McCormick, Evidence §§ 285 & 286 (6th ed. 2006).

2. *Antiquated requirements. Robertson*, which does not follow the modern dimensions of the exception, accurately reflects the requirements for the admission of business records under the common law of its day. Which among *Robertson*'s requirements became particularly onerous to litigants as businesses increased in size and complexity and modified their record-keeping practices in response? Doesn't *Robertson*, which excluded erroneous extra charges, suggest that the modern, more relaxed requirements may entail some loss in accuracy?

3. *"Original entries."* A requirement that the record contain "original entries" obviously raises problems of interpretation. Should the books of a law firm, prepared from the time sheets submitted by various attorneys, be admissible in an action to recover a fee? What if the various attorneys prepare their time sheets weekly from notations on their desk calendars? What is the underlying justification for the original entry requirement? Is its relaxation warranted by the nature of modern bookkeeping procedures and mandated by the advent of computer records?

OLESEN v. HENNINGSEN

Supreme Court of Iowa, 1956.
77 N.W.2d 40.

Peterson, Justice. There is only one question in this case: was it reversible error for the trial court to admit in evidence a long distance telephone ticket on which was shown the time of the placing of a call?

[Plaintiff brought suit to recover damages for personal injuries sustained when the car he was driving struck the rear of a wagon load of corn which had been temporarily parked on a public highway by the defendant Simonson. The wagon was owned by the defendant Henningsen. At the time of the collision, no lighted red tail lamp was being exhibited on the rear of the wagon, and a principal issue of fact in the case was whether the collision had occurred at a time of day at which exhibition of such a light was required by Iowa statute. The jury found in favor of the defendants, and plaintiff appealed.]

The evidence in the case centered around the question as to whether or not it was earlier or later than 30 minutes after sunset when the collision occurred. There was a slight conflict as to the time of sunset. Each side had secured a report from the weather bureau and one report placed sunset at 4:45 and the other report placed it at 4:54.

The issue urged by appellant is that the trial court erred in admitting a certain telephone ticket, on which was stamped the time of a call. It appeared on the ticket that a long distance telephone call was placed from the Olesen farm residence near Graettinger to Emmetsburg to call the sheriff about the accident. It was not in dispute that the call was placed when plaintiff was brought home after the accident. The evidence was offered by defendants and the ticket showed that the call had been placed at 5:45 p.m. It was the claim of defendants that this was some evidence as to the accident having occurred prior to one half hour after sunset. Defendants also urge that it constituted an impeachment of the testimony of plaintiff's father and mother as to Richard being brought home at 6:05 p.m. The question of impeachment was settled by the verdict of the jury.

The testimony in connection with the call from the Olesen home to the sheriff at Emmetsburg is in substance that Mrs. Harry Fink was the operator at Graettinger, and that she kept the books and had charge of all records of the telephone office of Graettinge—Telephone Company. She testified that she held that position on November 17, 1950, the date involved in this case. When a long distance call came in for Emmetsburg she testified that the Graettinger operator made a report of the call and the long distance operator at Emmetsburg also made a record of the call, together with the time of the call and the length of the conversation. The Emmetsburg ticket as to the call was sent to Bell Telephone Company at Des Moines for record and was then sent back to Mrs. Fink, who checked it with her ticket, and then made it a part of the records of the office. This is the ticket offered in evidence. The Graettinger ticket was delivered to the customer with the charges for the month. Mrs. Fink does not testify that she handled the call. The chief operator at Emmetsburg supported the testimony of Mrs. Fink. She testified that it would be impossible to tell what operator at the Emmetsburg office handled the call, but as chief operator she had charge of the long distance records. Although she had not made the ticket, she identified it, and verified the time. In one part of the testimony they testified that the ticket was a part of their permanent records, but they also stated that the records were not necessarily permanent. However, the trial of the case was nearly three and one half years after the date of the telephone call, and the Graettinger operator and bookkeeper still had the ticket, so this in itself would be evidence of reasonable permanency of the records.

* * *

IV. Evidence as to long distance telephone tickets, railway-ticket records or hospital records is not the same as evidence concerning a book account. It does not need the same type of technical proof as the statute requires for proving an account, as set out in § 622.28. The elements necessary for admission of a telephone ticket in a case such as this, are identification by one or more telephone employees who either make or have supervision and charge of the records, and who know the ticket to be a genuine part of the records of the company, and who can testify it was made at or about the time shown thereon. The evidence submitted in this case meets this test. The trial court did not commit reversible error in admitting the telephone ticket. The question of admission of telephone tickets under the circumstances as herein offered has not heretofore been directly before this court. Some comparable matters have been considered, such as railroad-ticket records and hospital records. * * * There must be elements of precaution involved, because the admission creates an exception to the hearsay rule.

* * *

American Law Institute Model Code of Evidence, Rule 514 on page 270 provides as follows:

> "A writing offered as a memorandum or record of an act, event or condition is admissible as tending to prove the occurrence of the act or event or the existence of the condition if the judge finds that it was made in the regular course of a business and that it was the regular course of that business for one with personal knowledge of such an act, event or condition to make such a memorandum or record *or to transmit information thereof to be included in such a memorandum or record,* and for the memorandum or record to be made at or about the time of the act, event or condition or within a reasonable time thereafter." (Emphasis supplied.)

A comparable subject of hospital records was considered at length in Gearhart v. Des Moines R. Co., supra [21 N.W.2d 571]. In this case the court states:

> "The witness did not make any part of the records but testified as to the manner in which they were made and that they were made by the nurses and doctors in charge of the patient." One nurse testified as to part of the entries, but other entries were made by other nurses and doctors who did not testify. The court further states:

> "It is apparent that hospital records cannot be governed by the same rules or principles as applied to books of account nor admitted under our statute relating to such entries."

In this case the court based a substantial part of its argument upon provisions and quotations from Wigmore on Evidence.

Wigmore announces some tests, as quoted in the Gearhart case, supra, which apply in this case. In Wigmore on Evidence, 3d Ed., Volume V, § 1422, p. 204 it states as follows:

> "Further, in generalizing, the author states there is 'ample authority in judicial utterances for naming the following different classes of reasons underlying the exceptions:
>
> " 'a. Where the circumstances are such that a sincere and accurate statement would naturally be uttered, and no plan of falsification be formed.
>
> " 'b. Where, even though a desire to falsify might present itself, other considerations, such as the danger of easy detection or the fear of punishment, would probably counteract its force.
>
> " 'c. Where the statement was made under such conditions of publicity that an error, if it had occurred, would probably have been detected and corrected.' "

Exception "a" pertains to this case. The two operators were wholly disinterested witnesses. The circumstances were such that sincere and accurate statements were uttered. The evidence is such that it is clear no falsification plan was formed.

The greatest objection to evidence of this type is lack of opportunity for cross-examination, but the court quotes from Wigmore stating that "common sense and experience have from time to time pointed them out as practically adequate substitutes for the ordinary test" of cross-examination.

* * *

Several Federal Circuit Courts have approved the admission of long distance telephone tickets. The question has usually arisen in criminal cases, but the theory involved in cases of this type was analyzed and stated in the case of Valli v. United States, 1 Cir., 94 F.2d 687, 693, as follows:

> "While formerly at common law such evidence may not have been admissible under the hearsay rule, the law, however, is not static and the impossible is not required in these days of complicated business to meet the rules of evidence adopted when earlier and simpler methods of doing business were customary. With a business like that of the New England Telephone & Telegraph Company requiring many employees, who make records of hundreds of calls daily, if litigants were compelled to summon each employee engaged in making every record requiring proof, it would render the rules of evidence as originally recognized at common law an obstruction to justice instead of a means of promoting it. Funk v. United States, 290 U.S. 371, 381 * * *. We think it was within the sound discretion of the trial court to admit such evidence offered by the witness

Buddington, especially since much of the evidence offered by him was corroborated by other testimony in the case."

In this case there is other testimony corroborating the information on the telephone ticket.

V. The argument and citations of attorneys for appellant are largely directed to specific identification of documents of evidence and to evidence necessary for proof of book accounts. Their argument is also directed along the line of the distinction between admission of evidence in states that have adopted what is known as Uniform Business Records as Evidence Act and the states which have not adopted same. Iowa has not adopted such an act. However, in view of the general statements of law, and decisions in Iowa heretofore cited, it is not necessary that evidence such as the long distance telephone ticket involved herein, be based on legislative enactment.

* * *

The judgment rendered, in accordance with the decision of the jury, is affirmed.

Affirmed.

Notes and Questions

1. *Earlier formulations.* The Uniform Business Record as Evidence Act, referred to by the court in the *Olesen* case, provided in pertinent part as follows:

> § 1. Definition.—The term "business" shall include every kind of business, profession, occupation, calling or operation of institutions, whether carried on for profit or not.
>
> § 2. Business Records.—A record of an act, condition or event, shall, in so far as relevant, be competent evidence if the custodian or other qualified witness testifies to its identity and the mode of its preparation, and if it was made in the regular course of business, at or near the time of the act, condition or event, and if, in the opinion of the court, the sources of the information, method and time of preparation were such as to justify its admission.

The Uniform Act was adopted in more than half the states. Its substance was incorporated in Uniform Rule of Evidence 63(13) (1953). The essential features of the Act are incorporated in Federal Rule 803(6). See generally Kwestel, The Business Records Exception to the Hearsay Rule—New is Not Necessarily Better, 64 Mo.L.Rev. 595 (1999).

2. *Scope of "business records."* Cases recognize an enormous scope in what is a record made in the regular course of activities covered by the exception. United States v. McPartlin, 595 F.2d 1321 (7th Cir.1979) (combination appointment calendar and business diary); Stone v. Morris, 546 F.2d 730 (7th Cir.1976) (report of incident involving prisoner by prison counselor to staff psychiatrist); United States v. Keane, 522 F.2d 534 (7th Cir.1975) (letter between officials of local governmental units); United States v.

Kingston, 971 F.2d 481, 486 (10th Cir.1992) (loan counselor's notes of conversation with customer); Department of Pub. Safety & Correctional Servs. v. Cole, 672 A.2d 1115, 1123–24 (Md.1996) (videotape of removal of prisoner from his cell). This trend is clearly demonstrated in the admission of records of personal business activities. For instance, in Keogh v. C.I.R., 713 F.2d 496, 499–500 (9th Cir.1983), the court held that a black-jack dealer's personal diary recording his tips at a Las Vegas casino was a business record. The court acknowledged that the diary was not a business record of the casino but found it was kept in the course of the dealer's own business activity or occupation. Moreover, records are covered even if such business activity is illegal. See United States v. Hedman, 630 F.2d 1184, 1197–98 (7th Cir.1980) (diary recording illegal payoffs); United States v. Lizotte, 856 F.2d 341, 344 (1st Cir.1988) (calendar with notations of daily illegal drug sales). However, personal records that are kept for non-business reasons do not qualify under the exception. Compare Clark v. City of Los Angeles, 650 F.2d 1033, 1037 (9th Cir.1981) (216–page diary recording encounters with police and city officials not business record since not used in witness' business of selling new and used merchandise), with Sabatino v. Curtiss Nat'l Bank of Miami Springs, 415 F.2d 632 (5th Cir.1969) (personal check record).

3. *Liberal definition of foundation witness.* Under Rule 803(6), the foundation for admission of the business record may be shown by the testimony of the custodian of the record, or it may be established by another qualified witness. Courts have construed rather broadly the types of individuals who may lay a sufficient foundation. See *Keogh*, note 2, supra, 713 F.2d at 500 (wife of blackjack dealer laid adequate foundation to show regularity of entries recording tips in husband's diary); United States v. Veytia–Bravo, 603 F.2d 1187 (5th Cir.1979) (Bureau of Alcohol, Tobacco, and Firearms agent laid adequate foundation for regularity of records kept by defunct firearms dealer where records kept pursuant to federal statute); United States v. Jenkins, 345 F.3d 928, 935–36 (6th Cir.2003) (concluding that postal inspector was qualified to lay foundation for express mailing labels because directly familiar with record keeping system at specific post office even though not employed there).

4. *Foundation by witnesses from another business.* Individuals who, for example, receive records will often not be able to establish the necessary foundation for records from the shipper's business because they do not have knowledge of their method of preparation and cannot verify their accuracy. See NLRB v. First Termite Control Co., 646 F.2d 424 (9th Cir.1981). There is some debate among the cases as to whether the receiving business' reliance on the preparer's records is sufficient foundation, but the better view is that, while reliance is an important part of establishing trustworthiness, it is not alone sufficient. See State v. Radley, 804 A.2d 1127, 1132 (Me.2002); 2 McCormick, Evidence § 292, at 318 (6th ed. 2006). Place of employment is not decisive if the witness has the requisite knowledge to establish the required foundational facts. See Phoenix Assocs. III v. Stone, 60 F.3d 95, 101–02 (2d Cir.1995) (partnership's accountant had sufficient knowledge).

5. *Certification alternative.* Rule 803(6) allows the foundational facts required for admission under the Rule to be provided, not by a witness, but

by a certification authorized by law (e.g., Rules 902(11) or 902(12)). Because these provisions were only enacted in 2000, the case law interpreting them is not extensive. However, the cases generally accept as sufficient certifications tracking the specific terms of the Rule. See, e.g., DirecTV, Inc. v. Murray, 307 F.Supp.2d 764, 772 (D.S.C.2004) (relying on the precise terms of the certification to find e-mails admissible as created timely and kept in the regular course of business). They also enforce the notice requirement. See Latman v. Burdette, 366 F.3d 774, 787 (9th Cir.2004) (excluding records, *inter alia*, because requirement of written notice or opportunity to challenge was not met). Whether the courts will look behind a facially sufficient tracking of the Rule's requirements is unclear, but it is occasionally suggested. See Rambus, Inc. v. Infineon Techs. AG, 348 F.Supp.2d 698 (E.D.Va. 2004). They exhibit some willingness, when challenged, to examine whether the certifying party is a "custodian or other qualified witness." See *Latman*, 366 F.3d at 786–87; *Rambus*, 348 F.Supp.2d at 702–03. See also Chapter 11, Section A, supra.

The Supreme Court's decisions in *Crawford v. Washington* and *Davis v. Washington*, Chapter 13, Section C, supra, excluding "testimonial" statements make certification of business records in criminal cases problematic. However, application of this new confrontation jurisprudence outside the specific situations covered by *Crawford* and *Davis* is unclear, and beyond recognizing the questionable constitutionality of admitting such statements, confident conclusions cannot be reached.

UNITED STATES v. DE GEORGIA

United States Court of Appeals, Ninth Circuit, 1969.
420 F.2d 889.

HAMLEY, CIRCUIT JUDGE. Richard Allen De Georgia appeals from a judgment of conviction, entered on a jury verdict, for violating 18 U.S.C.A. § 2312 (Dyer Act). The offense involved a 1968 Mustang automobile allegedly stolen from the Hertz Corporation, in New York City, and thereafter driven to Tucson, Arizona. The car was recovered from De Georgia on September 9, 1968.

* * *

Defendant confessed in writing that he stole the automobile from the vicinity of John F. Kennedy Airport, New York, on or about July 2, 1968. However a confession does not constitute adequate proof of an element of an offense unless, as to that element, the confession is corroborated by other admissible evidence. While the Government did produce other evidence designed to corroborate the confession with regard to the element in question, defendant contends that this other evidence was inadmissible hearsay and his trial objection thereto should have been sustained.

The evidence offered by the Government in corroboration of defendant's confession that the Mustang was a stolen vehicle consisted of the testimony of Tony Gratta, the Hertz security manager for the company's New York zone. Gratta produced documentary evidence establishing that the Mustang was owned by Hertz, that it was rented to Edward P. Sweeney from John F. Kennedy Airport on June 28, 1968, and that Sweeney returned it to a Hertz station at the airport on June 30, 1968.

Gratta testified, in effect, that the vehicle was not rented or leased by Hertz after that date and therefore was a stolen vehicle when it was taken from the Hertz lot at the airport sometime after June 30, 1968. Gratta based his testimony that the Mustang had not been rented or leased by Hertz after June 30, 1968, upon information he obtained from the Hertz master computer control in Gratta's New York office.

According to Gratta, Hertz does not keep a running written business record of its rental and lease transactions but maintains this information in a computer system. Information concerning all automobile rental and lease agreements is fed into computer consoles located at each Hertz terminal and may be retrieved at the master computer control in Gratta's New York office. He explained that, under this system, one can check the master control to determine when and where a particular vehicle was last rented and when it was returned.

On July 26, 1968, Gratta received information from the Hertz office in Lincoln, Nebraska, that led him to believe that the Mustang might have been stolen. He thereupon checked the master computer control in his office and ascertained that the automobile in question had been returned to the Hertz office at the New York airport on June 30, 1968, and that there was no subsequent rental or lease activity recorded. Gratta testified that this indicated that the vehicle had been stolen.

Counsel for defendant objected to the admission of this evidence upon the ground that it was hearsay. As amplified in his motions for judgment of acquittal and in his briefs on appeal, counsel believes that the evidence was hearsay because it amounted to an assertion by those who placed rental and lease information into the Hertz computer system (and who were not called as witnesses) that no such transaction involving the Mustang occurred after June 30, 1968.[25]

This view finds support in the writings of Professor Wigmore. He has expressed the view that the absence of an entry concerning a particular transaction in a regularly-maintained business record of such transactions, is equivalent to an assertion by the person maintaining the record that no such transaction occurred. 5 Wigmore, Evidence (3d Ed.) §§ 1531, 1556, pages 392, 410.

But, assuming that the evidence was hearsay, this does not conclude the matter. There are many exceptions to the hearsay rule, one of which is the business records exception which, in the federal courts, is legisla-

25. Counsel did not make any point of the fact that the records examined by Gratta in reaching this conclusion were maintained in a computer system rather than in a running written business record of rental and lease transactions. In any event, paragraph (a) of 28 U.S.C.A. § 1732, which is the part of the Federal Business Records Act which concerns us here, does not require that, to be admissible, the record must be in writing. That paragraph involves the admissibility of "any writing *or record,* whether in the form of an entry in a book *or otherwise,* made as a memorandum or record of any act, transaction * * *." (Emphasis supplied.)

tively declared in the Business Records Act, 28 U.S.C.A. § 1732.[26] See Phillips v. United States, 356 F.2d 297, 307 (9th Cir.1965). Professor Wigmore believes that negative testimony of the kind described above, based upon what regularly-maintained business records do not show, is admissible hearsay as a corollary to the exception that records made in the regular course of business are admissible. Wigmore, ibid.

A contrary view was stated in Shreve v. United States, 77 F.2d 2, 7 (9th Cir.1935), as one of several alternative reasons for reversing a district court judgment. * * *

All of the other United States Courts of Appeals which have passed upon the matter have held such evidence admissible. This is also the rule by statute in at least five states. This rule of admissibility was proposed in the Uniform Rules of Evidence, Rule 63(14), as drafted by the National Conference of Commissioners on Uniform State Laws, and approved by it at its annual conference in 1953. The Uniform Rules were also approved by the American Bar Association in 1953.

The rule that such evidence is admissible has also been proposed by the Committee on Rules of Practice and Procedure of the Judicial Conference of the United States. * * *

Regularly-maintained business records are admissible in evidence as an exception to the hearsay rule because the circumstance that they are regularly-maintained records upon which the company relies in conducting its business assures accuracy not likely to be enhanced by introducing into evidence the original documents upon which the records are based.

In our view, this same circumstance offers a like assurance that if a business record designed to note every transaction of a particular kind contains no notation of such a transaction between specified dates, no such transaction occurred between those dates. Moreover, in our opinion, that assurance is not likely to be enhanced by the only other means of proving such a negative; that is by bringing into court all of the documents involving similar transactions during the period in question to prove that there was no record of the transactions alleged not to have occurred, and calling as witnesses all company personnel who had the duty of entering into transactions of that kind during the critical period and inquiring whether the witnesses remembered any additional transactions for which no record had been produced.

As applied to the case now before us, this alternative method of proving the negative would have been singularly burdensome and unrewarding. An enormous volume of rental and lease contracts would have had to be brought into court. In addition, the Government would have been required to call as witnesses every Hertz employee who might have consummated a lease or rental of the Mustang during the period between June 30, 1968, the date the car was returned after its last recorded rental, and at least July 26, 1968, the date that Gratta first

26. [The text of the act is shown in Yates v. Bair Transport, Inc., infra. Ed.]

received information that the car was stolen. These employees would have had to be asked to state from memory whether, out of all of the lease and rental transactions which they had entered into during that time, there was any rental of this particular Mustang. Recourse to the Hertz computer avoided these difficulties.[27]

We are in accord with the rule permitting admission of such hearsay evidence * * * which rule is supported by the weight of modern authority. With the knowledge and approval of all of the members of the court in active service, we therefore disapprove the holding in *Shreve* that such evidence is inadmissible.

It follows that Gratta's testimony to the effect that the Mustang was a stolen vehicle when it was transported across state lines after July 2, 1968, was properly received in evidence and provides adequate corroboration of defendant's confession to the same effect.

In his reply brief defendant argues, for the first time, that reception of Gratta's testimony violated the best evidence rule which required that the business records be introduced into evidence.

No such objection having been made in the trial court, we decline to consider the contention here.

Affirmed.

ELY, CIRCUIT JUDGE (concurring). [Omitted.]

Notes and Questions

1. *Hearsay exception for no record.* The Federal Rules define a separate hearsay exception, Rule 803(7), for admitting the absence of a "business records" to prove the "nonoccurrence or nonexistence of the matter." The facts of *De Georgia* show its use.

2. *Changing with the times.* Compare the approach to the calling of available witnesses and the keeping of records in *De Georgia*, after the dawn of the computer age, and that in *Robertson*, which involved a much less complex business organization, a simpler society, and a hearsay exception that was at an earlier stage of development.

27. While, as stated above, it is immaterial that the business record is maintained in a computer rather than in company books, this is on the assumption that: (1) the opposing party is given the same opportunity to inquire into the accuracy of the computer and the input procedures used, as he would have to inquire into the accuracy of written business records, and (2) the trial court, as in the case of challenged business records, requires the party offering the computer information to provide a foundation therefor sufficient to warrant a finding that such information is trustworthy.

In our case defendant had a full opportunity, upon cross-examination, to inquire into the company practice of feeding information as to all car rentals and leases into the computer, and as to the accuracy of the computer in retaining and retrieving such information. The Government presented foundation evidence as to input procedures used. While the Government did not produce expert testimony as to the mechanical accuracy of the computer, it did establish that it was sufficiently accurate so that Hertz relied upon it in conducting its business. We need not decide whether this was an adequate foundation, because defendant raised no question in the trial court as to the mechanical accuracy of the computer.

POTAMKIN CADILLAC CORP. v. B.R.I. COVERAGE CORP.

United States Court of Appeals, Second Circuit, 1994.
38 F.3d 627.

KEARSE, CIRCUIT JUDGE:

Defendants B.R.I. Coverage Corp. *et al.* (collectively "BRI"), licensed commercial insurance brokers, appeal from so much of a judgment of the United States District Court for the Southern District of New York, Thomas P. Griesa, *Chief Judge,* as dismissed BRI's counterclaims against plaintiffs Potamkin Cadillac Corp. *et al.* (collectively "Potamkin") for $776,368 in insurance premiums allegedly advanced by BRI to insurers on behalf of Potamkin. The district court adopted the recommendation of a special master that BRI's counterclaims be denied because BRI failed to prove that it had advanced those premiums. On appeal, BRI contends principally that the district court erred in excluding a document on which it relied to prove its claims and that, in any event, Potamkin had admitted that BRI advanced the premiums in question. * * *

We reject BRI's contentions and affirm the judgment of the district court. * * *

I. BACKGROUND

Potamkin, a group of corporate entities engaged in the sale, lease, and servicing of automobiles, retained BRI as its insurance broker in 1980. In 1987, the relationship soured, and Potamkin commenced the present action * * * . Potamkin alleged that defendants had defrauded it through a scheme that included charging for insurance coverage that was not provided; charging "service fees" supposedly in lieu of commissions, while concealing percentage commissions in the premium charges it billed to Potamkin; and overstating premiums and converting payments made by Potamkin. BRI denied Potamkin's allegations and counterclaimed to recover amounts allegedly owed by Potamkin, including amounts for premiums allegedly advanced by BRI to insurance companies, for which Potamkin had never reimbursed BRI ("unreimbursed premium advances").

In November 1991, after four years of protracted and acrimonious discovery, the action came to trial. * * * The trial was terminated when the parties entered into a stipulation * * * leaving for adjudication only (a) an accounting with respect to Potamkin's claims for return of premiums, unapplied payments, overbillings, and overpayments, and (b) BRI's counterclaims for, *inter alia,* unreimbursed premium advances. [Both Potamkin and BRI submitted to the court evidence and summaries in support of their claims and agreed to appointment of a special master.]

A. The Proceedings Before the Special Master

* * * In support of its counterclaims, BRI relied primarily on an accounting history prepared by the computer department of B.R.I. Cov-

erage Corp. (the "company"), allegedly detailing all unreimbursed advanced premiums (the "Potamkin History" or the "History"). The affidavit of Edward DeLuca, the company's controller and the head of its accounting department, described the History's contents and compilation. DeLuca stated that the History "represent[ed] all business transacted between [the company] and the Potamkin organization over the course of the entirety of the[ir] relationship," and had been prepared "several years ago" by the company's computer department "by extracting information concerning the transactions from [the company's] computer history tapes." (Affidavit of Edward DeLuca, dated December 3, 1991 ("DeLuca Affidavit"), ¶¶ 7, 2.) DeLuca stated that this process required the computer department to program its computer system "to scan the history tapes, extract the pertinent information concerning the transactions between the parties," and create a printout. (*Id.* ¶ 2.) His affidavit was silent as to why the History had been prepared, what documents were the sources for the computer tapes from which the History had been prepared, and why, despite Potamkin's requests covering such documents, the tapes themselves had not been produced during the four years of discovery.

The DeLuca Affidavit stated that though DeLuca had found no "material financial improprieties" in the History (*id.* ¶ 9), a "test sample review" comparing parts of the History to the company's open ledger records had revealed a number of "keypunch errors, misapplication of cash or billings among policies, and policies mislabeled as unassigned. * * *

Potamkin, in support of its own claims and in support of its defenses to BRI's counterclaims, relied primarily on some of the evidence proffered by BRI. For example, Potamkin argued that portions of the History constituted admissions by BRI of Potamkin's payment of certain premiums.

Both sides also produced expert opinion evidence. BRI submitted affidavits of an independent accountant opining that the History was largely correct. Potamkin submitted reports of two academics opining that the History was self-serving and that BRI had not established the document's reliability.

After reviewing the presentations, the special master made tentative findings and circulated a draft report to the parties. Seeing that the special master intended to recommend denial of all of BRI's counterclaims for unreimbursed premium advances, BRI, with the master's permission, moved for reconsideration of the draft, arguing for the first time (a) that the History was presumptively reliable as a business record admissible under Fed.R.Evid. 803(6), and (b) that Potamkin had admitted in its complaint that BRI had made the pertinent premium advances on Potamkin's behalf.

B. The Recommendations of the Special Master

In June 1993, the special master submitted to the district court his final report recommending the granting of certain of Potamkin's claims and the denial of all of BRI's counterclaims. (Recommendation of the Special Master ("Recommendation").) As to the counterclaims for unreimbursed premium advances, the master rejected BRI's contention that Potamkin had admitted those claims (Recommendation at 46–47), and concluded that the evidence produced by BRI was "insufficient to prove that it advanced moneys on behalf of Potamkin" (*id.* at 45).

* * *

The master rejected BRI's contention that the History was admissible, and should be deemed reliable, as a business record. He found that "[f]ar from being a contemporaneous business record, the Potamkin History was prepared at the request of counsel." (*Id.* at 47.) He noted that in a November 1989 deposition, BRI had taken the position that the History was privileged as attorney work product. (*Id.*) He found that none of the affidavits submitted by BRI established that the History was a business record. Although the DeLuca Affidavit described the History as having been prepared from BRI's historical computer tapes, the master found that there was "no evidence presented of what information was the source of these computer tapes and indeed, the tapes themselves have apparently never been produced, despite their request by Potamkin." (*Id.* at 48.)

In sum, though the special master found that, where pertinent, the History could be relied on by Potamkin as admissions of BRI to support claims asserted by Potamkin (*id.* at 16), and though he gave some weight to the History in considering BRI's defenses against claims by Potamkin (*id.* at 45), he concluded that "the Potamkin History, by itself, is not sufficient to support BRI's claims against Potamkin * * * particularly * * * in the absence of any explanation for the failure to submit checks" (*id.* at 45–46). BRI had failed to meet its "burden of presenting competent evidence that it paid the money it seeks reimbursement for." (*Id.*) * * *

C. *The Findings of the District Court*

* * *

Judgment was entered in favor of Potamkin in accordance with the recommendations of the master. This appeal followed.

II. Discussion

On appeal, BRI principally pursues the contentions that its Potamkin History should have been admitted as a business record and that Potamkin admitted that BRI had paid the premiums for which BRI here seeks reimbursement. We find no merit in its contentions.

A. *The BRI History*

The party proffering evidence has the burden of showing that the prerequisites for its admissibility are met. The district court's findings as to whether those prerequisites have been met may not be overturned unless they are clearly erroneous. *See, e.g., Gentile v. County of Suffolk,* 926 F.2d 142, 151 (2d Cir.1991); *United States v. Maldonado–Rivera,* 922 F.2d 934, 957 (2d Cir.1990). "The findings of a [special] master, to the extent that the court adopts them, shall be considered as the findings of the court," Fed.R.Civ.P. 52(a), and cannot be set aside unless they are clearly erroneous, *Mentor Insurance Co. v. Brannkasse,* 996 F.2d 506, 513 (2d Cir.1993). "Where there are two permissible views of the evidence, the factfinder's choice between them cannot be clearly erroneous." *Anderson v. Bessemer City,* 470 U.S. 564, 574 * * * (1985).

Rule 803(6) of the Federal Rules of Evidence excepts from the operation of the hearsay rule, *see* Fed.R.Evid. 802, any

> memorandum, report, record or data compilation, in any form, of acts [or] events * * * *made at or near the time by,* or from knowledge transmitted by, a person with knowledge, *if kept in the course of a regularly conducted business activity,* and if it was the regular practice of the business activity to make the memorandum, report, record or data compilation, * * * unless the source of information or the method or circumstances of preparation indicate lack of trustworthiness.

Fed.R.Evid. 803(6) (emphasis added). A business record may include data stored electronically on computers and later printed out for presentation in court, so long as the "original computer data compilation was prepared pursuant to a business duty in accordance with regular business practice." *United States v. Hernandez,* 913 F.2d 1506, 1512–13 (10th Cir.1990); see also Notes of Advisory Committee on 1972 Proposed Rules of Evidence. Data prepared or compiled for use in litigation are not admissible as business records. *See, e.g., Palmer v. Hoffman,* 318 U.S. 109, 114 * * * (1943). Thus, a document that constitutes attorney work product, *i.e.,* material prepared by or at the instance of an attorney during or in anticipation of litigation and reflecting the attorney's thought processes, *see, e.g., Hickman v. Taylor,* 329 U.S. 495, 510–11 * * * (1947), is not a business record within the meaning of Rule 803(6).

In all cases, "the principal precondition to admission of documents as business records pursuant to Fed.R.Evid. 803(6) is that the records have sufficient indicia of trustworthiness to be considered reliable." *Saks International, Inc. v. M/V "Export Champion",* 817 F.2d 1011, 1013 (2d Cir.1987). The determination of whether, in all the circumstances, the records are sufficiently reliable to warrant their admission in evidence is left to the sound discretion of the trial court. *See, e.g., id.; United States v. Lavin,* 480 F.2d 657, 662 (2d Cir.1973).

We see no error in the findings of the special master, which were adopted by the district court, that BRI did not show that its Potamkin History met the prerequisites for admissibility as a business record within the meaning of Rule 803. In concluding that BRI had not met its burden of showing that the History was prepared from original computer data compiled in accordance with regular business practice, the court was entitled to take into account BRI's refusal, despite discovery requests, to produce the computer tapes from which DeLuca asserted the History had been compiled. Further, the DeLuca Affidavit disclosed that the testing of the History showed that it contained inaccuracies resulting from, *e.g.*, keypunch errors, misapplication of cash or billings among policies, mislabeling of policies, and miscodings. Whether or not these errors were corrected, the fact that they were made suggests that the History required significant selection and interpretation of data, not simply a downloading of information previously computerized in the regular course of business. The view that the document was not prepared in the ordinary course of business was further supported by BRI's prior statements, recorded in a deposition transcript, that the History in fact constituted its attorney's work product.

* * *

Finally, we note that BRI contends that the special master could not reject the History as proof of BRI's payments on Potamkin's behalf because he relied on that document in granting certain claims of Potamkin. This argument is unsound. Assertions by a party in documents it has prepared and offers into evidence are admissible against it as admissions, *see* Fed.R.Evid. 801(d)(2)(A), and hence are evidence on the basis of which the court may make findings of fact. *See, e.g., United States v. Bedford Associates,* 713 F.2d 895, 905 (2d Cir.1983) (statements in answers to interrogatories or in proposed findings of fact are admissions admissible against the party that made them); *Bertha Building Corp. v. National Theatres Corp.,* 248 F.2d 833, 836 (1957). Such statements are nonhearsay admissions, however, only when offered against, not by, the party that made them.

* * *

Conclusion

We have considered all of BRI's contentions on appeal and have found them to be without merit. The judgment of the district court is affirmed.

Notes and Questions

1. *Computer records.* Courts have come to treat computer records routinely under the basic requirements of business (or government) records. See United States v. Vela, 673 F.2d 86, 90 (5th Cir.1982) (records received despite no specific showing that computers generating them were in proper working order—"computer evidence is not intrinsically unreliable"); United States v. Salgado, 250 F.3d 438, 453 (6th Cir.2001) (ruling that "government is not required to present expert testimony as to the mechanical accuracy of the computer where it presented evidence that the computer was sufficiently accurate that the company relied upon it in conducting its business"); United States v. Catabran, 836 F.2d 453, 458 (9th Cir.1988) (question regarding accuracy of printouts based on allegations of incorrect data entry or operation of computer program treated like similar claims for other types of business records); People v. Martinez, 990 P.2d 563, 581–82 (Cal.2000)

(admission of computer records under the hearsay rule for government records has no prerequisite of testimony regarding acceptability, accuracy, maintenance, and reliability of hardware or software). The unfortunate English experience with a detailed statute governing the admissibility of computer records, described as "a morass of drafting," is discussed in Newark & Samuels, Civil Evidence Act 1968, 31 Mod.L.Rev. 668, 670 (1968).

2. *Timeliness requirement and printouts.* The creation of a printout to be used in evidence raises a set of issues under Rule 803(6) that barred admissibility in *Potamkin* but typically do not pose great obstacles to admission. These questions include: Does such a printout satisfy the Rule's requirement that it be "made at or near the time" of the act or event? Is such a printout prepared in the regular course of business? Is it a suspect "litigation record"? For routine records, the timeliness issue usually disappears when focus is placed on the time of data entry rather than its retrieval. See United States v. Russo, 480 F.2d 1228, 1240 (6th Cir.1973). The last two questions are in fact inter-related. Unlike the situation in *Potamkin*, if the printout is simply ordering existing data rather than creating new information or, although done in this instance for evidence purposes, is the type of record that is part of the ordinary business routine, it should not be treated as suspect. See United States v. Sanders, 749 F.2d 195, 198 (5th Cir.1984) (contrasting programs that "only orders it [the data] out" rather than "sorting, compiling or summarizing information"); 4 Mueller & Kirkpatrick, Federal Evidence § 446, 510 (2d ed. 1994) (test should be whether producing the printout is part of the business routine that gives basis for assuring reliability).

3. *Sources.* 3 Bender, Computer Law ch. 6 (1992); Horning, Electronically Stored Evidence: Answers to Some Recurring Questions Concerning Pretrial Discovery and Trial Usage, 41 Wash. & Lee L.Rev. 1335 (1984); Johnston, A Guide for the Proponent and Opponent of Computer–Based Evidence, 1 Computer L.J. 667 (1979); Peritz, Computer Data and Reliability: A Call for Authentication of Business Records Under the Federal Rules of Evidence, 80 Nw.U.L.Rev. 956 (1986); Singer, Proposed Changes to the Federal Rules of Evidence as Applied to Computer–Generated Evidence, 7 Rutgers J. Computers, Tech. & L. 157 (1979).

YATES v. BAIR TRANSPORT, INC.

United States District Court, Southern District of New York, 1965.
249 F.Supp. 681.

TENNEY, DISTRICT JUDGE. The respective parties herein request of the Court a ruling prior to trial on the admissibility of two proffered items of evidence: firstly, a police blotter report concerning the instant accident, and, secondly, medical reports of various doctors who examined plaintiff in connection with a prior Workmen's Compensation claim arising out of the accident.

The parties have stipulated that if the reporting officer were called he would testify that the police blotter was prepared by him in the regular course of his duties and filed with the Police Department in accordance with his and their regular practice and procedure. If the officer were called, it is further agreed that he would also testify that the photostatic copy was authentic. Plaintiff accordingly argues that a sufficient foundation has been laid for the admissibility of the report without the necessity of calling the police officer.

The Federal Business Records Act, 28 U.S.C.A. § 1732 (Supp.1964), provides:

> "§ 1732. Record made in regular course of business: photographic copies.
>
> (a) In any court of the United States and in any court established by Act of Congress, any writing or record, whether in the form of an entry in a book or otherwise, made as a memorandum or record of any act, transaction, occurrence, or event, shall be admissible as evidence of such act, transaction, occurrence, or event, if made in regular course of any business, and if it was the regular course of such business to make such memorandum or record at the time of such act, transaction, occurrence, or event or within a reasonable time thereafter."[28]

It further provides that "[a]ll other circumstances of the making of such writing or record [i.e., a record kept in the ordinary course of business] including lack of personal knowledge by the entrant or maker, may be shown to affect its weight, but such circumstances shall not affect its admissibility." * * *

A copy of the police blotter report has been supplied to the Court. Therein the ownership of the vehicle in question is set forth. In addition, the details of the accident are enumerated. The officer, as stated in the report, was not an eyewitness to the accident; in addition, under the heading of names and addresses of witnesses there appears the entry "none". Accordingly, it may be assumed that the information set forth in the report was supplied either by the driver of the truck, a helper, or the plaintiff; however, this is an assumption not based on any affirmative proof.

In spite of the apparent clarity of the language in both statutes to the effect that the fact the entry is based on lack of personal knowledge of the entrant goes to weight rather than admissibility of a record kept in the ordinary course of business, the Courts and commentators have seemingly taken a different view of the metes of this exception to the hearsay rule.

Professor McCormick has summed up the state of the law as follows: "Thus the statements of by-standers recorded in a policeman's report of accident * * * would be denied admission as business records to show the facts reported * * * ." McCormick, Evidence § 286 at 602–03 (1954). * * *

28. [The federal act, which was the Commonwealth Fund Act, has been repealed and superseded by Fed.R.Evid. 803(6). Ed.]

It is clear that Johnson v. Lutz, 253 N.Y. 124, 170 N.E. 517 (1930) would preclude the admissibility of statements by bystanders given to a police officer at the scene of the accident.

"Where, however, the informant to the entrant of the record is under no duty to anyone to make a truthful account of the facts thus recorded, the record will not be admissible as proof of such facts. Johnson v. Lutz, 253 N.Y. 124, 170 N.E. 517 (Ct.App.1930) (report of policeman as to accident based on information from bystander witness * * *). Aside from Wigmore [5 Wigmore, Evidence § 1530a (3d ed. 1940)], no competent authority in the field and few courts have dissented from this qualification obviously basic to the rationale of the business entry exception (citing cases and Law Review articles)." Fagan v. City of Newark, 78 N.J.Super. 294, 188 A.2d 427, 440 (App.Div.1963).

* * *

> Despite [some] criticism of the Johnson case, the limitation it imposes seems sound and in accord with the basic philosophy of the business entry statutes. These acts were intended to make admissible records which because made pursuant to a regular business duty, are presumed to be reliable. The mere fact that recordation of third party statements is routine, taken apart from the source of the information recorded, imports no guaranty of the truth of the statements themselves. There is no reason for supposing an intention to make admissible hearsay of this sort. So to construe these statutes would make of them almost limitless dragnets for the introduction of random, irresponsible testimony beyond the reach of the usual tests for accuracy. Johnson v. Lutz did not ignore the statutory language making personal knowledge unnecessary, but merely emphasized that the presumption of reliability attaches only to statements made entirely in the course of business.
>
> A record which contains the hearsay statements of volunteers [be they bystanders or participants under no duty to impart the information] then, does not by operation of the business record statutes become admissible to prove the truth of those statements." Note, *Revised Business Entry Statutes: Theory & Practice,* 48 Colum.L.Rev. 920, 926–27 (1948).

The following reconciliation between the statutory language and the clear weight of authority appears correct:

"This [the statutory language stating that lack of personal knowledge of the maker or entrant goes to weight rather than admissibility] could be interpreted as abolishing the requirement of first-hand knowledge by one whose job is to know the facts. The more reasonable interpretation, however, is to read 'entrant or maker' as meaning the recorder only and thus merely making clear that one who makes the record on reports of others need not know the facts without broadening (beyond the probable intent of the drafters) the content of this hearsay exception to embrace records founded on reports by one who has no business duty to know the facts." McCormick, supra, § 286 at 602. * * *

Moreover, if the policeman testified in court, his testimony that a bystander told him that the accident occurred thusly would be hearsay and if not within one of the exceptions, inadmissible. Why a different result should be reached where the policeman writes what the bystander said instead of testifying to it, is not readily apparent. * * *

In analyzing these cases, however, it must be borne in mind that there are numerous exceptions to the hearsay rule and that an utterance, while not properly admitted under one exception, may very well be admitted under another.

"It should be recognized, of course, that apart from the business entry statutes there are numerous exceptions to the hearsay rule—e.g., those covering statements regarding present mental or physical conditions, admission, declarations against interest, spontaneous declarations, statements or dying declarations. A record of volunteer hearsay may be admissible as proof of the facts stated where such an exception exists. * * * [T]he statutes are applicable only in admitting the first step of hearsay, while the second step is admitted because a further exception wholly independent of business rules is appropriate." 48 Colum.L.Rev. at 928–29. * * *

[T]he Business Records Act overcomes the initial hurdle to the admissibility of evidence, but goes no further. Thus the hearsay statement (of a volunteer) contained in the police officer's report is no more admissible than the testimony of the police officer on the stand as to the hearsay statement made at the scene of the accident. If the making of the statement itself is relevant, it can be proved both by the report, which is a record kept in the ordinary course of business, as well as by the in-Court testimony of the officer. However, if the report is offered to prove the truth of the statement contained therein, the statement must either have been made in the regular course of business of the person making it, or must have an independent ground of admissibility such as an admission, etc., the same as the in-Court testimony of the officer as to the statements made, offered to prove the truth of what was said, must have an independent ground of admissibility, since all that can be shown under the Business Records Act is that in the regular course of business of the officer he wrote that X made the following statement to prove the truth of the fact that X made the statement, not the proof of the facts contained in the statement.

Accordingly, without knowing who made the statements and under what circumstances they were made, an insufficient foundation has presently been laid upon which to admit the proffered report over objection.

We next proceed to the second class of proffered documents—the reports of various doctors who examined plaintiff.

* * * Plaintiff wishes to introduce the reports of Doctors Youmans, Guthrie, Lewis, Fleck and Richman into evidence in lieu of calling them as witnesses, and has requested a pre-trial ruling as to their admissibility.

It appears from ¶ 4C of the Pre–Trial Order herein that all the parties agreed as to the authenticity of the medical reports which are now being proffered. It further appears from the reports themselves, and it can very easily be verified, that Doctors Guthrie and Youmans examined plaintiff on behalf of [the defendant's insurance carrier], that Doctor Richman examined plaintiff on behalf of Interboro Mutual Indemnity Insurance Company,[29] and that Doctors Fleck and Lewis were plaintiff's treating physicians. Accordingly, the reports have been sufficiently authenticated. Compare Pellegrini v. Chicago Great Western Ry., 319 F.2d 447, 455 (7th Cir.1963).

In ruling on the admissibility of the documents, the reports will be grouped, based on the identity of the party on whose behalf the report was prepared.

* * *

That the report of Drs. Youmans and Guthrie was prepared in the ordinary course of the business of both doctors is indicated by the Court of Appeals decision in White v. Zutell, 263 F.2d 613 (2d Cir.1959), which involved a medical report made by a specialist who had examined the plaintiff on behalf of the defendant's insurance carrier.

In sustaining the admissibility of the report, the Court stated: "The making of this report was clearly a part of this specialist's 'business'; indeed that is what he was commissioned to do. And it bears its own inherent guaranty of being what it purports to be—a detailed report of what he found medically upon examining the subject. That it might come up in the course of litigation does not affect this guaranty, unless to enhance it; what would be the use of such a report except to aid in fixing legal damage?" *Id.* at 615.

As stated in McCormick, Evidence § 287 at 604 (1954): "[W]ell reasoned modern decisions have admitted in accident cases the written reports of doctors of their findings from an examination of the injured party when it appears that is the doctor's professional routine or duty to make such report." But, it is argued, all the doctors' reports were prepared specifically for litigation (whether before the Workmen's Compensation Board, or in this suit) and at a time when the motive to misrepresent was present and the reports thus lack the trustworthiness necessary to permit their introduction. Palmer v. Hoffman, 318 U.S. 109 * * * (1943) is cited in support of this argument.

In Palmer v. Hoffman, supra, the Court was concerned with the likely untrustworthiness of materials prepared specifically by a prospec-

29. [Dr. Richman's status with relation to the parties to the litigation was unclear. See infra. Ed.]

tive litigant for courtroom use (see United States v. New York Foreign Trade Zone Operators, 304 F.2d 792, 797 (2d Cir.1962)), and thus held that the mere fact of regularity of preparation would not in itself be enough to justify the use of the evidence. The Business Records Act was interpreted in Palmer as facilitating the "admission of records which experience has shown to be quite trustworthy." 318 U.S. at 113 * * *.

Accordingly, what must be found in the case at bar is an added element of trustworthiness which will counterbalance the fact that these reports were prepared in clear anticipation of litigation. With respect to the reports of Doctors Guthrie and Youmans, this added element is present.

> "In Pekelis v. Transcontinental & W. Air Inc., 187 F.2d 122 (2 Cir.1951), we held that the district court was erroneous in refusing to admit the plaintiff's offer of certain accident reports prepared by boards set up by the defendant airline to investigate the crash of one of defendant's airplanes. We interpreted the decision in Palmer v. Hoffman to exclude accident reports only when they were prepared for use in litigation or when there was other indicia of their untrustworthiness. The Pekelis reports, the court pointed out, '* * * were against the interest of the entrant when made, * * * were clearly not part of a story cooked up in advance of litigation in the disguise of business records' and were offered as evidence by the party opposing the one which had had the reports prepared. 187 F.2d at 130.
>
> "In Korte v. New York, N.H. & H.R.R., 191 F.2d 86 (2 Cir. 1951), another accident case, the district court had admitted certain doctors' reports, offered by the plaintiff, which had been prepared at the request of the defendant railroad. We affirmed the district court. Again, we pointed out that the decision in Palmer v. Hoffman was directed against the admission of hearsay evidence prepared for a litigious or other self-serving purpose. The court in Korte doubted whether the Palmer v. Hoffman rationale extended to reports made by independent doctors. Regardless of this, the Korte court stated that its holding could rest on Pekelis, where it had been held that reports offered by the party adverse to the party for whom the reports were prepared were admissible."

United States v. New York Foreign Trade Zone Operators, 304 F.2d at 798.

Thus the thrust of both opinions supports the admissibility of a doctor's report made in the regular course of business (when litigation was on the horizon) "when offered by one other than the entrant or one for whom the entrant is then working, i.e., the carrier * * *." Rotondi v. McLellan, 194 F.Supp. 415, 417 (E.D.N.Y.1961). * * *

Thus in the case at bar the fact that litigation involving Liberty Mutual was pending when these three reports were made, if anything, enhances the trustworthiness of the documents, since it is the plaintiff, not the defendant, who seeks their introduction (i.e., the party whose interest is adverse to that of the party on whose behalf the reports were made.) * * * Accordingly, I am inclined to overrule the objection to the report of Doctors Youmans and Guthrie.

* * *

[T]he situation with respect to the reports of the doctors employed by plaintiff is different than that of defendant's doctors (Doctors Guthrie and Youmans) and warrants a different result, since statements by them would (if statements by defendant's doctors can be deemed admissions) be self-serving with no added degree of trustworthiness. They are thus statements made on behalf of a party by persons more inclined to favor that party's position, and the fact that they were made for the purposes of litigation causes me sufficient concern to refuse to admit them at this time.

* * *

Accordingly, where, as here, there is no counterbalancing force to the desire to promote the self-interest of the party on whose behalf the report was made, discretion dictates that the objection at this time be sustained and plaintiff be required to call Doctors Lewis and Fleck. Insofar as Doctor Richman is concerned, his status is not clear with respect to the parties involved in the litigation, and with respect to his report there may not be present this added element of trustworthiness. Therefore, I will place him in the latter group of doctors employed by plaintiff and hold his report at this time inadmissible as well. * * *

So ordered.

Notes and Questions

1. *Common ground between business and government records*. The first part of the *Yates* opinion that involves the police report would be treated today as a governmental record under Rule 803(8) rather than as a "business record" under Rule 803(6). Its analysis of the exclusion of statements by persons outside the organization (the *Johnson v. Lutz* issue) remains quite solid. Governmental records are examined in the next section.

2. *Hearsay within hearsay. Yates* discusses the admission of multiple layers of hearsay, which in some situations is dealt with by multiple hearsay exceptions under Rule 805, see Section M, infra, and in others by the single exception of business records. As *Yates* notes, if each of the multiple layers of hearsay involve people within the business with a "business duty," then they are all admissible under the instant exception. However, if someone outside the business makes one of the statements (e.g., a bystander), then Rule 805 is involved and the statement cannot be received for its truth without another exception (e.g., excited utterance). United States v. Sparkman, 235 F.R.D. 454, 460 (E.D.Mo.2006) (recognizing the distinction between two levels of hearsay when the source and the recorder are not the same person and the source is not acting in regular course of business, and a single level of hearsay under business records when, although different people, both the source and the recorder are acting within the regular course

of business). Assuming an exception exists for the outsider's statement, note that the person within the business must have some business interest in hearing and recording the statement accurately. See Commonwealth v. Harris, 41 A.2d 688 (Pa.1945) (examining whether description of attacker should be admitted when contained in hospital record).

3. *Verification.* As to requiring that persons furnishing information, as well as those recording it, be in the routine of the "business," consider United States v. Lieberman, 637 F.2d 95, 100–01 (2d Cir.1980), where the trial court had admitted a hotel registration card under Rule 803(6).

> Lieberman's objection to the admission of the hotel guest card was that the lines showing the guest's name and address had been filled in by the guest, not the hotel's employee. This objection missed the mark. We do not view the applicability of the business records exception as depending on the purely formal matter of whether the guest supplies the information by writing it on the card, or by stating it so that it may be written on the card by the employee. The latter process would not suffice to make the business records exception applicable to prove the identity of the guest unless the employee were able in some way to verify the information provided * * *. By the same token, however, if such verification is obtained by the employee, we see no reason why the guest card that has been filled in by the guest himself would not qualify as a business record and thus be admissible for the truth of its statements.

See also United States v. Vigneau, 187 F.3d 70, 75–77 (1st Cir.1999) (ruling inadmissible defendant's name as sender on Western Union "To Send Money" forms since he was not part of business and company's practice was not to verify identity).

4. *Ad hoc showing of lack of trustworthiness.* Rule 803(6) provides that a statement that meets the formal requirements of the Rule may be excluded if "the source of the information or the method or circumstances of preparation indicate lack of trustworthiness." As is generally required, the proponent of the evidence initially bears the burden of establishing that the statement meets the Rule's requirements, and this language, which begins with "unless," then places the burden of demonstrating lack of trustworthiness on the party opposing admission. See, e.g., Shelton v. Consumer Prods. Safety Comm'n, 277 F.3d 998, 1010 (8th Cir.2002).

5. *Trustworthiness undercut by preparation for litigation.* In some cases, such as *Olesen v. Henningsen*, supra, the business that prepared the record has no interest in the litigation, but in others, such as with the doctors in *Yates*, the entity preparing the record has a recognizable interest in the litigation. Lack of trustworthiness may be shown in a number of circumstances, and one given particular attention is that the record was prepared for litigation purposes. See Peat, Inc. v. Vanguard Research Inc., 378 F.3d 1154, 1159–61 (11th Cir.2004) (excluding document prepared in response to discovery request by party to identify trade secrets allegedly misappropriated because prepared not in the regular course of business but for litigation); Echo Acceptance Corp. v. Household Retail Servs., Inc., 267 F.3d 1068, 1090–91 (10th Cir.2001) (excluding business correspondence that district court found constituted legal posturing drafted by lawyers in antici-

pation of litigation); Paddack v. Dave Christensen, Inc., 745 F.2d 1254, 1258–59 (9th Cir.1984) (audit reports ordered by trustees of trust account only upon suspicion of deficiency were prepared for litigation and lacked trustworthiness); United States v. Williams, 661 F.2d 528, 531 (5th Cir.1981) (memorandum estimating value of company's trailer stolen three years earlier made by head of maintenance department lacked trustworthiness because it was not prepared in course of regularly conducted business but rather for trial); Pan–Islamic Trade Corp. v. Exxon Corp., 632 F.2d 539, 560 (5th Cir.1980) (memorandum drafted for purpose of preventing cancellation of contract prepared for litigation and lacked trustworthiness).

6. *Admissible "litigation records."* The fact that a record may have value in the event of litigation does not, however, automatically exclude it from the exception as untrustworthy. In Lewis v. Baker, 526 F.2d 470 (2d Cir.1975), the court admitted as a business record an accident report prepared by railroad employees shortly after plaintiff's injury. In spite of the fact that the report was offered on behalf of the defendant railroad, the court found no lack of trustworthiness. The individual employees who prepared the report were neither personally involved in the accident nor potential targets of the suit, and such reports were regularly prepared both in response to federal regulations and because of their utility to the employer in preventing future accidents.

7. *Hospitals as businesses.* Hospital records may contain a variety of entries, as in United States v. Bohle, 445 F.2d 54, 61 (7th Cir.1971):

> It contains material in the nature of a case history consisting largely of statements made by Bohle and third parties, principally his mother, and recorded by members of the hospital staffs. It also contains records concerning the treatment given Bohle and concerning observations made of him which require no special skill and as to which there is little likelihood of disagreement among trained observors [sic]. Finally, Exhibit A contains diagnoses, and similar judgment opinions, of Bohle's condition prepared by those who attended him while he was hospitalized.

The court in *Bohle* reached the conclusion that different treatment is required depending upon the nature of the entry. Rule 803(6) specifically includes opinions or diagnoses within its scope and draws no distinction based on their objective or judgmental character. Does this mean that all opinions are admissible under the Rule or does the court retain discretion to exclude those that are questionable under the trustworthiness rubric? Some commentators argue that courts can require the testimony of the expert before admitting the record in situations where the opinion is especially contestable. See 5 Weinstein's Federal Evidence § 803.08[6][b] (2d ed. 2006); 2 McCormick, Evidence § 293, at 321–22 (6th ed. 2006).

8. *Diagnoses and opinions.* In general, expert opinions in business records should not be admissible if the person rendering the opinion is unqualified or the topic is not a proper one for expert testimony. 2 McCormick, Evidence § 287, at 307 (6th ed. 2006). It makes little sense that an opinion that could not be received under Rule 702 if the expert testified, for example, were admissible from the same individual through a business

record. See related discussion of expert opinions that are part of evaluative reports in Section F, infra, following *Bridgeway*.

Whether the party who offers the record or the opponent who would challenge it bears the burden of proving issues regarding expertise is not entirely clear, and perhaps which party has the burden should not receive uniform treatment. Courts have reached different conclusions. Compare United States v. Licavoli, 604 F.2d 613, 622–23 (9th Cir.1979) (no inflexible rule that qualifications be affirmatively established, but trial judge has discretion to exclude opinion where qualifications are seriously challenged), with Forward Communications Corp. v. United States, 608 F.2d 485, 510–11 (Ct.Cl.1979) (opinions that are not part of factual reports of contemporaneous events but are prepared for the purpose of stating or supporting expert opinions are inadmissible unless preparer testifies and establishes qualifications). Which approach is more consistent with the general structure of Rule 803(6)? Perhaps a sensible pattern can be seen in pre-Rules cases involving diagnostic entries contained in hospital records. They have frequently been admitted, at least where the entrants are shown to be members of the hospital staff, with the competency of the doctor presumed from the position held. See Allen v. St. Louis Pub. Serv. Co., 285 S.W.2d 663 (Mo.1956). A similar presumption appears to attach to technicians whose laboratory findings are incorporated in such record. See Webber v. McCormick, 164 A.2d 813 (N.J.Super.1960). But, a presumption of competency may not be appropriate for records of privately practicing physicians. See Falcone v. New Jersey Bell Tel. Co., 236 A.2d 394 (N.J.Super.1967).

SECTION F. PUBLIC RECORDS AND REPORTS

FEDERAL RULES 803(8), (9) & (10)

CHESAPEAKE & DELAWARE CANAL CO. v. UNITED STATES

Supreme Court of the United States, 1919.
250 U.S. 123.

[Action by the Government to recover dividends claimed to be due and unpaid on shares of stock held by it in defendant corporation.]

MR. JUSTICE CLARKE delivered the opinion of the court: * * *

The government produced a witness who testified that he, in conspiracy with another employee of the Canal Company, embezzled the amount of these dividends, and that, to conceal their crime, they placed in the files of the Canal Company, from which they were produced in evidence, forged drafts purporting to have been drawn by Assistant Treasurers of the United States upon the treasurer of the Canal Company for payment of these dividends, and also what purported to be receipts therefor. This witness testified that until 1886, when he left the employ of the Canal Company, no notice of the declaration of the three dividends in controversy had been sent to the government, as had been the practice when earlier dividends were declared; that until that time no payment of them had been made, and that the names signed to the drafts and receipts were fictitious.

The government also produced the notices by the Canal Company of the declaration of each of the fourteen earlier dividends and the record of the payment of them.

To supplement this evidence the books were produced in evidence, the admission of which is assigned as error.

Employees of the Department of the Treasury, who produced the books, testified: that they were records of the Department, compiled by authority of law under the direction of the Secretary of the Treasury, and were the volumes in daily use by officials and employees in the discharge of their duties; that part of them were printed from the original records of miscellaneous revenues, in which such dividends would be classed, while others were printed compilations from books not of original entry, and the testimony was that the volumes produced were intended to, and the witnesses believed did, show all of the miscellaneous receipts and disbursements of the government from 1848 to 1914. They showed the receipt by the government of fourteen dividends paid by the Canal Company prior to those in controversy, and the witnesses testified that a careful search made by them failed to discover any record in the books of the receipt of any of the three dividends sued for. There was an elaborate description of the method employed by the Department of the Treasury in keeping its accounts, and of the necessarily contemporaneous character of the original entries, which it is not necessary to rehearse. The copies produced were printed by the Public Printer.

The objection is that these are not books of original entry, and that they are not certified as copies of public records are required to be by Rev.Stat. 882, Comp.Stat.1916, § 1494, 3 Fed.Stat.Anno.2d ed. p. 197.

It is enough to say of this last contention that although the books admitted were printed from written public records, they were so printed by authority of law, and were produced from the custody of the Department of the Treasury, where they were used as original records in the transaction of the daily business of the Department, and therefore they did not require certification.

They were public records, kept pursuant to constitutional and statutory requirement. Constitution of the United States, Article 1, § 9, cl. 7; Act of Congress, approved September 2, 1789, * * * Thus, their character as public records required by law to be kept, the official character of their contents, entered under the sanction of public duty, the obvious necessity for regular contemporaneous entries in them, and the reduction to a minimum of motive on the part of public officials and employees to either make false entries or to omit proper ones, all unite to make these books admissible as unusually trustworthy sources of evidence. * * * Obviously such books are not subject to the rules of restricted admissibility applicable to private account books. The considerations which we have found rendered the books admissible in evidence as tending to prove the truth of the statements of entries contained in them also make them admissible as evidence tending to show that because the receipt of the dividends was not entered in them, they were not received, and therefore were not paid. The evidence may not be as persuasive in the latter case as in the former, but that it was proper evidence to be submitted to the jury for the determination of its value we cannot doubt. Such books so kept presumptively contained a record of all payments made, and the absence of any entry of payment, where it naturally would have been found if it had been made, was evidence of nonpayment, proper for the consideration of the jury. * * *

* * *

The judgment of the Circuit Court of Appeals is affirmed.

Note

Public official requirement. Rules 803(8)(A) & (B) create an exception for records and reports made by public officers or agencies pursuant to a statutory authorization or mandate. The Rule does not directly authorize admission of statements made by private individuals to public officials. It also does not provide a blanket exception for statements by private individuals to public officials even when those statements are made pursuant to statutory duty, although a limited exception is created under Rule 803(9) for records of vital statistics.

UNITED STATES v. QUEZADA

United States Court of Appeals, Fifth Circuit, 1985.
754 F.2d 1190.

John R. Brown, Circuit Judge:

In this appeal from a conviction under 8 U.S.C. § 1326 for illegal reentry after deportation, appellant challenges the admission of certain evidence at his bench trial. We review the proceedings below, find that properly admitted evidence sufficiently supports the conviction, and affirm.

Background

Appellant Oscar Ramos Quezada, an illegal alien, was deported from this country on April 25, 1982, pursuant to a warrant of deportation (Form I–205) issued by the United States Immigration and Naturalization Service (INS). Seven months later, on November 17, 1983, a Border Patrol officer arrested Quezada at the El Paso County Jail, where he was incarcerated on a public intoxication charge. Quezada was subsequently indicted by a federal grand jury for illegally reentering the country after having been previously arrested and deported, in violation of 8 U.S.C. § 1326. After a bench trial, he was convicted and sentenced to a prison term of two years, all but six months of which were suspended in lieu of supervised probation.

At trial, the principal part of the government's case was devoted to proving that Quezada had been "deported and arrested" as required for conviction under the statute. In order to establish these statutory requisites, the government called as a witness Border Patrol Agent David Meshirer. Agent Meshirer first testified that he had been designated the custodian of appellant's immigration file. The government then used the witness to introduce its exhibits.

Two exhibits are of particular importance in this appeal. The first is INS Form I–205, the warrant of deportation which authorized the deportation of appellant. The second, INS Form I–294, is a letter to appellant in his native language, warning him of the penalties for illegal reentry after deportation. Both exhibits were admitted into evidence over appellant's objections.

The testimony of Agent Meshirer also figures prominently in this appeal. His testimony described the use and function of the INS forms put in evidence. First, he explained that on the back of Form I–205 are spaces to be filled out by the deporting officer, as well as a space for the thumbprint of the deportee. Agent Meshirer also observed that the back of Form I–205 reflected that appellant had been deported on April 25, 1982, and that this deportation had been witnessed by an immigration officer whose signature appeared on the exhibit. Finally, he pointed out a thumbprint on the back of the exhibit, which subsequent testimony established to be that of appellant.

Agent Meshirer next testified as to the normal procedure followed in executing warrants of deportation. He stated that when a person has been ordered deported, an immigration officer will pick up the deportee, fill in the blanks on the back of the warrant, and sign the warrant as having witnessed the departure. He also testified that in the course of a normal deportation, the deportee's right thumbprint is taken. As to Form I–294, the letter informing the deportee of the penalties for illegal reentry, Agent Meshirer observed that it is given to the deportee along with a copy of the warrant of deportation. Thus, according to this testimony, the deported individual is fully apprised of the fact of his deportation, and that he is subject to criminal penalties for illegal reentry.

* * *

Discussion

Appellant urges that the evidence below was insufficient to prove the "arrest" necessary for prosecution under 8 U.S.C. § 1326, as that term has been interpreted by this court. In *United States v. Wong Kim Bo,* 466 F.2d 1298 (5th Cir.1972) *rehearing denied,* 472 F.2d 720 (5th Cir.1972), we discussed that term as it fits into the scheme of the statute in question. First, we observed that there are five elements which the government must prove in order to obtain a conviction for illegal reentry after deportation: [i] that defendant was an alien; [ii] that he was "arrested" and [iii] "deported" as those terms are contemplated by the statute; [iv] that he was subsequently found within this country and [v] that he did not have consent from the Attorney General to reapply for admission. *Id.* at 1303.[30]

We next turned to an analysis of the "arrest" requirement. After examining the legislative and Congressional purpose underlying the Act, we concluded that an "arrest" under the statute is accomplished by service on the alien of the warrant of deportation, thus providing the requisite notice to trigger criminal sanctions for illegal reentry thereafter. *Id.* at 1304–05. This notice is critical, we observed, for it insures that criminal sanctions are not imposed for reentry where the alien does not know that he has previously been officially deported. *Id.* at 1304.

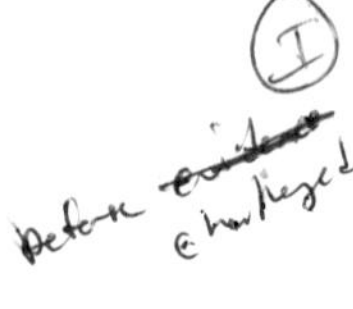

The argument presented on appeal is that the government failed to prove that appellant was actually served with a warrant of deportation issued by INS. This argument implicates important questions respecting the use of public documents in criminal proceedings * * *.

DOCUMENTARY EVIDENCE

Initially, our attention is drawn to the question of the admissibility of INS Form I–205, the warrant of deportation. This document is crucial to the government's case, as it contains virtually all of the information proving appellant's prior arrest and deportation. Thus is implicated F.R.Evid. 803(8)(B), the public records exception to the hearsay rule, which provides as follows: * * *

> (8) Public records and reports. Records, reports, statements, or data compilations, in any form, of public offices or agencies setting forth * * * (B) matters observed pursuant to duty imposed by law as to which matters there was a duty to report, excluding, however, in criminal cases matters observed by police officers and other law enforcement personnel.

Two principal reasons underlie this exception to the general rule excluding hearsay: the presumed trustworthiness of public documents prepared in the discharge of official functions, and the necessity of using such documents, due to the likelihood that a public official would have no independent memory of a particular action or entry where his duties require the constant repetition of routine tasks. *See generally,* 4 D. Louisell and C. Mueller, Federal Evidence, Public Records § 454.

Despite this policy favoring the admissibility of public records, Congress was also obviously concerned about the use of such documents in criminal cases. In an apparent attempt to avoid a collision between the hearsay rule and the confrontation clause of the Sixth Amendment, Congress excluded from the public records exception "in criminal cases matters observed by police officers and other law enforcement personnel. * * * "Rule 803(8)(B). In so doing, however, Congress did not make clear whether the Rule was designed to exclude all reports made by a

30. Of these five elements, appellant challenges only the second, whether or not he was properly "arrested."

government employee which are offered against a criminal defendant, or whether only certain types of reports were intended to be excluded.

While some courts have inflexibly applied the Rule 803(8)(B) proscription to all law enforcement records in criminal cases, *see, e.g., United States v. Oates,* 560 F.2d 45, 83–84 (2d Cir.1977), we are not persuaded that such a narrow application of the rule is warranted here.[31] The law enforcement exception in Rule 803(8)(B) is based in part on the presumed unreliability of observations made by law enforcement officials at the scene of a crime, or in the course of investigating a crime:

> [o]stensibly, the reason for this exclusion is that observations by police officers at the scene of the crime or the apprehension of the defendant were not as reliable as observations by public officials in other cases because of the adversarial nature of the confrontation between the police and the defendant in criminal cases.

Senate Report No. 1277, 93d Cong.2d Sess., *reprinted in* [1974] U.S.Code Cong. & Ad.News 7051, 7064. Thus, a number of courts have drawn a distinction for purposes of Rule 803(8)(B) between law enforcement reports prepared in a routine, non-adversarial setting, and those resulting from the arguably more subjective endeavor of investigating a crime and evaluating the results of that investigation. *See, e.g., United States v. Orozco,* 590 F.2d 789, 793–94 (9th Cir.1979) (admitting computer records of license plates on cars crossing the border due to non-adversarial setting in which information was gathered); *United States v. Union Nacional de Trabajadores,* 576 F.2d 388, 390–91 (1st Cir.1978) (admitting Marshal's return of service); *United States v. Grady,* 544 F.2d 598 (2d Cir.1976) (admitting reports on firearms serial numbers for Northern Ireland law enforcement agency on basis that they were records of a routine function).

Under this analysis, a warrant of deportation was deemed properly admissible in a § 1326 action in *United States v. Hernandez–Rojas,* 617 F.2d 533 (9th Cir.1980). The Ninth Circuit there concluded that the notations on the warrant indicating the defendant's deportation were the result of a ministerial, objective observation, and thus had none of the subjective features of reports made in a more adversarial setting, such as an investigation of a crime scene. *Id.* at 535.

We find the reasoning of these cases persuasive. This circuit has recognized that Rule 803(8) is designed to permit the admission into evidence of public records prepared for purposes independent of specific litigation. *United States v. Stone,* 604 F.2d 922 (5th Cir.1979) (Rule

31. While we cited *Oates* with approval in *United States v. Cain,* 615 F.2d 380 (5th Cir.1980), that case is not contrary to our decision today. First, we cited *Oates* only for the proposition that a document inadmissible under Rule 803(8)(B) may not be received in evidence merely because it satisfies Rule 803(6), the exception for business records. *Id.* at 382. Further, unlike the case here, the public record at issue in *Cain* reported actual criminal activity on the part of the defendant. Finally, the *Cain* court apparently was not faced with a situation in which the very number of cases handled by the government agency made reliance on such records an administrative and evidentiary necessity. * * *

803(8)(A)). In the case of documents recording routine, objective observations, made as part of the everyday function of the preparing official or agency, the factors likely to cloud the perception of an official engaged in the more traditional law enforcement functions of observation and investigation of crime are simply not present. Due to the lack of any motivation on the part of the recording official to do other than mechanically register an unambiguous factual matter (here, appellant's departure from the country), such records are, like other public documents, inherently reliable. *See Smith v. Ithaca,* 612 F.2d 215, 222 (5th Cir.1980) (records trustworthy where recording official has no reason to be other than objective).

We further believe that the warrant of deportation in this case establishes the service required by *Wong Kim Bo.* Appellant's thumbprint on the warrant indicates that the warrant was presented to him prior to departure. Additionally, testimony of Border Patrol Agent Meshirer conclusively established the authenticity and reliability of this record of deportation. *See* F.R.Evid. 901(b)(7). He testified that the warrants of deportation are kept in the normal course of business of the INS. Trial Transcript at 11. He further testified that the warrants of deportation are kept as a matter of course with the individual file maintained for each alien being processed. *Id.* at 9–10. This testimony clearly indicated the extent to which such records are relied on by the INS in its day-to-day operations.

Moreover, in a case like the one at bar, the absolute necessity of proving the government's case through the use of public records is unquestionable. In the years 1977–1981, the INS processed for departure from the country, on average, more than 1,000,000 aliens annually. In 1981, more than 260,000 aliens were processed in the State of Texas alone, with over 6,000 of those having been officially deported. Given these numbers, it is unlikely that testimony by an INS officer as to the deportation of a particular individual could be based on anything other than recorded observations, with such testimony being merely cumulative to the more reliable written record of deportation.

We thus conclude that the warrant of deportation, containing appellant's thumbprint and indicating the date and location of his deportation, sufficiently established the arrest requirement contemplated by the statute. Given the overwhelming number of immigration cases processed each year, the INS must be permitted to rely on such records to establish certain elements of a violation of § 1326.

* * *

Affirmed.

Notes and Questions

1. *Admissibility of "ministerial" records.* As *Quezada* notes, a number of other courts have disagreed with United States v. Oates, 560 F.2d 45, 83–84 (2d Cir.1977), as to its extremely broad reading of the exclusion of public

reports when offered against a criminal defendant under Rule 803(8)(B). The clear majority view is that the Rule does not bar use of "ministerial" as opposed to "investigative" reports. Is this a sensible result? See Alexander, The Hearsay Exception for Public Records in Federal Criminal Trials, 47 Albany L.Rev. 699, 716–17 (1983) (finding "the majority view" preferable and consistent with legislative intent). In getting a sense of the distinction between ministerial and adversarial records, compare United States v. Brown, 315 F.3d 929, 931 (8th Cir.2003) (admitting information from Secret Service database on location of counterfeit bills with same serial numbers because records were both objective and not adversarial in that they were not collected in anticipation of defendant's trial) with United States v. Orellana–Blanco, 294 F.3d 1143, 1150 (9th Cir.2002) (ruling that interview with INS agent about nature of marriage was adversarial in nature, rather than ministerial or objective observation, and therefore not admissible under Rule 803(8)(B) against the defendant).

2. *Limitations on police records as business records.* Substantial pre-Federal Rules authority supported the admissibility of police reports under the hearsay exception for business records. Annots., 77 A.L.R.3d 115, 31 A.L.R.Fed. 457. *Oates* reasoned that, since a public report is not admissible against a criminal defendant under Rule 803(8) by virtue of Congress' explicit prohibition, the same document may not properly be received under Rule 803(6). The reasoning of *Oates* that Rule 803(6) should not provide a "back door" method of admitting statements by the police against criminal defendants has been generally followed. See, e.g., United States v. Cain, 615 F.2d 380, 382 (5th Cir.1980). See also Alexander, note 1, supra, 47 Albany L.Rev. at 723 (agreeing generally with this aspect of *Oates*). However, if the declarant testifies, courts frequently find the prohibition, which is seen as protecting confrontation rights, inapplicable. See United States v. Sokolow, 91 F.3d 396, 404–05 (3d Cir.1996); United States v. Hayes, 861 F.2d 1225, 1230 (10th Cir.1988).

3. *Police records and other exceptions. Oates* also argued that a public report may likewise not be admitted under any other hearsay exception. 560 F.2d at 78. Some courts have disagreed and admitted statements under several other exceptions, principally based on the declarant's presence on the stand. See United States v. Arias–Santana, 964 F.2d 1262, 1264–65 (1st Cir.1992) (police report, which is generally inadmissible against criminal defendant, may be admitted as a prior consistent statement under Rule 801(d)(1)(B)); United States v. Sawyer, 607 F.2d 1190, 1193 (7th Cir.1979) (prohibition inapplicable to Rule 803(5) when police officer testifies). But others follow *Oates* in this regard. See United States v. Pena–Gutierrez, 222 F.3d 1080, 1086–87 (9th Cir.2000) (ruling that law enforcement reports are not admissible under Rule 803(5) because they are admissible only under Rule 803(8)). Statutory construction arguments have also been used to permit alternative admission. See United States v. Metzger, 778 F.2d 1195, 1201–02 (6th Cir.1985) (prohibition not included in Rule 803(10), an exception equally specific to Rule 803(8), and therefore *Oates* argument is not applicable).

4. *Laboratory reports in criminal cases.* United States v. Baker, 855 F.2d 1353, 1359–60 (8th Cir.1988), presents a more general challenge to *Oates* in holding a police department lab report, made on a routine basis,

admissible against the criminal defendant. See also United States v. Rosa, 11 F.3d 315, 331–33 (2d Cir.1993) (restriction meant to focus on police officers, accusers, and adversaries and not to public servants who have no law enforcement duties). A number of state courts have ruled in favor of admitting routine laboratory or similar reports against the defendant following analysis similar to that in *Quezada*. See, e.g., Ealy v. State, 685 N.E.2d 1047, 1054–55 (Ind.1997) (autopsy report admissible because not prepared for advocacy purposes); State v. Dilliner, 569 S.E.2d 211, 215–17 (W.Va.2002) (finding intoxilyzer accuracy report admissible as governmental record in criminal case). Again, however, other states disagree. See State v. Sandoval–Tena, 71 P.3d 1055, 1058–59 (Idaho 2003) (holding police crime lab report inadmissible as either governmental or business record).

5. *Admission by the defense of government reports against the prosecution and the unfortunate wording of Rule 803(8)(B).* While 803(8)(C) allows admission of evaluative reports if offered by the defense against the government, Rule 803(8)(B), if read literally, would exclude law enforcement reports even when offered by the criminal defendant. In United States v. Smith, 521 F.2d 957 (D.C.Cir.1975), the court concluded that the Rule should not be read to prohibit admission of reports offered by the defendant since such a reading was inconsistent with the obvious legislative intent. Accord United States v. Versaint, 849 F.2d 827, 831 (3d Cir.1988). But see United States v. Sharpe, 193 F.3d 852, 868 (5th Cir.1999) (treating exception as excluding records under Rule 803(8)(B) when offered against the government in accord with its literal wording). *Sharpe*'s "plain meaning" analysis is criticized in 2 McCormick, Evidence § 296, at 332 n.22 (6th ed. 2006).

BRIDGEWAY CORP. v. CITIBANK

United States Court of Appeals, Second Circuit, 2000.
201 F.3d 134.

CALABRESI, CIRCUIT JUDGE:

Bridgeway Corp. ("Bridgeway"), a Liberian corporation seeking to enforce a final judgment rendered by the Supreme Court of Liberia, appeals from the district court's decision denying Bridgeway's motion for summary judgment and granting, *sua sponte,* summary judgment in favor of the nonmoving party, Citibank. The district court held * * * that the evidence in the record established, as a matter of law, that the Liberian judicial system was not "a system that * * * provide[s] impartial tribunals or procedures compatible with the requirements of due process." *Bridgeway Corp. v. Citibank,* 45 F.Supp.2d 276, 288 (S.D.N.Y. 1999). We affirm.

I. BACKGROUND

Overview of Liberian History

This appeal derives from an action by Bridgeway to enforce a money judgment against Citibank entered by the Supreme Court of Liberia on July 28, 1995. Because the merits of this case turn on the events surrounding the Liberian civil war during the first half of the 1990s, it is helpful to provide a brief overview of those circumstances before proceeding to discuss the case. * * *

From 1980 to 1989, Samuel Kanyon Doe headed a Liberian government marked by corruption and human rights abuses, as well as by rampant inflation. In 1989, a group of dissidents seized power and, in 1990, executed Doe. Doe's death marked the beginning of a violent seven-year civil war. By 1991, Liberia was in effect ruled by two governments: one controlled Monrovia, the capital, while the other controlled the remainder of the country. Following several short-lived cease fires, a formal peace accord was signed in August 1995. After another outbreak of violence in 1996, elections were held in July 1997. In August 1997, Charles Taylor was inaugurated and the 1986 Constitution was reinstated.

Throughout the period of civil war, Liberia's judicial system was in a state of disarray and the provisions of the Constitution concerning the judiciary were no longer followed. Instead, under an agreement worked out among the warring parties in 1992, the Supreme Court was reorganized, with various factions each unilaterally appointing a specified number of justices. The U.S. State Department Country Reports for Liberia during this period paint a bleak picture of the Liberian judiciary. The 1994 Report observed that "corruption and incompetent handling of cases remained a recurrent problem." The 1996 Report stated that, "the judicial system, already hampered by inefficiency and corruption, collapsed for six months following the outbreak of fighting in April."

In 1997, before elections were held, the leaders of the various factions acknowledged that the integrity of the Supreme Court had been compromised by factional loyalties since 1992 and agreed that the Court would have to be reconstituted so that it might gain the legitimacy that would enable it to resolve successfully disputes that might arise concerning the elections. The members of the Court were therefore dismissed and new members were appointed based on the recommendations of the Liberian National Bar Association.

This Case

* * * For many years Citibank maintained a branch in Monrovia, but it closed that branch in January 1992 and completely withdrew from Liberia by 1995. As required by Liberian law, Citibank, before withdrawing, formulated a plan of liquidation, which was approved by the National Bank of Liberia. According to this plan, funds were to be remitted by Citibank to Meridian Bank Liberia Ltd., in order to meet Citibank's obligations to depositors. Citibank alerted its customers to its plans so that they could withdraw their funds. On April 21, 1995, the National Bank of Liberia indicated by letter that Citibank had satisfactorily completed the liquidation plan and was no longer licensed to do business in Liberia.

Bridgeway had an account at Citibank's Liberian branch with a balance of $189,376.66. In November 1992, Bridgeway brought suit in

Liberia against Citibank, seeking a declaration that Citibank was obligated to pay Bridgeway its balance in U.S. (rather than Liberian) dollars. In August 1993, the trial court ruled in favor of Citibank. The court found that, under Liberian law, a person may not refuse to accept Liberian dollars for the discharge of an obligation unless there is an express agreement to the contrary and that Liberian law gives the Liberian dollar a par value equal to the value of the U.S. dollar. The trial court also found that under Bridgeway's contract with Citibank, the latter had the right to decide the currency in which a withdrawal would be paid. Bridgeway appealed to the Liberian Supreme Court, which reversed the lower court's decision and entered judgment for Bridgeway.

Bridgeway filed suit in New York state court to enforce the Liberian Supreme Court judgment, and Citibank removed the case to the federal district court. When it became apparent that Citibank was going to defend itself by challenging the legitimacy of the Liberian judicial system, Bridgeway moved for summary judgment—arguing that Citibank was estopped from questioning the fairness of the Liberian judiciary. But the district court denied that motion and, *sua sponte,* granted summary judgment for Citibank. Specifically, the court found that, as a matter of law, Liberia's courts did not constitute "a system of jurisprudence likely to secure an impartial administration of justice" and that, as a result, the Liberian judgment was unenforceable in the United States. *See Bridgeway,* 45 F.Supp.2d at 287. Bridgeway now appeals.

II. Discussion

[The court found no error in the trial court's action to grant summary judgment *sua sponte* against the moving party and found no merit in Bridgeway's argument that by voluntarily participating in litigation in the Liberian courts Citibank was estopped from challenging the impartiality of those courts.]

Fairness of Liberian Courts

* * *

Burden

The parties strenuously dispute who bears the ultimate burden of proof with respect to the fairness of the Liberian judicial system. Although there are cases in which the question of the burden might be significant, it does not ultimately matter here. Accordingly, we express no opinion on it. Even if Citibank were to bear both the burden of production and that of persuasion, it has come forward with sufficiently powerful and uncontradicted documentary evidence describing the chaos within the Liberian judicial system during the period of interest to this case to have met those burdens and to be entitled to judgment as a matter of law. Thus, the U.S. State Department Country Reports presented by Citibank indicate that the Liberian judicial system was in a state of disarray, as do, more subtly, the affidavits by Citibank's Liberian counsel, H. Varney G. Sherman.

The only evidence Bridgeway has introduced in support of its position are three statements by Liberian attorneys. * * * The first statement concerns the design of the Liberian judicial system, but says nothing about its practice during the period in question.[32] The second, in addition to suffering from the same defect as the first, does not even discuss the Liberian judicial system directly. And the third is purely conclusory. *See Kulak v. City of New York,* 88 F.3d 63, 71 (2d Cir.1996) ("[C]onclusory statements, conjecture, or speculation by the party resisting the motion will not defeat summary judgment.").

Evidence

Summary judgment cannot be granted on the basis of inadmissible evidence. *See* Fed.R.Civ.P. 56(e). And Bridgeway raises many objections to the evidence relied upon by the district court in determining that Liberia's courts were, as a matter of law, unlikely to render impartial justice. Although the parties argue over a variety of different pieces of evidence, in the absence of any proof supporting Bridgeway's position, we need only consider whether Citibank adduced admissible evidence in sufficient amount to make the district court's decision regarding the performance of the Liberian judiciary during the civil war be supportable as well as uncontroverted. In fact, all of the district court's conclusions concerning this issue can be derived from just two sources: the affidavits of H. Varney G. Sherman ("Sherman affidavits") and the U.S. State Department Country Reports for Liberia for the years 1994–1997 ("Country Reports" or "Reports").

* * *

The district court also relied quite heavily on the Country Reports. Bridgeway argues that these Reports constitute excludable hearsay. Citibank replies that the Reports are admissible under Federal Rule of Evidence 803(8)(C), which allows the admission of "factual findings resulting from an investigation made pursuant to authority granted by law, unless the sources of information or other circumstances indicate lack of trustworthiness." *See* Fed.R.Evid. 803(8)(C).

Rule 803(8) "is based upon the assumption that public officers will perform their duties, that they lack motive to falsify, and that public inspection to which many such records are subject will disclose inaccuracies." 31 Michael H. Graham, Federal Practice and Procedure § 6759, at 663–64 (Interim ed. 1992). " 'Factual finding' includes not only what happened, but how it happened, why it happened, and who caused it to happen." *Id.* at 689. The rule therefore renders presumptively admissible "not merely * * * factual determinations in the narrow sense, but also * * * conclusions or opinions that are based upon a factual investigation." *Gentile v. County of Suffolk,* 926 F.2d 142, 148 (2d Cir.1991).

32. Evidence concerning the design of a judicial system might be sufficient, in the absence of countervailing evidence. But where a party presents evidence concerning the actual practice of a judicial system, evidence about design is not likely to create a genuine issue of material fact.

In order to fit within the purview of Rule 803(8)(C), the evidence must (1) contain factual findings, and (2) be based upon an investigation made pursuant to legal authority. Once a party has shown that a set of factual findings satisfies the minimum requirements of Rule 803(8)(C), the admissibility of such factual findings is presumed. The burden to show "a lack of trustworthiness" then shifts to the party opposing admission. *See Ariza v. City of New York,* 139 F.3d 132, 134 (2d Cir.1998).

In this case, there is little doubt that the Country Reports constitute "factual findings." Moreover, the Reports are certainly gathered pursuant to legal authority: federal law requires that the State Department submit the Reports annually to Congress, *see* 22 U.S.C. §§ 2151n(d), 2304(b) (1994 & Supp.1999). They are therefore presumptively admissible.

Bridgeway attempts to rebut this presumption by arguing that the Reports are untrustworthy, and it points to language in the State Department's description of their preparation. The State Department says that "[w]e have given particular attention to attaining a high standard of consistency despite the multiplicity of sources and the obvious problems related to varying degrees of access to information, structural differences in political and social systems, and trends in world opinion regarding human rights practices in specific countries." Although this constitutes a frank recognition of the shortcomings intrinsic in any historical investigation, it does not amount (as Bridgeway argues) to an admission of the lack of trustworthiness required to reject the admissibility of these documents.

When evaluating the trustworthiness of a factual report, we look to (a) the timeliness of the investigation, (b) the special skills or experience of the official, (c) whether a hearing was held and the level at which it was conducted, and (d) possible motivation problems. *See* Fed.R.Evid. 803(8)(C) advisory committee's note. With the exception of (c), which is not determinative by itself, *cf. id.* ([T]he rule * * * assumes admissibility in the first instance but with ample provision for escape if *sufficient negative factors* are present. (emphasis added)), nothing about the Reports calls into question their reliability with respect to these factors. The Reports are submitted annually, and are therefore investigated in a timely manner. They are prepared by area specialists at the State Department. And nothing in the record or in Bridgeway's briefs indicates any motive for misrepresenting the facts concerning Liberia's civil war or its effect on the judicial system there.[33] *See Bank Melli Iran v. Pahlavi,* 58 F.3d 1406, 1411 (9th Cir.1995) (relying on Country Reports in granting summary judgment on the issue of the fairness of Iranian courts).

33. One could certainly imagine situations in which motivational problems might plausibly be present (e.g., a country report on an avowed enemy or a significant ally of the United States), but Bridgeway has raised no such doubts here. Accordingly, we express no views on the admissibility of country reports in those circumstances.

In addition to its reliance on the Sherman affidavits and the Country Reports, the district court took judicial notice of historical facts drawn from a variety of sources. *See Bridgeway,* 45 F.Supp.2d at 278 n.2. Bridgeway objects to this. Even if we agreed with Bridgeway's objection, we would affirm the district court's decision because the facts of which the district court took judicial notice were merely background history and of no moment to the ultimate determination of the fairness of Liberia's courts during the period of the civil war. The information in the district court's opinion concerning the functioning of the Liberian courts during the war is drawn (or could easily be drawn) entirely from the Sherman affidavits and the Country Reports, both of which were clearly admissible.

* * *

Having found all of Bridgeway's contentions to be without merit, we AFFIRM the judgment of the district court.

Notes and Questions

1. *Scope of "investigative reports."* In *Bridgeway*, the court describes the scope of "investigative reports" under Rule 803(8)(C) to properly include not only "factual determinations in a narrow sense" but also "conclusions or opinions that are based upon a factual investigation." While it cites an earlier Second Circuit case for this proposition, the authority for this broad view of the scope of such reports is the United States Supreme Court decision in Beech Aircraft Corp. v. Rainey, 488 U.S. 153 (1988). In that decision, the Court resolved the split between the circuits, rejecting the narrow view that "factual findings" under Rule 803(8)(C) "did not encompass 'opinions' or 'conclusions' " and adopting the broader view that "factually based conclusions or opinions" are within its scope. 488 U.S. at 162. *Beech Aircraft* held such opinions and conclusions admissible as long as they: (1) are based on a factual investigation and (2) satisfy the Rule's trustworthiness requirement. Id. at 170.

2. *Reliance on unreliable data.* In addition to the four factors listed in *Bridgeway* to determine whether the report lacks trustworthiness, reliance upon unreliable data is sometimes treated almost as a fifth factor. However, reliance on hearsay does not necessarily result in exclusion. For example, in Kehm v. Procter & Gamble Mfg. Co., 724 F.2d 613, 618 (8th Cir.1983), Proctor & Gamble challenged the admission of epidemiological studies conducted by the Center for Disease Control on the toxic shock syndrome. It based its challenge to the evidence, *inter alia*, on the preparer's lack of firsthand knowledge of the data used. In rejecting the company's argument, the court stated, "We agree with the district court that once a report is conclusively shown to represent findings of a public agency made pursuant to an investigation authorized by law, the central inquiry becomes whether the report is trustworthy." The court placed the burden on the party opposing admission to demonstrate untrustworthiness beyond the mere fact that the report relied in part on hearsay. See also Robbins v. Whelan, 653 F.2d 47 (1st Cir.1981) (Department of Transportation report on automobile stopping distances admissible despite reliance on data provided by automo-

bile manufacturers of which the agency had no firsthand knowledge because other factors helped insure trustworthiness).

On the other hand, when the report relies upon unverified evidence or when it depends on the data of parties whose motivation may be questionable and merely repeats that data without independent evaluation, the weakness of the underlying data may render the report inadmissible. See, e.g., United States v. Jackson–Randolph, 282 F.3d 369, 381 (6th Cir.2002) (agreeing with exclusion of examiner's report that relied on testimony of witness with motive to lie because unreliable); Barlow v. Connecticut, 319 F.Supp.2d 250, 258 (D.Conn.2004) (excluding report because based largely on unreliable hearsay). Whether this provision allows the court to exclude the evidence because it simply doubts the result is questionable. See Blake v. Pellegrino, 329 F.3d 43, 48 (1st Cir.2003).

3. *Guidance from rules on expert witnesses.* Where opinions or conclusions are reached, the principles of Rules 702 and 703 are helpful in determining admissibility. The lack of expertise of those preparing the report may be critical. See Jenkins v. Whittaker Corp., 785 F.2d 720, 725–27 & n.18 (9th Cir.1986) (Investigative reports were properly excluded where they included opinions rendered by investigators without expertise: "it would be anomalous if [the investigator's] opinions were allowed into evidence as part of a report that is not subject to cross-examination when [he] lacked the expertise to testify to those same opinions at trial where he *could* be cross-examined."). See also Matthews v. Ashland Chem., Inc., 770 F.2d 1303, 1309–10 (5th Cir.1985) (report properly rejected where record revealed no special skill or experience of fire investigator who prepared report). Also, the data upon which the investigator relies must be of a satisfactory character. See Faries v. Atlas Truck Body Mfg. Co., 797 F.2d 619 (8th Cir.1986) (where state trooper performed incomplete personal investigation and relied upon potentially interested eyewitnesses, report lacked trustworthiness, and under Rule 703, trooper's testimony was inadmissible because not based on information reasonably relied upon).

4. *Final report requirement.* Reports that are tentative, are merely accumulations of information rather than the conclusion of a government agency, or do not reflect a comprehensive investigation may also be rejected. City of New York v. Pullman Inc., 662 F.2d 910, 914 (2d Cir.1981) (interim report subject to revision and review does not constitute agency finding under Rule 803(8)(C)); Toole v. McClintock, 999 F.2d 1430, 1434–35 (11th Cir.1993) (proposed as opposed to final FCA findings lack the type of trustworthiness anticipated under the Rule); United States v. Mackey, 117 F.3d 24, 28–29 (1st Cir.1997) (report not admissible that simply repeated statement of third party without assessing its accuracy); Koonce v. Quaker Safety Prods. & Mfg. Co., 798 F.2d 700, 720 (5th Cir.1986) (report did not involve hearing or comprehensive investigation and lacked trustworthiness).

5. *Other admissibility concerns.* In Chandler v. Roudebush, 425 U.S. 840, 863 n.39 (1976), the Supreme Court ruled that administrative findings of racial discrimination are admissible under the Rule in a subsequent federal trial de novo. Does this mean that the findings are per se admissible in non-jury trials under Title VII? Are there additional concerns that might warrant exclusion when the report is offered in a related civil rights action

tried before a jury? The circuits are in some conflict on these issues. See Barfield v. Orange County, 911 F.2d 644, 649–50 (11th Cir.1990) (discussing positions of courts, which most often afford the trial judge some discretion in determining whether to admit the findings).

6. *Sources.* Grossman & Shapiro, The Admission of Government Fact Findings Under Federal Rule of Evidence 803(8): Limiting the Dangers of Unreliable Evidence, 38 U.Kan.L.Rev. 767 (1990).

SECTION G. UNAVAILABILITY

FEDERAL RULE 804(a)

UNITED STATES v. MacCLOSKEY

United States Court of Appeals, Fourth Circuit, 1982.
682 F.2d 468.

MURNAGHAN, CIRCUIT JUDGE:

* * *

Count Two of the indictment charged MacCloskey and others (the same alleged coconspirators as in Count One) with conspiracy to obstruct the administration of justice by killing Steve Lansley, a potential government witness (by blowing him up with dynamite), in violation of 18 U.S.C. §§ 371, 1503 and 844(d). * * *

MacCloskey appeals his conviction raising a number of contentions * * * [, including his contention] that the district court's failure to admit prior testimony of a key defense witness, Patsey Elaine Edwards, [at a voir dire hearing] was prejudicial error.

* * *

ADMISSION OF EDWARDS' PRIOR TESTIMONY

* * * [W]e are of the opinion that a new trial is required because MacCloskey was improperly denied the complete testimony of his major defense witness, Patsey Elaine Edwards.

Edwards was originally indicted with MacCloskey and others for conspiring to murder Lansley and Skaggs. At the beginning of the trial, which commenced on January 19, 1981, the defense made known its intention of calling Edwards as a defense witness. Before trial, MacCloskey's attorneys were advised by the federal prosecutor that the indictment against Edwards would be dropped prior to the commencement of MacCloskey's trial. On January 21, 1981, the U.S. Attorney, David Smith, telephoned Edwards' attorney, Michael Greeson. In essence, Smith told Greeson that he would be well-advised to remind his client that, if she testified at MacCloskey's trial, she could be reindicted if she incriminated herself during that testimony. The attorneys defending MacCloskey were apprised of the conversation (presumably by Greeson) the same evening.

The next morning defense counsel brought the conversation containing Smith's warning to the attention of the trial court. Later that afternoon, Edwards agreed to testify out of the jury's presence in a *voir dire* hearing. She was warned of her *Miranda* rights by the trial judge before she testified. She nevertheless testified and was cross-examined by the U.S. Attorney. Reduced to its basics, her testimony was that she knew nothing about any scheme to kill either Skaggs or Lansley and that MacCloskey never discussed the matter with her. In short, the testimony contradicted [the testimony of the government's informant, Pete Honeycutt,] of Edwards' involvement and was completely exculpatory of both her and MacCloskey. After the *voir dire* hearing, the indictment against Edwards was dismissed.

On January 26, the day the defense began its case, MacCloskey's counsel advised the trial court that they had been advised that Edwards might not testify on advice from an attorney identified as Gary Vannoy.

On January 27, defense counsel told the trial judge that they had been advised by Edwards and her attorney that Edwards would invoke her Fifth Amendment privilege. They requested a *voir dire* if she so invoked her rights. In addition, defense counsel requested that, if she refused to testify, her prior *voir dire* testimony be admitted pursuant to Fed.R. of Evid. 804.

The trial judge stated that if she invoked the Fifth Amendment he would not pursue the matter because he felt that he had no right to determine whether a person was properly pleading the Fifth Amendment. In addition, he refused to admit Edwards' prior testimony because it was his belief that a person's testimony was not "unavailable," as required by Rule 804, merely because the person has invoked the Fifth Amendment. Thereafter, Edwards was called to the stand by the defense and she answered many questions in the jury's presence but refused to answer some questions, invoking the Fifth Amendment. She had testified in great detail to virtually identical questions at the *voir dire* held earlier that week and at that time she answered all the questions which she subsequently refused to answer at trial.

Before cross-examination by the prosecutor, *voir dire* was held. Edwards said that she truthfully testified at the *voir dire* earlier in the week. She testified that she nevertheless now was invoking the Fifth Amendment because she was afraid that her indictment would not be dismissed.[34] She stated she was not concerned about incriminating herself but was not testifying because her attorney told her that the U.S. Attorney's office suggested that she had "better remember the privilege of the Fifth Amendment." At that point, defense counsel moved for a mistrial on the ground that MacCloskey had been denied the use of his witness as a result of the prosecutor's call. In addition, defense counsel renewed their motion that the prior *voir dire* testimony be admitted

34. This is an inaccurate statement on her part. Her indictment had been dismissed on January 22, about a week earlier. Nonetheless, her fear of reindictment lingered.

pursuant to Rule 804. Both motions were denied. After the evidence closed, Edwards' former attorney, Michael Greeson, testified, out of the presence of the jury, concerning the details of the phone call he received from Mr. Smith.

The defense sought to get Edwards' prior testimony (which was exculpatory to both her and MacCloskey) into evidence under Fed.Rule of Evid. 804, [which requires that the declarant must be unavailable] * * *. No dispute existed that the *voir dire* testimony could be admitted under the Rule if Edwards was found unavailable. Rule 804(a) defines unavailability as including situations in which the declarant:

> (1) is exempted by ruling of the court on the ground of privilege from testifying concerning the subject matter of his statement; or
>
> (2) persists in refusing to testify concerning the subject matter of his statement despite an order of the court to do so.

* * *

The district court refused to admit the prior testimony of Edwards on the erroneous ground that Edwards' invocation of her right against self-incrimination did not render her unavailable. The law is clear that a witness is unavailable under Rule 804(a)(1) when he invokes the Fifth Amendment privilege and the claim is sustained by the trial court. *See, e.g., United States v. Zurosky,* 614 F.2d 779, 792 (1st Cir.1979); *United States v. Toney,* 599 F.2d 787, 789–90 (6th Cir.1979).

The Rule requires, however, that the court first rule the declarant exempt from testifying on the ground of privilege. We think the requirement was met when the district judge informed counsel that, if Edwards pleaded the Fifth Amendment, the judge "would not pursue it;" i.e. would allow Edwards to stand mute, because he thought he did not have the authority to determine whether she was properly invoking the Fifth Amendment. That view was also erroneous. *See, e.g., Roberts v. United States,* 445 U.S. 552, 560 n.7 * * * (1980) ("It is the duty of a court to determine the legitimacy of a witness' reliance upon the Fifth Amendment."); *United States v. Klauber,* 611 F.2d 512, 514 (4th Cir.1979) ("The right to invoke the Fifth Amendment as to any question put is not absolute. The trial judge in appropriate cases may determine that a foundation for invocation of the Fifth Amendment does not exist."); McCormick, *Handbook of the Law of Evidence* § 139 at 293 ("[T]he court itself has the obligation to determine whether the refusal to answer is in fact justifiable under the privilege.").

Arguing that a witness can be unavailable under Rule 804 only if he *properly* invokes the Fifth Amendment, the government contends that Edwards waived her Fifth Amendment privilege by virtue of her testimony during the *voir dire* and at trial. *See Rogers v. United States,* 340 U.S. 367 * * * (1951). We think the government is, as a general proposition, correct in asserting that a witness must properly invoke his Fifth Amendment right for him to be unavailable under Rule 804(a)(1).[35]

Nevertheless, we still think reversible error occurred. Assuming Edwards waived her Fifth Amendment privilege during either her *voir dire* testimony, her trial testimony or both,[36] the trial judge should have compelled her to testify.[37] If she still refused to testify after being ordered to do so and threatened with contempt if she did not, she would be unavailable under Rule 804(a)(2) and her *voir dire* testimony then should have been admitted under Rule 804(b)(1). Of course, if she testified because of the court order, her complete testimony would have been before the jury.

Edwards was the primary defense witness. The testimony she gave in the first *voir dire* was detailed and contradicted, or offered innocent explanations to, Honeycutt's damaging testimony. In short, her *detailed*

35. We could find only one case which overturned the admission of evidence under Rule 804 because the trial court erroneously upheld a witness' Fifth Amendment privilege. In *United States v. Mathis,* 559 F.2d 294, 298 (5th Cir.1977), the court ruled that a witness who improperly invoked a privilege was not unavailable under Rule 804(a)(1).

The commentators suggest that the privilege must be properly invoked for a witness to be unavailable under Rule 804(a)(1). *See, e.g.,* 4 D. Louisell & C. Mueller, *Federal Evidence* § 486 at 1027–29. (Unavailability under Rule 804(a)(1) is established "where a witness properly claims his constitutional privilege against self-incrimination. * * * Where a claim of privilege by a witness is erroneously sustained, a finding of unavailability based thereon is also erroneous.").

Note, however, that the case does not fall within Rule 804(a)(2) because, instead of ordering Edwards to testify, the district judge made clear that he would not so order her. If we address the problem in terms of what should have been done, however, if the judge had ordered Edwards to testify, and she then refused, she would have been unavailable under Rule 804(a)(2). 4 J. Weinstein & M. Berger, *Weinstein's Evidence,* ¶ 804(a)[01] ("If the declarant refuses to testify * * * by erroneously relying on a privilege * * * he is rendered unavailable [under Rule *804(a)(2)*].") (Emphasis added).

36. The fact that she testified at the *voir dire* hearing does not, by itself, mean that she waived her Fifth Amendment privilege. The privilege is waived only if the prior testimony revealed incriminating facts. *See, e.g., McCarthy v. Arndstein,* 262 U.S. 355, 359 * * * (1923). * * * Of course, once incriminating facts are voluntarily revealed, "the privilege cannot be invoked to avoid disclosure of the details." *Rogers v. United States,* 340 U.S. 367, 373 * * * (1951).

Edwards' *voir dire* testimony was *exculpatory* to both her and MacCloskey. Arguably, she never waived her Fifth Amendment rights. Since we decide that Edwards' complete testimony should have come in, in one form or another, whether she waived her privilege or not, we choose not to parse her testimony for what parts, if any, constituted a possible waiver.

37. We think that the best procedure to follow after a witness has improperly invoked the Fifth Amendment or any privilege in such a situation, is to issue an order, outside of the jury's presence, directing him to testify and admonishing him that his continued refusal to testify would be punishable by contempt. *See United States v. Zappola,* 646 F.2d 48, 54 (2d Cir.1981); 4 D. Louisell & C. Mueller, *Federal Evidence* § 486 at 1033 ("[I]t is obvious that the trial judge should in fact advise the witness that his continued refusal will put him in contempt of court and subject him to incarceration or other punishment."). The Advisory Committee notes for Federal Rule of Evidence 804(a)(2) support this approach. "A witness is rendered unavailable if he simply refuses to testify * * * despite judicial pressures to do so." The language of Rule 804(a)(2) is implicitly to that effect.

The government argues that, once it was obvious that Edwards was not properly invoking her Fifth Amendment rights, defense counsel should have specifically requested that she be compelled to testify. Since the trial judge had previously indicated incorrectly that he did not have the authority to determine whether she was properly invoking her rights, such a request would have been futile. * * *

testimony was vital to MacCloskey's defense. Since the evidence against MacCloskey was not overwhelming and consisted largely of Honeycutt's testimony concerning Edwards' statements and actions, we are unable to say that the error was harmless.

* * *

Reversed and Remanded.

Notes and Questions

1. *Necessity.* When the declarant is unavailable, as is required under the exceptions found in Rule 804(b), the choice is between receiving no evidence and admission of the hearsay evidence, rather than between ideally presented evidence and imperfectly presented evidence. Unavailability of the witness obviously adds nothing to the trustworthiness of his or her extrajudicial statement. With regard to former testimony, the unavailability requirement, which originally was perhaps only satisfied by the witness' death, now may be met by other types of unavailability, such as claims of privilege, inability to locate, and insanity. 5 Wigmore, Evidence §§ 1402–1410 (Chadbourn rev. 1974).

2. *Judicial ruling on privilege.* Rule 804(a)(1) defines a witness to be unavailable where the witness "is exempted by ruling of the court" on the grounds of an asserted privilege. Does this language mean that the witness must formally invoke a privilege and the court rule favorably? An affirmative answer is clearly indicated by the Advisory Committee Note: "A ruling by the judge is required, which clearly implies an actual claim of privilege must be made." See United States v. Pelton, 578 F.2d 701, 709–10 (8th Cir.1978) (unavailability not established by proffer that witness' counsel would advise witness to assert Fifth Amendment). In some instances, however, the validity of the claim is so certain that the court may dispense with formal invocation. See, e.g., United States v. Lieberman, 637 F.2d 95, 103 (2d Cir.1980) (declarant, a defendant in the case, could not even be called by government to the stand and was therefore unavailable); United States v. Chan, 184 F.Supp.2d 337, 341 (S.D.N.Y.2002) (accepting representation by lawyers for coconspirators).

3. *Refusal to testify as alternative to privilege.* When the judge rules against the existence of a privilege and the witness persists in his or her refusal to testify, unavailability is established whether or not the appellate court determines the privilege claim was properly made. In *MacCloskey,* the appellate court notes that, where a claim of privilege is denied by the trial court, the court should order the witness to testify before finding the witness unavailable because of refusal to testify under Rule 804(a)(2). While the trial judge's misunderstanding of the law removed this issue from *MacCloskey,* an order to testify is generally considered a prerequisite when the claim of privilege is properly denied and the witness persists in her refusal to testify based on that erroneous claim. See State v. Finney, 591 S.E.2d 863, 866–67 (N.C.2004) (ruling that reluctant witness not unavailable where she never definitively refused to testify and sufficient effort was not made by the court to determine persistence in resistance to testimony); Sapp v. Commonwealth, 559 S.E.2d 645, 650–51 (Va.2002) (holding that witnesses' general-

ized statements of concern for their safety was insufficient to establish unavailability as the result of refusal to testify, and concluding that at "bare minimum" court must order the witnesses to testify and should carefully consider contempt order).

4. *Immunity.* The claim of privilege under the Fifth Amendment, which renders the declarant unavailable, is eliminated when the government grants immunity. Under special circumstances, a criminal defendant may be able to compel the granting of immunity and thereby make the witness available. See United States v. Bahadar, 954 F.2d 821, 825–26 (2d Cir.1992).

CAMPBELL v. COLEMAN CO.

United States Court of Appeals, Eighth Circuit, 1986.
786 F.2d 892.

DIANA E. MURPHY, DISTRICT JUDGE.[38]

Minor plaintiffs July A. Campbell and James E. Campbell, by and through their next friend, Janet M. Campbell, brought this action for strict liability against defendant The Coleman Company, Inc. (Coleman), alleging that they were severely burned because of a defective gasoline lantern. A jury trial was held and a verdict returned in favor of Coleman. * * *

[Plaintiff claimed that the two Campbell children were injured when a lantern manufactured by Coleman exploded as a result of its defective manufacture, a claim they supported by expert testimony.]

Coleman has a different theory of the case. It contends that the lantern ignited after Johnnie Lee Hayes had filled it with gasoline, that he threw the burning lantern out of the house, and that it accidentally hit the children. At the start of its case, Coleman informed the trial judge that it had subpoenaed Hayes but failed to locate him. It therefore proposed to call three witnesses to testify to out-of-court statements made by Hayes. Over plaintiffs' objection, the trial court permitted these witnesses to testify under the "statements against interest" exception to the hearsay rule, Fed.R.Evid. 804(b)(3).

The first of these witnesses, Jerry Lee Davis, was a neighbor who drove the children to the hospital. He testified that at the hospital he asked Hayes what had happened. He reported that Hayes "said something about he lit the lantern after he just filled it up and they lit it and they had it outside and it blowed up, that's all I know." Transcript, Vol. III, p. 7. Davis added: "[H]e [Hayes] lit it and he set it down there and then it blowed up and then he threw it to the yard or whatever." Transcript, Vol. III, p. 8.

The second witness was Lilly Salts, a sister of Mildred Warren. Salts testified that she drove to the Warren home and asked Hayes what happened and he told her that the lantern had "blew up." Salts was not sure whether Hayes said at that time whether the lantern was in the

38. [S]itting by designation.

house or whether it was on the front porch when it exploded. Salts also stated that Hayes told her that "he was putting unleaded gas in this Coleman lantern so they would have a light and it blowed up * * * [h]e said he pitched it out the door * * * [h]e said the little girl was in the line of fire." Transcript, Vol. III, p. 18.

The third witness was Morgan Pruett, who testified to a conversation with Hayes which apparently took place about one week after the incident. "He told me that he filled up the lantern, and was filling it up, and I understand him to say he overfilled it or something and he lit it, it caught on fire, and he picked it up and threw it out in the yard." Transcript, Vol. III, p. 46. Pruett said that Hayes did not tell him where the kids were when he threw the lantern, and he [Pruett] thought the kids were burned when the lantern blew up as it hit the ground. Plaintiffs moved to strike Pruett's testimony about the conversation on the ground that the statements attributable to Hayes were not against his interest within the meaning of the rule. The court denied the motion.

* * *

The record indicates that both sides attempted to subpoena Hayes without success. At the time of trial, neither side knew where he was. Coleman had taken his deposition, but it was not introduced at trial. In his deposition, Hayes testified that he was in the yard when he saw the children were on fire and the lantern was shooting flames from its upright position on the front porch. He said he then picked up the lantern and threw it into the yard. He denied ever making any contradictory statements as to how the plaintiffs were burned.

II. Discussion

Plaintiffs contend that the trial court erred in admitting the out-of-court statements of Hayes as exceptions to the hearsay rule under Fed.R.Evid. 804(b)(3). They claim that the requirements of the rule were not met as Hayes was not "unavailable" and several of his statements were not against his interest.

* * *

Before a statement against interest may be admitted, the proponent of the evidence must demonstrate that the declarant is "unavailable." *United States v. Pelton,* 578 F.2d 701 (8th Cir.1978). Rule 804(a)(5) provides that a declarant is "unavailable" if "absent from the hearing and the proponent of his statement has been unable to procure his attendance (or in the case of a hearsay exception under subdivision (b)(2), (3) or (4), his attendance or testimony) by process or other reasonable means." This subsection is concerned with the absence of testimony, rather than the physical absence of the declarant. *See generally* H.R. 1597, 93d Cong., 2d Sess. 12 (1974), U.S.Code Cong. & Admin.News 1974, p. 7051; Cotchett and Elkund, *Federal Courtroom Evidence,* 163 (1984). Hayes was absent from the trial, but his testimony was available. Coleman had taken his deposition on July 5, 1984, eight

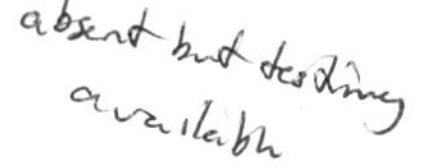

months before trial. Since Hayes was not unavailable within the meaning of Rule 804(a)(5) and (b), his hearsay statements could not be admitted under the "statement against interest" exception in Rule 804(b)(3).

Coleman argues that plaintiffs failed to make a timely objection and conceded Hayes' unavailability. The record indicates, however, that plaintiffs objected to the admission of the hearsay statements with enough specificity. Plaintiffs did not dispute that Hayes himself was unavailable at trial, but they informed the court several times that the deposition of Hayes was available. To be sure, the objection could have been phrased in a more clear manner. The repeated references to the deposition were sufficient, however, to focus the trial court's attention on the nature of the unavailability requirement in Rule 804.

Coleman next argues that even if the trial court erred in admitting the hearsay statements, it was harmless error. We cannot agree. At the close of plaintiffs' case-in-chief, no evidence had been introduced from which Coleman could have argued that plaintiffs' injuries were caused by the negligent actions of a non-party. Introduction of the inadmissible hearsay created a substantive defense for Coleman, allowing it to present to the jury another explanation for plaintiffs' injuries. Admission of the testimony enabled the jury to consider improper evidence in deciding causation, one of the central issues. Plaintiffs were thereby prejudiced. Nor can we find that the error is harmless because testimony about Hayes' prior statements would have been admissible to impeach him. Before the statements could have been admitted under this alternative theory, Coleman would have first been compelled to produce Hayes or read his sworn deposition testimony. If the deposition had been read, the jury would have heard Hayes flatly denying that he caused plaintiffs' injuries. The deposition would have corroborated plaintiffs' theory of the case. The jury also would have been instructed that the prior inconsistent statements were not received to prove the truth of the assertions, but only for impeachment purposes. *See United States v. Rogers,* 549 F.2d 490, 497 (8th Cir.1976). Thus, the circumstances under which the testimony about Hayes' statements could have properly come in would have been very different than those under which it was actually presented. The fact that some of the testimony might ultimately have been admissible for impeachment purposes does not mitigate the prejudice to the plaintiffs. The admission of the hearsay statements under Fed. R.Evid. 804(b)(3) was therefore reversible error.

* * *

[Reversed and remanded.]

Notes and Questions

1. *Limited deposition requirement.* The requirement that a party use a deposition of an unavailable witness applies only if unavailability arises under Rule 804(a)(5) and applies only to the admission of testimony under

the exceptions covered by Rules 804(b)(2), (3), and (4). Why the requirement is not imposed for prior testimony (Rule 804(b)(1)) is easily understood; there is no argument for the superiority of one type of prior testimony (a deposition) over another.

Should the deposition requirement be applied to bar admission of hearsay by a presently unavailable declarant who was available for a deposition while the litigation was pending but was not deposed? Although rarely raised in the cases, it is possible that a deposition must be attempted if the declarant is outside the subpoena power of the court but at a location where the declarant could be deposed, and if not done, other hearsay will be excluded. See 1337523 Ontario, Inc. v. Golden State Bancorp, Inc., 163 F.Supp.2d 1111, 1120 (N.D.Cal.2001) (holding failure to attempt to take deposition of witness who could not be compelled to attend because living in another state barred receipt of statement against interest because testimony was not unavailable); 4 Saltzburg, Martin & Capra, Federal Rules of Evidence Manual § 804.02[3], at 804–10 (9th ed. 2006) (arguing for such a requirement). Other courts have appeared cold to the requirement. See United States v. McHan, 101 F.3d 1027, 1037 (4th Cir.1996) (hearsay admitted under Rule 804(b)(5) not excluded under Confrontation Clause despite government's failure to depose unavailable witness it knew was approaching death); United States v. Yonkers Contracting Co., Inc., 701 F.Supp. 431, 433–34 (S.D.N.Y.1988) (no requirement of taking deposition before death of terminally ill declarant).

2. *Degree of "permanency" of infirmity required.* Subsection (a)(4) defines as unavailable persons who are unable to testify because of illness or infirmity. Issues arise under these provisions concerning the degree of permanency required of the disabling condition. When the disability is apparently temporary, the trial court may be required to grant a continuance. See United States v. Faison, 679 F.2d 292 (3d Cir.1982) (trial court abused discretion in failing to grant continuance since witness, who was hospitalized with heart attack, was important witness against defendant). In United States v. Amaya, 533 F.2d 188, 191 (5th Cir.1976), the court set out a general standard that "[t]he duration of the illness need only be in probability long enough so that, with proper regard to the importance of the testimony, the trial cannot be postponed." Several commentators have suggested that, because of the Confrontation Clause, the standard must be applied in a much more exacting fashion in criminal cases where hearsay from an unavailable witness is offered against the defendant. 2 McCormick, Evidence § 253, at 169 (6th ed. 2006); 5 Weinstein's Federal Evidence § 804.03[5][b] (2d ed. 2006).

3. *Testimony as to lack of memory.* Lack of memory must be established by the declarant's testimony. See State v. Thoma, 834 P.2d 1020, 1025 (Or.1992). The Rule is silent on the nature of proof required for other types of unavailability. See In re Complaint of Bankers Trust Co., 752 F.2d 874, 888 (3d Cir.1984) (counsel's representations of physical infirmity held insufficient in absence of affidavit from witness). When unavailability is predicated on the lack of memory, loss of memory about some details covered by the statement is not sufficient. State v. Miller, 408 S.E.2d 846, 849–50 (N.C. 1991).

4. *Discretion in judging adequacy of effort.* The trial court has substantial discretion in determining that the party seeking to admit an absent witness' statement has been unable to secure this testimony by process or other reasonable means under Rule 804(a)(5). See Bailey v. Southern Pac. Transp. Co., 613 F.2d 1385 (5th Cir.1980) (trial court has discretion to accept counsel's assertion that witness was not subject to process and opponent has burden of demonstrating an abuse of that discretion). That discretion is not unbounded, however. See Perricone v. Kansas City S. Ry., 630 F.2d 317, 320–21 (5th Cir.1980) (trial court erred in finding absent witness unavailable where opponent was able after trial easily to locate witness through telephone listing).

5. *Non-impact of Crawford.* While Crawford v. Washington, 541 U.S. 36 (2004), profoundly changed much of confrontation law, see Chapter 13, Section C, supra, the requirements respecting when a witness is unavailable appear unchanged.

6. *Implicit impact of Confrontation Clause.* The effort that must be exerted to find or secure the presence of the declarant may differ between criminal and civil cases. The Advisory Committee Note refers to Barber v. Page, 390 U.S. 719 (1968), a Confrontation Clause case, for the standard for reasonableness of efforts to secure declarants. That standard, either as a matter of rule interpretation or as required by the Confrontation Clause, applies when statements are offered against the criminal defendant. See United States v. Kehm, 799 F.2d 354, 360 (7th Cir.1986). In civil cases and in criminal cases when the statement is offered against the prosecution, there is some authority that the "inability to procure the declarant's attendance by reasonable means is equivalent to inability to serve a subpoena." 5 Weinstein's Federal Evidence § 804.03[6][a] (2d ed. 2006). But see Kirk v. Raymark Indus., Inc., 61 F.3d 147, 165–65 (3d Cir.1995) (ruling expert witness in civil case not unavailable despite being beyond subpoena power where party failed to offer normal witness fee and request attendance).

7. *Effect of "unclean hands."* Rule 804 states that, where the proponent of the witness' statement procured or wrongfully caused the absence, a witness is not unavailable. Where the party procures unavailability, the Rule disables the party from admitting hearsay under Rule 804 even though the actions were not "wrongful." See United States v. Bollin, 264 F.3d 391, 414 (4th Cir.2001) (defendant could not assert his Fifth Amendment privilege and then claim unavailability). However, refusal of the government to grant immunity, which would eliminate unavailability under the Fifth Amendment, is not treated as causing the unavailability. See United States v. Dolah, 245 F.3d 98, 102–03 (2d Cir.2001).

Where the conduct is wrongful, it will frequently not only bar admission of hearsay by the party who is responsible for rendering the declarant unavailable, but also affirmatively permit admission of statements by that declarant against him or her under Rule 804(b)(6). See Section K, infra.

8. *Unavailability under other rules.* In addition to Rule 804(b)(1), depositions are admissible under the terms of the Federal Rules of Civil and Criminal Procedure. Under Rule 802, if admissible under such rules or under federal statute, the prior testimony is separately admissible. See Advisory

Committee Note to Rule 802. These separate rules and statutes frequently impose conditions different than the evidence rules for admission of what would otherwise constitute hearsay. For example, "unavailability" under Federal Rule of Civil Procedure 32(a)(3)(B) permits admission of a deposition where the witness is 100 miles from the place of trial or is out of the United States, unless the party offering the deposition secured that absence. Thus, the unavailability requirement for former testimony generally under Rule 804 is more demanding than the unavailability requirement for former testimony of a witness in the form of a deposition under Civil Procedure Rule 32. Is the difference justified?

SECTION H. FORMER TESTIMONY

FEDERAL RULE 804(b)(1)

UNITED STATES v. FELDMAN

United States Court of Appeals, Seventh Circuit, 1985.
761 F.2d 380.

WISDOM, SENIOR CIRCUIT JUDGE.

This case presents the question whether a deposition taken in an earlier civil proceeding is admissible in a later criminal prosecution. The defendants were found guilty of several counts of wire fraud from practices in connection with the sale of precious metal futures. The government's case relied heavily on the deposition of a former business associate taken without any cross-examination in an earlier civil proceeding. On appeal, the defendants argue that the admission of this deposition violated [the hearsay rule] * * *.[39] We agree and accordingly reverse.

I. FACTS AND PROCEEDINGS BELOW

The defendants, Richard Feldman and Richard Martenson, were upper echelon managers in First Guaranty Metals ("FGM"), a Florida corporation engaged primarily in investing in leveraged futures contracts in precious metals. Herbert Sanburg, who was later to provide the government with abundant testimony against Martenson and Feldman, was president of FGM, although the testimony at trial shows that Sanburg was less involved in the daily operations of the firm than Feldman. Sanburg left FGM in August 1979.

During the gyrations of the precious metals market from July 1979 through January 1980, FGM retreated from its prudent policy of fully hedging customer orders[40]; the company also began to have increasingly

39. The defendants also argued that admission of the deposition violated their rights under the Confrontation Clause, and the court, in an omitted portion of the opinion, agreed. [Ed.]

40. When FGM and a customer entered a leverage contract, it was to be "hedged", or backed, by FGM's purchase of the physical metal or by a contract to purchase metals equal to the amount that the customer had purchased. This hedging by FGM would insure that FGM could either pay profits or deliver the metal should the customer wish. * * * Customers valued FGM's great "spreads" between the prices at which a customer could buy and sell the same commodity on a given day. FGM's customers lost money. The company filed for bankruptcy on January 29, 1980. On January 30, 1980, FBI agents searched FGM's offices under a warrant. The same day, the Commodity Futures Trading Commission ("CFTC") filed a complaint against FGM alleging that the company defrauded customers by its salesmen's misrepresentations concerning hedging and prices. CFTC sought to freeze the assets of FGM and to obtain its profits.

As part of this "disgorgement" action, CFTC sought the deposition of the three defendants in its case: Sanburg, Feldman, and Martenson. Each party received notice of the depositions through counsel. Neither Feldman nor Martenson attended the Sanburg deposition, nor did their attorneys represent them at the deposition. Sanburg, however, had agreed with the government the day before his deposition to testify against Feldman and Martenson in return for a promise that Sanburg himself would not be a target of any later legal proceedings. This agreement between Sanburg and the government was not disclosed for almost a year, until just a short time before Feldman's and Martenson's criminal trial. At the time of Sanburg's deposition, the government had not returned a criminal indictment against any party in connection with FGM. Sanburg, whom the government knew to be terminally ill, died less than a month after his deposition.

On December 17, 1981, ten months after Sanburg gave his deposition, the U.S. Attorney in Chicago returned an indictment charging Richard Feldman and Richard Martenson with mail fraud in violation of 18 U.S.C. § 1341 (1982), wire fraud, *id.* § 1343, and fraudulent bullion transactions, 7 U.S.C. §§ 13(b), 23(b) (1982). In an order and memorandum of May 28, 1981, the district court ruled that it would admit the Sanburg deposition if the government could establish that Sanburg and the present defendants were parties in the civil case in which the deposition was taken; that the defendants were represented by counsel at that time; and that the defendants received notice of the deposition and were afforded an opportunity to be present. On November 1, 1981, the district court conducted a hearing on the admissibility of the deposition. The court admitted the deposition on the grounds that the defendants had an adequate opportunity to appear at the Sanburg deposition, that the defendants knew what Sanburg would say, and that the defendants were represented by counsel and were parties to the civil litigation for which the deposition was taken. The deposition became the centerpiece of the government's prosecution.

On October 4, 1982, a grand jury returned a superseding indictment [adding] a RICO charge, 18 U.S.C. § 1962(c) (1982) * * *. The court entered acquittals on the transaction counts, and the jury returned guilty verdicts on all remaining counts. * * *

policy of hedging because of the security hedging provided. Salesmen for FGM were informed that FGM was one of the few fully hedged companies handling commodity investments.

II. Discussion

A. *Use of a Civil Deposition in a Subsequent Criminal Proceeding*

Numerous courts have approved the admissibility of a transcript of pre-trial proceedings when the declarant was cross-examined during the prior proceedings. *Ohio v. Roberts,* 1980, 448 U.S. 56 * * * ; *Phillips v. Wyrick,* 8 Cir.1977, 558 F.2d 489, 496 * * * ; *United States ex rel. Gayden v. McGinnis,* N.D.Ill.1983, 574 F.Supp. 661. Generally, the *opportunity* to cross examine the declarant at the prior proceeding is sufficient. "The actual use then made of the opportunity becomes a matter of defense strategy, and deliberate trial tactics do not ordinarily exact constitutional protection." *Phillips,* 558 F.2d at 496. Several courts have therefore admitted the transcript of a witness's testimony from a preliminary hearing even though the witness was subject to a less searching cross-examination than would have been the case at trial. *United States ex rel. Haywood v. Wolff,* 7 Cir.1981, 658 F.2d 455, 461–62 * * *.

The government, relying on this line of cases, urges us to affirm the district court's admission of Sanburg's deposition. In *Phillips,* for example, the defendant's 15–year–old accomplice, Chris Brownfield, testified as a witness for the prosecution during a preliminary hearing before a magistrate. The defendant was represented by counsel at the preliminary hearing, and had the opportunity to cross-examine Brownfield. When the case came to trial, Brownfield invoked his privilege against self-incrimination, and refused to answer any substantive questions. The State called the assistant prosecutor who had conducted the preliminary hearing. This prosecutor summarized Brownfield's testimony (no stenographer was present at the preliminary hearing), which corroborated the victim's trial testimony. The jury convicted Phillips, who pursued his appeal through the state courts and then brought a habeas petition in federal court.

The Court of Appeals for the Eighth Circuit allowed the introduction of the testimonial reconstruction of Brownfield's testimony. The Court found that there was no violation of the Confrontation Clause because Brownfield's statement had been made under oath in a "truth-inducing" courtroom atmosphere before "a judicial tribunal"; Phillips was represented by counsel at the hearing and had the opportunity to cross-examine both Brownfield and the prosecutor; and Phillips had the opportunity to call witnesses to counter any discrepancies in the prosecutor's reconstruction of Brownfield's testimony. *Phillips,* 558 F.2d at 494–95.

We find that *Phillips* is not controlling for two reasons. First, the co-defendants Feldman and Martenson did not have a meaningful opportunity to cross-examine Sanburg during his deposition. Although it is true that Feldman and Martenson had notice of the deposition, at the time of Sanburg's deposition the co-defendants had no knowledge of the agreement between the U.S. Attorney and Sanburg that Sanburg would not be the subject of the grand jury investigation. Nor did they have any formal notice of criminal proceedings against them, and the evidence discloses that the grand jury investigation had not commenced when Sanburg was deposed. Feldman and Martenson had no reason to suspect that Sanburg would incriminate them on criminal charges. In these circumstances, mere notice of the deposition does not constitute the opportunity, in any real sense, for Feldman and Martenson to cross-examine Sanburg. In *Phillips,* by contrast, the defendant had been indicted before the hearing and therefore knew or should have known that his accomplice might incriminate him on criminal charges.

There is another distinguishing factor. Because no criminal indictment had been entered in the present case, the co-defendants would not have had the issues framed with sufficient clarity to allow for an intelligent cross-examination even if the defendants had been present during Sanburg's deposition. To contrast again with *Phillips,* the defendant knew at the time of Brownfield's interrogation of the specific charges that he was to defend against.[41]

In admitting Sanburg's deposition, the district court relied on *United States v. Ricketson,* 7 Cir.1974, 498 F.2d 367 * * *. In *Ricketson,* the defendant challenged the admission of the deposition of the owner of some stolen goods regarding the value of the goods. In admitting the deposition, the court held: "Ricketson's counsel was given full opportunity to cross-examine [the deponent]. This opportunity came after notice that the deposition was being taken for use at trial—an advantage Green's counsel did not have in *California v. Green* [1970, 399 U.S. 149 * * *]. The defendant was present at the deposition to assist his counsel." *Id.* at 374. Here, counsel had no notice that Sanburg's deposition was going to be used in a criminal trial. In fact, the defendants were not indicted until almost a year after the notice of the deposition was delivered. We therefore find *Ricketson* and similar cases inapposite.

* * *

Inadmissibility Under Fed.R.Evid. 804(b)(1)

Under Fed.R.Evid. 804(b)(1), the testimony or deposition of a witness taken in another proceeding is admissible if the party against whom the testimony is now offered had "an opportunity and similar motive" to examine the witness.

41. The government urges us to find a waiver of Feldman's and Martenson's right to cross-examination because the two defendants were "aware of Mr. Sanburg's severe illness and could not be certain that Mr. Sanburg would be available for subsequent depositions or testimony." Appellee's brief at 27. Assuming that the defendants did know that Sanburg had cancer, there is no basis to infer the defendants knew that Sanburg was *terminally* ill. We decline to predicate the waiver of a constitutional right in a criminal trial on a layman's prognosis. Even if the defendant knew at the time of the deposition for a certainty that Sanburg would soon die, the testimony would still be inadmissible if, as here, the [other] proceedings were sufficiently different from the original proceedings that the deposition failed to pass the "similarity of motive" requirements of Fed.R.Evid. 804(b)(1) or the "indicia of reliability" test of the Confrontation Clause.

Fed.R.Evid. 804(b)(1) requires that a defendant have sufficient notice and opportunity for cross examination. Putting aside the question of notice,[42] Feldman and Martenson did not have the opportunity to cross-examine Sanburg. Mere "naked opportunity" to cross-examine is not enough; there must also be a perceived "real need or incentive to thoroughly cross-examine" at the time of the deposition. *United States v. Franklin,* D.D.C.1964, 235 F.Supp. 338, 341. At the time of Sanburg's deposition, the defendants Feldman and Martenson were not adverse parties to Sanburg. There was no reason for Feldman or Martenson to believe that Sanburg, who was a co-defendant in the CFTC action, would testify against them on criminal charges. Both Feldman and Martenson had chosen not to defend in the CFTC's civil suit, and they could reasonably expect that Sanburg, who had left the company well before its demise, would chose to do the same. It is undisputed that not until after the deposition were Feldman and Martenson informed of the non-subject agreement between Sanburg and the government. The defendants therefore did not make a meaningful waiver of their right to cross-examination.

Fed.R.Evid. 804(b)(1) also requires that even if Feldman and Martenson had sufficient notice and opportunity to cross-examine Sanburg, they must have had a "similar motive to develop the testimony by direct, cross, or redirect examination." In determining whether a party had such a motive, a court must evaluate not only the similarity of the issues, but also the purpose for which the testimony is given. *Zenith Corp. v. Matsushita Electric Industrial Co.,* E.D.Pa.1980, 505 F.Supp. 1190, 1251, *aff'd in part, rev'd in part,* 3 Cir.1983, 723 F.2d 319. Circumstances or factors which influence motive to develop testimony include "(1) the type of proceeding in which the testimony is given, (2) trial strategy, (3) the potential penalties or financial stakes, and (4) the number of issues and parties." *Id.* at 1252. Consideration of the second and third criteria persuades us that under Fed.R.Evid. 804(b)(1)'s "similarity of motive" test, Sanburg's deposition was inadmissible in the criminal trial.

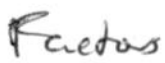

Sanburg's deposition was taken in a civil proceeding and ultimately used in criminal prosecution. It is well-settled that strategies for civil and criminal trials may differ greatly. As one court has observed, in antitrust litigation where the defendants faced criminal prosecution and later civil proceedings and the plaintiffs sought to admit into the civil

42. It is not clear that the defendants received proper notice as required in CFTC's litigation under Fed.R.Civ.Pro. 30(b). The government gave notice of Sanburg's deposition about a week before the deposition, but then rescheduled it twice in the next few days. Apparently the government attorneys left messages with secretaries. We do not decide the question whether such practices conform to the "reasonable notice" requirement of Fed.R.Civ.Pro. 30(b) because of the view we take in this case of the question of "similarity of motive" and because of the scant development of the question of notice on appeal. We therefore also decline to decide whether this notice should have conformed to Fed.R.Crim.Pro. 15, as is commonly required when the government intends to preserve evidence for a later criminal prosecution. *See United States v. Benfield,* 8 Cir.1979, 593 F.2d 815.

proceeding a witness's cross-examined deposition taken in the criminal suit:

> "[S]uccessive defendants do not always share the same interests when defending against claims which arise out of the same circumstances. For instance, in the antitrust field, a defendant in a criminal trial may be motivated in its defense to protect itself against liability by implicating other defendants—perhaps defendants who have pled *nolo contendere* to the same criminal charges."

In re Screws Antitrust Litigation, D.Mass.1981, 526 F.Supp. 1316, 1319. The court therefore ruled that the deposition failed to qualify for admission under Fed.R.Evid. 804(b)(1).

Here Feldman and Martenson pursued opposite strategies in the civil and criminal trial. Neither of the defendants contested CFTC's motion for a permanent injunction or ancillary relief. Their strategy was not to contest any CFTC's claims. In the criminal case, by contrast, the defendants vigorously sought to prove their innocence.

The admission of Sanburg's deposition also fails under the third criterion enunciated in *Zenith,* that is, whether the "potential penalties or financial stakes" are similar. In the civil proceeding, neither Feldman nor Martenson had any exposure to personal liability. Martenson had severed his ties with FGM before its demise. Feldman, who was still associated with FGM upon its bankruptcy, nevertheless was willing to let the government obtain the declaratory and injunctive relief it sought, and his attorney allegedly offered to enter a consent judgment on behalf of Feldman several months before the deposition. It appears from the record that both Feldman and Martenson had little personal or financial stake in CFTC's litigation. It is understandable that neither party attended Sanburg's deposition in that case. In the subsequent criminal proceeding, however, the defendants faced, and received, fines and imprisonment.

The Supreme Court has recognized that a criminal defendant's liberty is "an interest of transcending value." *In re Winship,* 1970, 397 U.S. 358, 363 * * *. As the Court observed: "The accused during a criminal prosecution has at stake interests of immense importance, both because of the possibility that he may lose his liberty upon conviction and because of the certainty that he would be stigmatized by the conviction." *Id.* The stakes at the time of the Sanburg deposition—disgorgement of a trading company's profits—were quantitatively less and qualitatively different from the stakes in the criminal trial. *See also Zenith Radio Corp. v. Matsushita Elec. Ind. Co.,* E.D.Pa.1980, 505 F.Supp. 1190, 1251 n.77, *aff'd in part, rev'd in part,* 3 Cir.1983, 723 F.2d 319, where the court observed that "[a] discrepancy in the financial stakes involved in the two cases may also affect motive. An action in small claims court may not be defended with the same vigor as an action where considerably more is involved."

The Seventh Circuit has recently applied these criteria in determining the admissibility in a later criminal proceeding of a deposition from an earlier criminal case. See *United States v. Pizarro,* 7 Cir.1983, 717 F.2d 336, 349, holding that the testimony of an unavailable witness is admissible if the statements were "subject to the scrutiny of a party interested in thoroughly testing its validity." In *Pizarro,* the government moved successfully during the defendant's third trial to exclude as hearsay a co-defendant's testimony at the second trial. That testimony implicated a third party rather [than] the defendant, Pizarro, as the source of heroin in a drug distribution network. *Id.* at 348. The district court concluded that the government had been unable to develop fully the co-defendant's identification at the second trial. The district court denied the introduction of this exculpatory testimony at Pizarro's third trial because the codefendant was unavailable at the later trial. *Id.* at 349. Relying on the "similarity of motive" test in Fed.R.Evid. 804, the Court of Appeals reversed:

> " 'If the party against whom [the testimony is] now offered is the one *against* whom the testimony was offered previously, no unfairness is apparent in requiring him to accept his own prior conduct of cross-examination or decision not to cross-examine.' Consequently, our inquiry under this exception focuses not on the extent of cross-examination at the former proceeding, but on whether the party's handling of the testimony was 'meaningful in light of the circumstances which prevail[ed] when the former testimony [was] offered.' "

Id. (quoting Fed.R.Evid. 804 advisory committee) (emphasis and alterations in *Pizarro*). The Court then found that the government had the motivation during the second trial to demonstrate that the co-defendant, Rodriguez, was not telling the truth when he identified the third party rather than Pizarro as the heroin supplier: "This testimony was not only highly damaging to their case against Pizarro, but also went to the issue of Rodriguez's credibility, which the government itself contends was the ultimate issue in [the second trial]." *Id.*

It is true that *Pizarro* is not squarely on point because the testimony was taken in a criminal proceeding and then offered in a retrial of the same charges. *Id.* at 340. Here, Feldman and Martenson were under indictment by CFTC at the time of Sanburg's deposition only for violations of 7 U.S.C. § 6o(1) (1982). The government sought to introduce the deposition in a later criminal prosecution alleging wire fraud and mail fraud. Our holding today, however, is consistent with the rigorous test established by the *Pizarro* court that the testimony be "subject to the scrutiny of a party thoroughly interested in testing its validity." *Pizarro,* 717 F.2d at 349. We have simply elaborated on that test by applying an analysis based on similarity of motive and of stakes. Judged by this expanded test, the two defendants reasonably lacked the motive to cross-examine Sanburg at his deposition.

Finally, the government has argued that the Trustee's questions to Sanburg count as cross-examination. The Trustee, however, seemed more interested in the movement of FGM's assets than in fraudulent

sales practices. He was uninterested in discrediting Sanburg, which would have been of utmost importance to the co-defendants. In any event, the Trustee's questions cannot be deemed to have the same measure of scrutiny or the same focus as questions that would have come from a criminal defendant. In short, no one at the Sanburg deposition had the requisite stake in the proceeding that would be necessary for them to be deemed a predecessor in interest to the criminal defendants, and those who did have the requisite stake had no reason to suspect that they should be there. We hold that the deposition fails to pass the test of Fed.R.Evid. 804(b)(1) and that Sanburg's deposition from the civil suit was not admissible under Fed.R.Evid. 804(b)(1). * * *

III. Conclusion

The Sanburg deposition was the heart of the prosecution's case against the co-defendants. At the time of the deposition, however, no criminal charges were pending against Feldman and Martenson, they had no reason to suspect that they should cross-examine Sanburg, and there was no party at the deposition who could be deemed a predecessor in interest to Feldman or Martenson. The trial court therefore erred in admitting the deposition under Fed.R.Evid. 804(b)(1). * * * We therefore reverse the convictions of the defendants. * * *

Notes and Questions

1. *Satisfying hearsay protections?* Are depositions and former testimony actually hearsay under conventional definitions? Wigmore was the leading proponent of the view that prior testimony should not be classified as hearsay. 5 Wigmore, Evidence § 1370 (Chadbourn rev. 1974). United States v. Inadi, 475 U.S. 387, 394 (1986), took a very different perspective, figuratively treating former testimony as a particularly inferior form of hearsay from the perspective of the Confrontation Clause. It required a showing of unavailability for this type of hearsay while eliminating the requirement for coconspirator statements: "former testimony often is only a weaker substitute for live testimony." What is a sensible justification for limiting admissibility of former testimony since it has been previously subjected to cross-examination when considered purely as a matter of hearsay policy? See 2 McCormick, Evidence § 301, at 344 (6th ed. 2006) (antipathy to trial by presentation of prepared statement, perhaps?).

2. *Similarity of motive, not identity of issues.* While some rigid formulations of the exception for prior testimony have required identity of issues in the two proceedings, even before the Federal Rules the trend was to require substantial rather than technical identity. Rule 804(b)(1) imposes no direct requirement concerning identity or similarity of issues. Rather, the Rule requires that the party against whom the testimony is offered have a similar motive to develop the testimony. "Since identity of issues is significant only in that it bears on motive and interest in developing fully the testimony of the witness, expressing the matter in the latter terms is preferable." Advisory Committee Note to Rule 804(b)(1). See also 2 McCormick, Evidence § 304, at 353 (6th ed. 2006). See, e.g., United States v. Licavoli, 725 F.2d

1040, 1048 (6th Cir.1984) (almost identical issues in state criminal prosecutions that formed predicate acts for federal RICO prosecution provided similar motive for cross-examination); United States v. Poland, 659 F.2d 884, 896 (9th Cir.1981) (testimony offered at hearing on defendant's motion to suppress identification evidence admissible at trial since motive of cross-examination at hearing was to challenge the reliability of the identification); Commonwealth v. Sena, 809 N.E.2d 505, 515–16 (Mass.2004) (finding that additional evidence regarding new witness at subsequent trial did not substantially affect motive to challenge witness at the first trial as to what he saw).

3. *Emphasis on opportunity.* Whether the opportunity and motive for cross-examination at a preliminary hearing in a criminal case or at a discovery deposition in a civil case is sufficient to permit admission of the testimony has been frequently litigated. As a general matter, courts have ruled that testimony from such prior proceedings is admissible in spite of some rather obvious differences in tactical and strategic interests at those proceedings as contrasted with the interests at trial. See, e.g., United States v. Avants, 367 F.3d 433, 444 (5th Cir.2004) (finding preliminary hearing in 1966 state case admissible in 2003 civil rights prosecution); DeLuryea v. Winthrop Labs., 697 F.2d 222, 226–27 (8th Cir.1983) (deposition); People v. Zapien, 846 P.2d 704, 728–30 (Cal.1993) (preliminary hearing).

4. *Major limits on cross-examination.* Restrictions on the scope or extend of cross-examination at the prior proceeding may render the testimony inadmissible. See United States v. Jackson, 335 F.3d 170, 177–78 (2d Cir.2003) (holding statements by defendant during plea colloquy inadmissible because the Rule directs that examination be conducted by the court rather than the prosecutor and prosecution questioning is limited and typically perfunctory); United States v. Smith, 231 F.3d 800, 817 (11th Cir.2000) (finding opportunity to cross-examine inadequate where witness asserted Fifth Amendment privilege during government's cross-examination); In re Complaint of Paducah Towing Co., 692 F.2d 412, 418–19 (6th Cir.1982) (opportunity to cross-examine held inadequate where conducted by nonlawyer in administrative proceeding and where both redirect examination and opportunity to impeach witness were improperly limited). At the same time, the courts have held that the opportunity for cross-examination need not be unbounded. United States v. King, 713 F.2d 627, 630 (11th Cir.1983) (limitations imposed by court on cross-examination at prior trial were reasonable and permitted "adequate" or "meaningful," if not unlimited, cross-examination).

5. *Unimportance (but not irrelevancy) of actual motivation.* Courts generally pay little attention to arguments that the party's actual motivation differed at the prior proceeding. A frequent response to such arguments is that "tactical decisions" or "selection of a trial strategy" are not considered sufficient to eliminate the motive for cross-examination. United States v. Pizarro, 717 F.2d 336, 349 (7th Cir.1983); United States v. Zurosky, 614 F.2d 779, 793 (1st Cir.1979). However, as reflected in *Feldman*, the greater the facial dissimilarity between the issues, the more likely the court is to examine the adequacy of the party's actual motivation. See Hannah v. City of Overland, Missouri, 795 F.2d 1385, 1390–91 (8th Cir.1986) (prosecutor in

homicide case lacked significant motive to challenge testimony of witnesses at civil deposition that posed little threat to government's case).

6. *Application to grand jury testimony.* In United States v. Salerno, 505 U.S. 317 (1992), the Supreme Court rejected the argument that grand jury testimony of a declarant who asserts a Fifth Amendment privilege at trial should be automatically admissible against the government under the principle of "adversarial fairness," regardless of whether the prosecutor could be shown to have had a "similar motive" when examining the witness before the grand jury. The Court believed it was not free to alter the literal terms of the Rule's requirements. Id. at 322. On remand, the Second Circuit rejected any automatic position about the similarity of the prosecutor's motivation before the grand jury and at a subsequent trial, considering that inquiry to be fact specific in each case. United States v. DiNapoli, 8 F.3d 909, 914 (2d Cir.1993) (en banc). On the particular facts of *DiNapoli*, the court found the motive to be dissimilar and excluded the hearsay. Id. at 915. However, in some cases, exculpatory grand jury testimony has been found admissible against the government. See United States v. Foster, 128 F.3d 949, 955–56 (6th Cir.1997).

DYKES v. RAYMARK INDUSTRIES, INC.

United States Court of Appeals, Sixth Circuit, 1986.
801 F.2d 810.

ENGEL, CIRCUIT JUDGE.

National Gypsum Company appeals a judgment entered against it after a jury awarded plaintiffs $300,000.00 in compensatory damages and $200,000.00 in punitive damages for injuries suffered by Mr. Eulis Dykes from exposure to asbestos-containing products while on the job.

* * *

Eulis Dykes worked as a plasterer at Gilbert Plastering Company in Knoxville, Tennessee, from 1947 through the mid–1960's. He used the spray gun method of applying plaster which involved using an applicator attached to a hose immersed in liquid plaster. The acoustical plaster he used in some of his work contained asbestos. The district court expressly found that on several occasions Mr. Dykes was exposed to Gold Bond Sprayolite, an acoustical plaster manufactured by National Gypsum. * * * [Around 1965, he] became a utility mechanic at Union Carbide. His work at Union Carbide included some plastering as well as the replacement of asbestos pipe insulation and asbestos boiler linings. The trial court found that Mr. Dykes' last possible exposure to asbestos was in 1967, and this finding is not challenged on appeal. He left Union Carbide in 1982 after he was diagnosed as suffering from mesothelioma, a form of chest cancer associated with the inhalation of asbestos. Mr. Dykes died from complications of his disease in November 1983, shortly after the present suit was filed in the district court.

* * *

SUFFICIENCY OF EVIDENCE OF PUNITIVE DAMAGES.

Punitive damages are available under Tennessee law for conduct "involving fraud, malice, gross negligence or oppression * * * or where a wrongful act is done with a bad motive or so recklessly as to imply a disregard for social obligations. * * * " *Island Container Corp. v. March,* 529 S.W.2d at 45. Mrs. Dykes attempted to meet this standard by establishing that National Gypsum was aware of the dangers of asbestos exposure during and after her husband's exposure but did nothing to protect or inform employees of those dangers. She also attempted to establish that National Gypsum suppressed studies and reports documenting the risks associated with asbestos exposure. The parties do not dispute the trial court's finding that the last possible year in which Mr. Dykes was exposed to asbestos is 1967.

National Gypsum challenges * * * the admission by the trial court of * * * the deposition of Dr. Kenneth Wallace Smith, the medical director of the Johns–Manville Corporation from 1953 to 1966 * * *.

Dr. Kenneth Wallace Smith joined Canadian Johns–Manville in 1942 as a medical officer, became medical director there in 1946 or 1947, corporate director in 1951, and in 1953 he became the medical director for Johns–Manville Corporation. He held that post until 1966. Dr. Smith was deposed on January 13, 1976, in relation to the case *DeRocco v. Forty–Eight Insulation, Inc.,* Nos. 7880, 7281 (Pa.Ct.Common Pleas, Allegheny County 1974). The entire deposition was read into the record before the jury in the present case.

National Gypsum objects to the admission of Dr. Smith's testimony on the ground that it is hearsay, and is inadmissible former testimony under Rule 804(b)(1) * * *

There is no dispute that Dr. Smith's deposition was not previously offered by or against National Gypsum. Absent these circumstances, former testimony of an unavailable declarant is admissible only if National Gypsum can be said to be a "predecessor in interest" to Johns–Manville, against whom the deposition was originally offered.

The Sixth Circuit addressed this same issue with respect to *this same deposition* in *Clay v. Johns–Manville Sales Corp.,* 722 F.2d 1289 (1983). There, the issue was whether Dr. Smith's deposition was admissible against Raybestos–Manhattan, which likewise was not a party in *DeRocco.*

In *Clay,* our court speaking through Judge Edwards adopted the Third Circuit's construction of Rule 804(b)(1) and the following language:

> While we do not endorse an extravagant interpretation of who or what constitutes a "predecessor in interest," we prefer one that is realistically generous over one that is formalistically grudging. We believe that what has been described as "the practical and expedient view" expresses the congressional intention: "if it appears that in the former suit a party having a like motive to cross-examine about

> the same matters as the present party would have, was accorded an adequate opportunity for such examination, the testimony may be received against the present party." Under these circumstances, the previous party having like motive to develop the testimony about the same material facts is, in the final analysis, a predecessor in interest to the present party.

722 F.2d at 1295 (citing *Lloyd v. American Export Lines, Inc.,* 580 F.2d 1179, 1185 (3d Cir.1978)).

In a more recent decision, *Murphy v. Owens–Illinois, Inc.,* 779 F.2d 340 (6th Cir.1985), our court, speaking through Judge Kennedy, upheld the exclusion of the same deposition of Dr. Smith involved in *Clay* and involved here when it was offered to show the state of the art against a manufacturer which withdrew from the asbestos product market in 1953. We there held that although the company was a predecessor in interest under Rule 804(b)(1) and *Clay,* the admissibility of Dr. Smith's deposition must still be subject to the balancing test of Rule 403, Fed.R.Evid. * * *, to determine whether its relevance was out-weighed by its prejudicial effect. Since in *Murphy* we agreed with the district judge that the particular circumstances were different from those in *Clay,* we upheld his exclusion there of Dr. Smith's deposition. Judge Kennedy for the court in *Murphy* recognized as *stare decisis* the continuing viability of *Clay.* She characterized its holding as having "collapsed the two criteria, i.e., whether the defendant was a predecessor in interest, and whether he had an opportunity and similar motive to develop the testimony by cross-examination into one test." 779 F.2d at 343. We view the net effect of *Clay* and *Murphy* as holding that in our circuit the fact of being a predecessor in interest is not limited to a legal relationship, but is also to be determined by the second aspect of the test under the rule: whether the defendant had an opportunity and similar motive to develop the testimony by cross-examination. In the instant case, the record shows that the trial judge was familiar with *Clay* and that he had examined the deposition before he concluded that the Smith deposition ought to be admitted. He further held that any differences in the interests of the defendants here and the defendants in *DeRocco* was a matter of degree but did not affect his decision that they were sufficiently similar to justify the use of the Smith deposition.

We might normally be concerned with the ruling of the trial judge here. We do not view our decision in *Clay* as establishing the admissibility of Dr. Smith's deposition for all purposes in all asbestos cases. *Clay* did not rule the deposition admissible as a matter of law. It only held that it was the type of deposition which was subject to the application of Rule 804(b)(1), and thus should have been admissible under the particular facts in *Clay.* While we agree with *Clay* that a realistic application of the rule is to be preferred over one which is formalistically grudging, we believe also that the preferred approach in determining admissibility is for the attorneys to present to the court and for the court to consider the circumstances under which the original deposition was taken so that a full understanding of the motives in the first case can be obtained. Some of the motives of the defendants can be understood from the very limited cross-examination which appears in the Smith deposition, but very little otherwise is shown in our record or is shown either in *Clay* or in *Murphy*.

What is more important, however, is the question of potential prejudice that can accrue to a defendant against whom a deposition is introduced which the defendant never had an opportunity to adequately refute. Under such circumstances, we think it is incumbent upon counsel for the defendant when objecting to the admissibility of such proof to explain as clearly as possible to the judge precisely why the motive and opportunity of the defendants in the first case was not adequate to develop the cross-examination which the instant defendant would have presented to the witness. Thus, we would have been much more impressed with the defense's objections had they articulated before the trial court in the first instance, and later before us, precisely what lines of questioning they would have pursued. While National Gypsum here points to certain areas of difference between its situation and that of Johns–Manville, much of its argument before us was not presented to the district court, nor are we told precisely what lines of questioning National Gypsum would have pursued had it had the opportunity. We do not doubt that the trial judge here understood that he was not bound as a matter of law to admit the document in every case and we do not doubt he would have carefully considered any such factors, if they existed and had been pointed out to him at the time. We believe that it was the responsibility of National Gypsum to make this showing in the district court if it wished later to seek a retrial in which the evidence was to be excluded.

We further comment that we are aware of the great risk which might normally attend the use of a deposition of an expert who is no longer available for cross-examination. Expert witnesses all too often may be obtained on any subject and may speak with great authority and express opinions very wide in scope. When they are not adequately cross-examined, even though an opportunity is present, experts are often prone to create too heavy an aura of authoritativeness. Further, it should rarely be necessary to use the purely opinion testimony of an expert who testified in an entirely different case; and the dangers are correspondingly great that, where there exists a wide variety of opinion, an alert attorney may simply search out expert testimony which he conceives to be favorable to his cause and which he knows to have been made by a witness who is no longer, through death or otherwise, available to testify. Obviously, Rule [804] is not designed to deprive the opposite party of the historic right of cross-examination; rather, it is intended to permit parties to employ proof and testimony which is essentially reliable, cannot be effectively obtained in any other manner, and whose relevancy and probity is such that its introduction outweighs the possible prejudicial value which may result from denying cross-examination.

Here, the testimony of Dr. Smith is not so much the testimony of any expert who is giving opinions, as it is the testimony of a very knowledgeable person who was aware of the historical development of the specialized subject matter under examination. We believe that the very limited cross-examination of which the counsel in the original *DeRocco* case availed itself reflects its correct conclusion that most of Dr. Smith's testimony did relate to historical facts and was of a type which was not subject to refutation. Indeed, nothing in the argument before us or before the district court challenges the accuracy of the historical statements made by Dr. Smith, and for this additional reason we believe it was not an abuse of discretion for the trial judge here to have admitted the deposition. As observed by Judge Kennedy, "Smith, as former Medical Director of the leading manufacturer of asbestos-containing products, was in a unique position to discuss the scope of knowledge available to the industry during his 20–year tenure at Johns–Manville." *Murphy,* 779 F.2d at 343.

* * *

[Remanded on damages issue.]

Notes and Questions

1. *Progression of party identity requirement.* "Identity of parties" has been, on occasion, given as a requirement for admission of prior testimony. However, the modern trend, as reflected in Rule 804(b)(1), is to eliminate such a requirement in a number of situations. See 2 McCormick, Evidence § 303, at 341–42 (6th ed. 2006). First, there is no requirement of mutuality. Only identity of the party against whom the testimony is offered is required. See Bailey v. S. Pac. Transp. Co., 613 F.2d 1385, 1390 (5th Cir.1980) (testimony by plaintiff in another civil action against the railroad concerning malfunctioning signal light admissible in second suit against same defendant). Also, where the party against whom the prior testimony is offered is in privity with a party in the prior proceeding, the testimony is admissible. Creamer v. Gen. Teamsters Local Union 326, 560 F.Supp. 495, 499 (D.Del. 1983) (owner of company is predecessor in interest to company).

An arguably distinct rationale covers cases where the government is placed in a position akin to the predecessor in interest when its public duty is to protect private interests. See In re Master Key Antitrust Litig., 72 F.R.D. 108, 109 (D.Conn.1976) (unique relationship between government's antitrust suits and private actions that follow); Lloyd v. Am. Export Lines, Inc., 580 F.2d 1179, 1185–86 (3d Cir.1978) (testimony at Coast Guard inquiry admissible because of community of interest between victim of assault and Coast Guard, which has overlapping duty to protect both private interest of alleged victim and public interest in unimpeded merchant marine service). The line of cases culminating in *Dykes* relies heavily upon the *Lloyd* case. Was the extension proper?

2. *Party identity issues in civil cases. Dykes* teaches that the predecessor-in-interest language should not be applied too strictly, but it concerned a rather unique situation. Does *Dykes* mean that testimony offered against

similarly situated but entirely separate parties is freely admissible? Consider the following: Suppose two bus passengers are injured in a collision and file separate actions against the bus company. Should the testimony of a witness called by the defense in the suit of the first passenger be admissible against the second passenger, the witness having become unavailable? *Dykes* suggests that protection against unfairness is provided by giving the new party the opportunity to explain why cross-examination was not adequate. See also Horne v. Owens–Corning Fiberglas Corp., 4 F.3d 276, 283 (4th Cir.1993) (employee opposing admission must point up distinctions not evident in earlier litigation involving different employees that would preclude similar motive); O'Banion v. Owens–Corning Fiberglas Corp., 968 F.2d 1011, 1015 (10th Cir.1992) (finding no harm in admitting prior testimony where opponent offered no basis to find prior examination inadequate). Does this opportunity provide sufficient protection against unfairness to the opponent of the evidence given that the alternative is the total loss of the evidence (witness is by definition unavailable), which may lead to unfairness to the other party?

3. *Criminal cases.* When evidence is offered against the defendant in a criminal case, the "predecessor in interest" concept has no place. Under Rule 804(b)(1), the defendant must have been a party in the prior proceeding. "Another party, no matter how closely allied in interest or motive, will not do." 5 Weinstein's Federal Evidence § 804.04[6] (2d ed. 2006). Whether the predecessor-in-interest concept applies when the statement is offered against the government is subject to debate. Compare United States v. McDonald, 837 F.2d 1287, 1291 (5th Cir.1988) (open question), with United States v. Peterson, 100 F.3d 7, 12–13 (2d Cir.1996) (assuming admissibility only if federal prosecutor controlled state prosecution or had opportunity to develop testimony). See also 2 McCormick, Evidence § 303, at 350–51 (6th ed. 2006) (exclusion probably not intended by Congress and may violate due process under some circumstances).

4. *Sources.* Falknor, Former Testimony and the Uniform Rules: A Comment, 38 N.Y.U.L.Rev. 651 (1963); Martin, The Former–Testimony Exception in the Proposed Federal Rules of Evidence, 57 Iowa L.Rev. 547 (1972); Weissenberger, The Former Testimony Hearsay Exception: A Study in Rulemaking, Judicial Revisionism, and the Separation of Powers, 67 N.C.L.Rev. 295 (1989).

SECTION I. DYING DECLARATIONS

FEDERAL RULE 804(b)(2)

SHEPARD v. UNITED STATES

Supreme Court of the United States, 1933.
290 U.S. 96.

MR. JUSTICE CARDOZO delivered the opinion of the Court.

The petitioner, Charles A. Shepard, a major in the medical corps of the United States Army, has been convicted of the murder of his wife, Zenana Shepard, at Fort Riley, Kan., a United States military reservation. The jury having qualified their verdict by adding thereto the words "without capital punishment" (18 U.S.C. § 567 [18 USCA § 567]), the defendant was sentenced to imprisonment for life.

* * *

The crime is charged to have been committed by poisoning the victim with bichloride of mercury. The defendant was in love with another woman, and wished to make her his wife. There is circumstantial evidence to sustain a finding by the jury that to win himself his freedom he turned to poison and murder. Even so, guilt was contested, and conflicting inferences are possible. The defendant asks us to hold that by the acceptance of incompetent evidence the scales were weighted to his prejudice and in the end to his undoing.

The evidence complained of was offered by the government in rebuttal when the trial was nearly over. On May 22, 1929, there was a conversation in the absence of the defendant between Mrs. Shepard, then ill in bed, and Clara Brown, her nurse. The patient asked the nurse to go to the closet in the defendant's room and bring a bottle of whisky that would be found upon a shelf. When the bottle was produced, she said that this was the liquor she had taken just before collapsing. She asked whether enough was left to make a test for the presence of poison, insisting that the smell and taste were strange. And then she added the words, "Dr. Shepard has poisoned me."

The conversation was proved twice. After the first proof of it, the government asked to strike it out, being doubtful of its competence, and this request was granted. A little later, however, the offer was renewed; the nurse having then testified to statements by Mrs. Shepard as to the prospect of recovery. "She said she was not going to get well; she was going to die." With the aid of this new evidence, the conversation already summarized was proved a second time. There was a timely challenge of the ruling.

She said, "Dr. Shepard has poisoned me." The admission of this declaration, if erroneous, was more than unsubstantial error. As to that the parties are agreed. The voice of the dead wife was heard in accusation of her husband, and the accusation was accepted as evidence of guilt. If the evidence was incompetent, the verdict may not stand.

1. Upon the hearing in this court the government finds its main prop in the position that what was said by Mrs. Shepard was admissible as a dying declaration. This is manifestly the theory upon which it was offered and received. The prop, however, is a broken reed. To make out a dying declaration, the declarant must have spoken without hope of recovery and in the shadow of impending death. The record furnishes no proof of that indispensable condition. So, indeed, it was ruled by all the judges of the court below, though the majority held the view that the testimony was competent for quite another purpose, which will be considered later on.

We have said that the declarant was not shown to have spoken without hope of recovery and in the shadow of impending death. Her illness began on May 20. She was found in a state of collapse, delirious, in pain, the pupils of her eyes dilated, and the retina suffused with blood. The conversation with the nurse occurred two days later. At that time her mind had cleared up, and her speech was rational and orderly. There was as yet no thought by any of her physicians that she was dangerously ill, still less that her case was hopeless. To all seeming she had greatly improved, and was moving forward to recovery. There had been no diagnosis of poison as the cause of her distress. Not till about a week afterwards was there a relapse, accompanied by an infection of the mouth, renewed congestion of the eyes, and later hemorrhages of the bowels. Death followed on June 15.

Nothing in the condition of the patient on May 22 gives fair support to the conclusion that hope had then been lost. She may have thought she was going to die and have said so to her nurse, but this was consistent with hope, which could not have been put aside without more to quench it. Indeed, a fortnight later, she said to one of her physicians, though her condition was then grave, "You will get me well, won't you?" Fear or even belief that illness will end in death will not avail of itself to make a dying declaration. There must be "a settled hopeless expectation" (Willes, J. in Reg. v. Peel; 2 F. & F. 21, 22) that death is near at hand, and what is said must have been spoken in the hush of its impending presence. Mattox v. United States, 146 U.S. 140, 151 * * * ; 3 Wigmore on Evidence, §§ 1440, 1441, 1442, collating the decisions. Despair of recovery may indeed be gathered from the circumstances if the facts support the inference. Carver v. United States, supra; Wigmore, Evidence, § 1442. There is no unyielding ritual of words to be spoken by the dying. Despair may even be gathered, though the period of survival outruns the bounds of expectation. Wigmore, § 1441. What is decisive is the state of mind. Even so, the state of mind must be exhibited in the evidence, and not left to conjecture. The patient must have spoken with the consciousness of a swift and certain doom.

What was said by this patient was not spoken in that mood. There was no warning to her in the circumstances that her words would be repeated and accepted as those of a dying wife, charging murder to her husband, and charging it deliberately and solemnly as a fact within her knowledge. To the focus of that responsibility her mind was never brought. She spoke as one ill, giving voice to the beliefs and perhaps the conjectures of the moment. The liquor was to be tested, to see whether her beliefs were sound. She did not speak as one dying, announcing to the survivors a definitive conviction, a legacy of knowledge on which the world might act when she had gone.

The petitioner insists that the form of the declaration exhibits other defects that call for its exclusion, apart from the objection that death was not imminent and that hope was still alive. Homicide may not be imputed to a defendant on the basis of mere suspicions, though they are the suspicions of the dying. To let the declaration in, the inference must be permissible that there was knowledge or the opportunity for knowledge as to the acts that are declared. Wigmore, § 1445(2). The argument is pressed upon us that knowledge and opportunity are excluded when the declaration in question is read in the setting of the circumstances. [Authorities omitted.] The form is not decisive, though it be that of a conclusion, a statement of the result with the antecedent steps omitted. Wigmore, § 1447. "He murdered me," does not cease to be competent as a dying declaration because in the statement of the act there is also an appraisal of the crime. State v. Mace, 118 N.C.1244, 24 S.E. 798; State v. Kuhn, supra. One does not hold the dying to the observance of all the niceties of speech to which conformity is exacted from a witness on the stand. What is decisive is something deeper and more fundamental than any difference of form. The declaration is kept out if the setting of the occasion satisfies the judge, or in reason ought to satisfy him, that the speaker is giving expression to suspicion or conjecture, and not to known facts. The difficulty is not so much in respect of the governing principle as in its application to varying and equivocal conditions. In this case, the ruling that there was a failure to make out the imminence of death and the abandonment of hope relieves us of the duty of determining whether it is a legitimate inference that there was the opportunity for knowledge. We leave that question open.

[The Court determined that the statements to the nurse were not admissible under other hearsay exceptions.]

Reversed.

Notes and Questions

1. *Relaxing standard. Shepard*, which was decided long before the development of the Federal Rules, is generally consistent with the requirements of Rule 804(b)(2). However, the Rule's provision, "believing that the declarant's death was imminent," is somewhat less emphatic than the "swift and certain doom" of *Shepard*. Cases decided over the past two decades have slightly relaxed the previous extremely demanding standard, see, e.g., Burks v. State, 876 S.W.2d 877, 901 (Tex.Crim.App.1994), perhaps in recognition of the increasing effectiveness of modern medicine. See Johnson v. State, 579 P.2d 20, 25 (Alaska 1978); 2 McCormick, Evidence § 310, at 365 (6th ed. 2006). As *Shepard* states, the declarant's belief that death is imminent need not necessarily be proved by his or her direct statements of that belief. It may also be established circumstantially by evidence such as the apparently fatal nature of the wounds or statements made to the declarant by others. McCormick, supra, at 366. However, the burden is on the party offering the statement to show declarant's recognition of the dire nature of the situation, see United States v. Lawrence, 349 F.3d 109, 117 (3d Cir.2003) (ruling statement inadmissible under exception where no statements by medical staff or police indicated declarant was going to die and all medical statements were upbeat), and dire medical evaluations that are neither obvious nor communicated are sufficient, see Bell v. United States, 801 A.2d 117, 126–27 (D.C.2002) (excluding statements by patient whom medical staff understood had little chance of recovery where not shown that he under-

stood more than that his condition was serious and perhaps fatal or that visible nature of the injuries conveyed that he assuredly would die).

2. *Application to atheists?* Lack of religious belief in a hereafter on the part of the declarant would seem to require exclusion of his or her declaration if the guarantee of trustworthiness is theological. The Advisory Committee Note suggests that "powerful psychological pressures" provide an alternative guarantee of trustworthiness. Is this guarantee sufficient? Does necessity for the statement provide the additional justification that renders this exception rational? Some common law authority permits lack of religious belief to be used to impeach the credibility of the declaration. Annot., 16 A.L.R.411, 415. Does Rule 610, which prohibits admission of evidence of religious beliefs to impeach credibility, have an impact on such impeachment?

3. *Concern about trustworthiness.* Courts and commentators have remained concerned about the reliability of dying declarations, recognizing that (1) powerful human motivations such as revenge or favoritism do not necessarily cease to have sway as death approaches, (2) the condition of the declarant may distort the reliability of the statement, and (3) the statement may be the product of prompting by interested questioners. See Quick, Some Reflections on Dying Declarations, 6 How.L.J. 109, 111–12 (1960); 5 Weinstein's Federal Evidence § 804.05[1] (2d ed. 2006).

4. *Applicability outside homicide cases.* Standard doctrine in this country for many years limited dying declarations to those of the victim in homicide prosecutions. Thus, dying declarations of the victim in a prosecution for rape were held inadmissible where death resulted from a fever following the birth of a child so conceived, Hansel v. Commonwealth, 84 S.W.2d 68 (Ky.1935), and where another victim died from ingesting the same poisonous liquor, People v. Cox, 172 N.E. 64 (Ill.1930). Dying declarations were also held generally inadmissible in civil cases. Carver v. Howard, 280 S.W.2d 708 (Ky.1955). Federal Rule 804(b)(2) permits admission of dying declarations in civil cases generally and in homicide prosecutions. As proposed, the Rule would have admitted such statements in all criminal cases, but concerns about reliability of statements under this exception, see note 3, supra, prompted the House of Representatives to limit its application in criminal cases to homicide prosecutions where the need for the statement was considered greatest. Under the wording of the Rule, must the declarant be the homicide victim for the statement to be admissible, or can the declarant survive in a multiple victim case where one victim is killed?

5. *Belief, rather than death, required.* While death will frequently render the declarant unavailable when statements are admitted under this exception, the Rule does not require that death actually ensue—only that the declarant believe that it is imminent.

6. *Exculpatory statements.* In the nature of things, the declarations ordinarily are damaging to the accused. However, if the statement is helpful to the accused, it may be received if it otherwise meets the requirements of the exception. State v. Proctor, 269 S.W.2d 624 (Mo.1954); Commonwealth v. Plubell, 80 A.2d 825 (Pa.1951).

7. *Subject matter limitation.* Under common law development, the subject matter of the declaration was usually limited to the circumstances

surrounding the killing, but the interpretation of the scope of that limitation provided opportunity for "prolific quibbling." 5 Wigmore, Evidence § 1434, at 284 (Chadbourn rev. 1974). Perhaps typical under the common law was the exclusion of a reference to previous threats by the accused. State v. Chaplin, 286 A.2d 325 (Me.1972). While still limiting the subject matter of the statement to reduce the dangers of fabrication, the modern trend under the Federal Rule is more liberal and admits statements concerning the "cause or circumstances" of the declarant's apparently impending death. See 4 Mueller & Kirkpatrick, Federal Evidence § 495, at 808 (2d ed. 1994) (arguing that prior threats admissible under Rule 804(b)(2)).

8. *Death by suicide.* Should a suicide note ever properly qualify for admission as a dying declaration? See State v. Satterfield, 457 S.E.2d 440, 447–50 (W.Va.1995) (admitting suicide note). But see United States v. Angleton, 269 F.Supp.2d 878, 882–87 (S.D.Tex.2003) (ruling that suicide notes were inadmissible because unrelated to cause or circumstances of death and because of doubt that the declarant believed death would be swift and certain when the statements were made since it was unknown precisely when the notes were written).

9. *Sources.* Jaffee, The Constitution and Proof by Dead or Unconfrontable Declarants, 33 Ark.L.Rev. 227 (1979); Liang, Shortcuts to Truth: The Legal Mythology of Dying Declarations, 35 Am.Crim.L.Rev. 229 (1998); Quick, Some Reflections on Dying Declarations, 6 How.L.J. 109 (1960).

SECTION J. STATEMENTS AGAINST INTEREST

FEDERAL RULE 804(b)(3)

HASKELL v. SIEGMUND

Appellate Court of Illinois, Third District, 1960.
170 N.E.2d 393.

[Haskell recovered a judgment for $35,000 against Siegmund for injuries sustained from the latter's driving of an automobile owned by Peterson. He then sought by appropriate ancillary proceedings to collect the judgment from Peterson's liability insurance company. Liability under the policy depended upon whether Siegmund was driving with Peterson's permission. Following the accident, Klophel, an investigator for the insurance company obtained statements from Peterson to the effect that he had given Siegmund permission to use the automobile. The insurance company appeals from a judgment entered on a verdict against it.]

REYNOLDS, JUSTICE. * * * Peterson died before trial of the garnishment action. Siegmund, who was 19 years old at the time of the accident, left Peterson's employ shortly after August 6, 1955. He was thereafter convicted of the crime of forgery and was incarcerated. Neither Peterson nor Siegmund testified at either trial. * * *

* * * Peterson's written statements to Klophel that he loaned the 1942 Chevrolet to Siegmund were admissible as declarations against his

pecuniary interest, a well established exception to the hearsay rule. * * * The tests for admissibility of declarations against pecuniary interest are set forth in German Insurance Co. v. Bartlett, 1900, 188 Ill. 165, 173, 58 N.E. 1075, 1077:

> "* * * (1) The declarant must be dead; (2) the declaration must have been against the pecuniary interest of the declarant at the time it was made; (3) the declaration must be of a fact in relation to a matter concerning which the declarant was immediately and personally cognizable; and (4) the court should be satisfied that the declarant had no probable motive to falsify the fact declared."

Peterson's statements to Klophel meet these tests: (1) Peterson was dead at the time of the trial below. (2) It is presumed that one who is driving another's vehicle is the owner's agent. Parrino v. Landon, 1956, 8 Ill.2d 468, 470, 134 N.E.2d 311, 313; Howard v. Amerson, 1st Dist. 1925, 236 Ill.App. 587, 593–594. Hence, when Peterson stated that he owned the car being driven by Siegmund on the night of the accident, Peterson was exposing himself, *prima facie,* to liability for Siegmund's negligence. (3) Peterson had personal knowledge of the circumstances under which he gave the car to Siegmund. (4) No proof was adduced as to any reason why Peterson should falsify for a part-time employee, who did not even return to work after the accident.

* * *

Judgment affirmed.

Notes and Questions

1. *Admissions and against interest statements compared.* The distinction between statements against interest and admissions of a party should clearly be noted. Statements against interest require that the declarant be unavailable, he or she must have personal knowledge of the matters asserted, and the statement must be against the declarant's interest when made. These are not requirements of admissions. On the other hand, admissions must have been made by a party and must be offered by the opposing party, while the statement against interest exception applies to any declarant and may be offered by either party. 2 McCormick, Evidence § 316, at 375 (6th ed. 2006).

2. *How against interest?* What should satisfy the against-interest test? There are at least three possibilities: (1) that the facts stated be against interest; (2) that the statement itself create an obligation; or (3) that the declarant be creating evidence which may be used to his or her detriment. Furthermore, how should we evaluate the mental attitude of the declarant—by actually attempting to ascertain it or by setting up some kind of reasonable person standard? Consider Commonwealth Life Ins. Co. v. Clarke, 123 S.W.2d 811 (Ky.1938) (an action on a life insurance policy defended on the ground of suicide, holding it error to exclude a declaration of the insured that he had shot himself since the policy was still effectively his

property under a reservation of right to change the beneficiary). The cases are generally far from clear when closely scrutinized as to theory.

3. *What interests?* As to the nature of the interest involved, Rule 804(b)(3) is broadly drawn, and while excluding statements incurring social disapproval, the Rule "occupies the entire area developed by the common law except for some of the more fanciful English decisions in tenancy cases." 2 McCormick, Evidence § 317, at 378 (6th ed. 2006). Substantial issues will still remain, however, as to whether the statement in question is sufficiently contrary to such interest that "a reasonable person in the declarant's position would not have made the statement unless believing it to be true." See, e.g., Donovan v. Crisostomo, 689 F.2d 869, 876–77 (9th Cir.1982) (statements of alien workers that they did not work overtime not admissible under Rule 804(b)(3) since workers might feel it was in their interest to claim they were properly paid to avoid wrath of employer that might result in their deportation); State v. Lynch, 854 A.2d 1022, 1036–39 (R.I.2004) (concluding that statement by 14–year-old male of consensual sex was not against his interest, despite financial implications given that his partner became pregnant, considering the greater likelihood that statement was made to avoid more substantial criminal liability).

4. *Sources.* Jefferson, Declarations Against Interest: An Exception to the Hearsay Rule, 58 Harv.L.Rev. 1 (1944); Morgan, Declarations Against Interest, 5 Vand.L.Rev. 451 (1952).

KNAPP v. ST. LOUIS TRUST CO.

Supreme Court of Missouri, 1906.
98 S.W. 70.

GANTT, J. This is an action to contest the validity of the will of Mrs. Margaret Gaffey. The grounds of contest were and are that the testatrix at the time of executing the alleged will was not of sound and disposing mind and memory and was under undue influence. * * *

As the case must be reversed it is proper that we should note another assignment of error, to-wit: That the circuit court improperly held that the entries in the account book of Dr. McWilliams were only admissible for the purpose of showing that at certain dates the doctor made certain charges for visits to Mrs. Gaffey. It is insisted by the learned counsel for the plaintiff that these entries were admissible as evidence of the other fact stated therein, to-wit, the nature of the disease for which he treated Mrs. Gaffey. Dr. McWilliams, who made the entry, was shown to be dead. The first entry is a fair sample of the others and was in this form:

"1890. Mrs. Marg. Gaffey, 5886 Cabanne Place:

June 24, Hyperaemia of Brain, 1 visit and med. $2.00

June 24, By cash paid .... $2.00"

In Higham v. Ridgway, 10 East 109, the proposition now urged by the appellant received great consideration by the court of King's Bench in 1808. In that case the question was as to the date of the birth of a child. There was offered in evidence an entry from the book of a man mid-wife, in which he had entered a charge, stating the services, and acknowledged the receipt of the payment. It was objected to and discussed at great length by counsel pro and con, and it was held by the court, all the judges concurring, that the entry was admissible as evidence of the birth and the time, as well as of the receipt of the payment. Lord Ellenborough, C.J., said: "I think the evidence here was properly admitted upon the broad principle on which receivers' books have been admitted; namely, that the entry was made in the prejudice of the party making it. * * * It is idle to say that the word *paid* only shall be admitted in evidence without the context, which explains to what it refers."

Le Blanc, J., states: "But here the entries were made by a person who, so far from having any interest to make them, had an interest the other way; and such entries against the interest of the party making them are clearly evidence of the fact stated, on the authority of Warren v. Greenville, and of all those cases where the books of receivers have been admitted." * * * In 16 Cyclopedia of Law and Procedure, p. 1218, it is said: "Declarations against interest are not only received as evidence of the fact directly asserted, but of incidental facts fairly embraced within the scope of the declaration." In view of this practically unanimous statement of the rule, we think that the entries were admissible not only for the purpose of showing that at certain dates Dr. McWilliams rendered medical services to Mrs. Gaffey, and was paid therefor, but also for the purpose of showing that he treated her for hyperaemia of the brain and for softening of the brain and paralysis, and the circuit court erred in holding otherwise.

For the errors noted, the judgment of the circuit court is reversed and the cause is remanded for a new trial in accordance with the views herein expressed.

WILLIAMSON v. UNITED STATES

Supreme Court of the United States, 1994.
512 U.S. 594.

[Justice O'Connor, for six justices, delivered the opinion of the Court as to Parts I, II–A, and II–B. Justices Scalia, Ginsburg (for four justices), and Kennedy (for three justices) filed concurring opinions.]

Justice O'Connor * * *.

In this case we clarify the scope of the hearsay exception for statements against penal interest. Fed. Rule Evid. 804(b)(3).

I

A deputy sheriff stopped the rental car driven by Reginald Harris for weaving on the highway. Harris consented to a search of the car, which revealed 19 kilograms of cocaine in two suitcases in the trunk. Harris was promptly arrested.

Shortly after Harris' arrest, Special Agent Donald Walton of the Drug Enforcement Administration (DEA) interviewed him by telephone. During that conversation, Harris said that he got the cocaine from an unidentified Cuban in Fort Lauderdale; that the cocaine belonged to petitioner Williamson; and that it was to be delivered that night to a particular dumpster. Williamson was also connected to Harris by physical evidence [in the car] * * *.

Several hours later, Agent Walton spoke to Harris in person. During that interview, Harris said he had rented the car a few days earlier and had driven it to Fort Lauderdale to meet Williamson. According to Harris, he had gotten the cocaine from a Cuban who was Williamson's acquaintance, and the Cuban had put the cocaine in the car with a note telling Harris how to deliver the drugs. Harris repeated that he had been instructed to leave the drugs in a certain dumpster, to return to his car, and to leave without waiting for anyone to pick up the drugs.

Agent Walton then took steps to arrange a controlled delivery of the cocaine. But as Walton was preparing to leave the interview room, Harris "got out of [his] chair * * * and * * * took a half step toward [Walton] * * * and * * * said, * * * 'I can't let you do that,' threw his hands up and said 'that's not true, I can't let you go up there for no reason." 'Harris told Walton he had lied about the Cuban, the note, and the dumpster. The real story, Harris said, was that he was transporting the cocaine to Atlanta for Williamson, and that Williamson was traveling in front of him in another rental car. Harris added that after his car was stopped, Williamson turned around and drove past the location of the stop, where he could see Harris' car with its trunk open. Because Williamson had apparently seen the police searching the car, Harris explained that it would be impossible to make a controlled delivery.

Harris told Walton that he had lied about the source of the drugs because he was afraid of Williamson. Though Harris freely implicated himself, he did not want his story to be recorded, and he refused to sign a written version of the statement. Walton testified that he had promised to report any cooperation by Harris to the Assistant United States Attorney. Walton said Harris was not promised any reward or other benefit for cooperating.

Williamson was eventually convicted of possessing cocaine with intent to distribute, conspiring to possess cocaine with intent to distribute, and traveling interstate to promote the distribution of cocaine * * *. When called to testify at Williamson's trial, Harris refused, even though the prosecution gave him use immunity and the court ordered him to testify and eventually held him in contempt. The District Court then ruled that, under Rule 804(b)(3), Agent Walton could relate what Harris had said to him: "The ruling of the Court is that the statements * * * are admissible under [Rule 804(b)(3)], which deals with statements against interest." * * * Williamson appealed his conviction [and the Court of Appeals affirmed].

II

A

The hearsay rule, Fed. Rule Evid. 802, is premised on the theory that out-of-court statements are subject to particular hazards. The declarant might be lying; he might have misperceived the events which he relates; he might have faulty memory; his words might be misunderstood or taken out of context by the listener. And the ways in which these dangers are minimized for in-court statements—the oath, the witness' awareness of the gravity of the proceedings, the jury's ability to observe the witness' demeanor, and, most importantly, the right of the opponent to cross-examine—are generally absent for things said out of court.

Nonetheless, the Federal Rules of Evidence also recognize that some kinds of out-of-court statements are less subject to these hearsay dangers, and therefore except them from the general rule that hearsay is inadmissible. One such category covers statements that are against the declarant's interest: "statement[s] which * * * at the time of [their] making * * * so far tended to subject the declarant to * * * criminal liability * * * that a reasonable person in the declarant's position would not have made the statement[s] unless believing [them] to be true." Fed. Rule Evid. 804(b)(3).

To decide whether Harris' confession is made admissible by Rule 804(b)(3), we must first determine what the Rule means by "statement," which Federal Rule of Evidence 801(a)(1) defines as "an oral or written assertion." One possible meaning, "a report or narrative," Webster's Third New International Dictionary 2229, defn. 2(a) (1961), connotes an extended declaration. Under this reading, Harris' entire confession—even if it contains both self-inculpatory and non-self-inculpatory parts—would be admissible so long as in the aggregate the confession sufficiently inculpates him. Another meaning of "statement," "a single declaration or remark," *ibid.*, defn. 2(b), would make Rule 804(b)(3) cover only those declarations or remarks within the confession that are individually self-inculpatory. See also *id.*, at 131 (defining "assertion" as a "declaration"); *id.*, at 586 (defining "declaration" as a "statement").

Although the text of the Rule does not directly resolve the matter, the principle behind the Rule, so far as it is discernible from the text, points clearly to the narrower reading. Rule 804(b)(3) is founded on the commonsense notion that reasonable people, even reasonable people who are not especially honest, tend not to make self-inculpatory statements unless they believe them to be true. This notion simply does not extend to the broader definition of "statement." The fact that a person is making a broadly self-inculpatory confession does not make more credible the confession's non-self-inculpatory parts. One of the most effective ways to lie is to mix falsehood with truth, especially truth that seems particularly persuasive because of its self-inculpatory nature.

In this respect, it is telling that the non-self-inculpatory things Harris said in his first statement actually proved to be false, as Harris himself admitted during the second interrogation. And when part of the confession is actually self-exculpatory, the generalization on which Rule 804(b)(3) is founded becomes even less applicable. Self-exculpatory statements are exactly the ones which people are most likely to make even when they are false; and mere proximity to other, self-inculpatory, statements does not increase the plausibility of the self-exculpatory statements.

We therefore cannot agree with JUSTICE KENNEDY's suggestion that the Rule can be read as expressing a policy that collateral statements—even ones that are not in any way against the declarant's interest—are admissible. Nothing in the text of Rule 804(b)(3) or the general theory of the hearsay Rules suggests that admissibility should turn on whether a statement is collateral to a self-inculpatory statement. The fact that a statement is self-inculpatory does make it more reliable; but the fact that a statement is collateral to a self-inculpatory statement says nothing at all about the collateral statement's reliability. We see no reason why collateral statements, even ones that are neutral as to interest, should be treated any differently from other hearsay statements that are generally excluded.

Congress certainly could, subject to the constraints of the Confrontation Clause, make statements admissible based on their proximity to self-inculpatory statements. But we will not lightly assume that the ambiguous language means anything so inconsistent with the Rule's underlying theory. See *Cooter & Gell v. Hartmarx Corp.*, 496 U.S. 384, 394–395, 408–409 (1990). In our view, the most faithful reading of Rule 804(b)(3) is that it does not allow admission of non-self-inculpatory statements, even if they are made within a broader narrative that is generally self-inculpatory. The district court may not just assume for purposes of Rule 804(b)(3) that a statement is self-inculpatory because it is part of a fuller confession, and this is especially true when the statement implicates someone else. "[T]he arrest statements of a codefendant have traditionally been viewed with special suspicion. Due to his strong motivation to implicate the defendant and to exonerate himself, a codefendant's statements about what the defendant said or did are less credible than ordinary hearsay evidence." *Lee v. Illinois*, 476 U.S. 530, 541 (1986) (internal quotation marks omitted); see also *Bruton v. United States*, 391 U.S. 123, 136 (1968); *Dutton v. Evans*, 400 U.S. 74, 98 (1970) (Harlan, J., concurring in result).

JUSTICE KENNEDY suggests that the Advisory Committee Notes to Rule 804(b)(3) should be read as endorsing the position we reject—that an entire narrative, including non-self-inculpatory parts (but excluding the clearly self-serving parts), may be admissible if it is in the aggregate self-inculpatory. The Notes read, in relevant part:

> "[T]he third-party confession * * * may include statements implicating [the accused], and under the general theory of declarations against interest they would be admissible as related statements * * *. [*Douglas v. Alabama*, 380 U.S. 415 (1965), and *Bruton v.*

> *United States*, 391 U.S. 123 (1968)] * * * by no means require that all statements implicating another person be excluded from the category of declarations against interest. Whether a statement is in fact against interest must be determined from the circumstances of each case. Thus a statement admitting guilt and implicating another person, made while in custody, may well be motivated by a desire to curry favor with the authorities and hence fail to qualify as against interest * * *. On the other hand, the same words spoken under different circumstances, e.g., to an acquaintance, would have no difficulty in qualifying * * *. The balancing of self-serving against dissenting [sic] aspects of a declaration is discussed in McCormick § 256." 28 U.S.C. App., p. 790.

This language, however, is not particularly clear, and some of it—especially the Advisory Committee's endorsement of the position taken by Dean McCormick's treatise—points the other way:

> "A certain latitude as to contextual statements, neutral as to interest, giving meaning to the declaration against interest seems defensible, but bringing in self-serving statements contextually seems questionable * * *. [A]dmit[ting] the disserving parts of the declaration, and exclud[ing] the self-serving parts * * * seems the most realistic method of adjusting admissibility to trustworthiness, where the serving and disserving parts can be severed." See C. McCormick, Law of Evidence § 256, pp. 551–553 (1954) (footnotes omitted).

Without deciding exactly how much weight to give the Notes in this particular situation * * *, we conclude that the policy expressed in the statutory text points clearly enough in one direction that it outweighs whatever force the Notes may have. * * *

B

We also do not share JUSTICE KENNEDY's fears that our reading of the Rule "eviscerate[s] the against penal interest exception," or makes it lack "meaningful effect." There are many circumstances in which Rule 804(b)(3) does allow the admission of statements that inculpate a criminal defendant. Even the confessions of arrested accomplices may be admissible if they are truly self-inculpatory, rather than merely attempts to shift blame or curry favor.

For instance, a declarant's squarely self-inculpatory confession—"yes, I killed X"—will likely be admissible under Rule 804(b)(3) against accomplices of his who are being tried under a co-conspirator liability theory. See *Pinkerton v. United States*, 328 U.S. 640, 647 (1946). Likewise, by showing that the declarant knew something, a self-inculpatory statement can in some situations help the jury infer that his confederates knew it as well. And when seen with other evidence, an accomplice's self-inculpatory statement can inculpate the defendant directly: "I was robbing the bank on Friday morning," coupled with someone's testimony that the declarant and the defendant drove off together Friday morning, is evidence that the defendant also participated in the robbery.

Moreover, whether a statement is self-inculpatory or not can only be determined by viewing it in context. Even statements that are on their face neutral may actually be against the declarant's interest. "I hid the gun in Joe's apartment" may not be a confession of a crime; but if it is likely to help the police find the murder weapon, then it is certainly self-inculpatory. "Sam and I went to Joe's house" might be against the declarant's interest if a reasonable person in the declarant's shoes would realize that being linked to Joe and Sam would implicate the declarant in Joe and Sam's conspiracy. And other statements that give the police significant details about the crime may also, depending on the situation, be against the declarant's interest. The question under Rule 804(b)(3) is always whether the statement was sufficiently against the declarant's penal interest "that a reasonable person in the declarant's position would not have made the statement unless believing it to be true," and this question can only be answered in light of all the surrounding circumstances.

C

In this case, however, we cannot conclude that all that Harris said was properly admitted. Some of Harris' confession would clearly have been admissible under Rule 804(b)(3); for instance, when he said he knew there was cocaine in the suitcase, he essentially forfeited his only possible defense to a charge of cocaine possession, lack of knowledge. But other parts of his confession, especially the parts that implicated Williamson, did little to subject Harris himself to criminal liability. A reasonable person in Harris' position might even think that implicating someone else would decrease his practical exposure to criminal liability, at least so far as sentencing goes. Small fish in a big conspiracy often get shorter sentences than people who are running the whole show, see, e.g., United States Sentencing Commission, Guidelines Manual § 3B1.2 (Nov. 1993), especially if the small fish are willing to help the authorities catch the big ones, see, e.g., *id.*, at § 5K1.1.

Nothing in the record shows that the District Court or the Court of Appeals inquired whether each of the statements in Harris' confession was truly self-inculpatory. * * * [W]e therefore remand to the Court of Appeals to conduct this inquiry in the first instance.

* * *

JUSTICE SCALIA, concurring.

* * * [A] declarant's statement is not magically transformed from a statement against penal interest into one that is inadmissible merely because the declarant names another person or implicates a possible co-defendant. For example, if a lieutenant in an organized crime operation described the inner workings of an extortion and protection racket, naming some of the other actors and thereby inculpating himself on racketeering and/or conspiracy charges, I have no doubt that some of those remarks could be admitted as statements against penal interest. Of course, naming another person, if done, for example, in a context where

the declarant is minimizing culpability or criminal exposure, can bear on whether the statement meets the Rule 804(b)(3) standard. The relevant inquiry, however—and one that is not furthered by clouding the waters with manufactured categories such as "collateral neutral" and "collateral self-serving"—must always be whether the particular remark at issue (and not the extended narrative) meets the standard set forth in the Rule.

JUSTICE GINSBURG, * * * concurring in part and concurring in the judgment.

I join Parts I, II–A, and II–B of the Court's opinion. I agree with the Court that Federal Rule of Evidence 804(b)(3) excepts from the general rule that hearsay statements are inadmissible only "those declarations or remarks within [a narrative] that are individually self-inculpatory." As the Court explains, the exception for statements against penal interest "does not allow admission of non-self-inculpatory statements, even if they are made within a broader narrative that is generally self-inculpatory"; the exception applies only to statements that are "sufficiently against the declarant's penal interest 'that a reasonable person in the declarant's position would not have made the statement unless believing it to be true * * * ' "

Further, the Court recognizes the untrustworthiness of statements implicating another person. A person arrested in incriminating circumstances has a strong incentive to shift blame or downplay his own role in comparison with that of others, in hopes of receiving a shorter sentence and leniency in exchange for cooperation. * * *

Unlike JUSTICE O'CONNOR, however, I conclude that Reginald Harris' statements, as recounted by DEA Special Agent Donald E. Walton, do not fit, even in part, within the exception described in Rule 804(b)(3), for Harris' arguably inculpatory statements are too closely intertwined with his self-serving declarations to be ranked as trustworthy. Harris was caught red-handed with 19 kilos of cocaine-enough to subject even a first-time offender to a minimum of 12 1/2 years' imprisonment. * * * He could have denied knowing the drugs were in the car's trunk, but that strategy would have brought little prospect of thwarting a criminal prosecution. He therefore admitted involvement, but did so in a way that minimized his own role and shifted blame to petitioner Fredel Williamson (and a Cuban man named Shawn).

* * *

To the extent some of these statements tended to incriminate Harris, they provided only marginal or cumulative evidence of his guilt. They project an image of a person acting not against his penal interest, but striving mightily to shift principal responsibility to someone else. See *United States v. Sarmiento–Perez*, 633 F.2d 1092, 1102 (C.A.5 1981) ("[The declarant] might well have been motivated to misrepresent the role of others in the criminal enterprise, and might well have viewed the statement[s] as a whole—including the ostensibly disserving portions—to be in his interest rather than against it.").

For these reasons, I would hold that none of Harris' hearsay statements were admissible under Rule 804(b)(3). * * *

JUSTICE KENNEDY, * * * concurring in the judgment.

I

* * * There has been a long-running debate among commentators over the admissibility of collateral statements. Dean Wigmore took the strongest position in favor of admissibility, arguing that "the statement may be accepted, not merely as to the specific fact against interest, but also as to every fact contained in the same statement." 5 J. Wigmore, Evidence § 1465, p. 271 (3d ed. 1940) (emphasis deleted); see also 5 J. Wigmore, Evidence § 1465, p. 339 (J. Chadbourn rev. 1974); *Higham v. Ridgway*, 10 East. 109, 103 Eng.Rep. 717 (K.B. 1808). According to Wigmore, because "the statement is made under circumstances fairly indicating the declarant's sincerity and accuracy," the entire statement should be admitted. 5 J. Wigmore § 1465, p. 271 (3d ed. 1940). Dean McCormick's approach regarding collateral statements was more guarded. He argued for the admissibility of collateral statements of a neutral character; and for the exclusion of collateral statements of a self-serving character. For example, in the statement "John and I robbed the bank," the words "John and" are neutral (save for the possibility of conspiracy charges). On the other hand, the statement "John, not I, shot the bank teller" is to some extent self-serving and therefore might be inadmissible. See C. McCormick, Law of Evidence § 256, pp. 552–553 (1954) (hereinafter McCormick). Professor Jefferson took the narrowest approach, arguing that the reliability of a statement against interest stems only from the disserving fact stated and so should be confined "to the proof of the fact which is against interest." Jefferson, Declarations Against Interest: An Exception to the Hearsay Rule, 58 Harv.L.Rev. 1, 62–63 (1944). Under the Jefferson approach, neither collateral neutral nor collateral self-serving statements would be admissible.

Enacted by Congress in 1975, Rule 804(b)(3) establishes a hearsay exception for statements against penal, proprietary, pecuniary, and legal interest (and does not distinguish among those interests). The text of the Rule does not tell us whether collateral statements are admissible, however. * * *. The Court resolves the issue, as I understand its opinion, by adopting the extreme position that no collateral statements are admissible under Rule 804(b)(3). * * * The Court reaches that conclusion by relying on the "principle behind the Rule" that reasonable people do not make statements against their interest unless they are telling the truth, and reasons that this policy "expressed in the statutory text" "simply does not extend" to collateral statements. * * *

With respect, I must disagree with this analysis. All agree that the justification for admission of hearsay statements against interest was, as it still is, that reasonable people do not make those statements unless believing them to be true, but that has not resolved the long-running debate over the admissibility of collateral statements, as to which there is no clear consensus in the authorities. * * * The Rule's silence no more incorporates Jefferson's position respecting collateral statements than it does McCormick's or Wigmore's.

II

Because the text of Rule 804(b)(3) expresses no position regarding the admissibility of collateral statements, we must determine whether there are other authoritative guides on the question. In my view, three sources demonstrate that Rule 804(b)(3) allows the admission of some collateral statements * * *.

First, the Advisory Committee Note establishes that some collateral statements are admissible. In fact, it refers in specific terms to the issue we here confront: "[o]rdinarily the third-party confession is thought of in terms of exculpating the accused, but this is by no means always or necessarily the case: it may include statements implicating him, and under the general theory of declarations against interest they would be admissible as related statements." * * *

Second, even if the Advisory Committee Note were silent about collateral statements, I would not adopt a rule excluding all statements collateral or related to the specific words against penal interest. Absent contrary indications, we can presume that Congress intended the principles and terms used in the Federal Rules of Evidence to be applied as they were at common law. * * * Application of that interpretive principle indicates that collateral statements should be admissible. "From the very beginning of this exception, it has been held that a declaration against interest is admissible, not only to prove the disserving fact stated, but also to prove other facts contained in collateral statements connected with the disserving statement." Jefferson, 58 Harv.L.Rev., at 57; see also McCormick § 256; 5 J. Wigmore, Evidence § 1465 (3d ed. 1940). * * *

There is yet a third reason weighing against the Court's interpretation, one specific to statements against penal interest that inculpate the accused. There is no dispute that the text of Rule 804(b)(3) contemplates the admission of those particular statements. Absent a textual direction to the contrary, therefore, we should assume that Congress intended the penal interest exception for inculpatory statements to have some meaningful effect. * * * That counsels against adopting a rule excluding collateral statements. As commentators have recognized, "the exclusion of collateral statements would cause the exclusion of almost all inculpatory statements." Comment, 66 Calif.L.Rev. at 1207 * * *

I note finally that the Court's decision applies to statements against penal interest that exculpate the accused as well as to those that inculpate the accused. Thus, if the declarant said, "I robbed the store alone," only the portion of the statement in which the declarant said "I robbed the store" could be introduced by a criminal defendant on trial for the robbery. See Note, Declarations Against Penal Interest: Standards of Admissibility Under an Emerging Majority Rule, 56 B.U.L.Rev. 148, 165, n.95 (1976). That seems extraordinary. The Court gives no justification for such a rule and no explanation that Congress intended the exception for exculpatory statements to have this limited effect. See *id.*, at 166 ("A strict application of a rule excluding all collateral statements can lead to the arbitrary rejection of valuable evidence").

III

Though I would conclude that Rule 804(b)(3) allows admission of statements collateral to the precise words against interest, that conclusion of course does not answer the remaining question whether all collateral statements related to the statement against interest are admissible; and if not, what limiting principles should apply. The Advisory Committee Note suggests that not all collateral statements are admissible. The Note refers, for example, to McCormick's treatise, not to Wigmore's, for guidance as to the "balancing of self-serving against dis[serving] aspects of a declaration." * * * McCormick stated that "[a] certain latitude as to contextual [i.e., collateral] statements, neutral as to interest, giving meaning to the declaration against interest seems defensible, but bringing in self-serving statements contextually seems questionable." McCormick § 256, p. 552. McCormick further stated that, within a declaration containing self-serving and disserving facts, he would "admit the disserving parts of the declaration, and exclude the self-serving parts" at least "where the serving and disserving parts can be severed." *Id.* § 256, p. 553. It thus appears that the Advisory Committee Note, by its reference to (and apparent incorporation of) McCormick, contemplates exclusion of a collateral self-serving statement, but admission of a collateral neutral statement.

* * *

Notes and Questions

1. *Collateral statements in civil cases. Knapp* and *Higham v. Ridgway*, cited in *Knapp* and by Justice Kennedy in *Williamson*, reflect a longstanding practice of receiving collateral statements in civil cases. Collateral statements were not an issue in criminal cases until relatively recently because statements against penal interest were until then excluded from the exception. While the Supreme Court in *Williamson* recognized special concern with the trustworthiness of collateral statements that incriminate another, its analysis should also exclude collateral statements in civil contexts as well. See Silverstein v. Chase, 260 F.3d 142, 146–48 (2d Cir.2001) (applying *Williamson* analysis in civil case and finding collateral statements inadmissible).

2. *Separating different parts.* Does *Williamson* mean that the self-serving and disserving parts of the statement must always be severed? Is it ever impossible to do? Given that she joined the part of Justice O'Connor's opinion that requires severing the two types of statements, why does Justice

Ginsburg then argue that the inculpatory statements must be excluded because they "are too closely intertwined with his self-serving declarations"?

3. *Impact of identity of hearer on reasonable belief.* The requirement of Rule 804(b)(3) is written in terms of the reasonable person in the position of the declarant, requiring that such a person believe the statement to be against interest. One factor logically important in determining whether the declarant believed the statement against interest is the identity of the person to whom the statement was made. However, the fact that the statement was made to a friend, who might be expected (or hoped) to keep the damaging information secret, is typically not considered to eliminate the disserving quality of the statement. See, e.g., United States v. Lang, 589 F.2d 92, 97 (2d Cir.1978) (statement admitting crime against interest when made to undercover agent whom the defendant thought was a confederate). As *Williamson* indicates, a different view is taken when the statement also implicates another and is made to persons known to be police officers. Statements incriminating another have obvious potential benefits for the declarant in bargaining with authorities.

4. *Corroboration requirement for exculpatory statements.* Under Rule 804(b)(3), in addition to being against interest, statements exculpating the accused are not to be admitted unless "corroborating circumstances clearly indicate the trustworthiness of the statement." The legislative history shows that Congress recognized the potential unfairness of excluding statements that exculpated the defendant but feared fabricated confessions, and it added this requirement to guard against manufactured evidence. Some courts have applied rather exacting corroboration requirements and thereby excluded exculpatory statements. See, e.g., United States v. MacDonald, 688 F.2d 224 (4th Cir.1982). See generally Tague, Perils of the Rulemaking Process: The Development, Application, and Unconstitutionality of Rule 804(b)(3)'s Penal Interest Exception, 69 Geo.L.J. 851 (1981). The corroboration that is appropriately required goes beyond a minimal level, but it should not be made unrealistically severe. 5 Weinstein's Federal Evidence § 804.06[5][b] (2d ed. 2006).

The Federal Rules Advisory Committee has proposed several versions of an amendment to Rule 804(b)(3) that, parallel to the requirement of corroboration for exculpatory statements, would require corroboration for inculpatory statements as well. The proposal was derailed by the Supreme Court's decision in Crawford v. Washington, 541 U.S. 36 (2004), which has the effect of excluding many of the most problematic inculpatory statements by co-participants to investigating officers because they are clearly testimonial. Is such a provision still appropriate after *Crawford*? See Capra, Amending the Hearsay Exception for Declarations Against Penal Interest in the Wake of *Crawford*, 105 Colum.L.Rev. 2409 (2005) (arguing rule revision is still needed).

5. *Impact of Williamson.* After *Williamson*, it seems safe to say that fewer statements against interest, both inculpatory and exculpatory, will be admitted. However, is Justice Kennedy correct that from the statement "I robbed the store alone," only "I robbed the store" could now be introduced

by a criminal defendant on trial for that robbery? Does the addition of the word "alone" add to the incriminating nature of the statement? Is it "collateral"? On the other hand, arguments can be made that statements inculpating others should be admissible. See United States v. Manfre, 368 F.3d 832, 841–43 (8th Cir.2004) (admitting statements made to fiancee when declarant not under threat of prosecution and to friend in setting where no incentive to shift blame); United States v. Barone, 114 F.3d 1284, 1294–99 (1st Cir.1997) (arguing that statements implicating others are self-incriminating in showing insider's knowledge). Moreover, Justices O'Connor and Scalia argued that statements incriminating others might be against the declarant's interest by implicating him in a larger conspiracy. When might that larger conspiracy argument, which is often available, be rejected? See United States v. Mendoza, 85 F.3d 1347, 1351–52 (8th Cir.1996) (statements inculpating higher up that only confirm facts of crime already known held to be currying favor and ruled inadmissible). Is the typical ("reasonable person") criminal likely to anticipate being charged with conspiracy?

6. *Impact of Crawford.* Even if the statements of co-participants implicating others in criminal activity satisfy the requirements of this hearsay exception, to be admitted against the defendant in a criminal case, they must not violate the Confrontation Clause. After Crawford v. Washington, 541 U.S. 36 (2004), such statements made to the police while in custody will generally be found testimonial and excluded unless meeting one of the limited *Crawford* exceptions. This change in Confrontation Clause analysis has had a profound effect on this particular type of hearsay, and Supreme Court dissatisfaction with the failure of the earlier doctrine under Ohio v. Roberts, 448 U.S. 56 (1980), to exclude such statements appears to have been a major motivating factor in jettisoning that doctrine. See *Crawford*, 541 U.S. at 63–64 ("The unpardonable vice of the *Roberts* test, however, is not its unpredictability, but its demonstrated capacity to admit core testimonial statements that the Confrontation Clause plainly meant to exclude * * * [—] accomplice statements implicating the accused."). Some statements of this type, if made to private individuals, for example, may not be considered testimonial and therefore would not be covered by *Crawford*. See United States v. Manfre, 368 F.3d 832, 838 n.1 (8th Cir.2004) (finding *Crawford* inapplicable to statements made to fiancee and to friend).

7. *Impact on state law.* Although *Williamson* is not binding on the states, a number have adopted its analysis for their hearsay exception for statements against interest. See McCormick, Evidence § 319, at 385 n.17 (6th ed. 2006). Prior to *Crawford*, the result was likely influenced by the Supreme Court's decision in Lilly v. Virginia, 527 U.S. 116 (1999), where the Supreme Court ruled that admission of statements that fell within Virginia's exception for statements against interest, even though the parts laid sole blame on an accomplice, violated the Confrontation Clause. Id. at 146–48 (Rehnquist, C.J., concurring). After *Crawford*, one may expect somewhat less interest in following *Williamson* since such hearsay based analysis has little impact on Confrontation Clause analysis.

SECTION K. ADMISSION THROUGH FORFEITURE OR BECAUSE OF WRONGDOING

FEDERAL RULE 804(b)(6)

UNITED STATES v. DHINSA

United States Court of Appeals, Second Circuit, 2001.
243 F.3d 635.

MESKILL, CIRCUIT JUDGE:

This appeal arises out of the prosecution of appellant Gurmeet Singh Dhinsa (Dhinsa) in connection with his role as leader of the Singh Enterprise, a racketeering organization centered around a chain of gasoline stations owned and operated by Dhinsa throughout the New York City area. [After a lengthy trial, the jury convicted Dhinsa of twenty-one offenses, including conspiracy to commit murder in aid of racketeering, murder in aid of racketeering, and obstruction of justice murder. He was sentenced to multiple terms of life imprisonment.]

On appeal, Dhinsa [argued, *inter alia*, that] the district court erred by admitting the hearsay statements of two murder victims pursuant to *United States v. Mastrangelo,* 693 F.2d 269 (2d Cir.1982), and its progeny, and Fed.R.Evid. 804(b)(6).

* * *

Dhinsa was the self-professed leader of the "Singh Enterprise," a vast racketeering organization built around a chain of fifty-one gasoline stations that Dhinsa owned and operated throughout the New York City metropolitan area under the name "Citygas." The enterprise was funded by a pump-rigging scheme that overcharged Citygas customers through the use of an elaborate electronic device located beneath the gasoline pumps at the various Citygas stations. Operated via remote control, the rigging mechanism overcharged each customer by about six to seven percent on each purchase. During the enterprise's ten year existence, the pump-rigging scheme generated tens of millions of dollars, which were used, *inter alia,* to bribe public officials, purchase weapons and carry out crimes of violence aimed at protecting the enterprise's operations and its profits.

As the leader of the Singh Enterprise, Dhinsa maintained an "inner management circle" consisting of his cousin Gulzar Singh (Gulzar), his brother Gogi Singh (Gogi) and Citygas employee Babu Singh (Babu). Gulzar and Gogi supervised and trained the Citygas employees on the pump-rigging scheme, and, along with Babu, collected proceeds from the various Citygas stations and assisted Dhinsa in carrying out his violent criminal activities. Equally vital to the enterprise's operations were Antonio and Otilio Galvan, the designers of the pump-rigging mechanism and Marvin Dodson (Dodson), Walter "Jazz" Samuels (Samuels) and Evans Alonzo Powell (Powell), the group of hitmen employed by Dhinsa in connection with the murders of former Citygas employees Manmohan Singh (Manmohan) and Satinderjit Singh (Satinderjit).

Manmohan and Satinderjit were both murdered on Dhinsa's orders. Prior to his death, Manmohan made numerous inquiries, and confronted various members of the Singh Enterprise, about the July 1995 disappearance of his brother Kulwant, a Citygas employee. Dhinsa ordered Satinderjit murdered after learning that he was cooperating with police regarding, *inter alia,* Kulwant's disappearance, Manmohan's murder, and the enterprise's pump-rigging scheme. * * *

The Murders of Manmohan and Satinderjit * * *

Dhinsa was convicted for his role in the murders of Manmohan and Satinderjit * * *. Each was targeted by Dhinsa because of his active or potential cooperation with the police. Although their stories differ, they share a common theme—each posed a threat to the continued operation of the Singh Enterprise and the millions of dollars of profits generated each year by the enterprise's criminal activities.

The events leading up to Manmohan's murder began with the disappearance of his brother Kulwant in July 1995, when Kulwant was observed getting into a Citygas truck with Dhinsa's cousin Gulzar and Gulzar's brother Gurdial Singh (Gurdial). In March 1997, Manmohan was marked for death after he confronted Dhinsa and other key members of the Singh Enterprise about their involvement in Kulwant's disappearance. Around that same time, Dhinsa arranged to meet with Dodson across from the gas station where Manmohan worked and instructed Dodson to kill Manmohan. Operating on Gulzar's identification, Dodson returned to Manmohan's gas station armed with a gun supplied by Dhinsa and in a Citygas truck driven by Powell. After accompanying Manmohan to an office area at the station under the pretext that he needed a can of oil, Dodson ordered Manmohan to kneel down near a bench and proceeded to fire two shots into the back of Manmohan's head, killing him. Dodson and Powell then drove to Dodson's apartment, where Dodson changed his clothes and telephoned Dhinsa to inform him of the murder. Dhinsa paid Dodson $4,000 for the murder and instructed him to take the Citygas truck to a body shop located at one of Dhinsa's gas stations in order to have it repainted.

At Manmohan's funeral, the police initiated contact with Satinderjit, who offered to cooperate with police about Manmohan's murder, Kulwant's disappearance and the Citygas pump-rigging scheme. Satinderjit also made efforts to contact Dhinsa's brother Gogi, who was a suspect in a 1991 homicide. Satinderjit persuaded Sarvjeet, a witness to that homicide, to cooperate with the police. Apparently aware of Satinderjit's involvement with the police, Dhinsa (identifying himself as "Gurmeet Singh") made two threatening telephone calls to Julie Uberoi (Uberoi), Satinderjit's girlfriend, stating that he would kill Satinderjit and Uberoi if Satinderjit continued to inquire into his business or cooperate with the police.

In May 1997, Satinderjit informed the police that Gogi would be at the Citygas corporate offices in Brooklyn, New York. Based on that information, Satinderjit and Sarvjeet accompanied the police to the Brooklyn offices, presumably to identify Gogi. After Gogi arrived and was identified by Sarvjeet, police entered the Citygas offices and arrested Gogi. Also present were Dhinsa's cousin Gulzar and Babu, a Citygas employee, both of whom were arrested on weapons charges relating to guns found inside the building. During a sweep of the Brooklyn offices, police uncovered two handguns and a bullet proof vest inside a Citygas armored van. A trace of one of the handguns revealed that it was part of a shipment of handguns stolen in 1996. Dhinsa arrived a short time later and was also arrested on weapons charges. Following his arrest, Dodson testified that Dhinsa purchased firearms from him on two previous occasions.

After posting bail, Dhinsa contacted Dodson and ordered that Satinderjit, who he believed was a cooperating witness against Gogi, be killed. Dhinsa provided Dodson with photographs of Satinderjit and his car and a printout of Satinderjit's license plate and home address. On Dhinsa's order that Satinderjit be killed as soon as possible, Dodson maintained surveillance outside Satinderjit's home for an opportunity to commit the murder. During that time, Dodson regularly reported his progress to Dhinsa.

* * *

Growing impatient with Dodson in light of court proceedings pending against Gogi, Dhinsa instructed Dodson to kill Satinderjit within a few days. On June 18, 1997, Dhinsa telephoned Dodson from Satinderjit's neighborhood and arranged for Dodson, Samuels and Powell to meet him across from Satinderjit's home. By early afternoon, the trio arrived at Satinderjit's home and met Dhinsa. Dhinsa supplied them with a Citygas van and instructed Samuels and Powell to go to a nearby Citygas station to have the van's license plates changed. Earlier, Dhinsa telephoned Santokh Singh (Santokh), a Citygas mechanic, instructing him to change the van's license plates. When Samuels and Powell arrived, Santokh replaced the van's New York license plate with a Pennsylvania license plate. When Samuels and Powell returned, they noticed Dhinsa in his car, and Dodson and another person in a separate car, both parked across the street from Satinderjit's home.

Dhinsa's plan was set into action when Satinderjit and his cousin Kirpal Singh emerged from Satinderjit's home and entered Satinderjit's livery cab. Dodson positioned himself around the corner of Satinderjit's home, armed with a handgun purchased by Dhinsa a few days earlier. When Satinderjit attempted to drive away, Powell (Samuels had exited the van a few minutes earlier) drove the Citygas van alongside Satinderjit in order to block his exit and to provide Dodson sufficient time to get into position. Dhinsa, also present at the scene and driving a black Lexus sedan, apparently blocked Satinderjit's car from behind. As Satinderjit pulled around the Citygas van and turned the corner, Dodson approached Satinderjit, who was seated in the driver's seat. Dodson fired multiple shots at Satinderjit, killing him on the scene. Kirpal, crouched below the dashboard, was not killed.

After the shooting, Dhinsa instructed Dodson and Powell to follow him to a nearby Citygas station, where they were later joined by Samuels. When Dodson and Powell arrived in the Citygas van, Dhinsa instructed Santokh to replace the van's license plate. Dhinsa later met up with Dodson, Samuels and Powell at Dodson's residence, at which time he congratulated them on their success and paid them each $5,000.

* * *

Fed.R.Evid. 804(b)(6) and the Admission of Mastrangelo Evidence

Dhinsa argues that the district court erred by admitting out-of-court statements of Manmohan and Satinderjit, offered through numerous prosecution witnesses, as proof of Dhinsa's involvement in the murders of the declarants. The gravamen of Dhinsa's objection is that the admission of hearsay statements introduced as proof of the declarants' murders rather than about past events or offenses Dhinsa allegedly committed violated Fed.R.Evid. 403 and Fed.R.Evid. 802, and, more importantly, his right to confront the witnesses against him as guaranteed by the Sixth Amendment. Thus, Dhinsa raises three related arguments under *Mastrangelo* and Fed.R.Evid. 804(b)(6) on appeal: (1) Rule 804(b)(6), which codifies the *Mastrangelo* rationale, limits the admission of hearsay statements to past events or offenses committed by the defendant about which the declarant could testify, and not as proof of the declarant's murder; (2) the district court failed to assess independently the reliability of the declarants' statements in accordance with *Lilly v. Virginia,* 527 U.S. 116 * * * (1999) (plurality opinion); and (3) the district court failed to find, as required under Fed.R.Evid. 804(b)(6), that Dhinsa intended to procure the unavailability of Manmohan and Satinderjit. Further, Dhinsa argues that the court's admission of *Mastrangelo* evidence under the circumstances of this case "cannot be deemed harmless error." We consider the merits of these arguments *seriatim.*

1. *The Confrontation Clause and the Waiver–By–Misconduct Doctrine*

* * *

Although the confrontation right is of constitutional dimension, it is not absolute, *see Maryland v. Craig,* 497 U.S. 836, 847–48 * * * (1990) ("[W]e have repeatedly held that the Clause permits, where necessary, the admission of certain hearsay statements against a defendant despite the defendant's inability to confront the declarant at trial."), and may be waived by a defendant through a "knowing and intentional relinquishment." *United States v. Houlihan,* 92 F.3d 1271, 1279 (1st Cir.1996).

* * * These cases recognize that although the right of confrontation is an essential trial right, it may be waived by the defendant's misconduct.[43]

Consistent with that principle, this Court, as well as a majority of our sister circuits, have also applied the waiver-by-misconduct rule in cases where the defendant has wrongfully procured the witnesses' silence through threats, actual violence or murder. *See, e.g., United States v. Cherry,* 217 F.3d 811, 814–15 (10th Cir.2000) (murder) * * *. Recognizing that "[s]imple equity" and "common sense" justify a defendant's forfeiture of his confrontation rights under circumstances where he wrongfully procures the witnesses' absence, the D.C. Circuit held:

> It is hard to imagine a form of misconduct more extreme than the murder of a potential witness. Simple equity supports a forfeiture principle, as does a common sense attention to the need for fit incentives. The defendant who has removed an adverse witness is in a weak position to complain about losing the chance to cross-examine him. And where a defendant has silenced a witness through the use of threats, violence or murder, admission of the victim's prior statements at least partially offsets the perpetrator's rewards for his misconduct. We have no hesitation in finding, in league with all circuits to have considered the matter, that a defendant who wrongfully procures the absence of a witness or potential witness may not assert confrontation rights as to that witness.

White, 116 F.3d at 911. Relying on the maxim that "the law [will not] allow a person to take advantage of his own wrong," *Mastrangelo,* 693 F.2d at 272 (quoting *Diaz v. United States,* 223 U.S. 442, 458 * * * (1912)), in *Mastrangelo* and cases following, we have reaffirmed the principle that, where a defendant wrongfully procures the silence of a witness or potential witness, he will be deemed to have "waived his sixth amendment rights and, *a fortiori,* his hearsay objection" to the admission of the declarant's statements. *Id.* at 272. * * * We extended that principle to situations where "there was [no] ongoing proceeding in which the declarant was scheduled to testify." *Miller,* 116 F.3d at 668; *see also Houlihan,* 92 F.3d at 1279–80. The application of *Mastrangelo* under these circumstances is both logical and fair since a contrary rule "would serve as a prod to the unscrupulous to accelerate the timetable and murder suspected snitches sooner rather than later." *Houlihan,* 92 F.3d at 1280.

2. *Whether* Mastrangelo *and Fed.R.Evid. 804(b)(6) Contain a Subject Matter Limitation*

Fed.R.Evid. 804(b)(6), made effective December 1997, codified the waiver-by-misconduct doctrine as an exception to the hearsay rules by permitting the admission of hearsay statements "offered against a party

43. [Although this case was decided under the *Ohio v. Roberts* approach to confrontation, its conclusion is consistent with that reached in *Crawford v. Washington,* see Chapter 13, Section C. Ed.]

that has engaged or acquiesced in wrongdoing that was intended to, and did, procure the unavailability of the declarant as a witness." Fed. R.Evid. 804(b)(6); *see also United States v. Ochoa,* 229 F.3d 631, 639 (7th Cir.2000). Under Rule 804(b)(6), "a party forfeits the right to object on hearsay grounds to the admission of a declarant's prior statement when the party's deliberate wrongdoing or acquiescence therein procured the unavailability of the declarant as a witness." Fed.R.Evid. 804(b)(6) advisory committee's note to subdivision (b)(6) * * *.

By its plain terms, Rule 804(b)(6) refers to the intent of a party to procure the unavailability of the *witness,* and does not, as Dhinsa contends, limit the subject matter of the witness' testimony to past events or offenses the witness would have testified about had he been available. *See Emery,* 186 F.3d at 926 ("[Rule 804(b)(6)] contains no limitation on the subject matter of the statements that it exempts from the prohibition on hearsay evidence."). This interpretation is supported by the underlying purpose of the waiver-by-misconduct doctrine—"that a defendant may not benefit from his or her wrongful prevention of future testimony from a witness or potential witness." *Id.* * * * Adoption of Dhinsa's proposed limitation would limit the proof against him—the very result that the waiver-by-misconduct doctrine seeks to remedy. *See Emery,* 186 F.3d at 926. Further, we have declined to read in such a limitation in our pre-Rule 804(b)(6) decisions dealing with *Mastrangelo* evidence, permitting statements made by the declarant to be admitted where the murder of the declarant was one of the charged offenses. *See, e.g., Miller,* 116 F.3d at 667–69 (hearsay statement of murdered drug supplier made to his wife) * * *. Because Rule 804(b)(6) was intended to codify the waiver-by-misconduct rule as it was applied by the courts at that time, * * * it is reasonable to conclude that Rule 804(b)(6) did not intend to create a subject matter limitation where one did not previously exist. *See Cherry,* 217 F.3d at 816 ("We * * * read the plain language of Rule 804(b)(6) to permit the admission of those hearsay statements that would be admissible under the constitutional doctrine of waiver by misconduct.") * * * .

In sum, based on the plain language of Rule 804(b)(6) and the strong policy reasons favoring application of the waiver-by-misconduct doctrine to prevent a party from profiting from his wrongdoing, we hold that Rule 804(b)(6) places no limitation on the subject matter of the declarant's statements that can be offered against the defendant at trial to prove that the defendant murdered the declarant.

3. *The Requirements Under* Mastrangelo *in Light of Rule 804(b)(6)*

By its plain terms, Rule 804(b)(6) requires a finding that the defendant acted with the intention of making the declarant unavailable as a witness. This conclusion is not disputed by the parties. A number of cases decided after Rule 804(b)(6) became effective have also read in an intent requirement. *See, e.g., United States v. Johnson,* 219 F.3d 349, 355–56 (4th Cir.2000) ("[Defendant] murdered [the witness] at least in part to procure the unavailability of the only witness to his murder.");

Emery, 186 F.3d at 926 ("[Rule 804(b)(6)] establishes the general proposition that a defendant may not benefit from his or her wrongful prevention of future testimony from a witness or potential witness."). Thus, consistent with our pre-Fed.R.Evid. 804(b)(6) precedent, we now hold that, prior to finding that a defendant waived his confrontation rights with respect to an out-of-court statement by an actual or potential witness admitted pursuant to Rule 804(b)(6), the district court must hold an evidentiary hearing outside the presence of the jury in which the government has the burden of proving by a preponderance of the evidence that (1) the defendant (or party against whom the out-of-court statement is offered) was involved in, or responsible for, procuring the unavailability of the declarant "through knowledge, complicity, planning or in any other way," *Miller,* 116 F.3d at 668; and (2) the defendant (or party against whom the out-of-court statement is offered) acted with the intent of procuring the declarant's unavailability as an actual or potential witness. *See* Fed.R.Evid. 804(b)(6) advisory committee note to subdivision (b)(6) (adopting the preponderance of the evidence standard required under Fed.R.Evid. 104(a) "in light of the behavior the new Rule 804(b)(6) seeks to discourage."); *accord Houlihan,* 92 F.3d at 1280 ("We * * * hold that when a person who eventually emerges as a defendant (1) causes a potential witness's unavailability (2) by a wrongful act (3) undertaken with the intention of preventing the potential witness from testifying at a future trial, then the defendant waives his right to object on confrontation grounds to the admission of the unavailable declarant's out-of-court statements at trial."). *But see Emery,* 186 F.3d at 926 (holding that a trial court is not required to hold a 804(b)(6) hearing outside the presence of the jury but, instead, can admit the hearsay evidence "at trial in the presence of the jury contingent upon proof of the underlying murder by a preponderance of the evidence"). The government need not, however, show that the defendant's sole motivation was to procure the declarant's absence; rather, it need only show that the defendant "was motivated *in part* by a desire to silence the witness." *Houlihan,* 92 F.3d at 1279; *see also Johnson,* 219 F.3d at 356. As Rule 804(b)(6) and our prior precedents do not require such a finding of sole motivation, we decline to read one into the rule. "Further, in order to avoid the admission of facially unreliable hearsay, the district court should undertake a balancing of probative value against prejudicial effect in accordance with Fed.R.Evid. 403." *Miller,* 116 F.3d at 668 (internal quotation marks omitted). "The district court's findings after a hearing will not be disturbed unless they are clearly erroneous, and we are particularly hesitant to disturb the court's determinations when they are based on its evaluation of the credibility of witnesses." *Thai,* 29 F.3d at 814.

4. *Lilly v. Virginia*

Dhinsa argues that the application of the waiver-by-misconduct rule to allow the admission of hearsay statements of a declarant as evidence of that declarant's murder by the defendant is inconsistent with the Supreme Court's recent decision in *Lilly v. Virginia,* 527 U.S. 116 * * *

(1999) (plurality opinion). In response, the government argues that Dhinsa waived his confrontation rights by murdering the declarants and, therefore, the *Mastrangelo* evidence is not subject to the *Lilly* test. We find the government's argument persuasive.

* * *

This does not, however, mean that the declarant's statements will be admitted automatically. As discussed *supra,* after the district court finds by a preponderance of the evidence that the hearsay statement is admissible under Fed.R.Evid. 804(b)(6), it must still perform the balancing test required under Fed.R.Evid. 403 "in order to avoid the admission of facially unreliable hearsay." *Thai,* 29 F.3d at 814 * * *. Thus, while a finding that a statement may be admitted under Rule 804(b)(6)—resulting in a waiver of the defendant's confrontation rights and hearsay objections—renders the *Lilly* test inapplicable, the district court must still balance the probative value of the evidence against its prejudicial effect in accordance with Rule 403.

5. *Application of Harmless Error Analysis to Violations of the Confrontation Clause and the Present Case*

Dhinsa argues that the district court's failure to make a finding that he intended to "eliminate the declarant[s] as * * * witness[es]" prior to the admission of the *Mastrangelo* statements was not harmless error. Dhinsa further argues that the admission of such evidence was not harmless under the present circumstances. We disagree.

* * *

With respect to Manmohan, Dhinsa feared that Manmohan would go to the police regarding Dhinsa's involvement in Kulwant's disappearance. This fear was well founded in light of Manmohan's repeated confrontations with Dhinsa and other members of the Singh Enterprise in which he accused them of being responsible for his brother's disappearance. Dodson also testified that Dhinsa ordered Manmohan murdered because he had "seen [Dhinsa] and Gogi shoot somebody, and the police [were] getting close to the guy." Thus, Dhinsa believed that Manmohan posed a threat to the Singh Enterprise and to Dhinsa and Gogi personally by his cooperation with the police. *See, e.g., Houlihan,* 92 F.3d at 1280–81; *Thai,* 29 F.3d at 815 (defendant motivated by declarant's cooperation with police).

With respect to Satinderjit, the evidence presented at trial established that Satinderjit was in fact cooperating with the police at the time Dhinsa ordered Dodson to kill him, providing police with information regarding Manmohan's murder, Kulwant's disappearance and the Citygas pump-rigging scheme. Satinderjit's active involvement with the police is evidenced by his presence at the May 1997 raid of the Citygas offices in Brooklyn, New York during which Dhinsa, Gogi and other members of the Singh Enterprise were arrested. Dodson testified that Dhinsa ordered Satinderjit murdered because he was "a witness against his brother." Dodson also testified that Dhinsa was upset that he was taking too long to murder Satinderjit and ordered Dodson to act quickly since Satinderjit was "supposed to go to see the [g]rand [j]ury." Powell and Samuels, the other members of the group of hitmen hired by Dhinsa, similarly testified that Dhinsa wanted Satinderjit murdered quickly to prevent him from testifying against Gogi and himself. Dhinsa also made threatening calls to Manmohan warning him to cease his efforts to locate his brother and similar calls to Uberoi, Satinderjit's girlfriend, warning her that they would both be shot "if [Satinderjit] did not stop messing around with his case and did not stay out of his business." Thus, there was sufficient support in the record to establish that Dhinsa murdered Manmohan and Satinderjit because he believed that they both had knowledge concerning his criminal activities, as well as those of other members of the Singh Enterprise, and, therefore, could cooperate in a police investigation targeting Dhinsa and the Singh Enterprise. *See Thai,* 29 F.3d at 815. We also find that the admission of these statements under Rule 403 did not constitute an abuse of discretion. *See United States v. Gelzer,* 50 F.3d 1133, 1139 (2d Cir.1995). * * * Accordingly, the district court's admission of the *Mastrangelo* evidence relating to statements made by Manmohan and Satinderjit should not be disturbed.

* * *

Notes and Questions

1. *Wrongful intent.* Rule 804(b)(6) requires an intent to procure the absence of the witness. It also requires "wrongdoing" to procure that result, but as the Committee Note states, wrongdoing need not necessarily involve criminal conduct. See United States v. Scott, 284 F.3d 758, 763–64 (7th Cir.2002) (concluding that "wrongdoing," which the Advisory Committee states need not be a criminal act, also need not include murder, physical assault, or bribery, but would be satisfied by coercion, undue influence, or pressure to silence testimony).

2. *Murder to eliminate witness(es). Dhinsa* rules that the hearsay statements may be admitted not only as to the crimes as to which the witness would have testified but also to criminal conduct, such as murder, through which the witness' absence was procured. The exception does not, however, apply to the murder of all potential witnesses. By its terms, the Rule should be inapplicable to a murder committed during a robbery for the purpose of overcoming the victim's physical resistance. The Committee Note states that it "applies to actions taken after the event to prevent a witness from testifying." In many cases, the wrongful conduct will occur long after the original crime (the event) when the witness' identity becomes known to the defendant. Would the exception apply to a murder committed during a robbery if the perpetrator killed the victim in order to eliminate any witnesses? What is the result if the purpose is to both overcome resistance and to eliminate a potential witness?

3. *No trustworthiness requirement.* Rule 804(b)(6) operates under the rationale of forfeiture rather than the typical mix of trustworthiness and

necessity involved in most hearsay exceptions. As a consequence, it requires no explicit showing of trustworthiness, and *Dhinsa* holds no such showing is required under the Confrontation Clause as well. See United States v. Scott, 284 F.3d 758, 765 (7th Cir.2002) (ruling that, to the extent the unreliability challenge depends on lack of cross-examination, admission under wrongdoing renders that objection unavailing). A somewhat related examination is required under Rule 403, which considers probativity, a factor that rests in part on trustworthiness. However, the review under Rule 403 is a forgiving one, requiring admission of evidence unless its probativity is substantially outweighed by its prejudicial impact.

4. *Procedures for finding intent.* In line with preliminary factfinding generally under the hearsay rules, this Rule requires the trial court to find the required intent, for example, by a preponderance of the evidence. As *Dhinsa* discusses, the circuits differ on whether this finding must be made before admission and outside the presence of the jury or whether the evidence may be admitted conditionally upon subsequent proof of the requisite facts. While *Dhinsa* holds that the trial court must hold a hearing outside the presence of the jury prior to admitting hearsay under this exception, the Eighth Circuit rejects this requirement. See United States v. Emery, 186 F.3d 921, 926 (8th Cir.1999).

5. *Procurement "through others."* Action "through others" producing unavailability may be directly arranged by the defendant. Direct proof of procurement is often difficult to obtain. Thus, it is important that actions that may be "counted against" the defendant, which can be done (1) if actions taken by coconspirators, (2) if the wrongful procurement was within the scope and in furtherance of the conspiracy, and (3) if it was reasonably foreseeable as a natural consequence of the conspiracy. Several courts have held that such indirect involvement of the defendant in the declarant's unavailability of the type that satisfies conspiratorial liability for such unavailability (frequently through murder) is sufficient. See, e.g., United States v. Thompson, 286 F.3d 950, 963 (7th Cir.2002).

6. *Relationship to Confrontation Clause.* In Crawford v. Washington, 541 U.S. 36, 62 (2004), the Supreme Court stated that "forfeiture by wrongdoing," which the Court had previously recognized, remains an exception under *Crawford*'s new mode of analysis because it is not based on a questionable reliability judgment but instead extinguishes the right on equitable grounds. While both the constitutional doctrine and the hearsay rule may share the same name, their requirements may well prove to be different. The federal hearsay exception's requirements are clearly not met simply by showing that the defendant made the declarant unavailable through wrongful acts, such as by killing the witness. By contrast, several courts have ruled that wrongful actions that procure absence, such as killing the declarant, operate as a forfeiture of confrontation rights under *Crawford*. See, e.g., United States v. Garcia–Meza, 403 F.3d 364, 370–71 (6th Cir.2005); State v. Meeks, 88 P.3d 789 (Kan.2004).

7. *Antecedents and state adoptions.* Prior to the addition of Rule 804(b)(6) to the Federal Rules in 1997, some courts had admitted hearsay when a party wrongfully caused the declarant's unavailability under the theory of waiver or forfeiture of hearsay and Confrontation Clause objec-

tions. See United States v. Smith, 792 F.2d 441, 442 (4th Cir.1986); Steele v. Taylor, 684 F.2d 1193, 1202 (6th Cir.1982); Kroger, The Confrontation Waiver Rule, 76 B.U.L.Rev. 835 (1996). See generally Birdsong, The Exclusion of Hearsay Through Forfeiture by Wrongdoing—Old Wine in a New Bottle—Solving the Mystery of the Codification of the Conception into Federal Rule 804(b)(6), 80 Neb.L.Rev. 891 (2001); Flanagan, Forfeiture by Wrongdoing and Those Who Acquiesce in Witness Intimidation: A Reach Exceeding its Grasp and Other Problems with Federal Rule of Evidence 804(b)(6), 51 Drake L.Rev. 459 (2003).

A handful of states have adopted a form of this hearsay exception by rule or court decision. See 2 McCormick, Evidence § 253, at 174 & n.61 (6th ed. 2006).

SECTION L. CATCHALL OR RESIDUAL EXCEPTION

FEDERAL RULES 807 (FORMERLY 803(24) & 804(b)(5))

DALLAS COUNTY v. COMMERCIAL UNION ASSUR. CO.

United States Court of Appeals, Fifth Circuit, 1961.
286 F.2d 388.

WISDOM, CIRCUIT JUDGE. This appeal presents a single question—the admissibility in evidence of a newspaper to show that the Dallas County Courthouse in Selma, Alabama, was damaged by fire in 1901. We hold that the newspaper was admissible, and affirm the judgment below.

On a bright, sunny morning, July 7, 1957, the clock tower of the Dallas County Courthouse at Selma, Alabama, commenced to lean, made loud cracking and popping noises, then fell and telescoped into the courtroom. Fortunately, the collapse of the tower took place on a Sunday morning; no one was injured, but damage to the courthouse exceeded $100,000. An examination of the tower debris showed the presence of charcoal and charred timbers. The State Toxicologist, called in by Dallas County, reported the char was evidence that lightning struck the courthouse. Later, several residents of Selma reported that a bolt of lightning struck the courthouse July 2, 1957. On this information, Dallas County concluded that a lightning bolt had hit the building causing the collapse of the clock tower five days later. Dallas County carried insurance for loss to its courthouse caused by fire or lightning. The insurers' engineers and investigators found that the courthouse collapsed of its own weight. They reported that the courthouse had not been struck by lightning; that lightning could not have caused the collapse of the tower; that the collapse of the tower was caused by structural weaknesses attributable to a faulty design, poor construction, gradual deterioration of the structure, and overloading brought about by remodeling and the recent installation of an air-conditioning system, part of which was constructed over the courtroom trusses. In their opinion, the char was the result of a fire in

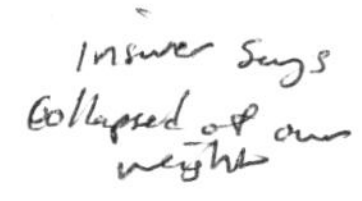

the courthouse tower and roof that must have occurred many, many years before July 2, 1957. The insurers denied liability.

The County sued its insurers in the Circuit Court of Dallas County. As many of the suits as could be removed, seven, were removed to the United States District Court for the Southern District of Alabama, and were consolidated for trial. The case went to the jury on one issue: did lightning cause the collapse of the clock tower?

The record contains ample evidence to support a jury verdict either way. The County produced witnesses who testified they saw lightning strike the clock tower; the insurers produced witnesses who testified an examination of the debris showed that lightning did not strike the clock tower. Some witnesses said the char was fresh and smelled smoky; other witnesses said it was obviously old and had no fresh smoky smell at all. Both sides presented a great mass of engineering testimony bearing on the design, construction, overload or lack of overload. All of this was for the jury to evaluate. The jury chose to believe the insurers' witnesses and brought in a verdict for the defendants.

During the trial the defendants introduced a copy of the Morning Times of Selma for June 9, 1901. This issue carried an unsigned article describing a fire that occurred at two in the morning of June 9, 1901, while the courthouse was still under construction. The article stated, in part: "The unfinished dome of the County's new courthouse was in flames at the top, and * * * soon fell in. The fire was soon under control and the main building was saved. * * * "The insurers do not contend that the collapse of the tower resulted from unsound charred timbers used in the repair of the building after the fire; they offered the newspaper account to show there had been a fire long before 1957 that would account for charred timber in the clock tower.

As a predicate for introducing the newspaper in evidence, the defendants called to the stand the editor of the Selma Times–Journal who testified that his publishing company maintains archives of the published issues of the Times–Journal and of the Morning Times, its predecessor, and that the archives contain the issue of the Morning Times of Selma for June 9, 1901, offered in evidence. The plaintiff objected that the newspaper article was hearsay; that it was not a business record nor an ancient document, nor was it admissible under any recognized exception to the hearsay doctrine. The trial judge admitted the newspaper as part of the records of the Selma Times–Journal. The sole error Dallas County specifies on appeal is the admission of the newspaper in evidence.

In the Anglo–American adversary system of law, courts usually will not admit evidence unless its accuracy and trustworthiness may be tested by cross-examination. Here, therefore, the plaintiff argues that the newspaper should not be admitted: "You cannot cross-examine a newspaper."[44] Of course, a newspaper article *is* hearsay, and in almost

44. This argument, a familiar one, rests on a misunderstanding of the origin and the nature of the hearsay rule. The rule is not an ancient principle of English law recog-

all circumstances is inadmissible. However, the law governing hearsay is somewhat less than pellucid.[45] And, as with most rules, the hearsay rule is not absolute; it is replete with exceptions. Witnesses die, documents are lost, deeds are destroyed, memories fade. All too often, primary evidence is not available and courts and lawyers must rely on secondary evidence.

* * *

We turn now to a case * * * in which the court used an approach we consider appropriate for the solution of the problem before us. G. & C. Merriam Co. v. Syndicate Pub. Co., 2nd Cir., 1913, 207 F. 515, 518, concerned a controversy between dictionary publishers over the use of the title "Webster's Dictionary" when the defendant's dictionary allegedly was not based upon Webster's dictionary at all. The bone of contention was whether a statement in the preface to the dictionary was admissible as evidence of the facts it recited. Ogilvie, the compiler of the dictionary, stated in his preface that he used Webster's Dictionary as the basis for his own publication. The dictionary, with its preface, was published in 1850, sixty-three years before the trial of the case. Ogilvie's published statement was challenged as hearsay. Judge Learned Hand, then a district judge, unable, as we are here, to find a case in point, for authority relied solely on Wigmore on Evidence (then a recent publication), particularly on Wigmore's analysis that "the requisites of an exception to the hearsay rule are necessity and circumstantial guaranty of trustworthiness." Wigmore on Evidence, §§ 1421, 1422, 1690 (1st ed. 1913). Applying these criteria, Judge Hand held that the statement was admissible as an exception to the hearsay rule:

nized at Runnymede. And, gone is its odor of sanctity.

Wigmore is often quoted for the statement that "cross-examination is beyond any doubt the greatest legal engine ever invented for the discovery of the truth". 5 Wigmore § 1367 (3d ed.). In over 1200 pages devoted to the hearsay rule, however, he makes it very clear that: "[T]he rule aims to insist on testing all statements by cross-examination, *if they can be.* * * * No one could defend a rule which pronounced that all statements thus untested are worthless; for all historical truth is based on uncross-examined assertion; and every day's experience of life gives denial to such an exaggeration. What the Hearsay Rule implies—and with profound verity—is that all testimonial assertions *ought to be* tested by cross-examination, as the best attainable measure; and it should not be burdened with the pedantic implication that they must be rejected as worthless if the test is unavailable." 1 Wigmore § 8c. In this connection see Falknor, *The Hearsay Rule and Its Exceptions,* 2 U.C.L.A.L.Rev. 43 (1954). * * *

45. "The fact is, then, that the law governing hearsay today is a conglomeration of inconsistencies, developed as a result of conflicting theories. Refinements and qualifications within the exceptions only add to its irrationality. The courts by multiplying exceptions reveal their conviction that relevant hearsay evidence normally has real probative value, and is capable of valuation by a jury as well as by other triers of fact. This is further demonstrated by the majority view that inadmissible hearsay received without objection may be sufficient to sustain a verdict. Most statutes regulating procedure before administrative tribunals make hearsay admissible. And it is by no means clear that the administrative official ordinarily presiding at a hearing has more competence to value testimony than has a jury acting under the supervision of a judge. The numbers of cases tried before juries as compared with the number tried before judges without juries and before administrative tribunals, is small indeed." ALI Model Code of Evidence, p. 223 (1942).

> "Ogilvie's preface is of course an unsworn statement and as such only hearsay testimony, which may be admitted only as an exception to the general rule. The question is whether there is such an exception. I have been unable to find any express authority in point and must decide the question upon principle. In the first place, I think it fair to insist that to reject such a statement is to refuse evidence about the truth of which no reasonable person should have any doubt whatever, because it fulfills both the requisites of an exception to the hearsay rule, necessity and circumstantial guaranty of trustworthiness. Wigmore, §§ 1421, 1422, 1690 * * *. Besides Ogilvie, everyone else is dead who ever knew anything about the matter and could intelligently tell us what the fact is. * * * As to the trustworthiness of the testimony, it has the guaranty of the occasion, at which there was no motive for fabrication." 207 F. 515, 518.

The Court of Appeals adopted the district court's opinion in its entirety.

The first of the two requisites is necessity. As to necessity, Wigmore points out this requisite means that unless the hearsay statement is admitted, the facts it brings out may otherwise be lost, either because the person whose assertion is offered may be dead or unavailable, or because the assertion is of such a nature that one could not expect to obtain evidence of the same value from the same person or from other sources. Wigmore, § 1421 (3d ed.).

The fire referred to in the newspaper account occurred fifty-eight years before the trial of this case. Any witness who saw that fire with sufficient understanding to observe it and describe it accurately, would have been older than a young child at the time of the fire. We may reasonably assume that at the time of the trial he was either dead or his faculties were dimmed by the passage of fifty-eight years. It would have been burdensome, but not impossible, for the defendant to have discovered the name of the author of the article (although it had no by-line) and, perhaps, to have found an eye-witness to the fire. But it is improbable—so it seems to us—that any witness could have been found whose recollection would have been accurate at the time of the trial of this case. And it seems impossible that the testimony of any witness would have been as accurate and as reliable as the statement of facts in the contemporary newspaper article.[46]

The rationale behind the "ancient documents" exception is applicable here: after a long lapse of time, ordinary evidence regarding signatures or handwriting is virtually unavailable, and it is therefore permis-

46. Cf. Rule 63(4) of the Uniform Rules of Evidence: "If the declarant is unavailable as a witness, a statement narrating, describing or explaining an event or condition which the judge finds was made by the declarant at a time when the matter had been recently perceived by him and while his recollection was clear, and was made in good faith prior to the commencement of the action [is admissible.]" Cf. also the Massachusetts Hearsay Act: "No declaration of a deceased person shall be excluded as evidence on the ground of its being hearsay if it appears to the satisfaction of the judge to have been made in good faith before the beginning of the suit and upon the personal knowledge of the declarant." Mass.Acts 1898, c. 535.

sible to resort to circumstantial evidence. Thus, in Trustees of German Township, Montgomery County v. Farmers & Citizens Savings Bank Co., Ohio Com.Pl.1953, 113 N.E.2d 409, 412, affirmed Ohio App., 115 N.E.2d 690, the court admitted as ancient documents newspapers eighty years old containing notices of advertisements for bids relating to the town hall: "Such exhibits, by reason of age, alone, and unquestioned authenticity, qualify as ancient documents." The ancient documents rule applies to documents a generation or more in age. Here, the Selma Times–Journal article is almost two generations old. The principle of necessity, not requiring absolute impossibility or total inaccessibility of first-hand knowledge, is satisfied by the practicalities of the situation before us.

The second requisite for admission of hearsay evidence is trustworthiness. According to Wigmore, there are three sets of circumstances when hearsay is trustworthy enough to serve as a practicable substitute for the ordinary test of cross-examination: "Where the circumstances are such that a sincere and accurate statement would naturally be uttered, and no plan of falsification be formed; where, even though a desire to falsify might present itself, other considerations, such as the danger of easy detection or the fear of punishment, would probably counteract its force; where the statement was made under such conditions of publicity that an error, if it had occurred, would probably have been detected and corrected." 5 Wigmore, Evidence § 1422 (3d ed.). These circumstances fit the instant case.

There is no procedural canon against the exercise of common sense in deciding the admissibility of hearsay evidence. In 1901 Selma, Alabama, was a small town. Taking a common sense view of this case, it is inconceivable to us that a newspaper reporter in a small town would report there was a fire in the dome of the new courthouse—if there had been no fire. He is without motive to falsify, and a false report would have subjected the newspaper and him to embarrassment in the community. The usual dangers inherent in hearsay evidence, such as lack of memory, faulty narration, intent to influence the court proceedings, and plain lack of truthfulness are not present here. To our minds, the article published in the Selma Morning–Times on the day of the fire is more reliable, more trustworthy, more competent evidence than the testimony of a witness called to the stand fifty-eight years later.

We hold, that in matters of local interest, when the fact in question is of such a public nature it would be generally known throughout the community, and when the questioned fact occurred so long ago that the testimony of an eye-witness would probably be less trustworthy than a contemporary newspaper account, a federal court, under Rule 43(a), may relax the exclusionary rules to the extent of admitting the newspaper article in evidence. We do not characterize this newspaper as a "business record", nor as an "ancient document", nor as any other readily identifiable and happily tagged species of hearsay exception. It is admissible because it is necessary and trustworthy, relevant and material, and its admission is within the trial judge's exercise of discretion in holding the hearing within reasonable bounds.

Judgment is affirmed.

BOHLER-UDDEHOLM AMERICA, INC. v. ELLWOOD GROUP, INC.

United States Court of Appeals, Third Circuit, 2001.
247 F.3d 79.

BECKER, Chief Judge.

This is an appeal by defendant Ellwood Group, Inc., (Ellwood) from a final judgment entered against it by the District Court for the Western District of Pennsylvania in favor of plaintiff Uddeholm Tooling AB (Uddeholm). This complicated commercial case emerges from the disintegration of a joint venture entered into by Ellwood, a Pennsylvania corporation in the business of forging steel ingots into various components of heavy machinery, and Uddeholm, a Swedish company that produces specialty tool steels. Uddeholm brought numerous claims against Ellwood, including breach of contract, breach of fiduciary duty, misappropriation of trade secrets, and civil conspiracy. Resolution of this appeal requires us to address a number of questions of Pennsylvania contract, business tort, and damages law, along with two questions on the application of the Federal Rules of Evidence.

[The portions of the opinion treating issues other than the admission of a hearsay statement have been omitted.]

EVIDENTIARY CHALLENGES

* * * We review the District Court's evidentiary rulings for abuse of discretion. *See Walden v. Georgia–Pacific Corp.,* 126 F.3d 506, 517 (3d Cir.1997).

The Jonsson affidavit

The District Court admitted into evidence portions of an affidavit of Bo Jonsson, a former President of Uddeholm, under Federal Rule of Evidence 807, the catchall exception to the hearsay rule. Jonsson attested to the affidavit in 1994 and died in 1996, before the trial. Uddeholm used the affidavit to counter assertions by Ellwood about what transpired at certain directors meetings that Jonsson attended in a representative capacity for Uddeholm. Rule 807 provides that

> [a] statement not specifically covered by Rule 803 or 804 but having equivalent circumstantial guarantees of trustworthiness, is not excluded by the hearsay rule, if the court determines that (A) the statement is offered as evidence of a material fact; (B) the statement is more probative on the point for which it is offered than any other evidence which the proponent can procure through reasonable efforts; and (C) the general purposes of these rules and the interests of justice will best be served by admission of the statement into evidence. However, a statement may not be admitted under this exception unless the proponent of it makes known to the adverse

party sufficiently in advance of the trial or hearing to provide the adverse party with a fair opportunity to prepare to meet it, the proponent's intention to offer the statement and the particulars of it, including the name and address of the declarant.

Ellwood argues that the District Court's admission of the Jonsson affidavit under Rule 807 was error, because Rule 807 is meant to be used only in the rare case, which, it argues, this is not. *See United States v. Bailey,* 581 F.2d 341, 347 (3d Cir.1978) (stating that the residual hearsay exception is "to be used only rarely, and in exceptional circumstances," and is meant to "apply only when certain exceptional guarantees of trustworthiness exist and when high degrees of probativeness and necessity are present").[47] Specifically, Ellwood takes issue with the District Court's findings that the Jonsson affidavit was exceptionally trustworthy and that it was more probative than any other evidence that Uddeholm could present.

While Ellwood is correct that Rule 807 should only be used in rare situations, the District Court made careful and extensive findings in support of its conclusion that this was such a situation. * * *. First, the District Court ascertained that the requirements of Rule 807 were met. The court specifically found that

- the affidavit was offered as evidence on a material fact, namely the parties' course of dealings, which bears upon the interpretation of the Agreement;
- the affidavit was more probative on the point for which it is offered than any other evidence which the proponent could procure through reasonable efforts: it was highly probative because Jonsson was the only representative of Uddeholm on the EUS board of directors at the time in question, and, as such, this evidence was the only evidence that Uddeholm could present to counter the Ellwood's allegation that Uddeholm understood the Agreement to permit sales to third parties and reimbursement for those sales;
- the general purpose of the rules, fairness and the administration of justice, would be served by admitting the affidavit, because it would assist the jury in determining the truth;
- there was sufficient notice to Ellwood that it would be used, as Uddeholm proffered the affidavit months prior to trial, and there was argument and briefs filed on the issue.

47. Before 1997, the residual hearsay exceptions in the Federal Rules of Evidence were contained in Rules 803(24) and 804(b)(5). In 1997 the Rules were amended and these two residual exceptions were combined and transferred to the new Rule 807. "This was done to facilitate additions to Rules 803 and 804. No change in meaning is intended." Fed.R.Evid. 807 advisory committee's note. *Bailey* addressed the old residual hearsay exceptions contained in Rules 803(24) and 804(b)(5), but because Rule 807 is simply the combination of these rules, *Bailey*'s holding applies to the current Rule 807 as well. The same is true of other pre–1997 cases on the residual hearsay exceptions that are cited in this Section.

The District Court found that the following factors also militated in favor of admitting the Jonsson affidavit:

- Ellwood had ways to rebut the affidavit: its witnesses were present at the meetings discussed therein, and these witnesses could present their testimony, while Uddeholm's only witness to these meetings (Jonsson) was dead;
- the affidavit was trustworthy because: (1) the declarant was known and named, (2) the statement was made under oath and penalty of perjury, (3) the declarant "was aware of the pending litigation at the time he made the declaration and thus knew that his assertions were subject to cross examination," (4) the statements were based on personal observation, (5) the declarant was not employed by the plaintiff at the time of the statements, and thus had no financial interest in the litigation's outcome, (6) the affidavit was corroborated, partially, by minutes of directors meetings (some statements Jonsson said were made match others' notations), and (7) his position and background qualified him to make the assertions.

The District Court then acknowledged that Rule 807 should only be used sparingly, but opined that this affidavit presented "a rather unique combination of circumstances where a material fact can be proved only through one method, or, in this case, rebutted by only one method." The court was also swayed by the fact that it was Ellwood that first argued that Uddeholm knew of Ellwood's interpretation of the Agreement because Jonsson must have gained this knowledge at the directors meetings; the only way Uddeholm could rebut this claim was via Jonsson's affidavit, given that he was not available to testify.

These findings are sufficient for us to hold that the District Court did not abuse its discretion when it admitted the Jonsson affidavit under Rule 807. In *Copperweld Steel Co. v. Demag–Mannesmann–Bohler,* 578 F.2d 953 (3d Cir.1978), this Court upheld a district court's admission of a similar item—a memorandum prepared by a lawyer of an executive who was later killed—on a weaker showing by the district court under the predecessor rule to Rule 807 (Rule 804(b)(5)). *See id.* at 964. We therefore hold that the admission of the Jonsson affidavit was not error.

Notes and Questions

1. *Trustworthiness factors.* Trustworthiness under the catchall exception involves the circumstances under which the declarant made the statements and his or her incentives to testify truthfully. The factors that may establish such trustworthiness are so varied that providing useful categorization is difficult, but some factors repeatedly found to be important are:

> whether the declarant had a motivation to speak truthfully or otherwise; the spontaneity of the statement, including whether it was elicited by leading questions, and generally the time lapse between event and statement; whether the statement was under oath; whether the declar-

ant was subject to cross-examination at the time the statement was made; the relationship between the declarant and the person to whom the statement was made; whether the declarant has recanted or reaffirmed the statement; whether the statement was recorded and particularly whether it was videotaped; and whether the declarant's firsthand knowledge is clearly demonstrated.

2 McCormick, Evidence § 324, at 405–07 (6th ed. 2006). See also 4 Saltzburg, Martin & Capra, Federal Rules of Evidence Manual § 807.02[4], at 807–7—807–9 (9th ed. 2006) (providing lengthy list of factors supporting trustworthiness). Whether the reliability of the report of the hearsay statement is an appropriate factor is subject to dispute between the circuits. Compare Huff v. White Motor Corp., 609 F.2d 286, 293 (7th Cir.1979) (inappropriate), and 2 McCormick, supra, at 407 (inappropriate), with United States v. Bailey, 581 F.2d 341, 349 (3d Cir.1978) (proper), and 4 Graham, Handbook of Federal Evidence § 807.1, at 642 (6th ed. 2006) (considering certainty that statement was made, including evaluation of in-court witness).

2. *Meaning of "not specifically covered"; Is a "near miss" bad or good for admissibility?* When a statement fails to meet the requirements of a hearsay exception, should that not mean it is excluded? On the other hand, when a statement is offered under the residual exception, one of its characteristics is that the statement is "not specifically covered by Rule 803 or 804." Should there be a difference in treatment depending on whether the statement appears to fall within a category governed by a specific rule but fails to qualify versus a statement that is unlike any of the specific exceptions? Is it a favorable factor for admission of a statement that fails to qualify that it just barely missed admission under one of the specific rules, or is the fact that it is a "near miss" a factor disqualifying the statement?

In a concurring opinion in United States v. Dent, 984 F.2d 1453, 1465 (7th Cir.1993), which concerned the admissibility of grand jury testimony, Judge Easterbrook argued that the language of the catchall "reads more naturally if we understand the introductory clause to mean that evidence of a kind specifically addressed ("covered") by one of the four other subsections must satisfy the conditions laid down for its admission, and that other kinds of evidence not covered (because the drafters could not be exhaustive) are admissible if the evidence is approximately as reliable as evidence that would be admissible under the specific subsections." That is not, however, the dominant position. See, e.g., United States v. Laster, 258 F.3d 525, 530 (6th Cir.2001) (rejecting exclusionary argument that had been suggested in an earlier opinion in the circuit); People v. Katt, 662 N.W.2d 12, 18–23 (Mich. 2003) (rejecting "near miss" exclusion after extensive discussion).

The term "near miss" is sometimes applied to the above argument or a slight extension of it. It is occasionally used by courts to deny admissibility under the catchall exception, but the predominant use is to provide support for admissibility. Courts have frequently found statements admissible where the statement narrowly misses qualifying under one of the specific exceptions, and the court determines by analogy, that the statement has substantial guarantees of trustworthiness, almost satisfying the "equivalent circumstantial guarantees of trustworthiness" requirement of the catchall. See United States v. Valdez–Soto, 31 F.3d 1467, 1471 (9th Cir.1994); State v.

Anderson, 695 N.W.2d 731, 749 (Wis.2005); 4 Graham, Handbook of Federal Evidence § 807.1, at 669 & n.30 (6th ed. 2006). A few courts have followed Judge Easterbrook's analysis and held that, where a specific exception is available and the evidence "misses" admission under its requirements, the residual exception should be rejected. See Acme Printing Ink Co. v. Menard, Inc., 812 F.Supp. 1498, 1527 (E.D.Wis.1992).

Is there at least a little possible common ground between these approaches when legislative intent of the drafters gives concrete indication that failure to satisfy a specific exception demonstrates a lack of trustworthiness? Compare United States v. Bailey, 581 F.2d 341, 349 n.12 (3d Cir.1978) (rejection by Congress of exception for statements of recent perception gives guidance as to whether similar statement has equivalent trustworthiness to other Rule 804(b) exceptions), with Robinson v. Shapiro, 646 F.2d 734, 742 n.6 (2d Cir.1981) (rejection of recent perception exception meant only that Congress was unwilling to admit all such statements, not a legislative intent to exclude any statements if offered under appropriate circumstances through the residual exception).

3. *Corroboration?* Can corroborating evidence establishing the accuracy of the statement be used to establish trustworthiness under the catchall rule? Idaho v. Wright, 497 U.S. 805 (1990), would appear to answer the question "no." While *Wright* decided an issue under the Confrontation Clause, see Chapter 13, Section C, supra, its conclusion that "particularized guarantees of trustworthiness" "include only those [circumstances] that surround the making of the statement and that render the declarant particularly worthy of belief" rested on "the rationale for permitting exceptions to the general rule against hearsay." *Id.* at 819. In *Wright*, the Supreme Court appeared to endorse not only a Confrontation Clause theory, but also a hearsay rationale, that excludes corroboration as a source of trustworthiness. 4 Graham, Handbook of Federal Evidence § 807.1, at 656 (6th ed. 2006); 2 McCormick, Evidence § 324, at 408 (6th ed. 2006). But see United States v. Valdez–Soto, 31 F.3d 1467, 1470–71 (9th Cir.1994) (corroborating evidence may be used to establish trustworthiness under the catchall hearsay exception where Confrontation Clause concern is satisfied by declarant's availability for cross-examination); United States v. McGrath, 39 M.J. 158, 165–67 (C.M.A.1994) (declining to construe *Wright* as excluding corroboration from hearsay analysis without further clarification by the Supreme Court).

4. *Impact of declarant's unavailability.* The catchall exception under Rule 807 covers both situations where the declarant is available (formerly 803(24)) and where he or she is unavailable (formerly 804(b)(5)). One clear difference between these situations is that an unavailable declarant cannot testify, which might in general suggest a greater likelihood to receive the hearsay because it is more "necessary." Courts have treated the significance of the declarant's availability in very different ways. Some have ruled that, with available declarants, the requirement that the statement be "more probative on the point for which it is offered than any other evidence which the proponent can procure through reasonable efforts" is difficult to meet because the available declarant could give live testimony as an alternative to the hearsay statement. See United States v. Mathis, 559 F.2d 294, 298–99 (5th Cir.1977); State v. Smith, 337 S.E.2d 833, 846 (N.C.1985). This concern

should not apply where the statement, as is often the case with the exceptions under Rule 803, is clearly superior in terms of its trustworthiness to the testimony of the declarant at the time of trial. The *Dallas County* case, presented at the beginning of this Section, provides an example of this latter situation. Other courts have taken a different tack and have concluded that, where the declarant is available and does testify, the required showing of trustworthiness is more easily met. See, e.g., United States v. Leslie, 542 F.2d 285, 290 (5th Cir.1976); United States v. Iaconetti, 406 F.Supp. 554, 559 (E.D.N.Y.), aff'd, 540 F.2d 574 (2d Cir.1976).

5. *Analyzing "necessity."* On the question of whether the hearsay statement satisfies the requirement of Rule 807(B)—that the statement must be more probative on the point than other available evidence—courts have used different methods of analysis. For example, in United States v. Simmons, 773 F.2d 1455, 1459 (4th Cir.1985), the court found the hearsay more probative than other available evidence by balancing the trustworthiness of the hearsay against the cost of alternative proof. It held that the government was not required to assemble witnesses from across the country to establish the state in which the weapons had been manufactured, given the likely accuracy of standard government "trace forms" completed by the manufacturer. In United States v. Welsh, 774 F.2d 670 (4th Cir.1985), the court held that the requirement is not met simply because an unavailable declarant is a more credible witness than the witness who would otherwise testify for the government. And in United States v. Vretta, 790 F.2d 651, 658–59 (7th Cir.1986), the court held that the statement may be more probative than other available evidence, even if some other nonhearsay evidence is available on the issue when the hearsay statements complete the picture of a pattern of conduct otherwise not established.

6. *Application to grand jury testimony.* Prior to the Supreme Court's decision in Crawford v. Washington, 541 U.S. 36 (2004), a number of courts had admitted grand jury testimony under the cathcall exception. See, e.g., United States v. Earles, 113 F.3d 796 (8th Cir.1997). Although *Crawford* does not change the hearsay analysis, it makes the hearsay analysis irrelevant because grand jury testimony is undeniably testimonial and therefore excluded by the Confrontation Clause.

7. *Children's cases.* Another general area where courts have rather liberally used the catchall exception involves the statements of children who are the victims of sexual offenses. Relying upon research that shows children are unlikely to fabricate claims of sexual abuse and corroborating circumstances, such as knowledge about anatomy and sexual functioning typically foreign to one of tender years, many courts have found the statements trustworthy. See, e.g., United States v. Dunford, 148 F.3d 385, 392–94 (4th Cir.1998); United States v. NB, 59 F.3d 771, 775–78 (8th Cir.1995); State v. McCafferty, 356 N.W.2d 159, 164 (S.D.1984). Whether the witness' availability should weigh heavily against admission is subject to some disagreement. Compare United States v. Cree, 778 F.2d 474, 478–79 (8th Cir.1985) (young child need not be unavailable and prosecution not required to call child as witness before testimony concerning sexual assault admissible under catchall exception), with State v. Fearing, 337 S.E.2d 551 (N.C.1985) (child must be unavailable before testimony meets requirement that it be more probative than other available evidence). *Crawford* will have an impact in cases of this

type, although statements by children are generally not as clearly testimonial.

About half the states have followed a different course and created a new exception for statements of youthful victims of sexual abuse where the statement is shown to bear indicia of trustworthiness. See, e.g., State v. Myatt, 697 P.2d 836 (Kan.1985). These statutes create for child abuse cases an exception that, like the catchall exception, allows the court to find trustworthiness from any available factor. See generally Mosteller, Remaking Confrontation Clause and Hearsay Doctrine Under the Challenge of Child Sexual Abuse Prosecutions, 1993 Ill.L.Rev. 691, 698–99.

8. *Admission not so rare.* As the two preceding notes suggest, the drafters' admonition that the residual hearsay exceptions should "be used very rarely, and only in exceptional circumstances" has not been followed. Evidence is rather frequently admitted under the catchall exceptions in federal litigation, and they have been used more heavily in criminal than in civil cases. Raeder, The Effect of the Catchalls on Criminal Defendants: Little Red Riding Hood Meets the Hearsay Wolf and Is Devoured, 25 Loy.L.A.L.Rev. 925, 933–34 (1992).

9. *Notice requirement.* Rule 807 requires that the proponent of the evidence provide notice to the adverse party of the particulars of the statement and the identity of the declarant to allow a fair opportunity to meet the statement. Generally, courts have interpreted this notice requirement flexibly. See, e.g., Furtado v. Bishop, 604 F.2d 80, 92 (1st Cir.1979). However, courts have occasionally demanded strict compliance with the notice requirement. See United States v. Ruffin, 575 F.2d 346, 358 (2d Cir.1978). See generally Grant, The Pre–Trial Notice Requirement of Federal Rule of Evidence 803(24), 36 Drake L.Rev. 91 (1986–87).

10. *Sources.* Beaver, The Residual Hearsay Exception Reconsidered, 20 Fla.St.U.L.Rev. 787 (1993); Black, Federal Rules of Evidence 803(24) & 804(b)(5)—The Residual Exceptions—An Overview, 25 Hous.L.Rev. 13 (1988); Fenner, The Residual Exception to the Hearsay Rule: The Complete Treatment, 33 Creighton L.Rev. 265 (2000); Lewis, The Residual Exception to the Hearsay Rule: Shuffling the Wild Cards, 15 Rut.–Cam.L.J. 101 (1983); Nance, The Wisdom of *Dallas County*, in Evidence Stories 307 (Lempert ed., 2006); Raeder, The Hearsay Rule at Work: Has It Been Abolished De Facto by Judicial Discretion, 76 Minn.L.Rev. 507 (1992); Rand, The Residual Exceptions to the Federal Hearsay Rule: The Futile and Misguided Attempt to Restrain Judicial Discretion, 80 Geo.L.J. 873 (1992); Sonenshein, The Residual Exception to the Federal Hearsay Rule: Two Exceptions in Search of a Rule, 57 N.Y.U.L.Rev. 867 (1982).

SECTION M. NOTES ON OTHER SELECTED EXCEPTIONS AND MISCELLANEOUS PROVISIONS

Notes and Questions on Federal Rules 803(16), (18) & (22)

A number of other hearsay exceptions are defined under Rules 803 and 804 besides those discussed above. These include:

1. *Ancient Documents* (Rule 803(16)). This exception permits the admission of documents that have been in existence twenty years or more. Traditionally, the ancient document doctrine established only authenticity and did not constitute a hearsay exception. See, e.g., Town of Ninety Six v. Southern Ry., 267 F.2d 579 (4th Cir.1959), Chapter 11, Section A, supra. The rationale for the hearsay exception is somewhat related to the authentication theory. As to both, it is unlikely that witnesses will be available or will reliably recall the events recorded. Trustworthiness is supplied by the requirements that the statement must be in writing and that it must have been created years earlier, presumably long before the beginning of litigation. See generally 2 McCormick, Evidence § 323 (6th ed. 2006).

2. *Learned Treatises* (Rule 803(18)). This exception adopts the position long advocated by many of the major commentators that learned treatises should be admissible substantively and should not be limited to use for impeachment purposes. 6 Wigmore on Evidence §§ 1690–92 (Chadbourn rev. 1976).

The Rule requires that the treatise be established as a "reliable authority." This can be done by the expert's reliance on the treatise during direct examination or, when used in the cross-examination of the expert, by that witness' admission, the testimony of another expert, or judicial notice. In order to reduce the possibility of over-valuing or misunderstanding the treatise, the Rule permits the treatise only to be read to the jury and not to be received as an exhibit. See generally 2 McCormick, Evidence § 321 (6th ed. 2006). In addition to "published treatises, periodicals, or pamphlets," the learned treatise exception may also encompass videotapes prepared by authoritative sources. Constantino v. Herzog, 203 F.3d 164, 170–73 (2d Cir. 2000). Note that while the Federal Rules permit learned treatises to be used, not only to impeach an expert's testimony, but also to be admitted for their truth as an exception to the hearsay rule, some states continue to limit their use to affect credibility, either for impeachment, see Michigan Evidence Rule 707, or to support the opinion of the expert, see Aldridge v. Edmunds, 750 A.2d 292, 296–98 (Pa.2000). See also Chapter 12, Section E(10) (discussion in connection with *Freshwater v. Scheidt*).

3. *Judgment of Felony Conviction* (Rule 803(22)). The Rule permits the admission of a conviction for a crime punishable by imprisonment of more than a year to prove any fact essential to the judgment. Limiting the Rule to crimes carrying a potential punishment of felony grade is intended to exclude from the Rule's operation minor offenses where the motivation to defend is "often minimal or nonexistent." Advisory Committee Note to Rule 803(22). The Rule only authorizes the conviction to be admitted as an item of evidence and does not accord it binding effect. Furthermore, in order to avoid conflict with the Confrontation Clause, Rule 803(22) prohibits use of the conviction of a third party to establish a fact against a criminal defendant.

Notes and Questions on Rules 805 & 806

Rules 805 and 806 map out an important procedural framework for certain aspects of the application of the hearsay rules.

1. *Rule 805—Double hearsay.* Rule 805 makes explicit the unassailable position that, where a statement that is itself hearsay contains another hearsay statement, the entire statement may be admitted if both parts of it are admissible because they either satisfy a hearsay exception or they are excluded from the hearsay rule, as are admissions of parties and prior inconsistent statements used for impeachment purposes. See, e.g., Wright v. Farmers Co–Op, 681 F.2d 549 (8th Cir.1982) (statement of employee admissible as admission of party's agent and document containing it admissible as business record of insurance adjuster who secured the statement). See also discussion in Section E, supra, following the *Yates* case.

2. *Rule 806—Practical difficulties of impeaching "virtual" witness.* Rule 806 permits the opponent of a hearsay statement to attack the credibility of its declarant to the same extent as would have been permitted if the declarant had testified at trial. The opponent also may call the declarant to the stand and examine him or her concerning the statement in the manner permitted during cross-examination. A difficulty with the Rule in practice arises when the government introduces the statements of codefendants as statements of coconspirators. Can one defendant impeach the testimony offered by the non-testifying codefendant by offering his prior convictions? Compare United States v. Bovain, 708 F.2d 606 (11th Cir.1983) (giving affirmative answer), with United States v. Robinson, 783 F.2d 64 (7th Cir.1986) (sustaining trial court's exercise of discretion against permitting impeachment). Similarly, how is the prohibition in Rule 608(b) against use of extrinsic evidence affected when the hearsay declarant is unavailable and therefore cannot be asked about the "bad act" on cross-examination? See United States v. Saada, 212 F.3d 210, 221 (3d Cir.2000) (ruling that the prohibition is not modified by Rule 806 but finding a conflict between the circuits). See generally Condray, Evidence Rule 806 and the Problem of Impeaching the Nontestifying Declarant, 56 Ohio St.L.J. 495 (1995); Douglass, Virtual Cross–Examination: The Art of Impeaching Hearsay, 34 J.Mar.L. & Com. 149 (2003); Douglass, Beyond Admissibility: Real Confrontation, Virtual Cross–Examination, and the Right to Confront Hearsay, 67 Geo.Wash.L.Rev.191 (1999); Sonenshein, Impeaching the Hearsay Declarant, 74 Temp.L.Rev. 163 (2001).

3. *Rule 806—Implications of the impeachment rationale.* Rule 806 treats the declarant as a witness when a hearsay statement is admitted. If the statement is not admitted for its truth, such as to explain why the person hearing the statement took an action, impeachment of the declarant is not appropriate. See United States v. Arthur Andersen, LLP, 374 F.3d 281, 292 (5th Cir.2004). Conversely, use of prior testimonial statements for the limited purpose of impeaching the declarant under Rule 806 should constitute an exception to the Confrontation Clause under Crawford v. Washington, 541 U.S. 36, 59 n.9 (2004) (recognizing an exception to the confrontation right when statements are not admitted for their truth); Le v. State, 913 So.2d 913, 940–43 (Miss.2005) (applying this principle).

Topic VI
PRIVILEGE

Chapter 15[1]

PRIVATE PRIVILEGES

SECTION A. INTRODUCTION

STATE v. 62.96247 ACRES OF LAND

Superior Court of Delaware, 1963.
193 A.2d 799.

LYNCH, JUDGE.

* * *

There are many exclusionary rules of evidence that are intended to withhold evidence which is regarded as unreliable or regarded as prejudicial or misleading, but rules of privileged communications have no such purpose. Such rules of privilege preclude the consideration of competent evidence which could aid in determining the outcome of a case, and privilege in no way can be justified as a means of promoting a fair settlement of disputes.

Privileges have been traced to the Roman law, where the basis for exclusion was the general moral duty not to violate the underlying fidelity upon which the protected relation was built.[2]

At early common law, the obligations of honor among gentlemen were advanced as the basis for maintaining silence[3], however, in 1776 the House of Lords made it clear that the communicant was the holder of the privilege and the policy was to protect his interests.[4] Some courts

1. Throughout this chapter some footnotes from the cases and materials have been omitted; others have been renumbered. [Ed.]

2. Radin, The Privilege of Confidential Communication Between Lawyer and Client, 16 Calif.L.Rev. 487 (1928).

It was written long ago, Gospel of St. Matthew, Chap. 6, 24th verse:

"No man can serve two masters; for either he will hate the one, and love the other; or else he will hold to the one, and despise the other. * * * "

3. 8 Wigmore, Evidence, § 2286 (3d Ed. 1940).

4. Duchess of Kingston's Case, 20 How. St.Tr. 586; Notable British Trial Series (Melville ed. 1927); see also City and County of San Francisco v. Superior Court, 37 Cal.2d 227, 231 P.2d 26, 25 A.L.R.2d 1418 (1951) (to preclude the humiliation of the patient that might follow disclosure of his ailments); Woernley v. Electromatic Typewriters, 271 N.Y. 228, 2 N.E.2d 638 (1936) (to prevent the physician from disclosing information which might result in humilia-

have justified a particular privilege in the interest of justice,[5] public health[6] or some similar goal.[7]

Thus, the duty of the confidant of nondisclosure of confidential communications is imposed to protect the reliance interest of the communicant, with an assent of the community. This reliance interest is protected because such protection will encourage certain communications. Encouraging these communications is desirable because the communications are necessary for the maintenance of certain relationships. It is socially desirable to foster the protected relationships because other beneficial results are achieved, such as the promotion of justice, public health and social stability. These goals are promoted in furtherance of a well-organized, peaceful society, which in turn is considered necessary for human survival.

Note and Questions

The foregoing statement is a succinct summarization of the generally accepted concept underlying the recognition of relational privileges in the present day. It is a concept that has proved strongly attractive to American legislators (though somewhat less to American judges) and a greater or lesser number of privileges adorn the statute books of every state.

How effective is an evidentiary privilege likely to be in promoting the types of confidences that society deems desirable? It is doubtful whether anyone can, or at least should, feel confident in answering this question since a satisfactory answer is arguably discoverable only through the use of empirical research techniques that have only begun to be applied to the problem. In the face of this uncertainty might it be argued that at least some of the currently widely recognized privileges actually should be viewed as resting on some other alternative basis?

The Federal Rules of Evidence, as proposed by the Supreme Court, Prop. Fed.R.Evid., 56 F.R.D. 183 (1973), contained a set of rules on privilege that attempted to codify several well-entrenched common law privileges while rejecting others either that were fixtures of the common law or of the statutory schemes of most states. Specifically, the proposed rules codified the private privileges concerning communications between attorney and client, psychotherapist and patient, spousal testimony, and to clergy, as well as

tion, embarrassment, or disgrace to the patient); Annesley v. Earl of Anglesea, 17 How.St.Tr. 1139, 1225 (1743) (inability of client to carry on his own legal business).

5. Anderson v. Bank of British Columbia, 2 Ch.D. 644 (1876); Greenough v. Gaskell, 1 Myl. & K. 98, 103 (1833) ("But it is out of regard to the interests of justice, which cannot be upholden, and to the administration of justice, which cannot go on without the aid of men skilled in jurisprudence * * * .")

6. "To open the door to the disclosure of secrets revealed on the sickbed, or when consulting a physician, would destroy confidence between the physician and the patient, and, it is easy to see, might tend very much to prevent the advantages and benefits which flow from this confidential relationship." Edington v. Mutual Life Ins. Co., 67 N.Y. 185, 194 (1876) [sic].

7. "* * * the reason of the rule for excluding the confidences between husband and wife * * * is found to rest in that public policy that seeks to preserve inviolate the peace, good order, and limitless confidence between the heads of the family circle so necessary to every well-ordered civilized society." Mercer v. State, 40 Fla. 216, 227, 24 So. 154, 157 (1898).

several privileges concerning governmental activities. Glaringly absent from the proposed rules were privileges for marital communications and for communications generally between physicians and patients. Congress ultimately rejected the codification and substituted current Rule 501, which leaves the development of privileges either to the federal common law, or, where state law supplies the rule of decision, to state law.

Among the many criticisms of the privilege rules proposed by the Supreme Court were those directed to the elimination of the privileges referred to above. As part of his criticism of the Supreme Court proposals, one prominent legal academic set forth a rationale for privileges significantly different from the traditional one:

BLACK, THE MARITAL AND PHYSICIAN PRIVILEGES—A REPRINT OF A LETTER TO A CONGRESSMAN[8]

1975 Duke Law Journal 45, 48, 49–50.

Let me first consider the near-elimination of the marital-confidentiality privilege (Rule 505). There remains a narrow privilege in proceedings where one spouse is a criminal defendant. Aside from this, the meaning of the Rule (made entirely clear in the Advisory Committee's comments) is that, however intimate, however private, however embarrassing may be a disclosure by one spouse to another, or some fact discovered, within the privacies of marriage, by one spouse about another, that disclosure or fact can be wrung from the spouse under penalty of being held in contempt of court, if it is thought barely relevant to the issues in anybody's lawsuit for breach of a contract to sell a carload of apples. It ought to be enough to say of such a rule that it could easily–even often–force any decent person–anybody any of us would want to associate with–either to lie or to go to jail. No rule can be good that has that consequence–that compels the decent and honorable to evade or to disobey it. It seems clear to me that this Rule trenches on the area of marital privacy so staunchly defended by the Supreme Court, and especially by the late Mr. Justice Harlan's concurrence in *Griswold v. Connecticut*, [381 U.S. 479 (1965)]; certainly it is arguable that it does so. Even if *Griswold* had never been decided, it would be an entirely viable contention that the "scheme of ordered liberty," sanctioned in much earlier cases, forbade this nearly complete destruction of the privacy of marriage, in the interest of the conduct of ordinary litigation.

* * *

Hardly less grave is the invasion of central human privacy involved in the root-and-branch abolition of the physician-patient privilege. The question here is not only whether people might be discouraged from making full communication to physicians, though it seems flatly impossible that this would not sometimes happen–a consideration which would in itself be enough to make incomprehensible the absolute subordination

8. Copyright © 1975 Duke Law Journal. Reprinted by permission. [Ed.]

of this privacy interest to any trivial interest arising in litigation. But evaluation of a rule like this entails not only a guess as to what conduct it will motivate, but also an estimate of its intrinsic decency. All of us would consider it indecent for a doctor, in the course, say, of a television interview, or even a textbook, to tell all he knows, naming names, about patients who have been treated by him. Why does this judgment of decency altogether vanish from sight, sink to absolute zero, as soon as somebody files any kind of a non-demurrable complaint in a federal court? Here, again, can a rule be a good one when the ethical doctor *must* violate it, or hedge, or evade?

Note and Questions

Is Professor Black's articulation of a privacy rationale the only reasonable alternative to the utilitarian rationale set forth by Judge Lynch, above, that can be put forward as the basis for the law of evidentiary privileges? Consider the lively debate between the student editors of the Harvard Law Review, Comment, Developments in the Law—Privileged Communications, 98 Harv.L.Rev. 1450 (1985), and the authors of 23 Wright & Graham, Federal Practice and Procedure § 5422.1 (West 2000 Supp.).

For a thorough and thoughtful discussion of the various rationales for evidence privileges, see Imwinkelried, The New Wigmore: Evidentiary Privileges ch. 5 (2002). Professor Imwinkelried suggests a humanistic theory of privilege that emphasizes autonomy—the creation of privacy enclaves with particular types of consultants to enable the citizen to make more intelligent, independent life preference choices. Id. § 5.3.3.

Consider whether the comments of Professor Black apply to any or all of the privileges considered in this chapter. If such considerations are applicable to existing privileges, do they also suggest the creation of privileges not so commonly recognized such as communications between parents and children? How about communications between lovers or good friends?

Professor Black's argument assumes a compulsion to testify in a whole range of legal actions, including the most mundane. Should the same considerations apply in cases involving serious crime or devastating personal injury? Should the value of privilege, whether based on considerations of privacy, protection of a relationship or any other reason, be weighed against the particularized need in a particular litigation? What effect would such an uncertain privilege have on the considerations giving rise to the privilege?

SECTION B. HUSBAND–WIFE

TRAMMEL v. UNITED STATES

Supreme Court of the United States, 1980.
445 U.S. 40.

MR. CHIEF JUSTICE BURGER delivered the opinion of the Court.

We granted certiorari to consider whether an accused may invoke the privilege against adverse spousal testimony so as to exclude the

voluntary testimony of his wife. 440 U.S. 934 (1979). This calls for a re-examination of Hawkins v. United States, 358 U.S. 74 (1958).

I

On March 10, 1976, petitioner Otis Trammel was indicted with two others, Edwin Lee Roberts and Joseph Freeman, for importing heroin into the United States from Thailand and the Philippine Islands and for conspiracy to import heroin in violation of 21 U.S.C.A. §§ 952(a), 962(a), and 963. The indictment also named six unindicted co-conspirators, including petitioner's wife Elizabeth Ann Trammel.

According to the indictment, petitioner and his wife flew from the Philippines to California in August 1975, carrying with them a quantity of heroin. Freeman and Roberts assisted them in its distribution. Elizabeth Trammel then travelled to Thailand where she purchased another supply of the drug. On November 3, 1975, with four ounces of heroin on her person, she boarded a plane for the United States. During a routine customs search in Hawaii, she was searched, the heroin was discovered, and she was arrested. After discussions with Drug Enforcement Administration agents, she agreed to cooperate with the Government.

Prior to trial on this indictment, petitioner moved to sever his case from that of Roberts and Freeman. He advised the court that the Government intended to call his wife as an adverse witness and asserted his claim to a privilege to prevent her from testifying against him. At a hearing on the motion, Mrs. Trammel was called as a Government witness under a grant of use immunity. She testified that she and petitioner were married in May 1975 and that they remained married.[9] She explained that her cooperation with the Government was based on assurances that she would be given lenient treatment.[10] She then described, in considerable detail, her role and that of her husband in the heroin distribution conspiracy.

After hearing this testimony, the District Court ruled that Mrs. Trammel could testify in support of the Government's case to any act she observed during the marriage and to any communication "made in the presence of a third person"; however, confidential communications between petitioner and his wife were held to be privileged and inadmissible. The motion to sever was denied.

At trial, Elizabeth Trammel testified within the limits of the court's pretrial ruling; her testimony, as the Government concedes, constituted virtually its entire case against petitioner. He was found guilty on both the substantive and conspiracy charges and sentenced to an indeterminate term of years pursuant to the Federal Youth Corrections Act, 18 U.S.C.A. § 5010(b).

9. In response to the question whether divorce was contemplated, Mrs. Trammel testified that her husband had said that "I would go my way and he would go his." (App., at 27).

10. The Government represents to the Court that Elizabeth Trammel has not been prosecuted for her role in the conspiracy.

In the Court of Appeals petitioner's only claim of error was that the admission of the adverse testimony of his wife, over his objection, contravened this Court's teaching in Hawkins v. United States, 358 U.S. 74 (1958), and therefore constituted reversible error. The Court of Appeals rejected this contention. It concluded that *Hawkins* did not prohibit "the voluntary testimony of a spouse who appears as an unindicted co-conspirator under grant of immunity from the Government in return for her testimony." 583 F.2d 1166, 1168 (C.A.10 1978).

II

The privilege claimed by petitioner has ancient roots. Writing in 1628, Lord Coke observed that "it hath been resolved by the Justices that a wife cannot be produced either against or for her husband." 1 Coke, A Commentarie upon Littleton 6b (1628). See, generally, 8 J. Wigmore, Evidence § 2227, (McNaughton rev. 1961). This spousal disqualification sprang from two canons of medieval jurisprudence: first, the rule that an accused was not permitted to testify in his own behalf because of his interest in the proceeding; second, the concept that husband and wife were one, and that since the woman had no recognized separate legal existence, the husband was that one. From those two now long-abandoned doctrines, it followed that what was inadmissible from the lips of the defendant-husband was also inadmissible from his wife.

Despite its medieval origins, this rule of spousal disqualification remained intact in most common-law jurisdictions well into the 19th century. See 8 Wigmore, § 2333. It was applied by this Court in Stein v. Bowman, 10 L.Ed. 129, 13 Pet. 209, 220–223 (1839), in Graves v. United States, 150 U.S. 118 (1893), and again in Jin Fuey Moy v. United States, 254 U.S. 189, 195 (1920), where it was deemed so well established a proposition as to "hardly requir[e] mention." Indeed, it was not until 1933, in Funk v. United States, 290 U.S. 371, that this Court abolished the testimonial disqualification in the federal courts, so as to permit the spouse of a defendant to testify in the defendant's behalf. *Funk*, however, left undisturbed the rule that either spouse could prevent the other from giving adverse testimony. Id., at 373. The rule thus evolved into one of privilege rather than one of absolute disqualification. See J. Maguire, Evidence, Common Sense and Common Law, at 78–92 (1947).

The modern justification for this privilege against adverse spousal testimony is its perceived role in fostering the harmony and sanctity of the marriage relationship. Notwithstanding this benign purpose, the rule was sharply criticized. Professor Wigmore termed it "the merest anachronism in legal theory and an indefensible obstruction to truth in practice." 8 Wigmore, § 2228, at 221. The Committee on the Improvement of the Law of Evidence of the American Bar Association called for its abolition. 63 American Bar Association Reports, at 594–595 (1938). In its place, Wigmore and others suggested a privilege protecting only private marital communications, modeled on the privilege between priest and penitent, attorney and client, and physician and patient. See 8 Wigmore, § 2332 et seq.[11]

These criticisms influenced the American Law Institute, which, in its 1942 Model Code of Evidence advocated a privilege for marital confidences, but expressly rejected a rule vesting in the defendant the right to exclude all adverse testimony of his spouse. See American Law Institute, Model Code of Evidence, Rule 215 (1942). In 1953 the Uniform Rules of Evidence, drafted by the National Conference of Commissioners on Uniform State Laws, followed a similar course; it limited the privilege to confidential communications and "abolishe[d] the rule, still existing in some states, and largely a sentimental relic, of not requiring one spouse to testify against the other in a criminal action." See Rule 23(2) and comments. Several state legislatures enacted similarly patterned provisions into law.

Hawkins

In Hawkins v. United States, 358 U.S. 74 (1958), this Court considered the continued vitality of the privilege against adverse spousal testimony in the federal courts. There the District Court had permitted petitioner's wife, over his objection, to testify against him. With one questioning concurring opinion, the Court held the wife's testimony inadmissible; it took note of the critical comments that the common-law rule had engendered, id., at 76, and n.4, but chose not to abandon it. Also rejected was the Government's suggestion that the Court modify the privilege by vesting it in the witness spouse, with freedom to testify or not independent of the defendant's control. The Court viewed this proposed modification as antithetical to the widespread belief, evidenced in the rules then in effect in a majority of the States and in England, "that the law should not force or encourage testimony which might alienate husband and wife, or further inflame existing domestic differences." Id., at 79.

Hawkins, then, left the federal privilege for adverse spousal testimony where it found it, continuing "a rule which bars the testimony of one spouse against the other unless both consent." Id., at 78. Accord, Wyatt v. United States, 362 U.S. 525, 528 (1960).[12] However, in so doing, the Court made clear that its decision was not meant to "foreclose whatever

11. This Court recognized just such a confidential marital communications privilege in Wolfle v. United States, 291 U.S. 7 (1934), and in Blau v. United States, 340 U.S. 332 (1951). In neither case, however, did the Court adopt the Wigmore view that the communications privilege be substituted *in place of* the privilege against adverse spousal testimony. The privilege as to confidential marital communications is not at issue in the instant case; accordingly, our holding today does not disturb *Wolfle* and *Blau.*

12. The decision in *Wyatt* recognized an exception to *Hawkins* for cases in which one spouse commits a crime against the other. 362 U.S., at 526. This exception, placed on the ground of necessity, was a longstanding one at common law. See *Lord Audley's Case,* 123 Eng.Rep. 1140 (1931); 8 Wigmore § 2239. It has been expanded since then to include crimes against the spouse's property, see Herman v. United States, 220 F.2d 219, 226 (C.A.4 1955), and in recent years crimes against children of either spouse, United States v. Allery, 526 F.2d 1362 (C.A.8 1975). Similar exceptions have been found to the confidential marital communications privilege. See 8 Wigmore, § 2338.

changes in the rule may eventually be dictated by 'reason and experience.' " 358 U.S., at 79.

III

A

The Federal Rules of Evidence acknowledge the authority of the federal courts to continue the evolutionary development of testimonial privileges in federal criminal trials "governed by the principles of the common law as they may be interpreted * * * in the light of reason and experience." Fed.Rule Evid. 501. Cf. Wolfle v. United States, supra, 291 U.S., at 12 (1934). The general mandate of Rule 501 was substituted by the Congress for a set of privilege rules drafted by the Judicial Conference Advisory Committee on Rules of Evidence and approved by the Judicial Conference of the United States and by this Court. That proposal defined nine specific privileges, including a husband-wife privilege which would have codified the *Hawkins* rule and eliminated the privilege for confidential marital communications. See Fed.Rule of Evid., Proposed Rule 505. In rejecting the proposed rules and enacting Rule 501, Congress manifested an affirmative intention not to freeze the law of privilege. Its purpose rather was to "provide the courts with the flexibility to develop rules of privilege on a case-by-case basis," 120 Cong.Rec. 40891 (1974) (statement of Rep. Hungate), and to leave the door open to change. See also S.Rep. No. 93–1277, 93d Cong., 2d Sess., 11 (1974); H.R.Rep. No. 93–650, 93d Cong., 1st Sess., 8 (1973),[13] U.S.Code Cong. & Admin.News 1974, p. 7051.

Although Rule 501 confirms the authority of the federal courts to reconsider the continued validity of the *Hawkins* rule, the long history of the privilege suggests that it ought not to be casually cast aside. That the privilege is one affecting marriage, home, and family relationships—already subject to much erosion in our day—also counsels caution. At the same time we cannot escape the reality that the law on occasion adheres to doctrinal concepts long after the reasons which gave them birth have disappeared and after experience suggests the need for change. This was recognized in *Funk* where the Court "decline[d] to enforce * * * ancient rule[s] of the common law under conditions as they now exist." 290 U.S., at 382. For, as Mr. Justice Black admonished in another setting, "[w]hen precedent and precedent alone is all the argument that can be made to support a court-fashioned rule, it is time for the rule's creator to destroy it." Francis v. Southern Pacific Co., 333 U.S. 445, 471 (1948) (Black, J., dissenting).

13. Petitioner's reliance on 28 U.S.C.A. § 2076 for the proposition that this Court is without power to reconsider *Hawkins* is ill founded. That provision limits this Court's *statutory* rulemaking authority by providing that rules "creating, abolishing, or modifying a privilege shall have no force or effect unless * * * approved by act of Congress." It was enacted principally to insure that state rules of privilege would apply in diversity jurisdiction cases unless Congress authorized otherwise. In Rule 501 Congress makes clear that § 2076 was not intended to prevent the federal courts from developing testimonial privilege law in federal criminal cases on a case-by-case basis "in light of reason and experience"; indeed Congress encouraged such development.

B

Since 1958, when *Hawkins* was decided, support for the privilege against adverse spousal testimony has been eroded further. Thirty-one jurisdictions, including Alaska and Hawaii, then allowed an accused a privilege to prevent adverse spousal testimony. 358 U.S., at 81, n.3, (Stewart, J., concurring). The number has now declined to 24.[14] In 1974, the National Conference on Uniform States Laws revised its Uniform Rules of Evidence, but again rejected the *Hawkins* rule in favor of a limited privilege for confidential communications. See Uniform Rules of Evidence, Rule 504. That proposed rule has been enacted in Arkansas, North Dakota, and Oklahoma—each of which in 1958 permitted an accused to exclude adverse spousal testimony.[15] The trend in state law toward divesting the accused of the privilege to bar adverse spousal testimony has special relevance because the law of marriage and domestic relations are concerns traditionally reserved to the states. See Sosna v. Iowa, 419 U.S. 393, 404 (1975). Scholarly criticism of the *Hawkins* rule has also continued unabated.

C

Testimonial exclusionary rules and privileges contravene the fundamental principle that "the public * * * has a right to every man's evidence." United States v. Bryan, 339 U.S. 323, 331 (1950). As such, they must be strictly construed and accepted "only to the very limited extent that permitting a refusal to testify or excluding relevant evidence has a public good transcending the normally predominant principle of utilizing all rational means for ascertaining truth." Elkins v. United States, 364 U.S. 206, 234 (1960) (Frankfurter, J., dissenting). Accord, United States v. Nixon, 418 U.S. 683, 709–710 (1974). Here we must decide whether the privilege against adverse spousal testimony promotes

14. Eight states provide that one spouse is incompetent to testify against the other in a criminal proceeding * * * . Sixteen states provide a privilege against adverse spousal testimony and vest the privilege in both spouses or in the defendant-spouse alone * * * . Nine states entitle the witness-spouse alone to assert a privilege against adverse spousal testimony * * * . The remaining 17 states have abolished the privilege in criminal cases * * * .

In 1901, Congress enacted a rule of evidence for the District of Columbia that made husband and wife "competent but not compellable to testify for or against each other," except as to confidential communications. This provision, which vests the privilege against adverse spousal testimony in the witness spouse, remains in effect.* * *

15. In 1965, California took the privilege from the defendant-spouse and vested it in the witness-spouse, accepting a study commission recommendation that the "latter [was] more likely than the former to determine whether or not to claim the privilege on the basis of the probable effect on the marital relationship." See Cal.Evid. Code §§ 970–973 and 1 California Law Revision Commission, Recommendation and Study relating to The Marital "For or Against" Testimonial Privilege at F–5 (1956). * * *

Support for the common-law rule has also diminished in England. In 1972 a study group there proposed giving the privilege to the witness-spouse, on the ground that "if [the wife] is willing to give evidence * * * the law would be showing excessive concern for the preservation of marital harmony if it were to say she must not do so." Criminal Law Revision Committee, Eleventh Report Evidence (General), at 93.

sufficiently important interests to outweigh the need for probative evidence in the administration of criminal justice.

It is essential to remember that the *Hawkins* privilege is not needed to protect information privately disclosed between husband and wife in the confidence of the marital relationship—once described by this Court as "the best solace of human existence." Stein v. Bowman, 13 Pet., at 223. Those confidences are privileged under the independent rule protecting confidential marital communications. Blau v. United States, 340 U.S. 332 (1951). The *Hawkins* privilege is invoked, not to exclude private marital communications, but rather to exclude evidence of criminal acts and of communications made in the presence of third persons.

No other testimonial privilege sweeps so broadly. The privileges between priest and penitent, attorney and client, and physician and patient limit protection to private communications. These privileges are rooted in the imperative need for confidence and trust. The priest-penitent privilege recognizes the human need to disclose to a spiritual counselor, in total and absolute confidence, what are believed to be flawed acts or thoughts and to receive priestly consolation and guidance in return. The lawyer-client privilege rests on the need for the advocate and counselor to know all that relates to the client's reasons for seeking representation if the professional mission is to be carried out. Similarly, the physician must know all that a patient can articulate in order to identify and to treat disease; barriers to full disclosure would impair diagnosis and treatment.

The *Hawkins* rule stands in marked contrast to these three privileges. Its protection is not limited to confidential communications; rather it permits an accused to exclude all adverse spousal testimony. As Jeremy Bentham observed more than a century and a half ago, such a privilege goes far beyond making "every man's house his castle," and permits a person to convert his house into "a den of thieves." 5 Rationale of Judicial Evidence 340 (1827). It "secures, to every man, one safe and unquestionable and ever ready accomplice for every imaginable crime." Id., at 338.

The ancient foundations for so sweeping a privilege have long since disappeared. Nowhere in the common-law world—indeed in any modern society—is a woman regarded as chattel or demeaned by denial of a separate legal identity and the dignity associated with recognition as a whole human being. Chip by chip, over the years those archaic notions have been cast aside so that "[n]o longer is the female destined solely for the home and the rearing of the family, and only the male for the marketplace and the world of ideas." Stanton v. Stanton, 421 U.S. 7, 14, 15 (1975).

The contemporary justification for affording an accused such a privilege is also unpersuasive. When one spouse is willing to testify against the other in a criminal proceeding—whatever the motivation—their relationship is almost certainly in disrepair; there is probably little in the way of marital harmony for the privilege to preserve. In these circumstances, a rule of evidence that permits an accused to prevent adverse spousal testimony seems far more likely to frustrate justice than to foster family peace.[16] Indeed, there is reason to believe that vesting the privilege in the accused could actually undermine the marital relationship. For example, in a case such as this the Government is unlikely to offer a wife immunity and lenient treatment if it knows that her husband can prevent her from giving adverse testimony. If the Government is dissuaded from making such an offer, the privilege can have the untoward effect of permitting one spouse to escape justice at the expense of the other. It hardly seems conducive to the preservation of the marital relation to place a wife in jeopardy solely by virtue of her husband's control over her testimony.

IV

Our consideration of the foundations for the privilege and its history satisfy us that "reason and experience" no longer justify so sweeping a rule as that found acceptable by the Court in *Hawkins*. Accordingly, we conclude that the existing rule should be modified so that the witness spouse alone has a privilege to refuse to testify adversely; the witness may be neither compelled to testify nor foreclosed from testifying. This modification—vesting the privilege in the witness spouse—furthers the important public interest in marital harmony without unduly burdening legitimate law enforcement needs.

Here, petitioner's spouse chose to testify against him. That she did so after a grant of immunity and assurances of lenient treatment does not render her testimony involuntary. Cf. Bordenkircher v. Hayes, 434 U.S. 357 (1978). Accordingly, the District Court and the Court of Appeals were correct in rejecting petitioner's claim of privilege, and the judgment of the Court of Appeals is affirmed.

Affirmed.

MR. JUSTICE STEWART, concurring in the judgment.

Although agreeing with much of what the Court has to say, I cannot join an opinion that implies that "reason and experience" have worked a vast change since the *Hawkins* case was decided in 1958. In that case the Court upheld the privilege of a defendant in a criminal case to prevent adverse spousal testimony, in an all-but-unanimous opinion, by Mr. Justice Black. Today the Court, in another all-but-unanimous opinion, obliterates that privilege because of the purported change in perception that "reason and experience" have wrought.

The fact of the matter is that the Court in this case simply accepts the very same arguments that the Court rejected when the Government

16. It is argued that abolishing the privilege will permit the Government to come between husband and wife, pitting one against the other. That, too, misses the mark. Neither *Hawkins,* nor any other privilege, prevents the Government from enlisting one spouse to give information concerning the other or to aid in the other's apprehension. It is only the spouse's testimony in the courtroom that is prohibited.

first made them in the *Hawkins* case in 1958. I thought those arguments were valid then, and I think so now.

The Court is correct when it says that "[t]he ancient foundations for so sweeping a privilege have long since disappeared." * * * But those foundations had disappeared well before 1958; their disappearance certainly did not occur in the few years that have elapsed between the *Hawkins* decision and this one. To paraphrase what Mr. Justice Jackson once said in another context, there is reason to believe that today's opinion of the Court will be of greater interest to students of human psychology than to students of law.

Notes and Questions

1. *"Marrying the witness into silence."* See also the English case of Hoskyn v. Metropolitan Police Comm'r, 2 W.L.R. 695 (H.L.(E.) 1978), where the House of Lords found a victim who had married the accused two days before trial was not compellable to testify. As illustrated by a case such as *Hoskyn*, the *Trammel* decision does not of itself render impossible the time-honored practice of "marrying the witness into silence." Should this practice be prevented and, if so, by what rule? Proposed Federal Rule 505, which would have codified the spousal testimony privilege, excepted matters occurring prior to marriage. See also United States v. Clark, 712 F.2d 299 (7th Cir.1983). Uniform Rule 504, dealing with the same privilege, contains no such limitation, and the holding of the *Clark* case has been rejected, at least in dicta, by the Seventh Circuit. See United States v. Byrd, 750 F.2d 585, 590 (7th Cir.1984); United States v. Lofton, 957 F.2d 476, 477 (7th Cir.1992). See also A.B. v. United States, 24 F.Supp.2d 488 (D.Md.1998) (noting that *Clark* has been relegated to the status of an isolated artifact by later Seventh Circuit cases). Should the rule be different if the marriage is a sham? See Osborne v. State, 623 P.2d 784 (Alaska 1981); Annot., 13 A.L.R.4th 1305.

2. *Requirement of a valid marriage.* Given the rationale for excluding adverse spousal testimony, should a valid marriage constitute a *sine qua non* of the privilege? Most courts have held that it should. See, e.g., United States v. Snyder, 707 F.2d 139 (5th Cir.1983); United States v. Lustig, 555 F.2d 737 (9th Cir.1977). By whom and by what standard should the existence of marriage be ascertained? See Chapter 1, supra.

3. *Exceptions.* Various exceptions exist to the spousal privilege. Some, but not all, courts recognize an exception where the spouses were joint participants in the crime. Compare United States v. Van Drunen, 501 F.2d 1393 (7th Cir.1974) (joint participants exception to privilege), with United States v. Ramos–Oseguera, 120 F.3d 1028 (9th Cir.1997) (no joint participants exception). Most jurisdictions provide that the privilege does not exist where one spouse is charged with a crime against the person or property of the other or against a child of either. See, e.g., United States v. Allery, 526 F.2d 1362 (8th Cir.1975).

4. *Scholarly debate.* Some commentators advocate abolition of the adverse spousal testimony privilege in its entirety. See Medine, The Adverse Testimony Privilege: Time to Dispose of a Sentimental Relic, 67 Or.L.Rev. 519 (1988). Others take an opposite tack, believing that the Court went too

far in *Trammel* in precluding the defendant/spouse from claiming the privilege. See Mullane, *Trammel v. United States*: Bad History, Bad Policy, and Bad Law, 47 Me.L.Rev. 105 (1995). Still others see the existence or nonexistence of the privilege as an important cultural statement of how our society views marriage and call for a continued study of the issue. See Regan, Spousal Privilege and the Meanings of Marriage, 81 Va.L.Rev. 2045 (1995). See also Ortiz, Making Marriage, 81 Va.L.Rev. 2157 (1995), and Williams, The Adverse Testimony Privilege, Inalienable Entitlements, and the "Internal Stance:" A Response to Professor Regan, 81 Va.L.Rev. 2167 (1995).

5. *The other privilege.* As indicated in *Trammel*, the spousal or testimonial privilege involved in that case is a very different rule from the rule that provides a privilege for confidential communications made during the marriage. The next case discusses that other privilege.

UNITED STATES v. ESTES

United States Court of Appeals, Second Circuit, 1986.
793 F.2d 465.

VAN GRAAFEILAND, CIRCUIT JUDGE:

Kenneth Estes appeals from a judgment of the United States District Court for the District of Vermont convicting him, after a jury trial before Judge Franklin S. Billings, Jr., of violating 18 U.S.C. § 1623 by testifying falsely before a grand jury concerning his involvement in a theft. For reasons hereafter assigned, we reverse the conviction and remand for a new trial.

Appellant's principal contention on appeal is that testimony of his former wife, Lydia, concerning confidential communications between them was introduced erroneously before both the grand jury and the trial jury. * * *

On February 23, 1982, the Purolator Armored Car Service, for whom appellant worked as a driver-guard, was the victim of a $55,000 theft. Appellant's estranged wife, Lydia, testified willingly before the grand jury and at trial that appellant returned home on the day of the theft carrying a motorcycle bag full of money. In response to Lydia's inquiry, appellant told her that he had taken the money from Purolator. Lydia also testified that she helped appellant count the money and hide a portion of it behind a stair panel. At a subsequent time, she "laundered" some of the money by exchanging small bills for larger ones.

Appellant contends that all of Lydia's testimony should have been excluded on the ground that it involved the disclosure of confidential communications between them. The district court rejected this contention, citing cases from other circuits which hold that "confidential marital communications concerning ongoing criminal activity are not protected by the privilege" and opining that this is likely to be the rule followed by the Second Circuit. * * * The district court's very statement of the rule shows, however, that it does not apply to the most damning testimony given by Lydia, viz., that appellant brought home a bag of money and told her that he had taken it from the Purolator truck.

At that time, the theft of the money had been completed and Lydia's involvement could be only as an accessory after the fact. *United States v. Barlow,* 470 F.2d 1245, 1249, 1252–53 (D.C.Cir.1972). Lydia could not become such an accessory until she knew that the theft had taken place. *Id.* at 1252; 18 U.S.C. 3. The communication to her of that knowledge was a necessary precursor to her involvement and therefore could not have been made as part of an ongoing joint criminal activity. Under the normal evidentiary rule applicable to confidential marital communications, this portion of Lydia's testimony should not have been admitted. *See Blau v. United States,* 340 U.S. 332 * * * (1951). To the extent that *United States v. Neal,* 743 F.2d 1441 (10th Cir.1984) * * * (1985), the case upon which the Government places main reliance, holds to the contrary, we decline to follow it.

* * *

Normally, the confidential communication privilege extends only to utterances and not to acts. *Pereira v. United States,* 347 U.S. 1, 6 * * * (1954); * * * Testimony concerning a spouse's conduct can be precluded upon the spouse's challenge only in the rare instances where the conduct was intended to convey a confidential message from the actor to the observer. *United States v. Mitchell,* 137 F.2d 1006, 1009 (2d Cir.), *aff'd on reh'g,* 138 F.2d 831 (1943); * * * *United States v. Lewis,* 433 F.2d 1146, 1150–51 (D.C. Cir.1970) (per curiam). The counting, hiding and laundering of the money conveyed no confidential message from appellant to Lydia. Acts do not become privileged communications simply because they are performed in the presence of the actor's spouse. *United States v. Lustig,* 555 F.2d 737, 748 n.13 (9th Cir.1977). "Nor does it appear that the essential qualities of communication and confidentiality flow automatically from the fact that the act seen by the other spouse is one that connotes criminal conduct." *United States v. Lewis, supra,* 433 F.2d at 1151. Lydia's testimony concerning the handling and disposition of the money, much of which was done by Lydia herself, was properly heard by both the grand and petit juries.

Assuming for the argument that one or more of appellant's acts which followed the original disclosure of his theft might be construed as additional confidential communications of wrongdoing, we agree with so much of the opinion in *United States v. Neal, supra,* 743 F.2d at 1446–47, as would support the district court's holding that Lydia's testimony concerning those acts was admissible as evidence of joint criminal activity. There are a number of cases, including *In re Grand Jury Subpoena United States,* 755 F.2d 1022 (2d Cir.1985) * * *, which refuse to apply the "partnership in crime" exception to the marital testimonial privilege. However, because an accused cannot invoke marital testimonial privilege to prevent his or her spouse from testifying, *Trammel v. United States,* 445 U.S. 40 * * * (1980), those cases have little precedential significance where the spouse chooses to testify voluntarily. Although an accused does have the right to object to spousal testimony which violates confidential communications privilege, a number of circuits, in addition to the Tenth Circuit which decided *United States v. Neal, supra,* refuse to recognize that right where the testimony is not given under compulsion and the communications in question were made in furtherance of unlawful joint criminal activity. *See, e.g., United States v. Sims,* 755 F.2d 1239, 1240–43 (6th Cir.1985) * * * . Indeed, our own decision in *In re Grand Jury Subpoena United States, supra,* suggests that a joint participation exception makes sense in the context of the marital confidential communications privilege. 755 F.2d at 1027.

There is sound reasoning behind these holdings. As we stated in *In re Grand Jury Subpoena United States, supra,* 755 F.2d 1022, public policy may militate against subjecting a marriage to the possible disruptive influence of compelled adverse spousal testimony. However, testimonial privileges "must be strictly construed and accepted 'only to the very limited extent that permitting a refusal to testify or excluding relevant evidence has a public good transcending the normally predominant principle of utilizing all rational means for ascertaining truth.' " *Trammel v. United States, supra,* 445 U.S. at 50 * * * (quoting *Elkins v. United States,* 364 U.S. 206, 234 * * * (1960) (Frankfurter, J., dissenting)). The above-cited courts which recognize the "partnership in crime" exception to the confidential communication privilege believe that greater public good will result from permitting the spouse of an accused to testify willingly concerning their joint criminal activities than would come from permitting the accused to erect a roadblock against the search for truth. We agree.

For all the reasons above stated, we hold that Lydia's testimony concerning appellant's initial disclosure of his theft should not have been admitted but that it was not error to admit the balance of Lydia's testimony dealing with the handling and disposition of the stolen money.

* * *

The judgment of conviction is reversed and the matter is remanded to the district court with instructions to grant appellant a new trial.

Notes and Questions

1. *Difference from spousal testimony privilege.* In what respects does the privilege applied in the principal case differ from that recognized in *Trammel v. United States*? Would a *Trammel*-type privilege have been of any value to the defendant in the principal case?

2. *Acts as communications.* As to whether acts performed by one spouse come within the scope of a "communications" privilege, compare the holding of the principal case with Shepherd v. State, 277 N.E.2d 165 (Ind.1971) (communication privilege applicable to husband's observation of defendant's driving a car). Many courts support the more expansive view reflected in cases such as *Shepherd.* 1 McCormick, Evidence § 79 (6th ed. 2006). Cases are collected in Annot., 10 A.L.R.2d 1389. Even in jurisdictions limiting the privilege to communications rather than acts, certain acts without words may be viewed as communications. See, e.g., United States v. Bahe, 128 F.3d 1440 (10th Cir.1997).

3. *Confidentiality.* In what instances will communications between spouses possess the confidentiality universally required for application of the communications privilege? It is often stated that inter-spousal communications are "assumed" to be confidential, Wolfle v. United States, 291 U.S. 7 (1934), but it is clear from the decisions that a variety of factual patterns, if present, will destroy the presumption. Thus threats to harm or kill the spouse if he or she "talks" are frequently held incompatible with "reliance on the confidence which exists between husband and wife." See, e.g., People v. Dudley, 248 N.E.2d 860 (N.Y.1969). Similarly, the question whether privacy from eavesdropping was reasonably to be expected at the locus of the conversation may be determinative. North v. Superior Court, 502 P.2d 1305 (Cal.1972). The known presence of third persons generally precludes confidentiality, and this has been held true even where the third person is the minor child of the spouses. See, e.g., People v. Sanders, 457 N.E.2d 1241 (Ill.1983) (communication in presence of children, the eldest 13, not privileged). For additional cases, see Annot., 39 A.L.R.4th 480.

4. *Revelations to third persons.* It will sometimes occur that a spouse, whose testimony would come within either the adverse spousal testimony privilege or the privilege for marital communications, has revealed matters to some other person. If otherwise admissible and unprivileged, would testimony from such a third person violate the adverse spousal testimony privilege? Wigmore believed that it should. See 8 Wigmore, Evidence § 2232, at 225–26 (McNaughton rev. 1961). See also Imwinkelried, The New Wigmore: Evidentiary Privileges § 6.6.5 (2002), where the author examines both sides of the issue, but ultimately reaches the same conclusion as Wigmore. But see United States v. Archer, 733 F.2d 354 (5th Cir.1984) (third party could testify to spouse's statement); State v. Burden, 841 P.2d 758 (Wash. 1992) (same).

5. *Marital disharmony.* Should marital disharmony that has not yet resulted in a divorce decree serve to remove the privileged character of communications between the spouses? Compare United States v. Roberson, 859 F.2d 1376 (9th Cir.1988), with People v. Vermeulen, 438 N.W.2d 36 (Mich.1989). What problems arise under a rule that the privilege is terminated by marital discord short of divorce? See Blazek v. Superior Court, 869 P.2d 509 (Ariz.Ct.App.1994).

6. *Crime or fraud exception.* Should the marital communications privilege be qualified by a crime or fraud exception as advocated by the dissent in the principal case? Remember that some, but not all, courts engraft such an exception onto the adverse testimony privilege. See Note 3 following *Trammel v. United States.* Are there differences between the rules that would call for the existence of such an exception in one privilege but not the other. See discussion in 2 Saltzburg, Martin & Capra, Federal Rules of Evidence Manual § 501.02[8], at 501–78—501–79 (9th ed. 2006). Many courts, including all federal circuits to address the question, have held that such an exception should apply to the marital communications privilege, although the test for determining when the exception applies has varied from circuit to circuit. See, e.g., United States v. Marashi, 913 F.2d 724 (9th Cir.1990) (statements made in furtherance of criminal activity); United States v. Hill, 967 F.2d 902 (3d Cir.1992) (commission of a crime in which both spouses are participants); United States v. Evans, 966 F.2d 398 (8th Cir.1992) (exception

limited to communications regarding "patently illegal activity"). Does the creation of a crime or fraud exception effectively abolish the communications privilege? See United States v. Neal, 743 F.2d 1441, 1448 (10th Cir.1984) (Logan, J., concurring).

UNIFORM RULES OF EVIDENCE

RULE 504. SPOUSAL PRIVILEGE.

(a) Confidential communication. A communication is confidential if it is made privately by an individual to the individual's spouse and is not intended for disclosure to any other person.

(b) Marital communications. An individual has a privilege to refuse to testify and to prevent the individual's spouse or former spouse from testifying as to any confidential communication made by the individual to the spouse during their marriage. The privilege may be waived only by the individual holding the privilege or by the holder's guardian or conservator, or the individual's personal representative if the individual is deceased.

(c) Spousal testimony in criminal proceeding. The spouse of an accused in a criminal proceeding has a privilege to refuse to testify against the accused spouse.

(d) Exceptions. There is no privilege under this rule:

(1) in any civil proceeding in which the spouses are adverse parties;

(2) in any criminal proceeding in which an unrefuted showing is made that the spouses acted jointly in the commission of the crime charged;

(3) in any proceeding in which one spouse is charged with a crime or tort against the person or property of the other, a minor child of either, an individual residing in the household of either, or a third person if the crime or tort is committed in the course of committing a crime or tort against the other spouse, a minor child of either spouse, or an individual residing in the household of either spouse; or

(4) in any other proceeding, in the discretion of the court, if the interests of a minor child of either spouse may be adversely affected by invocation of the privilege.

SECTION C. ATTORNEY-CLIENT AND "WORK PRODUCT"

DENVER TRAMWAY CO. v. OWENS

Supreme Court of Colorado, 1894.
36 P. 848.

[Action by passenger for personal injuries allegedly sustained in alighting from a cable car.]

MR. JUSTICE ELLIOTT delivered the opinion of the court.

* * *

Mr. C.V. Mead, an attorney at law of several years in Denver, was called as a witness for defendant. He testified that shortly after the accident, plaintiff came to his office and that he had a talk with her "about the facts of this case." He was then asked to state what that conversation was.

Plaintiff's counsel being permitted to first cross-examine, the witness testified that the conversation between himself and plaintiff was in his "professional capacity;" that she was consulting him "as an attorney in relation to her case."

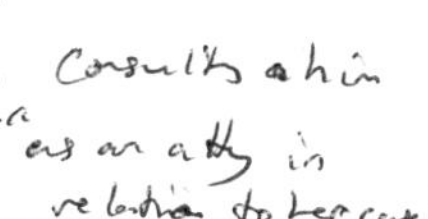

On further examination in chief he stated that he had never before seen plaintiff on professional business; that she had never been a client of his before that time; that the relation of attorney and client never existed between them prior to that time; that she did not pay nor agree to pay any retainer fee; that there was no talk about fees or compensation, and no contract or agreement with her at all.

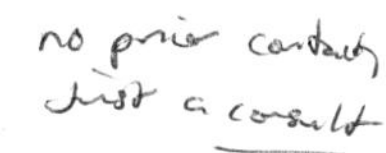

The witness was then asked if he made any charge against plaintiff for the consultation. This was objected to as immaterial, and the objection was sustained.

Counsel for defendant then stated to Mr. Mead the substance of plaintiff's testimony as to the manner in which she had been injured, and thereupon asked if plaintiff's statement to him as to the occurrence resulting in her injury was materially or substantially different from what she had thus testified. The court sustained plaintiff's objection to the testimony thus sought to be elicited. These rulings are assigned for error.

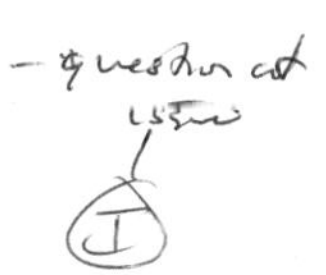

At common law *professional communications* between an attorney and his client relating to the business affairs of the latter were privileged. Lord Brougham states the reason of the rule as follows:

> "The foundation of this rule is not difficult to discover. It is not (as has sometimes been said) on account of any particular importance which the law attributes to the business of legal professors, or any particular disposition to afford them protection, though certain-

ly it may not be very easy to discover, why a like privilege has been refused to others, and especially to medical advisers.

> "But it is out of regard to the interests of justice which cannot be upholden and to the administration of justice, which cannot go on without the aid of men skilled in jurisprudence, in the practice of the courts, and in those matters affecting rights and obligations which form the subject of all judicial proceedings. If the privilege did not exist at all, every one would be thrown upon his own legal resources. Deprived of all professional assistance, a man would not venture to consult any skillful person, or would only dare to tell his counselor half his case. If the privilege were confined to communications connected with suits begun, or intended, or expected, or apprehended, no one could safely adopt such precautions as might eventually render any proceedings successful, or all proceedings superfluous." Greenough v. Gaskell, 1 My. & K. (7 Eng.Ch.) 103.

According to one author the rule had its origin in the fact that at common law parties were not competent witnesses in their own behalf, and could not be compelled to disclose facts known only to themselves. Weeks on Attorneys, § 142. The general rule now being that parties are competent witnesses, and that they may be compelled to testify in civil cases, it is urged that the rule in regard to professional communications should be relaxed. *Cessante ratione, cessat lex.* There would be some force in this argument if the rule rested alone upon the common law; but we have a statute passed long after parties were made competent witnesses in this state, which reads as follows:

> "An attorney shall not, without the consent of his client, be examined as to any communication made by the client to him, or his advice given thereon in the course of professional employment." Gen.Statutes, § 3649.

When a party invokes the protection of the statute, it should not be unduly extended or restricted, but should be fairly construed and applied according to the plain import of its terms so as to effectuate its intent and purpose. The statute is intended for the benefit of the client, not the attorney.

In determining whether or not an attorney should be required or permitted to testify to a conversation between himself and another person without the consent of the latter, the test is: Had such person at the time of the conversation employed the attorney in his professional capacity in respect to the subject-matter of the conversation? If yes, the testimony would not be admissible; otherwise, it would be. It becomes necessary, therefore, to determine whether plaintiff had employed Mr. Mead in his professional capacity as attorney at the time of the conversation inquired about.

To constitute professional employment, it is not essential that the client should have employed the attorney professionally on any previous occasion. Such a limitation of the rule would bear hard upon a person involved in legal controversy for the first time, and also upon an attorney with his first cause. It is not necessary that any retainer should have been paid, promised, or charged for; nor are such matters of any importance except as they may tend to show whether the attorney was or was not professionally employed; neither is it material that there was a suit pending at the time of the consultation, nor that the attorney consulted did not afterwards undertake the case about which the consultation was had.

If a person, in respect to his business affairs or troubles of any kind, consults with an attorney in his professional capacity with the view to obtaining professional advice or assistance, and the attorney voluntarily permits or acquiesces in such consultation, then the professional employment must be regarded as established; and the communication made by the client or advice given by the attorney under such circumstances is privileged.

An attorney is employed—that is, he is engaged in his professional capacity as a lawyer or counselor—when he is listening to his client's preliminary statement of his case, or when he is giving advice thereon, just as truly as when he is drawing his client's pleadings, or advocating his client's cause in open court. It is the consultation between attorney and client which is privileged, and which must ever remain so, even though the attorney, after hearing the preliminary statement, should decline to be retained further in the cause, or the client, after hearing the attorney's advice, should decline to further employ him. The general rule undoubtedly is that a breach of professional relations between attorney and client, whatever may be the cause, does not of itself remove the seal of silence from the lips of the attorney in respect to matters received by him in confidence from his client. Foster v. Hall, 12 Pick. 89; Hunter v. Van Bomhorst, 1 Md. 504; Cross v. Riggins, 50 Mo. 335. * * *

Affirmed.

Note

See generally Fried, The Lawyer as Friend: The Moral Foundations of the Attorney–Client Relation, 85 Yale L.J. 1060 (1976); Hazard, An Historical Perspective on the Attorney–Client Privilege, 66 Cal.L.Rev. 1061 (1978).

5 BENTHAM, RATIONALE OF JUDICIAL EVIDENCE 302

(J.S. Mill, Ed.1827).

When, in consulting with a law adviser, attorney or advocate, a man has confessed his delinquency, or disclosed some fact which, if stated in court, might tend to operate in proof of it, such law adviser is not to be suffered to be examined as to any such point. The law adviser is neither to be compelled, nor so much as suffered, to betray the trust thus reposed in him. Not suffered? Why not? Oh, because to betray a trust is treachery; and an act of treachery is an immoral act.

An immoral sort of act, is that sort of act, the tendency of which is, in some way or other, to lessen the quantity of happiness in society. In what way does the supposed cause in question tend to the production of any such effect? The conviction and punishment of the defendant, he being guilty, is by the supposition an act the tendency of which, upon the whole, is beneficial to society. Such is the proposition which for this purpose must be assumed. Some offences (it will be admitted by every body) are of that sort and quality, that the acts by which they are punished do possess this beneficial tendency. Let the offence in question be of the number: it is of such only as are of that number that I speak. The good, then, that results from the conviction and punishment, in the case in question, is out of dispute: where, then is the additional evil of it when produced by the cause in question? Nowhere. The evil consists in the punishment: but the punishment a man undergoes is not greater when the evidence on which the conviction and punishment are grounded happens to come out of the mouth of a law adviser of his, than if it had happened to come out of his own mouth, or that of a third person.

But if such confidence, when reposed, is permitted to be violated, and if this be known, (which, if such be the law, it will be), the consequence will be, that no such confidence will be reposed. Not reposed?—Well: and if it be not, wherein will consist the mischief? The man by the supposition is guilty; if not, by the supposition there is nothing to betray: let the law adviser say every thing he has heard, every thing he can have heard from his client, the client cannot have any thing to fear from it. That it will often happen that in the case supposed no such confidence will be reposed, is natural enough: the first thing the advocate or attorney will say to his client, will be,—Remember that, whatever you say to me, I shall be obliged to tell, if asked about it. What, then, will be the consequence? That a guilty person will not in general be able to derive quite so much assistance from his law adviser, in the way of concerting a false defence, as he may do at present.

Except the prevention of such pernicious confidence, of what other possible effect can the rule for the requisition of such evidence be productive? Either of none at all, or of the conviction of delinquents, in some instances in which, but for the lights thus obtained, they would not have been convicted. But in this effect, what imaginable circumstance is there that can render it in any degree pernicious and undesirable? None whatever. The conviction of delinquents is the very end of penal justice.

Notes and Questions

1. *Attacks on the privilege.* Frontal attacks on the attorney-client privilege are not limited to the nineteenth century. See the different, but equally scathing, attack on both the attorney-client and the work product privileges in Fischel, Lawyers and Confidentiality, 65 U.Chi.L.Rev. 1 (1998). What rebuttal is there to Bentham's attack? Wigmore was somewhat more sympathetic to the privilege, arguing in essence that Bentham's points were well taken only with regard to a certain proportion of cases. He argues that

the privilege may serve a more valid societal function in a civil case where right and wrong are not so clear. 8 Wigmore, Evidence § 2291 (McNaughton rev. 1961). But he concludes his lukewarm defense with the observation that the benefits of the privilege are "all indirect and speculative; its obstruction is plain and concrete."

2. *Other rationales.* Are there other, better arguments for the privilege than those suggested by the *Denver Tramway* case? Is there a need for a free flow of information between lawyer and client even when the client is in fact guilty of a crime or misconduct? Do considerations of privacy or personal autonomy, as suggested in by Professor Black and the following notes in Section A of this chapter, come into play with regard to this privilege? What impact might the elimination of the privilege have on how clients view their lawyers? On how they view the judicial system? See also Freedman, Lawyers' Ethics in an Adversary System (1975); Fuller, The Adversary System, in Talks on American Law 30, 32–38 (1961).

SWIDLER & BERLIN v. UNITED STATES

Supreme Court of the United States, 1998.
524 U.S. 399.

Chief Justice Rehnquist delivered the opinion of the Court.

Petitioner, James Hamilton, an attorney, made notes of an initial interview with a client shortly before the client's death. The Government, represented by the Office of Independent Counsel, now seeks his notes for use in a criminal investigation. We hold that the notes are protected by the attorney-client privilege.

This dispute arises out of an investigation conducted by the Office of the Independent Counsel into whether various individuals made false statements, obstructed justice, or committed other crimes during investigations of the 1993 dismissal of employees from the White House Travel Office. Vincent W. Foster, Jr., was Deputy White House Counsel when the firings occurred. In July 1993, Foster met with petitioner Hamilton, an attorney at petitioner Swidler & Berlin, to seek legal representation concerning possible congressional or other investigations of the firings. During a 2–hour meeting, Hamilton took three pages of handwritten notes. One of the first entries in the notes is the word "Privileged." Nine days later, Foster committed suicide.

In December 1995, a federal grand jury, at the request of the Independent Counsel, issued subpoenas to petitioners Hamilton and Swidler & Berlin for, inter alia, Hamilton's handwritten notes of his meeting with Foster. Petitioners filed a motion to quash, arguing that the notes were protected by the attorney-client privilege and by the work-product privilege. The District Court, after examining the notes in camera, concluded they were protected from disclosure by both doctrines and denied enforcement of the subpoenas.

The Court of Appeals for the District of Columbia Circuit reversed. In re Sealed Case, 124 F.3d 230 (1997). While recognizing that most courts assume the privilege survives death, the Court of Appeals noted that holdings actually manifesting the posthumous force of the privilege are rare. Instead, most judicial references to the privilege's posthumous application occur in the context of a well-recognized exception allowing disclosure for disputes among the client's heirs. Id., at 231–232. It further noted that most commentators support some measure of posthumous curtailment of the privilege. Id., at 232. The Court of Appeals thought that the risk of posthumous revelation, when confined to the criminal context, would have little to no chilling effect on client communication, but that the costs of protecting communications after death were high. It therefore concluded that the privilege was not absolute in such circumstances, and that instead, a balancing test should apply. Id., at 233–234. It thus held that there is a posthumous exception to the privilege for communications whose relative importance to particular criminal litigation is substantial. Id., at 235. While acknowledging that uncertain privileges are disfavored, Jaffee v. Redmond, 518 U.S. 1, 17–18 (1996), the Court of Appeals determined that the uncertainty introduced by its balancing test was insignificant in light of existing exceptions to the privilege. 124 F.3d, at 235. The Court of Appeals also held that the notes were not protected by the work-product privilege.

The dissenting judge would have affirmed the District Court's judgment that the attorney-client privilege protected the notes. Id., at 237. He concluded that the common-law rule was that the privilege survived death. He found no persuasive reason to depart from this accepted rule, particularly given the importance of the privilege to full and frank client communication. Id., at 237.

Petitioners sought review in this Court on both the attorney-client privilege and the work-product privilege.[17] We granted certiorari, 523 U.S. 1045 (1998), and we now reverse.

The attorney-client privilege is one of the oldest recognized privileges for confidential communications. Upjohn Co. v. United States, 449 U.S. 383, 389 (1981); Hunt v. Blackburn, 128 U.S. 464, 470 (1888). The privilege is intended to encourage "full and frank communication between attorneys and their clients and thereby promote broader public interests in the observance of law and the administration of justice." Upjohn, supra, at 389. The issue presented here is the scope of that privilege; more particularly, the extent to which the privilege survives the death of the client. Our interpretation of the privilege's scope is guided by "the principles of the common law * * * as interpreted by the courts * * * in the light of reason and experience." Fed.Rule Evid. 501; Funk v. United States, 290 U.S. 371 (1933).

The Independent Counsel argues that the attorney-client privilege should not prevent disclosure of confidential communications where the client has died and the information is relevant to a criminal proceeding. There is some authority for this position. One state appellate court,

17. Because we sustain the claim of attorney-client privilege, we do not reach the claim of work-product privilege.

Cohen v. Jenkintown Cab Co., 238 Pa.Super. 456, 357 A.2d 689 (1976), and the Court of Appeals below have held the privilege may be subject to posthumous exceptions in certain circumstances. In Cohen, a civil case, the court recognized that the privilege generally survives death, but concluded that it could make an exception where the interest of justice was compelling and the interest of the client in preserving the confidence was insignificant. Id., at 462–464, 357 A.2d, at 692–693.

But other than these two decisions, cases addressing the existence of the privilege after death—most involving the testamentary exception—uniformly presume the privilege survives, even if they do not so hold. See, e.g., Mayberry v. Indiana, 670 N.E.2d 1262 (Ind.1996); Morris v. Cain, 39 La. Ann. 712, 1 So. 797 (1887); People v. Modzelewski, 611 N.Y.S.2d 22, 203 A.D.2d 594 (1994). Several State Supreme Court decisions expressly hold that the attorney-client privilege extends beyond the death of the client, even in the criminal context. See In re John Doe Grand Jury Investigation, 408 Mass. 480, 481–483, 562 N.E.2d 69, 70 (1990); State v. Doster, 276 S.C. 647, 650–651, 284 S.E.2d 218, 219 (1981); State v. Macumber, 112 Ariz. 569, 571, 544 P.2d 1084, 1086 (1976). In John Doe Grand Jury Investigation, for example, the Massachusetts Supreme Judicial Court concluded that survival of the privilege was "the clear implication" of its early pronouncements that communications subject to the privilege could not be disclosed at any time. 408 Mass., at 483, 562 N.E.2d, at 70. The court further noted that survival of the privilege was "necessarily implied" by cases allowing waiver of the privilege in testamentary disputes. Ibid.

Such testamentary exception cases consistently presume the privilege survives. See, e.g., United States v. Osborn, 561 F.2d 1334, 1340 (C.A.9 1977); DeLoach v. Myers, 215 Ga. 255, 259–260, 109 S.E.2d 777, 780–781 (1959); Doyle v. Reeves, 112 Conn. 521, 152 A. 882 (1931); Russell v. Jackson, 9 Hare 387, 68 Eng. Rep. 558 (V.C.1851). They view testamentary disclosure of communications as an exception to the privilege: "[T]he general rule with respect to confidential communications * * * is that such communications are privileged during the testator's lifetime and, also, after the testator's death unless sought to be disclosed in litigation between the testator's heirs." Osborn, 561 F.2d, at 1340. The rationale for such disclosure is that it furthers the client's intent. Id., at 1340, n.11.[18]

18. About half the States have codified the testamentary exception by providing that a personal representative of the deceased can waive the privilege when heirs or devisees claim through the deceased client (as opposed to parties claiming against the estate, for whom the privilege is not waived). See, e.g., Ala.Rule Evid. 502 (1996); Ark.Code Ann. § 16–41–101, Rule 502 (Supp.1997); Neb.Rev.Stat. § 27–503, Rule 503 (1995). These statutes do not address expressly the continuation of the privilege outside the context of testamentary disputes, although many allow the attorney to assert the privilege on behalf of the client apparently without temporal limit. See, e.g., Ark.Code Ann. § 16–41–101, Rule 502(c) (Supp.1997). They thus do not refute or affirm the general presumption in the case law that the privilege survives. California's statute is exceptional in that it apparently allows the attorney to assert the privilege only so long as a holder of the privilege (the estate's personal representative) exists, suggesting the privilege terminates when the estate is wound up. See Cal.Code Evid.Ann. §§ 954, 957 (West 1995). But no other State has followed California's lead in this regard.

Indeed, in Glover v. Patten, 165 U.S. 394, 406–408 (1897), this Court, in recognizing the testamentary exception, expressly assumed that the privilege continues after the individual's death. The Court explained that testamentary disclosure was permissible because the privilege, which normally protects the client's interests, could be impliedly waived in order to fulfill the client's testamentary intent. Id., at 407–408 (quoting Blackburn v. Crawford, 3 Wall. 175, 18 L.Ed. 186 (1865), and Russell v. Jackson, supra).

The great body of this case law supports, either by holding or considered dicta, the position that the privilege does survive in a case such as the present one. Given the language of Rule 501, at the very least the burden is on the Independent Counsel to show that "reason and experience" require a departure from this rule.

The Independent Counsel contends that the testamentary exception supports the posthumous termination of the privilege because in practice most cases have refused to apply the privilege posthumously. He further argues that the exception reflects a policy judgment that the interest in settling estates outweighs any posthumous interest in confidentiality. He then reasons by analogy that in criminal proceedings, the interest in determining whether a crime has been committed should trump client confidentiality, particularly since the financial interests of the estate are not at stake.

But the Independent Counsel's interpretation simply does not square with the case law's implicit acceptance of the privilege's survival and with the treatment of testamentary disclosure as an "exception" or an implied "waiver." And the premise of his analogy is incorrect, since cases consistently recognize that the rationale for the testamentary exception is that it furthers the client's intent, see, e.g., Glover, supra. There is no reason to suppose as a general matter that grand jury testimony about confidential communications furthers the client's intent.

Commentators on the law also recognize that the general rule is that the attorney-client privilege continues after death. See, e.g., 8 Wigmore, Evidence § 2323 (McNaughton rev. 1961); Frankel, The Attorney–Client Privilege After the Death of the Client, 6 Geo.J.Legal Ethics 45, 78–79 (1992); 1 J. Strong, McCormick on Evidence § 94, p. 348 (4th ed. 1992). Undoubtedly, as the Independent Counsel emphasizes, various commentators have criticized this rule, urging that the privilege should be abrogated after the client's death where extreme injustice would result, as long as disclosure would not seriously undermine the privilege by deterring client communication. See, e.g., C. Mueller & L. Kirkpatrick, 2 Federal Evidence § 199, pp. 380–381 (2d ed. 1994); Restatement (Third) of the Law Governing Lawyers § 127, Comment d (Proposed Final Draft No. 1, Mar. 29, 1996). But even these critics clearly recognize that established law supports the continuation of the privilege and that a contrary rule would be a modification of the common law. See, e.g.,

Mueller & Kirkpatrick, supra, at 379; Restatement of the Law Governing Lawyers, supra, § 127, Comment c; 24 C. Wright & K. Graham, Federal Practice and Procedure § 5498, p. 483 (1986).

Despite the scholarly criticism, we think there are weighty reasons that counsel in favor of posthumous application. Knowing that communications will remain confidential even after death encourages the client to communicate fully and frankly with counsel. While the fear of disclosure, and the consequent withholding of information from counsel, may be reduced if disclosure is limited to posthumous disclosure in a criminal context, it seems unreasonable to assume that it vanishes altogether. Clients may be concerned about reputation, civil liability, or possible harm to friends or family. Posthumous disclosure of such communications may be as feared as disclosure during the client's lifetime.

The Independent Counsel suggests, however, that his proposed exception would have little to no effect on the client's willingness to confide in his attorney. He reasons that only clients intending to perjure themselves will be chilled by a rule of disclosure after death, as opposed to truthful clients or those asserting their Fifth Amendment privilege. This is because for the latter group, communications disclosed by the attorney after the client's death purportedly will reveal only information that the client himself would have revealed if alive.

The Independent Counsel assumes, incorrectly we believe, that the privilege is analogous to the Fifth Amendment's protection against self-incrimination. But as suggested above, the privilege serves much broader purposes. Clients consult attorneys for a wide variety of reasons, only one of which involves possible criminal liability. Many attorneys act as counselors on personal and family matters, where, in the course of obtaining the desired advice, confidences about family members or financial problems must be revealed in order to assure sound legal advice. The same is true of owners of small businesses who may regularly consult their attorneys about a variety of problems arising in the course of the business. These confidences may not come close to any sort of admission of criminal wrongdoing, but nonetheless be matters which the client would not wish divulged.

The contention that the attorney is being required to disclose only what the client could have been required to disclose is at odds with the basis for the privilege even during the client's lifetime. In related cases, we have said that the loss of evidence admittedly caused by the privilege is justified in part by the fact that without the privilege, the client may not have made such communications in the first place. See Jaffee, 518 U.S., at 12; Fisher v. United States, 425 U.S. 391, 403 (1976). This is true of disclosure before and after the client's death. Without assurance of the privilege's posthumous application, the client may very well not have made disclosures to his attorney at all, so the loss of evidence is more apparent than real. In the case at hand, it seems quite plausible that Foster, perhaps already contemplating suicide, may not have sought legal advice from Hamilton if he had not been assured the conversation was privileged.

The Independent Counsel additionally suggests that his proposed exception would have minimal impact if confined to criminal cases, or, as the Court of Appeals suggests, if it is limited to information of substantial importance to a particular criminal case.[19] However, there is no case authority for the proposition that the privilege applies differently in criminal and civil cases, and only one commentator ventures such a suggestion, see Mueller & Kirkpatrick, supra, at 380–381. In any event, a client may not know at the time he discloses information to his attorney whether it will later be relevant to a civil or a criminal matter, let alone whether it will be of substantial importance. Balancing ex post the importance of the information against client interests, even limited to criminal cases, introduces substantial uncertainty into the privilege's application. For just that reason, we have rejected use of a balancing test in defining the contours of the privilege. See Upjohn, 449 U.S., at 393; Jaffee, supra, at 17–18.

In a similar vein, the Independent Counsel argues that existing exceptions to the privilege, such as the crime-fraud exception and the testamentary exception, make the impact of one more exception marginal. However, these exceptions do not demonstrate that the impact of a posthumous exception would be insignificant, and there is little empirical evidence on this point.[20] The established exceptions are consistent with the purposes of the privilege, see Glover, 165 U.S., at 407–408; United States v. Zolin, 491 U.S. 554, 562–563 (1989), while a posthumous exception in criminal cases appears at odds with the goals of encouraging full and frank communication and of protecting the client's interests. A "no harm in one more exception" rationale could contribute

19. Petitioners, while opposing wholesale abrogation of the privilege in criminal cases, concede that exceptional circumstances implicating a criminal defendant's constitutional rights might warrant breaching the privilege. We do not, however, need to reach this issue, since such exceptional circumstances clearly are not presented here.

20. Empirical evidence on the privilege is limited. Three studies do not reach firm conclusions on whether limiting the privilege would discourage full and frank communication. Alexander, The Corporate Attorney Client Privilege: A Study of the Participants, 63 St. John's L.Rev. 191 (1989); Zacharias, Rethinking Confidentiality, 74 Iowa L.Rev. 352 (1989); Comment, Functional Overlap Between the Lawyer and Other Professionals: Its Implications for the Privileged Communications Doctrine, 71 Yale L.J. 1226 (1962). These articles note that clients are often uninformed or mistaken about the privilege, but suggest that a substantial number of clients and attorneys think the privilege encourages candor. Two of the articles conclude that a substantial number of clients and attorneys think the privilege enhances open communication, Alexander, supra, at 244–246, 261, and that the absence of a privilege would be detrimental to such communication, Comment, 71 Yale L.J., supra, at 1236. The third article suggests instead that while the privilege is perceived as important to open communication, limited exceptions to the privilege might not discourage such communication, Zacharias, supra, at 382, 386. Similarly, relatively few court decisions discuss the impact of the privilege's application after death. This may reflect the general assumption that the privilege survives—if attorneys were required as a matter of practice to testify or provide notes in criminal proceedings, cases discussing that practice would surely exist.

to the general erosion of the privilege, without reference to common-law principles or "reason and experience."

Finally, the Independent Counsel, relying on cases such as United States v. Nixon, 418 U.S. 683, 710 (1974), and Branzburg v. Hayes, 408 U.S. 665 (1972), urges that privileges be strictly construed because they are inconsistent with the paramount judicial goal of truth seeking. But both Nixon and Branzburg dealt with the creation of privileges not recognized by the common law, whereas here we deal with one of the oldest recognized privileges in the law. And we are asked, not simply to "construe" the privilege, but to narrow it, contrary to the weight of the existing body of case law.

It has been generally, if not universally, accepted, for well over a century, that the attorney-client privilege survives the death of the client in a case such as this. While the arguments against the survival of the privilege are by no means frivolous, they are based in large part on speculation—thoughtful speculation, but speculation nonetheless—as to whether posthumous termination of the privilege would diminish a client's willingness to confide in an attorney. In an area where empirical information would be useful, it is scant and inconclusive.

Rule 501's direction to look to "the principles of the common law as they may be interpreted by the courts of the United States in the light of reason and experience" does not mandate that a rule, once established, should endure for all time. Funk v. United States, 290 U.S. 371, 381 (1933). But here the Independent Counsel has simply not made a sufficient showing to overturn the common-law rule embodied in the prevailing caselaw. Interpreted in the light of reason and experience, that body of law requires that the attorney-client privilege prevent disclosure of the notes at issue in this case.

The judgment of the Court of Appeals is

Reversed.

JUSTICE O'CONNOR, with whom JUSTICE SCALIA and JUSTICE THOMAS join, dissenting.

Although the attorney-client privilege ordinarily will survive the death of the client, I do not agree with the Court that it inevitably precludes disclosure of a deceased client's communications in criminal proceedings. In my view, a criminal defendant's right to exculpatory evidence or a compelling law enforcement need for information may, where the testimony is not available from other sources, override a client's posthumous interest in confidentiality.

We have long recognized that "[t]he fundamental basis upon which all rules of evidence must rest—if they are to rest upon reason—is their adaptation to the successful development of the truth." Funk v. United States, 290 U.S. 371, 381 (1933). In light of the heavy burden that they place on the search for truth, see United States v. Nixon, 418 U.S. 683, 708–710 (1974), "[e]videntiary privileges in litigation are not favored, and even those rooted in the Constitution must give way in proper circumstances," Herbert v. Lando, 441 U.S. 153 (1979). Consequently, we construe the scope of privileges narrowly. See Jaffee v. Redmond, 518 U.S. 1, 19 (1996) (SCALIA, J., dissenting); see also University of Pennsylvania v. EEOC, 493 U.S. 182, 189 (1990). We are reluctant to recognize a privilege or read an existing one expansively unless to do so will serve a "public good transcending the normally predominant principle of utilizing all rational means for ascertaining truth." Trammel v. United States, 445 U.S. 40, 50 (1980) (internal quotation marks omitted).

The attorney-client privilege promotes trust in the representational relationship, thereby facilitating the provision of legal services and ultimately the administration of justice. See Upjohn Co. v. United States, 449 U.S. 383, 389 (1981). The systemic benefits of the privilege are commonly understood to outweigh the harm caused by excluding critical evidence. A privilege should operate, however, only where "necessary to achieve its purpose," see Fisher v. United States, 425 U.S. 391, 403 (1976), and an invocation of the attorney-client privilege should not go unexamined "when it is shown that the interests of the administration of justice can only be frustrated by [its] exercise," Cohen v. Jenkintown Cab Co., 238 Pa.Super. 456, 464, 357 A.2d 689, 693–694 (1976).

I agree that a deceased client may retain a personal, reputational, and economic interest in confidentiality * * * . But, after death, the potential that disclosure will harm the client's interests has been greatly diminished, and the risk that the client will be held criminally liable has abated altogether. Thus, some commentators suggest that terminating the privilege upon the client's death "could not to any substantial degree lessen the encouragement for free disclosure which is [its] purpose." 1 J. Strong, McCormick on Evidence § 94, p. 350 (4th ed. 1992); see also Restatement (Third) of the Law Governing Lawyers § 127, Comment d (Proposed Final Draft No. 1, Mar. 29, 1996). This diminished risk is coupled with a heightened urgency for discovery of a deceased client's communications in the criminal context. The privilege does not "protect disclosure of the underlying facts by those who communicated with the attorney," Upjohn, supra, at 395, and were the client living, prosecutors could grant immunity and compel the relevant testimony. After a client's death, however, if the privilege precludes an attorney from testifying in the client's stead, a complete "loss of crucial information" will often result, see 24 C. Wright & K. Graham, Federal Practice and Procedure § 5498, p. 484 (1986).

As the Court of Appeals observed, the costs of recognizing an absolute posthumous privilege can be inordinately high. See In re Sealed Case, 124 F.3d 230, 233–234 (C.A.D.C.1997). Extreme injustice may occur, for example, where a criminal defendant seeks disclosure of a deceased client's confession to the offense. See State v. Macumber, 112 Ariz. 569, 571, 544 P.2d 1084, 1086 (1976); cf. In the Matter of John Doe Grand Jury Investigation, 408 Mass. 480, 486, 562 N.E.2d 69, 72 (1990) (Nolan, J., dissenting). In my view, the paramount value that our criminal justice system places on protecting an innocent defendant should outweigh a deceased client's interest in preserving confidences. See, e.g., Schlup v. Delo, 513 U.S. 298, 324–325 (1995); In re Winship, 397 U.S. 358, 371 (1970) (Harlan, J., concurring). Indeed, even petitioners acknowledge that an exception may be appropriate where the constitutional rights of a criminal defendant are at stake. An exception may likewise be warranted in the face of a compelling law enforcement need for the information. "[O]ur historic commitment to the rule of law * * * is nowhere more profoundly manifest than in our view that the twofold aim of criminal justice is that guilt shall not escape or innocence suffer." Nixon, supra, at 709 (internal quotation marks omitted); see also Herrera v. Collins, 506 U.S. 390, 398 (1993). Given that the complete exclusion of relevant evidence from a criminal trial or investigation may distort the record, mislead the factfinder, and undermine the central truth-seeking function of the courts, I do not believe that the attorney-client privilege should act as an absolute bar to the disclosure of a deceased client's communications. When the privilege is asserted in the criminal context, and a showing is made that the communications at issue contain necessary factual information not otherwise available, courts should be permitted to assess whether interests in fairness and accuracy outweigh the justifications for the privilege.

A number of exceptions to the privilege already qualify its protections, and an attorney "who tells his client that the expected communications are absolutely and forever privileged is oversimplifying a bit." 124 F.3d, at 235. In the situation where the posthumous privilege most frequently arises—a dispute between heirs over the decedent's will—the privilege is widely recognized to give way to the interest in settling the estate. See Glover v. Patten, 165 U.S. 394, 406–408 (1897). This testamentary exception, moreover, may be invoked in some cases where the decedent would not have chosen to waive the privilege. For example, "a decedent might want to provide for an illegitimate child but at the same time much prefer that the relationship go undisclosed." 124 F.3d, at 234. Among the Court's rationales for a broad construction of the posthumous privilege is its assertion that "[m]any attorneys act as counselors on personal and family matters, where, in the course of obtaining the desired advice, confidences about family members or financial problems must be revealed * * * which the client would not wish divulged." * * * That reasoning, however, would apply in the testamentary context with equal force. Nor are other existing exceptions to the privilege—for example, the crime-fraud exception or the exceptions for claims relating to attorney competence or compensation—necessarily consistent with "encouraging full and frank communication" or "protecting the client's interests." * * * Rather, those exceptions reflect the understanding that, in certain circumstances, the privilege " 'ceases to operate' " as a safeguard on "the proper functioning of our adversary system." See United States v. Zolin, 491 U.S. 554, 562–563 (1989).

Finally, the common law authority for the proposition that the privilege remains absolute after the client's death is not a monolithic body of precedent. Indeed, the Court acknowledges that most cases merely "presume the privilege survives," * * * and it relies on the case law's "implicit acceptance" of a continuous privilege * * * . Opinions squarely addressing the posthumous force of the privilege "are relatively rare." See 124 F.3d, at 232. And even in those decisions expressly holding that the privilege continues after the death of the client, courts do not typically engage in detailed reasoning, but rather conclude that the cases construing the testamentary exception imply survival of the privilege. See, e.g., Glover, supra, at 406–408; see also Wright & Graham, supra, § 5498, at 484 ("Those who favor an eternal duration for the privilege seldom do much by way of justifying this in terms of policy").

Moreover, as the Court concedes * * * , there is some authority for the proposition that a deceased client's communications may be revealed, even in circumstances outside of the testamentary context. California's Evidence Code, for example, provides that the attorney-client privilege continues only until the deceased client's estate is finally distributed, noting that "there is little reason to preserve secrecy at the expense of excluding relevant evidence after the estate is wound up and the representative is discharged." Cal. Evid. Code Ann. § 954, and comment, p. 232, § 952 (West 1995). And a state appellate court has admitted an attorney's testimony concerning a deceased client's communications after "balanc[ing] the necessity for revealing the substance of the [attorney-client conversation] against the unlikelihood of any cognizable injury to the rights, interests, estate or memory of [the client]." See Cohen, supra, at 464, 357 A.2d, at 693. The American Law Institute, moreover, has recently recommended withholding the privilege when the communication "bears on a litigated issue of pivotal significance" and has suggested that courts "balance the interest in confidentiality against any exceptional need for the communication." Restatement (Third) of the Law Governing Lawyers § 127, at 431, Comment d; see also 2 C. Mueller & L. Kirkpatrick, Federal Evidence, § 199, p. 380 (2d ed. 1994) ("[I]f a deceased client has confessed to criminal acts that are later charged to another, surely the latter's need for evidence sometimes outweighs the interest in preserving the confidences").

Where the exoneration of an innocent criminal defendant or a compelling law enforcement interest is at stake, the harm of precluding critical evidence that is unavailable by any other means outweighs the potential disincentive to forthright communication. In my view, the cost of silence warrants a narrow exception to the rule that the attorney-client privilege survives the death of the client. Moreover, although I disagree with the Court of Appeals' notion that the context of an initial client interview affects the applicability of the work product doctrine, I do not believe that the doctrine applies where the material concerns a client who is no longer a potential party to adversarial litigation.

Accordingly, I would affirm the judgment of the Court of Appeals. Although the District Court examined the documents in camera, it has not had an opportunity to balance these competing considerations and decide whether the privilege should be trumped in the particular circumstances of this case. Thus, I agree with the Court of Appeals' decision to remand for a determination whether any portion of the notes must be disclosed.

With respect, I dissent.

Notes and Questions

1. *More on rationale.* Does the Court's opinion in the *Swidler & Berlin* case shed any further light on the reasons behind the attorney-client privilege? Is the Court's posthumous recognition of the privilege based on the utilitarian notion that the continuation of the privilege after death fosters better communications between lawyer and client or considerations of privacy or some of both? See generally Broun, The Story of *Swidler & Berlin v. United States*, in Evidence Stories 127 (Lempert ed., 2006).

2. *Constitutional limitations?* The majority brushes off the dissent's concern that a continuation of the privilege after death may deprive a criminal defendant of a full defense to a crime by suggesting that there may be constitutional limits on the privilege in some circumstances. In what circumstances could you foresee a constitutional challenge to the exercise of the privilege? See Chambers v. Mississippi, 410 U.S. 284 (1973); Davis v. Alaska, 415 U.S. 308 (1974). Might not those same considerations apply in the case of the exercise of the privilege before the death of the client?

3. *Using evidence obtained as a result of a breach of an evidentiary privilege.* The courts have generally held that evidence derived from a breach of an evidentiary privilege such as the attorney-client privilege is admissible. See, e.g. Nickel v. Hannigan, 97 F.3d 403, 408–09 (10th Cir.1996) (even if attorney's testimony should have been suppressed because of the attorney-client privilege, evidence derived from that testimony should not have been suppressed). See Mosteller, Admissibility of Fruits of Breached Evidentiary Privileges: The Importance of Adversarial Fairness, Party Culpability, and Fear of Immunity, 81 Wash.U.L.Q. 961 (2003).

UPJOHN CO. v. UNITED STATES

Supreme Court of the United States, 1981.
449 U.S. 383.

JUSTICE REHNQUIST delivered the opinion of the Court.

We granted certiorari in this case to address important questions concerning the scope of the attorney-client privilege in the corporate context and the applicability of the work-product doctrine in proceedings to enforce tax summonses. With respect to the privilege question the parties and various *amici* have described our task as one of choosing between two "tests" which have gained adherents in the courts of appeals. We are acutely aware, however, that we sit to decide concrete cases and not abstract propositions of law. We decline to lay down a broad rule or series of rules to govern all conceivable future questions in this area, even were we able to do so. We can and do, however, conclude that the attorney-client privilege protects the communications involved in this case from compelled disclosure and that the work-product doctrine does apply in tax summons enforcement proceedings.

I

Petitioner Upjohn manufactures and sells pharmaceuticals here and abroad. In January 1976 independent accountants conducting an audit of one of petitioner's foreign subsidiaries discovered that the subsidiary made payments to or for the benefit of foreign government officials in order to secure government business. The accountants so informed Mr. Gerard Thomas, petitioner's Vice–President, Secretary, and General Counsel. Thomas is a member of the Michigan and New York bars, and has been petitioner's General Counsel for 20 years. He consulted with outside counsel and R.T. Parfet, Jr., petitioner's Chairman of the Board. It was decided that the company would conduct an internal investigation of what were termed "questionable payments." As part of this investigation the attorneys prepared a letter containing a questionnaire which was sent to "all foreign general and area managers" over the Chairman's signature. The letter began by noting recent disclosures that several American companies made "possibly illegal" payments to foreign government officials and emphasized that the management needed full information concerning any such payments made by Upjohn. The letter indicated that the Chairman had asked Thomas, identified as "the company's General Counsel," "to conduct an investigation for the purpose of determining the nature and magnitude of any payments made by the Upjohn Company or any of its subsidiaries to any employee or official of a foreign government." The questionnaire sought detailed information concerning such payments. Managers were instructed to treat the investigation as "highly confidential" and not to discuss it with anyone other than Upjohn employees who might be helpful in providing the requested information. Responses were to be sent directly to Thomas. Thomas and outside counsel also interviewed the recipients of the questionnaire and some 33 other Upjohn officers or employees as part of the investigation.

On March 26, 1976, the company voluntarily submitted a preliminary report to the Securities and Exchange Commission on Form 8–K disclosing certain questionable payments. A copy of the report was simultaneously submitted to the Internal Revenue Service, which immediately began an investigation to determine the tax consequences of the payments. Special agents conducting the investigation were given lists by Upjohn of all those interviewed and all who had responded to the questionnaire. On November 23, 1976, the Service issued a summons pursuant to 26 U.S.C.A. § 7602 demanding production of:

> "All files relative to the investigation conducted under the supervision of Gerard Thomas to identify payments to employees of foreign governments and any political contributions made by the Upjohn Company or any of its affiliates since January 1, 1971 and to determine whether any funds of the Upjohn Company had been improperly accounted for on the corporate books during the same period.
>
> "The records should include but not be limited to written questionnaires sent to managers of the Upjohn Company's foreign

affiliates, and memoranda or notes of the interviews conducted in the United States and abroad with officers and employees of the Upjohn Company and its subsidiaries." App. 17a–18a.

The company declined to produce the documents specified in the second paragraph on the grounds that they were protected from disclosure by the attorney-client privilege and constituted the work product of attorneys prepared in anticipation of litigation. On August 31, 1977, the United States filed a petition seeking enforcement of the summons under 26 U.S.C.A. §§ 7402(b) and 7604(a) in the United States District Court for the Western District of Michigan. That court adopted the recommendation of a magistrate who concluded that the summons should be enforced. Petitioner appealed to the Court of Appeals for the Sixth Circuit which rejected the magistrate's finding of a waiver of the attorney-client privilege, 600 F.2d 1223, 1227, n.12, but agreed that the privilege did not apply "to the extent the communications were made by officers and agents not responsible for directing Upjohn's actions in response to legal advice * * * for the simple reason that the communications were not the 'client's.'" Id., at 1225. The court reasoned that accepting petitioner's claim for a broader application of the privilege would encourage upper-echelon management to ignore unpleasant facts and create too broad a "zone of silence." Noting that petitioner's counsel had interviewed officials such as the Chairman and President, the Court of Appeals remanded to the District Court so that a determination of who was within the "control group" could be made. In a concluding footnote the court stated that the work-product doctrine "is not applicable to administrative summonses issued under 26 U.S.C.A. § 7602." Id., at 1228, n.13.

II

Federal Rule of Evidence 501 provides that "the privilege of a witness * * * shall be governed by the principles of the common law as they may be interpreted by the courts of the United States in light of reason and experience." The attorney-client privilege is the oldest of the privileges for confidential communications known to the common law. 8 Wigmore, Evidence § 2290 (McNaughton rev. 1961). Its purpose is to encourage full and frank communication between attorneys and their clients and thereby promote broader public interests in the observance of law and administration of justice. The privilege recognizes that sound legal advice or advocacy serves public ends and that such advice or advocacy depends upon the lawyer being fully informed by the client. As we stated last Term in Trammel v. United States, 445 U.S. 40, 51 (1980), "The attorney-client privilege rests on the need for the advocate and counselor to know all that relates to the client's reasons for seeking representation if the professional mission is to be carried out." And in Fisher v. United States, 425 U.S. 391, 403 (1976), we recognized the purpose of the privilege to be "to encourage clients to make full disclosures to their attorneys." This rationale for the privilege has long been recognized by the Court, see Hunt v. Blackburn, 128 U.S. 464, 470

(1888) (privilege "is founded upon the necessity, in the interest and administration of justice, of the aid of persons having knowledge of the law and skilled in its practice, which assistance can only be safely and readily availed of when free from the consequences or the apprehension of disclosure"). Admittedly complications in the application of the privilege arise when the client is a corporation, which in theory is an artificial creature of the law, and not an individual; but this Court has assumed that the privilege applies when the client is a corporation, United States v. Louisville & Nashville R. Co., 235 U.S. 318, 336 (1915), and the Government does not contest the general proposition.

The Court of Appeals, however, considered the application of the privilege in the corporate context to present a "different problem," since the client was an inanimate entity and "only the senior management, guiding and integrating the several operations, * * * can be said to possess an identity analogous to the corporation as a whole." 600 F.2d, at 1226. The first case to articulate the so-called "control group test" adopted by the court below, City of Philadelphia v. Westinghouse Electric Corp., 210 F.Supp. 483, 485 (E.D.Pa.1962), reflected a similar conceptual approach:

> "Keeping in mind that the question is, Is it the corporation which is seeking the lawyer's advice when the asserted privileged communication is made?, the most satisfactory solution, I think, is that if the employee making the communication, of whatever rank he may be, is in a position to control or even to take a substantial part in a decision about any action which the corporation may take upon the advice of the attorney, * * * then, in effect, *he is (or personifies) the corporation* when he makes his disclosure to the lawyer and the privilege would apply." (Emphasis supplied.)

Such a view, we think, overlooks the fact that the privilege exists to protect not only the giving of professional advice to those who can act on it but also the giving of information to the lawyer to enable him to give sound and informed advice. See *Trammel,* 445 U.S., at 51; *Fisher,* 425 U.S., at 403. The first step in the resolution of any legal problem is ascertaining the factual background and sifting through the facts with an eye to the legally relevant. See ABA Code of Professional Responsibility, Ethical Consideration 4–1:

> "A lawyer should be fully informed of all the facts of the matter he is handling in order for his client to obtain the full advantage of our legal system. It is for the lawyer in the exercise of his independent professional judgment to separate the relevant and important from the irrelevant and unimportant. The observance of the ethical obligation of a lawyer to hold inviolate the confidences and secrets of his client not only facilitates the full development of facts essential to proper representation of the client but also encourages laymen to seek early legal assistance."

See also Hickman v. Taylor, 329 U.S. 495, 511 (1947).

In the case of the individual client the provider of information and the person who acts on the lawyer's advice are one and the same. In the corporate context, however, it will frequently be employees beyond the control group as defined by the court below—"officers and agents * * * responsible for directing [the company's] actions in response to legal advice"—who will possess the information needed by the corporation's lawyers. Middle-level—and indeed lower-level—employees can, by actions within the scope of their employment, embroil the corporation in serious legal difficulties, and it is only natural that these employees would have the relevant information needed by corporate counsel if he is adequately to advise the client with respect to such actual or potential difficulties. This fact was noted in Diversified Industries, Inc. v. Meredith, 572 F.2d 596 (C.A.8 1977) (en banc):

> "In a corporation, it may be necessary to glean information relevant to a legal problem from middle management or non-management personnel as well as from top executives. The attorney dealing with a complex legal problem 'is thus faced with a "Hobson's choice." If he interviews employees not having "the very highest authority" their communications to him will not be privileged. If, on the other hand, he interviews *only* those employees with the "very highest authority," he may find it extremely difficult, if not impossible, to determine what happened.' " Id., at 608–609 (quoting Weinschel, Corporate Employee Interviews and the Attorney–Client Privilege, 12 B.C.Ind. & Comm.L.Rev. 873, 876 (1970)).

The control group test adopted by the court below thus frustrates the very purpose of the privilege by discouraging the communication of relevant information by employees of the client to attorneys seeking to render legal advice to the client corporation. The attorney's advice will also frequently be more significant to noncontrol group members than to those who officially sanction the advice, and the control group test makes it more difficult to convey full and frank legal advice to the employees who will put into effect the client corporation's policy. See, e.g., Duplan Corp. v. Deering Milliken, Inc., 397 F.Supp. 1146, 1164 (SC 1974) ("After the lawyer forms his or her opinion, it is of no immediate benefit to the Chairman of the Board or the President. It must be given to the corporate personnel who will apply it.").

The narrow scope given the attorney-client privilege by the court below not only makes it difficult for corporate attorneys to formulate sound advice when their client is faced with a specific legal problem but also threatens to limit the valuable efforts of corporate counsel to ensure their client's compliance with the law. In light of the vast and complicated array of regulatory legislation confronting the modern corporation, corporations, unlike most individuals, "constantly go to lawyers to find out how to obey the law," Burnham, The Attorney–Client Privilege in the Corporate Arena, 24 Bus.Law. 901, 913 (1969), particularly since compliance with the law in this area is hardly an instinctive matter, see, e.g., United States v. United States Gypsum Co., 438 U.S. 422, 440–441 (1978) ("the behavior proscribed by the [Sherman] Act is often difficult to distinguish from the gray zone of socially acceptable and economically justifiable business conduct").[21] The test adopted by the court below is difficult to apply in practice, though no abstractly formulated and unvarying "test" will necessarily enable courts to decide questions such as this with mathematical precision. But if the purpose of the attorney-client privilege is to be served, the attorney and client must be able to predict with some degree of certainty whether particular discussions will be protected. An uncertain privilege, or one which purports to be certain but results in widely varying applications by the courts, is little better than no privilege at all. The very terms of the test adopted by the court below suggest the unpredictability of its application. The test restricts the availability of the privilege to those officers who play a "substantial role" in deciding and directing a corporation's legal response. Disparate decisions in cases applying this test illustrate its unpredictability. Compare, e.g., Hogan v. Zletz, 43 F.R.D. 308, 315–316 (N.D.Okla.1967), aff'd in part sub nom. Natta v. Hogan, 392 F.2d 686 (C.A.10 1968) (control group includes managers and assistant managers of patent division and research and development department) with Congoleum Industries, Inc. v. GAF Corp., 49 F.R.D. 82, 83–85 (E.D.Pa.1969), aff'd 478 F.2d 1398 (C.A.3 1973) (control group includes only division and corporate vice-presidents, and not two directors of research and vice-president for production and research).

The communications at issue were made by Upjohn employees[22] to counsel for Upjohn acting as such, at the direction of corporate superiors in order to secure legal advice from counsel. As the magistrate found, "Mr. Thomas consulted with the Chairman of the Board and outside counsel and thereafter conducted a factual investigation to determine the nature and extent of the questionable payments *and to be in a position to give legal advice to the company with respect to the payments.*" (Emphasis supplied.) Pet. App. 13a. Information, not available from upper-echelon management, was needed to supply a basis for legal advice concerning compliance with securities and tax laws, foreign laws, currency regulations, duties to shareholders, and potential litigation in each of these areas. The communications concerned matters within the scope of the employees' corporate duties and the employees themselves were sufficiently aware that they were being questioned in order that the corporation could obtain legal advice. The questionnaire identified

21. The Government argues that the risk of civil or criminal liability suffices to ensure that corporations will seek legal advice in the absence of the protection of the privilege. This response ignores the fact that the depth and quality of any investigations to ensure compliance with the law would suffer, even were they undertaken. The response also proves too much, since it applies to all communications covered by the privilege; an individual trying to comply with the law or faced with a legal problem also has strong incentive to disclose information to his lawyer, yet the common law has recognized the value of the privilege in further facilitating communications.

22. Seven of the 86 employees interviewed by counsel had terminated their employment with Upjohn at the time of the interview. App. 33a–38a. Petitioner argues that the privilege should nonetheless apply to communications by these former employees concerning activities during their period of employment. Neither the District Court nor the Court of Appeals had occasion to address this issue, and we decline to decide it without the benefit of treatment below.

Thomas as "the company's General Counsel" and referred in its opening sentence to the possible illegality of payments such as the ones on which information was sought. App. 48a. A statement of policy accompanying the questionnaire clearly indicated the legal implications of the investigation. The policy statement was issued "in order that there be no uncertainty in the future as to the policy with respect to the practices which are the subject of this investigation." It began "Upjohn will comply with all laws and regulations," and stated that commissions or payments "will not be used as a subterfuge for bribes or illegal payments" and that all payments must be "proper and legal." Any future agreements with foreign distributors or agents were to be approved "by a company attorney" and any questions concerning the policy were to be referred "to the company's General Counsel." App. 165a–166a. This statement was issued to Upjohn employees worldwide, so that even those interviewees not receiving a questionnaire were aware of the legal implications of the interviews. Pursuant to explicit instructions from the Chairman of the Board, the communications were considered "highly confidential" when made, App. 39a, 43a, and have been kept confidential by the company.[23] Consistent with the underlying purposes of the attorney-client privilege, these communications must be protected against compelled disclosure.

The Court of Appeals declined to extend the attorney-client privilege beyond the limits of the control group test for fear that doing so would entail severe burdens on discovery and create a broad "zone of silence" over corporate affairs. Application of the attorney-client privilege to communications such as those involved here, however, puts the adversary in no worse position than if the communications had never taken place. The privilege only protects disclosure of communications; it does not protect disclosure of the underlying facts by those who communicated with the attorney:

> "The protection of the privilege extends only to *communications* and not to facts. A fact is one thing and a communication concerning that fact is an entirely different thing. The client cannot be compelled to answer the question, 'What did you say or write to the attorney?' but may not refuse to disclose any relevant fact within his knowledge merely because he incorporated a statement of such fact into his communication to his attorney." City of Philadelphia v. Westinghouse Electric Corp., 205 F.Supp. 830, 831 (E.D.Pa.1962).

See also *Diversified Industries,* 572 F.2d, at 611; State v. Circuit Court, 34 Wis.2d 559, 580, 150 N.W.2d 387, 399 (1967) ("the courts have noted that a party cannot conceal a fact merely by revealing it to his lawyer"). Here the Government was free to question the employees who communicated with Thomas and outside counsel. Upjohn has provided the IRS with a list of such employees, and the IRS has already interviewed some 25 of them. While it would probably be more convenient for the Govern-

23. See magistrate's opinion * * *: "The responses to the questionnaires and the notes of the interviews have been treated as confidential material and have not been disclosed to anyone except Mr. Thomas and outside counsel."

ment to secure the results of petitioner's internal investigation by simply subpoenaing the questionnaires and notes taken by petitioner's attorneys, such considerations of convenience do not overcome the policies served by the attorney-client privilege. As Justice Jackson noted in his concurring opinion in Hickman v. Taylor, 329 U.S., at 516: "Discovery was hardly intended to enable a learned profession to perform its functions * * * on wits borrowed from the adversary."

Needless to say, we decide only the case before us, and do not undertake to draft a set of rules which should govern challenges to investigatory subpoenas. Any such approach would violate the spirit of F.R.E. 501. See S.Rep. No. 93–1277, 93d Cong., 2d Sess., 13 ("the recognition of a privilege based on a confidential relationship * * * should be determined on a case-by-case basis"); *Trammel,* 445 U.S. at 47; United States v. Gillock, 445 U.S. 360, 367 (1980). While such a "case-by-case" basis may to some slight extent undermine desirable certainty in the boundaries of the attorney-client privilege, it obeys the spirit of the Rules. At the same time we conclude that the narrow "control group test" sanctioned by the Court of Appeals in this case cannot, consistent with "the principles of the common law as * * * interpreted * * * in light of reason and experience," F.R.E. 501, govern the development of the law in this area.

III

Our decision that the communications by Upjohn employees to counsel are covered by the attorney-client privilege disposes of the case so far as the responses to the questionnaires and any notes reflecting responses to interview questions are concerned. The summons reaches further, however, and Thomas has testified that his notes and memoranda of interviews go beyond recording responses to his questions. App. 27a–28a, 91a–93a. To the extent that the material subject to the summons is not protected by the attorney-client privilege as disclosing communications between an employee and counsel, we must reach the ruling by the Court of Appeals that the work-product doctrine does not apply to summonses issued under 26 U.S.C.A. § 7602.

The Government concedes, wisely, that the Court of Appeals erred and that the work-product doctrine does apply to IRS summonses. Gov.Br., at 16, 48. This doctrine was announced by the Court over 30 years ago in Hickman v. Taylor, 329 U.S. 495 (1947). In that case the Court rejected "an attempt, without purported necessity or justification, to secure written statements, private memoranda, and personal recollections prepared or formed by an adverse party's counsel in the course of his legal duties." Id., at 510. The Court noted that "it is essential that a lawyer work with a certain degree of privacy" and reasoned that if discovery of the material sought were permitted

> "much of what is now put down in writing would remain unwritten. An attorney's thoughts, heretofore inviolate, would not be his own. Inefficiency, unfairness and sharp practices would inevitably develop

> in the giving of legal advice and in the preparation of cases for trial. The effect on the legal profession would be demoralizing. And the interests of the clients and the cause of justice would be poorly served." Id., at 511.

The "strong public policy" underlying the work-product doctrine was reaffirmed recently in United States v. Nobles, 422 U.S. 225, 236–240 (1975), and has been substantially incorporated in Federal Rule of Civil Procedure 26(b)(3).[24]

As we stated last Term, the obligation imposed by a tax summons remains "subject to the traditional privileges and limitations." United States v. Euge, 444 U.S. 707, 714 (1980). Nothing in the language of the IRS summons provisions or their legislative history suggests an intent on the part of Congress to preclude application of the work-product doctrine. Rule 26(b)(3) codifies the work-product doctrine, and the Federal Rules of Civil Procedure are made applicable to summons enforcement proceedings by Rule 81(a)(3). See Donaldson v. United States, 400 U.S. 517, 528 (1971). While conceding the applicability of the work-product doctrine, the Government asserts that it has made a sufficient showing of necessity to overcome its protections. The magistrate apparently so found, Pet. App. 30a. The Government relies on the following language in *Hickman*:

> "We do not mean to say that all written materials obtained or prepared by an adversary's counsel with an eye toward litigation are necessarily free from discovery in all cases. Where relevant and nonprivileged facts remain hidden in an attorney's file and where production of those facts is essential to the preparation of one's case, discovery may properly be had. * * * And production might be justified where the witnesses are no longer available or may be reached only with difficulty." 329 U.S., at 511.

The Government stresses that interviewees are scattered across the globe and that Upjohn has forbidden its employees to answer questions it considers irrelevant. The above-quoted language from *Hickman*, however, did not apply to "oral statements made by witnesses * * * whether presently in the form of [the attorney's] mental impressions or memoranda." Id., at 512. As to such material the Court did "not believe that any showing of necessity can be made under the circumstances of this case so as to justify production. * * * If there should be a rare situation justifying production of these matters, petitioner's case is not of that

24. This provides, in pertinent part:

"[A] party may obtain discovery of documents and tangible things otherwise discoverable under subdivision (b)(1) of this rule and prepared in anticipation of litigation or for trial by or for another party or by or for that other party's representative (including his attorney, consultant, surety, indemnitor, insurer, or agent) only upon a showing that the party seeking discovery has substantial need of the materials in the preparation of his case and that he is unable without undue hardship to obtain the substantial equivalent of the materials by other means. In ordering discovery of such materials when the required showing has been made, the court shall protect against disclosure of the mental impressions, conclusions, opinions, or legal theories of an attorney or other representative of a party concerning the litigation."

type." Id., at 512–513. See also *Nobles,* supra, at 252–253 (White, J., concurring). Forcing an attorney to disclose notes and memoranda of witnesses' oral statements is particularly disfavored because it tends to reveal the attorney's mental processes, 329 U.S., at 513 ("what he saw fit to write down regarding witnesses' remarks"); id., at 516–517 ("the statement would be his [the attorney's] language, permeated with his inferences") (Jackson, J., concurring).[25]

Rule 26 accords special protection to work product revealing the attorney's mental processes. The Rule permits disclosure of documents and tangible things constituting attorney work product upon a showing of substantial need and inability to obtain the equivalent without undue hardship. This was the standard applied by the magistrate, Pet. App. 26a–27a. Rule 26 goes on, however, to state that "[i]n ordering discovery of such materials when the required showing has been made, the court shall protect against disclosure of the mental impressions, conclusions, opinions or legal theories of an attorney or other representative of a party concerning the litigation." Although this language does not specifically refer to memoranda based on oral statements of witnesses, the *Hickman* court stressed the danger that compelled disclosure of such memoranda would reveal the attorney's mental processes. It is clear that this is the sort of material the draftsmen of the Rule had in mind as deserving special protection. See Notes of Advisory Committee on 1970 Amendment to Rules, reprinted in 48 F.R.D. 487, 502 ("The subdivision * * * goes on to protect against disclosure the mental impressions, conclusions, opinions, or legal theories * * * of an attorney or other representative of a party. The *Hickman* opinion drew special attention to the need for protecting an attorney against discovery of memoranda prepared from recollection of oral interviews. The courts have steadfastly safeguarded against disclosure of lawyers' mental impressions and legal theories * * * ").

Based on the foregoing, some courts have concluded that *no* showing of necessity can overcome protection of work product which is based on oral statements from witnesses. See, e.g., In re Grand Jury Proceedings, 473 F.2d 840, 848 (C.A.8 1973) (personal recollections, notes and memoranda pertaining to conversation with witnesses); In re Grand Jury Investigation, 412 F.Supp. 943, 949 (E.D.Pa.1976) (notes of conversation with witness "are so much a product of the lawyer's thinking and so little probative of the witness's actual words that they are absolutely protected from disclosure"). Those courts declining to adopt an absolute rule have nonetheless recognized that such material is entitled to special protection. See, e.g., In re Grand Jury Investigation, 599 F.2d, at 1231 ("special considerations * * * must shape any ruling on the discoverability of interview memoranda * * * such documents will be discoverable

25. Thomas described his notes of the interviews as containing "what I consider to be the important questions, the substance of the responses to them, my beliefs as to the importance of these, my beliefs as to how they related to the inquiry, my thoughts as to how they related to other questions. In some instances they might even suggest other questions that I would have to ask or things that I needed to find elsewhere." Pet. App. 13a.

only in a 'rare situation' "); cf. In re Grand Jury Subpoena, 599 F.2d, at 511–512.

We do not decide the issue at this time. It is clear that the magistrate applied the wrong standard when he concluded that the Government had made a sufficient showing of necessity to overcome the protections of the work-product doctrine. The magistrate applied the "substantial need" and "without undue hardship" standard articulated in the first part of Rule 26(b)(3). The notes and memoranda sought by the Government here, however, are work product based on oral statements. If they reveal communications, they are, in this case, protected by the attorney-client privilege. To the extent they do not reveal communications, they reveal the attorneys' mental processes in evaluating the communications. As Rule 26 and *Hickman* make clear, such work product cannot be disclosed simply on a showing of substantial need and inability to obtain the equivalent without undue hardship.

While we are not prepared at this juncture to say that such material is always protected by the work-product rule, we think a far stronger showing of necessity and unavailability by other means than was made by the Government or applied by the magistrate in this case would be necessary to compel disclosure. Since the Court of Appeals thought that the work-product protection was never applicable in an enforcement proceeding such as this, and since the magistrate whose recommendations the District Court adopted applied too lenient a standard of protection, we think the best procedure with respect to this aspect of the case would be to reverse the judgment of the Court of Appeals for the Sixth Circuit and remand the case to it for such further proceedings in connection with the work-product claim as are consistent with this opinion.

Accordingly, the judgment of the Court of Appeals is reversed, and the case remanded for further proceedings.

Chief Justice Burger, concurring in part and concurring in the judgment.

I join in Parts I and III of the opinion of the Court and in the judgment. As to Part II, I agree fully with the Court's rejection of the so-called "control group" test, its reasons for doing so, and its ultimate holding that the communications at issue are privileged. As the Court states, however, "if the purpose of the attorney-client privilege is to be served, the attorney and the client must be able to predict with some degree of certainty whether particular discussions will be protected." * * * For this very reason, I believe that we should articulate a standard that will govern similar cases and afford guidance to corporations, counsel advising them, and federal courts.

The Court properly relies on a variety of factors in concluding that the communications now before us are privileged. * * * Because of the great importance of the issue, in my view the Court should make clear now that, as a general rule, a communication is privileged at least when, as here, an employee or former employee speaks at the direction of the management with an attorney regarding conduct or proposed conduct within the scope of employment. The attorney must be one authorized by the management to inquire into the subject and must be seeking information to assist counsel in performing any of the following functions: (a) evaluating whether the employee's conduct has bound or would bind the corporation; (b) assessing the legal consequences, if any, of that conduct; or (c) formulating appropriate legal responses to actions that have been or may be taken by others with regard to that conduct. See, e.g., Diversified Industries, Inc. v. Meredith, 572 F.2d 596, 609 (C.A.8 1977) (en banc); Harper & Row Publishers, Inc. v. Decker, 423 F.2d 487, 491–492 (C.A.7 1970), aff'd by an equally divided Court, 400 U.S. 348 (1971); Duplan Corp. v. Deering Milliken, Inc., 397 F.Supp. 1146, 1163–1165 (SC 1974). Other communications between employees and corporate counsel may indeed be privileged—as the petitioners and several *amici* have suggested in their proposed formulations—but the need for certainty does not compel us now to prescribe all the details of the privilege in this case.

Nevertheless, to say we should not reach all facets of the privilege does not mean that we should neglect our duty to provide guidance in a case that squarely presents the question in a traditional adversary context. Indeed, because Federal Rule of Evidence 501 provides that the law of privileges "shall be governed by the principles of the common law as they may be interpreted by the courts of the United States in light of reason and experience," this Court has a special duty to clarify aspects of the law of privileges properly before us. Simply asserting that this failure "may to some slight extent undermine desirable certainty," * * * neither minimizes the consequences of continuing uncertainty and confusion nor harmonizes the inherent dissonance of acknowledging that uncertainty while declining to clarify it within the frame of issues presented.

Notes and Questions

1. *Sources.* See generally Rothstein, *Upjohn v. United States:* The Story of One Man's Journey to Extend Lawyer–Client Confidentiality and the Social Forces That Affected It, in Evidence Stories 151 (Lempert ed., 2006).

2. *State decisions.* Note that the Supreme Court's decision in *Upjohn* is predicated on common law and not upon federal constitutional grounds. Accordingly the decision does not compel state abandonment of the control group test, which was widely followed prior to *Upjohn.* Although many states have adopted the *Upjohn* approach, see Southern Bell Telephone & Telegraph Co. v. Deason, 632 So.2d 1377 (Fla.1994), some states have continued to adhere to their earlier standard. Consolidation Coal Co. v. Bucyrus–Erie Co., 432 N.E.2d 250 (Ill.1982). Compare Uniform Rules of Evidence 502, infra.

What problems arise from recognition of different forms of the privilege by state and federal courts? See McCormick, Evidence § 76 (6th ed. 2006).

One state court, attempting to minimize such problems by affording "rough comparability with federal common law," Samaritan Foundation v. Goodfarb, 862 P.2d 870 (Ariz.1993), found its solution quickly nullified by legislative action. See Ariz.Rev.Stat. § 12–2234.

3. *Empirical study.* An interesting (and rare) empirical study of the actual operation of the privilege in the corporate context is Alexander, The Corporate Attorney–Client Privilege: A Study of the Participants, 63 St. John's L.Rev. 191 (1989) (proposing that the privilege for non-control group employees be only a qualified one).

4. *Other problems in the corporate context.* Among the many problems raised by application of the attorney-client privilege in the corporate context some of the most troublesome concern the question of who should be viewed as representing the corporation in a variety of situations. Should the privilege be available to management in a derivative stockholders action? See Garner v. Wolfinbarger, 430 F.2d 1093 (5th Cir.1970) (privilege held by management but may become unavailable upon stockholder showing of "good cause"). See also Saltzburg, Corporate Attorney–Client Privilege in Shareholder Litigation and Similar Cases: *Garner* Revisited, 12 Hofstra.L.Rev. 817 (1984); Friedman, Is the *Garner* Qualification of the Corporate Attorney–Client Privilege Viable after *Jaffee v. Redmond*, 55 Bus. Law. 243 (1999). *Garner* has been extended to a variety of situations other than derivative suits. See, e.g., In re Occidental Petroleum Corp., 217 F.3d 293 (5th Cir.2000) (employees who were participants in stock ownership plan suing for breaches of fiduciary duty relating to the plan); Fausek v. White, 965 F.2d 126 (6th Cir.1992) (minority shareholders suing for own benefit rather than corporation's). Who should hold the privilege as between management and a trustee in bankruptcy? Commodity Futures Trading Comm'n v. Weintraub, 471 U.S. 343 (1985). Problems of this sort will obviously be compounded if the communicating employee asserts that he was also personally the client of the attorney.

5. *Work product privilege.* The *Upjohn* case involved the work product privilege as well as the attorney-client privilege. See 1 McCormick, Evidence § 96 (6th ed. 2006), for a comparison of these related, overlapping and often confused doctrines.

UNIFORM RULES OF EVIDENCE

RULE 502. LAWYER–CLIENT PRIVILEGE.

(a) Definitions. In this rule:

(1) "Client" means a person for whom a lawyer renders professional legal services or who consults a lawyer with a view to obtaining professional legal services from the lawyer.

(2) A communication is "confidential" if it is not intended to be disclosed to third persons other than those to whom disclosure is made in furtherance of the rendition of professional legal services to the client or those reasonably necessary for the transmission of the communication.

(3) "Lawyer" means a person authorized, or reasonably believed by the client to be authorized, to engage in the practice of law in any State or country.

(4) "Representative of the client" means a person having authority to obtain professional legal services, or to act on legal advice rendered, on behalf of the client or a person who, for the purpose of effectuating legal representation for the client, makes or receives a confidential communication while acting in the scope of employment for the client.

(5) "Representative of the lawyer" means a person employed, or reasonably believed by the client to be employed, by the lawyer to assist the lawyer in rendering professional legal services.

(b) General rule of privilege. A client has a privilege to refuse to disclose and to prevent any other person from disclosing a confidential communication made for the purpose of facilitating the rendition of professional legal services to the client:

(1) between the client or a representative of the client and the client's lawyer or a representative of the lawyer;

(2) between the lawyer and a representative of the lawyer;

(3) by the client or a representative of the client or the client's lawyer or a representative of the lawyer to a lawyer or a representative of a lawyer representing another party in a pending action and concerning a matter of common interest therein;

(4) between representatives of the client or between the client and a representative of the client; or

(5) among lawyers and their representatives representing the same client.

(c) Who may claim privilege. The privilege under this rule may be claimed by the client, the client's guardian or conservator, the personal representative of a deceased client, or the successor, trustee, or similar representative of a corporation, association, or other organization, whether or not in existence. A person who was the lawyer or the lawyer's representative at the time of the communication is presumed to have authority to claim the privilege, but only on behalf of the client.

(d) Exceptions. There is no privilege under this rule:

(1) if the services of the lawyer were sought or obtained to enable or aid anyone to commit or plan to commit what the client knew or reasonably should have known was a crime or fraud;

(2) as to a communication relevant to an issue between parties who claim through the same deceased client, regardless of whether the claims are by testate or intestate succession or by transaction inter vivos;

(3) as to a communication relevant to an issue of breach of duty by a lawyer to the client or by a client to the lawyer;

(4) as to a communication necessary for a lawyer to defend in a legal proceeding an accusation that the lawyer assisted the client in criminal or fraudulent conduct;

(5) as to a communication relevant to an issue concerning an attested document to which the lawyer is an attesting witness;

(6) as to a communication relevant to a matter of common interest between or among two or more clients if the communication was made by any of them to a lawyer retained or consulted in common, when offered in an action between or among any of the clients; or

(7) as to a communication between a public officer or agency and its lawyers unless the communication concerns a pending investigation, claim, or action and the court determines that disclosure will seriously impair the ability of the public officer or agency to act upon the claim or conduct a pending investigation, litigation, or proceeding in the public interest.

Notes and Questions

1. *Comparison with Upjohn.* Prior to 1986, Revised Uniform Rule of Evidence 502 embodied the "control group" test rejected in *Upjohn Co. v. United States*. The rule was amended in 1987 to track the *Upjohn* holding. Uniform Rule of Evidence 502 (amended 1986), Comment. To what extent does it do so? Are all aspects of the rule suggested by the *Upjohn* decision?

2. *Subject matter.* What should be the result if the subject matter of the corporate employee's communication to the corporate attorney has no connection with the employee's corporate duties? A subject matter limitation where the privilege is claimed for communications by corporate employees has frequently been advocated. See, e.g., D.I. Chadbourne, Inc. v. Superior Court, 388 P.2d 700 (Cal.1964). Would such a limitation invite unduly restricted applications of the privilege? In Leer v. Chicago, M., St. P. & Pac. Ry., 308 N.W.2d 305 (Minn.1981), the court first argued, conventionally, that "communications about events which are within the employee's knowledge simply because he witnessed an accident" should not be privileged. The court then applied this rule to deny privilege to statements of the members of a railway switching crew concerning a switching accident, stating that "the witnessing of an accident was not within the scope of the employees' duties."

3. *Representatives of the client.* Cases considering who is a "representative" of the client under rules similar to Uniform Rule 502 are collected in Annot., 66 A.L.R.4th 1227. Should the expansive definition of "representative of the client" now contained in Uniform Rule 502 apply, as the text of the rule would justify, to individuals as well as to corporate clients? Should it matter whether the communication concerns the principal's business or private affairs? In State v. Jancsek, 730 P.2d 14 (Or.1986) (en banc), the privilege was held inapplicable to a letter written by the defendant to a former employer which contained incriminating statements and empowered the addressee to secure legal representation. The court held that while the

terms of the statute (similar to Uniform Rule 502) would support availability of the privilege to a non-business entity, the legislative history did not.

Compare Sexton, A Post *Upjohn* Consideration of the Corporate Attorney–Client Privilege, 57 N.Y.U.L.Rev. 443 (1982) (suggesting that *Upjohn* may foreshadow the development of an "enterprise" privilege, extending to the non-managerial employees of labor unions, government agencies, partnerships, and other entities).

STATE v. PRATT

Court of Appeals of Maryland, 1979.
398 A.2d 421.

DIGGES, JUDGE.

The question presented by this criminal cause is one of first impression in this State, and yet, it involves "the oldest of the privileges for confidential communications"—that which exists between an attorney and his client. 8 J. Wigmore, *Evidence in Trials at Common Law* § 2290, at 542 (McNaughton rev. 1961). Stated succinctly, we are asked to decide whether this privilege was violated when, over objection, a psychiatrist, who was retained by defense counsel to examine his client in preparing an insanity defense, was permitted to testify at the instance of the prosecution. Because we conclude that this fundamental privilege was invaded, we will direct a new trial.

The factual background here is uncomplicated and may be briefly related. On the morning of October 23, 1976, respondent Margaret Melton Pratt, after a sleepless night during which she contemplated the taking of her own life, shot and killed her still-slumbering husband, William S. Pratt, in their Montgomery County apartment. After the shooting, the wife packed an overnight bag and drove to a friend's farm near Front Royal, Virginia, to visit the gravesite of her dog; she stayed several hours and then proceeded to a nearby motel to spend the night. The next morning Mrs. Pratt returned to her home and, after a short stay there, began driving aimlessly around the Bethesda–Rockville area. Realizing she would eventually be apprehended, the respondent went to the Montgomery County police and informed them of her husband's death. The officers, after verifying Mrs. Pratt's story concerning what had taken place, arrested her for murder.

* * *

Throughout the trial, Mrs. Pratt did not dispute that she had killed her husband but, instead, strenuously urged that she was insane at the time she fired the fatal shots. In support of her insanity plea, respondent presented two psychiatrists, Dr. Gerald Polin and Dr. Leon Yochelson, who testified that at the time of the act Mrs. Pratt was, in their opinion, suffering from a mental illness of such severity that she lacked substantial capacity to conform her conduct to the requirements of the law. *See* Md.Code (1957, 1972 Repl. Vol.), Art. 59, § 25(a). In rebuttal, the State produced three psychiatrists, all of whom agreed that the respondent was suffering from some degree of mental disorder when the shooting took place. Nonetheless, two of these medical experts testified that, under Maryland law, Mrs. Pratt was legally responsible for her act. Of these two, one, Dr. Brian Crowley, had examined the accused at the request of her attorney after being retained by him to aid in preparing support for Mrs. Pratt's insanity plea. It is the evidence given by Dr. Crowley, who testified during the trial at the request of the State and over the objection of the defense, that precipitated the controversy now before us. On appeal to the Court of Special Appeals, that court concluded that the permitting of Dr. Crowley's testimony violated the attorney-client privilege and ordered a new trial. *Pratt v. State,* 39 Md.App. 442, 387 A.2d 779 (1978). We agree.

In this State the attorney-client privilege, deeply rooted in common law and now memorialized in section 9–108 of the Maryland Code's (1974) Courts Article, is a rule of evidence that forever bars disclosure, without the consent of the client, of all communications that pass in confidence between the client and his attorney during the course of professional employment or as an incident of professional intercourse between them. *See Harrison v. State,* 276 Md. 122, 135, 345 A.2d 830, 838 (1975); 3 B. Jones, *The Law of Evidence* § 21:8–:10, at 762–71 (6th ed. S. Gard 1972); 8 J. Wigmore, *supra,* § 2292, at 554. The privilege is based upon the public policy that " 'an individual in a free society should be encouraged to consult with his attorney whose function is to counsel and advise him and he should be free from apprehension of compelled disclosures by his legal advisor.' " *Harrison v. State, supra,* 276 Md. at 135, 345 A.2d at 838 (quoting *Morris v. State,* 4 Md.App. 252, 254, 242 A.2d 559, 560 (1968)); *accord,* 8 J. Wigmore, *supra,* § 2291, at 545. While never given an explicit constitutional underpinning, the privilege is, nevertheless, closely tied to the federal, as well as this State's, constitutional guarantees of effective assistance of counsel and could, if limited too severely, make these basic guarantees virtually meaningless. *Harrison v. State, supra,* 276 Md. at 133–34, 345 A.2d at 837; *United States v. Alvarez,* 519 F.2d 1036, 1045–47 (3d Cir.1975); *see* U.S.Const., amend. VI; Md.Decl. of Rts., Art. 21.

Initially we observe that, given the complexities of modern existence, few if any lawyers could, as a practical matter, represent the interest of their clients without a variety of nonlegal assistance. Recognizing this limitation, it is now almost universally accepted in this country that the scope of the attorney-client privilege, at least in criminal causes, embraces those agents whose services are required by the attorney in order that he may properly prepare his client's case. Consequently, in line with the views of the vast majority of the courts in our sister jurisdictions, we have no hesitancy in concluding that in criminal causes communications made by a defendant to an expert in order to equip that expert with the necessary information to provide the defendant's attorney with the tools to aid him in giving his client proper legal advice are within the scope of the attorney-client privilege. *E.g., United States v. Alvarez, supra,* 519 F.2d at 1046 (psychiatrist); *United*

States v. Kovel, 296 F.2d 918, 922 (2d Cir.1961) (accountant); *People v. Lines,* 13 Cal.3d 500, 119 Cal.Rptr. 225, 232–35, 531 P.2d 793, 800–03 (1975) (psychiatrist); *accord,* 3 B. Jones, *supra,* § 21:15, at 786–87. *But cf. State v. Mingo,* 143 N.J.Super. 411, 363 A.2d 369, 370–71 (1976) (per curiam) (because defendant's handwriting exemplars not privileged communications, State's solicitation at trial of opinion of defense-hired graphologist as to identity of handwriting on note sent to assault victim not barred by attorney-client privilege). This is uniquely so in cases concerning the question of a criminal defendant's sanity, because the need of an attorney to consult with a qualified medical expert is paramount. Such a medical expert not only provides testimony that usually is necessary at trial to support an insanity defense, but also "attunes the lay attorney to unfamiliar but central medical concepts and enables him, as an initial matter, to assess the soundness and advisability of offering the defense * * * and perhaps most importantly, * * * permits a lawyer inexpert in the science of psychiatry to probe intelligently the foundations of adverse testimony." *United States v. Taylor,* 437 F.2d 371, 377 n.9 (4th Cir.1971).

The State here does not dispute the inclusion of psychiatric communications within the scope of the attorney-client privilege; instead, it contends that when Mrs. Pratt interposed a defense of insanity, she waived the privilege with respect to all statements she may have made to any medical expert, whether in her employ or in that of the State.[26] While there is little doubt that a client may waive this right to confidentiality, which may be done either expressly or impliedly, *see, e.g., Harrison v. State, supra,* 276 Md. at 136–38, 345 A.2d at 839; 8 J. Wigmore, *supra,* § 2327, at 634–39; *but see* 2 H. Underhill, *Criminal Evidence* § 333, at 841 (5th ed. P. Herrick 1956) (doubtful if any waiver of the privilege should be implied in criminal cause), we have been made aware of only one decision in which a court, the New York Court of Appeals, has held that raising the defense of insanity, without more, is a relinquishment of the attorney-client privilege as to communications between the client and his alienist. In its opinion the court justified its conclusion that a defendant's insanity plea waived the attorney-client privilege on the following basis:

> A defendant who seeks to introduce psychiatric testimony in support of his insanity plea may be required to disclose prior to trial the underlying basis of his alleged affliction to a prosecution psychiatrist. Hence, where, as here, a defendant reveals to the prosecution the very facts which would be secreted by the exercise of the privilege, reason does not compel the exclusion of expert testimony based on such facts, or cross-examination concerning the grounds for opinions based thereon. It follows that no harm accrues to the

26. In effect, the State asks us, by judicial decision, to create a waiver of the attorney-client privilege as the General Assembly has done by providing that, in the case of the psychiatrist/psychologist-patient privilege, if the patient "introduces his mental condition as an element of his claim or defense * * *," the privilege is waived. *See* Md.Code (1974, 1978 Cum.Supp.), § 9–109(d)(3)(i) of the Courts Article.

> defense from seeking pretrial psychiatric advice where an insanity plea is actually entered, for in such circumstances, the underlying factual basis will be revealed to the prosecution psychiatrist. (*People v. Edney,* 39 N.Y.2d 620, 385 N.Y.S.2d 23, 26, 350 N.E.2d 400, 403 (1976). * * *)

While there appears to be some logic, at least in a technical sense, to New York's highest court's reasoning, nonetheless we find that the chilling effect such a result would have upon a client's willingness to confide in his attorney or any defense-employed consultants requires that we align ourselves with the overwhelming body of authority and reject that court's conclusion. *See United States v. Alvarez, supra,* 519 F.2d at 1046; *United States ex rel. Edney v. Smith,* 425 F.Supp. 1038, 1039, 1053 (E.D.N.Y.1976) (dicta); *People v. Lines, supra,* 531 P.2d at 800–03, 119 Cal.Rptr. at 232–35; *Pouncy v. State,* 353 So.2d 640, 641–42 (Fla.Dist.Ct.App.1977); *People v. Hilliker,* 29 Mich.App. 543, 185 N.W.2d 831, 833 (1971); *State v. Kociolek,* 23 N.J. 400, 129 A.2d 417, 423–26 (1957).

Moreover, a further drawback to the New York rule is the prejudice inherent in disclosing to the trier of fact that the source of this adverse testimony is an expert originally employed by the defendant. This factor will almost certainly carry added weight with the jury, which usually is the prosecution's principal purpose for producing the defense-employed psychiatrist as a witness. *See United States ex rel. Edney v. Smith, supra,* 425 F.Supp. at 1053; Note, *Protecting the Confidentiality of Pretrial Psychiatric Disclosures: A Survey of Standards,* 51 N.Y.U.L.Rev. 409, 411 (1976). The potential for prejudice inherent in such evidence, as demonstrated by the State's closing argument to the jury in this case,[27] graphically illustrates that the attorney-client privilege protecting such potential testimony from disclosure should remain intact. Though the State points out that this Court previously has recognized the existence of a discretion in the trial court to permit the introduction of evidence concerning the employment posture of an expert because such evidence is frequently a useful factor in evaluating the credibility of the expert witness's testimony, *City of Baltimore v. Zell,* 279 Md. 23, 28, 367 A.2d 14, 17 (1977), that decision arose in a civil context and does not provide a persuasive basis for employing a waiver of the attorney-client privilege in criminal causes.[28]

* * *

27. Concerning the testimony of Dr. Crowley, the State's Attorney argued to the jury:

> Mr. Heeney [, the defendant's attorney,] said he was glad he didn't use Dr. Crowley. If Dr. Crowley had given a different opinion, Dr. Crowley would have been in here so fast it would have made your head spin and not in my case but in Mr. Heeney's case. *They hired Dr. Crowley.* Dr. Crowley was the first defense psychiatrist to see Mrs. Pratt. He said she did not lack substantial capacity * * * . *What do they do after that? They kept looking and finally they found him. How many people didn't show up here?* I don't know the answer to that. Were there any others we don't know about? I don't know. We know they found two. [(Emphasis added.)]

28. In reaching the result we do in this case, we confine our holding to criminal

* * * Breaching the attorney-client privilege in this situation also would have the effect of inhibiting the free exercise of a defense attorney's informed judgment by confronting him with the likelihood that, in taking a step obviously crucial to his client's defense, he is creating a potential government witness who theretofore did not exist. *Id.* The possible impact upon the federal and State constitutional rights of the defendant of a rule permitting such testimony further persuades us that we should be reluctant to hold there is a waiver, under the circumstances here, of the attorney-client privilege.

Accordingly, we affirm the judgment of the Court of Special Appeals, which comports with the ruling we make here.

Notes and Questions

1. *Insanity defense.* Courts are split on the issue of whether defendant presenting an insanity defense waives the attorney-client privilege as to nontestifying defense retained psychiatrists. In addition to *Pratt*, compare State v. Pawlyk, 800 P.2d 338 (Wash.1990) (privilege still applies), with United States v. Alvarez, 519 F.2d 1036 (3d Cir.1975) (no privilege). See generally Note, Witness for the Prosecution: Prosecutorial Discovery of Information Generated by Non-testifying Defense Psychiatric Experts, 62 Fordham L.Rev. 653 (1993).

2. *Waivers based on claims or defenses. Pratt* is extensively discussed and criticized in Saltzburg, Privileges and Professionals: Lawyers and Psychiatrists, 66 Va.L.Rev. 597 (1980). Professor Saltzburg advocates the view that raising the defense of insanity should, in effect, waive the attorney-client privilege insofar as it might cover psychiatric testimony from experts initially retained by the defense. Should the commencement of an action by the beneficiary of a double indemnity life insurance contract, contested on grounds of suicide, waive the attorney-client privilege as to statements by the deceased to his attorney? Martin v. John Hancock Mut. Life Ins. Co., 466 N.Y.S.2d 596 (Gen.Term.1983), held in the affirmative. On what ground, if any, can this result be justified?

Certain defenses, too, may if asserted waive the privilege. Not surprisingly, asserting a defense of advice of counsel waives the privilege. See United States v. Workman, 138 F.3d 1261 (8th Cir.1998).

causes and specifically reserve for another time the question of the scope of the attorney-client privilege when an attorney hires an expert to aid in the preparation of civil matters. Though an opponent called as his witness at trial an expert appraiser hired by his adversary in *City of Baltimore v. Zell,* 279 Md. 23, 367 A.2d 14 (1977), he did so without objection and thus, in *Zell,* the question of the impact upon the attorney-client privilege of allowing that testimony was not determined by this Court. For differing views among our sister states on this subject compare *People v. Donovan,* 57 Cal.2d 346, 369 P.2d 1, 5–7, 19 Cal.Rptr. 473, 477–79 (1962) (appraiser's opinion not covered by attorney-client privilege) with *State v. 62.96247 Acres of Land in New Castle County,* 193 A.2d 799, 810, 7 Storey 40 (Del.Super.Ct.1963) (attorney-client privilege bars party from compelling testimony of appraiser hired by opponent) and *Lindsay v. Lipson,* 367 Mich. 1, 116 N.W.2d 60, 62–63 (1962) (to allow physician hired by plaintiff in tort action to testify for defendant, over opponent's objection, violates attorney-client privilege).

3. *Work product privilege.* To what extent should the work product privilege bar access to expert testimony which will be used at trial? See Federal Rule of Civil Procedure 26(b)(4). See generally Imwinkelried, The Applicability of the Attorney–Client Privilege to Non–Testifying Experts: Reestablishing the Boundaries Between the Attorney–Client Privilege and the Work Product Protection, 68 Wash.U.L.Q. 19 (1990), where the author asserts that the attorney-client privilege applies to communications between the client and the psychiatrist but that only the work product privilege applies to the expert's other information. See also State v. Pawlyk, note 1, supra (work-product privilege also inapplicable); Friedenthal, Discovery and Use of Adverse Party's Expert Information, 14 Stan.L.Rev. 455 (1962); Graham, Discovery of Experts under Rule 26(b)(4) of the Federal Rules of Civil Procedure, 1976 U.Ill.L.F. 895.

HENKE v. IOWA HOME MUT. CAS. CO.

Supreme Court of Iowa, 1958.
87 N.W.2d 920.

LARSON, JUSTICE. The principal issue involved in this appeal is whether correspondence, reports and communications are confidential and privileged between an insurer and the attorney employed by it to defend an insured in litigation resulting from an automobile accident insofar as it pertains to that litigation.

Plaintiff brought an action at law asking damages against the defendant, an automobile liability insurance company, referred to herein as the insurer, for bad faith and negligence in failing to settle two cases against plaintiff within the limits of the policy and in which judgment was rendered against him in an amount greatly in excess of the limits of the policy. After the issues were resolved, plaintiff filed an application asking for an order directing the defendant company to produce for plaintiff's inspection, copying, or photostating "all letters, correspondence, reports, communications and copies of the same," concerning the two previously tried cases in Floyd County, Iowa. Defendant's resistance was on the sole ground that each and every item which plaintiff asked an order to produce "is privileged" under the laws of the State of Iowa, and is therefore not available to plaintiff for his use in the trial of this cause.

In its ruling the court found that the insurer employed a Mason City law firm in accordance with its obligation under an insurance contract with plaintiff's decedent, to defend in any action for damages resulting from such an accident; that said firm did defend the administrator in the trial of the two cases, and further that said firm "did defend and represent both parties, that is E.W. Henke, Administrator, and Iowa Home Mutual Casualty Company in the two cases against * * * E.W. Henke, Administrator."

The trial court then said: "The Court finds that this being true, the letters and documents which the plaintiff in this cause wishes to inspect, copy or photostat, are not privileged," and it entered an order for the defendant to deposit within fifteen days with the clerk, for inspection, copying or photostating by plaintiff, *all letters, correspondence, reports, communications* and *copies* of same, concerning the causes of action heretofore mentioned, sent by the defendant company to the Mason City attorneys who tried the cases, and received by the company from said attorneys, as it concerned the two causes of action already tried. * * *

I. Defendant denies there is any attorney-client relationship between a lawyer, hired by an insurer and who defends the insured under the terms of the insurance policy, and the insured. The contention is without merit. * * *

II. We have consistently held that when two or more parties consult an attorney for their mutual benefit, the testimony as to the communications between the parties or the attorney as to that transaction is not privileged in a later action between such parties or their representatives. In our latest reference to this matter in England v. England, 243 Iowa 274, 282, 51 N.W.2d 437, 442, we said:

> "Notwithstanding section 622.10, Code 1950 (now 1954), I.C.A., prohibiting testimony as to confidential communications, (the attorney's) testimony would have been admissible since, as (he) testifies, he acted as adviser to both plaintiff and defendant who went together to his office, if indeed he was more than primarily a scrivener of the deeds."

The rule is quite clear that to constitute a privileged communication to an attorney there must be some element of confidence imposed in the attorney himself, and for him to accept that relationship it must be apparent that the transaction or his action in relation thereto is for the mutual benefit of the parties, knowingly and willingly seeking his professional services.

It is true that in most, if not in all, of our previously-decided cases, both parties went together to the attorney for advice and guidance. Defendant vigorously contends that even if insurer and insured were both clients of one attorney in regard to the actions, the confidential nature of their respective communications with the attorney must be respected and be held privileged unless (1) they are made in the presence of the other, or (2) are made with the intent that they be communicated. Such exceptions to the confidential nature of attorney-client communications, if adopted, might be justified as waivers. * * *

While there is respectable authority holding that communications between joint clients and their attorney are not privileged on the basis of waiver, Allen v. Ross, 199 Wis. 162, 225 N.W. 831, 64 A.L.R. 180; State v. Rogers, 226 Wis. 39, 51, 275 N.W. 910, and other cases cited in annotation, 22 A.L.R.2d 662–664, we are convinced there is a more compelling reason the general rule prohibiting disclosures of information received in confidence by one of two or more joint clients in regard to a transaction for their mutual benefit, is not privileged. It is simply that if it appears the secret or imparted communication is such that the attorney is under a duty to divulge it for the protection of the others he has undertaken to represent in the involved transaction, then the communication is not privileged. It would be shocking indeed to require an attorney who had assumed such a duty to act for the mutual benefit of both or several parties to be permitted or compelled to withhold vital information affecting the rights of others because it involves the informant. * * * The rule is based on much firmer ground than waiver, that of duty, loyalty and fairness, as well as on substantial public policy.

In the fast-moving economic world of today it seems desirable and proper to permit and encourage the consultation of an attorney by several parties on matters or transactions in which they have joint and mutual interests, although in almost every such case there is a potential conflict of interest and, if and when it develops, that lawyer cannot and should not try to render further service or advice therein.

In the case of Kilgo v. Continental Casualty Co., 140 Ark. 336, 215 S.W. 689, we find a situation somewhat in reverse of the case at bar. There the insured communicated the information to the attorney representing both the insured and insurer, in a personal damage action, that his former statements given the insurance company were false. That communication was held not privileged and the attorney's testimony concerning same admissible in an action between the parties and their representatives or assigns. * * *

Such being the case before us, we conclude the trial court was correct in holding that the papers requested were not as between the parties confidential, and that the claim of privilege was invalid.

Affirmed.

Notes and Questions

1. *Communications between insured and insurance company.* Should communications between an insured and representatives of his or her insurance company be privileged as against third persons? Compare Asbury v. Beerbower, 589 S.W.2d 216 (Ky.1979) (privileged), with Varuzza v. Bulk Materials, Inc., 169 F.R.D. 254 (N.D.N.Y.1996) (no privilege). Should it matter with whom the insured communicates—an attorney, claims representative, outside adjuster? Cases dealing with the existence of the privilege in a variety of situations involving the insured and insurer are collected in Annot., 55 A.L.R.4th 336. If not within the attorney-client privilege, should work product protection apply? See Menton v. Lattimore, 667 S.W.2d 335 (Tex.App.1984).

2. *Presence of third persons.* The presence of a third person who is not an agent of either the client or the attorney is usually taken as an indication of lack of confidentiality, precluding the application of the privilege. Mitchell v. Towne, 87 P.2d 908 (Cal.Ct.App.1939); People v. Buchanan, 39 N.E. 846 (N.Y.1895). However, the cases have been generous in including within the privilege agents employed in effecting the communication. Thus State v. Loponio, 88 A. 1045 (N.J.1913), applied the privilege to communications by an illiterate accused to a fellow prisoner who acted as his amanuensis in writing a letter for the purpose of retaining a lawyer. What about the presence of the client's family members during the conference with the

attorney? Compare United States v. Bigos, 459 F.2d 639 (1st Cir.1972) (presence of father did not vitiate privilege), with Cafritz v. Koslow, 167 F.2d 749 (D.C.Cir.1948) (sister's presence destroyed privilege).

3. *Joint defense or common interest.* Meetings between clients and their lawyers planning a joint defense or the exchange of statements between attorneys representing different parties with a common interest have generally been held not to constitute a waiver of attorney-client privilege applicable to the statements in the first instance. See, e.g., United States v. McPartlin, 595 F.2d 1321 (7th Cir.1979); Continental Oil Co. v. United States, 330 F.2d 347 (9th Cir.1964). But see United States v. Evans, 113 F.3d 1457 (7th Cir.1997) (common interest did not arise until after meeting with attorney); Vance v. State, 230 S.W.2d 987 (Tenn.1950) (meeting not for purpose of planning a joint defense). If there is a common interest, will communications between clients concerning their legal representation outside the presence of the attorney for either be privileged? The court in United States v. Gotti, 771 F.Supp. 535 (E.D.N.Y.1991), suggested that there would be no privilege.

4. *Inadvertent disclosure.* Conventional doctrine dictates that disclosure of privileged matter to third persons, and particularly opponents in litigation, constitutes waiver. See Unif.R.Evid. 510 (1999). However, the realities of modern discovery practice, in which thousands of documents may be required to be produced, obviously raise unprecedented possibilities of inadvertent disclosure. Should waiver automatically result from even inadvertent disclosure, or should additional conditions be attached? Courts, including the federal circuits, are divided on the issue. There are at least three different approaches. A significant number of courts take the position that a disclosure waives the privilege regardless of the circumstances. See, e.g., International Digital Systems Corp. v. Digital Equipment Corp., 120 F.R.D. 445 (D.Mass.1988). The fewest number of cases take the approach that there is no waiver so long as the disclosure is inadvertent. See Mendenhall v. Barber–Greene Co., 531 F.Supp. 951 (N.D.Ill.1982). A significant and growing number of courts take a balanced approach to the issue—the existence of waiver depends on the circumstances, especially the degree of care taken to prevent disclosure of privileged matter and the existence of prompt efforts to retrieve the document. See Lois Sportswear, U.S.A., Inc. v. Levi Strauss & Co., 104 F.R.D. 103, 105 (S.D.N.Y.1985). Which is the best approach? See generally Marcus, The Perils of Privilege: Waiver and the Litigator, 84 Mich.L.Rev. 1605 (1986); Kiker, Waiving the Privilege in a Storm of Data: An Argument for Uniformity and Rationality in Dealing with the Inadvertent Production of Privileged Materials in the Age of Electronically Stored Information, 12 Rich.J.L. & Tech. 15 (2006). The Federal Rules of Evidence Advisory Committee has drafted a proposed rule (proposed Fed.R.Evid. 502) that takes the balanced approach to the issue. Its proposal has been submitted for public comment. See http://www.uscourts.gov/rules, Standing Committee Action, June 2006.

5. *Partial disclosure.* Waiver will generally not result from disclosure of the underlying facts, but only if the communication itself is disclosed. Commonwealth v. Goldman, 480 N.E.2d 1023 (Mass.1985). Should disclosure of a portion of the communication result in waiver of the privilege with respect to the remainder? Should the answer depend upon whether the

partial disclosure is made judicially or extrajudicially? See von Bulow v. von Bulow, 828 F.2d 94 (2d Cir.1987); Marcus, note 4, supra. Proposed Fed. R.Evid. 502, note 4, supra, provides that a waiver extends to undisclosed communication or information "concerning the same subject matter only if that undisclosed communication or information ought in fairness to be considered with the disclosed communication or information."

UNITED STATES v. KENDRICK

United States Court of Appeals, Fourth Circuit, 1964.
331 F.2d 110.

PER CURIAM.

This is an appeal from the District Court's decision denying, after hearing, the petitioner's motion under 28 U.S.C.A. § 2255 to vacate an illegal sentence on the grounds that the petitioner was incompetent to stand trial. * * *

The Government's case consisted of the testimony of counsel appointed by the Court to represent the petitioner at his trial in 1960 and of the F.B.I. Agent who arrested him. Both of these witnesses testified to the extent of their contacts with the petitioner and stated over objection from petitioner's present counsel that in their opinion he was sane and competent to stand trial. * * *

We do not agree with the petitioner that the testimony of his trial counsel should have been excluded at the post-conviction hearing on the basis of the attorney-client privilege.

We need not now consider whether the assertion that he was incapable of effective communication and cooperation with trial counsel is a waiver of the attorney-client privilege on the ground that the petitioner has flung open the curtain of secrecy which otherwise would conceal his actual communications. Nor need we enter the controversy as to whether such an assertion is always so necessarily an implicit attack upon the competence of trial counsel as to amount to a waiver of the privilege to the extent necessary to enable trial counsel to defend himself and his reputation. See Gunther v. United States, 97 U.S.App.D.C. 254, 230 F.2d 222 (1956); cf. United States v. Wiggins, 184 F.Supp. 673 (D.C.1960); United States v. Bostic, 206 F.Supp. 855 (D.C.1962). We do not here consider the question of waiver on either ground, for the attorney's testimony was well within an established exception to the privilege.

Communications made in confidence by a client to his attorney are protected by the attorney-client privilege. It is the substance of the communications which is protected, however, not the fact that there have been communications. Excluded from the privilege, also, are physical characteristics of the client, such as his complexion, his demeanor, his bearing, his sobriety and his dress. Such things are observable by anyone who talked with the client, and there is nothing, in the usual case, to suggest that the client intends his attorney's observations of such matters to be confidential.[29] In short, the privilege protects only the client's confidences, not things which, at the time, are not intended to be held in the breast of the lawyer, even though the attorney-client relation provided the occasion for the lawyer's observation of them. See generally VIII Wigmore, Evidence (McNaughton Revision) § 2306.

Here the attorney testified to just such nonconfidential matters. Petitioner, the attorney testified, was responsive, readily supplied the attorney with his version of the facts and the names of other people involved, was logical in his conversation and his reasoning, and appeared to know and understand everything that went on before and during the trial. No mention was made of the substance of any communication by client to attorney; the witness testified only about his client's cooperativeness and awareness.

All of the matters to which the attorney testified are objectively observable particularizations of the client's demeanor and attitude. Made at a time when neither client nor lawyer manifested any reason to suppose they were confidential, they were not within the privilege. Certainly, the client was then making no secret of his capacity, or want of capacity to communicate with his attorney and to cooperate in his defense.

It is suggested that, in these circumstances, adequate cross-examination of attorney-witness might require the petitioner to inquire into the substance of his communications. That is speculative, however. Effective cross-examination need not go so far. And, if difficulty inheres in the situation, it is no more than if the question were the client's sobriety or inebriety at the time of an otherwise unrelated consultation. If the attorney who testifies his client's hair was blonde when she consulted him had confused her with another client, inquiry as to the substance of the communication might be the only effective means of revealing his confusion, but his testimony is not drawn within the privilege on that account.

We have not heretofore considered this particular question when it was contested, but we have tacitly assumed that the trial attorney may be examined as to such matters, indeed, that the postconviction court should seek such light as the trial attorney can throw upon the question. United States v. Pledger, 301 F.2d 906 (4 Cir.1962); United States v. Taylor, 303 F.2d 165 (4 Cir.1962); United States v. McNicholas, 298 F.2d 914 (4 Cir.1962). Our tacit assumption does not foreclose reconsideration, but after thorough reconsideration in this contested case, we adhere to it.

However persuasive the highly relevant testimony of the attorney, which we now hold properly received, it does not militate against our conclusion that a further hearing should be held to inquire into the

29. Particular circumstances may alter the rule. If the client reveals to the attorney a physical defect, usually concealed by clothing, which may be relevant to the attorney's representation of him, it well may be a confidential and protected communication.

petitioner's medical history, diagnosis, treatment and response after his reception in Atlanta. * * *

The judgment is vacated and the case remanded for further proceedings in accordance with this opinion.

Vacated and remanded.

SOBELOFF, CHIEF JUDGE, and J. SPENCER BELL, CIRCUIT JUDGE (concurring specially).

In full accord with the majority in vacating the judgment and remanding the case, we nevertheless cannot agree that the attorney's testimony was admissible in the proceeding under review, or that it should be admitted in the proceedings to follow.

We agree that an attorney may testify as to "facts observable by anyone," but we refuse to accept the characterization of the lawyer's testimony here as merely reporting "facts observable by anyone." If nothing were involved beyond observations open to anyone, it is doubtful that the attorney would have been called to the stand. His testimony was desired for a purpose more far-reaching. Any expression as to the client's mental competency necessarily embraced more than facts observable by anyone; it comprehended conclusions drawn in the course of an association that is uniquely regarded in the law.

The lawyer's observations were inextricably intertwined with communications which passed between him and his client. It cannot be said that the testimony was confined to nonconfidential matters. This being so, the well-established privilege which protects the client against disclosure was violated. * * *

Consider the practical difficulty that arises when an attorney is permitted to testify on such an issue as the section 2255 hearing presented. The attorney testifies baldly that his client was "cooperative" and mentally competent. No meaningful cross-examination is possible without inquiring what his client said to him and what he said to his client. The client finds himself on the horns of a dilemma: Either he must forego raising the issue of his incapacity or he must surrender the protection of the privilege the law accords him—a choice he should not have to make. The lawyer's conclusory opinion thus stands without possibility of effective challenge.

The new hearing which the court awards the appellant will, therefore, do him little or no good.

Notes and Questions

1. *Litigation between attorney and client.* The privilege has generally been viewed as inapplicable in an action by an attorney to recover a fee, or by a client to recover damages for the attorney's malpractice. See 1 McCormick, Evidence § 91 (6th ed. 2006). See also Uniform Rule of Evidence 502(d)(3), supra. Should institution of such a malpractice action simultaneously waive the privilege in litigation between the client and third parties

concerning the same subject matter? See Industrial Clearinghouse v. Browning Mfg., 953 F.2d 1004 (5th Cir.1992).

2. *Client's location.* Should the privilege apply to preclude an attorney's testimony that he informed the client as to the time and date of a required court appearance? See State v. Breazeale, 713 P.2d 973 (Kan.Ct. App.1986) (holding testimony not privileged). What of an attorney's testimony concerning the whereabouts of the client? Fellerman v. Bradley, 493 A.2d 1239 (N.J.1985) (denying privilege on facts but stating that a client's address may be privileged in some circumstances).

IN RE GRAND JURY INVESTIGATION NO. 83-2-35 (DURANT)

United States Court of Appeals, Sixth Circuit, 1983.
723 F.2d 447.

KRUPANSKY, CIRCUIT JUDGE.

Attorney Richard Durant (Durant) appeals a finding of contempt for failure to disclose to the grand jury upon order of court the identity of his client. On March 1, 1983, Special Agent Edwards (Edwards), of the Federal Bureau of Investigation (FBI), visited Durant's office and explained that the FBI was investigating the theft of numerous checks made payable to International Business Machines, Inc. (IBM). He advised that a number of the stolen checks had been traced and deposited into various banking accounts under names of non-existent organizations, at least one of which included the initials "IBM". Edwards produced a photostatic copy of a check drawn upon one of these fictitious accounts which check was made payable to Durant's law firm. Upon FBI inquiry, Durant conceded that this check for $15,000 had been received and endorsed by his firm for services rendered to a client in two cases, one of which was "finished" and the other of which was "open". Durant refused to disclose the identity of his client to whose credit the proceeds had been applied, asserting the attorney-client privilege.

Durant was subpoenaed to appear before the grand jury the following day, March 2, 1983, where he again refused to identify his client, asserting the attorney-client privilege. The government immediately moved the United States District Court for the Eastern District of Michigan for an Order requiring Durant to provide the requested information. At a hearing that same afternoon, Durant informed the court that disclosure of his client's identity could incriminate that client in criminal activity so as to justify invoking the attorney-client privilege. Citing to the court: *In re Grand Jury Appearance (Michaelson),* 511 F.2d 882 (9th Cir.1975); *Baird v. Koerner,* 279 F.2d 623 (9th Cir.1960). Durant additionally stated that "I do not know any of the facts about this theft or anything else", and suggested that the requested information should be obtained through other methods.[30] The court adjudged

30. Durant stated:

I should add that if the facts as the agents have discussed them with me are correct and there is a substantial number of checks flowing around the city, all those checks come back to the drawee bank with bank endorsements on the back. It should be, it seems to me, equally

that the privilege did not attach and ordered Durant to identify his client. Upon refusal to comply with this Order, Durant was held in contempt. Further proceedings (e.g. bond) were stayed until March 16, 1983, and subsequently stayed until March 22, 1983.

In an obvious attempt to ascertain the identity of Durant's client in an alternate manner, the United States issued a second subpoena to Durant on March 9, 1983, ordering him to appear before the grand jury on March 16, 1983, and produce * * * [certain] documents * * * Durant moved to quash this subpoena duces tecum, again asserting the attorney-client privilege. At the March 22, 1983 hearing on this motion, Durant re-asserted that production of the subpoenaed documents could implicate his client in criminal activity. He additionally observed that the FBI had admitted before Durant and the district court judge in-chambers that an arrest would be effected by the FBI immediately following disclosure.[31] * * *

The Court was informed that disclosure of the requested information would not only implicate Durant's client in criminal activity, but it would implicate that client in the very criminal activity for which legal advice had been sought.

> COURT: Do you contend and do you submit that the disclosure of the information which is sought by this subpoena, quote, would implicate your client in the very criminal activity for which legal advice was sought?
>
> MR. DURANT: Yes, Your Honor, I do.
>
> COURT: Other than—in what way do you contend that it would?
>
> MR. DURANT: Sir, I'm in a catch–22 position again. I can't tell you. If I tell you, I have explained things that my client obviously doesn't wish to be disclosed.
>
> COURT: All right.

Durant failed to move the court for an *ex parte in camera* submission of evidence or testimony to establish that his client had indeed sought legal advice relating to past criminal activity involving theft of IBM checks. Nor did the district court, *sua sponte,* suggest an *ex parte in camera* submission of evidence to probe Durant's blanket statements.

The United States then introduced the check into evidence in support of the proposition that it was improbable that Durant's client

possible, without violating the attorney-client privilege, for the agents to find out who presented, who cashed and to trace the money through normal commercial channels, to say nothing of the fact that who opens the mail at IBM now obviously becomes of significant importance.

31. Durant stated:

I would remind the Court that when, through the courtesy of the Court, we had a session in-chambers with the members of the FBI present, as well as the U.S. Attorney and myself, the FBI members specifically said—I can't remember which one—specifically said that as soon as we get the name of that client, we are going to arrest the client * * * .

had engaged Durant's services to defend against impending charges of theft. A notation on the lower left hand corner of the check stated "corporate legal services". The United States observed "That doesn't say anything about crimes committed or to be committed or legal services in connection with criminal matters. It is 'corporate legal services'; no suggestion of any criminal investigation." It was additionally noted by the government that the FBI had not initiated the investigation nor had it been informed of the theft of the IBM checks until March 1st, approximately two weeks *after* the check had been received by Durant. Durant offered the following rebuttal:

> I don't know when IBM knew it (i.e. knew that checks had been stolen), but Mr. Edwards, when he appeared at my office, told me that it did involve checks from IBM, and I said that on March 2nd, when I appeared here.
>
> I think the mere fact that the check says for "corporate legal services" when it has been admitted by the U.S. Attorney that such a corporation doesn't even exist, it is a fictional entity, doesn't deny what I am representing to the Court.

The district court, opining that the issues joined in the first and second subpoenas served upon Durant were "essentially the same", withheld a decision of Durant's motion to quash the second subpoena duces tecum pending appellate resolution of the court's contempt Order of March 2, 1983.

Confronting the applicability of the attorney-client privilege as urged by Durant, it is initially observed that the privilege is recognized in the federal forum. See: *Fisher v. United States,* 425 U.S. 391 * * * (1976); Rule 501, Federal Rules of Evidence. * * *

The federal forum is unanimously in accord with the general rule that the identity of a client is, with limited exceptions, not within the protective ambit of the attorney-client privilege. *See: In re Grand Jury Proceedings (Pavlick),* 680 F.2d 1026, 1027 (5th Cir.1982) (en banc) * * * [32]

The Circuits have embraced various "exceptions" to the general rule that the identity of a client is not within the protective ambit of the attorney-client privilege. All such exceptions appear to be firmly grounded in the Ninth Circuit's seminal decision in *Baird v. Koerner,* 279 F.2d

32. This general rule applies equally to fee arrangements:

> In the absence of special circumstances, the amount of money paid or owed to an attorney by his client is generally not within the attorney-client privilege. *In re Michaelson,* 511 F.2d 882, 888 (9th Cir. 1975); *see In re Grand Jury Proceedings,* 517 F.2d 666, 670–71 (5th Cir.1975). The receipt of fees from a client is not usually within the privilege because the payment of a fee is not normally a matter of confidence or a communication. *United States v. Hodgson,* 492 F.2d 1175 (10th Cir. 1974). This Court has held that ministerial or clerical services of an attorney in transferring funds to or from a client is not a matter of confidence protected by the attorney-client privilege. *United States v. Bartone,* 400 F.2d 459 (6 Cir. 1968).

United States v. Haddad, 527 F.2d 537, 538–39 (6th Cir.1975).

623 (9th Cir.1960). In *Baird* the IRS received a letter from an attorney stating that an enclosed check in the amount of $12,706 was being tendered for additional amounts due from undisclosed taxpayers. When the IRS summoned the attorney to ascertain the identity of the delinquent taxpayers the attorney refused identification asserting the attorney-client privilege. The Ninth Circuit, applying California law, adjudged that the "exception" to the general rule as pronounced in *Ex parte McDonough,* 170 Cal. 230, 149 P. 566 (1915) controlled:

> The name of the client will be considered privileged matter where the circumstances of the case are such that the name of the client is material only for the purpose of showing an acknowledgement of guilt on the part of such client of the very offenses on account of which the attorney was employed.

Baird, supra, 279 F.2d at 633. The identity of the *Baird* taxpayer was adjudged within this exception to the general rule. The Ninth Circuit has continued to acknowledge this exception.

> A significant exception to this principle of non-confidentiality holds that such information may be privileged when the person invoking the privilege is able to show that a strong possibility exists that disclosure of the information would implicate the client in the very matter for which legal advice was sought in the first case.

In re Grand Jury Subpoenas Duces Tecum (Marger/Merenbach), 695 F.2d 363, 365 (9th Cir.1982). * * * This exception, which can perhaps be most succinctly characterized as the "legal advice" exception, has also been recognized by other circuits. *See: In re Walsh,* 623 F.2d 489, 495 (7th Cir.1980); *In re Grand Jury Investigation (Tinari),* 631 F.2d 17, 19 (3d Cir.1980). Since the legal advice exception is firmly grounded in the policy of protecting confidential communications, this Court adopts and applies its principles herein. *See: In re Grand Jury Subpoenas Duces Tecum (Marger/Merenbach), supra.*

It should be observed, however, that the legal advice exception may be defeated through a *prima facie* showing that the legal representation was secured in furtherance of present or intended continuing illegality, as where the legal representation itself is part of a larger conspiracy. *See: In re Grand Jury Subpoenas Duces Tecum (Marger/Merenbach), supra,* 695 F.2d at 365 n.1. * * *

Another exception to the general rule that the identity of a client is not privileged arises where disclosure of the identity would be tantamount to disclosing an otherwise protected confidential communication. In *Baird, supra,* the Ninth Circuit observed:

> If the identification of the client conveys information which ordinarily would be conceded to be part of the usual privileged communication between attorney and client, then the privilege should extend to such identification in the absence of other factors.

Id., 279 F.2d at 632. Citing *Baird,* the Fourth Circuit promulgated the following exception:

> To the general rule is an exception, firmly bedded as the rule itself. The privilege may be recognized where so much of the actual communication has already been disclosed that identification of the client amounts to disclosure of a confidential communication.

NLRB v. Harvey, 349 F.2d 900, 905 (4th Cir.1965). *Accord: United States v. Tratner,* 511 F.2d 248, 252 (7th Cir.1975); * * * The Seventh Circuit has added to the *Harvey* exception the following emphasized caveat:

> The privilege may be recognized where so much of the actual communication has already been disclosed [*not necessarily by the attorney, but by independent sources as well*] that identification of the client [*or of fees paid*] amounts to disclosure of a confidential communication.

United States v. Jeffers, 532 F.2d 1101, 1115 (7th Cir.1976) (emphasis added). The Third Circuit, applying this exception, has emphasized that it is the link between the client and the *communication,* rather than the link between the client and the possibility of potential criminal *prosecution,* which serves to bring the client's identity within the protective ambit of the attorney-client privilege. *See: In re Grand Jury Empanelled February 14, 1978 (Markowitz),* 603 F.2d 469, 473 n.4 (3d Cir.1979). Like the "legal advice" exception, this exception is also firmly rooted in principles of confidentiality.

Another exception, articulated in the Fifth Circuit's *en banc* decision of *In re Grand Jury Proceedings (Pavlick),* 680 F.2d 1026 (5th Cir.1982) (*en banc*), is recognized when disclosure of the identity of the client would provide the "last link" of evidence:

> We have long recognized the general rule that matters involving the payment of fees and the identity of clients are not generally privileged. *In re Grand Jury Proceedings, (United States v. Jones),* 517 F.2d 666 (5th Cir.1975); see cases collected *id.* at 670 n.2. There we also recognized, however, a limited and narrow exception to the general rule, one that obtains when the disclosure of the client's identity by his attorney would have supplied the last link in an existing chain of incriminating evidence likely to lead to the client's indictment.

Id. at 1027. Upon careful consideration this Court concludes that, although language exists in *Baird* to support validity of *Pavlick's* "last link" exception,[33] the exception is simply not grounded upon the preservation of confidential *communications* and hence not justifiable to support the attorney-client privilege. Although the last link exception may promote concepts of fundamental fairness against self-incrimination, these concepts are not proper considerations to invoke the attorney-

33. Although *Baird* observed in passing that disclosure of the identity of the clients "may well be the link that could form the chain of testimony necessary to convict [the taxpayers] of a federal crime", 279 F.2d at 633, the Court repeatedly emphasized that the retention of the attorney and remission of a check to the IRS was tantamount to a *communication* or admission from the clients to the attorney that "they had not paid a sufficient amount in income taxes some one or more years in the past". *Id.*

client privilege. Rather, the focus of the inquiry is whether disclosure of the identity would adversely implicate the confidentiality of communications. Accordingly, this Court rejects the last link exception as articulated in *Pavlick.*

Turning to the facts at bar, it is observed that Durant asserted three justifications for invocation of the attorney-client privilege. First, at the March 2 hearing, he stated that disclosure might possibly implicate the client in criminal activity. As this justification has no roots in concepts of confidentiality or communication, it cannot be advanced to support an abdication of the general rule that identity of a client is not privileged. Second, at the March 22 hearing, Durant informed the Court that the FBI had informed him that an arrest would be effected upon disclosure of the identity of Durant's client. This is simply an assertion that disclosure would provide the last link of evidence to support an indictment as articulated in *Pavlick*—a precedent which is herein rejected.

Third, at the March 22 hearing, Durant submitted that disclosure was justified under the "legal advice" exception embraced by the Ninth Circuit. Seeking to invoke this exception, it was incumbent upon Durant to "show that a *strong possibility* exist[ed] that disclosure of the information would implicate the client in the very matter for which legal advice [had been] sought in the first case". *In re Grand Jury Subpoenas Duces Tecum (Marger/Merenbach), supra,* 695 F.2d at 365 (emphasis added). A well recognized means for an attorney to *demonstrate* the existence of an exception to the general rule, while simultaneously preserving confidentiality of the identity of his client, is to move the court for an *in camera ex parte* hearing. *See: In re Grand Jury Witness (Salas),* [695 FP.2d 3594, 362 (5th Cir. 1982)]; (proper procedure to establish existence of "legal advice" exception was to make an *in camera* showing); *In re Grand Jury Empanelled February 14, 1978 (Markowitz), supra,* 603 F.2d at 474 (referring to procedure to be employed by an attorney who asserts Fifth Amendment privilege); *In re Grand Jury Subpoena (Slaughter),* [694 F.2d 1258, 1260 n.2 (11th Cir. 1982)] (United States requested in its subpoena that any averred privileged matters be deleted and the original copy retained intact for possible *in camera* inspection by the district court); *In re Walsh, supra,* 623 F.2d at 494 n.5; *United States v. Tratner, supra,* 511 F.2d at 252.

Since the burden of establishing the existence of the privilege rests with the party asserting the privilege, it is incumbent upon the attorney to move for an *in camera ex parte* hearing if one is desired. In the action *sub judice,* Durant failed to so move. Rather, he rested on his blanket assertion that his client had initially sought legal advice relating to matters involving the theft of IBM checks. Such unsupported assertions of privilege are strongly disfavored. *See: United States v. Cromer,* 483 F.2d 99, 102 (9th Cir.1973); *United States v. Davis,* 636 F.2d 1028, 1044 n.20 (5th Cir.1981); *In re Grand Jury Witness (Salas), supra,* 695 F.2d at 362. Further, it is pertinent to observe that at the first hearing on March 2 Durant had expressly disavowed knowledge of the existence of stolen IBM checks. This statement significantly diminishes the credibility of

Durant's subsequent March 22 representation that his client had indeed engaged Durant's services for past activity relating to stolen IBM checks. Accordingly, Durant clearly failed to satisfy his burden of demonstrating a "strong possibility" that disclosure of the identity of his client would implicate that client in the very matter for which legal advice had been initially sought.

Last, it is observed that Durant did not represent to the district court that disclosure of the identity of his client would amount to a disclosure of a confidential communication. *See: NLRB v. Harvey, supra; United States v. Jeffers, supra.* Not having advanced this exception to the general rule, it follows axiomatically that Durant failed to satisfy the burden of establishing its existence. Nor does the record suggest the viability of this exception so as to justify a remand.

In sum, Durant has failed to establish the existence of any exception to the general rule that disclosure of the identity of a client is not within the protective ambit of the attorney-client privilege. Therefore the Contempt Order of the district court issued against Durant is hereby AFFIRMED.

Notes and Questions

1. *Client identity.* As suggested by the principal case, the leading decision in Baird v. Koerner, 279 F.2d 623 (9th Cir.1960), has given rise to a miscellany of exceptions to the general rule that client identity is not protected by the privilege. For criticisms of these derivatives of *Baird,* see Comment, Developments in the Law—Privileged Communications, 98 Harv. L.Rev. 1450, 1522–24 (1985) (suggesting that protection vel non of client identity should depend essentially upon the client's intent in seeking legal services). See also In re Grand Jury Subpoenas, 803 F.2d 493 (9th Cir.1986) (characterizing *Baird* facts as "unique" and holding privilege inapplicable to protect identity of anonymous payer of fees for criminal defense because no legitimate attorney-client relationship was shown to exist between fee-payer and attorney; alternate holding); United States v. Goldberger & Dubin, 935 F.2d 501 (2d Cir.1991) (holding neither federal nor state attorney-client privilege exempted attorneys from federal statutory obligation to report cash fee payments in excess of $10,000); Goode, Identity, Fees, and the Attorney–Client Privilege, 59 Geo.Wash.L.Rev. 307 (1991); Annot., 84 A.L.R.Fed. 852.

2. *Confidentiality distinguished.* The attorney-client privilege must be distinguished from the rule governing a lawyer's professional conduct that requires that information received in the course of a lawyer's representation of a client be kept confidential. What differences might you suspect there are between a rule that governs whether a court can compel the disclosure of communications between lawyer and her client and a rule governing a lawyer's professional obligation to keep such communications secret? See Model Rules of Professional Conduct, Rule 1.6. A useful contrast of the differences between the privilege rule and confidentiality imposed by the rules of professional conduct is contained in Zacharias, Privilege and Confidentiality in California, 28 U.C.Davis L.Rev. 367 (1995).

Both rules may be implicated by the problem suggested in the principal case, which arises when physical evidence, or the key to its discovery, is delivered by the client to the attorney. Is the attorney under legal or ethical obligation to deliver the evidence to the authorities and, if so, what use may the latter make of it at trial? Is it possible to separate the "communication" of a murder weapon, effected by its delivery to the attorney, from the evidentiary entity itself? For helpful treatments of these and related questions, suggesting somewhat contrasting responses, see Lefstein, Incriminating Physical Evidence, The Defense Attorney's Dilemma, and the Need for Rules, 64 N.C.L.Rev. 897 (1986); Saltzburg, Communications Falling Within the Attorney–Client Privilege, 66 Iowa L.Rev. 811 (1981). Discussions focusing primarily upon the ethical problems arising from possession of the client's guilty secrets are found in Noonan, The Purposes of Advocacy and the Limits of Confidentiality, 64 Mich.L.Rev. 1485 (1966); Callan & David, Professional Responsibility and the Duty of Confidentiality: Disclosure of Client Misconduct in an Adversary System, 29 Rutgers L.Rev. 332 (1976). A further complicating factor has appeared in the form of required reporting statutes. See Mosteller, Child Abuse Reporting Laws and Attorney–Client Confidences: The Reality and the Specter of Lawyer as Informant, 42 Duke L.J. 203 (1992). See also discussion in Chapter 2, note 2 after *Napue v. Illinois*, supra.

IN RE SEALED CASE

United States Court of Appeals, District of Columbia Circuit, 1997.
107 F.3d 46.

RANDOLPH, CIRCUIT JUDGE:

This appeal arises out of ongoing grand jury proceedings. The grand jury is investigating violations of federal election laws. The record is sealed. The appellant is a corporation, which we shall call the "Company." The Company refused to produce two subpoenaed documents, for which it was held in contempt. One of the documents is a memorandum from a Company vice president to the president, with a copy to the Company's general counsel. The memorandum reflects a conversation between the vice president and the Company's general counsel about campaign finance laws. The Company withheld it on the basis of the attorney-client privilege. The other document is a memorandum written by the general counsel, apparently at the request of outside counsel. The Company withheld it on the basis of the attorney-client privilege and work product immunity.

The district court examined both documents *in camera* (*see United States v. Zolin,* 491 U.S. 554 * * * 1989)), and, without deciding whether they were covered by the privilege or the work product doctrine, ordered the Company to turn them over. The court found that the crime-fraud exception applied because of these circumstances. In late June 1994, the Company's political action committee contributed the maximum amount permitted by law to a former candidate for federal office who was seeking to retire his campaign debt. The vice president wrote his memorandum and had his discussion with the general counsel in early

August 1994. Later in the same month, the vice president called two individuals who did business with the Company and asked them to contribute to the former candidate. The individuals and their wives made the contributions. After several weeks had passed, the vice president authorized checks to be drawn from his department's budget to reimburse these individuals not only for the amount of their contributions, but also to make up for the additional taxes they would incur from reporting the reimbursement as income. The vice president's solicitation may have been permissible but, according to the government, this use of corporate funds was illegal.

The other subpoenaed document—the general counsel's memorandum to the file—was written more than a year later. It mentions dates in November 1995, and according to the Company's appellate counsel, recites actions the Company took to correct the vice president's use of corporate funds to reimburse the donors.

In addition to appealing from the order to produce the documents and the contempt citation, the Company appeals the district court's order compelling the vice president to testify in the grand jury about a late August 1994 meeting between him, the Company's president, and its general counsel. The participants at the meeting discussed certain facts and the general counsel gave legal advice about federal election laws. In the grand jury, the vice president—who had been granted immunity—invoked the attorney-client privilege on behalf of the Company. Again, the district court ruled that the crime-fraud exception applied and ordered him to testify about the late August 1994 meeting. The vice president then signed an affidavit stating that he would honor the court's directive. The court stayed its order pending the outcome of the Company's appeal.

I

We will take up first the vice president's early August 1994 memorandum and his meeting in late August 1994 with the president and general counsel. Both the memorandum and the meeting, as the Company sees it, are covered by the attorney-client privilege. Since the district court has yet to pass on this question, we will assume the Company is correct. The "privilege of a witness," Fed.R.Evid. 501 tells us, is "governed by the principles of the common law as they may be interpreted by the courts of the United States in the light of reason and experience." Those principles recognize the importance of maintaining the confidentiality of attorney-client communications in order to promote the rendering of legal services. In modern society, legal advice and assistance is often essential. To provide effective representation, attorneys need "full and frank" disclosures from their clients. *Upjohn Co. v. United States,* 449 U.S. 383, 389 * * * (1981). Clients, it has been thought, might not be forthright if their lawyers could be turned into witnesses against them or if they could be forced to disclose their conversations with their lawyers.

The relationship between client and counsel may, however, be abused. And so the attorney-client privilege is subject to what is known as the crime-fraud exception. Two conditions must be met. First, the client must have made or received the otherwise privileged communication with the intent to further an unlawful or fraudulent act.[34] *In re Sealed Case,* 754 F.2d 395, 399 (D.C.Cir.1985) (*Sealed Case II*); *United States v. White,* 887 F.2d 267, 271 (D.C.Cir.1989). Second, the client must have carried out the crime or fraud. In other words, the exception does not apply even though, at one time, the client had bad intentions. Otherwise "it would penalize a client for doing what the privilege is designed to encourage—consulting a lawyer for the purpose of achieving law compliance." *See* Restatement of the Law Governing Lawyers § 142 cmt. c, at 461 (Proposed Final Draft No. 1, 1996).[35]

The privilege is the client's, and it is the client's fraudulent or criminal intent that matters. A third party's bad intent cannot remove the protection of the privilege.[36] For example, a stenographer hired to record a meeting between an attorney and a client might intend to use his notes to commit some kind of crime—say extortion—but the contents of the meeting would not therefore cease to be privileged. Otherwise, existence of the attorney-client privilege would be unpredictable and the interest of "full and frank communication" between client and counsel would be undermined. *See Upjohn Co.,* 449 U.S. at 389 * * *.[37]

As the party seeking to overcome the privilege, the government had the burden of showing that the crime-fraud exception applied to the memorandum and the meeting. What was the nature of that burden? Here we encounter some confusion. This court and others have described the required showing in terms of establishing a "prima facie" case. *See, e.g., Sealed Case II,* 754 F.2d at 399. The formulation can be traced to the Supreme Court's opinion in *Clark v. United States,* 289 U.S. 1, 14

34. In nearly all cases, a client's innocence will bar application of the crime-fraud exception. We say "nearly all" because there may be rare cases—this is not one of them—in which the attorney's fraudulent or criminal intent defeats a claim of privilege even if the client is innocent. *See, e.g., Moody v. IRS,* 654 F.2d 795, 800–01 (D.C.Cir.1981); *In re Impounded Case (Law Firm),* 879 F.2d 1211, 1213–14 (3d Cir. 1989).

35. To this the Restatement drafters added: "By the same token, lawyers might be discouraged from giving full and candid advice to clients about legally questionable courses of action." *Id.* This seems to us rather doubtful. Why would a lawyer put his client–and himself–at such risk? Fully advising the client may prevent possibly unlawful action. On the other hand, if the lawyer gives less than "full and candid" advice, the client may rely on it, wind up violating the law and thus lose the privilege anyway. A lawyer representing such a client would have reason to be concerned about his own personal civil and criminal liability. Rather than discouraging full advice, that prospect plus the danger to the client provides a strong incentive for the lawyer to advise the client clearly and firmly.

36. Of course, in many cases, a third party's access to a communication may destroy the confidentiality required for the attorney-client privilege, *see, e.g., In re Sealed Case,* 877 F.2d 976, 980 (D.C.Cir. 1989) (*Sealed Case III*), but that is a separate problem.

37. At least one district court seems to have said that anyone's use of a communication to further a crime or fraud defeats the attorney-client privilege, regardless of the innocence of the attorney and the client. *See Duttle v. Bandler & Kass,* 127 F.R.D. 46, 53, 55–56 (S.D.N.Y.1989). We think this is incorrect.

* * * (1933). The problem is, as the Supreme Court mentioned in *Zolin,* 491 U.S. at 563 n.7 * * * , that "prima facie" evokes the concept, familiar in civil litigation, of shifting the burden from one party to another. Yet it is altogether clear where the burden in these cases lies–on the party invoking the crime-fraud exception. In terms of the level of proof, is a "prima facie showing" a preponderance of the evidence, clear and convincing evidence, or something else?

Our opinion in *Sealed Case II* contains this answer: "The government satisfies its burden of proof if it offers evidence that if believed by the trier of fact would establish the elements of an ongoing or imminent crime or fraud." 754 F.2d at 399. We appended a footnote to this statement explaining that although the Second Circuit had "framed the test in terms of probable cause to believe that a crime or fraud had been committed and that the communications were in furtherance thereof" (*see In re John Doe Corp.,* 675 F.2d 482, 491 & n.7 (2d Cir.1982)), there was "little practical difference" between that standard and the one just quoted from *Sealed Case II.* 754 F.2d at 399 n.3. We confess some difficulty in understanding why the differences between the two formulations were considered slight, but there is no reason to dwell on the matter. It is apparent here that the government failed to make the sort of probable cause showing the Second Circuit would demand, or the showing *Sealed Case II* contemplated.[38]

The critical consideration is that the government's presentation had to be aimed at the intent and action of the client. It was not enough for the government to show that the vice president committed a crime after he wrote his memorandum and attended the late August meeting with Company counsel. The holder of the privilege is the client and, in this case, the client was the Company, not the vice president. Unless the government made some showing that the Company intended to further and did commit a crime, the government could not invoke the crime-fraud exception to the privilege.

As to the late August meeting, the government's evidence reveals that the participants discussed campaign finance laws. That is not enough. One cannot reasonably infer from the meeting that the Company was consulting its general counsel with the intention of committing a crime, or even that the vice president was then doing so. Companies operating in today's complex legal and regulatory environments routinely seek legal advice about how to handle all sorts of matters, ranging from their political activities to their employment practices to transactions that may have antitrust consequences. There is nothing necessarily

38. *Zolin* left the standard of proof question for another day. The Supreme Court decided only that the crime-fraud exception need not be established entirely with independent evidence; that courts may review allegedly privileged materials *in camera* in order to determine whether the crime-fraud exception applies, 491 U.S. at 565–70 * * * ; and that before "engaging in *in camera* review * * * , the judge should require a showing of a factual basis adequate to support a good faith belief by a reasonable person that *in camera* review of the materials may reveal evidence to establish the claim that the crime-fraud exception applies," *id.* at 572 * * * (internal quotation marks and citation omitted).

suspicious about the officers of this corporation getting such advice. True enough, within weeks of the meeting about campaign finance law, the vice president violated that law. But the government had to demonstrate that the Company sought the legal advice with the intent to further its illegal conduct. Showing temporal proximity between the communication and a crime is not enough. *Sealed Case II,* 754 F.2d at 402; *In re Grand Jury Subpoenas Duces Tecum,* 798 F.2d 32, 34 (2d Cir.1986).

Moreover, from the material before the district court, there was no way of knowing or even guessing whether the vice president was on a frolic of his own, against the advice of Company counsel, when he reimbursed the donors with corporate funds. The government suggested at oral argument that even if he was, the Company still could be held criminally liable. There are circumstances under which corporations are responsible for the crimes of their agents. * * * But neither in this court nor in the district court did the government offer anything in terms of evidence or law to support the idea that the Company bore criminal responsibility for the acts of this officer. * * * The government therefore did not sustain its burden. In so holding, we express no view on the Company's ultimate criminal liability. The law of corporate criminality is not well developed in this circuit. Given the government's complete failure to address the subject, this is not the case to develop it.

Many of the same points can be made about the vice president's memorandum. Like the district court, we have examined this document, which the Company submitted *in camera* and *ex parte.* From the memorandum and the other information the government presented, all that can be discerned is that the Company's vice president and its general counsel discussed federal election laws in early August 1994, perhaps at the suggestion of the Company's president. The memorandum reflected that discussion. Again, given the need for corporations and their officers to seek legal advice about activities like political contributions, there is nothing suspect about this discussion. And the fact that the vice president broke the law weeks later does not, without more, demonstrate the validity of the government's assumption that the Company intended or probably intended to further that crime.

II

This brings us to the second of the two documents the Company withheld. We have examined the document. It is a memorandum by the Company's general counsel, written to the file and relating to matters that occurred one year after the vice president's illegal action. As Company counsel seemed to agree at oral argument, the document is covered by work product immunity rather than the attorney-client privilege. The protection for attorney work product is broader than the attorney-client privilege, but less absolute. Work product immunity covers not only confidential communications between the attorney and client. It also attaches to other materials prepared by attorneys (and their agents) in anticipation of litigation. *Cf.* Fed.R.Civ.P. 26(b)(3). Like the attorney-client privilege, work product immunity promotes the rendering of effective legal services. *See Hickman v. Taylor,* 329 U.S. 495, 510–11 * * * (1947). And as with the privilege, the interests in favor of work product immunity are overcome when the client uses the attorney to further a crime or fraud. *See In re Sealed Case,* 676 F.2d 793, 811, 812 (D.C.Cir.1982) (*Sealed Case I*); 1 Scott N. Stone & Robert K. Taylor, Testimonial Privileges § 2.11, at 2–67 & n.284 (2d ed. 1993) (collecting cases).

With respect to work product immunity, the crime-fraud exception calls for a somewhat different inquiry than with the attorney-client privilege. The focus is not on the client's intent regarding a particular communication, but on the client's intent in consulting the lawyer or in using the materials the lawyer prepared. The question is: Did the client consult the lawyer or use the material for the purpose of committing a crime or fraud?[39]

In light of these principles, the government's argument for invoking the crime-fraud exception goes nowhere. As is apparent from the nature of the inquiry, the crime-fraud exception for work product immunity cannot apply if the attorney prepared the material after his client's wrongdoing ended. *See, e.g., Zolin,* 491 U.S. at 562–63 * * * ; *Sealed Case II,* 754 F.2d at 402; *In re Grand Jury Subpoena 92–1(SJ),* 31 F.3d 826, 831 (9th Cir.1994); *In re Federal Grand Jury Proceedings 89–10(MIA),* 938 F.2d 1578, 1581 (11th Cir.1991). Here, the general counsel wrote the memorandum long after the vice president committed the offenses. The government points out that work product might still be in furtherance of a crime or fraud even if the client's original offense was complete. The client could be using the attorney to cover up or conceal his first crime. The trouble is that the government has made no such allegation here and, even if it did, we have spotted nothing in the record that would support it. And if the government cannot show that the Company or any of its officers tried to or intended to cover up the vice president's illegality, it surely cannot show that the Company used its general counsel for that purpose.

* * *

The district court decided this case by assuming that the meeting and the memoranda fell under either the attorney-client privilege or the work product doctrine and then finding that the crime-fraud exception applied. Since we disagree with the district court's conclusions regarding the crime-fraud exception, we reverse and remand the case.

Notes and Questions

1. *Procedure for determining existence of crime-fraud exception.* As noted in the principal case, the procedure for determining whether a

39. So long as the client had the requisite intent, the proposed Restatement removes work product immunity—but not the attorney-client privilege—even if the client never carries out the crime or fraud. *Compare* § 132 with § 142 of the Restatement of the Law Governing Lawyers, *supra.* Why the crime-fraud exception differs in these two contexts is not explained in the draft's commentary or in the reporter's notes.

communication comes within the crime-fraud exception to the attorney-client privilege was established for the federal courts in United States v. Zolin, 491 U.S. 554 (1989). Chapter 1, supra. The judge may inspect documents *in camera* when there is a "factual basis adequate to support a good faith belief by a reasonable person" that such an inspection "may reveal evidence to establish the claim that the crimc-fraud exception applies." Id. at 572. See 1 McCormick, Evidence § 95 (6th ed. 2006). For state treatments of the issue see, e.g., First Union Nat'l Bank of Florida v. Whitener, 715 So.2d 979 (Fla.Dist.Ct.App.1998); State ex rel. Nix v. Cleveland, 700 N.E.2d 12 (Ohio 1998).

2. *Work product privilege.* The court in the principal case considers the crime-fraud exception to be applicable to both the attorney-client and the work product privileges. However, it notes that there has been a difference in application of the exception between the two privileges where the client never in fact commits the crime or fraud. The court did not explain the difference. Can you? For a case holding that the crime-fraud exception does not apply to a state created work product privilege, see Menton v. Lattimore, 667 S.W.2d 335 (Tex.App.1984).

3. *Intentional torts.* Should the crime-fraud exception also apply to communications in furtherance of intentional torts other than fraud? Some courts have so held. See, e.g., Recycling Solutions, Inc. v. District of Columbia, 175 F.R.D. 407 (D.D.C.1997); Horizon of Hope Ministry v. Clark County, Ohio, 115 F.R.D. 1 (S.D.Ohio 1986). *Contra* Motley v. Marathon Oil Co., 71 F.3d 1547 (10th Cir.1995).

4. *The Bentham criticisms.* To what extent are the criticisms leveled by Jeremy Bentham, above, at the attorney-client privilege adequately addressed by recognition of a crime or fraud exception? To what extent are Bentham's criticisms not met by such an exception? Should the exception have been applied to permit the attorney's testimony in *Denver Tramway v. Owens*?

SECTION D. ADDITIONAL PRIVILEGES

IN THE MATTER OF MYRON FARBER

Supreme Court of New Jersey, 1978.
394 A.2d 330.

MOUNTAIN, J.

In these consolidated appeals The New York Times Company and Myron Farber, a reporter employed by the newspaper, challenged judgments entered against them in two related matters—one a proceeding in aid of a litigant (civil contempt), the other for criminal contempt of court. The proceedings were instituted in an ongoing murder trial now in its seventh month, as a result of the appellants' failure to comply with two *subpoenas duces tecum,* directing them to produce certain documents and materials compiled by one or both of these appellants in the course of Farber's investigative reporting of certain allegedly criminal activities.

Farber's investigations and reporting are said to have contributed largely to the indictment and prosecution of Dr. Mario E. Jascalevich for murder. * * *

I

The First Amendment

Appellants claim a privilege to refrain from revealing information sought by the *subpoenas duces tecum* essentially for the reason that were they to divulge this material, confidential sources of such information would be made public. Were this to occur, they argue, newsgathering and the dissemination of news would be seriously impaired, because much information would never be forthcoming to the news media unless the persons who were the sources of such information could be entirely certain that their identities would remain secret. The final result, appellants claim, would be a substantial lessening in the supply of available news on a variety of important and sensitive issues, all to the detriment of the public interest. They contend further that this privilege to remain silent with respect to confidential information and the sources of such information emanates from the "free speech" and "free press" clauses of the First Amendment.[40]

In our view the Supreme Court of the United States has clearly rejected this claim and has squarely held that no such First Amendment right exists. In Branzburg v. Hayes, 408 U.S. 665 * * * (1972), three news media representatives argued that, for the same reason here advanced, they should not be required to appear and testify before grand juries, and that this privilege to refrain from divulging information, asserted to have been received from confidential sources, derived from the First Amendment. Justice White, noting that there was no common law privilege, stated the issue and gave the Court's answer in the first paragraph of his opinion:

> The issue in these cases is whether requiring newsmen to appear and testify before state or federal grand juries abridges the freedom of speech and press guaranteed by the First Amendment. We hold that it does not. [Branzburg v. Hayes, supra, 408 U.S. at 667 * * * (1972).]

In that case one reporter, from Frankfort, Kentucky, had witnessed individuals making hashish from marijuana and had made a rather comprehensive survey of the drug scene in Frankfort. He had written an article in the Louisville Courier–Journal describing this illegal activity. Another, a newsman-photographer employed by a New Bedford, Massachusetts television station, had met with members of the Black Panther movement at the time that certain riots and disorders occurred in New

40. The First Amendment of the United States Constitution reads as follows:

> Congress shall make no law respecting an establishment of religion, or prohibiting the free exercise thereof; or abridging the freedom of speech, or of the press; or the right of the people peaceably to assemble, and to petition the Government for a redress of grievances.

Bedford. The material he assembled formed the basis for a television program that followed. The third investigative reporter had met with members of the Black Panthers in northern California and had written an article about the nature and activities of the movement. In each instance there had been a commitment on the part of the media representative that he would not divulge the source of his article or story.

By a vote of 5 to 4 the Supreme Court held that newspaper reporters or other media representatives have no privilege deriving from the First Amendment to refrain from divulging confidential information and the sources of such information when properly subpoenaed to appear before a grand jury. The three media representatives were directed to appear and testify. The holding was later underscored and applied directly to this case by Justice White in a brief opinion filed in this cause upon the occasion of his denial of a stay sought by these appellants. He said,

> There is no present authority in this Court either that newsmen are constitutionally privileged to withhold duly subpoenaed documents material to the prosecution or defense of a criminal case or that a defendant seeking the subpoena must show extraordinary circumstances before enforcement against newsmen will be had. [New York Times and Farber v. Jascalevich, 439 U.S. 1317, [1322] * * * (1978)]

We pause to point out that despite the holding in *Branzburg,* those who gather and disseminate news are by no means without First Amendment protections. Some of these are referred to by Justice White in the *Branzburg* opinion. See 408 U.S. at 681–2 * * * . They include, among others, the right to publish what the press chooses to publish, to refrain from publishing what it chooses to withhold, to seek out news in any legal manner and to refrain from revealing its sources except upon legitimate demand. Demand is not legitimate when the desired information is patently irrelevant to the needs of the inquirer or his needs are not manifestly compelling. Nor will the First Amendment sanction harassment of the press. These do not exhaust the list of such First Amendment protective rights.

The point to be made, however, is that among the many First Amendment protections that may be invoked by the press, there is not to be found the privilege of refusing to reveal relevant confidential information and its sources to a grand jury which is engaged in the fundamental governmental function of "[f]air and effective law enforcement aimed at providing security for the person and property of the individual * * * " [408 U.S. at 690 * * *]. The reason this is so is that a majority of the members of the United States Supreme Court have so determined.

Faced with this conclusion, appellants appear to argue that Justice Powell's concurring opinion in *Branzburg* somehow fails to support this result. The argument is without merit. We do not read Justice Powell's opinion as in any way disagreeing with what is said by Justice White. But even if it did, it would not matter for present purposes. The important and conclusive point is that five members of the Court have all reached the conclusion that the First Amendment affords no privilege to a newsman to refuse to appear before a grand jury and testify as to relevant information he possesses, even though in so doing he may divulge confidential sources. The particular path that any Justice may have followed becomes unimportant when once it is seen that a majority have reached the same destination.

Thus we do no weighing or balancing of societal interests in reaching our determination that the First Amendment does not afford appellants the privilege they claim. The weighing and balancing has been done by a higher court. Our conclusion that appellants cannot derive the protection they seek from the First Amendment rests upon the fact that the ruling in *Branzburg* is binding upon us and we interpret it as applicable to, and clearly including, the particular issue framed here. It follows that the obligation to appear at a criminal trial on behalf of a defendant who is enforcing his Sixth Amendment rights is at least as compelling as the duty to appear before a grand jury.

II

The Shield Law[41]

In Branzburg v. Hayes, supra, the Court dealt with a newsman's claim of privilege based solely upon the First Amendment. As we have

41. The term "shield law" is commonly and widely applied to statutes granting newsmen and other media representatives the privilege of declining to reveal confidential sources of information. The New Jersey shield law reads as follows:

Subject to Rule 37, a person engaged on, engaged in, connected with, or employed by news media for the purpose of gathering, procuring, transmitting, compiling, editing or disseminating news for the general public or on whose behalf news is so gathered, procured, transmitted, compiled, edited or disseminated has a privilege to refuse to disclose, in any legal or quasi-legal proceeding or before any investigative body, including, but not limited to, any court, grand jury, petit jury, administrative agency, the Legislature or legislative committee, or elsewhere:

a. The source, author, means, agency or person from or through whom any information was procured, obtained, supplied, furnished, gathered, transmitted, compiled, edited, disseminated, or delivered; and

b. Any news or information obtained in the course of pursuing his professional activities whether or not it is disseminated.

The provisions of this rule insofar as it relates to radio or television stations shall not apply unless the radio or television station maintains and keeps open for inspection, for a period of at least 1 year from the date of an actual broadcast or telecast, an exact recording, transcription, kinescopic film or certified written transcript of the actual broadcast or telecast.

Unless a different meaning clearly appears from the context of this act, as used in this act:

a. "News media" means newspapers, magazines, press associations, news agencies, wire services, radio, television or other similar printed, photographic, mechanical or electronic means of disseminating news to the general public.

b. "News" means any written, oral or pictorial information gathered, procured, transmitted, compiled, edited or disseminated by, or on behalf of any person engaged in, engaged on, connected with or employed by a news media [sic] and so procured or obtained while such required relationship is in effect.

c. "Newspaper" means a paper that is printed and distributed ordinarily not less frequently than once a week and that contains news, articles of opinion, editorials, features, advertising, or other matter regarded as of current interest, has a paid circulation and has been entered at a

seen, this claim of privilege failed. In *Branzburg* no shield law was involved. Here we have a shield law, said to be as strongly worded as any in the country.

We read the legislative intent in adopting this statute in its present form as seeking to protect the confidential sources of the press as well as information so obtained by reporters and other news media representatives to the greatest extent permitted by the Constitution of the United States and that of the State of New Jersey. It is abundantly clear that appellants come fully within the literal language of the enactment. Extended discussion is quite unnecessary. Viewed solely as a matter of statutory construction, appellants are clearly entitled to the protections afforded by the act unless statutory exceptions including waiver are shown to apply. In view of the fundamental basis of our decision today, the question of waiver of privilege under the Shield Law need not be addressed by us.

III

The Sixth Amendment[42] and its New Jersey Counterpart[43]

Viewed on its face, considered solely as a reflection of legislative intent to bestow upon the press as broad a shield as possible to protect against forced revelation of confidential source materials, this legislation is entirely constitutional. Indeed, no one appears to have attacked its facial constitutionality.

United States post office as second class matter.

d. "Magazine" means a publication containing news which is published and distributed periodically, has a paid circulation and has been entered at a United States post office as second class matter.

e. "News agency" means a commercial organization that collects and supplies news to subscribing newspapers, magazines, periodicals and news broadcasters.

f. "Press association" means an association of newspapers or magazines formed to gather and distribute news to its members.

g. "Wire service" means a news agency that sends out syndicated news copy by wire to subscribing newspapers, magazines, periodicals or news broadcasters.

h. "In the course of pursuing his professional activities" means any situation, including a social gathering, in which a reporter obtains information for the purpose of disseminating it to the public, but does not include any situation in which a reporter intentionally conceals from the source the fact that he is a reporter, and does not include any situation in which a reporter is an eyewitness to, or participant in any act involving physical violence or property damage. [N.J.S.A. 2A:84A–21 and 21a].

42. The Sixth Amendment of the United States Constitution reads as follows:

In all criminal prosecutions, the accused shall enjoy the right to a speedy and public trial, by an impartial jury of the State and district wherein the crime shall have been committed, which district shall have been previously ascertained by law, and to be informed of the nature and cause of the accusation; to be confronted with the witnesses against him; to have compulsory process for obtaining witnesses in his favor, and to have the Assistance of Counsel for his defence.

43. Article 1, ¶ 10 of the Constitution of the State of New Jersey reads as follows:

In all criminal prosecutions the accused shall have the right to a speedy and public trial by an impartial jury; to be informed of the nature and cause of the accusation; to be confronted with the witnesses against him; to have compulsory process for obtaining witnesses in his favor; and to have the assistance of counsel in his defense.

It is however, argued, and argued very strenuously, that if enforced under the facts of this case, the Shield Law violates the Sixth Amendment of the Federal Constitution as well as Article 1, ¶ 10 of the New Jersey Constitution. These provisions are set forth above. Essentially the argument is this: The Federal and State Constitutions each provide that in all criminal prosecutions the accused shall have the right "to have compulsory process for obtaining witnesses in his favor." Dr. Jascalevich seeks to obtain evidence to use in preparing and presenting his defense in the ongoing criminal trial in which he has been accused of multiple murders. He claims to come within the favor of these constitutional provisions—which he surely does. Finally, when faced with the Shield Law, he invokes the rather elementary but entirely sound proposition that where Constitution and statute collide, the latter must yield. Subject to what is said below, we find this argument unassailable.

The compulsory process clause of the Sixth Amendment has never been elaborately explicated by the Supreme Court. Not until 1967, when it decided Washington v. Texas, 388 U.S. 14 * * * had the clause been directly construed. Westen, *Confrontation and Compulsory Process: A Unified Theory of Evidence for Criminal Cases,* 91 Harv.L.Rev. 567, 586 (1978). In *Washington* the petitioner sought the reversal of his conviction for murder. A Texas statute at the time provided that persons charged or convicted as co-participants in the same crime could not testify for one another. One Fuller, who had already been convicted of the murder, was prevented from testifying by virtue of the statute. The record indicated that had he testified his testimony would have been favorable to petitioner. The Court reversed the conviction on the ground that petitioner's Sixth Amendment right to compulsory process had been denied. At the same time it determined that the compulsory process clause in the Sixth Amendment was binding on state courts by virtue of the due process clause of the Fourteenth Amendment. It will be seen that *Washington* is like the present case in a significant respect. The Texas statute and the Sixth Amendment could not both stand. The latter of course prevailed. So must it be here.

Quite recently, in United States v. Nixon, 418 U.S. 683 * * * (1974), the Court dealt with another compulsory process issue. There the Special Prosecutor, Leon Jaworski, subpoenaed various tape recordings and documents in the possession of President Nixon. The latter claimed an executive privilege and refused to deliver the tapes. The Supreme Court conceded that indeed there was an executive privilege and that although "[n]owhere in the Constitution * * * is there any explicit reference to a privilege of confidentiality, yet to the extent this interest relates to the effective discharge of a President's powers, it is constitutionally based." 418 U.S. at 711 * * * . Despite this conclusion that at least to some extent a president's executive privilege derives from the Constitution, the Court nonetheless concluded that the demands of our criminal justice system required that the privilege must yield.

> We have elected to employ an adversary system of criminal justice in which the parties contest all issues before a court of law. The need

to develop all relevant facts in the adversary system is both fundamental and comprehensive. The ends of criminal justice would be defeated if judgments were to be founded on a partial or speculative presentation of the facts. The very integrity of the judicial system and public confidence in the system depend on full disclosure of all the facts, within the framework of the rules of evidence. To ensure that justice is done, it is imperative to the function of courts that compulsory process be available for the production of evidence needed either by the prosecution or by the defense. [United States v. Nixon, supra, 418 U.S. at 709 * * * .]

It is important to note that the Supreme Court in this case compelled the production of privileged material—the privilege acknowledged to rest in part upon the Constitution—even though there was no Sixth Amendment compulsion to do so. The Sixth Amendment affords rights to an accused but not to a prosecutor. The compulsion to require the production of the privileged material derived from the necessities of our system of administering criminal justice.

Article 1, ¶ 10 of the Constitution of the State of New Jersey contains, as we have seen, exactly the same language with respect to compulsory process as that found in the Sixth Amendment. There exists no authoritative explication of this constitutional provision. Indeed it has rarely been mentioned in our reported decisions. We interpret it as affording a defendant in a criminal prosecution the right to compel the attendance of witnesses and the production of documents and other material for which he may have, or may believe he has, a legitimate need in preparing or undertaking his defense. It also means that witnesses properly summoned will be required to testify and that material demanded by a properly phrased *subpoena duces tecum* will be forthcoming and available for appropriate examination and use.

Testimonial privileges, whether they derive from common law or from statute, which allow witnesses to withhold evidence seem to conflict with this provision. This conflict may arise in a variety of factual contexts with respect to different privileges.[44] We confine our consideration here to the single privilege before us—that set forth in the Shield Law. We hold that Article 1, ¶ 10 of our Constitution prevails over this statute, but in recognition of the strongly expressed legislative viewpoint favoring confidentiality we prescribe the imposition of the safeguards set forth in Point IV below.

IV

Procedural Mechanism

Appellants insist that they are entitled to a full hearing on the issues of relevance, materiality and overbreadth of the subpoena. We agree. The trial court recognized its obligation to conduct such a hearing,

44. Compare the informer's privilege where disclosure of identity may sometimes be required. State v. Milligan, 71 N.J. 373, 365 A.2d 914 (1976); State v. Oliver, 50 N.J. 39, 231 A.2d 805 (1967); Roviaro v. United States, 353 U.S. 53 * * * (1957).

but the appellants have aborted that hearing by refusing to submit the material subpoenaed for an *in camera* inspection by the court to assist it in determining the motion to quash. That inspection is no more than a procedural tool, a device to be used to ascertain the relevancy and materiality of that material. Such an *in camera* inspection is not in itself an invasion of the statutory privilege. Rather it is a preliminary step to determine whether, and if so to what extent, the statutory privilege must yield to the defendant's constitutional rights.

Appellants' position is that there must be a full showing and definitive judicial determination of relevance, materiality, absence of less intrusive access, and need, prior to any *in camera* inspection. The obvious objection to such a rule, however, is that it would, in many cases, effectively stultify the judicial criminal process. It might well do so here. The defendant properly recognizes Myron Farber as a unique repository of pertinent information. But he does not know the extent of this information nor is it possible for him to specify all of it with particularity, nor to tailor his subpoena to precise materials of which he is ignorant. Well aware of this, Judge Arnold refused to give ultimate rulings with respect to relevance and other preliminary matters until he had examined the material. We think he had no other course. It is not rational to ask a judge to ponder the relevance of the unknown.

* * *

The judgment of conviction of criminal contempt and that in aid of litigants' rights are affirmed. Stays heretofore entered are vacated effective as of 4:00 p.m., Tuesday, September 26, 1978.

[The concurring opinion of HUGHES, C.J., and the dissenting opinions of PASHMAN, J., and HANDLER, J., are omitted. The dissents contended that the procedure followed was inadequate.]

Notes and Questions

1. *The New Jersey aftermath.* Following the decision in the principal case the New Jersey legislature amended the state shield law in an attempt to afford the broadest protection possible to newspersons consistent with the Sixth Amendment. See N.J.S.A. 2A:84A–21.1 et seq. The amended statute codified the tripartite showing required by *Farber* for penetration of the qualified privilege, but it also mandated that such a showing must be made *before* even an *in camera* inspection is ordered. Despite the observation in the principal case that such a requirement would "effectively stultify the judicial criminal process," the court subsequently acceded to the legislative will. State v. Boiardo, 414 A.2d 14 (N.J.1980). The resulting balance between First and Sixth Amendment concerns is criticized in Comment, Sixth Amendment Limitations on the Newsperson's Privilege: A Breach in the Shield, 13 Rutgers L.J. 361 (1982).

2. *Other state statutes.* State statutes conferring the privileges are common. See Morele, Evidentiary Privilege for Journalists' Sources: Theory and Statutory Protection, 51 Mo.L.Rev. 1 (1986). Where extant, they have

typically received broad interpretation. Henderson v. People, 879 P.2d 383 (Colo.1994) (en banc) (privilege extended to pilot's knowledge of flight plan of news helicopter from which police officer observed marijuana plants).

The Commissioners on Uniform State Laws decided to abandon consideration of a uniform news gatherer's privilege, being unable to agree on either the content of or need for such an act. Uniform Laws Commissioners at Work, 61 A.B.A.J. 1399 (1975).

3. *Federal cases.* Despite the Supreme Court's rejection of a constitutionally based privilege in Branzburg v. Hayes, 408 U.S. 665 (1972), most federal courts, noting that this rejection did not command an absolute majority of the Court, have undertaken to recognize a qualified privilege penetrable upon bases much the same as those set out in *Farber.* See, e.g., United States v. Cuthbertson, 651 F.2d 189 (3d Cir.1981); Shoen v. Shoen, 5 F.3d 1289 (9th Cir.1993). In the federal courts, the requirements of relevance and need have been seen as heightened in civil cases. See Baker v. F & F Inv., 470 F.2d 778 (2d Cir.1972); Silkwood v. Kerr–McGee Corp., 563 F.2d 433 (10th Cir.1977). Compare Maressa v. New Jersey Monthly, 445 A.2d 376 (N.J.1982) (holding New Jersey privilege "absolute in the context of a libel action").

A few federal circuits have refused to recognize even a qualified privilege in connection with grand jury proceedings. See In re Grand Jury Proceedings, 810 F.2d 580 (6th Cir.1987); In re Grand Jury Proceedings, 5 F.3d 397 (9th Cir.1993). See generally Note, Journalist's Privilege: When Deprivation is a Benefit, 108 Yale L.J. 1449 (1999).

4. *The newsperson's privilege and the headlines.* Not surprisingly, claims of privilege by news people often involve situations of intense public interest—with reporters willing to suffer time in jail for contempt rather than divulge information concerning hot news stories. See, e.g., In re Grand Jury Subpoena, Judith Miller, 438 F.3d 1141 (D.C.Cir.2005) (court rejected argument on both constitutional and common law grounds that identity of sources for stories concerning disclosure of Valerie Plame as a CIA operative was confidential; grand jury subpoena had to obeyed). For a further discussion of this incident, see Nestler, Comment, The Underprivileged Profession: The Case for Supreme Court Recognition of the Journalist's Privilege, 154 U.Pa.L.Rev. 201 (2005). See generally Larsen, Note, The Demise of the First Amendment–Based Reporter's Privilege: Why This Current Trend Should Not Surprise the Media, 37 Conn.L.Rev. 1235 (2005).

5. *What about bloggers?* Who is a newsperson or journalist entitled to the protection of any privilege? For two different solutions to the question of who can claim protection, compare Alexander, Looking Out for the Watchdogs: A Legislative Proposal Limiting the Newsgathering Privilege to Journalists in the Greatest Need of Protection for Sources and Information, 20 Yale L. & Pol'y Rev. 97, 130 (2002) (claimant must have a substantial connection with an established news organization and the end product must be found to include information of public interest or concern) with Berger, Shielding the UnMedia: Using the Process of Journalism to Protect the Journalist's Privilege in an Infinite Universe of Publication, 39 Hous.L.Rev. 1371, 1411 (2003) (any individual engaged in "journalism" should be protected by journalists' shield laws; "An individual is 'engaged in journalism'

when he or she is involved in a process that is intended to generate and disseminate truthful information to the public on a regular basis.'').

6. *Sixth Amendment questions.* For discussions of the problem of reconciling testimonial privilege with the requirements of the Sixth Amendment, see Hill, Testimonial Privilege and Fair Trial, 80 Colum.L.Rev. 1173 (1980); Westen, Reflections on Alfred Hill's ''Testimonial Privilege and Fair Trial,'' 14 U.Mich.J.L.Ref. 371 (1981); McCormick, Evidence § 76.2 (6th ed. 2006).

JAFFEE v. REDMOND

Supreme Court of the United States, 1996.
518 U.S. 1.

JUSTICE STEVENS delivered the opinion of the Court.

After a traumatic incident in which she shot and killed a man, a police officer received extensive counseling from a licensed clinical social worker. The question we address is whether statements the officer made to her therapist during the counseling sessions are protected from compelled disclosure in a federal civil action brought by the family of the deceased. Stated otherwise, the question is whether it is appropriate for federal courts to recognize a ''psychotherapist privilege'' under Rule 501 of the Federal Rules of Evidence.

I

Petitioner is the administrator of the estate of Ricky Allen. Respondents are Mary Lu Redmond, a former police officer, and the Village of Hoffman Estates, Illinois, her employer during the time that she served on the police force. Petitioner commenced this action against respondents after Redmond shot and killed Allen while on patrol duty.

On June 27, 1991, Redmond was the first officer to respond to a ''fight in progress'' call at an apartment complex. As she arrived at the scene, two of Allen's sisters ran toward her squad car, waving their arms and shouting that there had been a stabbing in one of the apartments. Redmond testified at trial that she relayed this information to her dispatcher and requested an ambulance. She then exited her car and walked toward the apartment building. Before Redmond reached the building, several men ran out, one waving a pipe. When the men ignored her order to get on the ground, Redmond drew her service revolver. Two other men then burst out of the building, one, Ricky Allen, chasing the other. According to Redmond, Allen was brandishing a butcher knife and disregarded her repeated commands to drop the weapon. Redmond shot Allen when she believed he was about to stab the man he was chasing. Allen died at the scene. Redmond testified that before other officers arrived to provide support, ''people came pouring out of the buildings,'' App. 134, and a threatening confrontation between her and the crowd ensued.

Petitioner filed suit in Federal District Court alleging that Redmond had violated Allen's constitutional rights by using excessive force during the encounter at the apartment complex. The complaint sought damages under Rev. Stat. § 1979, 42 U.S.C. § 1983, and the Illinois wrongful-death statute, Ill. Comp. Stat., ch. 740, § 180/1 *et seq.* (1994). At trial, petitioner presented testimony from members of Allen's family that conflicted with Redmond's version of the incident in several important respects. They testified, for example, that Redmond drew her gun before exiting her squad car and that Allen was unarmed when he emerged from the apartment building.

During pretrial discovery petitioner learned that after the shooting Redmond had participated in about 50 counseling sessions with Karen Beyer, a clinical social worker licensed by the State of Illinois and employed at that time by the Village of Hoffman Estates. Petitioner sought access to Beyer's notes concerning the sessions for use in cross-examining Redmond. Respondents vigorously resisted the discovery. They asserted that the contents of the conversations between Beyer and Redmond were protected against involuntary disclosure by a psychotherapist-patient privilege. The district judge rejected this argument. Neither Beyer nor Redmond, however, complied with his order to disclose the contents of Beyer's notes. At depositions and on the witness stand both either refused to answer certain questions or professed an inability to recall details of their conversations.

In his instructions at the end of the trial, the judge advised the jury that the refusal to turn over Beyer's notes had no "legal justification" and that the jury could therefore presume that the contents of the notes would have been unfavorable to respondents. The jury awarded petitioner $45,000 on the federal claim and $500,000 on her state-law claim.

The Court of Appeals for the Seventh Circuit reversed and remanded for a new trial. Addressing the issue for the first time, the court concluded that "reason and experience," the touchstones for acceptance of a privilege under Rule 501 of the Federal Rules of Evidence, compelled recognition of a psychotherapist-patient privilege. * * * "Reason tells us that psychotherapists and patients share a unique relationship, in which the ability to communicate freely without the fear of public disclosure is the key to successful treatment." * * * As to experience, the court observed that all 50 States have adopted some form of the psychotherapist-patient privilege. * * * The court attached particular significance to the fact that Illinois law expressly extends such a privilege to social workers like Karen Beyer. * * * The court also noted that, with one exception, the federal decisions rejecting the privilege were more than five years old and that the "need and demand for counseling services has skyrocketed during the past several years."

The Court of Appeals qualified its recognition of the privilege by stating that it would not apply if, "in the interests of justice, the evidentiary need for the disclosure of the contents of a patient's counseling sessions outweighs that patient's privacy interests." * * * Balancing those conflicting interests, the court observed, on the one hand, that the evidentiary need for the contents of the confidential conversations was diminished in this case because there were numerous eyewitnesses to the shooting, and, on the other hand, that Officer Redmond's privacy interests were substantial. * * * Based on this assessment, the court concluded that the trial court had erred by refusing to afford protection to the confidential communications between Redmond and Beyer.

The United States Courts of Appeals do not uniformly agree that the federal courts should recognize a psychotherapist privilege under Rule 501. Compare *In re Doe,* 964 F.2d 1325 (C.A.2 1992) (recognizing privilege); * * * Because of the conflict among the Courts of Appeals and the importance of the question, we granted certiorari. 516 U.S. 930 (1995). We affirm.

II

Rule 501 of the Federal Rules of Evidence authorizes federal courts to define new privileges by interpreting "common law principles * * * in the light of reason and experience." The authors of the Rule borrowed this phrase from our opinion in *Wolfle v. United States,* 291 U.S. 7, 12 (1934), which in turn referred to the oft-repeated observation that "the common law is not immutable but flexible, and by its own principles adapts itself to varying conditions." *Funk v. United States,* 290 U.S. 371, 383 (1933). See also *Hawkins v. United States,* 358 U.S. 74, 79 (1958) (changes in privileges may be "dictated by 'reason and experience' "). The Senate Report accompanying the 1975 adoption of the Rules indicates that Rule 501 "should be understood as reflecting the view that the recognition of a privilege based on a confidential relationship * * * should be determined on a case-by-case basis." S.Rep. No. 93–1277, p. 13 (1974) U.S.Code Cong. & Admin.News 1974, pp. 7051, 7059. The Rule thus did not freeze the law governing the privileges of witnesses in federal trials at a particular point in our history, but rather directed federal courts to "continue the evolutionary development of testimonial privileges." *Trammel v. United States,* 445 U.S. 40, 47 (1980); see also *University of Pennsylvania v. EEOC,* 493 U.S. 182, 189 (1990).

The common-law principles underlying the recognition of testimonial privileges can be stated simply. " 'For more than three centuries it has now been recognized as a fundamental maxim that the public * * * has a right to every man's evidence. When we come to examine the various claims of exemption, we start with the primary assumption that there is a general duty to give what testimony one is capable of giving, and that any exemptions which may exist are distinctly exceptional, being so many derogations from a positive general rule.' " *United States v. Bryan,* 339 U.S. 323, 331 (1950) (quoting 8 J. Wigmore, Evidence § 2192, p. 64 (3d ed. 1940)). See also *United States v. Nixon,* 418 U.S. 683, 709 (1974). Exceptions from the general rule disfavoring testimonial privileges may be justified, however, by a " 'public good transcending the normally predominant principle of utilizing all rational means for ascertaining truth.' " *Trammel,* 445 U.S., at 50(quoting *Elkins v. United States,* 364 U.S. 206, 234(1960) (Frankfurter, J., dissenting)).

Guided by these principles, the question we address today is whether a privilege protecting confidential communications between a psychotherapist and her patient "promotes sufficiently important interests to outweigh the need for probative evidence * * * ." 445 U.S., at 51. Both "reason and experience" persuade us that it does.

III

Like the spousal and attorney-client privileges, the psychotherapist-patient privilege is "rooted in the imperative need for confidence and trust." * * * . Treatment by a physician for physical ailments can often proceed successfully on the basis of a physical examination, objective information supplied by the patient, and the results of diagnostic tests. Effective psychotherapy, by contrast, depends upon an atmosphere of confidence and trust in which the patient is willing to make a frank and complete disclosure of facts, emotions, memories, and fears. Because of the sensitive nature of the problems for which individuals consult psychotherapists, disclosure of confidential communications made during counseling sessions may cause embarrassment or disgrace. For this reason, the mere possibility of disclosure may impede development of the confidential relationship necessary for successful treatment. As the Judicial Conference Advisory Committee observed in 1972 when it recommended that Congress recognize a psychotherapist privilege as part of the Proposed Federal Rules of Evidence, a psychiatrist's ability to help her patients

> " 'is completely dependent upon [the patients'] willingness and ability to talk freely. This makes it difficult if not impossible for [a psychiatrist] to function without being able to assure * * * patients of confidentiality and, indeed, privileged communication. Where there may be exceptions to this general rule * * * , there is wide agreement that confidentiality is a *sine qua non* for successful psychiatric treatment.' " Advisory Committee's Notes to Proposed Rules, 56 F.R.D. 183, 242 (1972) (quoting Group for Advancement of Psychiatry, Report No. 45, Confidentiality and Privileged Communication in the Practice of Psychiatry 92 (June 1960)).

By protecting confidential communications between a psychotherapist and her patient from involuntary disclosure, the proposed privilege thus serves important private interests.

Our cases make clear that an asserted privilege must also "serv[e] public ends." *Upjohn Co. v. United States,* 449 U.S. 383, 389 (1981). Thus, the purpose of the attorney-client privilege is to "encourage full and frank communication between attorneys and their clients and thereby promote broader public interests in the observance of law and administration of justice." *Ibid.* And the spousal privilege, as modified in *Trammel,* is justified because it "furthers the important public interest in marital harmony," 445 U.S., at 53. See also *United States v. Nixon,*

418 U.S., at 705; *Wolfle v. United States,* 291 U.S., at 14. The psychotherapist privilege serves the public interest by facilitating the provision of appropriate treatment for individuals suffering the effects of a mental or emotional problem. The mental health of our citizenry, no less than its physical health, is a public good of transcendent importance.[45]

In contrast to the significant public and private interests supporting recognition of the privilege, the likely evidentiary benefit that would result from the denial of the privilege is modest. If the privilege were rejected, confidential conversations between psychotherapists and their patients would surely be chilled, particularly when it is obvious that the circumstances that give rise to the need for treatment will probably result in litigation. Without a privilege, much of the desirable evidence to which litigants such as petitioner seek access—for example, admissions against interest by a party—is unlikely to come into being. This unspoken "evidence" will therefore serve no greater truth-seeking function than if it had been spoken and privileged.

That it is appropriate for the federal courts to recognize a psychotherapist privilege under Rule 501 is confirmed by the fact that all 50 States and the District of Columbia have enacted into law some form of psychotherapist privilege. We have previously observed that the policy decisions of the States bear on the question whether federal courts should recognize a new privilege or amend the coverage of an existing one. See *Trammel,* 445 U.S., at 48–50; *United States v. Gillock,* 445 U.S. 360, 368, n.8 (1980). Because state legislatures are fully aware of the need to protect the integrity of the factfinding functions of their courts, the existence of a consensus among the States indicates that "reason and experience" support recognition of the privilege. In addition, given the importance of the patient's understanding that her communications with her therapist will not be publicly disclosed, any State's promise of confidentiality would have little value if the patient were aware that the privilege would not be honored in a federal court. Denial of the federal privilege therefore would frustrate the purposes of the state legislation that was enacted to foster these confidential communications.

It is of no consequence that recognition of the privilege in the vast majority of States is the product of legislative action rather than judicial decision. Although common-law rulings may once have been the primary source of new developments in federal privilege law, that is no longer the case. In *Funk v. United States,* 290 U.S. 371 (1933), we recognized that it is appropriate to treat a consistent body of policy determinations by state legislatures as reflecting both "reason" and "experience." *Id.,* at 376–381. That rule is properly respectful of the States and at the same time

45. This case amply demonstrates the importance of allowing individuals to receive confidential counseling. Police officers engaged in the dangerous and difficult tasks associated with protecting the safety of our communities not only confront the risk of physical harm but also face stressful circumstances that may give rise to anxiety, depression, fear, or anger. The entire community may suffer if police officers are not able to receive effective counseling and treatment after traumatic incidents, either because trained officers leave the profession prematurely or because those in need of treatment remain on the job.

reflects the fact that once a state legislature has enacted a privilege there is no longer an opportunity for common-law creation of the protection. The history of the psychotherapist privilege illustrates the latter point. In 1972 the members of the Judicial Conference Advisory Committee noted that the common law "had indicated a disposition to recognize a psychotherapist-patient privilege when legislatures began moving into the field." Proposed Rules, 56 F.R.D., at 242 (citation omitted). The present unanimous acceptance of the privilege shows that the state lawmakers moved quickly. That the privilege may have developed faster legislatively than it would have in the courts demonstrates only that the States rapidly recognized the wisdom of the rule as the field of psychotherapy developed.[46]

The uniform judgment of the States is reinforced by the fact that a psychotherapist privilege was among the nine specific privileges recommended by the Advisory Committee in its proposed privilege rules. In *United States v. Gillock,* 445 U.S., at 367–368, our holding that Rule 501 did not include a state legislative privilege relied, in part, on the fact that no such privilege was included in the Advisory Committee's draft. The reasoning in *Gillock* thus supports the opposite conclusion in this case. In rejecting the proposed draft that had specifically identified each privilege rule and substituting the present more open-ended Rule 501, the Senate Judiciary Committee explicitly stated that its action "should not be understood as disapproving any recognition of a psychiatrist-patient * * * privileg[e] contained in the [proposed] rules." S.Rep. No. 93–1277, at 13, U.S.Code Cong. & Admin.News 1974, pp. 7051, 7059.

Because we agree with the judgment of the state legislatures and the Advisory Committee that a psychotherapist-patient privilege will serve a "public good transcending the normally predominant principle of utilizing all rational means for ascertaining truth," *Trammel,* 445 U.S., at 50, we hold that confidential communications between a licensed psychotherapist and her patients in the course of diagnosis or treatment are protected from compelled disclosure under Rule 501 of the Federal Rules of Evidence.

46. Petitioner acknowledges that all 50 state legislatures favor a psychotherapist privilege. She nevertheless discounts the relevance of the state privilege statutes by pointing to divergence among the States concerning the types of therapy relationships protected and the exceptions recognized. A small number of state statutes, for example, grant the privilege only to psychiatrists and psychologists, while most apply the protection more broadly. Compare Haw. Rules Evid. 504, 504.1 and N.D. Rule Evid. 503 (privilege extends to physicians and psychotherapists), with Ariz.Rev.Stat. Ann. § 32–3283 (1992) (privilege covers "behavioral health professional[s]"); Tex. Rule Civ. Evid. 510(a)(1) (privilege extends to persons "licensed or certified by the State of Texas in the diagnosis, evaluation or treatment of any mental or emotional disorder" or "involved in the treatment or examination of drug abusers"); Utah Rule Evid. 506 (privilege protects confidential communications made to marriage and family therapists, professional counselors, and psychiatric mental health nurse specialists). The range of exceptions recognized by the States is similarly varied. Compare Ark.Code Ann. § 17–46–107 (1987) (narrow exceptions); Haw. Rules Evid. 504, 504.1 (same), with Cal. Evid.Code Ann. §§ 1016–1027 (West 1995) (broad exceptions); R.I. Gen. Laws § 5–37.3–4 (1995) (same). These variations in the scope of the protection are too limited to undermine the force of the States' unanimous judgment that some form of psychotherapist privilege is appropriate.

IV

All agree that a psychotherapist privilege covers confidential communications made to licensed psychiatrists and psychologists. We have no hesitation in concluding in this case that the federal privilege should also extend to confidential communications made to licensed social workers in the course of psychotherapy. The reasons for recognizing a privilege for treatment by psychiatrists and psychologists apply with equal force to treatment by a clinical social worker such as Karen Beyer.[47] Today, social workers provide a significant amount of mental health treatment. See, *e.g.,* U.S. Dept. of Health and Human Services, Center for Mental Health Services, Mental Health, United States, 1994, pp. 85–87, 107–114; Brief for National Association of Social Workers et al. as *Amici Curiae* 5–7 (citing authorities). Their clients often include the poor and those of modest means who could not afford the assistance of a psychiatrist or psychologist, *id.,* at 6–7 (citing authorities), but whose counseling sessions serve the same public goals.[48] Perhaps in recognition of these circumstances, the vast majority of States explicitly extend a testimonial privilege to licensed social workers. * * * We therefore agree with the Court of Appeals that "[d]rawing a distinction between the counseling provided by costly psychotherapists and the counseling provided by more readily accessible social workers serves no discernible public purpose." 51 F.3d, at 1358, n.19.

We part company with the Court of Appeals on a separate point. We reject the balancing component of the privilege implemented by that court and a small number of States. Making the promise of confidentiality contingent upon a trial judge's later evaluation of the relative importance of the patient's interest in privacy and the evidentiary need for disclosure would eviscerate the effectiveness of the privilege. As we explained in *Upjohn,* if the purpose of the privilege is to be served, the participants in the confidential conversation "must be able to predict with some degree of certainty whether particular discussions will be

47. If petitioner had filed her complaint in an Illinois state court, respondents' claim of privilege would surely have been upheld, at least with respect to the state wrongful-death action. An Illinois statute provides that conversations between a therapist and her patients are privileged from compelled disclosure in any civil or criminal proceeding. Ill. Comp. Stat., ch. 740, § 110/10 (1994). The term "therapist" is broadly defined to encompass a number of licensed professionals including social workers. Ch. 740, § 110/2. Karen Beyer, having satisfied the strict standards for licensure, qualifies as a clinical social worker in Illinois. 51 F.3d 1346, 1358, n.19 (C.A.7 1995) * * * .

48. The Judicial Conference Advisory Committee's proposed psychotherapist privilege defined psychotherapists as psychologists and medical doctors who provide mental health services. Proposed Rules, 56 F.R.D., at 240. This limitation in the 1972 recommendation does not counsel against recognition of a privilege for social workers practicing psychotherapy. In the quarter century since the Committee adopted its recommendations, much has changed in the domains of social work and psychotherapy. See generally Brief for National Association of Social Workers et al. as *Amici Curiae* 5–13 (and authorities cited). While only 12 States regulated social workers in 1972, all 50 do today. See American Association of State Social Work Boards, Social Work Laws and Board Regulations: A State Comparison Study 29, 31 (1996). Over the same period, the relative portion of therapeutic services provided by social workers has increased substantially. See U.S. Dept. of Health and Human Services, Center for Mental Health Services, Mental Health, United States, 1994, pp. 85–87, 107–114.

protected. An uncertain privilege, or one which purports to be certain but results in widely varying applications by the courts, is little better than no privilege at all." 449 U.S., at 393.

These considerations are all that is necessary for decision of this case. A rule that authorizes the recognition of new privileges on a case-by-case basis makes it appropriate to define the details of new privileges in a like manner. Because this is the first case in which we have recognized a psychotherapist privilege, it is neither necessary nor feasible to delineate its full contours in a way that would "govern all conceivable future questions in this area." *Id.,* at 386.[49]

V

The conversations between Officer Redmond and Karen Beyer and the notes taken during their counseling sessions are protected from compelled disclosure under Rule 501 of the Federal Rules of Evidence. The judgment of the Court of Appeals is affirmed.

JUSTICE SCALIA, with whom the CHIEF JUSTICE joins as to Part III, dissenting.

The Court has discussed at some length the benefit that will be purchased by creation of the evidentiary privilege in this case: the encouragement of psychoanalytic counseling. It has not mentioned the purchase price: occasional injustice. That is the cost of every rule which excludes reliable and probative evidence–or at least every one categorical enough to achieve its announced policy objective. In the case of some of these rules, such as the one excluding confessions that have not been properly "Mirandized," see *Miranda v. Arizona,* 384 U.S. 436 (1966), the victim of the injustice is always the impersonal State or the faceless "public at large." For the rule proposed here, the victim is more likely to be some individual who is prevented from proving a valid claim–or (worse still) prevented from establishing a valid defense. The latter is particularly unpalatable for those who love justice, because it causes the courts of law not merely to let stand a wrong, but to become themselves the instruments of wrong.

In the past, this Court has well understood that the particular value the courts are distinctively charged with preserving—justice—is severely harmed by contravention of "the fundamental principle that ' "the public * * * has a right to every man's evidence." ' " *Trammel v. United States,* 445 U.S. 40, 50 (1980) (citation omitted). Testimonial privileges, it has said, "*are not lightly created nor expansively construed,* for they are in derogation of the search for truth." *United States v. Nixon,* 418 U.S. 683 (1974) (emphasis added). Adherence to that principle has caused us, in the Rule 501 cases we have considered to date, to reject new privileges, see *University of Pennsylvania v. EEOC,* 493 U.S. 182

49. Although it would be premature to speculate about most future developments in the federal psychotherapist privilege, we do not doubt that there are situations in which the privilege must give way, for example, if a serious threat of harm to the patient or to others can be averted only by means of a disclosure by the therapist.

(1990) (privilege against disclosure of academic peer review materials); *United States v. Gillock,* 445 U.S. 360 (1980) (privilege against disclosure of "legislative acts" by member of state legislature), and even to construe narrowly the scope of existing privileges, see, *e.g., United States v. Zolin,* 491 U.S. 554, 568–570 (1989) (permitting *in camera* review of documents alleged to come within crime-fraud exception to attorney-client privilege); *Trammel, supra* (holding that voluntary testimony by spouse is not covered by husband-wife privilege). The Court today ignores this traditional judicial preference for the truth, and ends up creating a privilege that is new, vast, and ill defined. I respectfully dissent.

* * *

III

Turning from the general question that was not involved in this case to the specific one that is: The Court's conclusion that a social-worker psychotherapeutic privilege deserves recognition is even less persuasive. In approaching this question, the fact that five of the state legislatures that have seen fit to enact "some form" of psychotherapist privilege have elected not to extend *any form* of privilege to social workers, * * * ought to give one pause. So should the fact that the Judicial Conference Advisory Committee was similarly discriminating in its conferral of the proposed Rule 504 privilege * * * . The Court, however, has "no hesitation in concluding * * * that the federal privilege should also extend" to social workers, * * * and goes on to prove that by polishing off the reasoned analysis with a topic sentence and two sentences of discussion, as follows (omitting citations and nongermane footnote):

> "The reasons for recognizing a privilege for treatment by psychiatrists and psychologists apply with equal force to treatment by a clinical social worker such as Karen Beyer. Today, social workers provide a significant amount of mental health treatment. Their clients often include the poor and those of modest means who could not afford the assistance of a psychiatrist or psychologist, but whose counseling sessions serve the same public goals." * * *

So much for the rule that privileges are to be narrowly construed.

Of course this brief analysis—like the earlier, more extensive, discussion of the general psychotherapist privilege–contains no explanation of why the psychotherapy provided by social workers is a public good of such transcendent importance as to be purchased at the price of occasional injustice. Moreover, it considers only the respects in which social workers providing therapeutic services are *similar* to licensed psychiatrists and psychologists; not a word about the respects in which they are different. A licensed psychiatrist or psychologist is an expert in psychotherapy–and that may suffice (though I think it not so clear that this Court should make the judgment) to justify the use of extraordinary means to encourage counseling with him, as opposed to counseling with one's rabbi, minister, family, or friends. One must presume that a social worker does *not* bring this greatly heightened degree of skill to bear, which is alone a reason for not encouraging that consultation as generously. Does a social worker bring to bear at least a significantly heightened degree of skill–more than a minister or rabbi, for example? I have no idea, and neither does the Court. The social worker in the present case, Karen Beyer, was a "licensed clinical social worker" in Illinois, * * * a job title whose training requirements consist of a "master's degree in social work from an approved program," and "3,000 hours of satisfactory, supervised clinical professional experience." Ill. Comp. Stat., ch. 225, § 20/9 (1994). It is not clear that the degree in social work requires *any* training in psychotherapy. The "clinical professional experience" apparently will impart some such training, but only of the vaguest sort, judging from the Illinois Code's definition of "[c]linical social work practice," viz., "the providing of mental health services for the evaluation, treatment, and prevention of mental and emotional disorders in individuals, families and groups based on knowledge and theory of psychosocial development, behavior, psychopathology, unconscious motivation, interpersonal relationships, and environmental stress." Ch. 225, § 20/3(5). But the rule the Court announces today–like the Illinois evidentiary privilege which that rule purports to respect, ch. 225, § 20/16–IS not limited to "licensed clinical social workers," but includes all "licensed social worker[s]." "Licensed social worker[s]" may also provide "mental health services" as described in § 20/3(5), so long as it is done under supervision of a licensed clinical social worker. And the training requirement for a "licensed social worker" consists of either (a) "a degree from a graduate program of social work" approved by the State, or (b) "a degree in social work from an undergraduate program" approved by the State, plus "3 years of supervised professional experience." Ch. 225, § 20/9A. With due respect, it does not seem to me that any of this training is comparable in its rigor (or indeed in the precision of its subject) to the training of the other experts (lawyers) to whom this Court has accorded a privilege, or even of the experts (psychiatrists and psychologists) to whom the Advisory Committee and this Court proposed extension of a privilege in 1972. Of course these are only *Illinois'* requirements for "social workers." Those of other States, for all we know, may be even less demanding. Indeed, I am not even sure there is a nationally accepted definition of "social worker," as there is of psychiatrist and psychologist. It seems to me quite irresponsible to extend the so-called "psychotherapist privilege" to all licensed social workers, nationwide, without exploring these issues.

Another critical distinction between psychiatrists and psychologists, on the one hand, and social workers, on the other, is that the former professionals, in their consultations with patients, *do nothing but psychotherapy*. Social workers, on the other hand, interview people for a multitude of reasons.

* * *

Thus, in applying the "social worker" variant of the "psychotherapist" privilege, it will be necessary to determine whether the information provided to the social worker was provided to him *in his capacity as a psychotherapist,* or in his capacity as an administrator of social welfare, a community organizer, etc. Worse still, if the privilege is to have its desired effect (and is not to mislead the client), it will presumably be necessary for the social caseworker to advise, as the conversation with his welfare client proceeds, which portions are privileged and which are not.

Having concluded its three sentences of reasoned analysis, the Court then invokes, as it did when considering the psychotherapist privilege, the "experience" of the States–once again an experience I consider irrelevant (if not counter-indicative) because it consists entirely of legislation rather than common-law decision. It says that "the vast majority of States explicitly extend a testimonial privilege to licensed social workers." * * * There are two elements of this impressive statistic, however, that the Court does not reveal.

First—and utterly conclusive of the irrelevance of this supposed consensus to the question before us—the majority of the States that accord a privilege to social workers do *not* do so as a subpart of a "psychotherapist" privilege. The privilege applies to *all* confidences imparted to social workers, and not just those provided in the course of psychotherapy. In Oklahoma, for example, the social-worker-privilege statute prohibits a licensed social worker from disclosing, or being compelled to disclose, "*any information* acquired from persons consulting the licensed social worker in his or her professional capacity" (with certain exceptions to be discussed *infra,* at 1939). Okla. Stat., Tit. 59, § 1261.6 (1991) (emphasis added). The social worker's "professional capacity" [in Oklahoma] is expansive . * * *

Thus, in Oklahoma, as in most other States having a social-worker privilege, it is not a subpart or even a derivative of the psychotherapist privilege, but rather a piece of special legislation similar to that achieved by many other groups, from accountants, see, *e.g.,* Miss. Code Ann. § 73–33–16(2) (1995) (certified public accountant "shall not be required by any court of this state to disclose, and shall not voluntarily disclose," client information), to private detectives, see, *e.g.,* Mich. Comp. Laws § 338.840(2) (1979) ("Any communications * * * furnished by a professional man or client to a [licensed private detective], or any information secured in connection with an assignment for a client, shall be deemed privileged with the same authority and dignity as are other privileged communications recognized by the courts of this state").[50] These social-worker statutes give no support, therefore, to the theory (importance of psychotherapy) upon which the Court rests its disposition.

50. These ever-multiplying evidentiary-privilege statutes, which the Court today emulates, recall us to the original meaning of the word "privilege." It is a composite derived from the Latin words "privus" and "lex": private law.

Second, the Court does not reveal the enormous degree of disagreement among the States as to the scope of the privilege. It concedes that the laws of four States are subject to such gaping exceptions that they are " 'little better than no privilege at all,' " * * * so that they should more appropriately be categorized with the five States whose laws contradict the action taken today. * * * In adopting *any* sort of a social-worker privilege, then, the Court can at most claim that it is following the legislative "experience" of 40 States, and contradicting the "experience" of 10.

But turning to those States that do have an appreciable privilege of some sort, the diversity is vast * * * .

* * *

Thus, although the Court is technically correct that "the vast majority of States explicitly extend a testimonial privilege to licensed social workers," * * * that uniformity exists only at the most superficial level. No State has adopted the privilege without restriction; the nature of the restrictions varies enormously from jurisdiction to jurisdiction; and 10 States, I reiterate, effectively reject the privilege entirely. It is fair to say that there is scant national consensus even as to the propriety of a social-worker psychotherapist privilege, and none whatever as to its appropriate scope. In other words, the state laws to which the Court appeals for support demonstrate most convincingly that adoption of a social-worker psychotherapist privilege is a job for Congress.

* * *

The question before us today is not whether there should be an evidentiary privilege for social workers providing therapeutic services. Perhaps there should. But the question before us is whether (1) the need for that privilege is so clear, and (2) the desirable contours of that privilege are so evident, that it is appropriate for this Court to craft it in common-law fashion, under Rule 501. Even if we were writing on a clean slate, I think the answer to that question would be clear. But given our extensive precedent to the effect that new privileges "in derogation of the search for truth" "are not lightly created," *United States v. Nixon,* 418 U.S., at 710, the answer the Court gives today is inexplicable.

In its consideration of this case, the Court was the beneficiary of no fewer than 14 *amicus* briefs supporting respondents, most of which came from such organizations as the American Psychiatric Association, the American Psychoanalytic Association, the American Association of State Social Work Boards, the Employee Assistance Professionals Association, Inc., the American Counseling Association, and the National Association of Social Workers. Not a single amicus brief was filed in support of petitioner. That is no surprise. There is no self-interested organization out there devoted to pursuit of the truth in the federal courts. The expectation is, however, that this Court will have that interest prominently—indeed, primarily—in mind. Today we have failed that expectation, and that responsibility. It is no small matter to say that, in some cases, our federal courts will be the tools of injustice rather than unearth the truth where it is available to be found. The common law has identified a few instances where that is tolerable. Perhaps Congress may conclude that it is also tolerable for the purpose of encouraging psychotherapy by social workers. But that conclusion assuredly does not burst upon the mind with such clarity that a judgment in favor of suppressing the truth ought to be pronounced by this honorable Court. I respectfully dissent.

Notes and Questions

1. *Further development of the privilege.* As is apparent from the principal case, unlike the comparable privilege existing in most states, the federal psychotherapist privilege is a judicial creation. The dimensions of the federal privilege are now being developed through the judicial process. See, e.g., Barrett v. Vojtas, 182 F.R.D. 177 (W.D.Pa.1998) (privilege did not apply where examination ordered by public officials); Speaker v. County of San Bernardino, 82 F.Supp. 2d 1105 (C.D.Cal.2000) (mandatory counseling sessions within privilege; privilege exists so long as patient believes counselor was a psychotherapist). See generally Amann & Imwinkelried, The Supreme Court's Decision to Recognize a Psychotherapist Privilege in *Jaffee v. Redmond*, 116 S.Ct. 1923 (1996): The Meaning of "Experience" and the Role of "Reason" Under Federal Rule of Evidence 501, 65 U.Cin.L.Rev. 1019 (1997); Note, Courville, Rationales for the Confidentiality of Psychotherapist—Patient Communications: Testimonial Privilege and the Constitution, 35 Hous.L.Rev. 187 (1998).

2. *Persons covered.* The dissent in the principal case is particularly concerned about the expansion of the privilege to cover social workers. Even under the majority view of the privilege, should there be a limit as to which counselors are covered by the privilege? If so, on what should that limit be based? Licensing? Education? See United States v. Schwensow, 942 F.Supp. 402 (E.D.Wis.1996) (privilege did not apply where communications made to persons who were not physicians, psychotherapists, counselors or social workers); Poulin, The Psychotherapist–Patient Privilege After *Jaffee v. Redmond*: Where Do We Go From Here?, 76 Wash.U.L.Q. 1341 (1998).

3. *General physician-patient privilege in the states.* Approximately forty states recognize a general physician-patient privilege in addition to a psychotherapist privilege. The privileges vary substantially among the states. Most provide that the privilege is absolute, with specific exceptions. See Cal. Evid. Code §§ 990–1007. Others provide for a qualified privilege, such as North Carolina Gen. Stat. § 8–53 (disclosure may be required by a judge if "necessary to a proper administration of justice"). Remember that, in the principal case, the Court rejected a qualified psychotherapist's privilege and instead opted for an absolute privilege. What are the advantages and disadvantages of a qualified privilege? See generally 1 McCormick, Evidence ch. 11 (6th ed. 2006).

4. *General physician-patient privilege in the federal courts.* As did the proposed Federal Rules of Evidence governing privilege, the federal courts have uniformly rejected a general physician-patient privilege. See, e.g.,

United States v. Bercier, 848 F.2d 917 (8th Cir.1988). What is the rationale for rejecting a general physician-patient privilege, while accepting a psychotherapist-patient privilege? See the criticism of such a choice in 25 Wright & Graham, Federal Practice and Procedure § 5522 (1989) and the proposal for a general physician-patient privilege in the federal courts, modeled after the privilege created in *Jaffee* in Broun, The Medical Privilege in the Federal Courts—Should It Matter Whether Your Ego or Your Elbow Hurts?, 38 Loy.L.A.L.Rev. 657 (2004).

UNIFORM RULES OF EVIDENCE

RULE 503. [PSYCHOTHERAPIST][51] [PHYSICIAN AND PSYCHOTHERAPIST] [PHYSICIAN AND MENTAL–HEALTH PROVIDER] [MENTAL–HEALTH PROVIDER]-PATIENT PRIVILEGE.

(a) Definitions. In this rule:

(1) A communication is "confidential" if it is not intended to be disclosed to third persons, except those present to further the interest of the patient in the consultation, examination, or interview, those reasonably necessary for the transmission of the communication, and persons who are participating in the diagnosis and treatment of the patient under the direction of a [psychotherapist] [physician or psychotherapist] [physician or mental-health provider] [mental-health provider], including members of the patient's family.

[(2) "Mental-health provider" means a person authorized, in any State or country, or reasonably believed by the patient to be authorized, to engage in the diagnosis or treatment of a mental or emotional condition, including addiction to alcohol or drugs.]

[(3) "Patient" means an individual who consults or is examined or interviewed by a [psychotherapist] [physician or psychotherapist] [physician or mental-health provider] [mental-health provider].]

[(4) "Physician" means a person authorized in any State or country, or reasonably believed by the patient to be authorized to practice medicine.]

[(5) "Psychotherapist" means a person authorized in any State or country, or reasonably believed by the patient to be authorized, to practice medicine, while engaged in the diagnosis or treatment of a mental or emotional condition, including addiction to alcohol or drugs, or a person licensed or certified under the laws of any State or country, or reasonably believed by the patient to be licensed or certified, as a psychologist, while similarly engaged.]

(b) General rule of privilege. A patient has a privilege to refuse to disclose and to prevent any other person from disclosing confidential

51. [The language in brackets was provided by the drafters to give jurisdictions options when adopting this privilege. Ed.]

communications made for the purpose of diagnosis or treatment of the patient's [physical,] mental[,] or emotional condition, including addiction to alcohol or drugs, among the patient, the patient's [psychotherapist] [physician or psychotherapist] [physician or mental-health provider] [mental-health provider] and persons, including members of the patient's family, who are participating in the diagnosis or treatment under the direction of the [psychotherapist] [physician or psychotherapist] [physician or mental-health provider] [mental-health provider].

(c) Who may claim the privilege. The privilege under this rule may be claimed by the patient, the patient's guardian or conservator, or the personal representative of a deceased patient. The person who was the [psychotherapist] [physician or psychotherapist] [physician or mental-health provider] [mental-health provider] at the time of the communication is presumed to have authority to claim the privilege, but only on behalf of the patient.

(d) Exceptions. There is no privilege under this rule for a communication:

(1) relevant to an issue in proceedings to hospitalize the patient for mental illness, if the [psychotherapist] [physician or psychotherapist] [physician or mental-health provider] [mental-health provider], in the course of diagnosis or treatment, has determined that the patient is in need of hospitalization;

(2) made in the course of a court-ordered investigation or examination of the [physical,] mental[,] or emotional condition of the patient, whether a party or a witness, with respect to the particular purpose for which the examination is ordered, unless the court orders otherwise;

(3) relevant to an issue of the [physical,] mental[,] or emotional condition of the patient in any proceeding in which the patient relies upon the condition as an element of the patient's claim or defense or, after the patient's death, in any proceeding in which any party relies upon the condition as an element of the party's claim or defense;

(4) if the services of the [psychotherapist] [physician or psychotherapist] [physician or mental-health provider] [mental-health provider] were sought or obtained to enable or aid anyone to commit or plan to commit what the patient knew, or reasonably should have known, was a crime or fraud or mental or physical injury to the patient or another individual;

(5) in which the patient has expressed an intent to engage in conduct likely to result in imminent death or serious bodily injury to the patient or another individual;

(6) relevant to an issue in a proceeding challenging the competency of the [psychotherapist] [physician or psychotherapist] [physician or mental-health provider] [mental-health provider];

(7) relevant to a breach of duty by the [psychotherapist] [physician or psychotherapist] [physician or mental-health provider] [mental-health provider]; or

(8) that is subject to a duty to disclose under [statutory law].

Note on the Clergy–Communicant Privilege

Though some authorities have questioned the existence of a clergy-communicant privilege at common law, it would appear that such a privilege was recognized before the Reformation and only dropped from view after that era had substantially reduced the importance of confession in England. Yellin, The History and Current Status of the Clergy–Penitent Privilege, 23 Santa Clara L.Rev. 95 (1983). Whatever its recognition at common law, the privilege is now recognized by statute in all but three states. 8 Wigmore, Evidence § 2395 (McNaughten rev. 1961). The statutory forms vary widely, however, and it has been said that "there is no typical clergy privilege statute." Mitchell, Must Clergy Tell? Child Abuse Reporting Requirements Versus the Clergy Privilege and Free Exercise of Religion, 71 Minn.L.Rev. 723 (1987). Similarly the justifications advanced for the privilege have varied. See Reece, Confidential Communications to the Clergy, 24 Ohio St.L.J. 55 (1963).

Problems arising from attempts to invoke the privilege have frequently centered on who is a "clergyman," Annot., 101 A.L.R.5th 619, and what types of communications are covered, Annot., 93 A.L.R. 5th 327. See also Kuhlman, Communications to Clergyman—When Are They Privileged?, 2 Val.U.L.Rev. 265 (1968).

Many of the priest-penitent statutes incorporate the requirement that the communication, to be privileged, must be made "in the course of discipline enjoined by the church or denomination" of the clergyman. Should this language be construed to extend the privilege only to communicants of a church in which confession is required? Compare In re Swenson, 237 N.W. 589 (Minn.1931) (holding the quoted statutes not to be so restricted), with Sherman v. State, 279 S.W. 353 (Ark.1926). See also State v. Martin, 959 P.2d 152 (Wash.Ct.App.1998) (language interpreted as requiring only that clergy member be required by the member's religion to receive the confidential communication and to provide spiritual counseling).

What of the constitutionality of any priest-penitent privilege, even one available to members of all denominations and sects? See Smith, The Pastor on the Witness Stand: Toward a Religious Privilege in the Courts, 29 Cath.Law. 1 (1984); Stoyles, The Dilemma of the Constitutionality of the Priest–Penitent Privilege, 29 U.Pitt.L.Rev. 27 (1967).

Note on Miscellaneous Statutory Privileges

A state by state survey of various and sundry evidentiary privileges can be found in Imwinkelried, The New Wigmore: Evidentiary Privilege, App. D (2002).

Among the more common statutory privileges listed by Professor Imwinkelried is the accountant-client's privilege, existing in more than half the states.

Increased awareness of the problems facing victims of rape has found expression not only in rules such as Fed.R.Evid. 412, but in advocacy for, and occasional adoption of, a rape victim-counselor privilege. See Comment, Rape Victim—Crisis Counselor Communications: An Argument for an Absolute Privilege, 17 U.C. Davis L.Rev. 1213 (1984).

A parent-child privilege has been adopted by statute in at least three states, Idaho Code § 9–203(7); Minn.Stat.Ann. § 595.02(j); Mass.Gen.L. ch. 233, § 20; though appeals for the judicial creation of such a privilege have been almost universally rejected. See In Re Grand Jury, 103 F.3d 1140 (3d Cir.1997) (listing cases rejecting the privilege). The literature, generally in support of some form of the privilege, is extensive. A representative selection includes Coburn, Child–Parent Communications: Spare the Privilege and Spoil the Child, 74 Dick.L.Rev. 599 (1970); Stanton, Child–Parent Privilege for Confidential Communications, An Examination and Proposal, 16 Fam. L.Q. 1 (1982); Kraft, The Parent–Child Testimonial Privilege: Who's Minding the Kids?, 18 Fam.L.Q. 505 (1985) (advocating non-traditional privilege protecting child as opposed to parent testimony); Schlueter, The Parent–Child Privilege: A Response to Calls for Adoption, 19 St. Mary's L.J. 35 (1987).

Creation of still other privileges has been advocated, Nejelski & Lerman, A Researcher–Subject Testimonial Privilege, 1971 Wis.L.Rev. 1085; Delgado & Miller, God, Galileo, and Government: Toward Constitutional Protection for Scientific Inquiry, 53 Wash.L.Rev. 349 (1978). For a tentative suggestion that creation of a librarian-patron privilege might be sought, together with discussion of several incidents giving rise to the idea, see 1 American Libraries 749 (1970).

Chapter 16[1]

PRIVILEGES DESIGNED TO SAFEGUARD GOVERNMENTAL OPERATIONS

SECTION A. STATE SECRETS AND EXECUTIVE PRIVILEGE

UNITED STATES v. REYNOLDS

Supreme Court of the United States, 1953.
345 U.S. 1.

MR. CHIEF JUSTICE VINSON delivered the opinion of the Court.

These suits under the Tort Claims Act arise from the death of three civilians in the crash of a B–29 aircraft at Waycross, Georgia, on October 6, 1948. Because an important question of the Government's privilege to resist discovery is involved, we granted certiorari. 343 U.S. 918.

The aircraft had taken flight for the purpose of testing secret electronic equipment, with four civilian observers aboard. While aloft, fire broke out in one of the bomber's engines. Six of the nine crew members and three of the four civilian observers were killed in the crash.

The widows of the three deceased civilian observers brought consolidated suits against the United States. In the pretrial stages the plaintiffs moved, under Rule 34 of the Federal Rules of Civil Procedure,[2] for

1. In the cases and materials throughout the chapter, some footnotes have been omitted and others have been renumbered. [Ed.]

2. "Rule 34. *Discovery and Production of Documents and Things for Inspection, Copying, or Photographing.* Upon motion of any party showing good cause therefor and upon notice to all other parties, and subject to the provisions of Rule 30(b), the court in which an action is pending may (1) order any party to produce and permit the inspection and copying or photographing, by or on behalf of the moving party, of any designated documents, papers, books, accounts, letters, photographs, objects, or tangible things, not privileged, which constitute or contain evidence relating to any of the matters within the scope of the examination permitted by Rule 26(b) and which are in his possession, custody, or control; or (2) order any party to permit entry upon designated land or other property in his possession or control for the purpose of inspecting, measuring, survey-

production of the Air Force's official accident investigation report and the statements of the three surviving crew members, taken in connection with the official investigation. The Government moved to quash the motion, claiming that these matters were privileged against disclosure pursuant to Air Force regulations promulgated under R.S. § 161.[3] The District Judge sustained plaintiffs' motion, holding that good cause for production had been shown. The claim of privilege under R.S. § 161 was rejected on the premise that the Tort Claims Act, in making the Government liable "in the same manner" as a private individual, had waived any privilege based upon executive control over governmental documents.

Shortly after this decision, the District Court received a letter from the Secretary of the Air Force, stating that "it has been determined that it would not be in the public interest to furnish this report. * * * " The court allowed a rehearing on its earlier order, and at the rehearing the Secretary of the Air Force filed a formal "Claim of Privilege." This document repeated the prior claim based generally on R.S. § 161, and then stated that the Government further objected to production of the documents "for the reason that the aircraft in question, together with the personnel on board, were engaged in a highly secret mission of the Air Force." An affidavit of the Judge Advocate General, United States Air Force, was also filed with the court, which asserted that the demanded material could not be furnished "without seriously hampering national security, flying safety and the development of highly technical and secret military equipment." The same affidavit offered to produce the three surviving crew members, without cost, for examination by the plaintiffs. The witnesses would be allowed to refresh their memories from any statement made by them to the Air Force, and authorized to testify as to all matters except those of a "classified nature."

The District Court ordered the Government to produce the documents in order that the court might determine whether they contained privileged matter. The Government declined, so the court entered an order, under Rule 37(b)(2)(i),[4] that the facts on the issue of negligence

ing, or photographing the property or any designated object or operation thereon within the scope of the examination permitted by Rule 26(b). The order shall specify the time, place, and manner of making the inspection and taking the copies and photographs and may prescribe such terms and conditions as are just."

3. 5 U.S.C.A. § 22:

"The head of each department is authorized to prescribe regulations, not inconsistent with law, for the government of his department, the conduct of its officers and clerks, the distribution and performance of its business, and the custody, use, and preservation of the records, papers, and property appertaining to it."

Air Force Regulation No. 62–7(5)(b) provides:

"Reports of boards of officers, special accident reports, or extracts therefrom will not be furnished or made available to persons outside the authorized chain of command without the specific approval of the Secretary of the Air Force."

4. "Rule 37. *Refusal to Make Discovery: Consequences.*

"(b) Failure to Comply With Order.

"(2) *Other Consequences.* If any party or an officer or managing agent of a party refuses to obey * * * an order made under Rule 34 to produce any document * * * , the court may make such orders

would be taken as established in plaintiffs' favor. After a hearing to determine damages, final judgment was entered for the plaintiffs. The Court of Appeals affirmed, both as to the showing of good cause for production of the documents, and as to the ultimate disposition of the case as a consequence of the Government's refusal to produce the documents.

We have had broad propositions pressed upon us for decision. On behalf of the Government it has been urged that the executive department heads have power to withhold any documents in their custody from judicial view if they deem it to be in the public interest.[5] Respondents have asserted that the executive's power to withhold documents was waived by the Tort Claims Act. Both positions have constitutional overtones which we find it unnecessary to pass upon, there being a narrower ground for decision. * * * .

The Tort Claims Act expressly makes the Federal Rules of Civil Procedure applicable to suits against the United States.[6] The judgment in this case imposed liability upon the Government by operation of Rule 37, for refusal to produce documents under Rule 34. Since Rule 34 compels production only of matters "not privileged," the essential question is whether there was a valid claim of privilege under the Rule. We hold that there was, and that, therefore, the judgment below subjected the United States to liability on terms to which Congress did not consent by the Tort Claims Act.

We think it should be clear that the term "not privileged," as used in Rule 34, refers to "privileges" as that term is understood in the law of evidence. When the Secretary of the Air Force lodged his formal "Claim of Privilege," he attempted therein to invoke the privilege against revealing military secrets, a privilege which is well established in the law of evidence.[7] * * *

* * * [T]he principles which control the application of the privilege emerge quite clearly from the available precedents. The privilege belongs to the Government and must be asserted by it; it can neither be claimed nor waived by a private party. It is not to be lightly invoked.[8] There must

in regard to the refusal as are just, and among others the following:

"(i) An order that the matters regarding which the questions were asked, or the character or description of the thing or land, or the contents of the paper, or the physical or mental condition of the party, or any other designated facts shall be taken to be established for the purposes of the action in accordance with the claim of the party obtaining the order * * * ."

5. While claim of executive power to suppress documents is based more immediately upon R.S. § 161 * * * , the roots go much deeper. It is said that R.S. § 161 is only a legislative recognition of an inherent executive power which is protected in the constitutional system of separation of power.

6. 28 U.S.C.A. (1946 ed.) § 932; United States v. Yellow Cab Co., 340 U.S. 543, 553 (1951).

7. Totten v. United States, 92 U.S. 105, 107 (1875); Firth Sterling Steel Co. v. Bethlehem Steel Co., 199 F. 353 (D.C.E.D.Pa. 1912) * * * .

8. Marshall, C.J., in the *Aaron Burr* trial, I Robertson's Reports 186: "That there may be matter, the production of which the court would not require, is certain. * * * What ought to be done, under such circumstances, presents a delicate question, the discussion of which, it is hoped, will never be rendered necessary in this country."

be a formal claim of privilege, lodged by the head of the department which has control over the matter, after actual personal consideration by that officer. The court itself must determine whether the circumstances are appropriate for the claim of privilege, and yet do so without forcing a disclosure of the very thing the privilege is designed to protect.[9] The latter requirement is the only one which presents real difficulty. As to it, we find it helpful to draw upon judicial experience in dealing with an analogous privilege, the privilege against self-incrimination.

The privilege against self-incrimination presented the courts with a similar sort of problem. Too much judicial inquiry into the claim of privilege would force disclosure of the thing the privilege was meant to protect, while a complete abandonment of judicial control would lead to intolerable abuses. Indeed, in the earlier stages of judicial experience with the problem, both extremes were advocated, some saying that the bare assertion by the witness must be taken as conclusive, and others saying that the witness should be required to reveal the matter behind his claim of privilege to the judge for verification.[10] Neither extreme prevailed, and a sound formula of compromise was developed. This formula received authoritative expression in this country as early as the *Burr* trial.[11] There are differences in phraseology, but in substance it is agreed that the court must be satisfied from all the evidence and circumstances, and "from the implications of the question, in the setting in which it is asked, that a responsive answer to the question or an explanation of why it cannot be answered might be dangerous because injurious disclosure could result." Hoffman v. United States, 341 U.S. 479, 486–487 (1951). If the court is so satisfied, the claim of the privilege will be accepted without requiring further disclosure.

Regardless of how it is articulated, some like formula of compromise must be applied here. Judicial control over the evidence in a case cannot be abdicated to the caprice of executive officers. Yet we will not go so far as to say that the court may automatically require a complete disclosure to the judge before the claim of privilege will be accepted in any case. It

9. [Duncan v. Cammell, Laird & Co., [1942] A.C. 624,] at pp. 638–642; cf. the language of this Court in Hoffman v. United States, 341 U.S. 479, 486 (1951), speaking to the analogous hazard of probing too far in derogation of the claim of privilege against self-incrimination:

"However, if the witness, upon interposing his claim, were required to prove the hazard in the sense in which a claim is usually required to be established in court, *he would be compelled to surrender the very protection which the privilege is designed to guarantee.*" (Emphasis supplied.)

10. Compare the expressions of Rolfe, B. and Wilde, C.J., in Regina v. Garbett, 2 Car. & K. 474, 492 (1847); see 8 Wigmore on Evidence (3d ed.) § 2271.

11. I Robertson's Reports 244:

"When a question is propounded, it belongs to the court to consider and to decide, whether any direct answer to it can implicate the witness. If this be decided in the negative, then he may answer it without violating the privilege which is secured to him by law. If a direct answer to it *may* criminate himself, then he must be the sole judge what his answer would be. The court cannot participate with him in this judgment, because they cannot decide on the effect of his answer without knowing what it would be; and a disclosure of that fact to the judges would strip him of the privilege which the law allows, and which he claims."

may be possible to satisfy the court, from all the circumstances of the case, that there is a reasonable danger that compulsion of the evidence will expose military matters which, in the interest of national security, should not be divulged. When this is the case, the occasion for the privilege is appropriate, and the court should not jeopardize the security which the privilege is meant to protect by insisting upon an examination of the evidence, even by the judge alone, in chambers.

In the instant case we cannot escape judicial notice that this is a time of vigorous preparation for national defense. Experience in the past war has made it common knowledge that air power is one of the most potent weapons in our scheme of defense, and that newly developing electronic devices have greatly enhanced the effective use of air power. It is equally apparent that these electronic devices must be kept secret if their full military advantage is to be exploited in the national interests. On the record before the trial court it appeared that this accident occurred to a military plane which had gone aloft to test secret electronic equipment. Certainly there was a reasonable danger that the accident investigation report would contain references to the secret electronic equipment which was the primary concern of the mission.

Of course, even with this information before him, the trial judge was in no position to decide that the report was privileged until there had been a formal claim of privilege. Thus it was entirely proper to rule initially that petitioner had shown probable cause for discovery of the documents. Thereafter, when the formal claim of privilege was filed by the Secretary of the Air Force, under circumstances indicating a reasonable possibility that military secrets were involved, there was certainly a sufficient showing of privilege to cut off further demand for the documents on the showing of necessity for its compulsion that had then been made.

In each case, the showing of necessity which is made will determine how far the court should probe in satisfying itself that the occasion for invoking the privilege is appropriate. Where there is a strong showing of necessity, the claim of privilege should not be lightly accepted, but even the most compelling necessity cannot overcome the claim of privilege if the court is ultimately satisfied that military secrets are at stake.[12] *A fortiori*, where necessity is dubious, a formal claim of privilege, made under the circumstances of this case, will have to prevail. Here, necessity was greatly minimized by an available alternative, which might have given respondents the evidence to make out their case without forcing a showdown on the claim of privilege. By their failure to pursue that alternative, respondents have posed the privilege question for decision with the formal claim of privilege set against a dubious showing of necessity.

12. See Totten v. United States, 92 U.S. 105 (1875), where the very subject matter of the action, a contract to perform espionage, was a matter of state secret. The action was dismissed on the pleadings without ever reaching the question of evidence, since it was so obvious that the action should never prevail over the privilege.

There is nothing to suggest that the electronic equipment, in this case, had any causal connection with the accident. Therefore, it should be possible for respondents to adduce the essential facts as to causation without resort to material touching upon military secrets. Respondents were given a reasonable opportunity to do just that, when petitioner formally offered to make the surviving crew members available for examination. We think that offer should have been accepted.

Respondents have cited us to those cases in the criminal field, where it has been held that the Government can invoke its evidentiary privileges only at the price of letting the defendant go free.[13] The rationale of the criminal cases is that, since the Government which prosecutes an accused also has the duty to see that justice is done, it is unconscionable to allow it to undertake prosecution and then invoke its governmental privileges to deprive the accused of anything which might be material to his defense. Such rationale has no application in a civil forum where the Government is not the moving party, but is a defendant only on terms to which it has consented.

The decision of the Court of Appeals is reversed and the case will be remanded to the District Court for further proceedings consistent with the views expressed in this opinion.

Reversed and remanded.

MR. JUSTICE BLACK, MR. JUSTICE FRANKFURTER, and MR. JUSTICE JACKSON dissent, substantially for the reasons set forth in the opinion of Judge Maris below. 192 F.2d 987.

Notes and Questions

1. *Uncertainty on conclusiveness of executive determination of privilege.* In *Reynolds,* the Supreme Court provides inconsistent indications as to whether the trial court must accept as virtually conclusive the executive determination of privilege or whether it has the right to determine independently the validity of the claim on the basis of an *in camera* inspection. In Ellsberg v. Mitchell, 709 F.2d 51 (D.C.Cir.1983), the court of appeals, while recognizing the dangers involved, stated the test for determining whether an *in camera* inspection should be conducted as follows:

> Whether (and in what spirit) the trial judge in a particular case should examine the materials sought to be withheld depends upon two critical considerations. First, the more compelling a litigant's showing of need for the information in question, the deeper "the court should probe in satisfying itself that the occasion for invoking the privilege is appropriate." Second, the more plausible and substantial the government's allegations of danger to national security, in the context of all circumstances surrounding the case, the more deferential should be the judge's inquiry into the foundations and scope of the claim.

13. United States v. Andolschek, 142 F.2d 503 (C.A.2d Cir.1944); United States v. Beekman, 155 F.2d 580 (C.A.2d Cir.1946).

709 F.2d at 58–59 (quoting *Reynolds*, 345 U.S. at 11).

The court then dealt with the requester's argument that a decision by the court based solely upon an *ex parte in camera* inspection was inadequate. It concluded that in ruling upon the validity of the claim, the court should not permit the requester's counsel to participate in the *in camera* proceedings since "our nation's security is too important to be entrusted to the good faith and circumspection of a litigant's lawyer (whose sense of obligation to his client is likely to strain his fidelity to his pledge of secrecy) or to the coercive power of a protective order." 709 F.2d at 61. However, the court concluded that the government should be required to provide as complete a public account of the materials as possible to assist adversary analysis of the claim:

> [T]he trial judge should insist (1) that the formal claim of privilege be made on the public record and (2) that the government either (a) publicly explain in detail the kinds of injury to national security it seeks to avoid and the reason those harms would result from the revelation of the requested information or (b) indicate why such an explanation would itself endanger national security. * * * [B]efore conducting an *in camera* examination of the requested materials, the trial judge should be sure that the government has justified its claim in as much detail as is feasible (and would be helpful) without undermining the privilege itself.

Id. at 63–64. See also Northrop Corp. v. McDonnell Douglas Corp., 751 F.2d 395, 401 (D.C.Cir.1984) (describing court's determination of whether to conduct *in camera* inspection as application of "sliding scale").

2. *Limited judicial role. Reynolds* has been "extensively mined" for its analysis of the role of the judge in military or diplomatic secrets cases. 1 McCormick, Evidence § 110, at 489–90 (6th ed. 2006). "Whatever material is considered by the court the standard applied is whether there exists a reasonable danger that disclosure will damage national security. If this danger is found, the privilege is absolute and is not affected by the extent of the litigants need for the confidential information." Id. § 110, at 53. All other governmental privileges are qualified. As will be seen throughout the rest of the Chapter, these cases necessitate a greater role for the judiciary, which must weigh the competing interests of government secrecy against a litigant's interest in obtaining the evidentiary information. *In camera* inspection of the disputed evidence is often the means of accomplishing this task, but it "is not a necessary or inevitable tool in every case. Others are available." EPA v. Mink, 410 U.S. 73, 93 (1973) (noting that the agency may sometimes satisfy its burden by means such as a detailed affidavit or oral testimony).

3. *Government invocation of privilege where non-party.* As *Reynolds* notes, the state secrets privilege may be invoked only by the government. There are often significant consequences when it does so. Where the government is not a party, the result in most instances is as if the witness possessing the evidence were dead—the evidence is simply unavailable. *Ellsberg,* note 1, supra, 709 F.2d at 64. In some circumstances, the impact may be far more drastic. In Fitzgerald v. Penthouse Int'l, Ltd., 776 F.2d 1236 (4th Cir.1985), the court held that, where trial of a libel action would require proof of the truth or falsity of classified materials, the government's

invocation of the state secrets privilege required dismissal since litigation would compromise military secrets. See also Farnsworth Cannon, Inc. v. Grimes, 635 F.2d 268 (4th Cir.1980) (en banc) (where plaintiff possessed materials protected by state secrets privilege and highly relevant to claim, dismissal required to prevent litigation pressures from causing party to reveal secrets).

4. *Government invocation of privilege where civil defendant.* Where the government is a civil defendant, the results remain essentially the same as if it were not a party: there is no direct penalty for invoking the privilege, and the evidence is treated simply as unavailable. "The rationale for this doctrine is that the United States, while waiving its sovereign immunity for many purposes, has never consented to an *increase* in its exposure to liability when it is compelled, for reasons of national security, to refuse to release relevant evidence." *Ellsberg,* 709 F.2d at 64. In some circumstances, the government may be able to use the materials submitted *in camera* to establish a defense. See Molerio v. Federal Bureau of Investigation, 749 F.2d 815, 825 (D.C.Cir.1984) (summary judgment properly granted against plaintiff when privileged information provided *in camera* established a valid defense). See generally Comment, 29 Wake Forest L.Rev. 567 (1994).

5. *Government invocation where civil plaintiff or criminal prosecutor.* When the government is the moving party as civil plaintiff or prosecutor in a criminal case, assertion of privilege may result in direct sanctions. In a civil case, dismissal of the government's complaint will frequently be required but will not always be an appropriate remedy. Compare United States v. Cotton Valley Operators Comm'n, 9 F.R.D. 719 (W.D.La.1949), aff'd by equally divided court, 339 U.S. 940 (1950) (dismissal appropriate remedy), with Republic of China v. Nat'l Union Fire Ins., 142 F.Supp. 551 (D.Md.1956) (dismissal inappropriate). In the criminal context, when the government denies the defendant information material to the defense or bearing directly on the merits of the charge, dismissal is appropriate. United States v. Reynolds, 345 U.S. 1, 12 (1953). While changing neither the state secrets privilege nor the consequences of the government withholding classified materials, the procedures followed when such information is withheld is now governed by the Classified Information Procedures Act. 18 U.S.C.App. § 1, et seq.

6. *Classified material in criminal defense.* Criminal defendants will on occasion, chiefly in espionage cases, possess classified information they contend must be revealed in the presentation of their defense. A defendant in such circumstances has the ability to place the government in the position of continuing the prosecution at the cost of the revelation of state secrets. This situation, which may arise either from the bogus claims of the unscrupulous or through wholly proper efforts of counsel to present a defense, is given the label "graymail." This problem was a principal reason for passage of the Classified Information Procedures Act (CIPA). CIPA has been part of several recent high profile cases. See United States v. Noriega 117 F.3d 1206, 1215–17 (11th Cir.1997) (former Panamanian strongman arguing unsuccessfully that intelligence work performed for the United States should have been admitted at trial); United States v. Ho Lee, 90 F.Supp.2d 1324 (D.N.M.2000) (rejecting espionage defendant's argument that CIPA was unconstitutional as applied to him).

CIPA establishes procedures to litigate such claims in an effort to remedy one of the critical inadequacies of the then existing procedures, the lack of opportunity for the government to obtain an advance ruling concerning admissibility of the classified material. Prosecutors often cited this feature of the law as the reason they dismissed charges rather than risking disclosure of the information at trial. CIPA provides that a defendant must give advance notice to the prosecution if he or she intends to disclose classified information in connection with litigation of the criminal trial. The court then holds an *in camera* hearing to determine issues involving relevance and admissibility of the classified information. As a consequence of the hearing, the court may deny the defendant the right to disclose the information or, if it finds disclosure proper, order, at the government's request, that either a statement admitting relevant facts or a summary of the specific information be received as a substitute for the classified information. See United States v. Moussaoui, 382 F.3d 453, 471–82 (4th Cir.2004) (finding dismissal not appropriate sanction for government refusal to produce enemy combatant witness where substitutes for testimony were adequate). If the court denies the government's request to accept a substitute, upon objection by the Attorney General, the court orders the defendant not to disclose the information and either dismisses the charges or fashions other appropriate relief.

The prospect of a defendant's use of state secrets may justify resort to unusual procedural devices to protect the privileged information. In Loral Corp. v. McDonnell Douglas Corp., 558 F.2d 1130 (2d Cir.1977), the court upheld the trial court's action in striking a jury trial demand where the litigation involved large amounts of classified material. The case involved an action by a subcontractor producing classified equipment for the Air Force against the prime contractor for breach of contract. Both parties already had access to the classified material, and the court pointed out that the Department of Defense would grant security clearance to the judge and magistrate to whom the case was assigned but that such a course was not feasible with respect to jurors. See also Halpern v. United States, 258 F.2d 36 (2d Cir.1958). These unusual steps may be preferable to the option of dismissing the action.

7. *Sources.* 2 Imwinkelried, The New Wigmore: Evidentiary Privileges, ch. 8 (2002); Askin, Secret Justice and the Adversary System, 18 Hastings Const.L.Q. 745 (1991); Brancart, Rethinking the State Secrets Privilege, 9 Whittier L.Rev. 1 (1987); Gardner, The State Secret Privilege Invoked in Civil Litigation: A Proposal for Statutory Relief, 29 Wake Forest L.Rev. 567 (1994); Pilchen & Klubes, Using the Classified Information Procedures Act in Criminal Cases: A Primer for Defense Counsel, 31 Am.Crim.L.Rev. 191 (1994); Schmidt & Dratel, Turning the Tables: Using the Government's Secrecy and Security Arsenal for the Benefit of the Client in Terrorism Prosecutions, 48 N.Y.L.Sch.L.Rev. 69 (2003/2004); Stacy, The Constitution in Conflict: Espionage Prosecutions, the Right to Present a Defense, and the State Secrets Privilege, 58 U.Colo.L.Rev. 177 (1987); Stracher, Eyes Tied Shut: Litigating for Access under CIPA in the Government's "War on Terror," 48 N.Y.L.Sch.L.Rev.173 (2003/2004); Tamanaha, A Critical Review of The Classified Information Procedures Act, 13 Am.J.Crim.L. 277 (1986).

UNITED STATES v. NIXON

Supreme Court of the United States, 1974.
418 U.S. 683.

MR. CHIEF JUSTICE BURGER delivered the opinion of the Court.

* * *

On March 1, 1974, a grand jury of the United States District Court for the District of Columbia returned an indictment charging seven named individuals[14] with various offenses, including conspiracy to defraud United States and to obstruct justice. Although he was not designated as such in the indictment, the grand jury named the President, among others, as an unindicted coconspirator. On April 18, 1974, upon motion of the Special Prosecutor, * * * a subpoena *duces tecum* was issued pursuant to Rule 17(c) to the President by the United States District Court and made returnable on May 2, 1974. This subpoena required the production, in advance of the September 9 trial date, of certain tapes, memoranda, papers, transcripts or other writings relating to certain precisely identified meetings between the President and others. The Special Prosecutor was able to fix the time, place and persons present at these discussions because the White House daily logs and appointment records had been delivered to him. On April 30, the President publicly released edited transcripts of 43 conversations; portions of 20 conversations subject to subpoena in the present case were included. On May 1, 1974, the President's counsel, filed a "special appearance" and a motion to quash the subpoena, under Rule 17(c). This motion was accompanied by a formal claim of privilege. At a subsequent hearing, further motions to expunge the grand jury's action naming the President as an unindicted coconspirator and for protective orders against the disclosure of that information were filed or raised orally by counsel for the President.

On May 20, 1974, the District Court denied the motion to quash and the motions to expunge and for protective orders. 377 F.Supp. 1326 (1974). It further ordered "the President or any subordinate officer, official or employee with custody or control of the documents or objects subpoenaed," id., at 1331, to deliver to the District Court, on or before May 31, 1974, the originals of all subpoenaed items, as well as an index and analysis of those items, together with tape copies of those portions of the subpoenaed recordings for which transcripts had been released to the public by the President on April 30. The District Court rejected jurisdictional challenges based on a contention that the dispute was nonjusticiable because it was between the Special Prosecutor and the Chief Executive and hence "intra-executive" in character; it also rejected the

14. The seven defendants were John N. Mitchell, H.R. Haldeman, John D. Ehrlichman, Charles W. Colson, Robert C. Mardian, Kenneth W. Parkinson, and Gordon Strachan. Each had occupied either a position of responsibility on the White House staff or the Committee for the Re-election of the President. Colson entered a guilty plea on another charge and is no longer a defendant.

contention that the judiciary was without authority to review an assertion of executive privilege by the President. The court's rejection of the first challenge was based on the authority and powers vested in the Special Prosecutor by the regulation promulgated by the Attorney General; the court concluded that a justiciable controversy was presented. The second challenge was held to be foreclosed by the decision in Nixon v. Sirica, 159 U.S.App.D.C. 58, 487 F.2d 700 (1973).

The District Court held that the judiciary, not the President, was the final arbiter of a claim of executive privilege. The court concluded that under the circumstances of this case the presumptive privilege was overcome by the Special Prosecutor's prima facie "demonstration of need sufficiently compelling to warrant judicial examination in chambers * * * ." 377 F.Supp., at 1330. The court held, finally, that the Special Prosecutor had satisfied the requirements of Rule 17(c). The District Court stayed its order pending appellate review on condition that review was sought before 4 p.m., May 24. The court further provided that matters filed under seal remain under seal when transmitted as part of the record.

On May 24, 1974, the President filed a timely notice of appeal from the District Court order, and the certified record from the District Court was docketed in the United States Court of Appeals for the District of Columbia Circuit. On the same day, the President also filed a petition for writ of mandamus in the Court of Appeals seeking review of the District Court order.

Later on May 24, the Special Prosecutor also filed, in this Court, a petition for a writ of certiorari before judgment. On May 31, the petition was granted with an expedited briefing schedule, 417 U.S. 927 (1974). On June 6, the President filed, under seal, a cross-petition for writ of certiorari before judgment. This cross-petition was granted June 15, 1974, 417 U.S. 960 (1974), and the case was set for argument on July 8, 1974.

* * *

[The Court overruled jurisdictional objections that were based on lack of a final and appealable judgment in the absence of an adjudication of contempt and on lack of a case or controversy since the dispute was within the Executive Branch. The Court also overruled the claim that Criminal Rule 17(c) had not been satisfied.]

IV

The Claim of Privilege

A

* * *

Notwithstanding the deference each branch must accord the others, the "judicial power of the United States" vested in the federal courts by Art. III, § 1 of the Constitution can no more be shared with the

Executive Branch than the Chief Executive, for example, can share with the Judiciary the veto power, or the Congress share with the Judiciary the power to override a presidential veto. Any other conclusion would be contrary to the basic concept of separation of powers and the checks and balances that flow from the scheme of a tripartite government. The Federalist, No. 47, p. 313 (C.F. Mittel ed. 1938). We therefore reaffirm that it is the province and duty of this Court "to say what the law is" with respect to the claim of privilege presented in this case. Marbury v. Madison, supra, 1 Cranch, at 177.

B

In support of his claim of absolute privilege, the President's counsel urges two grounds one of which is common to all governments and one of which is peculiar to our system of separation of powers. The first ground is the valid need for protection of communications between high government officials and those who advise and assist them in the performance of their manifold duties; the importance of this confidentiality is too plain to require further discussion. Human experience teaches that those who expect public dissemination of their remarks may well temper candor with a concern for appearances and for their own interests to the detriment of the decision-making process.[15] Whatever the nature of the privilege of confidentiality of presidential communications in the exercise of Art. II powers the privilege can be said to derive from the supremacy of each branch within its own assigned area of constitutional duties. Certain powers and privileges flow from the nature of enumerated powers; the protection of the confidentiality of presidential communications has similar constitutional underpinnings.

The second ground asserted by the President's counsel in support of the claim of absolute privilege rests on the doctrine of separation of powers. Here it is argued that the independence of the Executive Branch within its own sphere, Humphrey's Executor v. United States, 295 U.S. 602, 629–630; Kilbourn v. Thompson, 103 U.S. 168, 190–191 (1880), insulates a president from a judicial subpoena in an ongoing criminal prosecution, and thereby protects confidential presidential communications.

However, neither the doctrine of separation of powers, nor the need for confidentiality of high level communications, without more, can sustain an absolute, unqualified presidential privilege of immunity from judicial process under all circumstances. The President's need for complete candor and objectivity from advisers calls for great deference from the courts. However, when the privilege depends solely on the broad, undifferentiated claim of public interest in the confidentiality of such

15. There is nothing novel about governmental confidentiality. The meetings of the Constitutional Convention in 1787 were conducted in complete privacy. 1 Farrand, The Records of the Federal Convention of 1787, xi-xxv (1911). Moreover, all records of those meetings were sealed for more than 30 years after the Convention. See 3 U.S.Stat. At Large, p. 475, 15th Cong. 1st Sess., Res. 8 (1818). Most of the Framers acknowledged that without secrecy no constitution of the kind that was developed could have been written. Warren, The Making of the Constitution, 134–139 (1937).

conversations, a confrontation with other values arises. Absent a claim of need to protect military, diplomatic or sensitive national security secrets, we find it difficult to accept the argument that even the very important interest in confidentiality of presidential communications is significantly diminished by production of such material for *in camera* inspection with all the protection that a district court will be obliged to provide.

The impediment that an absolute, unqualified privilege would place in the way of the primary constitutional duty of the Judicial Branch to do justice in criminal prosecutions would plainly conflict with the function of the courts under Art. III. * * * To read the Art. II powers of the President as providing an absolute privilege as against a subpoena essential to enforcement of criminal statutes on no more than a generalized claim of the public interest in confidentiality of nonmilitary and nondiplomatic discussions would upset the constitutional balance of "a workable government" and gravely impair the role of the courts under Art. III.

C

Since we conclude that the legitimate needs of the judicial process may outweigh presidential privilege, it is necessary to resolve those competing interests in a manner that preserves the essential functions of each branch. The right and indeed the duty to resolve that question does not free the judiciary from according high respect to the representations made on behalf of the President. United States v. Burr, 25 Fed.Cas. pp. 187, 190, 191–192 (No. 14,694) (CCVa.1807).

The expectation of a President to the confidentiality of his conversations and correspondence, like the claim of confidentiality of judicial deliberations, for example, has all the values to which we accord deference for the privacy of all citizens and added to those values the necessity for protection of the public interest in candid, objective, and even blunt or harsh opinions in presidential decisionmaking. A President and those who assist him must be free to explore alternatives in the process of shaping policies and making decisions and to do so in a way many would be unwilling to express except privately. These are the considerations justifying a presumptive privilege for presidential communications. The privilege is fundamental to the operation of government and inextricably rooted in the separation of powers under the Constitution.[16] In Nixon v. Sirica, 159 U.S.App.D.C. 58, 487 F.2d 700 (1973), the Court of Appeals held that such presidential communications are "presumptively privileged," id., at 717, and this position is accepted by both parties in the present litigation. We agree with Mr. Chief Justice Marshall's observation, therefore, that "in no case of this kind would a

16. "Freedom of communication vital to fulfillment of the aims of wholesome relationships is obtained only by removing the specter of compelled disclosure * * * [G]overnment * * * needs open but protected channels for the kind of plain talk that is essential to the quality of its functioning." Carl Zeiss Stiftung v. V.E.B. Carl Zeiss, Jena, 40 F.R.D. 318, 325 (D.C.1966). * * *

court be required to proceed against the President as against an ordinary individual." United States v. Burr, 25 Fed.Cas., at 192.

But this presumptive privilege must be considered in light of our historic commitment to the rule of law. This is nowhere more profoundly manifest than in our view that "the twofold aim [of criminal justice] is that guilt shall not escape or innocence suffer." Berger v. United States, 295 U.S. 78, 88 (1935). We have elected to employ an adversary system of criminal justice in which the parties contest all issues before a court of law. The need to develop all relevant facts in the adversary system is both fundamental and comprehensive. The ends of criminal justice would be defeated if judgments were to be founded on a partial or speculative presentation of the facts. The very integrity of the judicial system and public confidence in the system depend on full disclosure of all the facts, within the framework of the rules of evidence. To ensure that justice is done, it is imperative to the function of courts that compulsory process be available for the production of evidence needed either by the prosecution or by the defense.

Only recently the Court restated the ancient proposition of law, albeit in the context of a grand jury inquiry rather than a trial,

> " 'that the public * * * has a right to every man's evidence' except for those persons protected by a constitutional, common law, or statutory privilege, United States v. Bryan, 339 U.S. [323], at 331 (1950) * * * ." Branzburg v. [Hayes] United States, 408 U.S. 665, 688 (1972).

The privileges referred to by the Court are designed to protect weighty and legitimate competing interests. Thus, the Fifth Amendment to the Constitution provides that no man "shall be compelled in any criminal case to be a witness against himself." And, generally, an attorney or a priest may not be required to disclose what has been revealed in professional confidence. These and other interests are recognized in law by privileges against forced disclosure, established in the Constitution, by statute, or at common law. Whatever their origins, these exceptions to the demand for every man's evidence are not lightly created nor expansively construed, for they are in derogation of the search for truth.[17]

In this case the President challenges a subpoena served on him as a third party requiring the production of materials for use in a criminal prosecution on the claim that he has a privilege against disclosure of confidential communications. He does not place his claim of privilege on the ground they are military or diplomatic secrets. As to these areas of Art. II duties the courts have traditionally shown the utmost deference to presidential responsibilities. In C. & S. Air Lines v. Waterman

17. Because of the key role of the testimony of witnesses in the judicial process, courts have historically been cautious about privileges. Justice Frankfurter, dissenting in Elkins v. United States, 364 U.S. 206, 234 (1960), said of this: "Limitations are properly placed upon the operation of this general principle only to the very limited extent that permitting a refusal to testify or excluding relevant evidence has a public good transcending the normally predominant principle of utilizing all rational means for ascertaining truth."

Steamship Corp., 333 U.S. 103, 111 (1948), dealing with presidential authority involving foreign policy considerations, the Court said:

> "The President, both as Commander-in-Chief and as the Nation's organ for foreign affairs, has available intelligence services whose reports are not and ought not to be published to the world. It would be intolerable that courts, without the relevant information, should review and perhaps nullify actions of the Executive taken on information properly held secret." Id., at 111.

In United States v. Reynolds, 345 U.S. 1 (1952), dealing with a claimant's demand for evidence in a damage case against the Government the Court said:

> "It may be possible to satisfy the court, from all the circumstances of the case, that there is a reasonable danger that compulsion of the evidence will expose military matters which, in the interest of national security, should not be divulged. When this is the case, the occasion for the privilege is appropriate, and the court should not jeopardize the security which the privilege is meant to protect by insisting upon an examination of the evidence, even by the judge alone, in chambers."

No case of the Court, however, has extended this high degree of deference to a President's generalized interest in confidentiality. Nowhere in the Constitution, as we have noted earlier, is there any explicit reference to a privilege of confidentiality, yet to the extent this interest relates to the effective discharge of a President's powers, it is constitutionally based.

The right to the production of all evidence at a criminal trial similarly has constitutional dimensions. The Sixth Amendment explicitly confers upon every defendant in a criminal trial the right "to be confronted with the witnesses against him" and "to have compulsory process for obtaining witnesses in his favor." Moreover, the Fifth Amendment also guarantees that no person shall be deprived of liberty without due process of law. It is the manifest duty of the courts to vindicate those guarantees and to accomplish that it is essential that all relevant and admissible evidence be produced.

In this case we must weigh the importance of the general privilege of confidentiality of presidential communications in performance of his responsibilities against the inroads of such a privilege on the fair administration of criminal justice.[18] The interest in preserving confidentiality is weighty indeed and entitled to great respect. However we cannot conclude that advisers will be moved to temper the candor of their remarks by the infrequent occasions of disclosure because of the

18. We are not here concerned with the balance between the President's generalized interest in confidentiality and the need for relevant evidence in civil litigation, nor with that between the confidentiality interest and congressional demands for information, nor with the President's interest in preserving state secrets. We address only the conflict between the President's assertion of a generalized privilege of confidentiality against the constitutional need for relevant evidence in criminal trials.

possibility that such conversations will be called for in the context of a criminal prosecution.

On the other hand, the allowance of the privilege to withhold evidence that is demonstrably relevant in a criminal trial would cut deeply into the guarantee of due process of law and gravely impair the basic function of the courts. A President's acknowledged need for confidentiality in the communications of his office is general in nature, whereas the constitutional need for production of relevant evidence in a criminal proceeding is specific and central to the fair adjudication of a particular criminal case in the administration of justice. Without access to specific facts a criminal prosecution may be totally frustrated. The President's broad interest in confidentiality of communications will not be vitiated by disclosure of a limited number of conversations preliminarily shown to have some bearing on the pending criminal cases.

We conclude that when the ground for asserting privilege as to subpoenaed materials sought for use in a criminal trial is based only on the generalized interest in confidentiality, it cannot prevail over the fundamental demands of due process of law in the fair administration of criminal justice. The generalized assertion of privilege must yield to the demonstrated, specific need for evidence in a pending criminal trial.

D

We have earlier determined that the District Court did not err in authorizing the issuance of the subpoena. If a President concludes that compliance with a subpoena would be injurious to the public interest he may properly, as was done here, invoke a claim of privilege on the return of the subpoena. Upon receiving a claim of privilege from the Chief Executive, it became the further duty of the District Court to treat the subpoenaed material as presumptively privileged and to require the Special Prosecutor to demonstrate that the Presidential material was 'essential to the justice of the (pending criminal) case.' United States v. Burr, 25 Fed.Cas., at 192. Here the District Court treated the material as presumptively privileged, proceeded to find that the Special Prosecutor had made a sufficient showing to rebut the presumption, and ordered an in camera examination of the subpoenaed material. On the basis of our examination of the record we are unable to conclude that the District Court erred in ordering the inspection. Accordingly we affirm the order of the District Court that subpoenaed materials be transmitted to that court. We now turn to the important question of the District Court's responsibilities in conducting the *in camera* examination of presidential materials or communications delivered under the compulsion of the subpoena *duces tecum.*

E

Enforcement of the subpoena *duces tecum* was stayed pending this Court's resolution of the issues raised by the petitions for certiorari. Those issues now having been disposed of, the matter of implementation will rest with the District Court. "[T]he guard, furnished to [the President] to protect him from being harassed by vexatious and unnecessary subpoenas, is to be looked for in the conduct of the [district] court after the subpoenas have issued; not in any circumstance which is to precede their being issued." United States v. Burr, [25 F.Cas. pp. 30, 34 (No. 14,692d) (CC Va.1807)]. Statements that meet the test of admissibility and relevance must be isolated; all other material must be excised. At this stage the District Court is not limited to representations of the Special Prosecutor as to the evidence sought by the subpoena; the material will be available to the District Court. It is elementary that *in camera* inspection of evidence is always a procedure calling for scrupulous protection against any release or publication of material not found by the court, at that stage, probably admissible in evidence and relevant to the issues of the trial for which it is sought. That being true of an ordinary situation, it is obvious that the District Court has a very heavy responsibility to see to it that presidential conversations, which are either not relevant or not admissible, are accorded that high degree of respect due the President of the United States. Mr. Chief Justice Marshall sitting as a trial judge in the *Burr* case, supra, was extraordinarily careful to point out that:

> "[I]n no case of this kind would a court be required to proceed against the President as against an ordinary individual." United States v. Burr, 25 Fed.Cas. pp. 187, 192 (No. 14,694).

Marshall's statement cannot be read to mean in any sense that a President is above the law, but relates to the singularly unique role under Art. II of a President's communications and activities, related to the performance of duties under that Article. Moreover, a President's communications and activities encompass a vastly wider range of sensitive material than would be true of any "ordinary individual." It is therefore necessary in the public interest to afford presidential confidentiality the greatest protection consistent with the fair administration of justice. The need for confidentiality even as to idle conversations with associates in which casual reference might be made concerning political leaders within the country or foreign statesmen is too obvious to call for further treatment. We have no doubt that the District Judge will at all times accord to presidential records that high degree of deference suggested in United States v. Burr, supra and will discharge his responsibility to see to it that until released to the Special Prosecutor no *in camera* material is revealed to anyone. This burden applies with even greater force to excised material; once the decision is made to excise, the material is restored to its privileged status and should be returned under seal to its lawful custodian.

Since this matter came before the Court during the pendency of a criminal prosecution, and on representations that time is of the essence, the mandate shall issue forthwith.

Affirmed.

MR. JUSTICE REHNQUIST took no part in the consideration or decision of these cases.

Notes and Questions

1. *Sources on United States v. Nixon.* Berger, Executive Privilege: A Constitutional Myth (1974); Cox, Executive Privilege, 122 U.Pa.L.Rev. 1383 (1974); Freund, Foreword: On Presidential Privilege, in The Supreme Court, 1973 Term, 88 Harv.L.Rev. 13 (1974); Symposium, United States v. Nixon: Presidential Power and Executive Privilege Twenty–Five Years Later, 85 Minn.L.Rev. 1061 (1999); Symposium: United States v. Nixon, 22 UCLA L.Rev. 1 (1974).

2. *Executive privilege in recent presidencies.* During President Clinton's second term, a variety of privilege claims made their way from the White House into the legal system. See Clinton v. Jones, 520 U.S. 681 (1997); *In re* Lindsey, 148 F.3d 1100 (D.C.Cir.1998); *In re* Sealed Case, 121 F.3d 729 (D.C.Cir.1997); *In re* Grand Jury Subpoena Duces Tecum, 112 F.3d 910 (8th Cir.1997). See Kelley, The Constitutional Dilemma of Litigation Under the Independent Counsel System, 83 Minn.L.Rev. 1197, 1201–15 (1999) (briefly summarizing the Clinton privilege claims and their resolution). For direction, the courts often looked to *Nixon* and two United States v. Burr decisions (25 F.Cas. 30 (C.C.D.Va.1807) & 25 F.Cas. 187 (C.C.D.Va.1807)), cited in *Nixon*. See Yoo, The First Claim: The Burr Trial, *United States v. Nixon*, and Presidential Power, 83 Minn.L.Rev. 1435 (1999) (discussing *Burr* cases, their historical context, and their use in *Nixon* and the Clinton cases). During the Bush presidency, see Cheney v. United States Dist. Court, 542 U.S. 367 (2004) (ruling that separation of powers argument could be raised without first invoking executive privilege).

3. *Analysis of claim of executive privilege. In re* Sealed Case, 121 F.3d 729 (D.C.Cir.1997), is the most comprehensive judicial treatment of executive privilege since *Nixon* and also extensively examines the deliberative process privilege, treated in the next principal case. *In re Sealed Case* deals with White House documents related to allegations that former Secretary of Agriculture Mike Espy improperly accepted a gift. The Office of the Independent Counsel (OIC) sought all relevant White House documents. The White House provided several documents but withheld others under claim of privilege.

> * * * [A]t the OIC's request, the White House produced a privilege log identifying the date, author, and recipient of each document withheld as well as a general statement of the nature of each document and the basis for the privilege on which the document was withheld. This privilege log indicated that 84 documents were withheld on grounds of the deliberative process privilege, with one document additionally withheld on grounds of attorney-client privilege. In a later draft of the privilege log, the White House lists the privilege basis of all 84 documents as being "executive/deliberative privilege."
>
> The OIC negotiated with the White House for access to the withheld documents for several months, finally filing a motion to compel production on June 7, 1995. The White House resisted the motion, arguing that the withheld documents came within both the privilege for presidential communications, recognized in *United States v. Nixon*, 418 U.S. 683

(1974) (*Nixon*), and the deliberative process privilege that protects the deliberations and decisionmaking process of executive officials generally. After a hearing on the motion to compel, the district court ordered the White House to produce the withheld documents for *in camera* review and the White House complied. Each document produced was accompanied by an *ex parte* cover sheet that explained the purpose of the document. The OIC also made an *ex parte* submission justifying the grand jury's need for the documents. On September 30, 1996, the court denied the motion to compel. The memorandum opinion accompanying the denial quoted from *Nixon* to the effect that the "generalized assertion of privilege [for presidential communications] must yield to the demonstrated, specific need for evidence in a pending criminal trial," 418 U.S. at 713, but then concluded that the White House had properly asserted the claimed privileges in this case. In reaching this conclusion, the court stated that it had carefully reviewed the documents, but did not discuss the documents in any further detail and provided no analysis of the grand jury's asserted need for the documents.

121 F.3d at 735–36.

On appeal, the D.C. Circuit analyzed the issues as follows:

While the presidential communications privilege and the deliberative process privilege are closely affiliated, the two privileges are distinct and have different scopes. Both are executive privileges designed to protect executive branch decisionmaking, but one applies to decisionmaking of executive officials generally, the other specifically to decisionmaking of the President. The presidential privilege is rooted in constitutional separation of powers principles and the President's unique constitutional role; the deliberative process privilege is primarily a common law privilege. *See* [*Nixon v. Fitzgerald*, 457 U.S. 731, 753 & n.35 (1982)]. Consequently, congressional or judicial negation of the presidential communications privilege is subject to greater scrutiny than denial of the deliberative privilege. * * *

In addition, unlike the deliberative process privilege, the presidential communications privilege applies to documents in their entirety, and covers final and post-decisional materials as well as pre-deliberative ones. Even though the presidential privilege is based on the need to preserve the President's access to candid advice, none of the cases suggest that it encompasses only the deliberative or advice portions of documents. Indeed, *Nixon* argued that the presidential privilege must be qualified to ensure full access to facts in judicial proceedings, thereby assuming that factual material comes under the privilege. 418 U.S. at 709; *but see* LARKIN, [FEDERAL TESTIMONIAL PRIVILEGES] § 6.01 at 6–1 [(1996)] (asserting, without explanation, that the presidential privilege does not "protect purely factual material"). There is no indication either that the presidential privilege is restricted to pre-decisional materials. GSA cautioned that the privilege only applies to communications made in the process of arriving at presidential decisions, but by this we believe the Court meant that the privilege was limited to materials connected to presidential decisionmaking, as opposed to other executive branch decisionmaking, and not that only pre-decisional materials were covered.

433 U.S. at 449. Nor would exclusion of final or post-decisional materials make sense, given the *Nixon* cases' concern that the President be given sufficient room to operate effectively. These materials often will be revelatory of the President's deliberations—as, for example, when the President decides to pursue a particular course of action, but asks his advisers to submit follow-up reports so that he can monitor whether this course of action is likely to be successful. The release of final and post-decisional materials would also limit the President's ability to communicate his decisions privately, thereby interfering with his ability to exercise control over the executive branch.

Finally, while both the deliberative process privilege and the presidential privilege are qualified privileges, the *Nixon* cases suggest that the presidential communications privilege is more difficult to surmount. In regard to both, courts must balance the public interests at stake in determining whether the privilege should yield in a particular case, and must specifically consider the need of the party seeking privileged evidence. But this balancing is more ad hoc in the context of the deliberative process privilege, and includes consideration of additional factors such as whether the government is a party to the litigation. Moreover, the privilege disappears altogether when there is any reason to believe government misconduct occurred. On the other hand, a party seeking to overcome the presidential privilege seemingly must always provide a focused demonstration of need, even when there are allegations of misconduct by high-level officials. In holding that the Watergate Special Prosecutor had provided a sufficient showing of evidentiary need to obtain tapes of President Nixon's conversations, the Supreme Court made no mention of the fact that the tapes were sought for use in a trial of former presidential assistants charged with engaging in a criminal conspiracy while in office. *Accord Senate Committee*, 498 F.2d at 731 (noting that presidential privilege is not intended to shield governmental misconduct but arguing that showing of need turns on extent to which subpoenaed evidence is necessary for government institution to fulfill its responsibilities, not on type of conduct evidence may reveal); *contra* 26A WRIGHT & GRAHAM, [FEDERAL PRACTICE AND PROCEDURE] § 5673, at 53–54 (quoting *Senate Committee's* not-a-shield language and arguing that allegations of misconduct qualify the privilege, but not addressing *Senate Committee's* comment that need showing turns on function for which evidence is sought and not on conduct revealed by evidence).

These differences between the presidential communications privilege and the deliberative privilege demonstrate that the presidential privilege affords greater protection against disclosure. Consequently, should we conclude as to any document that the presidential privilege applies but that the OIC has demonstrated a sufficient showing of need, there is no reason to examine whether the documents also come under the deliberative process privilege. *A fortiori*, if release is required under the presidential privilege, it will certainly be required under the deliberative process privilege. Hence, we would need to address application of the deliberative process privilege as to any document only if we determine that the withheld document is not subject to the presidential privilege.

121 F.3d at 745–46. After a review of the precedents, the court stated:

> Based on our review of the Nixon cases and the purpose of the presidential communications privilege, we conclude that this privilege extends to cover communications which do not themselves directly engage the President, provided the communications are either authored or received in response to a solicitation by presidential advisers in the course of gathering information and preparing recommendations on official matters for presentation to the President. The privilege also extends to communications authored or solicited and received by those members of an immediate White House advisor's staff who have broad and significant responsibility for investigating and formulating the advice to be given to the President on a particular matter. We also hold that in order to overcome a claim of presidential privilege raised against a grand jury subpoena, it is necessary to specifically demonstrate why it is likely that evidence contained in presidential communications is important to the ongoing grand jury investigation and why this evidence is not available from another source.

Id. at 757.

Applying these principles to the case at hand, the court found "that all of the documents withheld by the White House here are subject to the presidential communications privilege," and as a result, it did not need to determine whether the documents would qualify for the "deliberative process privilege." Id. at 758. The court then balanced the presidential communications privilege against the OIC's "demonstration of need," id. at 759, and concluded that

> the OIC has demonstrated sufficient need in order to overcome the presidential communications privilege in regard to evidence of statements made by Espy or his counsel and contained in the withheld documents, and that the OIC should be given an opportunity to make out a sufficient showing of need in regard to other evidence more generally. On remand, the district court should identify and release specific items of evidence that might reasonably be relevant to the grand jury's investigation into the potential false statements charge. If the court deems any additional showing of need presented by the OIC to be sufficient, it should also identify any new items of information that merit release. We are submitting a sealed appendix to assist the district court with its review. * * *
>
> This case forces us to engage in the difficult business of delineating the scope and operation of the presidential communications privilege. In holding that the privilege extends to communications authored by or solicited and received by presidential advisers and that a specified demonstration of need must be made even in regard to a grand jury subpoena, we are ever mindful of the dangers involved in cloaking governmental operations in secrecy and in placing obstacles in the path of the grand jury in its investigatory mission. There is a powerful counterweight to these concerns, however, namely the public and constitutional interest in preserving the efficacy and quality of presidential decisionmaking. We believe that the principles we have outlined in this

> opinion achieve a delicate and appropriate balance between openness and informed presidential deliberation.

Id. at 762. Accordingly, it reversed the District Court's decision.

4. *Sources on executive privilege.* Chemerinsky, Constitutional Law: Principles and Policies § 4.3 (2d ed. 2002); 2 Imwinkelried, The New Wigmore: Evidentiary Privileges § 7.6 (2002); Rozell, Executive Privilege: The Dilemma of Secrecy and Democratic Accountability (1994); Miller, Congressional Inquests: Suffocating the Constitutional Prerogative of Executive Privilege, 81 Minn.L.Rev. 631 (1997); Ray, From Prerogative to Accountability: The Amenability of the President to Suit, 80 Ky.L.J. 739 (1991–92); Shane, Legal Disagreement and Negotiation in a Government of Laws: The Case of Executive Privilege Claims Against Congress, 71 Minn.L.Rev. 461 (1987); Symposium, *United States v. Nixon*: Presidential Power and Executive Privilege Twenty–Five Years Later, 83 Minn.L.Rev.1061 (1999); Symposium: Executive Privilege and the Clinton Presidency, 8 Wm. & Mary Bill of Rts.J. 535 (2000). For further discussion of Clinton and "executive privilege," see Miller, Presidential Sanctuaries after the Clinton Sex Scandals, 22 Harv.J.L. & Pub. Pol'y 647 (1999); Turley, Paradise Lost: The Clinton Administration and the Erosion of Executive Privilege, 60 Md.L.Rev. 205 (2001).

5. *English developments.* Lederman, The Crown's Right to Suppress Information Sought in the Litigation Process: The Elusive Public Interest, 8 U.B.C.L.Rev. 272 (1973); Cappalletti & Golden, Crown Privilege and Executive Privilege: A British Response to an American Controversy, 25 Stan. L.Rev. 836 (1973).

DEPARTMENT OF THE INTERIOR AND BUREAU OF INDIAN AFFAIRS v. KLAMATH WATER USERS PROTECTIVE ASS'N

Supreme Court of the United States, 2001.
532 U.S. 1.

JUSTICE SOUTER delivered the opinion of the Court.

Documents in issue here, passing between Indian Tribes and the Department of the Interior, addressed tribal interests subject to state and federal proceedings to determine water allocations. The question is whether the documents are exempt from the disclosure requirements of the Freedom of Information Act, as "intra-agency memorandums or letters" that would normally be privileged in civil discovery. 5 U.S.C. § 552(b)(5). We hold they are not.

I

Two separate proceedings give rise to this case, the first a planning effort within the Department of the Interior's Bureau of Reclamation, and the second a state water rights adjudication in the Oregon courts. Within the Department of the Interior, the Bureau of Reclamation (Reclamation) administers the Klamath Irrigation Project (Klamath Project or Project), which uses water from the Klamath River Basin to irrigate territory in Klamath County, Oregon, and two northern California counties. In 1995, the Department began work to develop a long-term operations plan for the Project, to be known as the Klamath Project Operation Plan (Plan), which would provide for allocation of water among competing uses and competing water users. The Department asked the Klamath as well as the Hoopa Valley, Karuk, and Yurok Tribes (Basin Tribes) to consult with Reclamation on the matter, and a memorandum of understanding between the Department and the Tribes recognized that "[t]he United States Government has a unique legal relationship with Native American tribal governments," and called for "[a]ssessment, in consultation with the Tribes, of the impacts of the [Plan] on Tribal trust resources." App. 59, 61.

During roughly the same period, the Department's Bureau of Indian Affairs (Bureau) filed claims on behalf of the Klamath Tribe alone in an Oregon state-court adjudication intended to allocate water rights. Since the Bureau is responsible for administering land and water held in trust for Indian tribes, 25 U.S.C. § 1a; 25 CFR subch. H., pts. 150–181 (2000), it consulted with the Klamath Tribe, and the two exchanged written memorandums on the appropriate scope of the claims ultimately submitted by the United States for the benefit of the Klamath Tribe. The Bureau does not, however, act as counsel for the Tribe, which has its own lawyers and has independently submitted claims on its own behalf.

Respondent, the Klamath Water Users Protective Association is a nonprofit association of water users in the Klamath River Basin, most of whom receive water from the Klamath Project, and whose interests are adverse to the tribal interests owing to scarcity of water. The Association filed a series of requests with the Bureau under the Freedom of Information Act (FOIA), 5 U.S.C. § 552, seeking access to communications between the Bureau and the Basin Tribes during the relevant time period. The Bureau turned over several documents but withheld others as exempt under the attorney work-product and deliberative process privileges. These privileges are said to be incorporated in FOIA Exemption 5, which exempts from disclosure "inter-agency or intra-agency memorandums or letters which would not be available by law to a party other than an agency in litigation with the agency." § 552(b)(5). The Association then sued the Bureau under FOIA to compel release of the documents.

By the time of the District Court ruling, seven documents remained in dispute, three of them addressing the Plan, three concerned with the Oregon adjudication, and the seventh relevant to both proceedings. * * * . Six of the documents were prepared by the Klamath Tribe or its representative and were submitted at the Government's behest to the Bureau or to the Department's Regional Solicitor; a Bureau official prepared the seventh document and gave it to lawyers for the Klamath and Yurok Tribes. * * * .

The District Court granted the Government's motion for summary judgment. It held that each document qualified as an inter-agency or intra-agency communication for purposes of Exemption 5, and that each was covered by the deliberative process privilege or the attorney work product privilege, as having played a role in the Bureau's deliberations about the Plan or the Oregon adjudication. * * * The Court of Appeals for the Ninth Circuit reversed. 189 F.3d 1034 (C.A.9 1999). It recognized that some Circuits had adopted a "functional" approach to Exemption 5, under which a document generated outside the Government might still qualify as an "intra-agency" communication. See *id.,* at 1037–1038. The court saw no reason to go into that, however, for it ruled out any application of Exemption 5 on the ground that "the Tribes with whom the Department has a consulting relationship have a direct interest in the subject matter of the consultations." *Id.,* at 1038. The court said that "[t]o hold otherwise would extend Exemption 5 to shield what amount to ex parte communications in contested proceedings between the Tribes and the Department." *Ibid.* * * * We granted certiorari in view of the decision's significant impact on the relationship between Indian tribes and the Government * * * , and now affirm.

II

Upon request, FOIA mandates disclosure of records held by a federal agency, see 5 U.S.C. § 552, unless the documents fall within enumerated exemptions, see § 552(b). "[T]hese limited exemptions do not obscure the basic policy that disclosure, not secrecy, is the dominant objective of the Act," *Department of Air Force v. Rose,* 425 U.S. 352, 361 (1976); "[c]onsistent with the Act's goal of broad disclosure, these exemptions have been consistently given a narrow compass," *U.S. Department of Justice v. Tax Analysts,* 492 U.S. 136, 151 (1989) * * * .

A

Exemption 5 protects from disclosure "inter-agency or intra-agency memorandums or letters which would not be available by law to a party other than an agency in litigation with the agency." 5 U.S.C. § 552(b)(5). To qualify, a document must thus satisfy two conditions: its source must be a Government agency, and it must fall within the ambit of a privilege against discovery under judicial standards that would govern litigation against the agency that holds it.

Our prior cases on Exemption 5 have addressed the second condition, incorporating civil discovery privileges. See, *e.g., United States v. Weber Aircraft Corp.,* 465 U.S. 792, 799–800 (1984); *NLRB v. Sears, Roebuck & Co.,* 421 U.S. 132, 148 (1975) ("Exemption 5 withholds from a member of the public documents which a private party could not discover in litigation with the agency."). So far as they might matter here, those privileges include the privilege for attorney work-product and what is sometimes called the "deliberative process" privilege. Work product protects "mental processes of the attorney," *United States v. Nobles,* 422 U.S. 225, 238 (1975), while deliberative process covers "documents reflecting advisory opinions, recommendations and deliberations comprising part of a process by which governmental decisions and policies are formulated," *Sears, Roebuck & Co.,* 421 U.S., at 150 (internal quotation marks omitted). The deliberative process privilege rests on the obvious realization that officials will not communicate candidly among themselves if each remark is a potential item of discovery and front page news, and its object is to enhance "the quality of agency decisions," *id.,* at 151, by protecting open and frank discussion among those who make them within the Government, see *EPA v. Mink,* 410 U.S. 73, 86–87 (1973); see also *Weber Aircraft Corp., supra,* at 802.

The point is not to protect Government secrecy pure and simple, however, and the first condition of Exemption 5 is no less important than the second; the communication must be "inter-agency or intra-agency." 5 U.S.C. § 552(b)(5). Statutory definitions underscore the apparent plainness of this text. With exceptions not relevant here, "agency" means "each authority of the Government of the United States," § 551(1), and "includes any executive department, military department, Government corporation, Government controlled corporation, or other establishment in the executive branch of the Government * * *, or any independent regulatory agency," § 552(f).

Although neither the terms of the exemption nor the statutory definitions say anything about communications with outsiders, some Courts of Appeals have held that in some circumstances a document prepared outside the Government may nevertheless qualify as an "intra-agency" memorandum under Exemption 5. See, *e.g., Hoover v. U.S. Dept. of Interior,* 611 F.2d 1132, 1137–1138 (C.A.5 1980); *Lead Industries Assn. v. OSHA,* 610 F.2d 70, 83 (C.A.2 1979); *Soucie v. David,* 448 F.2d 1067 (C.A.D.C.1971). In *United States Department of Justice v. Julian,* 486 U.S. 1 (1988), JUSTICE SCALIA, joined by JUSTICES O'CONNOR and WHITE, explained that "the most natural meaning of the phrase 'intra-agency memorandum' is a memorandum that is addressed both to and from employees of a single agency," *id.,* at 18, n.1 (dissenting opinion). But his opinion also acknowledged the more expansive reading by some Courts of Appeals:

> "It is textually possible and * * * in accord with the purpose of the provision, to regard as an intra-agency memorandum one that has been received by an agency, to assist it in the performance of its own functions, from a person acting in a governmentally conferred capacity other than on behalf of another agency—*e.g.,* in a capacity as employee or consultant to the agency, or as employee or officer of another governmental unit (not an agency) that is authorized or required to provide advice to the agency." *Ibid.*

Typically, courts taking the latter view have held that the exemption extends to communications between Government agencies and outside consultants hired by them. See, *e.g., Hoover, supra,* at 1138 ("In determining value, the government may deem it necessary to seek the objective opinion of outside experts rather than rely solely on the opinions of government appraisers"); *Lead Industries Assn., supra,* at 83 (applying Exemption 5 to cover draft reports "prepared by outside consultants who had testified on behalf of the agency rather than agency staff") * * * . In such cases, the records submitted by outside consultants played essentially the same part in an agency's process of deliberation as documents prepared by agency personnel might have done. To be sure, the consultants in these cases were independent contractors and were not assumed to be subject to the degree of control that agency employment could have entailed; nor do we read the cases as necessarily assuming that an outside consultant must be devoid of a definite point of view when the agency contracts for its services. But the fact about the consultant that is constant in the typical cases is that the consultant does not represent an interest of its own, or the interest of any other client, when it advises the agency that hires it. Its only obligations are to truth and its sense of what good judgment calls for, and in those respects the consultant functions just as an employee would be expected to do.

B

The Department purports to rely on this consultant corollary to Exemption 5 in arguing for its application to the Tribe's communications to the Bureau in its capacity of fiduciary for the benefit of the Indian Tribes. The existence of a trust obligation is not, of course, in question, see *United States v. Cherokee Nation of Oklahoma,* 480 U.S. 700, 707 (1987); *United States v. Mitchell,* 463 U.S. 206, 225 (1983); *Seminole Nation v. United States,* 316 U.S. 286, 296–297 (1942). The fiduciary relationship has been described as "one of the primary cornerstones of Indian law," F. Cohen, Handbook of Federal Indian Law 221 (1982), and has been compared to one existing under a common law trust, with the United States as trustee, the Indian tribes or individuals as beneficiaries, and the property and natural resources managed by the United States as the trust corpus. See, *e.g., Mitchell, supra,* at 225. Nor is there any doubt about the plausibility of the Government's assertion that the candor of tribal communications with the Bureau would be eroded without the protections of the deliberative process privilege recognized under Exemption 5. The Department is surely right in saying that confidentiality in communications with tribes is conducive to a proper discharge of its trust obligation.

From the recognition of this interest in frank communication, which the deliberative process privilege might protect, the Department would have us infer a sufficient justification for applying Exemption 5 to communications with the Tribes, in the same fashion that Courts of Appeals have found sufficient reason to favor a consultant's advice that way. But the Department's argument skips a necessary step, for it ignores the first condition of Exemption 5, that the communication be "intra-agency or inter-agency." The Department seems to be saying that "intra-agency" is a purely conclusory term, just a label to be placed on any document the Government would find it valuable to keep confidential.

There is, however, no textual justification for draining the first condition of independent vitality, and once the intra-agency condition is applied,[19] it rules out any application of Exemption 5 to tribal communications on analogy to consultants' reports (assuming, which we do not decide, that these reports may qualify as intra-agency under Exemption 5). As mentioned already, consultants whose communications have typically been held exempt have not been communicating with the Government in their own interest or on behalf of any person or group whose interests might be affected by the Government action addressed by the consultant. In that regard, consultants may be enough like the agency's own personnel to justify calling their communications "intra-agency." The Tribes, on the contrary, necessarily communicate with the Bureau with their own, albeit entirely legitimate, interests in mind. While this fact alone distinguishes tribal communications from the consultants' examples recognized by several Courts of Appeals, the distinction is even sharper, in that the Tribes are self-advocates at the expense of others seeking benefits inadequate to satisfy everyone.[20]

As to those documents bearing on the Plan, the Tribes are obviously in competition with nontribal claimants, including those irrigators represented by the respondent. App. 66–71. The record shows that documents submitted by the Tribes included, among others, "a position paper that discusses water law legal theories" and "addresses issues related to water rights of the tribes," App. to Pet. for Cert. 42a–43a, a memorandum "contain[ing] views on policy the BIA could provide to other governmental agencies," "views concerning trust resources," *id.*, at 44a, and a letter "conveying the views of the Klamath Tribes concerning issues involved in the water rights adjudication," *id.*, at 47a. While these documents may not take the formally argumentative form of a brief, their function is quite apparently to support the tribal claims. The Tribes are thus urging a position necessarily adverse to the other claimants, the water being inadequate to satisfy the combined demand. As the Court of Appeals said, "[t]he Tribes' demands, if satisfied, would lead to reduced water allocations to members of the Association and have been protested by Association members who fear water shortages and economic injury in dry years." 189 F.3d, at 1035.

The Department insists that the Klamath Tribe's consultant-like character is clearer in the circumstances of the Oregon adjudication, since the Department merely represents the interests of the Tribe before a state court that will make any decision about the respective rights of the contenders. Brief for Petitioners 42–45; Reply Brief for Petitioners

19. Because we conclude that the documents do not meet this threshold condition, we need not reach step two of the Exemption 5 analysis and enquire whether the communications would normally be discoverable in civil litigation. *See United States v. Weber Aircraft Corp.*, 465 U.S. 792, 799 (1984).

20. Courts of Appeals have recognized at least two instances of intra-agency consultants that arguably extend beyond what we have characterized as the typical examples. [*E.g.*] *Public Citizen, Inc. v. Department of Justice,* 111 F.3d 168 (C.A.D.C. 1997)[;] * * * *Ryan v. Department of Justice,* 617 F.2d 781 (C.A.D.C.1980) * * * . We need not decide whether either instance should be recognized as intra-agency * * * [because] the intra-agency condition excludes, at the least, communications to or from an interested party seeking a Government benefit at the expense of other applicants.

4–6. But it is not that simple. Even if there were no rival interests at stake in the Oregon litigation, the Klamath Tribe would be pressing its own view of its own interest in its communications with the Bureau. Nor could that interest be ignored as being merged somehow in the fiduciary interest of the Government trustee; the Bureau in its fiduciary capacity would be obliged to adopt the stance it believed to be in the beneficiary's best interest, not necessarily the position espoused by the beneficiary itself. Cf. Restatement (Second) of Trusts § 176, Comment *a* (1957) ("[I]t is the duty of the trustee to exercise such care and skill to preserve the trust property as a man of ordinary prudence would exercise in dealing with his own property * * * ").

But, again, the dispositive point is that the apparent object of the Tribe's communications is a decision by an agency of the Government to support a claim by the Tribe that is necessarily adverse to the interests of competitors. Since there is not enough water to satisfy everyone, the Government's position on behalf of the Tribe is potentially adverse to other users, and it might ask for more or less on behalf of the Tribe depending on how it evaluated the tribal claim compared with the claims of its rivals. The ultimately adversarial character of tribal submissions to the Bureau therefore seems the only fair inference, as confirmed by the Department's acknowledgement that its "obligation to represent the Klamath Tribe necessarily coexists with the duty to protect other federal interests, including in particular its interests with respect to the Klamath Project." Reply Brief 8; cf. *Nevada v. United States,* 463 U.S. 110, 142 (1983) ("[W]here Congress has imposed upon the United States, in addition to its duty to represent Indian tribes, a duty to obtain water rights for reclamation projects, and has even authorized the inclusion of reservation lands within a project, the analogy of a faithless private fiduciary cannot be controlling for purposes of evaluating the authority of the United States to represent different interests"). The position of the Tribe as beneficiary is thus a far cry from the position of the paid consultant.

Quite apart from its attempt to draw a direct analogy between tribes and conventional consultants, the Department argues that compelled release of the documents would itself impair the Department's performance of a specific fiduciary obligation to protect the confidentiality of communications with tribes. Because, the Department argues, traditional fiduciary standards forbid a trustee to disclose information acquired as a trustee when it should know that disclosure would be against the beneficiary's interests, excluding the Tribes' submissions to the Department from Exemption 5 would handicap the Department in doing what the law requires. Brief for Petitioners 36–37. And in much the same vein, the Department presses the argument that "FOIA is intended to cast light on existing government practices; it should not be interpreted and applied so as to compel federal agencies to perform their assigned substantive functions in other than the normal manner." *Id.,* at 29.

All of this boils down to requesting that we read an "Indian trust" exemption into the statute, a reading that is out of the question for reasons already explored. There is simply no support for the exemption in the statutory text, which we have elsewhere insisted be read strictly in order to serve FOIA's mandate of broad disclosure,[21] which was obviously expected and intended to affect Government operations. In FOIA, after all, a new conception of Government conduct was enacted into law, " 'a general philosophy of full agency disclosure.' " *U.S. Department of Justice v. Tax Analysts,* 492 U.S., at 142 (quoting S.Rep. No. 813, 89th Cong., 1st Sess., at 3 (1965)). "Congress believed that this philosophy, put into practice, would help 'ensure an informed citizenry, vital to the functioning of a democratic society.' " *Ibid.* (quoting *NLRB v. Robbins Tire & Rubber Co.,* 437 U.S. 214, 242 (1978)). Congress had to realize that not every secret under the old law would be secret under the new.

The judgment of the Court of Appeals is affirmed.

It is so ordered.

Notes and Questions

1. *General scope.* The "deliberative process" privilege covers opinion or evaluation that the agency sought to keep confidential prior to finalization of the policy decision. The privilege in general does not cover the mere reporting of objective facts. However, factual information that "reflects or reveals the deliberative process of the agency is protected." 1 McCormick, Evidence § 108, at 484 (6th ed. 2006).

2. *Maintaining the intra-agency or inter-agency requirement.* In *Klamath*, the Supreme Court feared that an opposite ruling would "drain[] the first condition"—that the evidence be intra- or inter-agency—"of independent vitality." Would this fear be realized given the Tribe's unique fiduciary relationship to the government?

3. *Relationship of privilege to FOIA exemption.* The decision in *Klamath* notes that the deliberative process privilege is "said to be incorporated in FOIA Exemption 5." In 1966 Congress enacted the so-called Freedom of Information Act (or Right to Know Act). No standing or special need is required to invoke the provisions of the Act. The Act provides that each agency shall make available to the public information subject to nine exemptions, including Exemption 5, which are listed in the next note.

The principal distinction between Exemption 5 and the deliberative process privilege has been explained as follows:

21. The Department does not attempt to argue that Congress specifically envisioned that Exemption 5 would cover communications pursuant to the Indian trust responsibility, or any other trust responsibility. Although as a general rule we are hesitant to construe statutes in light of legislative inaction, see *Bob Jones Univ. v. United States*, 461 U.S. 574, 600 (1983), we note that Congress has twice considered specific proposals to protect Indian trust information, see Indian Amendment to Freedom of Information Act: Hearings on S. 2652 before the Subcommittee on Indian Affairs of the Senate Committee on Interior and Insular Affairs, 94th Cong., 2d Sess. (1976); Indian Trust Information Protection Act of 1978, S. 2773, 95th Cong., 2d Sess. (1978). We do so because these proposals confirm the commonsense reading that we give Exemption 5 today, as well as to emphasize that nobody in the Federal Government should be surprised by this reading.

> FOIA does not address the question of admissibility of evidence, and therefore Exemption 5 should not be considered a congressional enactment of the deliberative process privilege, even though it may incorporate the rationale of the privilege. FOIA protects materials subject to "routine disclosure" by the government. Any material that is protected by a privilege, whether absolute or qualified, is clearly not subject to routine disclosure under FOIA. In other words, once the government makes a prima facie showing for invoking the privilege, analysis under FOIA Exemption 5 stops and does not proceed to the balancing of interests. This is an important distinction between the deliberative process privilege and FOIA. While a litigant's need for information may be sufficient to override the privilege, such need would not remove that information from the category of material that is normally privileged. Therefore, while FOIA may properly be viewed as defining the maximum limits of the privilege, the privilege itself should be interpreted as being somewhat less protective than Exemption 5.

Jensen, Note, The Reasonable Government Official Test: A Proposal for the Treatment of Factual Information Under the Federal Deliberative Process Privilege, 49 Duke L.J. 561, 580–81 (1999).

4. *FOIA exemptions.* The Freedom of Information Act (FOIA) was originally enacted in 1966 as an amendment to the Administrative Procedure Act. The exemptions, now found in 5 U.S.C. § 552(b)(1), are as follows:

> This section does not apply to matters that are—
>
> (1) (A) specifically authorized under criteria established by an Executive order to be kept secret in the interest of national defense or foreign policy and (B) are in fact properly classified pursuant to such Executive order;
>
> (2) related solely to the internal personnel rules and practices of an agency;
>
> (3) specifically exempted from disclosure by statute (other than section 552b of this title), provided that such statute (A) requires that the matters be withheld from the public in such a manner as to leave no discretion on the issue, or (B) establishes particular criteria for withholding or refers to particular types of matters to be withheld;
>
> (4) trade secrets and commercial or financial information obtained from a person and privileged or confidential;
>
> (5) inter-agency or intra-agency memorandums or letters which would not be available by law to a party other than an agency in litigation with the agency;
>
> (6) personnel and medical files and similar files the disclosure of which would constitute a clearly unwarranted invasion of personal privacy;
>
> (7) records or information compiled for law enforcement purposes, but only to the extent that the production of such law enforcement records or information (A) could reasonably be expected to interfere with enforcement proceedings, (B) would deprive a person of a right to a fair trial or an impartial adjudication, (C) could reasonably be expected

to constitute an unwarranted invasion of personal privacy, (D) could reasonably be expected to disclose the identity of a confidential source, including a State, local, or foreign agency or authority or any private institution which furnished information on a confidential basis, and, in the case of a record or information compiled by criminal law enforcement authority in the course of a criminal investigation or by an agency conducting a lawful national security intelligence investigation, information furnished by a confidential source, (E) would disclose techniques and procedures for law enforcement investigations or prosecutions, or would disclose guidelines for law enforcement investigations or prosecutions if such disclosure could reasonably be expected to risk circumvention of the law, or (F) could reasonably be expected to endanger the life or physical safety of any individual;

(8) contained in or related to examination, operating, or condition reports prepared by, on behalf of, or for the use of an agency responsible for the regulation or supervision of financial institutions; or

(9) geological and geophysical information and data, including maps, concerning wells.

5. *Exemptions as maximum limits of privilege.* While designed to make information available to the public generally, and to the mass media in particular, the Act has clear relevance to matters of governmental privilege. It defines what may be termed the maximum limits of any privilege for governmental information, for if the information is available to the public generally, it would be anomalous to prohibit the use of that information in litigation on the ground of an evidentiary privilege. On the other hand, the fact that the information is not generally available, while giving some insight into a relevant legislative judgment that the information is sensitive and not generally disclosable, does not necessarily mean that access to such evidence for litigation purposes will be denied since the need of the litigant may be substantially greater. 1 McCormick, Evidence § 108, at 482 (6th ed. 2006). Consistent with this view, the Court in United States v. Weber Aircraft Corp., 465 U.S. 792, 802 n.20 (1984), made clear that particularized need in litigation may require discovery in connection with the litigation process but that possibility does not authorize disclosure under the Act.

6. *Machin privilege under Exemption 5.* In *Weber*, note 5, supra, 465 U.S. at 799–800, cited in *Klamath*, respondents "sought discovery of all Air Force investigative reports pertaining to [an airplane] accident." Id. at 796. The Air Force claimed exemption from disclosure under the so-called *Machin* privilege (from Machin v. Zuckert, 316 F.2d 336 (D.C.Cir.1963)), which protects confidential statements to air crash investigators, and from Exemption 5. The Ninth Circuit reversed a lower court ruling in favor of the Air Force, arguing that while "the requested documents were intra-agency memorandums within the meaning of Exemption 5 and that they were protected from civil discovery under the *Machin* privilege," they were not covered under FOIA since "the statutory phrase 'would not be available by law' did not encompass every civil discovery privilege but rather reached only those privileges explicitly recognized in the legislative history of the FOIA." *Weber*, 465 U.S. at 797–98. The Supreme Court in turn reversed the Ninth Circuit on the basis that

> the legislative history of Exemption 5 does not contain the kind of compelling evidence of congressional intent that would be necessary to persuade us to look beyond the plain statutory language. Because of the difficulty inherent in compiling an exhaustive list of evidentiary privileges, it would be impractical to treat the legislative history of Exemption 5 as containing a comprehensive list of all privileges Congress intended to adopt. Rather, the history of Exemption 5 can be understood by means of "rough analogies." EPA v. Mink, 410 U.S. 73, 86. The legislative history of Exemption 5 indicates that Congress intended to incorporate governmental privileges analogous to the *Machin* privilege. That history recognizes a need for claims of privilege when confidentiality is necessary to ensure frank and open discussion and hence efficient governmental operations. * * * The *Machin* privilege was recognized for precisely this reason. Thus, the *Machin* privilege is sufficiently related to the concerns expressed in the legislative history that we cannot say that the legislative history demonstrates that the statute should not be construed to mean what it says with respect to the *Machin* privilege.

465 U.S. at 802–03.

How can this aspect of *Weber* be reconciled with the Court's assertion near the end of the *Klamath* opinion that "[a]ll of this boils down to requesting that we read an 'Indian trust' exemption into the statute"? Why does the Court in *Klamath* rule out such a reading?

7. *Meaning of "memorandum."* For a comprehensive presentation of the often inconsistent treatment of what has and has not counted as "memorandum" under Exemption 5, see Annot., 168 A.L.R.Fed. 143.

8. *Sources.* Weaver & Jones, The Deliberative Process Privilege, 54 Mo.L.Rev. 279 (1989); Wetlaufer, Justifying Secrecy: An Objection to the General Deliberative Privilege, 65 Ind.L.J. 845 (1990); Note, The Reasonable Government Official Test: A Proposal for the Treatment of Factual Information Under the Federal Deliberative Process Privilege, 49 Duke L.J. 561 (1999); 2 Imwinkelried, The New Wigmore: Evidentiary Privileges § 7.7 (2002); 1 McCormick, Evidence § 108 (6th ed. 2006); 3 Weinstein's Federal Evidence §§ 509.23 & 509.24 (2d ed. 2006); 2 Mueller & Kirkpatrick, Federal Evidence §§ 224–25 (2d ed. 1994).

SECTION B. PROCEEDINGS OF PETIT AND GRAND JURIES

TANNER v. UNITED STATES

Supreme Court of the United States, 1987.
483 U.S. 107.

JUSTICE O'CONNOR delivered the opinion of the Court.

Petitioners William Conover and Anthony Tanner were convicted [after jury trial] of conspiring to defraud the United States in violation of 18 U.S.C. § 371, and of committing mail fraud in violation of 18 U.S.C. § 1341. * * *

The day before petitioners were scheduled to be sentenced, Tanner filed a motion, in which Conover subsequently joined, seeking continuance of the sentencing date, permission to interview jurors, an evidentiary hearing, and a new trial. According to an affidavit accompanying the motion, Tanner's attorney had received an unsolicited telephone call from one of the trial jurors, Vera Asbul. App. 246. Juror Asbul informed Tanner's attorney that several of the jurors consumed alcohol during the lunch breaks at various times throughout the trial, causing them to sleep through the afternoons. *Id.,* at 247. The District Court continued the sentencing date, ordered the parties to file memoranda, and heard argument on the motion to interview jurors. The District Court concluded that juror testimony on intoxication was inadmissible under Federal Rule of Evidence 606(b) to impeach the jury's verdict. The District Court invited petitioners to call any nonjuror witnesses, such as courtroom personnel, in support of the motion for new trial. Tanner's counsel took the stand and testified that he had observed one of the jurors "in a sort of giggly mood" at one point during the trial but did not bring this to anyone's attention at the time. *Id.,* at 170.

Earlier in the hearing the judge referred to a conversation between defense counsel and the judge during the trial on the possibility that jurors were sometimes falling asleep. During that extended exchange the judge twice advised counsel to immediately inform the court if they observed jurors being inattentive, and suggested measures the judge would take if he were so informed:

> "MR. MILBRATH [defense counsel]: But, in any event, I've noticed over a period of several days that a couple of jurors in particular have been taking long naps during the trial.
>
> "THE COURT: Is that right. Maybe I didn't notice because I was—
>
> "MR. MILBRATH: I imagine the Prosecutors have noticed that a time or two.
>
> "THE COURT: What's your solution?
>
> "MR. MILBRATH: Well, I just think a respectful comment from the Court that if any of them are getting drowsy, they just ask for a break or something might be helpful.
>
> "THE COURT: Well, here's what I have done in the past—and, you have to do it very diplomatically, of course: I once said, I remember, 'I think we'll just let everybody stand up and stretch, it's getting a little sleepy in here,' I said, but that doesn't sound good in the record.
>
> "I'm going to—not going to take on that responsibility. If any of you think you see that happening, ask for a bench conference and come up and tell me about it and I'll figure out what to do about it, and I won't mention who suggested it.
>
> "MR. MILBRATH: All right.

"THE COURT: But, I'm not going to sit here and watch. I'm—among other things, I'm not going to see—this is off the record.

"(Discussion had off the record.)

" * * * [T]his is a new thing to this jury, and I don't know how interesting it is to them or not; some of them look like they're pretty interested.

* * *

"And, as I say, if you don't think they are, come up and let me know and I'll figure how—either have a recess or—which is more than likely what I would do." Tr. 12–100–12–101.

As the judge observed during the hearing, despite the above admonitions counsel did not bring the matter to the court again. App. 147.

The judge also observed that in the past courtroom employees had alerted him to problems with the jury. "Nothing was brought to my attention in this case about anyone appearing to be intoxicated," the judge stated, adding, "I saw nothing that suggested they were." *Id.,* at 172.

Following the hearing the District Court filed an order stating that "[o]n the basis of the admissible evidence offered I specifically find that the motions for leave to interview jurors or for an evidentiary hearing at which jurors would be witnesses is not required or appropriate." The District Court also denied the motion for new trial. *Id.,* at 181–182.

While the appeal of this case was pending before the Eleventh Circuit, petitioners filed another new trial motion based on additional evidence of jury misconduct. In another affidavit, Tanner's attorney stated that he received an unsolicited visit at his residence from a second juror, Daniel Hardy. *Id.,* at 241. Despite the fact that the District Court had denied petitioners' motion for leave to interview jurors, two days after Hardy's visit Tanner's attorney arranged for Hardy to be interviewed by two private investigators. *Id.,* at 242. The interview was transcribed, sworn to by the juror, and attached to the new trial motion. In the interview Hardy stated that he "felt like * * * the jury was on one big party." *Id.,* at 209. Hardy indicated that seven of the jurors drank alcohol during the noon recess. Four jurors, including Hardy, consumed between them "a pitcher to three pitchers" of beer during various recesses. *Id.,* at 212. Of the three other jurors who were alleged to have consumed alcohol, Hardy stated that on several occasions he observed two jurors having one or two mixed drinks during the lunch recess, and one other juror, who was also the foreperson, having a liter of wine on each of three occasions. *Id.,* at 213–215. Juror Hardy also stated that he and three other jurors smoked marijuana quite regularly during the trial. *Id.,* at 216–223. Moreover, Hardy stated that during the trial he observed one juror ingest cocaine five times and another juror ingest cocaine two or three times. *Id.,* at 227. One juror sold a quarter pound of marijuana to another juror during the trial, and took marijuana, cocaine and drug paraphernalia into the courthouse. *Id.,* at 234–235. Hardy noted that some of the jurors were falling asleep during the trial, and that one of the jurors described himself to Hardy as "flying." *Id.,* at 229. Hardy stated that before he visited Tanner's attorney at his residence, no one had contacted him concerning the jury's conduct, and Hardy had not been offered anything in return for his statement. *Id.,* at 232. Hardy said that he came forward "to clear my conscience" and "[b]ecause I felt * * * that the people on the jury didn't have no business being on the jury. I felt * * * that Mr. Tanner should have a better opportunity to get somebody that would review the facts right." *Id.,* at 231–232.

The District Court, stating that the motions "contain supplemental allegations which differ quantitatively but not qualitatively from those in the April motions," *id.,* at 256, denied petitioners' motion for a new trial.

The Court of Appeals for the Eleventh Circuit affirmed. 772 F.2d 765 (1985). We granted certiorari * * * to consider whether the District Court was required to hold an evidentiary hearing, including juror testimony, on juror alcohol and drug use during the trial, and to consider whether petitioners' actions constituted a conspiracy to defraud the United States within the meaning of 18 U.S.C. § 371.

II

Petitioners argue that the District Court erred in not ordering an additional evidentiary hearing at which jurors would testify concerning drug and alcohol use during the trial. Petitioners assert that, contrary to the holdings of the District Court and the Court of Appeals, juror testimony on ingestion of drugs or alcohol during the trial is not barred by Federal Rule of Evidence 606(b). Moreover, petitioners argue that whether or not authorized by Rule 606(b), an evidentiary hearing including juror testimony on drug and alcohol use is compelled by their Sixth Amendment right to trial by a competent jury.

By the beginning of this century, if not earlier, the near-universal and firmly established common-law rule in the United States flatly prohibited the admission of juror testimony to impeach a jury verdict. See 8 J. Wigmore, Evidence § 2352, pp. 696–697 (McNaughton rev. ed. 1961) (common-law rule, originating from 1785 opinion of Lord Mansfield, "came to receive in the United States an adherence almost unquestioned").

Exceptions to the common-law rule were recognized only in situations in which an "extraneous influence," *Mattox v. United States,* 146 U.S. 140, 149 (1892), was alleged to have affected the jury. In *Mattox,* this Court held admissible the testimony of jurors describing how they heard and read prejudicial information not admitted into evidence. The Court allowed juror testimony on influence by outsiders in *Parker v. Gladden,* 385 U.S. 363, 365 (1966) (bailiff's comments on defendant), and *Remmer v. United States,* 347 U.S. 227, 228–230 (1954) (bribe offered to juror). See also *Smith v. Phillips,* 455 U.S. 209 (1982) (juror in criminal trial had submitted an application for employment at the District Attorney's office). In situations that did not fall into this exception for external influence, however, the Court adhered to the common-law rule against admitting juror testimony to impeach a verdict. *McDonald v. Pless,* 238 U.S. 264 (1915); *Hyde v. United States,* 225 U.S. 347, 384 (1912).

Lower courts used this external/internal distinction to identify those instances in which juror testimony impeaching a verdict would be admissible. The distinction was not based on whether the juror was literally inside or outside the jury room when the alleged irregularity took place; rather, the distinction was based on the nature of the allegation. Clearly a rigid distinction based only on whether the event took place inside or outside the jury room would have been quite unhelpful. For example, under a distinction based on location a juror could not testify concerning a newspaper read inside the jury room. Instead, of course, this has been considered an external influence about which juror testimony is admissible. See *United States v. Thomas,* 463 F.2d 1061 (C.A.7 1972). Similarly, under a rigid locational distinction jurors could be regularly required to testify after the verdict as to whether they heard and comprehended the judge's instructions, since the charge to the jury takes place outside the jury room. Courts wisely have treated allegations of a juror's inability to hear or comprehend at trial as an internal matter. See *Government of the Virgin Islands v. Nicholas,* 759 F.2d 1073 (C.A.3 1985); *Davis v. United States,* 47 F.2d 1071 (C.A.5 1931) (rejecting juror testimony impeaching verdict, including testimony that jurors had not heard a particular instruction of the court).

Most significant for the present case, however, is the fact that lower federal courts treated allegations of the physical or mental incompetence of a juror as "internal" rather than "external" matters. In *United States v. Dioguardi,* 492 F.2d 70 (C.A.2 1974), the defendant Dioguardi received a letter from one of the jurors soon after the trial in which the juror explained that she had "eyes and ears that * * * see things before [they] happen," but that her eyes "are only partly open" because "a curse was put upon them some years ago." *Id.,* at 75. Armed with this letter and the opinions of seven psychiatrists that the letter suggested that the juror was suffering from a psychological disorder, Dioguardi sought a new trial or in the alternative an evidentiary hearing on the juror's competence. The District Court denied the motion and the Court of Appeals affirmed. The Court of Appeals noted "[t]he strong policy against any post-verdict inquiry into a juror's state of mind," *id.,* at 79, and observed:

> "The quickness with which jury findings will be set aside when there is proof of tampering or *external* influence, * * * parallel the reluctance of courts to inquire into jury deliberations when a verdict is valid on its face. * * * Such exceptions support rather than undermine the rationale of the rule that possible *internal* abnormalities in a jury will not be inquired into except 'in the gravest and most important cases.' " *Id.,* at 79, n.12, citing *McDonald v. Pless, supra,* 238 U.S., at 269 (emphasis in original).

The court of appeals concluded that when faced with allegations that a juror was mentally incompetent, "courts have refused to set aside a verdict, or even to make further inquiry, unless there be proof of an adjudication of insanity or mental incompetence closely in advance * * * of jury service," or proof of "a closely contemporaneous and independent post-trial adjudication of incompetency." 492 F.2d, at 80. See also *Sullivan v. Fogg,* 613 F.2d 465, 467 (C.A.2 1980) (allegation of juror insanity is internal consideration); *United States v. Allen,* 588 F.2d 1100, 1106, n.12 (C.A.5 1979) (noting "specific reluctance to probe the minds of jurors once they have deliberated their verdict"); *United States v. Pellegrini,* 441 F.Supp. 1367 (E.D.Pa.1977), aff'd, 586 F.2d 836 (C.A.3 1978) (whether juror sufficiently understood English language was not a question of "extraneous influence"). This line of federal decisions was reviewed in *Government of the Virgin Islands v. Nicholas, supra,* in which the Court of Appeals concluded that a juror's allegation that a hearing impairment interfered with his understanding of the evidence at trial was not a matter of "external influence." *Id.,* at 1079.

Substantial policy considerations support the common-law rule against the admission of jury testimony to impeach a verdict. As early as 1915 this Court explained the necessity of shielding jury deliberations from public scrutiny:

> "[L]et it once be established that verdicts solemnly made and publicly returned into court can be attacked and set aside on the testimony of those who took part in their publication and all verdicts could be, and many would be, followed by an inquiry in the hope of discovering something which might invalidate the finding. Jurors would be harassed and beset by the defeated party in an effort to secure from them evidence of facts which might establish misconduct sufficient to set aside a verdict. If evidence thus secured could be thus used, the result would be to make what was intended to be a private deliberation, the constant subject of public investigation—to the destruction of all frankness and freedom of discussion and conference." *McDonald v. Pless,* 238 U.S., at 267–268.

See also *Mattox v. United States,* 146 U.S. 140 (1892).

The Court's holdings requiring an evidentiary hearing where extrinsic influence or relationships have tainted the deliberations do not detract from, but rather harmonize with, the weighty government interest in insulating the jury's deliberative process. See *Smith v. Phillips,* 455 U.S. 209 (1982) (juror in criminal trial had submitted an application for employment at the District Attorney's office); *Remmer v. United States,* 347 U.S. 227 (1954) (juror reported attempted bribe during trial and was subjected to investigation). The Court's statement in *Remmer* that "[t]he integrity of jury proceedings must not be jeopardized by unauthorized invasions," *id.,* at 229, could also be applied to the inquiry petitioners seek to make into the internal processes of the jury.

There is little doubt that post-verdict investigation into juror misconduct would in some instances lead to the invalidation of verdicts reached after irresponsible or improper juror behavior. It is not at all clear, however, that the jury system could survive such efforts to perfect it. Allegations of juror misconduct, incompetency, or inattentiveness, raised for the first time days, weeks, or months after the verdict seriously disrupt the finality of the process. See, *e.g., Government of Virgin Islands v. Nicholas,* 759 F.2d, at 1081 (one year and eight months after verdict rendered, juror alleged that hearing difficulties affected his understanding of the evidence). Moreover, full and frank discussion in the jury room, jurors' willingness to return an unpopular verdict, and the community's trust in a system that relies on the decisions of laypeople would all be undermined by a barrage of post verdict scrutiny of juror conduct. See Note, Public Disclosures of Jury Deliberations, 96 Harv.L.Rev. 886, 888–892 (1983).

Federal Rule of Evidence 606(b) is grounded in the common-law rule against admission of jury testimony to impeach a verdict and the exception for juror testimony relating to extraneous influences. See *Government of Virgin Islands v. Gereau,* 523 F.2d 140, 149, n.22 (C.A.3 1975); S.Rep. No. 93–1277, p. 13 (1974), U.S.Code Cong. & Admin.News 1974, p. 7051 (observing that Rule 606(b) "embodied long-accepted Federal law").

Rule 606(b) states:

> "Upon an inquiry into the validity of a verdict or indictment, a juror may not testify as to any matter or statement occurring during the course of the jury's deliberations or to the effect of anything upon his or any other juror's mind or emotions as influencing him to assent to or dissent from the verdict or indictment or concerning his mental processes in connection therewith, except that a juror may testify on the question whether extraneous prejudicial information was improperly brought to the jury's attention or whether any outside influence was improperly brought to bear upon any juror. Nor may his affidavit or evidence of any statement by him concerning a matter about which he would be precluded from testifying be received for these purposes."

Petitioners have presented no argument that Rule 606(b) is inapplicable to the juror affidavits and the further inquiry they sought in this case, and, in fact, there appears to be virtually no support for such a proposition. See 3 D. Louisell & C. Mueller, Federal Evidence § 287, pp. 121–125 (1979) (under Rule 606(b), "proof to the following effects is excludable * * * that one or more jurors was inattentive during trial or deliberations, sleeping or thinking about other matters"); cf. Note, Impeachment of Verdicts by Jurors—Rule of Evidence 606(b), 4 Wm. Mitchell L.Rev. 417, 430–431 and n.88 (1978) (observing that under Rule 606(b), "juror testimony as to * * * juror intoxication probably will be inadmissible"; note author suggests that "[o]ne possibility is for the courts to determine that certain acts, such as a juror becoming intoxicated outside the jury room, simply are not within the rule," but cites no authority in support of the suggestion). Rather, petitioners argue that substance abuse constitutes an improper "outside influence" about which jurors may testify under Federal Rule of Evidence 606(b). In our view the language of the Rule cannot easily be stretched to cover this circumstance. However severe their effect and improper their use, drugs or alcohol voluntarily ingested by a juror seems no more an "outside influence" than a virus, poorly prepared food, or a lack of sleep.

In any case, whatever ambiguity might linger in the language of Rule 606(b) as applied to juror intoxication is resolved by the legislative history of the Rule. In 1972, following criticism of a proposed rule that would have allowed considerably broader use of juror testimony to impeach verdicts, the Advisory Committee drafted the present version of Rule 606(b). Compare 51 F.R.D. 315, 387 (1971) with 56 F.R.D. 183, 265 (1972); see 117 Cong.Rec. 33642, 33645 (1971) (letter from Sen. McClellan to Advisory Committee criticizing earlier proposal); *id.,* at 33655 (letter from Department of Justice to Advisory Committee criticizing earlier proposal and arguing that "[s]trong policy considerations continue to support the rule that jurors should not be permitted to testify about what occurred during the course of their deliberations"). This Court adopted the present version of Rule 606(b) and transmitted it to Congress.

The House Judiciary Committee described the effect of the version of Rule 606(b) transmitted by the Court as follows:

> "As proposed by the Court, Rule 606(b) limited testimony by a juror in the course of an inquiry into the validity of a verdict or indictment. He could testify as to the influence of extraneous prejudicial information brought to the jury's attention (e.g. a radio newscast or a newspaper account) or an outside influence which improperly had been brought to bear upon a juror (e.g. a threat to the safety of a member of his family), but he could not testify as to other irregularities which occurred in the jury room. Under this formulation a quotient verdict could not be attacked through the testimony of juror, *nor could a juror testify to the drunken condition of a fellow juror which so disabled him that he could not participate in the jury's deliberations.*" H.R.Rep. No. 93–650, pp. 9–10 (1973), U.S.Code Cong. & Admin.News 1974, p. 7083 (emphasis supplied).

The House Judiciary Committee, persuaded that the better practice was to allow juror testimony on any "objective juror misconduct," amended the Rule so as to comport with the more expansive versions proposed by the Advisory Committee in earlier drafts[22] and the House passed this amended version.

22. The House version, which adopted the earlier Advisory Committee proposal, read as follows:

> "Upon an inquiry into the validity of a verdict or indictment, a juror may not testify concerning the effect of anything upon his or any other juror's mind or emotions as influencing him to assent to or dissent from the verdict or indictment or concerning his mental processes in connection therewith. Nor may his affidavit or evidence of any statement by him indicating an effect of this kind be received for these purposes." H.R. 5463, 93d Cong., 2d Sess. (1974).

The Senate Judiciary Committee did not voice any disagreement with the House's interpretation of the Rule proposed by the Court, or the version passed by the House. Indeed, the Senate Report described the House version as "considerably broader" than the version proposed by the Court, and noted that the House version "would permit the impeachment of verdicts by inquiry into, not the mental processes of the jurors, but what happened in terms of conduct in the jury room." S.Rep. No. 93–1277, p. 13 (1974), U.S.Code Cong. & Admin.News 1974, p. 7060. With this understanding of the differences between the two versions of Rule 606(b)—an understanding identical to that of the House—the Senate decided to reject the broader House version and adopt the narrower version approved by the Court. The Senate Report explained:

> "[The House version's] extension of the ability to impeach a verdict is felt to be unwarranted and ill-advised.
>
> "The rule passed by the House embodies a suggestion by the Advisory Committee of the Judicial Conference that is considerably broader than the final version adopted by the Supreme Court, which embodied long-accepted Federal law. Although forbidding the impeachment of verdicts by inquiry into the jurors' mental processes, it deletes from the Supreme Court version the proscription against testimony 'as to any matter or statement occurring during the course of the jury's deliberations.' This deletion would have the effect of opening verdicts up to challenge on the basis of what happened during the jury's internal deliberations, for example, where a juror alleged that the jury refused to follow the trial judge's instructions or that some of the jurors did not take part in deliberations.
>
> "Permitting an individual to attack a jury verdict based upon the jury's internal deliberations has long been recognized as unwise by the Supreme Court.
>
> * * *
>
> "As it stands then, the rule would permit the harassment of former jurors by losing parties as well as the possible exploitation of disgruntled or otherwise badly-motivated ex-jurors.
>
> "Public policy requires a finality to litigation. And common fairness requires that absolute privacy be preserved for jurors to engage in the full and free debate necessary to the attainment of just verdicts. Jurors will not be able to function effectively if their deliberations are to be scrutinized in post-trial litigation. In the interest of protecting the jury system and the citizens who make it work, rule 606 should not permit any inquiry into the internal deliberations of the jurors." *Id.,* at 13–14, U.S.Code Cong. & Admin.News 1974, p. 7060.

The Conference Committee Report reaffirms Congress' understanding of the differences between the House and Senate versions of Rule 606(b): "[T]he House bill allows a juror to testify about objective matters occurring during the jury's deliberation, such as the misconduct of another juror or the reaching of a quotient verdict. The Senate bill does not permit juror testimony about any matter or statement occurring during the course of the jury's deliberations." H.R.Conf.Rep. No. 93–1597, p. 8 (1974), U.S.Code Cong. & Admin.News 1974, p. 7102. The Conference Committee adopted, and Congress enacted, the Senate version of Rule 606(b).

Thus, the legislative history demonstrates with uncommon clarity that Congress specifically understood, considered, and rejected a version of Rule 606(b) that would have allowed jurors to testify on juror conduct during deliberations, including juror intoxication. This legislative history provides strong support for the most reasonable reading of the language of Rule 606(b)—that juror intoxication is not an "outside influence" about which jurors may testify to impeach their verdict.

Finally, even if Rule 606(b) is interpreted to retain the common-law exception allowing post verdict inquiry of juror incompetence in cases of "substantial if not wholly conclusive evidence of incompetency," *Dioguardi,* 492 F.2d, at 80, the showing made by the petitioners falls far short of this standard. The affidavits and testimony presented in support of the first new trial motion suggested, at worst, that several of the jurors fell asleep at times during the afternoons. The District Court judge appropriately considered the fact that he had "an unobstructed view" of the jury, and did not see any juror sleeping. App. 147–149, 167–168; See *Government of Virgin Islands v. Nicholas,* 759 F.2d, at 1077 ("[I]t was appropriate for the trial judge to draw upon his personal knowledge and recollection in considering the factual allegations * * * that related to events that occurred in his presence"). The juror affidavit submitted in support of the second new trial motion was obtained in clear violation of the District Court's order and the court's local rule against juror interviews, MD Fla.Rule 2.04(c); on this basis alone the District Court would have been acting within its discretion in disregarding the affidavit. In any case, although the affidavit of juror Hardy describes more dramatic instances of misconduct, Hardy's allegations of *incompetence* are meager. Hardy stated that the alcohol consumption he engaged in with three other jurors did not leave any of them intoxicated. App. to Pet. for Cert. 47 ("I told [the prosecutor] that we would just go out and get us a pitcher of beer and drink it, but as far as us being drunk, no we wasn't"). The only allegations concerning the jurors' ability to properly consider the evidence were Hardy's observation that some jurors were "falling asleep all the time during the trial," and that Hardy's own reasoning ability was affected on one day of the trial. App. to Pet. for Cert. 46, 55. These allegations would not suffice to bring this case under the common-law exception allowing post verdict inquiry when an extremely strong showing of incompetency has been made.

Petitioners also argue that the refusal to hold an additional evidentiary hearing at which jurors would testify as to their conduct "violates the sixth amendment's guarantee to a fair trial before an impartial and *competent* jury." Brief for Petitioners 34 (emphasis in original).

This Court has recognized that a defendant has a right to "a tribunal both impartial and mentally competent to afford a hearing." *Jordan v. Massachusetts,* 225 U.S. 167, 176 (1912). In this case the District Court held an evidentiary hearing in response to petitioners' first new trial motion at which the judge invited petitioners to introduce any admissible evidence in support of their allegations. At issue in this case is whether the Constitution compelled the District Court to hold an additional evidentiary hearing including one particular kind of evidence inadmissible under the Federal Rules.

As described above, long-recognized and very substantial concerns support the protection of jury deliberations from intrusive inquiry. Petitioners' Sixth Amendment interests in an unimpaired jury, on the other hand, are protected by several aspects of the trial process. The suitability of an individual for the responsibility of jury service, of course, is examined during *voir dire.* Moreover, during the trial the jury is observable by the court, by counsel, and by court personnel. See *United States v. Provenzano,* 620 F.2d 985, 996–997 (C.A.3 1980) (marshal discovered sequestered juror smoking marijuana during early morning hours). Moreover, jurors are observable by each other, and may report inappropriate juror behavior to the court *before* they render a verdict. See *Lee v. United States,* 454 A.2d 770 (D.C.App.1982) (on second day of deliberations, jurors sent judge a note suggesting that foreperson was incapacitated). Finally, after the trial a party may seek to impeach the verdict by nonjuror evidence of misconduct. See *United States v. Taliaferro,* 558 F.2d 724, 725–726 (C.A.4 1977) (court considered records of club where jurors dined, and testimony of marshal who accompanied jurors, to determine whether jurors were intoxicated during deliberations). Indeed, in this case the District Court held an evidentiary hearing giving petitioners ample opportunity to produce nonjuror evidence supporting their allegations.

In light of these other sources of protection of the petitioners' right to a competent jury, we conclude that the District Court did not err in deciding, based on the inadmissibility of juror testimony and the clear insufficiency of the nonjuror evidence offered by petitioners, that an additional post verdict evidentiary hearing was unnecessary.

* * *

[Affirmed. Remanded on other issues.]

JUSTICE MARSHALL, with whom JUSTICE BRENNAN, JUSTICE BLACKMUN, and JUSTICE STEVENS join, concurring in part and dissenting in part.

Every criminal defendant has a constitutional right to be tried by competent jurors. This Court has long recognized that "[d]ue process implies a tribunal both impartial and mentally competent to afford a hearing," *Jordan v. Massachusetts,* 225 U.S. 167, 176 (1912), "a jury capable and willing to decide the case solely on the evidence before it." *Smith v. Phillips,* 455 U.S. 209, 217 (1982). If, as is charged, members of petitioners' jury were intoxicated as a result of their use of drugs and alcohol to the point of sleeping through material portions of the trial, the verdict in this case must be set aside. In directing district courts to ignore sworn allegations that jurors engaged in gross and debilitating misconduct, this Court denigrates the precious right to a competent jury. Accordingly, I dissent from that part of the Court's opinion.

I

At the outset, it should be noted that petitioners have not asked this Court to decide whether there is sufficient evidence to impeach the jury's verdict. The question before us is only whether an evidentiary hearing is required to explore allegations of juror misconduct and incompetency.

The allegations of juror misconduct in this case are profoundly disturbing. * * *

II

Despite the seriousness of the charges, the Court refuses to allow petitioners an opportunity to vindicate their fundamental right to a competent jury. The Court holds that petitioners are absolutely barred from exploring allegations of juror misconduct and incompetency through the only means available to them—examination of the jurors who have already voluntarily come forward. The basis for the Court's ruling is the mistaken belief that juror testimony concerning drug and alcohol abuse at trial is inadmissible under Federal Rule of Evidence 606(b) and is contrary to the policies the Rule was intended to advance. * * *

In this case, however, we are not faced with a conflict between the policy considerations underlying Rule 606(b) and petitioners' Sixth Amendment rights. Rule 606(b) is not applicable to juror testimony on matters *unrelated* to the jury's deliberations. * * *

It is undisputed that Rule 606(b) does not exclude juror testimony as to matters occurring before or after deliberations. See 3 D. Louisell & C. Mueller, Federal Evidence § 290, p. 151 (1979) * * * . But, more particularly, the Rule only "operates to prohibit testimony as to *certain* conduct by the jurors which has no verifiable manifestations," 3 J. Weinstein & M. Berger, Weinstein's Evidence ¶ 606[04], p. 606–28 (1985) (emphasis added); as to other matters, jurors remain competent to testify. See Fed.Rule Evid. 601. Because petitioners' claim of juror misconduct and incompetency involves objectively verifiable conduct occurring prior to deliberations, juror testimony in support of the claims is admissible under Rule 606(b).

The Court's analysis of legislative history confirms the inapplicability of Rule 606(b) to the type of misconduct alleged in this case. As the Court emphasizes, the debate over two proposed versions of the Rule—the more restrictive Senate version ultimately adopted and the permissive House version * * * , focused on the extent to which jurors would be permitted to testify as to what transpired *during the course of the* *deliberations themselves.*[23] Similarly, the Conference Committee Report, quoted by the Court * * * , compares the two versions solely in terms of the admissibility of testimony as to matters occurring during, or relating to, the jury's deliberations: "[T]he House bill allows a juror to testify about objective matters occurring during the jury's deliberation, such as the misconduct of another juror or the reaching of a quotient verdict. The Senate bill does not permit juror testimony about any matter or statement occurring *during the course of the jury's deliberations.*" H.R.Conf.Rep. No. 93–1597, p. 8 (1974), U.S.Code Cong. & Admin.News 1974, p. 7102 (emphasis added). The obvious conclusion, and the one compelled by Rule 601, is that *both* versions of Rule 606(b) would have permitted jurors to testify as to matters not involving deliberations. The House Report's passing reference to juror intoxication during deliberations * * * is not to the contrary. Reflecting Congress' consistent focus on the deliberative process, it suggests only that the authors of the House Report believed that the Senate version of Rule 606(b) did not allow testimony as to juror intoxication during deliberations.[24] * * *

Even if I agreed with the Court's expansive construction of Rule 606(b), I would nonetheless find the testimony of juror intoxication admissible under the Rule's "outside influence" exception.[25] As a common sense matter, drugs and alcohol *are* outside influences on jury members. Commentators have suggested that testimony as to drug and alcohol abuse, even during deliberations, falls within this exception. "[T]he present exception paves the way for proof by the affidavit or testimony of a juror that one or more jurors became intoxicated during deliberations. * * * Of course the use of hallucinogenic or narcotic drugs during deliberations should similarly be provable." 3 Louisell & Mueller, Federal Evidence, § 289, pp. 143–145 (footnote omitted). See 3 Weinstein & Berger, Weinstein's Evidence, *supra,* ¶ 606[04], pp. 606–29—606–32 ("Rule 606(b) would not render a witness incompetent to testify to

23. Proponents of the more restrictive Senate version were reluctant to allow juror testimony as to irregularities in the process by which a verdict was reached, such as the resort to a "quotient verdict." See, *e.g.,* 120 Cong.Rec. 2374–2375 (1974) (statement of Rep. Wiggins) * * * .

As the Court explains, * * * the Senate rejected the House version because it "would have the effect of opening verdicts up to challenge on the basis of what happened during the jury's *internal deliberations,* for example, where a juror alleged that the jury refused to follow the trial judge's instructions or that some of the jurors did not take part in deliberations." S.Rep. No. 93–1277, p. 13 (1974), U.S.Code Cong. & Admin.News 1974, p. 7060 (emphasis added). * * *

24. H.R.Rep. No. 93–650, p. 10 (1973), U.S.Code Cong. & Admin.News 1974, p. 7083 ("Under this formulation a quotient verdict could not be attacked through the testimony of a juror, nor could a juror testify to the drunken condition of a fellow juror which so disabled him that he could not participate in the jury's deliberations").

25. The sole support for the Court's cramped interpretation of this exception is the isolated reference to juror intoxication *at deliberations,* contained in the House Report, quoted *supra* * * * . The source for the reference is a letter to the House Subcommittee, to the effect that the version of the Rule adopted by the Senate would not allow inquiry into juror consumption of alcohol during deliberations. * * * In a subsequent letter, the writer dropped any reference to the question of intoxication, focusing exclusively on the issue of quotient verdicts. * * * Moreover, this reference is hardly dispositive. * * * None of the subsequent Committee Reports make any allusion to juror intoxication.

juror irregularities such as intoxication * * * regardless of whether the jury misconduct occurred within or without the jury room"). The Court suggests that, if these are outside influences, "a virus, poorly prepared food, or a lack of sleep" would also qualify. [483 U.S.] at 122. Distinguishing between a virus, for example, and a narcotic drug is a matter of line-drawing. Courts are asked to make these sorts of distinctions in numerous contexts; I have no doubt they would be capable of differentiating between the intoxicants involved in this case and minor indispositions not affecting juror competency.

The Court assures us that petitioners' Sixth Amendment interests are adequately protected by other aspects of the trial process: *voir dire*; observation during trial by the court, counsel, and courtroom personnel; and observation by fellow jurors (so long as they report inappropriate juror behavior to the court before a verdict is rendered). * * * Reliance on these safeguards, to the exclusion of an evidentiary hearing, is misguided. *Voir dire* cannot disclose whether a juror will choose to abuse drugs and alcohol during the trial. Moreover, the type of misconduct alleged here is not readily verifiable through nonjuror testimony. The jurors were not supervised by courtroom personnel during the noon recess, when they consumed alcoholic beverages and used drugs. Hardy reported that he and his three companions purposely avoided observation. They smoked marijuana and used cocaine first in a municipal parking garage and later "[d]own past the Hyatt Regency" because it was "away from everybody." App. 218, 222.

* * *

I dissent.

Notes and Questions

1. *Litigating effect of improper influence. Tanner* deals only with the issue of whether the testimony concerning "substance abuse" constitutes an "improper outside influence" available to impeach the jury's verdict. Even where an event is considered admissible as an outside influence, a juror may still not testify concerning the effect of that influence upon his or her mind under Rule 606(b) and long-standing case law. See, e.g., Mattox v. United States, 146 U.S. 140, 149 (1892). Accordingly, if evidence is admitted, the court must determine whether a new trial should be granted based upon objective circumstances. See, e.g., United States v. Vasquez, 597 F.2d 192, 194 (9th Cir.1979) (where file containing inadmissible evidence left in jury room, court examined prejudicial potential of information, period of time file left in room, and extent of exposure to jurors, but could not consider subjective effect on jurors). This means that direct testimony regarding the prejudicial impact of the outside influence will generally be unavailable, and as a result, the burden of proof regarding prejudice and presumptions of prejudice take on special importance in determining the outcome. The Supreme Court has on several occasions addressed improper outside influences: Remmer v. United States, 347 U.S. 227, 229 (1954) (any private communication about matter pending before jury is presumptively prejudi-

cial, placing burden on government to show harmlessness), and Smith v. Phillips, 455 U.S. 209 (1982) (defendant has opportunity to prove actual bias of juror who applied for employment with district attorney's office during trial). Lower courts have struggled with precisely what these cases mean with respect to the burden of proof and presumptions. See United States v. Maree, 934 F.2d 196, 201 (9th Cir.1991) (where extraneous material about the case is submitted to jury, defendant receives a new trial if the court finds a "reasonable possibility" that the material could have affected the verdict, but where *ex parte* contacts do not pertain to the law or facts of the case, a new trial is to be granted only if the court finds "actual prejudice"); Stockton v. Virginia, 852 F.2d 740, 743–44 (4th Cir.1988) (*Remmer* creates presumption of prejudice where third party communicates with a juror about the case and neither *Tanner* nor *Phillips* eliminates that presumption).

2. *Racists comments.* If the internal deliberations of the jury, as reported by one of the jurors after the verdict of guilty, included extremely racist remarks by jurors in a case involving a minority defendant, would the rationale of the *Tanner* Court hold? If not, what rationale might be used? See Developments in the Law: Race and the Criminal Process: VII. Racist Juror Misconduct During Deliberations, 101 Harv.L.Rev. 1595 (1988). For an argument that jury deliberations are too secretive and should be transcribed and made part of the record, see Ruprecht, Are Verdicts, Too, Like Sausages?: Lifting the Cloak of Jury Secrecy, 146 U.Pa.L.Rev. 217 (1997).

3. *False or incomplete answers on voir dire.* Where a juror fails to respond fully and truthfully to questions on voir dire, are the limitations of Rule 606 inapplicable? See Urseth v. City of Dayton, 680 F.Supp. 1084 (S.D.Ohio 1987). Is a new trial justified on a lesser showing of prejudice? See McCoy v. Goldston, 652 F.2d 654 (6th Cir.1981).

4. *Interviewing jurors.* In *Tanner,* the Supreme Court noted that the trial judge denied counsel's motion to interview jurors. If counsel is prohibited from interviewing jurors, how is misconduct to be discovered? With regard to the practical problem of discovering whether improprieties occurred that might serve as grounds for setting aside a verdict, compare United States v. Moten, 582 F.2d 654 (2d Cir.1978) (recognizing that notice must be given to the court and opposing counsel before jurors are contacted and that district court has the power to order that all post-trial investigation be conducted under judicial supervision), with Model Code of Professional Responsibility DR 7–108(D) (1998) (prohibiting the questioning of jurors only where done for the purpose of harassing or embarrassing juror or influencing future jury service). The Model Rules of Professional Conduct have no provision dealing with this issue. See generally 3 Mueller & Kirkpatrick, Federal Evidence § 254 (2d ed. 1994); 3 Weinstein's Federal Evidence § 606.06 (2d ed. 2006).

5. *2006 Amendment.* In 2006, Rule 606(b) was amended to clarify that juror testimony could be received to prove that there was a mistake made in entering the verdict on the verdict form.

6. *Sources.* Alschuler, The Supreme Court and the Jury: Voir Dire, Peremptory Challenges, and the Review of Jury Verdicts, 56 U.Chi.L.Rev. 153 (1989); Cammack, The Jurisprudence of Jury Trials: The No Impeachment Rule and the Conditions for Legitimate Legal Decisionmaking, 64

U.Colo.L.Rev. 57 (1993); Crump, Jury Misconduct, Jury Interviews, and the Federal Rules of Evidence: Is the Broad Exclusionary Principle of Rule 606(b) Justified?, 66 N.C.L.Rev. 509 (1988); Diehm, Impeachment of Jury Verdicts: *Tanner v. United States* and Beyond, 65 St. John's L.Rev. 389 (1991); Mueller, Jurors' Impeachment of Verdicts and Indictments in Federal Courts Under Rule 606(b), 57 Neb.L.Rev. 920 (1978); ABA Standards for Criminal Justice, Trial by Jury, Standard 15–5.7 (3d ed. 1996).

DOUGLAS OIL CO. OF CALIFORNIA v. PETROL STOPS NORTHWEST

Supreme Court of the United States, 1979.
441 U.S. 211.

MR. JUSTICE POWELL delivered the opinion of the Court.

This case presents two intertwined questions concerning a civil litigant's right to obtain transcripts[26] of federal criminal grand jury proceedings. First, what justification for disclosure must a private party show in order to overcome the presumption of grand jury secrecy applicable to such transcripts? Second, what court should assess the strength of this showing—the court where the civil action is pending, or the court that acts as custodian of the grand jury documents?

I

Respondent Petrol Stops Northwest is a gasoline retailer unaffiliated with any major oil company. In 1973, it operated 104 service stations located in Arizona, California, Oregon, Washington, and several other States. On December 13, 1973, respondent filed an antitrust action in the District of Arizona against 12 large oil companies, including petitioners Douglas Oil Company of California and Phillips Petroleum Company. In its complaint, respondent alleged that on January 1, 1973, there had been a sharp reduction in the amount of gasoline offered for sale to it, and that this reduction had resulted from a conspiracy among the oil companies to restrain trade in gasoline, in violation of §§ 1 and 2 of the Sherman Act. 26 Stat. 209, 15 U.S.C.A. §§ 1, 2. As a part of this conspiracy, respondent charged, petitioners and their codefendants had fixed the prices of gasoline at the retail and wholesale distribution levels in California, Oregon and Washington.

Respondents Gas–A–Tron of Arizona and Coinoco also independently sell gasoline through service stations they own or lease. Unlike respondent Petrol Stops Northwest, however, their operations are limited to the vicinity of Tucson, Ariz. On November 2, 1973, Gas–A–Tron and Coinoco filed an antitrust complaint in the District of Arizona naming as defendants nine large oil companies, including petitioner Phillips Petroleum Company. Like respondent Petrol Stops Northwest, Gas–A–Tron and Coinoco alleged that as of January 1, 1973, their supply

26. "Transcripts" is used herein to refer to the verbatim recordings of testimony given before a grand jury.

of gasoline had been sharply reduced, and attributed this reduction to a conspiracy to restrain trade in violation of the Sherman Act. The specific charges of illegal behavior asserted by the two retailers substantially paralleled those made by Petrol Stops Northwest in its complaint, and included an allegation that the defendants had fixed the price of gasoline at the wholesale and retail levels.

Although the issues and defendants in the two actions were substantially the same, the cases were assigned to two different judges in the District of Arizona. In February 1974, respondents served upon petitioners a set of interrogatories which included a request that petitioners state whether either of their companies at any time between January 1, 1968, and December 14, 1974, had had any communication with any of their competitors concerning the wholesale price of gasoline to be sold to unaffiliated retailers. Petitioners also were asked to produce any documents they had concerning such communications. Petitioners responded that they were aware of no such communications, and therefore could produce no documents pertinent to the request.

In the meantime, the Antitrust Division of the Department of Justice had been investigating since 1972 the pricing behavior on the West Coast of several major oil companies including petitioners. See App. 26. As part of this investigation, employees of petitioners were called to testify before a grand jury empanelled in the Central District of California. The Government's investigation culminated on March 19, 1975, when the grand jury returned an indictment charging petitioners and four other oil companies with having conspired to fix the price of "rebrand gasoline" in California, Oregon, Washington, Nevada, and Arizona. The indictment alleged that the price-fixing conspiracy had begun in July 1970 and had continued at least until the end of 1971.

Although initially all six defendants charged in the criminal indictment pled not guilty, by December of 1975, each had pled *nolo contendere* and was fined $50,000. Before changing their pleas, petitioners, acting pursuant to Fed.Rule Crim.Proc. 16(a)(1)(A), asked the District Court for the Central District of California to give them copies of the transcripts of testimony given by their employees before the grand jury. Their request was granted, and it appears that petitioners continue to possess copies of these transcripts.

In October of 1976 respondents served upon petitioners requests under Fed.Rule Civ.Proc. 34 for production of the grand jury transcripts in petitioners' possession. Petitioners objected to the requests for production, arguing that the transcripts were not relevant to the private antitrust actions and that they were not likely to lead to any admissible evidence. Respondents did not pursue their discovery requests by making a motion in the Arizona trial court under Fed.Rule Civ.Proc. 37 to compel discovery. * * * Rather, they filed a petition in the District Court for the Central District of California asking that court, as guardian of the grand jury transcripts under Fed.Rule Crim.Proc. 6(e), to order them released to respondents. An attorney from the Antitrust Division of the

Department of Justice appeared and indicated that the Government had no objection to respondents' receiving the transcripts already made available to petitioners under Fed.Rule Crim.Proc. 16(a)(1)(A). He suggested to the court, however, that the real parties in interest were petitioners, and therefore that they should be given an opportunity to be heard. The California District Court accepted this suggestion, and petitioners participated in the proceedings as parties adverse to respondents.

After briefing and oral argument, the court ordered the Chief of the Antitrust Division's Los Angeles Office "to produce for [respondents'] inspection and copying all grand jury transcripts previously disclosed to Phillips Petroleum Company or Douglas Oil Company of California or their attorneys relating to the indictment in United States v. Phillips, et al., Criminal Docket No. 75–377." App. 48–49. The production order was subject, however, to several protective conditions. The transcripts were to "be disclosed only to counsel for [respondents] in connection with the two civil actions" pending in Arizona. Furthermore, under the court's order the transcripts of grand jury testimony "may be used * * * solely for the purpose of impeaching or refreshing the recollection of a witness, either in deposition or at trial" in the Arizona actions. Finally, the court forbade any further reproduction of the matter turned over to respondents, and ordered that the material be returned to the Antitrust Division "upon completion of the purposes authorized by this Order."

On appeal the Ninth Circuit affirmed the disclosure order. 571 F.2d 1127 (1978). The Court of Appeals noted that under United States v. Procter & Gamble Co., 356 U.S. 677 (1958), a party seeking access to grand jury transcripts must show a "particularized need." In evaluating the strength of the need shown in the present case, the Ninth Circuit considered two factors: the need for continued grand jury secrecy and respondents' need for the requested material. The court found the former need to be insubstantial, as the grand jury proceeding had concluded three years before and the transcripts already had been released to petitioners. As to respondents' claim, the court conceded that it knew little about the Arizona proceedings, but speculated that the transcripts would facilitate the prosecution of respondents' civil suits: Petitioners' answers to the 1974 interrogatories concerning price communications with competitors appeared to be at odds with their pleas of *nolo contendere* in the California criminal action.

II

Petitioners contend that the courts below erred in holding that, because the grand jury had dissolved and the requested material had been disclosed already to the defendants, respondents had to show only a "slight need" for disclosure. According to petitioners, this approach to disclosure under Fed.Rule Crim.Proc. 6(e) is contrary to prior decisions of this Court indicating that, "a civil litigant must demonstrate a compelling necessity for specified grand jury materials before disclosure is proper." Brief for Petitioners 16.

We consistently have recognized that the proper functioning of our grand jury system depends upon the secrecy of grand jury proceedings. See, e.g., United States v. Procter & Gamble, 356 U.S. 677 (1958).[27] In particular, we have noted several distinct interests served by safeguarding the confidentiality of grand jury proceedings. First, if preindictment proceedings were made public, many prospective witnesses would be hesitant to come forward voluntarily, knowing that those against whom they testify would be aware of that testimony. Moreover, witnesses who appeared before the grand jury would be less likely to testify fully and frankly, as they would be open to retribution as well as to inducements. There also would be the risk that those about to be indicted would flee, or would try to influence individual grand jurors to vote against indictment. Finally, by preserving the secrecy of the proceedings, we assure that persons who are accused but found innocent by the grand jury will not be held up to public ridicule.[28]

For all of these reasons, courts have been reluctant to lift unnecessarily the veil of secrecy from the grand jury. At the same time, it has been recognized that in some situations justice may demand that discrete portions of transcripts be made available for use in subsequent proceedings. See, e.g., United States v. Socony–Vacuum, 310 U.S. 150, 233–234 (1940). Indeed, recognition of the occasional need for litigants to have access to grand jury transcripts led to the provision in Fed.Rule Crim.Proc. 6(e)(2)(C)(i) that disclosure of grand jury transcripts may be made "when so directed by a court preliminarily to or in connection with a judicial proceeding."[29]

27. Since the 17th century, grand jury proceedings have been closed to the public, and records of such proceedings have been kept from the public eye. See Calkins, Grand Jury Secrecy, 63 Mich.L.Rev. 455, 457 (1965). The rule of grand jury secrecy was imported into our federal common law and is an integral part of our criminal justice system. See Costello v. United States, 350 U.S. 359, 362 (1956); United States v. Johnson, 319 U.S. 503, 513 (1943). Rule 6(e) of the Federal Rules of Criminal Procedure codifies the requirement that grand jury activities generally be kept secret, by providing that,

> "A grand juror, an interpreter, a stenographer, an operator of a recording device, a typist who transcribes recorded testimony, [or] an attorney for the Government * * * shall not disclose matters occurring before the grand jury, except as otherwise provided for in these rules. * * * A knowing violation of rule 6 may be punished as a contempt of court."

Although the purpose for grand jury secrecy originally was protection of the criminally accused against an overreaching Crown, see Calkins, Grand Jury Secrecy, supra, with time it came to be viewed as necessary for the proper functioning of the grand jury. * * *

28. In United States v. Procter & Gamble, 356 U.S. 677, 681–682, n.6 (1958), we said that the reasons for grand jury secrecy had been summarized correctly in United States v. Rose, 215 F.2d 617, 628–629 (C.A.3 1954):

> "(1) To prevent the escape of those whose indictment may be contemplated; (2) to insure the utmost freedom to the grand jury in its deliberations, and to prevent persons subject to indictment or their friends from importuning the grand jurors; (3) to prevent subornation of perjury or tampering with the witnesses who may testify before the grand jury and later appear at the trial of those indicted by it; (4) to encourage free and untrammeled disclosures by persons who have information with respect to the commission of crimes; (5) to protect innocent accused who is exonerated from disclosure of the fact that he has been under investigation, and from the expense of standing trial where there was no probability of guilt."

29. Fed.Rule Crim.Proc. 6(e) provides in full:

In United States v. Procter & Gamble, supra, the Court sought to accommodate the competing needs for secrecy and disclosure by ruling that a private party seeking to obtain grand jury transcripts must demonstrate that "without the transcript a defense would be greatly prejudiced or that without reference to it an injustice would be done." 356 U.S., at 682. Moreover, the Court required that the showing of need for the transcripts be made "with particularity" so that "the secrecy of the proceedings [may] be lifted discretely and limitedly." Id., at 683. Accord, Pittsburgh Plate Glass Co. v. United States, 360 U.S. 395, 400 (1959).

In Dennis v. United States, 384 U.S. 855 (1966), the Court considered a request for disclosure of grand jury records in quite different circumstances. It was there held to be an abuse of discretion for a district court in a criminal trial to refuse to disclose to the defendants the grand jury testimony of four witnesses who some years earlier had appeared before a grand jury investigating activities of the defendants. The grand jury had completed its investigation, and the witnesses whose testimony was sought already had testified in public concerning the same matters. The Court noted that "[n]one of the reasons traditionally advanced to justify nondisclosure of grand jury minutes" was significant

"(e) Secrecy of Proceedings and Disclosure—

"(1) General Rule.—A grand juror, an interpreter, a stenographer, an operator of a recording device, a typist who transcribes recorded testimony, an attorney for the Government, or any person to whom disclosure is made under paragraph (2)(A)(ii) of this subdivision shall not disclose matters occurring before the grand jury, except as otherwise provided for in these rules. No obligation of secrecy may be imposed on any person except in accordance with this rule. A knowing violation of rule 6 may be punished as a contempt of court.

"(2) Exceptions.—

"(A) Disclosure otherwise prohibited by this rule of matters occurring before the grand jury, other than its deliberations and the vote of any grand juror, may be made to—

"(i) an attorney for the government for use in the performance of such attorney's duty; and

"(ii) such government personnel as are deemed necessary by an attorney for the government to assist an attorney for the government in the performance of such attorney's duty to enforce Federal criminal law.

"(B) Any person to whom matters are disclosed under subparagraph (A)(ii) of this paragraph shall not utilize that grand jury material for any purpose other than assisting the attorney for the government in the performance of such attorney's duty to enforce Federal criminal law. An attorney for the government shall promptly provide the district court, before which was impaneled the grand jury whose material has been so disclosed, with the names of the persons to whom such disclosure has been made.

"(C) Disclosure otherwise prohibited by this rule of matters occurring before the grand jury may also be made—

"(i) when so directed by a court preliminarily to or in connection with a judicial proceeding; or

"(ii) when permitted by a court at the request of the defendant, upon a showing that grounds may exist for a motion to dismiss the indictment because of matters occurring before the grand jury.

"(3) Sealed indictments.—The Federal magistrate to whom an indictment is returned may direct that the indictment be kept secret until the defendant is in custody or has been released pending trial. Thereupon the clerk shall seal the indictment and no person shall disclose the return of the indictment except when necessary for the issuance and execution of a warrant or summons."

Although Fed.Rule Crim.Proc. 6(e) was amended in 1977, all parties agree that the changes do not bear upon the issues in the present case.

in those circumstances, 384 U.S., at 872 n.18, whereas the defendants had shown it to be likely that the witnesses' testimony at trial was inconsistent with their prior grand jury testimony.

From *Procter & Gamble* and *Dennis* emerges the standard for determining when the traditional secrecy of the grand jury may be broken: Parties seeking grand jury transcripts under Rule 6(e) must show that the material they seek is needed to avoid a possible injustice in another judicial proceeding, that the need for disclosure is greater than the need for continued secrecy, and that their request is structured to cover only material so needed.[30] Such a showing must be made even when the grand jury whose transcripts are sought has concluded its operations, as it had in *Dennis.* For in considering the effects of disclosure on grand jury proceedings, the courts must consider not only the immediate effects upon a particular grand jury, but also the possible effect upon the functioning of future grand juries. Persons called upon to testify will consider the likelihood that their testimony may one day be disclosed to outside parties. Fear of future retribution or social stigma may act as powerful deterrents to those who would come forward and aid the grand jury in the performance of its duties. Concern as to the future consequences of frank and full testimony is heightened where the witness is an employee of a company under investigation. Thus, the interests in grand jury secrecy, although reduced, are not eliminated merely because the grand jury has ended its activities.[31]

It is clear from *Procter & Gamble* and *Dennis* that disclosure is appropriate only in those cases where the need for it outweighs the public interest in secrecy, and that the burden of demonstrating this balance rests upon the private party seeking disclosure. It is equally clear that as the considerations justifying secrecy become less relevant, a party asserting a need for grand jury transcripts will have a lesser burden in showing justification. Accord, Illinois v. Sarbaugh, 552 F.2d 768, 774 (C.A.7 1977); U.S. Industries Inc. v. United States District Court, 345 F.2d 18, 21 (C.A.9 1965); 1 C. Wright, Federal Practice & Procedure § 106, at 173 (1969). In sum, as so often is the situation in our jurisprudence, the court's duty in a case of this kind is to weigh carefully the competing interests in light of the relevant circumstances and the standards announced by this Court. And if disclosure is ordered, the court may include protective limitations on the use of the disclosed material, as did the District Court in this case. Moreover, we emphasize that a court called upon to determine whether grand jury transcripts

30. As noted in United States v. Procter & Gamble, 356 U.S. 677, 683 (1958), the typical showing of particularized need arises when a litigant seeks to use "the grand jury transcript at the trial to impeach a witness, to refresh his recollection, to test his credibility and the like." Such use is necessary to avoid misleading the trier of fact. Moreover, disclosure can be limited strictly to those portions of a particular witness' testimony that bear upon some aspect of his direct testimony at trial.

31. The transcripts sought by respondents already had been given to the target companies in the grand jury investigation. Thus, release to respondents will not enhance the possibility of retaliatory action by employers in this case. But the other factors supporting the presumption of secrecy remain and must be considered.

should be released necessarily is infused with substantial discretion. See Pittsburgh Plate Glass Co. v. United States, 360 U.S. 395, 399 (1959).

Applying these principles to the present case, we conclude that neither the District Court nor the Court of Appeals erred in the standard by which it assessed the request for disclosure under Rule 6(e). The District Court made clear that the question before it was whether a particularized need for disclosure outweighed the interest in continued grand jury secrecy. See App. 53–55. Similarly, the Court of Appeals correctly understood that the standard enunciated in *Procter & Gamble* requires a court to examine the extent of the need for continuing grand jury secrecy, the need for disclosure, and the extent to which the request was limited to that material directly pertinent to the need for disclosure.[32]

III

Petitioners contend, irrespective of the legal standard applied, that the District Court for the Central District of California was not the proper court to rule on respondents' motion for disclosure. Petitioners note that the Court of Appeals and the District Court both purported to base their decisions in part upon the need for use of the requested material in the civil antitrust proceedings pending in Arizona. This determination necessarily involved consideration of the nature and status of the Arizona proceedings, matters peculiarly within the competence of the Arizona District Court.

* * * The federal courts that have addressed the question generally have said that the request for disclosure of grand jury minutes under Rule 6(e) must be directed toward the court under whose auspices the grand jury was impanelled. * * * Indeed, those who seek grand jury transcripts have little choice other than to file a request with the court that supervised the grand jury, as it is the only court with control over the transcripts.[33] * * *

It does not follow, however, that in every case the court in which the grand jury sat should make the final decision whether a request for

32. As petitioners point out, the Court of Appeals did say that, because of the circumstances, "the party seeking disclosure should not be required to demonstrate a large compelling need," and that a "minimal showing of particularized need" would suffice. In a different context, these statements could be read as an unjustified lowering of the standard of proof required by *Procter & Gamble* and *Dennis*. We cannot say, however, that the Court of Appeals applied an incorrect standard in view of the circumstances of this case and the discussion thereof in the opinion below.

33. As we have noted, by virtue of a prior order petitioners have possession of the transcripts sought by respondents. * * * We were informed at argument by counsel for the Government that under the terms of that order, the transcripts were to be returned upon completion of the criminal proceeding in the Central District of California and were to be used only for purposes of defending against the criminal charges in that case. * * * It appears, therefore, that if the District Court in Arizona had the authority to order disclosure by the petitioners, this power was derived from petitioners' unlawful retention of the transcripts. Indeed, as the Government suggests, it is questionable whether the Arizona District Court properly could have ordered production of the documents in direct violation of the California District Court order.

disclosure under Rule 6(e) should be granted. Where, as in this case, the request is made for use in a case pending in another district, the judges of the court having custody of the grand jury transcripts will have no first-hand knowledge of the litigation in which the transcripts allegedly are needed, and no practical means by which such knowledge can be obtained. In such a case, a judge in the district of the grand jury cannot weigh in an informed manner the need for disclosure against the need for maintaining grand jury secrecy. Thus, it may well be impossible for that court to apply the standard required by the decisions of this Court, reiterated above, for determining whether the veil of secrecy should be lifted. * * *

In the present case, the District Court for the Central District of California was called upon to make an evaluation entirely beyond its expertise. The District Judge readily conceded that he had no knowledge of the civil proceedings pending several hundred miles away in Arizona. App. 58. Nonetheless, he was asked to rule whether there was a "particularized need" for disclosure of portions of the grand jury transcript and whether this need outweighed the need for continued grand jury secrecy. Generally we leave it to the considered discretion of the District Court to determine the proper response to requests for disclosure under Rule 6(e). See Pittsburgh Plate Glass Co. v. United States, 360 U.S. 395, 399 (1959). We have a duty, however, to guide the exercise of discretion by district courts, and when necessary to overturn discretionary decisions under Rule 6(e). See, e.g., Dennis v. United States, 384 U.S. 855 (1966).

We find that the District Court here abused its discretion in releasing directly to respondents the grand jury minutes they requested. Appreciating that it was largely ignorant of the Arizona civil suits, the court nonetheless made a judgment concerning the relative needs for secrecy and disclosure. The court based its decision largely upon the unsupported assertions of counsel during oral argument before it, supplemented only by the criminal indictment returned by the grand jury, the civil complaints, and petitioners' response to a single interrogatory that appeared to be inconsistent with petitioners' *nolo contendere* plea in the criminal case. Even the court's comparison of the criminal indictment and the civil complaints did not indicate unambiguously what, if any, portions of the grand jury transcripts would be pertinent to the subject of the Arizona actions, as only some of the same parties were named and only some of the same territory was covered.

The possibility of an unnecessary breach of grand jury secrecy in situations such as this is not insignificant. A court more familiar with the course of the antitrust litigation might have seen important differences between the allegations of the indictment and the contours of the conspiracy respondents sought to prove in their civil actions—differences indicating that disclosure would likely be of little value to respondents, save perhaps as a mechanism for general discovery. Alternatively, the courts where the civil proceedings were pending might have considered disclosure at that point in the litigation to be premature; if there were to be conflicts between petitioners' statements and their actions in the criminal proceedings, the court might have preferred to wait until they ripened at depositions or even during testimony at trial.

Under these circumstances, the better practice would have been for the District Court, after making a written evaluation of the need for continued grand jury secrecy and a determination that the limited evidence before it showed that disclosure might be appropriate, to have sent the requested materials to the courts where the civil cases were pending. The Arizona court, armed with their special knowledge of the status of the civil actions, then could have considered the requests for disclosure in light of the California court's evaluation of the need for continued grand jury secrecy. In this way, both the need for continued secrecy and the need for disclosure could have been evaluated by the courts in the best position to make the respective evaluations.[34]

We do not suggest, of course, that such a procedure would be required in every case arising under Rule 6(e). Circumstances that dictate the need for cooperative action between the courts of different districts will vary, and procedures to deal with the many variations are best left to the rulemaking procedures established by Congress. Undoubtedly there will be cases in which the court to whom the Rule 6(e) request is directed will be able intelligently on the basis of limited knowledge to decide that disclosure plainly is inappropriate or that justice requires immediate disclosure to the requesting party, without reference of the matter to any other court. Our decision today therefore is restricted to situations, such as that presented by this case, in which the District Court having custody of the grand jury records is unlikely to have dependable knowledge of the status of, and the needs of the parties in, the civil suit in which the desired transcripts are to be used.

The judgment of the Court of Appeals is reversed, and the case remanded for further proceedings consistent with this opinion.

[Justice Rehnquist's concurring opinion is omitted.]

MR. JUSTICE STEVENS, with whom THE CHIEF JUSTICE and MR. JUSTICE STEWART join, dissenting.

Although I join all but the last nine paragraphs of the Court's opinion, I cannot agree with the conclusion that the District Judge sitting in the Central District of California should not have granted access to the grand jury transcripts subject to the conditions stated in his order. More fundamentally, I do not share the Court's readiness to review the District Judge's exercise of his broad discretion in this matter in the absence of any allegation of egregious abuse on his part and in the face of the confirmation of his conclusion by the Court of Appeals.

* * *

34. Because the District Court for the Central District of California did not have the knowledge necessary to make an evaluation of the relative needs for secrecy and disclosure, we express no view whether on these facts a court with such knowledge properly could have ordered release of the requested transcripts.

Notes And Questions

1. *Principles of grand jury secrecy.* The common law principle of grand jury secrecy, noted in *Douglas Oil,* has been codified in Rule 6(e) of the Federal Rules of Criminal Procedure as well as numerous state statutes and rules. For a comprehensive treatment of issues of grand jury secrecy, see 2 Beale et al., Grand Jury Law and Practice ch. 5 (2d ed. 2006).

2. *Procedures for determining disclosure.* Effective in 1983, Federal Rule of Criminal Procedure was amended by adding subsections (3)(D) & (E) to codify and amplify the procedural aspects of *Douglas Oil.* Under these provisions, a petition for disclosure must be filed in the district where the grand jury is convened. Except when the hearing is *ex parte*, which may in some circumstances occur when the government seeks disclosure, notice and a reasonable opportunity to be heard is to be provided to the government and to the parties in the other judicial proceeding. Unless that court can reasonably obtain sufficient information concerning the other judicial proceeding to determine if disclosure is proper, it must transfer the petition to the district court where that case is pending. The transferring court is to forward, together with the material sought to be disclosed, a written assessment of the need for continued secrecy.

3. *Witness disclosure.* Federal Rule of Criminal Procedure 6(e) does not prohibit a witness who testifies before the grand jury from revealing his or her own testimony. See, e.g., In re Grand Jury Investigation (Lance), 610 F.2d 202, 217 (5th Cir.1980). However, if the witness declines to provide the information, the party seeking the information generally has no right to compel disclosure. In re Swearingen Aviation Corp., 605 F.2d 125, 127 (4th Cir.1979). Moreover, principles restricting discovery in connection with criminal litigation may even prevent disclosure. In re Application of Eisenberg, 654 F.2d 1107, 1113 (5th Cir.1981). When the witness does not wish to disclose his or her testimony, is it appropriate to consider the witness as holder of the privilege?

4. *Showing required for disclosure. Douglas Oil* requires a civil litigant to show "particularized need" before obtaining information from a grand jury investigation for use in connection with another judicial proceeding. Related issues arise when government attorneys, other than those handling the grand jury investigation, seek grand jury information for use in connection with enforcement activities by an administrative agency or in civil litigation where the government is a party. The Supreme Court has held generally that many of the same principles apply to disclosure to other government attorneys as apply in private civil litigation under *Douglas Oil.* In United States v. Baggot, 463 U.S. 476 (1983), the Court held that disclosure in connection with a civil tax audit was not "preliminar[y] to or in connection with a judicial proceeding" under Fed.R.Crim.P. 6(e)(3)(C)(i) and therefore was not authorized under the Rule. In United States v. Sells Eng'g, Inc., 463 U.S. 418 (1983), it held that attorneys in the civil division of the Justice Department were not entitled to automatic disclosure of grand jury information under Rule 6(e)(3)(A)(i), which permits disclosure to "attorneys for the government," but rather they must obtain the transcripts by court order upon a showing of particularized need under Rule 6(e)(3)(C)(i). Howev-

er, in United States v. John Doe, Inc. I, 481 U.S. 102 (1987), the Court relaxed the strictness of its earlier rulings. First, it held that the same government attorney who conducted the grand jury investigation involving potential criminal antitrust violations could use the grand jury information in connection with a resulting civil antitrust action without demonstrating particularized need since continued use did not amount to disclosure under the Rule. Second, the Court recognized that the concerns underlying grand jury secrecy are "implicated to a much lesser extent when the disclosure merely involves Government attorneys," id. at 112, thereby rendering the required showing less onerous when disclosure is sought for a related government civil enforcement action than for private civil litigation.

5. *Meaning of particularized need.* For an extended treatment of the factors examined by courts in determining "particularized need" as required by *Douglas Oil* for disclosure, see 2 Beale et al., Grand Jury Law and Practice § 7:12 (2d ed. 2006).

SECTION C. INFORMERS

McCRAY v. ILLINOIS

Supreme Court of the United States, 1967.
386 U.S. 300.

MR. JUSTICE STEWART delivered the opinion of the Court.

The petitioner was arrested in Chicago, Illinois, on the morning of January 16, 1964, for possession of narcotics. The Chicago police officers who made the arrest found a package containing heroin on his person and he was indicted for its unlawful possession. Prior to trial he filed a motion to suppress the heroin as evidence against him, claiming that the police had acquired it in an unlawful search and seizure in violation of the Fourth and Fourteenth Amendments. See Mapp v. Ohio, 367 U.S. 643. After a hearing, the court denied the motion, and the petitioner was subsequently convicted upon the evidence of the heroin the arresting officers had found in his possession. The judgment of conviction was affirmed by the Supreme Court of Illinois, and we granted certiorari to consider the petitioner's claim that the hearing on his motion to suppress was constitutionally defective.

[On the hearing of the motion to suppress, the two police officers who had arrested and searched petitioner testified that they had done so pursuant to a tip from an informer who had told them that petitioner had narcotics on his person and could be found in the area of 47th and Calumet Streets. Both officers further testified that the same informer who had supplied the information which led to petitioner's arrest had on numerous previous occasions supplied them with information concerning narcotics activities which had proved accurate and which had led to convictions. On cross-examination of the officers, petitioner's counsel attempted to elicit the informer's identity but was prevented from doing so when prosecution objections to this line of questioning were sustained.][35]

There can be no doubt, upon the basis of the circumstances related by Officers Jackson and Arnold, that there was probable cause to sustain the arrest and incidental search in this case. Draper v. United States, 358 U.S. 307. Unlike the situation in Beck v. Ohio, 379 U.S. 89, each of the officers in this case described with specificity "what the informer actually said, and why the officer thought the information was credible." 379 U.S., at 97. The testimony of each of the officers informed the court of the "underlying circumstances from which the informant concluded that the narcotics were where he claimed they were, and some of the underlying circumstances from which the officer concluded that the informant * * * was 'credible' or his information 'reliable.'" Aguilar v. Texas, 378 U.S. 108, 114. See United States v. Ventresca, 380 U.S. 102. Upon the basis of those circumstances, along with the officers' personal observations of the petitioner, the court was fully justified in holding that at the time the officers made the arrest "the facts and circumstances within their knowledge and of which they had reasonably trustworthy information were sufficient to warrant a prudent man in believing that the petitioner had committed or was committing an offense. Brinegar v. United States, 338 U.S. 160, 175–176; Henry v. United States, 361 U.S. 98, 102." Beck v. Ohio, supra, 379 U.S. 91. It is the petitioner's claim, however, that even though the officers' sworn testimony fully supported a finding of probable cause for the arrest and search, the state court nonetheless violated the Constitution when it sustained objections to the petitioner's questions as to the identity of the informant. We cannot agree.

In permitting the officers to withhold the informant's identity, the court was following well-settled Illinois law. When the issue is not guilt or innocence, but, as here, the question of probable cause for an arrest or search, the Illinois Supreme Court has held that police officers need not invariably be required to disclose an informant's identity if the trial judge is convinced, by evidence submitted in open court and subject to cross-examination, that the officers did rely in good faith upon credible

35. "Q. What is the name of this informant that gave you this information?

"Mr. Engerman: Objection, Your Honor.

"The Court: State for the record the reasons for your objection.

"Mr. Engerman: Judge, based upon the testimony of the officer so far that they had used this informant for approximately a year, he has worked with this individual, in the interest of the public, I see no reason why the officer should be forced to disclose the name of the informant, to cause harm or jeopardy to an individual who has cooperated with the police. The City of Chicago has a tremendous problem with narcotics. If the police are not able to withhold the name of the informant they will not be able to get informants. They are not willing to risk their lives if their names become known.

"In the interest of the City and the law enforcement of this community, I feel the officer should not be forced to reveal the name of the informant. And I also cite People vs. Durr.

"The Court: I will sustain that.

"Mr. Adam: Q. Where does this informant live?

"Mr. Engerman: Objection, your Honor, same basis.

"The Court: Sustained."

information supplied by a reliable informant. This Illinois evidentiary rule is consistent with the law of many other States. In California, the State Legislature in 1965 enacted a statute adopting just such a rule for cases like the one before us:

> "[I]n any preliminary hearing, criminal trial, or other criminal proceeding, for violation of any provision of Division 10 (commencing with § 11000) of the Health and Safety Code, evidence of information communicated to a peace officer by a confidential informant, who is not a material witness to the guilt or innocence of the accused of the offense charged, shall be admissible on the issue of reasonable cause to make an arrest or search without requiring that the name or identity of the informant be disclosed if the judge or magistrate is satisfied, based upon evidence produced in open court, out of the presence of the jury, that such information was received from a reliable informant and in his discretion does not require such disclosure." California Evid.Code § 1042(c).

The reasoning of the Supreme Court of New Jersey in judicially adopting the same basic evidentiary rule was instructively expressed by Chief Justice Weintraub in State v. Burnett, 42 N.J. 377, 201 A.2d 39:

> "If a defendant may insist upon disclosure of the informant in order to test the truth of the officer's statement that there is an informant or as to what the informant related or as to the informant's reliability, we can be sure that every defendant will demand disclosure. He has nothing to lose and the price may be the suppression of damaging evidence if the State cannot afford to reveal its source, as is so often the case. And since there is no way to test the good faith of a defendant who presses the demand, we must assume the routine demand would have to be routinely granted. The result would be that the State could use the informant's information only as a lead and could search only if it could gather adequate evidence of probable cause apart from the informant's data. Perhaps that approach would sharpen investigatorial techniques, but we doubt that there would be enough talent and time to cope with crime upon that basis. Rather we accept the premise that the informer is a vital part of society's defensive arsenal. The basic rule protecting his identity rests upon that belief.
>
> * * *
>
> "We must remember also that we are not dealing with the trial of the criminal charge itself. There the need for a truthful verdict outweighs society's need for the informer privilege. Here, however, the accused seeks to avoid the truth. The very purpose of a motion to suppress is to escape the inculpatory thrust of evidence in hand, not because its probative force is diluted in the least by the mode of seizure, but rather as a sanction to compel enforcement officers to respect the constitutional security of all of us under the Fourth Amendment. State v. Smith, 37 N.J. 481, 486, 181 A.2d 761 (1962).

If the motion to suppress is denied, defendant will still be judged upon the untarnished truth.

* * *

"The Fourth Amendment is served if a judicial mind passes upon the existence of probable cause. Where the issue is submitted upon an application for a warrant, the magistrate is trusted to evaluate the credibility of the affiant in an *ex parte* proceeding. As we have said, the magistrate is concerned, not with whether the informant lied, but with whether the affiant is truthful in his recitation of what he was told. If the magistrate doubts the credibility of the affiant, he may require that the informant be identified or even produced. It seems to us that the same approach is equally sufficient where the search was without a warrant, that is to say, that it should rest entirely with the judge who hears the motion to suppress to decide whether he needs such disclosure as to the informant in order to decide whether the officer is a believable witness." 42 N.J., at 385–388, 201 A.2d, at 43–45.

What Illinois and her sister States have done is no more than recognize a well-established testimonial privilege, long familiar to the law of evidence. Professor Wigmore, not known as an enthusiastic advocate of testimonial privileges generally,[36] has described that privilege in these words—

"A genuine privilege, on * * * fundamental principle * * *, must be recognized for the *identity of persons supplying the government with information concerning the commission of crimes.* Communications of this kind ought to receive encouragement. They are discouraged if the informer's identity is disclosed. Whether an informer is motivated by good citizenship, promise of leniency or prospect of pecuniary reward, he will usually condition his cooperation on an assurance of anonymity—to protect himself and his family from harm, to preclude adverse social reactions and to avoid the risk of defamation or malicious prosecution actions against him. The government also has an interest in nondisclosure of the identity of its informers. Law enforcement officers often depend upon professional informers to furnish them with a flow of information about criminal activities. Revelation of the dual role played by such persons ends their usefulness to the government and discourages others from entering into a like relationship.

"That the government has this privilege is well established and its soundness cannot be questioned." (Footnotes omitted.) 8 Wigmore, Evidence § 2374 (McNaughton rev. 1961).

In the federal courts the rules of evidence in criminal trials are governed "by the principles of the common law as they may be interpreted by the courts of the United States in the light of reason and

36. See 8 Wigmore, Evidence § 2192 (McNaughton rev. 1961).

experience."[37] This Court, therefore, has the ultimate task of defining the scope to be accorded to the various common law evidentiary privileges in the trial of federal criminal cases. See Hawkins v. United States, 358 U.S. 74. This is a task which is quite different, of course, from the responsibility of constitutional adjudication. In the exercise of this supervisory jurisdiction the Court had occasion 10 years ago, in Roviaro v. United States, 353 U.S. 53, to give thorough consideration to one aspect of the informer's privilege, the privilege itself having long been recognized in the federal judicial system.[38]

The *Roviaro* case involved the informer's privilege, not at a preliminary hearing to determine probable cause for an arrest or search, but at the trial itself where the issue was the fundamental one of innocence or guilt. The petitioner there had been brought to trial upon a two-count federal indictment charging sale and transportation of narcotics. According to the prosecution's evidence, the informer had been an active participant in the crime. He "had taken a material part in bringing about the possession of certain drugs by the accused, had been present with the accused at the occurrence of the alleged crime, and might be a material witness as to whether the accused knowingly transported the drugs as charged." 353 U.S., at 55. The trial court nonetheless denied a defense motion to compel the prosecution to disclose the informer's identity.

This Court held that where, in an actual trial of a federal criminal case,

> "the disclosure of an informer's identity * * * is relevant and helpful to the defense of an accused, or is essential to a fair determination of a cause, the privilege must give way. In these situations the trial court may require disclosure and, if the Government withholds the information, dismiss the action. * * *
>
> "We believe that no fixed rule with respect to disclosure is justifiable. The problem is one that calls for balancing the public interest in protecting the flow of information against the individual's right to prepare his defense. Whether a proper balance renders nondisclosure erroneous must depend on the particular circumstances of each case, taking into consideration the crime charged, the possible defenses, the possible significance of the informer's testimony, and other relevant factors." 353 U.S., at 60–61, 62 (Footnotes omitted.)

The Court's opinion then carefully reviewed the particular circumstances of Roviaro's trial, pointing out that the informer's "possible testimony was highly relevant * * * ," that he "might have disclosed an entrapment * * * ," "might have thrown doubt upon petitioner's identity or on the identity of the package * * * ," "might have testified to petitioner's possible lack of knowledge of the contents of the package that he 'transported' * * * ," and that the "informer was the sole

37. Rule 26, Fed.Rules Crim.Proc.

38. See Scher v. United States, 305 U.S. 251; In re Quarles & Butler, 158 U.S. 532; Vogel v. Gruaz, 110 U.S. 311.

participant, other than the accused, in the transaction charged." 353 U.S., at 63–64. The Court concluded "that, under these circumstances, the trial court committed prejudicial error in permitting the Government to withhold the identity of its undercover employee in the face of repeated demands by the accused for his disclosure." 353 U.S., at 65.

What *Roviaro* thus makes clear is that this Court was unwilling to impose any absolute rule requiring disclosure of an informer's identity even in formulating evidentiary rules for federal criminal trials. Much less has the Court ever approached the formulation of a federal evidentiary rule of compulsory disclosure where the issue is the preliminary one of probable cause, and guilt or innocence is not at stake. Indeed, we have repeatedly made clear that federal officers need *not* disclose an informer's identity in applying for an arrest or search warrant. As was said in United States v. Ventresca, 380 U.S. 102, 108, we have "recognized that 'an affidavit may be based on hearsay information and need not reflect the direct personal observations of the affiant,' so long as the magistrate is 'informed of some of the underlying circumstances' supporting the affiant's conclusions and his belief that any informant involved '*whose identity need not be disclosed* * * * was "credible" or his information "reliable."' Aguilar v. Texas, supra, 378 U.S., at 114." (Emphasis added.) See also Jones v. United States, 362 U.S. 257, 271–272; Rugendorf v. United States, 376 U.S. 528, 533. And just this Term we have taken occasion to point out that a rule virtually prohibiting the use of informers would "severely hamper the Government" in enforcement of the narcotics laws. Lewis v. United States, 385 U.S. 206, 210.

In sum, the Court in the exercise of its power to formulate evidentiary rules for federal criminal cases has consistently declined to hold that an informer's identity need always be disclosed in a federal criminal trial, let alone in a preliminary hearing to determine probable cause for an arrest or search. Yet we are now asked to hold that the Constitution somehow compels Illinois to abolish the informer's privilege from its law of evidence, and to require disclosure of the informer's identity in every such preliminary hearing where it appears that the officers made the arrest or search in reliance upon facts supplied by an informer they had reason to trust. The argument is based upon the Due Process Clause of the Fourteenth Amendment, and upon the Sixth Amendment right of confrontation, applicable to the States through the Fourteenth Amendment. Pointer v. Texas, 380 U.S. 400. We find no support for the petitioner's position in either of those constitutional provisions.

The arresting officers in this case testified, in open court, fully and in precise detail as to what the informer told them and as to why they had reason to believe his information was trustworthy. Each officer was under oath. Each was subjected to searching cross-examination. The judge was obviously satisfied that each was telling the truth, and for that reason he exercised the discretion conferred upon him by the established law of Illinois to respect the informer's privilege.

Nothing in the Due Process Clause of the Fourteenth Amendment requires a state court judge in every such hearing to assume the arresting officers are committing perjury. "To take such a step would be quite beyond the pale of this Court's proper function in our federal system. It would be a wholly unjustifiable encroachment by this Court upon the constitutional power of States to promulgate their own rules of evidence * * * in their own state courts * * * ." Spencer v. Texas, 385 U.S. 554, 568–569.

The petitioner does not explain precisely how he thinks his Sixth Amendment right to confrontation and cross-examination was violated by Illinois' recognition of the informer's privilege in this case. If the claim is that the State violated the Sixth Amendment by not producing the informer to testify against the petitioner, then we need no more than repeat the Court's answer to that claim a few weeks ago in Cooper v. California:

> "Petitioner also presents the contention here that he was unconstitutionally deprived of the right to confront a witness against him, because the State did not produce the informant to testify against him. This contention we consider absolutely devoid of merit." 386 U.S. 58, at 62.

On the other hand, the claim may be that the petitioner was deprived of his Sixth Amendment right to cross-examine the arresting officers themselves, because their refusal to reveal the informer's identity was upheld. But it would follow from this argument that no witness on cross-examination could ever constitutionally assert a testimonial privilege, including the privilege against compulsory self-incrimination guaranteed by the Constitution itself. We have never given the Sixth Amendment such a construction, and we decline to do so now.

Affirmed.

MR. JUSTICE DOUGLAS, with whom THE CHIEF JUSTICE, MR. JUSTICE BRENNAN and MR. JUSTICE FORTAS concur, dissenting.

* * *

In Roviaro v. United States, 353 U.S. 53, 61, we held that where a search *without a warrant* is made on the basis of communications of an informer and the Government claims the police had "probable cause," disclosure of the identity of the informant is normally required. In no other way can the defense show an absence of "probable cause." By reason of Mapp v. Ohio, supra, that rule is now applicable to the States.

In Beck v. Ohio, 379 U.S. 89, 96, we said:

> "An arrest without a warrant bypasses the safeguards provided by an objective predetermination of probable cause, and substitutes instead the far less reliable procedure of an after-the-event justification for the arrest or search, too likely to be subtly influenced by the familiar shortcomings of hindsight judgment."

For that reason we have weighted arrests with warrants more heavily than arrests without warrants. See United States v. Ventresca, 380 U.S. 102, 106. Only through the informer's testimony can anyone other than the arresting officers determine "the persuasiveness of the facts relied on * * * to show probable cause." Aguilar v. Texas, 378 U.S. 108, 113. Without that disclosure neither we nor the lower courts can ever know whether there was "probable cause" for the arrest. Under the present decision we leave the Fourth Amendment exclusively in the custody of the police. As stated by Mr. Justice Schaefer dissenting in People v. Durr, 28 Ill.2d 308, 318, 192 N.E.2d 379, 384, unless the identity of the informer is disclosed "the policeman himself conclusively determines the validity of his own arrest." That was the view of the Supreme Court of California in Priestly v. Superior Court, 50 Cal.2d 812, 818, 330 P.2d 39, 43:

> "Only by requiring disclosure and giving the defendant an opportunity to present contrary or impeaching evidence as to the truth of the officer's testimony and the reasonableness of his reliance on the informer can the court make a fair determination of the issue. Such a requirement does not unreasonably discourage the free flow of information to law enforcement officers or otherwise impede law enforcement. Actually its effect is to compel independent investigations to verify information given by an informer or to uncover other facts that establish reasonable cause to make an arrest or search."

There is no way to determine the reliability of Old Reliable, the informer, unless he is produced at the trial and cross-examined. Unless he is produced, the Fourth Amendment is entrusted to the tender mercies of the police. What we do today is to encourage arrests and searches without warrants. The whole momentum of criminal law administration should be in precisely the opposite direction, if the Fourth Amendment is to remain a vital force. Except in rare and emergency cases, it requires magistrates to make the findings of "probable cause." We should be mindful of its command that a judicial mind should be interposed between the police and the citizen. We should also be mindful that "disclosure, rather than suppression, of relevant materials ordinarily promotes the proper administration of criminal justice." Dennis v. United States, 384 U.S. 855, 870.

Notes and Questions

1. *Validity and wisdom of balancing test.* Despite the narrowly divided vote in *McCray*, its balancing test has remained the law, almost without challenge. For strong criticism of the opinion, see Grano, A Dilemma for Defense Counsel: *Spinelli–Harris* Search Warrants and the Possibility of Police Perjury, 1971 U.Ill.L.F. 405. See generally Quinn, *McCray v. Illinois*: Probable Cause and the Informer's Privilege, 45 Denv. L.J. 399 (1968); 2 Imwinkelried, The New Wigmore: Evidentiary Privileges § 7.3 (2002); 2 LaFave, Search and Seizure § 3.3(g) (4th ed. 2004); 1 McCormick, Evidence § 111 (6th ed. 2006).

2. *Alternative of in camera inspection.* Where an informer's identity is relevant to the existence of probable cause for an arrest or search without a warrant, the dissenting Justices suggest that the choice available is between allowing cross-examination of the informer and entrusting the Fourth Amendment to the "tender mercies of the police." A number of courts have concluded that an *in camera* examination by the court offers an intermediate alternative between disclosure and accepting blindly the word of the officer. See, e.g., United States v. Moore, 522 F.2d 1068, 1072 (9th Cir.1975) ("The *in camera* procedure provides an equally-acceptable accommodation of the competing interests of the Government and the accused * * * [where] the question is whether a law enforcement officer has lied."). Does this procedure adequately protect the defendant's interest since cross-examination will not be possible in the absence of defense counsel? Compare Quinn, note 1, supra, 45 Denv. L.J. at 420 (arguing that procedure is ineffective without cross-examination), with Grano, note 1, supra, 1971 U.Ill.L.F. at 447 (arguing that, since the issue at the suppression hearing is limited to whether the officer lied, *in camera* proceedings are sufficient).

3. *Procedures for in camera inspection.* State v. Casal, 699 P.2d 1234, 1238 (Wash.1985) (en banc), sets out procedures for the *in camera* proceedings: (1) the prosecutor may be present but defendant and counsel are strictly excluded; (2) defense counsel may submit written questions to be asked by the court; (3) a transcript shall be prepared for appellate review; and (4) precautions are to be taken to protect the informant. See also People v. Darden, 313 N.E.2d 49, 52 (N.Y.1974). Would it not be appropriate to permit the attendance of defense counsel under a protective order? See United States v. Anderson, 509 F.2d 724, 729–30 (9th Cir.1974) (approving counsel's presence); State v. Russell, 580 S.W.2d 793, 794 (Tenn.Crim.App. 1978) (same). But see 2 LaFave, Search and Seizure § 3.3(g), at 215 n.458 (4th ed. 2004) (arguing that most informants will not believe that defense counsel will keep their identities confidential from the defendant). See also State v. Richardson, 529 A.2d 1236, 1241 (Conn.1987) (expressing concern that requiring informer to attend any hearing entails substantial risk of disclosure of identity).

4. *Showing required for in camera inspection.* An *in camera* inspection clearly need not be held in every case. What is the nature of the showing that the defendant must make in order to require such a hearing? Professor LaFave argues that the showing should not be onerous:

> [B]ecause the protection-of-informer-anonymity interest and protection-against-police-perjury interest do not collide head on as they do when he questions whether full disclosure of the informant's identity should be made, it should not take much to prompt the suppression hearing judge to order such a hearing. If the defendant "has fairly put in issue" the existence of the informant, whether the officer's report of the informer's prior reliability is truthful, or whether the officers recitation of what the informant told him is correct, then an in camera hearing should be held.

2 LaFave, Search and Seizure § 3.3(g), at 217 (4d ed. 2004). See also People v. Vauzanges, 634 N.E.2d 1085 (Ill.1994) (court may order *in camera* hearing if it doubts the credibility of the affiant with respect to the existence of the

informant). But see People v. Luttenberger, 784 P.2d 633 (Cal.1990) (imposing rather onerous standard for *in camera* hearing).

5. *Privilege in civil cases.* The privilege is also available in civil cases. See, e.g., Hoffman v. Reali, 973 F.2d 980 (1st Cir.1992); Coughlin v. Lee, 946 F.2d 1152 (5th Cir.1991); Holman v. Cayce, 873 F.2d 944 (6th Cir.1989); Cullen v. Margiotta, 811 F.2d 698 (2d Cir.1987).

6. *Privilege for surveillance location.* Courts have developed an analogous privilege applicable to police surveillance locations. United States v. Green, 670 F.2d 1148 (D.C.Cir.1981); Bueno v. United States, 761 A.2d 856 (D.C.2000); Commonwealth v. Lugo, 548 N.E.2d 1263 (Mass.1990); State v. Garcia, 618 A.2d 326 (N.J.1993). The government's strongest interest is in insuring the safety of private citizens who permit the police to use their property. United States v. Harley, 682 F.2d 1018, 1020 (D.C.Cir.1982). For limitations on this privilege, see United States v. Foster, 986 F.2d 541, 542–44 (D.C.Cir.1993). For a contrary view, see State v. Darden, 41 P.3d 1189, 1196–97 (Wash.2002) (ruling that no surveillance location privilege exists under state statutory or common law and that the court has no authority to create such a privilege).

Index

References are to Pages

References are to Pages

References are to Pages

References are to Pages

†

Praise for the Author

"Judith Kay is a prolific writer who has published wonderful love stories, including a trilogy, "Love Takes a Chance." Her newest release is non-fiction entitled, Unspoken-ness, a collection of stories that offer a perspective on grief—on life and living, and death and dying. These stories are sure to touch many lives. Judith Kay also promotes other authors by carrying their books at her terrific brick and mortar store, JK Books & Gifts in Iowa. Check out her work store at https://www.facebook.com/JudithKayWrites."

-Laurie Fagen, Author, Blogger, Podcaster, Artist
www.readlauriefagen.com

"Judith Kay's writing style uses real life experiences to connect with the reader. The narrative includes the main character's thoughts, drawing the reader hungry for more with the turn of each page. Her scenes are so vivid you see them play in your mind as if watching a movie, and the characters are so real that you would recognize them if they walked down the street or lived in your own neighborhood. The combination of a family drama intertwined with new a new romance is relatable, practical, and applicable to life. You will find yourself laughing and crying all at once, sometimes within the same chapter. Judith Kay's passion for storytelling is evident in all of her writing. It will not disappoint."

-Wendy Olinger, Senior Editor

Contents

1 *Mind Over Body*

Samira

The room began to lighten with the first signs of daylight. Samira lay perfectly still watching him sleep. *This is my house. My bed. But he's not my husband.* Just the same, his steady breathing was almost comforting. *I was afraid I'd forgotten how to be with a man.* Memories from the night before proved otherwise. *Was that me? Or was it the wine working its spell?* Samira closed her eyes and allowed his touch to permeate her memory. She caught herself the instant before she fell back to sleep. *Somehow, I think it is safer to get up than allow him to awake with me still in bed.*

Steam from the shower filled the bathroom. Samira stepped into the steady stream of the rain shower hoping to diffuse the uneasiness of the morning. *It seems like so long ago.* She tipped her back and let her hair fall wet against her back. *Time used to pass like that… hours that melted into timelessness.* The rich scent of shampoo mixed with the steam. *I let him take me to a place I purposely banished from memory.* Ever so gently the man in her bed lured her away from motherhood into womanhood.

Samira turned under the water like a ballerina as she rinsed her hair. *His kiss, that touch, it all rushes back.* A sudden mix of emotions emerged, causing Samira to swallow hard to prevent new tears from spilling over. *Dear God, what have I done?* One part longed for more of the same. The other scolded her vulnerability and lack of willpower.

The rhythm of the water reinforced the shame that was beginning to rise. *Now what I am supposed to do? I made a promise to raise the girls first, then pursue my own interests.* Samira stepped out of the shower and toweled dry. *So, is this me pursuing my own interests? Or is it me toying with my aloneness?*

The man in Samira's bed had rolled onto his stomach and stretched out between the sheets. *How can he sleep so soundly while the voices in my head are screaming?* She slipped a V-neck t-shirt over her head and adjusted her wet hair. *The fact of the matter is, I made a cognitive decision to sleep with him.* She shook her head at her own lack of discernment.

Samira stepped into a pair of khaki shorts wondering why she was so drawn to this man. *I don't even know his last name, for Heaven's sake.* She silently studied him in the mirror as she brushed her hair.

Signs of a morning beard darkened his chiseled cheekbones. *There's more silver in his hair than I noticed before.* Tan lines over his shoulders indicated he'd worn a tank top outside in the sun. *He's handsome even in his sleep.* Samira shook off a tingle of excitement that ran the length of her spine. *There are so many things I wish I knew about him.* She flipped her hair over her shoulders. *Or maybe it's easier if I don't know.*

Wooden slats in the dining room window cast patterned sunlight across the kitchen floor. Samira pressed the brew button on the Keurig. Seconds later, she lifted her favorite mug to her lips and leaned against the counter to survey the remnants of the night before. Dirty dishes were stacked on the counter. Unfamiliar keys were on the dining room table. A designer sports jacket hung over the back of a dining room chair.

When was the last time I felt so comfortable with a man? Goose bumps prickled her skin when she recalled the moment, she crossed the line and surrendered to spontaneous foreplay.

It was with Tom. Right here in this house, and in the same bed. The consequences of her decision suddenly seemed very threatening. *What do I say to the man who serenaded me all the way to my bed...to the man who is not my husband?*

Samira sipped the coffee. *Something tells me he won't be as intimidated by this morning's circumstances as I am.* That thought was instantly maddening. *I've worked hard to protect myself from these feelings.* She started to load the dishwasher more out of habit than anything else. *Who is he to waltz into my life and shatter my defenses?* She rinsed the plates and put them in the racks. A single drop of wine was peacefully resting on the bottom of his glass. Samira watched as the deep red drop stretch slowly toward the drain.

I closed the door to romance and intimacy so long ago. Her memory skipped back to another candlelit dinner. *I served wine with that dinner too, but at least my date was my husband.* She dipped her finger into the leftover wine in the other glass then placed her finger on her tongue. *What made me so willing?*

Samira returned to her bedroom. He was still in the same position, content in his morning slumber. *What do I tell the girls when they ask me what I did on my date? And Norma. What do I tell her when she asks what I did all weekend while the girls were away?* She took note of the clock on the nightstand. Without thinking, she straightened a framed photo of her and Tom.

I'm sure Mrs. Barnes has already spotted his truck in my driveway and Lord knows she will talk. And my brother would have some words of wisdom for me under these circumstances. But these thoughts weren't nearly as accusing as the one that nagged the hardest: *What would my parents say if they knew I slept with a man I hardly even know?*

Samira crossed the bedroom and gathered his clothes off the floor. *He said he had a late morning appointment.* Her eyes moved back to the clock. *But it's only seven.* She carefully draped his pants over an easy chair. He was still sound asleep. *Even if it's not Tom, it's kind of sexy to have a man in my bed.* She decided to let him wake on his own.

Back in the kitchen the coffee had cooled considerably. *What kind of appointment do you schedule on a Saturday morning?* Samira warmed her coffee in the microwave before taking a seat on a barstool at the island. *I don't even know what he does for a living.*

Sex always comes with obligation. Samira cringed at the voice in her head. *Tom said that to me the night he proposed.* She shuddered at her immediate circumstances. *What if I've created a new obligation for him?* The keys to his truck were within reach. Samira fingered them thoughtfully. *Or have I created an obligation for me?*

Several minutes passed as she considered the ramifications of the morning. *Once he's awake, I'll offer him breakfast, and then he can simply be on his way.* She brewed a second cup of coffee. *I'll be hospitable but firm.* She silently refused to become anyone's obligation.

2 The Morning After

Joseph Phillip

J.P. Ralston rolled into the empty space next to him and raised his arms over his head. *What time is it?* It wasn't unusual to awake in an unfamiliar bed. He checked the time on his watch. *Seriously?* He confirmed the lateness of the hour with the digital clock on the nightstand. *Shit. No way you're going to make the driving range before going to the office now.*

He searched the room for his clothes. *In all my experience, I've never had a woman pick up my clothes for me.* After a trip to the bathroom, he pulled the button-down shirt over his shoulders. His phone was on the chair next to his pants. He swiped to check messages.

Mike, Denise, and the ex-wife. He took time to view the one from Denise. "Affidavits arrived. See you at 10 AM." J.P. laid the phone on the nightstand and stepped into his pants. *Ten o'clock should be doable.*

He shook his head. *Gut feeling told me to leave while I still had the power to make that decision.* He slipped his foot into a shoe. *But it was all good.* He smiled at the recollection of the entire evening. *In fact, it was incredibly good.*

J.P. leaned over to tie his shoes and came face to face with a photograph. The woman was smiling her gorgeous smile, but her arms were wrapped around another man. *Who the hell is he?* The picture tied a knot in J.P.'s stomach. *I know she was not wearing a ring. I always check that.* He couldn't help but look at the picture again. *How long ago* was *that was taken?* His eyes cautiously scanned the room in search of evidence. *Maybe I don't want to know who he is.*

Sunlight flooded the front rooms as J.P. stepped out of the bedroom. She was sitting at the island with her back to him. *Why did she let me sleep so late?* J.P. took in her quiet presence as he buttoned his shirt.

Samira glanced over her shoulder. "How long have you been standing there?"

"How long have you been awake?"

"You first."

J.P. grinned. "Long enough." *She's more beautiful in the morning than she is at night.* He smoothed the wrinkles in his dress shirt with his hands. "You?"

"Long enough."

And she's quick too. J.P. had to smile at the rhetorical remark.

"Would you like coffee?"

Common courtesy told J.P. to stick around long enough to be polite. *But the gut feeling is usually right.* "No thanks."

"Do you *ever* drink coffee?"

J.P. rolled the cuffs on his shirt and tucked the shirttail inside his dress pants. "Rarely."

"Really." Her voice was full of curiosity. "You *rarely* drink coffee, yet you invited me to the Café Ole Coffee Shop? Twice."

You didn't seem the type to invite to a bar. "Stranger things have happened."

"Hmmm," she sipped her coffee. "Not to me." She climbed off the stool and turned toward the kitchen. "What else can I get for you then? Orange juice? A glass of milk?"

J.P. watched her graceful moves. *In retrospect, it's a damn good thing she was already out of bed before I woke up.* He weighed his options. "Orange juice." *Breakfast is cordial but I never eat first thing in the morning.*

"Cereal? Toast?"

"Cereal." *I've already wreaked havoc with Mike this morning anyway.*

J.P. dared to glance around the room. *No other signs of the man in the photo.* The tidiness and tranquility of the house brought a sense of steadiness. *She's very settled here.* Subconsciously, he drummed his fingertips against the granite countertop of the kitchen island. *The last thing she needs is me meddling in her personal life.*

"The cereal is on the turntable next to the sink." The sound of Samira's voice pulled his thoughts back to the present.

I should probably just go. "Samira—" Her name felt strange rolling off his tongue. *Did I pronounce that right?*

She turned with a look of anticipation.

I don't usually have trouble reading a woman's thoughts, but nothing is registering. "I don't have a lot of time—" Something in her eyes stopped him mid-sentence.

"Don't let me keep you." She set the orange juice and glasses on the breakfast bar.

Shit, Ralston. J.P. took a deep breath. *I'll play this scene out and see where it goes.*

"You're not keeping me." *Cereal won't take long anyway.* He opened the cabinet expecting healthy bran cereals. *This is interesting.* "So, what's your preference? Tony the Tiger, Toucan Sam, or the Silly Rabbit?"

Samira's eyes widened.

Maybe not the health food nut I thought her to be.

"Oh, anything is fine." Color was rising in her cheeks.

Let's see what we have here. J.P. scanned the colorful boxes. "Best hidden picture game in the cupboard." He slid the box over the counter then sat down on the stool next to her.

Samira's face was crimson with embarrassment.

J.P. grinned. "What's the matter? You don't like the silly rabbit?"

"No." She shook her head. "I just didn't realize that's all I had in the pantry."

Let's see where she goes with this one. "Are you saying you don't normally eat cereal in the morning?" J.P. poured cereal into both bowls. *I like the fact she's a little off center.*

"Rarely."

He poured the milk. "And do I understand correctly that you don't eat cereal even though you offered it to me?"

"Stranger things have happened."

She's damn quick. "Not to me." J.P. shared his easy smile. *Touché.* He turned the box around and placed it between their bowls. "Last one to find the hidden rabbit does the dishes."

The momentary light-heartedness relieved the awkwardness of the morning.

"It's been a million years since I read the back of a cereal box." J.P. pushed the empty bowl across the smooth countertop. "Silly rabbit anyway."

"I think you cheated."

Gutsy woman to challenge me. J.P. leaned into the countertop and tipped the box on its side. He directed her eyes to the bottom edge with his finger.

"I knew it."

Humored by the interaction, J.P. watched Samira set her empty bowl aside. The moment they made eye contact, she looked away.

Her eyes are intense. But I still can't read her thoughts. No reason to fight the clock now. He leaned back into the armed barstool. *Mike's already halfway through a bucket of balls.*

"What time is your appointment?"

No personal discussions with a new woman. It's a cardinal rule.

"You did say you had to be somewhere, didn't you?" Samira stepped off the barstool and carried the orange juice to the refrigerator.

Her hips moved with such grace that J.P. caught himself undressing her with his eyes.

Ignore her body and play by the rules. "Yeah, I need to report in at the office around ten."

Samira returned to the breakfast bar and motioned for his empty bowl. A moment of silence passed between them.

"How long will you work today?"

J.P. picked up the empty juice glasses and followed her to the sink. "Until I get the job done." *Why are you answering these questions? Next thing you know she'll be expecting you to call when you're done.* He was very aware of potential expectations. *Don't set her up for failure, Ralston.* He watched her avoid his eyes again.

She set the bowls in the sink and turned around for the glasses. Their hands touched, causing them both to hold the moment.

"Shall I call you later?" *You know better than to go there, Ralston.*

New tension was suddenly present.

Samira quickly wiped her hands on a towel. Her response didn't come right away. She pushed her hair back from her forehead and forced a smile. "If you like."

One moment she's joking around over a cereal box and the next she's holding her thoughts. The sudden resistance in the woman's disposition was puzzling. *I hate this part of the morning after.* J.P. sighed. *Especially when she's so damned tempting.* He watched her put the milk away. *I should have skipped breakfast for the driving range.*

"Listen, Samira..."

This time when she turned, she held his eyes. "I don't want to make you late."

Fair enough. That gives me permission to be on my way. J.P. lifted his sports jacket off the dining room chair. Samira followed only as far as the end of the table. The expression on her face was suddenly transparent to the mixed emotions of the morning.

She really is beautiful. And last night was one of the most incredible experiences of my life. An onslaught of thoughts rushed his mind. *Except for the part when she cried. I'm not sure what that was all about.* There was a thoughtful pause. *Unless it has something to do with the guy in that photo.*

J.P. caught himself. "About last night—"

"It's okay." Samira looked away as her voice trailed off in an open-ended thought.

I seriously doubt that. J.P. swallowed the wave of guilt that stuck in his throat. *I think I'm the one responsible for her confusion.* Instead of making an exit, J.P. walked back to where she was standing. *Be careful but be honest.* Slowly, he ran his fingers through the ends of her dark hair. She stiffened slightly.

"Look, Samira," *Say the words, Ralston. Tell her she was unbelievable.* "Thank you for last night." J.P. was instantly disappointed. *That is NOT what I wanted to say.* He wanted to tell her how incredible the night had been for him. He wanted to tell her how beautiful she was. *I don't understand her tears in the moment, but she was incredible last night.*

J.P. caught her chin as it fell and gently lifted her face with his hand.

Samira closed her eyes and slowly turned her face away. His lips met her cheek.

Damn. Deflated and now equally confused, J.P. turned toward the front door.

"Phil."

The sound of his name stopped him. *Phil.* J.P. turned around in time to see his keys take flight. *What caused me to introduce myself as Phil?* He reached but missed the catch. The keys crashed loudly against the hard floor. *I haven't used my given name in years.* He scooped the keys up off the floor and nodded a silent thanks.

A perfect spring morning met him on the other side of the door. *Yep, I should have been on the driving range.* The sound of his name sounded in his ears again. *It sounds foreign, but it feels natural coming from her.* He stepped off the wooden planks of the porch with nothing more than an over-the-shoulder look to see if Samira was following. *Nope, not there.* He confirmed Mike's cell number vibrating on his cell phone before climbing into his pickup. *I'm going to skip the interrogation and call him back later.*

J.P. rolled down his window. Samira was watching him through the open door. *That's the face that made me use my first name.* He couldn't remember a time when he was so taken by a woman's beauty. *Nor can I remember a time when I've been so tormented by a woman's unpredictable candor.* Suddenly, the freedom of the day lost its attraction.

J.P. drew a deep breath and closed his eyes for a quick moment. When he opened them, she was gone. A solid door sealed the confusion over the whole situation.

3 Reflections

Samira

Samira watched until Phil's truck was out of sight. *I used to stand here, and watch Tom drive off to work every morning.* She could feel Mrs. Barnes watching from across the street. *But back then I didn't feel such an urgent need for privacy.* She calculated how long it would take for the elderly neighbor to circulate the news. *Just what I don't need.*

Something needs to speak louder than the silence resonating in this house. With a single command, Samira told the Alexa speaker to play her favorite station. *J.S. Bach. That should help.* She stopped to straighten a stray magazine on the coffee table, but her thoughts were still in the bedroom. She stepped into the hallway but hesitated at her bedroom door.

Samira Cartwright, you always make your bed. No exceptions. *Except today. Everything is out of order.* Her thoughts were reeling. So much had happened in a short two-week time. Routine habits were tainted with the anticipation that he might call; she couldn't stay focused on daily tasks. *And now even my house is in disarray because of him.*

Samira tucked her hair behind her ears. *I really don't know that much about him, yet there's a strange sense I am not his first overnight affair.* Samira reached for the top sheet. *Sometimes it's like I've known him forever.* She pulled the sheet tight across the mattress. *And then the next moment he's like a total stranger.* As she straightened the pillows, she ran her hand over the pillowcase where Phil had rested his head. *He certainly slept like he was comfortable here.* Samira stretched for the comforter at the foot of the bed. Her nightgown was hanging on a hook, untouched.

Without warning her conscience won out. Samira pushed the comforter all the way onto the floor and grabbed for the top of the sheets. A mix of emotion surged as she stripped the entire bed. *I gave him so much last night.*

Samira plopped down on the edge of the bare mattress and hugged Phil's pillow to her middle. *Face it, girl. You gave him everything.* She caught a whiff of his after shave on the pillowcase. She had never invited a man back to her house. *Not even the man I married.* Samira breathed in his scent again. *This morning I feel so vulnerable but last night that didn't come through at all.*

Baffled by her boldness and frustrated by the confusion, Samira smoothed the pillow on her lap and carefully placed it at the head of the bed. *I'm not ready to wash his pillowcase yet.* She gathered the bathroom towels and added them to the pile of bedding.

As she turned around, she caught her own reflection in the mirror. *Who are you?* The woman she thought she knew so well looked back with a questioning expression.

"What?" Samira spoke out loud to herself. "I had a wonderful evening. There is no reason to be ashamed." She ran a brush through her long dark hair, purposefully avoiding eye contact with herself. *I'm glad he stayed.* She stopped brushing her hair momentarily. *But I'm also glad he's gone.* Tom's picture caught her attention. Subconsciously she turned his wedding band on her right hand. Her own wedding rings were hanging over a hook with laced ribbon.

She recalled her wedding night with Tom in this same room. *I was so scared that night.* The brush caught on a tangle. Samira worked the knot until the brush moved freely again. *But I never told Tom.* She studied his face in the frame. *Did he know how scared I was?*

Samira's thoughts skipped forward in comparison. *I wasn't as scared last night.* Controlled passion permeated every touch. *Oh, how I'd love to have his touch all over again.* A sudden uneasiness in the comparison caused Samira to turn Tom's photo so he wasn't looking directly at her. *Is it really his touch? Or am I still missing Tom?*

Until today Samira had never considered altering her lifestyle. *After Tom was gone, I just never allowed myself to think about having another man in my life.* She had grown extremely comfortable raising her girls as a single parent. *Maybe too comfortable.*

But considering last night, everything had changed. *Oh, Dear God, he made me feel alive again.* Samira ran her hand over his pillow. *I've been just a mom for so long now.*

But she also knew moving into a relationship with a man was not in the master plan. She felt selfish for wanting him to stay and guilty for enjoying him so much. *He didn't resist my seduction, but if this isn't something new for him, how do I know if last night meant anything at all to him?* A new surge of guilt swept over her. *What if I'm simply part of his weekend entertainment?*

"Just keep busy," she spoke out loud. "Do whatever it takes to keep your mind busy."

Disgusted with her mix of emotions, Samira carried the bedding to the laundry room and sorted it into whites and colors. *Maybe my confusion will wash away too.* She started the washer.

"I don't want my mind to be in as much disarray as this house."

The light on the answering machine blinked four new messages but Samira walked on by. She stepped into the garage to recycle the wine bottle, but something stopped her.

"Valpolicella Classico from Sartori." The Italian rolled off her tongue nicely. With a hesitancy she couldn't explain, Samira set the bottle on the floor next to the crate. Sunlight flooded the garage as the overhead door opened. Samira shaded her eyes as she headed toward the mailbox.

"Nice day to be out and about."

Ah, Mrs. Barnes. I knew she was watching. "Beautiful day." *Maybe she didn't notice.* "Your petunias are starting to bloom nicely."

"Petunias are the easy ones." Mrs. Barnes straightened her back with a great deal of effort and peered out from under the wide brim of her straw hat. "Have you had company today?"

I knew it, I knew it, I knew it. Samira mindlessly flipped through the mail. "Enjoy the sunshine, Mrs. Barnes." *Maybe she'll forget.*

"Thank you. You do the same."

Dear God, please make her forget. Samira shook her head and picked up the wine bottle on her way back through the kitchen door. *And while you're at it, maybe you can make me forget last night too.* She smacked the stack of mail onto the counter harder than necessary. *And what in the world am I doing saving this stupid wine bottle?* Nonetheless, it fit into a perfect spot next to the dish drainer under the sink. She thought again. *No, don't make me forget. I need to remember.*

The telephone rang, startling Samira. She caught the knuckle of her finger in the cupboard door. "Hello?" Samira squeezed her hand into a fist to help diffuse the throbbing.

"Hi Mama. What are you doing?"

"Oh Krissy. Hi. I'm just tidying up around here." Samira was jolted back into motherhood. *And trying to ignore Mrs. Barnes.* "What are you doing this morning?"

"Hang on while I switch to speakerphone."

Samira listened as her daughters discussed the features on their grandmother's cell phone.

"There. Can you hear us now?"

"We're both here."

In the background Samira could hear the clatter of dishes and running water.

Obviously, they are in Norma's kitchen.

Kara's voice came on the line with her sister. "Hey, Mama. I wish you were here."

I really don't belong there. "Have you heard from Aunt Ellen yet?"

"Gramma doesn't think she's going to make it home in time." Krissy sounded disappointed. "Grampa says she has to work so she'll have to celebrate later."

Ellen always has to work.

"What did you do last night?" Kara asked excitedly.

"Yeah, how did it go on your—" Krissy was whispering loudly.

"Shhh," Samira quieted her daughters. *Let's not have this conversation on the speakerphone broadcasting into Norma's kitchen.* "We'll talk about it when you get home, okay?"

"Okay," Krissy answered. "Is he cute?"

"Krissy, please, not now." *But yes. I would say he is extremely attractive.*

"Sorry, Mama," Krissy giggled. She changed subjects as quickly as she'd asked the question. "I can't believe Aunt Donna and Uncle Vern have been married for fifty years. That's like forever. You should see the cake Gramma ordered for them."

"Gramma says there will be a houseful tomorrow," Kara interrupted. "We are going to serve the punch."

As the girls rattled on, Samira pictured Tom's family in her mind.

"I think we're going over to swim this afternoon." Krissy brought Samira's thoughts back to the conversation. "We have to get the salads done first so everything is ready to go. Gramma says she can't relax until everything is perfect for the party."

"Gramma wants to talk to you," Kara interjected. "I miss you, Mama."

Before Samira could say goodbye to her daughters, Norma Cartwright was on the line. "Samira, dear, how are you? Did you have a nice evening at home last night? We're so pleased to have the girls with us here and I'm sure you could use the peace and quiet at your house for a few days too. Have you thought any more about joining us tomorrow afternoon?"

Samira took advantage when Norma took a breath. "I think I'll just stay here." She glanced around the living room. The keys and the sports coat were nowhere in sight. *At least the evidence is gone.* "There are several things I need to catch up on. But thank you for the invitation just the same."

"That's fine, dear. We just don't want you to feel left out. Well, honey, we need to wrap up this kitchen work so we can get over to the pool. We'll be fine here, don't you worry about us. Thanks for the call."

The girls called me, Norma. Samira shook her head at her mother-in-law's comments. Before she could reply, Norma said her goodbye and the line went dead.

She tilted her head and stared at the phone in her hand. *It's good for Krissy and Kara to remain active in their grandparents' lives, but I'll take the liberty to distance myself, thank you very much.*

The music had switched to a Minuet. Samira gave the voice command to turn it off. The only sound in the house now was the gentle hum of the washing machine. She picked up her book from the breakfast bar and retreated to the rattan sofa in the sunroom. She curled up against the floral throw pillows and opened the story to the marked page.

Why can't I stop thinking about him? This time she didn't fight it. Samira closed her eyes and sank further into the cushions. *I can still feel the way he held me as we danced in the living room.* He was such a gentleman. She replayed the moment Phil broke from a kiss and suggested maybe he should leave while he could still claim an ounce of willpower. *No way.* She chuckled out loud. *There was no way I was going to let him leave by that time.* His gentle resistance gave way to her seduction.

Samira opened her eyes and stared at the living room floor where they'd danced. *I allowed my heart to speak louder than my head.* She drew her legs tighter to her chest and rested her chin on her knees. *Despite all the promises I made to myself.* She sat reflecting on the tears that spilled over as this man she'd only just met brought her back to a place she had missed so desperately yet been so afraid to seek. *Intimacy. I'd all but forgotten.*

Stop it, stop it, stop it. The inner voice was screaming in her head. Samira sat up on the edge of the sofa and piled her hair on top of her head with both hands. His words sounded again, "*Thank you for last night...*"

They were few but they were perfect. She hadn't realized until this moment how desperately she'd needed to hear them. *I hope he was sincere.* She pictured his face when he stopped to make eye contact. *He seemed sincere.* She shook her hair loose. *I didn't dare kiss him.* Now Samira was standing. *I had to separate my desires from my confusion somehow.*

Samira's eyes searched the room. *I stepped out of my comfort zone and took a chance. But what did I take a chance on? Myself?* The perfect order was suddenly unbearable.

"Okay, girlfriend," she spoke out loud to herself. "You have got to get out of this house."

4 *Fragments*

Joseph Phillip

The house phone was ringing when J.P. Ralston stepped out of the shower. Shifting gears from Samira had been more difficult than he'd anticipated.

Another ring. *Yeah, yeah, hang on.*

Chase, J.P.'s black Labrador, moved out of the way as he reached for the phone next to his bed. *This better be quick. I'm already late for the office.*

"This is J.P."

"J.P., buddy."

Mike.

"I stopped by on my way home last night, but you weren't there. You owe me one now. I fed Chase for you." He continued to ramble. "Who was the broad? Haven't seen her around before."

Ah, the dreaded interrogation. "About this morning—"

"Hope she was worth it. It's not every day I get stood up by my best friend." Mike forced an air of self -pity with a heavy sigh. "Well?"

I really don't have time for this right now. "Why the hell are you calling my house phone?"

"Because you're obviously not answering your cell. So, what's the deal with missing the driving range?"

"I just didn't get up in time, that's all."

"Yeah, right. Gut feeling says you didn't have any trouble getting up." Mike laughed heartily. "Who's the chick anyway?"

I've already ignored gut feelings this morning. J.P. fastened his watch on his wrist as he talked. "When did you see her?"

"I was at the bar when you waltzed her in at the club last night. Taking a big chance bringing a new face into that arena. Stirred up quite a fuss among the waitresses, I might add."

Should have known he'd be at the bar. J.P. half listened. His mind was already on the affidavit waiting on his desk.

"Where'd you meet a broad like that?"

I don't like his inference. "The lady, if you don't mind."

Mike chuckled. "She looks way out of your league."

"Thanks for your vote of confidence." J.P. sorted through a laundry basket for a pair of clean socks. "At the library."

Mike laughed loudly into the phone. "Yeah right. Where'd you really pick her up?" He was still laughing.

"No shit." He identified matching socks. "And I didn't pick her up. I invited her to dinner."

"You sure didn't stick around long for asking her to dinner. By the time I made my way across the room you'd split."

"Hey, Mike, I hate to cut you off, but I'm late for the office."

"What you hate is coughing up details." Another hearty laugh filled the phone. "Tell you what, I'd be more than willing to check in on your *lady* while you're at the office."

There was a slight pause. "Hell, I won't even charge you for the service."

"You touch the lady, and you die, good buddy," J.P. checked his watch again. "But you might check in with Denise this afternoon. We need your signature on an affidavit—"

"I'll check in with Denise in exchange for more particulars on the *lady.*" Mike interrupted playfully. "Where'd you end up for dinner?"

J.P.'s patience was growing thin. "Her place." *No more details on Samira just yet, Mikey.* "The paperwork arrived late yesterday."

Mike's tone was firm when he cut in again, "No details, no favors, Counselor. And by the way, it's Saturday. Screw the affidavit. I'll be on the green by the time you get out of the office. Look me up later."

~~~~~~~

J.P. ascended the outdoor staircase two by two. The red brick of the building radiated with heat from the morning sunshine.

"Mornin' boss." Denise looked up from her computer screen. "Nice you could make it in *around* ten."

Denise's naturally blue eyes appeared greener with the help of colored contacts. Her auburn hair showed signs of new highlights.

"New do?"

She acknowledged the compliment with a nonchalant gesture of her hand. "Nice try but you're still late."

J.P. reviewed the stack of mail.

"I don't have the affidavits yet."

"No, they're on my desk. I haven't looked at them yet." *I've been a little distracted.* "And chances are good we won't see Mike until Monday anyway."

"He'll need to sign before we can move forward."

I know, I know.

Denise fastened some messages to a clipboard then guided her boss's eyes about halfway down the top sheet with an artificial fingernail. "Mr. Hughes has already called this morning needing specifics on his father's Estate. You'll want to call him back today as he's leaving for London on Sunday."

"Tomorrow?"

"Yes, Boss." Denise frowned. "This is Saturday."

J.P. motioned for her to continue.

"You have a message from someone named Mary. She said something about an engagement or something on Friday night. She talked like you had already committed so you might want to check your calendar."

J.P. ran the name through his mind but couldn't put a face with it. "Do you know her? "

"Nope. This one didn't come through me."

"Did she leave any particulars?"

"No bust size or anything." Denise continued. "More importantly, the Mid-America Corporation left a message right before I came in that you should call Mr. Stephenson right away."

J.P. tapped the clipboard with his fingertips. "Call Mr. Hughes and tell him we'll have the documents ready for his review by one o'clock." J.P. moved into his own office. "This estate is taking more time than I'd hoped, Denise. How long will he be out of the country?"

"I'll ask for his timeline." Denise answered from the other room. "This is the very reason we stopped handling estates, Boss. Remember?"

I remember. "We won't make a habit of it." J.P. sat down in his high-backed leather chair and rolled up to the mahogany desk. With the click of a button, he booted his computer and listened to the hard drive whir into action. "The only reason we're assisting with this
~~~~~~~

estate..."

"...Is because Lloyd Hughes played such a huge part in setting up your private practice." Denise finished his sentence. "I know that story."

Satisfied, J.P. continued in a professional mode. "Let's get Mr. Stephenson on the line and see what's on his mind this fine day."

"What should I do about Mary?"

I have no idea who this Mary chick might be. J.P. wrinkled his face in thought. "Let it slide. If it's important, she'll call back."

Soon after his divorce, J.P. learned it was wiser and more conducive to filter his personal calls through Denise. His home number was unlisted and most of his social calls went through Denise. *And it happens to work very well this way.*

"Mr. Stephenson's on line two."

Without hesitation, he picked up the phone to greet his newest client. "Mr. Stephenson, J.P. Ralston here. How can I be of service?"

"J.P., I appreciate you getting back to me on the weekend like this." The executive sounded quite serious. "It seems our on-line system was hacked overnight. I don't have a full report from the technicians yet, but it appears the firewalls failed. Some accounts have been accessed and considerable assets seem to be misplaced."

J.P.'s adrenaline started to pump. *This doesn't sound good.*

"We may need legal counsel as the day progresses."

J.P. went over his morning agenda in his mind. "I can be there by noon, Mr. Stephenson. Is that soon enough?"

"Noon should be fine." There was a slight hesitation. "In fact, make it one o'clock. That will give the technicians another hour to reboot the system after we close for business." Mr. Stephenson addressed a third party then returned to the conversation on the telephone. "Meet me in the main board room, J.P."

"Let's get this Hughes file moving, Denise." He looked up to see his paralegal standing in the doorway ready for action.

"This is Saturday, remember? I want to be home by lunch."

"As long as this report is ready for Hughes, you're out of here at noon as promised. We're going to need permission from city hall to copy these plat maps." He handed Denise two cylindrical containers. "I have the plots and landmarks noted in the diagrams. Hughes will need copies of each page as well as documentation on the boundary lines."

Denise took the canisters. "I'll be at city hall as soon as the doors open Monday morning."

"I'd like to go over the precincts with the city attorney before we deliver to Hughes."

Denise was already on task. "What is the difference in the property tax if the city is right about the property lines?"

"A few hundred thousand dollars. Enough to make it a worthy discussion." The attorney skimmed a document as he spoke. "The key is to find the actual date Lloyd Hughes closed the purchase. If he closed before the city incorporated the township, the family is off the hook."

The boundary information Samira located on the library's computer was inconclusive. *But she gave me enough information to lead the city to believe we have the actual dates of incorporation, whether they're exact or not.* J.P. was still confident he could convince the city to lower the settlement.

Without another word, J.P. closed the door between the offices. He donned his rimless glasses and began to settle into the case. He'd spent several long weeks searching for specific information to secure a position against the city on behalf of the Hughes family. *The information from Samira gives us a fighting chance to win this case.* Another thought intruded. *I wonder if I have a chance with her.* He pushed that thought aside.

A vibration against the attorney's waist indicated a new call on his cell phone. Slightly frustrated at an interruption, he waited a few minutes before checking the message. *Janet. That's the last person I need to talk to this morning.* J.P. cringed at the thought of a confrontation with his ex-wife.

It wasn't until after the Hughes report was compiled that J.P. turned his attention back to the call. Reluctantly he pressed the speed dial on his desk phone.

"It took you long enough to call back." Janet sounded anxious.

Gotta love the attitude.

"I tried to call you at home. Where are you now?" Janet's tone already carried accusations.

"Believe it or not, Jan, it's a busy day at the office. Is there a specific reason for this call?" J.P. forced a business response.

"I wouldn't bother you if it weren't important."

Really? That comes as a surprise to me.

"I'm in over my head with James and we need to talk. I've probably waited too long but kept thinking I could handle it but now I just don't know, and Bruce is tired of—"

"Whoa, whoa, slow down." J.P. ran his hand through his hair. "One thing at a time."

"We have to talk, Phil. This can't wait any longer."

Everything is always overly dramatic and urgent when it comes to Janet. J.P. gave her permission to speak her mind.

"Not on the phone, for crying out loud. This is serious."

J.P. fingered the pile of research on his desk and ran the next forty-eight hours in his mind. The Hughes Estate had to be ready for deposition by mid-week and it was sounding like Mid-America could use up every other free moment. *No. I'm not leaving town this weekend.*

"Casework has dibs on my time, Jan. It's either now or sometime next week. Take your pick."

Several moments of silence followed the response.

"Can you even listen now, Phil? Or is your mind too full of legal issues to care?"

The attorney slowly turned the leather chair away from the stack of papers on his desk. "I can listen." *Momentarily.*

There was a heavy sigh into the phone. "I don't know when you last talked to the boys," she finally began. "But James and I have been locking horns lately." There was a slight hesitation. "Actually, Bruce and James have been going at it for quite some time now; maybe since Christmas; maybe even since last summer..."

That would explain the distance I felt with James on the phone awhile back.

"His choice of friends has been terrible, his grades have bottomed out, and he insists on running his own life." Janet choked back a sob as she continued. "He left last night."

Phil waited for an explanation, but nothing came. "What do you mean, *he left*?"

"He walked out the door." Now Janet's voice was cracking. "Bruce said if he walked out, he couldn't come home." Janet hesitated slightly. "And ...and ...he didn't."

Phil closed his eyes and leaned forward & rested his elbows on his knees. "Look, Jan, James must have some issues to work through. I wouldn't get too worked up about it yet."

"Too worked up?" Janet screamed into the phone. "You didn't hear their words, Phil. We told him to choose between his family and his friends and he didn't come home."

J.P. ignored a tap on the door.

"Have you talked to his friends? Someone knows where he is."

"I've called everywhere. He's nowhere to be found..."

"Who have you talked to?"

"I'm going to call the cops."

"Don't call the cops, Janet." Phil rose from his chair and removed his reading glasses.

"Call Jennie Johnson. Chances are good she'll know where he is."

"Jennie Johnson.?" The shriek in Janet's voice caught Phil off guard. "That little tramp?"

Herein lies the biggest part of the problem. Obviously, they don't approve of his girlfriend. "Careful, Jan. She's tramping around with your son. She probably has a good idea where to find him if he's not with her."

"So, help me," Janet warned. "If I find him with her..."

Case closed. "For Christ's sake, Janet. Do you want him home or not?" J.P. waited for his question to settle. "If you want James home, then it will be in your best interest to not condemn him before you find him." *No wonder he walked out.*

J.P. motioned for Denise to come on into his office. "Make some calls and call me back when you know something more concrete. But don't call the cops." *The last thing James needs right now is for the authorities to get involved.* He pointed to Denise's answer on the clipboard.

"Good God, Phil, I have enough phone numbers for you to fill a book. Which number am I supposed to use?"

"Use the cell." *Eventually they all reach me.* "I'm tied up in a meeting with a client early this afternoon."

"That's great. I can always count on you to be tied up."

Time to end this phone call. "Call me when you know something."

There was an abrupt click as the call ended. *I hate the miles between me and the boys.* Worse yet he hated that James was in trouble at home. *But I wouldn't want to live any closer to Janet either.*

J.P. took a deep breath and exhaled very slowly. The Café Ole` coffee shop at the end of the alley was alive with the approaching rush of the Saturday brunch crowd. *Add this fiasco to my caseload and I'll be lucky to find another noon hour at the coffee shop.*

Time passed but J.P. Ralston was lost somewhere between fatherhood and broken relationships. He detested Janet's accusation of being preoccupied with work, but at the same time, he realized the truth in that statement all too well.

"Anything I can do?" Denise appeared at his side. "It's 12:30."

The only thing J.P. wanted her to do in that moment was reach a woman on the phone; one he thought might understand. *Samira.* He remembered the uncluttered order of her home. *My life is anything but in order.*

"Unfortunately, not." *Hell, I don't even know where I stand with her after this morning. If I stand with her at all.* He looked up into the tinted eyes of his assistant. "I need to get over to Mid-America. I'll finish these files when I get back."

Denise nodded in understanding.

~~~~~~~

J.P. returned to his office a little over an hour later. *What's Denise still doing here?* He pushed open the glass door planning to address the violation of the Saturday noon deadline. He was surprised to find a young man standing with his back to the door. Denise was obviously in the middle of a lengthy discussion. *Who's she talking to?*

"Oh, J.P.," Denise seemed relieved to see her boss. "This is..."

"Uh, uh, R-r-rick." The young man hung his head as he spoke. He stuck his arm straight out.

J.P. took the card from his fingertips and turned it over. *What's he doing with one of my business cards?*

A worn Hard Rock Café t-shirt hung loosely from the boy's shoulders and his baggy shorts showed signs of long-time wear. J.P waited for the young man to speak again but nothing happened.
~~~~~~~

"Would you like to sit down?"

"N-n-no thank-you." Rick glanced up then immediately looked back to the floor again. "Ah-h-I, I have J-James in my c-car."

What the hell? "Here?"

"Y-yes, sir." Rick's lanky arms remained pinned to his side. "In my c-car."

J.P. tried to gather his thoughts. "Denise, get Janet on the phone."

"N-n-no sir. J-James s-said to get him h-here."

J.P.s' eyes went from Denise to Rick then back to Denise. "Hold off a minute." He held out his hand to stop Denise from dialing. "Take me to him, Rick."

J.P. found his youngest son crumpled over in the back seat of an old sedan. The headliner hung low, barely missing the top of James's hair. The car reeked of alcohol and cigarette smoke. J.P. held his breath and pushed James upright into the seat. The boy opened his eyes a crack then closed them again.

"James." There was no response. *I need to get him out of here.* J.P. turned around and faced Rick, who was now standing next to a woman who was just as lanky and awkward. *But first I need any information he might have.*

He took a long hard look at the woman. She held a burning cigarette between two fingers. Her thin hair was uncombed, and her flimsy dress clung to her stark frame.

Rick avoided eye contact, staring into the space between him and the well-dressed attorney. "Th-this is my m-mom."

J.P. was anxious to get James out of the car but forced himself to remain calm.

"I'm James's father." *Where in God's name did James connect with these people?* "J.P. Ralston."

"I think he's going to be okay." The woman spoke gently despite her rough appearance. "But he had a hard night."

J.P. stared at his son, obviously hung over. *What happened to him?* He looked back into the tired face of the woman. "Tell me your name again?"

"Rita." She took a long draw on the cigarette.

"Rita." J.P. repeated the name as he organized his thoughts. "How did James end up with you?" He ran his hand through his hair.

"J-Jennie called m-me to come get him," Rick began hesitantly. "Th-they went to the p-party at the p-ark." His eyes were focused on his friend in the car.

It was all J.P. could do to wait on Rick's stuttered words. *Just talk to me, kid.*

"H-he was m-messed up r-really bad. J-Jennie said h-he c-can't go home."

The woman flicked her cigarette butt onto the pavement and ground it out with the toe of an old shoe. *She looked like she might have something more to say.*

J.P. nodded silent permission for her to speak.

"James is a good boy, Mr. Ralston. Th-this is just a bad time for him." Rita's southern accent was more evident now. "Rick went and got him an' brought him down home. When I got home from work, we got him here to you." Rita hesitated. "He told us to get him here."

J.P.'s mind was racing. "Rick, what were they doing at the party?"

Instantly the boy grew more uncomfortable. He wiped his hands on his ragged shirt and exchanged a frightened look with his mother. She encouraged him to speak.

"It was a r-regular party, sir." Rick stared at his feet. "B-but J-Jennie says there was a f-fight...a bad'n." Rick's eyes moved to his friend again. "Th-that's all she said."

J.P. deliberated Rick's response. *Define regular party. Are we talking alcohol? Drugs? What's that term mean, anyhow?* "Was James in a fight, Rick?"

The young man gasped uneasily and froze in place. "If'n he was ah-ah-I don' know 'bout it." Rick stammered around. "Jennie says he drank too much too fast."

"Mr. Ralston," the mother interjected. "We just picked the boy up. He slept for a while then told us to bring him here." Her eyes softened as she looked over at James in the back seat of her car. "He had a bad night and needs a place to stay 'til he can go home again." She sighed. "Jennie says he can't go home now."

No, he can't go home to Janet, and it sounds like I need to talk to Jennie if I want any specific information. J.P. took a deep breath and began to process what little information he had.

"Rick, do you see that coffee shop at the end of the alley?"

The boy followed J.P.'s finger and nodded.

J.P. opened his wallet. "I need you to go there and ask for a large black coffee to go." Intentionally, he reached for the bony hand of the young man and placed a twenty-dollar bill in his palm.

Without speaking Rick took off in an awkward stride toward the Café Ole. J.P. turned back toward the mother. "Rita, I need to go back upstairs and talk with my assistant. I'll bring my truck around to get James in a few minutes." He hesitated on another thought. "Is there anything I can get for you?"

Rita reached through the open window for a carton of cigarettes. She shook her head as she lit up. "I'll wait here."

J.P. pulled his truck around to the front of the office building. James was almost six and half feet tall. *He's not exactly easy to maneuver in this condition.*

Rick handed J.P. a large, steaming Styrofoam cup with a lid. J.P. placed the cup in a holder on the console. He was quite surprised to see Rick offer the change.

"Oh, no, keep it." J.P. closed the door on his son. Reaching once again for his wallet, he extracted two more bills and laid them in Rick's open hand. "Thanks for getting James down here. James is lucky to have you for a friend." *Damn lucky* J.P. considered his son's condition. *He could have been left for dead alongside of the road somewhere.*

Rita stepped forward and expressed a word of thanks.

It's no doubt been awhile since she's had a couple of extra fifties.

"That's not necessary, Mr. Ralston."

"It's the least I can do." *If I had more on me, I'd give it to them.*

"He's a good boy. We just wanted him to be safe."

J.P. pulled a pen out of his shirt pocket and scribbled his cell number on the back of a new business card. On another card, he asked Rick to write his own phone number.

"Ah-h-I h-hope he's okay," Rick said meekly, glancing in James's direction.

J.P. followed the gaze and shared the same concern. *The worst of it may come after the hangover.*

Denise appeared with a stack of bound files and placed them behind the driver's seat. She made a face when the stench of James's condition hit her nose. She exchanged a worried glance with her employer.

I know. J.P. silently acknowledged her fear. "He'll be alright."

Saying that is one thing. J.P. took a long, hard look at his battered son slumped against the seat belt. *Believing it is another.*

5 Everything is Changing

Samira

Without a direct plan, Samira drove to the Maple Street Library and parked in her reserved space. *Next week would have a smoother start if I could get a little more paperwork off my desk.* Mrs. Haddock was redesigning the information board in the entryway when Samira arrived.

"Miss Samira." The grandmotherly woman shook a finger at her supervisor. "Whatever are you doing here? This is your day off."

Samira quieted the assistant librarian with her finger. "I'm only here to pick up some paperwork." She slipped around the edge of the circulation desk and unlocked the door to her office. *I wouldn't mind working an hour if I had the office to myself.* "I'm not planning to stay."

Mrs. Haddock followed Samira. "Something tells me your girls are away this weekend."

Samira pursed her lips as she flipped through the stack of mail on the corner of her desk. *Nothing that can't wait until Monday.*

"If they were home, you'd be busy with them somewhere instead of searching for something to keep you busy here."

Samira sighed. "You're right. Krissy and Kara are away this weekend." She smiled gently at the woman in the doorway. "I was just out and about and thought I'd pick up the finance reports for one more review before Tuesday's board meeting." *Anything to keep my mind busy.*

Mrs. Haddock rearranged her over-permed hair with her hands. "You really need to enjoy your time off, Miss Samira. I'm sure you have the reports in fine order already."

"Thank you, Helen." Samira slipped the reports into a manila envelope and with a swift twist, secured the string around the round plastic button. "Have you been busy today?"

Mrs. Haddock shook her head and nodded toward the window. "No ma'am. Too nice of a day for the library to be crowded. I have managed to catch up on the odd jobs however." She stepped aside as Samira closed the office door.

"The bulletin board out front looks great," Samira complimented. "It's nice to have a day to get caught up."

The wrinkles along Mrs. Haddock's mouth formed into a smile and her soft brown eyes twinkled slightly. "Thank you, Miss Samira. Have a nice afternoon and change things up a bit. Maybe do something for yourself."

"You do the same." Samira waved with car keys in her hands. *Change things up. Now there's an interesting piece of advice.*

The car was hot from sitting those few minutes in the sun. Samira cracked the sunroof and turned on the air conditioner. *I have no intention of working on library spreadsheets today.* She backed out of her parking space and turned in the direction opposite her house. *But they will be handy if I need a mental distraction later.*

Several blocks passed before Samira realized she didn't have a destination in mind. *I could take Helen's advice and do something for me.* She turned left onto the main thoroughfare and drove toward the new shopping mall. *Last night was for me.* Samira smiled quietly to herself. *My only deadline is meeting Susan at the Civic Center at seven thirty.* She checked her watch. *Plenty of time.*

~~~~~~~

"May I help you?" a salesclerk spoke from behind a rack of clearance items.

Samira's mind was a million miles from the merchandise. "Oh, no, I'm just looking today."

"Are you looking for yourself or for someone else?"

Am I shopping for someone? "Myself, I guess."

"Well," the short, stocky woman pushed a pair of big glasses up on her nose. "You shouldn't be looking in the clearance area. The new summer line is over here." She motioned for Samira to follow. They stopped in front of brightly colored fabrics and summer accessories. "This is where you should be shopping."

It's certainly more cheerful over here. Samira smiled and began to search the size 10 racks. *I really don't need anything new.* She pulled a skirt off the rack and held it out for a better view. *But then again, I haven't purchased anything new since...* Samira's eyes looked far into the distance at nothing. *Since I can't remember when.*

Before she realized it, Samira was in front of a three-way mirror in the dressing room. Assorted colors garnished an ankle-length skirt hanging gracefully from her waist. Samira piled her hair on top of her head so she could see the back view of the sleeveless sweater.

"It's definitely you."

Samira made eye contact with the same salesclerk. "I don't know." She turned around. "I love the skirt." She ran her hands over the broomstick pleats and admired the splashes of color against the navy background. "But I'm not so sure about the top. I really prefer a jeweled neckline and this fuchsia isn't doing much for me."

The stocky salesclerk took a hold of the edge of the skirt. The design took on a new dimension when the pleats were erased. "You're right about the hot pink. Not doing much for you. But I think the V- neckline is fine." She dropped the hem and allowed the skirt to fall naturally once again. "The new Vanderbilt twin sets are the answer. The colors are much softer."

Wearing the merchandise, Samira followed the woman back onto the sales floor. The clerk held up an open weave crocheted tank.

"Yellow?"

The woman held it up to Samira's face. "Yellow or the neutral taupe." She held another color over the edge of the skirt. "They both compliment your olive complexion."

"The open weave seems a bit risqué for me." Samira was already searching for another option.

"Just try it on," the clerk encouraged. "I think you'll be pleasantly surprised. It's not as revealing as it appears."

Samira reached for the taupe sweater and returned to the dressing room. Once again, she admired the new outfit. *Much better color and she's right, the sweater is very elegant.* She turned in the mirror and put her hands against her stomach to flatten it. Samira turned around again. *Just for fun, I think I'll take it home.*

The clerk folded the sweater in tissue paper at the checkout counter and slipped it into a paper shopping bag with the skirt. "You do know about the Memorial Day Shopping Extravaganza coupons, don't you?"

"No, I don't believe I do." Samira tapped her debit card and followed the prompts to complete the transaction.

"You earn one coupon for every item purchased anywhere in the mall all day." The woman slid two coupons across the counter. "You can use them at the food court or movie
~~~~~~~

theaters until five o'clock Monday afternoon of next weekend." She adjusted her large glasses. "If you don't get them used then you can keep them for the Labor Day weekend specials. Or if that doesn't work out, use them at the fall Bridal Fair." She smiled. "The trick is remembering where you put them if you save them that long."

"My daughters love the Bridal Show." Samira stashed the red coupons in the bill compartment of her wallet. "I bring them every year."

"There you go. Don't forget where you put them." The lady made direct eye contact. "How old are you daughters?"

"Thirteen and fourteen."

"I'd never have guessed. You look so young and in love." The clerk handed the bag over the counter. "Enjoy your new outfit ma'am."

Young and in love? Samira blushed. *That's an interesting observation. But I do feel like my cheeks are glowing today.* She glanced in the three-way mirror as she passed by on her way back to the main concourse. *It's only been two weeks since I met him, and things are already changing.* Samira shifted the bag from one hand to the other as she waited in line for frozen yogurt. *I just hope I haven't set myself up for disappointment.*

Her thoughts returned to the circumstances of the morning. *I should have kissed him.* She ordered a small cone and a glass of water. *But I might not have stopped with one kiss, and where would that have landed me?* Samira found an empty bench and sat down. *Back in bed, that's where I'd have ended up.* She caught a drip on the back of the cone with her tongue. *Tom was right. Sex always comes with obligation.* She thought some more. *I don't know if I'm ready for that yet.*

~~~~~~~

Back at the house Samira remade her bed and started a second load of laundry. There were still a couple of hours before she had to meet Susan at the Civic Center. *It's the last chamber concert of the season.* She unpacked her new clothes and hung them on the closet door while she put things back in order. Tom's picture was still turned sideways on the dresser. She started to turn it back then thought again. *I don't want to face him every time I brush my hair.*

Samira sat down on the edge of her bed. *It feels good to sit down for a bit.* She stretched out on top of the quilted comforter and inhaled the trace of aftershave from the pillowcase. As she closed her eyes, the passion in Phil's touch came alive. *How sweet that he waited for my permission.* She allowed her mind to revisit the way he moved his hand into the small of her back. *But surely by then he knew I was going to follow through.*

~~~~~~~

Samira opened her eyes with a start. The digital clock read seven-o'clock. She checked her watch to be sure she wasn't dreaming. When the two matched, she moaned out loud. *There's no way I can be on time now.* A quick change of clothes and slight touchup to her makeup sent Samira out the door on the run.

Susan grabbed Samira by the arm as she traded her car keys for a valet ticket. *I knew she would be frantic.*

"Where have you been? I was beginning to get worried." Susan was directing Samira toward the auditorium as she spoke. "I called your house, and you weren't there so I called your mother, and you weren't there either."

"You called my mother?"

"Not really."

Thank goodness.

"I just wondered if that's where you were." Susan was still guiding Samira by the arm. They crossed the formal lobby before Samira brought Susan to a halt in mid-stride.

"We can't go in during a number."

A tuxedo clad usher held his finger up for them to be quiet.

"I about freaked when you weren't here. You're never late, Samira. Are you feeling alright?"

"I'm fine, really, Susan." Samira tucked a stray hair behind an ear. *How much do I want to tell her?* "I went shopping this afternoon at the new mall then went home and took a nap. I just overslept, that's all." Samira shrugged her shoulders.

Susan's mouth fell open and her bright blue eyes lit up in disbelief. "You went shopping alone? Without the girls?"

The usher motioned again for them to talk more quietly.

Susan put her hands on her wide hips and lowered her voice. "No way. You never go shopping. Especially alone."

I know she'll be totally surprised with this piece of information. "I even bought a new outfit." She leaned away when Susan tried to put her hand against Samira's forehead. *Maybe I'll have an occasion to wear it soon.*

"Something's wrong," Susan stated. "Is there something you're not telling me?" Susan tried to put the back of her hand on Samira's forehead again.

Samira leaned back and gently pushed Susan's hand away. *If you only knew. But Susan is not the one to talk to about Phil.* Samira considered her options. *Then again, maybe I shouldn't bring him up to anyone until I know if I'm going to see him again.*

The sound of muffled applause from within the auditorium beckoned a safe reprieve from the pending conversation. When the usher opened the doors, the women entered the aisle-lit concert hall.

~~~~~~~

Samira breathed in the fresh evening air outside the civic center.

"Are you hungry?" Susan pulled a lightweight jacket over her shoulders. "Samira?" Susan sounded irritated. "Are you feeling alright? You are quite distracted tonight."

"Oh, really, I'm fine," Samira lied.

"You don't look very fine."

"I was just thinking about the concert."

Susan's blonde hair bounced as she shook her head. "It was okay, but not the best. We've had finer performances this season, don't you think?"

Samira brushed a strand of long hair from her face. "Maybe." With a deep breath she changed the subject. "Don't you just love the crisp rush of the spring air?"

"I'm a little cool myself." Susan studied her friend's face carefully. "You parked with the valet, right?"

Samira flipped her parking ticket between her fingers.

"They're open until eleven. Let's grab something to eat then I'll drop you back here." Susan started for her car.

"Wait, Susan, I don't want to keep you from your family." *And I don't know if I'm up to a meal with Susan.*

"Nonsense." Susan linked her arm in Samira's and started for her car again. "It's girls' night out, remember?"

A young couple walked by holding hands. Samira watched them cross the street and disappear around the corner. *I don't remember what it feels like to belong to someone like that anymore.*

Susan was following Samira's eyes. "Did you see someone you know?"

"No."

"Well, you sure were intent on watching something." Susan shook her head. "I don't know what to think about you sometimes, Samira."
~~~~~~~

Why do I let her control me like this? Samira skipped a step to pace Susan's sudden urgency.

Susan drove a few blocks and pulled into a neon-lit diner. The line at the door hinted at a long wait, but the hostess assured them it would only be a few minutes before a table would be available. Samira crossed her arms uncomfortably over her stomach. *I am hungry, but not in this noisy setting.* Her eyes followed lime green and orange neon lines around the top edge of the diner. *Dear God, make this meal pass quickly.*

As promised, they were seated within a few minutes.

I just want something light to hold me over.

Susan looked over the top of her menu. "You're not going to get a salad, are you?"

I wish it didn't make so much difference to Susan what I eat and don't eat. When the waitress came to take their order, she ordered a Chinese Chicken Salad with a glass of water.

"Always watching your diet," Susan mused. "Just once I'd love to see you sink your teeth into a big juicy steak. "I need a few more minutes," she told the waitress.

"I'm not watching my diet. I just don't like to eat heavy before going to bed." Slightly annoyed, Samira shifted in her seat. *It is so loud in here.*

"At least you can go home and go to bed." Susan emptied her thoughts. "I'll have to check on Joey when I get home, put the house back together, and I'm sure Sam will want to get personal in bed." She tilted her head to one side. "Then maybe I'll be able to go to sleep." Susan slapped the menu down on the table and waved for a waitress.

Samira tried to remember what it was like to be a wife and a mother at the same time. It was hard to step back into those shoes. *But I don't ever remember not wanting private time with my husband.*

"How do you do it?" Susan looked Samira directly in the eyes. "You always seem to have everything under control."

Susan has no idea who I am anymore. "For one thing," Samira had to raise her voice to be heard over the music and the televisions playing above them. "I don't have a little one to care for anymore." *For another thing, I've sacrificed a personal agenda.* She hid a smile. *Except for last night.*

The waitress delivered a huge plate of onion rings. Susan pushed the plate into the center of the table. "Dig in. I can't eat all these by myself."

Samira declined the offer politely.

"There you go, watching your diet again." Without warning, Susan changed subjects. "Did I tell you Sam signed me up for golf lessons this summer? He says that's the only place we're ever going to be able to hold an uninterrupted conversation so it's time I learned to swing a club." She continued to talk with a mouthful. "I think there's still room in the class if you'd like to join me."

Golf? That's one of the few personal details I do know about Phil. He plays golf. Samira turned a bite of salad on her fork. "Thanks, but I'll be busy enough with the girls' activities. They're going to babysit for my brother's kids this summer."

"How many kids do they have now anyway?"

"Three," Samira smiled gently at the thought of her nieces and nephew. "Bonnie is just finishing first grade, Lizzie will go into Kindergarten next year and baby Mark just turned two."

"Holy-moly, no wonder they need your girls to babysit." Susan tipped her head. "And what's up in your life? Anything tall dark or handsome?"

Samira almost choked on a bite of salad. "Why would you ask?" *Surely, she doesn't know about last night.*

"Because," Susan stopped talking to take a bite of shrimp. "If you're not seeing anyone, I have someone I think you should meet."

Oh good, she doesn't know.

"Would that be a yes or a no?"

That would be a definite NO. Samira avoided eye contact and rested her fork against the edge of the glass plate. "I don't know Susan." She composed her thoughts. "I'm really not in the market for a man right now." *Unless it's with Phil again.*

"Nor will you ever be." Susan's tone was accusing. "You need to step out of your comfort zone, sister. It's time to experience life outside of your house for a change." Susan pushed her now empty plate aside and motioned for the waitress to pick it up. "Greg is really cute, he's a gentleman, and he's easy to get along with. I'll have him call you then you can make a decision."

"I really don't want him to call me, Susan," Her mind was reeling with memories of another time Susan set her up on a blind date. *I could live without that kind of humiliation again.* "I just prefer to manage my own affairs. Or lack thereof." *Is that what I just started? An affair?*

"Honest, he's a really nice man, Samira. You might like him and fall in love or something. Then we could do family things together like we used to." Susan realized her words too late. "I'm sorry. That didn't come out exactly like I'd planned."

I know. Samira's eyes were fixed on the back of the booth behind Susan. *Everything always goes back to our family outings together.*

"Of course, we could do some things together without a man too," Susan tried to smooth the tension that hung between them. "It's just hard for Sam to hang out without another guy, that's all."

It's just like Susan to point out the obvious. Samira shook her head as she took a bite of salad. *That was a long time ago. I wish she could let it be.*

The next thing Samira knew, Susan was fishing for her car keys. "Are you finished? The baseball game is probably about over, and I promised Sam I'd be back about then."

The salad on Samira's plate was only half eaten. She set her fork aside and wiped her fingers on a napkin. *This would be the answer to the prayer for a quick meal, I guess.* She nodded. *Even if I'm not finished, going home alone is surely better than sitting in this crowded diner with Susan.*

Samira silently longed for someone she could really visit with. *I used to have a lot in common with Susan Olinger.* She extracted cash from her billfold for a tip and slid it under the edge of her plate. *But even this friendship is changing.* When she realized Susan hadn't left anything for the waitress, she added two more bills to her own.

6 *Stuck*

Joseph Phillip

J.P. half carried James into the house and took him directly to the bathroom. Without much resistance, he stripped James down to his underwear and maneuvered him into the shower. *God, I hate to do this.* J.P. turned the faucet. *But it's the only way to revive him.* Seconds later, cold water rained down on his son's weakened body.

James screamed obscenities at the top of his lungs. *At least he's saying something.* J.P. loosened his hold. James slid down the wall and landed in a sitting position. *What the hell?* J.P. stared at a single golden hoop hanging through his son's belly button. *James, we have a long way to go.* J.P. closed the bathroom door, leaving James to sober up alone.

Chase barked announcing a visitor before J.P. could change out of his wet clothes.

Mike, no doubt. I wondered how long it would be before he'd look me up. He unbuttoned his dress shirt as he made his way back to the kitchen.

"Hey, man, most people shower with their clothes off." Mike helped himself to a glass of water. "Denise told me you'd be here." He downed the water in one gulp. "What the hell are you doing home? I figured the Mid-America leak would keep you occupied all afternoon."

J.P. slipped out of his wet shirt and draped it over the back of a kitchen chair. "It's James." He nodded toward the closed bathroom door. "I left him in a cold shower." He started down the hall toward his bedroom. "How do you know about Mid-America?"

"James?" Mike followed J.P. into the short hall and stopped in the bedroom doorway. "How'd he get here?"

"When did you talk to Denise?"

"A few minutes ago."

"At the office?" *Why is she still at the office?*

"Yes, at the office. I figured you'd be involved with Stephenson somehow." He pointed an accusing finger at J.P. "By the way, I signed that affidavit. Now you owe me two."

"Two? Where'd you get two?"

"I fed your orphaned dog last night. That was one. And signing an official document on a Saturday is another. That's two."

Mike always keeps score. J.P. shook his head. *Denise should have been home before I got back from Mid-America.*

"So, what's the scoop with James?" Mike crossed his arms and leaned on the bedroom door frame.

"Long story." J.P. dug through a pile of folded laundry on a chair. "How much time do you have?"

Mike leaned on the door frame. "Give me the abbreviated version."

J.P. changed into a worn sleeveless tee shirt and gym shorts as he recapped the major points. "...so, now he's in the shower sobering up."

He passed Mike in the doorway and headed back to the kitchen. Mike followed.

"Now I'm stuck here for the rest of the day." J.P. untwisted the tie on a loaf of bread. "Did you eat?" *I'm starving.*

"Yeah, I ate at the club." Mike straddled the back of a kitchen chair. "Who's tending to Mid-America if you're here this afternoon?"

J.P. opened the refrigerator to find the fixings for a sandwich. His mind was still on James. "His timing could have been a little better." J.P. opened a jar of mayonnaise. *He didn't answer my question.* "So, how do you know about Mid-America?"

Mike beat his hands against the tabletop in a rhythmic pattern. "One of our clients is missing some assets." He grinned. "I figured you were called in for legal counsel." Mike reached for a bag of potato chips.

"I thought you said you ate."

"I did." Mike fingered a chip. "I doubt James stopped to think about *your* timing when he walked out on his mother."

"Still pisses me off." J.P. stacked cheese slices and leafed lettuce on top of cold cuts. *The whole deal with Janet pissed me off.* "I've already met with Mr. Stephenson. There's not much he can do until Monday morning." He leaned on the counter and took a bite of his sandwich. "What are you doing off the course already?"

Mike helped himself to another chip. "I played golf with the mayor and this new guy named Sammy-O. Only nine holes this round. For the record, I'm playing them again on Wednesday."

Must be nice to have time to play golf whenever you want. "What kind of a name is 'Sammy-O?'"

"Don't know, but he's a damned good golfer. Still beat 'em by four strokes." Mike wiggled his thick, blonde eyebrows and grinned. "Strictly business though."

"If this Mid-America case rolls, it's likely I'll need assistance. Think you guys might have an intern to spare for a couple-three weeks?"

"Hey, hey," Mike interrupted the professional conversation. "I think a little congrats is in order here. I gave up a whole Saturday to challenge our fair mayor."

Half a Saturday. "Was the mayor keeping score?"

"Nope."

I didn't think so.

"I need to stop by the office on my way home. I'll talk to Vince and see who might be available." Mike grinned. "On second thought, I have a new little gal who's sharper than a pin. How much experience are you looking for?"

"In what category?"

"How much work you want to get done?" Mike rose from his chair to refill the empty water glass. "But I don't have anybody like that model you picked up."

Bobbie Jo Sommers. J.P. finished chewing. "She picked me up, remember?"

Mike grinned fictitiously. "Oh, yeah. I forgot that detail. What was it she offered you again? S-N-S-A?"

J.P. returned the sly smile. *Good memory, Mikey.* "Sex—no strings attached." He laughed at the recollection. *And damned good sex too. But the SNSA was her rule.*

"How do you get so damned lucky?"

That time I happened to be in the right place at the right time. "Must be my looks."

"Certainly isn't intelligence."

J.P. displayed a choice finger but held the verbal assault. "What's wrong with the one shacking up at your place?"

"Strings and plenty of them."

He always ends up with pushy women who take advantage of his good nature.

"I gotta get that one figured out." Mike filled his water glass again. "Anyway, the modeling chick...what was her name?"

"Sommers. Bobbie Jo Sommers."

"Yeah. Bobbie Jo Sommers. I saw her picture on the cover of a magazine."

J.P. pointed to a stack of mail. "Halfway down."

Mike started through the stack. "The girl at the office looks pretty experienced. Maybe a nine and a half. Great boo—"

"Spare me the stats." J.P. interrupted the physical description. *I don't need a distraction. I need a make-shift attorney.* "Who else you got?

Mike pulled the cover model from the stack and whistled. "She does have a body, now, Counselor." He flipped through the lingerie catalog. "She should have made a killing with this release."

Every release.

"What exactly do you need assistance with?"

"The Hughes case will be ready for court next month and there's a couple smaller cases that need attention." He finished the last bite of the sandwich.

"Shit, J.P. You've never backed away from a nine and a half before. What's up with you?" Mike shot an accusing look in J.P.'s direction.

He's right. The thought of anyone new who wasn't Samira suddenly wasn't appealing. *But I don't know if I like Mike taking notice.* He turned away from the observation. *But Samira obviously comes with strings attached.*

"Okay, let me check it out." Mike let J.P. off the hook. "I'm thinking Derek Danielson. He's done with school, preparing for the bar." His eyes twinkled. "But this other gal—"

A loud crash in the bathroom interrupted the conversation. Both men stared down the hall at the closed bathroom door.

I forgot James was here.

Mike winced. "He must have hit it pretty hard, huh?"

"Plenty hard." J.P. closed his eyes and squeezed the bridge of his nose with his thumb and forefinger. *I just hope he made it to the toilet.*

Mike put a firm hand on his friend's shoulder. "Go easy on him, J.P. It's his first offense."

"It's his first *public* offense."

"Do you know that for a fact?"

"According to his mother—"

Mike looked J.P. square in the eye. "Then he's innocent until proven guilty."

I have my doubts.

"At least give him a towel or something." Mike was headed for the back door. "He's probably freezing to death. God, I hate it when you don't bring me a towel."

I remember the last time I sobered Mike up in a cold shower. That was a long, hard night. "Women have a way of bringing men to their knees over a toilet."

"Do you think James is involved with a girl?"

"Oh yeah." J.P. pictured the girls in his mind. "Jennie Johnson. She's a trip."

James was heaving again.

"Look, I'm going to take off and let you deal with James." Mike unlatched the screen. "Let me know if you need any help with Mid-America. I'll be around the rest of the weekend and my official day off is Monday, you know."

An official day off is the fringe benefit of sharing a partnership with Vince Barringer. The door banged loudly as Mike made his exit.

~~~~~~~

Is there anything else that can go wrong today? J.P. unclipped the leash from Chase's collar when they reached the path that paralleled the creek. The phone call back to Janet had been anything but pleasant and James hadn't exactly been cooperative either. *But at least he's sleeping it off now.* Familiar scenery passed at a steady pace as Chase and J.P. ran in sync.

God, he's only fifteen years old. How did he end up like this? Sweat ran down J.P.'s back and sides. *Josh always seems to have his act together, but James follows a different path.*

J.P. had been out of his boys' lives for a long time. In fact, he couldn't remember the last
~~~~~~~

time James and Josh had been inside his house. *It's just like Jan to wait until things are out of control to hand off to me.*

J.P. snapped his fingers. Chase followed him over the walk bridge to the concrete path on the other side of the creek. He stopped running long enough to reattach the leash. "Too many weekend walkers over here for you to run free."

He wiped the sweat off his face with the front of his shirt. *A few more blocks and I'd be in Samira's neighborhood.* J.P. shook his head. *But no reason to bother her with James passed out in the guestroom.*

~~~~~~~

Invigorated, J.P. set the stack of research files on top of his desk. *I need to get this Hughes case done before Mid America picks up pace.* He removed his shirt and used it to mop up the sweat on his face and arms. He skimmed the contents of the research again. But nothing was sinking in.

So, what do I do with James? Being a dad didn't come as naturally as he'd hoped. *Hell, I didn't have time to even plan to be a dad.* But then time passed. *I never really grew into it over time either.* He thought some more. *Being a dad meant spending time with a woman who made me miserable.*

As J.P. sat down in front of the television, Samira's living room came to mind. *She seems to have her life in order.* He pictured her daughter's school photos on the wall. *Obviously, she has solid relationships with her kids.* Another picture came into his mind. *Who the hell knows who the man in the bedroom photo is?* That thought was slightly unsettling. *Mike might be right. I need to be careful where I socialize with this one.*

~~~~~~~

It was late into the night before J.P. heard James moving.

"Need some help?"

James was sitting in a heap on the bathroom floor. The blanket from the bed was wrapped loosely around his shoulders.

James was weak and hung over. "I throw up, but nothing happens." Silent tears stained his face.

"Your stomach is empty, but your muscles don't know that yet," J.P. knelt and offered his son a tissue. The attorney in J.P. Ralston was slowly giving way to the father James needed. "It's going to take some time for this one to wear off, James." He studied his son's weary face. "How's your head?"

"Pounding." James blew his nose. "I don't even know which way is up."

J.P. flipped on the overhead light to get a better look at his son. *I don't know if his eyes are black from drinking or from fighting.* James cursed and put his head between his knees.

"Why don't you go back to bed? You'll feel better lying down."

J.P. offered a hand to help pull him up. James refused the assistance and staggered to his feet on his own weakened power.

Have it your way.

James stumbled to the kitchen and collapsed into a kitchen chair, still wrapped in the blanket. Carefully, he rested his head in his hands.

J.P. placed the Styrofoam cup from the Café Ole in the microwave and waited for it to heat. When it was good and hot, he placed it on the table directly in front of his son.

"I'm not going to drink that shit."

"It's better than the last shit you drank, and the caffeine will help the headache."

James pushed the cup away, almost causing it to spill.

Stubborn, just like his mother. "You can either drink it or I'll pour it in. Your choice." J.P. waited.

James squinted his eyes against the light of the kitchen. He stared at the cup for a long time. Eventually he took a sip, swearing as it burned his mouth. He took a few more sips then pushed it away again. "It's not helping my head."

"Give it time, it will." *Trust me. I know.* The Café Ole logo on the side of the cup caused emptiness in J.P.'s stomach. There was supposed to be a woman on the other side of that logo. *I probably should have called her tonight.* He wondered what the consequences of that might be.

~~~~~~~

A few short hours of sleep were all J.P. could find. His mind was consumed with questions he needed to ask James or Josh. At the same time, he was already starting to process the next step for Mid-America. He rolled over again, disgusted that sleep wouldn't come. He finally climbed out of bed resigned to the fact that he might as well begin the day. Chase was still fast asleep on the rug. James was breathing heavily and steadily. *Best he just sleeps it off.* He poured a glass of orange juice and stepped outside to retrieve the Sunday paper.

J.P. was at his desk when the room darkened slightly. James filled the entire door. *He's grown since I spent time with him.* The Ralston men studied one another for a moment. *He looks like a little kid stuck in a six-foot-four-inch body.*

"Hungry?"

James leaned heavily on the doorframe. "Not exactly."

He needs nourishment. "You should eat something." J.P.'s voice was low but controlled. "There are English muffins in the cupboard, but if you don't want that then try some dry toast. You need something in your stomach."

James nodded once then leaned forward and put his head in his hands.

Several moments of silence passed between them before J.P. spoke again.

"A hot shower wouldn't be a bad idea either."

Now James looked his father directly in the eye and tightened his jaw. "A *hot* shower would be a hell of a lot better than the one you put me through."

"You can choose the temperature of the water when you can stand on your own power." J.P. kept a close watch on his son. "Look, James, I don't know what happened up in Harrisonburg the other night but before this day is out, we need to get to the bottom of it."

James looked away. The circles under his eyes gave insight to the pain in his temples.

"Why don't you get something in your stomach and shower up?" J.P. remembered his promise to his ex-wife. "And before you and I sit down to sort through this mess, you owe your mother a phone call. Do you have your cell phone with you?'

"I don't think so."

J.P. pointed to the phone on the kitchen wall. He let that bit of information sink in. "Your clothes are still in the washer, so you'll have to find something around here that fits."

James stuck out his foot and examined the lack of length in the borrowed pair of sweatpants he was already wearing.

I know. He has a good inch and a half of height on me already. J.P. rose from his chair. "Don't forget the phone call."

J.P. took note of the dread in his son's eyes as he stared at the telephone. *I don't blame him. I wouldn't want to call her either.*

J.P. knew another phone call that needed consideration. *Samira's probably up by now, but I don't know if a Sunday morning call is a wise decision or not.* The attorney traded one file folder for another. *Besides, I don't know what I'd say to her.* He opened the cover of the file but didn't recognize the contents. *There was no way to read her thoughts.* J.P. closed the folder and leaned back in his chair. *Mike might be right again. She may be out of my league.*
~~~~~~~

7 Out with It

Samira

The organ prelude beckoned parishioners into the sanctuary. Samira reached the top step at her parents' church. *I'm not getting here any too early.* She spotted her parents already seated in their regular pew near the front. *Mama and Daddy will be surprised to see me this morning.* Samira politely sidestepped a few friendly greetings then slipped in beside her father.

The familiar words of the old hymn came easily. Samira blended her clear soprano voice perfectly with her father's tenor harmony. *I love singing with daddy.* She bowed her head as the pastor offered the invocation. *Sometimes I miss the tradition and familiarity of this place.*

It felt good to be tucked in the nook of her father's arm. *I always feel complete here.* But as she recited the prayer of confession, Samira no longer felt so confident. *Maybe I shouldn't have come here after all.*

Samira studied the stained-glass windows. *I used to love looking at these windows as a child.* She observed the patterns and the colors. *The angles in the glass remind me of my comforter.* Samira squirmed in the pew. *Dear God. This is NOT the place to be thinking of that.* She felt her father's hand rest a little heavier than necessary against her shoulder. *Daddy used to do that to keep me still when I was little.* Samira grew self-conscious. *Am I that restless?*

A wave of relief rushed over as Samira stood for the final hymn. It was good to be standing. Raymond's voice sang out in clear tenor harmony once again, but this time it was all Samira could do to open her mouth.

There is no way Daddy would approve of Friday night. She sang a few words. *Phil is too intense for my father.* The song ended. *But I see some of Daddy's traits in Phil too.* She bowed her head for the benediction. *Like his work ethic.*

Without warning, hands and faces began to surround Samira. Warm welcomes and well wishes from old family friends flooded from every direction.

"It's so good to see you."

"Welcome home, Samira."

"Where is your family this morning?"

Samira pasted a smile on her face and patiently answered questions and exchanged handshakes in the aisle. *I know they mean well, but this is a little overwhelming.* She searched the room with her eyes, hoping to locate her parents. *Where's my father when I need him?*

"It's good to see you, Samira."

Of all the people I thought I might run into this morning, David was not one of them. Samira tried to appear composed. *I thought he quit coming to church soon after he and I—.* Samira corrected herself. *Well, soon after I stopped seeing him.*

"It's good to see you, David." She forced another smile.

Immediately following Tom's passing, David took it upon himself to try to fill the vacancy in Samira's life. *His intentions were good.* Samira shook her head at the sudden recollection. *And I know he was a good friend of Tom's, but…*

"Uh-hem." A woman cleared her throat.

David laid his hand on her shoulder. "Samira, this is my wife, Melanie."

Oh, good. David found a wife. Samira offered her hand and a word of congratulations on the expectant baby. *I wonder if she knows about me.* Samira listened impatiently as Melanie rattled on and on about their expectant child. *I really didn't mean to hurt him.*

"Samira, dear."

Thank you, Mama. Get me out of here.

"I see you've met Melanie."

"Just now." Samira smiled again. "And their news is exciting too." "It's a boy," David announced proudly.

"It is very exciting, isn't it?" Ashleigh smiled genuinely. "Your father is waiting outside, dear." Ashleigh started to lead Samira down the aisle toward the double doors at the back of the sanctuary. "Do take care of Melanie, now David."

Thank goodness. Samira held on to her mother's hand just like she had as a child. *I just wasn't ready to see anyone else.* Samira sighed. *And David wasn't the one I needed.*

Ashleigh laughed heartily as she stepped into the narthex. "Everyone is always glad to see you. They don't mean to be overbearing."

Samira looked directly into her mother's dark eyes. *Mama grows more beautiful every day.* Her once dark hair was now streaked with gray and white. Samira had inherited her mother's chocolate brown eyes and tall frame.

"You look radiant this morning, Mama."

"Why, thank you, dear." Ashleigh's olive complexion glowed from within. "I had a feeling you might show up here with the girls away for the weekend." She smoothed a long strand of loose hair back from her face and skillfully tucked it into the bun at the nape of her neck.

I don't want to ask. But I do want to know. "When did David come back to church?"

"It's been a while," Ashleigh thought out loud. "Ever since he got married. A couple of years anyway." She touched Samira on the shoulder. "I know it is still hard for you to see him."

"Really, it's alright." David aside, the sooner she was out of this church, the better. *It's just strange to be back sitting among old memories again.*

Samira shaded her eyes and spotted her father waiting patiently in the shade of an old oak tree. *He looks quite spry in his sports jacket and dress slacks.* His hair had also grayed over the years but as far as Samira was concerned, he hadn't aged at all. Raymond's hazel eyes sparkled with delight as his hands connected with Samira's.

"It's good to have you here this morning, Princess. And you're coming for lunch I presume?"

"Of course." *I have nothing else on my agenda.* "I expected Wes and Pam to be here with the kids."

Raymond looked deep into Samira's eyes.

Oh, Daddy, don't do that.

"Weston said something about Pam being away this weekend. I'm assuming he'll join us for lunch."

Ashleigh was already headed down the sidewalk.

Daddy knows me too well. Samira started to follow her mother but hesitated in her father's gaze. *He's wondering why I couldn't sit still.*

~~~~~~~

Every room of Ashleigh's house was adorned with freshly cut flowers.

"The lilies are beautiful, Mama." *And they smell good too.*

"They're in full bloom now." Ashleigh fingered the bouquet as she passed by the dining room table. "Would you like some coffee? Almond spice, made just this morning."

Samira knew the house well for she had grown up in this very place. Without hesitation she crossed the white painted kitchen and retrieved two cups from the
~~~~~~~

cupboard. *Everything is always in its place.*

"Lunch smells wonderful." Raymond shared a contented smile with his daughter. "Weston left a message that he and the children will be here for lunch."

As always.

Ashleigh nodded her head with approval. "I was almost sure he wouldn't attempt to feed the children Sunday dinner on his own."

"Where is Pam this weekend?" Raymond accepted a cup of coffee from his daughter. "Thank you, Princess."

"Pam went to Springfield with some girlfriends for the weekend." Ashleigh sipped her coffee. "Weston said she needed the time away."

I'm sure she did. Being at home with three little ones all day long definitely merits a weekend away. Samira enjoyed the aroma of the coffee as much as the flavor. *Although I'm not sure I personally ever took any time like that for myself when my girls were little.* Samira smiled at the recollection. *I always took Tom with me and left the girls here.*

"So, Princess," Raymond addressed his daughter gently. "Tell me, what's new in your life?"

"Well," Without thinking, Samira started to mention the new man in her life. *No wait.* She took a quick sip of coffee. "I can't think of anything in particular." *I have never withheld anything from my parents before.*

The simple fact that she'd had an affair over the weekend caused new anxiety. *My parents would not approve.* Samira sighed into her coffee. "Nothing new, I guess. Just the same old routine." *I've never had anything to withhold from them before.*

"When do you expect the girls home?" Ashleigh turned her attention back to her daughter.

Samira recovered quickly. "This evening." She set her coffee cup on the counter and opened the cupboard to set the table. *They are probably on their way over to the clubhouse for the anniversary party as we speak.* "Norma and Dale will bring them back sometime after supper."

"I'm sure they're having a grand time with all of their relatives." Ashleigh glanced in her daughter's direction. "You'll have to get some plates from the dishwasher." Ashleigh checked the meat in the oven. "Did you go to the chamber concert with Susan last night?"

Samira nodded her head as she counted out seven forks and seven spoons. *But that may very well be the last time I go anywhere with Susan.*

"We called Friday night to see if you wanted to join us for dinner at Twin Hills. Did you get our message?"

Twin Hills? That's where Phil took me first, but we couldn't get a table. Samira dropped a table knife against the white tiled floor. *Running into my parents would have been a disaster.* She leaned over to pick up the knife.

"Well, anyway," Ashleigh continued. "Since you didn't answer we went ahead. Wonderful meal. Ed and Phyllis met us there—"

"Who?" Samira turned around suddenly. *Who did she say?*

"Ed and Phyllis Jones," Raymond clarified over the top of the Sunday paper. "You know Ed..."

Samira didn't hear the rest of the sentence. *Oh. I thought she said she met Phil.*

"Samira?"

"What."

Ashleigh laughed a jolly laugh. "I don't know what's gotten into you, dear, but I need the serving bowl from the hutch. Would you mind getting it for me?"

The bang of a door followed by hurried little footsteps announced the grandchildren. *Thank God.*

"Granny, Granny."

Samira watched her mother's eyes dance as she greeted her youngest granddaughters with a group hug. The little girls squealed with delight as their grandfather lifted them off the floor. *I remember when Daddy used to do that to me.* Samira finished setting the silverware around the table.

"Where's your father?"

"Coming in a minute," Bonnie, the oldest, answered. "He couldn't get Mark out of the car seat."

Wes always has trouble working gadgets.

Lizzie giggled and climbed into her grandfather's lap at the kitchen table.

Samira's brother appeared in the kitchen doorway carrying his youngest child. Mark's little blonde head was resting heavily against his daddy's shoulder. Without permission, Samira reached for the toddler.

Mark leaned into Samira's hands without thinking twice.

"How's my little Mark?" Ashleigh asked her grandson.

The boy turned his face away from the attention. *Let's go rock, Little Man. Did you just wake up?* She snuggled her nephew noting how much he had grown since she'd last held him. As he closed his eyes against her shoulder, Samira ran a finger through a lock of curls. Softly, she kissed the top of his head and nudged the chair into a rocking motion.

Tom wanted a little boy. She imagined herself as a new mother again. *We would have tried again if—* Little Mark sighed heavily indicating fresh sleep. *Well, anyway.* Samira caressed Mark's soft hair as she continued to cradle him in her arm.

~~~~~~~

Casual conversation followed dinner as Samira helped her mother clear the dishes. She could see her nieces through the French doors playing on the swing set with their grandfather.

"Sorry about barging in on you, Sis," Weston apologized as he sorted through the Sunday paper. "I didn't realize you had plans to be here *without* the girls."

"Since when do you have to be sorry about showing up here with the kids?" Samira closed the dishwasher and started the wash cycle.

Wes continued to shuffle the papers. "I know you don't get much time alone with the folks, that's all."

Today is not the day to be alone with the folks anyway.

"What happened to the business section?"

"Your father had it in the sunroom." Ashleigh answered as she entered the kitchen. "Look who I found sitting in the middle of the crib." She skillfully maneuvered about the kitchen carrying little Mark on her hip.

Wes disappeared into the sunroom and sank into the floral cushions of the couch. Samira watched him settle into the business news.

Weston always reads the business news first. Samira spent some time on the lawn admiring her mother's flowerbeds. Brilliant color accented every corner of the yard. *It's no wonder I love gardening.* She returned to the air-conditioned house through the sunroom.

Wes lowered the newspaper and addressed his sister. "I thought about calling you to help with the kids yesterday morning, but Mom said you had a day to yourself."

"You could have called. I was home." *Why do I make myself so available?*

"That's alright. Turned out Mom was home." Wes went back to his newspaper.

That's good. I had company anyway. Samira straightened some gardening magazines on the coffee table.

"So, what's new in your life?"

Why is everyone suddenly so interested in my life? She put her hands to her face when she felt her cheeks fill with color.
~~~~~~~

"Obviously, you've got something to share." Wes's eyes twinkled at his sister.

Samira rolled her eyes. "It's just the sun." *Wes knows I'm lying.*

"What do you say we go for a walk?"

"Maybe I don't feel like walking." Samira headed for the kitchen.

"Isn't it a beautiful day?" Ashleigh exclaimed.

"It's a great day for a *walk.*" Wes followed his sister with interest. His untied shoestrings tapped against the tile.

"Don't you have someplace to be?" Samira poured a glass of iced tea for herself. *If I tell anyone anything, it will be Wes. He already knows I have something to tell.*

Wes shook his head and held an empty glass under the pitcher.

"Weston," Ashleigh called from the table. "Can you get Mark out of the highchair for me?"

Wes left his glass on the counter and went to assist his mother.

Maybe he'll forget about going for a walk. She watched little Mark toddle off toward the family room. *But if I'm going to talk to him, I don't want to talk here.* Samira stepped into her loafers and started out the front door.

"Hey, where are you going?"

"For a walk."

Wes scrambled to tie his shoes. He caught up to Samira at the end of the driveway.

"My ears are on little sister."

Samira set the pace and avoided eye contact. "What if I don't have anything to tell you?" *But I know the words are going to tumble.*

Wes lengthened his stride to keep pace. "You always have something to tell me. I'm your confidant, remember?" He caught his breath and took a few more steps. "Might as well spill it."

Samira kept her eyes glued to the sidewalk. *I need to talk to him, but I don't want him to know all the details.*

"Okay, then I'll guess." He took a stab. "Somebody you met through Susan?"

How frustrating. "I don't need Susan to find a date."

"Okay, so you found him on your own. What else you got?"

How does he know already that this is about a man? "Close. I think I might have a man in my life." Samira glanced to the left, then to the right before stepping into an intersection.

"Short? Fat? Skinny?"

Perfect in all those departments. "Handsome, tall, tender, funny..." *Taller than Tom.*

"Whoa, whoa, whoa. Handsome and tall are good. Go back to the tender part." *Wrong adjective.* "We danced, we talked..."

"And?"

I need to tell him to clear my conscience. "And I let him stay."

They kept walking.

Why isn't he saying anything?

"It's not like I just let him stay, I mean," Samira searched her words, but nothing was coming to mind. "I've been seeing him a few weeks now." *Well, a couple of lunches and a date or two at a coffee shop, if you call that seeing someone.* Unintentionally, Samira's pace slowed a little.

"I'm not passing judgment, Sis."

Why not? You usually do.

"So, how long have you known him? Is he married?"

Samira slapped her brother hard on the arm. *No. He's not married.* "Divorced. Has two teenage boys who live with their mother." *I can't believe he asked me that.*

"Where'd you meet him?"

"At the library."

"What's he do for a living?"

"He's an attorney. I think."

"You think? You should know. Successful?"

Now he's going to pass judgment. "I don't know." Samira threw her hands up. "He drives a pickup, has designer labels in his suit coats."

"Smoker? Party animal?"

"Wes. You said you weren't passing judgment." Samira paused briefly at the curb and waited for a car to pass before she started across the street. *I hardly know enough about him to answer these questions.*

"I'm not passing judgment on you, but he's another matter. So come on, out with it."

It's not like I didn't expect Wes to ask questions. "Alright. But only one more question." Samira ran her hand through her hair, which had fallen out of the clip. "Non-smoker, plays golf, don't know anything about his personal life, and he drinks Italian wine."

"Last inquiry. History with women?"

Samira stopped mid-stride. Wes stopped a few steps in front of her.

Why would he ask me that? "Frankly, Wes, I didn't ask, and he didn't offer." She pushed her hair back again.

"I just don't want you to get hurt."

How can I possibly get hurt if I don't have any expectations? Samira turned a shoulder to her brother. *Sometimes I get tired of being protected and babied.*

"It's been a long time, Sis."

"I know," Samira interjected. "But I—" She searched for an explanation. "I really had a good time." *I don't want to make eye contact with my brother.*

Samira pulled her head back as Wes removed her sunglasses.

"Just go slow, okay?" He paused momentarily. "Life's too short not to take a chance, but be careful, alright?"

Why do I feel like he can see right into my soul?

Samira recalled her brother's advice when she'd decided not to see David anymore. "You once told me to look for somebody with passion."

Wes rolled his eyes, "Passion yes. Lust, no. You've got a lot to offer, Sis. I don't like the idea of some guy taking advantage of you."

He's not just some guy. "I invited *him* to stay." *At least I don't think so anyway.*

"That doesn't mean he had to accept the invitation." Wes frowned. "He could have kissed you goodnight and made his exit."

It's not like he didn't try. "Maybe I didn't want him to leave." *Now there's a confession if I've ever had one.*

"You haven't known him that long. I'd just appreciate him more if he took his time getting you in bed, that's all."

He took his time once we were in bed. Samira caught that thought. *But that's not a detail I'll share with anyone. Not even my brother.*

Wes put his hands on his hips and looked past his sister into the distance. "Truce, okay?"

That means we can't discuss this matter in the same way again. Samira nodded once. *Truce.*

Wes was looking hard into his sister's eyes.

I hate hearing what he has to say. She looked away to relieve the tension. *But I do feel better having spilled my guts.*

Wes wrapped his arm around his sister's neck. For just a moment Samira rested her cheek against his shoulder. She could feel his heart beating hard in his chest.

"You're really out of shape if you can't pace me on a walk." Samira changed the subject as she put her sunglasses back on.

"That was hardly a walk." He nudged her around and they started back in the direction from which they had come. "I'd call that an almost-sprint."

Comfortable silence walked with them for a short distance.

"So, you'll call if you need me?"

"Hopefully, I won't have to call."

"But know I'll answer if you do."

Thank you, Wes.

8 History Repeats Itself

Joseph Phillip

J.P. sat across from his son in the dining room at Twin Hills Golf Club. James fingered a French fry.

"You're not eating much." *He needs the nourishment after being so sick.*

James shrugged his shoulders. His face was solemn and the circles under his eyes were still dark and sunken. "I'm not that hungry."

J.P. wiped his mouth on a paper napkin and leaned back in the chair. *I'd still like a little more information before he goes back home.*

"Look, James," *Go easy, Counselor.* "I need to understand what happened the other night. I'm working with a blank slate here and can't be of much help to you if I don't know the facts."

The burger sat cold and untouched on the restaurant plate.

I've never known James not to eat. J.P. weighed his options. *Obviously, open-ended questions aren't working.* "Exactly how did Rick know to come pick you up?"

James was instantly on the defense. "I don't know."

That's the same answer I got last night. Trying to sound more patient than he felt, J.P. probed further, "You don't know, or you don't remember?"

James glared at his father and set his jaw. "I don't know, *and* I don't remember."

"Listen, James." *This shouldn't be so hard.* "I'm not mad, I'm just in the dark. I need to know the circumstances so I can help mediate between you and your mother and Bruce."

James suddenly slammed his fist into the table. "Just leave Bruce out if it. All right? I don't want anything to do with that bastard."

J.P. studied his son's face. *Obviously, hit a nerve.* He motioned to the server across the room. *Let's see what else I can get.*

"All right." He signed the ticket for lunch. "We don't have to bring him into it."

Reluctantly, James followed his father toward the front desk. J.P. stopped in his tracks. *Wouldn't you know she'd be on duty today?* His eyes landed on the girl working behind the counter.

"My card please." *She knows my name even if I can't remember hers.*

The girl pretended not to notice him. J.P. waited. He knew James was watching with interest. *It would help if I could at least recall her name.* Once again J.P. addressed the young woman. "J.P. Ralston."

"Heard you been out of town." She tapped the edge of his membership card on the counter. Her short brown ponytail bobbed as she spoke, but her eyes were full of spite.

It would also help if she were wearing a staff name badge. J.P. chose his words carefully. "I've been working." *I'd have never picked her up if I'd known how resentful she was going to be.* J.P. reached for the card, but she pulled it back and very slowly slid it through the magnetic reader.

She squinted her eyes into an accusing look. "Is that your rehearsed excuse for broken promises?"

"I don't make promises."

She placed the card flat on the counter between them but didn't remove her hand.

I wrote the policy about touching an employee while on duty. He knew the security camera was focused on the registration desk. *I'm not going to take her bait.* Eventually, she removed her hand so J.P. could have his card.

James broadened his step to catch up with his father. "What did you do to piss her off?"

Now there's a sudden change from his sorry attitude. J.P.'s stride was resolute. *Just my luck James would witness that.* He weighed his options again, but this time the stakes were higher. *If I want answers from him, I'd best be honest.*

"I slept with her." J.P. stopped in the middle of an empty parking space. "Once." *But I told her up front not to expect anything more.* J.P. pushed his hands into the pockets of his khaki shorts and looked into his son's gray eyes. *I never thought I'd be looking up at my own son.*

"She looked pretty wicked, Dad." James curled his mouth into a slight smile. "She didn't look that bad in bed, did she?"

J.P. gave his son a look that told him not to tread much further. "To be perfectly honest, I don't remember." *I took her to dinner, got what I wanted, and was on my way.* He took a deep breath and looked off into the distance. "It's not something I'm proud of and I don't plan to let it happen again." *At least not with her.*

James ran his tongue over his bottom lip. "She sure knew how to ruffle your feathers though, didn't she?"

J.P.s patience was spent. *Enough discussion about my private life.* He took a step closer to his truck. "We have exactly two hours to get our butts to your mother's living room. Do you want to ride with me, or shall I call her to pick you up?"

James opened the door of the truck and climbed inside. "I'll ride with you." He was still visibly humored.

~~~~~~~

J.P. found himself sitting in a worn easy chair in Janet's living room. The discussion was not producing any results.

"We really can't finish this until Bruce gets home," Janet reiterated.

J.P. watched James close his eyes at the mention of Bruce's name. *I've got to get to the bottom of this.*

"I don't know what's keeping him," Janet admitted out loud. "He's usually home by now."

It's Sunday night. Where could he possibly be?

Janet was pacing the living room floor. *There's more gray in her hair than the last time I saw her.* He watched Janet's eyes fall on their son who was slumped into an old sofa.

"And you still have semester exams to take if you want to be promoted out of the sophomore class." There was an edge in her voice.

James crossed his arms and shrugged his shoulders.

I'm beginning to think maybe he honestly has no memory of anything from Friday night.

Josh waved a rolled newspaper in his father's direction. Disgusted with the lack of progress with Janet and James, J.P. joined Josh in the kitchen.

"Page three, lower left corner." Josh pointed.

J.P.'s eyes came to rest on the sheriff's report.

Late Friday evening, area residents reported a brawl at the picnic area in Madsen Park. By the time authorities arrived on the scene the perpetrators had fled, but in their haste, they left a broken picnic table and park bench. Anyone with information concerning the incident should contact the sheriff's department."

"James?"

"Most likely," Josh replied half interested. "And his buddies."
~~~~~~~

"Your mother know?"

"Probably not." Josh shrugged. A phone rang in the living room. "I doubt she's read the paper today."

Janet appeared in the kitchen doorway holding her hand over the phone. "It's Bruce. He can't be home until late."

J.P. checked his watch. *It's already late, damn it.* "How late?"

"Nine-ish."

Shit. I still have a couple hours of road time. "What's the hold up?"

Janet spoke back into the phone, but he could tell from the way she was hiding her face that she had no control.

J.P. looked beyond Janet at his son on the couch. *James doesn't even want the bastard involved.* "Then we'll finish up without him."

"You can't," Janet covered the mouthpiece. "Bruce needs to be involved in these discussions."

Bullshit. J.P. knew he had to stay. *I told James I'd see him through this.* But at the same time, he could have easily walked away. He ran his hand through his hair.

Janet laid her phone on the counter. "He's stuck with a client. That shouldn't be totally foreign to you, J.P."

He's an insurance agent. Reschedule the freakin' appointment.

"He says he'll be here as soon as he can break free." Janet sighed uneasily.

Prove to me he's even with a client. He watched Janet leave the room.

"I don't want to be here all night." J.P. spoke out loud without thinking. He looked at Josh. "Nothing personal. I can just think of some places I'd rather be."

"Missing a hot date, Dad?" Josh took a playful stab at his father.

"No."

But I can think of one I probably should have called. His thoughts rewound to the open-ended suggestion to call Samira when he was finished at the office Saturday. *It wouldn't have taken much to just pick up the phone.*

"I thought maybe you had somebody in waiting," Josh wiggled his eyebrows.

"Not this time, Joshy."

"Too bad." Josh hopped off the kitchen counter. "I have one meeting me in town in a few minutes if I can find a ride."

J.P. grinned at his son. *Now there's a subtle suggestion if I've ever heard one.*

He followed Josh into the living room and turned his attention back to James. *I'll try him one more time.* "Surely you can recall one of the issues between you and your mother before you left the house the other night?"

The teenager clung to his silence. *Come on, James. Just talk to me.* J.P. took a long breath.

"Grades." Josh answered for his brother. "That was one of the issues." He glanced at his brother for consent to continue. "They didn't think he should be going out with his friends because of his grades."

"I had all my homework done."

He's defensive, but at least we have a starting point. J.P. looked between his sons hoping for a breakthrough.

"They just don't want me going out, period. Had nothing to do with my grades." James looked away. "Doesn't matter what I want to do, they keep me under lock and key anyway."

J.P. looked to Josh for confirmation. The older brother tipped his head to the side and shrugged one shoulder as if he couldn't dispute the accusation.

Janet returned to the room.

She looks like hell warmed over.

"After Bruce gets home, we can decide how to manage the next few days," she announced.

The easiest thing to do is to tell the boys to pack and take them home with me until the dust settles. He thought about that possibility. *If it settles.* Something was telling him there was more domestic unrest than he cared to know. *Damned if I'm going to sit cooped up here while we wait.*

"You still need a ride to town, Josh?"

"Are you serious?" Josh was obviously surprised.

Janet's shot a sharp look of warning across the room. "You can't take him to town."

"Why not?"

"Because Bruce isn't even here yet."

"Jan, it's not even seven o'clock."

"Josh has no business being in town tonight."

Josh rolled his head back in unbelief.

More bullshit. "We'll be back around nine." *But I hate to leave James here.*

"That will give James time to study," Josh suggested.

"Good." J.P. looked at his son on the couch. "He'll have a head start." He tossed his keys to Josh. "We'll be back."

James made a defiant exit up the stairs.

"J.P." Janet's voice was sharp. "Josh doesn't have any business going into town. It's Sunday night."

The door at the top of the stairs slammed loudly.

What is she so afraid of? "Did you ask him if he had plans tonight?"

Janet scoffed. "He can't have plans if he doesn't have a ride."

"Well, he has a ride. So now he can have some plans." *Case closed.*

"Don't you walk out that door on me."

J.P. opened the door for his son. "We'll be back."

Once inside the truck, J.P. let out a deep breath. "What's up with the Sunday night bullshit?"

"She's always like that. If she doesn't want to drive us into town, then we can't go." Josh started his father's pickup and carefully pulled out of the driveway onto the gravel road.

These boys need some transportation of their own. I can't believe they're held hostage in their own house.

"She's always been that way," Josh explained. "She worries too much or something."

She's too damn controlling. J.P. decided to change the subject. "So, who's the hot date?"

"You'll see," Josh smiled his father's smile. "She'll be there pretty soon."

They parked on the town square where a large group of teenagers were already gathered. The custom Dodge pickup drew a crowd. He watched closely but didn't see Josh paying attention to anyone in particular. *But he sure is having fun showing off my truck.* J.P. stepped away and allowed him the glory of the spotlight. *Looks like a harmless crowd.*

J.P. scanned the parking lot. Three other students were mingling on the far side of the parking lot. One face was familiar.

Rick. J.P. studied him long and hard before deciding to be sociable. *He's not an active player here, but he doesn't appear to be an outcast either.*

"Hey Rick." He recognized the old sedan that had delivered his son to Joplin.

Rick looked up, made brief eye contact, and then looked away again. "H-hello Mr. Ralston."

"School's about out for the summer, huh?"

Rick nodded, then looked away again.

"What do you plan to do with all your free time, Rick?"

The young man stuffed his hands deep into his baggy shorts and dropped his head nervously. "I-ah-ah- I go work where m-my mom works."

I wish he weren't so self-conscious.

"I-is J-James home?" This time Rick looked directly at J.P. and for once, held his eyes there for a few seconds.

"Briefly," the father reported. "I don't know how long he'll be around, but he's at home tonight." *My guess is he'll be better off staying with me for a little while.*

Rick raised his chin in a half nod. "Ah-I'd hoped h-he was okay."

A squeal of tires interrupted the lagging conversation. J.P. watched a rusted out pickup fish tail into another parking lot a few blocks away.

Rick watched too. When they could no longer see the truck, Rick spoke up. "Th-that's some of J-james' friends."

No shit?

"J-Jennie's prob'ly over th-there."

This may be my opportunity to glean some information. "If Josh asks," J.P. peered into the distance. "Tell him I went for a walk. I'll be back."

Dusk was setting in as J.P. approached the small crowd of high school students. He hung in the shadows and evaluated their disposition before making his presence known. *Takes guts to make out in the bed of a pickup in public.* J.P. looked away from the couple heavily involved in personal activity.

You've got nothing to lose, Counselor. J.P. stepped out of the shadows. A few eyes glanced in his direction, but no one spoke. *I can be patient.* J.P. scanned the faces. *They look lost.* He waited some more. *I've seen this same look on James.* A petite, bleached-blonde girl wearing a skimpy mid-drift top was in the center of the gathering. She was wearing a hoop in her belly button that closely resembled that of his son's.

I'll take a stab. He watched her step forward, flaunting her heavy bust as she moved. *Jennie Johnson.*

One by one the teenagers began to pay attention. Someone exhaled a vaping device.

Gutsy, considering not one of them is of age in the first place. J.P. put up his hand in silent refusal. He leaned against a faded Pontiac. "Anyone here know James Ralston?"

Time passed but no one answered. *I'll just wait this one out.*

"Who's asking?" A muscular young man with a tattoo on his bicep emerged from behind the old pickup with a young girl wrapped around his arm.

At least James isn't sporting a tattoo. Well, as far as I noticed. "His father."

Low murmurs passed among the crowd and a few students started to walk away.

The girl in the mid-drift top took a step forward. "You're his dad?"

Yep, Jennie Johnson.

"I didn't know he had a dad." The streaked ponytail that hung off the back of her head bounced with the front of her shirt. "But I know him. Is he okay?"

With the raising of that question everyone seemed to freeze. Even the kids who were walking away stopped moving.

Let's string them along and see how much they're willing to give. J.P. looked directly at Jennie Johnson. "For the most part, but he's not out of the woods yet."

A sigh of relief rippled through the teenagers.

Jennie asked another question. "Is he home?" She flicked ashes from a burning cigarette then put it between her lips and inhaled as she waited for an answer.

"Briefly." J.P. answered carefully. He slowly made eye contact with each person in the group. "In order for me to help James, I need some information about what happened at Madsen Park. And I need it tonight."

Most of the eyes fell away from him and new murmurs rose from the crowd. *No one's going to fink on a friend in public.*

The tattooed boy spoke again. "Is he in trouble?"

He looks older than the rest of these kids. J.P. shook his head. "I just need to understand what happened, that's all." He reached for his wallet and extracted a business card. "This is my cell number." He jotted the numbers across the back of the card. "I'll answer until midnight."

The attorney left the card on the back of the Pontiac and walked away in the opposite direction from which he'd come. *We'll see if anyone has the nerve to call.* He circled the block on foot and arrived back at the bandstand where he'd left Josh.

Josh took his father by the arm and turned him slightly. J.P. thought maybe he was going to direct his attention to the crowd down the street. But instead, Josh nodded his head toward a group of girls sitting on the bandstand.

His hot date. "Which one?"

"The one in the middle."

Her long blonde hair was brushed to a glossy shimmer. *A lot different than the one his brother hooked up with.*

"That's the one I want to ask out."

J.P. frowned at his son. "What's the hold up?"

"I'm just waiting for the right time." Josh's eyes were fixed on the girl. J.P. bumped him in the ribs.

"Hey, Josh."

Josh returned to his previous conversation as if he'd never left.

He's got a good head on his shoulders. Too bad he's so shy with the girls. Jennie Johnson's figure flashed in his mind. *Well, maybe being shy isn't all bad.*

His thoughts were interrupted by a vibration against his hip. *That was faster than I expected.* J.P. checked the caller I.D. *It's a Harrisonburg number.*

"J.P. here."

"Is this James's dad?" A girl's voice was on the other end of the line. J.P. pressed the device hard into his ear so he could hear better.

"It is."

"I was in the parking lot but I'm home now." The voice stopped for a moment.

This may be my only willing witness.

"I know what happened the other night."

Bingo.

"It's not James's fault that he got so drunk. There was a fight at home or something and Jennie went over to get him." The girl was noticeably nervous. "One of the guys thought it would help him to have a drink, but it didn't. He just got wilder and wilder and kept drinking more beer." The tension was becoming more evident. "We couldn't get him settled down, so Marcus dropped a Valium in his beer."

She stopped talking.

Valium? "And then what happened?"

"And then James went ballistic. He started jumping around and breaking things up. I got really scared and Jack made me leave...everybody started running away." J.P. heard the girl choke and realized she was crying. "Jack said he passed out and wouldn't get up." She choked out a sob. "Everybody thought he was dead."

Put her mind at ease. "He's not dead, but he was pretty sick." *Does she know anything else?* "Is there anything else you can tell me?"

The girl didn't respond right away.

She needs to know my intentions. "No one will know you've talked to me tonight. I'm just trying to help James."

"Well, there is something, but I don't think I should tell. Jennie will kill me if she finds out."

"She won't find out. You have my word." J.P. listened closely.

The next sentence was only three words long, but it took all of J.P.s breath away. The father replayed it in his mind. It fell the same the second time.

"Jennie is pregnant."

Nooooooo! The voice inside of J.P.'s head was so loud he put his hand over the other ear. The call disconnected, but the statement was still reverberating in his mind.

The pierced belly button and full bust line seemed like a cheap trick considering this information. *Now what?* He was stunned beyond belief. *This is exactly how I ended up with their mother.* His eyes dared to look down the street again. *Only I was 25, not 16 years old.* J.P. put his hand on his forehead. *And I wasn't nearly old enough.*

The longer J.P. thought about it, the angrier he got. *Goddam. We've talked about this. I've even put the prevention in his hand.* Suddenly the silence concerning the weekend events wasn't enough.

I've been calm and I've been patient. But my patience is spent. J.P. was tired of James' attitude. He was tired of Janet's controlling demands. But most of all he was tired of not having all the pieces to the puzzle.

It is time to end this charade. J.P. made sure Josh had a ride home and then set out to finish what he'd come up there to do in the first place. *And I'm going to start with the one who has the answers.*

9 The Threat of Exposure

Samira

When Norma Cartwright sets a time, she rarely misses the mark. Today was no exception. At exactly seven o'clock, Dale and Norma's Cadillac pulled into the driveway. *Here we go.* Samira took a deep breath, donned a smile, and opened the front door.

"Samira, dear." Norma exploded into the front room close on Kara's heels. Samira accepted the loose embrace from her former mother-in-law. Norma was still wearing her dress clothes. "It's so good to see you."

You just saw me Friday. "Come on in."

"We had a grand time, just a grand time." Norma clapped her hands together, her colored golden hair shining. "The girls are turning into young women right before our very eyes." She tipped her head and admired the girls at length. "But we so missed you."

It's just as well I stayed home. Samira greeted Dale with less exuberance. He looked more comfortable in shorts and a plaid shirt.

"Thanks, Grampa," Krissy reached up to hug her grandfather as he set her bag next to the door. Next, she turned and hugged her mother.

I'm glad to have the girls back home. Samira savored the moment.

"Iced tea?"

"No thank you, nothing for me," Norma answered. "Krissy tells us your garden is starting to bloom. We'd love to have a peek."

Dale raised his forefinger to interrupt his wife. "I might have a sip of tea, Samira," he indicated politely with his gentle southern accent. *His eyes remind me so much of Tom.* She couldn't help but return his smile.

"Right this way," she motioned for Dale to follow her to the kitchen. "Krissy, go ahead and take Gramma out back. We'll be along shortly."

Samira took her time. "How have you been, Dale?"

"We've been mighty busy this week. But other than that life is treating us well." He took a long drink. "How about you, Samira?"

"Things are adjusting into the summer just fine."

"You're looking good," Dale complimented. His blue eyes twinkled.

Just like Tom's used to do. "Thank you." She tucked her hair behind her ear. *Krissy has their eyes.*

"Dale, dear," Norma called. "You must see this floral heaven."

Samira watched Dale tip his head. "After you," he said with a quiet smile.

"It gets more beautiful out here every year," Norma complimented. She was sitting in the plastic lawn chair, her legs comfortably crossed. "You really should submit this work of art to a home and garden magazine, dear." She waved her hands over the area. "Really you should."

But if I were selected, I'd have photographers and reporters all over my sanctuary. Samira admired her work. *I prefer to keep it to myself, thank you.*

"You should have been at the party, Mama." Krissy's eyes were bright with excitement. "There were so many people there."

I wouldn't have known anyone outside the immediate family.

"We counted like over a hundred cards in the basket at the end of the day and all of the cake was, like, gone." Krissy shook her head. "But it was a blast."

"It was a grand success," Norma added. Thank you so much for letting the girls join us. We just love showing them off."

As well you should. Anytime."

"We took lots of photographs." Norma announced.

"Gramma says she'll send them to us as soon as she gets them back."

"I'll send them in for prints right away."

"Mama, Mrs. Barnes is here," Kara called from the back door.

Mrs. Barnes? What in the world is she doing here? Samira exhaled slowly as she rose from the wooden garden bench. *Mrs. Barnes hasn't paid a personal visit in quite a while now.* Reluctantly, Samira left her guests in the garden to greet her neighbor in the kitchen.

Mrs. Barnes held out a plate with her bronze hands. "I won't stay long because I know you have company."

And chances are good she even knows who they are.

"I brought you some fresh cookies. I thought you might be able to use them with the girls coming home and all."

Samira reached for the plate. *I should have known Mrs. Barnes would know the exact moment the girls arrived home.*

"It's not a problem to double the recipe, you know. Just as easy to make a double batch as a single." Mrs. Barnes glanced around the room as if searching for evidence. "I can't stay long," the woman repeated as she patted her bluish gray hair. "Mr. Barnes is waiting for me, you know."

"Here," Samira removed a plate from the cupboard. "Let me transfer the cookies over so you can take your plate back home." *That way she won't have a ready excuse to make a second appearance.* Samira carefully stacked the cookies on her own plate. *The only time Mrs. Barnes pays a visit is when there's neighborhood gossip in the making.*

Mrs. Barnes didn't waste any time. "Did your brother get a new vehicle?"

Exactly what I thought. Samira handed over the empty plate. *The sooner I get her back across the street, the better off we'll all be.* Kara was suddenly involved in the conversation.

"What? Uncle Wes got a new car?" She snatched a warm cookie as she crossed the kitchen. "I didn't know that."

"No, Uncle Wes didn't get a new car."

"Who got a new car?" Krissy piped as she entered the kitchen from the other direction.

She went directly to the pitcher on the counter and refilled her grandfather's tea glass.

Mrs. Barnes was politely waiting for an explanation.

"No one has a new car." Samira corrected.

"I just thought the pickup must be your brother's. I haven't seen it around before." The old lady baited the conversation with skill.

Oh, Mrs. Barnes, you do know something about timing, don't you? "A friend came by, that's all." *I hope Norma and Dale stay in the garden.*

"It's a good thing you're an early riser," Mrs. Barnes quipped. "He came by a might early for an ordinary visit."

Samira saw Krissy raise her eyebrows at her sister. They stifled a giggle. The mother sent a look of warning to her daughters.

Let's try this. "How's Mr. Barnes? Is he over his cold?"

Mrs. Barnes' eyes danced. "I was up with him several times in the night through the weekend, but he's doing much better now." The neighbor nodded once. "Thank you for asking." With that the elderly lady turned toward the kitchen door.

She obviously made her point.

"I won't keep you any longer. I know your company is waiting. Somewhere—."

Samira watched Mrs. Barnes scan the room again.

"They're out back in the garden," Kara clarified without being asked.

No, we're not going to invite Mrs. Barnes to the garden. Samira opened the door to the garage for Mrs. Barnes to make her exit just as Norma came in through the laundry room entrance.

"Is she gone already?" Norma quipped.

Samira put her hand over her heart as it pounded in her chest.

Norma crossed the dining room and looked out over the white painted slats in the windows. "Why, she needn't run off like that on our account."

Yes, she did, trust me. Samira looked out to be sure Mrs. Barnes was safely across the street. "She just wanted to bring us some cookies." She placed the plate of warm snacks on the breakfast bar. Dale helped himself but Norma put her hand over her stomach.

"Oh, Samira dear, none for me," she lamented. "I ate more than my share at the reception."

"Everybody did." Kara agreed. "The food was so good. Gramma did a good job putting it all together." Her daughter changed the focus. "What did you have for lunch, Mama?"

Caught off guard, Samira had to remember. "Oh, I ate with Papa Ray and Granny." *And Wes and the kids.*

"I'm sure they appreciated your visit," Norma added.

She probably thinks I went over there simply to avoid Tom's family gathering. Samira caught that thought. *Well, I kind of did.* "When will Ellen be home next?"

Dale's eyes lit up with the mention of his daughter.

"She'll be home for three weeks next month," the grandfather answered quickly. He winked at Krissy across the breakfast bar. "I'm sure she'll come get the girls to spend a few days."

From there the conversation flowed more smoothly, relieving the knots in Samira's stomach. *If they overheard anything about an early morning visitor, they certainly aren't letting on.*

Krissy was hot on the topic as soon as Dale and Norma were gone. "Was it your friend's truck that was here, Mama?"

I should have known Krissy wouldn't forget. "Yes, it was Phil's." *At least she waited for her grandparents to leave.* She started to cover the cookies with plastic wrap, but Kara grabbed another one.

"He must be an early riser too, then?" Krissy followed her sister's lead and swiped another cookie from the plate. "So, is he?" She started to follow her mother toward the hallway.

I don't really know, but he seemed quite content sleeping in. "Do you have homework?" Samira took a stack of clean towels out of the linen closet and headed for her bedroom.

"Mo-ther. We don't have homework the last week of school." Kara's interjection showed signs of agitation.

"Was Daddy an early riser too?" Krissy asked, close on her mother's heels.

Where did that come from? Samira stopped in the doorway to her bedroom and faced her daughters. She closed her eyes and tried to stabilize the congestion in her mind.

"I think Mama needs a minute," Kara suggested out loud. She tapped Krissy on the shoulder.

"So, is he cute?" Krissy's eyes twinkled.

I guess they're not going to let me off the hook. Unwilling to jeopardize the memories still lingering in her bedroom, Samira decided to put the towels away in the main bathroom.

"WE-LL?" Krissy was impatiently perched on her knees with her freckled arms hanging over the back of the couch.

I knew they would be curious. I didn't know they were going to be this demanding.

"She's blushing," Krissy whispered loudly across the room to her sister.

Samira touched her cheeks. They were hot with color.

"Yep, he's cute," Krissy assumed. "He must not drive a sports car."

"No," Samira answered quietly, her thoughts still somewhat distant. "He drives a pickup."

"A pickup?" Kara exclaimed. "What kind of a guy drives a pickup?"

A complex, sophisticated, professional. Samira was surprised to hear such reluctance in Kara's voice. *Why does it matter what he drives anyway?*

"Well, he's actually very nice." *Why am I defending him?* "And he has a great smile." *But it's already Sunday night and I haven't heard a word from him.*

Kara rolled her eyes and flopped into the easy chair with her legs dangling over the edge. Her brown eyes met her mother's. "A pickup truck sounds like some kind of farmer or something."

"Or someone who hauls a lot of stuff," Krissy thought out loud. "How tall is he?"

Samira couldn't help but smile. "He's taller than me by a couple-three inches. I'd guess around six-two."

"Wow. That's taller than Daddy, isn't it?"

I forget how curious they are about Tom when they've spent time with his family.

"Your daddy was almost six feet," she remembered for the girls. *But not quite because when I wore two-inch heels, I was taller than him.*

"He doesn't wear cowboy boots, does he?" Kara asked with skepticism.

"No cowboy boots." *Just designer clothes.* Samira chuckled. *Kara would appreciate that more than Krissy.*

Before any more questions were asked, the telephone rang. Both girls scrambled to answer but Kara got there first and quickly handed it over to her sister.

"Hurry up," Kara warned. "I want to call Paula."

Krissy took the telephone and disappeared into her bedroom.

"Everyone else in my class has a cell phone. I swear I'm the only one in my class without a phone of my own." Kara disappeared down the hall.

I feel a little like the girls. When the phone rings, I hope it's for me. At the same time, she preferred not to take a call from Phil in front of the girls. *But honestly, I haven't felt the need to invest in cell phones just yet.*

~~~~~~~

Long after Krissy and Kara were asleep, Samira still paced between the kitchen island and the dining room. To keep busy, she moved most of her houseplants to the sunroom. When that job was complete, she folded a load of laundry and then unloaded the dishwasher. She tried to read the newspaper but couldn't bring her mind to rest on any one topic.

The light on the answering machine had been flashing the entire weekend. *I might as well clear them before starting a new week.*

"Samira, it's your mother. Ed and Phyllis Jones are meeting us for dinner. Daddy and I would like for you to come along if you don't have any plans." *Ed and Phyllis Jones.* Samira chuckled at her reaction to the name earlier in the day.

The machine continued. "Samira. Where in heaven's name are you? I'm calling your mother." *Susan, Susan.* An unfamiliar male voice started the third message. *Oh, wow. Maybe he did call.* Samira leaned over the counter to listen more closely. "Uhm...hello. My name is Greg. Susan Olinger gave me your number thinking you might have an interest in going out with me...so give me a call if you're free...I'll leave my number and you can..."

Oh, for Heaven's sake. Samira didn't wait for the message to finish. She pressed the delete button and held it down until the machine protested with a loud buzz. *I can't believe Susan gave out my phone number AFTER I asked her not to.*
~~~~~~~

Samira was angry at her friend's betrayal. *How many times do I have to say no?* She looked out the kitchen window as she turned down the lights. *Is it that important to her and Sam that I have a man in my life?* A light still shone in Mrs. Barnes' front room. *I wish I understood her insistence that I find someone.* As she watched, the light across the street went out. *I knew Mrs. Barnes was paying attention Friday night.* There were times when a neighbor's attentiveness was a blessing, but today was not one of those times.

Emotionally exhausted, Samira retreated to her bedroom. *Just a week or so ago I was quite content reading my books and tending to my family.* Samira released the clip in her hair and let the ends fall haphazardly over her shoulders. *I didn't ask for him to interrupt my life.* The dresser drawer opened with ease. She selected a clean nightshirt from the folded pile. *Did I?* She couldn't remember praying for a relationship. *I used to pray that prayer, but somewhere along the line I knew it wasn't meant to be.*

Samira leaned into the pile of pillows on her bed and opened her book. The ring of the telephone startled her. *Maybe that's Phil.*

"Hey Sis,"

It's just Wes. He sounds tired.

"Did I wake you?"

"I wish," Samira admitted. "I'm tired, but I can't get still enough to sleep."

"It's probably the caffeine in all that coffee."

Samira leaned heavily into the pillows and propped her head up. "That would be too easy." She sighed heavily. "What bids your call?"

"Just wondering how your day panned out," Wes hinted. "Did he call?"

It's nice that Weston cares. Still, she didn't want her brother to catch her disappointment. With noted effort, Samira strengthened her voice. "No, not today." *Or yesterday.*

"Were you expecting he might?"

Samira pulled her hair back from her face with her free hand. "We didn't part with any plans," she answered honestly. *Or if he had any, I squelched them by leaving the decision to call in his court.*

"I was just wondering," Wes stated simply. Are you okay with that?"

I can't lie. He knows anyway. "I don't know yet." Samira sank deeper into the pillows.

"I'm sorry, Sis." Wes was sincere. "I thought maybe he'd take time to check in."

He's setting me up in case Phil decides not to call again.

"I know," Samira sighed. Maybe tomorrow." *Maybe.* Yet she was afraid to hope too hard.

"Well, hang in there, alright?"

"Alright." Samira promised. "I'll do my best."

"I'll talk to you tomorrow. Call if you need me."

Samira smiled into the phone. "Thanks."

Once Samira hung up, the room became extremely silent. Hollowness crept into her heart. It was a feeling she hadn't felt in a long while and the memories that came with it were distant, yet painstakingly familiar.

Now that I've discovered that innermost part of me again, I don't know if I can go back. Samira turned off her reading lamp. *I don't know if I want to go back.*

She burrowed down into her covers. *I took a chance.* His scent was still evident on her pillow. *I just hope this isn't my last chance.*

10 The Score that No One Tallied

Joseph Phillip

The screen door banged loudly behind J.P. as he entered Janet's living room without knocking. Bruce and Janet were sitting at the kitchen table. They stopped talking and stared at J.P.

Janet frowned. "You should knock."

Don't give me any shit, Jan. "Where's James?"

"Still in his room. We need to talk first."

J.P. headed for the staircase.

"You don't have a right to go up there," Janet yelled. "We need to talk to you first, J.P."

The time for talking is over. Two by two he ascended the stairs and stopped in front of the only closed door in the hallway. The door was locked from the inside.

"James, open the door." He wrapped the back of his hand against the hollow wood.

Nothing happened.

"J.P., leave James alone and come back down here." Janet was frantic when she reached the top of the stairs. Bruce was close on her heels.

You don't have the answers I need. J.P. pounded harder. "Open the door James, or I'll open it for you." He could feel the force in his own voice, but this time he didn't even try to hold back.

"For heaven's sake, J.P." Janet touched J.P.'s arm.

Don't touch me. "Back off Jan and let me get to the bottom of this."

"Bruce and I were just talking, and we think…"

"I don't give a damn what either one of you think." J.P. banged on the door again. "James, open up."

J.P. grabbed for the knob, but before he could apply any pressure, it turned in his hand.

James stood on the other side, defensive, and erect. A pair of earphones blared music into his ears.

"Get your shoes on, we're going out."

James flopped back onto his bed and cranked the volume.

J.P. could feel his anger boiling. He physically removed the earphones and set his jaw. "I said we're going out."

"J.P. don't—" Janet started to plead.

I have one issue to resolve, and it does not concern you, Janet. J.P. held a long hard stare with his son.

James finally had to look away.

"Get your shoes on." James didn't move. "Now."

"You can't threaten anyone in this house."

J.P. turned and looked at the face that had spoken. *Hamilton finally has enough gumption to open his mouth.* "I didn't threaten anyone." *Yet.* He looked back at James. "Move."

James looked from his mother to his father, then back to his mother who was now crying. He finally reached for his shoes and slipped his size fourteen feet inside.

"Outside." *I want him as far out of Hamilton's earshot as possible.*

J.P. prodded his son onto the front porch and stayed on his heels until they were standing in the driveway next to his truck.

My patience is spent.

James mirrored his father's angry glare.

"I have a few things to say to you James, and it's high time you listened and listened hard." J.P. was talking through clenched teeth and his eyes were narrowly focused on his son.

James looked away.

"Look at me when I'm talking to you, James."

Defiantly James turned back to his father and locked glares again.

"It doesn't sound like you have a welcome bed to sleep in at this house anymore." J.P. began his opening argument. "Up until a few minutes ago you were welcome at my house, but you have some unfinished business in this town and it's high time you leveled with me."

The look on James's face told J.P. that he now knew more details than James had ever planned to tell.

James squared his shoulders and set his jaw. "Since when have you been so goddamned interested in my life?"

J.P. held his ground and answered with force. "Since you arrived on my doorstep too hungover to stand on your own power, that's when."

James spit on the ground in front of his father's shoe. J.P. grabbed for his son's arm, but a right hook caught him under the edge of his ribs.

Holy shit. The father lunged forward and caught his breath. *He delivers a solid punch.* J.P. looked sideways in time to dodge the next swing. *You want to fight James Ralston?* J.P. blocked the next punch. *You'll be sorry you ever took that first swing.*

Niceties were over and the tensions that had been building translated into pure rage. J.P. found himself delivering punches as fast as he was receiving them. He could hear Janet screaming in the background, but it took everything he had to defend against the bent-up anger in his son.

J.P. took a hit high on the cheekbone.

Obscenities flew as flesh and bone connected in ugly blows. There was a vengeance between the Ralston men as blood mixed with tattered emotions. Neither cared who won or lost. This was a battle to earn respect and to settle a score neither had tallied over the years.

Get him down for the count. J.P. was tiring quickly, and he knew he had to take James now or forfeit his dignity. With a final thud, J.P. knocked the legs out from under his son. Off balance and unable to catch himself, James crashed hard onto the gravel. J.P. pinned his son to the ground and used his legs to lock the hold.

Finally, James surrendered.

"You listening now?" J.P. could feel blood running down the side of his cheek. *Jesus, Ralston, what have you done?*

James looked at his father through teary eyes. His nose was bleeding and the look on his face showed stark confusion. J.P. didn't let up on the pressure holding him down. *Let's get this out once and for all.*

"It's one thing to go around screwing up your own life, James," J.P. was winded, but he was determined to close the argument. "But when you manage to screw up someone else's life, that's another story." He stopped talking to spit blood out of his bleeding mouth. "No son of mine will engage in that kind of activity and walk away without taking responsibility." Looking hard into his son's eyes. "Do you hear me?"

James tried to bite his bottom lip, but it was too swollen. He nodded in understanding and let his head fall back against the gravel.

J.P. struggled onto his knees, but James rolled into a fetal position and sobbed quietly. *What kind of a father are you?* J.P. closed his eyes to combat the guilt. There was a scuffle on the gravel. He opened his eyes to see Josh kneeling over his brother. When their eyes connected Josh looked confused and betrayed.

There may not be anything left to fight for. J.P. pressed his hands into his thigh to keep his balance. What had once been anger was now bitter remorse. He watched Josh and Janet help James up off the ground.

Back inside the house J.P. cleaned his wounds in the bathroom while Janet tended to James in the kitchen. J.P. leaned into the mirror and examined the cut on his cheekbone. A cold compress took some of the sting away, but nothing took away the hurt in his heart. *Never in a million years did I think I'd lose control of my temper like that with my own kids.*

Bruce stopped in the doorway. "You want me to wrap that fighting fist for you?"

I don't need any assistance from that bastard. J.P. refused the assistance. Upon closer examination he decided the cut could stand a few stitches. *I just hope the tooth that cut my hand is still intact.* He wrapped his fist with a damp rag.

Janet's eyes were swollen from crying. James had his head tipped back against his mother who was nursing his nose and lip, which were both still oozing blood.

J.P. looked at his son and then looked away. Shame came over him like a blanket. He sensed an unspoken respect between him and James that hadn't been there before. *But that's a hell of a way to find it.*

Josh was seated at the table. He held his head low and refused to make eye contact with his father. *It wasn't that long ago I conceded to Janet's demand for custody.* He forced his eyes back into the faces of both of his boys. *Now my chances of even having a decent conversation with them is in jeopardy.*

Spent from the fight and emotionally drained, there was still business that needed attention. J.P. knew he had to stay to see it through. Every muscle in his body ached and complained as he eased into a chair. Patiently he waited until James and Janet were able to converse.

Tensions were high in the discussion that followed. It was obvious James would not be allowed to stay with Janet and Bruce. *That leaves me.* J.P. thought about that for a moment. *I have no business becoming a parent at this stage in the game.* He studied his son's beaten face. *But I don't think either one of us have much choice in the matter now.*

Late into the night, it was finally agreed that James would stay with Janet long enough to take his semester tests. After that he was headed for Joplin.

Bruce started to get up from the table.

J.P. motioned for Bruce to stay put. "Wait a minute."

"It's late. I'm going to bed."

"There's still two items of unfinished business." J.P. spoke quietly. *We're all tired.* He waited for Bruce to sit back down. *But we need to get everything on the table.* Cautiously, he addressed his son one more time.

"Concerning Jennie Johnson."

James looked away. Josh covered his face with his hands.

"Jennie Johnson is a slut." Bruce accused.

Shut up, Hamilton.

Janet began to speak but J.P. put his hand out to stop her. "Any suggestions, James?" *He knows exactly what I'm talking about.*

Everyone waited as James prepared to respond. His lip was quite swollen by this time and his eyes were starting to darken.

The last hangover isn't even going to register compared to the headache he'll have in the morning.

James dropped his head and mumbled. "She says it's not mine."

"Doesn't think what's yours?" Bruce demanded without permission.

Go easy, Hamilton. We've been through enough already.

James squirmed in his chair. J.P. gave silent permission for him to answer the question.

"The baby." His voice was almost inaudible.

Bruce bolted, tipping his chair over backwards. "You bastard. This is my house." Bruce announced wildly. "And if you knocked up white trash like Jennie Johnson then your ass isn't—"

J.P. stood at the opposite end of the table in defense of his son. He stole a look at Janet and saw her hands come to her mouth in astonishment, but she didn't move.

"Sit down, Bruce."

"You're not in a courtroom, Ralston," Bruce retorted. "You have no right to order me around in my own house."

"Sit down." *You have no right to threaten my son.*

Janet pulled on Bruce's arm. Tears were once again streaming down her face. Reluctantly, Bruce reset his chair and eventually sat back down. He was visibly angered.

"How do you know, James?"

James shrugged his shoulders and hung his head. "I only slept with her once."

Again, Bruce sprang from his chair. "How many times do you think it takes?"

Janet's face softened as she made eye contact with J.P. "Only once," she whispered. Her eyes softened as they connected with J.P.'s. "Only once."

J.P. looked away quickly. He and Janet were all too familiar with the situation at hand. Josh sat at the table as living evidence to that fact. Blurred memories of his ancient past threatened to rock his focus. *That's one mistake I never wanted to pass on to my kids.*

It's out there now. J.P. reviewed the situation and decided to move things forward. *Whether it's his or not, we can work through the details later.* There was only one more item that needed addressed.

J.P. spoke calmly. "James, there's a plea in yesterday's paper from the sheriff's department asking for information regarding the incident in Madsen Park." He waited for James to make eye contact. "Before you can take up residence with me, you need to pay a visit to the sheriff's office and tell them what you know."

Janet gasped. "How can you just stroll into town and know all this about my son?"

OUR son, Janet. J.P. watched Josh and James exchange a knowing look. *That's what I thought. Both still know more about Madsen Park than they're letting on.*

J.P.'s defenses wanted to attack Janet's lack of attention to their sons. *Just stay focused, Ralston, and wrap this up.* "When you give a report of the incident, you'll have to sign a document." He waited for both boys to show attentiveness before continuing. "I expect you to have a copy of that statement with you when you arrive at my house later this week." J.P. rose from his chair and tapped the tabletop with his fingertips. "We'll deal with Jennie Johnson on another agenda."

"I'll deal with Jennie Johnson right now." Bruce was standing again.

J.P. squared his shoulders. "No. You won't." He held Bruce's eyes long enough to let him know who was in charge. *And if I have my way, you won't deal with either of my sons again.*

J.P. needed fresh air. His entire body ached from the fight and his head was pounding from the emotional fatigue. He stepped onto the front porch.

Without permission, Bruce Hamilton followed. He stood with his back to J.P. and lit a cigarette. "He's a tough kid, Ralston." Bruce exhaled the smoke. "You handled him well."

J.P. didn't feel like dealing with Bruce. *Not now or ever again.* "I didn't *handle* anything."

"Let's just say you got your point across," Bruce snickered and puffed on the cigarette again. "The boy is messed up."

That boy you're talking about is my son. J.P. drew a deep breath to control his temper. *It wouldn't take much to take you out, Hamilton.*

"You should let me wrap your hand. It looks pretty rough."

I don't need your rhetoric.

"The last few months around here have been quite a challenge. You have no idea how much shit James has brought into our lives." Bruce took another drag on his cigarette.

His sentiments are much the same for you.

"He's all but flunked out of school. He never comes home at night. And he's hanging out with a bunch of punks."

Give me one thing that would motivate him to come home to this confine. J.P. was still holding his tongue. *My patience is waning.*

Bruce turned around and leaned against the railing. "I have no time for a kid like that in my life."

Nor do I have time for you, bastard. J.P. considered his options. *It's time for closing arguments.*

"You know, Hamilton, I've tolerated the way things are because I figured it was better for the boys if I didn't interfere. I thought it was more important for them to have family stability than a regular visitation schedule with me. Recent discussions with my boys lead me to believe I was dead wrong. I should have stepped in when I knew they were dealing with your egotistical, self-righteous, arrogance months ago. I should have exercised the rights of shared custody and stayed involved in my boys' lives." Now J.P. faced Bruce Hamilton. "I don't know what's going on around here, but something isn't adding up. I'm here to tell you, I'll get to the bottom of it."

Bruce started to speak but J.P. didn't allow a single word. "Understand that from this point forward *all* decisions concerning Josh and James will not concern you."

"If that's the case, then they don't have a right to live under my roof." Bruce shouted in retaliation.

"So be it." J.P. wasn't going to back down. "I'll do whatever it takes to secure stability in my sons' lives, even if it means removing your authority."

Bruce flicked a cigarette butt off the edge of the porch. "You can't do that without a court order."

Consider it done. J.P. considered the ramifications. *Let's see how long he's willing to live without the child support payments.* "Stay away from my boys, Bruce." J.P. felt the depth of his concern rise from somewhere deep within. "They deserve better than you."

He'd finished his argument and was ready to take whatever steps were necessary to remove Bruce Hamilton from immediate custody. J.P. turned to walk away and came face to face with his beaten son. *How long has he been standing there?*

James pursed his swollen lips. The look in his eyes was weary and dejected.

What are you doing, J.P? As badly as he wanted to, he couldn't force his eyes away from James. *The marks on his face are from my fists.* James was crying out in silent desperation.

My God, James. I am so sorry. Every ounce of energy that was left in J.P. screamed for him to put his arms around the boy.

James glanced sideways and broke the silent communication.

"We're going to get through this," J.P. assured his son quietly. *I wish Hamilton would go back inside and leave me alone with my son.*

James nodded as his eyes came to rest on his father's. J.P.'s heart broke with the anguish that was in his son's expression.

He lifted his uninjured hand and placed it on James's shoulder. "We will. I promise."

"I thought you didn't make promises." James spoke the truth solemnly.

He heard what I told the girl at the desk. J.P. took in a long breath and held it there for a long moment. "I do when it's important." *This is different, James.* "This is important."

James nodded once, but avoided eye contact with J.P.

J.P.'s eyes looked over James's shoulder. Josh was standing in the doorframe. His eyes were also mournful and sad. *I might as well have beaten him too.* James went back in the house. If there was communication between the boys in the doorway, J.P. wasn't aware.

Josh moved as his brother passed by. *He hurts as much as James does.* The door slammed again. Josh disappeared behind the screen door without speaking.

And maybe I do too. All the mistakes of his past piled up in his heart. *I thought I had it made with the boys living up here and me working to pay off the divorce and alimony, providing for them according to the law, and putting money away for when they'd finally be free to come and go according to their own agenda.* J.P. tucked his injured hand under his other arm to help deaden the pain. He hadn't realized how long he'd looked forward to the day when James and Josh could make their own decisions about his presence in their lives.

I'm right back where I started seventeen years ago facing the repercussions of the same bad decision. Time passed. *The road I've been on led me right back to the trap I fell into the first time around.*

Standing there alone under the vastness of the universe, J.P. felt considerably insignificant. *Heaven's about the only thing that can save me now.* A single streak of light fell from the sky. J.P. watched it plummet and obliterate into the darkness. *And I'm not putting much hope in that anymore either.*

He made his way down the sidewalk to his truck without saying goodbye to anyone. When he glanced back at the house, James was standing in an upstairs window watching. A new thought occurred. *He may be stuck in a trap too.* J.P. climbed into the driver's seat. *He deserves a chance.* He started the engine and turned the truck around in the driveway. *What if I'm his last chance?*

11 First Aid

Samira

He said he didn't have much time but wondered if I could meet for lunch. Samira replayed their conversation as she walked the three short blocks from the library to her house. *He just wants to talk.* The librarian walked around a little, red tricycle that was parked haphazardly in the middle of the sidewalk. *I wish I knew what he wants to talk about.* She looked both ways before crossing the street. *Of course, I'll make time. I always do.*

Samira stopped at the mailbox. *It would be nice to know where Mrs. Barnes is about now.* She pressed the keypad to open the garage door. *Bill, bill, advertisement, and three fashion magazines. How do these publishers get my name and address, anyway?*

Leftovers were easy to reheat. *A minute in the microwave and we have a full- blown meal.* Samira set two plates on the eating bar at the island. *I hope he's not disappointed I wanted to meet here instead of the Café Ole.* She checked the clock. It was a few minutes before twelve. *It would be so crowded and busy there over the noon hour.*

There was a knock at Samira's front door. *He has yet to be late.* She wiped her fingertips on a kitchen towel. *Breathe.* The door opened to the man she'd only seen in her dreams for the past several nights. He didn't speak and she didn't move.

He looks just as inviting as he did the last time.

"May I come in, Pretty Lady?"

He said that Pretty Lady thing again. "Oh, yes." She opened the door further. "I'm sorry."

"I thought maybe you'd changed your mind."

"About what?"

"About lunch."

Out of habit, Samira relocked the door. *Oh, lunch. What is the matter with me?* "Not at all." *Why am I so nervous?* "Come on in." Her hands were balmy with sweat. *He's clean-shaven but the fresh bruise on his cheekbone looks sore.*

"Are you afraid of intruders?" Phil tapped the lock on the door.

Just breathe, remember? She inhaled slowly through her nostrils and decided to speak the truth. "Maybe more afraid of an intrusion."

"Yeah—" Phil's eyes scanned the room uncomfortably. "Maybe I shouldn't be invading your lunch hour like this."

"Oh, no." Samira caught the misunderstanding instantly. "I mean, from my neighbor." She pointed through the wooden blinds in the dining room window. "I have an elderly neighbor, well, Mrs. Barnes, who doesn't know the word *knock*." Her eyes went back to the bruise on Phil's cheek. *I wonder what happened.*

Phil was nodding. "The one I waved to a minute ago."

I knew she'd be watching. "Yes. That would be Mrs. Barnes." Samira glanced out the window. "I just don't want her paying me an unexpected visit." *Lunch. You should offer him lunch.* Samira tucked her hair behind her ears. "It is lunchtime though. You're probably starving."

"I don't have a lot of time but wanted to see you for a few minutes."

A quick lunch is better than not seeing him at all. "How about ham and scalloped potatoes? Just takes a few seconds." Samira put the casserole dish in the microwave. "Would you like a salad?"

"You don't have to serve me."

I'm more nervous today than I was last weekend.

Phil smiled a genuine smile. "Here." He handed over an empty plate. "You do whatever you do with the potatoes, and I'll fill the glasses. Deal?"

Deal. "The glasses are in..."

"...the cupboard to the right of the sink." Phil finished her sentence. When Samira turned around Phil was already holding two glasses.

"Water for the lady?"

"Yes, please." *I can't believe he remembered.* Samira breathed in deeply, enjoying the scent of his aftershave. *He smells like my pillowcase.* When he turned toward her, she once again took notice of his cheek.

"Have you cleaned your cut?"

Phil glanced at her, then looked away. "I've showered. Does that count?"

"Not really." *It needs some attention.* She waited for him to finish filling the glasses. When he turned toward the breakfast bar, she studied it more closely. "It really should be cleaned. It will heal better."

Phil raised his eyebrows and shook his head again. "It doesn't hurt anymore."

"It looks like it does." The microwave beeped. Samira checked the casserole, but it wasn't ready yet. She pushed the reset button.

"Believe it or not," Phil touched the cut with his fingers. "It looks better than it did."

Then it needs cleaned. "Wait here," Samira touched him briefly on the arm as she left the kitchen. She went to the hall closet. *Here's everything I need. Hydrogen peroxide, cotton swabs, and a box of bandages.*

"Whoa, girl. What are you thinking?"

"I'm going to clean your wound." She set the items on the breakfast bar. "It won't hurt." She reached for his hand. "And it won't take but a minute." She gently pulled on his hand for him to sit down. Phil tensed and yanked it away.

I must have overstepped my bounds. Samira took a step back.

Reluctantly, he put his hand to his chest. It was wrapped in a soiled bandage.

The beep of the microwave interrupted the silence that hung between them.

"Okay, so this one hurts a little."

"I'm sorry." Samira apologized. *I have a feeling there's more to this story than I might want to know.*

"It's not your fault." Much to Samira's amazement, Phil took a step toward the barstool. "You're sure it won't hurt?"

"Not much." *If he's willing, they do need some attention.*

Phil sat down at the breakfast bar, even though his eyes still showed signs of distrust.

Samira poured a small amount of peroxide into a bowl and carefully dipped a cotton swab, studying the cut on Phil's cheek as she did so. Gently, she pressed the swab against his cheekbone and held it there for a few seconds. "Doin' okay?"

"Would it matter?"

He's very tense. Samira touched her fingertips against his other cheek hoping to steady his nerves. The smoothness of his cheek sent shivers up her spine.

"Yes, it would." She removed the swab and examined the cut again. "It will heal faster if it's clean." She used the swab to clear away the dried blood around the edges. "To be honest, I'm more concerned about your hand." *I hate to think what's hidden under there.* "Did you consider seeing a doctor?"

"Didn't even cross my mind."

Why am I not surprised?

"Maybe you could just kiss it and make it better."

"I could, but that might not make it any better."

"I'd be willing to give it a shot."

Samira tried to ignore the chemistry that was building. She used her fingernails and gingerly removed the band aide. The wound underneath was still open. Phil flinched as she adjusted his hand against the counter. *If I didn't know better, I'd guess he was wounded in battle.*

"Where'd you learn first aid"

"My mother is a retired registered nurse. In fact, she's a retired emergency room nurse." Samira looked into Phil's eyes. "If she were here, she'd be dragging you in for stitches." She surveyed the cut on his hand again. "This one is deep."

The muscles in Phil's jaw line flexed as Samira removed the last bit of bandage.

"I'm almost afraid to ask, but what did your father do?"

"Finance and Business." Samira flattened Phil's hand against the counter.

"I'm glad he wasn't a surgeon." Phil inserted a moment of lightheartedness into the moment.

Samira was sincerely concerned about the lack of medical attention. "This one might hurt a little." She eased the swab into the cut.

Phil's jovial spirit faded quickly as the peroxide penetrated the wound.

Samira apologized when he caught his breath, but she didn't remove the swab. *He asked a personal question. I'll do the same.* "Who was the victim?"

Several seconds passed.

"What makes you think it was a *victim*?"

I wonder if he always answers a question with another question. "I'm assuming he fought back." She removed the cotton swab and started to soak another.

"Really," Phil started to pull his hand away. "You don't need to do it again."

"The second won't hurt as much because the nerve endings are primed." Gently, Samira took a hold of Phil's fingers and repositioned his hand. "Almost done." This time when the peroxide penetrated, Phil didn't respond.

"How bad was the other guy?" *I don't know if he's holding out because of the pain, or because he doesn't want to talk about it.*

Phil drew a deep breath and let it out slowly. "My hand hit his teeth about the same time his fist connected with my cheekbone."

Samira held pressure on the open sore. "Is he alright?" She looked up from the wound into his eyes. *The anguish in his eyes is far worse than the pain in his hand.*

Phil stared at his hand. When he answered, his voice was very low. "The *other guy* was my son."

Oh, Phil.

Without further prompting, Phil filled in the details of his weekend, ending with the fight with James.

No wonder he hasn't called. Samira finished cleaning the cut as she listened. Using a butterfly bandage, she pulled the flesh together as best she could. *It could still stand a few stitches.*

Phil summarized the situation. "So, he'll be arriving on my doorstep with a suitcase tonight." He stopped talking and looked at Samira. "I haven't been a full-time father in more than ten years." His face was contemplative. "And to be perfectly honest, I haven't the slightest idea where to begin."

The worrisome look in Phil's eyes captured Samira's empathy. "You've already begun." There were many questions she wanted to ask but she knew the noon hour was quickly slipping away. "Just go slow. You'll both have some adjustments to make, but everything will come together. But right now, we need to get some food in your stomach."

Samira turned for the microwave, but Phil pulled her into a full embrace. This time when he started to kiss her, Samira didn't turn him away.

"Aren't you hungry?"

"Not anymore." He kissed her again. "At least not for lunch."

Without warning, Phil suddenly let go. He didn't push away, he just released his hold on her.

Oh, my. Samira watched him raise a cell phone to his ear. *Did it ring?*

Phil checked his watch against the display on the cellular phone. "I need to check in at the office." He pressed a button. "It will just take a minute."

Samira pushed the reheat button on the microwave. She listened over the hum of the microwave.

"Yeah, Denise, it's me...what time?"

Who's Denise?

"I'm still at lunch...no, I can be there...call the city attorney and reschedule for morning...any word from Benson and Barringer?"

He reminds me of Wes when he's in a business mode. She carried the steaming food to the breakfast bar.

"...It could run late but I'll still check in before I leave for home...,"

Samira continued to listen.

"...Anything else? ...She did? ...tell her I'll be there...no, just tell her to meet me at the office..."

He never says goodbye at the end of a phone call. "Busy day?"

"Busy week."

I'm beginning to think his entire life is scheduled to the hilt. "It's okay if you eat and run," Samira offered. "I need to get back to work too."

Phil sat down on the same barstool and picked up a fork with his uninjured hand.

That's funny, he ate with his right hand the other night. The playfulness of the previous moment was long gone. *His mind has moved on to the afternoon agenda.*

"Thanks for the first aide, Samira," Phil offered between bites. He held out his injured hand and examined the new bandage. "I'll certainly look more presentable at this afternoon's meeting."

"Your cheek looks better too. You still might want to have a doctor look at your hand."

Phil interrupted. "Nah, it will be alright." He nodded his head in approval. "Feels better already."

Something tells me he doesn't even have a primary care physician. She could feel his eyes on her as she finished taking a bite of potatoes.

"What?" She asked as she laid her fork alongside of her plate.

Phil was leaning back in the armed stool with his hands behind his head. "I was just thinking," he grinned slightly. "Last time I left with an agenda and now I show up with the same scenario." Phil rose from his chair. "I'm damn lucky you're so accommodating. Especially on short notice like this."

I'm glad we didn't go to the Café Ole.

"You don't have to be so kind." He refilled his water glass and took a drink before returning to the breakfast bar. "But I do appreciate the hospitality." He stopped right next to her. "I really wanted to call before today—"

"That's okay." *Under the circumstances.* "You were obviously a little distracted."

Without waiting for permission, Phil bent down and gently kissed her on the lips. *If this is his thanks, I like it.*

"There's a chair with my name on it in a conference room across town." Phil's voice was smooth and quiet.

Samira stood up and allowed Phil to kiss her again. But this time he didn't stop. His bandaged hand moved up her back on the inside of her shirt.

"Then you'd best be on your way." *I don't want him to start what he can't finish.* This time Samira was close enough to feel the vibration between her stomach and Phil's hip. *So that's how he knows he has an incoming call.*

Reluctantly, he slid his hand out of her blouse. His eyes were suddenly distant.

"Duty calls?" Samira was somewhat relieved for the interruption. *I really don't want to make him late.*

"Unfortunately."

Samira noted a look of regret. "Don't let me keep you."

Phil put the phone to his ear. As he turned away, he ran his hand through his hair.

Samira waited. *He is so intense.*

There was an awkward silence when Phil turned back around.

"Thanks for lunch, Samira." There was a hint of hesitation. "And for the medical attention."

Samira's eyes re-examined the cut on his cheek. *It does look much better.* She stood completely still as Phil's arm gently pulled her in. Instinctively, she closed her eyes and returned his tender kiss.

"I'll call you," he whispered.

I wonder how soon.

His lips brushed her forehead briefly before he walked toward the front door. He stopped long enough to unlock the deadbolt.

Samira watched. He crossed the length of the porch and climbed into his pickup. His stride was confident. *He's already focused on work.*

He isn't anything like the man in my prayers. She had pictured a man with a typical nine to five workday. *Or maybe a schoolteacher who worked the same kind of hours as me.* She'd pictured someone more settled, and maybe even more adjusted. *I imagined a family man.*

But Phil is none of these things. He's restless, over committed to his work, and insecure about being a dad. He's as professional as he is rugged. Samira shook her head as she cleared away the lunch dishes. *He's so far from the man I had painted in my mind.*

Samira started down the driveway headed back to work. *What is it about him that draws me?* She glanced across the street. *No visible sign of Mrs. Barnes.* She crossed the second street. *So why do I only want more of him if he isn't what I'd hoped for?* His aftershave was still fresh in her memory.

I'm drawn to his restless nature. A smile crept across her face. *Yes, I am. There is something exceedingly romantic about a man who can't settle down.* She thought about his busy schedule. *Or maybe about a man who won't settle down.* Samira waited for a car to pass before crossing the intersection.

As she walked through the entryway of the library, her eyes passed over the rows upon rows of organized books and periodicals. *Maybe it's time for something less predictable and orderly for a change.* A shiver crept up her spine as she considered the answers to the questions. *Maybe it was his intrusion I feared when I locked the door.*

12 House Arrest

Joseph Phillip

J.P. was still deep in thought over Mid-America as he climbed the steps to his office. Evidence against the hackers was piling up and the documentation of the crime was complete, but the board of directors was frustrated with the investigative reports. *The authorities are not moving fast enough.* It was becoming obvious that additional examination would be necessary over and above that of the local precinct. *Because nothing is leading to an arrest.*

"You were a bit distracted over the lunch hour." Denise handed the communications clipboard to her boss immediately upon his arrival.

"I was behind closed doors." His eyes scanned the telephone messages. *Too many personal calls.*

"I'm sure you were." She pointed at his hand. "You must have decided to see a doctor."

Better than a doctor.

"The Hughes Corporation needed an RSVP for a dinner party before two o'clock."

"How did I respond?"

"You accepted for you and a guest. You'll be sitting with Christopher and his wife at the head table the night after they return from England."

"When?"

"Three weeks from Friday in Springfield." Denise turned to her computer and pulled up J.P.'s calendar on the screen.

"Business or otherwise?" J.P. set the clipboard back on Denise's desk. "And who's on the guest list?"

"Formal business, it sounds like you'll be overseeing the prenuptials. It's their daughter's engagement party. I'll inquire about the guests." Denise turned and faced her employer. "Should I secure an escort?"

"That won't be necessary." *I'll make that call myself this time.*

"I could call *Mary*?" Denise exaggerated the name. "She called again, by the way. She sounded like she might like to see you again."

"Screw Mary." *I still can't put a name with a face.*

"I'm assuming you already took care of that." Denise followed him into his office. "What do I do with the rest of these phone calls?"

The attorney sat down in his chair. "Call the vet back and schedule Chase for vaccinations." J.P. picked up a pen and jotted down his concerns about the incomplete investigation for Mid-America. His eyes went back to Denise in the doorway. *Why is she still standing there?*

"Any instructions for the rest of the phone messages?"

J.P. stopped writing and looked directly at his assistant. *I don't have any desire to talk to any of them.* He considered the names on the list. *But I don't know why I can't tell Denise that.*

She was still waiting.

J.P. made another note concerning Mr. Stephenson's case. *You don't want to tell her because you know she's going to give you shit about it.* "You can let them go."

Denise opened her green eyes wide and put her hands on her hips. "You don't even want me to call one for the Hughes party?"

"No."

"You don't happen to have a steady or something now, do you, Boss?"

I do not have a steady. J.P. chose not to respond. *She's right. Normally I'd be all over that list looking for a date.* "What's on for the rest of the week?"

Denise disappeared for a minute and returned with the clipboard. "Okay, I've put off all the low priority items until the Mid-America case is underway. We have a court date for the Hughes hearing in two weeks." She looked up from her notepad. "I expect they'll settle before that though, don't you?"

"The city will do whatever it takes to avoid negative publicity with the Hughes family. I'm sure city hall is working on a compromise." Another thought entered his mind. "However, it might not hurt to have a representative at the city council meeting next week."

"I'll clear my calendar." Denise jotted a reminder on the corner of the paper. "Derek Danielson from Benson & Barringer will be here to interview in an hour and Mike left a message about a special investigator?"

"Our honorable police department isn't impressing me with Mid-America's computer glitch. Benson and Barringer have an inside track on a private investigator, but I want to talk to Mike again before we hire." *The sooner the better.*

"I'll see if I can get him on the phone."

"Very well. Give me five minutes to recap the board meeting." He checked his watch. "How long before Janet gets here with James?"

"She said she'd be here around six. Derek Danielson will be here in about forty-five minutes now."

"Before I talk to him, brief him on a couple business law case studies."

Denise was taking notes. "I can do that. Obviously, you want an intern to actually work this time and not just follow you around to social engagements?"

J.P. ignored her insinuations. *Although the last two interns were less for legal assistance and more for my personal agenda.*

"And what about James? Is he coming to stay?" Denise stopped writing.

"He could be here for the better part of the summer." *Just thinking that makes me nervous.* "Depends on how fast Mike gets to the paperwork." *I'm more comfortable unraveling the online heist at Mid-America than I am trying to figure out how to be a father to a wayward fifteen-year-old.*

Denise smiled. "Personally, I find it rather interesting that becoming a full-time father has you turning down dates."

I may get more mileage out of James than I thought. J.P. glanced in Denise's direction. "That will be all, Denise."

The peace that came with the closed door was a welcome reprieve to the madness of the previous twenty-four hours. J.P. stretched his arms into the air then locked his hands behind his head. *You think I'd be anxious to get on with this case.*

He found the Maple Street Library number in cell history and tapped the call button. "Ms. Cartwright, please." A few moments later Samira's voice filled his ear. "Samira, it's J—" *No, she doesn't know me as J.P.* "Phil. Do you have a minute?"

"I was just about ready to leave for home."

Which means she probably gets off about this time every day. He mentally filed that information for future reference. "Should I wait and call you there?"

Samira gave permission for him to continue.

"I just got back to the office and learned I have a dinner engagement in Springfield in about three weeks." J.P. moved the computer mouse to pull his calendar onto the screen. "I'd like to take you as my guest if you're free." *And I hope she is.* J.P. tapped his pen against the legal pad as he waited for a response.

"What's the date?"

Tell me you can make it. His eyes scanned the Fridays until he spotted the Hughes engagement. "Looks like the seventeenth."

The silence on the other end of the phone was not as encouraging as J.P. had hoped. "But if you already have plans, I understand—"

"No, no," Samira replied quickly. "It's nothing like that. Can I let you know?"

"Sure, no problem." *How soon?* "Should I give you a call later?"

"Give me a couple of days."

J.P. waited. But no further explanation followed. *A couple of days before I call you again, or before you can give me an answer?*

The call ended without any clear direction. *I should have waited to call her at home.* He was used to immediate answers. *This woman, as beautiful as she is, has issues making decisions.* Even this morning when he called to take her to lunch, he had no intention of ending up at her house. *But she wasn't very eager to meet at the cafe.*

J.P. admired the clean bandage on his hand again. He could feel her body against his as he remembered the way she returned his kiss. *I couldn't have done that at a restaurant.*

Maybe I gave her too much personal info. He jotted a few notes on the pad concerning Mid-America, but his train of thought was elsewhere. *I don't know what made me open up like that.* His pen went over the letters of his notes again. *She's obviously easier to talk to than any woman I've been out with in the past.* J.P. shook his head. *Correction. She's the only woman I've ever discussed personal matters with.*

~~~~~~~

Derek Danielson turned out to be a promising prospect for legal assistance. J.P. rose from his chair and offered a handshake. Derek rose also, towering over the senior attorney by several inches.

"Any way I can be of service, Mr. Ralston."

"Be here in the morning and we'll put you to work." J.P. stepped back from the table. "And call me J.P." *Everyone else does.* He corrected his thought. *Well, almost everyone.*

"Very well, sir." His glasses made his eyes look smaller than they really were.

He's eager to work. That's a good sign. "Denise will brief you on the case work at hand."

"Yes, sir."

We've got to lose the sirs.

The smile on Derek's face gave away his excitement. J.P. buzzed for his assistant. *I don't know if I've ever hired a male intern.* Denise appeared instantly.

"Denise, Mr. Danielson will be starting in the morning. Is there anything you need to go over with him before he leaves today?"

"Yes, I do. And your son is here, J.P."

He's early. J.P. followed Denise and Derek Danielson into the outer office. Janet was sitting cross-legged in a winged-back chair looking quite out of place. James had his back to the office, looking out the window over the street down below.

James turned around slowly. J.P. took a long, deep breath. *The bruises around his eye are from my fist.* J.P. motioned for them to join him in his own office.

"How'd it go at school today?" He cleared the interview files from the table behind his desk.

James lowered himself into the corner chair. "Fine."

"Any specifics?"

James shrugged. "Took the semester tests and came home."

"James only had two tests today, so he was out early." Janet was still standing in front of J.P.'s desk. "So, we're here a little early."
~~~~~~~

"I noticed." J.P. ran his hand through his hair and sat down at the table. "Have a seat, Jan." *It's hard to focus on family matters when this casework is screaming for my attention.*

"James has a paper to show you." Janet sat down at the table across from James. "He and Josh went down to the sheriff's office and told them what they knew about the Madsen Park incident."

We could have reviewed that later, but since she brought it up, we might as well get it over with. J.P. motioned for James to hand over the papers. They were crumpled and tattered.

He quickly skimmed the contents of the legal-sized papers. *I'd prefer to discuss this with James in private.* "It appears everything is in order."

"Nothing is in order if you read the whole thing." Obviously agitated, Janet rose from her chair and crossed her arms.

A buzzer sounded on his desk. "Excuse me, J.P. Can you take a call on two?"

Denise wouldn't interrupt if it weren't important. He walked to his desk and picked up the receiver hoping to hear Samira's voice.

"I have a meeting set up with Sparky, J.P."

It's Mike.

"He's willing to listen, but he doesn't want to meet downtown. I set it up at Mona's Cafe just south of the city."

J.P. turned his back to his ex-wife. "This isn't the best time." *James's affidavit needs my attention.*

"Best time for what?" Mike asked into his ear. "To hire the best cyber spy in the world?"

"No, to discuss the possibilities." *Maybe Mike will read between the lines here. And what the hell kind of a name is Sparky anyway?*

"Well, excuse me for interrupting, but Sparky needs a confirmation within the next two minutes, or he'll split."

"Split what?"

"Town, that's what." Mike laughed. "Do you want him or not?"

Sparky. The attorney considered the name again. *His credentials are outstanding.* "I don't know."

"Trust me, J.P. This is the P.I. you want. He's ex-KGB. His skills are second to none and he won't settle for anything less than goal. You tell him what you need, and he'll deliver."

J.P. had no reason to not trust Mike, but at the same time *Sparky* seemed a bit far-fetched to be real. "Does he speak English?"

"Si ` , si ` ," Mike replied seriously. "Along with probably five or six other languages."

All I need is English. "Where's Mona's?"

"Tenth and Collyer. Eight tomorrow morning I already cleared that with Denise."

J.P. glanced at the schedule that was still up on his computer screen. *Sure enough, M. B. at Mona's is typed right into the agenda.* "Eight?" *Why so early?*

"Do you need a wake-up call?"

"No, I'll be there."

Janet was impatiently pacing the length of his office.

I've got to get her out of here. J.P. turned his attention back to the paperwork from the sheriff's office, but this time he put on his glasses. He wasn't sure what he was looking for, but it seemed complete. Without looking up, J.P. turned to the second page. James Ralston's signature was scrawled on the bottom line followed by Janet's signature.

"Did you have to go with him today?"

"Yesterday," Janet corrected. "And no, I didn't take him down there. They called me to come over."

J.P. looked from his ex-wife to his son.

"Your ingenious suggestion for James to go talk to the cops now has charges filed against him."

"Charges?" The attorney in J.P. looked at his son over the top of his glasses. "What kind of charges?"

"It's all there in those papers," Janet continued. "Now he's under arrest. Juvenile house arrest until he can see the judge a week from Thursday."

"What else can you tell me, James?" J.P. sat down at his desk and waited.

"I wouldn't fink on my friends, so they are holding me accountable, whatever that means." James shrugged, keeping his eyes anywhere but on his father.

J.P. removed his glasses and squeezed the bridge of his nose. *This isn't exactly the way I wanted to begin my custody stint.* Janet was rattling on and on. *God, I wish she'd shut up.* She finally stopped talking and looked at him as if maybe there should be a response of some kind.

"What do you want me to say?"

"You weren't even listening."

How can I listen and think at the same time?

"Do you even care what the rules are?"

"Rules for custody or the arrest or what?" *What I need to do now is get this paperwork over to Mike.*

"You figure it out yourself," she said through clenched teeth. "I came all the way down here, waited for you to get out of yet another meeting, just so I could talk to you about this, and you still don't care enough to hear what I have to say."

J.P. couldn't deny the fact that he'd tuned her out, and he was fairly sure he couldn't convince her that he did care. *But given the set of circumstances, there's nothing I can do until he goes before the judge anyway.*

"Look, Jan, if he's under house arrest, then he's under house arrest. We can't change that before he goes to court."

"Do you know exactly what that means?" She didn't wait for an answer. "That means he must be in the presence of a parent or guardian twenty-four-seven unless he has a job. If he has a job, he has to sign in and out with a designated supervisor even when he goes to the bathroom." The pitch of Janet's voice was getting higher as she spoke. "He cannot be out of sight from an adult for one minute for the next ten days."

Okay. J.P. thought about that information. *That's a little overwhelming.* Considering the current casework, the attorney could see some issues arising. *Then we'll find him a job, so I know where he is all day long.* The father leaned back into his leather chair and took a deep breath. *And Denise is going to hate the fact that she's legal guardian number two.*

"Then we'll deal with it." *It's time to end this conversation.* "At least James went down to the precinct and reported what he knew." *Or at least part of what he knows.* "You're off the hook, Jan. You can go home. I'll pick Josh up at the usual meeting place on Saturday morning."

Janet blinked the tears out of her eyes, obviously surprised at the dismissal. J.P. appreciated the moment of silence as she gathered her thoughts.

"His things are in my car."

J.P. reached his right hand into his front pocket, careful not to rub too hard against the fresh bandage. He handed his truck keys to James. Without a word James followed his mom out of the office.

"Denise. Can you get Ernie McElroy on the phone for me?"

"At the club?"

"Yeah. You know him, the maintenance manager." *Surely, he has something James can do around there.*

"Will do."

"Then I need to talk to Mike again as soon as you can locate him." *He's probably already at the gym.* J.P. checked his watch. *Looks like I won't get a workout in today.*

"Line two, boss. Ernie."

"Ernie, I need a favor. My son is moving in with me for a while and he needs a job. Have anything out there he can give you a hand with?"

The elderly voice of the long-time employee at the club was thoughtful. "Well, I can surely find something for him to do. How old is he, J.P.?"

"Fifteen. And he's big—six four and about one-ninety." J.P. thought again. "And he's an athlete." He waited while Ernie thought again.

"How soon is he gonna be here?"

"He's here now. The sooner he's employed the better."

"I could use him in the mornings to pick up golf balls off the driving range. After that he can help the mowers out on the green. Can you have him out here by five thirty?"

J.P. glanced at the clock reluctant to give up another minute of the quickly passing afternoon. "I can run him over right now. How long do you need to keep him?"

Mr. McElroy chuckled. "Five thirty in the mornin,' J.P."

"In the morning?" *Shit. I thought eight o'clock was early.* "Do you know how long it's been since I've seen five thirty at that end of the day?"

"That's the beginning of the day," Ernie chuckled again. "Not the end. Have him over here and I'll see to it he gets a good workout."

J.P. wrapped up the details of the arrangement and thanked Ernie for his help. By the time he was finished with the phone call James was back upstairs in the office.

James pointed at the clean bandage on his dad's hand as he tossed the truck keys across the room. "You go see a doctor or what?"

J.P. admired the bandage. "A friend doctored me up over the lunch hour." *I don't think I've ever referred to a woman as a friend.*

"It looks damn serious now. You end up with stitches?"

J.P. shook his head. He could see evidence of the split in James's lip and the darkness of his eyes gave indication that he was also still recovering. "How are you?"

James shrugged his shoulders. "Alright, I guess. A little sore."

Denise buzzed the desk.

Probably Mike.

"Mr. Hughes, J.P. Line one."

J.P. picked up the call without hesitation.

"J.P., this is Jeffrey Hughes."

Must be calling about real estate. Christopher Hughes would be calling about the estate matters. "How can I be of service?"

"I'm needing some information on a real estate tycoon in Joplin. He goes by the name of Sean Bridges. Do you know him?"

"I know the name but nothing specific." J.P. turned to a clean sheet of paper. "But we can do some snooping around. Something specific you're looking for?"

"He's contacted us regarding an industrial tract for sale northwest of the city."

The city of Joplin has shown interest in that same tract. Across the bottom edge of a legal pad, he wrote: *Sean Bridges.*

"We need to understand Bridges' motives before we move forward."

J.P. nodded his head into the phone. "I'll see what I can do, Mr. Hughes. Are you working on a timeline?"

"As always, J.P.," Mr. Hughes' tone was dead serious. "Do what you can."

"We'll do." *But I'm hesitant to take on another assignment.* J.P. ran his hand through his hair. *But it is the Hughes Corporation, just the same.*

"We appreciate your assistance."

J.P. shook his head as he hung up the phone. *Derek Danielson isn't coming on board any too soon.*

"Denise, what do you know about a Sean Bridges?"

"He owns and operates Bridges Property Management. Why?" She appeared in the door between the offices.

"Jeffrey Hughes wants the run down on him as soon as humanly possible. Anything you can get on him."

"I can put Danielson on it first thing in the morning."

"I'd rather have it today." *I'm going to owe her for this one.* "And if you can find anything on the industrial tract for sale on the edge of town, we could use that too."

"The one out by the airport?"

"That's the one."

"The city is considering it for airport expansion. It will no doubt be on the agenda for next week's council meeting."

I know. "Get the low down. Anything you can find could be useful." J.P. spun around in his chair and reached for the newspaper folded on the credenza. He pulled out the real estate section and handed it to his son along with a yellow highlighter. "Mark every listing you can find with Bridges Property Management or Sean Bridges as the agent."

James spread the paper out across the conference table behind his father's desk and went to work. The additional assignment at the end of the day rewound J.P.'s mind back to the weekend before.

"Hey, Denise, what were you doing here late Saturday afternoon?"

"Oh, I finished the report for the Lloyd Hughes Estate so we could get it off in time Monday."

Shit. I forgot all about finishing that report. "Did we get it over there in time?"

"Of course."

I owe her big time. "I'll make it up to you."

"A simple thank you would suffice, but I'm always up for a cash bonus." Denise flashed a quick smile and disappeared through the doorway. "I hate to add excitement to your day but while you were on the phone with Mr. Hughes, another call came in."

"And that would be from?"

Denise grinned but didn't answer.

Don't make me play games, Denise. "Who was it?"

"I don't know much about her," Denise started. "But she called earlier and wondered why you didn't call back. She's in the area this weekend."

Obviously not Samira. "Out with it." J.P. opened the Mid-America file in his hand.

Denise came back and stood between the offices momentarily. "Bobbie Jo Sommers." She instantly disappeared around the corner.

The attorney stared at the empty doorway. *Just who I don't need making an appearance.* Leaving the folder on his desk, he followed Denise.

"What'd you tell her?"

"That you were behind closed doors."

"Very funny." *I didn't figure I'd see Bobbie Jo anytime soon.*

"Seriously," Denise added. "I told her you'd call when you got a free moment." She handed him a memo with Bobbie's phone number.

Doesn't look like I'll be any too free this weekend. He remembered the house arrest. *Or any time soon.*

"Who's Bobbie Jo Sommers?" James asked as he was reviewing the real estate listings.

Surprised by his son's inquiry, J.P. tried to shrug it off. "A girl I ..." *I what? I didn't exactly date her. I just spent a week in her bed.* "I was with a while back." The details of the affair were still fresh in the attorney's memory. *Let's change the subject.* "What are you finding on Bridges?"

"Nothing yet." He didn't look up from the paper. "So, you might have a hot date this weekend then?"

"Doubtful." *But she does have a figure that will stop you in your tracks.* He pictured Bobbie's lingerie shot in his mind. *But the last time she was in town I lived alone.* Another pretty face came into focus. *And the last time she was in town, I didn't know Samira Cartwright.*

J.P. tried to concentrate on the case in front of him. *What is it with this Cartwright woman? She didn't even accept my invite to the Hughes' engagement.* The one-sided conversation continued. *Face it, Ralston, she's so far out of your league. Maybe you should walk away while you still can.*

13 Drama

Samira

The Cartwright girls danced anxiously waiting for their mother to finish a phone conversation. *For heaven's sake, what is so important that they can't wait another minute?*

"Guess what. Guess what happened after school today." They giggled simultaneously.

"What? What?" *I don't know what's triggering their excitement, but I do know it's about time for us to meet my parents for dinner.*

Kara nudged Krissy in the arm.

"Well?" *Spit it out, girls.*

"Kara has a boyfriend."

A boyfriend? "Really?" *Oh my. I don't know if I'm ready for this.* Samira's excitement instantly turned into nausea.

Kara's skin turned a dark crimson. "Well, maybe not a boyfriend yet, but he asked me out."

Asked her out.

Krissy hugged her sister. "This is so exciting. I can't wait to tell Tiffany."

Samira removed Krissy's freckled arms from around Kara's neck. "What's his name?"

"His name is Ryan and he's so cute. He's Rona's brother and he's in high school and everything." Before Kara could take a breath, Krissy spilled. "He wants Kara to go to the movies with him Saturday."

Ryan. "Saturday?" *Knowing his name doesn't help me feel better about this.*

"You should see him, Mama. He's—"

Samira held out her palm. "Thank you for the report, Krissy, but I would rather discuss the details with your sister." *Alone.*

The telephone rang into the excitement. Krissy pounced on the receiver and quickly disappeared behind a closed door. *Okay. We have about twenty minutes to figure this out.* Samira studied Kara's face. *She's waiting for my permission.*

"This is very big news, Kara." Samira sat down in the desk chair. "Ryan." *Wow. Is Kara old enough to date?* "Is he really in high school?"

"Going into the tenth grade." Kara's eyes were dancing. "But Mama, I am going into the ninth grade, remember?"

It doesn't seem possible. Samira studied her daughter's excited face. "Do I know Regan?"

"Ryan."

"I mean the sister."

"Rona."

"Rona. Do I know her?"

"Rona Parkison. They live on Walnut Street not too far from the old depot." Kara's face lit up. "The movie starts at 2:00 Saturday. It's PG-13 and his parents can pick me up and—"

"Oh, Kara." Samira interrupted. She stood up and ran her hand through Kara's hair. *She is so beautiful.* She hugged Kara more to buy time to gather her thoughts than anything else. *And growing up so fast. How do I know this Ryan won't take advantage of her?*

"Can I think about this through dinner?"

"You're not going to talk to Uncle Wes about it first, are you?"

"Why do you ask that?"

Kara dropped her voice. "I don't know. It just seems like you always talk to him about these kinds of things first. I don't want him involved in my private life this time."

I can appreciate that. "Then I won't talk to Uncle Wes. But let me think it through, okay?"

~~~~~~~

The restaurant was busy when Samira and the girls arrived. *We all have our assigned places to sit, as always.* Her parents sat one at each end of the table. *They're kind of like bookends to our lives.* But the chair opposite Samira was empty. *It's not like Wes to miss a family gathering.*

"I'm going to order for Wes." Pam was getting Mark situated. "He said he'd be along in a few minutes."

As soon as the waitress had taken everyone's order, Papa Ray was right on task. "Let's see the end of the year grade cards." He was beaming at his granddaughters.

Both grandparents examined the report cards with animated enthusiasm. Samira felt her father put his hand over hers. *That's daddy's way of telling me how proud he is of my girls.*

Samira's mind slipped back to the conversation with Phil earlier in the week. *I don't know what I'd do if one of my girls was having issues in school.* She unfolded her napkin and put it on her lap when the waitress delivered her salad. *I am so thankful my girls take their studies seriously.*

Ah, here comes Wes. Samira glanced at Pam, who was busy feeding Mark croutons from her salad. *She'll feel better when Wes gets in his seat.* It felt strange having one empty chair. *I remember the first time we came here after Tom was gone.* She forced that memory from her mind. *I'm glad Wes's chair won't stay empty.*

They were halfway through the main course before Samira was addressed in conversation.

"You've been awfully quiet this evening, Sis." Wes was looking across the table into his sister's eyes.

Samira shrugged. "I didn't mean to be."

"Something on your mind?"

Plenty. Samira shook her head and forced a smile. She could feel Kara watching her. "I'm just enjoying the chatter, that's all." Now she could feel her father's eyes on her as well. *Why do I always feel so transparent with Daddy and Wes?* She wiped her mouth with the napkin.

Wes nodded but Samira knew he didn't buy her explanation. *Nor did Daddy.* She added a pad of butter to the baked potato. *And Kara is scared to death I'm going to talk to Wes about her social agenda.* The butter melted quickly. *That's kind of how I feel. Melted from the inside out.*

~~~~~~~

The stars were faintly visible in the sky beyond the city lights. *It's a beautiful night.* Samira walked along the sidewalk in front of the restaurant. It was warm enough she didn't need a jacket. She watched her brother help fasten the children into their car seats.

If I don't discuss Kara's social issues with Wes, where do I turn for advice? For a moment, Samira wished Tom could be there to celebrate the end of another school year with his daughters. *Sometimes I wish he were here to help me through these parenting decisions too.* A new thought entered her mind. *I wonder what he would say about Kara wanting to date a high schooler.*

"The girls' grade cards are very impressive indeed," Raymond spoke quietly.

"They had a good year. I just can't believe this will be their last year together at the middle school." Samira liked the way her father put his arm around her shoulder.

"They wouldn't be nearly so well adjusted without your guidance, Princess." A genuine smile crossed his face. "You're doing a fine job with them."

"Thank you, Daddy." *Does he know I'm struggling with a parenting issue tonight?* Samira followed his eyes to where her daughters were standing. *He must know, or he wouldn't have said that.*

"Sometimes it's really hard, Daddy." *My biggest issue is making a decision about my own dinner invitation before I can deal with Kara's.*

"I know it is." Raymond pecked his daughter on the cheek with his soft lips. *That's exactly how Phil kissed my forehead when he left the other day.* Samira smiled and glanced at her father. *No wonder it feels so natural when Phil does that. It's just like Daddy.*

"Sorry I was late to dinner." Wes apologized as he stepped up onto the sidewalk.

Wes is talking to Daddy, not to me.

"Everything alright at the bank, Weston?" Raymond dropped his hand from Samira's shoulder and tucked it into his front pocket.

They rarely discuss business outside the office.

"A little hectic, but under control." Wes answered casually but Samira knew he was thinking otherwise. "Just happened to have an early meeting that ran late."

"Unusual for a Friday afternoon, isn't it?"

Wes nodded. "First time in a long time."

Krissy and Kara joined their mother.

Wes grinned broadly at his nieces. "I didn't know if I'd see you two here tonight. Won't be long and we'll be adding chairs for boyfriends at this end of the school year dinner."

The comment was made in complete innocence, but the look on Kara's face wrongly accused her mother of discussing private issues with her uncle.

"It's not our social schedule you have to worry about, it's Mama's. She's been—"

Krissy. Please don't bring me into this. She stopped her daughter with her eyes.

Wes ruffled Krissy's hair. "Your mother deserves a little personal time, don't you think?" He winked at his sister.

Samira could feel her father's eyes studying her face as it reddened against the night sky. *It's not time to talk to my parents about Phil.* But she did know if she chose to accept an evening invitation to Springfield, she would need a place for the girls to stay the night.

"I was thinking I might take Pam out tomorrow night."

Samira wondered if Wes changed the topic of conversation for her benefit.

"It's been a while since we've had a moment alone."

Pam did seem unusually quiet at dinner. "Do you need help with the children?"

"Maybe," Wes admitted. "If you're free."

Krissy turned abruptly and faced her mother with a pouting lip.

"Your father and I could take the children for a while," Ashleigh volunteered as she joined her family. "We'll be through with the hospital auxiliary function around five."

Something tells me Wes would rather not accept that offer.

"That's okay, Mama," Samira assured. "We don't mind, do we girls?" *Maybe Wes and Pam would reciprocate the favor if I do decide to go to Springfield.*

Kara rudely pulled her mother's arm toward the car. "It's getting late, and we still have some…" Kara whispered the next word, "…*discussing* to do."

Samira fastened her seatbelt as Krissy let loose. "How come we're always the babysitters when Uncle Wes decides he needs a night out?"

"They just went out for dinner together tonight," Kara added.

Believe me, it's not the same. Samira sighed and turned her car into the night traffic.

"But we start babysitting Monday. Maybe we don't feel like sitting with them tomorrow too." Krissy sighed obnoxiously. "You didn't even ask us." Krissy's annoyance was relentless, and her irritation showed. "How come Uncle Wes always plans on us to stay with the kids? Granny offered too."

Enough. "I offered, Krissy. Wes is more comfortable with us coming to the house than he is taking all three kids to Granny's for the night."

Kara clarified the statement, "Why is Aunt Pam more comfortable with us than Granny? You've always trusted Papa Ray and Granny to be our overnight babysitters, right Mama?"

Except when I go with Phil to Springfield. She reviewed that thought. *Does that mean I'm leaning toward accepting?*

Tensions ran high back at the house. It was late and Samira was emotionally drained from analyzing her own pending date. *Now I must factor in a date for my daughter too.* Samira pulled the clip out of her hair. *How am I supposed to navigate this?*

"You talked to Uncle Wes, didn't you," Kara pulled a brush through the length of her hair.

Samira gathered the stray towels and pulled the hamper drawer out far enough to deposit the dirty laundry.

"No, Kara, I haven't spoken to anyone about Ryan."

"Then why did he say he thought we might not come to dinner because we'd have a date?" Kara squeezed toothpaste onto her toothbrush and mindlessly laid the tube on the counter.

Samira moved the toothpaste and the hairbrush into a drawer. "Wes just knows you're growing up. One of these days Papa Ray will call to schedule the end of the year dinner party and you'll have to tell him you can't make it because you have other plans." *I just hope that day doesn't come any too soon.*

Kara spit into the sink. "Well, he sure talked like he knew something." She wiped her mouth on a towel and left it on the counter.

Instantly, the mother hung the towel back on the holder. Kara rolled her eyes. "Will you stop cleaning up?"

"I just want it tidy in the morning."

"Well, I'm not done in here yet." Kara's voice was sharp. "So, have you made any decision yet?"

"I'd like to talk to Ryan's parents first."

"Did you read the movie review? I left it on the dining room table."

"Yes. I read it. The movie is not the problem. I am concerned about the company. I don't know anything about them." *And you're only fourteen.*

Kara left the bathroom in a huff. Samira followed. *It's usually Krissy who speaks her mind. Not Kara.*

"Just let me call them in the morning, okay?"

"You're making a bigger deal about this than you need to."

I don't mean to. I just want to be sure. "I'll call first thing." *And I'm the mother so that gives me the prerogative to make deals out of issues.* She watched Kara organize the piles of school paraphernalia on her bed. "I'm sorry I can't give you an immediate answer, Kara. This is all new to us. We have to work through it together."

Kara carried a stack of notebooks to her desk, her long hair shimmering in the light. "I know. All my friends can go to the movies with boys. But I have to keep waiting for an answer."

"All of your friends are not you."

"You can't protect me forever, Mama."

Samira sat down on the edge of her daughter's bed. *Well, that pretty much says it all.*

Kara immediately retracted her remark. "I'm sorry, Mama. I didn't mean to hurt your feelings."

Samira bit her bottom lip. *Am I overly protective of them?* Samira's thoughts went back to Phil's analysis on his son's family life. *I'd rather have Kara mad at me for caring too much than wondering if I cared at all.*

"We'll discuss this again in the morning when I'm not so tired, okay?" Samira's voice faltered a little as she spoke to her daughter.

Kara nodded meekly as her mother left the room.

It had been a long, full day. Samira dimmed the lights in the front room and picked up her book from the coffee table. The house was still and peaceful, just the way she liked it at this hour. The steady light on the answering machine haunted her as she climbed into bed. *Phil has a way of not being very predictable.* On one hand his spontaneity was quite erotic. On the other, it drove her crazy.

Maybe I'm making a big deal out of my own issue for no reason. Samira pondered that for a moment. *Why did it have to fall on the seventeenth? Any day but my anniversary.*

Kara's only going into the ninth grade. She fingered the novel on her lap. *Daddy made me wait until I was 17 before I could date and even then, I wasn't allowed to date without a group of friends.*

Samira's eyes fell on her husband's face in the photograph on the nightstand. *What I wouldn't do to have you here tonight.* She turned his wedding band on her right hand. *Tom would not be intimidated by these situations.* Samira moved her hand across the empty pillow.

Slowly, as if in a dream, another man's face appeared in her mind. She tried to dismiss the vision. *What if Phil needed an answer right then?*

Nothing felt right. *Am I more upset because I couldn't decide on my own issues? Or because I don't feel qualified to give Kara an answer.* A single tear slipped out the corner of her eye and rolled down her cheek. *I can't even give a response to my own invitation. How am I supposed to know how to answer Kara?*

Without warning, Norma's voice loud and clear in Samira's memory. They were at the hospital the day Tom died. *"Samira, promise us you won't take Tom away from them."*

I haven't taken their father away from them. Samira looked around the room. His pictures still graced the shelves. *His memory is alive and well. They will always know their father.* Samira rolled her neck from side to side. *Maybe that's part of the problem. I will always know their father too. But he can't complete me anymore.* She blinked away another tear. *What happens when the girls grow up and get lives of their own? Dear God, am I wrong for wanting to be with Phil again?*

Her memory rewound to lunch with Phil. She felt his hand slip up the inside of her blouse. *Phil's a grown man and he made that move without permission.* That thought made Samira shudder. *What will Kara do if that happens to her?*

Maybe I'm out of sorts with the girls because I'm out of sorts with myself. After Kara's outburst this afternoon, there was no doubting her resentment against Wes having input on her life. *There was a point in time I would have used Susan as a motherly sounding board, but even that relationship is slipping.*

That thought alone spurred an entirely new set of questions:

She arranged the pillows against the headboard and opened the book to the marked page. *I am allowing myself to take a chance with a man.* The words on the page blurred. *Do I dare take a chance and let Kara go on a solo date with a high school boy?* Samira closed the book and set it aside. *It shouldn't be so hard.*

14 Heart to Heart

Joseph Phillip

"Sit for a minute, Phillip." Aunt Maggie's wrinkled hand patted the leather cushion on the sofa. "It's been a long time since we've talked."

It has been a long time. J.P. stopped in the kitchen doorway. *It sure feels good to be at the ranch.*

"These fellas need their sleep if they want to be at the lake by dawn, Maggie Jean." Uncle Roy was turning out the lights as he spoke.

Maggie waved him off with her hand. J.P. watched his sons disappear around the staircase landing. "Night, Dad."

Aunt Maggie smiled sweetly. "I see so much of your father in Joshua."

"Hate to admit it, but I see a lot of me in that boy too." J.P. relaxed into the sofa. "Kind of frightening."

"Don't be so hard on yourself." Maggie's eyes were still on the empty staircase. "Josh has your best qualities. And you both have Joe's smile."

A yellowed photograph of his parents hung on the wall next to Maggie and Roy's wedding picture. For a moment, J.P. recognized the man in the frame.

"Do you ever think about looking him up?"

"Nope." *No reason to.* "Not anymore. He had his chance and didn't show."

"That was a long time ago, Phillip. Time may have changed him over the years."

I don't want to waste my weekend talking about the Captain.

"How tall is James, now? Do you think six-four?"

"About." *I'm right at 6'2.* "I never thought I'd be looking up at my boys, Aunt Maggie."

"I've looked up to everybody all my life. But the Ralston genes do run strong."

There were several moments of comfortable silence. J.P. could feel himself settling into Joseph Phillip.

"James says he's spending the summer with you."

"He doesn't have much choice." J.P. rested his head on the back of the sofa. "James and Janet..." *No, that's not right.* "James and Bruce aren't seeing eye to eye on much these days."

"It will be good for you to spend the time with James. He needs you."

I hope. "It's going to take some getting used to."

"Of course, it will, Phillip." Maggie rocked back and forth in the platform rocker as she visited. "Lord knows how badly your boys have needed you over the years."

If the Lord knows, he hasn't gone out of his way to inform me.

"You don't give yourself enough credit as a father, Phillip."

Here comes the pep talk. He waited but she didn't say any more for a while.

"I've heard from your father, Phillip. He would like to see you. Bobby went..."

"Out to see him over Christmas." J.P. completed the sentence. "I know, he told me."

"He has some things of your mother's he'd like to give you," Maggie continued. "I know it's hard, but he's an old man now." Maggie paused. "He took the Navy business very seriously, Phillip. Too serious if you ask me. But just the same, he would like to mend some fences."

I know she means well, but I have no feelings of sentiment for my father. No matter how old and decrepit he might be.

"Bedtime, Maggie Jean." Uncle Roy appeared on the landing.

"Well, anyway, I don't want to spoil your time at home, but I'll put the letter on the desk. It will be there if you want to read it." Maggie reached out and patted her nephew on the knee. "You look tired, son. I imagine those boys will have you out of the sack before daybreak."

"Your bag's at the top of the stairs, Phillip." Uncle Roy stepped off the last step and turned for his own bedroom on the main level. "You comin' Maggie?"

"In a minute," she replied softly. "Anything I can do for you before I turn in?"

Aunt Maggie always used to ask me that at bedtime. J.P. shook his head.

The short, round woman wriggled out of her rocker. She walked behind the sofa and squeezed J.P.'s shoulders as she passed. "Good night, dear. The guest suite is ready if you like."

"Thanks, Aunt Maggie, but I think I'll bunk in the back room." He looked into her gray blue eyes. "It's nice and quiet down there."

"It's quiet everywhere here, Phillip. But I made your old bed too, just in case."

J.P. watched the platform rocker as it swayed back and forth and then slowed to a stop. The grandfather clock chimed ten times. *She's right. It is quiet here. No traffic. No sirens.* The only audible sound on the main floor was the steady sway of the pendulum on the clock.

Time passed. J.P. contemplated the letter on Maggie's desk. *I have no desire to contact the man who took my mother away.*

Slowly, J.P. pulled himself off the sofa and turned off the only remaining light. He made his way up the wrap-around staircase. As promised, his bag was waiting at the top. James was stretched out over the entire length and width of the double bed in the first room down the hall. *I have no idea what I'm going to do with that boy for the rest of the summer.* A glint of light reflected off the rhinestone earring in his son's ear. *I wonder what made him do that?*

The only light shining at the end of the hall was under the crack of the bathroom door. J.P. passed Josh's empty room. He turned the switch on the bottom of the wall sconce. *Nothing has changed.* The bed was still against the far wall and the walnut dresser was still in its place next to the window. He set his bag down and reached behind his head to remove his t-shirt. *Sleep is going to come easily.*

There was a slight tap on the open door. *Josh.* "Too early to be turning in?"

"Way early." Josh flopped into the worn swivel rocker.

"James didn't have any trouble calling it a night." J.P. sat down on the end of the double bed. The stitched pattern of the old quilt top felt familiar under his hands.

"James never has trouble sleeping."

"Probably growing."

"Maybe." Josh shrugged casually. The Ralston men studied one another in comfortable silence.

"It's good to have you guys here, Josh."

"It's been a while, huh?"

"Too long." *Since Thanksgiving last year.* "Too many miles..."

"...and too many schedules."

J.P. looked away. *I know. Caseload.*

"We were beginning to think you might not make it this afternoon."

I should have watched the clock closer. "I didn't realize I was running that late until your mother pointed it out."

Josh rolled his eyes. "You missed the bulk of her pointing." He eyed his father carefully. "I tried to call you when shit hit the fan with James last weekend. I figured you were at the driving range with Mike or something."

J.P.'s mind went back to breakfast with Samira that morning. "I missed that driving range appointment with Mike too."

"Heck, if you stood Mike up, I don't feel nearly as slighted."

"I didn't say I stood him up."

"But you didn't say you didn't either." Josh grinned. "So, you were working right?"

Not exactly. "I went in around ten."

"I tried calling the house."

J.P. remembered the three calls on his ID that morning. That must have been Josh calling on his mom's phone.

"Late night, then?" Josh leaned forward and rested his elbows on his knees.

The father couldn't deny the insinuation.

"That's what I thought. All nighter?"

Some dates I might brag about, but Samira is more of a treasure than a trophy.

"Speak now or forever hold your peace." Josh's eyes were twinkling. "Should have known it was a girl that held you up."

Why should I have to answer to a seventeen-year-old anyway?

Josh was suddenly serious. "So, you know a lot about girls, right Dad?"

"Not nearly as much as I wish I knew." *I still can't read Samira's thoughts.*

"You never seem to have any trouble finding one."

That's true. "But that doesn't mean I know much about them. Finding a girl is one thing; keeping her is another." *Not that I've wanted one around for long at a time anyway.*

"Good point." Josh laughed a little.

"What's so funny?"

"You're track record with women. You don't stay with one woman too long at a time, do you?"

Let's not go there "Do you have something specific in mind for this line of questioning?"

Josh's blue eyes became solemn. "I'd love to have specifics to talk about, Dad." The young man sighed heavily and sank deeper into the old chair. "Most of the guys I hang out with have steady girlfriends and plenty of specifics to go with. I'm lucky to have a date on Friday nights."

What about that blonde he pointed out to me in the parking lot? "If the girls are turning you down, Josh—"

"That's not it." Josh was visibly flustered. "That's not it at all. I don't even know what to say when I have the chance to ask somebody out."

J.P. thought back to his own tongue-tied episode with Samira the day he went back to the library looking for her. "You might come by that more honestly than you think, son."

"You always know what to say, Dad. Same with James. He could have several dates every weekend if he wanted." Josh's voice faded away and he closed his blue eyes.

"You're wrong, Joshy." J.P. decided to confess his blunder. "I tripped over my tongue so bad that I invited a woman out for coffee."

Josh opened his eyes and looked doubtingly at his father. "You don't even drink coffee."

"Case in point. This lady was so gorgeous, I forgot everything I'd planned to say and ended up inviting her for coffee."

"You're a lawyer, Dad. You always know what to say."

J.P. popped his son on the arm with the back of his hand. "I have notes in the courtroom, Josh. Seriously, I felt like a fool."

"So, how did you get over it?"

"I ordered a Coke."

"No, about the knowing what to say stuff."

"Nothing. I'm still not over it." *I have never been so nervous asking a woman out. Ever.*

"No, I mean how'd you finally learn to ask a girl out? You do it all the time now."

Oh. Josh thinks this happened in the past. He shook his head and ran his hand through his hair. "This just happened a couple of weeks ago, Josh." *Shit, I've known her less than three weeks and already she's messing with my mind.*

"What?" Josh chided. "Mr. Sly fumbled a date? Like, recently?"

I don't know if I appreciate his sudden interest or not. "You're not going to tell this story to your mom, are you?"

"Nah, I never tell mom your good stories."

Wonder what he does tell her then. "Here's the deal. I think the reason I stumbled around and forgot what I was going to say is because this lady was so incredibly pretty—"

"You mean like sexy?"

Sexy? "No..." *Yeah. Sexy is a good word.* "Well, okay." J.P. couldn't hide his boyish grin. "She's just a really classy lady."

Josh motioned with his hands for his dad to continue.

Why am I explaining this to Josh? "Anyway, I was kind of short with her at the library one afternoon while she was helping me research a case." *No. I was very impatient with her.* "I was working against the clock and didn't give her much credit for the research she produced. But after I left, I couldn't stop thinking about her. A few days later I decided to go back and apologize for the way I'd acted and officially thank her."

"No doubt. Did she remember you when you went back?"

That's an interesting question. J.P. opened his mouth to say something, but nothing came out. *I have no idea if she did or not.*

Josh leaned in further. "Well?"

"It's really weird," J.P. admitted. "When I went back to the library, I didn't see her anywhere and I didn't know her name. So, I'm standing there trying to describe her to this old woman behind the counter when suddenly she just appeared right there in front of me." J.P. could see her just as plain in his mind now as if she were standing in his room right then.

"And?"

"And nothing." J.P. laughed at his own lack of poise. "I couldn't think of a thing to say." *And I don't think I ever apologized either.* "I think she finally introduced herself or something and I asked her out for coffee."

Josh was laughing. "That blows me away. You always have something to say."

"Your mother is the one who always has something to say." *I don't know why I'm talking to him about this.* "I use notes, remember?"

"Even with girls?"

"Not with every girl, Joshy, just the really pretty ones." J.P. walked over to the dresser and started to unpack his bag.

"I hear that." Josh flopped onto his father's bed. Suddenly he became serious again. "There's this girl in our school. Her name's Amy and she's new this year. She's the one I showed you in the parking lot." Josh paused momentarily. "I wanted to ask her to prom but never got the words to come out of my mouth."

"Maybe you should have asked her out for coffee." *It saved my ass.*

"Maybe." Josh was thinking. "But you always have a date, Dad, so you must know how to ask a girl out."

"Getting a date is one thing, Josh. Getting knocked off your feet by a woman is an entirely different story." *Is that what Samira did to me?* That thought took J.P. by surprise. *I think she did.* "This woman is different somehow. I can't explain it and I can't deny it." His voice was softer when he spoke again. "Somehow you just know she's the one you have to ask out, so you fumble around and do what it takes to get the job done."

"So, are you saying this is *the* one?"

J.P. looked his son directly in the eyes. "Hell, I don't know. But I figure if I can't stop thinking about a woman before I even know her name, I have nothing to lose by asking her out." *Funny to hear those words come out of my mouth.* J.P. shook his head.

"So?"

"So what?"

"Did she go out for coffee?"

"She did." J.P. grinned. "And we went out to dinner a few nights later."

"Now I *know* why you didn't answer the phone Saturday morning." Josh slapped his hand against the mattress in victory. "I knew I could get it out of you."

He baited me. J.P. put his hands on his hips and studied his son. *And I fell for it.*

"So, I guess I just have to open my mouth, even if I do make an ass out of myself like you did, huh?" Josh climbed off the bed and stood directly in front of his father.

I did not make an ass out of myself. Did I?

"You crack me up." Josh turned for the door. "Morning's going to come too soon. 'Night, Dad."

That's it? A little father-son dialogue then 'night dad? He stepped into the hall and watched Josh disappear behind a door. *Good night, Josh.*

J.P. finished undressing and climbed into the freshly made bed. *Even the sheets smell like cedar.* The conversation with Josh replayed in his mind. *I know I didn't make an ass out of myself.* The grandfather clock struck eleven times in the distance. *Or if I did, it didn't seem to faze her.* J.P. rolled over into the empty space in the bed. *What I wouldn't do to fill this space with Samira tonight.*

15 The Prick of the Thorn

Samira

Just because I can't talk to my brother about Kara's love life doesn't mean I can't talk to him about my own. She picked up a business magazine and flipped through the pages without reading anything. *I can't believe I've let this decision take over every waking thought.* Samira put the magazine back down on the small table. *And I can't imagine what's keeping Wes on a Sunday afternoon.* Samira's hands were sweating as she paced the floor of her brother's office. *I liked Daddy's office better.* Samira glanced at the walnut accent table next to the bookcase. *The furniture is too heavy for this sunny room.* She stopped in front of the full-length windows overlooking downtown.

"Samira." Wes appeared in the doorway. "Sorry to keep you waiting."

She turned to face him. *He's trying to look enthusiastic, but the fact is, he's exhausted.* Samira was surprised to see him still in his church clothes. "I didn't mean to interrupt."

"Interrupt? I'm here on a Sunday afternoon of a holiday weekend."

He's busy. "This really isn't important, Wes. You can just call me later if you like." *But I hope he lets me stay.*

Wes was shaking his head. "Nonsense. Here, take a load off." He motioned for Samira to sit down. "You want a drink or something?"

Samira watched her brother pour himself a small glass of alcohol from a cupboard behind his desk. *I don't think I've ever seen Weston fix himself a drink in the middle of a Sunday afternoon.*

"So, what's on your mind, Sis?" Weston took a seat in the winged-back chair.

Here goes. "You told me to call if I needed you, right?"

"I'm answering." Wes sipped his drink.

Samira couldn't sit down. *Just get it out there.* She leaned on the edge of her brother's massive desk. "It's about the seventeenth." *I wish he already knew what I was going to say so he could finish my sentences.* "I've been invited out for an evening in Springfield."

"Okay." Wes was frowning. "And you're here to what? Ask my permission?"

"I don't know, exactly." Her fingers tapped the edge of the desk. "It's a big step for me, I guess."

"Help me out here, Sis. I'm assuming it's with the same guy."

Samira nodded.

"What exactly did he invite you to?"

"He called it a dinner engagement." *I don't know much more than that.*

Wes opened his palms to the ceiling. "Maybe I'm missing the gist, but dinner shouldn't be threatening." He shrugged his shoulders. "I think you should go, Sis. Obviously, he thinks highly of you if he's inviting you to join him on business."

I hadn't thought of it that way.

"Seriously," Wes added. "I'd be extremely cautious of taking someone along to meet with my clients. He probably is to."

"Do you think he's meeting with clients?"

"Samira." Wes stood up and put his hands on his hips. "You said he was a lawyer, right? So, I'd assume a dinner engagement might include a client." Wes raised his eyebrows.

"I guess so." *I want him to talk me out of it.* "But it's clear over in Springfield. We're talking about an entire evening here. It's not like I can leave work, get ready to go, and then be home by midnight."

"Look," Wes squared his sister's shoulders and looked her in the eye. "You're not exactly up against Cinderella's curfew here." He narrowed his dark eyes. "I don't know what's eating at you, but you're going to have to get over it before you make a decision."

Someone tapped on the open door. Samira watched her brother cross the room and exchange information with a short balding man.

"Hey, Sis, I need to initialize the mainframe computer so they can reboot. It won't take long."

That's okay. I'll wait. Samira studied her right hand. *My finger feels naked without Tom's ring. I didn't think I'd ever take it off.* Her mind tripped back to the day in the hospital when the nurse removed it from her husband's finger before surgery. *He told me to keep it safe.* She touched the faint line it had made around her finger. *I didn't know it would be the last time he'd have it on.*

Samira sank into the chair her brother had been sitting in. *What is it that's really holding me back?* She thought for a moment. *Wes is right. I should be honored he invited me on a business engagement.* She held her hand out at arm's length and studied her ringless finger. *And it's not that I don't want to be with him again.*

Suddenly the chair was too confining. Pam's picture was smiling back at her from the corner of Weston's desk. *June seventeenth has always been reserved for my husband.* Samira fingered the frame around the photo. *I don't know if I can give myself to any other man on that night.*

She walked back to the window. The sidewalk below her brother's second story office window was amazingly lifeless. *If I accept the invitation, then I accept the potential that comes with being alone with Phil.* She breathed in deeply. *And if I don't accept, then I remain locked in my past without any potential at all.*

"So?"

Samira jumped at the sound of her brother's voice.

"What'd you decide?" Wes proceeded to sit down in his oversized executive's chair.

Samira wrapped her arms around her middle and shrugged her shoulders. *I feel silly needing his approval.* Wes studied her face until she looked away.

"Samira," he said gently, "If you're looking for my blessing, you have it. Pam and I will even keep the girls for the night, so you don't have to worry about watching the clock. Besides, we owe you one for watching our kids last night." Wes tipped his head to the side. "But if you're looking for my consent, I can't give that to you."

Samira closed her eyes. *Of course not. No one can give me permission except the voices inside my head.* Very slowly Samira realized her brother was standing right next to her. Without asking, he cradled his arms around her from behind and pulled her into his chest.

"It's still the seventeenth of June, Wes."

"I know."

"That was our anniversary."

"I know."

"Any day but that one."

"You know, Sis, just because you're going to dinner with a man who isn't Tom doesn't make you any less of a mother or wife."

How can I be sure?

"And if the evening turns into breakfast again, you'll know it's time to let the past be the past. Your time with someone else will not erase your memories with Tom. I promise."

"But what will the girls think?"

"How will they know?"

"How will they know what?"

"Whatever it is you're trying to hide from them." Wes squeezed his sister harder.

"They'll know what the date is on the calendar."

"So?"

"So, it's not with their dad."

"It can't ever be with their dad again, Samira. Accept that fact and move on. It's time to live for your future instead of idling in the past. Take a chance. See where it leads."

Samira pressed the back of her head into her brother.

"Look at me." Wes turned Samira around to face him. "You need to get over whatever obstacle you've created. You're a beautiful woman with a whole life ahead of you." Wes ignored the intercom buzzer on his desk. "Maybe going out with someone new on your original wedding date has some sort of symbolic significance. Maybe it doesn't. But you can't keep your heart in the past and ever expect to share your future with anybody new."

Samira didn't like the implication. *But he's speaking the truth.*

"Pam and I will keep the girls that weekend. The whole weekend if you like. We'll be glad to have them around and you'll be glad to not have them around. Okay?"

"But you're the one who said to go slow, Wes."

Wes didn't break eye contact. "You are."

This time when his intercom buzzed, Wes responded, leaving his sister to her own thoughts.

~~~~~~~

If is becoming a bigger word than I imagined possible. Samira cleared the dinner dishes still contemplating what she would tell Phil *if* he called for an answer. *I was gone most of the afternoon and he still didn't call.* Deep down she wondered why he'd never offered his phone number to her. *Maybe it's a control thing.*

When the dishes were done, she stepped into the sanctuary of her back yard. The aroma of fresh flowers was invigorating. She breathed in through her nose and allowed her senses to be filled. The Magnolia was in full bloom. Samira followed the brick walkway to the bed of roses in the center of her garden. A tiny pink bud begged for her attention. *It's so beautiful.* Gingerly Samira fingered the flower.

It must take a lot of courage to open such fragile petals to the world. I'd be scared to death.

She sat down along the raised edge of the rose bed. *Maybe that's what's really holding me back.* She touched the pink bud again. *What happens if I take that chance and things don't work out? Then what?*

"What happens if you open up and the wind blows your petals all over the yard?" Samira spoke out loud to the flower. "But if you ever want to share your blossom, you have to let go and open up."

Samira stayed in the garden for several minutes of contemplative solitude. *Life wasn't always so complicated.* Tom had swept her off her feet and asked her to marry him before she even had a chance to tell her parents she was in love. *Not that they didn't know that from the way I talked about him and spent time with him.* Saying yes to Tom's marriage proposal was a given—something she knew she was supposed to do. *Why is it so difficult to say yes to a simple dinner invitation fifteen years later?*

But Tom is gone. She fingered the tiny rosebud again. *Forever. Maybe it's time to let go and move forward.*

As Samira released the rose bud her finger caught on a thorn. Dark red blood oozed from the wound and stained the pink petals. She applied immediate pressure to the wound. *That's exactly what I fear might happen.* A slight throb caused her to press the wound harder. *I'm afraid the old wounds will open, and I'll be hurt all over again.* She felt badly for staining the rosebud with her blood. *But this time if I get hurt, Krissy and Kara will suffer too.*
~~~~~~~

Samira dared to look at her finger. The bleeding had stopped but there was a mark where the thorn had penetrated her skin. *What if the bleeding in my heart doesn't stop that easily?*

"Mama."

Samira looked back toward the house. Krissy was standing at the back door waving her arms.

"Mrs. Barnes wants to know if you can take her to the store."

Of course, I can take Mrs. Barnes to the store. I have nothing better to do. Samira sighed. "Tell her I'll be over in a few minutes."

She stood up and inhaled deeply. The fragrance of the roses was thick. *I'll never know what new love is like if I don't take the chance.* The now stained rosebud looked so vulnerable at the end of the long stem. "I think I know how you feel." Samira spoke to the bud. "I just hope I don't get stained like you."

16 *The Catch of the Day*

Joseph Phillip

An obnoxious clanging brought an abrupt end to J.P.'s slumber. He rolled over in Aunt Maggie's bed and moaned.

"Rise and shine. Didn't you hear the breakfast bell?"

Is that what that noise was?

James threw his body weight into his father's bed. "You're missin' Aunt Maggie's grub."

"Do you know what time it is?"

"Time to fish."

The hands on his wristwatch indicated four thirty. *No fish is worth losing this much sleep over.* Reluctantly, J.P. forced his legs over the side of the bed. *This is supposed to be vacation.* The faint aroma of bacon hinted at a big breakfast. *Breakfast before dawn doesn't feel like rest or relaxation.*

Maggie's voice called up the stairs.

"No time for a shower this morning, Phillip. Roy's afraid the sun's going to beat you to the lake."

I only fish at this ungodly hour to appease Uncle Roy and the boys. J.P. ran his hand over a second-day beard. *And I'd feel a hell of a lot better with a quick shower.* Instead, he heeded Aunt Maggie's advice and rinsed his face with cold water.

After breakfast, the boys and Chase piled into the bed of Uncle Roy's faded blue pickup.

"Open your eyes, son." Uncle Roy bellowed as they bumped down the gravel road. "You're going to miss the sunrise."

J.P. put on his dark sunglasses and closed his eyes. "There will be others."

"Not on this day."

He's way too chipper for me at this hour.

"Now sit up and take notice." With a flip of his calloused hand Roy tapped J.P.'s arm then pointed toward the sky. "There's a hawk up there scouting out morning grub."

J.P. leaned forward in the seat and removed his sunglasses pretending to watch the hawk. Then he closed his eyes behind the glasses again.

The sky was just starting to turn pink as Uncle Roy pulled to a stop under a grove of cottonwood trees.

"A boy can't come of age unless he's experienced the dawn at the lake."

I oughta be of age by now. J.P. had to smile at his uncle's consistency. *Never once have we skipped a fishing trip during a summer visit.* He helped the boys unload the gear.

"Sit back and watch carefully, men. I'm going to show you how to catch the best fish of the day on the first cast." Uncle Roy was preparing his line.

Josh shook his head as he made his first cast. "If you catch the biggest fish of the day first thing, I'll clean it for you." He grinned boyishly at his great uncle. "Deal?"

Roy nodded once and adjusted his fishing hat. Skillfully, he dangled his rod over the edge of the dock and made some mysterious maneuvers with his elbows and hands.

"What's he doing?" James asked with caution.

He always makes those moves. "He's getting ready to reel in the catch of the day," J.P. whispered.

"Oh. Riiight."

J.P. searched the tackle box for the perfect bait. *It's all Greek to me.* He fingered a brightly colored orange and yellow fly.

"What's the matter, Dad?" James poked his finger into the miniature box. "Can't bait a hook?"

It's hardly a fish I care to bait, J.P. thought to himself. *Wrong species.* He allowed James to bait his hook, then cast his fly line with rusty skill. J.P. sat down on the dock and leaned into a sturdy support post. The sunlight sparkled on the water like glitter.

Now this is one view I wouldn't mind sharing with Samira. Never once had he considered bringing a woman to the ranch. *Where did that thought come from?* He'd always figured that would interfere with the little time he had with Josh and James. *Besides this is my escape.* The thought lingered. W*onder if the boys would like to share their territory with two junior high girls?* J.P. contemplated that possibility. *Probably not.*

Then again, their next regular trip would be in July. He might throw out the possibility just to see what she said. *Shit, J.P., you don't even know if she's going to Springfield with you yet. Maybe you should only make one invitation at a time.*

A sudden scurry of activity drew J.P. back to the dock.

"Here she comes, boys." Uncle Roy had a snag on his line. Whatever was on the end of the line wasn't going to give up easily. Roy worked the rod and reel with expertise. "Well, don't just stand there, give me a hand."

Chase barked at the excitement as James and Josh both grabbed for the rod. Between the three of them they hauled in a feisty bass.

Roy stood tall holding the line a few inches above the fish. "Now there's a beaut' of a fish, fellas." He cut the line and smiled broadly. "Let me see you match this."

"What'daya think she weighs, Uncle Roy?" James was admiring the catch.

Roy suspended the fish in midair. The scales glistened in the morning sunlight as the fish flipped in resistance. "Four, maybe five pounds," he estimated. "Joshy, you might want to sharpen your knife."

Josh moaned and picked up his own rod again.

Somehow J.P. couldn't see Samira getting much enjoyment out of a slimy bass, but he smiled at the possibility of sharing the story.

In the solitude of the morning, J.P.'s thoughts bounced back to the letter on Aunt

Maggie's desk. *Eventually I'll read the letter out of respect for Aunt Maggie.* He didn't have that much respect for the Captain. Too many burned bridges between him and his father. *Joseph Phillip.* Most people earn the right to be called by their name. *To date, the Captain hasn't earned any honors for being a family man. Why's he trying to start now?*

James disappeared for a bit leaving Josh in charge of his rod. J.P. watched his youngest son walk along the edge of the woods and disappear. *I suppose if he's still under house arrest, I should follow him.* At the same time, he was quite comfortable with his legs tanning in the morning sunshine. *I'll cut him some slack.* By the time James returned, Josh had landed a catfish.

"Whose rod was it on?"

Josh shrugged his shoulders. "Doesn't matter. I reeled it in either way."

James grabbed for his rod, but Josh pulled it out of arm's reach. James slipped on the wet dock and stumbled toward the edge of the lake. He came up swearing and swinging at his brother.

"There'll be none of that on my fishing trip," Uncle Roy warned. He kicked a small item toward James. "Seems you might have lost something there, boy."

James exchanged a quick look with his brother and snatched it up. He pulled his baseball cap low to avoid eye contact with his father.

J.P. ran his hand through his hair and rested his weight against a wooden post. He didn't see what the item was, but he did see the exchange of silent communication between the brothers. *I wonder what other secrets he's hiding underneath that cap?*

By the time the sun was high in the sky, Uncle Roy was taking inventory. "A catfish, a walleye, two blue gills, and a beaut' of a bass." Roy removed his fishing hat and wiped the sweat on his brow with the back of his hand. "Should be enough for grub tonight."

"What time is it, Uncle Roy?" James asked.

"Time to head back to the ranch. Church starts in an hour and Maggie Jean won't want me to go smellin' like a fish."

James narrowed his eyes. "Are we goin'?"

Roy shrugged. "That's up to you."

I think I'll stretch out in the hammock between the Ash trees instead of sitting on a hard pew. J.P. knew he should encourage the boys to go with Aunt Maggie. *But it's hard to make them go if I'm not.* He looked out over the water. *I vowed after Mom's funeral to never set foot inside a church building again.* A red-tailed hawk dove at the water and came back up carrying a fish in its talons. *No reason to break that vow now.*

"The fish are probably done biting till nightfall, anyway, aren't they Uncle Roy?" Josh was reeling in his line.

Roy watched the hawk fly off. "Chances are good they've gone deep." He reached into the creel with his bare hands and pulled out the first catch of the day. "We have just enough time to clean these before heading out."

Josh moaned out loud.

"And you thought the old man would forget, didn't ya?" James chided from the edge of the dock.

J.P. quieted the younger brother with a motion of his hand. "What do you say we start packing up the gear?"

Obediently, James pulled his line in and started to gather the tackle boxes and equipment. "Are we keeping the rubber boot?"

Roy was already bent over Josh, guiding his knife with his experienced hand. He answered without looking up. "We keep every catch."

I have a catch I want to keep too. It seemed a little too soon to be making that assumption. *Why is this woman so fresh in your mind this morning, Ralston?*

James tossed the boot on top of the pile and headed for the truck.

I wonder how much I'd have to pay James to remove his earring before introducing him to Samira.

That's it, J.P. told himself. *You have way too much time on your hands out here in the wide-open space.* He folded Roy's lawn chair and leaned it against the post. *You need to quit thinking about her.* J.P. looked out across the lake. *If there ever was a place to behold, this is it.* The water gave a rippling reflection of the sky.

J.P. looked back at the fish cleaning lesson. Josh took a deep breath and held it in as Uncle Roy led him through the steps. Roy would make a cut in a smaller fish, and then Josh would copy in the bass. *Who's coming of age this time? Josh or Uncle Roy?*

James returned to the dock and peered over his brother's shoulder.

"Hey, Joshy. You missed a spot over there."

Without speaking, Josh leaned back throwing his body weight into his brother. James went sailing off the edge of the dock into the cold lake. Caught up in the excitement, Chase bounded into the water as well.

J.P. leaned back on his heels and watched as James surfaced. He was spitting water and spouting obscenities at his brother. *Josh made his point.* J.P. didn't dare laugh.

Josh ignored the lack of affection and finished cleaning the bass. James swam back to the dock and hoisted his soaked body out of the water.

"Seems to me you might want to save your advice 'til you're a little closer to shore," Uncle Roy looked up over his photo gray lens.

James swore again and glared in his father's direction. J.P. watched with interest as he removed his shirt. He fingered the contents of his pocket then disgustedly wrung it out over the water. *Eventually, I'll have to investigate that stash.* James leaned against the post and removed his high-top shoes. When he straightened up, sunlight reflected from the hoop through his belly button. *I will never understand what possessed him to do that.*

James looked away defiantly as he passed his father on the dock.

"Asshole," James retorted.

"Fool." Josh evened the score.

~~~~~~~

Back at the house, J.P. fingered the plain white envelope on Aunt Maggie's desk. Shaky handwriting addressed *Margaret Jean Tennison.* The return address was a pre-printed label from the Captain's residence in Lexington, Virginia.

"Ready, Dad?" Josh clamored down the wooden stairs. "James is already outside."

I'm ready for a nap. J.P. tapped the bottom edge of the envelope firmly against the desktop. "Yeah, I'm coming."

The door closed with a solid thud leaving J.P. alone in the room. *Twenty-five years. That's how many years separate us.* He remembered sitting alone at the rail station in St. Louis an entire day waiting for the Captain to step off a train. That moment never came. *Nor did an apology that explained the absence.* That was the day Joseph Phillip Ralston, II dropped his first name.

But today is not the day to dig up old wounds. He left the letter on the desk and joined his sons on the front porch. They drew straws to determine who carried the backpack first then headed into the state park that led them back toward the lake. At first the conversation was limited, but as the men hiked, the silence dissipated.

"Remember when we used to camp out here when we were little?" Josh asked. "We carved our names in a tree trunk somewhere around here."

James pointed to a downed tree. "I remember Uncle Bobby helping me climb over that trunk." He stepped over the tree with ease and rolled it enough to clear the walkway.

"You'd probably have to help Uncle Bobby over it now," Josh commented with a laugh. The boys scouted about until they found their names in the side of a Maple tree.

"That tree has grown since we were here last," J.P. observed out loud. He reached out and ran his fingers over the rugged letters.

"What's Uncle Bobby doing these days, anyway?" James started back toward the path.

"He's still in Boston working telecommunications." J.P. stepped over a small limb. "He'd like for us all to come out this summer if we can find a mutual date."

"Like with a girl?" James asked.

"No," J.P. chuckled. "Like on the calendar."

"Be more fun with a date."

Chase bounded by his master in pursuit of a chipmunk. The boys took off after the dog. Moments after they dipped out of sight, Josh called back.

"Dad. Look down there." He pointed over the edge of a hill. "I thought the lake was a lot further out than this."

J.P. laughed as he caught up to his son. "It is when your legs are short." James was already at the water's edge throwing a stick into the ripples for Chase to retrieve. "This is the best camping site on the property." J.P. remembered days gone by. "Kindle, shade, water, fish." He momentarily lost track of time.

"I remember when Uncle Bobby pushed mom off the end of that dock." Josh chuckled.
~~~~~~~

J.P.'s eyes landed on the end of a worn wooden ramp. "Bobby didn't push your mother into the lake. She stepped back too far and lost her footing."

"Tell that to Mom," James retorted. "She's still pissed."

"That's the same trip we caught too many fish, and the game warden made us throw some back," Josh recalled.

"Same trip you got a fishhook[12] stuck in your thumb and we had to quit fishing to take you to the hospital," James reminded. "You about ruined the whole weekend.'

Josh examined his thumb as if looking for remnants of the scar.

J.P. silently remembered a time he had to carry James on his shoulders because his legs were too tired to walk that far. *Where does the time go?* Crouching down, he picked up a small stone. As he turned it in his hand, his mind wandered back to times at the lake with Janet. The early memories were full of adventure and new experiences. The last trips to the lake were tainted with hollow conversations and hurtful accusations.

I brought the family up here hoping to mend that relationship. J.P. shook his head. *Nothing I did by that time was going to satisfy Janet.*

He straightened his body and squeezed the rock in his hand. It was warm from the afternoon sun. *How can something so hard have any warmth at all?* Somehow, he knew that his heart had hardened with the ruling of the divorce decree. *Joint custody is a sham.* Instead of challenging the paperwork and fighting the system, J.P. forfeited his scheduled rights to see his sons. *At the time I thought it would keep things more peaceful for the boys if I stayed out of the picture.*

J.P. pulled his arm back and threw the rock far into the water.

That was ten years ago. Seeing his almost grown boys stretched out in the sun on the wooden planks conjured feelings of regret. *I should have gone to bat for them.* He felt out of touch in ways he couldn't describe. *Hell, they don't even know who I am. All they know about me is what Jan and Bruce have told them over the years.*

Tired of fleeting thoughts, J.P. called his boys back to shore and headed them off in another direction. Forty-five minutes later they arrived at the top of a bluff overlooking the lake.

"Out of breath, old man?" James teased.

"Hardly." It felt good to be out on the terrain. J.P. removed the backpack from around his shoulders and passed it off to his youngest. James opened the zippered pouch and took a long drink from the water bottle. Without waiting for permission, Josh stretched out on the leaf-laden lawn under the trees.

"So, talk to me. What do you guys do when you're home?" J.P. joined them on the ground.

James handed out peanut butter sandwiches and homemade cookies from Aunt Maggie's lunch stash. Both boys remained silent for a moment.

Josh finally spoke. "Well, we aren't home all that much, Dad. Between school and games and other stuff, we aren't there much."

"There isn't much time between school and games, so we usually just hang out with friends after school." James added between bites. "If we don't have a game, we have practice and that usually runs late."

"Your practice runs late," Josh corrected. He looked at his father. "James always sticks around longer than everyone else."

"So, exactly what does 'hanging out' consist of these days?" *I'm curious.* "I'm out of the loop."

James winked at his father. "We wouldn't have to hang out so much if we had a car of our own."

J.P. took a bite of an apple and ignored his son's comment. *I hear you. If Janet and Bruce would allow it, they'd already have their own transportation.* J.P. nudged his son for an answer.

Realizing he wasn't off the hook, James filled in some blanks. "Okay, so sometimes we play cards, do video games."

"Homework," Josh added. He rolled his eyes at his brother. "One of us did our homework."

James shrugged.

"Someday you'll wish you'd have done your homework," Josh remarked under his breath.

James put up his fists in an imaginary fight. "Ooooo, go ahead. Take a stab, Joshy."

J.P. kicked his youngest son gently in the foot. He tossed an apple core into the shaded woods. *J.P. knew the answer to the next question but decided to ask it anyway.* "Do you two hang out with the same friends?"

Simultaneously James answered the same, but Josh answered different.

That's interesting. J.P. raised his eyebrows.

"Well, some of them are the same," James offered. "Not all of them."

Josh climbed up off the ground. He bumped his brother harder than necessary. "Not many are the same. We usually go our separate ways after school then meet up with Mom for a ride home." By this time Josh was headed back to the trail.

There's more dissention in the ranks than I thought. J.P. didn't like where it might be leading. "You two need to stick together. Whatever the circumstances. Alright?"

James stood up and stretched his arms toward the sky. "Just like you and Uncle Bobby used to do, right?"

J.P. laughed a little. "I looked out for Bobby because he had a way of not looking out for himself." *In more ways than one.*

Josh ignored the humor, but James related. "So that's what big brothers are for, huh?" James held his hands out for his brother to return a high five.

Josh turned away leaving his brother's hands hanging in midair.

"Lighten up, Joshy."

J.P. placed his forefinger and thumb between his lips and let out a shrill whistle.

"Dad!" James retorted.

Chase bounded out of the woods and beat his master's leg with a wagging tail.

"Just calling my dog." *And ending the sibling assault.* J.P. reached down and patted Chase with his hand, but his eyes were on Josh who had already started down the other side of the bluff.

~~~~~~~

The boys challenged J.P. to a game of basketball late in the day. Uncle Roy carried the old metal lawn chairs off the porch and positioned them at the edge of a concrete apron in front of the barn while the boys rolled the portable hoop into position.

J.P. played a few rounds then dismissed himself. *I don't want to wait any longer.* All afternoon he'd fingered his phone in his pocket. He found the number in his contacts and pushed the button. No one answered.

"Did you leave a message?"

J.P. spun around on his heels, unaware that Josh had followed him. He shook his head as he pushed END on the cell.

"No message."

Josh wiggled his eyebrows. "How's she gonna know ya called if you didn't leave a message?"

"How do you know I'm calling a her?"

"Just a hunch," Josh teased. "A little late to be makin' a call, don't you think?"

I don't know if I like where this might be heading. "Your definition of late and hers might not be the same."

"Told you it was a her." Josh pointed his finger at his father. "Never know. Leaving the right message might make all the difference."

"A difference between what?"

"How will you know if you don't leave a message?" Josh crossed his arms over his chest and leaned against the truck.

"Alright, alright. I'll call back and leave a message if you'll leave me alone." *I could live without the badgering.*

Josh nodded eagerly in anticipation.

J.P. fumbled with his phone. "Maybe you could go over and wait on the porch or something."

Josh smiled brightly. "I'd rather wait here." He pointed at the phone. "You know, Dad, You don't have to redial on a cell phone if you're calling the same number twice in a row."

I know that. J.P. deliberately turned away from Josh. *I was hoping to buy a little time.*

One ring.

I prefer not having an audience and I hate answering machines.

Two rings.
~~~~~~~

The sun was getting low in the sky. J.P. looked back toward the barn and caught a glimpse of James dribbling a layup across the ready-made court. He pointed for Josh to join his brother.

Three rings.

"Maybe later," Josh antagonized. "I'd rather wait for you."

Four rings.

What if she doesn't want to talk to me? After all, even Mike thought she looked a little out of my league.

"Hello?"

The voice on the other end caught J.P. by surprise and he failed to respond.

"Hello?"

J.P. cleared his throat. "Hey, Samira, it's me, J...Phil." J.P. swallowed hard and tried to ignore Josh, who was now doubled over in laughter. "I didn't think you were going to answer."

"Oh, Phil." There was amusement in her voice when she spoke again. "You called but didn't expect me to answer?"

How does she do this to me? J.P. was flustered. *And it doesn't help that Josh is laughing hysterically.* "Well, not exactly. I mean, I called a few minutes ago but you didn't answer," J.P. looked up at the sky and took a deep breath. "So, I didn't think you'd answer this time either." *She gets me totally worked up and she's two hours away on the other end of a phone.*

Samira laughed. "Well, I didn't make it to the phone a minute ago, but you didn't leave a message either."

"No, I guess I didn't," J.P. confessed. "Are you busy?" *Because I could call back later.*

"I was outside watering the roses." There was a pause on the line. "Are you home?"

"No, no, I'm up at my aunt's ranch." J.P. dug his shoe into the gravel. "I just thought I'd check in."

"I didn't realize you were leaving town."

J.P. ran his hand through his hair. "No, I guess I didn't tell you." *Should I have told her?* He tried to ignore Josh who was now mimicking his every move. *Maybe I should explain.* "I bring my boys up here every year at this time. We come up here and fish and hang out for the long weekend."

"You go, Dad." Josh yelled from the tailgate of the pickup.

I wish he'd go away. "You won't believe what I'm doing now."

"Are you underestimating me?"

J.P. was taken aback by Samira's candor. "No, not at all." *I would never underestimate her.* "But any self-respect I might have had I've lost to my son."

Josh laughed loudly and pointed at his father.

"Anyway, we did a little fishing earlier and spent some time out on the trail."

"Catch anything?"

The only thing I want to catch is you, Pretty Lady. "There's nothing out here I'd like to catch."

Samira played along. "I thought maybe you'd tell me a big fish story. Like Moby Dick."

Moby Dick. I haven't heard that title since undergrad literature class. "Hemmingway?"

"Melville, Herman."

"World Lit?"

"American."

Damn.

Josh was getting a little too much enjoyment out of his father's conversation. *I need to know what she's thinking about Springfield, but I'm not going to bring it up with Josh standing here.* "I'll have to brush up on my authors."

"I could help you do that."

"I'd like that." J.P. grinned. "Listen, it's good to—" *To hear her voice.* "Be in touch." *Why don't my words come out?* "I'll be back sometime Monday."

"I'll be around."

Is that an invitation or just information? "I'll give you a call."

"I'd like that."

There's a little confirmation, anyway. There was a long pause. *So how do I end this now?* Josh was making faces and imitating his father with exaggerated movements.

Samira finally spoke. "So, I'll talk to you then?"

I'd like to do more than talk. "Yeah, I guess so."

With that Samira said her goodbye and left J.P. hanging in front of his son. J.P. tossed his phone into the grass and immediately lunged in Josh's direction.

Josh was bent over in laughter. "That's the best entertainment I've had in a looooong while." he gasped.

J.P. wrestled Josh to the ground playfully. *I had no idea he had this much strength.* With more than a few quick turns, J.P. finally twisted Josh's arm into the small of his back.

"I give, I give." Josh surrendered but he was still laughing.

J.P. released the hold and rolled over onto his back, exhausted from the romp but invigorated by the success of his phone call.

"You really like her, don't you Dad?"

J.P. closed his eyes and put his hand over his forehead. *Yeah. I think I do.*

A sharp jab in the ribs made J.P. catch his breath.

"Well? Do you or not?"

J.P. propped himself up on his elbows. "Do I what?"

"Like her."

Humored by Josh's insistence, the father smiled his easy smile.

"You must really like her if you can't even talk about her." Josh offered a hand to help his dad up off the ground.

J.P. accepted the assistance. *Just say it.*

"Chicken."

I am not a chicken. "Okay. I admit it. I like her." J.P. trotted to catch up to his son.

"A lot," Josh added. He lengthened his stride.

J.P. caught up to Josh with ease. "Maybe."

Josh laughed out loud and ran onto the court. "Chicken."

"I thought the basketball game was called HORSE," Uncle Roy bellowed from his lawn chair.

"It is." Josh accepted a pass from his brother. "It's Dad." The boy turned and shot the ball through the hoop. "He's the chicken."

Roy laughed. "Your father's only a chicken when it comes to women."

What? J.P. stopped in the middle of the court and threw his arms out to his sides. *Where does he get the gall to say that?*

"Dad."

A pass bounded off J.P.'s shoulder. He retrieved the miss and took the ball to the basket. *Score.* One quick pass and James made a shot over his brother's attempted block.

"Well?" Josh dribbled the ball back out to center court.

"Okay." J.P. stole the ball from his son and took it in for an easy layup.

Josh rebounded. "Just say it, chicken."

"Say what?"

"A lot."

He's relentless. J.P. blocked Josh's shot. *But I am not chicken.*

"A lot." He leaned over to catch his breath. "Satisfied?"

Josh laughed. "Yeah. For now."

Well, I'm not. J.P. stepped aside and allowed his boys to jockey for the shot. *I'd like to know what she's thinking about Springfield.*

17 The Sanctuary

Samira

Samira surveyed the flowerbed with a gardener's scrutiny. *If I keep at it, I should be able to finish weeding these two small beds before dusk.* She pointed to the wheeled work cart.

"Krissy, would you hand me my gloves and trowel, please?"

Krissy obeyed silently.

I love how every season brings new life to this garden. In the aftermath of Tom's death, Samira created a sanctuary where she could experience a continuous life cycle. Everything from the small pool and fountain to the brick walkway worked toward that goal.

"So, tell me more about the last day of seventh grade." *It's hard to believe my youngest daughter is already going into eighth grade.*

Krissy settled into a green patch of grass. "Let's see, where did we leave off?" She thought for a minute. "Tiffany and Renee were really nervous that the boys would sit by them at lunch time, so we ate our picnic lunch early and hurried outside." Krissy stopped. "Do you know Gramma gets really nervous too?"

Where did that thought come from? Samira glanced at her daughter.

"She kept clicking her fingernails on the hymnal during church. Grampa says she gets that way when something important is in her mind."

The narrow spade in Samira's hand turned the dirt around the dahlias. *Norma is always slightly on edge,* Samira thought to herself. *Interesting Krissy noticed.*

"Once Uncle Steve and the cousins arrived, Gramma seemed to relax. Did I tell you that Aunt Donna wore a bright red dress and made Uncle Vern wear a tie with his suit? They all looked so proper and everything." Krissy pulled her knees up to her chest. "Why do people make such a big deal out of being married for fifty years anyway?"

"Because fifty years is a very long time to have a relationship with one person." Samira tapped the trowel on the edge of the flowerbed. "Anymore, even five- and ten-year anniversaries are something to celebrate."

"Do you think you and Daddy would have made it to fifty if he hadn't been sick?"

Wow. I didn't expect to go into that tonight. "Yes, I do. We knew when we said our marriage vows that it was a forever thing."

"Well, until the death and parting thing anyway."

That would be the finality of it all, wouldn't it? Many months had passed without a direct conversation about Tom. *I wonder if Krissy is thinking about June seventeenth like I am.* The anniversary remembrance was marked on every calendar in the house.

"Your Daddy liked to celebrate, Krissy." Samira leaned further into the flowerbed to reach the far side. "We celebrated every year in style, he made sure of it." *He always made me feel so special on our anniversary.*

Krissy rested her chin on her knees seemingly lost in thought for a moment. "That's pretty cool." She grinned. "I must get my party attitude from him, huh?"

Samira chuckled. "That and many other traits." *Like your quick wit and talkative nature.* She finished her work and sat down on the edge of the raised bed. *And her little freckled face and crystal blue eyes. Those are her father's too.* "You most certainly have his zest for life."

Krissy giggled and started to get up. "Does that mean I can go to the mall with Tiffany tomorrow night then?"

Samira shook her head. "The trip to the mall has nothing to do with this conversation."

Kara's voice called from the house.

"Over here," Samira waved a garden glove but didn't bother to stand.

"Mama, there's someone at the door for you," Kara called.

"Who is it?" Krissy skipped toward the house with enthusiasm.

Samira checked her watch. *Almost eight. I'm not expecting anyone.* She kicked off her garden shoes outside the kitchen door and stepped inside with bare feet. Krissy was standing at the kitchen island staring at the door.

Samira looked from her daughter to the guest. *Oh my.*

"I tried to call but the line's been busy."

Kara ducked her head at the mention of the busy signal.

Phil shared an easy smile. "So, I decided to stop over on my way across town."

Krissy cleared her throat obnoxiously.

Wow. With a quick exhale of breath, Samira tried to gather her thoughts. *Whew. Okay, regroup.* She had hoped Phil would check in when he got home. *But it didn't occur to me he might just drop in.* She smoothed her old t-shirt with her hands. *I must look like a wreck, just coming in from the garden and all.*

"So?" Krissy prompted.

"Yes," Samira's eyes were locked with Phil's. *Of course, I should introduce the girls.*

Phil ran his hand through his hair and shook his head once. "Maybe I should have waited for the line to clear."

"No, it's okay." *I doubt Kara would have been off the phone before bedtime anyway.* She swallowed again and tucked a lock of loose hair back into her ponytail. *Just focus.* "Let me introduce you. Krissy, Kara, this is Phil." Samira still hadn't taken her eyes off the man. "Phil, this is Kara."

Kara had been studying Phil's face, but now she looked away shyly.

"And this is Krissy," Samira continued. *And I'm still Samira. I think.*

Krissy tried to stifle a giggle when Phil acknowledged her by name.

Samira left her gardening gloves on the kitchen island and started across the room. *Just act casual and breathe.* "Phil has been fishing with his boys this weekend."

"Well, that would definitely explain the whiskers," Krissy blurted.

Phil rubbed his chin as if just remembering he hadn't shaved in several days.

Krista. Samira watched Kara send a daggered look across the room at her sister. *I never know what she's going to say.* Krissy's eyes were full of orneriness.

Phil flashed an easy smile in Krissy's direction. *I love that smile.* She felt the color rise in her cheeks.

Kara's dark brown eyes reflected more maturity than her sister. "We're very pleased to meet you, Phil." She looked at her mother. "We'll be in my room if you need us."

"We will?" Krissy's expression indicated total surprise. She waved to the visitor as her older sister took her arm and drug her toward the hallway. "Bye Phil."

Thank God for Kara. She knows I'm a nervous wreck. Samira hid her face in her hands. "I am so sorry."

"No need to be," Phil leaned back on his heels and stuck his hands in his pockets. "I should have called first."

"That's okay, really." Samira started to explain. "I just hadn't prepared them to meet you, that's all." She melted under his gaze. *No, I hadn't prepared me to share you.* Silence lingered between them.

"I was thinking I should have called more for your sake." Phil's voice was gentle when he spoke.

Obviously, he noticed too. "Maybe so." Samira sighed heavily. *Where's my manners? I should offer him coffee. Oh no…* "Something cold to drink?"

"I'm alright," Phil assured. He glanced over his shoulder. "But I might take some water out to Chase. I left him in the truck."

"In the truck?" Samira's reaction was genuine. "Invite him in."

"Oh, no." Phil started to explain. "You don't want him in here. He's been at the lake all weekend. He's in serious need of a bath."

What a terrible thing to say. Samira stepped over to the window and adjusted the wooden shutters so she could see the driveway. "Nonsense. It's silly to leave someone in the truck. Bring him in for a drink."

"Oh, wait."

Samira frowned when Phil laughed.

"Chase is my dog."

Chase is his dog? Dumbfounded, Samira stared at the rugged man in her entryway. *I didn't know he had a dog.* Suddenly, the realization became very humorous, and she burst out laughing. *He's more inviting by the minute.* Samira covered her mouth with her hand and tried to compose herself. *Now that's funny.* "Maybe you could just let him into the back yard then," She stifled a laugh.

Phil obliged and met Samira in the garage with his canine friend. *And he's a big dog too.* Chase bolted into the backyard. Samira closed the walk-in door and crossed the yard to the pool. *I'll give him some fresh water.* She bent down and turned a faucet near the ground. A spray of water burst into the air at the far side.

"I don't have a bucket or a bowl out here." Samira could feel Phil watching her with growing interest.

"This will work just fine."

She watched as his eyes took in the garden.

"What a sight for sore eyes."

Samira assumed he was talking about the landscape. She touched a leaf on a flowering tree as she spoke. "This is my hideaway. I love it out here. I planted this garden when —" *Wait. I've never talked to another man about my husband.* "Well, anyway," she tried to refocus. "There is something in bloom in every season." *He probably doesn't care much about flowering trees and rose bushes.*

When she looked up, she realized Phil's eyes were fixed directly on her. Samira crossed her arms over her middle trying to ignore the attraction that was building. Chase found the pool and noisily helped himself to a long drink.

Change the subject. "So how was your weekend?"

Phil moved slightly closer to Samira as he answered. "It was good to get away but it's good to be back just the same."

Samira cleared her throat. "I meant with your boys." She glanced over her shoulder wondering where her daughters were.

Phil thought for a moment. "A weekend is hardly enough time, but it was good to hang with them for a while." He grinned and ran his fingers over his scruffy beard. "I guess I took my sabbatical seriously."

Despite the beard, Samira couldn't help but notice how well the cut on Phil's cheekbone was healing. "I don't mind." *The rustic look is rather sexy.*

"The beard or the dropping in?"

"Your cheek looks better." *Of course, it will probably show up more when he's clean-shaven.*

Phil reached up and touched the wound. "Not bad, huh?" He held his hand out for Samira to examine. "Even this one is healing up pretty good."

Samira noticed the dark scab. *There will be scar when that one heals.* "Does it still hurt?"

When Phil didn't answer, she looked up.

Without waiting for permission, he took a step closer and drew Samira into his body. *No wait.* Passion took over in a heartbeat and there was no way Samira was going to ignore it now. She succumbed to his kiss and enjoyed the prickly whiskers against her cheek. *This is definitely okay.* Samira wrapped her arms around Phil's waist and kissed him again.

Screams from the garden entrance brought a sudden halt to the intimate moment. In an instant, Samira's personal desires were shattered by motherhood defenses.

"There's a big black dog in the yard." Krissy raced past her mother and Phil. "Did you see it?" She continued to search around the flowerbeds. "How did it get in here anyway?"

Phil separated himself from Samira. With a snap of his fingers Chase appeared obediently at his side. Samira listened through a filtered ear as Phil introduced his dog to Krissy.

"You didn't tell me he had a dog."

There are many things I didn't tell you. Samira looked out across the garden. *And there are many things I still don't know.* Samira put her hands in her hair. *I just need a moment to compose myself.* Somehow, she managed to suggest that her daughter wait back inside the house.

"I'd rather stay out here and play with Chase." Krissy rubbed the dog's head. "Obviously, no one told him about the 'no dog' rule."

Phil smiled guiltily.

Samira rolled her eyes at her daughter's accusation. "No *stray* dogs allowed." *Why doesn't she just go back inside?* "Chase hardly appears to be a stray." *Although I don't think I've ever had a dog in my backyard before.* Samira tried to remember.

Samira watched Phil's eyes scan the garden. "He's definitely not a stray, but he could probably find something to dig up." He bent down and looked Krissy in the eyes. "Krissy, thanks for telling me about the dog rule."

Oh, no. Don't let Krissy spoil everything. Samira started to interrupt but Phil stopped her with the motion of his hand.

"Maybe you should take him back through the garage and put him in my truck."

"Okay." Krissy bounced off the ground. "Do you think he'll go with me?"

Phil snapped his fingers twice and Chase stood at attention. The master gave a command with his hand and the canine obeyed.

That's amazing how the dog responds to Phil's hand commands. "I'll meet you inside, Krissy," Samira called as her daughter disappeared. *He handled that exceptionally well.* "Thank you." *for talking to Krissy like that.*

Several feet now separated them.

"Thank you."

"I meant for giving Krissy something to do," Samira avoided Phil's eyes. *It's too dangerous to look at him again.* Her stomach was churning. *He makes me do things I shouldn't do. It's almost like I don't have any control.* Suddenly her life seemed extremely complicated. *I can't let him do that to me when the girls are around.*

"I know what you meant."

And I know what you meant too. Samira looked high into the branches of the magnolia tree. *And it was good for me too. You're welcome.*

Phil took a step toward her, but Samira took a step to keep her distance. *What if passion is all there is to this?* Her heart pounded hard in her chest. She wondered how much of the kiss Krissy had witnessed. *Worse yet, I wonder what she'll tell her sister? Or her friends?*

Phil sighed heavily. "Look, Samira—"

I've disappointed him again. "I know," she interrupted. "It just seems so soon." *Too soon for what, Samira?* She struggled to find balance between womanhood and motherhood. *Given your history, anytime is going to be too soon.* She glanced at the house. "I should probably get back inside." *It's too soon to juggle Phil with the girls at home. That's all.* She wasn't convinced.

Phil nodded but the look on his face gave insight to his own confusion.

"I'm sorry," Samira whispered. "This isn't the way I had things pictured." *Not even close.*

"It's alright." Phil's voice was low when he spoke.

No, it's not. Samira was doubtful. Nothing seemed right anymore. "I think I have some things to figure out." *I could easily let him in if I were single and looking for a companion.* Every ounce of her being wanted to continue what they had started. *But I'm not single. I must make sure the man I bring into my life is good for my girls too.* "I am so sorry." *Or do I just have to make sure I'm ready?*

Samira could feel his eyes on the back of her shoulder as he spoke. "Take your time, Samira." There was a slight pause. "I can wait."

I don't know how long it will take to figure me out. Several awkward moments separated their thoughts. *And I still owe him an answer on the Springfield thing.* Samira took a deep breath. *If it's even still open for invitation.*

Phil spoke again. "Why don't you give me a call when you're ready."

Samira looked out across her garden. "With school just getting out things could be quite hectic." *I can't believe I'm making excuses. I waited all week for him to call and now I don't even know how to talk to him.*

"Like I said," Phil interrupted. "Take your time." He ran his hand through his hair. "I'll be around."

I don't want him to be around. Samira stared at the brick walk under her bare feet. *I want him to be right here.* She wanted so desperately to be cradled in his arms yet held firm to her defenses. *I should just ask him about Springfield and get it off my mind.* When he stepped closer, she felt her heart skip a beat. Looking up, she met his dark blue eyes again. *This is just too risky.*

Ever so gently Phi placed his hand under her ponytail and kissed her on the forehead.

Samira closed her eyes. *Just like my father.* She watched Phil turn and head for the gate. *I really don't want him to leave like this.* She couldn't bring herself to speak and he didn't say a word until he reached the exit.

"Be in touch, Samira."

Be in touch? Samira bit her bottom lip. *That's it? He walks away and leaves the ball completely in my court.* Guilt engulfed Samira as the gate closed between them. *How can I possibly be a good mother while I'm dying to share my innermost being with a man that isn't their father?*

Everything about this man felt right yet the exact things felt terribly wrong. *What right does he have to waltz into my life and conjure up all those feelings I buried so long ago?* Samira fought against her conscience. *How can he bring me so much pleasure and cause me so much distress at the same time?* Samira stretched her chin to the heavens. *He can make decisions too. What if he decides he can't wait long enough for me to be ready?*

O dear God, what am I supposed to do? Samira whispered. She bent down and turned off the water spicket. Instantly, the fountain stopped flowing.

~~~~~~~

"He's really cute." Krissy commented as her mother tucked her into bed. "You didn't tell us he had a dog."

"I didn't know he had a dog until tonight, Krissy."

"Does he always have a beard?"

"Not that I know of."

"Nice truck. Does he have a car too?"
~~~~~~~

"I don't know."

"How old are his kids?"

Samira's patience with the questions was growing thin. "I just don't know yet, Krissy." The mother tried not to sound edgy. *But I don't know any of these things.*

"It's kind of hard to learn everything about one another after just one date," Kara added from the doorway to her sister's room.

Two coffee shop dates, dinner, and an overnight, Samira silently corrected.

"Right, Mama?"

Samira pulled the top cover over her youngest daughter and quickly pecked her on the cheek. "We're just starting to get to know one another." *But if I don't hurry up and reply, he may move on.*

"I can still smell his aftershave. He smells alright for coming home from camping."

Oh, good grief. His scent is on me. Samira ignored the comment and turned off the light as she left Krissy's room.

"I hope he comes back," Krissy chimed as the room went dark.

I hope he calls first.

Kara turned off her light and slipped under the covers of her own bed. "He looked like a mountain man."

What kind of comment is that? Samira sat down on the edge of the bed, watching Kara's face in the dimly lit room. "He'd been camping for several days. The last time I saw him he was clean shaven and very professional looking."

Kara's eyes widened. "I can't picture him that way."

Samira smiled. *I don't mind the rustic look.* "Well, maybe you'll have a chance to meet him under different circumstances." *Kara always has trouble visualizing.* She smoothed Kara's long dark hair back from her face.

The fourteen-year-old turned onto her side. *She's done talking for the night.* Relieved to be off the hook, Samira left the room.

What made Tom's name almost fall out of my mouth when I was talking to Phil anyway? It didn't seem like the natural thing to do, yet at the same time it was right there. *The entire garden was created in Tom's memory. But I've never talk to anyone about that.* Being able to give life to something new every season was therapy in and of itself. *Why I felt compelled to say something about it tonight is a mystery.*

Samira slipped into her nightshirt. In front of the bathroom mirror, she washed her face with cool water and toweled dry. The texture of the towel reminded her of Phil's beard against her cheek. *I feel awful that I pulled away from him like that. And then I couldn't even explain.* Krissy's questions echoed in her mind. *I'd like to know the answers to those questions too.*

With a book in hand, Samira climbed into bed. The words on the page read easily under her eyes, but they weren't sticking. Reluctantly she closed the novel and turned out the light. But even in the dark of the room there was no peace of mind.

Oh, God, have I sacrificed too much already? The prayer fell silently into the night. *Is it all right for me to seek solace with a man that isn't Tom?* Samira hugged her pillow and closed her eyes tight. *I don't know if I have the strength to be with someone again. And I really don't know if I have the endurance to survive if I turn out to be his passing phase.*

There was no sanctuary in the hollow of the night.

18 The Waiting Game

Joseph Phillip

Mr. Stephenson stood facing the window overlooking downtown. His back was to the board of directors. The meeting had been in session most of the morning. *It is high time to decide so I can be on with my day.*

J.P. removed his glasses and spoke into the silence of the room. "Either we take a chance on the new discoveries from Sparky, or we sit the week out waiting on local authorities." He waited but there was no immediate response. "The deciding factor is how quickly you want to move the investigation forward."

"How are the local investigators going to take it when they know we've undermined their efforts?" Mr. Stephenson looked worried when he turned around.

J.P. pushed his chair away from the table. *He is one of the most conservative clients I've ever served.* "Two things, Mr. Stephenson. First, we are not undermining an investigation. We are enhancing the timeline. Second, hiring a private investigator is going to communicate that you're serious about finding the suspects." *It doesn't make sense not to move forward with Sparky.* "The longer we wait, the less chance there is of an arrest. Bottom line."

A buzzer on the intercom interrupted the meeting. Mr. Stephenson nodded for a board member to answer. "For you Mr. Ralston."

For me? J.P. rose from his seat and identified himself to the caller.

"It's Denise, Boss." Her voice was energetic. "Sparky checked in. He thinks he's found the missing link. He needs access to the mainline server at closing."

Perfect timing. J.P. covered the mouthpiece and addressed Mr. Stephenson. "Sparky's found the link he was looking for. He needs access to the server at closing. Is that a possibility?"

Mr. Stephenson narrowed his eyes in thought. *Come on, just make a decision. We need to make this work.* Slowly Mr. Stephenson's head nodded once.

"Send him over, Denise."

"Sparky's weird about that, you know," she reminded. "Stay on the line. Let me ask him for a specific time."

Why is she calling on their phone anyway?

"He needs access before they close out today's business."

"On site?"

"Nope. Told you. He's weird about that. He prefers to work from a remote site but to do that, he'll need new access codes."

Whatever that means. J.P. shook his head. He'd never worked with an investigator as intense and secretive as Sparky. *I wonder if I'm going to have to pay him in unmarked bills.*

"Mr. Stephenson," J.P. addressed his client who was once again looking out the window. "We'll need new access codes so Sparky can access the server before the close of business today."

A single nod gave silent approval.

"Tell Sparky it's a go."

"Will do," Denise confirmed. "And by the way, your cell phone isn't on."

It's not? J.P. felt his phone through his jacket pocket.

"You might want to fix that as you leave the meeting."

If I ever get out of the meeting. J.P. hung up the telephone feeling a new sense of energy. *If Sparky pans out as successful as Mike promised, I'll owe the biggest favor of my life.*

Mr. Stephenson picked up the telephone and notified his technicians to allow access to the investigator.

I have never known a businessman to be so slow to make decisions. J.P. spoke to each board member as they parted ways.

"You're making the right decision, Mr. Stephenson."

Mr. Stephenson nodded but avoided eye contact. "I hope so."

What is it going to take to earn his trust?

"I don't like not knowing and I like waiting even less."

I understand the waiting part. J.P. activated his cell phone before repacking the contents of his briefcase. "We should have a good report in the morning." *With any luck.* "I'll be in touch."

Mr. Stephenson's face was still contemplative. "I appreciate your attentiveness, J.P."

What is it about him that feels so familiar? "Not a problem." J.P. exchanged a handshake before Mr. Stephenson left the room. *I can't believe how long that meeting lasted.* J.P. exited the building through a back doorway. *Shouldn't have been that difficult.* He unlocked his truck with the remote. *Either we hire the private investigator, or we don't.*

The downtown library was busy with the noon hour activity when J.P. drove by. *I wonder if Samira ever has business at the downtown site.* The same thought made him mad. *Considering her inability to make a decision, it's just as well you keep your mind on your work.* He turned the corner at the Café Ole and followed the alley to his private parking space. The café was busy too. *I'd passed that place a million times without giving it a thought until I invited Samira there.* Again, he caught his thoughts. *Give it up, man. She may not even call you back.*

"Hey, Boss."

Denise was at her desk when J.P. entered. Derek was busy in front of a computer in the makeshift workspace in the corner.

J.P. addressed Denise. "Nice work with Sparky. Did he leave any indication about what he was thinking?"

Denise shook her head as she handed over the message board. "Nope. He's very secretive, you know. Kind of like he lurks in the shadows of some crime movie or something." She wiggled her shoulders from side to side. "I'd love to meet him and get his autograph when this is all said and done."

J.P. skimmed the messages. "He's not very social. Doubt if he's much into signing his name for a fan." He returned the clipboard to Denise's desk and addressed the first message on the list. "What's the scoop with Christopher Hughes?"

Denise followed J.P. into his office. "His secretary emailed that you should be receiving documents from England concerning the affair in Springfield."

"What kind of documents?" J.P. removed his sports coat and hung it over the back of a chair.

"She didn't say."

"Find out." *I knew I'd be on official business once I returned the RSVP.* "I'd prefer to work that evening in the know—without surprises."

"In that case," Denise continued. "She also indicated that the guest suite was reserved in your name at the convention center complex. Sounds like it could be a late night."

J.P. tried to ignore the pit in his stomach. *I can't even get Samira to decide on dinner, let alone an overnight.*

"Are you sure you don't need me to secure a date for the evening?"

You mean night, so you'd might as well say it. "No." He tried to tame his tone. *I'll give her a few more days to reply.* "That won't be necessary."

"Not even a backup?"

J.P. balanced his weight on his fingertips as he leaned slightly into his desk. *Read my lips, Denise.* "I said, no."

"There's no word from a Sean Bridges," Denise changed the subject without further harassment. "We did have a call back from a Jessica Hutchison who says she's a senior associate for the Bridges Property Management Group. Should I call her back?"

The attorney sorted a short stack of piles into order of priority for the afternoon. "If she's the only connection then we'll have to run with it." He opened a file marked *Hughes Estate.* "Any word from the city attorney on possible settlement?"

"Nothing yet. Should I call him?"

"Let's wait him out."

"How long?"

"Give him until Thursday. They should be able to make a decision by then." *Which is more than I can say about Samira. I don't think she has a timeline.*

"You're out of town for a juvenile court hearing on Thursday. Don't forget." Denise tapped her pen on the clipboard. "When did James get back?"

"Yesterday." *I left him at home long enough to run up here to pick up a file and to make a personal stop.*

"Is he working at the club today?"

J.P. glanced at his watch. "For a few more hours." *Short hours at that.* "Did Mike call about the hearing?"

"Yes, Mike called." Denise tapped the edge of the clipboard. "I was getting to that. He says he'll brief you on the way up there. You're scheduled at eleven, but Mike says they run late so plan to be bored."

I can think of a million places I'd rather be than sitting in the lobby at juvenile court. "Anything else?"

"Not at the moment, which is probably just as well since you're a little on edge." She started to leave the office. "Derek and I can manage the Thursday agenda if you're worried about that. And he's doing a fine job so far, in case you're interested." Denise turned in the doorway and faced her boss. "If there's something else eating at you then it might be in your best interest to either resolve the issue or let me in on it so I can fix it for you."

J.P. sat at his desk staring at the closed door between the offices. He hadn't even spoken to Derek Danielson who was diligently managing the case overload. *And now I only have three short hours before James is done at the club.* He fingered the files on his desk. *What the hell am I supposed to do with him while I continue my workday?* Irritated with the new responsibility, J.P. opened the army green folder as if a new bit of information might jump off the page concerning the boundary issues between the city and Lloyd Hughes estate.

And what exactly is Christopher expecting of me in Springfield? That thought was irritating as well. *I don't mind managing their business affairs.* The Hughes Corporation was his biggest and most profitable client. *But they've managed to blur the lines with this estate and now their daughter's engagement.*

J.P. turned his attention back to the file in hand. *All I need is one historical, dated document that proves the township was unincorporated in 1912 to close this file for good.* That document had yet to be discovered.

"Mr. Hughes, Christopher," Denise's voice sounded on the intercom. "Line two."

Damn it, I didn't want to talk to him. J.P. closed his eyes for a minute. *A simple explanation from Hughes' personal secretary would have sufficed.*

"Mr. Hughes, J.P. Ralston here. How can I be of service?" *There are times I'd prefer not to make myself so available.*

"J.P., it's good to hear your voice. I understand you have questions concerning your role in Springfield. Are you concerned about the accommodations?"

"The invitation and the accommodations are quite satisfactory, Mr. Hughes. However, I can only meet your expectations when I am informed of my duties." He drummed his fingers against his desk in anticipation of the client's response.

Mr. Hughes chuckled. "This is the very reason I have you on board, J.P. You're the best in the business."

Skip the niceties, Christopher. Let's get down to business.

"It seems our family attorney, I'm sure you remember Sebastian—"

"Very well, sir." *Sebastian and I have our differences.*

"Sebastian will be tied up here in Great Britain, unable to make the Springfield engagement. I'd appreciate you looking over my daughter's prenuptials so we can make it official at the ceremony."

I despise family law. J.P. closed his eyes and pressed his fingertips into his forehead. *But this is Christopher Hughes.*

"It would be a great favor to the family, J.P.," Mr. Hughes continued to thicken his plea. "No one would appreciate it more than Mrs. Hughes and myself."

"Who prepared the agreement?" *Tell me it wasn't Sabastian.*

"Sebastian and the legal representation of the betrothed."

Figures.

"I would appreciate your taking time to go over it, you know, make sure everything is in order."

Maybe he doesn't trust Sebastian either. "I'm assuming you'll need it notarized as well?"

"If it's not too much trouble, J.P."

It was suddenly obvious that Mr. Hughes wanted the agreement signed and notarized without Sebastian's presence. *I wonder how many of my own documents have been proofed and edited by Sebastian over the years?*

"Very well, Mr. Hughes. I'll review the agreement so it can be notarized that night." He took a deep breath knowing full well how tedious and time consuming it could become.

"Fine, fine, J.P.," Mr. Hughes sounded into the telephone. "As you know, we've reserved the private suite for you and a guest at the civic center so plan to stay the night. I'll be sure it is well stocked."

"That won't be necessary, Mr. Hughes." *I don't even know if she's going to accept the invite to dinner yet.*

"Just the same, we'll plan on you staying." It was obvious the businessman was turning his thoughts to other matters. "The documents should reach you by the weekend. We'll be in touch."

Damn it. J.P. had known Stephanie Hughes since she was born, and she had yet to be denied anything she wanted. *Including the Duke of Ellington.*

He's twice her age, J.P. guessed. With that thought came another. *I wonder how old Samira is anyway.*

The attorney slammed a folder hard against his desk. Every time he turned around Samira was creeping into his thoughts. *I should have told Denise to secure a date for the seventeenth.* He left his desk and stepped into his private bathroom. Trying desperately to clear his thinking, he turned the ceramic handle on the faucet and cupped his hands to catch the cold water. He rinsed his entire face.

I have never left the ball in a woman's court. J.P hid his face in a dry towel for several moments. *What was I thinking? She can't even relax enough to kiss me, let alone pick up the phone to call.* J.P. left the towel hanging over the edge of the sink. *No woman has ever been so appealing and downright maddening at the same time.*

J.P. grabbed his sports coat and headed for the front door of his office.

"Boss?"

"I'll be at the gym."

"It's only two o'clock."

I know that. This workout is for me.

"Leave your phone on so I can call you if I hear from Sparky." Denise paused. "Or should I not call you?"

J.P. held the door open with one hand. "Only if you deem it necessary." *There is no reason to be short with Denise.* When he turned to look at her it was obvious, he'd hurt her feelings.

I should probably apologize. But J.P. Ralston wasn't in the business of making apologies. Instead, he turned away and stepped out into the hot afternoon sunshine. *The sooner I'm at the gym the better off we'll all be.*

19 Meet Mike

Samira

"Are you going to lunch, Miss Samira?" Mrs. Haddock located the head librarian in the research center.

Samira had been at the computer all morning. "Oh, is it lunchtime already?"

"Any luck yet?"

"No. Nothing." *How frustrating.*

"Anything I could help you with?"

Samira shook her head. "I'm looking for a phone number."

"Who is it for honey?" Mrs. Haddock adjusted her bifocals to read the computer screen."

"I don't really know." *I can't believe I slept with a man who isn't showing up in a phone listing.* "Why don't you go ahead and take lunch, Helen. I'll go when you get back."

"It seems to me it would help to have a name if you're looking for a number to go with it." Mrs. Haddock patted Samira on the shoulder. "Good luck. I'll be back at one."

Samira was relieved to be alone with the computer again. *He said to call when I was ready.* Her eyes skimmed the professional listing again. *Well, I don't know if I'm ready or not, but I'd at least like to be able to call him.*

"Attorneys. Lawyers. Legal Advice. Nothing." Samira's finger tapped the mouse. *This isn't that big of a town. He shouldn't be so hard to find.* She opened the Chamber of Commerce site. *No Phil. No Phillip. No anything.* She closed the site. *It would have been helpful for him to leave a number.*

There was a tap on the door. "Samira? Are you busy?"

Busy. But not successfully so. Samira turned in the steno chair. "Oh, Kelly. Hi. Come on in." The green eyes of Kelly Davis were a sharp contrast to her dark red hair. "What brings you to Maple Street Library? School is out for the summer."

Kelly smiled and sat down in a chair across from Samira. "I know. You'd think a schoolteacher would hide from books all summer long."

"What can I help you with?"

"Well," Kelly hesitated, but her eyes were still bouncing with energy. "I'm here on a personal matter with a professional motive."

Samira raised her eyebrows.

Kelly reached around her head and unbound her naturally curly hair. "I need some informational books on American Government, maybe something on US History."

"Government?" Samira rose from her chair. *But you're Krissy's English teacher.* "Do you have a new teaching assignment?"

"Oh, no. Nothing like that." Kelly re-wrapped her hair with an elastic band. "You know Brian Wilson, right?"

"Mr. Wilson. The science teacher." *Serious. Single. I know who he is.*

"Yes." Kelly followed Samira into the main library. "He's invited me on a continuing ed trip this summer. For two weeks. All the way to Washington D.C. and back."

This must be the personal part. "Do continuing ed credits in Social Studies count for English teachers?"

"Only if I fill out the paperwork correctly." Kelly giggled. "That would be the professional part of my visit today.

"Government and history are over here." *Kelly is taking a two-week vacation with Brian Wilson. Interesting.*

Kelly ran her hand over a bookshelf as they walked through the historical section. "We'll go through Philadelphia on the way out, so any history on the sites there would be helpful too."

Samira slowed to a stop and began skimming the spines. "You know, the high school library has a vast collection of historical books on Washington D.C."

"Oh, I know." Kelly interrupted. "But I'd prefer Mrs. Billings not get wind of my trip with Brian."

Understood. I can appreciate that.

"Not that we shouldn't be going together, but—" Kelly pretended to skim the titles with Samira.

"You don't have to explain, Kelly." Samira pulled a big colorful book off the shelf. "Start with this one. It's a pictorial directory of the nation's capital." She pulled another. "And this one has more documentation."

Kelly took both books with interest. "So, what about you, Samira? Do your summer plans include a man?"

Taken aback, Samira turned and stared at Kelly Davis. *Where did that question come from?*

Kelly waited. "Well?"

I don't know Kelly all that well. But I don't see any harm in talking to her either. "I don't know yet." Samira took a deep breath. "I've had a couple of encounters with a man here lately, but I have no idea where it's going. If anywhere." *Encounters? What kind of a word is that?*

Kelly tipped her head playfully and then leaned toward Samira as if she had a secret to share. "I have to be honest. Krissy told me you had a hot date a week or so back."

A hot date? Samira shook her head. *Why am I not surprised by that?*

"Don't be mad at her," Kelly cautioned. "She was so excited for you, Samira." Kelly shook a few loose curls back away from her face. "So how did it go?"

A genuine smile appeared on Samira's face without hesitation. "It went well, I think."

But I can't even be myself with him when the girls are home. "But you know, Kelly, it's really hard to have a man with my life the way it is." *Do I really want to share this with a woman I only kind of know?*

"Maybe you're trying too hard."

What is she talking about?

Kelly reached across and touched Samira's hand. "What's the worst-case scenario?"

Kelly just told me she's driving halfway across the country and spending two weeks with Brian Wilson. Samira crossed her arms over her stomach.

"Think about it. What's the worst thing that could happen? You'll end up liking him and then it wouldn't work out?"

What's the worst thing? That I already do like him. That he's too intense for my father. That he'll have nothing in common with Wes. That he's not enough of a family man for my mother? "I really don't know. There's just so much to juggle and think about and plan around."

"And you're the only one who knows. Right?"

Knows what?

"I mean, you probably haven't been able to talk to him about any of the complications or anything, so it's all just stuck in your head." Kelly was looking Samira right in the eyes.

Amazing how she can read my thoughts. Samira looked away. *Susan used to be able to do that.* "I guess I'm just afraid to get my hopes up." *Maybe afraid to get the girls' hopes up, too.* That last thought hit the nail on the head. *Plain and simple, I don't feel like getting hurt. And worse yet, I'm not ready to get the girls' hopes up only to have them crash with me if things don't work out.*

Kelly began to walk as if she realized the conversation had gone deeper than Samira was ready to share. "Let me see, how can I say this and not come across sounding too simplistic?"

Samira followed, hoping Kelly could relieve her mind.

"Let me say it this way," Kelly turned back and looked at Samira again. "The only way he can break your heart is if you put it out there for him to take."

Samira translated the comment back through her mind slowly: *The only way he can break my heart is if I put it out there for him to take.* She stood stock still for several moments. *Do I want to take that risk?*

"You're the only one who knows, so you're the only one who can make that decision," Kelly added through the opposite side of a bookshelf.

So, let me ask her this. "How is it with Brian Wilson?"

"It's not." Kelly picked up another book. "I mean, we have a great time together and I enjoy his company but he's just not the forever type." She laughed a little, "I have a hard time picturing myself settling in for life with anybody, but especially with Brian." She continued to talk as her hand pushed her bushy curls back again. "Personally, I think Brian found this continuing ed trip so he could show me how adventurous he is." Kelly smiled casually. "But he's really not that way at all." She shrugged her shoulders. "But I have yet to get a better offer so I'm going to go explore the world, spend some more time with him, and see where it all goes from there."

She's so nonchalant about the whole affair. "Isn't it uncomfortable spending time with him if you know he might not be the one you want to end up with?"

Kelly laughed. "Only if I let it be." She set the books down on a study table and once again refastened her hair. "I figure I can either stay inside my room for the rest of my life or put my heart out there to test the water. Who knows? It might lead somewhere if I give it a chance. Or it might not." She cocked her head with a brilliant smile. "My guess is you'll be glad you gave him a chance."

I'll have to revisit this conversation later. By myself.

~~~~~~~

Kelly Davis left with an armload of books about the same time Mrs. Haddock came back to work. *The only way he can break your heart is if you put it out there for him to take.* A sudden urgency took over Samira's need to reach Phil. *What if Kelly Davis is right?* She informed her assistant that she might not be back right on time. *If I can't find him in a phone listing, maybe I can find him at Twin Hills Country Club where he attempted to take me for dinner.*

Samira's heart pounded hard in her chest as she opened the full-length glass doors of the athletic club. *I am totally OUT of my comfort zone.*

"Excuse me."

The girl behind the desk stopped folding towels and made eye contact.

Samira smiled. "I'm wondering if you might be able to assist me. I'm looking for someone who is a member here."

"We have a lot of members' ma'am." Her dishwater blonde ponytail flipped over the top of her head when she bent over to pick up a fallen towel. "Does this person have a name?"

Samira cleared her throat. "Well, yes he does, but I'm not sure I have it right." Her palms were sweating profusely. *I can't believe I don't even know his whole name.* "His first name is Phil and I think he's an attorney."

The desk attendant grinned mischievously and focused her blue eyes directly on Samira. "Phil?" The girl laughed. "That's interesting."

What's interesting? Samira decided not to ask. "Do you know him?"

"Oh, I know him." She moved a stack of folded towels to the shelf behind her.

Samira took a deep breath. "Well, I've been trying to get in touch with him—"

The girl interrupted. "You and every other woman around here." She popped her gum. "Try Ralston." The girl snapped a towel. "I hear he's out of town but with him you never know if that's a fact or not."

Samira wiped her hands on her thighs. *Well, he told me he'd be around.* The voices inside her head were screaming for her to leave. *I've come this far, I'm not going to give up*
~~~~~~~

quite that easily.

"Ralston, thank you." Still watching the girl, Samira continued with hesitation. "Would it be alright if I left a message for him here?"

The attendant glanced sideways at Samira. "Plenty of women ask for him but we're not his answering service. You can leave a message, but no promises he'll ever see it."

I don't know what I was expecting, but this wasn't it.

"Here's a piece of paper if you dare to give it a shot." The girl sneered. "Last I knew his weekends were booked through November."

Through November? What is she talking about? Samira didn't dare inquire about the nature of the bookings. *Maybe this wasn't a good idea.*

"If you're not already on his weekend agenda the chances of getting in now are slim to none." The girl snapped another towel and forced a laugh. "And I'd say your chances of getting in with him are probably slimmer than most. You seem a little out of his league."

Now Samira knew she had made the wrong decision. The pit in her stomach was quickly rising to her throat. *I hope to God she's talking about the wrong man.*

Samira pushed the paper back toward the girl without speaking and turned to leave. *I made a terrible mistake in coming here.* Samira felt exposed from the inside out. *I should have known better than to go out on a limb like this.*

Samira's eyes were already focused on the parking lot on the other side of the glass doors.

"Excuse me, ma'am?"

Samira stayed focused on the exit.

"Miss?" A man caught up to her and touched her arm.

Dear God, is he talking to me? She pulled her arm away from his touch.

"I didn't mean to startle you."

He is talking to me. Samira looked up into dancing blue eyes.

"I really am sorry to be so rude," the man offered gently. "But I couldn't help overhearing your conversation with the attendant. I apologize for her inappropriate behavior." He continued to explain. "I'll see to it that her manager is aware of this most uncomfortable situation."

Maybe he works here. Samira glanced at the bartender across the room. *But I'd think he'd be wearing a uniform or a nametag or something.*

"Would you mind?" The man motioned toward the empty lounge. "I'd like to visit if you have a moment."

Samira hesitated, but something about the energy in his eyes made her oblige. She stepped into the lounge and allowed him to lead her to the bar. He pulled up a barstool and sat down so he was just under Samira's eye level.

"My name's Mike, Mike Benson." He offered his hand.

Mike Benson. I don't know a Mike Benson. Samira examined his long, curly blonde hair and bushy mustache. *He'd better not be trying to pick me up.*

"Do I understand that you're looking for someone in particular?"

He eavesdropped on my conversation. Samira crossed her arms. *I should have just stayed at the library.*

The man folded his hands on his lap. His eyes were still fixed directly on hers. Samira shifted her weight against his gaze.

"I really am sorry."

He should be. Samira took a step toward the door.

"No. Wait, please. I know about everyone who comes through here," the man offered in a gentle tone. "I thought I might be able to deliver a message."

Mike Benson. Samira was still skeptical. *How do I know I can trust him?*

"Look," Mike tried to explain. "I have a feeling you're looking for a good friend of mine." When Samira didn't respond he offered the name. "Did I hear you mention Phil Ralston?"

At least he knows the name. With Phil's name out in the open, Samira breathed a slight sigh of relief. *And he doesn't seem to be derogatory about it either.* She returned his inquisitive glance. *I should probably say something.* She took a deep breath.

"Yes." she finally admitted. "I was supposed to call him but haven't been able to find a phone number." Samira looked around the room finally. *This is the same bar where Phil and I waited for a table that didn't materialize.*

"Somehow, that doesn't surprise me." The man laughed and shook his head making his blonde curls bounce. "I've known J—"

Who?

"—Phil Ralston longer than I can remember." Mike wiggled his eyebrows. "Let's see, I went to undergraduate school with him, roomed with him in law school, and work hard to keep him in line. I'll be seeing him later today."

So, he is a lawyer. Samira studied the man in front of her. *Maybe Mike is too. Although he isn't as clean cut as Phil.*

A broad smile peaked out from under the scruffy mustache. "Anyway, I have a feeling he'd like to hear from you."

I'm so relieved to hear him say that. Samira smiled back, thankful that she might finally be a step closer to locating Phil.

Mike almost laughed out loud. "My buddy has a way of forgetting himself in the presence of a pretty lady."

Pretty lady? Samira put her hand to her face when she blushed. *Does he know Phil called me that?* "Well, I would like to talk to him. If I could get a number or something."

"That's no problem." Mike moved his hands for the first time since sitting down. Samira could feel the depth of his thoughts as he studied her face. "I'd be glad to give him a message."

Samira glanced over her shoulder. "The girl said he was out of town."

Mike followed her eyes to the front desk. "That girl is highly misinformed." He left the barstool and walked across the room. Samira watched Mike exchange a few words with the bartender and return with a pad of paper and a pencil.

"Here you go." Mike handed her the paper and pencil. "Any message you want will be personally delivered at the earliest possible convenience."

That's nice of him. Samira signed her name. *Even if his approach was rather abrupt.* Underneath her name she wrote one word: *Ready.* "Just ask him to call me." *He has my number.*

Much to Samira's dismay, Mike opened the paper and read the note. "Pronounce your name for me."

"Samira."

"Very pretty." Mike refolded the paper. "I'll see that he gets this." He stashed it in the hip pocket of his dress shorts. "Anything else I can do for you, Samira?"

Samira could feel her cheeks burn with color as his eyes penetrated hers.

"Buy you a drink? Give you a ride home?" Mike's eyes twinkled. "Anything? I'm at your service."

How does he look at me like that? It's like he's seeing through me. "Just deliver the message, Mr. Benson." She could feel her voice shake a little as she spoke.

Mike crossed his heart with his hand and then patted his hind pocket. "You have my word, Miss Samira."

I hope so. With a word of thanks, Samira turned to leave. She could feel Mike Benson's eyes on her all the way to the front door. *I hope he delivers the message soon.* She didn't breathe a sigh of relief until she reached the safety of her car and even then, she was short of breath. *Not only does Phil take my breath away, but his friend has a way of doing the same thing.*

As she drove back across town, Samira replayed the meeting with Mike Benson. *He's an interesting character. I wonder if he's a lawyer too. Must be if he roomed with him in law school.* She also wondered how much of the conversation with the attendant he'd overheard.

"You and every other woman," the girl had said. It was hard to know how to interpret that remark. *"And your chances of getting in with him are probably slimmer than most."* Mike had said the girl was misinformed, but the comment still hurt.

Samira's mind went back to that magical Friday night. *He was so patient and so gentle. I can't imagine him any other way.* She desperately wanted to dismiss any unprecedented concerns. *The girl had to be thinking of someone else.* Samira pulled into her parking space at the library. *Or is it possible she's one of Phil's weekend agendas?*

A new train of thought entered Samira's mind as she ascended the steps to the front entrance. *Maybe there's a reason I can't locate a phone number.*

20 *The Confession*

Joseph Phillip

"Hey, Mike, my man." The kitchen door slammed behind J.P. Mike was in the living room with a major league baseball game streaming on the television. Empty pizza boxes graced the coffee table where Mike's stocking feet rested.

"Hey man." Mike lifted his tall frame off the leather sofa. "How'd it go?"

"Very well, thank you."

They exchanged a high five as J.P. passed through the corner of the living room.

"I take it Sparky impressed the heebie-jeebies out of the Mid-America board?"

"You have such a way with words, Mikey." J.P. set his briefcase on the table in his office. "Sparky was right on the mark. Where's James?"

Mike pointed toward the bedroom. "We watched the first four innings waiting on the pizza. He ate. We talked. Then he crashed."

J.P. scanned his computer screen for messages from Denise. "Did he eat much?"

"You doubt a growing boy's appetite? He put away enough pizza to feed an entire baseball team."

Nothing from Denise. That's a good sign. "What'd he talk about?" J.P. loosened his tie and unfastened the top button on his dress shirt.

"Do I look like a fink?" Mike ignored the question. "What's the scoop with Mid-America?"

Let's get the chaff out of the air. "What's the connection between Mid-America and your client?"

Mike twisted his first two fingers around each other.

That's what I figured. "In that case, my discoveries are confidential." J.P. raised his eyebrows. "All I can say is there should be enough evidence for an arrest." *Eventually.* He removed his suit coat and draped it over the back of his desk chair.

Mike seemed satisfied.

"No raw confessions out of James, huh?"

"Nada. We talked baseball, basketball, and a little football. I walked him through tomorrow's hearing in detail. I think he'll do fine before the judge." Mike turned his head toward the television and followed scores as they scrolled across the bottom of the screen. "Damn, the Cubs are two runs up on the Cards." He returned to the previous conversation. "He sure has the hots for Jennie Johnson. Talked about her a lot. Gut feeling says he's holding out the truth on her account."

J.P. pulled his tie completely off and hung it over the suit jacket. "Could be. Did he happen to mention she's knocked up?"

"Shit." Mike's face turned serious. "James?"

"He doesn't think so. Says she talked to him about that possibility *before* they got it on." J.P. unbuttoned a cuff on his shirt and began to roll it over his wrist. "How's that going to play into his testimony?"

Mike chewed on his mustache for a minute. "I'll definitely need to address that with him *before* he goes in." He paused for a moment. "The last thing we need is a surprise on the witness stand."

"No shit." *We've had enough surprises.* He rolled his other cuff out of habit.

"Hey," Mike's eyes twinkled with orneriness. "Speaking of having the hots for a girl, what did ya do to piss off the little gal who works the front desk?"

"What *little* gal at what desk?"

"The dishwater blonde who works check-in at the club."

J.P. pictured the girl in his mind. *She just doesn't go away, does she?*

"She had some choice words to describe your weekend behavior." Mike distorted his face. "In fact, she seemed to think you were out of town this week."

J.P. squinted his eyes as he pictured the girl in his mind again. Ever so slowly, a nametag came into focus. "Oh my god. His palm met his forehead. "That's the mystery Mary." He shook his head. "She's been calling but I couldn't put a face with that name for the life of me."

"Go on..."

I've already had to tell this story once.

"Counselor?"

"Oh, I was supposed to have a date or something with her last weekend. Denise dealt with it." *I still have no recollection of promising her anything after our first meeting.*

"So, you've been out with her then?"

"Once." J.P. tried to act casual. "I took her to a business dinner when I needed to impress potential clients."

"Were they impressed?"

"I didn't get the job if that's what you're after."

Mike pumped up his chest and blocked the doorway so J.P. couldn't pass through. "That's not what I'm after."

Maybe I can distract him. "Wouldn't you rather hear more about the Mid-America link?"

"Not anymore. This Mary story is very intriguing. Let's finish this saga first."

There is no escaping Mike's interrogation.

Mike laughed and allowed J.P. to exit.

"Look, there's not that much to tell," J.P. headed for the kitchen. "I had her once. No big deal. I couldn't even remember her name for Christ's sake." J.P. tipped a wineglass in Mike's direction.

"None for me, thanks." Mike grinned. "I have a few plans of my own later tonight." Mike straddled a kitchen chair and rested his chin on his fist. "Nothing like *Bobbie Sommers* though."

There is no one like Bobbie Sommer, my friend. "You have a hot date on a Wednesday night?"

"Since when were weeknights ruled out?" Mike shook his head full of hair. "Besides, it's one of the few nights Rachel isn't at my place."

At least I don't bring them home with me. "Mikey, that is one item of business you need to take care of." J.P. removed a cork from an already opened bottle of wine.

"It's on my list of things to do."

He doesn't want to face Rachel's wrath. J.P. could feel Mike's eyes on his back. "What exactly is it you want out of me, Counselor?"

"Let's see." Mike tapped his hand against the table. "How about the name of my interception at the club this afternoon and meal expenses for pizza with James?"

What interception is he talking about? J.P. reached for his wallet and tossed a twenty on the table. "It's all I've got on me. Float me the rest until morning."

Mike folded the bill and stashed it in the pocket of his T-shirt. He smiled broadly. "Okay, are you ready?" His blue eyes glistened with anticipation of a new story. "This is one you're going to want to hear."

Ah, Mikey, you're always good for a story. J.P. eased himself into the chair across the table and enjoyed the smoothness of the wine as it went down. "Anytime, Mikey, I'm listening." He offered a silent toast with his glass.

"Okay, get this. You know I was at the club today, right?"

"Playing golf with the mayor again."

"Rematch you know."

"Okay."

"And Sammy-O."

"Whoever."

"Remember the new guy I played with a couple of weekends ago?"

J.P. took another drink. *Unnecessary details, good buddy.*

"Anyway, I'm on my way out the front door and this *lady* walks up to the desk and asks if she can leave a message for you."

What do you mean, lady?

"Mary was working. What a bitch. She bad mouthed you so bad. I couldn't take it." Mike stopped the story and pointed an accusing finger. "You really need to learn how to let them down easy. You're killing your reputation, man."

Better than allowing one I don't even like to live in my house. J.P. flipped a choice finger back at Mike. *I'll handle my affairs my own way, thank you.*

Mike ignored the gesture. "So, anyway, this lady is trying to leave a message and Mary is carrying on. She spouted off something about you being out of town and being booked until November or something."

Let's cut to the chase. "So, I'm assuming you intercepted the message?"

"Right. So now you owe me another one." Mike rose from his chair and approached the counter. "I think I might have that glass of that wine after all."

You're funny, Mike. J.P. patiently watched while his friend poured a glass of Merlot.

"And the message is?"

Mike leaned on the counter directly behind his friend's chair. "Please call."

Give me a break. J.P. looked over his shoulder. "That's it? You set me up for a *please call?*"

"Yep." Mike's eyes danced wildly. "I got her name too." Mike reached for his hip pocket. "If you can't remember her name, I'd be hap—"

Holy shit. J.P. bolted from the chair and grabbed Mike by the shirt. "Samira."

Mike held the wine glass high to keep from spilling. "Good god, J.P. You don't have to fight me for it."

J.P. smoothed Mike's shirt. *I should probably explain.* "I've been waiting for her to call all week."

"Relax, man." Mike took a folded piece of paper out of his pocket. "It's only Wednesday. And it would help if you'd leave a number." Mike sat back down in the chair at the table.

My number should be in her call history. J.P. opened the note and ran this thumb over the ink. *Ready.* Samira's handwriting was fluid and graceful across the paper. *Ready for what?*

"Same one from two weekends ago, right?"

"Yeah," J.P. leaned against the counter. "Same one."

"Well?"

I'm not talking to him about Samira. "Well, what?" He couldn't hide the smile on his face or the color in his cheeks.

Mike's tone softened. "She's quite a catch, J.P. Be advised to take care sporting her around the club."

Maybe so, J.P. thought to himself. *She is not my usual date.*

"Look, good buddy, I'd love to stick around and hear the rest of the story, but I need to take a shower before I meet up with my date." He reached into his shirt pocket and removed the twenty-dollar bill. Deliberately, he stuck it in the empty wine glass. "Thanks for the drink and congrats on the progress with Mid-America."

"It's almost ten."

"She promised to wait."

I hope Samira is still waiting too. "What time are we leaving in the morning?"

"Eight and I'll be on time," Mike promised. "Oh, by the way, James said Ernie is picking him up at 4:45 to work for a couple of hours before we leave. He wants to come home and clean up before we head north so you'll need to retrieve him about seven."

"Hey, Mike?"

The rambunctious attorney turned around at the back door and rested his forearm against the top of the refrigerator.

"Thanks for hanging out with James tonight."

"And for making that awesome interception."

"And for the interception."

"And for hooking you up with Sparky."

Yeah, and for that too. "And for Sparky."

Mike waved off the appreciation. "You owe me at least four favors, good buddy. And believe me, you'll pay."

J.P. grinned at Mike's insistence on keeping score.

"I'll see you at eight." Mike stepped outside. "And next time you want a pretty woman to call you back, leave your number."

She really couldn't retrieve my number? J.P. ran his hand through his hair. *I'm surprised she went out to the club looking for me.* The last drop of wine in the bottom of Mike's wine glass was working its way into the corner of the folded bill. *That took guts.* J.P. pulled the money out of the glass with two fingers. *Same Merlot I served Samira at her house.* The note was laying on the counter. J.P. ran his fingers over Samira's name. *Payback on this one's going to be hell.*

J.P. didn't want to wait any longer to talk to Samira. He reached for his cell phone as he sank into the oversized leather chair. *I already know her number, which is frightening considering Denise usually makes these calls for me.* As he pressed the call button, J.P. felt a presence and remembered he wasn't alone. He looked into the gray-green eyes of his son. *She'll have to wait.* He disconnected the call before it rang.

James lowered himself into a chair. "How was the meeting?"

"It went well. Good progress on the case tonight." *Nice he asked.* "How'd it go with Mike?"

James leaned his head against the wall behind him. "Okay, I guess. He says the meeting with the judge could be intense."

"Are you worried about that?"

"Maybe."

I'll prompt him, see where he goes with it. "The best way to handle this whole deal is to come clean, James. It's possible the authorities already know the details from Madsen Park, so holding out isn't going to gain you any points with the judge." The father folded his hands and allowed James time to think about that. *Just ask the question.* "Do you know what happened, James?"

For the first time in over a week, James nodded with affirmation.

I knew he did.

James looked away. Then came the long-awaited confession. "It's Jack's baby, the one Jennie is pregnant with."

Jack? "Isn't he Gina's boyfriend?" *The one who called my cell phone?*

"Yeah. How do you know Gina?"

J.P. had forgotten James didn't know he'd made an appearance to his friends. "It's a long story. But how does that work with Jack?" *I'm not sure I want an answer to that question.*

"It's complicated."

"Try me."

James took in a deep breath. "Jennie slept with Jack to get some goods."

Well, she got the goods. "Then Jack needs to be responsible for the baby."

"If Jennie tells him about the baby, then, well..."

Spit it out, James. No use holding out now.

"Well, Jack is the one who supplies the booze and other goods. If Jennie tells him about the baby, Jack will pull out of town and Jennie will be left high and dry." James shrugged his shoulders.

She's already left high and dry. "Define *goods*, James?"

For a brief second James made eye contact with his father. *I've seen that look before. It's the same way he looked at Josh that night in Janet's kitchen and again on the dock the morning we were fishing.*

James shrugged his shoulders again.

It's a look asking for trust. "Here's the deal." J.P. leaned forward and put his elbows on his knees. "Keeping secrets right now is not going to help Mike plead your case. We need the truth to give you fair representation." James was looking at the floor.

James lowered his voice. "But anything I say can or will be used against me, right?"

J.P. nodded slowly. "Basically." *But there's more.* "But it can also work in your favor." The father knew what else needed to be spoken. *Just say it, Ralston.* J.P. inhaled very deeply. "But that only holds true in the court of law, James. Whatever you tell me," *If I say this out loud, then I must abide by it.* "I won't hold it over your head."

"You won't be mad at me?"

That's not what I said. "I said I won't hold it against you—once it's out there you and I will deal with it together. I won't throw it back in your face." *Like Bruce does.*

A few more moments of silence separated the men.

"Jack gets us whatever we want," James confessed. "Booze, smokes, vapes..."

"Anything else?"

"Maybe."

"Like what?"

"Like whatever anyone asks him to get."

"Specifically?"

James rose from his chair. "Pills."

"What kind of pills exactly?" *This could get serious fast.* J.P. followed his son into the kitchen. "Are you in possession?" *Of course, he is. He had it at the lake.*

"Maybe." James stopped in the hall that separated the kitchen from the guest room.

J.P. spoke very calmly. "What are we dealing with, James?"

"They're mostly pain-killers. Like leftovers people don't need anymore." James sighed. "I don't take them, but I carry them around so if somebody asks, I have some to give them." James avoided eye contact. "Jack calls me "The Keeper." It's kinda what makes them want me around."

Opioids. J.P. ran his hand through his hair. *I don't know what I expected, but this isn't the confession I'd hoped for.* He knew what had to happen. "Whatever you've got, James, it has to go to the judge tomorrow."

"But I'll get busted."

"We'll both get busted if you don't turn them in."

"But Dad, you don't understand." "No, James, this time I call the shots." *And then I must let it go if I'm going to maintain any kind of trust with this kid in the future.*

Slowly James turned toward his bedroom. J.P. followed and watched James dig his hand deep into the over-sized duffel bag. It came out holding a large Ziplock bag of unmarked prescription containers. James studied it a moment before handing it over to his father.

"Is this all of it?"

James nodded silently.

"You're not holding any back?"

"That's it."

"This will change the outcome of your hearing tomorrow, son." J.P.'s heart ached as he thought about the potential ruling. "You'll be looking at a summer of probation." *Could be facing juvenile time.* "Maybe longer." *Probably longer.* "The judge will most likely order an immediate drug test on you."

"I'm clean." James responded immediately. "Honest, dad. I just keep them. I don't take them. I don't even know what they are."

I have no reason not to believe him. J.P. studied the contents of the bag.

"What about Jennie?"

He's got to let her go. "It's not your responsibility unless you got her pregnant."

"And what if I did?"

Don't be the hero, James. "If you did, then we deal with it." J.P. watched his son's eyes closely. "But if you know for sure it's not yours, then you need to let it go."

James sat down on the edge of the bed and placed his elbows on his knees. "It's Jack's. She told me before we had sex. She'd already done one of those tests and everything."

"Then she's going to have to figure it out."

"But I'm her friend."

"Friends get friends help."

"But what if she doesn't want anyone to know?"

"Somebody has to know, James."

"Why?"

He really doesn't get this, does he? J.P. knelt so he was eye level with his son. "Because there's a baby involved James. A human being. You just can't let that fact go untold. Eventually everyone is going to know anyway."

"She says she'll take care of it."

"Maybe she will, maybe she won't." J.P. hesitated before finishing his thought. "But your responsibility as a friend is to see she gets the proper assistance either way. Letting people think it's your baby isn't going to let her off the hook. Either way, she's pregnant." *She needs more help than you can give her, James.* "As a friend, it's not your job to protect her. She needs your support to do the right thing."

James leaned forward and tucked his head between his knees.

I wish I could rewind this story and make it all go away.

When James looked up, his eyes were damp. "If I do that, she's not going to see me again."

"Probably not." *Which would be my preference given the current set of circumstances.*

There was a long period of silence as the Ralston men each processed their own thoughts. *Maybe he just needs to think this through on his own.* Just as J.P. reached the hall James spoke again.

"Then I need to call her, Dad. I need to tell her what I'm going to do."

That takes courage. J.P. handed his son the cell phone. Then he closed the bedroom door to give James's privacy.

I might as well call Mike with the new information. He used the phone in the office and left a message on the voice mail. *I thought his confession would relieve my mind somehow. But this is a lot to take in.*

J.P turned off the lights in the living room and sank into the leather sofa. The television flickered in the darkness, but there was no motivation to turn on the sound. He stared at the screen.

James appeared and took a seat in the chair adjacent to his father.

"Did Mike tell you I'm going in to work for a while in the morning?"

J.P. nodded.

"I figured I could pick up a few bucks before we leave town. I'll just do the golf balls then call you for a ride."

That's fine. J.P.'s brain and emotions had grown numb. "Did you talk to Jennie?"

"Yeah."

There were no other words between them. *Really there's nothing left to say.*

James started to leave the room, then paused in the doorway. "I'm sorry, Dad."

I am too, James. The sports scores scrolling on the television screen were repetitious. *Sorry for leaving you to fight your own battles.*

J.P. clicked off the television and turned to face his son. But the space in the doorway was empty, just like the space in his heart.

21 *Just Say the Words*

Samira

I was only gone for a few minutes. Samira listened to the short message again. Phil's smooth baritone voice sent excited shivers up her spine.

"Is the machine broken or something?" Kara leaned over the counter next to her mother.

"Oh, no, nothing's broken." Samira was embarrassed to be caught. "I just couldn't hear the last message very well."

Kara started to reach. "Turn up the volume."

Oh, no. Don't push play. Samira grabbed Kara's arm abruptly. "I've got it now." In the same motion she picked up the notepad where she'd written Phil's phone number.

"Are you sure there's not something else on the machine you need to hear?" Kara looked sideways at her mother.

"No, nothing else." Samira could feel sweat beads forming on her forehead. *I feel like a teenager.*

"If you had a cell phone like most adults do these days, you could get your messages anytime all day long and be able to save them instead of writing them down."

Samira shook her head. "Thank you for that insight but I don't think I'm ready for that yet. *Besides, if I had a cell phone, then the girls would think they needed their own too. As it is, I still have screen-less conversations with my daughter.*

"You will never be ready for a cell phone." Kara rolled her eyes. "Whatever, Mama."

I wish she wouldn't use that word.

"Uncle Wes isn't going in early tomorrow, so we don't need to be at their house until you leave for work." Samira watched her daughter tie her hair in a knot at the back of her head as she talked. "After lunch we're going to meet Paula and Renee at the pool. Aunt Pam said she could drop us off."

Samira was listening, but it was hard to keep her mind away from Phil's message. *I just want to listen one more time.* "I'll pick you up at the pool after work then."

Samira watched as Kara disappeared into the hallway. *Thank God she didn't push play.* She stared at the little machine. *He said he'd be home this evening.* Then glanced at the clock and decided to wait a while longer before returning the call. To pass the time she flipped through a magazine. Next, she watered the plants in the kitchen windowsill. When that was finished, she checked the clock again. *I used up a whole four minutes.*

I feel like a schoolgirl with a new crush. She decided to water the flowers in the front yard. *It's been two days since I gave the note to that guy named Mike.* Samira adjusted the garden hose. *But I haven't talked to Phil since I pushed away from him in the garden.* Mindlessly, she pulled a small weed out of the flower bed. *I want to tell him I've decided to go to Springfield.*

Back inside the house, thirty minutes had passed. *It's officially evening now.* But when Samira picked up the receiver, Kara was talking to a friend. It was much later before she retreated to her bedroom and dialed the numbers. *It's ringing.* Samira wiped her sweaty palms on her bedspread.

"Joe's pizza."

I know I dialed correctly. She double checked the numbers.

"Will this be dine in, or carry out?"

Samira was still studying the series of numbers written on the notepad.

"Well? Are you going to order or not?"

Don't tell me it's the wrong number. Disappointment was settling in quickly. "I'm sorry. I think I have—"

A different voice came on the line. "This is J.P."

J.P. isn't the man I was hoping for either. "I think I've misdialed."

"No, wait."

Is this the same voice on my answering machine? You should ask for Phil.

"Who's this?"

I'm not giving him my name until I know who it is. "I'm calling for Phil Ralston."

There was a delayed pause. "This is Phil."

It is? Samira pressed the phone harder into her ear. *He seems very distracted.* "This is Samira."

There was a different tone in the voice when he spoke again. "Hey, Pretty Lady," he replied with recognition, but he still sounded preoccupied. "Hang on a minute, okay?"

This is almost as crazy as the Mike Benson thing. She took a deep breath. *Talking to this man on the phone should not be so nerve wracking.* She leaned into the pillows on her bed. *But nothing with Phil ever seems normal.*

"Samira."

Now I recognize his voice.

"Sorry about that. James answered while I was outside with the dog. He had no business picking up like that."

Oh, that was James. Samira almost laughed at the prank. "He caught me off guard that's all."

"I imagine he did." There was a slight pause on the line. "Hey, I got your message."

Now that was a whole other experience. Samira thought to herself. "I was hoping your friend would deliver it." *I was hoping he was really your friend.*

"Mike's a good messenger."

He certainly has a style of his own. "He seemed trustworthy enough." *At least once I got to talking with him.* "Calling is difficult without a telephone number."

"My fault. I assumed you could pull it from your caller ID."

Confused, Samira pushed her hair out of her face. *I didn't think about that.*

"I shouldn't have assumed."

Samira wished she could see Phil's face.

"Your note says you're *ready.*"

Whatever that means. Samira subconsciously twisted her hair with her fingers. *Maybe he'll explain not being listed in a telephone directory.* She took a deep breath. "About next weekend," she forced her voice to sound stronger than she felt. "Ready or not, I've been thinking, and I'd like to try to go with you." *I mean, I do want to go...*

Phil didn't reply immediately.

Samira waited. *Phil?*

He didn't reply at all.

Samira removed the phone from her ear and made sure it was still powered on. *He's still not responding.* A sudden panic set in. *What if he found another date?*

"That is if the invitation is still open." *Please still be open.*

Still nothing. A few seconds later a dial tone buzzed in her ear.

Stunned, Samira stared at the receiver in her hand. The pit that was already in her stomach felt like erupting. A wave of emotion seemed to rise from the tips of her toes and form a lump in her throat.

Samira put her head in her hand and leaned her shoulder into the arrangement of pillows. *What kind of a response was that? Did he find someone else? Why wouldn't he at least respond?* Samira didn't know if she was angry or hurt, or both. What she did know was that he was very confusing and very frustrating. *He drives me crazy.*

Samira climbed off the bed. She grabbed a damp washcloth and began to wipe down the bathroom counter. When the phone rang, she chose not to answer. *Surely one of the girls will pick up.* Samira ran the cloth under the faucet and rinsed it out.

"Mama."

Samira ignored Krissy.

"Where are you?" Krissy's voice was getting closer. She appeared in the bedroom. "Oh, there you are." She smiled a mouthful of braces and wiggled her eyebrows. "The phone is for you, but I can't find the other phone."

Samira pointed to her bed. Krissy cheerfully clicked it on and handed it over.

"I'll give you some privacy." Krissy slowly closed the bedroom door.

Privacy. Like that's really what I need here. Samira inhaled deeply, trying desperately to control the emotions that were on the brink of spilling over.

"Hello."

"Samira, it's Phil. The battery went dead on the phone."

Oh, really? Samira didn't know if she believed him or not.

"I had it on the charger before you called, but obviously it wasn't a full battery yet."

"I thought maybe you hung up on me." *I can't believe I just said that to him.*

"Not a chance."

Samira's anger began to fade into relief, which faded into more confusion. She sat down on the edge of her bed and waited through an awkward pause.

"Samira, what are you doing right now?"

Just talking to you. "Not much." *Unfortunately.*

"Listen, this phone thing isn't working out very well." Phil was obviously thinking out loud. "And James and I could use a little space. Can I just come over for a few minutes?"

Right now? The mother's defenses started to kick in. "The girls are home."

"I know. I just talked to one of them."

Oh, yeah. I guess he did. Do I want him to be here with Kara and Krissy home again? Samira took note of the late evening sky out her bedroom window.

"I don't have to stay long."

He sounds disappointed. Samira resigned to her self-imposed fears. "Okay, for a few minutes." *He's right about the phone part not working out very well.* Deep down she was excited to see him in person. *And I did wish I could see his face while he was talking to me.*

"Give me twenty minutes to get across town."

~~~~~~~

Twenty minutes didn't sound like a long time, but now that she was waiting, it seemed to take forever. *I'll meet him outdoors.* Her heart raced and the sweat in her palms went from hot to cold the minute she realized he was approaching the front door.

Samira opened the door before Phil had a chance to ring the bell. He grinned boyishly and tipped his head in greeting. She couldn't help but return the smile.

This is silly. I'm a grown woman and he's a grown man. It shouldn't be so uncomfortable inviting him into my own house. Instead, she stepped out onto the porch. *If I don't turn on the porch light, maybe Mrs. Barnes won't notice us out here.*

Samira turned her back to the invisible neighbor and leaned against the wooden railing. *It doesn't matter what he wears. He still takes my breath away.*

"So, you really didn't hang up on me?" Even as the words fell, Samira was surprised to hear them come out of her mouth. *The cut on his cheek is almost completely healed.*

"No ma'am, I did not hang up on you." Phil's eyes were intense. "But your conversation
~~~~~~~

with James wasn't fair." He made a worried face. "There's a lot of things I didn't calculate into fatherhood."

I don't think he knows how to be a father yet. "How did the meeting go today?"

"How do you know about that?"

She stifled a smile as she realized he'd answered a question with a question. *That's Phil's trick.* "You said you had an out-of-town meeting concerning your son during the day, but you'd be back this evening."

Phil's face was still blank.

"On my answering machine."

"Oh yeah." The look on his face showed a hint of humor but the tone of his demeanor took on a serious front. "The meeting."

Samira waited. *Maybe I shouldn't have asked. He seems uncomfortable.*

"The meeting was a court appearance." Phil's eyes looked out across the yard. "It wasn't all bad news, I guess."

A court appearance? This is more serious than I thought. "Is everything alright?"

"Well, let's see," Phil counted on his fingers. "How do I put this?" He looked at the porch ceiling for a minute. "James has been with me ten complete days now and my schedule is completely challenged, my homelife is nonexistent, and I'm beginning to feel like a full-time chauffeur. And all this before he took a job at the club that starts at five in the morning." Phil looked past Samira into the distance behind her. "And, in addition, he is now under my custody for the remainder of the summer, facing several hours of community service, and answering my phone without permission." His dark blue eyes settled on Samira's. "Let's just say it's a test I'm not sure I can pass."

I'm sure it is. Samira held his eyes. "And how is James adjusting?"

"I don't know." A slight grin appeared on his lips. "I guess I hadn't thought much about how James is taking it all." He shrugged his shoulders and stuffed his hands into the pockets of his shorts. "He seems to be getting on alright far as I can tell."

Obviously, he is out of practice. "You'll both adjust over time." *But if he works at it, I think he'll make a fine father.* Samira smiled gently.

"Hope so." Phil cocked his head to the side and studied Samira's face. "But I didn't come here to talk about James." The hue of his eyes darkened. "I came here to talk about you."

Samira felt immediately awkward again. She scooted onto the porch railing and balanced her weight with her toes wrapped around the spindles. *I'd rather talk to him about his life than mine.* "What might there possibly be to talk to me about?"

"No," Phil corrected. "Not talk to you about—I want to talk *about* you." He took a step to the side and sat down in the wooden rocker. He leaned forward and placed his elbows on his knees. "I'd like to take you to Springfield with me."

The directive caught Samira slightly off guard, but she was determined not to let it show. "And why do you want to take me?" *I'd really like to know the answer to that question.*

"Because, Pretty Lady,"

Pretty Lady? I love the way he calls me that.

"Because you are the lady I desire."

That was it.

Is he going to say something else? She was more stunned with this statement than she was when the dial tone sounded in her ear.

"The question seems to be whether or not you want to go along." Phil slowly leaned back into the chair.

Oh. His phone must have died before he heard me. Samira's heart was pounding hard against her sternum and her breath was shallow and weak. *And evidently, he hasn't found another date.*

She stared at Phil without answering.

"Well?"

"I do." *I really do.*

Phil's seriousness faded into an easy smile. "I'm really glad to know that." He rose from the chair and took two steps toward Samira. He stopped immediately in front of her. There was just enough space between them that she could have moved away had she chosen to. When she didn't, Phil stretched his arms against the porch supports on either side of her.

His presence, his body language, his easy smile—everything draws me in. Afraid to move, Samira stayed frozen in place. The firmness of his biceps flexed as he leaned in closer.

And this is the man I desire.

About the time Samira was seriously thinking about kissing him, the porch light unexpectedly flooded the entire area.

What in the world? Samira covered her face with her hands.

Krissy exploded onto the front porch. She seemed just as surprised to see Phil and Samira as they were to see her.

"Oh, my." Krissy exclaimed. "I didn't know you were out here, Mama." The girl put her hands to her face.

Phil stepped back and silently acknowledged Krissy's presence.

"Krissy." *Krissy how could you do this?*

"Did I just talk to you on the phone?" Krissy was looking at Phil.

Oh, Krissy. Don't empty your mind now.

Phil concurred.

"Then why are you here now?"

Now Samira was humiliated.

"Because I wanted to talk to your mother in person instead of talking to her on the phone." His tone was gentle, and his eyes were soft as he looked at Krissy.

Wow. Samira liked the way he looked at her daughter. *Obviously, he's not afraid to hold his own with her.*

"Did you bring your dog this time?" Krissy's eyes went to the truck.

Phil knelt and balanced on the balls of his feet. "No, I didn't. Maybe next time." He raised his eyebrows in humored acceptance of the interruption. Samira had to look away.

"Oh." Krissy looked back to her mother. "Um, well, anyway, I couldn't find you in the garden, so I came out here." She was seldom at a loss for words and Samira found it interesting that Krissy was searching for them now. "Tiffany called and wants to know if I can go over Saturday afternoon."

Samira shook her head. "Can we discuss this in a few minutes, Krissy?" Shifting into motherhood with Phil sitting right there was very awkward. *Or am I uncomfortable shifting out of womanhood with Krissy right here?* Whatever the case, Samira refused to succumb to a repeat scenario like the disaster in the garden. She forced herself to remain on the railing and did her best to appear unaffected by Krissy's abrupt interruption.

"Yeah, sure," Krissy answered. She turned to go back in the house and then turned back around toward her mother. "Should I tell Kara you're out here?"

Samira chuckled at Krissy's confusion. "If you want to." *I wish she'd turn off the light.*

Samira realized she was holding her breath. She attempted to let it out slowly, but her heart was beating so fast she almost couldn't contain the nervous excitement.

Phil was chuckling. "She's a ball of fire, isn't she?"

"That's one way to describe her."

Phil's eyes were once again focusing on Samira's. He stood up and faced Samira again.

Obviously, he remembers where we left off.

"About Springfield," Phil continued. "If you're comfortable staying the night, there are accommodations available at the Civic Center Complex. If you'd rather drive back late that night, then I don't have a problem with that either." Phil lowered his voice a little more.

"However, you're most comfortable."

I'm most comfortable wherever he is, and my girls aren't. A chill ascended the length of Samira's spine as Phil's hand ran over her left shoulder and down her arm.

"I'll let you think on that, and you can let me know."

I do appreciate the advanced permission to think it through. "At least I have your number this time."

Phil displayed an easy smile, but his eyes were watching her hand. "Did you really not have my number on your caller ID?"

Samira shook her head. "I don't think my phone saves a call history."

"We might have to see about getting you a personal cell phone, so you don't have to share anymore." Phil grinned mischievously.

Samira rolled her eyes. "Why does everyone think I need a cell phone?" *Although, under these circumstances it would be nice not to have to wait my turn.*

Phil locked his eyes with hers. "Food for thought. But I do feel better knowing you can reach me whenever you want now." His voice trailed off as he lifted her right hand off the rail.

Samira allowed him to link his fingers between hers. Unable to speak, she just nodded, wondering if he'd notice she was no longer wearing the wedding band. She could feel his thighs between her knees as he leaned in closer. Despite her personal promise to not ruin another intimate moment, Samira was horrified at the thought of Mrs. Barnes watching from across the street. *I wish the lights were off.*

Very gently Phil's lips touched her forehead. Samira wanted so desperately to answer the initiation, but she couldn't. She rested her head heavily into Phil's cheek.

"Very well, then."

He knows I'm not going to kiss him out here. I hope he's okay with that.

"You can let me know." He squeezed her fingers in his, touched her on the temple with his lips once again, and then turned and walked away.

Samira couldn't make her legs move. She sat frozen in place on the porch rail.

No longer had Phil backed out of the driveway than Krissy and Kara were on the porch. *I knew they were watching.*

"Did you see the way he looked at you?" Krissy asked.

"Mama. He is so good looking," Kara added.

"Why didn't you tell us he was coming?"

"Is he coming back?"

"You should have kissed him."

"Enough." Samira left the security of the porch rail, even though she felt weak in her knees. She waved her hands toward the door. "Back in the house before Mrs. Barnes hears you two."

"Like she didn't see everything anyway," Krissy sneered.

Great. Samira shooed her daughters behind the front door and turned off the outside light.

"What was he doing here?" Kara asked all too seriously.

That tone deserves an honest answer. Samira bit her bottom lip as she walked to the kitchen. Safe behind the island, she turned and faced her daughters.

"He wanted to ask me out."

"I hope you said yes after the way he did that," Kara's voice trailed off.

"Did what?"

"Well, came over here and *everything.*"

Krissy butted in, "Like what is *everything,* Kara?"

"Girls," Samira interjected. "It's really not that big of a deal, is it? He just wanted to invite me to a business dinner, that's all." *But it's more than that.*

Krissy giggled and grabbed her mother's arm. "And you said yes, right?"

Samira simply nodded. Krissy threw her arms around her mother. "Oh, this is really exciting. What are you going to wear?"

What am I going to wear? Samira sat down on a barstool. "I haven't any idea." *What do you wear to a business dinner?*

She observed her daughters with caution. Krissy's exuberance was quite unnerving. But as she looked into Kara's eyes, she saw a shadow of doubt. *Or maybe it's a feeling of betrayal somehow.*

Krissy flitted off into the bedroom. Samira questioned Kara with her eyes.

"Really, I'm glad you're going."

"Are you sure?"

"It's okay." Kara's dark eyes were contemplative. "I think he really likes you."

"You do?" *How do you know?*

"Well, the way he looks at you and all," Kara tried unsuccessfully to explain. "And he just seems really gentle, like, well, not like the mountain man guy who was here the first time."

Yep, they were watching. Samira smiled softly.

"Do you want to go out with him again?"

"Yes, I do."

Kara nodded once. "Then I think you should go."

Samira hadn't realized how badly she needed her daughter's blessing. "Thank you, Kara." *Maybe she just needs to feel involved.* "Maybe you can help me decide what to wear,"

Kara nodded in affirmation then quietly slipped away into her bedroom.

~~~~~~~

Because you are the lady I desire. Phil's words replayed again and again in Samira's mind. There wasn't the slightest hesitation in his voice when he answered her inquiry. *I like the sounds of that.*

A manly shower-fresh scent was still apparent in the air when Samira stepped back onto the front porch. Either that or the scent was on her again somehow. *He shared just enough personal information to make me feel trustworthy. He spoke to me directly, so I know he's sincere. And he touched me just enough to show me he cares.* And he was the gentleman she'd experienced that first night together. *Just as I hoped he would be.*

He's complex. Samira leaned into the support post and allowed the weight of her body to slide down into a sitting position on the top step. *He's intense and demanding, but in a gentle sort of way.* For a moment it didn't matter if Mrs. Barnes was watching or not. *And he called me Pretty Lady. Daddy would like that about him.*

A gentle breeze blew her hair away from her face. *Now I really know how the little rose bud in my garden feels.* She rested her head against the post. *Absolutely scared to death.*
~~~~~~~

22 More to Come

Joseph Phillip

J.P. was oblivious to the twenty minutes back across town. Three things had him totally stumped. First, she led me right into another personal discussion before I realized what was happening. Then she dared to ask me why I want to take her to Springfield. J.P. scratched his head. No woman has ever asked me why I invited her on a date.

What's up with that? J.P. looked both ways at an unmarked intersection. *And then to answer her like that. Any word but desire. For god's sake you're a lawyer, Ralston. Use your vocabulary.*

He turned off the ignition in his driveway. *I have worked damn hard to call my life my own. Until a few weeks back I had a perfect world where I could come and go and think and do as I please.* The entire house was ablaze with lights. *Now I have a son who needs a father.* The next thought all but paralyzed his independence. *And I think I have a woman who might need me too.*

J.P. closed his eyes and pressed his head into the headrest. *It has nothing to do with that. What if I'm the one who needs her?* He opened the door. *Now that is a frightening thought.*

J.P. Ralston had never needed anything or anyone to make his life complete. He reminded himself of that as he subconsciously patted the dog who was there to greet him in the driveway.

"Chase. I have never let anybody have this much control over me." He snapped his fingers for Chase to follow him to the back door. *But the way she was sitting there tonight, there isn't much I wouldn't do for her.*

James was sitting on the kitchen counter with the telephone wedged between his ear and his shoulder. He was munching on of a bag of pretzels.

I hate it that she has this much control over me.

"It's for you." James spoke through a mouthful.

J.P. took the phone but was irritated to have his private thoughts interrupted. He covered the mouthpiece. "Who is it and why are all the lights on?"

"Mom and I were kinda tied up on the phone. Couldn't reach the switches." James crossed the kitchen and turned off the hall light before disappearing into the living room.

J.P. waited a few seconds before putting the receiver to his ears. *It's almost impossible to shift gears to Janet.* He cleared his throat.

"Jan, what's up?" *I spent all day at the courthouse with her. Hard to tell what she wants now.*

"It's a little late to be running errands, isn't it, J.P.?" Janet was picking a fight. "I've been on the phone with James for a while now."

I am not going there tonight, Janet. "Then you should be all caught up." J.P. helped himself to a pretzel. "What can I do for you?"

Janet was speaking but the voice J.P. heard in his ear was Samira's. *I do.* He shuddered at the recollection. *She said those words without even a slight hesitation.*

"Holy shit." J.P. spoke out loud.

"What's the matter now?"

J.P. stood stock still in his kitchen trying to clarify what had happened. *I do is not a phrase I'd ever planned to hear again.* Samira was clear and fresh in his memory. *But at the same time, the way she was sitting there was totally erotic.* J.P ran his hand through his hair. *Given my vulnerability, I might have replied with a commitment I am nowhere near ready to make.*

"J.P.?"

Who the hell is on the other end of this phone call? "Jan."

"Have you heard anything I've just told you?"

This is not Samira. J.P. decided Janet wasn't worth the effort. He had more important things to contend with. *Namely a pretty lady across town who is threatening my independence.*

"Look, Jan, it's getting late, and it's been a long day for all of us." *I've got to get her off this phone.* "Let me call you back in the morning."

"I'll be at work in the morning."

"So, will I. I'll call you from there."

"What do I do about Jennie Johnson until then?"

J.P. tried to remember what his ex-wife had just told him. *Nothing. I didn't hear a thing she said.* "Is it an emergency?"

"Good god, J.P.," Janet sneered. "I don't know how you can possibly function with clients when you can't even communicate for one minute on the telephone."

Doesn't sound like there's anything pressing. "I'll call you in the morning." *Spare me the verbal assault.* "Sleep well, Jan." Without waiting for a formal close to the conversation, he put the handset back on the charger.

I do. The quiet confidence in Samira's voice was still the same.

Damn it. She's so far out of my league. He opened the refrigerator. *I need something to slow down these thoughts.*

James pulled a t-shirt off over his head as he entered the kitchen. He stopped in the doorway and made an exaggerated effort to turn off the living room light behind him. "I'm turning in. Four thirty comes mighty early."

Hope I'm asleep by then.

"Thanks for bringing my bike down, Dad. That's going to make it easier to get around during the day."

For both of us. J.P. acknowledged the appreciation in a single nod. He twisted the cap off a cold Corona.

James grinned.

"What?"

"I don't know what she did to you in that short amount of time but whatever it was, she did it up good."

Who? Your mother? J.P. lifted the bottle of beer to his lips.

James continued to observe his father.

"What the hell is that supposed to mean?" J.P. sat the bottle against the counter a little harder than necessary.

"Nothing," he stated with the same sly smile. "But your eyes are all glazed over, and you act like you—"

"Like what?"

"Like maybe there's more to come."

"More of what?"

"More of whatever it was you didn't get tonight."

He's not talking about his mother. J.P. watched his son vanish around the corner. J.P. rubbed his eyes with his fingertips. *If that had been Mike, I'd have had a few choice words for him.*

"Good night, Dad," James called from the bedroom. "I'll see you when you get to the gym for your workout."

A door closed the space between the father and son.

Any other night he would review a case or catch Sports Center on ESPN. Tonight, his mind was too busy to attempt either. He lowered himself into the oversized armchair in the living room and propped his feet up on the coffee table. Sitting there in the dark he allowed Samira's dark eyes to penetrate his again.

There's more to come. But she's the one who's calling the shots.

He took another drawl on the bottle.

One kiss wouldn't have done it tonight. There's no way I could have stopped with that.

Chase lumbered into the room and rubbed against his master's leg.

Maybe that's why she wouldn't look at me.

J.P. was at the bottom of the bottle before another cognitive thought emerged.

Obviously, she's going to want more than I've had to give in the past. He thought about that for a while. *How much of me am I willing to give her?*

The empty bottle looked out of place on the coffee table.

Or maybe it's me. Maybe I'm the one wanting more than I've had in the past.

Chase sighed heavily indicating a deep canine slumber.

What is it about her that keeps me from walking away? J.P. asked himself the question as he rose from the chair. *God knows the smartest thing to do is turn and run like hell.*

The brew was doing its job. *I might be able to relax enough to get some sleep eventually.* He left the bottle on the coffee table and turned off the lights in the kitchen. The house was quiet.

On his way into the hall, he cracked the door on the guest bedroom. *I guess this is his bedroom now.* J.P. watched his son sleep for a few minutes. *He must be tired after the long day in court.* An unopened duffel bag sat at the foot of the bed. *Just because the marriage ended didn't give me any right to believe that fatherhood ended with it.* J.P. closed his eyes for a moment. *He's a good kid. I just hope we can figure this mess out together.*

J.P. removed his clothes and brushed his teeth. *Everything is ready for tomorrow.* He checked the alarm clock before turning off the light next to his bed.

He should have been able to surrender to the day. But as the darkness consumed him, J.P. could see the seductive, contented face of the woman on the porch as clear as day.

No doubt there's more to come. He rolled onto his back and put his hands under his head. *But her 'more' and mine may be in different playing fields.*

Chase made his way through the dark and found the dog bed in the corner.

I want to be able to give her what she needs, but what if I don't have what it's going to take? Time ticked off the clock.

23 Getting to Know You

Samira

Samira took a mental inventory. *Casual clothes for Saturday daytime, a change in case the day fades into evening, and a cotton nightgown.* Samira held the gown at arm's length. *No. Not a cotton nightgown. Too conservative.*

The top drawer on the dresser was still open. *How about a long nightshirt?* Satisfied, she added it to the wardrobe collection on her bed. *I don't want to over pack, but I also want to have everything I might need.* She would wear her dress shoes and pack sandals. *The only thing I know for sure is that the evening party is formal.*

Samira removed the plastic from the only formal dress she owned. She held it against her by the hanger and surveyed the tea length in the full mirror. *This is better than wearing one of Pam's.* She turned to the side. *It's more me.*

At least it still fits. The last time she'd worn it was to an officer's ball when Krissy was three or four. *That was a long time ago now.*

Commotion in the other room drew Samira out of the bedroom.

"We're home, Mama." Krissy skipped across the living room to greet her mother. Bonnie and Lizzie were close on her heels.

Lizzie grinned and batted her big blue eyes at her aunt. "We're going to help you get a date."

"Mark is asleep," Kara informed. "Aunt Pam is going to put him on my bed." She moved her little cousins out of the way so Pam could make her way through with the sleeping toddler.

"How long before Phil gets here?" Krissy asked.

Samira's eyes went directly to the clock on the kitchen wall. "He said four o'clock or shortly thereafter." *And he has yet to be late.*

"Great." Krissy exclaimed. "We have exactly an hour to turn you into Cinderella."

Samira sighed as she made eye contact with her sister-in-law. *Does she have any idea how nervous I am?*

"Why don't you let your mother and me get organized, then we'll come get you to help with the finishing touches." She motioned for Samira to follow her to the bedroom while Kara and Krissy busied themselves with the little girls.

"Thank you."

"No problem. I could take them all over to the pool, so you have more time to get ready by yourself." Pam pushed the bedroom door closed.

Samira shook her head and started to pack her clothes into an overnight bag. "No, I think it's important the girls are here when he comes." She tucked her still-damp hair behind an ear. "And I'm glad you're here too. I'm a little nervous." *Correction. I'm terrified.*

Pam laughed as she eased into the chair. "I can understand that. So, show me. What did you decide to wear?"

Samira pointed to the black dress on the closet door. "I tried them all on, but Kara settled on this one and I think she's right. It's simple, it's plain..."

"And it's you," Pam interjected. "But I bet Krissy went for the sequined gown."

"Funny you would know that." Samira had to laugh. "That girl is the queen of fashion."

"They're both excited that you're going away. That's all they've talked about this week."

Samira sat down on the edge of the bed. "It feels really strange, Pam. Sometimes everything feels out of sorts with this guy, and then in the next minute everything feels really right." *I have a boatload of emotions with him.* "It's really hard to explain."

"Maybe there's more to him than meets the eye," Pam suggested. She rose from the chair and lifted the dress off the hanger. "Finish packing and let's get you into this dress. I can't wait to see it on."

~~~~~~~

Samira stood stock still in front of the bathroom mirror while Krissy and Kara rolled her long dark hair into a French roll and fastened it securely with a transparent comb. *It's pretty.* A few strands at a time Kara formed the loose ends around her face into long vertical curls with the curling iron. *But I don't know.*

"Perfect." Krissy looked at her mother in the mirror.

Almost too perfect.

"Now, add these and you're set." Very carefully Krissy fastened a strand of pearls around the jeweled neckline of the dress. Samira stood up, inserting a pair of dropped pearl earrings as she moved.

"Where are your shoes?" Krissy sounded almost panicked. "It's almost time for him to get here. Don't you feel like you're going to a prom?"

Samira noticed the clock next to her bed. *Krissy's right. Almost four o'clock.* "I don't know. I never went to the prom."

Krissy shook her head. "A mother who didn't go to the prom. Every girl should get to go to the prom."

"Maybe this is Mama's prom." Kara was studying her mother in the mirror.

Krissy left the room in search of her mother's dress shoes.

"So, what do you think?" *Be honest, Kara. I'm counting on you.*

Kara walked completely around her mother, taking care to notice every detail. She stopped and straightened the bow at the waistline in the back.

"Honestly?"

"Of course." *Please.*

"The hair needs something." Kara made a worried face. "You need to do something because it doesn't look like you."

Thank you. Loosening only the top edge of the comb, Samira reached underneath the twist and released the ends. The loose ends cascaded over the top of the rolled bun. *Much better.*

"Now that looks more like you," Kara admitted. "What do you think, Krissy?"

"That's it." Krissy put Samira's shoes on the floor. "Now, step into your shoes and let's go show Aunt Pam."

The girls hurried out to find their aunt, but Samira stayed in the bathroom. The woman in the mirror looked vaguely familiar, like maybe someone she had once known. She sucked in her stomach against the fitted bodice. *It's snug.* Samira smiled. *Control top panty hose aren't hurting anything either.* She leaned into the mirror and touched up her lipstick with a finger.

When the doorbell rang, her heart skipped at least two beats. *I don't know if I'm ready.* This time when Samira put her hand over her stomach it was to stop the fluttering of butterflies. *I can't believe I'm going away overnight with a man.*

"Mama. Come on." Kara whispered through the bedroom door.

Samira crossed the bedroom trying to look more confident than she felt. Every nerve in her body was on edge but she didn't want that to show. She stopped and made eye contact with Pam before stepping into the living room. Little Mark was perched on his
~~~~~~~

mother's hip. Pam smiled brightly and nodded her approval.

Breathe, Samira. Breathe. The dress shoes sounded against the hard wood floor as she crossed the room to greet her date. *There he is. Tuxedo shirt. Formal pants.* Samira smiled. *And he always rolls the cuffs on his sleeves.* A bowtie hung loosely around Phil's neck. *I should have known he wouldn't be completely dressed.*

When their eyes met, neither spoke.

"Auntie, you're so pretty." Six-year-old Bonnie was standing between Phil and Samira. Her hands glided over the satin fabric of the skirt.

Samira touched the girl's blonde curls. "Phil," she motioned toward Pam with her hand. "I'd like you to meet my sister-in-law, and little Mark." Then she pointed her finger playfully at her niece who was peering over the back of the sofa. "And this is Lizzie."

"And me. What about me?"

"Yes," Samira smiled at the hem of her dress. "This is Bonnie."

Phil acknowledged the woman at the breakfast bar, but Samira knew he was mostly watching her. She excused herself to get her things. Kara followed her all the way to the bedroom.

"I put your hairbrush and lipstick in the bag. Do you have everything else?"

"I hope so." Samira looked into her daughter's eyes. "I feel really strange." Samira realized her honesty, but it was too late.

"You're just nervous like it's your first date." Kara sounded mature beyond her years. "Once you get out of here, you'll feel fine." Kara zipped the overnight bag. "You look so pretty, Mama."

"Really?" Samira glanced at the full-length mirror.

"Really." Kara patted her mom's shoulder. "Wait right here and don't move." She returned a few seconds later with a bottle of body glitter.

"Oh, Kara, I don't know..." *But I don't want to disappoint her either.*

"Just a little across your shoulders." Gently Kara rubbed the gel into her mother's skin. "It's the perfect touch. You'll dazzle him for sure now."

Kara carried her mother's bag and set it down at the front door.

"I think I'm set."

"Mama, the phone is for you," Krissy announced. "Should I take a message?"

Samira looked to Phil. *Who in the world?* He indicated that she had time. She walked back to the desk and took the phone from her daughter.

"It's Susan."

Oh no. Not Susan. "Hello?" *I should have had Krissy take a message.*

"Hey, girl," Susan was full of energy on the other end. "Sam and I have this great evening planned for tomorrow night, but we need a fourth. A man he's golfing with tomorrow has invited us to dinner. Sam says he needs a classy date, so naturally I thought of you."

"Oh, that's very kind of you, but I have plans." *It feels good to tell Susan I'm busy.* "I'll have to pass this time."

Susan went into recruitment mode immediately. Samira shook her head and rolled her eyes at Pam.

"I'm sorry, Susan," Samira finally interjected. "I really need to go. I have someone at the door." A few more brief exchanges were made before Samira was finally able to hang up the phone.

Krissy was engaged in conversation with Phil when Samira turned around. *Lord only knows what Krissy is telling Phil.* "I'm sorry."

Phil shrugged his shoulders as if the interruption didn't bother him.

"You're going to have a great time," Krissy announced. The girl turned back to Phil. "So, you'll probably have her home by?" her voice trailed off in a question.

Phil's eyes sparkled at Krissy's candor. "Whenever she's ready to come home."

I'm so glad he's patient with Krissy.

"Ready?" Phil reached for her bag and opened the door. *He needs to get out of here.* She turned and told her daughters and Pam goodbye. *And so do I.*

"Have a great time, Mama." Kara handed her mother a small black purse and a folded shawl.

Samira couldn't hide her excitement. She flashed a full smile at her daughters and stepped through the door. She walked around the front of Phil's pickup and waited as he opened the door for her to get in. Their eyes met as he reached around to place her bag in the extended cab.

Samira swallowed hard. Her back was against the open door, and she could feel his presence move somewhere deep within. *Am I really going to have him all to myself until I'm ready to come home?*

Phil stood there with his hand on the top corner of the window. "You are a sight to behold, Pretty lady." His eyes looked her up and down. "If we didn't have an audience standing in that front room window and another one sitting on that porch swing across the street, I'd kiss you right now."

Samira smiled and rolled her eyes. *Now I know he's noticed Mrs. Barnes.* When he took a hold of her hand to help her into the truck, her heart skipped another beat. As soon as he closed her door, she let all her air out so she could breathe more steadily.

"Honestly, Samira," Phil said as they started down the street. "You take my breath away." He glanced in her direction when they stopped at a red light. "I don't know if I can focus on business with you along."

Samira looked out the window to hide her blush. Before she could speak, Phil was lifting a cellular phone to his ear. *Did he make a call, or did someone call him?*

"J.P. here."

There's that name again. Samira listened. *Obviously, someone called him.* She saw him check his watch. "We'll hit traffic this time of day so I'm just going to head out...no, I haven't, I'll stop on the way out of town...you're going to have to transfer the file when it comes in then..."

I wonder who's on the other end. The tone in his voice had changed dramatically and everything was business now.

"...I'll call you as soon as we're settled...I know, I don't appreciate this last-minute review either...can you make changes from this end if need be? ...alright, I'll go through it as quickly as I can...Use the business center...Alright, keep me informed...I'll call from Springfield."

Phil didn't say goodbye, he just clicked off the phone. "The client I am representing has made some last-minute changes. It's been a scramble to get document finalized." Phil turned off a main thoroughfare and started into an older neighborhood lined with quaint brick houses. "I need to stop at home to pick up my bag and let the dog out one more time before we leave town."

He's taking me to his house. Samira nodded, not sure how or if she was supposed to respond. *He's obviously tuned into the business at hand.* They turned into an alley, which led to a driveway. He parked the truck under a carport.

"Let me get the dog out of the way before you come in."

Chase. Samira waited while Phil disappeared into the house. *So, this is where he lives.* He returned a few seconds later and led the black Lab around the corner of the house and through a gate. Samira's eyes examined the quaint, brick house with interest. *I expected something bigger.*

Phil opened her door. "The coast is clear." Samira took his hand as she stepped out of the truck and then followed as Phil led her to the side door.

"I just need to grab a couple of things. Make yourself at home."

Like that is really going to happen. She looked around the dated kitchen. *No dishwasher.* The light pine cupboards with their round stainless-steel handles were obviously original to the sixty's era of the house. A sports coat hung over the back of a kitchen chair with the plastic cover from the cleaners piled on the table. *It's very quaint.*

She dared to cross the room and peek into the living area which opened into what appeared to be another room. *I wonder what books are on his shelves.* Samira admired the brick fireplace. *A tv and a stereo. Nothing too extravagant.* A matching leather couch and chair were the only pieces of furniture except for a coffee table laden with newspapers and magazines. *More simplistic than I imagined.*

"Let me check the email one more time then I'll be ready to head out." Phil returned to the kitchen with an overnight bag. "Come on in." He motioned for her to follow him into the other room. "It's nothing fancy but it's a roof over my head."

Samira stepped through the arched doorway into the living room. Windowpane linoleum changed to a low piled carpet. Glass French doors separated the living area from the office. One magazine on the coffee table was a sports journal, but the one next to it was a glamour magazine. *Why would a bachelor have a woman's fashion magazine on his living room table?* Then Samira remembered James. *Maybe that's something teenage boys are into.* She recognized the Vanity Fair periodical from the subscription at the library. *A bit risqué for my taste.*

As she stood there still not speaking, Phil's hand touched her arm. A shiver went down her spine and she turned to face him. His face was serious.

"This is for you." In his hand was a long-stemmed pink rosebud. Samira could smell it even before he handed it to her.

She put it to her nose. *It's like the timid little rosebud in my garden.* However, the rose she held in her hand had already begun to open.

"It's beautiful."

"And so are you." Phil was looking into her eyes. "We don't have an audience now."

No, I guess we don't. Without waiting for further permission, Phil kissed her gently on the lips. Samira didn't know how long the kiss lasted, but the next sensation she was aware of was his hand against her bare back right above the satin bow. She allowed him to hold her closer than necessary. The room seemed to spin around her. *He makes me feel so alive.*

When she looked up into his face, she noticed a smudge of lipstick. His skin was smooth and silky under her fingertips when she wiped it away. *I like it when he shaves late in the day.*

Phil chuckled and pulled her in tight against him, hugging her with both arms. As he started to kiss her again, a telephone rang. He hesitated to let her go, but by the third ring he'd stepped around the corner into the kitchen and answered the phone in the charger.

At least I can tell the girls we are not the last household in town with an old-fashioned landline phone. Samira took a deep breath. *It's probably just as well the phone rang. I don't know if we could have stopped on our own.* She smoothed her skirt as she listened to yet another one-sided conversation.

"Josh, what's up? You guys make it up there alright? ...Are you worried about Bruce? ... Where's your mother? ...No, I don't want to talk to her." Several seconds of silence passed as Phil continued to listen. Samira could see his shoulder blades tense through the back of his dress shirt. "Oh, for Christ's sake, put James on the phone." Phil ran his hand through his hair. "Then put your mother on."

Feeling like she was intruding, Samira stepped further into the living room and picked up the *Vanity Fair.* A scantily dressed model graced the cover. *Her smile is bigger than the lingerie she's wearing.* Irritation was evident in Phil's voice when she listened in again.

"You get one phone call this weekend, Jan, and this is it."

Samira waited.

"It's comforting to know he's been there less than an hour and you're already at odds with him ...No, you listen. James is up there for two and a half days. You can either pick up where you left off, or you can take the high road and attempt to build some bridges....Jan, I'm not finished yet. Just remember, whatever you choose is what you live with for the rest of the weekend because I'm not coming up there to settle any discrepancies."

Several more seconds of silence passed. Samira mindlessly thumbed through the magazine and set it back on the table. *I wish I knew how to help him. He doesn't need any family problems going into a business meeting.*

"...listen, I have got to hit the road. I'm already pushing the clock. You're the mother, Jan. If you force the issue right off the bat you face a living hell until James leaves again... That's all I have to say about the whole damn thing."

Samira cringed. *This is a side of him I have yet to know.* She sat down on the arm of the big chair and waited until she knew Phil was off the phone. When he didn't come for her, she dared to find him.

Phil was facing the window with his back to the kitchen. His hands were shoved deep into his front pockets.

He must be so torn right now. "I'm sorry." *He seems to be trying hard to make things work with James, but it doesn't sound like it's going so well on the other end.*

Samira waited. Very slowly, Phil turned and faced her. *His thoughts are so far away.* She waited until she was sure he knew she was there and then crossed the kitchen to where he was standing. *I know he's hurting, but I also know he has a schedule to keep.* "Is there anything I can do?"

The hue of his eyes had darkened considerably. Phil shook his head slowly and looked away. *He is so tense.* Samira slowly moved her hands from his wrists all the way to his shoulders. "You're just going to have to trust everything is going to be alright until you get back." She didn't know enough about James's home situation to offer anything more than that. Samira touched Phil's face with her fingertips. The close shave exaggerated the tension in his jaw.

This time when their eyes met Samira saw the soul of a father. Very slowly Phil embraced her, drawing her whole body into his. *It's different from the way he held me in the living room.* This time Samira could feel passion beyond what words could describe. She put her arms around him and held him until he was ready to let go.

~~~~~~~

It took a few minutes to break the ice again once they were back inside the truck. Samira watched the scenery change from Joplin's city limits to the open highway.

"That Krissy of yours is quite a talker."

"Krissy has a way of not knowing when it's best to talk and when it's best to be still."

"She's entertaining." Phil was nodding his head. "She tells me you went to school in Springfield."

I wonder what other pertinent information Krissy shared without my permission. "Oh, she did?"

"Undergraduate?"

"And library science."

"SMSU?"

"I started at Drury. Finished at Southern Missouri State but I didn't go straight through." She stopped not knowing exactly how much of her history she wanted to share. *I'd have finished a year earlier had I not met Tom.*

"So, you know Springfield pretty well then?"
~~~~~~~

That was a long time ago. "The city has changed a lot since then." *I've changed a lot since then. Everything has changed since then.* She didn't realize how lost she was in her own thoughts until Phil spoke again.

"What's on your mind, Pretty Lady?"

That was the third time he had called her *Pretty Lady.* Several things ran through her mind, but the biggest question was the one she decided to voice.

Here's my opportunity. "I'm curious," Samira grinned at Phil. "Who is J.P.?"

Phil threw his head back with an easy smile. "Fair question." He signaled to pass another car. "Joseph Phillip." Phil looked from the road back to Samira. "My father was Joe. I'm just Phil. My clients know me as J.P."

"Who should I know you as this evening?"

Phil looked over at her with that same easy smile. "You have my permission to know me as anyone you like."

I'm not sure which one of you to know. Another thought crossed Samira's mind and she decided to voice it before she lost her confidence. "You're not exactly easy to find in a phone listing."

Phil raised his eyebrows but didn't look at Samira. "Is that so?"

Samira nodded. "I didn't find any of your names in the directories."

"That's because I'm not in them."

He's purposefully avoiding eye contact now.

"Keeps my life simpler." Now he looked at her. "Unless there's a pretty lady trying to reach me."

Well, at least he admits to having an unlisted number.

Without any further explanation he changed subjects. "So where are your girls staying the weekend?"

The weekend, or the night? We agreed on a night. "They're staying at my brother's house until I get home."

"The brother that is married to the sister-in-law at your house this afternoon?"

Samira picked up the playfulness that first drew her to this man. "That's the one."

She felt his eyes on her face and dared to glance in his direction. The rolled shirt cuffs and loose bow tie brought a comfortable charm to the formal apparel. There was something sexy about a man in a tuxedo—*or at least part of a tuxedo.*

Samira could feel Phil's impatience in the traffic as they approached the city limits. She fingered the five-leaf pattern on the rose.

"Traffic is one reason I don't live in the city."

There was a long pause in conversation as they changed lanes.

Just then an over-anxious driver honked and forced a shiny red sports car between Phil's truck and another car. *Something in the way he set his jaw makes me think Phil kept those thoughts to himself.*

"I hope you aren't disappointed in this evening's affairs, Samira." Phil was shifting into more of a business mode as they approached downtown. "Until I get my hands on my client's documents and get a feel for what I'm up against, I don't really have a clue how much personal time I'm going to have." Phil ran his hand through his hair.

He does that when he's thinking.

"My goal will be to finish with the business as efficiently as possible so..."

"You don't have to explain," Samira interrupted. "I know this is a work night for you." She turned the rose between her fingers.

Phil stretched his arm over the back of the seat and touched the back of her neck with his fingertips.

"Well, let me put it this way..."

Samira tipped her head slightly to defer a shiver as it crept up her spine. Just the touch of his hand was enough to trigger anticipation.

"I have yet to attend a business meeting that's lasted all night." Phil didn't take his eyes off the road.

There's an expectant invitation if I've ever heard one. Samira studied Phil's profile. *I wonder if I'll ever know Phil without J.P.?* She thought about that for a moment. *I think he's more accustomed to being J.P. without having to be Phil.*

24 A Line of Questioning

Joseph Phillip

J.P. reread the email from Denise. *There's barely enough time to double check the amendments in the prenuptial agreement before reporting to Mr. Hughes.* For just a quick moment his eyes wandered from the laptop to the woman curled into the velvet wing chair. *She seems content.* He forced his eyes back to the computer screen. *Wish I could say the same for me.*

Concentrate, Ralston. J.P. couldn't help it. He glanced in her direction again. The wispy dark curls framed her face perfectly. *I wonder what's in that tablet that holds her attention so long at a time.*

An abrupt knock against the motel door snapped the attorney back to attention.

"Your document, Mr. Ralston." A motel employee handed J.P. a document when he opened the door.

"Thank you, Barbara." He tipped the woman with a folded bill then closed the door promptly. When he turned around the woman who had been lost in her own world was now studying him carefully. *What?* He returned to his seat at the high counter where a barstool acted as an office chair.

No matter how hard I try, I still can't read her thoughts. J.P. pulled the lengthy document from the file folder. *I'm just going to ask and see where it goes.*

"What's on your mind, Pretty Lady?"

The attorney laid the unneeded sheets aside and dared to look at his date, who was still watching his every move. When their eyes met, her attention went back to the tablet on her lap.

The telephone on the desk sounded a double ring. *Mr. Hughes, no doubt.* He could feel Samira's eyes on him once again. *Once I pick up that phone, I'm on the Hughes time clock until who knows when.* His eyes met Samira's. *She could be thinking anything.* He picked up the phone.

"Mr. Hughes, J.P. here."

"Very well," Christopher's strong voice sounded into the receiver. "I trust your drive over was uneventful."

Except for the event sitting in that chair. J.P. had to turn away from Samira so he could think straight. "It was, thank you." *Get the formalities out of the way.* "And you have outdone yourself with the accommodations, Mr. Hughes." J.P.'s eyes passed over the fully stocked beverage refrigerator. He stopped on Samira's quiet presence again.

"Good, good. Do you have a copy of the amended agreement?"

"I'm on the final review now. It looks good." *I'd still like to take one more look though.*

"You know Mrs. Hughes and I appreciate you doing this for Stephanie on such short notice, J.P. We'll see to it you are well compensated."

The price I pay working on site for Hughes family business is calculated in time. Most generally he could spare the time, but with this particular lady in his room, J.P. was wishing he had less business commitments and more time for personal discovery.

"Hors d'oeuvres and cocktails are being served before dinner."

In other words, he expects me to be there.

"I'll finalize the review and be right down, Mr. Hughes."

The call ended without a formal conclusion. *Unfortunately, it's time to make a public appearance.* When he turned to tell Samira, it was almost time to go, she was no longer seated in the chair.

He ran his hand through his hair. *I really don't have the time for this final review.* J.P. typed a quick text back to his assistant.

Is it good to go?

A few moments passed. J.P. could hear water running in the other room.

Looks good to me. Denise returned the text. *I didn't find any errors and the changes we made are correctly documented.*

Then I'm rolling with it. He tapped the arrow to send the message.

I'll be at home. Call me if something comes up. -D

The attorney closed the apps on his phone and rose from his chair. He started to unroll his cuffs. *I don't know what fragrance she's wearing but it's enticing.* She was now standing only a short distance from the counter.

"You didn't answer my question, Pretty Lady." J.P. grinned as he pulled his tuxedo jacket over his shoulders.

Samira didn't blink and her expression was more serious than J.P. preferred. *The last woman I brought to a Hughes engagement ended up spending the evening at the bar. I picked her up after dinner.* He fastened his cuffs. *But I don't want this one out of my sight.*

She's still thinking something. J.P. raised his eyebrows and waited for the response she seemed to be weighing in her mind.

Samira put her elbows on the back of the high-backed stool. "How did you know the attendant's name at the door?"

J.P. smiled. *That wasn't even close to what I thought might be on her mind.*

"Do you know her?"

"No, I don't." He straightened his jacket and clicked the mouse to shut down his laptop.

"Do you know the concierge?"

"No."

"Then how did you call them both by name?"

I think I'll keep her guessing. "Maybe that's for me to know and you to wonder about." J.P. taunted with a twinkle in his eye.

Samira crossed her arms over the black satin evening gown. "And how did you know who was going to be on the other end of that phone call?"

That one I can answer. J.P. placed the revised agreement back in the file folder and laid it carefully in his briefcase.

"Because, Pretty Lady, I knew Mr. Hughes would call as soon as he was aware of my arrival."

Samira's eyes indicated a hint of understanding.

"Anything else?"

Her look was still serious. "You still haven't answered my first two questions, Mr. Ralston."

She'd be good in litigation. "Mr. Ralston?" *Sounds mighty formal if you ask me.* He closed the lid on his briefcase and secured the latches.

"They all seem to know your name."

"So, they do." J.P. thought for a moment. "But you don't have to use that name."

"You said I could call you whatever name I wanted."

"Yes, I did." *Damn, she's quick.*

"So, the hotel employees call you by name, yet you don't know them?"

Maybe I should share my secret, so I don't piss her off. The attorney grinned through his response, "Only by their name badges."

Samira's mouth curled into a slight smile.

"Satisfied?"

"Not yet."

Me neither, Pretty Lady. That part is yet to come. "Well, the Hughes party is beginning, and I believe it's time to make our appearance." He opened the room door and waited for Samira. She took her time crossing the threshold. *The end of the Hughes business won't come any too early tonight.*

Samira hesitated slightly at the doors of the glass elevators. J.P. wondered if the motion bothered her.

"No, it's not the motion."

I don't dare take a hold of her yet. Samira's slight figure was held tight by the satin dress. *But I would like to read her mind.*

"I'm curious about this elevator." Samira turned slightly and looked down the extravagant lobby. J.P. followed her eyes. "Why are there only four floor options when there are at least twelve or fourteen floors in the complex?"

I've had other woman in this same elevator and not one of them has ever paid attention to that detail.

The carriage stopped but the doors didn't open. J.P. realized Samira was holding the door closed with the button on the control panel. *Oh, that's very funny.* J.P. reached for the hand holding the button.

Samira stopped him with her free hand. "Not until you answer my question."

So that's how she's going to play the game. "Which question do you want me to answer first?"

Samira raised a single eyebrow. "As long as you answer with something other than another question, you may have your pick."

There wasn't a doubt in J.P.'s mind that he would be held captive until he answered. He wanted to kiss her. *But I know better.* "The Hughes family has exclusive rights to seven suites in this complex."

He started to reach for her hand again.

Samira stopped him again. "But that doesn't tell me why I can only choose from four floors."

"I wasn't finished yet, but I thought the people waiting outside the elevator might be getting impatient." J.P. held her eyes. *Or is she holding mine?*

Samira smiled as she continued to wait.

She knows she has me in a corner now. "Okay," J.P. had to laugh. "All seven suites are located on the seventh floor." He watched Samira glance at the open balconies to the seventh level. "This elevator has access to the ground floor where we are now, the conference rooms on the second floor, and to the executive's club on the top level."

Very gently J.P. removed her hand from the elevator button and guided her steps with his hand on her waist. The people who were waiting to use the elevator were impatiently looking Samira and J.P. up and down.

"You sure know how to draw a crowd."

"I wouldn't have to stall if you would answer more directly." Samira's voice was playful.

J.P. laughed out loud. *She does keep me guessing.*

"I'm serious." Samira had a playful glint in her eye.

"Good evening, Mr. Ralston." A young man working a counter next to the elevator greeted the attorney.

J.P. nodded in acknowledgement.

Samira's eyes came back to his. "You're not wearing a nametag."

"Anything else you would like to ask before we go down to the ballroom?" J.P. folded his hands over the handle on his briefcase and waited patiently for a response. *I'd rather get the line of questioning out of the way before we meet the Hughes family.*

Samira didn't back down. "So, how do they all know your name?"

J.P. leaned in close to Samira's ear and lowered his voice. "Because, Pretty Lady, when I'm under the employ of the Hughes brothers everybody knows who I am." He straightened his back and looked into Samira's now smiling eyes.

This is entertaining, to say the least. "Anything else?"

"No, Mr. Ralston." Her chocolate brown eyes were dancing with a new energy now. "I think I'm just beginning to understand."

The space that separated the couple was less than an arm's distance, but to J.P. Ralston it could have been a mile. *Beginning to understand what?*

Tuxedo-clad men escorting high-society women graced the corridor. J.P. slowed his step when Samira's eyes stopped on a painting in the hallway.

"What do you see?" *I've been down this hallway before and never even noticed the artwork.*

"It's by Phillippe De Champaigne." Samira was carefully studying the canvas. "I've never known his oils to be in the public domain like this."

J.P. also studied the painting. "Nor have I." *But she sure uses a nice accent when she says that name.* He suddenly wished he knew exactly who De Champaigne was so he could converse knowledgably.

Without further reference to the artist, Samira turned her attention to other paintings. J.P. walked beside her as they made their way slowly to the next display. *What is going on in that beautiful mind of hers?*

"Mr. Ralston, Sir?"

J.P. turned to face the voice. Several couples in ceremonial formals were making their way to the ballroom but none seemed to be looking for anyone.

A hotel employee suddenly appeared at his side. Slightly out of breath, the young man in uniform extended a linen envelope toward the attorney's hand.

"J.P. Ralston?"

I have no idea what this is. The attorney nodded a silent identification.

"This is for you."

J.P. took the envelope expecting the messenger to disappear. Instead, the employee stood at attention as if he were waiting for an immediate reply.

J.P. turned the envelope in his hand. His name was scrawled across the front in a woman's handwriting. *Not correspondence from the Hughes family.* Curious, he opened the tab. A loose object fell into his hand. J.P. turned it over and read silently. *Admit One. Private Viewing. Runway Seating. Table Ten. June 18th, 8 PM.* The handwritten message simply read: *I'm free after the show. 516.*

Bobbie Jo Sommers. J.P.'s heart skipped a beat under his tuxedo shirt. *June 18th is tomorrow.* Instinct told him to turn around and scan the lobby, but experience told him to put the note back inside the envelope and show no immediate reaction.

"Is something the matter?" Samira's soft voice was sincere as she touched his arm.

The last thing I need this weekend is a skeleton jumping out of my closet. J.P. folded the note around the ticket and stashed the entire envelope in his interior jacket pocket. Guests were beginning to form a line at the entrance to the ballroom. *I know she's probably watching me.* The hotel employee was still there. *Waiting for a response he's not going to get.*

J.P. looked the employee directly in the eye. "There is no reply at this time." The young man nodded before disappearing into the crowd.

J.P.'s heart was in his throat. He knew he was being watched and most likely being watched very carefully.

Samira's eyes showed signs of concern. J.P. remembered her question.

"Everything is fine." *Not.* He glanced down the hall that led in the opposite direction of the ballroom. "But I do need to make a quick call before meeting my client." J.P. reached for his cell phone and unlocked the screen. A single button sent the call through. *Come on, pick up the phone, Denise.* Needing to distance himself from his date, J.P. turned slightly away. Samira took the hint and stepped away. J.P. widened the distance with a few more steps. *Now I have two women watching me.*

"Hey boss, what's up?"

"More than I bargained for." *God, I hope she knows something.*

Denise interrupted. "The agreement is in complete order. All you should have to do is make sure the proper people sign on the proper lines—"

"I know," J.P. stopped the review. "I know that." *Of all times for Bobbie Jo to show up.* "I need to know if I had any messages from Bobbie Sommers today."

"Bobbie Sommers? No. Why?"

J.P. turned in a half circle and dared to scan the lobby area. "Because she's in this building." When he turned back, he caught sight of Samira several yards down the corridor studying another painting. Her quiet presence summoned a guilty conscience. "Can you reach her to tell her I'm working this weekend? All weekend."

"All I can do is leave a voicemail. She never picks up. Should I do that?"

The pit in J.P.'s stomach was getting bigger by the moment. *A good stiff drink wouldn't hurt anything.* "Do something." He glanced back toward Samira. "The last thing I need is her on my tail this weekend." *Shit. What am I saying? She's already on my tail.*

"Obviously, your mystery date accepted."

Not now, Denise.

"I'll do what I can but after that you're on your own. Anything else?"

That's all I can ask. Samira was making her way toward him now. She seemed to glide along the carpet.

J.P. ran his hand over his breast pocket to be sure the incriminating envelope was tucked deep within. "It's better than nothing." He disconnected the call without saying goodbye.

The evening ahead was suddenly looking far more complicated than he'd anticipated. *Just conducting business with this Pretty Lady by my side is enough.* But now the S-N-S-A escort was lurking around a corner.

Samira smiled slightly, sending chills all the way up J.P.'s spine. *Just get her in the ballroom.* He ran his hand through his hair and took a long, deep breath. When he offered his arm, Samira accepted. They fell into step behind the others waiting in line for the engagement party. *Why would Bobbie Jo Sommers be in Springfield?*

"There are two by Philippe De Champaigne," Samira noted out loud.

Two what? J.P. turned his head and glanced at the sophisticated woman who had her hand loosely around his sleeve. *Oh, paintings.* "Really?" *I had no idea.*

Samira's dark eyes caught his. "Really."

She knows I have no idea what she's talking about.

"Oh, J.P." Mrs. Christopher Hughes was suddenly wrapping her ring-clad hands around his neck. "It's bloody good of you to be here." She hugged the attorney without permission.

J.P. breathed a welcome sigh of relief as they stepped out of the public arena into the private Hughes event.

25 Prom Night

Samira

Samira could feel Phil's hand against the small of her back. *It makes me feel like I belong with him when he touches me like this.* He addressed the woman inside the door by name. *Mrs. Hughes is a woman of high society. Sequined gown, diamond earrings and choker.* Samira felt plain and simple in comparison.

"J.P., Christopher was so pleased you could squeeze us in," Mrs. Hughes gushed through a British accent. She continued to talk as she again hugged Phil around the neck. "You will be at Stephanie's wedding, won't you?"

A wedding?

J.P. accepted the ceremonial embrace. "You're looking more beautiful all the time, Mrs. Hughes."

He avoids her questions too. J.P.'s hand was once again against Samira's back.

"I'd like to introduce Samira Cartwright."

Mrs. Hughes opened her eyes wide. "My, my, J.P." Her deep red lips parted into a broad smile as she reached for Samira's hand. "Ms Cartwright, we are very pleased to have you joining us this evening." The woman waved at someone behind Samira and then turned her attention back. "Do help yourself to the bar and mingle, do mingle. Lots of people to meet." With more seriousness she looked at the attorney. "Christopher will be most delighted to see you."

Samira felt Phil's hand touch her own. *I'll gladly take his hand.* She smiled and nodded to Mrs. Hughes. "I'm honored to meet you."

Samira was relieved when they turned toward the ballroom activity. "Exactly what does the 'my, my' refer to?"

Phil rolled his eyes. "What does anything she says mean?" He seemed uninterested in Mrs. Hughes' disposition. "Elizabeth Hughes is, well, let's just call it eccentric. You'll see by the end of the night."

She does have a way with words. Phil was zigzagging around linen wrapped tables. *He must have spotted Mr. Hughes.* A server carrying an empty tray stopped in front of them.

"May I bring you something to drink, Mr. Ralston?"

Even the waitress knows his name. When her eyes connected with his she realized she was supposed to order a cocktail.

I don't know protocol.

"Two club sodas on the rocks."

Thank you. Samira smiled at the server. *I wonder if Phil ever drinks while he's working.*

As they approached a large gathering of people, Phil moved his hand to gently guide her by the waist. *I like the way he takes care of me.*

"Christopher Hughes is standing on the far side of that circle." Phil was speaking quietly as he moved her toward a group of tuxedoed executives. "He's talking to his brother, Jeffrey. The man on his right is the company's Chief Financial Officer."

Samira's eyes studied the businessmen with care. *Evidently the other three men are not pertinent.* When the elder Hughes spotted J.P., he nodded and immediately excused himself from the men.

"J.P." Mr. Hughes called with an outstretched hand. "J.P., I appreciate your efforts to be here." Right away his sparkling brown eyes stopped on Samira. "And it appears you've outdone yourself tonight, Counselor."

With gentle pressure against the small of her back, Phil moved Samira a step closer to the executive. "Mr. Hughes, Samira Cartwright."

Samira extended her right hand expecting to shake but the balding man raised it to his lips instead. "Welcome, welcome." He released her hand. "Have you met Elizabeth?"

Well, that is most flattering. "Yes, a few moments ago."

"Very fine," the man assured. "We'll be dining together a little later." He motioned with his hand. "J.P., if I might have a few words."

Samira felt a sudden urge to dismiss herself from the pending conversation. She moved with Phil to the edge of the room. His hand was still against her back when she leaned closer to speak into his ear.

"I'm going to step aside." *I don't think I belong in this conversation.*

Phil started to shake his head. "I'll be back." Samira excused herself politely. *Something tells me Phil doesn't want me wandering too far off.*

The private ballroom was even more elegant than the lobby of the hotel. Samira marveled at the artwork and décor. *Krissy was right about this being my prom.* Samira's eyes took in the extravagant attire of the guests. *And this is much more entertaining than spending my anniversary night alone with a book.* Diamonds and rubies accented women's hands and earlobes and glitzy dresses shimmered in the indirect lighting.

"Your drink, ma'am." The waitress appeared out of nowhere.

"Oh, thank you." *I can't believe she found me amongst all these people.* The girl handed her a cocktail glass. *And without Phil.* Her eyes went immediately back across the room where her date raised his glass in her direction. *Obviously, he's still keeping an eye on me.*

The soda was refreshing. Samira wound her way to the self-serve buffet and picked up a china plate. *It's been an awfully long time since lunch.* She selected a few slices of cheese.

Across the table, another woman was filling a plate full of appetizers. Her hair was piled high on top of her head and her gloved hands displayed large diamond rings on the outside of the gloves. *Now that is an interesting way to wear your jewelry.* When the woman looked up, Samira expected an older face than the one that met her.

"Are you here for the bride or the groom?" The woman spoke with a foreign accent.

Oh. Am I supposed to have a role here? "The bride, I guess." *But honestly? Neither.*

"Beautiful girl," the lady said as she continued to fill a plate. "She's marrying a duke, you know. I hear they will settle in Wales."

Maybe it's best not to say anything than to try to carry on a conversation about something I know nothing about.

"It's a bloody shame the last one didn't work out, it is. Stephanie could have lived a life of pure luxury had she married the ambassador. Oh, what was his name?" The woman looked to the ceiling as if something up there might trigger the memory. "Shit. I can't remember his name."

Oh my. I didn't expect that.

The woman continued to heap food onto the little plate. "I can't remember, but you know who he was, the old ambassador from France. He wanted her for show. Stephanie should have done it. He would have given her whatever she wanted." Without further conversation, the woman noticed someone more familiar on the other side of the serving table and immediately engaged in a new conversation.

Samira realized she was still staring at the gloved woman and quickly turned away. She wasn't sure what was more astonishing—the woman's sudden use of profanity in the middle of an otherwise straight conversation, or her initiation of family gossip at the serving table. *So much more entertaining than I'd imagined.*

She added a few crackers to her plate and stepped away from the table. Orchestra members were tuning their instruments near the dance floor. She was still thinking about the young woman when she felt a familiar hand against her bare back.

"Hey, Pretty Lady. You didn't have to leave." Phil helped himself to a piece of cheese on the edge of her plate. "You should have stayed. I don't think you should be mingling around by yourself."

"Well, Mr. Ralston, I'm perfectly comfortable alone in a crowd." She offered him another piece of cheese. *I've spent half of my life alone in a crowd.* Phil took a hold of her wrist and guided the cheese to his mouth. Samira laughed as he took a bite from her fingertips.

"Next time I'll let you know if you need to step aside. Otherwise, stick with me."

I appreciate his concern, but I'm more comfortable mulling around in a crowd alone than I am engaging in a conversation that doesn't pertain to me.

Samira noticed Mrs. Hughes at the head table. She removed two name cards from the table altogether and handed them to a hotel employee, using her hands to make her instructions clear. *Obviously, the woman knows what she wants and isn't afraid to make it happen.*

"Do you know everyone at this table?" Samira asked as they gathered to be seated for dinner.

She watched as Phil's eyes scanned each face standing in the vicinity.

"Not one," he answered with a matter of fact. Then he grinned at Samira. "With the exception of you and the Hughes."

Mrs. Hughes was reaching toward them as she made her way around the table toward Samira and Phil. "J.P.," she addressed them as she walked. "Do sit over here. I've seated you next to Christopher." The woman ran her hand over the back of a draped chair. With a brilliant smile she turned to Samira. "And you, my dear," She touched Samira's shoulders lightly. "You will sit next to me."

Oh, please don't separate me from Phil. Phil immediately took her hand. She forced a smile for the hostess.

"Right here, Ms Cartwright."

Mrs. Hughes touched the chair next to the one she had indicated for Phil. *Oh good.* Samira realized what had happened. *Interesting. Mr. and Mrs. Hughes have us sandwiched between them.*

Elizabeth started to step away then whispered into Samira's ear, "Is a pity he hasn't put a ring on your finger." She smiled and stepped away as if she hadn't said a word.

Eccentric may be an understatement.

Phil pulled out the chair for Samira to take her assigned seat as a server appeared and placed a lettered name card next to her plate. Ms. Cartwright. *Impressive. Mrs. Hughes must have taken care of that detail a few moments ago.* She caught sight of the hostess a few tables over hugging yet another guest.

Tête-à-tête flowed easily among the dinner guests at the head table. It turned out most of those sitting with the Hughes were members of the prospective groom's family. *That must be the bride and groom over there.* It seemed odd they were sitting alone without their families. She glanced around the room full of strangers. *There is much I don't understand about this event.*

At her own table, Samira listened to chatter about the wedding plans, the stock market, and the unpredictable weather in Wales. Mrs. Hughes' comment concerning a ring on her finger was still fresh in her mind as she allowed her own thoughts to crowd out the table conversation.

"How are you doing?" Phil asked when there was a break in business discussion.

"Very well, thank you." When her eyes met his, she realized how serious he was. "Honest." she added. *I'm just here as an observer, and a very patient one at that.* She gently touched his leg under the table for assurance.

Samira watched as Phil passed his fork from his right hand to his left. *Is he right-handed or left-handed?* Samira vowed to pay closer attention.

A trumpet fanfare announced the honored couple as the final dinner dishes were cleared by the wait staff. The entire room full of guests rose from their chairs. Phil helped Samira with her chair. *I wonder what happens next.*

Christopher Hughes motioned for Phil to follow him.

Wait. Where are they going?

"I'll be back."

Obviously, all business now. Samira followed Phil with her eyes. He stepped onto a platform with Mr. Hughes.

What are they going to do up there? Samira felt deserted.

"It was so good of J.P. to come tonight, Ms. Cartwright."

I wonder if Mrs. Hughes senses that I'm a little uneasy.

"Our family attorney stayed behind in England so J.P. will notarize the agreement."

She's explaining on my behalf. Samira turned her attention back to the stage. *I appreciate that.*

Mr. Christopher Hughes spoke into the microphone. "It is with a great deal of pride that I introduce to you my daughter, Stephanie Elizabeth Hughes, and her betrothed, Sir William Bradford Cottingham, the fourth."

The fourth? Thunderous applause filled the large ballroom and for the first time Samira got a good view of the bride to be. *Very petite and much younger than I'd imagined.* Dressed less extravagantly than her mother, Samira guessed Stephanie to be more reflective of her father's character. The groom was considerably older than the bride. *I wonder if this marriage is arranged. Or are they truly in love*? From what she could tell there was no outward sign of affection between them. *But then again, how do you show affection in front of such a crowd?*

"Please do be seated," Mr. Hughes suggested to the assembly. As he continued to offer words of praise to his daughter, Mrs. Hughes turned back to Samira.

"I was thinking about tomorrow evening," the woman whispered loudly over her husband's speech. As if just having a revelation, the woman scanned the room and quickly flagged a server.

I'd think she might want to hear what her husband was saying.

Mrs. Hughes whispered something in the waiter's ear then settled back into her chair. "Just sit tight a moment."

As if I had anywhere to go. The father of the groom was now speaking. His wife, who was sitting next to Mrs. Hughes, appeared to be attentive to the speech. Samira watched as the two fathers shook hands and then took turns signing an agreement that was placed before them on the podium. J.P. Ralston and another man signed the agreement. *The bride and groom look like statues on a cake.* Samira felt a tinge of sadness for the couple. *It's like they don't have any say for themselves in this matter.*

Without warning, the trumpet fanfare cut loose again. Samira jumped. She put her hand to her chest to steady her nerves. Four trumpeters were obviously playing according to cue. Behind them, seated on the far side of the dance floor, a chamber orchestra was preparing to play. *Everything is formally orchestrated.*

"About tomorrow..." Mrs. Hughes patted her hand against the table.

What about tomorrow? Samira turned her attention back to Mrs. Hughes. *I like her accent.*

"The Springfield Symphony is performing Copeland's Fanfare in its entirety in the auditorium." Mrs. Hughes picked up the conversation just like there had not been a break in thought. "I was thinking, if you were still in town, J.P. should escort you." Mrs. Hughes' eyes lit up with enthusiasm. "Now I know J.P. might prefer to find other entertainment, but it wouldn't hurt him, wouldn't hurt him a bloody bit, to sit in on the orchestra." With that she placed two tickets to the symphony in front of Samira. "Give these to him and see what he says."

Tomorrow night? I don't think we'll still be in town.

"Do you know the Fanfare?"

"The Fanfare for the Common Man?" *I assume.*

"I knew it," the woman exclaimed as she started to rise. "You are a gem, Ms Cartwright. Do talk to J.P. about the concert." She put the tickets directly in Samira's hand. "Now keep these close. If you don't use them, it's no loss. But we'll all be sitting together in the box. The ushers will know from the tickets."

"J.P.," Mrs. Hughes announced Phil's return to the table. "You need to step it up for this pretty lady." She patted the attorney on the arm then turned to address addressed another guest.

Before Samira could speak, Christopher Hughes was at their side. "Thank you, kindly, J.P. I trust you'll take care of the agreement until morning."

"It will be in the hotel safe, Mr. Hughes."

"Very well, then we'll see you first thing tomorrow. I'll be interested to learn more about Bridges' property. He's sending a representative with a diagram. Jeffrey will be most interested as well."

It sounds as if Phil might have an appointment yet tomorrow. I wonder if he knew that.

Mr. Hughes took Samira's hand. "And you have been most gracious to share the counselor with us this evening, Ms Cartwright."

And maybe again in the morning? She smiled and acknowledged the host as he kissed her hand again.

"Now, don't stay up too late," Mr. Hughes advised with a twinkle in his eye. "First thing tomorrow in my conference room."

He has his own conference room?

"Yes sir, Mr. Hughes."

Phil doesn't seem any too pleased to have another commitment. Samira studied his face when he looked away.

The orchestra had started to play while Mr. Hughes was talking. Samira mentally tuned into the Mozart minuet. She assumed from the conversation with Mrs. Hughes that her date would not be interested in the orchestra. *But it would be fun to step onto the dance floor.*

This time when a waitress stopped to take a drink order, Phil ordered a Jack Daniels and Coke.

He must be off duty. He looked to Samira for a request.

"I'm fine." *Although a cup of coffee would be nice.*

"Wine? Champagne?"

Samira shook her head with a quiet smile. *My last experience with a glass of wine left me fuzzy in the head.*

"Bring the lady a cup of coffee." Phil gave the instruction with authority.

Samira touched her hand to her heart. *How did he know to do that?* The Mozart melody was still playing in the background. *That was sweet of him.* She took a step closer as Phil slipped his hand around her waistline.

"Would you be so kind as to honor me with a dance?"

I thought he might not ask. Samira allowed him to guide her through the tables and crowds of people to the edge of the dance floor. Every pore of her being came alive as Phil took her right hand in his left. As she looked up into his eyes, she was suddenly aware how much taller Phil was than Tom. *It used to make Tom uncomfortable when I wore these shoes.* She relaxed into her date's embrace. *I stood exactly even with Tom in these heels.*

Every time Samira glanced away, Phil's eyes remained on hers. *This just might be my prom.*

The first number ended, but Phil didn't move toward the edge of the dance floor. Instead, he stood still, holding her slightly closer than necessary. His eyes were only focused on her.

He's so intense.

"Where'd you learn to dance?"

Samira could feel his body against hers. "My father." *Who doesn't even know I'm here tonight.* The fleeting thought caught her off guard. "And you?"

"You're a good lead."

I know better than that. Phil's steps came naturally with gentle authority. *He does know how to flatter me.*

~~~~~~~

Samira stood in front of the mirror over the bathroom sink. She loosened the comb the girls had placed so carefully in her hair. Shaking her head slightly, the hold released. Her dark locks tumbled over her shoulder.

Phil stepped into the reflection behind her and placed a glass of wine on the counter.

He is not my husband, but he is the one I want to be with tonight.

Ever so gently, Phil ran his hand across the front of the fitted satin dress. Passionate signals radiated all the way through Samira. *I hope he doesn't notice how hard my heart is beating.* She continued to remove her jewelry despite his seductive attention.

He took a sip from his own wine glass. The bow tie was long gone, and his pleated shirt was unbuttoned to the waist with the sleeves rolled twice. *Just like they were earlier in the day.* As she reached for the second earring, Phil's lips followed her hands. He kissed her gently behind the ear. *I love the way he draws me in.*

"I'm assuming you're officially off duty now."

"I was off duty the moment Hughes indicated a morning meeting." He kissed her on the neck again.

Samira tipped her head allowing his playfulness. "What time in the morning?"

"Nine."

"At least you were right about the meeting not going all night." *Maybe one sip of the wine won't hurt anything.*

"That leaves all night for our own business." Phil reached around and set his glass where hers had been. Without asking for permission, he slowly unzipped the dress.

No, the wine isn't going to hurt a thing. Samira took another sip. "But Mr. Hughes said not to stay up too late."

Phil's blue eyes met hers in the mirror. "What I choose to do on my own time is none of Hughes' business." His look was suddenly firm.

Now there's a lesson to be learned. Samira logged the moment into memory. *Once he's off duty, there's no reason to bring up business until he does again.* She set her glass down on the counter. *But I'm almost positive I can lure him back.* Samira turned toward her date and initiated a kiss that lingered longer than she expected.

There is nothing I want more than to ease his tension and make him forget his worries. For the first time Samira realized she wanted to give him more than an evening affair. *I want to give him something so lasting nothing can compare.*

"Tell you what," Samira spoke softly into his ear. "If you'll be so kind as to find a light for those candles," she pointed through the doorway into the sitting room. "I'll run a hot
~~~~~~~

bath in that big tub." Phil's eyes looked over her shoulder into the luxurious bathroom.

Hughes' business is finished for the night.

26 Blurring the Lines

Joseph Phillip

Sunlight was illuminating every corner of the hotel bedroom when J.P. opened his eyes. *Who opened the curtains?* It took a moment to recall his locale but didn't take any time at all to remember the woman with whom he had spent the night.

J.P. rolled over under the covers and found Samira sitting next to him against a pile of pillows. A tablet was leaning on her bare thighs. *She's totally oblivious to everything except whatever is holding her attention in that device.* He was slightly humored by the way she could totally escape reality without going anywhere. When her eyes wandered to his face he grinned.

"How long have you been awake?"

J.P. touched her arm with the back of his finger. "How long have you been lost in that tablet?"

Samira rested her head against the ornate headboard. "Do you always answer a question with a question?"

What kind of a question is that? He wiggled his eyebrows and lifted the tablet. "What's so intriguing that it pulls you in so deep?"

"You did it again."

Did what? "Do you like reading from a tablet?"

Samira's eyes got big, but she didn't speak that thought. "I prefer a real book, but it was easier to bring the Kindle this trip."

"I prefer hard copies, hands down. What's the book?" J.P. ran his hand up her leg and stopped at the edge of the Kindle."

"*I Know this much is True.* It's for the literary club review. From Oprah's list." Samira ran her hand over the screen. "Do you know it?"

You know how much is true? "Are you an Oprah fan?"

"There you go again, answering questions with a question." Samira closed the cover on the Kindle. Her dark brown eyes were deep in thought.

She's not going to let me off the hook until I answer. "No, I can't say I'm familiar with that one." He put his arm under his head. "Read it to me."

The woman smiled slightly. "I doubt if you'd like it."

How does she know if I'd like it or not? He chuckled. "Too deep for me?"

"It's very complex."

Does that mean I'm too shallow to follow the storyline?

Samira unfolded her legs. "Are you hungry?"

Not for breakfast. "What time is it?" When she didn't answer he looked up. An accusing look was gazing back at him. *Ah. I answered her question with a question.* "No, not yet." *She's paying attention.*

"A little after eight." Samira set the tablet aside. "There are pastries on the counter when you're ready to eat."

J.P. sat up on the edge of the bed. *There weren't any pastries in the room last night.* "Where'd they come from?"

"Downstairs." Samira crossed the room. She was wearing a long nightshirt and her hair looked damp from a shower.

She is one inviting woman.

"From the continental breakfast bar."

"You went down there by yourself?"

Samira stopped in the doorway and turned around. "Of course, by myself."

Her coy smile gave J.P. the chills. *She's bold.* "Wearing that?"

"That's for me to know and you to wonder about." She turned and stepped out of sight.

J.P. laughed. *Touché. She doesn't miss a beat.* "I'm going to jump in the shower."

"I'll be here." Samira's attention went back to the story in the Kindle.

J.P. found Samira in the same spot when he returned. *I don't think I've ever opened all the curtains in a hotel room.*

"How late were you going to let me sleep?"

Samira looked up from the book and tipped her head. "I was going to finish the chapter and then wake you."

So exactly how long would that have been? He watched her tap on the screen before closing the cover. *I could skip the meeting and lay back down with her for a while.* J.P. stopped her from going into the kitchen. He wanted to tell her how incredible she had been the night before. *She has a way of taking my words away.* Instead of speaking, he ran his fingers through her damp hair and kissed her. Samira responded without hesitation. *Everything about her is inspiring.* Instinctively, one of his hands dropped over her hip as the other moved up her side.

Without warning, Samira removed his hand from her shirt. J.P. held her close despite her sudden resistance. *Whoa, Pretty Lady, we've been here on the morning after and this time I'm not going to let you walk away.*

"I don't want to make you late." She was gently resisting his embrace.

Mr. Hughes would have to understand. He tried to kiss her again but, this time she wasn't as receptive. "Wouldn't be the first time."

That was all it took. Samira put her palms against his bare chest and pushed away.

What in the...? "That's not what I meant, Samira. I meant I've been late before, not that you made me late."

"Mr. Hughes said nine o'clock. He's expecting you." She tucked her hair behind an ear.

Screw Christopher Hughes. There was no indication of a morning agenda when I agreed to a Friday night business engagement. J.P. ran his hand through his hair. *Now she's on edge.*

J.P. returned to the bedroom to finish dressing. *I'm known for calling my own shots. In fact, Miss Samira Cartwright, I like showing up at the last possible minute to avoid idle conversation.* But that wasn't the way the statement had sounded. *She's holding me to a schedule I never agreed to.*

J.P. picked up a pastry on his way out the door. *Since she went to the trouble of bringing breakfast.* "I'll be in the Hughes conference room on the second floor." The tension from the moment before was still evident. *Hope it dissipates before I get back.* "With any luck this won't last more than an hour." Samira was now curled into the corner of the oversized sofa. *She's the most tempting woman I've ever known.* J.P. studied her carefully. *And the most unpredictable too.*

"I'll be here when you get back."

I'm counting on that. He started to leave and realized she might want the room key. *Hell, she's already used it once this morning.* "I'll have to call you to come back up." *There's a first, Ralston. Calling my own room to get back in.* J.P. gathered his files and briefcase off the makeshift desk at the kitchen bar.

"I don't have any plans to leave the room." Samira's voice was quiet. "All the entertainment I need is right here." She lifted the Kindle slightly.

That's amazing in and of itself. J.P. appreciated her offer. *But I think I'll leave it anyway.* He tapped the key card on the countertop. "I'll just ring the room when the meeting is over."

Samira nodded.

Why am I so hesitant to leave her here? J.P. took one last look at her before he closed the door. *Although I don't think she's going to miss me much.*

He pulled the door closed with weighted regret. Everything about last night had been so perfect, more fulfilling than he had imagined. *She's gorgeous, simple, and intelligent.* He pushed the elevator call button. *No, take back the simple part.* J.P. rubbed his eyes with his thumb and middle finger in thought. *Complex. She's definitely complex.* He stepped into the glass carriage and leaned against the golden handrail. *And she scares the hell out of me.*

Christopher Hughes met J.P. as the elevator door opened. The attorney took a deep breath and forced his mind to shift gears.

"Good morning, chap." Mr. Hughes clasped his hand with a business handshake. "Sean Bridges sent his assistant. She's inside with Jeffrey. Help yourself to some coffee and I'll be right in."

I'd prefer to meet with Bridges in person. J.P. continued to listen, but his mind went immediately back to the woman in his room. *She drives me crazy.*

He opened the conference door and found Jeffrey Hughes leaning over a table-sized diagram. The woman standing on the far side of the table was quite young. It took only a moment for J.P. to realize the hem of her skirt was just below table height. *I wonder what kind of impression Bridges is trying to make on the Hughes Corporation.*

The woman crossed the room with an outstretched hand. *I seriously doubt if she's wearing much under that double-breasted jacket.*

"Jessica Hutchison." Her green eyes accentuated her dark complexion. Her short dark hair was stylish and thick. *Not bad for a real estate assistant.*

"J.P. Ralston." He returned the handshake and set his briefcase on the table. The woman followed him to where Jeffrey was standing.

"This is the property the Hughes Corporation is considering."

I can see that. J.P. put on his reading glasses and scanned the enlarged plat map. He walked all the way around the table trying to get a feel for the lay of the land. *If this is the property I think it is, the view is skewed.*

"Ms. Hutchison, where is the airport in relation to this property?"

Christopher Hughes joined them at the table with a steaming cup of coffee.

Miss Hutchison walked around the table and leaned over the top of the map. *I was right. Not much on under that jacket.* Her bright red fingernails clicked against the tabletop as she pointed to the top right-hand corner.

"The airport is here." She tapped her nails against the map again. "The proposed commercial development site is just west of there."

J.P. chose to ignore the busty cleavage hanging over the map. *I beg to differ.* He walked around the map again and then moved it a quarter of a turn. *She's either misinformed or she's trying to mislead my clients.* "South is here." *I know that for sure.* He put his finger on the top right-hand corner. "That puts the airport over here." He rested his other finger on the exact opposite corner and looked to Miss Hutchison. *Let's see where she goes with this.*

When she finally spoke, she was slightly flustered. "If you look at it this way," She tried to turn the map back the way she had it on the table, but J.P. held it down.

"Let's view it true to direction." Without further delay he gave an overview of the entire area on behalf of his clients. *The city is looking at this same piece of property for airport expansion.* The more he looked, the more discrepancies he noticed. *I'm not convinced this map gives accurate dimensions either.* Denise had briefed him otherwise. *And I trust Denise over this Miss Hutchison.*

"Mr. Hughes," J.P. addressed Christopher knowing Jeffrey was also attentive. "I'd advise we take a look at this property from another diagram before moving forward." *Let's look at the map provided by city hall.*

Christopher crossed his arms and stroked his chin in thought. "Jeffrey?"

"I agree. I'd like to fly over and take a look from the air."

"Very well," Christopher stated. "We appreciate your time this morning, Miss Hutchison, but we won't be needing your assistance any longer." Christopher shook her hand. "Tell Mr. Bridges we will be in touch."

On another occasion, I might be inclined to follow up with an assistant like this. J.P. watched her turn away slightly irritated. *But this morning I have other interests.* Without asking permission, he began to roll the diagram.

"I can do that." There was a bite in her tone.

J.P. released the document into Ms. Hutchison's hands. *A little touchy this morning.* He set the canister on the tabletop to hurry her along. *Seems to be going around.*

Once Miss Hutchison was on her way, Christopher and Jeffrey Hughes were ready to work on their father's estate. *I wish I had something concrete to offer them.* J.P. still needed that one document to seal the case. *I'll just put it out there so they can chew on their options.*

"We don't have enough evidence on either side to take your father's estate before a jury." J.P. sat down in a chair across from the Hughes brothers. "If you're serious about commercial development in Joplin it will be wise to offer fair settlement against the back taxes and call it done."

"Our intention is to move commercial development into the city within the next year. You know that J.P. How much are we talking in settlement?" Christopher was looking him directly in the eye.

J.P. set his jaw. "They're still too high, but if the city is willing to drop the base to around two hundred and fifty thousand, I'll advise you counter them with half that in cash."

"That's still a hundred twenty-five, J.P.," Jeffrey stated. "We're talking about a city property line that was not even established until eight years after my father purchased it."

"I understand, but at the same time, there's no sufficient evidence to prove where the actual boundary was when Lloyd signed the deed. If you refuse to pay anything and we end up in court, the risk is high. Chances are good the jury will rule in favor of the city." J.P. waited for that information to settle in. "That ruling could potentially hamper any future development in Joplin."

"I say we do it," Christopher announced. "I'd like to have a commercial complex going up over there within six months. The longer this estate drags out, the longer it slows expansion."

J.P. observed the brothers exchange a look that indicated there would be more discussion behind closed doors. *Jeffrey's not convinced.*

"Talk it over." J.P. stood up. "Then get back to me. I can meet with the city attorney as early as Monday morning." J.P. shifted the point of discussion. "And I'll be back to you with more information concerning Sean Bridges." He looked directly at Jeffrey Hughes to let him know that topic was not forgotten. "We're still investigating pertinent out of state transactions that may or may not impact potential business with his company. As soon as we have the details, I'll let you know."

"And what about the plat map?" Jeffrey leaned back in the chair. "You obviously weren't comfortable with the diagram Miss Hutchison brought along."

He pegged that. "You're right, I'm not impressed. The dimensions were exaggerated, and the directions seemed off." He thought about the way she had the map turned on the table. "Something doesn't measure up."

"Sometimes they enlarge the details for easier reading," Christopher pointed out.

"Sometimes. But that's not it." *I have a feeling Ms. Hutchison is hiding something.* "Tell you what, I'll get a copy of the abstract from the courthouse Monday. Let's look it over together. It will surprise me if Miss Hutchison was even showing you the same piece of land."

"Interesting." Christopher punctuated the thought.

Jeffrey Hughes was finished with business for the day. He thanked J.P. for his time and politely excused himself from the table. Christopher also rose from his chair.

"J.P., it's been mighty good of you to give so much of your weekend on our behalf." He made eye contact. "If you don't have anything else planned for tonight and tomorrow, feel free to stay on. We'll pick up the tab."

As always. J.P. offered a word of thanks.

"Seriously, J.P.," Christopher stopped at the door and turned around with an obvious twinkle in his eye. "May I make a suggestion? The lady by your side last night, maybe you should latch onto this one."

Define latching on. J.P. closed his briefcase but refused to look Mr. Hughes in the eye.

"I advise you do whatever it takes to keep her happy. She'll serve you well." Mr. Hughes winked. "Don't mess it up. It could be your last chance."

Last chance at what? "Who's the counselor here?" J.P. reached for the house phone next to the door.

"Need a lift?" Christopher grinned.

"Only picked up one keycard."

Mr. Hughes opened the door and motioned for J.P. to follow. They stopped at the private elevator. "Mr. Ralston is my guest," Christopher told the man behind the small desk.

A moment later the carriage arrived.

"I imagine she'll answer a knock at the door." Christopher started to walk away. "Think about what I said, J.P."

I'm thinking already. He stepped into the elevator. *Thinking about what Mike said about her being out of my league. Thinking about what Elizabeth Hughes said about stepping it up for her. Now Mr. Hughes says she might be my last chance. Thinking about the way I could have taken advantage of her this morning.*

Trouble is, hanging on to a woman is not one of my strongest traits. He was still thinking when the elevator stopped at the seventh floor. J.P. stepped off the elevator. His mind was full of unanswered questions. *I don't like the way she gets into my psyche.* No woman had ever affected him like this. *Normally I can keep business and pleasure separated.* He could see her in his mind's eye. *But she has a way of blurring the lines.*

He tapped on the door to his suite. *Or am I the one blurring it all together?*

Momentarily the door opened. J.P. took in Samira from head to toe. *She's doing it again.* She had changed into a long flowing skirt and an open weave sweater. J.P. noticed the contour of her collarbones. *She's standing right here, and I can't think of a thing to say.* His eyes traced the veins in her hands. *Even her feet look sexy in those crisscrossed sandals.*

She's the one blurring the lines.

27 A Bucket of Balls

Samira

"Would you like to come in?" Samira cocked her head and grinned playfully.

Phil finally crossed the threshold but was still contemplative. *He's watching me, yet I can't hold his eyes.*

"Did you finish your book?"

That's not the question he has on his mind. Samira closed the door and watched him set his briefcase on the bar stool. *Maybe he's still thinking about the meeting.* "No, but I found a good stopping point."

Phil opened the laptop and pushed a button.

"How was your meeting?"

"So, what is your usual Saturday morning routine?"

I should have known he'd do that question thing again. "You first."

"Okay." Now Phil made eye contact. "I'd say fair."

When he left for the meeting, he was mostly Phil. Now there's more of J.P. Ralston.

"The first part was not to my satisfaction, but the remainder covered some solid territory." Phil was watching something on the computer screen. "Your turn."

For what? Samira almost forgot. *Oh. Saturday morning.* She grinned at the mundane answer that was about to fall from her lips. "Laundry."

"Every Saturday?"

Samira nodded once. "Every Saturday, first thing. Then I'm done for the weekend." *Very boring, isn't it?* She waited for him to type something into the computer. *I have nothing to lose by posing the question.* "And what is your usual Saturday morning routine?"

This time Phil answered without hesitation. "I usually hit a bucket of balls at the driving range with a friend." Phil seemed very intent on completing whatever he was doing on his computer.

At least he didn't answer with another question. Samira slid onto the barstool next to his briefcase. *I wonder if his friend is Mike Benson.* Samira got an idea. "Is there a driving range here?"

"Do you golf?"

There, he did it again. She crossed her arms.

The knowing grin on Phil's face gave insight to the realization. "I'm sure there is."

I do like that easy smile. The hair on Samira's arms tingled when his blue eyes connected with hers. *I'd like to spend more time with Phil before our time is up.* "I'm curious as to what is entailed in *hitting a bucket of balls.*"

Phil laughed out loud. It was the same easy laugh she remembered from their first night together.

Maybe he's starting to relax. "Are you officially off duty now?"

Phil ran his hand through his hair and looked away. "I am as soon as I check in with the office."

Samira stepped off the barstool. "I'll finish packing while you wrap things up." *Obviously, it's hard for him to shift gears.*

Most of her things were already in the overnight bag. *I'll give him some time to clear his mind.* She pulled a clear plastic bag over her evening gown and laid it across the bed. Then she went into the bathroom to get her hairbrush. *How does he keep track of his things when they're all over the place?* Instinctively, Samira organized Phil's toiletries on the counter.

The pink rose was the last thing to go in her bag. She put it to her nose. *Even without water it continued to open.* She ran her fingertips over the silky petals. *It doesn't seem so afraid to face the future now.*

When Samira turned around Phil was sitting in a chair across the bedroom. Samira jumped. "I didn't know you were in here." *How long has he been watching me?*

Phil folded his hands and leaned forward as if he was going to say something important. Samira waited. *He has that unsure kind of look in his eye again.* She sat down on the bed next to her dress.

"You really want to go to a driving range?"

That's not what he's thinking. "Sure. You can show me your normal Saturday morning routine." *It is surely more exciting than laundry.*

His eyes were walking her up and down. She had to break the silence. "What are you really thinking?" *Maybe I don't want to know.*

Phil walked over to where Samira was sitting. He moved the dress to the side and sat down next to her.

Now what's he going to do?

"What am I thinking?"

Is he mocking my question?

He put his hands on the edge of the bed and leaned forward. "I'm thinking I have this absolutely stunning woman in my room who wants to go to the driving range."

That's it? Samira took a quick breath. *That doesn't feel like what he's thinking.* "Or we could get a bite to eat if you like." *I don't think he's thinking about golf or food.*

"Are you hungry?"

Samira admired his tanned profile. "A little." *I'm famished.* She had eaten long before Phil was even awake. "Are you?"

Now he turned his face and looked at her. *That's the same look he had in his eyes before he got ready for his meeting with Mr. Hughes.*

"Yeah, I'm hungry." Phil was watching her closely now.

I meant hungry for food.

Very slowly he put his arm against her lower back. His other hand gently reached up under her ear.

If I return his kiss, I might not get lunch. At the same time, she could feel herself melting into the same passion she'd initiated the night before. *Then again, lunch can wait.* Samira closed her eyes and allowed Phil to take the lead.

~~~~~~~

Samira could see the entire lobby below. *I'm standing in this glass room, and no one down there knows how I just spent the last hour.*

The elevator began to descend. *He's still watching me.* The doors opened onto the main level. Samira hesitated, but Phil politely waited for her to exit first. *Always a gentleman.* Their hands brushed in passing. Her mind went back to their intimacy. *In every possible way.*

"I need to touch base with Antonio at the concierge desk," Phil informed. He was sorting through a small stack of notes and hotel cards in his hand.

Antonio must be wearing a nametag. "Are you sure they'll bring the luggage?"

Phil smiled his easy smile. "It will be in the truck before we are, trust me." He ran his tongue over his bottom lip. "Mr. Hughes would have it no other way."

I'm beginning to like this Mr. Hughes.

Phil put his hand behind Samira's back to guide her. "I'll wait over by the paintings." *I*
~~~~~~~

need a moment to gather myself.

"Anything you wish, Pretty Lady." Phil selected a single envelope from his collection. "I'll just be a minute."

That's all I'll need. Samira turned and walked toward the gallery. *I can't believe I survived June seventeenth. And I made love to a man who is not my husband.* As she neared the fountain, she could hear a piano in the distance. *Schumann, I think.* She followed the music. *And strangely enough, I don't feel any guilt.* Samira stopped to admire one of Champaigne's paintings again. She felt like her feet weren't even touching the floor. *He handles me so...* She stared at the painting hoping to find the word she needed to complete that thought. *He's so passionate and strong...and patient.* Her own reflection revealed a glow Samira didn't recognize in her own face. She laughed out loud at the realization. *He completes every part of me somehow.*

Samira turned around. *I want to see him from over here.* Her eyes went immediately to the concierge's desk. *Where did he go?* The music stopped for a minute. When it started again, Samira didn't recognize the piece. *I should probably go back.*

A marquee at the entrance to the auditorium announced the Springfield Symphony. *Oh.* Samira remembered the tickets from Mrs. Hughes. *I need to get these to Phil so he can return them.* Samira opened her purse to the bill compartment. *I put them right next to the food court tickets from the mall.*

Once again, Samira's eyes scanned the area. *I don't think he said he was going anywhere else, did he?* She could feel the smile that was still radiating on her face. *I wonder how far away the Café is. I'm starving.* Phil was nowhere near the concierge's desk.

Oh, there he is. Samira started in his direction. *Don't forget to give him the tickets.* Suddenly, she realized Phil wasn't alone. *And the woman he's talking to is certainly not one I'd want to compete with.* Samira slowed her steps. *And he certainly seems engaged.*

Maybe he doesn't want me in that conversation. Samira noted the woman's youth and contemporary attire. *She looks vaguely familiar.* Samira couldn't help but stare. *Where have I seen her?*

The glow in Samira's face faded. *I don't know who she is, but Phil certainly seems to know her.* She watched him nod his head in conversation. When the woman reached out and touched Phil's face, Samira looked away.

She squeezed the symphony tickets in her hand and turned around. *Maybe he should just come find me when he's finished doing whatever it is he's doing.* There was a sitting area in the far corner of the room. *If I had my Kindle, I could just wait over there.*

Samira felt lost. She wandered reading various marquees. *This is a busy place. Every ballroom has a booking for tonight.* She read some more. *There's even a Runway show for Victoria's Secret. That's crazy.* Samira had to concentrate to keep her eyes away from Phil and that girl. *What kind of people buy tickets to a lingerie runway show?*

Time seemed to stand still. Phil was still talking to the girl. *They're not any of my business.* Samira forced her eyes in the opposite direction. *Well, she is not any of my business, but I would like to think Phil might be.*

Eventually she felt a familiar hand against her back. *Finally.* Samira took a deep breath. *Do I bring her up, or let it go?*

"Samira." Phil spoke her name quietly. "That took longer than I expected."

I noticed. Samira glanced over his shoulder wondering if his companion was still there.

"I bumped into someone I haven't seen in a while."

He admits to knowing her.

"I stopped to get caught up on her news."

He's not trying to hide her.

"I didn't mean to take so long."

Probably not.

"But now I know the luggage beat us to the truck."

He's more anxious than he was earlier. Again, Samira looked over his shoulder, but there was no sign of the girl. She hesitated when he started to slip his hand into hers.

"An old friend then?" *She's hardly old enough to be an "old" friend.*

Phil's blue eyes came to rest on hers, but he didn't answer right away.

I shouldn't have asked. Samira looked away. *I have no right to be jealous.* She watched Phil look around the room. *Is he looking for her too?*

"That was unfair, Samira." Phil ran his tongue over his bottom lip. "I should have..."

No, I'm out of line.

"...introduced you."

Introduced me? Samira started to shake her head. *No. I just made love with you. I have no desire to meet a woman as gorgeous as her before my feet even touch the floor.*

Phil was looking very unsure of himself.

"I'm sorry," Samira apologized. "It's none of my business." *I'm overreacting.* She started to take the hand that he'd offered. *I still have Mrs. Hughes' tickets.* "Oh, here." Samira opened her hand. "I have some tickets for tonight's—"

"Tickets for what?" Phil's tone was suddenly defensive.

This is all very confusing.

Phil took the tickets out of her open hand.

"Mrs. Hughes gave them to me last night." *Maybe I shouldn't have brought them up.* "They're for the Springfield Symphony. I thought if we weren't using them, we might leave them so Mrs. Hughes could give them to someone else." Samira wiped her now sweaty palms on her skirt. *If things weren't awkward over that girl, they sure are now.*

Samira watched Phil tap the tickets against his other hand. Momentarily his eyes ascended the open balconies of the hotel above them. *What tickets did he expect?*

Phil puckered his lips thoughtfully. "Mrs. Hughes," he stated simply. "She's always, well, giving something away."

That is nowhere near what he's really thinking.

"We could use the tickets tonight if you like." Phil suddenly seemed relieved.

Still in town at eight o'clock? Samira tried not to appear too anxious. *That would put me home too late to pick up the girls.*

Phil held the tickets out for her to take again. "It's up to you, Pretty Lady. If you want to go, then, we'll make it happen." His voice was sincere, and his blue eyes were once again focused only on her.

He called me Pretty Lady again. Samira was relieved now. "I'd love to go. But maybe another time. I'm thinking I should be home to the girls by then."

Phil hesitated as if contemplating his next thought. "Very well. I'll leave these with Antonio for Mrs. Hughes."

This time I'm going with him to see the Concierge. Phil explained the situation to Antonio and then turned to face Samira.

"About that friend. It is your business."

No. He really doesn't have to go there. "You don't have to explain." *Oh wow. They brought his truck around AND put the luggage inside?* She watched Phil tip the parking attendant.

"Maybe not." Phil offered his hand as Samira stepped onto the running board. "But just to set the record straight—"

Please don't disappoint me now. Samira held her breath. *Not today.*

"You're still the lady I desire."

Thank you. When he closed the door, she breathed a sigh of relief. *That's all I need to know.*

~~~~~~~
~~~~~~~

Samira found herself standing next to a set of golf clubs in the warm sunshine. *I feel so much better with food in my stomach.*

"This, Pretty Lady, is a bucket of balls." Phil held up a wire bucket bulging with golf balls.

"So it is." *I've never seen so many golf balls in one place before.* "What exactly do you do with them?"

Phil set the bucket on the ground and finished putting his wallet away. "Well, I'm going to position them on a tee and then practice my swing."

I wonder if this is what Susan does at her lessons. Men and women were coming and going along the sidewalk. *Everyone is dressed the same and they're all wearing funny shoes.*

"Do you take your golf clubs everywhere you go?"

"Are you...?"

He's going to ask me a question.

"Almost."

Nope. He caught himself. Samira smiled.

"You really don't golf then?"

Samira shook her head and smiled. "Nope, no golf. My brother plays though. In fact, he built a house in the middle of the new golf community south of town."

"He lives in Country Club Estates then?"

I really don't like admitting my brother lives in a gated community. She nodded. *That's all he needs to know about my brother.*

There was a bench behind the green strip where golfers were practicing. "I'll watch from here."

She watched Phil select a club from his bag. He placed a white ball carefully on the ground. Samira observed casually. "Okay, Tiger, show me what you've got." Phil gave her a sideways look. *I already know what he's got.*

Several strokes later Phil turned directly toward her. "You want to give this a shot?"

Oh. No. Not me. "I don't think so. I'd rather watch you." *In fact, I rather like watching him.*

Phil walked over to the bench and took her by the hand. "Come on, I'll help you."

Susan would love this. Reluctantly, Samira perched the dimpled ball on the tee according to Phil's instruction. The next thing she knew Phil was moving her feet with his own. *What's he doing?* Her sandaled feet looked out of place compared to the other golfers.

"About shoulder width apart."

He's really going to try to coach me through this. Samira moved her feet a little.

"Alright, close enough." He handed her a club. "Now, take the iron with your left hand."

"This is an iron?" *It doesn't look like the iron I use on my clothes.*

"Yes."

Now he knows how little I know about golf. The club felt clumsy in Samira's hands. *It's heavier than I expected.*

"Are you right-handed or left?" Phil was looking at Samira's hands.

I've been wondering that about Phil since I met him. "Are you right-handed or left-handed?"

Phil shook his head. "I golf left-handed."

That doesn't really answer my question. "Do you do everything left-handed?"

"No, Pretty Lady, I don't."

"Do you eat left-handed or right?"

"Right, why?"

"Just wondering." Samira thought again. "Which hand do you write with?"

"My left," Phil ran his right hand through his hair. "Which way do you hold a club?"

"I don't." *I'm not a golfer, remember?*

Samira noticed the man next to them. He appeared to be listening in on their conversation. When he saw Samira looking at him, he looked away.

Is he laughing at me?

Phil squared Samira's shoulders and tipped his head to look her in the eye.

Wes does that to me when he wants me to listen.

"Are you right-handed or left?"

"Right-handed." *I am listening. I was curious.* "For everything."

"Okay then," Phil attempted to hide his easy smile. "Then you need to stand on the other side of the ball."

"Why?" Samira was confused. "You stand over here."

"But I swing left-handed. You're going to swing right-handed." Again, he started to position her feet.

This is not my turf. I came here to watch Phil in his comfort zone.

Phil returned to his golf bag and began to sort through his clubs.

I wonder if Susan has this much trouble. "How do you know if it's left or right if you're standing sideways to the ball?"

"Trust me."

The man next to them was also sorting through his clubs. *Obviously neither one of them know what they're looking for.*

"Here." The man handed Phil one of his own clubs. "Try this. It's my wife's. It might fit her a little better."

Phil accepted the club with a word of thanks.

Does Phil know him? He's not wearing a nametag.

Phil returned to Samira and once again adjusted her stance.

"I want you to hold your hands like this." Phil demonstrated.

"But this isn't even your club." *This may be more trouble than it's worth.*

"No, but it fits you better and now you can swing the right way."

He's obviously not going to give up.

"Okay, watch."

"Do you know him?"

Phil shook his head. "Not yet."

"Are you going to know him?" *Does he get to know everyone he meets? Maybe it's a form of networking for work.*

Phil was still serious.

Humor him and pay attention.

She studied the way Phil's fingers were clutching the club. When he handed it to her, she imitated him perfectly.

"Nice." Phil reached for her hands. "Choke up on it a little."

I have no idea what he means.

"Grip lower on the handle."

Oh. She moved her hands slightly and gained a nod of approval. The next thing Samira knew, Phil was standing behind her with his arms wrapped around hers. He placed his hands over her grip.

I like this part.

"We're just going to get a feel for the swing." Phil started to rock the club back and forth to the side of the ball.

This is strange. "I thought we were supposed to *hit* the ball." *Why is he laughing?* When she started to turn her head, Phil wouldn't let her move.

Phil's in charge. Samira turned her attention back to the ball.

"First we need to get a feel for the swing." Phil continued to hold her in position. "Can you feel the weight of the club?"

"I can feel something." *But it's not the club.* She felt funny standing in this long row of regular golfers. *I'm the only lady wearing a long skirt and sandals.* And as far as she could tell, she was also the only one receiving personal coaching.

"Now we're going to feel the ball with the club. Feel that?"

"Maybe." *What exactly am I supposed to be feeling for?*

Suddenly, Phil forced the club back and took a swing. Much to Samira's surprise, the ball went flying towards a flag.

Samira looked on in amazement. "How do you know which ball is yours?"

Phil let go of her hands and stepped out of her stance. "Just keep your eyes on the ball."

Sounds easy enough. Samira scanned the grassy field stretched out before her. "How'd we do?"

Phil gazed out over the field with his hands on his hips. "I've done better."

Phil was chuckling but the gentleman next to them was doubled over laughing.

"I think I'm a better spectator."

"You are—" Phil started to say something and stopped. His eyes were dancing with renewed energy. "What do you say we bag these balls and find something else to do?"

I don't care what he does with the balls, but I do want him to finish his sentence. "I'm what?"

Phil lifted the club out of Samira's hands and returned it to its owner with a word of thanks.

"No problem." The man placed another ball on the tee. "Best entertainment I've had in a long time."

Oh, that's nice. Samira put her hands on her hips. *I didn't come here to be his entertainment.*

"Play these out on me." Phil set the bucket of balls down beside the man.

I'm not going until he finishes his sentence. Phil returned to the platform and nudged Samira.

"After you finish your sentence."

"Let's walk."

I'll walk, but he's not off the hook.

"Well?" They were headed for the parking lot.

Phil lifted his golf clubs over his shoulder. "You are—"

What? Finish your sentence.

"Absolutely amazing."

I seriously doubt that's what he was going to say.

"What made you want to come here, anyway?"

Samira's face broke into a coy smile. "I thought maybe I'd find Phil here."

"Did you?"

Parts of him. "There was less of J.P. Ralston here than at other places."

Phil was thinking. He put his clubs in the bed of his truck and snapped the tarp.

The only place I didn't experience J.P. was in his bed. He was all Phil there. Samira allowed him to open her door. *At least I think that's who he was then.* She climbed into the seat.

"Come here."

Where? I'm already here.

He wiggled his finger for her to move closer.

Why?

Phil pushed a loose hair out of Samira's face and tucked it behind her ear.

Oh. Samira succumbed to his kiss. *This is all Phil Ralston.*

28 No Answer

Joseph Phillip

J.P. sat in his own office as Mike reviewed the latest charges pressed against his son.

"These charges are damn serious, J.P." Mike flipped the document in his hand and skimmed the second page. "Assault and battery with premeditated intent? If Hamilton takes James to court, they could try him as an adult."

I'm very aware of the allegations. In fact, he'd watched as James was cuffed and forced into the back seat of the squad car. *Then all I could do was stand there while they booked him into the county jail.* J.P. didn't move. His eyes were fixed on the coffee shop at the end of the alley.

Mike was still studying the indictment. "If there is an upside here, it's the fact that James refused to talk to anyone without his attorney present."

True statement. "I was surprised they let me into the interrogation room."

"I'm surprised they released James into your custody."

"I didn't give them much choice."

"Somehow that doesn't surprise me." Mike's voice trailed off as he continued to read. He turned another page. "What'd you find on Bruce, Denise? Anything useful?"

Denise presented a short stack of memos. "He's been picked up for public intoxication and driving under the influence several times in the last six months. Other than that, I didn't find much." She handed the paperwork over to Mike, but her eyes were glued to her employer. "When did you know there was trouble in Harrisonburg?"

J.P. shrugged his shoulders and took a deep breath. "Josh called on my way home from Springfield and told me Bruce and James were at odds. I hadn't planned to get him until Sunday night, but Josh was insistent, so I went on up." J.P. ran his hand through his hair. "When I arrived, there was a sheriff's car and an ambulance in the driveway."

Mike spoke up. "Did Josh give any indication of a motive for the blow up?"

"Maybe you should ask Josh."

"I will. Don't worry. I have a few questions for Janet too." Mike reviewed the memos from Denise. "Is Hamilton's license suspended?"

"I'll run that report and find out." Once again, her eyes were on J.P. She waited patiently. "Is there anything else I can do?"

"Well, let me go to work on it." Mike was calm. "I'll see how far I get with Hamilton's attorney and Janet. I'll catch up with you later if I need anything more. As it stands, James won't appear in court until Thursday. That gives us a couple of days to build a case." Mike lifted his sturdy frame off the conference table where he'd been sitting. "You going to be alright?"

J.P. nodded with false confidence. "I'm fine. James will be at the club with Ernie McElroy until one of us picks him up."

Mike puckered his bushy mustache. "Alrighty then." Mike nodded his head. "Don't let the boy out of your jurisdiction and avoid any contact with your ex-wife until you hear from me. I'll find you later and let you know what's up."

It's a hell of a lot easier to be an attorney than it is a father. The last thing J.P. needed on a busy Monday morning was more trouble concerning James. *I should have known it was too soon for him to go back up there.*

Denise tapped her pen against the edge of the communication clipboard as she re-entered the office. "You have exactly one hour before meeting with the city attorney. Are you up for it?"

J.P. nodded again. *Anything to keep busy.*

Denise continued. "There's no indication they've lowered the settlement as of yet." She checked the item on the list. "You meet with Mr. Stephenson at one o'clock. No board members, just Stephenson, one on one."

"Do you have an update on the case?" J.P. was sitting at his desk fingering through a stack of file folders.

"Third file down," Denise informed without looking. "Sounds like you'll be out of the office all day on Thursday. Mike says there's no way around it."

I hate the fact James must face the judge again. "So be it." J.P. surrendered. "What's the rest of today look like?"

"Before you came in a Jessica Hutchison called from Bridges Property Management. She's requested a private consultation concerning the property for the Hughes Corporation."

"That's the Bridges rep I met Saturday morning in Springfield. I'm not impressed so far." *Not impressed with her business anyway.* "Give her an early lunch, nothing more. No plat maps. I'd like to see the authentic documents without her edits." He pulled the Mid-America file out of the stack. "Any chance you can get a copy of the tract in question from the courthouse today?"

"I can call ahead for you to pick it up after you meet with the city attorney."

"That works." *Just take care of business.* "Anything else pressing?"

"One more," Denise hesitated.

She looks concerned. "Spit it out."

"Bobbie Sommers called this morning. She's in town and wants to see you tonight."

Shit, Ralston. You should have told her you were unavailable when you had the chance. Slowly he shook his head. "Can't do it." *Not after the weekend I just spent with Samira.* J.P. thought again. *But I don't necessarily want Denise knowing that either.* "I need to give James my full attention tonight."

"She didn't leave a number," Denise informed. "The message said she'd stop in this afternoon."

That's just great.

"You know, boss," Denise's tone softened. "If you have a steady or something, I can head off some of these calls before they—"

I don't know if I have a "steady. "That won't be necessary." *At least for the time being.* He touched the computer keyboard and cued the monitor.

Denise slid forward in her chair. "Forty-five minutes before meeting Miles. He'll be in the third-floor conference room at the courthouse. Sparky is already in Baltimore. He's supposed to call in before noon today."

"Noon our time or Baltimore time?"

"I didn't ask. Does it matter?"

J.P. watched as she walked away. "No, I was just curious."

Denise tapped her acrylic fingernails on the brass door handle. "Let me know when I should start forwarding Miss Sommers' calls to Mike."

J.P. closed his eyes for a moment. *God, she knows me well.* When he looked back at the door, Denise was gone. *SNSA. Bobbie Jo Sommers.* The attorney opened Sparky's update and skimmed the overview for Mr. Stephenson. *Something tells me that's not the case with Samira.* He tried to concentrate on the file again. *I don't know exactly what my intentions are with her.* His mind went over the abrupt ending to his weekend. *It just stopped.*

I kissed her goodbye twice. Once inside her house when he carried her bag in and then again in the doorway as he was leaving. *How hard would it have been to ask when I could see her again?* He turned the page absent-mindedly. *Because, Counselor, your mind was on the chaos in Harrisonburg.* He turned another page. *I should have at least told her how much I enjoyed the weekend.*

J.P. closed the file on his desk confident he could plead his case with Mr. Stephenson despite the distractions playing with his mind. *I've always known my intentions with other women.* He ran his hand through his hair and removed his glasses. *Kiss them and keep them guessing.*

Most dates he could kiss goodnight and walk away. *But Samira is not like that.* He pictured her in the evening gown. *I walk away but somehow she stays with me.*

J.P. closed his door before dialing the Maple Street Library. He asked for Samira. *I should at least explain why I needed to leave so quickly Saturday night.*

"I'm sorry, sir, she is on the other line. Would you like her voice mail?"

J.P. declined. *I don't know what I was going to say in person, and I hate voice mail.*

~~~~~~~

An hour later, J.P. was across a conference table from three city council representatives. Miles Johnson, the city's attorney, was acting as the mediator.

"You're missing the point, J.P.," Miles reiterated for a third time. "You know fair and square that Lloyd Hughes owed tax money for all those years he owned that property. We're not willing to negotiate anything less than the taxes due."

J.P. sat back in his chair. *I've argued this point numerous times. They should be ready to settle.* He looked his colleague in the eye. "We've been over this. I don't disagree. Lloyd owed property tax, Miles." He pointed to the deed on the table between them. "And the Hughes brothers do not have an issue paying what was due in 1959. But they are not going to pay for damages beyond the lost tax. Period." J.P. ran his finger down the left-hand column of the page. "Do the math. If Lloyd were sitting here in this room right now, he'd write you a check for a hundred twenty-five thousand and close the deal. That's what was due at the time that property sold." *Never mind that the attorneys in charge of the sale happened to misprint the back tax in 1962 and forget about the fact that the paperwork for the new owner was misplaced for two years following the close of the sale.* "Lloyd was a sound businessman. He always paid his debts."

"Well now he owes closer to half a million," a councilman interjected. "If you seriously think we're going to let the Hughes Corporation walk away for less than a quarter of that, think again."

Miles held his hand to stop the council member from saying anymore but it was too late.

What does this council have against the Hugh Corporation? "The only way you can come up with five hundred grand is if you charge out under commercial tax. When Lloyd purchased that tract, it was still residential, and it remained residential until 1968 at which time the name on the deed was not Lloyd Hughes." *I am sick and tired of reminding them of that fact.* "You are still missing the point." *I'm going to lay it on the line. I have nothing to lose, and my patience is spent.* "The issue at hand is not about back taxes. The crux of this matter lies in future commerce in Joplin." J.P. looked Miles in the eye. "If you stick them for the whole amount against the estate now, the opportunity to gain economic development from the Hughes Corporation in the future is nonexistent."

A councilman spoke up. "We've seen healthy economic development for years without support from the Hughes Corporation. Why should we be concerned about their money now?"

I could name twenty or thirty commercial developments in Joplin funded by the Hughes Corporation. "You might verify that information before taking it before a jury,
~~~~~~~

councilman." J.P. looked back to Miles. "Call me when you're ready to settle."

Done. I've said my piece. They can take it before the jury for all I care. J.P. lifted the deed off the table and placed it in his briefcase. "Good day, gentlemen."

All we need is one printed document—one stinking document would close this deal in a heartbeat. His mind was reeling.

J.P. stepped into the marble hallway and opened his phone. *Three calls. Denise. Mike. Janet.* He scrolled through a list of numbers and pressed the one he needed most.

"Samira Cartwright, please."

"She's in a meeting. May I take a message?"

No. J.P. disconnected the call. *I don't know why I'm thinking about her right now anyway.* J.P. stepped outside into the hot sunshine. *Business before pleasure. You know the rule.*

"Counselor."

J.P. stopped and turned around.

"Where's your head, man? I've been trying to catch you since the second floor." Mike grinned through his bushy mustache.

"What brings you to the courthouse?"

"Hughes."

"They settle?"

"Not yet."

"Think they'll hold out for a jury?"

"I hope not."

"You don't sound any too confident, J.P." Mike wiggled his eyebrows over the top of designer sunglasses. "Where's the scrap in the dogfight?"

"I prefer fair settlement over scraps, Mike."

"I didn't know if you had anything left in you when I left your office this morning."

J.P. looked away. "That makes two of us."

"Hang in, good buddy. We'll get to the bottom of this." Mike's curly hair bobbed when he nodded. "I talked to Hamilton's attorney. So far, no dope, but gut feeling tells me there's more to the story. I'll stay on it."

Mike opened a new pack of chewing gum. "Meet me at the club at six o'clock. Maybe I'll have something by then."

J.P. silently refused the gum. "Alright." *I need a good, hard workout.*

"So, tell me, Counselor," Mike paused. "You never filled me in on your romantic weekend with the classy chick."

"Lady."

Mike wrapped his tongue around the gum. "*Lady.*" He grinned. "Okay. So, how was she?"

"Good." *Incredible.*

Mike chewed on his gum. "That's it? Just good?"

He's not getting any details. "Yeah. It was a good weekend." He tried to shrug it off. "We had a good time." *I couldn't put her into words if I tried.* J.P.'s mind tripped back to the moment he looked down from the podium and saw her visiting with Mrs. Hughes. *She's sophisticated and smart and…*

Mike laughed out loud. "I kept your dog for a 'good' weekend?" Mike laughed again. "Next time, call Denise. If I'm going to dog sit, I want more than a *good* report."

J.P. checked the ID on a new incoming. *He knows I'm holding out.*

Mike started to walk away. "I'll take the silence as an indication that things went better than *good.* In the meantime, I'm late for an appointment, good buddy. Six o'clock, alright? We have a lot of ground to cover with James before Thursday."

J.P. slid his thumb across his phone and answered a call from Denise. *Why is it so hard to talk to Mike about Samira?*

~~~~~~~

Mr. Stephenson looked tired and concerned as J.P. took a seat in his office. This was their first private meeting since the discovery of the hacker's damage. *He acts like we've already been defeated.* He watched Mr. Stephenson pour a cup of coffee.

"Mr. Stephenson, the news is good. The suspects are in custody. We should be able to summon a grand jury fairly quickly."

"Coffee?"

Is he listening to me? J.P. declined.

Slowly, Mr. Stephenson crossed the room and sat down in a big leather chair adjacent to J.P. *Something about him seems more familiar to me than usual.*

"There are many things I have yet to understand, J.P." Mr. Stephenson was reserved. "I have read the latest update, but I don't understand why we can't just charge the suspects with a crime and take them through the normal court proceedings."

"It's a complicated case." *Go slow enough he can follow and quick enough he won't change his mind.* "The whole nature of the case is complex. For instance, if these suspects would have physically robbed the bank at gunpoint and escaped with the 1.8 million there would be physical evidence to trace. As it is, the suspects broke into the bank in cyberspace. There are no fingerprints, no videotapes, no witnesses that we are aware of, and no bundles of money to uncover."

"I understand all that." Mr. Stephenson set his cup on the walnut table. "But why Baltimore? Wouldn't it be easier to bring the suspects here for court appearances?"

"That's complicated too." *How do I explain this?* "Exactly where did the crime take place? The only part of the robbery that happened here in Joplin is the part we can see on the computer screen. Funds were moved from one account to another over wire. No one came inside this building and actually touched a machine to make that happen." *At least not as far as we know.* "Furthermore, the suspects are believed to have worked it from their home in Maryland." *I'll let him chew on that for a second.* "As inconvenient as it seems, the crime was actually committed in another state, therefore, the judicial system has to try them in Maryland."

Mr. Stephenson took a deep breath and folded his hands. "What exactly does that mean for me and my employees?"

In other words, how much expense is involved traveling back and forth. "It will be necessary for Mid-America to have a presence on the East Coast, no doubt about that. But we'll try to schedule the appearances before the court as conveniently as possible. My assumption is we will be allowed to video conference in for most appearances."

Mr. Stephenson lifted his tall, lean frame out of the chair and walked across the room. He folded his arms and turned back to face J.P. "Explain to me again, the involvement of the other law firm."

"With the board's approval, Benson and Barringer will come on board to assist with litigation." J.P. followed his client to the window and looked down over the main street. "Vince Barringer and Mike Benson are the best in the business, Mr. Stephenson. You can't hire any two attorneys better equipped for federal prosecution. Each one of us will oversee one phase of the trial, which will give Mid-America the upper hand. Vince Barringer is licensed in Maryland. He will work the case from Baltimore. Mike will work the case from here with the assistance of Denise Burke. And my roll will be to keep your best interests at the forefront of every decision."

Mr. Stephenson nodded once but he was obviously still deep in thought. "And Ms Burke, what exactly is her role?"

"Denise Burke is my personal assistant. She is communication central." *Among about a million other tasks that she performs to the "nth" degree.*
~~~~~~~

A long silence separated J.P. from his client. *What is it about him today? It's something about the way he's just standing there looking out the window. Or maybe the way he's holding his cup?*

"Very well, then. We'll talk to the board in the morning. I'm sure they will support moving forward with the grand jury."

"We can't move forward without the grand jury, Mr. Stephenson. This jury will decide if there is enough evidence to indict the suspects. Without the indictment, there cannot be a verdict of guilt."

"I understand, J.P., I read the report." This time when Mr. Stephenson's eyes met J.P. he seemed more at ease. "I do appreciate your efforts in the case. I realize these requests are above and beyond your normal responsibilities to Mid-America."

Whatever it takes, Mr. Stephenson. "I'm glad I can be of service." *For the most part.*

By the time he was finished with Mid-America business it was late in the afternoon. J.P. returned to the parking lot with his mind already skimming the evening agenda with James and Mike. *No free time to speak of in the immediate future.* He pushed the redial button on his phone.

Damn it. Busy. *Again.*

~~~~~~~

Derek Danielson was standing at Denise's desk when J.P. returned to the office. Denise glanced at the clock and then back at her boss.

"James just called to be picked up. Should I send Derek or are you available?"

J.P. nodded a greeting to the intern as he passed through to his own office. "You tell me." *It seems strange it takes three adults to keep track of one teenager.*

"You stay."

J.P. heard Denise give the order but had no idea to whom it pertained. *Me or Derek?* He sifted through a small stack of folders while he waited for more direct instructions.

"Hey boss, did you pick up the plat map at the courthouse?"

Damn it. I knew I was forgetting something. J.P. slapped a folder onto his desk.

"I'll take that as a no." Denise appeared in the doorway. "I sent Derek to pick up James. You and I have some unfinished business to wrap up before you leave for the day."

I have business of my own I'd like to wrap up. J.P. sat down in his chair as Denise made her way toward his desk with the message clipboard. *But she's not answering a phone.*

"First things first." Denise made eye contact. "This Bobbie chick is starting to piss me off. Either I get rid of her for you, or you do it yourself. She has stopped in twice and called at least three times this afternoon. She acts like you're going to be just as excited to see her as she is to see you. And from the look on your face, my guess is otherwise." Denise took a seat and crossed her legs.

I don't know what to do with Bobbie Jo Sommers.

"Obviously, we're not going to make much progress on that topic." Denise checked her list. "Next item. Jessica Hutchison. Lunch tomorrow or Wednesday? You need to tell me what time and where. I'll call her back. She's promised 'information you will be pleased to see'."

I'll believe that when I see it. J.P. ran his hand through his hair but did not verbally respond.

"I know you're upset about James, Boss, and you have a right to be. But at the same time, you still have work to do. You know, like an agenda to keep?"

I don't like the tone in her voice. J.P. started to retaliate but was met with firm resistance.

"Look, I'm hanging on to more than a few loose ends and they're starting to fray at the ends. Either you give me some direction, or you end up with the threads as they unravel when I go home."
~~~~~~~

I hear what she's saying, but I can only juggle so much. Let's fix one of the issues.

"Tell Hutchison Wednesday, eleven o'clock at the pub across the street from Mid-America."

"O'Flannigan's?"

"That's the one. I'll be with Stephenson and the board of director's starting at nine. We need to get a hold of Benson and Barringer and set an appointment for them to meet with Mid-America as soon as they can spare an hour."

Denise made a note on the corner of the notepad. "Very well. Now we're getting somewhere. Are they officially on the case now? "

"As soon as we get the board's approval, hopefully on Wednesday morning."

Denise made another note. "J.P., Derek is doing a fine job on the Andrews case, but I think he could use a little mentoring. I've been giving him all the attention I can spare, but he needs a little encouragement from the expert."

I don't need another assignment right now. "I can do that."

"Today?"

"If you think it's that urgent."

Denise stood up. "Maybe tomorrow when you come in you can leave the bullshit at home." She continued to attack as she left the room. "We all feel the caseload, Boss, but you act as though maybe you'd rather be somewhere else."

Maybe I would. J.P. walked around his desk and closed his office door slightly harder than necessary. *The city didn't budge on their charges against Lloyd Hughes. Something about Mr. Stephenson wasn't right today. The plat map I need is still at the courthouse. My son is now facing assault charges. And as if all that isn't enough, the goddamned line is still busy. Would it be all that difficult for her to pull the plug on a landline and invest in a cell phone?*

J.P. stepped into his private bathroom to relieve himself. *There is no reason for me to take it out on Denise. And I know I need to be spending more time with Derek.* But another entire day had passed, and he still hadn't been able to reach Samira.

That's it, isn't it Ralston? He continued to talk to the reflection in the mirror above the sink. *You're pissed because she's not answering your calls.* J.P. Ralston wasn't used to not getting what he wanted when he wanted it. *If you had any sense at all you'd back out now—before you're in too deep.* J.P. shook his head. *Unless I'm already in that deep.*

That thought gave him the chills. J.P. turned the doorknob and stepped back into his office. Denise was waiting by the door between the offices. *I don't like the look in her eyes.*

"Someone to see you, boss."

Shit.

J.P.'s eyes started at the stacked heels and continued up the long, shapely legs to the edge of a short leather skirt. A casual belt hung loosely around her waist and a tight cotton tank clung to the curves of her breasts. Long brown curls rested silently over her shoulders and the neutral lip color faded into a sultry smile.

"Hello, Bobbie."

"You're a hard man to track down, J.P. Ralston." Bobbie swung her hip in his direction and crossed her arms under her heavy bosom.

"I'll hold your calls, *Mr. Ralston.*" Denise mocked the cover model's tone as she silently closed the door.

The one time I broke my own rule and brought a woman to my office. J.P. looked over the cover model again. *I'm still paying for that mistake.*

"What can I do for you, Bobbie?"

Bobbie Jo took a step toward J.P.

Wrong question.

"You can do anything you want for me. We didn't seem to have any trouble finding things to do the last time we were together."

I really don't need this today. J.P. sat down in his chair. Bobbie propped her hip on the corner of his desk and leaned her heavy chest into his personal space. She touched his hand with a long fingernail.

Exactly what do I do with her now? Temptation was readily available. *But there's a woman across town...*

"What do you say, J.P.?"

...who's not answering her phone.

Bobbie Jo ran her finger under J.P.'s chin.

Do I dare take a chance here? J.P. tried to push that thought away. Ever so slowly he allowed her to link her fingers in his.

Bobbie leaned closer and kissed his earlobe.

There was a time when she was a game for me. J.P. tipped his head and allowed the cover model to tease him with her foreplay. *She was something I desired but didn't want to keep.*

Instinctively, J.P. stood up into Bobbie's space. He took a step forward as she slid into the center of his desk. He dared to run his hand across her thigh to the hem of her skirt. *I know the shape of her breasts and the scent she's wearing.*

Bobbie Jo put her hands in J.P.'s hair. *And I know the brand of her lingerie.* There wasn't anything about her J.P. Ralston didn't remember. *She is for the taking right here and now if I choose.*

The slit in the already short skirt revealed what little Bobbie Jo was wearing underneath. She was right there, but J.P. didn't readily participate.

"J.P., if I didn't know any better," Bobbie cocked her head dramatically, "I might think you were putting me off."

Am I? The attorney was waiting on his instincts to kick in. *It wouldn't take much to release some tension.*

Seemingly unaffected by J.P.'s lack of participation, Bobbie proceeded to wrap her legs around his thighs. She tilted her head and let her long curls fall to one side.

"Remember the last time we used this desk?"

I remember.

Very slowly Bobbie moved into position and began to finger J.P.'s belt. "I was surprised to see you in Springfield."

No more surprised than I was to get that runway ticket.

"I thought you'd join me in my room."

"I was only in town for a short time." *Why can't I tell her the truth?*

She began to unfasted the buckle. "But I'm here now. And I won't take long."

Everything about her is sexy and fresh.

Bobbie wrapped her body around his as their lips met.

J.P. closed his eyes, but the woman who came into view was not the one with her arms around his neck.

Walk away, Ralston. Before it's too late. As Bobbie's lips touched his again, the intercom on his desk buzzed. Bobbie hesitated just long enough for J.P. to unwrap her legs from around his thighs.

Denise spoke into the intercom. "You have a call on line four."

We don't have a line four. J.P. picked up the intercom line.

"Had enough?" Denise spoke firmly.

J.P. considered his answer carefully.

"Boss? I need an answer."

I can't believe what I'm about to do. "Yes."

"Thirty seconds, J.P. That's all I'm giving you."

The attorney stepped out of Bobbie Jo's reach. "That will be fine." He stared at the closed door between the offices. The model moved toward him and ran her fingers through his hair. J.P. stopped the motion with his free hand.

Denise offered a suggestion. "Derek has just returned with your son."

Timing is everything. "Very well. Send him in."

"Which one?"

I don't care. "Danielson." He refastened his belt.

Bobbie was still standing next to J.P. when Derek made an unprepared entrance.

J.P. recovered quickly. "Have a seat, Mr. Danielson."

Derek looked from J.P. to the cover model, then back to J.P. Obviously unsure of what else to do, he took a seat at the conference table.

"That will be all, Bobbie Jo." J.P. nodded toward the door. *I hope this decision doesn't come back to bite me.*

Denise appeared in the doorway and motioned for Bobbie Jo to make an exit. "Will there be anything else for Miss Sommers?"

"Nothing else." *I can't believe I'm doing this.*

Bobbie Jo flipped her hair over her shoulder and smiled wryly. As she walked by, her hips didn't swing quite like they had. *Funny. Her scent isn't even appealing anymore.*

Denise followed Bobbie out.

J.P. pulled up to the conference table where Derek was waiting for further instructions. *What the hell just happened here?* He took a breath and put his glasses on. "Okay Derek, show me where you're at with..." *What case is he working again?*

"The Andrews case." Denise returned to his office and finished his sentence. "I closed the last case for you, Boss."

I bet she did. J.P. opened the file. *Someday I'll ask her for the verdict.*

29 A Jealous Streak

Samira

Samira ran her ink pen over the letters she'd already written. *Noon. O'Flannigan's Pub. Across from MidAmerica building.* "Sure, I can be there." *But I was supposed to have lunch with Krissy, Kara, and Susan's girls.*

"You know where Mid-America is, right?"

Everyone knows where the Mid-America building is. "Of course."

"The pub is right across the street from their parking lot." Phil informed. "Just tell the hostess you're there to meet me."

No doubt he'll know her name.

"Once you get there, I'll wrap up my appointment and we can grab a bite to eat somewhere else."

"Wouldn't it just be easier to stay there for lunch?"

"I'd rather not."

Okay. Her ink pen made another pass over the notation. *That seems a little strange.*

"Still there?"

Samira smiled into the phone. "Still here." *I love the sound of his voice.*

"Alright, I'm on my way into a meeting. I'll see you in a couple of hours, okay?"

He is all J.P. today.

"I'll be there." *But my next call isn't going to be so pleasant.* She hung up the receiver and ran her hand over the cover of a magazine on her desk. *It's the same periodical that was on Phil's coffee table.* The scantily dressed model on the front was smiling back at her. Samira turned to the cover story and read the lead.

Supermodel, Bobbie Jo Sommers, is the newest member of the Victoria Secret Family.

Samira took a deep breath. *That's the same woman Phil was talking to in Springfield.* There was no mistaking that face. *Or that body, for all that matters.* The article highlighted the Bobbie Sommers' success story then moved into more hype about the live runway shows the company was sponsoring around the country. *I don't understand the motive behind putting lingerie on live models in public.*

Samira remembered the way the model had touched Phil's face. *My assumption is they're more than just acquaintances.* Samira turned back to the cover photograph. *It's certainly a body that has never had babies.* Samira sighed. *But not one I care to compete with either.*

Samira opened her desk drawer and pulled out the local phone directory. *Now that I know his name, I wonder if I can find him in the directory.* She opened the yellow pages to the A's. *Attorneys.* She ran her fingernail over the listings. *There's a Benson and Barringer. I would guess that to be Mike Benson's practice.* Samira's eyes continued to search the page. *There he is.* She tapped the page. *Ralston, J.P., Business Law.*

Samira flipped to the white pages. *Let's see what we can find here.* Several passes over the R's revealed an absence for J.P. Ralston or anything of that nature. *Nope.* She closed the heavy book. *So, the number I have on the back of his business card must be private.*

"Miss Cartwright," Helen Haddock poked her head around the door. "Should I take the dated periodicals downstairs for you?"

"That's okay, Helen, I'll get them in a few minutes."

She fingered the numbers on the telephone but didn't dial right away. *What do I tell the girls and Susan?* Samira thought for a moment. *They're going to be disappointed I'm canceling lunch with them.* She dialed her brother's home number.

Kara answered.

Here goes nothing. "Hi Kara, it's Mom."

"I know," Kara acknowledged. "The library number is on the caller ID. What's up? Aunt Pam's in the shower. Should I have her call you back?"

"Actually," Samira hesitated slightly. "I called to talk to you or Krissy." She paused again. "Something has come up at lunch. I'm not going to be able to meet with Susan and the girls at the park."

"So that means you won't be meeting us either then."

"That's right, Kara. I'm sorry. We'll have to reschedule."

"Like that's going to happen. Susan only has this week off from work, you know. That's why she set up the picnic for today."

"I know, Kara, I..." *How do I tell her I'm going to meet Phil instead?* "Maybe Susan can meet tomorrow. I'll call her at home and see what she thinks."

"She's going to be really mad."

Kara's *probably right about that.*

"You know how she thinks you're always avoiding her these days? This is just going to make it worse."

The words on the notepad were starting to blur as Samira's pen ran over and over them. "Maybe it won't be as bad as you think." *We can hope.*

"Whatever."

Whatever. I hate that word. Samira promised to call Kara back after talking to Susan.

It really shouldn't be so hard to talk to a girlfriend. Samira carried the periodicals to the basement. *If Susan were a real friend, she would understand without any explanation.* She sorted the magazines into alphabetical order and stacked them on the worktable for her staff to file later. *This is her week off, not mine.* Samira re-thought that statement. *Heck, if Susan knew I was dumping the picnic for a man she'd be ecstatic.* Samira pulled the magazine with Bobbie Jo Sommer's article out of the stack and decided to take it back to her office.

Time was passing. *Now I don't have any choice but to call Susan.* Her hands were sweating when she lifted the receiver to dial.

Four rings later, voicemail picked up. *Oh good. I'll just leave a quick message.*

The last hour of the morning passed very quickly. "I'll be back sometime early this afternoon, Helen."

"Take your time, Miss Cartwright. Enjoy the picnic with your girls."

There's a guilt trip if I've ever known one. Just as Samira climbed into her car, Susan pulled into the parking space next to her. *What is she doing here?*

"Wait," Susan hurried around the front of her car. She leaned over, her short, bobbed hair bouncing with every move. "Why don't you just ride with me and then I'll drop you off on my way back home?"

Now what do I tell her? "Didn't you get my message?"

Susan stood up straight and let her hand rest against Samira's open car door. "What message?"

"I called about an hour ago, maybe a little more." *Well, more like forty-five minutes ago.* "Something has come up, Susan. I need to be downtown in a few minutes."

Susan waved her hand in dismissal. "Well, that's alright. I'm a little early anyway. I was just in the neighborhood. Go on downtown and then meet us when you're done."

Samira realized the misunderstanding. "Not for the library, something else." She took a deep breath. "I don't know when I can break free."

"You mean I hired a sitter for Joey so we could have a mother daughter picnic and now you don't know if you're going to make it or not?" Susan was instantly frustrated. "My girls are already over there."

"I'm sorry, Susan. I tried to reach you as soon as I knew." *But I really need to be going. Downtown parking over lunch is going to be a nightmare.*

"Did you call your girls?"

Oh no. I can't believe I didn't call them back.

Susan put her hands on her thick waist. It was obvious she was mad. "Alright. I'll get Krissy and Kara just like we'd planned." Susan adjusted her wristwatch. "No clue when you'll be done?"

Nothing seems right now. Samira was so torn. *But I've waited three days to hear from Phil. I didn't want to let him down either.*

"I'm picking up Joey at one thirty so if you're done by then, stop by, alright?"

The pit in Samira's stomach grew heavy as she drove downtown. She circled the Mid-America parking lot without any luck. *Phil said noon, and he sounded like he meant noon straight up.* Reluctantly, she circled around behind the three-story building and parked in a reserved parking space. *I don't usually do this.* She stuck her reserved parking pass on the rearview mirror. *But without it, I'm never going to find a place to park.*

O'Flannigan's Pub was dark compared to the bright sunshine. It took a moment for Samira's eyes to adjust even after removing her sunglasses.

"Just one for lunch?"

Angelina. She's wearing a name tag. "Oh, no." Phil's instructions replayed in Samira's mind. "I'm here to meet Phil," *No wait.* "J.P. Ralston."

The hostess nodded knowingly. "Right this way."

Samira's khaki skirt and plain tee didn't compare to the business-clad men and women gathered in the bar. *Why does it feel like everyone is watching me?*

Very few guests were in the dining area when the hostess held out her arm toward a table in the far corner. Samira could see Phil's profile against the window. He was sitting across from a woman. *But not the model from the magazine. Thankfully.*

It only took a moment for Phil to notice her. Samira could feel the intensity of his thoughts from across the room. *There is something powerful about his presence.* Phil rose from his chair and motioned for her to come closer.

Samira tuned into the conversation as she stepped closer.

"If you'll excuse me," J.P. was speaking to the woman who still had her back to Samira. "Tell your employer I'll be more interested when he starts conducting business in person."

"But Mr. Bridges is rarely in town—"

She doesn't seem as interested in ending this discussion as Phil does.

"I understand." J.P. was addressing the woman directly. "When he gets back into the area, call my assistant and I'll make myself available."

Without any reserve, Phil took Samira's hand. "Shall we?"

Sure. Samira nodded as her fingers interlocked with his. *It feels good to touch him again.* She kept her eyes on Phil even though she was dying to get a better look at the woman he was deserting. *J.P. is very intense this noon hour.*

Samira skipped a step to keep up as J.P. led her out of the dining room. More people had gathered for lunch and a line was beginning to form at the hostess' desk. Phil stopped briefly and exchanged a few remarks with the girl behind the counter. *I bet he tips her.* Phil handed the young woman a folded bill. *Sure enough.*

J.P. led Samira from the central air of the pub into the hot sunshine. *His thoughts are somewhere between that meeting and his next one. I can tell.* They walked about halfway down the block before speaking.

"It's good to see you."

Samira thought back to the scene at the restaurant. "I feel like maybe I interrupted."

But I feel worse for standing up Kara and Krissy.

J.P.'s eyes were still focused on the sidewalk ahead. He shook his head slightly. "Don't. She had an hour to make her case and failed to provide anything substantial."

But she seemed a little distraught.

"But you," J.P. slowed his steps and turned to look at Samira. "You made your case simply by walking across that room."

"Was I late?" *I didn't mean to be late.*

"No. You were right on time. Thanks for the rescue."

Oh. He set me up to be his excuse to leave.

"You were extremely sexy walking across the dining room."

"I should have changed out of these clothes." *And would have with more advanced notice.*

J.P. moved his hand to her waist and pulled her closer as they continued to walk. *Just like he did in Springfield.*

"You don't have to change a thing."

People were gathered at the corner waiting for the walk light to signal. *I wonder if I know anyone here.* It hadn't been that long ago that she'd longed for a man's hand to hold. *But today, in broad daylight, walking along this familiar sidewalk, I don't know if I should...* Samira stopped her thoughts. *Springfield is one thing. In Joplin, it's another.*

Phil turned toward her. *Please don't kiss me here. Not in public.* Samira forced a smile when Phil caught her eyes.

"What are you thinking, Pretty Lady?"

Now I sense more of Phil, and less of J.P.

He cocked his head and patiently waited for her answer.

I'm thinking I should be at a mother -daughter picnic. Samira bit her bottom lip, thankful for her dark glasses. "I'm thinking you promised me lunch." *I should tell him about the picnic.*

"Then by all means, let's find a place to eat."

When the light changed, Phil slipped his hand back into hers.

"I believe there's a deli on the next block with a gourmet coffee shop."

Sounds good to me.

"Great sandwiches, but I can't speak for the coffee. You'll have to be the judge of that."

Coffee is good. Samira nodded. *A deli won't take long. I might still have time to swing by the park on the way back to the library without having to make up too much time at the end of the day.*

Samira stood in the crowded lunch line. *I really do feel plain and simple compared to all these businesswomen in heels.*

"Anything you like." Phil nodded toward the menu.

First things first. Samira ordered a Cappuccino. Next, she ordered half a club sandwich with mayo but no pickles. She sat down in a wire chair to hold the table while Phil waited on the order.

"Samira Stephenson?" An unfamiliar voice called a familiar name. *No one has called me that for a long time.*

Oh, wow. "Ricardo." Samira rose from her chair and greeted him with both hands. "It's Samira Cartwright now." She stepped into a quick hug with her former classmate.

"So, it is. So it is." A huge smile crossed his dark complexion. "It's been a long time. Missed you at the last reunion. Are you still in the area?"

"Yeah, it has been a long time. The reunion fell during a difficult time." Samira's mind went back to the spring Tom had been so sick. *Ricardo. It's so good to see his smile again.* "And yes, I'm still living here in Joplin. Same house and everything." *Well, almost everything. Everything but my husband.*

"You're looking great, Samira." Ricardo took the liberty of walking all the way around her despite the busy patio. "Life must be treating you well."

Samira followed Ricardo with her eyes as he circled her. "I'm good, Ricardo." *I really am.* "What about you?"

Ricardo's eyes lit up as he caught sight of something behind her. "Still in Joplin. Still a pharmacist at the hospital. Still scouting out new prospects and the one approaching your table is quite nice." Ricardo grinned and nodded toward Phil.

Samira suddenly realized she was caught standing between two men. *Wouldn't Susan love this?* Then she realized what Ricardo was insinuating.

Phil stuck out his hand. "I don't believe we've met." His tone was all business.

"Oh, I'm sorry." Samira recovered her hospitality. "Ricardo Martinez. We graduated together. And Ricardo, this is—" *Which name do I introduce him by?*

"J.P. Ralston." Phil turned back toward Samira. "There's a table inside if you want to move in where it's cooler."

Samira returned Ricardo's ornery grin. "Do you want to go inside?" *After all, he's the one wearing the business suit.*

Samira watched Phil remove his suit jacket and hang it over the back of his chair. He proceeded to roll his shirt cuffs. *He always rolls his cuffs twice.*

"No, I'm fine." Phil's dark blue eyes studied the intruder. "Will you be joining us, Ricardo?"

Ricardo was standing with his arms crossed, eyeing the attorney carefully.

Oh, Ricci. You never know what he's going to say next.

"No, no, but thank you for the invitation. Maybe another time." Ricardo winked at Samira. He reached for Samira's hands again and when she reciprocated, he leaned in and whispered in her ear. "When you're finished with him, send him my way. He looks like a dream."

Samira rolled her eyes and grinned. "I'm thinking I might keep this one for myself."

"Can't say I blame you." Ricardo flashed his million-dollar smile in Phil's direction and raised a hand. "Nice to meet you J.P. Ralston." Ricardo hesitated.

Samira watched him study Phil's physique once more. *Oh, please. Don't say anything more.*

"Do take good care of Miss Samira. She's a doll. A real doll." Ricardo's eyes passed over Samira again. "It was good to bump into you, my friend. Look me up at the pharmacy sometime. Let's catch up."

That would be entertaining. Samira pulled up to the table and watched Ricardo set out across the busy city street.

Phil unwrapped his sandwich. "So, Ricardo was a classmate then?"

"Yes."

"And obviously you knew him well?"

"Yes." Samira took a sip of the cappuccino. *He sounds a little concerned.* "We were good friends."

Phil nodded. He looked like he might ask another question but instead sunk his teeth into his sandwich.

"I haven't seen him for a long time." Samira added more for her own thought than for Phil's information.

"He didn't act like much time had passed."

I could have asked a few more questions in Springfield but chose to take the high road, Mr. Ralston. "What makes you say that?"

Phil avoided any kind of eye contact.

If I didn't know better, I'd think he was a little jealous.

"He didn't hold much back when he saw you."

For the first time, Samira realized Phil had been watching her while she waited at the table. "Because he hugged me?"

"That and the way he looked at you. And I don't know that he needed to whisper in your ear."

Samira was smiling and she knew that was irritating Phil too. *He's jealous.* She put her fingers over her mouth to finish chewing before she spoke. *He really doesn't like someone else paying attention to me, does he?* "That's just Ricci." She remembered Ricardo from years ago. "He's always been that way."

Phil nodded again but this time he was looking directly at her. "Did you like the way he was looking at you?"

Did you like the way that model touched you in the lobby? "No, Mr. Ralston, you have it all wrong." Samira waited on purpose. *Let's see how he responds to this.* "I liked the way he was looking at you."

"What's that supposed to mean?"

Samira tipped her head and raised an eyebrow. "He was far more interested in you than he was in me." Phil's eyes were full of doubt. *He's going to freak.* "Seriously. Would you like to know what he whispered in my ear?"

Phil leaned back in his chair. "I don't know if I do or not."

Okay, then. Samira picked up her sandwich again.

"So, what did he say?"

I knew he'd have to know. "Are you sure you want to know?"

"I asked, didn't I?"

He did. She put her sandwich back on the wrapper. "When he whispered in my ear, he told me to send you his way when I'm done."

Phil put his elbows on the table. The look in his eyes told Samira he didn't want to believe what he was hearing. "You're full of sh—"

Samira pointed her finger at Phil and stopped his sentence. "I know Ricardo," she reminded. "And I know he liked what he saw."

"You know what?"

"What?"

Phil was searching for words.

He's speechless.

He refused to make eye contact. "You drive me crazy."

"Is that a good crazy, or a bad crazy?" *I should probably know before I tease him again.*

"I don't know yet." Phil held his sandwich with one hand, but he didn't take a bite. "I can usually figure out what a woman is thinking, but you never cease to amaze me."

"That's funny," Samira replied immediately. "Because I've always felt like my emotions are completely transparent." *I don't think I've ever voiced that to anyone outside of my own family.*

"You're wrong, Pretty Lady." J.P. shared his easy smile. "Emotions, maybe. But you hold your thoughts and I'm not exactly sure what to do about that." He took another bite of his lunch.

I do not hold my thoughts. Samira realized her internal defenses all too well. *Okay, so maybe I do. Sometimes.* She looked up the street in the direction of the Mid-America building. *He just finished what I started.* She decided to change the subject. "Where do you usually have lunch in the middle of a busy week?"

"What makes you think this is a busy week?"

There he goes, answering a question with another question. "You just sounded busy when you called. And you looked busy when I arrived at O'Flannegan's." *I might as well just state those facts.*

Phil nodded. "You're right. It's been busy and looks like it's going to continue to be that way for a while. That's why I thought maybe we could catch a quick lunch today."

At least he said quick. Samira remembered the picnic. *Maybe I still can pop in on the girls for a few minutes.*

"Your week must be a bit hectic as well."

"What makes you say that?" *Few people ever refer to my life as busy.*

"Well, let's see," Phil took a drink of water. "It seems Monday you were either in meetings or on the phone when I tried to reach you during the day. Then your line was busy all evening. Yesterday they said something about you being downtown most of the day."

So, he did try to call. "For training." *I should explain.* "I was teaching a new software program." *At least he tried to find me.* "So, I guess I was busier than sometimes."

"Have you ever considered investing in a cell phone?"

Samira couldn't believe her ears. "It's a daily conversation with the girls. But I haven't taken that plunge yet." *Is he inquiring so he has instant access to me?*

"Just curious." Phil took another bite of sandwich. "That might solve the busy signal problem on your landline."

I don't exactly understand his motive for making this suggestion. "Up until a few weeks ago, it was rare I ever received a personal call." *Maybe he simply wants a more private conversation?* Samira wiped her fingers on a napkin.

When she looked up, Phill was looking right at her. "What?"

"It's really good to see you, Samira."

He said my name this time. Despite the warm day, goose pimples formed on Samira's arm.

Phil's voice was gentle. "I didn't know if you could break free in the middle of the day, but I know my next two days are jam packed. I was hoping you could spare a few minutes."

He spoke with such honesty Samira almost forgave herself for deserting her daughters. "I didn't feel like—"

Samira waited but Phil didn't complete his sentence. *No, please don't leave me hanging again.* She took the last bite of her sandwich and waited some more, but he didn't say anything. She caught Phil stealing a glance at his watch.

"Where are you parked?"

I don't want him to know I have a reserved parking permit. "At the end of the block."

Phil crumpled his wrapping with his hands and offered to take her trash as well. Samira obliged. Instinctively, she picked up his sports coat and handed it to him upon his return.

"Thanks."

I hate it when he leaves his thoughts hanging like this.

"I'm assuming the end of the block this way?" Phil pointed toward the Mid-America building.

Samira nodded. Without speaking they started to walk in that direction at a slower pace than they had arrived. Phil didn't offer his arm or try to take her hand this time. He was obviously deep in thought.

Cars passed by on the busy street, and the sidewalk was bustling with people heading back to their downtown office. But Phil still wasn't speaking.

I don't know if I should try to extract those thoughts or just leave him alone.

They were almost back to the stoplight when Phil finally broke their silence.

"I've been thinking." He was contemplative. "Saturday night didn't go quite like—"

Like what?

"I don't know, like it should have."

I thought about inviting him to stay a little while, but he seemed anxious to go. "Which parts should have gone differently?"

Phil ran his tongue over his bottom lip. "Like maybe the part where I kissed you but didn't ask when I could see you again." J.P.'s eyes were focused in the distance. "Because I've decided I don't like not knowing when our paths will cross again."

Neither to do I. The walk signals flashed but Phil didn't follow the rest of the pedestrians across the street. "Then I guess it's a good thing you called this morning."

"I didn't know if…" Phil hesitated. "Well, anyway, I was glad you were in the office to take a call. Next time maybe we could plan a little further in advance."

"I'm glad you called."

Another group of people were gathering at the corner to wait for the light to change again.

"I'm glad to hear that because at first I wasn't sure you wanted to come." Phil looked away as he spoke those words as if maybe he didn't want a direct response.

He deserves to know. "You're right. But it didn't have anything to do with you." Samira took the liberty to touch his elbow where it was bent holding his jacket. "I'm supposed to be at a picnic with my girls right now. They're still waiting on me." *And if I were to be completely honest here, I'd tell him I'd just discovered his Springfield friend on the cover of a magazine. But I'm not quite ready to be that honest.*

This time when the light changed, his hand guided her to follow the crowd. "Well, I was preoccupied when I left on Saturday too. I'd heard from the boys and things weren't going well up at their mother's."

I knew something wasn't right. "You should have said something," she replied sincerely. "We could have been home earlier."

"That was the call I took on the way home, so being earlier wouldn't have helped any. I just had a hard time shifting gears."

Samira caught his eyes for a moment.

"I feel bad I couldn't give you my full attention."

Did you give the girl in the magazine your full attention? Samira caught her thoughts. *That's not fair. I need to let him off the hook.*

"Truce then?" She offered her right hand.

Phil questioned her with his eyes.

"You were distracted Saturday and I was distracted today. We cancelled one another out." She offered her hand again. "Truce."

Phil grinned as he slowly offered his right hand to seal the deal. "Truce." They shook but Phil didn't let go. "But before you get too far away this time, I was thinking maybe we could go out for dinner one night this weekend."

The light changed and this time they crossed to the side of the street in the shade.

"Maybe," Samira answered with caution. "After standing Krissy and Kara up for lunch today I need a little time to redeem myself. Can I check with the girls and see which night they're going to the movies?"

"Do you think they'll forgive me for stealing you away this noon?"

"Maybe." *Then again, who knows? They're teenage girls.*

"James has another court appearance day after tomorrow. Barring any major changes in parental requirements I should be able to break free either night."

I wonder if these are new charges. "I'm sorry, Phil. I hope things will go his way in court."

"There's no way to know how the judge is going to rule. This time James is just going to have to live with the consequences." Phil seemed to stop in mid-thought. "But there's nothing I can do about it now."

He always hesitates when he's discussing his family with me.

They slowed to a stop in front of O'Flannegan's Pub.

"Well, we're back where we started."

Samira thought for a moment. "I think we made a little more progress than that."

Phil shared his easy smile, but he didn't speak.

"Should I call to let you know about the weekend?"

He nodded slowly. "You might have to leave a message if I don't pick up."

He mentioned it so I think I'll ask. "Did you leave me any messages when you tried to call?"

Phil shook his head and looked away. "I hate voice mail."

"But you want me to leave you a message if you don't pick up?" Samira grinned, knowing she was teasing him again.

Phil returned her smile. "If you had a cell phone, I could send you a quick text and you'd know to call me back later."

Samira raised her eyebrows. "Point noted." *But if I get a cell phone for me, the girls will expect phones of their own and I don't know if I'm ready for that yet.* She could feel his eyes trying to see through her dark lenses. Out of courtesy she removed her sunglasses.

"If we didn't have an audience—"

"You'd kiss me right here on the sidewalk?"

Phil nodded with a grin.

Samira leaned closer and let his lips touch her temple. *I love the way he does that.* The tenderness of his lips sent ripples of pleasure all the way to the tips of her toes.

"You'll call me then?"

"I have your number this time."

An awkward silence held their thoughts. J.P. finally checked his watch.

"Yeah, me too. I should be getting back." *Or stopping to check on the girls and Susan.* She started to step away but couldn't help the next thought from falling. "I'm sorry I teased you about Ricardo."

Phil shook his head and grinned at the recollection. He put his hands out in warning. "Just make sure he keeps his distance, alright?"

"From you or from me?"

"From both."

Nice we ended on a lighter note. Samira unlocked her car. *Obviously, he has a jealous streak.* She slid behind the wheel. *He didn't want me out of his sight in Springfield either.* She started her car and backed out of the reserved parking area. *Just the same, I don't mind him staking a claim on me if he'll let me do the same on him.* Samira checked for oncoming traffic and then pulled into the four-lane street. *And eventually I'm going to need to know the whole story behind the woman on the magazine cover.*

But that was a conversation for another day.

30 *Before the Judge*

Joseph Phillip

"My car would've gotten us here faster." Mike climbed the steps to the courthouse two by two. "Saved on gas too."

"As it is, we're right on time." J.P. followed his friend. *Less time to sit around waiting our turn.*

"Is there a crime in being early?"

I've spent my entire career in a courthouse, but never once thought I'd be in one to defend my son. Twice.

James caught up. "I don't think your Corvette would have held us all."

"All the more reason to leave your dad at home." Mike grinned mischievously,

It's probably a good thing he didn't offer. J.P. started to open the oversized door to the ancient entry hall, but Mike's hand brought it to a sudden halt.

What? J.P. looked into Mike's reflective lens.

"Whatever happens in here, I'm the attorney. You're the dad. Are we clear?"

He knows my temper, my motives, and my tongue. J.P. could feel James watching him.

Other people were trying to pass through the door. *James has the best counsel.* He exchanged a resolute look with his son. *Today he needs a father.*

Mike let go of the door and they crossed the threshold into family court.

"We meet with social services first." Mike was already scanning the crowd. "Why don't you guys go stand in that line while I check things out inside."

I hate standing in lines. J.P. knew Mike was still trying to find a way to have the charges against James either dropped or reduced. J.P. led his son toward the door marked Department of Human Services.

"How are you doing?" J.P. wanted to sound like a father. *But I feel more like an attorney.*

"I'm alright. I guess." James leaned heavily into a marble wall. "I could live without this shirt though." He made a pass over his chest with his hands.

He's only talking about the shirt because he doesn't want to talk about what's really on his mind.

"You should try wearing one every day." J.P. smoothed his own shirt.

"You couldn't pay me to wear your shirts every day."

"I get paid to wear them."

James laughed. "Yeah, I guess you do."

"Do you know why Mike wanted you to dress up?"

"To improve my image." James raised his eyebrows in a facetious air of authority.

Not quite. "He wants you to make a good first impression on the judge."

"Same judge, isn't it?"

"Yes, but it helps to lose the tough-guy image."

"I feel stupid."

J.P. bumped his son playfully with his elbow. "You look good."

Mike reappeared in the hallway. There was a purpose in his step that made J.P. meet him halfway. Mike took James by the sleeve and directed him toward a conference room door. The first one was occupied but the second one was empty.

Mike's eyes were alive with energy. *He knows something.* J.P. could sense a sudden surge of adrenalin.

"James." Mike was direct. "Tell me exactly what you're going to tell the judge about the actual fight with Bruce."

James questioned his counsel. "Just like you told me to?"

"I told you to tell the truth." Mike reminded. "Tell me, right now, word for word what happened during the fight."

James took a breath. "He—"

"Who's he?"

"Bruce."

"Use his name in court. Continue."

They've been over this.

"Bruce shoved mom into the kitchen table and then he yelled at me to stay out of the argument."

"Were you involved in the argument before that?"

"I'd told him to leave mom alone."

Mike was holding eye contact. "Was there any dialogue between the two of you before you told him to leave your mother alone?"

"No."

"Okay, go on."

What's Mike looking for?

"He," James stopped and corrected himself. "Bruce pushed Mom into the table and told me to stay out of the argument then he started toward Mom again. When he raised his arm to hit her, I laid him out."

"Define 'laid him out'."

I can personally testify to what he means by laying somebody out. The father checked the scar on his hand for proof.

James shrugged seemingly unaffected by Mike's insistence on using the right words. "Knocked him down."

"Better. And that was it, right?"

James nodded. "Yeah."

"Did he take a swing at you?"

"He didn't have a chance."

"Had he hit your mom before you walked in?"

"I don't know," James answered honestly. "Josh and I got home in the middle of the fight."

"Don't call it a fight in court. Call it an altercation."

I still don't know what Mike's thinking.

"Where did you hit him?"

"Bruce?"

Way to correct your counsel, James.

"Yes. Where did you hit Bruce?"

"Under the edge of his ribs with my right fist."

Yeah, that's the punch I know.

"One punch?"

James nodded. "One punch. He went down like a—"

"No explicates in court, James. Just the facts."

"One punch."

I need to know what's up. "What's with the clarification?"

Mike slid a hip onto the polished conference table. "Bruce is in there all bandaged up like an accident victim. His hand is wrapped and he's wearing this brace thing around his rib cage." Mike made a motion with his hand.

"On the outside of his clothes?"

Mike nodded. "His eye is all bruised up too."

"That's odd."

"Exactly." Mike agreed. "My guess is he's going to try to make it sound like he and James had a knock down drag out fight when in truth James took one swing in defense of his mother's safety." Mike stroked his mustache.

"Is Janet in there?"

"Not yet." Mike stood up and lifted his cell phone from his suit pocket.

Ah. He's going to summons Janet to testify now. J.P. checked his watch. *There's still time to make that happen.*

James suddenly looked concerned.

"Just tell them the truth, James. That's all you can do." *And hope your mother has the guts to do the same.*

James nodded as he lowered himself into a wooden conference chair.

~~~~~~~

An hour and a half later J.P. found himself sitting alone in a chair along the back wall of the courtroom. *At least the hearing is closed to the public.* But sitting there in the back row he didn't feel helpful whatsoever. *I certainly don't feel like an attorney, and I barely feel like a father.* He glanced at his son. *He looks confident enough.* J.P. took a deep breath. *James shouldn't even be here.*

J.P.'s eyes went to his ex-wife. Janet was sitting a row behind Bruce with her head bowed. *She looks scared out of her mind.* J.P. recognized the little old lady Janet used for legal counsel. *She's the same witch who demoralized my character before a judge even though it wasn't me that stepped outside the boundaries of marriage.*

The proceedings began. Bruce was called to the stand to state his case. It was all J.P. could do to sit in his chair without making a verbal objection. *The ONLY thing that's keeping me quiet is the promise I made to Mike before we came in here.* The more questions Bruce answered, the more dramatic he got. *Half this stuff is irrelevant to the charges.* J.P. shifted in his seat and folded his arms hard against his chest. *Counsel is leading the witness, for god's sake.*

Mike began his cross-examination. "How many times did James make physical contact to your ribs?"

Bruce held his head high. "I can't remember. Once I was down everything got all blurry and—"

"How many times did James hit you, Mr. Hamilton?"

Hold him to it, Mike.

"One time that I remember."

"How many bones did he actually break?"

There was a long silence in the courtroom.

Bastard. J.P. leaned forward and sat on his hands to keep from crossing the bar. *I could take him out right here and now.*

"Mr. Hamilton, you are required to answer the question." The judge spoke with authority.

"There are no broken bones but—"

"Thank you." Mike interrupted Bruce's explanation.

"How long would you say the conflict between you and James lasted?"

Again, there was a moment of silence.

"Let's see if we can narrow it down, Mr. Hamilton. Would you say five minutes or less than five minutes?"

He'll fall flat on his face with this one.
~~~~~~~

"Less than five minutes."

Thank you.

"And Mr. Hamilton, who placed the call to the authorities to summons the law enforcement and an ambulance to your residence?"

Who the hell cares who called for help? J.P. watched Bruce lower his head. When he answered, his voice was too low to be heard.

"Please speak into the microphone, Mr. Hamilton." The judge folded her arms.

"I made the call." Bruce raised his head. "But—"

"There are no further questions."

Now I know why he's the attorney and I'm the father.

James took the stand calmly and with confidence. *Mike has either prepared him extremely well, or James is extraordinary under pressure.*

The prosecuting attorney crossed his wrists behind his back.

"Can you describe for the court your mother's state of mind during the argument?"

"Objection, Your Honor." Mike rose from his seat. "Counsel is asking my client to speculate."

The judge raised her hand. "I'll allow it."

You can do it, James. J.P. fixed his eyes on his son. *Just tell them the truth.*

The judge allowed time for James to think his answer through.

"I walked into the middle of the altercation. She seemed to be upset, but I don't think she was hurt."

By the time Mike took the floor to restate the most important issues J.P.'s mind was no longer in the courtroom. He'd slipped years into the past. *What was I? Six or seven at the time?* He'd taken a running leap at his own father to stop a verbal assault on his mother. In his memory he could still taste his father's blood as he sunk his half-grown permanent teeth into the Captain's shoulder. *I paid for that attack with solitary confinement in Uncle Roy's barn.*

"Objection, Your Honor." Bruce's lawyer drew J.P.'s mind back into the courtroom. "Counsel is leading the witness."

The judge puckered her lips in thought. "I'll allow it. I believe the questioning is valid."

Mike restated his original question with caution. "Is this the first incident of physical attack from your husband, Mrs. Hamilton?"

When did they call her to the stand? J.P. ran his hand through his hair and watched Janet bow her head.

"You are required to answer the question, Mrs. Hamilton," the judge urged.

J.P. shifted in his chair. *I forfeited my visitation rights with Josh and James thinking it would give them more stability at home.* He still felt responsible for Janet's decision to separate. *I figured if I stayed out of their lives as much as possible that would give them one less thing to contend with.* Now, as he waited on Janet's answer with the rest of the courtroom, J.P. sunk deeper into his own self-doubt.

"Yes." Janet finally answered the question. "This is the first time my husband has attacked me in any physical way." Her eyes were moist when she looked up.

She's lying. J.P. studied his ex-wife's face.

Cross-examination did not reveal any new information. Seemingly satisfied, Mike informed the judge that there were no more questions.

When the judge dismissed Janet from her seat, she made brief eye contact with J.P.

It doesn't matter if she told the truth or not. Josh and James have options. J.P.'s eyes moved to Bruce Hamilton. *She's stuck with him anyway you look at it.* He tried to feel sorry for her, but he couldn't. *Hamilton undermined my marriage and won the bride.* That was a fact forced upon J.P. long ago.

Following Janet's testimony, the judge clapped her mallet hard on the podium. "The court will be in recess for twenty minutes. I will see counsel in my chambers."

Mike turned in his chair and gave a nod of approval. *Obviously, Janet's testimony got the judge's attention, just like Mike had hoped.*

As soon as Mike and the prosecuting attorney disappeared behind closed doors, J.P. moved to the seat directly behind his son.

James lowered his head. "Mike says this is a good sign."

"It is," J.P. assured. "The judge sees major discrepancies in the accounts. She needs to ask some more questions before making a ruling."

James nodded. Momentarily the boy's eyes scanned the room. *He's studying Hamilton.*

"I didn't give him that black eye," James whispered. "He looks like me the day after my fight with you."

J.P. recalled Bruce's exact words. "*He came at me like a wild animal.*"

Very slowly J.P. realized that the fight scene Bruce had described was the one between him and James. "Holy shit." J.P. spoke the words out loud. James was staring at his father. "Are you thinking what I'm thinking?"

"I think so."

That pisses me off. "What's the motive behind that?" J.P. dared to look in Bruce's direction. *That's exactly what he did. He described my fight with James.*

"Mom looks really scared."

She knows the truth.

"All rise." The bailiff's voice announced the judge's return. As the people rose from their chairs, J.P. moved back to his seat at the back of the room.

"The charges against James Allen Ralston have been dismissed for inconclusive evidence." The judge wrapped her mallet against the podium.

That was that. The next case was announced without any further discussion.

J.P. fell into step behind James and Mike. Janet was also making her way up the aisle. Politely, but without speaking, J.P. waited for her to pass before making his own exit.

Mike turned seemingly unaware of Janet's presence. "James and I have some business to attend to with DHS, then we have a quick meeting with Janet and her attorney."

Why the hell do we have to meet with them? Mike led James away. Suddenly, J.P. realized he was standing alone with his ex-wife. *This could be interesting.*

"James didn't give him the black eye." Janet spoke without prompting. She was looking into the empty hallway.

What did she just say?

"I did." Janet sighed. "Last night."

Janet, this is not the time nor the place to make that kind of a confession. The attorney in J.P. told him not to speak a word.

"Bruce has it in for Jennie Johnson's dad. I think he's trying to take it out on James or something." Janet's confession came but not without cost. Her eyes were damp, and her hands were shaking.

J.P. looked around. *Let's not share the real testimony and be overheard in public.* There was an empty conference room not too far from where they were standing. Without speaking, J.P. led Janet into the room.

"Is this what you do for all your clients?" Janet asked with new sarcasm.

She just spilled her guts. Now she's going to attack? "I don't recall you ever being my client."

"I was on a lower priority list than your clients." She sat down in a chair.

I promised Mike…

"You never made time for me."

J.P. leaned on the back of a chair. *Nope, I'm not going to let that one go.* "That was partly by your choice, Jan."

"Maybe." Janet found a tissue in her purse and blew her nose. "You're the only one who still calls me Jan."

"I met you as Jan, I believe." *Where did that come from?* "Would you prefer I call you Janet?"

"No, that's all right." The look in her eyes told J.P. her thoughts were far away. "I still wonder what we could have done to remedy our differences for the boys' sake?"

My legal counsel would not approve of this conversation. J.P. glanced through the open door. *Maybe coming in here wasn't such a good idea.* J.P. ran his hand through his hair. "Look, we've been over that a million times. We can't go back and recreate what didn't happen so let's just leave it where it is."

"I know," Janet wiped her nose again. "But sometimes I wish I would have given you a little more time to come around. I was so sure you didn't want to be with me I hurried things along so I could get on with my life."

Quit playing the martyr, Jan. J.P. wasn't moved by her tears nor taken by her honesty. *I need to get out of this conversation.* He started toward the door hoping for an escape.

"Phil?"

Phil?

J.P. stopped at the sound of his name. For a moment, he heard another woman's voice. When he turned around that face faded back into Janet's.

"Would you have been more willing to reconcile had you not known of my involvement with Bruce?"

That question caught J.P. completely off guard. "Your involvement with Bruce was your choice. How I responded had nothing to do with your decision to end whatever was left of our relationship."

"But Bruce looked at me differently than you did, Phil. He talked to me. And he didn't always have to rush off to some meeting."

J.P. widened his stance. "I'd have treated someone else's wife differently too, Jan." The attorney could feel his blood pressure rising but decided against leaving the room. "And how the hell do you think his wife felt when she found out about you? Did you ever stop to put yourself in her shoes?"

Janet rose from her chair, but it didn't change her height much. "Their marriage was over long before I ever entered the picture," she looked J.P. in the eye. "Maybe ours was too."

"Our marriage was over the day I came home and found you in my bed with another man." *That's a day I'll never forget.* "You made your choice."

"But you didn't even fight for me." Janet's eyes were wide with accusation. "You could have at least acted like you wanted me back. Maybe I just wanted to win your attention back. Did you ever think of that?"

Promise or no promise, she's going to hear me out this time around. "You won my attention, Jan." J.P. started into his closing argument. "Your decision to sleep with my client in my bed was enough indication. There was nothing more I needed to understand about your feelings for whatever was left of our marriage."

J.P. walked completely around the table and faced his ex-wife. *I've spoken these words a million times in my mind.* He balanced his weight on the tabletop with his fingertips.

"Until that day I would have gone to bat for our marriage. I'd have bent over backwards to give our boys a fighting chance at a family. But I was not going to stoop low enough to take my wife back after she willingly climbed onto another woman's husband. The choice you made is the one we've all learned to live with, Janet Hamilton. And now you get to live with that bastard for the rest—"

"Counselor."

Mike.

"May I have a word with you?"

J.P. took one last look at his ex-wife. The tears that had formed in her eyes were now spilling onto her cheeks. *I waited ten years to speak those words. Now that they're out, I'm content to let them lie.*

Mike was walking very quickly toward the front doors of the courthouse. "I don't know what in hell's name was going on in there, and to be honest I don't care if I ever know," Mike continued to walk. "But I need you to pull yourself together and get a grip before you sign the paper with the judge that says you are now legal guardian of your sons." Mike's pace didn't slow as he pushed the heavy door open into the sunshine.

J.P. stepped outside, glad to be out of the building—glad to be out of Janet's presence. His mind was reeling with memories that hadn't surfaced for years.

"Damn it, J.P., I leave you alone with the woman for five minutes and you're engaged in a domestic discussion from eons ago."

"How much did you hear?"

"Enough to know you were out of line."

"She opened the can of worms—"

"I don't give a shit who opened what." Mike made hard eye contact. "You're the dad today. Did you forget? James needs a father and you're on the verge of denying him any hope of stability."

"I didn't forget."

"Then act like it." Mike straightened J.P.'s shoulders. "Whatever was going on in that room is ancient history. Let it go."

J.P. tried to pull free of Mike's hands. *She had no right to bring that bastard into my bed!*

"You hear me?" Mike's voice was calm but firm. "Let it go. Walk it off. Run it off. Do whatever you gotta do to get it out of your system because in twenty minutes you're going to stand before the judge and sign for custodial rights. They need you to be in a stable presence of mind."

"What do you mean *they*?"

"I'm putting both Josh and James on the custodial papers. Josh can decide where he wants to live, but you're going to have legal rights for both until DHS is done with the case." Mike released his hold on J.P.'s shoulders. "Twenty minutes and she's a timely judge." Mike lifted his wrist so J.P. could check the time.

J.P. took a deep breath.

"Be in her chambers in twenty minutes and leave the baggage behind." Mike started to go back inside the building but turned with one last instruction. "And you don't have permission to talk to *anyone* between now and then. You hear?" Mike disappeared behind the heavy door.

J.P. wished for his running shoes and a pair of shorts. *I didn't involve myself with the intent of becoming a fulltime father.* He started down the stairs toward the parking lot. *But James doesn't have anywhere else to go either.*

Shit. He stopped walking in the shade of a maple tree. *Just like she controlled the circumstances in the divorce, she's controlling them again.* J.P. put his hands on his hips. *Things didn't work out so well for her with Bruce, so once again she's tampering with my life.*

J.P. noticed Janet's Oldsmobile drive into the parking lot. *Josh must be out of school.* In a moment's time Josh was out of the car headed for the courthouse. *He's a good kid.* Josh ascended the steps two at a time. *He deserves better than he's getting.* Josh disappeared into the building. *They both deserve better.* J.P. sighed heavily. *But how am I supposed to work them into my schedule after all this time?*

It was almost time to meet the judge. *As much as I'd like to spend more time with the boys, signing for custody now feels like wicked revenge.* J.P. began back up the concrete staircase. *It's like Jan finally has me right where she wants me.* He opened the heavy doors and stepped out of the sunlight into the dimly lit hallway of the courthouse.

31 *The Setup*

Samira

Even though it's Saturday, I'm glad I went in to work for a while. Samira stepped into the kitchen from the garage and came face to face with her daughters. *It feels good to get a head start on next week already.*

"We got the towels folded and put away." Krissy's eyes were hopeful.

"And I unloaded the dishwasher," Kara added. "And dusted the living room for good measure."

Wow. They really worked for this privilege.

"And," Krissy emphasized the word. "We got the downstairs ready for a sleepover complete with air mattresses and everything."

Step aside, ladies. Samira waved her hands. The girls backed up into the kitchen as their mother moved forward. "I'm impressed."

"Please, please can we go to the movies and then have Paula and Renee spend the night, Mama?" Krissy's hands were folded like a prayer.

"You promised if we got our chores done while you were at the library..."

I know what I promised. "Have I ever not followed through on a promise?" *And it is nice to have a head start on the housework too.* "Thank you for going the extra mile too. Go ahead and call the girls."

Neither girl budged. *So why are they not racing for the telephone?* Samira raised an eyebrow.

"We called them already." Krissy freckles all bunches together when she wrinkled her face. "And Susan said you were going to help her pick out fabric for her curtains."

"She said she'll be here in an hour or so to pick us up." Kara added carefully.

"Oh, she did, did she?" Samira sighed. *I knew there would be repercussions for missing the picnic, but I didn't know it would entail spending an entire Saturday afternoon with Susan.* Now there was no backing out.

Samira sank into the sofa and pulled a throw pillow onto her lap. "I don't feel like being Susan's decorator today." *Or any other day, really.*

"At least she's taking you out to dinner while we're at the movies," Kara pointed out.

Which nullifies any chance of having dinner tonight with Phil. Samira sighed. *Again.* Meals with Susan were stressful for a variety of reasons. *All I want to do right now is unwind for a few minutes.* When the phone rang Samira chose to let the girls answer.

"It's for you, Mama," Krissy announced with a smile. "And I don't think you're going to want to miss it."

Probably Susan. "Hello?"

"She's quite a chatter box."

Phil. Samira put her hand to her forehead and pushed her hair back from her face. "Yes, she is. I'm sorry about that."

"No need to be." Phil paused. "Sounds like your evening is a little tied up though."

"Oh, so you know my social agenda, do you?" The question slipped out of Samira's mouth before she realized her tone. "What did Krissy tell you?"

"That you have a hot date."

"No way." Samira was immediately on her feet. *Surely that's not what Krissy said.*

"Not really." Phil was laughing. "I just wanted to get your reaction."

Well, he got one. "That's not fair," Samira sat back down.

"Probably not." There was a slight pause. "I didn't get you called back yesterday. I forgot I had to make an appearance at a study session for my intern. That appearance lasted until almost midnight."

He doesn't sound any too thrilled about that. "How'd he do?"

"Do with what?"

"The studying."

"Oh."

He always seems to be surprised when I ask a personal question.

"They did fine. There's four of them working together. Derek should pass without any trouble." The business tone that had slipped into Phil's voice shifted again. "So, you're all booked up tonight, huh?"

Samira sat back down and drew her knees into her chest allowing the cushions on the sofa to close in around her. "I'm afraid I am." *But not by choice.* "This is payback for the picnic I skipped mid-week."

"Paybacks are hell."

Samira nodded into the phone. "You have no idea."

"Well, I need to get some work done at the office in preparation for next week anyway. Just thought we might be able to catch a bite to eat somewhere."

"If I understand correctly, we're doing a little shopping, and then meeting up with Susan's husband for dinner while the girls are at the movies this afternoon." Samira twisted her hair in her fingers.

There was a delay in Phil's response. "Are you free later on?"

Samira shook her head slowly. "The girls are having a double slumber party." On a second thought she added, "But you're welcome to stop over."

"At a slumber party?" Phil sounded surprised. "I don't know if that's a good idea or not."

"Well," Samira considered the alternative of not seeing Phil at all. "You can think about it. They'll be downstairs eating snacks and watching movies."

"I'll give you a call when I'm wrapping up at the office."

It seemed like Phil wanted to talk about something more, but as had happened before, the telephone just didn't seem to be close enough. *I feel badly I had to turn him down for this evening. He sounds lonely. Or maybe he's tired.*

She was just ready to put the phone back on the charger when Susan rang the back doorbell and let herself into the kitchen. *So much for my down time.*

"Ready to go, girlfriend?" Susan looked anxious. "Joey is with my mother, Sam is on the golf course and the girls are in the van. Where do you want their sleeping bags?"

Samira pointed to the laundry room. "Right there is fine. They're sleeping downstairs so they can have their privacy." *And maybe so I can have mine.*

Krissy and Kara appeared in the living room. *My goodness. Make up. Hair done. Different clothes. Must be a serious shopping spree.* The girls looked so much older all done up. *Won't be long and there will be boys picking up Krissy and Kara for the movies.* That thought sent a shudder up Samira's spine. *I'm not ready for that.*

~~~~~~~

Samira followed behind Susan at the fabric store. *It's a beautiful day.* She ran her hand over a patterned bolt. *I could be in my garden.*

"What do you think?" Susan tossed a sofa pillow onto a swatch of fabric. "Is it close enough?"

No. That's not it. "Not if you want the greens to match."
~~~~~~~

Susan was impatiently turning the fabrics over and over. *A few more mismatches and she'll make the decision whether the fabrics match or not.*

An electronic version of the William Tell Overture sounded. Susan flopped her oversized purse onto a fabric table and began to dig for the ringing cell phone. *The best-suited fabric for the project is over here.* Samira pulled a perfect match from the rack and unrolled a yard to get the effect.

This is the one I would choose. Samira carried the bolt back to where Susan was standing. *But convincing Susan will be another issue.* The sofa pillow matched the colors perfectly. *I knew it.*

"Oh, do you think?" Susan sounded doubtful. "I'd pictured a solid."

"Everything else in your living room is a solid. A pattern will add texture and depth." Susan shook her head. "Your living room could be on HGTV. Mine will be lucky to have matching greens." The woman turned the bolt this way and that. "But I trust your opinion. You're the decorator. But Sam's going to hate it."

Samira could have lived without the rhetoric reply. *Why does she even bring me along if she really does not want my opinion?*

"Speaking of Sam," Susan continued without realizing the insult. "He's off the course now so we can meet him as soon as we're ready."

Samira checked her watch. The movie was just starting. *This is going to drag on way too long. I can feel it coming.*

"We'll go eat and then come back for the girls," Susan rambled on as she carried the decorative fabric to the service counter. "Twelve yards, please," she told the clerk. "Did I tell you Sam's new golf partner was eating with us?"

What? "Tonight?" *I should have known a Saturday evening outing with Susan would include a set up.*

"In a few minutes." Susan paid the clerk. "It's no big deal or anything so don't get all worked up about it. I haven't met him yet either."

But I don't want to meet him. Anxiety set in on the way to the restaurant. Susan chattered on and on about her golf lessons but Samira's efforts to act interested were in vain. *I hate it when she does this to me.*

Susan barged into the dining area. Samira followed with sweaty palms and a nervous stomach.

"Relax, girlfriend." Susan patted Samira's arm. "I'm sure you'll like him. Sam talks about him all the time."

I wish they wouldn't talk about me. A few moments passed before Sam appeared. He waved across the room as the hostess escorted them toward the table.

"He looks like a dream." Susan chirped.

I don't even want to look. Samira put her hand on her stomach. *These setups are always a disaster.* Samira arranged a cloth napkin on her lap. *I don't even have my own transportation, so I'm stuck here.* She took a long drink of water trying to hide behind the glass.

"Hey Samira." Sam gave Samira a squeeze around the shoulders.

Samira forced a smile. *It's always good to see Sam.*

"Susan, this is my golf partner."

Samira's eyes widened as she recognized the face. *What are the chances?* She put her almost empty glass back on the table.

"And this is our friend, Samira Cartwright." Sam continued the introductions. "Ladies, meet Mike Benson."

Susan gushed an overly friendly greeting and invited Mike to sit down next to Samira. Contrary to Susan's suggestive motions, Mike chose the chair across from Samira. Susan mimed for Sam to switch places, but Sam was oblivious.

Samira dared to glance over the top of her menu. Mike wiggled his bushy eyebrows and returned a boyish grin from under his full moustache. *Obviously, he remembers me.* Samira looked back to the menu, but nothing was coming into focus. *If I had any appetite before, it's vanished.*

"That's breakfast," Sam whispered. "Dinner is over here." Without permission Sam turned the menu pages then went back to his own menu.

I need to focus. Samira inhaled very slowly. She could feel Mike's eyes on her again. *I hope he doesn't let Sam and Susan know we've met before.* She emptied her water glass. *Why am I suddenly so thirsty?*

Are you ready to order?" A waiter knelt beside the table and made eye contact with Samira. She opened her mouth to speak.

"Just bring me the Club Sandwich with fries. Ranch dressing on the side, please." Susan closed her menu and handed it across Samira to the waiter. The waiter jotted a note on his pad then looked back to Samira.

I have no idea what I want. "Go ahead," she told Sam quietly.

Sam and Mike both placed their orders while Samira scanned the choices again.

"How about an Italian Grilled Chicken salad?"

"Would you like the sandwich with fries, Ma'am?"

Samira shook her head at the waiter. "No thank you."

"She's always watching her diet," Susan announced as if Samira couldn't hear. "But just look at her figure. You wouldn't think she'd need to be worried at all, would you?"

She's always making remarks about my eating habits. Samira handed the menu to the waiter. Her shoulders were now stiff with tension. *What I really need is a glass of water.*

Mike stopped the waiter before he walked away. "Could you please refill the lady's water upon your return?"

That was very insightful of him. Samira thanked Mike with her eyes, and he nodded slightly in return. *It's rare someone takes care of me, especially when Susan is involved.*

Dinner conversation was mostly about golf. Samira listened. *I don't know enough about golf to offer anything anyway.* Samira took another drink of water. *However, I do know more now than I did a few weeks back.*

"You haven't eaten much," Susan pointed out as she pushed her clean plate to the center of the table.

My appetite faded when you mentioned a guest at dinner. Samira glanced across the table. *And it dissipated completely when the guest turned out to be Mike Benson.*

Sam tried to smooth over Susan's frankness, but it just magnified the issue. *I wish they wouldn't talk about me while I'm sitting right here.* Mike winked over the marital discussion going back and forth across the table.

Samira was relieved when Susan's telephone finally rang. Just like before, she flopped the heavy bag onto the corner of the table and began to dig.

There's a whole other reason to not have a cell phone. It seems so rude to be interrupted at any given moment by a phone call.

"Sorry, Samira." Sam apologized as Susan stepped away. "She just doesn't think before she speaks."

"Actually, she speaks what she thinks," Samira corrected gently. "It's okay." *That's just Susan. Unfortunately.*

Sam patted Samira's hand. "You're too forgiving."

Sometimes.

"Sam, are you finished?" Susan returned to the table and leaned over the back of her chair to pick up her purse. "Mom has to leave and needs us to pick Joey up before we get the girls from the movie."

Sam frowned and waved his hand over his plate. "I wouldn't mind finishing." There was new tension in his voice.

Now even Sam is uncomfortable in front of his friend.

"Where's your car?"

"At the club." Sam took a bite.

"I can drop you off there on my way to Mom's."

And my car is home in my garage.

"I guess I can be ready," Sam sounded disgusted. He rolled his eyes at Mike as he pushed his chair back from the table. "What about you, Samira, are you...?"

"Oh my god." Susan remembered out loud. "I forgot you were with me too. I told Mom I'd be there in a few minutes."

"I can take her home, not to worry." Mike jumped into the conversation.

The lump that had been in Samira's stomach immediately lodged in her throat. *Oh, no. That's not okay.*

"Are you okay with that?" Susan asked abruptly.

No.

"I'm okay with it," Mike answered. "You guys go do what you have to do, and I'll take care of the lady."

He's called me 'lady' twice now.

Sam grinned at his friend. "Are you sure?"

If I didn't know better, I'd think Susan had this planned.

Mike stood when Sam stood. "It's not a problem, really." He winked at Samira. "I don't mind at all."

Sam walked backwards, eyeing his friend. They exchanged a thumbs up sign.

"Sam will bring the girls by after the movies, all right Samira?" Susan hollered over her shoulder as she walked away.

"As if you've had a say in any of this." Mike added as he returned to his dinner. "She's a character."

Samira blinked in unbelief. "I'm sorry." *What just happened here?* "I can call my brother for a ride. He lives close."

"Nonsense," Mike interrupted. "Relax and enjoy your meal. I'll run you home."

Samira surveyed the situation. *I don't know what it is about Mike Benson, but I trust him.* She thanked him and went back to lunch.

Mike flagged the waiter. "Would you care for anything to drink?"

You know, I would. "Iced tea would be very nice."

Mike ordered a cold draft along with the tea. "So, how have you been, Samira?"

I'm not particularly good at small talk. "I've been good." *I wonder if he knows I've been to Springfield with Phil.* "Summertime is always an adjustment at my house but we're settling in."

"Are you a schoolteacher?"

"No, I work at the Maple Street Library, but my girls are out of school for the summer. Their freedom seems to affect my schedule." *I haven't given out that much information to a man in a long time.* Samira glanced at Mike and found his blue eyes twinkling with energy.

"How old are your girls?"

"Thirteen and fourteen."

"I can understand why your life gets a bit hectic in the summer then." Mike smiled easily. When his beer arrived, he took care to enjoy the first sip.

"How do you know Sam and Susan?"

Samira wiped her fingers on a napkin. "Let's see, I've known them since, well, I guess since Kara, my oldest, was in preschool. Our girls are the same ages. They were good family friends while—" Samira pictured park picnics with Tom and the girls. "I've known them a long time." She immediately forced the memories back into the archives.

Mike nodded as he took another drink from his draft. He sat the beer on the table and leaned into the table.

"So, what brings you to dinner with them tonight?"

Samira was somewhat overwhelmed with all the questions. *At least he's easy to talk to.* "That's a good question." *I wondered that myself.* "I think I'm here as a result of a guilty conscience."

"Really," Mike seemed intrigued. "Do tell."

Samira had to smile at his demeanor. *This is kind of like a personal counseling session.* "I stood Susan up at a mother-daughter picnic earlier in the week so tonight I'm paying my dues."

Mike opened his arms to the space around the table. "I don't see any mothers with daughters here."

True statement. She was beginning to enjoy his company. "Okay, then let's just say I was strong-armed into dinner with her and Sam. You just happened to come along as a surprise."

"Ditto." The curls on the top of Mike's head bobbed when he nodded his head. "I think we were set up."

Samira set her salad to the side. *I think I'm getting full.* "You may be exactly right about that."

Mike cocked his head in thought. "I don't know much about Sam and Susan, but I have this friend. I'm thinking you might know him. He has many aliases. Phil Ralston?"

"Another being J.P. Ralston?"

"One in the same," Mike continued. "I know him well. If he knew I was sitting here with his date, he'd kick my ass."

I wonder if he knew Phil and I had hoped to have dinner together tonight. "What do you think we should do about that?"

Mike leaned into the table again. "I'm thinking when we leave here, I take you straight to your house and we forget we ever saw one another. I happen to like my ass as it is."

Samira laughed. *Surely, he's exaggerating.*

"No, seriously, Samira." Mike's face became very earnest. "He'll beat the shit out of me if he thinks I stole his date tonight. Trust me on this one."

He must have known. "Maybe I could talk to him for you." Samira ate a crouton from the salad. *It's the least I could do.*

"Here." Mike handed his cell phone to Samira.

I was joking.

"When he answers, get me off his hit list."

What in heaven's name am I going to say if he answers?

"Mike, what's up?"

Oh, he thinks I'm Mike. "This is Samira."

There was a long pause.

"Samira Cartwright." *I don't think this was such a good idea.*

Mike leaned back in his chair attentive to the conversation. "Tell him we're having a drink together."

I think not.

"That's not the number on the I.D."

Caller ID? Samira took a deep breath. *He knows I'm with Mike.* "I guess not." She looked at Mike. "Here, I'll let you talk to him."

Mike shook his head and moved out of reach. "You said you'd talk to him for me, remember?"

This is getting complicated. Samira gave Mike a look of warning as she put the phone back to her ear.

"Where the hell are you?" Phil's voice sounded more forceful.

I don't want to make him mad. "T-Bone's Family Restaurant."

"I thought you handed off to Mike." Phil's tone had changed dramatically. "Why T-Bone's?"

"It's a long story," Samira began. "I'm here with Mike because my girlfriend had to leave. He's going to take me home."

"Told you he'd be pissed." Mike shook his head.

I don't like being in the middle of this friendship.

"I thought you were busy tonight." Phil sounded irritated.

It's not what he's thinking. "I was, with Susan," Samira reminded back. "I just didn't know she was going to leave me here."

"Are you headed home now?"

He sounds so serious. "I think so." She looked at Mike. "Are we going home now?"

"Sure. If that's in the best interest of my well-being." Mike crossed his arms.

I wonder where Phil is. She decided to ask. "Where are you?"

"At the office." Phil hesitated a moment. "I need to finish what I'm working on then I'll meet you at your house."

"You don't have to do that." *I'd hoped he'd come by tonight, but not because he didn't trust me.* "I'll be fine."

"He's going to meet us at your place, isn't he?"

How does Mike know that?

"I knew he wouldn't trust me."

"Here, maybe you should talk to Mike." Samira stood up and handed Mike the phone. "I'll be right back." *I'm not going to give him the chance to back away again.*

A few minutes later Samira stepped out of the ladies' room to find Mike paying for her meal.

"Please, let me get it." She opened her purse.

Mike returned his wallet to his back pocket. "Too late," he stated. "Besides, I'll bill it to J.P. anyway." With that Mike wiggled his eyebrows and motioned toward the exit. "My guess is we have about five minutes to get to wherever it is you live before I'm accused of kidnapping or something far worse."

Samira was humored by Mike's inference to Phil's jealousy. When he opened the door on a shiny red sports car, she stopped in her tracks. *This is a far cry from Phil's practical pickup truck.*

Mike's hand guided her into the leather seat. "Stay low and remember, you don't know me."

Samira laughed. *He's actually quite funny.*

The drive across town was speedy and a bit too careless for Samira's taste. *But at least I can say I've lived to tell the story.* She pointed to her driveway.

"Here you are, Samira Cartwright, delivered to your house as promised." Mike pulled the emergency brake between the bucket seats. "I'd walk you to your door but am afraid that would not be in my best interest."

Samira thanked Mike for the ride. "And for dinner." She fumbled for the door handle.

"Here, sit tight." In a flash Mike was at her side opening the door for her.

Just as Mike took her hand to help her out of the low seat, another car pulled into the driveway. Kelly Davis smiled her brilliant smile and greeted Samira.

"I brought the girls over from the movies. I hope that's all right." Kelly popped out of her car and flipped her seat forward. Three teenage girls bounded out of the backseat and Krissy climbed out of the front.

"We made her scoop the loop with the top down." Krissy informed as she eyed the man standing next to Samira.

"What happened to Sam?" *I thought he was going to bring the girls home.*

"We didn't see him anywhere and the crowd was thinning," Kelly answered with a matter of fact. "I didn't want them standing around in an empty parking lot without a phone."

Yet another reference to the need for mobile phones. "When did you get home from your trip?"

"Monday." Kelly pushed the driver's seat back into position.

"How'd it go?" Samira was honestly interested.

"Fine."

"My car can do that too," Mike jumped into the already confusing conversation.

Oh, I forgot about Mike.

"Do what?" Kelly asked.

"That top-down thing."

I should introduce him to Kelly.

"Really?" Kelly put her hands on her hips and turned into the breeze to blow the curls off her face. "Prove it."

"Do we know him?" Krissy asked her mother.

No. No one knows Mike.

"Yeah, we know him. That's Mike. Dad's golf partner." Paula answered.

Paula and Renee know Mike?

"Thanks for the ride, Miss Davis." Paula turned directly to Samira. "Can I use your phone? I think I should call Dad and tell him to never mind about picking us up."

"Sure." *I guess*

Mike was busy unfastening clips along the edge of the windshield. With the push of a button, the white vinyl top lifted into the air and began to fold automatically into the space behind the seats.

That's amazing.

"Not bad, *Mike.*" Kelly emphasized his name as she reacted to the challenge. "But I bet your car can't do this." She climbed in behind the steering wheel and cranked up the sound system.

It's Aida. My favorite opera.

Mike crossed his arms and leaned back on his heels. "Miss Davis,"

Apparently, they don't need an introduction now.

"I can name that tune in 3 miles."

"Do you mind?" Kelly was looking at Samira.

"Mind what?"

Kelly removed the band holding her hair and immediately wrapped it back into a bun. "He said he could name the tune in three miles. I'm inclined to take him up on it."

"Oh. No. He's not with me."

"But she was with me." Mike jumped into his car. "Let me park in the street. I'll be right back."

Kelly turned the volume down on the sound system. "If he guesses *Giuseppe Verdi,* then he's worth hanging onto. But he's going to have to be able to spell the first name correctly." Kelly climbed into the driver's seat. "I'll let you know how he does." Kelly flashed her bright smile.

Samira suddenly realized what Kelly was thinking. "He's really not with me." She watched Mike get out of his car. "He just gave me a ride home."

"And it was my pleasure." Mike opened the passenger door. "I must say, I've played golf. Played just today in fact. But I can't say that I've ever ridden in one."

"Buckle your seat belt," Kelly instructed. "Three miles to name the tune and the composer and I'll bring you back."

Mike waved a hand into the open air above the windshield. "Tell our mutual friend I'm sorry I couldn't stick around."

Kelly put her little black car into reverse. "We'll be back."

Take your time. Samira started for the house. *That was quite a set up.* She picked up the newspaper off the porch. *Both of them.*

~~~~~~~

Samira had been home quite some time before headlights pulled into her driveway. *That was a long three miles.* She leaned into the kitchen window. *Nope, I know that truck now.*

Phil stopped just inside the front door. "Who's little black car?"

Samira craned her neck around the doorframe. *What do you know?* The top was up on Kelly's car, and it was now parked in front of her house. Mike's car was nowhere to be seen. *I wonder when they made that exchange.* She closed the door. *I bet Mrs. Barnes is having a hay day with all this activity.*

"It belongs to my girlfriend." Samira closed the door. "But not the girlfriend who made me go to dinner." *I think I'll leave that story in Mike's court.*

"Have you eaten?"

"No, I haven't." Phil closed the door and followed Samira to the kitchen. "But obviously you ate with my best friend."

Samira felt bad. "Mike and I were both set up. Neither of us knew what Susan and Sam were up to. It just turned out that way."

"So, when I talked to you earlier you really had no idea about the dinner plans?"

Samira shook her head. "I knew I was stuck going to dinner with Susan and Sam. But had no idea they had ulterior motives."

Phil helped himself to a glass of water. "You should never be *stuck*, Samira. Just tell them if you don't want to be there."

Easier said than done. "Susan has a way of weaving me into her plans."

Phil nodded and refilled the water glass. "Mike said she was a trip. I just don't like that they strong-armed you into a dinner without full disclosure."

Samira smiled at the way he was looking out for her. "Dinner with Susan is stressful even without a setup. But you're right, I do need to speak up for myself more than I do." *Especially when Susan is involved.*

Phil glanced around the room.

"The girls are downstairs with their friends."

"It took me longer to finish up than I thought." Phil was attempting to explain his delay in arriving. "I trust Mike delivered you in a timely fashion."

Samira smiled. "Very much so," she assured. "Straight home, no detours or anything." *However, he was a little liberal on the neighborhood stop signs.*

"Mike's a good guy." Phil's eyes were now focused on her every move.

I wonder what he's really thinking. Samira offered leftover tacos.

"Sounds good to me. Did you make them?"

"Yesterday. Sorry they're not fresh off the stove." Samira extracted a covered dish from the refrigerator. "Mike seemed to think you might not appreciate his assistance tonight, Mr. Ralston. He was worried you might try to rearrange his features somehow." Samira placed the taco meat in the microwave and pushed the reheat button.

Phil swiveled in the barstool as Samira walked toward him with a plate and silverware. He intercepted her at the waist and pulled her in tight against him.

"Mike knows not to mess with my territory." Phil's eyes were softer than they'd been a moment earlier. "You are a sight for sore eyes tonight, Pretty lady."

His territory? Samira crossed her wrists behind his neck. *Then I'm guessing Mike also knows I went to Springfield.* "I wouldn't want to create a rift between friends." *I think I'm*
~~~~~~~

going to kiss him.

Samira closed her eyes and allowed his lips to touch hers not only once, but more than once. By the time she was aware of footsteps on the stairs, the tacos needed reheated again. Samira reluctantly backed away and reset the microwave. *Just breathe and act normal.*

Four girls appeared in the kitchen.

"Are you cooking tacos, Mama?" Krissy sniffed the air. "They smell great. Are there more?"

"No more tacos, but plenty of chips and salsa." She poured some chips into a wooden bowl and handed Kara an already opened jar of salsa. *Back downstairs, please.*

"Can we have melted cheese?" Kara asked.

I guess.

"Here," Krissy took the chips and salsa from her sister. "You melt the cheese. We'll take this downstairs."

"Do we know him?" Renee asked. She was looking at Phil, who was watching the activity from his seat at the island.

"It's not Mike." Paula announced.

Nope. Not Mike.

"No, that's Phil." Krissy punctuated. "Hi Phil. These are our friends." The young teen held the wooden bowl over the island. "Would you like some chips?"

Phil helped himself to a chip and nodded a silent thanks.

Samira took the tacos out of the microwave. Kara took the liberty of heating the jar of cheese.

"Did we know you were coming by?" Krissy asked Phil.

Phil shook his head. "I was in the neighborhood."

"And you thought you'd stop by?" Krissy finished his sentence. "You should have called first, we could have waited to start the movie so you could join us."

He is not here to watch your movie. Samira was silently wishing for the girls to disappear back to the basement.

"I thought I'd stop to visit with your mom for a bit." Phil was grinning at Samira.

He obviously knows I'm out of my league here with him and the girls and the commotion.

"Okay then." Paula turned toward Kara. "Bring the cheese when it's ready."

Like mother like daughter, Samira thought to herself. *Paula is going to have all of Susan's lack of tact.*

By the time the girls went back downstairs, Phil was checking his phone.

I don't want him to have to leave. Samira noticed the clock on the wall. It was after ten o'clock.

"James," Phil informed. "I left him on a basketball court with my intern. They were supposed to text me when they were done."

"Do you need to pick him up?" *I hope not.*

Phil put the phone back on his hip with a natural ease. "No, Derek is dropping him off at the house. The text is my way of knowing they're on the way."

"Is James still under adult supervision?"

"To some degree." He was finished with the plate of food, but he wasn't moving away from the bar.

"How did things go for him on Thursday?" Samira slid onto the stool next to Phil. *He looks so tired.*

Phil sighed. When he spoke, his voice was distant. "Things went all right. Mike managed to get the immediate charges against James dropped, but an investigation is still pending."

Oh, yes, Mike is also a lawyer. Samira surmised. *That would account for way he questioned me at the dinner table.*

"All things considered, we're better off now than we were before the hearing."

"And that's good, right?"

"The only thing better would be if I didn't have to get back home to be a father right now." Phil's eyes reflected a gentle honesty.

Samira smiled softly and touched Phil's arm. Motherhood was not exactly her first choice in the given moment either.

"This parenting thing is a full-time job."

His eyes look heavy. "We'll just have to find our own time."

"With the kids or without?"

I was thinking without. "Why do you ask?"

Phil pulled Samira's barstool closer to his and rested his arm behind her. "I have to go out of town on business the first part of this week, but when I get back, I was thinking I'd take my boys up to my aunt and uncle's ranch." Samira could feel Phil's fingertips in her hair. "I was thinking maybe you might bring Krissy and Kara and join us."

Go out of town with my girls? With Phil and his boys? Samira ran her calendar in her mind. "That's the fourth of July weekend."

"I know." Phil's eyes were serious. "I take the boys up there every year."

And I spend every year celebrating Kara's birthday and watching fireworks with my family.

"Since you missed their little picnic thing on my account, I thought maybe we could make it up to them."

Samira considered her options. *This is a matter for family discussion.*

"Where exactly is this ranch?"

"North of Macon. It borders Mark Twain State Park."

I've never been that far north. Samira tilted her head in thought. "And what kinds of things do you do while you're there?" *Because I'm not an out-doorsy kind of person.*

Phil smiled quietly. "We eat really well because my aunt is a great cook. We sleep well because it's quiet there. We hike and fish and ride horses sometimes. Sometimes we take a dip in the lake." Phil raised his shoulders. "Basically, whatever you want to do." He winked. "You can read your book for long periods of time without any interruption if that's what you choose to do."

Samira smiled. *I like the way he thinks of me.* "I'll talk to the girls." *Hard to tell what their reaction will be.*

"You can let me know." Phil seemed to be shifting gears. "I fly out tomorrow afternoon and get back late Wednesday. I won't leave for the ranch until after work on Friday."

Samira avoided eye contact, but she nodded her head. *What I'd really hoped was to see him maybe tomorrow afternoon when he isn't so tired, and it wasn't so late.*

Phil lifted her face to his and she returned his kiss again. This time he didn't hang on. When she walked him to the door, she could feel the weight of unspoken thoughts lingering between them.

"Be in touch, all right? My cell phone rings even when I'm out of town."

At least I have permission to call. "Hurry back."

"Only three days."

Three long days.

He kissed her on the forehead then turned and walked out the door.

He has no idea how much comfort that little kiss brings me.

Samira waited until he drove away before she closed the door. Kelly's car was still parked out front. *It must be nice to have such freedom.*

Suddenly the restraints of parenthood seemed overwhelming. Samira leaned heavily on the door with her face in her hands. The emptiness deep inside echoed the reality of her singleness. *My desires taunt me even more when he's here and I can't have him.*

"More chips, Mama."

Until I met Phil, I was simply a mom, and I made that enough. Samira slowly lifted her weight off the door. *But now I've crossed a line.*

Samira refilled the wooden bowl with tortilla chips.

"Did Phil leave already?" Krissy asked innocently.

"Yeah, he went home to..." *He went home to be a dad.*

Krissy tipped her head in anticipation.

"It was getting late."

"Too bad he couldn't have stayed longer." Krissy turned toward the basement steps again. "Thanks for the chips."

'Too bad' is an understatement. Samira gathered Phil's dinner dishes. *I have a feeling he needs me too.* Girlish laughter echoed up the stairwell. *How will we ever be able to fulfill our needs for one another and still carry out the responsibilities of parenthood?* She rinsed the dirty dishes. *Things could get complicated very quickly.*

32 Settled In

Joseph Phillip

Josh grinned. "Relax, Dad. She's still back there."

"I know." J.P. had to look anyway. *Just to make sure she's still following in her car.*

"I'll let you know if she drops out of my mirror." Josh was driving his father's pick up. "We're not that far out now anyway."

That's true. J.P. was glad Josh was driving. *This has been a hellacious week.* "You and James got along alright with Derek then?"

"He's cool." Josh answered with a shrug. "I can see why you needed me around to chauffeur James during the daytime." Josh raised his eyebrows. "You got him scheduled tight enough?"

"That's so I can keep track of him." He looked at James, sound asleep in the seat behind him.

"Do you really need to know where he is at five in the morning?"

"Yep." *The earlier he gets up, the earlier he goes to bed at night.* "But Derek did alright?"

"I like having Derek stay over better than hanging out at Denise's place while you're out of town."

Denise would agree. If he looked exactly right, J.P. could see Samira's car in the right-hand mirror. *Samira sounded excited to be coming up here when I talked to her on the phone.* He watched her car in the distance. *But her disposition in person wasn't as promising.*

"You can sleep if you want to, Dad." Josh was looking at his father.

Do I look that tired? "That's alright—" *But it would feel good to close my eyes for a little while.*

"I'm going to get you to the ranch either way. You might as well take advantage."

J.P. studied his son. *He's confident. He's dependable.* The father adjusted his seat to tilt a little further back. *And he's got a good point.* J.P. closed his eyes.

~~~~~~~

The engine shifted into a lower gear. *Are we there yet?* J.P. forced himself awake. James was stirring too.

"Slow down on the gravel. The dust will make it harder for Samira to follow." J.P. gave the instruction as he moved his seat back into the upright position.

Josh obeyed and let off the accelerator. "What kind of a name is Samira, anyway?"

The kind of name for a pretty lady. "I don't know."

"Never heard it before."

Me neither. J.P. twisted in his seat to stretch his back muscles. He was relieved to finally be arriving at the ranch. *I just hope bringing Samira here with her daughters is a good idea.* J.P. watched the dust behind his truck drift off into a field. *Something in the way she looked at me today tells me she's having second thoughts.*

Josh turned into the lane and followed the drive to the end of the sidewalk. J.P. watched Samira pull her car in behind. *And here comes Aunt Maggie. She's always happy to see us, even if we bring an entourage of strangers into her house.*

"Oh Phillip," Aunt Maggie gushed. "It's so good to see you." She threw her arms into the air so J.P. could give her a hug. "Uncle Roy went into town for supplies."
~~~~~~~

Supplies. J.P. shook his head slightly. *You'd think they lived in the outback or something.* He watched Samira climb out of her car. *Uncle Roy probably went to town to get a gallon of milk.* Krissy and Kara joined their mother in the driveway. *I still can't believe I brought a woman, and her daughters, to the ranch.* J.P. ran his hand through his hair.

James purposely bumped his father's arm as he walked past. "She looks a little uptight."

I hate to admit it, but he's right. He watched his big black Lab take another lap around the barnyard. *At least the dog is happy to be here.*

"Maybe she's just nervous," Josh added with a firm pat to his father's broad shoulders.

We can only hope.

J.P. took a deep breath and opened his arm to Samira as she stepped up next to him. *If the tension in her shoulders is any indication, I'd say she's more than a little on edge. Let's get the introductions out of the way.* "Samira, this is my aunt, Maggie."

"And these must be your beautiful girls," Aunt Maggie exclaimed. "Welcome to the ranch."

J.P. took the liberty to properly introduce Krissy and Kara to Aunt Maggie. *They only spent a couple of minutes with the boys.* J.P. decided to reintroduce James and Josh as well.

"This looks like a blast." Krissy's eyes were wide with wonder. "Do we get to sleep in that big cabin?"

At least one of them has a sense of adventure.

"Absolutely," Aunt Maggie answered with a hearty laugh. "Come on inside. The boys can show you around."

James tilted his head at his father in silent protest. The father raised an eyebrow in warning.

"Alright." James sighed. "Come on." He waved his arm for Krissy and Kara to follow him into the house.

Thank you. J.P. watched Krissy skip up the sidewalk to catch up. *Where's Kara?*

J.P. turned around and found her face to face with her mother. Kara's arms were crossed, and she wasn't showing any signs of Krissy's enthusiasm whatsoever.

This could be trouble. He observed the two women exchange a nonverbal point of contention. *This is no doubt half of Samira's problem.*

"I bet you're famished," Aunt Maggie clapped her hands. "I made cherry pies this afternoon." She turned toward the house. "Come on in, we'll get the bags later."

Samira had already opened her trunk. *I guess she's going to get her bags now. The least I can do is help carry them inside.* There were only two bags for the three women.

"You pack lighter than any women I've ever traveled with," J.P. innocently noticed out loud.

"And how many women might that be?"

Where did that come from?

Samira lifted the first bag from the trunk.

"Here, let me help you."

"That's alright," Samira stopped J.P. from helping. "We'll get them."

Alright. J.P. pulled his hand back. *This is certainly a new side of her.* He watched Kara take one of the bags and start for the house. *We can hope she loses the attitude.*

Kara dropped her bag at the end of the sidewalk and impatiently crossed her arms.

I could offer to fix Kara's attitude. He glanced in Samira's direction. *Or I could stay out of it and give her some space.* J.P. decided on the latter. He walked back to his truck and began to unsnap the tarp. *What the hell?* He watched Josh pick up Kara's bag. *She's following him into the house.* Now Samira was waiting on him.

J.P. lifted his own duffel out of the truck. It felt strange to carry his own bag but not hers. *But she had her chance and turned it down. I'll be damned if I'm going to offer again.* He opened the front door. Before crossing the threshold, he took one last purposeful breath of fresh air. *Just in case the walls start to close in.*

"Go on up, honey," Aunt Maggie was talking to Samira. She waved her hand toward the wrap-around staircase. "Your room is straight at the top of the stairs. Just make yourself right at home." Aunt Maggie smiled warmly at Phil. "I'll have your pie ready when you come back down."

As soon as Samira was around the bend in the staircase Aunt Maggie spoke. "It's okay, Phillip. She just needs to get settled. Why don't you come on in and have some pie?"

Obviously, Aunt Maggie is aware of the tension too. He stared at the staircase. *Cherry pie doesn't even sound good now.*

"I think I'll go close up the barn." *Anything to get out of this house till this dust settles.*

"Oh nonsense. Roy will be back in a jiffy. You just come on in and relax a bit." Aunt Maggie headed for the kitchen.

Relax? J.P. dropped his bag at the bottom of the stairs then made an exit through the front door. *I don't know if that's possible.*

"Dad." Josh's voice stopped J.P. in the open door. "Aren't you coming in for pie? It's still warm and Aunt Maggie has homemade ice cream to go with."

"I'll be back." *Eventually.* "You guys go ahead." *Don't wait on me.* He watched Kara follow Josh into the kitchen. *Whatever Josh did to win her over seems to have eased her attitude.* He could still feel the sting of Samira's tone. *But there's still an attitude to contend with at the top of the stairs.*

J.P. stepped out onto the porch. *It's a little damp, but not too cool yet.* He placed his foot on the porch railing and stretched one leg and then the other. *The sooner I work off my own stress, the sooner the weekend can begin.*

Chase fell into step as J.P. picked up his pace. *A good, hard run won't hurt a thing.* By the time he reached the lake, J.P. was in full stride. The sun was just starting to dip over the horizon casting an orange glow onto the water.

J.P. slowed to a stop. He leaned over and put his hands on his knees. Chase bounded on by and rushed directly into the cool water. The canine returned a few moments later soaking wet. J.P. took off back toward the house. *Before Chase has a chance to shake himself dry.*

At least she has her own car in the case she decides she can't stick around. J.P. slowed his pace as he approached the barn. Sweat was pouring off his body, but he felt better having spent his own energy. *What made me invite her here anyway?* He pulled his shirt off over his head and used it as a sweat rag. *Had I anticipated the attitude, I'd have skipped the notion.*

Once inside the barn, J.P. leaned into the wall and stretched his hamstrings. *Maybe she'll decide she can't stay.* J.P. changed his stance and stretched the other leg. *And what's with the cheap shot about how many women I've traveled with anyway?*

Chase trotted into the barn and greeted the horses before heading back out into the twilight. *I'll finish choring for Uncle Roy while I'm out here.* J.P. started toward the horse stalls to close the windows. *Don't know if I'm ready to face her yet anyway.* Instead of opening the gate, J.P. simply lifted himself over the metal rungs. *She pisses me off.* He stopped to greet Claire and allowed the old mare to nuzzle her soft nose into his hand. *Women. There's a breed I have yet to master.*

J.P. thought he heard Chase. *I don't want him to startle the horses.* He turned to slow the dog's approach, but instead came face to face with the brown eyes of the woman he'd deserted at the house.

Samira.

She stopped walking.

She is beautiful. He turned away long enough to close the wooden shutter over the open window. *But I don't have the slightest idea what makes her tick.* When he turned around Samira hadn't moved. *And she sure knows how to piss me off.* She was still watching him. *What am I supposed to do with her now?*

J.P. slowly lifted himself back over the gate. Several yards separated them. *The last attempt to communicate with her didn't exactly go well.*

"What's on your mind, Pretty Lady?" *As if that's something I really want to know right now.* He tried to sound less irritated than he felt.

Samira's head fell forward, and she put her hands behind her back. He watched as she gathered her thoughts. When she looked up her face was serious.

She probably told her girls to meet her in the car.

"I came to..."

Just get it over with, then we can both get on with our weekend. J.P. draped his arm over the gate and stared at the wall on the far side of the barn.

"Well, I came to apologize. I'm sorry. I was out of line."

That's not what I was expecting. J.P. listened to Samira's apology replay in his mind. *Tell her she doesn't have to be sorry.* J.P. opened his mouth to speak, but she was moving toward him, and he couldn't force any words to officially form.

"This has been a really stressful week," Samira was explaining as she walked. "And then Kara, well—"

You don't have to explain anything to me.

"Kara and I are experiencing some differences in opinions, and, well..." Samira stopped walking just a few feet from the stall. "I'm just sorry, that's all."

Chase suddenly lost attentiveness in the discussion and quickly darted back outside.

Say something. Anything, Ralston. J.P. finally found his tongue. "You don't have to be."

"Yes, I do." Samira threw her head back and shook her hair off her shoulders.

Don't do that, Samira. The summer breeze coming in through Toby's window was cool against J.P.'s bare, damp chest. *Hard to stay pissed at her if she's sorry.* J.P. crossed his arms to divert a shiver.

Samira's eyes were still low when she spoke again. "Maybe we could start all over. You know, pretend like we're just arriving or something," Samira suggested. Her serious face was fading into a girlish grin.

At least she's not packed to leave. J.P. decided to play along. "Like go back to the driveway again?"

"Well, maybe not quite that literally, but at least start our time together all over." Samira's hair was gently blowing in the breeze.

I could easily keep her alone in the barn with me for the rest of the night. "Welcome to the barn, Miss Cartwright." J.P. put his foot on the bottom rung of Toby's gate and swung his leg to the other side. *The further I stay away from her, the better chance she has of making it back to the house with her clothes on.* "I'd like for you to meet Toby." J.P. patted the horse's shoulder as he walked across the stall. "And next door is his mate, Claire." J.P. reached to pull the window closed.

Samira stepped up to the stall. When J.P. walked back to the fence, Toby followed. He stuck his big horse nose over the top of the gate. Obviously startled, Samira took a step backwards.

J.P. folded his arms on the top of the gate and watched Samira through the top two rungs. *She's out of my league.* Her brown eyes sparkled in the dim lights of the barn. *Gorgeous. Complex. And plain irritating sometimes.*

"Very pleased to meet you," Samira told the big brown stud. "And the same for you, Claire." Her eyes turned to the old mare.

Chase bounded in with a quick bark and gave Toby a start. The big horse tapped his hooves quickly in place. Samira jumped as well.

"Whoa, boy." J.P. steadied Toby with his hand.

The barn suddenly filled with an obnoxious, husky singing voice, "Oh give me a home where the buffalo roam...and the deer and the ante..." Uncle Roy stopped mid lyric. He stared at Samira.

Uncle Roy, you are a trip. J.P. climbed out of the stall and offered his uncle an open hand. "Uncle Roy, this is Samira."

Uncle Roy let out a hearty laugh. "Well, she gave me a start, she did." The old man wrapped his big hand around his nephew's. "What happened to your shirt, boy?"

"I took it off after my run." *Probably does look a little misleading.* He glanced at the nail where he'd left it hanging and noticed it was no longer there. Next thing he knew Roy was handing it over.

"Best to keep your clothes on," Roy winked. "Mighty pleased to meet you ma'am," the wise old uncle nodded a greeting to Samira. "You've got a couple of good-looking girls in my kitchen."

J.P. shook out his shirt, but it was saturated in sweat. *I have no intention of putting this thing back on.*

"Let me get the grain sack ready for morning then I'll close her up the rest of the way." Uncle Roy looked at J.P. "I hear Aunt Maggie's cherry pie calling your name, so you won't want to tarry."

Now the pie sounds good. J.P. reached for Samira's hand and led her into the barnyard. Josh and James almost had their tent assembled in the yard.

"Did Uncle Roy find you?" The voice came from inside the tent.

"Yeah, he did." *I can't tell their voices apart anymore.* He pulled back the flap to see which of his sons had spoken. James was standing right inside. He grinned. Josh appeared from around the outside corner.

"Hey, Dad," Josh looked frustrated. "Can you hold this stake? The ground is so hard I can't get it pounded in far enough." J.P. followed Josh to the darkest side of the yard. "I can't hold it and keep it taunt at the same time."

J.P. tossed his shirt into the grass and knelt to get a good grip. He gave a big tug. The first time nothing happened, but Josh indicated for him to pull it tighter. Just as the hammer connected with the stake, the opposite corner pulled loose collapsing the entire structure.

Samira laughed out loud.

It is good to hear her laugh. Maybe we can salvage this rendezvous after all.

But the boys weren't laughing, and they weren't appreciative of Samira's humor either. James climbed out of the canvas ready to accuse his brother.

"He did it." Josh pointed to his father.

J.P. threw his hands out in surrender. "All right," he told the boys as he stood up again. "Here." He handed Josh one corner and James another. "Samira, are you honed up on your camping skills?"

Samira wasn't laughing now.

This will be good for her. J.P. walked around and handed her a third corner. "Hold this. He picked up the small sledgehammer and claimed the fourth corner. "Okay, pull." Two of the tent corners pulled tight, but the third was hanging loosely in the breeze.

"Hey, Samira, you're supposed to hold on when we pull," Josh teased.

Samira was once again pulling her corner and the look of determination on her face told J.P. she was going to give it a good shot.

Alright, let's try it again. He gave them the indication to pull it again. This time he was able to get his stake in the ground without anyone letting go.

The next two corners staked quickly. *This old tent might be useable again.* J.P. moved around to the last corner and told Samira to pull it tight. As she did, J.P. hooked a stake through the loop and proceeded to pound it into the ground. *One more strike ought to hold it.*

It was almost secure when Samira let out a scream and let go of the string.

What the hell? J.P. looked in time to see Josh dive over the stake and break Samira's fall. *They're both going down.*

"Hey, get this thing off of me." James was yelling from somewhere in the heap of canvas.

Now Samira was laughing hysterically.

At least she's laughing. J.P. located the sledgehammer in the pile of rubble. *But I have no idea what triggered that.*

"What happened?" James asked as he beat the tent off his body.

A dripping wet Chase was sitting in the darkness with his head low in embarrassment.

"Looks like the mutt did a little fishing." Josh pointed. A partial fish was laying on the ground next to Chase's foot. "He didn't mean to scare you. He was just showing off his catch."

Samira pushed her hair out of her face and took a step away from the wet dog. When she backed up, she bumped into J.P. That made her jump again.

Easy there, Pretty Lady.

Samira caught her breath and laughed again.

This trip might be more than either one of us bargained for. Just touching her made his entire body tingle.

"All right." James spoke with force. "That's it. The tent goes up come hell or high water." Without hesitation he took the hammer from his father and handed it to Samira. "You knocked it down, so you get to put it back up."

No. You're not putting Samira in the middle of this. J.P. reached for the hammer, but Samira held it off to the side where he couldn't reach.

"No." J.P. wasn't going to let her pound the stakes into the ground. *Especially in the dark.*

"Do you doubt my ability?"

Is she challenging my authority? J.P. put his hands on his hips.

Josh slapped his dad on the arm. "Sounds like a challenge to me, Dad."

I would never doubt her ability. Her judgment maybe. But never her ability. J.P. was beginning to enjoy the game. *Okay, Pretty Lady. If you have something to prove, who am I to stand in your way?*

James took charge and pulled the first string back out into the grass. "Here you go, Samira. I'll put the stake through the loop, you pound it into the ground."

Samira followed the instructions, and the first corner went up without a hitch.

J.P. watched, surprised. *He trusts her more than I do.*

Samira did the same with Josh's string and by the time she was around to the far side James was holding the third stake. J.P. listened as the hammer connected with the metal stakes three, then four times.

Not bad. I must say she has—

"Oh, no."

What now?

"Look out." One of the boys sounded distressed, but J.P. didn't know which one. "Oh, man. Are you all right?"

J.P. wasn't going to wait any longer. He let go of his corner and hurried around to where the boys were hovered over Samira. *What is going on?* J.P. still couldn't see what was wrong. *Back off.* He pushed Josh out of the way and dropped one knee to the ground. Samira was sitting on the ground, and she appeared to be laughing, but it was too dark to tell for sure. He started to reach for her hand but the next thing he knew, the tent was coming down over the top of both him and Samira.

And this time it isn't Samira's fault. J.P. caught his balance in a full straddle over her and held out his arms to keep the canvas from separating him from Samira.

Samira covered her head with her hands. "I think we've been set up."

Is that what's going on here? J.P. realized the situation too late. He took advantage of the private moment and stole a kiss from the lady on the ground before James and Josh pretended to rescue them.

J.P. couldn't see Samira's face very well, but he could feel her. *And she feels mighty inviting.* He took her hand in his and gently pulled her into a sitting position. James and Josh were working to uncover them from the topside, all the while exchanging staged bickering.

J.P. was half straddling Samira when the canvas lifted. He looked up into the thick lens of Uncle Roy's glasses. *Where the hell did he come from?* It seemed like a long time before Roy broke the mutual stare.

Suddenly Roy handed a damp t-shirt back to J.P. "I thought I told you to keep your clothes on, boy."

J.P. took the shirt. *Where does he get off telling me when to get dressed anyway?*

With that Roy straightened his back and clapped his hands together.

"James, get me that hammer and let's get this thing staked to the ground. The sun is going to be up before you ever get your heads on a pillow."

James handed the sledgehammer to his great uncle. "At least he's going to let us have a pillow."

What I wouldn't give to stay concealed under that tarp. J.P. helped Samira all the way to her feet.

"Shouldn't we help them?" She was still stifling a laugh.

I think Uncle Roy has it under control.

~~~~~~~

J.P. showered before accepting Aunt Maggie's invitation for cherry pie. The house was quiet when he descended the stairs. A single piece of pie was waiting on the kitchen table. Phil grabbed a fork out of the drawer then carried his plate into the living room. *Where'd the kids go?* No one was in sight. *Aunt Maggie could win contests with this recipe.* He watched Samira across the room while he savored another bite. The tension from earlier in the evening had dissipated. *Maybe she finally settled in.*

When the pie was gone, J.P. set the empty plate on the coffee table. Without permission, he walked up behind Samira and wrapped his arms around her middle. She was facing a wall full of family photos.

"Are the girls asleep?"

"They're in bed but I doubt they're sleeping yet. It takes Kara a long time to settle down." Samira laid her head back against his shoulder.

"Is she doing any better?"

J.P. kissed her hair. *I like the way she feels against me like this.*

"I never know about her," Samira admitted. "One minute she's fine, the next she's in a tiff about something or the other." She leaned forward so J.P. loosened his hold. "Maggie turned in for the night. I don't know where your uncle went."

J.P. nodded toward the staircase. "Their light is out. Uncle Roy will be up with the sun so I'm sure he's down for the count."

"Who's this?" Samira's manicured fingernail pointed to an old photo on the wall.

I don't feel much like facing these old pictures tonight. "That's my mother, and that's Maggie."

"And this must be your father," Samira guessed. "Strong resemblance in the cheek bones and smile." Samira tilted her head away from J.P. "Josh must have a lot of Ralston genes too."
~~~~~~~

It's a curse. J.P. tried to dismiss the derogatory thoughts. *He'll be hell bent on ambition and miss the same things in life I have.* He started to back away.

Samira caught J.P.'s hand. "No, come back. I want to meet the others."

Why? "No, you don't."

"Yes, I do," Samira tugged on his arm. "I love family pictures."

J.P. shook his head. *There's no reason to spend time on them. They're hardly family.*

"Please?" Samira pouted her lip.

J.P. considered his options. *How can I turn her down now?*

"Let me guess," Samira studied the prints. "This is definitely Josh so I'm assuming this is little James following along behind."

J.P. nodded.

"Who's with them?"

"That's my brother's oldest daughter, Alicia."

"Where do they live?"

"New England."

"Younger or older brother?"

"Younger." *I should have called him when I was out there this week.*

J.P. watched Samira study another set of photos. *She could ask me anything right now and I'd answer.*

"She's beautiful." Samira lifted his parent's wedding picture off the table. "What's her name?"

Yes, she was. "Leona."

"Leona."

I like the way she said mom's name.

Samira's eyes admired the photo some more. "Was he in the service?"

J.P. nodded the answer as he moved toward the old leather sofa. "Career Navy."

Samira set the photo back down where she'd found it and picked up another. "Who's this with you?" She carried the framed photo to where J.P. was sitting.

J.P. knew who it was without looking. "That's my brother."

"Who's car?"

"Mine." *This is ancient history.* He shifted on the sofa. "That was a '69 Impala. Great car." *I loved that car.*

"Who's the girl?"

She would have to ask. J.P. looked at the photo again even though he didn't need to. *I didn't love her.* "Well—" *Let's not reopen the discussion about how many women I've traveled with.* "I don't have any sisters—"

"I assumed as much," Samira sat down on the edge of the sofa. "What happened to the car?"

J.P. took the frame out of Samira's hands and set it down on the coffee table. *Pick a different picture.* "I sold it to make a dent in expenses during law school."

"How long did you have it?"

"Longer than I had the girl." *Let's see what she makes of that.*

Samira's elbow caught him under the ribs.

Hey. J.P. grabbed for her hand, but she was too quick. "True statement."

J.P. watched Samira fold her hands. "It's really nice here, Phil. I'm glad you invited us."

I like the way she says my name too. "I'm glad you decided to come." *And glad you didn't decide to leave.*

A comfortable silence separated their thoughts for a moment.

"To be honest—"

You don't have to tell me if you don't want to.

"It was really hard with the girls and all." Samira's eyes were distant. "And my brother too."

Why would her brother care if she went away for the weekend?

"Kara's birthday is this weekend, so she wanted to stay home and be with her friends."

That would explain the sour attitude upon arrival.

"And my brother—"

Yeah, let's hear about this brother of yours.

Samira hesitated. "I don't know. This is all just very new for us, that's all." She was looking across the room at nothing in particular.

Me too. He'd never once brought a woman to the ranch. *Bringing someone here is new for me too. Except for Janet.* But she was his wife before she ever set foot in the cabin.

But Samira is still holding her thoughts on her brother. J.P. wondered what made her so concerned about her brother's opinions. *Let's see where she goes with this.* "I'm feeling a little guilty here, Samira. Last week I interfered with a mother-daughter picnic and now you tell me I pissed off your brother too?"

"Maybe."

Shit. She didn't have to be so honest.

"But he's the forgiving type."

A faraway look in Samira's eyes caught J.P.'s attention. *I don't know what triggered it, but I've seen that look before.* Very carefully he moved closer to her. *She had that same look the morning I was leaving her house.*

"What's really on your mind, Pretty Lady?"

Samira tucked her hair behind her ears with both hands. "I think I'm getting really sleepy."

Doubtful. J.P. hated the way she held her thoughts. *She may be tired, but that wasn't what was in her eyes.* He ran a finger under the edge of her tank top and continued over her bare shoulder. She didn't move away so he linked his fingers through hers. Samira allowed him to pull her into a standing position.

"May I tuck you in for the night, Miss Cartwright?"

She answered with her chocolate brown eyes.

Of course, this time her thoughts are loud and clear. Damn.

"But you may kiss me goodnight."

There's an invitation I'm not going to refuse. Very gently he brought her into him. *She completes me in ways I've never known.* When she laid her head against his shoulder, J.P. gathered her in completely. *I could hold her like this all night.* Slowly he rocked her back and forth until he felt her lips on his cheek.

"Good night, Mr. Ralston. Sleep tight."

J.P. watched Samira disappear around the bend in the staircase. *She takes my breath away.* He sank into the sofa.

Chase sighed heavily in his sleep. J.P. sighed too but it wasn't a sigh of sleepiness. It was a sigh of contentment that he hadn't known before. It was a sigh of satisfaction he hadn't anticipated. *It feels good to be settling in here.* The pendulum in the grandfather clock swayed with a steady beat. *I can't remember the last time I felt this much at peace.*

Good night, Samira Cartwright.

33 Need vs Want

Samira

Morning brought a peaceful awakening. Samira lay silently in her bed and soaked up the sunshine that was pouring in through the window. The hand sewn quilt showed fading from sunlight of days gone by. *Being here is like stepping back in time.* She slid out from under the covers and opened her door a crack. *It appears no one else is awake yet.* She decided to take advantage of her own bathroom, but even after showering, her watch still only read six thirty.

This is my favorite way to start the day. Samira opened her book. *Except for a cup of coffee.* She sank into a worn swivel rocker and propped her feet up on the low footstool. She was well into the second chapter before a tap at the door drew her out of the story.

"Come in." Samira looked up at the rugged man who had once stood in her living room. *Unshaven and still a bit sleepy, he's more than just a bit inviting.*

"Mornin' Pretty Lady," Phil's voice was low and quiet. "Did you sleep well?"

Samira had to smile. *I dreamt of you all night long.* She closed the book on her thumb. "I did, thank you." Samira rested her head against the back of the easy chair. "You're up early." *Phil's eyes are bluer than sometimes.* She wondered what made them change hues like they did.

Phil came on into the room and sat down on the corner of the already made bed. Samira pulled her knees in tighter. *It's hard to keep that promise to myself with him sitting here in my bedroom.* Samira replayed the reasoning in her mind. *But I can't afford to compromise my judgment with the girls here.*

"I couldn't sleep anymore." Phil shaded his eyes in mock seriousness. "The sun was in my eyes." He grinned slightly. "No one's up yet." His eyes moved to the window overlooking the ranch. "Except Uncle Roy. He's probably out choring."

Samira had to steady her breathing on purpose.

"If you're not too far into that book I was thinking maybe we could walk down to the waterfront."

"I could probably find a bookmark."

~~~~~~~

No one was more excited to be on an early morning outing than Chase.

He's so full of energy. Samira watched the dog zigzag across the path, back and forth. Wildflowers dotted the tall grassland. They had only walked a short distance before Samira caught sight of the water. The iridescence shimmer on the horizon took her breath away.

"It's really something, isn't it?"

I've never seen anything like it. The sun-glittered water stretched as far as Samira could see. "It's beautiful."

Without asking, Phil linked his fingers in hers.

How can one tiny touch stimulate every ounce of my being? Samira didn't pull her hand away. *But I am not going to let myself go there this weekend. Too risky.*

Listen to the birds singing their morning songs. It was still a distance before they reached the water's edge. *I can smell flowers mixed in with the wet grass.*
~~~~~~~

No words were spoken. Nor did they need to be. It was as if everything that could be said was simply understood. *I wish I could bottle this moment and keep it forever.*

The shore was rustic, without a formal shoreline. Flowering trees peaked in and out of the deep green pines surrounding the lake. Phil led Samira right to the point where the water met the land. Without missing a step, he leaned down and picked up a thick stick. *What's he going to do with that?*

Chase came bounding out of the wooded area. Phil let go of Samira's hand and stepped into the water.

Obviously, he doesn't care if his shoes get wet.

With purposeful effort, Phil raised the stick behind his head and then threw it far into the water. Chase took off like a bullet. He darted to the end of a wooden dock and took a flying leap into the water. Samira laughed. *This is obviously a game Chase and his master have played before.*

Samira removed her sandals and stepped into the water next to Phil. *The sun is warm, but the water is cool.* She shook off a slight shiver.

Samira watched Phil hunt another stick. Just as Chase reached the shore, he tossed the second stick into the water, but not quite as far as the first.

*He's never been so...*There was a quiet spirit in him that piqued her interest. *So what?* The way he moved and worked with Chase was tranquil and tender. *It's very much like the way he moves with me in intimate moments.* Phil was waiting for Chase to return. *He's perfectly at ease. Nothing to prove and nothing to lose when he's out here.*

The third time Phil threw a stick into the water it didn't go far from shore at all. Chase swam right to it and obediently brought it back. However, this time the dog didn't stay in the deeper water. He dropped the stick at his master's feet. Phil leaned down to pick it up about the same time Chase decided to shake dry. Phil cried out in disgust as he raised his arm against the canine shower.

Now that's funny. Samira laughed right out loud. She couldn't help it. The stillness of the morning was suddenly awakened. Chase barked happily before taking off down the dock again.

"You find this funny?" Phil dried his face with his shirt.

"Very." She turned around to see Chase take another fearless leap off the dock. *And I must say, I've never seen a dog have so much fun.*

Without warning, Phil's strong arms had Samira in a full embrace, and it felt as natural as the water lapping against her ankles. *I don't even know if my feet are even still on the ground.* She felt suspended in midair by something more magical than anything she'd ever known. *I want to stay like this forever.* Samira wrapped her arms tight around Phil's neck.

As Phil completed a full turn, her toes skimmed across the shallow water again. She closed her eyes and allowed his kisses to take her back to the dreams she'd left in her bed at the break of dawn.

Chase rudely interrupted the tender moment by brushing his saturated fur against Samira's bare legs. *Oh, he's cold and wet.* Samira danced her feet in the water so Chase would back away.

Phil laughed as he released his hold.

What a healthy, contented laugh that is. It drew Samira in even deeper. *Don't let me go yet.* She laughed right out loud, thrilled to be a part of his morning.

"One more time, boy." Phil took a stick out of Chase's mouth and threw it deep into the meadow.

Now that was a good idea. Samira knelt in a grassy spot to put her sandals back on. *There is so much passion and electricity right now.* She looked over at Phil on the shore. He was still watching Chase.

He is passionate and tender and handsome and...and intense. Samira needed to walk away to stop the voices in her head. *Very intense.* They were loud and they were suggesting things she wasn't going to allow. *And I like all those parts.* Samira glanced over her shoulder. *He should scare me, but he doesn't. He should be too much to handle, but he isn't. He should be everything I'd never need, but he's not.*

She ducked under a low branch of a Red Bud tree. *When I prayed for a new someone in my life, I prayed for someone more traditional. I didn't pray for intense and passionate and...*

She stopped and turned around. Phil was jogging to catch up. *He is everything I'll ever need.* She returned his smile. *Oh my. Where did that thought come from?* Chase took off headed back toward the house.

"There you are, Chase." Krissy opened her arms to the dog as he dashed toward her. "Oh. Ick." She wrinkled her nose. "Where have you been?"

"We took Chase down to the lake." Phil answered softly.

"He must like to swim or something."

"And chase sticks." Samira was watching the dog roll on his back in the grass.

Phil was also watching the dog. "That's how he got his name."

"It's a verb."

Phil frowned slightly. "What's a verb?"

"His name." *Did I state that thought out loud?* "Most names are a noun."

"Well," Krissy put her hands on her hips. "Now it is a noun because it's his name."

Phil waved his hand to stop the conversation.

"Is Kara up yet?" *I have no idea what we're going to find to keep her satisfied all day long.*

Krissy shrugged her shoulders. "I'll go check." She quickly disappeared inside the house.

"She's a free spirit." There was amusement in Phil's eyes as he said that.

That's one way to describe her. "Definitely."

"And Kara?"

Now Samira shook her head. "Much more like her mother. Calculated and deliberate." *Set in her ways.*

Phil leaned into the porch support. "They both have some of your best qualities. Don't cut yourself short."

Kara has more of me in her than Krissy. Samira sighed as her thoughts tripped back to the day before. "Kara was not very happy with me yesterday." Phil looked interested so she continued. "Somewhere along the line she decided she was going to stay home. In fact, she made arrangements to stay with my parents without my permission." *And that was the first my parents knew I was going away for a couple of days.*

"Obviously, you convinced her otherwise."

"Let's not say convinced." Samira recalled the harsh words exchanged during the late day argument. "Mandated, maybe."

Phil ran his hand through his hair in thought.

I wonder if he knows he does that thing with his hair?

"Well, I guess I can see her point. How many perks can there be on a holiday weekend in a totally strange place with totally strange people?"

And a man that Kara still isn't too sure about. "So, what do you do when your boys don't want to do things with you?" *Any advice would be helpful now.*

Phil studied the grass in the yard as if he were watching it grow. When he finally answered the tone in his voice was distant. "I don't know." Phil's eyes connected with Samira for just an instant. "I haven't had them any too much in recent years. Our times together are determined by a schedule that fits someone else's agenda."

He sounds so sad. Until then it hadn't occurred to her that this strong, able man could be manipulated in any way. *He must have a lot of hurt buried down deep inside.*

"I know their mother struggles with them not following her rules and plans though. It's tough, you know. They have their friends and their plans, and we have ours. We want them to be independent yet conform at the same time." Phil shrugged his shoulders. His eyes were looking at the tent where his boys were still sleeping. "I haven't been a father for a long time so this custody thing with James is a challenge."

The look on his face indicated the same worry and concern she felt.

"I guess I just blunder through and hope I can remember the basics of parenting."

Samira shook her head in disagreement. "It's more than that." *I'm not sure where this is going, but I think he's missed the point.* "I don't believe you ever actually stopped being a father. Just because James and Josh didn't live with you doesn't mean you weren't their father."

"But I didn't have a say in their decisions and activities."

"But you were still their father. You still had their love in your heart, and they had yours in them. No one can take that away." Samira touched Phil's arm. "They know you differently than anyone else simply because they're a part of you. And because of that, you're already becoming that father you think you've forgotten how to be." *I hope he followed that.*

Phil wasn't saying anything. He was deep in thought.

I hope I didn't say something wrong.

"Good mornin' young'uns."

Samira jumped at the sudden interruption. Phil's uncle appeared from around the corner of the porch. Krissy was close on his heels. *How funny. He's calling me and Phil the 'young'uns.'*

"We're going to gather eggs," Krissy announced. "Kara is up but she didn't want to go to the henhouse."

I don't blame her. Uncle Roy was swinging a wire basket. *He reminds me of a character in a Norman Rockwell painting.*

"Do you want to come?"

"Oh, no thank you." Samira immediately refused the invitation.

"I wasn't talking to you, Mama." Krissy pointed at Phil. "I mean him. Are you coming or what?"

Phil shared an easy smile with Samira. "I guess I'm going to the henhouse."

"You don't have to."

"Oh yes I do." Phil started across the grass. "I am not going to pass up a perfectly good invitation from a Cartwright woman?"

At least he qualified the Cartwright part. Samira instantly scolded herself. *He's been such a gentleman. Why do you doubt his character?* She opened the front door of the cabin. *Because I still need to know more about the woman on the cover of that magazine.*

The magazine was in her car. *I wish I could just let it go, but I can't.* The only thing left to do was talk about it, and there was only one person with whom she could do that, and he was on his way to the henhouse with her daughter. *And then again maybe I'm just making way too much out of it.*

Phil's aunt called from the kitchen and offered a cup of coffee. *Now that's an invitation I can't refuse.*

~~~~~~~

Much to Samira's dismay, Kara's discontentment permeated into the afternoon.

"Here's the deal," Kara pointed out. "You said we'd come up for a night or two. There's nothing more for us to do here, so we might as well go home."

"James says there are fireworks here tomorrow night," Krissy piped up from the porch swing. Her legs were crisscrossed, and a magazine dangled over her knees.
~~~~~~~

"Big deal." Kara rolled her eyes.

Samira's patience was being tried and she didn't like the trapped feeling closing in around her. *I'd even hoped, against all odds, that maybe, just maybe, Krissy, and especially Kara, would find something in Phil that captured their interest.* If the truth were known, Samira had even prayed that they might come to understand more why she needed this man in her life. *But that prayer has yet to be answered.* The cabin door closed behind her.

Kara took one last stab. "Well, there's nothing to do here."

"What do you mean, *nothing to do*?"

Phil's challenge surprised Samira. *Now what?* Kara wasn't used to being confronted by anyone, let alone a man.

Kara frowned and crossed her arms in defense. "At least I can't *think* of anything to do." Her dark eyes were studying Phil with caution.

Phil looked out across the lawn into the distance. "The boys and I are going to hike the Woodcutter's Trail down to the waterfront. Maybe you'd like to come along."

Please go with them, Kara. It would be so good for you.

"Can I come?" Krissy hopped up and left the magazine upside-down in the swing.

"Sure." Phil glanced in Krissy's direction. "But you'll need to change into long pants. The grass along the trail is long and scratchy."

Krissy was off in a flash.

Come on, Kara. Go. Take him up on the offer.

"How far is it?" Kara finally asked into the silence.

Phil tilted his head in contemplation. "Maybe an hour and a half total. Forty-five minutes each way."

Just do it, Kara.

"We can cut it short if you get tired," Phil offered casually.

That will do it.

Kara was instantly defensive. "I won't have any trouble keeping up."

"Only one way to find out."

Now there's the response of an experienced father if I've ever heard one. Samira thought again. *Either that or the response of an experienced attorney.*

Kara narrowed her eyes. "Whatever." She disappeared behind the door.

Oh, how I hate that word.

Phil questioned Samira with his eyes.

"I hate that word."

"Whatever?"

"That's the one."

"It's all in the way you interpret it."

Samira shook her head. "It's all in the way it's meant to be taken."

Phil draped his arm over the mother's shoulder. "*Whatever.*"

She jabbed him in the ribs with her elbow but had to smile at his jibe. *He thinks this is funny.* Samira sighed with relief. *But I do like the way he baited Kara.*

Time passed but neither the boys nor the girls came outside.

"Wonder what they found to do in there?" Phil checked his watch.

All was quiet inside the house except for hushed conversation coming from Uncle Roy's game room. The door was open. Samira could see Josh sitting on the floor next to the pool table. Krissy was sitting next to him. *At least Krissy changed her clothes.* She tuned into the conversation best as she could.

"There's some cards missing." One of the boys sounded concerned.

"What's missing?"

I can't tell their voices apart.

A few moments passed without an answer. "The ace and the king of spades."

"I say they're cheating."

"We are **not** cheating." Krissy's voice was serious.

This doesn't sound good.

Samira started for the game room, but Phil motioned for her to stay still. *He doesn't seem nearly as concerned as I feel.*

"Show your cards," one of the boys demanded.

"All of them." The other voice followed.

A few more moments passed.

"Stand up."

"There. Happy now?" Krissy mouthed back. "I'm standing."

What is this about?

"Not yet." One of the boys spoke.

Samira watched Josh climb up off the floor. "Turn around."

"Told you we're not cheating," Krissy taunted. "See? No cards."

"Now you, stand up."

Kara, I assume.

"I say she's wearing them."

Suddenly Phil bolted from his parental eavesdropping.

What triggered that sudden reaction?

One of the girls squealed, but Samira couldn't tell which one it was.

"That's enough." Phil called the game with a single command. "Put her down."

Put who down?

"They're cheating." One of the boys complained.

"I don't care who's playing fair and who's not. Put her down." Phil's voice was forceful.

Samira stepped into the doorway just in time to see James and Josh set Kara back down on the floor. *What in heaven's name is going on in here?* As Kara put her feet out to catch her balance, two playing cards fell to the floor.

"I knew it." James darted for the cards. "She *was* wearing them."

"Kara Elizabeth." Krissy snapped. "I can't believe you'd do that."

"That means we win the bet," Josh surmised. "You two owe us big time."

Kara's arms were crossed, and her face was red.

Why would Kara cheat? Samira didn't know what to make of her daughter's behavior. *And what are they betting on anyway?*

"And paybacks are hell," James added, with a slight challenge in his voice.

"Watch the language," Phil instructed.

Thank you.

"I sent you in here to get ready for Woodcutter's trail a while ago. What happened to that plan?"

Krissy jumped into the chaotic conversation. "They said we had to play Hearts to see who was going to carry the gear. The losing team had to carry the heaviest packs."

Leave it to Krissy to air the grievance. Samira crossed her arms. *Let's see how the father handles this.* She watched James try to make an exit into the garage.

"Hold it." Phil's voice reverberated in the room.

Obviously, he's not going to let it go.

"Kara, if you're going, you need long pants." Phil pointed toward the stairs. "Krissy, if you're going you need to round up Chase and meet me in the driveway."

Samira stepped aside as the girls passed her in the doorway.

"James and Josh, you know damned good and well there isn't any 'gear' to carry down the trail."

"Uh, Dad, there's a lady present. You might want to, uh, you know, the language."

Phil put his hands on his hips and took a step toward his boys. They both took a step closer to the garage exit. "Make a run for that door and you'll meet me on the other side."

Josh threw his hands into the air. "Honest, Dad, we just invited the girls into a friendly game of cards. Low stakes, no kidding."

Phil pointed a finger at Josh. "You, get the water bottles, and you," he pointed at James. "I want to see you out back."

Josh ducked his head in respectful defeat and passed by Samira without speaking. Much to her dismay, she watched Phil lead James out through the garage door.

I hope he doesn't blame James any more than the others. Samira felt an uneasiness rise in her stomach. A few minutes later Phil returned alone.

I wonder what happened to James. Samira was still standing in the same spot unsure of what she should do or say.

Kara descended the stairs wearing jeans and a fresh t-shirt.

"I'll be out in a minute." Phil turned around and hollered toward the kitchen. "Josh."

"Yeah, yeah. I'm on my way." Josh rounded the corner with an armload of filled water bottles." He avoided eye contact with Samira as he passed through.

Phil leaned on the banister and crossed his arms. "I didn't mind the friendly interrogation until the boys assumed she was *wearing* the cards."

He's trying to explain but I still don't understand. "What is that supposed to mean?"

Phil looked at her in disbelief. "That means they thought Kara was hiding the cards in her clothes somewhere."

"And that means?"

"That means the boys were dead-bent set on finding the cards no matter where she'd stashed them."

"Are you serious?" Suddenly Samira understood the insinuation. "Only a man would even think of that."

"Only a woman would think to hide them there."

Phil started for the door.

Hey. "What's that supposed to mean?"

"Take it any way you like, Samira, but I wasn't going to have my boys conducting a body search on your daughter." Phil opened the door.

"They would do that?"

Phil kept walking. "Only if they thought it would prove their point."

Samira thought for a moment. *They did have a point to prove, I guess.* The door closed between her and Phil. *I wonder where Kara hid them anyway.* The door opened again.

"Did you want to come with us?"

Samira laughed at Phil's sudden afterthought. "I'd prefer to stay here with my book."

Phil nodded. "That's what I assumed."

I'm glad he made that assumption. Samira stepped over to the window and watched as they headed out. *Together they could be a handful.* Samira saw Phil take a playful punch at one of the boys followed by a gentle attack from her youngest daughter.

God help him. It's probably just as well I stay here. Maybe this is the outing Kara needs. Samira climbed the staircase to her room and located her book. *And maybe this is the peace of mind I need too.* She curled into the armchair where she'd started her day.

The story was the same, but her frame of mind had changed. *I don't know how long I can resist him.* Even though it startled her to watch Phil take charge of the children, she still found herself drawn to him. *What is it about him that makes me want him so badly?*

Or is it more of a need than a want?

That thought struck Samira. *At least while I want him, I am still in control of my actions. However, if I need him—* Samira shifted in the chair and closed her book. *Oh, dear God, if I need him then I'm afraid it's out of my hands.* Another thought emerged. *If I need him, that raises the stakes.* She leaned her head into the old chair. *Am I ready to take that chance?*

34 Horsing Around

Joseph Phillip

J.P. could hear Aunt Maggie chattering as he crossed the living room.

"I worry about him. He works too hard and takes life so seriously. He's very much like his father in that way, but he has his mother's love of nature and her understanding of people..."

Aunt Maggie, do you have to air all your concerns for me?

"Oh, Phillip." Aunt Maggie was quite surprised. "I didn't hear you come in. How was the trail today?"

Nice cover, but it's too late. J.P. cast an accusing look on his little old aunt.

"We were just having a dandy visit." Aunt Maggie avoided his eyes.

"I'm sure you were." *I really don't appreciate her analysis of me.* Samira's face was quiet when their eyes connected.

"Here," Maggie walked around the oversized kitchen table. "Denise called an hour or so ago. She needs you to call her back as soon as you can."

J.P. took the paper from Aunt Maggie and read the phone number. *She's at the office? On July 4th? What's up with that?* Work hadn't crossed his mind since arriving at the ranch and the thought of it now was invasive. *I'd better get her called.*

"And Bobby called to find out when you are going back out east."

How did my brother know I was out east in the first place? J.P. cast another accusing look at his aunt.

"We were outside. The message said to call in later." Aunt Maggie offered to refresh Samira's cup of coffee.

Dear Aunt Maggie. Without any further discussion, J.P. went to get his phone out of the truck.

Kara and Krissy were balanced in the hammock between the Ash trees when J.P. crossed the front porch. He had to smile. *They remind me of their mother with their noses in a book.* Across the barnyard, James and Josh were involved in a one-on-one basketball match.

J.P. unplugged the charger and pushed the auto dial. *No answer at the office. I'll try her cell.* This time Denise picked up.

"Hey boss. Happy fourth of July. Sparky called."

"Good news?"

"He has key witnesses lined up for interviews in Baltimore."

J.P. watched James dribble a layup.

"So, what do you want me to do, Boss?"

How can I be a father when I have business dragging me back to Baltimore?

"I can get you out late tomorrow." Denise was obviously focused. "What airport do you want to fly out of?"

Samira appeared on Aunt Maggie's porch. *And how am I supposed to maintain any kind of connection with that pretty lady when I can't even stay home for a week?*

"Boss?"

"Joplin. I need to get James settled again before I leave." *And figure out what to do with him while I'm gone.*

"Derek is available to help. I already talked to him."

Damn, she's good. J.P. was watching Samira walk toward him. *And she's even better.*

"Hello?" Denise called J.P.'s attention back to the phone.

"Yeah, go ahead." *What was she telling me?*

"The only flight out is through St. Louis at eight o'clock. Puts you in late but Sparky can pick you up and get you to the motel."

I really don't want to talk about work today.

"That will give you all morning to prep. However, that also means a private hopper out of Joplin."

Do what you need to do, Denise. I need off this phone.

"J.P.?"

"That's fine." The attorney ran his hand through his hair. "Anything else?"

"No. I guess not."

"Okay then. I'll most likely talk to you from Baltimore next."

Really? "Most likely." J.P. greeted Samira with his eyes. "I'll talk to you at some point tomorrow." He half-listened to Denise's final instructions. "That will be fine." J.P. tossed his phone back inside the truck.

"Did you get your calls returned?" Samira was close enough to touch.

"Only the urgent one. The other one can wait."

"Is everything alright?"

Yes. He could lie but somehow that didn't feel right. *No. Everything is not all right.* J.P. sighed. "Not exactly." *She's not going to like this.* "Sounds like I have to leave town again tomorrow night."

"But that means the case is progressing, right?"

"That would be correct."

Samira turned slightly and glanced back over her shoulder. "Then that's good news, right?"

"Right." *Let's not talk about my work today.* "The travel just makes for short weeks at home." *Leaving town hasn't been an issue in the past.*

He noticed Samira's eyes watching her daughters in the hammock. "Your girls seem more content now." *Especially Kara.*

"I think they're both enjoying themselves finally." Her eyes came back to his. "Thank you for taking Kara on the hike. She had a great time once she decided there was something to do after all."

"Maybe she just needed to quit thinking about the options she left at home."

"Maybe." Samira pushed her hair out of her face. "We'll get up early tomorrow and head back in time to spend time with my brother's family tomorrow afternoon."

And maybe her mother needs to stop thinking about her options at home too. J.P. closed the door of his truck. *But at least she's staying the night again.*

"Is everything alright with James?"

Why would she ask that? "Is there something I should be aware of?"

Samira shook head and put her sunglasses on. "Oh, no. I was a little worried when you said you wanted to talk to him in private."

She pays attention to every detail. "No worries. I needed him to run down to the barn to tell Uncle Roy where we were headed."

"So where did you go on the hike?"

J.P. pointed beyond the barn. "Do you want to see?"

"How far is it?" Samira sounded hesitant.

Like mother, like daughter. "We can ride faster than we can walk." *Toby would be up for an evening stroll.* "But you'll need to change into jeans."

Samira agreed to change and promised to meet J.P. in the barn.

This may be the only time I have alone with her before she leaves. J.P. had the stud saddled before Samira appeared in the doorway. Samira's steps slowed as she realized what he was suggesting.

J.P. smiled to himself. *You'll be fine. Trust me.*

Uncle Roy appeared from the back of the barn. "Toby, it looks like you're in for a treat." He ran his calloused hands over the saddle and checked the bridle with skill. "You'd best lower the stirrups, Phillip," Uncle Roy suggested without looking up. "I was the last one in the saddle."

J.P. followed the advice without questioning.

"Shall we saddle up Claire?" Uncle Roy adjusted his thick glasses and looked toward Samira.

No thanks. I'd rather have her with me. J.P. shook his head.

"I don't know about this," Samira shook her head. "I thought you meant riding like in the truck."

"Are you headed down the trail?" Uncle Roy asked.

J.P. nodded as he ducked under Toby's neck to adjust the other stirrup. *Roy will set her straight.*

"The truck won't go down that trail, ma'am." Uncle Roy patted Toby's shoulder. "But this ole' boy will take you there in no time." He motioned for Samira to come closer.

I wonder if she's ridden before.

Samira removed her sunglasses. "Are you sure?"

"Absolutely." Roy answered.

I'm not going to give her enough time to change her mind. J.P. put his left foot in the stirrup and swung his right leg over the saddle with ease. He grinned at Samira's doubtful look.

"But he's so big."

"He's no bigger than he was when he was standing here next to you," Roy commented with honest misunderstanding. "And he'll be the same size when you get back off too."

"I didn't mean, Phil."

Good ol' Uncle Roy.

"Climb up the fence one rung and then put your left foot in here."

J.P. moved his foot so Uncle Roy could position the stirrup for Samira to use.

Roy helped Samira balance on the metal fence. "That's right. Now put your left foot in here."

Samira did as she was told but it was obvious, she was nervous.

"You're doing fine. Now, swing your other leg over the back of the saddle."

J.P. reached out his hand. With a great deal of uncertainty Samira locked her left hand in his.

Toby stood stock still as Samira's weight landed behind the saddle.

Good boy. J.P. was impressed that she'd mounted without putting up a bigger fight. *She's too stubborn to not rise to a challenge.*

"That was good."

"I'd call it a little awkward."

J.P. tapped his heels gently into Toby's side and the big, old stud started down the path.

"Where do I hold on?"

J.P. chuckled. She was gripping his t-shirt with both hands. He put his hand over hers more for comfort than instruction. "Wherever you want."

"What do I do with my feet?"

"Whatever you do," J.P. instructed. "Don't kick the horse."

"Why?"

"He'll take off on a full run." He could feel Samira's grip tighten with that remark. *Easy girl.*

Toby's steady gate took the couple all the way to the cove where J.P. had hiked with the kids. The longer they rode, the less frightened Samira seemed to be. *At least she's not clutching her fists anymore.* However, he could feel Toby's resistance to the slow pace.

"Patience, boy, patience." As they reached a shady spot near the water, J.P. pulled back the reins. *I know how he feels. Patience isn't one of my best qualities either.* "Whoa, boy." The horse stopped immediately. *We could turn around and go right back.* J.P. considered the other option. *Or we could dismount here and spend a little time without company.* With a few encouraging words he finally convinced Samira to dismount with his assistance. J.P. put his own foot back in the stirrup and dismounted as well.

Samira pushed her jeans over her knees. "It feels funny to walk now."

J.P. led Toby to the edge of the water and allowed the horse to drink. *Tell me about it.* He dropped the reins and allowed Toby the freedom to graze on the tall grass.

J.P. turned around to find Samira sitting against the trunk of a large tree. *This woman is beautiful in any setting.* Her face was serious when she made eye contact.

"How often do you come here?"

His initial hope for a moment of intimacy was diffused by her cautious demeanor. *Maybe Aunt Maggie's shared a little too much.* J.P. crouched down so he could see her eyes.

I have nothing to hide here. "I used to bring the boys up every holiday but we're down to about three times a year if we're lucky. I doubt I'll have them back up here before Christmas now."

Samira looked surprised. "You should come more often. Your aunt really enjoys your company."

Aunt Maggie has been sharing information that is better left alone.

"Do you ever come without the boys?"

J.P. shook his head more at Aunt Maggie's liberty than at Samira's question. "Rarely. It's hard enough to get away when Josh and James are available."

Samira was studying his face.

Now what's she thinking? J.P. looked over at Toby who was contentedly pulling at the long grass with his teeth.

Let's see how she responds to this. "Where's your escape, Samira? Where do you like to take your girls?"

"I don't take them many places." Her eyes were distant. "We spend holidays with my family and they're all right there in town."

"No vacations or getaways?" *Is she that much of a homebody?*

"I'm pretty content just to stay home." With that, Samira stood up and walked over to where Toby was eating grass. "What about you? Any other hideaways?"

J.P. followed. *So much for taking advantage of some private time.* He tried not to let his disappointment show, but as she stood there in the sunlight it was all he could do to not take a hold of her. *I have no idea where this conversation is headed.*

"If I do get out of town there is usually a business connection of some sort."

Samira had her back to him when she asked the next question. "Do you travel alone?"

Something is obviously on her mind. J.P. wasn't sure how he should respond. *Might be time to head back to the ranch.* He decided to guard the answer until he had a better feel for her motive.

"Once in a while I have the opportunity to take someone along," he answered carefully. *Take Springfield, for example.* "Generally, I travel solo."

Samira turned and faced him.

There's that same distant look she had last night.

"It's really strange for me to be here with you this weekend." Samira ran her hands through her hair and lifted it off her shoulders. "I mean, and don't get me wrong, Phil, but to be here with you and have the girls along and all, it's very much out of my comfort zone."

Maybe she's feeling guilty for not being home with her family.

"I don't think I told you," Samira dropped her hair. "But the decision to go to Springfield was a really big step for me. To leave town to spend a night with a man in a hotel, well, that was a really difficult decision for me to make."

That explains why it took her so long to respond. "I'm glad you decided to go." J.P. pulled a fox tail out of its shaft.

Samira smiled briefly. "Oh, I am too." Then her eyes dropped. "I had some personal issues to overcome that night, but I'm glad I—"

You what? J.P. was chewing on the end of the foxtail.

Samira turned completely away from him.

Why is she bringing this up now? J.P. wished he could see her face because he wasn't sure how to respond. *Maybe she just needs to know how much that night meant to me.* He walked up behind her and ran the fuzzy end of the grass over the back of her neck.

"What you shared with me that night is still with me, Samira." He wanted desperately to turn her around but resisted the temptation.

"I gave you everything."

"I know."

Samira interrupted his thought by stepping out of reach.

Now what?

She took a few short steps and turned around. "Do you?"

I thought I did, but maybe not. J.P. weighed his options. *I have no idea what she's talking about.* Toby was working his way closer to the water, but there was no way J.P. was going to walk over to bring him back right then. *I'm going to plead the fifth.*

She turned toward the lake and let the breeze blow her hair off her face. "It's just that I haven't done that for very many others."

Holy shit, Ralston. Whatever it is she's given you, you'd best know how to reciprocate. He knelt and picked up a flat rock. *Because the way she's standing there in the breeze is a silhouette of pure desire.* J.P. flung the rock across the water. *There isn't much I wouldn't give to find a soft grassy spot where we could get comfortable together.* He watched the rock skip three times before disappearing into the lake.

"Three. That's how many times I've given myself away."

Away for what?

Samira's eyes were fixed on the place where the rock sank. "Obviously with my husband. One time as a result of bad judgment. And then you." She paused. "That's it. Three."

She's talking about more than sex. J.P. tried to listen between the lines. *She's talking about something far deeper than that.* He rubbed his face in his hands. *I've given those parts away too many times to count.* When he lifted his eyes out of his hands, Samira was standing directly in front of him.

No. That's not true. I've never given anyone as much as I've already given her.

Samira's dark eyes were focused directly on his. "Maybe you should take me back to the house, cowboy," her voice was tender. "I think I'm dangling way too close to the point of no return."

And that's a bad thing? "Do I go against your better judgment?" *I don't think I really want her to answer that question.*

Samira looked past J.P. toward the water. "Let's just say you test my boundaries."

She's only had sex with three men in her life. Ever? J.P. was running that reality through his mind. *That's impossible. A woman this beautiful? There has to be more than three. Doesn't there? And I've never spent the night in the same house with a gorgeous, available woman without making sexual contact.* J.P. corrected himself. *That is until last night.*

"My hope is—"

What is that hope, Pretty Lady?

"The third time is a charm."

I'm the third.

Samira continued. "My fear is otherwise."

What the hell is that supposed to mean? J.P.'s thoughts were reeling as she started to kiss him. *This is the moment I've been anticipating for two days.* J.P. wrapped his arms around Samira's waist. *But now I'm playing on her terms.* He felt the curves of her body in his hands. *Hell, I don't even know how to define her terms.*

Her words sounded again. *My fear is otherwise...*

Fear of what? J.P. allowed her to kiss him again but this time he wasn't as anxious to respond. The passion he'd waited on so patiently was suddenly more ominous than enticing. *I'd love to give her everything she needs, but my gut feeling tells me I don't have whatever it is she's expecting.*

Samira's fingertips ran over his day-old beard, and she pressed her face into his shoulder. *God, Samira. If I had it, I'd give it to you in a heartbeat.* J.P. held her tight fearing if he let go, she might not be there at all.

Toby's nose brushed the back of J.P.'s shoulder. He let go of Samira when she jumped at the nearness of the horse.

There is no way I'm going to take anything else from her without clarifying her expectations. "I think Toby's thinking about supper."

Samira's eyes were cloudy, and J.P. could feel her pulling away. *I can't afford to take advantage of her any longer.* Samira was trying to appear unscathed by the confession, but J.P. knew better. "Maybe we should go back."

"And I suppose we have to *ride* him back?" She was studying the stirrup again.

I wish I knew exactly what she wants from me. J.P. decided he needed more time to think. *But I don't want her to know I'm thinking.*

"Yes, Pretty Lady." J.P. avoided her eyes. "We're going to ride him back, but this time you're going to drive."

Samira backed away quickly. "I don't know the first thing about riding a horse." She looked at Toby. "And he's so big."

"Up you go." He knelt and started to pick up Samira's left foot.

"But what about you?"

"I'm getting on behind you." *So, I can think without being observed.*

Samira shook her head.

"Do you trust me?"

With that, Samira took a deep breath and nodded her head.

Trust is a start.

Samira put her left foot in the stirrup and allowed J.P. to push her on into the saddle. Even when Toby stepped sideways, Samira sat tight.

At least she's determined once she makes up her mind. J.P. mounted behind the saddle and placed the reins in Samira's hands. The diversion of the riding lesson relieved the tension that had built between them. *Given a choice I would make her third time all she needs it to be.* J.P. tapped his heels into Toby's sides. *But what happens if I don't have all she's hoping for? What then?*

J.P. guided Samira's hands and legs with his own as Toby ambled up the trail toward the ranch. *Given my history and temperament, I don't know if I can play by her terms.* Suddenly his desires for Samira were shadowed by a threat to his independence. *I don't know if I'm ready to give that much.*

~~~~~~~
~~~~~~~

The rhythmic click of the Grandfather Clock was the only sound in the house when Samira appeared at the bottom of the stairs. Freshly showered and wearing only her nightshirt J.P. caught himself once again fighting instinctive tendencies. *Why does she tempt me like this then keep me at bay?*

Samira crossed the room and sank into the corner of the cushy leather sofa. "Big day," she stated simply. "The fireworks were really pretty over the lake."

J.P. was sitting on the floor leaning against the matching chair.

"Did the girls like them?"

Samira curled her feet underneath her hips. "I think so. They were thinking of their little cousins watching fireworks without them."

She's the only woman I know who purposefully doesn't show me what she's wearing underneath. J.P. nodded for lack of a better response.

"Are you tired?"

The question came out of context. J.P. wasn't sure if he looked tired or if Samira was thinking he should be after the day's activities. He rested his elbow on his knee. "A little."

Samira's eyes were soft as she studied his face. *She didn't allow me to tuck her in last night so I'm not holding out hope for tonight either.*

"You look sleepy."

"Maybe more relaxed than sleepy." *And extremely spent in the mental capacity.*

"Tell me about your parents, Phil." Samira's eyes had moved to Joe and Leona's wedding photo on the wall. "What happened to them?"

Do we have to go there? J.P. followed her eyes as he took a deep breath. There wasn't that much to tell really, yet at the same time he rarely allowed himself the memories. He subconsciously ran his hand through his hair.

"There's not much to know." *Or at least not much I want to tell.* He flipped a newspaper upside down for no reason at all. "My mother raised my brother and me on her own for the most part. Joe was in the Navy my whole life, so I didn't know much of him." *Nor do I care to know him now.*

"Where did they meet?"

"Virginia Beach, Virginia." J.P. knew the story like he knew his own life. But sharing it was another thing. He decided to cut the dramatic details. "My mom was out there visiting her oldest sister, Naomi. She ended up staying out there until they were married the next year."

Samira curled deeper into the sofa and rested her head against the back. "Love at first sight?"

J.P. shook his head. "Doubtful." He couldn't imagine his father knowing anything about love. *I wonder how much Aunt Maggie has already told her.*

Samira's eyes were on the photo again. "What happened to them?"

J.P. studied his bare feet against the pattern of the area rug. "My mother died in a plane crash the summer I turned twelve." J.P. took a breath. *God, I hate those memories.* "And the Captain," J.P. glanced at the man's face in the photograph. "My father is in Virginia. Retired Navy now."

There was a long, silent span of time between that statement and Samira's next comment. When she spoke, her voice was almost inaudible.

"Do you see him?"

J.P. shook his head. *There's no reason to see my mother's husband.* She was gone and as far as Joseph Phillip Ralston, II was concerned, the Captain was gone too.

"I'm so sorry, Phil." Samira's eyes reflected deep compassion.

Suddenly his thoughts were too intimate for sharing. *Move on.* "No need to be. That was a long time ago." He leaned back on the chair again and crossed his ankles on the rug.

But since she opened the door, I think I'll follow suit. He studied her, wishing he could touch her. "So, what's your story, Samira?" *Tell me about your husband.* "What did *he* do for a living?"

"Tom?"

Yeah, Tom. J.P nodded.

"He was a city police officer."

"How did you meet him?"

Samira smiled slightly. "I was set up. I met him during his last year at the academy through a mutual friend."

J.P. watched her eyes dance with the memory for a quick moment.

"My friend Susan invited him to dinner. That's the same friend, incidentally, who also invited me and your friend Mike to dinner last week." Samira raised a single eyebrow to punctuate the confession.

J.P. raised his eyebrows in response. "She must be some friend." *Still pisses me off they had dinner without me.*

"She tries."

"What happened to...Tom?" *Why is it so hard for me to say his name?*

Samira's eyes dropped. Suddenly J.P. wished he hadn't asked anything at all.

"You don't have to answer."

"It's okay." Samira shook her head slowly. Her hair fell around her face. "Tom died of cancer. Kara was eight and Krissy had just turned six." She tucked her hair behind both ears.

I had no idea. "That must have been really hard." *Harder than anything I've been through.*

Samira didn't respond right away. Her thoughts were obviously somewhere in the distant past.

I didn't mean to make her cry.

"I'm sorry." She wiped her cheeks with her fingertips. "I haven't talked to anyone about that for a long time."

Without permission J.P. eased onto the couch next to Samira. She didn't resist when he slipped his arm behind her shoulders. *I understand that all too well.* He stroked her hair, grasping for words that might make everything all right again. *There are no words.* He pulled her in against his body and kissed the top of her head.

"He tried to hang on." Samira's voice was distant. "But in the end the cancer won." J.P. felt her lungs expand against him. "That was six years ago now."

"That's a long time ago."

Samira's head moved back and forth against his shoulder. "In some ways. In other ways it seems like yesterday."

Time passed but no other words were spoken. The Grandfather Clock chimed at eleven o'clock but neither Samira nor J.P. moved. They were kindred in spirit. Neither spared from life's injustice and heartache. They had both been left to face their futures alone.

The outside door clicked loudly causing J.P. to sit up unexpectedly. Samira also sat up, both just awakened from a light sleep. J.P. watched James pass through the living on his way to the bathroom. *How long was I asleep?*

Samira leaned forward on the sofa. She was obviously trying to get her bearings as well. J.P. pushed the hair back from her face. Her eyes turned toward the staircase.

"I'll walk you up." He offered his hand. His shirt was still warm where she had fallen asleep against him. *The last thing I want to do is leave her alone in a cold bed.* Samira took his hand. *But just the same, I'll respect her wishes.*

J.P. climbed into his own bed drained from the day's activities and fatigued by the memories that plagued his weary mind. He rolled over on his side and checked his alarm. *She's an early riser if I ever met one.*

In the moment before drifting off to sleep, the crack in the bedroom door widened. Thinking he might already be dreaming, J.P. rubbed his eyes. *She's still here.* He laid perfectly still, for fear if he moved the apparition would disappear.

Silhouetted by the moonlight trickling in the window, he continued to watch as she undressed and slipped silently into his bed.

This is my chance to make sure her third time is a charm.

~~~~~~~

J.P. awoke the next morning unaware of when Samira had gone back to her own room. He pulled on his jeans from the day before and stepped into the hall. *Her door is ajar.*

Samira lay sound asleep under one of Aunt Maggie's quilts. The sunlight was just starting to warm her room. J.P. stood silently in the doorway and observed her slumber.

She'd given him everything once again. *It's so different than any woman I've ever been with.* There was something about the way she needed him. Something about the way she gave herself over to him. *It's so much more than I've ever received from anyone else.* Her dark hair fanned across the cotton pillowcase.

Not once have I known a woman like I've known Samira Cartwright.

Samira lay perfectly still as J.P. watched. *Mike says she's out of my league, but I'm beginning to think I need to take a chance on her and see where this goes.*
~~~~~~~

35 An Angel in Disguise

Samira

Samira pulled the laced curtains back from the window so she could get a better view. Phil was jogging toward the house, Chase leading the way. *I love the way he interacts with his dog.* There was a gentleness about him that was not always apparent in other relationships. Samira watched as he stopped to stretch. *I wonder if he runs every day.*

I should probably pack my things before going downstairs. The weekend had been more fulfilling than she'd anticipated. *But there are still so many things I wanted to talk to him about. Like the woman on the magazine cover.* She glanced at the picture on the cover before setting it aside. *But it sounds like Phil is flying out for business somewhere out east.*

Samira glanced out the window again. Phil was headed up the sidewalk, shirtless and sweaty from the early morning run. *He really does take his sabbaticals seriously. He hasn't bothered to shave since we arrived.* She grabbed the magazine. *I'll pack later so I can catch him before he gets in the house.*

"Well, good morning, Pretty Lady." Phil skipped the bottom step and joined her on the wooden porch.

Even in his sweat-drenched body he's still the most inviting man I've ever known. "You're up nice and early this morning."

Phil grinned. "I thought I'd get my run in before it got too hot."

"It's already plenty warm."

"So it is." Phil put his hands on his hips and bent his neck in thought. *He's looking at me like he wants to say something.*

"So? What's on your mind?"

"I'm thinkin'—"

How funny that he can't put his thoughts into words sometimes. Samira walked past Phil and took a seat in the porch swing. *I'll just wait while he thinks.* Her feet dangled as she pushed it into motion.

Phil's eyes watched her all the way to the swing, but he didn't follow. When he finally did speak, he was shaking his head.

"I was thinking I either had the most incredible dream of my life last night or," he stopped talking again. His eyes were fixed on hers.

I want to hear him say it out loud. "Or?"

Phil took a step in her direction. "Or an angel visited me in my bed." He crouched down and leaned his back against a porch support.

An Angel? I've never been likened to an angel before. She had to break his gaze. "You must have been dreaming."

"Somehow I think I have evidence to prove otherwise."

Evidence? Samira felt her cheeks fill with color. *There was so much I wanted to give him.* She ran the night backwards in her mind. *I didn't feel right leaving him alone in his bed.* His dark blue eyes were watching her very closely. *But I couldn't have lived with myself had someone found us in there together.*

The model's picture on the magazine came into Samira's focus. *Maybe she isn't a discussion for today.* Fearing Phil might realize what she was holding, she quickly laid it aside, face down.

"You're welcome to stay as long as you like."

If I were here alone, or single without my daughters, I'd be very tempted. Samira shook her head slowly. *But staying on with Krissy and Kara isn't as appealing.* "I really can't stay. Once the girls are packed and ready, we'll need to start toward home."

Phil's eyes fell at that statement. "That's alright," he said as he stood. "It's been really nice having you here with me." His eyes scanned the outskirts of the yard. "I don't share this part of my life with too many people."

I'm honored to have shared it with him. Samira stepped out of the swing and joined Phil at the railing. "I'm really glad I came too." *I will forever cherish that magical moment out at the lake.* "And thanks for spending so much time doing things with the girls. They had a good time despite their initial misgivings." Samira leaned against the railing so she could see Phil's face.

He stretched a well-sculpted arm and balanced his weight on a high support beam. "I didn't mind. It was good to get to know them a little more."

"Your boys will probably be ready for them to go home."

Phil chuckled. "They'll probably miss Krissy's stories. She's a live wire out there on the trail."

"She's a live wire anywhere." As an afterthought she added. "I hope Kara behaved." *Lord knows her teenage attitude has been showing lately.*

Phil nodded slightly. "She has to work harder to have fun than her sister, but she does alright." His eyes met Samira's again. "Give her a good challenge and she'll rise to the occasion."

He's already figured Kara out.

Chase bounded onto the porch with something green hanging between his teeth. *I hope it's not another dead fish.* Samira pulled her legs up abruptly. *Go away.*

Phil tried to divert the dog's aggression with his knee, but Chase was too excited to share his treasure. Samira pulled her legs up even further. *Please. Make him stop.* Before she realized what was happening, she lost her balance and started to fall backwards.

In an instant, Phil had Samira's hand and was pulling her back toward him. He was still jockeying the dog with his foot but hung on long enough that Samira could catch her own balance again.

Thank goodness.

"Here, boy," Phil knelt. He steadied the dog with one hand and examined the object with another. "You are going to get your butt kicked if Aunt Maggie finds out about this."

I don't want to know. Samira closed her eyes and turned her face away, afraid to look.

Uncle Roy appeared from behind the corner of the house. "Keep that thief out of Aunt Maggie's garden."

Where'd he come from?

Samira watched Roy disappear behind the house again.

"A green tomato." Phil examined the object. "Or rather, what's left of it." He rubbed Chase between the ears. "That'll give you a belly ache, buddy." Phil tossed the juicy remnants of the tomato into the bushes along the front edge of the porch.

Samira took note of the bushes. *At least I'd have fallen there instead of onto the hard ground.* She tucked her hair behind her ears. When she looked up Phil was standing over her. *My knight in shining armor.* A slight shiver ran up Samira's spine.

"What are you thinking, Pretty Lady?"

"I think you just saved my life."

"I'm thinking maybe you just saved mine."

His beard is softer this morning than it was last night. She ran one hand up under his ear and let the other one rest against the bare, sticky skin on his lower back. *This is the part of him I want to take home with me.*

"Phillip." Aunt Maggie's voice called out a sharp interruption.

The kiss left Samira catching her breath. *Wow.* She pulled her hair back with one hand and held it in a ponytail.

"There's a phone call for you Phillip, dear," the aunt announced, seemingly oblivious to the intimate moment taking place on her porch.

Phone calls always alter Phil's demeanor.

"On your phone? Who is it?"

I hope it's not that Bobbie person again. Samira glanced at the magazine still laying on the swing.

"Well," Maggie looked apologetic. "It's Janet. I told her I'd see if you were back from your run yet."

Samira could see a sudden tension form across Phil's shoulder blades. *Case in point.* Samira remembered. *The same ex-wife that called his house as we were trying to leave for Springfield.*

Phil walked through the open door with purpose. It closed loudly behind him leaving Maggie and Samira on the porch.

So much for a private moment. The half-eaten tomato was stuck in the bushes. *That is disgusting.* "There's a book entitled, Fried Green Tomatoes," Samira recalled out loud. *Why did I say that out loud?*

"My mother used to fry up green tomatoes." Aunt Maggie responded as if she'd always been a part of that conversation. "I never much enjoyed them myself." Maggie wiped her wrinkled hands on her apron. "I should have told her Phillip wasn't back yet." Maggie's eyes were fixed on the solid door. "He's had such a nice weekend."

I hope it's nothing serious.

"I wonder what could be on her mind at this hour on a Sunday morning?" Maggie worried out loud. "Janet has a way of turning things sour for no reason, no reason at all." The old woman shook her head as she headed for the door. "I just hope Phillip doesn't let her change his mood. He's been so relaxed..." Maggie didn't stop talking as she opened the door into the house. "It's so good to see him so relaxed..." The woman continued to chatter as the door closed behind her.

I should check on the girls. She could see Phil in the kitchen, the phone to his ear. His back was to her, but Samira could sense the tension just the same. *Janet does have a way of pushing his buttons.*

Samira touched base with the girls then stopped in the guestroom to finish packing her own things. *It's harder to leave here than I thought it was going to be.* Her hair was almost dry now. She ran a brush through the length and then wrapped a quick bun with her free hand. Krissy was at the foot of the stairs where she set her bag down.

"I think you need to go after Phil, Mama. He's really mad and James is really going to get it."

What in the world? Samira's questioning eyes moved to Maggie's worried look.

"It's true, Samira. Whatever Janet had to say turned up the heat." Maggie was wiping her forehead with the back of her hand. "I'm afraid the weekend won't end as good as it began."

Samira didn't wait for Maggie to finish. *There's no reason for the weekend to end with tension that arrived in that phone call.* She opened the door and scanned the front yard. *He's headed for the tent.* There was determination in Phil's stride. *I'm going to have to hurry.* She recalled Phil's regret when he told her about his fight with James. *Surely there's a better way to handle whatever it is.*

Chase was sitting at attention on the top step of the porch. *This is serious if Chase isn't following his master.* Phil was almost at the tent. *I'm never going to catch him at this rate.*

Samira called out his name, but if he heard, it didn't slow his steps. "Phil." She called louder this time.

Phil stopped walking but didn't turn around.

Samira stopped a few feet from where Phil was standing. He had his hands on his hips and he was breathing heavily.

For whatever it's worth. "Phil?"

He turned around ever so slowly. His jaw was set, and his eyes were angry. *This is neither J.P. nor Phil.*

"Samira, don't—"

Don't what? Samira felt her confidence grow. *What does he think I'm here to do?*

"You don't know—"

I know he's too mad to confront his son. "Maybe there's another way to handle this."

"Handle what?" Phil snapped. "It's already started."

"But maybe you should—"

"Should what? Do you think you know these boys better than I do?"

I would never question his relationship with the boys. "Not at all, I just thought—"

"Thought what?" The irritation in his voice was showing more with every statement.

"If you'll let me finish."

"Finish? I'm going to finish what she started."

Now he was beginning to raise his voice. "Exactly my point. What she started has little to do with what you're about to do." Samira didn't appreciate his tone. *Phil's anger has nothing to do with the boys in that tent. That's obvious.* She put her hands on her hips and locked her eyes with his. "Maybe that's the point."

This time when Phil tried to interrupt, Samira wouldn't allow it. "No, hear me out." *He needs to cool down.* She was careful not to match his tone. "Whatever Janet said to you on the phone just now may have more to do with her control over you than it does with the boys." *I can't believe I just said that to him.*

"What the hell is that supposed to mean?" Phil set his jaw and lowered his head to make a stronger point. "You don't have any goddamned idea what she told me on the phone."

Well, there's no turning back now. "You're right about that, Mr. Ralston." *And there is no reason to swear at me.* "But I do know that she knows how to push your buttons and she's found just the one to gain your attention this morning." *I can't believe I'm standing up to him like this.* "And she also knows how to put an end to a perfectly good morning." Samira stopped talking. *I may as well put it all out there now.* "And there is no reason for you to raise your voice at me and even less reason for you to swear at me."

Phil was still staring her down, but Samira refused to let him intimidate her.

"And my suggestion, in the case you might be listening at all, is that you let that phone call go and enjoy that last few hours you have with your sons before you have to leave town on business again." *There. I spoke my piece.* Samira put her hand over her stomach hoping to relieve the pit that was forming.

Phil shook his head hard and glanced toward the tent. "I don't let things go." His eyes were steel gray. "If there's an issue that needs addressed then by God, we're going to address it."

Addressing it with God would be a better alternative than what you're about to do now. "Then address it on your time frame, not hers."

"What the hell is that supposed to mean?"

"You don't need to swear at me." Samira's patience was running thin. *Is this the same man I made love to in the dark of the night?*

Phil looked away.

"All I'm saying," *How do I speak the truth without setting him off more?* "Is that you need to get your thoughts in order before addressing the issues. Maybe she called on purpose to prompt a fight or something."

Phil threw his arms out. "Who are you? Some kind of authority on my ex-wife?"

I could live without his petty insinuations. She'd hit a nerve. *But if I back down now, the boys, or at least one of them, is in line for the next punch.*

"No, but something Maggie told me makes me—"

"Maybe Aunt Maggie needs to keep her thoughts to herself."

"She wasn't speaking directly to me," Samira interrupted. "And she only says what she does because she loves you."

Phil closed his eyes and let his head fall forward. He put his hands behind his neck. Samira waited but he didn't speak.

Now what do I do? Her heart was pounding hard in her chest and James and Josh were now watching from the unzipped screen of the tent. *I guess I'll make one last suggestion. He can take it or leave it.*

"Listen, Phil," Samira lowered her voice so the boys couldn't hear. "I just don't want you to have any regrets about the weekend."

Nothing else came to mind. *I guess that's all that needs to be said.* Samira turned toward the house. Maggie quickly ushered Krissy off the porch. *Obviously, they witnessed the whole thing.* Chase was still perched at attention on the top step. *Even his dog avoids his temper.*

"You did it, Mama." Krissy announced as Samira set foot inside the cabin. "You saved James from being in big trouble."

Samira pursed her lips. *We'll see.* "Why don't you run along and see how Kara is doing." She needed a minute to gather her own thoughts. When Krissy was out of sight Samira stepped back to the window where she'd watched Phil jog across the yard less than an hour before. *He went from being thoughtful, passionate, and incredibly irresistible to insanely angry in no time at all. I don't know.*

"You were very brave. Not many people dare to stop Phillip when he's in a rage like that." Maggie's voice was still shaking.

Samira turned to face Aunt Maggie.

"I've always sent Roy, but I didn't know where he was." Maggie caught a tear on her cheek with her fingertip.

The front door opened, and Josh stepped through. He greeted his great aunt with a natural smile. "What's for breakfast, Aunt Maggie? I'm about starved to death."

Samira looked back out the window. James was on his way to the house, but Phil was nowhere in sight. *Chase is gone too.*

After breakfast James and Josh convinced Samira to allow the girls one last jaunt to the waterfront before heading home. She helped Maggie clear the last of the dishes as the kids took off across the yard. Maggie was chattering on about something or the other when Phil's broad shoulders darkened the kitchen doorway.

Samira stopped wiping the table and studied his eyes. *They're not angry anymore.* She wanted so badly to touch him, but his stance still showed signs of tension. *And he's showered and shaved.*

Aunt Maggie changed subjects without taking a breath. "Oh, Phillip, I fixed you a plate —"

He waved his hand. "Thanks, but I'm not hungry right now, Aunt Maggie."

"You really should eat something, Phillip." Maggie wiped her hands on her apron and glanced in Samira's direction. "I'll just take these scraps out to Chase." The old aunt gathered the leftover sausages and made her way toward the front door.

Samira leaned against the sink. *I think I'll let him do the speaking this time.*

Phil walked across the kitchen and balanced his weight against one of Aunt Maggie's kitchen chairs. You didn't have to do that."

Oh yes, I did. Samira knew better. *Who knows what might have happened had I not stepped in.?*

"I didn't mean for Janet's phone call to involve you."

Phil's voice was apologetic, but he still hadn't said the two words Samira thought he might. "Better to involve me than the boys."

Phil shook his head slowly. "Not so."

Just say you're sorry and we'll be alright.

"You're right about one thing," Phil added. "Janet does know how to push my buttons and this morning was no exception."

At least he's admitting that much. Samira dried her hands on a dishtowel and crossed the room to where Phil was leaning. "You just need to remember you have control over the buttons." She brushed the dishtowel over his arm hoping to relieve the tension hanging between them.

Phil looked beyond her but didn't speak.

"I just didn't want you to say or do something to jeopardize the good times the boys had with you this weekend," Samira explained carefully. "They deserve a break from everyday pressures just like everyone else." *And I didn't want you to put a damper on what we shared this weekend either.*

Phil ran his hand through his hair.

He can't say it. Watching him try to cope with the awkwardness of the moment, Samira knew he wasn't going to be able to form the words of apology. *He is sorry. But he can't say it.*

"Are the girls packed?"

"They left their bag by the door."

"What time are you leaving?"

"As soon as the kids get back from the lake."

Phil nodded his head in understanding.

So, what do I say to him after this? Samira felt completely numb from the entire experience. *I might as well load the car and get ready to go.*

Phil followed her to the living room and picked up her bag. They walked to the car without speaking.

Samira could hear the kids' voices in the distance. *My time with Phil is growing short.*

"You deserve better," Phil announced out of the blue. He had his hands in his front pockets and was looking into the distance to a place Samira couldn't see.

Maybe, maybe not. She recalled the way he touched her the night before. *Most parts of you are perfect.*

"I didn't mean to swear at you."

Samira knew Phil was working toward an apology, but it was not forthright in coming.

"I...I wasn't mad at you, Samira."

"I know that."

"But that doesn't make it all right."

"I know that too."

"And you're right again. The issues Jan called about aren't as urgent as they seemed."

"I didn't think they were."

"I wish we could just start the morning over again."

Like the way we started our arrival again? "We could start around midnight maybe."

Phil's eyes suddenly returned to hers. The reminder of the night before caught him off guard. "That would be...well, yeah. I'd like that." His voice trailed off but the voices on the trail were getting closer.

"I'm sorry, Phil." She spoke his words and she knew it. Yet she couldn't stop them from coming.

"No, don't be." Phil's fingers lifted her hand. "There's nothing for you to be sorry about."

His eyes were searching hers, but she was afraid he wouldn't find the answer he needed. There was more to his unspoken apology—more than Samira could possibly begin to understand.

She allowed his lips to touch hers. Ever so gently he gathered her into a full embrace and held her just like he had at his house the night they were leaving for Springfield.

I can love him, but I can't give him what he needs most. What he needed was beyond her capability. *He needs to find himself somewhere amid this confusion.*

Phil let her go just as the kids appeared at the end of the trail.

The next few minutes were a blur of goodbyes and an exchange of hospitable thanks between Samira's family, and Maggie and Roy. Even Chase got in on the departing excitement delivering yet another green tomato just as Samira climbed into the driver's seat.

Phil threw it into the barnyard beyond the driveway. As the dog took off, Phil knelt at Samira's open door.

"I'll call you from out East."

Samira nodded. *I'd rather see him in person, but a phone call is a good start.*

"I don't know when I'll get a break but—"

"I'll be there when you're free." *There's no need for him to feel pressure from me too.*

Phil nodded. His eyes were full of unspoken thoughts, but it was obvious their time was up. He squeezed her hand as he stood up.

Samira started the engine just as Chase returned with the tomato again. This time it was dripping between his teeth. She laughed. *I don't mind leaving the ornery hound behind.* Samira dared to look in her rearview mirror before turning onto the gravel road in front of the ranch. Phil was still watching the car, his fingers tucked inside his front pockets. *Yes, he's everything I prayed for.* Dust from the road blocked her view of the driveway. *Yet he's so much more. What if he is my last chance at love?*

36 Bobby

Joseph Phillip

Uncle Roy's face appeared hidden behind his thick glasses. "If you ask me, that there looks like a woman you need to latch onto."

J.P. was trying to see Roy's face but couldn't make it out. "Uncle Roy, I don't know any more about latching onto a woman than I know about taming a lion."

"Seems to me the woman's not the one who needs taming."

Uncle Roy's words stung.

"She looks way out of your league, J.P."

"You might be the one who needs tamin'..."

"She could be your last chance..."

"...a little out of your league..."

"Mr. Ralston."

"The woman might not be the one who needs tamin'..."

The voices were getting louder and louder.

"Better be careful dragging her around..."

"Sir."

"You might need some taming..."

"Sir."

J.P. opened his eyes, but he didn't recognize the woman looking back at him. Her hand was on his arm. Uncle Roy's husky voice was still playing tricks in J.P.'s mind.

"We've begun our descent to the runway, Sir. Please put your seat all the way into the forward position."

Very slowly the roar of jet engines drowned out the voices from his dream. *That's the flight attendant.* J.P. leaned forward and rested his face in his hands. *If you're planning on hanging on to her, you need to get your shit together.* He pictured her face in his mind. *Samira.*

There were only two other people flying first class. He watched the stewardess prepare for landing. She looked over her shoulder and smiled in J.P.'s direction. *Nice looking girl, but the smile I'd like to see isn't hers.*

J.P. took the magazine out of the pocket in front of him. He was sure it was the same magazine Krissy and Kara had on the hammock. *And I know it's the same one Samira left lying on the porch swing.* Bobbie Jo Sommers smiled back at him.

The plane touched the runway once.

Why would Samira have this magazine?

There was a bump as the wheels touched the tarmac again.

And what does she know, if anything, about Bobbie Jo? He turned it over. *It's a newsstand copy. Not a subscriber.*

This time when the plane touched down it stayed. A few short minutes later the jetliner decelerated to a complete stop. *Maybe Samira saw more of Bobbie Jo in Springfield than I thought.* He left the magazine in the empty seat next to him.

Sparky was waiting along the wall outside the boarding area as promised. J.P. tucked his return ticket inside his jacket and stretched out his hand to greet the former KGB officer. Sparky made very brief eye contact and shook the attorney's hand only once.

"Der is a car waiting."

I can't believe I put my trust in a man of so few words. J.P. adjusted his shoulder bag and fell into step behind the bald little man. The air outside was smoggy and thick. *Gotta love Baltimore.* They walked to a waiting limousine. Instantly, two chauffeurs stepped onto the curb and opened the doors on either side of the car.

What the hell? J.P. watched Sparky walk to the far side. He barely had to bend over to climb inside. The uniformed chauffeur offered to take J.P.'s bag. He parted with his garment bag. *I think I'll keep my briefcase and computer.*

The doors closed and locked immediately. J.P. found himself facing Sparky. He turned in his seat and took note of the security glass between them and the drivers. Sparky poured a shot of vodka and offered one to his employer.

No thank you on the Vodka. "This is really nice." J.P. continued to examine the car. "Am I paying for this?"

Sparky suppressed a smile. "No, sur." He offered a toast in midair. "I have a good friend in area." Sparky's imperfect English accented his words. "Ah, but Hyatt Regency is very nice. Dat you do pay for. Tank you."

Must be a hell of a friend. "Denise tells me you have a full day planned."

Sparky's black bushy eyebrows raised considerably. "Ah, Denise is good vorker."

"She's the best. What time do we start in the morning?"

Sparky pointed a finger at his wristwatch. "Tomorrow is now today."

J.P. sighed. *I've just added an hour to what was already a long day.*

"Ve start at eight o'clock sharp. I vill brief you on the vay in."

That's good because I'm too tired to digest anything now. J.P. could see the reflection of the Hyatt's signage in the back window.

"Your key, sur."

J.P. accepted a business card-size envelope.

"I checked you in on the account." Sparky folded his hands politely. "Denise say she take care of everyting."

Wonder what else she's managing while I'm out here?

"I vill meet you in lobby at six thirty." The limousine slowed to a stop under the Hyatt's canopy.

"Six thirty?"

Sparky stepped out of the car. "Much briefing to do sur."

J.P. waited for the chauffeur to bring his garment bag.

"Four-tvelve." Sparky tapped his finger on J.P.'s room card. "Five-feefty." He tapped his own. "Good night, J.P."

Five fifty. I need to remember that. J.P. found himself standing alone outside the Hyatt Regency. He could hear airplanes taking off and landing somewhere not so far off. Traffic dotted the horizon with multicolored lights. There was nothing familiar about this place. Even the scattered thoughts in his own mind seemed unfamiliar.

Four-twelve. He entered the hotel and pressed the call button on the elevator. *I don't care what number the room is as long as I have a pillow for my head.*

~~~~~~~

The morning began right on time. Sparky was more than prepared for J.P.'s arrival. The briefing was detailed and exact. By the time they were interviewing potential witnesses, J.P. felt confident in the case. It was nearing lunchtime before J.P. checked his watch for the first time.

"You do good work, Sparky." He packed his briefcase. "I appreciate the time you've put in out here." *Very timely and complete.*

Sparky's face remained serious as he nodded acceptance. "Dis afternoon you vill meet the judge overseeing the case. You also vill meet the defense team."
~~~~~~~

"How long before the actual hearing?"

"Long lunch in Balteemoor." Sparky studied his watch. "Courthouse will close 'til two o'clock. Den da hearing start." The little man finished scribbling a note on a yellow legal pad. "I vill brief you over lunch."

Sparky had lunch scoped out at an upscale café not far from the courthouse. It didn't take but a few minutes for Sparky to launch into the new briefings.

Mike was right on the money with Sparky. He doesn't miss a beat.

"My vork here in Balteemoor is almost fineeshed." Sparky wiped his dark mustache with a cloth napkin. "Ve must get the suspects to agree to the plea bargain if ve are to know der employer."

Sparky's right. Without that, chances of identifying their employer are slim to none.

"Der is something more I need to discuss vith you," the investigator leaned in as if he had a secret to share.

J.P. leaned in too. *I hope it's not a major hidden expense—like a limo.*

"Mmmm, I don't know vhat to tink." Sparky scratched his chin. "But I tink der is another link to dis case."

"What kind of a link?"

The investigator knitted his brow as he thought. "I don't know yet. Der are many vires back and forth to Joplin still."

"Are you still monitoring the communication traffic?"

"Absolutely." Sparky seemed surprised to be questioned over that. "Alvays keep alert. Zometing is feeshy. Don't know vhat it is yet."

J.P. crossed his arms and watched the little man think. "Do you need to go back to Joplin to trace the link?"

"No. I don't think so. Caleefornia maybe. I maybe need to go to Caleefornia."

"California?" *How do I know he's not using this as a way for me to pay his way to the west coast?* "What's the connection there?"

"Mmm, lots of traffic to Caleefornia. Nothing from here to der anymore. All from here to Joplin to Caleefornia."

"And you think you could go out there and link somebody to this case?"

"Very posseeble."

Sparky is dead serious. J.P. studied the little man. *If this is a solid lead, we're going to have to slow the whole thing down to accommodate new evidence.* "How soon do you need to go out there?"

"Soon. Maybe tomorrow."

J.P.'s telephone rang. *Probably Denise wanting the latest update.* "This is J.P."

"Hey, hey. Big Bro. What brings you to the eastern sphere?"

J.P. hadn't heard Bobby's voice in a long while. He excused himself from the table and carried the phone outside the café. "How the hell do you know I'm on the East Coast?"

"Aunt Maggie doesn't keep family secrets."

"Don't have to tell me that." *I'm sure she shared a few with Samira.* "When did you talk to her?"

"This morning first thing. She says you're in Baltimore."

J.P. looked up at the street sign and gave an exact location.

"Get this. I'm in Newark on business. I can be down there by eight tonight, and we can find some seafood and catch up."

*I can make that work. It isn't every day I spend an evening with my brothe*r. "Eight o'clock it is then. I'm at the airport Hyatt. Meet me there."

"Will do. Hey gotta run."

J.P. slipped the phone back into his pocket. *It'll be good to see Bobby.* Sparky was waiting for him at the entrance to the café. "Let me pick up the tab."

"Ah, dis one is on me," Sparky spoke with appreciation. "You been very good to me on dis case."

J.P. stood at least a foot taller than his investigator. He had to chuckle as they walked side-by-side back toward the courthouse. "California, huh?"

"Yes, sur." They walked a few more lengths of the sidewalk before he spoke again. "And I think, if I am not meestaken, de links vill lead right back to Joplin again."

Interesting.

~~~~~~~

A pounding on the hotel door ended J.P.'s shower sooner than he'd hoped. He wrapped his lower body in a towel. Bobby's smiling face was looking back at him through the peephole.

"You said eight."

"So, I'm early. Is it a crime to be early?" Bobby stepped into the room with his usual vigor. Slightly shorter and less fit than J.P., he still smiled the easy Ralston smile. "Get your ass in some clothes and let's hit the streets, find some entertainment, eat some seafood, drink some ale."

I'm barely unwound from my case, damn it. Samira's smile was stuck in his memory. *And I also have a phone call I'd like to make before we leave.* "How'd you get my room number?"

"It was tricky, let me tell you. Had to read the computer screen upside down." Bobby stood on his tiptoes and indicated how he'd had to stretch his neck to see over the counter.

He's full of shit. The light was flashing on the hotel phone indicating a message. *He watched the desk clerk dial my room.* He shook his head and returned to the bathroom.

"How long did you wait downstairs?"

"Ten minutes before I decided to take matters into my own hands. Don't you ever check for messages?"

"I was in the shower for god's sake."

"Whoever's sake it was, you could have at least ordered me a drink while I waited," Bobby walked across the room and opened the curtain.

Samira opens curtains too.

"Aunt Maggie tells me you took a little family to the ranch." Bobby's voice was playful. "Don't mind if I go through your wallet to find her picture, do you?"

No picture but getting one's not a bad idea. J.P. watched in the mirror as his brother examined the contents of his billfold.

"No photo. But hey, you've got all the protection you could need for a night." Bobby flashed a set of condoms between his fingers. "That's my brother the attorney. Always prepared."

And that's my brother, Robert. J.P. shook his head. *Always full of shit.*

The Ralston brothers called for an UBER to take them to the reef. A live band entertained on the beach while cocktail waitresses worked the crowd. When they'd had their fill of happy hour ale, they made their way inside the restaurant.

"Steak and lobster." Bobby rubbed his oversized stomach with his hand. J.P. ordered the seafood platter and requested a bottle of house wine.

"So, how are Megan and the kids?" J.P. watched his brother fill the stemmed glasses.

"Fine, doing fine." Bobby shared the Ralston smile again. "Megan's accounts are still growing which keeps her on the cutting edge of investments. Besides that, she's awesome as always." Bobby grinned. "I'm not on the road quite as much as I used to be so I'm catching more ball games and school concerts. Makes me feel like a real dad for a change." His eyes grew more serious. "What about you? How often do you see the boys?"

J.P. tipped his head back slightly. *Ale on an empty stomach might not have been a good idea.* He lowered his head to stabilize his vision.
~~~~~~~

"Well, James is currently living with me so I'm finding out all over again what it's like to be a dad." J.P. turned the stemmed glass in his hands but didn't lift it off the table. "I just spent four days with Josh, and it sounds like he'll come down and stay a week once I get home."

"So, what's up with James? Did he finally grow wise to his mother's ways?"

Janet and Bobby never did exactly bond. "Something like that." *Bobby was too wild for Janet's taste and Janet too stale for his.* "He and Bruce aren't seeing eye to eye anymore."

"Like they ever did."

"Maybe not," J.P. concurred again. "The judge decided it best for James to not live at home this summer."

"What's that do to your lifestyle?"

"Puts a new twist on everything from what time I wake up in the morning to when I can take a shower without running out of hot water." J.P. rested his head on the back of the booth. "But James seems to be adjusting all right. He has a job at the golf club. That keeps him occupied most of the day."

The waitress delivered a loaf of warm bread and clam chowder.

With the soup dish pushed aside Bobby asked another question. "Well, Big Bro, what can you tell me about this *little family* that accompanied you to the ranch?"

The chowder and bread were taking the edge off the alcohol. J.P. tried to hide the grin that was forming on his face.

"Uh-huh." Bobby pointed a finger at his brother. "Aunt Maggie's hoping this is the one to settle you down."

Suddenly Uncle Roy's words replayed in J.P.'s mind. *You're the one who might need tamed.*

"So, give me the lo-down bro. What's she like? How long you known her?"

J.P. hadn't talked to anyone about Samira. Not even Mike. *Can't hurt to let Bobby in on Samira.* "I've known her a couple of months now."

"Just a couple of months, huh? She must be movin' pretty fast."

"Not really," J.P. admitted. "She actually moves rather cautiously."

"Smart woman." Bobby grinned with a hint of brotherly torment. "If she knows anything about you at all she's wise to move slowly—a snail's pace even."

How is it my past always seems to get in the way of my future? Bobby was still talking, but J.P.'s mind wandered back to the magazine he'd left on the airplane.

"So, she must be stunning if you're still showing interest after eight weeks."

Stunning is close. The confrontation in Aunt Maggie's front yard replayed in his mind. *Amazing is more accurate.*

"And she must have kids if you took a *family* to the ranch."

That's a question I can answer. "Two girls. Thirteen and fourteen, I think."

"Right between Alicia and Angie." Bobby pulled out his phone and pulled up photos of his daughters. "Alicia will be thirteen in the fall and Angie just turned fifteen."

"So that means Justin is driving?"

"He's a senior this year, Phil. Same as Josh, remember?" Bobby flipped some more frames and stopped on a photo of his son.

Wow. Josh is going to be a senior in high school. Suddenly J.P. was aware how quickly time was passing.

The waitress replaced the empty soup bowls with fresh salads. J.P. picked up his fork. *A little more food in my stomach won't hurt a thing.*

"So, if you were to propose tomorrow you think she'd accept?"

Bobby was never one to beat around the bush. J.P. took a bite. *Doubtful on the accepting part after yesterday's scene in the yard.*

"For being newly in love you don't seem to have much to say."

"Who the hell said anything about love?" *I'm a far cry from being in love, little brother.*

"Aunt Maggie said she looks at you like she loves you."

J.P. put his fork down and rested his elbows on the table. "Do you believe *everything* Aunt Maggie tells you?"

Bobby made the sign of the Boy Scout with his hand. "Everything. Scout's Honor."

The wine was suddenly looking inviting again. J.P. took a sip. Then he took another. The whole time Samira's silhouette in the bedroom was playing in his mind. *Give him enough to keep him satisfied.* "Let's just say we're still getting to know each other, and with all four kids, there's a lot to process." *Does she really look at me like that?*

"Bullshit," Bobby challenged. "You think I'm going to buy that?" He took another bite of salad. "It's written all over your face, big brother. She's got you wrapped around her little finger, and I bet you haven't even had the guts to tell her that yet."

Maybe she does, but I have no intention of telling her anytime soon.

"Don't wait too long, Phillip, 'cause gems like that don't stick around too long." Bobby raised his wineglass in a toast. "Here's to taking a chance on this one."

Another reference to taking a chance. J.P. raised his wine and felt the tingle as the glasses touched. *He's spoken his piece. I doubt he brings her up again.*

The seafood platter was more than J.P. could eat. He pushed his plate away and sat up straighter in the booth.

"I almost hate to bring this up," Bobby was still working on a lobster tail. "But I'm here and you're here so I'm just going to say it." Bobby laid the lobster pliers on the edge of his plate and lifted a piece of meat out of the shell with his fork.

Now what's he got on his mind?

"You know, you're only a couple of hours from the Captain out here. Maybe you could take an afternoon and drive down to see him."

Where the hell did that come from?

"Seriously, Phil. He'd like to see you and you're not that far out of the way." Bobby worked another bite of lobster.

"Since when have you become so chummy with the Captain?"

"I don't know," Bobby spoke carefully. "He and I are getting along these days. I went down at Christmas you know. I've taken Megan and the kids down there a couple of times now. He always asks about you."

"What do you tell him?"

"What's there to tell? You work hard. You play hard. Then when you get a break, you usually spend it with the boys."

J.P. sighed heavily. *I avoided this conversation with Aunt Maggie only to run head on into it with my brother.*

"You know, I don't officially have to be back in Boston until day after tomorrow. I could stay on and go down even tomorrow if—"

"No." J.P. interrupted the suggestion while he still could. "I have a flight out in the morning, and I really need to be getting back." *If I get in early enough, I could catch Samira before she gets off work, maybe meet her at the Café Ole.*

Bobby stopped chewing. He was looking directly at his brother. "You know, he's aged a lot and he's mellowed over time. You might actually have a decent conversation with him even if you'd just pick up the phone."

"I don't have anything to say to the Captain."

Bobby wiped his fingers on a napkin. "Maybe that's not the point anymore, Phillip. Maybe the Captain has some things he needs to say to you."

This is exactly the reason I choose to distance myself from my family. New tension hung over the table.

"Hey, it's your life. You're going to live it as you choose and honestly, that's okay with me."

At least he's still honest with me.

"But if you get a sudden urge to maybe pop in on the Captain sometime, know he won't turn you away at the door." Bobby offered another refill on the wine, but J.P. refused. *One more glass of wine is not going to help me in the morning.*

Bobby picked up a more positive conversation just as easily as he dropped the last one. When the UBER driver let them out under the Hyatt's canopy, J.P. offered his extra bed for the night.

Back in the room, J.P. listened as Bobby checked in at home. *She's got to know he's been drinking the way his words are slurring together.* J.P. tried to block out his brother's conversation. He flipped through Sparky's notes. *I don't need to hear what he's talking to Megan about anyway.* But still, he couldn't help but hear. *Every time I turn around Samira's smile is taunting me.* Bobby lowered his voice as he told his wife he loved her. *I don't know if I'm ready to say those words to her yet.*

I don't even know what those words mean for sure.

~~~~~~~

Morning came too early. J.P. left Bobby sleeping off the wine and ale. *Happy trails, little brother. We'll have to do this again soon.* His own head was still pounding from the effects of the alcohol the night before, but duty called, and he knew Sparky was waiting.

Denise had successfully changed Sparky's flight, so he was off to the west coast. J.P. looked around the airport for an empty chair. *Two hours to kill before boarding.* He needed to sit down and get his thoughts together.

Too much to drink and not enough sleep.

There were no available chairs in the boarding area, so J.P. went back to the main concourse. He leaned on a wall across from a large lighted map. The longer he stood there the more he was drawn to the coastline glowing on the wall atlas. He followed the main highway out of Baltimore with his finger.

Richmond Virginia. About a hundred and fifty miles. Plus, traffic. Damn. Probably three hours down there, then the drive back. That puts me back in late tomorrow instead of this afternoon. Immediately he dismissed the idea and returned to his stance along the wall.

"Maybe the Captain has some things he needs to say to you." Both Bobby and Aunt Maggie have spoken those words.

I wonder if they can get me out later tonight. J.P. fingered the return ticket in his hands. *Can't hurt to find out, I guess.* J.P. inquired at the ticket counter.

"Well, sir, coach is full, but first class has a few openings. You could probably get out standby." She ran her long fake fingernail over the screen. "The last flight out leaves at eleven fifty-three."

J.P. signed on the line to release his seat on the morning flight. *I hope to God I'm doing the right thing, here.* He retraced his steps to the main level and signed on another line to rent a car. *I'll just pop in, pop out, return the car, and fly home.*
~~~~~~~

37 The Analysis

Samira

Honeysuckle filled the garden with sweet aroma. *One more bed to water after this.* Samira adjusted the spray nozzle on the end of the garden hose and gently showered the herb garden. She'd stayed in the house after dinner hoping Phil might call. Now that it was almost dark, Samira wished she'd started earlier. *Because now the mosquitoes are starting to bother.*

Tidbits of conversation with Phil played in her mind. *He was just a little younger than Krissy is now when he lost his mom.* She couldn't imagine growing up without her own mother. *Such a tender age.* But at one time she couldn't imagine her life without Tom either. *I guess that's something we accept if it comes to pass.*

The fountain was making shallow ripples in the garden pond. Samira knelt and ran her fingertips through the cool water. *It reminds me of the lake.* As she listened to the running water, she allowed her mind to whisk her back to Phil's kiss. *I've never been kissed like that before. Not once.* She could still feel his whiskers brush up against her cheek.

"Guess who, guess who?" Krissy was on the run from the house carrying the portable phone.

Samira had only one guess.

"You're not going to believe this." Krissy announced with her hand over the mouthpiece.

Just hand me the phone, Krissy.

"Not yet," Krissy taunted. "First I need to know if we're busy Thursday and Friday."

"I don't know yet," Samira reached for the phone again. "Just let me have it."

"She doesn't know yet," Krissy said into the phone. "I don't think there's anything going on. I'll go ask Kara while you talk to Mama."

Ask Kara what? "Hello?"

"Samira. Hi. How are you? I'm surprised I actually caught you at home."

The woman's voice was not even close to the voice she'd hoped for. *I'm always at home.*

"It's Ellen. I had a chance to come home for a few days, so I hopped the first plane north and here I am."

Ellen. Samira tried not to sound too disappointed. "Ellen, how are you? When did you get in?"

"I'm great. Doing great."

She repeats everything just like her mother. Ellen was Tom's youngest sister. *Every time she comes home there's an array of festivities.*

"I came in this morning. Mom and I did some shopping and then I caught up with some friends for lunch."

And she's still a social butterfly, also like her mother.

"I was hoping to pick up Kara and Krissy for a few days at the end of the week."

Samira sat down on the edge of a raised flowerbed and subconsciously began plucking miniature weeds from between the hydrangeas. "I can't think of anything going on. The girls have been babysitting—"

"Oh, I know, for your brother," Ellen interrupted. "Yes, Krissy told me. Do you think they could spare the girls for a couple of days?"

"I'll call Pam and see if she has anything planned."

"Oh, would you do that? That would be so good. I have to leave on Monday, but I really want to spend some time with the girls."

It will be good for the girls to see her.

"I'm thinking Thursday and Friday for sure. Saturday if they're still putting up with me."

Samira promised to get back to Ellen with an answer. *But right now, I'd like to keep my phone line open.*

"Do call me right back, do that, will you honey?" Ellen's voice sounded more and more like her mother's. "I'll be sitting by the phone."

I'll call her back after I finish out here. Samira snipped a collection of fresh flowers. A *couple of carnations, a coneflower, three cheerful zinnias, a handful of daisies, and baby's breath for accent. Perfect.*

Krissy was on her way out as Samira was on her way in the kitchen door. They almost collided.

"Oh, Mama. What did you tell her?"

"I told her I'd call her back after we talked it over."

"So, what is there to talk about?" Krissy threw her freckled arms into the air. "Aunt Ellen is home. We are in slumber party heaven." She pointed toward the hallway. "Kara is like, in there packing her things."

There was still plenty of dirty laundry from their trip to the ranch. *I sincerely doubt they have enough clean clothes to pack.* "Ellen's thinking maybe Thursday and Friday. There's plenty of time to get your things together."

Kara joined into the conversation. "But we should call Aunt Pam first, right?"

"Exactly. Give her a call and make sure she doesn't have anything major planned." *And try not to talk too long, please.*

"Here, Mama," Krissy reached for the flowers. "I can put those in water for you."

Samira handed off the flowers then stepped into the laundry room to wash her hands. When she got back to the kitchen Krissy was busily arranging the fresh cut flowers. *She's using my wine bottle for a vase.*

"Krissy. Where did you get that bottle?" *Why did I ask that?*

Krissy stopped, bewildered. "Under the sink." She pointed to the open cupboard door. "I saw it down there once and thought it would make a pretty vase."

Samira started to reach for the bottle. *That wine bottle is from my first date with Phil.* As she reached for the bottle, she caught a glimpse of Krissy's saddened, confused face.

What is the matter with me? She wanted desperately to hide the wine bottle back in safekeeping, yet at the same time she didn't want to destroy Krissy's array. *How do I fix this now?* "Do you think they will all fit?"

Krissy shrugged her shoulders. "Maybe. You didn't let me finish."

"I'm sorry." *I overreacted.* But at the same time, that is a personal memory. "I'd just never thought of using it for flowers." Silently, Samira watched Krissy go back to work. A few moments later Krissy held up a small batch of leftover flowers.

"I think we should put these in another vase." Krissy scrunched her face. "Do I need to *ask* before I pick one out of the china cupboard?"

Samira closed her eyes as she shook her head. "No, go ahead." *A couple are just a tad too tall.* When Krissy turned her back to cross the room, Samira took the liberty of rearranging a couple flowers to give it a better balance.

"I knew you would do that."

"Do what?"

"That. Move the flowers." Krissy returned to the counter with a crystal bud vase. "You always do."

"I can't help it." Samira shrugged her shoulders. "It's in my nature."

"Just like Granny."

Funny, I just compared Ellen to her mother. "Yes, I do get that from Granny, don't I?"

Krissy giggled. "You get a lot of you from Granny." She turned the bud vase all the way around for her mother to admire. "What do you think?"

"Perfect," Samira announced. *Personally, I'd cut that carnation a shade shorter, but I'm going to let it go.*

"Really?" Krissy carried the smaller bouquet to the dining room table. "Thanks, Mama." She admired her work. "I'm going to check the flowers later and make sure you don't move any." She flashed a quick smile in her mother's direction.

Leave it, leave it, leave it, the mother told herself. *It's only a carnation in a vase.*

~~~~~~~

The entire evening passed without a phone call from Phil. Disgusted with her own impatience, Samira tried to relax. She was curled into the downstairs couch trying to watch a movie with the girls. They were totally engrossed but it was all Samira could do to sit still.

I'm sure he's tired after flying in late and then working all day. Samira glued her eyes to the television screen. *But he did say he would try to call.* The bright screen against the darkened room made Samira's eyes water. *He just didn't say exactly when he would call.* She rubbed her eyes with her fingertips. *But he is out there on business. I really shouldn't even expect to hear from him until he's home and caught up.*

"Are you crying, Mama?" Krissy leaned back against the sofa.

"No," Samira shook her head. "I'm not."

"Me neither," Krissy noted. Then she lowered her voice. "But I think Kara is. She always cries at this part."

Oh, so this is a rerun for them. Samira couldn't believe she was having so much trouble settling into the film. She took a sip from her coffee cup. *Cold. Any excuse to go upstairs.*

~~~~~~~

Kara climbed up onto her mother's bed and pulled her knees into her chest. "Look at this, Mama," the young woman ran her finger over a welted spot around her right ankle.

Samira adjusted her reading light to take a better look. "Does it hurt?"

"No, it just itches like crazy."

"Have you been putting something on it?"

Kara nodded. "The cream that Aunt Maggie sent home with me."

Aunt Maggie? Samira ran her hand over Kara's ankle. "It looks like a couple of bug bites have swollen together. If it's not better in a day or so we might want Granny to take a look."

Kara nodded. "I'll put some more cream on before I go to bed." She pulled her hair to one side and began to weave the long strands into a braid. "The next time we go to the ranch I want to sleep in the tent."

Now there's a complete turnaround. "The next time? You didn't want to go at all this time."

"I know," Kara smiled shyly. "But it wasn't as bad as I thought."

Well, let's hear the whole story. Samira laid her book face down on the comforter. "What was your favorite part?"

"Hmmmm," Kara finished braiding her hair and wrapped the end with a band from around her wrist. "Maybe the hike after the boys found the missing card."

"Hey, what was that all about anyway?"

Kara giggled. "James told us the loser had to carry the heaviest backpack and do chores with Uncle Roy."

Uncle Roy? She's talking like she's related to these people.

"I didn't know if he was serious or not. James is tricky that way. But I didn't want us to be caught out there in the barn scooping horse…well, you know."

"I know."

"But we were losing really bad."

Samira reached for her own hairbrush and began working it through her hair. "Did you really think you could win by cheating?"

Kara flipped her heavy braid behind her shoulder. "Just for a minute." She giggled again. "But it didn't really work out that way and the boys really soaked us down at the lake."

Amazing how that all worked out.

"But the hike down to the lake was fun too. It was really pretty up there, Mama. I wished you could have seen the view. You could see the whole lake from there."

I did see that view, but not with you.

Kara's eyes came back to her mother. "Phil's pretty nice." She thought for a minute. "And he's pretty funny too."

He's much more than that. "Funny like how?" *Tell me what you think, Kara.*

"Funny like you never know what he's going to say. And he's always teasing Josh and James." Kara's eyes lit up. "Oh, and he plays into Krissy's stories really good. You know how Krissy starts chattering on, right?"

Of course.

"Well, yeah, like Krissy would start into this long, drawn out story and Phil would constantly interrupt her. He would say things like, 'Then what?' and 'Tell me that part again' Krissy would get really flustered because she's just used to talking until, we tell her to hush. But Phil kept her on her toes. A few times she couldn't even remember what she was going to say, and she'd have to, like stop talking." Kara was smiling. "He wasn't mean or anything. He was just really funny with her."

Samira could picture Krissy's antics. *I'm so glad Krissy didn't scare him off with her babbling.*

Kara crisscrossed her legs and pulled her ankles in with her hands. "You really like Phil, don't you Mama?"

Oh wow. Am I ready to answer that question yet? She stared at her daughter who was watching her very closely.

"I mean, like, are you like going steady or anything?"

Does sleeping with him constitute going steady? Samira put her hand to her forehead and rested her elbow on her knee. "I don't know. I guess I hadn't really thought much about that yet."

"Well, he must like you if he asked all of us to go to the ranch and everything."

"True."

Kara drew an invisible design with her finger on the comforter. "And when he looks at you, he seems like he," Kara paused in thought. "Like maybe he really likes being with you or something." Now Kara's dark eyes met her mothers. "Do you like being with him?"

I can answer that question. "Yes, Kara, I like being with him." *I like it more than I want to admit.*

Kara was deep in thought. Several long seconds passed.

"He looks really different when he doesn't shave."

That's for sure. Samira liked the rustic, laid back Phil.

"I think he's funnier when he's just hanging out and not all dressed up for work and stuff."

Me too. "What makes you think that?"

Kara raised her eyebrows and shrugged her shoulders. "He's more serious when he's like dressed up. Like when we were getting ready to leave, he'd shaved and then he was all business-like again."

That's an interesting observation. And not so far off the mark. "By the time we were leaving Phil was already thinking about going back to work. He had to fly out to the east coast later that night."

"Yeah, I know." Kara slid to the edge of the bed. "Josh told us. That's why he and James were staying a few more days at the ranch." Kara stood up and stretched with a big yawn. "Does he have to go out of town a lot?"

Now there's a good question. "I don't know." *But it's something I might want to find out.*

"Well, anyways," Kara started walking toward the door. "It was fun to go up there. Maybe he'll invite us again sometime."

Maybe. If I ever get to talk to him again.

"By the way," Kara stopped in the doorway and turned back toward her mother. "You know that magazine you bought for us?"

It was for me.

"I can't find it. I thought I had it with my things but when I started getting stuff ready to go with Aunt Ellen, I couldn't find it."

That's because I took it so I could talk to Phil about the model on the cover. Samira suddenly remembered. *On the swing.* Her heart rate increased. *I left it laying on the swing.*

"What is it, Mama?"

Samira threw her legs over the side of the bed. "Are you sure you didn't get home with it?" *I can't believe I asked her that. I know exactly where I left it.*

"Pretty sure." Kara yawned. "I'll look again tomorrow. Good night, Mama. I'll see you in the morning."

Samira watched until Kara was completely out of sight before burying her face in her hands. *I had it with me all weekend just so I could talk to him about it, only to leave it out there for the whole world to see.* She made her way to the bathroom. *Now what? Do I ever ask him about it, or did he find it before he left? What am I supposed to do now?*

Samira brushed her teeth. *I bought it for the sole purpose of discussion. But that didn't come as easily as I'd hoped.* She wiped her mouth on the corner of a towel. *And then again, maybe I've just read something into it. Maybe that Bobbie has no relevance in his life whatsoever.*

Samira left her bedroom and walked the nighttime routine through the house. *But then again, why would she call and leave a message for Phil to be in touch the next time he went out east?* She turned off all the lights in the front part of the house except for the one under the kitchen counter. *A little light adds comfort.* She peeked out the window. *It looks like Mrs. Barnes is already in bed for the night.* She double-checked the deadbolt locks on both doors and set the alarm.

The house was perfectly quiet. *So, Kara thinks he's funny.* She lifted her feet off the floor and tucked them under her covers. *He is. But he's more than that.* She reached over the nightstand and touched the brass base of the lamp. The light gently faded away. *And I happen to like the non-shaven Phil too.* Samira closed her eyes wishing he could be there with her. *I like them both. Phil and J.P.* She was beginning to understand the difference between the two. *Maybe Aunt Maggie found the magazine and tossed it out.*

Samira sat straight up in bed and immediately touched the base of the lamp again. The room was illuminated at once.

Aunt Maggie?

Samira put her hand to her forehead. *Where did that come from? She is NOT my aunt.* Samira grabbed her book and left the bedroom. She curled into the throw pillows in the corner of the sofa. *He can permeate all my thoughts, yet he can't be here with me. In fact, he can't even seem to find the time to call me from wherever he is.*

Another series of thoughts came to mind. *What if he's out on the east coast with that magazine woman?* It didn't seem so far-fetched after hearing Maggie tell Phil to call her when he got out there again.

Surely not. Samira's logical side kicked in. *How could he possibly spend a weekend like that with me only to turn around and spend time with someone else?*

The model's figure formed in Samira's mind. *That's the drawing point, isn't it? There's no way I can compete with that.* She squeezed a couch pillow into her churning stomach. *If only I'd have asked the hard questions when I had the chance.* The series of events that followed Janet's phone call replayed in fast forward motion.

No, that wouldn't have been a good time either. And had I brought Bobbie up before that, he might not have kissed me at all. I'd rather have his kiss than his explanation. Samira climbed up off the couch. *You over analyze everything.* Instead of reading, she decided to balance her checkbook. *At least that won't take any emotional energy.*

It was long into the night before Samira made her way back to bed. And by that time, all her thoughts were exhausted.

38 *Joseph Phillip*

Joseph Phillip

The afternoon sunshine was beating through the windshield of the rented sedan. J.P. opened the car door and sat with one foot on the pavement and the other still inside the car. He scrutinized the row of brick houses along the narrow, tree-lined street. *Looks like the right address.* He compared the house numbers to the return address on the worn envelope. He'd had the first letter from the Captain with him ever since Aunt Maggie insisted he take it. *Never had a desire to open it.* But it was with him all the time just the same.

Maybe I should have eaten something. The knots in J.P.'s stomach threatened to cramp. *No, on second thought, confrontation is usually better on an empty stomach.* Too many unpleasant memories plagued the drive down the coast. *It must be about twenty-four years since I've been face to face with the Captain. That's a hell of a long time, Ralston.*

J.P. finally climbed out of the car. *This would be a good time for one of Sparky's vodka shots.* He left the letter in his seat with his sport coat. *No reason to make this more formal than necessary.* He locked the car with the key control. *And no reason to drag it out either. Short and sweet and I'm on a plane to St. Louis.*

J.P. ascended the steps and raised the brass knocker. He turned and faced the front yard. A bronze golden eagle glistened in the afternoon sun at the top of a high flagpole. *Not even a breeze today.*

There was no answer. *This might make the visit even easier. I could leave my business card and be gone.*

Just the same, I drove all this way. J.P. struck the knocker twice more. He moved to the edge of the porch and watched a pair of sparrows hop across the manicured lawn.

Very slowly, the heavy wooden door opened. A small, elderly man of Asian origin stood on the other side. *Who is he?* J.P. rechecked the house numbers. *They're the same.*

"Yes, Sir?" The elderly gentleman bowed slightly.

J.P. eyed him carefully. *Might as well get it over with.* "I'm here to see Captain Joe Ralston."

The little man looked J.P. up and down with pursed lips. "Do you have an appointment? Sir."

"No, I don't.." *Do I need an appointment to see my own father?* "Does the Captain only work by appointment?" *That would be one way to get out of here without a confrontation.*

"No, sir." The little man bowed his head momentarily. "Who shall I tell him is calling?"

Enough with the sirs. "Tell him his son is here to see him."

"Yes, Sir."

J.P. stepped off the porch as the man disappeared behind the closed door. *I don't know if this was a good idea or not.* His stomach was still churning.

Momentarily, the door opened again. "The Captain will be up to meet you, sir." The Asian man disappeared.

J.P. judged the distance to the rented car. *There's still time to make an exit.* Deep down he knew he wouldn't leave, but the sting of being stood up an entire day at the St. Louis train station was suddenly fresh in his memory. *It wouldn't take much to get back in that car and drive away.*

The door opened again but J.P. couldn't bring himself to turn around. Footsteps crossed the porch, but J.P. refused to face his father. *I have nothing to say to him.*

Short and sweet. J.P. heard the Captain walk down the steps. *I've made my appearance.* The Captain crossed in front of his son. *He's a lot broader than I thought he would be at his age.* He walked straight and tall with his hands behind his back. *He's got to be over 80 by now.*

The Captain held his head high as their eyes connected.

I came here to see him. J.P. remained silent. *Surely, he can think of something to say.*

The Captain's clean-shaven face was leathered and worn but his eyes were still the same blue.

He really doesn't look much different than I remember. A long silence occupied the space between the Ralston men.

Finally, the Captain opened his mouth. "Joseph. Joseph Phillip."

J.P. glanced over the top of his father's shoulder into the empty street. No one had called him Joseph since...*since I don't know when.* It didn't sound right. *That name doesn't fit any more now than it did when I was growing up.* It was a name J.P. never grew into.

He knew his father's eyes were on him, but he couldn't think of anything decent to say. *What do you say to the man who chose not to show up after promising you the world for your eighteenth birthday?*

"Joseph." The aging Captain spoke the name again. "It's good of you to come."

Is it? You don't look exceedingly pleased to see me. With his hands still inside his pants pockets, J.P. realized he was slightly taller than the Captain. *He used to be the tallest man I knew.*

The Captain didn't offer a handshake or any other form of greeting. His hands were tucked tightly behind his back. "You look good, Joseph. You're taller, more fit than your brother."

Does that have a bearing on my inheritance? J.P. caught his thought and tried to dismiss the negative connotations. He stood still as the Captain walked all the way around him as if passing an inspection of sorts.

"What brings you to my quarters?"

What the hell is that supposed to mean? J.P. turned around to find his father facing away lighting a cigarette. *Does he think I'm here for my benefit?*

J.P. cleared his throat. "A letter, I guess."

The Captain nodded as he exhaled smoke through his nostrils. "The one to Maggie?"

J.P. nodded back.

"Did you read it?"

"No."

"I assumed as much." The Captain took another draw.

This is going nowhere. J.P. was beginning to plan his exit. *He can keep his goddamned assumptions to himself.* He looked up to find his father watching him very closely.

"Come on in. I'll introduce you to Tayshaun." With that the Captain started back up the steps to the porch. He motioned for J.P. to follow with a cigarette between his fingers.

I am not here to meet his friends. "Look," J.P. glanced toward the rental car. "You don't have to entertain me or show me around." *I don't even know why I am here.* He ran his hand through his hair. "I had business in the Baltimore area and hooked up with Bobby. He thought..." *Shit, do I tell him this was Bobby's idea? No.* "He offered to drive down with me but—"

"You don't have to explain anything to me, Joseph." The Captain's eyes were surprisingly gentle. "It's good of you to come." He finished the cigarette and stepped on the butt. With ease, the Captain leaned over and picked it off the porch floor.

I came this far. I might as well go inside. An awkward silence followed them. *Nothing feels right about being here.*

He stepped inside his father's house. It was sparsely furnished but the walls were covered with photographs, recognition plaques and honorary medals. *Wow. That's a lot of memorabilia.*

"What can I get you to drink?" The Captain had stepped behind a make-shift bar.

Anything to calm my nerves. "J.D. and Coke."

Nothing more was said. The Captain put the drink in his son's hand and lifted his own glass to his weathered lips.

The whiskey burned all the way down. *I wonder what he's drinking.*

The Captain sank into an oversized leather recliner in the corner of the room.

His furniture looks a lot like mine.

Leather bound books lined the walls of the adjacent room. *Has he read all these books, or are they only for show?* J.P. sat down on the edge of an ottoman. Much to his surprise the coffee table between him and his father was covered with photos. *There's James and Josh and all of Bobby's kids.* A glass top protected the prints.

"Maggie sends them to me periodically."

J.P. looked closer. *Some of these are more recent than what I have.*

"You have a set of good-looking boys, Joseph." The Captain's eyes were a darker blue than they had been outside in the sunshine. "Do you go by Joseph?"

I have a feeling he already knows the answer to that question. J.P. took another sip of the drink before answering. "No, I don't." The moment of truth was about to be known. Professionally I use my initials. Aunt Maggie still uses my middle name." *Along with a few close friends.* Samira's face came into his mind's eye with that thought. *And I like the way she says my name.*

"Phillip." The Captain seemed to be mulling that over in his mind. "Your mother would have preferred Phillip over Joseph anyway." He blinked slowly.

And how would you know that or anything else about my mother? J.P. narrowed his eyes at his father. *All you cared about was climbing the ranks.*

"Leona." The Captain looked deep into his drink. "I still think about her every day." He held his glass up toward the wall behind J.P. "She's there in my thoughts all the time."

Mom is all over that wall. J.P. stood up for a closer look.

"I have something I want to show you." The Captain rose from his chair and disappeared into another room.

J.P. took the liberty to look even closer. Some of the shots of his mother were familiar. *But most of these I've never seen.* His eyes studied her face and her hair and her hands. *I remember everything about her.* J.P.'s memory was lingering somewhere between the past and the present.

The little Asian man appeared silently and set a tray of cookies on the photo-strewn coffee table.

"Thank you, Tayshaun." J.P. heard his father's voice. "This is my son, Joseph Phillip. He goes by Phillip."

J.P. turned and faced the elderly man who folded his hands and bowed his head in silent greeting.

"Tayshaun is from the Philippines. We've been together since sixty-eight."

J.P. nodded. *That's a long time for my father to maintain a relationship of any kind.* He took another sip of the whiskey before turning his eyes back to the photos on the wall.

"She was a beautiful woman," the Captain spoke again. "Here." His able hands took the cover off an old shoebox. "I told Maggie I had some things that belonged to your mother. They're all here."

That's not why I'm here. "You don't need to give me anything of hers."

"Hear me out," the Captain continued. "I gave a few things to Robert at Christmastime. These are yours. I didn't trust the U.S. Mail."

You don't trust the U.S. Mail? Now that's funny. But J.P. really didn't want anything of his mother's. *I don't want any of his baggage.*

The Captain lifted a stack of banded envelopes. "These are the letters Leona wrote to me over the years. I sorted them so you and Robert could get a feel for her thoughts while you were back in Missouri with her."

And where were you in the world while we were back there? The whiskey was starting to mess with his mind on an empty stomach. J.P. helped himself to a plain cookie from the tray.

"And these I saved thinking you might have a use for someday." The Captain hesitated before opening an old envelope. "I gave the other set to Robert." He poured the contents out in his hand and examined them as if for the last time. "These are her wedding rings, Joseph." He held them out for his son to take. "She'd want you to have them."

J.P. set his glass down on the table, but he couldn't bring himself to accept the rings. *They're not mine and they don't represent anything that has ever been part of my world.*

"You should give them to Bobby."

"Robert has the anniversary set. These belong to you."

I don't want them. "I didn't come here to take her stuff."

The Captain raised his eyes and met his son face to face. "And I didn't invite you here to argue about it."

"You didn't invite me here period."

"Maybe you should have read the goddamned letter."

J.P. set his jaw. "It wasn't addressed to me." He watched the Captain turn away.

Behind his father he took note of more military honors. *Action in World War II, Korea, and Vietnam.* Another series of honors mentioned Captain Joseph Phillip Ralston's advisory roles in Desert Storm. Photos lined the walls with pictures of the Captain shaking hands with various presidents and other public figures.

All this yet he couldn't find any time to check in at home. J.P. didn't want a part of anything that was written in those letters. *They're not addressed to me either.* The whiskey on an empty stomach was taking full effect and J.P.'s temper was playing into it with ease.

"I don't know who Leona was to you, Captain. She was my mother and at some point, in time I didn't get her back." J.P. scanned the photos of her again.

The Captain kept his back to his son, but his voice was strong when he spoke.

"Neither did I. She didn't want to raise a family on military bases, so we made the decision not to have children. But during one of the most memorable nights of my life she conceived. And at that point in time, I gave her up for you and later for Robert because that was the way she needed it to be."

That's bullshit. J.P. balanced his weight with his hand against one of the bookcases. *Nothing is making sense.*

The Captain turned and walked back to the leather chair leaving the wedding rings and letters in the cardboard box for J.P.'s taking.

"So that's it?" J.P. addressed his father from the dining room. "I drive all the way down here and walk away with Leona's thoughts and her rings."

"That's it." The Captain didn't show any emotion.

No apology for leaving us out there? No explanation for the flight that never made it home? No excuse for not getting off the train in St. Louis?

J.P. fingered the banded letters. *Hell, I came all this way and gave up my flight home. I'd might as well take the box and be done with it.* He haphazardly replaced the lid on the box and started for the front door. *At least he won't be able to accuse me of never coming.*

But there was one obstacle yet to cross. *I have to walk in front of him to get to the front door.* J.P. tucked the box under his arm but couldn't force his feet to walk across the room.

"It was still good of you to come, son."

J.P. couldn't help but look at his father. *Why do I recognize the look in his eyes now?*

"If you don't have to rush right off, I'd like to take you to dinner." The Captain was studying his son's face. "It might be good to mix a meal with that whiskey."

The last thing I need to do now is get stuck socializing with the Captain at some Navy hangout.

"Nothing fancy. A good crab dinner and you'll be on your way." The Captain rose from his chair. "What do you say? My treat."

On the other hand, food won't hurt anything either. Especially before a long drive.

The Captain summoned Tayshaun to bring his car around. J.P. was surprised to see a late model Lincoln pull up out front. *Maybe an old Cadillac, but never a new Lincoln.* The display lit up when the Captain's cell phone automatically connected through Bluetooth. *Who would've known the Captain would have all the latest technology in his car?*

They drove into the country and stopped at what appeared to be a little shack. J.P. eyed the sign out front warily. *Mobley's Crab House. Looks like a hole in the wall.*

"It might not look like much, but Mobley fixes up the best crabs on the Eastern Coast." The Captain was obviously aware of J.P.'s demeanor. "Trust me."

Trusting you is not something I've ever done in the past. The attorney in J.P. was still very leery of the entire situation. *I don't like the way the Captain is trying to warm up to me and I don't like the fact that I'm still in Virginia when my flight is leaving from Baltimore.* Nevertheless, he allowed his father to order a bucket of crab legs with the complete works.

It felt strange to be sitting across a table from a man he knew only from pictures and stories and distant memories. *I don't ever remember having a meal with the Captain.* J.P. watched. The Captain passed his fork from his left hand to his right. *That's odd. I wonder which hand he writes with.*

"You've done very well for yourself, Phillip."

J.P. took note of the Captain's purposeful use of his preferred name.

"What made you choose law school over something else?"

"Money." J.P. answered honestly. "At the time of decision, I went for the wage."

The Captain smiled for the first time. It was the same easy smile J.P. recognized in Josh. "Good motivator." He took a generous bite of crabmeat. "What made you stay in law?"

That's an interesting question. "I like to win and I'm good at it."

This time the Captain all but laughed. And then he did something that caught J.P. completely off guard. The Captain ran his hand through his thick gray hair. *I do that all the time.*

"I like your spunk, Phillip. That's what makes you a successful attorney."

Since he's asking questions, maybe I'll ask a few of my own. "What made you stay in the Navy?"

The Captain looked out from under his eyebrows. "I liked winning too and I was good at it."

That's not a fair answer.

"But I lost a few too." With that, the Captain concentrated on his dinner for a moment. "Eventually winning doesn't mean as much in light of the losses."

About that time J.P.'s phone rang. *Of course, it would ring now.* He excused himself from the conversation as politely as possible.

"This is J.P."

"Where the hell are you?" Denise sounded frantic on the other end. "I have called every airline from here to the East Coast."

"Virginia. I'm in Virginia." *Didn't I call her?* "I'm flying in standby late tonight."

"Business endeavor or otherwise?"

Otherwise. J.P. answered in his mind. *No, it's more than otherwise. It's a little of everything.*

"So Sparky is in L.A. and you're in Virginia and I am totally in the dark here. You were supposed to be in a meeting with Jeffrey Hughes and Sean Bridges an hour ago."

Sean Bridges? When did she arrange that meeting? J.P. excused himself from his father's table. Once outside, he briefly granted permission for Denise to do whatever it was she needed to appease Jeffrey Hughes and then explained that he was going to have to call her back. *I hate to do that to her, but I can't leave him sitting in there either.*

J.P. returned to the table, surprised by his sudden concern for his father.

"Business as usual?"

"Business anyway," J.P. admitted. "My assistant was expecting me back a couple of hours ago."

"Do you need to be back yet today?" The Captain checked his vintage military wristwatch. "It's an hour earlier there."

I'm aware of the time change. "I fly out standby tonight. Business will resume then." *If Denise is still talking to me.* J.P. considered the ramifications of missing a meeting with Jeffery Hughes. *And if the city of Joplin hasn't cut all ties with the Hughes brothers for tampering with the city's new economic development plan.*

"But you know as well as I do that business runs smoother when you're there to direct the traffic." The Captain shared the easy Ralston smile again. "I know that look on your face. You're scheming."

He doesn't know anything about me. "What look?"

"The one I see in the mirror." The Captain mimicked his son's serious face.

I've seen that look in the mirror too. This time J.P. had to share the smile. *And I've seen it in Josh and James from time to time.* It was something Aunt Maggie always referred to as being in the Ralston genes.

A little while later J.P. watched his father sign for dinner. *Left-handed. I always wondered why I did some things right-handed and other things with my left.* Now he knew. *Another Ralston gene.*

~~~~~~~

Back at the Captain's house, J.P. picked up the cardboard box with less hesitation than he had before.

The Captain was in the kitchen making a phone call. J.P. took the liberty to once again admire the numerous photos of his mother. *She looks so happy.* The pictures above the Captain's desk included faded prints of him and Robert from days gone by.

"Jos—, I mean, Phillip," the Captain corrected mid-sentence. "I can get you out in an hour."

I need to be headed out now if I'm going to make my flight. It took a little over two hours to drive down here and I'll need to check in for stand-by—

"On a flight." The Captain clarified. "There's a Fed Ex flight scheduled for takeoff at nineteen hundred. I can get you clearance into St. Louis."

What's he doing? I don't need to be his charity case.

The Captain squared his shoulders. "This is something I can do, Phillip," his eyes had turned a steel blue.

There were a lot of things he couldn't do. *Like go back in time and fix the broken and missing parts.* J.P. ran his hand through his hair. *Now I'll think of the Captain every time I do that.* Bobby's words suddenly replayed in J.P.'s mind, *"Maybe it's what the Captain needs to say to you."*

"All right. If it will make you feel better." J.P. resigned. *That saves me the drive back to the city.*
~~~~~~~

The Captain's face remained solemn. "It would. I want to do this for you."

J.P. granted permission for his father to follow through. Arrangements were made to have the rental car picked up at the house. The next thing J.P. knew, they were on their way to the airport. *I'm amazed how quickly the Captain is granted access to restricted areas simply by flashing his smile and his VIP badge.*

The Captain parked his car under the nose of a Federal Express jetliner. As soon as he stopped, uniformed men opened the car doors and escorted the Captain to the plane with proper salutes along the way.

Impressive.

A seasoned officer presented the Captain with official paperwork granting permission to board. Without any hesitation, the Captain handed his key fob over to the officer. *Obviously, they know the routine.*

Now this almost beats the Hughes' perks at the Hyatt in Springfield. J.P. was slightly humored at the military's insistence on proper ritual.

The Captain led the way up the stairs to the open door on the jetliner. Three uniformed crewmen were saluting his father with highest regard. The Captain returned the salute and then put the men at ease. He handed over the paperwork and introduced his son using his full name.

"Joseph Phillip Ralston, the second." The Captain stood straight and tall.

I'll be damned. For the first time in J.P.'s life, he felt slightly honored to be his father's son.

"You will have to pass security. Sir." J.P. realized the crewman was speaking to him. He had no idea what security entailed but he agreed. Immediately, the crewmen took his garment bag and briefcase including his computer. *They don't seem to be concerned about the contents of the box the Captain is holding.*

J.P. lifted his arms as a metal detector scanned his entire body. He obediently removed his shoes when asked. And he showed them two forms of identification without resistance. When the crew was satisfied, they stamped the paperwork and informed the Captain of clearance.

Only then did the Captain proceed on into the cabin. Much to J.P.'s surprise, the airliner seats occupied only a few short rows. A partition stopped the view to the back of the aircraft. Only three other men, all in uniform, occupied the cabin.

The Captain underwent the same security measures as his son and then took a seat in the first row and indicated that his son should sit next to him.

What's he doing? "Are you flying to St. Louis too?"

"On the contrary, I am flying all the way to St. Louis and back." The Captain watched his son carefully. "The last flight carrying a family member never made destination."

My mother's flight home.

"This time I'm going to make sure the boys at home get their father back."

The Captain's presence thwarted J.P.'s wayward thoughts. No longer did he question the relevancy of his visit here. The old man was doing what he could. *And he's willing to go down with the craft if, for whatever reason, it doesn't make destination.*

J.P. sat down in the spacious seat next to his father. But there were more than two boys waiting back home. *And she's a damn good reason to make it home.*

There was no service crew aboard the jetliner. No one told him to buckle his seat belt. No one told him to straighten the back of his seat. But when the jet engines revved J.P. did those things anyway. He noticed the Captain doing the same.

They were high in the sky before either of them spoke.

"Two other officers lost their wives in that same flight," the Captain remembered out loud. "Eventually the others remarried but Leona was all I ever needed. She's been enough for me over the years." His eyes had softened considerably. J.P. could feel the jetliner settle into cruising altitude.

J.P. listened as his father shared his most treasured memories. Stories of his mother's visits to bases all over the world filled J.P.'s mind with new insight on the long-distance relationship that sustained both his father and mother for the better part of their marriage.

"She was the only thing that kept me going in the heat of combat."

J.P. dared not look at his father while he talked for fear of ruining the stream of memories that triggered some of his own treasured thoughts. Once, when J.P. looked at his father's hands, he realized the Captain was holding Leona's rings.

"I'd raised up a lot of those boys by the time we got to Nam, Phillip."

J.P. was surprised to hear his name mentioned in that sentence. *I figured by now he'd forgotten he was even speaking to me.*

"Sailing into the sea without most of my crew that night was one of the hardest things I ever had to do, next to putting your mother on a flight home every time my furlough was up."

In the archives of recollection, J.P. remembered his father being home two, maybe three times during his childhood.

"But the hardest thing I ever did was walk away from you boys on that Missouri farm." The Captain stopped talking and J.P. almost wondered if he had to compose himself before continuing. "Leona stood there proud and strong, holding your hands in hers."

That was the day I left teeth marks in his shoulder. The scar on his hand reminded him of another boy who needed a father.

The Captain ran his hand through his hair. "I went out there to bring Leona and you boys back to Virginia, but Leona would have nothing of it. She knew what you needed." The Captain took a long pause. "You were better off without me there, Phillip."

It's almost like he's read my thoughts.

"I was brash and impatient and out of my territory. You needed your mother and her family more than you needed me."

That's exactly what I've told myself concerning Janet's insistence on taking custody of the boys. J.P. pressed his head back into the comfortable seat. *They needed their mother more than they needed me.*

"Then after she was gone, I was glad you and Robert were already comfortable with Maggie and Roy. They were your family more so than I ever could be."

That's enough. J.P. closed his eyes and tried to lose himself in the roar of the jets. *I don't want to hear anymore.* But now the Captain was turning in his seat to face him.

"The last time I saw you," the Captain nodded his head indicating a clear memory. "You were leaning on the railing at the train station."

So, he was there.

"You were so handsome and strong and confident."

Like hell I was. All I wanted was for you to step off that train and take me somewhere far away from that Missouri farm.

"I watched you for a long time before deciding you were better off without my interference."

J.P. started to shake his head, but the Captain continued.

"You had a future where you were. You didn't need me coming in there passing judgment and making suggestions. And that's exactly what I'd have done." The Captain leaned back in his seat once again. "No. You were better off there without me."

You're wrong, Captain. I needed you more that day than either one of us realized. Subconsciously, J.P. could feel the jetliner decrease in speed. *We don't have much time left.*

"Here," the Captain lifted J.P.'s hand off the armrest. Without any discussion he pressed Leona's rings into his son's hand.

J.P. closed his hand around them, honored to have them in his possession.

Several minutes later the Ralston men stood shoulder to shoulder at the top of the stairs. The sultry night air of summer in St. Louis was heavy.

"It was good flying with you, son."

J.P. shared his easy smile. "First class will never be the same."

The Captain mirrored his son's smile.

J.P. adjusted his garment bag on his shoulder as they started to descend the steps. Once on solid ground, a band of Federal Express employees surrounded the Captain in honorary regard. The Captain acknowledged them as he continued to walk his son to a waiting car.

"Where do you need to go?"

"St. Louis International will have a hopper down to Joplin." J.P. started to put his bags in the backseat when a uniformed woman silently offered to take them for him. *Now this is service.*

The Captain looked apologetic. "I'm afraid we don't fly directly into Joplin, but this driver will get you over to the connection."

J.P. was astounded at the service. Especially on such short notice. He looked up planning to offer a final thanks to his father, but the look on the Captain's face indicated there might be more. J.P. waited.

The Captain looked at the ground. "Winning is good, Phillip. But some things in life aren't worth losing. Some things you can't play to win." His father's eyes were clear and serious when he looked up. "Son, no matter how good you are at winning, there may come a time when winning isn't enough."

I've never heard him call me 'son' until today.

"I hope you find the one who will give you enough that the need to win will lose its power."

Give me enough that the need to win will lose its power...

"It was good of you to come, Phillip." The Captain placed the cardboard box in J.P.'s hands.

My hands look just like his.

Without an invitation, the Captain wrapped his arm around his son's shoulder and gave him a good solid pat of approval.

I don't think he's ever done that to me before either. J.P. returned the gesture. *But it feels right.* He watched his father turn and cross the tarmac, obviously aware of where he needed to go to fly home. The Captain turned around when he reached a waiting vehicle. Standing straight and tall, he saluted his son.

He didn't have to do that. J.P. acknowledged his father's salute with a broad smile and a nod of the head. *But I'm glad he did.*

39 Around the Table

Samira

Samira clicked the remote control in her hand and displayed the final slide in the PowerPoint presentation. *The goal is to expand the online services at the library.* She had spent several weeks in preparation for today's meeting with the board of trustees. *Be careful not to let them divert the attention to other areas also in need of funding.*

Following a brief question and answer session, the board thanked Samira and began proceedings to adjourn. *I can't wait to get out of here.* She fastened the button on her suit jacket to calm the butterflies in her stomach.

"Miss Cartwright," a board member offered his hand. "Congratulations on the recent successes at Maple Street. Things are going very well. You keep it up and they're going to want you directing business downtown."

Samira accepted the compliment graciously. *It's nice to be recognized, but I prefer the branch down the street from my house.*

"Well done, Samira, as usual." The board chair adjusted her wire-rimmed glasses. "I appreciate your time this afternoon."

"This was important," Samira pointed out. "It's time to see this proposal through."

"And that you did." The businesswoman knit her brow in thought. "We'll make our presentation to the board of supervisors in a week. I'll be sure to call you as soon as we hear anything back."

"Thank you, Geraldine." Samira returned a firm handshake.

It's over, it's over, it's over. And I am so relieved. Not only was Samira finished speaking in front of a crowd, her days of research and number crunching could now turn to more exciting events. *Like preparing for the sculptor who's coming in for seminars next week.* Samira was totally lost in her own thoughts as she left the conference room.

"Hey Pretty Lady."

There's only one person who would have spoken those words. She turned but didn't see anyone. *I'm probably just hearing things.*

The next time she heard them, she stopped walking. *That must be Phil.* She adjusted her purse on her shoulder and turned all the way around.

J.P. Ralston was standing just a few feet away. *He's clean-shaven, in a three-piece suit, and carrying a briefcase.* Samira almost didn't recognize him. *He must be working.*

J.P. was holding a pair of glasses. "What brings you all the way to city hall on this fine afternoon?"

Last I knew he was still on the east coast somewhere. Suddenly she wondered how long he'd been back and why he hadn't called. *I should be furious.* Despite her disappointment, Samira couldn't help but smile. *I'm still glad to see him.* "Business."

Phil lifted his chin slightly in understanding.

"And what brings you to city hall this afternoon?"

"Business." Phil returned the smile.

At least he didn't answer with another question. They were still standing several feet apart.

Phil's eyes came alive with energy. "But given an opportunity we could change that."

"Really?" *What makes you think I'd be willing to take that opportunity?* "And what would you change it to, Mr. Ralston?"

"Strictly pleasure."

Samira's cheeks suddenly burned with embarrassment. *I wonder if anyone heard that.*

Phil gently took a hold of her elbow and guided her across the foyer to a recessed doorway.

"You gave an incredible presentation in there. I am impressed."

Samira was taken aback. "In where?"

"In that meeting."

I was so nervous. "You were watching me?" *He had no right to eavesdrop without my knowing.*

"The door was ajar."

Samira glanced toward the conference room. Sure enough, there was a full-length pane of glass in the door. *It's a good thing I didn't know that at the podium.* She tried to dismiss the subject. *It was nerve wracking enough without knowing Phil was watching.* "When did you get back?"

"Very late Tuesday night."

Samira watched Phil recalculate his answer.

"No, it was more like early Wednesday morning come to think about it."

And it's Thursday already. "Did you have a good trip?"

"Let's just say it wasn't at all what I'd planned but—"

He's not telling me everything.

"It was fruitful in several facets."

Phil's eyes were distant as he completed his sentence.

In personal or professional facets?

"I didn't get you called."

"I noticed." Samira tried not to sound hurt. "But that's okay." *I guess.* She thought again. *But if he's not going to call, then he shouldn't tell me he might.*

Phil ran his hand through his hair. "I've been booked solid."

"You don't have to explain."

"Does it help if I thought about calling every night?"

"A little." Samira smiled shyly. *How difficult is it to pick up the phone?* Out of the corner of her eye she caught him checking his watch.

"I need to be going," she offered. "I have a few things to finish up at the library before picking up the girls from the pool."

"Yeah, me too." Phil's eyes were searching hers as if he had more to say. "I meet with the city attorney here in about two minutes and Miles is rarely late."

A sudden thought occurred. *Unless he's too busy.* "Are you *booked* for dinner?"

"Tonight?"

Yes, tonight. "Six-thirty. You can eat and run if you need to. *"Anything just to spend some time with him.*

Phil checked his watch again. Samira could tell he was beginning to shift into a full business mode. *He's probably too busy.*

"I can give it a shot," Phil lifted his shoulders slightly. "It may depend on the results of this meeting."

"Fair enough," Samira let him off the hook. "I'll set the table at six-thirty. But leftovers warm in the microwave anytime." *It doesn't really matter what time he gets there.*

"Fair enough," the attorney echoed her words. "I'll see what I can do."

"Are the boys with you?" *I can set plates for them too.*

Phil checked his watch again. "Not until tomorrow."

He really needs to go.

When the door across the way opened, Phil politely excused himself. "I'll shoot for six-thirty."

What I wouldn't give for that door to be ajar so I could watch him in action.

~~~~~~~

Back at the library Samira sorted through a stack of mail as she updated Mrs. Haddock and Daphne, their newest assistant, on the afternoon meeting.

"Now maybe we can get back to our regular agenda," Mrs. Haddock commented. She started to leave the office but stopped in the doorway. "Oh, by the way, Ms. Cartwright," she nodded her head toward the circulation desk. "The ladies from the historical society were here. They left a stack of resources they've decided not to use in their display. They wanted to know if there was a way to catalog and file them here with the other city historical records."

"I can take a look." Samira hadn't realized how much energy she'd poured into the presentation. *I'm exhausted.* The historical documents were sitting on the corner of the counter. Samira pulled a high stool next to the pile and sat down.

She skimmed them with half interest and laid them aside as she sorted. *Hmmm. What's this?* Something near the bottom of the pile caught Samira's eye. *It looks incredibly old.* It was a leather-bound book with yellowed pages. Very carefully Samira opened the cover. In antiquated script penmanship she read:

Diary of Mr. David C. Montgomery, Mayor of Joplin. 1933-39.

Ever so carefully Samira turned the pages. *It appears to be a log of the mayor's daily appointments and schedules.* Some paragraphs were complete sentences. Others were fragmented thoughts and lists of things to be done. *Was this left in this pile on accident?*

"It's four o'clock, Miss Cartwright." Mrs. Haddock pointed at the clock. "I can take these to your office for tomorrow if you like."

It is time to be going. Samira ignored the clock. *But there are several references in here to Mr. Lloyd Hughes.* She continued to turn the pages. *Without a doubt, Lloyd Hughes is the name I searched extensively for Phil on his initial visit to the library. I should remember.* She ran her finger down the spine. *I typed it into the search engine enough times. I wonder if it's the same Hughes family from Springfield.*

Samira gathered her purse to leave for the day. She was almost to the front door when she decided to go back for the diary. *If Phil is still working on the case, that book might be of significance. He can thumb through it, and I'll bring it back tomorrow.*

~~~~~~~

I don't know what I was thinking. Samira scolded herself as she washed the seeds out of a green pepper. *How could I forget about Ellen picking up the girls tonight?* She placed the pepper on a cutting board and ran a sharp knife through it. Once sliced, she began chopping it into smaller pieces. *Phil does that to me. He scrambles my thoughts.*

"What's for supper?" Krissy reached for the cookie container.

"Company." *Oh, for heaven's sake.* "Stir fry."

"Who's the company?" Krissy

"I'd prefer you hold off on snacking until after supper. We're going to eat pretty quick here."

"With who?"

Samira glanced out the kitchen window and momentarily wondered if Mrs. Barnes would be watching the driveway all evening.

"Hel-lo." Krissy leaned into her mother's face. "I'm waiting."

"With Phil."

"Cool. He can meet Aunt Ellen."

I hope NOT. Samira caught her thought. *That's the last thing I need.* Suddenly Samira regretted the dinner invitation altogether. *I am not ready for Tom's family to know about Phil.* "He's going to eat and run." *I hope.* "I doubt he'll still be here by the time Ellen arrives."

Krissy squeezed her shoulders together. "She said around eight thirty or nine. Oh, I can't wait to see her." The girl wrinkled her nose when Samira took the skin off an onion. "Whew. That's strong." She stepped away from the counter. "Too bad we can't find that fashion magazine. We wanted to show Aunt Ellen those custom fingernail designs. I bet she could do something like that for us."

That magazine. Samira blinked her eyes at the onion. *Too bad I left it in such a precarious place.*

"Do you know where else it might be, Mama?"

Samira wiped an eye with the back of her hand. "I don't have it." *Anymore.*

Krissy sighed heavily. "Well, we had it at Aunt Maggie's, but I don't think we brought it home."

There it is again. This time from Krissy. *Aunt Maggie.*

"What about James?" Krissy was headed for her bedroom. "Is he coming?"

"No," Samira answered as she chopped the onion. "I assume James and Josh are still at Aunt Maggie's." *Oh, for Pete's sake. She is NOT any relation to us. None.*

"I'm packed and ready to go." Kara flopped onto the sofa. "If my friends call, just tell them I'm with Aunt Ellen."

Samira noticed the excited grin on her daughter's face.

"I can't wait to see her."

Ellen. She had somehow retained a magical effect on the girls. *That's probably because she still lives in a world of make-believe herself.* Samira checked the rice. *Ellen may never grow up.*

"Kara, could you set the table please?"

Tom would be glad his sister still brings so much joy to the girls.

"Oh, for four." Samira corrected the number of plates in Kara's hands. "We'll need one more."

"Oh, really?" Kara reached for another plate. "And who might the other plate be for?"

Samira turned away to hide her smile. "Phil."

"Is that why you keep looking out the window?"

"I'm not looking out the window."

Kara laughed. "Yes, you are. Every time you do something you look out the window to see if he's here yet."

Samira looked out the window. "Well, he's not." But Mrs. Barnes was working in her front yard. *That's convenient.*

By the time Phil's truck was pulling in the driveway, dinner was almost on the table. Samira wanted it to be ready so he could just eat and go if he needed. *I am the one who needs him to eat and run.*

"Oh wow." Krissy flew across the living room to the front door. "He brought Chase." Without any hesitation she opened the door and welcomed Phil with a happy greeting.

He had changed but he was still wearing slacks and a long-sleeved shirt with the cuffs rolled twice. *He looks more at ease now.* Samira enjoyed the way he interacted with Krissy. *But I miss his beard, just the same.* She watched Krissy take Chase down the front sidewalk and into the garage. Phil let himself into the front room.

"Hey, Pretty Lady."

Samira smiled. *I love the way he says that.* "Hey."

Phil closed the door. When she turned around with the hot food, he was standing in her kitchen. She paused for a moment, holding the hot dish between two hot pads. Phil took it from her and set it on the table.

"Okay, I think we're all set. I'll get the girls."

"No, wait," Phil intercepted her. Without asking permission he kissed her once on the lips.

He can't find time to call, but he can steal a moment to kiss me. Samira felt her frustration dissipate into desire. *But I can't stay here like this.* She wrapped her arms around his waist and allowed him to kiss her again. *We're on a deadline.*

"More business than pleasure?"

He knows I'm on edge. "Possibly." *He has no idea what I'm up against tonight.* "What can I get you to drink?"

Phil leaned against the kitchen counter. "Water is fine."

Samira filled a glass with ice cubes. Just as she reached for the faucet, she caught her hand on the edge of the sink. "Damn."

"Did you break a nail, Mama?" Kara asked the question as she entered the room. She looked at Phil. "Mama only swears when she breaks a nail."

Samira was examining her fingernail.

"Let me see." Phil tried to take her hand.

"No, it's okay." *It's nothing, really.*

Phil didn't back down. Instead, he raised her hand and examined the notched fingernail. "It doesn't look too bad," he commented almost with a tease. "Can I kiss it and make it better?"

I don't appreciate the sarcasm. If that's what it is. She pulled her hand away from his. "No, that won't make it better."

Phil kissed it anyway then offered to finish filling the glasses for dinner. Samira was slightly embarrassed by the petty issue. *It's just a fingernail.* She called Krissy to dinner.

Phil headed Chase back outside when Krissy came in. "He's been with Mike for a couple of days so he's more rambunctious than usual. I probably should have left him at the ranch with the boys."

"Oh, no." Krissy interjected. "Don't make him stay out. Can't he stay in here while we eat?" She stepped around the dog and folded her hands in prayer before her mother. Please, please, please? I can put a rug on the floor like Aunt Maggie did and he'll stay right on it. I bet you he will."

There's that Aunt Maggie again. Samira glanced at Phil to see if he'd noticed. *If he heard it, he isn't letting on.*

"He'll be alright outside."

Samira put her hands on her hips. "He can stay if he'll stay on the rug."

"Oh, thank you, thank you, thank you." Krissy squealed. She hugged her mother around the neck then quickly turned to the dog and gave the 'Stay' command Phil had taught her at the ranch.

I can't believe I just gave into a plea for a dog. With that settled, they gathered around for the family meal. *Four around the table again.* Samira passed the chicken. *It used to be like this with Tom.*

Conversation flowed easily between Phil and the girls. He quizzed them about their experience at the ranch. Then he asked them about their week of babysitting. *If this pattern continues, he'll ask them about this coming weekend, and I don't want him to know that Ellen is on her way.*

Samira was somewhat relieved when the telephone rang. It was easier to avoid the subject of in-laws than it was to try to explain.

"Mama, it's for you," Kara announced casually. She handed the phone to her mother. "It's Uncle Wes and he says he needs you." Kara leaned over and whispered. "But you can't leave right now."

Samira excused herself from the table. *Well, Kara's right. He can't have me right now.*

She put the phone to her ear feeling awkward talking to her brother while Phil was within earshot.

"Hey, Sis," Wes' sounded concerned. "I got called back to the office, but Pam is home with the kids. Are you busy?"

Busier than usual. Samira glanced at Phil. "We're eating dinner."

"Well, we don't need you right now."

Oh, Wes, please don't need me at all tonight.

"But I need to get back to the bank for a while and Pam needs to pick up some allergy prescriptions for Mark before morning. Could you fill the gap? It won't take too long."

Samira wondered why Pam couldn't have remembered that earlier in the day. *Like maybe this morning while the girls were still there to watch the kids.* "I don't know Wes," she turned her back to the table. "The girls are going with Ellen later this evening. I need to be here until they leave."

"The pharmacy is open until ten," Wes encouraged. "Even for just a few minutes would help tremendously."

But he's my brother. I can't turn him down. "Alright, I'll call you after Ellen leaves."

Before Samira had a chance to sit down again, Kara attacked. "He wants you to go over there to watch the kids tonight, doesn't he?"

Let's not have this discussion in front of Phil. Samira tried to head it off. "Maybe later, for a short time."

"You should just tell him no, Mama."

Krissy jumped right in. "Besides, you can't leave until Aunt Ellen gets here anyway." The girl smiled through her braces. "He'll just have to figure this one out on his own."

Even if it's not fair, they aren't going to talk about Wes that way. "Girls," Samira was standing next to her chair. "He doesn't call that often and he doesn't need me for that long. I don't know that you should be making decisions for me—"

"But you can't leave before Aunt Ellen gets here."

"And you can't leave with company here."

"And you shouldn't have to go back over there anyway."

The onslaught of accusations came simultaneously. Kara stood to make her point clearer than Krissy.

This is a fiasco. Samira held her hands out to stop the girls from saying anymore but they were both talking at the same time.

Ouch. Samira covered her ears. The shrill whistle came out of nowhere. The girls immediately stopped talking and Chase bound his way from the laundry room to his master's side.

"Sit." Phil commanded.

And all three Cartwright women took their seats.

Phil chuckled. "I was talking to the dog, but I guess it works both ways." He pushed away from the table and folded his arms. "If I'm hearing correctly,"

I can't believe I sat down at a command meant for a dog.

Phil continued without permission. "Your mother has a decision to make concerning her evening agenda. If you two aren't going to be here, I'm not sure you have a say in how she chooses to spend her time."

Krissy and Kara looked at each other guiltily. Kara lowered her head.

"If you need to go Samira, I could stay for a short time."

I don't know if I like him having input on my family decisions. "No, you're not going to stay while I go to my brother's." She caught the tone in her voice and backed off. "What I mean is, he doesn't need me right away and maybe by later he won't need me at all." Samira searched for words of explanation. "And I need to be here with the girls anyway." *Ellen is coming. Remember?*

Phil pulled back up to the table and picked up his fork. When he made eye contact with Krissy, she burst out laughing.

"How funny." Krissy doubled over. "We sat down with the dog."

It's not funny. Samira didn't appreciate Krissy's humor and she was frustrated with the way the whole evening was going. *This isn't anything like I pictured when I invited Phil to dinner.* Samira sighed. *I'm tired and Kara obviously has her feelings hurt.* The mother's eyes fell on the dog sitting on her dining room floor. *Who invited him in here?* She picked up her fork again. *And as if that isn't enough, I also still need to find a fingernail file.* She avoided Phil's questioning eyes. *What else could possibly go wrong?*

The phone that rang next came from Phil's hip. *If he carries a phone with him all the time, there really isn't an excuse for not calling me.*

"This one I need to take." Phil pushed away from the table. "If you'll excuse me." Phil snapped his fingers. Chase followed his master obediently out the back door.

Samira was relieved for the moment of privacy. She wanted desperately just to be herself. *But it never seems to work that way. There are always too many things to juggle.* She tried to take a bite of supper. *Like Ellen's arrival later tonight.*

That thought had no more played in Samira's mind than Krissy was out of her chair bolting for the front door. "It's Aunt Ellen."

No. No, not yet. Samira threw her hands over her head. *Nothing is working out right.*

Ellen made her usual boisterous entry, with compliments and hugs and questions for the girls. Both Krissy and Kara were instantly entertained and amused by Ellen's attention.

Samira rose from her chair and greeted Ellen properly—with a hug and a warm welcome. She couldn't help but return the natural hospitality despite the nervous cramp in her stomach.

"Have you eaten?" *Please say you're not hungry.*

"I had a late lunch so I'm good." Her eyes scanned Samira's front rooms. "Absolutely gorgeous what you've done with the place, Samira. Absolutely." Ellen clapped her hands together. Her freckled face beamed with joy at seeing the girls. "Come here you two." Another group hug followed. "I can't believe how much you've grown." Ellen put her hands on top of Krissy and Kara's heads. "We're going to have to do something about your school wardrobe before I bring you home. I bet you've outgrown everything from last year." Ellen's smile froze as she looked back toward Samira.

Samira followed Ellen's eyes to the kitchen. *Oh my God. Phil.*

"I don't believe we've met," Ellen offered her hand as she crossed the room headed toward Phil. Her long floral skirt brushed the hardwood floor as she walked.

Phil was standing next to the island silently observing the situation.

How long has he been standing there?

"J.P. Ralston." Phil introduced himself with reserve.

Samira hid her face in her hands. *This is the last thing I needed. She's two hours early for Pete's sake.*

"I'm Aunt Ellen. And I'm here to kidnap these two teenagers for a couple of nights." Ellen turned back toward the table. "Don't let me interrupt your dinner." Ellen pumped her eyebrows in Samira's direction.

You've already interrupted our dinner.

"Go ahead and finish and then we'll go." Ellen clapped her hands toward the table. "Come on, eat up. We have an agenda to plan."

The girls obediently sat back down at the table. Samira quietly apologized to Phil for Ellen's intrusion.

Phil was watching the woman as he spoke. "That's alright." The acceptance sounded forced. "That phone call was a client. There's a new development in a case so I need to meet him downtown in a few minutes."

Samira was glad to have him leaving yet disappointed that he couldn't stay. *I don't know what I want anymore.* She watched Phil tell the girls goodbye and bid them a good time with Ellen. He politely acknowledged Ellen as he excused himself.

I feel terrible for putting everyone in such an awkward position. She followed him onto the front porch. *Oh. Wait.* Samira remembered the diary. "I brought something home from the library for you." Samira was already on her way to her car. "It will just take a second."

A moment later she returned with the book. Phil was standing with his truck door already open. "I ran across this at the library today." *Mrs. Barnes is nowhere in sight, but no doubt watching, nonetheless.* "I don't know if you're still looking for information on Lloyd Hughes or not, but his name is mentioned in this diary several times."

Phil accepted the book with sudden interest.

"It's not exactly my property yet so I need it back right away."

Phil was carefully turning the worn pages as he listened. "I'll take a look."

Samira knew from his tone he had once again shifted into a business mode. *I don't think he's ever totally off duty.* Phil briefly thanked her for dinner and promised to bring the book back as he climbed into his truck.

Oh, I wish he didn't have to go. Samira tried to hide her disappointment. She rejoined her daughters and Ellen at the dinner table. Phil's plate sat cold and only half-eaten. *He didn't even get to finish.*

"Here," Ellen took Samira's plate and carried it into the kitchen. "Let me reheat that for you. I'm sure it's cold by now."

Samira folded her hands on her lap. "Thanks." *But I'm not even hungry anymore.*

40 *Status*

Joseph Phillip

Mike climbed into the passenger's seat. "What's the status if the honorable Mr. Stephenson jeopardized the case by allowing that intern to snoop around today?"

J.P. slid his key into the ignition. "I don't know. It's not like him to be so careless. I told him *no one* logs onto a computer without a complete background check and employee clearance." *I wonder what made him allow that university student on the mainframe anyway?*

"So now what, Counselor?" Mike cracked his window.

"We wait for the reports, I guess." J.P. stopped at a red light. "Sparky will be pissed if we blew his cover tonight."

"How long before he checks in?"

"Tomorrow." The light turned green. "He was hoping to be on a flight back here by tomorrow afternoon."

"We'll see about that now." Mike shook his head. "Stupid mistake on Stephenson's part."

Stupid mistake is an understatement. "With all the complexities of this case, you'd think Stephenson would be wary of letting anyone new on his mainframe."

"Maybe he was trying to keep things as normal as possible. It's a community service to allow these students to intern at the bank. Stephenson probably assumed it's all legitimate."

"Fact of the matter is, two minutes later and we'd have been in the middle of Sparky's security test."

"Fact of the matter, Counselor, is that we were on task quick enough to get her off before security was jeopardized."

Makes me nervous. "Did he seem distracted to you tonight?" J.P. pulled into the parking lot next to Mike's Corvette.

"A little." Mike unbuckled his seat belt. "His wife called a couple of times before you got there. Maybe there's friction on the home front."

Maybe. But that's no excuse for exposing the whole investigation.

"We're on for tomorrow afternoon at the club, right?"

"Aside from an act of God." J.P. hadn't been to the gym all week. *I'm ready for a good solid workout.* "Meet me at five. The boys are getting home tomorrow night."

"Five, good buddy. Both boys?" Mike opened the truck door, but he didn't get out.

"Both. Josh is staying the weekend. I'll take him back on Sunday." *I've got to get those boys transportation so they can get themselves around.*

Mike nodded in understanding. "Hey, what would it cost me to borrow your work horse Saturday during the day?"

J.P. narrowed his eyes. "What do you need my truck for?"

"Helping a friend move."

"In with you?"

"No, I still have baggage there." Mike lowered his head to look out the windshield. "Can't seem to get all of Rachel's stuff to wherever it is Rachel has gone."

"Maybe you should use my truck to move her stuff out before you haul someone else's stuff." *He's way too lenient with his women.*

Mike climbed out of the truck and leaned over to make eye contact. "I wish it were that easy."

Mike looks tired. Not his usual disposition.

"She's a bitch to get rid of. Lesson learned. Can we trade vehicles at the driving range?"

J.P. nodded. "If I make it. I've got major shit going down between Hughes and our beloved city attorney."

"So, I hear."

I should have known Mike would have the low down from city hall already.

"I'll put in a good word for you."

"I'd prefer to use my own words, thanks."

Mike laughed. "Have it your way, Counselor." He started to close the door then leaned down once again. "You headed home?"

J.P. glanced at his watch. *If it's not too late, I'd like to go back to Samira's.*
"I don't know yet."

Mike puckered his moustache. "Well, ya know? It's been a good, what, four days since you saw her?"

Not exactly, I had dinner with her. Well, half of dinner, anyway.

"Catch her in the right mood and who knows what she'll give you."

Save the sarcasm, Mikey. J.P. flashed a choice finger in Mike's direction.

"Precisely what I had in mind." Mike laughed out loud as he closed the door. He patted the truck as he walked away.

~~~~~~~

Samira's house was dark except for a glow of light in the kitchen window. *I should probably call instead of knocking on the door unannounced.* J.P. reached for his phone. *Especially if she's home alone.* As he waited for an answer, he turned the worn journal from Samira over on the seat of his truck. *Nineteen thirty-three. Too early. The Hughes transactions took place closer to '39 and '40.*

Samira's voice was quiet when she answered.

"Did I wake you?"

"Almost." Samira yawned. "But that's okay."

"Are you in bed already?"

"I was reading. Did you forget something?"

I like thinking about her in bed. "Not that I know of." *My hands were empty when I went in earlier.*

"Where are you?"

J.P. smiled. "Closer than you might think."

"How close?"

Not close enough. "In your driveway."

Samira laughed. "Did you come back for your dog?"

J.P. threw his head back in disbelief. *I can't believe I didn't even miss him.* "That's unbelievable."

"I'll let you in through the garage."

J.P. took in Samira from head to toe. *Freshly brushed hair. Long nightshirt.* She led the way inside. *This is a far cry to the professional businesswoman I saw at city hall this afternoon.*

J.P. carried the journal back into the house with him. *The documents I need will be dated much later than this.* He set the book on the counter and greeted Chase who was obediently sitting on the rug in the laundry room.

She didn't have to bring him inside. "You could have left him outside."

"In here I knew where he was and what he was into." Samira crossed her arms over her middle. "I wondered if you'd remember."
~~~~~~~

"You should have called."

"You were in a meeting." She tipped her head. "I was going to wait and call later."

Not many women would give me that much leeway.

"How was the meeting?"

"It could have gone smoother." *How much can I tell her and still be honest?* "I have some backtracking to do in the morning to make sure the evidence stayed intact."

"I'm sorry." Samira's reply was sincere. "That makes it hard when you've already been out of town, doesn't it?"

"It doesn't make it any easier."

Samira pushed her hair out of her face with both hands. "Can I get you anything?"

She could get me about anything, and I'd be satisfied. J.P. made Chase stay on the rug with a silent hand command. "You don't have to wait on me."

"Maybe I don't mind," Samira tilted her head and waited for an answer.

I am hungry. "Any chance there's any dinner left?"

"Chances of that are pretty good." Samira turned toward the refrigerator. "I noticed you didn't get to finish."

I usually try to finish what I start—especially where she is concerned. He watched Samira fill a plate with leftovers. *She's very much at home in her own space.*

"I didn't mean to rush off like that." *I should try to explain.* "I thought I had a longer block of time when I got here. But my investigator moved the time frame unexpectedly."

"That's alright," Samira removed a fork from a kitchen drawer and handed it to J.P. "I didn't know Ellen was going to arrive so early either."

J.P. noticed dark circles under her eyes. *I don't think I've ever seen her so tired before.*

"I'm sorry about her intrusion."

J.P. washed his hands in the kitchen sink. "Who exactly is Ellen, anyway?"

Samira handed the warmed plate to J.P. He leaned against the counter and took a bite of the stir-fry chicken. *It's just as good this time as it was earlier.*

"Ellen is Tom's younger sister." Samira dropped several ice cubes into an empty glass. "She lives in Tampa, so we don't see her often but when she comes home, she always makes time for the girls." She turned around. "You can sit down and eat if you like."

Standing through a meal isn't as unusual as she might think. "I don't know what you put in this, but it's excellent." He took another bite and pulled out a barstool. *I could get used to meals like this.*

"I don't know what got into the girls tonight," Samira put her hands over her face "They were wound tight."

J.P. chuckled. *I love the way they all sat down when I whistled.*

"It's really not funny." Samira's voice was low. She slid onto the barstool next to him. "I feel bad."

I wonder if she's been crying.

"Hey, you've had some challenging moments with me, right?" *Like that less than desirable confrontation in Aunt Maggie's yard.* "Let's just chalk it up for water under the bridge."

Samira moved her head in a nod, but she didn't speak.

"So, how did the rest of your evening go?"

Samira put her elbows on the counter and crossed her wrists. "I went over to my brother's house for a little while. He never has to work late." She paused. "Or at least he never used to have to work late."

J.P. watched Samira think for a moment.

"To be honest, I think my sister-in-law just needed to get out of the house and away from the kids for a little bit by herself." Samira sighed. "She was pretty stressed out. I got two of their three kids bathed and to bed before she got back."

"That's impressive." *No wonder she looks tired.*

"I haven't been home too long."

Another question had been on J.P.'s mind all day. "Tell me more about your presentation this afternoon."

Samira raised her eyebrows. "It's over." There was a hint of relief in her voice. "I really don't like speaking in front of crowds."

"If you don't mind my saying, you seemed to handle it with a great deal of professionalism."

Now Samira frowned. "How long were you watching me?"

"Only from the first slide all the way to the end."

Samira didn't say anything. She seemed to be lost in her thoughts.

She doesn't give herself enough credit. "You were very polished, Samira."

"I spent about six weeks getting ready. We are in desperate need of more computer stations in our online center. To make that happen, I have to ask for money and that's always a hard thing for me to do." She was studying her fingernails. "Today's presentation was a request for funding."

"How much do you need?"

"About sixteen thousand dollars for the complete expansion."

I can think of several business owners who might be inclined to support such a cause. "So, what happens next? Do they allocate the funds?"

"Oh, no." Samira's dark eyes met his. "This was just the board of trustees. They must make a recommendation to the board of supervisors and then we wait to see what they decide. The funds aren't budgeted for this year, so my guess is they'll approve the proposal for the next fiscal year."

J.P. finished the last bite of vegetables. "What other avenues of income do you have?"

"Private donations and gifts." Samira tucked her hair behind her ear. "But we don't have enough designated funds in those accounts for such a large project. And at this point, growing in stages doesn't reduce the number of customers waiting in line for a computer every day."

Maybe I'll probe around and see what kind of interest I can generate. J.P. started to get up, but Samira had his plate and was already on the way to the sink. *She really doesn't need to wait on me.*

He watched her put his plate in the dishwasher. *She still looks tired.* "How long are the girls staying with Ellen?" *That probably sounds like a leading question.*

"I don't know." Samira wiped the counter with a dishcloth. "Ellen is a free spirit. She's thinking she'll keep them at least two nights." Samira stopped and made eye contact. "Are you finished for the night?"

Either finished or just getting started. He gently pushed her hair behind a shoulder. "I'm finished working if that's what you're asking."

Samira took a step closer. J.P. wasn't going to turn her away. When he opened his arms, she stepped into them willingly.

"I'm glad you came back." She rested her head against his shoulder.

"Thanks for supper." J.P. kissed her hair. "Both times."

He felt Samira's head move against him in acceptance, but she didn't let go. *I can stay like this as long as she wants.* When she finally pulled away slightly, he noticed her cheeks were damp.

What's up with the tears? "Hey, Pretty Lady," J.P. lifted her chin with his fingertips and kissed her gently. "What's on your mind?"

Samira closed her eyes for a moment. "I'm just really tired."

I doubt it's that simple.

"The presentation downtown today took a lot out of me." Samira nodded as if she were trying to convince herself. "Then my brother needed me, and I was already really tired, but he doesn't ask very often so I felt I needed to be there for him."

J.P. wiped another tear with his thumb.

"And the girls," Samira sighed and looked away. "They were totally out of line at supper —"

Let her off the hook here. "They didn't bother me. Kids will be kids."

"I know." Samira lowered her head. "But then Ellen showed up early and I really hadn't planned—" she held her hair back with one hand. "Well, I hadn't exactly told Tom's family that I was seeing someone."

J.P. couldn't resist. "You are?"

There was sudden hurt in Samira's eyes. "Sometimes I don't know."

Bad timing, Ralston. J.P. wrapped his arm around her neck and pulled her in against him again. *Am I seeing someone?*

Samira wiped her cheek again. "And—"

Shit. I don't know if I can survive any more 'ands' tonight.

Samira's voice was noticeably quiet. "I can't give you what you came back for tonight."

Here we go. When he tried to see her eyes, she turned away. *What does she assume I'm here for?* He tried to read her thoughts. *Nothing.*

J.P. pushed his weight off the counter. "Help me out here, Samira." *Don't put her on edge.* "What do you think I came here for?" He ran his hand through her silky hair. "I came for my dog, and it appears getting him back won't be a problem." He stroked her hair again. "And I came for dinner. Twice. And that was excellent both times." He could feel Samira's shoulders stiffen. "And I came here to see you."

Samira walked completely around the island and stopped next to the dining room table. In the dimly lit room, her face was shadowed. J.P. had to strain to see her eyes.

"Then maybe I can't give what I want tonight." She crossed her arms over her middle. "And that was a really selfish thing to say."

Me or her? Who's being selfish? J.P. ran his hand through his hair. *This is why I don't get in too deep. Unspoken expectations.*

"I can't sleep with you tonight, Phil." Samira confessed from across the room.

What's she talking about?

"It would seem—" Samira's voice trailed off for a moment. "It would seem with the girls gone and James not back yet—"

No. Let's not make any assumptions here. "Listen." *For whatever it's worth.* "It's been a long day for both of us. What do you say we just call it a night?" *Then I can go home with my dog, and she can get some sleep.*

Samira looked away. "I'm sorry."

Why is she always sorry? "No need to be." J.P. crossed the room to where she was standing. "Come on, I'll tuck you in."

Samira shook her head. "You don't have to do that."

"Maybe I want to."

"I know." Samira looked up into his eyes. "But then you have to go." She sighed. "And that's a really selfish thing to say too."

"No, it's not." *Why does she think that's selfish?*

"I don't want you to go, but I'm not in a position t—" Again, Samira's voice trailed off.

It suddenly hit him. *Oh. She's can't have sex tonight. That's it? She's worried about that?* "Who said I had to go?"

Tears were forming in Samira's eyes again.

I must say this will be a first for me. "My dog is here. I've had supper. And my work is done for the day." *Or at least can be done.* "With the exception of a toothbrush I have everything I need until morning."

Samira took him by the hand and led him into her bedroom. J.P. looked around. *She moved his picture.* She disappeared into the hallway and returned with an unopened toothbrush.

He tapped the sealed box on her shoulder. "You're amazing." *In every way possible.* Samira closed the bathroom door between them.

I guess this is my invitation to stay. J.P. sat down on the edge of the bed and united his shoes. *Tom's picture is on the table by the door.* He looked at his watch. *It's only ten.* He read the title of Samira's book on the bedside stand.

Samira returned and sat down on the edge of the bed. He watched her divide her long hair into three strands.

"I'm supposedly leading the literary club discussion on that book next week." Samira explained without being asked. Her fingers wove her hair in and out with expertise. "But I have a long way to go to be ready."

"I doubt it will take you too long." *Every time I've seen her, she's been in a different book."*

"Reading for me and reading for group discussion are two different things."

"How do you do that?"

"Read for discussion? I have to outline and analyze the main plots and—"

"No, do this." He lifted her hair with his hand.

"My mother taught me when I was little. She still braids her hair every night." She smiled gently.

That's the first genuine smile I've seen out of her all night.

"I braid my hair when I know I don't want to wash it the next morning." Samira got up and walked across the room. As she turned off the lamp she leaned over and straightened J.P.'s shoes.

She'd get mighty tired of putting my bedroom in order every night. J.P. used Samira's bathroom and left the toothbrush on the counter to use again in the morning. *If I'm still here in the morning.* He still wasn't completely convinced he was staying the night. *Maybe I'll just stay until she goes to sleep. It's still early for me.*

Samira was under the covers when J.P. returned. He unbuttoned his shirt as he crossed the room.

"Phil?"

I like the way she says my name. He glanced over his shoulder as he sat down on the bed. Her hand ran across his shoulder blades. *And I like the way she touches me.*

"What exactly did you do while you were out East?"

I wonder where that came from. J.P. stretched out next to Samira and propped his head up with one hand.

"Well, let's see," *What's her motive for asking that question?* "I interviewed about fifteen possible witnesses. I met the judge and staff overseeing the case. I interviewed suspects in jail. Twice." *Is she looking for something else?* "Why?"

Samira's head was resting heavily in her pillow. "No reason, really." She yawned. "But earlier when I asked you about your trip you seemed, well, maybe a little distracted or something."

J.P. remembered. *I was thinking about the Captain.*

"See?" Samira lifted her head slightly. "You just did it again."

She reads me well. He ran his tongue over his bottom lip in thought. *If there's anyone I could talk to about the Captain, it's Samira.*

"I went to see my father before I came home." *I still can't believe I did that.*

"How is he?"

J.P. had to chuckle at his answer. "He's old." He pictured the Captain saluting him at the airport. "Older than I expected." *Much older.* "But he's good. He's strong and active and..."

By the time J.P. stopped talking about his experience with his father, the clock read eleven o'clock. Samira was still listening, but she was starting to drift into sleep.

"How are you?"

J.P. thought for a moment. "I don't know yet." *Funny she would ask that.* "I don't know." He answered the second time more for himself.

Samira ran the back of her hand over J.P.'s cheek. Very slowly she cupped his face in her hands and kissed him gently on the lips.

"It's good that you went." She kissed him again. "But tonight, I'm glad you don't have to go." Samira rolled over and reached for the light. "When should I wake you in the morning?"

J.P. pulled the backside of Samira's body closer to him. *I think that means I'm staying all night.* The covers separated them, but he wasn't sure he was ready to stay in bed yet. *I need to sort out this Mid America mess out before I can sleep.*

"I'll need to go home and shower."

"And drop off your dog."

"Oh yeah." J.P. remembered. *Chase.* He laid his head on the pillow next to Samira's. "Better have me up by seven."

"Okay." Samira whispered. Her breathing was getting heavier.

J.P. lay in the bed awake long after Samira had drifted off to sleep. His mind sorted through the evening meeting with Mr. Stephenson. Unable to sleep, J.P. slid off the edge of the bed and followed the light to the kitchen. *Does she always leave the counter lights on at night?* He poured a glass of orange juice. An empty wine bottle was sitting next to the sink. J.P. turned it toward the light. *That's interesting. Surely, she didn't keep it on purpose.*

Another thought haunted him. *Am I really seeing her?* He rinsed his glass and set it next to the sink. *I guess maybe I am.* He'd claimed a bachelor status even before his divorce was final. *If I'm seeing her, am I still single?* As he crossed the kitchen the dated journal caught his eye again. *Maybe I'll take that in for Denise to review, just in case.*

He sat down on Samira's sofa and clicked the remote control for the television between the built-in bookcases. He muted the sound and flipped channels until he found Sports Center. *Single maybe.* J.P.'s mind was still churning while final scores scrolled across the bottom of the screen. *But I wouldn't exactly consider myself eligible anymore.* He continued to process. *At least not to anyone but her.* His eyes wandered from the tv to the hallway that led back to her bedroom.

"Sometimes I don't know." J.P. replayed Samira's words in his mind. *Sometimes I don't know either. But what I do know is that woman has a hold on me I can't shake. Maybe I don't want to shake it. But if I'm not shaking her off, does that mean I'm falling for her?*

He turned off the television. *The Cubs lost. Again.* There were files in need of review out in the truck, but J.P. had no desire to retrieve them in the dark of the night. *I'm too tired to process anymore anyway.*

J.P. went back to the bedroom where Samira was sleeping soundly. She hadn't moved since he'd climbed out of bed. *I could probably go on home, and she wouldn't know the difference until morning.* He admired the serenity of her face in the dimly lit room. *But there's no way I am going to leave this pretty lady alone in her bed.*

J.P. draped his shirt and pants over the chair in the bedroom and slid under the sheets next to Samira. As he pressed his body into hers, Samira moved closer and linked her fingers into his, pulling his arm around her middle as she settled back in.

I'm beginning to think she may be all I need. J.P. thought about what his father had told him concerning his mother. *But what if I don't have what it takes to win?*

Another thought crept in as he drifted into sleep. *She may very well be my last chance.*

41 Principle Matters

Samira

Samira ran her index finger over the sculptor's picture. "His name is Fabiano Uberti." *That fingernail could use a little more filing.* She examined the nail she'd chipped the night before.

"He looks like a dream." Daphne fanned her hand in front of her face. "I have to make sure my husband doesn't come over while he's working here."

Samira studied the black and white press photo. "He looks like an artist." She turned the photo over and read the press release again. *Or maybe I'm just not looking anymore.* That thought caught Samira completely off guard. *I hope I didn't say that out loud.* Daphne's eyes were still glued to the photograph. *Back to business.*

"Here's a copy of the room layout. We'll need to have the conference center in order by noon." Samira placed the diagram on her desk. "Is Jim in?"

"Pretty soon, Mrs. Haddock interjected. "He's at lunch right now."

"Let me know when he gets back." *Jim is the best. It won't take him long to set up the room.* "Mr. Uberti will be here with his agent to survey the facility in a few minutes. Is there anything else you can think of before his arrival?"

"Have we ever hosted an international artist?" Daphne asked the question while she was still drooling over the photo.

Mrs. Haddock shook her head. "We've hosted lots of national artists, but never an international sculptor."

"This should be very educational." *I, for one, am ready to learn about a new art form.*

Fabiano Uberti arrived precisely at the top of the hour. Samira shook his hand. *Now I see why Daphne was so taken by his photograph.* Dark curls framed his olive features giving a greenish tint to his almost blue eyes.

The agent moved quickly and spoke without making eye contact. "We would like to tour the facility. The entire facility if you don't mind."

I'd guess him to be about, what, mid-forties, maybe. Samira studied the artist's features. *But his modern suit gives him a very contemporary look.*

"We want to see everything." Fabiano waved his arms out into the room.

Everything? Samira graciously offered a cup of coffee before beginning the tour. *I'll show him everything he needs to see.* She started with the online center and then worked her way around the entire main floor. The final stop was in the conference center. Jim had returned from lunch and was already starting to move tables and chairs to transform the room into a sculptor's studio.

Fabiano's eyes walked the entire perimeter of the room. "De light is, what shall I say? It is very soft." His Italian accent was apparent in his speech.

Samira suggested Jim open the blinds, but the artist stopped her.

"No, no, soft is good." He crossed his arms over his chest. Samira listened for several minutes as he conversed in Italian with his agent.

This is fascinating, even if I can't understand a word they're saying.

"Excuse me, Miss Samira." Helen Haddock was standing in the doorway. "I'm sorry to bother but I need you to take a phone call."

That's odd. Helen is quite capable of managing most telephone calls. Samira frowned in question.

"It's someone inquiring about an old journal, but I don't know what journal she's referring to. She is under the impression you might know."

Samira thought for a moment. *The mayor's diary from 1933. But a woman?* She left Mrs. Haddock with the guests.

"This is Miss Cartwright. How may I help you?"

"Yes, sorry to interrupt your work," the woman's voice in Samira's ear was extremely professional. "My name is Denise Burke."

How do I know this name?

"I'm employed by J.P. Ralston, attorney at law. J.P. handed me a journal from a former Joplin city mayor dating back to 1933. Do you know the book?"

Yes, I know the book. And I know J.P. Ralston. But I don't know Denise Burke. Yet.

"This document contains information pertinent to a case we are currently trying to close, but J.P. is under the impression you need it back right away."

"That's correct." *I can't believe the book I gave J.P. might be useful.*

"In order for this document to be used as evidence in court we need physical accessibility. Is there a way we can check it out from the library under an extended agreement?"

Not until it's cataloged. "That diary is actually the property of the local historical society," Samira started to explain. "We haven't cataloged it into the system for public viewing yet." *And even if it were already in the system, it would be held as reference material only.*

"I see." There was a slight pause. "So, there is no way we could keep it here for a few days?"

It was left in my care, which puts my reputation and working relations with the historical society on the line. "I'm sorry, Ms Burke." Samira knew the rules. "Until we have it cataloged in the system, it needs to physically be here in the Maple Street facility."

"Is it possible the book might be somehow *misplaced* until about this time next week?"
Misplaced? I don't misplace items left in my care.

"We only need it long enough to prove a point. Then we can return it in time to be *found.* And in the meantime, we can guarantee its safety and protection."

"I'm sorry." Samira was watching the sculptor across the room. It appeared he was preparing to leave the building. "I will need the book back right away." *Then I can get it cataloged properly so they can use it.* "I can call you as soon as it becomes accessible to the public."

The tone in Denise's voice made it obvious she was not pleased with Samira's decision.

But I really need to get back to my guests. Samira hung up the phone. *At least she agreed to be in touch.* As she crossed the library, another thought crossed her mind. *I should have asked her how soon I could expect it back.*

A short hour later Mrs. Haddock stuck her head in the conference room door again. This time Samira was leaning over a table reviewing the room layout with Jim.

"Oh, Miss Samira, there is trouble. You need to come quickly." She waved her hand for Samira to follow.

What in the world? A uniformed police officer was standing at the circulation desk. "Go ahead with our plans, Jim." *Is it a friend of Tom's?* "I'll be right back."

"Good afternoon. Ms. Samira Cartwright, I presume?"

Samira acknowledged her identity and offered her hand in greeting.

"If I might have a minute of your time?"

Of course. Samira escorted him into her office and closed the door. *I don't recognize him.* Through the glass wall she could see the frightened look on Helen's face.

"How may I help you?" Samira sat down in the chair behind her desk, but the policeman remained standing. He handed her a piece of paper.

"You have been served."

Samira examined the paper, not understanding.

"I have a subpoena from attorney J.P. Ralston for a historical book entitled, Diary of Mr. David C. Montgomery, Mayor of Joplin. 1933."

What? Samira was stunned. *What right does he have to stand here and order over historical records that aren't even available to the public yet? But that's not the half of it.* Samira was instantly angry. *I can't believe Phil would make such a demand without at least talking to me first.*

"Do you have this book in your possession Ms Cartwright?"

"No, I don't." *Why would Phil make such a demand on me? He hasn't even talked to me about it yet.* "I believe Mr. J.P. Ralston has possession of that book."

"His office believes it is here in your building."

Then his office is playing games because I just talked to Denise Burke. Samira pushed away from her desk. *I don't appreciate the way he's chosen to handle this.* She opened her office door and addressed her assistants.

"Ladies, the officer is here for a historical journal from a former city mayor. It belongs with the historical—"

"Oh." Daphne interrupted. "Is it really old?"

Samira tipped her head slightly. *How would Daphne know about the journal? I haven't shown it to anyone yet.*

"I'm sorry," Daphne began to explain. "I didn't know what to do with it." She reached under the counter and handed the journal over to Samira. "It was in the drive through book return but you were busy with Jim so I couldn't ask right then."

So, this is Ms Burke's idea of being in touch? Samira took a deep breath. *I asked Helen and Daphne knowing that book was at Phil's office.* She turned around and faced the officer. *Now I have no choice but to turn it over.*

"This book," Samira started to explain. "Is between ownerships. It was recently donated to the library for historical purposes only and I am not comfortable allowing you to take it off the premises without permission from the historical society."

"This book is needed by a court of law, Ms Cartwright."

"I understand," Samira clutched the diary with her hands. "But at the same time, it needs to be officially documented and cataloged before it leaves here."

"How long will that take?" The officer crossed his arms.

Samira sighed. She could feel the agony of defeat already starting to settle in her stomach. "Well today and tomorrow we're getting ready for the resident artist to move his studio into the conference center."

"If you prefer, you can wait in jail while your staff prepares for the artist in residence."

Samira opened her eyes wide. *Is he threatening me?* She stared at the officer. *I was married to a police officer long enough to know my rights.*

"Excuse me," Samira read his name badge for the first time, "Officer Centralis. I do believe I have rights above and beyond what you have indicated, and I would be willing to discuss them with your superior officer."

"You have twenty-four hours to turn the evidence over to the courts. After that, your presence will suffice in its place." Officer Centralis turned for the door. "Thank you for your time this afternoon, Ms Cartwright."

Samira was furious. Absolutely livid.

Mrs. Haddock came into the office, her eyes wide with worry. "What do we do now, Miss Samira? No one has ever come in here wanting a book that bad."

"I'll tell you what we do now," Samira returned to her desk and pulled the bookmark out of her Clancy novel. "We call the attorney who ordered that subpoena." She flipped the bookmark over on her desk. Phil's phone numbers were written on the backside in pencil. Without a moment of hesitation, she picked up the phone and dialed the number next to the lower case "c." *Let's see if he's answering his cell phone this afternoon.*

"J.P. Ralston."

I know this voice. Pure business. "J.P. Ralston, Samira Cartwright."

"Samira?"

"Yes, Samira." She could hear voices in the background.

His tone changed slightly. "Hey, Pretty Lady, what can I do for you?"

"What can you do for me?" *I'll tell you what you can do for me.* "You can tell your friends at the precinct that my books are not eligible for court orders. And furthermore, you can tell them that I am not substituting in its place."

"Whoa. What are you talking about?"

I am NOT playing any more legal games. "The officer that just left here expects me to hand over the historical diary by this time tomorrow. I told you I don't have formal custody of this book yet. There's no way I'm releasing it to the court. You could have handled this much differently."

"What diary?"

"Come on, Phil." Samira pounded her hand against the top of her desk. "You know what book I'm talking about. Your office ordered the subpoena."

"You received a subpoena from my office?"

"From your office. I have it right here on my desk. Would you like me to read it to you? Your signature is on the line."

"Look, I'm in the dark here."

He can sound as confused as he wants. I'm not buying it.

"I haven't been in the office since first thing this morning and I'm about to step into jury selection right now—"

"J.P. Ralston, Attorney at Law. It's right on the line, Phil. But the book isn't leaving this premise. I loaned it to you in confidence and told you I needed it back right away. We haven't even cataloged it yet for heaven's sake." *I have never been so furious.*

"Samira," Phil's voice was shifting again. "The bailiff is calling me. I need to go. But let me do some checking and I'll get back to you. Alright? Don't panic. Maybe there's just a misunderstanding or something."

Misunderstanding? Samira's thoughts were coming a million miles a minute. *And he has to go?*

"I'll call you back, alright?"

Is that anything like your assistant being in touch? "The sooner the better Mr. Ralston." *And who ever this Denise Burke is, she'd best be ready to face the music as well.*

~~~~~~~

The rest of the afternoon passed in a blur. The sculptor's agent returned to oversee the preparations in the conference center and a woman from the historical society dropped by to discuss the items she had delivered a few days earlier. On top of all that, Samira's mother called and invited her to dinner to celebrate Pam's birthday.

Maybe I don't feel like celebrating a birthday right now. Just the same, Samira knew she would make an appearance for dinner.

Samira hung up the telephone from talking to her mother and looked through the glass wall to see J.P. Ralston enter the building through the front doors. *Nice he can make a personal appearance.* She watched him cross the room. *All business. Definitely J.P. Ralston. None of Phil in that walk.*

Samira folded her arms and allowed Mrs. Haddock the formalities of showing him to her office.
~~~~~~~

"Mr. Ralston."

"Samira." Phil pulled a chair up to the front of Samira's desk. "We need to get this issue over the journal cleared up."

"You first." *Let's hear this explanation.*

"First," Phil held up one finger. "I was not involved in the decision that sent a subpoena to your office today." Phil was looking her right in the eye. "Had I known how valuable the journal was going to be to the Hughes' case I would have discussed it with you in advance of legal action."

I hoped that would be the case.

"Second," Phil held up two fingers. "I can close the case with the book you put in my hands."

"Which you subsequently placed in someone else's hands."

"Right." Phil didn't deny that fact. "Here's the deal. We summoned a jury today to hear the case beginning Monday morning at nine. I can avoid a jury trial and negotiate fair settlement with the city this weekend *if* I can show them the evidence in those dated documents."

Samira wasn't satisfied. *He has no idea what I've been through this afternoon. Not only did I have to face an officer of the law, but I also had to defend my own rights.* "Do you know what happened here this afternoon?"

"I'm presuming a local authority delivered the subpoena requesting the book." Phil sat back in his chair.

"Before that." *Let's tell him the whole story.*

"No, I don't know what happened before that."

Samira picked up the book from the top of the lateral filing cabinet behind her desk. She placed it on the desk directly in front of her. "I was tricked."

"How so?"

"I received a call from Denise Burke."

"That's my paralegal and personal assistant."

"I assumed as much." *I've heard you on the phone with her.* "Denise Burke asked if your office could keep the book for a while longer."

"That's because I told her it had to be back to you today."

"Very well." *Just hear me out.* "I told her we needed to catalog the book before it could be made available to the public."

"Which means we don't have access to it in the physical form for a few days, correct?"

"Correct."

"Denise actually insinuated that I might *misplace* the book for a week, until your office could return it to me."

Phil didn't respond one way or the other.

"I'm sorry, but my reputation is on the line, and I am not known for 'misplacing' anything—especially something of that magnitude. I told her that was not a possibility."

The attorney opened his hands in silent affirmation of her decision. "So, what's the problem?"

What's the problem? "That was shortly after one o'clock. At three-ten a uniformed officer arrived here demanding that journal. I told him it was already in your custody." She held the book up for Phil to see. "And guess what? One of my librarians finds *this* book in the return cart."

Phil narrowed his eyes. "Looks to me like Denise returned the book like you requested."

"No." Samira could feel her blood pressure rising. *Don't you dare side with Ms Burke.* "She returned the book to trap me. I can't very well turn it over if it's not in my possession, right?"

"Right."

"So now that it's here, I have to physically hand it over."

"Right again."

"You don't get it do you?"

"Get what?" Phil slid to the edge of his chair. "We need the book to close the deal. If you have it and we need it, we either ask to borrow it for a period of time, or we have to obtain legal permission to gain custody." His eyes were a steel blue as he explained.

I have only seen those eyes once. In Aunt Maggie's driveway when he was headed for James in the tent.

"It's a matter of having the right piece of evidence at the right time, Samira."

"Is it?" Samira held his glare. "Does it make any difference that this book doesn't even belong to the library yet or that my reputation is on the line if something happens to it while it's *missing*?"

"Okay."

Samira crossed her arms. *All it will take to clear this up is an apology for the way I was taken advantage of by both Denise Burke and the police officer.*

"Here's the deal. I've spent a solid eight months searching for the very evidence that is handwritten in that journal. If you're not going to allow it to be used for the purpose of aiding this case, then yes, I take legal action to obtain the evidence needed to get the job done. It's that simple."

This is anything but simple. Samira couldn't believe her ears. *There's no way this is the same man that woke up in my bed this morning.* She was angrier now than she was when the officer threatened her. *What happened to his tenderness and his compassion?* As confusing as this encounter was, protecting that diary suddenly seemed to take precedence over everything else.

"It's not that simple, Mr. Ralston." Samira crossed her arms again. "I was told that if I don't hand over the book for your case, that I would be taken into custody."

"According to the law, the person blocking the evidence from being obtained has an obligation to respond one way or another."

Let's get this straight. "Are you saying you would allow me to go to jail in order to get your hands on this journal?" Samira held the book up between them.

"It doesn't have to be that way, Samira. You're missing the point."

"I'm missing the point?"

"Hear me out." Phil stood up and walked around to the end of her desk. He knelt so he was just under her eye level. "Denise could have handled this differently, but she didn't. I left the book for her to review this morning. She ran across the exact dates and transactions that have been under scrutiny since the beginning of February concerning Lloyd Hughes' estate."

His eyes are so intense I can't even look away.

"If the case goes to court, it's highly probable the jury will side with the city. If I can keep it out of court and prove the case using that document tomorrow morning, or even first thing Monday morning, then the city gets fair settlement, and we can finally close the estate."

I don't want an explanation. Samira frowned. *I want an apology.* "You didn't answer my question. The officer stated I would go to jail if I didn't hand over the journal. Would you allow that to happen?"

"Would you withhold the evidence?"

"Don't answer a question with a question."

"Then don't ask me to make a judgment call against my own case."

The attorney stood up and ran his hand through his hair. "What's the worst thing that could happen if you allowed me to borrow that book?"

"The worst thing?" *Besides the fact that you've challenged my integrity.* "The book belongs in this facility. It was placed under my care, and I will protect it until it's cataloged properly or until I have permission to do otherwise."

"Then who do I need to call?" Phil's frustration was beginning to show. "Give me a name and a number and I'll make the call."

"It's not that easy."

"To ask permission to borrow a book from the library?"

"No, to remove a historical reference item from the library."

"Excuse me?" Phil put his hands on his hips and walked around Samira's desk again. "If the Maple Street Library doesn't even have full custody of the book yet, how can you withhold the name of the person who can grant permission for the book to leave here?"

Samira leaned back in her chair. *If I give him the name, he'll make the call and get permission to use the book, there's no doubt about that.* She studied his face. *The part I don't understand is if he would allow me to be arrested if I refused to turn it over to the authorities.*

"So where do I stand in all of this, Phil?"

The attorney ran his tongue over his bottom lip. "You're standing between me and the one piece of evidence that will close this case."

He could have thanked me for finding the evidence in the first place. Samira waited but he didn't say anymore. *He could admit that ordering a subpoena was an overreaction to something a simple personal request might have solved.* Samira considered his last option. *Or he could have apologized and asked how we might remedy the situation.*

He was watching her very closely.

But he didn't choose to do any of those things. "So that's it?" Samira stood. "I'm just a roadblock for the final goal?"

Phil shook his head. "Look, Samira...you don't see..." his tone had softened, but his eyes were still intense.

"No, I see very clearly." She leaned over her desk for a yellow sticky note. "Business before pleasure."

"Samira, wait."

In an instant, she scribbled down the name of the lady from the historical society. *If he has the resources to order a subpoena, then he also has the resources to find the phone number.* "This should take care of your dilemma."

There was a long hesitation before Phil reached out and removed the note from the end of Samira's finger. His eyes were suddenly very dark, and he held them low.

"I'll make the call."

"I'll wait to hear back then."

Inside Samira's chest her heart was screaming to let him off the hook. *All he had to do was say he was sorry.* Her head was holding firm. *I've given him every part of me, yet he can't drum up the courage to apologize. Now it's a matter of principle.* Samira put the book behind her desk again. *He'll either realize he shouldn't have put me in the middle of his case, or he'll win the ruling.*

Phil opened her office door. Very slowly he turned around.

I don't want him to see how much this hurts me. Samira looked away. *Just go.* She started to shuffle a stack of papers. When she looked up again, Phil was leaving the building.

42 Endings or Beginnings

Joseph Phillip

"Let me get this straight." J.P. put his fingers to his temple and closed his eyes as he attempted to understand Sparky's report. "If the money never left Joplin, then exactly how did the suspects turn up in Baltimore?" He opened his eyes.

Sparky was standing across the room with his hands tucked deep into his pants pockets.

"Ah, listen carefully, J.P." He raised his dark eyebrows. "De suspects in Balteemore are still de ones who moved de monies." His face showed no expression. "But, I am led to beleev dat de money vas used right here in Joplin somehow."

"So that means the suspects are working for someone here locally?"

"Zat is my assumption." Sparky walked back to the small conference table and removed several sheets of paper from his briefcase. "I've traced every communication to and from de Mid-America computer mainframe." He pointed a finger at an email address on the top of the first sheet. "Dis address is fictional. It does not exeest. But dis one," Sparky indicated another address on the sheet. "Dis one answers in Caleefornia."

"How do you figure all this out?" Denise asked the question as she looked up from taking notes.

"Ah." Sparky broke into a bright smile from under his moustache. "Dat is only for Sparky to know."

Denise returned the smile about the same time a bell rang announcing someone entering the front door.

Derek Danielson removed his glasses and rubbed his eyes with his thumb and forefinger. "So, in reality, this investigation is just beginning."

After the interviews in Baltimore, I was sure I could indict the suspects on reasonable doubt. J.P. sighed. *If Derek is right, we've just barely scratched the surface of this case.*

Sparky seemed to understand their concern. "Nothing is ever as simple as it seems, J.P." The investigator rubbed his shiny head. "But, ve vill get the job done."

What do I tell Mr. Stephenson in the meantime?

"Hey, Boss?" Denise inquired from the other room. "I think you should come out here."

J.P. stepped into the front office. She handed him the Mayor's diary.

Damn it. "I thought I told you to cancel that subpoena." *This book is causing more trouble than it's worth.* J.P. was instantly angry.

"I did," Denise confirmed. "I called and cancelled late Friday afternoon." Denise sorted through a small stack of papers on her desk. "Here's the fax confirmation."

J.P. took the paper out of her hand. "Then where the hell did this come from?"

"A lady just dropped it off."

A Lady? J.P. immediately started for the door. "What lady?"

"A little gray-headed lady came in here and laid it on my desk."

"Just now?"

"Yeah, just now." Denise put her hands on her hips. "What's up with you anyway, Boss? First you tell me to skim the info to see if anything is pertinent. When I realize we can close the case using this evidence and go after the book you all but fire me for doing my job. And now you don't believe me when I say a lady just dropped the book off again?"

J.P. stopped in the open door. *The old woman from the library.* He ran his hand through his hair. *Having this book in my possession changes the dynamics of the nine o'clock court appearance considerably.*

"Call the judge and ask for a continuance," J.P. ordered. His mind shifted into high gear. "Tell him I'm sure we can settle without a jury."

Denise sat down in her chair and picked up the telephone.

"Derek," *Let's get one thing off my plate.* "I need you to work with Sparky for the rest of the day. Maybe even the rest of the week. Give him whatever he needs to keep this investigation moving forward. Maybe we can have some answers by Friday."

Sparky stroked his moustache. "Maybe by de end of de day."

Wishful thinking.

Derek gathered his file folders and started for the door. "What do I tell Mike and Vince at the eleven o'clock meeting?"

J.P. sat down at his own desk. "I'll try to reach Mike right now." The attorney reached for his telephone. "Chances are good you won't have an eleven o'clock with Benson and Barringer." He dismissed his intern without any further instructions. The clock read a few minutes past eight. *I've never known a private investigator who called meetings so early in the morning.*

"Mike Benson, please." J.P. opened a file folder on his desk.

"I'm sorry, he's not in yet. May I take a message?"

J.P. remembered the hour. "No message," he replied quickly. With the same intensity he pushed another button on the phone. This time Mike picked up.

"Rise and shine, Counselor."

"I'm up, already," Mike answered with forced enthusiasm. "And I'm finally done with your truck. I can bring it by on my way to the office."

I'm sick of driving that little sports car. "Took you long enough."

"She had a lot to move."

"I hope she's worth it." *And I hope she treats him better than the last one.* "Sparky just finished briefing his investigation out west. He thinks the Mid-America scandal is still active here in Joplin. And, more importantly, he thinks the monies are being laundered right here under our noses."

"Do tell."

"I've given Sparky full use of Derek for the rest of the week to see what they can uncover. That puts everything out east on hold and makes for some interesting conversations with Stephenson later today. Any chance you can sit in on that meeting."

"I'm free after ten. I'll drop your truck off in a few minutes."

"Keep it for now. I'll meet you at the gym at noon and bring you up to date on Sparky's report before meeting Stephenson at two."

"Noon is good."

J.P. buttoned the cuffs on his shirt. In full stride, he grabbed his suit coat off the back of a chair. "I'll be at the courthouse."

"I put the copies for the city attorney in your briefcase in the file marked *diary.*"

Thank you.

"Do we need to recognize the fact this book came back?"

I don't know. J.P. tapped the edge of the worn diary against Denise's desk. *She didn't answer her phone Friday night.* The weekend replayed in his mind. *I spent all day Saturday on the golf course with Hughes and the city planning commissioner trying to negotiate the misunderstanding that took place while I was out of town.* J.P. closed his briefcase. *And spent most of Sunday at Mid-America with Sparky.* He sighed. *And today is Monday.* The weekend was over. *And I haven't talked to her since the less than pleasant encounter in her office.*

"Shit."

"Gut feeling says something in the form of an apology might be in order. What do you want me to do, Boss? Send flowers or write a letter?"

Deep down inside J.P. knew what Samira wanted more than anything was to hear from him. *Tucking my tail isn't exactly my style.* He checked his watch. *And I'd better get moving or I'll be late to the courthouse.*

What the hell. "Both. And make the flowers roses."

"Roses?" Denise sounded surprised. "I'm thinking I might deliver them in person just to see who's on the other end."

J.P. caught the end of that statement as he stepped out onto the concrete balcony outside his office door. He turned around and retraced his tracks. "Just have them delivered." *The last thing I need is Denise agitating Samira further.*

~~~~~~~

"Your keys, Counselor." Mike tossed them into J.P.'s gym locker.

J.P. dropped them in his gym bag.

"Christ, I had to park at the back of the parking lot." Mike opened his locker and began to unbutton his collarless dress shirt. "That beast is so big I couldn't fit into the spaces up here."

J.P. put his toe on the edge of the bench to tie his shoe. "It was big enough to haul someone's shit though, wasn't it?"

Mike pulled a Nike tank top on over his head. "That it was." He held out his hand. "By the way, I believe you have my keys."

J.P. returned to his locker and removed the Corvette keys from his pants pockets. "Where'd she move to?"

"From the Bridges condos out by the airport to an apartment closer to the school where she teaches."

"Too much noise or what?"

Mike shook his head. "Nope. Not that simple." He sat down on the bench and tied his shoes. "She didn't like the new manager at the condos. Seems the complex was sold a month or so ago and she didn't appreciate the new corporate rules concerning where she could and could not park her Golf."

J.P. eyed his colleague warily. "How do you park a golf?"

Mike wiggled his eyebrows. "Much like you park my Corvette—very carefully and close in so you don't have to walk a mile to your destination."

"What do you know about Bridges Property Management? Anything?" *Be helpful if Mike has some firsthand intel on the infamous Mr. Bridges.*

"New in town about a year ago. Aggressive with new acquisitions. And from what I know from a recent former tenant, hard ass all the way around."

Nothing I didn't already know. "I'll see you out there."

J.P. was deep in his own thoughts when Mike entered the racket ball court.

"I hate to break the news, but my new racket ball partner is going to bump you in thirty minutes." Mike slammed the little blue ball into the far wall with his racket.

"You've replaced me with a woman?" J.P. raised the racket in his left hand and returned the serve without any trouble.

"Yep." Mike took his turn again. "Not unlike the way you stood me up in exchange for a *lady's* company at the driving range."

J.P. ducked as the ball bounced back toward his head.

Mike missed the return. "How is your *lady* anyway?" He served a second ball into the wall.

"Pissed." J.P. returned the serve with more power than necessary. "Denise served a subpoena for a historical document from her library before I could intervene." He dodged
~~~~~~~

left so Mike could make the play. When the ball came back, he hit it again, but it skimmed the sidewall and stopped the play action.

Mike wiped the sweat from his face with his arm. "You sent a subpoena to Samira without warning?"

Oh yeah. I forgot Mike knows Samira. He picked the little blue ball up off the floor and hammered it into the wall with his racket. "Yep."

"Shit."

"Shit." J.P. echoed.

Several volleys were exchanged without comment. The first game was played and scored. Without a break in play J.P. served the second game. When there was finally a short break in volley, J.P. used the bottom of his shirt to wipe his face.

"But you've kissed and made up, right?"

J.P. served again. "Not exactly."

Instead of returning the serve Mike caught the ball with his free hand. "Excuse me?"

"Not yet." J.P. motioned for Mike to give him the ball. "That's game point."

"That's bullshit." Mike closed his hand over the ball. "You let a case rest between you and Samira?"

Basically.

Mike bounced the ball against the wooden floor and caught it again. "Your head is harder than this floor, good buddy." Mike was sounding serious. "You want my advice?"

This time when the ball bounced J.P. hit it out from under Mike's hand with his racket. "No."

"Screw you then." Mike let the ball rebound off the ceiling.

Since when does Mike Benson back away from sounding his own advice? J.P. missed the return. The ball bounced wildly against the glass behind him. *I do feel a little guilty about it if that helps anything.*

Mike adjusted the sweatband around his head. "You have less than five minutes to brief me on Sparky's investigation."

Fine. If he doesn't want the rest of the story with Samira, then he doesn't get it. The ball hit J.P. in the chest before he had a chance to return it.

"That's game. Again." Mike put his hands on his knees to catch his breath. "You lose."

Again. J.P. looked up to see a cheerful, redhead smiling down upon them from above.

"Three minutes. What's the scoop on Stephenson?"

Suddenly Mid-America has little bearing on my life. J.P. stated the three main points of Sparky's discoveries in brief sentences.

"So, it's basically in Stephenson's best interest to sit it out and wait to see where the monies turn up?" Mike straightened his back. Sweat was running off his face and dripping onto the floor.

"Basically."

"I can lean him in that direction." Mike waved at the redhead above them to come on down. "All said, what we thought was close to being the end is actually only the beginning?"

"That's what it looks like." J.P. started for the door. "Two o'clock."

"I'll be there."

"Shower first." J.P. stepped into the cooler air of the corridor. The red-headed woman was making her way down the steel staircase.

"Hey, Counselor." Mike called from behind the glass.

What?

"Call the lady. She may be your last chance."

Last chance at what? J.P. stripped in the locker room and made his way to the shower. *For all I know, what was just beginning with Samira might be closer to the end.*

~~~~~~~

J.P. sat with his truck backed into the parking space two spots down from Samira's car. *I might not be able to read her thoughts, but she is predictable to some degree.* J.P. opened the Mid-America file across the console and began to document his mental notes from the meeting with Mr. Stephenson and the board president. *I know she gets off work at four.*

As anticipated, Samira appeared on the front steps of the library a little past four o'clock. *Who's the guy?* There was a man with her, and he was talking to Samira using big hand motions. Samira was laughing. *She certainly seems to be enjoying the conversation.*

I can wait. J.P. finished notating his meeting and closed the file folder, but Samira had only advanced two steps toward the sidewalk. *And he's still talking to her.*

Who the hell is he? The longer he watched, the more irritated it made him. *I could just leave, and she'd never know I was here.* The man on the steps made a slight advance toward Samira. *Or I could get out of the truck and introduce myself.*

Just as he reached to turn the key in the ignition, the man turned and went back inside the library. J.P. watched Samira descend the remaining stairs. Now it was decision time. *Do I get out of the truck or let her leave?*

Just talk to her. J.P. opened the door of the truck and stepped onto the concrete of the parking lot. Samira looked up into his face with a bright smile.

I have missed that smile.

The smile quickly dissipated.

But this may be the last time I see it.

Samira glanced over her shoulder toward the front door of the library. "Phil." She tucked a loose hair back into her bun at the back of her head. "I didn't expect to see you here." She held her hand over her eyes to block the sun. "Have you been here long?"

J.P. decided to lie. *It will ease the tension to some degree.* "Not long."

"I got the note and the roses," Samira's dark eyes were looking directly into his. "I'm assuming they came from the office."

He'd hoped Denise sent them from him. *Obviously not the case.* "Thanks for the book."

"Maybe you can close the case now."

She's still distant and cautious. J.P. nodded. "Maybe." *Not that I blame her.* "I guess that would be the goal."

Samira nodded.

"So how was your day?" *Maybe she'll tell me who the man is.*

"Great." Samira removed her hand from her forehead. "Today was a really good day."

Not a hint of insight. "Good start to the week then?"

"Lots better than last week." Samira turned away from the direct sunlight, but she kept her eyes on him. "Is there something I can do for you, Phil?"

I have a million things I want to tell her and don't even know where to start. He started to run his hand through his hair, but Samira reached out and stopped the motion with her hand.

"You don't have to answer." Her face was suddenly concerned.

"No, I do have to answer." *Say it, Ralston.* "I am here to offer..." *an apology.* "Well, let's just say I was out of line." He looked beyond Samira into the row of bushes in front of her parked car. "And to answer your question, no, I wouldn't have let you go to jail in place of gaining custody of the book."

There. J.P. took a deep breath. *I answered that question.*

Samira's hand fell from his arm. "That takes a load off my mind."

Gotta love the sarcasm. "I don't know if we can go back and start this one over."

Samira's eyes were low. "I don't know either, Phil. This one is complicated."

The pit in J.P.'s stomach tightened. "I'd like to take you to dinner." *Or go anywhere to be*
~~~~~~~

alone with her for a while.

Samira shook her head. "I can't, Phil. Not tonight." She adjusted the strap on her purse. "I promised Mrs. Barnes I'd take her to the grocery store after work, which is now."

Phil watched as she fidgeted with her fingernail.

"And tonight, I'm coming back here to work with our guest artist."

Guest artist? J.P. glanced over his shoulder. *Is that who she was talking to?* "It doesn't have to be tonight." *I'd make myself free anytime to be with her.* J.P. watched her look away. *But the damage may already be done.*

Samira crossed her arms over her middle.

She looks nervous. "I just want a chance to—" J.P. stuffed his hands in his pockets. "To make amends, Samira. I was wrong."

"I know." Samira agreed quickly. "And maybe I was wrong too." Her eyes were scanning the parking lot. "Maybe I was wrong for assuming too much."

How is it I can read these thoughts? "No—" *I don't like the way this is headed.*

"I'm sorry, Phil. But I do have to pick up Mrs. Barnes or she'll be calling out here looking for me." Samira checked her watch. "And I don't want to be late getting back either."

If anyone knows a time crunch, it's me. But gut feeling says she's putting me off. J.P. weighed his options knowing his time was waning. *You can either lay it on the line with her right here, Ralston, or get in your truck and drive away.*

Always before J.P. Ralston had walked away. *But I've never lost anything I ever missed.* He inhaled deeply. *And I'm already missing her.*

J.P. opened his mouth. "I never meant to hurt you, Samira." *Why can't I just say it?* J.P. lowered his head. "I'm sorry too." *There. I said it.*

"I know, Phil." Samira's voice was just above a whisper. "But this one is going to take a little getting over." She paused briefly. "And I don't know..."

Here it comes.

"...if I can give you what you need."

J.P. closed his eyes. *There she goes blaming herself again.* "You already give me what I need, Samira."

"Then I don't know if you have it in you to accept."

The reality of that statement hit like a ton of bricks. *Mike told me she was out of my league.* J.P. stood stock still as Samira kissed her fingertips and then pressed her fingers into his cheek. The emotions he felt were too strong for words and too powerful for a reaction of any kind. *She reads me like a book.* He held Samira's hand to his cheek until she gently pulled it away.

"I need to be going." Samira turned toward her car. "Mrs. Barnes is waiting."

J.P. stood stock still watching Samira drive away. *She may be in a league all her own.* Numbness rose from his toes and stopped in his chest. *Maybe it's better this way.* He walked slowly toward his truck. *I knew it was risky taking a chance like that.* He started the engine and turned the air conditioner all the way up. *In fact, I knew better and let her in anyway.*

He pulled onto the main street unaware of the traffic. *What in the hell is that supposed to mean?* He stopped at a red light and came face to face with himself in the rearview mirror. The hollow gaze was vaguely familiar, but it was one J.P. Ralston didn't want to claim.

I have no desire to go back. The car behind him honked bringing his thoughts back to present. *But if my last chance just walked out of my life, what's the point?* The car honked a second time. *Get off my tail, asshole.* J.P. flipped his middle finger at the driver in his mirror. *Dammit. I shouldn't have let myself get involved.* He moved through the green light but had no idea where he was going from there.

43 Newsworthy

Samira

A caption in the business section caught Samira's eye as she cleared miscellaneous papers from her mother's table: ***Hughes Family Estate Closes with Fair Settlement.*** *So, the diary I found for the defense paid off after all.* Samira leaned over the paper to read the details:

> The estate of the late multi-millionaire, Lloyd Hughes, of Springfield, Missouri, reached a settlement with the city of Joplin. After many months of discrepancy, legal representation from the law office of J.P. Ralston was able to prove the estate did not owe back commercial tax as originally charged. The city of Joplin agreed to settlement of $125K in residential tax owed since 1944...

"Well, well," Samira's father entered the kitchen unannounced. "How's my girl?"

Samira greeted him with a hug. "Hi Daddy." Two little blonde girls caught up with happy squeals. "Where did you find these two?"

"I didn't find them," Raymond rubbed their heads. "They found me." With that he sent them towards the sun porch. "I bet Granny's in the garden."

"She is." Samira confirmed. "We needed a tomato for supper."

"Then you're staying?" Raymond filled a coffee cup.

Samira nodded. *Seems like I've been here a lot lately.* "Are we keeping Bonnie and Lizzie?"

"I'll take them home after dinner." Raymond was eyeing his daughter with care.

He knows I'm not exactly myself. To avoid being quizzed she went back to clearing the table.

"Your mother will want to eat in the dining room since the little girls are staying too." It wasn't long before Kara was in the kitchen helping Papa Ray set the table.

I just want a moment to finish that article. As soon as everyone was busy, Samira skimmed the details and focused on the summarizing paragraph.

> The settlement was accepted by the now reigning brothers of the highly successful Hughes Corporation, with headquarters in Springfield. "This one has been a long time in coming to a close," said legal representation, Mike Benson. "Everyone involved feels the settlement is fair and in the best interest of the city as well as the Hughes family. "It's a win-win." Miles Kelton, Joplin city attorney, expressed similar sentiments, "We are pleased with the outcome."

Mike Benson?

"What's caught your attention there, Sugar?" Raymond was leaning over his daughter's shoulder.

"Oh, Daddy." Samira jumped at the interruption. "I was just skimming the news."

Raymond looked doubtful. "I don't know that I've ever seen you take much interest in the business news." He shuffled some papers. "Now the Arts and Entertainment section sounds more like you. Have you seen it yet?"

I wonder why Phil didn't close the Hughes Estate.

Raymond opened another paper over the top of the business news. "Here." He pointed a finger at the boxed announcement in the corner. "Now this is newsworthy." Samira followed along as her father read aloud: "The sculpture gallery of Fabiano Uberti, Artist in Residence, is now open to the public at the Maple Street Library until the end of August. Uberti's work is known the world over for its keen sense of reflective expression and life-like features. This is a must-see display. For a private showing or seminar with Uberti, please contact the library during business hours."

Raymond stopped reading and looked up at his daughter.

"And it's not a bad photo of him either. Most newspaper photos don't come out so clear."

"This one happens to be a press copy, so it's made especially for newspapers and such." Samira explained. *The original is still on my desk.*

"How's he working out? Are you getting a lot of traffic?"

Samira smiled. "Yes, Daddy. Lots of tours and on-lookers." She tucked her hair behind an ear. "And here's a little piece of information," she taunted her father on purpose. "Guess who he asked to be his model for his in-house piece?"

Raymond crossed his arms and puckered his lips in thought. "I only know one woman beautiful enough for that honor."

"No." Krissy interrupted. "He picked Mama." She threw her arms into the air. "Can you believe it? My mother is a model."

Thanks, Krissy.

Raymond laughed heartily. "That is quite an honor, Princess."

I love the way Daddy still calls me Princess. He's never given that up. Even though Tom used to think it was childish.

"And I trust you are living up to his expectations."

Samira crossed the kitchen as she spoke. "I simply show up wearing the same style of clothing from the day before, take my position, and read while he works." She checked the meatloaf in the oven for her mother.

"Isn't it marvelous, Raymond?" Ashleigh appeared from the sunroom with two big, ripe tomatoes. "Our daughter is a model for a world-famous sculpture." She removed a large bowl of tossed salad from the refrigerator and handed it to her husband. "We need to go over tomorrow and see his work."

"Indeed." Raymond was still watching Samira with great interest.

Samira closed her eyes against the penetration of her father's thoughts. *Please don't ask any hard questions today, Daddy. I'm too tired.*

~~~~~~~

Kara and Krissy offered to take their little cousins to the park behind the church after dinner. The house was suddenly incredibly quiet. Samira slipped to the back of the house where oversized windows in her father's study overlooked the back yard. *Daddy's read every word on every page of every book in this room.* She ran her hands over the covers of the books on the shelves.

I have needed the tranquility of this room for a while now. Without an invitation, Samira curled into her father's reading chair and rested her chin on her knees. Through the window she could see her mother gathering an armful of cut flowers.

"I thought I might find you here." Papa Ray's shoes tapped softly on the hardwood floor.

Samira smiled gently. *I was half-hoping he'd come looking for me.* "It's quiet back here, Daddy."

Raymond took a seat on the loveseat adjacent to his daughter. He crossed his legs and followed her gaze into the back yard. "Is there a storm going on inside your pretty little
~~~~~~~

head, Samira?"

Rarely did Raymond address his daughter using her first name. *Now I know he is reading my thoughts.* "I didn't realize how consuming it would be to have this sculptor in, Daddy. He is a quiet man, but at the same time he is very demanding of my time and attention."

Raymond nodded his head once. His eyes were on Samira. But her eyes were still in the back yard.

"Being a still life model is hard work then?"

Samira rested her head on the chair. "He only works on the in-house piece after hours, so I've had some late nights." *Later than I am used to anyway.*

"Surely not alone."

"Oh, no." Samira waved her hand to calm her father. "Either Jim, our maintenance man, or one of my assistants has been in the building every time I've gone back for a sitting." Samira replayed the past few days in her mind. "But they're tiring of the overtime too."

"How much longer before he doesn't need a live model?"

"He's almost done with me." *But there is somebody else I'd rather be with.*

Raymond linked his hands behind his head.

He is satisfied with my answers.

When he spoke again so soon, Samira was caught completely off guard.

"And what about the man who stole your heart, Princess? Are you able to work him into your modeling schedule?"

How does Daddy read me like that? Samira pulled her knees tighter to her chest. *The whole summer has passed, and I have never mentioned Phil to my parents.* She avoided her father's eyes completely. "Daddy," she tried to brush him off. "What makes you think someone stole my heart?"

"I'm your father, Sugar. The glow on your face tells me there is a man in your life that means something special. But the pain in your eyes tell me it must not be as easy as you'd hoped."

Transparency. Samira hated it when her family could read her so easily. She flipped her hair off the side of her shoulder. "It's not." *This is the part you were not going to tell him, remember?* "He's a really busy man." *Just don't say anything to incriminate Phil before Daddy meets him.* "It's hard for him to separate work and personal time." *Why am I defending him?*

"Not exactly a family man then?"

Daddy is going to trigger my emotions. I can feel it coming.

"I wouldn't say that." Samira thought for a moment. "He's a father so that takes up his time and energy too. And he owns his own business so that takes most of the rest of him."

Raymond puckered his lips in thought. "I guess we know the repercussions of running your own business, don't we Ashleigh?"

Samira wasn't aware that her mother had joined them. *I wouldn't be surprised if they arranged this time alone with me.*

Ashleigh sat down and patted Raymond's leg. "We love having you, dear,"

But obviously they've noticed I'm hiding out over here. "Sometimes it's easier to be here than to wait for the phone to ring." *There. I said it. They shouldn't need any more information on Phil or any other part of my life.* Samira could feel her chest tightening. *But I really don't think he's going to call.*

"Waiting is difficult," Ashleigh admitted. "Very difficult." She patted Raymond's leg again. "Is he good for you, dear?"

Samira inhaled very deeply. She pulled her hair back in her hand and held it there. "He's passionate, intense, and playful, all at the same time." She let go of her hair. "He's really good with the girls and he takes me places and treats me like a queen." Samira felt a smile form on her lips. "And he has this really great smile." *And I love the way he calls me Pretty Lady.*

"Yes," Ashleigh smiled genuinely at her daughter. "We've heard some things from Krissy."

Of course, they have. She uncurled her legs and set her feet on the floor. "I like everything about him." A tear threatened to spill onto her cheek. *The only part I don't like is the way he used me to leverage his evidence for a case.*

Raymond leaned forward and put his hand on his daughter's knee. "Then why the tears, Sugar?"

He hasn't called me since that day in the library parking lot. Samira couldn't hold them in anymore.

In the distance she could hear Krissy and Kara returning with the little girls. Ashleigh silently excused herself.

"Oh, Daddy," Samira put her face in her hands. "I like everything about him. Everything." She reached for a tissue and held it to her nose. "But he scares me."

"In what way, darling?"

Samira found a smile through her tears. "Not like you might think." She wiped her nose again. "He scares me because I don't know if I can handle all of him." She thought some more. "And because if I give him my whole heart, I'm afraid he won't know what to do with it." *Am I afraid of being hurt?*

"He doesn't know love yet, Daddy. Not like I do anyway." Another thought occurred to her. "Sometimes he's so focused on his work that I can't get to where he is even though I'm right there in the same room." *Like that day in my office.* "Yet if he'd just quit trying so hard to make it work—" Samira bit her bottom lip. *Love might have a fighting chance.* "I don't know what to think anymore." Samira blew her nose. *But I do know I really miss him.* "What am I going to do, Daddy?" *I need to know what to do because I miss all of him.*

Raymond didn't wait any longer. He slid forward onto his knees. In one fell swoop he gathered his daughter completely into his arms.

Just hold me, Daddy, because I already gave him my whole heart and it hurts so deep. She allowed her father to caress her hair and hold her until she gained composure.

Raymond let her sit back in the chair again. He moved a small footstool and sat down at Samira's feet.

"Well, Princess," he began. "It sounds to me like you need to share all this with him." Raymond was looking directly into his daughter's eyes. "You have the gift to read a person's soul, Samira. You understand people in ways that most miss. He might not know what to do with you either."

Samira could see her father's face through her tears. *Only Daddy could remind me of my own intensity without hurting me.*

"You're going to have to tell him how you feel and then give him the freedom to make the decision." Raymond's brow was wrinkled in concern. "And his decision might not be the one you're hoping for, Sugar."

Is that what I'm afraid of? Samira pushed her hair back again. *I am afraid if I call him, he might not know how to handle me either.* "I know." She choked another sob.

"I'm sorry you have to go through this." Raymond's eyes were soft. "Taking a chance at love never comes easily."

"Nope," Samira wiped her face in her hands. "It never does."

"I wish I could do it for you, Samira."

"I know, Daddy." She forced a tearful smile. "Thank you."

"Do we know this man?"

Samira had kept her parents in the dark on purpose knowing it would be easier to let him go without their judgement. *They still don't need to know who he is.* "I don't think so." *It will be better if they do not know him.*

"Is he from around here?"

Samira nodded. "But his family is from northern Missouri."

Raymond seemed satisfied with that little bit of information.

"I'll be okay," Samira wrapped her arms tight around her middle to get a grip on her emotions. *I hope.*

Raymond nodded with assurance. "I know you will. You're a strong woman like your mother." He rose from his low seat and offered his hands to help Samira out of the chair. "You'll come out of this better for it either way." The father embraced his daughter as she accepted his assistance.

Samira inhaled her father's aftershave. *I wish I were a little girl again so Daddy could carry me into my room and tuck me in for the night without a worry in the world.*

"Why do things have to be so complicated, Daddy?"

"I don't know, Princess." Raymond stroked her hair as he answered. "But sometimes you have to fight harder than others." He kissed her hair.

Suddenly reminded of Phil's kisses, Samira closed her eyes. *I fought hard the last time and I lost.* Memories of Tom's last days flitted through her mind. *What if I don't have the fight in me this time?*

Everything will be alright."

I don't know if Daddy actually spoke those words out loud or just thought them hard enough, I heard him. Samira nodded against her father's shoulder.

~~~~~~~

Monday morning came all too soon. Spent from the emotional outlet the day before, Samira still felt tired. *I just can't seem to get caught up on my sleep.* But her emotions were intact, and the busyness of the library schedule was a welcomed retreat. Samira raised her elbows as an entourage of day care children skipped around jockeying for a front row seat.

"There's plenty of space, children," Daphne assured. The assistant gathered a wayward group of students with her arms and began to guide them to the viewing area.

Fabiano Uberti was waiting patiently to speak to the children. He positioned himself on a tall stool and folded his hands in his lap. Surprisingly, his quiet presence drew the attention of the children, and they began to settle down.

"Isn't it amazing how he does that?" Daphne asked of the artist.

"Does what?"

"Quiets them down without even speaking," Daphne was totally amazed by just about everything Fabiano had done during his three-week stay. *She is so smitten by him. Only a few more days and he'll pack his presentation and sculptures and be on his way.*

But Samira admired the way he worked with children too. *Most of all I admire the way he can capture someone's emotion and carve it into his work.* Her eyes moved to the incomplete sculpture sitting on a worktable behind Fabiano. What started out as a block of hard, formless clay was now a shapely character resembling Samira's body. But more than that, the shape of the eyes and the position of the head allowed Samira to see a glimpse of her own soul.

"Miss Samira," Mrs. Haddock whispered from the conference room doorway. When Samira looked up, Mrs. Haddock moved her hand for Samira to follow. "There's a gentleman here who would like to see you in person."

The last visitor Helen interrupted an important meeting for turned out to be a police officer.

"He looked important," Mrs. Haddock explained. "So, I seated him in your office."

Samira's eyes went immediately to the backside of a balding businessman. She didn't recognize him at first. But as she stepped into her office, the gentleman stood and greeted her with a warm smile. Samira offered her hand and instead of shaking, he raised it to his
~~~~~~~

lips.

"Mr. Hughes," Samira was quite surprised to see him. "Would you care for a cup of coffee?"

"No, no, Miss Cartwright." He took a seat.

"I am here to return something of great value." Christopher Hughes opened his suit jacket and removed a worn journal. "I understand you are the mastermind who uncovered the winning piece of evidence to close my father's estate."

"A mastermind might be a stretch," Samira corrected honestly. "But I did happen to run across it about the same time the evidence became pertinent." *I wondered if I'd ever see that book again, but I never expected it to be hand delivered by Christopher Hughes.* She accepted the book without hesitation.

Mr. Hughes smiled. "My brother and I certainly appreciate your role in this project. As you might already know, my father's estate has been tied up in legal battles ever since his passing." The gentleman's face grew more serious. "That journal allowed a fair settlement over what could have been an economic challenge for the company." Christopher Hughes rose from his chair. "We are in the notion to repay you for your help, Miss Cartwright."

Oh, no. Samira put her hands out to stop the man from speaking. "That certainly won't be necessary."

"On the contrary." Mr. Hughes was reaching for his interior pocket again. "You saved my brother and I several hundred thousand dollars by discovering that journal." The man removed a sealed envelope. "It is our understanding that the library accepts donations on behalf of individuals. Is that correct?"

"We do." *Accepting payment on behalf of the library is another story.* "We accept designated gifts in memory of individuals if the family has a specific wish. Or we also accept undesignated gifts and allow the library board to use the gifts where they are most needed at the time."

Samira walked around her desk and opened a drawer. A glossy flier stated all the different ways individuals and businesses might make donations to the library. Mr. Hughes looked over the pamphlet with interest.

"This gift would be designated." He thought for a moment. "And we would like to give it in memory of our father, the late Lloyd Hughes."

"He was a very generous man from what I understand."

"He was indeed." Christopher punctuated the compliment. "Do you have a suggestion on the designation, Miss Cartwright?"

Samira's heart skipped a beat. *In all my years as the head librarian of the Maple Street Branch, no one has ever asked how I might designate a gift.* Immediately her thoughts went to the needs of the online center. Without hesitation Samira indicated that possibility.

"I would be interested to know more about this online center," Mr. Hughes replied with enthusiasm. "Is it on site?"

Samira offered Mr. Hughes a personal tour of the center. While she walked him through the area, she restated most of the points she had presented to the board of trustees. *It's a good thing I worked so hard on that PowerPoint presentation.* It felt good to be able to say the words with such confidence.

As they made their way back to her office Mr. Hughes once again fingered the sealed envelope. He complimented Samira's informative tour as he began to open the flap. "Is it possible that our father's memoriam might be placed in the center?"

"I'm sure we could arrange for that, Mr. Hughes." Samira's heart was pounding hard in her chest. *Anything you wish.*

"That would be very nice." Christopher Hughes handed Samira a check made out to the city with the Maple Street Library as the recipient. The check was for twenty thousand dollars. "Do you think this might get the board of directors moving on the project a little quicker?"

"Oh, Mr. Hughes," Samira swallowed hard so her excitement would gush all at once. "This is a very generous donation for the cause."

"My father would be pleased to know he is still propelling the city of Joplin into the future." Mr. Hughes stooped to pick up his briefcase.

Samira remembered the formalities. "I have some papers for you to fill out in order to make this official."

Christopher Hughes produced a business card without so much a turn of his hand. "Just fax the forms to my secretary. She will take care of everything." The gentleman smiled genuinely. "Once again, my brother and I appreciate your intervention immensely. If there are ever other ways we might be of assistance, please don't hesitate to let us know."

I have never had this kind of experience in my entire life. The next thing Samira knew Christopher Hughes was gone and she was left holding a check that would more than complete the online project.

Fabiano Uberti tipped his head in Samira's direction as she glanced at the class through the glass windows. *Can he see my excitement from over there?* Samira felt like doing cartwheels all the way back to the circulation desk. She returned the artist's smile but ignored his silent invitation to join him. Instead, she headed for the back room to find Mrs. Haddock. *Mr. Uberti will just have to wait.*

44 *Tough Love*

Joseph Phillip

Denise rattled off the phone messages. "I know it's getting late for a Friday, but Jessica Hutchison from Bridges Property is expecting to hear from you yet today. I checked the city council notes and it looks like they're set to close on the airport property next week. Her call may be in reference to that."

J.P. nodded as he skimmed the other messages. "What's from the Maple Street Library?"

"A woman called and asked for you. When I offered to take a message, she said she'd try back later." Denise shrugged her shoulders. "Nothing more than that."

"She leave a name?"

"No name."

"Get her on the phone for me," J.P. dropped the clipboard on Denise's desk. *I haven't talked to Samira in over two weeks.*

"She didn't leave a name, Boss. Who should I ask for?"

"Ask for Miss Cartwright."

"The same one I ordered a court subpoena on?"

J.P. shot his assistant a wary look. *That single document altered my entire life.*

"Very well."

J.P. unpacked the contents of his briefcase onto the conference table behind his desk. *What am I supposed to say to her after so much time has passed?*

Denise called from the outer office. "Miss Cartwright on line two, Boss."

J.P. reached for the phone. *Just act casual.* He took a long, deep breath and exhaled slowly before pushing the button to connect.

"This is J.P." *That was anything but casual.*

"This is Samira."

"Samira. *It's good to hear her voice.* "How are you?"

There was a slight hesitation on Samira's part. "I'm fine."

Is she fine?

"How are you?"

Swamped. Tense. Stressed. Insane without you. "Fine."

"Does your assistant make all of your calls for you now?"

It didn't even occur to me to dial the phone myself. "Only when I'm on the fly," he lied again hoping to redeem himself.

"Are you short for time?"

Damn it. Nothing is coming out right. "No." J.P. could feel tension in his chest. *Just relax and talk to her.* "Not anymore."

"That's good." Samira sounded relieved. "I know this might be short notice, but I received a gift today and I was thinking that if you had some time tomorrow—"

Name the time, Pretty Lady.

"I'd like to share it with you."

"What exactly do you have in mind?" *Dinner? Candlelight?*

"Lunch."

Lunch?

"I was hoping maybe you could meet me for lunch."

"Okay." *Whatever she wants.* "I can make that happen." *With minimal rearranging.*

"Good."

Maybe she is ready to kiss and make up.

"Do you know where McClelland Park is?"

"At Shoal Creek?" *There is no place out there to eat.*

"Yes." Samira's voice was suddenly filled with renewed energy. "I'll be at the west parking lot at noon."

"Noon tomorrow." *I wish I knew what's on her mind.*

"And I'll bring the lunch."

"Like in a picnic?"

"Is that alright?"

"That's good." *It's not exactly a candlelight dinner, but it will work.*

"Then you'll be there?"

I wouldn't miss it. "I'll be there."

Samira said goodbye but then caught J.P. with a parting thought. "Oh, Phil?"

Man, I like the way she says my name.

"Next time maybe you could make the call yourself."

J.P. closed his eyes. "I can do that." *She could have called my cell. I would have answered.*

He hung up feeling the same distance he'd felt the day she left him in the library parking lot. *She is way out of your league.* Mike's words echoed again in J.P.s memory.

"Noon tomorrow?" Denise questioned as she entered the office with a note stuck to the end of her finger. "Do I need to add that to your calendar?"

"No." J.P. read the note. *Jessica Hutchison.* "I won't need a reminder."

"Be careful there, sport," Denise warned with a hint of sarcasm. "I think you're already booked at noon tomorrow."

This time my personal agenda comes first. "Then make adjustments."

"She sounds smart."

"She is."

"I don't think she liked me making the contact."

"She didn't."

"Do you need me to remind you of that in the future?"

"No." J.P. looked hard into Denise's eyes. "That will be all."

"What about Derek's study group?"

"When?"

"Noon tomorrow."

Shit. J.P. put his head in his hands. *He's only a week from the bar exam.* "Fix it."

"As in reschedule?"

"Yes, Denise. Reschedule the study." J.P. could feel the force in his voice.

"Maybe I should remind you that this study group includes more than just Derek." Denise started to return to her own office. "And you sited the study group as one of the reasons you sent James home for the weekend."

I sent James home so I could have some peace of mind. J.P. Ralston had been inundated with the Mid-America case and Hughes business since the afternoon he last saw Samira. *My patience is growing thin.* "Just fix it, Denise."

Denise turned around in the doorway. "The last time you told me to *fix* something, I got my butt chewed for sending Mike to close your case." She clicked her fake fingernails on the doorframe. "Therefore, I'd prefer if you'd be a little more explicit this time."

She's right. But I couldn't close a case after spending a night with a bottle of Jack Daniels. "Tell Derek I can't make it at noon. In fact, I don't know exactly when I'll get there but tell him I'll stop by as soon as I am finished with my noon appointment."

"That I can do. Thank you for the clarification."

"Remind me again why I put up with you."

"Because I'm one of the few people in your life that can save your ass and your case all in the same day."

Point well taken. J.P. cued his computer screen to check the remaining items on his agenda. "Can you get—"

"Jessica Hutchison on the phone?" Denise finished the question. "Done."

And because she's the only person in my life who reads my mind and puts up with me anyway.

"Line one, Boss."

J.P. picked up the phone prepared to listen to a new sales pitch aimed at the Hughes Corporation. He was right on the money with that assumption. *But the business Jessica Hutchison offers isn't nearly as high on my priority list as the business scheduled for tomorrow noon.*

~~~~~~~

The newspaper reiterated mostly old news from the day before. J.P. laid it aside as he finished off a glass of orange juice. This was the first morning he'd had completely alone in his own house since James had moved in. The unusual stillness was as much a surprise as it was a welcomed retreat. *No music playing in the background and no one sitting in front of my computer.*

Instead of meeting Mike at the driving range, J.P. stretched out, then headed down the bike path in a full stride. Chase ran dutifully alongside his master. J.P. had been doing his workouts at the gym, which left Chase home without regular exercise.

"That's really not very fair, is it boy?" J.P. talked to the dog as they crossed the bridge at the end of the path. The steady rhythm of the run matched the evenness of his breathing. *I'm getting too old to give myself over to the bottle like that.* He stopped long enough to attach the leash. *Takes me too long to recover anymore.*

Chase spotted a squirrel in the distance. "Whoa boy. Let it go." J.P. gripped the leash tighter. *I'd feel more confident going into lunch knowing Samira's motives.* He shortened his stride to begin the cool down. *I don't know if she's ready to move on, pick up where we left off, or just call the whole thing off.* He slowed to a stop in front of his house. *Good run, Chase.* He unclipped the leash and let the dog into his backyard. *I could live with picking up where we left off or moving forward.* J.P. stretched his hamstrings. *But I don't think I want to call the whole thing off.*

~~~~~~~

It didn't take but a moment to spot her. J.P. parked where he could watch her without being seen. *She looks very much at peace with her book like that.* Samira was sitting cross-legged on a low park bench. *How does she get her hair to stay up like that?* J.P. stood next to his truck admiring her for a long time. *I still can't read one single thought.*

Samira's eyes met his long before he reached the bench. They were full of energy. *I have missed those dark eyes.*

"Hey Pretty Lady."

Her smile came naturally. "Mr. Ralston. It's good of you to come."

Funny. Those are the same words my father said to me in Virginia.

"Are you hungry?" Samira closed her book.

For you? Yes. Famished. He wanted to touch her but did not feel the same sentiments from Samira.

"I brought lunch but it's over there." She pointed to the edge of a hill.

I would follow you about anywhere right now, Samira Cartwright. J.P. spotted a checkered blanket stretched over the grass in the shade of an old maple tree. A picnic basket offered a silent invitation.

"This is the best view of the river."

J.P. watched her eyes scan the area.

"It's especially beautiful down here in the fall when the trees are in full color."

The only view I need is right here.

Samira sat down and patted the space next to her.

There is an invitation I won't refuse.

A sudden array of cold cuts appeared. Then a bowl of red grapes. Then a bag of cookies. J.P. watched in amazement as Samira turned the area between them into a summertime buffet. Her quiet smile made him chuckle out loud.

Samira looked up. "What's so funny?"

J.P. shook his head. *You are funny. You just prepare this little meal like no time has passed between us at all.*

"I don't know that I've ever known you to not speak." Samira popped a grape in her mouth and offered one to J.P.

I hope this is a peace offering. "I don't know what to say to such a pretty lady." His eyes moved from her face to her hands where she was busy preparing a piece of bread for a sandwich. *Say something, Ralston.* "It's really good to see you, Samira." *And it is.*

"It's been a while."

"Seventeen days."

Samira stopped spreading the mayonnaise, but she didn't look up. *I wonder if she's kept track too.* He watched as she prepared her next thought.

"What would you like in your sandwich? Turkey or ham?"

"Both."

"Lettuce? Cheese?"

"I want it all." *Including the lady preparing it for me.*

Samira proceeded to lay the cold cuts over the bread. "Maybe that's part of the problem." She made brief eye contact.

Either she's picking up where we left off, or she's about to call it off.

Samira handed him the sandwich without saying anymore.

Not moving forward yet. J.P. held the bread in his hands. *I'd be perfectly satisfied to skip lunch and just have her.*

He waited to take a bite until Samira made her own sandwich.

If we're picking up where we left off, I might as well ask the question. "I noticed in the paper you were sponsoring a guest artist." *I also noticed the photo in the paper matched the face talking to her in the parking lot.* "How's that working out?" *I may not want to know the answer.*

Samira smiled easily. "It's working out really well."

Just my luck. J.P. took a bite despite the pit that was slowly forming in his stomach.

"Fabiano is good with the children and has a way with the older generation as well." Samira's eyes scanned the horizon briefly. "Not all of our guest artists are so adaptable."

Fabiano. J.P. said the name in his mind with resentment. *I don't like the way her eyes change when she says his name.*

"I read the paper too. I see the Hughes estate settled with the city."

J.P. swallowed. *Chances are good she also knows I wasn't present for the closing.* "It's good to have that case off my desk."

"The article mentioned Mike Benson." Samira wiped her mouth on a paper napkin. "Don't they interview you after cases?"

Yep. She knows. J.P. ran his tongue over his bottom lip. "I don't usually interview very well." *Which is true. But I know she wants an explanation.* A guilty conscience forced him to expand further. "I wasn't present when it settled."

Samira's eyes were gentle when she looked at him. "I'm sorry. I know it was a long time in coming."

Why does she apologize like that? Does she know I was deep into a bottle of Jack Daniels over my last meeting with her? "It was my own fault. I wasn't in any shape to be there that morning."

Samira didn't inquire any further and J.P. didn't offer any more explanation.

"One of your clients stopped to see me yesterday." Samira's face was suddenly bright.

I'm listening. "One of *my* clients?" *Maybe one I called pertaining to the funding for the library.*

"I think so. Mr. Christopher Hughes."

Professional training kept J.P. from showing the shock. *That wasn't one of the calls I made.* "Mr. Hughes?"

"I was quite surprised to see him myself."

How is it she reads me like a book, and I can't get one single thought from her?

"He returned the mayor's diary."

"No kidding?" *How the hell did he get his hands on that? And who told him it belonged to the Maple Street Library?*

"No kidding." Samira offered a homemade cookie, which J.P. readily accepted. "And he made a donation to the library for helping settle his case."

"Mr. Hughes is a generous man." J.P. tried to sound casual. *Someone shared confidential information without my knowledge.*

"Generous enough to pick up the tab for the new online system at the library," Samira concluded. "I'm thinking I might owe you a commission on the gift."

That's a hefty gift. J.P. gathered a handful of grapes. "Not me."

"Your office, then?" Samira took a grape out of his hand.

"Not that I'm aware of." *I seriously doubt Denise was involved in that.* "But I'm not surprised that Mr. Hughes searched you out. That sounds like something he would do."

Samira was eyeing J.P. carefully.

She really thinks I sent Mr. Hughes over with the money. "Honest." J.P. put his hands up. "I did not have any knowledge of Mr. Hughes' intention." He shrugged his shoulders and offered another grape.

"You didn't even mention it to him?"

No, but I should have. "Not a word."

"Well, we're going to set up a memorial in his father's honor." Samira tried to hide her smile. "With his donation and a few that have come in since my presentation, we should be able to get started on the project much sooner than I'd anticipated."

"What's your completion goal?" *It's fun to see her so excited.*

She squinted her eyes into the branches of the tree above them. "Well, let's see, my original goal was to have it done by the time school started, but that's only a couple of weeks out now." She rearranged her legs and leaned back on one arm. "So now I'm hoping for the first of the year."

J.P. wished he could accelerate the project for her. *I could write her a check, but I have a feeling that's not what she's wanting from me.*

"How are the boys?" Samira offered another cookie.

Might as well fess up on that. "James wants to play football with Josh again this year."

"So that means he's going back to his mom's?"

He's gone. Practice has already started. "He's going to give it a shot." *It's not what I advised, but it's what he decided to do.*

Samira's eyes showed compassion. "And how are you doing with that?"

J.P. sighed. "I don't know yet." *I don't like it.* "I was getting used to having him around." *Turned out ok to be needed at home.* "We'll see if it lasts."

"I'm sure it's a tough adjustment." Samira tucked her feet up under her long skirt.

"Tougher than I anticipated." J.P. finished the cookie. "And your girls? What are they doing to use up the rest of their summer?"

Samira shook her head. "That's a really good question." She looked off into the distance. "I've had a lot of overtime with Fabiano on site. I don't feel like I've been a particularly good mom these past few weeks."

She could never be a bad mom. "Give yourself a little credit." J.P. wished he could touch her but wasn't sure if the invitation were open. "I'm sure the girls understand."

"Maybe." Samira ran her finger over J.P.'s forearm sending excitement all the way to his toes.

Be careful, Pretty Lady. Touch me like that and I might not be able to control my instincts. J.P. opened his hand to hers. I know what she wears to bed at night and how quickly a glass of wine affects her defenses, but I still don't know what she's thinking.

Samira's eyes were thoughtful, almost serene when she looked up at him.

"There's a boardwalk that follows the creek."

In the back of his mind J.P. knew he needed to touch base with Derek's study group. *But there is no way I'm turning down this invitation.* He helped Samira load the picnic into her car and then followed her down the hill toward the river.

The only sounds were the gentle tumble of the shallow creek and the birds in the trees. *Obviously, she's been here before.* J.P. watched Samira carefully. *There's something on her mind.*

He followed her lead and joined her when she sat down on the boardwalk. She crossed her legs and reached her hand into the water. A mature weeping willow shaded the walkway from the hot afternoon sun.

"I miss talking with you."

"I do too." *I just hope I'm ready to listen.* He was afraid to look at her for fear he'd read something in her eyes he didn't want to see.

"I never know if I should call or not." Samira's voice was quiet. "I know you're busy."

I'm never too busy for her.

"And I know how much your work means to you."

Does my work mean that much to me? J.P. thought about it for a moment. "Maybe that's part of the problem. Maybe that's all I know."

Samira bumped him with her shoulder.

Is that an invitation to touch her back?

"That's not true."

"What? That my work isn't all I do?"

"No, that it's all you know." Samira looked out across the water. "You know a lot more than that."

Here goes nothing. "I don't know much about hanging on to a pretty lady," He was afraid to say it out loud, yet just as scared not to say it at all. "I don't know much about that."

"Maybe not," Samira looked over her shoulder at him. "But you know how to handle a pretty lady and I've missed that too."

I've missed that part too. J.P. couldn't resist. He lifted his hand and ran his fingertips down her arm. *More than she knows.* "What do you think we should do about that?"

Very slowly Samira leaned into J.P.'s side. With guarded reserve he allowed her body to rest against him. *There is nothing I want more than to hang on to this.*

"I don't know."

That's the part I'm afraid of.

"I think we need to work on the hanging on part." Samira looked up into his eyes.

I can't resist that look. The kiss that followed left J.P. speechless. *But why do I feel like it could be the last?*

Samira suddenly pulled away and climbed to her feet. "I didn't mean for that to happen."

"You don't have to fight it." J.P. stood as well. *Please don't fight it, Samira.*

She crossed her arms and closed her eyes. "Yes, I do," she answered quietly. "I do."

The last time she said those words to me I didn't know how to take them. A chill ran up his spine. *But this time they're even more confusing.*

Samira's now open eyes pleaded with him. "I do because—" She searched for words. "Because I need to know where you stand." She squeezed her shoulders together. "I need to know where I stand." She looked away. "I'm not very good at open-ended relationships and before—" Samira stopped talking and turned away.

"Before what?" *This is why she's out of my league. Her expectations are out of my reach.*

"Before I give any more of me," Samira turned back around and faced J.P. "I need to know your intentions."

I don't have any intentions. J.P. put his hands in his pockets and studied the motion of the water as it passed under the boardwalk. *What the hell is she asking for? A proposal or something?* "Samira, if I knew for sure what it would take to hang on, I'd give it to you on a silver platter." *Anything to hang onto what we had.*

"Hanging on doesn't mean you always give something away."

J.P. hung his head in dreaded anticipation. "Maybe not, but there isn't anything I wouldn't give to hang on to you."

"I need you to hang on for yourself, Phil. Not for me. I need you to want me for your sake, not mine."

What's she insinuating? When J.P. looked up, Samira was facing the river. *Is she asking me to give up everything I've worked for?* He didn't like the growing tension. *She's stating her thoughts. I'm going to state mine.*

"Look, Samira, I worked really hard to call my life my own." J.P. stared at her back. "And until you came along, I was extremely secure in the world I created for myself." *No matter how I say this, it's going to come out wrong.* "And to be perfectly honest, I've never let anyone have this much control over me."

Samira turned her face into the breeze, but she didn't turn all the way around.

"A long time ago I swore I'd never compromise my efforts again. So, I don't know what to tell you, Samira. All I know is how to give you the parts of me that are the most easily detached from what I do." *And that's obviously not enough for her.* "Maybe you need to be free of me so you can live your own life." *But I hope to God I'm wrong.*

"I do live my own life. Everyday." Samira moved a step closer to him. "That's the easy part. But a huge part of me is incomplete and you—"

First, she tells me she wants me to need her, and then she says she can't live without me. "I'm not getting a real clear picture of what you're expecting of me here." *But if she wants total commitment, I can't do that.* "I play by my own rules and always have. That's my problem. But if you're asking me to change the rules, I don't know if I can do that." *If I knew how, I would. But I tried that once and failed.* J.P. crouched on the balls of his feet and reached for a foxtail that was growing up between the slats in the board. *Open-ended relationships are safer. Period.*

"Maybe your rules are what keeps you at a distance. Have you ever thought of that? Maybe you're so afraid of hurting you're also afraid to love. What you and I have shared doesn't come along every day, Phil."

No, it doesn't, but demanding more of me isn't the way to keep it coming. "I've told you, it's the only way I know." *I am not afraid of hurting and seriously doubt I know how to love anymore.* "The things that come with a relationship don't come as easily for me as you might think."

"Maybe you make them too hard."

"I don't make them at all, that's part of the problem." *Just put it out there. She can take it or leave it.* "As much as I'd love to be able to promise you the moon, I can't even promise to make it home for dinner on any given night, Samira."

"Dinner can be re-heated."

"Not all dinners." *I've been down that road before. That's why I don't make promises anymore.*

J.P. felt Samira turn away from him. *No, we're not going to end like this.*

"What exactly do you want me to say?" *Tell me and I'll say it.*

Samira's eyes were damp when she faced him again.

Now she's crying.

Her voice was surprisingly calm when she spoke. "I don't want you to say anything."

"Then what do you need from me?" *Mike told me she was out of my league.*

She wiped a tear with her fingertips. "I just need to know if you love me."

If I love her? "You think that's all you need, but it won't be enough."

"You're wrong, Phil." Samira was quickly gaining her composure. "It's not enough because you won't let it be. You work so hard to keep your life compartmentalized to the point you don't let anyone in. But you don't have to work that hard for me."

"No, I do work hard. That's what I know." J.P. ran his hand through his hair. "I work hard to win and I'm good at winning."

"I am not a trophy to be won, Phil." Samira's tears had stopped. "You don't have to win me."

Then I am out of my league.

Samira sighed. "I don't really know where I stand at the moment, but I think I have a better idea of where you stand."

"Then maybe you could enlighten me because I'm still in the dark here."

"I know."

Phil could feel her slipping away.

"But you're the only one who can find you."

J.P. turned his face toward the motion of the water wondering what he should do or say next. When he turned back to Samira, she was halfway up the hill headed toward the parking area.

The rushing creek seemed louder than it had earlier. *Tell me who am I, Samira, because I don't think I know anymore.*

The pain that started in J.P.'s heart radiated through his entire body. *I don't know what this feeling is.* He put his hand on his chest. Very slowly, the colors of the world faded into hues of gray and white. *It can't be as simple as just loving her.*

Nothing was making sense. J.P.'s eyes went to the crest of the hill. *There's got to be more to it than that.* Suddenly nothing else seemed to matter. *Dad said there are some things you can't play to win.* He buried his face in his hands. *I don't know what to do if I'm not playing to win.*

45 Stained Glass

Samira

Samira looked into the eyes of the artist.

"May I touch you?"

Fabiano had called her back to the library for one final modeling session. *He says it's time to put the finishing touches on the face.*

Samira nodded silent permission.

Fabiano Uberti gently touched her jawbones with his hands and positioned her face much like he had done in earlier sessions. Samira held her head exactly as he placed it.

"Mmmmm." Fabiano studied Samira's face thoughtfully. "I fear zhat I waited too long, Miss Samira." He tilted his head to the side as he raised a small scalpel to the terracotta figurine. "Zhe light I knew in your eyes is not zhere anymore." Very carefully the artist made a slight mark. "Zometing is different, hmmm?" Fabiano looked from his work back to Samira's face, then back to the figurine again.

I feel badly that I can't give him what he's worked toward all this time. The better part of a month had passed since she first sat in this position for him. During that time, the lump of clay had taken on a life form. Samira studied the shape of the hands and the angle of the shoulders as Fabiano worked in silence.

He's exceptionally good. The figurine was in a sitting position with one knee up and one knee down. *He has captured my form.* Locks of hair were shaped into a loose weave at the nape of the neck, and one hand was holding an open book against the lower knee. The other hand was resting to the side.

"No need to respond if you don't want to." Fabiano continued to work. "Your silence speaks its own thoughts."

Forgetting her pose, Samira moved to the edge of the table and folded her hands in her lap. The transparency of her emotions seemed more evident in Fabiano's presence than with anyone else. *Even than with Wes or Daddy.*

Fabiano described the exuberance he saw in her eyes when he first mentioned the possibility that Samira might be his model. *That was the day he followed me outside and talked to me on the steps.* But there was more to that day than Fabiano's invitation to model. *Little did I know Phil was waiting for me too.* She thought some more. *And little did I know this was the sculpture Fabiano would choose as his feature piece at the auction.*

Caught up in the initial excitement, Samira couldn't refuse. *But now I wish I could take it all back.*

Fabiano looked into her eyes with great intensity. "I once thought maybe marble for the finished work. Ah, but now," he puckered his chin in thought. "Now maybe bronze to capture the sadness of your soul."

Maybe I don't want my soul captured.

"Yes, bronze. Bronze sets the stage for you now." Fabiano tipped his head indicating for Samira to turn hers slightly toward the light.

Remembering her purpose, Samira obliged. *I'll be glad to go home tonight.* "How long does it take to finalize a sculpture once you are finished carving?"

"She speaks but does not answer." Fabiano smiled quietly at the clay figure. "I must fire it next. When zhat is complete it will take a couple of days for the bronzing." The artist smiled with his eyes. "But don't you worry, Miss Samira, it will be ready in time for the auction."

"I'm not worried." *I trust him.*

"Maybe not about zhat," Fabiano replied casually. "But worried you are. Or saddened by zometing near to your heart." He stopped and admired his work for a moment.

Hopefully, he is this intuitive with all his models.

"Your spirit is wounded tonight. Yes?"

Samira bowed her head. *Very much so.*

"Tis not good for a woman to keep it all inside." Fabiano stopped working and walked to the table where Samira was sitting. He held out his hand.

Unsure of what he was going to do, Samira hesitated to give him hers.

"Let me show you zometing." He invited her to follow his thoughts.

Reluctantly, Samira put her hand in his and walked with him to the lobby where the finished pieces were on display.

"Look into zhere eyes." Fabiano released Samira's hand. "Tell me what you see." Samira looked into the faces of each piece. *An old lady in a swing. A child pulling a wagon. A girl holding a kitten. A mother and a daughter. A boy with a fishing pole. It is in their eyes.* Fabiano had captured the spirit of each model in his work. *I can see it.* She looked over the top of the display directly into Fabiano's anticipation.

"Do you know?"

Samira looked away.

"If you know what it is, you must say it to make it real." Fabiano walked around the display. His presence was strong. "You will feel better to say it out loud, Miss Samira."

Samira looked once more into the eyes of the lady in the swing. "It's love."

"Ah, yes." Fabiano slowly put his hands out as if he might embrace her. Samira didn't know if she should move away or not. "And I fear it is love zhat has left your eyes." In his eccentric kind of way, the artist reached out to Samira's face and positioned it like he had done many times in previous weeks. "Once it was zhere, but tonight it is gone." He gently held one hand against her cheek. "Do you zhink it will come back?"

Samira tried to look away, but his eyes held hers with a powerful gaze. She moved her head against his hand. "Not this time." She could see Phil's face clearly in her mind. *He's so confused yet so convinced that he has to do*[15] *something more to win me.*

Fabiano's hand moved to Samira's arm. "I am very zorry." He spoke with compassion.

Somewhat surprised by the artist's empathy, Samira allowed him to squeeze her hand. "Thank you, Fabiano." Her eyes moved back to the woman on the swing. Aunt Maggie's porch swing came to mind. *Even that day I could sense conflict in his spirit.*

Jim appeared in the back of the library. Samira dropped Fabiano's hand as she watched him weave his way through the sitting area toward the lobby.

"All of these pieces go downtown on Monday, right?"

"Everyting." Fabiano waved his hand over the area. "Zhe ones in zhe studio will go too. I will tell you zhe ones we will sell and zhe ones we will keep."

"Very well." Jim seemed satisfied. "It's getting late, Miss Samira. Are you finished for the evening?"

Samira looked to Fabiano for an answer.

"Yes. We are finished for tonight." Fabiano was looking directly at Samira when he answered.

"Let me know when you're ready to leave and I'll lock the doors behind you. I'm going to run the buffer over the entryway after you go."

Samira thanked Jim as he turned to walk away. She could feel Fabiano's eyes still watching her as Jim disappeared behind the rows of books in the back of the library.

"I am finished working for zhe night," Fabiano informed quietly. "May I take you to dinner, Miss Samira?"

Caught completely off guard, Samira instantly put her hand to her chest. *This wouldn't be a good night to keep my company.* Another thought seemed to urge an acceptance.

"As a way to thank you for modeling," Fabiano clarified.

Samira tried desperately to coincide logic with her thoughts. *Go to dinner with this passionate artist who just put the finishing touches on a sculpture of me?* "I don't know," she began to sort her thoughts out loud. Samira checked her watch. It was nearing eight o'clock. "I would need to check in with my girls."

Fabiano looked back toward the conference room where his work was still visible. "And I would need time to clean up here. Maybe an hour?"

Samira calculated how long it would take her to get home and visit with the girls and then freshen up. She was still wearing the clothes she'd worn to meet Phil. "I could meet you in an hour or so." *I have no idea what's motivating me to accept.*

Fabiano's eyes lit up with new excitement. "Do you know the bistro zhat is in zhe old hotel?"

"Andres?" A mental picture of the old inn formed in her mind. "It's French, you know."

"Hmmm, yes. I know." Fabiano kissed his fingertips into the air. "Zhe French have a way with entrées." He leaned in toward Samira. "In an hour zhen?"

Tipping her head in agreement, Samira confirmed the time, still wary of her underlying intention. Her mind played out the possibilities as she gathered her purse from her office. *I feel like I have something to prove. If Phil doesn't need me, then I should be open to new offers.* She located Jim in the back and informed him of her departure.

Samira crossed the parking lot with random thoughts boggling her mind. *But at the same time, I just walked away this afternoon. Isn't it a little too soon to be going out with someone else?* The sun was just dropping over the horizon as Samira pulled into her driveway. *And Fabiano is leaving town in a week. He's not someone I could ever form a long-term relationship with anyway.*

Samira raised a hand to the invisible Mrs. Barnes. Without looking she knew the old woman was somewhere within viewing distance on the other side of the street. *Maybe the fact that Fabiano is leaving town makes him even more appealing.* That thought caught Samira totally unaware. *If he's leaving, then whatever happens with him tonight leaves with him in a week.*

Samira put her hand to her forehead before opening the door into the kitchen. *I just need the voices to stop before I talk to Krissy and Kara.*

It's a good thing the girls are home tonight. Dim lights flickered in the basement stairway indicating they were probably watching a movie. *I need them for accountability.* She knew her defenses were being challenged by Fabiano's presence. *And he is quite handsome in an artistic kind of way.* She pushed Phil's face out of her mind. *Mix Fabiano's looks with his talent and his passion, and I might have a hard time resisting another invitation.*

Samira stopped in her tracks. *This time you have gone too far.* She buried her face in her hands and took a long, deep breath. *No. Absolutely not.* She sat down at the breakfast bar.

You, Samira Cartwright, could have about any man you wanted if you allowed yourself the freedom. Her eyes went to her daughter's school pictures on the bookshelf across the room. *But that's not who you want to become.*

Samira kicked her shoes off and listened as they made a hollow thud against the hard floor. *Dinner at Andre's would be romantic simply due to the atmosphere. But dinner is the only option. Nothing more.* Her thoughts tripped back to Fabiano's comment about the finishing glaze on the figurine. *Bronze is a better choice than marble.*

~~~~~~~

Sunday morning arrived much sooner than Samira hoped. She rolled over and checked
~~~~~~~

the time on the alarm clock. It was after seven. She closed her eyes and put the back of her hand over her forehead. She was in her own bed, wearing her own nightshirt, and she was alone. *Completely alone. Just as I will be for the rest of my life.*

Samira wished she could stay in bed for the rest of the day. There was no motivation to get up. No underlying hope for a future with a whole family again. *Nothing left to make me think I could ever be whole again either.* She pulled the covers up over her shoulder as she turned over on her side and dozed off to sleep again.

"Yoo-hoo. Good morning, Mama." Krissy pounced on the end of her mother's bed then crawled up to the empty pillow. "Time to wake up sleepy head. Granny is expecting us at her church this morning, remember?"

Samira moaned at the recollection. *I'd rather just stay here.*

"Did you stay out all night?" Krissy had her head perched on a bent elbow.

"I came in about midnight." *Much later than I'd planned.*

"Did you have a good time?"

"It was okay," Samira yawned. She rolled over to face the freckled face of her youngest daughter. *It was actually very awkward.*

"Was it like a real date?" Krissy wasn't looking at her mother as she asked the questions. "Like, I mean, did he take you to dinner and pay for your meal and then walk you to your car and kiss you goodnight?"

The mother thought for a moment before answering. "Yes, he paid for my dinner and walked me to my car and he," *Yes, he kissed me, but it didn't feel right. It was all wrong.* "—kissed my hand." Samira felt terrible lying to her daughter. *But it just didn't feel right.*

The initial shock in Krissy's eyes blinked in guarded unbelief. "So, he didn't really kiss you then, right?"

Samira frowned. "I would call that a gentleman's kiss." *He wanted it to be real. But it wasn't.*

"Not like the real thing though?" Krissy popped up off the bed. "That's a relief." She turned toward the bedroom door. "It's almost eight. You're going to be the one hurrying for a change."

Is she really relieved? Samira buried her head in her pillow. *She has her hopes set on Phil.* She tried to forget. *I did too for a while.*

~~~~~~~

Samira sat next to her father during church like she'd done a million times before. Throughout the service her mind played games with her heart. While the minister delivered the morning message, Samira pondered the events of the previous evening.

He would have kissed me again had I given him permission. But even now she could feel his narrow lips on hers. *It just wasn't right.* There was no doubt in her mind that she left him disappointed in the parking lot. *Dinner was fabulous—bon appetite without the mass of an American meal. The wine was a treat. His stories were enchanting. His attentiveness was flattering.*

Samira stood with the rest of the congregation at the announcement of the last hymn. *But there was something missing.* She opened the hymnal in her hands and began to sing the familiar words. *I wasn't drawn into his presence like I am—or was,* Samira instantly corrected that thought, *with...* It was hard to even think his name. A few stanzas later her father reached over and turned the page to the correct song. *...with Phil.*

The sanctuary was almost empty when Samira's mother remembered her flower vase downstairs.

"I'll go get it and meet you outside."

Samira watched her mother exit through the glass doors into the narthex. As she walked along the aisle, she ran her hand over the aged, oak pews. The wood was smooth
~~~~~~~

with regular wear. As Samira neared the back, she noticed a light in the chapel.

No one was in the room. Samira reached for the light switch that was higher on the wall than usual. *Daddy used to have to pick me up so I could reach this switch.* As the light clicked off, sunlight poured through a stained-glass window casting a kaleidoscope pattern onto the neutral carpet. *That's beautiful.* Samira moved toward the center of the room. Her eyes followed the ray of light back to the window. Cut glass revealed figures of men and women joined in a circle, their faces gazing upwards toward a radiant ray of sunlight. Beyond the yellow streaks of glass was the figure of a descending dove. The glass seemed to shimmer in the sunlight as Samira studied the dove.

What I wouldn't do for that peace dove to touch me right now. I spent the better part of the past six years telling myself I could make it on my own, believing that I wasn't meant to be with a man. The light changed slightly illuminating the golden rays of light again. *But I was wrong. I was wrong to believe that. It was wrong to let myself want to be alone.*

The light changed again and the people holding hands in the glass seemed to dance in a syncopated pattern. *I isolated myself from the world around me—from the world I used to know. I thought if I just stayed home, I wouldn't be able to meet anybody.* Samira justified her actions. *But there's a huge difference between meeting just anyone and meeting the one you know loves you better than all the rest.* Samira felt her spirit tremble somewhere deep within her soul. *How can I expect to be content now that I've known that kind of love again?*

A slight movement in the room caused Samira to catch her thoughts. The window instantly lost the animation. Staring at the now two-dimensional glass, Samira felt a presence move closer to her.

"It's a beautiful piece." The voice spoke from behind.

Pastor Bill. Samira turned around slowly. His once dark hair was all white, yet he still held the merriment in his eyes that had once reminded Samira of Santa Claus.

"I've seen it come to life more than once, but it always seems to fade back into the single pane eventually."

Samira looked back to the window. The light had changed drastically, and the window no longer appeared to have any resilience at all. *I see what he means.*

"Did you see the dove in the stained glass?" The pastor walked slowly into the room. "You can only see it when the light is just perfect." He squinted his thoughtful eyes toward the top corner. "But it's not there now."

Samira looked too, expecting to see it descending right where it had been a few moments before. *Where did it go?*

"I've come to understand the movement of the dove to be a message of peace because I've only been able to see it when my soul was deeply troubled." The pastor turned and faced Samira directly. "And I sense maybe this is a good day for the dove to appear for you, Samira."

Samira questioned his observation with her eyes.

"I was watching you this morning." The wise, aging man looked deep into her eyes. "I've known you since you were born, and I know from the pain in your eyes that you are working through something very difficult." The pastor raised his hand and gently placed it on Samira's shoulder. "Let's give it to the Lord in prayer."

Samira obediently bowed her head as her lifelong pastor prayed openly and without contempt for her to find the peace her soul was seeking. Moved by the depth of his perception, Samira remained still for several moments following his amen.

"I've known that peace before," she finally admitted. "But it seems like it's been a long, long time."

The pastor folded his hands against his suit coat buttons. "It's not as far away as you might think," he assured gently. "Look inside yourself, Samira, it is there, waiting for you to recognize it." The pastor paused. "Just like the dove in the window, Love is still within even though you can't see it."

Samira shook her head. "It wasn't enough."

"Maybe you've overlooked its purpose."

"I chose to put it there and I can choose to take it out." Samira retaliated.

"You can't choose love. Love chooses you."

"It must have made a wrong choice then because it isn't going to happen." Samira could feel a tinge of bitterness in her words.

The pastor looked back toward the window causing Samira's eyes to follow. The sunlight outside had moved again and the menagerie of colors in the cut glass were bright with intensity.

"Love doesn't make a wrong choice, Samira."

It did this time.

"Once the love is in your heart, you don't have a right to take it out." The pastor crossed his wrists behind his back. "You can deny it, but you can't remove it."

What am I supposed to do with it if I can't remove it? The chapel was completely silent. *Even the people in Fabiano's statues have love in their eyes.*

"And since you can't make it go away, you might as well accept it. Ironically enough, once you fully acknowledge it's there, you will understand its purpose." With that the pastor tipped his head in Samira's direction. "It's a chance you have to take." His eyes twinkled in a silent revelation and then he made an exit through a single door along the far wall of the chapel.

I have always wondered where that door leads. Samira's eyes went back to the window again. The transparent dove flickered into motion and then faded back into the stained glass as quickly as it had appeared.

I can deny it, but I can't make it go away. Samira thought for another moment. *Does he mean I have to accept the love I have for Phil even if I don't understand its purpose?* She turned away from the window and started for the door back into the main part of the church. *I know it's there because I feel it, and it hurts.* Her hand went to heart.

Another understanding slowly came into focus. *Or maybe I'm supposed to keep loving Phil even if he doesn't have the capacity to reciprocate.*

Samira heard her mother call her name.

"Coming." Samira took one more look at the window. The white dove flitted into motion again, then faded instantly. *Fabiano may have captured my wounded spirit in bronze, but I feel more like that stained glass, disjointed and one dimensional.* When the light changed, the glass came to life momentarily once again. *One moment I am a free spirit, letting Love tease me with foreplay and anticipation, and then the circumstances change, and I fade back into my safe, secure, lonely little world.*

"Samira?" Ashleigh stepped into the chapel bewildered. "Are you coming dear?" Her eyes went beyond her daughter to the mystical glass. "It's a beautiful piece, isn't it? Stained glass is dependent on light. Without it the glass is a flat canvas. But once the sun shines through it takes on a life of its own." Ashleigh's eyes came back to her daughter.

Even Mother notices how the light makes the window work. Samira followed Ashleigh all the way to the parking lot. *But I feel like I'm the one who's stained this morning.* She covered her eyes with her sunglasses. *I'm afraid there won't be enough Light to bring me back to life.*

46 Decisions

Joseph Phillip

J.P. tucked his tie between two shirt buttons as he leaned over the chair. Sparky was monitoring online transactions at Mid-America.

"Dis is the vire I am vaiting for." The detective pointed his finger to a series of numbers moving along the top of the computer screen. "I predict dis transaction vill move from the holding company in Balteemor to Mid-America vithin a few minutes."

J.P. had no idea how Sparky had traced the transaction. *Nor do I have an inkling how it might relate back to the online tampering that took place at the beginning of the summer.* All J.P. knew was that it was high time to be discovering concrete evidence.

Sparky lunged forward. His eyes were fixed directly on the computer screen, but his hand was scribbling out a line of numbers as they crossed the screen.

He is an amazing little man.

"Vatch dis." Sparky keyed a command that opened another window. He leaned back in the steno chair and crossed his arms.

What am I watching? J.P. stared at the screen. *What are these numbers?* Clearance was granted from another computer in the building, and then suddenly a sizable dollar amount appeared followed by an account number. *Whatever they are, the box says the transaction completed.*

Sparky jotted down the information and keyed in another code. "Ah-ha. Just as I tought." He put the end of his stubby pencil to his lips. "Look at dis, J.P."

I'm looking.

"Look closer," Sparky encouraged. "See dis? Ve just vatched dis deposit come in over the wires from Balteemor." The detective tapped the pencil against the glass of the oversized screen. "But see? Today is not June fifth."

J.P. looked again. *Sure enough. It says June 5th.* "Are you sure it's the same transaction?"

"Positive." Sparky reached for the phone and dialed an extension. J.P. listened as he talked with a computer technician working on the mainframe. "He vill be right over."

When the technician arrived with the report, the student intern was close on his heels.

What the hell is she doing here? J.P. shook his head. *That's the same student Stephenson allowed on board without security clearance earlier this summer.*

Sparky eyed the young woman and extended his hand. "I don't believe ve've met."

Sparky knows exactly who she is.

"Celia Monroe." She returned the handshake.

"And what brings you to my computer room?"

He means surveillance unit.

"What do you mean?"

This could be interesting.

"You tapped into my line."

Ms Monroe shifted her weight from one foot to the other. "I don't know what you're talking about."

"Ah, I beleev you do, Ms. Monroe." Sparky turned the page on the report and waited.

J.P. noticed that the color beginning to drain from the woman's face.

"I...I wasn't even working on a computer."

Sparky raised his thick eyebrows and addressed the technician. "Vas Ms. Monroe vorking vith you den?"

The technician seemed surprised to suddenly be involved in the conversation. "Uh, No, sir. Miss Monroe works in accounting. She followed me here after I picked up this report from the printer."

"Did you suspend the system like I requested?"

The technician affirmed the action.

"Den ve vill see in a moment who vas logged onto the system during de last few minutes." Sparky continued to skim the report in his hands. The only sound in the room besides the hum of active computers was the ticking of the wall clock above the door.

This is good. J.P. leaned against a computer workstation and waited. *I'd say Sparky has a tiger by the tail.* A long minute passed before another employee stuck her head in the door.

"I have the report you ordered, Sir."

"Tank you very much." Sparky walked across the room and took the stack of papers from her hands. "Dis report vill tell me vhat I need to know." He began to skim and then looked up at the spectators in the room. "Oh, I am zo zorry. Do you vait on me? You may go now."

The computer technician excused himself quickly. But Miss Monroe hesitated. Her eyes were wandering back and forth from Sparky to the stack of papers he'd left on the computer desk.

"If you vant to read dem, go ahead," Sparky spoke without looking up. "You von't find vhat you are looking for."

Miss Monroe suddenly turned toward the door.

"Vhat time are you leaving today Ms. Monroe?" Sparky asked the question cautiously.

"I have been leaving at three o'clock, why?"

"No reason."

J.P. closed the door behind her.

"Dis is Sparky."

J.P. turned to see the little investigator talking into the telephone again.

"Yes, der is zometing. Keep an eye on Ms. Celia Monroe. Tell me de moment she leaves de building."

J.P. checked the clock above the door. *One thirty.* Curiosity was about to get the best of him. *I'd love to know what Sparky suspects.*

"Ah, yes, J.P. Patience. In due time I vill tell you."

J.P. smiled. *Funny he reads my thoughts.*

"In de meantime, you can tell Mr. Stephenson zhat de missing monies are back where zhey belong." The investigator put his hand up in a firm stop. "But. De must remain untouched and unmanipulated until I give de signal. Understood?"

J.P. was shocked. "All of the monies are recovered?"

"Every penny."

"Are you sure?"

"Yes. I am sure." Sparky's eyes were reading the report in his hands. "And I am sure Miss Monroe is de one hired to validate de transaction." He turned a page and smiled at the security camera in the corner above their heads. "Ve vill see."

"Hired by who?"

"Ah. Patience." Sparky worked his bushy black eyebrows. "Ve must be patient."

The telephone on the desk rang once and Sparky answered.

But I am not a very patient man, Sparky.

"Just as I tought." The investigator hung up the telephone and gathered both reports into one pile. "I must go. Ms. Monroe is leaving de building and I need to know where she is going." The investigator smiled with his lips closed and raised his bushy eyebrows. "I vill leave you to Mr. Stephenson."

Sparky made a quiet exit through a security entrance, but J.P. took the stairs two flights up and knocked against the open door to the president's office.

Mr. Stephenson looked up and motioned for the attorney to enter. "Any luck, J.P.? Sparky seemed confident something important was going to happen today."

J.P. took a seat in the leather chair across from Mr. Stephenson. "And Sparky is rarely wrong."

Mr. Stephenson leaned forward on his desk and crossed his arms.

What is it about his eyes that seem so familiar? "The missing monies have been returned to their original accounts, Mr. Stephenson. They came in from a holding company in Baltimore about a half an hour ago. Sparky has a wiretap on the accounts and has asked that they not be manipulated in any way until he gives the okay. He has already notified mainframe security so they're aware of the situation."

"Are you telling me the money came back?"

"That's what it looks like."

"That's incredible."

"Indeed." *Laundered, no doubt, but back just the same.*

"So, what's next? Does he know where the money has been or how it came back?"

J.P. patted his hands against the arms of the big chair. "I don't know exactly what Sparky knows, but professional instinct tells me he knows enough that your case against the hackers in Baltimore may be bigger than we originally imagined."

Mr. Stephenson stood up and walked over to the window overlooking downtown. "Amazing. It blows my mind that the money can disappear and reappear in these accounts without anyone here being aware of the transactions. And it is even more puzzling that a remote computer somewhere in the world can enter into my systems and deploy data without anyone in this building granting access."

It will be interesting to see where Ms. Monroe is going. "We need to stay out of the way and let Sparky finish the investigation."

"How long are you thinking, J.P." Mr. Stephenson poured himself a cup of coffee and started back toward his own desk. "May I get you anything?" J.P. watched the president open a flask and pour a shot of something into the coffee.

That's interesting. I wonder what he's drinking. "No thank you." Mr. Stephenson sat back down at his desk. "I don't have a time frame from Sparky yet. Obviously, we don't have much control of the situation currently. Patience is the best we have to offer." *I can't believe I'm the one advising patience.*

Mr. Stephenson nodded. "Well, it's easier to be patient knowing the funds are back where they belong. Should I notify the investors?"

"Not yet." J.P. advised. "We need to let everything settle so Sparky can validate the trace, which should eventually help lead us to the mastermind behind the crime."

Mr. Stephenson put his hand to his face. "It's very slow going, isn't it?"

"That it is, Mr. Stephenson. That it is." *No one is more tired of waiting than me.*

"I appreciate you sitting in on yesterday's board meeting, J.P." Mr. Stephenson held his coffee cup out in an informal toast. "I know you had other things you could have been doing." He took a sip. "So, tell me. What are your thoughts? The property is prime development land, but Mid-America is never going to use it. We have plenty of room for growth right here where we are and, to be honest, I like being in the heart of downtown. Even if we were to put up a branch, we wouldn't need nearly that much land." Mr. Stephenson was interrupted by a buzz on his phone. He held out a finger to excuse himself for a moment and pressed a button.

"Your wife on line 3, sir."

"If you'll excuse me, I need to take this call," Mr. Stephenson rose from his chair and crossed the room to another telephone.

J.P. watched Mr. Stephenson greet his wife and check his watch simultaneously. The attorney's eyes landed on a large, framed photo of Mr. Stephenson and his wife. *She's pretty enough but she looks young compared to him.* J.P. had noticed the photo before but never paid much attention. But today he studied it more closely. *She looks vaguely familiar, but I haven't the slightest idea where I'd have seen her.*

"...I might actually be out of here in a decent time today...I'll come home first then we can go over together..."

I wonder what it's like to have to stop working to take a call from a wife. For a moment, his mind pictured Samira's gentle smile. *But it's not likely you'll ever have the chance to find that out.* J.P. caught his mental slip. *Nope. Not going back there.* He walked over to the full-length window and peered down upon the activity of the business district. His eyes followed the sidewalk to the law offices of Benson and Barringer. He thought about Mike's partnership with Vincent Barringer.

Early on, J.P. had advised against Mike's decision to join a law firm fearing it might limit opportunities. *But twelve years later Mike's doing very well for himself. And he's able to enjoy some freedom too.* J.P. sighed and dropped his hands into his front pockets. *That's another chance that has no doubt passed me by.*

"I apologize for the interruption, J.P." Mr. Stephenson joined him at the window. "At any rate, how would you advise the board concerning that piece of land?"

J.P. faced the executive. At one time J.P. would have been eager to share his opinion but today he didn't feel the usual surge of energy that came with that opportunity. "I say if you're not going to use it for expansion, then you have two options. You either develop it for industrial or commercial lease, or you sell it." *Plain and simple.*

Mr. Stephenson nodded his head slowly. "I agree. But of the two options, what is your advice?"

Hughes will be more than interested, especially since they lost the final bid on the airport property. The attorney's mind continued to strategize. *I also know how slow Mid-America's board of directors move with big decisions. It would take them months, if not years, to develop the land into anything profitable for their own benefit or the benefit of the city.*

J.P. nodded his head. "I'd sell."

Mr. Stephenson chewed on his bottom lip and squinted his eyes in thought. "Would you list it through an agency?"

J.P. shook his head. "Not with that particular tract. If you're interested enough to sell, I might be able to drum up some interest." *Two phone calls. One to Denise. The second to Jeffrey Hughes.*

There was more thoughtful silence between the two professionals. Finally, Mr. Stephenson spoke again. "How long do you think it would take to find a buyer?"

The attorney smiled to himself. *A lot less time than it's taking to track down a computer hacker.* "I'd say within a week." *By morning.*

"Really?" Mr. Stephenson sounded surprised. He returned to his desk for his coffee cup. "I'm impressed."

Wait until he knows who is interested. Then he can be impressed.

"Tell you what," the president stood next to his chair. "Why don't you go to work on a buyer, and I'll go to work on the board and together let's see if we can't at least advance one item of business toward closure."

J.P. could hear the hopefulness in Mr. Stephenson's voice. *He's bored with the lack of progress on the hacker's case too. We all are.*

"Sounds like a good plan."

Mr. Stephenson stuck out his hand. "Then it's a go. I'll call a board meeting for first thing Monday morning."

"And I'll see what interest I can stir up before I go home tonight." J.P. returned the firm handshake.

"Can I offer you a word of advice, J.P.?"

Do I look like I need advice?

"No need to spend all night working on this. You've put in plenty of hours for Mid-America these past weeks. Take some time for yourself."

Is there something else I should be doing?

"Seriously." Mr. Stephenson's face was solemn. "Go home. Take a load off for a night."

Maybe my attitude is beginning to show. Lately he'd been fed up with the lack of forward motion in the hacker's case. And now Sparky was off on a new wild goose chase that only made limited sense. *Not to mention the fact that my personal life took a hit this week too.*

"Maybe I will." *More likely, I'll go back to the office and work late into the evening. With James only around every other weekend now, there's little motivation to go home early.*

~~~~~~~

J.P. found Denise on the telephone when he walked into his office. She pushed a button on the base and smiled brightly at her boss.

"Lucky me," she quipped. "Or maybe I should say, lucky you."

J.P. stopped in front of her desk. *Probably neither.*

"You missed the initial onslaught of information from Sparky, but you're here in time to make a decision on this call."

"When did you talk to Sparky?"

"Just now. He's on his way back to Mid-America with new information on this Celia chic. And for your information, he's taking a cop back to the computer lab with him."

Now I'm interested.

"But more on that in a second." Denise tipped her head. "Jessica Hutchison is on line two. She has a dinner invitation for you at Bridges' Condominiums for later this evening."

"What's her motive?" *Those are the same condos Mike's friend moved out of a couple of months ago.*

"She says she has information from her broker that might interest you."

J.P. started to walk away. "Six months ago, I might have been interested."

"Then that's a no?"

"Yeah." *It might be worth checking out.* He went back to Denise's desk. "I don't know. What time?"

"Like that would matter?"

It might. "Find out."

Denise picked up the phone and inquired as to the nature and time of the engagement. Once again, she asked the party to hold. "Eight o'clock. She says you can expect to meet other real estate gurus as well."

"Are those her words or yours?"

"Mine," Denise smiled. "Are you in or not?"

"Get an address."

"I'll take that as an affirmative."

J.P. removed his suit jacket and hung it over the back of a conference chair in his own office.

"I don't think your little librarian would appreciate you having dinner with this Hutchison woman." Denise was carrying a yellow sticky note when she entered J.P.'s office.

And maybe that's none of your business.

"She sounds a bit too flirtatious to be serious about a business setup."

"Maybe that's just her nature."
~~~~~~~

"And maybe it's her nature to undermine any future you might have in a halfway decent relationship."

"What the hell is that supposed to mean?" J.P. felt new tension in his shoulders. He unbuttoned a shirtsleeve and started to roll his cuff.

Denise stuck the note on the edge of his desk. "That means you might want to practice saying 'no' all the way over there and avoid any alcohol she might offer."

J.P. was irritated at Denise's sudden concern over his personal discernment. He read the address on the note. *That's new condominiums on the edge of town.*

"Seriously, Boss," Denise continued. "I don't know if you should take a chance with her."

"Since when have you been so concerned about my personal life?"

"Since you had someone you might want to keep."

Had would be the magic word here. "Like you know a hell of a lot about keeping someone."

Denise's face fell, and she set her jaw. "For your information, Phillip Ralston, I have kept a relationship for the better part of thirteen years. Just because I don't have a ring on my finger doesn't mean I don't know how to hang on to what I have."

She's right. J.P. felt a sting deep inside. *She's been with Jerry far longer than I've ever been with any given woman.*

Denise turned abruptly to leave the room.

"I'm sorry." J.P. found himself apologizing, which felt terribly out of character. "I shouldn't have said that."

Denise stopped in her tracks. "You're right, you shouldn't have." She turned around briefly. "I think, if you're finished with me for the day, I'll go on home."

Maybe I should take the night off and go home too. J.P. sat down in his chair and put his head in his hands.

"I'll see you Monday." Denise closed the door between the offices much harder than necessary.

J.P. shifted the files on his desk from one side to the other. *Hughes, Mid-America, Sparky. Shit. Denise didn't fill me in on Sparky's update.* He thumbed through another stack of folders. *Derek's casework for review.*

There was a lot to be done. He could work all night and still not be finished. *But I'm certainly finished with one thing. Samira.* J.P. leaned back in his chair. *And maybe with Denise if I don't watch it.* The attorney loosened his tie. Chances of getting Jeffrey Hughes on the line now were very slim. *I should have talked to him before business closed today.*

A bell rang announcing someone's arrival through the front door. *Or Denise's departure.* Either way J.P. had to check. He opened the door to an empty office. The computer was shut down and the coffee maker was off for the weekend. Denise's desk was cleared in a very permanent kind of way. *Even Derek's desk is less scattered than usual.* J.P. sat down on a winged chair in the waiting area and put his feet on the chair across from him.

James isn't even at the house waiting for me to get home. Football practice had started in Harrisonburg. *I won't see either one of the boys before Labor Day weekend now.*

Several minutes passed. And then a full hour went by. There was nothing motivating J.P. to go home. *And there's not much motivating me to go back to work either.* When he finally did go back to his desk the pile of folders turned his stomach.

You need to eat, Ralston. But eating alone at the club again wasn't appealing and fixing something at home had even less pull. J.P. opened a desk drawer and began to file the folders in the proper places for the night.

The attorney considered the offer from Jessica Hutchison. *But then again, if Denise is right, you could end up in a compromising position.* He unrolled his cuffs and fastened the buttons. *On the other hand, what are you compromising? Everything you hoped for walked away at Shoal Creek.*

I should heed her advice and stay away from Bridges Condos. He selected a sports coat from the armoire next to the bathroom door. *There might be some action at the club tonight.* He started for the door then turned back and snagged the yellow sticky note from the edge of his desk. *Just in case.*

The Golf Club was loud and crowded when he arrived. He greeted several clients as he made his way to the bar. *I'll order dinner.* Without asking, the bartender put a JD and Coke in front of J.P. He put it to his lips as he turned around to face the room.

"You ordering dinner tonight, J.P.?" A familiar waitress stopped to take his order.

Carrie Powers. He took another drink. "I don't know yet. Give me a few minutes."

She disappeared into the crowd.

Every table J.P.'s eyes fell on had two people dining together. *Is that normal? Or am I just wishing Samira were here?* Another couple passed by.

"J.P." The man stuck out his hand. "Haven't seen you in a long while. Are you golfing in the mayor's tournament Labor Day weekend?"

Adam Bishop. I helped him secure the real estate for his printing business. J.P. returned the handshake. "How's business, Adam?" *No, I'm not giving up Labor Day weekend to golf with the mayor.*

J.P. half listened as the businessman gave him a quick run-down of his current accounts. *The businessman I need to be talking to tonight is Jeffrey Hughes.* Before he stepped away, he put his hand around the woman who'd been standing next to him. "This is my fiancé, Madeline."

"J.P. Ralston." He nodded a greeting at the woman, who smiled in return. *Even Adam Bishop has a date tonight.* Suddenly the thought of staying at the club to eat was not inviting at all. He waved at the bartender to bring his tab.

"Must have big plans tonight if you're stopping with one already, J.P." Carrie put her hands on her hips.

J.P. motioned for her to hand him his ticket.

Carrie rang him out at the register and returned with a single piece of paper. The attorney signed on the line. "It is Friday night, after all."

The waitress grinned. "You've never been one to waste a good Friday night."

There was a time I waited for her Friday shift to finish so we could have our own activities. But that was a long time ago. He left the ticket on the counter and put the pen back in his shirt pocket. He wished he were headed to Samira's for dinner around her table with Krissy and Kara. *But dinner wouldn't be enough.* J.P. felt his world fading into black and white again. *If I don't have to fight to win her over, then what am I supposed to do?* He crossed the parking lot and unlocked the door to his truck. *Give it up, Counselor. That chance has passed you by.*

The yellow sticky note stared back at J.P. when he climbed into the truck. *What the hell. I'll drive over and check out the party and then go home. If I can score dinner and a base figure for Mid-America's property in the same sitting, then I'm one up on the never-ending to-do list on my desk.*

The decision was made. *Let's see what's on Jessica Hutchison's agenda.*

47 The Cry of the Heart

Samira

The atrium at city hall was a buzz of activity as the final preparations were being made for the fundraiser auction. *Promote literacy.* Samira straightened the sign. *A few more hours and this event is a done deal.*

The library board sponsored this auction at the end of every summer. Throughout the year, local artists and artists in residence donated their work. Samira surveyed the artwork. *Good quality and an excellent selection.*

"Everything looks great, Sis." Wes nodded his approval. "Is that statue on the pedestal supposed to be you?"

Samira glanced at Fabiano's work, now covered with a bronze finish. "You have to ask?"

"No, it looks like you." Wes chewed on his bottom lip a moment. "Did you pose for him like that?"

"What do you mean like *that?" Just say it, Wes.*

"Well," Wes raised his eyebrows. "Without anything on."

Samira avoided eye contact. "No." *I suppose everyone is going to think that.* "I posed in that position with my clothes on. Fabiano imagined the rest."

Wes shook his shoulders uncomfortably. "What did the folks think?"

"They didn't comment one way or another." *It's just art, and he never saw me naked.* At first it had seemed like a great idea. *But I agreed under the influence of some powerful wine.*

"The auctioneer is ready," Daphne informed her supervisor.

"I'll be right over."

"I'll let you get back to work," Wes offered.

"Are you staying?"

Wes's eyes traveled toward the front doors of the building. "Yeah, I'm staying. Pam will be here in a few minutes with the kids. We'll keep Kara and Krissy with us until it's over."

At least I won't have to worry about where my girls are the whole time.

The atrium was beginning to fill with people holding black and white bidding numbers attached to a long stick. *This is a much larger crowd than I remember from a year ago.* Some had taken seats in the rows of chairs while others stood. An air of anticipation permeated the room and conversations reverberated in the exhibit hall.

Jim appeared at Samira's side. "Everything is ready, Miss Samira. Can I get you anything? A cup of coffee maybe?"

Samira's anxiety level was higher than usual. *It must be my adrenalin.* "How about a cappuccino, Jim?"

"A cappuccino it is." He turned toward the coffee vendor along the back wall.

Samira checked her watch and gave a nod to the board president. *I'm glad she's the mistress of ceremonies.* It was time for the auction to begin. *That's one job I would not want.* Introductions were made and credit was given to the appropriate parties. When Samira's name was mentioned, the head librarian felt her face turn completely red. *I wouldn't mind if they'd just leave my name out of the program.* She covered her cheek with her hand.

"For you, Miss Samira." Jim returned with a Styrofoam cup steaming with rich cappuccino. "Great crowd tonight."

The Café Ole. The logo on the cup caught Samira off guard.

"Is everything alright?" Jim looked concerned.

"Oh, yes, fine, thank you." She turned the cup in her hand. *Where in the world did he get this?* "It takes a huge team effort—"

"With a diligent leader." Jim tipped his cap to the librarian. "I'll be in the back if you need me."

I couldn't do this event without him. Samira listened to a detailed description of the first item. *Here we go.* The auctioneer cried out the first call. *I didn't realize the Café Ole won the bid to set up here tonight.* Samira took a sip.

Across the way Samira could see her parents standing with Wes and Pam. *Krissy and Kara probably aren't too far away.* As usual, Pam had the little girls dressed to the hilt. *If there is one thing Pam loves, it's social outings.* That thought led Samira to another one. *Pam would have loved the high society party in Springfield.* She forced her mind back to the auction.

Time passed as the auctioneer cried on. Charcoal drawings, paintings, pottery, weaving—every kind of medium was for sale. A spotlight illuminated a table lamp accentuated
with a leaded glass shade. Samira listened and watched as inconspicuous bidders pushed the dollar amount past a thousand dollars.

"Excuse me, ma'am?"

Samira turned and faced Mike Benson.

"I understand this is your gig."

"Hello, Mr. Benson." *My gig? Mike has such a way with words.*

"Hello, Samira." Mike stood tall. "What exactly are we raising money for today?" The tall attorney whispered over the auctioneer as his eyes studied the crowd.

"Sold."

Samira's eyes landed across the way on her brother. He tucked his bidding number under his arm. *Surely, he didn't pay that much for the lamp.* She remembered the question. "We're raising support for the literacy program to aide underprivileged children."

"Impressive," Mike nodded slowly. His eyes moved from the crowd back to Samira. "You bring in a wide array of Joplin society."

I'm not the one who brings them in. Samira looked away. "It's the quality of the artwork that brings the crowd."

"But every show needs a professional at the top."

And Mike Benson is a professional flatterer. Samira tucked a loose strand of hair behind her ear. *I'm not in the mood for chit chat.* "What brings you to the art auction, Mr. Benson?"

Mike grinned. "Nothing. I've been in court and stopped here to pick up some paperwork. Seems I happened upon this grand gala by accident."

"You should look around, maybe there's something here for your office." Samira half listened as the next item for sale was described in detail through the speaker overhead.

"I thought about that." Mike squinted his eyes. "There's only one piece here that interests me."

Samira felt the lead. *But I am not going to give him the satisfaction of taking the bait.*

Mike crossed his arms over his designer suit. "Right there in the middle. Can you see it?" He nodded his head carefully. "That bronzed statue caught my eye."

I'm sure it's just a coincidence. Samira caught her breath. *There's no way he could know it's a replica of me.*

"There's rumor that the artist in residence just finished that piece." Mike's eyes were alive with energy.

"Last week." *Saturday evening.*

"He's good. I like his other pieces too, but that one is different."

It's bronzed, unlike the others. Samira shifted her weight uncomfortably. She really didn't want to talk about it. *Not with Mike Benson.*

"It's almost as if, I don't know..." Mike's voice trailed off in thought. "Like Uberti captured a broken heart."

Surprised first that Mike used Fabiano's last name and secondly that he read right into her. Samira put her hand to her face. She tried to remember if she'd talked to Kelly Davis about modeling for Fabiano. *I didn't, but that doesn't mean Krissy didn't. I wonder how long Mike was in the atrium before making his presence known to me?*

"At any rate, it's a beautiful work of art," Mike summarized. His quiet tone shifted gears. "So how are you, Samira?"

Totally taken aback by his candor, Samira closed her eyes.

"I was sorry to hear...well...that things went the way they did."

So how long has it been since Mike talked to Phil anyway? It's only been a few weeks.

"You look good."

I always do. I have to. Samira straightened her back. *It's my job to put up a front and look good, at least on the outside. Everyone expects me to be strong and happy.* "Thank you," Samira whispered as the auctioneer announced the sale of an oil canvas.

"Our mutual friend would be jealous of this little meeting."

Probably not anymore. "That's funny," Samira decided to play the game. "I've never known Kelly to be the jealous type."

Mike pointed his finger at Samira. His face was more serious than she'd expected. "Me neither," he agreed with a long gaze into her eyes. "I was thinking of the other mutual friend."

"How is he?" *I can't even say his name.*

Mike hesitated.

He doesn't know what to say either.

"Overworked and taking life way too seriously." Mike wiggled his eyebrows playfully. Then his face got serious again. "He's taking the boys to meet Bobby at the ranch over Labor Day weekend. A little R and R won't hurt him."

Samira had to look away. *Why would Mike bring Bobbie into this conversation?*

"He'd probably rather be in different company given the opportunity."

Does he always need company? Samira crossed her arms against her now knotted stomach. "Then it's good he can get away from work for a few days." *Maybe he should stay away.*

Mike puckered his bushy moustache. His eyes were fixed on Samira.

I am not going to give him the satisfaction of eye contact.

"I guess if I'm going to be a serious bidder I need to register."

Samira could feel some tension building. "The registrar is at that booth by the coffee vendor." *But I doubt he'll follow through with a purchase.*

"Thanks," Mike nodded but he didn't move. "It's good to see you, Samira."

She didn't respond because she couldn't swallow the lump that had formed in her throat.

"Take care of yourself." Mike turned to go but stopped and faced her again. "If there's anything I can do, don't hesitate." Mike took one last glance at Samira then made his departure.

The next item went up for bid. A set of colorful, oversized ceramic pots drew hushed exclamations from the crowd. *How am I supposed to take care of myself when every thought trips back to the man who is now taking Bobbie to the ranch?* Samira looked back over her shoulder, but Mike was gone. Across the way she could see his tall frame weaving in and out of the bidders. *Good he's leaving.*

A sudden sadness came over the librarian. *It took me all week to muster up a positive front.* But deep down her heart was still empty. Samira worked her way to the opposite side of the atrium. All the chairs were taken, and a large swarm of onlookers lined the back of the bidding area. *How is it I always end up feeling so alone in a crowd?* She stood in the middle of the most populated area.

A large spray of dried flowers sold for a hundred-dollar bill. A black and white photo of a park bench at City Park brought fifty. An origami mobile auctioned for seventy -five.

"Things are selling so high." Susan Olinger pushed her way through to Samira's side between items. "I can't believe someone would actually pay seventy-five dollars for a little mobile like that." The woman's blonde hair bobbed against her shoulders. "But it's all for a good cause I guess." Susan applauded with the crowd when another small item sold.

Susan is always so critical, but I know she's here to support me.

"Samira," Susan whispered. She wiggled her finger for Samira to bend down to listen. Samira bent her neck slightly. "When I came in, I saw Sam's golf partner here. The one who took you home that one time."

Samira straightened back up. *I know.* She didn't need Susan's meddling today. *Especially with Mike Benson.*

"He was over there." Susan pointed across the room. Samira grabbed Susan's arm to keep her from placing an illegal bid. A man standing next to them showed signs of annoyance. *It is always hard to keep Susan under control.*

"Here," Susan reached up and patted the bun at the back of Samira's hair. "You should freshen up a bit in case he sees you." The next thing Samira knew Susan was handing her a tube of lipstick and a mirror. *Susan. Stop it.*

"Just wait here," Susan instructed. "I'll see if I can find him."

He's long gone by now. But she can knock herself out looking.

The auctioneer was nearing the end of the sale. Only Fabiano's sculptures remained. Samira listened intently as the first item was described. She'd given her father firm instructions. Of the two pieces for sale, this was the one she wanted. *It reminds me of Aunt Maggie, who isn't even my aunt.* The old woman sitting in the swing. *I told Daddy no more than two hundred dollars. This can be my contribution to the reading program for the year.*

The auctioneer started the bids at seventy-five dollars, instantly shattering Samira's hope of securing this sculpture. Immediately it soared to three hundred and topped out at three-hundred and fifty dollars. Samira couldn't see her father from where she was standing, and she was glad of that. *If he even gets a glimpse of my face, he'll know I'm disappointed.*

Samira tried to console herself. *Some things just aren't meant to be. Maybe I'm not supposed to keep anything of Fabiano's around.* She challenged her personal motive for wanting one of the sculptures in the first place. *The less I think of his seductive initiation, the sooner I can move on.*

But standing there in the middle of that throng of people, Samira suddenly felt totally and completely alone. The applause at the close of that item reverberated loudly in her mind.

A firm hand gripped Samira's shoulder. *Thank God for Weston.* It was a hand that read her thoughts from afar and came to stand by her as the final sculptures were auctioned off.

The mistress of ceremonies described a finished Uberti figurine of a little boy with his fishing pole. Hushed approval rose above the crowd. Bidding began again.

Without permission, Samira leaned into her brother's side. He tightened his hug. The terra cotta fisherman sold for four hundred dollars. People around Samira gasped.

"How'd you book Uberti?"

"I called his booking agent," Samira answered honestly. "His work was in an advertisement for an international art show in Springfield. I just dialed the number."

The final item up for bid was the bronzed statue of the woman. Again, the crowd responded enthusiastically. Unable to stand the tension, Samira put her hands to her mouth. She felt Wes reach his inside suit pocket for his bidding number.

"No, don't."

"Dad told me to."

"I don't want you to."

"But you're not Dad."

"I don't want him to either."

"He can't. He's outside entertaining Lizzie and Bonnie."

Samira could feel panic in her chest. She didn't want to draw attention to herself or anyone in her family. *I want someone to buy my sculpture and take it far away where I won't be reminded of Fabiano.*

The description stopped and suddenly the auctioneer was crying out in fifty-dollar increments. Wes listened and watched but didn't enter a bid until the two-hundred fifty-dollar cry.

"Wes, please." Samira grabbed his bidding arm. *Dear God, please don't let him buy that statue.*

There must have been something urgent in her plea because Wes took his eyes off the auctioneer and looked down into his sister's eyes. Samira moved her head slowly from side to side. Wes let the next several bids go by without taking his eyes off of her. He finally put his number back inside his coat.

Thank you. Samira breathed a sigh of relief. Wes put his arm around her again. *What I would do for Harry Potter's invisibility cloaks so I could hide.*

The auctioneer's cries continued to climb until they were well over a thousand dollars. Some buyers were starting to hesitate, and others were dropping out completely.

This is amazing.

"Dad's max was a thousand," Wes whispered in Samira's ear.

At least it wasn't me that prevented Daddy from getting his prized piece. At the same time, she was in shock that the bid was still climbing.

The auctioneer slowed the rhythm of his cry as two lone bidders rose to the occasion. Samira could feel Wes's fingertips grip her shoulder. *He's nervous too.*

"Who are they?" Samira asked her brother.

"The one on the left owns a gallery in Springfield. He's purchased several items today. I don't recognize the other."

The crowd gasped when the auctioneer reached two thousand dollars. Neither bidder seemed ready to back away. The gallery owner nodded his head to raise a hundred dollars, but before the other man could respond, a single voice rang out from the crowd.

"I bid five thousand dollars."

Samira turned her head toward the voice.

Every person in the room seemed to catch their breath simultaneously. Even Weston stared in disbelief.

The auctioneer paused until he had confirmation of a legitimate bid.

"The bid stands at five thousand dollars." The auctioneer offered the two remaining bidders a chance to raise again.

"Who is it?" Samira whispered to her brother.

Wes shook his head. "I can't tell."

"Going once...going twice..." Samira closed her eyes. *We have never sold a single piece for that much. Ever.*

"Sold. Five thousand dollars buys Uberti's latest work."

The auctioneer's gavel echoed into the microphone. Thunderous applause filled the atrium.

Unbelievable.

The crowd began to disperse but Samira remained frozen in her tracks. She suddenly needed to know who purchased her sculpture.

Wes frowned. "Are you alright, Sis?"

She nodded, unable to explain.

"That's a lot of money for one piece of art," someone exclaimed as they walked past. The library board president stopped and congratulated Samira by shaking both hands at once. Other well-wishers congratulated her too. But she couldn't concentrate. *I still need to know who purchased the bronze statue.*

"I'm going to close out," Wes told his sister between congratulatory wishes.

Samira was surprised he had made a purchase. "What did you buy?"

"The leaded lamp," Weston smiled, "For my office."

"You paid over a thousand?"

Wes smiled. "Pam said it was for a good cause."

It is, but oh my goodness.

Samira tried to see who was claiming her piece of art, but so far it was still sitting on the display in the middle of the make-shift gallery. The entire crowd was in motion. Some people were leaving, others were mingling casually, while yet others were in line to finalize their purchases. But no one seemed to be claiming the bronze statue.

It was late into the evening before the crowd thinned completely. As always, Samira stayed until the very last patron was gone before giving the okay for her crew to clean up the display area. The auctioneer and his staff were finalizing the details of the sale as well. The bronze statue still held its place on the pedestal in the middle of the atrium. *It's the only item left unclaimed.* Samira eyed it carefully.

"I must congratulate you, Miss Samira." The auctioneer's voice sounded tired after a long afternoon of crying. "This was a huge success." He held his hands out in exclamation. "Your reading program should flourish this year."

Samira thanked the man graciously for his donation of time and energy to the project as well.

"It's the least I can do. You taught my granddaughter to read, remember?"

Samira remembered the shy little girl very well. *She's probably almost ten years old by now.*

"We'll do it again next year." The auctioneer's wife promised. "We will get the check over to city hall by the middle of the week. It's going to be at least double over last year's auction."

"The owner of the biggest art gallery in Springfield was here." One of the staff members began to explain. "He didn't hold anything back. If he wanted a piece, he went home with it."

"There were a couple of other dealers here too." The auctioneer was packing up the last of the paperwork.

Samira couldn't resist. *I must know.* "Who purchased the last Uberti?"

The two staff members exchanged a quick look but neither spoke. The auctioneer nodded his head and smiled slightly. "The final bidder has asked to remain anonymous, Miss Samira."

That's not fair. Samira felt like she'd sold her soul to a total stranger. Her heart pounded hard in her chest. "Is that legal?" Samira tried not to sound as alarmed as she felt.

"I'm afraid it is," the auctioneer's wife answered with a sigh. He made that request when he registered so it's very legal."

"We're all finished, Miss Samira." Jim interrupted the moment. "What should we do with the remaining item?"

"The buyer has made arrangements to pick it up at a later time." The auctioneer explained cautiously, as if he sensed Samira's concern. "We'll crate it and keep it under lock and key until that time."

"Very well." Jim seemed pleased. "Then we're going to take the display props back to the museum and be done for the night."

Somehow Samira managed to respond to Jim. She also managed to drive herself to her brother's house where her parents and Krissy and Kara were waiting to congratulate the success of the auction. She even forced her way through follow-up conversations with her family concerning details about the auction. But all the while she fought against the unknown answers in her head.

Who bought my sculpture? And why in heaven's name did Mike Benson torment me so openly about Phil taking Bobbie to the ranch?

~~~~~~~

Back at her own house, Samira felt the fatigue of the day closing in around her. *It certainly didn't take Phil long to replace me.* Her mind's eye could see the model's body on the cover of the magazine wearing nothing but a skimpy thong. *Or maybe he never really intended to give her up for me in the first place.*

Samira finished the day in her own kitchen. The girls had retired to their rooms even though Samira was sure they were both still awake. She leaned over and peered through the window above her sink. *It looks like Mrs. Barnes has turned in for the night.*

She wiped the counter off. *You already wiped it down.* Samira always cleaned and cleaned some more when her mind couldn't rest. *Just stop.*

I should have known better than to pose for Fabiano. But how was I supposed to know he could capture my soul in that work? She rinsed the dishrag. Again. *And how was I supposed to know a complete stranger was going to take me home?*

Samira left the light on above the counter and moved into the dining room. She rearranged the flowers in the middle of the table and then straightened the placemats.

And who is Mike Benson to come along and tell me that Phil decided to take Bobbie whatever her name is to the ranch for a long weekend?

She fluffed the pillows on the sofa with a heavy hand. Without hesitation she turned to the coffee table and picked up a magazine the girls had left out of place. *If I've told them once, I've told them a thousand times to put these back when they're finished.* Disgusted with the little bit of clutter, Samira flopped the periodical toward a basket in the corner of the room. The back page caught on the edge and fell to the floor. Samira bent over to put it more securely in its place. A full-page advertisement for the famous lingerie company was looking back at Samira.

Great. So now she's not only plastered in magazines with hardly any clothes on, but she's also strutting her stuff all over a runway for the whole world to see.

Fabiano's sculpture came into mind again. *Oh, who am I to judge?* Samira sat down in the corner of her sofa and pulled her legs to her chin. She wrapped her arms around her ankles. *Whoever took me home in the form of a bronze statue thinks I posed that way for Fabiano Uberti too.* Samira put her forehead on her knees and closed her eyes.

A blanket of shame closed in around her. *It started out so innocent. But the more time I spent in position for him, the more his imagination worked through my good intentions.*

And it's not like I didn't know it. Samira covered her entire face with her hands. *I knew exactly what he was doing with me in his mind, and I actually found it flattering at the time.* Samira's heart grew heavier with each thought. *And the only reason he wined and dined me at dinner was to gain permission to undress me in the final moments of his stay in Joplin.*

The rhythm of the auctioneer's cry was once again alive in Samira's mind. *The reason he wined and dined me was to undress me in real life.* Darkness completely overcame Samira
~~~~~~~

even though there was still a light in the kitchen. *I led him on by going to dinner and then stood him up in the parking lot unsatisfied.* Tears were beginning to dampen Samira's hands. *But he won in the end, didn't he? No matter who took that work of art home, Fabiano got the last word.*

Time passed but Samira didn't move. Images of her statue danced with the model in the magazine, playing tricks on her mind. Even after the tears stopped, the fragmented thoughts still taunted.

Feeling as if she was no longer alone, Samira lifted her face. *Kara.*

"Mama?" Kara approached her mother slowly, as if she could sense the delicate condition of her emotions.

Samira inhaled deeply. She felt numb as she shifted her weight against the sofa cushions. Kara sat down next to her.

"I saw Miss Davis's boyfriend at the auction tonight. He was talking to you."

"His name is Mike Benson."

"Miss Davis says he knows Phil."

"He does." Samira swallowed hard. Neither of her girls had mentioned Phil's name since she'd told them she would no longer be seeing him. *Kara must still be thinking about him too.*

A long silence occupied the space between mother and daughter. Kara finally lifted her feet off the floor and curled into her mother's side. Samira put her arms around Kara's shoulders and pulled her in tight. *Just hold me, darling, okay?* Tears ran down her cheeks into Kara's silky hair.

"I miss you, Mama."

I miss me too, Samira cried in her heart. *I miss all of me.* She hugged her daughter tightly, hoping Kara's presence could stop the shadows of Phil's image from playing in her mind. *We danced here in this very room.* Samira remembered the candlelight and the music. *Did I lead him on like I did Fabiano?*

Kara didn't move. "Is there anything I can do, Mama?"

The mother shook her head and allowed the tears to fall openly. "No, baby. I have to get through this one on my own."

"Krissy and I prayed for you tonight." Kara put both arms around her mother's shoulders.

Samira nodded in approval. *That's the only way I'll ever get through this. He's the only one who can heal this broken heart.*

"Everything's going to be alright," Kara assured with more confidence than her years. "I know it is."

Samira forced her head to move in a nod. "I hope so." *I really hope so.*

48 *Old Habits*

Joseph Phillip

J.P. parked his truck between a new BMW and a shiny black Mercedes. It was eight o'clock exactly. *Just the way I like it—right on time.*

Jessica Hutchison met him at the door wearing a short black skirt and a sleeveless white top that plunged deeply at the chest. *She's more casual than I've seen her in other settings.*

"Mr. J.P. Ralston," Jessica extended her arm into the room. "I'm sure you'll find this evening to your pleasure."

I'm here to observe, learn and leave. J.P. allowed Jessica to take his sports coat. He inventoried the guests as he rolled the cuffs on his shirt. *Mr. and Mrs. Armstrong from Armstrong Construction. Clark Roberts, an architect from Springfield. Alan Goldstein from city council.*

"There's a self-serve bar just around the corner," Jessica announced. "Make yourself comfortable until the caterers are ready for dinner."

J.P. poured a glass of wine and helped himself to the crackers and cheese.

"J.P., good to see you. It's been a long time." Clark Roberts was extending a hand.

"That it has." J.P. returned the handshake. "What brings you to Bridges Condominiums tonight?"

"Miss Hutchison is presenting Bridges' proposal for the new condo development on the south side of town."

J.P. frowned. "On the south side? What development ground is available down there?"

"It's a tract overlooking Shoal Creek."

Shoal Creek? J.P.'s mind instantly tripped back to the boardwalk with Samira. His still empty stomach turned uncomfortably.

"At any rate, I'm looking forward to tonight's proposal." Clark Roberts lifted a brandy glass to his lips.

J.P. was caught off guard. "What proposal?"

Clark leaned in closer as if he might have a secret to share. "You must be working for the Hughes Corporation tonight?"

No, sir. I'm working for myself. J.P. forced the thoughts of Samira from his mind and traded the wine in for a whiskey and coke. "No, I'm not working for Hughes or anyone else tonight. What kind of proposal are you talking about?"

Clark wrinkled his brow. "Miss Hutchison is revealing the model for the Shoal Creek development. I assumed Hughes sent you here to take notes."

J.P. shook his head. "I'm here because Miss Hutchison invited me to dinner." *That didn't come out right.* Just as quickly as the words were spoken, J.P. regretted having said them. "I mean, she thought there would be some kind of benefit for me here tonight."

"Any benefits she has to offer might be worth showing up for." Clark wiggled his eyebrows from behind his glass.

A few months back, that kind of a comment wouldn't have bothered J.P. In fact, it might have even fueled more incentive to pursue extracurricular activities. But tonight, the comment toted an unfamiliar sourness. J.P. looked across the room at Jessica. She was very much in control of her party, and she was quite easy to look at as well. *Maybe I should change the subject.*

"What's your relationship with Sean Bridges?"

Clark puckered his lips. "I've never met Sean Bridges. The only contact I have with the company is through Miss Hutchison."

That's interesting. J.P. was beginning to seriously wonder if Sean Bridges actually existed. His eyes took inventory of the guests again. *Tom Jones is in real estate. Mary and Kurt Walters are commercial contractors, two of the best in the business. Richard...oh, what is his last name?* J.P. stared at the casually clad businessman across the room. *He's in marketing and sales.*

Jessica tapped a spoon on a water glass. J.P. kept an eye on the guests as they took their seats. *The only player missing in this lineup is an investor.* Jessica patted the chair next to her. *How convenient.*

Introductions were made while the caterers served. *Everyone seems to be aware of Jessica's purpose here tonight except me.* The hostess dropped her napkin. As she leaned over to pick it up, she ran her hand across J.P.'s thigh. A few moments later she took the liberty of brushing her hand over his when she reached for a fork. *If I didn't know better, I'd say she's trying to lead me on.*

The room was getting warm. *Denise warmed me about the alcohol.* The main course conversation flowed without J.P.'s input. He listened and took mental notes. *But nothing seems important.* When the caterers brought dessert, J.P. excused himself from the table.

I don't know what I'm doing here. The dinner conversation replayed in his mind. *I don't care what they decide to do with Shoal Creek and care even less about Jessica.* He stepped outside onto an oversized deck. J.P. leaned his hip into the railing. He could see Jessica preparing a presentation board in the sitting area. *If my sports coat weren't inside, I'd have half a mind to make an early exit.*

Clark Roberts stuck his head outside. "Time for the presentation, J.P. Can I refill your drink?"

I'm driving. "Sure." *What the hell does it matter?*

J.P. followed the architect back inside. He stood behind the sofa so he could see everyone in the room at once.

"Let's begin with the property itself," Jessica began the dissertation. With the press of a button on the wall, the lights in the room dimmed and an oversized television screen turned from blue to green and then a full-scale production began to run.

The video opened with shots of the boardwalk along the creek under the canopy of trees. *I know that area all too well.* The voice on the television chattered on, but J.P. didn't hear anything. All he could make out was the replay of Samira's parting moment. *She just needed to know if I loved her.* The trees were swaying in the breeze on the screen. *I should have gone after her.* J.P. could still see her disappear over the top of the hill. *I shouldn't have let her go that easily.*

There was a pause in the presentation. Jessica turned the ceiling lights up a notch. "What do you suppose this tract of land would be worth if it were located in the heart of downtown?"

J.P. tuned in. *Here's a piece of information I can use for Mr. Stephenson.*

"How much land are we talking about?" J.P. asked from the back of the room.

Jessica looked doubtingly at him. "If you were paying attention at all..."

I wasn't.

"...you would know we're talking about 15 acres."

"How much of the land would actually be developed into residential housing?" Kurt Walters, the contractor asked.

"Exactly half." Jessica motioned toward a miniature model of the proposed development sitting on the large coffee table. "The other half would be divided between commercial services and common grounds."

"Seven and a half acres of residential development ground near downtown would run close to a million dollars." Tom Jones, the local real estate agent spoke up. "And the same in commercial could run double."

So, five acres of commercial development could bring somewhere around three hundred and fifty.

"But wouldn't commercial development in Shoal Creek pull business away from established local merchants?" The marketing director questioned the motives forthright.

Hayes. That's his last name. J.P. finally remembered. *Richard Hayes.*

Councilman Goldstein put his nose in the air. "It's not our intent..."

What's with the 'our' part of the claim? J.P. made a mental note.

"...to take business away but rather to establish services that might not otherwise be convenient to folks living that far out of the way."

Tom Jones stood and walked around to the backside of the sofa where J.P. was standing. "Shoal Creek isn't that far out of the way. I don't see why anyone would expect commercial services down there."

Jessica turned the model on the table, positioning the commercial development side was closest to the guests. "We feel strongly that commercial services and conveniences enhance the motivation for sales. When people know they can stop at the dry cleaners or get a quick cup of coffee three blocks from home on their way to or from work, they are more inclined to make a move."

"It also creates a bigger market to bring people in from outside areas," the councilman added.

J.P. finished the last of his drink. *Since when does he know so much about this development? You'd think he'd be more interested in developing something inside the city limits. Let's see what he knows.*

"Where are the city limits in relation to this development?" J.P. walked closer to the model as he spoke.

Jessica Hutchison eyed him warily.

"If the property is within city limits—"

"It's not." Clark Roberts spoke up. "When I made the drawings, I had to check with city hall for code requirements. Shoal Creek butts up to the city but it's unincorporated."

Jessica wasn't about to let that conversation go any further. "And as a result, the million dollars we could be investing in this caliber of property will run only about half that. That leaves more for commercial development."

If Bridges develops residential and commercial property outside the city limits, then the city gains nothing in taxes or otherwise. J.P. didn't like what he was hearing. *But they're trying to market this proposal as if it is in city limits.* He reviewed the recent case facts between Lloyd Hughes' estate and similar taxing issues with the city.

"Don't get the wrong idea, J.P.," Councilman Goldstein attempted to explain. "The city has been trying to incorporate this area for years."

Trying to develop or trying to incorporate it? There are two different motives here.

Hushed discussion began to permeate the room. *Nothing like opening Pandora's box.* Questions flew back and forth about the city's involvement over the proposed development. Jessica and Alan Goldstein replied with well-rehearsed answers. *I'd venture to say that I asked the one question Bridges hoped wouldn't be voiced.*

J.P. listened to the discussion as it heated up. The longer he listened the more he wondered exactly what role the councilman was playing. *If the property in question is not within the city limits, then Goldstein shouldn't have any business at this party.*

Mr. and Mrs. Armstrong finally had enough. They excused themselves and explained they would need more information before making a final decision concerning their involvement. Richard Hayes followed quickly behind them.

One by one the guests began to explain their reason for needing to leave. J.P. was ready as well. He reached for his jacket, but Jessica Hutchison held his arm.

"Do you have to rush off?"

J.P. ran his free hand through his hair. *Denise warned me about this as well.*

"I was hoping to give you a guided tour of the premium condominiums." Her hand moved from his arm to his waist. "It won't take too much of your time."

But I'm not in the market for a premium condominium. There was just enough alcohol in him that his defenses were low. But common sense screamed at him to decline the invitation.

Jessica turned away as quickly as she'd appeared. Alan Goldstein was at the door. He and Jessica exchanged a few hushed words. J.P. removed his coat from the hanger and pulled it across his shoulders. As he stepped closer to the door, the councilman's glance turned to a definite sneer.

That confirms the hunch I had to not vote for him. Without another word, he passed through the front door onto the porch.

"Wait," Jessica Hutchison was close on his heels. "Are you sure you can't stay, J.P.?"

J.P. turned and faced the woman. *She's unbuttoned her shirt further.* Her sultry smile was tempting. *Walk away, Counselor.*

"No." J.P. took a deep breath.

"No, you're not sure or no you can't stay."

Both. J.P. looked the woman up and down like he'd done with a thousand women in the past. *She's something I could get interested in.* But she packed a lot of ammunition at the same time. *I don't know her motive. Play by the rules.* J.P. tried to hold firm. *Always know the motive. That was one reason playing with Bobbie Sommers had been so satisfying. I knew the objective up front. Sex. That was it.* J.P. stared at the exposed cleavage. *She's tempting. But she has a hidden motive.*

"No, I can't stay."

Jessica pouted her bottom lip. J.P. looked beyond her at the councilman who was still standing in the door. *The look on his face tells me he's already had her.*

"I'm really sorry," the woman touched the back of her finger to J.P.'s chest. "The master suite is a sight to behold."

I'm sure it is. "Thanks for dinner."

"I'm sorry you didn't want dessert." Jessica was still touching him.

The sound of high heels clicked behind him on the sidewalk. Jessica's eyes suddenly turned from flirtation to concern. J.P. turned to see who was coming. The woman on the sidewalk was digging in her purse. She looked up into J.P.'s face.

It looks like the intern from Mid-America.

"Excuse me." The woman continued along the way. Councilman Goldstein wrapped his arm around her shoulders the moment she stepped onto the porch. The door, which had been standing open to this point, closed with a solid thud.

Now that's interesting. J.P. wished the woman would turn around so he could see her face through the window. *Maybe I should stick around.*

Jessica seemed to be reading his thought. "Maybe another time then." Without offering anything more, she crossed the porch and went inside. A few seconds later the outside lights clicked off.

So much for dessert. J.P. stood on the dark sidewalk only a moment longer. He knew the supposed identity of that woman. *She says she's Celia Monroe.* And he knew Jessica Hutchison still had to prove that Sean Bridges existed. *I'm beginning to doubt his existence more all the time.*

Now the attorney wished he'd have settled for a single drink. *It's hard to keep all these details straight.* He started to walk to his truck, which was the only vehicle in the main parking lot now. *Obviously, Goldstein and Jessica are working this Shoal Creek deal together somehow.* He climbed into the driver's seat. *And now I know Celia Monroe is connected to them as well.* J.P. turned the key in the ignition. *What I don't know is what my role was at this party.*

The attorney reviewed the silent communications he'd observed between Jessica and Alan Goldstein. *Hutchison wanted me there for reasons beyond sex because there's no doubt in my mind, she was going to get that from Goldstein whether I stuck around or not.*

J.P. drove out of the condominium complex back into the city. *I wonder if Goldstein's high society wife knows where he is and who he's with tonight.* The attorney was only a few blocks from his office. *So, what was her purpose inviting me into that circle?*

It was late, but not too late. J.P. weighed his options. *I could go on home, or I could go back to the office.* But he wasn't tired, and he didn't feel like working anymore. J.P. checked the clock on the dashboard. *And Mike's probably not alone.*

Old habits were tempting. J.P. parked his truck in the parking lot behind Jimmy's Bar. He left his suit coat behind and entered the familiar pub from the rear entrance just like he'd done a thousand times before.

"J.P., ol' buddy." Jimmy called from behind the bar. "I haven't seen you in months." The experienced bartender slapped a napkin down in front of a barstool. "You drinkin' the usual?"

"Make it a double," J.P. slid onto a stool. The air was thick with the smells of alcohol and pub food. The crowd around the pool table was rowdy.

Jimmy filled a shot glass with expertise. "What's been keepin' you away, partner?"

I can always count on Jimmy for decent counsel. "A pretty lady."

Jimmy spun his head around toward the back door. "I don't see her taggin' along. Where'd 'ya leave her?"

J.P. downed the shot but didn't answer. *I wish it were that simple.*

"Or did she leave you?" Jimmy crossed his arms and leaned his big, black body back on his heels. His bald head glistened with sweat.

"Something like that."

"So, what, we're talkin' three months? Maybe four since you've graced my establishment?" Jimmy refilled the shot.

Somewhere in there." J.P. took another drink.

The bartender shrugged his shoulders and snapped a bar towel in J.P.'s direction. "Not bad, J.P. Considering your record, I'd say that's one of the longest stints you've done in a while." Jimmy threw his head back in laughter. "Drink up, counselor. There's more where that one came from."

J.P. knew Jimmy was talking about the drink. *But chances of finding another woman like Samira are slim to none.* What used to be friendly counsel felt more like a hit below the belt. Before J.P. finished his drink, Jimmy had another ready.

"Look over there." Jimmy took the empty glass and nodded his head toward the pool table. "See that brunette? A free drink says you can take her home."

J.P. shook his head.

Jimmy nodded excitedly. "Then two free drinks say she can take you home." He slapped his hands against the solid wood of the bar. "And three says that by morning she'll make you forget all about that pretty little lady on your mind."

The whiskey was beginning to take full effect. J.P. turned on the stool and looked at the brunette playing pool.

"The only way to forget that pretty lady is to get back on the pony and ride," Jimmy counseled with a glint in his eye.

"She alone?"

"She is now. The guy she came with left with someone else over an hour ago."

Jimmy knows a good setup when he sees it. The attorney glanced around the crowded room. No one looked familiar, which was just the way he liked it. *But then again, nothing looks familiar anymore.*

Several shots later J.P. moved to a stool closer to the pool table. It didn't take long for the friendly brunette to make her move. Within the hour Jimmy gave a thumbs up. J.P. followed the woman out the front door to her car.

She talked to him all the way to the hotel. *I have no idea what she's talking about.* He gave her cash to pay for the room and waited until she came back with the key.

J.P. didn't remember going inside the room. What he did remember was her coming out of the bathroom wearing only a garter belt and stockings. *I don't even know her name.* The woman straddled his body on the bed and started to unbutton his shirt. Her face was deep into his stomach before he felt an impulse to make her stop.

Confused by the alcohol as much as his own emotions, J.P. excused himself to the bathroom. He closed the door and leaned against it with his full weight. *What the hell is wrong with you, Ralston?*

The voices inside his head were as vague as the reflection in the mirror. Jessica Hutchison's face flashed through his mind. Then Bobbie Sommers. And then Samira's. J.P. closed his eyes tight to make the images go away. *Any other time it wouldn't matter who was climbing on board.* He buried his face in his hands. *But tonight, it matters, and I don't know why.*

A sharp knock against the door startled J.P.

"Are you okay in there?"

Shit Ralston, you don't even know where you are. "Yeah, in a minute." *Does she have a name?* J.P. ran cold water into his hands and rinsed his face. *Of course, she has a name. Everybody has a name.* He pressed his face into a dry towel. When he looked up, he didn't recognize the man in the mirror.

Fatigue and confusion looked back at J.P. Ralston. He stared at the blank look. His father's steel blue eyes reflected a loneliness that he'd never allowed himself to claim. But tonight, there was proof of that aloneness in the mirror. *Samira.* Very slowly he realized exactly what he'd let walk away. *Dear God, I didn't want her to walk away. The depth of his hurt pierced his heart.*

"Mister. I have a surprise for you out here."

I still don't know who she is, but I know she's annoying.

J.P. opened the door to the waiting woman. She was still topless, laying on her side on the bed. When he stepped into the room she sprang to where he was standing and wrapped her arms around his neck.

"I didn't think you were ever going to come out of there." Her lips touched J.P.'s neck.

Disgusted, J.P. pulled away. She moved with him. *Just give me some space, woman.* Finally, he unlocked her hands from behind his neck and backed away. He picked up her shirt.

"Here." J.P. struggled to find words as much as he struggled to keep his footing. The entire room was swimming around his head by now.

"Oh, you don't have to do that," the woman assured. "I'm good for whatever you want. And I won't tell a soul."

J.P. shook his head as he put his hand to his throbbing temple. "I'm not in any kind of shape for this." As much as he tried to control his speech, he could still hear the words running together.

The woman took her shirt, but she didn't put it on. Instead, she pushed her chest into his. "But I am, so you don't have to be."

"Look, this was a mistake." *My whole damn life is a mistake.* "You're going to have to leave."

Much to J.P.'s relief, the woman backed away slightly. But the relief was only temporary, for the next thing he knew her hand slapped into the side of his face.

What'd she do that for? J.P. closed his eyes against the sting on his skin. *I gave her permission to leave.*

In an instant, the woman was behind the closed bathroom door. J.P. didn't care where she was as long as she wasn't against him. *I just need her to go away.* He sat down on the desk chair and put his head between his knees. He could hear the fast rhythm of the woman's chatter behind the door. *I don't give a shit what she's saying, I just want her to go away.*

She emerged fully dressed holding a cell phone to her ear. She didn't speak to J.P., and he didn't offer any words to her either. She simply marched through the room and made a swift exit, all the while talking into her telephone.

"Good." J.P. tried to stand up. "Whoever she is, she's gone."

He started for the door, but his stomach had other plans. The next thing he knew he was hanging over the toilet.

~~~~~~~

J.P. awoke on a bed that wasn't his own and in a room he didn't recognize. He tried to sit up, but his head hurt too bad to move. Through blurred vision he finally decided it was around four o'clock. *Four in the morning? Or four in the afternoon?* J.P. forced himself onto his stomach and closed his eyes again.
~~~~~~~

49 Charades

Samira

Krissy dropped her backpack onto the dining room table with a loud thud. "Homework. I can't believe it. It's only the first week of school and I'm loaded." She wrinkled her freckled nose. "English, math, AND reading."

Math. Samira wasn't looking forward to Krissy's math homework. *Last year was hard enough, even with Kara's help.*

"I need you to sign on the line so I can play volleyball." Kara smoothed a piece of paper flat against the table.

"Do you need a physical in order to play sports again this year?" Samira signed her name in blue ink.

"The clinic is holding them next week."

"When does practice start?"

"Monday." Kara unpacked the rest of her bag. "And speaking of Saturday, are we doing anything?"

"Were we speaking of Saturday?"

"I guess not." Kara clarified. "But I was *thinking* about Saturday."

Samira watched her daughter break into a bright smile. *She's growing up all too fast.*

"Maybe I could go to the movies Saturday night?"

"And let's see if I can guess who else will be there." Krissy interjected. "Could it be, Aaron Taylor?"

Kara's instant blush gave away the answer.

So much for Ryan Parkison. Samira sighed. *No matter how hard I try, I won't be able to keep the boys from calling.*

Krissy sprang from her chair when the phone rang. "I'll get it."

"So, can I?" Kara's face was expectant.

How can I deny that smile? "I suppose."

Kara pantomimed a silent YES.

"It's for you, Kara. Guess who."

Without hesitation, Kara swiped the phone from her sister and disappeared into her bedroom.

"Boys." Krissy opened the refrigerator. "Who needs them?"

That won't last much longer. Samira carried a pile of clean laundry to her bedroom. *Boys. Who needs them?* She passed by Tom's picture on the cedar chest. *Me, I guess.* No matter how hard she'd tried to forget the feelings she had for Phil, they just weren't going away. *They're not even beginning to fade.*

Samira fingered Tom's rings as she passed by the ribbons hanging on the wall. *Still. I think I'm more inclined to being married as opposed to being a single mom. I just talked myself out of it for a while.* She took off her skirt and hung it on a hanger. *But that doesn't mean I'm going to go searching for someone else either.* She took off her pantyhose and put them in the hamper. *It's not like I was even looking before. He just happened into the library, and I fell for his invitation for a cup of coffee.* Samira unbuttoned her shirt and added it to the dirty laundry too. She felt a smile curl her lips. *A cup of coffee he didn't even drink.*

A knock at the bedroom door interrupted Samira's thoughts. "Mama? Miss Davis is here."

Kelly Davis? "I'll be right out." *That's interesting.* Samira dressed quickly. *I wonder what's on her mind.*

"Sorry I didn't call first," Kelly apologized right away. She was leaning over the newspaper on the dining room table.

Samira waved her hand. "You don't have to call before coming to my house." "What can I get you? Lemonade? Tea?"

"Lemonade would be great."

"How was your first week of school?" Samira asked the question as she prepared two glasses of cold lemonade.

"Full." Kelly smiled. "But we're off to a good start. I love my summers, but I love teaching too. I missed the kids."

Samira motioned toward the sunroom. Kelly took a seat in the rattan loveseat and pulled one leg up underneath. "How are you, Samira?"

"I'm good." Samira used her rehearsed response. "I'm glad for the school routine too." She took a drink. "But I can't say I miss the kids. It's nice having the library back after the summer programs." *Especially after Fabiano.*

Kelly's green eyes danced. She set the glass down on the end table and rewrapped her bulging curls back into a bun. "You do well to run as many programs as you do, Samira. And the paper reported that the art sale was a huge success a few weeks ago. You should feel good about that."

I do. Kind of. Samira simply nodded at the compliment. *I still don't know who bought my statue.*

"I was out of town that week," Kelly informed without being asked. "But Mike was there. He found it to be exceptionally well organized."

Mike Benson. "We talked briefly."

Kelly was watching her carefully. "So how are you really?"

Samira forced a smile, but she couldn't meet Kelly's eyes. "I am good." *How do I express my thoughts without sounding pathetic?* "But it hasn't exactly been easy."

Kelly's voice softened. "I'm really sorry, Samira. I know you might have liked things to work out differently."

Samira shrugged. "Maybe. But then again, you know, maybe it's all for the best this way." She glanced over her shoulder toward the living room. "Relationships take a lot of energy. As it is, I can focus more on the girls now." *Even though they don't seem to be needing me as much as they used to.* "Kara signed up for volleyball so that means weaving in another schedule."

"I thought Kara might want to play junior varsity this year. I know she had a lot of fun last year."

I wonder why Kelly is really here. "I'm still getting used to the idea that she's really in high school." Samira shook her head. *It seems like only yesterday that they were babies.*

Kelly smiled quietly but didn't offer any further comment.

"What about you?" Samira dismissed the melancholy moment. "Obviously, you're still seeing Mike Benson."

Suddenly Kelly leaned forward and put her elbows on her knee. "I am. He's so much more fun than Brian Wilson." Kelly's eyes sparkled.

Samira had to agree. *The science teacher never seemed like Kelly's type.*

"He's funny and he's spontaneous and yet he's really caring too." Kelly's eyes widened as she grinned. "And so far, he's remained very loosely attached, which gives me a lot of freedom. He comes and goes as he pleases, and I do the same. But we are in daily contact and have a really good time when we're together." Kelly leaned back again. "I like it this way."

Samira had to appreciate Kelly's honesty. *More straightforward than I could ever be.* "Any future plans tucked away in there?"

With that question, Kelly burst into melodic laughter. "I'm playing racket ball with him in the morning and golfing with him on Sunday. If I don't beat Mike too badly at his own games, I expect I might get dinner out of at least one of those outings." Kelly laughed again. "That's about as far as the future goes right now."

But don't you wish for more? Samira didn't understand Kelly's lack of long-term thinking. *She's just a few years younger than me. I'd think she'd want to know what's in store beyond Sunday afternoon.* "Mike seems like a really great companion."

"Mike is a really good friend." Her voice became more serious. "He's loyal to a fault." She poked her finger at an ice cube in the lemonade. "Once he's attached, Mike has a hard time letting go." Kelly's eyes passed over Samira's. "And to be perfectly honest, he sent me here today to check on you."

"Me?" *Why would he do that?* Samira was stunned. "Why me?"

"Because he's worried about you." Kelly unfolded her legs. "And to be honest, so am I." She licked her lips. "I just haven't seen you out and about lately. Not even at church."

"I don't even know Mike."

"I know." Kelly was watching Samira closely. "But Mike has this knack for feeling people out and I think he's right that you're really, well, how do I say this? I just know that you must be hurting still, that's all."

"I've been over to my parents' church a couple of times recently."

"It's okay, Samira. You don't have to explain."

Several moments of silence separated them. *What am I supposed to say now?* Samira sipped her drink.

Kelly knitted her brow. "You know, I've met J.P. a couple of times now. In fact, I've even taken a few days of dog duty when both he and Mike had to leave town on business."

"You took care of Chase?"

"Afraid so. Long story." Kelly put her hands over her knees. "For being a lawyer, he doesn't communicate his thoughts completely. At least not his personal thoughts. He is probably highly effective in the courtroom, but he puts up a huge front when it comes to his personal territory."

Samira listened carefully. *If there's a point here, I don't want to miss it.*

Kelly shrugged her shoulders. "For what it's worth, and I don't want to sound petty or anything like that, but I just think—"

"Mama?" Krissy stepped through the French doors into the sunroom. "Mrs. Barnes wants to know if you can take her to the store tonight."

Can't it wait? Agitated at the interruption, Samira turned to face her daughter. "Is she here?"

"No, she just hollered across the street." Krissy grinned. "I told her yes."

"Then why are you asking me?"

"Because I thought you should know."

Of course, I'll take Mrs. Barnes to the store. I'm so good at taking care of everyone else's needs. Samira half listened as Krissy babbled on with Miss Davis about a few school issues before disappearing back around the corner.

Kelly smiled. "Believe it or not, Samira, I miss Krissy when I don't see her all the time."

"That's very kind of you."

"Well, it's a true statement. She makes me think and she makes me laugh all at the same time." Kelly finished the lemonade. "But as I was saying about J.P...."

Phil. J.P. Samira thought about his names. *Mr. Ralston. Why did he introduce himself to me as Phil, yet he is J.P. to Kelly and Mike?*

"What he said to you and what he meant might have been two different things." Kelly looked confused for a minute. "I mean, I don't know how things actually ended with you two, but the little I've been around him the more I'm inclined to believe that J.P. thought he was making the best decision *on your behalf* when in reality he wasn't."

Samira put her hand to her head. *I don't know exactly where Kelly is headed with this conversation, but I'm not in any position to renew hope in whatever I had with Phil.*

"For whatever it's worth, Samira, I know through Mike, and Mike has a really good sense for things like this—especially with J.P., I know he didn't mean to hurt you."

I know that. I've known that all along. He was setting me free so his life issues wouldn't interfere with mine. He was letting me go to separate me from his past. He watched me walk away so he didn't have to wonder if I'd stop loving him at some point in the future.

"And I'm sure that I have probably not communicated very clearly myself, but I'm still really sorry things didn't work out." Kelly's eyes were sincerely apologetic.

Samira appreciated Kelly's efforts, even if the words didn't help take the hurt away. *But it hasn't helped the emptiness in my heart.*

"I wish there was something more I could do."

"Me too." Samira sighed. "But that's okay. This is something I have to get through on my own."

Kelly started to say something and then hesitated. "Well, I'm already out here on a limb," she admitted. "And you can tell me to shut up at any time, but your last statement might be completely wrong."

Samira opened her eyes wide. Then she frowned.

"I disagree. I don't think you have to work through these kinds of things on your own. I think if you'd just let someone else in on your pain, you'd find out that you might heal a lot quicker." Kelly wrinkled her nose obviously afraid she'd said too much.

Samira wanted to walk away, but she couldn't. *Kelly is a guest in my home. I will treat her with respect.* But at the same time, Samira strongly disagreed. She'd always held back her personal struggles. I'm a strong woman. She'd come through a lot already. *And I will get through this too.*

Somehow Samira finished the conversation with Kelly. And a little while later she managed to take Mrs. Barnes to the grocery store and back. After supper she retired to her garden while the girls entertained themselves with friends on the telephone and on the computer. The summer vines needed trimmed, and it was time to clear away the dying branches of the rose bushes.

Samira worked diligently. Dusk was fast approaching, and she'd really hoped to be finished in this area of the yard before the weekend. *But then again, I don't know what the hurry is. It's not like you have anything going on over the holiday weekend.* Samira worked the pruning shears with ease. One after another, dead branches tumbled into the dirt. *Nor is it likely you'll encounter a knight in shining armor to rescue you from this Garden of Eden.* She trimmed another bush. *You really need to stop reading those medieval novels.*

A falling branch caught on a trellis. Without thinking Samira grabbed hold to pull it loose. A sharp pain shot through her hand. Quick examination showed an over-sized thorn from the rosebush protruding from her finger through the garden glove. Samira immediately removed the thorn, but blood was already soaking through. *So much for finishing tonight.*

Samira held her finger under cold running water in the laundry room sink. It hurt, but it wasn't as bad as she'd suspected. *Only a little puncture.* She heard the walk-in garage door close and assumed one of the girls had been out front. Samira turned her finger. *I think it's going to be alright.* She turned off the faucet and turned toward the kitchen just as her brother stepped through the entrance.

"Wes." Samira gasped. "You startled me."

"I knocked, but no one answered. Is your doorbell working?"

Samira shrugged.

"Obviously, your telephone is working. It's been busy all evening. Eventually you're going to have to break down and get a cell phone. You know that right?"

He's probably right. The throb in her finger was still prominent. Samira went on through the kitchen to get a band aide out of the hall closet.

"Let's see," Wes reached for Samira's hand. "What'd you do?"

Samira explained.

"You did this through a pair of gloves?"

"It was a big thorn."

"I guess." Wes examined the wound carefully. "Do you think Mom should take a look at it?"

"No." Samira didn't want her mother examining a cut from a thorn. She held still as Wes wrapped the band aide around her finger. "See? It's better already." *It still hurts.* "So, what brings you to my neighborhood, Wes?" *He has something on his mind, or he wouldn't be here.*

"Are you busy in the morning?"

Babysitting. I knew it. Just because I don't have anything planned on my personal agenda doesn't mean I want to spend it babysitting. "I don't know yet, why?"

Wes turned a page in the newspaper, which was still open across the dining room table. "Here. Did you read this?" He pointed a finger. Samira walked back around the table to see what had his attention. "Shoal Creek. Are you tuned into this at all, Sis?"

Samira had heard mumblings from patrons at the library but didn't know the details. *I don't want anything to do with Shoal Creek. Nothing at all.*

Wes straightened his back and put his hands in his front pockets. "Alan Goldstein wants to bulldoze the entire area for development." He shook his head in disbelief. "I don't understand it."

Samira pretended to skim the article as Wes attempted to sort through his thoughts. "Mid-America is getting ready to sell the property on that end of town. And no doubt, whoever buys it will develop it for commercial investment. But Shoal Creek isn't protected by city code. I'm afraid they'll destroy the natural beauty of the area."

The picture in the paper showed the boardwalk along the creek. *A little further down was where I sat with...well anyway.* "They want to take out all these trees?" Samira ran her hand over the full-color photo. The trees in the picture were still green, but in a few short weeks they would be turning to rich shades of autumn. *They shouldn't take the trees out.*

"Every last one if I'm understanding correctly." Wes leaned over the paper again. "Here," He rested his finger on a paragraph at the end. "There's a town hall meeting on Tuesday for citizens who wish to protest Goldstein's plan."

Samira was still confused. "Why isn't city council fighting against Councilman Goldstein's ideas?"

"Because Shoal Creek isn't within the city's limits."

Oh wow. Without the protection of the city, this could be devastating for the whole area. "You mean it's not protected by parks and rec regulation or anything?"

"Apparently not." Wes stuffed his hands back in his pockets. "Right now, it's privately funded. But if Goldstein gets a hold of it, Shoal Creek as we've known it will be no more."

"Are you going to the town hall meeting?"

Wes nodded. "But tomorrow another member of city council is offering a guided tour of Shoal Creek for those interested in trying to protect the area from being destroyed."

"And you want to go to that?" That's why he needs me to babysit.

"Yes." Wes answered forthright. "But I want you to go with me."

Samira was taken aback. *I can't go back to Shoal Creek. It's too soon.*

"Come on, Sis. I need your input. I'm willing to fight this thing, but I need you there to see the natural beauty for me. I'm going to look at it through the eyes of an investor. You're going to see it as a gardener."

Samira crossed her arms over a now churning stomach. "I can't, Wes."

"What could you possibly have going on in the morning?"

"What business is that of yours?"

"I didn't mean it that way," Wes tried to apologize. "This is something I would like to see you sink your teeth into, that's all."

Suddenly his motive was clear. "You want me to adopt this project?"

"You'll want to if you go down there and take a look."

"I know what it's like down there."

"I know you do. That's why I want you to go on this tour with me and hear what they have to say about Goldstein taking it all away."

"I have plenty on my mind without taking on a city council member," Samira retorted. "Do you think I don't have enough to keep me busy or something?"

"I know what's on your mind, Sis, and you need to let it go."

So that's it, isn't it? Even my own brother is here to help me get over this man I should never have had in the first place.

"I can live without your advice." *Wes is my brother. Unlike Kelly Davis, I can walk out on him.* She turned for the door.

"Where do you think you're going?"

"I left my pruning shears in the rose bed."

"Get them later."

"I'm getting them before it gets dark."

"You have enough lights out there to make it look like daytime if you flip a switch."

Samira let the door slam harder than necessary as she marched into the garden. *This is my retreat.* Not even Wes's snide remark about her outdoor lighting could take away the hallowed presence in her garden.

The door slammed again. Samira looked back. Wes was following her.

He has no right to come here and taunt me with an ecological issue to distract me from whatever it is I choose to hide behind.

Samira reached for her clippers, careful not to bump the newly fallen stems from the rose bushes. *If I only knew exactly what I was hiding behind.*

"Just stop it, Samira." Wes's voice was stern. "Stop the charade and the lies you're telling yourself and face the music once and for all."

Samira refused to face him.

"You work so hard at being strong and able and secure, Sis, but you're no stronger than the rest of us." Wes paused but he didn't move any closer. "You don't have to be perfect and secure. Hell, you don't even have to be happy." He paused again. "But there's a bunch of us out here in the real world waiting for you to come back around, and it's about high time you give up your pride and admit that things didn't go the way you'd planned."

"I didn't plan."

"Then you hoped," Wes corrected immediately. "We all feel badly about the way things ended. But as long as you're shutting yourself off from the world, we can't help."

Samira hung her head. Dead limbs from the rose bushes were scattered at her feet and on the sides of the raised beds. She knew how quickly those branches would dry up and disintegrate now that they were cut from the mother bush. *Just like me. It wouldn't take much for me to disintegrate right now either.*

"It was just a matter of time, Wes," Samira started to speak her thoughts. "I needed more commitment than he could give."

"Maybe you can't manipulate everything like you want to. Maybe some things have to evolve on their own."

"I took a chance and look what happened."

"You took a chance and look what you'd never have known had you not tried?"

"Like what?"

"Like the fact that you have the capacity to love someone again."

Samira closed her eyes. "But it was all wrong. I made some hasty decisions."

"Yeah, well, love will do that to a person. No reason to beat yourself up for that one."

Now Samira turned around and looked up into her brother's dark eyes. "But Wes, I let him move me in ways I'd forgotten I could be moved."

"And it was a very good thing."

"No. It wasn't. Because I almost let it happen again with someone else for all the wrong reasons."

"The artist?"

I knew Weston figured that one out. She hung her head in shame.

"So what? I figure he's halfway around the world with another project working his art into someone else's soul by now." Wes reached out and put his hand on his sister's head. "It's your soul I'm concerned about."

You and everyone else it seems. "Dang it, Wes. I don't want to talk about this." She gripped the shears tightly. "I'm tired of thinking about it. I'm tired of replaying the good memories in my head only to have them end in disappointment. I'm tired of being nice and being happy." Samira sighed heavily. "I'm even tired of pruning the vines."

"Then it must be time to take off the mask and just be yourself." Wes let go of her head. "So, how are you now, Sis?"

"Mad."

"Good, now we're getting somewhere."

The dark cloud that had been shadowing Samira's ability to move suddenly lifted. She opened her mouth and breathed in the thick, humid air of the evening.

"So, will you go with me in the morning?"

It feels good to be free. Samira didn't know exactly what had happened, but she suddenly knew there were better days ahead.

"I guess." She nodded her head. "I don't have anything better going on."

Wes smiled a genuine smile. "You should vent more often, Samira." He wrapped his elbow around his sister's neck. "It does you good to vent."

Is that what it is? Samira walked back to the house tucked inside her brother's arm. *Somehow, I think it's more than that.*

Samira waved goodbye to her brother as he backed his van out of the driveway. *Does my love for Phil have to stop because he can't accept it?* She turned to go back inside. *I think I can love him still, even if he doesn't know how to love me*. Somehow there was new freedom in that realization. *Maybe this is what Pastor Bill was trying to tell me.*

50 Letters and a Name

Joseph Phillip

J.P. opened the door to the outside. Bright sunshine flooded the dark motel room burning his eyes. He put his hand to his forehead and took in the surroundings of the building. *Second floor balcony.* The sign over the parking lot lit up one letter at a time. W-E-L-C-O-M-E T-O T-H-E C-A-P-R-I.

He scanned the parking lot as best as he could against the sunlight. *That's what I figured.* No truck. *Not that I could drive it anyway.* He closed the door and sat down in the chair at the desk. Surprisingly, he was still dressed. *But I have no idea how I arrived in this hellhole.*

J.P. reached for his cell phone. *Nothing.* He pressed the restart button again. *Dead battery.* He ran his hand through his hair and leaned back into the chair. *Just my luck.* The clock on the desk read 1:22. *Obviously P.M.*

The numbers on the desk phone blurred as J.P. struggled to recall Mike's phone number. *Shit, Ralston.* Ever so slowly he pushed the buttons one at a time, hoping against hope that a familiar voice would answer.

"Mike Benson at your service."

Relieved, J.P. pressed the phone hard into his ear. "Mike."

"Hey, good buddy, where are you man?"

J.P. put his pounding head in his other hand. "At the Capri."

"Are you alone?"

"As far as I know."

"Do you need a ride?"

"Yeah." It hurt his head just to speak out loud.

"Anything I can bring you?"

J.P. closed his eyes. "A clean shirt and a quart of milk."

"Alright. Here's the deal. I'm on the green at the 4th hole. It's going to take me a while to get down there. Are you going to be alright for a while longer?"

"Yeah." *I'm going to lay back down.*

"What room?"

I have no idea what room I'm in.

"J.P.?"

"I don't know."

"Check the door."

J.P. set the receiver on the desk and pushed himself off the chair. He opened the door long enough to read the number. He staggered back to the phone. "211."

"Sit tight. I'll be there as soon as I can."

I'll be here. J.P. looked around the room. *I guess.* It was cheap and dingy. The curtains hung haphazardly, and the furniture was dated and worn. *Nothing like waking up at the gates of hell without a rope to hang onto.*

J.P. stretched out on the musty bed and closed his eyes.

A loud thud brought him back into consciousness. He tried to sit up, but his muscles didn't respond.

"Holy shit, J.P.," Mike emerged from the bathroom.

Has he been here awhile or is he just arriving? J.P. put the back of his hand over his forehead.

"Let's get you out of this flophouse."

"How'd you get in here?"

Mike offered a helping hand. "I paid for the extra day, and they gave me a key to come find you." Mike tossed a large metal key on the desk.

The blood-curling ring sent a throbbing pulse through his temples.

"Sorry." Mike apologized. "Here, change out of that."

I know. I'm a mess. J.P. attempted to unbutton his soiled dress shirt, but his fingers wouldn't work.

"Jesus, J.P." Mike unbuttoned his friend's shirt. "Put this on and let's get you the hell out of here."

J.P. shrugged out of the dirty shirt and exchanged it for a clean t-shirt. Mike grabbed the cell phone off the desk and picked up the dirty shirt. "Did you have anything else with you?"

J.P. tried to remember, but nothing came to mind. He shook his head slowly.

Mike nodded toward the door.

Without speaking, J.P. forced himself off the low bed. It took a few seconds to get his bearings, but eventually he followed Mike onto the balcony and down the concrete stairs.

"How'd you get my truck?"

"Jimmy called." Mike opened the door and walked around to the driver's side. "He thought you might not want it towed first thing this morning."

"Jimmy who?"

Mike started the engine and adjusted the air conditioner vents. "Jimmy, the bartender." He opened a quart of milk and handed it to J.P. "The bartender who bragged up the brunette he sent you away with."

J.P. took a drink of milk without any discussion. *I remember a little about being at Jimmy's bar. But I don't have any recollection of a brunette.* The motion of the moving vehicle was causing J.P.'s stomach to work against him. He grabbed the armrest with all the strength he had left.

"You gonna make it or do I need to stop?"

J.P. couldn't answer. He just shook his head and closed his eyes again.

They drove in silence for a while.

"I called your aunt, so she knows not to expect you this morning."

J.P. squeezed his eyes tight. *Oh shit. I was supposed to be at the ranch this weekend with Bobby's family.*

"Whad'ya tell her?"

Mike turned the truck into the sun. J.P. closed his eyes against the glare.

"I lied through my teeth."

What do you tell her in a case like this?

"I told her you were in the middle of a case and couldn't break free quite yet." Mike looked back to the road. "You owe me double for that one." Mike continued to explain. "She said Bobby and his family got in yesterday and are looking forward to seeing you."

Not today. Not like this.

Once inside his house, J.P. sat in a kitchen chair and watched as Mike let Chase back inside and checked for telephone messages.

"Sparky's on a hot trail, J.P." Mike paused. "You do remember Sparky, don't you?"

J.P. managed a nod. *Kind of.*

"He tried reaching you last night on your cell without any luck. I'm going down to your office with him this afternoon. We're going to set a trap for—"

J.P. knew Mike was trying to brief him on a case, but he was talking way too fast for comprehension.

"Shit, J.P." Mike headed for the door. "Sleep it off. I'll be back later. And don't forget to call your aunt."

The slam of the screen door caused J.P. to grab his head again.

~~~~~~~

The sun was still shining when J.P. awoke. This time he was in his own bed. Chase was asleep on the rug by the bedroom door. J.P. rolled over and sat up. *Ten o'clock.* J.P. read the clock again. *Ten o'clock what?*

It doesn't matter what day it is anymore. J.P. took his time getting into a hot shower. His beard had grown considerably but there was no motivation to shave. Instead, he rested his hands on the top of the shower stall and let the hot water pound against his aching muscles.

Dressed only in a pair of sweatpants, J.P. found his way to the kitchen and let Chase into the back yard. *I'm hungry but I don't dare eat too much.* He filled a glass with water, drank it down and then filled another. *I wonder where Mike is.* J.P. leaned into his kitchen window. *The truck's here so he must have had a way to get home.*

J.P. carried a piece of dry toast to the living room and sat down on the couch. Thursday's paper was still open on the coffee table. He flipped it over and found the remote control. With a click the television turned on to ESPN pregame show. *It must be Sunday.* J.P. rubbed his rugged face in his hands. Mindlessly he watched the commentators on television give their opinions of the NFL lineups for the day. Some days he might care. *But not today.* He clicked off the tv and went into his office.

Message lights flashed on his computer and his cell phone indicating several messages. Mike must have plugged in my phone. He moved a small stack of papers to the side and uncovered a reminder to call the boys before heading up to the ranch. *Shit, Ralston. You can't even hold yourself together long enough to make an appearance at the ranch.*

Disgusted with himself, he went back to the bedroom and put on his running shoes. Unsure of his strength, J.P. decided to take Chase out on the street instead of down the walking path. *I don't need to go far, but I do need to get outside and breathe in the fresh air.*

Thirty minutes later J.P. returned to the house sweaty and tired, but somewhat refreshed. He drank another glass of water and returned to his desk. *I need to call Aunt Maggie.* J.P. picked up the phone but couldn't force himself to dial. *She's the one person I can't lie to.* He put the phone back down. *I have no idea how I'm going to fix this one.*

The shoe box from his father caught his eye. He carried it into the living room and sat down on the sofa. Trying not to be too curious, J.P. flipped off the lid and picked up a bunch of banded letters. Some had red, white, and blue stripes around the edge indicating airmail delivery from days gone by. Others were plain envelopes with colorful stamps in the corners. But all were yellowed with age.

J.P. allowed his fingers to unwrap a stack. He sorted through taking note of the postmarks and addresses. They'd been delivered all over the world at different times. One envelope caught his eye. It was dated October 22. *Mom's birthday.* J.P. removed the contents. *Mom's handwriting was so beautiful.*

> Dear Joe, It's my birthday. Can you believe I'm 28 years old today? I received your package a week ago, but Maggie won't let me open it until tonight. That will be the highlight of my day.
>
> The skies are blue in Missouri today. I took the boys over to Maggie's early this morning and we busied ourselves making birthday cake for tonight's party. What I wouldn't give to save you a piece. Angel food from scratch. Your favorite. The Langford's and Annabelle Campbell are joining us at Maggie's for dinner. After
~~~~~~~

> that we'll play cards and celebrate with cake and ice cream. Joey is so excited about the shindig. He knows there will be kids to play with and candles on the cake.
>
> Little Bobby is cutting teeth this week. Poor little guy is miserable most of the time. I stayed up with him rubbing his gums until he fell asleep on my lap last night. Maggie helped me with him this morning. A few more days and those two-year molars should be through the gums. That will make all the difference. Roy took Joey fishing this afternoon so I could rest. But I wanted to get a quick note off to you before I lay down.
>
> Joe, I've been thinking about our time together in Washington a few weeks back. We were so fortunate to be able to steal a few precious hours. I can still feel your arms around me and sometimes when I'm up with the baby in the night I can sense your steady breathing next to me once again. I miss you more than I can express, but I love you even more than that. The thought of you facing the heat of the battle is almost more than I can bear some days. But then I say my prayers and I know you are safe in God's care once again. I don't doubt God's protection over your life—not for one minute. And I don't want you to doubt it either. Know that wherever you are and whatever you're facing, that God is between you and the enemy.
>
> I must go for now. Bobby will be awake before my head ever hits a pillow. But you are in my heart and in my prayers. I will write after the party tonight. And then again in the next day or so. I love you, Joe Ralston. Don't you ever forget that.
> ~Leona

"Leona." J.P. spoke his mother's name out loud. *God, I miss her still.*

After that, the letters came one right after another. Constant news from home bridged the distance between the Ralston boys and their father. And every letter was punctuated with words of loving, tender care. J.P. felt his eyes well up with tears when he read about his mother's pride when he won his first boy scout medal. *I remember that day.* And he felt his stomach knot when he read about Bobby's close call with a neighborhood dog. *Yeah, I remember that day too.*

His emotions became one with his mother's words until he could no longer separate himself from their history. Aunt Maggie's constant presence in his upbringing became more apparent and for the first time in his life he realized how attentive his mother was to their every need.

> Joey started kindergarten today, Joe. You should have seen him all dressed up in his shorts and button shirt. I walked him all the way to school with a brilliant smile for the little guy. But I cried all the way home, Joe. Why is it we cry when something so wonderful is happening? I don't understand any of it. I was the first mother at the school when the day was done.

J.P. remembered his mother crying that day. He remembered her lingering hug before she turned away to walk back home.

> I took Joey to the doctor today. It seems the spots on his back are poison ivy. Must have been from an outing with Roy...

> *And a nasty case of it too,* J.P. recalled. *Missed a whole week of school getting over that.*

> Joey came home from school today with a black eye. I couldn't imagine what had happened. But the other boy's mother didn't hesitate to call and fill in my curiosity. I never liked that little boy anyway. He's such a bully...

Timmy Houston. And I took him down too. J.P. still felt the satisfaction of that moment.

> Joey asked me about the Navy today, Joe. He worries about you—wonders where you are and if you're safe. I tell him only the Navy and God know where you are in the ocean. And I tell him God is watching out for your safety. He prays for you every night before bed.

J.P. put the letter down on the coffee table. He didn't remember ever saying a prayer for his father. *But I remember praying.* He remembered praying for his mother to come back. He remembered begging God to fix the plane crash so his mother could come home again. And he remembered taking off into the woods at a full stride toward the lake screaming at God for taking her away. But he didn't remember any prayers after that. *There wasn't anything more to pray for.*

Scenes from his childhood, of his mother's funeral, of his father standing alone at a distance at the graveside. Memories of Aunt Maggie's ranch and of playing games with Roy in the living room. Scenes playing catch with Bobby in the backyard at the house where they lived in town. And a single memory of the time he decked his brother for asking his sweetheart to the spring dance.

J.P. dropped his head between his knees and locked his fingers behind his head. He tried to shut out the flood of memories that were now coming at him faster than his mind could possibly comprehend.

He laughed at the last memory. *Damn it. I had my heart set on Suellen Jackson, but she chose my scrawny little brother over me.* He shook his head at the recollection playing in his mind. *And if I'm not mistaken, Bobby got about what he deserved out of that night.*

Chase nudged his master gently, bringing J.P. back to the present. J.P. accepted the affection and returned the favor with a firm grip around Chase's broad shoulders. "Well, ol' boy. What do you think?" J.P. looked his dog in the eye. "I think it's about time this sorry, old master of yours got his shit together."

Chase cocked his head to the side with canine interest.

"I've spent my whole life fighting wars I can't win." J.P. sighed. "I haven't been able to win against any odds, ol' boy, but I gave it a fair shake."

With that command, Chase put his front leg in the air. J.P. smiled. He shook Chase's paw with satisfaction.

J.P. went to the sink and filled a water glass. *I couldn't win my father's attention. And I couldn't win my mother back. And I couldn't even win custody of my boys.* He swallowed the water in one long drink. "But I could win in court." J.P. made the announcement to his dog who was now standing at attentive anticipation. "And for a hell of a long time that's been enough."

Back in his bedroom, J.P. opened his top dresser drawer and removed the envelope that contained his mother's wedding rings. A single marquee diamond graced the engagement ring while the band held a row of twelve smaller cut diamonds. J.P. turned the rings in his hand. They were small compared to his own fingers.

His father's words replayed in his head. *"She's all I ever needed."*

And he's all she ever needed. J.P. accepted that realization for the first time in his life. He'd always assumed his mother suffered great hardship over his father's commitment to the Navy. *But her letters tell me something different.*

"She knew what was best for you boys." The Captain's face was resolute when he'd made that statement. *Obviously, he trusted her to let her stay home like that time and time again.* J.P. put the rings back in the envelope. *I don't think I've ever trusted anyone that much. Not even Mike.*

There was a sudden urge to be near his mother. J.P. pulled an old t-shirt from his drawer and grabbed a change of clothes and his shaving kit. His duffel bag was packed in less than five minutes.

As he turned for the door, he snapped his fingers to summon his dog.

"Come on, Chase. We have a reservation at the ranch."

J.P. drove in silence, unaware of the passing time. The miles passed under his tires as childhood memories continued to play in his mind. Close to three hours later J.P., turned his truck off the main highway onto a low maintenance gravel road. Dust rolled in his rearview mirror, but J.P. didn't mind. *I haven't been here for a million years.* He knew exactly where he was going. *When was the last time I was here anyway?* He brought the truck to a stop in the shade of a massive oak tree overlooking a deep valley. *I came here after the Captain stood me up at the depot.*

Chase bounded out of the truck excited to have new territory to explore. But J.P. sat stock still in the driver's seat. His eyes passed over the rows of headstones. *I came here that day so she could fix the broken parts.*

J.P. took his time. He walked the row all the way to the far fence and then turned and faced his mother's epitaph. A beloved wife and mother. Leona Elena Ralston. The space next to his mother's was incomplete. Joseph Phillip Ralston. An American Bald Eagle graced the corner of the tombstone.

He stood staring at his father's name and for the first time in his life, Joseph Phillip Ralston felt no bitterness. *I'm not even angry.* There wasn't even bottled resentment shouting false accusations at the father he never knew. The grown boy knelt and put his hand on the cool marble that marked his mother's place of burial.

"I'm sorry, Mom." J.P. could feel tears well up in his eyes. "I didn't know. I didn't know how much you loved him." J.P. thought again. "Hell, I didn't think you loved him at all. And I didn't know how much he depended on you back home either." J.P. took a deep breath as his tears spilled over and mixed into his whiskers. "I just didn't know."

Chase passed by with his nose to the ground. "I've spent my whole life fighting for the love I never knew you had. I figured if you didn't get it then I didn't deserve it either." J.P. sat down on the grass and pulled his knees to his chest.

Time passed.

All I've ever known, or at least all I remember knowing, is that I didn't have what it took to bring my father home. Ever. And the few times he was home, he wasn't the father I wanted him to be.

J.P. stared at the sandblasted eagle on the stone. *Eventually I took matters into my own hands. Figured if he didn't need me, then I didn't need him either.* He wiped his nose on the back of his hand. *But the things I thought I needed never brought me any lasting satisfaction either.*

He recalled his college days of carousing and partying. *But Mike had a sense for the finer things in life.* J.P. smiled and leaned back on his hands. *Still does. He'd let me flail, then he'd reel me back in. Somewhere in there I figured out I could win at something, so I latched on and curtailed the party life long enough to get into law school.*

J.P. noticed a hawk circling high in the sky. *Then that ordeal with Janet. That was just a stupid mistake. I never intended to get her pregnant. And I never intended to love her either. But I think I did for a while.* He remembered some happy moments. *It's hard not to love the woman who gives birth to your own flesh and blood.*

He leaned all the way back on his elbows so he could watch the hawk. "But you know what?" J.P. spoke into the space between him and his mother's tombstone. "Even though I gave her all I had, it still wasn't enough."

The hawk made one last circle then lifted toward the heavens. *I wasn't the man she hoped I'd be. I had to finish law school and pass the bar. And then I went to work for Lloyd Hughes so I could pay off my school loans.* Chase padded by in the overgrown grass. *Hughes became my escape from the onslaught of discontent and demands Janet unloaded on me every night.* J.P. nodded his head. *Hughes was probably the best thing that happened to me back then.*

"You're wrong."

J.P. sat up in the grass. He looked around to see if anyone else was there because he knew the words he'd heard in his head were not his own.

What do you mean, I'm wrong? He directed the question to the unseen voice.

"Joshua Thomas and James Allen Ralston."

J.P. picked a long blade of grass and twisted it in his fingers. Slowly he began to understand. *Yeah, they're the best things that ever happened to me. But I couldn't be the father they needed either.*

"You're wrong again."

"I am not wrong again." Now J.P. was standing, screaming into the valley. "I tried, but I couldn't make their mother love me back."

J.P. could see James's face in his rearview mirror the day he left him standing in the driveway. *God, don't make me go back there.* He closed his eyes, but the image wouldn't leave. *Don't you know I tried to make that work?*

Guilt and remorse conjured up scenes of angry tantrums and irresponsible decisions.

"But you didn't have to win their love, did you?"

Again J.P. looked around for the voice, but this time he knew it came from somewhere deep within. *No, I didn't.* He rubbed his damp eyes with his hands. *But I was afraid if I accepted it, I wouldn't be able to live up to their expectations either.*

Suddenly aware of his immediate surroundings again, J.P. snapped his fingers. Chase stopped digging at the base of a fencepost and trotted up to his master's feet. "You don't require very much of me, do you boy?" J.P. knelt beside his dog. "A little exercise, a scoop of chow, and a bucket of water. That's all you need."

"But people," J.P. dug his hand into Chase's thick fur as his thoughts shifted again. "People are different than that." *To make people happy you have to do all kinds of things that don't work the way you think they might.* He continued to massage the dog's shoulder. *Janet needed me to be someone I wasn't and when I didn't fit that mold, she found someone that did. So, I figured he was probably the one the boys needed too.*

The big black dog rolled over on his back. "Yeah, I'll rub your belly if you'll rub mine." *It's a great concept, but it's no rule to live by. I simply prefer to take care of my own endeavors. It's safer that way.*

"And you can control it."

Now J.P. was beginning to recognize the voice in his head as something more powerful than his own thoughts. *Is that what it is? Control?* He puckered his lips in thought. *No, it's not control. It's a mask to protect myself from those who want me to be someone or something else.*

It's not Joseph Phillip Ralston, II that answers to Christopher Hughes, nor it is Joseph Phillip that wins in court.

The attorney's eyes fell on the engraved letters again. *Joseph Phillip Ralston. I wanted to be just like him—independent, strong, brave, brash.*

Chase flopped over onto his feet and wagged his tail. *But I didn't like who he turned out to be in real life or in my mind, so I gave up the name and became J.P. Ralston, Attorney at Law.* J.P. picked up a short stick and tossed it into the air. Without a moment's hesitation, Chase took off after it.

I must admit, J.P. does damn well for himself. He considered his court record. *But the satisfaction of winning isn't as motivating as it used to be.* J.P watched his dog retrieve the stick. *Joseph Phillip II must have more to learn about life.* Suddenly Samira's sweet smile appeared in his mind. *And she may be the one thing I can't fight to win.* He took the stick out of Chase's mouth.

By now J.P. wasn't surprised to hear the voice inside his head speak again. *"Maybe she's the reason there's no fight left in you."*

Chase jumped against J.P.'s knees and knocked him off balance. When J.P. rolled into the grass, the dog took advantage.

"Quit it." J.P. pressed against the ninety-pound dog with his arm. He couldn't help but laugh. "Chase. Stop." J.P. tried without success to deter Chase's wet tongue from licking his face. The master finally gave in. Chase barked excitedly and pounced at his master, thrilled at the spontaneous wrestling match.

"You win, boy," Phil rolled into a fetal position to protect himself from the dog's happy attack. "I'm all yours. You win. I don't want to play this game anymore."

Bottled tears of guilt and regret welled up in J.P.'s eyes and ran onto his face. Despite Chase's affection, J.P. couldn't hold them back any longer. *I don't want to play this game.* He took advantage of a lull in Chase's attack and pushed himself into a sitting position. Chase nudged him again, but this time J.P. was ready. He tossed the stick into the air, relieved to have his canine friend occupied with something other than him.

God, I've spent over half my life fighting battles I couldn't even see. But I don't want to do that anymore. Chase returned with the stick, but this time he stretched out in the grass, seemingly content to be still for a moment. J.P. wiped his face with the hem of his shirt.

Exactly what did the Captain mean when he wished for something of sustenance to take away my will to win.

Chase was panting hard, and the birds had begun to sing their nighttime songs.

No, he didn't wish for something to take away my will to win. The color of the sky was fading into a darker blue. *He said he hoped I'd find something of sustenance so the need to win would lose its power.*

Suddenly life didn't seem to be an empty chasm. For the first time, Joseph Phillip Ralston felt an invisible weight lift from his chest. *So, the will to win isn't the driving force. Or at least it shouldn't be.*

Time passed again. But how much time passed, J.P. didn't know. But he was aware when the sun began to drop lower in the sky. And he was also aware that Chase was now sleeping in the grass next to him."Exactly what I am supposed to do now?" J.P. questioned his dog in the stillness of the moment. "What do I do if I'm not playing that game anymore?"

And then, in an echo of his mother's thoughts, he heard her voice inside his head again. *Know that wherever you are and whatever you're facing, God is between you and the enemy.*

The enemy has been in my own mind. The realization came slowly. *The enemy has been talking me out of the life meant for Joseph Phillip Ralston, II.* With that thought came the assurance that maybe, just maybe, there was a bigger purpose to his life than winning women and court battles. *And maybe I haven't been fighting these battles alone all this time.*

J.P. stood up and let his eyes take in the beauty of the valley before him. *If the Captain trusted her, then I need to trust her too. I think I can do that. I can trust her.*

But as he walked away, he knew that he was trusting more than the words of his beloved mother. He was trusting in her belief that God was between him and his self-imposed enemy. *All this time I thought God was the enemy.*

The master snapped his fingers. His dog appeared obediently at his side. "Come on, Chase. Let's see if Aunt Maggie has any supper left." He opened the driver's door and waited for Chase to bound across the console to the waiting passenger seat. "And we'd better hurry up because we've got a lot of explaining to do when we get there." *Especially to Bobby. There's no way he'll let me off the hook.*

J.P. felt good making a showing at the ranch. *It would be far too easy to just head back home and chalk the whole damn weekend up to another lost bygone.* But this time J.P. knew there was more to it than that. *I owe it to the boys.* He thought again. *No, I owe it to myself.*

He put the truck into reverse. *I need to show my ragged face and give them whatever is left of me.*

But as he started to back away, another thought caused him to take one last look at the valley below. J.P. put his foot on the brake and held it there. He squinted into the distant sky that was now fading into shades of lavender and orange. *My God, what have I done? What if I just let the last prayer of a chance walk out of my life? What if she's the sustenance I need to take away the power of winning?* In his mind's eye, J.P. could still see Samira walking up the hill away from him.

He heard Chase sigh a heavy breath indicating a deep canine sleep. Very slowly J.P. understood the full implications of his decision not to go after Samira at Shoal Creek.

A single prayer formed on his lips. *Dear God, give me another chance.*

51 Making Contact

Samira

"What's the matter, Mama? You look confused." Kara passed by the dining room table.

Samira pushed her hair to the back of her head. "I am." She turned the page of the document she was trying to understand. "I think I need an interpreter to understand all this legal jargon." She was exasperated. *I've been through this paperwork about Tom's trust three times, and I still don't understand.* "I have to sign these papers before the end of the month, but I don't want to sign them if I'm not sure what I'm signing."

"Maybe you could call someone to help you."

Krissy looked up from her math homework. "Let's see, who might we know that's a lawyer?" She grinned. "Miss Davis knows someone. We could ask her to ask him."

Mike did say to call if I needed anything. "No. I'll figure it out. I just need to focus more."

"You could make an appointment with Papa Ray's lawyer if it's still confusing," Kara made another suggested.

Funny thing. He's the attorney that sent these papers. "Thanks for your concern, ladies, but I'll figure it out." She looked first at Kara and then at Krissy. *They don't believe me.* "Really, I will." With that Samira closed the document and stashed it back in the legal sized envelope. *Later, when I'm alone.*

Kara poured a glass of milk then pulled out a chair adjacent to her mother. "I have to turn this in tomorrow, and I don't know who to write on the line." Kara handed a single sheet of paper to her mother. "It's for Career Development class."

Annual Career Exploration Banquet.

Kara looked defeated. "I don't know who to invite. Everybody is taking someone with really exciting careers, and I don't have a clue who I should take."

"What's the assignment?"

"We're supposed to invite an adult with a career the we would like to learn about. There's this big banquet and all the adults are introduced and then we divide up into smaller groups and learn about people's careers that might interest us. Then the next day we are supposed to write a report on our favorite ones."

That doesn't sound so bad. "So, what careers interest you?"

Kara rolled her eyes. "That's not it, Mama. Don't you see? I don't have anyone to invite."

"Like, you mean, you don't have anyone you *want* to invite," Krissy interjected.

"No one with an exciting career." Kara crossed her arms. "Danielle is taking her father who's a medical technician. Kacey is taking her uncle who designs bridges. Jennifer's dad is in publishing and he's going."

"Is anyone taking a librarian?" Krissy was still working on her math.

"No. But everyone is taking their dad."

"I thought Kacey's uncle was going."

"He is, but he's a guy, isn't he?"

"Don't moms have careers too? Or aunts?"

"Not my friend's moms." Kara's impatience with her sister was showing.

Samira listened trying to understand more fully. *What is really bothering Kara?* "Uncle Wes and Papa Ray are in banking. I'm sure they would represent the career world from a male's perspective if you wanted."

"I don't want to take them. Banking is boring."

"What about Miss Davis's boyfriend? He's a—" Krissy tried again.

"I don't even know him."

Krissy shrugged her shoulders at her mother.

"What career would you like to represent that night, Kara?" Samira was searching for helpful insight.

"I don't know." Kara stood up and walked to the kitchen. "Something exciting and challenging and helpful."

"Like a nurse? Granny was an emergency room nurse. That's pretty exci—"

"No." Kara's voice was sharp. "That's a woman and all my friends are taking men."

Okay, she's not interested in a woman's career tonight. "Name a career that interests you then."

Kara dropped her eyes and lowered her voice. "Like someone in law enforcement."

She's thinking of her father.

"Cool." Krissy seemed to like that idea. "Just like Daddy."

Just like Tom. Samira clarified in her mind. *But she can't take him.* She watched her daughter's face fall. *I don't know if I can fill this void for her.*

"What about that guy from Granny's church that worked with Daddy? Do you remember him?" Krissy was determined to find a date for her sister now.

Samira knew exactly the man in Krissy's memory. *But David is NOT an option.* She couldn't stand the idea of even contacting him again. *Besides, his wife just had a baby.*

Kara sat down in one of the barstools at the kitchen island. "No, not him." Her eyes were still low.

Krissy shrugged her shoulders again and pushed her math notebook toward her mother. "Here. Done. Will you check these for me while I shower, please?"

I hope I can do the math enough to check them. So far this year she'd kept up with Krissy's assignments, but they were into new algebra, and it was getting more and more difficult with each assignment.

Krissy left her pencil on the table and headed for the hallway. "I'll let you know if I think of anyone else, Kara. Okay?"

I know what Kara's thinking, but I don't know how to help. "I'm sorry you can't take your father, Kara."

The young woman looked away. "Yeah. Me too." She took a deep breath. "It just seems like all my close friends have a dad to take. Kacey is taking her uncle, but she's not someone I hang around with much. Tia and Brittney at least have stepdads to take. I don't even have that."

"There's still a couple of weeks before the actual banquet," Samira pointed out. "What if I call the teacher and tell her we're working on this and will have an answer by the end of the week?"

"For one thing," Kara began to correct her mother. "The teacher is a guy. Mr. Wilson. And for another, I don't want anyone to know I don't have anyone to take."

You just don't have the one you want to take. "So how can I help?" *I had no idea Brian Wilson was teaching this class.*

Kara slid off the stool and started to walk away. "I don't know if you can, to be honest."

And I don't know if I can either.

Without another word Kara disappeared behind the door to her bedroom.

"Too bad Phil didn't stick around. He'd have been a great date," Krissy surprised her mother from behind. She was wrapped in a towel. "Forgot my sweats. They're in the washroom." She tiptoed across the hard floor to the laundry room and returned carrying a folded sweat suit in her arms. As she passed by the desk, she answered the ringing telephone.

Samira took her empty coffee cup and walked away from the table. *They've both talked about the lack of a father's presence in our lives lately.* Prior to her relationship with Phil, neither Kara nor Krissy had ever mentioned wanting a father-figure in their lives. *Obviously, they've gotten a glimpse of what things could be like with a dad around now too.*

Samira rinsed her cup in the kitchen sink. *But it isn't likely to happen.* Still, she felt awful about Kara's predicament. *Maybe one of Kara's teachers would go with her. Or maybe we could ask Pastor Bill.*

"Mama, the phone is for you." Krissy passed the cordless phone over the island.

Samira had been so lost in her thoughts she already forgotten that the phone had rung.

"And it's a man." Krissy punctuated with a loud whisper.

Samira frowned. "Hello?"

"Miss Cartwright? My name is Marty Brown. I'm on staff out at the university."

Marty Brown. Samira was sure he was calling to raise funding for the school. *Maybe he could go to the banquet.*

"I apologize for calling you at home, but under the circumstances we thought it might be more professional this way."

Yep, he's asking for money.

"We have been made aware of your work at the Maple Street Library and the more we hear, the more interested we are about talking to you concerning an opening we are anticipating at the end of this year."

He's not going to ask me for money?

"Before the university foundation launches a broader search for a program director, we wondered if you might be willing to meet with us?"

A moment of silence passed before Samira realized she was supposed to reply.

"Exactly what are you asking of me?" *I don't understand.*

Marty Brown cleared his throat. "We would like to interview you for the opening."

Samira laughed. "Me? But I have a job." *This is quite humorous.*

"That's why we thought it better to call you at home."

He's serious. She put her hand to her mouth. "Oh, my. This is quite interesting." Samira needed to think. *Did he say program director?* "Do you know I'm a librarian?"

"Yes, Ma'am. But we are impressed by what you've accomplished with the Maple Street branch." The voice paused. "We would appreciate your taking the time to visit with us in the near future."

They're impressed with my success at the auction, that's all. Samira tilted her head in thought. "How near are we talking into the future?"

"As soon as next week if you have the time."

No, Samira. You need to think about this before answering. You always think about these kinds of things before answering, remember? "Is there a way I can think about this and call you back with an answer?"

Mr. Brown sounded more serious when he spoke again. "It would be better if we could go ahead and set up a time to meet. There will be plenty of time for questions then."

Samira couldn't believe her ears. No one ever told her she couldn't think about something important before she answered. *They want to interview me for a job I'm not even seeking.*

"Miss Cartwright?"

"I guess that will be alright."

"This is very good," Marty Brown confirmed. "Shall we say Tuesday evening at seven o'clock? That would be one week from tonight."

Samira checked the activity calendar on the kitchen wall. "My daughter has a volleyball scrimmage until 7:30."

"Would eight o'clock be better?"

He's not going to back down, is he? "Eight o'clock is better. Where exactly should I meet you?"

"We'll be in the meeting room at the university library. Just tell them at the desk who you are, and someone will show you the way."

Samira listened as Marty Brown gave her a few more details about the possible position and then he reiterated the meeting time and place before ending the call.

"Who was that?" Kara asked as she returned to the kitchen.

Samira didn't know how to answer. *I certainly don't want anyone to know about this yet.* She flipped her hair over a shoulder. "It was someone from the university. They want to talk to me about the programs at the Maple Street Library." *Which isn't exactly untrue.*

"Sounds serious," Kara replied half-heartedly. She picked her library book up off the table and returned to her bedroom.

It is serious, I think. Samira leaned over the math book to check Krissy's problems, but her mind was still on the telephone conversation. The last time she'd been offered a job when she wasn't looking, she took it. *And I still have that job.*

~~~~~~~

Eight days later, Samira sat fidgeting in a folding chair next to her brother. *This is a huge meeting. A much larger crowd than I anticipated.* She turned her head to hear Councilman Goldstein restate his case concerning Shoal Creek.

"Development of that property could mean huge revenue for the surrounding area. The longer we delay this decision the longer before we will see any profit."

"Thank you, Councilman." The mayor interrupted Alan Goldstein politely.

Wes put his hand on Samira's knee. She stopped bouncing her heel against the floor.

"The fact is, we as a council do not have a right to make a decision on this property..." another councilmember began an explanation, but Samira's mind was wandering.

The university offer is so different from what I do now, yet it sounds intriguing. I wouldn't be in the library, but I could use the library resources to build a program for the foundation. She glanced at her brother wishing for his full attention to process the opportunity with him. *But I'm not even looking for a job. Remember? I have a good job. And I'm right in the middle of our new online project.*

"The city attorney has advised us to proceed with caution, Mr. Goldstein." The mayor spoke deliberately. Samira could feel the tension rise in the room. "There will be no more discussion over property outside the city limits. However, development plans for the same tract of land will be heard by the county commissioner at next week's public hearing."

Loud whispers permeated the overcrowded room. Samira leaned forward in her seat as the mayor dismissed the forum.

"Now that was a heated debate," Wes announced. "I don't see how Goldstein can push this through the county commission without public support."

I don't know either, but I only came here to talk to Wes about more personal matters.

"Weston."

Samira turned her head to see a suit-clad businessman reach to shake her brother's hand. Wes returned the greeting and engaged in politics while the crowd began to close in around Samira. *Now I'm going to have to wait even longer for his attention.*

She made her way to the room divider then turned and scanned the room. *Standing here I can see the whole room and keep an eye on my brother.* Samira's eyes stopped on Mike Benson. He was standing on the far side of the room obviously deep in discussion with a small group of people. *He's the last person I'd expect to find in this crowd.*

Although Samira tried to keep her eyes away from Mike, she couldn't help it. *Just a glance.* Her eyes passed over that side of the room again. But Mike had moved slightly to
~~~~~~~

one side and Samira looked directly into the face of J.P. Ralston. He was wearing a business suit and tie and his dark blue eyes were focused directly on her.

Oh, my goodness. Samira caught her breath, but she couldn't look away. If Phil had been engaged in conversation, he wasn't saying anything now. He was just standing there. His jaw was set deep in thought.

"Ms Cartwright." A man about her same height offered his hand. Samira looked into his face and recognized him.

"Mr. Brown." *I hope he's not expecting a response. I just interviewed with him last night.* Samira forced a smile and returned the handshake.

"You can call me Marty. This issue over Shoal Creek has created quite a stir among the community," Mr. Brown continued.

I wonder what business Phil has here.

"Are you in favor of Goldstein's proposal?"

Samira knew better than to speak her thoughts about a public proposal in a public arena. *Especially with someone who has the potential to become my employer.* "I am still drawing my conclusions."

"I see." Marty Brown studied her face carefully. "I trust you are still considering our position."

"I am." *Now maybe he'll let me be. Besides, I'm not ready to discuss anything about the interview until I talk with my brother.* Marty Brown was standing square in front of her view to the far side of the room. *And I will also talk to my parents, although I know Daddy will want me to spread my wings and take the job.*

Mr. Brown nodded politely. "Very well. I look forward to hearing from you then."

Good. He's gone.

Samira immediately looked back to the far wall, but there was no one there whatsoever. Wes was still talking in the same spot Samira had left him, but there was no sign of Mike Benson or Phil Ralston anywhere. *I know they were both there a minute ago.* Suddenly the room became very warm.

It looks like Wes is going to be awhile. Samira stepped into the corridor where it was cooler. Several clusters of concerned citizens were still discussing the impact of the Shoal Creek debate.

"Buenas tardes, Senorita."

It wasn't the voice she'd hoped for, but she stopped walking and turned around anyway.

"Do you speak to all the ladies in Spanish, Mr. Benson?" Samira found him looking quite smart and professional in a double-breasted, pinstriped suit. *No tie though. He seems to like these collarless shirts instead.*

"Only the really pretty ones." Mike puckered his bushy blonde mustache in a playful manner that made Samira forget he was wearing a suit. "I'm surprised to see you at such a heated political extravaganza."

"You just never know where I might appear."

"Obviously." Mike grinned. "We're representing some clients tonight, in case you're wondering."

"I wasn't," Samira lied. "But thank you just the same."

Mike opened his mouth to say something, but his eyes shifted to a spot just beyond her. His tone changed dramatically. "If you'll excuse me."

Samira turned to see where Mike's eyes had gone. Standing just a few short feet from her was J.P. Ralston. He had his phone to his ear, but his eyes were watching her. He seemed taller than she'd remembered. *Or is it the suit? Much more conservative than his friend.* Whatever it was, there was something different about him. *Now what do I do?*

Phil finished the call. Samira wondered where Wes was, but she was too close to Phil to turn away now.

"It's good to see you." Phil spoke into the space that separated them.

Samira smiled shyly. She couldn't help it. "And you."

"Are you coming, Boss? I'm picking up Sparky—" A woman wearing a black pantsuit and high heels was fast approaching the attorney from behind. Samira watched the woman slow to a stop. Her eyes went from the attorney to Samira and back again. "J.P." she tapped a long fingernail on the face of his watch. "Three minutes."

"I'll be there." J.P. acknowledged the woman's insistence with a silent gesture. Without another word she turned and started off in the direction from which she'd come.

"Busy night?" Samira decided it would be best to let him off the hook. *Maybe that's why Mike told me they were working, so I wouldn't be disappointed.*

Phil closed the space between them by taking a few short steps in her direction. "I didn't expect to see you here."

"Funny, that's what Mike said as well." *But I am disappointed he has to go, just the same.* Samira watched Phil run his hand through his hair.

"I'd like to say great minds think alike but that would be an understatement in Mike's case."

Samira inhaled deeply. *I've never been good at small talk.* She wanted to ask him how the boys were and if he was okay. *I want to know everything about him. But this isn't the time or the place.*

"I'm on my way out of town on business."

Phil was sounding more like an attorney than Samira wanted him to. "Don't let me keep you." *This is the attorney I need to help me with the legal papers on my desk.*

"We're headed to the airport now." Phil nodded, but it was obvious he was either still deep in thought or completely distracted by business matters. "It is really good to see you, Samira."

He spoke my name instead of calling me, Pretty Lady. "It's too bad you have to go."

J.P. looked beyond Samira into the distance of the corridor. "Maybe some time we..." His voice trailed off in an unfinished thought.

Samira could hear the woman in high heels coming toward them again. "Maybe we could." *She's intent on keeping him on schedule.* "I'm not hard to find." *If I'm still working at the Maple Street Library.* The click of the high heels on the polished floor was getting closer.

Phil held his hand out in acknowledgement of the time. His eyes were a darker shade of blue when he looked back at Samira.

"Then maybe I'll come find you."

"I would like that." *I hope he means that.*

Phil looked away. "I'm glad to know that, Samira."

When he looked into her eyes, she could see a thousand unspoken words. "Don't let me keep you." *He said my name again.*

Phil nodded. "I'm sorry," he hesitated a moment, then turned to go. "Until then?"

"Until then." Samira gave silent permission for Phil to be on his way.

The main part of city hall had cleared considerably. Samira watched the woman at the end of the hall wave her arm for Phil to hurry. He picked up his pace into a gentle jog and disappeared through the glass doors into the dark of the night.

I wonder where he's flying off to.

"Hey, Sis, sorry I took so long," Wes apologized as he came up behind Samira. His eyes followed hers to the double doors. "Are you ready to go? The girls are probably starting to wonder where you are."

Wes conversed freely about the debate all the way back to the house. Instead of asking for his opinion on the job at the university, Samira decided to engage with her brother concerning the debate against Councilman Goldstein.

After bumping into Phil, I don't know if I want Weston's opinion. Or even Daddy's for that matter.

If there was even a remote possibility that Phil Ralston might come find her, Samira didn't want to jeopardize his effort by taking another job. *Or maybe I'm just looking for an excuse to turn it down.*

Wes was still talking about the City Council Meeting, but Samira's thoughts were a million miles away. *Phil seemed different somehow. Like his defenses were down, unlike our last meeting at Shoal Creek.*

52 The Facts of the Matter

Joseph Phillip

J.P. ducked his head as he slid into Mike's Corvette. "Are we set to go?"

"As far as I know," Mike took off diagonally across the parking lot.

"What about Chase?"

"Kelly's checking on him."

"Are you sure?"

"Of course, I'm sure."

J.P. snapped his seatbelt into place. "I should have boarded him."

"Kelly doesn't mind. She'll let him out on her way to school in the morning and put him back in when she gets done at the gym at night." Mike patted his hands against the steering wheel while he waited at a red light. J.P. could see the taillights of Denise's car driving away on the other side of the intersection.

"Do we have the case documents?"

"Denise has them. Sparky wants to prep us as soon as we get in the air."

"What are your thoughts on Goldstein?" *The entire proposal seems preposterous if you ask me.*

Mike glanced in his rearview mirror. "I don't know yet. It's fishy but I can't put a finger on it."

"Everybody knows the county planning commission will shut him down cold, so I don't know why the mayor is letting it get blown out of proportion now."

"Our fine mayor is going to let the voices speak. He always does."

Always. J.P. thought this might have been one time the mayor should have shut down public opinion before it got out of hand.

Mike interrupted J.P.'s thoughts. "Well, how'd it go?"

J.P. looked sideways at his friend. *He's not talking about Goldstein anymore.* "How'd what go?"

"In there. With Samira."

"What's it to you?" *I don't like the way Mike can converse so easily with a woman whose name I can barely speak.*

J.P. could feel the sudden acceleration as Mike shifted into a higher gear. "Is it a crime to ask a personal question?"

No, it's not a crime, it's just that I didn't know what to say to her. "Ask away. You didn't have any trouble striking up a conversation with her."

"Hell, it didn't appear that you were going to open your mouth. I figured one of us should be polite and acknowledge her presence."

"Josh called about the football game this weekend. I was going to finish talking to him then talk to her." *If she was still there.*

"Could have fooled me." Mike sounded disgusted. "So, what did you say to her?"

J.P. watched the white line of the highway streak by the side of the car. "Not much you can say in three minutes or less."

Mike pulled the Corvette into the parking lot at the airport. Denise and Sparky were already walking across the parking lot toward the entrance. "You either say nothing or you say it all."

Great. J.P. opened the door. *Then chances are good I said absolutely nothing.* He heard the alarm set on the Corvette as he walked away. "I told her I'd look her up." *And I will.*

Mike caught up to J.P. on the sidewalk. "When?"

As soon as I get back. "Why? Are you going to ask her out if I don't?"

"Maybe not me, but if you don't, guaranteed, someone else will."

What's this maybe shit? J.P. knew that fact very well. *I know she's one of the hottest commodities on the market.* But there was business at hand, and he needed to clear his mind of everything that didn't pertain to the case. *That's the only way I know how to work.*

The attorneys met Denise at the top of the stairs of the chartered jet. She handed Mike a Tablet and gave J.P. a newly assembled folder.

Mike took note of J.P.'s notebook. "One of these days you need to accept the fact that documents are more accessible electronically."

"I prefer the hard copy so I can take notes." *I hate reviewing court docs on a screen.* J.P followed Mike into the cabin of the chartered jet.

"Face it, Mike, J.P. is never going to change." Denise pointed to Mike's tablet. "Vince will meet us at the airport. He wants these documents memorized by then."

Derek was already fastening his seat belt.

"Don't wait too long to look up the lady," Mike whispered as J.P. began to settle into a seat facing him.

I just need to get through this case. Then I'll be able to give her my full attention. He settled into his seat. *Or maybe I should call her in the morning at work.* He clamped the thick metal tongue of the seatbelt in place. *At least then she'd know I was serious. I have every intention of looking her up, but maybe I didn't communicate that very well.*

J.P. opened the file folder as the jet engines prepared for takeoff. He skimmed the updated reports from Vince Barringer. *But it was damn nice to see her tonight.* He could still see her in his mind's eye. *Damn nice in every way possible.*

Sparky wasted no time. Once the jet was at cruising altitude, the little investigator stood at the front of the aircraft and indicated for everyone to follow along.

"As you know, ve are at the heart of dis investeegation," Sparky informed with his hesitant, broken English. "Ve must be exactly prepared in de morning." He knitted his bushy, black eyebrows. "De Balteemore suspects have taken the plea. De evidence is weighted against dem." Sparky made eye contact with all four team members in the plane. "Dey know who is de culprit behind the Mid-America heist and it is time for dem to tell us."

"By now Vince should know who the mastermind is." Mike leaned his head into the airplane seat facing J.P. "Do you know who it is, Sparky?"

The little man raised his eyebrows. "I tink zo."

"Are you going to share that information with us?" *I hate playing Sparky's waiting game.*

"De suspects are vorking for the same person as Celia Monroe."

"Celia, the student banker at Mid-America?" Derek asked.

"Dat is de one," Sparky assured.

"Celia, othervise known as Melinda Lynn Jones," Sparky paused and allowed the newly revealed alias to hang in the air. "And I beleev J.P. knows who she is vorking vith because he bumped into her at a party."

J.P. frowned. *I went to a party with Celia Monroe?* He looked over at Mike.

"The dinner party," Denise realized out loud. She leaned across the aisle toward her boss. "You went to that dinner party with Jessica Hutchison. That must be where you saw her."

Sparky nodded his head once.

"I didn't go *with* Jessica Hutchinson."

"When did all this transpire?" Mike cast an accusing look in J.P.'s direction.

Give it up, Counselor. I didn't do anything with anybody.

Denise filled in the blanks. "That Friday night. Late dinner."

Mike focused harder. "That Friday night before the Sunday I picked you up?"

That would be the one.

"Jimmy said it was an unknown party."

"It was." *As far as I know.* J.P. still remembered very little about that night.

"She approached you as you vere leeving." Sparky tried to give a hint.

"As I was leaving where?"

"De party."

"What?" *Was he following me?* "How do you know that?"

"Ah."

J.P. unbuckled his seat belt and shifted uncomfortably. *Don't 'ah' me now, Sparky.* "My suspect vas under surveillance, but you appeared dere too."

Denise laughed out loud.

"Bag it, Denise," J.P. instructed.

"Told you he was good," Mike interjected. "As good at investigation as Vince is at interrogation." Mike pointed his finger at his friend. "Imagine that. Our investigator finds his own employer at the scene of a surveillance."

J.P. flipped Mike a choice finger. *What's up with Mike's sudden disgust with my personal life?* J.P. forced his mind to remember the dinner party. *That dinner party is what initiated this city-wide discussion concerning Shoal Creek.* His mind's eyes followed Celia Monroe up the stairs onto the wooden porch of the condominium office suite. *Now I remember, Celia passed through the door right past Alan Goldstein and Jessica Hutchison.*

"And who does Miss Hutchison vork for?" Sparky continued to lead J.P.'s memory.

"Sean Bridges."

"Beengo."

The plane bounced slightly in an air pocket.

Mike leaned forward in his seat. "Bingo what, Sparky? Jessica Hutchison works for Bridges. We know that. Does Celia Monroe, or whatever her other name is, work for him too?"

"Tomorrow ve vill know for sure. Tonight ve only speculate."

"We don't even know who the hell Sean Bridges is." *I've been trying to land a face-to-face meeting with that man since the onset of issues between Hughes and the city.*

Sparky raised one eyebrow. "But, ve know dat Bridges needed monies to make land purchases for his developments. And ve know dat Jessica Hutchison is pushing for more development, but I tink dat is just a red herring."

"You think Bridges is funding the Shoal Creek proposal?"

"No, I tink de Shoal Creek proposal is designed to turn your attention avay from de facts of the matter." Sparky was looking directly at J.P. "De more interest you show to the Shoal Creek development, de less dey tink you vill pay attention to de on-going investeegation for Mid-America."

J.P. closed his eyes. *So, the mastermind is right under my nose, watching my every move, hoping to lead me astray?*

"Dis one is very compleecated, J.P.," Sparky knitted his brow again. "I tell you everyting, but only when it is time."

"Do I know Sean Bridges, Sparky?" *I need to know who he is.*

Now even Denise was leaning in to hear the answer.

"I beleev you do."

Denise cocked her head to the side in thought. "We've never met him face to face. The only person we know who has seen him in the flesh is Jeffrey Hughes."

"When in God's name did Hughes meet him?" J.P. demanded.

"While you were out gallivanting somewhere off the shores of the eastern coast with another unknown party."

Enough accusations. "I was gallivanting with my Father."

"Holy shit, J.P." Mike looked shocked. "Why didn't you tell me?"

"Because it wasn't relevant." J.P. stood up. *I hate it when I'm accused of things I didn't do.*

"I figured you'd connected with Bobbie Jo Sommers." Denise informed. "She called looking for you that day."

Am I ever going to lose that woman? He rubbed his temple with his fingertips. *She's the biggest red herring I've ever encountered.*

"Sparky," J.P. addressed the investigator directly. "How do I know Sean Bridges?"

"You ate dinner with him at his own dinner party." Sparky leaned on the seat and crossed his hairy arms over his chest.

J.P. forced his mind back to the guest list. *The Armstrongs were there, that architect, Clark Roberts, Tom Jones in real estate.* So far, these guests didn't seem to have any direct relation to Sean Bridges. *Had I realized the impact that meeting had on this case, I'd have ended that night much differently.*

"Who is it?" J.P. continued to run the guests through his mind. *That marketing and sales guy who works with Hutchison. Hayes, Richard Hayes.* "Bridges wasn't there that night, Sparky. I wasn't introduced to him whatsoever."

"Dat's because you already know him."

There was only one other person there that night besides Hutchison. "Alan Goldstein."

"Two beengos." Sparky's eyes flashed like lightning. "And I tink he vants you fighting against Shoal Creek for the city's interests instead of vorking dis case."

Now Mike was standing too. "Are you sure, Sparky?"

Sparky had to look way up to see the faces of both attorneys. "Only speculation tonight, remember? Tomorrow ve learn for sure."

Denise spoke up again. "Then what's the scoop in California? What cover did you find out there?"

"Dat is vhere the holding company kept de funds. A real estate company is de umbrella to cover the holding company's assets. Ingenious, but quite simple."

"That makes perfect sense," Derek finally remarked from his seat. "Bridges only needed funding long enough to purchase the land out by the airport. When the land sold to the city, the money was returned in hopes that no one missed it."

That's pretty good coming from an intern.

"But it took longer to close on the property by the airport than Bridges thought it would. Mid-America discovered the missing funds in the meantime." Mike continued.

"Greed."

Everyone's eyes turned to Sparky for an explanation.

"De airport property vas a done deal until Bridges found a higher bidder."

The Hughes Corporation.

"Den he tried to make more dan vas coming to him. De delay created just enough time for Mid-America to run quarterly reports. Vhen dey deescovered de money vas gone, dey reported it." Sparky shook his head sadly. "Greed."

"And you really think Sean Bridges is one in the same as City Councilman, Alan Goldstein?" *He's been on city council a long time to be under an alias.*

Mike sat down in another seat. "I don't doubt it, J.P. Look at what Goldstein was doing tonight at the forum? He knows he's proposing something totally against public opinion. He's creating a stir big enough that the media and city government are going to be totally focused on Shoal Creek when the Mid-America case comes to a peak."

Hutchison invited me to the party to distract me from the Mid-America investigation. That was her hidden motive.

"Tomorrow ve vill know everyting," Sparky reminded. "But tonight, ve must try to rest."

Rest? With information like this banging around in my head? J.P. sat down again and tried to settle into his own thoughts. He couldn't even close his eyes without Samira's face appearing.

And God, she looked good. Not good like I need to have her, but better than that. Like I... J.P. closed his eyes to find the right word. *...like what?*

He opened his eyes and looked around the cabin. His closest comrades were all in the air with him. Derek's face was illuminated by the screen of his tablet. Everyone else in the small cabin was at least pretending to be asleep. Even Mike seemed extremely relaxed.

But Mike can go to sleep at the drop of a dime. These are the people who know me the best, put up with me, repeatedly save my ass, work my agenda, and yet the only face in my mind when I close my eyes is Samira's.

Alan Goldstein's involvement in the Mid-America case caught J.P.'s thoughts again. *This could turn out to be the biggest case in my entire career. I should be strategizing and preparing. Normally I would be.*

He closed his eyes again. Samira was still there. He wondered how she was getting along, and if Kara had decided to play volleyball. He wondered why Samira attended the Shoal Creek forum. *Mostly I wonder if she's missed me as much as I've missed her.*

Face it, Ralston. J.P. put his face in his hands. *You can't even have sex with anybody else now that you've had her. You tried and it didn't work. She's the only one you want.* J.P. turned in his seat. *But it's more than that. It's lots more than that.* J.P. stretched his legs. *Until I met her, I thought a woman was something to be won, but this woman is something to behold.* He pressed his head into the high-backed, leather seat.

There used to be this feeling of victory every time I mastered a new woman, especially if there was a little competition for her attention. I won Samira, but there wasn't any victory march. J.P. laid the folder aside. *It's like she's a part of me all the time now. I thought if I let her walk away that I'd be able to just pick up my life where I left off. But it's not working out that way.*

I'm really tired. He squeezed his eyes shut tight and tried to lose himself in the roar of the engines. *Ralston, tomorrow you're going to wake up, that is if you ever get to sleep, and lead this legal team into an opportunity that could turn into a whale of a case. You should be ecstatic.*

But he wasn't. The case was right within reach and J.P. Ralston knew exactly what he needed to do to blow it wide open. *With the suspects taking the plea bargain and testifying against the mastermind of this heist, I've got the world by the tail.* J.P. thought about the possibilities. *It's still going to take some doing, but with Vince and Mike onboard, we should be able to nail them without a shadow of doubt.*

J.P.'s thoughts shifted again. *But she's right there too.* He pictured Samira's contemplative face. *It's like I don't live alone anymore—like she's one of my missing pieces. I know this case. I know the potential impact it has on my future.* The prospects were extremely enticing. *But what about the potential with Samira? What bearing does she have on my future?*

J.P. rubbed his weary face in his hands. *I knew something was different about her that first night. What I didn't know then was how she was still going to be affecting me now. She was so fragile that night. Always is. It wasn't like I was having sex with someone new. I know that feeling. It was more like the night moved with us somehow...like I'd known her my whole life.*

J.P. wished he weren't trapped in an airplane. *I thought if I ever found the perfect match there'd be a flash of light or something to alert all the senses to move in that direction.* J.P. remembered her fresh scent. *And it's not like I have to out draw someone who's shooting for her too.* His eyes studied Mike's sleeping face. *Unless Mike knows something I don't.*

Derek turned off the reading light above his seat creating a new degree of darkness in the cabin. *But it wasn't like that at all.*

The drone of the small jet consumed J.P. for a while. In his mind he was with Samira at the waterfront again—*Or was she with me?* Her dark eyes and subtle smile brought a sense of deep contentment he'd never known with a woman. *It's more than simply being together —not just standing there together, but immersed in one another's...what? What is it?*

"A soulmate."

The thought came out of nowhere. J.P. lunged forward in his seat. *Who said that?* He looked around but no one was sitting near him.

The walls of the plane seemed to be closing in. J.P. stepped into the space that separated him from the other seats. There was no escaping the thoughts of Samira. *Or is it her thoughts in my mind?* She felt just as close to him now as she had been when he kissed her at the edge of the lake. *Or did she kiss me?*

There was nowhere for J.P. to go. He walked to the back of the short jet and took a seat against the bathroom wall. His mother's letters to the Captain were fresh in his mind again. *She was all he ever needed because she prayed him through. That's what she kept saying in her letters.* At first that thought felt foreign. But the more J.P. pondered the notion, the more it made sense.

If there is a God above, then He's the only one that could have kept them connected over the miles and through the years. He considered the hardships his parents must have faced during those times. *Only something that big could have connected them like that.*

J.P. closed his eyes again and tried without success to relax with the hum of the engines. "*Samira is praying you through.*"

Once again J.P. was on his feet. Again, no one was there, but the words were so clear in his mind he was sure someone in the plane had spoken to them. J.P. checked every passenger. They were all asleep. He sat back down in the same seat.

Maybe she is. Maybe that's why she feels close enough to be right here with me right now. Somehow that thought was very comforting. J.P. inhaled deeply and closed his eyes. *I would like that—if she were right here with me.*

~~~~~~~

J.P. awoke as the small plane bounced onto the runway in Baltimore. Vince would pick them up and take them immediately into preliminary meetings. The deposition was scheduled for nine o'clock and there was still much preparation to do.

The new case facts swirled in J.P.'s mind as he descended the steps of the small aircraft. He breathed in the smell of jet fuel and hot rubber as he pulled his suit jacket over his shoulders.

"This is the big day, Counselor," Mike slapped his colleague on the shoulder, obviously refreshed and ready for the day ahead. "If all goes well, we should leave here ready for pretrial hearing and thus launch the beginning of the end to a very powerful case."

How does he wake up all chipper and clear minded? J.P. was still groggy from the abbreviated night. He could see Vince waiting in a black Escalade along the fence of the private runway.

I know this case inside and out. The new evidence felt solid, and J.P. felt confident they could advance at a very rapid pace. Despite the familiar pump of adrenalin in his veins, he couldn't feel the underlying drive that always came with new energy in a big case.

The fact of the matter is, Counselor, Vince opened the door to the waiting vehicle. *The facts of the case don't matter as much as the matter of fact back home.* Samira's smiling face appeared in his mind as J.P. slid across the bench seat so Sparky could sit next to him.

And she's a very comforting matter of fact.
~~~~~~~

53 *Wearing Hats*

Samira

The book club ladies were mingling in her living room. Samira took silent attendance. *Everyone's here tonight.* She surveyed the women she'd shared books with for over a decade. *We represent four generations of female perspectives.* Pam was one of the youngest in the group.

Mrs. Haddock clapped her hands together. "Gather around, ladies. Let's get started."

Samira had her furniture arranged around the fireplace. The women were all finding a place to sit.

"I started another pot of coffee." Pam sat down in the chair next to Samira. "It will be ready shortly."

What would I do without Pam?

Mrs. Haddock began the discussion with a short review from the New York Times.

Helen always does such a great job when she leads. Samira listened as the women began to talk about the novel. *Their faces are familiar, and their thoughts are intriguing, but aside from that, we don't really know one another very well.* Samira half-listened to their comments.

One of the women turned to Samira. "What are your thoughts? Did you enjoy the story?"

I've never held my opinions from this group. "Personally?" The ladies turned their attention to Samira. "No. I have to say I didn't enjoy it very much. I found myself skipping here and there over parts that didn't hold my attention." *But that might have been my unsettled spirit more than the book itself.*

"That's exactly how I felt," someone chimed in. "It just didn't grab me like most best sellers."

The phone rang in the middle of the discussion. *The girls will get it.* It only rang once. *I knew they'd pick up.* Samira tried to turn her attention back to conversation. *How is it every time the phone rings now I wonder if it's going to be Phil looking me up.* She listened to Pam make a point. *I thought I was over waiting for the phone to ring.*

Usually, Samira was more involved in the conversation, but not tonight. Her mind jumped from work to Krissy's schoolwork to the job offer from the university. Nothing held her attention very long, except for her chance meeting with Phil.

He was so serious that night. She took a sip of her coffee. *And he was still very intense.* She replayed their brief conversation in her mind again. *I should be terrified of a man like that.* Samira smiled. *But I'm not.* She frowned. *At least I don't think I am.*

The corporate conversation was beginning to divide into smaller groups.

I'm not afraid of Phil, but J.P. Ralston might be another story. I get irritated with J.P., but I am not intimidated. She placed her cup on the coffee table and sighed. *I hate to get my hopes up though.*

"Do you think she ever really understood the motive behind his denial?"

Samira looked around. *Are they talking to me?* "Whose denial?"

"Jonathan's." Pam grinned. "Francine's lover."

"Oh." Samira remembered the topic at hand. "Oh him. No. Francine was too worried about her own motives. She didn't have the capacity to figure Jonathan out."

One of the ladies sitting across from Samira shook her head. "We were wondering if the author had a clue, not Francine. But I agree with you, Samira. Francine was totally self-absorbed from the very beginning."

Oh.

"Don't you think that's one of the reasons the book didn't hold our attention?"

Maybe it's time to warm their coffee. When Samira headed for the kitchen, Pam followed.

"I can't believe I answered like that."

"Me neither." Pam bumped her sister-in-law with her hip.

"I don't know where my mind is tonight." *Well, yes, I do.* "Not only did the book not hold my attention, but the conversation isn't either."

Pam chuckled. "Let's play hostess. Maybe they'll burn themselves out of chit-chat and go home early."

Samira jumped when the phone rang again. Krissy came flying up the stairs into the kitchen with the portable phone. Samira lifted the coffee pot above her head to avoid a collision. Krissy all but ran through the dining room then slid in her sock feet into the hallway.

"Must be an important call."

Must be.

Krissy tip-toed back into the dining room, this time without the telephone. Her cheeks were a bright red.

Very curious behavior. But when have I ever known Krissy to act normal in front of an audience?

~~~~~~~

"It didn't turn out too bad," Pam spoke as she helped Samira clean up. "I was expecting the discussion to end on a negative note, but Mrs. Haddock did a good job bringing it back around."

Samira lined up the cups up in the dishwasher. "That's Helen's gift. She knows how to bring people together."

"She brought almost everyone together at the end," Pam rinsed the dishrag under a running faucet. "Everybody except for our hostess."

Me? "Why do you say that?" Samira poured the remaining coffee into her own cup.

"I don't know," Pam grinned. "Maybe the way your thoughts seemed to be a million miles away tonight—like you were thinking of someone."

"Is it that obvious?"

"Not to anyone else in the room. But I'd venture to say I know you better than most of these women."

Transparency. "That you do." *Helen probably noticed too.*

"Sometimes it's nice to be with a group of women who don't know you very well yet appreciate you for who you are." Pam ran the dishrag over the countertop. "But you are always who you are. You don't wear masks Samira. And tonight, I know you were nowhere near this room for the better part of the evening."

She read me like a book. "Maybe not."

"Definitely not."

"What's his name?"

"I don't know, Pam."

"You don't know his name?"

"No, I know his name, but I don't know if I want to talk about him."

"Do we know him?"

"No."
~~~~~~~

"Have you known him long?"

"Awhile now."

"Has he asked you out yet?"

"Not in a while."

Pam paused. "So, you've been out with him already?"

And a lot more than that with him.

"Obviously, you'd like to go out with him again. Has he asked you again?"

I don't want to lead her astray. "No." Samira sighed. "It's the same guy I was seeing in the summer. I bumped into him last night for the first time in a while."

Suddenly Pam looked concerned. "He didn't restore any hope, did he?" She recovered the accusing remark quickly. "I don't know all the facts, but Wes told me that things didn't end up like they...well, like they should have."

Samira leaned against the counter. "I don't know what I hoped for before."

"Yes, you do." Pam answered immediately. "You hoped for the opportunity to complete your family again."

Is that it? Samira hadn't thought of it quite that simply. *Am I simply hoping for a man to complete my family again?* "Maybe I hoped for someone to take care of me again."

"Oh, Samira. There's nothing wrong with that." Pam put her hand on Samira's shoulder. "In fact, I'd say it's rather healthy to wish for someone who reciprocates your love. Someone who cares for you like you care for him. Don't you think?"

"Maybe." *But what I hoped for and what happened were two different things.* "It just caught me off guard to bump into him like I did."

"But that's all it was, right?"

"Right." *Pam is still worried about me.* "We just talked for a couple of minutes then he had to go."

"It's probably better that way."

Krissy poked her head around the corner. "Is the coast clear?"

"Except for me, everyone is gone." Pam cocked her head. "What's up?"

"Oh, nothing." Krissy disappeared again.

"Something is definitely up." Pam sat down on a stool next to Samira on at the island. "Your mom is having Mark's birthday dinner Friday night. Did she call you?"

"Yes. She left a message late last week."

"And you'll be there, right?"

It's not like my calendar is bulging with other commitments. "Of course, we'll be there."

Krissy hurried through the kitchen going the other way.

What is she doing with my laptop?

Pam watched with curiosity. "They're up to something."

"They'll be back." *One of them won't be able to keep a secret for very long.* In fact, Krissy returned almost immediately with Kara close on her heels.

"Mama, we need you to come over here." Krissy gently tugged on her mother's arm. "There is someone that wants to talk to you."

"Did the phone ring?" *I didn't hear the phone ring.*

"Not just now," Kara answered from the computer. "But earlier it did."

What are they up to?

"Give me just a minute," Kara typed on the keyboard a minute and then clicked on the mouse a few times. "Okay. I think I have it ready."

"Have you ever done messenger?" Krissy asked.

By this time Pam had joined them at the computer desk.

"No."

"It's really easy," Kara began to explain. "You just type like you're talking to someone. Then you hit Enter and the message sends right to the other person so they can type right back." Kara stood up and indicated for her mother to sit down in the steno chair.

"Who called earlier?" Pam asked casually.

Krissy couldn't hold it in anymore. "James."

"James who?" Samira asked quickly.

"James. You know, Phil's James." Kara clarified.

James Ralston?

"He called to see if you were on Facebook. I told him I could set you up on my account after the women were gone." Kara leaned over the computer keyboard and clicked the mouse. "So here. You can use my messenger."

They put me on Kara's Facebook?

Pam was humored. "And who might James be?"

"Mom's old boyfriend's son." Krissy shrugged her shoulders.

"Well, he's not that old," Kara corrected. "But he's the son of the man Mama dated for a while." Kara wrinkled her face at her mother. "Is it okay to explain him like that?"

I guess. The computer played a faint tone and a screen popped up.

Hey, pretty lady.

"Oh, my gosh, he's online." Krissy squealed.

"James?" Pam asked.

"No. Phil. James called to get Mom on Facebook so his dad could talk to her. And he actually did it." Krissy was excited.

Samira's heart was pounding hard in her chest.

"Are you going to say something back?" Kara sounded concerned.

"I don't know what to do."

"Type, for heaven's sake. Say anything." Krissy was getting frantic. "If you don't answer he'll think you're not on."

Not on what?

"Just say anything," Kara encouraged with more patience than Krissy.

Hey back.

Samira's fingers were shaking. Krissy reached over and pushed the Enter key.

Are you busy?

Not at the moment. Samira remembered to press enter this time.

Can you talk?

Can I type or can I talk? Samira glanced at her over-interested audience.

"Girls." Pam sprang into sudden action. "Let's put the furniture back where it goes and get this day wrapped up so I can go home."

Thank goodness. For a few minutes. Samira typed back.

I've been doing a lot of thinking about that question you asked me.

Exactly what question is he referring to? Refresh my memory.

The one about needing to know if I loved you.

Oh my.

Another line of dialog popped up before she could respond. I'd like to revisit that question when I get back if you have the time.

Obviously, he's not home yet. Where are you now?

I'm at the ranch with the boys. No phone connection tonight, but James got me on the Internet. I'll be back tomorrow.

Samira reviewed the next day in her mind. I'll be home tomorrow after work.

I'm not free until Friday and then it's complicated. Are you free Friday night?

Except for the family birthday party. I could be.

If you are, I'd like to take you to the boys' football game.

Football? I was hoping for something more intimate. I don't know anything about football. *Why isn't he saying anything? Oh. Press Send.*

Football is secondary. I was thinking the drive up to the game might be a good time to talk.

Okay. *Talking is a good idea.*

I'll call you when I'm out of my last meeting.

Okay. Is there anything I need to know about football games before I go?

Dress warm, it's supposed to be cold.

It's not exactly what I expected for an answer, but okay.

"What's he saying?" Krissy asked as she and Pam pushed the easy chair back into its normal position.

Samira answered without thinking. "He invited me to a football game."

"Cool. Very cool." Krissy sounded excited. "Are you going to go?"

Oh, wait. I don't want Krissy involved in this conversation. "Hold on, Krissy, let me finish this."

"But you don't even like football." Kara chimed in.

Just let me concentrate. Samira waved her hand for her girls to be still. I'll dress warm.

I'll call you as soon as I'm free. Late in the afternoon probably.

Another chat bubble appeared on the screen, a message to Kara from somebody named "Sweet Anthony."

"Kara, come take care of this. Someone else is trying to talk to you."

Kara appeared at her mother's side instantly. When she saw the name, she quickly closed the window. She shrugged her shoulders. "I don't know why he always pops in on me like that."

It's a boy, obviously. "Can you talk to more than one person at a time?"

"Oh yeah." Kara was nodding her head. "But go ahead and finish up."

Suddenly Samira felt vulnerable. *Messenger does not feel very private.* She had to reread Phil's last comment again before replying.

I'll be home.

Nothing happened. *Oh, press enter. Again.*

Sounds good. Sleep tight, Pretty Lady.

I doubt I'll be able to sleep at all now. You do the same.

It's hard to sleep with you in my mind all night long.

Funny, he has the same effect on me. I'll talk to you Friday then.

Friday.

"When's the game?" Krissy passed by the computer.

"Friday."

"Friday?" Kara interrupted. "That's when we're going to Granny's for supper. Remember?"

Samira turned all the way around in her chair. *I know.*

"If I were your mother and had a chance to spend the evening doing something new and entertaining, I think I would have to choose the evening out." Pam winked at Samira.

"But it's Mark's birthday." Krissy added with a hint of drama. "Don't you think she should go eat cake and sing the song for her nephew?"

Pam looked knowingly at her sister-in-law. "I think your mother needs to follow her heart."

Samira appreciated Pam's permission to miss the family gathering. *I just hope my folks and Wes feel the same way.* She turned the chair around to face the computer again. In light gray type along the bottom of the message screen it read: James Ralston is offline.

Samira brushed her fingers over the keyboard wishing he weren't so far away. *But at least he looked me up.* She smiled at the computer screen. *And he called me Pretty Lady again.*

Pam finished tidying up and headed toward the coat closet. "If I were you, I'd go to the game Friday night."

"Thank you for understanding," Samira spoke candidly. "He just wants to talk and I'm ready for that too."

Pam patted her sister in law's arm. "Why don't you let me get the girls after school and keep them for the night. Then you won't have to worry about what time you get home."

"You want my girls on Mark's birthday?"

"Think about it, Samira. Having the girls around might actually give Wes and me some desperately needed time alone." Pam winked. "This is the same guy that arrived on your doorstep in a partial tuxedo, right?"

Samira smiled. "That's the one."

Pam opened the door. "I'd be willing to go just about anywhere with him." She paused with another thought. "But go slow, okay? I don't want you to get hurt again."

"Me neither." Samira spoke honestly. "I think we need to talk some things through first and see where we end up."

Krissy was hot on her mother's trail as soon as Pam was out of sight. "Does this mean you're dating Phil again, Mama?"

"No." *I don't want to get their hopes up again. Or mine for that matter.* "We're going to watch Josh and James play football and talk. We're definitely not dating." She tried to sound and appear calm and in control. *Even though my heart is pounding in my chest.*

"Well," Krissy flopped over the back of the sofa and landed out of sight on the cushions. "If you hurry up and go steady with him again, Kara could take Phil to that banquet party. I think a lawyer would make an interesting career guest."

I forgot all about Kara's dilemma over that. "Have you thought any more about who you want to invite, Kara?"

"Yes." Kara looked directly at her mother. "I've decided I want to take you."

Krissy popped up over the back of the couch.

"But I thought all your friends were taking their dads."

"They are. But you're like a mom and a dad to me. And I've decided I'm okay with that."

Oh, Kara, I've waited a long time to hear those words. Samira walked across the room and pushed Kara's silky hair back from her face. "And I would be honored to be your guest at the banquet."

Kara smiled and leaned her cheek into her mother's hand.

"Even if I am a boring librarian." *Unless I have a new job by then.*

"You are a lot of things, Mama," Kara stated. "But you are NOT boring." She sat up straight in the barstool. "You'll probably give the best career talk of the whole night."

Krissy shook her head as she left the room. "You guys are too mushy for me."

"Did Krissy tell you who the other phone call was from?" Kara was whispering.

Samira whispered back. "No. Who?"

"Ben Applegate." Kara raised her eyebrows. A boy actually called Krissy."

That is amazing. Too bad Pam's not here to tease Krissy about that now.

Krissy returned. "What?"

"Oh, nothing." Kara smiled at her mother. "I'm really glad you want to go with me to the career banquet."

"And I'm glad you decided to invite me."

"We'll be a great team."

~~~~~~~

Samira was left to her own thoughts as she prepared for bed. *There's the decision about the university job offer.* She'd hoped to discuss it with Wes and her parents at dinner Friday night. *But now that's not going to be a possibility.* She changed into a long nightgown and returned to the kitchen to turn down the lights for the night. *I don't know why I want to talk to them about the university, really. They'll want me to take it, and I don't think that's what I*
~~~~~~~

really want to do.

Samira passed by the computer and realized she was nervous about being with Phil again. *Maybe more excited than nervous.* Samira clicked the mouse to shut down the computer. *No, definitely nervous. It's like having a first date all over again.*

I'm glad I got to talk with him. Samira turned off the living room light. *But the best part of my day is having Kara invite me to her career banquet.*

I like being the Pretty Lady almost as much as like being both a mother and a father to my girls. She glanced at her face in the mirror as she passed through her bedroom. *It's kind of fun to wear all these hats and still feel like me.*

54 Coming Clean

Joseph Phillip

Tension was high in the conference room at Benson and Barringer's Law firm. J.P. sat at the foot of the table directly opposite a federal agent.

Who would have known Mid-American's scandal was going to intersect with an FBI investigation?

"Gentleman," the agent cleared his throat. "And lady." He paused again. "I must say I am impressed with the amount of research you have compiled regarding the business of Sean Bridges, but I am here to tell you this is an overly complex case. I've been on his trail for over six years now and I still don't have enough hard evidence to prove his guilt."

"But you do agree that Sean Bridges is definitely Alan Goldstein." *He only shares enough information to keep us out of his way.*

The agent's eyes were steel blue when he answered. "Yes, this time. He has many aliases. And many accomplices."

I need to understand further. "But so far none who were willing to testify against him, correct?"

"Pardon my doubt, Mr. Ralston, but it is going to take more than two witnesses to put Sean Bridges, currently a.k.a. Alan Goldstein, behind bars for any length of time. He has a monopoly of underground banking scams, including laundering in this particular case."

"How many witnesses will it take?" Mike spoke up.

"More than two." The agent began to close his briefcase.

Mike didn't back down. "Define more. Are you talking six? Twelve? Twenty-four?"

"Mr. Benson, I know what you're thinking because I've studied his puppets personally. He pays them extremely well and hides them even better when he's done with them. The best we can do right now is keep a close eye on your local suspects." The agent snapped the latches. "And it is extremely important that your knowledge of this case be kept entirely confidential. One slip and we both lose him."

"Excuse my ignorance, Agent Roderick," Vince leaned forward in his chair. "But based on the evidence we can provide, it would seem the court could at least detain him while you finished the job."

"I have boxes full of evidence that could have detained the man." Agent Roderick rose from his chair. "Our goal is to put him away. Not detain him."

"Then our goal is the same," Vince pointed out. "What more would you need from us in order to file federal charges?"

Agent Roderick didn't back away. "I need affidavits stating direct involvement in this given case. In addition, I need hard evidence, be it computer files, banking files, signatures, video surveillance, anything that links Goldstein, aka Bridges, back to the current case."

Vince was nodding in understanding. "The current case being the scam within the Mid-America accounts."

"As you know, the events of the Shoal Creek proposal are also linked somehow. We are watching him with extreme caution." Agent Roderick's eye passed over the attorneys.

Vince was thoughtful. "Would you agree that Goldstein's biggest obstacle concerning Shoal Creek is raising funding?"

"It's not as simple as you're thinking, Mr. Barringer. Like I said, I have boxes of evidence, but attaining it in a timely fashion is the missing link to date. By the time we've been able to gather enough information to press charges, he manages to wrap up the loose ends and move on to another job under a new name."

He's already moved on to a new job. Shoal Creek. But this time he's moved on within the same community.

"But you said earlier he always appears to start a new job to distract the officials before the original scam is completed, right?" Mike was thinking out loud.

"That has been his pattern to date."

"And we believe he is hoping to distract us from the original scam right now, which would lead us to believe with even more confidence that his work with Mid-America is almost complete."

"I don't disagree, Mr. Benson." Agent Roderick was still standing. "But to hold his interest with the Shoal Creek proposal, he's going to need considerable revenue. My prediction, based on history, is that once the final transactions are complete at Mid-America, any possibilities with Shoal Creek will dissipate immediately."

What about this? "From what you described to us concerning previous scams, Bridges never followed through with the red herring. In other words, the distraction served its purpose and then he walked away, correct?"

"That is correct." Agent Roderick seemed uninterested.

But agent Roderick doesn't know Bridges' tendencies as well as Sparky does. "What if the funding became available for Shoal Creek? Do you think he would attempt to keep the Shoal Creek proposal alive?"

"What would be his motive?" The agent frowned. "He's already profited on job A. Why jeopardize his identity further by trying to force another lump sum within the same infrastructure?"

Nope. Roderick does not know Bridges. "For the sake of speculation, let's say he did secure funding to develop Shoal Creek. With that said, do you think it's possible to catch him in the act of laundering?" *Let's see where he goes with this.*

"In the act?" The agent looked doubtful.

"For example, what if we made it possible to catch him in the act of a direct transaction?"

Now the agent frowned. "You humor me, Counselor. His work is invisible. It happens in cyberspace."

Some of it happens in cyberspace. The rest happens through his trusty accomplices.

"Again, why would he jeopardize his identity by putting his undercover operation at risk again so soon?"

Greed. Sparky said it. "For the sake of speculation."

"I would encourage you to call me if you run across something that sure."

At least he left the door open.

The meeting broke up quickly with that last remark.

The FBI's been monitoring Sean Bridges' involvement at Mid-America for almost eight months now. J.P. watched Agent Roderick shake hands with Vince. *I'd place my vote of confidence in Sparky's investigation over the FBI any day.*

Denise followed J.P. out of the conference room and down the hall. "I'll have these notes ready in the morning."

"I'll be in late since I'm going up to the boys' game tonight." J.P. turned around to make eye contact. "So, don't stay up all night getting them ready."

"Thanks, but I'd rather type them while they're fresh in my mind." Denise stopped in Mike's office long enough to pick up her coat. "Didn't you just get back from up north?"

"Yeah. Last night. Went up to the ranch and met the boys for Josh's birthday."

"Good God, J.P. You were only home from Baltimore for two days." Denise let J.P. hold her coat as she slipped her arms through. "How soon are you leaving? Should I pick up a sandwich for the road."

It is getting late. J.P. checked his watch. "Within the hour." *And I need to make a phone call along that line as well.* "I'll get something on my way out of town but thanks for the offer." "What time tomorrow, J.P.?" Vince was removing his necktie, apparently headed out for the day. His assistant was close on his heels.

"Let's make it one o'clock."

"One o'clock, Betty." Vince nodded his head. "Alright. I'm going to pick my kids up here in a few minutes, but I think you might be on to something, J.P. Let's hash it out tomorrow and get it on paper."

Mike was sitting on the corner of his desk. "I think you're on to something." Mike mimicked his partner. "Do you really think Sparky can set the trap?"

"If anyone can, Sparky is the man."

"Wouldn't that piss off the FBI if a former KGB agent produced proof for their case?" Mike laughed. "I think it's worth a shot." He spun off the desk and landed in his leather executive's chair. "So, you're still headed up north again?"

J.P. nodded in the affirmative. "I'd rather stay here and work on the case." *But the company is too good to turn down.*

"The case will be here tomorrow."

"Yeah."

"Mike," a petite assistant knocked on the open door. "Kelly is on the line. Can you still meet her at 5:00?"

Mike gave two thumbs up.

"Dinner?"

"Racket ball."

J.P. shook his head. "Then dinner?"

"Only if she's buying."

There's no way I'd let a woman pay my way.

"Excuse me again," the assistant interrupted. "If you have a minute, she wants to talk to you. Line four."

Mike exploded into the phone. "Of course, I have a minute."

J.P. turned away to give Mike a moment of privacy. *Not that Mike knows that much about privacy.* His eyes passed over a statue on the bookshelves. *I've never noticed that before.* He walked closer. *A nude woman, reading a book.* J.P. took the liberty to move it a quarter of a turn. *Look at that.* He studied the bronzed piece further. *Her hair is in a knot like—*

"What do you think?" Mike appeared at J.P.'s side.

J.P. didn't take his eyes off the statue. "Is it new?"

"Brand new. And it's an original too."

Mike has always had an eye for art, but I've never known him to be interested in sculpture.

"Do you recognize anything?"

"Where'd you get it?"

"At an art auction."

"Where?"

"At city hall."

"Who did it?"

"Who did it or who is it?"

It looks like Samira. J.P. stared at his friend. "Why do you have it?'

"Because I knew you wouldn't want anyone else to have it."

"What the hell is that supposed to mean?"

"Think about it, good buddy. Your woman sitting on anyone else's shelf just didn't seem right."

Then it is Samira. J.P. looked at her again. "How'd you get it?"

"I outbid the artist himself."

I don't understand. "What artist?"

"The one who formed this body." Mike gently ran his hand over the statue. "He wanted it bad, man."

The statue or her? "What'd it run you?" *Wait. I knew that artist was on the make with Samira the day I saw him on the library steps.*

Mike laughed his hearty laugh and walked away. "You don't want to know."

"Yes, I do." J.P. left the statue and followed Mike across the office.

"No, trust me on this one."

"Come on, Mike. I'll write you a check."

Mike put his hands out and stopped J.P.

"Here's the deal." He crossed his arms. "You figure out what you need to do to win Samira back, and I'll let you have it for free."

J.P. didn't like being blackmailed. *And I don't like being denied something I want either.* "You can't do that."

"Ah. But I can." Mike wasn't backing down. "That's the deal. Take it or leave it. Just be thankful she's on my shelf instead of entertaining Fabiano Uberti."

"Fabiano Uberti is –"

"Spare me the explicates, Counselor. Win her back and the lady in bronze is all yours."

J.P. ran his hand through his hair. *Mike's going to win this one.*

"And I tell you what, I won't even hold this favor for payback."

He's serious. "You really think I did her wrong, don't you?" *I don't know if I want to hear his answer.*

"I think you forced your trump card assuming she'd tag along for the ride."

"But you're the one who said she was out of my league."

"She is. Or at least she was." Mike puckered his moustache in thought. "But you've demonstrated progress in your character here lately." Without hesitation Mike pushed a button on his cell phone and handed it to J.P. "She's probably home."

"Why the hell is her number in your phone?"

"Because, good buddy, someone has to look out for her when her man isn't paying any attention."

Point well taken. The phone rang in J.P.'s ear. *Mikey doesn't know I've already made contact.* J.P. had the upper hand now.

"Samira, it's Phil." J.P. watched Mike listen with interest. "I told you I'd call" *Mike is doubtful, I can tell.* "I should be there to pick you up in about," he checked his watch. "In about 45 minutes."

After she hung up, J.P. handed the phone back to Mike.

"You're taking her to a football game?"

"You're playing racket ball."

Mike shrugged his shoulders under his long blonde curls. "Okay. I give. Get the wrinkles ironed out and she can grace your shelf."

"Does she know you have it?"

"Highly unlikely."

"Who did your bidding?"

"Some thugs I met in the parking lot."

"You're full of shit."

"Yeah, I am." Mike smiled. "Clint Barr was with me. He works here. I had him do the dirty work."

J.P. only needed one more answer. "What was your cap?"

"I told Clint to come home with the prize."

"How much, Mikey?" *I really want to know what he paid.*

"More than Uberti was willing to pay."

"How much?"

"More than you keep in your checking account."

"How much?"

"Five grand."

"Holy shit, Counselor."

"She's worth it, isn't she?"

"Five grand?"

"But it's an original Uberti."

That's its only drawback. J.P. admired the work again. "Now I do owe you."

"No, you owe *her*." Mike folded his arms as he sat down in his chair. "And if you don't get your ass out of my office, you're going to make us both late."

~~~~~~~

Despite the chill in the air, J.P.'s hands were sweating when he rang Samira's doorbell. *It feels like our first date, or something.* His heart skipped a beat when the doorknob turned.

"Come on in," Samira covered the mouthpiece on the telephone as she answered the door. "I'll just be a minute."

J.P. stepped inside. *I didn't know if I'd ever be back here.* Samira motioned for him to follow her.

"Okay, Daddy, I'll call you in the morning when I get up." She crossed the kitchen and removed the lid on a crock pot. He started to decline the offer. *But I am hungry, and it does smell good.*

"Chicken and dumplings." She handed him a ladle. "Go ahead."

J.P. helped himself. Before he reached the crockpot, Samira had a glass of ice water ready.

"No, I don't have a number where I can be reached." Samira was still talking into the phone. "But I won't be gone all night."

J.P. reached for his cell phone. *She can give him this one.* He pushed a button to display his own number.

"Oh, wait," Samira corrected. "Here's a number you can call if you need anything."

J.P. took a bite as Samira read his number off.

"I know, I am too. Yes, I talked with Wes...I will...You have fun tonight too..."

Makes me a little uncomfortable she has to explain herself to her father. He must not be pleased she's leaving town.

"Sorry," Samira apologized as she hung up the phone. "I'm missing a family birthday dinner tonight for the first time ever." She put both of her hands in her hair. "My father is having a hard time with it."

That puts me in the middle of another family discrepancy. "Excellent dumplings, by the way."

"Thanks." Samira still looked distracted. "It's easy and I figured you'd need something quick."

Does she always plan ahead like this? J.P. leaned on the counter with his bowl. "What about you?"

"I ate already." Samira turned off the crockpot. "Before Daddy called."

J.P. processed his next thought as he ate. *Mike says I owe her a fair shake.* "You know, Samira, if you need to go to the family dinner—"

"Oh, no. It's okay."

"We can do this another time," J.P. finished his sentence.
~~~~~~~

"Can we?" She looked doubtful. "I'm okay with it. But Daddy doesn't know what to do with an extra plate at the table."

J.P. took another bite. "I don't like the idea of ruffling your father's feathers." *Any grown woman who still calls him Daddy obviously has a tight relationship with the man.*

"Thank you." Samira sighed. "But I've made up my mind. My girls are taken care of, and my brother doesn't mind. It's his son's birthday. Maybe we should just go before I talk myself out of it again."

"Are you sure?" J.P. stepped aside as Samira rinsed his dishes and placed them in the dishwasher.

"Yes." Samira dried her hands on a dishtowel. "Let me get my coat." She locked the deadbolt on the front door then picked up a long woolen coat from the back of the sofa.

She still looks stressed.

Once inside the pickup there was no place to hide from the thoughts that were bouncing around in his head. *I've wanted to talk to her for so long now, I don't know where to begin.* They spent the first several miles in small talk about Krissy and Kara's activities and James and Josh's busy lives. Then several miles passed in silence as J.P. worked up the nerve to open the real conversation.

When he finally opened his mouth to speak, Samira started to say something at the exact same time.

"Go ahead."

"No, that's okay. You go."

"Ladies first."

Samira looked away. "I was just thinking," she paused in thought. "I didn't know if we'd ever be alone long enough to talk again."

I had that same feeling. "That's my fault." J.P. decided to let her off the hook. "I have a nasty habit of not knowing how to sustain healthy relationships."

"Do you think what we had was a relationship?"

J.P. thought for a moment. *We had sex. We had dinner. I couldn't focus on work because of her. Still can't focus.* He glanced in her direction. "I'd have to answer in the affirmative. Do you think otherwise?"

"Sometimes I don't know," Samira leaned her head into the headrest. "It was definitely more than a one-night stand, but I can't exactly decide if it was a full-blown relationship or not. Everything moved so fast for a while and then it suddenly stopped."

"I didn't mean for it to stop like that."

"That was my fault. I got in a hurry to—"

"No, you didn't."

"Hear me out." She put her hand on the console. "I pressed you for answers you didn't have yet. I should have been more patient."

"And I should have given you more of my time." *I have a hard time separating work from home.* J.P. thought for a moment. *That's the main reason I couldn't stay married. At least according to Janet.*

They rode with their own thoughts for a mile or so.

"Tell me about the game tonight."

Is she asking that to pass time, or because she doesn't want to talk about us? "It's away. Against one of their biggest rivals. According to Josh, it should be a good game." *Might as well give her the rest of it.* "Last I knew Aunt Maggie and Uncle Roy were planning to drive over so we may see them there." He noticed a slight smile on Samira's face with that comment. "I didn't talk to them today, but that was the plan last night." *Oh yeah.* "And it's possible Bobby might be there too. If the work schedule played out the way—"

Sudden tension caused J.P. to stop talking in mid-sentence. *What caused that?*

Samira turned her shoulder away from him.

He drove a way further before asking the dreaded question. "Is it something I said?"

"Maybe."

Great.

"There's something I've needed to talk to you about and should have talked to you about a long time ago, but it just never seemed like the right time."

I love hidden agendas. "I'm all ears." *Might as well get it over with.*

"Well, I seem to have a knack of running into your friend Mike."

"I've noticed."

"Either that or he has the knack of running into me." Samira fidgeted in her seat. "But one of the last times I talked to him he told me Bobbie was going to be at the ranch over Labor Day weekend."

J.P. frowned. *Why would she be concerned over that? And why would Mike share my personal agenda without my permission?*

Samira wasn't saying anything.

"And you're upset because?" *She's looking at me as though I should already know the answer to that question.* "For whatever it's worth, that weekend left a lot to be desired." *It's probably better to fess up than muddy the waters at this point.*

"This is a really hard thing to say out loud," Samira spoke with a great deal of caution. "But I need to get it out of my system, and to be honest, you're the only one I can say it to."

Shit, Ralston, here it comes. J.P. gripped the steering wheel.

"I didn't appreciate knowing that someone else had already taken my place."

"Taken your place how?"

"I mean, maybe I jumped to a few conclusions, but the time I spent with you at your aunt's ranch meant something to me."

"And to me."

"Then why would you turn around a few short weeks later and take somebody else to that same place."

Samira stopped talking, but J.P. kept listening.

So, she didn't want me to take my brother and his family to the ranch? He hoped she'd explain more because he was missing a big part of something she wasn't explaining. *To my knowledge, no one has ever felt slighted by my brother's presence. Well, except for Janet.* He glanced at Samira and found her watching him very carefully. *Does she know about the brunette from Jimmy's bar?*

"Am I speaking out of turn here?"

I don't know. "No, I don't think so." *I can cross-examine a witness on the stand with great success. But I have no idea what to say to her.* "I don't know exactly what you want me to say."

Samira's eyes dropped, telling him even saying that was a mistake.

Come on, Ralston. Get a clue, would you? He forced his mind back to that weekend to see if he'd missed any incriminating details. *Maybe I just need to come clean.*

"I'm not sure how much Mike shared with you, but I didn't even make it up to the ranch until late Sunday and I had to have the boys back to their mother by nightfall on Monday." *And I'm not sure James has forgiven me yet for my absence that weekend.*

"I spent a day and a half with them and Bobby and then drove back home." He looked over to see if her body language had relaxed any. Her arms were crossed. *Obviously, that didn't help.*

You're damn lucky she can't walk out on you now. Samira was looking out her window, but he knew she was still listening. *Just lay it out there. I have nothing to lose now.* J.P. reran the entire weekend in his mind. *Either that or I have everything to lose.*

"Alright." *Lose the defensiveness.* "Here's what I remember from that weekend. Do you want the short version or the whole nine yards?"

Samira shrugged.

The whole thing. "I left the office late Friday afternoon and attended a business dinner that ended up pertinent to my highest priority case." *Even if I did have ulterior motives at the onset of that party.* He decided that was all she needed to know about that appointment.

"On my way home, against my better judgment, I stopped in at an old hangout, one I hadn't been to in several months now."

Samira was still staring out her window.

Might as well spill it. "The old hangout is a bar I used to frequent. But I haven't been there, well, since I met you, I guess." *I didn't realize Samira was the reason I quit going to Jimmy's.*

"I hooked up with an old friend, the bartender, actually, who fell into step with my old habits and set me up with a woman at the pool table." *Tell her the rest.* J.P. stared at the windshield. "And if it matters at all, I'd had way too much to drink by then."

Samira still hadn't looked at him. *I really don't want to tell her about this part.*

"And to be perfectly honest," *This may be the end of what could have been.* "I don't remember much else until I woke up in a place I shouldn't have been without transportation and had to call our now mutual friend, Mike, for a ride home."

There, it's out there for whatever she wants to make of it. "But if it matters to you at all, I couldn't do what I set out to do there." *How honest do I dare be?* J.P. drew a deep breath. "I didn't..." The words wouldn't come.

Samira turned in her seat.

Sure, now she's going to look at me. "I didn't have sex with her." He couldn't force himself to look at Samira. *I might as well finish it now.* "And to my recollection, I don't think I even kissed her." *My guess is I made a shitty date that night.*

"What about Bobbie?"

Who is she referring to? Now he looked at Samira. "Bobby who?"

Samira wrung her gloves in her hands. "I should have asked you about her earlier. I'd planned to talk to you at the ranch, but like I said, it didn't happen and..."

Bobbie Jo Sommers. "But you took her magazine to the ranch, didn't you?"

"Yes. And I felt stupid. Like I was prying into your private life somehow. But when Mike said you were taking her to the ranch I—"

Whoa. "Wait, wait, wait." *I need to get off this highway.*

"I took the magazine so I could ask some questions."

"Just, wait, Samira." *Shit. I just confessed to a weekend she didn't even know about.* J.P. took the next exit ramp and pulled off to the side of the road.

"I didn't know how to bring her up without sounding pathetic." Samira was sitting as close to the door as possible.

Let's get this cleared up once and for all. "Bobby—the one at the ranch, was my brother, Robert. I didn't take the model in the magazine to Aunt Maggie's."

The look on Samira's face was mixed. *Is she relieved, or doesn't she believe me?*

"But I saw you with her in Springfield."

J.P. ran his tongue over his bottom lip. *I knew Bobbie Jo was trouble there, but I didn't know how much Samira witnessed.* This was far more serious than he'd imagined it could be. *You have no choice but to come clean now, Ralston.* J.P. put his hands behind his head and leaned as far back into the truck seat as possible. "Bobbie Jo Sommers is a model."

"I know. I did my research. In fact, I get those magazines in the mail every month or so."

She is out of my league. "Alright." *I'll give her credit for doing her homework.* "I met her at a club after some kind of a fashion show her agency put on at the mall last spring."

"Probably the spring bridal show."

Does she want me to tell this story or not? "Maybe, I don't know. I didn't go to the show, I met her afterwards."

"That's the show the chamber sponsored in the spring."

"Okay. Then that's the one she was in town for." J.P. took a breath. "Do you want me to finish this or not?"

Samira was completely facing him now. "Go on."

"At any rate, Bobbie—that would be Bobbie Jo, and I hit it off and spent some time together while she was in town. Then later in the spring I spent a week with her in Mexico." *I never thought I'd share that information with Samira.*

Samira slid to the edge of the seat.

So now what? Is she going to get out or what?

Samira did not speak.

"And that's it." *Besides the fact Bobbie was incredible in the sack and a handful in the gentleman's club.* "That's how I know her."

Samira blinked but she still didn't speak.

I wish she'd say something. "And if it matters, and I'm thinking it might..." *Maybe I don't want her to say anything.* "I haven't spent any time with her since then." The scene at his office suddenly came to mind. "Wait, before I get myself in any deeper, let me clarify that. She did come by the office when she was in town mid-summer, but I let her know I was seeing someone and sent her away." *Or at least Denise let her know.*

"So, the meeting in Springfield was what then?"

"Chance. What do you want from me? I didn't plan it if that's what you're thinking." J.P. was finished being accused of something he hadn't done. "I didn't know she had a show going on there, and she didn't know I had meetings with the Hughes Corporation."

"Had you known, would you have still invited me to go along?"

If that isn't a loaded question, I've never heard one. J.P. leaned on the driver's door and thought for a minute. "Here's the bottom line, Samira, take it or leave it." *I doubt this is what Mike had in mind when he suggested I win her back.* "I invited you to Springfield because I wanted to spend time with you. I wanted to get to know you better and thought that would be a good way to do it." The memories of his time with her in the hotel came back easily. "And I have no regrets."

"And Bobbie?"

And Bobbie. That could prompt about a million different responses.

Samira was still solemn. "You told me you were going to the concierge's desk, but when I turned around, you were talking to her, and then—" She took a deep breath and looked away. "And then she touched you and it made me wonder. I guess I needed to know."

J.P. ran his hand through his hair. *Tell her the truth.* "Listen. That whole happenchance meeting was awkward for me too." A few moments of silence passed. "With Bobbie I have a few regrets." He nodded in new understanding. "When I took her to Mexico, my only motive was sex. She was easy to look at and had no attachments." He ran the memory through his mind. "And, I'll be perfectly honest with you here," *I'm to the point now I really don't care what she's thinking.* "Bobbie Jo and I had a good time together." *And incredible sex.*

"And now?" Samira was not looking at him.

"And now?" J.P. scanned the roof of his vehicle hoping to find words to finish his thoughts. "Bobbie Jo was before I met you." *I have never told a woman what I'm about to tell her.* There was a lot of risk in his next series of thoughts. *She can either hear me out or shut me down.*

"Samira," *How do I explain this?* "Before I knew you, I lived alone and led a life that was all mine. I did whatever I pleased whenever I wanted to do it. But you've given me something no woman has ever offered before." *Be careful, Ralston. This could sound extremely shallow.* "I don't know if I can even explain."

Samira sighed.

"When I'm with you something moves deep within me." *Deeper than I've felt anything move in my entire life.* "Hell, even when I'm not with you, I'm moved by your presence. And lately you haven't even been part of my life, yet you're in my thoughts and my decisions, and habits—" J.P. looked at her hands resting uneasily in her lap. "No one has ever permeated my every waking and sleeping thought like you do, Samira. I'm still single and I still live alone, but it's like you're here with me all the time." J.P. felt his hand move to his chest. "No one has ever made a lasting impact on me before." *I hope she's taking this the right way.* "Every time I close my eyes, you're right there with me." *And God, she's so beautiful.*

Tell her. J.P. heard the voice in his head loud and clear, but he hesitated.

Samira's head was bowed when J.P. finally dared to look at her again. He couldn't tell if she was deep in thought or crying. Very slowly he reached over and brushed the hair away from her face. "You, Samira Cartwright, are the most beautiful woman I've ever known."

She still didn't look at him. "The same is true of you. Even when I'm not with you, you're with me. But I didn't know where I belonged, or if I belonged."

J.P. was watching Samira very carefully. "Maybe it's more of a belonging and we both missed the point."

"Maybe." Samira's voice was almost inaudible.

I've said everything I know to say. He remembered his earlier confession. *And then some.* J.P. glanced at his watch and then back to Samira. *We'll be lucky to make the start of the game now.* "If you want me to, I can take you back home." *I don't know what else to offer.*

Samira slouched into the seat. "If you take me home, I won't get to see Maggie and I won't get to meet your brother, Bobby."

I don't care what we do anymore. His emotions were spent. J.P. had never been that transparent with a woman. Ever. *At least she's not screaming obscenities at me.* "Whatever you want to do. It's your call."

"I'm sorry," Samira tucked her hair behind an ear as she apologized.

"No, we're not going there," J.P. shook his head. "This whole thing is far more complicated than it should be but we're not going to be sorry over it." *I hate apologies with no blame.* "It's just one huge misunderstanding on many different levels."

"Then if we're not going to be sorry, we can't rehash it in the future."

"What the hell is that supposed to mean?"

Samira looked spent too. "It means we call a truce." She turned her face toward him. "That means it's water under the bridge. We leave this whole misunderstanding right here along the side of this road and move forward."

I don't like the idea of permanent closure. "And move forward into what?"

"That question brings us back to the whole point of this road trip."

J.P. hated games. "I have no idea what you're talking about."

"Think about it, Mr. Ralston."

J.P. almost smiled at Samira's use of his formal name. *She's going to make her point now.*

"In that Facebook thing we did the other night with the help of our children, you told me you wanted to revisit the question from Shoal Creek." She tipped her head. "Here we are."

But I've just aired all my bullshit. How do I answer a question like that now?

Samira offered her right hand to seal the truce.

Reluctantly, J.P. offered his right hand and shook on the agreement. "So, what are you suggesting, Pretty Lady?" *Even though she's tired, she's still the most beautiful woman I've ever known.*

"I think we have a game to catch, that's what I'm suggesting."

"Are you sure?"

Samira nodded.

J.P. put the truck into gear. A wave of relief washed over him. It was as if he'd been set free from a burden he didn't know he carried.

"So, tell me more about Bobby."

There's no way in hell I'm going back there again. "Be specific."

"Your brother."

"Maybe we should call him Robert."

"So, tell me more about Robert."

That I can do. "He's in telecommunications, lives out east with his wife, Megan, who's an investment broker. They've got three kids..."

55 *New Beginnings*

Samira

Phil pointed to a glow in the sky. "My guess is that would be the stadium."

"You've never been here before?"

"Not here." He turned the truck in the direction of the lights. "On average I miss more games than I see each season."

I can't imagine missing any of the girls' activities. "Is it alright to leave my purse in the car?"

Phil opened the console.

Samira laid her purse inside. *This way I don't have to keep track of it on the bleachers.* She slid out of the truck. *I wish I weren't so tired.*

"Ready?"

"Sure." *My family is probably just sitting down to dinner about now.*

"Watch your step." Phil took her elbow as they stepped up onto a wooden bridge that led them across a ditch.

It feels good to have him touch me. Even if we are separated by coats.

"That'll be eight dollars, sir." The man at the entrance held out his hand.

Phil handed over a fifty-dollar bill.

The gatekeeper frowned. "I can't break this sir. They've already taken my money pouch."

Phil is a little on edge. "I have a ten in my purse."

"How close can you come?"

"Well, let's see," the ticket taker counted some ones. "If I give you my twenty and all my ones, I'm still short."

Phil held out his fifty. "Keep the change."

"Well, then I won't have any change for the next person." The man seemed frustrated. "There's a convenience store a block down the road. They'll have plenty of change for you there."

"But I'm here now and I'd like to get in to watch my boys play ball before any more time ticks off the clock."

I could fix this. "Just let me get my purse."

He shook his head. "Here, give me a twenty and as many ones as you can part with, then donate the rest to the cause."

The gentleman sighed. "I don't feel right about it." He took the fifty with a great deal of hesitation. "Here's my twenty. If I give you ten ones then I've shorted you and that just isn't right, mister."

"Am I complaining?"

He's used to getting what he wants.

"Well, I'm sorry about that and I'm sorry they took my extra programs too. They'll have some of those at the concession stand."

"That's just great."

Samira turned her collar up to block the cold north wind. *A ten- dollar bill would have eliminated the issue.* She watched Phil accept the shortchange.

"You'd think they could break a freakin' fifty-dollar bill."

Phil stopped and read the scoreboard. Samira looked too. *First quarter. No points on the board yet.* They walked to the edge of the visitor's bleachers.

"Uncle Roy will be seated at the fifty-yard line about halfway up the bleachers." Phil's eyes were searching the crowd.

He's so tense. Samira watched him for a moment. *Maybe I should have had dinner with my parents.*

Phil guided Samira with his hand on her waist.

"Over here."

Samira looked up to see Aunt Maggie waving her hands. *There's a familiar face.* The people on the end of the row began to shift so Samira could pass through. Phil held her arm as she stepped over the knees of the people between her and Aunt Maggie.

"My, my." Aunt Maggie exclaimed. "I didn't expect to see you here tonight." Aunt Maggie lifted the corner of an old quilt. "Move down, Roy, so Samira can be warm with us."

I didn't mean to make such a stir.

Phil crouched in the aisle so people in the stands could see around him. *I feel bad I'm in here and he's over there.* She felt Aunt Maggie's hand pat her leg.

"How are you, darlin'? We missed you over Labor Day."

Oh, wow. I didn't expect to begin with that discussion. Samira chose to keep things simple. "I'm doing well, thank you." *But it's nice to be missed just the same.* Samira looked out over the football field. "What numbers are we watching for?"

Uncle Roy leaned over Maggie. "James is on the offensive line. See him? He's wearing a number twenty-four jersey." Roy pointed with his gloved finger. "But Joshy, we can't see him so good. He's on the far side lined up as a receiver. We'll see him in a minute. Look for number eighty."

"Oh, honey, you can't really see too much from way up here." Maggie adjusted the quilt. "We just come here to support the team and pretend like we know what's going on."

At least I'm not the only one who doesn't know the game.

There was another break in play and the entire team left the field. *Where are they going?* People around Samira began to move around too. Phil took the opportunity to squeeze in directly behind Samira. He put his hands on her shoulders as he settled in. Samira straightened her back. *I think I'm going to like him sitting behind me like this.*

"Hey, bro. Nice you could make it."

There's a familiar tone in that voice.

"Are you going to introduce me?"

Must be Bobby.

Samira leaned back as Phil spoke into her ear. "Meet *Robert*."

Funny. She smiled in Robert's direction.

"Bobby, Samira Cartwright." Phil finished the introduction.

Maggie chimed right in. "She's such a nice girl, Robert." She turned and patted her nephew's knee. "It's good to see you, too, Phillip." Maggie's face beamed with a genuine smile.

Aunt Maggie sure loves these boys. Samira ran her gloved hands over the patchwork quilt covering her lap. *But it would be warmer at home.*

Maggie caught her studying the pattern on the quilt. "My sister made this a million years ago."

Samira gave the worn blanket more deliberate attention. *It reminds me of the quilt on the bed at the ranch.* "Do you quilt, Maggie?"

"No, I left the sewin' to my sisters." Maggie wriggled a little under the cover. "I took to the kitchen."

And a fine cook she is. "How many sisters do you have?"

Maggie waited to answer until the crowd around them finished a cheer. "There were four of us. We were alphabetized youngest to oldest. Leona, me, Naomi, and Opal. In that order." Maggie nodded her head. "Naomi is the quilter. Leona used to sew too."

Leona. Samira remembered the photo in Maggie's living room. *Phil's mom.*

"This here is a log cabin pattern," Maggie explained further. "But it's so worn and patched you can't really tell anymore."

Samira admired the miniature stitches. *It's cozy at any rate.*

Aunt Maggie chattered on as they watched the game. When the buzzer rang, the crowd began to disperse around them. Samira felt Phil stand.

What's he doing?

"It's halftime." Phil explained without being asked. "We're going to go try to catch the boys when they come back from the locker room. Do you want anything from concessions?"

Samira couldn't think of anything.

"We'll bring you a cup of coffee." Robert smiled the easy Ralston smile.

Strong resemblance. Samira had to smile back.

Robert tapped his uncle on the shoulder. "Come on, old man, let's go find those boys."

It's funny how they call Uncle Roy old man.

"I'm going to walk down to that bathroom." Maggie wiggled out from under the blanket too. "Do you mind sitting here with our things?"

Samira suddenly felt very vulnerable. In the distance she could see Phil and Robert walking towards the school. *I'm glad volleyball is an indoor sport.* She pulled the quilt in tighter around her legs. *I wonder how the birthday party is going.*

A man wearing a long coat and a wool hat was making his way up the bleachers toward her. *I wonder who that is.* He walked on the empty seats and stopped right where Samira was sitting. Without asking for permission, he sat down next to Samira in Maggie's spot.

"I'm sorry," Samira tucked the quilt in around her legs. "Someone is sitting there."

"No one is sitting here right now."

I don't like his arrogance. "But she is coming back." *I wish he would go away.* Samira looked around hoping someone was on their way back.

"Not to worry." The man had a sly grin on his face. "I came up here to talk to you for a minute."

Well, I don't have anything to say to you.

Without warning, the man slid his hand under the blanket and put it on Samira's knee.

Samira instantly slid into the empty space next to her. *What does he think he's doing?*

"You're pretty jumpy for being a companion of J.P. Ralston's."

What business does he have knowing I'm with J.P. Ralston? "I have no idea what you're talking about." Samira spoke through clenched teeth. *If Aunt Maggie's purse weren't on the other side of that quilt, I'd walk away.*

"Of course, you don't know." The man leaned in closer. "I've been watching you. You seem mighty refined to be in J.P.'s company."

He's disgusting.

The man picked at his teeth with a toothpick. "I happen to know a little about the man who is escorting you tonight and feel obligated to offer a word of warning."

Samira turned away. *I don't need advice or anything else from this man.* The man slid closer to her again. *I'm going to have to get out of here.* She started to stand, but a woman carrying a bag of popcorn and a steaming Styrofoam cup returned and took a seat one row behind Samira. *I don't know her either, but at least I feel less vulnerable now.*

Samira slid even further onto the metal seat. Much to her horror, the man moved when she did. When he leaned in to speak again, Samira could smell alcohol on his breath.

"You are out of line."

"I'm not out of line any more than J.P. is." The man gazed into Samira's eyes. "His idea of a relationship is to love 'em and leave 'em. Think about that the next time he gets you in the sack."

This time when the man put his hand on her knee, Samira bolted from her seat. Strong arms caught her in the aisle, but coffee spilled over the bleachers because of the collision.

"Whoa there, girl."

Samira's heart was pounding hard in her chest, and she knew if she said anything at all that tears would spill out of her already damp eyes. Samira was unaware of anything other than the sheer terror of the man still sitting on Maggie's blanket.

"It's okay." The calming tone of his voice caught Samira's attention. She looked up into Robert's concerned face.

Oh, thank you, God. Samira put her gloved hands to her face. "I don't know who he is..." Samira tried to explain, "...but he's..."

"Shhh," Robert put his arm around Samira's shoulders and pushed her head into his chest. "That's Bruce Hamilton." Robert whispered into her ear. "And I don't doubt you for a minute."

Who's Bruce Hamilton?

"What the hell?" Phil stopped a few steps below where Samira and Robert were blocking the stairs.

Robert let Samira go. "We've had a brief encounter with—" He nodded his head. Samira watched Phil's eyes go from Robert to the man sitting on Maggie's blankets. *I have never seen his eyes like that.* The look frightened Samira. But the face of the woman hurrying up behind Phil was just as frightening.

"Get your ass off those blankets and out of the stands," Phil demanded.

The man crossed his arms and raised his eyebrows.

"Hold this." Robert handed Samira the half empty coffee cup. She watched Robert turn and face his brother. Phil tried to step around Robert.

Oh, no. He's going to get physical.

"Phillip, this isn't your ballgame." Robert was speaking very calmly. "You're here to support James and Josh, not make a scene in their stands." He took a sideways step blocking Phil's view.

The woman standing behind Phil put her hands on the back of Phil's coat. "Don't do anything stupid."

Samira could hear trembling in the woman's voice.

"I didn't know he was coming over here, or I would have warned—"

Who is she?

Phil stepped out of the woman's hold. His eyes were full of fire.

Samira looked around. The football team was beginning to gather on the sidelines again and the stands were beginning to fill up. She could see Maggie making her way back across the grassy lawn between the bathroom and the bleachers. *This could get ugly.*

"Don't do it, Phillip," Robert warned quietly. "He's not worth the price you'd pay."

Uncle Roy was now standing at the bottom of the steps and appeared to be aware of the conflict. He put his hand out to keep Maggie from starting up the stairs.

Phil's eyes were a cold blue and his jaw was set. Samira had seen that look only one other time. *And that time he was on his way to reprimand James for something his mother—.* Suddenly Samira realized who the woman was behind Phil. *So that must be Janet's husband.* She looked back at the man who was still inviting a fight simply by his stubborn presence. *They know exactly how to push Phil's buttons.*

He's creepy. No wonder James has trouble living with him.

"I only touched her a couple of times," the man purposefully explained to the audience gathering in the stands. "I don't know what he's all worked up about."

He touched me to provoke, Phil.

Phil took a quick step toward the man.

Oh, oh. We're not going to do this. "Excuse me," Samira held the coffee cup out to the woman sitting in the bleachers. "Would you hold this?" Without waiting another second, she stepped between Phil and Bruce Hamilton. *Now what am I going to do?*

"Don't get in the middle of this."

"I'm already in the middle." Samira took a deep breath. "But he came up here to provoke you. We're going to take the high road and walk away."

Phil's eyes moved to Samira. *Hold his eye contact.*

"He's the biggest bastard in the county." Phil's voice was loud enough most of the people gathered around heard.

"I know." *And I believe you.* She stepped into Phil's personal space. "But this isn't the time or the place to make that fact known." She flattened her hand against his coat. Her voice was almost whispering when she spoke again. "Just walk with me off these bleachers and let Bobby deal with him."

Phil set his jaw again, but he kept his eyes on hers.

"Come on." Samira added a little pressure to his side and much to her relief, Phil moved with her. Together they stepped over the fallen quilt.

Samira dared to turn around, but only long enough to confirm Robert was indeed going to handle whatever was left of the conflict. She had to skip several steps to catch up with Phil who was now headed out into the open lawn.

I have no idea what Phil's mindset is now, but I'm glad he didn't follow through with whatever he was thinking back there.

Phil stopped walking when he reached the chain-linked fence that separated the parking area from the stadium.

"He's an asshole."

"I know."

"I hate him."

"I understand."

"I should have cleaned his clock when I had the chance."

I can't agree with that one. "You did the right thing."

"I let him steal my family away. Is that the right thing?"

Oh, I didn't know that's what he was talking about. "No. But you can't win battles by beating people up."

"He's no fighter."

Especially when he's drunk. "Not in that condition."

"What condition?"

Do I tell him or not?

Phil stopped right in front of Samira and addressed her directly. "What condition are you talking about?"

I'm not going to lie to him now. "He's been drinking." *And he's creepy.* Samira watched Phil's eyes go back to the stands. "He's not in his right mind." *Even though I'm not sure he'd be any better in a sober state.* Samira shuddered at that thought.

She watched Phil's face. *His mind is suddenly a million miles away.* She turned her back to the wind and pulled her hood up.

Samira watched two full minutes tick off the scoreboard in addition to the time the clock was stopped completely. A few times she heard the fans in the stands cheer. But Phil's eyes stayed in the distance with his thoughts.

Samira wrapped her arms tighter around her middle trying to keep warm. The wind was stiff. *I could be sitting in front of my father's fireplace but instead I'm here with this man I hardly know, waiting for him to say something. Anything.* In the stadium light his face looked more chiseled than usual.

Ever so slowly, Phil's thoughts came back to the present. "I'm sorry."

That's the most sincere thing he's ever said to me. Samira waited but he didn't say anymore. "No harm done." *Except for frostbite in my toes.*

"No, I mean," Phil's thoughts were still more distant than Samira realized. "I'm sorry for not being in my right mind." He ran a bare hand through his hair.

His eyes were cloudy when he looked at Samira again. *Has he been drinking too?*

Phil put his hand back in his pocket. His eyes were turned toward the playing field now. "I haven't been a father to those boys for over half of their lives."

Samira stepped closer so she could be sure to hear.

"I've had opportunities and backed off because I thought I was doing the right thing by letting Janet and that bastard raise them as a family. But I was wrong."

Samira saw number twenty-four run off the field to the sidelines.

"You know, I met my father a few weeks back."

I remember.

"I mean, I knew him, but I didn't understand who he was while my mother was alive." Phil's eyes were focused somewhere deep in the distance. "I always thought he was a Navy brat out there saving the world while his wife and kids were struggling along back on the Missouri homeland."

Phil paused and Samira waited. "But I was wrong about that too. The Captain and my mother had an understanding between them that allowed them to raise us up according to what my mother thought was best. It turns out he's the one who gave us up to make her happy."

I had no idea.

"The result is, I never really knew my dad. But I thought I did, and I held a grudge against him for too long. Somehow in the distance of their relationship there was a strong bond of...I don't know how to explain it, but something held them together even when they were apart."

Maybe like a bond of love?

"But now... now I understand that what was between my parents was the reality of something I've never personally known."

The hue of Phil's eyes softened drastically when he looked at Samira.

"Until maybe now."

I think he's addressing the question from Shoal Creek.

"You've changed me, Samira."

He said my name.

"I wasn't in my right mind, so to speak, the Friday and Saturday of Labor Day weekend." Phil looked away and ran his hand through his hair again. "I wasn't any better off than the bastard in the stands."

So that's what happened the night he was supposed to be with his family.

Samira watched Phil chew on his bottom lip a minute. "I put a case at risk, exposed my professional reputation again, and jeopardized the trust between me and James that I spent the entire summer establishing."

The lump in Samira's throat was finally too big to swallow. *At least now I know he was drinking the night I thought he was at the ranch with that magazine model.* She could feel the weight of Phil's realization before he was even finished. *But he's still a better man than Janet's creepy husband.*

"I've spent my whole life getting even." Phil looked away. "But I don't think that matters anymore."

When he looked back to Samira, she felt it was time to say something. "Then what does matter, Phil?" *I hope that's the right question.*

Phil rubbed his face in both hands, then slowly reached out and pulled Samira into his chest. "You matter a whole hell of a lot."

Samira allowed his embrace to warm her from the inside out.

"And if you really want to know the truth, you also scare the shit out of me."

"Maybe you have much the same effect on me." Samira lifted her face so she could see his. *Although it's doubtful I would ever phrase it quite that way.* She'd never known anyone with such depth of character, both destructive and constructive. *Nor have I known a man who beats himself up so badly over fatherhood.* Samira pressed her face into his chest again. She wished she could feel his heart beating, but his coat was too thick. *How will I ever explain him to Daddy?*

"I owe you a cup of coffee."

Samira made a worried face. "Just don't leave me alone again, okay?"

Phil draped his arm over Samira's shoulder and started toward the concession stand. "Highly unlikely I'll ever leave you alone again."

That sounds promising.

Robert intercepted their route. He removed his stocking hat and knelt on one knee before them on the gravel walkway. "My hat is off to you, Lady Samira. In my entire life I've never seen anyone handle my brother with such grace."

"Get up, Bobby." Phil kicked his shoe at his brother's bent knee.

Bobby stood up. "She's a keeper, big brother."

"Yeah, I know."

Phil answered with such confidence that Samira's heart skipped a beat.

"The coffee is on me."

Robert handed the first cup to Samira and the next one to Phil. Samira was stunned to see Phil accept. *I've never known him to drink a cup of coffee. Ever.*

"It's always a pleasure to bump into your ex-wife and her entourage, Phillip." Bobby snapped a lid on his cup and then turned to do the same for Phil and Samira.

"Is it now?" Phil allowed his brother to cover the coffee. *So that must have been Phil's pre-game tension.* Samira noted that there was no tension in Phil's voice at all when Janet was mentioned this time. *Maybe we've made some progress here after all.*

"She has always held me in such high esteem." Bobby rolled his eyes at Samira. He lifted his cup in a toast. "Here's to new beginnings."

"To new beginnings." Phil raised his cup. When his eyes passed over Samira's they stopped.

She allowed Phil's quiet gaze to penetrate. *He's still serious, but the earlier torment is gone.* She lifted her cup. *Maybe if he's coming to terms with his past, he'll be able to move into his future.*

"Yes. To new beginnings."

56 *Freedom*

Joseph Phillip

J.P. clicked the computer mouse and waited for the document to print while Samira changed into his clothes. *At least she agreed to come home with me.* He took the papers out of the printer tray and sorted them back into numerical order. *Even if she stipulated her own terms.*

"I found some hot chocolate mix," Samira called from the kitchen. "Do you have cups?"

"Yeah. Somewhere." *Where are they?* "Try the cupboard next to the stove." He carried his papers out to the living room. *I really need to go over Denise's notes at least once before morning.*

"Plenty of alcohol, but no cups."

I know I have some somewhere.

"Found them." A few minutes later Samira appeared in the archway between the kitchen and living room. She was wearing a pair of his sweatpants and a long-sleeved t-shirt James had left behind.

And she looks damn good.

Samira set one of the mugs down amidst the scattered newspapers on the coffee table.

"Sorry about the mess. Maria didn't come in today."

Samira lifted her cup to her lips. "Who's Maria?"

Let's get this one out in the open from the get-go. "My housekeeper."

"She doesn't pose for magazine covers or anything like that, does she?"

J.P. had to smile. "No, I doubt Maria has even been considered for a cover shot." He pictured the elderly Hispanic woman in his mind. "But she does stop in a couple times a week to tidy up and do my laundry." J.P. looked around his front room. *It's been worse.* "She's probably glad James isn't here."

"Do you miss him?" Samira curled into the corner of the sofa and pulled her knees to her chest.

"Sometimes." J.P. spoke honestly. "But right now, my casework is heavy enough that he's better off playing football and sticking to a familiar routine." *Or am I just talking myself out of fatherhood again?*

Samira nodded and sipped the hot chocolate.

She looks tired. J.P. looked back to the notes. *I should get this done so we can call it a night.* He felt Samira's feet slide in between him and the couch. *It feels good to have her touching me.*

J.P. finished his review of Denise's notes. Much to his surprise, Samira hadn't spoken a word while he was reading. *She's either that tired or extremely polite.* He dug a pencil out from under the corner of a newspaper. *Most likely the latter.* He jotted a quick note: How much does Goldstein need to purchase Shoal Creek? He stacked the papers on the coffee table.

"Finished?"

"For now." *Tomorrow will be a long day at the office.*

J.P. stood up and offered a hand to Samira. She accepted and allowed him to assist her off the couch. J.P. went back into his office. *If I were alone, I'd go over the FBI report one more time.* He glanced in Samira's direction. *But I am certainly not alone.*

As he turned out the overhead light in the office, Samira became silhouetted in the doorway. *I don't know if I want to play by her terms.* He'd never had a woman stay the night in his own home.

"What are you thinking?"

"I'm thinking," *How honest should I be here?* "That your terms are going to be difficult to keep."

"And I'm thinking if you don't put me to bed, I'm going to fall asleep standing up."

"Putting you to bed won't be a problem. But not undressing you? That could be a challenge."

J.P. crossed the kitchen and checked the lock on the back door. *She did my dishes.*

"Do you leave a light on at night?"

"No. Why?"

Samira shrugged. "I always leave a dim light in the kitchen. It makes me feel peaceful."

"Would you be more comfortable if I left one on?"

"No, I'm okay." Samira yawned. "Do you have that toothbrush you promised me?"

"I put it on the counter." He pointed to the bathroom off his bedroom.

J.P. took a deep breath and held it in as Samira disappeared behind the closed bathroom door. He exhaled as slowly as he'd breathed in. *How do you put a woman like that in your own bed and not finish what you're dying to start?* He reached behind his head and grabbed his sweatshirt. He pulled it off with one swift tug and tossed it into the dirty clothes hamper. *After all the crap at the game, it's amazing she even agreed to come home with me.*

J.P. opened his top dresser drawer looking for a t-shirt. The worn envelope his father had given him was folded along the edge. He poured the contents out in his hand. *Mom's wedding rings.* J.P. turned the diamond so he could see it in the dim light of the room. *Some things in life aren't worth losing.* His father's words played in his mind. *There may come a time when winning isn't enough.*

J.P. closed his hands around the rings and looked at the closed bathroom door. *She's not worth losing but if winning isn't enough, then what is?*

The door opened and Samira stepped out into the light. Her hair resting over her shoulders. *Just like in Springfield.*

"Your turn." Samira stepped into the bedroom. "Which side do you usually sleep on?"

J.P. shook the rings in his hand. "Both."

Samira raised her eyebrows. "Well, tonight you need to pick a side."

"I pick your side." *She can think on that for a minute.* J.P. closed the bathroom door before she had a chance to retaliate.

He laid his mother's rings on the shelf. *Geez, Ralston. You look tired.* He ran his hand over his chin and decided not to shave until morning. He took care of business and brushed his teeth. When he left the room, he took the rings with him again.

Samira was already curled up under the covers. Her hair fanned the entire pillowcase.

Someday these rings are going to mean something. J.P. set the rings on the nightstand as he sat down on the edge of the bed. Samira's hand touched the base of his neck, then moved slowly down the length of his spine sending signals to every nerve ending in his body.

"You're making your terms very difficult." *But I'm not playing to win her. Am I?*

"Don't put a shirt on."

I don't put anything on to go to bed. "I don't know if I can leave anything on under the circumstances." *Maybe she'll grant me permission.*

Her hand moved to his waist. "But you promised."

J.P. turned so he could see her. "That I did." He pulled the covers down and slid between the sheets next to her. *She took off the sweatpants.* "You should know, this is the hardest promise I've ever had to keep."

Samira's fingertips touched his cheek. "I like it when you don't shave."

"I like it when you talk to me in bed." J.P. dared to pull her closer to him. He had yet to kiss her tonight, but he was afraid a single kiss would only make it harder to keep his promise.

"Turn off the light."

J.P. clicked the switch at the bottom of the lamp like he did every night. But tonight, he had a woman to hold. *An incredibly special woman.*

His eyes adjusted to the darkness of the room. *I want to watch her fall asleep.*

"Did your aunt make the quilt?"

"What quilt?"

"The one we're laying under." Samira moved closer. Her hands were against his bare chest.

Oh. "Yeah, I guess she did." *I'd never stopped to think about who made this quilt.*

"Aunt Maggie said her sisters are the quilters."

"Naomi and my mother. They were the sewers." *Why do I know that piece of information right now?*

"I know. It's very cozy under your family quilts."

It's not the quilt making it cozy.

"Do you remember the first time you slept with me?"

How could I forget? "Every detail."

"I was so scared."

J.P. ran his fingers through her hair. "You didn't seem scared."

"I was. I was terrified I'd forgotten how to make love to a man."

He still couldn't explain the way she moved him. *She's the first woman I have ever made love with.*

"And then the next morning I was afraid I'd never see you again." Samira completed her confession.

"Is that why you wouldn't let me kiss you?"

Samira's head was instantly off the pillow. "No." She sat up and put her face in her hands. "I didn't want you to remember that part."

J.P. laughed at her reaction. "I remember all the parts."

"Even the part when I cried?"

Yeah, that part too. He nodded knowing she could see him well enough to see his answer.

"I'm sorry I didn't kiss you when you left the next morning. I didn't mean to hurt you." Samira pushed her hair back over her shoulder. "I was afraid of being hurt."

I wondered what that was all about. "If it makes you feel any better, I felt guilty for staying that night."

"Why?" Samira was laying down again with her head propped up on an elbow.

"Because I felt like I was taking advantage of you."

"But I invited you to stay."

"I know." He could see her dark eyes searching his in the dark. "And I wanted to stay." *You might as well lay it out there.* "But I was afraid I wasn't ready for a woman like you."

Samira rolled onto her back and put her arms over her face. "I hate it when people say that about me."

Now J.P. was up on his elbow. "When they say what?"

"*A woman like you.*" Samira threw her arms into the air. "What is that supposed to mean anyway? It's like I can't be who I am because I'm like *that.*"

"Come here." He took a hold of her hand and pulled her back toward him. "I'll tell you about the woman like you." He slid one of his legs between hers, pulling her tight against him. "There is only one woman like you. You're compassionate and beautiful. You're spirited and sophisticated, independent, and strong—"

Samira began to shake her head and tried to pull away.

"I'm not finished yet." *And she needs to hear me out.* "But at the same time, you're stubborn and vulnerable and extremely sexy. And if you want to know the whole of it, I didn't know if I could handle all you had to offer that night."

"I am not stubborn."

J.P. smiled in the dark. "Oh, yes you are, Pretty Lady."

"Strong-willed, maybe, but not stubborn."

"I beg to differ." *This is kind of fun.* He moved his hand up the inside of the t-shirt and felt her tenderness against his hand. *She's not wearing anything underneath this shirt.*

"You promised."

"Yes, I did." *But the promise only stipulated sex. She didn't mention anything about making love.* J.P. pressed his pelvis into hers as their lips touched. Consumed by her presence in the darkness he kissed her again. And then again.

But you promised. J.P. heard his conscience through the heat of the passion. *Oh shit.* As much as he hated to, he knew this was a promise he had to keep.

Samira was lost in her own passion. J.P. felt her bare legs rise over his body. Straddling his hips, she started to remove the t-shirt.

I owe her my integrity if nothing else. J.P. moved his hands up her thighs and hung on to the hem of the shirt. Her eyes searched his. "I have a promise to keep."

Samira pulled on the shirt again, but J.P. held it tight. He sat up into her and wrapped his arms all the way around her. "These are your terms, Pretty Lady." *Not terms I'd agree to for anyone else.*

"Maybe I changed my mind."

And she says she's not stubborn. "Maybe you did," J.P. allowed her to kiss his neck. "But I'm a man of my word." *And I'm not going against my better judgment like I did the first time I was with her.*

Samira stopped kissing him and threw her head back. J.P. held her body weight as she fell away from him. *I could work my way down this pose.*

She was smiling playfully when she leaned forward again. J.P. caught his breath as she ran her hands through his hair.

"Then just kiss me goodnight."

I don't have to because you're kissing me. J.P. opened his eyes expecting to find himself standing in the shallow waters of the lake at Aunt Maggie's ranch. He'd always attributed the power of that kiss to Samira's passion. *But it's more than that. It's more of a power between us.* Samira eased off his lap. *I've felt chemistry before. But this is even more evocative than that.*

J.P. watched as she turned her back to him and slid her legs back under the covers that had almost fallen off the end of the bed. J.P. grabbed the quilt and pulled it over Samira's shoulder. Then he pulled her into him and wrapped his arm around her middle.

What I wouldn't do for this sensation to last a lifetime. Her body warmed him from the inside out. *Some things aren't worth losing.*

"Phil?"

"Yeah?" He linked his fingers with hers under her breasts.

"Next time can I stay under your terms?"

J.P. chuckled. *Anything you wish, Pretty Lady.*

~~~~~~~

Morning came with clarity of mind and a rejuvenated spirit. J.P. awoke early. *I'm going to let her sleep.* He dressed as quietly as possible and took Chase out the kitchen door,
~~~~~~~

stopping it before it banged shut. Completely consumed with thoughts of Samira, he started off in a jog and worked up to full stride. *How is it that I feel more committed to this woman than I've ever felt before yet at the same time I feel completely free?* The gravel crunched under his running shoes. *I don't feel like I have anything to prove.*

By the time he reached the turnaround point at the bridge, he was ready to get back to her. He removed his sweatshirt and tied it around his waist. *It took me all of ten years to bring a woman home to stay with me. I don't want her to wake up alone.* J.P. threw a large stick into the timber for Chase to retrieve before he took off again.

Samira was just beginning to stir when J.P. returned to the bedroom. He watched as she rolled over and opened her eyes. *She's just as beautiful in the daylight as she is in the moonlight.*

"Mornin,' Pretty Lady."

"What time is it?"

"Almost eight."

Samira sat up with an abrupt jerk.

"Too early or too late?" He removed his sweaty t-shirt.

Samira was climbing out of bed. "I told my father I'd call him when I got up."

"Go ahead." J.P. pointed to the phone by the bed. He sat down on the edge of the chair and removed his running shoes and socks. *Does she call him every morning?*

"No, you don't understand." Samira pushed her hair back out of her face with both hands.

I have no idea why this is so important. At the same time, he was humored by the way she was standing there.

"I'm usually up long before this. Daddy would have expected my call before now."

Then call him. "Tell him you slept in." *Which is exactly what she did.*

"But what if he's already been to the house to check on me?"

He would do that? J.P. stood up and used the damp t-shirt to wipe his face again. "How will you know if you don't try to get a hold of him?"

"What do I tell him?" Samira put her hands on her hips, obviously in a state of panic.

I don't know if it's healthy for me if she's this concerned about her father after one of the best nights of my life.

Samira was still looking panicked.

J.P. reached over and handed the handset to Samira. "Dial the number and get the facts before you set yourself up for something that might not even have happened."

Samira looked at him and then at the phone. "I guess you're right." She started to push the numbers on the keypad then stopped. She looked up at J.P. like maybe she didn't want him listening.

J.P. threw his arms out to his sides. "Alright, I'm going to take a quick shower while you sort this out." *I'd rather not hear what she tells him anyway.*

Samira's face softened. "I'm sorry."

"Don't be." *What is it with her father anyway?* He started to run water in the sink. While the temperature of the tap warmed, he lathered his face. *I don't know if I want to know the answer to that question.* J.P. adjusted the faucet to a slow stream and ran the razor over his cheek with his left hand like he did every morning. *A simple "good morning" would have sufficed.*

There was a faint tap on the door.

"Come in."

Samira's dark eyes peeked through the crack.

I could tell her there's another bathroom. J.P. passed the razor from his left hand to his right and started down the other cheek. Samira was still watching him in the reflection.

"You can come in." He stopped shaving long enough to focus on her eyes in the reflection. She stepped all the way through the door, still wearing James' shirt. It hung just below her panty line. *Too bad it's not a little shorter.*

"Have you been out already?"

He rinsed the blade under the running water. "Chase and I went on our morning run."

"I didn't mean to sleep so long."

J.P. lifted his chin in the reflection and ran the razor over the edge of his jaw line. "Didn't do any harm, did it?" *I hope everything's in order with her father.*

"I guess not." Samira put the lid down on the toilet and sat down. "Daddy wasn't looking for me yet, thank goodness. He's a worrier."

Obviously. J.P. rinsed his blade again. He could feel Samira's eyes on him.

"I told him I'd be over for brunch in an hour or so."

"Works for me. I need to be at the office by then anyway." He turned off the water and set the razor in its place by the medicine cabinet.

"These were on your bedside table."

J.P. watched her in the reflection.

"They look old."

They are. "They were my mother's. Dad gave them to me when I went to see him."

"They're beautiful. What a great keepsake." Samira held them out for J.P. to take. "It's still awhile before an hour is up."

He set the rings on the windowsill. *So, what's she suggesting*? He decided not to give her the satisfaction of eye contact. Instead, he buried his face in a dry towel and wiped the remaining shave cream off his face. Before he looked up again, Samira's arms were around his middle from behind. *I'm going to need a cold shower instead of a hot one.*

"I'm glad you're a man of your word." Samira tucked her fingers under the waistband of his shorts.

I'm not so sure I'm as grateful. "What about your terms of agreement?" He put the towel over the edge of the sink and turned around to face her. *I am not going to terminate an agreement without reading the face of the one who drafted the conditions.*

Samira's hands moved over his bare shoulders and locked behind his head. "The terms of the original agreement ended at daylight," she said slowly. "And as far as I'm aware, no new terms have been set for the new day."

J.P. ran his hands over her hips. No panties. *Now there's a silent invitation if I've ever known one.*

"I'd hate to keep you from your family again." *The last thing I need to do is piss off her father before brunch.*

"Krissy wasn't even awake yet, and Mama and Kara had gone to the store for eggs."

J.P. ran his hand up her backside and cupped it behind her ear right before he kissed her.

Samira broke the kiss gently. She took his hand and almost on tiptoe, led him back to his bed.

This time when she reached to remove the t-shirt, he didn't stop her like he had before.

"What time do you have to be at the office?"

J.P. could feel her hand against the small of his back.

"It doesn't matter." *Nothing is going to rush this moment.* He'd waited for it for too long. He felt the curves of her body with his hands as he kissed her again. *Nothing has ever felt this right.* He rolled slowly onto his back, pulling her with him as he moved.

"I don't want to make you late."

She's still talking to me in my bed. J.P. pulled her leg over his hips and moved her back into the same position he'd experienced in the darkness of the night. "You won't."

Samira leaned over him and balanced her weight on her forearms. He enjoyed the sensation of her hair when it brushed against his bare chest. He didn't dare close his eyes for fear he'd miss the passion in her dark eyes.

"I think we've been this far before."

The desire J.P. was hoping to see in her eyes was overshadowed by a fresh playfulness that brought an easy smile to his lips. She kissed his smile.

We have, but this time it's daylight and I can see all of you. He allowed her next kiss to linger. *And I like everything I see.* J.P. sat up into her just as he'd done the night before, but this time, he didn't have to hold back. The delayed response of the moment was sweeter than it would have been had they rushed into it the night before. J.P. realized that fully as the warmth of her body consumed his entire being.

She is very much worth the wait. J.P. pulled her slightly forward and moved gently within her. *Without a doubt, she's all I'll ever need.*

57 *In Pursuit of Victory*

Samira

The afternoon had been long, and it wasn't over yet. Samira leaned into the mirror in the lady's room to reapply her lipstick. She hoped it would make her look fresher than she felt. *Another hour,* she told herself. *Then I can go home and get off my feet.*

It was Thursday. She'd spent all morning on the telephone confirming the library events for the next quarter in preparation for the noon board meeting. *That meeting lasted way longer than I anticipated.* Now she was at the high school gym waiting for Kara to play her fourth volleyball match.

A loud buzzer from the gym announced the start of another game. Samira inhaled deeply and gave her reflection a weary nod. *Smile.*

"Samira. Come here."

Oh no, not Susan. Samira stopped in her tracks. *Be polite but firm.* Much to her dismay, Susan was pulling a man by his coat sleeve. *How does he always seem to show up?*

"Look who I found wandering the halls." Susan was proud of her catch.

"I wasn't exactly wandering," Mike Benson raised his bushy eyebrows at Samira. "I'm late and have a feeling I might be too late."

"Oh, don't be silly. It's never too late." Susan was still pulling on his arm.

Poor Mike. He doesn't need Susan's meddling. "Mike Benson," Samira stuck out her hand. "It's good to see you again." His hair was wet. *He obviously walked in the rain.*

Susan let Mike's arm go and clapped her hands together. "Oh, and you remember each other too. How perfect." She reached with both hands and straightened Samira's suit jacket from the bottom. "Well, I'll let you two chat. Take your time. I'll keep stats on Kara for you." Susan began to walk away slowly. Twice she turned around and made encouraging gestures in Samira's direction.

Mike rolled his neck from side to side. "She's a case, isn't she? I think she gave me whiplash."

He's obviously here to see Kelly. "May I help you find your date?" *I just talked to her a few minutes ago. Funny, she didn't mention Mike.*

Mike adjusted the loose watch around his wrist. "Well, let's see. I told her I'd be here forty minutes ago."

Samira stepped aside so a group of high school girls could pass by. "She's probably watching the game."

Mike seemed distracted. He pushed a button on his cell phone and put it to his ear. "I didn't know there was a game today." He sounded rushed. "Hang on."

Samira looked through the open gym door. Kara was still sitting on the bench next to her coach. *I don't want to miss her game.* Her eyes went on up into the bleachers and stopped on her mother. *And I told Mama I'd be right back.* Samira tuned into Mike's end of the telephone conversation.

"...No, trust me and just come in here a sec, alright?" Mike's voice was forceful. He punched another button on his phone and dropped it into his suit pocket. "Our mutual friend is sitting outside in my car."

"Phil is here? At the school?" *Really?*

"It's a long story, but he's without transportation and I'm without my date so we're both a little stressed. Is she in there?" Mike nodded toward the gym.

"Probably."

Mike's face was already searching the bleachers. "What are you doing here anyway?"

"It's my daughter's game." Samira looked back into the gym. Kara was still on the bench. *Fortunately.*

"Miss Samira, you may have just saved my hide and my date." Mike Benson looked from the crowd back to her. "If that red-headed English teacher is still talking to me when I finally work my way to the top of those stands, I owe you a favor."

"You don't owe me anything." Samira knew Kelly was patiently waiting. *She's not the type to be bent out of shape over a late appointment.*

There wasn't a minute's hesitation in Mike's step. He stopped inside the door, paid his entrance fee, then took off in full stride for the bleachers. *I wonder if he's been here before.* Samira watched Mike climb effortlessly to the very top of the stands where he bent one knee on the bleacher in front of Kelly. *There goes the explanation and dramatic apology.*

Her eyes went back to the game just in time to see Kara trade places with another player. *That's my girl.* She showed the red mark on her hand to the door attendant, then stepped inside so she could see better.

They put her in to serve. The ball left Kara's hand and bounced near the baseline of the opposing court. *12-13.* The line judge rolled the ball under the net and Kara served again. *13-13. Nice going.* Samira clapped with the crowd. *14-13. You go, Kara.* The next serve went into play and the home team lost the serve.

"She's good."

Samira's eyes went to Mike in the stands. *I don't know if I'm ready to face that voice in public.* She turned and faced Phil who was standing several feet directly behind her. *Especially in a public that includes my mother.*

"She gets her athletic ability from her father."

"She gets her poise from her mother."

The ball was back in play. "Not hardly." *I really want to watch this. 14-15. Come on, girls.* Samira could feel Phil's presence move closer. "Tom had nerves of steel." She remembered well. "That's what made him so valuable on the police force." *14-16. Win the serve back, ladies.* She was relieved to see Kara's coach call timeout. "They play the best of five. This is game four."

"Poise and nerves are two different things." Phil picked up the conversation. "And the poise she gets from you. It's very becoming."

Samira blushed. She stepped out of the doorway, hoping her mother wasn't paying any attention. *Or Susan for that matter.*

Mike Benson appeared suddenly.

"I hate to prolong this situation," Mike tried to apologize. "But it seems my date would like to stay and watch the end of this match." Mike's face was extremely serious. "And being the gentleman I am, I'm inclined to give her the benefit of my presence through the remainder of this game."

The look on Phil's face was total frustration, yet the way Mike addressed him was very comical.

These two are funny together.

Phil looked from Mike to Samira, and then back again. "Counselor, it would seem that you've forgotten one major detail of a promise you made earlier today."

Mike crossed his fingers behind his back so Samira could see. "And what promise might that have been?"

"The promise that you would run me back to the office immediately following the afternoon meeting."

Phil is far more serious than Mike realizes.

Mike continued to hold his hand behind his back. "The stipulation to that promise was that the meeting needed to end on time." The damp curls on Mike's head bobbed as he talked. "Seeing as how you were in charge of that ever-so important business maneuver, it would seem you should have ended it in a timely fashion to accommodate the original agreement."

Samira was trying to concentrate on the game, but with Mike's final comment, she burst out laughing.

"Then give me the keys to your car and I'll come back and get you."

He really wants to go.

"By the time you get back to the office, the game will be over, and I'll be ready for my car again. What's another twenty minutes anyway?"

"Maybe your date could drop you off at my office to pick up your car when this whole thing is over."

"Here, tell you what, Counselor,"

Samira listened to Mike's voice amidst the crowd noise.

"Let's just call this a return favor. You owe me a couple of doosies anyway and this one will only cost you a few minutes of your time."

"Mike, come on," Phil was beginning to plead. "I have a shit load of paperwork to complete by morning and you know it."

Samira continued to listen.

"You'd take a dinner break and work out, right?"

"Later."

"Just consider this an early break."

"I don't see a place to eat anywhere near this volleyball game."

"Ah, you're just not looking hard enough."

Samira turned around just in time to see Mike place a green bill in Phil's hand.

"There's a concession stand down that hall. I passed it when I was looking for Miss Davis." Mike sounded very matter of fact. "And I'm almost certain the popcorn was fresh."

Mike turned and spoke to Samira. "He'll be fine. He just needs to unwind a minute. Way too intense today, but gut feeling tells me he doesn't have anything smaller than a fifty in his wallet." With that statement, Mike made a swift departure.

Samira's eyes followed him all the way to the top of the bleachers where Kelly was contentedly watching the game. *Interesting Mike knows Phil only carries large bills. But I need to be paying closer attention.* Despite that desire, she turned just long enough to make eye contact with Phil again. His face showed signs of obvious irritation.

"This is the third time I've been stranded today." He ran his hand through his damp hair. "And to be honest, my patience is about shot."

I understand. Noise from the crowd took her eyes back to the scoreboard. *If Kara weren't playing, I'd drive him myself. 20-18. And Paula is serving.*

"Do you want to take my car?"

For the first time since he'd walked into the building, Phil's face looked hopeful. But then he seemed to have a second thought. "Then how would you get home? It's raining. And it's a hell of a long walk."

"My mom is here. She can take us home." *I don't know how I'll explain that to her, but I'm sure she'll give us a ride.*

"My truck should be back at the office by now."

Phil started to explain but Samira's attention shifted back to the game. Paula lost the serve, and the opponents were tied again. *I really need to get off my feet.* "Do you want to sit down for a minute?"

Phil looked blankly into the gym, then ran his tongue over his bottom lip. "Sure." He threw his hands out in surrender and started to follow Samira.

"Excuse me, sir. That will be three dollars." The ticket taker held out her hand.

Phil handed over the bill Mike had given him and waited for change.

That was easier than changing a fifty.

Phil sat down beside Samira.

I wonder if anyone in this crowd will recognize J.P. Ralston. She lifted her feet out of her dress shoes and placed her nylon toes on the bleacher in front of them. *That feels better.*

And Kara is serving again. Samira sat on her hands and watched as Kara served the first point. *22-20. They must win by two.* "If they win this game, they'll play one more to fifteen." *23-20.*

"Hey there, stranger." Krissy was suddenly seating herself directly in front of them. "Where did you come from?" Krissy's friend plopped down directly in front of Samira. "Tif, meet Phil. Phil, Tif—short for Tiffany but she hates her real name."

Krissy hasn't seen Phil since the ranch, yet she picks up like they just left off.

Phil yanked Krissy's ponytail playfully. Samira looked in time to see his easy smile. "Pleased to meet you, Tif. I understand about the name thing." Phil played the game politely. He winked at Samira.

Kara missed the serve, and the opponents took over again. Samira buried her face in her hands more in reaction to Krissy's arrival than to Kara's missed serve.

"Don't worry, Mama, they'll get it back." Krissy nodded toward the home team. "See? Christine Jackson is up next. She'll ace the next serve."

First, they must win the serve back.

"I'm starving." Krissy held out her hand. "Can I have some money, please, please?"

"Krissy, it's less than an hour before we get home."

"But my stomach can't wait an hour."

Can't she just leave me be until after the game? Samira thought again. *That's a very selfish thing to think.* She reached for her purse. *And they're tied again. I can't stand it.*

"Here," Phil took Krissy's hand and pressed Mike's change into her palm. "Go. Be happy."

"Oh, my gosh." Krissy squealed. "You're awesome. Thanks." Without a moment's hesitation, Krissy threw her arms around Phil's neck and hugged him.

In front of God and everybody. "How much did you give her?"

"Two bucks."

"That's it?" Samira was shocked. *She thinks he's awesome for two bucks.*

"That's it, why?"

"Because she's never reacted that way when I've given her money." Samira watched as Christine Jackson aced a serve over the net. 24-23. The crowd went wild causing Samira to wish she weren't sitting in a busy gym. *I can't even hear myself think. And thinking would be helpful right now.*

"That's game."

"There's one more." Samira stated over the cheers. "For the match."

"I figured as much."

She remembered her offer. "Are you sure you don't want to take my car?"

Phil looked over his shoulder. Samira looked too. *Mike and Kelly don't look like they're ready to leave yet.* The people in the stands around them sat back down in their seats.

"You know, if you really don't mind, I'd be inclined to do just that."

"I don't mind," Samira reached for her purse. *Anything to relieve his tension.*

"I can call you later or stop by so you can take me back to my truck."

Whatever works for him. "That's fine." Samira handed him her keys. "I'm in the second row on the south side."

Phil nodded. "You're sure you're okay with this?"

"Positive." *I'll think of something to tell Mama.*

"Then I'll give you a call in a while." Phil thanked her and started to stand up.

"Wait." Krissy was suddenly present again. "Don't go yet."

Samira followed Krissy's backward glance and spotted her mother walking directly toward them. *Oh, Krissy, how could you?* The clock on the gymnasium wall was ticking off a ten-minute break between the games. *That's way too much time.*

Phil waited politely as Krissy helped her grandmother onto the bottom bleacher. "Here they are, Granny." Krissy was beaming from ear to ear. "Phil, this is my grandmother, Ashleigh."

Samira closed her eyes. *Why am I so embarrassed for Mama to meet Phil?*

"And Granny, this is Phil, the one I've been talking to you about."

The one she's been talking to Mama about. Samira opened her eyes to see Phil kindly greet her mother. *He is very gentle, yet professional, and calm. And sexy.* The last thought caught Samira totally off guard.

Phil excused himself from the introduction very casually and then turned to face Samira again. He held out her car keys. "I'll be in touch later."

Okay. Samira nodded. She was so tongue-tied now she didn't know if she would ever recover. *And there's still five minutes of break.*

"I'm going to go to the restroom, Samira," her mother patted her knee. "I'll be right back."

Krissy disappeared as quickly as she'd appeared leaving Samira to her own thoughts. The whole turn of events was too much too fast.

"Would you just look at him, Samira?" Susan was talking loudly as she made her way down the bleachers.

She's just what I don't need.

"I can't believe it. But I think we've lost your window of opportunity." Susan was thoroughly disgusted. "Just look at the way he's talking with Miss Davis. You'd think he's known her for some time the way they are carrying on."

Samira turned around and made eye contact with Kelly and Mike. They waved and she waved back. *Maybe that will keep Susan out of my love life for a while.*

"I'm telling you Samira, the way you scare them off, it's safe to say that you're going to end up an old maid." Susan's eyes went to the top of the bleachers again. "He was quite the catch and you screwed it up." Susan continued down the bleachers without fully stopping.

Thank you, God, for taking her away.

"This is an exciting afternoon." Ashleigh took her a seat next to Samira. The teams had switched sides and now the serving position for the home team was right in front of Samira and her mother. "Kara didn't think they would have a chance and just look at the way they're playing."

But what she's saying and what she's thinking are two different things. Samira knew her mother meant well. *The excitement she's referring to is more than the game.*

I might as well tell her the truth. "I didn't know Phil was going to be here."

"I assumed as much," Ashleigh's eyes were on the game. She clapped with the crowd as the home team scored a point. "I'm sure you might have wanted me to meet Phil in a different setting, but it's alright honey." She clapped again when they scored. "He seems like a very nice man."

I can always count on Mama to hold her thoughts until she processes them further. Samira tried to concentrate on the game, but it was difficult to think about volleyball when the man she loved had just appeared at her daughter's game. "He rode over here with his best friend, but his friend decided to stay for the rest of the match. Phil needed to get back to work so I loaned him my car."

"That was very nice of you, dear." Ashleigh smiled politely. "So, you and the girls will need a ride home?"

Samira nodded.

"I can stir up some beef and noodles quick after the game and you won't have to fix a meal."

Samira's first reaction was to decline, but the thought of not having to put a meal on the table was very inviting. On a second thought she accepted the invitation.

Ashleigh clapped again. "Wonderful. Your father will be home by then. We've been missing you."

Kara was next to serve.

I know, ever since I missed the birthday party. Samira put her elbows on her knees and rested her chin in her hands. *Had I known how long they'd hold that over my head, I might have made a different decision.* Samira watched her daughter drop a serve near the baseline, scoring for her team again. *But then again, I'd have missed that whole night and the next morning with Phil.* Samira forced her attention back to her mother's voice.

"Where does this Phil work, honey?"

"He's an attorney. He has his own practice." Now Samira was glad for the noise of the crowd.

Ashleigh nodded slightly. Her salt and pepper hair was tucked back into a loose bun at the nape of her neck. "He looks very professional. And a very nice smile too."

But you should see him in the morning when he hasn't shaved and he's all sleepy and unaware. Samira smiled. "Yes, he does have a great smile, doesn't he?"

"And he makes you smile." The mother looked directly into her daughter's eyes. "I haven't seen you smile like that in a long while, Samira."

Samira looked back to the game. "Like what?"

"I'm your mother, Samira." Ashleigh also looked back to the game. "I know your expressions and the one you wore in the doorway over there was a genuine smitten look."

She was watching me. Samira sighed, once again very aware of her transparency. *It's just as well Krissy brought her over now.*

"Just be careful, dear."

Samira closed her eyes. *I know Mama's going to finish that thought.*

"It seems he could spare a few minutes to finish a freshman volleyball game."

Samira rocked back with her hands against the bleachers. She had no desire to hear the rest of the observation.

They don't even know Phil yet, so I don't dare defend him.

"Now I just hope they can hang on." Ashleigh's excitement for Kara's team was sincere.

I hope I can hang on.

They finished the match. *15-10. Excellent game for freshmen girls.* The season was almost over already. *They've come so far this year.* Samira stood to applaud with the rest of the crowd. Just the thought of putting her feet back in her heels made her feet hurt again.

"Do you want to stop at home and change?"

Oh, thank you. "That's a good idea. My feet are killing me."

"You look tired, dear." Ashleigh stepped down a bleacher. "I'll go get my coat and meet you in the hall."

I am tired. I've been tired since last weekend when I stayed up too late Friday night. Reluctantly she slipped her foot back inside the leather pump.

"Am I correct in assuming that our mutual friend made an independent departure?"

Mike Benson was standing on the gym floor in front of Samira. Kelly was a few feet away chatting with a group of parents. "Yes, he did."

"Sorry about that." Mike folded his hands in front of his jacket. "I thought maybe he'd relax and stick around a few more minutes if I stayed."

"That's okay." Samira started to walk toward the steps, but Mike offered his hand. She accepted and stepped down off the bleacher seats. "This is a lot for Phil and me to juggle."

Mike was listening with his eyes.

"It's like, I don't know." Samira buttoned her suit jacket. "When we're alone together we're great. Everything is good." She thought a minute more. "But then when other people are around, we're on guard somehow and it's not very comfortable for either one of us."

Mike was nodding his head and smiling gently. "I know. You'd think with J.P. being an attorney and all he'd be great in a crowd, but he's a natural solitude seeker."

Kelly was still visiting as Samira and Mike started toward the door into the hallway. "And so are you."

"Do you think?" *Boy, he reads me like a book.* In the distance she could see Krissy talking with her grandmother.

"Pretty sure about that." Mike wiggled his eyebrows and without looking away he lifted his arm for Kelly to step under.

How did he know she was coming? The sunny smile of the English teacher made Samira smile.

"He couldn't take the crowd, could he?"

"That's okay."

"Do you need a ride home?"

"What the hell?" Mike was stunned. "He took your car?"

"I offered." Samira corrected. "He needed to go, and I needed him to be gone." Her eyes went back to her mother. *As much as I love my mother, how do I explain this intense, passionate man?*

"I saw you hand over the keys," Kelly admitted. "I'm going with Mike. You can have my car."

"Oh no." Samira was surprised at the offer. "My mom will take us home. We're just waiting on Kara."

"Are you sure?"

"Positive." *For the most part.* Samira thanked her friend for the offer. *That's far more than Susan would have ever done for me.*

"Okay, then we're out of here. We have a racket ball court with our name on it," Mike announced. "Catch you later?"

"More than likely." Samira was surprised how often she bumped into Mike.

Kara emerged from the locker room, changed and ready to relive the game. All the way home, Samira participated in the excitement of the big win with guarded detachment.

My greatest victory will be winning Phil over to my parents. He's going to challenge everything they've ever imagined for me and the girls.

58 *Belonging*

Joseph Phillip

The garage door was open when J.P. arrived at Samira's house. He pulled her Camry inside and turned off the engine. The headlights of his pickup pulled in behind him. Mike's Corvette was parked in the street at the end of the driveway.

"I can't believe you let a girl drive your car." J.P. snagged his truck keys out of the air.

"She either drove my car or your truck."

"You made the right decision." J.P. grinned. "You and Kelly seem to be getting on."

Mike shook his head. "I don't know what you're talking about. We're strictly business, nothing more." He pointed toward the house. "But that one in there, she's one to be getting on with."

"I'll take care of my own business, thank you." J.P. was slightly humored. "Thanks for bringing the truck."

"It's the least we could do after the mess at the school." Mike narrowed his eyes in thought. "Contrary to what you might be thinking, I really had no idea Samira would be there."

Mike doesn't apologize often. "I know. No harm done."

"I know, but, well, it just didn't go like I thought it might."

"It's a done deal, good buddy." J.P. nodded toward Mike's car. "Kelly's waiting." "Alrighty then."

He's either stalling, or his woman has put him up to something.

"Kelly and I were talking."

Here it comes.

"We'd like to go out with you and Samira Saturday night after Stephenson's cocktail party. You know, take them along for the party then maybe have dinner somewhere."

We don't take our women out together, Mikey. Remember our rules? J.P.'s first instinct was to decline the offer. "I don't take women with me on local business, Mikey."

"I usually don't either, but this is only a cocktail party with Stephenson." He shrugged his shoulders inside the bulky sweatshirt. "I'm planning to take Kelly."

"You're taking Kelly over me?"

"Maybe, but it's not like we have an official role there. We're making an appearance strictly for a professional presence. So, I thought I'd invite her along. If you invited Samira, then we could make a quick appearance at the gathering and then find a decent dinner somewhere."

Kelly put him up to this. J.P. still didn't like the idea, but Mike was speaking so earnestly J.P. couldn't bring himself to say no. "Let me talk to her about it."

"That's fine, take your time." Mike was getting anxious. "But we're set for tomorrow, right?"

"Yeah, everything is a go. Sparky will be in position early in the morning at Mid-America. The Hughes Corporation is sending their CFO with the deposit at ten. Everything after that should be a cakewalk."

"Do you really think Bridges is going to take the bait?"

"We have nothing to lose by trying."

"Gotta like it." Mike clapped his hands together. "Hey, that property closing between Hughes and Mid-America was sweet." Mike patted J.P. hard on the shoulder. "That's a business fusion Joplin's been needing for too long."

Considering Bridges almost severed the relations between the city's business world and Hughes last summer, this is a very amazing turn of events. "Things are starting to come together." *I finally feel like I'm making progress after a long summer of setbacks.*

"I can't believe you kept it quiet long enough to pull it off."

Easier said than done. Mike was starting to fidget. J.P. was amused.

"So, I guess I'll see you tomorrow then?"

"Don't let me keep you, Counselor."

Okay." Mike started for his car. "I'm going to go then."

The look on Mike's face made J.P. laugh out loud. *He's either extremely anxious to be alone with Kelly, or he's scared to death.*

Mike turned around as he reached the end of the driveway. "Don't forget to ask about Saturday."

I can't believe he's letting his girl chauffeur him in his own car. That's nuts. If it's my truck, I'm going to drive it.

All three Cartwright women were gathered at the dining room table. Samira had changed from her business suit into a warmup outfit. *She looks far more comfortable, but the suit was a nice touch.*

"Hey ladies." J.P. pushed the garage door button as he stepped into the kitchen.

"Hey." Samira looked up and forced a tired smile. "Come on in." She stood up. "Can I get you something?"

Always a hostess. "No, I'm fine, thanks." *The fireplace is a nice touch tonight.*

"Did you eat supper?"

Dinner. Remember to ask her about dinner. "Yeah, I did. On the way back to the office." J.P. looked back to the girls. Kara had moved closer to her sister. Krissy had her face buried in her hands.

"We're struggling with last minute homework." Samira explained the situation wearily. "I didn't think to ask them about homework before I accepted my mother's invitation to dinner. So now we're cramming it in last minute."

It looks serious. "What are we working on?"

Samira closed her eyes. "Math. And it's math beyond me." She opened her eyes again. "Kara is trying to check them so we can do the next problem. She only has three left."

He leaned over the girls. "Having any luck?"

"Not really," Kara replied. "I get two different answers every time."

"Let's see," J.P. sat down in another chair and motioned for Kara to slide the book over. Krissy looked up. *Poor kid's been crying.*

"Only the even numbers." Kara ran her hand over the problems.

J.P. took his reading glasses out of his interior jacket pocket.

"I didn't know you wore glasses." Krissy seemed to perk up.

"Only when the numbers on the page are too small to see with normal eyes." J.P. wiggled his eyebrows at Krissy. He read the problem in the text and compared it to Krissy's work as he rolled the cuffs on his shirt. *She's set the problems up backwards.* He could feel Krissy watching him.

"You look very distinguished wearing glasses."

"Why thank you." *They make me feel old.* He picked up the pencil on the table and wrote out the numbers on a piece of scratch paper.

"You play a wicked game of volleyball, Kara."

Kara's face lit up immediately. "Thanks. Were you there?"

"I saw part of a game."

Kara launched into a recap of the final game as J.P. worked the problem in his head.

"Keep practicing and you'll be the clinch server on varsity." *There, that's the way the problem should look.* "Okay, Krissy, take a look at this," J.P. turned the book so she could see what he'd done. "You need to rearrange your problem to look like this. You had the formula backwards. You can get the answer that way, but it will take a lot longer."

He watched Krissy study the numbers.

"I'm going to go shower and get ready for bed, okay, Mama?" Kara pushed her chair back under the table.

There she goes, calling Samira Mama again. It's very southern.

"Can you work it from here?"

"I think so." Krissy took the pencil and went to work.

J.P. turned around to see Samira sitting on a stool at the kitchen island. Her head was bent over a pile of papers, seemingly deep in thought. Krissy finished the problem and turned the paper back around.

J.P. checked the answer against his own. "That's right." He pointed to the next one. "Now set this one up the same way."

"We're only doing the evens."

"I know, do the odd ones for practice."

Krissy's swollen eyes challenged him. "But I can't check the answers in the back on the odd ones."

"I have the answers, Krissy."

"Where?"

J.P. chuckled. "In my head." He pointed to the next problem. "It's only going to take a minute." J.P. leaned back in his chair and linked his fingers behind his head. "I'll wait."

"You're crazy." Krissy went back to work.

No, Mike is crazy. I'm just a hard ass.

"Maybe you can help Mama with her papers while I'm working on this."

He looked over his shoulder at Samira. *Does she have homework too?* J.P. left his glasses on the table and stepped around to see what she was working on. "Math?"

Samira sat up straight and pushed the papers away. "It's nothing really."

"It's due tomorrow, isn't it? You said you needed a lawyer to figure it out." Krissy made the statement without looking up.

Samira closed her eyes again. "Yes, it's due tomorrow, Krissy. Thanks for your concern."

She's wishing Krissy would mind her own business. J.P. put his hands against Samira's shoulders and pressed his thumbs into the base of her neck.

Tense. Very tense. Samira pulled her hair over a shoulder and allowed him to continue the massage. *If we didn't have company, I could do her whole body.* He couldn't help but notice the return address on the legal sized envelope. *Cramer? I thought he retired.*

"Done with that one." Krissy pushed the book to the end of the table.

J.P. returned to the dining room table for his glasses. He checked her work. "Good. Do the next three."

"The next three in a row or just the next three even?" Krissy turned her crystal blue eyes up to his.

It's getting late. "Even."

"Good." Krissy bent over her book with renewed understanding. "Then I'll be done." J.P. watched her write a set of numbers. "It's easier this way."

"This is the correct way, that's why it's easier."

"Well, it works anyway."

Samira picked up her papers and carried them to the table. "I do need a lawyer to figure these out." She pulled out a chair and sat down. There is a lot of legal jargon that I don't understand." Her dark eyes met his with a sense of surrender.

J.P. sat back down in the same chair. "Well, let's see, I happen to know a good attorney who might be able to help you, but I think he's on a date right now." *Remember to ask her about dinner on Saturday.* He pulled his telephone off his belt. "But I might be able to reach him if you really need assistance." J.P. rested his elbows on his knees and swiped his thumb over the screen.

Samira took the phone out of his hand.

"That isn't exactly the one I had in mind."

"You're a lawyer, aren't you?" Krissy asked the question as she pushed her paper toward J.P.

"You know, Krissy, I am." He started to check the math in his head.

"Then maybe you could just do it for her."

I love the way she just puts it out there. J.P. couldn't hide his smile. *She's a handful, but I like the spunk.* "You set it up right but did the math wrong." J.P. turned the paper around again. "Check your sums."

"Oh, great." Krissy took the paper back. She found her error and fixed it. "Is that better?"

J.P. read upside down. "That's the right answer. Is that better?"

"You mess with my mind."

J.P. laughed out loud. *Any mind as busy as hers needs a challenge.* "Two more and you're done."

"Good, because I'm tired."

So is your mother. J.P. looked back at Samira who was quietly watching the exchange between him and her daughter. "I really don't mind."

"Krissy?" Samira looked confused.

"No, looking at your papers." He opened his hand. *I don't really want her working with Cramer anyway. He's clueless about ninety percent of the time.* "What are we looking at?"

Samira put her elbows on the table and rested her chin in her hands. "I get these once every year or so concerning the girls' Trusts from Tom's estate."

"Tom was my dad." Krissy clarified.

"I have to agree to the changes, sign, and return in the envelope provided by tomorrow to avoid penalties."

"You don't have to agree." *She doesn't have to agree to anything if she doesn't want to.* "And there shouldn't be any penalties."

"I do if I don't know what the other options are," Samira explained. "That's where I'm stuck."

Krissy spun her paper around again. "Done. And I double checked the math this time."

She's quick.

"I'm going to go get ready for bed while he checks them."

"I know it's the end of the day, Phil." Samira touched his arm. "You don't have to read this if you don't want to."

It's the least I can do for a Pretty Lady. "I don't mind." *Besides, I owe her a favor.* He set the legal papers aside to check Krissy's math. "It's what I do, you know." He circled a wrong answer.

"I do know, but you're off the clock."

"A good attorney is never off the clock."

"Really?" Samira sounded doubtful. "Does that mean I'll get a bill in the mail later?"

Only if I mention the favor to Denise. "Yeah. It'll read, *services rendered.*" J.P. refused to look at Samira's face.

"Mr. Ralston."

"Yes ma'am?" J.P. could feel the tension lift. But Samira didn't respond right away. She was biting her bottom lip and her face was thoughtful. *I don't know if I should interrupt her thoughts or not.*

Krissy reappeared wearing flannel pajamas. "How many did I miss?"

"One."

"Good." She picked up the pencil. "Easy one, too." She made the correction. "That's the kind of mistake that costs me points in tests."

"Work the problem, then double check your math." *I feel more like a father than I do an attorney.* J.P. thought about that for a minute. *Now there's a frightening thought, Mr. Ralston.*

Samira was still watching him.

"What?" *Talk to me, Pretty Lady.*

Krissy put her math book away.

"I'll keep that a minute," J.P. snagged the pencil before Krissy put it away.

"I just realized something."

J.P. leaned back in his chair and stretched his legs out far enough to touch her sock feet with his. "Can you share that realization?" *Now I feel like an attorney again.*

"Not just yet," Samira pulled her feet away and stood up. "I'm going to see if Kara is in bed yet." She disappeared in the hallway leading to the bedrooms.

"I'll wait."

"You already said that once." Krissy was gathering up the stray homework items off the table.

"I'm a man of my word, then, right?"

Samira was suddenly in the archway of the hall again. She tipped her head to the side just enough to let J.P. know he'd been heard. *I'll keep my word anytime, but especially whenever that lady is involved.*

"Good night, Phil," Krissy was following in her mother's footsteps. "Thanks for the popcorn at the game and for the help with my math. Next time I'll call you before I stress out."

And I'll answer. "Anytime, Krissy. Sleep tight."

"You too," Krissy said with a yawn.

J.P. picked up Samira's papers and the pencil and took them to the sofa. He tried to turn on a lamp, but nothing happened.

"Oh, it's on the Alexa." Krissy was packing up the last of her homework.

J.P. didn't understand.

"The lamp." Krissy zipped her backpack. "Alexa. Turn on the sofa lamp."

The light illuminated immediately.

Interesting. The woman doesn't own a cell phone, but she programs her lights to a computer. He glanced through the papers from Tom's trust. *These don't look too intimidating.* He skimmed the first part. *She just needs to make an educated decision and sign. You'd think Cramer could take time to at least walk a client through the options instead of just mailing them out for a signature.*

A phone rang but J.P. didn't respond. *It's not my house.*

It rang again.

"Is this your phone?"

Kara was walking toward him. The phone in her hand rang again.

Oh hey, it is my phone. J.P. checked the I.D.

"James."

"Yeah. Dad."

He set the papers aside. "What's up?" *He sounds defeated.*

"Not much."

"Are you home?"

"Not yet. I'm at a friend's house waiting for Mom to pick me up."

J.P. checked his watch as he removed his reading glasses. It was nearing ten o'clock. *You'd think she could pick them up in a timely manner.*

"What's up for your weekend?"

I gotta remember to ask Samira about Saturday. "I'm working, that's about it. Might have plans Saturday evening. Might not." *But I hope I do.*

"All night plans?"

Only by God's grace. "Doubtful." J.P.'s eyes followed Samira across the room. She stopped at the kitchen sink.

"Josh and I were thinking about coming down after the game."

"Come on down." He watched Samira dim the kitchen lights. *Smells like she's brewing a cup of coffee.* "Do you need me to pick you up?"

"Don't know yet." James's voice was more distant than usual. "I'll find out and call you."

"Is everything alright?" *Something doesn't sound right.*

"Yeah, for the most part." There was a long pause on the other end. "I just need to get out of here for a while."

"Where's your game?"

"Home."

"I'll come pick you up if need be." *I don't like the tone of his voice.* He fingered the papers as Samira curled up in the corner of the sofa. "Just say the word." *God, she is beautiful.* He was listening to James, but his eyes were on Samira as she sipped a cup of coffee. *How can she drink coffee this late in the day?*

"Well, it looks like Mom's headlights. I'd better go."

He's only told me half of what's on his mind. "James, call me back tomorrow, alright?"

"Alright."

"Hang in."

"Yeah, I will. Later."

"Later." A few seconds later the call disconnected.

Samira's toes pressed into the side of his thigh. "James?"

"James." J.P. closed his phone and set it on the coffee table. "He's ready for a break."

"I can understand that."

I guess she can. Bruce Hamilton is a bastard. "I need to get the boys transportation so they can come and go as they please."

"Do you think James can stick it out a whole year?" Samira's eyes were genuinely concerned.

Doubtful. "I don't know." *But what would I do with him down here all the time?*

Samira wrapped both of her hands around the mug. "You'll figure it out when the time comes."

How does she know what I'm thinking?

"You really don't have to look over those papers. I know it's late."

"It's late for you," J.P. corrected. *I'm usually checking Sports Center on ESPN about now.* He glanced at her silent television screen. *I don't think I've ever seen her watch tv.* "I'm usually home in front of the television reviewing a pile much deeper than this." He put his glasses back on and flipped the front page over the clip at the top. "Besides, I'm halfway through it already."

"That's amazing in itself," Samira set her cup on a ceramic coaster. "I've lost sleep just trying to get through the first page."

J.P. rubbed her feet with his hand. "This I can do." *It would be easy to do more than her feet.* "Just don't ask me to fix your sink or change the oil in your car."

Samira laughed unexpectedly.

"What?"

"You're so funny."

"No, I'm serious." J.P. corrected. "I don't do plumbing or cars."

"But you do this." Her hand slapped the papers hard.

"Yes, I do."

"That's funny."

No, it's not. He felt Samira's fingertips against his scalp. *And neither is that. If she wants me to get through this, she's going to have to stop doing that.*

J.P. skipped a page. *Let's just cut to the chase.* "Here, this is the part you need to understand." He leaned forward so Samira could follow along. "Do you want the girls to have access to the funds at age twenty-one or twenty-five. And," J.P. moved his finger across a line so she could see where he was reading. "Do you want to specify what they can and cannot use the money for?"

"That's it?" Samira sounded unsure.

"Basically. There are more investment options, but you'd need to talk to a professional investor before making any changes there." *Too bad my sister-in-law lives so far away.* "Your other option is to check this box and request an extension on the deadline so you can make a more educated decision." *I should do a little research as to why the Trust requires an annual review. It should have been set in stone when it was opened.*

Samira looked directly into J.P.'s eyes with that remark. "I do have a decision to make." There was a sudden heaviness in her remark.

"Not tonight."

"No, I do, really." Samira picked up her coffee cup and sat back into the corner of the sofa again. "And earlier I realized you're the one I've been needing to talk to about it."

Oh, this is the revelation from a few minutes ago. He set the papers down again. "Alright." *Personal or business?* He set his glasses on top of the papers and rubbed the bridge of his nose with his thumb and forefinger. *I still need to ask her about Saturday night.*

Samira stared into her coffee cup like J.P. had seen her do many times before.

I can wait. Again.

"When I got home tonight there was a message on my machine from Mr. Marty Brown."

Who the hell is that? J.P. had to work hard not to be defensive at the mention of a man's name. *And what does he have to do with her?*

"Do you know him?"

"No, I can't say that I do."

"Well, he needs an answer by tomorrow afternoon," Samira unfolded her legs and left the sofa. J.P. followed her with his eyes to the dining room table where she started to straighten the loose papers leftover from Krissy's homework.

"And I don't know what to tell him." Samira sorted the papers and tossed the scratch into the trashcan by her desk.

What is she talking about? It took all of J.P.'s patience to wait. *This is one time I could use Krissy's input to move things along.* Unable to stand the suspense, J.P. left the sofa too. Samira started to wipe down the island counter with a rag. J.P. put his arms around her and stopped the motion.

"The counter is clean." *Very clean.* "And I can't be of much assistance to you if I don't know what you're talking about."

"I know." Samira leaned heavily in his arms.

Obviously, I'm going to have to ask questions to get the answers.

"What do you know?"

"I know that the counter is clean." Samira lobbed the damp rag toward the sink. "I already wiped it off."

J.P. couldn't help but smile in disbelief. *I was hoping for a subject matter on the previous conversation.* Her hesitation was beginning to make him wonder if Mr. Marty Brown had personal interests in Samira. *I'm not going to take a chance.*

"What kind of decision, Samira?" J.P. loosened his hold around her middle.

Samira's dark eyes were sad. "He offered me a job at the university."

What university? "And this is a bad thing?" *Usually, a job offer is more exciting than she's letting on.*

"No." Samira frowned. "Well, yes." She rolled her eyes. "I don't know if it is or not."

"Come on." J.P. couldn't take her indecision anymore. He took her by the hand he led her back to the living room where he sat her down in the easy chair. J.P. sat down on the coffee table directly in front of her. "Talk to me. Start at the beginning."

He watched Samira take a deep breath. "Normally, I talk these things through with my brother, but I already know his advice, so I decided not to tell him about the offer."

Okay, it's not the beginning, but at least she's talking.

"And I always talk about things like this with my parents, but I know their answer too."

"So, you didn't bring it up with them either?"

"No." Samira looked straight into his eyes. "Because now I know you're the reason I can't talk to them."

How do you end up in the middle of these things, Ralston?

"It's a really nice offer, Phil. It's more money, a nice office, a generous expense account, and exciting potential."

I'm still waiting.

"But I like what I do now. In fact, I really like what I do now. I know what's expected of me and I'm comfortable. There's no hidden agendas and nothing to take me out of my comfort zone, and I like it that way."

She doesn't want to change jobs. "So, what's the issue?"

"Until tonight I didn't know. But now I understand."

Understand what?

Samira folded her hands tightly and leaned forward in the chair. "I understand that you accept me just like this." She flung her hands out to her side. "Just like I am." Her eyes lit up a little. "I don't have anything to prove to you because you don't demand that of me."

Is this a good thing?

"Don't you see?" She started to stand up.

No, let's not wipe down an already clean counter again. He gently put his hands on her hips and guided her back into the chair.

"Mr. Marty Brown learned about me from several different sources within the infrastructure of my supervisory board. He decided I was the one he wanted to direct the fundraising programs for his alumni foundation. So, suddenly he has this idea of who I am and what I can do for him."

Makes sense. She's got a clear picture of Brown's motives.

"But I'm not the person he thinks I am. I'm a librarian who loves her work." Samira put her hands in her hair. "I really like what I do, in spite of my misgivings with this last guest artist."

Uberti. I knew he was trouble from the get-go.

"But, if I talk to my brother about it, he's going to tell me I'm boring and too safe, yet he's not much better than me. He's Mr. Conservative from the word go. Still, he'd think I was a fool for not taking the extra money and the challenge and at least giving it a whirl." Samira crossed her arms. "And my parents, well, they would encourage me to follow my heart. But really what they want me to do is follow my heart if it leads to the same conclusions they come to." She was talking extremely fast. "And my decision might not be the same as theirs." Samira rolled her eyes.

I've seen Kara do that hundreds of times.

"Don't get me wrong, they'd support my decision, but I know for a fact that after I'm out of ear shot, they'd talk about their disappointment in me because I didn't do what they preferred." Samira sighed and hung her head. "What kind of support is that?"

Agreed. She's onto something here.

"But not you, Phil." Now she looked into his face. "Not you. You say, 'what's the problem?' And there isn't one really. Because you trust me to be myself."

This is an amazing one-sided conversation. J.P. took Samira's hands. They were perfectly manicured as always. "Samira, this is the you I know. I don't want you to change a thing."

"Wow." Samira sighed. "I don't think anyone has ever said that to me and meant it." Her fingers gripped his tighter.

"You gotta be who you are, Pretty Lady. Even if it goes against someone else's notions."

Samira nodded.

How far can I take this without going too far? "Look. There's going to come a time when you'll break away from your family's expectations and live according to your own rules and your own ideas. In fact, over time my guess would be that they'd learn to trust your instincts more."

Samira's hands were still holding on for dear life. "Do you think?"

"I do." J.P. said those words again. "Yeah, I do." *In more ways than you know, I do.*

Samira's eyes were damp, but he knew her well enough by now that he knew she wasn't going to let them spill over into tears. "Then I do, too."

Now this is intense. Yet the hopefulness that had filled Samira's eyes brought another thought. *Why do they think they have a right to make decisions for her?*

Samira sighed again. "And then there's this." She let go of J.P.'s hands and climbed out of the chair. She disappeared into the hallway and returned with an opened shipping box. Samira set it on the table. "Ellen sent these. It arrived the day before yesterday but I'm not sure how I feel about it."

J.P. lifted the packing materials. *iPhone.* "For the girls?"

Samira removed another bulky wad of paper. "Three."

"Remind me. Ellen is?"

"Tom's sister. The girls' aunt."

I don't understand. "Why would she send you three iPhones?"

Samira sighed heavily. "I'm guessing the girls told her they wanted cell phones, and this is Ellen's way of granting their wish." Samira fished a handwritten note out of the bottom of the box.

J.P. read silently.

> *Samira, dear. These are for you and the girls. Mom and Dad are going to add you to their cell phone plan. The phones are activated and ready as soon as you turn them on. I hope you don't mind. Think of it as an early Christmas present. I thought it would help you keep track of these busy young women. Love, Ellen.*

He looked up at Samira who was still standing next to the coffee table. "Your thoughts?"

"The girls were at school when the box was delivered so I haven't told them about the phones yet." Samira started to tidy up some stray magazines on the end table. "I have held out on getting cell phone on purpose. Every student who comes through the library has their face buried in their phone screens." She plopped into the corner of the sofa. "I don't know. Sometimes it would make communications easier, but I just don't know if I'm ready."

I don't like the idea that her phones are on her former in-law's cell plan.

"Do the boys have phones of their own? I didn't see them with phones up at the ranch."

"Yeah. There's limited cell phone coverage at the ranch. But they've been on my plan for a while now." *How honest can I be with her about my concerns?*

"I don't know the first thing about a cell phone plan, except that adds an expense to my budget." Samira looked defeated. "But mostly I don't know if I like Ellen making this decision for me."

At least she recognizes the dilemma. J.P. sat down in the middle of the sofa. "I don't disagree at all, Samira. Ultimately, it's your call."

Samira nudged him with her stocking feet at the unintended pun.

J.P. put his hand over her foot. "Seriously though. If you don't want the girls to have phones yet, send these back."

Samira tipped her head back and ran her hand through her hair. "But it's Ellen. She's always buying something for the girls. I've never had to reject a gift from her. I don't know how she'll take it." Samira puckered her mouth in thought. "Nor do I know what Norma will say when I tell her I don't want to be on their phone plan."

Exactly. J.P. took a deep breath. *Why does she let so many people play into her decisions?* I guess you could get a cell plan of your own, then it would be more like a thanks but no thanks, as opposed to a direct rejection."

Samira closed her eyes and shook her head. "Not a bad idea, Counselor. But I don't think I have it in me to make a decision on anything tonight." She leaned forward and repacked the phones, including the note. "Maybe tomorrow."

J.P. ran his hand down her side and rested it against her hip as she sat next to him. "If you need help learning about how the cell plans work, I'm sure Denise would be willing to coach you. She manages—"

There was sudden tension in the room. "I know firsthand how Denise manages your business."

I forgot about the subpoena. J.P. decided to diffuse the unnecessary stress. "Trust me on this. The day will come when you'll know Denise better. You'll learn to appreciate her, I promise."

Samira looked over her shoulder doubtingly.

"Come here, Pretty Lady." J.P. pulled Samira toward him. Without asking permission he kissed her gently on the lips.

"I don't want you to leave," Samira whispered between kisses.

No more than I want to go.

Samira pulled away from his kiss. "I mean ever." The look in her eyes was completely sincere.

A slow realization surfaced from somewhere deep within. "I know." He ran his tongue over his bottom lip. "Me either." *I have no desire to spend the rest of my days across town in a house by myself knowing she's over here.* "We might have to figure this whole thing out."

Samira's face was suddenly full of light. J.P. laughed at her bright smile and reveled in the way her eyes scanned the room as if a whole new concept were developing in her mind.

"I want to show you something." J.P. stood up and slipped his hand into his front pocket. Mixed in with loose change and keys, he felt his mother's wedding rings.

"I've been thinking about this for a while now, but, uh," J.P. couldn't believe he was about to say the words he'd rehearsed a million times in his mind since leaving the ranch.

Samira opened her hands. "The same rings from your nightstand."

I forgot she's already seen these. "My mother's wedding rings." He placed the two separate rings in Samira's hand and watched as she turned them gently in her fingers. "She was everything my father ever needed even though they lived thousands of miles apart for the whole of their marriage. It's taken me most of my life to figure that out." J.P. inhaled very deeply. "I came extremely close to letting the only thing I ever needed walk out of my life, and I'm not willing to make that mistake twice."

Samira's eyes were full of wonder when she looked up into his.

You'd better say it now, Ralston, before you lose your nerve. J.P. took a deep breath. "When the time is right, I'd like to put another set of rings on your finger." *Nothing has ever seemed so right.*

Samira was still studying the rings in her hand, but now her eyes were moist. *I don't think she's going to be able to hold the emotion in this time.*

"That is, if she'll have me." *Not exactly how I rehearsed, but it's out there now.*

There were no words or sounds whatsoever. Samira simply rose from the sofa and wrapped her arms tightly around his waist and held him.

J.P. reciprocated, completely consumed by her presence. "It's taken me a hell of a long time to understand, Samira," J.P. spoke quietly as he held her. "But I know you belong to me."

She held on tighter.

"It doesn't matter where I am or what I'm doing, you are everything I'll ever need." J.P. heard her sniffle. *Yep, the tears spilled over.* "I'm willing to take a chance if you are."

Samira nodded her head against his shoulder.

He kissed her gently on the top of her head. *Is that a yes?*

59 Viewing Rights

Samira

The cashier behind the counter radiated a familiar smile. "Well, hallo." The southern accent brought a smile to Samira's face. "Ya'll haven't been in for a bit."

"No, I haven't."

"But I bet you'd like a Cappuccino."

"Yes, thank you." *I feel connected to this woman even though I don't know her name.*

"Are you meeting that handsome Joe in a few minutes?"

Does she know his name, or is she just using Joe as a catch phrase? "As a matter of fact, I am." *We haven't been here for a long time. I'm surprised she remembers.*

"I was afraid maybe it didn't work out between ya'll, but I musta been wrong." She placed a lid over the steaming beverage and snapped it into place. "Shall I just put this on his tab? I 'member how he likes to take care of you and all."

He does like to pick up the tab, doesn't he? "That would be fine." *But I didn't know he kept one at the Café Ole.*

"I see ya'll's table is vacant too." The woman pointed to the front corner.

Boy, she does remember us. Samira thanked her again. She opened her Kindle against the wrought iron tabletop and picked up where she'd left off.

A chapter later, Samira looked up into Phil's deep blue eyes.

"Am I late?"

"No, I'm early."

"I knew that." Phil sat down in the chair across from her. "It's been a while since we've graced this place."

"But the cashier remembered me."

"Of course, she did. You're not easy to forget." Phil smiled easily. "Besides. Shondra and I have a special agreement."

Samira raised her eyebrows on purpose. "Shondra?"

Phil placed his right hand over his chest. "It's on the nametag."

"Of course." *I should have known.* "What kind of an agreement might you have with your friend, Shondra?"

"She keeps the tab. I pay the bill."

"You're just lucky I'm a light eater."

"No, I'm just lucky." Phil leaned across the table. Samira was sure he was going to kiss her, but his lips only touched her forehead. "What can I get you?"

"I was thinking of the French Onion soup."

"Anything else?" Phil was already headed for the counter where people were beginning to wait in line.

Samira shook her head as he walked away. *I like the way he takes care of me, even when he's not here. He makes me feel important.* She tried to go back to her book but had trouble concentrating. *More later.* She powered off the tablet.

Phil returned with two bowls of soup and a glass of water. He set the tray between them and went back to the counter for napkins. *I bet he tips Shondra well for taking care of me.* Samira smiled at that thought. *No wonder she remembers me.*

Samira dipped a metal spoon into the rich soup. *I've missed this place.* But mostly, she'd missed the company. "Did you sleep well last night?"

"Not really." Phil stirred chicken and noodles around in a bowl. "It's hard to be content knowing you're across town alone in another bed."

"Well, it's better than thinking I'm not alone in another bed." *I couldn't resist.*

Phil's feet wrapped around hers under the table unexpectedly. "That is not an option, Pretty Lady." The hue of his eyes darkened a shade with that comment.

"No, it's not, but I had to say it." *It doesn't take much to make him jealous.* She savored her first bite of broth. *But I really don't mind him staking his claim on me either.*

"How was your morning?"

"Well, I called Mr. Marty Brown and officially declined the offer."

"And how does that make you feel, Ms Cartwright?"

I don't feel guilty. I don't feel responsible. "Very free, thank you for asking."

"Then you made the right decision." Phil raised his water glass to her in an unofficial toast.

"Are the boys coming down tonight?"

"It sounds like it." Phil was nodding his head. "Jan is going to meet me halfway."

He didn't sound defensive when he mentioned her name this time.

"I've got somebody checking into a car for them. Hopefully, I can give them a little travel independence and relieve myself of making those late-night trips north."

"Are they staying the whole weekend?" *Before I extend the invitation, I need to know what his weekend looks like.* She broke a saltine cracker in half and dipped it into the broth.

"I'll meet Jan again Sunday night, unless the boys have a car by then."

I think getting the boys a car is a good idea. "Well," *I have no idea how he's going to react.* "My mother has invited you and the boys for Sunday dinner." *This certainly takes us into new territory.*

Phil stopped chewing and looked doubtingly in her direction. "Why would she do that?"

Samira scanned the perimeter of the small café. "Let's see, maybe she's curious to know more about the man with whom her only daughter has been spending time." Samira blew gently on the soup in her spoon. "Or maybe she is just trying to be hospitable to a man she's only briefly met at a volleyball game."

Phil finished chewing the cracker that was already in his mouth.

"More than likely it's both," Samira clarified. "She called me this morning and made the invitation."

"You're going to be there, right?"

Samira laughed. *I would never send him in there alone.* "Yes. And Krissy and Kara too."

"Alright." Phil wiped his fingers on a paper napkin. "I'll go if you'll go."

"I'll RSVP in the affirmative then." She tipped her head to one side. "My mother is a wonderful hostess."

"Based upon what I know of her daughter, I don't doubt that for a minute." Phil complimented easily. "Is this a formal occasion?"

That's an interesting question. "I don't know." Samira frowned in thought. "I guess we'll all be coming from church, but Mama won't expect you to be dressed up." She thought some more. "No, just come as you are."

Phil shook his head and grinned mischievously. "Probably not. You don't know my normal Sunday morning attire."

If it's anything like his Saturday morning attire, I like it. "I can promise you one thing, Mr. Ralston," Samira set her empty bowl off to the side. "You won't go away hungry."

Phil ran his tongue over his bottom lip. "You always leave me just a little hungry because I always go away wishing for more."

"I was speaking of the meal."

"I was speaking of you." Phil stacked his empty bowl underneath hers and began to gather the used napkins.

He must have a tight schedule. He told me last night he might not have a lot of free time. She helped him gather what little trash was left on the table.

"Do you have a few more minutes?"

So, maybe a tight schedule isn't the urgency. Samira checked her watch. "A few."

"I have something I want to show you."

Now I'm curious. "Okay."

"Not here." He picked up the tray full of dishes. "Let's go for a walk."

What in the world? Samira picked up her coat as she stood up. A moment later Phil was holding it while she slipped her arms into the sleeves. *He's always a gentleman. Always.*

It must not be far. His truck was nowhere in sight, and he wasn't wearing a coat other than his sports jacket. *The same one he had on last night.*

Without hesitation Phil linked his fingers between hers. An alleyway led to the back of an office building. Samira noticed Phil's truck at the far end of a small parking area.

Where in the world is he taking me? Samira walked with him up a flight of concrete stairs. At the top she read the cursive lettering across a glass door. *J.P. Ralston, Attorney at Law.*

So, this is his office. There was something urgent in his step that accelerated her adrenalin as well. He held the door open for her.

That's the woman I saw at the Shoal Creek public meeting.

The woman looked up and began speaking at the same time. "Oh, hey, Boss, can you take a call from Sparky? He's been calling your cell but—" Suddenly the woman's greenish brown eyes stopped on Samira. "Oh, sorry."

Phil was very much in a business mode. "Yeah, I need to talk to him." He left Samira's side and reached for the phone.

"Sparky, J.P., what's going on?"

Sparky? Now there's an interesting name. Samira crossed her wrists and smiled at the lady.

"Excuse me, I didn't know J.P. had company." The woman rose from her seat and offered to take Samira's coat. "Can I get you something? A cup of coffee maybe?"

"No, I'm fine, but thank you." Samira allowed the woman to hang her coat on a brass hook along the wall. *This is an elegant room. Very formal and highly professional.* She scanned the sitting area. *A few plants would make it more inviting.*

"I'm Denise Burke. I don't believe we've met."

She's the one who issued the subpoena on Lloyd Hughes' diary. Now I can put a name with a face.

"Samira Cartwright." Samira exchanged a firm handshake with the woman. Denise's eyes widened as she identified herself.

She's older than I imagined, but obviously highly efficient.

Phil was still talking on the phone.

"Would you like to sit down?"

He shook his head in Denise's direction.

A gentle bell rang as the door to the outside opened. A tall, slender man walked in with a hand full of file folders. He nodded a silent greeting to Samira.

Samira tuned into Phil's phone conversation. "...Derek is here now...Alright...We'll get on it and I'll see you in a few minutes."

Obviously, this will be a short visit. Samira watched Denise sort through folders from the young man.

"Derek," Denise addressed him without looking up. "This is Samira Cartwright."

The young man turned and greeted Samira properly. "Very pleased to meet you." He shook her hand. "Derek Danielson. Have you been helped?"

"Undoubtingly." Denise sounded sarcastic.

Oh my. Samira watched Phil send a silent look of warning toward Denise.

Denise smiled at Derek. "She's here with the boss."

That's funny that she calls him 'the boss.' Maybe she doesn't know which of his names to use either.

Phil handed the phone back to Denise. "He's going to walk you through the plan."

Denise looked surprised. "What plan?"

"This one." Derek handed her an open file folder.

I'm impressed with the way they're all on the same line of communication.

"Why me?" Denise raised her eyebrows in Phil's direction.

"Because I'm busy." Phil motioned for Samira to follow, but his eyes were still on his secretary. "Give me ten and hold the calls."

Samira's shoes left an imprint in the plush carpeting as she crossed the room toward an open door.

"Ten and counting." Denise covered the mouthpiece on the phone and addressed Phil one more time. "Derek's on his way back over there. Do you need him to take anything?"

Phil allowed Samira to step into the interior office before he answered Denise's question. "No, I'll be right behind him."

"I'll believe that when I see you leave."

Phil closed the door behind them. *If he's bothered by her remarks, he's not letting on.*

"She's a damn good paralegal." Phil answered without being asked. "But she speaks every thought that crosses her mind." He smiled easily.

I wouldn't put up with it, but obviously he's used to it. Samira dared to let her eyes travel around the book lined office. *Very elegant yet quite simple at the same time.*

"So, this is where you spend your time."

"And plenty of it." Phil concurred. "But that phone call considerably diminished my lunch hour."

Samira heard new urgency in Phil's voice. "Don't let me keep you."

"You're not keeping me." Phil took Samira by the hand and led her to the window behind his desk. "But I want you to see something."

She followed his gaze down the alley to the Café Ole. Samira laughed out loud. *The café is in full view from anywhere in his office.* "Now I know why you knew the name of a coffee shop so quickly that first time you invited me out."

"Exactly." Phil seemed pleased that he'd given away his secret. "These last few months when I've been sitting here at my desk, I've been wishing you could meet me over there again."

Samira watched him run his hand over the glossy edge of a conference table that matched the rest of his furniture. Her eyes went from the tips of his fingers to a single object on the table.

"Oh, dear God." Samira put her hand to her mouth. *That's my statue.* She couldn't speak. Nor could she take her eyes off it.

"It's an original, so I've been told."

Samira forced her eyes to his. *Doesn't he know Fabiano carved that of me?*

"It's quite a find, isn't it?" Phil was studying Samira's face.

He must know. Samira swallowed hard but there was an air pocket stuck in her throat. She swallowed again.

"It's a beautiful work of art." He admired the bronzed statue openly, running his fingertips over the woman's head and following the form of her body all the way down her back.

Samira backed up and sat down in a chair. *I need to explain.* "She didn't pose that way."

I mean, I didn't pose that way.

"It looks very natural to see her reading." Phil's eyes were on the sculpture.

"No, I mean, like..." *I mean, it's totally obvious the statue is nude.* "...like *that.*"

"But that's the way I like her."

He does know it's me.

Phil turned the figurine one half turn. "But here's the biggest mystery of the whole work." He pointed to the bundle of hair at the nape of the statue's neck. "How does she get it to stay like that all day long?"

At least now I know where I am. Samira threw her head back and let all her tension out with one long sigh.

"I knew Uberti was trouble that day in the parking lot."

He must have been watching me with Fabiano longer than I realized.

"What I didn't know was his plan to carve you like this." Phil turned the statue another quarter of a turn, revealing the obvious nudity.

Samira shook her head. "It really wasn't like that, Phil. He didn't see me like that." She rose from the chair and touched Phil's arm. "Not once."

"But he wanted to."

I am going to come clean. "You're right. He did want to. And he tried. But..." *Samira took a deep breath at the recollection.* "...but I couldn't. I'd already known you. And he wasn't you."

Phil was looking at the statue. "How did you get this way then?"

Samira put her finger to her lips as she thought. "I gave him permission to undress the statue under the influence of some very powerful wine."

Very slowly Phil looked into her eyes. "And that's it?"

"Well," *Do I dare tell him?* "He did try to kiss me goodnight."

Phil turned her to face him. "And how did that work out?"

Samira smiled into his eyes. "Not very well for him."

Phil wrapped his arms around her shoulders. "Not one of the three, then?"

She shook her head slowly and stepped closer. "No. You are my third." Samira searched his eyes. "And with any luck, final."

"I am the lucky one, remember?" Phil drew her completely in.

Samira was consumed by the passion in his kisses and the tenderness of his touch. When he released his hold, Samira had to remind herself of her surroundings.

How does he do that to me? She touched the bun at the back of her head to see if it was still in place. She remembered his agenda and the urgency for a diminished noon hour. *But I must know...*

Phil turned the figurine back around on the table and admired it with genuine interest.

"How?" *How do I ask this?* "Who?" She put her hand to her forehead to try to organize her thought. "Where did it come from?"

Phil's eyes were intense. "She was here when I came in this morning."

"No." *I don't mean your secretary.* "I'm talking about the sculpture."

"So am I." Phil cupped Samira's face in his hands gently and kissed her again. "I said, she was here when I came in this morning."

I don't like not understanding. There had been too much mystery with this piece of art already. "But where was it before it came here?"

Phil smiled softly. "It was in good hands."

Oh my gosh. "Mike had it then, didn't he?" *It's so obvious now. He had it all along.*

Phil didn't answer, but he didn't deny Mike's ownership either. "I had to earn the right to own it."

It was Samira's turn to smile now. *Mike must have raised the stakes.* "And what exactly were the stakes?"

Phil grinned and wiggled his eyebrows. "Someday, Pretty Lady, we'll go there. But right now, I have a business associate in need of my input on a very big case, and I have an assistant out there who doesn't know the word knock. And if I stay in here alone with you one more minute, you're going to be more like that statue than you ever intended to be."

Samira took a step away from Phil's presence. *And I'm afraid I might not fight against the notion either.* When Phil started to kiss her again, Samira put her fingers gently over his lips.

He laughed right out loud.

It is so good to see him laugh like that. Samira walked around to the front of his desk, forcing even more space into the passionate moment.

A buzzer sounded somewhere in the room, startling Samira.

"That's my ten-minute warning."

More like twenty.

He was still chuckling. "I failed to carry through on a promise last night and I don't want to jeopardize a friendship, so I need to follow it through now."

I have no idea what he's talking about. She lifted her purse off the corner of the desk and wrapped her hands through the straps.

"I have a business engagement here in town tomorrow late in the afternoon."

Samira watched Phil open a hidden armoire on the wall. He selected a necktie. Without looking in a mirror, he slid it under his collar and began to tie it.

I know that pattern. I used to tie that knot for Tom.

"Mike and Kelly have invited us out to dinner following the business engagement."

Oh, I can't stand it. Without asking permission, she intercepted the motion of Phil's hands and finished the knot in a perfect Windsor. *That's nice.* But the satisfaction vanished as she ran her schedule through her mind. *I told Wes I'd babysit Saturday evening.*

Phil opened a door and stepped into a bathroom. "Thanks. It looks good." He came back out. "So, what do you think about dinner?"

Samira felt a familiar pang in her stomach. *I really do need to distance myself further from my family.* "What time?"

Phil shrugged his shoulders and adjusted the knot to fit better. "I don't know. Not before eight."

That's late, but maybe not late enough. "I'm going to have to check." She hated turning him down. *Besides, it would be gun to go out with Mike and Kelly.* "I've promised my brother a few hours of childcare tomorrow afternoon and evening." Samira bit her lip. *But maybe I can talk Kara and Krissy into taking over later.* "Let me see what I can work out."

"It doesn't matter to me either way." Phil seemed satisfied. "Don't knock yourself out over it. If it works, we'll go. If not, we'll meet up with them another time." He reached for the brass handle on the solid door between the offices. "I'll call you tonight and let you know what's up with the boys, alright?"

I like being behind this closed door with him. Samira closed her eyes and allowed him to kiss her one more time before he opened the door to the outside world. *But I like being in any room with him, even if it's a noisy volleyball game.* She smiled into his eyes.

"Pretty Lady, you need to leave my office before we're busted." Phil opened the door slowly and Samira stepped through.

"Ten minutes?" Denise was sitting at her desk typing away on a computer keyboard. "I'll open some windows to let the steam out of your office."

Samira watched Phil flash a middle finger in his assistant's direction. Much to her own surprise, Samira had to stifle a laugh.

"Denise. This pretty lady needs some assistance choosing a cell phone plan for herself and her daughters. Any chance you can work that into your agenda?"

Denise didn't look up from her work. "Would that be an individual plan, or another set of lines on your business plan?"

Oh, wait. Individual.

"Doesn't matter," Phil answered. "Whenever you have time." He opened the door to the outside. "Talk to you tonight."

Samira nodded, realizing he was going to make an exit whether she was following or not.

"Not today, Miss Cartwright, but I have your number. Let's talk cell phones early next week?" Denise was looking at Samira as if she needed an answer.

"Of course," Samira stammered. No hurry." *I guess this means I can return the iPhones to Ellen and let her know we are already on a plan. Or going to be on a plan. Or something.*

Samira felt a lilt in her step all the way back to her car.

He's the only one who should have that statue. Because he's the only one with viewing rights. Samira knew she was smiling on the inside as well as on her face. *And other rights.* She closed her eyes with that thought. *My parents would be horrified.* She pressed the button on her key fob to unlock her Camry. *As if they haven't figured it out already.*

Samira slid behind the wheel of her car. *I need to remember to thank Mike for looking out for me.* She started the engine and backed out of the parking space. *Unless he was simply looking out for Phil.* Samira laughed out loud as she pulled into traffic. *What on earth is my father going to think of this man? He's nothing like they would choose for me. He's too passionate. Too spontaneous.*

She stopped at the red light next to the Mid-America parking lot. *Oh, and then there's Wes who's going to drill him about investments and personal issues.* Samira waited for the light to change. *God help us.* Slowly she followed the car in front of her across the intersection. *But they're just going to have to get over their hang-ups, because this time my decision is made. I'm keeping him.*

60 Meet the Parents

Joseph Phillip

J.P. sat down hard on the bench at the end of the gym and wiped the sweat off his face with the tail of his t-shirt. *I'm getting too old for this.* He leaned forward and placed his elbows on his knees to catch his breath.

"You in, Dad?" James yelled from the center of the basketball court.

J.P. shook his head and motioned for someone else to go in for him. *Three games back-to-back and I'm done.* He wiped his face again. *I used to be able to go all morning.* J.P. watched as Josh and James worked the offense.

"Good morning, J.P."

That voice is way too cheery for me. He looked up as Kelly Davis sat down next to him.

"You're up and at 'em early for a Saturday."

Tell me about it. "The boys wanted to play ball."

Kelly's eyes went to the action under the hoop. "Which one is yours?"

"Two of them are mine." *It feels good to claim them both.* J.P. pointed. "Josh is a senior. He's taking the shot." *Damn. He should have had that.* "And James recovered his rebound." *Nice shot, James.*

"How old is James?"

"He's a sophomore." *Turning sixteen soon. He needs his license.*

Kelly flashed her sunny smile. "Good looking boys. I bet it's fun having them around."

More than I realized. "Yeah, it's good to have them around the house."

"Hey, what did you and Samira decide about dinner tonight?"

J.P. shook his head. "She had plans with her family. We'll catch you another time." *It's just as well with the boys being here.*

"Samira is very faithful to her family."

Is she telling me that on purpose?

"But faithful to a fault, sometimes."

Yep. She said that for my benefit, obviously. J.P. refused to go there. *Tomorrow could be interesting though.* Sunday dinner didn't quite seem like his style. *I fit in better at a cocktail party like Stephenson is having tonight.*

"We'll try again."

Since she's sitting here, I might as well ask a few questions of my own.

"What brings you to the club so early this morning?"

Kelly laughed heartily. "This isn't early. It's after nine."

It's after nine? I need to shower so I can check Sparky's progress over at Mid-America.

"I'm meeting a girlfriend for aerobics here in a few minutes."

I wonder if she ever takes a break. "How many times a week do you work out?"

Kelly was watching the game on the court. "I do cardio every day. What about you?"

I thought I was asking the questions. "I'm in the weight room with Mike three times a week."

"What about cardio? That's what your heart needs, you know."

Yes, I know. J.P. stood up to give indication he was about finished chatting. "I run a few times a week with Chase."

Kelly stood up too. "That's funny. You run with Chase." She grabbed a handful of her bushy curls and pulled them into a wrap behind her head. "That's like having two verbs and no subject."

Who else compared my dog to a verb? J.P. put his hands on his hips. *It was Samira and one of the girls at the ranch. What's up with women and verbs?*

Kelly started to walk away. "Sorry I won't see you tonight but have a good time at the cocktail party."

J.P. nodded. *Obviously, Mike's not taking her to Stephenson's party either.*

The locker room was starting to fill up with Saturday morning regulars. J.P. grabbed a towel and a bar of soap and headed for the showers. *Too many short nights this week.* J.P. was tired. *I could live without the social outing tonight.* It was just one more thing on his agenda. *But Mr. Stephenson is developing into a fine client. He's at least worth an appearance.*

J.P. checked the clock on the wall of the athletic club. *If I hurry, I'll get to Mid-America about ten then don't have to be back here to get the boys until noon.* He adjusted the temperature of the water in the shower. *Then maybe we can get this issue of transportation underway.*

~~~~~~~

The security guard at Mid-America's back entrance recognized J.P. before he presented his identification. Ever since Sparky moved the makeshift surveillance unit into a secured area, badges had become standard procedure. J.P. slid his badge through the magnetic reader on the door.

Sparky was sitting in front of two large computer monitors.

"What do you know this morning, Sparky?"

"Tings seem to be right on schedule." Sparky pointed to an in-house security screen. "Our suspect, Celia Monroe requested to vork overtime today. Ve vill see vhat she is up to."

J.P. could see the suspect at work in every angle of her cubicle. *It's amazing how detailed we can get.* "Any other activity?"

"Monies from de new account are secure. Quarterly reports ran at the close of business yesterday. And now ve vait."

Waiting is always the hardest part.

Sparky swiveled in his chair. "Mr. Stevenson came by dis morning. He said I should come to his house tonight for a drink." The little man stood up and refreshed a cup of coffee. "Dat all depends on vhat is going on inside de mainframe."

"I understand." *Besides, I hired you to work this case. Not make social appearances.* J.P. didn't like the idea of his private investigator mingling with Joplin business society.

Sparky continued as if J.P. hadn't spoken. "Our suspect vill be dere. I tink she is going dere for an alibi." His eyes went back to Celia Monroe on the screen. "And if dat is de case, den I vill need to be here."

Up until now J.P. had assumed Stephenson's cocktail party was simply to celebrate the sale of property and new business relations between Mid-America and The Hughes Corporation. "Stephenson didn't plan this party as a distraction, did he?"

Sparky eyes became animated. "On da contrary, it turns out de party is timed perfectly to be a distraction. But Mr. Stephenson doesn't know dat yet."

At least that gives me a little more incentive to show up and mingle.

"Vhile ve have time, shall ve go over da chain of command once again?"

"I'm at your beck and call, Sparky."

The investigator pulled up a chair and opened a well-worn folder. "It vill vork like dis-"

J.P. sat down and watched as Sparky moved his hand over the typewritten page, complete with English misspellings.

"De monies vill be authorized from dis building. Computer number seventy-two."

The only in-house computer, other than Sparky's, enabled to authorize this account.
~~~~~~~

"Our friends in Balteemore are standing by."

The one-time suspects, now working undercover to save their own asses in court.

"When notified, dey vill transfer de funds to de holding company in Caleefornia."

The one disguised as a real estate company.

"At vhich time ve vill trace de transaction back to dis system and prepare to secure de account from further tampering zo dey cannot even attempt to move de monies back."

In the event they get skittish. "Is this the first time Bridges has attempted to move funds from the same institution more than once?"

Sparky shook his head. His eyes were still fixed on the schematic in the folder. "No. He's tried it before, *but...*" Sparky accented that little word by raising his right pointer finger. "...at least according to de FBI reports, by de time the transaction was complete, Bridges suspected a tail and cancelled." Sparky turned a few loose pages of notebook paper in the folder. "Dat happened at least two times."

"Third time's a charm." *In more ways than one.*

"Ah, ve are dangling sizeable revenue. Bridges is no fool. De money vill talk, and he vill move cautiously at first. When he is sure of clearance, click-click, ve seal de account."

If you say so, Sparky. J.P. still didn't understand how Sparky had been able to track all the details of the online hoist in the first place.

~~~~~~~

Late in the afternoon J.P. found himself leaning over his bathroom sink with a razor. He'd tried to call Samira, but no one had answered. *The more I think about it, the more I think I should add Samira and the girls on my cell account.* But for now, it was time to be thinking about the cocktail party.

"So, Dad." James was laying sideways across his father's bed. "Did you ask mom if you could buy us a 4-Runner this weekend? Or are we going to, like, totally surprise her when we pull in the driveway with it."

J.P. rinsed his razor. "I told her you were driving yourselves home in your own vehicle." *I don't ask my ex-wife for permission on anything.*

"That is so sweet." Josh hollered from the hallway. "I can't believe we finally have a little freedom."

"Don't abuse it." J.P. glanced at James in the mirror. "Do you hear me?"

Josh appeared in the bathroom doorway. "Loud and clear, Dad." He grinned. "Thanks."

It's the least I can do for them.

"So, you really don't care if we go to the movies tonight?"

J.P. rinsed the shave cream out of the blades. "Depends on what movie you're planning to see."

"It's rated R, but I'm seventeen," Josh reminded. "Action flick. Stallone."

"Which theater?"

"The new one at the mall."

"Ten-thirty curfew. I'll be home by then." He made eye contact to secure the deadline.

"Cool." James jumped off the bed. "And we don't have to call for a ride home, right?"

"Not if you take the 4-Runner." J.P. could see the excitement on the boys' faces in the reflection of the mirror. *It feels good to trust them.* "Temporary plates are prone to scrutiny."

"I have yet to have a traffic violation," Josh offered.

But the excitement of a new vehicle can change all that. J.P. wiped his face in a towel. "Just don't test it. That truck can go away as fast as it appeared." He stepped out of the bathroom. James and Josh gave silent understanding. "Ten thirty."

"When do you have to leave?"

J.P. glanced at the digital clock next to his bed. "Mike's picking me up in a few minutes."

"Any dinner plans?" James rubbed his stomach.
~~~~~~~

Oh yeah. They probably need to eat. J.P. opened his wallet. "Order a pizza."

"Or we could drive through somewhere." Josh hinted.

Either way they take my cash. J.P. grinned at his boys. "Suit yourself." The series of whoops and hollers that followed were well worth the permission granted.

J.P. finished dressing. He hadn't worn his tux since the weekend in Springfield with Samira. It seemed strange to be putting it on for such a brief engagement. *I'll be there an hour at the most. Just long enough to take guest attendance and make good on the public appearance for Stephenson.*

James appeared in the bedroom doorway again. "I'd think with a getup like that you'd have a date or something."

One would think. "She's busy with her family tonight."

"No other options, huh?"

"Nope." *I might as well fess up.* "And to be honest, I'm not really looking for another option."

James balanced his weight on the top of the doorway with his forearms. "So, you and Samira must be a couple now, huh?"

The father straightened his bow tie in the reflection. *I hadn't exactly thought of it that way.* "I guess maybe so."

"Sweet." James gave his father two thumbs up. "She's good for you."

"Do you think?"

"Oh, yeah. She keeps you, like, way mellow." James grinned. "You're not as irritable with her around."

Not as irritable, huh? J.P. laughed. "That is a good thing, then." He lifted his tuxedo jacket off the dry cleaner's hanger. "We're having dinner at Samira's parents' house tomorrow."

James made a face with that news. "Why would we do that?"

"Because it keeps peace in the family." *Her family. I could live without family relations.* J.P. thought again. *Hell, I do live without family relations.*

"Wait till I tell Josh." James started to leave but turned around. "You look hot, Dad. You deserve a date. Maybe you should call her again."

I tried that. J.P. had dialed Samira's number only to get the answering machine right after they got home with the new truck. "The tux is to impress a client or two."

"You're call."

"Whoa." Mike entered through the kitchen door. "Nice wheels."

"Nice duds." James circled Mike.

"When do I get my ride?"

Josh fished the keys out of his pocket. "Name the time."

Mike pounded the counter in a rhythmic pattern. "How about when I bring your Dad back?"

"What time will that be?"

Mike shrugged his shoulders. "Movie night for you guys, eh?"

"Sylvester Stallone." Josh grinned. "Since you and Dad didn't find dates, you have to go out together, huh?"

"I'm taking your ol' man so he doesn't feel stupid being there alone." Mike lowered his voice and turned away from J.P. "My hot date is after this business affair."

Josh raised his eyebrows.

The phone on J.P.'s hip rang. He checked the caller ID before answering. "Sparky, this is J.P. What's up?"

"Ve have activity on the new account. Vhen are you going to de party?"

"We're on our way now." J.P. made eye contact with Mike.

"I need you to keep a close eye out for our honored guests. Vatch for Goldstein, Jessica

Hutchison, and our Celia Monroe. Dhey are de most important."

I can do that.

"Ve need to know vhat time dey come and vhat time dey go." Sparky finished giving the instructions and then disconnected the call without any further discussion.

"Alright, guys," J.P. clapped his hands together. "Ten-thirty. Be here. No later. And one stop before the movie to eat."

J.P. put his hands in the air and met James's open palms with high fives as he started to leave the house. *It's fun to set them free.*

He followed Mike out the kitchen door and climbed into the low seat of the Corvette. *I wouldn't want to slide into this thing every day of my life.*

"I brought you a present," Mike reached behind his seat and fished out a plain paper bag. He handed it to J.P. as he buckled his seat belt. "Couldn't resist."

"What is it?"

"Had your name written all over it."

J.P. didn't like the way Mike was avoiding eye contact. *It's a DVD.* He turned it over and read the title. "Meet the Parents."

"I thought you might want to watch it after I bring you home."

Up until this moment the thought of meeting Samira's parents hadn't bothered J.P. too much. He read the title again. "You're full of shit." *Should I be concerned?*

Mike laughed heartily.

"There's been some activity on the new Mid-America account. Sparky needs us to inventory the crowd and note arrival and departure times."

"Very cool," Mike widened his eyes as they pulled into Mr. Stephenson's neighborhood. "The usual suspects?"

J.P. felt the engine slow as Mike geared down. "Goldstein, Hutchison, and Monroe."

There was a line of guests entering Mr. Stephenson's house when Mike turned the corner. "We can do that." Mike had slowed way down. "It's not hard to find this place but finding a place to park might be another story."

J.P. surveyed the gated community that surrounded the newest golf course in the area. *Big houses. Fancy cars.* The three-story brick house was impressive. *Stephenson isn't as conservative as he lets on.* The clock on the dashboard indicated five-twenty. *Fashionably late along with the rest of the guests.*

Mr. and Mrs. Stephenson greeted Mike and J.P. at the front door with great enthusiasm. "I've heard a lot about your legal counsel in these past days," Mrs. Stephenson announced with a handshake. As her eyes met J.P.'s, she started to speak and then stopped. Mr. Stephenson made a formal introduction, seemingly unaware of her hesitation.

J.P. looked at the cheerful blonde. *I know her face from the picture in his office.* He studied her face again. *But I've seen her somewhere else.* He followed Mike further into the house but glanced back for one more look at Mrs. Stephenson. *Face it, Ralston. You could have met her in one of a million places.* Their eyes connected again. *I know she's seen me. I can read that much from her face.*

Mike bumped J.P. in the arm with his elbow. "The Hughes brothers seem right at home."

J.P. looked into the formal living room just off the entryway. *I'll make my presence known.* Christopher and Jeffrey Hughes were mingling among the gathering crowd. *Casual conversation like this saves phone calls later.*

"Any news today?" Christopher asked under his breath.

J.P. knew the businessman was talking about Sparky's surveillance at Mid-America. *But Sparky says no public conversations on the topic.*

"Nothing yet." *I'll check in with our little investigator a little later.*

"Oh, J.P.." Mrs. Hughes appeared from around a corner with her arms spread open wide. "It's so good to see you." She initiated a ceremonial hug, which J.P. returned formally. Her eyes scanned the room behind him. "Where is that beautiful woman I met in Springfield? She is with you, isn't she?"

J.P. ignored Mike's accusing look. "No, she's not here tonight."

"But she is *with* you, tell me she is." Mrs. Hughes looked over her wire-rimmed glasses.

She's as eccentric as ever. J.P. watched as his best friend made a silent escape from the conversation. *Good, he can scout out the crowd while I entertain the Hughes.*

"Elizabeth," Christopher Hughes cautioned his wife.

J.P. smiled. "That's alright." He made eye contact with the high society woman. "Yes, she's just not here tonight."

"Oh, wonderful, wonderful." Elizabeth Hughes threw her arms out to her sides again. "I knew you could keep her if you would just step it up a bit." J.P. watched her hurry over to a corner table and reached for a small black purse. "Here," she said returning with something in her hand. "I've had this for her ever since I last saw you in Springfield. Would you be so kind as to deliver this for me?"

It was a new audio release of the Springfield Symphony in concert. *Leave it to Mrs. Hughes to drop a subtle reminder of the concert we missed.* His eyes scanned the room hoping to catch a glimpse of Mike somewhere in the crowd.

Mrs. Hughes chattered on. "She didn't get to go hear the live symphony that night. They were performing Copland." J.P. was humored. "And they played very well, I must say."

If she's trying to make me feel guilty, it's not going to work. J.P. thanked her for the gift and promised to give it to Samira at his earliest convenience.

Christopher Hughes interrupted his wife's conversation, almost as if he had news of his own to flaunt. "I paid Miss Cartwright a visit of my own on behalf of my father's estate," he publicized the information without reserve.

I'll handle this one with care. "I understand you were able to assist with a new addition to the library."

Christopher nodded. "A fine woman, J.P. Do encourage her to call if the library has needs in the future."

I didn't realize Samira had made such an impression on the Hughes. J.P. noticed Denise and Derek at the front door and excused himself from the Hughes' company. *I could stand for a few more minutes with Christopher, but under the circumstances, I think it's best to leave Mrs. Hughes to mingle with someone else.* J.P.'s eyes happened upon Mrs. Stephenson again. *She's awfully familiar.*

Mike reappeared before J.P. could get to Denise. "Mixed crowd here tonight," he reported. "High society, low society, and great servers." Mike held a mixed drink out for J.P. to take. "This is for you."

"What is it?"

Mike sipped his own drink. "Your usual. JD and Coke."

I would usually hold off while I'm working, but it is a cocktail party after all. J.P. accepted the drink anyway. Across the room he noticed Celia Monroe mingling through the crowd with another bank employee. *Interesting.* He noted the time as Sparky had requested. *Five forty-five.*

"Two city council members and the mayor are in the other room." Mike held his glass out toward the room behind the kitchen. "Gorgeous two-story fireplace in the family room." He sipped his drink again. "You need to check this place out."

"Not exactly as conservative as I'd expected."

"Quite extravagant, I'd say," Mike complimented the décor. "They say he is heir to his father's throne."

J.P. turned around so he could see the people mingling behind him. Mr. Stephenson's father was engaged in conversation with a group of people just inside the French doors of what appeared to be an office. "He already has the throne. His father retired from Midland Mortgage four years ago, at which time Midland Mortgage and American Savings merged." *There's a couple of my clients over there.* "Young Mr. Stephenson has been in the driver's seat since then. His father has input through the board of directors."

"Impressive," Mike stared at J.P.'s historical account. "You've done your homework, J.P. Ralston."

J.P. smiled and nodded his head toward a woman in the far corner. "Now there's a familiar face, Mikey." Derek was on the make with a woman dressed in a tight-fitting black mini skirt and revealing blouse.

J.P. watched Mike's eyes widen with the recognition. *Now I know why he didn't bring Kelly here.*

"Rachel Radakovich." Mike whistled quietly through his teeth. "She's still a looker, isn't she?" Mike grinned broadly under his mustache. "I do know how to pick 'em don't I?"

It suddenly occurred to J.P. that he didn't recognize anything extremely sexy about Kelly Davis. *At least not like the one standing over there.*

"Looks like Derek is wanting a piece of Rachel tonight." Mike finished his drink.

J.P. watched Derek on the make. "Think we should tip him off?"

Mike shook his curly head. "I say let him figure it out on his own. He'll be a better man for it."

J.P. laughed. *I seriously doubt she made Mike a better man for any of the shit she handed him.*

Denise wasn't far away and for the first time J.P. realized Jerry was with her. "I need to talk to Denise a minute." He excused himself from Mike's company and joined Denise mid-conversation with an editor from the Tribune.

J.P. offered his hand to Denise's long-time companion. "Jerry, it's good to see you. How's the beat?" *Denise and Jerry have been together longer than I've worked with Denise.*

Jerry's crew cut and button-down shirt gave him an ultra-conservative appearance. "It's good, J.P. And your office never seems to be too far out of the loop of current affairs."

J.P. smiled. Jerry was always good to keep the media focused on the positive side of the law. *But, I'd think, after all this time, he would want something a little more permanent with his woman.*

"You've done well to keep up with the riff-raff surrounding Shoal Creek." J.P. spoke in recognition of Jerry's recent press concerning the venture. *And there may be more to that story soon.*

"Shoal Creek has some interesting twists. Do you think Goldstein can pull it off?"

Ask me again in a week. "It's hard to tell. Just keep your ears open and your eyes peeled."

Jerry raised a cocktail to his lips. "I always appreciate an insightful tip."

"Anytime I can be of service." He raised his glass to meet Jerry's toast. But when the whiskey went down it burned more than usual. J.P. swallowed hard, trying not to choke on the drink. *Who in the hell mixed this anyway?*

J.P. glanced at the entryway and immediately recognized the guest entering the front door. Despite Sparky's warning, he really didn't think he'd have the guts to show his face in this crowd. J.P. checked his watch. *Six o'clock straight up. Interesting.* But even more interesting was the guest's companion. *Jessica Hutchison.* J.P. watched Mr. and Mrs. Stephenson greet them just as they had all the others.

Now I need to stick around until they leave. J.P. was very intrigued by their appearance. *If he is indeed aka Sean Bridges, then Jeffrey Hughes is going to know him by that name.* J.P. turned around and searched the room for the younger Hughes brother.

The attorney wound his way through to the far door of the formal living room and entered an oversized kitchen that overlooked the family room. The outside wall was all glass overlooking the golf course and lake. Mr. Stephenson senior was entertaining yet another band of businessmen. *He is very comfortable working the crowd.*

J.P. continued into the family room. *There's Jeffrey.*

J.P. made his way up to Mr. Hughes and turned around so he could see Alan Goldstein in the kitchen.

"You've done a fine job with the business details between the corporation and Mid-America, J.P." Jeffrey complimented J.P. before he had a chance to speak. "I want you to know we appreciate all you do for us." The executive sipped the drink in his hand. "You know, if you ever change your mind and decide you want to give up a private practice, you have a place with us."

Nice offer, but it won't happen. J.P. thanked Mr. Hughes for the kind words. *I'd lose too much independence working for one client.* J.P. thought again. *And I'd be bored out of my mind.*

"Mr. Hughes," J.P. changed the subject. "Help me out. There's a man in the kitchen I recognize, but I can't place his name. I'm thinking you did some business with him while I was out of town last summer."

J.P. watched Mr. Hughes narrow his eyes to scan the faces of the guests in the kitchen.

Black suit, black tie, just like everyone else in the room.

"Oh, yes, I see," Jeffrey was focused on the middle of the crowded room. "I can't see all that well, but it appears to be that real estate broker who wanted to sell us the airport tract."

That would be the one.

"He goes by Bridges, I think."

Jeffrey went on to describe the details of the meeting J.P. had missed. But the only detail he needed was the one he already had. *Hands down Jeffrey Hughes will testify in a court of law if I need his witness.*

A short, blonde woman had captured Mike Benson in the kitchen. She had a hold of his arm and was attempting to move him toward the entryway. Mike raised his drink toward J.P. like a distress flag.

I should probably try to rescue him. J.P. stepped into the kitchen and wound his way over to his best friend.

The blonde bob the woman was sporting bounced against her shoulders as she spoke. "I gave you her phone number. Did you even call her?"

"Not yet," Mike answered, obviously trying to wrap up the conversation. "Susan, have I introduced you two yet?" He nodded toward his best friend. "This is J.P. Ralston."

Who the hell is she? J.P. questioned Mike with his eyes.

"J.P., you remember my golf partner from last summer? Sammy-O, right?"

J.P. nodded more to accommodate his friend than to recall the golf partner.

"This is his wife, Susan." Mike lifted his arm trying to be free of her hold. "Susan, this is my best friend."

The woman tugged on Mike's suit coat again. "Sam is over here. You should come say hello and then I really need you to call my friend. She's not here tonight but I'm sure we could call her."

She could stand to learn some professional protocol. "Counselor, if I might have a word." *She needs to take a hike.* J.P. nodded toward the doorway into the formal dining room.

Mike downed the rest of his drink. "Maybe another time," he told the woman.

He's way too polite. I'd have told her to go to hell.

Mike finally pulled free of the woman's grip and followed J.P. into the dining room. "She is a case, J.P." He looked over his shoulder. "She knows Samira and somewhere along the line she decided I needed to hook up with her."

J.P. stopped walking and turned around to get a better look at the woman, who was now engaged in another conversation. *In that case, I think I will tell her where to go.*

"She's not worth it, good buddy. Trust me." Mike bobbed his curly head. "I'm going to get another drink. You want one?"

J.P. examined the partial drink still in his hand. "Yeah, but not as strong. That last one was bitter."

Mike blinked in disbelief. "Since when did you complain about a drink being too strong?"

He's got a point. But it was wicked. J.P. shrugged his shoulders. "I'm going to make a round and see if our honored guests are still on site."

J.P. watched and waited. Jeffrey Hughes was engaged in conversation with Mr. Stephenson, and Jessica Hutchison was mingling with Celia Monroe. He scanned the room looking for the councilman but didn't see him anywhere.

Mike appeared looking more animated than usual.

Derek must have gotten a bite out of Rachel.

"You are not going to believe this," Mike started talking before he even reached J.P. "You've got to see this." He started to lead J.P. back through the throng of formally clad people.

"You're not going to believe this either." *Wait until I tell him we have our eyewitness.*

"No, me first this time." Mike had a hold of J.P.'s elbow. "Is that still your first drink?"

"Yeah." J.P. made a face. "What'd they put in it?"

"Whisky and Coke. I already told you that." Mike was leading J.P. back through the living room. They passed the French doors that led into an oversized study.

"Well, it's plenty strong."

"I didn't notice anything wrong with mine." Mike stopped at the bottom of a grand staircase. "Seriously, when was Jack Daniels ever too strong for you?"

I don't know. J.P. stared into his drink. *But it tastes like hell.*

"Take a look up there."

J.P. followed Mike's eyes up the stairs. "Where?"

"On the wall."

"What were you doing up there?" J.P. noted a gallery of photos hanging on the wall.

"Mingling." Mike nudged his shoulder. "Go up to the landing and take a good hard look at the picture on the left."

J.P. felt stupid going up the stairs. *No one else is up there.*

"Just go." Mike nudged him again. "That whiskey will taste better once you see what I saw."

What the hell? Reluctantly, J.P. made his way up to the first landing. He stopped and glanced at the photograph on the left. *Looks like Stephenson's wedding picture.* He turned around and shrugged his shoulders at Mike.

"Look closer." Mike was coming up the stairs now.

Before he turned back to the picture, Mike had his finger on a bridesmaid.

J.P. looked once. Then he looked again. Then he reached for his glasses.

"Don't bother." Mike stopped J.P.'s hand. "It's her."

J.P. looked again, stunned. *What is Samira doing in Stephenson's wedding picture?* He suddenly wondered if she might be in the crowd. *No, she had family obligations tonight.* "What the hell?"

Mike shrugged his shoulders under his blonde curls. "I don't know, but if you like, being the friend that I am, I could make some inquiries."

I need to know. He gave Mike permission to ask some questions.

Suddenly it didn't seem important that Jessica Hutchison was there with Alan Goldstein, or whoever that man claimed to be. And it didn't matter if Rachel Radakovich was on the make with Derek. Celia Monroe's presence no longer had an impact on J.P.'s agenda either. *The ONLY thing that matters right now is the relationship between Samira and the Stephenson family.*

"Got it." Mike came up from behind and handed J.P. another drink.

"I don't need it." J.P. declined.

"Trust me, you need it." Mike handed it over anyway. "This is one time you should have done your homework."

I always do my homework. He declined the drink.

"Take it. Trust me. You'll need it." Mike lowered his head and looked out from under his bushy eyebrows.

J.P. took the drink. "What's the scoop?"

"You're not going to believe it when I tell you."

"Try me."

"Take a drink first. It will help."

Just give me the freaking information.

Mike waited stubbornly.

Oh, fine. J.P. sipped the drink. It was just as bitter and hard as the last one. He made a face and wiped his mouth on the back of his hand.

Mike was nodding his head eagerly. "He's her brother."

"Who?"

"Stephenson."

What?

"Do I have to spell this out?" Mike took J.P. back to the photo. "Samira Cartwright, your woman in waiting, is the honorable Weston Stephenson's sister. Get the picture?"

J.P. stared at the photograph. *Oh, my god. That's the familiar look I see in his eyes when he questions my judgment.* He looked closer. *And he's the brother who'd tell her to take a job for the money.* The realizations were starting to come faster than J.P. could control. *And it was probably his kid's party Samira missed last weekend.*

"Counselor?" Mike interrupted the onslaught of connections that were blinding J.P.'s vision. "Are you alright?"

J.P. couldn't answer. He lifted the whiskey to his lips and drank it down. All the way down. And it burned all the way to his toes, but J.P. Ralston was too stunned to notice.

Mr. and Mrs. Stephenson were still greeting incoming guests near the front entryway a few feet from where Mike and J.P. were standing. *And I know I've seen her face somewhere other than on Stephenson's desk—and oh holy shit, their kids. I know his kids. They were at Samira's house when I picked her up to go to Springfield.*

Mike pounded J.P. hard on the back. "Breathe, buddy, breathe."

"J.P." a voice greeted from behind. "Counselors, I'm glad you could make it." J.P. turned to face the voice but when he went to shake hands, he realized he had a glass in each one. Totally embarrassed, J.P. tried to stack the empty glass under the full one. Much to his relief, Mike held out a hand. J.P. handed the full one to his friend and then offered his hand in greeting.

"Great party." *Stupid thing to say. But what do I say to the father I dared to piss off before brunch last Saturday morning?* J.P. swallowed hard as the handshake released.

"It's wonderful to have the Hughes brothers with us as well. They are going to be fine contributors to city commerce."

"Indeed." J.P. had noticed the similarities between the Stephenson men before, but to put Samira into the mix was overwhelming. *Do I need his permission to date his daughter?* Reality set in. *And I've done far more with her than simply take her to dinner. Shit.* J.P. swallowed hard.

"Harold Reinholdt is here from Reebok. He is one of our most highly esteemed investors. You should introduce yourself if you get a chance." Raymond Stephenson discreetly pointed out the executive across the room.

Funny. I wonder if Mr. Stephenson would be so eager to endorse my services if he knew what

I've been doing with Samira.

Raymond Stephenson excused himself, leaving J.P. to his confusion. Mike put the full glass back in J.P.'s hand. Without thinking, J.P. raised it to his lips and drank it down.

"Damn." J.P. choked. "This is a nasty drink."

Mike frowned and shrugged his shoulders. "It's your usual, man. What's up with you and the Jack Daniels?"

Everything is up with me. Suddenly the room felt very crowded. *This puts a whole new twist on meeting the parents.*

61 *Family*

Samira

Krissy grinned and rolled her eyes. "I know why you want to sign on to your Facebook account. You want to see if Phil messaged you."

Samira waved her hands for Krissy to move out of the chair. "I won't be here long." *I just want to see if he wrote in today.* She still couldn't believe she'd let the girls create a Facebook account. *Never in a million years did I see myself with a personal account on social media.* In the background, Samira could hear little Mark crying. *He's getting sleepy.* Samira accessed her account from her parents' computer.

No new messages. She sighed. *I know I talked to him yesterday, but it seems like longer.*

"I don't know what to do with Mark." Kara looked exasperated. "Granny has the girls in the tub, and I can't make him happy."

Samira signed off. "I'll take him." She gave her seat up to Kara. *She'd rather be chatting with her friends right now anyway.*

Mark was laying in the middle of the family room floor sucking his thumb when Samira got to him. His little eyes were puffy from crying.

"Come here, little guy," Samira put him over her shoulder. *Two years old already.* Samira stooped to pick up his blanket. *My how time flies.*

Samira could hear joyful screeches coming from behind the bathroom door. *I bet Mama's as wet as the girls by now.* She crossed her parent's bedroom and eased onto the platform rocking chair. Very gently she turned Mark, so he was leaning against her. "You, little fella," Samira whispered to her nephew, "Need to close your eyes."

Samira began to hum. *Just like I used to do for the girls.* The words to the song played in Samira's mind even though she didn't sing them out loud. Little Mark snuggled in. He was asleep almost before Samira finished the first stanza. *Sometimes I miss these quiet moments at the end of the day.* Mark had a new little boy haircut. *I miss his curls too. Tom always hoped we'd have a little boy someday, but I'm not sure he would have approved of a Mama's boy.* She cuddled Mark closer. *But that's exactly what my little boy would have been.*

Samira stayed in the rocking chair until the house was quiet from bath time. She was just starting to get up when her mother came to find them.

"He's getting to be a handful, isn't he?" Ashleigh held out her hands.

"I can get him, Mama." Samira shifted Mark's weight against her shoulder and carried him across the room to the crib. *Sweet dreams, little guy.*

A Bach Invention was playing on the smart speaker when Samira joined her mother in the kitchen again. Ashleigh handed her daughter a cup of coffee. "I do appreciate your assistance tonight, dear. I can take care of the kids, but it's so much easier when your father is home to assist."

"What time do you expect Daddy home?" Samira looked at the clock. It was well past eight o'clock. *I could be getting ready for a dinner date right now.*

"Oh, anytime. He didn't think he would be too late." Ashleigh leaned across the kitchen counter and wiped it clean with a damp rag.

It's already clean, Mama. Samira almost laughed out loud. *Funny, that's what I did when my mind was busy the other night. Just like my mother.*

"I think everything is ready for tomorrow. The salads are in the refrigerator, the meat is seasoned and ready to put in the oven, and the green bean casserole is mixed and ready to bake. All I have to do in the morning is make the bread and peel the potatoes." Ashleigh smiled at her daughter.

"I wish you'd let me bring something," Samira offered again. "I really don't mind."

"You are bringing the guests."

"And lots of them." Krissy appeared in the kitchen. Without asking permission, she helped herself to an apple out of the fruit basket on the counter. "Three, to be exact."

"Tell me again, how old are the boys?" Ashleigh started to count out plates.

"Josh is a senior. What is he, Mama? Seventeen?" Krissy was talking between bites.

"I think he's eighteen." Samira watched Krissy pick a piece of apple from between her braces. "Be careful, Krissy. I'd like those brackets in place when we see the orthodontist this week."

"I know. I want to get these things off my teeth." She took another bite. "James is going to be sixteen like next month or something." The girl took another bite and smiled at her mother. "I hope you have lots of food because they'll eat a lot." Krissy chewed for a moment. "And they are big boys. James is taller than his dad."

Ashleigh chuckled. "There will be plenty."

Mama will have more than enough food for all of us.

Kara stuck her head around the corner. "The girls want to watch *Pete's Dragon.* Is there enough time before bed?"

"That's a long one." *But that's the one Krissy always picked too.* "Bonnie and Lizzie might fall asleep before it's over."

"Fine with me." Kara disappeared as quickly as she'd appeared.

"I never know what she's thinking anymore."

Ashleigh's eyes were warm when they met her daughter's. "And you may never know again." She cocked her head to the side as she counted out silverware.

"Am I really that hard to read?" *I always feel so transparent.* Samira picked up the stack of plates and carried them to the dining room table.

"You're not hard to read, dear, I just never know exactly what you're thinking." Ashleigh joined her daughter in the dining room.

"You should have gone over to Wes and Pam's party tonight, Mama." Samira started to space the plates evenly around the oversized oak table. "The girls and I could have stayed with the kids."

"Not with so much to do." Ashleigh looked around her spotless house. "No, I am more comfortable getting things ready for tomorrow. Your father will represent us both."
She smiled genuinely. "You know how I feel about social gatherings anyway." She followed her daughter, placing the silverware in appropriate positions alongside the plates.

Mama loves social gathering if she's the one in charge. She finished arranging the plates, but there were two left over. Samira started back to the kitchen.

Ashleigh stopped placing silverware and studied the table. "Oh, wait, dear. We need to shift the side plates to add two more."

Samira silently named off the guests as she counted the plates already on the table. "There are eleven plus Mark's highchair."

"I know, but I decided to seat the little girls out here with us."

Wait. She watched as Ashleigh made room for the extra two plates. She counted again in her head. *Eleven. Right?*

Ashleigh pointed. "One here, and one there."

"Phil only has two boys."

"Yes, I know." Ashleigh smiled sheepishly. "But I invited Pam and Wes to join us. With the party going on at their house tonight, Pam won't have time to put a meal together." Ashleigh turned away. "Besides, two more at the table just helps complete the picture."

Complete what picture? Samira was irritated. "You should have told me." *Now I have no way to inform Phil of the changes. Meeting my parents is one thing. Meeting my entire family is another.*

"I didn't think about it until just tonight." Ashleigh went back to setting the silverware. "I couldn't leave them out."

Why not? Samira sighed heavily.

"I don't understand, Samira." Ashleigh finished with the silverware. She opened a drawer on the hutch and extracted a stack of cloth napkins. "It only made sense." She began folding them into shapes on the corner of the table.

Samira left the dining room. *Mama always says, if you can't say anything nice, then don't say anything at all. It's not fair for Phil to walk in unaware of the extra guests.*

"Do you need to call and let him know your brother and sister-in-law will be joining us?"

"It won't do any good now," Samira answered. "I won't talk to him before morning."

"You can call from here if you like."

Nice gesture, Mama, but it won't work. "He's out for the evening." *On a date I should have accepted.* "I won't talk to him before he gets here."

"Isn't he meeting us at church?"

Church? Oh, heaven's NO. Samira put her hands on her hips. She couldn't believe her mother expected her to invite Phil and the boys to church. *I wasn't even planning on going to church in the morning.*

"He does go to church, doesn't he?" The mother skillfully hid her face behind her coffee cup.

Church? No, not Phil. Samira crossed her arms. *Now I suppose Mama is going to pass judgment before she even really gets to know him.* "I don't know."

"I thought that would be one of your priorities when you started dating someone."

It's not exactly like I planned to meet this man, Mama. Samira started to wipe down the counter. *Stop. The counter is already clean.*

"So, he had plans tonight?"

He has a name, you know. "Yes." Samira had to guard the bite in her tone. "Phil had a business engagement tonight."

"On a Saturday night?

Samira glared at her mother. "Wes has a business engagement tonight and Daddy went over there."

"But it's not a regular business affair. I'd say it's more of a social event. Wes hosted the party to celebrate one of his newest clients at the bank."

"That's business." Samira couldn't help but raise her voice a notch. "Phil is a highly professional businessman. I'm sure he is meeting with important clients tonight too."

Ashleigh met her daughter's glare with soft eyes. "I'm sure that's right, dear." She lowered her head slightly. "I didn't mean to upset you."

Now I'm glad she doesn't know exactly what I'm thinking. Samira looked away. *But I know what she's thinking, and I don't appreciate her passing judgment so soon. He's not going to be who they want him to be anyway.*

"Krissy tells us he's a lawyer."

Phil. Learn his name, please. "Phil has a private practice here in town."

"I wonder if your father knows him?"

"Highly unlikely."

"Well, I'm sure he's a very good lawyer." Ashleigh's voice was soft.

How does she do that? She knows I'm upset, yet she softens her tone and takes the conversation back to a neutral zone every time.

Ashleigh offered to fill Samira's cup again, but Samira politely refused.

"We're all looking forward to spending time with Phil and his family."

We are, are we? Samira rinsed her cup in the sink. *At least she used his name.*

"Weston was quite concerned about you when it didn't work out between you and Phil a while back."

How nice of Wes to break confidentiality.

"I think it will help ease his mind if he can sit and visit with this man in your life."

Now we have the real reason Mama invited Wes and Pam to dinner. It had little to do with their personal agenda. In fact, it has everything to do with mine. Samira decided to go out on a limb.

"I just hope you haven't set your expectations too high, Mama." She watched her mother's face carefully. "I like Phil a lot." *More than I'd like to admit.* "He makes me laugh." *He makes me cry.* "He supports my decisions." *He lets me think for myself.* "He's always a gentleman." *Especially when we're alone together.* "And he seems to enjoy spending time with Krissy and Kara." *Just as much as I enjoy being with James and Josh.* "I don't want you to be disappointed in him because he doesn't go to church or because he chooses to work on a Saturday evening."

Ashleigh leaned her hip on a kitchen stool. Her face was serene and thoughtful.

"Phil's a very good man, Mama." *I like everything about him.* Samira felt her face redden as she continued to explain. *Even if he tends to lose his temper.* "I don't want you to be worried about me." *He's good for me because he needs me in ways I didn't realize I could be needed.* "I want you to be happy for me." *He makes me whole again.*

The mother placed her coffee cup on the granite countertop. "We are happy that you're dating again, Samira. We just don't want to see you get hurt."

"I figure that's a chance I have to take." *But I'm not dating again. I'm keeping Phil.*

Ashleigh's eyes questioned her daughter. "There may be other chances to love someone again, dear. You just haven't been open to that possibility."

Samira searched her mother's eyes. "But what if this is my last chance?"

"Don't be silly, Samira." Ashleigh waved her hand in dismissal. "There will always be another chance. It just seems that love shouldn't have to be hurtful."

Wes must have shared more than I thought. Samira surrendered the battle. *It hurts just as much to not have anyone at all.* It was almost ten o'clock. *Why doesn't anyone understand that?* "If you're all set for tomorrow, I think I'll take the girls home."

"That's a good idea." Ashleigh crossed the kitchen and turned off the overhead lights so all that shone was a glow from under the cabinets. "Will you meet us here or at church?"

I dim the lights at my house just like Mama does at her house. "I told Phil my car would be parked in your driveway, so I guess I'll meet you here."

Ashleigh followed her daughter into the living room. "I want to leave a little early so try to be here around nine."

I guess we're going to church with them in the morning. Samira sighed. *Just once I'd love to make my own decisions.*

~~~~~~~

The church service lasted much longer than Samira's patience. *I only came this morning to deter any repercussions later.* Even the familiar hymns stuck in her throat.

I can't believe I'm this worked up about Phil meeting my parents. She passed the offering plate. *He is so independent, yet committed and passionate about his work.* She studied her father's profile in the stillness of the sanctuary. *And in that way, he's not so much different from Daddy.* She stood with the congregation to sing the traditional doxology.

Samira's mind was still wandering during the morning message. Wes and Pam were
~~~~~~~

seated across the aisle and one row up. Samira watched her brother draw Pam closer to him in the pew. *Wes would tell me to follow my heart. But he'd also tell me to be cautious and not to give away too much before I knew for sure.*

Samira's mind tripped back to the ranch. For a moment she could see Phil walking up Aunt Maggie's sidewalk after his morning run. She felt her mouth curl into a silent smile. *No, his passion isn't just in his work. It's in the way he walks. It's in his voice and in his smile.* Samira remembered his arms around her as they rode Toby back to the house together. *It's in his anger as much as it's in his kisses.* She squeezed her arms around her middle. *I hope they can see all that about him.*

Samira admired her mother's loose bun at the back of her neck. *They wouldn't be so critical except for the fact that they worry about me way too much.* Samira bowed her head at the pastor's invitation.

Maybe it's because we love you so much. That thought came out of nowhere. Samira lifted her head to see who was thinking the inaudible thought. Very gently, Samira felt her father's hand slip under hers. She returned the loving gesture by linking her fingers over his.

Oh, Daddy, you always know me the best. Samira continued to hold her father's hand as they stood to sing the last hymn. *I just want you to give Phil a chance.* Raymond let go of her hand and instead wrapped his arm around her shoulder.

Samira allowed him to pull her close as he sang. "Amazing Grace, how sweet the sound, that saved a wretch like me..."

Maybe that's what we need at dinner today. Samira joined in. *Amazing Grace.*

Ashleigh didn't waste any time exiting the sanctuary. She had a family dinner to put on the table and no one was going to slow her efforts. Samira skipped a step to keep up with her mother's stride.

"I'm thankful the table is set already," Ashleigh commented as she unlocked the Cadillac. "We can fill the glasses and pop the bread in the oven and everything else should be ready."

Samira motioned across the churchyard for Krissy and Kara to hurry. *They're going to have to walk in the rain if they don't hustle.* Krissy waved back and pointed to Wes and Pam. Samira understood. *That way they can help with the kids.* She climbed into the backseat while her father took the seat next to Ashleigh.

"Mama is on a mission, Daddy."

"Don't I know it." Raymond laughed as he fastened his seatbelt. "If it weren't so drizzly, we could walk our backyard path home."

Samira smiled. *I loved those walks with Daddy as a child.* Her eyes followed the path they'd walked together hundreds of times over the years.

Ashleigh was in high gear the moment they entered the house. Samira watched her mother stop in the entrance hall and rearrange a bouquet of fresh cut flowers. *It won't matter, Mama. I doubt Phil and the boys would have noticed if one stem were too long.*

"Twenty minutes is all we need on the rolls."

Samira looked at the grandfather clock next to the bouquet. *Plenty of time.* Still, she couldn't keep her eyes from going back to the dining room windows. She'd parked her Camry in the driveway before church, just like she'd promised. *As if Phil can't read street addresses.*

Wes and Pam's van pulled in the driveway while Samira was putting ice in the glasses. *Here we go.* Samira tried to steady her nerves, but her hands were shaking. *For Pete's sake, it's only your brother.* Samira thought again. *No, it's more than that.*

Suddenly the aroma of freshly baked bread mixed with the smell of burning wood. Samira smiled. *Daddy built a fire in the fireplace.*

"Thank you, Daddy."

"You're welcome, Princess." Raymond kept poking at the fire. "It's just cool enough I thought a little fire might help warm our spirits."

I wonder if he knows I'm a wreck over all this. Samira returned to her task. *Probably.*

The hall was suddenly filled with happy commotion. "Leave your shoes at the door." Pam ushered the little girls in out of the rain. "We don't want to get Granny's carpet muddy." Samira watched Pam remove Lizzie's coat.

Wes ducked in out of the rain carrying little Mark under a blanket. The moment the door closed, Mark pulled the cover off his head.

"Boo." He cooed at his father.

Samira smiled as she took Mark. "Let's get you out of those wet clothes."

Wes removed his trench coat and hung it on the hall tree. "I imagine his diaper is about as wet as my raincoat." He held his hands out to take Mark back, but the toddler leaned back into the security of his aunt's shoulder. "Since when did I play second fiddle to my little sister?" Wes poked the little boy in the tummy with his finger playfully. "So, are you excited for us to meet this man in your life, Sis?"

Samira tugged on the sleeve of Mark's jacket and pulled it off one arm. "I don't know if I can call it excitement." *More like nervous anxiety.*

"It can't be that bad, can it?" Wes leaned back on his heels. "You've been seeing him long enough now I'd think you'd be ready to let us in on your secret."

"Maybe." *He's not really a secret.* Samira pulled Mark's coat completely off and hung it on the hall tree.

"Why the worried face?"

There he goes, reading my emotions again. "I just want you to like him, that's all."

"Sis, I trust your judgment." Wes squeezed her arm. "Relax."

Easier said than done. "I'll go change him." *I really don't mind.*

Samira changed her nephew's diaper with ease. *Just like riding a bike, little Mark. You never forget how to change a diaper either.* He was content and playful as she carried him back down the hall into the main part of the house.

Wes was standing with the front door open when Samira came around the corner. She overheard her brother's voice.

"Hey what can I do for you? We're just getting ready for a family dinner."

That sounds funny. Samira stepped into the entrance hall. Her eyes met the visitor behind the door.

Phil.

"I'm actually not here to see you."

He's letting in the cold air. "Come on in." Samira made the invitation much to her brother's dismay.

Wes moved over and allowed Phil to step inside. "Then you're here to see my father?"

Why would he be here to see Daddy? "Wes," Samira tried to set Mark on the floor, but he was holding on to her necklace. She straightened again and loosened his hold on the sterling chain.

"I'll get Dad."

I really don't understand. "I'm sorry I didn't get you told earlier. Did you get my Facebook message?"

Phil shook his head.

"Phone message?"

He shook his head again.

Samira sighed. Mark was examining her earring. "I tried to warn you ahead of time. I'm sorry."

hil looked concerned. "It's an amazing turn of events. To be perfectly honest, I'm not sure how we missed it."

How we missed the fact that my mother invited Wes and Pam to dinner? Samira pulled her head away from Mark's busy little hands. *He's more nervous than I thought he would be.*

"My mother didn't tell me until last night, so I didn't have much time to inform you."

Phil shrugged. "It's probably just as well I didn't know any sooner."

Probably. One sleepless night is plenty for me. Suddenly Samira missed James and Josh. "Are the boys coming?"

Phil turned around and ducked to see through the leaded glass windowpane. "Yeah, they should be here shortly. I came from the office so they're meeting me here."

"Did you get them a car?" *I could be hospitable.* "Can I take your coat?"

"Looks like your hands are full." Phil slipped out of his leather jacket. "I did. We'll see if it relieves any weekend travel stress."

Samira took the coat with her free hand and hung it on the hall tree. "This is Raymond Mark. But we just call him Mark." *One introduction out of the way.* Mark was trying to get Samira's necklace in his mouth. "Come on in."

Samira's eyes locked with Phil's for an extended moment. She could feel his presence moving somewhere deep within her soul. *Oh, I know that look and it makes me nervous.* "His little hands are so busy." *Please don't kiss me here.*

Mark finally lost interest in his aunt's jewelry. Samira took advantage of the moment and quickly put him on his feet. "Where's Papa Ray?" Mark balanced for a moment before wobbling off toward the living room.

"Why there you are." Pam appeared from the dining room with a happy smile. "I wondered what happened to my little guy. I missed you last night." She knelt long enough to get a hug from Mark as he passed by. When Pam stood up, she was surprised to find a visitor in the hall.

"So that's where I've seen you before." Pam exclaimed. "I knew I'd seen you somewhere, but I couldn't figure it out." Samira watched her sister-in-law shake Phil's hand without reserve.

"Same." Phil nodded his head. "It didn't dawn on me either."

"I was at the house..."

"When I picked up Samira once."

"Exactly." Pam was nodding her head as well. "Samira you should have told me."

Told you what? Samira looked over her shoulder to see her father and brother crossing the living room. Her father was removing the gloves he always wore when he worked with firewood.

"J.P. Ralston."

How does Daddy know that name?

Raymond stuck out his hand in greeting. "This is a surprise." Raymond was smiling but Samira knew he was all business. "What can we help you with?"

Help him with? Samira was confused. "Daddy, this is Phil."

"I know J.P., Princess." Raymond excused his daughter's introduction gently.

Not J.P., Phil. I know him as Phil. Well, most of the time. Her father was waiting for a response. *Maybe they do know each other from the business world.*

"I'm here to see Samira," Phil tucked his hands in the front pockets of his khaki pants.

Raymond seemed worried. "Is something the matter?"

"Not that I know of." Phil looked to Samira who in turn looked to her father.

"He's here for dinner." *He knows Pam. Does he know my father?*

"Dinner?" Wes looked confused.

The doorbell chimed, causing a stir of commotion behind them. Krissy appeared out of nowhere and made a beeline for the door. "Hey guys." She turned around with a bright smile. "Oh, hey. When did you get here?" She stopped long enough to address Phil. "Here." Krissy was holding out her arms. "I'll take your coats."

"Papa Ray, this is Josh, and this is James." Krissy turned toward Phil. "And I guess you guys have already met, right?"

"Yeah," Wes looked at Phil. "We've met."

Not officially. I don't know what's going on here.

"Great." Krissy turned toward the boys. "This is my uncle Wes, and my grandfather, Raymond Stephenson." Without waiting for another second, she grabbed James by the sleeve. "Come on. Come meet my grandmother and aunt."

Maybe I should just let Krissy make all the introductions.

Bonnie and Lizzie came flying down the hallway hot on Krissy's heels.

"Be careful." Samira tried to slow them down, but it was too late. They knocked little Mark onto his knees. He was instantly in a full-blown cry, but the girls ran a full circle eight pattern between Phil and Samira preventing her from helping Mark.

"Girls, please," Wes tried to gain control of the situation, but by then the girls were clear across the living room. He turned back toward Phil and Samira and apologized.

"Doesn't bother me."

He looks uneasy.

And Samira was still completely in the dark.

"So, let me get this straight," Wes pointed his finger at Phil. "You're here to eat dinner with my sister?"

"I believe that was the invitation."

Raymond crossed his arms. His eyes were focused on his daughter. "You should have told us you invited J.P. Ralston to dinner, Princess."

Sometimes I wish he wouldn't call me Princess. Besides, I didn't make any of the invitations. Mama made them all.

"This is quite a shock."

Phil's trying to smooth things over, but it's not his fault. "I tried to get a hold of Phil last night so he would know everything, but we missed each other, so here we are." Samira threw her arms out to her side.

"Here we are, indeed." Raymond motioned toward the living room. "Come on in. Fine young men you have with you."

They didn't get two steps into the living room before Bonnie and Lizzie were the center of attention again.

"No running in the house." Krissy gave instruction from somewhere out of sight.

Samira put her face in her hands. *This is NOT at all what I was expecting.*

Pam was starting to fill the water glasses from a crystal pitcher. "Samira, he's much more handsome in khakis and a denim shirt than he was in half a tux."

I know. But I liked the tux too. She could see Phil in the living room. He was examining a toy with little Mark. *It's strange to see him interacting with a toddler.*

Samira caught Phil's glance and returned a nervous smile.

Ashleigh stepped into the dining room and removed her apron. "I think everything is ready." Her eyes passed over the table. "Shall we gather the family?"

Family. Samira's eyes went directly to the man sitting in her parents' living room. *That takes on a whole new meaning when you add the three of them to all of us.*

62 *Dessert*

Joseph Phillip

J.P. turned the plastic truck in his hands. *Mark.* The little boy who had given it to him had totted off to get another object. *They said his name was Mark.* The fire in the fireplace was warm. *Nice ambiance, anyway.* But even the fire didn't ease his nerves. *I still can't believe I missed this vital family connection.*

"So, J.P.," Weston Stephenson was sitting in the easy chair. "I had no idea you were the one my sister was, um..."

Sleeping with?

"Seeing." Wes smiled a little. "How long have you known her?"

I don't know what she wants them to know and what she wants to keep to herself. J.P. set the toy truck down on the floor. "Since last summer." *Vague answers are better than no answers at all."*

"No kidding?"

No kidding.

J.P. watched Mr. Stephenson's wife cross the room behind him.

"I just assumed," Mr. Stephenson stopped talking to help Mark with a toy.

Extremely awkward here. J.P.'s eyes skimmed the spines of the books lining the wall between the living and dining rooms. *Copperfield, Melville, Dickens, Kipling, Twain. Well-read people.* Mark toddled over and pushed a stuffed rabbit into J.P.'s hand. *I don't know what to do with a person this size.*

"Anyway, I just assumed the lawyer my sister was seeing was one I didn't know."

At least you knew my profession. That's more she told me about you. J.P. had to remind himself not to be defensive. *After all, she did say she tried to warn me.*

"So, what is your intent?" Wes shrugged his shoulders. "I mean, do you have plans?"

I have plans to eat dinner with her family. J.P. didn't like the insinuating tone. *I don't know how to answer that question.*

Mark's little hands were starting to examine the buttons on J.P.'s shirt. *He sure is an inquisitive little thing.*

Wes's dark brown eyes reflected the same depth of thought as his sister's. "Well, at least I know she's been in good hands."

J.P. didn't dare look up. *What he means is at least he knows whose hands she's been in.*

"J.P." Raymond entered the living room unannounced. "I had a wonderful visit with Christopher Hughes last night. Fine gentleman."

J.P. leaned back in his chair and made eye contact. *It's his house. He can set the tone.*

"Tell me, how do you know the Hughes brothers?" Raymond sat down on the sofa.

Is this a professional interview or a personal one? J.P. weighed his options. *Either way my answers could be used against me.*

"I went to work for Lloyd Hughes—"

"The brothers' father?" Wes interrupted.

"That's right. Lloyd hired me right out of law school. I worked directly with the Hughes Corporation until I went into private practice." *Seems like a long time ago.*

"Well, I'm impressed with their knowledge in commerce and their interest in local business development." Raymond narrowed his eyes in thought. "They're a fine asset to Mid-America."

The Hughes are fine assets to anyone they deem worthy. J.P. recalled their business history. *Don't do anything to piss them off.* "Keep Hughes happy, and they'll perform well for Mid-America."

Weston raised an eyebrow behind his newspaper.

He heard me.

"Didn't you take my sister to a Hughes event in Springfield awhile back?"

Interesting that he knows that. "Last summer." Samira's image in the hotel bathtub suddenly came into vision. "That was a major event."

"I remember she had to find formal wear and get her hair done and everything."

I remember the black dress as it came off. J.P. tried not to grin. "Christopher Hughes announced his daughter's engagement that night."

"Were you there on business or pleasure?"

Now there's a loaded question. Business until midnight, then strictly pleasure. "I was under the Hughes' employ to oversee the prenuptials." J.P looked from one Stephenson to the other and matched their corporate tone.

Wes frowned momentarily.

"Where'd you go to law school, J.P.?" Raymond fired another question.

The only answers he's going to get today are the ones on my resume. "Columbia."

"University of Missouri?"

"Yes, sir." *He already knows the answers to some of these questions.*

Raymond's look was sincere. "Why a private practice over joining a firm or continuing with a corporation?"

He knows my work ethic. This is a personal question. "I prefer to be in control of my casework and my clientele." *Take it or leave it. I don't play well with others.*

"It takes guts to set out on your own," Weston pointed out.

"More discipline than guts." *Anything else you want to drill me on while I'm at your disposal?* Mark had wandered into the middle of the living room and was busily scattering a stack of professional magazines into disarray.

By now the aroma of fresh bread was permeating the entire house. *Reminds me of Aunt Maggie's.* J.P. watched Raymond straighten the stack of periodicals. *He tidies up, just like his daughter.*

Raymond lowered his head. "J.P., what are your feelings concerning Councilman Goldstein's plans for Shoal Creek?"

I had no idea what to expect here today, but Shoal Creek never crossed my mind. J.P. leaned forward and put his elbows on his knees. *Sean Bridges?* "I think he's climbing an uphill battle." *He doesn't have enough revenue to make it happen. Yet.* Little Mark bounced the stuffed rabbit happily over J.P.'s hands.

"But what do you think about the actual development plans? Do you think people would eventually buy into property down there?" Weston almost sounded hopeful the plan might really work.

J.P. shook his head. *Doesn't matter what his master plan projects.* "I don't think he'll get that far." *Especially if he falls into the electronic trap that's set in the basement of your bank later today.*

"Alan Goldstein is a new name to these parts. He came to town about six years ago and the next thing we know he's holding a seat in city government." Raymond was obviously puzzled. "I wonder where he came from?"

California. "Out of state." *With illegal cyberspace ties all over the nation.* "Somewhere out west, I've heard."

Two little girls went blazing through the front room full speed ahead. Raymond reached out and snagged one of them around the waist with his arm. J.P. was sure the child was going to be reprimanded, but instead Raymond pulled her into his lap and tickled her until she couldn't breathe.

This isn't exactly like I'd pictured Samira's father. I expected a man of high integrity, but I didn't expect it to be Raymond Stephenson.

Weston still had his nose behind the Sunday paper.

J.P. could see Samira arranging food on the dining room table. She blushed when he caught her eye. *I like being able to draw that response from her without saying a word.*

"All right, fellas, gather the troops. I think we're ready to eat." Ashleigh emerged from the kitchen. *She is a very elegant woman.* J.P. admired the way she motioned everyone to the dining room with a graceful turn of her hand. *Samira certainly has her mother's grace.* Ashleigh smiled. *And her dark eyes.* When those dark eyes fell on J.P., he couldn't hold them. *It's like she's reading something beyond my thoughts.*

J.P. started to stand up, but little Mark was leaning on his leg. *What do I do with him?* Mark raised his arms to be picked up. *Well, alright.*

"Come on, little fella." J.P. held his finger out and Mark took a hold. "Let's go eat."

I don't know when the last time was that I had contact with a person this small.

"Are you Auntie's boyfriend?" One of the little girls was pulling on J.P.'s pants.

J.P. stopped walking and studied the little girls' face. *How do I answer that?* "I guess maybe I am."

The girl rolled her little blue eyes and put her hands over her mouth. Then she spun around and disappeared.

"Lizzie, let's go wash up." Krissy grabbed hold of the back of the girl's shirt and guided her toward the hallway. "Mark goes in the highchair."

She wants me to put him in there? Wes was still behind the newspaper and his mother was nowhere to be seen. J.P. looked from Mark to the highchair. *It doesn't look all that complicated.*

Mark walked right up to his chair and then turned and put his chubby little arms up for J.P. to pick him up. *I don't have a clue what I'm doing.*

J.P. looked around hoping to find Samira. No one was there so he crouched down to Mark's eye level. "Here we go, little fella." Mark didn't weigh anything like J.P. expected. He lifted him off the ground without any effort at all. *James was probably the last little guy I picked up like this.* Yet he couldn't recall a single moment holding either one of his boys for any length of time at all. *I worked too hard blocking those memories.* J.P. pulled his head away when the little boy tried to grab his ear. *It wasn't exactly the most gratifying time of my life.*

"Oh, here, let me help you." Mr. Stephenson's wife appeared out of nowhere. J.P. watched her skillfully remove the tray on the highchair. "I'll buckle him in for you."

"Well, well, well," Krissy announced her arrival. "Look who found you." She was speaking to the toddler.

More like, who found me. J.P. observed Mark in the chair. *Kinda like riding in a car but you don't go anywhere.*

"Where do you want to sit, Pam?" Ashleigh was helping the older of the two girls into a chair.

Pam. Her name is Pam. J.P. dared to look closer at her face. *She's got to be a good ten years younger than Stephenson.*

"Why don't you put the girls between you and me." Pam arranged the crystal water glasses away from the little girls.

Krissy purposefully bumped into J.P. as she passed. *Thank God for Krissy.* He caught her ponytail enough to give it a slight tug. Krissy stuck out her tongue before scooting around the edge of the table.

"Krista, is that any way to treat our guests?" Ashleigh disciplined gently.

What is up with this Krista business? J.P. winked at Krissy.

"He started it, Granny."

J.P. felt his own cheeks warm as Mrs. Stephenson's dark eyes fell on him. *Are they always this formal?* J.P. ran his hand through his hair. *A retired nurse. And a very intense retired nurse at that.*

"J.P., why don't you sit here next to Samira." Ashleigh put her hand on the back of a polished chair at the corner.

I bet she kept an orderly emergency room too. J.P. watched Samira help the little girl into a chair and push her up to the table. *I like the way her skirt sways when she moves.* J.P. ran his hand through his hair again. *I shouldn't be thinking about her skirt with her father in the room.*

"Weston." Ashleigh called into the living room. "You can finish the business section later. Come and find your seat."

Weston. J.P. watched the man rise from his chair and sheepishly make his way into the dining room. *He looks more like a Mr. Stephenson than a Weston.*

"A word to the wise," Weston spoke to J.P. as he started for a chair.

Obviously, he knows where he is going to sit.

"My mother doesn't allow any business talk at the table." Weston raised his eyebrows. "Mealtime is sacred."

Considering the company, that's a good thing to know. J.P. stood behind his assigned seat and waited for the others to sit down first. *Mrs. Stephenson has this all planned out.* When Samira appeared at his side, he automatically pulled out her chair.

"Well, J.P., it is an honor to dine with you." Raymond took the seat at the head of the table.

"Indeed." J.P. pulled his chair up to the table. *What do I say, non-business related to the father of the woman…?*

"I don't want to sit here." One of the little girls was whining.

J.P. found himself sitting between Samira and her father. *Holy shit. I'm dining with him, but I'm sleeping with her.*

"Bonnie, just sit still," her father instructed.

"No. I want to sit by him." She climbed off the chair and pointed at Josh across the table. Her father put her back on the chair.

Raymond Stephenson was patiently waiting for his granddaughters to get situated.

I wonder if he'd be that calm if he knew where his daughter was last Saturday morning?

"It's okay, Wes." Pam seemed to have a calming effect on her husband. "Do you mind?" She looked across the table at Josh.

Josh shrugged his shoulders. "I'm cool."

Bonnie was instantly on the move. She eagerly climbed onto the chair between James and Josh.

"Now we can pray," she announced happily.

We're going to pray? J.P. swallowed hard. *Of course, we're going to pray.*

Kara was the last one to sit down. "I guess that puts me over here."

She looks less than pleased to be sitting by Krissy. J.P.'s. eyes circled the faces. *I don't think I've ever sat at a family table that would hold this many people at once.*

Samira's mother was seated closest to the kitchen door. She spread her hands, and everyone followed suit, linking fingers. J.P. bowed his head according to the family tradition, but his senses were instantly triggered when Samira touched his hand.

I'd love to be holding more than just her hand. Those thoughts dissipated instantly when Raymond Stephenson took his other hand. *I don't like being in the middle.* J.P. had a hard time concentrating on the prayer.

"I understand we have some football players dining with us," Raymond passed the roast beef to his son. "What positions do you play?"

Josh took a roll out of the basket and passed it to Samira. "Wide receiver."

James accepted the green bean casserole from Ashleigh and helped himself to a generous serving. "Offensive line."

"Cheerleader." Krissy added cheerfully.

"You cheer for volleyball," Kara corrected.

"I know." Krissy passed the potatoes.

"What's your record so far this year?" Raymond seemed genuinely interested.

Both boys looked up to see who was being addressed. And then they answered in unison. "Five and two."

J.P. took a helping of everything that was passed.

"What's the forecast for the rest of the season?" Weston jumped into the conversation.

Josh shrugged his shoulders. "We have one more competitive opponent. The other three should be easy wins."

"Last game of the season will be the toughest one," James added. "Excellent dinner, by the way."

Ashleigh thanked the young man with a warm smile.

J.P. was more than a little surprised to hear the compliment come out of James so naturally. *Could be a result of too much takeout pizza.*

Just as Weston had foreshadowed, there was no business discussion at the table whatsoever. But conversation flowed easily among the family members. Every grandchild was given equal opportunity to share.

These people listen to each other. Even the little girls were well-mannered while the others talked around them. *And they're all polite too.* He tried to remember. *James and Josh never knew this kind of family continuity. Still don't.*

"I think Mark is about ready for his nap." Ashleigh started to remove the highchair tray. "Shall I take him?"

Nothing better than a Sunday afternoon nap after a great meal. J.P. glanced at the sleepy eyes. *He's trying to stay awake.* The rolls passed again, so J.P. helped himself to another. *Almost as good as Aunt Maggie's.*

"I'll take him." Pam pushed away from the table calmly. "That way I can change him before I lay him down."

Pam. I need to remember her name. He watched the women work together to free Mark from the straps that held him in.

Ashleigh sat back down in her chair. "I bumped into Ginny O'Brien at the grocery store yesterday."

Who? J.P. didn't hear very clearly. He looked up when no one responded right away.

"We were waiting in line at the meat counter together."

Surely, she didn't say who I thought she said.

Weston frowned across the table. "Do we know Ginny O'Brien?"

A wave a relief passed over J.P. *I thought she said, Jimmy the bartender.* J.P. wiped a drop of sweat from his forehead with his napkin.

"Well, she knows us." Ashleigh filled in the blank. J.P. watched her eyes stop on Samira. "We used to play cribbage together. Ginny sits on the board of directors at the university."

J.P. could feel Samira's sudden tension without even touching her. *She never told them about the job offer.* The look on Ashleigh's face told him the cat was just about to be let out of the bag. *Here it comes.* He reached under the table and patted Samira's thigh in silent support.

"I remember Ginny," Raymond lifted his fork as he spoke. "Short woman. Kind of plump?"

"Well, yes," Ashleigh agreed. "She tells me the university contacted Samira about a possible position."

"No kidding," Weston was instantly interested. "A position as in a job?"

Samira nodded.

"That's great, Sis." Weston was obviously excited. "What kind of a position?"

"Mama has a job already." Kara interjected. "And it's a really good one."

Fine point, Kara.

"That doesn't mean she isn't open to new opportunities," Weston pointed out. "What's it about?"

Mr. Stephenson likes thinking for his sister. J.P. noticed Samira fidgeting with her silverware. "It's a not-for-profit position within their alumni association. Sales and marketing for the most part."

Fundraising and events.

"Full time? Part time? Out with it, Sis. This sounds like something you might need to explore."

Samira's eyes scanned the table. "James, would you please pass the butter?" She sliced the end of the stick.

She doesn't have anything to put butter on.

"I don't know, Wes." Samira was still holding the knife with the butter, obviously flustered.

She'd be a mess on a witness stand. J.P. pulled his bread in half. Without saying anything he placed it in Samira's free hand. *I need to teach her to think on her feet.*

"Thank you." Samira stared at the bread. Then she stared at J.P.

He smiled his easy smile. *Good luck with the interrogation.*

Samira buttered the bread. "I thought about it for a long while, but I'm not in the market for a new job."

J.P. watched her take a bite of his bread. When she finished chewing, she finished the thought. "I turned them down."

"Already?"

Obviously, her brother isn't too thrilled about that.

"How can you make that decision without weighing the advantages?"

By this time Krissy and James had a conversation going on of their own, which was good because it took some of the tension out of the adult discussion. J.P. finished his last bite of potatoes. *It'd be nice if someone came to her rescue.*

The little girls were finished eating. First one asked to be excused, and then the other. It didn't take but a moment for Krissy and Kara to follow suit.

Amazing how they all carry their plates to the kitchen. I can't even get the boys to throw away an empty pizza box. He looked around the table. His boys were still finishing their dinner. But no one else was eating anymore. All eyes were on Samira. *No wonder she has trouble making decisions for herself.*

Samira finished her bite of bread, so J.P. silently offered her his other half.

"I did weigh the advantages." She was obviously in mid-thought, but she stopped talking to take the bread.

"But the disadvantages added up faster than the advantages." Samira took a bite. For the first time she looked across the table at her brother with confidence.

He crossed his arms. Not a good sign.

"I'd think you'd at least want to bring it up for discussion first."

"I did."

J.P. decided to finish eating. *This may be the last meal I ever eat in this house if they find out she discussed it with me.*

"When?"

He approaches his own decisions at a snail's pace but expects his sister to let him weigh in on her decisions.

Raymond Stephenson put his hand gently against his son's shoulder, but his eyes fell on his daughter.

Pick a side, Mr. Stephenson. Which one are you going to support?

"Do you know how difficult it is to get on staff at the university?" Weston was looking at his father but was obviously talking to his sister. "There is a waiting list a mile long of people who would like to be employed out there?"

I know what I'd like to say. J.P. glanced in Wes's direction. *But gut feeling says to hold my tongue.*

"I can name three people right off the top of my head who would give their right arm to teach at the university."

But this wasn't a teaching job. This was sales and marketing.

Weston shot an irritated look across the table at his sister. Samira lowered her head.

Enough. J.P. made his decision. *Time for the closing argument.* "That's good." He wiped his mouth on a cloth napkin. "If there are that many people waiting to get on board, they won't have any trouble finding the right person to fill the vacancy."

Samira's eyes widened, but she didn't speak. Instead, she lifted her water glass and took a drink. J.P. watched Weston's eyes go from his father to his mother, but no one chose to speak.

Case closed.

"I'm sorry, Samira." Ashleigh folded her hands politely. "I was wrong to bring Ginny up at the table."

Samira's voice was steady when she spoke. "There just wasn't a good time to bring it up for discussion." Without hesitation she touched Josh on the arm. "Does that new vehicle out in front of the house happen to belong to you?"

Nice recovery.

Suddenly the boys were animated and alive again.

And good confidence too, even if she is faking it. He put his arm over the back of Samira's chair, making sure to touch her shoulder as he did so. *She's coachable.*

Samira's father was instantly involved in the new conversation and Ashleigh was beginning to gather dirty dishes at her end of the table.

J.P. felt his phone vibrate on his belt. The grandfather clock read almost one-thirty. *This could be Sparky.* He thought again. *Or it could be Janet.* The phone vibrated a second time. This time J.P. quietly excused himself from the table. He stepped into the living room and answered.

Check the Caller ID. "What's going on, Sparky?"

"Dere is activity as ve speek. I beleev de monies vill be moved to de holding company vithin de hour."

I'd like to see this go down with my own eyes. "We need to notify Agent Roderick."

"Denise has done dat already."

Chances are good this phone call will put an end to the family affair. J.P. glanced around the room. *But if this surveillance plays out it will also put an end to Sean Bridges.*

"If you vant to vatch, you vill need to arrive quickly."

"Alright." J.P. spoke with hesitation. "I'll see what I can do."

The call ended without a formal goodbye. All eyes, including Pam's, were on him when he re-entered the dining room. *Obviously not a family that approves of business calls in the middle of Sunday dinner.* Nonetheless, J.P. could feel his adrenalin starting to pump.

I should take Stephenson with me. J.P. sat back down on his chair knowing he couldn't stay there long. *He's going to need to understand this chain of events to be able to report to his board of directors.* Samira's hand brushed his leg under the table. *How does she do that? One little touch sets off every nerve ending in my body.*

"Is everything alright?" Weston was gathering his plate and silverware.

I haven't been one to mince words up to this point. No reason to do so now.

"Hey, Dad." Josh was standing in the entryway door. "James and I are taking Kara and Krissy for a ride in the 4-Runner. Be back in twenty."

J.P. looked at Samira.

"They have my blessing." Samira rose from the table.

J.P. Ralston fixed his eyes on the bank president. "Mr. Stephenson,"

"Wait." He shook his head. "Under the circumstances, I think *Wes* would be in order."

Wes. It didn't sound right. *He's my client.* J.P. felt Samira's presence as she walked behind his chair. *This could get complicated.*

"Okay, Wes," J.P. stumbled over his tongue a little. *I'm going to break the cardinal rule and talk business at the table.* "That was Sparky."

Wes was suddenly very alert.

"He is picking up some activity on the new account."

Samira had returned from the kitchen for more dishes. *I hate to run out on her, but the impact of this is huge.*

Wes was serious. "Do we need to go down there?"

"Boys," Raymond Stephenson jumped in. "This is Sunday. Surely there is someone else who can go."

"Go where?" Ashleigh asked the question innocently enough.

"Downtown," Wes answered quickly.

"To the bank?" Pam sounded irritated. "Today?"

Shit.

"Oh, Weston," his mother was talking again. "This is Sunday, son."

"I know what day it is." Wes sounded defensive.

And all the while the clock is ticking.

"It shouldn't take too long, should it?" Wes started to carry his plate into the kitchen.

"No way of knowing." *Let's not mislead them.*

Samira returned for the third time. "No way of knowing what?"

J.P. picked up his own plate and silverware and followed Wes.

"How long this might take."

"Might what take?" Samira looked confused.

J.P. put his plate in the stack with the others. "We need to run down to the bank."

"Now?" She looked surprised.

"Yeah." *Come on Samira, give me the go ahead. I need this.*

"The bank isn't even open." Samira poured leftover green beans into a smaller container.

Good point. "That's precisely why we need to get down there." *Only one computer is running in the entire building other than Sparky's. It's critical we monitor everything that happens in the next few minutes.*

Samira frowned at her brother. "Can't it wait until tomorrow?"

J.P. threw his head back. *I can't believe how many people are involved in this conversation.*

Wes was shaking his head. J.P. could see his focus shifting as well. "No, this isn't something we can control."

"Who's we?"

"The legal team." Wes wasn't backing down. "I need to see what J.P. is building here so I can explain it to my board on Monday."

Samira was still frowning, but now she was looking at Phil. "J.P.?"

That would be me. "Maybe it won't take long." *It could take a split second. Or it could take the rest of the day. Shit. I can't lie to her.* "This is business, Samira. And I need to be there.

It would be a great advantage to have Mr. Stephenson..." J.P. corrected himself, "Wes down there with me."

"You need to be at the bank?" She was obviously confused.

"As soon as possible."

"Do you bank there?"

What is she talking about? "No."

Samira looked worried.

This is taking way too long.

Raymond carried the breadbasket and an empty casserole dish into the kitchen. "If J.P. Ralston says he needs to be down there, then I think we should let him go."

Let me go? J.P. shook his head. *Excuse me?* He looked back at Samira who now had her face hidden behind her hands.

"I won't be all day." J.P moved her hands with his. *I hope.* The emotion behind her eyes was almost ready to spill over. He bent his knees to be at her eye level. *I can't leave her like this.* He lifted her chin with his forefinger. "What's the matter, Pretty Lady?"

"I don't understand."

"Don't understand why I have to go to work?" *Make it quick, Ralston.*

"And why does my brother have to go with you?"

She's not making any sense. J.P. wanted to close his eyes to think. But he was afraid to look away. *How do I make this any clearer without breaking confidentiality?*

"I'm going down to check on the case at Mid-America. Once the meeting is over, I can come back."

Weston walked past and tapped J.P. on the shoulder. "I'm ready when you are."

J.P. nodded but he didn't take his eyes off Samira's.

"What case?"

"The Mid-America case." *This shouldn't be so hard.*

"You're on a case?"

I'm always on a case. That's what I do. "Yes." *Make it clear.* "I'm representing Mid-America on a case and the lead investigator needs me down there to monitor some activity."

Samira's emotion spilled out of her eyes and onto her cheek.

Don't cry, Samira. He wiped her tear with his thumb.

"You're my brother's attorney?"

No, he's my client. Or at least his company is my client. "Yes."

"That's how you know my brother?" Now the tears were coming in a stream.

J.P. was the one who didn't understand now. "Yes."

"Why didn't you tell me?"

How could she not know this? "Because I didn't know until last night."

"How did you know last night?"

"Because I went to a party at his house and saw a picture of you on his wall." *Good God. I'd rather be having this conversation in private. The whole damn family is gathered around.*

"Princess—"

Princess?

Raymond was butting into J.P.'s conversation. *I can handle my own business. And what's with the Princess?*

"J.P. Ralston is our attorney down at the bank. Didn't you know that?"

"You went to his party while I was babysitting his kids?" Samira was questioning Phil with a sadness he'd never heard in her voice.

You were babysitting his kids? J.P. moved his hand from her face to her shoulders.

Samira pulled completely away from his touch. "How could you not know that Wes was my brother?"

Maybe because you are so damned secretive about your private life. J.P. took a deep breath. *I didn't mean that. There was just no reason for this discussion to come up.* "I don't know." *How was I supposed to know you were a Stephenson?* J.P. took a step back and ran his hand through his hair. "You said you tried to let me know." *Why are all these people standing here?*

"I tried to let you know my brother and his wife were coming for dinner." Samira wiped her face with her fingertips.

Okay. J.P. still didn't get it. *Oh, God I need to be going.* The phone vibrated again. "I didn't check any messages."

"Is that my fault?" Samira was still crying.

"Sis," Wes reached out and touched her shoulder, but she pulled away abruptly. "I've been working with J.P. on a particular incident down at the bank for months now."

"Am I the only one here who doesn't know what's going on?" Samira was openly frustrated.

"No, dear. I'm afraid I don't know either." Ashleigh was quietly confused as well.

"I think I know."

Everyone's eyes turned to Pam.

"I think J.P. Ralston has been working for Wes."

For the bank.

"And I think Phil has been dating Samira."

I don't know if we can officially call it dating.

"But I don't think J.P. knew Wes was Samira's brother."

Not until last night.

"And it's obvious Samira didn't know Phil was working at Mid-America." Pam shrugged her shoulders. "At least until now."

At least.

Samira still had tears in her eyes, but when she looked at J.P., he could see a hint of something that wasn't there before.

"So, you just found out too?"

There was so much he wanted to explain, but J.P. didn't know where to start. *I just figured she knew when she said she left a message.* He nodded his head once.

"Well, this is a small world, isn't it?" Ashleigh seemed relieved to know the details, even if she didn't fully understand.

"But if you don't mind," Wes was getting impatient. "I need to take my attorney and get moving or we may both lose our jobs."

"Go." Ashleigh waved the men out of her kitchen. "Go do what you have to do so you can come back for dessert."

There's more to this meal? Suddenly J.P. remembered his manners. "Thank you for..."

"Go." For a quick moment, Ashleigh's eyes were the exact reflection of her daughters. "You can thank me later. Sounds like you have work to do."

Wes appeared with J.P.'s coat. "If we're coming back here together, you might as well ride over with me."

J.P. slid his arms into his jacket. *I hate riding with someone else.*

"Phil?"

He stopped and turned all the way around. Samira was right behind him. Her eyes looked exhausted from fatigue of the misunderstanding.

"Are you coming back for dessert?"

She looks so frail and so beautiful all at the same time. J.P. couldn't help but smile. *I don't care whose house I'm standing in.*

"Come here." He reached for her hand. When she reciprocated, he pulled her all the way to him. J.P. whispered in her ear, "I'll come back if you'll be my dessert."

The tears in her eyes suddenly glistened with new understanding. And much to his surprise, Samira kissed him. Gently at first. But then with more passion. Not once. And not twice. But three times. Right there in her parent's dining room.

The impact of Sparky's activity on the Bridges' accounts suddenly had little relevance. He laughed out loud and returned Samira's embrace. For the first time in his life, Joseph Phillip Ralston understood that some things were more important than all the rest.

"J.P. are you coming?"

I know I'm coming right back here for dessert when this is all said and done. He stole another quick kiss, then reluctantly let Samira go.

J.P. followed Wes out into the dismal weather, but J.P. Ralston didn't notice the rain or the clouds. The only thing he noticed was the freedom he felt somewhere deep inside. *A freedom like I've never known before.*

63 The Defense

Samira

Samira ran her hands over the front of her skirt. She watched through the dining room window as Wes covered his head and ran all the way to the driveway. *If Phil minds the rain, he's not letting on.* Samira watched him walk calmly to Wes' van.

I didn't plan to kiss him. Samira smiled. *But I couldn't stop either.* She heard his whisper again. *"I'll come back if you'll be my dessert."*

Samira began to gather the remaining odds and ends. Salt and pepper shakers. Loose silverware. *Anything to keep my thoughts private and my hands busy.* She took a step toward the kitchen and bumped into her father. *Oh. How long has he been there?* His hands were tucked deep inside his pants pockets and his eyes were studying her very carefully.

Instantly, Samira's cheeks reddened, and her heart began to pound against her sternum. She had to look away. *I haven't done anything wrong.* She set the miscellaneous tableware down on the buffet. *Was he standing there when I kissed Phil?*

Her father's voice was calm and gentle when he spoke. "You should have told us you were seeing J.P. Ralston, Princess."

Samira chose not to face her father. "I didn't know it mattered so much." *Besides, I don't know him as J.P. Ralston.*

Raymond Stephenson puckered his lips in thought. "He's a very powerful man, Samira."

Powerful? Samira frowned. "How so?"

"Come with me."

Samira watched her father cross the dining room and start down the hall. *No, Daddy. Not today.* She knew he was going to his study. *But he's my father so I'll go with him.*

Raymond opened a drawer in the bureau and sat down in his chair. Very intentionally he selected a large envelope and pulled out the contents.

What's he doing? Samira watched her father flip the corners of the pages until he found the exact set of papers. He put that set aside and the rest went back in the envelope.

The father patted the seat next to him. "Here, Sugar." He placed his reading glasses on the end of his nose and tipped his head to read through the lenses.

Reluctantly Samira sat down. She had no idea what her father was thinking, nor did she have a clue what the papers might reveal about Phil. *But the way he's acting, they could be incriminating.* She curled into the corner of the loveseat.

Raymond folded a few pages back over the stapled corner and turned the packet so Samira could see. "This is a list of cases J.P. Ralston has successfully closed on behalf of his clients in the past five years, many of them before litigation was required." Raymond indicated multiple pages. "Then, we get to the cases that closed unsuccessfully during the same amount of time." Raymond revealed a single sheet of paper. He handed the whole packet to his daughter.

I still don't understand. Her eyes skimmed the list of businesses and individuals J.P. Ralston had represented. *Wow.* She turned to the second page. She was surprised how many names she recognized. *These are big businesses. Or at least people with a lot of money.*

"He's a very powerful man, Samira."

"He's powerful because he wins cases?" *And why does Daddy have a list like this anyway?*

With a record like this, I'd think he'd be making an extremely sound living.

Raymond shook his head slightly as he gazed over his glasses into his daughter's eyes. "He's powerful because he knows how to get his way."

Suddenly Samira didn't want to see any more of the list. *I feel like I'm spying on him.* She flipped back to the top page. *But if he's as successful as this printout shows, his lifestyle sure doesn't reflect his earnings.* She smoothed the papers flat. The top sheet was a copy of J.P. Ralston's resume. *Or at least his house is humble enough.* She reviewed the furnishings of his house in her mind. *He doesn't even have a dishwasher.*

Samira frowned. "Daddy, why do you have these?" *But I guess Maria washes his dishes.*

"Because we hired him to represent Mid-America." Raymond lifted the large envelope off the bureau. "These are the attorneys we didn't hire."

Samira couldn't help it. She had to read further. *Business, corporate, probate, wills, trusts, real estate, lawsuit matters. I didn't realize he did all of that. No wonder he could help me with the paperwork for Tom's trust.*

"He seems to be very capable." Samira continued to read. *Education, Bar Admissions, Professional Activities, Community Involvement.*

"J.P. is very capable." The father linked his hands over his crossed knee. "That is, capable of overseeing the legal matters for the bank."

Now Samira looked up at her father. *I don't appreciate his tone.* "What exactly are you suggesting, Daddy?"

"I'm not suggesting anything. But it occurs to me that you might not be aware of his reputation."

His legal reputation looks rather good. Samira ran her hand over Phil's resume. *Is Daddy talking about his personal reputation?*

"Companies hire him because they want to win. Right or wrong, they expect J.P. Ralston to bring them out of the thick on top." The business tone in Raymond's voice was very apparent. "That's why the board hired him for Mid-America. We knew he could get the job done." Now the father's eyes softened a degree. "My fear is he may very well use those same powers to win my daughter."

Am I a prize to be won? Samira looked away from her father's eyes. They were too deep. Too personal.

"So, is Mid-America right for hiring him if he wins for the wrong reasons?"

"That's not the point, Samira." Raymond lowered his head a degree. "Mid-America needs their rights protected and J.P. Ralston has the credentials to make that happen."

"But you just insinuated that J.P. Ralston will do whatever it takes for the victory, right?"

Raymond nodded. "According to his resume and references, yes."

Samira skimmed the front page of the case history again. *I am simply amazed at all he has accomplished since law school.* She sighed. "Remember when I told you I didn't know if I could handle all of him?"

"Yes. And had I realized J.P. Ralston was the man you were referring to, I would have advised you differently."

But you didn't know so now you must hear me out now. "You told me I needed to tell him how I felt inside," Samira reminded. "So, I did." She didn't want to look at her father. "And you know what happened? I expressed my feelings to Phil. But I was answered by J.P. Ralston." *Maybe you should just level with him.* "Daddy, I don't know J.P. Ralston as well." She handed the resume packet back to her father. "In fact, it doesn't even sound right when you call him J.P. I know him as Phil Ralston." *And it took me forever to even find his last name.* "I met him as Phil and that's who I've come to know. His business life is a segment I'm not as familiar with."

"That's just it, Princess." Raymond leaned forward to make his point. "What about his other life? There isn't a businessman in Joplin who doesn't know J.P. Ralston. And I can assure you, there are plenty that would prefer not to do business with him."

"Then why did you hire him?"

"Because we knew he could manage the multi-faceted legalities at the bank."

Then the ones who don't like him must have been on the other side of his cases.

"So, the fact that I am seeing him is a bad thing?"

"No. Not necessarily." Raymond took a deep breath and removed his reading glasses. "Samira, I trust J.P. Ralston to get to the bottom of the business issues at the bank. Hands down, he is the man for the job." Raymond sighed again. "But I don't know if I want my daughter in those same hands. We did thorough research before we hired him, and his personal reputation is not as—"

"As what, Daddy?" Samira knew her father was searching for a polite word.

"Let's just say his personal life has some blemishes." Raymond looked directly at his daughter. "I don't want you to be one of his affairs. You said yourself that he scares you."

He does. "But he scares me because there is so much of him to understand. Not because of the way he treats me or anything like that." Samira closed her eyes as she searched for the right words. "He scares me because I don't know if I can be all he needs me to be for both Phil and J.P." *They can be two totally different people sometimes.* "Am I making any sense at all?"

"You are telling me the man you love and the man that works for Mid-America are two different personalities. I don't see that as healthy."

Did I say I loved him? "But it's not exactly like that." Samira was frustrated at her own lack of understanding. "Phil Ralston is a very..." *Choose your adjectives carefully, Samira.* "... sensitive, quiet, caring man. But J.P. is strictly business. He thinks in business terms and acts with authority and is quick to judge..." *yet he can be angry in an instant.*

"He has no right to pass judgment." Raymond snapped.

"I didn't say he passed judgment." Samira corrected her father firmly. "I meant that he's quick to make decisions." *And he'll defend a case to its death—even if I'm caught in the middle.*

"But you don't know him that well."

"I know him well enough to know that what we have together is an amazing connection."

"Connecting what, Samira?"

"Connecting everything." Samira heard her voice raise a notch. "We connect as parents. We connect as people, as a couple." *Stop. Don't go any further.*

"J.P. Ralston will connect with someone as long as he is in charge and getting his way."

"Maybe in business, Daddy, but I've not experienced any kind of manipulation from him." *Well, except for when he filed a subpoena against me.* Samira remembered that all too well. *But I stood my ground. He didn't budge my decision.* She gave herself credit for standing strong.

"Yet. Not yet maybe." Raymond was obviously worried. "It's just a matter of time."

Samira couldn't believe her ears. Her father had never spoken so candidly to her about anything. Everything inside silently screamed to defend the man. But something in her father's face caused Samira to hold her tongue. She pulled both knees up under her skirt.

"Don't you see, Princess?" Raymond leaned forward on his elbows. "I see the way you look at him and I know you think he's good for you. But he's a man..."

"...of his word." Samira finished her father's sentence. "He's been nothing less than a gentleman with me."

Raymond became quiet. Samira could feel his eyes on her as she watched the rain run down the outside of the windowpane.

"He let me go, Daddy." Samira leaned her head into the back of the loveseat. "I told him how I felt about him. And do you know what he told me?" Her eyes followed a single raindrop all the way from the top of the glass to the bottom. "He told me he wasn't fit for a woman like me." Samira hugged her knees tighter. "He told me he couldn't make it home for dinner all the time and that I deserved better than that. He told me he was too intense, and he had a hard time separating his work from his personal life." *At least that's what he meant.* "And he allowed me to make my choice."

Samira looked at her father. "And I walked away."

Raymond dropped his eyes to the floor. "I'm sorry we have to talk about this."

"I'm not." Samira swung her feet to the floor. "I'm not, Daddy." She touched her father's knee. "I lived without him for almost three months." *I need him to understand.* "But I wasn't really living anymore. Don't you see? He honored my decision. He didn't even try to talk me out of it. But I made the wrong decision."

"Kind of like the university decision, then?"

"No. Nothing like that." *How can he compare a life decision with a job offer?* "No. What Phil and I have together is bigger than a career option." Samira searched for words again. "He makes me laugh. Do you know how long it's been since I had someone to really laugh with, Daddy?"

Raymond was listening.

"He takes time to help Krissy with her math. And he asks Kara about her ballgames. And he wants to know how my day went." *But there's so much more.* "And I trust him. I trust him for the whole of who he is, both in the business world and in his personal life." A commotion in the hall let Samira know Josh had returned with the girls. "Just like you trust him to oversee Mid-America's legal affairs."

An intense silence permeated the room.

Tell him what you need. He's not going to know if you don't spell it out. Samira took a deep breath. "Daddy, I need you to get to know Phil. J.P. aside, there's a man that you don't yet know."

Raymond was chewing on his bottom lip. Samira knew he was trying to decide how to respond without hurting her feelings. When he finally spoke, his words were soft.

"I guess the things you know him by wouldn't be listed on a resume."

Samira smiled at her father's wit. "No. But his clients might be able to list some of those qualities." *Like the Hughes brothers, for instance.*

"I don't know about that yet," Raymond replied. He patted his daughter's knee. "But I trust you, Samira."

Footsteps were coming down the hall toward the study.

"Thank you, Daddy."

Raymond's eyes were sincere.

"Here you are." Krissy exploded into the book-lined room. "Josh is wondering who owns the chess set in the sunroom."

Samira smiled again. *Daddy won't be able to turn down a game of chess on a Sunday afternoon.*

"I reckon that would be me." Raymond rose from his chair.

"I told him no one played until they played against you." Krissy poked her grandfather in the arm.

"How did you get to be so smart?"

"It just comes naturally," Krissy quipped.

Samira watched her father and Krissy disappear into the hall arm in arm. *Sometimes I think he loves me too much.* She stood up and crossed her arms over her middle. *But really, I wouldn't want it any other way.* Phil's resume was face up on the bureau. Samira returned it to its place inside the envelope with the others. *You can't judge a man by what it says on a piece of paper.*

The rain had intensified considerably. The sky was very dark now and thunderclaps were coming closer together. Samira found her mother and Pam visiting in the living room. She could hear the dishwasher running in the kitchen and the dining room table was wiped to a high gloss.

"Sorry I didn't help you clean up." Samira curled into the corner of the sofa.

"You had more important matters at hand," Ashleigh observed.

Maybe. I didn't really have a choice. Daddy kind of dictated that whole situation.

"Samira. I owe you an apology." Ashleigh's dark eyes came to rest on her daughter. "I did not bring my friend Ginny into dinner conversation to put you on the spot."

Samira started to shake her head. *It wasn't her fault. I should have told them earlier.*

"You know how we like to catch up on the news around the table." Ashleigh's face was quite serious. "We'd heard from all the grandchildren so I thought you might need a way to bring your news to the forefront. I didn't realize you'd already made a decision."

Well, at least now I understand she wasn't intentionally trying to incriminate me. Samira reached back and removed the clip from her hair. *Why is it I can always speak my mind to Daddy, but when it comes to Mama, I can't ever seem to find the right words?* Samira's hair fell against her shoulders in a bunch.

"I knew from the start I was not designed for the job at the university." She shook her hair loose with her fingertips. "But I went and heard what they had to say and then made my decision."

"I'm sure you made the right choice, Samira." Pam's face was sincere. "You're always so cautious."

Always? Samira thought of her quick decision to allow Fabiano to carve her in the nude. *Not always.* "Can you see me organizing fundraising events and giving motivational speeches on a regular basis?" *I would be miserable.*

"Yes." Pam spoke up very quickly.

Samira rolled her eyes. *No way.* "You're very kind, Pam, but I don't think so. I'm lucky to survive the art auction once a year."

"Speaking of the auction, did you ever find out who purchased that statue of you?" Pam's eyes were alive with new energy.

Samira was speechless. *What do I tell her?* She rearranged her hair again. *Do I want them to know Phil has me on his table?* She felt her cheeks warm with color. *No. I don't want them to know.*

"It's the oddest thing. Someone would pay that much for it and then remain anonymous." Pam shrugged her shoulders.

Ashleigh was watching her daughter carefully. "It was a beautiful work of art."

If only I'd have told Fabiano to leave my clothes on. Samira stopped herself from smiling. *But now that I know who has the piece, I really don't mind.*

"Hey, Mama." Kara came up behind her mother and touched her shoulder. "Can you help James? He's stuck on his homework."

"Sure." *Anything to get out of this discussion.* Samira slid forward and stood up. *But at least now I know what Phil bought with some of his hard-earned cash.* She couldn't help but smile now. *Unless Mike really did make the purchase.* Suddenly Samira wondered about that entire turn of events. *Someday I'm going to ask for the whole story.*

James was slouched into the corner of the bench at the kitchen table.

"What are we working on?"

His eyes were doubtful. "English." He leaned forward and put his elbows on the table. "I have a book report due tomorrow." He tapped his pencil on his textbook. "And it sucks."

Samira smiled and sat down. "Have you read the book?"

"Yeah. For the most part. I didn't get some of it, but I read the whole thing."

"Do you have the book with you?" *It would be helpful if he brought it along.*

James shook his head. "No. I thought I did, but it's not in my backpack. All I have is the assignment sheet." He handed the syllabus over to Samira.

She skimmed the instructions. *Overview, Summary, Basic Themes, Plot, Dilemma, Resolution, Personal Interpretation and Application, Conclusion.* "What's the name of the novel?" *We could run down to the library and get a copy since he didn't bring it with him.*

James sat up into the tall back of the wooden bench. "Something about a Yankee in a King's Court, or something."

"Oh. By Mark Twain." Samira knew that one well.

"Maybe." James narrowed his eyes in thought. "Yeah, that sounds right. But the only Yankees I know play baseball in New York."

Samira smiled. *His father had a hard time with Moby Dick if I'm remembering right. That was Melville, not Hemmingway.* "Follow me." Samira led James into the living room where they turned and faced a large bookcase. "Watch this." She ran her hands along the spines of the well-read books until she came to the T's. "Twain, Mark." She followed the titles and stopped on the one they needed. "A Connecticut Yankee in King Arthur's Court."

James pulled it off the shelf. "Yeah. That's the one." His eyes passed over the massive collection. "That's amazing."

Instead of taking James back to the kitchen table, she had him join her in front of the fireplace. *Much cozier and relaxing in here.* "Grab your notebook and a pencil. Let's see if we can rock this out."

"Can I help?" Kara joined her mother on the floor.

"Sure." Samira handed Kara a piece of paper. "Let's help James get some notes on paper for his report due tomorrow."

"Tomorrow?" Kara looked directly at James. "At least we're not the only ones who wait till the last minute to get big projects done."

James stretched out on his stomach in front of the fire as Samira started to walk him through the assignment. "Overview. Start with the title."

Obediently, James went to work. Between Kara's insightful questions and Samira's coaching, James seemed to be relaxing. Time passed as they worked their way through the novel. By the time they were to the part where James could add his own interpretation, he was understanding how the themes could relate to his own situations and issues.

"There you go, James." Samira patted him on the shoulder. *Wow. His shoulders are much more developed than I expected.* "I think you've got it." Her memory tripped back to the summer. *No wonder his father had a few injuries from the fight.* Samira thought again. *But Phil isn't exactly a lightweight either.*

"Coffee Samira?" Ashleigh was pouring a fresh cup.

"Please." It gave Samira great satisfaction knowing she had repaid a favor to his father.

Josh came into the kitchen rubbing his face in his hands. "Excellent chess player out there, man. Boggles my mind."

"But you played a fine game, son." Raymond was obviously pleased with his competition. "Who taught you how to play?"

"Dad at first but after I started beating him, my uncle Roy tweaked my strategy."

"Someday I would like to play against your uncle Roy."

You might just meet your match in Uncle Roy, Daddy. It suddenly felt perfectly comfortable to know Roy and Maggie as an aunt and uncle.

"Uncle Roy is intense at the chess board," James interjected. "His games last for hours."

The grandfather beamed. "Every perfect chess game is meant to last hours."

Ashleigh put a cup of hot coffee in front of her daughter. Samira breathed in the rich aroma with anticipation. *Nothing like a fresh cup of coffee to warm the spirits.*

A sudden flash of lightning caused the electricity to flicker. Screams could be heard from another room.

Raymond turned and headed for the basement stairs. "Don't want those girls to be frightened if the lights go out."

"Did Dad say what time he was coming back?" Josh was sitting on the footstool in front of the recliner.

Samira shook her head. "I don't think he knew."

"He said he was coming back for dessert," Ashleigh answered.

That's not all he said about dessert. Samira didn't like Josh's worried look. "Do you need to talk to him?"

"He probably forgot we had to leave today," James added. He was still working on his assignment.

Surely, he wouldn't forget that, would he? Samira thought about Phil's one-track mind when it came to business. *Well, he might.* "Should you call him?"

"Maybe." Josh was thinking. "I don't want to leave too late. Mom's already not happy we're driving home alone."

Samira looked out the window. *I can certainly understand her concern.* "I hope the rain lets up."

"Me too."

"Why don't you call him. Tell those boys the peach cobbler is just about ready to come out of the oven." Ashleigh looked concerned.

"So, that's what I smell." Kara entered the kitchen from the dining room. Bonnie was close on her heels.

"The lights went out." The little girl was animated. "Even the tv went off."

Samira watched Josh pull his cell phone out of his pocket and push a button. *It does seem convenient to simply make a call whenever you want.* She tuned into the one-sided conversation.

"Dad. Yeah, they went out for a second and came back on...only once...When are you coming back? No, but James and I need to be headed home pretty soon..."

Samira watched Josh turn toward the window.

"No, it's still coming down hard...okay, I'll call her when you get here...How much longer? ... Mrs. Stephenson says the peach cobbler is just coming out of the oven..." Josh covered the mouthpiece with his hand. "He wants to know if you have ice cream."

"Of course."

"Yes." Josh went back to the telephone conversation. "Alright." Josh put his phone back in his pocket. "He says they had to shut down because of the lightning so they should be here in a few minutes."

I wouldn't want to be in that building without electricity. Samira shuddered at the thought. Another flash of lightning announced the thunderous clap that followed. Bonnie screamed again, causing everyone in the room to jump.

"Come here, Pumpkin." Raymond picked up his granddaughter with ease and moved toward the middle of the room.

In other words, Daddy doesn't want anyone near the windows with all this lightning.

"Finished?"

James pushed his notebook book toward Samira. "Pretty close."

"Should I look it over?"

"Yeah." James looked pleased. "Hope you can read my writing."

Samira took the notebook and began to read the different parts of the assignment. "There is nothing wrong with your handwriting, James." *In fact, it's very neat.* It suddenly occurred to her that James was holding his pencil in his left hand. "Which hand do you write with, James?"

"Left." James looked uneasy. "That's why my letters slant the wrong way."

"There's nothing wrong with the way your letters slant," Samira encouraged. "Which hand do you eat with?"

"Both." Krissy quipped as she entered the room eating a banana.

"Krista." Ashleigh reprimanded.

"Well, he does when he's really hungry."

James lunged, but Krissy darted just out of reach. "I hold silverware in my right hand."

Samira smiled. *Just like his father.* His personal analysis of the story was short and to the point. *That's interesting.*

James climbed off the floor and followed Krissy into the kitchen.

"Samira, if things ever become more permanent between you and Phil, or do you call him J.P.?" Pam stopped in mid-thought. She had Mark perched on her hip.

"Phil." Samira closed the notebook.

"Between you and Phil, you're going to have your hands full."

Josh accepted a glass of orange juice from Ashleigh. "No, she's not. I can handle Krissy, no sweat."

"That's exactly my point." Pam laughed.

Samira tapped the eraser of the pencil against the hearth. From where she was sitting, she could see James and Krissy across the living room and Josh at the kitchen counter. And Kara was in the dining room on the other side. For the first time, she could see the makings of a family on a broader scale.

Brothers would be good for my girls. Samira studied Josh's face. *He looks so much like his father.* Her eyes traced his young cheekbones. *Sisters probably wouldn't hurt the boys' perspectives either.* Samira was suddenly aware of Josh's status. *Although he'll be off to college by this time next year.* That thought caused her to stop and think about how fast her own children were approaching that age.

Samira gathered the remnants from the homework and returned the novel to its place in the bookcase. Then she joined Kara in the dining room leaning over a piece of paper.

"What is it?" Samira studied the image sketched in colored pencil.

"It's the sky over Granny's garden before it rained hard. I drew it after church when it was still just sprinkling."

Samira looked again. She could recognize approaching clouds in the distance behind an array of flowers. *She has a gift.* "Kara, it's very good."

"I'm going to take it to my art teacher tomorrow." She cocked her head to the side in thought. "You're really happy today, aren't you Mama?"

Samira thought for a minute. "Well, I guess I'm not in a bad mood."

"No, not like that." Kara lifted her drawing off the table. "I mean, like, you just seem really safe and content or something."

Funny that Kara would say that. Samira looked into her daughter's dark eyes. *Funnier still that she noticed.*

"I think it's because Phil is here." Kara looked around the dining room. "Or, I mean, was here." Her eyes came back to her mother. "He makes you happy, doesn't he?"

There was nothing Samira could do about the smile that was forming on her lips. It came so naturally and so easily. "I think he must." She tucked her hair behind her ears and tried to look away.

"I remember when you were so sad." Kara's was deep in thought. "I didn't know if we'd ever get you back when you stopped seeing him."

I didn't realize how much those days affected my girls. "I'm so sorry, Kara."

"I'm glad he's back." Kara smiled slightly.

"Really?"

"Really. He makes you happy."

Samira pushed Kara's hair behind her shoulder. *I needed to hear that.*

"And Phil seems pretty happy when he's around you too." Kara pulled her own hair away from her face. "Actually, when you're around he kind of forgets everyone else is here."

Samira frowned.

"Don't be mad. It's just what happens." Kara shrugged her shoulders. "It's actually kind of funny."

"Daddy, Daddy, Daddy, Daddy." Lizzie came bouncing into the dining room, interrupting the intimate conversation. *I don't know if we'll get back to this talk again.* She wished for more time alone with Kara.

Samira looked up in time to see Wes run from the driveway to the shelter of the front porch. He stopped in front of the door and blocked Samira's view through the window. A few moments later, Samira heard the front door open, but not before another strike of lightning took the electricity for good.

Phil stood in the entry hall, soaked from the pouring rain. The only light came from the window behind him. Samira studied his form as he removed his jacket and hung it on the hall tree.

Despite the lack of electricity, Ashleigh was still in top form. "Let me get some towels."

Phil lowered his head and ran both hands through his hair. Samira felt her heart stop the moment his eyes connected with hers. His easy smile warmed Samira from her head to her toes.

"Hey, Pretty Lady."

He makes me more than simply happy. The man in the hall was familiar, yet something about him caused Samira to search his eyes for a deeper identity.

Ashleigh returned quickly and handed over two small towels. Wes took his and playfully dried Lizzie's dry hair before using it on himself. But Phil just stood there. Samira knew he had taken in all of her from the bottom up. She'd felt the movement of his eyes on her body and now they were once again looking deep into her eyes.

He still scares me. Samira inhaled very deeply. *But I need him to keep me satisfied.*

"Peach cobbler by the fire," Ashleigh announced with authority. "Who wants ice cream?"

Samira felt the entire family move toward the kitchen. Happy conversation and playful exchanges were loud in her ears. But Phil didn't move. He stayed in the entry hall just watching. Very slowly he ran the towel over the back of his neck and dried his face.

This is the Phil Ralston I know and love. He's quiet and peaceful, and yet he's so intense, all at the same time. Samira grinned playfully. *And I think he's thinking about dessert.*

"Samira?" Ashleigh poked her head around the corner. "Ice cream?"

"No thank you."

"Phil?"

"Absolutely."

Samira watched Phil's eyes go from her to her mother. Now he was moving toward her.

He didn't speak, he simply took her hand when she reached. The warmth of his skin penetrated Samira's senses. Goose pimples formed on her arms and the back of her neck. As she took a step toward the kitchen, Phil let go of her hand and draped his arm over her shoulder. *Just like he did at the driving range in Springfield.* She pressed her head into his shoulder as they moved together. Very briefly his lips touched her temple, but he still never said a word.

Samira couldn't hide the smile that was begging to be shared. *Daddy still kisses me like that.* Everything felt right. *Everything.* She stepped out from under Phil's arm when she entered the kitchen. It was then she realized her father's watchful eye upon them.

Raymond offered a single serving of peach cobbler to his daughter. *I should have known Daddy was watching us again.*

"Phil?"

Samira's heart skipped another beat. But this time it was for love of her father. *Oh, Daddy.* She grabbed his arm and pecked him on the cheek. "You're the best, Daddy."

Raymond winked at his daughter, but his eyes went right back to Phil. "Ala mode, right?"

"Yes, sir." Phil accepted the plate overflowing with cobbler and ice cream. Samira watched him exchange an appreciative glance with her mother. "This is just the way I like it."

Me too, Samira concluded. She looked from her mother to her father and at last, to Phil. *This is just the way I like it too.*

64 *Linguistics*

Joseph Phillip

The next three weeks were a flurry of activity as the Mid-America case came to a head. The jury foreman dismissed the session for a two-hour lunch break. J.P. checked his watch. *That gives us just enough time to review with Sparky and prep Agent Roderick one final time.* He reviewed the morning testimonies. *Celia Monroe, our two ingenious hackers from Baltimore, and Jessica Hutchison.* He was pleased with the way things had gone so far. *Hutchison's the only one who needed to consult with her attorney, but if she's been shacking up with Goldstein as I suspect, then she has the most to lose no matter how the court rules.*

Vince caught up with J.P. as they exited the courtroom. "Genius decision, Counselor. What made you lean toward a grand jury summons in the first place?"

"Expediency more than anything." The attorneys crossed the street to the civic center plaza. "If Agent Roderick is right about Goldstein's disappearing acts, then we don't have much time to detain him."

"Here's the part that still boggles my mind," Mike's eyes were narrowed in thought. "Goldstein moved to Joplin seven years ago and wasted no time marrying Angelica Juervas. If he were already on the run, or at least involved in these other laundering operations, why would he hitch himself to a prominent society figure like Angelica?"

It's obvious, isn't it? "To hide away. No one's going to look for a professional thief in society's spotlight."

"I suppose not." Mike was still baffled. "But why take up relations with someone else if you've got the society queen by the tail?"

"Maybe he didn't like playing by the queen's rules." Vince ran a room key through the magnetic strip at the private elevator.

I don't like playing by anybody else's rules.

Denise and Sparky had transformed the Hughes' suite into command central.

"Lunch is on the counter." Denise didn't look up from her computer screen. "We've eaten so you go ahead."

Vince and Mike removed their suit jackets and hung them in the closet next to the door. J.P. hung his on the back of a high barstool and rolled his shirt sleeves.

"How did it go dis morning?" Sparky perched himself on a stool and crossed his hairy arms over his chest.

"Very well." Vince answered without hesitation. "The witnesses were very cooperative."

Sparky raised his stubby chin toward the ceiling. "Dey must be. Dey have everyting to lose."

"Jessica Hutchison didn't like answering questions concerning Goldstein." Mike accepted a clipboard from Denise.

Put yourself in her shoes. If she testifies against him, she loses her cohabitation ticket. J.P. sank his teeth into a club sandwich. *If she testifies on our behalf, she reduces her charges. Either way you look at it she loses.*

Denise handed a clipboard to Vince. "Betty needs you to check in at the office before you go back into session."

"Denise, what am I supposed to do with this call from Kelly? Should I call her back?"

This stint with Kelly Davis is lasting longer than I anticipated.

"She said you could call her cell phone between twelve twenty and one o'clock or leave a voice message at home." Denise pointed. "I wrote that down on the bottom of the note."

"So, you did, Ms Burke. Forgive me for missing that ever so obvious notation."

"I charge double for repeating information," Denise handed another clipboard to J.P. "No news is good news from Derek. He's managed all the incoming calls." Denise tapped a fingernail on a specific message.

Call Bobby. I know. Aunt Maggie told me he'd be calling about Thanksgiving.

"That's the only one of urgent matter." Denise made eye contact. "Derek says it's getting more urgent each day."

Since when was Thanksgiving so urgent for my brother?

Denise lowered her voice. "Have you decided how to navigate the Stephenson-Cartwright connection? It would be a shame for the media to exploit whatever it is you have going with the librarian."

I'll deal with that issue in private, thank you very much.

"I'm telling you, Boss. I talked to Jerry this morning. He senses some kind of a storm brewing. You'd best take care of business before your business takes care of you."

"Does she really charge double?" Mike spoke to J.P. under his breath. "How do you afford to keep her?"

"I get it right the first time."

"Sometimes." Denise straightened up the dishes from lunch. "The information that's about to leak could cost you more than double."

I heard you the first time, Denise.

"Hey, J.P." Mike covered the mouthpiece on his cell phone. "What time you figure we'll be out of the courtroom tomorrow afternoon? Four? Five?"

"At the latest." *The afternoon kicks off with Sparky, followed by the investment officers from California. Then we'll hear from Jeffrey Hughes.* J.P. nodded his head in satisfaction. "Yeah. Closing arguments should be done by close of day."

"Cool." Mike disappeared behind a bedroom door.

Unless Sparky's testimony takes longer. Then that puts closing arguments first thing Monday morning.

Mike reappeared. "Kelly's thinking about driving over after school."

"Why?"

"Counselor. It's a night on the town. Where's your sense of adventure?"

At home. I'd rather be on my way to see Samira.

"So, here's what we're thinking. You and Samira still owe us a night out."

We do?

"You turned us down the night of Stephenson's party."

How does he keep track of everything?

"Kelly is going to invite Samira to join us for dinner."

Samira won't accept. She'd rather I come home.

"It's only dinner." Mike grinned. "Then the evening is all yours."

Plan all you want, Mikey. She won't do it.

~~~~~~~

Testimony went as planned the next morning and the court proceeding commenced without any surprises. The attorneys packed their briefcases at the end of the day, satisfied with the way things were progressing.

"You sealed the indictment with Jeffrey Hughes. His testimony brought down the house." Mike offered a high five.
~~~~~~~

J.P. was smiling. *That was a damned good way to end the day wasn't it.* "By the time we're into our main course, Sean Bridges, alias Alan Goldstein, should be behind bars."

"And as usual, Sparky knew exactly where he'd be."

"He's an amazing investigator." J.P. nodded his head in approval. "He'll be invaluable as we prepare for trial."

"You owe me for that one too."

I will never get out of debt with Mike.

"Anything you weren't satisfied with?" They crossed the intersection at the green light.

"I don't know." J.P. rewound the testimonies in his head. "I don't like Hutchison's hesitations." *It's a damn good thing I walked away from that dinner party when I did.*

"She'll burn her own bridges."

"As in *Sean Bridges*?"

"Most likely." Mike pointed at a sign further up the street. "Kelly made reservations at The Chardonnay."

I can't believe Samira accepted this invitation. J.P. examined the elegant script on the sign. *Looks nice enough.* "I suppose I have to speak French and leave my tie on?"

"Just for that, I'll let you buy dinner." Mike held the door open for J.P. "American Express is an international language, isn't it?"

"I'll buy your dinner after we win the case."

"Fair enough." Mike approached a short man with a waxed moustache.

"Bienvenue au Chardonnay. Avez-vous une réservation?"

I was just kidding. I didn't think they'd really speak French.

"Welcome to the Chardonnay," the host started to translate.

Mike interjected, "Oui. Quatre à diner sur le balcon supérieur. Benson et Ralston."

"Ampèreheure, oui. Vous voici. Y a-t-il d'autres qui vous joignent ?"

I get the oui. But everything else is Greek to me.

"Oui. Nous avons deux dames nous joindre. Vous pouvez les montrer à notre table quand elles arrivent." Mike answered again.

Okay, this time I picked up the dames. I know what they are.

"Très bien. Redressez de cette façon, svp."

J.P. followed Mike up a set of decorative wrought iron stairs.

"Frederick sera avec vous sous très peu."

"Merci." Mike thanked the host. "He says our server will be with us shortly."

I could use a cold draft. J.P. slid up to the table.

"So, what do you think?"

"Very classy." *Not exactly my style.* "How'd you know about this place?"

"Kelly knew about it." Mike wiggled his eyebrows. "She's got a knack for fine dining."

No doubt. "And I suppose the two of you can converse in French as well as Italian and Spanish,"

"Oui." Mike grinned. "L'italiano di Kelly's potrebbe usare una poco più pratica. Ma il suo francese è molto fluent."

I have no idea what he just said.

"In other words," Mike continued. "She needs to work on her Italian. But her French is fluent enough."

"You two must be getting on fairly well these days."

"Pourquoi vous inquiétez-vous ?" Mike raised his bushy, blonde eyebrows in a question.

I'll take a stab. "Because she's still hanging around and you don't seem to be wishing she'd go away."

Mike's eyes lit up. J.P. turned to see what had caught his attention.

Very timely.

"Let's just say I have no desire to see anyone else in the near future."

Fair enough. J.P. rose from his chair as Kelly and Samira approached. *And let's just say I have no desire to see anyone else at all.* He took Samira's hand as she stepped up to the table. 'Hey Pretty Lady." *She's more beautiful every time I see her.*

Samira smiled quietly and allowed him to kiss her on the forehead.

"Samira?" Mike pulled out her chair.

Kelly was already seated.

It's like time stands still when she walks into a room.

A tuxedo-clad waiter appeared at the table. "Bonsoir, dames et messieurs. Mon nom est Frederick. Je serai votre serveur ce soir. Est-ce que je piu vous commencer au loin par quelled chose de la liste de vin ? "

Samira raised her eyebrows at her date.

"We'll let Mike manage the formalities."

"Wine, J.P.?" Mike handed him the list. "You choose, I'll order."

J.P. skimmed the list. *Merlot, Petit Bistro.*

Mike nodded and placed the order.

"Ainsi que ce soit." Kelly conversed with the waiter easily. "Veuillez commander l'immersion d'artichaut et d'épinards de Parmesuan."

That's great. Now we have two French- speaking parties at our table.

"He'll be back with the wine." Mike translated again. Then he turned back to Kelly. "Le chardonnay est très amusement. Excellent choix pour diner, Mlle Davis."

"Much obligé, M. Benson."

"Some things we won't understand." J.P. admired the way Samira's black dress wrapped its way around her body and disappeared under the tablecloth. The only language I need to know is hers.

"Very enchanting." Samira made eye contact.

"The company or the setting?"

"Both."

The waiter returned with four wine glasses and a bottle of wine. He poured a sample into a single glass. J.P. went through the ceremonial gestures before taking a sip. "Very good." *Smooth and rich.*

"Les apéritifs seront dehors momentanément." The waiter carefully filled the remaining glasses.

"May I offer a toast?" Mike lifted his glass. "To friendships and the future."

Friendships and the future, huh? J.P. lifted his glass. *I figured he'd toast the indictment.* "To friendships and the future," Kelly repeated.

The wine is exceptional.

Samira was studying the menu.

I could just order her for the rest of the night. Samira blushed when their eyes connected. *I like being able to do that without saying a word.*

"Queest-ce que je peux apporter à votre pour le dîner ?"

J.P. listened to Mike order their entrees in French. *I'll order for us in English.*

"Your French is very impressive." Samira smiled across the table.

It's annoying if you ask me.

"You should hear his Italian and Spanish." Kelly was patting Mike on the arm.

"I've experienced a little of his Spanish."

What the hell? J.P. shot a wary look at his friend.

Mike put his hands up in defense. "Only in public, man. I've never said a foreign word to her in private."

Now Kelly was frowning at Mike.

"I swear." Mike frowned at J.P. "See what you started?"

"I didn't say a word."

"How did your day turn out?" Kelly changed the subject.

I'd rather not discuss this case with Samira here. It is her brother's case. I have enough issues between Samira and my client as it is. If Denise is right about the media picking up on that, I don't need the Tribune publishing my private affairs.

"...Wouldn't you think, Counselor?"

"Think about what?" *I have no idea what they're talking about.*

"Well," Kelly explained. "I talked to Samira, and we planned ahead just in case."

"In case of what?"

Mike was leaning toward his date in a playful manner.

"In case you were off duty." Kelly smiled brightly. "We don't have to go back until tomorrow unless you guys need to go back tonight."

"Vous dites-vous pouvez-vous rester la nuit avec moi dans la suite luxueuse d'hôtel, madame ?"

Obviously, Kelly is the only one who can understand that.

"If you don't want to stay over tonight, I can go back." Samira's eyes were searching J.P.'s.

"Go back where?"

"Home." Samira shrugged her shoulders. "Either way is fine with me. I don't want to put you out."

Either way? Is she planning to stay in Springfield tonight?

"Oui." Kelly spoke into the middle of the table. "Then it's settled. We'll all stay over and go home in the morning."

"But I don't want to impose." Samira was still speaking only to J.P.

Where did I get lost in this conversation? "You're not imposing." *They are.* "Do you want to stay tonight?" *If she wants to, I'm not going to turn her away.*

"Only if you do."

Only with her. Not them. "What about Krissy and Kara?"

"Pam and Wes have them."

I don't know if I like my client knowing who I'm with and where I am.

The waiter appeared at their table again, this time carrying a tray full of entrees. "Bon appetite." He presented each meal with a dramatic flair.

"Est-ce que je peux vous apporter toute autre chose ?"

Mike took inventory of the table.

"Rempliriez-vous svp son verre de l'eau ?"

"Devons-nous diner?" Mike picked up a steak knife and a fork. 'Shall we dine?"

"Oui." Samira answered in French, catching everyone off guard.

That was good. J.P. took a bite of his steak. *Does she speak French, or is she just playing along?*

"Rumor has it the library is putting in a new online system this fall." Mike purposefully engaged Samira in conversation.

Samira rested her knife on the edge of her plate. "We are. It's exciting, but I'll be glad to be finished with the construction. It's a mess to work around."

"But it's going to be really nice when it's done," Kelly chimed in. "You guys need to stop and see it sometime."

J.P. watched Samira take a drink of water. *She hasn't touched her wine.*

"You know, Mike, I've had something on my mind for quite some time now," Samira began cautiously.

This could be interesting.

Mike wiggled his eyebrows and tipped his head in a playful manner. "Maybe we can help ease your pretty little mind."

"I'm thinking that might be a possibility."

Where's she headed?

"For the longest time I didn't know who won the final bid at the art auction."

"Exactly what art auction are you referring to, ma'am?"

Spare us the drama, Counselor.

"I'm referring to the art auction at city hall. You remember. The one to raise money for the reading program."

"Oh, yes. *That* art auction." Mike was nodding knowingly now. "How might I be of assistance?"

"Until that day, I didn't know anonymous bidding was allowed at a public auction."

"Really? I wasn't aware of that either."

Fess up, Mikey. She's got the tiger by the tail.

"That surprises me since you turned out to be the final, *anonymous* bidder."

"That surprises me too since I left moments after talking to you."

Samira raised her eyebrows. "Then you must have friends in high places."

Now Mike was shaking his head. "I wouldn't exactly call it a high place, but I do have friends who are willing to assist me with worthy causes." Mike wiped his mouth and moustache with a cloth napkin. "Did the current owner happen to tell you what the stipulation was for entitlement to that piece?"

Leave it be, Mikey.

"No, I'm not aware of any stipulations." Now Samira was looking at J.P.

"Let's see, maybe you'd like to tell the rules of the bargain." Mike hid behind his wine glass.

"There was a bargain?" Samira tipped her head.

Oh, Mikey. You'll pay for this later. J.P. avoided Samira's eyes. *How do I explain this?*

"Go on, Counselor." Mike raised his glass in encouragement.

There's no way around this now. "Mike wouldn't allow me access to the statue until I figured out how to win you back."

"Am I a prize to be won?"

The sharpness in Samira's tone caught J.P. off guard. *Maybe I have more to lose here than I thought.* His father's words were suddenly making sense. *Some things in life aren't worth losing.* He sighed heavily. *Anything I say at this point can or will be used against me.*

Samira's eyes were doubtful.

This must be what the captain meant when he said sometimes winning isn't enough.

"Let me clarify," Mike stepped in. "I had my doubts that our mutual friend had given you a fair shake." Mike waited for Samira to make eye contact before he continued. "So, I made him get his shit together before he could have access to the art."

I don't know if that helped or hindered. J.P. passed his fork from his left hand to his right. *She's not responding.*

"And I must say, I think J.P. has done rather well untucking his tail, don't you think, Samira?" Kelly was totally focused on Samira.

Even Kelly knows we're in over our heads this time. J.P. continued to watch Samira, but she wasn't looking in his direction.

"Est-ce que tout est bien ?"

How long has he been standing there? The waiter looked on hopefully.

"Any complaints?" Mike translated.

Yeah, the topic of this conversation.

"Excellent, merci." Mike dismissed the waiter politely.

Dinner continued, but the lightness of the evening was lost. J.P. was glad to finally get his check. *It's time to end this charade.*

"We're going to walk the French Quarter," Kelly announced.

"You're more than welcome to join us," Mike assured. "Or you're free to meet up with us to get Samira's luggage later."

I fulfilled my end of the deal by having dinner with them. "Why don't you call the suite when you get back to the hotel?" *I'd prefer a little warning before they make an appearance.*

"Fair enough. Merci." Mike thanked the waiter as he delivered a steaming cup of coffee to Samira. "In the meantime, we'll find some entertainment of our own."

Why don't you do that? J.P. reviewed his ticket. *Ten to one, Mike put the wine on his tab.* He put a charge card in the pocket of the leather pouch. *That would be correct.* He smiled to himself. *Now I'll probably owe him for that too.*

Mike put his hand on Samira's shoulder as he stood. "Samira, thanks for the privilege of dining with you. We'll have to do it again soon."

If I ever recover from the comment about winning her back. "Kelly." J.P. stood and offered his hand. "You have my condolences on the rest of your evening."

"On the contrary, we'll get on just fine." Kelly smiled brightly. "We'll call you in a while, Samira."

I'm sure they won't have any trouble getting it on. J.P. grinned to himself as he sat back down.

Samira's disposition was still contemplative. "Mike is a good friend, isn't he?"

J.P. watched Mike and Kelly make an exit on the main level. "Yes, he is." *The best.*

"Kelly really enjoys his company."

J.P. rested his eyes on his date. "They must be good for each other." He watched Samira sip the coffee.

"I'm sorry about the wine," Samira turned the still full glass with her fingertips. "And I shouldn't have brought the statue up like that."

"It's no problem." *There's no reason for her to apologize about anything.*

"Well, there is, really." Her dark eyes were sad.

J.P. watched her stare into her coffee cup. *Her brother does that when he's thinking.*

"The last time I dined in a French restaurant I gave a man permission to do something I regretted later."

I have never taken her to a French restaurant. He thought again. *Unless she's talking about the Café Ole, but they don't serve wine.* Now he was curious. *Who took her to a French restaurant?*

Samira was deep in thought.

J.P. waited.

"I didn't want the wine making any decisions for me tonight."

I don't like the direction this might be headed.

Samira spoke with a faraway look in her eye. "Fabiano Uberti took me to the Bistro 712 the last night he was in Joplin."

J.P. swallowed hard. *How does he keep coming back into these conversations?*

"I allowed the wine to...well, I just had a little more than I should have."

Probably no more than the Jack Daniels I had that night. But I was alone.

"That's the night I gave him permission to—"

To what? She said she didn't have sex with him.

"To undress the clay model." Samira took another drink of the coffee. "He talked me into it before I realized what the repercussions could be. I didn't think about my statue being on display for the whole world to see." She rolled her eyes but refused to look at J.P. "I posed with my clothes on. The whole time. But at the last minute he used his imagination."

I need to clear her conscience. "As you know, I had my reservations about Uberti from the get-go. But I give him credit for capturing you in the sculpture. Clothes on or off, it's a beautiful piece, Samira."

Samira looked away. "I just didn't think it all the way through." When she made eye contact, it was brief.

"Honestly speaking, as your attorney," J.P. made sure Samira heard that comment before he continued, "I don't appreciate the way he took advantage of you."

Samira started to speak, but J.P. stopped her with his hand. "Hear me out. He knew exactly what he was doing when he offered the wine. Gut feeling says when you turned him down, he used the statue as his replacement."

"I admit that thought did cross my mind. He kissed me in the parking lot, but he was hoping for more." Samira's eyes were low.

J.P. lifted her chin with his fingers. "Well, now the bronzed figurine, in all of its beauty and mystery, belongs to me. Mike outbid the artist to be sure it didn't leave with Uberti."

"I wondered."

"I know." J.P. smiled gently. "And now you know too. It's only a piece of art, but the woman it represents is beautiful, and strong, and smart." J.P. drew her in a little closer. "And incredibly sexy."

With that, a slight smile formed on Samira's face." You're the only one who should have the sculpture."

"I'd rather just have you." J.P. grinned.

"That is a wish I might be able to grant." Samira reached for her purse. "By the way, I have something for you. Unless Denise already told you."

"Told me what?" J.P. finished his glass of water.

"Here." Samira placed a cellular phone on the table between them. "Denise made time to help me at the phone store this week."

I forgot about that item of business. "Did she get you and the girls set up?" JP. picked up the phone. *It's identical to mine.*

"She did. But you didn't need to add me to your plan, Phil. I am perfectly able to take care of my own expenses."

I told Denise I didn't care either way. "Here's the deal. I can write it off. You can't." He smiled and handed the phone back to Samira. "Send me a text and I'll save your number."

Samira made a face at the phone in her hand. "If I knew for sure how to do that, I'd gladly send it over. I need one of the girls to teach me."

J.P. opened the screen and found the app with ease. Without asking permission, he sent a message to his phone. When he opened his own phone, the number was already saved under *Samira Cartwright.* "Denise must have programmed you into my contacts already."

Samira finished the last of her coffee. "I really appreciate the way she took time to help me. I know it was an intense week for you guys and she still squeezed me in."

"She's the best paralegal in the business." J.P. stood to help Samira with her chair.

"She was on top of every detail." Samira allowed J.P. to take her hand as she stood. "And you know what?"

J.P. stole a quick kiss. "What."

"Denise apologized for ordering the subpoena. She felt bad that it caused so much trouble."

So, did I. "To answer your question from that intense, awkward conversation. No. I would not have allowed you to go to jail."

Samira brushed her forehead with the back of her hand. "Well, that's a relief." She playfully nudged J.P. in the ribs. "I was humbled by her apology. All said, I learned a lot from her and enjoyed getting to know her a little better."

"That's good, she's my next closest confidant next to Mike." *Which is a true statement.* "She reads me like a book and keeps me on the straight and narrow as far as I'll allow." *She saves my cases and my ass, even when I don't deserve it.*

"You do have a couple of good friends. And tonight's experience was fun with Mike and Kelly and all the French."

They stopped at the front door where J.P. helped Samira with her coat.

"I'm ready when you are." Samira was starting to relax.

I'm ready, you just say the word. "Did you have anything in particular in mind?"

Samira raised an eyebrow. "Dessert maybe."

I'd almost given up on dessert. He took a deep breath as he studied Samira's chocolate brown eyes. "I've been thinking about this dessert since dinner at your parents' house."

"Me too." Now Samira's smile was sincere.

The walk back to the civic center was comfortably quiet. Without any resistance Samira allowed him to gather her in tighter than necessary. *This must be what the captain meant about my mother being enough.* J.P. closed his eyes as he kissed her hair. *Because right now she's enough just like this.*

"I really don't mind if you need to get home tonight."

And give up an entire night with this beautiful woman? "You're the only reason I wanted to get home." *But I didn't figure we'd have a chance to be alone even then.*

"Really?"

"Really."

"Kelly told me it was my call."

J.P. considered Samira's situation as they crossed the courtyard. "Are you comfortable staying?"

She stepped into the revolving door with him. "I think so. It was strange because this time Wes and Pam know who I'm with."

I know exactly how she feels.

"It took Wes a little bit to get used to the idea that I was spending the night with his attorney."

This is obviously a difficult situation for all of us. "Would you be more comfortable if we went back home?"

Samira gently shook her head. "No. I want to stay."

I'm glad to hear her say that out loud. "So, you're okay knowing that your family knows you're here with me." *She's studying the artwork again.*

"I told them I was coming over to meet you for dinner."

Maybe she is trying to distance herself from her family a little more. J.P. swiped his room card for the private elevator. Especially with her father being who he is.

Samira's hand suddenly slipped out of J.P.'s. *What the...?*

"Good evening, J.P."

J.P. spun around and faced the voice. *Stacked heels, short skirt, tight sweater. Holy Shit. Where did she come from?*

"I've been trying to reach you all week." Bobbie's eyes were sultry.

She's been drinking. Her presence caused a knot to form in J.P.'s stomach. *Obviously, this is the "Bobby" call that was getting more urgent by the day.*

The elevator doors opened, and J.P. stepped aside. *Denise tried to warn me, but Derek spelled it wrong in the email.* He glanced at Samira, who had now taken several steps away from him. *This isn't at all what she's thinking.*

"J.P., I thought we had something special."

If she were sober, I could at least reason with her. J.P. jerked his head away as Bobbie tried to touch his ear like she did before in this very same lobby. "S-N-S-A was your call, Bobbie Jo. And it ended a long time ago." *Like in April, when I left you at a photo shoot in Mexico.*

"But baby," Bobbie Jo cooed. "I thought you'd always save a little piece for me."

"Good evening, J.P." Vince Barringer stepped off the elevator.

"Vince." *This isn't what it looks like.* J.P. glanced in Samira's direction, but she wasn't there.

Bobbie took a step toward J.P. "She left."

Who left?

"She doesn't stand a chance next to me." Bobbie ran her hand along J.P.'s arm.

That's it. J.P. turned all the way around. *Samira Cartwright is my last chance, and I don't want to screw this up again.* Samira was nowhere to be seen. *Come on, Pretty Lady. Give me a chance to explain.* Panic began to set in. *Dear God, don't let this be the end.*

65 *Staking a Claim*

Samira

Where in the world is he going? She started to follow, but Phil was moving too fast. She watched Bobbie Jo Sommers and her friends get on the elevator. *Good. Maybe they'll leave him alone now.*

Phil turned both ways in the lobby. Samira smiled. *I've seen him speechless before. But I've never seen him completely frazzled.* She crossed her wrists and waited patiently. *He'll notice me eventually.*

Intuition proved successful. When Phil turned all the way around, she was in full view. Very slowly he started into the courtyard where Samira was standing. *I could meet him part way, but I think I'll let him come all the way over here instead.* She grinned playfully. *That way Bobbie will be able to see us.*

"I didn't know where you were." Phil sounded more like J.P. Ralston when he spoke.

That's the same thing he said to me at the Hughes party. "I didn't go very far." *I was within earshot.*

Phil stopped a short distance from Samira. "I still didn't know where you were."

Samira closed the space between them with a single step. "Well, I'm here now."

"I owe you an explanation—"

"No, you don't."

"Yes, I do." Phil put his hand out. "That was unfair and unexpected."

Three stories above, Samira could see the model and her friends leaning over the balcony making provocative motions with their bodies. *Perfect. They're just where I want them.*

"She's the last person—"

"Phil." *Having those women up there is kind of like having Mrs. Barnes watching, only here I don't have anything to hide.* "I called a truce on this topic. Bobbie whatever her name is, is not open for further discussion."

"I still need to explain."

"Truce." Samira took a hold of his tie. "That means the case is closed. You explained before and unless something has changed, there's no reason to rehash it."

Samira could feel him trying to read her motives. *He'll never read me on this one.*

"Truce." She moved her hands along his sides on the inside of his jacket.

"I'm sorry, Samira."

I think that's the second time he's apologized to me.

"I'm really sorry."

Samira smiled knowing full well they still had an audience up above. "I know." She pressed her body against his and moved her hands to guide him even closer. *Let's show them who gets the last chance.* Without waiting for permission, Samira kissed him on the lips. At first Phil didn't respond, but it didn't take him long to change his mind.

This is kind of fun. She felt Phil's arms pull her in even closer. *He has no idea I'm staking my claim.* Samira didn't pull away and Phil didn't offer to let her go either.

"Whoa, whoa, whoa. Break it up."

Mike.

"For God's sake, this is why you have a room."

Samira caught her breath and turned into the crook of Phil's arm. She smiled at the women on the balcony. *He's mine, Bobbie Jo.*

Mike was shaking his head. "What's with you two anyway? Don't you have any sense of ethic responsibility here?"

Samira could still feel the excitement of Phil's body against her hip.

"Back from your walk already?"

Nice try, changing the subject.

Kelly appeared at Mike's side with a brilliant smile. "I figured you two would be in the room by now."

"They need to be." Mike shook his head again. "You wouldn't believe what I just caught them doing in the lobby."

Kelly cast an accusing look in Samira's direction.

Guilty as charged.

"We're on our way."

"Well, so are we." Mike lifted a strap off his shoulder. "We're headed out so here's Samira's bag."

"You mean went to my room without calling first?" Phil was teasing and Samira knew it.

Mike didn't miss a beat. "After what I just witnessed, I'm not sure you'd have made it to the room without my intervention." He handed Samira's bag to Phil. "This little lady of yours packs lighter than any woman I've ever traveled with."

Hey. That's what Phil told me at his aunt's ranch last summer.

"I know." Phil put the bag over his free shoulder. "What do you mean you're headed out?"

I thought the plan was for us to stay over.

"Headed out, like nos estamos yendo. You know, Nous partons de la ville. In other words, see ya later." Mike lifted his hand in the air in a fictitious wave. "We decided to sleep at home. We have a racket ball court reservation at the club first thing in the morning."

Samira opened her eyes wide. *Kelly knew I'd never arrange a night out of town like this on my own, so she did it for me.* She dared to make eye contact with Kelly. *It's been a long time since a girlfriend took it upon herself to look out for me.*

"Now this is an interesting turn of events." Phil still had his arm around Samira's waist. "If I didn't know better, I'd think maybe you two planned this all along."

"J.P., you never know any better so you might as well give it up while you're ahead." Mike's eyes were suddenly wide with wonder. He turned his head and followed a group of women with his eyes.

She got the picture. Samira knew Mike had spotted the scantily dressed models.

"Uh, Counselor," Mike looked panicked. "Might I have a word with you? In private?"

Oh, now this could be interesting.

Phil let go of Samira. "No need to."

"But, uh, I would strongly advise a moment in confidence." Mike was now looking directly at Phil.

Obviously, Mike knows Bobbie. But he doesn't know I know.

"Like now." Mike insisted.

Phil was starting to laugh. "I'm good."

"Not good enough."

"For what?"

"For a surprise of this magnitude." Mike took Phil's arm. "It will only take a second." He started to pull Phil away from Samira.

Samira decided to play her card. *The only one I have.* "Is that how long it takes to define S-N-S-A?" *I have no idea what that stands for, but I'd love for these two clowns to explain it to me.*

Both Mike and Phil froze and stared at Samira.

Samira raised an eyebrow.

"What's SNSA?" Kelly chimed in. "And who were those girls that walked by?"

It must be something more revealing than I presumed.

"It's a dry-cleaning term," Mike answered quickly. "Starch, non-stain..."

"Aerosol." Phil finished.

Now they're scrambling.

Kelly put her hands on her hips. "I've done a lot of business at the dry cleaners over the years, and I don't ever recall having the option of no stain aerosols."

Kelly's on to them too. Samira crossed her arms and cast a look that indicated the dupe was up.

"Aerosol?" Mike squished his face.

Phil shrugged his shoulders. "It was the first thing that came to mind."

"I told you. You never know better." Mike shook his head. "Next time let me finish my own sentence."

"And you would finish with?" Kelly was tapping her foot.

Mike looked at Phil and Phil look back at Mike.

It's possible this is the one time we will ever witness both able attorneys speechless at the very same time.

"We used to be better at this."

"No, we just used to be faster. Much faster," Mike answered without looking at the women. "J.P., did I tell you what we saw as we walked through the French Quarter after dinner?"

"No, I think that conversation was interrupted."

These two are quite the pair.

"I don't think they're buying it." Mike glanced in Samira's direction.

"I feel terribly out of practice."

"We are out of practice." Mike was starting to laugh. "And we're old."

"Hey, hey." Kelly interrupted the play. "You two might be old, but we happen to be quite young and spry. If you're too old and out of practice to finish what you started, Samira and I may have to find some younger, more refined dates for the rest of this affair."

This is an affair?

"Okay, okay. You've got us over a barrel." Mike winked at Phil. "Let's just tell them what it means so we can get on with our evening."

Dessert is resting on this one last explanation, Counselor.

Phil motioned for Mike to speak first.

"It's a sex word," Mike lowered his voice. "I don't know if we should talk about it in public."

Kelly leaned toward Mike in playful retaliation. "After what you witnessed from these two love birds, I don't think it's going to matter if you talk about sex in public."

Samira blushed all the way to her toes. *I only did that to stake my claim.*

"Your call, Miss Davis."

You're on, Mr. Benson."

These two make a great couple.

Mike faced his date. "Sex. No strings..."

Sex, no strings what?

"Shit." Mike swore. "I can't remember the rest."

"Try harder," Kelly encouraged.

"Attached." Phil answered.

"Yeah. That's it. Sex, no strings attached."

No way.

"You've got to be kidding." Kelly laughed loudly. "That's what that means?"

"You insisted." Mike reminded.

"You should have lied." Kelly suggested. "That's disgusting."

"We tried—"

"But we're terribly out of practice," Phil added.

"With the sex part or the lying?" Kelly asked.

Wow. Kelly's just going to put it all out there, isn't she?

"Both." Mike and Phil answered in unison.

"Now that was damn good." Mike commented under his breath.

"Not bad, Mikey. Maybe we haven't lost our touch completely."

Mike and Phil exchanged a high five.

Samira laughed right out loud. *They're just too funny together.*

"Enough already." Kelly pointed her finger. "All sex has strings attached. I'd think you'd both know that by now."

"It does?" Mike had a look of total surprise plastered on his face.

"Mr. Benson, your ride home balances on the remainder of this conversation."

"Ah, Kelly. I didn't mean it, really." He turned to face J.P. "Look, I'd love to stay and see the next chapter of your heated affection, but it's been a hell of a long day and my ride is leaving."

"Call me tomorrow, Samira," Kelly reached out and squeezed Samira's arm. "And enjoy the rest of your *uninterrupted* time together."

Now I know for sure Kelly set me up intentionally. "Thanks, Kelly."

"Anytime." Kelly grabbed Mike by the hand. "Good night, J.P."

"Kelly." Phil nodded in their direction. "Counselor."

Mike turned around and waved his free hand. "Goodnight, John Boy."

Phil was shaking his head when he turned back to face Samira. "A twenty-dollar bill says Mike either finished the wine by himself, or they found another nightcap on their way back here."

"I'm not really a gambling woman," *But I sure seem to take a lot of risks with Phil.* "But, if I had to gamble tonight, I'd say you're pretty close to the mark."

"Right on the mark." Phil reached for Samira's hand and took a step toward the private elevator.

"The Hughes' suite?"

"The Hughes' suite." The doors opened. "So where did you run off to, Pretty Lady?"

He really doesn't like me out of his sight. Samira looked down on the courtyard. "Over there," she pointed. "I went to see the paintings while you took care of business. I thought you'd be more comfortable if I stepped away." She could feel Phil's eyes on her even though she wasn't looking at him.

"You didn't have to do that."

"Yes, I did." Samira turned and faced him. "Is that really what the SNSA comment referred to?" She fell into step as Phil started to walk.

"Yep."

That's unbelievable.

"After you, Pretty Lady." Phil opened the door to the suite.

I remember every detail about the night we spent here. Phil's things were packed and organized on the foot of the bed. "Mike must not have told you Kelly and I had made arrangements to stay tonight."

"Let's just say Mike withheld pertinent information." Phil set Samira's bag on the bed next to his.

I'd put a twenty-dollar bill on the table that says he's going to hang the jacket over the chair and roll the cuffs on his sleeves. Much to her surprise, Phil hung the jacket on a hanger and loosened his tie. *That's why I'm not a gambling woman.*

"What are you thinking, Pretty Lady?" Phil was removing his tie.

Samira stepped into his personal space and began unbuttoning his dress shirt. "I'm thinking this is the first time I've spent an entire evening with J.P. Ralston."

"Really?"

She pulled his shirt tail out and unbuttoned the last button. "Really."

"What makes you think that?" Phil slid the tie out from under his collar and draped it around Samira's neck.

"It doesn't match my outfit." *He's still very much in a professional mode.* "Are you tired?"

Phil shook his head and slipped out of his shirt. "Why?"

He answered a question with another question. "You're just really quiet." *I can't believe he hung up his shirt too.* Samira handed him the tie.

"I'm just waiting on you to answer my question, that's all."

Samira frowned. "What question?" She stepped out of her shoes and sat down on the edge of the bed.

"What makes you think you just spent an entire evening with J.P. Ralston?" Phil unzipped his shaving kit.

Samira thought for a minute. "Well, let's see, for starters, you refused a refill on the wine after only one glass. I've only seen you do that when you were officially on duty."

"Tonight, I was following your lead."

Oh, he's going to pin that one on me. "That was very thoughtful of you." *Let's see where he goes with this one.* "J.P. Ralston is the only man I know who can be spotted and picked up by a supermodel at the entrance to an elevator in a fancy hotel."

Phil was squeezing toothpaste onto his toothbrush. "And I walked away so I could spend the rest of my evening with you."

"And I must say you did so with a great deal of integrity."

Phil put a toothbrush in his mouth and disappeared into the bathroom. The door closed for a few minutes.

Samira stretched out sideways across the king-sized bed. *I always feel small on a bed this size.*

Phil asked another question upon his return. "Anything else?"

Only one more thing, J.P. Samira propped her head up on an elbow. "I've never seen Phil hang up a coat and a tie." *I don't think he has an answer this time.* "Ever."

Phil was shirtless. He stretched out on his stomach between Samira and the luggage. "Maybe there's some other things J.P. Ralston needs to hang up."

Samira assumed he was still playing the game. "Like what?" She ran her fingertips down the length of his spine.

"Like anything that hinders what you and I could have together." Phil turned his face toward hers. "Like casework and cover models."

I don't know how serious he is, but he seems to be contemplative. Samira thought for a moment as she continued to move her hand over his bare shoulder.

"You don't have to give up anything for me." *Well...* "Except the supermodel."

"Maybe I have to give it up for me." Phil rolled onto his side and ran his hand over Samira's shoulder. He linked his fingers into hers. "I think I need to give some things up for me so I can be more of who I need to be for you."

This is exactly the point I was trying to make at Shoal Creek. "And what exactly does that mean, Mr. Ralston?"

Phil looked deep into her eyes. "That means I need to be less of J.P. Ralston and more of Joseph Phillip."

So, there's even more of him to know than I realized. "I don't think I know Joseph Phillip very well, yet."

"Maybe we can get to know him together." Phil leaned in close.

Maybe we can. Samira closed her eyes as Phil kissed her. *If this is the introduction, then so far, I like him very much.* She rolled onto her back and allowed Phil's body to press into hers.

"J.P. did a great job staking my claim in the courtyard." Samira ran her fingers over Phil's check bone. "Once he understood I was serious, he didn't seem to mind being kissed like that in public."

The grin that appeared on Phil's face made the spontaneous moment even more worthwhile.

"Let's talk about that. J.P. didn't mind much, but it was totally out of character for the Samira Cartwright I've known."

It was Samira's turn to smile. "I think the audience on the third balcony brought out an ornery streak in me."

"What audience?"

He's looking into my eyes, but I know he's thinking about other body parts. "Bobbie Jo and her friends were in full view over your left shoulder. I decided to give them a little something to talk about."

"Now that's funny." Phil laughed easily. "I didn't know you had it in you to be so forthright and impulsive."

Samira shared the laughter. "Does it bother you?"

Phil pulled away slightly.

Maybe that was the wrong question.

"No. But I do have one major concern," Joseph Phillip turned serious again. He put his knee over her leg as he talked.

I like the way he's communicating. "And that would be?"

Phil kissed her gently on the lips.

Samira wrapped her arms around Phil's neck.

"My dog." He spoke between kisses.

"Derek is taking care of him," she snuck an answer into the foreplay.

Suddenly Phil was laughing.

"What?" Samira moved with him as he started to sit up.

"I know Derek is taking care of him right now." Phil pulled her up beside him on the edge of the bed.

Then what? Samira didn't want the playful moment to end.

"But what about him in the long term?"

What is he talking about? "Derek?"

"No." Now Phil was shaking his head. He stood up and helped Samira to her feet.

"What?" *And why are we standing up?*

Phil put his hands under Samira's ears and turned her face toward his and kissed her again. "What about Chase when Joseph Phillip gets his act together?"

"I don't think Chase will mind knowing Joseph Phillip."

"Chase is probably the only one who knows Joseph Phillip completely." Phil skillfully unzipped Samira's dress.

She could feel his hands against her bare back. *I like where this is leading, but I'm still not sure about the dog.*

"I can give up a lot of things, Pretty Lady," Phil kissed her again. "But I don't think I can give up my dog."

"Oh, Phil." Samira pushed away slightly. "Is that what you're afraid of? Do you think you have to give up Chase to have me?"

Phil pulled her back in. "My dog and your backyard are not exactly a match made in heaven."

He does have a point. Samira put her arms around Phil's neck. "But if our match is made in heaven, don't you think everything else will fall into place?"

"Can you learn to live with a dog and a husband?"

A husband? Samira's heart skipped a beat. *Is he proposing?* "If that's what it takes to gain a husband, I'm sure I could make adjustments." Her dress was hanging loosely around her body.

"Then I'd like to make a proposal." Phil linked his hands behind Samira's waist.

For some reason I never pictured this moment like this. She held her breath.

"I'd like to propose that you, Samira Stephenson Cartwright, become my wife."

Oh, Dear God. This is the answer to my prayers. And all I had to do was agree to take in his dog.

"Pretty Lady, you are everything I need."

"Everything?"

Phil's face was radiating the same joy Samira was feeling. "Absolutely everything." With that statement he drew her into his body. "You are the lady I desire."

"And you are the only one I desire, Joseph Phillip Ralston." Samira confessed between his kisses.

"Then you accept my proposal?"

Samira rested her head against Phil's bare shoulder. "Yes, I accept." She could feel his heart beating against her collarbones.

A few moments later Samira stepped out of her dress and allowed Phil to remove the remaining articles of clothing. *He's always a gentleman.* She pushed the covers back on the bed and watched her future husband finish undressing as she slid between the crisp sheets. When he joined her, his hands were warm and smooth against her hips.

She gave silent permission for him to continue. *I don't know that I've ever seen his eyes so intent.* The depth of his focus caused Samira to melt even further into his spell. Phil's lips were soft against her skin and his hands had a magical effect as he continued to discover her.

If this is Joseph Phillip, then he's the one I want to know more.

Very slowly Samira opened the whole of her being to his.

Phil spoke as they became one. "I love you, Samira Stephenson."

Samira didn't dare close her eyes. "And I love you, Joseph Phillip." *More than I even knew was possible.*

~~~~~~~

The next afternoon found Samira in her brother's family room. She could see the kids playing in the backyard through the wall of glass.

"Well, this is certainly an unexpected turn of events," Raymond Stephenson spoke with trepidation.

It's not unexpected if you're me.

Weston was staring out the window.

I wish he'd say something. Anything.

"It's like we've been hung out to dry."

That's not what I wanted him to say. Samira was totally disgusted with her brother. *Maybe he should have just stayed quiet.* Samira glanced into the kitchen wishing Pam would come to her rescue. *Or Mama, or anyone.*

"Well, not exactly hung out to dry," Raymond attempted to comfort his son. "J.P. just said he wasn't going into litigation. He'll still provide legal counsel as we proceed into trial."

Wes cast an accusing look at Samira.

You'd think he could be happy for me. But he's too caught up in the business at the bank.
~~~~~~~

Samira crossed her arms over her middle. *How was I supposed to know Joseph Phillip was going to give up litigation to free J.P. Ralston?* She felt her heart sink lower into her stomach.

Samira's mother appeared at the sliding glass door with Mark on her hip. "Weston, could you bring me a dry diaper please?"

"Where's Pam?"

Oh, for Pete's sake. "I'll go get a diaper." *So far no one has seemed even remotely happy for me.* Pam was folding towels at the top of the stairs.

"Have you told the girls yet?"

At least someone is interested. "Not yet. Phil's boys are coming down tonight. We wanted to talk to all four of them together."

"Well, of course." Pam snapped a towel. "Are you excited?"

Obviously, she can't tell by looking. "I was until I came over here." Samira stepped into the nursery and took a diaper out of the bag next to the changing table. "Had I known Wes and Daddy were going to blame me for their attorney pulling out of litigation, I'd have stayed home."

Pam wrinkled her face empathetically. "I know. It doesn't seem fair, does it?" She folded her arms. "Maybe it won't be as disastrous as they're thinking."

"Maybe." *I'm sure Benson and Barringer will carry them just fine.*

"Did he give you a ring yet?" Pam reached for Samira's left hand.

"Not yet. He has an appointment for us with a private jeweler in Springfield next week. I think it's someone he knows through the Hughes brothers." Samira studied her empty ring finger. *It wasn't that long ago I took Tom's ring off.*

Pam was genuinely interested. "That is so romantic, Samira. I can't wait to see what you two pick out."

Samira went back downstairs and handed the diaper over to her mother.

"Thank you, dear." Ashleigh's face showed signs of concern.

I highly doubt she's concerned about Mark. Samira could hear her father and Wes talking in the office. She turned her head so she could make out their words.

"Dad, we hired J.P. because we knew he'd get the job done."

"And he did, Wes. He exposed an underground laundering business right under our noses."

"But the job is not finished."

"He didn't say he wouldn't help. He just said he wasn't going to litigate."

"Why? Because it conflicts with his personal life?"

"No, because it conflicts with your personal life."

What is that supposed to mean, Daddy? Samira watched her mother fasten Mark's britches.

"Since when has my attorney had the right to determine my rights to privacy?"

Samira could hear the change in her father's tone. "Since he decided your sister was more important than a case, Weston."

Phil told them that? Samira put her hand to her heart.

"There you are little fella. Run and play." Ashleigh put Mark on his feet and watched as he toddled back outside. "We won't have too many more nice days to play outside."

"No, we won't." Samira hadn't taken notice of the beauty of the day. She jumped a little when her mother put her hand on her shoulder.

"You're going to have to be patient with them, Samira." Ashleigh nodded toward the office door. "This news is quite unsettling for the business."

Go on, Mama. Tell me you're happy for me, despite the Mid-America crisis. Samira watched her mother's thoughtful face.

"Thanksgiving is really quite soon. Are you sure you shouldn't wait a little longer?"

Samira put her hands in her hair. *Why am I even here?* "Does it matter that Phil's family will be here then?"

"This is an important event, Samira." Ashleigh walked across the kitchen and put the wet diaper in the trash. "Surely they wouldn't mind coming back again."

They just don't get this, do they? Samira spun around on her heels. *There is no reason for us to wait.* She picked up her purse by the front door. *The only thing waiting will do is keep us apart when we're ready to be together.* Samira put her hand on the front door handle. *Why can't they see this?*

"Where are you going?" Ashleigh was following a few steps behind her daughter.

"I don't know." *And even if I did, I wouldn't tell anyone.*

"Don't go, Samira." Ashleigh's voice was pleading. "We still need to talk about some things."

"Talk to Daddy. And Wes." Samira turned around in the open door. "Obviously, what I have to say isn't nearly as important as their issues today."

Samira took one last, long look at her mother before she closed the door.

66 *Breaking News*

Joseph Phillip

I've never done this to him, so I don't know how he's going to react. Mike was sitting at his desk with his hands folded in silent thought.

Time was passing, but Mike still wasn't speaking. He finally made eye contact with J.P.

"I can't believe you're walking away from federal litigation. This is the biggest case of our lives, J.P."

"I have to, Mike." J.P. leaned forward in the chair. "I don't have any choice."

"Yes, you do." Mike stood and walked across the room. You could wait until after trial to tie the knot."

"It's not that simple."

"She's not pregnant, is she?"

"No, for God's sake, Mike." *It only took once to learn that lesson.* "No." *I can't believe he even said that.* "But there's no reason for us to wait. I don't want to go home alone at night anymore. And I don't want to wake up alone either."

"Surely you could figure it out."

"You're right, I could figure it out." J.P. crossed the room and faced his best friend. "But I'm tired of figuring it out."

Mike's eyes softened a little.

"I can't have this case and Samira too. You know that as well as I do. The conflict of interest is too risky." J.P. thought some more. "Even if I wasn't going to marry her, I'd need to pull free of one or the other until after trial."

"You don't make things easy, do you J.P.?"

"Not this time."

"Not ever. Face it, good buddy, you're a hard ass all the way around."

At least he's loosening up. There for a while I thought he was going to blow.

"That puts Vince in position for opening arguments. When do you want to talk to him?"

"The sooner the better. Goldstein's arrest will make Sunday headlines. It won't take long for legalities to follow." *At least he's thinking strategy.* "And I'll leave Denise and Derek at your disposal."

"And Sparky."

"And Sparky." J.P. chuckled. "He was yours to begin with."

"I know. You still owe me for that one." Mike turned and faced his friend. "I'm happy for you man, but I didn't think about it pulling you off Mid-America."

"Neither did I." *I've spent my whole career striving for a case of this magnitude.* "But it has to be, Mikey."

"Yeah, I know." Mike stuck out his hand.

J.P. hesitated. When he put his right hand into Mike's he received a genuine handshake.

"Hats off to you, buddy. I don't think I could do it."

Do what? Get married?

"I'd have to finish the job first, then go back and pick up the relationship."

Things change, my friend. "I'd have said the same six months ago." J.P. shrugged.

"There's no doubt in my mind I could go in there and win this case, Mikey. But this time winning isn't enough."

"She's not worth losing, is she?"

"No, she's not." *I wonder if he's thinking the same thing about Kelly.* "Some things you can't play to win."

"Amen, brother." Mike raised his head in a thoughtful gesture. "So, what? You going to stand before the judge or do the whole walk down the aisle thing?"

"It's her call." *Makes no difference to me as long as the end result makes her my wife.*

"Unbelievable." Mike turned back toward his desk. "How'd Stephenson take the news?"

Which one? "Not very well." *Neither one of them, really.*

"I assumed as much." Mike sat down in his chair and rolled back up to his desk. "How'd you go about it?"

"I went to see her parents first."

"That was noble of you."

"Samira's got this tight little family thing going. I figured I'd best be in the clear with her father before making her my wife." *The last thing I need to do is piss him off.*

"You really asked *permission* to marry her?"

"Basically." *But not in so many words.* "I just told them—"

"Them?"

"Yeah, her mother was there too."

"No shit?"

"No shit." J.P. grinned. "I asked for their blessing on my proposal and told them I'd take good care of her."

"I was asking about how the Stephenson's took the news about litigation." Mike laughed. "But my buddy, the elusive, uncommitted, J.P. Ralston, not only proposed to a woman who has him wrapped around her little finger, but he even asked her parents for her hand in marriage." Mike laughed again as he made eye contact with his friend. "This really is too much, J.P."

I know.

"Oh, hell." Mike picked up his cell phone. "I need to find Vince and tell him what's up." The attorney pushed a button. "Shall we say three o'clock?"

"That's good." J.P. checked his watch. "The boys are coming down tonight, so I'll want to be out of here by about four thirty."

"Sure, play the family man now." Mike held out his hand to stop J.P. from responding. "Hey Vince. We have some late-breaking news on the Mid-America case. Our trusted colleague has pulled out of litigation so he can marry the Stephenson heir."

How is it Mike can make something with life-changing implications sound so trivial with a simple flip of his tongue? J.P. ran his hand through his hair.

"No, I'm not joking. He's standing right here in my office looking more guilty than Goldstein feels. We're thinking the three of us need to sit down yet today to go over business before the media gets wind of the arrest...No. Goldstein's held without bail...it's a done deal if you ask me...We're aiming for three o'clock...Good. See ya then."

Mike hung up the phone. "It's a date. Be back here at three."

"Sounds like Vince took it with a grain of salt." *Getting Vince to work on a Saturday isn't always an easy task.*

"You know Vince, he's steady. He knows the media hype is coming too." Mike rose from his chair. "I guess congratulations are in order, Counselor."

"Thanks."

"Tell Denise I appreciate her willingness to stay on board."

I'll tell her, after I tell her my news.

"You haven't told her yet, have you?"

"I will." J.P. cringed.

Mike pressed a finger into J.P.'s chest.

"Honest. She's next on the list." *Like as soon as I leave here.* "Unless you'd be willing to talk to her for me."

Mike grinned and shook his head full of curls. "You don't pay me enough to deliver that kind of news to Denise. She's all yours, good buddy. And spare me the details."

Mike answered his phone when it rang.

Kelly. The look on his face is a dead giveaway.

"I'm outta here." J.P. waved on his way out the door. "I'll be back at three." *I wonder how long it will be before ol' Mikey takes the plunge?* Once inside his truck, J.P. pressed an autodial on his cell phone. *Hard to tell where I'll find Bobby.*

"Bobby, it's your brother."

"I'll be damned. You actually returned my call."

Maybe that message was Bobby after all. "Did you call?"

Familiar laughter filled J.P.'s ears. "Yeah. Several times. I'm bringing the whole fam-damily out for Thanksgiving. Did Aunt Maggie tell you?"

"I caught wind of something along that line." J.P. turned onto Main Street. "How much flexibility do you have that weekend?"

"Flexibility is the name of the game, big brother. What do you have in mind?"

Plenty. "I was thinking maybe you could bring your brood down to Joplin to attend my wedding."

"Holy shit, Phillip."

No kidding. The more times I hear myself say that out loud, the more surprised I am all the way around.

"You mean like in three weeks?"

Is that all it is? "Three weeks." *Wow. That's going to go fast.*

"Same girl, right?"

"Same one."

"We'll be there." Bobby was laughing again. "I knew she was a keeper when her finesse saved your ass in the bleachers."

That was a nice save, wasn't it? J.P. pulled into his personal parking place. "I knew before that."

"No doubt you did."

"I'll send the details through Aunt Maggie." J.P. locked his truck.

"Wait, Phil. There's one more thing."

There always is. J.P. started up the stairs.

"Did Aunt Maggie happen to mention that the Captain is coming with us?"

"With you where?" J.P. unlocked the door to his office.

"To Thanksgiving."

I think he's serious. "To Aunt Maggie's?"

"Yeah, to Maggie's."

"No. She didn't happen to mention that major detail."

"I thought you might want a heads up."

That sheds new light on the weekend.

"Phil?"

"Yeah, I'm still here."

"That may play into your plans to a degree."

"To a major degree." *It didn't occur to me to invite the Captain.*

"Why don't you process that for a while and get back to me, so I know how to proceed, alright big brother?"

"Alright." J.P. turned on the lights and booted the computers.

"I'm headed into a tunnel. Call me back later."

"Will do, Bobby." A click on the line alerted J.P. that the call had dropped.

The makeshift office from Springfield was in boxes around the office. *At least they got things unloaded.* J.P. looked around the room. *I wonder how hard it's going to be to convince Denise I'm doing the right thing.* The message clipboard was waiting on J.P.'s desk.

"Bobby called. Return the call." J.P. ran his hand through his hair. *Maybe it was my brother.* He set the clipboard back down on his desk. *If that's the case, then it was strictly happenchance to bump into Bobbie Jo in Springfield. How unlikely is that?*

"J.P.? Are you here?"

Denise. I should have known she'd come in to organize today.

"I thought I'd come in and unpack the Mid-America files so we could get a clean start on Monday." Denise met her boss in the doorway between the offices. "When did you get back? Derek said he fed your dog last night."

At least I know she's been in touch with Derek today. "We came back early this morning."

"We? Who's we?" Denise disappeared into her own office.

"I came back with Samira."

"Oh really?" Denise lifted a file box onto the counter in the workroom. "That's a pretty risky thing to do considering her connection to Mid-America."

There's a segue if I've ever had one. J.P. lifted the second box onto the counter for her. "About that connection," *I have no idea how she's going to take this.* "I've resigned from Mid-America's prosecution team."

"Yeah, right." Denise tucked her hair behind an ear. "Tell me something I can believe, Boss."

J.P. took a stack of file folders out of the box and sorted them into two piles on Derek's desk. "Believe it or not, it's true."

Denise put her hands on her hips. "This is federal prosecution, J.P. You don't just walk away."

"You do if there's a conflict of interest that could jeopardize the integrity of the case." *Or the integrity of the relationship.* He accepted a small stack of files from his assistant.

"In that case you stop seeing her until after trial, right?"

"Not in this case." He waited until Denise looked at him. "In this case I'm pulling out of litigation."

"You can't do that, Boss. You have too much riding on the outcome."

"I already did because I have too much riding on it." *Personally, and professionally.*

All the color drained from Denise's face. The sorting stopped as she processed the news. After a few moments, she stepped away from the counter and sank into one of the winged backed chairs in the waiting area. "So that's it? We're done? Mid-America just stops after all this?"

J.P. sat down in the chair adjacent to Denise. "Not exactly. I'm done with litigation. But I'm staying on as legal counsel for Mid-America until the end of the trial. However, you are still on the case, as is Sparky, and Derek if he's needed." *She's listening, but she doesn't want to hear this.* "I personally won't have direct involvement in the trial."

"How can you do this?" Denise's eyes showed signs of betrayal. "All this time and effort and you're just going to walk away?"

Tell her the rest, Counselor. "I'm not exactly walking away, I asked Samira to marry me, Denise."

Stunned silence permeated the room. Denise didn't say anything. In fact, she didn't react in any way whatsoever.

This is worse than waiting on Mike. At least I had confidence that Mike would come around.

Very slowly Denise rose from the chair and walked over to her desk. "So just like that, you decide to cancel your ticket to federal litigation and get married." She flashed an accusing look in J.P.'s direction. "All for the little librarian?"

"Not exactly *just like that,*" J.P. defended. "I've given it a great deal of thought."

"Your thoughts obviously didn't include me or the practice."

"That's not true, Denise." *I didn't anticipate this.* "I weighed all the options, I just didn't happen to include anyone else's opinion, including Samira's. We can't afford to put the case at risk over a relationship, and I can't afford to put my relationship with Samira at risk over a case either." *Especially after the way she reacted to the subpoena over the Hughes' diary.* "But nothing else around here will change." *Except for fewer weekends and holidays at the office.*

"We'll see about that over time." Denise's tone was sarcastic. "So now I report to Mike and Vince. Is that what I'm hearing?"

J.P. shook his head. "No, you don't report to them any more than you report to me. You're on the case with them. You're a part of the team."

"Somehow I can't see either one of them buying into that." Denise sat down in her chair with an air of defeat.

J.P. knelt in front of Denise's desk to be just below her eye level. "They can't win the case without you." *And that's the truth of the matter.* "Hell, I couldn't even win it without you, Denise. You're the best paralegal in the business. They need to secure the court's favor and you're the only one who has enough skill and tact to make that happen."

Denise looked across the desk doubtfully. "But it's not the same. You won't be there reading my mind."

"I'll be there, I just won't be at the bench."

"You're really going to go through with this aren't you?"

I already have. "I am." *As far as I'm concerned, the only thing left are the formalities.*

Denise sighed and rearranged a few loose papers.

"It will be okay, Denise." J.P. stood up and walked around the desk. "I'm not going anywhere, and neither are you."

Denise looked up.

Is she crying?

"Can you guarantee that for me, Boss, because I'm feeling a little slighted here."

"You have my word."

Denise rolled her eyes.

"Have I ever let you down before?"

Denise blinked.

Yep, she's crying.

"No."

"Then I won't this time either."

Denise forced a quick smile. "So, what now? Business as usual?" The phone rang. She checked the ID. "It's for me."

I knew she would take it hard. I just didn't know she'd take it personally. J.P. sat down in his chair and turned around very slowly. *What am I supposed to be doing if I don't have trial prep on the top of the pile?* The cell phone on his belt vibrated.

J.P. picked up knowing it was James. "What's up?"

"Hey Dad, we're headed out. Should be there in a couple of hours."

"Tell your brother to drive carefully and call me if you need anything along the way."

"Like gas?"

"Get gas before you leave town."

"We already did that. I was just messing with you."

It's good to hear him laugh.

"Oh, and Josh says we'll need food."

"Save up, we're going out to eat with Samira and the girls tonight."

"Alright. We'll see you at the house."

"Be safe and keep the shiny side up, alright?"

"Will do. See you soon."

J.P. disconnected the call. *You know, Ralston, it feels good to be called Dad.* He fingered the phone in his hand. *It wouldn't hurt to call mine and let him know what's going on.*

J.P. opened his briefcase and pulled out the worn envelope. Once again J.P. scanned the aged handwriting on the lined paper. *It's more a note of appeal than a letter.* He turned the paper over in his hand. *He just wanted to plead his case with me one more time.* J.P.'s eyes stopped on the footer underneath the formal signature. Very slowly he tapped the numbers on the cell phone.

J.P. took one long breath before sending the signal. Two rings sounded in the attorney's ear. Then three. *Maybe he's out for the afternoon.*

"Captain Joe."

The crisp baritone voice resonated in J.P.'s ear. "Captain, this is J.P."

There was no immediate response.

"Your son."

"I know. Joseph Phillip."

More Joseph Phillip today maybe than yesterday or the day before that.

"I didn't expect your call."

Nor did I expect to be calling. J.P. ran his hand through his hair. "I talked to Bobby today. He says you're thinking about joining us for Thanksgiving." *Seems odd I'd say it that way. I've missed more Thanksgivings than I've made over the years.*

"Robert invited me, and Maggie agreed." The Captain sounded reserved.

I should put his mind at ease. "That's good. You'll get to meet my boys." *They're eighteen and sixteen years old and don't even know the Captain exists.*

"I'm looking forward to that, Phillip."

I need to tell him what's been running through my mind. J.P. drew a deep breath. "I've been thinking a lot about what you told me on the tarmac in St. Louis."

The Captain seemed to be listening so J.P. continued.

"You told me there might come a time when winning wouldn't be enough."

"I remember."

"Well," J.P. paused to gather his thoughts. "I'm there."

"We all get there eventually." The Captain paused as if he was still thinking. "What are you going to do about it?"

J.P. chuckled at his father's direct reply. "There's only one thing to do."

"What's that?"

He seems genuinely interested. "I'm going to marry the one thing in life that isn't worth losing." J.P. couldn't help but smile. He ran his hand over Samira's bronzed statue on his desk. *She looks almost as good in bronze as she does in nothing at all.*

"I'm happy for you, son. I hope she's all you'll ever need."

"She is." *I like the way he calls me son.* J.P. could picture his father's face. *He's probably looking at one of my mother's pictures as he says that.* "I'd like to have you join us that day if you're up for a road trip from the ranch down to Joplin."

"Are you thinking around Thanksgiving?"

"I am."

"I'd like that very much."

So, would I. "I'll get the details up to Aunt Maggie and we can go from there."

"Very good." The Captain's voice was stronger now. "You be in touch now, you hear?"

"I will." But there's more. "Hey Dad?"

"Yes?"

It feels as good to call him 'Dad' as it does to be called that. "Thanks." *For the advice.*

"You're welcome, Phillip. You take care now."

He used my preferred name. "You do the same and we'll see you in a few weeks."

Denise was standing in J.P.'s office when he ended the call. *She looks mellow enough. Maybe she'll surrender the fight.*

"Your dad, huh?"

"Yeah." *Believe it or not.* "He's coming out for Thanksgiving."

"For the *wedding*?" Denise started to organize the loose papers on J.P.'s desk.

"For Thanksgiving. But we're thinking we might use that holiday to everyone's advantage." *Especially our own.*

Denise nodded. "Well, let me know if you need anything. I'd be glad to help."

I don't think I've ever seen her so sad. "Are you okay?" J.P. walked around his desk and stopped her from sorting unimportant papers.

"Yeah, I'm fine. I just never thought..." Denise flipped her short hair behind her ear. "... well, you know. Who would have guessed you'd be getting married before me?"

So, that's what all this is about. He sat down on the edge of his desk.

"It's just that—" Denise was searching for words. "That I could always justify my situation against your...what should I call it?" She tapped her acrylic fingernails on the desk. "Your elusiveness to commitment."

Is that what that was? J.P. had to stifle a smile. *That's what Mike called it too.*

"But if you're getting married then that leaves me without a comparison and it makes my situation with Jerry seem very, well, hollow."

"Jerry's a good man, Denise." *And you're a good woman.* "Maybe you need to decide what you need from one another."

"I don't know if we know anymore." Denise blinked away a tear. "We've been like this for so long that I don't know if there's a definition of need. It's all a matter of convenience and comfort levels now. Stepping out of them seems like a huge threat to whatever it is we've established."

J.P. thought about Denise's common law status and realized her quandary. *I need more than a common law commitment from Samira just as much as she needs more from me.*

"But I am happy for you." Denise reached out and touched J.P.'s arm. "Samira seems like a really nice lady."

"She is." *And she's a hell of a lot more than that too.* J.P. put his hand over Denise's. It's not very often Denise is this candid with me.

"I guess this means I can burn the little black book in my desk drawer, huh?" The glint in Denise's eye seemed more in character.

J.P. stood up and shook his head. "You're not off duty yet. Derek is coming along. He may need your scheduling services."

"Speaking of Derek,"

She's starting to shift back to business.

"He's losing the lease on his apartment. Right now, he's living in one of the Bridge's condos." She started back toward her own office and stopped in the doorway. "Bridges' Property Management isn't exactly the most stable place to be paying rent now. But maybe, if you're moving out of your place, he could rent your house."

Am I moving? That thought caught J.P. off guard. *Yeah, I guess maybe I am.*

Denise frowned. "You are moving in with her, aren't you?"

"I don't know," J.P. was humored by his own lack of forethought. "I guess I hadn't thought much about that." *The only thing that matters is sealing my proposal to Samira.*

"Well, think about what you want to do. Derek has until the first of December to make a decision." She clicked her nails on the doorframe. "Are you going to be here much longer?"

Now she's starting to sound like the Denise I know and depend on. "No. I need to be back over at Benson and Barringer at three."

"Do you need me to be there?"

I don't need her to be there, but maybe she needs to be there for herself. "Are you free? I don't want to mess up your whole Saturday."

"No, I'm good. If you need me, I'll go with you and keep you men in order."

J.P. nodded his head. "Three o'clock straight up." He thought again. "And here's the deal, I need to be out of there no later than four thirty to meet the boys." *So, we can be on time for dinner with Samira.*

"I'll see to it that we're done by then."

I can always count on Denise to bust me out of a meeting.

"I assume our focus is a handoff from you to Vince?"

"Exactly." *Now she's talking.* "Vince will open. Mike will close."

"And Mike will cross-examine."

"Most likely." J.P. held out his hand. Denise slapped it with her palm. *Things are going to transition very easily.* He watched Denise open the main file for Mid-America. *Thanks, Denise.*

67 New Territory

Samira

Samira set the plastic shopping bag on the dining room table as she called the girls to join her. *I've resisted this commitment for so long. But Phil's right, it will help me stay in touch with the girls when we're all going different directions.*

"What time will Josh and James get here?" Kara was brushing her hair as she emerged from her bedroom.

Krissy appeared from the laundry room. "And why are we going out to eat instead of eating here?" Suddenly Krissy's eyes were alive with new energy. "Wow. What is in the bag? Did you go shopping for us?"

"Mama." Kara was reading the name printed on the bag. "Is this what I think it is?"

Samira took a seat at the head of the table and pointed to the chairs on either side of her. *This will take us into new territory.* "I did do a little shopping, but I had some help." She took the two phone boxes out of the bag.

"Are these for us, Mama?" Kara's eyes were alive with new interest.

"Yes. These are yours. And this one is mine." She laid her own phone on the table.

Krissy squealed with excitement. "Since when did you have a cell phone?"

"Since last week." Samira slid the new boxed phones toward her daughters but held her hand over the top so they couldn't pick them up. "These are actually gifts. And they come with a new set of responsibilities and some house rules as well."

Krissy and Kara were eagerly reaching for the boxes.

"Did you buy them for us?" Krissy had her hand over her mother's.

"No." *I'm still a little confused as to why Phil insisted our phones be on his plan.* "These are from Phil."

"Why would Phil buy us cell phones?" Krissy blurted out.

"Maybe he wants to keep track of us." Kara surmised.

"Or maybe he just wants to keep track of Mama, so he got us all connected." Krissy was giggling as she spoke.

That thought crossed my mind as well. Maybe this is one way he is staking his claim on me. "At any rate, you know I have some reservations about you having your own phones. We're going to give this a try and I expect you both to follow the rules and be respectful if we need to make some adjustments."

Krissy clapped her hands together. "Can we please open them?"

"In a minute." Samira made eye contact with both daughters. "First, understand there are parental controls on your phones."

"They're devices." Kara corrected.

"Excuse me?"

"The phone."

This could prove more difficult than I thought. "Whatever you want to call them, know I have access to your calls, your texts, and your browsing history."

"What's browsing history?" Krissy asked honestly.

Kara answered knowingly. "That's where we go on the Internet on our device."

"Wait. These phones have Internet too? That is so cool."

Denise told me it's unlimited data. "You will have to follow the phone rules at school as well as at home. The phones will stay in the kitchen at night, and we are not going to pause our family discussions or quiet time in exchange for screen time." *I just hope unlimited understands teenagers.*

Krissy was starting to bounce in her seat. "So, that means..."

"Mama doesn't want us to replace our conversations with our phones, Krissy. You know, if someone texts us and we are talking to Mama, then we don't stop the conversation to answer the text. Right Mama?"

"Right. I want us to use the phones as tools to stay in touch with each other and our friends, but I also want us to respect our quiet times here at home."

"We can do that, can't we Krissy?"

"Yes. We can. Now can we open them?"

"One more thing," Samira once again made eye contact. "I think it would be very nice if you thanked Phil."

Both girls were nodding in agreement.

"Okay." Samira lifted her hands off the boxes. "You may open them."

Samira watched as the girls unpacked their phones and began to explore the contents. They were still amid the excitement when Phil knocked on the kitchen door.

"Come on in," Samira called from the dining room.

James and Josh were close behind. Phil directed James to take Chase to the back yard through the laundry room. "Hey, Pretty Lady." He put his arm around Samira's shoulders and pulled her in for a quick hug. "I see you gave the girls their phones."

All four kids were already bent over the table exploring the new devices. The volume of the conversation had raised considerably as they compared and discussed the features and options.

"Who would have known a cell phone could bring so much excitement?" Samira shook her head. *I still hope this was the right thing to do.* "How'd it go with Mike and Denise?"

Phil sat down on a barstool at the kitchen island. "Took them both a little bit to come around to the idea, but they're on board now. I just came from a meeting with Benson and Barringer. We'll have a smooth handoff for litigation."

Samira leaned on the counter. "I was more worried about Denise than Mike. I knew Mike would be supportive. But I don't know Denise very well."

"You are right about that." Phil sighed. "She didn't like the news at first, but in the end, she offered to help with the ceremony."

"Really?" Samira raised her eyebrows. "That's more than I expected."

"It's all good. She's loyal." Phil narrowed his eyes. "How'd your family take our news?"

With that question Samira turned away. *Irritating if you ask me.* "Not as well as I'd hoped." She started to wipe down the counter and caught herself. *It's already clean.* "Daddy and Wes were completely consumed by the fact their attorney pulled out of litigation. The news that we had set a date for our wedding was not on their priority list."

"I figured as much," Phil was watching Samira from across the kitchen.

"And Mama thinks we're rushing things. She wants us to take more time to plan and do things right." Samira piled her hair on her head for a minute, then let it fall again.

"Sorry. I hoped you'd get more support than that." Phil walked over to where she was standing and put his hands on her shoulders. "You okay?"

Samira allowed his eyes to penetrate her. "I'm good." *There's nothing I want more than to become his wife.* She kissed him when he lifted her chin with his finger.

Krissy appeared in the kitchen. "You guys are disgusting." She grinned through her braces. "But look what we have." She waved her cell phone at Phil. "Thank you so much. This is like our dreams come true."

"Krissy, let me see your phone a minute."

"Why? Did I do something wrong?" She handed it over to Phil cautiously.

Phil tapped something into the phone, then handed it back to Krissy.

What in the world is he doing?

Krissy examined the phone. "Thank you. Now I have your number in my contacts."

It took me weeks to even find his number. But he hands it over to my daughter like it's public knowledge. She rolled her eyes at her fiancé.

Phil shrugged his shoulders.

Samira glanced at the clock on the wall. "Shall we?" *Dinner reservations are only 30 minutes out now. We should probably get the children told.*

Phil nodded. "With any luck, the only support we really need will come out of this entourage." He put his fingers between his lips and let out a shrill whistle to stop the boisterous activity over the new phones.

Samira jumped. *A little harsh, but it did stop everyone's chatter.*

"Hey. That's the same whistle you did when we all sat down with the dog." Krissy was laughing at the memory. "Do you remember, Mama?"

All too well.

Phil motioned the kids toward the living room. The girls were still exploring their new phones as they took a seat on the sofa together.

"Are we going to dinner somewhere?" James asked the question as he sat down in the easy chair.

"In a minute." Phil turned around and called Josh to join them.

"Why are we going out to eat, anyway?" Krissy looked up from her phone with a funny look on her face. "Usually Mama cooks us supper."

Samira took in the gathering with all four children present. *Sons. I have two stepsons sitting in my living room.* She thought about that for a minute. There's some more new territory to navigate.

"It's a celebration dinner," Phil answered Krissy.

"For what? Our new phones?"

"Krissy." Kara shot her sister a look of warning.

"Well," Samira sat down next to her daughters on the sofa. "We are getting married."

"No shit?" James let the explicit slip.

Phil pointed his finger at his son as Krissy burst into laughter.

Kara put her phone on the coffee table and made eye contact with her mother but didn't speak.

"So, you guys are serious?" Josh was leaning on the bookcase next to the television. "I mean, it's not like we didn't see it coming, but..."

"But, like, right?" Krissy turned to face her mom. "Like you guys are going to be husband and wife?"

"Yes. We are." Samira couldn't hide her smile. *I didn't know how they'd react.*

"This is so exciting." Krissy was alive with new energy. "So, like, you're going to be our step-brothers?"

James looked at his dad. "Holy shit."

"James." Phil's irritation with his son's lack of filters was evident in his tone.

"Sorry. This is just really big news."

"But it's good news." Josh came to the rescue. "Are you thinking sooner? Later? What are the plans?"

"Yeah. What are the plans?" Krissy was grinning from ear to ear.

"We'll talk about the details over dinner because our reservation is in a few minutes," Samira interjected. "But we wanted to share the news with all of you at the same time." *I wish Kara would say something. I can't read her thoughts.*

Krissy bounced off the sofa and headed for the kitchen. "Can I ride with you guys?" She was looking at Josh.

Josh looked to his dad.

"Tell you what, Krissy. You can ride back with us, but we need to run that hound home on our way to the club. Why don't you ride over with your mom and meet us there?"

Krissy was putting on a jacket. "Okay. But what's a hound."

"Chase." James answered as he pulled Krissy's ponytail. "The dog."

"Oh. That's good because he can't stay in Mama's garden if we're not here." Then another thought hit her. "Oh. My. Gosh. We are finally going to get a dog."

That's a whole other new territory. Samira was gathering her car keys and her purse.

Phil and the boys headed the dog out through the garage door with a promise to meet at the restaurant in a few minutes.

Samira watched Kara silently gather her purse and her new phone. "Are you okay?"

Kara nodded. "I'm fine." She put her jacket on without making eye contact.

"We're going to have brothers, Kara. Can you believe it? And a dog." Krissy was beaming. "I can't wait to tell Renee."

That will be another momentous bridge to cross. Samira gave a voice command, and the lights in her front room turned off. *Susan will not receive the news well because she's still wanting me to go out with Mike.*

~~~~~~~

It was a short drive to the Golf Club. Samira turned onto the long lane leading to the parking lot. *I haven't been here since I attempted to leave a message for Phil.*

"Are you serious, Mama?" Krissy was still bounding with energy. "We're eating at the Country Club? Are we members like Uncle Wes and Papa Ray now?"

"We are not members. But Phil is."

Samira walked up the steps to the restaurant with her daughters. *I really wish I knew what Kara was thinking.* As they approached, two staff members opened the oversized glass doors for them.

"Reservations tonight?" The host met them at the door.

"Yes. For six." Samira answered as her eyes adjusted to the dimmed light of the dining room. *This is the same place we couldn't get a table on our first date.* That thought made her scan the room to see if Mike was at the bar like he was the day he intercepted her message for Phil. *I didn't even know his name yet.*

"Name?"

Samira looked at the host wondering what he'd asked.

"The name on the reservation, Ma'am?"

"Oh yes." *Of course.* "Ralston." I wonder if I am going to be a Ralston too. *I guess I hadn't thought about my name yet.*

"This is really nice, Mama." Kara whispered, her eyes passing over the linen draped tables.

Krissy's eyes were wide with wonder. The host pulled out Samira's chair at the end of the table and motioned for the girls to sit on either side of her.

Kara tapped her sister on the shoulder. "Phil will probably want to sit there." She pulled out the next chair. "We should leave it for him."

She's so insightful for her age. Samira admired her oldest daughter with pride. *And even though she hasn't expressed any thoughts yet, I know she's forming them.*

"Samira."

Did someone just call my name? All three Cartwright women turned toward the voice.

"Samira. What are you doing here? And why are you at a big table?"

Susan. What in the world is she doing here? Before Samira could explain, Susan was pulling out the chair Kara had left open for Phil.

"If you add another chair, Sam and my mother can join you when they get here." Susan
~~~~~~~

was making herself at home. "I have never seen you here without your parents. When did you get a membership?"

Renee and Paula had caught up with their mother and were beginning to converse with Kara and Krissy.

"We didn't," Krissy answered. "Phil has one. We're here with him." She grinned at Renee. "You're not going to believe what Mama did today?"

We might as well get the news out there.

Krissy revealed her new cell phone. "She got us phones. Can you believe it? We are finally connected to the whole world."

And I was sure she was going to tell Renee I was getting married. Silly me.

"Samira."

Oh. I wasn't listening. "Yes?"

Susan stared at Samira. "I asked what you were having for dinner."

"Company." Samira looked Susan directly in the eye. "I am waiting for the rest of our dinner party."

"No worries. They will be along." Susan was skimming the menu.

Samira touched Susan on the hand. "We have guests coming, Susan. That's why we have a table for six."

Susan scanned the table and then looked at Samira again. "We should call Mike and see if he could join us. He has a membership here too because Sam golfs with him all the time." She looked around the room as if he were going to appear out of nowhere.

There's the only man I need to find here tonight. Samira smiled at her fiancé as he crossed the room with Josh and James following close behind.

68 Loose Ends

Joseph Phillip

"Is there someone else joining us for dinner?" Josh asked the question as they approached the table set for six that was already full.

"Not that I know of." J.P. was surprised to find the girls engaged in conversation with what looked like the friends from their slumber party weeks before. His eyes went to his new fiancé. "What the hell?" He spoke under his breath, but both James and Josh heard him.

"Who is she?" James was watching his father carefully. "You didn't...um...well, Dad... did you?"

J.P. realized the insinuation and shot his son a look of warning. "No. I didn't." *That's the pushy woman from Stephenson's party that was trying to set Mike up with Samira.*

"There are you." Krissy exploded out of her seat. "We wondered what was taking you so long." She hurried around the table and linked her arm around Josh's elbow. "Come say hello."

Krissy introduced the boys. "Paula and Renee are our friends. And Susan is their mother."

That's their mom?

Krissy started to pull out a chair to sit down. "And I guess she is sitting in your seat." Krissy nodded at Susan.

I see that. J.P. eavesdropped on Susan's story.

"Well anyways," Susan blurted. "I wanted Mike to call you from that party at your brother's house, but some guy was wanting to talk to him in private."

It's obvious Samira doesn't get to say much.

Krissy and Kara were excitingly sharing the wedding news with Susan's girls. "This is our celebration dinner." Kara explained. She looked up at Phil and held his eyes for a moment before speaking again. "Josh," Kara motioned toward the eldest brother. "And James will be our stepbrothers."

Kara seems to be taking our news in stride. J.P. watched her engage Josh in conversation right away as the boys pulled empty chairs over from another table. *Time will tell if that's honestly how she feels.* He turned back to the conversation at the end of the table. *That woman hasn't stopped talking since we arrived.*

Susan finally looked over her shoulder, obviously annoyed. "May I help you?"

She's speaking to me. "I believe you're sitting in my chair." *I really don't have much patience for her.*

"On the contrary, I believe I was here first."

J.P. and Samira exchanged a momentary glance.

"He's here to eat dinner with us." Krissy piped up from across the table.

Susan looked at Samira. "Did you invite him?"

"I believe he invited us."

"Well, she's busy." Susan went back to her previous conversation. She picked up a menu from the table. "Are you going to order, Samira? Or are you watching your weight today?"

J.P. dropped his hands into his pockets and leaned back on his heels. *I'll give Samira a couple minutes to dismiss this dame, then I'm closing the case.*

Samira cleared her throat to speak. "Susan—"

"You should try the filet, Samira. With the mashed potatoes. You could stand the extra protein and the starch wouldn't hurt you a bit either."

"Susan." Samira spoke very clearly. "I am having dinner with my fiancé and his family tonight."

Susan looked around the room. "What?"

Samira repeated herself.

"Susan." Krissy stood up and walked to the end of the table where Susan and Samira were sitting. "Mom is marrying Phil. Isn't that exciting?"

"Who is Phil?" Susan looked irritated.

"This is Phil." Krissy pointed to J.P. "He goes by a couple of names. But he's mom's fiancé. And tonight, we're celebrating their engagement."

Susan stared at Samira.

Maybe she finally ran out of things to say. J.P. rolled his eyes at his sons.

One of Susan's daughter's spoke from the far end of the table. "Mom, I think we should go. This is their party. Not ours."

Obviously annoyed, Susan pushed away from the table. "You're that guy from the party, aren't you?"

"One in the same." J.P. was still holding his tongue.

"Samira is much better suited for Mike Benson, my husband's golf partner." She started to slide back from the table but took one more stab at Samira. "You could have told me." Susan stood but did not act as if she was ready to make an exit. "Samira is a very picky eater and she's always watching her weight. I don't know that's she's going to be a good match for you. And I am expecting my husband to join us for dinner."

Samira started to speak but J.P. held out his hand.

Time to close this case. "I'm not sure what your relationship is to my fiancé, but I do know that you are out of line. Samira is perfectly capable of ordering her own meal and she deserves to order whatever she desires. And as far as Mike Benson is concerned, he is not nearly as available as you might think, and Samira is not available at all." *This woman needs to make an exit before I show her to the door.* "If you would have paused to take a breath, I believe Samira might have been inclined to share her news. As it is, you are free to go."

Susan flipped her hair, obviously offended. She looked to see if Samira was going to come to her defense. "Well, I never."

"Mom, I think we should go. Dad wasn't expecting us this early anyway." One of her daughters was trying to lead her away. "We'll talk later, Kara. Thanks for sharing your news and good luck to all of you."

As the girls got up, Josh and James started to move their borrowed chairs back to the empty table.

Susan stared at Samira for a few more moments before turning for the door. She looked back over her shoulder and took one last stab. "You're missing your chance with Mike Benson."

J.P. took a step in Susan's direction, but Josh quickly put his hand on his dad's shoulder. "At least your chair is available now."

All four of the kids stared at the exit door until Susan and the girls were out of sight.

"Well spoken, Dad." James gave his dad a high five across the table.

Even Kara seemed glad Susan was gone. "She can be so obnoxious. Kinda like Paula is sometimes."

Samira shook her head. "Sorry. She came through here looking for her mother and happened to invite herself to our dinner."

"Do not apologize for that woman," J.P. instructed.

"Fair enough." She raised her eyebrows and shrugged her shoulders. "Meet the friend who set me up with Mike last summer."

Now J.P. was shaking his head. "She is a lot of things, but a friend is not one of them." He felt Samira touch him on the hand. *Let it go, Counselor*. J.P. took a deep breath.

Krissy was taking the seat directly across from J.P. "So, that was fun. Can we order now? I'm starving."

Leave it to Krissy to clear the air. Phil waved for the server. *If I were in different company, I'd order a JD and Coke.* He looked around the table at what was beginning to look like a family. *I may never order my regular at dinner again.*

Comfortable conversation permeated dinner as Samira laid out the plans for the coming weeks.

She is stunning. Phil admired his bride to be as she talked to the children openly, answering their questions and navigating their teasing. *This is her most natural role—a mother first, then my wife.*

Samira was radiant as she explained the ceremony details to the children. "And we'd like you to all stand up with us."

"Oh. My. Gosh." Krissy was the first one to react. "Like at the wedding where he'll become your husband?"

Samira glanced at Phil. "Yes, Krissy."

"So that means we'll be the bridesmaids?" A look of sudden surprise came over Krissy's face. "And you'll like, become our stepdad."

That's funny, I hadn't exactly thought of myself as a stepdad. I'm just figuring out how to be a regular dad.

Krissy threw her hands into the air. "Always the bridesmaid, never the bride."

Maybe that's how Denise felt earlier today.

Suddenly Krissy had another thought. "Maybe we can go to the mall tomorrow. Isn't that where the big Bridal Fair is, Kara?"

Kara had her nose in her phone. "I think so." She swiped the screen. "Let me check. Yep. All weekend."

Samira was suddenly digging in her purse. "You know, I think I have tickets for free food court items."

This whole idea of adding three women to my life is going to be interesting. One mention of a shopping mall and I've lost them all.

"I found them." Samira held up some small colored tickets. "Who would have known when I got them over Memorial Day, I'd actually have a reason to be at the Bridal Fair six months later?"

No shit. I've only known her six months?

"Pretty cool you two are getting hitched," James locked his hands behind his head. "But it's not like we didn't see it coming."

Samira's eyes flew open wide.

"That's not what he means," Josh was trying to bridge the comment.

What did he mean?

"He means it was pretty obvious you two belonged together."

"Well, duh." Krissy exclaimed. "It's written all over them."

J.P. knew if he looked at Samira she'd blush. *I'll let her off the hook this time.*

Krissy had a sudden thought. "Where is your ring?" She hopped out of her chair and marched around to her mother's left side. "Did he give you a ring?" She reached for Samira's hand.

Leave it to Krissy to bring that up.

"What?" Krissy pounded J.P. on the shoulder. "Don't you know how it works? When you ask a woman to marry you, you're supposed to get down on one knee and put a ring on her finger."

"You watch too many Hallmark movies, Krissy." Kara spoke for the first time.

I wonder what she's really thinking.

"In real life it might not happen exactly like it does in the movies."

"But you are going to give her one, right Phil?"

There's a plan in place for that detail. "If that's what your mother wants."

"Well, of course she wants one." Krissy threw her hands into the air again. "Every woman wants a diamond. They're a girl's best friend, you know."

"Just like a dog is a man's best friend," James added.

We could have done without that. J.P. signed the ticket for dinner and handed it back to the server. "Let's finish this conversation back at the house." He stood and helped Samira with her chair.

"Which house?" Krissy asked. "Ours or yours?"

That's funny, I had that same realization earlier today. "Yours."

J.P. held the door for everyone, but Kara hesitated. *I have no idea how to communicate with this young woman.* J.P. held out his hand for Kara to pass by, but instead she turned and faced him.

And I thought Samira was intense.

"I think it's okay that you're marrying my mother." Kara's voice didn't waver. "She needs you more than you probably know."

Intense. But extremely insightful. "You know what, Kara? I need your mother about that much too."

The young woman didn't blink or move. "She was really sad when she wasn't with you." Kara spoke without pretense. "But she's been really happy again since you've been back."

Takes guts to speak her observations like this.

"But I don't want her to be hurt anymore."

That is a very bold thing to tell the man who is about to marry your mother. J.P. had to look away for a moment to compose his thoughts. "Kara," *I'm not exactly sure what to say but I think I'd better be as honest with her as she's daring to be with me.* "I love your mother more than I've ever loved a woman." He chose his words very carefully. "I'll do whatever it takes to be a good husband..."

"...and not hurt her anymore."

Okay. "And not hurt her anymore."

"Promise?" Kara raised her eyebrows.

She's just like her mother. "I promise." His eyes traveled through the glass door to Samira. *I had no idea she was standing there.*

"Cross your heart and hope to die?"

"Cross my heart and hope to die." He crossed his heart with his finger.

"Okay then." Kara turned around and joined the rest of the family in the parking lot.

J.P. followed Kara out the door.

"That's about all the approval you'll get out of her for the time being."

J.P. put his hand under Samira's hair and kissed her on the forehead. "Then that's about all I need for the time being." *That's plenty for starters.*

All four kids were standing at Phil's truck.

"Hey, Dad." Josh called out. "Throw me your keys. I'll take the girls home."

James put his hand over his dad's shoulder as they walked. "Give you and the lady a couple minutes alone."

Some of the staff from the Golf Club were walking across the parking lot. J.P. slowed his step to let one of them pass in front of him.

"Dad." James nodded in her direction. "Isn't that the...you know..."

Holy shit. Mary. Why would James remember her? He shot his son a look of warning. Then he observed Mary turn all the way around to look at Samira. *What is her problem?*

Samira's steps slowed as well, until she came to a complete stop. She looked from the staff member to J.P.

Surely, she doesn't know about that too, does she?

"Mama." Krissy broke the awkward silence. "Phil said we could ride with him on the way back."

"Let's take the truck and pick up Chase. Meet your mom back at your place." Josh was motioning for his dad to toss him the keys.

"I'm okay with it if you are," Samira spoke quietly, but her eyes were still watching the staff members as they made their way to their cars.

I'd rather drive my own truck. "Alright." He fished his keys out of his pocket and tossed them to Josh. "To the house long enough to get Chase then all four of you need to be back at Samira's place, pronto." J.P. checked his watch. "Twenty minutes, Josh."

"No worries, Dad. We got this," James assured. He winked at his father. "Text if you need more time."

Phil couldn't say the words on the tip of his tongue knowing it would offend the ladies in their company. Instead, he shook his head at his boys and waved them off with his hand. *I appreciate their efforts to give me a little privacy, but I need more than twenty minutes with this Pretty Lady.* He ran his hand through his hair as he turned to face his fiancé.

"I guess that leaves us." Samira held up her car keys. "Do you want to drive?"

J.P. reached for keys, but as he did, he pulled Samira in close. She laughed unexpectedly. *She staked her claim in Springfield. I can stake mine right here.* He heard the truck start and knew the kids were pulling out of the parking space. *But I also know there's another car over there that hasn't left yet.*

Samira was playing along. "If we didn't have an audience..." she put her hands around his waist inside his jacket.

God, I love it when she does that. "Audience or not." He kissed Samira right there in the parking lot. *I don't care if the whole world is watching.*

"Counselor."

Mike.

"You two are impossible." Mike and Kelly appeared out of nowhere.

Samira leaned into J.P.'s side. *I could keep her this close all night.* "What brings you to the Club tonight?"

"Dinner." Kelly answered. "We have a late reservation."

J.P. kissed Samira's hair.

Samira spoke quietly. "We just celebrated our news with the kids."

Mike looked around the parking lot. "I don't see any kids."

"They just left in my truck."

"Don't tell me you're stranded again," Mike wiggled his eyebrows at Samira.

She pointed at her car.

Kelly smiled brightly. "I think the last time you were stranded, I met Mike in your driveway." She linked her arm through Mike's. "We are very grateful for that setup and very happy for your news."

"Thank you." Samira leaned her head into J.P.'s shoulder. "We are too."

Mike nodded his head at Samira. "We won't keep you." He looked down at Kelly. "Shall we dine?"

Kelly beamed a brilliant smile. "See you two love birds again soon."

J.P. and Samira watched Mike and Kelly cross the parking lot.

"Did you set them up?"

Samira shook her head. "No. It was kinda strange. The night Mike took me home from my dinner with Susan and Sam, Kelly brought the girls home from the movies because they didn't have a phone to call Sam to pick them up."

That won't be an issue anymore. They'll be able to call when they need to.

"They met in my driveway over convertible tops and Aida."

"Over what?"

"They both have convertibles and sound systems. Aida was playing."

I have no idea what she's talking about. J.P. shook his head. "Whatever."

Samira pulled away. "I hate that word."

"Whatever?" He unlocked Samira's car and opened her door. *Come here, Pretty Lady.* He kissed her one more time before helping her into the car.

~~~~~~~

Back at the house, conversation was lively. The girls gave Josh and James a tour of the entire house, with Chase following every step.

They've seen more of Samira's house than I have.

Suddenly Chase was at full attention, staring at the front door. *What is it boy?* Chase let out a sharp bark announcing a visitor.

Samira put her hand over her heart, startled.

Going to need some canine house rules.

"Mama." Krissy called from the living room window. "Papa Ray and Granny are here."

The sudden look of shock on Samira's face caused J.P. to worry.

"What in the world?" Samira seemed to be addressing herself more than anyone else. "I hope they're not here to try to talk us out of this." She rolled her eyes at J.P. and put her hand on her forehead.

Surely, she wouldn't allow them to do that.

"I didn't expect my parents tonight."

"I knew that from the look on your face."

Samira sighed. "I don't know why they're here. But earlier I walked out on Mama before she had a chance to speak her piece."

That doesn't sound encouraging.

"What if they don't want me to get married?"

He shrugged his shoulders. "Who are you going to listen to?"

"You?"

J.P. shook his head.

"Them?"

Nope. He shook his head again but this time he looked deep into Samira's eyes.

"Me." Samira exhaled very slowly. I know. Listen to my heart."

"You know, Pretty Lady," J.P. lowered his voice as he put his hand on her shoulder. "There are things you'll hang on to all your life. But maybe, kinda like J.P., you need to let some of those things go so you can become my wife."

James passed by the parents, dragging Chase by the collar.

Samira looked over J.P.'s shoulder. "Why do things always have to be so complicated where my family is concerned?"

J.P. put his hand under her ear and kissed her forehead. "They don't." He winked.

The kids were entertaining the grandparents in the living room with animated conversation.

"I'm going to make a pot of coffee." Samira crossed the kitchen and began to run water into a carafe. "Would you like anything?"

She needs the coffee to calm her nerves, but I don't think she has anything strong enough for me tonight. Despite Samira's concerns, J.P. crossed the dining room and offered his hand to
~~~~~~~

JUDITH KAY

Raymond Stephenson. *Might as well get this over with.*

69 Sharing Secrets

Samira

Samira sat between Phil and her father, anxiously awaiting the close of the service. *Had I known Mama's intent was to invite us all to church today, I'd have steered her in another direction.* She opened the hymnal to the page indicated in the bulletin. *Church is something Phil and I can work through later.* Samira's eyes passed over the stained glass in the window at the end of the pew. *But I am glad he's here with me this morning.* She breathed in deeply, noticing a hint of Phil's aftershave. *Especially if we're going to have Pastor Bill officiate our wedding.*

"Please stand for the closing hymn." The song leader raised his arm for the congregation to rise.

Normally Samira would share her hymnal with her father. But today she was slightly confused. *Oh good. Daddy is going to share with Mama.* Across the way she could see Krissy and Kara entertaining Josh and James. *I hope they're behaving.*

Tom knew all these songs, but my guess would be that they are unfamiliar to Phil. Samira opened her mouth to sing the opening stanza. *As far as that goes, this entire setting is probably unfamiliar territory.* Her father's tenor harmony blended with the congregational voices. Samira smiled to herself. *I will never tire of hearing Daddy sing these songs.*

Samira bowed her head for the final benediction. As she looked down, it was obvious Phil didn't know what to do with his hands. He started to tuck them in his pants pockets, but Samira slipped her hand inside his.

"Amen." Raymond straightened his back. "It's always good to have you join us for worship, Princess." He pecked his daughter on the cheek. "And a nice treat to have you sitting with us this morning as well, Phil."

Daddy is making a genuine effort here. Samira suddenly wondered how she should introduce Phil when people came to greet her. *He has so many names to choose from.*

"J.P."

Samira turned to see old Mr. Price offer his hand in greeting.

"Glad to have you with us this morning."

Samira watched Phil exchange a handshake. "It's good to see you, Mr. Price. It's been a while."

How does Phil know my father's tailor?

"Anytime I don't need you is a good sign, don't you think?" The old man laughed cordially. "Are you here with Miss Samira?"

"I am."

Samira felt her cheeks warm when Phil looked at her.

"Excellent company, that young woman." Mr. Price winked at Samira causing her blush to intensify. "We should meet for lunch and catch up sometime."

Phil nodded his head. He was in direct eye contact with the elderly gentleman. "Give me a call and I'll work it in."

"Very well." The man turned and raised his hand in a silent wave.

Before Samira got to the end of the pew, another man had stopped her fiancé to visit. *How in the world do they know him?* She stepped into the aisle and turned to wait for Phil to join her. *Or maybe I should ask how he knows them?*

"Mama?" Kara was standing at her mother's side. "Can we ride to Papa Ray's with Josh? He offered to drive us."

Samira looked over Kara's shoulder at Phil's boys. Krissy was busy introducing them to other teenagers. "I guess." *This is a new phenomenon. I'm not used to having other drivers in the family.* Phil was still talking to the couple in the pew behind him. *And it won't be long before James has his license too.* "As long as he takes you straight to the house. No scooping the loop."

Phil finally joined her. The look on his face told Samira he was ready to be out of the crowd.

"How do they know you?"

Phil put his hand against Samira's waist and began to direct her through the mingling parishioners. "Clients."

Oh. I never considered that possibility. "Yours?"

"Mine."

"Pastor Bill said he'd meet us in the chapel when he's finished greeting the people." It was Samira's turn to guide Phil. She took his hand and led him around the end of the last pew.

"And Pastor Bill is?" Phil was looking around the room.

"He's the one shaking hands in the black suit at the door." *I keep forgetting Phil doesn't know this place.* "Pastor John gave the message this morning. He's new. But I've known Pastor Bill since I was a baby." *Or maybe I should say he's known me that long.*

Phil raised his chin giving indication he was following Samira's explanation.

"Come in here." Samira stepped into the chapel off the side of the sanctuary. "This is my favorite room." She closed the door behind them. "It's peaceful in here." *And if the light hits that window exactly right, maybe the dove will appear.* Phil looked less than comfortable. "Is something wrong?"

"No." Phil took the liberty to walk to the middle of the room. "But to be perfectly honest, I have a hard time finding anything peaceful inside a church building."

That doesn't surprise me. Samira smiled gently and met Phil in the middle of the room. "I guess if you're not used to it, a church can be kind of intimidating."

"I just never feel like I belong here." Phil's eyes were on the stained-glass windows.

I wonder if he even went to church as a child. "When I was little, I used to sneak in here to get away from all the grownups who always wanted to visit with me after the service." Samira chuckled. "Some of them are out there chatting away right now." *Like Mr. Price.* "They used to ask me all kinds of questions I never really wanted to answer so I'd come in here to escape the interrogation." *They still do that to me when I visit.* Samira was smiling at the memory. *I feel like I'm revealing all my secrets.*

"They have good intentions." Phil was looking around.

"They do, but if you're like me, you'd rather be in here where it's quiet and still." Samira glanced at the window hoping against all odds to see the dove flicker across the pane.

Phil nodded his head. "I must be a lot like you because it's much more comfortable in here than it is out there."

Samira pointed at a child-sized pew along the far wall. "I'd sit on that bench and stare at the window." She wanted desperately to tell Phil about the dove but was afraid to reveal the image before he had a chance to experience it for himself. "Sometimes, if I was very still, I could hear God talking to me."

Phil looked less than convinced.

Samira raised her eyebrow. "You don't believe me?"

"Somehow I do believe you." He ran his hand through his hair. "I can't say I've ever heard the voice of God."

Samira was curious. "So, what can you say then?" *I'd like to hear this side of Joseph*

Phillip.

Phil's eyes met hers again. "I can say I've heard a voice in my head, but I don't know I could attribute it to be The Voice." His eyes settled into the distance behind Samira.

"I remember one time I was in here by myself, and Daddy came to get me. I could still hear the grownups talking out there and I wasn't ready to leave." Samira's heart warmed with the memory. "Instead of picking me up and carrying me out like he usually did, Daddy sat down with me, and we stayed in here until I couldn't hear so many people talking." *I was probably about five or six years old then.* She could remember swinging her feet off the edge of the little pew. *Daddy prayed with me that day. I know he did even though he didn't say a word out loud.*

Phil dropped his hands into his pockets. "You'll have to read the letters my mother wrote to the Captain when Bobby and I were little." His eyes were distant yet focused. "My dad sent a box of them home with me and I finally gave myself permission to read some." Phil puckered his lips in thoughtful silence for a moment. "I didn't realize how much faith my mother had in those days."

Samira was standing only a short distance from Phil, but she could feel the distance of his thoughts. *That fact alone makes me think Phil and Bobby must have attended church as children.*

"She closed her letters by reminding the Captain that God was between him and the enemy." Phil's blue eyes came back to Samira's.

"And obviously He was. Your father certainly had great success facing the enemy over and over again."

Phil slowly nodded his head, but Samira doubted he was nodding in agreement.

"It's taken me awhile, but I think I misinterpreted the enemy's identity."

This is going much deeper than I expected. "Who did you think the enemy was?"

Phil's eyes darkened considerably.

Maybe I shouldn't have asked that.

"For a long time, I thought it was God." Phil's eyes went back to the window.

I've wondered from time to time if that's what he thought. "Can I tell you something very personal?"

Phil blinked slowly and cast his eyes back on Samira.

Samira put her hands on his waist under his open jacket. "I believe you are the answer to my prayers."

"Can I tell you something very personal?" Phil's voice was noticeably quiet.

She felt Phil take a deep breath and waited for him to exhale.

"I have come to realize that I've been my own worst enemy over the years. And it's a damn good thing you were praying because I don't think I'd have ever found you any other way."

"Oh, Phil." Samira caught her breath. *It took courage for him to share that secret too.*

"True statement, Pretty Lady." Phil's eyes were locked on hers. "Being back in a church service brought back a lot of memories this morning."

"Good memories, I hope." Samira watched his eyes search the room.

A single turn of his head indicated not all the memories were pleasant. "The last time I was in a church building was for my mother's funeral." Phil continued to avoid eye contact. "That was a long time ago."

"I'm sorry." Samira touched her fingers to his cheek.

"Don't be." Now Phil looked at her. "It feels right to be here with you."

"Ah, Samira." Pastor Bill entered through the double doors that led back to the sanctuary. "I knew I would find you here." He moved to the center of the room and reached out his right hand. "I'm Pastor Bill."

"Phil Ralston."

Interesting. Samira shared a look of surprise with her fiancé. *Not J.P. today?*

"Very pleased to meet you." Pastor Bill was motioning toward a small round table. "Shall we sit down for a moment?"

"I know this isn't the best time," Samira apologized to the pastor.

"Now, now," The elderly gentleman took a seat. "You're both here and I am here. This must be the perfect time."

Pastor Bill always knows how to put people at ease. Samira admired Phil's composure as he sat down in the chair next to her. *I wonder if we will ever revisit that conversation.*

"I was not surprised to get your call, Samira." Pastor Bill's eyes danced with merriment. "It wasn't so long ago we were here in this room leaning toward a glimpse of the future."

Is that what we were doing? Samira couldn't help but smile at his choice of descriptive words. *He's such a poet.*

"I sense you've found the peace you came seeking that day." Pastor Bill was looking only at Samira.

Subsequently, Samira realized Phil was also looking at her. "I believe I have." She felt her cheeks warm with her confession.

"I believe you have as well." Pastor Bill nodded in satisfaction. "Shall we get down to business then?"

Samira could see Phil run his tongue over his bottom lip and she knew he was humored by the conversation so far. *I just hope he holds that thought until we're out of this building.*

"I understand the two of you are planning to be married."

"And I..." Samira stopped to correct herself. "Or rather, we would like for you to perform the ceremony."

The minister's eyes twinkled again. "It would be my honor."

"We don't want anything as fancy as my mother is thinking," *I don't want to sound harsh, but I need to be honest.* "I'm thinking the best way to satisfy everyone is simply to have the ceremony after church."

"And how do you feel about this, Phil? Do you have any concerns about such a service?"

Phil was shaking his head. "My only concern is that I leave that day with this pretty lady as my wife. Everything else is of secondary priority."

"I know for a fact we can accommodate that." Pastor Bill smiled broadly. "And I know from our phone call that we don't have much time in which to prepare, but I would like to meet with the two of you at least once before the ceremony." The minister paused.

Of course, we would want to meet with Pastor Bill. Samira was nodding her head in agreement, and she sincerely hoped Phil could spare the time to meet with them too.

"As you know, it takes three to get married. And it takes three to stay married. It's important we remember to include the third and most important party in our preparation."

Phil tipped his head as if he were contemplating the pastor's comment.

Pastor Bill answered the silent question. "You, Samira, and God."

Much to Samira's relief, Phil smiled.

"Do you agree?"

"I do." Phil put his arm around the back of Samira's chair.

"Very well." The minister turned toward Samira. "As you may recall, I told you once that Love doesn't make a wrong choice. I trust you are ready to embrace its purpose for the greater good."

I am so thankful love doesn't make a wrong choice. She knew Phil was wondering what they were talking about. "I am." She answered easily. Without hesitation, she leaned into Phil's arm. *The warmth of his body permeated hers immediately.*

"Shall we say Thursday at seven then?"

Samira looked at Phil for approval. *His schedule is much more complicated than mine.*

"That works for me." Phil sat up straighter in his chair.

Phil must be about done with this conversation. "Thursday is good for me too." Samira also slid forward on her chair. *Now I'm glad Mama is cooking. I'm getting hungry.*

Pastor Bill rose from his seat and offered his hand to Phil one more time. Before he walked away, he squeezed Samira's shoulders with his aged hands. "Until then."

Samira watched her lifelong pastor walk the length of the chapel and disappear through the single door at the back. *In all my years of coming to this room, I still have no clue where that door leads.* For the first time in her life, Samira wondered what was concealed on the other side. *I'm going to investigate that one of these days.*

When her thoughts came back to the present, Phil was standing in front of the stained-glass window. Her eyes followed his to the very top.

Phil pointed to the top of the glass, but he didn't say anything.

"Did you see the dove?"

Phil nodded his head with excitement. "Yeah. Did you see it?"

"I just know it's there." Samira's heart was pounding in her chest. "Did the people dance?"

"I don't know about that," Phil studied the window again. "But I know I saw a dove swoop across the glass lengthwise."

Samira was excited with Phil's revelation. "Now you know why I used to sneak in here when I was little. It's the dove of peace. Pastor Bill says he's only known it to appear as a symbol of peace to troubled souls."

Phil laughed out loud. "Yeah, well, my soul certainly fits that category." He looked at the window again.

It's magical. "You can't make it happen, you just have to be patient and allow it come."

"That's interesting." Phil ran his hand through his hair. "I've spent most of my life forcing things to happen only to learn if I relinquish control, the best things in life come to me."

That's what Pastor Bill meant when he said Love would come to me.

"Trouble is, I'm not the most patient man in the world."

Samira put her arms around Phil's neck. "I would beg to differ. Joseph Phillip Ralston happens to be the most patient man I've ever known."

Phil grinned. "Some things are certainly worth the wait." He kissed her quickly. "Isn't somebody cooking lunch for us?"

"My mother." *But I'm not quite ready to go.*

"Then what are we waiting for?"

Peace maybe? Phil returned Samira's kiss, but it was obvious he was ready to leave. She let go and watched him cross the room toward the single door.

"Where are you going? We came in over here." Samira pointed to the double doors that led back to the sanctuary.

"I know, but the parking lot is out here." Phil pointed to the single door at the back of the room.

How does he know that? Samira decided to prove him wrong. "Okay, then I'll follow you." *It probably leads into the pastor's study or something.*

Much to Samira's surprise, the door led into a dark entry hall. She watched Phil turn another doorknob. When he opened the second door, sunlight flooded the entire area.

"Hey, how did you know that?" *All my life I've imagined a magical passageway to heaven behind this door.*

Phil allowed Samira to step outside first. "It's not too hard to figure out. When we parked, I noticed the main entryway and this one. I assumed from the inside that this one led back outdoors."

This is too funny. She scanned the parking lot for Phil's truck. "Where did you park?"

A funny look came over Phil's face. "I guess I didn't. Josh did."

Samira grinned at the realization. "And I came over with my parents." *Maybe this is more like a passageway to heaven than I originally thought.*

"So, we're stranded?"

"Better than stranded." Samira took him by the hand and started across the brown grass in the churchyard. "Now I get to show you one of my favorite secrets." Samira laughed into the sunshine. *I am so thankful I was patient enough to let Love come back to me.*

Phil followed without any reluctance whatsoever. Samira tucked herself into his arm. *Now I can show him some more of my favorite places.* Until today, this path had been reserved only for her father. *But today I get to share it with the man who loves me better than the rest. Maybe even better than Daddy.*

70 Last Chance at Love

Joseph Phillip

Mike patted the inside pocket on his suit coat. "Shit. I left the marriage license in my car."

J.P. slapped him on the arm. "Don't swear in here." He looked around the chapel. *I wonder if that dove is going to appear.* "Lightning is nearer striking here than anywhere else."

Mike laughed. "Okay, Counselor. But I still need to get outside to get your legal document."

J.P. pointed to the single door at the back of the room. "That leads to the parking lot and as far as I know you can come back in by the same route."

"A groom's room with a chicken exit." Mike nodded his head. "Gotta like it." He started for the door.

"Hey, Mike." J.P. waited for his friend to turn around. "You do have the rings, don't you?"

Mike's blonde curls bobbed on his head. "Not to worry." He held Samira's rings out for J.P. to see. "Right here in my hot little hand."

Just checking. Mike slipped quietly out the door. The congregation was still singing the last hymn. *Pastor Bill told me he'd come for me at the end of the service.* J.P. paced the length of the room. *I don't remember being this nervous the first time I got married.* He thought some more. *Fact is, I don't remember being this sober the first time around.* Samira's dark brown eyes came into focus in J.P.'s mind. *There's no way in hell, or heaven for that matter, that I'd do anything to jeopardize this day.*

The stained-glass window caught J.P.'s attention again. The sunlight was illuminating the image as it had before, but there was no animation. *He said it takes three to get married and it takes three to stay married.* J.P. ran his hand through his hair. *There may have been three present when I got married before, but I certainly didn't have three following the ceremony.*

The entire first year of his marriage to Janet had always been a blur. *I don't know how it all works, but I'll do whatever it takes to be the husband... "And father."* J.P. turned his head. A voice had sounded in his ear. *And father?* He smiled to himself. *I guess it's a package deal, huh?* The voice spoke again. *"That it is."*

J.P.'s eyes went to the top of the windowpane. *Maybe that's what Samira means by hearing the voice of God.* He chuckled slightly. *How in the hell do you know it from your own?*

Without warning, the light behind the window shifted and the image of a dove flitted across the glass toward the people who seemed to be dancing at the bottom of the design.

The dove of peace. He waited another moment hoping for the dove to appear again. *Peace for a troubled soul.*

Mike reappeared as silently as he'd slipped away. "Got it." He waved the paper in the air. "I'd hate to get out of here without all the right signatures."

That's not an option.

"Nice job with her rings," Mike was examining the diamond engagement ring and band with interest. "It's unique but classy all at the same time.

"It's the one she liked." *Wait 'til he sees it on her hand. That's where it really takes on her personality.* J.P. took the engagement ring out of Mike's fingers and studied it. "Once she saw this one, her mind was made up."

Mike grinned. "Do you have any idea how tightly you're wrapped around her little finger?"

J.P. gave the ring back to his best friend. "Yes, I think I do." *And I'm thinking I like it that way.*

"I can't believe you're actually going to let her put a ring on your finger." Mike slid on to the round conference table and crossed his ankles. "You fought tooth and nail to *not* wear a ring the first time around."

"Wrong woman." J.P. remembered that fight. *But I'll wear this Pretty Lady's ring.*

"Amen to that." Mike stroked his moustache. "I bet she picked out your ring too."

"She let me choose my own."

"Really?"

"Really." *Well, not exactly.* J.P. grinned. *I chose my own with her approval.* "I let her make the final decision."

"I figured as much." Mike was nodding his head knowingly. "How'd you land the appointment with Mark Schneider?"

"He does custom design work for Elizabeth Hughes." J.P. ran his hand through his hair. "Samira hit it off with Mrs. Hughes in Springfield that first time." *Still don't know how that happened.* "Elizabeth insisted I use her jeweler when she heard we were getting married."

Mike was examining the diamond ring again. "It's stunning. What'd you drop for the set?"

"You don't want to know." J.P. grinned.

"Oh, but I do." He held the ring up to the light. "Two karats total?"

"Closer to three."

"How much?"

"Almost ten grand." J.P. held out his hand. "This one was over half that, then add mine plus the rush charges."

"Your AmEx card is racking up some points these days."

J.P. examined the ring again then nodded with satisfaction. *She's worth it.*

Mike was suddenly contemplative. "You know, I think I owe you one, good buddy."

"I'm sure you do, but in light of everything I owe you—"

Mike shook his head. "Seriously, J.P. Hear me out." He looked J.P. square in the eye. "In the beginning of all this I assumed you didn't have a chance with Samira. You know, she had her life together, she was smart, she was steady." Mike chewed on his moustache for a moment. "You weren't ready for a woman like that. You were in a league of your own, working the courtroom, catering to your clients, enjoying your weekends."

"Things change, Mikey."

"Yeah, I know." Mike crossed his arms. "You've changed."

Yes, I have. "So, you're saying?"

"I'm saying I'm proud of you, brother. You broke free of the past and stepped into the present with, well..." Mike was thinking. "Well, with a dignity I haven't seen since I met you."

"Thanks. I think." J.P. was studying Mike's face. *What's he telling me here?*

"No, really, J.P. Think about it. You'd totally given up on love, then Samira came along and pushed you way out of your comfort zone. You came into this relationship kicking and screaming, but you took a chance and look what happened."

"She's my last chance, Mikey. I gotta make it count."

Mike grinned. "All will be well. No doubt in my mind."

I hope he's right. I don't want to mess this up.

Pastor Bill opened the double doors and stepped inside. "Almost time, gentlemen." He crossed the room wearing a full-length white robe.

No one said anything about the robe thing. J.P. glanced at Mike. *I just hope he keeps his observations to himself.*

"The ushers are rearranging a few things and making sure the family is seated appropriately." Pastor Bill patiently explained the slight delay. "When we get the signal that the women are ready, we'll enter the sanctuary and walk up the side aisle like we practiced yesterday."

Mike jumped up off the table. "This would be my cue to become a fly on the wall."

Mike is always Mike.

Pastor Bill turned back around and peered through the double doors.

Mike offered his hand, but as J.P. started to return the shake, Mike pulled hard and embraced J.P. "You're doing the right thing, Phil. Trust yourself on this one."

Trusting myself is a new thing these days.

Mike lowered his voice. "But you owe me big time for making me sit through church first."

J.P. laughed as he returned the embrace. "Fair enough."

"I'm going to give this rock in my pocket to Josh." Mike winked as he walked away.

"You have a good friend in that man," Pastor Bill observed out loud.

"The best."

"Few men are so fortunate.'

No one knows me as well as Mike Benson. J.P. couldn't pull his eyes from the minister's face. *He reminds me of somebody, but I can't quite place him.* When Pastor Bill smiled, J.P. realized who it was. *He reminds me of Santa Claus.*

"It is time, Phil. Are you ready?" Pastor Bill was now holding J.P. by the elbow.

"Yes, I am." He put his hand over his stomach to stop the butterflies.

The sanctuary looked more crowded than it had been. *That's Mr. and Mrs. Barnes.* The ushers were still helping an elderly couple up the aisle on the far side of the room. *Samira was worried they would be so far away they couldn't hear.* He glanced at the back of the sanctuary. *She probably made special arrangements to have them moved closer to the front.*

Pastor Bill waited for the elderly couple to be seated, and then led Phil up the side of the church. They took their places at the front of the center aisle.

As the music began to play, J.P. scanned the faces in the crowd. Samira's parents were seated in the same row as Aunt Maggie and Uncle Roy. *It's been a long time since I've seen Uncle Roy this dressed up.* The captain was seated next to Roy. His dress uniform was sharp and professional. *He looks good. And it's good to have him here.* Wes had Mark on his lap in the next row back. Bobby winked as their eyes connected. *It's a good thing he and Mike aren't seated anywhere next to one another.*

I wonder where the fly on the wall is. J.P. dared to search the room looking for Mike's smiling face. *There's Kelly.* She was at the back of the church watching through the glass. *Chances are good Mike's not too far out of her jurisdiction.*

The music changed. Suddenly James and Krissy were standing next to Kelly. *Oh, she must be the one giving directions.* He folded his hands over his tuxedo buttons and watched Krissy and James start up the aisle. James walked about halfway and then gave his father a big thumbs up. They shared the Ralston smile. *Leave it to James to cheer me on in my own wedding.*

Josh and Kara were close behind. *They look amazing all dressed up like this.* His sons had chosen black slacks with black collarless shirts. *Very professional. And these young women look like a million bucks in those fancy dresses.* J.P. considered the voice he'd heard in his head a few minutes earlier. *Any boy wanting to take them out will have to go through me first.*

"Are you nervous?" James whispered as he stepped into his place.

Not anymore. J.P. shook his head slightly.

Krissy was beaming a brilliant smile across her freckled face. "Here comes the bride." she whispered as she turned to take her place.

Breathe, Counselor. Breathe.

His eyes connected with Mike at the back of the church. Mike threw his hands high above his head and grinned back. *Behave, Mikey.*

Two little blonde girls appeared at the back of the aisle. Pam was still doting over their hair. With a little prompting Lizzie and Bonnie started to drop flower petals as they walked the aisle. *They look a lot like their mom all dressed up like that.*

His eyes happened to fall on Denise and Jerry as the little girls passed their pew. *She looks a little sad. She knows what she needs but doesn't know how to get there.*

Lizzie and Bonnie stepped up next to the pastor and turned around to face the congregation. Their faces beamed with joyous anticipation.

This time when the music changed the entire congregation stood. *Okay. Now I'm nervous.* J.P. took a deep breath and held it in. His bride stood at the back of the church wearing a dress he'd never seen before. *Dear God, she is the most beautiful woman I've ever laid eyes on.* J.P. glued his eyes to Samira as she walked toward him. *She's perfect.* The blush that appeared in Samira's cheeks told J.P. she knew exactly what he was thinking.

I don't know if I can wait for permission to kiss her or not. Even as J.P. exhaled, he didn't feel any relief in his lungs. *She's poised, confident...* It seemed like it took forever for Samira to reach his side. All the while he held eye contact. Samira's dark eyes penetrated. *...She's all I'll ever need.*

J.P. took a hold of her hands like they'd practiced. *Her palms are sweaty.*

"Dear Friends, we are gathered here in the presence of God to witness the marriage of Samira Susanne Cartwright and Joseph Phillip Ralston. Who gives this couple in holy matrimony?"

"We do." All four children responded as they'd been instructed.

The pastor smiled his Santa Claus smile and motioned for everyone to be seated. When they turned to face the minister, J.P. felt Josh's hand on his shoulder. *He knows I'm about ready to hyperventilate.* But Samira's dark eyes brought a calm over his whole being. *She does have a way with me like none other.*

Pastor Bill offered a prayer, but J.P. didn't close his eyes. *I don't want to take my eyes off her for one minute.*

"Repeat after me," the minister spoke quietly as he made brief eye contact with Phil.

Just go slow because I want her to hear every single word.

"I, Joseph Phillip Ralston, take you Samira Suzanne Cartwright, to be my wife..."

"To have and to hold..."

J.P. finished his vows, still holding Samira's eyes with his own. She was gripping his hands tightly as he spoke.

When it was Samira's turn to state her vows, she hesitated.

Just concentrate, Pretty Lady. We're almost finished here.

"I, Samira Suzanne Cartwright, take you Joseph Phillip Ralston, to be my husband."

For just a moment J.P. glanced over Samira's shoulder in his father's direction.

I do believe this is the first time in my life I've felt worthy of that name.

"To have and to hold..."

It suddenly felt exactly right that the Captain was seated in the same row as Aunt Maggie and Uncle Roy. J.P. swallowed an unexpected lump of emotion.

"...This is my solemn vow." Samira's eyes were damp, but they hadn't spilled over yet.

J.P. shared his easy smile with his woman. *Neither one of us likes being the center of attention.*

Pastor Bill seemed to be taking his time getting the rings from the children. He even stooped to show them to the curious Lizzie.

Just give us the rings and get on with the show. J.P. held out his hand as Pastor Bill placed the diamond in his hand. Obediently he repeated the words after the minister.

"I give you this ring...as a sign of my vow...and with all that I am...and all that I have... I honor you...in the name of the Father...and of the Son...and of the Holy Spirit."

It takes three to get married. The impact of that statement suddenly made sense. J.P slipped Samira's rings onto her finger. *I'm all yours, Pretty Lady.*

He held out his left hand and listened as Samira did the same for him. *She's the only one for whom I'd wear a ring.*

Samira finished without further prompting from the pastor. "...in the name of the Father, and of the Son, and of the Holy Spirit."

Her smile calmed every nerve in J.P.'s being. He knew the pastor was still talking, but he had no idea what he could possibly be saying. The moments began to blur, but eventually J.P. realized he was kissing his bride. *Did we wait for permission?* The next thing he knew the congregation was on their feet and applauding. Mike was standing at the back waving for J.P. and Samira to walk down the aisle.

"Did he announce us as man and wife?" Samira asked as they started to walk arm in arm.

"I don't have a clue." When he looked at Samira her cheeks were glowing.

At the end of the aisle J.P. turned his bride toward him and kissed her again. *In the name of the Father and the Son and the Holy Spirit.* He punctuated his vow. Samira's arms were wrapped around him on the inside of his jacket. *I like the way she does that.*

"A-hem." Mike interrupted the intimate moment by pulling the couple apart. "You're blocking traffic, Mr. and Mrs. Ralston."

Mr. & Mrs. Ralston. That has a nice ring to it. J.P. reluctantly allowed Mike to hug his bride. *Go easy there, fella, that's my wife.* He turned to face his sons who were already in line to embrace his bride.

"Way to go, Dad." Josh exchanged a high five with his father and then paused for a fatherly hug. "That was sweet."

Krissy turned around like a ballerina. "How do you like the dresses? We picked them especially for you."

"They're perfect." J.P. wrapped the young woman in his arms. *But only made perfect by the ladies wearing them.*

J.P. noted a few tears in the corner of Kara's eyes. He hugged her with both arms. Surprisingly, she hugged him back. *She is so much like her mother.*

"Welcome to the family." Weston Stephenson grasped J.P.'s hand. "I must say, this union is a win-win for the whole family."

A banker first. A brother second. "Indeed." J.P. accepted a warm embrace from Pam.

He looked beyond Pam's shoulder into the dark eyes of his new mother-in-law. *She does her hair the same way Samira does hers.*

"Ashleigh," he offered his hands, but the woman lifted her chin and kissed him on the cheek. She didn't speak, and J.P. didn't offer any words. But there was an understanding that passed between them. *How does she communicate like that?*

Raymond Stephenson stepped back and admired Samira. "It's not every day a father gets to see his beautiful daughter pledged in holy matrimony."

Samira was beaming at her father.

"I love you, Princess." Raymond hugged his daughter. "Don't you ever forget that."

J.P. knew Samira spoke, but he couldn't make out her words. *Surprisingly, she's not crying.* J.P. admired his bride's composure. *If anyone would make her cry, I'd think it would be her father.*

Raymond offered his hand to J.P. "Phil, I'm putting my daughter in good hands."

Now I am totally out of my league. J.P. nodded. *His expectations are higher than any I've ever had to earn.*

"In fact, I can't think of any hands I'd rather have her in." Raymond stepped closer and squeezed J.P.'s shoulder with his free hand.

"Thank you, sir." J.P. was completely serious. *He may always be Mr. Stephenson to me.*

The line kept moving and people continued to greet J.P. and Samira. *Surely, we're about done with this formality.*

The next hand wasn't unfamiliar, however. J.P. paused for a moment and then opened his arms to hug Denise. *I wish she wouldn't cry.*

"It was a beautiful ceremony," Denise sobbed. "Just beautiful."

J.P. lifted her chin with his finger. "You deserve the same."

Denise nodded. "I know. We've been talking." She wiped her eyes with a damp tissue. "I'll see you at the Stephenson's in a few minutes."

Jerry's handshake was sincere. "Congratulations, man. You've given us plenty to think about."

J.P. smiled. "Take all the time you need, but don't wait too long."

Jerry's eyes were thoughtful. "Thanks for the advice, Counselor."

"Phillip?" Aunt Maggie stretched out her arms. "I am so happy for you."

She's been crying, but her real tears will be shed in private.

"I knew God wasn't finished with you yet."

J.P. bent in half to hug his aunt. *And somehow, I knew she never stopped praying for me.*

J.P. embraced Uncle Roy.

"Well done, Phillip. I knew she was a keeper."

"Not before I did though." Bobby was ready for a brotherly hug. "You done good, big brother. Life has much in store."

J.P. greeted Bobby's family one after the other. Megan was also crying.

Why do people cry at weddings? J.P. looked at Samira. She was in a full body embrace and tears were streaming down her face. Captain Joe had his eyes closed as he hugged his new daughter in law.

That's intense. J.P. had to look away to keep his own emotions from overflowing. Time stood still as he made eye contact with his father.

The Captain saluted his son in military fashion. J.P. stood tall.

"I'm proud to call you my son, Joseph Phillip."

J.P. nodded once but the lump in his throat kept him from speaking. *And I'm proud to wear your name, Dad.*

The Captain held out his hand, but J.P. ignored the handshake and opened his arms.

"To hell with the Navy."

I think he waited to be last in line on purpose. J.P. hugged the Captain long and hard.

"Your mother would be proud." When they separated, the Captain's cheeks were wet. "That grandson of mine has offered to drive me to the Stephenson's for the reception after family pictures." Captain Joe wiped his face with a white handkerchief.

Family. I didn't realize how much I needed it. "That grandson of yours is mighty proud to be your chauffeur."

"The pleasure is all mine."

J.P. turned and watched Josh meet his grandfather. *I didn't realize how much Josh resembled my father.* Mike and Kelly were engaged in animated conversation just inside the door. *There's no reason to hold back, Mikey.*

And then Joseph Phillip turned and faced his new wife.

Her eyes were on her wedding rings. "They are so beautiful." She turned her rings to catch the light. "I can't stop looking at them."

"I can't stop looking at you." Phil cupped her face in his hands. "You are stunning, Mrs.

Ralston."

The new bride beamed with joy. "Well, we took a chance and here we are, Mr. and Mrs."

Phil lifted her hand to his lips. "And I will do everything in my power to give us a fighting chance."

"I'm all yours." Samira's hands linked around his waist inside of his jacket.

This pleasure is all mine. Joseph Phillip kissed his bride uninhibited by their surroundings. *She's everything I will ever need.*

Turn the page for a sneak peek:

A Fighting Chance, Book 2 in the series

1 *Good Morning* *Joseph Phillip*

The room began to lighten with the first signs of daylight. J.P. Ralston lay perfectly still watching her sleep. *This is not my house. Not my bed.* Her dark hair was fanned over the pillow. *But this is my wife.* He refrained from touching her. *I don't want to wake her.*

The activities from the day before blurred together. *And it's not because I was drinking this time.* J.P. pieced the memories together. *I remember watching her walk down the aisle and remember putting the ring on her finger.* He admired his own wedding band. *I never planned to wear a wedding ring again.* He turned it all the way around on his finger. *She has damn good taste. I may never take it off.*

The new bride stirred under the covers. *She has no idea how deep my commitment is. My 'I do' is her promise.*

Samira rolled over and opened her eyes slowly. "Good morning, Mr. Ralston."

"Good morning, Mrs. Ralston." *That has a nice ring to it.* He smiled as she yawned. *Now I can touch her.* Very gently he pushed her hair away from her face. "Did you sleep well?"

Samira nodded and smiled as she linked her fingers with his. "What time is it?"

"Does it matter?" *She hates when I answer a question with another question.*

"Maybe."

"A little after six."

Samira moved closer to her new husband. She ran her hand over his bare chest and laid her head against his shoulder.

As far as I'm concerned, I could stay in bed like this all day. J.P kissed her hair and pulled her in closer. *I remember kissing her at the altar.*

"It feels strange to not be going to work today."

Tell me about it. J.P. thought about his usual workday schedule. *It feels strange to not have a case breathing down my neck.*

"You're really quiet this morning." Samira pulled her head away far enough to look up at him. "Are you okay?"

"Never better, Pretty Lady." This time he kissed her lips. *The details from yesterday are vague. Everything ran together during the ceremony, but my memory of last night is crystal clear.* He kissed her again, this time rolling with her.

"Mr. Ralston, just because we aren't going to work doesn't mean there isn't work to be done."

"Nothing that can't wait." *How many mornings are we going to have like this? Alone. Without responsibilities.* "Unless you have an agenda I don't know about." J.P. snuck the comment in between kisses.

Samira shook her head slowly. "No agendas. Not today."

I'll take that as permission to proceed.

~~~~~~~

J.P. returned from his morning run very aware this would be one of his last days in his old neighborhood. He unclipped the leash and let the big black Labrador through the gate into the back yard. "You better enjoy your last days out here, Chase." J.P. looked out across the shaded yard. "I bought this place for you, good buddy. But now you're going to have a new spot." *And I hope he can learn to behave over there.*

The screen door slammed when J.P. stepped into the kitchen. *Never did get that door fixed.* He poured a glass of orange. *My morning routine is going to change drastically too. I hope I learn to adjust as well.* The clock on the wall read eight thirty. *I should have time to shower before Samira gets here.*

J.P. pressed play on a remote and cued the stereo as he closed the bathroom door. *I'm*
~~~~~~~

not going to work so I'm not going to shave. The music was loud even with the door closed. *I have never taken a week off from the practice.* He adjusted the water temperature before he stepped into the shower. *Not once. I never gave myself permission to take purposeful time off.*

Refreshed, J.P. dried off then wrapped the towel around his waist. The song had changed, but the music was still playing. *Sounds like the kitchen door. I really need to get that fixed.*

"Phil?"

"Back here," J.P. stepped into the hallway to greet his new bride. *She looks relaxed in blue jeans and that sweater, but she looks better in nothing at all.*

Samira shook her head. "Eighties rock? Really?"

J.P. turned the volume down with the remote. "And you would listen to?"

"Not eighties rock."

J.P. dug through a laundry basket. *I know there's a clean pair of jeans here somewhere.*

"You must have taken Chase on a run."

"What gave me away?" *I should probably find out what she notices if I'm going to live in her house.* He opened a dresser drawer for a pair of socks.

"The leash on the counter and your running shoes in the middle of the kitchen floor."

The leash is always on the counter. The song on the radio changed again. *Surely, she can relate to this one.* He turned the volume back up. "This is for you, Pretty Lady."

Samira tilted her head playfully. "The socks?"

"No, the song." *This is what we danced to in her dining room on our first date.* "She's Got a Way About Her." *She's blushing.* "You remember?"

"Of course."

"Billy Joel. 1982. Not bad. For the eighties, anyway."

"I thought you were referring to our first dance." Samira brushed her hand over his bare shoulder.

"I was." J.P. took her right hand in his left.

She allowed him to move with her to the music until the song ended. "I didn't realize you were so versed in music." There was a glint in her eye as she let go of his hand.

"Some verses are more meaningful than others." J.P. snuck a quick kiss.

Samira looked around the room. "Are you going to miss your place?"

"Truth be told, I bought it for the dog." J.P. removed the towel he was still wearing and started to get dressed. "But it's been a good spot."

"Seriously?" Samira was eyeing him carefully. "You bought a house for your dog?"

"You doubt me?"

"I do."

"That's what you said when you became Mrs. Ralston." *I remember the part when she said, 'I do.'*

Samira laughed. "No one buys a house for a dog."

"I do."

Samira smiled at his use of her words.

J.P. walked her to the window and opened the shade. "Look out there. That is a dog's wonderland. Shade, trees, squirrels, water. What more could he ask for?"

Samira was shaking her head when she looked back at him. "Only you would—"

J.P. didn't wait for her to finish the sentence. He intercepted her thoughts with a kiss.

"You need to get your clothes on before we forget our purpose here," Samira reminded.

"You said there was no agenda today." J.P. kissed her again. "And the girls are in school until when?" His phone vibrated on the dresser across the room.

"I thought you were taking this week off." Samira was frowning at the phone.

I said I wasn't going into the office unless there was an emergency. J.P. stepped away to check Caller ID. "That doesn't mean my phone won't ring." *Denise. I should probably answer.*

Samira turned back to the window.

She has her hair wrapped in that amazing little bun thing at the back of her neck. "Denise." *I may regret pushing this button.* "What's up on this gorgeous day?"

"Hey Boss. No news is good news from Benson and Barringer. I have everything in order for Derek until about noon. Do you want some help at the house?"

I do, but I don't know how Samira will take this. "Give me a minute. I'll call you back."

"You're not still in bed with your bride, are you?"

"I wish." *Honest statement.* "But let me check on some things and get back to you." He disconnected the call without a formal goodbye.

"Duty calls?" Samira turned around slowly.

J.P. shook his head. "Nope. Denise just offered to come help here at the house. She's free until noon."

"Is she off this week too?"

Denise is never off. "She's on the clock. But willing to clock in over here instead of at the office if we need her."

"Do we need her?" Samira raised her eyebrows.

J.P. grinned. "Not for what I had in mind."

"You are impossible, Joseph Phillip. Is that all you think about?"

"You don't make it easy," J.P. ran his hand down her back and pulled her tight against him. "We could skip the packing—"

Samira kissed him but removed his hand. "Do you need Denise to be here?"

Tread carefully, Ralston. This is new territory. "I don't *need* her here." *Although she is extremely efficient and task oriented.* "But she would be helpful." *It would be good for Samira to get to know her better too.*

The kitchen door slammed, announcing another visitor.

"Buenos Dias, señor." A cheerful voice called down the hallway.

"Señor?" Samira crossed her arms and looked accusingly at her husband.

Shit. "That would be Maria." *Is this Monday? She comes on Mondays.*

Samira brushed against him as she started for the bedroom door. "You're just lucky you have some clothes on, Mr. Ralston." Her voice was playful.

"No shit."

Mrs. Ralston turned around in the doorway and shot him another accusatory look.

I may be in the doghouse with Chase if I don't get my act together. J.P. fastened his jeans and pulled an old t-shirt over his head before joining his wife in the kitchen. *I'm going to take a chance and tell Denise to come on over.*

"Good morning, Maria. May I introduce you to my wife? This is Samira." *This is my first official introduction.*

"Felicidades señora." The short, round Mexican woman beamed at Samira. "Very happy for you." Maria was already starting to gather stray articles of clothing from the kitchen chair. "Lavar la ropa." She stooped to pick up the running shoes. "You are good for J.P., Miss Samira." Maria carried the stray articles of clothing down the hall toward the bedroom.

This could get complicated. J.P shrugged his shoulders at his wife who was shaking her head.

"How long have you had Maria?"

"She came with the house." *Honestly.*

"With the house you bought for your dog."

"Pretty much."

"J.P." Another voice called from outside.

"That would be Denise."

Samira frowned and put her hands on her hips. "Did you call her back?"

Not exactly. "I sent a text."

Denise let herself in the kitchen door but caught it before it slammed. "Hey Boss. You need to get that fixed before Derek moves in here."

I know. Along with a few other things.

"Judging from the look on your face, you won't mind if I have Jerry take a look?"

J.P. grinned. "Stick around here long enough, you'll have a whole list for Jerry." "I'll send you the bill." Denise turned her attention to Samira, who by this time had made her way to the living room. "Good morning to the new Mrs. Ralston. I brought you a present."

What kind of present would Denise bring for Samira?

Denise held up a steaming hot cup of coffee. "The girl at the counter said this is your favorite."

Very strategic, Denise. Her favorite beverage from her favorite coffee shop. The Café Ole logo was on the cup. *At least Denise is trying to build a relationship here.*

"Thank you." Samira accepted the steaming coffee graciously.

"Thank your *husband.*" Denise put emphasis on the new title with a glint in her eye. "I put it on his tab."

Denise is working hard to earn Samira's trust.

"I hope you don't mind that I'm here." Denise was talking to Samira. "I thought I might be able to help keep the Boss on task. If he's anywhere outside of the office, he has a hard time staying focused."

Samira glanced in J.P.'s direction. "I've noticed."

"Oh, here." Denise produced a pile of mail secured with a rubber band. "These were in Saturday's mail. Where shall I put them?"

J.P. was curious. "What are they?" *Denise always handles the mail. All of it.*

"They are all addressed to Mr. & Mrs. Ralston, so I am assuming wedding cards."

"I thought you told them no gifts."

Denise nodded. "I did. But maybe they wanted to send congratulations. They are all from clients."

J.P. looked at his bride. "Where do you want them?"

2 *Piecing Him Together* *Samira*

Samira took the stack of cards from Denise and put them with her purse on the kitchen table. *Why is he asking me? They're his clients.* As she set the cards down, she noticed a light blinking on her cell phone. Curious, she swiped her thumb across the screen to wake it up. *It's a text from Krissy.* Samira read silently: *Good morning, Mama. Miss you. See you tonight."*

J.P. looked over Samira's shoulder. "I told you cell phones would keep you in touch with the girls."

Samira nodded as she typed a quick text back to her youngest daughter. *I have to admit, they do make a difference.*

"Is Maria here?" Denise was looking at J.P.

J.P. nodded toward the back of the house.

"Perfect." Denise clapped her hands. "Where do you want to start?" She looked from J.P. to Samira, then back to J.P. "Are you sure you two are moving in together?"

Samira started to laugh. "I don't think we have any idea where to begin, Denise. It's probably a God-send you are here."

"Exactly why I thought I should pop over." Denise helped herself to a legal pad and a pen from J.P.'s office. "You only have me for a while, so let's get crackin'." She put her hands on her hips and surveyed the front room "It's probably best to go room by room, don't you think? Make decisions as we go."

She is going to be very helpful. "That's a good strategy." Samira surveyed the same space as Denise, but still had no idea how to start. Samira blew on her coffee through the plastic lid.

"Let's tackle the front room and the office while Maria is working in the back of the house."

Samira heard the washing machine start. *Does Maria always do Phil's laundry?*

"I've never been to your house, Samira, so tell me how much space you have."

Oh, wow. I haven't thought much about that in relation to moving some of Phil's things over there. She looked around the room again with new understanding. *I guess if he is truly moving in, some of this will come with him.* "There is plenty of room."

"Boss, what are you thinking? Keep the furniture? Take it with you? Leave it here? Sell it?"

Both women looked at the doorway between the kitchen and the living room, but Phil wasn't standing there.

"Boss?" Denise rolled her eyes at Samira. "I told you. He can't stay focused for two minutes when he's out of the office."

Where did he go? Curious, Samira stepped into the kitchen. Maria bustled down the hall and disappeared into the bedroom. *Not back there.*

"Found him." Denise called from the back door. "He's outside talking to Eduardo, Maria's husband."

Eduardo?

Denise was standing on the back step with the kitchen door open. "J.P., we're trying to get some decisions made here." The assistant looked at Samira and shook her head. "He's impossible."

Samira thought about his one-track mind earlier in the morning. "I have discovered that already."

"I'm sure you have." Denise motioned with her arm for J.P. to come back in the house. "He's never home when Maria and Eduardo are here. He's probably just catching up."

Maybe Denise can clarify a couple things for me. "Phil said Maria came with the house."

Denise nodded. "She did." She stepped back inside. The door banged loudly. "I'll get Jerry over here to fix that before Derek moves in."

I was hoping for a little more explanation than that.

"Maria and Eduardo lived across the street when J.P. bought the house." Denise continued. "She brought a basket of homemade tamales over his first night here and offered to be his housekeeper."

Ah. "How long has he lived here?"

Denise was starting to inventory the contents in the kitchen drawers. "He bought this place soon after his divorce." She stopped and counted on her fingers. "I guess it's been about 10 years now. He was looking for a place to give Chase room to run."

Maybe he wasn't exaggerating when he said he bought this house for his dog.

"He hired Maria and soon after Eduardo joined payroll doing the yard work and upkeep."

Denise opened an overhead cupboard and looked over at Samira. "Do you have any need for things like this?"

Samira surveyed the plates and unmatched drinking glasses. "Not really." *No wonder he doesn't need a dishwasher. He doesn't have enough dishes to fill one.*

"Can we be brutally honest here?" Denise leaned on the counter and made solid eye contact.

"Of course." *I guess.*

Denise held her hands out over the cabinets. "Do you think there is anything in here you will need at your house?" She opened another set of doors. "Oh, good God, J.P."

That cabinet was stocked full of various alcoholic beverages and mixes.

"No doubt, this will be the only content J.P. will want to keep from the kitchen." Denise tilted her head at Samira. "And my guess is, he'll take the grill. I seriously doubt he knows how to use any of these pots or pans."

She seems to know him very well.

Phil stuck his head in the door. "I'm going to run Eduardo down to pick up his mower. Be back in ten."

"J.P." Denise's tone was sharp. "Do you have a clue why we're here today?"

He grinned. "I believe so. But honest, I'll be right back." Phil caught the door before it slammed.

Something tells me Phil doesn't want to make these decisions today. Samira thought again. *Or maybe he simply doesn't have an opinion on what goes and what stays. I'll try to get some clarification.*

"No focus, whatsoever." Denise mumbled. "Let me give you a little insight." She opened the cupboard next to the stove. "The Boss doesn't cook. But he is a master griller. He drinks shakes for breakfast." Denise took the tub of protein shake mix out of the cabinet and set it on the counter. "Lunch, if he takes a lunch break, he usually eats out. And dinner is most often at the golf club because he hates to eat alone."

Somehow, I am not surprised by any of that information. Samira moved the shake mix to the table next to her purse. "So, if I take this to my house, he will be set for breakfast, lunch, and dinner."

"Yes." Denise smiled. "And if you want him to grill out for you, take his grill." She opened the drawer next to the refrigerator. "And his grilling utensils." She laid them with the shake mix.

Why does Denise know where everything is?

Denise stepped back into the living room. "You two can talk over the furniture in here. It's fairly new. Don't know if you have a place for it or not." She pointed to the bookcase. "He'll want his books, but my guess is he'll take those to the office." A funny look came over her face. "Do you think you'd use the sofa and chair at your place?"

Samira shrugged her shoulders. "Not unless he wants them in my downstairs tv room." *Unless he's really attached to them and wants them upstairs.* Samira ran her hand over the back of the chair. *But it doesn't match my décor.*

"Huh." Denise was obviously thinking. "Maybe we could take these to the office. He needs to do some updating there and it would be a nice change."

The office could use some renovating. Samira remembered her only visit there. *And it could use some plants to make it a little more inviting.* "How long ago did he move into his office?" *It's helpful to get some of this background information on my new hubby.*

Denise made a few notes on the legal pad. "Before he moved into this house. When I started working with him, he was basically living at the office." She looked up at Samira. "His marriage was a mess, and he had no reason to go home back then."

I can't imagine what he must have gone through.

Denise popped her gum. "About the time the divorce papers were served he started looking for a place to call home." She opened the cabinet under the tv. "Empty. That will be easy to pack."

Samira followed Denise into the office room.

"He bought this place so his puppy would have room to grow. But it never was home for J.P. More like a place to land when all of his other options were spent." Denise tipped her head. "It was cheap and move-in ready. He lives simply enough, it worked."

The kitchen door slammed.

"Denise, can you get—"

"Yeah, I'll get Jerry on that door tonight."

It's crazy how they finish one another's sentences like that.

"We finished the kitchen, Boss." Denise was writing on the legal pad. "Do you want to keep some of your things for Josh in case he needs them at college?"

College. I hadn't even considered the fact that Josh might be able to use some of these things next year at college. "I have storage space." Samira spoke up.

"You finished the kitchen without me?" Phil was taunting Denise and it showed in his tone.

"Didn't take much."

Samira stifled a laugh at Denise's sarcasm.

Phil opened the cupboard filled with the alcohol and mixers. "This moves. Everything else is expendable."

She pegged him on that.

"And the grill." Phil looked at Samira. "Do you have a grill?"

Samira shook her head.

"Then the grill goes. Need a decision on anything else?"

Again. Denise called it.

"I figure Derek will need a place to land by the end of the weekend. We can rent a storage unit if we need one," Denise outlined the deadline for the first time.

That's not necessary. "I have plenty of storage downstairs." She looked at Phil. *There are only a few leftover baby items in there right now.*

"Boss, you want to take a look at that and make some decisions, so I know what to do?" She made another note. "And what about taking the sofa and chair up to the office? Use it to update your space?"

Phil ran his hand through his hair. "That might work. Does Derek need it?"

"I say let him bring his own things in, J.P. He seems to be pretty well set."

"Works for me." Phil winked at Samira. "What else did you get done while I was gone?"

For the first time Samira realized he'd run Eduardo's errand on purpose. *Phil doesn't want to make these decisions.*

Maria piled clean towels on the kitchen table. "I go to store for you today, yes?" She was looking at Phil.

"Not today, Maria." Denise answered. "J.P. is moving to Samira's house this week, remember?"

Maria looked at Samira. "Ah. I go to store for you? Pick up Señor favorites? Yes?"

Samira frowned at Phil. *I prefer to do my own shopping.*

"Gracias, Maria." Phil thanked his long-time housekeeper. "Not today." He was talking to Maria, but his eyes were on Samira.

He knows I won't let her do my shopping.

Denise had moved back into the office. While she and Phil were discussing the items in there, Samira returned to the kitchen. She opened the only cupboard Denise hadn't. *Paper plates. Napkins. And plastic utensils.* She took another drink of her coffee.

Maria finished folding the towels. "Señor not need much." She disappeared down the hall with the towels stacked neatly, ready to put away.

Unbelievable. She noticed a check on the front of the refrigerator and stepped closer. *Why does Phil have a signed check on his fridge?* She lifted the corner enough to see a handwritten list on a sticky note. *His grocery list.* Now she understood. *Maria takes the check to the store when she does his shopping.*

Without warning, Phil grabbed Samira from behind, catching her off guard. He lifted her playfully.

This would be more fun if there weren't so many people here.

Denise joined them in the kitchen. "You two talk about the beds and decide what goes and what needs to be distributed someplace else." She looked around the kitchen once again. "I'm headed back to the office until you are officially ready to pack." Denise made eye contact with Samira. "Good luck keeping him focused the rest of the day." She started to leave. "Do you have my number?"

"I have the office number," Samira remembered the now worn business card she kept in her billfold.

Denise shook her head. "I'll text you my cell phone number, so you can save me in your phone. You never know when you might need me."

That's a scary thought. "Do you have my number?"

Denise held up her phone. "Yes, I do. I pay the bill."

Of course, she does. Samira looked over at her husband.

Phil shrugged his shoulders.

"How many people does it take to keep track of you?" Samira asked the question honestly.

"You don't want to know." Denise stopped the door from banging. "You know where to find me."

Maria appeared in the kitchen again carrying a bucket and mop. She set the bucket down and spoke several phrases to Phil in Spanish. Then she waved them away with her hands.

"We may have outstayed our Monday welcome." Phil was starting to move toward the door. "I think she wants to mop the floor."

Samira put her purse over her shoulder then picked up the shake, the grill utensils, and the wedding cards.

"Go, go, go." Maria was waving them out the door. "Quitarse los zapatos."

"Okay, okay." Phil was laughing as he held the door open for Samira. "We're outta here. And I'll take off my shoes when I come back."

Does he speak Spanish? Or simply know what she's referring to?

Phil unlatched the backyard gate and called Chase. The big black Lab came across the yard in a full run. He stopped short when Phil held out his hand like a stop sign.

He is well-behaved, I must admit.

"What do you think, Pretty Lady? Lunch?"

He always eats lunch out. Denise said so. "Can we take lunch down to Shoal Creek?" *I know we don't have great memories from there, but this is a chance to start fresh.* Samira's mind tripped back to their last picnic above the boardwalk. *The day I walked away, and he didn't come after me.*

"Like a picnic?"

Samira nodded. "It's a little cool, but still a nice day to be outside. The trees might still have some color."

"Whatever you wish, Mrs. Ralston." With a swift motion of his hand, Phil had his phone to his ear.

Did his phone ring?

"Let me grab the leash."

It's on the counter by the fridge.

When Phil opened the kitchen door to go back inside, Maria shooed him back out with a wet mop. She was carrying on in animated Spanish. Samira found it humorous that

Phil couldn't get back into his own house.

Chase was still sitting where his master had given the command.

"You're a good boy, Chase." The dog responded by tipping his tail in acknowledgement. "Never in a million years did I think I'd have a dog in my house." Chase perked his ears and tipped his head to the side. *Now that's kind of cute.*

Phil finally convinced Maria to hand him the dog leash. He held it up in victory as he descended the steps.

"Got it. Sandwiches will be ready for pick up from the deli in ten. I'll grab those on my way back to your place then we'll go find a spot at Shoal Creek."

Samira was confused. "Did you call ahead to the deli?" *Why would he have that number in his phone?*

"Kinda." Phil was a little sheepish. "I called Denise. She's on it."

You've got to be kidding. "Honestly, Mr. Ralston. You are so spoiled."

"So, I've been told." J.P. opened the door on his truck for Chase to jump into the back seat. "I'll pick up lunch and see you at your place."

We were supposed to be backing but we sure didn't get much done. New thoughts arose as Samira drove across town to her house. *How will we ever break him of Denise tending to his business?* She qualified that thought. *Both professional and personal.* She thought again. *And this whole thing with Maria and Eduardo is crazy. Phil doesn't have to do anything for himself if he doesn't want to.*

Samira passed by the library. *It doesn't look too busy over the noon hour.* She pushed the button and opened her garage door. *I wonder how things will transition when he only has me taking care of him. Maria, Eduardo, and Denise sure seem to take care of a majority of his daily responsibilities.* Samira climbed out of her car and walked to the mailbox at the end of the driveway.

"Afternoon, Miss Samira." A familiar voice called from across the street.

Samira raised a hand to the elderly neighbor. "Hello, Mrs. Barnes."

"Beautiful ceremony yesterday."

"Thank you." Samira smiled across the street. "I'm glad Mr. Barnes was feeling well enough to attend with you."

"We've never been to a wedding on a Sunday before." Mrs. Barnes shaded her eyes with her hand.

"I know it was a little unorthodox, but it seemed to be the best fit." *Everyone my parents wanted to invite was already at the church, and it kept things simpler.*

"Are you going to the store today?"

Of course, she needs to go to the store on the day after my wedding. And on one of my few days off too.

"If you're not, there's nothing pressing." The old lady baited her inquiry.

Samira opened the mailbox and folded the loose items in a magazine. "Not today. I'm sorry. Maybe tomorrow." She shaded her eyes to get a better look at her neighbor. "Is everything alright?"

"Oh yes, Miss Samira. See you tomorrow." Mrs. Barnes smiled from under her wide brimmed straw hat. "Have a nice day."

A thought struck Samira. *I wonder....*

To order the next book in the series, or discover more books and blogs by Judith Kay, visit:

www.judithkaywrites.com

www.amazon.com/author/judithkay

To order directly from the author call:
JK Books & Gifts: 515-581-9022
or email: judithkaywrites@gmail.com

Acknowledgements

From the depth of my heart I owe a huge thank you to those who have dedicated time and energy to the completion of this work. My brain never stops. It takes a whole village working around the clock to track my work!

To my husband, Craig, who continues to inspire and encourage me. He stays up late with me to edit, brainstorm, and rewrite. He gives up his recliner when I need more "room" in my writing aura to focus. He cheers me on no matter what, and loves me unconditionally. I owe him my life.

To Emily, my forever friend, who has enough faith for both of us. Emily has known my characters since they were sketches on the back of an envelope. She was with me in the days of instant-chat, (you know, before texting) reading a chapter or two behind me (when the chapters were still in rought draft format) offering advice and insight as the characters grew into the ones you now know in these pages. Emily's steadfast friendship, depth of wisdom, and listening heart have shaped me into the woman I am today. She is forever embedded into my life. I carry her heart in mine. My gratitude for her constant watch care and prayers over me is beyond what words can express. Emily is my gift from God and I am eternally grateful.

To Wendy, my administrative everything and my senior editor. She works late at the office, works from home, offers her technical and editorial support, shares her faith and friendship even when she's off the clock. I would be lost without her and thank God for her presence in my life.

To my friend Jenn, who has been with me on this project since the beginning of the move to independent publishing. I am forever grateful for her insight, her honesty, her humor, and her positive energy in every situation. Jenn is in my speed dial and always answers my call. I am forever indebited for her gift of time and expertise from the reader's perspective.

About The Author

Judith Kay

Judith Kay has spent her life observing, listening, questioning, accepting, challenging, and wrestling with life's toughest questions. Her writings reveal the answers, enmeshed in the tangled, sometimes messy analogies from everyday living.

Judith Kay's rural Iowa upbringing planted deep roots in core family values, a solid work ethic, and a humble spirit. These traits are personified in characters with deep convictions and heartfelt struggles. No stranger herself to disappointment, struggles, and grief, Judith Kay presents characters that wield their way into your heart, inviting you to seek your own answers along their journeys.

Moving fluently between works of fiction and non-fiction, life-changing implications draw you into Judith Kay's stories. Engaging dialogue includes the inner-most thoughts of her characters bringing an authenticity to them unlike most works of fiction. Her quick wit and keen sense of authenticity keep you engaged. Her characters stay with you long after the story has ended.

Praise For Author

5.0 out of 5 stars

Judith Kay had me hooked by the 2nd page of this sweet romantic novel. Her characters seem to leap off the page to become people you know and care about immediately. She has woven a beautiful romance between two very interesting and real people, while managing to introduce other characters and situations to keep you from putting this book down long into the night.

This is a book that is simplistic in its premise, but complicated and thought provoking in the situations that are presented. One of the things I appreciated about the book is although there are love scenes, Judith Kay lets the reader read between the lines and does not fill page upon page of the same hot & heavy stuff. It is more about the developing relationships & inner struggles of the people in the book.

I highly recommend this book for a fulfilling, light, believable and pleasant journey away from the stresses of everyday life. It is a long book - but I was not ready for it to end!

- MELANIE PATRICE

5.0 out of 5 stars

Fantastic read!
Reviewed in the United States on July 28, 2021

The characters and story were well developed, realistic, and relatable. The book draws you in and keeps you reading to see what happens next and if a happy ending is possible. The story is believable, emotional, and heartwarming. Could not put it down and felt that I knew the characters and was truly invested in the book. Contemporary fiction at its best!! Highly recommend!

- DENISE W.

5.0 out of 5 stars
Great Read!

Reviewed in the United States on June 28, 2021

Contemporary fiction at its finest. Samira and J.P. are strong, independent individuals who learn to trust and lean on each other as they discover companionship that completes their lives.

The author brings the characters to life with heart. As a reader, you become part of their challenges, get a glimpse into their past. and root for their future. You won't want to put the book down. A word of advice: Order the next two in the series before you finish the first.

-JENNIFER O.

5.0 out of 5 stars
Wonderful

Reviewed in the United States on July 8, 2021

I was captivated throughout the book. It told the real-life story of common family dynamics and how careers can put strains on relationships. It reveals what is important in life and the importance of keeping God first. I look forward to the next book in the series.

- VERIFIED AMAZON READER

5.0 out of 5 stars

I'd love to see this book turned into a movie!

Reviewed in the United States on November 5, 2021

This is not your average romance novel. There are multiple stories happening at once with fun twists and turns all tied together. The characters are super relatable, and the author does an amazing job at getting you in the character's minds. I can't wait to read the next one!

- VERIFIED AMAZON READER

"Author Judith Kay is a kind and compassionate Christian woman who writes from her heart. Her life experiences and education give an authentic voice to her works. Judith Ka's writing style captivates the reader all the way to a perfect, satisfying ending. She is also a skilled editor and publisher. Check out her services a www.judithkaywrites.com."

- BECK STANLEY, AUTHOR OF THE LAST WEEKEND OF SEPTEMBER.

Love Takes a Chance, A Trilogy

An unexpected romance, complex family relations, and unhealed wounds comingle as two single parents wrestle with their pasts, putting everything on the line for one Last Chance at Love.

Everyone deserves A Fighting Chance, but the stakes are higher when popular opinion threatens parental decisions and social agendas take precedence over house rules.

Love Takes a Chance, but everything must work together—Trust, Responsibility, and Intimacy. There is no margin for error.

Last Chance At Love, Book 1

Unexpected romance, complex family relations, and unhealed wounds comingle as two single parents wrestle with their pasts, putting everything on the line for one last chance at love.

Samira Cartwright is smart, she is steady, and she is very settled. Widowed much too young, Samira is raising her daughters as a single mother and running the programs at the local library. Her life is simple, safe, and predictable. Maybe too predictable!

J.P. Ralston's life is anything but simple. His professional reputation in the courtroom reflects great success, but his reputation with women speaks otherwise. Detached, untamed, and set in his ways, J.P. embarks upon new territory when research needed to close a case intersects with Samira's jurisdiction at the library.

As the romance intensifies, the stakes get higher. J.P. must come to term with his past. Samira must let go of what was to embrace what might be. All must be reconciled before they can take that one last chance at love.

A Fighting Chance, Book 2

A Fighting Chance, second book in the series, Love Takes a Chance, pursues the intense romance between Samira Cartwright and J.P. Ralston. They tumble into new territory with holy matrimony, but unwritten expectations come with tremendous responsibility. Marital bliss is threatened by teenage drama, demanding professional agendas, and a never-ending battle for intimacy.

When tragedy strikes, everything is on the line. Decisions must be made despite public and professional opinions. Crimson roses connect the past to the present.

Judith Kay weaves current issues and real to life emotions into an epic family story that tests loyalties, forces acceptance, and discovers the power of unconditional love. Life-changing forgiveness opens the way for new beginnings. Mr. and Mrs. Ralston draw you even deeper into their story, mind, body, and spirit. Will their Last Chance at Love be enough to give them A Fighting Chance?

Love Takes A Chance, Book 3

Love Takes a Chance, but everything must work together—Trust, Accountability, and Intimacy. Increased family responsibility takes its toll on career-minded professionals who jockey for positions both at home and at work. A demanding family activity schedule coupled with J.P.'s ever-increasing case load threatens the equilibrium Samira tries so hard to control.

As Samira spreads her wings, corporate politics skew her commitments. J.P. runs interference between truth and heresy in the best interest of all involved, his wife included. Mr. and Mrs. Ralston find themselves evolving as lovers, as parents, and as business partners. As the world presses in, there is no margin for error.

Judith Kay intertwines current family issues and real to life emotions into this epic drama that tests loyalties, forces acceptance, and discovers the power of unconditional love. Life-changing forgiveness open the way for new beginnings. Mr. and Mrs. Ralston draw you even deeper into their passion—mind, body, and spirit.

Books By This Author

Unspoken-Ness, A Perspective On Grief

Unspoken-ness offers a fresh perspective on living with grief. No stranger herself to disappointment, struggles, and sorrow, Judith Kay presents a collection of musings that digs deep into the heart speaking to those who have loved and lost and to those who have triumphed only to be disappointed. Not all prayers are answered on this side of heaven yet our survival hinges on how we navigate the path forward.

The deeper we love, the harder we grieve. That is a fact that cannot be changed. Life and death—living and dying go together. They cannot be separated nor does one exist without the other. Grieving is a natural response to loss and brokenness. There is no right or wrong way to comfort a grieving heart, but somehow, some way, life on this side of heaven must continue.

In her unique, heartfelt writing style, Judith Kay weaves her stories into your experiences. You will find yourself inspired, challenged, and affirmed. In the end, Unspoken-ness will leave you with hope for your own journey —living life changed.

Forward by Bob Waldron.

Household Faith

Household Faith is faith discovered in the midst of everyday living. It is honesty, questions, and guilt, with a few answers along the way. It is the realization that life isn't perfect. It is the laughter of a moment. It is understanding that children are our best teachers. It is the sleepless nights and the pure exhaustion of parenthood. But mostly, it weaves the questions into answers, the tears into joy, and the memories into our soul.

Household Faith is a collection of stories, memories, insights, and musings from everyday moments. Each story stands alone but also encompasses a bigger picture. Alone they capture a moment in time. As a collective work, they span a lifetime, connecting the present to the past and the past to the future. They are an offering, a glimpse of heaven, and a flicker of hope.

Devotional in style, but not necessarily designed to be read as individual segments, Household Faith reminds parents they are enough. It affirms grandparents and gives aunts and uncles permission to laugh. It strengthens the bond between siblings and drives home the fact that family often includes those who are not related by blood. It is a gift you give yourself as it transports you back and propels you forward all in one fell swoop. May the faith of this household become a window to yours.

Diagnosis Dementia ~ Prognosis Hope

Dementia care for a loved one walks the fine line between knowing it won't last forever and the absolute horror that the final outcome is death. The beginning is unforeseen, but the end is inevitable.

Diagnosis Dementia-Prognosis Hope is a touching memoir of a mother-daughter journey through their journey with Dementia, made all the worse with the timing of the COVID-19 pandemic. These stories capture the daily struggles, the momentary joys, and the complex challenges that compound the caregiving effort. Judith Kay speaks from the heart, sculpting each situation into hope-giving inspiration.

Seasoned with just the right amount of humor, this book is a must-read for caregivers, children of Dementia patients, and anyone who finds themselves involved with memory-challenged loved ones. Dementia is not an individual struggle. It is a family disease affecting every facet of daily living. Judith Kay presents an inspirational glimpse into the day-to-day memory-challenged world she navigated with her mother, unprepared, untrained, and overwhelmed. Each story stands alone, yet simultaneously intertwines with the past, all the while foreshadowing what is yet to come.

Livvie's Favorite Day & Livvie Loves Water

Two rhyming storybooks tell the antics of Olivia, our gray cat. Whimsical and colorful, these stories will become fast favorites for little readers.

Designed for small hands and complete with a dedication page for gifting.

Verses by Judith Kay. Illustrations by Craig Marshall.

Grandma K's Recipes

Who doesn't long for the comfort foods of days gone by?

Grandma K's Recipes is a collection of Midwestern favorites compiled between 1935 and the mid-1980s by Martha Koboldt, fondly remembered by her family as "Grandma K". Complete with her personal notes, these recipes are sure to bring back memories of your own family dinners and church potlucks.

Categories include everything from appetizers to desserts, main courses, vegetable dishes, salads galore, and so much more! Every recipe gives credit to the original recipe-holder, most derived from Madison County, Iowa. Grandma K's down-home-style cooking is a treasure to be passed along from our family to yours.

Living Life Changed Day Planner

The Living Life Changed Day Planner by Judith Kay is elegant, durable, and designed to capture the most important parts of each day. Designed with a woman in mind, it is perfect for the busy mom, businesswoman, entrepreneur, or college student. Every page includes a daily scheduler running from 6 AM until 10 PM. There is space to capture daily doses of gratitude, a to-do list, a hydration tracker, and a meal planner. The Living Life Changed Planner covers 365 days.

Living Life Changed Journal

The Living Life Changed Journal by Judith Kay is a perfect companion to the Daily Planner, or perfect as a stand along journal. There are 200 blank pages to capture thoughts, ideas, ponderings, drawings, or musings.

Every woman needs a pretty place to write down her dreams and goals. The Living Life Changed Journal is small enough to drop in your backpack but big enough to keep all your secrets safe.

Made in the USA
Monee, IL
24 March 2023

30333955R00299